Equity and Trusts
Seventh Edition

Alastair Hudson's *Equity and Trusts* is an ideal textbook for undergraduate courses on the law of trusts and equitable remedies. It provides a clear, current and comprehensive account of the subject through which the author's enthusiasm and expertise shine through, helping to bring to life an area of the law which students often find challenging.

Fully updated and revised, this Seventh Edition contains an analysis of *Jones v Kernott* and trusts of homes; a new treatment of dishonest assistance and unconscionable receipt; a full treatment of the law on super-injunctions; coverage of all of the trusts law cases precipitated by the collapse of Lehman Brothers; a reflection on women and equity, and the politics of trusts law; a new treatment of the *Hastings-Bass* principle; and analysis of over 200 new cases, the Charities Act 2011 and the Perpetuities and Accumulations Act 2009.

Equity and Trusts remains the most comprehensive and up-to-date coverage of the law of Equity and Trusts, while still a lively and thoughtful account of the issues raised by it. This book has been cited as being authoritative in the courts of numerous countries.

The seventh edition is supported by a companion website which includes:

- over 50 short podcast lectures by the author discussing and clarifying key topics from within the book, which cover an entire course;
- a set of brief video documentaries filmed on location which provide context and bring to life selected key topics;
- a brief introductory video presentation from the author introducing the viewer to the subject of Equity and Trusts and to the book in particular.

Review of a previous edition:

'One of the book's great strengths is its clear exposition of some very difficult areas of the law, moving seamlessly from points that puzzle students to points that puzzle practitioners. Other strengths are the breadth of its approach, the fact that it is extremely up to date, the freshness and vividness of its approach and its willingness to place equity in a wider context ... The student will enjoy a clear, lively and challenging account of the subject matter. The practitioner will find the book well worth consulting for its clear exposition of the basic principles and of their application in difficult areas.' – *New Law Journal*.

Alastair Hudson is Professor of Equity & Finance Law at the University of Southampton, and of Lincoln's Inn, Barrister. He is a National Teaching Fellow, Fellow of the Higher Education Academy, Fellow of the Royal Society of Arts, and was UK Law Teacher of the Year in 2008.

Equity and Trusts

Seventh Edition

Alastair Hudson

LLB LLM PhD (Lond.)

Professor of Equity & Finance Law
University of Southampton
National Teaching Fellow
Fellow of the Royal Society of Arts
Fellow of the Higher Education Academy
Of Lincoln's Inn, Barrister

Routledge
Taylor & Francis Group

LONDON AND NEW YORK

Seventh edition published 2013
by Routledge
2 Park Square, Milton Park, Abingdon, Oxon OX14 4RN

Simultaneously published in the USA and Canada
by Routledge
711 Third Avenue, New York, NY 10017

Routledge is an imprint of the Taylor & Francis Group, an informa business

First edition published by Cavendish Publishing 1999
Sixth edition published by Routledge-Cavendish 2010

British Library Cataloguing in Publication Data
A catalogue record for this book is available from the British Library

Library of Congress Cataloging in Publication Data has been requested.

ISBN: 978-0-415-68232-9 (hbk)
ISBN: 978-0-415-68233-6 (pbk)
ISBN: 978-0-203-10191-9 (ebk)

Typeset in Times
by RefineCatch Limited, Bungay, Suffolk

MIX
Paper from
responsible sources
FSC
www.fsc.org   FSC® C004839

Printed and bound in Great Britain by the MPG Books Group

Preface

Equity is a fascinating and subtle area of law; the law of trusts is by turns a technically progressive, practical and theoretically complex topic. This book constitutes a comprehensive analysis of both equity and the law of trusts, suitable for undergraduate and postgraduate courses, and (as suggested by reviews of the previous edition) it is widely used by legal practitioners and has been cited in the courts of several jurisdictions.

This subject has everything: birth, life, greed, sex, lies, truth, conscience, bitterness, vengeance and death – and then what comes after death. The rules of equity, and in particular the trust, are the ways in which English law deals with so many of these things. This book is meant to *teach* students and others interested in this subject, and to deal forthrightly with the issues which this subject raises: both subtle technical issues and contextual, social issues. To say that it is a teaching aid does not mean that it is not intended to be an academic or scholarly book. On the contrary I have had two aims in writing it: to explain the law of trusts in an accessible way and also to address all of the major academic debates that currently surround the complex principles of equity and the law of trusts. It explains the concepts by using easy-to-understand examples from real life, together with my 'cognitive reinforcement' teaching technique, and detailed analyses of the key cases and principles.

Important information for the student reader: how to read this book

It is important that you read this Preface before you start reading the rest of the text. It is then very important that you read the first two chapters, which will explain the vital underpinnings for the whole of the rest of the book.

This book has been written in a way that is slightly different from other trusts textbooks. Each chapter and each individual section begins with an overview of the relevant legal principles in that area. These summaries serve as a shorthand note of the discussion that follows. Importantly, they will give an outline of the subject matter to come. The secret to reading textbooks and cases is to know what the core legal principles are before you start to read. Without that knowledge you will find it very hard to understand the detail of the discussion. In this book each major principle is illustrated with a factual example to show how the ordinary world is understood through a trusts law analysis. That way, the discussion that follows will make more sense and the major issues will stand out more clearly.

After the summary, the remainder of the section will explain how those principles work. Those sections will be designed as problem-solving discussions – examining the real-life issues which have led to development of the law of trusts and the principles of equity.

Discussion will be primarily of the most significant cases, set against accounts of the academic analysis of each subject.

Equity and trusts is a topic in which it is possible for a student to score very high marks in essays and examinations because there are a number of very sophisticated ideas bound up in it. If you deal with them well, you will shine. Therefore, importantly for you, this text and its two companion websites include discussion of all of the major academic and judicial debates in the area (with a few more besides): there are podcasts on each individual topic, and full lectures online too. These ideas are usually considered towards the end of each chapter after the basic material has been explained at the outset. A glossary of essential terms is also supplied, which may prove useful in those dark early days.

The significance of the painting on the cover of this book

The painting on the cover of the paperback edition of this book shows us the possible after-effects of a trust on the lives of a young couple. The previous edition of this book bore the first in a series of six paintings called *Marriage à la Mode* which was painted by the English satirical artist Hogarth between 1743 and 1745. Hogarth was satirising the way in which the complacent rich of 18th-century English society lived their lives. That painting depicted a foolish old patriarch, the Earl of Squander, altering the trust which governed the ownership of his family's property down the generations so that his stupid son could marry the daughter of a wealthy merchant. All six paintings tell a story of how two young people receive a huge fortune by way of a trust before squandering it all and ending up dying in ignominy (he is stabbed by one of his wife's lovers and she dies in poverty). All six paintings in the *Marriage à la Mode* series are on permanent exhibition at the National Gallery in London. This story fits this book perfectly, and they are among my favourite paintings. The cover of this edition is a detail of the second painting in the *Marriage à la Mode* series of paintings, which is called 'The Tête-à-Tête'.

In this second painting, we see the newly-weds exhausted from a long night of carousing – albeit that they have not spent the night together (her table is laid only for one person, and the clock shows it is midday). So soon after their marriage he has been out all night and she has been entertaining a large party at their palatial home (just out of sight in the painting are the gaming tables which a servant is clearing away). Their wealth is dependent upon their trust: the house in which they live, the expensive ornaments and furniture, and all of the money that they have to spend, will be held on the terms of a 'settlement' (the formal name for this sort of trust) in the expectation that all of the property will be held on trust after their deaths for successive generations of their family. However, Hogarth's morality tale shows how they will nevertheless squander their family's wealth (even though, strictly speaking, the law of trusts should ensure that the trustees do not allow them to do so).

Hogarth filled the painting with tiny details that tell the story of the human drama which is being lived out behind the surface of this trust. If you look closely at the young husband's left pocket, you will see the lace cap of his lover from the night before poking out, with the little dog pulling at it. The little dog itself suggests an animal wildness in their fine home. The black mark on his face indicates syphilis. His wife's contented look is intended to show not only that she had had a raucous evening with her house party but also that she had a satisfying sexual experience. Just out of the frame in the detail on the cover is a servant clutching a stack of unpaid bills, who is rolling his eyes to the ceiling in dismay at the way in which the young couple are squandering their money. An over-turned chair also indicates the chaos in their lives, or possibly that her lover has just left in a hurry. One thing which always strikes me about this painting is how modern their faces look: on his face we can already see an exhaustion caused by his life of excess, his hands sunk deep into his pockets, a miserable look on his face; and in the inscrutable expression on her face we can see her excitement at being able at last to break out of the bonds of the demureness which society would have imposed on her before she was married. Her sitting position on her chair is far from demure. Similarly modern is their need to shop – for the expensive ornaments packed onto the mantel, for their expensive taste in Eastern curios among those ornaments, for their fine clothes, and so on. She is reading a book on gambling after a night effectively hosting a casino in their house. His broken sword lies (the broken tip is a positively Freudian metaphor) unbuckled by his feet and wrapped suggestively in a ribbon (suggesting that his manhood is spent and that he has been fighting). Hogarth was satirising a society which was concerned with money and with acquisition, and whose morality seemed to be slipping. These are still very modern complaints about 21st-century Britain.

The couple in the painting are living the high life on their trust fund, but when the money runs out then they will be destitute (because they have no other form of income). That the failure of a trust could ruin a family became a key driver in the strictness of trust law in relation to the duties of trustees and the liabilities of various other people discussed in Part 6 of this book in the event that any trust money should be lost. Literally an entire social class was dependent upon the proper management of the trusts which held their wealth. This was long before the Industrial Revolution transformed the social landscape in England. Such was the role of trusts law in Georgian England and beyond: the livelihoods of the upper classes were entirely dependent upon trusts. Trusts and the courts of equity controlled their access to wealth and security. Equity and trusts have continued to be very important in English law and in English life: they govern pensions, investment, rights to the home in many cases, and so much more. The cases we shall study are full of marriages, infidelities, lies, bankruptcy, drama, sex and death. Just like a series of Hogarth paintings. This book will try to explain this area of law to you with the same energy with which Hogarth hosed down the foibles of his countrymen.

The structure of the book

Part 1 is essential background material for the student reader, as it considers the fundamental principles of equity and explains the basic structure of the trust. No student of this subject will get far without a sure understanding of this basic material. Part 2 considers the nature of express trusts and the formalities necessary for their creation, which form the basis of all courses on express trusts law.

Part 3 considers the administration of express trusts and the responsibilities imposed on trustees by case law and by statute. The global financial crisis and the collapse of the US investment bank Lehman Brothers has given rise to a large amount of important case law on the certainties necessary to create a trust. As the author of *The Law of Finance*, it has been possible for me to synthesise the discussion of these fascinating but complex new cases with the relevant principles of financial practice and financial regulation. There continues to be a detailed discussion of the fiduciary duties of trustees, including significant developments in the principle in *Hastings-Bass* as a result of the decision of the Court of Appeal in *Pitt v Holt* and on the rights of beneficiaries to information from trustees.

Part 4 analyses resulting trusts, constructive trusts, equitable estoppel and the nature of fiduciary liabilities: these areas are central to the study of trusts law and also pivotal in the scholarly debates about equity, trusts and unjust enrichment. There has been a large amount of new case law, particularly in relation to the treatment of bribes and commercial joint ventures.

Part 5 considers the interaction of principles of trusts law and proprietary estoppel with equitable principles of unconscionability and family law in relation to the acquisition of rights in the home. Chapter 15 has been extensively updated to account for the decision of the Supreme Court in *Jones v Kernott* and its impact on the interpretation of the decision of House of Lords in *Stack v Dowden*. This is the most dynamic area of equity and trusts: the discussion sets out a categorisation of the various streams of case law both in England and elsewhere in the Commonwealth, before considering in detail the particular problems raised by equitable estoppel, relationship breakdown, human rights law and philosophical models of social justice.

Part 6 contains three chapters which consider the variety of claims available in relation to breach of trust: whether brought against trustees in person, or against persons who have unconscionably and knowingly received trust property or dishonestly assisted in a breach of trust, or to trace proprietary rights in equity or at common law. The chapter on dishonest assistance and unconscionable receipt has been completely re-cast to account for the burgeoning case law in this area, and to consider some of the fascinating theoretical and practical questions which it raises.

Part 7 considers the way in which commercial people use trusts and other equitable principles such as the floating charge and mortgages in their transactions. There is also a consideration of the nature of trusts law in international commercial practice. From this discussion emerges an account of the uncomfortable assimilation of general equitable doctrine into commercial activities juxtaposed with commerce's enthusiastic acceptance of some techniques found in express trusts and equitable charges.

Part 8 considers the welfare uses of trusts in the forms of occupational pensions schemes and charities. The chapter on Charities was completely re-written to account for the Charities Act 2006 in the last edition, it has been updated to account for the Charities Act 2011, and has been expanded in this edition to cater for new cases interpreting that legislation. The interaction between the old case law, which remains in force, and the new categories of 'charitable purpose' promises to be a fascinating area for the future.

Part 9 considers the established categories of equitable remedies – specific performance, injunctions, rescission, rectification and set-off for undue influence – as well as a comprehensive round-up of less conspicuous equitable remedies, including subrogation, account, equitable damages, remedies for breach of trust, and the appointment of receivers. Many of these equitable doctrines and remedies are frequently overlooked in the calls made by restitution lawyers to 'replace equity' with principles of unjust enrichment. What emerges from this discussion is a demonstration of equity at its purest: discretionary, imaginative and always in flux. For the first time there is a comprehensive discussion of the equitable doctrine of confidence and of the law relating to the award of super-injunctions.

Part 10 sets out in two short essays a compilation of the main themes of the book. First, a consideration of the theoretical underpinnings of the law of property as put to work in the context of trusts and equity; then the final chapter of the book considers the theoretical nature of equity and also examines the various meanings associated with the important term 'conscience' in this context. It has always been my aim to make this a progressive book as well as a comprehensive textbook: it is in these final chapters that I set out to achieve that goal most obviously.

Two companion websites – containing updates on all important cases

A library of further materials can be found at www.alastairhudson.com/trustslawtrusts-lawindex.htm, including extended essays on the nature of express trusts, of restitution of unjust enrichment, and of trusts implied by law, as well as essays on unit trusts, co-operatives and public interest trusts. That site has developed a large number of casenotes on new decisions reached by English and other courts between editions of this book. It also contains a number of short podcasts on issues of particular concern to students in examinations, videos explaining some knotty problems of trusts law, and issues which are of particular academic interest. All of my undergraduate lectures and many other podcasts besides from the academic year 2009–10 are available free of charge on that website too. My publishers maintain a companion website (www.routledge.com/cw/hudson) for purchasers of this book which is also updated periodically to account for new developments in equity and trusts: that website will continue to grow with essays, casenotes and commentaries on this and other areas of law and legal theory. This new edition was written in the period leading up to February 2012. It was written using the materials available to me at that time. References to approximately 250 new cases have been included in this edition, making it one of the most comprehensive treatments of this topic in print today. Updates on later developments will be made available on-line, as described before. Consequently, this book will remain as up-to-date as possible.

From Routledge, I would like to thank Fiona Kinnear for her ever-professional and always good-humoured help in the preparation of this book, and also Damian Mitchell for a thousand kindnesses. There are other people I would like to thank for help and comradeship which, while not necessarily directly connected to this book, were essential to its completion in many other ways: in no particular order but with boundless thanks – my colleagues Dr Helena Howe, Prof Geraint Thomas, and Prof Roger Cotterrell. As this book aims to show, nothing is perfect but thinking can make it seem so.

Alastair Hudson
Haywards Heath
Valentine's Day 2012

Guide to the Companion Website

Visit the *Equity and Trusts* Companion Website at http://www.routledge.com/cw/hudson to discover a comprehensive range of resources designed to enhance the learning experience for students of equity and trusts.

RESOURCES

Podcasts

Listen to a comprehensive series of short podcasts by the author covering an entire equity and trusts law course, discussing and clarifying key topics from the book, together with updating podcasts.

Essays

A range of essays discuss new developments and provide pathways into further research.

Video introduction

Familiarise yourself with equity and trusts through the author's introductory video presentation.

Vodcasts

Short videos in which the author explains some of the more complex issues arising in trusts law so that they make sense.

Documentaries

See key topics brought to life through a set of brief video documentaries filmed on location.

Additional material

Access Chapter 23 on 'Mortgages, charges and taking security' and Chapter 24 on 'Occupational pension funds' alongside further additional material.

Explore further

Access a link to the author's own site which features up-to-date casenotes, further reading and research essays on various areas of law with commentary and feedback for help in developing essay-writing skills as well as guidance for taking effective lecture notes.

UPDATES

Keep up to date with the latest developments in equity and trusts by reading the author's updates to the text on-line.

Outline contents

Detailed Contents

Glossary

Equity and trusts law is a language. Therefore, it is important for you to understand its vocabulary. This is a glossary of some of the main terms which arise in the early days of an equity and trusts course, especially in the older cases, together with appropriate cross-references to the text that follows where particularly important terms are considered in some detail.

Absolute title   ownership of all of the property rights, legal and equitable, in property.

Administrator   the person who administers the estate of someone who died without making a will.

Beneficial interest   a synonym for 'equitable interest'.

Beneficiary   as discussed in para 2.3.4, the person (or people) for whose benefit property is held on trust, such that they have the equitable interest in that property. The nature of the rights of beneficiaries is discussed in Chapter 4 in detail.

Bequest   a gift made under a will.

Certainty of intention   the requirement, considered in Chapter 3, that the settlor intended to create a trust, as opposed to something else. The court may infer the existence of an express trust from the circumstances: there is no obligation for the settlor to use any specific form of words nor to use writing to create a trust in all circumstances.

Certainty of objects   the requirement, considered in Chapter 3, that the beneficiaries of a trust or power must be sufficiently certain.

Certainty of subject matter   the requirement, considered in Chapter 3, that the property comprising the trust fund is sufficiently certain, i.e. that it must be separately identifiable from other property.

Cestui que trust   a Latin synonym for 'beneficiary'.

Chose in action   a form of intangible property, such as a debt, which constitutes an item of property in itself formed of the rights and obligations created between two (or more) parties.

Constructive trust   a trust created by operation of law (rather than by the conscious intention of the parties) when a person has knowledge of some factor affecting their conscience in relation to property, considered in Chapter 12.

Declaration of trust   the action performed by a settlor in creating a trust. In relation to some kinds of property, there are formalities for a proper declaration of trust; see Chapter 5. In relation to most property the settlor needs only to manifest an intention to create a trust.

Deed   a formal document signed and delivered as a deed (s 1 of the Law of Property (Miscellaneous Provisions) Act 1989) required, for example, to create a valid will (s 9 of the Wills Act 1837) and to effect a valid conveyance of land (s 53 of the Law of Property Act 1925).

Devise   a bequest, usually concerning land.

Equitable interest   a right in property classically recognised by the courts of equity.

Equity   as discussed in section 1.1 and thereafter, a system of rules developed to counter-balance the rigours of statute and common law by the Courts of Chancery so as to allow for fairness in individual cases. It is a legal technique based on ensuring the good conscience of the individual defendant.

Executor   a fiduciary under a will trust. (The feminine form is 'executrix'.)

Express trust   a trust created voluntarily by a settlor such that a trustee holds property on trust for a beneficiary or beneficiaries.

Injunction   an equitable remedy either requiring or precluding some action, considered in Chapter 27.

Intellectual property   copyright, patent and trade marks, being forms of chose in action constituting intangible property.

Inter vivos   some relation, such as a trust, taking effect while the settlor is alive. Literally, it is Latin for 'between living people'.

Legal title   the property rights acquired by a trustee which enable that trustee to manage and administer the trust fund for the benefit of the beneficiaries.

Legatee   a beneficiary under a will.

Next of kin   a person specified under the intestacy rules as being a deceased's nearest relative for the purposes of distributing the estate of a person who has died intestate.

Personal property   property other than land and intellectual property, such as chattels. Sometimes referred to as 'personalty'.

Personal representative   one who is appointed to administer a deceased's estate.

Real property   land; referred to as 'real property' because historically to acquire rights in land one had to bring a 'real action'; technically 'real property' does not include leases.

Rectification   an equitable remedy affecting an alteration to a contractual document to give effect to the parties' true intentions, considered in Chapter 28.

Rescission   an equitable remedy rendering void a contract, considered in Chapter 28.

Restitution   either the common law process of restoring specific property to its original owner, or more generally the contested principle of effecting restitution of unjust enrich-ment by way, *inter alia*, of subtracting that enrichment from the defendant.

Resulting trust   a trust arising to return an equitable interest in property automatically to its original owner where no trust has been created, or a trust arising in favour of a person who has contributed to the purchase price of property, as considered in Chapter 11.

Settlement   a synonym for trust in most circumstances, with a technical meaning in rela-tion to the law of taxation and under the now-repealed Settled Land Act 1925. Family settlements were the way in which wealthy families organised the ownership and use of property down the generations, and were often created on the marriage of family members.

Settlor   one who creates an express trust.

Specific performance   an equitable remedy enforcing the intention of the parties to a contract, considered in Chapter 26.

Subrogation   an equitable remedy permitting a person to sue on obligations originally owed to another person where the court considers it just to do so, considered in Chapter 30.

Testamentary   taking effect after death, such as a trust, for example, coming into effect by means of a will after a person's death.

Testator   one who creates a will, a settlor of will trusts. (The feminine form is 'testatrix'.)

Tracing   the process of identifying and recovering either specific or substitute property transferred in breach of trust, prior to the imposition of an equitable remedy to recover that property or its substitute, considered in Chapter 19.

Trust   defined in full in para 2.2.1, an equitable institution arising so as to require a trustee to hold property for the benefit of a beneficiary, or beneficiaries, arising either expressly at the instigation of a settlor or being implied by a court as a resulting trust or as a constructive trust.

Trustee   a fiduciary who holds property on trust for the benefit of a beneficiary or beneficiaries.

Unjust enrichment   an alternative explanation of some equitable claims and remedies; a doctrine which achieves restitution by means of the subtraction of an unjust enrichment which the defendant has acquired at the claimant's expense.

Vesting property   transferring property rights to a person.

Volunteer   one who receives property or a benefit without giving consideration for it.

Will   an attested document which provides for the manner in which the testator's property is to be divided on death, created in accordance with statute.

Table of cases

Table of legislation

Part 1

Fundamentals of equity and trusts

Chapter 1

Introduction – the nature of equity

1.1 THE FOUNDATIONS OF EQUITY

1.1.1 The nature of equity

Equity is the means by which a system of law balances out the need for certainty in rule-making with the need to achieve fair results in individual circumstances. An expression which has been commonly used to describe the way in which equity functions is that equity 'mitigates the rigour of the common law' so that the letter of the law is not applied in so strict a way that it may cause injustice in individual cases.[1] English equity does this by examining the conscience of the individual defendant.[2] Equity, then, is that part of English private law which seeks either to prevent any benefit accruing to a defendant as a result of some unconscionable conduct or to compensate any loss suffered by a claimant which results from some unconscionable conduct, and which also seeks to ensure that common law and statutory rules are not manipulated unconscionably. At its broadest, equity appears to imbue the courts with a general discretion to disapply statutory or common law rules whenever good conscience requires it;[3] however, in practice, modern equity is comprised mainly

---

1 *Earl of Oxford's Case* (1615) 1 Ch Rep 1, *per* Lord Ellesmere LC: 'to soften and mollify the extremity of the law'; *Lord Dudley v Lady Dudley* (1705) Prec Ch 241, 244, *per* Lord Cowper, LC: 'Equity is no part of the law, but a moral virtue which qualifies, moderates and reforms the rigour, hardness and edge of the law.' In Samuel Johnson's dictionary (first published in 1755), the 'chancery' is described as being 'The court of equity and conscience, moderating the rigour of other courts, that are tied to the letter of the law': this definition quotes the jurist Cowell's own definition in *The Interpreter*, a legal glossary of the time. Also, considered below, St German explained that 'equytie is ordeyned . . . to temper and myttygate the rygoure of the lawe' (1528–31), quoted in Plucknett and Barton (eds), 'St German's Doctor and Student' 91 *Selden Society*, London, 1974, 97. See also Lord Kaims' treatise *Principles of Equity*, 3rd ed, Edinburgh: Bell and Creech, 1778, 41 which uses the same expressions. See below the discussion of Aristotle's notion of equity at para 1.1.5 in relation to the rectification of legislation by equity.

2 *Earl of Oxford's Case* (1615) 1 Ch Rep 1.

3 This broad use of equity is rare in modern equitable practice, as we shall consider in this chapter and elsewhere throughout this book. See, for example, the discussion of *Jaggard v Sawyer* [1995] 1 WLR 269; [1995] 2 All ER 189 (para 27.1.1) where the Court of Appeal preferred to apply precedent closely rather than consider themselves to have a broad discretion to act as they saw fit under the terms of the Supreme Court Act 1981, s 50 which purported to permit them to grant interim injunctions in general terms. However, doctrines such as the principle that equity will not permit statute to be used as an engine of fraud (*Rochefoucauld v Boustead* [1897] 1 Ch 196: see para 1.4.13), the doctrine of secret trust (*McCormick v Grogan* (1869) LR 4 HL 82; *Jones v Badley* (1868) 3 Ch App 362; *Blackwell v Blackwell* [1929] AC 318: see para 6.1.4 below) and the doctrine of equitable estoppel (*Yaxley v Gotts* [2000] Ch 162: see para 13.1) operate expressly in contravention of the terms of Acts of Parliament with the general intention that no benefit be taken nor any loss suffered as a result of some unconscionable conduct.

of substantive and procedural principles which only permit the courts a limited amount of discretion.[4]

There are three different ways of understanding equity's role as part of the English legal system.[5] First, equity can be understood as the means by which English law ensures that the strict application of a common law or a statutory rule does not result in any unfairness when applied in a specific case. To this extent equity is a form of natural justice,[6] which means that it has a moral basis.[7] Equity's particular moral purpose was described by Lord Ellesmere in the *Earl of Oxford's Case*[8] as being to 'correct men's consciences for frauds, breach of trusts, wrongs and oppressions . . . and to soften and mollify the extremity of the law'.[9] This is a moral purpose in that it both prevents a defendant from taking unconscionable advantage of a situation and also in that it prevents the law from inadvertently permitting an unconscionable result. Secondly, equity can be considered, in its formal sense, as constituting the collection of *substantive* principles developed over the centuries by the Courts of Equity, principally the Court of Chancery,[10] to judge people's consciences.[11] In this sense, equity should be understood as being a code of technical, substantive rules and not simply as a reservoir of general, moral principles.[12] Thirdly, equity can be understood as comprising the *procedural* rules and forms of action developed by the Courts of Chancery over the centuries under the authority of the Lord Chancellor.[13] The main equitable principles are considered in

4 See, for example, the discussion of *Jaggard v Sawyer* [1995] 1 WLR 269, [1995] 2 All ER 189 (see para 27.1.1 below) which indicates the courts' reluctance to consider its powers to be broad discretionary powers even if their enactment by statute might suggest that they are capable of being applied in such a way.

5 In the final chapter of this book we will consider how other disciplines in the social sciences use the notion of equity in different senses.

6 *Lord Dudley v Lady Dudley* (1705) Prec Ch 241, 244, *per* Lord Cowper. See, in similar vein, Story, 1839, 1, drawing a parallel with the natural justice understood in Justinian's Pandects. The approach of seeing a Roman root to these ideas is rejected by Professor Maitland (1936, 6). Perhaps Professor Story's preparedness to identify a Romanic similarity between the natural justice root to equity and '*ius*' in the Roman sense used by Justinian is founded on American lawyers' affection for that sort of natural justice which is set out in the US Constitution.

7 See McGhee, 2005, paras 1–01 and 1–03, who identifies the moral base of equity while also considering the need for the legal conceptualisation of such moral notions as being based on specific principles. See also Spry, 2001, 1, who advances the proposition that 'equitable principles have above all a distinctive ethical quality, reflecting as they do the prevention of unconscionable conduct'.

8 (1615) 1 Ch Rep 1.

9 As St German described this underlying purpose: '. . . in some cases it is good and even necessary to leue the wordis of the law and to folowe that reason and Justyce requyreth and to that intent equytie is ordeyned that is to say to temper and myttygate the rygoure of the lawe', quoted in Plucknett and Barton (eds), 'St German's Doctor and Student' 91 *Selden Society*, London, 1974, 97. Or, to attempt a translation of my own into a more modern, English-legal vernacular: '. . . in some cases it is good and even necessary to deviate from the strict letter of the law and [instead] to follow what reason and justice require – which is the purpose for which equity is ordained – that is to temper and mitigate the rigour of statute and the common law'.

10 While we will focus on the Courts of Chancery as constituting the most significant Courts of Equity in this book, there were other courts (which are of no importance to the modern legal system) which also operated on equitable principles. After the Judicature Act 1873, the old courts of chancery were replaced by the High Court of Justice, although it could be said that the spirit of the old courts of chancery lived on in the Chancery Division of the High Court which was created by that Act.

11 *Earl of Oxford's Case* (1615) 1 Ch Rep 1.

12 The tendency to think of equity in terms of general principles as opposed to technical devices and strict case law rules was criticised by Vice-Chancellor Megarry in *Re Montagu's Settlement* [1987] Ch 264.

13 To emphasise the distinction between the second and third aspects of equity: the second aspect relates to substantive legal rules (such as the trust) whereas the third aspect relates to procedural rules and devices (such as interim injunctions).

section 1.4 below. It should be noted that these second and third aspects of equity differ from the apparent breadth of the first in that they constitute technical rules of law rather than abstract philosophical principles. It is common for English and Australian writers on equity to focus on these latter senses of equity in preference to a consideration of more philosophical notions of natural justice theory; although, it is suggested, an appreciation of these philosophical underpinnings is important if equity is to be understood as a collection of coherent principles and not simply as a ragbag of different doctrines.[14]

In all legal systems the following problem arises: how can we create general common law or statutory rules without treating some individual circumstances unjustly? In the context of the English legal system it is equity which performs this balancing act when set against the rigidity of the common law. In this regard, the work of the German philosopher Hegel has generated the following definition of equity:

> Equity involves a departure from formal rights owing to moral or other considerations and is concerned primarily with the content of the lawsuit. A court of equity, however, comes to mean a court which decides in a single case without insisting on the formalities of a legal process[15] or, in particular, on the objective evidence which the letter of the law may require.[16] Further, it decides on the merits of the single case as a unique one, not with a view to disposing of it in such a way as to create a binding legal precedent for the future.[17]

Hegel was one of the foremost philosophers of the last 200 years, not a lawyer, but this definition of the activities of equity in its legal sense is nevertheless particularly useful because it shows us how equity permits the achievement of 'fair' or 'just' results in situations in which the literal application of statute or common law might otherwise lead to unfairness or injustice. As mentioned, this summary should be treated with some caution because he wrote as a German philosopher rather than as an English lawyer; and yet, Hegel captures the fact that the court is concerned only with the merits of the case between the claimant and the defendant, and not necessarily with the broader context of the law. In this way the court can focus on reaching the best result in the circumstances even where a literal application of statute or common law might seem to require a different result.[18] Despite this ostensible flexibility, this book will consider some areas in which equity generally (and the trust in particular) seem to have become rigid institutions more akin to contract than to the underlying spirit of equity which treats each case as a unique one.[19]

14 This is the approach preferred by Professor Maitland in his lectures on 'Equity' published originally in 1909 and then revised posthumously in 1936 (see Maitland, 1936, 1). See also Loughlan, 2003, 3; Meagher, Heydon and Leeming, 2002, 3. Professor Martin distinguishes between the 'wide sense' of equity as opposed to its narrower 'legal meaning' where the legal meaning refers to the substantive principles applied and administered by the Courts of Chancery before 1873, in *Hanbury and Martin's Modern Equity*, 16th edn, 2001, London: Sweet & Maxwell, 3 (hereafter 'Martin, 2001'). Professor Pettit prefers a history of the courts of chancery and an analysis of the Judicature Act 1873 to an abstract definition of the term 'equity', *Equity and the Law of Trusts*, 9th edn, 2001, London: Butterworths (hereafter 'Pettit, 2001'). See, however, the approach taken by the current author of Snell's *Equity*, John McGhee QC, considered at fn 7 above, which is more in tune with the discussion in this book.
15 English equity, however, *is* also concerned with procedural and interlocutory matters.
16 See, for example, breach of trust in relation to which common law notions of causation play no part.
17 Hegel, 1821, 142, para 223.
18 Cf Dworkin, 1986.
19 See the discussion in Chapter 7 below.

The underlying argument of this book is that there is a need to understand the elegant simplicity of equity at the same time as the legal system is asked to consider questions asked of it by an ever more complex society. We shall see this development, for example, when we consider how equity allocates rights in the home between members of the same family.[20] That will require us to resist the siren call of those who argue for ever more formalistic tests for doctrines like the trust[21] which were originally formed in the grand tradition of equity by the Courts of Chancery. It has been said that certainty is the hallmark of every effective legal system,[22] but it is also true to say that chaos and complexity are the common characteristic of every problem which confronts such a legal system. People only go to court when their problems have become too difficult for them to sort out on their own. Therefore, I would suggest that equity's flexibility is important in ensuring that the law retains sufficient suppleness to cope with the social developments over which the court is asked to sit in judgment.

Equity and trusts are interesting subjects precisely because their inherent fluidity has enabled them to regenerate themselves regularly over time and yet their technical sophistication has provided lawyers with a range of techniques with which to achieve their clients' goals in a variety of circumstances. The fundamental principles of equity are part of a philosophical tradition which is identifiable in the thoughts of the ancient Greeks.[23] Nevertheless, it should be remembered that the English Courts of Equity have never expressly acknowledged that they are operating on any one philosophical basis, although, as will emerge throughout this book, it may appear that they do have such grand aspirations hidden within their judgments.[24] The development of equity through the cases has been far more pragmatic than that.

1.1.2 The scope of this book: equity and trusts

This book considers both the general doctrines and remedies which form part of equity, and more particularly the law of trusts. The general principles of equity are founded on the maxims which are considered in section 1.4 of this chapter. These maxims have informed the creation of equity over the centuries and continue to be important.[25] The principal equitable doctrine is that equity acts *in personam* on the conscience of the defendant, which means that the main focus of a Court of Equity is to consider whether or not the individual defendant has acted in good conscience.[26] The law of trusts was born out of equity's focus

---

20 See Chapter 15 and Chapter 17, which consider the flexibility of modern family law and human rights law when measured against the rigidity of much of property law.

21 Birks, 1989:1, 85; Beatson, 1991; Honoré, 2003, 15 *et seq.*

22 Eg, Oakley, 1997, 27.

23 See Thomas, 1976, 506. This tradition is considered in greater detail below and in Chapter 32.

24 A word on terminology. It is usual to refer to the jurisdiction of the courts of equity in the capitalised form 'Equity'; whereas the ideas which make up the principles of equity are often referred to instead in the lower case as 'equity', a usage which also appears in other social science. In this book the capitalised usage will be reserved for mention only of the system of courts making up the equitable jurisdiction. However, I will more generally use only the lower case to refer both to the jurisdiction, to the ideas which that jurisdiction has generated and also the general notion of equity as broadly akin to 'fairness' or 'just treatment' (as discussed in greater detail in the text).

25 See, for example, the continued significance of doctrines of conscience in the House of Lords in *Westdeutsche Landesbank v Islington* [1996] AC 669 and the maxim that equity looks upon as done that which ought to have been done in the Privy Council in *Attorney-General for Hong Kong v Reid* [1994] 1 AC 324.

26 *Earl of Oxford's Case* (1615) 1 Ch Rep 1.

on acting on conscience,[27] but the subsequent development of trusts law has reflected the increasing use of trusts in commercial transactions in which certainty has been considered to be an important requirement.[28] As a result, the ostensible flexibility of equity was displaced first by the development of the doctrine of precedent governing the application of equitable maxims and latterly by the increasing certainty required of doctrines like the trust. So, this book considers the law of trusts in great depth in recognition of the central importance of trusts in English law over the centuries. The remainder of the book is concerned with the other equitable doctrines and with understanding the trust as being a part of the equitable canon. Therefore, this chapter considers equitable maxims in the abstract before the next chapter introduces the trust concept.

1.1.3 Equity and trusts are based on conscience

As explained in the preceding paragraph, the most significant equitable doctrine is the trust, which forms the principal focus of this book: our focus will therefore divide between the law of trusts on the one hand and general equitable principles and remedies on the other. The most important case in relation to the development of equity and the trust in recent years was arguably that in *Westdeutsche Landesbank v Islington LBC*,[29] in which Lord Browne-Wilkinson addressed two main issues, aside from dealing with the appeal before him. First, he set out his version of the core principles of the law of trusts.[30] Secondly, he set about re-establishing traditional notions of equity as being at the heart of English trusts law. As opposed to the new principle of unjust enrichment developed (principally) by Lord Goff and a group of academics centred primarily in Oxford,[31] Lord Browne-Wilkinson has re-asserted a traditional understanding of the trust as being based on the conscience of the person who acts as trustee.[32] So, in *Westdeutsche Landesbank v Islington LBC*, his Lordship went back to basics with the first of his 'Relevant Principles of Trust Law':

(i)   Equity operates on the conscience of the owner of the legal interest. In the case of a trust, the conscience of the legal owner requires him to carry out the purposes for which the property was vested in him (express or implied trust) or which the law imposes on him by reason of his unconscionable conduct (constructive trust).[33]

As we shall see, the basis of the trust (and indeed the whole of equity) is concerned with regulating the conscience of a person where the common law might otherwise allow that person to act unconscionably but in accordance with the letter of the law.[34] Suppose, for example, that

---

27 *Westdeutsche Landesbank v Islington LBC* [1996] AC 669.
28 In relation to the increasing commercialisation of trusts law, see, for example, the discussion of *Target Holdings v Redferns* [1996] 1 AC 421 in para 21.2.2. As to the importance of certainty in the ordinary law of trusts see Chapter 3 generally and the authorities following *Knight v Knight* (1840) 3 Beav 148 discussed in that chapter.
29 [1996] AC 669.
30 See section 2.4.
31 See the work of Professor Peter Birks (in particular his *Introduction to the Law of Restitution* (1989) and *Unjust Enrichment* (2003)) and the literature which it has spawned.
32 This debate is considered in depth later in this book and summarised in Chapter 32. Alternatively you may choose to consult the essay at www.alastairhudson.com/trusts/restitution of unjust enrichment.
33 [1996] AC 669; [1996] 2 All ER 961, 988.
34 *Rochefoucauld v Boustead* [1897] 1 Ch 196: on which see para 1.4.13.

a defendant is permitted by a statutory provision, or a rule of common law, to receive a payment of money as a result of being red-headed. If the defendant had worn a red wig to fool the payer into thinking that she fell within the category of red-headed people, the common law might permit the defendant to keep the money on a literal interpretation of the rule. However, equity would prevent the defendant from manipulating that statute for fraudulent purposes on the basis that to allow the defendant to do so would be unconscionable.[35] *Westdeutsche Landesbank v Islington LBC*[36] re-asserts this basic principle of good conscience.[37] A substantial part of the argument of this book is that it is only the traditional equitable notion of focusing on the conscience of the defendant which can make trusts law coherent.[38]

1.1.4 The many senses of conscience

Conscience in equity

The task of establishing a meaning for the term 'conscience' will be, as we shall see throughout the course of this book, an interesting one. The genesis of the term 'conscience' in this context is in the early statements of the English jurists that the Courts of Equity were courts of conscience[39] and, more significantly, that the Lord Chancellor was the keeper of the monarch's conscience. The post of Lord Chancellor was frequently referred to as the position of 'Lord Keeper'[40] and, by way of example, Sir Christopher Hatton[41] in particular was known during his time in the position as being 'the Keeper of the Queen's Conscience' during a part of the reign of Elizabeth I. In other words, the rules of equity are historically taken to be the application of the monarch's personal power to dispense justice and to ensure that good conscience was enforced in that way. As is discussed in Chapter 32,[42] these Lords Chancellor were bishops and therefore the 'conscience' with which they were concerned was more a religious conscience than a legal conscience until the beginning of the 17th century.[43] The conscience which concerns equity now is a secular idea of conscience.

While Lord Browne-Wilkinson has stated the law as it exists today in *Westdeutsche Landesbank v Islington LBC*,[44] there are many reasons to comment on, and even criticise, that decision and the direction in which the substantive law has been pointed.[45] As will be explored below, there may be a number of contexts in which this standard of 'conscience' will not be easy to apply in all contexts. In particular, it is unclear whether or not a single standard can be created which will cater, for example, both for commercial cases involving cross-border financial transactions and for family cases involving rights to the home. If his

---

35 *Ibid*, exemplifying the principle that equity will prevent statute being used as an engine of fraud, discussed at para 1.4.13.
36 [1996] AC 669.
37 This author has considered that case in detail in another book: Hudson, 1999:1. Many of the themes in that book are rehearsed in this one.
38 See the essay which comprises Chapter 32 of this book in this regard.
39 As noted by Meagher, Gummow and Lehane, 2002, 3.
40 Thomas, 1976, 506.
41 Lord Chancellor from 1587–1591.
42 See in particular the discussion of the term 'conscience' in section 32.2.
43 The Lord Keeper appointed by James I was the first non-ecclesiastic: Thomas, 1976, 506.
44 [1996] AC 669.
45 Hudson, 1999:1.

Lordship did not intend to create a single standard but rather to erect a concept which will be applied differently in different contexts, it is not always immediately clear on what intellectual bases those different notions of conscience are to be constructed. This book seeks to explain how this jurisdiction of conscience should be understood today and how it operates in practice.

Nevertheless, the underpinning concept of that judgment is that equity is concerned with acting on the conscience of a defendant on a case-by-case basis.[46] That means equity is an ethical response which English courts will deploy in circumstances in which other legal rules would otherwise allow a defendant to act unconscionably. Equity will turn to the many claims and remedies considered in this book to address the rights and wrongs of such cases. One of the more sophisticated instruments in equity's armoury is the trust, which will form the main focus of this book and which is introduced in detail in Chapter 2.[47]

The idea of a conscience in general terms

Much of the confusion about the idea of conscience among modern commentators is based on two phenomena. First, those commentators tend to prefer a form of law which is rigid and laid out in a clear framework, even though it is the experience of every legal system that factual situations will always be generated which defy those tight rules and which instead require the courts to reach just conclusions in exceptional cases. What those commentators overlook is how equity operates in reliance both on 'high-level principles' (i.e. general principles which supply the general goals which the law is seeking to achieve, rather than detailed rules) and also on detailed rules which have been developed by centuries of precedent. Their caricature of equity as something which is entirely discretionary is simply a caricature. Second, those commentators fail to understand what a conscience is. Their assumption is that a conscience is an entirely random and entirely subjective phenomenon which is unique to each individual mind. That is not the view of psychiatrists or psychoanalysts. For example, Freud[48] and Jung[49] both conceived of the conscience as something which sits *outside* the conscious mind and calls the conscious mind to account. It is also a staple of English literature. Shakespeare's character The Fool in *King Lear* is the equivalent of a court jester, but that character was an important part of central European literature (from which Shakespeare borrowed) in that The Fool did not simply tell jokes or sing songs but rather acted as the King's conscience by telling him when he had acted foolishly or immorally or contrary to "nature". Importantly, this conscience is a separate person from the King himself: this was a metaphor for the way in which the conscience exists outside the conscious mind. If you think about how you experience your conscience, it is something which comes to you unbidden and which nags at you. You have no conscious control over the things which do or do not bother your conscience. The conscience is something which is formed objectively in large part, even if you experience it subjectively (after all, hopefully, no one can hear you wrestling with your conscience). The word 'conscience' is an amalgam of 'con' and 'science': literally,

---

46   As exemplified by *Earl of Oxford's Case* (1615) 1 Ch Rep 1.

47   Trusts fall into two types: express trusts (deliberately created for a variety of reasons which will be considered below) and trusts implied by law (comprising constructive trusts and resulting trusts which are imposed by the court on the basis of principles considered below). See para 2.2.3 below.

48   Freud, 1923 and 1930.

49   Jung, 1927.

'knowledge with', or rather knowledge of oneself with oneself. The conscience is experienced subjectively but it is generally understood as being formed objectively. From birth, through childhood and through one's adulthood, we all receive messages constantly about right and wrong from parents, schoolteachers, the media, the legal system, society at large, and so on. The conscience is the product of all of these objective stimuli being internalised so as to produce the individual conscience which we then experience as something deep within our own minds. But the fact that the conscience comes from objective stimuli – that is, from outside the mind – means that it is an entirely coherent proposition that the courts are entitled to judge the contents of a person's conscience. If the contents of the conscience come from the outside world, then it is appropriate for the courts to identify what one's conscience should have prompted one to do and to judge each individual defendant accordingly.

A good example of this arising in the law is the discussion of 'dishonesty' in Chapter 20, where the courts have struggled to decide whether they may objectively decide what a person should have done or whether the individual must be shown to have understood that their behaviour was dishonest. If it was accepted that the conscience which underpins equity is objectively constituted (and only subjectively situated) then it would be entirely appropriate to use an objective concept of what the defendant should have done in the circumstances. This idea of the nature of the conscience is explored in Chapter 32 in detail.[50]

1.1.5 Concepts of equity in ancient Greek philosophy

Professor Maitland, in lectures originally published early in the 20th century,[51] would have had us believe that equity is founded on 'ancient English elements' and rejected the idea that equity was taken from Roman law.[52] In truth, the provenance of the English courts of equity is a mixture of ecclesiastical law and a body of law which, as Maitland suggested, developed in terms of a line of precedent from 1557 onwards.[53] It seems that that is the most appropriate date because that is when the common law courts and the courts of equity began to diverge most clearly when the common law judges rejected Lord Chancellor Thomas More's offer to rein in his frequent issue of injunctions against decisions of common law courts if they would 'mitigate the rigour of the common law'. Before that time, there was some suggestion that the idea of conscience could be found even in the common law, as suggested by the remark 'conscience is aequum et bonum, which is the basis of every law',[54] even in the ancient common law. Nevertheless, the common law courts and the courts of equity began to diverge markedly from the mid-16th century onwards. However, the basis of equity as a counterpoint to the common law is not an idea which should be considered to be simply English. There are echoes of it in the ancient Greek philosophers when, as Douzinas tells us: 'Aristotle argued that equity, *epieikeia*, is the rectification of legal justice *nomos* in so far as the law is defective. Laws are general but "the raw material of human behaviour" is such that it is often impossible to pronounce in general terms'.[55]

---

50 See section 32.2.
51 These lectures were published in 1909 and exist now as Maitland, 1936 in a posthumous second edition.
52 Maitland, 1936, 6.
53 *Ibid*, 8.
54 Reported at Bro Abr *Estates* pl 78, cited by Baker, 2002, 107.
55 Extracts from Aristotle, *Ethics*, taken from Douzinas, 2000, 42.

Aristotle's *Ethics* described equity in the following terms:

> For equity, though superior to justice,[56] is still just . . . justice and equity coincide, and although both are good, equity is superior. What causes the difficulty is the fact that equity is just, but not what is legally just: it is a rectification of legal justice.[57]

In this way, Aristotle considered that equity provides a better form of justice[58] because it provides for a more specific judgment as to right and wrong in individual cases which rectifies any errors or similar unfairness which the common law or statute would otherwise have made. The superiority of equity, on Aristotle's account, emerges in the following passage which continues on from the last quoted passage:

> The explanation of this is that all law is universal,[59] and there are some things about which it is not possible to pronounce rightly in general terms; therefore in cases where it is necessary to make a general pronouncement, but impossible to do so rightly, the law takes account of the majority of cases, though not unaware that in this way errors are made . . . So when the law states a general rule, and a case arises under this that is exceptional, then it is right, where the legislator[60] owing to the generality of his language has erred in not covering that case, to correct the omission by a ruling such as the legislator himself would have given if he had been present there, and as he would have enacted if he had been aware of the circumstances.[61]

It is worth noting that Aristotle refers only to the role of a legislator here, and not to judge-made law in a common law system like that in England and Wales. However, the core point transfers perfectly well: if the common law or a statute has failed to anticipate a particular situation or if it would produce unfairness or allow unconscionability to persist without a remedy, then equity will intervene to correct that universal rule. Aristotle refers to these as 'errors' in the law, which is perhaps simply redolent of a different time when there was nothing like the volume of law nor the breadth of legal rights among all citizens which we see today. Modern society is simply far more complex than Aristotle could ever have imagined; so much so that equity is all the more essential in the modern world. Thus, equity exists to rectify what would otherwise be errors in the application of the law to factual situations in which the judges who developed common law principles or the legislators who created statutes could not have intended. It should be noted that English judges do not quote Aristotle as

---

56 The concept of justice in the work of Aristotle is too complex to consider here. In short, it divides between various forms of justice: justice in distribution, justice in rectification, justice in exchange and mean justice. On these categories of justice see Bostock, 2000; Leyden, 1985. Equity is presented in Aristotle's work as a flexible counterpoint to these formalistic attitudes to justice.

57 Aristotle, 1955, 198, para 1137a17, x.

58 A philosophically loaded term in the Aristotelian tradition but here limited to the context of legal justice as provided for by common law and statute.

59 That is, law aims to set down general principles and not to deal with individual cases.

60 Or judge, for our purposes. It is important to note that Aristotle was thinking about statutes as opposed to judge-made law, although his entire concept of equity assumes the presence of a judicial interpreter of those rules.

61 Aristotle, 1955, 198, para 1137a17, x.

an authority but for the early judges in courts of equity it can be expected that knowledge of Aristotle would have been a part of their education and therefore that those judges are more likely to have had ideas like Aristotle's as part of the warp and weft of their attitudes to law. For example, Lord Ellesmere held the following in the *Earl of Oxford's Case*: 'men's actions are so diverse and infinite that it is impossible to make a general law which may aptly meet with every particular and not fail in some circumstances'.[62] This, it is suggested, is almost identical to the passages quoted from Aristotle immediately above. Therefore, it would seem reasonable to argue that Aristotle's ideas have been one of the philosophical ingredients in the casserole that is equity.

What will be important in this discussion will be the extent to which equity can be concerned to achieve justice, or whether there is some context of 'justice' (as Aristotle suggests) which is outside the purview of equity. So it is that we will consider whether equity can be remodelled so as to achieve justice (in the terms that that concept is conceived by ancient philosophers like Plato and Aristotle)[63] or in terms of social justice as conceived by modern social theorists. Within this debate are potentially competing claims by human rights law and equity to constitute the principles on which the legal system will attempt to provide for fairness in litigation and in the dissemination of socially agreed norms.

1.1.6 Kant's notion of equity

The philosopher Immanuel Kant presented the following notion of equity (or '*aequitas*') in his *The Metaphysics of Morals*:[64]

> *Equity* (considered objectively) is in no way a basis for merely calling upon another to fulfil an ethical duty (to be benevolent and kind). One who demands something on this basis stands instead upon his right, except that he does not have the conditions that a judge needs in order to determine by how much or in what way his claim could be satisfied. Suppose that the terms on which a trading company was formed were that the partners should share equally in the profits,[65] but that one partner nevertheless *did* more than the others and so *lost* more when the company met with reverses. By *equity* he can demand more from the company than merely an equal share with the others. In accordance with proper (strict) right, however, his demand would be refused; for if one thinks of a judge in this case, he would have no definite particulars (*data*) to enable him to decide how much is due by the contract.

---

62 (1615) 1 Ch Rep 1, at 6.
63 See Morrison, 1995.
64 Kant, 1996, 390, para 6:234. Kant lived between 1724 and 1804. The *Metaphysics of Morals* was published in two parts in 1797, having been in preparation since about 1765. The reference here is to the most easily accessible version of this work in print at the time of writing. The emphases in the quoted passages are taken from the original.
65 It should be noted that the form of company considered is the joint stock company which existed also in English law, before the decision in *Saloman v A Saloman & Co Ltd* [1897] AC 22, whereby the members of the company were partners and the company's property was held on trust for the members as beneficiaries by the directors of the company: see Hudson, 2000:1, 107.

This conception of equity does not equate entirely with equity in English law.[66] English equity *does* operate by means of judicial *diktat* so as to require a defendant to act in good conscience and either to refrain from exercising some common law right or to grant some equitable right to the claimant. However, in the example set out by Kant in the passage quoted above, there is no reason to suppose that *in legal terms* there would be any requirement on the other partners to this trading venture to grant the claimant any greater right than he had agreed to by way of contract. Importantly, in this sense, English equity is not concerned to act fairly between people in the sense that everybody must be left entirely happy and have suffered no loss. It will not seek to be 'fair' in the general sense of that word, but instead will tend to deal only with limited categories of act: that is, those acts which are considered in this book. English equity is concerned to ensure that there has been no unconscionable behaviour but, for example, there is nothing *legally* unconscionable in making a profit from someone else's foolishness or naivety, provided that there has neither been any fraud nor undue influence exercised over that naive fool. Importantly, equity also acts on the basis of the doctrine of precedent, in particular in relation to the law on express trusts (as considered in the next chapter). Therefore, the idea of conscience which we will identify with English equity is one which is commercially aware and which may act differently in cases involving ordinary people acting in their private capacities as opposed to cases involving business people acting at arm's length from one another.[67]

So, English equity is not a general means by which people can protest that they have simply lost money or had their hopes dashed if there has not been any action by the defendant which the courts would consider to be blameworthy or unconscionable. What the substantive principles of equity may allow is a claim based on a form of unconscionable behaviour which English equity does recognise. So, for example, a valid claim recognised by the courts might be one brought by a claimant who was induced to invest in a business venture in reliance on a representation made to her by the other partners,[68] or if the other partners made a secret profit from the venture not disclosed to the claimant.[69] In this sense, in accordance with Aristotle's view of equity, the equitable court of conscience takes priority over the strict rules of a common law court.[70]

66 Kant also has a peculiar notion of equity as 'a princess who cannot speak'. This odd idea merges two themes which happen to recur in equity theory in England. First, that there is something 'feminine' about a form of legal thinking which reacts to circumstances by using high-level principles like 'conscience'. Second, the idea that equity reacts to circumstances where there is unfairness but cannot establish legal doctrines positively in itself. This second idea does not reflect English equity at all: equity has created the injunction, the trust, proprietary estoppel, the charge and many other positive, substantive legal doctrines which are considered in this book. Otherwise, this idea of equity as a princess is more arresting than meaningful.
67 See, for example, the discussion of equity of redemption of mortgages where ordinary people are protected against oppressive contractual devices imposed on them by banks and other mortgagees (*Fairclough v Swan Brewery* [1912] AC 565) or, on a different note, the avoidance of liability by a defendant based on its commercial status (*Polly Peck International v Nadir (No 2)* [1992] 4 All ER 769).
68 This may give rise to a claim in proprietary estoppel: see Chapter 13, especially *Gillett v Holt* [2000] 2 All ER 289.
69 This may give rise to a claim in constructive trust: see Chapter 12, especially *Boardman v Phipps* [1967] 2 AC 46.
70 Compare, in this regard, the equitable maxim that equity follows the law (in para 1.4.2) and the principle derived from *Earl of Oxford's Case* (1615) 1 Ch Rep 1 that equity may nevertheless override common law principles.

1.1.7 Equity as a moral virtue

The general principles of equity, in applying the letter of the law to the circumstances of individual citizens, pre-date the medieval Lords Chancellor through whose offices the various claims and actions applied in the modern Courts of Chancery were developed. It is important to recall that neither Aristotle nor Hegel are authorities in English law, nor have their ideas tended to be cited generally or directly by English judges as legal authorities.[71] However, they do provide an intellectual framework into which many approaches to equity can be placed. Study of the philosophy of the ancient Greeks was long a part of the intellectual furniture of the educated classes in England. Therefore, it should come as no surprise that there is some similarity between the writings of Aristotle on justice and the principles developed by the English judiciary over the centuries, even if one does not cite the other explicitly. Consider, for example, the following description of equity provided in 1705 by Lord Chancellor Cowper:

> Now equity is no part of the [common] law, but a moral virtue, which qualifies, moderates, and reforms the rigour, hardness, and edge of the law, and is an universal truth; it does also assist the law where it is defective and weak in the constitution (which is the life of the law) and defends the law from crafty evasions, delusions, and new subtleties, invested and contrived to evade and delude the common law, whereby such as have undoubted right are made remediless: and this is the office of equity, to support and protect the common law from shifts and crafty contrivances against the justice of the law. Equity therefore does not destroy the law, nor create it, but assist it.[72]

What is significant about this description of equity is that it considers equity itself to be a moral virtue. This is similar in tone to Aristotle's approach to equity as a means of preventing any unfairness which might otherwise result from the rigid application of formal legal rules. Perhaps it could be observed that Lord Cowper was speaking in a different age from that in which Lord Nottingham began the formulation of the more technically-minded equity which we know today.[73] However, it should not be forgotten that for many equity jurists, the assertion that its principles are 'an universal truth' is a very significant part of the legal concept of equity.[74]

Equity has a long tradition: this book will aim to highlight its remnants in its modern application. The text which follows will consider the modern uses of equity and in particular the core principles of equity to which modern courts still have recourse. The important first task is to consider the birth of those principles of equity before anything else will make any sense.

---

71 Cf *Jones v Maynard* [1951] Ch 572, 575, *per* Vaisey J, considering Plato's notion of equality; see para 1.4.8.
72 *Lord Dudley v Lady Dudley* (1705) Prec Ch 241, 244, *per* Lord Cowper LC. The same passage is cited similarly in Snell's *Equity*, 2, although attributed to Sir Nathan Wright LK.
73 A good example of this tension is the discussion of the speeches of Lords Browne-Wilkinson and Goff in *Tinsley v Milligan* [1994] 1 AC 340, considered in detail in para 11.4.6, where the former grants an equitable interest in property on a purely technical basis whereas the latter sought to deny such an interest on the basis that the claimant had committed immoral acts and therefore should not be granted equity's aid.
74 See, for example, a range of writers including Lord Kaims, *Principles of Equity*, 1778, 41; I Spry, 2001, 1; and McGhee, 2005, paras 1–01 and 1–03.

1.2 THE BIRTH OF EQUITY

1.2.1 The development of two systems: common law and equity

It is impossible to understand any part of English law without understanding English history first. Even the geographic jurisdiction covered by this discussion is the result of history. The genesis of English polity and the structure of its legal system are generally understood to be the result of the Norman invasion of 1066 by which William I seized control of the entire kingdom. The composition of that kingdom had itself been the result of hundreds of years of consolidation of warring tribes. The development of England and Wales as a single legal jurisdiction results from hundreds of years of wars of conquest fought by the insurgent English against the Welsh. Scotland retained its own, distinct legal system despite the Act of Union of 1707. Now, the history of any part of English law is always subject to debate because documentary proof of these matters is difficult to find. Professor Story, in his 19th century American history of equity,[75] describes the court of equity as being 'an original and fundamental court, as ancient as the kingdom itself'.[76] The role of a 'chancellor' is identified in the Roman law tradition as a form of secretary or chief scribe, and as an official used by the Saxon kings in England, and also across the Catholic church in the Roman tradition.[77] However, for present purposes, nothing will be gained by casting our historical net too broadly – instead, I shall begin with the events of the 11th century which are generally taken in our understanding of English law and equity as constituting a sufficiently significant breaking point in the historical chain.

The Norman Conquest is therefore vitally important. It forms the point in time at which the Normans introduced an entirely new legal system to England. This law was common to the whole of the kingdom. Arguably, it was the first time that the kingdom had had such a single legal system.[78] Hence the term 'common law' was coined to mean this new system of legal principle created by the English courts which was *common* to the entire realm, rather than being a patchwork of tribal customs applied unevenly. It is thought that the term 'common law' itself derives from the ecclesiastical term '*ius commune*' which was used to describe the law administered by the Catholic church.[79]

Henry II created the courts of King's Bench to hear matters otherwise brought before the Crown. From these early, medieval courts the principles of the common law began.[80] Rights were founded and obligations created as a result of the decisions of these early courts. There remained, however, a right to petition the King directly if it was thought that the decision of the common law court was unfair or unjust. So, for example, a tenant of land who was unjustly dealt with in the court of his local lord could seek a remedy directly from the King if he was unsatisfied with the decision of the court. For the monarchy this provided an important safeguard against the power of these courts by reserving the ultimate control over the administration of justice to the person of the monarch. However, the proliferation of suits

---

75 Story, *Equity Jurisprudence*, 1st edn, 1835; 13th edn, 1886.
76 Quoting Lord Hobart, *ibid*, para 40.
77 *Ibid*.
78 'Arguably' in the sense that some would point to King Alfred as having been the first to attempt to introduce a single system of law to much of England.
79 Maitland, 1936, 2.
80 It has been suggested also that the Lords Chancellor sat on the earliest common law courts, and so the jurisdiction of Courts of Chancery was as ancient as any other.

that were brought directly before the King eventually required the creation of a separate mechanism for hearing them. Otherwise the King would be permanently diverted from important matters like war, hunting and effecting felicitous marriages. It should also be remembered that, for these Norman kings, England was a distraction from their main business of protecting their lands in what is now France and elsewhere in Europe.

During the medieval period the position of Lord Chancellor was created, among other things, to hear those petitions which would otherwise have been taken directly to the monarch. The medieval Lord Chancellor was empowered to issue royal writs on behalf of the Crown through the use of the Great Seal, but gradually acquired power to hear petitions directly during the 13th and 14th centuries. As a result the Lord Chancellor's discretion broadened, until some lawyers began to comment that it had begun to place too much power in the hands of one person.[81] It is also interesting to note that the courts of equity did not necessarily concern themselves with strict legal rules at all but instead concerned themselves with inquiring specifically into the defendant's conscience: so, for example, Fortescue CJ declared in 1452 that '[w]e are to argue conscience here, not the law'.[82] Selden is reputed to have said: 'Equity is a roguish thing. For [common] law we have a measure . . . equity is according to the conscience of him that is Chancellor, and as that is longer or narrower, so is equity. 'Tis all one as if they should make the standard for the measure a Chancellor's foot.'[83] This statement implied that Lords Chancellor were thought to ignore precedent and to decide what judgments to make entirely in accordance with their own caprice. The Courts of Chancery were typically comprised only of the Lord Chancellor and his assistant, the Master of the Rolls, until 1813 when the first Vice-Chancellor was appointed.[84] Since that time the rules of equity, and in particular the rules relating to the law of trusts, have become far more rigidified[85] – a tendency which will be considered in detail in this book.[86]

The Lord Chancellor was a politician first and foremost. In truth, before Robert Walpole became the first Prime Minister in 1741, it was the Lord Chancellor who would have been considered the 'prime minister' to the Crown.[87] It was the Lord Chancellor who would summon defendants to appear before him to justify their behaviour. This jurisdiction of the Lord Chancellor, which was hotly contested, arose from the range of writs which he would serve even after a court of common law had given judgment: in fact, the Lord Chancellor would be concerned to ensure that the individual defendant had behaved properly and would not be seeking to overturn any *rule* of the common law. Nevertheless, by the time of James I it was required that the King intercede to decree once and for all that it was the Courts of Equity which took priority.[88] The early Lords Chancellor were all clerics: that is, they were bishops who were Keepers of the King's Conscience.[89] Latterly, the Lords Chancellor were secular appointments, some of whom were attracted to the post by the profits which were available to

---

81 For an account of the sort of issues which the office of Lord Chancellor created at this time see Thomas, 1976, 506.
82 Mitch 31 Hen VI, Fitz Abr, *Subpena*, pl 23, cited by Baker, 2002, 108.
83 *Table Talk of John Selden*, 1927.
84 There were no official, methodical law reports of Chancery cases before 1557: Maitland, 1936, 8.
85 Croft, 1989, 29.
86 See in particular Chapter 7.
87 Meagher, Heydon and Leeming, 2002, 3.
88 *Earl of Oxford's Case* (1615) Ch Rep 1.
89 Thomas, 1976.

the less scrupulous holders of the post. Indeed the Georgian Lords Chancellor used to charge for the award of the positions of Master in the Courts of Chancery. The Earl of Macclesfield, when Lord Chancellor, was convicted by the House of Lords of embezzling court funds in the early 18th century.[90] We should not allow the irony of a person who sat as the sole judge in the court of conscience accepting 'presents',[91] either from litigants or from people who wished to sit as judges, to escape us. By today's standards the courts in this period were very corrupt.

The writs that the Lord Chancellor served were processed by his administrative department known as the Chancery.[92] The Chancery was therefore simply an administrative department concerned with dealing with petitions sent to it by Parliament[93] and with sending out the monarch's writs under seal.[94] Over time, the Lord Chancellor personally began to hear all of the petitions which would ordinarily have been brought before the monarch. From this beginning, the role of the Chancellor expanded, particularly in the person of Cardinal Wolsey in the reign of Henry VIII. The Chancery emerged as a force in parallel to the Court of Star Chamber[95] particularly during those dark, intolerant days in English history surrounding the Reformation:[96] the former concerned with ordinary equity, and the latter with 'criminal equity'.[97] In time, the number of petitions brought before the Lord Chancellor became so numerous that a separate system of courts was created to hear those cases: the Courts of Chancery. It is thought that the Chancery was so called because its first room had a latticed partition known as a 'cancelli' – hence, after some minor adaptation of pronunciation and spelling, the term 'chancery' emerged.[98] Another explanation suggested by Coke was that it derived from the term 'cancellarius' relating to the cancellation of the King's letters patent.[99] It was in these Courts of Chancery that the principles of equity were developed. The position of Lord Chancellor has encompassed the constitutionally confusing roles of House of Lords judge, politically-appointed Cabinet minister and speaker of the House of Lords. This position has changed with the creation of the Supreme Court by means of the Constitutional Reform Act 2005. These changes have had no effect on the substance of equity.

90 See eg, Hibbert, 1957, 126.
91 As Baker refers to these payments: Baker, 2002.
92 These writs were subject to a subpoena which meant, quite literally, that the defendant was called to appear on pain of suffering a financial penalty for non-appearance.
93 In existence between 1485 and 1641 sitting in permanent session – unlike Parliament – and comprising both the Privy Council and the Chief Justices: thereby constituting the most important power base in the country and used to police the opinions and activities of the seditious or the otherwise untrustworthy.
94 In Hale's account, this was the beginning of the Chancery jurisdiction: see Story, 1886, para 42.
95 Baker, 2002, 101.
96 Any number of standard historical works will explain the level of religious intolerance and persecution of individuals through the reigns particularly of Henry VIII, Mary I and Elizabeth I. The Star Chamber seems to have commenced its activities some time between 1347 and 1487. The name 'star chamber' arose because this group sat in a chamber in Westminster with stars on the ceiling – hence 'star chamber'. At the outset this group dealt both with state matters and with pleas for justice. Its membership was the same as the monarch's Privy Council for most of its history. It is most (in)famous, however, for its activities in the early seventeenth century (most particularly in the 1630s) in persecuting alleged traitors and insurgents, both in trying and in executing them.
97 Maitland, 1936, 19, explaining that, fraud apart, Chancery took no interest in criminal matters, whereas Star Chamber had jurisdiction over many criminal and seditious practices.
98 Holland, 1945, 17.
99 Although, in truth, many courts gave effect to principles which will be defined as equitable in this book (ie, to promote fairness) outside the Courts of Chancery even before 1875: Meagher, Heydon and Leeming, 2002, 5.

1.2.2 The continuing distinction between equity and common law

In order to understand English law at the beginning of the new millennium it is vitally important to understand that there used to be two completely distinct sets of courts in England, and
therefore two completely distinct systems of law: common law and Equity.[100] This position
continued until the enactment of the Judicature Act 1873 which removed the need to sue in
common law courts for a common law remedy, and so forth. However, even though the
physical separation of the two codes of principles into separate systems of courts was
removed in 1873, the intellectual separation of the principles remains.

The distinction between equity and the common law was both practically and intellectually significant before the Judicature Act 1873. Before that Act came into full effect in 1875
it was necessary for a litigant to decide whether her claim related to common law or to
equity. To select the wrong jurisdiction would mean that the claim would be thrown out and
sent to the other court. So, if a claim for an equitable remedy were brought before a common
law court, that common law court would dismiss the claim and the claimant would be
required to go to the Court of Equity instead. This problem is explained in Charles Dickens's
Bleak House in the following way: 'Equity sends questions to Law, Law sends questions
back to Equity; Law finds it can't do this, Equity finds it can't do that; neither can so much
as say it can't do anything, without this solicitor instructing and this counsel appearing . . .'
And so it was that the litigant trudged disconsolately between the various courts seeking
someone who could deliver judgment on her claim. The result of the Judicature Act 1873
was that the *practical* distinction between common law and equity disappeared. However, it
is vitally important to understand that the *intellectual* distinction remains. As considered
below, there remains a division between certain claims and remedies which are available
only at common law, and other claims and remedies available only in equity.

The principles of equity remain subject to their own logic, and common law claims to
their own logic, even though all courts are now empowered to apply both systems of rules.
In practice, the Chancery Division of the High Court will still hear matters primarily relating
to trusts and property law, whereas the Queen's Bench Division of the High Court will hear
traditionally common law issues such as the interpretation of contracts or matters concerning
the law of tort. The reason for this allocation of responsibility has to do with the expertise of
the judges in each field, but it has resulted in the perpetuation of particular modes of thought
in the different divisions of the High Court.

The key point to take from this discussion is that nothing will make sense unless we
understand that there is an important distinction to be made between, on the one hand,
common law and, on the other, equity. The two systems operate in parallel but must not be
confused one with the other.

1.2.3 The impact of the distinction between common law and equity

The main result of the distinction between common law and equity is that each has distinct
claims and distinct remedies. Common law is the system which is able to award cash
damages for loss. This is the pre-eminent common law remedy, for example in cases
concerning breach of contract or the tort of negligence. On the other hand, a claimant seeking

---

100 Story, 1886, para 40.

an injunction must rely on equity because the injunction is an equitable remedy awarded at the court's discretion, in line with the specific principles considered in Chapter 31.

Suppose the following set of facts. Arthur enters into a contract with Sunderland Association Football Club (SAFC) to deliver five footballs to SAFC each Saturday morning before a home game, in return for payment of £1,000 in advance each month. Suppose that SAFC paid £1,000 in advance for delivery in August, but Arthur then refused to make the delivery. Suppose then that SAFC was required to spend an extra £1,000 to acquire those footballs from another supplier. SAFC have two issues to be resolved. First, SAFC will wish to recover from Arthur the £1,000 spent on acquiring footballs from the alternative supplier. Secondly, SAFC will wish to force Arthur to carry out its contractual undertaking or to repay the £1,000 paid in advance.

The first issue is resolved by a common law claim for damages to recover the £1,000 lost in acquiring alternative footballs.

The second issue, however, will be resolved by a claim for specific performance (an equitable remedy) of the contractual obligation to supply footballs. The second claim will be at the discretion of the court. If Arthur had gone into insolvency, it would be unreasonable, and legally probably impossible depending on the administration of the insolvency, to force Arthur to perform the contract. Alternatively, if it could be shown that both parties had been operating under a mistake as to the number of footballs to be provided, it might be that a court would think it unfair to enforce the contract. In such a situation, the equitable jurisdiction gives the court the discretion to award another remedy, even though the ordinary law of contract would suggest that the contract must be enforced once it is validly created. Equity may decide to order the contract void on grounds of mistake instead and thus rescind it.[101]

Therefore, it is necessary to make a distinction between common law and equity. The division might be rendered diagrammatically as shown in the table below. The detail of the available remedies is considered below and variously through this book. What is apparent from this list is that it is only in equity that it is possible to receive tailor-made awards of specific performance or rescission in relation to contracts, or to take effective control over property. The common law is organised principally around awards of money in relation to loss by means of damages, or recovery of specific, identifiable property by means of common law tracing, and the common law claim of 'money had and received' in relation to specifically identifiable payments of money. Therefore, the common law is concerned with return of particular property or with making good loss, unlike the more complex claims and remedies which are available in equity.

Common law	Equity
Examples of claims:	
Breach of contract	Breach of trust
Negligence	Tracing property
Fraud	Claiming property on insolvency
Examples of remedies and responses available:	
Damages	Compensation
Common law tracing	Equitable tracing

101 As considered in section 11.5.

Money had and received	Specific performance
	Injunction
	Rescission
	Rectification
	Imposition of constructive trust
	Imposition of resulting trust
	Subrogation
	Account
	Lien
	Charge (fixed and floating)
	Specific restitution

The impression we might take from this list is that equity is much more creative than the common law. The principal common law remedy is the award of damages, whereas equity has created many more remedies and doctrines.

1.2.4 The Judicature Act 1873

It is worth observing that before 1813 there was only one full judge for chancery matters: that was the Lord Chancellor. Consequently, it could take an enormously long time for a case to be heard before that one judge. The Lord Chancellor was assisted by the Master of the Rolls, who in time acquired judicial status.[102] It was only early in the 19th century that the weight of cases waiting to be heard by these two people led to the appointment of a Vice-Chancellor for the first time, and later to the appointment of two Vice-Chancellors. Through this passage of time, however, the popular conception of equity – and one which accords with the reality – was that the chancery courts were expensive and caused extraordinary delays. Charles Dickens's novel *Bleak House* was in part a polemic against the antiquated workings of the chancery courts, with its opening metaphor which presented those courts as being clouded in a dense fog, and an exploration of the hardship which endless chancery procedures caused to those people whose homes and wealth were dependent upon judicial decisions. It should also be recalled, as outlined above, that Lord Macclesfield was convicted of embezzlement while acting as Lord Chancellor and Lord Bacon was also found to have accepted 'presents' (which today we would consider to be bribes) in office.[103] So, the reputation of the chancery courts was far from spotless.

By 1873 pressure had built to change the court structure.[104] Two particular objectives were pursued: one to fuse equity and common law, and the second to reorganise the courts. Whereas there had previously been many different courts operating separately from one another (including probate courts, the Queen's Bench common law courts, and so on), the High Court was organised into a single court but with a number of divisions specialising in different areas: such as the Chancery Division, the Queen's Bench Division, and so on.

---

102   That is, the Master of the Rolls appeared at first to have been merely a clerk, later a judge in chancery matters, and after 1873 a presiding judge within the new Court of Appeal.

103   Bribes of this sort were taken from people wishing judicial office for themselves or some salaried post in the gift of the Lord Chancellor. It is more difficult to divine from the sources whether or not presents were also received from litigants. These were, nevertheless, criminal acts even at that time.

104   A very full account of this history is presented by Meagher, Gummow and Lehane, 2002, 41 *et seq*.

Briefly put, the fusion of common law and equity took the shape of permitting any court to award common law remedies or equitable remedies without the need to petition one particular court or another.[105] Instead proceedings were simply begun in the High Court. Similarly, the Court of Appeal became a single court (albeit with many judges) as opposed to having a separate Court of Appeal solely for equity matters. The Appellate Jurisdiction Act 1876 retained a right of appeal to the House of Lords. Significantly section 25 of the Supreme Court of Judicature Act 1873 provided:

> Generally, in all matters not hereinbefore particularly mentioned in which there is any conflict or variance between the rules of equity and the rules of common law with reference to the same matter, the rules of equity shall prevail.

Thus the principles of equity prevail over the principles of common law. The decision in the *Earl of Oxford's Case* thus received a statutory form. So, in cases like *Walsh v Lonsdale*[106] where there was a clash between a failure to comply with a common law rule as to the proper creation of a lease (which would have held the lease to be unenforceable) and the equitable doctrine of specific performance of contracts, it was held that the equitable principle of specific performance would give effect to the agreement to provide a lease.

The passage of this legislation was not without its own perturbations. This fusion of common law and equity raised concerns from many equity practitioners. Previously, practitioners and judges before the chancery courts had been specialists in equity. Now, or so the argument ran, there would be practitioners and judges dealing with the culturally different principles of equity who had only previously been trained in common law. Such people referred to this process of fusion of common law and equity as being, in truth, a confusion of common law with equity. Whether or not that has turned out to be the case can only be established from a study of the materials in this book. There has not, it is suggested, been any obvious step-change between the rigidification of the principles of equity under Lord Eldon and the decisions reached after the 1873 Act. Equity clearly functions now on the basis of the doctrine of precedent, but that is not due in particular to the 1873 Act. As considered below the intellectual sophistication necessary to reach judgments on the basis of conscience on a case-by-case basis and yet in accordance with general principles has emerged in the late 20th century and at the beginning of the 21st century, as considered at the end of the next section.

1.3 UNDERSTANDING EQUITY

1.3.1 Equity: an ethical construct

At its root, equity is concerned to prevent a defendant from acting unconscionably (literally, contrary to conscience) in circumstances in which the common law would otherwise allow the defendant to do so. To put that point another way, the courts will intervene to stop a fraudster, shyster or wrongdoer from taking advantage of the rights of another person. I rather like the term 'shyster' because it is vague enough to cover a broad range of people,

---

105   Judicature Act 1873, s 24.
106   (1882) 21 Ch D 9.

from those who may be deliberately committing fraud, to those who are not acting entirely honestly without being fraudulent, and even to cover those who are carelessly acting in a way which would do harm to others. In each case, the shyster is acting in a way which we would consider to be unconscionable. So we will use the term 'shyster' for present purposes to cover the perpetrators of all of those various activities.

Equity is therefore interfering to protect some underlying right of the victim either because of a contract with the shyster, or because the shyster has control over some property which is rightfully the victim's, or because we can assume that the actions of the shyster will affect the victim in the future in some way. In any of these cases, equity will attempt to intervene to stop the shyster from acting unconscionably. It will then impose a remedy which both prevents the shyster's wrongdoing and compensates the victim for any consequential loss.

Aside from the discussion of the manner in which this form of claim and remedy operates, there is a question as to the underlying purpose behind this code of principles. Evidently, there is an ethical programme at work here. Most civil code jurisdictions (such as France, Italy and Germany) have a different division in their jurisprudence which is aimed at reaching the same results. Typically on the model suggested by Roman law, they will divide between cases to do with consensual actions (akin to English contract), cases to do with wrongs (akin to English torts) and cases to do with unjustified enrichment. It is this final category which operates as a rough comparator to equity. To prevent unconscionable behaviour there is a catch-all category which enables a claimant to claim that something which would otherwise appear lawful on its face should nevertheless be declared void on account of some factor like fraud, mistake or misrepresentation. This distinction is the root of the ideological conflict between traditional trusts law and the law of restitution, considered in detail in the essays at the end of this book.[107]

1.3.2 Equity acts *in personam*

The core of the equitable jurisdiction is the principle that it acts *in personam*. That means that a Court of Equity is concerned to prevent any given individual from acting unconscionably. The Court of Equity is therefore making an order, based on the facts of an individual case, to prevent that particular defendant from continuing to act unconscionably. If that person does not refrain, she will be in contempt of court. The order, though, is addressed to that person in respect of the particular issue complained of. It is best thought of as a form of judicial control of that particular person's conscience.[108]

The study of equity is concerned with the isolation of the principles upon which judges in particular cases seek to exercise their discretion. It is a complex task to find common threads between different cases in which judges are reaching decisions on the basis of the particular facts before them. Therefore, it is always important for the student to *read* the leading cases and the anomalous cases in the law reports to understand *the reasons why* judges have reached particular conclusions.

---

107 Section 31.3.
108 The distinction between an *in personam* and an *in rem* action in this context is that an action *in personam* in equity binds only the particular defendant, whereas an action *in rem* would bind any successors in title or assignees from the defendant (other than the *bona fide* purchaser for value of any property at issue).

1.3.3 The nature of equity: paradox and cool jazz

The paradox at the heart of equity

Equity is paradoxical: it appears to grant the courts a large discretion to address unconscionability while at the same time it is governed by the doctrine of precedent. (This idea is explored in detail in Chapter 7.) Different doctrines within equity operate differently. For example, express trusts (considered in Part 2) are organised by reference to principles of certainty and the sort of rules which will be familiar from contract law; whereas doctrines like injunctions or equitable estoppel are avowedly open-textured and flexible. Nevertheless, both types of equitable doctrine are predicated on the doctrine of precedent and central principles identified by the higher courts (or occasionally by statute). Some commentators find these different aspects of equity difficult to understand. The truth is that equity is like cool jazz.

Equity is like cool jazz

In *Time* magazine,[109] a review of The Dave Brubeck Five described their brand of 'cool' jazz in the following terms:

> It is tremendously complex, but free. It flows along, improvising constantly but yet it is held together by a firm pattern. . . . The essence is the tension between improvisation and order; between freedom and discipline.

It seems to me that this is an ideal description of equity at its finest. Equity exhibits a tension between order and flexibility. To its denigrators, equity is disorganised, chaotic and unprincipled; to its adherents it exhibits clear patterns in compliance with subtle but meaningful principles. The adherents have simply understood the field better than its denigrators – they have understood the subtlety of its method. As Lord Jessel MR explained in *Re Hallett's Estate*,[110] equity is not beyond child-bearing: meaning that it is capable of creating new doctrines and, consequently, that it is capable of meeting new challenges in new ways. This is evident in the growth of doctrines such as constructive trusts and proprietary estoppel in recent years, and the invention of completely new doctrines such as the super-injunction. Each appears to operate entirely freely but in truth each is bound by clear principles which operate sensibly in practice.

The outcome, it is suggested, is like improvised jazz: a combination of ideas and techniques into a comprehensive whole, exhibiting both an order which is bound together by a particular kind of intellectual rigour and yet a freedom which is appropriate to the moment. Improvised jazz is not a completely random collection of notes played on a whim. Instead, jazz musicians respond to a firm pattern and to established musical understandings so as to create new expressions of their art in any given situation. Equity is similar. It is not simply a collection of random judicial pronouncements, but rather it is a body of jurisprudence which is organised around a nuanced and subtle application of a central principle of 'conscience'.

---

109 'The Man on Cloud No.7', *Time*, 8 November 1954.
110 (1880) 13 Ch D 696.

In consequence, it is tremendously complex because it is built on centuries of case law; but it is free in that the courts are able to generate new doctrines and to adapt or apply old ones when the circumstances or social norms require. In that sense it improvises constantly, but its use of case law precedent and the careful application of principle to individual circumstances ensures that it is held together by a firm pattern. Throughout a study of this subject, you will sense a tension between different judges, between different commentators and between different cases such that there will be innovation and improvisation in some circumstances, and rigid adherence to precedent in others. Understanding rules which are strictly adhered to (such as certainty of subject matter and certainty of objects in Chapter 3) and rules which permit fluidity (such as equitable estoppel, for the most part, in Chapter 13) is part of coming to understand the subject.

When one listens to good jazz, there is a large amount of freedom. Often some musicians hold a tight rhythm while other musicians are free to experiment and to follow their technically proficient impulses. In so doing, they are following established understandings of how the music works or using pre-existing musical phrases. So, by way of example, in Miles Davis's album *Sketches of Spain*,[111] Davis and his fellow musicians took their inspiration from well-known Spanish folk music and blended it into their jazz compositions. The recorded work was built on their own patterns and on the patterns of specific pieces of Spanish folk music, but so that Davis and others could improvise in ways which were in keeping with that general context. Miles Davis did not simply play random notes. Rather, years of practice and many long hours of those musicians playing together meant that they developed a musical language in which their improvisation could operate both coherently and fluently. That album was the third in a sequence which those musicians had produced for Columbia Records. There was improvisation but it was built on a musical language which they had developed; just as equity may appear to improvise but it is built on a legal language which has been developed by means of centuries of jurisprudence.

The same is true of language itself. In Chapter 7, I suggest that equity is very like the English language. For a non-native speaker, English appears to be a confusing series of idioms with very few formalised grammatical rules or taxonomies in the form of declensions and conjugations, unlike many continental European languages, for example. However, for a native English speaker, when someone breaks the subtle and numerous grammatical rules which actually do exist then that jars against the ear.[112] Non-native speakers can sometimes sling English idioms together randomly, and it is only the natural reticence of the English which stops them from interrupting and issuing a correction. The native English speaker assimilates the rules that do exist from birth, and similarly comes to absorb the more nuanced rules of good English from childhood. Equity is much the same. While on its surface it may appear to be less ordered than the common law,[113] in truth it is comprised of many principles and rules which will be closely observed by an equity specialist. In that sense it is quintessentially English, just like the English language.

---

111   Miles Davis, *Sketches of Spain*, Columbia Records, 1960.
112   Assuming that speaker is not a footballer, or in any way associated with professional football.
113   Although, it is suggested, the supposed orderliness of the common law is much over-hyped (consider the law on mistake in contract law, for example); and complaints about equity being disordered are usually made by those who have not immersed themselves in the culture of the subject sufficiently well.

1.3.4 Roots in trade and in the family

So the question arises: where do the morals underpinning equity come from? They are not morals in an avowedly political, or even an explicitly philosophical sense.[114] Rather, judges are generally careful to talk about 'legal principle' as though it were some arena of thought divorced from politics, philosophy and all of the other paraphernalia with which human beings seek to impose order on a chaotic world. Equity, and the trust in particular, has been developed primarily in relation to two contexts: trade and the family.

Trade and equity

The history of the city of London stands as a useful mirror to the development of equity. Having been abandoned when Boudicca razed the Roman city to the ground, it was the Saxons' development of London (or Lyndwych) as a trading port which saw the city grow in importance again. The Tudors, and in particular Henry VIII, were instrumental in promoting trade between England's capital city and other trading ports. London continues to flourish as a financial and commercial centre today due in no small part to the experience in such matters of the legal system and its personnel.

Consequently, the common law developed to regulate commercial transactions and so forth. At the same time, equity was required to develop to provide a means of resolving disputes which arose out of that commercial activity but which the common law was not able to manage. Therefore, many of the core principles of equity (considered immediately below) concerned the avoidance of transactions procured by means of fraud and so forth. The minimisation of fraud has remained a key principle of equity. It has also ensured that equity is less well-developed in areas which do not involve fraud or something akin to it. Much of the more difficult case law in the 1990s considered in detail in this book is founded on situations involving mistakes and misrepresentations which were not properly capable of being described as fraudulent. Equity has had more difficulty in applying its principles to morally ambiguous cases than to straightforward circumstances involving good old-fashioned lying and deceit. Indeed, when considering modern banking transactions it is very difficult to know whether or not a banker who knowingly makes a large profit from the inexperience or dim-wittedness of her counterparty ought to be considered to have acted unconscionably. It is far easier to find that she has acted in bad conscience if she can be proved to have lied rather than simply to have engaged in lawful but sharp business practice. However, this is probably just a result of the world having become more complex than any defect in equity.

The family and equity

The other context in which these rules have developed is that of the family. Much of the history of English law has seen one rule for the rich and another for the poor. Quite literally, there were once different courts for rich people and for poor people, so that the working class would not come to know of the imperfections in the characters of their supposed social betters. Many would say that the limited availability of legal aid and the high cost of court proceedings means that, even in the 21st century, there is effectively one law for the rich and another for the rest.[115]

---

114 Even though the roots of equity have been traced to major philosophical systems in section 1.1 above.
115 See Hudson, 1999:2, for a discussion of the modern context of these issues.

It was these well-to-do families, the principal focus of Jane Austen novels like *Pride and Prejudice*, who sought to use trusts and equity to organise succession to their family fortunes. Typically, wealthy families would arrange marriages between their offspring and then create family trusts to administer the property and dowries of each party to the marriage. The rules of the law of trusts therefore developed as a part of equity to administer these situations.

The House of Lords has raised the question in recent cases as to whether the existing principles of equity and trusts are suitable to cope with the broad variety of life in the modern world. As Lord Browne-Wilkinson expressed his view in *Target Holdings v Redferns*:[116]

> In the modern world the trust has become a valuable device in commercial and financial dealings. The fundamental principles of equity apply as much to such trusts as they do to the traditional trusts in relation to which those principles were originally formulated. But in my judgment it is important, if the trust is not to be rendered commercially useless, to distinguish between the basic principles of trust law and those specialist rules developed in relation to traditional trusts which are applicable only to such trusts and the rationale of which has no application to trusts of quite a different kind.

Similarly, Lord Woolf advocated 'a new test' in his speech in *Westdeutsche Landesbank Girozentrale v Islington LBC*,[117] with the aim of recognising the very particular commercial intentions of the parties to cross-border financial transactions in comparison with the concerns of the litigants in early cases involving trusts law which were typically concerned with family property. The question does have to be asked how well a single stream of equitable principles copes with all of the many kinds of issues which are brought before the courts, ranging from domestic disputes as to ownership of the family home to the resolution of very complex, international banking disputes. Lord Browne-Wilkinson in *Target Holdings v Redferns* suggested that rules concerning breach of trust, which were developed in relation to family trusts, may be inadequate to deal with commercial situations. This is not a line of thought which has arisen in many subsequent cases but it is nevertheless an important issue for the operation of equity.

Teleological morals – whose conscience?

So where does this moral code of equity come from? The answer is that it has been developed in England in accordance with the doctrine of precedent primarily as a judicial support for open markets and to enforce the wishes of the owners of property who wish to create trusts over them by policing the behaviour of trustees. That bald statement will require justification throughout this book. As outlined at the beginning of this chapter, Lord Browne-Wilkinson in *Westdeutsche Landesbank Girozentrale v Islington LBC*[118] underlined the focus of the trust on the conscience of the particular defendant in each case, or, more accurately, on the conscionability of that person's actions. It is important to note that in other cases, such as *City of London BS v Flegg*,[119] there are situations in which overarching policy concerns, such as the need to protect a viable market in property which favours the interests

---

116   [1996] 1 AC 421, 475.
117   [1996] AC 669.
118   *Ibid.*
119   [1988] AC 54.

of mortgagees, should take priority over the equitable property interests of those who live in such property. Therefore, the moral premises of equity and of property law are typically focused on their end-point: that is, on the practical results of any decision. The application of the applicable remedies therefore see the courts applying backwards from those results, in many cases such that the courts seem to be identifying the conclusion which they want to reach and thinking backwards (or, teleologically) from that point.[120] In considering the rules that populate this book, it is important to bear in mind the ideology on which these ideas are founded.

1.4 THE CORE EQUITABLE PRINCIPLES

Equity is based on a series of fundamental principles, which are reproduced here. As drafted they may appear to be a collection of vague ethical statements, some more lyrical than others. The twelve propositions set out below are culled, as a list, primarily from Snell's *Equity*.[121] At first blush, it is obvious that they are too vague to be meaningful in the abstract. They do not assert any particular view of the world other than that people should behave reasonably towards one another – hardly an alarming proposition in itself. They are rather like the Ten Commandments both in that they are capable of many interpretations and in that they constitute moral prescriptions for the values according to which people should behave. But they are not to be dismissed as merely lyrical pronouncements, because they are still applied by the courts. More to the point, it is entirely appropriate that our law should have a bedrock of morality in the form of these high-level principles.

Those principles are as follows:

(a) Equity will not suffer a wrong to be without a remedy.
(b) Equity follows the law.
(c) Where there is equal equity, the law shall prevail.
(d) Where the equities are equal, the first in time shall prevail.
(e) Delay defeats equities.
(f) He who seeks equity must do equity.
(g) He who comes to equity must come with clean hands.
(h) Equality is equity.
(i) Equity looks to the intent rather than to the form.
(j) Equity looks on as done that which ought to have been done.
(k) Equity imputes an intention to fulfil an obligation.
(l) Equity acts *in personam*.

I would also add to that list five further principles which cut to the heart of equity:

(m) Equity will not permit statute or common law to be used as an engine of fraud.[122]
(n) Equity will not permit a person who is trustee of property to take a benefit from that property *qua* trustee.[123]

---

120 Eg, *Attorney-General for Hong Kong v Reid* [1994] 1 AC 324, [1993] 3 WLR 1143.
121 Baker and Langan, 1990, 27; McGhee, 2000, 27.
122 Eg, see the discussion in *Rochefoucauld v Boustead* below at para 1.4.18.
123 Eg, see the discussion of *Westdeutsche Landesbank v Islington LBC* in Chapter 12.

(o) Equity will not assist a volunteer.[124]

(p) Equity abhors a vacuum.[125]

(q) A trust operates on the conscience of the legal owner of property.

It is worth considering each of these principles, briefly, in turn. The text which follows will highlight these principles in greater detail.

1.4.1 Equity will not suffer a wrong to be without a remedy

The following principle is at the very heart of equity: where the common law or statute do not provide for the remedying of a wrong, it is equity which intercedes to ensure that a fair result is reached.[126] In that sense, equity will not allow a wrong to be committed without there being some sort of remedy to address it. Hence, the scope for the courts to apply flexible doctrines like injunctions in any circumstance in which it is necessary to do justice between the parties.[127] Equity will intervene in circumstances in which there is no apparent remedy but where the court is of the view that justice demands that there be some remedy made available to the complainant.[128] Under a trust, as we shall see below, a beneficiary has no right at common law to have the terms of the trust enforced, but the court will nevertheless require the trustee to carry out those terms to prevent her committing what would be in effect a wrong against that beneficiary.

1.4.2 Equity follows the law – but not slavishly or always[129]

With the introduction of the system of petitioning the Lord Chancellor and the steady development of procedures by which applications could be made formally to the Court of Chancery, there was conflict between the courts of common law and the courts of Equity. That each set of courts applied its own rules in studied ignorance of the rules of the other is indicative of this conflict. Consequently it would have been possible for a court of common law and a Court of Equity to have come to completely different decisions on the merits of the very same case. Therefore, the question arose as to the priority which should be given to each subject in different circumstances.

It is significant that ever since the personal intervention of James I in the *Earl of Oxford's Case*,[130] the principles of equity have overruled common law rules. At this time Sir Edmund Coke had argued that common law must take priority over equity.[131] That is possibly a useful

---

124 Eg, see the discussion in Chapter 5.

125 Which is quite possibly why the Chancery courts are so dirty! Eg, see the discussion of *Vandervell v IRC* in Chapter 5.

126 Eg, *Sanders v Sanders* (1881) 19 Ch D 373, 381.

127 *Mercedes Benz AG v Leiduck* [1996] AC 284, at 308, *per* Lord Nicholls.

128 *Seddon v Commercial Salt Co Ltd* [1925] Ch 187.

129 *Graf v Hope Building Corp* 254 NY 1, 9 (1930), *per* Cardozo CJ.

130 (1615) 1 Ch Rep 1; (1615) 21 ER 485.

131 See *Heath v Rydley* (1614) Cro Jac 335, (1614) 79 ER 286; *Bromage v Genning* (1617) 1 Rolle 368, (1617) 81 ER 540.

isolation of language: the common law has 'rules' which are applied in *rigor juris*[132] more mechanically than the 'principles' of equity, which are necessarily principles governing the standard and quality of behaviour in a more subtle and context-specific way than abstract legal rules. It is, after all, the very purpose of equity that it enables fairness and principle to outweigh rigid rules in appropriate circumstances.

However, equity will be bound to follow statutes in all circumstances. Given the history of equity as a counterpoint to the common law, it will not typically refuse to be bound by rules of common law unless there is some unconscionability in applying a particular common law rule. For example, general common law rules, such as the rule that only parties to a contract will be bound by that contract, will be observed by equity. This principle that statute will be obeyed does not give the common law supremacy over equity in general terms – rather equity will have priority over non-statutory common law rules, as discussed below.

1.4.3 Where there is equal equity, the law shall prevail

In a situation in which there is no clear distinction to be drawn between parties as to which of them has the better claim in equity, the common law principle which best fits the case is applied. In that sense, where the equitable doctrines produce an equal result, then the common law prevails. So, in circumstances where two people have both purported to purchase goods from a fraudulent vendor of those goods for the same price, neither of them would have a better claim to the goods in equity. Therefore, the ordinary common law rules of commercial law would be applied in that context.

1.4.4 Where the equities are equal, the first in time shall prevail

Time is important to equity, reflecting, perhaps, its commercial element. Where two claimants have equally strong cases, equity will favour the person who acquired their rights first. In that sense, the first in time prevails. Thus, if two equitable mortgagees each seek to enforce their security rights under the mortgage ahead of the other mortgagee, the court will give priority to the person who had created their mortgage first.

1.4.5 Delay defeats equities

Another example of the importance of time in equity is the principle relating to delay. It is said that 'delay defeats equity' in the sense that too much delay will prevent access to an equitable remedy. The underpinning of the principle is that if a claimant allows too much time to elapse between the facts giving rise to her claim and the service of proceedings to protect that claim, the court will not protect her rights.[133] This doctrine of not allowing an equitable remedy where there has been unconscionable delay is known as 'laches'.[134] Some

---

132 An excellent expression for which I am grateful to Meagher, Heydon and Leeming, 2002, 6, where those authors also record the view of common lawyers that they had decided that they 'must not allow conscience to prevent your doing law', thus illustrating the divide between the common law mentality and the equitable mentality culled in large part from the ecclesiastics who served as Lords Chancellor.

133 *Smith v Clay* (1767) 3 Bro CC 639; *Fenwicke v Clarke* (1862) 4 De GF & J 240.

134 *Partridge v Partridge* [1894] 1 Ch 351, 359; *Habib Bank Ltd v Habib Bank AG (Zurich)* [1981] 1 WLR 1265.

modern cases have suggested that this doctrine should work on the basis of deciding where the balance of good conscience lies in the light of the delay.[135] Clearly, in any case it will depend on the circumstances how much time has to elapse before the court will decide that there has been too much of a delay.

1.4.6 He who seeks equity must do equity

Another theme in the general principles of equity is that a claimant will not receive the court's support unless she has acted entirely fairly herself. Therefore, in relation to injunctions, for example, the court will award an injunction to an applicant during litigation only where that would be fair to the respondent and where the applicant herself undertakes to carry out her own obligations under any court judgment. A Court of Equity will not act in favour of someone who has, for example, committed an illegal act.[136]

1.4.7 He who comes to equity must come with clean hands

Equity requires that a claimant comes to equity 'with clean hands' in the sense that that person must not have acted improperly or unconscionably if she is seeking an equitable remedy. As a development of the preceding principle of fairness, an applicant for an equitable remedy will not receive that remedy where she has not acted equitably herself.[137] So, for example, an applicant will not be entitled to an order for specific performance of a lease if that applicant is already in breach of a material term of that lease.[138] The principle means that you cannot act hypocritically to ask for equitable relief when you are not acting equitably yourself. It is important to look only to the 'clean hands' of the applicant; the court will not necessarily try to ascertain which of the parties has the cleaner hands before deciding whether or not to award equitable relief.

1.4.8 Equality is equity

Typically, in relation to claims to specific property, where two people have equal claims to that property, equity will order an equal division of title in that property between the claimants in furtherance of an ancient principle that 'equity did delight in equality'.[139] In that sense, the touchstone of equity is equality between the parties. In common with the discussion of Aristotle's view of justice and equity, Vaisey J has considered the doctrine of

---

135 *Nelson v Rye* [1996] 1 WLR 1378; *Frawley v Neill* (1999) *The Times*, 5 April.
136 *Nessom v Clarkson* (1845) 4 Hare 97; *Oxford v Provand* (1868) 5 Moo PC (NS) 150; *Lodge v National Union Investment Co Ltd* [1907] 1 Ch 300. Cf *Tinsley v Milligan* [1994] 1 AC 340; *Rowan v Dann* (1992) 64 P & CR 202.
137 *Jones v Lenthal* (1669) 1 Ch Cas 154; *Evroy v Nicholas* (1733) 2 Eq Ca Abr 488; *Quadrant Visual Communications v Hutchison Telephone* [1993] BCLC 442: that maxim cannot be excluded by agreement of the parties. Halliwell has misread this footnote to suggest that *Jones v Lenthal* is being used here as authority for the maxim that he who comes to equity must come with clean hands, whereas it is intended only to refer to authority for the proposition that equitable remedies may be denied to those who have acted inequitably, as is suggested in the text as written: Halliwell, (2004) Conv 439, 442. The identification of that case as a founding influence over this doctrine emerges, eg from Snell, 2005, 98.
138 *Coatsworth v Johnson* (1886) 54 LT 520; *Guinness v Saunders* [1990] 2 WLR 324.
139 *Petit v Smith* (1695) 1 P Wms 7, 9, *per* Lord Somers LC; see also *Re Bradberry* [1943] Ch 35, 40.

'equality is equity' in the following way: 'I think that the principle which applies here is Plato's definition of equality as a "sort of justice": if you cannot find any other, equality is the proper basis.'[140]

One early example of this principle in action was in the case of *Kemp v Kemp*,[141] in which the court could not divine from the terms of the trust which beneficiary was intended to take which interest and therefore resolved to divide the property equally between them. This principle has been extended in the case of trusts relating to homes by the Court of Appeal to mean that on the breakdown of long-standing marriages, where the parties have dealt with their affairs as though they are sharing all of the benefits and burdens, the parties will receive equal title in the family home.[142] However, it should be noted that the courts will typically seek to give effect to a trust settlor's intentions rather than simply divide property equally if at all possible, because in many situations equal division may be the last thing which the owner of property intended.[143]

1.4.9 Equity looks to the intent rather than to the form

It is a common principle of English law that the courts will seek to look through any artifice and give effect to the substance of any transaction rather than merely to its surface appearance.[144] In this sense, equity will consider the parties' intentions and not simply the form which any documents may have taken. Equity will not ignore formalities altogether – for example, in relation to the law of express trusts, equity is particularly astute to observe formalities[145] – but it will not observe unnecessary formalities.[146] As we shall see in Chapter 4, even where the parties do not use the expression 'trust' the courts will give effect to something which is in substance a trust as a trust,[147] and will strike down supposed trusts which are merely shams.[148]

1.4.10 Equity looks on as done that which ought to have been done

One of the key techniques deployed by the courts in recent years has been the principle that equity will consider that something has been done if the court believes that it ought to have been done.[149] In that sense, 'equity looks upon as done that which ought to have been done'. One of the older examples of this principle is that in *Walsh v Lonsdale*,[150] where a binding contract to grant a lease was deemed to create an equitable lease, even though the formal requirements to create a valid common law lease had not been observed. The rationale behind equity finding that there was a lease which could be effective was the principle

---

140 *Jones v Maynard* [1951] Ch 572, 575.
141 (1795) 5 Ves 849; (1795) 31 ER 891.
142 See *Midland Bank v Cooke* [1995] 4 All ER 562.
143 See, eg, *McPhail v Doulton* [1970] 2 WLR 1110; *Pettitt v Pettitt* [1970] AC 777; *Gissing v Gissing* [1971] AC 886.
144 *Parkin v Thorold* (1852) 16 Beav 59; *Midland Bank v Wyatt* [1995] 1 FLR 697.
145 *Milroy v Lord* (1862) 4 De GF & J 264.
146 *Sprange v Lee* [1908] 1 Ch 424; *Ranieri v Miles* [1981] AC 1050.
147 See *Paul v Constance* [1977] 1 WLR 527.
148 *Midland Bank v Wyatt* [1995] 1 FLR 697.
149 Although the principle dates back at least to *Banks v Sutton* (1732) 2 P Wms 700, 715.
150 (1882) 21 Ch D 9.

that the landlord was bound by specific performance to carry out his obligations under the contract and to grant a formally valid lease to the tenant. Therefore, it was held that the landlord ought to have granted such a lease. In the eyes of equity, then, the grant of the lease was something which ought to have been done and which could therefore be deemed (in equity) to have been done, with the result that a lease was created by equity.[151]

1.4.11 Equity imputes an intention to fulfil an obligation

This doctrine assumes an intention in a person bound by an obligation to carry out that obligation, such that acts not strictly required by the obligation may be deemed to be in performance of the obligation.[152] For example, if a deceased woman had owed a money debt to a man before her death, and left money to that man in her will, equity would presume that the money left in the will was left in satisfaction of the debt owed to that man. This presumption could be rebutted by some cogent evidence to the contrary, for example, that the money legacy had been promised long before the debt arose.

1.4.12 Equity acts *in personam*

As was considered above, it is a key feature of equity that it acts *in personam*.[153] This is an idea which will be explored in greater detail in Chapter 12 on constructive trusts.[154] This jurisdiction will operate on the individual defendant whether that individual is within or outwith the English jurisdiction. As Lord Selbourne stated the matter:

> The courts of Equity in England are, and always have been, courts of conscience, operating *in personam* and not *in rem*; and in the exercise of this personal jurisdiction they have always been accustomed to compel the performance of contracts and trusts as to subjects which were not . . . within their jurisdiction.[155]

The focus of a Court of Equity in making a judgment is to act on the conscience of the particular defendant involved in the particular case before it. Therefore, equity is acting against that particular person and not seeking, in theory, to set down general rules as to the manner in which the common law should deal with similar cases in the future. Of course, over the centuries, the courts have come to adopt specific practices and rules of precedent as to the manner in which equitable principles will be imposed, just as common law rules have developed by means of the application of the doctrine of precedent. This topic will, in effect, occupy us for much of the remainder of this book.

---

151 *Re Antis* (1886) 31 Ch D 596; *Foster v Reeves* [1892] 2 QB 255; *Re Plumptre's Marriage Settlement* [1910] 1 Ch 609.
152 *Sowden v Sowden* (1785) 1 Bro CC 582.
153 See para 1.3.2 above.
154 In relation to personal liability to account for breach of trust (*Royal Brunei Airlines v Tan* [1995] 2 AC 378) as well as in relation to the general jurisdiction of equity to police a person's conscience (*Westdeutsche Landesbank v Islington LBC* [1996] AC 669).
155 *Ewing v Orr Ewing (No 1)* (1883) 9 App Cas 34, 40. Cf *Duke of Brunswick v King of Hanover* (1848) 2 HLC 1; *United States of America v Dollfus Mieg et Cie SA* [1952] AC 318.

1.4.13 Equity will not permit statute or common law to be used as an engine of fraud

Equity will not allow a defendant to use a statutory principle so as to effect a fraud in relation to someone else. Slightly more lyrically, equity will not permit statute to used as an engine of fraud. While this principle is not strictly part of the list of equitable principles which is reproduced in the classic books such as *Snell's Equity*[156] or *Modern Equity*,[157] it does appear to form the basis for a number of cases in equity (particularly in the 19th century).[158] It is a good explanation of the general operation of equity in relation to common law and statute. Whereas equity will not usually contradict common law or statute (it is said), it will act *in personam* against the conscience of a defendant to prevent that defendant from taking inequitable advantage of another person.

The best example is probably the secret trust, considered in Chapter 6 below. Secret trusts arise in situations in which a person making a will has sought to create a trust without recording that intention or the terms of the trust in the will (hence the expression 'secret trust').[159] The Wills Act 1837 requires that the will be treated as containing all of the terms by which the deceased's estate is to be distributed. However, where one of the deceased's personal representatives (who was informed of that secret trust by the deceased person) seeks to ignore the terms of the secret trust by relying on the strict application of the Wills Act, equity will prevent that person from perpetrating what is effectively a fraud on the intended beneficiary of the property under the secret trust.[160]

1.4.14 Equity will not permit a person who is trustee of property to take benefit from that property as though a beneficiary

As considered in detail below, a trust is created by transferring the common law title in property to a trustee to hold that property on trust for identified beneficiaries.[161] A further fundamental principle of equity is that even though the trustee is recognised as being the 'owner' of the trust property by common law, the trustee is not to be permitted to take all of the rights in the property in her capacity as trustee. Rather, a trustee is required to hold the trust property on trust for the beneficiaries under the terms of the trust. This technique of both enabling and forcing one person to hold property for another person is a unique feature of English law (and of systems derived from English law).

1.4.15 Equity will not assist a volunteer

The principle that equity will not assist a volunteer occurs frequently in this book. In line with the commercial roots of many of these doctrines, equity will not assist a person who has given no consideration for the benefits which she is claiming. Therefore, someone who is the intended recipient of a gift, for example, will not have a failed gift completed by equity interpreting the incomplete gift to be a trust or some other equitable structure.[162] As will

---

156   Most recent edition by McGhee, 2000; 1st edn by Edmund Henry Turner Snell, 1868.
157   Most recent edition by Martin, 1997; 1st edn by Hanbury, 1935.
158   *Rochefoucauld v Boustead* [1897] 1 Ch 196; *Lyus v Prowsa Developments Ltd* [1982] 1 WLR 1044.
159   *Blackwell v Blackwell* [1929] AC 318; *Ottaway v Norman* [1972] 2 WLR 50.
160   *McCormick v Grogan* (1869) LR 4 HL 82.
161   *Fletcher v Fletcher* (1844) 4 Hare 67.
162   *Milroy v Lord* (1862) 4 De GF & J 264.

emerge from the discussion of trusts law in Chapter 2, beneficiaries under trusts are the only category of true volunteers who acquire the protection of equity exceptionally if a trust has been created.

1.4.16 Equity abhors a vacuum

In considering rights to property, equity will not allow there to be some property rights which are not owned by some identifiable person.[163] Thus, a trustee must hold property on trust for identifiable beneficiaries, or else there is no valid trust. Similarly, it is generally considered at English law that no person can simply abandon their rights in property – rather, that person retains those proprietary rights until they are transferred to another person. To do otherwise would be to create a vacuum in the ownership of property. The doctrine of resulting trusts can be understood as operating on this basis by ordering that property rights without an owner are deemed to 'result back' to the person who was their last owner.[164]

1.4.17 A trust operates on the conscience of the legal owner of property

The most significant of the equitable doctrines is the trust, under which a beneficiary is able to assert equitable rights to particular property and thus control the way in which the common law owner of that property is entitled to deal with it. The trust is considered in the next chapter. As will emerge, the key tenets of the trust are that the legal owner of property will be obliged to hold it on trust for any persons beneficially entitled to it where good conscience so requires: this can be due to an express declaration of trust, or to the imposition of a trust implied by law by the courts.[165] This principle is in line with the earliest reported cases on equity which were concerned to 'correct men's consciences', as will emerge in the next chapter.[166]

1.4.18 Equity and fraud

It would not be an exaggeration to suggest that many of the principles of equity are aimed at the avoidance of fraud, or the avoidance of the results of fraud. Many of the doctrines considered in this book will be orientated around the avoidance of fraud, whether by trustees, or in the doctrine in *Rochefoucauld v Boustead*[167] (considered in detail in Chapter 5), or in the operation of secret trusts (considered in Chapter 6). Lord Browne-Wilkinson in *Westdeutsche Landesbank Girozentrale v Islington LBC*[168] set out his view that the operation of the trust centres on the prevention of any unconscionable (as opposed to strictly 'fraudulent') act or omission. The notion of fraud here is different from that under, for example, the tort of deceit.[169] This indicates the increasing breadth of equitable doctrine beyond the category simply of straightforward fraud. Fraud remains difficult to prove, attracting a high standard

---

163 *Vandervell v IRC* [1967] 2 AC 291, HL.
164 *Ibid.*
165 *Westdeutsche Landesbank Girozentrale v Islington LBC* [1996] AC 669.
166 *Earl of Oxford's Case* (1615) 1 Ch Rep 1, *per* Lord Ellesmere.
167 [1897] 1 Ch 196.
168 [1996] AC 669.
169 *Derry v Peek* (1889) 14 App Cas 337.

of proof, and many actions which we may consider worthy of censure will not necessarily be fraudulent. So equity developed the canons of so-called 'constructive fraud' to cover situations in which there was not normal fraud but there were acts tantamount to fraud – an example of which is the exertion of undue influence on a person to procure their agreement to a contract.[170]

Nevertheless, the doctrine in *Rochefoucauld v Boustead*[171] is instructive in this regard. The doctrine is simply stated: statute and common law shall not be used as an engine for fraud. For example, if a rule of the common law were to state that no transfers of lollipops were to take place after 1 January 2001, but I knew full well that I had entered into a binding contract with X under which X paid me £1,000 on 31 December 2000 so that I would transfer my lollipop to him, it would be a fraud on X for me to seek to rely on the statute to allow me to keep my lollipop and X's £1,000. Under another principle of equity, the equitable interest in that lollipop would transfer automatically to X at the moment at which our contract was formed.[172] In these ways equity precludes me from relying on the fruits of my dastardly behaviour even though the common law or statute may permit me to do so. Equity operates to achieve a higher form of justice than that sought by the common law in individual cases. What is important is to understand the philosophy which underpins the activation of equity in such circumstances. That discussion is introduced in the following section.

1.5 PLACING EQUITY IN CONTEXT

1.5.1 The development of equity over time under the steerage of different judges

There are two general approaches to equity as a subject, as will emerge during the course of this book. The first view, typically held by those who have been schooled in the practice of chancery courts, is that equity possesses a laudable flexibility predicated on an understanding of equity's subtle principles: people who subscribe to this view consider that equitable discretion is a positive thing. The second view, typically held by those who have been schooled in the common law tradition rather than equity, is that equity's flexibility can lead to irrational and random decision-making and that equity would be better if it was reorganised so as to make it more akin to common law with its more rigid and more predictable rules. It is suggested that neither of these views has any complete claim to truth and that both of these views suggest mere caricatures of equity and of common law whereas in truth, both doctrines have elements of rigidity and elements of flexibility. As will emerge through this book, there are many principles of trusts law which resemble rigid common law doctrines – for example the requirements of certainty in the creation of an express trust – and there are others which appear to be based on broad judicial discretion but which are in truth predicated on a detailed understanding of the underlying principles – for example in areas such as equitable estoppel and common intention constructive trusts. A very clear history of equity is presented by Professor Baker[173] and an excellent, if older, history presented by Professor

170 *Barclays Bank v O'Brien* [1993] 4 All ER 417, considered in Chapter 20.
171 [1897] 1 Ch 196.
172 *Walsh v Lonsdale* (1882) 21 Ch D 9. See now *Neville v Wilson* [1997] Ch 144, which explains this principle on the basis of constructive trust.
173 Baker, *An Introduction to English Legal History*, 4th edn, Butterworths LexisNexis, 2002.

Story.[174] What follows here is a potted account of some of that history which will give us a flavour of the background to the discussion to follow in this book.

Through equity's history, then, there have been judges who have been enthusiasts for a broadly discretionary equity and judges who have scorned it. The most obvious example of this division of opinion arose in the *Earl of Oxford's Case*[175] which is the first case in the official reports of chancery cases. In that case there was a debate between Coke, the great common lawyer and chief justice of the King's Bench, and Lord Ellesmere, the then Lord Chancellor, as to whether it was the common law courts or the courts of equity which should take priority if both wanted to deliver judgments which contradicted one another. Coke had, for example, taken to releasing prisoners who had been committed by the Lord Chancellor for contempt of injunctions by using the old doctrine of habeus corpus. It was decided by King James I that it was the courts of equity which should take priority, and so Lord Ellesmere delivered his seminal judgment in that case (as quoted in para 1.1) to the effect that the purpose of equity is 'to correct men's consciences'. It is important to note that it required the King's intervention to decide which of the two legal jurisdictions was to take priority.

It was, of course, an odd situation which had permitted two streams of courts to exist in parallel, and therefore in conflict, in the first place. A part of the conflict between the King and the common law courts for some centuries had been whether or not the monarch was entitled to introduce new jurisdictions, such as the ever-expanding jurisdiction of equity and of the court of Star Chamber, or even to intervene in judicial decisions directly. Therefore, the primacy of equity over common law was not simply a technical legal question, it was also a matter of political controversy. It would be the equivalent now of the Queen seeking to reverse a decision of the Court of Appeal or seeking to direct the Court of Appeal which decision to reach: it would be unthinkable in a democratic society and would precipitate a constitutional crisis. Back in the early seventeenth century, at a time when the Catholic King James I[176] had succeeded the Protestant Elizabeth I to the throne – all part of an age-old and bloody conflict between Protestant and Catholic, and only a generation before the religious and political conflict that precipitated the English Civil War – it was a matter of tremendous significance that the common law judges were considered to be subordinate to the decisions of the monarch's principal minister, the Lord Chancellor.

After these overtly political events, the history of equity thereafter could be explained as being a history of the differing attitudes of different judges, some of whom were equity enthusiasts and some of whom were equity sceptics.

Sir Heneage Finch, better known as Lord Chancellor Lord Nottingham, is generally credited with bringing a large amount of orderliness to equity in the 17th century.[177] For example, it was Lord Nottingham who developed the principles of perpetuities which prevented devices like trusts from existing in perpetuity: importantly Lord Nottingham's developments simplified the law on perpetuities which previously had been caught between various different types of 'contingency'. The two volumes of Lord Nottingham's Chancery cases,

---

174 Story, *Equity Jurisprudence*, originally published in 1835; references are to the 13th edn in four volumes by
       Bigelow (ed) in 1886, taken from a reprint by Beard Books, 2006.
175 (1615) 1 Ch Rep 1.
176 While James I, later in his reign as King of England, persecuted Catholics, he was born to a Catholic mother,
       Mary, and was christened and raised as such.
177 E.g. *Cook v Fountain* (1676) 3 Swan 585.

published by the Selden Society, are a record of one man's determination to regularise the
disparate principles of earlier courts. This work was continued by Lord Hardwicke and Lord
Eldon, as subsequent Lords Chancellor. Lord Eldon, for example, pronounced that:

> The doctrines of this court ought to be as well settled, and made as uniform almost as
> those of the common law, laying down fixed principles, but taking care that they are to
> be applied according to the circumstances of each case. I cannot agree that the doctrines
> of this court are to be changed with every succeeding judge. Nothing would inflict on
> me greater pain, in quitting this place, than the recollection that I had done anything to
> justify the reproach that the equity of this court varies like the Chancellor's foot.[178]

This line of thought can be seen right the way into the 20th century where it was regularly
suggested that the courts would only activate equitable doctrines if they could be shown to
be predicated on clear authority and not simply because they appeared to be 'just' or 'right'
or 'conscionable'.[179] As is considered below, there is a suggestion that at the end of the
20th century and in the 21st century equity's heritage as a reservoir of good conscience is
nevertheless being reclaimed. However, for present purposes we shall concentrate on equity
in the post-Elizabethan period, that is from the 17th century onwards.

At this time there was no systematic reporting of court decisions like there is now.[180]
Different court reporters could produce very different accounts of what a judge had said in the
course of his judgment. There were very few books on law – and there were certainly many,
many fewer books than are available now, and the books which were available were not as
painstakingly referenced and researched as modern books. It is thought that the first book
concentrating solely on equity was Francis's *Maxims of Equity* published in 1727. Consequently,
it was difficult for legal principles to develop systematically. Principles therefore developed by
reference to vague maxims and half-remembered remarks of earlier judges – indeed it might
be a criticism of some legal historians that they attribute too much intellectual prowess to some
ancient judges whose decisions often contained little internal consistency and even less relation to early cases. Therefore, the work of someone like Lord Nottingham in seeking to regularise legal principle was very significant. Today, of course, we have electronic databases
giving access to every decision that is reached by the High Court, no matter how trivial in the
grander scheme of things, and there are many textbooks which have organised and categorised
the law into readily comprehensible categories. How things have changed.

Nevertheless, equity is constantly in flux, and constantly being developed. On the question of the level of reverence which we should accord to ancient precedents, Sir George
Jessel MR in the Court of Appeal in 1880 said the following:[181]

> It must not be forgotten that the rules of Courts of Equity are not, like the rules of the
> Common Law, supposed to have been established from time immemorial. It is perfectly

---

178 *Gee v Pritchard* (1818) 2 Swans 402, 414.
179 *Re Diplock* [1948] Ch 465, 481. See Lord Jessel MR in *Re National Funds Assurance Co* (1878) 10 Ch D 118,
     128: 'This court is not, as I have often said, a Court of Conscience, but a Court of Law'; meaning that courts
     of equity were bound by principles and precedent just like the common law courts.
180 Although in 1617 Lord Chancellor Bacon did appoint an official reporter to sit at his feet so as to record his
     judgments.
181 *Re Hallett's Estate* (1880) 13 Ch D 696.

well known that they have been established from time to time – altered, improved and refined from time to time. . . . We can name the Chancellors who first invented them, and state the date when they were first introduced into Equity jurisprudence; and, therefore in cases of this kind, the older precedents in Equity are of very little value. The doctrines are progressive, refined, and improved: and if we want to know what the rules of Equity are, we must look, of course, rather to the more modern than the more ancient cases.

So, here we have a call not to fixate on the heritage theme-park nature of some equity scholarship – instead we must have a gimlet-eyed focus on the modern applications of principle. Nevertheless, tracing some of the fundamental doctrines of equity, such as the notion of conscience, can only be done satisfactorily if one has an eye to history.

As for the ostensibly broad notion of 'conscience', back in the 17th century Lord Nottingham preferred to think of it as being a technical question. In *Cook v Fountain*[182] Lord Nottingham held that:

> With such a conscience as is only *naturalis et interna*,[183] this court has nothing to do; the conscience by which I am to proceed is merely *civilis et politica*,[184] and tied to certain measures: and it is infinitely better for the public that a trust, security, or agreement, which is wholly secret, should miscarry, than that men should lose their estates by the mere fancy and imagination of a chancellor.[185]

So, the idea of conscience was still in play but it was not a 'conscience' as that term was ordinarily understood; instead the form of conscience with which Lord Nottingham was concerned was a conscience that is a strictly legal and civil concept as opposed to a religious, moral or philosophical notion. This determined march towards regularisation of equity was very different from the attitudes of judges from earlier centuries who had concerned themselves solely with inquiring into the defendant's conscience, such that Fortescue CJ had declared in 1452 that '[w]e are to argue conscience here, not the law'.[186] So, Lord Nottingham held that a contract would not be rectified where it would be conscionable to do so because it was 'binding in conscience but not in equity': meaning that the two ideas, a general moral conscience and the technical rules of equity, were different things.[187]

Later judges also took as their goal the corralling of equity into more rigid rules. So, Lord Eldon hoped that he had introduced order and predictability to equity in his work as Lord Chancellor.[188] Indeed, many of the principles which we shall consider in detail in Part 2 of

---

182 (1676) 3 Swan 585, 600.

183 That is, 'arising naturally' and 'internal'.

184 That is, concerning 'civil law matters' and 'political matters'.

185 This is a reference to Selden's jibe that the principles of equity in their application seemed to change from Chancellor to Chancellor much as the length of his foot would vary from Chancellor to Chancellor: *Table Talk of John Selden*, ed Pollock, 1927, 43.

186 Mitch 31 Hen VI, Fitz Abr, *Subpena*, pl 23, cited by Baker, 2002, 108. It should be noted that this opinion was not without its dissenters, however. Many judges in chancery courts considered themselves to be operating on the basis of precedent and in accordance with legal principle as opposed to functioning on a purely case-by-case basis. See the *dicta* of Blackstone J quoted by Story, 1886, para 18.

187 *Honywood v Bennett* (1675) Nottingham Rep (73 Selden Society) 214.

188 *Gee v Pritchard* (1818) 2 Swan 402, 414.

this book relating to the formation of express trusts are still based on decisions of Lord Eldon and the judges of the Court of Appeal in Chancery, such as Turner LJ, in the early 19th century.

At the end of the 19th century, as was discussed in the preceding section, the Judicature Act 1873 rang enormous changes in the interaction between equity and common law. As Professor Maitland explained matters in his lectures (published posthumously)[189] by this time it could not be thought that equity and the common law were antagonistic to one another because equity was dependent upon the existence of common law – in effect, without common law rules on which to pass comment there would not have been equity. One is tempted to respond 'up to a point, Lord Copper'.[190] The history of equity and common law had been forged precisely by the determination of equity to establish itself as a competing jurisdiction within England and Wales, as discussed above, and not simply to carry on as the common law's shadow. In the modern era perhaps we could consider equity in this fashion. Even in the modern era, however, there are substantive doctrines like the trust, proprietary estoppel, injunctions, and so forth which are based solely on equity and which are not in any way parasitic on the common law – rather, they exist in their own right.

The first 60 or 70 years of the 20th century saw one trend (arguably among others) towards great rigidity in decision-making. Judges like Viscount Simonds, many of whose judgments we shall study in great detail in Chapters 3, 4 and 5,[191] were primarily concerned to interpret trusts literally and to invalidate trusts which had been imperfectly drafted. Trusts law in particular hardened into a system of rules which were reminiscent of the rigidity of the common law. This tendency is considered in detail in the essay that comprises Chapter 7.

However, the late 20th century also saw a liberalising tendency in the decisions of Lord Denning as he dominated the large flow of cases through the Court of Appeal, in his role as Master of the Rolls with the power to decide which cases he heard himself and which judges sat alongside him on the three person panel. When I studied law in the late 1980s and early 1990s many of the then recent decisions I was called upon to read were reversals of Lord Denning's liberalising doctrines such as 'the deserted wife's equity', promissory estoppel, and the proprietary effect of contractual licences. Lord Denning was perhaps one of the clearest examples of a 'pure equity' judge in that he was concerned to achieve 'fair' results no matter what the strict legal rules would seem to have required.

Lord Browne-Wilkinson has been presented already in this chapter as the modern judge who reclaimed and re-expressed the place of conscience at the centre of trusts law – a concept which will sustain much of this book. There were other judges who had referred back to trusts law's reliance on conscience from time to time but at the time that Lord Browne-Wilkinson gave judgment there had been a number of contradictory academic and judicial currents which had suggested different ideas, such as the Romanic idea of restitution of unjust enrichment. However, when we consider the full range of Lord Browne-Wilkinson's judgments in the field of equity – such as his decision in the High Court in *Re Barlow*[192] and

189   Maitland, 1936.
190   This expression is used by a newspaper editor in Evelyn Waugh's satirical novel *Scoop* in which that editor dare not disagree explicitly with the newspaper's proprietor, Lord Copper, and so instead of saying 'no' to his patron, the newspaper editor says 'up to a point, Lord Copper'.
191   For example, *Grey v IRC* [1960] AC 1; *Leahy v Att-Gen NSW* [1959] AC 457; *Oppenheim v Tobacco Securities* [1951] AC 297.
192   [1979] 1 WLR 278.

in the House of Lords in *Tinsley v Milligan*[193] – it emerges that he was no woolly-minded moralist, but that he was a pragmatist and, in *Tinsley v Milligan*, a careful technical thinker when identifying the source of a claimant's rights as opposed to denying that person a proprietary right because she was coincidentally involved in a criminal act which related at one remove to that property.

By contrast, Lord Goff gave a dissenting speech in *Tinsley v Milligan* which took the moral high line by suggesting that that claimant could not acquire any equitable rights in property which she had paid for because she had also committed a criminal offence: thus giving effect to an ancient equitable principle that one may not have an equitable remedy if one has acted unconscionably oneself. This view of Lord Goff's was ironic because it was Lord Goff's book, titled *The Law of Restitution* and published first in 1966 with Gareth Jones, which had begun a movement in English law which ultimately argued for a change in direction away from traditional ideas of equity.[194] Lord Goff can be identified in his judgments with a concern to achieve 'justice' in the broadest possible sense, for example in his dissenting speech in *Westdeutsche Landesbank v Islington*[195] and in *Tinsley v Milligan* or his speech in *White v Jones*;[196] in fact Lord Goff can be understood as having been by inclination an old-fashioned equity lawyer. By contrast again, it was Lord Millett who began to fly the flag for the modish principle of restitution of unjust enrichment in the House of Lords, picking up on all of the significant academic trends in the areas of this book which relate to trusts implied by law and breach of trust. The effect of this principle would have been to introduce even greater rigidity to those areas of equity which, even in the modern era, are still typified by their flexibility.

Among judges more recently at the time of writing it is a group of judges whose most prominent member is Lord Walker who are turning the clock backwards towards ideas of giving judgment so as to avoid unconscionability. So, for example, the development of proprietary estoppel by Walker LJ in *Jennings v Rice*[197] has signalled a return to courts awarding rights in property or to compensation on the basis that that is conscionable. The tendency to understand courts as having a general discretion to make orders, for example requiring disclosure of information relating to a trust fund, has appeared in Lord Walker's judgment in *Schmidt v Rosewood*.[198] His lordship's judgments in *Stack v Dowden*[199] and *Jones v Kernott*[200] have tended towards confusion rather than rationalisation. His judgments

---

193 [1994] 1 AC 340.
194 Unjust enrichment seeks to displace equity with a more rigid and much more limited and unimaginative system of doctrines. It is suggested in Chapter 31 of this book that restitution on grounds of unjust enrichment operates as a possible explanation of some equitable institutions but does not account for the whole range of equitable remedies present in English law. Unjust enrichment is concerned to isolate an enrichment in the hands of the defendant, to decide whether or not it is unjustly received, and then to reverse that enrichment if it is unjust. The House of Lords accepted the existence of a principle of unjust enrichment in *Lipkin Gorman v Karpnale* [1991] 2 AC 548 and in *Woolwich Equitable Building Society v IRC (No 2)* [1993] AC 573, but the scope for the operation of that principle has been greatly restricted by the decision of the majority of the House of Lords in *Westdeutsche Landesbank Girozentrale v Islington LBC* [1996] AC 669.
195 [1996] AC 669.
196 [1995] 1 AC 207.
197 [2003] 1 P&CR 100, [2003] EWCA Civ 159.
198 [2003] 3 All ER 76.
199 [2007] UKHL 17, [2007] 2 WLR 831.
200 [2011] UKSC 53, [2011] 3 WLR 1121, [2011] 3 FCR 495.

in relation to proprietary estoppel in *Cobbe v Yeoman's Row*[201] and *Thorner v Major*[202] were contradictory in many senses in that the former was very restrictive of the doctrine and latter much more traditional. However, what has disappeared almost completely in his lordship's judgments on trusts law is any reference to 'unconscionability', a concept which was central to cases like *Jennings v Rice*.

The presence of the former family law academic, Baroness Hale, in the House of Lords is also an intriguing presence for the future. Thus far, her judgments have been somewhat more restrained than her academic writing – which is something of a shame. Her judgment in relation to rights in the home in *Stack v Dowden*[203] caused more confusion rather than the conceptual revolution it hoped to precipitate; with the result that another judgment was required in *Jones v Kernott*[204] to conduct some undiscussed overruling of detailed elements of *Stack v Dowden* and the introduction of a new concept of 'fairness', again without explanation. So much was hoped for from this country's first female judge in the highest court, particularly when she was a well-known former academic too. These cases are discussed in Chapter 15. Her judgment in *Campbell v MGN*[205] in relation to super-injunctions was thoughtful and lively – suggesting a new kind of judge on the bench.

1.5.2 Equity in a broader context

The most honest approach is to accept that equity, in its English, legal sense, no longer has any single intellectual core in the form of a code or philosophy. Rather, it is something which must be observed in and assembled from the decisions of the Courts of Chancery down the ages: a stream of thought which has been resistant in the main to abstract philosophising. In this sense it does not have an intellectual pedigree of the sort which can be assembled for human rights thinking or for human rights law. Equity is *not divined* from philosophical foundations; rather, equity is *found* in the law reports, albeit derived on the basis of case law precedent and the principles set out earlier in this chapter. While that is true of equity up to now, this book will suggest that that is not sufficient for the future. In the notion of conscience mentioned frequently in Chancery decisions by judges like Lord Browne-Wilkinson, it is possible to detect broad parallels with the ideas of Plato[206] and Aristotle.[207] Consequently, it is by reference to this idea of conscience that it might be possible to manufacture an underlying philosophy for equity. The notion of conscience is itself one which can be traced into much ethical philosophy, as I attempt to do in Chapter 32, and it is in that soil that intellectual roots sufficient to cope with the challenges of the 21st century might yet be grown.[208] As yet the courts have been reluctant to explain what is meant by conscience, or how we might understand it as informing all of the principles of equity. Rather equity is currently comprised of its history rather than any particular ideas.

The outlines of equity's historical roots have been considered in this chapter. In truth, those historical foundations have much to do with an understanding of equity as merely a

201 [2008] 1 WLR 1752.
202 [2009] 1 WLR 776.
203 [2007] UKHL 17, [2007] 2 WLR 831.
204 [2011] UKSC 53, [2011] 3 WLR 1121, [2011] 3 FCR 495.
205 [2004] 2 AC 457.
206 Eg, *Jones v Maynard* [1951] Ch 572, 575, *per* Vaisey J.
207 See section 1.1.
208 See section 32.1.

reservation of power to the Crown, at the time when Henry II created a new court system, which subsequently devolved in practice to the Lord Chancellor. At the time of writing, the discussion of equity in all of the books has moved beyond any need to consider the ambit of monarchical power – only essays on constitutional law consider the continuing significance of the Royal Prerogative. And yet there is a need to understand the intellectual core of equity as being grounded in this royal power. In searching for any *historical* core to this jurisdiction we encounter the disputes about the comparative power of the ecclesiastics and the secular lawyers.[209] The creation of the post of Lord Chancellor and the rise of the Tudor Lords Chancellor have everything to do with political expediency and nothing to do with an early Enlightenment drive for a humanist management of claims for effective social justice; although today we would prefer to model our equity on the latter.

There is another paradox in equity. On the one hand we can be confident that equity exists so as to dispense Solomon's justice where the common law or statute would act in some way unfairly. On the other hand we might be nervous of equity as a means of permitting judicial legislation beyond the democratic control of Parliament. We are right to be concerned when such norms are developed by an unaccountable and powerful judiciary, even though we may consider many of their judgments to be perfectly desirable in their own contexts. It is in relation to equity that Ronald Dworkin's idealised judge Hercules would have most difficulty putting his integrity to work in finding the 'right answer'.[210] Any suggestion that the solution to questions of justice and equity can be decided by reference to some matrix of rule-application is doomed either to failure or to the generation of injustice. But for Hercules, equity does offer the possibility of being sufficiently free to reach the 'right' conclusion, and so to do justice between the parties to any particular case in the broadest possible sense.

As considered above, the roots of equity-type thinking are to be found in Aristotle's and Plato's discussions of justice.[211] What we are left with by Aristotle's determination, that circumstances must decide the appropriate rule and that concrete rules cannot always be set out in advance and then applied without pause for reflection, is that the justice of a decision can be evaluated only after the decision is made. As such, equity becomes a conversation in which the judgment is one communication within a larger discourse as to the shape of justice in society.

For this writer, equity is the place in which our society should discuss the ways in which we will provide procedural justice through the courts, as well as in the political system which generates statutory rights before they come to law. Equity should be concerned to ensure *equality of outcome* in individual cases so that there is fairness between litigants (applied more broadly through the legal system's web of advice and informal dispute resolution outside courts). Equity has a significant procedural role to play in ensuring that the application of legal rules in individual cases does not allow unfairness. To adopt the words of the great Welsh socialist Aneurin Bevan, equity as a tool of social justice will enable us to ensure that 'the apparently enlightened principle of "the greatest good for the greatest number" cannot excuse indifference to individual suffering'.[212] Equity forces us to consider the plight of the individual in this complex world and to save that individual from being caught up in the legal machine or exposed to irremediable suffering.

---

209 Thomas, 1976, 506.
210 Dworkin, 1986.
211 See section 1.1 above.
212 Bevan (1952), 1978.

Chapter 2

Understanding the trust

2.1 THE BIRTH OF THE TRUST

The trust is both the most important part of equity[1] and the greatest and most distinctive achievement performed by Englishmen in the field of jurisprudence,[2] according to the legal historian and equity specialist Professor Maitland. Whether or not that is true, the trust has certainly become a peculiarly English way of thinking. The trust concept, whether created deliberately by ordinary people or used by a court to remedy unconscionable behaviour, is one of the fundamental techniques with which English lawyers analyse the world. Its current form is an accident of English history and as much as part of that history as kings and queens, Magna Carta and the Gunpowder Plot.

The trust performs a very simple trick: it enables more than one person to have rights in the same property simultaneously. The trick is simple but it has complex ramifications. In short, the trust permits a division in the ownership of the trust property between a trustee and a beneficiary so that the trustee is compelled to act entirely in the best interests of the beneficiary in relation to the management of whatever property is held on trust.[3]

I will tell you the story of how the trust was born as it was first told to me: I think it is the best way of understanding the trust at this stage, although it is worth bearing in mind that it is impossible to prove when the first trust was created because it seems to have developed out of legal practice, but it certainly did not emerge from anything as obvious as a statute or a single judicial decision. The story goes like this. The earliest example of the trust occurred at the time of the early religious wars fought in the 12th century when Christian noblemen from Europe travelled to the Middle East on 'crusades'.[4] Typically, the crusader[5] would be away from England for some years and therefore needed to have his land tended in his absence.[6] It was essential that the person who was left in charge could exercise all of the powers of the legal owner of that land, such as deciding who would farm which part of the land and collecting taxes. However, the crusader wanted to ensure that he would be able to recover all of his rights of ownership when he returned from the war. Consequently, the idea

---

1 Maitland, 1936, 23.

2 *Ibid*, 129.

3 See section 2.5: including the extensive obligations of a fiduciary as described in *White v Jones* [1995] 1 AC 207 and *Bristol & West Building Society v Mothew* [1998] Ch 1, such as the duty not to make secret profits (*Keech v Sandford* (1726) Sel Cas Ch 61; *Boardman v Phipps* [1967] 2 AC 46); the duty to act fairly between all of the beneficiaries (*Stephenson v Barclays Bank Trust Co Ltd* [1975] 1 All ER 625); and the duty to account to the beneficiaries for any loss stemming from a breach of trust (*Target Holdings v Redferns* [1996] 1 AC 421).

4 This is the basis on which Professor Maitland explained the basis of the 'use' and latterly its successor concept the 'trust': Maitland, *Collected Papers*, vol ii, 403. See also Pollock and Maitland, 1895, 228; Holdsworth, 1945, 407 *et seq*. See also the very useful summary in Cheshire and Burn, 2000, 42 *et seq*.

5 An unfortunate word but nevertheless the word historians still use when describing this particular conflict.

6 Students of English history will know that at this time the crown of England was held in common with other lands by the Dukes of Aquitaine and therefore, even without the crusades, the people who were the ultimate owners of land in England spent most of their time outside the country in any event.

of split ownership of the property emerged, whereby the crusader was treated as the owner of the land by the courts of equity and the person left in charge was treated by the common law courts as being owner of the land.[7] Therefore, two categories of people had different types of right in the same property at the same time. So, the crusader had property rights which were only recognised by the courts of equity (and so that person had an 'equitable interest' in the land), whereas the person who looked after the land had rights which were recognised by the common law courts (and so that person is described as having 'legal title').

There are other stories about how the trust first came into existence, which may be linked to the one I was told. History is in truth a selection between different accounts of the past. One account locates the earliest trusts as being created for Franciscan monks. Franciscan monks took a vow of poverty and therefore could not own property. Consequently, if anyone wanted to give money to the order of Franciscan monks or to monks in a particular monastery it was necessary for someone else to hold that property for the benefit of the monks. It was important to ensure that the monks would have the use of the property and that this third party would not be allowed to take the property for herself: hence imposing the obligations of trusteeship on the person who held the property. Another account of the source of the trust places it in the Middle East in the 'waqf', a device which was used within Muslim families to provide for property to be held by one family member for the benefit of other family members who required charity.[8] It has been plausibly suggested that either the European crusaders[9] or the Franciscan monks brought this idea back to Europe with them.[10] An idea which has a pleasing circularity with my initial story of the European crusader whom we might believe learned of the waqf when in the Middle East. Indeed, it seems that the trust was found in many European countries like Italy before those countries adopted civil codes which obliterated their traces.[11] Yet another story starts with the fact that English law knew the 'use' before it knew the 'trust' – that much is accepted fact – and that the trust more specifically was developed by conveyancing lawyers in the seventeenth century around the time of the English Civil War in the 1640s to ensure that land would not be appropriated or misapplied by binding its trustees as to given courses of action over time. Indeed all of this seems at odds with the determination of historians at the turn of the 20th century that there was something quintessentially English about the trust.[12]

Whichever story is to be preferred they each have two common themes: first, more than one person has rights in the same property simultaneously but in such a way that one person is required to deal with the property entirely for the benefit of the other person; and, secondly, these trusts were developed by practical people trying to deal with practical problems, as opposed to being created by a legislator or a judge setting out all of the appropriate principles

---

7 Therefore, you might find it useful to think of the first breach of trust as having been the abuses wrought on the kingdom by King John when Richard the Lionheart left the kingdom in the care of his brother, John. Many of the fundamental principles of trusts law can therefore be illustrated by watching those Robin Hood films in which Richard the Lionheart eventually returns from captivity in Austria to reclaim his proprietary rights over his kingdom from his brother, eg, *The Adventures of Robin Hood*, starring Errol Flynn. It has been suggested that these crusaders may have developed the trust out of the Islamic waqf, which was a form of charitable institution used within families to support family members: see, eg, Lim, 2001.

8 See, eg, Lim, 2001.

9 Moffat, 1999, 26.

10 See Lim, 2001, 56.

11 Lupoi, 2000, 368.

12 See Maitland, 1936, 1. See section 32.5.2 on this point.

in advance. In truth in trusts law we have always been reacting to circumstance: every case and every statute has been seeking to order and to regularise whatever has already been done in practice. The purpose of books like this is to explain how these principles fit together and also how they should be understood as working in the future.

As we shall see later in this chapter, this division of ownership enables a large number of complex commercial and non-commercial uses of property to be carried on, ranging from the creation of pension funds and explaining ownership of the home through to taking security in international financial transactions and constructing sophisticated tax avoidance schemes. First, however, we shall set out a definition of the trust and then consider the various types of trust.

2.2 THE DEFINITION OF A TRUST

2.2.1 The definition of a trust

The following definition of a trust is given in Thomas and Hudson's *The Law of Trusts*:[13]

> The essence of a trust is the imposition of an equitable obligation on a person who is the legal owner of property (a trustee) which requires that person to act in good conscience when dealing with that property in favour of any person (the beneficiary) who has a beneficial interest recognised by equity in the property.[14] The trustee is said to 'hold the property on trust' for the beneficiary. There are four significant elements to the trust: that it is equitable, that it provides the beneficiary with rights in property, that it also imposes obligations on the trustee, and that those obligations are fiduciary in nature.

Trusts are enforced by equity and therefore the beneficiary is said to have an 'equitable interest' in the trust property (sometimes this right in a beneficiary is referred to as a 'beneficial interest'), whereas the trustee will be treated by the common law as holding the 'legal title' in the trust property, thus enabling the trustee to deal with the trust property so as to achieve the objectives of the trust.[15] In general terms we can observe that a trustee is the officer under a trust who is obliged to carry out the terms of the trust and who owes strict fiduciary duties of the utmost good faith to the beneficiaries.[16] The mechanics of the trust are

---

13 Thomas and Hudson, 2010, para 1.01. Footnotes within this quotation are footnotes from the original text. In that book, from pages 1 through 26, Thomas and Hudson analyse the effects of this definition in greater detail than is necessary at this stage of this book.

14 The nature of this form of 'conscience' has been the subject of scholarly debate for centuries. For jurists such as St German and for Sir Thomas More conscience bound the Lord Chancellor to follow the rules set out in the common law and conscience bound a trustee not simply to follow his own conscience but rather conscience bound a trustee to observe the wishes of his beneficiary (see, for example, *Gresley v Saunders* (1522) Spelman Rep 22–23). However, as the notion of conscience is rendered by Lord Browne-Wilkinson in *Westdeutsche Landesbank v Islington LBC* [1996] AC 669, there is a suggestion of a greater subjectivity in that a person will only be subject to the duties of a trustee if he knows of the matter which is said to affect his conscience: see para 27.01 in this regard in relation to constructive trusts arising on the basis of conscience.

15 The distinction between equity and common law was considered in Chapter 1, in section 1.2.

16 These fiduciary obligations are considered in detail in Part 3 of this book. The idea of good conscience requiring a trustee to act in the best interests of the beneficiary appears to have been present in *Gresley v Saunders* (1522) Spelman Rep 22–31.

considered in detail in section 2.3 below. Before that, however, we will turn our attention to consider the different forms of trust and how the different forms of trust come into existence.

2.2.2 The mechanisms by which the different forms of trust come into existence

The mechanisms by which trusts come into existence are described by Thomas and Hudson in *The Law of Trusts* in the following fashion:[17]

> A trust comes into existence either by virtue of having been established expressly by a person (the settlor) who was the absolute owner of property[18] before the creation of the trust (an express trust); or by virtue of some action of the settlor which the court interprets to have been sufficient to create a trust but which the settlor himself did not know was a trust (an implied [express] trust);[19] or by operation of law either to resolve some dispute as to ownership of property where the creation of an express trust has failed (an automatic resulting trust)[20] or to recognise the proprietary rights of one who has contributed to the purchase price of property (a purchase price resulting trust);[21] or by operation of law to prevent the legal owner of property from seeking unconscionably to deny the rights of those who have equitable interests in that property (a constructive trust).[22]

These various forms of trust are outlined in the next section; however, it will take much of the rest of this book to consider how they function in detail.

2.2.3 The different types of trust

There are four principal types of trust:[23] express trusts; resulting trusts; constructive trusts; and implied trusts, although implied trusts are rarely applied today.[24] We will focus in this short section on the three most significant types of trust in modern trusts practice: express

---

17 Thomas and Hudson, 2010, para 1.02. The footnotes in the quotation are footnotes from the original.
18 Such that the 'property' in question is best understood to be 'rights in property' and need not be absolute title in the property. Thus, a lease over land may itself be the subject matter of a trust even though it is not the largest property right in that land (*Keech v Sandford* (1726) Sel Cas Ch 61). An equitable interest in a trust may itself be the subject matter of a trust (*Re Lashmar* (1891) 1 Ch 258; *Grainge v Wilberforce* (1889) 5 TLR 436).
19 *Re Kayford* [1975] 1 WLR 279; *Paul v Constance* [1977] 1 WLR 527.
20 *Vandervell v IRC* [1967] 2 AC 291.
21 *Dyer v Dyer* (1788) 2 Cox Eq Cas 92.
22 *Westdeutsche Landesbank Girozentrale v Islington LBC* [1996] AC 669.
23 As suggested by Law of Property Act 1925, s 53(2).
24 That the fourth category of 'implied trusts' exists is suggested by its mention in s 53(2) of the Law of Property Act 1925 but that category is suggested to be an empty one for the most part unless the suggestion made by Thomas and Hudson, 2010, para 1.20 (as mentioned in this book in para 2.2.2 above) to the effect that 'implied trusts' should be taken to constitute express trusts which are created unknowingly by a settlor as in *Paul v Constance* [1977] 1 WLR 527, is adopted by the courts. Lord Browne-Wilkinson in *Westdeutsche Landesbank v Islington LBC* [1996] AC 669 referred to 'implied trusts'. This is an expression which is problematic in English law with some taking it simply to refer to 'resulting trusts' (which are considered in Chapter 11), while others feel that it ought to refer both to constructive and resulting trusts (an area which is dubbed in this book 'trusts implied by law' as opposed to 'implied trusts'). What was meant by this class of trusts was unsure when Sir Arthur Underhill wrote *A Practical and Concise Manual of the Law Relating to Private Trusts and Trustees*, 3rd edn, Butterworths, 1889, 12, suggesting that an 'implied trust' might be any of the categories just mentioned.

trusts, resulting trusts and constructive trusts. The most significant distinction between them is that express trusts can be created deliberately by a settlor (as considered in Part 2 of this book), whereas resulting and constructive trusts are implied by a court in appropriate circumstances (as considered in Part 4 *Trusts Implied by Law* of this book). Later in this chapter we will also draw some distinctions between trusts on the basis of the types of powers which they give to their trustees, and by reference to the purpose behind their creation. For the moment we will consider the three, principal types of trust.

Express trusts

Express trusts are trusts which are declared intentionally by the settlor.[25] Typically, the settlor will intend to settle specific property on trust for clearly identifiable beneficiaries, to be held by appointed trustees according to terms set out by the settlor.[26] However, there are situations in which the settlor might intend her actions without knowing that a lawyer would define those actions as constituting the creation of a trust.[27] For example, a settlor may intend both of her children to have equal access to the money left in her will without knowing that a lawyer would say she had thereby created a trust over that money in favour of her children. In such situations the court will find that an express trust has been created (as considered in Chapter 3).[28] It is necessary that the trust property is sufficiently identifiable[29] and that there is no uncertainty as to the identity of the beneficiaries (as considered in Chapter 3).[30] Similarly, legal title in the trust property must be transferred to the trustees before the trust can be effective.[31] These issues are considered in greater detail in Part 2 generally. In particular, Part 2 considers the possible distinctions between various forms of express trusts. Express trusts created under a formal instrument were also known as 'settlements', which was the source of the term 'settlor'.

Resulting trusts

Resulting trusts are implied by the court – they are not created intentionally by the settlor.[32] Resulting trusts arise in two situations, in the wake of the decision of the House of Lords in *Westdeutsche Landesbank Girozentrale v Islington LBC.*[33] First, where the settlor has transferred the legal title in property to a trustee but has failed to identify the person(s) who will take the equitable interest in the trust property, that part of the equitable interest which has not been settled on trust for an identified beneficiary will be held by the trustee on resulting

---

25 *Re Kayford* [1975] 1 WLR 279; *Paul v Constance* [1977] 1 WLR 527.

26 *Morice v Bishop of Durham* (1805) 10 Ves 522; *Milroy v Lord* (1862) 4 De GF & J 264; *Bowman v Secular Society Ltd* [1917] AC 406.

27 *Paul v Constance* [1977] 1 WLR 527.

28 *Ibid.*

29 *Re London Wine Co (Shippers) Ltd* [1986] PCC 121; *Re Goldcorp Exchange Ltd* [1995] 1 AC 74; *Westdeutsche Landesbank Girozentrale v Islington LBC* [1996] AC 669.

30 *Morice v Bishop of Durham* (1805) 10 Ves 522; *Knight v Knight* (1840) 3 Beav 148; *Knight v Boughton* (1840) 11 Cl & Fin 513; *Re Gulbenkian* [1968] Ch 126; *McPhail v Doulton* [1970] 2 WLR 1110.

31 *Milroy v Lord* (1862) 4 De GF&J 264.

32 Cf comments made by Lord Browne-Wilkinson in *Westdeutsche Landesbank v Islington LBC* [1996] AC 669 to the effect that resulting trusts come into effect as a result of the common intention of the parties, an idea confronted at para 11.1.3 in this book.

33 [1996] AC 669.

trust for the settlor.[34] The underpinning of this form of resulting trust is that where the equitable interest in property is not vested in another person, that equitable interest will 'jump back' to the settlor. This is an extension of the equitable principle that there cannot be a vacuum in the equitable interest in property.

Secondly, where a person contributes to the purchase price of property, that person acquires an equitable interest in the property.[35] The size of the equitable interest will be equal to the size of the contribution in proportion to the total purchase price of the property. Therefore, if a person contributes £20,000 to the purchase of an asset which cost £100,000, that person would acquire an equitable interest equal to one-fifth of the value of that property on resulting trust principles. Resulting trusts are considered in detail in Chapter 11.

Constructive trusts

A constructive trust arises by operation of law.[36] In circumstances in which a defendant has acted unconscionably, for example, in keeping a payment which she knows was paid to her by mistake, the court will consider the defendant to be a constructive trustee.[37] In the case of unconscionable receipt of property, the defendant will hold that property on constructive trust for the person properly entitled in equity to that property.[38] Therefore, if Dipali has retained money paid to her under a mistake, from the moment that Dipali is aware that the payment was made mistakenly, she will be treated by the court as being a trustee of that money.[39] Dipali will therefore hold the money on constructive trust for the payer as beneficiary.[40]

There are other contexts in which the courts will analyse a situation as giving rise to a constructive trust. In relation to family homes, as discussed in Chapter 15 of this book, where two or more people come to an arrangement as to the ownership of their home (possibly by allocation of responsibility for the mortgage, or as a result of more general conversations between themselves) the English courts will typically impose a constructive trust on those parties to give effect to their common intention.[41]

Other examples of the constructive trust are considered in more detail in Chapter 12 of this book.[42] There are situations in which a constructive trust will impose a liability on a defendant not to hold specific property on trust, but rather will impose an obligation to pay money to the other person.[43] These remedies are dubbed 'personal liability to account' and

---

34 *Vandervell v IRC* [1967] 2 AC 291, HL.
35 *Dyer v Dyer* (1788) 2 Cox Eq Cas 92.
36 On which see section 12.1.
37 *Westdeutsche Landesbank Girozentrale v Islington LBC* [1996] AC 669; *Paragon Finance plc v DB Thakerar & Co* [1999] 1 All ER 400.
38 *Ibid.*
39 *Westdeutsche Landesbank Girozentrale v Islington LBC* [1996] AC 669, particularly as explaining the decision in *Chase Manhattan Bank NA v Israel-British Bank (London) Ltd* [1981] 1 Ch 105.
40 *Ibid.*
41 *Lloyds Bank v Rosset* [1991] 1 AC 107, [1990] 1 All ER 1111; *Ivin v Blake* [1995] 1 FLR 70.
42 In particular, constructive trusts in relation to fiduciaries earning secret profits (*Keech v Sandford* (1726) Sel Cas Ch 61; *Boardman v Phipps* [1967] 2 AC 46) or receiving bribes (*Attorney-General for Hong Kong v Reid* [1994] 1 AC 324, [1993] 3 WLR 1143) or forming contracts to transfer property (*Neville v Wilson* [1997] Ch 144).
43 In particular, the claims for personal liability for knowing receipt of property in breach of trust or dishonest assistance in a breach of trust, as considered in Chapter 20: *Barnes v Addy* (1874) 9 Ch App 244; *Royal Brunei Airlines v Tan* [1995] 2 AC 378; *Twinsectra Ltd v Yardley* [2002] 2 AC 164, [2002] 2 All ER 377; *Dubai Aluminium v Salaam* [2002] 3 WLR 1913.

deal with situations in which the defendant has received trust property knowing it has been transferred away in breach of trust,[44] or has dishonestly assisted in the breach of trust.[45] The defendant, by definition, will not have that trust property still under her control (or else a constructive trust would be imposed directly over that property). Rather, the defendant's obligation is to make good the loss suffered by the trust.[46]

2.2.4 The structure of the rest of this chapter

In this chapter we will first consider the structure of express trusts in detail in section 2.3, including an overview of the various sub-categories of express trusts. This analysis will throw some light on the various people who participate in a trust and the nature of their respective rights and obligations. Then we will return to the fundamental principles of trusts law in section 2.4 which apply to resulting and constructive trusts as well as to express trusts. Then we consider the benefits and uses of trusts in section 2.5, varying between their commercial and their domestic uses. Finally we will distinguish the trust from other legal concepts in section 2.6.

2.3 EXPRESS TRUSTS – THE MAGIC TRIANGLE

2.3.1 How the express trust is structured

A description of an express trust might run as follows: a trust is created when the absolute owner of property (the settlor) passes the legal title in that property to a person (the trustee) to hold that property on trust for the benefit of another person (the beneficiary) in accordance with terms set out by the settlor. There are three legal capacities to bear in mind in the creation of a trust: the settlor, the trustee, and the beneficiary. These three capacities form the 'magic triangle'. The 'magic triangle' looks like this:

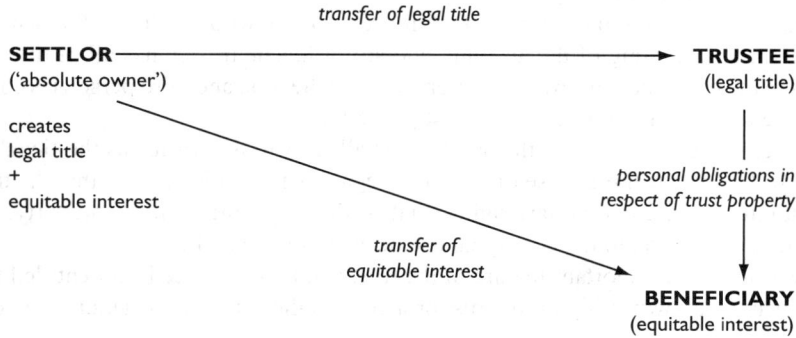

---

44 *Re Montagu* [1987] Ch 264; *Polly Peck International v Nadir (No 2)* [1992] 4 All ER 769.
45 *Royal Brunei Airlines v Tan* [1995] 2 AC 378; *Twinsectra Ltd v Yardley* [2002] 2 AC 164, [2002] 2 All ER 377; *Dubai Aluminium v Salaam* [2002] 3 WLR 1913.
46 *Ibid.*

2.3.2 The settlor

In the magic triangle, before the creation of an express trust, the settlor holds absolute title[47] in the property which is to be settled on trust. If the settlor does not hold the absolute title in the property rights which are to be settled on trust, then the settlor is incapable of creating a valid trust over them. The formalities for a valid declaration of trust are set out in Chapter 5. Provided that a trust has been validly declared, the legal title must be transferred to the trustees, as considered in Chapter 5.[48] The beneficiary acquires the equitable interest in the trust fund at that time.

Once a trust has been validly declared, the settlor ceases to have any active role in the trust.[49] A trust may be created entirely orally or it may be created by means of a carefully drafted trust instrument, as considered in Chapter 3. For example, if a settlor declared a trust over property just before her marriage in favour of herself, her husband and any prospective children, if the marriage failed, the settlor would not be entitled in her capacity as settlor to unwind the trust and recover the trust property.[50] Once a trust has been created, it remains inviolate. The only possible exception to this rule would be if the settlor were to reserve to herself some specific authority under the terms of the trust to unwind the trust, whether acting as trustee or enjoying the property as a beneficiary. The precise terms of the trust will be decisive, unless those terms transgress any rule of public policy.[51] In any event, it is likely that in such a situation, the person who acted as settlor would then reserve rights as a form of trustee rather than as settlor.

2.3.3 The trustee

On creation of a trust, the legal title in the trust property must be vested in the trustee and the property rights making up the trust fund must be held by the trustee on trust for the beneficiaries. Take the example of a trust created over a fund of £1,000 held in a current bank account. The legal title in that bank account will be vested in the trustee. In practice, this means that the trustee's name appears on the cheque book, the trustee is empowered to authorise transfers of any money held in that account, the trustee has a contract with the bank as to the administration of the bank account, it is the trustee who would sue the bank for any negligence in the handling of the account, and so forth. The trustee has all of the common law rights in the bank account. Any litigation between the trust and third persons is conducted by the trustee as legal titleholder in the trust property.

Therefore, in the remainder of this book we shall refer to the trustee as the 'legal owner' of property. This is a technical use of the term 'legal owner' which means that the trustee is vested with all of the common law rights (that is, the 'legal title') in the property. It is not being used in opposition to the colloquial use of the word 'illegal'.

However, the most important feature of the trust is that the trustee is not entitled to assert personal, beneficial ownership in the trust property. Rather, it is the beneficiary who has all

---

47   That is, all of the rights of ownership in the property: all the legal and all the equitable rights potentially held in that property.

48   See section 5.1 below.

49   *Paul v Paul* (1882) 20 Ch D 742.

50   *Ibid.*

51   Such as defrauding creditors: *Midland Bank v Wyatt* [1995] 1 FLR 697.

of the beneficial title in property, as considered immediately below. Therefore, suppose that Susan dies leaving a will which appoints Tabitha to hold a house on trust as trustee for her children. Tabitha will be the person whose name appears on the legal title to the property at the Land Registry. However, Tabitha would not be entitled to sell the property and keep the money for herself beneficially. Rather, she would be required to hold the sale proceeds on trust for the beneficiaries. In that sense, it is not her property.

Two important points arise. First, a practical point. It will always be important to consider the precise terms of the trust. As will become apparent throughout this book, the courts will tend to look very closely at the precise written terms of a trust or at the verbal expression of the settlor's intentions.[52] Therefore if, in the example above, Tabitha was required to hold the house on trust so that Susan's children could live there until the youngest of them reached the age of 18, Tabitha would be committing a breach of trust by selling the property before the child reached the age of 18. Consequently, not only would Tabitha hold the sale proceeds of the house on trust for the children, but she would also be required to pay compensation to the trust to make good any loss suffered by the trust fund from the breach of trust.[53] However, if the terms of the trust gave Tabitha a discretionary power to sell whenever Tabitha chose, then Tabitha would not have committed a breach of trust, *prima facie*, in selling the house.

Secondly, the trustee is required to hold the original trust property, or any substitute property, on trust for the beneficiaries. Therefore, unless there is something expressly to the contrary on the terms of the trust, a trust does not simply attach to specific property and that property only. Rather, the trust attaches to bundles of property rights which may be transferred from one piece of property to another. Suppose a trust with a defined purpose of maintaining a house for the beneficiaries with a power for the trustees to sell that house if the beneficiaries wish to move elsewhere. At the outset the original house is held on trust. When the house is sold, the trust attaches instead to the sale proceeds and then to the second house which is bought with that money. If the trust attached rigidly to one piece of property, it would be impossible for the beneficiaries to acquire rights in the second house because those rights would be stuck to the first house. In truth, a trust attaches to property rights and to value, not permanently to specific property. In this way a trustee can deal legitimately with the trust property by buying and selling it, and so on. This idea is considered in more detail below at para 3.4.3. What is important to bear in mind is that the particular property which makes up the trust fund from time to time may change; it is the trust fund in whatever form at any particular time which the trustees are required to hold on trust.

The precise obligations on the trustee are therefore to be found in the trust document itself. However, there are more general obligations on the trustee imposed by the general law of trusts. These issues are considered in more detail in Part 3 *Administration of Trusts*. Among the issues to be considered are the amount of information which trustees are required to give to beneficiaries, the manner in which the trust fund should be invested while it is being held on trust, the appointment or retirement of trustees, and the termination of the trust. As may have become apparent by now, much will depend upon the nature and terms of the trust. However, the most important types of express trusts are considered next.

---

52 *Fuller v Evans* [2000] 1 All ER 636.
53 *Target Holdings v Redferns* [1996] 1 AC 421, considered in Chapter 18.

Bare trust

A bare trust arises where the trustees hold property on trust for a single, absolutely entitled beneficiary. The beneficiary therefore owns the entire equitable interest in the trust fund. That means that the trustee has no discretion nor any obligation other than the stewardship of the trust property on behalf of that beneficiary. The beneficiary herself must not be subject to any contingency or encumbrance which will interfere with her equitable interest in the property. She will hold 100% of the possible equitable interest in that property. The trustee in such a situation is generally referred to as being a 'nominee'; that is, one who holds property in the name of another.[54]

Fixed trust

A fixed trust refers to the situation in which the trustees hold property on trust for a certain, defined list of beneficiaries. An example of such a class of beneficiaries would be: 'on trust for my two children Anna and Bertha.' The 'fixed' nature of the trust refers then to the fixed list of people who can benefit from the trust. The role of trustee is comparatively straightforward in this situation because the trustee is required simply to perform the terms of the trust slavishly.[55] The trustee has no meaningful discretion in the operation of such a trust.

Discretionary trust power and mere power of appointment

The settlor may want to give the trustees the flexibility to cope with unexpected future events by giving them some discretion. So, a *discretionary trust* gives some discretion to the trustee as to the manner in which property is to be distributed and/or the people to whom that property is to be distributed. Suppose a situation in which a settlor has three adult children and wishes to require that the trustees use as much of a fund of money as they may think appropriate to help whichever one of the children earns the least money in any given calendar year. The trustee has discretion to distribute the amount of money necessary to make good the child's lack of funds. The role of trustee is therefore more complicated than in respect of the fixed trust because the trustee is required to exercise some discretion, always ensuring that such exercise of her discretion remains permitted within the terms of the trust.[56] Suppose the settlor set aside a fund of money 'such that my trustee *shall* pay £5,000 per year out of that fund to whichever of my children has the greatest need of it'. In such a situation, the trustee is compelled to make the payment because of the inclusion of the word 'shall', but she has discretion as to which child will receive it.[57]

Alternatively, a settlor may decide that a trustee is to have a power of appointment between a number of potential beneficiaries so that the trustees are only required to make a payment out of a trust fund if they consider it to be appropriate. That means that the trustee is empowered to decide which people from among an identified class of beneficiaries are entitled to

---

54 See para 3.5.6 below.
55 See para 3.5.5 below.
56 See para 3.5.4 below.
57 The issue in such situations will often be whether or not the ambit of the trustee's discretion has been identified with sufficient certainty.

take absolute title in any property which is appointed to them by the trustees. Suppose then that the settlor sets aside a fund 'to be held on trust by Trustee with a power to appoint the sum of £10,000 to whichever of the Sunderland AFC first team has performed most consistently throughout the current season'. The trustee therefore has discretion to choose which of the identified class is to receive absolute title in that £10,000 per season, but unlike a discretionary trust power, the power of appointment does not require that any payment be made unless the trustee considers it to be necessary: because the trustee has a *power* to appoint that money, she will not be obliged to do so if she considers it inappropriate.[58] (The rights of beneficiaries in relation to discretionary trusts and powers of appointment differ from the rights of beneficiaries under bare trusts in the manner discussed in section 4.1.4 below, but those issues are not important at present.)

Accumulation and maintenance trust

A settlor may seek to create an endowment trust from which, for example, the needs and living expenses of the settlor's children are to be provided. Consequently, the principal responsibility of the trustee is to invest the trust property and then to apply it according to the needs identified in the terms of the trust. The beneficiaries have rights against the trustees to have the trust performed in accordance with the terms of the trust and to have property advanced for their benefit at the time identified in the trust (subject to any discretion vested in the trustees).

The significance of the trustees' powers and obligations being fiduciary in nature

The trustee is possessed of both powers and obligations, as just discussed. By 'powers' are meant a range of abilities and capacities set out in the terms of the trust possibly to hold the trust fund, to invest the trust fund in specified investments, to exercise their discretion between certain classes of beneficiaries and so forth.[59] By 'obligations' are meant duties contained in the terms of the trust which the trustee is compelled to carry out. It would be possible to invest a person with powers without that person necessarily being a trustee. It would be possible for one person to have rights and obligations in relation to property without necessarily being a trustee.

   The trustee is a form of what English lawyers term a 'fiduciary'. The expression 'fiduciary' is a difficult one to define with precision – a little like an elephant, we think we will know one when we see one, but we may have some difficulty in defining it in the abstract.[60] It is perhaps easier to list the four classic examples of fiduciaries: a trustee in relation to the beneficiaries; a company director in relation to the company; an agent in relation to the

---

58 *Breadner v Granville-Grossman* [2000] 4 All ER 705.
59 Thomas, 1998.
60 For example, the comedian Eddie Izzard defined an elephant as being 'an upside-down squirrel' in his *Definite Article* show.

principal; and a business partner in relation to other partners.[61] One commonly used definition of a fiduciary office was given by Millett LJ:[62]

> A fiduciary is someone who has undertaken to act for or on behalf of another in a particular matter in circumstances which give rise to a relationship of trust and confidence. The distinguishing obligation of a fiduciary is the obligation of loyalty. The principal is entitled to the single-minded loyalty of his fiduciary. The core liability has several facets. A fiduciary must act in good faith; he must not make a profit out of his trust; he must not place himself in a position where his duty and his interest may conflict; he may not act for his own benefit or the benefit of a third person without the informed consent of his principal. This is not intended to be an exhaustive list, but it is sufficient to indicate the nature of fiduciary obligations. They are the defining characteristics of the fiduciary.

Therefore, we know that the obligations of acting in a fiduciary capacity arise in circumstances in which one person has undertaken to act loyally in the affairs of another. The clearest example of a fiduciary is a trustee who owes duties not to take any unauthorised profit from her office of trustee, not to permit any conflict of interest between her own affairs and those of the trust, to act with impartiality among all of the beneficiaries to a trust, and so forth.[63] These obligations are discussed in detail in Chapter 8.

Broadly then, a fiduciary is one who owes legal duties of loyalty and utmost good faith in relation to another person. Yet, whether a fiduciary obligation exists in any specific set of circumstances is not always an easy question to answer.[64] In relation to a trustee carrying on trust business, once that trust is properly constituted, there will necessarily be a fiduciary relationship between trustee and beneficiary. The effect of there being a fiduciary relationship will be that the fiduciary will owe the beneficiary a range of obligations of good faith[65] and potential obligations to make good any loss suffered by the beneficiary:[66] it is an onerous role, as considered in Part 6 of this book, *Breach of Trust and Related Equitable Claims*. In other contexts it is less easy to know how far any fiduciary obligations will extend. Suppose that the trustee and the beneficiary leave a trust meeting and emerge into the open air. The beneficiary starts to cross the road unaware of the danger of oncoming traffic. At that point in time any obligation which the trustee owes to the beneficiary to pull her back onto the kerb is not a fiduciary duty. We may think that one human being owes another human being some indefinable, quasi-moral obligation to try to save her in such a situation, but whatever form that obligation may or may not take, it is not a fiduciary obligation. Similarly, a solicitor will

---

61   See the analysis of the concept of 'fiduciary' in the essay which comprises Chapter 14.

62   *Bristol & West Building Society v Mothew* [1998] Ch 1 at 18, *per* Millett LJ.

63   All of these principles are considered in Chapter 8 and more generally in Part 3 of this book.

64   For a discussion of this concept, see Chapter 14 of this book.

65   See the various expressions of these principles in *Keech v Sandford* (1726) Sel Cas Ch 61 and *Boardman v Phipps* [1967] 2 AC 46 relating to the obligations not to make secret profits nor to permit conflicts of interest; and *Tito v Waddell (No 2)* [1977] Ch 106 concerning the self-dealing and fair-dealing principles relating to trustees dealing on their own account with the trust property.

66   *Target Holdings v Redferns* [1996] 1 AC 421 concerning the obligations of the trustees to account to beneficiaries in relation to any breach of trust causing loss to the beneficiaries.

typically owe fiduciary duties towards a client in relation to the conduct of the client's legal affairs but not in relation to the client's choice of socks. Alternatively, a doctor may occupy a fiduciary position in relation to a patient's medical treatment but not in relation to the patient's choice of financial investments. It is all a matter of context.[67]

Therefore, as we will see, it will be necessary to examine the precise terms of any trust to decide what form of obligation is owed by the trustee in particular circumstances. In Chapter 3 we will consider the need for the settlor to make the identities of the beneficiaries sufficiently certain. In considering the tests for certainty of beneficiaries it will be necessary to distinguish between powers which are given to people in their personal capacities and powers which are given to people in fiduciary capacities. In Chapters 4 and 5 we will analyse the different rights of beneficiaries and the various mechanisms for constituting a trust respectively, each of which will require us to analyse closely the precise terms of any given trust. The particular fiduciary duties of the trustee in normal circumstances are considered in detail in Chapter 8. The ramifications of the breach of a fiduciary duty are considered in detail in Chapter 18.

2.3.4 The beneficiary

The rights of the beneficiary, as has emerged from the preceding discussion, will depend on the specific terms and nature of the trust. The beneficiary will always have a right to compel the trustees to carry out the terms of the trust. It is a necessary part of the law of trusts that there be some person for whose benefit the court can decree performance of the trust.[68] Furthermore, the beneficiary has proprietary rights in the trust property.[69] Thus, the beneficiary's equitable interest is a right in property. That property right forms part of the beneficiary's estate; but it does not form part of the trustee's personal estate. This has the important result that if a trustee were to go into insolvency, then the trust property would remain the beneficiary's property and would not fall to be distributed among the trustee's creditors. Therefore, trusts provide protection against an insolvency for their beneficiaries. If the trust property should be lost as a result of some breach of trust, then the beneficiary also has a right against the trustee personally to compensate the beneficiary's loss.[70] This right to equitable compensation operates over-and-above the beneficiary's proprietary rights.[71] The beneficiary's proprietary rights also permit her to trace after her property and to assert rights over any property by which the original trust property has been substituted[72] and against any

---

67   See the analysis of the concept of 'fiduciary' in the essay which comprises Chapter 14.

68   *Morice v Bishop of Durham* (1805) 10 Ves 522; *Bowman v Secular Society Ltd* [1917] AC 406, 441 by Lord Parker, as considered in Chapter 4 below. Cf *Medforth v Blake* [2000] Ch 86.

69   *Saunders v Vautier* (1841) 4 Beav 115; *Tinsley v Milligan* [1994] 1 AC 340, 371. The proprietary nature of these rights are discussed in detail in section 4.1.

70   *Clough v Bond* (1838) 3 My & Cr 490; *Re Massingberd's Settlement* (1890) 63 LT 296; *Nocton v Lord Ashburton* [1914] AC 932; *Target Holdings v Redferns* [1996] 1 AC 421. Breach of trust is considered in Chapter 18.

71   *Target Holdings v Redferns* [1996] 1 AC 421.

72   *Pilcher v Rawlins* (1872) LR 7 Ch App 259; *Re Diplock's Estate* [1948] Ch 465; *Westdeutsche Landesbank v Islington LBC* [1996] AC 669; *Boscawen v Bajwa* [1996] 1 WLR 328. The law of tracing is considered in Chapter 19.

people who participated in the breach of trust despite not being trustees.[73] Therefore, as we shall see in the course of this book, the beneficiary has a range of remedies available to her which will enable her to protect her rights under the trust.

Given these general propositions, beneficiaries will nevertheless occupy subtly different positions depending upon the terms of the trust under which they take their particular interests. The foregoing discussion of the varying types of trusts indicates not only that the precise obligations of the trustees will differ from case to case, but also that the rights of the beneficiaries will vary in quality.

The most important distinction will be between vested rights and rights which remain contingent on some eventuality provided for under the terms of the trust. Under a mere power of appointment, the beneficiary will have no vested rights in any property until the trustee exercises her power of appointment in favour of that beneficiary.[74] The right of the beneficiary is merely an unenforceable hope (or *spes*) that the trustee will decide to exercise her power in favour of that beneficiary.[75] A power of appointment does not give the beneficiary any right in the money: all that the beneficiary has is an unenforceable hope that the holder of the power will choose to benefit her. Under a discretionary trust, however, the beneficiary will not acquire a vested right in any particular property under the trust until the trustees' discretion is exercised in her favour – but significantly under a discretionary trust, the beneficiary will acquire a personal right in common with the other beneficiaries to ensure that the trustees observe the terms of the trust. A beneficiary under a discretionary trust has a right to require the trustees to consider her case fairly: that in itself constitutes some right in the trust property.[76] To decide which is which, the trusts lawyer is required to construe the words used by the settlor carefully: this point is considered in section 4.1.4.

It is important to note that beyond that personal claim against the trustee, the beneficiary will not have rights to any specific property under a discretionary trust before the trustee has exercised her discretion. This should be compared with a bare trust, under which the beneficiary will have equitable *proprietary* rights in the trust property from the moment at which the trust is created. This is simply because in a bare trust there is only one beneficiary; whereas in a discretionary trust there will be more than one person potentially with a right in the trust property. Under a bare trust there is no interest to compete with that of the bare beneficiary, therefore the right of the beneficiary is deemed to be vested in the trust fund itself. Similarly, where trust property is held 'on trust for A for life, remainder to B', it is A who will have a vested proprietary interest in the trust fund and a right to receive the income from the trust fund, whereas B will acquire a right to ensure that the trustees respect her rights to the property after A's death but no vested interest until A's death.

The most important principle in defining the nature of the beneficiary's entitlement is that set out in *Saunders v Vautier*.[77] A beneficiary who is absolutely entitled and *sui juris* (that is,

---

73 *Barnes v Addy* (1874) 9 Ch App 244; *Royal Brunei Airlines v Tan* [1995] 2 AC 378; *Twinsectra Ltd v Yardley* [2002] 2 AC 164; [2002] 2 All ER 377; *Dubai Aluminium v Salaam* [2002] 3 WLR 1913. The law on personal liability to account for participation in a breach of trust is considered in Chapter 20.

74 *Re Brooks' ST* [1939] 1 Ch 993.

75 *Ibid*. This passage was cited with approval and formed the basis of the decision in *World Group Europe Holdings plc v Bettina Vossberg* (2004) August 7, First Hall, Civil Court, Malta; Onor. Cuschieri.

76 *Re Ralli's WT* [1964] 2 WLR 144.

77 (1841) 4 Beav 115.

over 18 and not otherwise incapacitated) will be able to direct the trustees to deliver up the trust property to that beneficiary so that the beneficiary becomes absolutely entitled to it. Therefore, the beneficiary's greatest possible right is to be able to take control of this trust fund and to direct the manner in which the trustee is able to deal with it. However, in relation to discretionary trusts, for example, it is a difficult question to know whether or not the beneficiaries will be able to exercise such a power precisely before any identified property is appointed to them. This question is considered in detail in para 4.1.2. On the one hand, if there is a possibility either that there may be further members of the class of beneficiaries added in the future or if the trustees have a power to retain trust property, then the beneficiaries could not be said to have rights commensurate with the *Saunders v Vautier* principle;[78] by contrast, on the other hand, if the terms of the trust instrument mean that no further people can be added to the class of beneficiaries and if the trustees are required to exhaust the trust property, then the beneficiaries will be entitled to act together and so exercise *Saunders v Vautier* rights.[79] As will be clear by this stage, everything will depend upon the precise terms of any trust instrument.

Aside from the power given by *Saunders v Vautier*, the right which the beneficiary will have, even under a discretionary trust, is a right to compel the trustee to carry out her obligations in accordance with the terms of the trust. Significantly, this does not mean that the beneficiaries can direct the trustee as to which decisions to make nor the substance of those decisions, but rather that the beneficiaries are entitled to ask the court to police the manner in which those decisions are made, as considered in Chapter 8.

2.3.5 Distinguishing between 'people' and 'legal capacities'

It is important to distinguish between the human beings (or companies) involved in the formation of a trust and the capacities which those people occupy. The same human being can occupy a variety of different capacities in relation to the same trust. An example will make the point clear. It is possible that Sally, the absolute owner of shares in SAFC plc, may decide that she wishes to create a trust over those shares for the benefit of her immediate family. Therefore, Sally might declare that she will hold those shares on trust herself, as sole trustee, in favour of herself, her husband and her children. Therefore, Sally would be settlor, trustee and one of the beneficiaries. This is perfectly possible. It is vital, however, to remember that Sally acts in three different capacities simultaneously: settlor, trustee and beneficiary. Do not confuse the person involved with the capacity which they occupy from time to time.[80] This is a difficulty which even courts experience occasionally.[81] One person may be trustee and beneficiary, but in trusts law it is important to think of such an individual as two people – one a trustee and the other a beneficiary.

The only situation which would not be legally possible in trusts law would be that in which Sally held as sole trustee for herself as sole beneficiary. This is not possible because Sally would therefore hold all of the proprietary rights in the shares, and therefore should be considered still

---

78   *Gartside v IRC* [1968] AC 553, 606 *per* Lord Reid, 617 *per* Lord Wilberforce.
79   *Re Smith* [1928] Ch 915; *Re Nelson (note)* [1928] Ch 920.
80   *Re Brooks' ST* [1939] 1 Ch 993.
81   Eg, *Re Vandervell's Trusts (No 2)* [1974] 3 WLR 256.

to be the absolute owner of those shares without the need to consider issues of trust at all. Suppose Albert is the absolute owner of a car which he settles on trust for his benefit as absolutely entitled beneficiary: it would be a nonsense to suggest that such a trust was created, because in truth Albert has retained all of the rights in the car and therefore remains its absolute owner. It would, however, be possible for Albert to declare that he held the car on trust as the sole trustee for the benefit of himself and his children as beneficiaries because Albert would not then hold the *whole* of the equitable interest: part of it would be held by his children.

2.3.6 The distinction between the trust and civil law concepts of ownership

The trust is not naturally a part of the jurisprudence of civil code jurisdictions.[82] Before the trust was developed in English law, there was an institution known as the 'use'. This expression 'use' derives from the Latin '*ad opus*' meaning property held 'on behalf of' another person.[83] This was the principal difference between Roman law (or 'civilian') systems used in continental Europe (like those in France or Germany) and that developed in England: civilian systems recognised only one person as having outright ownership (or, '*dominium*') over property and all other people as having merely personal claims against the owner of that property.[84] Consequently, for a civilian lawyer, the distinction between rights *in rem* and rights *in personam* would mean that a right *in rem* was a claim to be the owner of land, whereas a right *in personam* would be a purely personal claim against the owner of the land claiming damages or perhaps some right to access the land in some way. That means that the holder of a right *in personam* in civilian legal systems has a claim against the owner of property, but no claim against the property itself.

By contrast, the English law of trusts recognises that while there will be some person who is the owner at common law of property, it may be that equity requires that common law owner to hold that land for the benefit of some other person. In effect, the English law of trusts accepts that there may be a right for someone other than the common lawyer owner *in the property itself*. Therefore, a beneficiary is able to assert rights against the trustee or any third person in relation to the property. At the same time, however, the trustee has legal title over the trust property and so can deal with the property in a way which enables her to carry out the terms of the trust. Consequently, as will emerge during this chapter and Part 2 of this book, the law of trusts recognises that one person, the *trustee*, is the common law owner of property but is required to hold that property on behalf of a *beneficiary* or a number of beneficiaries who are treated by equity as having rights in that property.

2.3.7 The use of trusts by English families through history

The painting on the cover of this book is part of Hogarth's *Marriage à la Mode* series, which depicted the aftermath of a patriarch amending the family settlement so as to account for the

---

82 Since the creation of the Hague Trusts Convention, however, a number of signatory states have adopted the trust into their jurisprudence: see para 21.2.5, which considers the recognition of trusts. It is only through this Convention that such jurisdictions have accepted the trust and that is why the text refers to the trust not being 'naturally' a part of such systems of law; although see Lupoi, 2000, 267 in relation to Italian law.

83 Maitland, 1936, 24.

84 *Ibid.*

marriage of his stupid son to the daughter of a rich merchant. The characters in the paintings squandered their wealth and died in poverty – exactly the sort of thing which family settlements were intended to avoid. The wealth of aristocratic and wealthy families in England was tied up in family settlements (which were trusts) which settled the rights of ownership and use of the various items of property belonging to a family: whether houses, money, income from investments, chattels and so on. It was common to create a 'fee tail' arrangement whereby property passed to the eldest male heir such that daughters would be effectively disinherited on the patriarch's death if they had not married.

This was the principal driving factor behind the plots of Jane Austen's novels *Pride and Prejudice* and *Sense and Sensibility* because the young women would lose their homes when their fathers died because they were bound by a fee tail arrangement which would pass the houses and chattels to male relatives on their deaths. Consequently, the race is on through those novels for the young women to find rich husbands to save them from penury. In Dickens's novels there are many similar arrangements: in *Bleak House*, for example, the Jarndyce children are anxiously waiting for the result of litigation in the case of *Jarndyce v Jarndyce* to know what interests they will have under a will and its related trusts created by a deceased relative. Family settlements became a way of protecting women in such families from the fate which almost befell Anne Elliott in *Persuasion* where a gold-digging young man tries to win her hand in marriage because property law at the time meant that he would then become the absolute owner of all of his wife's property. The only way of protecting wives from having their property passed absolutely to their husbands (because wives at the time became 'the shadows of their husbands' on marriage) was to provide that other people had rights under trust in that same property. Thus, an unscrupulous husband could not assert ownership of it because his wife did not herself have unencumbered ownership of it.

The fortunes of the wealthy in England and Wales were also dependent generally on the honesty of their trustees. We shall see in Part 6 of this book that the law on breach of trust is weighted heavily in favour of protecting the beneficiaries under a trust from the risk of losing their property as those people typically had no property other than the land and money left to them by their ancestors. Consequently, it is impossible to underestimate the social importance of the early decisions on family settlements which underpin so much of the law in the first six parts of this book. While other concerns have come into play latterly (such as the growth of pension funds and investment funds based on trust law, and the use of constructive trusts in international banking law cases), the roots of trusts law are in the determination of judges drawn from this same social class to protect the integrity of trusts funds and the families who literally depended on them.

2.4 FUNDAMENTALS OF THE LAW OF TRUSTS

2.4.1 The core principles of the trust

The most important judicial statement of the core principles of trusts law in recent times was made by Lord Browne-Wilkinson in *Westdeutsche Landesbank Girozentrale v Islington LBC*,[85] when his Lordship sought to set out the framework upon which the trust operates:

---

85 [1996] 2 All ER 961, 988; see also *HCK China Investments Ltd v Solar Honest Ltd* (1999) 165 ALR 680; *Lonrho Exports Ltd v Export Credits Guarantee Department* [1999] CL 158.

The Relevant Principles of Trust Law:

  (i)   Equity operates on the conscience of the owner of the legal interest. In the case of
        a trust, the conscience of the legal owner requires him to carry out the purposes for
        which the property was vested in him (express or implied trust) or which the law
        imposes on him by reason of his unconscionable conduct (constructive trust).

  (ii) Since the equitable jurisdiction to enforce trusts depends upon the conscience of the
        holder of the legal interest being affected, he cannot be a trustee of the property if
        and so long as he is ignorant of the facts alleged to affect his conscience . . .

  (iii) In order to establish a trust there must be identifiable trust property . . .

  (iv) Once a trust is established, as from the date of its establishment the beneficiary has,
        in equity, a proprietary interest in the trust property, which proprietary interest will
        be enforceable in equity against any subsequent holder of the property (whether the
        original property or substituted property into which it can be traced) other than a
        purchaser for value of the legal interest without notice.

Four things emerge from these *dicta*, and were set out in the definition of trusts set out in
para 2.2.1. Each is considered in turn in the following paragraphs.[86] The main points arising
from Lord Browne-Wilkinson's words can be broken down as set out in the following
sections.

2.4.2 The trust imposes equitable obligations on the conscience of the trustee

First, the source of the trustees' obligations are found in equity requiring that they act in
good conscience whether as a result of a settlor having created an express trust, thus obliging
the trustee to obey the terms of the trust in good conscience, or else a court having considered it appropriate to impose a trust in circumstances in which the trustee would otherwise
have been permitted to act unconscionably. As has already been said,[87] equity acts *in
personam* and thus operates on the conscience of the defendant.[88] The explanation of the
trust as an equitable institution is that the trustee receives property in circumstances in which

---

86 Aside from these *dicta* being the clearest statement in the decided cases of the nature of the trust, it is important
    to understand that much of what Lord Browne-Wilkinson says in *Westdeutsche Landesbank Girozentrale
    v Islington LBC* (and in other decisions), about resulting trusts and constructive trusts in particular, is consid-
    ered to be slightly heretical by some slightly heretical commentators, eg, Birks, 1996 and Chambers, 1997. This
    book will take issue with some of the things that are said by the various commentators, particularly in Parts 4
    and 6 (*Trusts Implied by Law* and *Breach of Trust and Related Equitable Claims*). So, before we launch into the
    analysis, one word of advice for the student reader. It is important to understand that different people have
    different points of view about the law. Nothing should be taken as being absolute truth. One must differentiate
    between those areas of the law of trusts on which there is concrete authority and those areas where there remains
    debate. At the next level, you must try to come to terms with those issues on which academics and judges disa-
    gree either with decided case law or with other academics and judges. The flexibility and fluidity of the applica-
    tion of the principles of trusts law is both the joy and the difficulty associated with the study of this subject.

87 See para 2.2.1 for a definition of the trust as acting on the conscience of the trustee, and para 1.4.12 above for
    the manner in which equity operates *in personam*.

88 Thomas Lewin, in the first edition of his seminal work *A Practical Treatise on the Law of Trusts and Trustees*,
    Maxwell, 1837 identified the birth of the trust as being in the avoidance of fraud by Chancery courts, and on
    page 2 that 'the parents of the trust were Fraud and Fear, and a court of conscience was the Nurse'.

it would be against conscience for her to refuse to be bound by the terms of that trust. The trust can take one of two forms:

(a) It might be an express trust under which a settlor has consciously and deliberately created a trust. In such circumstances, equity would not permit a trustee to seek to act in contravention of the terms of such a trust or to act more generally in bad conscience.

(b) Alternatively, the trust might be one imposed by the courts, instead of by a settlor, because it is considered that it would be unconscionable to allow a person who has acquired common law rights in property to continue to control that property without some judicial action being taken against her. Thus, Lord Browne-Wilkinson refers to these constructive trusts as being imposed on a person 'by reason of his unconscionable conduct'. Such a person has the role of 'trusteeship' imposed on her by the court, thus creating the obligations of trustee and beneficiary between that person and others.

As was considered in Chapter 1, it is a core feature of equity that it acts *in personam* against the defendant in the sense of judging whether or not she has acted in good conscience.[89] This is particularly so in relation to the trustee in a trust relationship.

Another well-known definition of a trust is that set out in *Underhill and Hayton on Trusts and Trustees* in the following terms:

> A trust is an equitable obligation, binding a person (called a trustee) to deal with property owned[90] by him (called trust property, being distinguished from his private property) for the benefit of persons (called beneficiaries or, in old cases, *cestuis que trust*), of whom he may himself be one, and any one of whom may enforce the obligation.[91]

From this definition, just as with the definition given by Thomas and Hudson above,[92] it is clear that the obligation is equitable. The obligation of conscience is not apparent on the terms of Underhill and Hayton's definition, unlike Thomas and Hudson's definition and the

---

89 *The Earl of Oxford's Case* (1615) 1 Ch Rep 1.

90 Interestingly, Professor David Hayton in a recent edition of Underhill and Hayton, 2002, 5, explains that he has altered Sir Arthur Underhill's definition of the trust slightly to recognise that the trustee is an *owner* of the legal title in trust property (on which see *Smith v Anderson* (1880) 15 Ch D 247 at 275, *per* James LJ) and not simply a person who has the trust property under his control: a person may have control of the trust property as a bailee or depositary for that property without having any legal title in it. The definition in previous editions had read: 'A trust is an equitable obligation, binding on a person (who is called a trustee) to deal with property over which he has control (called trust property, being distinguished from his private property) for the benefit of persons (called beneficiaries or, in old cases, *cestuis que trust*), of whom he may himself be one, and any one of whom may enforce the obligation.'

91 Underhill and Hayton, 2002, 3; cited with approval in *Re Marshall's WT* [1945] Ch 217, at 219; *Green v Russell* [1959] 2 QB 226, at 241. Professor Pettit adds to the end of this definition the following: '. . . or for a charitable purpose, which may be enforced at the instance of the Attorney-General, or for some other purpose permitted by law though unenforceable': Pettit, 2001, 25. The suggestion in *Snell's Equity* suggesting that there is no satisfactory definition of a trust was cited with approval in *Allen v Distillers Company (Biochemicals) Ltd* [1974] QB 384, as to which see the previous edition of Snell's *Equity*, 2000, 394, which it is suggested is unsatisfactorily defeatist.

92 Reproduced at para 2.2.1 above.

discussion in Chapter 1 of this book which would suggest that the notion of conscience is necessarily bound up in the concept of an 'equitable obligation'.[93]

What can also be observed about trusts, however, is that the importance which they have acquired over the centuries has caused the courts to develop a number of strict principles surrounding the manner in which they are created and operated, as is considered in detail in Parts 2 and 3 of this book. This tendency towards increased rigidity of principle – which will become apparent when we consider the requirements of certainty in Chapter 3 and of formalities in Chapter 5 – might suggest a movement away from a general notion of conscience as underpinning the trust. In truth the idea of conscience still governs the obligations of trustees even though it may appear to have been submerged at times behind the requirements of certainty and formality. This development emerges more clearly in the next paragraph.

2.4.3 For the beneficiary trusts create proprietary rights in the trust property and personal rights against the trustees

A trust must take effect over property in favour of a beneficiary

The trust is built on a combination of property law rules and personal obligations. First let us consider the proprietary aspects of the trust. As Lord Browne-Wilkinson held in *Westdeutsche Landesbank v Islington LBC* that '. . . in order to establish a trust there must be identifiable trust property'.[94] Thus, if a settlor purported to create a trust without having any rights in the trust property at the time of purporting to create that trust, there would be no valid trust created.[95] Once a trust is created, the trustee is required to hold the identified trust property on trust for the identified beneficiaries.[96] The trustee may not take any beneficial interest in the trust property,[97] unless the trustee is also a part of the class of beneficiaries in that particular trust, and must obey the terms of the trust.[98] The beneficiaries in their turn have proprietary rights in the trust property,[99] as is considered in detail in Chapter 4. Furthermore, if there is no beneficiary for whose benefit the property is held on trust, then the purported trust will simply not be valid.[100] Therefore, property law will deal with the manner in which the trust fund is treated.

Secondly, however, the manner in which the trustee is required to behave in relation to the beneficiaries in the exercise of her fiduciary duties is a matter concerning a system of

93 On this point, see also Thomas and Hudson, 2004, 14.
94 See para 2.4.1 above.
95 *Re Brooks' Settlement Trusts* [1939] 1 Ch 993. See also *Re Ralli's Will Trusts* [1964] 1 Ch 288 and the discussion in this book at section 5.3.
96 See *Milroy v Lord* (1862) 4 De GF & J 264.
97 See, eg, *Fletcher v Fletcher* (1844) 4 Hare 67, where a trustee sought to take beneficially a fund of money bequeathed to him with the intention that he was to have held it for the settlor's son, even though the trust in favour of the son did not appear *prima facie* to be valid.
98 *Clough v Bond* (1838) 3 My & Cr 490, 496.
99 *Saunders v Vautier* (1841) 4 Beav 115.
100 *Morice v Bishop of Durham* (1804) 9 Ves 399; *Bowman v Secular Society Ltd* [1917] AC 406; *Leahy v Attorney-General for NSW* [1959] AC 457. This precise form of wording, it is suggested, would be accepted even by Goff J in *Re Denley* [1969] 1 Ch 373 who was otherwise prepared to accept merely that there be some person with *locus standi* to enforce the trustees' obligations with only an indirect right to take some use or enjoyment from the trust property.

personal, equitable obligations. The obligations are equitable in that it is equity which recognises the rights of the beneficiaries. These obligations will stem from the proprietary rights of the beneficiaries in the trust property but go further than simply imposing proprietary obligations on the trustees. If the beneficiaries' rights were simply attached to the trust property, then if the trust fund were lost, the beneficiaries would similarly lose all of their rights. Therefore, to protect the beneficiaries' rights, the trustees are also taken to owe personal obligations to the beneficiaries to account to the beneficiaries for the value of the trust property in the event that the trustees commit some breach of trust.[101] This has the effect that the trustees are personally liable to pay into the trust fund an amount equal to any loss suffered by the trust, as considered in Chapter 18.[102] This obligation is over and above any rights of the trustees to specific recovery of the trust property[103] or to trace its value into the hands of third parties.[104] The distinction between personal and proprietary obligations is considered in greater detail next.

The division between property rights and personal obligations

The beneficiary under a trust will have rights in property (or, 'rights *in rem*') provided that she is validly a beneficiary with some rights vested in her at the material time. In English law, if the defendant owes only a personal obligation to the claimant (or, a 'right *in personam*') then the defendant will be liable either to pay damages at common law (in the form of a breach of contract or a tort) or to pay some equitable compensation in equity to the claimant (for example in relation to a breach of trust) in the event that that obligation is breached.[105] However, if the claimant can demonstrate a right in some property controlled by the defendant then the claimant can require that that specific property is delivered up in satisfaction of some breach of duty.[106]

This is the root of the distinction, for example, between being a secured or an unsecured creditor. Suppose that Anne has entered into a contract with Bridget which imposes fiduciary (or trustee-like) obligations on Bridget. Anne runs the risk that Bridget will go into insolvency such that if Bridget has breached that fiduciary obligation to Anne, Anne will not be able to recover any financial compensation from the insolvent Bridget. However, if Anne had some proprietary rights under a trust in property over which Bridget was trustee, then Anne could seize that property in satisfaction of the breach of obligation committed by Bridget without the need to concern herself with the insolvency.

The trust, whether express or implied, will grant proprietary rights to the beneficiary. Significantly, rights in property entitle the beneficial owner to title to the property regardless of the value of that property. Therefore, it is also preferable to retain title in property which is likely to increase in value instead of relying on Bridget's undertaking to pay damages under a personal claim. Conversely, if the property is likely to decrease in value, then it would be preferable to recover monetary compensation equal to the beneficiaries' loss

101   *Clough v Bond* (1838) 3 My & Cr 490; *Target Holdings v Redferns* [1996] 1 AC 421.
102   *Target Holdings v Redferns* [1996] 1 AC 421.
103   *Ibid.*
104   See the discussion of the law of tracing in Chapter 19.
105   *Target Holdings v Redferns* [1996] 1 AC 421.
106   *Ibid.*

measured at a level before the property decreases in value.[107] The trust therefore grants property rights in relation to obligations which would be considered to be merely personal obligations by common law.

The notion of the trust as a form of personal obligation on the trustee is considered in the following section. For the purposes of this discussion, it is important to consider the manner in which trusts purport to create proprietary rights in the beneficiary.

2.5 THE BENEFITS AND USES OF TRUSTS

Having outlined the nature of the trust, it is worth considering the reasons why settlors would choose to create trusts in the first place, before moving on to consider the detailed business of creating a legally valid trust.

2.5.1 Owning property but not owning property

The genius of the trust is that it enables one person, the trustee, to control property while vesting all of the ultimate entitlement to that property in another person, the beneficiary.

Family business

For people writing their wills, the trust device enables the appointment of executors who take the deceased's property as trustees of it until they carry out the obligations imposed on them under the will. Therefore, quite literally, it enables a person who cannot deal with their own property once they are dead to appoint another person to do it on their behalf. More to the point, the persons who are intended to benefit ultimately from this property are able to exercise control by means of the law of trusts over the trustees to ensure that the settlor's intentions are carried through effectively.

As considered already, the trust enables families to organise the distribution of property between family members. Complex family settlements enable rights in property to be settled for generations into the future (subject to what is said in Chapter 4 about the rules on perpetuities). Thus, large estates can be divided between children and the rights to each can be organised. The trustees are responsible for carrying out the terms of such a settlement. The beneficiaries are able to control their own rights and duties by suing the trustees to comply with the specific obligations set out in the settlement.

Commercial uses

The other primary use for the trust is to facilitate commercial transactions. A straightforward example of the commercial use of a trust was in the case of *Re Kayford*,[108] in which a mail order business took payment in advance from its customers before sending them the goods which they had ordered. Importantly, the customers' money was held in a bank account separately from the other money held by the company. The company went into insolvency

---

107 See section 18.3.6 generally in relation to the valuation of property.
108 [1975] 1 WLR 279.

and the question arose as to the ownership of the advance payments held in the bank account, which had been received from customers who had not received the goods they had ordered. The court held that a trust had been created over those advance payments in favour of the customers who had made pre-payments without receiving their goods.[109]

In commercial terms, this therefore becomes a core technique in taking security in a transaction. Where one party is concerned about the ability of the other party to perform its obligations, any property (including money) which is to be passed as part of the transaction can be held on trust until such time as both parties' contractual obligations have been performed.

Suppose the following set of facts. Choc Ltd is a company organised under English law, and resident in England, which manufactures 'Magic' chocolate bars. Each Magic bar requires sugar. Choc Ltd has decided to acquire sugar from Cuba, a corporation organised under Cuban law and resident in Cuba which grows and refines sugar. Choc Ltd is attracted by Cuba's competitive prices. The parties agree that Cuba will deliver x tons of sugar to England each month for £100,000. However, neither party has dealt with the other before. Choc Ltd bears the risk that Cuba will not deliver the sugar at all, or that the quality of the sugar would not be as specified in the contract. Cuba bears the risk that Choc Ltd will not pay £100,000 each month as per the contract, even though the sugar has been shipped from Cuba.

The parties might compromise on the following structure. Briefly put, a third party trustee will hold the property rights in both the money and the sugar until both are satisfied that the other party to the contract has performed its obligations as it is required to do under the contract. Cuba would insist that Cuba retains property rights in the sugar until the payment of £100,000 is made to it. Choc Ltd would insist that it retains title in its money until a quantity of suitable sugar has been delivered to it. The parties would therefore declare a single trust, with an independent third party to act as trustee. The trust fund would be made up each month of x tons of sugar and also of £100,000. The terms of the trust would be that the sugar would be held on trust for Cuba if Choc Ltd failed to make payment, but that it would be held on trust for Choc Ltd if payment was made. Similarly, the £100,000 would be held on trust for Choc Ltd until a suitable quantity and quality of sugar was delivered to Choc Ltd, at which time the equitable interest in the £100,000 would be transferred to Cuba absolutely.

This transaction is illustrated in the diagram below:

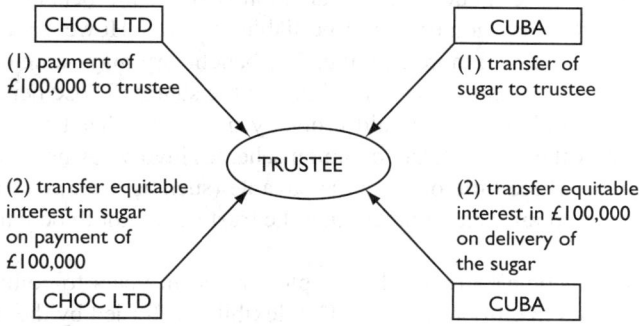

109 For example, in *Sendo International Ltd (In Administration)* [2006] EWHC 2935 (Ch), [2007] 1 BCLC 141 trusts were used to hold property for the benefit of two classes of creditors when a company went into insolvency. Those trusts were useful devices to manage the insolvent company's property while the administration of that insolvency was worked through.

The trust operates as a pivotal technique in the structure of many commercial transactions. Concerns about a counterparty's creditworthiness can be controlled by taking the equitable interest in property under a trust structure as indicated above. If the one party to the contract does not perform (that is, if Cuba does not deliver suitable sugar), the other party can recover the property which it transferred to the trust (that is, Choc Ltd can recover the £100,000 it had transferred to the trustee). It is common for parties to a contract, neither of whom has any connection with England and Wales, to use the English trust law structure to control their credit risk concerns.[110]

A central intellectual technique

The trust has become an important part of the way in which English lawyers look at property law. The proliferation of resulting and constructive trusts considered in Part 4 is evidence of the ubiquity of the trust. In any situation in which property is held by one person where it is considered improper for that person to assert unencumbered beneficial ownership of it, the cry will go up from English lawyers that the property must be considered to be held on trust. As this book progresses, the trust will emerge as the most common form of equity in action in a very broad variety of contexts.

2.5.2 Taxation of trusts

Trusts as a means of tax avoidance

One of the more common uses of the trust is as a means of tax avoidance. As considered above, the trust enables one person (the settlor) to have property held by another (the trustee) for the benefit of some other person (the beneficiary). Suppose that the property involved is a bundle of valuable shares which are expected to generate a large dividend annually. The shareholder will be liable to tax on those dividends. However, if those shares were transferred to a trustee to be held on trust for herself, the shareholder might then be able to say 'I do not have legal title in those shares and therefore I should not be liable to tax payable on any dividends paid in respect of those shares'.

As considered below, the modern law of taxation will tax the beneficial owner of the shares and therefore the shareholder would be liable to tax.[111] However, the shareholder/settlor may then be a good deal more cunning. The beneficiary may name other persons as beneficiaries and therefore claim to have no rights to the shares. Those beneficiaries might be the settlor's own children (who would probably not have other taxable income) or a company controlled by the settlor. Other common schemes involve using trustees resident in other tax jurisdictions where little or no tax is payable (such as the Cayman Islands or the British Virgin Islands) to raise an argument that the trust ought not to be liable to UK taxation in any event.

Tax statutes have become increasingly complex in recent years to combat these transparent attempts to avoid liability to UK tax. The flexibility afforded by the trust means that

110 For a discussion of how this might work in relation to financial contracts, see Hudson, 2002, 413.
111 *Baker v Archer-Shee* [1927] AC 844.

the ingenuity of lawyers practising in the field of taxation can be applied to construct ever more sophisticated structures to avoid the letter of the law. In response to this tax avoidance industry, HM Revenue and Customs has adopted the approach of promoting legislation that is targeted at very specific forms of avoidance. The more effective approach appears to be that developed by the courts to ignore any 'artificial steps' in such tax avoidance structures, so that the true substance of the transaction can be taxed without the sham devices of a tax avoidance scheme, which in itself can be thought of as an equitable doctrine.[112] However, there is nothing *per se* to prevent a person from ordering her own affairs in a way which reduces her liability to tax.[113]

Principles in the taxation of trusts

The difficulty with reference to the taxation of trusts is that there is more than one person with proprietary rights in the trust fund. This short section does not attempt to do more than outline some of the main principles involved in the taxation of trusts. Readers with a more specific interest are directed to books dealing with the taxation of trusts.[114]

The general principle is that it is the trustee who must account for any taxable income deriving from the trust property.[115] There are those who doubt that this authority does create quite such an all-embracing principle.[116] Where the trust is a bare trust (that is, a trustee holds as bare nominee for a single beneficiary absolutely), it is the beneficiary who is liable for taxable income generated by that trust.[117] It is suggested that this latter decision must be correct, otherwise a taxpayer liable to higher rate income tax would simply be able to create a number of trusts, each receiving a portion of the income belonging beneficially to the taxpayer but so that those portions fell below the threshold for payment of higher rate tax.

Different rules apply to accumulation and discretionary trusts. A special rate of tax is applicable to trusts under ss 686(1) and (1A) and also s 832(1) of the Income and Corporation Taxes Act (TA) 1988. The creation of settlements in which the settlor retains some equitable interest (however small) will typically be caught by anti-avoidance legislation. Therefore, where the settlor retains a benefit under such a discretionary or accumulation trust, the taxpayer will be liable for any difference between the rate of tax applicable to trusts and the taxpayer's own effective rate of tax.[118] Similarly, under inheritance tax rules, where a taxpayer makes a gift with a reservation of some benefit in that gift to herself, tax will be chargeable on the taxpayer's estate.[119] This is because the legislation assumes that a settlor who retains some interest for herself is doing so for the purposes of tax avoidance and that she is in fact intended to take the entire benefit ultimately. The Finance Act 2006 introduced

---

112 *Ramsay v IRC* [1982] AC 300; *Furniss v Dawson* [1984] 2 WLR 226. See most recently on the developing restriction of this doctrine in the unanimous decision of the House of Lords in *Barclays Mercantile Business Finance Ltd v Mawson* [2004] UKHL 51 to the effect that this principle is predominantly a principle of statutory interpretation dividing between technical and commercial uses of language.

113 See perhaps *Ingram v IRC* [1985] STC 835.

114 Thomas, 1981; Shipwright and Keeling, 1998; Tiley, 2001.

115 *Williams v Singer* [1921] 1 AC 65, *per* Viscount Cave.

116 *Reid's Trustees v IRC* (1926) 14 TC 512; Shipwright and Keeling, 1998, 401 *et seq.*

117 *Baker v Archer-Shee* [1927] AC 844.

118 TA 1988, s 687.

119 Finance Act 1986, s 102.

a new regime for inheritance tax over settlements. The reader is referred to the detailed, specialist literature on that topic.[120]

In the Finance Act 1995, a broad range of tax avoidance rules were introduced in relation to settlements by addition to Pt XV of the TA 1988. These provisions consolidated the piece-meal anti-avoidance legislation passed in connection with settlements hitherto. Within the technical tax term 'settlement' for this purpose fell 'any disposition, trust, covenant, agreement, arrangement or transfer of assets'.[121] The underlying intention of these provisions was to prevent tax avoidance in situations in which a settlor seeks to retain some benefit to herself under a settlement.[122] The tax position in relation to non-resident trusts is particularly complex and not within the compass of this book.[123]

2.6 THE DISTINCTION BETWEEN TRUSTS AND OTHER LEGAL CONCEPTS

The trust bears similarities to, and important distinctions from, other structures recognised by English law. Like the structures considered below, a trust does not have legal personality (that is, it does not exist independently like a human being or a company). Rather, there are formalities to be complied with so that it is possible to identify the structure as being a trust rather than something else.

2.6.1 Contract

A contract is a bilateral agreement (resulting from an offer,[124] an acceptance of that offer,[125] and consideration passing between the parties[126]). An express trust arises from the unilateral act of the settlor in declaring a trust.[127] There is no contract between settlor and trustee in ordinary circumstances. It will be the case that if a professional trustee is appointed (perhaps a bank or a solicitor), then the trustee will require payment from the settlor to act as trustee. In such circumstances there will be a trust and also a contract between settlor and trustee. However, the contract does not form a part of the trust – rather, it is collateral to it.[128]

A contract creates personal obligations between the two contracting parties. Those parties can therefore sue one another for damages for breach of contract,[129] or can sue for specific

---

120 See Venables, 2006.
121 TA 1988, s 660G.
122 *Ibid*, s 660(2).
123 See Venables, 1999, generally.
124 *Weeks v Tybald* (1605) Noy 11; *Lambert v Lewis* [1982] AC 225. See on the distinction between a contract of loan and a trust *Morley v Morley* (1678) 2 Cas in Ch 2, *per* Lord Nottingham; and *Twinsectra v Yardley* [2002] 2 WLR 802, 821, *per* Lord Millett.
125 *Butler Machine Tool Co Ltd v Ex-Cell-O Corporation (England) Ltd* [1979] 1 WLR 401.
126 *Rann v Hughes* (1778) 7 TR 350, 4 Bro PC 27.
127 *Paul v Constance* [1977] 1 WLR 527.
128 See the discussion at para 8.5.5.
129 *Tai Hing Cotton Mill Ltd v Kamsing Factory* [1979] AC 95.

performance to require that the contract be carried out.[130] The rights to damages arise in common law from the very existence of the contract. A contract also requires consideration, whereas a trust requires no consideration.[131]

In relation to a trust, there are personal obligations between trustee and beneficiary in relation to the treatment of the trust fund and the performance of the trustee's obligations under the trust.[132] The trustee will be liable to the beneficiary both to reinstate the trust fund and for compensation if there is any breach of trust.[133] The beneficiary is also entitled to require the trustee to carry out her obligations.[134]

Prima facie, then, there are some similarities in form between the trust and the contract in terms of the existence of personal obligations between parties. Nevertheless, there are three significant distinctions between contracts and trusts. First, a trust creates proprietary rights in favour of the beneficiaries and is therefore not restricted to personal claims for compensation.[135] Secondly, the obligations which arise in a contract are created by the common intention of the parties, whereas the trust obligations arise because equity acts on the conscience of the trustee (in relation to express trusts because a settlor has declared a trust). Thirdly, trusts impose fiduciary obligations in relation to specific property whereas contracts ordinarily do not.[136]

2.6.2 Bailment

The important element of the trust is that property is held by the trustee for the benefit of the beneficiary whereby the beneficiary acquires an equitable interest in the trust property. Therefore, a division occurs when the settlor declares the trust between legal and equitable title. That structure forms a useful comparison with the law of bailment – again a property law rule. In bailment, a person delivers property into the control of another person on the understanding that the property is to be returned to its owner. Thus, in a theatre, a member of the audience may leave a coat with the cloakroom attendant during the performance. There is no transfer of property rights. Rather, the theatre becomes bailee of the coat during the performance, on the understanding that physical possession of the coat is to be returned at the end of the performance. This may form part of the contract for the acquisition of the theatre ticket, or be the subject of a separate contract requiring payment for each garment left at the cloakroom, or it may be a purely gratuitous service offered by the theatre.[137]

Whatever form the bailment takes, it is essentially different from a trust in that a trustee acquires common law property rights in the trust fund. That the trustee acquires these property rights is essential to the functioning of the trust.[138] A bailee of property does not acquire any property rights in the objects put into her control.

---

130 *Hutton v Watling* [1948] Ch 26. Cf *Beswick v Beswick* [1968] AC 58.
131 See Underhill, 1889, p 3.
132 *Target Holdings v Redferns* [1996] 1 AC 421.
133 *Ibid.*
134 Beneficiaries who are absolutely entitled to the trust property, and acting *sui juris*, are empowered to direct the trustees to deliver the trust property to them: *Saunders v Vautier* (1841) 4 Beav 115.
135 *Saunders v Vautier* (1841) 4 Beav 115, considered at section 4.1 in detail.
136 With the notable exceptions of contracts of agency and partnership.
137 For a radical restructuring of this topic see McMeel, 'On the redundancy of the concept of bailment', in Hudson, 2004:5.
138 *Milroy v Lord* (1862) 4 De GF & J 264.

2.6.3 Agency

In an agency relationship, a principal instructs an agent to act on behalf of the principal.[139] This agency can take a number of commercial forms. Its legal form is that of a contract between principal and agent that the agent can act on behalf of the principal to effect a specific range of transactions. A typical commercial example would be a principal who bred thoroughbred horses instructing an agent 'to conduct a search for new horses in Yorkshire'. Such an agent would typically be empowered to acquire horses of a specified quality on behalf of the principal. The agent will therefore enter into contracts of purchase for such horses. The contract between principal and agent would then require the agent to buy that property for the principal.

The trust bears some superficial similarities to this agency arrangement. At first blush a trustee may appear to operate as a form of agent, dealing with the legal title in property according to the terms of the trust. However, there is not necessarily a contract between settlor and trustee,[140] nor between trustee and beneficiary. Furthermore, in an agency arrangement, a principal would not ordinarily acquire equitable interests in property acquired by the agent in the way that a beneficiary under a trust acquires equitable interests once the declaration of trust takes effect.[141] It may, however, be possible for the principal to assert that the contract of agency would transfer equitable rights by means of specific performance.[142]

The most significant similarity between trustee and agent is in relation to the fiduciary obligations created by each office. Trustees and agents owe fiduciary duties to the beneficiaries and principals respectively, precluding them from making unauthorised profits from their arrangements and so forth.[143] However, the most significant difference is that an agency arrangement is based primarily on the common law of contract, albeit imposing fiduciary obligations, whereas a trust relies on equitable control of the conscience of the common law owner of the trust property.

2.6.4 Gift

A gift involves the outright transfer of property rights in an item of property from an absolute owner of those rights to a volunteer (that is, someone who has given no consideration for the transfer). The recipient (or donee) becomes absolute owner of that property as a result of the transfer.

In some senses the beneficiary appears to occupy a similar position in relation to a trust in that the settlor transfers absolute title in property by dividing between the legal title vested in the trustee and the equitable interest vested in the beneficiary. In that sense, the settlor has transferred all of the property rights away from herself *qua*[144] settlor. The beneficiary is not required (by the general law of trusts) to have given consideration for that transfer. In that

---

139   Whether expressly by deed (*Berkley v Hardy* (1826) 5 B & C 355) or by inference from the circumstances (*Garnac Grain Co Inc v HMF Faure and Fairclough Ltd* [1968] AC 1130).

140   See the discussion of Langbein, 1995 at para 21.2.3.

141   See generally *Attenborough v Solomon* [1913] AC 76; *Re King's WT* [1964] Ch 542, [1964] 1 All ER 833.

142   *Walsh v Lonsdale* (1882) 21 Ch D 9.

143   On which see the discussion of fiduciary responsibility comprising Chapter 14.

144   That is, 'in the capacity of' settlor.

sense the beneficiary is a volunteer. One of the core equitable principles already considered is that equity will not assist a volunteer.[145]

However, the significant difference between a gift and a trust is that only legal title in the trust property is assigned to the trustee on the basis that that person is required to deal with the property for the benefit of the beneficiary.[146] In short, equity is acting on the conscience of the trustee in her treatment of the trust fund, rather than seeking to benefit a beneficiary.[147] By contrast, the beneficiary takes only an equitable interest in the property. Neither the trustee nor the beneficiary becomes the absolute owner of the trust property, unlike the recipient of a gift, who does become absolute owner of the property which comprised the gift. Furthermore, as we shall learn in later discussion,[148] if a donor intends to make a gift of property, then she will not be entitled to rely on the law of trusts to validate that transfer if it fails to take effect as a gift.[149] Therefore, the courts have established a clear distinction between these gifts and trusts.

2.6.5 Powers

Powers give the rightholder an ability to perform some action in the sense that the right-holder has a discretion. For example, a power such that 'Xena may pay £1,000' to whichever of a given class of people 'has the most need of it' would enable Xena to advance the money if she chose to do so, but would not compel any money to be paid at all. By contrast, a trust creates an obligation which the trustee is obliged to follow.[150] Therefore, a power creates a right but no obligation to perform a given act, whereas a trust imposes an obligation (albeit occasionally involving some discretion). There is one category of what is now understood to be a trust[151] which does grant the trustee some discretion as to the manner in which her trust obligations are to be performed: these are discretionary trusts (as considered above at para 2.3.3). In such situations, the trustee has a choice of actions open to her but she is obliged to carry out that choice, unlike a mere power.[152] For example, 'Xena shall pay £1,000 to which-ever of the beneficiaries has the greatest need of it' would oblige Xena to make the payment of £1,000, but with some discretion as to which beneficiary is to receive the money. The distinction between powers and trusts of this sort is considered in detail in section 3.5 below.

2.7 SOCIOLOGICAL ISSUES IN EQUITY AND TRUSTS

2.7.1 Introduction

This discussion is not intended to be a complete analysis of the interaction of equity and trusts law and the right of women and global politics. Instead it is intended simply to give

---

145 See para 1.4.15 above.
146 *Re Brooks' ST* [1939] 1 Ch 993.
147 *Westdeutsche Landesbank v Islington LBC* [1996] AC 669.
148 See section 5.1.
149 *Milroy v Lord* (1862) 4 De GF & J 264.
150 *Breadner v Granville-Grossman* [2001] Ch 523, 540, [2000] 4 All ER 705, 719, *per* Park J.
151 These powers were once known as 'powers in the form of a trust'.
152 *Burrough v Philcox* (1840) 5 My & Cr 72; *Re Weekes Settlement* [1897] 1 Ch 289.

some context for the discussion of the core principles of trusts law: both in relation to the way in which English property law has treated women historically and the significant role which trusts law is thought to play in the funding of international crime today. It is all too easy to consider trusts law as simply a parade of legal rules which are politically neutral. In truth, all law has complex effects in terms of gender, race, class and sex. A full sociology of trusts law has yet to be attempted. What can be understood about trusts law is that it has tended to be designed for the benefit of the moneyed classes historically; albeit that the doctrine of constructive trusts is expanding today in ways which apply to commercial and non-commercial situations in different ways. In the modern world economy, the same trusts models in various jurisdictions allow legitimate investments to be made (with pension funds being based on ordinary trusts principles at root) as well as enabling criminal organisations to shield their activities and to avoid regulatory oversight.

2.7.2 Women and trusts law

Introduction

This discussion is not intended to be a complete analysis of the interaction of equity and trusts law and the rights of women. Instead it is intended simply to give some context for the discussion of the core principles of trusts law (which are based mainly on 19th-century cases) so that our analysis of those cases will not overlook the extraordinary way in which English law has treated women. As mentioned above, it is all too easy to consider trusts law as simply a collection of rules which have no political context. In truth, all law has complex effects in terms of gender, race, class and sex. Trusts law was designed for the benefit of the upper classes historically. As Dicey put it,

> the daughters of the rich enjoyed for the most part the consideration and protection
> of equity; the daughters of the poor suffered under the severity and injustice of the
> common law.[153]

What this alluded to was the fact that women in rich families could have the protection of family trusts (in the form of complex 'settlements') which provided for their maintenance and income, if their settlor was thoughtful enough to have provided for them; whereas women in poor families would not have the benefit of trusts at all because they were poor and therefore could not afford the advice of expensive trusts lawyers, and in any event because their families had no property to settle on trust.[154] However, as we shall consider below, it is not entirely clear that equity, trusts law or property law generally did operate entirely for the benefit of women in all circumstances.[155] So, this section is concerned simply to identify some themes in the way in which equity, trusts law and the position of women over the centuries have interacted.

---

153 Dicey, *Law and Opinion in England*, quoted in Crane, 1965, 254.
154 EM Forster expressed a similar idea in *Howards End* to the effect that to trust is 'a luxury in which only the wealthy can indulge; the poor cannot afford it'.
155 See Auchmuty, 2001.

The limited rights of married women to property and other things

It is easy to think of 18th- and 19th-century trusts law as being a distant time with distant concepts, but that would be to overlook something important about equity and trusts. It is sometimes said that equity was the protector of women, and at one time there was some truth in this. If you were to read the Jane Austen novel *Persuasion*, Anne Elliot is at risk from a fortune-hunting suitor who appears to be wealthy and attentive; his goal is to marry her for her money because, at that time, when a couple married, all of the wife's property would become her husband's property. The metaphor which was used at the time was that the wife became the shadow of her husband. That innocuous idea in the Christian marriage concept that husband and wife become 'one flesh' takes on a very disturbing dimension when you realise that metaphorically the wife's flesh is taken to merge into her husband's so that she effectively disappears. The revered feminist theorist Simone Weil began her essay 'Human Personality' with the celebrated idea that:

> 'You do not interest me.' No person can say these words to another without committing a cruelty and offending against justice.[156]

This, in effect, was the impact of much English law in this area on women. The very fact that married women became merely the shadows of their husbands meant that they ceased to exist at all.[157] The law commits the cruelty of saying that those women are of no interest. They were robbed of the protection of law against their husbands. Their property rights evaporated as soon as they married. It is no wonder in those novels of yesteryear that the day of a woman's marriage is treated with so much hope and so much dread. It should be remembered that it was only comparatively recently that the concept of rape in marriage and of contracts being capable of being enforced between married people were accepted. This is an appalling state of affairs in a society which considered itself democratic from 1927 (when adult women finally acquired the right to vote). Married women had their property rights protected, after a fashion, by the Married Women's Property Act 1882, but the idea of a wife being the shadow of her husband was still haunting cases like *Caunce v Caunce*[158] in 1969. Even in a decision of the House of Lords in 1965 in *National Provincial Bank v Ainsworth*[159] the rights of wives were described by Lord Wilberforce by beginning with the following peculiarly old-fashioned concepts:

> For though the wife had (apart from dower) no proprietary interest at law or in equity, in her husband's property, she had certain rights against her husband by virtue of her status of marriage . . . a wife acquired the right to two things: the right of cohabitation

---

156 Weil, 1950, at 70.
157 It was observed by the legal historian Coke that in relation to a married man there were three types of people who had no rights against him: his wife, his children and his servants. Instead the man bore the seigneural obligations of 'the master' in relation to those people. Until things changed in the early 20th century, what we now call employment law was formerly known as the law on 'master and servant'.
158 [1969] 1 WLR 286.
159 [1965] AC 1175, [1965] 3 WLR 1, sub nom *National Provincial Bank v Hastings Car Mart Ltd* [1965] 2 All ER 472. The same case is referred to by different names in different law reports. In essence, the husband here used the company as a cypher for himself in an attempt to defeat his wife's claims to the family home.

with her husband and the right to support according to her husband's estate and condition. She could obtain against him, from the ecclesiastical courts, an order for restitution
of conjugal rights which, in its usual form, ordered him to take her home and receive her
as his wife and render conjugal rights – an order which could be enforced by attachment
for non-obedience . . . . her rights were not rights *in rem*, nor were they related to any
particular property; they were purely personal rights against her husband, enforceable
by proceedings against his person, which he could satisfy by rendering her conjugal
rights, i.e. by living with her and supporting her in a suitable home.[160]

The English are the perfect nation to have developed sexual innuendo as an art form[161] in that
they often appear to be talking about sex when they are not (e.g. 'satisfy by rendering her
conjugal rights' actually means providing her with a home), and they generally try to appear
not to be talking about sex when they are. The ecclesiastical courts would in essence order
that a marriage be consummated as well as that the wife be provided with an appropriate
home: in essence, the court would order that the couple have sex. In *Scott v Scott*,[162] for
example, a divorce was ordered on the basis that the wife was proved still to be a virgin after
the marriage on the basis of a medical examination. Otherwise, conjugal rights were 'enforceable by proceedings against his person', which sounds like a euphemism for something. The
wife had no rights in property; but rather only the earthier rights to be 'received as a wife'.
Quite who should be receiving whom is unclear here. The significant point is that the place
and nature of women was treated as being merely a maternal, sexual vessel and a property-
less person who needed to be supported by her husband.

Attitudes to women among judges even in the late 20th century

While that may sound like a relic from the middle ages which was being used to begin an
analysis of the modern law in the 1960s, the following idea from Lord Denning (quoted in
greater detail in Chapter 15) is instructive. It is to be remembered that it was Lord Denning
who strove to develop the 'deserted wife's equity' in the 1960s; albeit that it is difficult to
know whether to celebrate him for seeking to improve the lot of women, or whether to criticise him for being interested only in married women and then for treating them as weak
creatures in need of protection instead of being in need of rights. The following passage
comes from a book of his memoirs published in 1980 which presents a view of women
which subordinates them to men, and which carries the imprimatur of the principles of ecclesiastical law which informed *National Provincial Bank* and thus carries more than a whiff of
the old religion:

No matter how you may dispute and argue, you cannot alter the fact that women are
different from men. The principal task in life of women is to bear and rear children: and
it is a task which occupies the best years of their lives. The man's part in bringing up the

160 [1965] 3 WLR 1, at 31.
161 As a German character in *Blackadder Goes Forth* remarked: 'For us, the lavatory is a mundane and functional
     item. For you [the British], it is the basis of an entire culture'.
162 [1913] AC 417.

children is no doubt as important as hers, but of necessity he cannot devote so much time to it. He is physically the stronger and she the weaker. He is temperamentally the more aggressive and she the more submissive. It is he who takes the initiative and she who responds . . .[163]

There is really nothing to be added to that. It suggests a male judiciary, even when seeking to protect women, which nevertheless misunderstands that they are adult human beings and not infants. As the poet Philip Larkin pointed out, the sexual revolution and a profound revolution in British society began in the 1960s:

> Sexual intercourse began
> In nineteen sixty-three
> (Which was rather late for me)
> Between the end of the *Chatterley* ban
> And the Beatles' first LP.[164]

And yet even in 1965 the rights of women in their own homes (let alone the workplace and so on) were being considered in the peculiar fashion outlined above.[165]

Trusts sometimes denying rights to women and sometimes protecting women, and the novels of Jane Austen

If one were to go back further in time to the novels of Jane Austen (again, by way of illustration of the condition of women in the 18th and the early 19th century), the protagonists in *Pride and Prejudice* and in *Sense and Sensibility* are young women from genteel families who must find rich husbands because when their fathers die it is provided in the trusts which govern their entire families' lives that their home, the capital which produces their income and most of their chattels will pass to a specified male relative. The ancient device of an 'entailed' estate meant that when family settlements were created it was typically provided that the principal assets in the trust fund would pass down the male line. These were social norms which diminished the importance of women, which had hardened into legal techniques used widely in practice. It is difficult to read the opening chapters of either of those great Austen novels without a lump in the throat as one realises what the settlor has done to future generations of women in his family.[166] All of the plot of those novels spring from that idea of women being considered to be unworthy of receiving the family property by the settlors of their family settlements.

---

163 Denning, *The Due Process of Law,* 1980 at p.194.
164 Larkin, 'Annus Mirabilis', 1974. The '*Chatterley* ban' is a reference to the lifting of a ban on the DH Lawrence novel *Lady Chatterley's Lover* (originally published privately in Italy in 1928) which had previously been considered to have been obscene. Needless to say, sales of that novel in the wake of the ban being lifted were remarkable.
165 Admittedly, Larkin is not the best vehicle for arguing for a more enlightened understanding of the rights of women; but those lines do give a flavour of the history of the time and the changing social mores to which they bore witness.
166 The settlement in *Pride and Prejudice* is described in Chapter 7 of that book; that in *Sense and Sensibility* is described in Chapter 1 of that book.

And yet, while settlements might exclude women in many circumstances, it was the marriage settlement which came to the protection of married women. If property was settled on trust for the woman and also for other people in remainder, then it was not 'her' property and as such it could not be seized by her husband on their marriage. In Austen's *Persuasion* (considered above), if Anne Elliot had had her property settled on her during her life and then to other people in remainder, it would have been impossible for any future husband to have taken that property from her because it would have continued to be held on trust. The husband would only have been able to take any payments of income which the trustees advanced to her. To avoid that problem, the trustees could have been given a discretion as to the amounts which would be forwarded to Anne and as to the form in which property would be forwarded to Anne. The flexibility of the trust device meant that it could be used to protect women as well. If property was settled on trust for that woman then she would not be entitled to take it for herself, and therefore she could not pass it to her husband by operation of law: this meant that a settlor could ensure that his female descendants were protected from their husbands by locking their property into a settlement under the stewardship of a trustee. Of course, this meant that the woman was also dependent on the trustee and furthermore on the terms of the trust as set down by the settlor in the first place. Nevertheless, it protected them against the notorious stories of some husbands who would marry, take their wives' property and spend it on loose living (often with a mistress and living apart from their wives), before returning to the matrimonial home if the wife inherited any further money in the future.[167] The place of women in our society was extremely precarious, but the trust did offer the possibility of protecting them within the family, if the settlor and his advisors were sufficiently forward-thinking.

The changing morality of 18th-century England

Much popular culture at this time depicted women seeking to protect themselves from the precarious position in which they found themselves. Samuel Richardson's *Pamela, or Virtue Rewarded*, published in 1740, is sometimes claimed to be the first proper English novel (told in the form of a series of letters written by a young woman). It tells the tale of a virtuous young woman who resists the rapacious advances of her master before eventually marrying him and thus securing a good, virtuous life for herself. The morality of this story – which to a modern mind merely suggests that success for the virtuous young woman involves marrying a rich man who tried to assault her – is deeply troubling and at the same time is locked into a vision of 'Merrie Old England' as a society of patient virtues and happy endings. Exactly that sort of moral blindness affected property law, as rich husbands commonly took mistresses while property law allowed them to live off their rich wives' property.

There was some resistance to this sickly, rose-tinted vision of English society in the 18th century. In the Preface to this book we considered the changing morality which the artist Hogarth depicted in the painting (part of a sequence painted between 1743 and 1745) which adorns the cover of the seventh edition this book, with its very modern tale of acquisition, infidelity and ultimately financial ruin. It was a popular moral theme of the time which also appeared in Henry Fielding's novel *Shamela*, which mocked Richardson's *Pamela* by depicting a very modern young woman, of low class but high spirits, who went in search of

167 See Cretney, 2005.

a fortune by ensnaring a rich man so that she and her children would benefit from a well-stocked marriage settlement. As Shamela put it herself, 'a settled settlement for me, and all my heirs, all my whole life-time, shall do the business'. While this does depict the young woman as a gold-digger, what it also suggests is that English culture offered two choices to women at a time when trusts law was beginning to be drawn together as a coherent set of principles: assuming they could avoid poverty, they were either required to be submissive wives or scheming gold-diggers. Other examples of the latter category in English literature were Defoe's *Moll Flanders* and, a little later in time, the feisty Becky Sharp in Thackeray's *Vanity Fair*, who flirted her way steadily upwards in society until her bluff was finally called.

Rights of women to the home

The issues considered in Chapter 15 in relation to trusts of homes are significant in that they have tended to demonstrate a particularly gendered approach to trusts law, until developments begun by Waite LJ in *Midland Bank v Cooke*[168] took a more nuanced view of the situation. Cases as to the equitable ownership of the home between unmarried couples or home-sharers typically used to favour the breadwinner, who statistically would often have been a man.[169] There were estoppel cases (such as *Pascoe v Turner*[170]) or equitable cases (such as *Midland Bank v Cooke* or *Cox v Jones*[171]) which saw value in women's contribution to the home other than the purely financial and which therefore relied both on 'undertaking a survey of the entire course of dealing between the parties' and on avoiding unconscionability. Things have begun to change, in no small part due to the flexibility offered by equity and trusts law. In more recent cases in front of the highest courts – in *Stack v Dowden*[172] and in *Jones v Kernott*[173] – it has been the women who have been the higher earners in the relationship. Lady Hale identified a need for a new generation to move away from the presumption in the old cases that if a man transferred property to his wife then it was to be assumed that his intention was to make a gift to her because a man's role was to 'maintain' his wife. Significantly, the recent cases have been looking into the entire course of dealing between the parties, and taking into account non-financial contributions, instead of looking simply at the money that was contributed to the original purchase price. Perhaps now the position of women who are not able to contribute financially to the home is being recognised as a result of those recent decisions. A more significant cause of change, however, might be the more general presence of women in the workforce, which has had a patchy effect and which has had complex impacts on issues like childcare.

Residual judicial attitudes to women

In spite of these developments, even in the 21st century, the conceptualisation of women by a mostly male judiciary can still be troubling on occasion. An otherwise unremarkable case

---

168 [1995] 4 All ER 562.
169 See, for example, the test set out by Lord Bridge in *Lloyds Bank v Rosset* [1991] 1 AC 107.
170 [1979] 1 WLR 431.
171 [2004] 3 FCR 693.
172 [2007] UKHL 17, [2007] 2 WLR 831.
173 [2011] UKSC 53, [2011] 3 WLR 1121, [2011] 3 FCR 495.

(in that it tells us little about legal principle) which is discussed in Chapter 11 on resulting trusts is *Elithorn v Poulter*,[174] in which the claimant was referred to as 'Madeline' by Rimer LJ throughout the case – even though she paid the entire purchase price for a couple's house – while the defendant – who paid nothing in cash – was referred to throughout as 'Dr Elithorn'. This seems to reduce her by referring to her informally by her first name, while by comparison he is referred to formally by his surname and more particularly by reference to his highest university degree. Even more remarkably, it was held that the property should be deemed to be owned equally between them in spite of the fact that she had paid the entire purchase price up-front. These sorts of differences in the treatment of parties to litigation require constant close attention. In many of the older cases on trusts of homes, there was a tendency to dismiss work which wives had performed in bringing up children and running the home as being simply the sort of work which was expected from women and which could therefore be dismissed. These sorts of gendered attitudes are something which needs to be exposed and criticised. There is still a large amount of work to be done on equity and trusts law in considering the sociology and the politics of that law as it functions in practice in the world.

2.7.3 A politics of trusts law

The use of trusts to avoid tax and regulation

As is considered in Chapter 4 and in Chapter 21, trusts are commonly used in practice to avoid liability to tax. In particular complex trust structures are used in so-called 'offshore jurisdictions' and 'tax havens' to shelter the money of the rich from taxation and to shelter the assets of international criminal enterprises from regulatory oversight. A politics of trusts law would have to account, ironically, for the way in which structures which are built on conscience are used to facilitate crime and to avoid taxation. There are trusts practitioners whose sole role is to help their clients to use trusts to avoid taxation and consequently to prevent hospitals from being built, schools from being fully staffed, and universities from being fully funded in their home jurisdictions. The attitude of clients seeking to shelter their assets can be summed up by the attitude of the *haute bourgeois* Forsyte family in John Galsworthy's *The Man of Property*:

> . . . no Forsyte had as yet died; they did not die; death being contrary to their principles, they took precautions against it, the instinctive precautions of highly vitalized persons who resent encroachments on their property.[175]

What is particularly significant here is the *resentment* at the idea of encroachments on their property. Such encroachments would include the claims of Her Majesty's Revenue and Customs before and after death,[176] ordinary creditors ranging from the greengrocer to

174 [2008] EWCA Civ 1364.

175 J Galsworthy, *The Man of Property*, being Book 1 of *The Forsyte Saga, Vol 1 of The Forsyte Chronicles* (originally published by William Heineman, 1906; republished in Penguin Classics, 2001, p 12).

176 Similarly, in PG Wodehouse's novels and stories about Bertie Wooster and his valet Jeeves, there is regularly the mood music of Bertie's uncle, Tom Travers, protesting about the incursions of the Inland Revenue on his inherited wealth.

significant trade creditors, other family members or former spouses, and for the super-rich in the modern world also law enforcement agencies and statutory regulators.

Tax havens and their role in international crime

One example of this sort of trust is known as an 'asset protection trust'. The expression 'asset protection trust' refers to a set of techniques which are used to put assets beyond the reach of creditors, taxing authorities, regulators and others so that they are 'protected' from those people. Commonly, clients seeking to use asset protection trusts are either resident in high tax jurisdictions (such as the UK or the USA) or they are seeking to avoid regulatory or governmental oversight. A trust is used in this context so that the beneficial ownership of the target assets, which might otherwise be at risk, is obscured or allocated in such a way that the claimants will not be able to seize or interfere with those assets. It is a key part of the nature of any ordinary trust that a single item of property can be subjected to the rights of a variety of different legal and equitable owners such that each one of those owners can have different qualities of right in relation to the same item of property. An asset protection trust relies heavily on the malleability of the trust device.

Governments in developed countries began to grow impatient with these tax havens both from the perspective of the cost to their own exchequers and also in the light of concerns about global terrorism and other international criminal activities. Consequently, many of these 'tax havens' were affected directly in recent years by a renewed focus on the fiscal and national security consequences in the developed world of the tax advantages offered to wealthy investors by financial service providers in these tax havens (often subsidiaries of large investment firms and banks). Of particular concern is that international terrorist and other criminal organisations use trusts and other products in these jurisdictions to fund their activities. The Organisation for Economic Co-operation and Development (OECD) used four criteria to identify a 'tax haven'. First, the levying of no or only nominal taxes. Second, a lack of transparency so as to prevent the open and consistent implementation of tax laws and the preparation of appropriate accounting information. Third, the absence of laws or administrative practices which prevent the giving of relevant information (about no tax or only nominal tax being levied) to the appropriate agencies of other governments or supra-national bodies. Fourth, the absence of any substantial activities being carried on in the tax haven itself by entities which have the protection of that jurisdiction's laws (which in itself indicates that the jurisdiction is operating its practices solely to attract investment capital from those wishing to avoid regulatory oversight elsewhere).[177] The asset protection trust usually does nothing and the trustees may in reality be in London or New York, but the laws of that tax haven may permit the trust to be treated as though it is resident in that jurisdiction for tax and other purposes.

An important part of this development in the treatment of tax havens was the effect of two OECD reports. The first identified a list of thirty-eight 'unco-operative tax havens'. Those jurisdictions were cajoled into changing their laws, and into beefing up their regulatory arrangements and so forth as a result. No jurisdiction wanted to be identified as being a haven for criminal and other activities because there were political consequences from being

---

177 This fourth criterion was dropped in 2001.

treated in that way. Many commentators doubt that these changes have had a significant impact on the use of these trusts in practice.[178] The second report, which has been updated annually since 2000 under the title *Towards Global Tax Co-operation*,[179] surveys the tax and trusts laws and the administrative practices of a growing number of jurisdictions, not just those which were considered to be transparent in relation to the assets and activities within their jurisdictions. Thirty-five jurisdictions[180] which were originally identified on the OECD list in 1998 as being 'unco-operative tax havens' have since given undertakings[181] to implement transparency standards and to engage in the exchange of information with other jurisdictions for tax purposes.[182] The other jurisdictions have negotiated different treatment with the OECD.

The impact on real people

The impact of using trusts to avoid tax and regulation is a reduction in the amount of money available to the public exchequer, the greased wheels of international crime, and the consequent impact on social life in countries like the UK. However, the effect of trusts practice can be even more visceral and direct than that. For example, *The Guardian* newspaper ran a truly disturbing article on 17 October 2007, by Ashley Seager and James Lewis, under the headline 'How top London law firms help vulture funds devour their prey', accompanied by a genuinely frightening photograph of an emaciated child appearing to rest its head on the ground in fatigue while in the background a vulture sat on the bare earth watching. The article laid bare the way in which a particular kind of investment fund – so-called 'vulture funds'[183] – invested in 'distressed sovereign debt',[184] particularly the debt of countries in equatorial Africa. Typically this would be extremely poor countries, like Zambia at the time, which needed the money for the poor and starving in their own countries but which were obliged to pay high rates of interest on their borrowings. This practice involved buying the bonds issued by countries which later announced that they could not make repayments on those bonds: the bonds are therefore very cheap indeed and investors are keen to off-load them. The buyers of these bonds then litigate aggressively to seek pay-outs on those bonds in the hope of realising more money than the purchase price of the bonds. It was by using anonymous trust fund structures that financial institutions would buy up the investors' rights to those bonds. The net effect is that countries which are in real trouble – with people suffering from famine and disease – end up spending money which should be spent on helping their poor and their sick on making repayments to vulture funds on these bonds. It really is the unacceptable face of capitalism.

178 See Hudson, 2011 on asset protection trusts.
179 *Towards Global Tax Co-operation 2010*, OECD Publishing, 2010.
180 An original group of 38 jurisdictions had previously been identified as being non-co-operative 'tax havens' by the OECD in 1998.
181 Albeit that four of those jurisdictions did not do so at first: Andorra, Liechtenstein, Liberia and Monaco; and three other jurisdictions have been removed from the list of unco-operative tax havens: Barbados, Maldives and Tonga.
182 See www.oecd.org.
183 Hence the vulture being used in the picture accompanying the article.
184 As explained in the text, that is borrowings by a country which announces it cannot make repayment.

Unregulated trusts in these circumstances can become the vehicles for visiting misery on real people. The absence of conscience in this sort of activity is clearly stark. That a vehicle created originally in a court of conscience could be used for this sort of activity would seem like something from an internet conspiracy theory, if it were not for the fact that there are people in the City of London, on Wall Street, in Paris, Frankfurt and Tokyo, calmly planning to do this sort of thing every day of the week. This was a rare journalistic account of something which one knows anecdotally is going on all the time. It serves as a useful introduction into the geopolitics behind even the most banal areas of trusts law. One such example within trusts law is the law surrounding the ancient 'beneficiary principle', discussed in Chapter 4, where the issue of international trusts law is probed again. The financial institutions which operate these trust funds argue that the 'beneficiary principle' should be jettisoned so as to make their tax avoidance activities easier to organise and to market. Before launching into a consideration of the law of trusts, it is important to understand the context in which trusts can operate in practice in the real world, and to understand the political context in which this otherwise seemingly apolitical field of law operates.

Express trusts

Chapter 3

Certainty in the creation of express trusts

OVERVIEW

The main principles underlying this area of law are as follows:

To create a valid trust, the terms of that trust must be sufficiently certain. There are three forms of certainty which the courts require: certainty of intention to create a trust; certainty as to the subject matter comprising the trust fund; and certainty of the beneficiaries (or 'objects') of the trust or power in question:[1]

(a) *The settlor's intention to create a trust, as opposed to something else, must be clear. There is no requirement to use a specific form of words when dealing with trusts over property[2] other than land.[3] The court will be prepared to infer an intention to create a trust from the circumstances and the parties' conduct.[4] The same principles apply in relation to domestic, private situations as in relation to the insolvencies of large financial institutions.*

(b) *The trust fund must be identifiable.[5] A trust in which the trust property is mixed with other property, so that it is impossible to identify precisely which property is held on trust, will be invalid.[6] However, exceptionally, it may be that where the property is intangible property made up of identical units (such as ordinary shares of the same class), it may not be necessary to segregate the trust property from other property.[7] This exception is doubted by many academics. Recent cases in the wake of the collapse of US investment bank Lehman Brothers have put these competing principles at centre-stage in the largest corporate insolvency in history.*

(c) *To identify the beneficiaries, it is first necessary to identify the nature of the power which is being exercised. In relation to fiduciary mere powers and in relation to discretionary trusts, it is required that it is possible to say of any person claiming to be a beneficiary that that person is or is not a member of the class of beneficiaries.[8] Some exceptional cases have taken the view that the trust may be valid where it is possible to say that a substantial number of people do or do not fall within the class of beneficiaries.[9] In relation to a fixed trust, it is necessary to be able to draw up a complete list of all the beneficiaries.[10] There appears to be a distinction between failure of a trust on grounds of uncertainty as to the concept used to identify the class of beneficiaries, problems of proving yourself to be a beneficiary, problems of locating beneficiaries and problems of administrative*

---

1 *Knight v Knight* (1840) 3 Beav 148; *Knight v Boughton* (1840) 11 Cl & Fin 513.
2 *M'Fadden v Jenkyns* (1842) 12 LJ Ch 146.
3 Law of Property Act 1925, s 53(1)(b).
4 *Paul v Constance* [1977] 1 WLR 527.
5 *Re London Wine Co (Shippers) Ltd* [1986] PCC 121; *MacJordan Construction Ltd v Brookmount Erostin Ltd* [1992] BCLC 350; *Re Goldcorp* [1995] 1 AC 74; *Westdeutsche Landesbank Girozentrale v Islington LBC* [1996] AC 669; see section 3.4 below.
6 *Ibid.*
7 *Hunter v Moss* [1994] 1 WLR 452; *Re Harvard Securities Ltd* [1997] 2 BCLC 369.
8 *Re Gulbenkian* [1968] Ch 126; *McPhail v Doulton* [1970] 2 WLR 1110.
9 *Re Baden (No 2)* [1973] Ch 9.
10 *IRC v Broadway Cottages Trust* [1955] 2 WLR 552.

unworkability[11] – *only the first and last categories appear to invalidate the trust necessarily. Personal powers, on the authorities, will not be void for lack of certainty of objects. The case law has dealt with a variety of words and expressions which commonly cause uncertainty, as considered in this chapter.*

3.1 INTRODUCTION

When creating an express trust, it is important that the settlor act with sufficient certainty. There are three certainties required for the creation of a valid express trust.[12] The settlor must demonstrate a clear intention to create a trust as opposed to creating something else;[13] the trust property must be sufficiently segregated from other property so that the trust fund is certain;[14] and the people who are to benefit from the trust must also be identified with sufficient certainty.[15] These forms of certainty are commonly referred to, respectively, as certainty of intention, certainty of subject matter and certainty of objects. Without such certainty, the trust will be held to be void. When considering express trusts – that is, situations in which the settlor *intends* to create a trust – we should recognise that there will be cases in which the court may analyse the actions of the settlor as evidencing an intention to create an express trust even though she might not have understood that that was what she was doing.[16] Thus, when we talk about express trusts, we are concerned with any situation in which the settlor performs actions with an intention which equity will analyse as disclosing a sufficiently certain intention to create a trust.

3.1.1 The relationship of settlor, trustee and beneficiary

In the creation of an express trust, there is a relationship created between the three different capacities under the trust: settlor, trustee and beneficiary. This relationship has been considered already above in Chapter 2. The central question considered in this chapter is the certainty that is necessary before an express trust will be said to exist.

3.1.2 The settlor

The settlor does not have any further role to play in relation to the trust, in her capacity as settlor, once a valid trust has been created.[17] Of course, that does not mean that the *person* who created the trust cannot have a role; rather, that person cannot have a role *as settlor*. So, the person who acted as settlor may also appoint herself to be one of the trustees of the trust. This is another reminder of the importance of distinguishing between the individuals involved and the precise capacities in which they are acting from time to time. The person who acted as settlor can therefore not have a further role *as settlor* once the trust has been created. That person's role may now only be in the capacity of a trustee or a beneficiary, or possibly both.

---

11 *McPhail v Doulton* [1970] 2 WLR 1110; see para 3.5.4 below.
12 *Morice v Bishop of Durham* (1805) 10 Ves 522, at 539, *per* Lord Eldon.
13 *Knight v Knight* (1840) 3 Beav 148; *Knight v Boughton* (1840) 11 Cl & Fin 513.
14 *Re London Wine Co (Shippers) Ltd* [1986] PCC 121.
15 *IRC v Broadway Cottages Trust* [1955] 2 WLR 552; *Re Gulbenkian* [1968] Ch 126; *McPhail v Doulton* [1970] 2 WLR 1110.
16 *Paul v Constance* [1977] 1 WLR 527 – as considered in section 3.3.
17 *Paul v Paul* (1882) 20 Ch D 742.

In considering whether or not a trust has been created, it is important to uncover an intention on the part of the settlor to create a trust. To that extent, the behaviour and the words of the settlor may continue to have significance after the date at which a trust is said to have been created because it may show what her intention had been. As has been said in Chapter 2 above, the settlor may choose to create a trust with professional legal advice perhaps as part of creating a will, or as part of a complex commercial transaction. This conscious decision to create a trust will be comparatively straightforward – this chapter will consider the necessary manifestation of intention in such circumstances. However, the more difficult cases are those in which a person deals with her property in ignorance of the law of trusts but where she performs actions which the law of trusts would define as being a declaration of trust. In such situations, the actions of the settlor will be unconscious as to their precise legal character. For example, a person may say 'I intend this money to be as much yours as mine', and therefore indicate to a court that she intends to create a trust even though she is ignorant that that would be the legal effect of her actions.[18]

3.1.3 The trustee

For the trustee, there is the problem of knowing whether or not a trust has been created so that she is subject to the fiduciary duties of a trustee. The essence of the rules on certainty considered below is that the court must be certain as to the nature of the trustee's obligations so that the court is able to oversee them. As considered in Chapter 2 above, it is perfectly possible for a settlor to declare herself to be one of the trustees (or the sole trustee) of property of which she is also one of the beneficiaries. For example, if Anne wishes to declare a trust over money which she has won on the National Lottery for the benefit of herself and her family, it is possible for Anne to declare the trust (and therefore be settlor) such that she is sole trustee of the money for the benefit of herself and her children in equal shares.

In relation to a trust created as part of a complex commercial transaction, it will typically be the case that the trustees will be professionals (perhaps lawyers or accountants, or alternatively bankers) who are paid to act as trustees and who hold themselves out as having expertise in the management of trust money. In that situation, the precise terms of the trustees' obligations will usually have been set out in a trust instrument.[19] The trustees can therefore be very confident of what is expected of them. Unless there were some error in the drafting of the terms of the trust, it would be unusual for there to be much uncertainty in such a case.

However, where an ordinary member of the public, perhaps a grandmother, gives money to her son, saying 'I want you to keep this money to buy my grandchildren a new bicycle each for Christmas', the law may consider that to be a declaration of trust. The son would be deemed to be a trustee holding the money on the terms of a trust in favour of the grandchildren as beneficiaries. In such a situation, the son would not know what to do if, for example, one of the children was adamant that she did not want a bicycle but rather wanted a pair of in-line skates. Would the terms of the trust permit such a deviation from the grandmother's express instructions? In such a situation, without a fully drafted trust there would be uncertainty as to the precise nature of the trustee's obligations.

---

18 *Paul v Constance* [1977] 1 WLR 527.
19 Eg, *Armitage v Nurse* [1998] Ch 241. See the discussion of Trustee Act 2000 in this context in Chapter 8.

Furthermore, the trustee would not know what he was supposed to do with the money between receiving it from the grandmother and buying the Christmas presents. Would he be obliged to invest the money and generate the best possible return for the grandchildren as beneficiaries? This would be the obligation on a trustee in ordinary circumstances,[20] but it is unclear whether that principle ought to apply in this particular circumstance. A well-drafted trust instrument will make all of this clear: whereas informally created trusts will leave such matters to the court's interpretation. The Trustee Act 1925 and the Trustee Act 2000, considered in Part 3 of this book, provide the obligations which will be implied in such circumstances. For the moment, however, we will focus on how trusts come into existence. (A 'trust instrument' is a document containing all the terms of a trust; although, as will be explained in Chapter 5, no written instrument is required to create an express trust in ordinary circumstances.)

Therefore, as we consider more and more examples of express trusts, we will ask ourselves about the nature of the obligations which are imposed on the trustees and whether those obligations should be identical in all circumstances. Usually the answer will be found by analysing the precise terms in which the settlor expressed her intention.

3.1.4 The beneficiary

For the beneficiary, it is similarly important to be certain as to the existence and the terms of the trust. The rights owned by the beneficiary are best understood as being both powers to control the use of the trust fund by the trustee[21] and as constituting property rights in the trust fund under the principle in *Saunders v Vautier.*[22] That principle entitles the beneficiaries under a trust, provided that they constitute the entire beneficial interest in the trust fund and that they are all *sui juris* (that is, of suitable age and competence to act), to call for the trust fund to be transferred to them absolutely. Clearly, this power is capable of being exercised only in circumstances in which it is possible to know who all of the beneficiaries are.[23] Nevertheless, this principle establishes that the beneficiaries do have proprietary rights in the trust fund itself, and not simply personal claims against the trustees.

Similarly, it is important that the trustees know the identity of the beneficiaries. For the courts, it is essential that the trust discloses both the identity of the beneficiaries and the terms on which those beneficiaries are entitled to take rights in the trust fund. Without such certainty, it would be impossible to control the conduct of the business of the trust.[24]

3.2 THE THREE CERTAINTIES

There are three forms of certainty which the courts require for the creation of a valid express trust: certainty of intention to create a trust; certainty as to the subject matter comprising the trust fund; and certainty of the beneficiaries (or 'objects') of the trust.

---

20 *Cowan v Scargill* [1985] Ch 270.
21 *Morice v Bishop of Durham* (1805) 10 Ves 522; *Re Denley's Will Trusts* [1969] 1 Ch 373.
22 (1841) 4 Beav 115.
23 The ramifications of the rule in *Saunders v Vautier* are considered below at para 4.1.2.
24 Section 3.5 below.

English law has a great affection for certainty: judges are concerned that the law promotes certainty in contracts, trusts and other dealings between persons. In terms of the trust specifically, the judges' concern is that the settlor makes her intention sufficiently certain so that the court will be able to direct the trustees how to act if there are problems with the administration of the trust. For the court to be able to make such directions, it is essential that it be certain:

(a) that the settlor intended to create a trust ('certainty of intention');
(b) which property is to comprise the trust fund ('certainty of subject matter'); and
(c) who the beneficiaries are ('certainty of objects').[25]

These forms of certainty are considered in turn in the sections which follow.

3.3 CERTAINTY OF INTENTION

> *It must be certain that the settlor intended to create a trust rather than to impose a merely moral obligation or to make a gift or do some other act which was not a trust. There is no requirement to use a specific form of words for trusts over personal property, although there are formalities for the creation of trusts over land. Therefore, given that there is no particular form of words which are to be used, the court will consider what the relevant parties' intentions were and will then find a trust if that satisfies those parties' intentions. The court will be prepared to infer an intention to create a trust from the circumstances of the case and from the parties' conduct. In short, if the owner of property demonstrates an intention either to share the beneficial ownership of property with some other person while remaining the owner at law of that property, or if the owner of property passes common law title in that property to some third party with the intention that beneficial ownership of it be held for some other person, then it is likely that there will be a trust inferred.*

3.3.1 What form of intention?

Conscious creation of a trust

It is important that the settlor intends to create a trust as opposed to creating merely a gift or some other device.[26] The simplest manifestation of that intention would be for the settlor to take advice from a solicitor and sign a formal declaration of trust in the form of a deed.[27] Such a written manifestation of a trust is referred to as a 'trust instrument'. As considered in

---

25 *Knight v Knight* (1840) 3 Beav 148, *per* Lord Langdale.
26 *Milroy v Lord* (1862) 4 De GF & J 264.
27 However, to remind ourselves that matters may be simple and that words may simply be taken to mean what they appear to mean on their face, the Australian High Court held in *Byrnes and another v Kendle* [2011] HCA 26, 14 ITELR 299 that the use of the term 'trust' by a husband in dealing with the matrimonial home indicated that he had intended to create a trust over it to the effect that he and his wife were tenants in common of it in equity. In that case a husband was somewhat disingenuously contending that he had not intended to create a trust which would benefit his former wife when clearly he had been. Law of Property (Miscellaneous Provisions) Act 1989, s 1.

Chapter 5, the creation of a written instrument will not be necessary in many cases,[28] but it does make it easy to prove that there is a trust.[29] A verbal expression of an intention to create a trust will be sufficient.[30] In such a situation, if the settlor consciously intended to create a trust, then there is no difficulty in establishing that there was sufficient certainty of intention.[31] The more difficult situations are where a settlor unknowingly behaves in a way which might have created a trust, or where the settlor leaves her intention ambiguous in the terms of a will or other document.

Express trusts based on inference by the court

The best example of this difficult situation is *Paul v Constance*.[32] Mr Constance left his wife to live with Mrs Paul. Constance received a court award of £950 for an injury suffered at work, subsequent to which Constance and Paul decided to set up a joint bank account. After visiting the bank, they were advised that the account should be set up in the name of Constance alone because the couple were not married. Therefore, Constance was the common law owner of the account. The £950 lump sum was paid into the account and formed the bulk of the money held in it. The couple also added joint bingo winnings to the account, and used some of the money to pay for a joint holiday. Importantly, evidence was also adduced at trial that Constance had said to Paul 'this money is as much yours as mine'.

Constance died. His wife sought to claim that the bank account belonged entirely to her deceased husband and that it therefore passed to her as his widow under the Intestacy Rules. Paul argued that the money was held on trust by Constance, as legal owner of the bank account, for both Constance and Paul as beneficiaries. Therefore, Paul argued, the bank account should pass to her as sole surviving beneficiary. The litigation was therefore the staple of soap operas: the spurned wife fighting against the new lover.

The court held that Constance had declared a trust over the money in the bank account. The reasoning was that the words 'the money is as much yours as mine' manifested sufficient intention that Constance would hold the property on trust for them both. Furthermore, that the couple had treated the money in the account as joint money was taken to be evidence of the intention to create a trust.

An interesting point arises from this case as an example of the law of express trusts. The court held that the trust was an *express* trust even though, in the words of the court, Constance was a man of 'unsophisticated character' who did not know he was creating a trust. In other words, you can create an express trust without knowing that there is a legal concept of trust. Instead, the court will consider your conduct and your 'real' intention in deciding whether or not you can be taken to have intended the creation of something which the court would interpret as being a trust. As Scarman LJ said, the words Constance did use, that the money was

---

28 There are, however, statutory exceptions which do require signed writing to create a trust, as discussed in Chapter 5, such as trusts of land: Law of Property 1925, s 53(1)(b).

29 See section 5.1 below.

30 For a demonstration that a verbal statement will be sufficient to create a trust, see *Moore v Williamson* [2011] EWHC 672 (Ch), [2011] 2 P&CR DG9 in which verbal assurances that a trust would be created over half the equity in a business were held to be sufficient to create a trust.

31 See, eg, *Slamon v Planchon* [2004] 4 All ER 407, [2004] EWCA Civ 799, where a trust was expressly declared over a property, in relation to the Leasehold and Urban Development Act 1993, s 10.

32 [1977] 1 WLR 527.

as much hers as his, 'convey clearly a present declaration that the existing fund was as much the plaintiff's as his own'.[33]

There are other cases which illustrate the English view that the court is uncovering an express trust rather than imposing a constructive trust. In *Re Kayford*,[34] a mail order company used to receive money from customers buying items from their catalogues before those items were sent to the customers. The customers therefore bore the risk that they had paid their money but that they might not receive the items for which they had paid. The mail order company realised that it was in danger of insolvency and therefore segregated all of its customer prepayments into a distinct bank account. Money was moved from that bank account only once the item had been sent to the customer. When the company did go into insolvency, the issue arose whether the money belonged to the company (and therefore would be distributed among the company's creditors) or whether it was held on trust for the customers (and therefore could be returned to them). The court held that the company's intention was to create a trust over the prepayments which had been manifested by transferring those prepayments into a separate bank account so as to shield them from the insolvency. This case illustrates the important role which the trust plays in protecting the beneficiary against the possibility of insolvency on the part of the trustee. The company, as legal owner of the bank account, was trustee. The customers were beneficiaries in the period between making a prepayment and receiving their items. Again, an express trust is uncovered from the parties' actions, without needing any conscious intention to create an express trust.

The finding of an intention to create a trust is based on the surrounding circumstances

In the previous section we saw that the court may infer the existence of sufficient certainty of intention to create an express trust from the circumstances, even if the parties involved were unaware that their actions would be interpreted by a court as suggesting an intention to create a trust. By extension from the previous discussion, the court may look at all the surrounding circumstances and decide that, on the facts, there is insufficient intention to create a trust. So, in *Jones v Lock*,[35] a father returned home from a business trip to Birmingham. He was scolded by his wife for not bringing back a present for his infant son. In what appears to have been a fit of pique, he went upstairs, wrote a cheque out in favour of himself as payee, came back downstairs, shouted 'Look you here, I give this to the baby', and thrust the cheque into the baby's hand. The issue arose whether there was a trust created over the cheque (or the money represented by the cheque) for the benefit of the baby. It was found that there had not been a perfect gift of the cheque (because it was made out in the father's name without having been endorsed in favour of the baby). The court held further that there was nothing to indicate an intention to create a trust of the cheque. Rather, the father's intention was either to make a gift, or simply to make a point to his wife (in which case he

---

33 An alternative approach, not used by the court in this case, could be that the court is imposing a constructive trust to prevent Paul being unjustly treated. This is closer to the way in which constructive trusts are used in the US, where they are seen as remedies to be used to reverse unjust enrichment. A US analysis of *Paul v Constance* might be that the wife would be unjustly enriched if Paul were denied her rights to the money in the bank account. (See the discussion in Chapter 31 and *Helga Stoeckert v Margie Geddes* [2004] UKPC 54.) Consequently, the US court could order the imposition of a constructive trust over the account to prevent any unconscionable denial of Mrs Paul's rights.

34 [1975] 1 WLR 279.

35 (1865) 1 Ch App 25.

intended nothing at all). Lord Cranworth found that the argument for a trust was merely an attempt to circumvent the failure to make an effective gift by advancing an argument for a trust. Therefore, he held that this imperfect gift could not be made effective by other means and that there had been no intention to create a trust here.

This principle appears most clearly from the words of Jessel MR in *Richards v Delbridge*,[36] where he held that 'If [a failed disposition] is intended to take effect by transfer [or 'gift'], the court will not hold the intended transfer to operate as a declaration of trust, for then every imperfect instrument would be made effectual by being converted into a perfect trust'. In that case, a businessman decided to transfer his business outright to a member of his family and sought to demonstrate this intention by an endorsement on the lease over the business premises. The gift was never perfected and therefore it was argued unsuccessfully in favour of the proposed transferee that the business should be treated as having been held on trust for him. The court held that the failed gift would not be effected by means of inferring an intention to create a trust. Here the intention had been to make an outright transfer (or, a gift), and not a trust (whereby the businessman would have held the legal title and only passed the equitable interest to his relative).

The use of the word 'trust' in an instrument or in a statute will not necessarily mean that a court will deem that to be a trust;[37] although that will be a likely inference, particularly if one person is holding property for the benefit of another. Where the Law Society was obliged by statute to create a fund to hold moneys when exercising its regulatory powers over solicitors, it was held that this should be understood as constituting a trust over those funds for the Society's statutory purposes and for the benefit of those entitled to the moneys.[38] This is the corollary of the principle in *Paul v Constance*: in that case it was found that even if the parties do not know what a 'trust' is, they may nevertheless be held to have created a trust if that is what a court would consider their intention to have meant; equally, just because parties do use the word 'trust' that does not mean that the court will necessarily find that they have created a trust if their true intention was really to do something else in legal terms. A close analysis of the circumstances of the case will be all-important. So, where r 43(3) of the Prison Rules 1999 obliges the governor of a prison to take all of a prisoner's cash from her on incarceration in a prison, it has been held that this rule did not make the governor a trustee of that property for the benefit of that prisoner.[39] The rules, on a close reading of them, only required that the prisoner's cash be paid into an account and credited to the prisoner: nothing in that wording suggested that the governor of the prison had the positive obligations of a trustee. Consequently, because there was no trust, the governor was not bound by any of the obligations usually incumbent on a trustee[40] to invest the trust property for the benefit of the beneficiary and so forth.[41] Therefore, when one person is obliged to hold property for another, it will not always constitute that person a trustee, particularly if it is not the parties' or the law's intention that such a person be encumbered with the usual obligations imposed on a trustee.[42]

---

36 (1874) LR 18 Eq 11.
37 *Tito v Waddell (No 2)* [1977] 1 Ch 106, 211, *per* Megarry V-C.
38 *Re Ahmed & Co* [2006] EWHC 480 (Ch).
39 *Duggan v Governor of Full Sutton Prison* [2003] 2 All ER 678.
40 See Chapter 8 generally in this regard.
41 This decision is interesting. It might have been held alternatively that the governor was a bare trustee for the prisoner so that the governor would not have been able to take any personal interest from the holding of cash.
42 The general duties imposed on a trustee are considered in Chapter 8.

The commercial context: whether or not there is sufficient certainty of intention

The courts will not only intervene to find the existence of an express trust in circumstances in which there are non-commercial people acting in their private capacities. While it may seem surprising, there are plenty of commercial situations in which the parties either do not turn their minds to the question whether or not there is an express trust declared over some property, or in which their commercial arrangements are so poorly constructed that it is impossible to know whether a trust was intended or not.[43] One example of the courts stepping in to decide whether the parties' intentions amounted to an intention to create an express trust is *Re Kayford*,[44] considered above,[45] in which case the parties' treatment of the property (segregating it into a separate bank account) led the court to decide that the best understanding of the company's intention was to declare a trust in favour of those customers who made prepayments. In that case Megarry J found that the parties' intention was to declare a trust over the money held in the separate bank account even though the parties did not explicitly declare a trust: rather, Megarry J analysed the circumstances and held that they disclosed something which a lawyer would consider to be an intention to create a trust.

The salient facts in *Re Kayford*, as explained by Megarry J, were these:[46]

> On 22nd November Monaco told the company that Monaco would have to go into liquidation unless it received further financial support. If this happened it would affect not only the company's ability to deliver the goods but also its solvency. The next day, 23 November, Mr Kay saw the company's accountants, who advised him to consult accountants specialising in matters of insolvency; and the same day Mr Wainwright of such a firm was consulted. He advised that a separate bank account should be opened by the company, to be called a 'Customers' Trust Deposit Account', and that all further moneys paid by customers for goods not yet delivered should be paid into this account and withdrawn only when the goods had been delivered. The object of doing this was so that if the company had to go into liquidation, these sums of money could and would be refunded to those who had paid them. This advice was accepted.

Megarry J considered that the question for him to answer was 'whether the money in the bank account . . . is held on trust for those who paid it, or whether it forms part of the general assets of the company'. As to the question of whether or not there would be any fraudulent preference under insolvency law, Megarry J held that: 'If one leaves on one side any case in which an insolvent company seeks to declare a trust in favour of creditors, one is concerned here with the question not of preferring creditors but of preventing those who pay money from becoming creditors, by making them beneficiaries under a trust.' As to the ease of finding the existence of an express trust in the circumstances, Megarry J held the following:

---

43 See eg *Don King Productions Inc v Warren* [2000] Ch 291.
44 [1975] 1 WLR 279.
45 See para 2.5.1 above. In *OT Computers v First National Tricity Finance* [2003] EWHC 1010 Pumphrey J held that where directors of a company, which later went into insolvency, had already created bank accounts with the purpose of paying money owed to suppliers into those accounts, then there was sufficient certainty to constitute a valid trust over those moneys held in those accounts, following *Re Kayford*.
46 [1975] 1 All ER 604, [1975] 1 WLR 279.

In *Re Nanwa Gold Mines Ltd*[47] the money was sent on the faith of a promise to keep it in a separate account, but there is nothing in that case or in any other authority that I know of to suggest that this is essential. I feel no doubt that here a trust was created. From the outset the advice (which was accepted) was to establish a trust account at the bank. The whole purpose of what was done was to ensure that the moneys remained in the beneficial ownership of those who sent them, and a trust is the obvious means of achieving this. No doubt the general rule is that if you send money to a company for goods which are not delivered, you are merely a creditor of the company unless a trust has been created. The sender may create a trust by using appropriate words when he sends the money (though I wonder how many do this, even if they are equity lawyers), or the company may do it by taking suitable steps on or before receiving the money. If either is done, the obligations in respect of the money are transformed from contract to property, from debt to trust. Payment into a separate bank account is a useful (though by no means conclusive) indication of an intention to create a trust, but of course there is nothing to prevent the company from binding itself by a trust even if there are no effective banking arrangements.

Thus all that was needed to establish an intention to create a trust was an intention to keep the beneficial ownership of the money for the benefit of the customer. The company receiving the money must take 'suitable steps on or before receiving the money' to establish a trust.

We come now to a somewhat unsatisfactory decision of the High Court just before Christmas 2006 on ostensibly similar facts: *Re Farepak Food and Gifts Ltd*.[48] This case dealt with a set of circumstances which were very similar to those in *Re Kayford* but the decision in *Re Kayford* was not cited before Mann J. Therefore, we must treat this decision with caution because it was decided *per incuriam* the judgment of Megarry J in *Re Kayford*, but it does nevertheless give us a different approach to the question of dealing with insolvent companies which purport to create a separate bank account for moneys received after the insolvency.

The *Farepak* litigation became, briefly, a cause célèbre in the British press in the lead-up to Christmas 2006. It was a Christmas story in which Scrooge seemed to win out, if you believe the tabloid account of the story.[49] The facts, briefly put, were as follows. Many thousands of low-income families participated in a Christmas fund whereby they contributed a few pounds each month throughout the calendar year so that they would have saved up a large amount by November to spend on Christmas presents, festive foodstuffs and so on. The Christmas food could be taken in the form of a Christmas hamper or presents provided by means of shopping vouchers. The Christmas fund was therefore a pool of shared moneys contributed by the various customers.[50] The Christmas fund was managed by a company, Farepak Food and Gifts

---

47   [1955] 3 All ER 219, [1955] 1 WLR 1080.
48   [2006] EWHC 3272 (Ch), [2007] 2 BCLC 1, [2006] All ER (D) 265 (Dec).
49   Much of the coverage in the Press centred on the question whether or not Farepak's bankers should have made good many of the losses suffered by its customer but for which it was not responsible. It seemed that the Press expected that, in a fit of Christmas cheer, the bank would step in to repay its customer – and in turn its many ordinary customers – what it had lost. It is not ordinarily the case that banks – or moneylenders like Scrooge – operate as charities in this manner. Such turned out to be the case in this instance.
50   I shall refer to this arrangement as a 'Christmas fund' although in truth it was a business operated commercially but a number of questions arise as to the nature of this club.

Ltd (hereafter 'Farepak').[51] Farepak went into insolvency. Farepak's directors decided to cease trading on 11 October 2006. Farepak went into insolvent administration on 13 October 2006. Before its insolvency, attempts were made to create a new bank account into which any further customer contributions to the Christmas fund would be paid so as to keep those further contributions separate from the other assets of Farepak. The principal question was whether or not these funds were to be deemed to be held on trust for the customers who contributed them. The background to the hearing of the case is interesting: the case was heard in one day before Mann J on 15 December and judgment was delivered on 18 December. It is important to note that this case came on as a matter of urgency before Mann J, with little time for the preparation of argument and little time for the delivery of judgment, because the parties' were seeking to have administration of this part of the Christmas fund decided before Christmas.[52]

It was argued in front of Mann J that the pattern of behaviour by the directors of Farepak and their purported declaration of trust constituted an express trust. There were two issues on the facts: one referring to whether or not there was sufficient certainty as to the property which was to be held on trust[53] which is referred to below, and the other relating to difficulty of finding the existence of an intention to create an express trust in a context in which there was an insolvency. It is this second problem with which we are concerned here. On the facts of the case Mann J held that it would be 'an obstacle at a practical level'[54] to enforcing such an express trust because that trust would be to elevate the status of the customers who paid amounts into the fund after administration into preferred creditors.

Personally, I fail to see the difficulty. There are three questions here. First, was there an express trust created? If there was such a trust created, then the customers who paid into the fund after administration began were 'preferred creditors'[55] not because of some unfair advantage they were given after the event but because a valid trust had been created in their favour. The second question[56] was really whether or not there was any point of insolvency law which should avoid such an express trust which was created after the company had ceased trading. The third question – which might disallow the finding of an express trust – was whether or not there was sufficient certainty of subject matter and sufficient certainty of objects. That is, on the facts is it sufficiently clear which customers' money was paid into the Christmas fund after administration began? If not – either through evidential uncertainty of beneficiaries or evidential uncertainty of subject matter – then the trust would be void. But the avoidance of the trust would not be void simply because of some queasiness about

---

51 Farepak retained the services of a large number of agents throughout the country. These agents were ordinary members of the public who sought the custom, for the most part, of friends and work colleagues. Thus, for the most part, the ultimate customers were members of the public who paid their contributions to people who were usually their friends or work colleagues, who in turn acted as agents of Farepak. It was made clear by Mann J that these 'Agents', as they were referred to in the customers' agreements with Farepak, were Farepak's agents and were not acting as agents for the customers.

52 [2006] All ER (D) 265 (Dec), [7] and [8].

53 The principal problem on the facts, as held by Mann J, was that the bank account into which the moneys were paid was incorrectly identified on the face of the trust instrument. However, Mann J held that on the facts this was a situation in which the trust instrument should be rectified and the correct account substituted for the incorrect one: following *Re Butlin* [1976] Ch 251.

54 [2006] All ER (D) 265 (Dec), [52].

55 A 'preferred creditor' is someone who has a right to specific property in the possession or control of an insolvent person when that person goes into insolvency, and so that preferred (or, 'secured') creditor is entitled to take that property regardless of the insolvency proceedings.

56 At which Mann J was prodding in para 52 of his judgment.

converting these post-administration customers from unsecured to preferred creditors. Rather, if the express trust was validly created on 11 December, then all of the post-insolvency customers were preferred creditors by dint of being beneficiaries under an express trust at the moment they paid money to the company. There is no question of reclassifying them as preferred creditors: rather, the court would have been realising for the first time that they had been secured creditors ever since 11 December.

The most unsatisfactory factor here is the omission of any mention of *Re Kayford* which is the most valuable authority in relation to the existence of an express trust in situations such as this. Setting up a separate bank account, as in the *Re Farepak* case, achieves the creation of an express trust in the opinion of Megarry J in *Re Kayford*. Suitable steps in creating a trust may take the form of setting up a separate bank account coupled with an intention to create a trust: on the facts of the *Re Farepak* case there was such an intention clearly manifested by the declaration of trust as well as the creation of a separate bank account. Therefore, it is suggested that, on the authority of *Re Kayford*, an express trust should have been found in *Re Farepak*.[57]

Another example of a question about certainty of intention was the case of *Don King Productions Inc v Warren*.[58] This case involved two famous boxing promoters. Don King was the leading boxing promoter in the USA and Frank Warren was the leading boxing promoter and manager in Europe. The two men formed a partnership agreement whereby they, and the companies which they controlled, agreed to exploit agreements with boxers in Europe for their mutual advantage. Under the terms of the 1890 Partnership Act and under the general English law on partnership, an ordinary partnership is not a separate legal person: rather, a partnership is a contractual agreement between persons to share profits and losses as part of a business enterprise.[59] Under the partnership agreements entered into in *Don King v Warren*, each partner was required to hold the benefit of any existing or future management agreements for the benefit of the partnership. Subsequently, one or more of the partners attempted to terminate the partnership agreement and sought to argue that certain management agreements did not fall to be included in the partnership property. The question arose whether the partners held the benefit of their management agreements on trust for the partnership.

For Frank Warren it was argued (on this point) that some of the management agreements were expressly provided not to be assignable and that the parties' intentions had not been to hold all agreements on trust for the partnership in any event, or certainly not after Warren's purported termination of the agreement. It was held by Lightman J at first instance that despite any particular provisions in the management contracts themselves, the intentions of the parties had been to hold the benefit derived from any such contracts on trust for the partnership. Thus, even though the contracts themselves were expressed to have been incapable of transfer (and so *prima facie* to have been incapable of forming the subject matter of a trust), it was held that any benefit received from them could be the subject matter of a trust

---

57 In a later case arising from the same facts, *Re Farepak Food and Gifts Ltd (in liquidation); Power and another (joint liquidators of Farepak Food and Gifts Ltd) v Revenue and Customs Commissioners and another* [2009] EWHC 2580 (Ch), [2010] 1 BCLC 444, it is taken by Warren J that Mann J in *Re Farepak Food and Gifts Ltd* [2006] EWHC 3272 (Ch) had imposed a constructive trust, whereas on a closer reading of his judgment he did not (see [2006] EWHC 3272 (Ch) at [43] and [44]): rather, Mann J clearly would have liked to have imposed a constructive trust but he felt that *Nestlé Oy* and the complexities of the case in front of him constrained him from doing that; he consciously 'regrets' the conclusion to which he is required to come in para [44].

58 [1998] 2 All ER 608, *per* Lightman J; affirmed [2000] Ch 291, CA.

59 Partnership Act 1890, s 1: that is, 'the relation which subsists between persons carrying on a business in common with a view of profit'.

and that this partnership arrangement evinced sufficient intention to create a trust. Lightman J made repeated reference to how poorly drafted the parties' agreements had been and how their frequent redrafting of their contracts had not made the position any clearer. This decision was affirmed in the Court of Appeal[60] – although that appeal focused primarily on questions of partnership law and less on questions of trusts. So, even in complex commercial situations, the court may infer an intention to create a trust.

The principle relating to certainty of intention applies to commercial and to non-commercial situations

Lord Millett summarised the principle relating to the identification of certainty of intention in the House of Lords in *Twinsectra Ltd v Yardley*:[61]

> A settlor must, of course, possess the necessary intention to create a trust, but his subjective intentions are irrelevant. If he enters into *arrangements* which have the effect of creating a trust, it is not necessary that he should appreciate that they do so; it is sufficient that he intends to enter into them.

Consequently, the court will infer the existence of a trust if the circumstances are the sort of circumstances which the court would interpret as constituting a trust. Such trusts will be express trusts, even if the parties did not know that that was what they were creating.[62] A little like a small child putting some food between two slices of bread: she may not know the word for what she has done, but she would nevertheless be taken by everyone else to have made a sandwich. This principle is true both of ordinary, day-to-day situations and complex, commercial situations.[63] Take the example of a tronc system for waiting staff tips in a restaurant.[64] A tronc system divides the tips evenly between the waiting staff. In *Annabel's (Berkley Square) Ltd v Revenue and Customs Commissioners*[65] a tronc system was operated whereby all cash tips left for waiting staff by customers were taken by a 'troncmaster', who was a senior member of the

60 Affirmed [2000] Ch 291, CA. See, interestingly, 'child trust funds' created by the Child Trust Funds Act 2004 which are themselves expressed to be incapable of transfer: *ibid*, s 4.
61 [2002] UKHL 12 at [71], [2002] 2 All ER 377 at [71], [2002] 2 AC 164. See also *Mills v Sports Direct Retail Ltd, Re Kaupthing Singer Friedlander* [2010] 2 BCLC 143, 158 adopting these dicta and those of Megarry J above. To the same end, in *Re Multi Guarantee Co Ltd* [1987] BCLC 257 at 266 Nourse LJ considered that this point turned on 'whether in substance a sufficient intention to create a trust was manifested by' the settlor.
62 This may seem counter-intuitive at first. After all, you might think, how can it be an 'express trust' if the parties did not know what they were doing would be called a trust by lawyers? The answer is that the parties were intending to do the things they did – in that sense the settlor's intentions were express intentions – and lawyers would place an interpretation on them to the effect that they constituted a trust.
63 *Re Lewis's of Leicester Ltd* [1995] 1 BCLC 428.
64 There are two ways of leaving tips in restaurants today: in cash, or by debit or credit card payment. Cash tips are passed into the tronc and divided up among the staff periodically in accordance with their entitlements, hours worked, etc. Some restaurant chains have taken to using the tips paid by way of payment card to pay part of the staff's wages (so as to meet minimum wage standards): importantly, those chains use these tips to offset the cost of their staff's contractual wage entitlements, not to pay them bonuses. Such tips are therefore not additional to the staff's wages but part of them in those restaurant chains. This is why it is important to ask your waiting staff whether they would prefer to have their tip in cash or paid by card: they will nearly always prefer to have it in cash so that they will be able to take it for themselves.
65 [2009] EWCA Civ 361, [2009] 4 All ER 55.

staff who was not acting on behalf of the employer but rather who held all of those cash tips before distributing them among the waiting staff periodically. An issue arose as to the nature of the troncmaster's duties when holding those cash tips before they were distributed. It was held that while the troncmaster held those cash tips he was holding them on trust for the other waiting staff. In essence, the troncmaster had legal title over those cash sums but they were held ultimately for the benefit of other staff, and therefore it was held that they were held on trust.

At the other end of the spectrum, in *Brazzill v Willoughby*,[66] Smith J considered the failure of the financial institution Kaupthing Singer Friedlander ('KSF'). This was one of a number of cases relating to failure of KSF. The old City of London merchant bank Singer Friedlander had been bought up by the Icelandic bank Kaupthing and transformed into 'KSF' before all of the booming Icelandic banks crashed in the global financial crisis of the autumn of 2008. Consequently, on the facts of this case, KSF would have been insolvent in October 2008 but for the support of the UK regulatory authorities.[67] KSF was regulated by the Financial Services Authority ('FSA') in the UK. The FSA had the power under the Banking (Special Provisions) Act 2008[68] to issue a 'supervisory order' to KSF, *inter alia*, to require KSF to set up an account with the Bank of England into which it would pay amounts to match any deposits made with it by its customers.[69] The purpose of this scheme was to ensure that there was money set aside to repay client deposits in case KSF did fail. Clause 2 of the supervisory order used the term 'trust' to describe this arrangement and the parties themselves also used the expression 'trust' to describe this arrangement; unfortunately the order did not make clear which deposits nor which customers were covered by this scheme and which were not. Issues arose as to whether or not there was in fact a trust in existence given this lack of clarity. It was held, following *Re Kayford*, that putting those sums into that account constituted a voluntary intention to create a trust on the part of KSF, even though it was made in accordance with the FSA's supervisory order.[70] Simply enough, setting aside funds in a separate account with the intention that they would be held for the benefit of identified

---

66 [2009] EWHC 1633 (Ch), [2010] 1 BCLC 673.
67 KSF was sold to ING, the Dutch bank, under the exercise of the statutory powers mentioned in the text. The statutory powers enabled the UK regulators to find a buyer for KSF and the reassurance offered by the statutory compensation scheme, which would reimburse any depositors who lost money, were both instrumental in keeping KSF from collapsing along with Kaupthing as a whole.
68 On which see Alastair Hudson, *The Law of Finance*, Sweet & Maxwell, 2009, 29–41.
69 Existing customers were protected by the Financial Services Compensation Scheme – on which see Alastair Hudson, *The Law of Finance*, Sweet & Maxwell, 2009, 9–58.
70 The facts of the case were more complex than the summary in the text, but there is no need to obscure the central point being made in the text about certainty of intention: this case did apply the principle in *Re Kayford*. There were two complicating factors. First, the supervisory order only required (in para 2(b)) equivalent amounts to be paid into that account and not the actual amounts themselves: it was held that there would be a trust over those equivalent amounts nevertheless. It is suggested that the FSA would have been better advised in requiring KSF to transfer the actual deposits received from customers into the Bank of England account so that there would have been no doubt as to which amounts were held on trust. Second, an issue arose on these facts as to some amounts (in excess of £140 million in total) which were not actually matched by payments into the Bank of England account: in practice, there was no issue on those amounts because the government took the view that it would recompense all depositors out of the Financial Services Compensation Scheme in any event. The confusion arose from the lack of clarity about which 'deposits' and which 'customers' were covered by the supervisory order. Smith J noted these shortcomings in the operation of the trust and the narrowness of the customer deposits which were actually matched by deposits in the trust account held with the Bank of England. This does not affect the main principle set out in the text and relate only to the extent of the trust on the facts of this case.

customers constituted a trust. Consequently, any sums paid into this account for identified customers were deemed to be held on trust. The simple point, therefore, was that an intention to set up a separate bank account for the benefit of customers will be taken to constitute a trust, and that such a trust will provide the beneficiaries with protection against the trustee going into insolvency. This complex commercial situation (it is hard to imagine one which could be more obviously commercial) was effectively decided by reference to the same concepts as were used at root in *Paul v Constance*.

Trusts over bank accounts

A number of issues arise in relation to the creation of trusts over the contents of bank accounts. It is not always the case that when one person receives another person's property there will be a trust. Importantly, it is a well-established principle of banking law that when a bank receives money from a customer and pays it into that customer's account, the bank receives an outright transfer of that money and so does not hold the deposited money on trust for the customer.[71] In *Foley v Hill* Lord Cottenham LC described the interaction of banker and customer in the following terms:[72]

> [M]oney placed in the custody of a banker is, to all intents and purposes, the money of the banker, to do with it as he pleases; he is guilty of no breach of trust in employing it; he is not answerable to the principal if he puts it into jeopardy, if he engages in a hazardous speculation; he is not bound to keep it or deal with it as the property of his principal; but he is, of course, answerable for the amount [as a debt], because he has contracted, having received that money, to repay to the principal, when demanded, a sum equivalent to that paid into his hands.

A banker therefore owes only personal obligations to its customers (that is, its depositors) when it receives their deposits. In that sense, money transferred to a bank is an outright transfer of money to the bank.[73] This conclusion was based on the court's analysis of the ordinary intentions of the parties to a banking contract. It would require an express agreement between the bank and the customer for the bank to be understood to be acting as a trustee: banks often do act as trustees, but only through special subsidiaries and only in limited circumstances, but not in relation to ordinary bank accounts. Thus, the court will look at the circumstances and infer the existence or non-existence of an express trust from those circumstances. So, more recently, where a defendant accepted money from a client as part of a hawala system that was held to negate the possibility of a trust. A hawala system is a money transfer system whereby the defendant took absolute title in the client's money subject to a contractual obligation to pay an equivalent amount of money through one of his

71 *Foley v Hill* (1848) 2 HL Cas 28; see generally Alastair Hudson, *The Law of Finance*, Sweet & Maxwell, 2009, para 30–04.

72 (1848) 2 HL Cas 28, 9 ER 1002, 1005. See also *Westminster Bank Ltd v Hilton* (1926) 43 TLR 124, 126, *per* Lord Atkinson to the same effect, identifying also that the banker acts as the customer's agent in relation to the payment and collection of cheques.

73 *Hirschhorn v Evans (Barclays Bank garnishees)* [1938] 2 KB 801, 815, *per* Mackinnon LJ. So a bank operating an account on behalf of a Lloyds insurance syndicate would not hold those moneys on trust (without something more in the arrangement to require that analysis): *Mann v Coutts & Co* [2003] EWHC 2138, [2004] 1 CLC 301.

agents in another currency to a person nominated by the client.[74] It was held that the well-understood basis for such money transfer arrangements was that the defendant took absolute title in the money and pooled all of the client money together with the intention of using it for trade. Sullivan J held that this was not a trust precisely because no money was set aside to the client's account. Instead this was considered to be more akin to an ordinary bank account, as considered above. The customer's remedy against the banker is a remedy based on ordinary contract law, not based on trust law.

The intention to create a trust in Mills v Sportsdirect.com *over share in financial transactions*

In the wake of the global financial crisis which had begun in the summer of 2007, the claimant in *Mills v Sportsdirect.com Retail Ltd*[75] sought to establish that it had a proprietary interest under a trust against Kaupthing Singer & Friedlander ('KSF', the same entity as was at issue in *Brazzill v Willoughby* above) before KSF's holding company went into insolvency at precisely 14.21 hours on 8 October 2008.[76] In essence, it was held that the parties had intended to create a trust over shares which the claimant had transferred to the defendant as part of a larger transaction because those shares had been held in a separate account. Therefore, when the defendant went into insolvency, it was held that the claimant had equitable proprietary rights in those shares which were therefore protected against the insolvency.

In more detail, the facts were as follows. Mills was one of the administrators of KSF. The claimant, Sportsdirect.com Retail Ltd ('SD'), had entered into a 'repo' transaction with KSF. A repo can be thought of as being a means for a financial institution to acquire securities in a hurry if it needs them to complete a transaction with one of its own customers: ordinarily in a repo transaction, securities[77] would be transferred between the parties in exchange for cash, and then securities of the same type would be transferred back and the cash repaid a few days later.[78] This sort of transaction is used in financial markets to get

---

74 *Azam v Iqbal* [2007] EWHC 2025, [2008] Bus LR 168.
75 [2010] EWHC 1072 (Ch), [2010] 2 BCLC 143.
76 Kaupthing was one of the Icelandic banks which crashed during the global financial crisis which began in 2007. It had bought the long-standing English merchant bank Singer Friedlander and created KSF as a result. When Kaupthing crashed, a part of KSF was sold to ING Bank further to the Banking (Special Provisions) Act 2008 and the remainder was put into administration. A large amount of difficult litigation was put in train by this collapse. Mills is one of the administrators of KSF. The concept of 'administration' refers to a mechanism in insolvency law to keep an entity operative after it has strictly gone into insolvency so that the business can be sold off or otherwise turned to account.
77 Or, alternatively, it can be used the other way around as a sort of very short-term loan whereby the lender pays money to the borrower and in exchange the borrower transfers securities to the lender, and then the parties reverse their payments a few days later. The term 'securities', in this context, relates to financial instruments such as transferable shares and bonds traded on regulated markets like the London Stock Exchange.
78 The text attempts to simplify the facts. They were quite complex and turned on the nature of the financial products involved. The 'repo' was documented under a standard market agreement known as the Global Master Repurchase Agreement ('GMRA'). A repo, as discussed in Hudson's *The Law of Finance*, para 50–14, is a transaction which involves a seller transferring securities to a buyer in return for cash, with the seller agreeing in turn to repurchase securities of the same type at a specified price at a specified time in the future from the buyer. The point of this transaction is that the seller is able to acquire cash in exchange for a short-term transfer of the securities, and then to have replacement shares transferred to it later. Think of it as being like pawning your securities: you get money in the short term, but you have to buy your securities back at a pre-determined

a hold of securities quickly or to get cash loans on a short-term basis.[79] The legal question is as to the rights which the seller has to the securities before they are transferred back to it. Ordinarily, the securities would be transferred outright between the parties without the seller retaining property rights over them. However, the transaction in *Mills v Sportsdirect.com* was structured slightly but significantly differently from an ordinary repo transaction because SD was concerned about the financial position of KSF.[80] The parties' representatives[81] had agreed that, in this situation, SD would transfer shares outright to KSF and then KSF would pass legal title in those shares to a nominee, Sinjul Nominees Ltd, which would then hold the shares.[82] The legal question was then as to the terms on which Sinjul held those shares: specifically, the question was whether or not a trust had been created with Sinjul as trustee in favour of SD. The terms of this transaction were discussed between the representatives of each party but it was unclear what the outcome of their discussion was before the parties transferred the shares.[83] The question for Lewison J was whether or not a trust had been effected over those shares in favour of SD. In essence, if this had been an ordinary repo, in which the seller retained no rights in the securities, then there would not have been a trust; but the specific feature of this transaction was that the shares had been

price a few days later. These repo markets are thought to be very useful in financial practice because it provides 'liquidity' for investment banks and similar institutions in the sense that they can borrow money easily using their securities as collateral, or they can get securities easily if they need to conduct other transactions.

79 If a bank needs a short-term loan, it will sell securities in exchange for cash, and then buy the securities back at a contractually agreed date in the future. Alternatively, an investment may need securities of a specified kind to fulfil a transaction and so it will buy those securities from another firm on a short-term basis by means of a repo and then transfer back securities of the same type a few days later. The repo market is a short-term mechanism for banks to 'borrow' money or securities on a private basis off-exchange. Financial institutions operate many of their trading activities on a short-term basis in which using short-term devices of this sort appears to be more useful than long-term loans or the many formalities involved with trading on exchanges. The risk, of course, is that markets will move adversely during the transaction so that the cost of re-acquiring the securities rises or falls sharply. Occasionally, firms are caught out catastrophically in this way.

80 Importantly, in an ordinary repo transaction the seller does not receive back the very same securities which were transferred originally, but rather the seller receives back securities of the same type at the end of the transaction. This means that there is no trust ordinarily over the original securities which are transferred to the buyer because the other party is entitled to deal with those securities, provided that the buyer transfers back securities of the same type at the end of the transaction. This means that the seller does not retain proprietary rights in the shares which are transferred away in the first place. The repo in this instance was enhanced by a collateral agreement, which is simply a means of securing payment which is too complex for this discussion and unnecessary for the decision in this case: see Hudson, *The Law of Finance*, Chapter 45 generally for a description of collateral arrangements.

81 SD acted through a broker and other advisors, and KSF acted through its own traders and in-house professionals. The transaction was conducted at some speed and, as is common on trading floors, there were uncertainties about its terms during the negotiation process.

82 The effect of this holding by Sinjul was that Sinjul was only transferring equitable interests in the shares when they moved. Such dispositions of an equitable interest do not, however, require signed writing under s 53(1)(c) of the Law of Property Act 1925 because there is an exception in the case of collateral arrangements under Financial Collateral Arrangements (No 2) Regulations 2003, SI 2003/3226, reg 4(2).

83 It is common for traders acting on behalf of parties such as this to discuss the commercial terms of these sorts of transactions but for important legal details to be overlooked in the pressured environment of transacting. This sort of pressure is discussed in Chapter 8 of Hudson, *The Law on Financial Derivatives*, 2012 and in Hudson, *The Law of Finance* at para 17–26. See *Peekay Intermark Ltd v Australia and New Zealand Banking Group Ltd* [2005] EWHC 830 (Comm); reversed at [2006] EWCA Civ 386.

transferred into a specific account held by Sinjul which appeared to be intended beneficially for SD.[84]

In deciding this case, Lewison J began with first principles. As already discussed, the most important case on the finding of a trust in circumstances in which a trust is said to exist in a case where the legal owner of property has gone into insolvency is the decision of Megarry J in *Re Kayford Ltd*.[85] Lewison J relied in particular on the following passage from the judgment of Megarry J:

> The sender may create a trust by using appropriate words when he sends the money (though I wonder how many do this, even if they are equity lawyers), or the company may do it by taking suitable steps on or before receiving the money. If either is done, the obligations in respect of the money are transformed from contract to property, from debt to trust. Payment into a separate bank account is a useful (though by no means conclusive) indication of an intention to create a trust, but of course there is nothing to prevent the company from binding itself by a trust even if there are no effective banking arrangements.[86]

It was considered by Lewison J to be important that KSF could be shown to have had an appropriate intention to create a trust when putting money aside in a separate account with Sinjul Nominees Ltd. Lewison J found on the facts that the understanding which was reached with the broker acting for SD with KSF was that (using the vague expressions used by the parties themselves) shares would be transferred into 'SD's box' within the holdings held by Sinjul so that those shares would be 'ringfenced' and so that 'you [SD] would own those shares outright'.[87] Under this repo transaction, SD was required to pay for this transfer of shares. SD was particularly keen that the shares were transferred away from KSF's beneficial ownership. Lewison J concluded that when the broker and KSF agreed that payment would be made by SD for the shares, then their intention was that the shares would be segregated into a distinct account before payment was made for those shares.[88] It was understood that the purpose of this transaction was 'to keep the shares out of the hands of KSF's creditors'.[89] Therefore, Lewison J held that when all of these factors were taken together there was a trust over the shares at the time that these elements of the transaction

---

84 The factual details were a little more complicated than they have been presented in the text above for ease of reference. The shares were held in uncertificated form on the CREST system (which means that legal title in those shares was identified by an entry on an electronic register as opposed to being identified by the issue of a physical certificate). The logistical elements of the transaction were effected by means of numerous conversations between the traders and brokers involved. In essence, in the wake of the collapse of Lehman Brothers the brokers acting on behalf of SD were concerned to make sure that the shares were put beyond the reach of the creditors of KSF in the event that the ultimate holding company in Kaupthing bank went into insolvency along with other Icelandic banks.

85 [1975] 1 WLR 279.

86 [1975] 1 All ER 604 at 607, [1975] 1 WLR 279 at 282. See also *Re Multi Guarantee Co Ltd* [1987] BCLC 257 at 266, Nourse LJ; *Twinsectra Ltd v Yardley* [2002] UKHL 12 at [71], [2002] 2 All ER 377 at [71], [2002] 2 AC 164, *per* Lord Millett.

87 [2010] EWHC 1072 (Ch), [2010] 2 BCLC 143, para [59]. Of course under a trust, the beneficiary would not own the shares 'outright', but rather would own only an equitable interest in them.

88 [2010] EWHC 1072 (Ch), [2010] 2 BCLC 143, paras [63] and [73].

89 [2010] EWHC 1072 (Ch), [2010] 2 BCLC 143, para [63].

were complete.[90] The timing was critical given that the insolvency of the entity could be established with such precision.

3.3.2 Moral obligations or trusts?

Making the distinction

There is a subtle difference between merely imposing a moral obligation on a person who is the recipient of property such that a trust will not be created and imposing formal, fiduciary obligations on that person such that they become a trustee over that property. As was said at the start of this book, the trust is based on the court's control of the conscience of the trustee. However, it is possible for one person to impose a moral obligation on another person in relation to the use of property without that necessarily constituting a trust. For example, I may ask you to watch my car for a few minutes, with the words 'take very good care of it, I will hold you responsible for any damage to it', without meaning that you become a trustee of that car. All I want in this example is that you watch the car – I do not intend you to acquire any property rights in it nor to deal with it for anyone else's benefit – and therefore the only obligation I can have imposed on you is a merely moral obligation to watch the car as you promised to do.

It is possible, therefore, as part of making a gift to someone, that the donor will seek to impose a moral obligation on them. When a parent gives a child money to buy a book as a reward and says 'don't spend it all on sweets', that does not make the child a trustee of the money. Instead the child is under a moral (rather than a legal) obligation to use the money to buy a book. The expression generally used by the courts to distinguish between a declaration of a trust and a moral obligation is to define merely moral obligations as setting out 'preca-tory words'. Merely 'precatory words' do not create substantive trust obligations.

In short, the nature of the intention is to be inferred from all the circumstances. In *Re Adams and Kensington Vestry*,[91] a testator left property to his wife (W) by will 'in full confi-dence that she would do what was right by his children'. It was argued on behalf of the children that the moral obligation imposed on W in the will created a trust. However, it was held that the property passed to W absolutely. The court interpreted the statement in the will to have added only a moral obligation on the wife to use the money in a way which would

---

90 There are two problems with this judgment. First, what is not clear, as considered below in relation to certainty of subject matter, is whether the shares had been segregated for there to have been a trust, or whether under the terms of this understanding between the parties that there had been payment made before the trust took effect. Second, Lewison J ended his judgment by noting that no argument had been made before him as to whether or not this transaction constituted a breach of the insolvency law anti-deprivation principle (see the decision of the Supreme Court in *Belmont Park Investments Pty Ltd v BNY Corporate Trustee Services Ltd* [2011] UKSC 38, [2011] 3 WLR 521). In essence, during an insolvency, no unsecured creditor nor any other person is entitled to take assets away from the insolvent person so as to reduce the amount of property available to the unsecured creditors, unless a device such as a valid, pre-existing trust entitles assets to be moved in that fashion (in which case the beneficiaries of that trust would not be unsecured creditors.) Either of these problems might have meant that a trust was not found between the parties but they were not considered in detail. The Supreme Court consid-ered another case claim in relation to just such an insolvency question in *In re Kaupthing Singer & Friedlander Ltd (No 2)*, joined with *Mills v HSBC Trustee (CI) Ltd*, [2011] UKSC 48, [2011] Bus LR 1644.
91 (1884) 27 Ch D 394.

benefit the children and not to place her under an obligation to hold that money as trustee for the children. Where a statement is analysed as being merely a statement of wishes in this way, it will not have the force of a trust.

On the other hand, in *Comiskey v Bowring-Hanbury*,[92] the testator left property by will to his wife subject to a provision for equal division amongst his nieces on his wife's death. The precise words of the bequest were that the property was left to the wife 'in full confidence that . . . she will devise it to one or more of my nieces as she may think fit'. Therefore, on the face of it, there would appear to be a merely moral obligation on the part of the wife to benefit the testator's nieces. However, it was held that there was an executory gift over the whole of his property which was intended to give those nieces some rights in that property under a trust. In part this was due to the fact that there was no property segregated from the rest of the testator's estate which could have been identified as being for the benefit of the nieces alone. Therefore, it was held that the wife should be prevented from dealing with that money as though she were entitled to it absolutely beneficially. Thus, the court found that the testator's intention was to give the nieces property rights from the moment that the will came into effect. Therefore, his wife did not take that property absolutely subject to a merely moral obligation to take care of her deceased husband's nieces; rather, she was subject to the obligations of a trustee and the property was held on trust for her for life and then in remainder to her nieces equally.

Identifying certainty of intention in the interpretation of wills

There has been a development in the attitude of the courts to the interpretation of words, particularly in relation to wills. In 1858, the estates of deceased persons began to be administered by the Courts of Chancery rather than by the ecclesiastical courts. In consequence, there was a change in judicial policy which sought to construe all testamentary gifts to be valid wherever possible, and therefore removed much of the problem of certainty of intention. However, subsequent judicial policy, including cases like *Re Adams and Kensington Vestry*[93] considered above, took the view that the court should examine the true intention of the testator and not simply imply an intention to create a trust in all circumstances where property was left other than as a straightforward gift.

In *Re Hamilton*,[94] Lindley LJ held that the approach taken by the court ought to be to 'take the will you have to construe and see what it means, and if you come to the conclusion that no trust was intended you say so . . .'. In other words: 'Don't simply assume there is a trust – look at the will and decide whether or not there is sufficient intention to create a trust.' This approach was approved in *Re Williams*[95] and in *Comiskey v Bowring Hanbury*.[96] It is suggested that the courts will adopt the approach set out by Lindley LJ in *Re Hamilton*[97] and consider each situation on its own terms and in its own context.

92 [1905] AC 84.
93 (1884) 27 Ch D 394.
94 [1895] 2 Ch 370.
95 (1877) 5 Ch D 735.
96 [1905] AC 84. This was doubted by Wynn-Parry J in *Re Steele's WT* [1948] 2 All ER 193 – the latter preferring the older approach of assuming a trust in general terms set out in *Shelley v Shelley* (1868) LR 6 Eq 540.
97 [1895] 2 Ch 370.

Even accepting that there has been a more interpretative approach adopted by the courts since *Re Hamilton*, it still may not be easy for the reader to isolate a clear distinction between the cases of *Re Adams and Kensington Vestry*[98] and *Comiskey v Bowring-Hanbury*[99] considered above. In relation to the law on express trusts, it is often the case that the final decision in the case will turn on two factors. First, a very close reading of the wording of a trust document: this is particularly true in older cases, leading up to the decisions of judges like Viscount Simonds in the 1950s.[100] After that time, many of the next generation of judges began to take a more purposive approach to interpreting trust documents. That means, they were more prepared to interpret documents in a way which made them valid rather than void. In cases involving testamentary trusts, the judges would often seek to maintain the validity of the trust because the settlor was no longer alive and therefore was incapable of rewriting the terms of the trust so as to make them valid.[101] Second, a consideration of the circumstances surrounding the creation of the trust: in many situations, the settlor will not have made her intentions clear, and therefore the court may look at the more general situation of the parties. For example, if a testator had already made provision for a particular beneficiary in her will, the court may decide that a further provision could not have been intended to confer additional benefit on that person. It would be unusual for this second aid to construction to be applied completely in the absence of a close reading of the words of the trust.

In relation to the cases already mentioned of *Re Adams and Kensington Vestry* and *Comiskey v Bowring-Hanbury*, the court decided that in *Adams*, the testator intended to give the property entirely to his wife and trusted her to deal with it appropriately. A number of cases have taken expressions which provide that the recipient of a gift will take the property 'in full confidence' that it will be used for the benefit of another person to constitute a merely moral obligation.[102] Similarly, instances suggesting that the testator 'wishes or requests' that something be done with the property by the recipient of the gift have not been held to constitute sufficient intention to declare a trust.[103] For a review of these cases, see *Swain v Law Society*.[104]

On the other hand, in *Comiskey*, the court decided that the testator had intended his nieces to acquire some rights in his property from the moment of his death, or of making the will, rather than requiring them to rely on his widow – even though the bequest was couched in terms that the testator had 'full confidence' in his wife. And so it was that in *Re Steele's WT*,[105] a trust was found to have been created based on a 'request' made by the testator of the legatee.

Perhaps one distinction between the two cases of *Adams*[106] and *Comiskey*[107] is a perception that a mother is more likely to ensure the well-being of her own children, and therefore

98   (1884) 27 Ch D 394.
99   [1905] AC 84.
100   See, for example, *Leahy v Attorney-General for NSW* [1959] AC 457; *Grey v IRC* [1960] AC 1.
101   This shift in attitude is considered in more detail in the discussion of cases like *Leahy* v *Attorney-General for NSW* [1959] AC 457 and *Re Denley* [1969] 1 Ch 373 in Chapter 4.
102   *Re Adams* (1884) 27 Ch D 394; *Re Hutchinson and Tenant* (1878) 8 Ch D 540; *Mussoorie Bank v Raynor* (1882) 7 App Cas 321; *Re Williams* (1877) 5 Ch D 735.
103   *Re Hamilton* [1895] 2 Ch 370; *Hill v Hill* [1897] 1 QB 483; *Re Connolly* [1910] 1 Ch 219; *Re Johnson* [1939] 2 All ER 458.
104   [1983] 1 AC 598.
105   [1948] 2 All ER 193.
106   (1884) 27 Ch D 394.
107   [1905] AC 84.

can be trusted to take the property absolutely beneficially whilst still providing for those children; whereas a widow might not be so concerned to see to the well-being of her deceased husband's nieces, preferring to care for some other family members instead. Often, the only real distinction between two cases (where it is not an obvious difference in principle or a question of very different factual situations) will be whether or not the court has been convinced by the witnesses during trial, or whether or not sufficient evidence could be brought before the court to prove a particular argument in a particular situation.

The law of trusts is frequently to do with the passions, greed and expectations of ordinary human beings. It cannot always be reduced to rigid legal principles. The beauty of equity lies in its ability to deal flexibly with such circumstances.

3.3.3 Intention to create a trust, not something else

Charges and trusts

As considered above, the primary commercial use of the trust is to allocate rights in property between commercial people as part of larger transactions. In many situations, it will be a difficult problem to decide whether it is a trust which has been created or merely some other form of quasi-proprietary right, like a charge. In *Clough Mill v Martin*,[108] that very problem arose. A manufacturer of yarn supplied a clothes manufacturer with yarn. The clothes manufacturer used the yarn to make clothes – that is, the yarn ceased to exist as yarn but rather became cloth which was incorporated into clothes. The supplier wanted security for the contractual payments to be made to it by the clothes manufacturer. Therefore, the supplier wanted to retain title in the yarn until it was used to create clothes, and then to have rights in the clothes themselves. That aim was incorporated into the contract between the parties. In this way, the supplier hoped that if the manufacturer went into insolvency, the supplier would be able to recover either the unused yarn or finished clothes up to the value of the contractual obligation which the clothes manufacturer owed to it.

Subsequently, the clothes manufacturer did go into insolvency without having made full payment to the supplier. The question arose whether or not the supplier could claim to have proprietary rights in the stock of clothes still held by the manufacturer. The supplier sought to rely on the term of the contract which gave it rights over those finished clothes – the main issue was whether the supplier's rights were as a beneficiary under a trust or in some other, lesser form. A number of analyses were possible. The supplier argued that the yarn and the clothes were held on trust for it until such time as it received payment. In effect, the supplier's argument was that the contract obliged the clothes manufacturer to recognise proprietary rights in the supplier over that yarn on trust. The problem with this argument on these facts was that because the property itself would change as new clothes were made and other clothes sold off during the course of the manufacturer's business, all the supplier could have was a floating charge over the stock of clothes, as opposed to a fixed right (as in a trust) over any particular clothes. A floating charge is a charge that has an identified value but which attaches only to a fluctuating pool of property and not to any particular item.[109] So, a floating

---

108 [1984] 3 All ER 982.
109 See para 23.2.2 below.

charge would not give the supplier proprietary rights in any particular items, as a trust would have done, but only a right of an identified maximum value against the total stock of clothes.

It was held by Goff LJ on a close analysis of the contract between the parties that a mere charge was created because of the difficulty which would arise if more than one seller sought to assert a like right against the supplier. His Lordship meant that if more people brought claims than there was property to go round, the trust would have been meaningless because no claimant could have identified which property was held on trust for them alone. As considered below in relation to certainty of subject matter,[110] it is important that the property which is to be held on trust is clearly identifiable and segregated from all other property.[111] By contrast, a floating charge does not attach to any specific property but rather takes effect over a range of property. Therefore, the intention of the parties as expressed in their contract on these facts was interpreted by the Court of Appeal to be an intention to create a charge over property rather than a trust. This case illustrates how the court will look at the circumstances and decide which analysis seems most appropriate.

Trust used as a sham device will not be a valid trust

When a purported trust is in fact a sham intended to achieve some ulterior purpose then that trust will not be valid. Sham trusts are used to avoid liability to tax by pretending that property is held on trust,[112] or frequently so as to attempt to put property beyond the reach of creditors in an insolvency. There are a number of cases considered in Chapter 11 on resulting trusts in which the absolute owners of property have sought to disguise their ownership of that property, perhaps to avoid creditors, by purportedly transferring it to other people with the intention of recovering the property in the future, perhaps when their creditors have given up the chase. Frequently, these have been unlawful attempts to put property beyond the reach of creditors – often by putting that property into the names of family members. (In Chapter 11, we will consider whether or not those property owners are entitled to recover their title in that property in circumstances in which the transfer was illegal.) In these cases, the parties purported to create a trust so as to shield their property from their creditors (contrary to insolvency law).

One such case which is an instructive example at this point is *Midland Bank v Wyatt*,[113] in which Mr Wyatt sought to protect himself against the possibility of business failure by settling the family home on trust for the benefit of his wife and his daughter. In time Mr Wyatt's business went into insolvency owing money to the claimant bank. Mr Wyatt sought to rely on the purported declaration of trust. However, it transpired that neither his wife nor his daughter had been told of the trust. Significantly, when Mr Wyatt had separated

---

110 See para 3.4.1 below.

111 *Re Goldcorp* [1995] 1 AC 74.

112 So, in Canada in *Marquis-Antle Spousal Trust v R* 2009 TCC 465, 12 ITELR 314 a taxpayer concocted a complex scheme to avoid capital gains tax by purportedly creating a discretionary trust in Barbados into which shares would be passed before being sold to his wife who would in turn sell them to third parties. It was held that no valid trust was created because the structure in Barbados was being used solely as an agent and not as a genuine trust, in part because the legal title in the property was never vested in the trustee in Barbados, in part because documentation relating to the trust had been backdated for tax purposes, and because it was effectively a sham intended to avoid capital gains tax.

113 [1995] 1 FLR 697.

from his wife, his wife's solicitors had not been informed of the existence of the trust when calculating the wife's beneficial interest in property held under the divorce settlement. Therefore, the court held that the trust had been a sham, the sole purpose of which had been an attempt to put property beyond the reach of Mr Wyatt's creditors and not to organise the equitable interest in the family home.

Thus, it is possible that the courts will look behind the creation of a trust to see whether or not the trust is, in truth, a sham. Indeed, in the context of revenue law, the courts have long been prepared to look beyond 'artificial steps' in the organisation of people's affairs, whether in relation to trusts or otherwise so as to give effect to the substance of the transaction.[114] Similarly, in land law, the courts will not give effect to terms in an occupation agreement which are a sham in that they seek to give the impression that the occupant has merely personal rights under a licence rather than proprietary rights under a lease.[115] Therefore, the concept of disallowing shams is not at all unusual. In line with the fundamental tenets of equity, someone seeking to prove a trust must come to equity with clean hands, and also that equity looks to the parties' real intent and not merely to the form in which they have dressed up their transaction: consequently, a trust will not be enforced if it is in truth a sham.

In defining what is meant by a 'sham', Diplock LJ held in *Snook v London and West Riding Investments Ltd* that:

> it means acts done or documents executed by the parties to the 'sham' which are intended by them to give to third parties or to the court the appearance of creating between the parties legal rights and obligations different from the actual legal rights and obligations (if any) which the parties intended to create . . . for acts or documents to be a 'sham', with whatever legal consequences follow from this, all the parties thereto must have a common intention that the acts or documents are not to create the legal rights or obligations which they give the appearance of creating. No unexpressed intentions of a 'shammer' affect the rights of a party whom he deceived.[116]

Therefore, a sham is a scheme of action which seeks to create the impression that the state of affairs is x whereas it is actually y.[117] This is frequently done in relation to trusts by the creation of documentation which is not intended to have any real effect on the parties although its literal drafting suggests that the position is something else. So, in *Hitch v Stone*,[118] Arden LJ observed that the court will not be limited to a simple reading of any documentation but rather will 'examine external evidence',[119] and the court will also consider whether or not the parties subjectively intended to create different rights and obligations from those contained in the documentation.[120] Thus, if the parties signed two differently worded letters dealing

---

114   See the slew of recent cases on the general, meandering case law principles concerning tax avoidance, eg, *Ramsay v IRC* [1981] STC 174; *Furniss v Dawson* [1984] 2 WLR 226; *Fitzwilliam v IRC* [1993] STC 502; *McGuckian v IRC* [1997] STC 908; *MacNiven v Westmoreland Investments Ltd* [2001] STC 327; *Barclays Mercantile Business Finance Ltd v Mawson* [2004] UKHL 51.
115   *Street v Mountford* [1985] 2 WLR 877.
116   *Snook v London and West Riding Investments Ltd* [1967] 2 QB 786, 802.
117   *Stokes v Mardner* [2011] EWHC 1179 (QB); *Soutzos v Asombang* [2010] EWHC 842 (Ch), [2010] BPIR 960, Newey J.
118   [2001] STC 214.
119   *Ibid*, 229.
120   *Ibid*.

with exactly the same circumstances in two completely different ways, it would be inferred that the parties intended to use whichever of these pretences seemed more convenient from time to time and therefore that the entire arrangement constituted a sham.[121] What is important is that the parties intended to deceive others, as opposed merely to having organised their affairs in an advantageous manner:[122] therefore it will be a sham to pretend that a husband owns property when in fact the property is used entirely by the wife as part of her business activities so as to reduce her liability to tax, but it will not be a sham if property is settled on a discretionary trust but genuinely used and held as discretionary trust property even if it has a beneficial tax effect.

It has been held that for a bankrupt person to purport to have his family home settled on trust for other members of his family so as to put it beyond the reach of his creditors would be a sham trust and so invalid.[123] In cases in Australia and New Zealand a notion of 'alter ego trusts' has arisen where the settlor is able to replace the trustees and control the trust so it operates simply as an alter ego of the settlor: where that permits a sham to be carried on (for example, where the property is used *de facto* as though the absolute property of the settlor, while purporting to be held for the benefit of some other person) then the trust will be invalid.[124]

What is not clear on the authorities is whether all of the parties to a transaction must realise that it is a sham,[125] or whether it is sufficient that only one of the parties knew that it was a sham and thus that the other parties were dupes.[126] It is suggested that it is sufficient that one controlling mind procures a sham transaction and uses other parties as dupes for there to be in fact a sham transaction.[127] In line with the core equitable principle that equity looks to the substance rather than the form, the courts will therefore ignore a sham transaction and give effect to the parties' real intentions – this may involve the effective undoing of a trust.[128] As considered in Chapter 11 in relation to *Midland Bank v Wyatt* (as outlined above), this tendency is particularly marked in relation to insolvency where the defendant has sought to put property beyond the reach of her creditors.[129]

3.3.4 How to identify an intention to create an express trust

The preceding discussion may have made the possibility of identifying an express trust seem further away than before. Whereas Chapter 2 presented the express trust as a simple matter of establishing three actors (settlor, trustee and beneficiary), the cases considered so far in

---

121 *Minwalla v Minwalla* [2004] 7 ITELR 457.

122 *Scott v Federal Commissioner of Taxation (No 2)* (1966) ALJR 265, 279, *per* Windeyer J.

123 *Re Reynolds* [2007] NZCA 122, 10 ITELR 1064, New Zealand Court of Appeal.

124 *Ibid; Public Trustee v Smith* [2008] NSWSC 397, 10 ITELR 1018, Supreme Court New South Wales.

125 *Snook v London and West Riding Investments Ltd* [1967] 2 QB 786, 802, *per* Diplock LJ.

126 *Midland Bank v Wyatt* [1995] 1 FLR 697.

127 In *Wrexham AFC Ltd v Crucialmove Ltd* [2006] EWCA Civ 237 the Court of Appeal appeared to support a doubt that a trust could be treated as a valid trust if it had been proved at trial to have been created in bad faith. In that case a small group of individuals had sought to use an insolvent football club as a front behind which they would acquire the freehold over the football ground from a brewery which owned it, and then through their control of the club they intended to develop the land for their own profit. They had purported to settle some of the club's assets on trust to facilitate the fiction that they were acting throughout in the best interests of the club. This, it is suggested, is akin to a finding of a sham trust.

128 See para 1.4.9.

129 Eg, Insolvency Act 1986, s 423.

this chapter have demonstrated that it will often be difficult to know whether or not there is a trust at all. However, what we should do at this juncture is to pause and go back to first principles: a trust will be said to exist in situations in which it would be unconscionable for the legal owner of property to deny the rights of other people in that property.[130] From that central principle, this and the next section will draw together these cases.

Identifying an intention to create multiple rights in property

The decision in *Don King Productions v Warren*[131] demonstrates two things. First, even in the most high-profile and complex of transactions, the parties and their legal advisors may well leave their intentions uncertain. In consequence, it will be a matter for the court to inter-cede and decide whether or not their true intention was the creation of a trust. The second point flows from the first: a trust will be declared to exist in circumstances in which property is held by one person but in such a way that other people were also intended to have rights over that property at the same time. For a trust to exist, one person must hold the legal title in the property (and so act as trustee) in circumstances in which it would be unconscionable for that person to deny that other people also have rights against the property, rather than purely against the legal owner personally (and so be beneficiaries).

So, in *Paul v Constance*,[132] there was an express trust found where it was clear that Mrs Paul was intended to have rights against the money in the bank account at the same time as Mr Constance. Or, to put that another way, it would have been unconscionable for Mr Constance or his administrator on death to overlook Mrs Paul's rights in that money. In *Don King*,[133] the partners entered into a contract which pledged the benefit of their manage-ment contracts to the partnership. Those partnership contracts demonstrated an intention that while, for example, Mr Warren might have entered into a management contract with a boxer, it was intended that any benefit derived by Mr Warren from that management contract was to be held on trust for the partnership. Or, to return to first principles, it would have been unconscionable for Mr Warren to have denied the rights of the other partners in the fruits of any new management contract.

Intention to impose a merely moral obligation, not a trust

If the settlor's intention is an intention merely to impose a moral obligation on someone, this will not be sufficient to impose a trust over that person. In those cases in which a merely moral obligation has been found, as considered above, the courts analysed the nature of the promise made by the settlor in all the surrounding circumstances. The circumstances are all important. Clearly the court would look first at the precise terms of the will to discern the testator's intention. As we have seen in the cases considered above,[134] the courts will also look to surrounding factors outside the terms of any written instrument. For example, assume a situation in which a testator has died leaving children. If the children were infants at the time of death, the court would assume that their surviving parent would intend to do the best

---

130 *Westdeutsche Landesbank Girozentrale v Islington LBC* [1996] AC 669.
131 [1998] 2 All ER 608, Lightman J; affirmed [2000] Ch 291, CA.
132 [1977] 1 WLR 527.
133 [1998] 2 All ER 608.
134 See para 3.3.1 above.

for them, and so would be content to treat the spouse as being the absolute owner of the testa-tor's property. However, if the children were being left in the care of someone who was not their biological parent, it may be that the court would be more likely to read the testator's intention to be to vest the children themselves with rights in the property, so that their inter-ests could be more effectively protected by deeming them to be beneficiaries under a trust. So, in situations in which, having heard all of the evidence and having read the terms of a will closely, the court decides that the testator intended his wife should take the property absolutely subject only to a moral obligation that she think about how best to benefit their children, there would not be a trust because there would be no intention that *the children* have any immediate proprietary rights in the deceased's estate.[135]

Intention to make a gift, not a trust

If the absolute owner of property intends to make a gift of all of her rights in that property, then this intention cannot be interpreted to be an intention to create a trust. A gift is an outright transfer of all of the owner's rights in property to the donee such that the donee becomes the absolute owner of that property. By contrast, a trust requires that the legal title in the property is vested in trustees and the equitable interest in the beneficiaries. A trust may be created by the owner declaring herself to be the trustee of property for her children without the need to make any transfer of the legal title; rather, the declaration of trust automatically transfers the equitable interest to the beneficiaries, thus leaving only the legal title with the mother as trustee. As is considered in detail in Chapter 5,[136] an intention to create a gift which fails for some reason cannot be rescued by interpreting the owner's intention to have been a trust.[137] So, if Richie promises to make a gift of money to Eddie but then Richie changes his mind, Eddie will not be able to argue that Eddie should be deemed to have created a trust over that money on the grounds that it would be unconscionable to renege on his promise: because Richie intended to make a gift, Richie could not have demonstrated an intention to create a trust.[138]

3.3.5 Analysing the possible interpretations of transfers of property

Having considered in general, analytical terms the distinctions between various forms of activity which will and which will not create a trust, it might be useful at this juncture to consider the most common interpretations of the situation in which property is transferred by one person to another with the intention of benefiting some third party. All of the analyses considered in this section have been examined earlier in this chapter: this section is merely intended to be a summary of them. There are five broad, possible constructions of the situa-tion in which Ana has transferred property to Bartholomew with an obligation to make a payment to Christopher:

(a) *Bartholomew takes absolutely beneficially*: that is, Bartholomew is deemed to have been the recipient of a gift such that Bartholomew takes absolute title in the property. This

---

135 *Re Adams and Kensington Vestry* (1884) 27 Ch D 394.
136 See para 5.3.1 below.
137 *Milroy v Lord* (1862) 4 De GF & J 264.
138 *Richards v Delbridge* (1874) LR 18 Eq 11.

situation might be like that in *Re Adams and Kensington Vestry*,[139] in which Ana left property to Bartholomew 'in full confidence' that Bartholomew would ensure Christopher's well-being, but without imposing a trustee's obligation on Bartholomew in relation to the property. No trust would be created.

(b) *Bartholomew takes subject to a charge*: that is, Bartholomew has use of the property but is subject to Christopher's right to seize that property if Bartholomew fails to make payment to Christopher. Such a charge could either be in relation to fixed property, or might be a floating charge over a pool of property. As with *Clough Mill v Martin*,[140] where there is no identified property which is segregated from other property and held solely for Christopher's benefit, but rather where Christopher's rights take effect over a large pool of property the contents of which differ from time to time, Christopher will have merely a floating charge over that pool of property. Alternatively, where Ana has lent money to Bartholomew to acquire a house for Bartholomew's occupation, the right is more likely to be a fixed charge over the house such that Ana (or Christopher) can seize the house should Bartholomew fail to repay the loan.[141] No trust would be created.

(c) *Trust in favour of Christopher*: that is, Ana is deemed to have declared a trust in favour of Christopher, with Bartholomew acting as trustee of the property. Where Ana intends that Christopher is to acquire some proprietary rights against the trust property immediately on the declaration of the trust, there will be a trust created in Christopher's favour. Alternatively, it may be that Ana has a demonstrable intention that Christopher acquire equitable proprietary rights against the property on the satisfaction of some contingency (such as reaching the age of 18), in which case, there will be a trust in favour of Christopher, with Christopher's rights vesting on the satisfaction of the contingency. A trust would be created.

(d) *Bartholomew is under a personal obligation to Christopher*: that is, Bartholomew may owe no fiduciary or trustee obligation to Christopher but bears some non-legal, moral responsibility towards Christopher in relation to the property. Alternatively, suppose that Ana and Christopher entered into a contract with Bartholomew such that Ana left property for safekeeping with Bartholomew before Christopher came to collect it.[142] In such a situation, Bartholomew would owe an obligation under the contract with Ana and Christopher to deal with that property in accordance with the contract. Banks frequently act as custodians of valuable property for commercial people under their contracts – for example, collateral transactions under banking contracts.[143] This would be a personal obligation under contract rather than a proprietary obligation under a trust.

(e) *Creation of a condition subsequent that Bartholomew must pass to Christopher if Bartholomew fails to pay*: that is, akin to an action for breach of contract, there is a contractual (or personal) obligation on Bartholomew to make a payment or transfer of property in the event that Bartholomew fails to perform the contract. It may be part of an agreement that Bartholomew will pass property to Christopher in the event that Bartholomew fails to pay. Again, this obligation would be a personal obligation rather than one based on trusts law.

---

139   (1884) 27 Ch D 394.
140   [1984] 3 All ER 982.
141   See section 23.1 below.
142   See also the discussion of bailment at para 2.6.2 above.
143   Hudson, 2006, Ch 12.

There is no quicker means of deciding which model is the most appropriate in any factual circumstances than working out which of the analyses fits the situation best – or test all five analyses and see which seems closest to the facts. So you will have to wrap a cold towel round your head and consider the parties' intentions (or read the terms of any written instrument if there is one) over and over until you can decide which interpretation is the most appropriate in the circumstances.

3.4 CERTAINTY OF SUBJECT MATTER

The trust fund must be identifiable. A trust in which the trust property is mixed with other property so that it is impossible to identify precisely which property is held on trust, will be invalid. However, it appears that where the property is intangible property made up of identical units (such as ordinary shares of the same class), it will not be necessary to segregate the trust property from other property. This exception is doubted by many commentators.

3.4.1 Introduction

The requirement of 'certainty of subject matter' is a requirement that the property which is intended to constitute the trust fund is segregated from all other property so that its identity is sufficiently certain. If the trust fund is not sufficiently segregated, with the result that there is no certainty of subject matter, then the trust will fail.[144] The problem of certainty of subject matter therefore relates to the problem of identifying the property that constitutes the trust fund. The trust is a combination of obligations between trustee and beneficiary, and of property rights in the trust fund. This conception of the trust was discussed in Chapter 2.[145] Therefore, it is important that if there are to be property rights and responsibilities over a trust fund, that fund must be identifiable, or else it would not be possible for the court to know which property is to be administered in accordance with the terms of the trust. So, the problem considered in this section of this chapter is the need to know precisely which property is intended to be subjected to the trust.

In most cases, it will be obvious what is meant when a testator says 'I leave my first edition copy of John Fowles's *The Magus* to be held on trust for my husband.' Assuming the testator had only one copy of that book, then both his intention to create a trust and the property which was intended to be held on trust will be obvious. This would not be so if he had more than one first edition copy of *The Magus*. If there were two copies of that book, and it was clear that the settlor only intended for one of them to be held on trust, then it would be necessary for the settlor to identify which copy was to be settled on trust and which copy was to remain absolutely her own. If the settlor failed to identify which copy was to be held on trust and which copy was to remain hers absolutely then there would be uncertainty as to which property was to be held on trust and therefore the trust would fail. So, it will be necessary for the settlor to demonstrate an intention to create a trust, and then also an intention to create a trust over specified property.

There may be more complicated circumstances than the examples involving *The Magus* which were just discussed. Suppose that the settlor has a large amount of money held in a

---

144   *Re London Wine Co (Shippers) Ltd* [1986] PCC 121; *Re Goldcorp* [1995] 1 AC 74.
145   See the discussion of these concepts in paras 2.4.2 and 2.4.3 above.

single bank account which she wants to settle in part on trust for her children and in part for herself absolutely. If the settlor intended to create a trust for the benefit of her children and to hold her own money entirely separately, then this mixture of moneys in a single bank account would mean that the trust in favour of her children would be void for uncertainty of subject matter. Therefore, we have to consider how the settlor could resolve this uncertainty. The simplest approach in these circumstances would be as follows: the settlor would have to create a new bank account and pay into that new bank account only the money which is to be held on trust for her children: once that is done there will be sufficient certainty of subject matter, provided that no other money is mixed up in this account. An alternative approach in this situation would be to create one trust and to specify that it is the whole of the fund which is to be held on trust for the beneficiaries and for the settlor herself, and then give the trustee a power to select precisely which property is to be allocated to which beneficiary. There is nothing wrong with giving a trustee the power to select which property should be advanced to which beneficiary, provided that it is clear from the outset which property is to be held on trust and therefore over which property the trustee may exercise her powers as trustee. The imaginative use of trustee powers over a general fund will escape many of the problems of uncertainty of subject matter.

The difficulty arises when the settlor manifests an intention to create a trust and identifies the intended beneficiaries with sufficient precision, but nevertheless fails to identify which property is meant to be held on trust. Suppose a situation in which a settlor decided that he wished to hold on trust three of his collection of 12 vintage racing cars for the benefit of his grandchildren. In that situation, if the settlor failed to specify which three out of the total holding of 12 racing cars were to be held on trust, the trust would be invalid for uncertainty of subject matter because the trustees would not be able to know which three cars were to be held on trust.[146] Therefore, as a general rule, failure to segregate the intended trust property from all other property will lead the trust to be void.[147]

Similarly, if the settlor wished to settle £30,000 on trust for his three grandchildren in equal shares, but did not identify which £30,000 out of his total fortune of £2 million was to form the trust fund, then the trust would also be void.[148] Interestingly, it is not necessary for the £30,000 itself to be divided into three separate parcels of £10,000 for each grandchild, because the trustees will hold the entire £30,000 for the three beneficiaries as joint tenants under a single trust provided that the fund of £30,000 is itself sufficiently certain. However, as will emerge below, it remains a contentious issue whether the same rule applies to intangible property as applies to tangible property.[149]

The simplest example of this principle on the decided cases considering certainty of subject matter is *Re London Wine Co*.[150] In that case, creditors of a vintner's business sought to claim that their contracts for the purchase of wine ought to grant them proprietary rights in wine held in the vintner's cellars. However, Oliver J held that the creditors would only be entitled to assert proprietary claims as beneficiaries under a trust over any wine held in the cellar if each creditor could demonstrate that particular, identifiable bottles of wine had been

---

146 *Re Goldcorp* [1995] 1 AC 74; *Anthony v Donges* [1998] 2 FLR 775.
147 *Re London Wine Co (Shippers) Ltd* [1986] PCC 121; *Re Goldcorp* [1995] 1 AC 74.
148 *MacJordan Construction Ltd v Brookmount Erostin Ltd* [1992] BCLC 350; *Westdeutsche Landesbank Girozentrale v Islington LBC* [1996] AC 669, at para 3.4.3 below.
149 *Hunter v Moss* [1994] 1 WLR 452; *Re Harvard Securities Ltd* [1997] 2 BCLC 369.
150 *Re London Wine Co (Shippers) Ltd* [1986] PCC 121.

segregated from the general stock held in the cellar and held separately to their account. If so, those identifiable bottles of wine would be held on trust for the claimant. However, if that wine had not been so segregated (whether in breach of contract or not), there would not be any proprietary rights over any wine held in the cellar. On these facts there had been no such segregation and therefore there was no trust. This approach is referred to here as being 'the orthodox approach'.

As Oliver J put the matter in *Re London Wine*:

> I appreciate the point taken that the subject matter is a part of a homogenous mass so that specific identity is of as little importance as it is, for instance, in the case of money. Nevertheless, as it seems to me, to create a trust it must be possible to ascertain with certainty not only what the interest of the beneficiary is to be but to what property it is to attach.

His Lordship was therefore not careless in coming to this conclusion but rather acknowledged that property rights must attach to some property and may not simply exist in thin air.

Re London Wine draws on a line of old cases.[151] By way of example, in *Sprange v Barnard*,[152] a testatrix provided that property would be left to her husband to use absolutely but that 'the remaining part of what is left, that he does not want for his own wants and use' was to be held on defined trusts. It was held that this statement was too uncertain for the trust to take effect over any part of the property because the property was not sufficiently clearly identified by the expression 'the remaining part of what is left'.[153] Similarly, in *Palmer v Simmonds*,[154] a testatrix left 'the bulk of her estate' on certain trusts. It was held that the subject matter of this trust was too uncertain by dint of the vagueness of the expression 'the bulk'. For a trust to be valid, the settlor must make the subject matter of the trust certain.

3.4.2 The application of the orthodox approach

The *London Wine* case was followed in an appeal to the Privy Council in *Re Goldcorp*.[155] That case affirmed the principle that property must be separately identified before it can be held on a valid trust. The facts in *Goldcorp* appear to be complicated at the outset. However, they are easily laid out with a touch of simplification so as to illustrate the key principles. For the purposes of this discussion, there were three classes of claimant: that is important. The added complexity is the result of counsel for the complainants attempting to use a host of sophisticated, imaginative arguments to support their clients' cases.

Re Goldcorp concerned a gold bullion exchange which went into insolvency. The exchange acted for clients in acquiring bullion for them. It also offered a further service in

---

151 *Harland v Trigg* (1782) 1 Bro CC 142; *Wynne v Hawkins* (1782) 1 Bro CC 142; *Pierson v Garnet* (1786) 2 Bro CC 226; *Sprange v Barnard* (1789) 2 Bro CC 585; *Palmer v Simmonds* (1854) 2 Drew 221; *Choitheram International SA v Pagarani* [2001] 1 WLR 1.
152 (1789) 2 Bro CC 585.
153 However, rather than hold the entire bequest invalid, the rule in *Hancock v Watson* [1902] AC 14 (considered at para 3.4.4 below) was applied so as to uphold the validity of the gift in favour of the husband and merely invalidate the trust.
154 (1854) 2 Drew 221.
155 [1995] 1 AC 74; *Associated Alloys Pty v CAN* (2000) 71 Aus LR 568.

which it acted as depositary for the bullion which clients asked it to buy. Typically, the exchange's standard-form contracts with its clients required the exchange to buy and hold physically all of the weight of bullion specified in the clients' orders, rather than merely acknowledging an obligation to acquire that bullion in the future should the buyer ask for delivery of the bullion.[156] Therefore, the exchange was contractually bound to hold the whole of any client order physically in its vaults. However, the exchange slipped into the practice which is common among financial institutions which fall into insolvency: it only took physical delivery of as much bullion as it usually needed to satisfy customers' day-to-day needs. It therefore broke its contracts by failing to buy all of the bullion in the order. When the exchange went into insolvency, it did not hold enough bullion to satisfy its clients' orders, even though it had taken their money.

The claimants were clients of the exchange who were seeking to demonstrate that bullion was held on trust for them as a result of their contracts with the exchange. In consequence, they sought to avoid the exchange's insolvency by having themselves accepted as being secured creditors under the trust.[157] The first category of claimants had proprietary rights in specifically identifiable holdings of bullion which the exchange had actually acquired physically to match its customers' orders. This class of claimant was successful in demonstrating that they had equitable proprietary rights in that particular bullion because that bullion had been segregated and was therefore identifiable. Segregation in this instance meant that the successful claimants' bullion was held physically apart from all other bullion within the vaults – whether in safety deposit boxes, or caged off separately in some other way from the bulk of unsegregated bullion held by the exchange. Those claimants satisfied the requirement of certainty of subject matter.

The second class of clients did not have their bullion segregated from the bulk of bullion held by the exchange. Therefore, they were not able to identify a particular stock of bullion in the vaults and show that it was held on trust for them. Rather, all they could show was a contractual entitlement to an amount of bullion bearing a specific monetary value but which was otherwise unidentifiable. This category of claimants did not satisfy the requirement of certainty of subject matter and therefore acquired no rights under a trust.

Counsel for the second class of clients attempted to raise a number of different arguments to support their contention that a trust had been created in favour of their own clients, all of which arguments failed for the same reason. First, they argued that the exchange had entered into contracts to provide a specific type and quantity of bullion, so that their clients acquired rights under the doctrine of specific performance against the exchange. Therefore, they contended, their clients ought to have received equitable rights in the bullion, akin to the doctrine in *Walsh v Lonsdale*.[158] However, Lord Mustill held that the property was nevertheless unidentifiable, and therefore there could be no equitable proprietary rights because there was no identifiable property to which they could have attached. Secondly, counsel argued

---

156 This is common practice: typically clients are only investing in bullion and so never take delivery of it because they intend to sell it as soon as its market price increases. Therefore, exchanges often take their clients' money, acknowledge that they owe the clients a given amount of bullion if delivery of it is ever requested, and hold only as much bullion as is needed on any normal trading day.

157 In terms of trusts law, a beneficiary under a trust will be a secured creditor of a trustee in the event that the trustee goes into bankruptcy. Such a secured creditor is entitled to have its property held separately from the remainder of the bankrupt's estate which is divided among the unsecured creditors.

158 (1882) 21 Ch D 9.

that there should have been proprietary estoppel rights on the basis that the exchange had represented to their clients that they would hold bullion for them, in reliance on which their clients had paid money. Again, Lord Mustill refused to apply the estoppel doctrine on the basis that there was no specific, segregated property over which those equitable proprietary rights could bite in any event.

The third category of claimant, an individual, highlights the rigid nature of this rule. He had placed an order to buy maple leaf gold coins – a rare form of coin of which the exchange would not usually carry a large stock. This customer, Mr Leggatt, made a large order for those coins and agreed that the exchange would keep them in its vault on safe deposit. There were, therefore, a handful of coins which the exchange ordinarily held, mixed in together with the large order of coins acquired for Mr Leggatt. The claimant could demonstrate that the exchange would not have bought the unusually large number of these coins for any other customer. Unfortunately for the client, those coins had not been separated from all the coins and bullion held by the exchange. Consequently, Mr Leggatt's coins were not identifiable as being the property belonging to Leggatt distinct from the exchange's other coins. Therefore, the logical conclusion is that the rule revolves not simply around it being logistically *possible* to identify the property, but rather that the property itself *has actually* been segregated for the purpose of subjecting it to the trust arrangement. Suppose I contract to buy 1,000 coins from an exchange which ordinarily holds six such coins: there would therefore be 1,006 of these coins in the exchange's vaults. If my 1,000 coins are mixed with the six coins, then there will not be sufficient certainty of subject matter for me to have an equitable interest under a trust in those coins. My 1,000 coins would need to be separated from the exchange's six coins for me to have such an equitable interest under a trust in the 1,000 coins.

3.4.3 An exception for fungible or for intangible property?

There is potentially a distinction in the foregoing principle between property which may be identified without segregation, and property which is entirely fungible (such as sugar or liquids) and therefore incapable of separate identification, or intangible (such as shares or patents).[159] In general terms, there is no reason why the orthodox approach considered above should not apply equally to intangible property as to tangible property. The principle in *Re London Wine* was also applied by the Court of Appeal in *MacJordan Construction v Brookmount*,[160] where a claim arose as to a trust over a bank account. In that case, under the terms of a construction contract, stage payments owing to a sub-contractor were to be paid on given dates.[161] Amounts of money had been paid into one large bank account during the performance of the construction contract, but the stage payments owing to the sub-contractor had not been segregated from other amounts held in that account. It was argued on behalf of the sub-contractor that money owed to it ought to have been deemed to have been held on trust for it. It was held that for the formation of a valid trust over those moneys, it would have been necessary to segregate any money which was to be held on trust from

159 *Re Staplyton Fletcher Ltd* [1994] 1 WLR 1181.
160 [1992] BCLC 350.
161 Given the size of the amounts payable under large construction contracts, rather than pay the entire sum either at the start or at the end, the amounts are paid periodically during the life of the contract.

other money in the bank account by paying that money into a new bank account.[162] Therefore, it was held that a trust over intangible property in the form of money in a bank account would require segregation before it could be made subject to a trust.

While *MacJordan* would appear to speak for the orthodox approach, the decision of the Court of Appeal in *Hunter v Moss*[163] reached a different conclusion in relation to the formation of a trust over fungible, intangible property. In that case, an employee of a company was entitled to 50 shares out of 950 shares held by the employer under the employee's contract of employment. The employer did not transfer the shares to the employee, nor were any attempts made to identify those shares which were to be subject to the arrangement. The issue arose as to whether or not the employee could assert that he had proprietary rights over 50 shares. If we were to apply the rule in *Goldcorp*[164] to these facts, there would be no valid trust over the shares because it would be impossible to know which 50 shares out of the total holding of 950 shares were to be held on trust.

Dillon LJ took a different approach in *Hunter* from that set out in *Goldcorp* and held that there was a valid trust over the shares. There appear to have been two underlying motivations for this decision, beyond the detailed arguments considered below. The first was that the finding of a trust would enforce the terms of the employment contract between the parties; and the second was that it made no practical difference which 50 shares were subject to the trust given that there is no qualitative difference between one ordinary share and another ordinary share (provided those shares are of the same class and in the same company). In essence, the Court of Appeal appeared to hold that it was not necessary to segregate the property comprising the trust fund if the property was intangible property, like ordinary shares, with each unit being indistinguishable from another unit (an approach which was approved in *Re Harvard Securities Ltd*[165] following *Hunter v Moss*, considered below). There are three notable features of the judgment.

The first notable feature is the way in which Dillon LJ justified the theoretical possibility of creating trust rights over a collection of identical property. Dillon LJ cross-referred the rights of the claimant in *Hunter v Moss*[166] with the position of an executor on a testator's death. The point he made was that there was a situation in English law in which a trustee is entitled to enforce a trust over unsegregated property. That situation was the position of an executor holding property as trustee of a will trust. His Lordship explained that on the testator's death, the executor is required to distribute the property between the legatees, even if the testator had not indicated which beneficiary was required to acquire interests in which property; rather, it was argued that the executor is required to divide the general fund of property between the legatees. From this premise, Dillon LJ held that it was impossible to say that there was no situation in which the law permitted trusts over unsegregated property. Having established that the rule requiring segregation was not an absolute rule, Dillon LJ felt sufficiently empowered to find a trust on the facts before him.

The objection to this line of reasoning is that an executor occupies a very different position from an *inter vivos* trustee. The executor acquires legal title in all of the deceased's

---

162 However, it should be noted that on the facts of the case it was not established that there had been sufficient intention to create a trust in any event.
163 [1994] 1 WLR 452.
164 [1995] AC 74.
165 [1997] 2 BCLC 369.
166 [1994] 1 WLR 452.

property, with a power to make division of property in accordance with the terms of the will as the personal representative of the deceased, whereas the *inter vivos* trustee acquires nothing more than legal title in those assets which the settlor makes subject to the trust. The executor stands in the shoes of the deceased person with the power to distribute all the property attaching to the deceased's estate at death almost as though she were the deceased person – that is what it means to be an executor or a personal representative. In essence it is always known which property is to be dealt with under a will trust: that is, all of the testator's property. Therefore, it is open to the executor (in a situation in which the settlor is unable to resettle the property) to allocate title between items of property. The *inter vivos* trustee, on the other hand, is entitled to exercise the rights of legal title only over that property which is subject to the trust. That is the heart of the problem: the *inter vivos* trustee cannot know which property falls under her remit, whereas the executor knows that she has title in the whole of the property formerly vested in the testator, and so there cannot be uncertainty of subject matter in this instance.

The second notable feature of the decision in *Hunter v Moss* is the manner in which Dillon LJ distinguished *Hunter* from the *London Wine* case.[167] It is typically said that Dillon LJ sets out an express test that there is a difference between tangible and intangible property. In fact he does not make any such affirmative statement; rather, he distinguishes the *London Wine* line of cases so that he is entitled to uphold Moss's rights on the facts before him. It is the obvious conclusion to draw that Dillon LJ must have meant to make a distinction between tangible and intangible property.[168] However, it is difficult to see how far that distinction can extend – as considered below. What Dillon LJ actually held was that, after having considered *Re London Wine*, 'that case was concerned with the allocation of title in chattels whereas this case is concerned with a declaration of trust over shares'. In effect, the difference is between a question of property law as to who takes what rights in which chattels and a different question as to whether or not there has been a valid declaration of trust over shares. Admittedly Dillon LJ's meaning is somewhat elliptically expressed. However, his words are clearly not the same as setting out an explicit test that there must be a distinction made between tangible and intangible property.[169]

There are cases in which a distinction has been made between tangible and intangible property. At first instance in *Hunter v Moss*,[170] Judge Rimer QC did refer to US decisions which held that there may be some forms of chattel like bushels of wheat which are in effect indistinguishable (and therefore which require no certainty of subject matter)[171] and cases involving intangibles.[172]

Among the English cases there has been one decision which has applied the rule apparently drawn from the Court of Appeal in *Hunter v Moss* that there is one rule for intangible property and another rule for tangible property: that is, the decision of Neuberger J in *Re Harvard Securities (Holland v Newbury)*.[173] In *Harvard Securities*, a dealer in financial securities held securities as nominee for his clients. While the terms of the contracts suggested

---

167 [1986] PCC 121.
168 Although one might think that his lordship was trying very hard not to make that the distinction.
169 Clarke, 1995; Martin, 1996.
170 [1993] 1 WLR 934.
171 *Caswell v Putnam* (120 NY 154).
172 *Richardson v Shaw* 209 US 365 (1908); *Busch v Truitt* (1945) LA No 19256, 27 November.
173 [1997] 2 BCLC 369.

that the dealer held the securities on bare trust for each of his clients, the securities were not numbered and were not segregated. In consequence, none of the clients was able to identify which securities were held on bare trust for which client. Neuberger J distinguished *Re Wait*,[174] *Re London Wine*[175] and *Re Goldcorp*[176] on the basis that those cases concerned chattels, and considered himself obliged by the doctrine of precedent to apply *Hunter v Moss*[177] because that case similarly concerned intangible securities. It was therefore held that the trusts were not invalid for uncertainty of subject matter because the securities were intangible property and therefore did not require segregation.

A further feature is to understand the legal principle for which *Hunter* could be said to be the law. It is the case that *Hunter* is a Court of Appeal authority for the proposition that there are circumstances in which it is not necessary to segregate property for it to be held validly on trust. By contrast, *Goldcorp* is persuasive authority only, being a decision of the Privy Council. However, *Hunter* appears to be an unsatisfactory authority.

In Australia, a decision of the Supreme Court of New South Wales in *White v Shortall*[178] explicitly rejected the approach taken by Dillon LJ in *Hunter v Moss*. In *White v Shortall* the parties entered into a contract whereby (amongst other things) the defendant was to declare a trust over a total holding of 1,500,000 shares such that the claimant would acquire an equitable interest in 222,000 of those shares. The argument was raised that, like *Hunter v Moss*, a distinct trust could take effect over just the 222,000 shares. There had been no segregation of those shares from the entire 1,500,000 shareholding. The court upheld the validity of the trust but explicitly disavowed the rationale in *Hunter v Moss*. Instead, the inference which the court took from the facts was that a single trust took effect over the entire holding of 1,500,000 shares such that the trustees had a power to elect which 222,000 shares out of that entire shareholding were to be treated as being held for the claimant. This avoided the problem of certainty of subject matter because the trust took effect over the identified fund of 1,500,000 shares, but there was no need to segregate out 222,000 shares under a separate trust if the trustees were to have a power to split off that number of shares from the valid trust fund: therefore, the claimant had an equitable interest in the large trust equal to 222,000 shares and the defendant was deemed to have an equitable interest equal to the remaining shares. In effect, the claimant and the defendant were treated as being beneficiaries under one trust in the ratio 1,500:222. (This idea is discussed in more detail below.)

The Supreme Court of New South Wales dismissed the arguments used by Dillon LJ in *Hunter v Moss* when purporting to justify granting a trust in that case. Dillon LJ sought to justify dispensing with the need for certainty of subject matter on the basis that most of the authorities had concerned chattels and on the basis that executors of a will trust do not know the property which they are to hold on trust and yet such trusts are valid. Neither argument holds water in that executors know that they hold on trust any property owned by the testator at the time of death, and that there is no reason in principle for distinguishing between tangible and intangible property except that it led conveniently to the answer Dillon LJ wanted to reach and only if one ignored the earlier decision of the Court of Appeal in

174 [1927] 1 Ch 606.
175 [1986] PCC 121.
176 [1995] AC 74.
177 [1994] 1 WLR 452.
178 [2006] NSWSC 1379.

MacJordan v Brookmount.[179] The judgment in *Hunter v Moss* is therefore a slender reed on which to base an argument that trusts over intangible property do not require certainty of subject matter. Doctrinally, it is suggested that the decision in *Hunter v Moss* is wrong and should not be relied upon; the alternative analysis in *White v Shortall* (if one wishes to elude *Re Goldcorp*) is more satisfying.

Problems with the approach in Hunter v Moss

There are a number of problems with the decision in *Hunter v Moss*. Three important issues arise. First, *Hunter v Moss* ignores the manner in which the logic of English property law requires that there be specific and identifiable property which is the subject of the property right.[180] Thus, when considering rights in an asset like a share which is held on a register, the property right involved is not the share (because that is a piece of property which is distinguishable from other shares) but the chose in action represented by the entry on the register (because that is a transferable right between the shareholder, the registry and the company).[181] Effecting a trust over a chose in action makes segregation of the property a more abstract exercise than in relation to tangible property, but as a representation of title (such as an entry on a share register), being able to identify which property is held on trust and which property is not so held is no less important.

Secondly, it was open to the Court of Appeal to decide that there had been a valid trust created only because there were sufficient shares to satisfy the claim. The Court of Appeal could not have decided the same way on the facts of *Goldcorp* because there were more claims than there was property to satisfy them. If there is a distinction to be made between cases in which it would be valid to hold one trust valid despite insufficient segregation and another trust invalid on grounds of insufficient segregation, that distinction would be between cases where the legal owner of that property is solvent or insolvent, and not between tangible and intangible property. In the event that the legal owner of property is insolvent, a range of concerns to do with achieving justice between unsecured creditors arises. The *pari passu* principle beloved of insolvency lawyers[182] requires that no unsecured creditor is advantaged ahead of any other unsecured creditor – equality is equity in that context. However, where the legal owner of property is solvent, it would be possible to argue that it does not matter whether or not the property is sufficiently segregated provided that there is some legal obligation between the parties whereby the legal owner is required to account to the claimant for some equitable interest in the property under contract or otherwise. Provided no other person's interests would be affected by such an equitable interest (such as in relation to the *pari passu* principle), then there is no harm in enforcing the trust. If the interests of another person were affected only as a result of the doctrine of notice, that is where the arrangement fails to acknowledge the existence of some pre-existing right in the property in some third party, that (it is suggested) is a question of breach of some other duty and not a question of certainty of subject matter.

179 [1992] BCLC 350.
180 *Westdeutsche Landesbank Girozentrale v Islington LBC* [1996] AC 669, *per* Lord Browne-Wilkinson, expressly approving *Re Goldcorp*.
181 Hudson, 2000:1.
182 See perhaps *Re Whitaker* [1901] 1 Chap 9; *Re BCCI (No 8)* [1995] Ch 46; *Stein v Blake* [1996] 1 AC 243, HL.

Thirdly, it is difficult to see why there ought to be a specific rule for intangible property. It is possible for tangible property potentially to be subject to the same principle that applies to intangible property. The US case of *Caswell v Putnam*[183] points out that bushels of wheat are to all intents and purposes indistinguishable (provided that they are of the same weight and of roughly the same quality). With reference to other tangible property, for example, mass manufactured products in which one unit is unidentifiable from another unit of property, there is no reason to suggest that a different rule should be applied to them than is applied to intangible property. In relation to a fund of 1,000 ball bearings (that is, tangible and identical metal objects), it can make no more difference if any 500 are separated out than it would matter if 500 shares were separated out from a total holding of 1,000 shares. Therefore, the distinction made on the basis of tangible and intangible property is spurious. The better distinction (if one must be made) is that outlined above in relation to solvent and insolvent trustees.

Certainty of intention in relation to the property

There is the further question of distinguishing between problems caused by uncertainty as to the identity of the trust property itself and uncertainty as to which beneficiary is intended to have beneficial interests in which trust property. Where the settlor fails to make the beneficial interests plain, that property will be held on resulting trust for the settlor.[184]

In two further cases, similar issues arose. In *Re Golay Morris v Bridgewater and Others*,[185] it was held that a provision that a 'reasonable income' be provided out of a fund could be held to be valid if one could make an objective measurement of what would constitute a reasonable income in any particular case. A contrary approach was shown in *Re Kolb's Will Trusts*,[186] in which the testator had directed trustees in his will to invest in 'blue chip' stocks. On these facts, Cross J held that insufficient power had been given to the trustees to decide what was meant by 'blue chip'. A possible distinction between *Golay* and *Kolb* might be to examine whether or not on the facts of any particular case the trustees have sufficient power to enable them to decide which property is intended to fall within the trust fund and which property should not.

Where the trust fails for uncertainty of subject matter, no trust will have been properly created because there was no fund of property ever impressed with a trust.[187] This latter proposition derives from the necessity that there be property over which the trust takes effect – where there is no such property, there can never be said to have been a trust at all. Where it is the identity of the beneficiaries which is uncertain, the trust fund may well be impressed with a trust and the trustee be subject to fiduciary obligations, but the settlor will receive the equitable interest in such property on resulting trust.[188]

183 (120 NY 154).
184 *Boyce v Boyce* (1849) 16 Sim 476.
185 [1965] 1 WLR 969.
186 [1962] Ch 531.
187 *Westdeutsche Landesbank Girozentrale v Islington LBC* [1996] AC 669.
188 *Vandervell v IRC* [1967] 2 AC 291, HL.

An explanation based on 'achieving equity'

One possible further distinction which could be drawn between *Goldcorp* and *Hunter v Moss* is that in *Goldcorp* the court was concerned solely with the allocation of property rights, whereas in *Hunter v Moss* the court was concerned to prevent the employer from benefiting from a breach of contract. In the former case, the court's principal concern was to administer the insolvency of the exchange by allocating property rights between the competing claimants. As such, an approach based on rigid certainty was appropriate because it was only possible to justify giving any claimant rights in property (and thus depriving other creditors of part of the money properly owed to them) if that claimant could have proved with certainty a right in the property claimed. In the latter case, the employer was contractually bound not only to pay a salary to the employee but also to transfer to that employee a given number of shares. Therefore, the court could have said that the employer in *Hunter v Moss* had not come to equity with clean hands – that is, that the employer should not have been entitled to rely upon the strict rules of certainty of trusts as a means of enabling him to commit a breach of contract.

Therefore, the approach in *Hunter v Moss* is probably best explained by seeing it as a case where the court failed to follow the prevailing precedent because it was concerned to do justice between the parties. That is very much within the spirit of equity as a means of reaching the 'right' result. The court in *Goldcorp* was similarly concerned to do justice between the parties, but that necessitated the rigid application of the prevailing orthodoxy because of the exchange's insolvency so that no one unsecured creditor should be advantaged over the other unsecured creditors. What is interesting here is that while the principles of trusts law are becoming ever more rigid and more akin to the rules of contract at common law, there is a substratum of equity at work which sees judges prepared to overlook the application of the rigid rules of trusts law when there is some more general issue of fairness between the parties at stake. It is almost as if the ancient principles of equity were needed to achieve fairness where the modern principles of trusts law produce unfairness. An example of the courts reaching back into those ancient principles, dusting them down and putting them to work in new contexts. A form of postmodernism in equity perhaps?[189]

The approach in commercial law

The detail of the rules of commercial law and their interaction with the law of trusts are considered in Chapter 21. In outline terms it can be observed at this juncture that the approach which the law of sale of goods and the law of carriage of goods by sea take to rights in property is occasionally different from that under ordinary property law. Take, for example, a ship sailing from Calcutta carrying cotton for delivery in London at Tilbury Docks. The shipment will, typically, contain more cotton than is necessary for the seller to meet one buyer's order. It may be that the shipment contains cotton to meet the seller's obligations to three buyers. Under the law of carriage of goods by sea, a number of issues arise. The principal concern is as to which of the parties (seller, shipper, or buyer) bears the risk of the cotton being lost at sea or otherwise damaged before delivery to Tilbury Docks. Under

---

189 'Postmodernism' is defined by Jameson, 1991, to include a pastiche of older ideas or styles by adapting them to new situations or contexts, often ironically – particularly in relation to architecture.

general principles of the law of sale of goods, where a contract specifies that one party or the other bears the risk of a cargo being lost, then it is that person who shall bear the cost of replacing the value of the goods so as to give effect to her obligations under the contract of sale.[190] So, if the buyer takes the risk, then the buyer must pay the purchase price to the seller no matter what, and if the seller takes the risk, then the seller must still deliver goods of like kind at her own expense to the buyer.[191]

However, suppose that the shipment was lost and that the buyer's contract contained a provision that the cotton should be deemed to be held on trust for the buyer until delivered at Tilbury Docks. The issue faced by the buyer under ordinary principles of trusts law would be that the cotton contracted for is mixed with cotton intended for delivery to other people and therefore there would not be a valid trust over that cotton.

In general terms the approach of the case law to questions of the creation of trusts in commercial situations is the same as that for ordinary property situations. So, for example, in *Re Wait*,[192] it was held that when the claimant had rights to 500 tons of wheat out of a total shipment of 1,000 tons carried from Oregon, that claimant had no proprietary rights to any 500 tons out of the total 1,000 tons held by the shipper at the time of his bankruptcy because no such 500 tons had been segregated and held to the claimant's order. In short, the claimant had only a contractual right at common law to be delivered 500 tons of wheat, but no equitable proprietary right in any identified 500 tons.

However, in cases like *Re Staplyton*,[193] there are clear distinctions drawn between rules of commercial law and norms of ordinary property law in relation to a store of wines kept in warehouses by a vintner for its customers but where those bottles of wine were not marked as being held for any particular customer. Following the decision in *Re London Wine*, there could have been no question that any customer took rights in any particular bottles of wine – rather, all customers should have had only the rights of unsecured creditors against the entire stock of wine. Nevertheless, in *Re Staplyton*, Judge Baker QC applied *dicta* in *Wait* and in *Liggett v Kensington*[194] to the effect that contracts to carry or store goods for another do not necessarily create equitable interests in such goods. But the judge applied s 16 of the Sale of Goods Act 1979 to find that the wine claimed by the plaintiff was sufficiently 'ascertainable' for the purposes of commercial law.

Therefore, the approach taken by the application of commercial law statute is different from the position under ordinary principles of the law of trusts. As a result of the Sale of Goods (Amendment) Act 1995, the effect of *Re Goldcorp*[195] would be nullified in relation to contracts for sale of goods. The 1995 Act created ss 20A and 20B of the Sale of Goods Act 1979.[196] In relation to a sale of a 'specified quantity of unascertained goods',[197] if the goods form part of a bulk which is itself identified and if the buyer has paid the full contractual price for those goods,[198] then 'property in an undivided share in the bulk is transferred to the

190   *Martineau v Kitchling* (1872) LR 7 QB 436, 454, *per* Blackburn J.
191   Eg, *Healy v Howlett & Sons* [1917] 1 KB 337.
192   [1927] 1 Ch 606.
193   [1994] 1 WLR 1181.
194   [1993] 1 NZLR 257.
195   [1995] AC 74.
196   Sale of Goods (Amendment) Act 1995, s 1(3).
197   Sale of Goods Act 1979, s 20A(1).
198   *Ibid.*

buyer'[199] so that 'the buyer becomes an owner in common of the bulk'.[200] So, if three buyers were entitled to 100 tons each out of a shipment of 300 tons of cotton, then they would be deemed at common law to be owners as tenants in common of one-third of whatever cotton was held on board ship. That that cotton is held at common law means that there is no need for segregation of the property so as to give effect to a trust (because the beneficiaries' rights under a trust would take effect in equity). Therefore, in relation to sales of goods (as with the contracts at the heart of the *Goldcorp* litigation), all of the purchasers would be deemed to be tenants in common in accordance with the proportionate size of their contractual entitlements by the 1979 Act. Therefore, the buyer would be able to rely on the 1979 Act to grant her a common law proprietary right in the cotton as a tenant in common with the other buyers who have rights against the entirety of the shipment. This principle, it is suggested, operates as a statutory exception to the general principles of the law of trusts and of the law of property.

The approaches of commercial law to these questions are considered further in Chapter 21.

The problem of after-acquired property

One further problem arises in relation to certainty of subject matter. That problem relates to the situation in which a person undertakes to create a trust on Day 1 on the basis that the trust fund will be property which will be acquired on Day 2. This issue is considered in detail in section 5.6. In short, the question as to whether or not there was a valid trust created on Day 1 would depend on whether or not the promisor had a vested right in the property purportedly settled on trust at the time of making the declaration on Day 1.[201] Allied to the question of whether or not a valid trust is created is the further question as to the identity of the property which is settled on the terms of the trust. In theory, such a trust is valid provided that the property can be identified (on the terms set out above in this section) and provided that the settlor had a sufficient proprietary right at the time of purporting to create the trust.[202]

New types of property: constituting trusts over non-transferable assets

It is a difficult question to know what will constitute 'property' capable of being held on trust in some circumstances. This interesting question as to the essential nature of 'property' versus 'non-property' is considered in detail in Chapter 31. It is often said that the key defining feature of property is that it be transferred to another person.[203] That thesis is no longer English law, however. To explain why this is the case will require a little background. It has become a feature of modern commercial life that people borrow money more than they used to, and that people frequently use their future cash flows as collateral when borrowing money. Indeed, information about anticipated, future cash flows are generally the best material which a bank and other commercial people have when deciding whether or not to enter into a transaction with someone: whether or not that person will have any money tomorrow

---

199   *Ibid*, s 20A(2).
200   *Ibid*.
201   *Re Brooks' ST* [1939] 1 Ch 993; *Re Ralli's WT* [1964] 2 WLR 144; *Williams' Trustees v IRC* [1947] AC 447.
202   *Tailby v Official Receiver* (1888) 13 App Cas 523; *Re Lind* [1915] 2 Ch 345; *Performing Rights Society v London Theatre* [1924] AC 1; *Norman v Federal Commissioner of Taxation* (1963) 109 CLR 9.
203   See, for example, Penner, 1997, 105.

is a key part of their profitability in a fast-paced commercial world. Commercial people therefore like to be able to enter into transactions whereby they use their future cash flows as collateral. Indeed, this issue is connected to the issue considered in the previous paragraph, which is considered in greater detail in section 5.6.

In *Vandepitte v Preferred Accident Insurance Corporation of New York*[204] the Privy Council accepted that when a father took out a motor insurance contract in his own name it would be possible for that contract to be held for the benefit of another person and for it to be held on trust, even though the terms of the contract limited rights to sue in the law of contract to the father alone. Therefore, the principle was accepted that the benefit of a contract may itself be property. There has been a slew of cases dealing with assets which are not transferable but which may nevertheless constitute property. This point was accepted in *Barbados Trust Co v Bank of Zambia*[205] where a financial instrument provided that assets could only be transferred to given types of entity: even though the claimant was not one of those types of entity, it was nevertheless held possible for the benefits to be derived from that instrument to be capable of forming the subject matter of a trust in favour of that person.[206]

As considered earlier in this chapter, in *Don King v Warren* the cash flows which were expected to be earned from boxing promotion contracts could be the subject matter of a trust, even though the terms of the boxing promotion contracts provided that the contracts themselves could not be transferred to any other person. Therefore, the benefits of these contracts could be held on trust. Lightman J considered the principle in *Vandepitte* and in particular the argument that to find the existence of a valid trust over non-transferable assets would be to circumvent the contractual provision that the benefit not be transferred. Lightman J held that the court would be careful in its application to commercial cases but that such a property right was nevertheless possible. In *Swift v Dairywise*[207] milk quotas which were non-transferable entitlements to sell milk were nevertheless found to give rise to benefits which themselves would constitute property. Similarly in *Re Celtic Extraction*[208] government licences to do works and dispose of waste were also expressed to be non-transferable, but the benefits which derived from them were capable of constituting property.

3.4.4 Certainty of subject matter in testamentary and other trusts

By separating this section from the foregoing discussion it is not suggested that there are different principles operating in general terms for testamentary trusts and floating charges; rather, there are complex conclusions in this context which follow from the logic of the rule requiring certainty of subject matter which has been considered above. There are three possible results of a trust being found to be void for uncertainty of subject matter. First, the trust is completely void and the property is held for the settlor on resulting trust. Or, secondly, the rule in *Hancock v Watson*[209] validates other parts of a will in spite of the invalidity of a particular trust power on grounds of uncertainty. Or, thirdly, the power is interpreted not

---

204 [1933] AC 70 (PC).
205 *Barbados Trust Co Ltd v Bank of Zambia* [2006] EWHC 222 (Comm), [2006] 1 Lloyd's Rep 723, para [58].
206 See also *Law Debenture Trust Corporation v Elektrim Finance NV* [2006] EWHC 1305 (Ch), [2006] All ER (D) 97 (Jun).
207 [2000] 1 All ER 320.
208 [1999] 4 All ER 684.
209 [1902] AC 14.

to be a trust power but rather some other form of power not subject to a requirement of certainty – such as a floating charge.

The rule in Hancock v Watson

The rule in *Hancock v Watson*,[210] derived from *Sprange v Barnard*[211] and *Lassence v Tierney*,[212] provides for a particular means of allocating property on death where a trust fails. The rule provides that in circumstances in which property has been left to a legatee as an absolute gift but subject to some trust which has failed, the legatee takes the property absolutely.

This proposition might be best illustrated by an example. Suppose that a testator had left 'all my money to Brian absolutely but so that any money he does not need will be held on trust for my cousin Vinny'. In that situation, the testator has made an absolute gift of the money in favour of Brian but subject to a trust over a part of that money. On the terms of the trust in this example, the subject matter of the trust in favour of Vinny is too uncertain and will therefore be held to be void. It might have been expected that on failure of the trust the entire gift ought to fail and the property be held on resulting trust for the estate as part of the testator's residuary estate. However, the rule in *Hancock v Watson*[213] enforces the absolute gift and merely avoids the trust power which was held invalid on grounds of uncertainty of subject matter: so Brian takes the sole beneficial interest in all of the money as legatee.

So, in the case of *Sprange v Barnard*,[214] a testatrix had left property to her husband 'for his sole use', subject only to a provision that 'all that is remaining in the stock, that he has not necessary use for, to be divided equally between [named beneficiaries]'. It was held the trust power over 'all that is remaining' was void for uncertainty because it could not be known what was necessary for the husband's use. Therefore, the husband took the property absolutely beneficially. Similarly, in *Palmer v Simmonds*,[215] a testatrix had left money to her husband for 'his use and benefit' subject to a trust to take effect on the husband's death 'to leave the bulk of my residuary estate' to named relatives. This trust over 'the bulk' of the deceased wife's estate was held void for uncertainty of subject matter. In consequence, the husband took his wife's estate absolutely beneficially free from the trust. In both cases, the principle embodied subsequently in the rule in *Hancock v Watson* provided for the gifts to continue in effect, even though the trusts attached to them were held to have been void for uncertainty.

Floating charges

A purported trust in relation to 'the remaining part of what is left' has been held insufficient to support the finding of a valid trust over property, on the basis that it was insufficiently certain which property was being referred to.[216] The alternative analysis of such provisions

---

210   *Ibid.*
211   (1789) 2 Bro CC 585.
212   (1849) 1 Mac & G 551.
213   [1902] AC 14.
214   (1789) 2 Bro CC 585.
215   (1854) 2 Drew 221.
216   *Sprange v Barnard* (1789) 2 Bro CC 585; see para 23.2.2 below in relation to floating charges generally.

is then that they create a mere floating charge, such that the person seeking to enforce the arrangement would acquire only a right of a given value which related to a general pool of property without that right attaching to any particular part of it. Such a structure would be weaker than a proprietary trust right in the event of an insolvency because no identified property is held outside the insolvent person's estate in the insolvency proceedings.

The case of *Clough Mill v Martin*[217] has already been considered above in relation to the necessary intention to create a trust.[218] In that case, a supplier of yarn had entered into a contract with a clothes manufacturer under which the supplier was granted proprietary rights in any unused yarn and, significantly, in any clothes made with that yarn until it received payment from the clothes manufacturer. It was held by the Court of Appeal that there was insufficient intention to create a trust of any particular stock of clothing. In part, the court considered the fact that the identity of the property over which the supplier's proprietary rights were to have taken effect changed from time to time and that those proprietary rights took effect over a stock of property larger than the value of the rights which the supplier was to have received. In consequence, on the proper construction of the contract the supplier was found to have merely a floating charge over the stock of clothes from time to time rather than a vested beneficial interest under a trust.

3.4.5 Certainty of subject matter, insolvency and the law of finance

Introduction: from certainty to crisis

This section considers how the same principles of certainty of subject matter which were considered above apply to financial transactions, and how they have been significant in litigation following the global financial crisis of 2007 to 2009.[219] Many of these cases flow directly from the seismic shock caused by the insolvency of the US investment bank Lehman Brothers, which transformed a financial crisis into a global economic catastrophe. There is no need to become disorientated by the complexities of the financial instruments at issue in these cases because we are concerned with the same simple principle as outlined above: that is, to what extent must the subject matter of a trust be segregated before the trust will be valid. (I have explained the details of those financial instruments in another book if you really need to know.[220]) For present purposes I have tried to explain the facts of these cases as briefly as possible so as to focus on the trusts law principles at issue. This has necessitated streamlining the facts of the cases, the detail of the regulations, and the discussion of judgments which ran into hundreds of pages in some instances. The objective here is to see how the same certainty of subject matter principles have been used to decide complex cases involving the failure of huge investment banks as are used to decide ordinary, non-commercial cases. All of the securities, shares, money and other financial instruments discussed in this section are intangible items of property.

In essence, each of these cases involves the insolvency of a financial institution and the creditors of that organisation seeking to prove that there was property held on trust for them

---

217 [1984] 3 All ER 982.
218 See para 3.3.3 above.
219 For an overview of the crisis, see Alastair Hudson, *The Law of Finance*, Sweet & Maxwell, 2009, Chapter 32.
220 Alastair Hudson, *The Law of Finance*, Sweet & Maxwell, 2009.

so that they would have equitable interests which would survive the insolvency. In each case, the problem which has arisen is that the financial institution which has gone into insolvency has a large number of accounts to which money and shares have been allocated, but it is not clear whether or not the contents of those accounts have been segregated sufficiently clearly so as to constitute valid trusts. We will begin with an overview of how financial institutions – referred to as 'investment firms' in the jargon – operate their accounts, and by giving a little background to some of the relevant markets. This is background information which may help to understand the discussion of the decided cases, but it is less important than the principles at issue in those decided cases about certainty of subject matter in the sections to follow.

The context in which 'investment firms' hold assets

The global financial crisis, which began in earnest in the summer of 2007, but which entered a new dimension with the insolvency of the huge US investment bank Lehman Brothers in September 2008, will continue to generate litigation far into the future. At present, one of the principal streams of litigation for the purposes of trusts law relates to creditors of insolvent financial institutions seeking to argue that they had property held on trust by that financial institution so that they ought to be treated as secured creditors in the insolvency. Importantly, in cases of insolvency, if assets are found to be held on trust by the insolvent entity then the trust preserves those assets for the creditor as a beneficiary of that trust; whereas if there is no valid trust then those assets are free to be distributed evenly among the unsecured creditors of the insolvent entity. Part of demonstrating the existence of a trust clearly is to demonstrate certainty of subject matter, even though financial institutions operate very large numbers of accounts for various purposes at once. Consequently, the liquidators and the administrators of these entities (both of which are types of official appointed under UK insolvency law in relation to insolvent companies in different circumstances[221]) also require the courts to confirm the equitable ownership of any assets held by the insolvent entity.

Importantly, insolvency law maintains two principles strictly: first, that all unsecured creditors should be treated alike and that no unsecured creditor should be given any advantage over the others ('the *pari passu* principle');[222] and, second, that assets should not allowed to be taken from an insolvent person's estate so that they are unavailable in the administration of the insolvency ('the anti-deprivation principle').[223] What these principles mean for trusts law is that the courts will be careful not to allow trusts to be inferred on only slight evidence because that would segregate assets away from satisfying the claims of other unsecured creditors. By the same token, Lehman Brothers was such a cataclysmic collapse – involving impacts on financial markets directly and indirectly worth hundreds of billions of dollars – that the courts have tended to take purposive interpretations of the financial regulations and of trusts law so as to maintain order in the unwinding of that investment bank in its insolvency. Therefore, while the demonstration of the existence and validity of any trust

---

221 See Alastair Hudson, *Understanding Company Law*, Routledge, 2010, Chapter 13 for an overview of the complexities of corporate insolvency principles and mechanics.

222 *Re BCCI (No 8); Morris v Rayner Enterprises Inc, Bank of Credit and Commerce International SA (No 8)* [1997] 4 All ER 568, [1998] AC 214.

223 *Belmont Park Investments Pty Ltd v BNY Corporate Trustee Services Ltd* [2011] UKSC 38, [2011] 3 WLR 519.

must be clear in cases of insolvency,[224] we will see the traditional principles being adapted differently by different judges here. Some very forceful judgments by High Court judges such as Briggs J have been reversed by the Court of Appeal simply because the Court of Appeal did not like the effect of the outcome on the unwinding of Lehman Brothers.

Financial institutions can be, from a lawyer's perspective, extremely casual in the way in which they deal with securities, cash and other assets deposited with them; this is even though those institutions are bound by strict regulations dealing with client assets in the UK, as considered below. Financial Services Authority ('FSA') regulation required that banks like Lehman Brothers should segregate their clients' money, in part to protect clients against the bank's own insolvency. This should have meant that the regulations created trusts in favour of investment bank clients. However, as will emerge from the cases discussed below, it was a feature of Lehman Brothers' business model that they just did not do this. As a result, many clients were seeking to establish that there were trusts in their favour when in truth Lehman Brothers had just lumped all of the cash and the securities held for itself and for its clients into the same general accounts. Nevertheless, as will emerge, some of the courts were concerned to uphold the regulatory trusts in spite of the lack of clear segregation. It is sometimes said that 'hard cases make bad law' – this expression means that difficult factual scenarios can force judges to make unfortunate statements about the law so that they can reach the best outcome on those facts. In many cases, that is a good description of what is happening here.

So, why would an investment bank knowingly breach its regulatory obligations for years at a time? For 'investment firms' (that is, financial institutions which trade on financial markets as opposed to high-street banks which take deposits from individuals and small enterprises[225]) there is a cost in keeping assets in segregated accounts on trust and consequently a preference instead for using assets to generate a profit in the short term. An investment banker generally takes the view that it is better to invest cash or other assets in the short term than have them sitting unused in an account. For example, so-called 'repo' and 'stock-lending' markets are used heavily by investment firms to 'lend' their assets out to third parties in return for cash and then to repurchase (hence the name 'repo') those assets a few days later.[226] If an investment firm holds securities then it would rather sell them and then buy back similar securities when it needs them in the future (even if that is only a few days away) than just hold onto them. (These markets were considered above in relation to certainty of intention in *Mills v Sportsdirect.com Ltd.*) However, from a property lawyer's perspective, what is happening in those repo transactions is that the investment firm is transferring those securities outright to a third party in return for cash, and the third party has a purely contractual obligation to return assets of a like kind (but not the same, identical assets) at a date in the future. In this way, the investment firm is able to access cash by using its

224 On these principles see Alastair Hudson, *The Law on Financial Derivatives* (5th edn, Sweet & Maxwell, 2012), Chapter 13 generally.

225 In the financial regulatory jargon, a financial institution which is regulated by the Financial Services Authority for the conduct of investment business (as opposed to ordinary deposit-taking, banking business) is known as an 'investment firm', even though the term 'firm' in legal parlance refers specifically to a partnership and not to a corporate entity with separate personality.

226 See Alastair Hudson, *The Law of Finance*, Sweet & Maxwell, 2009, Chapter 50 for an analysis of these financial techniques; and *Beconwood Securities Pty Ltd v Australia and New Zealand Banking Group Limited* [2008] FCA 594 for an admirably clear definition of these market instruments.

securities, while speculating on the future value of those securities,[227] and the third party is able to access securities in a hurry to satisfy its own needs. For an investment firm it is uneconomic to have securities sitting unused in a trust account when those assets could be turned to account in the meantime (a process known as 'rehypothecation' among bankers). In large investment banks like Lehman Brothers there were many, many subsidiary companies, all of which owned securities and cash, or which were holding securities or cash for clients; so Lehman Brothers used to pool all of these assets together and invest them, and then buy in replacement assets whenever the clients wanted delivery. Investment banks liked to keep everything 'liquid' and to maximise their use of the assets they held. Once the financial crisis hit, however, it was impossible to find replacement assets because the 'credit crunch' meant that no one would deal with anyone else in case they went into insolvency.

This is all terrifying for a property lawyer because the clear risk with repo transactions is that the third party who acquires the securities will be unable to return assets of a like kind, or more generally that the market might seize up so that there are no securities available for the third party to buy on the open market.[228] The principal risk is that the investment firm itself may go into insolvency in a situation in which it has sold all of the securities to third parties, at a time when it therefore has no assets segregated clearly to the account of any individual customer. This is a good example of the way in which financial market practice progresses at a great pace ahead of the preferences of the traditional lawyers who service those markets. It would be preferable, from the legal perspective of customers depositing securities or other assets with the investment firm, if the investment firm held those assets in a segregated trust account, but ordinarily financial institutions will refuse to do this unless a fee is paid for that service. In this sense, however, traditional banking practice has always been that a bank would become the absolute owner of any property deposited with it, as opposed to being a trustee of its customer's ordinary deposits.[229] It is only if the parties consciously declare a trust and require that the trust assets are held in a separate account that there will be a trust over that money.[230] Therefore, trusts and ordinary investment banking practice are not natural bedfellows – which is what prompted the litigation.

The principle in outline

The possible legal principles dealing with certainty of subject matter are very clear in their outline; the problem is that different judges simply disagree as to which one should be used in practice. As considered above, the traditional approach is exemplified by the decision of the Court of Appeal in *MacJordan v Brookmount* to the effect that money held in a bank account must be held in a segregated account before it can form the subject matter of a

---

227 When the investment firm lends its securities, it is taking a speculative position either that the market value of those securities will move so that it will have received more money for those securities than they were worth on the 'repurchase date', or that it will receive a repurchase of securities which have increased in value for a pre-determined lower amount, or that it will be able to turn the cash more successfully to account before being required to repurchase those securities.

228 What also happens is that the price of those securities might increase sharply on the open market so that the third party suffers a loss in replacing them. Alternatively, the price of the securities may move so that the investment firm receives assets worth comparatively little at a later date.

229 *Foley v Hill* (1848) Cas 28, 9 ER 1002.

230 *MacJordan Construction Ltd v Brookmount Erostin Ltd* [1992] BCLC 350; *Re Global Trader Europe Ltd (in liquidation)* [2009] EWHC 602 (Ch), [2009] 2 BCLC 18.

trust.[231] By contrast, the *Hunter v Moss*[232] approach considered that it was not necessary to segregate 50 shares from a general holding of 950 shares to establish a trust over those 50 shares. So, in relation to assets held in an account, no segregation would be necessary. All of the securities and the money considered in these cases are intangible assets. The New South Wales Supreme Court took the view in *White v Shortall*[233] that *Hunter v Moss* was not to be followed and instead found on the facts in front of it that there was an intention to declare a trust over the entire fund in favour of all of the people entitled to distributions from that fund. These principles have been developed in subsequent cases. There are four particularly significant cases in this context which have emerged from the financial crisis.

Money in bank accounts and breach of regulatory obligations: Re Global Trader
and Re Lehman Brothers (Europe) Ltd

Money held in a bank account is in truth not 'money' held anywhere, but rather it is a debt in relation to which the bank owes the depositor an amount equal to the value of the deposit.[234] In this sense, 'money' in a bank account (often somewhat inaccurately referred to as 'cash') is an intangible item of property.[235] The traditional approach to money held in a bank account is exemplified by the decision of the Court of Appeal in *MacJordan v Brookmount*.[236] That principle is that a purported trust would fail on grounds of uncertainty of subject matter if the claimant was seeking to establish proprietary rights in relation to an unidentified, unsegregated portion of money held in a general bank account which contained various sums owed to many different people.[237]

The decision of Park J in *Re Global Trader Europe Ltd (in liquidation)*[238] related to derivatives transactions (in the form of 'contracts for differences'[239] and spread-betting[240]) conducted with a financial institution, Global Trader, which went into insolvency. Global Trader, in essence, held money in accounts for the benefit of its many different customers; some of those accounts were segregated and others were not. (It is worth remembering that a financial institution operates huge numbers of accounts for its many different clients, and so in practice some accounts will be operated differently from others.) As in *Re Goldcorp*, in

---

231 *MacJordan Construction Ltd v Brookmount Erostin Ltd* [1992] BCLC 350.
232 [1994] 1 WLR 452.
233 [2006] NSWSC 1379.
234 When you deposit money with a bank, you become a creditor of the bank because the bank owes you money equal to the amount of your deposit. The account constitutes a mere debt (that is, a chose in action) because the bank takes absolute title in the deposit (rather than being trustee of it) and owes you merely a personal obligation to pay you money of equal amount rather than the actual money which you deposited: *Foley v Hill* (1848) Cas 28, 9 ER 1002.
235 For a consideration of what is meant by the term 'money' in finance law, see Alastair Hudson, *The Law of Finance* (Sweet & Maxwell, 2009), Chapter 2, ranging from the views of Aristotle, Simmel and Marx to reflections by Charles Dickens, Borges and others, as well as considering case law principles.
236 [1992] BCLC 350.
237 *MacJordan Construction Ltd v Brookmount Erostin Ltd* [1992] BCLC 350.
238 *Re Global Trader Europe Ltd (in liquidation); Milner and another (liquidators of Global Trader Europe Ltd) v Crawford-Brunt and others* [2009] EWHC 602 (Ch), [2009] 2 BCLC 18.
239 Ie financial instruments which speculate on the movements between different market rates: for example, speculating that the Bank of England 'base' interest rate will remain lower than the return on the FTSE-100 share index.
240 Ie betting on movements in different financial markets.

relation to one class of claimant in particular, Global Trader failed to segregate their money from other money so that it was not possible to identify which money was held for the benefit of which customer in relation to those funds. Other customers of Global Trader were luckier because funds had actually been segregated to their account and therefore trusts could be found in their favour. Park J held, in general terms, that there could not be a trust over any part of a fund in favour of any particular customer if that fund had not been segregated from other property and identified as being held to the account of that particular customer.

That was the general principle although the facts in *Global Trader* were slightly more complicated. The principal complicating factor was that FSA regulation, in the form of the Client Assets Sourcebook ('CASS'), required that Global Trader should hold client assets in segregated funds, unless a customer had agreed to an 'opt-out' from the regulations.[241] In none of the cases considered so far in this chapter has there been regulation requiring that funds be held on trust for clients. The second complicating factor was that different customers had been treated in different ways in practice by Global Trader; however, the details of those various customers' positions are not significant for present purposes because we want to keep our attention on the trusts law principles.

For the purposes of the certainty of subject matter principle it is sufficient to understand that there were therefore several classes of customers falling, roughly, into two groups: those with the protection of CASS ('the CASS customers') and those who had opted out of CASS. It was argued on behalf of the CASS customers that Global Trader should be deemed to have held those funds on trust for its customers. However, because Global Trader had not performed its regulatory obligations scrupulously in favour of all of its customers, there was in fact a shortfall in the segregated funds which should have been put aside for those CASS customers. Global Trader had simply failed to put sufficient money into the accounts which should have been held for them.

Consequently, Park J held two things. First, those CASS customers could only have proprietary rights to the extent that there were actually funds segregated to their account. So, if that customer was entitled to £150,000 but only £100,000 had actually been put in a segregated account for them, then they could only have a trust over the £100,000 actually held in a segregated account in their name. They would have a purely personal claim as an unsecured creditor for the remaining £50,000 owed to them in this example. Of course, those CASS customers then tried to argue that Global Trader should hold other money on trust for them. Therefore, secondly, Park J held that the CASS customers had no proprietary rights to any other property owned by Global Trader to top up their segregated funds to the level they should have been at that time. If those amounts were not actually segregated for their account then they could not pretend nor argue that other money should be deemed to be held on trust for them. In relation to the customers who had opted out of CASS, it was held that there would be no trusts in their favour where they could not identify any segregated funds held to their account specifically.[242]

---

241 Customers might opt out of CASS for numerous reasons, one of which might be to avoid a fee associated with the maintenance of a trust account and another of which might be to make transactions simpler.

242 It was held that where moneys had passed into the general accounts of the company then those parties might be able to trace into those general bank accounts, provided that those assets were identifiable as the traceable proceeds of property owned in equity by them: that is an area of equity which is considered in detail in Chapter 19.

Following *Re Global Trader*, in *Re Lehman Bros International (Europe)(No 2)*[243] J considered the poorly drafted regulations in Part 7 of the FSA rulebook CASS ('CA 7'),[244] which both required that client assets were held on trust and yet at the same time permitted financial institutions to elect to operate a single, running account holding all of the clients' assets and the institution's own assets in that same general account prior to amounts being segregated to the accounts of individual customers. Lehman Brothers tended to operate general accounts and was slow to segregate client money. The regulations required that client money must be held on trust but it was unclear on what basis that trust came into existence: when the money was received, or when segregation was actually effected by the bank. However, the regulations were unclear as to the nature of this statutory trust, the time at which it took effect and the property over which it took effect. When Lehman Brothers went into insolvency, the question arose, *inter alia*, as to whether or not a valid trust had been imposed over the moneys held in this general account in favour of clients. (Matters were complicated by the fact that Lehman Brothers had been breaching its regulatory obligations about the segregation of client money for many years.)

It was held that even though the regulations provided that there should be deemed to be a trust over client money, nevertheless the regulations (under CASS 7) also permitted the financial institution to hold property in this general account with only a contractual obligation at that time to account to its clients.[245] Briggs J held that until the money was segregated there could not be a trust over it in favour of any given client. If money was actually held in a segregated account for a given client then there could be a valid trust over that segregated money in favour of that client. Otherwise, the client would be required to advance a tracing claim (as considered in Chapter 19) to identify the traceable proceeds of any given client's money in any general account; this would require forensic accounting[246] to trace the flow of the clients' moneys through the various accounts in practice.[247]

In a supplementary judgment,[248] Briggs J held that, even though the bank would consider itself to be holding money for clients without allocating that money to specific clients, the

---

243 [2009] EWHC 3228 (Ch), [2010] EWHC 47 (Ch), [2010] 2 BCLC 301. See also the supplemental judgment of Briggs J at [2010] EWHC 47 (Ch).

244 See, for example, *ibid*, para [178] and [179]. The CASS regulations were created further to the EU Markets in Financial Instruments Directive ('MiFID') principles which obliged Member States to create arrangements in their domestic regulations whereby client money was segregated from other money. For a discussion of MiFID, see Alastair Hudson, *The Law of Finance*, Chapter 7 and Chapter 10.

245 Briggs J took the view that due to defects in the drafting the regulations seemed to create a charge rather than a trust due to the lack of segregation, at para [178]. The regulations were so poorly drafted that it was unclear whether this permission to operate general accounts was intended as a temporary measure before the bank effected segregation; or whether banks were permitted in effect to operate general accounts permanently and then to effect segregation whenever they got around to it. The purpose of these regulations was a fudge between protecting customers through segregation of funds, and yet allowing banks a little leeway to operate their accounts in a way that was convenient for them. The mistake, it is suggested, was in failing to draft sufficiently tight regulations which required instant segregation of client money into distinct accounts – something which can be done simply on computer in a bank's operations area by allocating an account number to any given holding of assets.

246 Forensic accounting is a specialist branch of that profession which is expert in the difficult business of tracing payment flows through electronic bank accounts, shell companies and other similar devices.

247 Moreover, it was held that the regulations could not make an exception to the principle of insolvency law that no unsecured creditor could be advantaged over any other unsecured creditor.

248 In essence, Briggs J was called upon to consider another aspect of this same case shortly after giving judgment as considered immediately above. Both of these impressive judgments were then appealed to the Court of Appeal together.

:d to hold that money on trust for clients for whom that money was
[249] (This, it is suggested, stretches the *Goldcorp* principle almost to
. makes this interpretation acceptable is that it can be identified which
: which group of clients prior to being allocated to them, and therefore
.dentification to make a trust possible over that general fund for those
.eneficiaries in the shares indicated by their contracts with the bank.)
.dgments of Briggs J were appealed to the Court of Appeal together (under
the ... *nan Brothers International (Europe)(in administration) v CRC Credit Fund
Ltd*).[250] The Court of Appeal took the view that the CASS 7 regulations should not be interpreted as requiring segregated funds for each client before a trust could come into existence,
but rather that the regulations should be interpreted as intending the creation of 'a single trust'
which took effect over the central pool of property held by the bank for all of its clients who
fell under CASS protection.[251] All of these judgments turned in part on general principles of
trusts law but they were concerned more particularly with very detailed readings of the very
poorly drafted provisions of CASS 7. Indeed very little case law was cited. In essence, then,
the Court of Appeal held that the regulations should be interpreted as providing for the creation of one large trust under which all the CASS customers had equitable interests (with those
equitable interests being based on their contractual rights against the bank).

So, the Court of Appeal considered that a single, large trust was created. It is worth
unpacking the reasoning which brought the court to that conclusion, contrary to the decision
of Briggs J. Arden LJ held that the regulations intended the creation of a trust, but that the
terms of that trust were left undefined, with the result that the general law of trusts must
supplement the regulations. In other words, the regulations were so vague that the court was
required to interpret what the terms of that trust should be, just as the Court of Appeal in
Paul v Constance had been required to interpret the existence and terms of a trust between
'unsophisticated people' in their private lives. In interpreting the particular regulations at
issue[252] it was held that the trust was intended to take effect on receipt of the clients' moneys,
as opposed to coming into existence only when the money was segregated to the account of
a particular client.[253] Following on from that finding, the Court of Appeal had to explain how
a trust which came into effect on receipt of moneys operated: their answer was to find that it
was a large, single trust for all the relevant clients as beneficiaries. In large part, the reason
for the Court of Appeal reversing this part of the judgment of Briggs J was that they took a
more purposive approach which identified the underlying purpose of CASS 7 as being to
protect investors.[254] Consequently, given that the provisions of CASS 7 were ambiguous as

---

249 [2010] EWHC 47 (Ch).

250 [2010] EWCA Civ 917.

251 *Ibid*, at [125], *per* Arden LJ: '. . . the statutory trust created by CASS 7.7 is a single trust. It is not a series of
individual trusts, one for each client.' This had the fortunate effect of creating a trust from the outset which
protected all investors from that time. Thus the judgments of Briggs J are reversed on this particular point. Sir
Mark Waller offered a neat summary of the difference in approach of the Court of Appeal to the judgment of
Briggs J, including the observation that the result to which Briggs J came was 'unsatisfactory' even though the
judgment was 'very impressive', at [241].

252 The regulatory rulebook in CASS 7 is simply too long and complex to be worth considering here in detail. The
relevant regulations are reproduced as an appendix to the very full judgment of Arden LJ.

253 [2010] EWCA Civ 917, at [104] and [105], *per* Arden LJ, and at [193] *per* Lord Neuberger.

254 *Ibid*, at [181], *per* Lord Neuberger.

to the nature of the trust which they imposed, it was held that it would be appropriate to take the analysis which offered the best protection to investors.[255] That necessitated the finding of a large, single trust which covered all CASS customers, as opposed to disappointing many customers who had not been fortunate enough to have had money segregated to their account.

What is missing from the judgment of Arden LJ is any analysis of the case law on certainty of subject matter. It is suggested that this is because the finding of a single, large trust means that the subject matter is taken to be all of the money in the pool, with the client's beneficial interests being in amounts provided for in their contracts with the bank, and because the Court of Appeal's principal focus was on the best interpretation of the statutory trust created by the regulations. In effect, the Court of Appeal was using the sort of thinking that was used in *White v Shortall* (considered above) so as to come to a convenient conclusion on the facts. In essence, if you are free to interpret the terms of the statutory trust, then why not interpret it in the most convenient way possible for everyone involved? Exactly the same sort of issue relating to the client money practices of Lehman Brothers arises in the next section of this chapter.

After the completion of this seventh edition, the Supreme Court upheld the decision of the Court of Appeal on slightly different grounds (at [2012] UKSC 6, [2012] Bus LR 667). In essence, the Supreme Court approached this case strictly on the basis of the interpretation of the 'statutory trust' in the CASS regulations and of the EU Markets in Financial Instruments Directive on which they are based, and not on the basis of general trusts law as it is considered in this book (eg Lord Clarke, para [110]); albeit that CASS 'is erected on the foundation of the general law of trusts' [para 84] according to Lord Walker. The majority, primarily through the judgment of Lord Dyson, chose to adopt an interpretation which offered the largest amount of protection to the largest possible number of clients of the bank (eg Lord Dyson at para 148). In that sense, this decision tells us nothing about general trusts law and as such should not be interpreted as having affected it. It was held by the majority that because the regulations require that 'all' client money is to be held on the statutory trust, then segregation would not be a pre-requisite for a client to participate in the allocation of the sums held by Lehman Brothers because all sums are necessarily held on the terms of the statutory trust anyway. Lord Dyson acknowledged the difficulties (or, in truth, chaos) which this would cause in allocating amounts between clients of the bank on this basis. Lord Walker effectively offered a dissenting judgment when he doubted the large 'single trust' trust approach [at para 82]. At one point Lord Walker held that 'a trust without segregation is a very precarious form of protection' which could be taken to be an acceptance that such a trust is a possibility in English trusts law, or else as a reason for rejecting the possibility of such a trust. Interestingly, Lord Walker held that 'the majority's decision [in the Supreme Court] makes investment banking more of a lottery than even its fiercest critics have supposed' [para 85] because the absence of a need for segregation means that it is unknowable which client will get how much property from the general pool of property in advance. Lehman Brothers itself was correctly criticised by judges at all levels for its 'shocking underperformance' and its regulatory non-compliance 'on a truly spectacular scale'. That none of these issues have yet led to criminal prosecutions is an affront to our jurisprudence and to the rule of law itself. (A full discussion of this appeal will appear on www.alastairhudson.com in the 'trusts law' area.)

---

255   However, Arden LJ explicitly left open the question as to whether there would be a breach of trust if the running account had been at any stage of a lesser value than the total claims against the bank on behalf of its customers, [2010] EWCA Civ 917, at [70].

Securities held within investment banking groups: Re Lehman Brothers
International (Europe) (In Administration)

This section also relates to the internal asset management practices and the insolvency of the
huge US investment bank Lehman Brothers as they arose in *Re Lehman Brothers International
(Europe) (In Administration)*.[256] This is a different case from the Lehman Brothers cases
considered immediately above, albeit that the issues also relate to certainty of subject matter.
When Lehman Brothers went into insolvency in September 2008, aside from nearly
destroying the entire global financial system, issues arose as to whether or not there would
be a trust over unsegregated securities held by one of its subsidiaries, 'LBIE'. The securities
were 'unsegregated' in the sense that they had not been assigned to separate accounts and
instead were held instead in one large pool. That subsidiary acted as a central depository for
all of the securities held by other Lehman Brothers subsidiaries in one particular part of the
world. When Lehman Brothers went into insolvency it was important to decide who owned
the securities held by the subsidiary and whether they could be deemed to have been held on
trust for the various claimants. In essence, the conclusion was very simple, and yet worrying:
the Court of Appeal in *Re Lehman Brothers International (Europe)(In Administration)*[257]
followed *Hunter v Moss*[258] without explaining why, and without considering the case law in
any detail. Instead, it appeared to be convenient, in the context of both the largest corporate
bankruptcy in history and the largest financial crisis in history, to hold that the parties would
have the property rights they wanted, even though there had been a conscious failure over
about twenty years within Lehman Brothers to segregate any of the property purportedly
held on trust and even though the purported trustee had been able to deal with that supposed
trust property so as to make profits for itself. It is suggested that both of these elements
should have prevented a trust being found on grounds respectively of uncertainty of subject
matter and the lack of any clear certainty of intention to create a trust as opposed to a floating
charge. We shall consider this decision in greater detail.

   The failed US investment bank Lehman Brothers, which collapsed with such appalling
consequences for the world economy in September 2008, had a number of unusual (and
some downright unacceptable) business practices.[259] One of its practices was at issue in *Re
Lehman Brothers International (Europe) (In Administration)*[260] before the Court of Appeal,
on appeal from a decision of Briggs J.[261] For reasons which are too complicated to consider
here, Lehman Brothers was in the practice of settling all of its securities dealings in various
jurisdictions across all its many subsidiary entities by transferring all of those securities to a

---

256 [2011] EWCA Civ 1544.
257 *Ibid.*
258 [1994] 1 WLR 452.
259 The most infamous of its practices related to the 'Repo 105' account through which Lehman Brothers was in
     the habit of transferring US$50 billion of its liabilities to third parties, in exchange for a hefty fee, at the time
     when its accounts were prepared so that its balance sheet appeared to be US$50 billion better than it would
     otherwise have been, before taking those liabilities back onto its books after its accounts had been completed.
     This transaction is explained in detail in the Anton Valukas Report titled 'In re Lehman Brothers Holdings
     Inc' for the United States Bankruptcy Court Southern District of New York (Chapter 11 Case No 08-13555),
     11 March 2010, especially at p 6.
260 [2011] EWCA Civ 1544.
261 [2010] EWHC 2914 (Ch).

single entity for each region:[262] the relevant 'hub' subsidiary to which it transferred all of those securities in relation to the UK was 'LBIE'. However, rather than segregating securities into different accounts within LBIE, Lehman Brothers simply passed all of the securities into a single, unsegregated account and conducted the bank's complex dealings from there.[263] Those securities could then be used in 'repo' transactions (of the sort explained above). The Lehman Brothers organisation went into insolvency on 15 September 2008. Questions then arose as to the equitable ownership of the securities held by LBIE. As emerged from the finding of facts at first instance, the organisation of these holdings was, to quote Lloyd LJ, 'a mess'. At first instance it was held that the shares were held on trust as part of a beneficial tenancy in common with the other rightholders. In essence, Briggs J sought to rely on the analysis in *White v Shortall* to find a valid trust on the facts in front of him but without really demonstrating that the facts in front of him were the same as the facts in *White v Shortall*. The matter was then appealed to the Court of Appeal.

Lloyd LJ simply concluded, without presenting a reasoned argument of his own beyond summarising the arguments of others, on two bases. First, that 'there is no ground for saying that the trust could not take effect in law because its subject-matter lacked certainty',[264] with the result that a trust was found. However, this does not explain whether the requirement of certainty of subject matter is being rejected in general or whether there is found to be sufficient certainty on these facts. Moreover, this trust takes effect in equity, not 'in law'. Second, his lordship held that 'it seems to me clear that . . . an approach involving the use of a trust binding on LBIE in favour of the affiliate was adopted';[265] although all that this assertion does is to assert that there should have been a trust, but not whether or not one was actually created.[266] The Court of Appeal followed *Hunter v Moss* and purportedly applied the conclusion in *White v Shortall* but without delving into that case to identify whether or not the cases were sufficiently similar. This judgment does little to analyse the clear rejection of *Hunter v Moss* in *White v Shortall* and the weight of journal commentary which similarly rejects it. There is nothing in the judgment to indicate why *Hunter v Moss* is to be preferred to *MacJordan v Brookmount*, nor indeed why any one case is to be preferred to any other.

---

262 In essence, this was a sort of internal clearing house through which all of those securities could be bundled up together and invested. Global banks like Lehman Brothers are in constant motion: when New York went home, the Tokyo subsidiaries and personnel took over, when Tokyo went to bed then the London subsidiaries and personnel took over, and when London leaked home on the Underground then New York took over again. No securities and no cash would be allowed to sit still in accounts: instead, they would all be invested so as to keep earning profits. The central clearing entity would then transfer any securities or cash that were needed to the relevant subsidiaries when they were needed. You must remember that this involved millions of transactions and thousands of people, like an enormous beehive made of computers and money. The problem was that the central clearing entity structure in Lehman Brothers operated general accounts and not segregated accounts.

263 LBIE entered into 'repo' and 'stock lending' transactions with those securities, in essence to make money from them before the other subsidiaries or customers needed them. Those transactions are explained in Alastair Hudson, *The Law of Finance*, Sweet & Maxwell, 2009, Chapter 50. This contributed to the securities being treated as a single lump of securities and not being segregated to the accounts of the various customers or subsidiaries who would be entitled to them.

264 [2011] EWCA Civ 1544, [75].

265 [2011] EWCA Civ 1544, [75].

266 Somewhat unsatisfactorily, Watkins LJ held in *R v Clowes (No 2)* [1994] 2 All ER 316 at 325 that: 'As to segregation of funds, the effect of the authorities seems to be that a requirement to keep moneys separate is normally an indicator that they are impressed with a trust, and that the absence of such a requirement, if there are no other indicators of a trust, normally negatives it. The fact that a transaction contemplates the mingling of funds is, therefore, not necessarily fatal to a trust.'

The holdings in LBIE were enormous and constantly changing – as is typical in an investment bank dealing with securities. Lehman Brothers had such poor control over its accounts
that the securities were simply held as a single mass and the contributors to that mass had their
entitlements within that mass recorded in its operations systems. This is not the same as having
property rights in any given securities. It is the very antithesis of a trust. At best, the customers
and other subsidiaries could be said to have the rights under a floating charge because not only
was the precise holding of securities of any one customer uncertain, but whether or not LBIE
would have those securities in its possession (as opposed to having been lent out or sold to third
parties) was a matter of chance. The argument runs as follows. LBIE was able to hold a
changing, fungible pool of securities which it was entitled to use for its own account. LBIE was
required to account both to other subsidiaries of Lehman Brothers and to its customers periodically. Importantly, however, LBIE was not required to account for the specific securities which
it had received but rather it was required to account only for securities of like kind (as would
be required by the use of those securities for repo and stock-lending transactions). Consequently,
the arrangement was in truth a floating charge over a changing pool of assets and not a trust at
all. This had been the analysis in the decision of the Court of Appeal in *Clough Mill v Martin*[267]
(considered above) in which a supplier of fabric purported to take security rights over the
general stock into which that fabric was passed by a clothes manufacturer as it used the fabric
in its business of manufacturing clothes. Given that the manufacturer had the right to use the
fabric and to sell the clothes made with that fabric to its customers in the ordinary course of its
business, Goff LJ held that the proper analysis of the parties' arrangement was not a trust but
rather a floating charge so that the supplier's rights were of an identified value over the general
stock of clothes from time to time.

So LBIE would seek to deal with those securities and to put them to work: repo and stock-
lending transactions by definition involve the outright transfer of the securities involved.[268]
Therefore, it cannot logically be said that any given property is being held on trust for two
reasons: first, because LBIE was entitled to deal with that property on its own account for its
own benefit, and second, because no property was segregated to the account of any third
person at any time. It is not enough for the judges to seek to protect commercial people such
as investment banks by giving them property rights when they want them; in truth Lehman
Brothers was simply involved in shoddy practice when their business as a bank was supposed
to be the maintenance of accounts. Their systematic failure in this context from the 1990s
through to their collapse in 2008, a period of about 20 years, demonstrates that they did not
consider it important enough to ensure that there were segregated property rights for any of
their subsidiaries or for their customers, and therefore there was no intention sufficient to
create a trust during this period. Even the risk of facing a large regulatory charge for failing
to organise their securities property did not lead to the internal task force appointed within
Lehman Brothers to consider this problem and create a system in which assets were held
separately from the accounts of the various customers.[269]

It is suggested that the decision of the Court of Appeal in *Re Lehman Brothers International
(Europe)* is a bad decision, and one hopes it will in time be considered by the Supreme
Court. It is bad in that it is poorly argued in relation to the authorities stacked against *Hunter*

267 [1984] 3 All ER 982, [1985] 1 WLR 111.
268 Eg *Beconwood Securities Pty Ltd v Australia and New Zealand Banking Group Limited* [2008] FCA 594.
269 Investment banks often take the view that it is worth paying a fine and keeping a profitable practice in opera-
     tion in breach of regulations.

v Moss, bad in that *White v Shortall* is misappropriated for this purpose, and bad in that the finding of a trust is the wrong analysis on trusts law principles for the reasons given above: the purported trustee was acting in a way in which a trustee may not act with a trust fund and there had been neither segregation for the claimants nor any clear intention to hold the entire fund on trust for any claimants to it as tenants in common (or else the internal working party would undoubtedly have formalised such an arrangement). In *White v Shortall* it had been held that there had been a clear intention on the facts to provide each customer with a right as a beneficiary in the entire fund as a tenant in common in equity with the other rightholders against that fund: but on the facts in *Re Global Trader* and in *Re Lehman Brothers International (Europe)* it is suggested that there was nothing on the facts which suggested that the employees creating those accounts had had any such conscious intention. The reason for finding as the Court of Appeal did was that it conveniently produced a trust which could be used in the insolvent administration of Lehman Brothers to distribute assets among the bank's customers. It is a good example of a hard case making bad law.

While these two streams of authority cannot be satisfactorily reconciled, it is suggested that the weight of judicial authority should be with the *Re Goldcorp* line of cases.[270] The poor internal practices in financial institutions should not encourage the English courts to bend clear principles of trusts law so as to patch over the cracks when those financial institutions go into insolvency.

3.4.6 A question as to which property needs to be segregated

The unprogrammed development of trusts law

The law of trusts is a subject which has grown rapidly outwards from its original beginning as a convenient means of recognising that more than one person could have various forms of property rights simultaneously in respect of the same piece of land.[271] Over time, the trust was applied to cases not involving land. New challenges to the logic of the trust over land were met by judicial ingenuity through which legal principle sought to keep pace with a changing world. In this sense, the law of trusts has developed as an accident of history. As such, the law of trusts was conceived as a reaction to circumstances and not out of immutable principle.[272] By the 19th century, it became imperative that some certainty was introduced to the law of trusts beyond the haphazard development of rules to match new cases and new forms of property, and so the principles of certainty were developed. Given this rolling development of the law and an attempt to entrench principle firmly between the mid-19th and mid-20th century, it is unsurprising that there will come situations in which the logic of the law will stretch so far and no further, for example, in relation to certainty of subject matter. Nevertheless, there can be conceptual problems with applying this ostensibly simple rule, particularly when those rules were created originally with land in mind – particularly given that a holding of land is usually easy to render certain – rather than more complex forms of intangible property like shares and money in bank accounts.

---

270 *Westdeutsche Landesbank v Islington LBC* [1996] 1 AC 669.
271 See section 2.1 above and para 7.1.1 below.
272 Except in relation to the general principles of equity as outlined in section 1.1.

Understanding which property must be certain

The essay which comprises Chapter 31 of this book considers the overlap between property law and trusts law. There is one particular problem which occasionally causes confusion in relation to certainty of subject matter. Certainty of subject matter requires that the fund which is to be held on trust must be segregated from all other property and must be segregated from any property held on the terms of another trust. So, suppose that Jerry wants to create a trust over £99,000 in favour of his friends George, Elaine and Cosmo. If Jerry has all of his money in one bank account and there is £200,000 in that bank account, then there will be no certainty of subject matter because it cannot be known which £99,000 out of that mixture of £200,000 is intended to be held on trust.[273]

If Jerry does create a new bank account in which the £99,000 which is to be the subject matter of the trust is deposited separately from all other money, then there will be a valid trust because the £99,000 is segregated and so is sufficiently certain. Suppose that Jerry drafts his trust so that 'the £99,000 shall be held equally for each of George, Elaine and Cosmo'; we might be concerned that we do not know which £33,000 is to be held for which of the three beneficiaries. However, there is no problem here as far as trusts law is concerned. All that is required is that the £99,000 which is to be the subject matter of the entire trust is segregated from all other property. Within that trust fund, however, it is perfectly permissible for the trustees to decide which money is to be advanced to which beneficiary.

Equally, in relation to a trust 'to hold £10,000 on trust for my two children in equal shares', there is no argument raised that the trust is void because neither child can know precisely which £5,000 out of the total £10,000 forms their equal share. Rather, we would accept that the trustees have a power to divide the fund in two and pay half each to each beneficiary. What needs to be certain is that the entire fund of £10,000 is sufficiently identifiable and not that the money constituting any particular interest within the fund is similarly identifiable.

While no argument is raised in that situation just considered, if the settlor were instead to have declared 'I hereby declare two trusts over this £10,000 such that £5,000 shall be held on trust for my only son and £5,000 on a separate trust for my only daughter', that would potentially raise the *Goldcorp* problem of knowing which £5,000 was to be held for which child because the parent would now be creating two entirely separate trusts which would require entirely separate subject matter. In this second situation, neither trust fund is certain – rather, both funds have a claim to half of the whole £10,000.[274]

Alternatively, if the settlor had declared 'I hereby declare two trusts over my bank account such that half shall be held on trust for my only son and half on trust for my only daughter' immediately before going bankrupt, the court might well have taken a stricter approach because of the claim of the unsecured creditors in that bankruptcy.[275] If the trust had provided 'I hereby declare two trusts over the £10,000 in my bank account such that £5,000 shall be held on trust for my only son and £5,000 on trust for my only daughter' when there was only £7,500 at the

273   *MacJordan v Brookmount* [1992] BCLC 350.

274   Alternatively, it is possible that a court might be prepared to order that the trustees simply make a division of the total fund in line with the principles advanced in *Hunter v Moss* [1994] 1 WLR 452 and *Re Harvard Securities Ltd* [1997] 2 BCLC 369 and decline to apply the rule in *MacJordan v Brookmount* [1992] BCLC 350 (that a fund of money held in a bank account must be segregated to be the subject matter of a trust).

275   See the discussion of Insolvency Act 1986, s 423 in para 11.4.6 below and the powers of the courts to recover property put beyond the reach of creditors in expectation of bankruptcy.

date of bankruptcy, then it is likely that the court would apply the rule in *Goldcorp*[276] to protect the bankrupt's creditors (particularly if it was thought that the trusts had been created simply to put the money beyond the reach of those creditors).[277] What the settlor should have done was to declare one single trust over the £10,000 in favour of her son and daughter in equal shares because then the subject matter of this single bank account would have been identifiable.

Mistake in identifying the fund

There will not be a failure of a trust simply because the property which was intended to have been held on trust was mistakenly identified in the trust instrument. Instead the court may order the equitable remedy of rectification to rectify the trust instrument so that the correct property is identified in the trust instrument.[278] The rationale behind this principle is easy to identify: if a settlor mistakenly records in a trust instrument that she wishes 'my money in bank account number 110' to be held on trust when she only had one bank account and that account had the number '100', then it should not be open to some third person to claim that there was no trust created over bank account '100' simply because of a mere typographical error or some similar sort of trifling mistake. The court must be convinced that it was a straightforward error and that the settlor's intention to declare a trust over the alternative fund is clearly made out. So, in *Re Farepak Food and Gifts Ltd*[279] Mann J considered a situation in which a company's directors had created a separate bank account into which customers' prepayments for goods and services were to be paid after the company had gone into insolvent administration. The company's directors created a trust instrument so as to declare a trust over these moneys in favour of those customers but the trust instrument recorded the wrong account number. From the evidence it was clear that the new account was the one which had been created expressly for the purpose of bringing this trust into being. Consequently, Mann J was prepared to find that it was clearly the settlors' intention that it was the new account which had been intended to be mentioned in the trust instrument and therefore held that the trust instrument should be rectified so as to record the details of the new account on grounds that there had been a simple error here. There is no question of uncertainty of subject matter here: rather the parties were certain as to the subject matter of the trust but made a simple error in recording that property in the trust instrument.

The underlying purpose of certainty of subject matter

The purpose of the rules on certainty of subject matter is to ensure that the trustees know over which property the trust takes effect. Once the trust fund is sufficiently certain, there is no problem in principle with allowing the trustees to decide which property is paid out of that fund to which beneficiary, in the same way that the trustees can decide which money is used to invest in shares, which money is used to invest in land, and so forth.

Thus, there is no doubt that interest earned on a fund of money will be added to the fund and subjected to the ordinary terms of the trust.[280] Consequently, when interest is earned on a trust

---

276 [1995] AC 74.
277 This, however, raises different questions as to 'sham trusts': see paras 3.3.3 above and 11.4.6 below.
278 *Re Butlin* [1976] Ch 251.
279 [2006] All ER (D) 265 (Dec).
280 Assuming here that there is no express trusts provision which would require that it be dealt with differently.

fund over money, that interest is simply added to the trust fund without anyone inquiring which beneficiaries are entitled to that interest. The interest is deemed to pass into the capital of the fund unless there is some express provision to the contrary. Suppose there is a trust over a fund of money with a power for the trustees to invest in shares. When the money is spent to acquire the shares, the rights of the beneficiaries attach to the shares once the trustees have secured an assignment of them: there is no suggestion that when the money is spent, the beneficiaries' rights have no property to which they can attach. Nor is there any suggestion of the trust's invalidity simply because the money held on trust is used to buy shares – rather, the shares are deemed to pass into the trust fund and to be held along with the other trust property.

3.5 CERTAINTY OF OBJECTS

There must be sufficient certainty as to the 'objects' (or, beneficiaries) of a trust or a power, or else that trust or power will be void. There are different tests for certainty of objects in relation to different forms of trust or power. Therefore, to decide whether or not it is possible to identify the beneficiaries of a trust or power with sufficient certainty it is first necessary to identify the nature of the power which is being exercised. It is important, therefore, to distinguish between: fixed trusts; discretionary trusts; fiduciary mere powers; and personal powers.

In relation to a fixed trust, it is necessary to be able to draw up a complete list of all beneficiaries.

In relation to fiduciary mere powers and discretionary trusts, it is required that it is possible to say of any person claiming to be a beneficiary that that person is or is not a member of the class of beneficiaries. Some exceptional cases have taken the view that the trust may be valid where it is possible to say that a substantial number of people do or do not fall within the class of beneficiaries.

In relation to personal powers, the authorities suggest that there will be no invalidity on grounds of uncertainty of objects. It is suggested that on principle this is the better approach because personal powers do not impose fiduciary obligations on the holder of the power.

There appears to be a distinction between uncertainty as to the concept used to identify the class of beneficiaries, problems of proving yourself to be a beneficiary, problems of locating beneficiaries and problems of administrative unworkability – only the first and last categories appear to invalidate the trust of necessity.

3.5.1 Introduction

The question at issue

A trust will be void if the 'objects' of that trust (meaning, the 'beneficiaries' of that trust) are uncertain. The principles dealing with certainty of objects relate to the need for the trustees to be able to know the identity of the beneficiaries under a trust because, in turn, the court cannot know whether or not trustees have exercised their powers properly if there is uncertainty as to the people who stood to benefit from that trust. Thus, it is said that it is important that the courts have someone in whose favour they can decree performance of the trust[281] and that the identity

---

281   *Morice v Bishop of Durham* (1805) 10 Ves 522.

of the beneficiaries must be certain so that the court can police the performance of the trustees properly (as considered below). If there were some dispute as to the manner in which the trustees should deal with the trust property, then the court would need to be able to take control of the management of the trust, but it cannot do this if there is some uncertainty as to the identity of the beneficiaries.[282] Consequently, any trust which is uncertain as to its beneficiaries will be void. The 19th century authorities assumed that the court would be required to divide the property equally between members of the class of objects in such a situation and therefore the old case law used to require that a complete list of the objects could be prepared:[283] the modern case law provides for a range of different tests dependent upon the type of power that is at issue.[284] In particular, in the modern authorities, we should consider that the court has an inherent discretion to administer trusts and, if the court is to carry out this discretion properly, it must be possible for the court to know with certainty who the objects of a trust or a power are.[285]

A 'power' is a responsibility imposed on a person, which might be part of a trust or which might stand alone, which grants that person a power to do whatever the terms of their power permits them to do with property and so forth.[286] The law on powers is distinct from the law on trusts, although the two concepts come close together in relation to the law on certainty of objects, as will emerge in the discussion to come.

The problem which is considered in this section is this: what level of certainty must there be as to the identity of the class of beneficiaries for a trust to be held valid? The question is whether the objects of the trust or power are sufficiently certain. The law relating to certainty of objects developed into its current form as a result of the merging of some of the tests relating to different types of powers and trusts in two House of Lords decisions in the 1970s: however, this area of the law still has different tests for different types of trust and power.[287]

This subject is best approached in the following way: first, identify the nature of the trust or power at issue. The choice is broadly between fixed trusts, discretionary trusts, fiduciary mere powers (including powers of appointment) and purely personal powers – the distinction between these forms of power and trust is considered in detail below. Secondly, apply the test for certainty of beneficiaries appropriate to that type of power or trust. In many circumstances, that test may appear overly strict and may produce a seemingly unfair result. Therefore, thirdly, consider the alternative cases which present a possible means of circumventing the strictness of those main tests, after you have considered whether or not the trust or power would be valid on the basis of the leading case. Fourthly, after analysing all of the above, consider one of the means of resolving the uncertainty bound up in these powers and trusts. This structure should guide the reader through the analysis of any problem relating to uncertainty of objects.

---

282 *IRC v Broadway Cottages* [1955] Ch 20, 30, *per* Jenkins LJ.
283 *Kemp v Kemp* (1801) 5 Ves Jr 849; *Morice v Bishop of Durham* (1805) 10 Ves Jr 522.
284 See variously *IRC v Broadway Cottages* [1955] Ch 20; *Re Gulbenkian* [1968] Ch 126; *McPhail v Doulton* [1970] 2 WLR 1110; *Re Hay's Settlement Trusts* [1981] 3 All ER 786.
285 *Re Manisty's Settlement* [1974] Ch 17, 27, [1973] 2 All ER 1203, 1211, *per* Templeman J; approved in *Schmidt v Rosewood Trust Ltd* [2003] 3 All ER 76, 88–89, [2003] UKPC 26, [42], *per* Lord Walker, both drawing on *Morice v Bishop of Durham* (1805) 10 Ves 522, 539, [1803–13] All ER Rep 451, 458, *per* Lord Eldon LC. See para 8.4.3 below for a full discussion of this case.
286 The leading text dealing with the law on powers is Thomas, *Powers*, 2nd edn, Oxford University Press, 2012.
287 *Re Gulbenkian* [1968] Ch 126; *McPhail v Doulton* [1970] 2 WLR 1110. See also [1984] Conv 304 (Martin) and 307 (Hayton).

The distinction between trusts and powers[288]

Trusts impose obligations on a trustee which the trustee is required to perform in obedience to the terms of that trust:[289] breach of such obligations will render the trustee personally liable to account to the beneficiaries for any loss suffered and thus to restore the value of the trust fund if the original trust property cannot be recovered.[290] Equally significantly, under a trust the beneficiary acquires proprietary rights in the trust property.[291] The trustee owes fiduciary obligations to the beneficiary further to the trust.[292]

By contrast, an ordinary power which is not in the form of a trust obligation, creates no such proprietary rights in any beneficiary but may impose fiduciary obligations on the holder of the power: such powers are referred to as 'mere powers' because they create no trust. There are two forms of power, for our purposes. The first form is a fiduciary power which gives the holder of the power the ability to do an act – for example, to pay money to one of an identified class of people – but which does not require that the holder of the power do anything. The second type of power is a power which is given to a person otherwise than as a fiduciary. The distinction between taking a power as a fiduciary and not as a fiduciary is that a fiduciary is required to act in the utmost good faith and is prevented from acting capriciously or irrationally, whereas the holder of a non-fiduciary power is not bound in this way.[293]

The distinction between the various forms of power is considered in greater detail below. At this stage it is sufficient to understand that a mere power may be exercised over a fund of money or other property so that it can be paid out (or 'appointed') to an identified class of people (or, 'objects'), but without obliging the holder of the power to make any such payment. An ordinary trust will oblige the trustees when and how to make transfers out of the trust fund to the beneficiaries. Between ordinary trusts imposing obligations on a trustee and mere powers granting an ability to advance property, there are 'powers in the form of a trust' which impose obligations on trustees but nevertheless give the trustees some discretion as to the manner in which their duties are to be performed. Such powers 'in the form of a trust' are known as 'discretionary trusts' in the modern jargon. Indeed, it is common to combine in one trust instrument many fixed and discretionary trusts, together with mere powers of appointment, so that the trustees are given a broad range of powers and duties both to achieve the settlor's wishes and yet also to provide for sufficient flexibility to cope with unexpected circumstances.

There is one principal distinction between mere powers and all forms of trusts: that relates to the entitlements which the objects of the various powers have. The object of a mere power has no right to any property until the holder of the power exercises her discretion and decides to make a payment to that object. By contrast, a beneficiary under even a discretionary trust has a right to compel the trustee's proper exercise of the power and also may have a proprietary right in the property over which the trustee is empowered to exercise her discretion.[294]

Combinations of different types of power and trust may be used by a settlor in a single trust instrument so as to achieve her goals. An example might help to make this combination

---

288 The most authoritative discussion of these principles is to be found in Thomas, 2012, paras 2.61–2.75.
289 *Westdeutsche Landesbank v Islington LBC* [1996] AC 669.
290 *Target Holdings v Redferns* [1996] 1 AC 421.
291 *Saunders v Vautier* (1841) 4 Beav 115.
292 *Westdeutsche Landesbank v Islington LBC* [1996] AC 669.
293 *Re Hay's ST* [1981] 3 All ER 786.
294 See para 4.1.2 below for a detailed discussion of the proprietary rights of beneficiaries and of the objects of mere powers in this context.

of different powers and trusts more comprehensible. Suppose that a settlor, Jane, wishes to provide for her husband, her two business partners, her two adult children, and her four sisters by means of a large settlement. Her intentions in relation to each of these people may be different, even though they will be set out in a single settlement. She may wish to create a bare trust in favour of her husband so that he is the only beneficiary in relation to some property she identified as being held for him exclusively: for example, the family home. She may wish to provide that some business assets are held for her business partners equally: in this sense she will impose a fixed trust so that the trustees are simply obliged to hold these business assets for the two partners equally. In relation to her children, she may want to require that the trustees pay money out to her children each year but she may also want the trustees to have a discretion as to which child is entitled to more money in any given year depending on how their fortunes fare in the future: therefore, she may require that the trustees make a payment to each child annually but she may decide to leave it up to the trustees to decide exactly how much each child should receive depending on their circumstances from year to year. This would be a discretionary trust which requires the trustees to make a payment each year but which nevertheless gives them scope to decide exactly how much that payment should amount to. Finally, Jane may decide that she wants to give her trustees the power to make a payment to any of her sisters if that sister is in serious financial difficulties: consequently, the trustees would be given a mere power such that they 'may' appoint a maximum amount of money to any sister who was in great financial difficulties but so that the money would otherwise be retained in the trust. The settlement we have constructed in this example contains a bare trust, a fixed trust in equal shares,[295] a discretionary trust, and a power to appoint money in favour of a total of nine different beneficiaries in relation to four separate funds of property. Because Jane cannot keep control over the property once it is settled on trust – even if she made herself a trustee she would still be bound by the terms of the trust – then she needs to construct a settlement which will be proof against future events. This combination of different types of powers and trusts can give the settlor great flexibility to ensure that her trustees will be able to cope with all sorts of eventualities in the future.

The most useful authority in this area is the judgment of Megarry VC in *Re Hay's ST*.[296] His Lordship presents a very clear discussion of the various forms of power in this area and gives clear indications of the applicable standards of certainty.[297] A discussion of these various powers and trusts follows in the next sections.

The example on which this section is based

It is important to decide on the facts of any case into which category the settlor's directions fall. In determining which type of power is created, there is no simpler method than reading the provisions of the trust closely to analyse the settlor's intention. It is possible for a settlor to create a trust and to give different people different types of power over the trust fund. The discussion

---

295 As to distributions among beneficiaries in 'equal shares', but equal shares between different groups, see *Sammut v Manzi* [2008] UKPC 58, [2009] 1 WLR 1834, where the court was required simply to apply the terms of the instrument.

296 [1981] 3 All ER 786.

297 For a wide-ranging scholarly discussion of trust powers, see the excellent book by Professor Thomas entitled quite simply *Powers*, 2012.

which follows will divide between the four main forms of trust by analysing a fictional trust provision. So, suppose the following provisions were included in a trust instrument:

I settle four separate amounts of £1,000 each to be held by T on trust for members of my family as follows:

Amount 1: so that T shall distribute all of the £1,000 equally to any of my grandchildren who have enrolled for a full-time university degree course before 1 October 2011, with the power to retain the whole of that £1,000 for the remainder beneficiary.

Amount 2: so that T may distribute all or part or none of the £1,000 to either of my daughters on their 40th birthday, with the power to retain the whole of that £1,000 for the remainder beneficiary.

Amount 3: so that T shall divide the £1,000 between any of my sons who become unem-ployed, with the power to retain the whole of that £1,000 for the remainder beneficiary.

Amount 4: so that X, as an old family friend, shall be entirely free in a personal capacity to pay as much of the £1,000 as he sees fit to any of my grandchildren whom he deems worthy of it, with the power to retain the whole of that £1,000 for the remainder beneficiary.

Any amount held in remainder shall be held on trust for my wife.

Each provision is analysed in turn in the discussion to follow as an example of the four main types of powers associated with a trust.

3.5.2 Fixed trusts

The nature of fixed trusts

A fixed trust refers to those situations in which the trust provision requires that the property be held for a fixed number of identified beneficiaries.[298] An example would be: '£10,000 to be held upon trust equally for the complete team of 11 Sunderland Football Club players who started the 1992 Cup Final at Wembley.' This is a fixed trust because the property is to be held 'equally' for this class of people such that it is necessary to know how many of them there are and who they are before the trust can be administered. It is only possible to divide property 'equally' if you know the number of people between whom that property is to be divided. In such a situation, it is necessary for the trustees to be able to produce a complete list of all the potential beneficiaries for there to be sufficient certainty as to the benefici-aries.[299] Thus, in the example given at the start of this section:

Amount 1: so that T shall distribute all of the £1,000 equally to any of my grandchildren who have enrolled for a full-time university degree course before 1 October 2011, with the power to retain the whole of that £1,000 for the remainder beneficiary.

---

298 See Thomas, 2012, para 3–03 *et seq.*
299 *IRC v Broadway Cottages* [1955] Ch 20.

The trustees are required to distribute the property equally and therefore they have no discretion about the amount of property to be held for each beneficiary: rather, the trustees are obliged to act in the limited manner so described. In such situations the trustee has only an obligation to act in the manner identified in the trust instrument but no discretion of any sort. The beneficiaries have proprietary rights in the equitable interest of the trust fund in accordance with the terms of the trust instrument.

The test for certainty of objects in relation to fixed trusts

In relation to establishing the certainty of objects under a fixed trust, it is necessary for the trustees to be able to compile a complete list of the beneficiaries, as required by *IRC v Broadway Cottages*[300] and by *dicta* of Lord Upjohn in *Re Gulbenkian*.[301] That means that the trustee must be able to name each possible beneficiary or to identify all of the members of the appropriate class. If there are any objects about whom the trustee could not be certain, or if the trustee is not able to compile such a complete list, then the trust will be void for uncertainty. If the identity of the membership of the class cannot be known until an identified time in the future at which the trust is to be performed, then that will be permitted provided that it will be possible to compile a complete list of the members of that class at that time.[302]

3.5.3 Fiduciary mere powers: the power of appointment

The permissive nature of fiduciary mere powers

The more difficult category is the situation in which a trustee, or some other person acting in a fiduciary capacity, is granted a 'mere power'[303] which is not a fully fledged trust obligation but which gives the holder of the power the *ability* to exercise that power without any obligation to do so. (For the purposes of this discussion, we shall describe the person entitled to exercise the power as being a 'trustee' for ease of reference.)[304] An example of a fiduciary mere power would be 'the trustee *may* advance £1,000 to X' as opposed to an example of a trust obligation which might read 'the trustee *shall* pay £1,000 to X annually'. In the former case, the trustee is able to pay £1,000 but is under no compulsion to do so, whereas the second example compels the trustee to pay £1,000 to X. However, the fiduciary exercising a fiduciary mere power cannot act purely capriciously in relation to that power. Rather, the trustee is under an obligation to exercise that power reasonably and to be able to justify its exercise. As Megarry VC put it in *Re Hay's ST*:[305]

---

300 [1955] Ch 20, 29, *per* Jenkins LJ; and also required at first instance by Wynn-Parry J at [1954] 1 All ER 878, 881.

301 [1970] AC 508, at 524. Cf Matthews (1984) Conv 22. Whereas *Re Gulbenkian* is a case dealing specifically with a mere power, Lord Upjohn did confirm that this was the test for certainty for fixed trusts.

302 *Swain v Law Society* [1981] 3 All ER 797, 822, *per* Fox LJ.

303 Also referred to as a 'power of appointment'.

304 This is so given that such mere powers may commonly be contained in trust instruments so as to qualify fixed trusts or to act in their own right, as well as existing at large.

305 [1981] 3 All ER 786, 791. That the court will not interfere with the competence of the trustees to make the decision to appoint property, provided that is done properly, emerges from *Breadner v Granville-Grossman* [2000] 4 All ER 705.

A mere power is very different [from an ordinary trust obligation]. Normally the trustee is not bound to exercise it, and the court will not compel him to do so. That, however, does not mean that he can simply fold his hands and ignore it, for normally he must from time to time consider whether or not to exercise the power, and the court may direct him to do this.

Therefore, we see the situation in which the trustee is given permission to exercise a power without an obligation; the trustee is obliged only to consider whether or not that power should be exercised.[306] It remains open to the trustee, however, to decide whether or not to exercise the power in fact. Importantly, this power-holder is required to act as a fiduciary. So, in contradistinction to a person exercising a purely personal power in a non-fiduciary capacity, the trustee is required to act responsibly. It is that responsibility which the court is able to review. Thus, in the following example, the trustee is permitted to exercise a power of appointment over a fund of £1,000 but does not bear an obligation to carry it out:

Amount 2: so that T may distribute all or part or none of the £1,000 to either of my daughters on their 40th birthday, with the power to retain the whole of that £1,000 for the remainder beneficiary.

There is a permission, evidenced by the word 'may', for the trustee to pay nothing at all or a maximum of £1,000 to any one of a class of beneficiaries as the trustee decides. The second half of the sentence creates a power over any money which is not paid to the daughters. Therefore, there is a mere power which acts as a condition precedent to the trust obligation to hold any residue for the remainder beneficiary.

The test for certainty of objects in relation to fiduciary mere powers

The leading case dealing with fiduciary mere powers is the decision of the House of Lords in *Re Gulbenkian.*[307] This case established a test which we shall refer to as the 'is or is not' test, which means that the trustees must be able to decide whether any hypothetical beneficiary is or is not within the class of objects. This rule is explained further below. *Re Gulbenkian* reversed the previous rule which had required the trustees to be able to draw up a complete list of beneficiaries:[308] this older approach had meant that, if it was not possible for the trustees to compile a complete list of the class of beneficiaries in advance of exercising the trust, then the trust would be held to be void. The majority of the House of Lords in *Re Gulbenkian* took a different approach. It was found instead that for a trust to be valid the trustees must be able to say of any postulant,[309] coming before the trustees claiming to be a beneficiary, that that person was either within the class of beneficiaries or was not within the class of beneficiaries. In short, to validate a fiduciary mere power you must be able to tell whether any given individual 'is or is not' within the class of objects.[310] As Lord Upjohn put it: 'the trustees, or

---

306 *Re Gestetner* [1953] Ch 672, 688 *per* Harman J.
307 [1968] Ch 126.
308 Cf *Re Gestetner* [1953] 2 WLR 1033.
309 A 'postulant', a term used in the cases, means a person claiming entitlement under a trust or a power, or a hypothetical person whose potential entitlement is at issue.
310 *Re Gulbenkian* [1968] Ch 785, 787, *per* Lord Reid.

the court, must be able to say with certainty who is within and who is without the power'.[311]
If there is even one person in relation to whom the trustees cannot decide whether or not she
falls within the class of objects, then the trust is invalid. This 'is or is not' test is consequently
still a strict test, whereby any uncertainty as to whether or not any hypothetical postulant is
or is not within the class of objects will invalidate the fiduciary mere power.

It may be helpful to take an example to illustrate how this test works. Suppose a fiduciary
mere power contained in a trust document which provided that 'the trustees may pay £10,000
to any of my good friends whom they shall deem worthy of it'. The problem of certainty of
objects here is bound up in the use of the expression 'my good friends'. We must establish
whether or not the objects of this power – the settlor's 'good friends' – are sufficiently
certain. The trustees are bound by the 'is or is not' test. Let us try and bring this test to life.
We should imagine the trustees sitting in a room behind a long desk facing the door. One by
one a hypothetical queue of people come into the room claiming to fall within the class of
objects. These claimants are 'the postulants'. For the power to be valid, the trustees must be
able to say of any person who may come through the door claiming to fall within the class
whether or not that person is indeed within or outside the class of objects. That means they
must be able to say with certainty either that each postulant is or that each postulant is not
within the definition of the class. If there is even one postulant about whom they could not
be certain, then the power will be void.

So, in relation to the term 'my good friends' if there is likely to be any conceptual uncertainty as to what is meant by the term 'good friends' then the power will be void. The cases
on the term 'good friends' are considered later in this chapter: but it is suggested that in
general terms that expression is likely to be uncertain because, even if the trustees can distinguish 'friends' from 'mere acquaintances' and so on, there is then the added problem of
knowing what a 'good' friend is as opposed to an 'ordinary' friend or a casual acquaintance,
and so on.

This 'is or is not' test is quite a strict one – even though it is slightly more relaxed than the
old 'complete list' test,[312] which we considered above in relation to fixed trusts. The application of the complete list test would invalidate any power for which it would be impossible to
produce a complete list of all of the objects of that power; whereas the 'is or is not' test
means that the trustees do not need to know the identity of all of the objects in advance and
instead may be able to wait to examine each postulant as circumstances arise. The reason for
this relaxation in the test for fiduciary mere powers in *Re Gulbenkian*[313] was that in relation
to mere powers the trustee is not compelled to carry out her duties under the trust.
Consequently, it was considered inconsistent to require the trustee to draw up a fixed list of
the potential beneficiaries in whose favour the discretion could be exercised when the trustee
was not necessarily even required to perform her power.

The case of *Re Gulbenkian* itself was concerned with the estate of Mr Gulbenkian,[314] who
had created a will to provide bequests for 'any person and his remoter issue . . . and any
person . . . in whose house or apartment or in whose company or under whose care or control
or by or with whom he may from time to time be employed or residing'. The question arose

---

311 *Ibid* at 794, *per* Lord Upjohn.
312 Considered at para 3.5.5 below.
313 [1968] Ch 126.
314 Nubar Gulbenkian was a famous figure in 1960s London. Alan Bennett, in his book *Telling Tales*, 2000, refers
     to an occasion on which he saw Nubar Gulbenkian emerging from his familiar gold-plated taxi in Bond Street.

whether or not this expression was too uncertain because it did not define the class of objects of the trust sufficiently clearly. On the facts of this case it was held that this provision was sufficiently certain.[315] Lord Upjohn rejected a test previously propounded by the Court of Appeal in *Re Allen*[316] to the effect that even if only one person could be demonstrated to have fallen within the test then the power should be held to be valid so that property could be distributed among those people who did satisfy the test.[317] Instead, Lord Upjohn approved a test outlined in *Re Gestetner*[318] to the effect that it must be possible for the beneficiaries to prevent the trustees applying the trust property beyond the scope of their powers. Consequently, this approach requires potential beneficiaries to be able to control the trustees and that to be able to control the trustees it must be known what the extent of the trustees' powers are. To know what the extent of the trustees' powers are, it must be possible to know whether or not any people to whom the trustees purport to transfer trust property are within the class of beneficiaries. And to know whether or not any given people fall within the class of beneficiaries the terms of the trust instrument must allow one to know whether or not any given postulant is or is not within the class of beneficiaries. It is only in the last paragraph of his speech that Lord Upjohn expressed unambiguous support for the 'is or is not' test; this expression was also used by Lord Reid. What we must do now, however, is to consider how subsequent cases have sought to manipulate the 'is or is not' test so as to validate powers which the judges considered to be worthy of preservation. In the discussion below, we consider some issues with the *Gulbenkian* decision; but before then we will consider some later decisions which have taken different approaches from *Gulbenkian on their own facts*.

Alternative approaches to certainty of objects in relation to fiduciary mere powers

The shortcoming of the *Gulbenkian* test is that trusts which are certain as to 99% of postulants may fail because 1% of postulants are of a sort which are difficult to reconcile with the definition of the class of objects provided for under the terms of the trust. In short, theoretical difficulties might lead to the avoidance of otherwise perfectly serviceable trusts. Needless to say, there have been subsequent cases in which the courts have sought to give effect to trusts which would have fallen foul of a literal interpretation of the 'is or is not' test.

The *Gulbenkian* test is a strict one on its own terms in that the presence of a single unallocated postulant means that the trust will be held invalid. However, in *Re Barlow*,[319] the court attempted to mitigate the full extent of that approach. In *Re Barlow*, a testatrix provided an option for any of her 'family or friends' to purchase paintings at a specially low price. Under a strict application of the *Gulbenkian* test, this trust would have failed for uncertainty on the basis that the class of beneficiaries (here in particular the problematic category 'friends') could not include or exclude all potential claimants. However, Browne-Wilkinson J held that the bequest was valid, on three bases. First, and most importantly, the bequest was construed by Browne-Wilkinson J as disclosing an intention to make a series of identical, individual gifts to anyone who could prove that they personally fell within the core of the

---

315   Thus overruling the decision of Harman J in *Re Gresham's Settlement* [1956] 1 WLR 573, [1956] 2 All ER 193, dealing with a very similar trust provision.
316   In the Court of Appeal [1968] Ch 126, 134E, [1967] 3 All ER 15, 18.
317   [1968] Ch 126, 133.
318   [1953] 2 WLR 1033.
319   [1979] 1 WLR 278.

beneficial class intended by the testatrix: therefore, the bequest was found to constitute a series of gifts and not a power nor a trust at all. If it was a gift then no problem of certainty of objects in trusts law arose at all: certainty of objects is only an issue if the structure in question is a trust, as opposed to something else. Thus, *Barlow* provides an analytical approach which mitigates the full effect of the strict 'is or is not' test where the court is able to construe the settlor's true intention to be to make a gift (or outright transfer) of property rather than a trust at all. Thus, we encounter a simple way of avoiding formalities required for the creation of a trust: structure or interpret the disposition otherwise than as a trust.

Secondly, Browne-Wilkinson J was also persuaded that, *on the facts of that case specifically*, the proposed distribution of property which the trustees were seeking the court's permission to make, was a reasonable one which would satisfy the testator's intention. Thirdly, his Lordship found that term 'friends' could be rendered conceptually certain as considered below in relation to the cases on the term 'friends'. We shall return to these second and third aspects of the judgment later: for now we should focus on the reclassification of the power as being a gift. The significance on the facts of this case of the power being held to be in fact a gift is that the problem of certainty of objects only relates to the law of trusts and the law on powers, it is not a problem in the law of gift. Consequently, Browne-Wilkinson J had reached a pragmatic solution to the problem of validating this particular bequest in spite of the rules as to certainty of objects: if it can be analysed as a series of gifts, then no question of trusts law arises.

There are potential problems with the approach adopted in *Barlow*. The primary problem relates to the distribution of a fixed number of paintings on the facts of that case, but could conceivably apply to other forms of property. Given that the trustees are entitled to distribute property to people about whose credentials they are satisfied, it is possible that further beneficiaries claiming also to be entitled will emerge after all of the property has been distributed. Therefore, the looser test creates the possibility that the trustees will begin to exercise their powers without having been required to conduct a comprehensive analysis of the objects of their power. The question therefore arises whether it would have been better to have had a fixed list approach where there is a finite amount of tangible property rather than entitlement to income derived from a capital fund.[320] The latter example would make it possible for other beneficiaries who only came to light subsequently to be added to the class of entitled beneficiaries. With reference to the former, the property may be extinguished before all the potential beneficiaries are satisfied. In short, the reason for the decision in *Barlow* was that there was not perceived to be any problem in these circumstances of more beneficiaries emerging. Rather, the court wanted to enable the trustees to make some distributions to those beneficiaries already identified.

3.5.4 Discretionary trust

The obligatory nature of a discretionary trust

The discretionary trust *requires* that the trustees exercise their discretion and carry out their power, rather than being a fiduciary mere power which enables (but does not require) the exercise of their trust obligations. In the following example, the terms of the trust provide that the trustee 'shall' exercise the discretion, thus making its exercise by the trustee compulsory:

---

320 See para 3.5.5 below.

Amount 3: so that T shall divide the £1,000 between any of my sons who become unem-
ployed, with the power to retain the whole of that £1,000 for the remainder beneficiary.

In this example, T is subject to a discretionary trust because the trust provides that 'T shall divide the £1,000': the word 'shall' indicates compulsion and thereby a discretionary trust power rather than a mere power. The further part of the provision, that T has the 'power to retain the whole of that £1,000', should be interpreted as being a mere power – that is, T is able to retain the £1,000 if she chooses but is not required to do so. Such combinations of powers are common in trust deeds to enable the settlor to provide for a suitable range of flexibility in the management and operation of the trust in the event that any one beneficiary subsequently comes to have more urgent needs than was the case when the settlor drafted the trust, particularly if the settlor then chooses to make herself a trustee as well, thus retaining ongoing practical control over the trust.

The leading case in relation to certainty of objects under a discretionary trust power

The leading case regarding the test for certainty in relation to discretionary trusts is the decision of the House of Lords in *McPhail v Doulton*.[321] Their Lordships adopted the *Re Gulbenkian*[322] test (the 'is or is not' test) for discretionary trusts. The tests for mere powers and discretionary trusts are therefore brought into line. As such, it is comparatively unimportant, for practical purposes, to attempt to draw any distinction between them. In practice, there is little substantive difference between the situation in which a trustee is exercising a permissive mere power and the situation in which the trustee is exercising a discretionary trust. In both circumstances, the trustee is prevented from acting totally capriciously and is obliged to consider the exercise of her power in accordance with the terms of the power itself. Therefore, the need to divide strictly between the two categories of power has waned slightly.[323]

The facts in *McPhail v Doulton*[324] were that payments were to be made in favour of 'employees, ex-officers or ex-employees of the Company or any relatives or dependants of any such persons'. The question of uncertainty surrounded the expression 'relatives and dependants' in particular. The issue arose as to the nature of the power and, importantly, as to the appropriate test to decide the question of certainty of beneficiaries. It was found that the application of the formerly applicable test in *IRC v Broadway Cottages*[325] required that a complete list of beneficiaries be capable of being drawn up by the trustees. However, requiring that there is no need for a complete list to be capable of being drawn up in advance, but rather that it be possible to say of any given postulant whether or not her case was sufficiently certain, would remove the uncertainty attached to trusts in favour of family or relatives in most circumstances.

The House of Lords in *McPhail v Doulton* adopted the 'is or is not' test set out in *Re Gulbenkian* in relation to discretionary trusts. Therefore, in considering the certainty of beneficiaries under a discretionary trust, it must be possible for the trustees to say of any

---

321   [1970] 2 WLR 1110.
322   [1968] Ch 126.
323   See Thomas, 2012, which is the most authoritative text on the question of trust and other similar powers.
324   [1970] 2 WLR 1110.
325   [1955] Ch 20.

postulant whether that person is or is not within the class of beneficiaries: if it is impossible to tell whether or not one individual falls within the class or not, that trust power fails. On the facts of the case, the House of Lords decided that the term 'relative' could be rendered certain if it were interpreted to mean 'descendants of a common ancestor', although this writer finds that expression every bit as confusing as the term 'relative'.[326]

Alternative approaches to the test in McPhail v Doulton

The use of the *Gulbenkian* approach in *McPhail* did therefore import the problem identified above in relation to *Gulbenkian*, that the presence of a single postulant who could not be categorised as being or not being within the class of beneficiaries would invalidate the trust. Consequently, the Court of Appeal sought to mitigate the effect of the *McPhail* decision in *Re Baden (No 2)*[327] to validate a trust which would otherwise have been invalid under the *McPhail* test. The case concerned (again) provisions relying on the vague term 'relative'. In accordance with *McPhail*, it was held that 'relative' could be explained (equally perplexingly) as referring to 'descendants of a common ancestor' and therefore rendered conceptually certain. However, it was acknowledged that there might nevertheless be evidential problems in connection with proving that individuals are or are not relatives (for example, in finding birth certificates) and also ascertainability problems in finding all the relatives who might have died or moved away.

All three judges in the Court of Appeal gave separate judgments: each attempted to paint a gloss on the decision in *McPhail* which would validate the trust before them. In the judgment of Stamp LJ, it was held that the definition of 'relatives' should be restricted to 'statutory next of kin' rather than 'descendants of a common ancestor' because the latter was too broad. This approach concentrates specifically on the facts – although it doubts the approach to the term 'relatives' which was followed in the House of Lords.

The judgment of Sachs LJ approached the matter very differently[328] by placing a burden of proof on the beneficiaries, rather than leaving it to the trustees to demonstrate that the trust was valid. In his Lordship's words: 'Once the class of persons to be benefited is conceptually certain it then becomes a question of fact to be determined on evidence whether any postulant has on inquiry been proved to be within it; if he is not so proved, then he is not in it . . .'[329] In short, the onus was placed on the claimants to prove themselves to be a 'relative' within the terms of the trust. If they could not, they were deemed not to be a relative. In this way, the literal meaning of the 'is or is not' test is preserved, even though the logic derived from *IRC v Broadway Cottages*[330] of requiring the trustees to demonstrate the validity of the trust is replaced by making the establishment of certainty simply a matter of evidence. Sachs LJ was careful not to seem to disagree with the House of Lords in *McPhail v Doulton* – rather, his approach preserved the literal force of that test but instead ensured that more trusts were likely to be validated on the basis that if a claimant cannot prove that she either is or is not within the

---

326 Who are one's common ancestors after all? Grandparents? Great-grandparents? A Christian might trace this back to Adam and Eve; an evolutionist to a single ape or microbe.

327 [1973] Ch 9.

328 From the outset of his judgment it was clear that Sachs LJ was annoyed that this case (which had been to the House of Lords already as *McPhail v Doulton*) had taken 12 years in total to reach the Court of Appeal.

329 [1973] Ch 9, 19.

330 [1955] Ch 20.

class of beneficiaries, then she will be deemed not to be within that class. Therefore, the test remains intact, but many more trusts are likely to be validated because of the reversal of the onus of proof. It should be borne in mind, as Sachs LJ made plain in his judgment, that this does not mean that every trust will be validated: there will still be trusts provisions which are so vague that it will be impossible to know what the concept embodied in the provisions was intended to mean in any event (as considered below in relation to 'conceptual uncertainty').

The judgment of Megaw LJ in *Re Baden (No 2)*[331] returned to the logic of the decision in *Re Allen*[332] in seeking to validate those trusts in which there are a substantial number of postulants about whom one can be certain. Megaw LJ held that the trust would be held to be valid despite some potential uncertainties as to a number of postulants, provided that there was a distinct core number of beneficiaries who could be said to satisfy the terms of the power: that is, the trust would be valid provided that there were a substantial number of postulants about whom one could be certain. The trust power would not be held to be void on the basis that there is a small number of postulants about whom the trustees are uncertain. The principal concern with the 'is or is not' test was the requirement that the trustees would be required, on a literal application of that test, to prove that someone 'is not' within the class of objects rather than focusing instead on the existence of an appreciable number of people who satisfy the class of objects.[333]

(It should not be forgotten that the approach set out in *Re Barlow*[334] above – that is, identifying in the settlor an intention to make a gift rather than a trust – could also be deployed in this context. Equally, there is no reason in principle why the arguments in *Re Baden (No 2)* could not be applied to fiduciary mere powers.)

Re-reading the 'is or is not' cases: what did Lord Upjohn mean to decide in Re Gulbenkian?

The purpose of this section is to drill down a little more deeply into the cases on certainty of objects relating to discretionary trusts and fiduciary mere powers. We will learn one important lesson in so doing: it is common for a case to be understood in later decisions and even in textbooks as having established a particular rule, when in fact the judge in that original case might not have meant that at all. It is a little like Humphrey Bogart in the classic, black-and-white film *Casablanca*, who is reputed to have muttered to the piano player in his favourite bar the words 'Play it again, Sam'. Latterly, Woody Allen made a film called *Play it Again, Sam* which imagined what it would be like to have Humphrey Bogart's character advising a young man on every step of his love life. Most impersonations of Humphrey Bogart have him saying 'Play it again, Sam' as he is supposed to have done in *Casablanca*. However, if you sit down to watch *Casablanca*, Humphrey Bogart does not actually say 'Play it again, Sam' at all.[335] Instead, the legend has grown up that that is what he said. A legend perpetuated by lots of television impressionists and by Woody Allen. This is the

331 [1973] Ch 9.
332 [1953] Ch 810.
333 [1973] Ch 9, 22.
334 *Re Barlow* [1979] 1 WLR 278.
335 At one stage Ingrid Bergman's character almost says this (she is mumbling, so it is difficult to hear exactly what she says but it is not exactly 'Play it again, Sam') and Humphrey Bogart's character says a few things to Sam about the music he is playing but never exactly 'Play it again, Sam'. It is the perfect black-and-white film for a rainy day. So is Woody Allen's film come to that.

legend of what Humphrey Bogart is supposed to have said in *Casablanca*; we are now going to consider the similar legend of what Lord Upjohn is supposed to have said in *Re Gulbenkian*.

I am going to suggest to you now that *Re Gulbenkian* is similar to *Casablanca* in that it is a case which is commonly understood to have established a given rule when on a closer reading it might not have done so. We have discussed the test established in *Re Gulbenkian* for certainty of objects in relation to mere powers as being the 'is or is not' test. However, when you go to read *Re Gulbenkian* in the original, it is not clear that that was what their Lordships intended to hold. What *is* clear is that Lord Wilberforce and the majority of the House of Lords in the subsequent case of *McPhail v Doulton* tell us that *Re Gulbenkian* must be taken as authority for creating the 'is or is not' test for certainty of objects under mere powers. Consequently, it is now correct to say that the test for certainty of objects in relation to mere powers is the 'is or is not' test because we must follow the most recent decision of the House of Lords. So, the legend of *Re Gulbenkian* is that it created the 'is or is not' test. But we must now look a little more closely at these cases.

To begin at the beginning, Lord Hodson had been one of the Court of Appeal judges in *IRC v Broadway Cottages* who had held that a complete list of objects was required for the validity of a fixed trust. In his speech in *Re Gulbenkian*, Lord Hodson supported the 'complete list test' in *IRC v Broadway Cottages* as being the most appropriate test for discretionary trusts, and in a sense for mere powers as well. Lord Hodson's particular concern was that the difference between trusts and powers should be maintained and that there was consequently a need for a stricter test for discretionary trusts than was needed for mere powers. The problem identified with the 'is or is not' test is that it does not require the fiduciary to know all of the members of the class before acting; instead, the trustees seem to have a power to limit their decisions to whichever objects of the trust actually turn up. Lord Guest concurred with Lord Hodson. However, both Lord Hodson and Lord Guest also concurred with Lord Upjohn.

For the bulk of Lord Upjohn's speech, his Lordship circled round the issues and seemed to express support for the 'complete list' test set out in *IRC v Broadway Cottages* at one stage, except in relation to mere powers. It is only in the last paragraph of his speech that he held unambiguously that it is necessary to know whether or not any given person is or is not with the class of objects. Therefore, Lord Upjohn did not in fact seem to express clear support for the 'is or is not' test to the exclusion of all other tests throughout his speech. Lord Reid used the expression 'is or is not' in his speech and Lord Reid criticised both the decision in *Broadway Cottages* for being too restrictive and this area of law in general for being over-burdened with technicality. Consequently we can see that Lord Reid supported the 'is or is not' test, whereas Lord Upjohn did not express his unequivocal agreement with it until the final paragraph of his speech. Furthermore, because *Re Gulbenkian* related only to powers, it is unclear which test Lord Upjohn intended to apply in cases involving discretionary trusts.

We then move on the decision of the House of Lords in *McPhail v Doulton* a short time later, in which Lord Upjohn did not appear. Instead it is Lord Wilberforce who suggested that Lord Upjohn's intention in *Re Gulbenkian* should be understood as having been to establish an 'is or is not' test for discretionary trusts as well as for mere powers. This point is important: it is Lord Wilberforce's interpretation that Lord Upjohn had meant to apply the 'is or is not' test and that he could be taken to have intended it to apply to discretionary trusts as well as mere powers, even though it is not absolutely clear that Lord Upjohn necessarily intended to hold anything of the sort on the face of his speech. When we come to the speeches of Lords Hodson and Guest in *McPhail v Doulton* we see that again they concurred with one another. Lord Hodson was clear in his opinion. As far as he was concerned, the only reason that he and Lord Guest had concurred with Lord Upjohn in *Re Gulbenkian* was because they had understood Lord Upjohn to be supporting the notion that the complete list test from *IRC v Broadway Cottages* was being applied to discretionary trusts (and arguably, on his Lordship's account, even to mere powers).[336] That is, the fiduciary would need to know all the objects in advance. Lords Hodson and Guest are in the minority in *McPhail v Doulton* and therefore the majority (following Lord Wilberforce) established two principles: first, that the test of certainty of objects for mere powers should be understood as being the 'is or is not' test; and, secondly, that the test of certainty of objects for discretionary trusts should also be the 'is or is not' test. This is important: those two judges were significant in establishing the majority in *Re Gulbenkian* but they did not think that Lord Upjohn was deciding what Lord Wilberforce has taken him to mean subsequently. Thus we have established a legend from *Re Gulbenkian*, even though it is not clear that the majority of the House of Lords in that case intended it to be the test for future cases.

There are two points of view about what precisely the 'is or is not' test might mean. This test has been explained already on the basis that it means that the trustees must consider whether or not any *hypothetical*, possible postulant would either fall clearly within or without the class. An alternative interpretation of the test, which makes it more likely to be satisfied, is that the trustees need only measure the certainty of objects on the basis of the postulants who *actually do come forward*. Lord Hodson considers that the test should refer to hypothetical postulants generally and that the test in relation to trusts (whether fixed or discretionary trusts) should be stringent. Lord Hodson believed that Lord Wilberforce was prepared to narrow the postulants to those people who actually turn up and ask the trustees to consider only them. Clearly, if the trustees only had to make their minds up about the people who actually appeared in front of them then it would be much more likely that the 'is or is not' test would be satisfied than if the trustees had to be satisfied about any possible, hypothetical postulant. It is suggested that the speech of Lord Upjohn does not suggest only considering those who actually come forward. The test is whether or not the trustees can be satisfied about who is within and who is without the beneficial class in general terms. That, it is suggested, relates to all possible hypothetical objects of the trust or power.

This is a unique feature of common law systems. Ideas go in and out of fashion over time. Understandings of what judges meant by the words they used can also change over time, unless those earlier judges make their meaning very clear indeed. Instead, during the course of a long judgment it is likely that a judge will express his ideas in many different ways with the result that, when we come to read those words many years later, we might be able to find different passages which appear to advance different points of view. Lord Upjohn's speech in *Re Gulbenkian* is a good example of this phenomenon: read it for yourself and identify passages which appear to support the *Broadway Cottages* test and other passages which appear to support the 'is or is not' test, and decide for yourself. In coming to write a legal textbook, I am required to set out the current position in trusts law. The current position must be that we follow the most recent House of Lords decision in *McPhail v Doulton* and its interpretation of the decision in *Re Gulbenkian*. However, as legal scholars, you and I must also be prepared to look a little more closely at what those judges actually said and what the underlying arguments seem to be.

---

336 Notably, Lord Hodson had appeared, *sub nom* Hodson LJ, in *IRC v Broadway Cottages*, so in the two House of Lords cases he was simply re-affirming (or so he believed) his concurrence with the complete list test in *Broadway Cottages*.

The rights of beneficiaries under discretionary trusts

The nature of the rights of the object of a discretionary trust is considered below in section 4.1.2.

3.5.5 Personal powers

The non-fiduciary nature of a personal power

A personal power is a power given to an individual without making that person subject to any fiduciary duty in relation to the exercise of that power.[337] An example of a personal power would be as follows, quoting from the example given above:

> *Amount 4: so that X, as an old family friend, shall be entirely free in a personal capacity to pay as much of the £1,000 as he sees fit to any of my grandchildren whom he deems worthy of it, with the power to retain the whole of that £1,000 for the remainder beneficiary.*

This power would be said to be a personal power in that it is explicit that X is to exercise his discretion not as a fiduciary, but rather as an ordinary person without the constraints of demonstrating that he has acted in accordance with the terms of fiduciary office (this is evident from the words 'entirely free in a personal capacity'). A power given to a person outside any fiduciary capacity entitles that person to act in any way that he sees fit within the law generally and within the terms of the power.[338] In this example, therefore, X can choose to pay all of the money to a favourite grandchild, but is not permitted to do anything which would be a criminal offence and is not empowered to pay more than the £1,000 which is available.

That a personal power may not be invalidated on grounds of uncertainty of objects

In the decision of Megarry VC in *Re Hay's ST*,[339] it was found that the holder of a personal power cannot have it invalidated on the specific ground of uncertainty of objects.[340] His Lordship held that 'it is plain that if a power of appointment is given to a person who is not in a fiduciary position, there is nothing in the width of the power which invalidates it *per se*', meaning that a personal power will not be void for uncertainty no matter how vague its terms may be. This point is echoed in *Re Wright*[341] where it was held that the holder of the power 'is entitled to prefer one object to another from any motive he pleases, and however capriciously he exercises the power the Court will uphold it'. The thinking behind this principle is that it is open to a holder of a personal power to exercise or not exercise that power precisely as she sees fit because it is a power which is personal to her and not a power which she holds further to any fiduciary office. This enables the holder of the power to act

---

337 *Re Hay's ST* [1981] 3 All ER 786.
338 *Ibid.*
339 *Ibid.*
340 However, if the holder of the power purports to act beyond the scope of that power then such excessive exercise will be void, on which see para 10.5.1.
341 [1920] 1 Ch 108, 118.

capriciously, without any need to justify the reasons for that decision. This situation should be compared with that of the holder of a fiduciary power, in that a fiduciary must reflect upon whether or not to exercise that power, as considered below. Similarly, the holder of a discretionary trust power must be assiduous in surveying the range of objects and may not act capriciously. The reason for a personal power not being justiciable on grounds of uncertainty of objects is simply that the holder of the power is not acting in a fiduciary capacity, by definition, and therefore there is no reason for seeking to control the objects in whose favour that person exercises their power as though the holder of the power was a fiduciary. This is the approach taken by David Hayton.[342]

In short, personal powers are not justiciable on the basis that the objects of the power are uncertain.[343] In the alternative, powers exercised by fiduciaries must not be exercised capriciously. In contrast with personal powers, it could be said that fiduciaries' powers are subject to 'negative justiciability': that is, if fiduciaries act improperly their powers will be declared null and void by the court, otherwise they will be permitted to do whatever they want.

The breadth of this principle must be clearly understood, however. Personal powers, like any other form of power, may be held to be void if the power is exercised in excess of its stated terms or if it is exercised so as to constitute a fraud on the power. So, for example, in relation to the excessive exercise of a power, if the power is a power to spend £1,000 on a given purpose, and if the holder of the power purports to spend £2,500, then the excessive portion of the exercise of that power will be void: that is, the £1,500 will be recoverable from the holder of the power. In relation to a fraud on the power, if the holder of the power purported to exercise the power so as to benefit someone who was evidently not intended to benefit from it (for example, such as the power holder herself without being permitted to do so by the terms of the power) then that purported exercise of that power would be void.[344] These are different issues from saying that a personal power may not be invalidated on the ground of the uncertainty of the identity of the objects of that power: it is a different matter altogether from certainty of objects.

There are commentators whose preference is for saying that personal powers must nevertheless be conceptually certain.[345] The basis for this argument is that if the holder of the power does not know what the terms of her power mean then it cannot be possible for the court to know whether or not that power has been exercised properly. However, if the power is a personal power to advance property between a testator's 'friends' then the holder of the power is not required to justify her actions as a fiduciary would have to and so can advance the property to people who are undoubtedly friends, even though there may be some other people about whom it is not possible to know with certainty that they are friends.[346] This is, in essence, the approach which Browne-Wilkinson J took in *Re Barlow*, as considered above: that is, the court may approve a scheme for the distribution of property even if there may be some uncertainty at the edges of the terms of the power. It could be said, of course, that this is just to unearth the *Re Allen* test in relation to questions of uncertainty of objects in relation to personal powers. The question would be as to personal powers which were drafted even more vaguely and about which it would be impossible to know who was intended to take a

---

342   Hayton and Mitchell, 2005, para 3–103. See also Emery (1982) 98 LQR 551, especially at 582.
343   *Re Leek* [1967] Ch 1061, 1076.
344   *Re Somes* [1896] 1 Ch 250, 255; *Palmer v Locke* (1880) 15 Ch D 294, 302.
345   See, for example, the breadth of arguments canvassed in Thomas and Hudson, 2010, para 4.29.
346   Emery (1982) 98 LQR 551; Thomas and Hudson, 2010, para 4.28.

benefit at all, such as 'subject to a personal power to distribute this property to nice people I have met during my lifetime': it is suggested. Notably, though, the *dicta* set out above from *Re Wright* and from *Re Hay's ST* do permit the holder of the power to exercise even these powers. While the alternative approach – suggesting that personal powers could be invalidated on grounds of conceptual uncertainty – may have some academic support, it can only apply in exceptional or marginal cases in any event. More significantly there is no clear judicial statement to support it; whereas the proposition that personal powers are generally not susceptible to justiciability in relation to certainty of objects does have the judicial support advanced above.[347]

Personal powers embedded in trust instruments

It is possible that there could be a category of personal power which empowers a person to decide on the destination of trust property.[348] For such a power to be a personal power, as opposed to a fiduciary power, that holder of that power must not be under any obligation to exercise nor to preserve it.[349] For example, if this power is exercisable only in default of trustees making some other appointment, then it may be a purely personal power if its exercise may not be necessary and especially if the holder of the power is not also a trustee. So, in *Mettoy Pensions v Evans*,[350] where a company was given 'absolute discretion' in a trust instrument as to the manner in which it was to deal with any surplus generated by a pension fund, then the company should be found to have only a personal power, as opposed to a fiduciary power, over the use of that money. On the facts, however, it was held that the trustees had to be acting in a fiduciary capacity. The rationale for arguing that this power was a personal power was that there may not have been any surplus generated by the pension fund and also because the company was empowered to act in its absolute discretion in deciding how to use that property, as opposed to being required to act within the strictures of fiduciary obligations when dealing with that property.[351] On the facts, however, trustees managing a pension fund were necessarily acting as fiduciaries, thus demonstrating the unlikelihood of finding that trustees are ever acting in a purely personal capacity.

3.5.6 Bare trusts

This category is not considered separately in the literature on this particular topic and is really a form of fixed trust for these purposes; however, it appears that we can make some more sense of the subject by dealing with it as a separate category. A bare trust is a trust under which the trustee holds property on trust for a single, specified beneficiary without any contingencies or terms governing the trust. Many trust obligations take this simple form. To consider the preceding trust obligations as the only possibilities is to ignore this more

---

347 There is a sense in which it could be an excessive exercise of a power to purport to appoint property to a person who is beyond the scope of the power, but what is clear is that Megarry VC was treating these concepts separately.

348 *Re Mettoy Pension Trustees Ltd v Evans* [1990] 1 WLR 1587, 1613, *per* Warner J. See also *Re Mills* [1930] 1 Ch 654; *Re Greaves* [1954] Ch 434.

349 *Re Mettoy Pension Trustees Ltd v Evans* [1990] 1 WLR 1587.

350 [1990] 1 WLR 1587.

351 *Ibid.*

straightforward category. Therefore, the remainder provision in the example given at the beginning of this section appears to be a clear example of a bare trust:

Any amount held in remainder shall be held on trust for my wife.

There is a contingency that amounts must be held over in remainder before the trust obligation operates. However, once amounts are held in remainder, T holds the property on bare trust for the settlor's wife. This obligation is straightforwardly categorised as a fiduciary obligation to hold that property for the benefit of the beneficiary. For a bare trust power to be sufficiently certain, it is simply necessary for the identity of that single beneficiary to be capable of being ascertained.

On the point of a 'remainder', it should be remembered that a remainder beneficiary is a beneficiary who takes absolute title in property after the death of the life tenant. So, in the following arrangement, '£1,000 to be held on trust for A for life, remainder to B', A is the life tenant entitled to receipt of the income derived from the trust fund, whereas B is a remainder beneficiary who has some rights during A's lifetime to ensure that the trust fund is not dissipated[352] but who becomes absolutely entitled to the fund after A's death. On the facts of the above example, the wife takes as a remainder beneficiary, meaning that she becomes absolutely entitled under a bare trust when all the other transfers have been completed. There is nothing uncertain about providing for the 'remainder' to be held on trust on the basis that the trustee will know what is left when the other gifts have been completed.[353]

3.5.7 Understanding the different approaches in the cases

The general approach of the cases

Thus far we have seen that there are a number of cases which appear to be in conflict. In short, the principal dispute on the cases is as follows. The leading cases, such as *Gulbenkian* and *McPhail v Doulton*, are concerned that the beneficiaries can only control the trustees by applying to the courts for a declaration as to whether or not a power has been exercised properly. The court can only know whether or not the power has been exercised properly if the terms of the trust or power are sufficiently certain for the purposes of that type of trust or power. By contrast, judges like Lord Denning, Browne-Wilkinson J in *Re Barlow* and the judges in *Re Baden (No 2)* have taken the view that one should seek to uphold testamentary bequests wherever possible if, on the facts of the particular case, it is possible to know that there are some people who will definitely fall within the class of beneficiaries, even if there are also some people about whom one might not be sure. The motivation behind this second line of authority is to ensure that the testator's wishes are given effect to so far as possible and to ensure that people who were clearly intended to take a benefit from the power or trust should not be denied property because the power or trust is poorly drafted. More technically, Lord Denning was concerned that the law relating to discretionary trusts should be brought into line with the treatment of conditions precedent and 'powers collateral' where the tests for certainty are less onerous.[354] It should be remembered, however, that these alternative

---

352 *Re Ralli's WT* [1964] 2 WLR 144; see para 5.4.2 below.
353 *Sprange v Barnard* (1789) 2 Bro CC 585, at para 3.4.4 above.
354 *Re Gulbenkian* [1968] Ch 126, 134; [1967] 3 All ER 15, 18, CA.

approaches have only emerged in exceptional cases and have been approved in courts which are junior to the House of Lords' decisions in cases like *Gulbenkian* and *McPhail v Doulton*. The leading cases remain the House of Lords' decisions.

Decisions on their own facts, where the circumstances permit

There is one trend in some of the cases which is worthy of mention. In spite of the seeming strictness of the case law principles, it is possible by reference to some of the authorities to convince a judge that even though a strict interpretation of the case law tests may lead to a trust or power being held void, nevertheless the trustees' proposed course of action in any particular factual circumstances is acceptable with the result that the trust should be held to be valid. So in *Re Barlow*, Browne-Wilkinson J was fortified in his view that the will trusts before him could be interpreted to be a series of gifts to be made by the trustees to people who were capable of being considered to be the testator's 'friends' because the trustees had clearly identified the manner in which they were proposing to distribute the property. Browne-Wilkinson J was satisfied both that these people were indeed friends of the testator and also that there would be no hardship caused to any third parties. For an example of this approach consider the following passage in which Browne-Wilkinson J held as follows, in considering whether or not the term 'friends' would be sufficiently certain:

> So in this case, in my judgment, there are acquaintances of a kind so close that, on any reasonable basis, anyone would treat them as being 'friends'. Therefore, by allowing the disposition to take effect in their favour, one would certainly be giving effect to part of the testatrix's intention even though as to others it is impossible to say whether or not they satisfy the test.

Similarly in *Re Gestetner*,[355] in spite of the ostensible rigidity of the case law principles, Harman J was prepared to accede to the trustees' proposed method of distributing of testamentary property because it satisfied the testator's objectives satisfactorily, even though the will was imperfectly drafted.

However, this should not be taken to mean that one can simply dispense with all of the legal principles. Even in these exceptional judgments the judges have agonised over the details of the earlier tests and only succumbed to the temptation to permit this level of flexibility when it could be justified in the circumstances of their cases.

3.5.8 Some particular words and expressions causing uncertainty

It will be useful to consider some other authorities on frequently-used words and expressions. The issue which confronts the court in each instance is whether or not the concept encapsulated by an individual word is sufficiently certain to define the class of objects or not. What can be derived from these authorities is that there is no evenly applied test, even in relation to the same concepts.

---

355 [1953] Ch 672.

The term 'friends' and similar expressions

The term 'friends' has been held sufficiently certain in some contexts but not in others. In *Re Gulbenkian* Lord Upjohn simply accepted, without discussion, that the word 'friends' was an axiomatic example of something that would be uncertain. In *Brown v Gould*,[356] a trust in favour of 'old friends' was found to have been invalid by Megarry J.[357] It was held that if the court cannot determine who an 'old friend' is, then the trustees will not be able to do so.[358] In general, the term 'friend' has been considered to be conceptually uncertain and therefore void, whether referring particularly to 'old friends' or 'dear friends' or some such similar expression.[359]

Nevertheless, cases decided under the influence of the *Re Allen*[360] approach to certainty of objects – to the effect that a trust should be valid if there were a substantial or sufficient number of people falling within the class on the facts of the particular case – have been prepared to find that if there were particular friends who could be taken to have been clearly intended to fall within the settlor's intention, then the power might be validated to that extent. In this vein, Megarry J has held:[361]

> Friendship . . . is a concept with almost infinite shades of meaning. Where the concept is uncertain, the gift is void. Where the concept is certain, then mere difficulty in tracing and discovering those who are entitled normally does not invalidate the gift.

So, in *Re Barlow*,[362] Browne-Wilkinson J was prepared to hold that the term 'friends' might be sufficiently certain in relation to testamentary bequests which entitled 'friends' to buy paintings from the trustees. While Browne-Wilkinson J found that the term 'friend' in general terms would be uncertain, his Lordship was nevertheless prepared to find in reliance on the test in *Re Allen*[363] that on the facts before him there were sufficient people who clearly would fall within the class of 'friends' in relation to that particular testator for the term to be validated.[364] Browne-Wilkinson J held that the term 'friend' could be rendered certain if it was taken to mean people who had a long relationship with the settlor, and whose relationship with the settlor was not built on business but rather on social contact. It is this writer's view that that approach does not necessarily answer all questions: for example, what is a 'long relationship'? In that latter case, there was no trust over the paintings in Browne-Wilkinson J's analysis because the bequest was taken to constitute an intention to enter into a series of discrete transactions equivalent to gifts.[365]

356 [1972] Ch 53.
357 Making reference to the unreported case of *Re Lloyds Trust Instruments*, 24 June 1970.
358 In relation to the uncertainty of the term 'friends' generally, see *Re Coxen* [1948] Ch 747; *Re Coates* [1955] Ch 495; *Re Gibbard* [1966] 1 All ER 273; *Re Gulbenkian* [1968] Ch 126; *Re Barlow* [1979] 1 WLR 278.
359 *Re Coates* [1955] Ch 495; *Re Gulbenkian* [1968] Ch 126.
360 [1953] Ch 810.
361 This extract is reproduced by Thomas, 1998, 100 and in *Brown v Gould* [1972] Ch 53, 57.
362 [1979] 1 WLR 278.
363 [1953] Ch 810.
364 Importantly, on the facts of that case, his lordship was prepared to find that it was clear whom the testator must have meant.
365 See also *Re Gibbard* [1967] 1 WLR 42: but note that this case was pre-*Gulbenkian*.

There is other judicial authority relying on the old case of *Re Allen*[366] which h... sought to validate fiduciary mere powers in favour of old friends, before the decisi... *Gulbenkian*[367] required that all such powers could only have sufficiently certain objec... could be said of any given postulant that that person is or is not with the class of beneficiar... So, in relation to the expression 'old friends' used as a description of a class of persons to b... benefited by a will, in *Re Gibbard*, Plowman J considered what might be meant by that term:[368]

> Suppose that the testator had been at prep school[369] with X and had gone on from prep
> school to public school with X, and then to university with X; each had become god-
> father to one of the other's children, perhaps lived in the same neighbourhood, perhaps
> belonged to the same club, perhaps played golf together, perhaps dined in each other's
> houses and had been doing that for fifty years. Could X, coming along and stating that
> that was the relationship between the testator and himself, fail to satisfy the description
> 'any of my old friends'? I should have thought that the answer was no. I should have
> thought that 'old friends' was a sufficiently precise test in the sense that there is no diffi-
> culty in envisaging cases where claimants might come along and establish beyond ques-
> tion that they would be eligible to use that expression.[370]

In the wake of *Re Gulbenkian*, however, this approach is insupportable. While it could be said of the particular individual spoken of by Plowman J that that person was an old friend, it would not be possible to say of anyone who came before the trustees that they were simi-larly an old friend. Such an approach as Plowman J suggests would only be possible if it were sufficient that the court find some people who fall within the class of objects.

The use of the term 'customers'

In *Sparfax v Dommett*,[371] a power in favour of 'customers' was held to have been invalid. Theoretically, it would have been possible to produce records or receipts to prove that indi-vidual postulants had been customers. However, what was not clear was whether to be a 'customer' you would have had to have purchased an item or a service, or whether one could simply visit a shop and be a 'customer' without making a purchase. The term was held to have been uncertain because these sorts of imponderables were left unclear.

The use of the term 'relatives'

As considered above, the term 'relatives' is one which has frequently been used by settlors in creating trusts. In *McPhail v Doulton*[372] – a case which was concerned only with the

---

366 [1953] Ch 810.
367 [1968] Ch 126.
368 [1966] 1 All ER 273, 279, [1967] 1 WLR 42, 48.
369 This is a reference to 'preparatory schools', which are private schools attended by some children before the
      age of 14 usually with the intention that those children will progress to English public schools thereafter.
370 And in these *dicta* we have a picture of the comfortable domesticity of the English upper classes.
371 (1972) *The Times*, 14 July.
372 *McPhail v Doulton* [1970] 2 WLR 1110.

ntification of the objects of a discretionary trust – it was suggested ould be taken to mean 'descendants of a common ancestor', a l for its ambiguity above.[373] When the facts of that same case were :ct question of whether or not the term 'relatives' could be consid- ntly certain, it was considered that the classes identified in the rning division of an estate on intestacy.[374] In further cases, the :qual shares' was interpreted to refer to statutory next of kin (as y Rules) so as to render it conceptually certain.[375] Similarly, the rendered sufficiently certain by taking it to mean 'descendants of every degree' albeit frequently restricted to referring only to children of the settlor.[376] The term may differ according to the context.[377]

3.5.9 Resolving the uncertainty: use of an expert or trustee discretion

Means of seeking to resolve uncertainty used in trust instruments

The preceding discussion has considered the strict tests applicable in cases of uncertainty and some decisions which have mollified the strict application of those tests. The purpose of this section is to consider the situation in which provisions have been added to the trust fund to enable the trustees to resolve any uncertainty in the trust by reference to experts or other designated individuals.

There are three common devices used by those drafting trusts to attempt to render certain provisions which would otherwise appear to be uncertain on their face. The first is to provide that some expert third party should be able to adjudicate on those persons who will or will not fall within the class of beneficiaries. The second is to give the trustees a power to decide who will or will not fall within the class in the event of any alleged uncertainty: this latter issue raising the question again whether such trustees are acting as fiduciaries or in a personal capacity when exercising such a power. The third is to provide, effectively, that the trustees have a discretion to appoint property to anyone in the world, in the hope that the power will be logically certain even if it will also be very broad. Each is considered in turn.

That some third person unconnected with the trust may be appointed as an expert

An example of the first approach for resolving uncertainty is to grant the trustees a power to appoint a third person to the role of arbitrator in the event of some uncertainty. Thus, in *Re Tuck's Settlement Trusts*,[378] Lord Denning held that a trust, which provided that money was left on trust for the benefit of such of the testator's issue who married into the Jewish faith, would be valid because the court (or the trustees) was able to ask the Chief Rabbi for advice as to the extent that there was uncertainty about any postulant. Importantly, in this context the question of whether or not a person was of the Jewish faith was something which could

---

373 See para 3.5.4 above.
374 *Re Baden (No 2)* [1973] Ch 9.
375 *Re Gansloser's WT* [1952] Ch 30; *Re Poulton's WT* [1987] 1 WLR 795.
376 See Thomas and Hudson, 2004, 111.
377 *Ibid.*
378 [1978] 2 WLR 411.

be answered definitively by reference to Jewish law (which has clear rules on who will be considered to be a member of that faith). So, this trust was valid because it was possible on its own terms to appoint an expert who would render the class of objects sufficiently certain. Other similar cases have included trust conditions such as a prohibition that the propositus 'must not marry someone of the Jewish faith and parentage',[379] in which case the 'parentage' part of the condition was held to be uncertain. Also, a condition that the propositus 'must remain Catholic' has been accepted as being sufficiently certain.[380] It is unclear whether or not these approaches will be accepted as general principles in future cases.[381] It is suggested that if the matters at issue are empirically demonstrable facts (such as a person needing to be suffering from a particular disease) or questions of law (such as whether or not a person is of a particular faith under Jewish law), then there ought to be no objection in permitting their validity because any uncertainty is removed by the decision of the specified expert.[382] By contrast, provisions which, for example, left it to a testator's solicitor to decide who were that testator's 'good friends' would be objectionable because it could not be known whether or not the term 'good friends' were conceptually certain, nor could the solicitor or any other person claim to be objectively an expert in such matters when compared, for example, with matters of scientific rigour which could be established empirically or objectively.

Clearly, these decisions are in conflict with the rigour of the decision in *McPhail v Doulton*.[383] The approach taken in *Re Barlow*[384] and in *Clayton v Ramsden*,[385] by comparison, was that in relation to conditions subsequent, whereby entitlement to be recognised as a beneficiary would be removed if that beneficiary subsequently failed to satisfy some condition (for example, that X shall be a beneficiary provided that she remains sufficiently tall), it would be enough to demonstrate the efficacy of the trust if a sufficient number of people could fall within it regardless of whether or not some individuals failed to satisfy a condition subsequent. Therefore, it was not considered necessary in those cases to demonstrate that it could be said of any given postulant that she did or did not fall within the category of beneficiaries. Thus, in *Re Barlow*, Browne-Wilkinson J held that gifts could be made to any propositus once that person could demonstrate that she fell within the category of beneficiaries: it would not matter that they might subsequently fail to satisfy a condition. Therefore, there does appear to be a different principle in relation to powers involving conditions subsequent when compared to conditions precedent in this sense.[386] The approach in *McPhail v Doulton*,[387] by dint of the 'is or is not' test, would have invalidated such objects clauses because it could not have been said whether or not any potential postulant would have fallen within or without the class of objects.

---

379   *Clayton v Ramsden* [1943] AC 320.
380   *Blathwayt v Baron Cawley* [1976] AC 397.
381   See Thomas, 1998, 135, para 3–117.
382   See *Re Tuck's Settlement Trusts* [1978] Ch 49, 62, [1978] 2 WLR 411, 424, *per* Lord Denning whereby the Chief Rabbi clause was considered to 'cure' the conceptual uncertainty.
383   [1970] 2 WLR 1110.
384   [1979] 1 WLR 278.
385   [1943] AC 320.
386   Underhill and Hayton, 2002, 82.
387   [1970] 2 WLR 1110.

That the trustees may not exercise their own unfettered discretion as though third parties

As to the second means of resolving uncertainty, by giving the trustees a power to decide on their own cognisance how to resolve any uncertainty, Jenkins J dismissed the general effectiveness of such provisions in *Re Coxen*[388] in the following terms:

> If the testator had sufficiently defined the state of affairs in which the trustees were to form their opinion he would not have saved the condition from invalidity on the ground of uncertainty merely by making their opinion the criterion.

Therefore, it will be difficult to resolve uncertainty simply by purporting to give such a general power to the trustees. However, his Lordship considered that if the testator 'had sufficiently defined' the basis on which the trustees were to exercise their judgment – so that it became effectively an objective or empirically demonstrable fact – then the provision may be valid. Such a narrow power would, it is suggested, remove any uncertainty in any event if it made the train tracks on which the trustee's discretion was to operate so clear and incapable of error. However, a discretion which cannot produce an uncertain result is, it is suggested, not a discretion which raises any problem of uncertainty of objects.[389]

The strict principle is the better one, it is suggested. This approach is in line with principle because if the trustees were able to exercise some unfettered discretion in this sense *qua* trustees, the court would not be able to know whether or not they had exercised their power properly. That the trustees are given an open power to resolve any uncertainty still leaves the circular problem of whether or not their power is for sufficiently certain objects in the first place. So, simply suggesting that the trustees can resolve any uncertainty will not render certain what is otherwise uncertain.[390] Rather, the settlor would have to be careful to appoint third parties either as experts (as under *Re Tuck's Settlement Trusts*[391] above), or in some other fashion as the holders of purely personal powers which would not be invalidated simply by reference to their width (as considered in relation to *Re Hay's ST*[392] above).

There is one further twist on this method of empowering the trust which might seem to provide a means of seeking to resolve uncertainty. This is to provide in the terms of the trust instrument that no term of the trust is to be deemed uncertain, but that any confusion in relation to a provision about which there appears to be uncertainty shall be resolved by a binding decision of the trustees. Nevertheless, the decision in *Re Coxen*[393] held that a concept was not made certain by leaving it to the trustees to decide who constituted, in that case, 'an old friend'. There are two reasons for this approach. The first is that there are no clear, justiciable criteria on which the court can review the trustees' decision if the beneficiaries choose to challenge it. Secondly, the court will typically be unwilling to allow those occupying the office of trustees to act as settlor also.[394] In short, while the decision would be clear, the

388 [1948] Ch 747.
389 If the trustees' discretion is on train tracks, then there is no scope for error or uncertainty, whereas if the trustees' discretion enables them to travel across an open field, then there is always the possibility of uncertainty.
390 *Re Jones* [1953] Ch 125, 130, *per* Dankwerts J; *Re Burton's Settlements* [1955] Ch 82, 95, *per* Upjohn J.
391 [1978] 2 WLR 411.
392 [1981] 3 All ER 786.
393 [1948] Ch 747.
394 *Re Brook's ST* [1939] 1 Ch 993.

criteria on which the trustees were to be judged would not and the courts could therefore have difficulty in reviewing their decision. Thus, in *Re Wright's WT*,[395] where a transfer of property was made to trustees to help institutions which the trustees considered had assisted the testator during his lifetime, that transfer was held to have been uncertain.

Granting the trustees wide powers

One further technique which has been used to resolve any risk of uncertainty is to give the trustees a power, for example, to advance trust property to 'anyone in the world' or to 'anyone whom the trustees consider appropriate'.[396] There is no objection to such a power being conferred on someone who is not a fiduciary.[397] The problem is with conferring such a power on a fiduciary. At one level, such a power is certain: the class of objects means anyone in the world. Therefore, it is conceptually certain. The issue is twofold. First, whether or not it is too broad a class to be administratively workable (as considered in the next section). Secondly, and more particularly, how can the court possibly judge whether or not such a power had been exercised properly? If the power can be exercised in favour of anyone in the world, then how can the court judge whether an advancement to a child in Bangladesh is more or less accept-able a use of that power than an advancement to a reindeer farmer in Lapland?[398]

In *Re Manisty's Settlement*,[399] there was a provision in the settlement to the effect that if a given event took place, the trustees could advance property to anyone in the world (effec-tively) except some of the testator's identified relatives. The purpose of such provisions is to ensure that if a particular event takes place which would have unfavourable tax consequences for the settlement and its beneficiaries, then this provision seeks to declare that none of those identified people can be objects of the power in the expectation that this will solve the tax problem. Templeman J held that there was no issue of uncertainty in the drafting of this provision because it could be said with certainty which relatives were and which were not excluded from the class of objects on these facts.[400]

This approach is logical,[401] but it is not without difficulty. In *Blausten v IRC*,[402] it was held that such a power could be void for uncertainty in general terms if the power was simply too wide for the court to be able to know with any certainty whether or not the trustees had exer-cised that power properly. As Buckley LJ put this point in *Blausten v IRC*, considering such powers in general terms:[403]

395 (1857) 3 K & J 419.
396 *Re Manisty* [1974] Ch 17, [1973] 2 All ER 1203. The two types of power here are typically either 'special wide powers' or 'intermediate wide powers'. For a discussion of these types of powers, see Thomas, 1998, para 6–39 *et seq*.
397 *Re Hay's ST* [1982] 1 WLR 202.
398 As the judges sometimes express this idea, is the fiduciary obliged 'to survey mankind from China to Peru?': *Re Gestetner* [1953] Ch 672, 688 *per* Harman J.
399 [1974] Ch 17, [1973] 2 All ER 1203.
400 Cf *Mettoy Pension Trustees Ltd v Evans* [1990] 1 WLR 1587, 1617, [1991] 2 All ER 513, 549, *per* Warner J, which took a broader view about the court's powers to intervene in relation to the administration of such powers beyond merely ensuring that the fiduciary had considered the exercise of her power appropriately.
401 In that logically, having excluded half a dozen people with certainty, we know who 'all of the rest of the people in the world' are. The problem is how can the trustees justify acting in favour of some people but not others?
402 [1972] Ch 256.
403 *Ibid*, 272.

If the class of persons to whose possible claims they would have to give consideration
were so wide that it really did not amount to a class in any true sense at all no doubt that
would be a duty which it would be impossible for them to perform and the power could
be said to be invalid on that ground.

Subsequently, in *Re Hay's ST*,[404] Megarry VC was asked to consider a power which could
be exercised 'for such persons . . . as the trustees shall . . . appoint except the settlor'. His
Lordship held that if the power was administratively workable,[405] and provided that the trustees considered the exercise of their power appropriately, then such a power need not automatically be void.

It is suggested that if the source of this area of law is to ensure that the court can exercise
its inherent power to administer a trust,[406] then it cannot be possible to know whether or not
a fiduciary has exercised a power properly if the power is expressed to be in such broad
terms: therefore, such powers should be held to be void for uncertainty.[407] (It should be
noted, as mentioned above, that Templeman J[408] and Megarry VC[409] have not themselves
seen anything wrong *per se* with the width of such powers.) This analysis would depend
upon the drafting of the trust provision and whether or not there are sufficient caveats
expressed in relation to that power so that the court can understand what would be a proper
and an improper exercise of that power. So, in *Blausten v IRC*, it was a requirement of the
exercise of the power that the prior agreement in writing of the settlor be given to any exercise of the power: therefore, it was held that this power was not so wide as to be invalid for
uncertainty because there would be some limit on its exercise and therefore it was in fact not
a clause for the benefit of everyone in the world.

3.5.10 The various forms of uncertainty

There is an important further means of analysing the ways in which powers may be found to
be valid or invalid: that is, the nature of the uncertainty. It appears that there are some forms
of uncertainty which will not, in themselves, cause the trust to be found invalid. A division
between the various forms of uncertainty has been made in the following way:[410]

(a) Conceptual uncertainty.
(b) Evidential uncertainty.
(c) Ascertainability.
(d) Administrative workability.

The point made in that article is that differing forms of uncertainty will or will not affect the
validity of a trust in differing circumstances. The acid test is that 'there must be sufficient

---

404 [1982] 1 WLR 202.
405 A concept considered in the next section.
406 *Schmidt v Rosewood Trust Ltd* [2003] 3 All ER 76.
407 As considered in the next section, it is also the case that such powers would be void for unworkability if the
     trustees were in fact to measure the comparative rights of everyone in the world.
408 *Re Manisty* [1974] Ch 17.
409 *Re Hay's ST* [1982] 1 WLR 202.
410 (1982) 98 LQR 551 (Emery). For a fuller discussion of these concepts see now Thomas, 1998, 91 *et seq.*

certainty for the trustees to execute the trust according to the settlor's intentions'. Adopting this division, each of these sub-divisions of uncertainty is considered in turn.

Conceptual uncertainty and the interpretation of objects clauses

The issue of conceptual uncertainty is the most fundamental in the validity of a trust or a power. The situation that is caught by this form of uncertainty is where the meanings of the words used in the trust are unclear.[411] Nevertheless, judges will not try to make trusts invalid, but rather they should 'judge the degree of certainty with some measure of common sense and knowledge and without excessive astuteness to discover ambiguities':[412] so if the matter is sufficiently certain for the purpose, then that should be enough. This was the approach which underpinned the *Re Allen*[413] approach, an approach which sought to validate objects clauses which were sufficiently comprehensible in their context. However, in the light of the strictness of the *Re Gulbenkian*[414] 'any given postulant' test, it is not clear that this approach is in the ascendant. Obviously, if the terms used are unintelligible to the trustees and the court, the trust cannot be carried out. It is conceivable that the uncertainty would arise because the settlor uses technical terms which the trustees cannot decipher – in such a situation, recourse might be had to the means for resolving uncertainty considered above. Alternatively, it might be that the words are familiar but so vague as to be incapable of effect. An example of this category would be 'friends of the settlor',[415] 'good customers',[416] 'pure-blooded Englishmen',[417] or 'useful employees'. In short, if it is found to be impossible to be certain of the concept, the trust fails.[418]

Evidential uncertainty

Aside from the problem of interpreting the concepts used in the trust, it is possible that it is simply impossible to prove as a question of fact whether or not a beneficiary falls within a class. Therefore, evidential uncertainty refers not to the meaning of the words involved, but rather to the question whether or not the claimant can *prove* that she falls within the class of beneficiaries. For example, a trust provision which entitled the holder of a season ticket to Sunderland Football Club in the season 2005/06 to a distribution from the trust fund on presentation of a ticket stub is conceptually certain. That is conceptually certain because we know what is meant by having been a season ticket holder in an identified season. However, for those season ticket holders who have lost their ticket stubs, it would be impossible to prove that they are genuinely beneficiaries. Therefore, their own claims would fail for evidential uncertainty because they would be incapable of proving that they fall within the class of beneficiaries, but the trust itself could be valid because the definition of the class of beneficiaries is sufficiently clear.

---

411 *Re Sayer* [1957] Ch 423, 432, *per* Upjohn LJ; *Re Hain's Settlement* [1961] 1 All ER 848, 853, *per* Upjohn LJ.
412 *Blathwayt v Baron Cawley* [1976] AC 397, 425, *per* Lord Wilberforce. See also *Hillas & Co v Arcos Ltd* (1932) 147 LT 503, 514, *per* Lord Wright in broadly similar vein.
413 [1953] Ch 810.
414 [1968] Ch 126.
415 *Re Coates* [1955] Ch 495; *Re Gulbenkian* [1968] Ch 126.
416 *Sparfax v Dommett* (1972) *The Times*, 14 July.
417 *Re Allen* [1953] Ch 810, 819, *per* Lord Evershed MR.
418 *Re Baden (No 2)* [1973] Ch 9.

Where it is impossible to prove whether or not potential beneficiaries succeed in falling within the category, this will *not* invalidate a trust or a power of appointment (in most circumstances).[419] This appears to be consistent with good sense. There is no reason to invalidate the trust simply because someone who falls within a perfectly comprehensible trust provision is not able to produce the proof necessary to demonstrate to the trustees that she is indeed within the class of beneficiaries. Given the underlying policy motivation to validate trusts wherever possible, that there are problems of evidence rather than concept, it would appear inappropriate to avoid the trust.

There may be factual situations, however, in which it would seem more appropriate to avoid the trust. Suppose, for example, that there is a bequest of season tickets at Sunderland Football Club to a person who sat in seat A40 because he saved the testator from falling 30 feet to the ground below on an identified afternoon. If it was impossible to prove who occupied that seat because his ticket was lost, that would make it impossible to carry out that trust obligation, but the trust could still be valid in theory because the settlor's intention is sufficiently clear. However, if it was impossible to prove who was in that seat, the trust may nevertheless fail because it is unworkable, and that property would lapse into residue as a consequence. The issue is therefore whether that trust should be held to be void on grounds of impossibility of proving entitlement, or valid because of its conceptual certainty. In the absence of a provision for transfer of the fund to a remainder beneficiary, it might be said that the trust fails and that the testator was intestate as to that property (so that the property would pass to the testator's next of kin under the Intestacy Rules).

As Jenkins LJ has held:[420]

> I must keep in mind the distinction between uncertainty as to the events prescribed by the testator as those in which the condition [governing any given object's right to take a benefit] is to operate (which is generally speaking fatal to the validity of such a condition) and difficulty in ascertaining whether those events . . . have happened or not, which is not necessarily fatal to such validity.

Thus, evidential uncertainty need not invalidate a trust nor a power, unless the circumstances make such invalidity reasonable.

Ascertainability

Linked to the last example of evidential uncertainty is the situation in which it is possible to understand the concept underlying the trust but it is impossible to find the beneficiaries. It might be impossible to find beneficiaries because they have died, or have remarried and changed names, or have moved abroad. This will not necessarily render the trust invalid.[421] It has been held by Wynn-Parry J that:

> mere difficulty of ascertainment is not of itself fatal to the validity of the gift. As has been pointed out, it is a matter of degree, and it is only when one reaches, on the

---

419   *Ibid.*
420   *Re Coxen* [1948] Ch 747, 760.
421   *Re Benjamin* [1902] 1 Ch 723; *Re Saxone Shoe Co Ltd's Trust Deed* [1962] 2 All ER 904; *McPhail v Doulton* [1970] 2 WLR 1110. Cf *Re Hooper's 1949 Settlement* (1955) 34 ATC 3; *Re Eden* [1957] 2 All ER 430.

evidence, a conclusion that is so vague, or that the difficulty is so great that it must be treated as virtually incapable of resolution, that one is entitled, to my mind, to say that a gift of that nature is void for uncertainty.

So, ascertainability will not in itself cause a trust or power to be avoided, unless the greater part of the trustee's obligations are so difficult to perform that the trust could be considered to be incapable of being validated.

Suppose, for example, that there is a bequest of season tickets at Sunderland Football Club to those people who sat in seats A40 and A41 on a particular afternoon. Suppose further that it was possible to read the records to see who occupied those seats, but impossible to locate them because they had moved to Australia without leaving a forwarding address. That would make it impossible to carry out that trust obligation. The issue is therefore whether it should be held to be void on grounds of impossibility of ascertaining the whereabouts of the beneficiaries, or valid because of its conceptual certainty. In the absence of a provision for transfer of the fund to a remainder beneficiary, it might be said that the trust fails and that the testator was intestate as to that property (so that the property would pass to the testator's next of kin under the Intestacy Rules). If neither of the occupants of those seats could be found, then none of the trust obligations could be performed. However, if the class of beneficiaries was to be 200 people who sat in that part of the stadium and it is only those last two people who cannot be found, then the trust could be validated in favour of the 198 people who can be found.[422]

Typically, the trustee's obligation will be discharged by placing advertisements in newspapers in which the beneficiary is thought likely to find them. Clearly, the size and nature of the bequest will tend to govern the lengths to which the trustees are required to go to locate the beneficiary. If it can be demonstrated that the trustees have taken sufficiently strenuous steps to find the lost member of the class of objects, then the court will order that the property be divided among the ascertained objects.[423]

Administrative unworkability

As a final extension of the preceding categories, it might be that the nature of the trust is such that it is impracticable for the trustees to carry out the settlor's wishes. If a trust were administratively unworkable, then that trust would be invalid. Lord Eldon held the following, in establishing the importance of the workability of the trust:

As it is a maxim that the execution of a trust shall be under the control of the court it must be of such a nature that it can be under that control: so that the administration of it can be reviewed by the court, or the court itself can execute the trust: a trust, therefore, which in case of maladministration could be reformed and a due administration directed.[424]

Consequently, part of the requirement that the objects of the trust be certain is a requirement that the trust be drafted so that it is possible to administer the trust in such a way that the court can judge whether or not that administration has been carried out properly.

---

422   *Re Benjamin* [1902] 1 Ch 723.
423   *Ibid.*
424   *Morice v Bishop of Durham* (1805) 10 Ves 522, 539.

Suppose, for example, that a fund of £10,000 is settled on trust to be distributed between 'all registered supporters of Sunderland Football Club who are naturally red-haired and more than six feet tall'. The concept is certain and it will be possible for any postulant to prove that he falls within the category. However, if the trustees are two ordinary individuals, it would be a large task for them to administer a settlement among such a potentially large group of people. If, for example, the trust referred to 'all people living in England and Wales who are naturally red-haired and more than six feet tall', that would clearly be a problem for two ordinary citizens to administer. Indeed, it would appear to be so great a task as to be administratively unworkable, such that it ought to be declared invalid.[425] Therefore, the scope of the trust may make the difference.

The nature of the trustees may make the difference. Suppose the following trust provision: '. . . £10,000 to be held upon trust for all retired coal miners who worked for British Coal in County Durham, still alive at 1 November 2010.' Clearly, the concept is certain enough. However, for ordinary members of the public acting as trustees, it would be difficult to administer this trust. Alternatively, if the trustees were also the trustees of the pension fund for miners in County Durham, it would be a far more straightforward task to access records held for retired miners and to distribute the funds accordingly. Therefore, it may be that it is the capacity and identity of the trustees from case to case which influences the workability of the trust power.

Therefore, where the requirements of the trust make it impossible for the trustees to perform their fiduciary obligations, this will invalidate the trust.[426] It should be noted that this principle applies to trust powers rather than to mere powers of appointment. Thus, in *R v District Auditors ex p West Yorkshire CC*,[427] a trust which would have had the effect of including within its class of beneficiaries 2.5 million people in West Yorkshire was held to be administratively unworkable. The terms of the trust would have included seeking to relieve unemployment in that region, assisting bodies that worked with problems experienced by young people in that region and the encouragement of better race relations. It was held that these objectives, coupled with such a broad geographic region and large body of beneficiaries, would be administratively unworkable and that the power was consequently void.

3.5.11 Conclusion

In conclusion, the following structure is the preferred means of dealing with problem questions in this area:

(a) identify the type of trust or power;
(b) identify which test applies to that type of trust or power;
(c) apply the means of eluding the strict test;
(d) are there any exceptions to that test for that type of trust or power?

The result of a trust failing is that the property is held on resulting trust for the settlor.

Therefore, this structure suggests that the student apply the leading case to the appropriate form of power, before using one of the alternative analyses advanced in either *Re Baden*

---

425   *McPhail v Doulton* [1970] 2 WLR 1110; see para 3.5.4 above.
426   *Ibid, per* Lord Wilberforce.
427   (1985) 26 RVR 24.

(No 2)[428] or *Re Barlow*.[429] At that second stage, the student might also consider Emery's division between the various forms of uncertainty and their respective effects on the validity of the trust. That structure might look something like the following diagram.

	Fixed trust	*Discretionary trust*	*Mere power*	*Personal power*
STAGE ONE: Identify the form of power				
STAGE TWO: Identify the test appropriate to that power	*IRC v Broadway Cottages* – preparation of a complete list of beneficiaries	*McPhail v Doulton* – the 'is or is not' test	*Re Gulbenkian* – the 'is or is not' test	*Re Hay's ST* – 'nothing in the width of the power will invalidate the trust'
STAGE THREE: Apply the means of eluding the strict test	None possible	*Baden (No 2)* – (1) reverse the onus of proof, or (2) a substantial number of certain beneficiaries is satisfactory	*Re Barlow* – construe the trust as a series of individual gifts	Not necessary – power cannot be invalid in any event
STAGE FOUR: Use an 'expert' to resolve uncertainty	*Re Tuck's ST* – unless irreconcilable conceptual uncertainty or administrative unworkability	*Re Tuck's ST* – unless irreconcilable conceptual uncertainty or administrative unworkability	*Re Tuck's ST* – unless irreconcilable conceptual uncertainty or administrative unworkability	Not necessary – power cannot be invalid in any event

Partial or total failure of the trust

It is said that where part of the gift fails, the whole gift must fail, to give effect to the settlor's intention.[430] However, there remains the problem of a complex trust in which only one out of a number of items of settled property is affected by the uncertainty. The issue would be that the failure of one disposition would lead to the invalidity of the entire settlement. As a point of trust drafting, it is important to include a *Cotman v Brougham*[431] type of clause to ensure that the failure of one part does not affect the validity of the rest. It appears that where there is a remainder provision, there is no objection to allowing a single part of the settlement to lapse into residue, so that the remainder of the trust can remain valid.

428 [1973] Ch 9.
429 [1979] 1 WLR 278.
430 *Re Gulbenkian* [1968] Ch 126.
431 [1918] AC 514.

In the case of *Re Leek*,[432] it was accepted in principle that a trust made up of many different powers could continue to be valid if the one offending (or void) power contained in that trust were simply removed. In effect, that single power would be struck out and the trust given effect without it. The question whether or not it is possible for one power within a complex trust to be declared invalid and for the rest to remain valid will depend upon the precise context of the trust. Suppose a testator intended to benefit two classes of beneficiary: the first class being his only child and the second class being his 'close friends'. Suppose that the will also provided for his only child to be his residuary beneficiary. In such a situation, there would be no principled objection to the bequest in favour of his 'close friends' being held void for uncertainty, but for the remainder of the trust to be upheld as being valid.[433]

However, suppose there is a different testator who intended to benefit his 'valued employees and his personal secretary' with 'equal gifts of no more than £10,000' each out of a total fund of £100,000 (that is, 'equal gifts' requires a fixed trust so that the trustees can know between how many people the fund is to be divided to achieve equal shares). The expression 'valued employees' would not be sufficiently certain under the complete list test.[434] But suppose the testator had had only one personal secretary during his entire career. It would be contrary to the intention of the trust to grant the whole £100,000 to the personal secretary, and therefore it would not be permissible to allow the trust to be valid in relation to the personal secretary's interest alone. Therefore, it is likely that the court would hold the entire trust power to be invalid. Although it might be that a particularly soft-hearted court would attempt to permit the personal secretary to be the beneficiary of a bare trust over £10,000 out of the fund of £100,000, once again this would raise the issue of certainty of subject matter.

432   [1969] 1 Ch 563.
433   Cf *Hancock v Watson* [1902] AC 14, at para 3.4.4 above.
434   *IRC v Broadway Cottages* [1955] Ch 20.

Chapter 4

The rights of beneficiaries and the beneficiary principle

OVERVIEW

A beneficiary under an ordinary express trust acquires equitable proprietary rights in the trust property as well as rights to demand an account from the trustee and to hold the trustee liable for any breach of trust. The principle in Saunders v Vautier *provides that if all of the beneficiaries are acting together and are* sui juris *then they may direct the trustees how to deal with the trust property. By contrast, the objects of mere powers have no proprietary interests at all until property is appointed to them. The nature of the rights of the objects of discretionary trusts are more complex because those objects may have no vested rights in any property until it has been appointed to them, except in relation to 'closed discretionary trusts'.*

It is a further requirement of the law of trusts that there must be some person with the rights of a beneficiary or else there will not be a valid trust: this is referred to as the 'beneficiary principle'. The 'beneficiary principle' requires that there be some person (individual or corporate entity) in whose favour the court is able to exercise the trust.[1] By contrast, a trust which is created to achieve some abstract purpose without any person entitled to take an equitable interest in the trust property as beneficiary will be invalid.[2] Therefore, it is necessary to distinguish between trusts for the benefit of people and trusts for the achievement of abstract purposes, where the former is valid and the latter invalid.[3] The exception to this rule is the charitable trust, discussed in Chapter 25. One particularly important example of this principle in action relates to transfers of property to unincorporated associations. A transfer of property to an unincorporated association must be structured correctly so that it does not constitute an invalid purpose trust.[4] There are a number of different ways of structuring such a transfer to make it valid: whether as a trust for the benefit of identified people, or as an accretion to the association's funds subject to contract, or as a transfer to the club's officers subject to a mandate to use that property in accordance with the association's purposes subject to contract, or as a gift to the members of the association. The transferor must avoid transferring the property to the officers of the association on trust to use for the abstract purposes of the association. The structure of any transfer of property to an unincorporated association must therefore be organised carefully to ensure that it is valid. On the termination of such an association, the individual members may acquire individual rights in the property held for the association.

With reference to trusts for the benefit of identifiable people, the trust must be subject to a maximum perpetuity or the trust will be invalid (rule against remoteness). Similarly, the beneficiaries must be able to acquire their interests within the perpetuity period (rule against inalienability). Under the case law before 1964, a large number of trusts were invalidated for falling foul of this rule. However, the Perpetuities and Accumulations Act 1964 created a mechanism by which trusts for the benefit of people without a provision to prevent them from lasting in perpetuity can nevertheless be deemed to be valid for a statutory perpetuity period.[5]

---

1 See Lord Grant MR in *Morice v Bishop of Durham* (1805) 9 Ves 399, 405 as expressed in this context in *Bowman v Secular Society Ltd* [1917] AC 406, 441 by Lord Parker.
2 *Leahy v Attorney-General for NSW* [1959] AC 457; *Re Grant's WT* [1979] 3 All ER 359.
3 *Re Denley* [1969] 1 Ch 373; *Re Lipinski's Will Trusts* [1976] Ch 235.
4 *Re Recher's WT* [1972] Ch 526.
5 Perpetuities and Accumulations Act 1964, s 3.

4.1 THE NATURE OF THE RIGHTS OF BENEFICIARIES IN THE TRUST FUND

4.1.1 The nature of the rights of beneficiaries as both proprietary rights and rights against the trustees *in personam*

It is a necessary part of any trust that there is a beneficiary capable of enforcing the trustees' performance of their duties under the trust.[6] This principle is known as the 'beneficiary principle' and forms the principal focus of this chapter from section 4.2 onwards. However, that proposition does not necessarily tell us very much about the nature of the rights of the beneficiary. Rather, it is the rule in *Saunders v Vautier*,[7] considered in this section, which demonstrates that ultimately each beneficiary has an equitable proprietary right in the trust property. There has been much discussion over the centuries as to the nature of the beneficiaries' rights: some suggesting that they are simply rights *in personam* (that is, personal rights akin to a mere debt) against the trustees and others suggesting that they are also rights *in rem* (that is, rights in property) exercisable against the trust fund.[8] It is suggested that the rights of the beneficiaries are to be understood as exhibiting two characteristics simultaneously: first, a proprietary right in the trust fund and, secondly, personal rights against the trustees in relation to the proper management of the trust's affairs.[9] In both cases it is equity which recognises the beneficiaries' claims against the trust property and against the trustees personally, whereas the common law merely recognises the trustees as being the owners of the trust property in the sense that the trustees hold the legal title in any property held on trust.

In terms of trusts theory, the beneficiary has rights against the trustee personally in the event that the trustee breaches her trust in some way.[10] In accordance with the most fundamental principles of equity, a court of equity will act *in personam* against the conscience of a defendant.[11] So, in the words of Lord Ellesmere in the *Earl of Oxford's Case*, 'the office of the Chancellor [acting through the courts of equity] is to correct men's consciences for . . . breach of trusts'.[12] As considered in Chapter 18, any trustee who commits a breach of trust will be subject to a personal obligation to replace any property lost to the trust or to pay over its equivalent value in cash.[13] Thus, the purpose of the entire equitable jurisdiction is to consider the defendant trustee, to act in judgment over the conscionability of her actions and to hold any trustee to account to the beneficiaries of a trust. In that sense the courts act *in personam*, but that expression should not be understood as restricting the beneficiaries' rights to purely personal rights against the trust.[14] Rather, since the 15th century, courts of equity have enforced the rights of a beneficiary under a trust not only against trustees but also against other people, provided that they had notice of the existence of the trust.[15] Included within the classes of people who cannot resist the proprietary rights of the

---

6 *Bowman v Secular Society Ltd* [1917] AC 406, 441, *per* Lord Parker.
7 (1841) 4 Beav 115.
8 For a more detailed account of this aspect of a beneficiary's rights, see Thomas and Hudson, 2004, 173.
9 See para 8.4.8.
10 *Target Holdings v Redferns* [1996] 1 AC 421.
11 See the discussion at section 1.1 above.
12 *The Earl of Oxford's Case* (1615) 1 Ch Rep 1. See also *Penn v Lord Baltimore* (1750) 1 Ves Sen 444.
13 *Target Holdings v Redferns* [1996] 1 AC 421.
14 See para 2.3.4 above.
15 See, for example, Yearbook 5 Edw IV, Mich pl 16, considered by Thomas and Hudson, 2004, 173.

beneficiaries are heirs of a trustee and volunteers who receive the trust property without giving consideration for it. Only a person who is a *bona fide* purchaser for value of the trust property without notice of the trust (otherwise known as 'Equity's darling') can take good title in the trust property:[16] and even then the beneficiaries' rights would consequently attach to the sale proceeds paid by the *bona fide* purchaser.[17] The beneficiaries' rights are therefore rights which attach to the trust property and protect the beneficiaries against the claims of third parties to that property. In consequence, the rights of the beneficiary should be understood both to be rights in the property comprising the trust fund as well as personal rights against the trustee. The following discussion considers the case of *Saunders v Vautier*,[18] which is generally taken, in English law, to establish the proposition that the beneficiaries' rights are rights in the trust property.

4.1.2 The principle in *Saunders v Vautier*

The principle itself

The rule in *Saunders v Vautier*[19] has been considered on numerous occasions already in this book – a large amount of attention to lavish on an otherwise unobtrusive decision from the mid-19th century but for its importance in describing the nature of a beneficiary's equitable interest. The principle which that case establishes is that all of the beneficiaries, constituting 100% of the equitable interest in a trust fund, provided that they are all *sui juris* and acting together, can direct the trustees how to deal with that trust fund. As Megarry J stated this proposition[20] in relation to the ability of beneficiaries using the rule in *Saunders v Vautier* to re-arrange the terms of a trust:

> If under a trust every possible beneficiary was under no disability and concurred in the re-arrangement or termination of the trusts, then under the doctrine in *Saunders v Vautier* those beneficiaries could dispose of the trust property as they thought fit; for in equity the property was theirs. Yet if any beneficiary was an infant, or an unborn or unascertained person, it was held that the court had no general inherent or other jurisdiction to concur in any such arrangement on behalf of that beneficiary.

As the principle is described by Prof Thomas:[21] 'an adult beneficiary (or a number of adult beneficiaries acting together) who has (or between them have) an absolute, vested and indefeasible interest in the capital and income of property may at any time require the transfer of the property to him (or them) and may terminate any accumulation.'

A simple example of the operation of the doctrine in *Saunders v Vautier* would be a bare trust (under which a trustee holds on trust for one absolutely-entitled beneficiary) under which that beneficiary could direct the trustees either to transfer the legal title to the

16   See *ibid*; and *Westdeutsche Landesbank Girozentrale v Islington LBC* [1996] AC 669.
17   *Westdeutsche Landesbank Girozentrale v Islington LBC* [1996] AC 669.
18   (1841) 4 Beav 115.
19   *Ibid*.
20   In *Re Holt's Settlement* [1969] 1 Ch 100, 111.
21   GW Thomas, *Powers*, 1998, 176. Applied in *CPT Custodian Pty Ltd v Commissioner of State Revenue* [2005] HCA 53, para [47].

beneficiary so as to make her the absolute owner of the property, or direct the trustees how to deal with the trust property, provided that the beneficiary was of sound mind and aged 18 or over. This rule extends to circumstances in which there is more than one beneficiary. In such a situation, *all* of those beneficiaries would be required to act together and all of them would be required to be *sui juris*. This would enable the whole of the beneficiaries under even a complex trust to call for delivery of absolute title in the trust fund from the trustees. Thus, the beneficiaries are able to override the settlor's expressed wishes as to the treatment of the trust property.

The significance of this principle is that it establishes that the beneficiary has a right in the trust fund itself and not merely personal claims against the trustees or against the settlor. Once the trust is declared and once the trust property has been vested in the trustees, it is the beneficiaries who have the whip-hand in relation to the treatment of the trust fund.

Applications of the principle

The case of *Saunders v Vautier*[22] itself concerned a testator who bequeathed £2,000 worth of East India stock on trust for Vautier. The trust provided that the capital of the fund should be held intact until Vautier reached the age of 25 and that the dividends from the stock should be accumulated with the capital. Vautier reached the age of maturity (at that time, 21 years of age) and sought delivery of the capital and dividends to him immediately rather than having to wait until he reached the age of 25. Lord Langdale MR held as follows:

> I think that principle has been repeatedly acted upon: that where a legacy is directed to accumulate for a certain period, or where the payment is postponed, the legatee, if he has an absolute indefeasible interest in the legacy, is not bound to wait until the expiration of that period, but may require payment the moment he is competent to give a valid discharge.

In short, even though the trust specifically provided that the beneficiary was not to be entitled to took the property until he reached the age of 25, it was held that the rights of the beneficiary take priority over the directions of the settlor. This right of the beneficiary was held to be capable of enforcement even though, in the submission of the residuary legatees, Vautier's interest was contingent on reaching 25 and therefore ought not to have been satisfied.

The rule in *Saunders v Vautier* has its roots in the principles relating to wills applied in the ecclesiastical courts, traceable through cases such as *Green v Spicer*[23] and *Younghusband v Gisborne*.[24] What is clear is that *Saunders v Vautier* was concerned with the rights of one beneficiary under a will. What is similarly clear is that subsequent cases have interpreted that decision so as to found the broader proposition that groups of beneficiaries, potentially even under discretionary trusts,[25] are entitled to call for the property or to require that the trustees

---

22 (1841) 4 Beav 115.
23 (1830) 1 Russ & M 395.
24 (1844) 1 Col 400.
25 *Green v Spicer* (1830) 1 Russ & M 395. The complexities associated with the nature of a beneficiary's rights under a discretionary trust are considered later in this chapter.

deal with the property in a manner which may appear tantamount to a variation of the existing trust.[26]

So, in *Re Bowes*,[27] a trust fund was created over £5,000 for the express purpose of planting trees on a large estate. Beneficiaries entitled under other provisions of that same trust were permitted to call for the fund reserved for the maintenance of trees so that they could alleviate the financial problems which they were experiencing at that time immediately. This approach was also applied by the Court of Appeal in *Re Nelson*,[28] where it was held that 'the principle [in *Saunders v Vautier*] is that where there is what amounts to an absolute gift it cannot be fettered by prescribing a mode of enjoyment'. In other words, where all of the equitable interest is settled for the benefit of a group of beneficiaries absolutely, that is tantamount to transferring title outright to them by means of an assignment. Similarly, in *Baker v Archer-Shee*[29] Lady Archer-Shee was the only life tenant, having an interest in possession, under her father's residuary estate with no other potential beneficiary in existence. Consequently it was held that Lady Archer-Shee would have been entitled under the principle in *Saunders v Vautier* to have directed the trustees how to deal with the trust property. Equally, Lady Archer-Shee was taxable on the income from the trust as though she was its absolute owner because this income was effectively held on bare trust for her.[30]

Similarly, in *Re Smith*,[31] a fund was held by the Public Trustee on discretionary trusts with a power to pay all or part of the capital and income to Mrs Aspinall and in the event of her death for Mrs Aspinall's three children in equal shares. Mrs Aspinall, her two surviving children (then of the age of majority) and the personal representatives of her deceased child mortgaged their interests with an insurance company. This had the effect of enabling the beneficiaries to borrow money against their equitable interests. The issue was whether the beneficiaries (effectively in the person of the insurance company) were entitled to call for the property. In the view of Romer J, where the trustees have a discretion as to the amount of the fund to be passed to one beneficiary and are also obliged to pass any remainder outstanding after exercising that discretion to other beneficiaries, where all of those beneficiaries present themselves to the trustees demanding a transfer of the trust fund, the trustees are required to make that transfer. The important point in this case was that those two classes of beneficiaries would constitute the whole of the equitable interest. In consequence, the trustees would be required to treat those beneficiaries 'as though they formed one person' absolutely entitled to the trust. That circumstance would be different from, for example, a beneficiary in the position of Mrs Aspinall approaching the trustees on her own and demanding for herself the whole of the trust fund, and would also be different from the situation in which the trustees had the express power to withhold some part of the trust fund from either class of beneficiaries in any event. In neither of these cases would the *Saunders v Vautier*[32] principle help the applicant, because she did not have the entire equitable interest in the former case and because the trustees had the power to defeat her interest in the latter.

26 These distinctions are considered below at para 4.1.5 below.
27 [1896] 1 Ch 507.
28 [1928] Ch 920.
29 [1927] AC 844.
30 See also *Archer-Shee v Garland* [1931] AC 212.
31 [1928] Ch 915.
32 (1841) 4 Beav 115.

Beyond the rule that beneficiaries representing the totality of the equitable interest can ask for delivery of the property, the decision in *Stephenson v Barclays Bank*[33] permitted a beneficiary to take delivery of her divisible share in the whole of the trust fund without needing to act together with the other beneficiaries: this approach would require that the property be capable of such division and that the beneficiary's precise entitlement is calculable. There are potential difficulties with this approach. Suppose a fund of money amounting to £100,000 in which five beneficiaries were expressed as having entitlement 'in equal shares'. Following *Stephenson*, one beneficiary would be entitled to call for £20,000 from the trustees. However, suppose that the rate of interest which the trustees could acquire for the fund fell as a result of the total capital falling below £100,000: would the loss of interest to the other beneficiaries be a ground for refusing that beneficiary's demand for delivery of her share? In *Lloyds Bank v Duker*,[34] a beneficiary was prevented from removing his part of the trust property because the removal of his portion from the total fund would have robbed the other beneficiaries of a majority shareholding in a private company. Therefore, it was held that the countervailing obligation to act fairly between the beneficiaries overrode the individual claimant's desire to realise his proprietary rights.[35]

4.1.3 The effect of beneficiaries having proprietary rights in the trust fund

Having examined the rule in *Saunders v Vautier*,[36] it is important to consider the more general theoretical importance of this principle. As considered above, Page Wood VC in *Gosling v Gosling*,[37] and subsequently the Court of Appeal in *Re Nelson*,[38] located the underlying rationale of the rule in the recognition that ultimate title in the trust fund is with the totality of the beneficiaries under the trust. That a trust is understood as vesting ultimate title with the beneficiaries is taken, then, by some of their Lordships as rendering trusts akin to gifts. A gift, of course, is an outright transfer of absolute title by donor to donee, whereas a trust transfers merely equitable title to the beneficiaries such that the settlor has necessarily stopped short of transferring absolute title immediately to them. This attitude does somewhat concertina together the different concepts of gift and trust: that is, to base the principle on an assumed intention on the part of a testator to make an absolute gift to beneficiaries ignores the fact that the testator chose to effect his intention as a trust rather than as a straightforward gift. Under the rule in *Milroy v Lord*,[39] equity will not give effect to gifts by means of trusts and vice versa – in short, one mode of transfer cannot be effected by another.[40] So, if the testator intended a gift, then a gift should be made, whereas if a testator created an express trust bounded in by express provisions making the legatees' rights subject to some contingency, that should not be subjected to the rule in *Saunders v Vautier*[41] because of some supposed analogy to a gift.

---

33 [1975] 1 All ER 625.
34 [1987] 3 All ER 193.
35 See para 8.3.9 below; *Tito v Waddell (No 2)* [1977] Ch 106.
36 (1841) 4 Beav 115.
37 (1859) John 265.
38 [1928] Ch 920.
39 (1862) 4 De GF & J 264.
40 See para 5.4.2 below.
41 (1841) 4 Beav 115.

The point made in those decisions is slightly more subtle than to say 'this trust should be described as a gift'. Rather, the point, as considered above, is that a transfer on bare trust is tantamount to vesting the entire interest in the beneficiary. By analogy, it is said, transferring property on trust means that all of those beneficiaries acting together constitute the entirety of the beneficial entitlement to the trust fund, and in consequence that the creation of such a trust is tantamount to making an outright transfer of the proprietary rights in the fund to those persons. On the one hand, this may be recognition of the practice (in cases like *Re Smith*)[42] of beneficiaries in selling or borrowing against their equitable interests.[43] On the other hand, this may correlate with the policy outlined above, that mid-19th century opinion considered it important that capital should circulate freely and therefore it was expedient that the beneficiaries should have control over the trust property to prevent it stagnating in the hands of the trustees.

Transferring power over the use of the trust fund to the beneficiaries reduced the influence of the settlor over the same property. As Harris put the matter, 'fidelity to the settlor's intentions ends where equitable property begins'.[44] To be more positive about the same issue, the beneficiaries acquire rights in the property making up the trust fund. They are ultimately, beneficially its owners. For the settlor intent on preventing the beneficiaries from unpacking her carefully crafted trust, it is important to structure affairs so that it is impossible for the beneficiaries to act together, or so that the trustees have rights to retain part of the trust fund such that the beneficiaries do not have all of the rights to it.

That the rule in *Saunders v Vautier* is a development peculiar to the English law of trusts is demonstrated by the American cases of *Brandon v Robinson*[45] and *Claflin v Claflin*,[46] which preferred to observe the wishes of the settlor rather than advance the rights of the beneficiaries.[47] It is a feature of English law that the beneficiaries are treated as the ultimate owners of the trust fund,[48] and not that the intentions of the settlor be closely observed and followed.

4.1.4 Issues as to the nature of the rights of the objects of specific types of trust

Introduction

So far in this chapter we have considered the general position under the principle in *Saunders v Vautier*. This is the proper description of the rights of beneficiaries in ordinary trusts. However, there are a number of specific types of trust in which it is not clear whether or not the principle in *Saunders v Vautier* provides a complete description of the rights of beneficiaries. The principal problem arises in relation to discretionary trusts – as discussed in Chapter 3 – in which it could be said that no objects of the trust can have any property rights whatsoever until the trustees have appointed some property to them. Much will depend

---

42 [1928] Ch 920.
43 Moffat, 1999, 251.
44 Harris, 1975:1, 2.
45 (1811) 18 Ves 429.
46 20 NE 454 (1889).
47 On which point see Moffat, 1999, 252.
48 *Curtis v Lukin* (1842) 5 Beav 147.

upon the precise terms of the discretionary trust. Similar issues arise in relation to the objects of fiduciary mere powers and unit trusts. This section, therefore, considers issues which go beyond the ordinary law of trusts and which stretch outside the usual discussion of the beneficiary principle. The new undergraduate reader may choose to pass over this material for the time being.

The nature of the rights of the objects of a discretionary trust

In relation to discretionary trusts, there is a question as to the nature of the rights which the objects of such a trust have. (It should be recalled that in relation to discretionary trust powers, we usually speak of 'objects' as opposed to 'beneficiaries'.) The central question is whether or not the objects of a discretionary trust could be said to have any proprietary rights in that trust property before the trustees exercise their discretion to allocate property to any one of them.[49] A discretionary trust requires that the trustees exercise a discretion in favour of a specified class of objects. The difficulties associated with identifying those objects were considered in section 3.4 above. The conceptual problem is as to the rights of the objects before the trustees exercise their discretion. Once the trustees' discretion has been exercised, then clearly the objects to whom identified property has been advanced will have absolute rights in the property which has been transferred to them,[50] whereas objects to whom no property has been advanced will have no rights in any property (assuming that the trustees have not breached any of their duties). Before the discretion is exercised, it could be argued that none of the objects has any rights in any identified property.[51] The effect of this argument would be that objects of discretionary trusts have no proprietary rights. However, it could be said that collectively they must constitute all of the people who could possibly acquire rights in the property at any time in the future. In consequence, it could be argued that all of the objects of the discretionary trust power – provided that they constitute all of the possible objects of that power and provided that they are all acting in concert – should be able to exercise the rights which the absolutely entitled beneficiaries would be entitled to under the principle of *Saunders v Vautier* under a fixed trust. The effect of this argument would be that all of the objects of a discretionary trust would have *Saunders v Vautier* rights and therefore that each object should be treated as having some sort of proprietary right in the trust property. Alternatively, a third argument might consider that the objects of the discretionary trust have a power to ensure that the trustees exercise their discretion properly. These arguments are considered in this section.

49 The general nature of beneficiaries' rights was explained in the following way: 'The beneficiaries' interests in a trust fund are proprietary interests in the assets from time to time comprised in the fund subject to the trustees' overriding powers of managing and alienating the trust assets and substituting others. On an authorised sale of a trust investment, the beneficiaries' proprietary interests in the investment are overreached; that is to say, they are automatically transferred from the investment which is sold to the proceeds of sale and any new investment acquired with them. . . . The beneficiaries' interest in the new investment are exactly the same as their interest in the old. They have a continuing beneficial interest which persists in the substitute.' Millett, 'Proprietary restitution' in Degeling and Edelman, *Equity in Commercial Law* (Law Book Co, 2005), 15. Cited in *Richstar Enterprises Pty Ltd v Carey (No 6)* [2006] FCA 814, para [17].

50 Assuming there is no claim for the recovery of that property by the other objects on grounds of breach of trust.

51 *Murphy v Murphy* [1999] 1 WLR 282; *Lemos v Coutts* (Cayman) Ltd (2006–07) 9 ITELR 616. Cf *Johns v Johns* [2004] NZCA 42, [2005] WTLR 529.

The elegant solution to these question, which has been proposed by Prof Thomas[52] and accepted by the Federal Court of Australia in *Richstar Enterprises Pty Ltd v Carey (No 6)*,[53] is that the proper analysis would depend upon whether the discretionary trust is open-ended or not. This is explained in Thomas on *Powers* in the following way:

> Thus, although an *individual* object of an exhaustive discretionary trust (and *a fortiori* in the case of a non-exhaustive one) cannot claim any part of the trust fund or its income (as the case may be) because he is not entitled to any interest in it unless and until the trustees exercise their discretion in his favour, and notwithstanding that the class of beneficiaries is a closed class, all the objects of such a discretionary trust, where the class is closed, may join together and collectively call upon the trustees to transfer the fund to them or deal with the property subject to the discretion as if they were the absolute owners thereof . . . Although, as Lord Reid pointed out in *Gartside v IRC*, two or more persons cannot have a single right unless they hold it jointly or in common, and the beneficiaries of a discretionary trust do not have such a right – indeed, they are in competition with each other and what the trustees give to one is his alone – it remains the case that, under the principle laid down in *Saunders v Vautier*,[54] such beneficiaries, as the persons for whom or in whose favour alone the trust property may be applied, have a right to terminate the trust and deal with the property as if it were their own.[55]

Therefore, an individual object has no property rights until property is appointed to her by the trustees. Rather, it can only be if the objects are acting together that they could possibly claim rights to property at all. The question is: in what circumstances could the collective rights of the beneficiaries grant them property rights in the discretionary trust property?

The answer is this: if the discretionary trust power obliges the trustees to exhaust all of the trust property by transferring it to the objects and provided that the complete class of objects can be defined, then the objects will be able to act together and rely on the principle in *Saunders v Vautier* to direct the manner in which the trustees are obliged to use the trust property.[56] Such a discretionary trust would be close-ended because the property would be required to be exhausted and it possible to know which people constitute the full membership of the class of objects. The objects of such a discretionary trust could have property rights in the trust property because that property must be divided between some of them and because it is possible to know who all the possible objects are so as to fall within *Saunders v Vautier*. This argument emerges from *Re Smith*:

> When there is a trust under which trustees have a discretion as to applying the whole or part of a fund to or for the benefit of a particular person, that particular person cannot come to the trustees, and demand the fund; for the whole fund has not been given to him but only so much as the trustees think fit to let him have. But when the trustees have no discretion as to the amount of the fund to be applied, the fact that the trustees have a

52 See Thomas, 1998, 6–268, and Thomas and Hudson, 2004, 184 *et seq*.
53 [2006] FCA 814.
54 (1841) Cr & Ph 240.
55 GW Thomas, *Powers*, Sweet & Maxwell, 1998, para 6–268.
56 *Re Smith* [1928] Ch 915; *Re Nelson (note)* [1928] Ch 920.

discretion as to the method in which the whole of the fund shall be applied for the benefit of the particular person does not prevent that particular person from coming and saying: 'Hand over the fund to me'.[57]

By extension, there are two circumstances in which this analysis would not apply. First, if the class of objects cannot be completely defined because there may be future, currently unknown members added to the class within the trust's perpetuity period. An example of this situation would be a provision in a trust instrument to the effect that the class of objects was defined as being 'any children of the settlor' at a time when the settlor was still alive and could therefore have further children in the future.[58] Secondly, if the trustees are not obliged to exhaust the whole of the trust property. This prevents there being property rights for the beneficiaries because, if the trustees were empowered to withhold some of the trust property and to appoint it to other objects, then it would not be possible for the objects of the discretionary trust power to assert that the whole of the equitable interest in that property was held for their benefit. This argument is conceived of by Parkinson and Wright in the following way:

> Since the trustees of a discretionary trust have no duty to make a particular distribution, or indeed any distribution to a specific individual, the rights of the beneficiaries are limited to compelling the trustees to consider whether or not to make a distribution in their favour and to ensuring the property administration of the trust. This is true even if the discretionary trust only has one beneficiary.[59]

This passage has been explained by the Federal Court of Australia in *Richstar Enterprises Pty Ltd*[60] as relating to non-exhaustive discretionary trusts and therefore as being in line with Thomas on *Powers* above, otherwise, it is suggested, it should be doubted.

Individual objects of a discretionary trust power will not have individual rights to any of the trust property because their rights are in competition with one another: that is, if object X receives trust property, then that is property which cannot be paid to object Y. Indeed, it has been suggested in one decided case, *Gartside v IRC*, that the distinct nature of each object's claims to the trust property means that no object can be recognised as having an interest in possession before any identified property has been appointed to her.[61] In this case, the issue was whether or not the object had an 'interest in possession' for estate duty purposes.[62] This analysis is particularly apposite if the trustees are not obliged to exhaust the whole of the trust property in favour of the objects of the power. If the class of potential objects remains open,[63] then even if there is only one object alive at the time, that person will not be able to exercise *Saunders v Vautier* rights because she could not prove that she would

---

57 *Re Smith* [1928] Ch 915, 918, *per* Romer J.
58 *Re Trafford's Settlement* [1985] Ch 34, 40, *per* Peter Gibson J.
59 Parkinson and Wright, 'Equity and Property' in Parkinson ed, *The Principles of Equity*, Law Book Co, 2003, 60, citing *Re Weir's Settlement Trusts* [1971] Ch 145.
60 [2006] FCA 814, para 26.
61 *Gartside v IRC* [1968] AC 553, 606, *per* Lord Reid, 617, *per* Lord Wilberforce.
62 See also *Re Weir's Settlement Trusts* [1971] Ch 145.
63 That is, if some future objects may yet join the class of objects.

constitute the entirety of the equitable interest in the trust property.[64] Nevertheless, in general terms, the logic of the *Saunders v Vautier* principle requires that all of the objects acting together will constitute the entirety of the potential equitable interest and that such a group may call for the trust property in circumstances in which the trustees are empowered to exhaust the whole of the fund and in which there cannot be any further members of the class of objects.[65]

So, then we have to consider what rights the objects of the discretionary trust have to control the trustees. As Lord Wilberforce in *Gartside v IRC*[66] put it:

> No doubt in a certain sense a beneficiary under a discretionary trust has an 'interest': the nature of it may, sufficiently for the purpose, be spelt out by saying that he has a right to be considered as a potential recipient of benefit by the trustees and a right to have his interest protected by a court of equity.

The key rights of all objects of all discretionary trusts, beyond the matters considered above, are therefore to have their claim to property under the trust considered by the trustees and to have that claim protected by the court against any abuse or breach of trust by the trustees in exercising their power.

The nature of the rights of the objects of a fiduciary mere power

The objects of a fiduciary mere power have only mere expectancies that they will have property appointed to them.[67] Consequently, they have no proprietary rights in any property before an appointment is made to them either individually or collectively.[68] This is a clear distinction from the discretionary trust power considered in the previous section. Under a discretionary trust power, the objects have some proprietary rights commensurate with being entitled under a trust, whereas objects under a mere power have no proprietary rights at all before the exercise of the appointment.[69] The rights of objects of a mere power are merely to have the power applied properly.[70]

The nature of the rights of participants in a unit trust

The nature of the rights of participants in a unit trust, a type of trust used for investment purposes, take a slightly different form albeit that they are based fundamentally on ordinary trusts law principles. This illustrates how those fundamental principles can be adapted for specific purposes. A unit trust operates as follows. The core element of the unit trust is its deed of trust. The trust fund (as provided by the participants) will be held on trust by a trustee but all investment decisions will be made by a manager. The manager (or managers) will usually be a management company. The manager will be empowered by the trust deed to

64 *Gartside v IRC* [1968] AC 553.
65 As before, this requires that the discretionary trust power be an exhaustive power.
66 [1968] AC 553, 617.
67 *Re Brooks' Settlement Trusts* [1939] 1 Ch 993.
68 *Re Gulbenkian* [1968] Ch 126; *Schmidt v Rosewood Trust Ltd* [2003] 2 WLR 1442, 1455.
69 *Ibid.*
70 *Ibid.*

acquire securities of a type specified in the trust deed. This power will be subject to a general duty to maintain a portfolio of investments to spread the risk of the total investment capital of the fund. Those securities are then held on trust by the trustees appointed in the trust deed. The trustees will usually be a company but will in any event be distinct from the manager. The fiduciary function is therefore divided between the investment management responsibilities of the manager and the custodian responsibilities of the trustee. The profits of the pooled capital is then allocated equally between the units held. The investor (or, participant) will be entitled to a pro rata cash return for each unit held. The question is as to the nature of the rights of the participants in a unit trust.

The High Court of Australia in *CPT Custodian Pty Ltd v Commissioner of State Revenue*[71] has considered the nature of the rights of investors in a unit trust which was created to invest in land. These investors under English law would be described as being beneficiaries under a trust; a similar approach is taken in Australia, only without the same statute in place.[72] Each investor acquired a proportionate number of the total 'units' issued by the unit trust depending on the size of its investment. The question, for the purposes of Australian land tax, was whether or not the investors owned proprietary rights in the land held by the unit trust. It was held that a court of equity could exercise its inherent jurisdiction to supervise the management of a trust on behalf of the investors without that necessarily meaning that the investors had proprietary rights in the underlying property.[73] In Australia, in *Charles v Federal Commissioner of Taxation*[74] it had previously been held that 'a unit under the trust deed before us confers a proprietary interest in all the property which for the time being is subject to the trust of the deed', so that whether or not the investors owned any profits held by the trustees would depend on the manner in which the trustees held those moneys. On the facts of *CPT Custodian Pty Ltd v Commissioner of State Revenue*, because the trust property could also be applied by the trustees to meet their own expenses then it could not be the case that the investors were solely entitled to trust property between themselves. This is akin, it is suggested, to saying that the investors are in the position of objects of a discretionary trust in that they do not know to which property they may become entitled in the future until some contingency is satisfied first. Moreover, it is suggested that this argument is akin to saying that no beneficiary is ever entitled to proprietary rights in any trust fund where the trustees are entitled to deduct amounts for their expenses: that is an unfeasible argument because it would destroy the notion that beneficiaries have equitable proprietary rights in the trust fund.

For the purposes of English trusts law, s 237 of the Financial Services and Markets Act 2000 provides that the property held for the purposes of a unit trust is 'held on trust for the participants' in that trust and therefore the question of whether or not there is a trust for the investors is answered by the statute in that the investors are necessarily the owners in equity of the property held for the purposes of the unit trust.[75] The statute provides: '"unit trust

---

71 [2005] HCA 53.

72 The nature of unit trusts is considered in Hudson, *The Law on Investment Entities*, 2000, Chapter 7; and in Thomas and Hudson, *The Law of Trusts*, 2004, Chapter 51, as was referred to by the High Court of Australia. As description of unit trusts taken from earlier editions of this book is also available on-line in the two web-sites supporting this book, as described in the Preface.

73 Relying on *Schmidt v Rosewood* [2003] 2 AC 709, 729, *per* Lord Walker.

74 (1954) 90 CLR 598, 609, *per* Dixon CJ, Kitto and Taylor JJ.

75 See GW Thomas and AS Hudson, *The Law of Trusts*, 2004, 1587 *et seq.*

scheme" means a collective investment scheme under which the property is held on trust for the participants.'[76]

It is suggested, therefore, in English law that the participants have proprietary rights against the unit trust property by virtue both of statute and of the rule in *Saunders v Vautier*[77] which permits the beneficiaries (provided that they are *sui juris* and absolutely entitled) to terminate the trust.[78] Therefore, the participant has (subject to any specific contractual, structural provision to the contrary) ultimately that kind of proprietary right,[79] when exercised in common with all the other participants, which is usually said to attach to a beneficiary under an ordinary English trust.[80]

4.1.5 Protective trusts

The purpose of protective trusts[81]

In consequence of the principles considered so far in this chapter, it is very difficult to structure a so-called 'protective trust' under English law. A protective trust is a trust which prevents an absolutely-entitled, *sui juris* beneficiary from taking absolute title to the trust property so that the beneficiary can be treated as having no vested title in that property. A settlor may wish to use such a protective trust for one of three general purposes. First, to prevent a beneficiary who is incompetent in some way from taking absolute title in property because they are not considered reliable enough to vest absolute title in property in them: for example, a drug addict who is feared incapable of resisting the urge to spend the whole of a trust fund on feeding her addiction. Secondly, to prevent the settlor from appearing to have title in property which otherwise the settlor would be required to give up to her creditors in insolvency proceedings: here the trust might be used in an attempt to make it seem that the trust property were owned beneficially by some other person. Thirdly, to prevent the settlor from appearing to be absolutely entitled to trust property for tax or other regulatory purposes.

Methods of seeking to establish protective trusts

The reason for the difficulty in structuring such protective trusts in English law is that an absolutely-entitled beneficiary can direct the trustees how to deal with the property (such that she will be considered to be the equitable owner of that property)[82] and consequently the courts will not permit a trust in favour of an absolutely-entitled beneficiary to deny proprietary rights in the trust property to that beneficiary.[83] In *Goulding v James*[84] the effect

---

76 See Alastair Hudson, *The Law of Finance*, Sweet & Maxwell, 2009, Chapter 52.
77 (1841) 4 Beav 115.
78 *Re AEG Unit Trust Managers Ltd's Deed* [1957] Ch 415. See Hudson, *The Law on Investment Entities*, 2000, Chapter 7; and in Thomas and Hudson, *The Law of Trusts*, 2004, Chapter 51.
79 *Baker v Archer-Shee* [1927] AC 844.
80 *Costa and Duppe Properties Pty Ltd v Duppe* [1986] VR 90; *Softcorp Holdings Pty Ltd v Commissioner of Stamps* (1987) 18 ATR 813.
81 See generally Thomas and Hudson, 2004, para 9–01 *et seq.*
82 *Saunders v Vautier* (1841) 4 Beav 115.
83 *Hunt-Foulston v Furber* (1876) 3 Ch D 285; *Re Dugdale* (1888) 38 Ch D 176; *Re Brown* [1954] Ch 39.
84 [1997] 2 All ER 239, 247, *per* Mummery LJ.

of the English law of trusts in relation to the principle in *Saunders v Vautier* was described in the following manner:

> The principle recognises the rights of beneficiaries, who are sui juris and together absolutely entitled to the trust property, to exercise their proprietary rights to overbear and defeat the intention of a testator or settlor to subject property to the continuing trusts, powers and limitations of a will or trust instrument.

The effect of the principle is therefore that it is very difficult to prevent beneficiaries from undoing the settlor's intentions unless the trust is carefully structured. Similarly, trusts law will prevent a beneficiary with vested equitable rights from denying property rights associated with that interest. The only certain way to ensure that the beneficiary does not have sufficient property rights would be to create equitable interests in favour of other beneficiaries so that the protected beneficiary acting alone would not be able to assume control of the trust property nor be deemed to have such a right of necessity. For example, the settlor may appoint herself as one of the beneficiaries and so retain a veto against the other beneficiaries being able to claim that they constitute the entirety of the equitable interest.

Furthermore, the settlor could seek to structure matters so that the beneficiary's interests are made subject to some condition precedent. For example, the trust may be structured so that the beneficiary only acquires rights in the property if the trustees exercise some power of appointment in her favour, as opposed to some other objects of a class of objects of that power, with the intention that the protected object of that power will have no vested rights in any trust property. Tax law[85] and insolvency law[86] have a number of clawback provisions which may deem the trust to be a sham intended only to avoid liability to tax or to account to insolvency creditors. In the USA, with the exception of Nebraska, the rule in *Saunders v Vautier*[87] is not applied, and therefore it is possible to have what are known as 'spendthrift trusts' whereby the beneficiary is prevented from demanding delivery of the trust fund from the trustee. It is also possible to use these structures so as to provide protection from one's own bankruptcy under English law. For example, if Arthur thought that he was at risk of bankruptcy, he might try to create a trust over his property whereby he is expressed either as having no vested property rights in the trust fund or as losing them at the moment of his becoming bankrupt.[88] Having no vested rights in the property means that it will not pass to one's trustee in bankruptcy in the event of insolvency.[89]

Also, building on the foregoing discussion of protection against insolvency, the settlor could seek to create a determinable interest which ended on the happening of a specified event. The structure of such a provision needs to be attended to carefully. If the trust sought to declare that Arthur's property rights would cease to be effective once he was declared bankrupt[90] or once

---

85 See generally the outline discussion of the tax treatment of discretionary trusts and tax avoidance structures in para 2.5.2 above.

86 Eg, Insolvency Act 1986, s 423.

87 (1841) 4 Beav 115.

88 Subject, that is, to what is said in Hudson, 2012 in relation to asset protection trusts and their limitation under insolvency legislation.

89 *Re Scientific Investment Pension Plan Trusts* [1999] Ch 53. Cf Welfare Reform and Pensions Act 1999, s 14(3).

90 *Re Burroughs-Fowler* [1916] 2 Ch 251.

it was transferred to a trustee in bankruptcy, then such provisions would be void.[91] If Arthur's interest became terminable on the happening of some other event, then it could be valid. So, in *Re Detmold*,[92] it was held unobjectionable to uphold a term in a marriage settlement which transferred the husband's entire interest to the wife in the event of his bankruptcy or the transfer of his share of the settlement property to a third person. In the modern context of bankruptcy, however, any device which seeks to put property beyond the reach of creditors in the expectation of bankruptcy will generally be unenforceable: such that structures used to put property beyond the reach of bankruptcy creditors would be capable of avoidance[93] and any protected interest under a trust would be liable to be forfeited in the event of bankruptcy.[94]

Section 33 of the Trustee Act 1925

Alternatively, s 33 of the Trustee Act 1925 provides a form of words for any trust which is expressed to be a 'protective trust'. In such a situation, if the principal beneficiary in receipt of the income under a trust 'does or attempts to do or suffers an act or thing . . . whereby . . . he would be deprived of the right to receive the same', then the trust property so designated will be held for the 'maintenance or support' of the people nominated in the trust for that purpose. This prevents, for example, the profligate wasting of property by a life tenant under a trust such that remainder beneficiaries would be left without their property. Such a structure will prevent the trustee in bankruptcy from taking possession of property which is required by s 33 to be held for the benefit of those nominated remainder beneficiaries.

The rationale for this principle is that the principal beneficiary is not the absolute owner of the property; therefore, it would be inequitable to allow his creditors in bankruptcy to take absolute title to the property. What might be more difficult, however, is a situation in which the protective trust was created with the sole purpose of avoiding the principal beneficiary's creditors through the device of expressing that principal beneficiary's next of kin to be entitled to take an interest in remainder. For example, in the case of *Midland Bank v Wyatt*,[95] the court held that a purported creation of a trust over the bankrupt's interest in the family home in favour of his wife and daughters would be held void as a sham where its sole purpose was to avoid those creditors and where the wife and daughters were evidently not intended to take possession of their putative rights.

4.1.6 Insolvency, trusts law and the rights of beneficiaries

Trusts provide protection against the insolvency of trustee and settlor in general

A beneficiary under a trust will have her equitable interest protected against the insolvency of her trustees, unless any of the legislative provisions considered in the next subsection

---

91   *Younghusband v Gisborne* (1846) 15 LJ Ch 355; *Re Sanderson's Trust* (1857) 3 K & J 497 (bankruptcy); *Brandon v Robinson* (1811) 18 Ves 429; *Re Dugdale* (1888) 38 Ch D 176; *Re Brown* [1954] Ch 39 (alienation to a third person).
92   (1889) 40 Ch D 585.
93   Insolvency Act 1986, s 423.
94   *Re Scientific Investment Pension Plan Trusts* [1999] Ch 53.
95   [1995] 1 FLR 697.

apply. It a very important feature of a trust used in commercial situations that if the trustee goes into insolvency then the trust fund is not distributed among the insolvent trustee's personal creditors because the trust fund is owned beneficially by the beneficiaries. Therefore, to seek protection against someone else's insolvency it is very useful indeed to have that insolvent person hold property on trust for you, or to have the court accept that the insolvent person should be treated as being a trustee (whether an express or a constructive trustee) for the claimant. Trusts provide protection against insolvency. As will emerge time and again throughout this book, people who have dealt with someone who has gone into insolvency will try to argue that the insolvent person should be treated as holding property on trust for them. By contrast, if the insolvent person merely owed them a debt (or, 'a personal claim') then the creditor would have no protection against that insolvency because there would be no property in which the creditor had rights. Consequently, the courts have become used to dealing with some fairly specious arguments to the effect that an express trust should be found even though many of the necessary pre-requisites for a trust (as discussed in Chapters 2 through 5) do not exist, or that a resulting or a constructive trust should be found even though the circumstances are not right (as discussed in Chapters 11 and 12). Consequently, insolvency is a context which arises again and again in relation to trusts law.

Insolvency legislation setting trusts aside

It is a salutary lesson to read a textbook on insolvency law and see how trusts are treated in that context as being ingenious devices to avoid insolvency law. In Chapter 3 we considered cases such as *Re Goldcorp*[96] and *Re Global Trader*[97] in relation to insolvent financial institutions and the need for the claimants to demonstrate that they were beneficiaries of those arrangements. However, there are provisions in the insolvency legislation which can operate so as to 'claw back' any property which was settled on trust solely for the purpose of avoiding insolvency creditors in anticipation of such an insolvency.[98] So, s 339 of the Insolvency Act 1986 provides that if a person enters into a transaction at an undervalue or gives 'a preference' to another person, then that transaction can be set aside. For this purpose, a 'transaction at an undervalue' includes any transaction entered into for no consideration (such as the ordinary declaration of a trust). The court may then make such order as it sees fit.

A similar provision is contained in s 423 of that Act, as discussed in section 11.4.7 below, relating specifically to the making of gifts or declarations of trust which can be set aside on the basis that they were intended to be used so as to defraud creditors, such that any property transferred in relation to them can be 'clawed back'.[99] The lesson from these provisions is that even if a purportedly valid trust is created in the expectation of an insolvency then the court may choose to set that trust aside if it was part of a transaction at an undervalue seeking to put property beyond the reach of the insolvent person's creditors. A good example of such

---

96   [1995] 1 AC 74.
97   [2009] EWHC 602 (Ch), [2009] 2 BCLC 18.
98   The decision of the Court of Appeal in *BNY Corporate Trustee Services Ltd v Eurosail-UK 2007-3BL* [2011] 1 WLR 2524 considers the legal principles in s 123 of the Insolvency Act 1986 on the identification of when an entity is to be deemed to be insolvent.
99   *Midland Bank v Wyatt* [1997] 1 BCLC 242.

a situation would be that in which the settlor created the trust knowing of the likelihood that she would soon go into insolvency in an effort to transfer her home and valuable chattels beyond the reach of her creditors. It was held in *Hill v Spread Trustee Co Ltd*[100] by the Court of Appeal that the grant of a security could constitute a transaction at an undervalue. Supplying a general principle, it was held by the Court of Appeal in *Agricultural Mortgage Corporation plc v Woodward*[101] that the court will look at the totality of the transaction, examine it realistically, and take into account the real value of the benefits and advantages accruing to either side, while always taking into account the underlying purpose of the transaction. This underlines, perhaps, the continued efficacy of the equitable principle that the court will always look to the substance of a transaction and not simply to its form, as was considered in Chapter 3 in relation to sham trusts (section 3.3.3).

The high-water mark of claw-back provisions was reached in *Re Butterworth*,[102] where a trader created a trust over his property before starting out in a new grocery business which failed a little over three years later. The Court of Appeal held that the trust was void for the purposes of the insolvency proceedings because it had been created so as to put the trader's property beyond the reach of his creditors in case his new business venture should fail. On this basis, albeit that that case was decided in 1882,[103] it can be very difficult to create a trust over one's own property which will be proof against one's own insolvency. This appears to be the opposite of the type of business practice which would emerge in 1897 in the wake of the decision of the House of Lords in *Salomon v A Salomon & Co Ltd*,[104] in which a boot-maker transferred his business assets, which he had previously owned himself absolutely, into a company such that the company was taken by the House of Lords to constitute a separate person from the boot-maker himself, with the result that the boot-maker would not be personally liable for the debts of his company. In *Midland Bank v Wyatt*[105] it was held that a trust would be set aside under s 423 of the 1986 Act where the trust that was purportedly created was a sham seeking simply to defraud the settlor's creditors.

These statutory provisions are all predicated ultimately on two common law principles, as has been confirmed in a recent decision of the Supreme Court. First, the '*pari passu*' principle requires that each unsecured creditor be put in the same position in the administration of the insolvency such that no preference is given to any one unsecured creditor over any other, as confirmed in the decisions of the House of Lords in *Stein v Blake*[106] and in *Re Bank of Credit and Commerce International SA (No 8)*.[107] Second, the 'anti-deprivation' principle prevents any assets being taken out of the estate of the insolvent person so that they are not available for distribution among the unsecured creditors, as confirmed in the decision of the Supreme Court in *Belmont Park Investments Pty Ltd v BNY Corporate Trustee Services Ltd*.[108] Consequently, the insolvency law context will need to be considered carefully when seeking to create a trust in practice to shield assets against insolvency.[109]

---

100 [2006] WTLR 1009.
101 [1995] 1 BCLC 1, [1994] BCC 688; *Barclays Bank v Eustice* [1995] 1 WLR 1238.
102 (1882) 19 Ch D 588.
103 That case related to a predecessor provision to s 423.
104 [1897] AC 22. See Alastair Hudson, *Understanding Company Law*, Routledge-Cavendish, 2011, Chapter 2.
105 [1997] 1 BCLC 242.
106 [1996] AC 243.
107 [1997] 4 All ER 568, [1998] AC 214.
108 [2011] UKSC 38, [2011] 3 WLR 519.
109 See generally Hudson, 2012, in relation to 'Asset Protection Trusts' for a much more detailed treatment of this area.

4.2 THE BENEFICIARY PRINCIPLE

For a trust to be valid, there must be an identifiable beneficiary which is either an individual or a company. If there is no such beneficiary, and consequently the trust is for the achievement of some abstract purpose, then the trust is void. Therefore, where there is a trust for the benefit of 'people', the trust will be valid, whereas a trust created to carry out an abstract purpose will be void, except in a group of anomalous cases.

The cases differ on what will constitute a 'people trust'. The traditional view preferred a literal interpretation of the terms of the trust: if there was no beneficiary, then the trust was simply void. This approach has been supported in more recent cases. The alternative approach suggests that as long as there is some direct or indirect benefit for some ascertainable beneficiaries who can bring the matter before the court in the event of a dispute, then that will be sufficient to satisfy the beneficiary principle.

It was a feature of the older cases involving trusts which satisfied the beneficiary principle that such trusts must nevertheless have been subject to a perpetuity period or else they would be void under the rules against perpetuities. Such 'people trusts' may now be rendered valid by the operation of the Perpetuities and Accumulations Act 1964, which enables the trustees to 'wait and see' if the trust is wound up within the perpetuity period. Where the trust is not so wound up, the 1964 Act provides a mechanism for bringing the trust to an end automatically.

None of these rules apply to charitable trusts. Charitable trusts are discussed separately in Chapter 25.

4.2.1 The nature of the beneficiary principle

The basis of the beneficiary principle

Two ideas are fundamental to the law on express trusts. The first idea is that the consciences of the trustees can only be controlled if there are beneficiaries who can bring the trustees to court when the trustees have failed to perform their obligations under the trust adequately.[110] Therefore, the courts insist on being able to take control of a trust in the event that there is some failure to perform the terms of the trust properly.[111] If there were nobody entitled to bring the trustees before the court by virtue of being a beneficiary, then the court would not be able to control the administration of the trust. In consequence, it is a requirement of English trusts law that there must be at least one beneficiary in whose favour the court can decree performance of the trust.[112] The second idea is that a trust requires that some property be held on trust for some person as beneficiary such that the beneficiary acquires a proprietary right in the trust property.[113] It is the beneficiary's proprietary right in the trust property which gives the beneficiary the *locus standi* to petition the court if the trustees fail to perform

---

110 The precise nature of the obligations of trustees is considered in detail in Chapter 8. The means by which trustees are held to account for breaches of their obligations are considered in Chapter 18.

111 *Morice v Bishop of Durham* (1804) 9 Ves 399, (1805) 10 Ves 522; *Bowman v Secular Society Ltd* [1917] AC 406.

112 *Ibid.*

113 *Saunders v Vautier* (1841) 4 Beav 115.

their duties.[114] In consequence, the so-called 'beneficiary principle' which we consider in detail in this chapter has become an essential feature of English trusts law.

The 'beneficiary principle' is a requirement that there must be an ascertainable beneficiary or beneficiaries for a trust to be valid.[115] The policy underlying this principle, and arguably the whole of the law of trusts,[116] is that there must be a beneficiary in whose favour the trust can be exercised by the court and that there must be beneficiaries with proprietary rights in the trust fund. The principle that there must be a beneficiary under a trust and that that class of persons must be sufficiently certain is generally taken to have been expressed most clearly in *Morice v Bishop of Durham*[117] in the words of Lord Grant MR:

> There can be no trust, over the exercise of which this court will not assume control . . . If there be a clear trust, but for uncertain objects, the property . . . is undisposed of . . . Every . . . [non-charitable] trust must have a definite object. There must be somebody in whose favour the court can decree performance.[118]

It is clear from these words that the court requires the existence of a beneficiary precisely because there must be a beneficiary who is able to keep the trustees in check by bringing any contentious matters before the court. Lord Eldon expressed the rationale behind the beneficiary principle as requiring also that the court be able to administer the trust if the trustees failed to do so or that the court be able to prevent maladministration of the trust.[119] In either circumstance, it was only considered possible for the court to maintain certainty and to ensure that trustees are observing the terms of the trust if there is a beneficiary capable of suing the trustees.[120] Given that the settlor disappears out of the picture once the trust has been properly created, there is no one else capable of policing the activities of the trustees other than the beneficiaries.[121]

In *Re Endacott*,[122] it was said, in relation to the beneficiary principle, that 'no principle has greater sanction or authority' in the law of trusts than that requiring the existence of a beneficiary. In the cases considered below, it will be seen that traditional judicial attitudes tended to invalidate trusts which did not satisfy the beneficiary principle on a literal interpretation of their provisions.[123] By contrast, more recent cases have tended to validate trusts provided

---

114 The beneficiary's *locus standi* in this context means the beneficiary's power to bring a matter to court based on her right as a beneficiary under the trust. If the applicant had no such right, then the court would not acknowledge her right to sue the trustees.

115 *Leahy v Attorney-General for NSW* [1959] AC 457, as explained by Goff J in *Re Denley* [1969] 1 Ch 373.

116 As was considered in Chapter 2.

117 (1804) 9 Ves 399; (1805) 10 Ves 522. It is possible that these *dicta* are directed at the requirement for certainty of objects (see Thomas and Hudson, 2004, 159). These *dicta* are rehearsed, however, by Lord Parker in *Bowman v Secular Society Ltd* [1917] AC 406, 441.

118 These sentiments are applied equally to the beneficiary principle in *Re Astor's ST* [1952] Ch 534, [1952] 1 All ER 1067 by Roxburgh J and in *Re Endacott* [1960] Ch 232, [1959] 3 All ER 562 by the Court of Appeal.

119 *Morice v Bishop of Durham* (1805) 10 Ves 522, 539.

120 *Re Astor's ST* [1952] Ch 534.

121 *Paul v Paul* (1882) 20 Ch D 742.

122 [1960] Ch 232.

123 *Leahy v Attorney-General for NSW* [1959] AC 457.

that there is some person or group of persons who could sensibly be said to be capable of controlling the trust by bringing matters to court.[124]

The policy against abstract purpose trusts

A trust which is *not* for the benefit of ascertainable beneficiaries is described as being a trust for the pursuit of an abstract purpose. Trusts for abstract purposes are void under English trusts law precisely because there is no beneficiary who can enforce the trustees' obligations before the court.[125] (It might be useful for you to think of the beneficiary principle as operating in addition to the rules on certainty of beneficiaries considered in Chapter 3: that is, all trusts require that there be ascertainable beneficiaries and it is the law on certainty of objects which tells us whether or not there are beneficiaries who are sufficiently ascertainable.)

It is feared that the absence of a beneficiary in abstract purpose trusts would have the effect of leaving the trustees at liberty to use the trust fund to pursue the purpose of the trust entirely as they saw fit, without the control mechanism of a beneficiary who is entitled to petition the court and so ensure that the trustees perform their fiduciary duties properly. Trustees are not entitled to use property for their own, personal benefit, nor are they permitted to use the property for any purpose other than the purpose specified by the settlor: without the possibility of the control of the trustees by the court, it would be possible for the trustees to abuse their powers in practice. Furthermore, if trusts for the carrying out of abstract purposes were allowed, the court would be required to oversee and validate the operation of such an abstract trust purpose without any guidelines as to how the trustees ought properly to act.

The other reason for avoiding abstract purpose trusts is that abstract purpose trusts may continue in existence in perpetuity. The courts have long thought that to have capital tied up in the fulfilment of an abstract purpose prevents that capital from circulating in the economy and consequently prevents it from being used to benefit people. The case law refers in part to 'the rule against remoteness of vesting', which is a reference to the problem of property not coming to vest in any beneficiary for an undetermined period of time. So, English property law will not enforce a trust of whatever kind which may last forever: this policy is encompassed in the rules against perpetuities and accumulations, which are discussed below in para 4.2.7.

An outline of the discussion to follow

There are two exceptions to the beneficiary principle: first, in relation to a few anomalous cases such as *Re Hooper*[126] which are considered below and, secondly, in relation to charitable trusts. Charities undertake activities which are considered by the law to be generally in the public interest and therefore statute creates an exceptional category for them.[127] In relation to disputes concerning charities, the Attorney-General sues in place of the beneficiary.

---

124   *Re Denley* [1969] 1 Ch 373; *Re Lipinski* [1976] Ch 235.
125   *Leahy v Attorney-General for NSW* [1959] AC 457.
126   [1932] Ch 38.
127   Charities are a case apart and considered in detail in Chapter 25.

The remainder of this section is therefore a discussion of the means by which the courts have sought to distinguish between those trusts which are for the benefit of persons and those trusts which are really only for an abstract purpose. For the purposes of this chapter we will define trusts which have ascertainable beneficiaries as being 'people trusts', and trusts which have no ascertainable beneficiaries and are therefore trusts for abstract purposes as being 'purpose trusts'. The first issue is therefore to decide whether a particular trust is a 'people' or a 'purpose' trust: whereas the former has identifiable beneficiaries, the latter does not. It will emerge from the discussion to follow that many of the cases are in conflict. Therefore, we shall consider each approach in turn. A summary of these principles is set out in para 4.2.9.

4.2.2 The strict approach to the beneficiary principle

The approach based on the avoidance of trusts lasting in perpetuity

The traditional, strict approach to the beneficiary principle took a literal interpretation of the trust instrument and sought to decide whether or not there was any logical, possible risk of the trust fund failing to vest in a person as beneficiary within a reasonable period of time. The principal concern of the cases before 1964, when the Perpetuities and Accumulations Act was enacted, was to prevent trusts for abstract purposes continuing in perpetuity. As considered in para 4.2.7 below, the case law developed a complex series of rules concerning the situations in which property could be said to vest in beneficiaries within a sufficient time. Many of these principles required that the trust terminate or that the trust property be vested in some beneficiary within an identified period of time or within the lifetime of some identified person: only in these ways could the courts be sure that the trust would indeed come to an end. In the quaint expression used by Viscount Simonds, any trust property which might vest outside such a time period would 'tend to a perpetuity' and therefore the trust would be void.[128] The approach of the courts was to search for lapses in the drafting of trust instruments and to be astute in finding trusts void for bearing the risk of continuing in perpetuity and for propounding an abstract purpose.

An example of this judicial enthusiasm might be the formerly leading case of *Re Wood*,[129] which concerned a trust created for the purpose of working gravel pits such that the profits were to be held on trust for identified family members of the settlor. On the basis that the drafting of the trust meant that it was nominally capable on its own terms of lasting in perpetuity, it was held to be void for remoteness of vesting.[130] This case is said to indicate the absurdity of the rule, because there would clearly have been a point in time at which the gravel would have been exhausted so that the trust would necessarily have ceased to have effect at some time in the future. Consequently, the case became known as the 'magic gravel pits' case on the basis that it appeared to assume that the gravel would continue to be dug forever. There were numerous other decisions in which infant children were considered

---

128 *Leahy v Attorney-General for NSW* [1959] AC 457.
129 [1894] 3 Ch 381.
130 In another case called *Re Wood* [1949] 1 All ER 1100 Harman J considered that a bequest for the purpose of paying money towards the BBC's 'This Week's Good Cause' would be void because the trust was simply considered to be too uncertain and because it disclosed no beneficiary, nor was it a charitable bequest.

capable of giving birth and elderly women similarly fertile. Slightly more lyrically this doctrine has also become known as the 'slaughter of the innocents', meaning the avoidance of otherwise perfectly acceptable trusts. The modern approach is enshrined in the Perpetuities and Accumulations Act 2009 (discussed below) which permits those cases which might theoretically continue beyond the perpetuity period to continue in full effect until the effluxion of the statutory perpetuity period.

The modern approach is contrary to the old law rule under which if the trust property *might have* vested outside the perpetuity period it was held invalid. Some irrational decisions were reached in the heat of this judicial witch-hunt for trusts provisions which could *possibly*, rather than those which would *probably*, have vested outside the period.

The approach based on identifying an abstract purpose without any benefit to any person

In the wake of the Perpetuities and Accumulations Act 1964 and its successor in 2009, provided that the trust is a trust for the benefit of an identified class of beneficiaries, a trust will not be held to be invalid automatically because there is some defect in its drafting which suggests that the trust might last in perpetuity. As considered below,[131] the 2009 Act introduces a perpetuity period if the trust does continue beyond the period of time permitted in the Act.[132] In relation to trusts which are not for the benefit of an identified class of beneficiaries, the beneficiary principle still holds any such purpose trusts void. It is important, therefore, to identify whether or not a trust is a people trust or a purpose trust.

The primacy of the strict approach to the beneficiary principle is evident from a number of other cases. Two examples will serve for present purposes. In *Re Astor's Settlement Trusts*,[133] a trust was created with the objective of advancing 'the preservation of the independence and integrity of newspapers'. The particular objective was the preservation of *The Observer* newspaper which the Astor family had been instrumental in creating. It was held that there was no beneficiary of such a purpose and furthermore that the purpose was in any event uncertain. Consequently, the purported trust was held to be void. Similarly, in *Re Shaw*,[134] the great socialist man of letters George Bernard Shaw had left money in his will to be applied in the creation of a new alphabet (with the ultimate objective of developing a new language which all of the peoples of the world could speak and so increase understanding and peaceable relations between them). It was held that this was a void purpose trust because there was no identifiable beneficiary. These cases clearly rest on the finding that there were no identifiable beneficiaries on their facts.

There will evidently be a number of situations in which it is unclear whether a purpose can be said to benefit people or to be simply an abstract purpose. While the trust might be intended to achieve some abstract purpose, it may nevertheless seem that there are some people who might take some indirect benefit from the trust. So, it could be argued that some people would 'benefit' in the broadest possible sense of that word from an independent newspaper or from world peace. In such a situation, it might be argued that that trust ought to be considered to be a people trust. However, that argument will not work. What is meant

---

131   See para 4.2.7 below.
132   Perpetuities and Accumulations Act 2009, s 7.
133   [1952] Ch 534, [1952] 1 All ER 1067.
134   [1957] 1 WLR 729.

by the trusts law use of the term 'benefit' is that there must be at least one person who can benefit in the sense of having some proprietary right in the subject matter of the trust thus giving that person a right to control the actions of the trustees. It is not enough that the trust would improve your life in some indirect way without you having a right in the trust property: only charitable trusts, considered in Chapter 25, are able to operate in this indirect, abstract fashion.[135]

For example, in *Re Nottage*,[136] a trust was purportedly created so that a cup would be provided for the best yachtsman in a yachting competition. The issue arose whether this trust could be said to benefit those people who were members of the yachting club, or whether it was simply a trust for the purpose of advancing the yachting competition at that club. It was held that the trust was not a people trust because its purpose was designed to improve yachting. Simply to say that it promoted competition among yachting enthusiasts was not sufficient to make it a purpose trust because there were no beneficiaries with any entitlement to the trust property under the *Saunders v Vautier*[137] principle. Consequently, the trust was held to be void as a purpose trust.

In the following section, we turn to consider the leading cases on the distinction between people and purpose trusts.

4.2.3 The distinction between 'people' and 'purpose' trusts

A 'people trust' is a trust the intention of which is to benefit identifiable people as beneficiaries,[138] as opposed to being focused on achieving some abstract purpose. If a trust qualifies as being a 'people trust', then it will satisfy the beneficiary principle and therefore be valid, whereas if a trust is a 'purpose trust', because it is created to pursue an abstract purpose without any identifiable beneficiaries, then it contravenes the beneficiary principle and will be void. Consequently, a trust to provide sports facilities for employees of a particular company will be a people trust because it provides some benefit for identifiable beneficiaries,[139] whereas a trust to preserve gravestones will be a trust for an abstract purpose and will therefore be void.[140]

In assessing the development of the applicable principles, two cases are compared in the following discussion: first we will consider the decision of the Privy Council in *Leahy v Attorney-General for NSW*,[141] where a gift in favour of an order of nuns was held void as a purpose trust; and secondly the decision of Goff J in *Re Denley*,[142] in which a bequest for the maintenance of an employees' sports facility was found to be a valid trust which was properly analysed as being for the benefit of people and not a purpose. These cases are frequently taken to be in opposition to one another, with *Re Denley* being taken to advance a modern approach. However, we shall attempt a reconciliation of the various approaches in para 4.2.9 below.

135 Cf *Leahy v Attorney-General for NSW* [1959] AC 457; *Re Denley* [1969] 1 Ch 373.
136 [1895] 2 Ch D 517.
137 (1841) 4 Beav 115.
138 You should recall that the definition of a 'legal person' includes both human beings and companies.
139 *Re Denley* [1969] 1 Ch 373.
140 *Re Endacott* [1960] Ch 232.
141 [1959] AC 457.
142 [1969] 1 Ch 373.

An example of the traditional, literalist approach: Leahy v Attorney-General for NSW

In the Privy Council appeal in *Leahy v Attorney-General for NSW*, property was left to 'upon trust for such order of nuns of the Catholic Church . . . as my executors and trustees shall select'. The trustees selected the non-charitable order of Carmelite nuns. This order of nuns was not a charity because the order was contemplative and therefore did not exhibit the necessary public benefit to be considered charitable.[143] The property in question was a large amount of land in New South Wales: a sheep station comprising 730 acres of grazing land and a single homestead comprising 20 rooms (and which we might suppose could have housed about two dozen nuns at a pinch).[144] The question was whether this trust for 'such order of nuns' was an abstract purpose trust for the benefit of the order of nuns or whether it could be construed to be a people trust for the benefit of the individual nuns who belonged to the Carmelite order. The decision of the Privy Council was that the bequest was in the form of a non-charitable purpose trust, being intended on its literal interpretation for the abstract purposes of the order rather than for the benefit of any individual beneficiaries. It was therefore held to have been void.

Viscount Simonds, delivering the leading opinion of the Privy Council, held that the trust was a void purpose trust. He had three main planks to his arguments. First, most significantly, the trust was expressed as being made to the *order* of nuns, for the furtherance of their communal purpose, rather than to any specified, individual nuns. Therefore, the trust was deemed to have been intended for the abstract purposes of the order. Secondly, and building on the first point, it was held that the terms of the trust being for the order of nuns would mean that the trust would be for the benefit of people who would become nuns at some time in the future, rather than being limited to members of the order at the time of making the trust, and therefore would 'tend to a perpetuity' and so breach the rule against remoteness of vesting. Therefore, he would have held the trust void for perpetuities on that ground.[145]

Thirdly, Viscount Simonds held that as a matter of logic it could not have been intended that 'immediate possession' of the rights of beneficiaries could have been taken by all the nuns in the order over a small homestead on a sheep farm. On a purely common sense basis, a worldwide order of nuns made up of thousands of members could not be said to benefit as individual beneficiaries from a gift of land containing a sheep station which could accommodate only about two dozen of their number. However, the issue of whether the land making up the rest of the sheep farm could have been developed or turned to account by the order was not addressed. Viscount Simonds also referred to a lack of evidence as to whether or not the order of nuns would have been able to wind itself up so that the property could have passed to the nuns as individual beneficiaries, in line with the *Saunders v Vautier*[146] principle. Moreover, his Lordship required that for a person to be a beneficiary under a trust, that person

---

143   *Thornton v Howe* (1862) 31 Beav 14; *Dunne v Byrne* [1912] AC 407.

144   No evidence was adduced as to how many nuns could have occupied the building at one time, but let us suppose two dozen nuns, assuming a sharing of bedrooms with other rooms for washing, cooking and religious observance. What is important is that the thousands of nuns making up the worldwide order of Carmelite nuns could not have occupied the building at one and the same time.

145   On the facts, a New South Wales statute came to the nuns' rescue to uphold the gift – even though they lost on the trusts point.

146   (1841) 4 Beav 115.

must be intended to take 'immediate possession' of her rights in property, something which his Lordship considered could not have been intended in relation to the Carmelite nuns.

Possible alternative interpretations of the facts in Leahy v Attorney-General for NSW

By contrast with the approach actually taken by the Privy Council, the question arises whether this bequest could have been seen as either a gift made to persons (as suggested by Viscount Simonds, and as accepted in the case of *Cocks v Manners*[147] considered below) rather than for a purpose or object; or alternatively as a gift for each and every member of the order individually.[148] Theoretically, it would have been possible for the testator to have made a gift[149] to those nuns who were at the time of the bequest members of the order of Carmelite nuns. Alternatively, it would have been possible to have made a gift subject to a condition precedent that the property be held on trust for present and future nuns, subject to a valid perpetuity period. The more difficult question is whether the Privy Council in *Leahy v Attorney-General for NSW* could have interpreted the intention of the testator to have been to make such a gift. Indeed, in *Cocks v Manners*,[150] an amount of money was settled on trust for the benefit of an order of nuns with the Mother Superior acting as trustee. The issue arose whether or not the provision in favour of the order of nuns ought to invalidate the transfer as creating a purpose trust. The court considered that the transfer was not intended for the purpose of supporting the order of nuns, but rather that the trust was found to be valid as a gift in favour of all the members of the order individually. Therefore, the beneficiary principle did not apply in that case.

Direct or indirect use or enjoyment of property: Re Denley

A decision which indicated a different interpretation in analogous circumstances to the case of *Leahy v Attorney-General for NSW* was the decision of Goff J in *Re Denley*,[151] in which case a sports ground was left for the recreational purposes of a company's employees. The trust provided that land 'be maintained and used as and for the purpose of a recreation or sports ground primarily for the benefit of the employees of [a] company and secondarily for the benefit of such other person or persons (if any) as the trustees may allow to use the same'.[152] The issue concerned the nature of the transfer either as a void purpose trust for the maintenance of a sports ground, or as a valid people trust in favour of the employees of the company. The decision of Goff J was that he could:

> see no distinction in principle between a trust to permit a class defined by reference to employment to use and enjoy land in accordance with rules to be made at the discretion of trustees on the one hand, and, on the other hand, a trust to distribute income at the

---

147 (1871) LR 12 Eq 574.
148 If the transfer were accepted as having been a gift to the individual members, then no question of trusts law would arise at all and therefore the beneficiary principle would not apply.
149 Subject to any applicable requirement for a perpetuity period.
150 (1871) LR 12 Eq 574. Cf *Re Smith* [1914] 1 Ch 937; *Re Ogden* [1933] Ch 678.
151 [1969] 1 Ch 373.
152 The certainty of objects issues here are resolved by looking at the company's payroll to ascertain the beneficiaries from time to time.

discretion of the trustees amongst a class, defined by reference to, for example, relation-ship to the settlor. In both cases the benefit to be taken by any member of the class is at the discretion of the trustees, but any member of the class can apply to the court to compel the trustees to administer the trust in accordance with its terms.

Thus, Goff J suggested that a trust in favour of the employees of a company was very similar to an ordinary discretionary trust. Consequently, his Lordship could see no problem with holding the trust to be valid. The facts of *Leahy v Attorney-General for NSW* were distin-guished as creating a trust for abstract purposes rather than for the practical benefit of the beneficiaries. It is submitted that this form of distinction is more convenient than completely satisfying. In truth, the two courts have different attitudes to the subject matter before them: one wanted to preserve the trust at all costs and the other did not. The decision in *Re Denley* decided that the strict approach of earlier authorities such as *Re Astor*[153] and *Re Endacott*[154] was confined to abstract purpose trusts (in which no human would take a direct benefit) and was not intended to include situations in which some identifiable humans would take a direct benefit from the trust's purpose. Consequently, the trust was held to be a 'people trust' such that it fell within the validating 'wait and see' provisions of the Perpetuities and Accumulations Act 1964.

In general terms, Goff J considered the best approach to be as follows:

> I think there may be a purpose or object trust, the carrying out of which would benefit an individual or individuals, where that benefit is so indirect or intangible or which is otherwise so framed as not to give those persons any *locus standi* to apply to the court to enforce the trust, in which case the beneficiary principle would, as it seems to me, apply to invalidate the trust, quite apart from any question of uncertainty or perpe-tuity. . . Where, then, the trust, though expressed as a purpose, is directly or indirectly for the benefit of an individual or individuals, it seems to me that it is in general outside the mischief of the beneficiary principle.

In short, the beneficiary principle will be deemed to be satisfied in circumstances in which there are identifiable beneficiaries who will take some benefit, even if that is only indirect, from the trust. That the beneficiaries can take an *indirect* benefit is important because it differs from Viscount Simonds's requirement that the people involved would have to take immediate rights in possession to qualify as beneficiaries under a valid trust. However, that is not to suggest that Goff J was supposing that we can ignore the beneficiary principle in future cases – far from it. As the passage quoted above requires, where the benefit is so intangible that those purported beneficiaries would not be able to bring the matter to court to control the activities of the trustees, then the trust will nevertheless be found to be invalid. What Goff J did do was to redraw the line at which trusts will be held valid or void – in effect making it easier to validate a trust than might have otherwise been possible.

Goff J identified other examples on the decided cases of money being used ostensibly for a purpose but being in truth for the indirect benefit of ascertainable people: these examples were an amount of money left on trust to maintain trees on land on which

---

153 [1952] Ch 534.
154 [1960] Ch 232.

human beneficiaries under the same trust lived[155] and also money left for the upkeep of gardens as being for the benefit of human beings dwelling on the land.[156] Therefore, it was held that there were other cases in which the prosecution of an ostensibly abstract purpose had nevertheless been upheld as being for the indirect benefit of ascertainable people.[157] However, it should be noted that these cases involved actions for the termination of those trusts so that the capital could be distributed among the human beneficiaries.

A closer comparison of the cases of Leahy v Attorney-General for NSW *and* Re Denley

What is difficult to see is why there are different results in *Denley* and in *Leahy*. In the abstract, the facts of the two cases are very similar. In both cases there are large areas of land containing few buildings. In both cases it would be impossible for all of the potential class of people who might use the land to occupy it at the same time. In both cases it is possible to identify all of the human beings who will benefit from the property. So, those are the similarities. In *Leahy*, it was ascertainable who the members of the religious order would be. Therefore, it could have been said that the land in New South Wales would have been used for their benefit as an order, with different individuals taking turns to use the land at different times. This would have been in exactly the same way that it was not required that all of the employees in *Denley* would have had to use the sports ground permanently and all together. Rather, groups of employees would use the sports ground from time to time in the manner made possible by the trustees. Therefore, there was an equal possibility in *Leahy* of seeing the gift in favour of the order of nuns as being in favour of the individuals making up the order, perhaps were it to be used as a retreat,[158] in the same way that the sports ground is taken to be for the benefit of the employees. As to the point about only a few nuns being able to use the sheep station, it is equally unlikely that all of the employees would have used the sports ground. Consequently, the more closely these two decisions are analysed, the more difficult it is to determine any substantive differences between them.

The different analytical possibilities are similar to the approaches canvassed in *Re Recher's Will Trusts*,[159] where transfers of property are made either for the benefit of the member of a society or for the purposes of a society more generally, rather than needing to be seen didactically as being either for the benefit of people or as being provided strictly for a purpose. Therefore, the answer to any future situation would be a matter of analysis on any particular set of facts.

As considered below, the decision of Oliver J in *Re Lipinski's Will Trusts*[160] doubted the logical correctness of the approach in *Leahy*. In that case, Oliver J held that a bequest to a social club, even where it appeared on its face to be an abstract purpose trust, ought to be held as being for the benefit of the membership provided that the members constituted a sufficiently certain beneficial class. Oliver J found that where the membership of the club

155 *Re Bowes* [1896] 1 Ch 507.
156 *Re Aberconway's Settlement* [1953] Ch 647.
157 *Re Harpur's WT* [1962] Ch 78.
158 A 'retreat' in this sense would be a place used by a religious community to visit from time to time to enable individuals to contemplate their faith.
159 [1972] Ch 526; see para 4.3.3 below.
160 [1976] Ch 235.

had control over the capital of the trust fund (meaning that they were able to dispose of it in any way they wished – similar to the position in *Saunders v Vautier*[161]) there was an even more compelling argument for holding that the trust was a valid trust: this case is considered below.

That is an argument with some force. The judicial principle behind the rule against inalienability is the feared economic consequences of tying property into trusts for long-term, abstract purposes.[162] The attitude of the judiciary in this context is therefore orientated around the notion of individual benefit from the trust, or of benefit being locked within a family. There has never been an argument raised that a trust for the education or the mainte-nance of young children would be void simply because it is based on a purpose. The reason why that trust has never been questioned is that the trust would clearly be for the benefit of those children. Similarly, there is no reason why a group of adults should not be able to join together and decide that they wanted to create a trust to achieve a common purpose – such as pooling money to pay wages to any of them who might become too unwell to work.

The question in principle, as suggested in *Re Denley* and in *Re Lipinski*, is therefore why it is necessary to invalidate trusts which are simply not expressed as being for the benefit of individuals even though their underlying purpose would benefit such people indirectly. In these cases, it was suggested that such purposes were unobjectionable in general terms and therefore that there was no good reason to be too astute in attempting to invalidate them. However, as considered in the next section, it is clear that the stricter approach is still taken in some cases.

The continued use of the strict approach

In spite of the foregoing discussion of *Re Denley*, it should not be thought that all decisions since *Leahy* have upheld trusts purposes as being valid. For example, in *Re Grant's Will Trusts*,[163] Vinelott J considered a testamentary transfer which was expressed to be made 'to the Labour Party Property Committee for the benefit of the Chertsey HQ of the Chertsey . . . Constituency Labour Party' or, if that constituency association should cease to exist, to be held for the purposes of the Labour Party's Property Committee nationally. The terms of the Labour Party's constitution laid down rigid rules as to the manner in which this money was to be used for the purposes of the Party as carried on in the appropriate constituency party.[164] Vinelott J found that the settlor's intention was to maintain this capital sum to provide a permanent endowment for the purposes of the Chertsey Constituency Labour Party and that it therefore constituted an abstract purpose trust which was consequently void. An alterna-tive analysis akin to *Re Denley* would have been that the money was intended to have been provided for the benefit of the individual members. Instead, a more literalist interpretation was given to this gift by Vinelott J on the basis that the testator appeared to intend a benefit for the present and future purposes of the association.[165] Vinelott J sought to limit the

---

161 (1841) 4 Beav 115.
162 *Bowman v Secular Society Ltd* [1971] AC 406.
163 [1979] 3 All ER 359.
164 The specified constituency had in fact ceased to exist by the time of the testator's death.
165 This analysis contrasts markedly with the Conservative Party which is found to be a single association, whereas the Labour Party has been found to be broken up into distinct associations, one in each constituency: cf *Conservative Association v Burrell* [1982] 2 All ER 1.

decision in *Re Denley* on the basis that his Lordship considered that *Re Denley* was a case involving ascertainable beneficiaries and therefore that no question of diluting the beneficiary principle arose because the trust in that case appeared to be a perfectly valid trust in which a complete list of the beneficiaries could have been compiled without difficulty.

An alternative analysis of the facts in *Re Grant's WT*, suggested by Underhill and Hayton,[166] is that the bequest could have been seen as being for the benefit of the individual members, with merely a super-added direction that those beneficiaries ought to use the money for the purposes of the local Labour Party. In effect this analysis is suggesting that the facts in *Re Grant's WT* could have been interpreted as being like those in *Re Denley* because there were identifiable individuals (the members of the association) who could have taken a direct or an indirect benefit from that property. For the reasons given above, Vinelott J did not consider that the terms of the constitution of the Labour Party permitted such an analysis on those facts. More generally, from a close reading of his judgment, Vinelott J was simply not supportive of the sort of approach taken in *Re Denley*.

Explaining the distinction between the cases

It is not easy to draw a distinction between *Leahy* and *Denley* which survives close scrutiny. As considered above, both cases involved a trust drafted on its face as though a purpose trust, involving land which was intended for the use of a group of persons too large to take immediate possession of it simultaneously. Yet Viscount Simonds in *Leahy* held his trust void, whereas Goff J in *Denley* held his trust valid. The difference is possibly attitudinal. The two judges came from different generations. Viscount Simonds, at the height of his career, was a great literalist – reading trusts provisions closely and holding the settlor to intend exactly what he said. On the other hand, Goff J was a younger judge at the beginning of his career in the late 1960s (as was Oliver J in *Lipinski*).[167] He was prepared to take purposive interpretations to validate trusts which would otherwise have been void. Such attitudinal shifts occur between generations – some ideas become less fashionable among judges. Oliver J was prepared to go to lengths unheard of by Viscount Simonds in validating a trust.

Another distinction can be drawn between Goff J and Viscount Simonds as to their respective opinions of the nature of the property involved in a trust. Viscount Simonds considered that a trust can take effect only where the beneficiaries are able to take immediate possession of rights in the land – it was his view that it could not have been intended that each of the nuns in the Carmelite order was to take possession of rights in a small homestead on a sheep station. Goff J was content that there be some person who would be able to bring any irregularities to court as one of the class of beneficiaries. There was no requirement in *Denley* that there be rights of possession taken by the objects of the trust – rather, it was enough to satisfy the beneficiary principle that some people would benefit either directly or indirectly from the trust.

What Goff and Oliver JJ have suggested, in effect, is that it ought to be possible to validate a trust which is indirectly for the benefit of individuals, even if it might appear on its face to be a trust for the achievement of a purpose. After all, the trust offers a means of pooling and using money which is owned by a number of people in common so that they can achieve

166 Underhill and Hayton, 2002, 106.
167 [1976] Ch 235.

their lawful, communal goals. In such a situation, it is difficult to see why, in principle, such activities ought to be robbed of the advantages offered by the law of trusts to enable citizens to organise their own affairs.

Oliver J goes so far in *Re Lipinski* as to suggest that he can see no reason why such a gift should fail. The suggestion is that the beneficiary principle is a technical interference in the ability of ordinary people to carry on perfectly lawful and socially desirable activities of forming associations and pooling their property to achieve their common ends. That the law of gift will validate such transfers of property, as is considered below,[168] means that it is only a part of technical trusts law which invalidates their purposes. However, as is considered in para 4.2.8 below, to overrule the beneficiary principle for the future would disturb the fundamental principle that the beneficiaries have equitable proprietary rights in the trust property and that they are liable to be taxed accordingly: to remove the beneficiary principle would make tax avoidance and regulatory avoidance easier with even more unfortunate consequences, as considered in para 4.2.8.

The form of property right necessary to constitute a person a beneficiary

The beneficiary principle is bound up with our discussion of the nature of a trust in Chapter 2, in which we considered the trust to be an amalgamation of property law rules governing the treatment of the trust fund and also a code of equitable obligations owed by the trustee to account to the beneficiary for their management of the trust property.[169] Where there is no human beneficiary, this relationship between a beneficiary capable of controlling the trustee and the trustee herself is absent. Therefore, there is an ideological objection to abstract purpose trusts, as well as the policy of preventing trusts from continuing in perpetuity, which is considered below.

The beneficiary principle is in line with the rights of the beneficiaries to the trust property as embodied in the principle in *Saunders v Vautier*[170] as discussed in para 4.1.2 above. The rule in *Saunders v Vautier* provides that all of the beneficiaries acting in concert[171] must be able to direct the trustees as to the manner in which they should deal with the property held on trust.[172] To achieve this, those beneficiaries must be clearly identifiable. This under-standing of the proprietary rights of beneficiaries was taken by Viscount Simonds to suggest that to be a beneficiary, it is a requirement that that person have vested rights in the trust property in possession.[173] Consequently, there could not be said to have been beneficial rights in favour of the members of the order of Carmelite nuns because it could not have been said, in Viscount Simonds's view, that the entirety of that worldwide order of nuns had been expected to go into immediate possession of beneficial rights in the sheep station. By contrast, however, Goff J took the view that it was sufficient to constitute the employees of a company as beneficiaries under a trust over a recreation ground if those employees were to have the use and enjoyment of that land; therefore, use and enjoyment would have been

---

168   See para 4.2.4.
169   See section 2.5 above.
170   (1841) 4 Beav 115.
171   Provided that they do constitute the entirety of the equitable interest in the trust property and that they are all *sui juris*.
172   See para 4.1.2 above.
173   *Leahy v Attorney-General for NSW* [1959] AC 457.

sufficient for a beneficial right in property as opposed to each employee taking immediate rights in possession over the sports ground.[174]

4.2.4 Where a transfer may be interpreted as constituting a gift rather than a trust

The discussion thus far has drawn a straightforward distinction between the people trust and the purpose trust. The approach in *Re Denley*[175] has clearly ushered in a means of validating more trusts than would otherwise have been possible under the approach taken by Viscount Simonds in *Leahy v Attorney-General for NSW*[176] or Vinelott J in *Re Grant's Will Trusts*.[177] The reader should already be developing a facility vital to trusts lawyers for looking around problems and finding other ways of structuring or interpreting our arrangements to reach the desired conclusions. Therefore, another means of eluding the beneficiary principle for trusts should be explored: that is, quite simply, structuring the disposition of property as an outright transfer (either under contract or by way of a gift) rather than as a trust.

This is demonstrated by the case of *Re Lipinski*.[178] This testamentary bequest was left for the benefit of an association in a form which appeared, at first blush, to be a purpose trust. The precise terms of the bequest of the testator's residuary estate were as follows: '. . . as to one half thereof for the Hull Judeans (Maccabi) Association in memory of my late wife to be used solely in the work of constructing the new buildings for the association and/or improvements in the said buildings . . .' In particular, the words '. . . to be used solely in the work of constructing . . .' make that bequest appear to create a trust for an abstract purpose, and the words '. . . in memory of my late wife . . .' were said by the claimants to create a permanent endowment.

However, Oliver J held that, on the precise wording of the bequest, the testator intended that the association take control of the capital completely. It was therefore possible for the association, if it considered it appropriate, to spend all of that capital at once in the construction and maintenance of the buildings. Oliver J was of the view that to make a bequest on terms which transferred control of the capital was equivalent to a transfer of absolute beneficial title or, in other words, was equivalent to making a gift of the money. Therefore, if the bequest could be interpreted as an outright gift rather than as a trust, there was no problem with the beneficiary principle because the beneficiary principle does not apply to gifts.

The approach which Oliver J took to the satisfaction of the beneficiary principle was even more wide-ranging than that of *Re Denley*. Having considered the speech of Viscount Simonds in *Leahy*, Oliver J held that:

> There would seem to me to be, as a matter of common sense, a clear distinction between the case where a purpose is described which is clearly intended for the benefit of ascertained or ascertainable beneficiaries, particularly where those beneficiaries have the power to make the capital their own, and the case where no beneficiary at all is intended

174 *Re Denley* [1969] 1 Ch 373.
175 [1969] 1 Ch 373.
176 [1959] AC 457.
177 [1979] 3 All ER 359.
178 [1976] Ch 235.

(for instance, a memorial to a favourite pet) or where the beneficiaries are unascertainable (as for instance in *Re Price*[179]).

In other words, a distinction is drawn between those cases in which, even though the trust power is drafted so as to seem like a purpose on its face, there is an intention to benefit people and cases in which there is no intention to benefit people.

Therefore, it would not be correct to say that Oliver J simply distinguished the case in front of him on the basis that it concerned a gift rather than a purpose trust. He did consider and criticise the approach in *Leahy*. He held that there ought to be a distinction drawn between the situation in which the purpose is intended 'for the benefit of ascertained or ascertainable beneficiaries, particularly where those beneficiaries have the power to make the capital their own' and the situation in which 'no beneficiary is intended [for instance, a memorial to a favourite pet] or where the beneficiaries are unascertainable'. Oliver J was suggesting that the beneficiary principle ought not to be applied in unincorporated associations[180] cases in a way that will tend to invalidate such dispositions by assuming that a disposition made in favour of such an association is necessarily to be taken to be for the purposes of that association. Rather, it was suggested that provided the membership of the association was sufficiently certain, a disposition to such an association ought to have been interpreted as being a valid people trust for the benefit of those members. That is particularly so when the membership as a beneficial class has a right to control the capital of the fund.

The distinction drawn by Oliver J is between a transfer to an association on trust which will benefit its members as being valid and a transfer to a trust for the maintenance of 'a useful monument to myself' as being void; however, Viscount Simonds in *Leahy* would have drawn the distinction between a trust which was for the immediate benefit of individuals taking immediate possession of their rights as being valid and a trust for present and future beneficiaries of a class as being void for tending to a perpetuity. The latter test would invalidate more trusts than the former.

A similar approach to *Lipinski* was taken in *Re Turkington*,[181] in which Luxmoore J held that where property had been left for the purposes of a Masonic lodge (an unincorporated association) to trustees who were also the sole beneficiaries, there had been in effect a gift made to the members of the lodge at the time. Oliver J also relied on this decision in *Re Lipinski*,[182] which he interpreted as being a case involving a power and not a purpose trust. He further referred to a stream of cases which had taken different approaches from the decisions in *Leahy* and in *Re Wood*.[183] All of these three cases concerned gifts with a statement from the donor as to the purpose for which the property was to be used. In each the gift was upheld as being valid on the basis that there were ascertainable beneficiaries who satisfied the beneficiary principle. These differences in approach demonstrate that what had previously been a matter of interpretation before *Denley* and *Lipinski* has now become a presumption of validity if there are people who may take direct or indirect benefit from the

---

179   [1943] Ch 422.
180   Ie, clubs and societies, like the Hull Judeans Maccabi Association: see section 4.3 below.
181   [1937] 4 All ER 501.
182   [1976] Ch 235.
183   [1949] 1 All ER 1100. That difference in approach was identified with cases like *Re Clarke* [1901] 2 Ch 110; *Re Drummond* [1914] 2 Ch 90 and *Re Taylor* [1940] Ch 481.

trust. The decision in *Re Grant's Will Trusts*[184] suggests that this approach does not command universal support.

4.2.5 Purpose trust or mere motive?

There are some cases in which the perpetuities and purpose trust rules appear to have been contravened but in which the courts have nevertheless interpreted the trust provision to connote only a motive behind the settlor's intention, rather than imposing a trust obligation, or as creating a gift rather than a trust. Suppose, for example, a settlor who intends property to be used for the benefit of specified individuals but who nevertheless creates a trust provision which denotes a purpose for which that property is to be applied. Such a provision might read: '£10,000 to be held by T upon trust to maintain a private library [therefore, not charitable] to enable my three children to study better for their A levels.' Cases of this sort are clearly a mixture of *Re Denley* trusts for the benefit of people but interlaced with an overriding obligation to carry out a particular purpose.

In *Re Bowes*,[185] it was held that the principle in *Saunders v Vautier*[186] (considered above)[187] could be applied so that the absolutely entitled beneficiaries acting together would be able to direct the trustees how to deal with the trust property. In *Re Bowes*, £5,000 was settled on trust to plant trees on a large estate. That provision would have constituted a purpose trust. However, the only two human beneficiaries under the trust were held to be entitled to direct the trustees to transfer the title in the money to the beneficiaries outright. Therefore, the purpose trust aspect was overlooked by the court in favour of upholding the validity of the trust in favour of the human beneficiaries.

Further examples of this judicial inventiveness occurred in a string of anomalous cases. *Re Osoba*[188] concerned a bequest in favour of the testator's widow 'for her maintenance and for the training of my daughter, Abiola, up to university grade and for the maintenance of my aged mother'. The court accepted the argument that this bequest for the training of Abiola was not a purpose trust but was, rather, an absolute gift to the three women with a merely moral obligation expressed in the trust.[189] In short, the settlor did not intend to create a trust in favour of Abiola, but rather to make a gift to her with an expression of how he would have liked the gift to be used.

Other cases include *Re Andrew's Trust*,[190] a decision of Kekewich J, in which a trust was created for the seven children of a clergyman once their education had been completed. Kekewich J held that the intention had not been to create a purpose trust but rather to make an absolute gift to the children with a statement of the settlor's motive in making the bequest.

A different problem may arise: suppose that such a purpose trust, with the intention to benefit individuals, has been created but that the objects of the trust become impossible before the trust can be performed. Thus, in *Re Abbott Fund*,[191] a fund was created in favour of two elderly ladies, and subscriptions were sought from the public. The purpose was not

184   [1979] 3 All ER 359, as considered above at para 4.2.3.
185   [1896] 1 Ch 507.
186   (1841) 4 Beav 115.
187   See section 4.1 above.
188   [1979] 2 All ER 393.
189   Cf para 3.3.2 above, where it was explained that a merely moral obligation will not constitute a trust.
190   [1905] 2 Ch 48. See also the discussion of *Re Grant's Will Trusts* below in para 4.3.3.
191   [1900] 2 Ch 326.

fully performed before the ladies died. It was held that the trust property remaining undistributed should be held on resulting trust for the subscribers.

By way of comparison, it is interesting to note that a similar approach was taken in *Re Gillingham Bus Disaster Fund*[192] in considering a subscription fund for which money was raised from the public in the wake of a bus crash. The victims of the crash did not require all of the money raised. The issue arose as to treatment of the surplus money. The court held that the surplus should be held on resulting trust for the subscribers. The potential problems with this form of resulting trust are considered below in Chapter 11.[193]

4.2.6 Anomalous purpose trusts which have been held to be valid

As is the case with much of English law, there are a number of situations in which the general rule is not observed by a number of anomalous cases. This is the case with the beneficiary principle. There are a few old cases in which settlements which were clearly purpose trusts were nevertheless held to have been valid. These rules have subsequently been held to be valid only on their precise facts on the basis that no further anomalies will be permitted.[194] In *Re Endacott*,[195] the Court of Appeal avoided a settlement of money for the purpose expressed by the settlor of 'providing some useful monument to myself'. While it might have been understandable to have avoided this settlement solely on the basis of extraordinary egotism, the court avoided the trust on the basis that it offended against the purpose trust rule. Further, the court drew the line at the exceptions to the beneficiary principle which had been made up to that point.

It is perhaps worth noticing that all the exceptions which have been accepted by the court thus far have been testamentary, indicating perhaps a judicial reluctance to avoid trusts in situations in which the settlor could not amend the trust provision. It is unlikely that an *inter vivos* trust would be similarly excepted, because if the trust is avoided the settlor can always effect the settlement again.

There are four anomalous cases. It should be noted that each of these cases would clearly offend against the beneficiary principle because there is no human beneficiary with *locus standi* to enforce the trust and the trusts are clearly created for the furtherance of abstract purposes. Sir Arthur Underhill referred to them as being based on 'concessions to human sentiment':[196] that is, they were trusts purposes allowed by the individual judges in question because they saw no harm in them. First, in relation to trusts for the maintenance of specific animals, where a trust is created to ensure that the animal is looked after.[197] Secondly, trusts for the erection or maintenance of graves and sepulchral monuments, such as trust for the maintenance of particular gravestones in churchyards.[198] Thirdly, trusts for the saying of Catholic masses in private (which would otherwise be non-charitable purposes because there is no public benefit derived from the activity).[199] Fourthly, trusts for the promotion and

---

192 [1958] Ch 300.
193 See also para 4.3.4 below.
194 *Re Endacott* [1960] Ch 232.
195 *Ibid.*
196 See now Underhill and Hayton, 2002, 111.
197 *Pettingall v Pettingall* (1842) 11 LJ Ch 176; *Re Dean* (1889) 41 Ch D 552.
198 *Re Hooper* [1932] Ch 38.
199 *Bourne v Keane* [1919] AC 815.

furtherance of fox-hunting, such as a trust to fund the maintenance of a particular hunt from which no specific individuals could be said to derive direct, personal benefit.[200]

It should be noted that these trusts will nevertheless be subject to the need for a perpetuity period or they will offend the rule against inalienability. The shortcoming with these trusts is evidently that there is no beneficiary who would be obviously capable of suing the trustees to control their conduct of the trust. In looking more closely at the decided cases, it is clear that the judges were more often than not motivated by the fact that these abstract purpose trusts had clear perpetuities provisions and therefore it would have been impossible for the trusts to have continued in perpetuity.[201] Alternatively, other cases involving, for example, the erection of a gravestone were not considered to create any risk of a purpose lasting in perpetuity because once the gravestone was erected, the purpose would then cease.[202] In the wake of the decision in *Re Endacott*,[203] we should recognise that these cases are wrong in principle and need not be applied in the future.

4.2.7 Perpetuities and accumulations

The principles in outline

The topic of perpetuities creates a number of problems for the validity of trusts, over and above the question of certainties. As considered above, a distinction must be made between trusts which are for the benefit of identifiable people and trusts which are created for a purpose. The reason being that the Perpetuities and Accumulations Act 1964 may validate people trusts which have no perpetuity provision, but not purpose trusts. This position has been amended further by the Perpetuities and Accumulations Act 2009, as explained below.

The principle against perpetuities is found in the judgment of Joyce J in *Re Thompson*[204] in the following terms:

> The rule against perpetuities requires that every estate or interest must vest, if at all, not later than 21 years after the determination of some life in being at the time of the creation of such estate or interest, and not only must the person to take be ascertained, but the amount of his interest must be ascertainable with the prescribed period.

In consequence, all equitable interests must vest within a perpetuity period of this sort under the case law principles. Statute has adapted those rules latterly. If the disposition was effected before 16 July 1964 then it is governed by the case law principle. However, if the trust came into effect after 16 July 1964, then it is governed by the Perpetuities and Accumulations Act 1964, considered below, to the effect that the parties 'wait and see' for a statutory limitation period whether or not the trust comes to an end. As a result of the Perpetuities and

200 *Re Thompson* [1934] Ch 342.
201 See in particular *Re Dean* (1889) 41 Ch D 552, *per* North J and *Bourne v Keane* [1919] AC 815, *per* Lord Buckmaster.
202 *Re Hooper* [1932] 1 Ch 38.
203 [1960] Ch 232.
204 [1906] 2 Ch 199, 202.

Accumulations Act 2009, dispositions which come into effect after that Act came into force on 6 April 2010 are governed by it.[205]

Explaining the rules on perpetuities – historical and cultural change

It is worth considering the reason for prohibiting purpose trusts continuing in effect in perpetuity. It should never be forgotten that the principles and policy which underpin property law, from the Law of Property Act 1925 to the common law, are based on a particular view of economics. The judiciary has long been aware of England's status as a trading nation. The birth of commercial law from the law merchant is testament to the expertise developed by English lawyers in reaction to the large amount of commerce within the jurisdiction or with other jurisdictions. The perceived necessity of creating property rules which do not prohibit this commercial flow is something which has loomed large in the collective judicial mind.

The stated purpose of the Law of Property Act 1925 was to facilitate the easy transfer of land and thus create an open market in real property.[206] A similar principle is the doctrine of maximum certain duration, which requires that leases must not continue in perpetuity on pain of being held unenforceable.[207] Similarly, the perpetuities rules prevent money and other property being tied up in trusts (which are not directed at the benefit of any particular individual), thus removing that capital from the economy.

In the mid-19th century, there was a change in judicial attitude both to use of money and to those forms of commercial undertakings which would be considered to be valid. The change in the intellectual landscape in the British Isles should not be underestimated. The utilitarianism of the Victorians established trade and investment for the common good as the pre-eminent goals of the rapidly expanding British Empire. In consequence, the turmoil of the South Sea Bubble (in which the economy had been profoundly shaken in 1720 by the failure of the South Sea Company) was forgotten and judges accepted that companies were not illegal contracts and subsequently, in 1897, in *Saloman v A Saloman & Co Ltd*,[208] that entrepreneurs acting through companies should have the benefit of distinct legal personality as well as limited liability granted to them by statute. In this changed cultural environment, the judiciary began to develop economic principles on which to build forms of trusts law and company law which were cast in the furnace of their time. Thus, the rules against perpetuities and tying property up in perpetuity were advanced and hardened – precisely because the country's new affection for commerce and economic expansion required that capital be kept moving and that old-fashioned trusts which tied money up in perpetuity should be invalidated. It is important in considering the rules on perpetuities and so forth that their roots even before this Victorian expansionism are recognised. Ever since the Statute of Mortmain (literally 'mort' + 'main', the hand of the dead) the courts have prevented settlers controlling the use of property through trusts from beyond the grave in perpetuity.

The two common law rules

In relation to perpetuities, there are two rules to be borne in mind. The first is the rule against remoteness of vesting, which requires that the interests of beneficiaries must vest within the

---

205 Perpetuities and Accumulations Act 2009 (Commencement) Order 2010, para 2 (SI 2010/37).
206 *City of London Building Society v Flegg* [1988] AC 54.
207 *Lace v Chantler* [1944] 1 All ER 305.
208 [1897] AC 22.

perpetuity period. The second is the rule against inalienability, which requires that income is not bound up in the trust outside the perpetuity period.

Forms of perpetuity clause

Where a trust for people has a perpetuities clause in it which provides for the trust to come to an end within a timeframe envisaged by the Perpetuities and Accumulations Act 1964, it is valid. The times envisaged by the Act are 'a life in being' plus 21 years, or 80 years. The peculiar 'lives in being' provisions were frequently used in trusts in the form of 'royal lives clauses', where the trust would be said to continue, for example, 'for the duration of the life of the youngest grandchild of Queen Elizabeth II plus 21 years'. While these clauses seem odd, they do at least ensure that there will be a period of time within which the trust will terminate. Death, after all, is the only thing in this life that is certain. Alternatively, the Act permits the use of a simple period of not more than 80 years.

The question then is what to do about trusts which do not contain a perpetuity clause. Before 1964, the trust would have been held to have been void. The answer after 1964 is provided by the Perpetuities and Accumulations Act 1964.

The effect of the Perpetuities and Accumulations Act 1964

The 1964 Act sought to ensure that many of the trusts invalidated by the common law would be effective. Therefore, rather than allow trusts which satisfied the beneficiary principle to be deemed invalid because of some possibility that they might continue indefinitely, s 3 of the 1964 Act provided that those trusts be assumed to be valid unless they ultimately proved to continue outside the statutory perpetuity period. Section 3(3) provides that:

> Where . . . a disposition . . . would be void on the ground that the right might be exercised at too remote a time, the disposition shall be treated . . . as if it were not subject to the rule against perpetuities and . . . shall be treated as void for remoteness only if, and so far as, the right is not fully exercised within that period.

Therefore, s 3 introduced the 'wait and see' provision, whereby the trustee is entitled to wait and see if the property does vest outside the perpetuity period. The trust is treated as being valid up to the end of the 'wait and see' period.

Section 1 of the 1964 Act creates a maximum, statutory perpetuity period of 80 years. A further issue then arises: how is the trust property to be dealt with at the end of the statutory perpetuity period? If the trust continues in operation at the end of that period, the class closing rules contained in s 4(4) of the 1964 Act are invoked. The effect of this guillotine provision is to say that no more beneficiaries become entitled to the property after the end of the statutory perpetuity period. Therefore, the trust fund is wound up and the proceeds of the winding up distributed among the surviving, currently-entitled beneficiaries.

One drafting device which is commonly used in trusts to elude the need to provide an express perpetuities clause is to use wording such as 'this trust shall continue in full force and effect as far as the law allows'. The effect of this provision is that the appropriate statutory perpetuity period is read into the trust provisions.

This mechanism was found to circumvent the perpetuity period problem in *Re Hooper*.[209]

---

209 [1932] Ch 38.

The Perpetuities and Accumulations Act 2009

The principal effect of the Perpetuities and Accumulations Act 2009 ('PAA 2009') is to create a new perpetuity period of 125 years. Clearly this greatly simplifies the law in this area for the future. The PAA 2009 does not apply to certain transactions involving charities[210] nor to transactions involving pension schemes.[211] Section 1 describes the ambit of the PAA 2009, subject to the notion in s 1(1) that '[t]he rule against perpetuities applies (and applies only) as provided by this section', in some of the poorest drafting seen this century, in describing the trusts and other instruments to which it will apply:

(2) If an instrument limits property in trust so as to create successive estates or interests the rule applies to each of the estates or interests.

(3) If an instrument limits property in trust so as to create an estate or interest which is subject to a condition precedent and which is not one of successive estates or interests, the rule applies to the estate or interest.

(4) If an instrument limits property in trust so as to create an estate or interest subject to a condition subsequent the rule applies to—
  (a) any right of re-entry exercisable if the condition is broken, or
  (b) any equivalent right exercisable in the case of property other than land if the condition is broken.

(5) If an instrument which is a will limits personal property so as to create successive interests under the doctrine of executory bequests, the rule applies to each of the interests.

(6) If an instrument creates a power of appointment the rule applies to the power.

Therefore, by inference, this Act applies to trusts with successive interests; to trusts subject to some condition precedent (such as 'the beneficiary must reach the age of 21'); to trusts subject to some condition subsequent (such as 'provided that the beneficiary does not marry'); to wills with successive interests; and to powers of appointment. Interestingly this provision does not say: 'this Act shall apply to trusts'. Nor does it say 'this Act shall apply to bare trusts'. However, it is suggested that the reference in s 1(1) to 'the rule against perpetuities' is to be read as a reference impliedly to all trusts and other instruments to which the rule against perpetuities in the case law and under the 1964 Act would previously have applied.

As to the new statutory perpetuity period which is created by PAA 2009, s 5(1) provides that:

The perpetuity period is 125 years (and no other period).

Section 5(2) provides that s 5(1) applies 'whether or not the instrument . . . specifies a perpetuity period; and a specification of a perpetuity period in that instrument is ineffective'.

---

210 Perpetuities and Accumulations Act 2009, s 2(2) and (3). Under (2) it is provided that: 'The rule does not apply to an estate or interest created so as to vest in a charity on the occurrence of an event if immediately before the occurrence an estate or interest in the property concerned is vested in another charity'; and under (3) it is provided that: 'The rule does not apply to a right exercisable by a charity on the occurrence of an event if immediately before the occurrence an estate or interest in the property concerned is vested in another charity.'

211 Perpetuities and Accumulations Act 2009, s 2(4). Under (5) it is provided that 'The exception in subsection (4) does not apply if the interest or right arises under — (a) an instrument nominating benefits under the scheme, or (b) an instrument made in the exercise of a power of advancement arising under the scheme.'

Consequently, the upshot of this legislation is that all other perpetuity periods become 125 years, whether or not they would otherwise have been valid. Thomas and Hudson question why shorter perpetuity periods which were valid under the case law principles should be transformed into this form of period.[212]

Section 6 provides for the starting point for measuring the period of 125 years: that is, the time at which the relevant instrument takes effect. Section 7 introduces a 'wait and see' provision in the sense that the trust is deemed not to be subject to the rule against perpetuities until the statutory period has expired and then any unused parts of the trust come to an end. Section 8 then introduces a 'class closing' rule to eliminate beneficiaries once the statutory perpetuity period has been reached. Section 18 provides that nothing in the Act affects the rule that 'limits the duration of non-charitable purpose trusts', which is a peculiar provision given that non-charitable purpose trusts which are not for the benefit of people are ineffective in any event: it is not a question of their duration, but rather their ineffectiveness.

4.2.8 Arguments suggesting that the beneficiary principle should be forgotten

There are many institutions which sell trusts services 'offshore',[213] primarily for tax avoidance purposes or to partition assets off from other entities. The trusts in such circumstances typically operate in the same way as mutual funds in that clients pay funds to the service provider and those funds are pooled with funds from other clients. This pooled money is then invested on behalf of all of the contributors to the fund. In ordinary circumstances, such an arrangement would be considered to provide each of the contributors with proprietary rights in the trust fund. However, to ensure that the contributors do not face any liability to tax attributable to their ownership of the fund, or to ensure that some other form of regulator does not learn of their partial ownership of the fund, the trust will be structured so as to suggest that none of the contributors to the fund owns any right in the trust property. Under the trusts legislation of many offshore jurisdictions, it is possible to have a trust without the beneficiaries needing to have any proprietary rights in the trust property. Such an analysis would not be possible under English law, because any structure purporting to be a trust in which there is no beneficiary with *locus standi* to enforce the trust would be void, as considered above.

It has been suggested[214] that if there were someone who was empowered to sue the trustees on behalf of the contributors to the fund, then that ought to satisfy the mischief of the beneficiary principle. This issue is considered in greater detail in Chapter 21.[215] For present purposes it is sufficient to observe two things. First, this suggestion would be ineffective under English law because a beneficiary is necessarily considered to have proprietary rights in the trust fund and the lack of any person with such rights renders any purported trust invalid. Secondly, the grounds on which this fundamental change in English trusts law is sought are repugnant to public policy. Change is sought by those in the offshore tax havens either to avoid liability to UK taxation or to avoid oversight by the Financial Services

---

212   Thomas and Hudson, *The Law of Trusts*, 2010, para 8.38.
213   By 'offshore' is meant that the jurisdiction is outside the UK, the USA and all similar, major jurisdictions. Often referred to as 'tax havens', such jurisdictions offer greatly reduced rates of tax (frequently involving the payment of only a small fixed fee by way of taxation) compared to most countries.
214   Hayton, 2001.
215   See also para 21.2.3 below.

Authority and other public, regulatory bodies. Particularly in the modern climate in which there are great fears about the funding of both international terrorism and international drug smuggling through clandestine bank accounts and financial arrangements, it is contrary to good sense to suggest that such arrangements should be facilitated by a change in English law. In either event, it is suggested that no change should be made to English law to achieve those ends. The role of the beneficiary principle in international trusts law practice is considered in para 21.2.4.

4.2.9 Summary of the case law approaches to the beneficiary principle

It is not possible simply to identify one approach on the cases as being correct and the others not; rather, different approaches will apply in different contexts. What is agreed on all of the preceding authorities is that a trust for the achievement of an abstract purpose, such as the erection of a memorial to a beloved pet, will be void.[216]

The more difficult cases are those in which there seems to be some intention to benefit some ascertainable people indirectly. Where the settlor expresses his intention to be to transfer property on trust 'for the benefit of' identified people, whether directly or indirectly, then that will be a valid people trust;[217] indeed, it has been suggested that there is no problem of an abstract purpose if there are identified beneficiaries specified in the terms of the trust.[218] In either case, there will be some person in whose favour the court can decree performance.[219] The difference in opinion is whether it is enough that there is merely some person in whose benefit the court can decree performance or whether that person must have some proprietary rights in the trust fund.[220] The latter point of view begins with the view that a beneficiary has that sort of proprietary right of immediate possession commensurate with the principle in *Saunders v Vautier*[221] in which beneficiaries representing the whole of the equitable interest can give directions to the trustees as to how the property should be used. Therefore, if property is expressed to be 'held on trust for the purpose of [an association]' or 'by the officers of the association for the purposes of the association', then that will be an abstract purpose trust and consequently void. In such a situation, there is little scope to interpret an intention to benefit some people as beneficiaries.

By contrast, Goff J in *Re Denley* suggested that it would be sufficient for there to be a people trust if there were some identifiable people who could take a direct or an indirect right in the property in the form of the use of enjoyment of that property. Alternatively, Oliver J in *Re Lipinski* suggested that there would be a people trust if there were ascertainable people – such as an implication that a transfer to a club is intended to be for the benefit of its members – or a gift if the members were given control over the capital of the transfer. It is this last view which is problematic. The distinction is between an understanding that the presence of some identifiable person who can hold the trustees to account will make the trust

---

216 *Leahy v Attorney-General for NSW* [1959] AC 457; *Re Denley's WT* [1969] 1 Ch 373; *Re Lipinski's WT* [1976] Ch 235.
217 *Re Denley's WT* [1969] 1 Ch 373.
218 *Re Grant's WT* [1979] 3 All ER 359.
219 *Morice v Bishop of Durham* (1805) 10 Ves 522; *Bowman v Secular Society Ltd* [1971] AC 406.
220 In this sense Vinelott J in *Re Grant's WT* [1979] 3 All ER 359 suggested that the decision of Goff J in *Re Denley's WT* [1969] 1 Ch 373 could be restricted to its facts or considered to be *obiter dictum* to the extent that it went beyond a finding that there was a trust for the benefit of identified people.
221 (1841) 4 Beav 115.

valid, and an understanding that for there to be such a person capable of holding the trustees to account, the trust must be drafted so as to make that sufficiently clear.

4.2.10 The application of the beneficiary principle to gifts made to unincorporated associations

The most significant application of the beneficiary principle, as already touched upon in the preceding sections of this section 4.2 of this chapter, is in relation to transfers of property to unincorporated associations. This particular issue is considered in detail in the next section of this chapter.

4.3 UNINCORPORATED ASSOCIATIONS

Gifts made to unincorporated associations must be structured correctly or else they will constitute invalid purpose trusts. There are a number of different ways of structuring such a transfer to make it valid: whether as a trust for the benefit of identified people, or as an accretion to the association's funds subject to contract, or as a transfer to the club's officers subject to a mandate to use that property in accordance with the association's purposes subject to contract, or as a gift to the members of the association. The transferor must avoid transferring the property to the officers of the association on trust to use for the abstract purposes of the association. The structure of any transfer of property to an unincorporated association must therefore be structured carefully to ensure that it is valid. On the termination of such an association, the individual members may acquire individual rights in the property held for the association.

4.3.1 Introduction

An unincorporated association is a group of people bound together by a contractual agreement but it is not a separate legal person (like a company). So when someone wants to give property to be used by the members of an association, they cannot give it to the unincorporated association itself because the association has no personality in law: instead, the property must be given to some person (either a human being or a company) to hold on behalf of the unincorporated association. This will itself cause problems because the person who holds the property for the association may be considered to be holding the property on the basis of an unenforceable purpose trust. There is a difficult boundary between making dispositions by way of a void purpose trust (which offends the beneficiary principle)[222] and making a disposition to an unincorporated association in a way that does not offend against the beneficiary principle.

4.3.2 What is an 'unincorporated association'?

The juridical nature of an unincorporated association

The first issue is to define what is meant by the term 'unincorporated association'. An association is a group of people who have joined together to form a club or society to pursue

---

222 Considered in section 4.2 above.

a common purpose, such as playing a sport together or indulging in some cultural activity. That they are 'unincorporated' means that they have not been incorporated as a company. A company has 'legal personality'[223] and therefore is able to own property in its own name, to enter into contracts in its own name and the rights of its members are controlled both by the Companies Acts as well as by the company's constitution,[224] whereas an *un*incorporated association can do none of these things. The best examples of unincorporated associations are social clubs not organised as companies. Most university law schools have some sort of law students' society which will organise social events, academic events and careers events with outside organisations: such societies are unincorporated associations to which the members pay subscriptions, they elect a committee to run the society, and they agree to abide by the terms of the society's constitution. Such a club or society itself, if not a company, will not have legal personality. That means that the club cannot own property in its own name; rather, property must be held in the name of some of its members on behalf of the club. Therefore, there is a risk that those members who hold the club property will appear to be trustees holding that property on trust for the purposes of the club. If that were the correct analysis, the trust might well be void for being a purpose trust.

Typically, the club will have membership criteria and will be subject to a constitution. The constitution will form a contract between members *inter se* who pay to join the club. A well-drafted constitution will set out not only the rights of the members, the means of selecting the club's officers and the way in which property collected is to be used, but will also provide for the manner in which property is to be divided if the club terminates.

The issues which will be considered in this section will deal, for the most part, with the rights of various members to the club's property, the various means by which property can be given to a club (by way of gift or otherwise) and the competing rights of members when the club is wound up. For the purposes of this section, we will assume such associations are not charities.

The most useful case on the nature of unincorporated associations is *Conservative Association v Burrell*.[225] This case considered the legal nature of the Conservative Party. When an individual joined the Conservative Party, she became a member of her local Conservative Association serving the constituency in which she lived and not the national Conservative Party. Each local Conservative Association held its own funds through its local officers. Because the national Conservative Party lacked a central organisation which controlled the local Conservative Associations, the national Conservative Party as a whole was not an unincorporated association. Rather, each local Conservative Association constituted a separate unincorporated association, because they had their own membership and their own rules. In comparison, the Labour Party has a central administrative function, centralised membership and centralised rules which apply to all members so that it is the central party to which members belong, although they are allocated to local, constituency areas and regions.[226] The Labour Party is therefore one single unincorporated association

---

223   *Saloman v A Saloman & Co Ltd* [1897] AC 22.

224   In relation to the companies, the constitution takes the form of the memorandum and articles of association, the minimum contents of which are controlled by statute.

225   [1982] 1 WLR 522.

226   See *Re Grant's WT* [1979] 3 All ER 359. The differences in structure tell us a lot about the differences between these two political parties: the Conservatives insist on local freedom to run local affairs, whereas the Labour Party has a centralised bureaucracy expressing the central principles with which the individual members interact. There is no information about the nature of the Liberal Democrats in the decided case law.

liable to corporation tax, whereas the Conservative Party is not. Unincorporated associations are therefore identifiable as being comprised of their own members, subject to a constitution or rules, such that the association is not a distinct legal person.

The reason why making transfers of property to unincorporated associations is problematic

As explained in the preceding section, an unincorporated association cannot own property on its own account. Therefore, if property is to be transferred for the benefit of such an association, that property must be transferred to a person who will hold that property for the association. It is usual for this person to be an officer of the association – such as its treasurer. If the treasurer is holding property for the association, then one analysis of that person's interaction with the association would be that she is a trustee of the property holding that property for the purposes of the association: if this is the proper analysis of the transfer, then that transfer will be void as having created an abstract purpose trust – something which is not permitted under the beneficiary principle as considered in section 4.2 above. Therefore, our focus in this section will be on identifying the ways in which property should be transferred so that the purposes of an association can be pursued but in such a way that a void abstract purpose trust is not created. The method we will use to identify the manner in which the transfer is being made is by analysing closely the terms on which that transfer is made. Consequently, the following sections analyse a variety of possible structures, explaining how each works and which will be valid and which will be void.

4.3.3   Possible constructions of transfers to unincorporated associations

There are a number of possible analyses of transfers to unincorporated associations depending on the facts of each case. There are subtle differences between each one, so it is important to analyse the individual transfer closely to identify which interpretation applies in each case. While there are a number of different shades of interpretation on the decided cases, there appear to be seven analyses based on the cases which are considered below:

(a) Outright gift, or assignment, to present members.
(b) Trust for present members.
(c) Trust for present and future members: endowment capital.
(d) Transfer to members as an accretion to the club's capital to be used in accordance with the club's constitution.
(e) Transfer subject to a mandate to use the property in accordance with the club's constitution.
(f) Trust for abstract, impersonal non-charitable purposes.
(g) Trust for charitable purposes.

It is worthwhile reminding ourselves of the problem. Unincorporated associations do not have legal personality and therefore are incapable of taking title in property. Therefore, transferring property to such an association (whether by outright gift or by means of a trust) creates the problem of ascertaining who is to take title in the property transferred. The property could either be held on trust, or alternatively transferred outright to the members as individuals. However, if the property is to be held on trust, there is a danger of creating a purpose trust which will be void under the beneficiary principle, as considered above. The only analysis which will necessarily render the transfer void is the analysis which finds that a given transfer is intended to be an abstract purpose trust. The other analyses have their own strengths and weaknesses, depending on the transferor's underlying objectives. In deciding which of the following analyses applies in any particular case, there is no simpler solution than to work through the analytical possibilities and see which applies most neatly to the facts in front of you. We shall consider the various possibilities in the sections to follow and consider in which circumstances each analysis would be appropriate. We shall suppose that the transferor of the property has not made her intentions clear and that therefore we are required to infer those intentions from the circumstances of the transfer of property to the unincorporated association.

(a) Outright gift, or assignment, to present members

The advantage of making a gift of property is that the trusts law concept of the beneficiary principle does not apply. If the donor of property intended that each of the members of the association was to have an item of property each absolutely, then this could be interpreted as being a series of small gifts, one to each member. Alternatively, it might be possible to see a large donation to a club as being one large gift of property which the members together take as tenants in common, just like the gift of money which was left in *Re Lipinski* to the Hull Judeans (Maccabi) Assocation. Indeed, the most straightforward means of transferring property to an unincorporated association is to make an outright gift to those members as individuals because a gift does not involve any of the complications associated with the beneficiary principle in trusts law. A 'gift' of property is synonymous with an 'outright transfer' of property or an 'assignment' of property. In each case, the transferor[227] is transferring away all of her rights in property to another person. For there to be an outright transfer, it must be the case that the transferor retains no property rights at all in the property. If the transferor did purport to retain any property rights *qua* transferor, then it would not be an outright transfer which had been made but rather some kind of conditional transfer or even a trust. Therefore, in using the terms 'gift' or 'outright transfer' in this section, we are considering the transfer of all of a person's rights in property to another person without any right to recover those property rights.[228] The term 'gift' is a common colloquial term for this kind of arrangement but it is being used in its strict legal sense here.

Let us take an example to illustrate the point. Suppose a gift of 11 Sunderland AFC replica kits is made to the New SAFC Supporters Association, at a time when that association has 11 members. If those kits were transferred outright to each of the individual members, so that each received one kit, that would be easily analysed as an outright gift of one kit to each of those members as individuals. Each member would take their own kit and acquire absolute title in it as a gift. Consequently, no question of the beneficiary principle arises. This analysis is possible because the property is of a kind which can be distributed easily between the members and on these facts there are exactly the same number of shirts as members. Therefore, there would be no reason to suppose that the transferor intended those shirts to be held on trust for the purposes of the association.

A more difficult example would involve property which cannot be divided up. Suppose then that the property which was transferred was the very football which was used in the

---

227   Also referred to as a 'donor' in relation to a gift.
228   That is, other than by some arm's length acquisition of the property by means of another, unconnected transaction.

1973 Cup Final, which was won 1–0 by Sunderland.[229] If such an item of property were transferred to the 11 members of the association, it would be unreasonable to suppose that each of them would take title in a separate piece of that property. In this instance the property is a single, precious object which would lose its intrinsic significance if it were cut up into eleven pieces, one for each member of the club. The more likely interpretation of the transferor's intentions would be that the football was to be held intact for the club's purposes. Therefore, it would need to be decided who would look after the property. At this point, it could be said that the transferor's intention was to have the football held on trust by an officer of the club – if there were no beneficiaries with rights in the football then the analysis would be a void purpose trust as in *Re Grant's WT*. Alternatively, it is possible that the transfer could be deemed to have been a gift which was made in such a way that all of the members are to be joint tenants of the absolute title in the football – perhaps leaving the football in a glass case in their club's meeting rooms. The advantage of this gift analysis would be that there is no beneficiary principle problem.

However, it will not always be entirely clear whether or not a gift is intended. From the discussion above of the decision of Oliver J in *Re Lipinski*,[230] we can glean the following proposition: if property is transferred on the basis of gift, rather than trust, then the rules of trusts relating to abstract purpose trusts will not apply. In particular, the analytical tool used by Oliver J is the idea that any transfer which grants the transferee complete control over the use of capital is tantamount to an outright gift of that capital. So, even if the transferor expresses her intention using words which suggest a declaration of a trust, then the court may still infer an intention to make a gift (as Oliver J did) if the beneficiaries acquire complete control of the capital. The argument is that if the transferee is entitled to spend the capital all at once, or to decide to use amounts periodically as she sees fit, then that has the same effect as making a gift of that property to the transferee.

The logic underpinning this idea is perhaps somewhat suspect. When the transferor has clearly intended to create a trust over property, it may be possible to argue that the trust is for the benefit of identifiable beneficiaries if it grants identifiable beneficiaries the right to use the capital entirely as they see fit. Therefore, it has the advantage that the problem posed by the beneficiary principle is removed. However, there is nothing to suggest that such a transfer ought not to be considered as a trust (albeit a trust for the benefit of identifiable beneficiaries) rather than as a gift. Control over the capital could equally well be explained as being a trust granting the beneficiaries the kind of property rights identified with *Saunders v Vautier*[231] whereby the beneficiaries have control of the trust fund as opposed to it being an outright gift.[232]

There is one further possible complication – where a gift is made contingent on some event, there may be an even narrower line between a gift and a trust. Suppose a gift made on the following terms: 'I give you this money provided that you pass your exams.' While that is an expression which might occur in the real world, it is unsatisfactory for the lawyer because the donor's intention is left unclear. It might be that the donor intends to give the money outright subject to a merely moral obligation to pass examinations. Alternatively, the donor may intend that no title is to pass in the money until the examinations are passed,

---

229 Ian Porterfield's strike and Jimmy Montgomery's double save will live long in the memory.
230 [1976] Ch 235; see para 4.2.3.
231 (1841) 4 Beav 115.
232 This latter view accords with the *dicta* of Oliver J in *Re Lipinski* [1976] Ch 235.

which would be a form of contingent gift under which transfer of title is contingent on the happening of some other event. As a further possibility, the donor may intend that she is to hold the money on trust for the donee on terms that the donee's rights vest only on passing the examinations. The short answer to this conundrum is that there is no right or wrong answer – rather, we must look at the circumstances and decide on what we think is the best interpretation of the donor's true intention.

(b) Trust for present members

A trust for the benefit of present members of the association would be a valid people trust, as in *Re Denley*. The restriction to present, as opposed to future, members removes any perpetuities problem. So, returning to the example used in the previous section, an alternative method of transferring the ball used in the 1973 Cup Final to the supporters club would be to declare a trust over the football such that it is 'held on trust by T for the benefit of those 11 persons who were the only registered members of the New SAFC Supporters Club as at 1 November 1998'. Using this express form of wording – 'for the benefit of those 11 persons', exactly as in *Re Denley* – would create a valid trust over the property for those current members as individuals.[233] Again, there is no suggestion that the property is the subject of a void purpose trust; rather, the members take the property immediately and have individual equitable interests. Therefore, on these facts all of the members acting together and *sui juris* would be able to direct the trustee how to deal with the property under the rule in *Saunders v Vautier*.[234] In this instance, the membership of the association is used to avoid any certainty of objects issue relating to the definition of the beneficiaries. The trust is structured for the benefit of those individual members rather than for the purposes of the association, thus making it a valid people trust as opposed to a void purpose trust. The one remaining issue arising from the trust provision, as drafted, would be the need for the inclusion of a perpetuities period.

Therefore, structuring the transfer correctly can alter the proper analysis of the donor's intentions. An advantage for the donor of using a trust structure would be the availability of the remedies for breach of trust and to recover property if the trustee should fail to comply with the settlor's wishes. A well-drafted trust instrument would explain clearly how the trustees were expected to behave so as to give effect to the settlor's wishes. By contrast, once a gift has been made, the donor has no control over the way in which the property is used. Therefore, there will be contexts in which a settlor will want to ensure that property is used in an appropriate, specified manner – in such contexts a trust is the best structure to employ. If a trust is to be used, then it must be structured appropriately so as to make it a valid people trust.

(c) Trust for present and future members: endowment capital

The difference between the trust for present members considered under (b) above and the endowment capital trust considered in this section is that an endowment capital trust intends

---

233   As accepted in *Re Grant's WT* [1979] 3 All ER 359.
234   (1841) 4 Beav 115.

that the property be locked into the trust so that income derived from the property is paid to the beneficiaries. Such a trust would be void for 'tending to a perpetuity' because endowment trusts ordinarily continue in existence for as long as there is capital left.[235] Suppose that the trust provision reads as follows: 'The football used in the 1973 Cup Final is to be held on trust so that the trustee must keep the ball on display and charge an entrance fee to members of the public to view the ball, and so that all such income generated is to be held on trust for the benefit of present and future members of the club.' There are three possible interpretations here.

The first would be that the trust is a trust for people (that is, the members of the association) which is capable of interpretation as lasting for a maximum perpetuity period, either if there is a perpetuity period included in the trust instrument or if the 1964 Act would impose one, so that there is certainty that the trust will be terminated.[236] The second is that the trust is a trust for people but invalid as offending the rule against remoteness of vesting. The issue is then whether or not the 1964 Act would operate to impose a statutory perpetuity period, thus validating the trust. The third is that the trust is deemed to be a trust for the purposes of the association, by virtue of supporting its present and future members, with the result that it would be a void purpose trust.[237]

Deciding which of these three analyses best fits any given set of facts would require a close reading of the terms of the trust instrument. A transfer will be interpreted to be a purpose trust if it is made 'for the present and future members' of the association because that wording suggests that the trust will continue forever, serving future members. The assumption is that where future members are also expressed as being entitled to the property, there cannot be an immediate, outright gift in favour of the current membership because that would militate against the rights of future members. The only viable analysis would be that there could only be a void trust for the purposes of the association in such a situation. Therefore, a transfer of property 'to be held upon trust by T for the purposes of the New Sunderland AFC Supporters Association' would be void as in *Leahy v Att-Gen NSW*. References to 'future members' are therefore best avoided in trust instruments, unless there is a clear perpetuities provision to specify the time at which future members would cease to be entitled to the trust property.

(d) Transfer to members as an accretion to the club's capital to be used in accordance with the club's constitution

Unincorporated associations usually operate by means of a contract between the members as to the rules of the association. Typically, officers of the association will be chosen, and those officers will maintain the property used by the association, raise subscriptions, admit new members and so forth. Consequently, property transferred for the benefit of the association may be placed under the control of the association's officers subject to the terms of the contract between the members in the form of their association's constitution. In such a situation, it is usual that a gift intended to be made to the association will pass into the

235 *Leahy v Attorney-General for NSW* [1959] AC 457; subject now to the effect of the Perpetuities and Accumulations Act 1964.
236 *Re Denley* [1969] 1 Ch 373.
237 *Leahy v Attorney-General for NSW* [1959] AC 457.

possession of the association's officers. An outright transfer on these terms will be valid if the property is intended to be held by the association's officers on the terms of the association's constitution as the agents of the association's membership and not as trustees under the law of trusts. The interpretation which is to be avoided is that those officers take the property as trustees under a void purpose trust. If contract law was the appropriate system of law to govern the transfer, then the beneficiary principle would not apply.

In *Re Recher's Will Trusts*,[238] a part of the residue of will trusts was to be held on trust for an anti-vivisection association which had ceased to exist. The issue arose as to the validity of the gift in any event, as if the association had still continued in existence. Briefly put, Brightman J held that this transfer could be interpreted to be an 'accretion to the club's fund' and that it would consequently fall to be administered in accordance with the terms of the club's contractual constitution: thus taking the transfer out of the ambit of the beneficiary principle. His Lordship held:[239]

> A trust for non-charitable purposes, as distinct from a trust for individuals, is clearly void because there is no beneficiary. It does not, however, follow that persons cannot band themselves together as an association or society, pay subscriptions and validly devote their funds in pursuit of some lawful non-charitable purpose. . . . Such an association of persons is bound, I would think, to have some sort of constitution; that is to say, the rights and liabilities of the members of the association will inevitably depend on some form of contract inter se, usually evidenced by a set of rules. In the present case it appears to me clear that the [members of the society] were bound together by a contract inter se. Any such member was entitled to the rights and subject to the liabilities defined by the rules. . . . In my judgment the legacy in the present case [to the society] ought to be construed as a legacy of that type, that is to say, a legacy to the members beneficially *as an accretion to the funds* subject to the contract which they had made inter se.

Brightman J is therefore suggesting that the beneficiary principle will not be an objection to the validity of a transfer of property to an unincorporated association if it is made under the law of contract as an accretion to the club's funds.[240]

Looking to the detail of his judgment, Brightman J held that it is possible for individuals to agree to deal between themselves as to a common purpose and to create a contract between themselves in the form of an association. Consequently, the use of their subscriptions and property committed under that contract could be controlled under the specific performance jurisdiction of the courts. Further, where there is no wording suggesting the creation of a trust, a transfer of property to that association should be read as an accretion to the capital collected for the association rather than creating immediate proprietary rights in favour of the members of the association.

Therefore, the interpretation which was applied to this bequest was that the property was transferred as an outright gift to members of the association as individuals, but held as an

---

238 [1972] Ch 526; *Artistic Upholstery Ltd v Art Forma (Furniture) Ltd* [1999] 4 All ER 277.

239 [1972] Ch 526, 538, [1971] 3 All ER 401, 407. Emphasis added by the author.

240 This approach was followed in *Universe Tankships Inc of Monrovia v International Transport Workers Federation* [1983] 1 AC 366, [1982] 2 All ER 67 and in *Artistic Upholstery Ltd v Art Forma (Furniture) Ltd* [1999] 4 All ER 277, *per* Lawrence Collins J.

accretion to the capital of the association. Consequently, the requisite officer of the associa-tion took possession of the property, even though it had been transferred to the members as individuals by way of gift. The use of the gift is then as an addition to the capital held by the association.

The treatment of the property, once it has become part of the capital collected for the association's purposes, is governed by the terms of the contract created by the members of the association between themselves. The transfer is deemed to be an outright transfer to the members of the association, albeit that the property is held by the association's officers on their behalf, and is to be used in accordance with the terms of the association's constitution. In broad terms, the members are therefore able to rely on provisions in their mutual contract to terminate the association and distribute the property between one another, as considered below. No question of trusts law generally, nor of the beneficiary principle specifically, arises where there has been a mere accretion to the funds of the association which is to be distributed in accordance with the terms of that association's constitution.

In deciding whether or not this *Re Recher* analysis is appropriate to any particular set of facts, we must consider the terms and the circumstances of the transfer closely. The donor should phrase his transfer as being 'an accretion to the association's general funds to be used in accordance with the terms of the association's constitution' for it to be held valid as in *Re Recher*. The donor should avoid using expressions such as 'the property is to be held on trust for the purposes of the association' because that would suggest the existence of a void purpose trust.

(e) Transfer subject to a mandate to use the property in accordance with the club's constitution as an agent of its members

Similarly to the preceding section, a mandate to use property in accordance with the terms of a club's contractual constitution would fall under contract law and not under the beneficiary principle in trusts law. Where property is transferred into the control of one person to pursue the purposes of the association, that person may be held to be an agent of the other members of the club rather than a trustee of property for the purposes of that association. Thus, in *Neville Estates v Madden*,[241] Cross J held that such a transfer could be interpreted to be:

> a gift to the existing members not as joint tenants but subject to their respective contrac-tual rights and liabilities towards one another as members. In such a case a member cannot sever his share. It will accrue to the other members on his death or resignation, even though such members include persons who became members after the gift took effect. It will not be open to objection on the score of perpetuity or uncertainty unless there is some-thing in its terms or circumstances or in the rules of the association which preclude the members at any given time from dividing the subject of the gift between them.

Therefore, a gift made subject to a mandate that the property be controlled in accordance with the constitution of the association will be valid and is to be administered strictly in accordance with those rules for the benefit of the membership generally. This arrangement takes effect at common law (therefore not creating any equitable proprietary interest in the

---

241 [1962] Ch 832, 849.

manner of an express trust) such that the club's officers are simply following a contractual instruction. That the property is used for the purposes of the association can be compelled by specific performance. A 'mandate' is a contractual direction which renders the person who is compelled to act on these instructions an agent of the person giving the direction. An example of a mandate would be an instruction given by a customer to her bank to make a payment by way of standing order out of her bank account to a third person such as her land-lord. In such a circumstance, the bank would be acting as an agent of its customer on the terms of the contract between them (in the form of the customer's bank account) but not as a trustee. The fact that this arrangement takes effect under contract law means that there is no problem with trusts law nor with the beneficiary principle as a result. As this approach was explained in *Conservative Association v Burrell* by Brightman LJ:[242]

> No legal problem arises if a contributor (as I will call him) hands to a friend (whom I will call the recipient) a sum of money to be applied by the recipient for political purposes indicated by the contributor, or to be chosen at the discretion of the recipient. That would be a simple case of mandate or agency. The recipient would have authority from the contributor to make use of the money, in the indicated way. So far as the money is used within the scope of the mandate, the recipient discharges himself vis-à-vis the contributor. . . . No trust arises, except the fiduciary relationship inherent in the relationship of principal and agent. . . . [If the contribution were made to an unincorporated association and paid to its treasurer then] the treasurer has clear authority to add the contribution to the mixed fund (as I will call it) that he holds. At that stage I think the mandate becomes irrevocable.

So, a payment to an unincorporated association could be interpreted as being a contribution to the association's general funds whereby the association's treasurer holds the property subject to a mandate to use it in accordance with the terms of the association's constitution. No trust arises in this context and therefore there is no problem with the beneficiary principle. The treasurer is simply the donor's agent under contract law principles. The significance of making that person an agent is that that person will bear the fiduciary obligations of an agent, and so the transferor can rely on their actions being controlled.

Again, one must look at the circumstances of the case and decide whether or not this is the best explanation of the donor's intentions. Did the donor intend that the recipient should simply use the property in accordance with the terms of the club's constitution and not that the recipient was to be a trustee of that property for the abstract purposes of the association? A donor would be well-advised to draft the terms of the transfer as 'an outright transfer subject to a mandate that the treasurer use the property in accordance with the terms of the association's constitution'. The donor should avoid using expressions such as 'the property is to be held on trust by the treasurer' which would suggest a void purpose trust.

(f) Trust for abstract, impersonal non-charitable purposes

The central issue considered above is that a purpose trust, which is not created for a charitable purpose, will be void because it offends against the beneficiary principle, as in *Leahy*

---

242 [1982] 2 All ER 1, 6.

v Att-Gen NSW and *Re Grant's WT*. If a transfer were interpreted to be an abstract purpose trust then it would be necessary to restructure that transfer in one of the ways indicated above, or for a court to be convinced to interpret that transfer in one of the other ways discussed above. The analysis of the transfer as being an abstract purpose trust is the worst possible result for the validity of the transfer, as is demonstrated by *Leahy v Att-Gen NSW* and *Re Grant's WT*. These cases have already been discussed in detail. Therefore, in this section we are concerned to identify some of the features of these cases which the transferor needs to avoid if her transfer is to be held to be valid.

A transfer is likely to be interpreted to be a trust if the transferor used expressions like 'the property is held on trust' and so forth. As is clear from *Re Lipinski*, however, using these sorts of expressions does not always lead to an interpretation of a transfer as being a trust if the court believes the true interpretation to be something else. Nevertheless, a transfer is likely to be interpreted as being a purpose trust where it is made 'for the present and future members' of the association, as in *Leahy v Att-Gen NSW*. The assumption is that where future members are also expressed as being entitled to the property, there cannot be an immediate, outright gift in favour of the current membership. Therefore, the transfer could not be interpreted to be an immediate gift as in (a) above. Consequently, the transfer will be interpreted as being held by the association's officers as trustees for the future members, as well as the present members, on the basis that a distribution of the property among present members would be contrary to the intention to benefit future members. Therefore, the transfer will be interpreted as a disposition for the purposes of the association, held on trust by the requisite officers, and therefore void.

For example, in *Re Grant's Will Trusts*,[243] a bequest was left to 'the Labour Party Property Committee for the benefit of the Chertsey HQ of the Chertsey & Walton Constituency Labour Party' or in default to the National Labour Party. Vinelott J held that the bequest should be interpreted as being intended to be held on trust for the Labour Party, despite the expression 'for the benefit of'. It was then held that the intention was to create an endowment (a permanent block of capital) to generate income for the local or national Labour Party. Consequently, the bequest was held to be void for perpetuity, as well as being void as a purpose trust.

(g) Trust for charitable purposes

The final possible analysis would be that the purpose of the trust is charitable. Where the trust is for a charitable purpose, the beneficiary principle does not apply nor does the perpetuity rule. The context of charitable trusts is considered in Chapter 25.

An example of these various analyses

The judgment of Lawrence Collins J in *Re Horley Town FC*[244] is a thorough survey of the possible analyses of property holdings by a small football club which was organised as an

---

243   [1979] 3 All ER 359, [1980] 1 WLR 360.
244   [2006] EWHC 2386.

unincorporated association and which had different categories of membership.[245] The question for us to consider now is how would we analyse a transfer of property to a football club, in this instance an unincorporated association. Let us consider the various possible analyses. A football club could be organised as a valid people trust for the benefit of its present members, and any future members within its perpetuity period, whereby those people are treated as being akin to the objects of a discretionary trust in that they are entitled to use the property as permitted by the club's management, as in *Re Denley*.[246] Alternatively, any property transferred to the club could be interpreted as being a gift made to the current members as tenants in common if they were entitled to dispose of the capital as they sought fit, or as a valid people trust with ascertainable members, as in *Re Lipinski*.[247] Alternatively, again, the club could be considered to be conducting an abstract purpose in providing for the playing of sport[248] in relation to which no person takes any proprietary rights and which is therefore void, as in *Re Grant's WT*.[249] The final analysis would be that any property passed to the trust is held in accordance with the terms of its constitution under the terms of the contract between the members as an accretion to the club's funds, as in *Conservative Association v Burrell*[250] or *Re Recher's WT*,[251] or as a gift to the members as joint tenants, as in *Neville Estates v Madden*.[252] Which analysis is the best analysis will depend upon a close reading of the club's constitution, if any, and a consideration of the nature of the property involved, as considered in the next section.

The potential importance of the nature of the property involved

As was suggested in the preceding discussions of the various forms of potential analysis of a transfer of property to an unincorporated association, it may well be that the form of property involved will have an effect on deciding which analysis is the most appropriate. If the property is a billiard table which is being transferred to the association, then it would be improbable that that table was expected to be divided up between the members so that they would saw it up and take home a piece of it each. Therefore, a court is more likely to find either that the members were to be owners of it as a gift as joint tenants or else that it was intended as an endowment to be held for the purposes of the club in perpetuity as a billiard table held intact for as long as possible. Alternatively, akin to the sports field in *Re Denley*, it could be argued that it is to be made available for the benefit of all of the members and so

---

245 Ultimately no conclusion is reached as to whether or not this association was based on a valid trust for the benefit of identifiable people as beneficiaries, or an association predicated on a valid contract to which property is added as an accretion to its funds, or a void trust without beneficiaries which was formed for the pursuit of an abstract purpose. The discussion in the judgment in this context was predicated on the three categories set out in *Neville Estates v Madden* [1962] Ch 832, a formulation which does not mention explicitly the possibility that the association is organised as a valid discretionary trust for the benefit of the members of the association as in *Re Denley* [1969] 1 Ch 373 (although that case is cited, over-much focus is paid to *Neville Estates v Madden*). The judgment is, otherwise, an excellent survey of the case law in this area.
246 [1969] 1 Ch 373.
247 [1976] Ch 235.
248 Something which was not a charitable purpose before the passage of Charities Act 2006, s 2(2)(g).
249 [1979] 3 All ER 359.
250 [1982] 1 WLR 522.
251 [1972] Ch 526.
252 [1962] Ch 832.

be the subject matter of a valid trust. If there were 24 members of the club and 24 small, valuable works of art were donated to the club, it might be possible to interpret this as an accretion to the club's property so that the members were entitled to vote in accordance with their constitution to divide those artworks between them and take one each: that the artworks are chattels numerous enough for equal division makes them susceptible to this analysis, as opposed to necessarily needing to be treated as being held on trust or as an accretion to the club's funds. It would be logically difficult to interpret a gift of a billiard table in the same way because it is unlikely that the transferor could have intended to have each member of the association saw off a piece of the billiard table to take home. It would be more likely that a billiard table was intended to be held for the purposes of the club in its clubroom in perpetuity: this analysis would suggest that this transfer was an invalid purpose trust. By contrast, money is a form of property which, because it is so easily divided into so many different lots or held together as a complete fund, can potentially be subjected to any form of analysis because of its malleable form. So, transfers of money could be susceptible to many different analyses and therefore more reliance is likely to be placed on the precise words used and intention evidenced by the transferor.

What is unclear about this model of property being granted to unincorporated associations is that it still does not explain who actually *owns* the property. To say that the property is held subject to a contract does not tell us, for example, who owns the legal title over the property and so should be recorded as such at the Land Registry in relation to land or as a signatory over the bank account in relation to money or whatever. For example, if property were transferred to the Trust Lawyers' Association, an unincorporated association, then the property would have to be transferred to some human beings in fact because if no individual or any other legal person was able to receive the property then it would go on resulting trust back to the transferor. If the property was land and was received by, for example, Tariq and Zena (the President and Treasurer of the Association respectively) then we would have to ask whether Tariq and Zena are to be registered as proprietors of the land at the Land Register, then that would tend to the analysis that they hold the property on a trust of land because they are not intended to be the beneficial owners of the property themselves. Arguing that the property is in some way 'held' further to the terms of the association's constitution does not explain who *owns* the land. The contractual analyses in *Re Recher* and in *Conservative Association v Burrell* are convenient in that they avoid the problems of the beneficiary principle, but they do not really solve the property law problems with transfers of property in this context. An initially more promising analysis is that the members of the association are joint tenants at common law of the property but that each member has only limited rights to use the property in accordance with the agreement constituted between the members in the form of the association's constitution: principally, this means that the members may not sever their shares in the property contrary to the terms of that constitution. The problem remains, however, that if the property were land, then only four members could be entered on the Land Register under the Law of Property Act 1925, so those four members become trustees for the remaining beneficiaries in any event, which brings us back to the original problem.

Answering problems in this area

Students often find this a challenging topic because it is very different from anything which they have studied before. The key is to remember that the legal principles remain set in stone. It is only the facts of different problems or the factual circumstances of cases which change. So, you must analyse the facts of each different case and decide which of the different legal models they most closely resemble. Consider the words which the transferor used: which legal model do they most closely resemble? Is there anything about the nature of the property involved which leads you to one model rather than another?

The various advantages and disadvantages of these various analyses could be understood by reference to the following diagram. In essence this table records each of the five key analyses which have been described in this discussion and asks (a) whether or not each will be valid; and (b) whether or not each provides the donor with sufficient control over the use of the property once it has been transferred to its intended recipient. In essence, if a transferor transfers property to a person then she will want to know that that property will be used for the purpose for which she transferred it originally, whereas it is possible that when the officers of the unincorporated association receive the property they may decide that they want to use it for a purpose which would not meet with the approval of the transferor. Therefore, the fiduciary offices (like trustee and agent) offer protection to the transferor in that the fiduciary is bound by her fiduciary duties to use the property appropriately, whereas if the property is the subject of a gift then the recipient acquires 'complete control' over it and is free to do whatever she wants with the property.

Various analyses of transfer to unincorporated association	Abstract purpose trust	'People trust'	Gift passing 'complete control'	An accretion to funds	Taking property as agent subject to mandate
Leading case exhibiting this analysis	Leahy v Att-Gen NSW	Re Denley	Re Lipinski	Re Recher	Conservative Association v Burrell
Valid or Void?	Void	Valid	Valid	Valid	Valid
Does the transfer retain control of money after transfer?	Yes, but void	Yes, because governed by trustee's fiduciary duties	No, because all title passes	No, because governed only by terms of association's constitution	Yes, because governed by agent's fiduciary duties
Is it clear who owns the property?	Yes, but void	Yes, held on trust	Yes	No	No

On each set of facts, having analysed (as discussed already in this section) which analysis best fits the facts of the situation, it is then important to advise a transferor as to which of the various possible structures offers the transferor the best combination of valid transfer and suitable control over the property. For example, if the transferor is also one of the officers of the association who will receive the property on behalf of that association, then having little control over the property once received would not bother her particularly; whereas if she had no control over that body then she may require some control over the recipient once the property is transferred to the unincorporated association. A lawyer's role is to advise her client on the best structure for her goals. However, it is important to note that it is not a lawyer's (nor a student's) role simply to assume that the analysis which suits the client best is the one which necessarily applies. Instead one must look at the circumstances and recognise which analysis honestly fits the circumstances, and if one has the luxury of being able to structure the circumstances before the property is transferred then one must ensure that the structure actually embodies the desired result. For example, if one wishes to seem most like *Re Denley* then one should use the precise formulation used in that case by Goff J.

4.3.4 Distributions on the winding up of an unincorporated association

Moribund associations – bona vacantia

One arcane set of rules surrounds the treatment of transfers of property to associations which subsequently cease to exist. As considered above, where subscribers contribute to a fund which becomes moribund and where it is possible to identify those subscribers, the property subscribed will be held on resulting trust for the subscribers. However, where it is not possible for the property to be held on such a trust, it passes *bona vacantia* to the Crown.[253] Therefore, if an association ceases to carry on any activities and has no members, the property held for that moribund association passes *bona vacantia* to the Crown, that is, to the Duchy of Cornwall.[254] This rule, it is suggested, is a reminder of the underlying logic of English property law that it is the monarch who ultimately owns all property in the jurisdiction: therefore, any unclaimed property reverts to the monarch. This may seem remarkable to the reader.

When winding up an unincorporated association it was held by Lewison J in *Hanchett-Stamford v Attorney-General*[255] that if there was still one member left of a moribund association then the property attributed to that association would not pass *bona vacantia* to the Crown. That much is in line with principle: where a member remains, the association is not completely moribund, even if it has stopped carrying on any activities. Interestingly, his Lordship considered that for the Crown to seize property in such circumstances would offend against that person's human rights to their property under the First Protocol of the European Convention on Human Rights.

Distributions among members on winding up

A number of problems arise on the termination of an association to do with the means by which the property belonging to the association is to be distributed. The first interpretation is that property should be returned to the person who transferred it to the association. As considered elsewhere,[256] this approach has been employed where the transfer has taken the form of a subscription to a purpose which cannot be carried out. The property is held on resulting trust if those subscribers can be identified. So, under the old authority of *Re West Sussex Constabulary's Widows, Children and Benevolent (1930) Fund Trusts*,[257] there were four categories of giving: substantial donations and legacies, money donated via collecting boxes, contributions from

253 *Westdeutsche Landesbank Girozentrale v Islington LBC* [1996] AC 669.
254 At present the income from the Duchy of Cornwall is paid directly to the Prince of Wales.
255 [2008] EWHC 330 (Ch), [2008] 4 All ER 323.
256 See para 11.2.4 below.
257 [1971] Ch 1.

members, and entertainment such as raffles and sweepstakes. First, where the makers of the donations were identifiable, the donations could be returned. It was held that where a legacy was made to an unincorporated association which subsequently became moribund, then that legacy would be held on resulting trust for the donor's estate. In relation to legacies, it was considered by Goff J that they were separately identifiable from the other property and therefore capable of being returned to their donors in a manner which smaller contributions, such as to collection tins, were not. Therefore, secondly, in the case of the collection boxes, it was held that it is impossible to return the property to the subscribers on the basis that their transfers of property were both outright gifts and made anonymously. Thirdly, contributions from members could be distributed in accordance with the rules of the association. Where the rules of the association were silent as to the redistribution of subscriptions to the membership, then those members would be taken to have received the services for which they had paid through their subscriptions. Fourthly, the proceeds of the entertainment were not capable of being returned to the people who participated on the basis that people who had contributed that money had received the entertainment they paid for and therefore had no right to the return of their property – their interaction had been based on contract and not on trust.

A second approach might apply where the transfer is an outright transfer such that there can be no suggestion that the transferor retains any title in the property. Where the property has been the subject of a gift or outright transfer, the transferor would not ordinarily retain any right.[258] Therefore, the property must be dealt with in accordance with the terms of the association's constitution, being the contract between the members.[259] In circumstances where the contract provides for the mechanism by which the trust property is to be distributed, the matter is considered to be one of contract in which equitable principles have no role. In *Re Bucks Constabulary Fund Friendly Society (No 2)*, Walton J held:[260]

> It is a matter, so far as the members are concerned, of pure contract, and, being a matter of pure contract, it is, in my judgment, as far as distribution is concerned, completely divorced from all questions of equitable doctrines.[261]

Therefore, the resulting trust is displaced as the means by which property is distributed on termination of the association by the law of contract. If the association contains rules as to the means by which the property held for the association is to be distributed, the members are bound by those contractual rules. There is a very important shift here between principles based on the law of property – by means of resulting trust – and principles based on contract, as in *Re Bucks Fund*. Where there is a contract between the members of the association, or between other people participating in entertainments organised by the association for fund-raising purposes, then the modern approach is to look to the enforcement of the terms of that contract in distributing the association's property. The motivation for this change in approach is that the membership of the association voluntarily subjugates its property rights to the terms of the association's constitution – itself a contract – and so should be held to the terms of that arrangement in the distribution of the association's property.

---

258 *Westdeutsche Landesbank Girozentrale v Islington LBC* [1996] AC 669.
259 *Neville Estates v Madden* [1962] Ch 832.
260 [1979] 1 WLR 936.
261 Followed in *Artistic Upholstery Ltd v Art Forma (Furniture) Ltd* [1999] 4 All ER 277.

That a resulting trust should not be implied where the claimant has already received all that he was contractually entitled to was doubted in *Davis v Richards and Wallington Industries Ltd*,[262] where employees sought to recover rights in surplus contributions to their occupational pension fund. Scott J considered that the employees contributing to a pension fund ought to be entitled to recover the surplus contributions to that fund in the event that it was wound up. This was doubted in *Air Jamaica v Charlton*,[263] where the Privy Council suggested that in cases of actuarial surpluses under occupational pension funds, the contributors were not automatically entitled to recover their over-contributions. These cases, it is suggested, relate specifically to the difficult questions relating to occupational pension funds which are considered in detail in Chapter 24:[264] surpluses in that context are actuarial calculations that the amount of money contained in a pension fund is more than is needed to meet the pensions requirements of the number of pensioners then contained in the fund.

Method of distribution where association's rules are silent

The further issue is which approach is to be taken if the association's constitution is silent on the matter of distributing the trust property. This was the situation in *Re Bucks Fund*: the fund was wound up and the question raised whether its property should be distributed between its surviving members, or whether it should pass to the Crown as *bona vacantia* once the association had become moribund. The association's constitution was silent as to the question of the distribution of the property. Walton J held that the proper approach was to distribute the property rateably between the surviving members, according to their respective contributions, rather than vacating it to the Crown.

One further problem arose in that case: what if there were different classes of membership? Suppose a gentlemen's club provided a restaurant and library service at a rate of £10 per week for those who lived in London, and at a rate of £5 per week for those who lived outside London. On the winding up of the club, those members who had paid £10 would claim entitlement to double the proceeds of the members who had paid only £5.[265] This was the situation in *Re Sick and Funeral Society of St John's Sunday School, Golcar*,[266] in which there were ordinary, adult members and child members of a society which provided sickness and death benefits. The members paid different subscriptions according to their age but otherwise took broadly similar services from the association. It was ordered by Megarry J that the property should be divided rateably among the surviving members on the winding up of the association, such that the adult members would receive full shares and the children only half-shares in proportion to their subscriptions. Now suppose a different situation in which there was another gentlemen's club providing residence for its members and a restaurant, such that there was a membership rate of £100 per week for those who lived on the premises permanently and a £50 per week rate for those who did not stay for more than three days per week. On the winding up of the association, the members who were permanent residents might not be entitled to double the property on the basis that they received a service

262 [1990] 1 WLR 1511.
263 [1999] 1 WLR 1399.
264 See para 24.5.2 below.
265 *Re Sick and Funeral Society of St John's Sunday School, Golcar* [1973] Ch 51.
266 *Ibid.*

from the club which was twice as large as the occasional residents. In this latter example, the permanent residents might be considered to have received a more extensive service in consideration for their greater payment such that they ought not to have any greater right to the association's property on its winding up.

Similarly, there might be disagreement between those who had been members for a longer period than others, or who had played a more active part in the activities of the association. Clearly, the permutations are endless. It is to be expected that the courts will seek to distribute property in the most commonsensical way possible. This perhaps illustrates the shortcomings of English property and trusts law, in that entitlement is frequently seen as attaching to specific items of property rather than being related to amounts of value in communal property which is better identified as being made up of claims against other persons, rather than being in claims *in rem*.[267]

A further problem relates to different categories of member having different types of voting rights in meetings of the association, and who may also have paid different amounts by way of subscription as considered before: should different voting rights lead to different rights in the club's property on a winding up? Megarry V-C held in *GKN Bolts & Nuts Ltd etc Works Sports and Social Club*[268] that the court should approach questions as to the winding up of unincorporated associations with the broad sword of common sense. In that case there was a clear distinction made in the club's rules between full members and other sorts of members such that only full members would be entitled to vote for a winding up of the association: consequently, it was held that only those members should be deemed to be entitled to participate in a winding up of that association so as to be entitled to receive its property absolutely beneficially.

In relation to the appropriate mechanism for winding up an unincorporated association whose members had different voting rights, Lawrence Collins J was asked to consider a club with full members, associate members, and temporary members in *Re Horley Town FC*.[269] His Lordship acknowledged that the division between different categories of member was less clear in his case than in the *GKN* case. The temporary members took out membership only on a one-off basis when they attended social events organised by the club – such as pub quizzes and that sort of thing: these temporary members had no rights to vote at any of the club's meetings. Associate members belonged to approved sports clubs of other sorts and took out membership for one year at a time, which permitted them to use the football club's facilities during that time: importantly, associate members had only limited rights to vote at association meetings during their membership. Full members had full voting rights during their membership which could last as long as the club lasted. In the event that the assets of the club were wound up it was found that the temporary members should receive no property because they were not entitled to vote for a winding up. Similarly, even though

267 This discussion is taken up in relation to tracing below in Chapter 19: *Barlow Clowes International Ltd (In Liquidation) v Vaughan* [1992] 4 All ER 22.

268 [1982] 1 WLR 774.

269 [2006] EWHC 2386. For those reasons who want a sense of what Horley is like, perhaps the following will help. Horley is near Gatwick Airport to the south of London. The well-known goth rock band The Cure were originally from Horley. On the *Faith* album (Fiction Records, 1981) there is a track 'Other Voices' which has lyrics which suggest to me what it would be like to live in Horley: 'It's just the noises of other voices / Pounding in my broken head' (lyric by Robert Smith).

associate members had limited voting rights, 'the associate members in the present case have no effective rights and it would be wholly unrealistic to treat the introduction of associate members by amendment of [the club's rules] as a transfer of the Club's property to them'. Therefore, only full members would be considered to be appropriate recipients of club property.[270]

However, the final paragraphs of the judgment are very unclear. The peni-penultimate clause[271] of the judgment proper provides that the Club's rules have no provision explaining how a winding up is to be conducted. Therefore, Lawrence Collins J held that:[272]

> The Rules do not specify how the Club's assets are to be distributed following dissolution. In the absence of any rule to the contrary, there is to be implied into the rules of the Club a rule to the effect that the surplus funds of the Club should be divided on a dissolution amongst the members[273] of the Club, and this distribution will normally be per capita among the members (irrespective of length of membership or the amount of subscriptions paid) but may reflect different classes of membership.

Ultimately, this question was adjourned for a further hearing.[274] The principal point which emerges is that one's category of membership will not necessarily entitle one to a greater or lesser share of the association's property than other categories of member.[275] If the terms of the club's constitution are expressly that there should be distribution in differential amounts then that is the method which must be followed.[276] Furthermore, in the judgment of Collins J it emerged that there will be differential distribution if that is the best analysis for the situation, for example if one category of membership did not have any rights to vote on matters such as distribution then it is not to be presumed that they should be entitled to participate in such a distribution.

A note on resulting trust

Chapter 11 considers the distribution of the proceeds of a trust which cannot be performed, or in relation to which there is surplus property. The approach had been taken in cases like *West Sussex* that property ought to be held on resulting trust for persons who had contributed to an unincorporated association, provided that such persons could be readily identified.[277] Subsequently, there has been a development in equity from the use of resulting trusts in

---

270   The judgment, annoyingly, decides to stop distinguishing between the three categories of member at this point and Lawrence Collins J instead simply refers to 'the members' from this point forwards, thus making it unclear precisely which members were intended to be covered.

271   [2006] EWHC 2386, [129].

272   *Ibid*.

273   However, it is not made clear here exactly which category of members is intended. From the previous paragraphs it seems likely that this is a reference to 'full members' only, but the final paragraph of the judgment leaves this question for a later date.

274   [2006] EWHC 2386, [132].

275   *Re Sick and Funeral Society of St John's, etc* [1973] Ch 51; *Re Bucks Constabulary, etc (No 2)* [1979] 1 WLR 936, 952; *Re GKN Bolts, etc.* [1982] 1 WLR 774, 778.

276   *Re Bucks Constabulary, etc (No 2)* [1979] 1 WLR 936.

277   *Re West Sussex Constabulary's Benevolent Fund Trusts* [1971] Ch 1.

situations like *West Sussex* towards a use of contract law thinking in cases like *Re Bucks*.[278] Equity was once eager to find resulting trusts to explain the return of title to the original owners of property. It is suggested (as considered in Chapter 11) that resulting trusts apply in situations in which the structure in which the legal title was originally held remains and that it is only the equitable interest which falls to be allocated. The thinking advanced in *Westdeutsche Landesbank*[279] sounds the death knell for more adventurous theories of the resulting trust by holding that once property is transferred under an intention that the recipient take absolute title, there is no resulting trust. This thinking is in stark contradistinction to the theories advanced by the restitution school.[280] In short, the resulting trust is displaced by an approach based on the law of contract.

It is suggested that the better approach for equity in any event in such circumstances ought to have been to require the parties to observe their contractual bargain (in the form of the association's constitution) rather than seeking to return title in property on resulting trust. The basis for this argument is that once a contract to transfer property is formed, the contracting parties are compelled to effect the transfer. This rule is clear under doctrines as varied as that in *Walsh v Lonsdale*[281] (that equity looks upon as done that which ought to have been done) and in *Westdeutsche Landesbank Girozentrale v Islington LBC*[282] (that a constructive trust be imposed where it would be unconscionable for the holder of the legal title to refuse to do so). In short, once the contract is formed, equity treats the equitable interest as having passed according to the terms of the contract. Therefore, it is not a question for resulting trust because the transferor loses title in the property *qua* original owner and acquires any proprietary rights only under the terms of the contract.

---

278 [1979] 1 WLR 936.
279 [1996] AC 669.
280 See section 31.3 below.
281 (1882) 21 Ch D 9.
282 [1996] AC 669.

Chapter 5

Formalities in the creation of express trusts

OVERVIEW

A valid declaration of trust over personal property will not require any formality, provided that it can be demonstrated that the settlor intended to create an immediate trust over the property.[1] In relation to property to be made subject to a trust on death, in relation to trusts of land,[2] and in relation to certain other property, there will be statutory formalities to be satisfied before a valid trust will be created.

The settlor must have had proprietary rights in the trust property at the time of purporting to create the trust; it will not be sufficient that the settlor acquires those property rights at some subsequent time.[3] For the effective constitution of the trust, the legal title in the trust fund must be transferred to the trustee.[4]

In cases of fraud, equity will not permit common law or statute to be used as an engine of fraud such that it may impose a trust even though there was no valid declaration of that trust.[5]

In cases where a property-holder has made an assurance to a claimant that she will acquire rights in that property, equitable estoppel will grant rights to that claimant if she can demonstrate that she has acted to her detriment in reliance on that assurance.[6] The precise remedy awarded is at the discretion of the court and may be either proprietary or personal.

The trust will not be used to perfect an imperfect gift, on the basis that equity will not assist a volunteer.[7] Where the intention was to make a gift, whether or not a gift was validly made will be decisive of the matter. The exceptions are as follows: cases of donatio mortis causa;[8] executors of the estates of persons to whom they owed debts will be deemed to have those debts discharged by way of gift;[9] the doctrine of proprietary

---

1 *M'Fadden v Jenkyns* (1842) 12 LJ Ch 146.
2 Law of Property Act 1925, s 53(1)(b).
3 *Re Brook's ST* [1939] 1 Ch 993.
4 *Milroy v Lord* (1862) 4 De GF & J 264.
5 *Rochefoucauld v Boustead* [1897] 1 Ch 196; *Lyus v Prowsa Developments Ltd* [1982] 1 WLR 1044.
6 *Gillett v Holt* [2000] 2 All ER 289; *Yaxley v Gotts* [2000] 1 All ER 711.
7 *Ibid.*
8 *Sen v Headley* [1991] 2 WLR 1308.
9 *Strong v Bird* (1874) LR 18 Eq 315.

estoppel will operate to prevent detriment being suffered by those to whom a promise of gift was made; and cases of fraud, as above.

Where a promise is made under covenant to the effect that the settlor will settle property which is to be acquired in the future, there will not be a valid trust. A valid trust will only be created if the settlor owned property rights in the trust property at the time of purporting to declare the trust. Otherwise, only the parties to that covenant will be entitled to enforce the covenant at common law for damages, or in equity by specific performance if they have given consideration for the promise.[10] Trustees who are parties to a covenant may not enforce that covenant,[11] unless the benefit of the covenant itself has been settled on trust.[12]

A disposition of an equitable interest must be effected by signed writing,[13] unless both legal and equitable title pass together from the trust.[14] Where a sub-trust is created, so that the beneficiary retains some office as sub-trustee, there is no disposition of the equitable interest – unless there is an outright assignment of that equitable interest.[15] An agreement to transfer the equitable interest has been held to transfer the equitable interest automatically on the specific performance principle, without the need for signed writing.[16]

INTRODUCTION

This chapter considers a broad range of issues to do with the creation of valid express trusts. In the previous chapters, we considered the fundamental nature of the express trust and the necessity of introducing certainty to the trust and some of the powers of the beneficiary. This chapter does three things. First, it sets out some of the contexts in which there are specific formalities to be satisfied in relation to the creation of a trust. Secondly, it considers the mechanics of setting the trust in motion by the proper transfer of the legal title in the trust fund to the trustee. The third element is then analysing further the distinction between gifts and trusts, covenants and trusts, and the complex question of dispositions of an equitable interest.

5.1 SPECIFIC FORMALITIES IN THE CREATION OF TRUSTS

A valid declaration of trust over personal property will not require any formality, provided that it can be demonstrated that the settlor intended to create an immediate trust over the property. In relation to property to be made subject to a trust on death, in relation to trusts of land, and in relation to certain other property, there will be statutory formalities to be satisfied before a valid trust will be created.

This first section considers the means by which trusts are to be created where the trust fund is a particular form of property. The main distinctions are between trusts in relation to land

---

10 *Cannon v Hartley* [1949] Ch 213.
11 *Re Pryce* [1917] 1 Ch 234.
12 *Fletcher v Fletcher* (1844) 4 Hare 67.
13 *Grey v IRC* [1960] AC 1.
14 *Vandervell v IRC* [1967] 2 AC 291, HL.
15 *Re Lashmar* (1891) 1 Ch D 258.
16 *Oughtred v IRC* [1960] AC 206; *Neville v Wilson* [1997] Ch 144.

and trusts in relation to personal property, and between testamentary and *inter vivos* trusts. There are two stages which are important in the constitution of a trust: first, a valid declaration of trust; and, secondly, the transfer of the legal title in the trust property to the trustee.

5.1.1 Declaration of trust

The first issue is the means by which a trust will be declared. The appropriate formal requirements will depend on the nature of the property which is to be held on trust.

Declaration of trust on death

Where the trust is declared on the death of the settlor, by means of her will, there are formalities under s 9 of the Wills Act 1837 to be complied with. Section 9 provides that:

> No will shall be valid unless –
>
> (a) it is in writing, and signed by the testator, or by some other person in his presence and by his direction; and
> (b) it appears that the testator intended by his signature to give effect to the will; and
> (c) the signature is made or acknowledged by the testator in the presence of two or more witnesses present at the same time; and
> (d) each witness either –
>   (i) attests and signs the will; or
>   (ii) acknowledges his signature, in the presence of the testator (but not necessarily in the presence of any other witness),
>
> but no form of attestation shall be necessary.

In short, the trust made under a will cannot be valid unless: it is in writing; it is signed by the testator; and it is also signed, or attested to, by two or more witnesses. Where these formalities are complied with, the will trust is valid. Failure to comply with these formalities will lead to a failure to create a valid will, or will trusts, and therefore the testator will die intestate.

Declaration of trust over land

There is a particular formality in relation to declarations of trust in respect of land. Section 53(1)(b) of the Law of Property Act 1925 provides that:

> (b) a declaration of trust respecting any land or any interest therein must be manifested and proved by some writing signed by some person who is able to declare such trust or by his will.

Briefly put, if a settlor wishes to declare a trust over land (or over any interest in some land, such as a lease or a beneficial right under a trust of land), then that declaration must be evidenced in written form and signed by someone who has a sufficient right in the property which is subject to the trust if it is effected *inter vivos*. Otherwise, a declaration of a testamentary trust over land must be created by means of a valid will.

Declaration of trust inter vivos over personal property

While there are formal requirements for the creation of trusts on death or in relation to land, there are no formalities required for an *inter vivos* trust of personalty.[17] Therefore, to create a trust over chattels, it is sufficient that there is an oral declaration of trust disclosing sufficient intention to create a trust.[18] There is, of course, always the practical difficulty of proving the existence of such a trust and of proving the terms on which the trust is created if that trust is not written down, because there will only be the testimony of witnesses on which the court can rely. This book is not, however, concerned with the law of evidence but rather with the types of action which will and will not create a valid express trust.

Many of the cases applicable in this area were considered above in relation to certainty of intention to create a trust, as considered in Chapter 3. In that chapter it was demonstrated that it is enough that the court can infer an intention to create a trust from the actions of the parties – there is not even a requirement that there be any particular form of words used to raise the finding of a trust. Thus, in *Re Kayford*,[19] a company which conducted a mail order business required customers either to pay in advance in full for their goods, or to pay a deposit for those goods. The company's accountants advised the opening of a customers' trust deposit account and paid into it all money paid by customers for goods which had not yet been delivered. It was held that the action of setting up a distinct account for those payments constituted the creation of an express trust over those moneys, so that when the company went into liquidation, those customers who had paid into that account but who had not yet received their goods were held to be equitable owners of the contents of the account. It was held that 'the property concerned is pure personalty and so writing, though desirable, is not essential'. Therefore, there is a properly constituted trust without the need for a written declaration of trust.

Also considered earlier in Chapter 3 was the case of *Paul v Constance*,[20] in which the use of the words 'the money is as much yours as mine' in relation to money paid into a bank account held only in one party's name was found to be sufficient intention to create an express trust of the account over which the individuals were equitable tenants in common. The court found that surrounding circumstances, such as joint use of the money and a lack of sophistication of the people involved, contributed to the impression that the individuals had intended the creation of a trust.

Therefore, it is clear that in relation to personalty, a general intention to create an express trust will be sufficient to constitute a declaration of such a trust. The settlor is not required to use any particular form of words because the court will infer that intention from the circumstances of the case.

5.1.2 A completely constituted trust cannot be undone

There is an important principle of the law on express trusts which states that a trust is inviolate once it has been created, unless the settlor builds something to the contrary into the terms of the trust. This means that a settlor cannot cancel a trust, nor recover the trust

17 *M'Fadden v Jenkyns* (1842) 12 LJ Ch 146.
18 *Paul v Constance* [1977] 1 WLR 527.
19 [1975] 1 WLR 279.
20 [1977] 1 WLR 527.

property, once the trust has been validly created.[21] Like so many of these rules of the law of trusts, it appears to have arisen at a time when trusts were being used primarily to effect large family settlements. When grand families succeeded in marrying their children off, they also negotiated the terms on which the property of each family would be made available to other relatives and descendants over time. There may have been situations in which the settlors may have decided that they preferred a trust to be cancelled if the marriage did not work, or there were no children, or the financial affairs of either family deteriorated. Nevertheless, once an *inter vivos* trust has been completely constituted, the settlor is not entitled to terminate it and recover the settled property, but rather the beneficiaries are entitled to enforce the trust. The beneficiaries have the right to enforce the trust even if they are volunteers. So, in *Paul v Paul*,[22] a husband and wife contributed property to a marriage settlement which was to have benefited both themselves and other people. Their marriage failed and so both husband and wife, *qua* settlors, sought to unravel the settlement. However, it was held that the trust, once constituted, cannot be unwound. The only way in which such a termination would be possible would be under the principle in *Saunders v Vautier*,[23] where the *beneficiaries* would be entitled to terminate the trust and call for the delivery of the trust fund (as considered at section 4.2 above) but not the settlor acting *qua* settlor. If a settlor wanted to retain a power to cancel the trust then such a revocable trust is possible, provided that an explicit power to that effect is included in the trust instrument. This will have a tax effect in most situations.

5.2 THE PROPER CONSTITUTION OF A TRUST

For the effective constitution of a trust, there must have been a valid declaration of trust and the legal title in the trust fund must be transferred to the trustee, or the settlor must have declared herself to be trustee.

5.2.1 The general principle governing the constitution of trusts

For a trust to be effective, it is necessary that the settlor must have demonstrated an intention to declare a trust over property in which she had property rights at the time of declaring the trust, and it is also necessary that the person who is to act as trustee takes the legal title in the trust fund. The question for this section of this chapter then is understanding the means by which legal title in differing forms of property is transferred to the trustee. The following are some of the more common forms of property discussed in this book and the particular means of transferring legal title in them. The remainder of this chapter is then concerned with isolating those situations in which legal and equitable title are suitably transferred from settlor to trustee and beneficiary respectively, and more particularly the situations in which such transfer mechanisms interact with gifts, contract, bailment and so forth.

The most definitive statement of the need to vest the trust property in the trustee is given in *Milroy v Lord*,[24] where Turner LJ held that:

---

21 *Paul v Paul* (1882) 20 Ch D 742.
22 *Ibid.*
23 (1841) 4 Beav 115.
24 (1862) 4 De GF & J 264.

in order to render a voluntary settlement valid and effectual, the settlor must have done everything which, according to the nature of the property comprised in the settlement, was necessary to be done in order to transfer the property [to the trustee] and render the settlement binding upon him. He may, of course, do this by actually transferring the property to the persons for whom he intends to provide, and the provision will then be effectual and it will be equally effectual if he transfers the property to a trustee for the purposes of the settlement, or declares that he himself holds it in trust for those purposes . . . but in order to render the settlement binding, one or other of these modes must, as I understand the law of this court, be resorted to, for there is no equity in this court to perfect an imperfect gift.

These *dicta* constitute the clearest statement of a comparatively straightforward principle that there can be no trust before legal title to the trust fund is transferred to the trustee. It should be remembered, however, that where the settlor intends to make herself sole trustee of the property, it is enough that she effects a valid declaration of trust because there is no need to transfer the legal title to another person. Therefore, if A wishes to create a trust such that she is herself trustee for the benefit of her children over property of which she is already the absolute owner, it is sufficient for her to declare herself trustee of that property and to declare that she holds it on trust for her children from that time forward because all title in the property is already vested in her.

5.2.2 The constitution of trusts over personal property

In relation to trusts of personalty, there are no formalities to be complied with before the trust fund is transferred to the trustee.[25] For shares to be transferred validly under statute such that a trustee is vested with the legal title in those shares, it is necessary that the shares be registered in the name of the trustee. In common with shares, copyrights and patents have their own particular formalities for the transfer of legal title in the property.

5.2.3 The constitution of trusts of land

As discussed above, declarations of trusts in relation to land must comply with s 53(1)(b) of the Law of Property Act 1925:

> a declaration of trust respecting any land or any interest therein must be manifested and proved by some writing signed by some person who is able to declare such trust or by his will.

The settlor need not execute a deed necessarily to create such a trust, although that is the most advisable way of ensuring that a proper settlement is created. It is sufficient if there is some writing, signed by the settlor, which provides evidence that such a trust has been created. An alternative possibility is that the settlor settles the property in her will. Where the trust is created by means of resulting or constructive trust, the formalities do not apply.[26] It

25 *M'Fadden v Jenkyns* (1842) 12 LJ Ch 146; *Milroy v Lord* (1862) 4 De GF & J 264.
26 Law of Property Act 1925, s 53(2).

should also be recalled that any contract for the sale of land or of any interest in land must be effected in writing such that all of the terms of the contract are contained in one document.[27]

Once a trust has been created over land then the provisions of the Trusts of Land and Appointment of Trustees Act 1996 govern the obligations of the trustees, the rights of the beneficiaries to occupy and otherwise deal with the land, and the circumstances in which a sale of the property can be ordered by the court. These provisions are considered in detail in Chapter 16.

The following section will consider the situations in which a claimant may seek to establish the existence of some equitable interest despite a failure to constitute the trust fund effectively.

5.2.4 The settlor must have a proprietary right in the trust property at the time of purporting to declare the trust

The settlor must have an appropriate interest in the trust property to create a valid trust

Before a settlor is able to create a valid trust over property, it is necessary that that settlor owns the proprietary rights in the property which she is purporting to settle on trust at the time of purporting to declare the trust. This point is made in *Norman v Federal Commissioner of Taxation* by Windeyer J[28] in the following way: '. . . it is impossible for anyone to own something that does not exist, it is impossible for anyone to make a present gift of such a thing to another person, however sure he may be that it will come into existence and will then be his to give'.

Just as a person cannot give something in which she has no interest, she cannot declare a trust over property in which she has no interest. At one level, it is clearly important that a person does not attempt to create a trust over property in which she has no interest at all. At another level, there is the problem posed by a settlor seeking to create a trust over property in which she expects to have a right at some point in the future. Similarly, it is said that a settlor cannot create a binding trust over property if the settlor does not have proprietary rights in that property *at the time of purporting to create the trust*. Importantly, a trust will not come into existence even if she does subsequently become entitled to that property.[29]

To illustrate this principle there are two very useful cases made up of similar, but crucially different, facts which serve to show how an intention to transfer property will not necessarily lead to the implication of a trust. In *Re Brooks' ST*,[30] there were two settlements over which a bank was trustee simultaneously. The beneficiary under one settlement, Arthur, had promised that any money he might receive from the first trust, over which his mother had a broad personal power of appointment, would be passed to the second trust. It is important that Arthur did not have any beneficial interest in the first settlement. Rather, he had a hope (or, a mere *spes*; or, a mere 'expectancy') that his mother would decide to exercise her wide power of appointment to pay money to him at some time in the future. He did not have beneficial rights which would have enabled him to sue his mother to enforce the transfer of

---

27 Law of Property (Miscellaneous Provisions) Act 1989, s 2.
28 (1963) 109 CLR 9, 24.
29 *Re Brooks' ST* [1939] 1 Ch 993.
30 *Ibid.*

money to him. In time it transpired that his mother did appoint money to him from the first trust. When the proceeds of the *spes* did arrive in Arthur's bank account, the bank effected an automatic transfer of that money in accordance with the promise which Arthur had made. Arthur sued the bank for the return of the money.

The issue arose whether or not Arthur had made a gift of the money. Clearly he had not. At the time of promising the money to the second trust, he had no rights in the money and he had not sanctioned the transfer to the account of the second trust when he did receive that money later. The further trusts law point was whether Arthur ought to be considered as having declared a trust over the money received from the first trust. It was held that there was only a mere *spes* at the time of the purported declaration of trust. Therefore, Arthur had had no proprietary rights *at the time of purporting to settle that money* over which he could have declared that trust. A mere *spes* is too insubstantial to be a property right.[31] Therefore, no trust had been created by Arthur.

The further point raised before the court was that the trustee was therefore appearing to act as the settlor here. On the basis that Arthur had never created a valid trust over the money, the only person who could have purported to create that settlement was the trustee bank. It was held to be impossible for a trustee to declare the terms of a trust. It is for the settlor to declare the trust, and it is for the trustee to carry out the terms of that trust. Even where the trustee was also the person who acted as settlor, acting *qua* trustee that person cannot declare the terms of the trust. Therefore, no valid trust was ever created by Arthur and therefore the intended beneficiaries acquired no rights to compel Arthur to transfer the money received from his mother's power of appointment to their trustees.

A similar case is *Re Ralli's WT*,[32] in which the facts were analogous with those in *Re Brooks' ST*. In *Ralli*, a daughter, Helen, had a remainder interest under a trust at the time when she purported to promise that any money received from that first trust would be settled on the second trust. The trustees were the same for both settlements and therefore those trustees sought to effect the promise automatically without waiting for Helen to ratify her earlier promise. Helen instead decided that she wanted to keep the money for herself after all. The question arose whether or not she was obliged to carry out her promise, and whether or not she had created a valid trust at the time of making that promise. The transfer and the new trusts were upheld, but the decision was *per incuriam Re Brooks' ST*. Despite *Ralli* having been decided in ignorance of *Brooks'*, it is possible to reconcile the judgments in the following way.

It was held that, because Helen had a remainder interest *at the time of the promise to settle the property*, she had an equitable proprietary right in the trust fund. The rights of a remainder beneficiary will constitute an equitable proprietary right in the trust fund because, *inter alia*, such a remainder beneficiary has a right to ensure that the trustees do not favour the life tenant to the exclusion of the rights of the remainder beneficiary.[33] Therefore, Helen had some property right which could be the subject matter of a trust, which meant that she could

---

31 Under *Tailby v Official Receiver* (1888) 13 App Cas 523, if there had been a contract for the transfer of the expectancy whereby Arthur, on these facts, had received consideration from the beneficiaries, then the equitable interest in that property would pass to those beneficiaries once Arthur received it on the basis that 'equity looks upon as done that which ought to have been done'. See also *Re Lind* [1915] 2 Ch 345; *Palette Shoes Pty Ltd v Krohn* (1937) 58 CLR 1, 26; *Re Andromeda Pty Ltd* [1987] 2 Qd R 134, 152.

32 [1964] 1 Ch 288.

33 *Tito v Waddell (No 2)* [1977] Ch 106.

validly declare a trust over it. Consequently, it was held that the validly declared trust must be carried out by compelling Helen to transfer the money to the trustees of the second settlement. The subtle difference between the two cases turns on the nature of the right which the settlor had *at the time of the purported declaration of trust* to decide whether or not there had been a valid declaration of trust. That there was some property right vested in the settlor in *Ralli* compelled the trust to be carried out, in accordance with *Paul v Paul*,[34] unlike *Re Brooks' ST*.

This point is evident in a number of other decided cases. So, in *Re Ellenborough*,[35] a woman purported to declare a trust over property which she hoped to receive in the future. It was held that no trust was created because, at the time of the purported declaration of trust, she had no right in the property.

The alternative approach to this area of law might be to suggest that the settlor ought, in good faith, to be bound by her promise to create a trust over property. It is possible that if property is left for an extended period of time as though it were held validly on trust, equity may decide that (in accordance with the equitable principle that delay defeats equity) the settlor ought not to be entitled to unwind the trust. For example, in *Re Bowden*,[36] a woman purported in 1868 to settle on trust any property to which she might have been entitled when her father died before she entered a convent to take holy orders. It was held that no trust was created because she had no right to any property belonging to her father (who was alive at the time of the purported declaration of trust) and therefore could not create a trust over any such property. Remarkably, on these facts the woman had not objected when the property had been taken on trust by the intended trustees while she had become a nun. All the parties had then carried on with this arrangement for about 65 years. However, Bennett J held that when property had been transferred to the trustees after her father's death in 1869, the woman could not claim in 1935 to have the property returned to her because the property had been treated as effectively settled for a period of over 60 years. Other cases asserting like ideas are *Re Adlard*[37] and *Re Burton's Settlements*.[38]

Alternative approaches to the requirement that the settlor must have had proprietary rights in the trust property at the time of purporting to declare the trust

There is one decided case in which a trust has been enforced contrary to the principle in *Re Brooks' ST*.[39] In *Re Antis*,[40] it was accepted by Buckley J that a term providing that all the property falling within a covenant 'shall become in equity subject to the settlement hereby covenanted' would constitute a trust before any proprietary right was received by the settlor. It is contended that this judgment is anomalous and contrary to settled principle. It is only in cases of estoppel, as considered below,[41] that such an arrangement could lead to the creation

---

34 (1882) 20 Ch D 742.
35 [1903] 1 Ch 697.
36 [1936] Ch 71.
37 [1954] Ch 29.
38 [1955] Ch 82.
39 [1939] 1 Ch 993.
40 (1886) 31 Ch D 596.
41 See para 5.5.3 below.

of a valid trust at a time when the purported settlor did not have any proprietary rights in the property.[42]

It may be that the trustees are entitled to recover damages from the promisor. In *Re Cavendish Browne*,[43] a testatrix purported to declare a trust over land to which she was not entitled at the time of the declaration. She entered into a covenant with her trustees that she would settle the property once it was received. The testatrix failed to vest title in the trustees on receiving rights in the land. It was held that the trustees were entitled to damages for the breach of the covenant at common law in the amount of the value lost to the fund to have been held by the trustees.[44]

5.3 EXCEPTIONS TO THE RULES OF FORMALITY

In cases of fraud, equity will not permit common law or statute to be used as an engine of fraud such that it may impose a trust even though there was no valid declaration of that trust. No formalities are required in relation to constructive trusts and resulting trusts under s 53(2) of the Law of Property Act 1925.

5.3.1 The operation of implied, resulting and constructive trusts

This section considers situations in which formalities are not required to invoke equitable doctrines akin to a trust. Any strict rule of formality is likely to generate unfortunate results in some circumstances. In relation to trusts law, the formal rules for the creation of express trusts may occasionally mean that no trust is created even though it would seem fair that there should be a trust. Consequently, equity has developed trusts implied by law, in the form of constructive trusts and resulting trusts, which will be imposed, broadly speaking, by the courts regardless of the need for formality to prevent unconscionable dealings with property, as considered in Part 4. Section 53(2) of the Law of Property Act 1925 creates an exception for trusts implied by law (whether resulting trusts or constructive trusts) from the rules as to a declaration of trust in relation to land and also the requirement for writing to effect a disposition of an equitable interest. It provides: 'This section does not affect the creation or operation of resulting, implied or constructive trusts.' Therefore, such trusts do not need formalities.

The courts may have recourse to such devices to prevent a defendant taking an unconscionable benefit where no formal trust was created.[45] The question of resulting trust is considered in detail in Chapter 11. There is an important overlap between the detail of the prevention of fraud doctrine and the occasional use of the resulting trust to prevent injustice. Thus, in *Hodgson v Marks*,[46] an elderly woman, Mrs Hodgson, was induced by her lodger,

---

42 The only means of ratifying this decision would be if the benefit of the covenant were deemed to be held on trust: *Fletcher v Fletcher* (1844) 4 Hare 67; see para 5.6.2 below.

43 [1916] WN 341.

44 See also *Williamson v Codrington* (1750) Belts Supp 215; *Clough v Lambert* (1839) 10 Sim 174; (1839) 59 ER 579; *Davenport v Bishop* (1843) 2 Y & C Ch Cas 451; *Fletcher v Fletcher* (1844) 4 Hare 67; *Cox v Barnard* (1850) 8 Hare 510; *Re Parkin* [1892] 3 Ch 510; *Synge v Synge* [1894] 1 QB 466; *Re Plumptre's Marriage Settlement* [1910] 1 Ch 609.

45 *Westdeutsche Landesbank Girozentrale v Islington LBC* [1996] AC 669, considered at section 12.1 below.

46 [1971] 2 WLR 1263.

Evans, to transfer the title in her house into his sole name. The motivation on her part had been to protect Evans, for whom she felt sorry, from her nephew who despised Evans (rightly it turned out) and who had expressed his intention to be to ensure that Evans received nothing after her death. There was an agreement between Mrs Hodgson and Evans that Evans would hold the property in such a way that Mrs Hodgson would be able to occupy it for the rest of her life, but importantly no formality for the creation of an express trust over land had been effected. Subsequently, Evans sold the property to a third party and disappeared with the proceeds.

The question arose as to whether the third party purchaser, who had acted in good faith, should acquire the property, or whether the old woman could maintain that the property was held on trust for her. It was held that the property was held on resulting trust for the elderly woman in accordance with her prior agreement with Evans. Thus, justice is seen to be done in relation to Mrs Hodgson, who would otherwise have lost her home to a confidence trickster, although perhaps not in relation to the third-party purchaser of the property, who had no reason to suppose he would not acquire good title.[47] It is, however, unsatisfactory that a resulting trust (as opposed to a constructive trust or estoppel) was used to grant her this right.

Therefore, in the imposition of express trusts, as with trusts implied by law, there are mixed issues of achieving justice and demonstrating an entitlement to specific property. The common root of all of these institutions in the conscience of the common law owner frequently leads to the courts deciding either to find an express trust on comparatively flimsy evidence,[48] or seeking to prevent the common law owner from acting unconscionably by means of a constructive trust even though there is ostensibly a common intention as to title in the property found on the facts.[49] Thus, to return to the core purpose of equity to mitigate unfairnesses which may be wrought by statute, such trusts implied by law will lead to the imposition of a form of trust without the need for formalities.

More usually, constructive trusts or proprietary estoppel are used by the courts in these situations. As considered in Chapter 12, if a defendant deals unconscionably with another's property, then the defendant will hold that property on constructive trust for the claimant.[50] Alternatively, where a defendant makes a representation to a claimant in reliance on which that claimant acts to her detriment, then the claimant will be entitled to a proprietary right or compensation on proprietary estoppel principles, as considered in Chapter 13.[51]

5.3.2 Fraud and unconscionability

The second context in which the creation of a trust without recourse to formality is important is fraud. This doctrine is a little more difficult to reconcile with the law of express trusts. The core equitable principle which is applicable in this circumstance is that 'statute cannot be used as an engine of fraud'. What this means is that a person will be precluded from relying

---

47 This principle is contrary to the ordinary rule that a *bona fide* purchaser for value without notice would acquire good title in the property bought: *Westdeutsche Landesbank Girozentrale v Islington LBC* [1996] AC 669. Cf Swadling, 2000.

48 *Paul v Constance* [1977] 1 WLR 527.

49 *Hodgson v Marks* [1971] 2 WLR 1263, although that case did relate to land with its own formalities.

50 *Westdeutsche Landesbank Girozentrale v Islington LBC* [1996] AC 669, considered at section 12.1 below.

51 *Re Basham* [1986] 1 WLR 1498; *Gillett v Holt* [2000] 2 All ER 289.

on her common law or statutory rights where to do so would enable her to carry out a fraud on another person.

This principle cuts to the very heart of the trust concept as an essentially equitable doctrine. If a trustee, the legal owner of property, were able to rely on her common law rights to the exclusion of all other obligations, this would enable her to misuse the property held on trust for the beneficiary. Where Xavier is trustee of land held on trust for Yasmin and Zena, Xavier is able as legal owner to take out a mortgage over land. Suppose then that Xavier purports to keep the loan money raised by way of mortgage for his own benefit, and refuses to make any of the repayments. The result would be that the mortgagee would repossess the land to discharge the loan. According to common law, the mortgagor Xavier is the owner of the loan moneys. However, equity will prevent Xavier from relying on that common law title to prevent Yasmin and Zena from asserting any rights over the mortgage moneys on the basis that common law would otherwise be used as an engine of fraud by Xavier. Therefore, this principle is at the heart of preventing trustees from misusing trust property and is also primarily concerned with imposing trustee obligations on fraudsters.

The clearest exposition of the rule was in *Rochefoucauld v Boustead*,[52] where P was a mortgagor of property which was sold by the mortgagee to D. D had orally agreed to hold the property on trust for P, subject to the repayment to D of the purchase price. However, D sold the land at a higher price to a third-party purchaser, but did not then account for the surplus in the sale proceeds to P. D then became bankrupt. The issue arose whether or not P could assert any right in the money which ought to have been paid to him by D but which had not been so paid. It was held that '. . . it is a fraud on the part of the person to whom land is conveyed as a trustee, and who knows it was so conveyed, to deny the trust and claim the land himself'. Here, parol (that is, oral) evidence was used to prove that the land was conveyed upon trust when D agreed that the property would be held on trust for P. Although there had not been a formal declaration of trust over the land, the court was determined to prevent a situation in which D would have been able to avoid the parties' common understanding that the land was to have been held on trust for P. Therefore, the court deemed there to be a valid trust to avoid the perpetration of a fraud.

The principle is similarly demonstrated in *Lyus v Prowsa Developments*,[53] where A sold land to B on the express understanding that B would hold the land on trust to give effect to a licence conferred by A on C. It was held, applying the principle against common law rights being used as an engine of fraud, that C acquired enforceable rights under trust against B to compel B to carry out the terms of that trust. In similar vein, it was held in *Bannister v Bannister*[54] that '[t]he fraud which brings the principle into play arises as soon as the absolute character of the conveyance is set up for the purpose of defeating the beneficial interest'. Therefore, the principle against permitting common law rights to be used as an engine of fraud is concerned to protect the person who is intended to receive the beneficial interest in that property, as well as to regulate the conscience of the common law owner of property.[55]

---

52 [1897] 1 Ch 196.
53 [1982] 1 WLR 1044.
54 [1948] WN 261.
55 See *Chaudhary v Yavuz* [2011] EWCA Civ 1314 considering this decision.

On this point, the court in *Gardner v Rowe*[56] held that a trust is unenforceable but not void in the period of time between the verbal declaration of trust and the writing necessary to satisfy the formalities for the creation of a trust. In that case, A had granted a lease to B on oral trusts for C. Such a trust over an interest in land required evidence in writing for it to be formally valid.[57] B then became bankrupt, but B executed a deed stating the terms of the trust on which the property was to have been held. It was held by the court, against the creditors in the bankruptcy, that there had been a valid declaration of trust prior to B's bankruptcy, such that his creditors had no claim to the lease. It should be noted that under the *Rochefoucauld* doctrine, B was bound by the terms of the trust from the time he took the lease. So, if instead A orally declared himself trustee of the land for C and provided written evidence only after his own bankruptcy, he would not be bound by the trust until the written evidence of that declaration. Therefore, his creditors would have had a claim to the land.[58]

The principle identified in this section is in line with the core principles of equity outlined in Chapter 1 that equity will act *in personam* against a person who would otherwise be permitted to commit an unconscionable act by the strict application of common law rules. Furthermore, this principle in relation to the creation of express trusts is in line with the principle set out by Lord Browne-Wilkinson in *Westdeutsche Landesbank v Islington LBC*[59] that the essential nature of the trust is its regulation of the conscience of the common law owner of property.

5.4 IMPROPERLY CONSTITUTED TRUSTS AND IMPERFECT GIFTS

The trust will not be implied so as to perfect an imperfect gift, on the basis that equity will not assist a volunteer. Where the intention was to make a gift, whether or not a gift was validly made will be decisive of the matter. The exceptions are as follows: cases of donatio mortis causa; *executors of the estates of persons to whom they owed debts will be deemed to have those debts discharged by way of gift; the doctrine of proprietary estoppel will operate to prevent detriment being suffered by those to whom a promise of gift was made; and cases of fraud.*

5.4.1 Introduction

As considered in section 5.2 above, for a trust to be properly constituted, it is necessary for the three certainties to be present when the settlor purports to declare the trust[60] and also for the legal title in the trust property to be vested in the trustees.[61] If these requirements are not met, then there is no valid trust created. This section considers those situations in which a trust has not been properly created and yet a claimant argues that there ought to be an effective trust nevertheless.

---

56   (1828) 4 Russ 578.
57   Law of Property Act 1925, s 53(1)(b).
58   This is always assuming that C had not acted to his detriment with reference to the land, thus claiming rights under proprietary estoppel: considered below at para 5.5.3.
59   [1996] AC 669.
60   The certainties of intention, subject matter and objects considered in Chapter 3.
61   See para 5.3.1 above.

There are two general situations in which this issue might arise. The first situation is that in which a person who was intended to be a beneficiary under a failed trust may seek to argue that the settlor who failed to create a valid trust is bound by good conscience to give effect to the intended beneficiaries' expectations that a trust would be created in their favour. So, even if the settlor fails to constitute a valid trust, the intended beneficiary may seek to argue that equity should provide her with property rights in the fund which was to have been settled on trust in any event.

The second situation arises when a person intends to make a gift of property but either changes her mind or fails to effect a transfer of that property to the intended recipient. The question, therefore, is whether an intention to make a gift of property (as opposed to a trust) can be enforced by arguing that the donor of the property is a trustee of that property on the grounds that it would otherwise be unconscionable for her to renege on her promise to make that gift. An intention to declare a trust arises in circumstances in which there is a division in the ownership of property between the legal title and the equitable interest in the manner considered in Chapter 2. By contrast, an intention to make a gift involves an intention to effect a transfer of absolute title in property from the owner of absolute title in that property ('the donor') to another person ('the donee'). The donor owes no fiduciary obligations to the donee in ordinary circumstances and the donee acquires no rights in the property until the transfer of absolute title takes effect. So, if Bernard promises to make a gift to Mani but then changes his mind, Mani may argue that in good conscience Bernard ought to be obliged to transfer the property and consequently Mani may argue that equitable title in the property should have passed on trust to Mani. However, equity will not assist someone who is the recipient of a benefit for which she has not given consideration unless there has been a validly constituted trust.[62] This rule is known as the principle that equity will not assist a volunteer. The best example of a volunteer in this context would be someone who expects to receive a gift but who has no proprietary rights in that gift and who has given no considera-tion for that gift. That equity will not assist a volunteer means that equity will not force the donor of the gift to make that gift if the donor decides not to make it.[63]

To explain the type of situation in which these issues may arise, consider the following set of facts:

> *Young Joey, aged six, is waiting for Christmas. It is November and he has been told by his mother that he must be good or else Santa Claus will not bring him any presents. Joey behaves himself impeccably in the lead-up to Christmas. He keeps his room tidy, helps his mother to wash up (when he remembers) and does all his homework. He there-fore has every expectation that he will receive the football boots for which he has asked.*

However, if his mother decides not to give him the pair of football boots which he has thirsted after for so long, then Joey has no legal remedy. Equity will not help him if he has given no consideration for those boots because as such he would be a mere volunteer. As will be considered below, if he had contributed to the purchase price, or possibly acted to his

---

62 *Re Brooks' ST* [1939] 1 Ch 993.
63 This rule indicates the increasing rigidity of the law concerning express trusts, which makes them appear to be more like contracts than the flexible equitable remedies from which they were born.

detriment in a meaningful way, then there would be a possibility of acquiring proprietary rights on equitable estoppel principles.[64]

Much of the discussion in this section returns to the discussion in Chapter 3 concerning the necessary intention to create a trust.[65] In those cases it was held that the intention of the transferor must be to create a trust. A general intention to benefit some other person will not be enough to create a trust. As held by Lord Jessel MR in *Richards v Delbridge*:[66]

> the settlor need not use the words 'I declare myself a trustee' but he must do something which is equivalent to it and use expressions which have meaning; for however anxious the court may be to carry out a man's intention, it is not at liberty to construe words other than according to their proper meaning.

As considered above, the courts will be prepared to infer an intention to create a trust in many situations, but they will not infer an intention to create a trust over property in circumstances in which the transferor actually intended to make an outright transfer of that property. So in *Milroy v Lord*[67] (as outlined above), Turner LJ held that:

> . . . to render the settlement binding, one or other of these modes [of transferring property to the trustee] must, as I understand the law of this court, be resorted to, for there is no equity in this court to perfect an imperfect gift.

Therefore, a claimant cannot rely on the law of trusts to effectuate an incomplete gift. However, as considered immediately below, there are situations in which equity may decide that it is contrary to conscience for the intended recipient to be denied any interest in the property.

5.4.2 Trusts and imperfect gifts

How do we decide whether an action of a transferor is to be classified as a trust or as something which is merely an imperfect gift? In general terms, it is not open to someone who wishes to show that they should have received title in property to argue that they are a beneficiary under a trust in circumstances in which they were expecting to be the recipient of a gift which was never completed.[68] There is a temptation for a lawyer attempting to enforce a gift which has not been made properly to argue that the donor in fact intended to create a trust over the property. So, for example, what if A intended to make a gift of 20 ordinary shares in SAFC plc to B but failed to register those shares in B's name, thus leaving the gift improperly made? B might seek to argue that A had intended to transfer those shares to B and therefore that A should be treated as having declared herself trustee over those shares for the benefit of B. A core rule of the English law of express trusts is that equity will not permit an action which was intended to be a gift to be validated by deeming

---

64 See para 5.5.3 below.
65 *Jones v Lock* (1865) 1 Ch App 25; *Paul v Constance* [1977] 1 WLR 527.
66 (1874) LR 18 Eq 11.
67 (1862) 4 De GF & J 264.
68 *Ibid.*

it to be a trust instead.[69] Therefore, in terms of vesting the trust property in the trustee, that a donor who fails to complete the gift already has legal title in that property will not suffice to demonstrate that that intended donor should be deemed to be a trustee of that property. Remember, this is still in the context of express trusts – we will consider trusts implied by law in Part 4 below.

5.4.3 The rule that equity will not assist a volunteer and its impact on imperfect gifts

Equity will not assist a volunteer. This principle means that equity will not assist a person to acquire rights if that person has not given consideration so as to acquire rights under contract: a 'volunteer' is a person who has not given consideration. The issue we shall consider in this section is whether or not a failure to make a complete, perfect gift can be rescued by deeming a trust to have been created over the property in question instead. Strictly speaking, beneficiaries under trusts will not have given consideration: however, equity assists beneficiaries once there has been a valid declaration of trust in their favour. Importantly, however, in relation to a mere promise to settle property at some point in the future, there will not have been any consideration given for the promise nor will a valid trust have been created because the intention here is merely a promise to create a trust in the future. Whereas, if consideration had been given in return for that promise then there would have been a contract created. Our limited concern for the moment is whether or not a failure to make a perfect gift can be saved by construing it instead to have been an intention to create a trust.

In the leading case in this area, *Milroy v Lord*,[70] a voluntary deed executed by Milroy purported to assign 50 shares to Samuel Lord upon trust for Milroy's benefit and in remainder to specified relatives (including the claimant). Lord was already acting as Milroy's agent under a general power of attorney (a fact which the claimant alleged made it seem as though Lord was already acting as a trustee). However, no transfer of the shares was registered in the company's books, as was required by the formalities for transferring shares under the law at the time; with the result that Milroy remained the legal owner of those shares and Lord acquired no legal title in them so as to make him a properly constituted trustee. Before a valid transfer could have taken place, this registration formality had to be complied with. This requirement of re-registration was the obligation of the transferor to complete before a transfer could be effective. The claimant sought to establish that a trust had been declared and that he had thereby acquired an equitable proprietary right in the shares. It was held that an ineffective transfer does not constitute a declaration of trust without there being a clear intention to create a trust in that way. Furthermore, to render a voluntary settlement valid and effectual, the settlor must have done everything which was necessary to be done to transfer the property and render the settlement binding upon him. That transfer must be performed in the manner appropriate for the property concerned. On these facts, no such transfer had been effected because the shares had not been re-registered and therefore no trust had been validly effected because legal title had not passed to the intended trustee. Therefore, one cannot try to argue for an express trust on the general basis of good conscience or failed gift if the settlor failed to vest legal title in the property in the trustee.

---

69 *Ibid.*
70 (1862) 4 De GF & J 264.

The decision of the Court of Appeal in that case was encapsulated in the following central statement of the law in this area (mentioned above but repeated here for ease of reference), when Turner LJ held that:[71]

> in order to render a voluntary settlement valid and effectual, the settlor must have done everything which, according to the nature of the property comprised in the settlement, was necessary to be done in order to transfer the property and render the settlement binding upon him . . . but in order to render the settlement binding, one or other of these modes [outright transfer, declaration of self as trustee, or transfer of property to a third party as trustee] must, as I understand the law of this court, be resorted to, for there is no equity in this court to perfect an imperfect gift. The cases, I think, go further to this extent: that if the settlement is intended to take effect by transfer, the court will not give effect to it by applying another of those modes. If it is intended to take effect by transfer, the court will not hold the intended transfer to operate as a declaration of trust, for then every imperfect instrument would be made effectual by being converted into a perfect trust.

Therefore, the court is adamant that a frustrated intention to make a gift will not be saved by re-interpreting it as an intention to create a trust.[72] This strict rule ensures an element of certainty in the law. Otherwise, the intention to create a trust might become a very vague notion which would be effectively moribund and available to perfect any imperfect gift. However, the doctrine has been applied more creatively in some of the more modern decisions considered below.

5.4.4 'Doing everything necessary', not an incompletely constituted trust

The principle in Re Rose

An issue arises in relation to the situation in which the donor has done everything necessary to transfer title in the property to another person but where that outright transfer (or, gift) has nevertheless not been completed. The question is: if the donor has performed all the acts necessary to be performed by her to complete the making of a gift, should the donor have been deemed to hold that property on trust for the intended donee from that moment of completing the necessary acts? It was held in *Re Rose*[73] that if the donor has done everything necessary for her to do to make the gift, then equity will deem an equitable interest in the relevant property to have passed automatically, even if the donee is a volunteer. This principle, it is suggested, is an exception to the rule that equity will not assist a volunteer, as considered in the previous section. This exception is considered in detail in the following section.

---

71 *Ibid.*
72 *Milroy v Lord* was followed more recently in Canada in *Marquis-Antle Spousal Trust v R* 2009 TCC 465, 12 ITELR 314 where a taxpayer sought to avoid capital gains tax by using a discretionary trust in Barbados but it was held that no valid trust was created inter alia because legal title was not vested in the trustee.
73 [1952] Ch 499.

The exception to the principle that equity will not assist a volunteer: doing everything necessary to transfer title

If a donor has done everything necessary for her to do to transfer title in property by way of gift, then an equitable interest in that property will pass even if the donor fails to complete all of the formalities necessary to complete that transfer. Confusingly, there are two separate cases in this area called *Re Rose*.[74] There are significant differences in the facts of those cases which enabled the courts to apply the rules quoted from *Milroy v Lord*[75] above to different effect. It is important to understand the narrow factual differences between *Milroy v Lord* and the two *Re Rose* cases, which can be the only reasonable explanation for the different decisions reached in those three cases. In *Milroy*, the agent had not completed all of the formalities necessary to achieve a transfer of the property; in *Re Rose* (1952),[76] Lord Evershed held that all of the actions *necessary to be taken by the transferor* to effect a valid transfer had been carried out, such that the court considered that it would have been against conscience for the donor to have sought to renege on his intention to make a transfer of the property.

In *Re Rose* (1949),[77] the testator had purportedly made bequests of shares in favour of a man called Hook, provided that Hook had not received those shares by transfer before Rose's death. Mr Rose had executed a voluntary transfer in respect of the shares which he had given to Hook: this transfer form constituted everything required of Rose to transfer the shares, but was not a completion of the transfer because there were further formalities to be performed by the company. The issue was whether the transfer of shares to Hook had taken effect under the ineffective *inter vivos* transfer form or under the terms of the will. As mentioned, the completion of this transfer form was the only formality which Mr Rose was required to carry out as transferor; however, the company's articles of association gave the board of directors power to refuse to register the transfer of shares. Therefore, the transfer was not complete until the board approved it. On the facts of *Re Rose* (1949), it was important for Hook to demonstrate that the transfer had taken effect before Rose's death to ensure its validity. The counter-argument was that there had been no transfer until ratification by the board of directors, and that there could be no suggestion of an express trust having been created because that would be to give effect to the intended bequest by other means not intended by the transferor.

However, Jenkins J held that because Mr Rose 'had done everything in his power to divest himself of the shares in question', the shares should be treated as having been passed to the legatee by the transfer and only perfected by registration. That Mr Rose could not have unwound the transfer once he had filled in the transfer form impressed the court that equitable title should be deemed to have passed.

In *Re Rose* (1952),[78] the registered owner of shares executed two share transfers, one in favour of his wife absolutely by way of gift and the other in favour of two people (including his wife) on trust. The shares were in a private company, which empowered the board of

74 [1949] Ch 78 and [1952] Ch 499.
75 (1862) 4 De GF & J 264.
76 [1952] Ch 499.
77 [1949] Ch 78.
78 [1952] Ch 499.

directors to object to the transfer of shares. Again, the transferor had completed all the formalities required of him; only ratification by the board of directors remained before the transfer was complete. The date of transfer was again important so that Rose's estate could demonstrate that the voluntary transfer had succeeded in passing an equitable interest in the shares to attract a lower rate of tax than would otherwise have been payable if the transfer had not taken effect until the date of ratification by the board. The argument for the Inland Revenue was that there was no transfer until ratification, as provided by company law, and that there could be no suggestion of an express trust having been created because that would be to give effect to the intended bequest by means not intended by the transferor.

The Court of Appeal in *Re Rose* (1952)[79] approved the decision in *Re Rose* (1949)[80] and held that the equitable interest in the shares had been transferred as soon as the transferor had completed all of the formalities which he was required to complete. The court sought to distinguish the case of *Re Fry*,[81] in which an American had been held to have failed to create a trust where he had filled in a transfer form in relation to shares in a private company but had not received the required consent of the Treasury to effect a valid transfer of those shares. In *Re Rose*, Jenkins J sought to suggest that the purported settlor in *Fry* had not done everything necessary to divest himself of the shares. However, it is difficult to see exactly which element remained outstanding in *Fry* which similarly had not been completed in *Rose*.

Understanding the principle at issue

A further complication is the rule which is derived from *Re Rose* (1952) on the basis that a trust (of some description) was created by transfer of the equitable interest in the property from the husband to his wife once he had done everything necessary for him to do to transfer the property. Lord Evershed's judgment was couched in the language of gift and not trust: his Lordship referred throughout to 'donor', 'donee' and 'gift' rather than to 'trust' or 'trustee'. Therefore, it is not immediately apparent how this judgment is authority for a proposition based on the law of trust. A partial answer is offered by Lord Evershed's explanation as to how title passed to Mrs Rose from her husband when he argued that after Mr Rose had purported to transfer title to his wife by doing everything necessary for him to do, it would have been inequitable for him to have reneged on that promise:

> if Mr Rose had received a dividend between [completion of the document and consent being granted by the board of directors] and Mrs Rose had claimed to have that dividend handed to her, what would Mr Rose's answer have been? It could no longer be that the purported gift was imperfect; it had been made perfect. I am not suggesting that the perfection was retroactive. But what else could he say? How could he . . . deny the proposition that he had . . . transferred the shares to his wife? . . . therefore the transfer was valid and effectual in equity from March 30, 1943, and accordingly the shares were not assessable for estate duty.

Therefore, it was argued that Mr Rose would have been compelled to hand over the dividend if one had been received between the time when he had done everything necessary for him

79 *Ibid.*
80 [1949] Ch 78.
81 [1946] Ch 312.

to do to transfer title and the date at which the company formally consented to the transfer of the shares. The reason why he is so compelled is not immediately obvious from these *dicta*. In the language of the 21st century, we would explain it as being contrary to good conscience for Mr Rose to refuse to acknowledge that an equitable interest had passed and in consequence that a constructive trust had been created over the shareholding. It is suggested that *Re Rose* should be understood as being either a constructive trust or a general equitable principle, but not an express trust.

Conceptually different applications of the Re Rose principle

Despite the conceptual difficulties identified with the *Re Rose* principle in the preceding paragraph, this decision has been followed in numerous other cases.[82] In *T Choithram International SA v Pagarani*,[83] a man lying on his deathbed sought to declare an *inter vivos* trust over his property. The settlor's intention was that he would be one of nine trustees over that property. However, the dead man failed to transfer legal title in the property to all nine trustees and, as a consequence, under the ordinary law of trusts, the trust would not have been validly constituted. Nevertheless, it was held that a valid trust was created over that property even though the deceased person had not transferred the legal title in the trust property to all nine trustees as trustees. The rationale given by the court was that the *Rose* principle could be applied so that the settlor could be taken to have done all that was necessary to create a trust and therefore that the equitable interest in his property should be taken to have passed automatically.

Subsequently, the Court of Appeal in *Pennington v Waine* has applied this principle (in following *Choithram*) so as to perfect a gift of shares in circumstances in which the donor had neither effected a declaration of trust over the shares nor done everything which was necessary for her to do to effect a transfer of the shares.[84] Here Ada Crampton wanted to transfer 400 shares in a private company to her nephew, Harold, and to have Harold made a director of that company. Ada completed a share transfer form which she sent to her accountant, Pennington, but Pennington failed to forward this form either to the company or to Harold. Consequently, due to the failure to deliver the form, no transfer of the shares was made to Harold. Ada subsequently signed a form consenting to Harold becoming a director of the company but by her will she transferred him insufficient shares for Harold to have a controlling shareholding in the company. If Ada had transferred the 400 shares to Harold before her death, then Harold would have had such a controlling interest in the company. It was held by Arden LJ (with whom Schiemann LJ agreed) that an equitable interest in those shares passed to Harold because it was considered that it would have been unconscionable for Ada to have refused to transfer those shares to Harold, whereas it was held by Clarke LJ that it was not necessary to have delivered the form to the company because the transfer took effect as an equitable assignment. It was clearly the view of the Court of Appeal that it had remained Ada's intention throughout her life to transfer these 400 shares to Harold and this influenced their Lordships' decision.

---

82   *Vandervell v IRC* [1967] 2 AC 291, HL; *Mascall v Mascall* (1984) 50 P & CR 119; *Brown & Root Technology v Sun Alliance and London Assurance Co* [1996] Ch 51. See also *Corin v Patton* (1990) 169 CLR 540.

83   *T Choithram International SA v Pagarani* [2001] 1 WLR 1. See also M Halliwell [2003] The Conveyancer 192.

84   *Pennington v Waine* [2002] 1 WLR 2075.

The decision in *Pennington v Waine* extends the *Re Rose* principle beyond its former boundaries where it could be demonstrated that the donor had indeed done everything necessary for her to have done to finalise the transfer. In *Pennington v Waine*, Clarke LJ accepted that the principle operated in general terms and that the equity identified by the Court of Appeal in *Re Rose*[85] was capable of such general application. It has been suggested that the *Rose* principle can be understood as being part of the more general principle that a court of equity should not be officious in defeating a gift.[86] So we might understand this to mean that the intention of the court in *Pennington v Waine* was to effect a gift and because courts of equity should not strike down gifts too eagerly, then the *Rose* principle could be extended so as to protect this gift.

However, in *Pennington v Waine,* there was not even such a concatenation of circumstances as there was in *Re Rose,* in that there had not been completion of all of the formalities necessary for the transferor to have performed. No completion of the necessary formalities had taken place on those facts. As such, the ordinary law of gift requires that the disponor be able to change her mind and to refuse to transfer the property, provided she does so before effecting the transfer. It is suggested that equity should not compel the transfer for two reasons. First, at what point should equity consider that it would be unconscionable for the disponor to recant her intention to make the gift? Could it be after she has told the other person of her intention to make the gift,[87] or when the property has been put in a condition so that it would be possible to transfer it (such as wrapping it or separating it from other property),[88] or when some of the legal formalities necessary for the transfer have been considered,[89] or when all of the legal formalities have been performed to effect the transfer?[90] In line with principle, it can only be on the happening of that last of these four possibilities that an equitable interest in the property can be said to pass, because that is the only approach which complies with *Re Rose* itself and because up until that point the donor would be able to renege on her intention to make the gift at common law. Secondly, the disponor had not performed all of the formalities necessary for her to perform to effect a transfer of absolute title in the property: therefore, equity is purporting to transfer an equitable interest in circumstances in which there has not been a transfer of title at common law nor a specifically enforceable transfer of such title and at a time when the recipient of the property is a mere volunteer.[91] A third point arises under company law: it is not clear – assuming the directors

---

85 [1952] Ch 499.

86 *T Choithram International SA v Pagarani* [2001] 1 WLR 1; *Pennington v Waine* [2002] 1 WLR 2075.

87 This cannot be the appropriate point in time because a person who is made a promise without giving consideration is a volunteer without any rights to compel the performance of the promise (absent proprietary estoppel).

88 Again, this cannot be the appropriate point in time because there is not necessarily the appropriate intention to make a gift of that property simply because it would be possible for the property to be transferred.

89 This cannot be the point given that by definition all of the necessary formalities have not yet been performed.

90 At last . . . I think we have reached it.

91 As a point of company law, it is not clear – assuming the directors or other shareholders have some right to resist the registration of the new shareholder – on what basis equity could recognise that title had passed to the claimant on the basis that the defendant had done everything necessary to transfer title (because at that time the claimant would be able to exercise *Saunders v Vautier* rights to compel the transfer of absolute title to herself) when under company law the board of directors retains the right to prohibit that transfer at all. Under the principle *nemo dat quod non habet*, the defendant could not claim to have such a title which could be passed to the claimant.

or other shareholders have some right to resist the registration of the new shareholder – on what basis equity could recognise that title had passed to the claimant on the basis that the defendant had done everything necessary to transfer title. Once equitable title is deemed to have passed the claimant would be able to exercise *Saunders v Vautier* rights to compel the transfer of absolute title to herself. However, under company law a board of directors with this power to refuse to ratify a transfer of shares prohibit that transfer.[92] This prohibition might be exercised by a board of directors precisely because they want to prevent a given person from acquiring shares in the company – for example to prevent a hostile takeover. Therefore, equity is subverting fundamental principles of company law by deeming an automatic transfer of property rights in shares when the company itself may still be entitled to resist that transfer at common law.

Similarly, in *T Choithram International SA v Pagarani*,[93] we have an unfortunate situation in which a deceased settlor – who could not therefore amend the nature of his affairs – failed properly to constitute the trust. That, it seems to me, could well have been an end of the matter. In such situations, of course, the court will prefer to give effect to the dead person's intentions rather than have a trust over particularly valuable property lapse into residue so as to benefit residuary legatees who were intended only to take any scraps left over from the administration of the dead person's estate and not to receive a large windfall in the form of property which the dead person had thought he had transferred elsewhere in his lifetime. In this vein, Lord Browne-Wilkinson held that '[a]lthough equity will not aid a volunteer, it will not strive officiously to defeat a gift'.[94] So, this is what the court is really doing, it seems to me, when it interpolates an equitable compulsion to deem property to have passed on the *Rose* principle in flat contradiction of the common law of gift: it is trying to give effect to a dying man's wish in spite of the technical rules. Nevertheless, on a literal interpretation of the principle in *Milroy v Lord*, it is not possible to support an incompletely constituted trust or to rescue a gift by another, artificial means. The dead man had not constituted the trust by transferring the legal title in the property to the trustees and so no trust had been properly created. Equity, however, will frequently find a way to produce a convenient answer in spite of the technical rules.

A return to the mainstream approach

A level of common sense has been re-introduced to this area of law by two recent decisions on the *Re Rose* principle. Whereas the courts in *Pagarini* and *Pennington* had both sought to find the *Re Rose* principle satisfied on the strictly incomplete facts in front of them, these recent decisions have returned to the ostensible strictness of the principle such that, even though the propositus had not been demonstrated to have changed his mind about making a transfer, the court would not find a transfer of the equitable interest if some act which that

92 This depends upon the nature of the company and the provisions of its articles of associations. By contrast, public companies which have their shares traded on the London Stock Exchange and which are entered on the Official List must ensure that their shares are freely transferable. It is commonly in relation to private companies that such provisions would be a part of the articles of association so as to prevent outsiders interfering with the company's affairs.

93 *T Choithram International SA v Pagarani* [2001] 1 WLR 1. See also M Halliwell [2003] The Conveyancer 192.

94 [2001] 2 All ER 492, 501.

person had been required to perform had not actually been performed. So, in *Kaye v Zeital*[95] the Court of Appeal refused to accept a finding at first instance that a transfer had taken effect even though the purported transferor had failed to do everything necessary for him to do. In that case the purported transferor had not provided the purported transferee with the share certificate nor any other documentation which, in relation to that company, she required to demonstrate that a valid transfer had been made in her favour.

In *Curtis v Pulbrook*,[96] Briggs J took the sensible approach that where a man had failed to transfer shares to his wife and daughter because he had not completed the transfer process, then the *Re Rose* principle could not be relied upon. His intention had been to make a gift of the shares, and yet he had neither completed a share transfer form nor sent the share certificates to the intended recipients. He then deposited documents which related to the shares in this company with his solicitors before leaving the UK to live with his new partner in Thailand; those documents did not contain a completed share transfer form. Therefore, at no stage had he done everything necessary for him to do to effect a transfer of the property. Furthermore, he had not been authorised to effect transfer of this sort to his wife and daughter in any event. Consequently, it was held that the principle in *Re Rose* had not been satisfied on these facts.[97] Moreover, it was held that there could not be a constructive trust because there was no evidence that the wife and daughter had suffered any detriment in these circumstances: although it is suggested that it is not clear that detriment is required for a constructive trust, so much as unconscionable activity on the part of the defendant trustee.[98] Briggs J did express the following view about the earlier cases, *Pagarini* and *Pennington*:[99]

> I reach [my] conclusion without any great comfort that the existing rules about the circumstances when equity will and will not perfect an apparently imperfect gift of shares serve any clearly identifiable or rational policy objective.

In other words, his lordship considered that the recent case law had not seemed to follow any clear principle. Briggs J summarised the decisions in the recent *Re Rose* cases as generating three bases on which the *Rose* principle would arise:[100]

> The first is where the donor has done everything necessary to enable the donee to enforce a beneficial claim without further assistance from the donor . . .[101] The second is where some detrimental reliance by the donee upon an apparent although ineffective gift may so bind the conscience of the donor to justify the imposition of a constructive trust . . .[102] The third is where by a benevolent construction an effective gift or implied declaration of trust may be teased out of the words used.[103]

---

95 [2010] EWCA Civ 159, [2010] 2 BCLC 1.
96 [2011] EWHC 167 (Ch), [2011] 1 BCLC 638.
97 *Pennington v Waine* [2002] 2 BCLC 448 and *Kaye v Zeital* [2010] 2 BCLC 1 applied.
98 See *Westdeutsche Landesbank v Islington* [1996] AC 669, at section 12.1 below.
99 [2011] EWHC 167 (Ch), [2011] 1 BCLC 638, [47].
100 [2011] EWHC 167 (Ch), [2011] 1 BCLC 638, [43].
101 *Pennington v Waine* [2002] 2 BCLC 448 at [55]–[56] and *Re Rose (decd), Rose v IRC* [1952] 1 All ER 1217, [1952] Ch 499
102 *Pennington v Waine* [2002] 2 BCLC 448 at [59].
103 *Ibid.* at [60]–[61], 'apparently based upon' *Choithram International SA v Pagarani* [2001] 2 All ER 492, [2001] 1 WLR 1.

What is interesting about this summary is that it does not reflect the precise rationale which Lord Evershed MR used in *Re Rose* itself, on the basis of unconscionability in reneging on the promise to make a transfer, as considered above. That aside, the first principle is the principle which can be divined from *Re Rose*, albeit not adopting the generally equitable approach in that case. While the *Re Rose* decision itself is used as authority for the 'constructive trust' argument, that idea is not broached at all in *Re Rose* itself. The third principle is not really a principle at all, but rather is a judicial determination to validate testamentary gifts wherever possible.

A modern explanation of the Re Rose principle

It is this writer's opinion that *Re Rose* is properly understood as a case of constructive trust. Given the Court of Appeal's decision, the argument must be that Mr Rose is deemed to have transferred equitable title in the shares because he had done everything in his power to transfer them away (in *Re Rose* (1952) transferring them partially onto trust), and that it would therefore be unconscionable for him to deny that that transfer created some proprietary rights in the claimant. In accordance with the definition of a constructive trust provided by Lord Browne-Wilkinson in *Westdeutsche Landesbank v Islington LBC*[104] that a constructive trust comes into existence from the moment the conscience of the trustee is affected by knowledge of some relevant fact, the contention must be that Rose was a trustee under a constructive trust over the shares. It is contended that there could not have been an express trust because Rose did not intend to create an express trust in the manner in which the court ultimately imposed one. To have held otherwise would be in conflict with *Milroy v Lord*,[105] as considered above.[106]

The weakness in this thinking is that, at common law, the transferor would be able to go back on the intention to transfer at any time before the transfer formalities were completed. In such a situation, the claimant would be required to rely on principles of equitable estoppel[107] or the avoidance of fraud[108] to insist that the transfer be carried through. Any rights flowing from that property, such as rights to a dividend, ought properly to pass to the common law owner unless either of those principles comes into play.

The main flaw in this doctrine is that it supposes an outright transfer has taken place in circumstances in which the transferor may well intend to retain for herself the right to renege on the transfer before the final formality is performed. It is significant that in *Re Rose* (1952),[109] Lord Evershed pointed out that title in the property was subsequently transferred as originally intended – it was only the time of the transfer for estate duty purposes that was at issue. The case of *Mascall v Mascall*[110] is instructive in this context because it concerned a father who had intended to transfer land to his son but, having done everything necessary for him to do, then sought to terminate the transfer before completion of the formalities by

---

104   See Chapter 12.
105   (1862) 4 De GF & J 264.
106   Oakley, 1997, 311 *et seq.*
107   *Yaxley v Gotts* [2000] 1 All ER 711.
108   *Rochefoucauld v Boustead* [1897] 1 Ch 196.
109   *Re Rose* [1952] Ch 499.
110   (1984) 50 P & CR 119.

the Land Registry because he had an argument with his son. The father contended that he should be entitled to terminate the transfer. However, the Court of Appeal held that because the father had done everything he had to do to transfer the property, he was not entitled to renege on the transfer.

The distinction between *Rose*[111] and some of the cases on perfecting imperfect settlements considered above, such as *Re Brooks' ST*,[112] must be that in *Rose,* the purported settlor had the property rights which he purported to transfer and that he evidenced sufficient intention to transfer them away such that he should be bound by that intention. Otherwise, the explanation for the *Rose* principle can only be found in constructive trust.

5.5 PERFECTING IMPERFECT GIFTS

As considered above, equity will not assist a volunteer. The implication for the law of trusts is that the courts will not therefore imply a trust simply to make good a gift which has not been validly made at common law. Trusts will not operate as a catch-all category merely to enforce promises or to reinforce merely moral obligations. That said, there are situations in which a gift which has not been validly made may be capable of enforcement by equity in particular circumstances. There are three contexts in which a gift will be perfected: *donatio mortis causa*; the rule in *Strong v Bird*;[113] and the doctrine of proprietary estoppel.

5.5.1 *Donatio mortis causa*

This category frequently confuses students – it is far more limited than it might otherwise seem. The doctrine of *donatio mortis causa* arose specifically to create an exception to the rule that a testamentary gift must be made properly or else it will not be effective. The gifts are gifts made during the donor's lifetime, made in expectation of immediate death, and which are intended to take effect on the donor's death. It is also important that the donor intends to 'give up dominion' to the property at the time of making his *donatio mortis causa*.[114] Thus, the donor must not intend to be able to deal with the property after the purported gift and must intend, in effect, to give up her rights to the property at that time.[115] This doctrine ordinarily only operates in cases of people acting in extremis.

For example, *donatio mortis causa* would cover a situation like that of a soldier lying dying on a battlefield, his head supported by a comrade as his life ebbs away, who then gasps 'I want my Sunderland AFC shares to be given to my second son'. That statement would not be sufficient to make an ordinary transfer of the shares because the formality of re-registering them under the Companies Act 2006 would not have been complied with. However, the doctrine of *donatio mortis causa* provides that such a gift will be enforceable because it was made in expectation of death in circumstances in which it would not have been reasonable to expect the purported donor to comply with the formalities for making a valid gift of the shares.

---

111 [1952] Ch 499.
112 [1939] 1 Ch 993.
113 (1874) LR 18 Eq 315.
114 *Wilkes v Allington* [1931] 2 Ch 104; *Re Lillington* [1952] 2 All ER 184.
115 *Re Wasserberg* [1915] 1 Ch 195; *Birch v Treasury Solicitor* [1951] Ch 298; *Woodland v Woodland* [1991] Fam Law 470, CA.

The Court of Appeal in *Sen v Headley*[116] considered facts which concerned a couple who had lived together for 10 years but had separated more than 25 years before the material time. One of the couple died of a terminal illness, but before death told his former partner (the plaintiff) that the house (with unregistered title) was hers and that 'You have the keys ... The deeds are in the steel box'. While it was argued against the plaintiff that she had always had keys to the house, such that the lifetime gift could have no further effect by way of gift, the plaintiff was successful in establishing her claim to the house because title deeds were essential in establishing title to unregistered land. There was no retention of dominion in this case because the deceased had not expected that he would return to the house, or that he would have been able to deal with it in any way before his death.

5.5.2 The rule in *Strong v Bird*

The rule in Strong v Bird *itself*

The rule in *Strong v Bird*[117] provides that if a debtor is named by the testator as an executor of the estate of the one to whom he owed the debt, that chose in action is discharged – in effect a gift is made of the amount of the debt. It is necessary that the donor intended to make an *inter vivos* gift of this property. The more modern rationale for the rule is that the executor cannot be expected to sue himself for the debt. The rule appears to be more convenient than real. The assumption is that if a person is made executor of an estate, the deceased must have intended to free the executor from any outstanding debts between them. The executor acquires all the deceased's rights to sue others, therefore the executor would be required to sue himself to recover the debt. While the rules relating to conflicts of interest would generally seem to apply to force the executor to withdraw or to act impartially, the law is content to excuse the executor from meeting the debt. It has also been held that gifts in relation to administrators should receive such immunity from a liability for the debt, even though this status has not been conferred on them by the deceased himself.

In relation to incomplete gifts, the rule in *Strong v Bird* means that where a deceased person intended to make a gift of property to another person without ever making a complete gift of it, if that intended recipient is named as executor of the deceased's estate, the gift is deemed to have been completed.[118] Clearly, the application of the rule to property other than debts is an extension of the *ratio* in *Strong v Bird,* but the rule holds good nevertheless. The rule has been extended in relation to administrators appointed to administer the deceased's estate in the case of intestacy.[119] It also applies to gifts of land.[120] It does not necessarily follow that the rule is appropriate in the context of administrators: you may be appointed as administrator of my estate, but I may also want to be paid what you owe me.

---

116 [1991] Ch 425.
117 (1874) LR 18 Eq 315.
118 *Re Stewart* [1908] 2 Ch 251.
119 *Re James* [1935] Ch 449; *Re Gonin* [1979] Ch 16.
120 *Re James* [1935] Ch 449.

Need for a continuing intention

Where the deceased person had an intention to benefit the claimant executor or administrator, but then changed that intention, the claimant will not be granted title in the property
at issue.[121] In *Re Gonin*,[122] a mother wished to pass her house to her illegitimate daughter on
death but had the (incorrect) notion that she could not do so because her daughter had been
born out of wedlock. Therefore, the mother wrote a cheque for £33,000 in her daughter's
favour. When her daughter was subsequently appointed administratrix of her mother's
estate, it was held that she could not claim title to the house because her mother had indicated
an intention to replace the gift of the house with a gift of money instead. Similarly, in *Re
Freeland*,[123] an intention to make a gift of a car was not supported by the rule in *Strong
v Bird* where the deceased had continued to use that car in apparent negation of any stated
intention to make a gift of it to the plaintiff executor.

Criticism of the rule in Strong v Bird

It does appear that the rule in *Strong v Bird*[124] has a fundamental conceptual weakness. The
executor is required to hold property on the trusts set out in the will. The executor therefore
has legal title in property vested in her to hold that property on trust for the legatees. There
can be no suggestion that the executor, in the capacity of executor, can have any equitable
title in the property. Rather, the role of executor/trustee is to protect the trust property for the
beneficiaries. And yet the rule in *Strong v Bird* does permit the executor to take a beneficial
interest in trust property. The benefit to the executor is the extinction of a debt which the
executor would otherwise owe to the deceased's estate.

It appears that the courts are allowing themselves to become hamstrung by the nature of
the property here. A chose in action owed by the executor is the same as any other piece of
property. There is a different rule if the property owed by the executor was a specific table
belonging to the deceased. Suppose, for example, that no perfect gift had been made of the
table but that it had passed into the control of the executor. In that circumstance, there could
be no argument other than that the table would be returned, beneficially, to the deceased's
estate and passed in turn to whichever legatee was entitled to it. However, because the property is a chose in action, the courts have adopted a different approach. It is suggested that this
distinction between tangible and intangible property is impossible to support. Furthermore,
the rule, even in relation to intangibles, ignores the fact that the deceased has taken no
express action to complete that gift.

The solution to the problem about the executor being required to sue herself can be
resolved by saying that a trustee is not permitted to act on the basis of any conflict of
interest.[125] Therefore, the executor ought to vacate the position of trustee so that this property
which comprises a part of the estate can be collected in with all the other property owned
beneficially by the deceased at the date of death. The rule is, of course, particularly arbitrary

---

121 *Re Gonin* [1979] Ch 16.
122 *Ibid.*
123 [1952] Ch 110.
124 (1874) LR 18 Eq 315.
125 *Keech v Sandford* (1726) Sel Cas Ch 61; *Tito v Waddell (No 2)* [1977] Ch 106.

in that it permits an administrator to benefit from this rule. By definition, the administrator is not a person whom the deceased intended to benefit by extinction of the chose in action because the administrator is appointed by the court and not by the deceased.

5.5.3 Proprietary estoppel and the enforcement of promises

Proprietary estoppel is a remedial doctrine which either seeks to compensate a claimant for detriment suffered as a result of relying on the representation made by the defendant or to give effect to the expectations raised by having so acted in reliance on a representation. The general nature of estoppel in equity is considered in detail in Chapter 13. Having considered the contexts in which equity will not involve itself in perfecting gifts, it is worth considering, albeit briefly, the context in which equity will provide a blanket claim in cases where the claimant has suffered some detriment in reliance on the promise that she would receive rights in property. By a circuitous route, this doctrine can therefore be seen as perfecting imperfect gifts in some contexts. The claim would appear to operate as follows. If Arthur had promised Bertha that he would transfer to her a valuable antique fireplace, knowing that Bertha had spent a large amount of money in having builders remove her old fireplace in the expectation that she could replace it with Arthur's fireplace, then even if Arthur failed to complete the gift, Bertha could argue that the fireplace be transferred to her due to her detrimental reliance on Arthur's representation. Thus, proprietary estoppel might have the indirect effect of completing an imperfect gift.

Thus, in *Pascoe v Turner*,[126] a man left a woman, with whom he had been in a relationship, but told her that the house and all its contents were hers. Interpreted as a gift, this was an incomplete gift of the house (in relation to which there would have needed to have been compliance with ss 52 and 53 of the Law of Property Act 1925) but a complete gift of the contents of the house (in relation to which there would have needed to have been no formalities). The woman sought to claim rights in the house on the basis of proprietary estoppel because she had carried out some peripheral improvements to the decorative order of the house. It was held that encouragement or acquiescence in improvements being made to the house led to the formation of an expectation in the woman of a property right. It was further found that to protect that right, it was necessary to complete the imperfect gift of the house by granting Turner the fee simple in the property, on the basis that it was the 'minimum equity necessary to complete the gift'.[127]

The clearest exposition of the modern doctrine of proprietary estoppel was set out in *Re Basham*,[128] in which there was merely oral evidence only of a gift of a house to a stepdaughter by her stepfather during his illness. Her claim was that she had been induced into thinking that by acting to help the dying man through his illness she would acquire an interest under her stepfather's will. Ultimately, the stepfather died intestate, and the intestacy rules would have passed the property to his nieces, who were his blood relatives. It was held that given that the stepdaughter had acted to her detriment in reliance on her stepfather's promise of a gift of the house, the doctrine of proprietary estoppel would pass the property to the stepdaughter rather than the nieces.

126 [1979] 2 All ER 945.
127 *Crabb v Arun DC* [1976] Ch 179.
128 [1987] 1 All ER 405.

In this way, proprietary estoppel operated to perfect the imperfect gift of the house, even though its primary aim had been to prevent the stepdaughter from suffering detriment.[129] This doctrine is in line with the underlying principle that equity will not assist a volunteer. In relation to proprietary estoppel, the claimant is not a volunteer due to the detriment suffered. There is therefore the question, considered in Chapter 13, as to the form of detriment which will be sufficient to recategorise the claimant as something other than a volunteer.

The question of equitable estoppel in relation to express trusts generally is considered in detail in Chapter 13.

5.6 COVENANTS AND PROMISES TO CREATE A SETTLEMENT OVER AFTER-ACQUIRED PROPERTY

Where a promise is made under covenant to the effect that the settlor will settle property which is to be acquired in the future, there will not be a valid trust if the settlor had no rights in the property at the time of purporting to create the trust. A valid trust will only be created if the settlor owned property rights in the trust property at the time of purporting to declare the trust. Otherwise, only the parties to the covenant will be entitled to enforce the covenant at common law for damages, or further to the Contract (Rights of Third Parties) Act 1999, or in equity by specific performance if they have given consideration for the promise. Trustees who are parties to a covenant may not enforce that covenant; unless the benefit of the covenant itself has been settled on trust, in which case a valid trust will have been created.

5.6.1 The problem of after-acquired property

A settlor must have proprietary rights in the property which is to be settled on trust at the time of purporting to declare a trust.[130] It has frequently happened in family situations that a person has made a promise to other family members that she will settle on trust for those family members some property which she expects to receive at some point in the future. This promise is usually made in the form of a covenant – that is, a contract under deed – which may be signed by the trustees or by the intended beneficiaries as well as by the settlor. However, if the settlor does not have any property rights in the property at the time of purporting to declare that trust, then there cannot be a valid trust.[131] The following question arises: if there is no valid trust, can the intended beneficiaries nevertheless sue on the covenant? Consequently, there is an interaction in this context between the law dealing with covenants and the law of express trusts. A covenant is a form of promise executed under a deed and is therefore a binding contract. Therefore, this area requires a discussion of contract law as well as trusts law. The principal issue is this: if Bernard makes a promise to Fran and Mani that in the future Bernard will settle property on Fran as trustee to hold it on trust for Mani as beneficiary, in what circumstances will that promise be enforceable? We will consider this situation, and these people, as we go through this section of this chapter. To bring this issue to life, consider the following set of facts:

---

129 *Lim v Ang* [1992] 1 WLR 113.
130 See para 5.2.4 above.
131 *Re Brooks' ST* [1939] 1 Ch 993.

David was a man in his late forties and a confirmed bachelor. He hoped that he would receive a legacy from his maiden aunt, who was still alive in 1998. David had no right to any property belonging to his aunt before her death and could get no right under her will until she died. In 1998, David made a promise to the trustees of a family settlement that he would settle any property he did receive from his aunt in the future on trust for his nieces. This promise was in the form of a deed of covenant (that is, a contract) between David and the trustees. In 1999, David was unexpectedly married after a whirl-wind romance. He and his new wife had a baby girl in 2000. David decided that he did not want to pass any property received from his aunt to his nieces because he now had a child of his own to care for. In 2001 his aunt died and left him £50,000.

The problem here is whether or not David will be required to observe the promise which he made in 1998. The various analyses are considered in detail in the discussion which follows, but an outline of the issues can be given at this stage.

The nieces in this example are volunteers – that is, they have given no consideration for the promise made by David. Following the equitable maxim that 'equity will not assist a volunteer',[132] the nieces would *prima facie* be entitled to nothing. However, if David has succeeded in declaring a valid trust, then he will be bound by the promise, because a trust once made cannot be undone.[133] The question as to whether or not David can have created a trust would depend on whether or not he had any proprietary rights in the money *at the time he purported to create the trust*: if David had no rights at that time, he could not have created a valid trust.[134] On these facts, David did not have any rights in the property at the time of purporting to create the trust – he had only a mere hope that he would receive some rights in the future – and therefore could not have created a trust.

The further question to arise would therefore be whether or not the trustees could enforce David's obligation under the deed of covenant. Again, equity will not permit enforcement by the trustees if the nieces are merely volunteers.[135] It would be necessary for the nieces either to have given consideration,[136] or to have been made parties to the deed of covenant[137] or to be identified as third parties entitled to benefit under the contract.[138] Otherwise, the nieces would be entitled to rely on equity only if they could assert that some other property had been settled on trust for them with the intention that the money received from the aunt was to be added to that trust.[139] These issues are considered below. First, we shall begin with a reminder of the principles as to whether or not a valid trust will have been created.

132 *Milroy v Lord* (1862) 4 De GF & J 264.
133 *Jefferys v Jefferys* (1841) Cr & Ph 138; *Paul v Paul* (1882) 20 Ch D 742.
134 *Re Brooks' ST* [1939] 1 Ch 993; *Re Ralli's WT* [1964] 2 WLR 144.
135 *Re Pryce* [1917] 1 Ch 234; *Re Kay* [1939] Ch 329; *Re Cook* [1965] Ch 902.
136 *Pullan v Koe* [1913] 1 Ch 9.
137 *Cannon v Hartley* [1949] Ch 213.
138 Contract (Rights of Third Parties) Act 1999.
139 This last idea is considered in the discussion of *Fletcher v Fletcher* (1844) 4 Hare 67 and *Don King Productions Inc v Warren* [1998] 2 All ER 608, *per* Lightman J; affirmed [2000] Ch 291, CA, at para 5.6.4 below.

5.6.2 To establish a trust the settlor must own the relevant property at the time of purporting to declare the trust

As was considered above in section 5.2.4, a settlor must own the relevant property rights at the time of purporting to declare the trust. If the settlor does not own those property rights at the time of purporting to settle them on trust, then there will not be a valid trust. This is important in relation to covenants to settle after-acquired property. If the settlor does have some rights in the property, then a valid trust will be declared and the beneficiaries will have rights against the settlor under the law of trusts to pass any property identified in the trust instrument into the trust fund. So, in *Re Ralli's WT*,[140] Helen was a remainder beneficiary under a trust who purported to declare a trust over any property in which she might become absolutely entitled in the future when the life tenant died. At the time of declaring this trust it was held that Helen did have some property rights, in the form of her remainder interest under the trust, so that she did create a valid trust at that time, with the consequence that when the life tenant did die some time later Helen was obliged to pass the property to which she then became entitled to her trustees on the terms of that trust. By contrast, in *Re Brooks' ST*[141] Arthur had only a mere hope that he would receive some property under a power of appointment at the time he purported to declare a trust over any property which he might receive in the future. Consequently, when there was some property appointed to him latterly, it was held that no valid trust had been created because at the time at which he had purported to declare that trust he had had no proprietary rights capable of constituting a trust fund.

Therefore, if a settlor purports to declare a trust over after-acquired property at a time at which she has no property rights, there will not be a valid trust declared and therefore the beneficiaries can have no equitable interests which are enforceable against her. In the following sections we shall consider what effect there can be on this principle if the settlor has not simply purported to declare a trust, but has gone further and entered into a covenant either with the beneficiaries or with the trustees under which she promised to settle any after-acquired property on trust.

5.6.3 The enforceability of a promise under covenant

This section considers the circumstances in which promises made by means of a deed of covenant or a contract will be enforceable. It should be remembered that a promise made in a deed of covenant will have the full force and effect of a binding contract (on the basis that a deed replaces the need for consideration).[142] In a distant past represented in the novels of Jane Austen, well-to-do families had arranged marriages (typically) such that the riches and standing of both families would be maintained. These marriages were forged in tandem with complicated settlements which allocated rights in the property of both families, providing for the rights of future generations as well as the married parties. As part of these agreements, it was common for the parties to enter into promises to settle property which might be received in the future on the terms of the matrimonial trust (or 'marriage settlement').

---

140 [1964] 1 Ch 288.
141 [1939] 1 Ch 993.
142 *Hall v Palmer* (1844) 3 Hare 532; *Macedo v Stroud* [1922] 2 AC 330.

Settlement cannot be unmade

Before considering the detail of the rules relating to covenants, it is worth reminding ourselves of the rules relating to the creation of trusts. Clearly, there may be situations in which the parties create marriage settlements, or other trusts, under which they promise to deal with property in a particular manner. However, it is possible that subsequent events may make the terms of the settlement appear to be unattractive. For example, in *Paul v Paul*,[143] where a couple who were parties to a complex marriage settlement subsequently sought to separate, the couple also sought to undo the marriage settlement and reallocate the property between themselves. It was held by the court that a settlement, once created, could not be undone.[144] The only circumstances in which the beneficiaries would be entitled to undo a trust would be in accordance with the rule in *Saunders v Vautier*,[145] whereby absolutely-entitled beneficiaries, acting *sui juris*, are empowered to direct the trustees to deliver legal title in the property to them. The further point which flows from this is that the trustees are not obliged to obey any directions which the settlor may seek to give after the trust has been constituted if those terms are outwith the terms of the trust.[146] Therefore, where trustees were vested with a discretionary power to provide for the maintenance of the settlor's children, the trustees were entitled to ignore the settlor's financial position when considering the exercise of their powers and not worry themselves that this might have the incidental effect of reducing the settlor's liabilities under a court consent order.[147]

Parties to the covenant can enforce the covenant

In relation to covenants to deal with property in a particular manner, the parties to the covenant are entitled to enforce the covenant under the ordinary principles of the law of contract. In the trusts context, the importance of a covenant would be as an obligation entered into by a person to settle specified property on trust for the benefit of other people. On the basis that there is no trust created, the covenant itself will give the parties to the covenant the right to sue to enforce the promise at common law, without the need for resort to the law of trusts. For example, where a person had undertaken by deed of covenant to settle property on his daughter, she would be entitled to enforce that obligation if she were a party to the covenant and consequently to receive an award of damages at common law.[148] It would be in the capacity of a party to the covenant that the daughter would be entitled to seek performance of the obligation in the covenant. However, she would not be able to sue on the promise in her capacity as a beneficiary under that trust, for the reasons given below.

Rights to specific performance are available only to those who have given consideration.[149] So, in *Pullan v Koe*,[150] the claimant was entitled to claim a right in contract where she had given consideration as part of a marriage settlement, and in consequence was entitled to

143 (1882) 20 Ch D 742.
144 *Paul v Paul* (1882) 20 Ch D 742.
145 (1841) 4 Beav 115.
146 *Fuller v Evans* [2000] 1 All ER 636.
147 *Ibid.*
148 *Cannon v Hartley* [1949] Ch 213.
149 *Pullan v Koe* [1913] 1 Ch 9; *Cannon v Hartley* [1949] Ch 213.
150 [1913] 1 Ch 9.

specific performance of the defendant's promise to settle after-acquired property on trust for her. If the claimant had not given consideration for the promise, then her only claim would be based on an entitlement to damages at common law if she were a party to the covenant. A deed of covenant does not require consideration because the use of a deed to create the contract is said to replace the ordinary need for consideration in a contract. Therefore, parties to deeds of covenant will frequently be volunteers because they will usually not have given consideration if they have simply signed the deed of covenant. Equity will not assist a volunteer – as considered above. Specific performance is an equitable remedy and therefore not available to volunteers because equity does not assist volunteers.[151] In the case of *Cannon v Hartley*,[152] a father entered into a covenant to settle after-acquired property on his daughter, amongst others. His daughter had given no consideration for this covenant, but she was entitled to damages at common law for breach of covenant when her father refused to transfer the property onto trust because she had been a party to the covenant. Her right to damages was predicated entirely on the basis that she had been a party to the covenant in that case. Significantly, the claimant in *Cannon v Hartley*[153] could only receive damages because she had not given consideration to become a party to the deed of covenant, unlike the claimant in *Pullan v Koe*[154] who had given consideration within the terms of a marriage settlement.

This rule has always struck this writer as unduly formalistic. To restrict the liability of a contracting party who has refused to observe the terms of the contract to a liability in damages does not necessarily permit the other contracting party to rely on a further non-cash benefit contained in the contract. The other party may prefer to have the contract performed rather than simply to receive cash damages. While it is a long-standing principle of equity that volunteers will not be assisted, what the principle in *Cannon v Hartley* does is to enable parties to a deed to renege on their obligations to perform the acts specified in the contract and limit their liabilities to cash damages. Another approach might be to argue that the defaulting party is acting unconscionably in relation to the property which ought to be transferred to the benefit of the other party to the deed.[155] Alternatively, if the claimant could demonstrate that she had suffered some detriment in reliance on the representation made in the deed of covenant, there might be a right to proprietary estoppel to reverse that detriment.[156] Here the dividing line between the law of trusts' affection for enforcing conscionable behaviour in relation to property and the formalistic application of the rule against benefiting volunteers is clear. Good conscience would generally favour performance of the promise. However, English law's preference for enforcing bargains (that is, arrangements where consideration passes) over mere promises (that is, representations without any consideration passing) means that the concept of 'good conscience' is subjugated to the commercial legal practice in favour of arm's length bargains.

Under contract law, it has been held that a contractual promise to transfer after-acquired property under a power of appointment will be subject to specific performance. So, under *Tailby v Official Receiver*[157] if there had been a contract for the transfer of any property

151 *Jefferys v Jefferys* (1841) Cr & Ph 138.
152 [1949] Ch 213.
153 *Ibid.*
154 [1913] 1 Ch 9.
155 *Westdeutsche Landesbank Girozentrale v Islington LBC* [1996] AC 669.
156 *Lim v Ang* [1992] 1 WLR 113 considered at section 14.7 below.
157 (1888) 13 App Cas 523.

which was received under a mere expectancy in the future then the equitable interest in that property would pass to those beneficiaries once the defendant received it. This decision is based on the equitable principle that 'equity looks upon as done that which ought to have been done'. It is significant that the claimant had tendered consideration to the defendant and therefore that the claimant was not a volunteer.[158] Because the defendant is not a volunteer, there is no breach of the principle that equity will not assist a volunteer. So, it is under the contractual doctrine of specific performance that the equitable interest passes, and not under trusts law.

Non-parties cannot enforce the covenant – pre-1999

In circumstances in which a person undertakes by means of a deed under covenant to settle after-acquired property on specified trusts, the beneficiaries will not have *locus standi* to enforce the promise unless they were parties to the covenant.[159] A person who is not a party to the covenant cannot enforce it. Where the covenant is effected between the settlor and the trustee, the trustee will be able to enforce it as a party to the covenant.[160] The issue of trustees seeking to enforce the covenant is considered below.

Contracts for the benefit of a third party – post-1999

In many civil code jurisdictions in continental Europe (where the trust does not exist generally as a legal concept), arrangements considered to be a trust under English law would frequently be understood in those civil code jurisdictions not as a division in property rights but rather as contracts for the benefit of third parties. So, if an absolute owner of property entered into an arrangement whereby her agents were to invest identified property with the intention of benefiting her children, that would probably constitute a contract between the owner of the property and her agents which was intended to benefit the children as third parties. Most non-Anglo-American jurisdictions see property rights as vesting in one person as owner with other people having merely personal claims in relation to the use of the property. This differs greatly from the English trust, in which the trustees and the beneficiaries all have varying forms of proprietary rights against the trust fund itself.

The enactment of the Contracts (Rights of Third Parties) Act 1999 has had the effect of introducing to English contract law the concept of a contract which reaches out beyond the common law rules of privity of contract to situations in which contracts are made specifically for the benefit of some third party on that civil code model. In relation to the issue of after-acquired property, the purported beneficiary will be able to enforce the contract if she is identified in the contract either personally, or as part of a class of persons for whose benefit the contract has been created.[161] The claimant is entitled to rely on all of the rights accorded

---

158 See also *Re Lind* [1915] 2 Ch 345; *Palette Shoes Pty Ltd v Krohn* (1937) 58 CLR 1, 26; *Re Androma Pty Ltd* [1987] 2 Qd R 134, 152.
159 *Cannon v Hartley* [1949] Ch 213.
160 *Beswick v Beswick* [1968] AC 58; *Pullan v Koe* [1913] 1 Ch 9. See also *Darlington BC v Wiltshire Northern Ltd* [1995] 1 WLR 68; *Panatown Ltd v Alfred McAlpine Construction Ltd* [2000] 4 All ER 97.
161 Contracts (Rights of Third Parties) Act 1999, s 1.

by contract law, including damages and specific performance – therefore, the contract takes effect at common law and in equity.[162]

The limits on the operation of the Act appear to be as follows. First, there must be a contract and not a mere promise. The promise made by the promisor must be in the form of a contract with consideration, or made under a deed. The principal argument against the operation of the 1999 Act in many situations would be that the promise made by the promisor to settle after-acquired property would not constitute a contract because typically there would be no consideration passing between the promisor and either the trustee or the purported beneficiary. In many commercial situations, there will be a commercial contract (into which the trust is incorporated), or there may be a contract between settlor and trustee in situations such as an occupational pension fund (as considered in Chapter 24). However, in relation to a formal contract of retainer between the settlor and trustee, it is unlikely that such a contract created to authorise the trustees' fees would specify a benefit for any beneficiary on its face. Further, it may be that an arrangement which will not create common law rights because there is no enforceable contract will grant rights in equity under either promissory or proprietary estoppel.[163]

Secondly, it is not clear to what extent the identified class of persons able to enforce the contract will correlate with the rules for certainty of objects in trusts law. To make the point another way: what is the class which must be identified? Will that level of certainty correspond with the trusts law rules for the identity of beneficiaries under, for example, a discretionary trust? It would seem sensible to suppose that if the class is sufficiently certain as a class of beneficiaries, it ought to be sufficiently certain for the purposes of the 1999 Act. What remains unclear, however, is whether or not the beneficiary would be required to have vested rights within the terms of the contract, or whether the Act would also apply to people who potentially fall within a class of objects of a mere power of appointment:[164] in the latter case, it could not be contended that the contract was for the benefit of the beneficiary because there was no vested interest on the part of the third party.

Thirdly, and perhaps most significantly, a contract may create personal rights and not necessarily proprietary rights nor fiduciary obligations. Suppose, therefore, that the promise made is a promise to transfer money – the claimant's entitlement is unlikely to be enforceable by specific performance because it is merely a money claim.[165] In consequence, the claimant receives only personal rights and not rights in property against that fund. However, if the contract provided the third party with rights in identified property (other than money), then there would be no principled reason to suppose that specific performance would not grant that third party rights in the property when received by the promisor.

It is important to remember that while a contract may also create a trust as a byproduct,[166] the contract itself will not *be* a trust in itself. A contract will not grant equitable title in property – only a trust, or a charge or a similar right will do that. A trust will give certain remedies which a mere contract cannot. The principal advantage of the trust over the

---

162   *Ibid.*
163   *Hughes v Metropolitan Railway* (1877) 2 App Cas 439; *Central London Property Trust Ltd v High Trees House Ltd* [1949] KB 130; *Combe v Combe* [1951] 2 KB 215; or in relation to proprietary estoppel, *Gillett v Holt* [2000] 2 All ER 289; *Yaxley v Gotts* [2000] 1 All ER 711.
164   *Re Brooks' ST* [1939] 1 Ch 993.
165   *South African Territories Ltd v Wallington* [1898] AC 309; *Beswick v Beswick* [1968] AC 58.
166   *Re Kayford* [1975] 1 WLR 279.

remedies available under contract law (principally common law damages and equitable specific performance) is that the trust will entitle the claimant to proprietary rights in that property which is held on trust. A beneficiary under a trust will be able to acquire preferential rights in an insolvency[167] and will be entitled to receive compound interest on amounts owing to it[168] rather than merely simple interest. Significantly, also, a trustee is bound by obligations of utmost good faith and prevented from allowing any conflicts of interest or the making of secret profits.[169]

The 1999 Act will replace many of the situations in which the case law has struggled to provide a remedy for the purported beneficiary in relation to after-acquired property. However, the foregoing discussion has highlighted some of the situations in which the 1999 Act will not have any application. It has also highlighted those senses in which the law of contract does not offer any better right to the claimant than the law of trusts. Indeed, if the claimant is seeking to claim rights in identified property, then a trust remains the most significant claim of all. The following sections consider the rights of the purported beneficiary and of the trustee to enforce the promise otherwise than under the law of contract.

5.6.4 Trustees seeking to enforce a promise to settle after-acquired property

This section considers the following problem. Suppose that a settlor expects to receive an allotment of ordinary shares in Sunderland AFC plc and that she undertakes by means of a deed of covenant with trustees to settle any shares received on trust for specified beneficiaries. If the settlor has only a mere *spes* in the shares at the time of the purported creation of the trust, there will not be a valid declaration of trust.[170] However, if the settlor had some equitable interest in the property at the time of the creation of the trust, there will be a valid trust over that equitable interest.[171] These issues have already been considered earlier in this chapter.[172]

Trustee not permitted to enforce the promise

The question arises as to the duties incumbent on the trustee to seek to enforce the covenant. The issue is the following. In circumstances where there is no valid trust, because the settlor had no equitable interest in the relevant property at the time of purporting to declare that trust, there is no right in the beneficiary to oblige the trustee to exercise those powers under the covenant. If the trustee were to sue under the covenant, as a party to that covenant, there would be no beneficiary for whom the property could be held on trust. It is not permissible for trustees to declare the terms of the trust.[173] Consequently, the court will not permit the trustee to sue for the property.[174] Indeed, the result of these cases is that the trustee must not begin such an action because that action would be struck out.

---

167 *Re Goldcorp* [1995] 1 AC 74.
168 *Westdeutsche Landesbank Girozentrale v Islington LBC* [1996] AC 669.
169 *Boardman v Phipps* [1967] 2 AC 46.
170 *Re Brooks' ST* [1939] 1 Ch 993.
171 *Re Ralli's WT* [1964] 2 WLR 144.
172 See para 5.4.2 above.
173 *Re Brooks' ST* [1939] 1 Ch 993.
174 *Re Pryce* [1917] 1 Ch 234; *Re Kay* [1939] Ch 329; *Re Cook* [1965] Ch 902.

The reason for this preclusion is that if the trustee did seek to enforce the covenant and sue for specific performance, the trustee would not be entitled to take a beneficial interest in that property as a mere trustee. Consequently, there would be a gap in the beneficial ownership, requiring that the equitable interest in the property be held on resulting trust for the settlor.[175] In general terms, English law will not permit a person to sue for property in circumstances in which the claimant would be required to hold that property on trust for the defendant in any event.[176] So, in *Re Kay's Settlement*,[177] a woman created a conveyance of property to herself for life and in remainder to other people while she was a spinster. The conveyance contained a covenant to settle after-acquired property. Subsequently, the woman married and had children. In later years she received property which fell within the terms of the covenant but to which she had had no entitlement at the time of creating the covenant. The woman refused to settle the property on trust in accordance with the covenant. It was held that none of the beneficiaries under the conveyance could establish any rights in the after-acquired property. The question arose whether or not the trustees, as parties to the covenant, could force the woman to settle the after-acquired property. In line with the earlier decision in *Re Pryce*,[178] it was held that the trustees should not be permitted to sue the woman under the terms of the covenant because the trust which they were seeking to enforce did not exist precisely because the woman had had no rights in the property at the time she had purported to create that trust. In the later case of *Re Cook*,[179] this idea hardened into a strict principle that the trustees ought not to be permitted to commence such litigation because it would be vexatious and wasteful. If the trustees were allowed to commence the litigation and enforce the covenant, there would be no trust on which the property could be held; because the trustees would not be entitled to take the property beneficially *qua* trustees, they would be required to hold the property on resulting trust for the original covenantor; therefore, the litigation would be wasteful because, even if successful, the trustees would be obliged to return the property to the defendant in any event.

This policy of avoiding wasteful litigation emerges in the case of *Hirachand Punanchand v Temple*,[180] in which a father sought to liquidate his son's creditors by reaching an agreement with them to pay off a percentage (but not the whole) of his son's debts as a full and final settlement of their claim against his son. The creditors agreed to the settlement proposed by the father and took the sum from him. However, the creditors, in contravention of their agreement with the father, sought to proceed against the son for the balance of the debt owing. It was held that the creditors would have been estopped from retaining title in any money they would have received from the son because it was in flat contravention of their agreement with the father. Consequently, the court refused even to allow the action to proceed, because any money won against the son would have been held on trust for the father. It is suggested that this thinking can be applied to the situation of trustees suing under covenants.[181]

---

175 *Vandervell v IRC* [1967] 2 AC 291, HL.
176 *Hirachand Punanchand v Temple* [1911] 2 KB 330; *Re Cook* [1965] Ch 902.
177 [1939] Ch 329.
178 [1917] 1 Ch 234.
179 [1965] Ch 902.
180 [1911] 2 KB 330.
181 Hayton, 1996.

A trust of the promise itself

The exception to the approach set out above appears in the decision in *Fletcher v Fletcher*.[182] A father covenanted with a trustee to settle an after-acquired sum of £66,000 (in 1844 an enormous sum of money) on his sons, Jacob and John. The property was passed to the trustee on the father's death. In reliance on the principles set out in the line of cases culminating in *Re Cook*[183] (above), the trustee contended that there had been no valid trust and that the trustee ought, therefore, to be absolutely entitled to the money. The court held, however, that the surviving beneficiary, Jacob, was entitled to sue under the terms of the trust on the basis that there had been property which could have been settled on the purported trust.

The property identified by the court in *Fletcher v Fletcher* was *the benefit of the covenant itself*. This single idea requires some short analysis. A covenant creates obligations. A party to the covenant can transfer the benefit of the covenant to another party, or borrow money using it as security. A covenant, in the same way as a debt, is a chose in action. A covenant can therefore be considered to be property in itself. Consequently, to enable the creation of a valid trust in circumstances in which a covenant is created obliging the settlor to settle after-acquired property on trust, the settlor would be required to settle the benefit of the covenant on trust for the beneficiary. That chose in action would be replaced by the subsequently acquired tangible property as the trust fund in time. This was the mechanism we should undertand the court as having used in *Fletcher v Fletcher* to justify the finding that there was a valid trust and thus to give the beneficiary a right to sue the trustee to force him to collect in the property to be settled on trust. In reality, it was to prevent the trustee's unconscionable claim to such an enormous sum of money.

In the case of *Don King v Warren*,[184] two boxing promoters entered into a series of partnership agreements whereby they undertook to treat any promotion agreements entered into with boxers as being part of the partnership property. It was held by Lightman J (and subsequently the Court of Appeal) that this disclosed an intention to settle the benefit of those promotion agreements on trust for the members of the partnership. This demonstrates a principle akin to that in *Fletcher v Fletcher*, whereby a contract was held to have been capable of forming the subject matter of a trust despite being incapable of transfer on its face. Further examples of the benefits of contracts or statutory licences being held on trust despite being incapable of transfer are the cases of *Swift v Dairywise Farms*[185] and *Re Celtic Extraction*.[186] In these two cases, the benefits of statutory licences which were not transferable from one person to another were held to be capable of constituting a trust fund despite the impossibility of transferring them.[187] Therefore, the point made in *Fletcher v Fletcher*,[188] that a trust can be declared over a chose in action, is one with modern support.

Suppose, as an illustration of this principle, that Arthur decides to settle property which he hopes will be advanced to him under a power of appointment at some point in the future.

---

182 (1844) 4 Hare 67.
183 [1965] Ch 902.
184 [1998] 2 All ER 608, *per* Lightman J; affirmed [2000] Ch 291.
185 [2000] 1 All ER 320.
186 *Re Celtic Extraction Ltd (In Liquidation), Re Bluestone Chemicals Ltd (In Liquidation)* [1999] 4 All ER 684.
187 Cf *Krasner v Dennison* [2000] 3 All ER 234 – restriction on transferability of annuity contracts did not prevent them vesting in a trustee in bankruptcy.
188 (1844) 4 Hare 67.

Therefore, Arthur decides to enter into a covenant with Tamsin, his appointed trustee, to the effect that he will settle any after-acquired property on trust for Gertrude. Some time later, Arthur is appointed a large sum of money. Given that he has no proprietary rights in the property at the time of making the covenant, he cannot create a valid trust.[189] Gertrude is a volunteer – in that she has given no consideration for Arthur's covenant – and therefore she cannot claim specific performance of the covenant to settle property in her favour. Gertrude is not a party to the covenant: if she had been, then she could have claimed common law damages for breach of Arthur's obligation.[190] However, if the covenant were worded such that Arthur undertook 'to hold the benefit of this covenant on trust for Gertrude immediately', then Arthur would have demonstrated a sufficient intention to create a trust of the covenant itself and so he would have created a valid trust at the time of making the covenant. Given that Arthur created a valid trust at that time, when he subsequently receives property under the power of appointment, that property passes on to the settlement in favour of Gertrude regardless of Arthur's change of heart.[191]

5.6.5 A summary of the principles discussed in this section

The principles considered in this section often challenge trusts law students. This section aims to summarise them and so draw them together. The question is whether or not a valid trust will be created by a promise (usually in the form of a covenant) made by Bernard that he will settle property which he hopes to receive in the future so that Fran will hold that property on trust for Mani. If Bernard had a proprietary right in the property at the time of purporting to declare this trust, then there will be a valid trust and Mani will be able to compel Bernard to transfer the property to Fran when he acquires it in the future so that Fran will hold it on trust for Mani.[192] Suppose, however, that Bernard decides to keep the property for himself when eventually he does receive it. If there is a valid trust created, then Bernard may not renege on it.[193] There is no need to pursue that particular hypothetical example any further because Mani has a good claim in trusts law.

However, if Bernard had no such property rights at the time of purporting to declare that trust, then Mani would have no immediate rights in trusts law because no trust would have been created.[194] Suppose that Bernard had made the promise to settle the after-acquired property in the form of a covenant: if so, Mani may have rights under contract law in the following contexts. If Mani had been a signatory to that covenant then Mani would be entitled at common law to sue Bernard for damages.[195] If Mani had given consideration for the promise then Mani would be entitled under contract law to sue for specific performance of the obligation to transfer the after-acquired property when it is received.[196] If the contract identified Mani as someone who was intended to take a benefit from it, then Mani would have rights under the Contract (Rights of Third Parties) Act 1999.

189 *Re Brooks' ST* [1939] 1 Ch 993.
190 *Cannon v Hartley* [1949] Ch 213.
191 *Fletcher v Fletcher* (1844) 4 Hare 67.
192 *Re Ralli's WT* [1964] 1 Ch 288.
193 *Paul v Paul* (1882) 20 Ch D 742.
194 *Re Brooks' ST* [1939] 1 Ch 993.
195 *Cannon v Hartley* [1949] Ch 213.
196 *Pullan v Koe* [1913] 1 Ch 9.

The question then arises whether or not Fran, assuming that she was a signatory to this covenant in her capacity as trustee, could sue on the terms of the covenant so as to compel Bernard to transfer to her the after-acquired property when Bernard receives it. Assuming still that Bernard had no property rights at the time of purporting to declare the trust, then there would not have been a valid trust in existence.[197] If there was no valid trust in existence, then Fran has no-one for whom she can hold the property on trust, even if she did sue Bernard to compel him to transfer that property across to her. Because there are no beneficiaries, on the basis that there is no trust, Fran would be holding the property for no-one: Fran could not keep it for herself beneficially because she was only ever intended to be a trustee in this example. It is not possible for Fran to hold property for no-one under English law. Therefore, Fran would have to hold the property on resulting trust for Bernard,[198] because there is no-one else who can take an equitable interest in it.[199] Consequently, the courts have held that Fran may not even commence litigation against Bernard under the covenant because it would be a waste of time (or, in the technical jargon, it would be vexatious litigation).[200]

The only way in which Mani could acquire an equitable interest under a trust in the after-acquired property – continuing the example in which there was no trust created originally and in which Mani had given no consideration – would be if it could be proved on the facts that Bernard had intended to declare a trust *over the benefit of the covenant itself*.[201] It is suggested that, to establish such a trust over the benefit of the covenant itself, Bernard would have had to have demonstrated that intention very clearly. If such a trust were created over the benefit of the covenant, then Mani would have rights as a beneficiary under a valid trust so that he could compel Bernard to settle the after-acquired property on trust with Fran when he does eventually receive it.

5.7 DISPOSITION OF EQUITABLE INTERESTS

A disposition of an equitable interest must be effected by signed writing as required by s 53(1)(c) of the Law of Property Act 1925, unless both legal and equitable title pass together from the trust. Where a sub-trust is created, so that the beneficiary retains some office as sub-trustee, there is no disposition of the equitable interest – unless there is an outright assignment of that equitable interest. In some cases, an agreement to transfer the equitable interest has been held to transfer the equitable interest automatically on the specific performance principle, without the need for signed writing.

5.7.1 The rule in s 53(1)(c) of the Law of Property Act 1925

The purpose of s 53(1)(c) of the Law of Property Act 1925 was twofold: first, to prevent hidden oral transactions in equitable interests defrauding those entitled to property; and,

---

197 *Re Brooks' ST* [1939] 1 Ch 993.
198 *Vandervell v IRC* [1967] 2 AC 291.
199 *Re Pryce* [1917] 1 Ch 234; *Re Kay* [1939] Ch 329.
200 *Re Cook* [1965] Ch 902.
201 *Fletcher v Fletcher* (1844) 4 Hare 67; *Don King Productions Inc v Warren* [1998] 2 All ER 608, affirmed [2000] Ch 291.

secondly, to enable trustees to know where the equitable interests are at any one time. Section 53(1)(c) provides that:

a disposition of an equitable interest or trust subsisting at the time of the disposition must be in writing signed by the person disposing of the same, or by his agent thereunto lawfully authorised in writing or by will.

Therefore, for a disposition of an equitable interest to take effect, the person who is making the disposition is required to make that disposition by signed writing. It has been held that a disposition made in two documents, when taken together, would be sufficient to satisfy s 53(1)(c).[202] The term 'disposition' is a wide one which incorporates a range of methods for transferring an equitable interest which will include gifts and sales of equitable interests but does not necessarily require that the equitable interest has been destroyed.[203] To disclaim an equitable interest[204] or to identify the person who should be entitled to one's equitable interest under a pension fund[205] is not to effect a disposition of such an interest. Notably, a *declaration* of trust does not constitute a *disposition* of an equitable interest because a declaration of a trust effects the *creation* of an equitable interest rather than a disposition of a pre-existing equitable interest.[206] Therefore, s 53(1)(c) does not apply to declarations of trusts.

Section 53(1)(c) of the Law of Property Act 1925 does not apply in relation to a financial collateral arrangement.[207] This is a transaction used to provide security in complex financial transactions, principally financial derivatives, where the parties transfer cash or securities to one another equal to the net exposure one party has to the other in relation to the mark-to-market value of any outstanding transactions between them.[208]

The most vital context in which s 53(1)(c) has operated on the reported cases is in relation to stamp duty. Stamp duty is a tax which is imposed on documents which effect transfers of certain types of property between persons. Therefore, the requirement that there be writing for a disposition of an equitable interest has the effect of requiring that there be a document, which in turn may create a liability to tax. Consequently, it became important for taxpayers in a number of situations to attempt to demonstrate that the transfer of their property took

---

202 *Re Danish Bacon Co Ltd Staff Pension Fund Trusts* [1971] 1 WLR 248, [1971] 1 All ER 486. See also *Crowden v Aldridge* [1993] 1 WLR 433, [1993] 3 All ER 603.

203 *Newlon Housing Trust v Alsulaimen* [1999] 1 AC 313, [1998] 4 All ER 1 in relation to the meaning of disposition under s 24 of the Matrimonial Causes Act 1973, following *Grey v IRC* [1960] AC 1 in that the equitable interest need not have been extinguished to have been disposed of.

204 *Re Paradise Motor Co Ltd* [1968] 1 WLR 1125, [1968] 2 All ER 625.

205 *Re Danish Bacon Co Ltd Staff Pension Fund Trusts* [1971] 1 WLR 248, [1971] 1 All ER 486; *Gold v Hill* [1999] 1 FLR 54.

206 See the *dicta* of Lord Browne-Wilkinson to this effect in *Westdeutsche Landesbank v Islington* [1996] AC 669: a creation of a trust also creates the equitable interest in property; the equitable interest does not sit latent in property before a declaration of trust, rather before the creation of a trust over property we should think only of there being absolute title in that property.

207 That s 53(1)(c) does not apply in relation to collateral arrangements is demonstrated by Lewison J in *Mills v Sportsdirect.com Retail Ltd* [2010] EWHC 1072 (Ch), [2010] 2 BCLC 143, as considered in Chapter 3.

208 Financial Collateral Arrangements (No 2) Regulations 2003 (SI 2003 No 3226) Art 4(2). See the discussion of these arrangements in Alastair Hudson, *The Law of Finance*, Sweet & Maxwell, 2009, para 45–01; and by the same author, *The Law on Financial Derivatives*, 5th edn, Sweet & Maxwell, 2012, Chapter 12 generally.

effect without the need for a written document. This would mean the avoidance of s 53(1)(c) and the concomitant avoidance of tax. The case law which was spawned by this desperation to avoid tax is therefore quite complicated.

It is interesting that the purpose of s 53(1)(c) was to promote certainty before a disposition would be considered to have been validly effected. However, the manner in which s 53(1)(c) has been used by the taxing authorities has been to say that a disposition must have been made in writing and therefore that it is a written document which *carries out* the disposition, rather than the document merely *providing evidence* of the disposition.[209]

5.7.2 Whether or not a transaction will fall within s 53(1)(c)

The issue is then one of deciding when a disposition will fall within s 53(1)(c) – and there-fore to decide how s 53(1)(c) can be avoided. The most straightforward judgment in this area is *Grey v IRC*.[210] This case is, in reality, a case of attempted tax avoidance in which the tax avoidance scheme was held not to work.[211] The taxpayer's plan was to transfer shares to his grandchildren without paying tax by creating a trust over them and simply moving the equitable interest in the shares so as to avoid the tax regulations.

The taxpayer, Hunter, created six settlements in 1949: five were separate trusts, one each for the benefit of his five grandchildren, and the sixth was for the benefit of then-living and future grandchildren. On 1 February 1955, he transferred 18,000 ordinary shares in a company to the trustees to hold on bare trust for Hunter. Then, on 18 February 1955, Hunter irrevocably directed his trustees to hold those shares on the terms of the 1949 settlements as to 3,000 shares each. Subsequently, on 25 March 1955, Hunter and the trustees together executed six written declarations of trusts in respect of the shares which, they contended, merely confirmed the oral direction of 18 February in written terms. Hunter's plan was to argue that the oral direction, rather than the documents, effected the transfer and therefore that no stamp duty should be payable.[212]

The question was whether the oral direction of 18 February was sufficient to transfer Hunter's interest in the shares, or whether it was required to have been done by signed writing. Hunter wanted to avoid signed writing because such a written transfer would have attracted *ad valorem* stamp duty. Instead, he wanted to demonstrate that his right in the shares ought to have been passed under the verbal direction of 18 February, thus avoiding the stamp duty.

The House of Lords, in the leading speech of Viscount Simonds, held that what Hunter was doing was making a disposition of his equitable interest. On the basis that the shares were held on trust for Hunter from 1 February 1955, he retained only an equitable interest in them. Therefore, it was said that he could only have been disposing of an equitable interest on 18 February. The House of Lords held that s 53(1)(c) of the 1925 Act therefore applied to require that the disposition be made in writing. The speech of Viscount Simonds repays some close attention. It is very short. Noticeably, his Lordship did not dwell on any of the niceties which will attract our attention in relation to later cases. Viscount Simonds was a

209 *Grey v IRC* [1960] AC 1.
210 *Ibid.*
211 See also *Baird v Baird* [1990] 2 AC 548, [1990] 2 All ER 300.
212 A similar argument was attempted in *Cohen & Moore v IRC* [1933] 2 KB 126.

clear-minded judge. In dealing with this case his Lordship was concerned solely with what the word 'disposition' means. It was argued on behalf of Hunter that the word 'disposition' should be given a narrow meaning drawn from early legislation based on the Statute of Frauds such that it would be limited to formal 'grants and assignments'. Viscount Simonds made his approach clear in the first sentence when he referred to the 'plain question' arising on the facts.[213] His Lordship held that if the word 'disposition' was 'given its natural meaning, it cannot, I think, be denied that a direction given by Mr Hunter, whereby the beneficial interest in the shares theretofore vested in him became vested in another or others, is a disposition'.[214] To put the same argument more simply: if Hunter's instruction means that the equitable interest starts with one person and then moves to another person, then there has been a disposition of it. If the interest moves, then it has been subject to a disposition. It was held that there was no reason in the statute to impose any more limited meaning on the word than that.[215] It is only in later House of Lords decisions that the scope of what might constitute a disposition is narrowed greatly.

The manner of the disposition looked something like this:

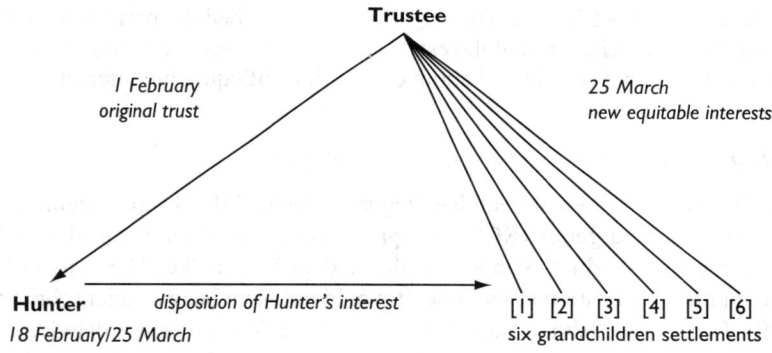

On the left side of the triangle is Hunter's original creation of a bare trust of the shares to be held on trust for himself by the Trustee. The base of the triangle depicts the attempt on 18 February to transfer his interest in the shares orally, and the successful transfer by means of signed writing on 25 March. The lines making up the right sides of the triangle depict the six 1949 settlements under which the equitable interest in the shares is then held after 25 March. The importance of the decision, as depicted in this diagram, is that Hunter had only an equitable interest at 1 February, and therefore was deemed to have attempted to

---

213 [1960] AC 1, 12.

214 *Ibid.*

215 It is an irony that in some dictionaries, the natural meaning given to the word 'disposition' is 'a person's personality or mood' or 'the arrangement of objects' (such as Michael Nyman's delicious piece of music 'The Disposition of the Linen' in *The Draughtsman's Contract* soundtrack). However, there is a contemporaneous meaning referring to 'the action of getting rid of or making over; bestowal by deed or will' in the two-volume *Shorter Oxford English Dictionary*. However, that this word has at least two natural meanings does make the purported logic of Viscount Simonds's approach seem a little less watertight.

make a disposition of that equitable interest when he directed his trustees to transfer the equitable interest in the shares to the 1949 grandchildren settlements. To achieve this goal under s 53(1)(c) would have required signed writing, thus attracting liability to stamp duty. The House of Lords therefore deemed the 18 February oral direction to be of no effect and therefore held that it was the written documentation of 25 March which effected the disposition: thus attracting stamp duty.

In the following section are considered a number of means by which Hunter might have restructured his tax arrangements to achieve this transfer without the need for signed writing. First, however, it is important to consider a different stream of cases in which the taxpayer benefited from a different approach to s 53(1)(c) adopted by a differently constituted House of Lords.

5.7.3 Transactions not within s 53(1)(c)

As set out above, it became important in many tax contexts to demonstrate that equitable property rights could pass without the need for a document. The collective mind of the tax lawyers was therefore focused on a means of transferring rights in property without the need for signed writing under s 53(1)(c). The litigation which probed the perimeters of the rule in s 53(1)(c) was that revolving around the estate of Mr Vandervell – a man who laid down his estate so that law students could learn about dispositions of equitable interests.

Transfer of equitable interest together with legal interest

In *Vandervell v IRC*,[216] Mr Vandervell had begun with the philanthropic intention to benefit the Royal College of Surgeons (RCS) and presumably ended with a profound hatred of lawyers. The means by which Vandervell decided to benefit the RCS was complicated. Given the high rates of taxation at the time, it would not have been efficient for him to have made a gift of cash after having paid tax on that cash. Therefore, he decided to transfer shares to the RCS, so that when the annual dividend was paid out to the shareholders that dividend would be paid in cash to the RCS in a more tax-efficient way. The shares themselves were originally held on trust for Vandervell as sole beneficiary by a bank as trustee together with Vandervell Trustee Co Ltd, a company which was wholly owned by Vandervell and used to manage his assets under this trust. Therefore, Vandervell himself had only an equitable interest in the shares.

The Inland Revenue argued in relation to s 53(1)(c) that Vandervell had failed to divest himself of his equitable interest through this arrangement because he had made a disposition of his equitable interest as a beneficiary of the trust and therefore required signed writing to make that disposition effective. Consequently, it was argued, the Vandervell settlement (and Mr Vandervell as beneficiary) retained the equitable interest in the shares, making him liable to taxation.

The House of Lords rejected the argument that Vandervell had not divested himself of his equitable interest in accordance with the requirements of s 53(1). It was held that where a beneficiary directs a trustee to move the entire absolute interest in property (that is, both

216   [1967] 2 AC 291, HL.

legal and equitable interests together) to new trusts, there does not need to be a separate disposition of the equitable interest under s 53(1)(c), and neither can the beneficiary be said to retain any of the beneficial interest. It was the court's unanimous view that s 53(1)(c) was not intended to cover dealings with the absolute title in property (that is, both legal and equitable together); rather, it was meant to cover dispositions of the equitable interest alone. Therefore, Vandervell won on the s 53(1)(c) point.

A number of other arguments were raised. It was suggested, in accordance with principles discussed elsewhere in this chapter, that perhaps Vandervell had done all that was required of him to divest himself of his rights in the shares. It was Lord Wilberforce who considered expressly whether or not the beneficiary had done all that he was required to do to divest himself of his equitable interest under *Re Rose*,[217] but he held that this simply begged the question as to what exactly the beneficiary was required to do to rid himself of that interest. The transaction in *Vandervell* can be represented by the following diagram:

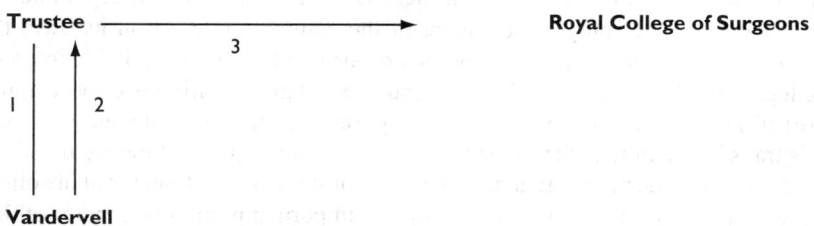

The three lines represent the three stages in the transaction. Line 1 represents the pre-existing Vandervell settlement on which the shares were held on trust for the benefit of Mr Vandervell. Line 2 represents the instruction given by Mr Vandervell to the Trustee that his equitable interest should be combined with the legal title, and that both should be transferred to the RCS. Line 3 represents the eventual transfer of legal and equitable title together. It is this transmission of absolute title in the property which is said to keep this arrangement outwith the scope of s 53(1)(c) because legal and equitable title passed together. The rationales given for finding that this transfer of legal and equitable title together does not constitute a 'disposition' of the equitable interest require some attention.[218] Lord Donovan took the view that if one had satisfied the formalities necessary to transfer the legal title, and if the two titles were to pass together, then there should be no further formality necessary (under s 53(1)(c)) to transfer the equitable interest.[219] Lord Wilberforce accepted that there was no need to have a separate formality for the transfer of the equitable interest if there was already clear compliance with the formalities for transferring the legal title (and if both titles were then to pass together). He argued for this state of affairs by reference to *Re Rose* (considered earlier in this chapter) by saying that because Mr Vandervell had done everything necessary for him to do to transfer legal and equitable title to the Royal College of Surgeons then

---

217 [1952] Ch 499.
218 Their Lordships focused primarily on the effect of resulting trusts in this context, but Lords Donovan and Wilberforce lavished some attention on the proper analysis of s 53(1)(c).
219 [1967] 2 AC 291, 317–8: (that is, 'In such a case I see no room for the operation of s 53(1)(c)').

the equitable interest should be considered to have passed automatically to the College.[220] Lord Wilberforce considered that the purpose of s 53(1)(c) was *merely to prove* who held the equitable interest; whereas Viscount Simonds in *Grey v IRC* seemed to consider that compliance with s 53(1)(c) in itself was required effectively *to carry out* the disposition of that equitable interest.

Now, it is noticeable that in *Grey v IRC* Viscount Simonds did not discuss any of these niceties. Indeed, it is possible that if Viscount Simonds had decided *Vandervell v IRC* then he would have found that because the equitable interest in the shares moved from Mr Vandervell to another person (the Royal College of Surgeons) then there had simply been a disposition of that equitable interest. It is a different, more modern House of Lords (many of whom had practised commercial law and who were therefore more accepting of these sorts of clever schemes) which is prepared to accept that Vandervell's scheme should avoid s 53(1)(c). So, what do we make of the analysis which *Grey v IRC* gives of s 53(1)(c) in the light of the decision in *Vandervell v IRC*? It is suggested, taking the two cases together, that *Grey* applies now only to cases in which there is no movement of the legal and equitable titles together, but rather only a movement of the equitable interest on its own: this is so because *Vandervell v IRC* is authority for the proposition that if the equitable interest passes with the legal title then s 53(1)(c) does not apply. So, signed writing is only required under s 53(1)(c) if the legal title is not passed to new trustees on new trusts and if the equitable interest is transferred alone; whereas signed writing is not required if the legal and equitable titles are passed together either to a different trust or by way of a transfer of absolute title.

However, Vandervell lost this case on another, important point. On transfer of the shares to the RCS, Vandervell was concerned that the Vandervell settlement be able to recover the shares once the dividend pay-out had benefited the RCS. Therefore, the transfer to the RCS was made subject to an option that the shares could be repurchased for £5,000. The problem was that the documentation did not make clear who would be entitled to exercise the option to repurchase the shares. The option constituted an equitable interest in the shares, but it was not made clear who was to be the owner of the equitable interest (given that the Vandervell Trustee Ltd was intended only to hold the option as a fiduciary): that gap in the ownership of the shares constituted by the option was the issue before the court. The House of Lords held that because there was no equitable owner specified over the option, that option must be treated as being held on resulting trust for the person who had it originally: in short, it was held on resulting trust for Mr Vandervell under the terms of the original Vandervell settlement. Therefore, because Vandervell had failed to divest himself of the whole of his equitable interest in the shares, the Vandervell settlement was held liable for tax in connection with them. This issue is considered in more detail in Chapter 11.

It had been unclear whether or not an option could have been held on resulting trust. The House of Lords was split on whether an option could be held on trusts which Vandervell would declare from time to time or that the option was held on trusts to be decided at a later date. It was held instead that where the legal owner vests the legal estate in a trustee before specifying the trusts, the trustee holds the property on resulting trust for the settlor until the trusts are declared – any declaration of those trusts will result in a disposition of that equitable interest under s 53(1)(c).

220 [1967] 2 AC 291, 330.

5.7.4 Declaration of a new trust by trustees or third party with dispositive powers

The *Vandervell* litigation had only just begun. The Inland Revenue intensified its efforts in the wake of a decision of the House of Lords in *Vandervell v White*[221] concerning the tax aspects of the transaction. As a result of that case, the issue arose as to treatment of the shares once the option to repurchase them had been exercised. This problem was confronted in *Vandervell (No 2)*,[222] a notoriously difficult case. At first instance, Megarry J delivered a seminal judgment on the operation of resulting trusts, which is considered in detail in Chapter 11. The issue was appealed to the Court of Appeal, where Lord Denning embarked on a remarkable intellectual odyssey to save the Vandervell estate from further exposure to taxation.[223]

The Inland Revenue was claiming that the executors of Vandervell's estate were liable to it for the beneficial interest in the shares when the Vandervell settlement repurchased under the option which had been held over in *Vandervell v IRC*.[224] Therefore, the executors had to bring an action against the trustees of the trusts to pay off the Inland Revenue. The trustees maintained that Vandervell did not own any rights in the shares after the transfer to the RCS, so that the children could benefit because no provision had been made for them in the will.

The Inland Revenue had pulled out of the litigation at the Court of Appeal stage, leaving a stepmother (claiming for the property to return to the Vandervell estate, in the person of the executors) trying to prevent the shares passing to the benefit of Vandervell's children by his first marriage who would take the property under the children settlement. (See, it's just like a soap opera: stepmother fighting with the stepchildren over the dead man's estate.)

The majority of the Court of Appeal held that (1) new trusts over the shares had been declared, and (2) even if they had not been declared, the executors would have been estopped from asserting their interest in the shares. This appears from the decision of Lord Denning. The root of the decision is that the option rights disappear once the option is exercised, leaving a question as to who should get the proprietary rights in the shares.

The two points need some careful examination. The declaration of the new trusts over the shares was by the trustees under the fiduciary capability identified by Lord Upjohn in *Vandervell v IRC*,[225] according to Stephenson LJ. In other words, because the option rights disappear, it is possible for the trustees to decide to whom the shares should pass beneficially. Clearly, this extraordinary proposition conflicts with the decision in *Re Brooks' ST*,[226] under which it was said that the trustee cannot declare entirely new trusts over the property – a trustee can only enforce the terms of the trust.

As to the second limb of the decision (that the trustees would have been estopped from refusing to pass the shares to the children settlement), it is unclear how the estoppel arises

---

221 [1970] 3 WLR 452.
222 [1974] Ch 269.
223 By the time of this appeal, Vandervell had died and the litigation was between Vandervell's children and their stepmother, whereby the children were seeking to argue that the shares had passed into a settlement created for their benefit whereas their stepmother was seeking to show that the shares returned to the Vandervell settlement, thus to Vandervell's estate and so to her personally as Vandervell's next of kin.
224 [1967] 2 AC 291.
225 *Ibid*.
226 [1939] 1 Ch 993.

here. The authority which is invoked for this estoppel is *Hughes v Metropolitan Railway*.[227] It is important to note, however, that *Hughes* is a case dealing with promissory estoppel which does not cater specifically for the presence or absence of rights in property. The clear impression is that Lord Denning was eager to find a 'just' solution to the practical problems of ending the Vandervell litigation once and for all, and allocating the deceased's property between the family members.

The following diagram indicates Lord Denning's analysis of the transaction and the movements in title in the various items of property:

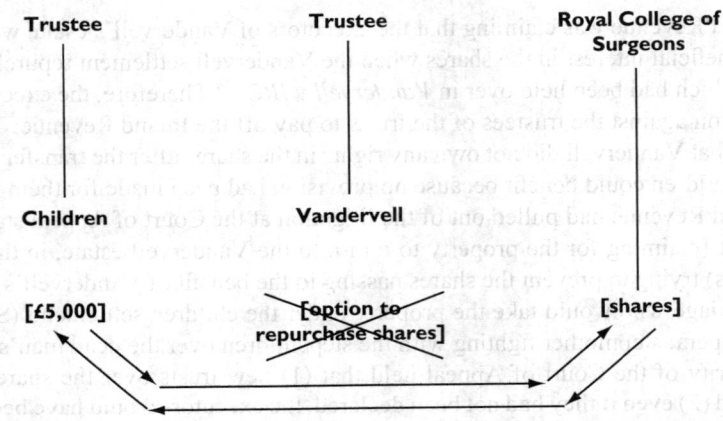

This transaction seems more complicated. The vertical lines show the pre-existing equitable ownership of each item of property. The RCS are equitable owners of the shares; the Vandervell settlement retains the equitable title in the option to repurchase the shares (remembering that the option is itself property); and the children settlement has the £5,000 in cash which is needed to exercise the option.

In Lord Denning's analysis, the option simply ceases to exist once it is exercised (which is why the diagram shows the option being crossed out). Therefore, Lord Denning finds that the question as to where the equitable title in the option rests is a matter for debate once the option rights have disappeared. Consequently, Lord Denning held that the children settlement must be deemed to acquire the equitable interest immediately on the basis that it is the children settlement which provides the money to exercise the option. Consequently, the bottom lines of the diagram show the money moving from the children settlement to the RCS, and the shares moving directly to the children settlement. Therefore, says Lord Denning, no property passes through the Vandervell settlement and there is no tax liability attaching to that settlement.

There is only one flaw with this theory: it is completely contrary to principle.[228] The better analysis, it is suggested, must operate on the basis of the diagram below:

227   (1877) 2 App Cas 439.
228   Stephenson LJ clearly had doubts about this approach: a criminal law specialist, he suggested in his judgment that he was being required to walk 'a dark and unfamiliar path' in deciding this case.

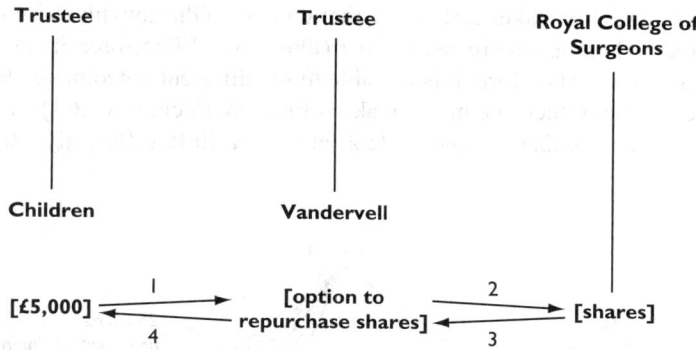

On the basis of this diagram we see a far more watertight analysis of the various transactions. Line 1 represents the transfer of the £5,000 from the children settlement. The proper analysis must be – because the money is being used to exercise the option, and because that option can only be exercised by the Vandervell settlement as equitable owner of the option – that £5,000 is transferred from one settlement to the other by way of gift, loan or contract. Whatever the legal analysis of the transfer of that £5,000, that is a legal relationship between the trustees of those two trusts only, which cannot bind the RCS because the RCS has never been made a party to it. The RCS has a subsisting legal relationship only with the Vandervell settlement by reference to the option to repurchase the shares – a contract between those two.

Therefore, on the exercise of the option, proprietary rights in the shares must be transferred to the Vandervell settlement, or else the RCS would be in breach of its contract to retransfer the shares to the Vandervell settlement on payment of £5,000. The rights represented by the option do not disappear. That option is itself property (in the form of a chose in action). Rather, the transfer of that piece of property leads necessarily to the acquisition by the Vandervell settlement of rights in other property (the shares themselves), as represented by line 2 (exercise of the option) and line 3 (transfer of the shares). It is then line 4 that represents the claim the children settlement may have against the Vandervell settlement, based on contract (or possibly some principle of estoppel or constructive trust) to transfer the shares to the children settlement. However, for tax purposes, it must be the case that the property is transferred via the Vandervell settlement, thus making the Vandervell settlement liable for tax.

5.7.5 Were *Grey v IRC* and *Vandervell v IRC* decided correctly?

The litigation on s 53(1)(c) can appear to be complicated, even though it revolves around a very simple idea concerning the need for writing in making dispositions of equitable interests.[229]

The analysis in this short section is derived from an article by Green.[230] It revolves around a close reading of the facts in the *Grey* and *Vandervell* decisions. Remember our realpolitik

---

229 If you think you have heard enough and you are worried about becoming horribly confused, you might decide to skip this next section. Those of you who are brave enough might persevere though. No pain, no gain.
230 (1984) 47 MLR 388.

thesis that some judges have taken restrictive, literal views of the law (like Viscount Simonds in *Grey*) whereas others are more permissive (like Lord Wilberforce in *Vandervell* and *Chinn v Collins* below). Therefore, it is possible to see different outcomes as being a result of comparative judicial reluctance not to make it too easy to elude s 53(1)(c). Building on that idea, Green suggests that we should look at *Grey* a little differently. Remember the diagram:

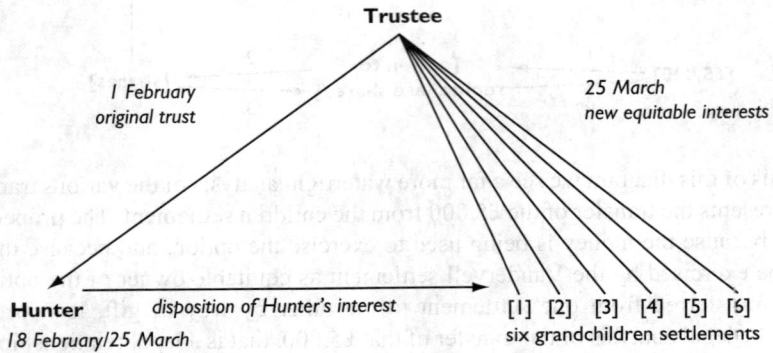

The complaint is that while the direction was given by Hunter to the Trustee to move the equitable interest, it would have been open to the court to find that there had in fact been a resettlement of the shares on new trusts, and not simply a disposition of the equitable interest. Possibly, the court was caught in deciding that the Trustee was the same human being, rather than saying the Trustee was acting in different capacities as trustee of seven different trusts. Therefore, perhaps Hunter should be deemed to have directed the trustee of his trust to transfer both legal and equitable title in the shares to the trustees of six different trusts. On that basis, the diagram would look as follows:

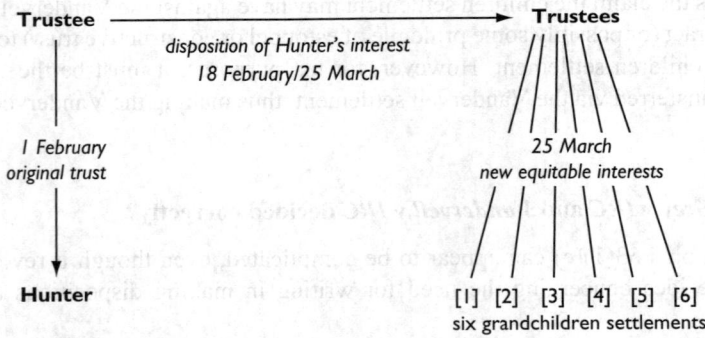

That is, the legal title and the equitable interest passing together from the Hunter trust to the six 1949 grandchildren settlements. Therefore, there ought to be no need for signed writing in line with the decision in *Vandervell v IRC*.

Similarly, it is not clear how the legal title for the shares in *Vandervell* is held at the outset. It is clear that Vandervell retained a part of the equitable interest in the shares, and therefore the whole of the equitable interest was not transferred with the legal title such that the RCS could have claimed to have had absolute title in the property. Therefore, the question arises: has Hunter made a partial disposition of his equitable interest, without transferring the whole in conjunction with the legal interest? Indeed, the bank and the Vandervell Trustee Co Ltd retain the legal title over that option as trustees for Vandervell – therefore, the whole of the legal interest had not transferred out of the Vandervell settlement.

The further problem is the identity of the trustee for Mr Vandervell. It would appear that the shares were held on trust for Vandervell by the bank under a bare trust. The right to exercise the option to buy back the shares was vested in Vandervell Trustee Co Ltd (VTCo, a company over which Vandervell had control which operated as a trustee for him). The issue with the option was that it was held by VTCo on trust but the identity of the beneficiary was not made clear – therefore, it was held that it was to be held on *resulting* trust for Vandervell. However, if the bank held as trustee of the shares at the outset, for VTCo to act as trustee of the option must mean that the property was not in fact held on resulting trust for Vandervell, because that would have required the bank to be the trustee of the option. Rather, if the option was held by VTCo, a trustee of a different trust, for Vandervell, then the option was held on a different express trust for Vandervell and not on resulting trust at all. Therefore, the analysis from *Grey v IRC* would seem applicable here because the bank remains the ultimate trustee in the sense of a custodian, in some capacity, of the shares even when they are transferred beneficially to the Royal College of Surgeons, with the result that it could only have been the equitable interest which moved in that case. This was not the analysis used by the House of Lords, but it is a possible analysis on the facts nevertheless.

Consequently, the Vandervell diagram might be as follows:

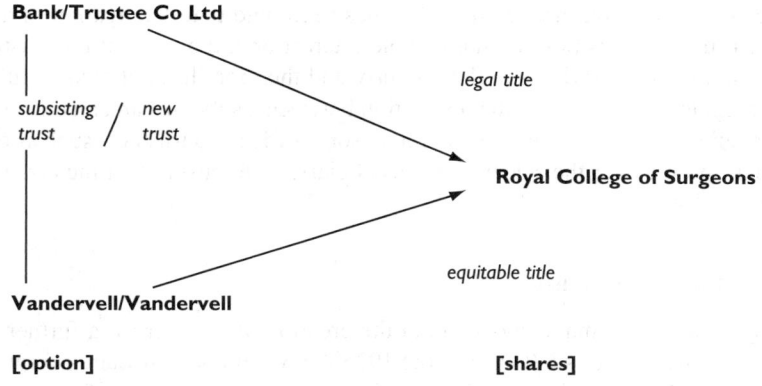

The following sections consider a number of means by which s 53(1)(c) is purportedly avoided.

5.7.6 Sub-trusts

There are a number of subtle shades of distinction between disposing of an equitable interest and creating a sub-trust. A sub-trust would include a situation in which the beneficiary under a trust agrees to hold a part of her own equitable interest on trust for another person. A little like a tenant holding rights on a subtenancy for a sub-tenant, the beneficiary under a trust can hold her equitable interest on sub-trust for a sub-beneficiary. This should be counterposed with an assignment of a tenancy in which the assignee would become the new tenant in place of the assignor; thus, a beneficiary who creates a sub-trust may be deemed to have made a disposition of all of her rights under the trust if the sub-beneficiary receives all of her equitable interest.

Therefore, the important element to a sub-trust is that the beneficiary retains some equitable right in the property held for her benefit under the trust, in contradistinction to the situation in which that beneficiary transfers absolutely all of her equitable rights in the trust property to the sub-beneficiary. By 'retaining some right' in the property is meant, for example, retaining some discretion as sub-trustee as to the amount of income to be paid to the sub-beneficiary from time to time. It is important that the beneficiary as sub-trustee retain some office to repel the argument that she has disposed of *all* of her rights in the property.

The situation in which the beneficiary transfers all of her rights to the sub-beneficiary is properly analysed as an assignment of the property. Such an outright assignment of all of the beneficiary's equitable rights would constitute a disposition of the trust property. The metaphor used in *Re Lashmar*[231] is that we can look through a bare trustee so that the beneficiary who is to act as 'sub-trustee' effectively drops out of the picture, having disposed of her equitable interest in favour of a new beneficiary so that the trustee is now effectively holding the property for the sub-beneficiary directly.

The question for the legal advisor which arises with reference to s 53(1)(c) of the Law of Property Act 1925 is whether the sub-trust constitutes a disposition of the entire equitable interest, or whether the beneficiary retains some rights so that it does not constitute such a disposition. As Lindley LJ put it, the question is whether or not 'the trustee had duties to perform' in her capacity as trustee, or whether she had no duties to perform such that the sub-beneficiary could 'look through her'.[232] It has been held that the creation of a sub-trust will not constitute a disposition of an equitable interest on the basis that the trustee retains some duties *qua* trustees or rights in the property and therefore has not made a full disposition of those rights.[233] To preserve the distinction between a sub-trust and an outright assignment, the beneficiary would be required to retain some office as a trustee – such as exercising a discretionary power over the selection of beneficiaries – to ensure that the arrangement is classified as a sub-trust.

5.7.7 Declaration of new trust

Following from the point made above about the creation of a sub-trust, a further means of avoiding the requirement of s 53(1)(c) of the 1925 Act would be to declare a new trust over the trust property. The question which arises is whether a declaration of a new trust by a beneficiary under an existing trust over that equitable interest would constitute a disposition of an equitable interest within s 53(1).

It should be recalled that a declaration of a new trust over property in which the settlor holds absolute title is not a disposition of an equitable interest; rather, that is the time at

---

231 (1891) 1 Ch D 258.
232 [1891] 1 Ch 258, 268, *per* Lindley LJ.
233 *Ibid; Grainge v Wilberforce* (1889) 5 TLR 436; *DHN Food Distributors Ltd v Tower Hamlets LBC* [1976] 1 WLR 852, [1976] 3 All ER 462.

which the settlor *creates* the equitable interest.[234] If the beneficiary under an existing trust terminates that trust (under *Saunders v Vautier*)[235] and declares new trusts over the property previously held on trust, that will not constitute a disposition of the equitable interest (as argued unsuccessfully in *Cohen & Moore v IRC*)[236] – a point considered in greater detail below.

Similarly, a variation of a trust under the Variation of Trusts Act 1958[237] will not constitute a disposition of an equitable interest within s 53(1)(c) requiring signed writing.[238] In *Re Vandervell (No 2)*,[239] Lord Denning held that the trustees were entitled to declare new trusts over the property held by the RCS. However, following the decision in *Re Brooks' ST*[240] it is said that it is impossible for trustees to declare new trusts over the trust property, in contradistinction to a formal variation under the 1958 Act, as considered by Megarry J in *Re Holt's Settlement*.[241]

It is only if the beneficiary directs the trustee that the property then held on trust is to be held on the same trusts but for a different person as beneficiary that there is a disposition of an equitable interest under s 53(1)(c).[242] In this context, it could be said that the analysis set out in *Grey v IRC*[243] is the one which future litigants will necessarily seek to avoid if they are trying to escape the need for signed writing, or if they are seeking to argue that an interest has passed when no signed writing was effected.

Assignment of equitable interests

It is clear that an equitable interest is capable of assignment. Where such an outright assignment takes place under which the equitable interest is still held on the terms of the same trusts, there will have been a disposition of that interest.[244] It is only if the assignment has been onto new trusts that no disposition will have taken place either because equitable title will have passed with the legal title,[245] or because there has been a formal variation of the trusts.[246] These points are considered further below.

Direction to trustees to hold on trust for another

A direction to bare trustees to transfer the beneficial interest in assets to other trustees of a separate settlement to be held on the trusts of that settlement constitutes a disposition of an equitable interest requiring s 53(1)(c) writing.[247] Alternatively, the beneficiary, if absolutely

234 *Westdeutsche Landesbank Girozentrale v Islington LBC* [1996] AC 669; *Grey v IRC* [1960] AC 1.
235 (1841) 4 Beav 115.
236 [1933] All ER 950.
237 Considered below in Chapter 10.
238 In *Re Holt's Settlement* [1969] 1 Ch 100.
239 [1974] Ch 269.
240 [1939] 1 Ch 993.
241 [1969] 1 Ch 100.
242 *Grey v IRC* [1960] AC 1.
243 *Ibid.*
244 *Ibid.*
245 *Vandervell v IRC* [1967] 2 AC 291.
246 *Re Holt's Settlement* [1969] 1 Ch 100.
247 *Grey v IRC* [1960] AC 1.

entitled, could exercise her rights under *Saunders v Vautier*[248] to direct the trustee to transfer both the legal and equitable title in the trust fund to new trusts.[249] This second approach would not constitute a disposition of an equitable interest under s 53(1)(c) because both legal and equitable title pass together. Remember, the principle in *Saunders v Vautier* permits all of the beneficiaries (provided they are *sui juris* and acting together) to direct the trustees how to deal with the trust property: including directing a termination of the trust. No case has yet held such a direction to be a disposition of such an equitable interest. However, Green argues that a declaration effected specifically over a trust of an equitable interest must amount to a disposition of that equitable interest (a proposition taken from the speech of Viscount Simonds in *Grey v IRC*).[250]

As an alternative means of avoiding the result in *Grey v IRC*,[251] Hunter would have been better advised to create a new trust and thus avoid *ad valorem* stamp duty. The appropriate steps would be orally to declare himself trustee of the shares alongside two existing trustees and then to retire from the position of trustee, leaving two others behind such that there would be no need to transfer the legal estate to a new trustee. The two remaining trustees would then prepare a document confirming that they held on the trusts originally declared by Hunter.

Automatic transfer under variation of trust

The question of varying trusts is considered in detail in Chapter 10. Under the terms of the Variation of Trusts Act 1958 and in line with the common law set out in *Chapman v Chapman*,[252] it is possible for the trustees and the beneficiaries to apply to the court for an order varying the terms of the trust. A number of questions arise in general terms: the main question is typically whether the variation canvassed in front of the court is merely a variation of the trust or rather a wholesale resettlement of the trust fund on new trusts. Deciding between those two options is a matter of degree. A further issue, which is more pertinent to the current discussion, is whether the variation of trust constitutes a disposition of an equitable interest by any beneficiary.

An example of this latter issue arose in *Re Holt's Settlement*.[253] An originating summons was served under the Variation of Trusts Act 1958, by which the settlor's daughter sought to surrender her life interest in one-half of the income of the trust so that she could both reduce her own liability to surtax and increase the entitlement of her children to the life interest. One question which arose was whether the mother's surrender of her life interest to her children constituted a disposition which required signed writing within s 53(1)(c) of the 1925 Act.

The doctrine in *Re Hambleden's Will Trusts*[254] stated that an order of the court permitting a variation automatically varied the trust without the need for any further action on the part of the trustees. This decision ostensibly contravened that in *Re Joseph's Will Trusts*,[255] in

---

248 (1841) 4 Beav 115.
249 *Vandervell v IRC* [1967] 2 AC 291.
250 [1960] AC 1.
251 *Ibid*.
252 [1954] 2 WLR 723.
253 [1969] 1 Ch 100.
254 [1960] 1 WLR 82.
255 [1959] 1 WLR 1019.

which case Vaisey J had held that it was necessary for the judge to include words in the court order permitting the trustees to alter the trusts, rather than acknowledging that the court order automatically had that effect. While this may appear to be a rule of little wider relevance, it was held in *Re Holt's Settlement* that the fact that the court order permitted the trustees to treat the trust as having been altered automatically meant that there was no need for the trustees to perform any formality to secure that variation. Consequently, the automatic effect of the order meant that the equitable interest passed to the disponor's children without the need for signed writing.

Therefore, a further means of eluding s 53(1)(c) is to acquire an order of the court permitting a variation of the trust in a manner which transfers the equitable interest from the beneficiary to another person. That order takes effect automatically without the need for signed writing.

5.7.8 Contractual transfer of equitable interest

The celebrated doctrine in *Walsh v Lonsdale*[256] set out an important facet of the interrelationship between common law and equity. That case concerned an agreement to grant a seven-year lease with rent payable in advance at the beginning of each year. No formal lease was ever created. However, the tenant went into occupation and began to pay rent quarterly in arrears, as though a tenant under a legal periodic tenancy. The issue arose whether the court should enforce the requirement for rent to be paid each year in advance on the basis that the agreement for a lease constituted an equitable lease,[257] or whether the court should give effect to the rent agreement established by the periodic tenancy. The court held that in situations in which an equitable and a common law analysis conflict, equity prevails, and therefore the contract for rent in advance would be effected in equity.

The further point raised by the doctrine of equitable leases is that where there is a contract to perform an action, the contracting party receiving the benefit of that action receives an equitable right of specific performance which entitles her to force the other party to carry out its contractual obligations. This rule operates on the basis of the equitable maxim 'equity looks upon as done that which ought to have been done'. Therefore, it is said that the contracting party acquires an equitable interest in any property which is to be transferred to her in accordance with the terms of the contract.

In terms of s 53(1)(c), this offers very exciting possibilities. The doctrine in *Walsh v Lonsdale* provides that an equitable interest in property passes automatically on the creation of a contract to transfer that property. In respect of dispositions of an equitable interest, this opens up the possibility that the equitable interest could be passed from one person to another without the need for signed writing. Thus, in *Oughtred v IRC*,[258] a mother and son sought to transfer the equitable interest in two parcels of shares which were held on trust for each of them. However, to have executed such a transfer in writing would have meant that the mother and son would have been subject to stamp duty. Therefore, they entered into an oral contract under which they sought to argue the equitable interest had passed before signed writing being effected. The judgment is slightly equivocal, particularly the speech of Lord

---

256 (1882) 21 Ch D 9.
257 *Parker v Taswell* (1858) 27 LJ Ch 812.
258 [1960] AC 206.

Jenkins, in that he finds there has been no case which prevents a subsequent written transfer being subject to stamp duty despite the purported previous transfer of the equitable interest.[259]

The more straightforward approach is summarised in the old case of *Lysaght v Edwards*.[260] Lord Jessel MR held expressly that contracts for the sale of land pass the equitable interest in that land before any signed writing which is effected subsequently.[261] Later, in *Chinn v Collins*,[262] Lord Wilberforce expressly approved the suggestion that the formation of a binding contract to transfer property automatically passed equitable interest in any property which was the subject matter of that contract without the need for any formality (other than any formality necessary to form a valid contract in those circumstances).[263] It is arguable that both of these judicial comments were *obiter dicta*. However, the modern authorities are clear that a contract to make a disposition is not a disposition in itself.[264] So in *Neville v Wilson*,[265] two shareholders had entered into a verbal agreement to the effect that the company should be wound up and the company's property divided between them in proportion to their shareholdings. It was held that by virtue of the binding agreement between the parties, the rights attaching to each of the parties' shares were held on constructive trust one for the other. There was therefore no need for signed writing to transfer these equitable interests.

5.7.9 Dispositions effected by trusts implied by law

As mentioned earlier, there is an exception from the general need for formalities built into s 53 by s 53(2) of the Law of Property Act 1925, in relation to trusts which are imposed by the court by operation of law rather than being purportedly express trusts. These issues are considered below in Part 4. In short, there are no formalities necessary where the court imposes such a trust.

It was held in *Chinn v Collins*,[266] in which the argument was put on the basis of constructive trust, that where a contract is made (that is, in circumstances in which an equitable interest is used to discharge a debt), a bare constructive trust will arise in favour of the party holding the chose in action. Similarly to the principle in *Walsh v Lonsdale*,[267] it is assumed by equity that everything which ought to have been done has been done. Therefore, where there is a contract to transfer an equitable interest in property, equity considers that the contract has succeeded in transferring equitable title in the property before any formal disposition of that interest is necessary.[268] Until the formal transfer of the interest is effected, the party obliged to transfer it under the terms of the contract is deemed to be constructive trustee of that property for the purchaser.

259 Followed in *Parinv (Hatfield) Ltd v IRC* [1998] STC 305.
260 (1876) 2 Ch D 499.
261 *Ibid*, 507.
262 [1981] AC 533.
263 *Ibid*, 548.
264 *Neville v Wilson* [1997] Ch 144.
265 [1997] Ch 144. An alternative view was taken in *United Bank of Kuwait plc v Sahib* [1997] Ch 107, 129; [1995] 2 All ER 973, 992, where Chadwick J held that he could not see that *Oughtred v IRC* created such a principle.
266 [1981] AC 533, 548.
267 (1882) 21 Ch D 9.
268 *Chinn v Collins* [1981] AC 533, 548, *per* Lord Wilberforce.

Therefore, the development which *Chinn v Collins* established was that the equitable interest transferred automatically on the basis of constructive trust, rather than by means of the somewhat convoluted rule in *Walsh v Lonsdale*. The constructive trust would arise on the basis that it would be unconscionable for the party obliged to transfer title under the contract to refuse to observe that contractual obligation.[269] The one advantage to this approach is that the doctrine in *Walsh v Lonsdale* depends on the availability of specific performance, whereas the constructive trust arises whether or not specific performance would be available. Therefore, in relation to contracts in which specific performance would not be available, the constructive trust device will permit the proprietary rights to be transferred automatically. The further advantage of the constructive trust is that it does not require any formality in its creation.[270]

The case of *Neville v Wilson*[271] approved the transfer of an equitable interest automatically on the creation of a contract between the transferor and transferee, on the basis that a constructive trust arose on creation of the contract which compelled the transfer of that equitable interest without the need for further formality. In that case, there was an agreement for the winding up of a company, in line with insolvency legislation. The issue which arose was whether the creation of the agreement meant that the rights attaching to the shares were held by each of the parties on constructive trust for the other party, or whether the liquidation of the company prevented such a transfer taking place. The Court of Appeal held that the creation of the agreement did cause the equitable interest in the shares to pass automatically on constructive trust.[272] Nourse LJ held that this was in line with the speech of Lord Radcliffe in the House of Lords in *Oughtred v IRC*[273] and also with Upjohn J in the same case, and also with *London and South Western Railway Co v Gomm*.[274] One point which is not considered in full is the transmutation in this doctrine from the rule in *Walsh v Lonsdale*[275] based on specific performance to a rule based on constructive trust thinking – that much is accepted without comment. It might be that the development of this area of law into concepts based on constructive trust simply marks a new trend in judicial thinking which values the apparent certainties of the law of trusts over the vague principles of equity as personified by 19th century cases like *Walsh v Lonsdale*.

5.7.10 Summary: analysing dispositions of equitable interests

Given the complexity of this subject, it is perhaps helpful to summarise the various possible analyses set out above. It is worth remembering that there remains an issue as to whether or not, on their own facts, *Grey v IRC*[276] and *Vandervell v IRC*[277] are correct.[278] The following nine points delineate the possible analyses:

269 Cf *Westdeutsche Landesbank Girozentrale v Islington LBC* [1996] AC 669.
270 Law of Property Act 1925, s 53(2): a proposition also accepted by Megarry J in *Re Holt's Settlement* [1969] 1 Ch 100.
271 [1997] Ch 144.
272 This approach was accepted in *Sahota v Bains* [2006] EWHC 131 (Ch).
273 [1960] AC 206.
274 (1882) 20 Ch D 562, *per* Lord Jessel MR.
275 (1882) 21 Ch D 9.
276 [1960] AC 1.
277 [1967] 2 AC 291.
278 Green (1984) 47 MLR 388; Harris (1975) 38 MLR 557.

(a) The core of the problem is the need for a disposition of equitable interest to be effected in signed writing.[279]

(b) Where there is a clear intention on the part of the beneficiary that her equitable interest is to be passed to another beneficiary, this requires signed writing under s 53(1)(c) to be effective.[280]

(c) The most straightforward means of avoiding s 53(1)(c) would be as follows. The whole interest in the property (comprising both legal and equitable title) must be transferred to new trustees in favour of new beneficiaries as in *Vandervell v IRC*.[281] Where this is achieved, it will not constitute a disposition of the equitable interest within s 53(1)(c). One explanation of this reasoning might be that the transfer of legal and equitable title together is analogous to the situation in which the absolutely-entitled beneficiary invokes her *Saunders v Vautier*[282] rights and directs the trustee to declare new trusts over the entire interest.

(d) Alternatively, where the beneficiary under an existing trust declares a sub-trust over that existing equitable interest, it is unclear under *Vandervell v IRC* whether a sub-trust can be created without the need for signed writing under s 53(1)(c). The analyses appear to find either that there has been the creation of a sub-trust in which the beneficiary retains some office as trustee and therefore has not disposed of the entire beneficial interest; or there has been a sub-trust created under which the beneficiary has passed on her entire equitable interest (and then drops out of the picture as in *Re Lashmar*)[283] requiring signed writing under s 53(1)(c).

(e) It has been accepted that the trustees might make a declaration of trust. Under the principle in *Re Brooks' ST*,[284] it was held that the trustees could not declare new trusts over the property themselves. However, in *Re Vandervell (No 2)*,[285] it was held that the trustees had the power to declare the trusts where there had been an express transfer of the property between trusts.

(f) Otherwise, in *Re Vandervell (No 2)*, there might have been a perfect gift made over the income derived from the trust property. Consequently, there would not be disposition of any equitable interest, unless some kind of proprietary estoppel can be proved as in *Re Basham*.[286] However, the estoppel invoked in *Vandervell (No 2)* is very dubious, invoking *Hughes v Metropolitan Railway*[287] (a case on promissory estoppel) as authority.

(g) More directly, the beneficiary could use her *Saunders v Vautier* rights in calling for the trust property (where *sui juris*, and absolutely entitled), or could direct the trustees to pay the income from the trust fund to another beneficiary.

(h) A variation of trusts under the Variation of Trusts Act 1958 will effect a disposition of an equitable interest without the need for signed writing.[288]

---

279 Law of Property Act 1925, s 53(1)(c).
280 *Grey v IRC* [1960] AC 1.
281 [1967] 2 AC 291.
282 (1841) 4 Beav 115.
283 (1891) 1 Ch 258.
284 [1939] 1 Ch 993.
285 [1974] Ch 269.
286 [1986] 1 WLR 1498.
287 (1877) 2 App Cas 439.
288 In *Re Holt's Settlement* [1969] 1 Ch 100.

(i)   In line with *Walsh v Lonsdale*,[289] the minority opinion in *Oughtred v IRC*[290] suggested that where there is a valid contract to sell an equitable interest, the vendor holds the property as constructive trustee of his equitable interest for the buyer, and therefore there is a disposition of the equitable interest without the need to comply with s 53(1)(c). Similarly, in *Chinn v Collins*,[291] Lord Wilberforce held that the equitable interest is transferred directly after the contract is created on the basis of constructive trust (as applied in *Neville v Wilson*).[292]

---

289   (1882) 21 Ch D 9.
290   [1960] AC 206.
291   [1981] AC 533.
292   [1997] Ch 144.

Chapter 6

Secret trusts

OVERVIEW

A secret trust arises when a testator wishes to benefit some person who cannot be named in the will; therefore the testator will ask a trusted confidant to agree to an arrangement whereby the confidant will receive a gift under the will ostensibly for her own benefit but which is in fact to be held on trust by that person for a third person who cannot be named in the will. Equity will enforce this arrangement as a secret trust so that the confidant cannot claim to be beneficially entitled to the property left in the will. The secret trust operates in spite of the provisions of the Wills Act 1837 and therefore illustrates equity's determination to prevent statute being used as an engine of fraud.[1]

Secret trusts fall into two main categories: fully secret trusts and half-secret trusts. Fully secret trusts arise in circumstances where neither the existence nor the terms of the trust are disclosed in the terms of the will. Oral evidence of the agreement between the testator and trustee is generally satisfactory. The settlor must have intended to create such a trust. That intention must have been communicated to the intended trustee. The trustee must have accepted the office and the terms of the trust explicitly or impliedly.[2]

For a valid half-secret trust, the settlor must intend to create such a trust. Further, the existence and terms of the trust must be communicated to the intended trustee before the execution of the will. The intended trustee must then accept the office of trustee and acquiesce to the terms of the trust.[3]

6.1 INTRODUCTION

The area of secret trusts raises interesting questions about the operation of equity in the law of trusts to achieve justice between the parties to litigation outside the strictures of legislation and common law.[4] In parallel with that, secret trusts raise a number of questions about the interaction between express trusts and the trusts implied by law which are considered in Part 4 of this book.

The significance of the secret trust for the purposes of this book more generally is that the secret trust demonstrates the willingness of equity to contravene straightforward statutory principles to achieve the result which the court considers to be in line with good conscience. A secret trust is a clandestine arrangement between a testator and a trustee which operates outside the terms of the will. As will emerge from the following discussion, equity enforces the settlor's true intentions to benefit a third party even though this is contrary to the provisions of the Wills Act 1837, which was itself based on long-standing principles of the old Statute of Frauds. A

---

1 Cf *Rochefoucauld v Boustead* [1897] 1 Ch 196.

2 *Ottaway v Norman* [1972] 2 WLR 50.

3 *Blackwell v Blackwell* [1929] AC 318.

4 It is also a good, old-fashioned equitable topic with lots of subtle distinctions made in the case law which are meat and drink for examiners.

worked example of a secret trust is given below at para 6.1.3. For present purposes it is necessary only to appreciate that a secret trust arises when a testator wishes, for whatever reason, to transfer the benefit of property to a person without specifying that person as a legatee under her will; in consequence, a confidant is asked to act as trustee for this secret arrangement under which the confidant ostensibly receives a gift under the will which the confidant is then expected to hold on trust for that third person. In this circumstance equity will enforce a trust in favour of that intended beneficiary in spite of such a trust *prima facie* breaching the Wills Act.

Equity's primary concern in developing the doctrine of secret trusts was to prevent the trustee from committing a fraud and attempting to keep the property left to the trustee under this clandestine arrangement for herself. One conceptual difficulty which emerges from this doctrine is that of deciding how to categorise the secret trust when faced with the various possibilities of express trust, constructive trust and a one-off rule based on equitable principles of preventing fraud.

6.1.1 The statutory background

The key feature of the secret trust is that it operates 'dehors the will' (that is, beyond the terms of the will itself) and in contravention of the provisions of the Wills Act 1837. Section 9 of the 1837 Act provides as follows:

> No will shall be valid unless –
>
> (a) it is in writing and signed by the testator, or by some other person in his presence and by his direction; and
> (b) it appears that the testator intended by his signature to give effect to the will; and
> (c) the signature is made or acknowledged by the testator in the presence of two or more witnesses present at the same time; and
> (d) each witness either –
>> (i)   attests and signs the will; or
>> (ii) acknowledges his signature, in the presence of the testator (but not necessarily in the presence of any other witness), but no form of attestation shall be necessary.

These provisions clearly set out the means by which a will is to be created if it is to be valid on death. Their purpose is to prevent frauds being perpetrated by people who might otherwise claim that they were entitled to property held in the deceased's estate. As a result of the 1837 Act, only those people who are identified in a properly executed will as having rights against the testator's property shall be entitled to receive such property on the testator's death. In the event that no will is effected, or if the will is invalid, the Intestacy Rules allocate title to the next of kin (those rules being effected under the Administration of Estates Act 1925).

However, the ramifications of these provisions are broader than that. If the testator wishes to alter the terms of her will, any alteration or any new will must conform to the provisions of the Act or else it will not be valid. Similarly, if the testator wishes to create some arrangement outside the precise terms of the will, that arrangement will be similarly invalid if it does not comply with the terms of the will.[5] Therefore, a secret trust (being an arrangement for the

5 *Re Edwards* [1948] Ch 440.

organisation of title in property after the testator's death outside the terms of the will) will be strictly invalid under the terms of the Wills Act 1837.

Equity takes a different approach and holds that a secret trust will be valid in equity if it is properly created. The requirements for the proper creation of a secret trust are considered below. On this basis, it is suggested that it is best to consider that the secret trust is a doctrine which seeks to provide justice in circumstances in which a literal application of the Wills Act would permit unconscionable behaviour on the part of the person intended to act as trustee of the secret trust.

6.1.2 Distinguishing between types of secret trust

It is important to distinguish between the two primary forms of secret trust. The distinction is important because the case law attributes different rules to each form of secret trust in different situations.

Fully secret trust

The first kind is the 'fully secret trust' – that is, a trust which is not referred to at all in the terms of the will. In such a situation the testator will have communicated the terms of the arrangement to the intended secret trustee. The property intended to pass to the beneficiary of the arrangement will then be left to the secret trustee without any mention being made in the will as to the reason why the property is being left to that secret trustee. As will emerge from the discussion to follow, it is often very difficult to prove the existence of a fully secret trust, unless the testator had mentioned the detail of the arrangement to someone else.

Half-secret trust

The second kind of secret trust is the 'half-secret trust' – that is, a trust which is mentioned in some form in the will. Importantly, the *existence* of the trust but *not its terms* are disclosed in the will. If all of the terms of the secret trust were disclosed it would be a testamentary trust and not a secret trust at all. The manner in which the half-secret trust is disclosed in the terms of the will differs from case to case. It may be that the testator provides: 'I leave the sum of £1,000 to Freddie for purposes which he knows all about.' That expression may disclose a half-secret trust, or it may simply indicate that the testator is grateful to Freddie for some particular kindness which he had performed in the past. Alternatively, the expression 'I leave the sum of £1,000 to Freddie to carry out my particular wishes as set out in my letter to him of 15 December 1998' is more likely to indicate a half-secret trust. It may be that such an explicit mention of another document may bring into play the probate doctrine of incorporation by reference, which would require that that letter be construed as forming a part of the will.[6]

One further point should be noted on the distinction between a fully secret trust and a half-secret trust. Given that so much turns on the division made between the two, it is important to note that in many circumstances it will be difficult to know whether the trust is fully secret

6   *In the Goods of Smart* [1902] P 238; *Re Jones* [1942] Ch 238; as interpreted by *Re Edwards' WT* [1948] Ch 440.

or half-secret. In relation to the example cited above – that 'I leave the sum of £1,000 to Freddie for purposes which he knows all about' – it could be said that that trust is fully secret if no one appreciates the significance of Freddie's knowledge. If Freddie is able to explain away those words as being something trifling and sentimental rather than as disclosing a fiduciary obligation imposed on Freddie, then the trust could be said to be fully secret. It would only be if the surrounding circumstances or something said by the testator to another person put them on notice of the existence (but not the terms) of the trust that it could be said to be half-secret. Therefore, words used by the testator may be susceptible to more than one interpretation. When creating strict divisions between categories of secret trusts that should be borne in mind.

Secret trusts on intestacy

There is potentially a third class of secret trust altogether. It is possible that a secret trust may arise to circumvent the Intestacy Rules. In a situation where a dying person was encouraged not to make a will and thereby to leave property so that it passes on intestacy, the dying person might agree with the person who would take title in his property as next of kin under the Intestacy Rules not to make a will on the basis that the next of kin would give effect to the dying person's wishes by way of secret trust. In such a situation, if the next of kin had induced the dying person not to make a will in reliance on his promise to give effect to the dying person's wishes, that next of kin would be required to hold the property received on trust for the intended beneficiaries.[7] This doctrine similarly prevents the recipient of property from perpetrating a fraud.

6.1.3 An example of a secret trust

A 'secret trust' is almost as exciting as its name suggests. A testator creates a secret arrange-ment which ostensibly benefits person X but with the real intention of benefiting person Y. Typically, the testator will not leave the property directly for the benefit of person Y in the will because to do so would be embarrassing. Alternatively, sometimes people prefer to live their lives in as complicated a way as possible and so are more comfortable in creating complex arrangements beyond their wills. To create a secret trust, a testator must form an arrangement with some person who is intended to act as trustee for a beneficiary not named in the testator's will. The testator will leave the property ostensibly to the trustee in the will to form the impression that the trustee is intended to take the property beneficially. However, the testator's true intention will be that the trustee is intended to hold the property on trust for the real beneficiary after the testator's death.

Suppose the following situation:

> *Bingo has learnt that he has a terminal illness and therefore needs to organise his affairs before death. Unfortunately, his personal life is a little complicated. He is married with children and therefore wishes to leave the bulk of his estate to his family for their maintenance. However, he has also had another child, Chloe, by an adulterous*

---

7 *Sellack v Harris* (1708) 2 Eq Ca Ab 46.

relationship with his mistress, Lottie. Therefore, he also wishes to benefit his mistress and illegitimate child. However, Bingo does not want to cause his wife any further distress after his death, and he knows he cannot leave any money to Lottie expressly in his will without his wife finding out. To enable him both to benefit his mistress and child and to keep that relationship secret from his wife, he decides to leave a large amount of money in his will ostensibly to his best friend Freddie so that Freddie can pass that money on to Lottie after his death. Freddie agrees to the arrangement in full knowledge of all of its terms. Consequently, Bingo dies leaving a fund of £100,000 to Freddie in his will.

This is indeed a 'secret' trust because the arrangement is something known only to Bingo and to Freddie. Its purpose is to make a disposition to Lottie and Chloe without having to identify either of them in the terms of the will. The Wills Act 1837 and the general law of probate would require that, for Lottie to take an equitable interest in any of Bingo's estate, Lottie would have to be specified expressly as a legatee under the will. As considered above in para 6.1.1, under s 9 of the Wills Act 1837 'no will shall be valid unless – (a) it is in writing and signed by the testator' and unless the signature is formally witnessed by two or more witnesses. Any other purported disposition after death which is not made in compliance with the 1837 Act is invalid under the law of probate. The purpose of a secret trust, however, is to prevent Freddie from asserting title to the fund of £100,000 which was never any of the parties' intentions that he should take beneficially. Therefore, the secret trust operates as an exception to the strict provisions of the Wills Act.

There are other problems with the manner in which the secret trust is created. It may be that some passing reference is made to the arrangement in the will. Suppose the following facts:

In 1998 Bingo made a will which was witnessed by Freddie. Bingo explained that he wanted Freddie to hold any property left to him on secret trust for Lottie, as before. Under the terms of the will Freddie was bequeathed a sum of £100,000 to use that sum 'in accordance with my desires which he knows all about'.

This arrangement would be a 'half-secret trust' on the basis that the existence of the trust is disclosed (or hinted at) in the will but the precise terms of the trust remain a mystery. This should be compared with the situation in which no reference at all to the secret trust arrangement is made in the will: a 'fully secret trust'.

In these circumstances one core principle operates to create the secret trust: it would be unconscionable for Freddie to assert beneficial ownership of that property in circumstances in which he knew that the property was supposed to be held on trust for Lottie. Therefore, it is an equitable response that requires Freddie to hold property on trust, even though his common law rights would appear to permit him to treat the property as his absolutely.

6.1.4 Explaining the role of the secret trust

The secret trust is included in this part of the book, within the discussion of the formation and nature of express trusts, primarily because the secret trust is most easily understood as an exception to the formal requirements in the creation of will trusts, as set out in s 9 of the Wills Act 1837. The original purpose of the doctrine of secret trusts in the early case law was to prevent statute or common law being used as an instrument of fraud,[8] for example, in situations in which the beneficiaries under a will received the property only on the understanding that they would hold it for someone else. In *McCormick v Grogan*,[9] Lord Westbury set out the basis of the secret trust as a means of preventing fraudulent reliance on common law or statutory rights:[10]

> The court has, from a very early period, decided that even an Act of Parliament shall not be used as an instrument of fraud; and that equity will fasten on the individual who gets a title under that Act, and impose upon him a personal obligation, because he applies the Act as an instrument for accomplishing a fraud. In this way a court of equity has dealt with the Statute of Frauds, and in this manner, also, it deals with the Statute of Wills.

Thus, the legal owner of property may be made subject to a 'personal obligation' in Lord Westbury's words (perhaps that is better rendered as a 'proprietary obligation' to act as a trustee) which requires that person to hold the specific property on trust for the person whom the testator had intended to receive an equitable interest in the property.[11]

One important facet of the early cases on secret trusts before *McCormick v Grogan*[12] (in relation to fully secret trusts) and *Blackwell v Blackwell*[13] (in relation to half-secret trusts) was that it was necessary for the claimant to demonstrate that the secret trustee was perpetrating a fraud by suggesting that the legacy left to her on the terms of the will was intended in fact for the claimant beneficially. The difficulty with proving fraud was that the standard of proof for fraud requires the claimant to prove almost beyond a reasonable doubt that the defendant was acting fraudulently.[14] With the advent of the more complex tests set out in *McCormick* and *Blackwell* respectively, the need to prove actual fraud was removed. The questions of evidence remain in two contexts, however. First, practically, it is frequently a difficult thing to prove the content of a secret arrangement between one person now dead and another person with a vested interest in denying that the arrangement ever existed. Secondly, the law of evidence, quite apart from the provisions of the Wills Act, throws up a number of problems considered below in para 6.4.6.

6.1.5 Mapping the discussion to follow

The following discussion is broken into five parts: (1) general principles surrounding the creation of a fully secret trust; (2) the rules relating to fully secret trusts; (3) the rules relating to half-secret trusts; (4) the probate doctrine of incorporation by reference; and (5) the various conceptual understandings of secret trusts.

---

8 *McCormick v Grogan* (1869) LR 4 HL 82; *Jones v Badley* (1868) 3 Ch App 362, 364; and *Blackwell v Blackwell* [1929] AC 318.
9 (1869) LR 4 HL 82.
10 *Ibid*, 97.
11 By 'personal obligation' is meant that equity requires him to act *in personam*.
12 (1869) LR 4 HL 82.
13 [1929] AC 318.
14 *Peek v Gurney* (1873) LR 6 HL 377; *Re Snowden* [1979] 2 WLR 654.

6.2 FULLY SECRET TRUSTS

Fully secret trusts arise in circumstances in which neither the existence nor the terms of the trust are disclosed in the terms of the will. Oral evidence of the agreement between the testator and trustee is generally satisfactory. The settlor must have intended to create such a trust. That intention must have been communicated to the intended trustee. The trustee must have accepted the office and the terms of the trust explicitly or impliedly.

6.2.1 Creating a valid, fully secret trust

As set out above, the term 'fully secret trust' refers to those trusts under which only the trustees and the settlor are aware of the existence of the trust and of the terms of the trust. In the circumstances envisaged by this section, property will have been left to a person under a will, or will have passed to him under the Intestacy Rules, without any other person being aware of the settlor's intentions. While the law had once required proof of a fraud on the part of the defendant, a more specific test has emerged from the cases considered below.

In the leading case of *Ottaway v Norman*,[15] Ottaway devised his bungalow, half his residuary estate and a sum of money to Miss Hodges for her to use during her lifetime, provided always that she was, in turn, to bequeath this property to the claimant after her death. She failed to do this in her will. Rather, she left the property by her own will to Mr and Mrs Norman. After Hodges's death the plaintiff brought an action against Hodges's executors claiming entitlement under secret trust principles to the property which had been left in Ottaway's will. Brightman J set out the elements necessary to prove the existence of a fully secret trust in the following terms:

> It will be convenient to call the person on whom such a trust is imposed the 'primary donee' and the beneficiary under that trust the 'secondary donee'. The essential elements which must be proved to exist are: (i) the intention of the testator to subject the primary donee to an obligation in favour of the secondary donee; (ii) communication of that intention to the primary donee; and (iii) the acceptance of that obligation by the primary donee either expressly or by acquiescence. It is immaterial whether these elements precede or succeed the will of the donor.

From *Ottaway* the following three-step test emerges, there must be: an intention to benefit the claimant-beneficiary; communication of that intention to the intended secret trustee; and acceptance by the secret trustee of that obligation. It was found on the facts of *Ottaway* that Hodges had known of Ottaway's intention and had acquiesced in it. Therefore, it was held that the bungalow and residuary estate should pass to the plaintiff. However, the money was not subject to the same obligation because the court found it difficult to see how this could have been done if Hodges was entitled to use the money during her lifetime, unless there was an implication that she had to keep Ottaway's money separate from her own.

Perhaps the easiest conceptualisation of what the court is really looking for, behind the three-stage test set out in *Ottaway*, appears in *Wallgrave v Tebbs*,[16] where it was held by

---

15 [1972] 2 WLR 50.
16 (1855) 25 LJ Ch 241.

Wood VC that where the secret trustee-legatee 'expressly promises' or 'by silence implies' that he is accepting the obligation requested of him by the testator then he will be bound by that obligation. The Wills Act will not interfere with the working of secret trusts in this way. The distinct components of the test (intention, communication and acceptance) are considered separately below.

6.2.2 Intention to benefit

Akin to the need for evidence of sufficient intention to create an express trust, the settlor of a secret trust must intend that the legal titleholder of property under a will (or intestacy) be trustee of that property for another.[17] Therefore, we are thrown back on many of the concepts considered in Chapter 3 in relation to certainty of intention in the creation of express trusts: that is, the distinction between an intention that one person is to hold property on trust for another person subject to fiduciary obligations, and an intention to create a merely moral, non-legal obligation that one person is expected to provide for the welfare of another person.

In circumstances where all that the deceased intended was to impose a moral obligation on the legatee as to the use of property, that will not be sufficient to create a secret trust.[18] In *Re Snowden*,[19] an elderly woman was unsure how to deal with her property on death. Therefore, she left the property to her elder brother with the words 'he shall know what to do'. It happened that her brother died only days later. The issue arose whether the brother had been subject to a secret trust in favour of the woman's niece and nephew. It was held by Megarry VC that the deceased woman had only intended to impose a moral obligation on him – an intention which could not be interpreted as imposing a positive trust obligation on her brother. Therefore, the property passed beneficially on the terms of her brother's will.

A further example of the question whether or not there was manifested sufficient intention to create a trust can be derived from *McCormick v Grogan*.[20] The facts are rather melodramatic. A testator executed a very short will in 1851 in which all of his estate was to pass to Mr Grogan. In 1854, the testator had contracted cholera and, knowing that he did not have long to live, he sent for Grogan. When Grogan arrived he was told by the testator that his will was in a desk drawer together with a letter instructing Grogan as to certain intended bequests. The letter contained the words: 'I do not require you to act strictly in accordance with the foregoing instructions, but rather I leave it entirely to your own good judgment to do as you think I would do if I was still living, and as the parties are deserving.' The claimant considered himself to have been both deserving and overlooked by Grogan, and therefore sought a declaration that he had a right under a secret trust in certain property. The House of Lords held that the testator had not intended to impose a trust obligation on Grogan, particularly in the light of the sentence in the letter to him quoted above which explicitly absolved Grogan of any trusteeship. Therefore, it was held that Grogan held the property subject only to a moral obligation to provide for the people mentioned in the letter. There was no secret trust under which the plaintiff could claim a benefit.

17　*Ottaway v Norman* [1972] 2 WLR 50, *per* Brightman J.
18　*Re Snowden* [1979] 2 All ER 172.
19　*Ibid.*
20　(1869) LR 4 HL 82.

6.2.3 Communication of the secret trust

The basic principles in relation to the communication and creation of fully secret trusts can be briefly stated. Where the settlor intends to create a secret trust, it is important that this intention is communicated to the trustee and that the terms of the secret trust are similarly communicated to her. Without such communication of the trust to the secret trustee there can be no trust.[21] Communication and acceptance can be effectuated at any time during the life of the testator. Under fully secret trusts there need be communication only before death. However, more complex issues fall to be considered.

The first question which arises is as follows: precisely what is it that must be communicated? That will depend on the nature of the property and of the testator's intention. In the event that the secret trustee is intended to take as bare trustee and hold a single item of property on trust for the beneficiary, there is no need for communication of the testator's intention that that property be held on bare trust. However, if there is more than one intended beneficiary, the identity of those various beneficiaries and the manner in which the property is to be distributed between them would also need to be communicated. A third scenario would be that in *Ottaway v Norman* itself, in which the secret trustee was entitled to use the property during her lifetime provided that she left that property to specified beneficiaries in her will. In such a situation it is necessary for the precise terms of the trust to be communicated to the secret trustee. The settlor must communicate both the existence of the secret and also as many terms of the trust as are necessary in the context.

The case law dealing with communication draws some distinctions between these contexts. In the case of *Re Boyes*,[22] the testator informed the intended trustee that he meant to leave property to him under a secret trust arrangement. The testator also informed the trustee that the terms of the trust would be communicated to the trustee before the testator's death. In the event, the terms of the trust were not communicated. After the testator's death, two unattested documents were found among the testator's effects which purported to direct the trustee to hold the property on trust for the testator's mistress and child. Significantly, it was unclear whether or not these unattested documents were sufficient to set out those terms as being the testator's final intention in the absence of any explicit communication of those terms to the secret trustee. Kay J held that presentation of these two unattested documents was insufficient to constitute communication of the terms of the trust to the trustee. The rationale given for this decision was that the trustee was not given the opportunity to refuse to act under the trust. Given the facts of this particular trust (that the testator wanted to benefit his unknown mistress and illegitimate child), the judge's approach in a decision handed down in 1884 was perhaps sensitive to the delicate position in which the trustee would be placed by compelling him to act to hold property in secret for the dead man's mistress and offspring.

In contradistinction to the strict approach taken in *Boyes*, that the trustee must be offered the chance to object to the office of trustee, there have been subsequent decisions which have held that communication of the terms of the trust might take place after the testator's death, provided that the trustee knew in general terms that he was expected to act as a trustee in receipt of the gift under the will. Thus, it has been held that while communication can ordinarily be made

---

21 *Ottaway v Norman* [1972] 2 WLR 50.
22 (1884) 26 Ch D 531.

orally or by letter from the settlor to the intended secret trustee, it can also be performed by means of a sealed envelope containing the terms of the trust given to the trustee (or made available to the trustee) before the testator's death (generally referred to as 'constructive communication'), with instructions not to open the envelope until after death.[23] In the case of *Re Keen*, the court took the view that the trustee was in a situation analogous to that of a ship sailing under sealed orders. In such a situation, the captain of the ship sets sail but is not permitted to know his orders until the time at which he is allowed to open the envelope which contains a document setting out his precise instructions. Therefore it is said that while the trustee does not know the precise detail of his fiduciary obligations, the means by which he can ascertain the terms of the trust are clearly known to him. It should also be acknowledged that the trust in *Re Keen*[24] was a half-secret trust disclosed on the terms of the will, and therefore the existence of the trust was more apparent to outside observers than that in *Boyes*.[25]

So, in *Boyes* the distinguishing factor must be supposed to have been that the trustee knew nothing of the terms of the trust before the settlor's death beyond the testator's general intention to create such a trust. The court's approach on the facts of that case appears to have been motivated by the fact that it was not clear that the two unattested documents were intended to stand for the terms of the trust, as well as the court's reservations about the trustee's inability to know the terms of the trust in time to refuse to accept the office of trustee. It appears that communication of both the intention and of the terms requires that the trustee must be able to know with sufficient certainty the terms of the trust before the death of the testator, an approach which was approved in *Moss v Cooper*[26] and also in *Re Bateman's WT*.[27]

6.2.4 Acceptance of the office of trustee

Following on from the decision of the court in *Keen*, the acceptance of the trustee to act as such is a vital pre-requisite to the imposition of the liabilities of a secret trustee on him. Two reasons for this rule are apparent. First, the basis of the secret trust was the avoidance of fraud on the part of the secret trustee, and therefore it is important that the secret trustee has accepted the office before such a standard can be imposed. Secondly, the trustee is to be given the opportunity to turn down the office, particularly given the sensitive nature of holding property in such circumstances. Communication and acceptance can be effectuated at any time during the life of the testator. However, communication can also be given by means of a sealed envelope given to the trustee before the testator's death, with instructions not to open until after death, subject to what was said in the foregoing section.[28]

The office of trustee under a fully secret trust can be accepted in one of two ways. In the words of Wood VC in *Wallgrave v Tebbs*:[29]

23   *Re Keen* [1937] Ch 236.
24   *Ibid.*
25   (1884) 26 Ch D 531.
26   (1861) 1 J & H 352.
27   [1970] 1 WLR 1463, which expressly approved *Re Keen*.
28   *Re Keen* [1937] Ch 236.
29   (1855) 25 LJ Ch 241.

> Where a person, knowing that a testator in making a disposition in his favour intends it to be applied for purposes other than his own benefit, either *expressly promises*, or *by silence implies*, that he will carry on the testator's intention into effect, and the property is left to him *upon the faith of that promise or understanding*, it is in effect a case of trust; and in such a case, the court will not allow the devisee to set up the [Wills Act].

The court's focus is on the question whether or not the actions of the trustee on being asked to act by the testator were sufficient to be said to have caused the testator to carry through his intention. Importantly, the trustee is not required to have expressly promised (although that will suffice to constitute acceptance); rather, it is enough that the trustee 'by silence implies' that he will act as trustee. Suppose, therefore, that a testator is lying sick in bed in full knowledge that he will soon die. He calls a close confidant to his bedside and in great secrecy explains his plans, and then asks: 'I know you will act as my secret trustee, won't you?' If the trustee remains silent and thereby allows the testator to believe that he has accepted the office then the trustee will be bound by the secret trust and not permitted to take the property beneficially.[30]

In *Wallgrave v Tebbs*[31] itself, a testator had left £12,000 'unto and to the use of Tebbs and Martin, their heirs and assigns, for ever, as joint tenants'. Oral and written evidence was presented to the court which demonstrated both that the testator had intended Tebbs and Martin to hold the property on secret trust and that the purposes of that trust were in breach of the Statute of Mortmain. At no time had the testator's true intentions been communicated to Tebbs or to Martin. In consequence, Tebbs and Martin sought an order from the court that they were entitled to take beneficial ownership of the property left to them by will. Wood VC held that they could indeed take beneficial ownership and were not required to act as trustees, because there had been 'no such promise or undertaking on the part of the devisees [Tebbs and Martin]' which could have constituted acceptance of the office. The significant point was that the two men had no knowledge of the intention to create a secret trust on the terms alleged, and therefore the gift on the face of the will took effect in their favour.

Where the terms of the trust are not disclosed, it has been held that the trustee must hold the property on resulting trust for the testator to prevent his own unjustified benefit.[32] Consequently, the trustee would hold the property for the next of kin under the Intestacy Rules. The question which arises then is whether or not this would unjustifiably benefit the next of kin, in that secret trusts normally operate to divert property from the normal beneficiaries because the testator had a genuine motive of benefiting concealed beneficiaries.

6.2.5 Consequence of the failure of secret trust

In the event that there is no validly created secret trust, it is important to understand the manner in which the property will be dealt with. One of two possibilities arises. If the intention of the testator is taken to be an intention to benefit the named legatee absolutely beneficially then the absence of a secret trust means that the legatee will take the gift absolutely.[33]

---

30 An approach approved in *Moss v Cooper* (1861) 4 LT 790.
31 (1855) 25 LJ Ch 241.
32 *Re Boyes* (1884) 26 Ch D 531.
33 *Wallgrave v Tebbs* (1855) 25 LJ Ch 241.

Alternatively, if the intention of the testator is that the legatee is intended to take the property only as a fiduciary, it would be inappropriate for the person to take the property absolutely beneficially. Instead the fiduciary would be required to hold the property on resulting trust for the testator's residuary estate.[34]

6.3 HALF-SECRET TRUSTS

For a valid half-secret trust, the settlor must intend to create such a trust. Further, the existence and terms of the trust must be communicated to the intended trustee before the execution of the will. The intended trustee must then accept the office of trustee and acquiesce to the terms of the trust.

6.3.1 Creating a valid half-secret trust

A half-secret trust is a trust under which the *existence* of the trust is disclosed in a document, such as a will, but the *terms* of the trust remain secret. The requirements for a valid half-secret trust were set out in *Blackwell v Blackwell*[35] by Lord Sumner, who held that there must be 'intention, communication and acquiescence' between settlor and trustee. In relation to half-secret trusts, Lord Sumner set out the core principles in *Blackwell v Blackwell*[36] in the following terms:

> The necessary elements [to create a half-secret trust], on which the question turns, are intention, communication and acquiescence. The testator intends his absolute gift to be employed as he and not as the donee desires; he tells the proposed donee of this intention and, either by express promise or by the tacit promise, which is satisfied by acquiescence, the proposed donee encourages him to bequeath the money on the faith that his intentions will be carried out.

Therefore, the test for a half-secret trust is very similar to that for a fully secret trust.[37] It was also held in *Blackwell* that there is no need for the plaintiff to prove actual fraud on the part of the defendant (or secret trustee).

6.3.2 Communication

Communication must be before or at the time of the execution of the will.[38] Lord Sumner held in *Blackwell* that '[a] testator cannot reserve to himself a power of making future unwitnessed dispositions by merely naming a trustee and leaving the purposes of the trust to be supplied afterwards'.[39] The rationale for this rule is that the trustee must know of the terms of the trust and be able to disclaim the obligations of trusteeship. Similarly, the testator is not

---

34 *Vandervell v IRC* [1967] 2 AC 291, HL.
35 [1929] AC 318.
36 *Ibid.*
37 *Ottaway v Norman* [1972] 2 WLR 50.
38 *Blackwell v Blackwell* [1929] AC 318.
39 *Ibid*, 339.

entitled to use the secret trust as a means of delaying the point in time at which he will finally decide the terms on which he wishes his estate to be left.

Where communication occurs after the will, the trust will fail and the legatee will hold on resulting trust for the residuary estate.[40] Therefore, there is a distinction between half-secret trusts and fully secret trusts in that the settlor must communicate before the execution of the will in the former, but need not communicate the existence or terms of the trust until the time of death in the latter.[41] Mee has pointed out that there is a different rule in the Irish cases, permitting communication at any time until death.[42]

6.3.3 Acceptance

The rules relating to acceptance of the obligations contained in half-secret trusts are similar to those for fully secret trusts. As with fully secret trusts, considered above, the intended trustee must accept the office of trustee and acquiesce in the terms of the trust. Similar issues arise as to the necessity of all trustees being aware of their obligations under the trust, as considered above. As seen above, in relation to half-secret trusts, Lord Sumner set out the core principles in *Blackwell v Blackwell*[43] in the following terms:

> [H]e tells the proposed donee of this intention and, either by *express promise* or *by the tacit promise*, which is satisfied by acquiescence, the proposed donee encourages him to bequeath the money on the faith that his intentions will be carried out [emphasis added].

Therefore, this test is in line with that in *Wallgrave v Tebbs*[44] for fully secret trusts. In that context Wood VC held that a person would be bound by a secret trust if he expressly promised or by silence implied acceptance of the terms of the trust. Those same sentiments are rendered in *Blackwell v Blackwell* as the trustee acting by means of 'express promise' or 'tacit promise'. It is required that the trustee acquiesce in the testator's proposed arrangement. It is this acquiescence which constitutes the root of the secret trustee's liability in equity to act as a trustee. One of the progressions in this area of the law in *Blackwell* was that it was no longer necessary to demonstrate that the trustee had committed fraud. Basing this area of law on fraud overlooked the foundation of the trustee's liability as being properly a proprietary obligation deriving from the acceptance of the trustee's instructions which are subsequently carried into effect on death.

6.3.4 Clash of doctrines – beneficiary attesting to the will

In the case of *Re Young*,[45] the juxtaposition between the requirements of the Wills Act 1837 and the rules as to secret trusts was made most clear. In *Re Young*, a secret trust was referred

---

40 *Re Keen* [1937] Ch 236; *Re Bateman's WT* [1970] 1 WLR 1463.
41 *Re Spence* [1949] WN 237.
42 Mee [1992] Conv 202; *Riordan v Banon* (1876) LR 10 Eq 469.
43 [1929] AC 318.
44 (1855) 25 LJ Ch 241
45 [1951] Ch 344.

to in the will. The terms of that secret trust were that the chauffeur would receive a legacy. The formal difficulty was that the chauffeur had witnessed the will and therefore ought to have been precluded from taking beneficially under that will in accordance with s 15 of the 1837 Act, which provides that 'if any person shall attest to the execution of any will . . . such devise . . . shall [against such person] be utterly null and void'.

It was held by Dankwerts J that the chauffeur could take validly in accordance with the terms of the secret trust. The underlying reason is that the 1837 Act necessarily has no part to play in the decision whether or not there is a secret trust, given that the rationale which underpins the doctrine of secret trusts that each secret trust necessarily operates in the face of the requirements of that statute. The stated *ratio* was that, when considering s 15 of the Wills Act with reference to a legatee who has witnessed the will, it might be that the beneficiary is actually taking as trustee under a secret trust and not beneficially so that the policy under the 1837 Act is not necessarily contravened.

6.4 GENERAL PRINCIPLES

This section introduces some specific issues which arise in relation to secret trusts, before turning to the detail of various intellectual approaches to the secret trust.

6.4.1 The problem with secret trusts

It seems to this writer that the subject of secret trusts cuts to the very heart of the nature of a trust, as discussed in para 6.6.5 below. A secret trust concerns the situation in which the settlor wishes to create a trust but, for various reasons, wishes to keep the matter secret from everyone except the trustee. The problem is, then, how is the trust to be proved? Typically, the settlor will create the trust secretly, disclosing the arrangement only to the intended trustee, before dying. Given the secrecy of the trust, it is perfectly possible that only the trustee knows of the existence of the trust. The property which was intended to make up the trust fund will then be transferred to the trustee by the settlor's will. To the rest of the world it will appear that an outright gift of that property has been made to someone, even though she was in reality intended to be only a trustee of it.

Presumably there are thousands of secret trusts which have come to nought because unscrupulous trustees have taken the property as though absolutely entitled to it, without disclosing the trust to another living soul. Alternatively, the will may give a hint, such as 'I leave my SAFC shares to Albert in accordance with my wishes already expressed to him', or the testator may refer in the will to a letter written to the trustee which explains the terms of the trust. All of these possibilities are considered below.

6.4.2 Trustee dies before the settlor

There is clearly a problem with secret trusts in that the person intended to take the property as trustee may predecease the settlor. In the general law of probate, if an intended legatee were to predecease the testator, the gift would lapse into the residue of the deceased's estate. Clearly, it would not be possible for the secret trust to take effect where the trustee was dead before the property vested in her. In such a circumstance, a fully secret trust would fail because the deceased secret trustee's personal representatives would not know of the trust and therefore would not be able to carry it out.[46] However, in the case of a half-secret trust, it will be possible for the deceased secret trustee's personal representatives to know of the existence of the trust and thereby to give effect to it, in spirit[47] if not in detail.[48]

6.4.3 Disclaimer of the trust

A further problem is that the secret trustee may seek to refuse to act as trustee. There are two possible approaches: either the property should be deemed to be held on trust for the beneficiaries in any event (although it would not be clear who would act as trustee); or the bequest is deemed to fail for want of a trustee such that property is deemed to be held on resulting trust for the deceased settlor's estate. It is possible for the secret trustee to disclaim the office of trustee, provided that the disclaimer is communicated to the settlor.[49] It appears that the secret trustee may disclaim the trust even after the death of the settlor, without invalidating the secret trust.[50] These issues are considered further below.

6.4.4 Where further property is added to a secret trust

It is important that, for a secret trust to take effect, the identity of the property is sufficiently certain. While this rule is also the case for express trusts generally, as considered in Chapter 3 in the discussion of the Privy Council decision in *Re Goldcorp*,[51] the issue is particularly difficult in relation to secret trusts. Under ordinary express trusts there is a requirement for certainty of subject matter so that the court and the trustees can know which property is held subject to the terms of the trust. This problem is intensified in relation to secret trusts because not only is there the issue of demonstrating which property is to be covered by the secret trust, but also there is the problem of proving that there is a secret trust in existence at all. Consequently, given the status of the secret trust as an exception to the Wills Act 1837, the courts have adopted a strict approach to the identity of the property comprising the trust fund in line with *Re Goldcorp*.

Thus, in *Re Colin Cooper*,[52] the testator communicated his intention to create a secret trust over a fund of £5,000. The testator then sought to add more money to that fund at a later date without communicating this intention to the trustee. The court upheld the rule that the identity of the property must be communicated to the trustee. Furthermore, it was held that any addition to the amount formerly orally settled was to be held on resulting trust for the testator's residuary estate, and was not to be held as part of the secret trust.

The rationale for this distinction, despite the fact that the property would have been sufficiently certain for the purposes of an ordinary express trust, is that the secret trustee did not know of the trust over the added moneys at the relevant time before the testator's death. As considered below, the necessity of communication of the terms of the trust before the

---

46 *Re Maddock* [1902] 2 Ch 220.
47 Ie, because the terms are not known to the personal representatives.
48 *Mallott v Wilson* [1903] 2 Ch 494.
49 *Re Maddock* [1902] 2 Ch 220.
50 *Blackwell v Blackwell* [1929] AC 318, *per* Lord Buckmaster.
51 [1995] AC 74.
52 [1939] Ch 811.

testator's death or before the execution of the will (depending on whether the trust is fully secret or merely half-secret) distinguishes the issue of certainty in relation to secret trusts from that in relation to ordinary express trusts. In relation to fully secret trusts it is said that it is sufficient that the terms of the trust be communicated to the trustee at any time before the testator's death. Therefore, the identity of the fund to be held on trust need not be made clear to the trustee either. On the other hand, in relation to a half-secret trust it is required that the terms of the secret trust be communicated to the trustee before the execution of the will. Therefore, in relation to a half-secret trust the identity of the trust property must be made known at an earlier date than in relation to a fully secret trust. Given that the half-secret trust will come into being (as will all secret trusts) only on the death of the testator, the identity of the trust property is required to be made plain at an earlier stage than would be necessary in relation to ordinary express trusts.

6.4.5 Secret trusts arising on intestacy

There is a tendency to assume that secret trusts arise solely in relation to wills. However, it is possible that a settlor may have purported to create a trust which was not revealed to any person other than the intended trustee without a will having been made. In such a situation, it would be possible for the settlor to die without leaving a will, but in a situation in which equity may regard the person in whom title is vested (on or before death) as being, in reality, a trustee of that property. Such situations are considered, for the purposes of this discussion, as falling within fully secret trusts on the basis that there is no will to disclose them.[53]

The form of secret trust supported in *Sellack v Harris*[54] arises in situations in which the person receiving property on intestacy under the Intestacy Rules in some way encouraged the deceased person to believe that by failing to make a will, and thus allowing property to pass to that person on intestacy, the recipient of the property would hold it on secret trust. This approach appears to be similar to a form of proprietary estoppel which binds the recipient of the property as a person who causes the deceased person to act in reliance on some assurance given (either expressly or impliedly) by the defendant. Unlike an ordinary example of proprietary estoppel, however, the benefit of the estoppel does not pass to the person who acted detrimentally in reliance on the assurance: in other words, it is the deceased person who acts in reliance and not the beneficiary under the secret trust (who is to all intents and purposes a volunteer). Further, an estoppel would bind the defendant only from the time of the court order, whereas the secret trust will bind the defendant from the moment of receiving the property in the knowledge of the deceased person's intention that the property be held on trust for the ultimate beneficiary.

6.4.6 Specific problems of evidence

As pointed out above, the principal practical problem associated with secret trusts is the fact that they are formed in secret and are therefore difficult to prove. There are other technical problems to do with the conflict between such informal arrangements and the formalities required by the law of probate.

---

53 *Sellack v Harris* (1708) 2 Eq Ca Ab 46.
54 *Ibid.*

The parol evidence rule

The parol evidence rule maintains that, in the general law of evidence, oral testimony cannot be introduced to contradict written evidence in the form of a will. Thus, it is possible that the court may hold that, in certain circumstances, the oral evidence of secret trust may not be enforced where such evidence is in direct contradiction of the terms of the will. For example, in *Re Keen*[55] a sum of money was left by will 'to be held upon trust and disposed of by them among such person, persons or charities as may be notified by me to them'. Contemporaneously with the creation of the will, the testator gave a sealed letter to one of the executors which was subsequently found to contain the name of a woman. However, the Court of Appeal held that the words in the will anticipated that the direction would be one given *in the future*, so that the letter passed at the same time as the will was executed could not have been the document referred to by the testator in the terms of the will. Consequently, the court held that the oral evidence of secret trust was in contradiction to the terms of the will. Therefore, the secret trust would not be enforced, such that the property passed to the residuary beneficiaries under the will.

This decision appears difficult and revolves around a literal (and somewhat pedantic) interpretation of the terms of the will. However, it does illustrate the importance of applying the precise terms of the will where there is a conflict between that document and some verbal communication to another person. It is difficult to know where to draw the line with this principle, given that secret trusts operate to contradict the rules for the formal creation of the will by definition. Clearly, the very purpose of the secret trust is that it does contradict the terms of the will by introducing other evidence to support the assertion that the testator did not intend a legatee to take property specified in the will beneficially.

Problems of evidence generally

Needless to say, in most circumstances, the central problem will necessarily be one of demonstrating that a dead person intended to create a trust when, by definition, there will be few surviving persons able to provide any direct evidence of that intention. It is clear that the standard of proof required of the person alleging the existence of a secret trust is therefore high. As Lord Westbury held in *McCormick v Grogan*:[56]

> being a jurisdiction founded on personal fraud, it is incumbent on the court to see that a fraud, *malus animus*, is proved by the clearest and most indisputable evidence . . . You are obliged, therefore, to show most clearly and distinctly that the person you wish to convert into a trustee acted *mala animo*. You must show distinctly that the testator or the intestate was beguiled and deceived by his conduct.

These *dicta* emphasise the result of the secret trust being based, classically, on the avoidance of fraud. In common with fraud claims, the standard of proof is therefore high.[57] This

---

55 [1937] Ch 236.
56 (1869) LR 4 HL 82.
57 *Re Snowden* [1979] 2 All ER 172.

recognises the reality of secret trusts claims: in most cases, the claimant will be alleging that the defendant is fraudulently asserting beneficial ownership of property which ought to have been held on trust for another person. However, the debate entered into at the end of this section as to the true nature of the secret trust (perhaps as an *inter vivos* express trust or a constructive trust) raises the question whether a burden of proof based on fraud is appropriate. More modern approaches would suggest that it is not.

A trustee cannot adduce evidence to demonstrate that he is entitled to take property beneficially (other than in a separate capacity) when he knows that he is to hold the property as trustee.[58] To allow such evidence would be to allow the defendant to perpetrate a fraud.[59] In certain circumstances it may be appropriate to decide whether the testator's intention was to create a trust, or merely a conditional gift or an equitable charge in relation to fully secret trusts.[60]

6.4.7 Secret trustees with different knowledge

Obligations on the secret trustees

The issue arose in *Re Stead*[61] as to the proper approach in cases where the testator leaves property to A and B on trust for X, where A and B are joint tenants of the legal title in the property, but in circumstances where A knows of the trust but B does not. It was held that where the testator has communicated his intention to A only before the date of the will and A accepts, both A and B are bound by the trust. However, where the testator has communicated his intention to A only after the date of the will and only A accepts, only A will be bound by the trust. The justification given for these approaches was that in the former case, the testator would be encouraged to make the bequest by A's acquiescence, whereas in the latter, the testator could not have been induced in that fashion.

However, it is perhaps difficult to understand the difference between the latter situation, where T is presumably similarly encouraged not to alter the bequest on the faith of A's acquiescence, even though B has had no opportunity to comment, and the former, where the situation is the same in all material respects. Perrins[62] has suggested that it would be better to assess whether or not the bequest was *actually* induced by the promise in either case,[63] rather than create general rules which make assumptions as to what the parties would do in practical situations.

In relation to a half-secret trust, where the trust expressly provides that the property is 'to be held in accordance with my terms which I have made known to them' but where communication is not made to all of the trustees, there will not be a secret trust imposed on all the intended trustees.[64] The secret trust would not take effect. Any person who received the

58 *Re Rees* [1950] Ch 284, CA; *Re Tyler* [1967] 3 All ER 389; *Re Pugh's WT* [1967] 3 All ER 337.
59 *Re Spencer's WT* (1887) 57 LT 519; *Re Williams* [1933] Ch 244.
60 *Irvine v Sullivan* (1869) LR 8 Eq 673; *Re Ford* (1922) 2 Ch 519.
61 [1900] 1 Ch 237.
62 Perrins, 1972.
63 *Huguenin v Baseley* (1807) 14 Ves Jun 273.
64 *Re Keen* [1937] Ch 236 and *Re Spence* [1949] WN 237.

property in the knowledge that he was intended merely to act as a fiduciary, and not to take the property beneficially, would hold that property on resulting trust for the testator's residuary estate. In relation to any legatees to whom communication had not been made, the bequest might take effect as an outright transfer,[65] assuming that it would be possible for those persons to take possession of that property separately from those legatees to whom communication had been made. The situation would be different if the will had provided 'to be held in accordance with the terms which I have made known to any one or more of them'.[66]

6.4.8 Time of the creation of the trust

It is generally assumed that a fully secret trust is constituted at the moment of the testator's death. This assumption is sensible. The trust must come into existence at some point in time. It must be possible to know at what moment the trustee becomes subject to the fiduciary duties of trusteeship. The sensible approach to providing for the date of death means that the most recent version of the will applies, passing legal title in the property to the secret trustee. Before that time, the trustee has no title in the property. (If the trustee had had title in the property, that would raise the question whether the trust was a normal *inter vivos* express trust, rather than a testamentary secret trust.)

However, there is the alternative authority of *Re Gardner*,[67] where Romer J held, controversially, that the gift is created at the date of the will, rather than at the date of death. Perhaps this decision is capable of explanation in that the court was evidently concerned to see property pass according to the wishes of the deceased. In that case, property had been left by a testatrix to her husband, subject to a secret trust in favour of her nephew and nieces. One niece predeceased the testatrix. Her executors sought to enforce her interest under the secret trust. Romer J held that the deceased niece had acquired her equitable interest in the property at the time the husband accepted the office of secret trustee, and not at the time of the testatrix's death.

It is suggested that the decision in *Re Gardner* cannot be correct in principle because the will could have been altered subsequently, thus revoking the secret trust. At law generally an absolute gift cannot be revoked. Therefore, the two approaches would be in straightforward contradiction. Furthermore, there would be problems if the intended donee predeceased the testator. Under the doctrine of lapse, where the beneficiary dies before the gift is made, the gift lapses and results to the settlor's estate to be distributed under the Intestacy Rules. This would not be possible if *Gardner* were correct because the property would already have passed to the deceased donee. The gift is not actually vested until the time of the testator's death and therefore the secret beneficiary had a mere *spes* at the time of her death.

6.5 THE PROBATE DOCTRINE OF INCORPORATION BY REFERENCE

The doctrine of incorporation by reference is a doctrine belonging, properly, to the law of probate. It relates to a situation where a testator expressly incorporates another, existing

---

65 *Wallgrave v Tebbs* (1855) 25 LJ Ch 241.
66 *Re Keen* [1937] Ch 236.
67 [1923] 2 Ch 230.

document into the will. For example, the will may provide 'I leave my season ticket to Sunderland AFC on the terms set out in a letter dated 14 October 2011 and concealed in my underpants drawer.' In this way, the letter becomes a part of the will even though the will does not set out the terms contained in that document. The law of probate gives effect to such devices, where they are sufficiently certain, to give effect to the testator's underlying intentions.[68]

6.6 CATEGORISING THE SECRET TRUST

There is a problem of categorising the secret trust. This book has left secret trusts among the express trust material because that is where the majority of commentators and judges seem to think secret trusts belong. But, to be honest with you, my heart is not in it. Some writers do maintain that secret trusts (particularly half-secret trusts) are a form of express trust. There are two streams to this argument: the traditional view and the modern view. Two other approaches are suggested: the 'split view' and the author's own.

It is important to note that the distinction between secret trusts as express or constructive trusts is an important one given that there are no formal requirements in relation to the creation of constructive trusts (through s 53(2) of the Law of Property Act 1925), whereas there are formal requirements for the creation of express trusts. Therefore, if the secret trust is found to be in truth an express trust, it would also need to satisfy the rules as to formalities considered in Chapter 5 above.

6.6.1 The traditional view

The traditional view is presented as the 'fraud theory'. As discussed above in this chapter, the fraud view tallies with the equitable doctrine illustrated in *Rochefoucauld v Boustead*[69] which precludes a person from relying on his common law rights to perpetrate a fraud. It is that equitable doctrine which explains the underpinning of the secret trust.[70] In *McCormick v Grogan*,[71] Lord Westbury set out the basis of the secret trust as a means of preventing fraudulent reliance on common law or statutory rights:[72]

> The court has, from a very early period, decided that even an Act of Parliament shall not be used as an instrument of fraud; and that equity will fasten on the individual who gets a title under that Act, and impose upon him a personal obligation, because he applies the Act as an instrument for accomplishing a fraud. In this way a court of equity has dealt with the Statute of Frauds, and in this manner, also, it deals with the Statute of Wills.

---

68 All that is required of the executors, in the example above, is to brave the testator's underpants drawer.
69 [1897] 1 Ch 196.
70 *McCormick v Grogan* (1869) LR 4 HL 82.
71 *Ibid.*
72 *Ibid*, 97.

These *dicta* acknowledge that, as a matter of historical fact, the doctrine was based on equity's concern to prevent fraud. That the secret trust is based on fraud also imports the higher standard of proof used in fraud cases than in ordinary civil cases.[73]

A problem with enforcing this traditional, fraud-based doctrine is the following: what is the named legatee (or secret trustee) supposed to do with the property? The issue is whether to hold the property on resulting trust for the settlor (or for the residuary estate once the settlor is deceased), or to pass it to the proposed beneficiary. There is a tension here between observing the wishes of the testator on the one hand, and satisfying the evidential burden for sufficient certainty in the creation of an express trust on the other. Furthermore, it is not clear whether the fraud is said to be perpetrated simply by the secret trustee seeking to assert beneficial title, or whether the fraud is properly a fraud perpetrated against either the settlor or the intended beneficiary.

The fraud theory is based on the trustee's unconscionable refusal to observe the terms of the secret trust agreed with the testator. Before the mid-19th century it was necessary to prove fraud before liability would be attached to the defendant as secret trustee. The doctrine operated to prevent the wrong committed by the defendant. As such a secret trust could be said to have been a form of restitution for wrongdoing or restitution to prevent unjust enrichment. However, the basis on which the doctrine operates is the imposition of a trust. Therefore, the mistake under which the fraud theory operates is in thinking that liability attaches as a result of fraud. It does not. Liability attaches on the basis of the proprietary obligation accepted by the defendant when the testator communicates his intention to the defendant: that proprietary obligation is assumed by the defendant when the testator dies and leaves the ostensible gift of property to the defendant in his will. The defendant is a trustee from the moment that his knowledge of the obligation which the testator wished to impose on him coincides with his conscience, preventing him from asserting absolute title to the property ostensibly left to him by will when the will comes into effect on the testator's death.

Two important points should be made. First, the obligation is a proprietary obligation immediately on the testator's death and not an obligation which arises as a result of the avoidance of fraud only when the beneficiary or some other person brings the matter to court.[74] Secondly, that obligation does not bind the defendant until the date of the testator's death because the testator could have changed his will or rescinded the secret trust arrangement at any time (logically) until death, or even thereafter by means of sealed instructions.[75] What is most important to recognise is that the obligation of the defendant arises on the basis of a trust and does not arise only when a claim of fraud is brought against him. Secret trusts are institutional and not remedial.

With that realisation, the fraud theory is based on weak foundations. It is true to say that equity will not permit the defendant to use the Wills Act as an engine of fraud, but it is also true to say that the defendant is deemed to be a trustee from the moment of the testator's death (if the requirements for the establishment of a secret trust have been satisfied). A more modern understanding of the use of the term 'fraud' in equity is as a synonym for the concept of 'conscience', as opposed to denoting the sense of 'fraud' used in the tort of deceit.

---

73 *Re Snowden* [1979] 2 WLR 654.
74 Rickett (1979) 38 CLJ 260.
75 *Re Keen* [1937] Ch 236.

However, all trusts arise on the basis of conscience and therefore that observation – even if 'fraud' should be read as meaning simply 'conscience' – does not help with the task of defining how secret trusts are to be categorised alongside other forms of trust. The question, then, is what form of trust is created.

6.6.2 The modern view

A more modern view of the nature of the secret trust is that the trust was created and declared *inter vivos* between the testator and the trustee, with the property vesting upon the death of the testator. This approach justifies the classification of the secret trust as a form of express trust. In short, it is argued that the testator sought to declare a trust while alive but did not completely constitute that trust until the point of death, when the will transferred title in the trust fund to the trustee. To complete the logic of this position, it is said that there could not be an express trust on death because that would be in contravention of the Wills Act – however, to balk at the application of the Wills Act in this context (as many of the proponents of this view seem to) is perhaps to forget the fact that secret trusts are intended to operate in contravention of the Wills Act in any event. Further, the express trust could not take place at the time that the testator communicates his plan to the trustee because no legal title vests in the trustee until the testator's death. Therefore, if the secret trust is to take effect as an express trust it must take effect as an executory trust – that is, a trust which takes effect at some designated point in the future. That designated point is the date of the testator's death.

However, an alternative analysis of this view is that the testator really intended to create a gift of property which is then being perfected by a trust, despite having been intended to take effect as a gift. This would conflict with the rule in *Milroy v Lord*[76] that a trust cannot be used to perfect a transfer which was intended to take effect by other means. Furthermore, this approach is objectionable on the basis that it requires the implication of an express trust which, by definition, was not required to comply with the formalities for the creation of an express trust. To attempt to analyse secret trusts as being express trusts appears to be a busted flush precisely because no such formally valid express trust was actually created. The secret trust arises when there has been an intention to create a secret trust, communication of that intention and acceptance by the trustee of that office. This does not require that there be satisfaction of the rules relating to express trusts as considered elsewhere in this book (see Part 2).

If the secret trust does not operate as an express trust then it falls to one of two alternative analyses. Either secret trusts are an exception to such formalities altogether (and constitute a one-off, *sui generis* rule of the law of probate), or they constitute a form of constructive trust (as considered below).

6.6.3 The split view

There is a third category of commentators who argue that fully secret trusts and half-secret trusts should be analysed differently one from the other: that is, that there should be a 'split view' of the two forms of secret trust. Oakley takes this approach.[77] In his view, fully secret

76 (1862) 4 De GF & J 264.
77 Oakley, 1997, 243.

trusts are better classified as constructive trusts, rather than as a form of express trust either avoiding fraud or effecting an *inter vivos* disposition. On the other hand, it is his contention that half-secret trusts are presented as being a species of express trust under which the reference made in the will to the existence of the trust provides sufficient evidence of the creation of an express trust.[78] The issue which is not addressed at this level is as to the formal requirements for express trusts. However, in relation to constructive trusts, s 53(2) of the Law of Property Act 1925 provides that there are no formalities necessary for the recognition of constructive trusts.

Martin is another proponent of the split view, but on a different basis from Oakley.[79] In explaining her split approach to the two forms of secret trust, Martin draws a different distinction between two types of secret trust which draws on the traditional view's determination to avoid fraud. The main plank of the argument is that by breaking secret trusts into two categories it can be seen that some secret trusts will operate to prevent fraud whereas others will not. The first category of secret trust would be those trusts which are mentioned in the will. It is said that in relation to trusts which are disclosed in the will there will be no fraud because a fiduciary duty is created simply by that mention in the will. The second category encompasses those secret trusts which are not mentioned in the will trust and in relation to which fraud is consequently more likely.[80] In line with the traditional view, this split view permits secret trusts to be imposed as a form of constructive trust to prevent fraud; whereas half-secret trusts are considered less likely to operate on that basis.

6.6.4 Secret trusts simply as an exception to the Wills Act

One further explanation of the operation of secret trusts would be, quite simply, that they constitute an exception to the Wills Act which defies straightforward definition. As Megarry VC stated the matter in *Re Snowden*:[81] 'the whole basis of secret trusts ... is that they operate outside the will, changing nothing that is written in it, and allowing it to operate according to its tenor, but then fastening a trust on to the property in the hands of the recipient.' It is not suggested that Megarry VC was subscribing to so Luddite a view as to suggest that secret trusts are simply 'something other' than the forms of trust considered in this book. What is suggested is that Megarry VC does put his finger on an essential feature of the secret trust: that it does not correlate easily with the existing rules concerning trusts and therefore its difference ought to be recognised as much as the possibilities of its complying with more general principles of English trusts law. What the following paragraph indicates is that it is only possible to correlate secret trusts with the broadest possible principles of the law of trusts: that is, that the conscience of the secret trustee will prevent that person from denying the office imposed on him once he receives a gift under the will.

78 *Re Baillie* (1886) 2 TLR 660.
79 Martin, 1997, 153.
80 *Ibid.*
81 [1979] 2 All ER 172, 177.

6.6.5 An alternative view – secret trusts and good conscience

Establishing the case for a composite view of all secret trusts as constructive trusts

The argument advanced here is this writer's own and is subtly different from those set out above. In short, it is contended that secret trusts are to be considered to be constructive trusts because they are imposed on the recipient of the testamentary gift where that person knows in good conscience that she is required to hold that property on trust for someone else. As outlined above, the secret trust cannot be considered to be an ordinary express trust because it does not obey the formalities for testamentary trusts; neither does it necessarily obey the formalities set out in cases like *Milroy v Lord*[82] or *Morice v Bishop of Durham*,[83] as considered in Chapter 5. Therefore, the secret trust falls to be considered either as a species of trust apart from all others, or as a form of constructive trust. These contentions are considered immediately below.

It is suggested that fully secret trusts are constructive trusts as contended by Oakley.[84] By definition there will not have been compliance with the formalities in relation to express trusts over land, shares or other such items of property if a trust is imposed over property for the benefit of A, when beneficial title in that property was explicitly allocated by will to B. A secret trust is not an express trust because it does not comply with the formalities necessary for such trusts; rather, it is imposed in line with the rules set out in *Blackwell v Blackwell*[85] and *Ottaway v Norman*.[86] Therefore, the fully secret trust must fall within the implied trusts in s 53(2) of the Law of Property Act 1925. There is no other satisfactory explanation for such a trust other than its being a constructive trust imposed to prevent the unconscionable actions of the legal owner of that property.

This leaves the half-secret trust unaccounted for. Rather than attempt to make out a case for half-secret trusts as constructive trusts at this stage, it would be profitable to analyse precisely what is meant by the term 'half-secret trust'. At root, there is only a subtle difference between the fully secret and the half-secret trust.

There will be only a shade of difference between a will containing the words 'I leave £100,000 to Fred', a will containing the words 'I leave £100,000 to Fred for reasons which he will understand', and another will containing the words 'I leave £100,000 to Fred to carry out purposes which I have communicated to him'. The first example is clearly a fully secret trust and the last is equally clearly a half-secret trust. The issue is as to the middle case. This could be said to disclose a half-secret trust if there had been discussions between Fred and the testator. Alternatively, it could be an acknowledgment of some close relationship between Fred and the testator which would cause the testator to leave £100,000 to Fred.

In short, there will be occasions in which the line between fully secret and half-secret trusts is difficult to draw. As considered elsewhere in this chapter, there will be situations in which there will be significant differences between the rules applied to fully secret and to half-secret trusts. Given the narrow line between the two forms of secret trust in many

---

82   (1862) 4 De GF & J 264.
83   (1805) 10 Ves 522.
84   See also the remarks of Nourse J in *Re Cleaver* [1981] 1 WLR 939.
85   [1929] AC 318.
86   [1972] 2 WLR 50.

situations, it would be unfortunate to seek to operate the two on different bases. However, the principle which will be common to judicial attitudes to all three forms of wording suggested above is that equity will not permit the secret trustee to benefit unconscionably from the testator's bequest. Controlling the conscience of the trustee is the key element in all circumstances – whether the case concerns a fully secret or a half-secret trust. The distinction between different forms of secret trust has more to do with evidential questions than with issues concerning the application of varying conceptual analyses to secret trusts.

As a result of the observation of this grey area between the established categories, there is no conceptual need to apply different rules to the two forms of secret trust – or, it is suggested, even to continue to distinguish between them. The tests for the creation of either form of trust have coalesced into very similar requirements of intention, communication and acquiescence/acceptance. It is only in relation to the time by which communication must be performed that there is any palpable distinction between them. What would be preferable would be for one single explanation for the operation of all kinds of secret trust to be isolated, given the tremendous overlap that exists between them and the arbitrary distinctions which may be created if that difference is maintained.

The argument based on constructive trust

In truth, what is happening when courts impose secret trusts is that they are imposing the office of trustee on the recipient of a gift on the basis that it would be unconscionable for that person to retain an absolute interest in the property. The primary motivating factor behind equity's response here is that the secret trustee is aware that she was not intended to take beneficial title in the property but rather to hold it on trust for another person. As considered above, there will be no finding of secret trust where the recipient had not had the testator's intention communicated to her and where that office had not been accepted.[87] Secret trusts will be imposed only on those who have knowledge of the unconscionability of retaining absolute title in the property.

Consequently, the imposition of a secret trust falls four-square within the test for a constructive trust as set out by Lord Browne-Wilkinson in *Westdeutsche Landesbank Girozentrale v Islington LBC*,[88] as considered in Chapter 12 below: that is, a constructive trust is imposed on a person who has knowledge of some factor affecting his conscience in relation to the use of property. Thus, the recipient of a testamentary gift who knows that he has acquiesced in an arrangement whereby the testator intended him to take that property in a fiduciary capacity only will be a constructive trustee of that property from the moment that legal title passes into his hands. In exactly that way, outwith the formalities for express trusts, equity imposes a constructive trust on anyone who accepts the office of secret trustee, whether that trust is disclosed in the will or not. As stated above, this is the only feature common both to fully secret and half-secret trusts. A secret trust therefore always conforms to a categorisation as a species of constructive trust which operates as an exception to the rules as to the creation of valid, express will trusts. That there is no need for any formality in the creation of constructive trusts is established by s 53(2) of the 1925 Act.

---

87 *Wallgrave v Tebbs* (1855) 25 LJ Ch 241; *Blackwell v Blackwell* [1929] AC 318.
88 [1996] AC 669.

The form of secret trust as constructive trust, not estoppel

The secret trust serves to highlight a further feature of the constructive trust as compared to the doctrine of proprietary estoppel. It may have occurred to the reader that the three-stage test of intention to benefit, communication and acceptance[89] bears some of the hallmarks of proprietary estoppel, in that the estoppel doctrine requires that there has been a representation promising a benefit in reliance on which the claimant acts to his detriment.[90] However, what is clear is that proprietary estoppel requires there to have been some detriment on the part of the claimant and that it will be, in general terms, estoppel's intention to prevent that detriment going uncompensated.[91] The doctrine of secret trusts is concerned to enforce the promise only obliquely – the primary purpose of the doctrine of secret trusts historically was always to prevent a fraud being committed by the person to whom the testamentary gift was made with the intention that the gift be held on trust for the concealed beneficiary. Secret trusts necessarily uphold the trustee's proprietary obligations under the trust and do not simply seek to compensate the claimant for the detriment which she has suffered. Therefore, the secret trust is similar to that model of constructive trust set out in *Westdeutsche Landesbank Girozentrale v Islington LBC*[92] which imposes a trust on the trustee from the moment he takes legal title in property which he knows is intended to be held on trust for another person.

The secret trust crystallises at the moment of the testator's death – that is, from the moment at which the will, and the secret trust contained within it, come into full force and effect. A constructive trust comes into existence from the moment when the defendant has knowledge of the factor affecting his conscience.[93] That is not quite true of the secret trust. The testator could reverse his intention to carry out the secret trust at any time before his death simply by changing his will. The constructive trust would typically come into existence at the later receipt of the trust property and the defendant's knowledge of the fiduciary duty imposed on the defendant: that is probably true of the secret trust too, in that the secret trustee is subject to the secret trust only from the moment of taking possession of the testamentary gift. This differs from proprietary estoppel, in that the estoppel rights come into existence only from the date of the court order prospectively and may not even grant property rights to the claimant.[94]

---

89 *Ottaway v Norman* [1972] 2 WLR 50.
90 *Re Basham* [1986] 1 WLR 1498.
91 *Lim v Ang* [1992] 1 WLR 113; *Walton Stores v Maher* (1988) 62 AJLR 110, (1988) 164 CLR 387. Although in truth there are exceptional decisions like *Pascoe v Turner* [1979] 2 All ER 945, in which the estoppel does appear to be enforcing the initial representation.
92 [1996] AC 669.
93 *Ibid.*
94 *Baker v Baker* (1993) 25 HLR 408.

Chapter 7

Essay – The nature of express trusts

7.1 THE BASES OF EXPRESS TRUSTS

7.1.1 The paradox at the heart of the law on express trusts

Equity is sometimes flexible and sometimes rigid

There is a paradox at the heart of the law on express trusts. On the one hand the trust is predicated on principles of equity which are in turn traceable to philosophical ideas of fairness and justice which were identified in Chapter 1 with Aristotle and others. On the other hand much of the law discussed in this Part 2 of this book to do with express trusts has been concerned with very technical ideas which have resembled common law principles of contract more than flexible principles used to achieve fair or just results at the whim of whichever judge is sitting to hear a case. Therefore, while we began this book with high-sounding talk of conscience, fairness and justice, we came quickly to concern ourselves with hard-nosed commercial practice or with technical rules used to allocate property between family members. In truth, when we peer a little more closely at the case law which we have considered in this Part 2 of this book there have been plenty of cases which have appeared to retreat into an approach which seemed far more like the approach favoured by Aristotle in refusing to apply strict rules of trusts law or of common law where that would generate injustice: so, we have considered how secret trusts circumvent the provisions of the Wills Act, how *Rochefoucauld v Boustead* prevented a defendant from relying on her strict legal rights to defraud the plaintiff, how *Hunter v Moss* sought to prevent the defendant from relying on a strict principle of trusts law to enable him to withhold property he was contractually obliged to transfer, and so on. There is, I would suggest, a conflict between some aspects of trusts which are concerned with the implementation of hard-and-fast rules and other aspects of equity more generally which are concerned with the appropriate application of principles of fairness to cases where those principles are considered to be more appropriate than the outcome of applying those hard-and-fast rules.

It is suggested later in this essay that this is bound up with the way in which the courts have been required to develop trusts law and equity. There was never a time at which a legislator sat down in England and set out all of the principles of trusts law in a statute. Similarly equity has never been described in such clear terms. Instead, both systems of law have developed pell-mell across the centuries on a case-by-case basis, albeit by reference to precedent. Frequently, judges have stopped to remind us of the intellectual foundations of what came before them and to map out the lie of the land ahead, but even those statements when they have come have only served to identify the particular prejudices of the time in which those words were spoken. So, the talk in the *Earl of Oxford's Case* in 1615 that equity exists to correct men's consciences has a slightly different echo in *Westdeutsche Landesbank v Islington* in 1996 when Lord Browne-Wilkinson is asked to adjudicate in a dispute between a large investment bank and a local authority.

How learning equity is very like learning the English language

I have a theory that there is something bound up even in the English language with this way of thinking. Some Englishmen (by which I mean to include women) like to think of themselves as being clear-headed and logical, such that they would like their law to be based on clear rules which everyone can learn and understand. Other Englishmen like to think of themselves as being caring and open-minded, and open to free expression of ideas, so that they would like to think of their law as being made up of principles which will guide private citizens when going about their lawful activities and which will constrain the unconscionable activities of others. The English language itself is a mixture of these contradictory currents. In fact I think that the nature of the English language is the best analogy for this complex structure of equity. The English language does have a number of rules and descriptions of its grammatical principles but, as anyone who has grown up learning a language like French or Italian or who has learned Latin will know, the English language does not have an organised system of endings and declensions and so forth like those other languages. Irritatingly, English also has an exception to almost every grammatical rule you learn. Also there are many English words which contain identical groups of letters but which are pronounced completely differently: for example 'cough', 'thought', 'borough', 'through' and so on. This leads many people to think that English has no meaningful grammatical rules and therefore that English can be spoken in any way one likes without worrying about grammar. However, there are many idioms and understood grammatical rules which will make a well-educated English person recoil in horror if a speaker breaks them. This is just like equity, I think. It may look like this is an area of law which is entirely concerned with random decisions by judges on a case-by-case basis according to what they think is 'fair' or 'conscionable', but in truth there is a very subtle understanding of how these various principles fit together, just like there is a very subtle understanding among the English-speaking peoples about how English grammar operates. Therefore, in trusts law, for example, we have a subtle mixture of hard-and-fast rules like certainty and the beneficiary principle, mixed with a fluid understanding of how other principles of equity may operate so as to disrupt the application of those hard-and-fast rules.

The English mind is therefore a mixture of strict rules and fluid principles, just like the English language. The same can be said of English private law. In this essay we shall think about how the law we have discussed so far in this book can be understood in that way. Hopefully this will help to pull all of this material into focus. We shall begin by thinking about the relationship between making gifts of property and making property available to other people through trusts in traditional trusts law.

7.1.2 Giving and time

Traditional trusts were concerned with the allocation of property rights, usually between family members, across the generations either during the parties' lifetimes or on the death of one of them. Consequently, there is a connection between giving and settling property on trust. Moffat suggests, with something of a metaphysical lilt, that 'a private trust is . . . a gift projected on the plane of time'.[1] What he means is that the trust constitutes a gift made by the settlor but it is not a gift which is perfected at one moment when possession of absolute title in that property passes to the beneficiary. Rather, an express trust operates over a period of time in transferring title from the settlor, via the stewardship of the trustee, to the beneficiaries of the arrangement. It should be pointed out that Moffat is not intending this remarkable expression to be a definition of the trust. Instead I am fixing on it precisely because it is such a powerful image; and therefore you should forgive me if what follows seems at first to be a little pedantic; but the image is so strong as to be deserving of close attention.

At one level Moffat is undoubtedly correct, and his reminder of the role of time here is very important. A trust is a stylised means of transferring title which has bound up in it the different roles of trustee and beneficiary. However, there are two aspects of the sentiment which would cause me to take issue with this statement as a definitive expression of the private trust. The first issue is with the term 'gift'. Trusts are often concerned with allocations of title in complex commercial situations. It would not be correct to say that commercial parties are making gifts (or outright transfers) of property in many of these situations. Rather, they are structuring the holding of title in property which is deployed for their common interaction (as considered in *Quistclose Investments v Rolls Razor*[2] and *Clough Mill v Martin*[3]). Alternatively, express trusts are often concerned with the allocation of property rights in circumstances in which the parties are unaware that they are creating trusts.[4] In any event, a trust is not a gift, properly so-called, precisely because an intention to make a gift will not be perfected by means of a trust.[5] What is true is that there is a general intention to pass title in property – which a lay person might well term a 'gift'.

The second complaint follows on from the first and takes issue with the suggestion that the express private trust operates on the basis of pre-meditated gift and not as a means of policing the conscience of the legal owner of property. As is clear from the leading speech of Lord Browne-Wilkinson in *Westdeutsche Landesbank Girozentrale v Islington LBC*,[6] the trust is founded on the conscience of the legal owner of property. This statement has an awkward

---

1 Moffat, 1999, 92.
2 *Quistclose Investments Ltd v Rolls Razor Ltd (In Liquidation)* [1970] AC 567.
3 [1984] 3 All ER 982.
4 *Paul v Constance* [1977] 1 WLR 527.
5 *Milroy v Lord* (1862) 4 De GF & J 264.
6 [1996] AC 669.

provenance. On the one hand it expresses the reason why, in principle, a trust would be enforced on a defendant.

However, in many situations the trust arises as a result of a will drafted by a testator creating a trust, or out of a contract which provides that X shall hold identified property for Y until specified contingencies occur: the creation of a trust usually derives from some other action of the parties which the law of property recognises as vesting an equitable interest in a set of claimants and merely legal title in other people as trustees. It is only in relation to breach of such obligations of property law norms, or in situations in which the parties do not understand that a trust is the proper analysis of their interaction, that an express trust could be said to arise on the basis of conscience as opposed to being merely explicable *ex post facto* as a control of conscience.

7.1.3 The role of equity as guardian of conscience

Moffat is right to remind us of the element of time. Trusts extend equity's control of conscience over time. It also reminds us that there are more elemental forces at work in relation to equity and trusts. To explain which elemental forces I mean, take the example of the ground-breaking work in theoretical physics in relation to chaos theory in the late 20th century. Whereas we had previously understood the physical world as being built on rigid building blocks called atoms, we now understand the world to operate on the basis of particles and waves of energy moving in more random ways: a phenomenon referred to as 'chaos theory'. And yet, this seemingly random activity at the sub-atomic level produces order: trees that grow towards the sun, solid rock, and so on. Within our atoms are gluons and quarks and other exotic phenomena which scientists are still discovering. Therefore, we could think of our strict legal rules, akin to our atoms, containing more chaotic but equally essential phenomena like equitable principles, akin to the sub-atomic particles, which seem to move in random patterns but which are essential to maintaining the fabric of the whole.[7] In this way we can think about equity as being an essential and integral factor in the maintenance of the overall fabric of the law. Equity is a form of energy which supplements the whole of private law and which is an essential part of its structure.

So the law of trusts, and equity more generally, are required to reconcile parties in conflict from a wide range of causes including wills, commercial contracts, and family disputes. It is suggested that the single idea of 'conscience' will solve all of those various disputes. Evidently the notion of conscience employed will be required to be different in each one of those contexts – but it is not apparent how we decide on the appropriate form of conscience to apply to such cases in the abstract. This ideal of good conscience is a useful way of describing the pattern which equity creates in resolving these disputes; but it is not a means by which the legal system ought to attempt to impose order on that chaos by shoe-horning different social problems into the same ill-fitting boots. As Dr Freud has told us, it is a human response to seek to impose order on chaos, but that is occasionally a symptom of some neurosis founded on our frustration at the fact that the world will just not comply with our desire for order.[8] Instead we must, at times, accept that chaos is the way of things and

7 Cohen and Stewart, 1994.
8 Freud, 1930.

permit our legal norms to reflect this. We must accept that not all of our private law can be reduced to simple rules: instead it is important that we retain an ability to reach the right result even if occasionally we might have to do so by means which go against the letter of the strict rules which we do have. Equity is as much a part of the law as the strict legal rules just as sub-atomic particles are as much a part of matter as the atom.

7.2 DIFFERENT TRENDS IN THE CASES

7.2.1 Formality

The principal way in which the law of trusts seeks to impose order on chaos is by means of legal formalities. Most of the formalities relating to the creation and constitution of trusts are based on the 1677 Statute of Frauds which was concerned to prevent fraudulent claims by people asserting rights to property to which they had no genuine rights.[9] The main problem identified by this legislation was the lack of evidence as to which person owned which rights unless claimants were required to produce written evidence of their entitlement before their claim would even be entertained by the courts. This approach was the basis for formalities as to declaration of trust over land, conveyance of rights in land, dispositions of equitable interests and the proper creation of wills.

That thinking has also informed much of the case law in this area. The rules as to certainty of intention, of objects and of subject matter are all based on the courts' need to be able to understand the settlor's intentions and thus to control the trustees' actions. Similarly, the beneficiary principle was founded such that the courts would be able to enforce the trust through the claims brought before them by beneficiaries. Indeed, for all the squabbling among the judiciary as to the precise scope of the beneficiary principle,[10] the only area on which all of their Lordships could agree was the foundation of the principle on the need for there to be some person who could bring the matter before the courts.

The cases making up the *Vandervell*[11] litigation, together with *Oughtred*[12] and *Grey*,[13] all demonstrate the way in which the law of trusts deals with innovative thinking to manipulate trusts law concepts. While the courts remain wedded to principles of certainty, the use of trusts law principles highlights the inherent flexibility in the core ideas. For each potential for tax liability, or for each argument that a trust might be invalid, there is a range of ways and means of avoiding those pitfalls. So, in relation to the void purpose trust,[14] it is possible to validate a trust intended in truth for abstract purposes by making gifts for the benefit of identified individuals,[15] by passing control of capital,[16] by making a transfer to an unincorporated association as an accretion to its funds[17] and so forth. Similarly, a disposition of an

---

9 Griffiths, 2003.
10 *Leahy v Attorney-General for NSW* [1959] AC 457; *Re Denley* [1969] 1 Ch 373; *Re Lipinski's Will Trusts* [1976] Ch 235.
11 [1967] 2 AC 291.
12 [1960] AC 206.
13 [1960] AC 1.
14 As discussed in Chapter 4.
15 *Re Denley* [1969] 1 Ch 373.
16 *Re Lipinski* [1976] Ch 235.
17 *Re Recher's WT* [1972] Ch 526.

equitable interest can be avoided by transferring that interest together with the legal title, or by terminating the trust and declaring a new trust, or by passing that interest under a specifically enforceable contract, or by varying the terms of the trust.[18]

What is interesting is the strict adherence to formality and the spirit of the legislation in decisions by Viscount Simonds in *Leahy*[19] and in *Grey v IRC*,[20] when compared with more purposive approaches taken by other judges in later cases. What this illustrates is a movement away from perceiving the law of trusts as being something to do with the strict observance of age-old rules and a shift towards enabling citizens to make use of trusts law techniques to achieve socially desirable goals. It would be wrong to try to think of the distinctions between these various cases as being capable of reconciliation one with another. The approach taken by Goff J in *Re Denley* and by Oliver J in *Re Lipinski* is simply different from that taken by Viscount Simonds in *Leahy*. Two different generations of judges had different attitudes to the role of the law, in exactly the same way that two generations of ordinary people would have different tastes in music. Viscount Simonds is concerned to see observance of the law for the law's sake; the next generation of judges prefers to permit people to use trusts provided that they do not transgress certain mandatory rules about the possibility of some beneficiary being able to enforce the trust in court.

The law of trusts should be seen as a developing literature in exactly the same way that one would study developments in the novel, fashion or film. As time passes new ideas come to the fore and replace old ideas. Many of the core decisions in this subject were settled in the mid–19th century. Consider how many pivotal cases were decided in the reign of Queen Victoria between 1837 and 1901: *Milroy v Lord* (1862), *Saunders v Vautier* (1841), *Fletcher v Fletcher* (1844), *Knight v Knight* 1840); *M'Fadden v Jenkyns* (1842), and in relation to company law *Salomon v Salomon* (1897) which held that companies were separate legal persons and not trusts at all. That timing is no surprise in itself. During the Victorian era it was commonplace to suggest that the commercial success of the British Empire in taking trade to the furthest corners of the globe had a profound effect on the opinions of the educated classes in England and Wales. As Norman Davies put it in his monumental history of *The Isles*,[21] during this period 'the centralised British Empire was still the largest economic unit on the world map, holding astronomic potential for further growth and development'. It would be churlish to suppose that the great developments in the formalisation of the express trust through certainties and perpetuities rules (which established the trust as a more useful commercial tool and which also identified the company as a distinct legal person better suited to raising capital for entrepreneurs) happened coincidentally during the same period as the British Empire was establishing itself as the world's leading economic power and as English law was establishing itself as the commercial world's lingua franca.

7.2.2 Redistribution of wealth

The law of trusts and the development of equity are two very important means by which the law absorbs more general, social agreements as to the sort of morality to which family and

---

18   As discussed in Chapter 5.
19   [1959] AC 457.
20   [1960] AC 1.
21   Davies, 1999, 642.

commercial life ought to conform. With the movement into an avowedly free capitalist society in which ordinary citizens are more than mere serfs under a feudal system (and arguably beyond that into a globalised society in which citizens have enforceable human rights), the central point of trusts law has changed. The certainties of the family settlement which devolved title in property down the generations for the landed gentry have given way to rules on perpetuities which prefer the free flow of capital to patriarchal domination.

In the pre-Victorian era, the trust had become an ever more important vehicle for the distribution of wealth between members of families on death or during life. In the late 20th century the trust became an increasingly important means of avoiding liability to tax by obfuscating the true ownership of property for tax purposes, or for the purposes of insolvency law. The decision in *Grey v IRC*,[22] and possibly even that in *Leahy*,[23] was caught in that gap between social change towards tax avoidance and so forth and a judicial reluctance to validate such arrangements through the agency of trusts law.

Moffat examines the interaction between inheritance tax, trusts and the distribution of wealth in the UK in detail.[24] The real difficulty in attempting to establish a picture of wealth distribution and the extent to which it is tied up in trusts is that express trusts are private and information is available only through the tax system. Similarly, it is not always possible to know whether trusts are created for tax avoidance, for the maintenance of property, for the use of a succession of individuals, or for the maintenance of particular individuals. What is clear is that, even given the rules on perpetuities, trusts do permit those sections of the population who are sufficiently well informed to organise their affairs both so as to minimise their liability to tax and so as to benefit future generations of their own relations.

7.2.3 Questions of technique

What the student should take away from the study of express trusts is an appreciation of the many pliable techniques which exist for the manipulation of trusts law for a number of purposes. Those purposes fall into two general categories. First, as a socially useful means by which ordinary citizens and corporations can organise the terms of their communal use of property. In Part 8, we shall consider the ways in which trusts and derivatives of trusts techniques are used to organise charities, pension funds, co-operatives and even (in a very particular manner) NHS trusts. Similar techniques based on the stewardship of property by a trustee for the ultimate entitlement of beneficiaries also form an important part of commercial agreements, as considered in outline in Chapter 2 and in more detail in Part 7.

Secondly, as a means of using trusts to elude or avoid legal problems. So, for example, the preceding discussion of the carrying on of dispositions of equitable interests, in ways which avoid the provisions of s 53(1)(c) of the Law of Property Act 1925, has indicated the manner in which trusts lawyers are able to structure their clients' affairs to achieve the desired effect. The same holds true for situations in which the client is not seeking to avoid some legal rule but rather to achieve an identified, desired effect. Therefore, a commercial contract between two multinational financial institutions dealing in financial derivatives, or between two sole

---

22 [1960] AC 1.
23 *Leahy v Attorney-General for NSW* [1959] AC 457.
24 Moffat, 1999, 76 et seq.

traders dealing in used cars, can be secured by providing that payment is held on trust until both buyer and seller are satisfied that the contract has been properly performed. The same trusts law techniques will apply, with suitable adaptations, to both circumstances. Express trusts law is therefore also about the development of tools with which lawyers can help their clients to achieve their goals.

With the increasing tightening of the formalities relating to the creation of express trusts, we might think that the trust is becoming ever more similar to the contract. As will become apparent in Parts 4–6, even in relation to trusts implied by law there is a tendency for the courts to generate increasingly rigid rules for the recognition of such trusts. As a result, much of the fluidity previously identified with the notion of 'conscience' has been lost. Indeed the rules of equity are becoming ever more reminiscent of the rules of the common law. The formalities necessary to create an express trust are similar to the three-stage test for the creation of a common law contract: offer/acceptance, consideration and intent to effect legal relations.

Equity ought to be about more than merely creating trusts by numbers. While the use of the express trust will become ever more institutionalised with its deployment in commercial contracts, will trusts and so forth, it should not be forgotten that this difficult concept of 'conscience' lies in the background. The question as to what constitutes good and bad conscience in different circumstances is a very real one, not necessarily with reference to the creation of such trusts but certainly in relation to the management and breach of such arrangements. The available remedies and equitable responses to contravention of the trust will differ in desirability from context to context. Therefore, this book takes the unusual step of dividing its later discussion between uses of the trust in commercial cases and in welfare-related cases.

In short, equity and trusts have a potentially far broader application than is at present allowed. The development of those principles will be a question of reading and applying the literature of equity and the literature of modern social theory to find the commonalities and dissonances between their shared use of English words like 'equity', 'justice' and 'efficiency', as discussed in Chapter 32.

7.2.4 Equitable estoppel and express trusts

One recurrent theme in the law relating to express trusts is the presence of equitable estoppel propping up situations in which express trusts are otherwise not available. These are contradictory currents, in truth. Equitable estoppel, in the form of proprietary estoppel, arises in situations in which the claimant has acted to his detriment in reliance upon an assurance made by the defendant.[25] The remedy supplied is at the discretion of the court. Typically it is such remedy as is necessary to achieve the 'minimum equity to do justice to the plaintiff':[26] this may result in a remedy which varies between a right to absolute title in the property at issue[27] and a purely personal claim to money.[28] What is most significant is that the

---

25 *Re Basham* [1986] 1 WLR 1498; *Yaxley v Gotts* [2000] 1 All ER 711.
26 *Crabb v Arun DC* [1976] Ch 179; *Yaxley v Gotts* [2000] 1 All ER 711.
27 *Pascoe v Turner* [1979] 2 All ER 945.
28 *Baker v Baker* (1993) 25 HLR 408.

purpose of equitable estoppel is to reverse the detriment suffered by the claimant. The remedy is therefore not simply that necessary to achieve the 'minimum equity to do justice to the plaintiff' but more precisely that necessary to achieve that justice by compensating the detriment suffered by the claimant.[29]

It is one of the principal tenets of the law of express trusts that equity will not assist a volunteer.[30] From that proposition flows a number of other rules. First, equity will not complete an incompletely constituted trust.[31] Therefore, a disappointed person who considered himself otherwise entitled to receive a gift could not argue that the donor ought to be deemed to have declared a trust over that property. That is, unless the donor had done everything necessary for her to do to divest herself of title in the property.[32] Secondly, no claimant will be entitled to assert title in property unless there has been a declaration of trust and until the trust has been constituted.[33] Thirdly, flowing from the second, no claimant will be entitled to claim rights under a trust unless the formalities necessary for the declaration of the trust have been performed.[34]

In all of these situations the main tenet of trusts law is that it is the intention of the settlor which is enforced by the court. As we have seen, there are issues concerning the interaction between the intentions of the settlor and the rights of the beneficiaries to assert rights under *Saunders v Vautier*[35] to call for the trust property and terminate the trust. However, it is the donative intention of the settlor which is carried out. Cases like *Paul v Paul*[36] and *Re Ralli's WT*[37] indicate that the settlor is not able to unpack the trust once it has been properly constituted, unless she has reserved to herself some express power to do so.

Where the trust is held to be invalid, the claimant may be able to claim rights under proprietary estoppel on the following basis. Where the settlor has not simply expressed a general intention to create a trust at some time in the future but has also made some assurance to the claimant that she will be a beneficiary under that trust, the claimant might argue that she acted to her detriment in reliance on that assurance. Clearly, it would be necessary for the claimant to demonstrate that she had in fact suffered some detriment in reliance on that assurance – as considered above, the appropriate remedy would be dependent on the nature and extent of that detriment. Assuming that the court considered a proprietary remedy was appropriate, the beneficiary might be entitled to a substantially similar right under equitable estoppel to that which would have been available if the trust had been properly constituted. In effect, then, equitable estoppel provides for a discretionary, reactive remedy which counter-balances the rigid rules of certainty required by the law of express trusts. Estoppel therefore fills a gap left by the increasingly institutional law of trusts to provide for justice in individual situations.

29 *Lim v Ang* [1992] 1 WLR 113.
30 *Milroy v Lord* (1862) 4 De GF & J 264.
31 *Ibid.*
32 *Re Rose* [1952] Ch 499.
33 *Milroy v Lord* (1862) 4 De GF & J 264.
34 See perhaps *Grey v IRC* [1960] AC 1.
35 (1841) 4 Beav 115.
36 (1882) 20 Ch D 742.
37 [1964] 2 WLR 144.

The law of trusts has developed a range of doctrines which validate trusts even though these general principles have not been obeyed: for example, constructive trusts, secret trusts, and the rule in *Strong v Bird*.[38] The doctrines of constructive trusts and secret trusts were developed to prevent unconscionable conduct and fraud. Their intention is distinct from that in estoppel. Estoppel prevents the claimant suffering detriment precisely as a result of the non-performance of some assurance given by the defendant, whereas the constructive and secret trusts doctrines protect the claimant against the defendant's unconscionable behaviour. There is clearly potential for overlap between these doctrines (as considered in *Yaxley v Gotts*).[39] The distinction, as discussed in Chapter 15 below, is that the constructive trust imposes a retrospective, institutional trust over property, whereas the estoppel claim grants either personal or proprietary claims prospectively on a discretionary basis from the date of the court order. Similarly, express trusts are concerned narrowly with property rights over identified property,[40] whereas estoppel is concerned more generally with the avoidance of detriment. Within the canon of equity, then, the doctrine of equitable estoppel is considerably more broadly based than the law relating to express trusts.

---

38 (1874) LR 18 Eq 315.
39 [2000] 1 All ER 711.
40 *Re Goldcorp* [1995] 1 AC 74.

Part 3

Administration of trusts

Chapter 8

The duties of trustees

OVERVIEW

The manner in which trustees are obliged to carry out their fiduciary duties is the core of the trust – the trustees owe those duties to the beneficiaries in relation to the trust fund. Statute provides for limited situations in which trustees who are incapable of performing their duties can be removed from office and other trustees appointed in their place.[1]

The duties of the trustees are manifold. The duties considered in this section are the following.

(1) The duties on acceptance of office relating to the need to familiarise oneself with the terms, conditions and history of the management of the trust. (2) The duty to obey the terms of the trust unless directed to do otherwise by the court. (3) The duty to safeguard the trust assets, including duties to maintain the trust property, as well as to ensure that it is applied in accordance with the directions set out in the trust instrument. (4) The duty to act even-handedly between beneficiaries, which means that the trustees are required to act impartially between beneficiaries and to avoid conflicts of interest. (5) The duty to act with reasonable care, meaning generally a duty to act as though a prudent person of business acting on behalf of someone for whom one feels morally bound to provide. (6) Duties in relation to trust expenses.

(7) The duties of investment, requiring prudence and the acquisition of the highest possible rate of return in the context. (8) The duty to distribute the trust property correctly. (9) The duty to avoid conflicts of interest, not to earn unauthorised profits from the fiduciary office, not to deal on one's own behalf with trust property on pain of such transactions

1 Section 8.2.

being voidable, and the obligation to deal fairly with the trust property. (10) The duty to preserve the confidence of the beneficiaries, especially in relation to Chinese wall arrangements. (11) The duty to act gratuitously, without any right to payment not permitted by the trust instrument or by the general law. (12) The duty to account and to provide information. (13) The duty to take into account relevant considerations and to overlook irrelevant considerations, failure to do so may lead to the court setting aside an exercise of the trustees' powers if they have committed a breach of trust in so doing.[2] The nature of the trustees' liabilities for breaching any of these duties are considered in Chapter 18.

The trustees bear only a limited obligation to give information to beneficiaries in relation to the administration and management of the trust fund and in relation only to that part of a trust fund in which they have a proprietary interest. Recent case law has emphasised the court's inherent discretion to make orders relating to the administration of trusts and therefore the access of beneficiaries to information may be enlarged in the future or alternatively it may continue to be exercised in accordance with traditional principles. Trustees are not obliged to disclose to beneficiaries any matter in relation to any exercise of their fiduciary discretion, nor are they obliged to disclose any confidential matter. The court reserves discretion as to the manner in which trustees exercise their powers, but not as to the content of any such decision unless there has been palpable wrongdoing.[3]

Trustees are entitled to have their liabilities for breach of trust and for the commission of any tort limited by the terms of the trust instrument. Such liability exclusion clauses are equitable devices and not contractual provisions. Trustees can limit their liability for negligence and gross negligence, but they may not limit their liability for dishonesty or fraud. There is a division in the authorities between a permissive approach to such exclusion clauses and an approach which prefers to limit them.[4]

The trustees may be controlled by the beneficiaries by means of an application to the court. The court has an inherent jurisdiction to make orders in relation to the administration of a trust. The court may make orders by way variously of (a) giving directions, (b) assuming administrative control, (c) judicial review (in a private law sense) of the trustees' actions, or (d) setting aside any decision of a trustee made by taking into account irrelevant considerations or failing to take into account relevant considerations.[5]

8.1 INTRODUCTION

It is a remarkable feature of the law of trusts is that there is no central statement of the duties owed by trustees in either a statute or in a single case; rather, there is a sense of the obligations borne by trustees which is expressed by the idea that trustees will bear those duties whenever conscience demands that they do.[6] There is no core of trusteeship in this sense but rather each example of trusteeship falls to be interpreted on its own terms.[7] There is a general

---

2 Section 8.3.
3 Section 8.4.
4 Section 8.5.
5 Section 8.6.
6 *Westdeutsche Landesbank v Islington LBC* [1996] AC 669.
7 *Cf Armitage v Nurse* [1998] Ch 241; Hayton, 1996.

sense of what it means to be a trustee which is then sensitive to the context of each trust instrument or to the context of each individual fiduciary office, and which is observable from the many decided cases in which the duties of trustees have been considered.

It should be borne in mind that there are two very different forms of trust at issue here. At one extreme there are trusts the terms of which are contained in carefully drafted trust instruments and which are managed by professional trustees, whereas at the other extreme there are informally created trusts or trusts without carefully drafted trust instruments whose trustees may not be professional trust managers. Carefully drafted trust instruments may well adapt or exclude some of the general principles of trusteeship which are considered in this chapter and in the succeeding chapters. Therefore, it should be recalled that any question as to the application of these principles in any given context will frequently be answered by an analysis of the trust instrument in question. In this chapter we will focus on the general principles and we will consider the extent to which it is possible to exclude general principles of trusts law in a trust instrument, whether those general principles were created by case law or by statute.

As we shall see in this chapter and in the two chapters to follow, there are many conflicting approaches to the duties owed by trustees on the decided cases. Some of this uncertainty is a result of the development of our understanding of the role of the trustee between the 19th century, when many of these principles were formalised for the first time, and the 21st century. Other difficulties are caused by the different contexts in which trustees may act: for example, the difference between professional and non-professional trustees, between trustees dealing entirely with family property and trustees managing large pension funds, between trustees of express trusts and trustees of trusts implied by law.

This chapter is organised as follows. First, a consideration of the manner in which trustees are appointed, removed and how they are treated by the trust.[8] Secondly, a survey of the general duties of trustees.[9] This section forms the focal point of this chapter and gives us our clearest understanding of the nature of trusteeship in express trusts. Thirdly, the particular nature of the trustees' duty to account to the beneficiaries and, more specifically, the particular types of information which the trustees are required to give to particular kinds of beneficiaries about the management of the trust. Clearly, if the beneficiary principle is to function effectively in practice so that the beneficiaries are able to hold the trustees to account for any shortcomings in their management of the trust, then it is important to know how much information the beneficiaries can demand from the trustees.[10] Fourthly, the important question of the trustees' right to limit or exclude their liabilities for negligence or breach of trust by the insertion of a term to that effect in the trust instrument.[11] Fifthly, an analysis of the way in which beneficiaries can control and set aside trustees' actions.

8.2 THE OFFICE OF TRUSTEE

The manner in which trustees are obliged to carry out their fiduciary duties is the core of the trust – the trustees owe those duties to the beneficiaries in relation to the trust

---

8 Section 8.2.
9 Section 8.3.
10 Section 8.4. See, eg, *Morice v Bishop of Durham* (1805) 10 Ves 522 and the requirement, considered in Chapter 4, that there must be a beneficiary in whose favour the court can decree performance.
11 Section 8.5.

fund. Statute provides for limited situations in which trustees who are incapable of performing their duties can be removed from office and other trustees appointed in their place. The forms of incapacity include death, infancy, mental ill-health, absence from the jurisdiction and unwillingness to act. Trustees have limited rights to remuneration for their services, to be reimbursed for their expenses and indemnified against certain liabilities assumed when acting on trust business.

8.2.1 The nature of the office of trustee

The scope of trusteeship in relation to express trusts

This section considers the nature of trusteeship. While, in truth, most of this book is a consideration of the nature of trusteeship and the rights of beneficiaries, this chapter focuses on the office of trustee itself and the manner in which legal persons become trustees and the general obligations which are owed by trustees unless something is provided to the contrary in the trust instrument. That the office of trustee is in truth an example of equity acting on the conscience of the legal owner of property was explored in Chapter 1. This chapter pursues that thinking into the detail of the office of trustee.

The personal obligations incumbent on a trustee in relation to a beneficiary were considered in part in relation to the enforcement of trusts in Part 2, and are also discussed in Chapter 9, Chapter 10 and in Part 6 of this book in relation to the liabilities of a trustee who commits a breach of trust. This chapter focuses on the nature of a number of those obligations specifically to do with the obligations of the trustee to communicate information to the beneficiaries and the manner in which trustees are required to carry out their duties.

Duties on acceptance of the office of trustee

Once a trustee has accepted the office of trustee, she is then bound by all of the terms of the trust instrument and, where applicable, by the requirements of the general law of trusts. These principles are considered at para 8.3.1 below.

Refusal to act as trustee

A person may refuse to act as a trustee and is perfectly entitled to refuse the entire office from the outset.[12] Equally, it is open to a trustee to limit her liabilities as a trustee[13] as well as to refuse to act in the first place.[14] If the trustee does limit or exclude her liabilities, then those liabilities are reduced or removed to that extent.[15] Acceptance will be proved clearly if the trustee either signs the trust instrument[16] or gives an explicit declaration of assent such as writing a letter to that effect.[17]

---

12 *Robinson v Pett* (1734) 3 Peere Wms 249, *per* Lord Talbot.
13 *Armitage v Nurse* [1998] Ch 241.
14 In the event that a person refuses to act as trustee then that person cannot in principle be said to be bound in conscience to act as a trustee.
15 This question is considered in detail in section 8.5 below.
16 *Jones v Higgins* (1866) LR 2 Eq 538.
17 *Vickers v Bell* (1864) 4 De GJ & S 274.

Nevertheless, two complications arise. First, what if the trustee accepts the office of trustee initially and then seeks to refuse that office subsequently? If the trustee has accepted the office of trustee and then seeks to repudiate it later, the refusal of the office is ineffective.[18] Instead the trustee (for such she will have become) would have to seek formally to disclaim the office, as considered below.[19]

The second problem in relation to refusal to act would arise if an individual had refused to act as trustee from the outset but had nevertheless come inadvertently into possession of the property which she was supposed to hold on trust. Suppose, for example, that a settlor thrust a valuable chattel into the hands of his intended trustee while on his deathbed and died before the intended trustee had a chance to request that the settlor appoint someone else as trustee. In such a situation, the trustee could not be bound by the office of trustee having repudiated the office but nevertheless should be treated as being either a bare trustee of the property, required to hold it until some other person can be found to act as trustee in her place, or as a bailee of the property to the same extent. What would be inequitable would be to hold that person liable to observe all of the terms of the trusteeship – as to investment of the property and so forth – as though she was actually bound to act as a full trustee.

Duties applicable in relation to trusts implied by law

What is unclear from the decided cases is the extent to which the rules considered below should be taken as applying to resulting and constructive trusts, which are considered in detail in Part 4. It is clear that the appointment and removal of trustees, and issues as to conflicts of interests and duties to give information, apply to trustees of express trusts. It is to be supposed that the same duties and obligations must be applied to trustees under resulting trusts and constructive trusts *from the date of the order* which confirms the existence of such a trust. What is more difficult is the extent to which such obligations should be deemed to have existed from the time that the trust came into existence but before the date of the court order.

The precise nature of such obligations remains unclear because there has been little discussion of them in the case law – frequently because the finding of a constructive trust or a resulting trust resolves questions as to title in the property in any event. It has been said that it would be 'a mistake to suppose that in every situation in which a constructive trust arises the legal owner is necessarily subject to all the fiduciary obligations and disabilities of an express trustee'.[20]

8.2.2 Appointment of trustees

It is possible for a trust instrument to create its own quasi-legislative framework for the powers of trustees and others to appoint or remove trustees. The validity of such provisions will depend upon any objections to them based on public policy. In the absence of any such

---

18 *Re Sharman's Will Trusts* [1942] Ch 311, 314. Refusal of probate even when a person has promised a testator that she would act will nevertheless be effective under the law of succession: *Doyle v Blake* (1804) 2 Sch & Lef 231, 239, *per* Lord Redesdale LC.

19 See para 8.5.2 below.

20 *Lonrho plc v Fayed (No 2)* [1991] 4 All ER 961, *per* Millett J.

provisions, the Trustee Act (TA) 1925 will apply. It is possible for a settlor to exclude the terms of the 1925 Act in whole or in part.[21] Therefore, the settlor may choose to create a different mechanism by which trustees are to be appointed to the office of trustee. This might be done, for example, to facilitate tax planning by enabling trustees resident in jurisdictions outside the UK to be appointed to the office of trustee.

Appointment of trustees

There is a statutory power of appointing new or additional trustees contained in s 36 of the TA 1925. Section 36(1) provides that it is possible to appoint new trustees in circumstances in which an existing trustee falls into one of the following categories: is dead; remains outside the UK for a continuous period of more than 12 months; desires to be discharged; refuses to act as a trustee; is unfit to act as a trustee; is incapable of acting as a trustee; or is an infant. In such circumstances, any person who is nominated by the terms of the trust to appoint a replacement, or failing that the remaining trustees (or the personal representatives of the last surviving trustee), may by writing appoint one or more other persons to be trustees in the place of the trustee who has fallen into one of these seven categories. In *Richards v Mackay*,[22] in a decision relating to the appointment of foreign trustees, Millett J held that 'where the trustees maintain their discretion . . . the court should need to be satisfied only that the proposed transaction is not so inappropriate that no reasonable trustee could entertain it'. Therefore, it is unlikely that a court will find that the appointment of trustees will be unenforceable unless there is some manifest defect in the course of action proposed by the trustees.

The statutory provisions further provide in s 36(2) of the TA 1925 that where a trustee has been removed under a power in the trust, a new trustee or trustees may be appointed as if that pre-existing trustee had been dead. Where the trustees have indeed died, a power of appointment given to that trustee is exercisable by the executors (or personal representatives) of the last surviving trustee.[23] In circumstances where there is a sole trustee, any person authorised by the trust to nominate a replacement trustee may appoint one or more additional trustees in writing.[24] Where a trustee is incapable pursuant to the Mental Health Act 1983, no new trustee can be appointed without an order to that effect being made under the Mental Health Act 1983.[25] Any appointees put into office under this s 36 are treated as having the same powers as if they had been originally appointed trustee.[26]

There is a distinction between 'unfitness to act' and being 'incapable of acting'. The concept of unfitness refers to whether or not the person in question is legally capable of acting, for example by being insolvent, and so it relates to whether or not she has the legal power to act as a trustee. By contrast, the concept of incapacity in this context refers more generally to being physically or mentally unable to carry out the duties of trusteeship. Therefore, a person in a coma would be incapable of acting as a trustee, whereas a person who had become bankrupt would be unfit to act as a trustee.

---

21 TA 1925, s 69.
22 [1990] 1 OTPR 1.
23 TA 1925, s 36(4).
24 *Ibid*, s 36(6).
25 *Ibid*, s 36(9).
26 *Ibid*, s 36(7).

Inherent judicial discretion

The court retains a power to appoint new trustees under s 41 of the TA 1925. That section provides that '[t]he court may, whenever it is expedient to appoint a new trustee or new trustees, and it is found inexpedient, difficult or impracticable to do so without the assistance of the court, make an order appointing new trustee or trustees . . .'.[27] Therefore, the court's own discretion does not require that it be necessary for the court to act, merely that it is considered to be 'expedient' on the basis of the difficulty in relying on some other mechanism. An example of such expediency is where one trustee is obstructing the proper administration of a trust by refusing to consent to the actions proposed by the other trustees. In such a situation, the court may deem it expedient to appoint a new trustee to enable the trust's purposes to be performed.

One of the most common reasons for making alterations in this way in practice is for the purposes of tax avoidance. In many circumstances, where the trustees are resident in a tax jurisdiction outside the UK, the trust will be treated as resident in that other jurisdiction and therefore not liable to UK tax. Consequently, a trust which has generated sizeable income or a taxable capital gain may wish to change its residence from the UK to another jurisdiction. The most straightforward method of achieving this is to appoint new trustees resident in that other jurisdiction and have the UK resident trustees withdraw.

On this issue, it was held in *Re Whitehead's WT*[28] that there was a distinction between exercise of a court discretion and a discretion belonging solely to the trustees. Where it is the exercise of the court's own discretion,[29] the court is unlikely to allow the appointment where the purpose of that appointment is the avoidance of tax. However, tax-saving is a valid consideration for trustees and therefore, where it is a matter for the trustees' own discretion, the trustees can act on a desire to minimise the tax exposure of the trust.[30]

Miscellaneous statutory powers of appointment

Under the supplemental provisions contained in s 37 of the TA 1925, the number of trustees may be increased so as to create a separate set of trustees (not exceeding four in number) for the purpose of holding a particular fund, especially where it is a complex trust structure or where the fund comprises many different types of property. In any event, where there is only one trustee at the creation of the trust it is not obligatory to appoint more than one trustee. However, a sole trustee shall not be appointed where that trustee would be unable to give a good receipt for the trust property.[31] There is sufficient evidence that there is a vacancy among the trustees in relation to a trust of land, provided that there is a statement in any trust instrument identifying one of the grounds in s 36(1) in relation to the existing trustees.[32] In relation specifically to trusts of land, s 19 of the Trusts of Land and Appointment of Trustees Act 1996 empowers all of the beneficiaries acting *sui juris* to give a written direction to the trustees to appoint or remove a trustee.

---

27 *Ibid*, s 41.
28 [1971] 1 WLR 833.
29 Eg, under the Variation of Trusts Act 1958, considered in Chapter 10 below.
30 Cf the discussion of the *Hastings-Bass* principle considered at para 8.3.13 below.
31 TA 1925, s 37(2).
32 *Ibid*, s 38.

In relation to the appointment of new trustees, the issue arises as to the manner in which property must be vested in the new trustees. Further to s 40(1) of the TA 1925, this vesting of the trust fund in the newly appointed trustees takes place automatically, provided that the appointment of the new trustees was effected by deed. This principle does not apply where the property is held by personal representatives and not by a trustee.[33] There are three exceptions to the s 40(1) principle set out in s 40(4). First, where the trust property is a mortgage of land, there is no automatic vesting because the mortgage deed will not make mention of the existence of the trust and it would become a complicated matter to ensure that redemption of the mortgage had been properly carried out. Secondly, in relation to a lease containing a prohibition on assignment without consent because the automatic transfer of the property to new trustees would defeat the purpose of that covenant against assignment without consent. Thirdly, in relation to shares and securities held on a register, because an automatic re-vesting of the property would defeat the statutory requirements for registration of the titleholder to effect a good transfer.

8.2.3 Principles governing dealings with the trust property

General questions relating to specific dealings with the trust property – whether selling it, allowing beneficiaries to occupy it or otherwise – are considered in Chapter 10.[34] Otherwise, the general principles which govern the manner in which trustees are required to bear in mind the interests of various beneficiaries and to avoid conflicts of interests, always governed by a general duty of care, are considered below in section 8.3.

8.2.4 The manner in which the trustees are obliged to act in general terms

The fundamental requirement of good conscience

Trustees are required to act in good conscience, at the most basic level.[35] This includes the avoidance of conflicts of interest between the trustees' personal interests and the interests of the beneficiaries.[36] The material considered in this chapter presents us with a map of those obligations which are generally said to impact on the trustees' consciences. What will emerge is that there is no single list of the obligations owed by trustees in general terms; rather, each trustee's obligations fall to be interpreted on the basis of that trustee's particular trust instrument or on the basis of the circumstances in which each trust was created (if there was no trust instrument or if the trust instrument was silent on a particular point).

The general duty of care and prudence

The general law of trusts has always required that a trustee acts with prudence and care.[37] This venerable principle has been adapted by statute into a general duty of care which is

---

33 *Re Cockburn's WT* [1957] 3 WLR 212.
34 See in particular section 10.1 below.
35 *Westdeutsche Landesbank v Islington LBC* [1996] AC 669.
36 See para 8.3.9 below.
37 See, eg, *Speight v Gaunt* (1883) 9 App Cas 1; *Learoyd v Whiteley* (1887) 12 App Cas 727.

considered in detail below.[38] Thus, whereas the trustees' duties are said to be based on a requirement of good conscience, the trustees' more precise duties are also to be considered in terms of duties of good management and fair dealing with the trust property. This does not mean that the idea of conscience is not important. Rather, it is the notion of conscience which imposes the office of trustee in the first place. Thereafter, in relation to express trusts, these duties of good management become significant and the duties of fair dealing become significant in relation to the operation of all trusts. The particular contexts in which these general principles are applied will emerge as this chapter progresses.

Trustees must act jointly; whether they are liable entirely jointly or severally

Where there is more than one trustee, those trustees are expected to act jointly.[39] Therefore, as a general rule, the trust property is required to be vested in the name of all of the trustees jointly, all of the trustees must receive any trust income, all of the trustees must give a receipt, and so forth. That said, however, there are circumstances in which the trustees need not act jointly. The trust instrument may permit some other means of proceeding without unanimity[40] or necessity may require that assets be registered in the name of only one of the trustees at a given time.[41] In such situations, however, the property must not be left in the hands of one or only a few of the trustees for longer than is necessary.[42]

Nevertheless, no individual trustee will be liable for any default which is the default individually of another trustee.[43] Therefore, as we shall see, it is a vexed business to know in which situations the trustees are considered to be responsible entirely as a collective entity and in which situations they bear only individual liability. Clearly this is important from the perspective of the beneficiaries. If the trustees are only liable for their own personal defaults, then the beneficiaries will only be able to proceed against any given trustee for breach of trust if it can be shown that that trustee was responsible for that breach; however, if the trustees are jointly liable, then the beneficiaries will be able to recover their losses from whichever trustee they choose and it will be a matter for the trustees to allocate liability between themselves.[44]

The nature of the trustees' liability for breach of trust

The nature of liability for breach of trust is considered in detail in Chapter 18. For present purposes it is sufficient to recognise the following. The trustees' principal obligation is to

---

38   See para 8.3.5.

39   *Luke v South Kensington Hotel Co* (1879) 11 Ch D 121; *Re Dixon* (1826) 2 GL & J 114; *Re Hilton* [1909] 2 Ch 548; *Re Whitely* [1910] 1 Ch 600; *Re Butlin's Settlement Trust* [1976] Ch 251.

40   TA 2000, s 11. For example, where only one trustee is to receive income on behalf of all of the other trustees: *Townley v Sherbourne* (1633) Bridg 35, 2 W & TLC (9th edn) 577; *Gouldsworth v Knights* (1843) 11 M & W 337.

41   *Consterdine v Consterdine* (1862) 31 Beav 330.

42   *Brice v Stokes* (1805) 11 Ves 319; *Re Munton* [1927] 1 Ch 262.

43   *Townley v Sherbourne* (1633) Bridg 35, 2 W & TLC (9th edn) 577. This principle was enshrined in the now repealed TA 1925, s 30(1) whereby trustees were liable only for their own acts and defaults. Although a trustee will be liable for any breach of trust of which she has knowledge or which she conceals or, obviously, in which she knowingly participates in some way: *Boardman v Mosman* (1799) 1 Bro CC 68. There will also be liability for failing to protect the interests of the beneficiaries in such a situation: *Brice v Stokes* (1805) 11 Ves 319; *Gough v Smith* [1872] WN 18.

44   Liability for breach of trust is considered in detail in Chapter 18, para 18.2.4.

account to the beneficiaries both in the sense of rendering accounts as to the value of the trust fund[45] and also to account in the sense of making good any loss caused to the trust by some breach of the trustee's obligations. Thus, if the trust suffers a loss which has some causal connection with a breach of trust committed by the trustees, then the trustees are obliged to restore the value lost to the trust.[46] The precise nature of the remedy owed by the trustee in such a circumstance is to account to the beneficiaries for the loss where this idea of accounting may take one of three forms: either recover any property which was lost to the trust by the breach of trust, or to restore the value of the trust fund in cash terms, or to pay equitable compensation for any loss suffered by the trust as a result of the breach of trust.[47]

8.2.5 Removal, death or retirement of trustee

Our focus now turns to the situations in which a trustee can be removed from office.

Voluntary retirement of trustee

It is possible for there to be a retirement of a trustee without a new appointment being made.[48] Where the trust itself contains a power permitting such retirement, that term is decisive of the matter. As considered above, the trustee may retire on the basis of one of the categories set out in s 36(1) of the TA 1925 (for example, unwillingness to act or absence from the jurisdiction).

Alternatively, a trustee who wishes to be discharged from the office of trustee will be deemed to have been discharged provided that there will remain two trustees or a trust corporation, and provided that the trustee has declared this intention by deed.[49] Two further caveats under that section exist to the effect that the remaining trustees must consent to the retirement, as must any person empowered by the trust deed to approve such retirement.

It is also possible for all of the *sui juris* beneficiaries acting together, when absolutely entitled, to consent to the retirement of a trustee. This is an extension of the rule in *Saunders v Vautier*[50] considered above.

Removal of trustee

Where there is an express power in the trust deed permitting the removal of the trustee by means of a specified mechanism in the trust instrument, that will be decisive of the matter (unless it is contrary to public policy). Commercial trusts will frequently contain an express provision for the alteration of the person who is to act as custodian of property. Typically, the commercial purpose would be to enable two commercial parties to appoint an alternative trustee. This change might be motivated by the cost of the trustee's professional fees. The

---

45 As considered below in section 8.4.
46 *Target Holdings v Redferns* [1996] 1 AC 421, considered in detail in Chapter 18.
47 *Ibid.*
48 The decision of a trustee to retire must be voluntary and must not have been induced by undue influence: *Daniel v Drew* [2005] WTLR 807.
49 TA 1925, s 39.
50 (1841) 4 Beav 115.

change might instead be motivated by a desire to make the trust emigrate to a different jurisdiction (perhaps for tax purposes) by appointing a trustee who is resident in another jurisdiction.

Under s 36(1) of the TA 1925, a trustee may be removed on the basis of one of the probanda set out in that subsection, as considered above. The court has jurisdiction under s 41 of the TA 1925 to appoint a new trustee and remove the former trustee. Alternatively, the court may exercise its inherent jurisdiction to remove a trustee where that is considered to be equitable. The court will consider the wishes of the settlor, the interests of all of the beneficiaries under the trust, and the efficient administration of the trust.[51] The court will typically be reluctant to consent to the appointment of trustees resident outside the jurisdiction without some undertaking to be bound by the decision of the court and therefore may remove such trustees where they are interfering with the proper administration of the trust.[52] Similarly, the court will be likely to remove a trustee whose personal interests conflict with the interests of the trust, particularly where that conflict is interfering with the proper administration of the trust. Thus, in *Moore v M'Glynn*,[53] a trustee was removed in circumstances where he set up a business in direct competition with the business interests of the trust. In relation to trusts of land, s 19 of the Trusts of Land and Appointment of Trustees Act 1996 empowers all of the beneficiaries acting *sui juris* to give a written direction to the trustees to appoint or remove a trustee.[54]

8.2.6 Right to remuneration

The trustee is entitled to be remunerated for any service to the trust even if that service could have been performed by a lay trustee (that is, someone not professionally qualified to carry out that task).[55] A trustee acting in a professional capacity is entitled to receive such remuneration as is reasonable in the circumstances.[56] Similarly, delegates may be remunerated on a basis that is reasonable in the circumstances.[57] The provisions as to remuneration of trustees apply only where they have not been expressly excluded by a trust instrument.[58]

8.2.7 Right to reimbursement and indemnity

A trust operates through the personality of the trustees: that is, a trust has no legal personality and therefore the legal title in its property must be vested in the trustees, contracts on behalf of the trust must be effected in the names of the trustees and so forth. In consequence, the trustees incur a range of liabilities in the ordinary conduct of the trust's affairs and the trustees will seek both to be reimbursed for expenses incurred as part of conducting these activities and also indemnified against any liability suffered while conducting those same

51 *Re Tempest* (1866) 1 Ch 485.
52 *Re Freeman's ST* (1887) 37 Ch D 148.
53 (1894) 1 IR 74.
54 See generally *Letterstedt v Broers* (1884) 9 App Cas 371, *per* Lord Blackburn. See also *Adam and Company International Trustees Ltd v Theodore Goddard* (2000) *The Times*, 17 March.
55 TA 2000, s 28(2).
56 *Ibid*, s 29(2), (3): providing the trustee is not a trust corporation or a charitable trustee, governed by the TA 2000, s 30.
57 *Ibid*, s 32.
58 *Ibid*, s 28(1).

activities. First, as to reimbursement, in relation to any expenses incurred while on trust business, the trustee is entitled to be reimbursed from the trust funds or to make payments in
pursuit of the trust's objectives out of the trust fund,[59] provided that such payments are not
made contrary to the terms of the trust.[60] The sorts of expenses which may be recovered
include travelling expenses,[61] expenses incurred in employing agents to perform trust activities,[62] the costs of taking legal advice,[63] and the costs of associated with new trustees famil-
iarising themselves with the trust's affairs.[64] Secondly, a trustee is entitled to payment in
relation to the provision of professional services[65] to the trust if there is a provision in the
trust instrument entitling her to receive such payment.[66] It is no objection to this right of
payment that the services in question could have been performed by a non-professional
trustee.[67] This right to payment can be excluded by the trust instrument.[68]

Thirdly, a trustee is entitled to be indemnified by the trust in relation to any contractual
obligation incurred on behalf of the trust.[69] Self-evidently, if the trustee were not so indemnified, then, by way of example, purchases made on behalf of the trust would need to be paid
for by the trustee personally: therefore, the trustee is evidently entitled to make that payment
out of the trust property[70] and to be indemnified against obligations arising from the contract
generally.[71] In accordance with principle, the trustees will only be entitled to be indemnified
against contracts which were entered into properly within the terms of their trusteeship and
not in relation to contracts which were entered into outwith their authority.[72] In relation to
any contracts entered into beyond the trustees' powers,[73] the trustees will be personally
responsible to satisfy any obligations owed to some third party. Equally, the trustees will be
entitled only to a partial indemnity to the extent that the trust instrument entitles them to

59 *Ibid*, s 31(1). This right to reimbursement has long been supported by the case law: see, eg, *Worrall v Harford*
   (1802) 8 Ves 4; and by subsequent case law dealing with successive statutes: *Re Earl of Winchilsea's Policy
   Trusts* (1888) 39 Ch D 168; *Holding and Management Ltd v Property Holding and Investment Trust plc* [1989]
   1 WLR 1313.
60 TA 2000, s 31(2).
61 *Malcolm v O'Callaghan* (1837) 3 Myl & Cr 52.
62 TA 2000, s 11.
63 *Macnamara v Jones* (1784) 2 Dick 587; *Smith v Dale* (1881) 18 Ch D 516.
64 *Re Pumfrey* (1882) 22 Ch D 255; *De Vigier v IRC* [1964] 2 All ER 907.
65 A person provides professional services if those services were provided in the course of a profession or business
   which is connected with the management of trusts: TA 2000, s 28(5); whereas a lay trustee is a person who is
   neither a trust corporation nor acting in the course of a profession or business: TA 2000, s 28(6).
66 TA 2000, s 28(1).
67 *Ibid*, s 28(2).
68 *Ibid*, s 28(1).
69 The notion of the trustee who is entitled to be indemnified in this way generally includes constructive trustees
   who hold property on proprietary constructive trust on the basis that if one seeks equity (by means of enforcing
   a constructive trust), then one must do equity (by means of permitting that trustee an indemnity against her
   expenses in the management of that property): *Rowley v Ginnever* [1897] 2 Ch 503. See also *Travis v Illingworth*
   [1968] WN 206.
70 See TA 2000, s 31(1)(b) in relation to the right to make payment even of the trustees' expenses out of the trust
   fund.
71 *Dowse v Gorton* [1891] AC 190; *Re Oxley* [1914] 1 Ch 604; *Vacuum Oil Co Pty Ltd v Wiltshire* (1945) 72 CLR
   319.
72 *Ibid*.
73 That is, any contracts entered into *ultra vires*.

enter into such a contract, for example, committing only a given proportion of the trust's assets to the satisfaction of that contract.[74] Similarly, in relation to the tortious liability of trustees, the trustees will be indemnified against any such liability provided that that liability was incurred in the proper performance of the trustee's duties.[75] However, to the extent that the trustee was acting outwith her duties, or to the extent that she was so acting without due diligence, then the trustee will not be indemnified.[76] Therefore, it is significant for the trustee to be entitled to an indemnity that the transaction into which the trustee had entered was authorised by the trust instrument.[77] An indemnity will only be permissible in circumstances in which the transaction was unauthorised if the transaction afforded a benefit to the trustees and if the court, in its general discretion, considers an indemnity to be appropriate.[78]

Difficult questions arise as to the allocation of trustees' expenses between various parts of the trust. For example, if trustees of a discretionary trust are acting for all parts of the trust at once, a question might arise as to whether those expenses should be allocated to the capital or to the income parts of the trust. The result for the objects of that particular part of the trust may be significant because the value of their interests will be reduced by the amount of the expenses. Lindsay J upheld the traditional principle that ordinarily it is the capital part of the trust which bears such general expenses which are not evidently directed to one particular part of the fund, and indeed suggested that there would need to be particular circumstances on the facts of any given case to justify a different analysis, in *Revenue & Customs Commissioners v Trustees of the Peter Clay Discretionary Trust*.[79] The principle is based on the idea advanced in *Re Bennett*[80] that if expenses were borne for the benefit of the entire trust estate then they were attributable to capital. This principle might be rationalised on the basis that if the expenses were borne for the benefit of the estate generally and for its long-term upkeep, then they were truly capital expenses because they would affect the capital value of the property. However, the answer might be different if, for example, money was spent on the upkeep of a house occupied by the life tenant under a trust which provided that no other beneficiary had a right to occupy that house and that the rights of the other beneficiaries were limited to an interest in shares: in such a set of facts it would be only reasonable to charge the trustees expenses in relation to the house to the life tenant's portion of the trust. Similarly, expenses borne for the purpose of the running of the trust on a day-to-day basis are more likely to be considered to best borne by the income part of the trust.[81] It may be

---

74 *Ex p Garland* (1803) 10 Ves 110; *Re Johnson* (1880) 15 Ch D 548; *Re Webb* (1890) 63 LT 545. So, for example, if the trustees were entitled to invest only one-half of the trust's assets in shares quoted on the London Stock Exchange and the trustees in fact invested three-quarters of the trust's assets in such shares, then the trustees would only be entitled to an indemnity in relation to two-thirds of the trust's investment in those shares.

75 *Flower v Pretchel* (1934) 159 LT 491.

76 *Ibid*; see also *Re Raybould* [1900] 1 Ch 199.

77 *Leedham v Chawner* (1858) 4 K & J 458; *Hosegood v Pedler* (1879) 66 LJ QB 18. Moreover, no further indemnity will be permitted if the trustee owes some personal obligation to the beneficiaries by way of breach of trust until that obligation is satisfied: *Jacubs v Rylance* (1874) LR 17 Eq 341.

78 *Vyse v Foster* (1872) 8 Ch App 309, 336; *Re German Mining Co* (1854) 4 De GM&G 19; *Re Smith's Estate* [1937] Ch 636.

79 [2008] 2 WLR 1052, Lindsay J.

80 [1896] 1 Ch 778. See also *Stott v Milne* (1884) 25 Ch D 710, as discussed in *Revenue & Customs Commissioners v Trustees of the Peter Clay Discretionary Trust* [2008] 2 WLR 1052, 1062.

81 *In re Duke of Norfolk's Settlement Trusts* [1979] Ch 37, 62, *per* Walton J.

possible also to divide expenses between income matters and capital matters on the principles set out above.[82]

Until the trustee's right to be indemnified is satisfied, the trustee has a lien over the trust fund[83] equal to the amount owed to her.[84] The trustee's lien takes priority over even the interests of the beneficiaries.[85]

8.2.8 Delegation of trustees' powers

In general terms, a trustee is personally liable, in conscience, for all of her own acts and defaults under the general law of trusts. In consequence, a trustee may not delegate her obligations as a trustee to some other person under the old case law[86] in line with the general principle *delegates non potest delgare*.[87] Nevertheless, statute does now permit delegation of trustees' powers in limited circumstances, as considered in section 10.2.

8.3 THE GENERAL DUTIES OF TRUSTEES

The duties of the trustees are manifold. The duties considered in this section are the following. (1) The duties on acceptance of office relating to the need to familiarise oneself with the terms, conditions and history of the management of the trust. (2) The duty to obey the terms of the trust unless directed to do otherwise by the court. (3) The duty to safeguard the trust assets, including duties to maintain the trust property, as well as to ensure that it is applied in accordance with the directions set out in the trust instrument. (4) The duty to act even-handedly between beneficiaries, which means that the trustees are required to act impartially between beneficiaries and to avoid conflicts of interest. (5) The duty to act with reasonable care, meaning generally a duty to act as though a prudent person of business acting on behalf of someone for whom one feels morally bound to provide. (6) Duties in relation to trust expenses.

(7) The duties of investment, requiring prudence and the acquisition of the highest possible rate of return in the context. (8) The duty to distribute the trust property correctly. (9) The duty to avoid conflicts of interest, not to earn unauthorised profits from the fiduciary office, not to deal on one's own behalf with trust property on pain of such transactions being voidable, and the obligation to deal fairly with the trust property. (10) The duty to preserve the confidence of the beneficiaries, especially in relation to Chinese wall arrangements. (11) The duty to act gratuitously, without any right to

---

82 As was suggested by Vinelott J in *Carver v Duncan* [1985] AC 1082, with the Court of Appeal focusing on the construction of the appropriate tax regulation.

83 This lien takes effect over both the capital and the income of the trust fund: *Stott v Milne* (1884) 25 Ch D 710; *Hardoon v Belilios* [1901] AC 118.

84 *Stott v Milne* (1884) 25 Ch D 710, 715; *Governors of St Thomas's Hospital v Richardson* [1910] 1 KB 271, 276. See now also *Balkin v Peck* (1998) 1 ITLER 717.

85 *Dodds v Tuke* (1884) 25 Ch D 617, 619; *Re Griffith* [1904] 1 Ch 807.

86 *Attorney-General v Glegg* (1738) 1 Atk 356; *Clough v Bond* (1838) 3 My & Cr 490; *Re Bellamy and Metropolitan Board of Works* (1883) 24 Ch D 387; *Re Flower and Metropolitan Board of Works* (1884) 27 Ch D 592.

87 That is, 'a delegate is not able to delegate'.

payment not permitted by the trust instrument or by the general law. (12) The duty to account and to provide information.

This section of this chapter considers the most significant general duties which arise in relation to the operation of a trust. Its importance for the flow of argument in this book is its explanation of the relationship between trustee and beneficiary. In the consideration of the conduct of the trust, it is possible to see the nature of the obligations between trustee and beneficiary most clearly. As considered in Chapter 2, the trust is comprised of property rules which relate to the treatment of trust fund, and also of personal obligations between the trustee and beneficiary. Those personal obligations were considered in relation to the enforcement of trusts in Part 2, and are also discussed in Part 6 in relation to the liabilities of a trustee who commits a breach of trust. This chapter focuses on the nature of a number of those obligations specifically to do with the obligations of the trustee to communicate information to the beneficiaries and the manner in which trustees are required to carry out their duties. This section identifies the most important of the trustee's general duties,[88] albeit that the discussion of some of these duties contains cross-references to more substantive discussions of those duties elsewhere in this chapter or elsewhere in this book.

8.3.1 Duties on acceptance of office

Once a trustee accepts the office of trustee, that trustee is bound by all of the obligations in the trust instrument.[89] The trustee may not consider that she is imbued with powers which are more extensive than those set out in the trust instrument,[90] except to the extent that the trust instrument is silent about some power which is granted to the trustee by the TA 1925 or 2000[91] or silent about some duty imposed by statute or by case law.[92] These principles are amplified in para 8.3.2 below. The trustee's obligations at the outset are composed of very general responsibilities and specific responsibilities.

The general responsibilities are for the trustee to familiarise herself with the terms of trust,[93] the nature of the property involved, the range of objects within the contemplation of the trust,[94] the identity of the other trustees,[95] to consult all of the documentation connected to the trust[96] (including the trust instrument, any documents relating to the exercise of any discretionary power or power of appointment, trust accounts, the scope of investments made by the trust,[97] statements of investment criteria and so forth) and to familiarise herself with

---

88 That is, duties provided under the general law as opposed to the more specific duties which may be identified in a trust instrument.

89 *Clough v Bond* (1838) 3 My & Cr 490, unless that would be to the apparent benefit of the beneficiaries and not in breach of some other mandatory rule (such as a rule of illegality).

90 *Ibid.*

91 This proposition, it is suggested, must be correct as a matter of principle within the scope of that legislation.

92 As before, it is suggested that this proposition must be correct as a matter of principle.

93 The costs and expenses of conducting this process of familiarisation may be recovered from the trust: *Re Pumfrey* (1882) 22 Ch D 255; *De Vigier v IRC* [1964] 2 All ER 907.

94 *Hallows v Lloyd* (1888) 39 Ch D 686, 691, *per* Kekewich J.

95 *Nestlé v National Westminster Bank plc* [1993] 1 WLR 1260, 1265.

96 *Tiger v Barclays Bank Ltd* [1952] 1 All ER 85.

97 *Nestlé v National Westminster Bank plc* [1993] 1 WLR 1260.

any other information pertinent to the management of the trust which is not recorded in documentary fashion.[98] Evidently, then, the first obligation of the trustee is one of general familiarisation with all of the issues connected to the management of the trust, both formal and informal matters connected to the management of the trust's affairs. If necessary the trustee is required to take legal advice as to the efficacy or legality of any action taken by the trustees in relation to the trust. What a trustee – whether a new trustee of an existing trust or a trustee of a new trust – cannot do is sit supinely by without investigating the nature and extent of her obligations as trustee. In general terms it is of some comfort to a trustee to know that any individual trustee will only be liable, in principle, for any matters of which she had or could have been expected to have had knowledge.[99] Nevertheless, it is important to bear in mind that a trustee will be liable for matters of which she could be expected to have knowledge: that is, as mentioned before, the trustee is obliged to find out information about her trusteeship and not simply to fail to investigate matters over which she is expected to exert control.[100]

The specific responsibilities of any trustee will come from two sources: first, any specific provisions of the trust instrument which impose particular duties on the trustee and, secondly, any duties which can be said to arise as a result of the context in which that person became trustee and the nature of the trust property. It will not be possible to consider here all of the possible provisions in any trust instrument which could ever come into existence; rather, we shall focus on some of the contexts which may influence these specific responsibilities. In general terms, it is the nature of the trust property and the composition of the class of trust objects which will be important. To begin with the trust property, the trustee is required to consider the nature of the property which is held on trust. The first duty is to ensure that the property is properly vested in the trustees.[101] The second duty will be dependent on the nature of that property. If the property is money, then the trustee will be required to consider the manner in which that money should be invested,[102] or to sell any property in a reasonable time which the trust requires her to sell,[103] or to distribute income and capital at appropriate times,[104] or to collect rents from land[105] and so forth. If the property requires maintenance (such as building work on land or taking legal proceedings to collect income owing to it)[106] or insurance[107] or other, similar actions in relation to it, then the trustee must perform those duties in good order.

---

98 *Mond v Hyde* [1999] QB 1097.
99 *Re Hurst* (1892) 67 LT 96; *Young v Cloud* (1874) LR 18 Eq 634.
100 See *ibid*, and *Mond v Hyde* [1999] QB 1097.
101 *Underwood v Stevens* (1816) 1 Mer 712; *Lewis v Nobbs* (1878) 8 Ch D 591.
102 See *Moyle v Moyle* (1831) 2 Russ & M 710, whereby, a little like the biblical parable of the talents, if a trustee simply holds onto the money for an unreasonably long period of time without investing that money, then she will be liable for failure to deal appropriately as a trustee with that property.
103 *Fry v Fry* (1859) 27 Beav 144; *Wentworth v Wentworth* [1900] AC 163.
104 *Hawkesley v May* [1956] 1 QB 304.
105 *Tebbs v Carpenter* (1816) 1 Madd 290.
106 *Buxton v Buxton* (1835) 1 My & Cr 80; *Re England's Settlement Trusts* [1918] 1 Ch 24.
107 *Re Godwin's Settlement* (1918) 87 LJ Ch 645.

8.3.2 Duty to obey directions of the trust

Each trustee is bound by all of the obligations in the trust instrument.[108] Failure to obey the terms of the trust will constitute a breach of trust.[109] In general terms, a trustee does not have powers which are more extensive than those set out in the trust instrument.[110] One clear exception to this principle arises in circumstances in which there is no trust instrument, or in circumstances in which the trust instrument is silent on a particular point. If the trustee is granted a particular power – such as the general power of investment[111] – by a statute, such as the Trustee Act 1925 (TA 1925) or the Trustee Act 2000 (TA 2000),[112] or alternatively if some duty is imposed on a trustee either by a statute or by case law, then it is suggested that that power or duty will be applicable to that trustee.[113] It is a general principle of the TAs 1925 and 2000, however, that the terms of those Acts may be excluded by a term in the trust instrument[114] and, impliedly at least, it is a principle of the general law of trusts that the liabilities of trustees may be excluded for all breaches of trust[115] which do not amount to dishonesty.[116] Where the trustees are bound by other legislative codes, for example, in relation to unit trusts or pension funds or more generally as to investment under the Financial Services and Markets Act 2000, then those statutory obligations may supplement or even override any terms of the trust instrument.[117] A failure to carry out any action required by the trust or the performance of an unauthorised action will constitute a breach of trust.[118]

8.3.3 Duty to safeguard trust property

The duty of safeguarding the trust property is fundamental to the notion of trusteeship and to the operation of trusts. Consequently, it can easily be understood that the trustees are responsible for ensuring that no harm comes to any property which they hold on trust. Thus, a trustee holding a house on trust would be required to ensure that the house was kept in proper repair, a trustee holding a horse on trust would be required to ensure that the horse was properly stabled, and so forth. To that extent, this duty will be dependent on the nature of the property. At this introductory level, we can understand the trustees' obligations as being an obligations to prevent the property from becoming broken, run-down or worthless.

However, there is a further dimension to this duty which imposes active obligations on the trustees to consider the best interests of the beneficiaries and so to consider the most appropriate way of maximising the utility or the value of the property, as applicable. Therefore, if

---

108   *Clough v Bond* (1838) 3 My & Cr 490, unless that would be to the apparent benefit of the beneficiaries and not in breach of some other mandatory rule (such as a rule of illegality).
109   *Clough v Bond* (1838) 3 My & Cr 490; as discussed in Chapter 18.
110   *Ibid.*
111   TA 2000, s 3.
112   This proposition, it is suggested, must be correct as a matter of principle within the scope of that legislation.
113   As before, it is suggested that this proposition must be correct as a matter of principle.
114   TA 1925, s 69; TA 2000, Sched 1, para 7.
115   *Armitage v Nurse* [1998] Ch 241.
116   *Walker v Stones* [2001] QB 902.
117   For example, in relation to unit trusts (Financial Services and Markets Act 2000, s 253) and pension funds (Pensions Act 1995, s 33), the exclusion of the trustees' liabilities for the investment of the trust property is prohibited by statute no matter what the provisions of the trust instrument may suggest.
118   Breach of trust is considered in Chapter 18.

the property is investment capital, then the obligations of the trustees are to obtain the most profitable investments[119] commensurate with the type of trust in question,[120] whereas if the trust's underlying objective is to provide accommodation for the beneficiaries, then the trustees' principal obligation will be to secure the maintenance and utility of the property so that it is fit for its purpose. In either case, the trustees have active duties to safeguard the trust property so that it remains suitable for the trust's objectives and may not simply watch over the property and preserve it from decay. So, if the trust property is comprised of money which is to be invested for the benefit of the beneficiaries, then the trustees will be required to consider the manner in which that money should be invested.[121] If the property were land and buildings which were rented out to tenants with a view to securing an income stream from those rents, then the trustees would be required to manage the property proactively by means of collecting the rents[122] or taking any necessary steps to enforce the beneficiary's rights generally over that land[123] or to insure the land appropriately.[124]

8.3.4 Duty to act impartially between beneficiaries

The general duty to act impartially between individual beneficiaries and between classes of beneficiaries

In general terms, a trustee is obliged to act impartially as between all of the beneficiaries.[125] At one level this requires the trustee to exercise fairness as between each beneficiary, showing no favour to any one; and at another level, this requires the beneficiary to act even-handedly as between different classes of beneficiaries.[126] It is suggested that the duty of impartiality is akin to the duty not to permit conflicts of interest, considered above, in that the trustee is expected to stand apart from partisan considerations as to the different entitlements of various classes of beneficiary to the fruits of the trust fund (income beneficiaries and life tenants) and to the fund itself (capital and remainder beneficiaries). As a fiduciary, the trustee is required to act in relation to each of the beneficiaries without any grace or favour, in the same way that the trustee must not take any personal advantage from the trust.

At its simplest level, then, the trustee is to treat each member of the same class of objects in the same way on the basis that each object has identical rights to all other members of the same class. The trustees are also required to act impartially between different classes of beneficiary and not simply between beneficiaries of the same class. The clearest example of the situation in which trustees have difficulty in acting impartially between different classes

---

119 *Cowan v Scargill* [1985] Ch 270.

120 *Nestlé v National Westminster Bank plc* [1993] 1 WLR 1260.

121 See *Moyle v Moyle* (1831) 2 Russ & M 710 whereby, a little like the biblical parable of the talents, if a trustee simply holds onto the money for an unreasonably long period of time without investing that money then she will be liable for failure to deal appropriately as a trustee with that property.

122 *Tebbs v Carpenter* (1816) 1 Madd 290.

123 *Buxton v Buxton* (1835) 1 My & Cr 80; *Re England's Settlement Trusts* [1918] 1 Ch 24.

124 *Re Godwin's Settlement* (1918) 87 LJ Ch 645.

125 *Stephenson v Barclays Bank Trust Co Ltd* [1975] 1 WLR 882; [1975] 1 All ER 625; *Cowan v Scargill* [1985] Ch 270; *Nestlé v National Westminster Bank plc* [1993] 1 WLR 1260.

126 The expression 'even hand' being that preferred in a number of cases: *Re Tempest* (1866) 1 Ch App 485, 487, *per* Turner LJ; *Re Lepine* [1892] 1 Ch 210, 219, *per* Fry LJ.

of beneficiary arises in relation to trusts in which there is a life tenant, entitled to the income of the trust, and beneficiaries in remainder, whose interest is in the capital of the fund. In such a situation, the trustee is obliged not to focus the investment and distribution of the trust fund on the generation of short-term income for the life tenant, when that would be to the detriment of the remainder beneficiaries who would depend on there being capital left in the trust fund.[127] However, even treatment need not mean that each object of a trust receives the same property under discretionary trusts, as considered below: rather each of them is entitled to equally impartial consideration.

Equally, it may be that one beneficiary satisfies a condition precedent to the vesting of some interest before any other beneficiary, in which case Walton J held the following in *Stephenson v Barclays Bank Trust Co Ltd*:[128]

> When the situation is that a single person who is *sui juris* has an absolutely vested beneficial interest in a share of the trust fund . . . he is entitled to have transferred to him . . . an aliquot share of each and every asset of the trust fund which presents no difficulty so far as division is concerned. This will apply to such items as cash, money at the bank or an unsecured loan, stock exchange securities and the like. However, as regards land, certainly in all cases, as regards shares in a private company in very special circumstances . . . the situation is not so simple, and even a person with a vested interest in possession in an aliquot share of the trust fund may have to wait until the land is sold, and so forth, before being able to call upon the trustees as of right to account to him for his share of the assets.

Thus, there may be forms of property which can be readily divided and transferred in part to one beneficiary without causing any loss to the other beneficiaries. A loss may be caused to the other beneficiaries by requiring a sale of the property earlier than would otherwise achieve the highest available price: in relation, for example, to land in the UK, a sale of a house in the 1960s would only have realised a few thousand pounds, whereas a sale of that same house in the 1990s would have realised many hundreds of thousands of pounds. Therefore, to distribute some forms of property early to one beneficiary may be to the detriment of future beneficiaries and so ought to be resisted.[129]

If a trustee has a mere power to appoint or advance property, or a similar power under a discretionary trust, then by definition this will require the trustees to grant property to one beneficiary and perhaps none to another, or to grant more to one beneficiary than to another, in the proper exercise of their power. This duty is therefore not a duty to treat all beneficiaries *equally*. If trustees were required to treat all beneficiaries absolutely equally, and so required by the case law to give them identical amounts of property in all circumstances, then that would make the exercise of most fiduciary powers impossible. By definition a settlor will often want the trustees to use any discretion granted to them under the trust instrument so as to do the best for the beneficiaries: this may involve digging one particular beneficiary out of trouble by advancing a large amount of money to her. If this is within the

---

127   *Re Barton's Trusts* (1868) LR 5 Eq 238.
128   *Stephenson v Barclays Bank Trust Co Ltd* [1975] 1 WLR 882, 889.
129   *Re Marshall* [1914] 1 Ch 192.

terms of their powers, then the trustees cannot be limited in their actions if it is what the terms of the trust provide. Therefore, what this principle should be taken to mean is that trustees must treat the objects of their powers impartially and in a manner which they can justify after the event. They should treat them *impartially* in the sense that no single beneficiary or group of beneficiaries should receive an unjustified benefit at the expense of the other beneficiaries. This is particularly difficult when the trustees have different classes of beneficiaries with competing claims to the trust capital: for example, some who are entitled to income during their lifetimes and others who are entitled to the capital only after the life tenants have died. Given the difficulties of resolving the competing interests of different classes of beneficiaries, in *Nestlé v National Westminster Bank*, Hoffmann J held that:

> A trustee must act fairly in making investment decisions which may have different consequences for differing classes of beneficiaries. . . . The trustees have a wide discretion. They are, for example, entitled to take into account the income needs of the tenant for life or the fact that the tenant for life was a person known to the settlor and a primary object of the trust whereas the remainderman is a remoter relative or stranger. Of course, these cannot be allowed to become the overriding considerations but the concept of fairness between classes of beneficiaries does not require them to be excluded. It would be an inhuman rule which required trustees to adhere to some mechanical rule for preserving the real value of capital when the tenant for life was the testator's widow who had fallen upon hard times and the remainderman was young and well-off.[130]

In consequence, this principle permits some reference to the precise issues which faced the trustee in the context of her own trust obligations and did not simply require that the trustee live up to an objective standard of proper performance. In pension funds there will be a huge number of beneficiaries potentially with competing interests in the trust fund: thus, the judges are aware of the need not to allow this rule to become too narrow. This elasticity in the principle was recognised by Chadwick LJ in *Edge v Pensions Ombudsman* in relation to a pension trust fund:[131]

> The so-called duty to act impartially . . . is no more than the ordinary duty which the law imposes on a person who is entrusted with the exercise of a discretionary power: that he exercises the power for the purpose for which it is given, giving proper consideration to the matters which are relevant and excluding from consideration matters which are irrelevant. If pension fund trustees do that, they cannot be criticized if they reach a decision which appears to prefer the claims of one interest – whether that of employers, current employers or pensioners – over others. The preference will be the result of a proper exercise of the discretionary power.[132]

---

130 *Nestlé v National Westminster Bank plc* [2000] WTLR 795, 802.
131 [2000] Ch 602, 627, [1999] 4 All ER 546, 567.
132 Similar sentiments were made at first instance by Scott V-C in *Edge v Pensions Ombudsman* [1998] Ch 512, to the effect that the duty to act impartially is not a straitjacket, although it does express the position that a trustee may nevertheless not act in a manner which unfairly prefers one beneficiary over another in breach of duty.

Therefore, this duty to act impartially does not necessarily mean that all beneficiaries are to be treated absolutely equally. Rather, trustees are not permitted to favour one class of beneficiaries or particular beneficiaries at the expense of other beneficiaries without good reason. Or, to make the same point positively, they can discriminate between different beneficiaries provided that they can justify their actions. Self-evidently, where trustees have a power to select between beneficiaries it would be impossible if the trustees were to be held liable for breach of trust simply because they exercised their power reasonably so as to appoint property to one beneficiary rather than another entirely within the terms of that trust or power.

Similarly, by analogy with *Chirkinian v Larcom Trustees Ltd*,[133] in relation to funds created not simply to provide employee pensions but to provide loans to employees as well, there would be no breach of trust simply because a trustee made a loan to a beneficiary within the terms of that trust.[134] So, even if that company went into insolvent liquidation subsequently, the trustees would not be required to recover that loan from the beneficiary to whom the loan was made on the basis (*inter alia*) that it constituted an unfair benefit to that particular beneficiary, provided that the loan had been made within the terms of the trustees' power to make such loans under the trust instrument. Equally, the trustees were not compelled to recover such a loan simply because there was subsequently an insolvency, unless the liquidator was seeking to recover the loan under insolvency law and had instructed the trustees to do that. On these facts that was not the case. Thus, a breach of trust will not be held to arise where the trustees are performing the terms of their trusteeship properly. Therefore, the context of the situation may mean that equality is not possible, and that absolute impartiality is not a practicable goal either, provided always that the trustees are exercising their powers properly.

This impartiality will be required of trustees by the courts unless there is some provision to the contrary in the terms of the trust instrument which requires that there be some different treatment.[135] That policy is clearly in line with a broader policy of applying the wishes of the settlor as manifested in the terms of the trust. Therefore, the case law rules are really a default setting in the absence of any express provisions set out by the settlor as to the treatment of the trust fund.

Allocations of assets between capital and income beneficiaries

There are always difficulties in knowing which forms of additional property realised by the trustees or settled onto the trust are to be added to capital and which are to be treated as being income: this is particularly significant where some beneficiaries are entitled to income and others only to capital. Generally, large increments to the trust fund are treated straightforwardly as additions to capital, rather than as bundles of future income to be applied to the life tenant's benefit.[136] However, where the property received has only taken the form of mere income (as with a bonus dividend paid on a share), they fall to be treated as income,[137] unless

133 [2006] EWHC 1917; [2006] WTLR 1523.
134 *Chirkinian v Larcom Trustees Ltd* [2006] WTLR 1523.
135 *Ibid.*
136 *Ibid.*
137 *Re Bouch* (1885) 29 Ch D 635.

they have been paid from a capital account (such as a share premium account).[138] Similarly, the addition of capital amounts to the account of a trustee, such as a reduction of capital by a company paid out to its shareholders, will be taken to form part of the capital of the fund.[139] A more difficult situation is that in which exceptional profits are generated in any given year of account: if realised from the disposal of capital assets, then they would belong to the capital account, whereas the generation of a large amount of income would ordinarily constitute income. In such a case, the court will look to the nature of the receipt in the trustees' hands.[140] In the absence of any such express provision, the life tenant will be entitled to the income generated by the fund, provided that there is no unauthorised discrimination in favour of the life tenant as against other beneficiaries.[141]

8.3.5 Duty to exercise reasonable care

The duty of care in the case law

The trustee's obligation in the 19th-century case law was to act as a prudent person of business would have acted if acting on behalf of someone for whom she felt morally bound to provide. Whereas it was held in *Learoyd v Whiteley*[142] that a trustee must act as a businessperson of ordinary prudence, this approach was modified in *Bartlett v Barclays Bank*,[143] in which it was held that trustees are permitted to take a prudent degree of risk but must avoid anything which amounts to 'hazard'. In the context of delegating authority to invest to some other person, the classic statement of the trustee's obligation was set out in the following terms in *Speight v Gaunt* in the decision of Lord Jessel MR:[144]

> It seems to me that on general trust principles a trustee ought to conduct the business of the trust in the same manner that an ordinary prudent man of business would conduct his own, and that beyond that there is no liability or obligation on the trustee.

Clearly, this may be a difficult test for a trustee to observe – particularly if that trustee is not acting in a professional capacity. As this concept was put by Megarry VC in *Cowan v Scargill*, the trustees are required to:

> take such care as an ordinary prudent man would take if he were minded to make an investment for the benefit of other people for whom he feels morally bound to provide.[145] This

---

138   *Hill v Permanent Trustee Co of NSW* [1930] AC 720.
139   *Ibid.*
140   *Re Doughty* [1947] Ch 263; *Re Kleinwort's Settlements* [1951] 2 TLR 91.
141   *Re Barton's Trusts* (1868) LR 5 Eq 238.
142   (1887) 12 App Cas 727.
143   [1980] Ch 515.
144   *Speight v Gaunt* (1883) 9 App Cas 1. See also *Brice v Stokes* (1805) 11 Ves 319; *Bullock v Bullock* (1886) 56 LJ Ch 221.
145   A rendering of the concept of prudence in relation to trustees in Guernsey, a Francophile system of law based on Norman law at root, is put somewhat more lyrically as an obligation to act 'en bon père de famille'; or, to put that into English, to act as though a good parent acting for his family. With all of the time-bound, gendered notions to one side, that gives a flavour of the trustee acting for someone for whom he or she felt morally bound to provide.

duty includes the duty to seek advice on matters which the trustee does not understand, such as the making of investments, and, on receiving that advice, to act with the same degree of prudence. Although a trustee who takes advice on investments is not bound to accept and act on that advice, he is not entitled to reject it merely because he sincerely disagrees with it, unless in addition he is acting as an ordinary prudent man would act.[146]

The approach taken here is that the trustees are to focus primarily on the protection and maintenance of the trust fund, whilst also allowing it to grow steadily.[147]

By contrast, Millett LJ in *Armitage v Nurse* suggested that he did not consider that there was a general duty on trustees to act with skill and care. The precise issue before the Court of Appeal in that case was whether or not a trustee could rely on a clause in the trust instrument which purported to exclude that trustee's liability for breach of trust caused by gross negligence. What Millett LJ held precisely was that 'I do not accept the further submission that [the trustee's] core obligations include the duties of skill and care, prudence and diligence'. This is surprising given that an obligation of prudence had long formed part of the case law on trustees' duties, as set out above. What Millett LJ was seeking to do was to reject the notion that trustees could not exclude their liabilities because there is some notional minimum level of obligations which all trustees must bear if there is to be a valid trust: his Lordship was doing this because in the case in front of him he was keen to ensure that trustees could have their liabilities excluded in the trust instrument without such clauses being held to be void. The detailed rules concerning trustee exemption clauses are considered below in section 8.5.1. What is important to note at this stage is that some modern judges – like Millett LJ – do not wish to allow the ordinary obligations on trustees to become too demanding so that the trust may become unattractive to commercial people because the obligations involved are too strict. Nevertheless, it is respectfully suggested that the case law had long contained a requirement of prudence and that the Trustee Act 2000 now contains a general duty of skill and care, as considered immediately below.

This principle requiring that the trustees act with care is considered in detail in relation to the investment of the trust property – the situation in which it is most significant – in Chapter 9.[148] While it may be that there has been a change in the judicial view of trustees' duties, the passage of the Trustee Act 2000 has changed the ordinary obligations of trustees from being based on 'prudence' to being based on 'reasonableness', as considered in the next section.

The limited statutory duty of care

The case law principles have been displaced in part by s 1 of the TA 2000, which provides that:

(1) Whenever the duty under this subsection applies to a trustee, he must exercise such care and skill as is reasonable in the circumstances, having regard, in particular –
    (a) to any special knowledge or experience that he has or holds himself out as having, and

---

146 *Cowan v Scargill* [1985] Ch 270, 289.
147 See the effect of this approach in *Nestlé v National Westminster Bank plc* [1993] 1 WLR 1260.
148 See section 9.6.

(b) if he acts as trustee in the course of a business or profession, to any special knowledge or experience that it is reasonable to expect of a person acting in the course of that kind of business or profession.

Therefore, the focus of s 1 of the 2000 Act is that the trustee must be held to a subjective standard of care commensurate with any knowledge or experience which she already has. The test is subjective in the sense that it is reactive to the trustee's own knowledge and experience, and the standard of care that is required will be a standard of care which is reasonable for someone with that knowledge or experience. If a trustee is foolish enough to represent herself as having knowledge or experience which she does not have, then the trustee is held to the standard of care appropriate to the knowledge and experience which she claimed to have had.[149] Similarly, if the trustee is an incompetent professional, then she will not be held to her low level of competence but rather to the level of competence which one ought to have been able to expect of such a professional.

There is nothing in the legislation which requires the trustee to act; as opposed to the case law which imposed a positive obligation to do the best possible for the beneficiaries.[150] Rather, the statutory duty of care applies only to the six categories of power identified in Sched 1 to the Act.[151] Those six categories of power are: investment; acquisition of land; the use of agents, nominees and custodians; compounding of liabilities; insurance; and dealing with reversionary interests.

This principle requiring that the trustees act with care is considered in detail in relation to the investment of the trust property in Chapter 9.

What is the effect of the Trustee Act 2000 on the case law standard of prudence?

The principal effect of the Trustee Act 2000 has been to shift the ordinary obligations of trustees from a requirement that they act *prudently* to a requirement that they act *reasonably*. This shift is subtle but significant. If a trustee is required to act prudently then that trustee is required to be cautious. When faced with a choice of options, the trustee must seek to be careful as opposed, for example, to taking a reasonable risk to make profit or to benefit the beneficiaries. By contrast, a requirement that a trustee act reasonably means that a trustee does not necessarily need to be cautious: instead when faced with a choice of options the trustee can take an acceptable level of risk provided that her actions are reasonable in the context. The remainder of the TA 2000, as considered in detail in Chapter 9, obliges trustees investing trust property to ensure that her actions are suitable, that they comply with modern standards of portfolio investment, and that they are based on appropriate professional advice. (It should be remembered that the TA 2000 will only signal a shift away from case law principles in relation to the investment of trusts in any event – the other areas will remain unaffected by the Act.) Thus, the need to act reasonably, as opposed to being careful, might seem to involve taking greater risks but they are informed risks which must be appropriate for the context. So, investing a pension fund involving millions of pounds will necessarily require

---

149 TA 2000, s 1(1)(a).
150 *Cowan v Scargill* [1985] Ch 270.
151 TA 2000, s 2.

the taking of reasonable investment risks to make large profits for all of the pensioners, whereas investing an elderly widow's few life savings reasonably will require the trustees to ensure that there is as little risk of losing those life savings as possible. Therefore, the test of reasonableness may require some trustees to behave prudently if the context so requires, but it also liberates other trustees to act more progressively on behalf of the beneficiaries without being pre-occupied by a high standard of obligation.

It is difficult to know how the TA 2000 will affect the case law principles. The remainder of this long chapter on trustees' obligations contains many hundreds of cases advancing the thirteen principal obligations of trustees. The TA 2000 will not affect most of those cases. What it might do is to signal to judges in the future that the culture in which trustees operate has become more liberal in that the trustees must be able to act reasonably, always within the confines of their obligations in the trust instrument, rather than having to act overly cautiously. The TA 2000 itself provides that its principles can be excluded by the trust instrument and therefore trustees will frequently limit their liabilities in practice in any event by ensuring that the settlor provides that the trustees can act as liberally as possible. The purpose behind the passage of the TA 2000 was to liberate trustees from the strictures of 'prudence' when investing trust property. Coupled with the approach taken by the Court of Appeal in *Armitage v Nurse* – which was, on the limited point of the existence of duties of prudence on trustees, contrary to earlier authority – this signals a potential shift in the nature of trustees' duties from a need for caution towards a need for trustees to be able to justify their actions as having been reasonable. What might be lost in this development, it is suggested, is the need to recognise that there is something special about the fiduciary obligations of trustees which ought not to be so diluted by removing many of the irreducible core of obligations on them, such as the duty to act with appropriate care and skill, before the device which we call a 'trust' is all but meaningless when compared to ordinary common law obligations like the contract.

8.3.6 Duties in relation to trust expenses

The trustee is entitled to be reimbursed for any expense and to be indemnified against trust expenses generally, as considered in para 8.2.7 above. There are complex questions, however, as to the allocation of expenses between different parts of the same trust fund. So, in *HMRC v Peter Clay Discretionary Trust*[152] an issue arose, in essence, as to whether or not the trustees of a discretionary trust could charge a part of their expenses relating to the capital portion of a trust fund to the income portion of that fund. Her Majesty's Revenue and Customs ('HMRC') objected to this charge being made against the income from the trust for tax purposes. It was held, in line with traditional principle, that charges incurred 'for the benefit of the entire estate' should be charged to capital.[153] The issue was whether or not there could also be a charge to income in this case. In the earlier authorities,[154] Sir John Chadwick considered, deciding whether or not an expense was for the benefit of the whole estate depended on whether or not it would benefit the entire estate, both the life tenant (the

---

152 [2009] 2 WLR 1353.
153 See *In re Bennett* [1896] 1 Ch 778 and *Carver v Duncan* [1985] AC 1082.
154 *Ibid.*

income beneficiary) and the remainderman (the capital beneficiary) in traditional settlements. Sir John Chadwick upheld the principle that if the work had been done for the benefit of the whole estate, both income and capital, then it would be chargeable to capital alone; however, because a part of the work which the trustees had done in this instance had been conducted exclusively for the income portion of the trust fund, then those expenses would properly be chargeable to the income portion of the fund alone.[155]

8.3.7 Duty to invest the trust property

The duties in relation to the investment of the trust property are considered in detail in Chapter 9. The law on investment of trusts is caught between an obligation on the trustees to secure the best performing investments available in accordance with the terms of the trust,[156] while balancing that quest for a high return with the general obligation to act prudently.[157] The tension between taking care and yet seeking the highest available return has developed into a modern requirement that trustees maintain a portfolio of investments whereby a breadth of investments will balance out the risks associated with any individual investment generating a loss.[158] The enactment of the TA 2000 has supplied a range of powers and duties for trustees when investing the trust property in the event that a trust instrument has no specific investment powers and duties to the contrary. The most significant statutory power is a general investment power for trustees whereby trustees have the investment powers of an absolute owner of the trust property.[159] This power displaces the greatly restrictive obligations contained in the now-repealed Trustee Investment Act 1961 which required a very conservative investment policy for trustees. The TA 2000 also requires trustees consciously to create standard investment criteria in the form of a set of principles by reference to which they will make their investments.[160] In making investment decisions, the trustees are also obliged to take professional advice.[161] When making investment decisions, the trustees are still governed by the general statutory duty of care.[162]

8.3.8 Duty to distribute the trust property correctly

Further to the trustee's duty to obey the terms of the trust[163] and the concomitant duty to avoid breaches of trust, the trustee must therefore obey any instructions as to the distribution of the trust property. Any failure to obey the terms of the trust will constitute a breach of

---

155 See now Law Commission, *Capital and Income in Trusts: Classification and Apportionment*, Law Com No 315, 2009, in particular as to the treatment of distributions from companies as constituting capital when received by a trust.
156 *Cowan v Scargill* [1985] Ch 270. See para 9.6.2 below.
157 *Speight v Gaunt* (1883) 9 App Cas 1, considered above at para 8.3.5 and, in relation specifically to investment of the trust property, at para 9.6.3 below.
158 *Bartlett v Barclays Bank Trust Co Ltd.* [1980] Ch 515. See generally section 9.6 on this development.
159 TA 2000, s 6(1). See para 9.3.1 below.
160 *Ibid*, s 4(1). See para 9.5.2 below.
161 *Ibid*, s 5(1). See para 9.5.3 below.
162 *Ibid*, Sched 1, para 1(b). See para 9.4.1 below.
163 *Clough v Bond* (1838) 3 My & Cr 490; considered at para 8.3.2 above.

trust, no matter what inducement there might have been to commit that breach,[164] although the beneficiaries will only be entitled to recover any property lost to the trust fund or to recover the value of any loss suffered as a result of the breach of trust.[165]

Aside from active breaches of trust, there are other forms of distribution which trustees must avoid. Trustees should only make distributions to beneficiaries who are *sui juris* and therefore able to give a good receipt for the property. Consequently, unmarried infants[166] and the insane may not give a good receipt because they are not *sui juris* at law. There are other contexts in which distribution may pose difficulties for trustees. After a divorce, a court order may have varied the terms of a family settlement and the trustees must therefore obey the terms of the court order rather than the original terms of the settlement.[167] When a beneficiary has died, the trustees should only release property to a personal representative if that representative can provide proof of entitlement to receive the property acceptable to English law;[168] otherwise the trustee will become a constructive trustee or executor *de son tort* of the wrongly distributed property.[169] In some circumstances it may not be known whether or not a beneficiary has died, in which case if there is no trace of that beneficiary for seven years, then the trustees are entitled to assume that she is dead,[170] although the trustees are supposed to seek actual proof of death before making any distribution on this basis.[171]

The general problem here is the problem of knowing which of a class of beneficiaries remains alive and who is therefore entitled to be considered either to receive property under a fixed trust or to be the object of some power held by the trustees. A similar form of this problem arises when the trustees seek to decide whether or not a given postulant still qualifies for membership of a class of objects of a trust or power. In general terms the trustees should protect themselves against any claim that they exercised their powers wrongly[172] by means of taking out an advertisement in the *Gazette*, and in a newspaper circulating in the district where any land at issue is situated, provided that the advertisement provides a mechanism for contacting the trustees and a deadline for such communication.[173] There is no obligation to

---

164   Therefore, the trustee will bear the principal liability even if she had been presented with a forged document by a person claiming entitlement to trust property: *Ashby v Blackwell* (1765) Eden 299; *Eaves v Hickson* (1861) 30 Beav 136. Cf *Re Smith* (1902) 71 LJ Ch 411.

165   *Target Holdings v Redferns* [1996] 1 AC 421.

166   Although a married infant may give a good receipt: Law of Property Act 1925, s 21.

167   Matrimonial Causes Act 1973, s 24; Family Law Act 1996, s 15, Sched 2, paras 1, 2 and 5.

168   As, for example, under the Power of Attorneys Act 1971, s 5.

169   *Smith v Bolden* (1863) 33 Beav 262; *New York Breweries Co Ltd v Attorney-General* [1899] AC 62.

170   *Re Watkins* [1953] 1 WLR 1323.

171   That is, seek a *Benjamin* order: *Re Benjamin* [1902] 1 Ch 723.

172   Provided that they comply with the procedure contained in Law of Property Act 1925, s 27, as considered next: *Re Letherbrow* [1935] WN 34 and 48; *Re Holden* [1935] WN 52. Not surprisingly, the trustees cannot ignore a claim of which they have notice simply because that beneficiary does not respond to the advertisement: *Markwell's Case* (1872) 21 WR 135. Although, just because trustees know of a claim, they may nevertheless not be able to find the beneficiary in question and therefore ought not to be liable provided that they have taken reasonable steps to find that person. In such a situation the trustees should seek a court order as to their best course of action: see para 8.6.2 below. For example, if a trustee has acted honestly and reasonably, then he may be excused for any breach of trust: TA 1925, s 61.

173   Law of Property Act 1925, s 27.

advertise in a foreign country if that is considered impracticable by the trustees.[174] An alternative means of protection is to seek the advice of counsel of 10 years' standing.[175]

8.3.9 Duty to avoid conflicts of interest

The general duty to avoid conflicts of interest

The trustee has an obligation not to permit conflicts of interest either between two competing fiduciary duties, or between the trustee's personal interests and the interests of the beneficiaries.[176] At one level, therefore, a trustee is not permitted to refrain from any action as trustee which would otherwise have been carried out, nor to take any action which would otherwise not have been performed, on the basis that the trustee's behaviour was motivated by a conflict between her personal interests and her countervailing fiduciary obligations.[177] However, it should be understood that the courts are not simply concerned to deal with conscious and deliberate conflicts of interest – for example, when a trustee intentionally seeks to make an unauthorised personal profit from the use of the trust property – but are concerned more generally to remove even the possibility that there might be any such abuse of fiduciary position by imposing a duty to avoid all potential, as well as actual, conflicts of interest. Therefore, at a second level, fiduciaries are obliged to refrain from any potential conflicts of interest. As is considered below, any benefit taken from such a conflict of interest will be held on constructive trust for the beneficiaries.[178]

The two key principles in this area are frequently described as the 'no conflict rule' and the 'no profit rule'[179] where the former rule prohibits fiduciaries from allowing any conflict between their personal interests and their fiduciary duties, and where the latter rule prohibits fiduciaries from profiting from their fiduciary offices. These two related principles have been described in the following fashion by Deane J in *Chan v Zacharia*[180] as being predicated on two separate themes:

> The first is that which appropriates for the benefit of the person to whom the fiduciary duty is owed any benefit or gain obtained or received by the fiduciary in circumstances where there existed a conflict of personal interest and fiduciary duty or a significant possibility of such conflict: the objective is to preclude the fiduciary from being swayed by considerations of personal interest. The second is that which requires the fiduciary to

---

174 *Re Gess* [1942] Ch 37.

175 Administration of Justice Act 1985, s 48(1).

176 *Tito v Waddell (No 2)* [1977] 3 All ER 129; *Re Thompson's Settlement* [1985] 2 All ER 720. This is equally true where accountants are advising both clients in a transaction and are therefore required to separate their activities by means of internal divisions (known as 'Chinese walls'); *Prince Jefri Bolkiah v KPMG* [1999] 1 All ER 517. Cf *Kelly v Cooper* [1993] AC 205 (estate agents).

177 *Clark Boyce v Mouat* [1994] 1 AC 428; *Nocton v Lord Ashburton* [1914] AC 932.

178 *Boardman v. Phipps* [1967] 2 AC 46.

179 See *Don King Productions Inc v Warren* [2000] Ch 291 and *In Plus Group Ltd v Pyke* [2002] 2 BCLC 201, 220; cited with approval in *Ultraframe UK Ltd v Fielding* [2005] EWHC 1638 (Ch), [2005] All ER (D) 397, [1305], *per* Lewison J.

180 (1984) 154 CLR 178, 198; cited with approval in *Don King Productions Inc v Warren* [2000] Ch 291; and in *Ultraframe UK Ltd v Fielding* [2005] EWHC 1638 (Ch), [2005] All ER (D) 397, [1305], *per* Lewison J.

account for any benefit or gain obtained or received by reason of or by use of his fiduciary position or of opportunity or knowledge resulting from it: the objective is to preclude the fiduciary from actually misusing his position for his personal advantage.

In either case, the trustee may be protected if she can show that she was authorised to act in the manner in which she did, as considered in the next section. Similarly, while the trustee cannot transact in a way which will accord any direct benefit to herself,[181] it may be possible for the trustee to sell trust property to a company in which the trustee is a mere shareholder without attracting liability.[182] This will preclude liability under the conflict of interest rule unless the trustee stands to make some substantial personal gain as a result of the company being substantially under his control[183] or in such a situation where the transaction itself involves a lack of probity.[184]

Trustee making unauthorised profits from the trust

In the event that the trustee makes any profit from the trust which has not been authorised by the terms of the trust, then the trustee is required to hold any such profits (and any property derived from those profits) on constructive trust for the beneficiaries, in accordance with any specific provisions of the terms of the trust.[185] If the trustee deals with the trust property in breach of trust and makes a loss, the trustee will nevertheless be required to make good the property and the loss to the trust fund.[186] These issues are considered in detail in Chapter 12[187] and Chapter 18.[188]

This rule is a strict rule which developed from the rule in *Keech v Sandford*,[189] in which case a trustee sought to renew a lease which previously he had held on trust for an infant beneficiary. The beneficiary, being an infant, was not able to take out the new lease in his own name and therefore the trustee took out the lease in his own name instead. It was held that the lease should be held on constructive trust for the beneficiary not because there had been any suggestion of fraud or unconscionable behaviour on the part of the trustee, but rather because the court considered that it should be astute to prevent even the possibility that there might be any unconscionable benefit taken by a trustee. This principle was expressed in the following manner by Lord Herschell in *Bray v Ford*:

> It is an inflexible rule of a Court of Equity that a person in a fiduciary position . . . is not, unless otherwise expressly provided, entitled to make a profit, he is not allowed to put himself in a position where his interest and duty conflict. It does not appear to me that

---

181 *Thompson's Trustee in Bankruptcy v Heaton* [1974] 1 WLR 605.
182 *Silkstone and Haigh Moor Coal Co v Edey* [1900] 1 Ch 167.
183 See, eg, *Farrar v Farrars Ltd* (1888) 40 Ch D 395.
184 Such as the auctioning of land at an undervalue by auction where only the trustee's spouse is present: *Tse Kwong Lam v Wong Chit Sen* [1983] 3 All ER 54.
185 *Boardman v Phipps* [1967] 2 AC 46; *Attorney-General for Hong Kong v Reid* [1994] 1 AC 324, [1993] 3 WLR 1143.
186 *Attorney-General for Hong Kong v Reid* [1994] 1 AC 324, [1993] 3 WLR 1143.
187 Section 12.5.
188 Section 18.1.
189 (1726) Sel Cas Ch 61.

this rule is . . . founded upon principles of morality. I regard it rather as based on the consideration that, human nature being what it is, there is danger, in such circumstances, of the person holding a fiduciary position being swayed by interest rather than by duty, and thus prejudicing those whom he was bound to protect. It has, therefore, been deemed expedient to lay down this positive rule.

The aim of this principle, then, is to prevent trustees from defrauding the trust by abstracting trust profits to themselves. It functions, in Lord Herschell's account, on the basis of a maudlin attitude to human nature by which it is supposed that all people, whether fiduciaries or not, are weak and will succumb to temptation if the law is not pitched at its strictest. In some cases it appears to operate harshly where trustees seek to make profits for the trust which the beneficiaries acting through that trust could not have made for themselves. One example of this situation was the case of *Boardman v Phipps*,[190] in which a solicitor took over the management of a trust which he had previously been advising. That solicitor contributed his own, personal money to a business plan, involving the acquisition of a majority shareholding in a private company. Subsequently, the solicitor realised a large personal profit in common with the beneficiaries of the trust who also realised a large profit – there was no suggestion that the solicitor had defrauded the beneficiaries, albeit that he could not demonstrate that sufficient information had been given to the beneficiaries so as to obtain authorisation from them for his course of action. Nevertheless, the majority of the House of Lords held that the trustee should hold all of his profits on constructive trust for the beneficiaries even though all of their Lordships agreed that he had not acted in bad faith.[191] Lord King LC in *Keech v Sandford* held that 'it is very proper that [this] rule should be strictly pursued, and not in the least relaxed, for it is very obvious what would be the consequence of letting trustees have the [trust property in their own names]'.[192]

Consequently, even in the absence of any proof of fraud or unconscionable behaviour, the trustee will be liable to hold any such profits on constructive trust for the beneficiaries.[193] The fiduciary may only be absolved from this obligation if the trust permits a particular form of profit (such as for a professional trustee to charge fees),[194] or if the fiduciary has sought authorisation for the profit,[195] or the person involved is held not to be in a fiduciary position at all.[196] However, it is not clear that authorisation will always generate permission to make profits or protection from liability for making such unauthorised profits,[197] whereas a right to

190 [1967] 2 AC 46.
191 The trustee was entitled to some equitable accounting to compensate him for his efforts in generating that profit for the trust.
192 (1726) Sel Cas 61.
193 *Boardman v Phipps* [1967] 2 AC 46.
194 On which, see para 8.2.6 above.
195 *Queensland Mines v Hudson* (1977) 18 ALR 1; *Prince Jefri Bolkiah v KPMG* [1999] 1 All ER 517. In *Brown v IRC* [1965] AC 244, it was suggested by Lord Reid that a trustee cannot keep any benefit taken from dealing with the beneficiaries unless he can 'show authority'.
196 *Re Biss* [1903] 2 Ch 40, as when a family business was passed to the defendant in a situation in which he was found by the Court of Appeal to owe no duties of good conscience to any other member of the family when renewing the lease over the business premises.
197 *Industrial Development Consultants Ltd v Cooley* [1972] 1 WLR 443; on which, see generally section 12.5 below.

receive payment or a finding that one is not a fiduciary will provide such absolution from liability.[198] This limitation on the defence of authorisation will obtain particularly if that authorisation has been sought merely from other trustees. In line with the idea of trusteeship being a bundle of obligations owed to the beneficiaries under the trust, simply obtaining the permission of other fiduciaries would not appear to be sufficient to avoid the ambit of the rule against profit from a fiduciary office.[199] However, receiving the permission, or affirmation, of beneficiaries will generally prevent any beneficiaries who gave such permission from seeking to enforce the rule against self-dealing, as considered next.[200]

The principle against self-dealing transactions

In a situation in which a trustee purports to deal on her own account with the trust property and especially if she takes a profit from such a transaction, not only will the trustee be required to hold that profit on constructive trust for the beneficiaries of the trust, but also the transaction itself may be set aside.[201] Previously we have considered the obligations of fiduciaries when making unauthorised profits from their office in general terms. The specific problem in relation to the self-dealing principle is that the trustees are purporting to deal with the beneficiaries of their fiduciary power as a third party, for example, when seeking to buy property from the trust. In that instance, the trustee would be acting simultaneously on behalf of the trust as well as acting on her own behalf. Such a transaction is considered to bear the risk that the trustee will acquire the property from the trust at an advantageous price and thus exploit the beneficiaries, although by the same token it might be argued on the facts of some cases that the price which the trustee obtains would have been the same price which the beneficiaries would have obtained on the open market and therefore that there is nothing wrong with the transaction.

Nevertheless, the prevailing strict approach on the leading authorities holds that the transaction is voidable, rather than automatically void, at the instance of the beneficiaries. On the basis of these authorities, there is no possibility that the courts will listen to arguments that the transaction caused no harm to the beneficiaries and therefore that the beneficiaries ought not to be permitted to avoid that transaction, the reason for this strict approach being to protect the beneficiaries from the 'danger' resulting from such a course of argument.[202] Consequently, it is possible for the beneficiaries to affirm the transaction after the event if they consider it to be in their interests so to do. The purpose of this rule is to prevent further conflicts of interest.[203] This rule had always been interpreted and

198 *Re Biss* [1903] 2 Ch 40.
199 *Regal v Gulliver* [1942] 1 All ER 378.
200 *Holder v Holder* [1968] Ch 353.
201 *Tito v Waddell (No 2)* [1977] 3 All ER 129, 141, *per* Megarry VC. See also *Newgate Stud Co v Penfold* [2004] EWHC 2993 (Ch).
202 *Parker v McKenna* (1874) 10 Ch App 96, 124, *per* James LJ. Indeed, his Lordship considered it necessary to secure 'the safety of mankind' by applying the strict version of this principle. That this is a general rule of policy has been affirmed by Vinelott J in *British Coal Corp v British Coal Staff Superannuation Scheme Trustees Ltd* [1993] PLR 303, 312.
203 *Re Brooke Bond & Co Ltd's Trust Deed* [1963] Ch 357; *Re Thompson's Settlement* [1985] 2 All ER 720; *Motivex Ltd v Bulfield* [1988] BCLC 104.

applied on a strict basis.[204] Lord Eldon expressed the strict approach to this principle in the following terms:[205]

> The purchase [of trust property by the trustee on his own account] is not permitted in any case, however honest the circumstances; the general interests of justice requiring it to be destroyed in every instance; as no Court is equal to the examination and ascertainment of the truth in much the greater number of cases.

It is a matter of policy that this principle is strictly observed.[206] Consequently, a fiduciary cannot ordinarily seek to argue that no substantial harm would be caused to the beneficiaries' interests by the transaction. So, it would not be open to the trustee to maintain that the price had been fixed by an independent third party or seemingly that the transaction had been effected through a third party.[207] In either case, the transaction would be voidable. In line with the principle in *Keech v Sandford*,[208] the courts are concerned to prevent the possibility of fraud.

Exceptionally, some flexibility was permitted in *Holder v Holder*,[209] when the Court of Appeal decided that it was possible for a court to inquire into the trustee's knowledge and intentions, and to decide on that basis that it was permissible for transactions in good faith to be affirmed by the court rather than being voidable. In that case, a testator's son had formally renounced his status as executor and (apart from some few initial activities) had taken no part in the administration of the estate. The son acquired the freehold to a farm of which he had formerly been tenant from his father's estate at auction. The price reached was greatly in excess of the reserve price. Consequently, the Court of Appeal held that the transaction should not be voidable on the grounds that the son had taken no substantive actions as trustee, nor had he benefited from any transaction at an undervalue as a result. It might similarly be wondered why a trustee who bought property from the trust at a standard market price – for example, a price fixed on a stock exchange – should not be entitled to enforce that purchase. This approach does, however, appear to be in conflict with the explicitly inflexible view of the House of Lords in *Boardman v Phipps*, where no evident advantage had been taken of the beneficiaries and no loss caused to those beneficiaries by a person who was not even an express trustee (but rather who became a constructive trustee by means of his meddling with the trust, or a 'trustee *de son tort*' as such a person is known).[210] The general principle in *Ex p Lacey*[211] was clearly to the effect that any transaction with the trust in which the trustee had

204 *Ex p Lacey* (1802) 6 Ves 625; *Ex p James* (1803) 8 Ves 337.

205 *Ex p James* (1803) 8 Ves 337, 345. See also *Ex p Bennett* (1805) 10 Ves 381; *Randall v Errington* (1805) 10 Ves 423; *Parker v McKenna* (1874) 10 Ch App 96.

206 *British Coal Corp v British Coal Staff Superannuation Scheme Trustees Ltd* [1993] PLR 303, 312, *per* Vinelott J.

207 *Wright v Morgan* [1926] AC 788. See also *Campbell v Walker* (1800) 5 Ves 678, 680, where the sale was made at a public auction and sold to the trustee for well above the reserve price: nevertheless, the *Lacey* principle was strictly applied.

208 (1726) Sel Cas Ch 61.

209 [1968] Ch 353.

210 [1967] 2 AC 46.

211 (1802) 6 Ves 625.

a personal interest would be voidable at the instance of the beneficiary. In *Holder v Holder*,[212] it was doubted by Harman LJ (in an *obiter* remark) whether the court was bound to apply the principle in *Ex p Lacey*[213] as a strict rule. In *Holder*, it was suggested that the mischief of the principle would not be affected where the trustee had ceased to act in effect as a trustee and therefore could not be deemed to be both the seller of the interest (on behalf of the trust) and also the buyer (on his own account). However, courts in subsequent cases have not interpreted *Holder* as casting any doubt on the general applicability of the *Lacey* principle.[214]

It is clear that the understanding of the self-dealing principle in the leading cases entitles the beneficiary to avoid any such transaction on the basis, set out in the *Keech v Sandford*[215] rule, that even the possibility of fraud or bad faith being exercised by the trustee is to be resisted.[216] Megarry VC in *Tito v Waddell (No 2)*[217] enunciated the self-dealing principle in the following terms – 'if a trustee purchases trust property from himself, any beneficiary may have the sale set aside *ex debito justitiae*, however fair the transaction'. The right of the beneficiary is therefore to set aside the transaction. There is no defence against the exercise of such a right that the transaction was entered into as though between parties acting at arm's length. The same principle applies to purchases by directors from their companies,[218] although most articles of association in English companies expressly permit such transactions.[219] So, where a director of a company which owned racehorses organised that some of those horses be sold to two partnerships in which he and his wife respectively had financial interests, it was held that these were self-dealing transactions.[220] Where the beneficiary acquiesces in the transaction, however, that beneficiary is precluded from seeking to have that transaction set aside.[221]

The strict application of the *Lacey* principle was demonstrated in *Wright v Morgan*,[222] in which a will bequeathed rights in property to a person who was both legatee and one of two trustees of the will trusts. The will permitted sale of the property to that legatee of the property. The legatee sought to transfer the property to his co-trustee subject to an independent valuation of the open market price for the property. The issue arose whether this transfer to the co-trustee should be set aside. It was held that the transaction was voidable even though there had been an independent valuation of the price.[223] The reasoning stated for applying the principle in spite of the independent valuation was that the trustees nevertheless could have delayed the sale and so applied a value which was no longer the open market value. Similarly, where fiduciaries acquired leases from a company and a partnership on their own account, it was held that those transactions were voidable at the instance of the beneficiaries of the powers.[224]

---

212 *Ibid.*
213 (1802) 6 Ves 625.
214 See, eg, *Re Thompson's Settlement* [1986] Ch 99.
215 (1726) Sel Cas Ch 61.
216 *Ex p Lacey* (1802) 6 Ves 625.
217 [1977] Ch 106.
218 *Aberdeen Railway Co v Blaikie Brothers* (1854) 1 Macq 461.
219 See Jaffey, 2000.
220 *Newgate Stud Co v Penfold* [2004] EWHC 2993 (Ch).
221 *Holder v Holder* [1968] Ch 353.
222 [1926] AC 788.
223 See also *Whelpdale v Cookson* (1747) 1 Ves Sen 9; *Sargeant v National Westminster Bank* (1990) 61 P & CR
     518.
224 *Re Thompson's Settlement* [1986] Ch 99.

The only advisable course of action for a trustee wishing to enter into such a transaction would be to acquire the leave of the court in advance of the transaction to acquire those interests. The court will require the trustee to demonstrate that the transaction is in the interests of the beneficiaries and that the trustee will not take any unconscionable advantage from the transaction.[225] It might be thought that such an application has the effect merely of adopting the *obiter* remarks of Harman LJ in *Holder v Holder*[226] to the effect that the court could treat the *Lacey*[227] principle as merely a rule of practice and accept as valid any transaction which was shown not to be to the unconscionable advantage of the trustee nor to the concomitant disadvantage of the beneficiaries.

Unsurprisingly, the trustee will not be able to avoid this principle simply by selling to an associate or a connected company or similar person, although the authorities on this point relate primarily to sales to relatives,[228] to nominees,[229] to the trustee's children[230] and to the trustee's spouse.[231] It is suggested that in any event, such a transaction would be a sham transaction and therefore capable of being set aside in any event[232] or treated as an attempt to effect a fraud on the power.[233]

The fair dealing principle

Where a trustee deals with a beneficiary's interest in the trust, or acquires that beneficiary's interest, there will be an obligation on the trustee to demonstrate fair dealing. Thus, in *Tito v Waddell (No 2)*, Megarry VC held:[234]

> if a trustee purchases the beneficial interest of any of his beneficiaries, the transaction is not voidable *ex debito justitiae*, but can be set aside unless the trustee can show that he has not taken advantage of his position and has made full disclosure to the beneficiary, and that the transaction is fair and honest.

Therefore, there is a burden of proof on the trustee to demonstrate both that no advantage was taken of the beneficiary, and that the beneficiary was made fully aware of the nature and the circumstances of the transaction. Where there is no disclosure to the beneficiary, therefore, the transaction will be set aside.[235]

The fair dealing principle is similar to the self-dealing principle considered immediately above. The fair dealing principle only validates acquisitions by trustees of the interests of their beneficiaries will be enforceable provided that the trustee does not acquire any

---

225 *Campbell v Walker* (1800) 5 Ves 678; *Farmer v Dean* (1863) 32 Beav 327.
226 [1968] Ch 353.
227 *Ex p Lacey* (1802) 6 Ves 625.
228 *Coles v Trecothick* (1804) 9 Ves 234 – which may be permitted where the transaction appears to be conducted as though at arm's length.
229 *Silkstone & Haigh Moor Coal Co v Edey* [1900] 1 Ch 167; *Re Postlethwaite* (1888) 60 LT 514.
230 *Gregory v Gregory* (1821) Jac 631.
231 *Ferraby v Hobson* (1847) 2 PH 255; *Burrell v Burrell's Trustee* 1915 SC 333.
232 See, eg, *Street v Mountford* [1985] 2 WLR 877; *Midland Bank v Wyatt* [1995] 1 FLR 697.
233 *Rochefoucauld v Boustead* [1897] 1 Ch 196.
234 [1977] 3 All ER 129.
235 *Hill v Langley* (1988) *The Times*, 28 January.

advantage attributable to his fiduciary office.[236] This principle also applies to fiduciary relationships such as acquisitions by agents of the interests of their principals.[237]

To demonstrate that the transaction was not procured as a result of any abuse of position the trustee will be required to demonstrate that no details were concealed, that the price obtained was fair and that the beneficiary was not required to rely entirely on the trustee's advice.[238] The fair dealing principle is necessarily less strict than the self-dealing principle because the trustee is able to seek justification of the former by demonstrating that the transaction was not procured in bad faith. It is an unconscious aspect of the principle nevertheless that the beneficiaries are required to authorise the transaction rather than permitting the trustee to act entirely alone: this accords with the principles on authorisation considered above. Where the beneficiary is an infant, the trustee will not be able to demonstrate that the beneficiary made an informed decision.[239]

Limitations on the 'no conflict' principle

The duty not to permit conflicts of interest has clearly been expressed as being a strict principle, particularly in cases in the early 19th century.[240] It is clear that a trustee may realise a personal profit if that is envisaged by the terms of the trust instrument.[241] There are, however, other judicial statements to the effect that there is some flexibility in this principle, provided always that it is remembered that its purpose is the protection of the beneficiaries.[242] One situation in which a trustee may be entitled to take a profit, then, is in a situation in which the settlor puts the trustee in a position in which the trustee, impliedly, is required to operate in the context of some conflict of interest.[243] So, consider a professional investment advisor, such as a stockbroker, who is appointed as trustee of a trust fund and who, to the settlor's certain knowledge, was already trustee of many hundreds of other trusts simultaneously. In that situation, the settlor would have put the trustee in a situation in which that trustee had to consider the competing needs of many beneficiaries under many different trusts and also to consider her own commissions and profits derived from recommending investment strategies to those various trusts. Equally, a stockbroker would, in line with modern market practice, sell to the trust securities which the stockbroker already owned and would possibly buy back from the trust those same securities when the trust sought to realise its profits, thus necessarily involving dealing with the trust on her own account. In such a professional situation, the trust instrument would usually contain provisions (at the insistence of the professional trustee) which permitted this ostensible conflict of interest and which would thus seek to limit the trustee's potential liabilities.[244]

---

236 *Chalmer v Bradley* (1819) 1 J & W 51; *Tito v Waddell (No 2)* [1977] Ch 106.
237 *Edwards v Meyrick* (1842) 2 Hare 60.
238 *Coles v Bradley* (1804) 9 Ves 234.
239 *Sanderson v Walker* (1807) 13 Ves 601.
240 Eg, *Ex p Lacey* (1802) 6 Ves 625.
241 *Sargeant v National Westminster Bank plc* (1990) 61 P&CR 518.
242 *Boulting v Association of Cinematograph, Television and Allied Technicians* [1963] 2 QB 606, 636, *per* Upjohn LJ.
243 *Sargeant v National Westminster Bank plc* (1990) 61 P & CR 518, 519, *per* Nourse LJ.
244 See para 8.5.1 below.

Nevertheless, it is suggested that there may be situations in which the transaction may not be to the detriment of the beneficiaries, but if the transaction is indeed a benign or even profitable one from the beneficiaries' perspective, then the beneficiaries can affirm the transaction if they choose to do so. If the beneficiaries do not choose to affirm the transaction, then it must be assumed that it is not considered by them to be in their best interests and therefore there is no good reason to dilute the 'no conflict' principle to protect the trustee from the obligation to reconstitute the trust fund. If the trustee requires protection, then the trustee can insist on terms to that effect being inserted in the trust instrument. Otherwise, the trustee cannot be under any doubt that self-dealing and other transactions will not be valid if the 'no conflict' principle is strictly enforced.

8.3.10 Duties of confidence and duties in relation to Chinese walls

One of the core duties of a fiduciary is a duty of confidence, which is coupled with the duty of loyalty.[245] In *Reading v R*,[246] Asquith LJ proposed the following summary of those circumstances in which a fiduciary relationship can be said to exist:

> a 'fiduciary relation' exists . . . whenever the plaintiff entrusts to the defendant property, including intangible property as, for instance, confidential information, and relies on the defendant to deal with such property for the benefit of the plaintiff or for purposes authorised by him, and not otherwise.

The essence of the fiduciary relationship is loyalty and consequently precludes the fiduciary from advancing his personal interests at the expense of, or in conflict with, the interests of the object of his fiduciary obligations.[247] Those sentiments have been expressed by Millett LJ in the following terms:

> A fiduciary is someone who has undertaken to act for or on behalf of another in a particular matter in circumstances which give rise to a relationship of trust and confidence. The distinguishing obligation of a fiduciary is the obligation of loyalty. The principal is entitled to the single-minded loyalty of his fiduciary. The core liability has several facets. A fiduciary must act in good faith; he must not make a profit out of his trust; he must not place himself in a position where his duty and his interest may conflict; he may not act for his own benefit or the benefit of a third person without the informed consent of his principal. This is not intended to be an exhaustive list, but it is sufficient to indicate the nature of fiduciary obligations.[248]

Therefore, a fiduciary (such as a trustee) must protect the confidence of his beneficiaries. That much has been considered already in relation to the obligation not to permit conflicts of

---

245 *Bristol & West Building Society v Mothew* [1998] Ch 1.
246 [1949] 2 KB 232 at 236.
247 On which see Chapter 29 on the imposition of constructive trusts in relation to the abuse of fiduciary office generally.
248 *Bristol & West Building Society v Mothew* [1998] Ch 1 at 18, *per* Millett LJ.

interest.[249] Briefly put, if a fiduciary earns a profits from the misuse of confidential information owned by a beneficiary without authorisation, then that profit is held on constructive trust by the fiduciary.[250]

One context in which the protection of confidential information is particularly significant is in relation to Chinese walls.[251] Chinese walls arise in circumstances in which an organisation is involved in acting on both sides of a transaction such that communication of confidential information owned by both sides to that transaction would ordinarily be possible between officers of that organisation in breach of the organisation's fiduciary duties of confidence to both parties. The clearest example of a Chinese wall would be the arrangement put in place when different departments within the same law firm are acting as advisors to two different companies who are negotiating a merger of their organisations. The Chinese walls relate specifically to the arrangements by which employees of that law firm are prevented from meeting so as to discuss the merger transaction, from seeing documentation relating to the other party's participation in the merger transaction, from accessing those parts of the firm's buildings where employees from the other department may work or store documents or even recreate, and from learning any confidential information in general terms. Clearly, to prevent the sharing of such information between fellow employees is a particularly complex business. Such a communication of confidential information would constitute a breach of the 'no conflicts' rule,[252] in that a conflict would be permitted between the interests of different beneficiaries, as well as general breach of the general duty of confidence to each of the beneficiaries involved. The law firm, to continue the earlier example, would be able to demonstrate that it did not bear any liability for any breach of confidentiality if effective Chinese wall arrangements were in place[253] – for example, if any exchange of information was made by the contumelious perseverance of employees in meeting outside the workplace. The arrangements need to be demonstrably thorough and designed specifically for those particular circumstances.[254] Chinese walls are considered in greater detail below in relation to the provision of information by trustees.

8.3.11 Duty to act gratuitously

In general trusts law, it is assumed that the trustee accepts her office voluntarily and it is assumed equally that she will not permit any conflicts of interest between the beneficiaries' interests and her own personal interests.[255] Consequently, it is assumed by the case law that the trustee will act without regard to payment.[256] It is suggested, however, in the modern context that this duty is of reduced value for two reasons. First, in commercial trusts practice, the trustees will be entitled to remuneration by the terms of the trust instrument. Secondly,

---

249 See para 8.3.9 above.
250 *Boardman v Phipps* [1967] 2 AC 46.
251 Chinese walls are considered in detail below at para 8.4.9.
252 See para 8.3.9 above.
253 *Galmerrow Securities Ltd v National Westminster Bank plc* [2002] WTLR 125.
254 *Bolkiah v KPMG* [1999] 2 AC 222.
255 See para 8.3.9 above.
256 *Robinson v Pett* (1734) 3 P Wms 249, 251.

as considered above, there are rights to remuneration and reimbursement of expenses in general terms.[257] Therefore, the main context in which this principle might be said to bite – that is, denying the trustees any sort of wage or emolument from their office – is circumscribed in most cases in which the duties are so onerous as to require such remuneration. Therefore, the significance of this principle in modern practice is as a recognition of the trustee's obligations to act loyally in the service of the beneficiaries in the manner required by their fiduciary office. In that sense, beyond questions of authorised remuneration, the trustee continues to act gratuitously.

8.3.12 Duty to account and to provide information

The trustees' obligations to account to the beneficiaries and the extent of the trustees' obligations to provide information to the beneficiaries are considered in section 8.4 below.

8.3.13 Duty to take into account only relevant considerations, and to achieve the trust's intended objective: the principle in *Re Hastings-Bass*

Introduction

Imagine for a moment how wonderful your life would be if you had a 'magic eraser' with which you could wipe out all of your poor choices in life, before going back and making those choices again. In the law of trusts, the 'principle in *Hastings-Bass*' seemed to offer trustees and their advisors just such a magic eraser in that they could ask the court to set aside any inappropriate exercise of their powers or discretions so that they could make their choices again. The principle in *Hastings-Bass* had acquired a life of its own in recent years as the judgment of Buckley LJ in the case of *In re Hastings-Bass*[258] itself was transformed by subsequent cases into a mechanism by which trustees who made errors in the exercise of their powers or discretions in relation to a trust fund, principally in the form of incurring unforeseen tax liabilities for those trusts, could effectively expunge their errors and have their actions set aside. For trusts law and tax professionals the doctrine in *Hastings-Bass* appeared to make it possible to undo any exercise of a trustee's powers or discretion which had an unforeseen consequence. As the principle had been developed by Warner J in *Mettoy Pension Fund Trustees Ltd v Evans*,[259] the court could set aside any such action of a trustee if the trustee had taken into account an irrelevant consideration or had failed to take into account a relevant consideration – such as a tax charge to the trust. Given that many trusts are used in practice for tax avoidance purposes, this rule was a very useful long-stop[260] if the trustees and their advisors failed to spot a future tax liability.

257 See paras 8.2.6 and 8.2.7 above.
258 [1975] Ch 25, [1974] 2 WLR 904, [1974] 2 All ER 193.
259 [1990] 1 WLR 1587, [1991] 2 All ER 513.
260 In cricket a 'long-stop' is a fielder who is placed a few yards directly behind the wicketkeeper so that if the wicketkeeper fails to stop the ball then the long-stop is there to provide cover for the wicketkeeper and stop the ball reaching the boundary. The principle in *Hastings-Bass* used to have this role in case trustees caused a loss to the trust in the exercise of their powers (like the ball getting past the wicketkeeper) by simply having the exercise of those powers reversed after the event.

Cases involving this principle have come thick and fast in recent years in reliance on the *Mettoy* approach to this principle. However, the decision of the Court of Appeal in the joined appeals of *Pitt v Holt* and *Futter v Futter*,[261] in the thorough judgment of Lloyd LJ, appears to have spoiled the party by restricting the operation of the *Hastings-Bass* principle to situations in which the trustees have committed a breach of trust, with the effect that mere errors or misunderstandings of the effect of an action would not be enough to have that action set aside. Incurring an unexpected tax liability will not in itself be a breach of trust. This is, as will be explained below, a great limitation on this principle, echoing a line of authority which began with *Abacus Trust v Barr*.[262] In essence, Lloyd LJ re-read the judgment of Buckley LJ in *Hastings-Bass* closely and decided that the development which began in *Mettoy* was a misreading of that case.

At the time of writing, however, the decision of the Court of Appeal in *Pitt v Holt* is to be the subject of an appeal to the Supreme Court. Therefore, this discussion retains an analysis of all of the relevant case law because the Supreme Court has yet to rule on the nature of this principle, even though many commentators take the view that the judgment of Lloyd LJ in *Pitt v Holt* has offered an authoritative restatement of the law.[263] The decision in *Pitt v Holt* will be presented as one of the two key arguments which run through this area of the law. In essence, those two arguments are: that *Hastings-Bass* should have a limited, negative interpretation placed on it such that a court may hold a trustee's actions to be voidable if it chooses to do so where there has been a breach of trust (as in *Pitt v Holt* and in *Abacus v Barr*);[264] or a more expansive, positive reading to the effect that beneficiaries are entitled to have their trustees' actions set aside where there have been irrelevant factors taken into account or relevant factors overlooked or mistakes made, regardless of whether or not there has been a breach of trust. As Lloyd LJ pointed out in *Pitt v Holt*, this appears to be a situation in which the dicta of Buckley LJ in *Hastings-Bass* were developed far beyond his lordship's original intentions by the decisions of later courts, especially in *Mettoy*.

The purpose of this principles: setting aside the exercise of the trustee's powers

The principles considered in this section permit the court to set aside trustees' actions or decisions in certain circumstances. At the most general level it would be contrary to principle if a trustee could misapply her powers so that trust property was misappropriated without the beneficiaries having any means of setting aside such a misapplication of the trustees' powers. The trustees would be liable to account to the beneficiaries for any loss

---

261 [2011] EWCA Civ 197, [2011] 3 WLR 19.

262 [2003] EWHC 114 (Ch), [2003] Ch 409, [2003] 2 WLR 1362, [2003] 1 All ER 763. Interestingly, the approach taken by Lightman J *Abacus Trust v Barr* was one which Lloyd J had disagreed with in *Sieff v Fox* [2005] EWHC 1312 (Ch), [2005] 1 WLR 3811, [2005] 3 All ER 693 but about which he later changed his mind (and there is no greater evidence of an honest intellect than that) in *Pitt v Holt*: that approach means that the trustee must commit some breach of duty (ie a breach of trust).

263 See, for example, the evidence led by Prof Paul Matthews in *In re R and S* [2011] JRC 117 as to English law in this regard being settled.

264 This book has always taken the approach that the narrow interpretation was preferable and that there was no reason for trusts law to provide a form of 'magic eraser' for the errors of trustees: that is why the law on breach of trust or the law of negligence or professional indemnity insurance exists – to allow beneficiaries to recoup the cost of their advisors and trustees causing them loss.

caused by a breach of trust.[265] Nevertheless, the beneficiaries may prefer to set the exercise of the trustees' power aside so that an appropriate exercise of that power can be applied instead of simply recovering compensation from the trustees. This would be so particularly if the trust property was intrinsically valuable and considered likely to increase in value in the future; merely recovering compensation for the property valued at the time of the breach of trust would not include the subsequent increase in the value of that property. In relation to discretionary trusts, for example, a misapplication of the trustees' power might have caused trust property to be paid to the wrong beneficiary or to beneficiaries who might not have been entitled to that property if the power had been properly applied. Alternatively, it may be that the trustee has not committed any breach of trust but, in exercising her powers properly, she has made a decision which the beneficiaries would prefer to have set aside. For example, if the trustees exercised their powers properly but, in so doing, exposed the trust to a large tax liability, the beneficiaries would prefer to have that decision set aside so that a more tax-efficient means of acting could be identified. So, in this section we are concerned to identify the ways in which beneficiaries may be able to set aside the exercises of trustees' powers. These principles are collectively referred to as the 'principle in *Re Hastings-Bass*'.

Taking into account relevant considerations and ignoring irrelevant considerations:
the principle in Hastings-Bass

Beneficiaries may be able to have the exercise of a power or a discretion by the trustees set aside if the trustees have taken into account irrelevant considerations or have not taken into account relevant considerations in so acting;[266] and provided that there has also been some breach of duty by the trustees.[267] The exercise of the trustees' power in such a situation is voidable at the instance of the court but not automatically void.[268] In reaching a decision as to the proper exercise of a trustee's power – and we are thinking here particularly of discretionary trust and fiduciary mere powers, rather than simply trust obligations[269] – there will be relevant considerations and there will be irrelevant considerations. Consider, for example, a discretionary trust power whereby a trustee was empowered to pay money for the maintenance of whichever of the homes of the settlor's adult children required building work at any time. Relevant considerations in relation to the exercise of this power might include the condition of the various buildings owned and occupied by those children, the urgency of any renovation work, or the relative wealth of the children and their ability to pay for their own repairs if the trust is short of funds. One important consideration, on the cases, would be any potential tax charge which the exercise of the power might incur. Irrelevant considerations

---

265 *Target Holdings v Redferns* [1996] 1 AC 421, considered in detail in Chapter 18.
266 *Re Hastings-Bass* [1975] Ch 25.
267 *Abacus Trust Company (Isle of Man) v Barr* [2003] 2 WLR 1362, 1370, para 24; *Burrell v Burrell* [2005] EWHC 245, [2005] All ER (D) 351; *Pitt v Holt, Futter v Futter* [2011] EWCA Civ 197, [2011] 3 WLR 19.
268 *Pitt v Holt, Futter v Futter* [2011] EWCA Civ 197, [2011] 3 WLR 19.
269 We are thinking particularly of discretionary trust powers and mere powers because fixed trust obligations will generally not be susceptible of misapplication since such an obligation usually only comprises a simple instruction to act in a particular way, whereas discretionary trust powers and mere powers give the power-holder a broader range of considerations to take into account or to ignore. Thus, a complaint about failing to take a consideration into account or about taking into account in irrelevant consideration is more likely to relate to a discretionary trust power or a mere power because they have more scope for such misapplications.

might include whether the trustees like some of the children more than others, whether the trustees would prefer to use the money to pay for holidays for the children, or whether the trustees consider the dilapidations to be the children's fault. If the trustees took into account only these irrelevant considerations or failed to take into account any of the relevant considerations, then the objects of that power would be able to petition the court to have the trustees' ultimate decision set aside.[270] Clearly there are two questions here: whether the factor was relevant or irrelevant, and the extent to which it was operative on the trustees in making their decision to act or not to act.

The question then is as to the precise nature of the court's powers in the event that the trustees have taken into account irrelevant considerations or failed to take into account relevant considerations. If a trustee failed to take into account a relevant consideration or took into account an irrelevant consideration, then two results ensue. First, the trustee may have committed a breach of trust by failing to perform her powers or her obligations properly.[271] Secondly, the beneficiaries are entitled to challenge the exercise of that power and to seek to have it set aside or otherwise administered by the court.[272]

Any analysis of this area must begin with the judgment of Buckley LJ in the case of *In re Hastings-Bass* from which this doctrine takes its name. The principle in *Hastings-Bass* was described in that decision in the following negative form[273] by Buckley LJ where:[274]

> a trustee is given a discretion as to some matter under which he acts in good faith, the court should not interfere with his action notwithstanding that it does not have the full effect which he intended, unless (1) what he had achieved is unauthorised by the power conferred upon him, or (2) it is clear that he would not have acted as he did (a) had he not taken into account considerations which he should not have taken into account, or (b) had he not failed to take into account considerations which he ought to have taken into account.

This is said to be a *negative*, limited form of the principle because the court is not required to take any action to set aside the action of the trustees but rather has a discretion whether or not it chooses to do so. Indeed, Buckley LJ clearly provided that 'the court should not interfere . . . unless' certain events had taken place, and even then the court had a discretion whether or not to intervene. This follows the principle that it is for the trustees to decide what actions to take in the performance of their duties, and that the court will only intervene in the event of some breach of duty. Thus, the court should not interfere with a trustee's exercise of a power unless it is clear either that the trustee has acted in breach of duty or unless she would not otherwise have reached the decision which she did reach. It is the second of these principles which does not explicitly require a breach of trust. Instead, all that seems to be required

---

270 *Re Hastings-Bass* [1975] Ch 25; *Scott v National Trust* [1998] 2 All ER 705; *Edge v Pensions Ombudsman* [2000] Ch 602.

271 This need not necessarily be so, it seems: the trustees may act properly but nevertheless fail to consider appropriate matters as they ought to be considered: *Burrell v Burrell* [2005] EWHC 245, [2005] All ER (D) 351.

272 *Re Hastings-Bass* [1975] Ch 25. Equally, the trustees could seek to set aside decisions which they regretted: *Breadner v Granville-Grossman* [2001] Ch 523, 543, *per* Park J.

273 As described by Mann J in *Burrell v Burrell* [2005] EWHC 245, [14].

274 [1975] Ch 25, 40.

is that the trustee would not have acted as she did if she had understood the ramifications of her actions – and that was sufficient to allow later courts to take this principle to mean that a breach of trust was not always required. Lloyd LJ gets around this problem in *Pitt v Holt* by finding that this summary of the principles is not part of the *ratio decidendi* in *Hastings-Bass*; whereas Warner J highlights this second principle in *Mettoy Pensions Trustees v Evans*.

Consequently this principle was put into a *positive*, broader form[275] by Warner J in *Mettoy Pensions Trustees v Evans*. It was this positive formulation of the principle which created the subsequent difficulties by allowing the courts in later cases to expand the principle beyond the narrow limits which Buckley LJ appeared to envisage for it in his first principle by building on the second principle. This positive interpretation was set out by Warner J in the following terms:[276]

> If, as I believe, the reason for the application of the principle is the failure by the trustees to take into account considerations which they ought to have taken into account, it cannot matter whether that failure is due to their having overlooked (or to their legal advisors having overlooked) some relevant rule of law or limit on their discretion, or is due to some other cause . . . . it is not enough that it should be shown that the trustees did not have a proper understanding of the effect of their act. It must also be clear that, had they had a proper understanding of it, they would not have acted as they did.

Therefore, Warner J removed any reference to a need for a breach of duty and instead based the principle on a mere failure by the trustees to account properly for irrelevant or relevant considerations (such as a likely tax charge) and also that the trustees would not have acted in the way they did if they had understood the effect of their actions. From this interpretation of what Buckley LJ had held in *Hastings-Bass*, as is considered below, subsequent cases were far more pro-active in setting aside the exercises of powers and discretions by trustees.

The decision of Lightman J in *Abacus Trust Company v Barr*[277] suggested, however, that it should be a requirement of any application of the principle in *Hastings-Bass* that the trustees must have committed a breach of trust, and not simply that irrelevant considerations have been taken into account or that relevant considerations have not been taken into account:

> In my view it is not sufficient to bring the rule into play that the trustee made a mistake or by reason of ignorance or a mistake did not take into account a relevant consideration or took into account an irrelevant consideration. What has to be established is that the trustee in making his decision has . . . failed to consider what he was under a duty to consider. If the trustee has, in accordance with his duty, identified the relevant considerations and used all proper care and diligence in obtaining the relevant information and advice relating to those considerations, the trustee can be in no breach of duty and its decision cannot be impugned merely because in fact that information turns out to be partial or incorrect. . . . [T]he rule does not afford the right to the trustee or any beneficiary to have a decision declared invalid because a trustee's decision was in some way mistaken or has unforeseen and unpalatable consequences.

---

275   As described by Mann J in *Burrell v Burrell* [2005] EWHC 245, [15].
276   [1990] 1 WLR 1587, 1624.
277   *Abacus Trust Company (Isle of Man) v Barr* [2003] 2 WLR 1362, [23].

The ramifications of this change in the direction of the principle are significant. The authorities after *Mettoy* had mostly taken the view that it was enough that the trustees had acted inappropriately (by failing to account for relevant considerations or by accounting for irrelevant considerations) without there to be any need for the trustee to have breached her obligations. If Lightman J were correct, then the principle would be a principle dependent on a breach of trust (that is, failing to consider something which one was under a duty to consider) and an alternative to a personal claim against the trustee for compensation.[278] Buckley LJ had originally provided that a demonstration that the trustee had acted in breach of duty was only one alternative means by which the principle could be put into effect.[279]

At the time, whether or not the principle in *Hastings-Bass* was to be considered to be dependent on proof of some breach of duty was a moot point.[280] In *Pitt v Holt*, as considered next, Lloyd LJ took the view that a breach of duty by the trustees was indeed required. Interestingly, when giving judgment in the High Court in *Sieff v Fox*[281] Lloyd LJ had doubted *Abacus Trust v Barr* and the idea that an exercise of a power or discretion by the trustees would be merely voidable and not automatically void, although in *Pitt v Holt* Lloyd LJ acknowledged that on reflection he had changed his mind, as well as holding that a breach of trust by the trustees should be a pre-requisite of the application of the doctrine.[282] *Pitt v Holt* and the other cases which had reined in the *Hastings-Bass* principle are considered next.

Limiting the principle in Hastings-Bass

In a very full judgment in the Court of Appeal in the joined appeals of *Pitt v Holt* and *Futter v Futter*,[283] Lloyd LJ considered the doctrine in *Re Hastings-Bass* and the related doctrine of mistake (which is considered below in section 8.3.14). In essence, the doctrine in *Hastings-Bass* was purportedly greatly limited by the Court of Appeal in *Pitt v Holt*. This was a decision of the Court of Appeal following other decisions of the Court of Appeal, and so strictly the status of this decision may be considered to be subject to affirmation by later cases – indeed, as mentioned, permission has been granted to appeal the decision in *Pitt v Holt* to the Supreme Court[284] – although it does appear that the consensus among the commentators is that it has clarified the law in this area and consequently that it now probably states the law correctly.[285]

What has been clear in the recent cases is that the *Hastings-Bass* principle is being steadily reduced in scope. Whereas once it was the favourite principle of Chancery counsel in

---

278 *Target Holdings v Redferns* [1996] 1 AC 421.

279 [1975] Ch 25, 40.

280 *Burrell v Burrell* [2005] EWHC 245, [22], *per* Mann J. In that case it was held that the principle could be invoked in either case because there had been a breach of duty. See also *Gallaher v Gallaher* [2004] EWHC 42, [2005] All ER (D) 177, [162] *et seq*, *per* Etherton J, where the same point is raised but not disposed of because it was not considered necessary to dispose of it on the facts.

281 [2005] EWHC 1312 (Ch), [2005] 1 WLR 3811, [2005] 3 All ER 693 – confusingly Lloyd LJ was still sitting in the High Court at this stage even though he had been elevated to the Court of Appeal at this point.

282 [2011] EWCA Civ 197, [2011] 3 WLR 19, at [30]

283 [2011] EWCA Civ 197, [2011] 3 WLR 19, [2011] 2 All ER 450, [2011] STC 809, [2011] Pens LR 175, [2011] BTC 322, [2011] WTLR 623, 13 ITELR 749.

284 [2011] 1 WLR 1977.

285 See, for example, the evidence led by Prof Paul Matthews in *In re R and S* [2011] JRC 117 as to English law in this regard being settled.

Lincoln's Inn, who considered that they could use it to reverse inadvertently costly errors made by trustees, especially in relation to the taxation of trusts, it is now being limited to a much narrower range of events. Three cases have been particularly significant in this regard.

First, it is limited to the acts and omissions of trustees and is not to be used in relation to inherent weaknesses in the trust instrument itself. The issue in *Smithson v Hamilton*[286] was an error in the drafting of the instrument which governed a pension fund. An application was brought to amend this rule in the trust instrument. However, Park J held in *Smithson v Hamilton* that the *Hastings-Bass* principle did not apply to the acts of settlors (such as mistakes in the drafting of a pension fund instrument) but rather only applied to the actions and omissions of trustees. Furthermore, Park J held that there would not be a general equitable relief for mistakes of this sort: what the parties were really seeking to do was to effect a rectification of the trust instrument, for which *Hastings-Bass* was an inappropriate mechanism, and mistake is governed by the doctrine in *Gibbon v Mitchell* (as considered below).

Secondly, in *Donaldson v Smith*[287] the scope of the principle in *Hastings-Bass* was limited to exercises of the trustees' discretionary powers and did not extend to the trustees' general power under the law of trusts to enter into contracts on behalf of the trust. This is a very significant limitation because it restricts the operation of *Hastings-Bass* to the discretionary powers of those trustees – such as powers to distribute £100,000 per annum to one beneficiary or to another – but not to other types of trust power.[288] This is a limit which should always have been understood as applying to this principle, even though many practitioners sought to extend it to cover the general actions of trustees, mistakes made by settlors in drafting the trust instrument causing the trustees to make mistakes, and so forth. The principle in *Hastings-Bass* had thus become a sort of 'magic eraser' for chancery practitioners.

The attitude of Her Majesty's Revenue and Customs is important in these cases, it is suggested, because these cases are predominantly concerned with using this principle to avoid liability to tax.[289] Unsurprisingly, the Revenue's view was that the *Hastings-Bass* principle had been extended far beyond its natural limits in the wake of the decision in the *Mettoy Pension Fund v Evans* case in which the principle was formulated in its 'positive' sense so as to require that the exercise of a power be set aside *in toto*.[290] All of which leads us to the restatement of this principle in *Pitt v Holt*, which is the third and most significant illustration of the limitation of the principle in *Hastings-Bass*.

The decision in Pitt v Holt

As outlined above, the decision of Lloyd LJ in *Pitt v Holt*, with which the other members of the Court of Appeal agreed, narrowed the principle of *Hastings-Bass* considerably by

---

286   [2008] 1 WLR 1453, [2007] EWHC 2900 (Ch). See Thomas and Hudson, *The Law of Trusts*, 20.63. See also
       Thorpe v Revenue and Customs Commissioners [2009] EWHC 611 (Ch) as to what will constitute the exercise
       of a trust power: so where a person who was both a trustee and a beneficiary sought to call for the trust it was
       only as a trustee that he could have given an instruction to a building society to demand delivery of legal title
       in the trust property, *per* Evans-Lombe J.
287   [2007] WTLR 421.
288   See Thomas and Hudson, *The Law of Trusts*, 20.62.
289   *Ibid*, 20.71 *et seq*.
290   See HMRC Tax Bulletin, Issue 83, June 2006, at 1292–4; www.hmrc.gov.uk/bulletins.

returning to the decision of Buckley LJ in the Court of Appeal in *Hastings-Bass* itself and subjecting it to a close re-reading. Lloyd LJ was careful to note that he was bound by the decision in *Hastings-Bass* but that the intervening decisions had all been decisions of the High Court alone; something which his lordship credited to the fact that the Inland Revenue had decided not to make itself a party to any of these later cases and that the parties had always been happy with the result they acquired before the High Court such that an appeal was never necessary. In part, what Lloyd LJ did in *Pitt v Holt* was to identify the *ratio decidendi* in *Hastings-Bass* as having been very narrow, and the summary of the principles set out by Buckley LJ as not forming a part of that *ratio decidendi*. It is suggested that this is to overstate the case because Buckley LJ was clearly summarising the points of law he had just developed, and therefore they had sprung from his consideration of the law necessary to reach his *ratio decidendi*. Nevertheless, in support of the approach taken by Lloyd LJ, there is no reason to read Buckley LJ as requiring a court to set aside a trustee's exercise of her powers; rather, Buckley LJ clearly held that the court could set aside the exercise of that power if it was considered to be appropriate. That is, the exercise of the power would be voidable if the court so decided, but it was not automatically void. In this vein, Lloyd LJ held in *Pitt v Holt* that:[291]

> 127. The cases which I am now considering concern acts which are within the powers of the trustees but are said to be vitiated by the failure of the trustees to take into account a relevant factor to which they should have had regard – usually tax consequences – or by their taking into account some irrelevant matter. It seems to me that the principled and correct approach to these cases is, first, that the trustees' act is not void, but that it may be voidable. It will be voidable if, and only if, it can be shown to have been done in breach of fiduciary duty on the part of the trustees. If it is voidable, then it may be capable of being set aside at the suit of a beneficiary, but this would be subject to equitable defences and to the court's discretion. The trustees' duty to take relevant matters into account is a fiduciary duty, so an act done as a result of a breach of that duty is voidable. Fiscal considerations will often be among the relevant matters which ought to be taken into account. However, if the trustees seek advice (in general or in specific terms) from apparently competent advisers as to the implications of the course they are considering taking, and follow the advice so obtained, then, in the absence of any other basis for a challenge, I would hold that the trustees are not in breach of their fiduciary duty for failure to have regard to relevant matters if the failure occurs because it turns out that the advice given to them was materially wrong. Accordingly, in such a case I would not regard the trustees' act, done in reliance on that advice, as being vitiated by the error and therefore voidable.

Significantly then, the court should only set the exercise of a power aside if the trustees had committed a breach of trust ('a breach of fiduciary duty'). It would not be a breach of trust simply to have taken professional advice and followed it, before realising that that advice had been incorrect or inadvisable. Such a situation could possibly involve a breach of trust, depending on the circumstances, but it would not be a breach of trust in itself. Indeed, for trustees to follow professional advice, in the context of their own trust and the exercise of their own discretion, is best practice.

The case of *Pitt v Holt* itself concerned a man who had suffered brain damage in an accident and in whose favour a receiver was appointed by the Court of Protection. The receiver created a discretionary trust as part of her plan for the man in her care, but failed to appreciate the inheritance tax consequences of that course of action. The joined appeal in *Futter v Futter* concerned a discretionary trust scheme in relation to which the trustees, in reliance on professional advice as to their best course of action, had failed to appreciate that there would be a capital gains tax charge.[292] In both cases, the trustees sought a court order to set aside their exercise of their powers. It was held on the facts in front of the Court of Appeal in *Pitt v Holt* and in *Futter v Futter* that the actions of the trustees would not be set aside in either appeal because neither set of trustees had acted in breach of trust, even though they had failed to appreciate their relative tax law positions. Both sets of trustees had taken appropriate professional advice, which had turned out to be incorrect or inadvisable in their circumstances, and therefore the trustees wished to reverse their decisions by having the court set them aside so that they could be made again with a clean slate. However, it was held that this had not involved the trustees in any breach of trust. They had taken advice and followed it, acting always in accordance with the terms of their powers. They would not have been capable of being sued for breach of trust on that basis. Therefore, having read *Hastings-Bass* closely, it was found that the doctrine could not be invoked. Furthermore, it was found that the court was not obliged to set the exercise of this power aside in any event because even if there had been a breach of trust the exercise of this power would have been merely voidable. It is suggested that it may be undesirable for a breach of trust to lead to merely voidable consequences and cleaner in many circumstances to have the exercise of that power be automatically void so that the beneficiaries can take action to recover any property passed from the trust without first requiring the decision of the court.[293]

The nature of the relevant and irrelevant considerations which have been considered to be significant

The key question, therefore, is how does one identify a factor, whether considered or ignored by the trustees, as being of sufficient relevance for the objects of the power to commence an action? The relevant and irrelevant considerations will differ from case to case depending upon the objectives and terms of any given trust, the nature and identities of the beneficiaries, the nature of the trust property and so forth. So, the considerations in relation to a single beneficiary may differ from the considerations applicable in relation to a power over a large class of potential beneficiaries.[294] It is also difficult to know whether or not the interests of other users of the trust or others who may take an interest in remainder ought to be taken into account.[295] Examples of considerations taken into account or not taken into

---

292 In the case of *Futter v Futter* the relevant partner in the firm of solicitors which had given this unfortunate advice to the trustees was named 'Mr Cutbill'. In these circumstances, one wonders whether or not he did.

293 For the approach in Jersey in the wake of *Pitt v Holt* see *In re R and S* [2011] JRC 117.

294 *Green v Cobham* [2002] STC 820.

295 See *Stannard v Fisons Pension Trust Ltd* [1991] PLR 225. Eg, the employer in relation to an occupational pension fund: *Re Imperial Foods Pension Scheme* [1986] 1 WLR 717; *Lock v Westpac Banking Corp* [1991] PLR 167.

account include a failure to take an up-to-date valuation of assets held in a pension fund before transferring assets between funds,[296] failing to take into account the fiscal conse-quences of a decision,[297] or failing to take the settlor's wishes into account correctly.[298]

The question then is to try to frame some sort of test which will help to understand from case to case what would constitute a relevant consideration which ought to be taken into account or an irrelevant consideration which ought not to be taken into account. In relation to relevant considerations which ought to have been taken into account by trustees when making a decision, most of the authorities have seized upon the idea that a consideration would have been relevant if it might have caused the trustee to make a different decision had she considered it.[299] This proposition has been explained in the following way by Lightman J in *Abacus Trust Co (Isle of Man) v Barr*:[300]

> [This principle] does not require that the relevant consideration unconsidered by the trustee should make a fundamental difference between the facts as perceived by the trustee and the facts as they should have been perceived and actually were. All that is required in this regard is that the unconsidered relevant consideration would or might have affected the trustee's decision, and in a case such as the present that the trustee would or might have made a different appointment or no appointment at all.

Lightman J proceeded to suggest four pre-requisites to a claim based on the *Hastings-Bass* principle necessary to set aside a trustee's actions: first, whether or not the trustee's actions were sufficiently fundamental; second, whether the trustee had failed to consider something which she was duty-bound to consider and failed to act with sufficient diligence in identi-fying that necessary information; third, whether the trustee was at fault for failing to give effect to the settlor's objectives; and fourth, whether the exercise of the power was void or voidable.

It has been suggested that this formulation of the principle, however, sets the barrier too low in that, in the view of dissatisfied objects of the power who had been overlooked by the trustees, too many purportedly relevant considerations might have been overlooked by the trustees.[301] If the barrier were set too low, then it would be too easy to challenge trustees' decisions and the management of some trusts might become mired in litigation between warring camps of beneficiaries each time the trustees make an appoint-ment of property.[302] The decision in *Pitt v Holt* solves a part of this dilemma by raising the general barrier to entry for beneficiaries seeking to have the exercise of a power set aside.

296 *Stannard v Fisons Pension Trust Ltd* [1991] PLR 225.
297 *Green v Cobham* [2002] STC 820; *Burrell v Burrell* [2005] EWHC 245 (inheritance tax).
298 *Abacus Trust Company (Isle of Man) v Barr* [2003] 2 WLR 1362.
299 *Re Hastings-Bass* [1975] Ch 25. Sir William Bass created a settlement on the marriage of the colourfully-named 'Captain Peter Robin Hood Hastings-Bass' to provide rights for a number of family members to the settled property. Questions arose as to whether or not estate duty was payable on the Captain's death, and whether the trustees were right to focus on the issue of estate duty when considering the exercise of a power of advancement which they held.
300 [2003] 2 WLR 1362, 1369.
301 [2003] PCB 173 (E Nugee); (2003) Trust Law Int 114 (B Green).
302 This argument is advanced by Thomas and Hudson, 2004, 385 *et seq*.

The court's response if the power was exercised in ignorance of a relevant
consideration or in contemplation of an irrelevant consideration

The issue then is as to the appropriate nature of the court's response if the power in question was exercised in ignorance of a relevant consideration or in contemplation of an irrelevant consideration. There are a range of possible judicial responses, each dependent on the extent to which the effect of the trustee's exercise of their power had deviated from the trust's intended objectives.[303] In general terms, it has been accepted that the incorrect exercise of the power should be voidable and not automatically void.[304] At one extreme the exercise of a power will be validated if the result was not 'substantially or essentially different from that which was intended',[305] whereas the exercise of a power of appointment would be invalidated if the trustees had not addressed their minds as to the impact of the law on the efficacy of the trust so that the trust's objective was not achieved at all.[306] Nevertheless, in *Re Hastings-Bass*,[307] the Court of Appeal would not avoid an exercise of a power to advance capital to the life tenant of a trust for creating benefits for the life tenant which were not within the trust's original contemplation when the exercise of that power had achieved the principal objective of saving death duties.

There is a way of thinking of the *Hastings-Bass* principle as being based on the court's supervision of the powers of fiduciaries.[308] On this basis, the court's response would be to validate the trustees' decision to the extent that it was valid and then to set aside only the excessive part. In this way, the principle derived from *Hastings-Bass* has been described as being limited only to a principle concerning the excessive exercise of a power.[309] On this narrow explanation, the entire exercise of the power should fail only if there is no possibility of drawing a distinction between the proper and the excessive execution of that power,[310] or alternatively where the exercise of the power fails to achieve the objectives of the trust (as though akin to the principles appropriate to a mistake of law).[311] To put this point another way: the court should consider the extent of the fiduciary's power and only set aside the exercise of that power to the extent that the taking into account of irrelevant factors, or the failure to take into account relevant factors, constituted an excessive exercise of that power. Consequently, the exercise of the fiduciary's power should be validated to the extent that it was within the proper limits of that power. So, in *Bestrustees v Stuart*,[312] Neuberger J held

303 As suggested by *Gilbey v Rush* [1906] 1 Ch 11; *Re Vestey's Settlement* [1951] Ch 209. On which, see Thomas and Hudson, 2004, 387.

304 *AMP v Barker* [2001] PLR 77, *per* Lawrence Collins J; *Hearn v Younger* [2002] WTLR 1317, 1338, [90], *per* Etherton J; *Abacus Trust Company (Isle of Man) v Barr* [2003] 2 WLR 1362, [28]–[33], *per* Lightman J; *Hunter v Senate Support Services Ltd* [2004] EWHC 1085. This discussion was raised in *Donaldson v Smith* [2006] All ER (D) 293 (May), para [52].

305 *Re Vestey's Settlement* [1951] Ch 209, 221, *per* Lord Evershed MR.

306 *Re Pilkington's Will Trusts* [1961] Ch 466, 489 (the effect of s 32 of the TA 1925); *Re Abrahams' Will Trusts* [1969] 1 Ch 463 (the effect of the rules against perpetuities and accumulations).

307 [1975] Ch 25.

308 For these purposes, a distinction can be drawn between a power of appointment – which takes effect in favour potentially of a class of objects – and a power of advancement – which can be exercised only to benefit that person who receives that advancement.

309 See Thomas and Hudson, 2004, 388, para 11.55; and see Thomas, 1998, 435.

310 On which see section 10.5 below.

311 See Thomas and Hudson, 2004, 388.

312 [2001] PLR 283.

that a purportedly retrospective alteration of the rules of a pension fund, where the trust instrument only permitted prospective alterations, should be permitted to the extent that it took effect prospectively and be set aside only to the extent that it was an excessive execution of that power.[313] A similar approach was contemplated in *Mettoy Pension Fund Trustees Ltd v Evans*[314] and in *Burrell v Burrell*.[315]

While this approach has attracted some judicial support, the mainstream of the law in this area has developed in a different direction such that it cannot be explained simply on the basis of the court's control of an excessive exercise of a power.[316] In the Court of Appeal's decision in *Re Hastings-Bass*, the more general proposition was accepted (in relation specifically to powers of advancement in that case) that an advancement would be set aside only if 'it could not reasonably be regarded as being beneficial to the person intended to be advanced'.[317] In the passage from Buckley LJ's judgment already quoted above, it was held that:

> the Court should not interfere with [the trustee's] action ... unless (1) what he has achieved is unauthorised by the power conferred upon him, or (2) it is clear that he would not have acted as he did (a) had he not taken into account considerations which he should not have taken into account, or (b) had he not failed to take into account considerations which he ought to have taken into account.[318]

The *Hastings-Bass* principle, therefore, appears to be formulated on a wide basis. So, in *Mettoy Pension Fund Trustees v Evans*,[319] it has been accepted by Warner J that this broader formulation relates generally to situations in which trustees have ignored relevant considerations or contemplated irrelevant considerations in general terms: their impact is not required to be materially and significantly in breach of the objectives of the trust before the exercise of that power can be set aside. Therefore, the court does not have to examine the width of the power and what would have constituted a proper exercise of that power; rather, it can consider in general terms whether or not the trustees would have acted in the way they did if they had considered relevant material or ignored irrelevant material.

The form of default by the trustee which will justify the application of the principle

Before the decision in *Pitt v Holt*, despite the breadth of the *Hastings-Bass* principle as suggested by the passage quoted from Buckley LJ in the preceding section, there was a division of opinion on the cases as to the precise meaning of this wide version of the principle. The distinction between these authorities has been explained[320] as being a distinction between

---

313 Applying Thomas, 1998.
314 [1990] 1 WLR 1587.
315 [2005] EWHC 245, [25], *per* Mann J.
316 *Mettoy Pension Trustees Ltd v Evans* [1990] 1 WLR 1587, 1622.
317 *Re Hastings-Bass* [1975] Ch 25, 40, *per* Buckley LJ.
318 *Ibid*.
319 [1990] 1 WLR 1587, 1622.
320 *Hunter v Senate Support Services Ltd* [2004] EWHC 1085, [172].

a 'might materially have affected [the decision] test'[321] and a 'would [have altered the decision] test':[322] that is, the former test only requires proof that if the trustee had accounted for the proper considerations appropriately, then it *might have* affected her decision, as opposed to the latter test requiring the claimant to demonstrate that it *definitely would have* affected the decision which the trustee made. The 'might have' test is an objective test, whereas the 'would' test is a purely subjective test.[323] This returns us to the alternative proposition in the passage quote above from the judgment of Lightman J in *Abacus Trust Co (Isle of Man) v Barr*[324] as to whether or not accounting for considerations properly would have made a 'fundamental difference' to the trustee's understanding of the facts. The approach taken by Lightman J does not fall down clearly either on the side of the 'might have' or the 'definitely would have' made a difference approach: rather, it seems to focus on the degree of importance which the true facts would have had in the making of the decision if they had been known to the trustees. It is suggested that, if anything, Lightman J is suggesting an objective approach whereby the court will examine whether or not the trustees ought to have reached a different decision because the true facts would have had such a high degree of significance in the administration of the trust that the trustees would have had to have reached a different decision.[325]

The principle in *Hastings-Bass* has been phrased slightly differently in *Sieff v Fox*[326] by Lloyd LJ (sitting in the High Court) in the following terms:[327]

> Where trustees act under a discretion given to them by the terms of the trust, in circumstances in which they are free to decide whether or not to exercise their discretion, but the effect of the exercise is different from that which they intended, the court will interfere with their action if it is clear that they would not have acted as they did had they not failed to take into account considerations which they ought to have taken into account, or taken into account considerations which they ought not to take into account.

Significantly, Lloyd LJ held in *Pitt v Holt*[328] that this account of the principles could not be accepted as being correct because it neither identified the need for a breach of trust nor that

---

321 *Stannard v Fisons Pension Trust Ltd* [1991] PLR 225, [39]. This form of test has been expressed in *Hearn v Younger* [2002] WTLR 1317, 1338, [86] by Etherton J to the effect that: 'a decision of trustees to exercise a discretion will be void if (a) the trustees have failed to take into account a material consideration, and (b) that consideration might have materially affected their decision.'

322 *Re Hastings-Bass* [1975] Ch 25.

323 *Hunter v Senate Support Services Ltd* [2004] EWHC 1085, [183].

324 [2003] 2 WLR 1362, 1369.

325 By contrast, it is suggested that a subjective approach would require the court to examine more closely the actual decision which those particular trustees would have made at the time and in the circumstances in which they made their original decision, taking into account the actual facts. The focus on the degree of significance of these matters to the trust appears to be an objective assessment of the circumstances. To be entirely subjective in a test in this context would, it is suggested, involve taking into account too many imponderables (would the trustees have understood the significance of those facts if they had known them, would they have been headstrong, would that have been their principal consideration at the time the decision was made, etc?).

326 [2005] EWHC 1312 (Ch), [2005] 1 WLR 3811, [2005] 3 All ER 693. Also *sub nom Re Bedford Estates; Sieff v Fox*.

327 [2005] EWHC 1312 (Ch), [2005] 1 WLR 3811, [2005] 3 All ER 693.

328 [2011] EWCA Civ 197, [30].

the exercise of the power was merely voidable and not automatically void.[329] On the facts of *Seiff v Fox*, property held on a discretionary trust was resettled on a new discretionary trust with unforeseen capital gains tax consequences. It was found that the trustees would have acted differently had they been aware of their mistake. Applying this notion in *Betafence v Veys*,[330] Lightman J held that the trustees of a pension fund in that case were free in the exercise of their discretion, and therefore that it must be demonstrated that those trustees would definitely have exercised their powers differently but for their mistake, and that on the facts in front of him it could not be so proved definitively, and therefore that their decision would not be set aside. Lightman J did ask whether or not this particular rule needed to be carried into pensions law, considering it perhaps to be an unnecessary refinement, but decided that it was a matter which could only be decided by an appellate court given the precedent of *Sieff v Fox* which faced his Lordship. The decision in *Pitt v Holt* appears to have resolved that issue, subject to appeal to the Supreme Court.

Examples of the *Hastings-Bass* principle being applied in the decided cases have tended to concern trustees who have not understood the tax effect of the decisions which they have made, with the result that the beneficiaries who sought to reverse those decisions had to demonstrate that it would have made a fundamental difference to the trustees' decisions if they had appreciated the actual tax effects of their decisions. So, where trustees failed to realise that a will trust and accumulation and maintenance settlements under their control formed a single, composite unit for capital gains tax purposes, it was held that the trustees' actions attracting capital gains tax should be set aside in their entirety because the trustees would not have exercised their powers in the way they had done if they had considered the tax implications correctly.[331] The same issue arose in *Sieff v Fox*,[332] where certain discretionary trusts were resettled on new discretionary trusts with unforeseen capital gains tax consequences, something which constituted a relevant consideration which ought to have been taken into account. Similarly, where trustees entered into a tax avoidance scheme which unbeknownst to them attracted liability to capital gains tax, their appointment of property under the avoidance scheme was held to have been void because it was considered of great importance that trustees consider the tax effect of any decision and that a failure on their part to appreciate the tax consequences on these facts constituted a failure to take into account a relevant consideration.[333]

Evidently, the principal use of the *Hastings-Bass* principle in modern trusts practice is in relation to tax avoidance. In effect, it grants a second bite of the cherry to trustees who have

---

329 In *Seiff v Fox* it could be understood that Lloyd LJ drew a distinction between cases in which the trustees were free as to the exercise of their discretion (that is, fiduciary mere powers principally, I would suggest) and cases in which the trustees are compelled to exercise their discretion (in the manner of discretionary trusts). In relation to 'mere power' cases it was held that trustees' decisions should only be set aside if they would definitely have acted differently but for the 'mistake'; whereas, in relation to 'discretionary trust' cases it was held that trustees' decisions should only be set aside if they merely might have acted differently but for the 'mistake'. The word 'mistake' is in inverted commas because that is how Lightman J described this test in *Betafence v Veys* [2006] EWHC 999 (Ch), para [72], although that is not exactly how Lloyd LJ phrased matters in the passage quoted above: Lloyd LJ referring simply to the trustees' '*not acting as they did* had they not failed to take into account considerations', as opposed to the trustees having positively made a mistake.
330 [2006] EWHC 999 (Ch); [2006] All ER (D) 91 (May), para [72].
331 *Green v Cobham* [2002] STC 820.
332 [2005] EWHC 1312, [2005] 1 WLR 3811, [2005] 3 All ER 693.
333 *Abacus Trust Company (Isle of Man) v Barr* [2003] 2 WLR 1362.

erroneously caused the beneficiaries to suffer a liability to tax. Therefore, it has become a principle which is deployed most frequently as a form of long-stop insurance for trustees who fail to take adequate professional advice as to the fiscal effects of their decisions or who fail to follow that advice properly. The beneficiaries are thus protected from the attentions of HMRC by the back door because the trustees' approach can be set aside and a different decision taken instead. Another approach would be to allow HMRC to recover the tax to which they would otherwise be entitled on the basis of revenue law and to leave the beneficiaries to proceed against the trustees in negligence or for breach of trust. It is not clear to this writer why the law of trusts should be quite so keen to permit tax avoidance in a context in which the common law would shift the burden to the defendant and/or her insurers. That HMRC chose to participate in *Pitt v Holt* was significant in bringing another perspective before the court on the operation of this principle.

Failure to exercise a discretionary power will render any act of the trustees a nullity

It has been held that a failure to exercise a discretionary power will render any act of the trustees of a discretionary trust a nullity. In *Betafence v Veys*[334] Lightman J held that it would be a nullity if trustees with a discretion failed to realise that they had such a discretion and so failed to exercise their discretion. In this regard Lightman J followed *Turner v Turner*,[335] a case in which trustees of a discretionary trust simply followed the directions of the settlor without appreciating that they had a discretion and so without exercising their discretion. Consequently, their actions were held to be a nullity and they were therefore required to exercise their discretionary power conscious of that power and in a manner appropriate to fiduciaries.

The error which gives rise to the doctrine in *Hastings-Bass* must be an error made by the trustees, not an error made by the settlor such as a mistake in the drafting of the trust instrument (for example, the scheme rules for a pension fund) nor an error made by some other person involved in the trust at a distance (such as the employer in relation to an occupational pension scheme).[336] Therefore, it was held in *Smithson v Hamilton*[337] that if a scheme rule in a pension fund failed to account for proper actuarial calculations, then that was not the fault of the trustees.[338] In such circumstances the proper remedy would not be to set aside the entire scheme under the *Hastings-Bass* principle, but rather to seek a rectification of the scheme rules.[339] In effect we could think of this as being a defect in the *creation* of the trustees' obligations as opposed to being some fault in the manner in which the trustees *carried out* their obligations.

Breach of trust compared with the Hastings-Bass *principle*

Liability for breach of trust arises in relation to a trustee where the trustee commits a breach of the terms of the trust or where the trustee commits a breach of a principle of the general law of trusts which is not excluded by the trust instrument (if there is one). Having

---

334 [2006] EWHC 999, [2006] All ER (D) 91 (May), para [73].
335 [1984] Ch 100.
336 *Smithson v Hamilton* [2008] 1 All ER 1216, Park J.
337 *Ibid.*
338 *Ibid.*
339 *Ibid.*

considered the principle in *Hastings-Bass*, it would be useful to consider the situation if a trustee simply failed to carry out her obligations at all. If a trustee fails to carry out a clear obligation set out in the terms of the trust then she commits a breach of trust, just as if she had performed an act which was prohibited by the terms of the trust.[340] There is also authority for the proposition that a failure to act in general terms constitutes a breach of trust if the trustee had an obligation to act under the terms of the trust.[341] This may impose liability for breach of trust on that trustee as considered in Chapter 18.

The broad understanding of the principle in *Hastings-Bass* which was established in *Mettoy* does something different, and that is why Lloyd LJ took against it in *Pitt v Holt*. On the *Mettoy* account of the test, if the trustee failed to exercise a power fully or failed to realise the breadth of that power, then the beneficiary might be able to have the exercise of that power set aside. So, for example, a trustee who failed to take into account a relevant consideration when exercising her power, such as failing to appreciate that she had a discretionary trust power, would have failed to exercise that power properly. Thus, if a trustee failed to appreciate that her powers contained a discretionary power and thus failed to consider the proper exercise of that power, then the purported exercise of that power would be null and void.[342] In that sense, the trustee would have failed to act. There remains a question, therefore, as to the extent of the principle of breach of duty which will trigger the doctrine in *Pitt v Holt*.

8.3.14 Mistake in the exercise of a trustee's powers

There is a principle which provides for the actions of trustees to be set aside on the grounds of mistake. As considered above, a trustee may make a mistake in the form of taking into account irrelevant considerations or failing to take into account relevant considerations: in such circumstances, the purported exercise of a power may be set aside on the basis of the principle in *Hastings-Bass*. However, it will not be sufficient for the implementation of that principle that a trustee simply made a mistake: rather, the trustee must have failed to take into account considerations which she was under a duty to consider.[343] Alternatively, there is clear authority that the beneficiaries of a pension may act on the basis of the principle in *Gibbon v Mitchell*[344] if the trustees have acted on the basis of a mistake and contrary to the intention of the settlors of, in that case, a pension scheme. The remedy is then the remedy of rectification of the trustees' decision. As Millett J held:[345]

> wherever there is a voluntary transaction by which one party intends to confer bounty on the other,[346] the deed will be set aside if the court is satisfied that the disponor did not

---

340 See, for example, *Turner v Turner* [1984] Ch 100.

341 *Ibid.*

342 *Meek v Bennie* [1940] NZLR 1. See generally Thomas, 1998, 309–24 on the improper exercise of powers.

343 *Ibid.*

344 [1990] 1 WLR 1304. See also *Re Butlin's Settlement* [1976] 1 Ch 251; *AMP v Barker* [2001] PLR 77; *Anker-Petersen v Christiensen* [2002] WTLR 313, 330; *Gallaher v Gallaher* [2004] EWHC 42, [2005] All ER (D) 177.

345 *Gibbon v Mitchell* [1990] 1 WLR 1304, 1309. This principle was approved in *Sieff v Fox* [2005] EWHC 1312 (Ch), [2005] 3 All ER 693.

346 Such as an occupational pension fund where the intention at issue is the intention of the employer.

intend the transaction to have the effect which it did. It will be set aside for mistake whether the mistake is a mistake of law or fact, so long as the mistake is as to the effect of the transaction itself and not merely as to its consequences or the advantages to be gained by entering into it.

The doctrine of mistake had become popular with chancery law practitioners because it also permitted the court to set aside the actions of trustees. The cases before *Pitt v Holt* tended to expand the doctrine. For example, in *Re Griffiths*[347] Lewison J extended the concept of the equitable jurisdiction to set aside a voluntary transaction on grounds of mistake much further than it could have otherwise have been intended to go in relation to a settlor who contracted lung cancer and died before the seven-year period which would have carried a transfer outside the charge to tax: it was held that the mistake was a mistake on the settlor's part as to whether he would live for seven years or not. It is a fundamental part of the human condition that we cannot know the time or nature of our passing from this mortal coil. To consider a misapprehension as to either of those things to be a mistake with legal consequences under *Gibbon v Mitchell* would seem to rob life of a little of its poetry.

This principle was also considered by Lloyd LJ in the joined appeals in *Pitt v Holt* and *Futter v Futter*, and was narrowed significantly. Lloyd LJ held the following:[348]

> 210. I would therefore hold that, for the equitable jurisdiction to set aside a voluntary disposition for mistake to be invoked, there must be a mistake on the part of the donor either as to the legal effect of the disposition or as to an existing fact which is basic to the transaction. (I leave aside cases where there is an additional vitiating factor such as some misrepresentation or concealment in relation to the transaction, among which I include *Dutton v Thompson*.[349]) Moreover the mistake must be of sufficient gravity as to satisfy the *Ogilvie v Littleboy*[350] test, which provides protection to the recipient against too ready an ability of the donor to seek to recall his gift. The fact that the transaction gives rise to unforeseen fiscal liabilities is a consequence, not an effect, for this purpose, and is not sufficient to bring the jurisdiction into play.

Therefore, a mistake must relate specifically to the *effect* of the transaction and not to its legal consequences. The point being made by Lloyd LJ is that the effect of an exercise of a discretion to advance money to Martha rather than Agatha would be that Martha became absolutely entitled to that money instead of Agatha; whereas the fact that the trust became chargeable with tax because of that advance would be a legal consequence of that action but not its principal effect. This distinction is perhaps better understood the other way around: misunderstanding the effect of tax law on the transaction may have the result of incurring a cost for the trust, but that is not the sort of mistake which the court will allow to set aside the action of the trustee on grounds of the equitable doctrine of mistake. It is a consequence but it is not an effect which will be legally actionable. On the facts in *Pitt v Holt* the claim based on mistake was therefore rejected. Longmore and Mummery LJJ concurred.

---

347 [2008] EWHC 118 (Ch), [2009] Ch 162, [2009] 2 WLR 394.
348 [2011] EWCA Civ 197, [210].
349 (1883) 23 Ch D 278.
350 (1899) 15 TLR 294, HL(E).

8.3.15 The effect of breach of duties

If the trustees commit a breach of trust, then those trustees will be liable to effect specific restitution of any property transferred away from the trust or to pay equitable compensation to the beneficiaries for any loss suffered as a result of that breach of trust.[351] The principles concerning breach of trust are considered in detail in Chapter 18.

8.4 THE TRUSTEES' DUTY TO PROVIDE INFORMATION AND TO ACCOUNT TO THE BENEFICIARIES

The trustees bear only a limited obligation to give information to beneficiaries in relation to administration and management of the trust fund and in relation only to that part of a trust fund in which they have a proprietary interest. Recent case law has emphasised the court's inherent discretion to make orders relating to the administration of trusts and therefore the access of beneficiaries to information may be enlarged in the future or alternatively it may continue to be exercised in accordance with traditional principles. Trustees are not obliged to disclose to beneficiaries any matter in relation to any exercise of their fiduciary discretion, nor are they obliged to disclose any confidential matter. The court reserves discretion as to the manner in which trustees exercise their powers, but not as to the content of any such decision unless there has been palpable wrongdoing.

8.4.1 Introduction

An important part of the ability of the beneficiaries to control the trustees is their ability to force the trustees to account to the beneficiaries by way of giving information to them as to the administration of the trust. The idea of the trustees accounting to the beneficiaries is considered in a subtly different sense in Chapter 18, in that the trustees are also required to account to the beneficiaries if there is any breach of trust: this means that the trustees will be obliged to compensate the beneficiaries for any loss to the trust out of their own pockets.[352] This section, however, focuses first on the obligation to account in the sense of the provision of information by the trustees to the beneficiaries, and then on the duty to render accounts giving an indication of the financial position of the trust. As to the general obligation to give information, it will become clear from the decided cases that there is a distinction drawn between cases of necessary confidentiality between trustee and settlor, cases concerning the trustees' exercise of their discretion as to the entitlement of beneficiaries to have interests in specific trust property, and cases concerning information as to the day-to-day management of the trust. There is no general obligation for the trustees to give full information to anyone who considers themselves entitled to an equitable interest under the trust.[353] The traditional English view is that access to information is limited to those with proprietary rights in the

---

351 *Target Holdings v Redferns* [1996] 1 AC 421.

352 *Ibid.* See Chapter 30 for a discussion of the remedy of account in general terms.

353 As impliedly accepted in *O'Rourke v Darbishire* [1920] AC 581; *Re Londonderry* [1965] Ch 918; unless the court chooses to exercise its inherent discretion as to the management of trusts, perhaps: *Schmidt v Rosewood Trust Ltd* [2003] 2 WLR 1442.

trust property to information relating specifically to the property in which they have rights.[354] However, an alternative approach has been mooted by the Privy Council which recognises the court's general discretion to supervise trusts and so to order access to information in favour of an applicant whenever it sees fit.[355] It may well be that in the future, application of these principles the courts decide to exercise their discretion in such a way that they adhere closely to the traditional English approach in any event.[356] These various approaches are considered below, beginning with the traditional English approach.

8.4.2 The limited duty to give general information as to the existence and nature of the trust

The trustees are required to inform *sui juris* beneficiaries of the existence and terms of a trust.[357] The requirement to inform the beneficiaries of the terms of the trust will necessarily involve disclosing to those beneficiaries the existence of their equitable interests, but there is no concomitant obligation to explain to the beneficiaries the meaning of those interests.[358] Perhaps this is a recognition of the potentially combative relationship between trustee and beneficiary in the event of some breach of trust, particularly in relation to pension funds.[359] The explanation given in the cases is that to give such advice to one beneficiary out of a class of beneficiaries might be to advantage that beneficiary over the other beneficiaries;[360] however, it does not explain why there should not be an obligation on trustees to give an equal level of information of that sort to all of the beneficiaries. It also recognises the fact that a trustee may be liable for any advice which is mistaken or which causes loss to the beneficiary. The trustees are not obliged, for example, to inform the beneficiaries of any breach of trust which comes to their attention.[361] The beneficiaries are entitled to know the names and addresses of the trustees, something which is important if the beneficiaries are to be able to contact the trustees in relation to the management of the trust.[362] In the event that some beneficiaries cannot be found, the trustees are only obliged to make reasonable efforts

354 *O'Rourke v Darbishire* [1920] AC 581; *Re Londonderry* [1965] Ch 918.

355 *Schmidt v Rosewood Trust Ltd* [2003] 2 WLR 1442.

356 On which, see *Crowe v Stevedoring Employees Retirement Fund* [2003] PLR 343; *Foreman v Kingstone* [2004] 1 NZLR 841.

357 *Hawkesley v May* [1956] 1 QB 304. See also *Re Emmet's Estate* (1881) 17 Ch D 142; *Re Lewis* [1904] 2 Ch 656. The duty is not a duty concomitantly borne by the settlor such that there is no ostensible obligation on the settlor to inform the trustees or the beneficiaries (*Fletcher v Fletcher* (1844) 4 Hare 67), although this squares oddly with the fact that if a trust has been validly created by a settlor, then that settlor is obliged to constitute the trust even if the settlor changes her desire to give effect to the trust (*Re Ralli's WT* [1964] 2 WLR 144; and see also the fact that the settlor may not undo a trust once it has been constituted as in *Paul v Paul* (1882) 20 Ch D 742).

358 *Hamar v Pensions Ombudsman* [1996] PLR 1, 10–11; *NGN Staff Pension Plan Trustees Ltd v Simmons* [1994] OPLR 1. See also *Tito v Waddell (No 2)* [1977] Ch 106, 242.

359 See, eg, *NGN Staff Pension Plan Trustees Ltd v Simmons* [1994] OPLR 1; *Hamar v Pensions Ombudsman* [1996] PLR 1, 10–11.

360 *Hamar v Pensions Ombudsman* [1996] PLR 1.

361 *Miller v Stapleton* [1996] 2 All ER 449, 463; *Hamar v Pensions Ombudsman* [1996] PLR 1; *NHS Pensions v Beechinor* [1997] OPLR 99; *Outram v Academy Plastics* [2000] PLR 283.

362 *Murphy v Murphy* [1999] 1 WLR 282.

to locate and inform the beneficiaries.[363] Other facets of the obligation to give information are considered in the paragraphs to follow.

8.4.3 The limited duty to disclose trust documents to those with a proprietary interest under the trust

No right of access to trust documents if the trust instrument precludes such access

The beneficiaries will have no right to trust documents if the trust instrument expressly precludes such access.[364] In principle, it could be seen that the beneficiaries' proprietary rights would be a bundle of rights which does not include access to information of specified kinds or information in general. What would be difficult in practice would be the situation in which beneficiaries require information to scrutinise the trustees' exercise of their powers but where the trust excluded the right to such access. The Privy Council decision in *Schmidt v Rosewood*[365] held that the court has an inherent discretion out of which access to information can be ordered; this may have the effect that the court can order access to information nevertheless. However, the position is different in relation to confidential information the disclosure of which will not be ordered in general.[366]

The traditional approach under English law

The general extent of the duty of trustees to disclose trust documents to beneficiaries, where there is no provision in the trust instrument dealing with such matters, was expressed by Lord Wrenbury in the following terms:[367]

> [A beneficiary] is entitled to see all the trust documents because they are trust documents and because he is a beneficiary. They are in a sense his own. Action or no action, he is entitled to access to them. This has nothing to do with discovery.[368] The right to discovery is a right to see someone else's document. A proprietary right is a right to access to documents which are your own.

Despite the apparent breadth of this statement, two issues arise. The first relates to the question 'who is a beneficiary?' in such circumstances, for example, in relation to the objects of discretionary trusts: this issue is considered in para 8.4.5. The second issue was raised by Lord Walker[369] to the effect that Lord Wrenbury's statement was appropriate on the facts of the case in front of him because the beneficiary in that case would have been entitled to the entire trust fund and therefore it would be right to say that he was also entitled to all of its

---

363 *Re Hay's Settlement Trusts* [1982] 1 WLR 202.
364 *Tierney v King* [1983] 2 Qd R 580; *Hartigan Nominees v Rydge* (1992) 29 NSWLR 405, 446.
365 [2003] 2 WLR 1442; Pollard, 2003.
366 See para 8.4.7.
367 *O'Rourke v Darbishire* [1920] AC 581, 626.
368 'Discovery' is the technical procedure during litigation in which the parties seek disclosure of information from one another.
369 *Schmidt v Rosewood Trust Ltd* [2003] 2 WLR 1442, 1457C.

documentation: however, his Lordship suggested that the question remains whether that position be the same in relation to a trust containing different classes of beneficiaries. It seems in accordance with principle that if a person does not belong to a particular class of beneficiaries entitled to a particular subset of the trust fund, then there is no reason to suppose that that person is entitled to see documentation relating to that subset of property:[370] this accords with Lord Wrenbury's logic because that person would not be the owner of those documents because she would not have any proprietary right in that property. So, for example, a beneficiary entitled only to the trust capital is not necessarily entitled to see documentation relating to the trust income.[371]

It has been said that it may be the case then that one beneficiary's desire for information may be disadvantageous to the other beneficiaries.[372] However, this statement is one with which this writer has some difficulty. It is difficult to see how simply providing information to a beneficiary could cause harm to another beneficiary, provided always that the trustees are exercising their powers properly; unless, perhaps, there is thought to be, for example, a risk of disclosing confidential account details relating to other beneficiaries. If the inquisitive beneficiary were able to pressure the trustees, as a result of receiving that information, into changing their minds so as to benefit her, then it would either be the case that the trustees had previously been exercising their powers inappropriately so as to disadvantage the inquisitive beneficiary or else that the trustees are latterly exercising their powers wrongly by advantaging the inquisitive beneficiary. It is not the provision of information which is problematic but rather the trustees' strength of character to ensure that they are exercising their powers properly throughout.

Indeed, the right to information being based on ownership of the property to which those documents relates is perhaps not the most appropriate basis for access to information. It may be that the capital beneficiary can only know whether or not the trustees are exercising their powers properly if that beneficiary has information about the management of the income portion of the trust fund. If the test remains one based on ownership, then the capital beneficiary is never entitled to know about the income portion of the trust. However, if the test recognised that someone who is validly a beneficiary under the trust is entitled to access to all documentation which affects her equitable interest in the trust, then that would be an approach which matched the beneficiaries' genuine interests more closely.

In *Re Londonderry*[373] the claimant sought copies of documents from the trustees in relation to a trust. The claimant was one of a class of beneficiaries who were the objects of a power of appointment over the trust's income. The trust capital had been exhausted in appointing property to the defendant: in effect, therefore, the claimant wanted information as to the trustees' decisions so that he could learn why the power of appointment had been exercised in favour of the defendant such that there was no capital left. The Court of Appeal (in particular Harman LJ) held that trustees were not obliged to give reasons for

---

370   *Re Tillott* [1892] 1 Ch 86, *per* Chitty J; *Re Cowin* (1886) 33 Ch D 179.

371   *Nestlé v National Westminster Bank plc* [2000] WTLR 795, 822; although in such a situation, it might be that the capital beneficiary wishes to know whether or not capital has been comprised in favour of generating more income such that the capital beneficiaries may argue that such documentation would give them vital information as to the probity of the trustees' management of their own property.

372   *Re Cowin* (1886) 33 Ch D 179, 197, *per* North J.

373   [1964] 3 All ER 855.

their decisions. Following on from the idea in *O'Rourke v Derbyshire* that a beneficiary is entitled to documents relating to a part of the trust over which one has property rights, Harman LJ held:

> If the [beneficiary] is allowed to examine [the minutes and agendas of trustees meetings], she will know at once the very matters which the trustees are not bound to disclose to her, namely, their motives and reasons. Trustees who wish to preserve their rights in this respect must either commit nothing to paper or destroy everything from meeting to meeting. . . .
>
> I would hold that, even if documents of this type ought properly to be described as trust documents, they are protected for the special reason which protects the trustees' deliberations on a discretionary matter from disclosure. If necessary, I hold that this principle overrides the ordinary rule. This is in my judgment no less in the true interest of the beneficiary than of the trustees. Again, if one of the trustees commits to paper his suggestions and circulates them among his co-trustees, or if inquiries are made in writing as to the circumstances of a member of the class, I decline to hold that such documents are trust documents the property of the beneficiaries. In my opinion such documents are not trust documents in the proper sense at all. On the other hand, if the solicitor advising the trustees commits to paper an aide-mêmoire summarising the state of the fund or of the family and reminding the trustees of past distributions and future possibilities, I think that must be a document which any beneficiary must be at liberty to inspect. . . . I cannot think that communications passing between individual trustees and appointors are documents in which beneficiaries have a proprietary right.[374]

I have two particular problems with this formulation. First, I do not understand why there is assumed to be a need for secrecy in such circumstances. The alternative view would be that if trustees act as fiduciaries then they must be accountable to the beneficiaries and therefore they must be transparent about their acts and omissions and thought processes. Secondly, if the beneficiaries do not have information as to the trustees' acts and omissions then they are robbed of the ability to bring proceedings against the trustees in the event of breach of trust because they cannot find out if there has been a breach of trust because they have no access to the appropriate information. It is to be remembered that the beneficiary principle (discussed in Chapter 4) requires that 'there must be some person in whose favour the court can decree performance': which in turn requires that the beneficiaries must have sufficient information to be able to seek proper performance of the trust.

The new analysis

The Privy Council in *Schmidt v Rosewood Trust Ltd*[375] suggested an alternative approach to understanding which beneficiaries are entitled to access to the trust documents. Rather than consider the beneficiary as being entitled on the basis of a proprietary interest, it was suggested instead that the power to order access to information is based on the court's

374   Ibid at 860.
375   [2003] 2 WLR 1442.

inherent jurisdiction to assume control of a trust and to supervise the actions of the trustees. Therefore, the court should be permitted to order access to information wherever appropriate. What this approach does not help with is in telling us which beneficiaries are entitled to access to which sorts of information and which beneficiaries are not so entitled. All the *Schmidt v Rosewood Trust Ltd* approach suggests is that one can apply to the court for an order seeking disclosure and that the court has a discretion as to which beneficiaries will be entitled to disclosure and which will not. It does not tell us which types of beneficiary have an entitlement to peruse trust documents as of right.[376]

8.4.4 Which documents constitute trust documents?

The right to access to information under the traditional approach is predicated on ownership of the trust property to which that information relates and therefore means that such owners are entitled to access to trust documents. To remind ourselves of what Lord Wrenbury held in *O'Rourke v Darbishire* on that point:[377]

> A beneficiary has a right of access to the documents which he desires to inspect upon what has been called in the judgments in this case a proprietary right. The beneficiary is entitled to see all trust documents, because they are trust documents, and because he is a beneficiary. They are, in this sense, his own.

The question is then as to the nature of documents which can properly be described as 'trust documents'. The contents of that category have been found to be incapable of precise definition. Trust documents in relation to a discretionary trust do not include documents relating to the basis on which the trustees have made their decisions as to the use of their discretion.[378] By contrast, a beneficiary is entitled to see all documents held by the trustee in her capacity as trustee[379] whether those documents relate to the creation of the trust,[380] receipts as to payments made by the trustees or on their behalf,[381] or advice received from counsel.[382] So, the beneficiary is entitled to see documents as to the management or condition of the trust, but not documents relating to the exercise of the trustees' decisions in relation to the management of the trust, as considered below.[383]

---

376 In *Schmidt v Rosewood* the claimant sought access to information on the basis that he was a beneficiary of two settlements of which his father was co-settlor and on the basis that (acting as his father's executor) his father had been a beneficiary of those settlements too. The trustees resisted disclosure on the basis that they contended that the claimant had no beneficial rights in either context. As set out in the text, the Privy Council decided that the court has an inherent discretion as to questions of disclosure, thus sidestepping the focus on the idea whether or not the claimant needed a beneficial right to acquire disclosure of information. Ultimately the matter was remitted to the court of first instance to find further facts.

377 [1920] AC 581.

378 *Re Londonderry* [1965] Ch 918, *per* Danckwerts LJ.

379 *Simpson v Bathurst* (1869) LR 5 Ch App 193, 202; *Bursill v Tanner* (1885) 16 QBD 1; *Re Cowin* (1886) 33 Ch D 179, 186; *Re Ojjeh Trust* [1993] CILR 348.

380 *Ex p Houldsworth* (1838) 4 Bing NC 386; *Bhander v Barclays* (1997/98) 1 OFLR 497.

381 *Clarke v Ormonde* (1821) Jac 108; *Re Elllis* [1908] WN 215.

382 *Devaynes v Robinson* (1855) 20 Beav 42; *Wynne v Humbertson* (1858) 27 Beav 421. But excluding any advice relating to the trustee's own personal liabilities: *Brown v Oakshott* (1849) 12 Beav 42.

383 See para 8.4.7 below.

The obligation to provide information (albeit of limited types) as to management accounts is an important part of the control of the trustee by the court and by the beneficiaries. Without such information it would be impossible in many circumstances to commence breach of trust claims, that is, the type of litigation dealt with in Chapter 18. What is clearly a limit on the power of beneficiaries is the lack of any entitlement to see documentation as to the rationale underpinning trustees' decisions or a right (in the absence of any such provision in the trust instrument) to receive reasons for trustees' decisions. So, under the *O'Rourke v Darbishire* approach, the objects of a discretionary trust are not entitled to know the reasons for the trustees' decision. This approach would deny the objects the information which they would need to commence proceedings, for example, under the *Hastings-Bass* principle on the basis that the trustees had taken into account an irrelevant consideration or had failed to take into account a relevant consideration.

By contrast with the decision in *O'Rourke v Darbishire*, the more recent decision of the Privy Council in *Schmidt v Rosewood Trust Ltd*[384] has suggested that there is no inherent right to disclosure of trust documents. As Lord Walker expressed this approach:

> no beneficiary . . . has any entitlement as of right to disclosure of anything which can plausibly be described as a trust document. Especially when there are issues as to personal or commercial confidentiality, the court may have to balance the competing interests of different beneficiaries, the trustees themselves, and third parties. Disclosure may have to be limited and safeguards may have to be put in place.[385]

Rather, the entitlement to disclosure of trust documents was held to be dependent on the discretion of the court as part of the court's general power to administer any trust. In the wake of the decision in *Schmidt*, which is of persuasive authority being a Privy Council decision, we will have to wait to see whether or not this new, narrower approach is used to displace the presumption that beneficiaries have an inherent right to consult trust documents relating to property in which they have proprietary rights.[386]

8.4.5 Who constitutes a beneficiary with a right to access to information?

If the right of access to information is predicated on equitable ownership of the property to which the information relates,[387] then anyone without such ownership would not be entitled to access to that information. This much was considered above. However, a further question arises: what does it mean to be a beneficiary in this sense? Does a person who is a member of a class of objects under a discretionary trust, but who has no vested right in any segregated property, constitute a beneficiary? Or is that person denied the status of being a 'beneficiary' for this purpose on account of the fact that she does not own vested property rights in any property? The answer suggested by Neuberger J is that the object of a discretionary trust is entitled to require that trustees provide information to him as to the value of the trust

---

384   [2003] 2 WLR 1442.
385   *Ibid*, 1463.
386   *O'Rourke v Darbishire* [1920] AC 581.
387   As in *ibid*.

property, the trust income, and the manner of the management of the trust fund.[388] Indeed, in *Re Ralli's WT*,[389] the rationale for considering that a remainder beneficiary was entitled to a proprietary right in the trust property, including its income, capable of founding a trust over that remainder interest was that the remainder beneficiary had some right at least to control the behaviour of the trustees.[390] Thus, the object of a discretionary trust would appear to have sufficient proprietary interest to entitle her to access to information relating to the management of that part of the trust.

More recently, however, the Privy Council has cast doubt on the general proposition that the object of a discretionary trust is entitled to access to trust documents as of right, preferring instead to hold that it is for the court in each case, as part of its inherent discretion to supervise the administration of a trust, to decide whether or not any given beneficiary is entitled to access to information.[391] Nevertheless, it has been held in Australia that the approaches in *Re Londonderry*[392] and *O'Rourke v Darbishire* continue to have effect even after *Schmidt v Rosewood* on the basis that the court's inherent discretion ought to favour those beneficiaries on the basis of their proprietary interest in the trust fund.[393] In New Zealand, *Schmidt v Rosewood* has been applied but in such a way as to recognise that the objects of discretionary trusts were entitled to access to information.[394] It is suggested that the *Schmidt v Rosewood* approach is unfortunate for two reasons. First, one cannot know if one has a right to access without incurring the expense of going to court. Secondly, it promotes secrecy on the part of trustees and militates against beneficiaries having that sort of access to information which makes the logic underpinning the beneficiary principle possible.[395] What is meant by this reference to the beneficiary principle is this: the logic of trusts law is that the conscience of the trustee is controlled by the court only if there is some person in whose favour the court can decree performance.[396] However, if the beneficiaries do not have access to trust information, then they cannot commence litigation and the court will therefore not be able to take control over the trustees' actions. Thus, the logic of trusts law threatens to collapse unless the beneficiaries have access to the necessary information. This idea is pursued below at 8.4.7 in relation to *Breakspear v Ackland*.[397]

8.4.6 No obligation on trustees to give reasons for their decisions

Trustees are required to give accounts and to provide details as to the decisions which have been made in accordance with the management of the trust.[398] The beneficiaries, or the class of objects of a power, are entitled to be informed of a decision, but are not entitled to be given

---

388 *Murphy v Murphy* [1999] 1 WLR 282.
389 [1964] 2 WLR 144.
390 See also *Stuart-Hutcheson v Spread Trustee Co Ltd* [2002] WTLR 1213; *Millar v Hornsby* (2000) 3 ITELR 81.
391 *Schmidt v Rosewood* [2003] 2 WLR 1458.
392 Considered below at para 8.4.7.
393 *Crowe v Stevedoring Employees Retirement Fund* [2003] PLR 343.
394 *Foreman v Kingstone* [2004] 1 NZLR 841.
395 On the beneficiary principle, see Chapter 4 generally.
396 See section 4.2.
397 [2008] 3 WLR 698.
398 *Re Londonderry* [1965] 2 WLR 229.

the reasons as to why that decision was taken.[399] The trustees may be required to disclose the material on which they based their decision, but they are not obliged to divulge their reasoning in reaching the decision that they did: this may have the effect that the trustees are not obliged to disclose any material on which they based their decision if that would reveal the reasoning behind their decision.[400] Where trustees fail to explain the reasons for their decision to exercise their discretion in a particular way, the court may set aside that decision or require reasons to be given.[401] In *Re Beloved Wilkes Charity*,[402] the trustees were required to select a boy from among a list of given parishes. They chose a boy not from one of those parishes but rather one who was the brother of a Minister who had sought help for his brother from one of the trustees. Lord Truro set aside the trustees' selection on the basis that it was done solely to benefit a person who had a nexus to the trustee and therefore was not a proper exercise of that power.

The court will look at the adequacy of reasons where they are given.[403] Written material which gives minutes of management of trust property should be disclosed to beneficiaries, but material relating to the exercise of discretions need not be.[404] It might be wondered why there is a difference in these two contexts. The rationale is that the former rule (concerning management of the trust fund) relates to professional management of the beneficiary's entitlement to the trust property, whereas the latter principle (concerning the exercise of discretion in connection with a discretionary trust) relates to a more fundamental question, in that such exercise of their discretion decides whether or not the beneficiary will have an interest in the trust at all. Therefore, a trustee is not obliged to disclose the reasons for making any determination as to the exercise of a discretion.[405]

8.4.7 No obligation to disclose confidential information

A further question might arise: are beneficiaries entitled to see a memorandum set out by the settlor giving her intentions with reference to the fund? In particular, should such a memorandum be disclosed if the settlor has expressed it to be confidential? Suppose the following set of facts: the settlor gave the trustees a memorandum set out by the settlor giving her intentions with reference to a power of appointment under the fund, and then the trustees told the claimant's sister that they would not make an appointment to her because of the terms of the memorandum. In just such a case in New South Wales, the majority of the court followed the decision in *Re Londonderry's Settlement*[406] in holding that the memorandum itself need not be shown to the beneficiary because it related to the exercise of the trustees' discretion;[407] rather, there is an implied obligation of confidentiality between trustee and settlor which would prevent the trustees from being obliged to disclose any such

---

399 *Hartigan v Rydge* (1992) 29 NSWLR 405.
400 *Ibid*, 445, *per* Sheller JA.
401 *Re Beloved Wilkes Charity* (1851) 3 Mac & G 440.
402 *Ibid*.
403 *Klug v Klug* [1918] 2 Ch 67.
404 *Re Londonderry's Settlement* [1965] 2 WLR 229.
405 *Wilson v Law Debenture Trust Corp plc* [1995] 2 All ER 337. See also *Tierney v King* [1983] 2 Qd R 580; *Stuart v Armourguard Security* [1996] NZLR 484; *Crowe v Stevedoring Employees Retirement Fund* [2003] PLR 343.
406 [1965] 2 WLR 229.
407 *Hartigan v Rydge* (1992) 29 NSWLR 405.

information. The rationale given by the Court of Appeal in *Re Londonderry* is that an obliga-tion to make disclosure to the members of a family, for example, might cause irreparable harm to family relations if the settlor had sought to benefit some family members at the expense of others.[408] Similarly, correspondence between the trustees and one or more of the beneficiaries may be considered to be confidential and so not to be capable of disclosure.[409]

In the Cayman Islands case of *Lemos v Coutts & Co*,[410] the *Londonderry* decision was also followed. Although a beneficiary may have proprietary rights to trust documents, it was held that such a right did not grant the beneficiary an absolute right to consult all documents. The court held that there may be categories of document which it is right to exclude from the beneficiaries. The right to see documents will be granted where they are evidentially important to the beneficiaries' case. The question, which is not answered by this approach, is whether the beneficiary should be allowed to see documents where there is no litigation pending.

In the wake of the Privy Council's decision in *Schmidt v Rosewood Trust Ltd*,[411] it may be that the court may consider it appropriate to exercise its discretion so as to order disclosure of confidential information. However, in general terms, it would be suggested on the basis of the older authorities that confidential information is ordinarily not the sort of information which is disclosed to beneficiaries. It was recognised by Lord Walker in *Schmidt v Rosewood* that 'no beneficiary (least of all a discretionary object) has any entitlement as of right to disclosure of anything which can plausibly be described as a trust document . . . [e]specially when there are issues as to personal or commercial confidentiality . . .'.[412] Nevertheless, if the power to order disclosure is now apparently at the discretion of the court as part of the court's inherent power to control the administration of the trust, then it would be open to a court to order such disclosure if, for example, it considered that non-disclosure was facili-tating a fraud to be perpetrated on one or more of the objects of a power. The court would be less likely to make such an order for disclosure, it is suggested, if a disgruntled object of a power were merely seeking to embark on a 'fishing expedition' in the hope of discovering something on which to base a claim against the trustees.

The question of a beneficiary's right to disclosure of information arose again in *Breakspear v Ackland*[413] when a beneficiary sought disclosure of a settlor's 'letter of wishes'. A letter of wishes is a letter sometimes written by a settlor which is not strictly binding on the trustees as a part of a trust instrument but which nevertheless records the settlor's wishes as to the way which the trustees should exercise any discretion or other power they have under the terms of the trust instrument. In this way, for example, a settlor might seek to avoid the tax conse-quences of leaving property to Xena by creating an open-ended discretionary trust under which Xena has no vested equitable interest, but nevertheless write a letter of wishes to her trustees so as to ensure that the trustees in practice will take certain matters into account when making their decision and that they will exercise their discretion so as to appoint the property to Xena. In *Breakspear*, Briggs J ordered disclosure of the letter of wishes on the facts of the

---

408   [1956] Ch 928, *per* Salmon LJ.
409   *Re Londonderry's Settlement* [1965] Ch 918.
410   (1992) Cayman Islands ILR 460.
411   [2003] 2 WLR 1442.
412   *Ibid*, 1463–64.
413   [2008] 3 WLR 698.

case before him. His Lordship followed the principle in *Re Londonderry* to the effect that the exercise of a trustee's 'discretionary dispositive powers' remained 'inherently confidential'[414] and therefore that a letter of wishes was similarly confidential in ordinary circumstances, except where the court considered that the circumstances and the best interests of the beneficiaries required it.[415] Briggs J identified the benefits of confidentiality in cases involving family illness and so forth; and thus, 'regardless of my own opinion',[416] downplays the general desire for more openness in trust dealings.[417] Nevertheless, after a lengthy review of the authorities from around the Commonwealth (with some circularity), his Lordship found that the question of awarding disclosure of this document was a matter for the trustees' discretion and not a question of whether or not the beneficiary had a proprietary right in the document. Thus the strict English authorities are interpreted by reference to decisions in Australia,[418] even though *Re Londonderry* is considered (with due deference to the doctrine of precedent) to remain good law.[419] Briggs J, however, considered that he needed to read the letter of wishes for himself and, with great secrecy as to its contents, decided that disclosure of the letter would be in the long-term benefit of the administration of the trust. He came to this view because he considered that disclosure would have been necessary in future litigation when the trustees would likely be required to seek the court's sanction for a scheme of apportionment of the property between the beneficiaries in any event.

His Lordship identified a weakness in the decision in *Schmidt v Rosewood* in that if the resolution of the question depended on the court's discretion, then trustees would be required to bring litigation on every occasion; and considered the old approach in cases such as *In re Beddoe*[420] that the trustees could always obtain the court's approval at 'modest expense' to be anachronistic given the cost of modern litigation. Ultimately, where Lord Walker departed from *Re Londonderry*, his comments were dismissed as being obiter dicta by Briggs J. This point was made in the text above: the *Schmidt* approach does require litigation for the parties to know where they stand. Briggs J identified a key tension in this area: on the one hand there is a traditional preference for confidentiality (which is likely to find favour among trustees), while on the other hand modern mores prefer openness in financial dealings as opposed to secrecy.[421] Much of the commentary in this area identifies that dichotomy. Briggs J considered himself bound by precedent and the confidentiality in *Re Londonderry*, but was evidently in favour of greater transparency in trust dealings. The principle remains that the trustees are advised to seek a court order before bringing or defending proceedings.[422]

---

414   *Ibid.* at 707.
415   On this basis a letter of wishes was not disclosed in Australia in *Hartigan Nominees Pty Ltd v Rydge* (1992) 29 NSWLR 405. See also *In re Rabaiotti's Settlements* [2000] WTLR 953, Jersey Royal Court; and *Countess Bathurst v Kleinwort Benson (Channel Islands) Trustees Ltd* [2007] WTLR 959, Royal Court of Guernsey: both of which applied the *Londonderry* principle to cases involving letters of wishes.
416   [2008] 3 WLR 698, 717.
417   *Ibid.* at 717.
418   In particular, *Hartigan Nominees Pty Ltd v Rydge* (1992) 29 NSWLR 405.
419   [2008] 3 WLR 698, 716 *et seq.*
420   [1893] 1 Ch 547.
421   See also Sir Gavin Lightman, 'The Trustees' Duty to Provide Information to Beneficiaries', [2004] PCB 23.
422   *Alsop Wilkinson v Neary* [1995] 1 All ER 431; *Bonham v Blake Lapthorn Linell* [2006] EWHC 2513 (Ch), [2007] WTLR 189; *Breadner Granville-Grossman* [2006] WTLR 411; *Three Professional Trustees v Infant Prospective Beneficiary* [2007] EWHC 1922 (Ch), [2007] WTLR 1631.

In similar vein it has been held in *Wilson v Law Debenture Trust Corpn plc*[423] that the trustees of a pension fund who had been given a discretionary power ought not to be required to disclose the reasons for their decisions precisely because the creators of the pension scheme could be taken to have granted the trustees that discretion precisely so as to minimise litigation, and thus that they should not be required to give reasons for their decisions. It is suggested that this is an odd reason for denying disclosure because it makes it effectively impossible for beneficiaries under the scheme to challenge decisions which are adverse to them and could therefore well provide an efficient smokescreen for inappropriate discrimination between beneficiaries, fraud and so forth.

8.4.8 The duty to render accounts

One of the trustees' most significant duties is the duty to render accounts to the beneficiaries as to their management of the trust's affairs. The accounts are required to give an accurate record of the trustees' management of the trust together with supporting documentation such as receipts.[424] This information must include, at the beneficiary's request, a valuation of the trust fund.[425] The beneficiaries are also entitled to have such trusts accounts and documents provided to their accountants[426] or legal advisors,[427] except for those sorts of documents to which those beneficiaries have no entitlement.[428] This duty cannot be excluded by the trust instrument because it is one of the core obligations of trusteeship.[429]

In this book we shall see the notion of rendering accounts appearing in three subtly different senses.[430] The duty to account to the trustees encapsulates not only the rendering of formal accounts in the fiscal sense, but also incorporates the sense of informing the beneficiaries about the manner in which the trustees have discharged their duties, in the way that a schoolmaster might demand that a naughty schoolboy 'account for his actions'. This notion of accounting also encapsulates the general obligation borne by the trustees to obey the terms of the trust and is the foundation of the liability for any breach of trust. Therefore, when we consider liability for breach of trust in detail in Chapter 18,[431] we shall consider the trustees' liability to account in the further sense of compensating the beneficiaries in cash for any loss occasioned to the trust fund by their breach of trust.[432] In the arcane language of

423 [1995] 2 All ER 337, *per* Rattee J.
424 *Springett v Dashwood* (1860) 2 Giff 521; *Burrows v Walls* (1855) 5 De GM & G 233; *Newton v Askew* (1848) 11 Beav 145.
425 *Armitage v Nurse* [1998] Ch 241, 261. See also *Re Tillott* [1892] 1 Ch 86; *Re Page* [1893] 1 Ch 304; *Ryder v Bickerton* (1743) 3 Swan 30n.
426 *Kemp v Burn* (1863) 4 Giff 348; *Re Cowin* (1886) 33 Ch D 179; *Re Londonderry's Settlement* [1965] Ch 918; *Schmidt v Rosewood Trust Ltd* [2003] 2 WLR 1442.
427 *Hawkesley v May* [1956] 1 QB 304.
428 On these categories of documents see the previous paragraphs of this section.
429 *Armitage v Nurse* [1998] Ch 241, 253, *per* Millett LJ.
430 For a general description see *Glazier v Australian Men's Health (No 2)* [2001] NSW SC 6.
431 See section 18.1.
432 This obligation arises in tandem with an obligation to effect specific restitution of any property taken from the trust: *Target Holdings v Redferns* [1996] 1 AC 421. This obligation includes a liability to costs resulting from a failure to keep proper accounts: *Eglin v Sanderson* (1862) 3 Giff 434; *Re Linsley* [1904] 2 Ch 785; *Re Den Haag Trust* (1998) 1 OFLR 495.

trusts law, any challenge to the accounts brought by the beneficiaries is done by way of 'falsifying and surcharging' those accounts. In modern parlance, we think of falsifying account as the process by which a trustee is subjected to a personal liability to account to the beneficiaries in cash or equivalent value for any loss suffered by the trust as a result of the breach of trust.[433] By contrast, surcharging accounts refers specifically to an argument that some asset ought to have been recorded in the trust accounts but has not been so recovered as a result of the trustee's failure to get the trust property in.[434] If the trustee has been guilty of wilful default in failing to get the trust property in, then the trustee will be liable for any property or value which might have accrued to the trust but for her wilful default.[435]

As to the detail of calculating the loss to the trust and the nature of the available remedies for breach of trust, you are directed to Chapter 18.

8.4.9 Fiduciary duties in relation to Chinese walls and confidential information

If a fiduciary were to earn personal profits from the misuse of confidential information belonging to a beneficiary, then that profit would be held on constructive trust for those beneficiaries. More generally the fiduciary may be liable for any loss caused to that beneficiary by means of compromising that confidential information. The obligations of a fiduciary are obligations of good faith, loyalty and confidence.[436] As such, the manner in which a fiduciary deals with confidential information belonging to a beneficiary is an important part of her fiduciary duties. There are two kinds of confidential information which should concern us here. The first kind would be confidential information which itself has a market value, such as knowledge of a secret ingredient or a formula used in a manufacturing process. This type of confidential information is recognised by intellectual property law as being property, akin to a copyright or a patent in that sense.[437] Thus, such property can itself be held on trust and so any misuse of such property by a fiduciary would give rise to liability for breach of trust and for any secret profits made by the fiduciary to be held on constructive trust.[438]

The second kind of confidential information of significance is knowledge of some private information as to the beneficiary's personal affairs. This sort of information might not be intellectual property, in the sense that it may not be capable of forming the subject matter of a trust in some circumstances, but misuse of such information by a fiduciary would constitute a breach of those fiduciary duties. An example of this second type of confidential information would be knowledge of the location of the beneficiary's secret, personal bank accounts and knowledge of the structure of the trusts and companies which hold the beneficiary's personal assets. Misuse of information of this type would similarly lead to liability for breach of trust, in relation to any loss which resulted to the beneficiary, and a

433 *Clough v Bond* (1838) 3 My & Cr 490, 496; *Knott v Cottee* (1852) 19 Beav 77; *Re Massingberd* (1890) 63 LT 296; *Wallersteiner v Moir (No 2)* [1975] QB 373, 397; *Target Holdings v Redferns* [1996] 1 AC 421.
434 *Bristol & West Building Society v Mothew* [1998] Ch 1, 17; *Bank of New Zealand v New Zealand Guardian Trust Co* [1999] 1 NZLR 664, 687.
435 *Partington v Reynolds* (1858) 4 Drew 253; *Coulthard v Disco Mix Club* [1999] 2 All ER 457.
436 *Re Coomber* [1911] 1 Ch 723, *Bristol & West Building Society v Mothew* [1998] Ch 1.
437 *Coco v AN Clark (Engineers)* [1969] RPC 41, 48, *per* Megarry J; *Douglas v Hello!* [2001] EMLR 199, 251, *per* Keane J. See Thomas and Hudson, 2004, para 29.29.
438 *Boardman v Phipps* [1967] 2 AC 46, as considered above.

constructive trust over any secret profits made from that misuse of confidential information.[439]

One particular context in which either form of confidential information might cause difficulties for fiduciaries is the context of litigation or advice given by professional advisors, such as solicitors or accountants, to their clients. The particular difficulty which arises in relation to complex litigation involving large corporate entities is that there are comparatively few law firms and very few accountancy firms which are sufficiently expert or technically capable of providing the necessary advice and services. In such situations, it is therefore common for large law firms or accountancy firms to be advising both parties to litigation. Evidently, there is the very real possibility of a conflict of interest or transmission of confidential information when employees of the same firm are advising both parties to litigation and are therefore in possession of a large amount of confidential information as to both parties' prospects for success, the details of their businesses and their tactics. That the same solicitors' firm, for example, acts for both sides in litigation is not, in itself, objectionable provided that both principals give their informed consent to such an arrangement.[440]

Consequently, the firms attempt to instate what are commonly known as 'Chinese walls' within the firm. The purpose of a Chinese wall is to segregate those employees who are advising one client from those employees who are advising the other client. There is no principle in English law to preclude a firm of solicitors from advising both parties to litigation or to prevent a firm of solicitors from acting in litigation against a former client,[441] although a firm cannot act both for and against the same client, unless that firm has the consent of both clients.[442] A good example of the sorts of techniques which are used are discussed in the case of *Bolkiah v KPMG*.[443] This is achieved, it is hoped, by programming the firms' security systems so as to deny employees advising client A from accessing any premises or part of the premises used by employees advising client B. This will include denial of access to photocopying facilities, restroom and refreshment facilities of such employees as well as their offices and other work areas. Usually, large firms will require different departments to work in different buildings and will prevent any employees moving from one team to another team. Employees are prevented from taking work home or even out of the office so that there cannot be any risk of loss or transmission of confidential information outside the office either accidentally or deliberately. A successful Chinese wall strategy will prevent the employing company or firm from being attributed with any knowledge acquired by employees; otherwise, if an employee of a firm had a requisite form of knowledge of confidential client information, then that knowledge would ordinarily be attributed to the employer, thus making the employer liable for any breach of duty.[444]

In *Bolkiah v KPMG*, the claimant Prince Jefri Bolkiah had been finance minister in Brunei and was a part of the Brunei royal family. In time, he fell from favour and sought advice

439 *Bolkiah v KPMG* [1999] 2 AC 222, [1999] 1 All ER 517.
440 *Marks & Spencer plc v Freshfield Bruckhaus Deringer* [2004] 3 All ER 773.
441 *Rakusen v Ellis Munday & Clarke* [1912] 1 Ch 831, [1911–13] All ER Rep 813.
442 *Bolkiah v KPMG* [1999] 2 AC 222, [1999] 1 All ER 517, 526h.
443 [1999] 2 AC 222, [1999] 1 All ER 517.
444 *Galmerrow Securities Ltd v National Westminster Bank plc* [2002] WTLR 125. Cf *Harrods Ltd v Lemon* [1931] 1 KB 157, demonstrating that ordinarily the knowledge of some wrongful or fraudulent design by one agent of a company or other organisation will generally be attributed to that company or organisation.

from the defendant accountancy firm. Subsequently, a Brunei state-owned entity, BIA, commenced litigation in relation to the claimant. BIA retained the defendant accountancy firm to advise it in relation to that litigation. The accountancy firm put in place the sort of Chinese walls just considered. When the courts came to consider the efficacy of the accountancy firm's arrangements, it was held that there were two principal problems with the operation of these Chinese walls in this case. The first problem was that the Chinese walls were the defendant's usual arrangements rather than being arrangements which were designed specifically for the circumstances of the particular litigation. The court was consequently unconvinced that the firm had done everything necessary to ensure that there was no transmission of confidential information within the firm. The second problem was that the Chinese wall arrangements failed in practice because there were movements of staff between the two departments such that there were employees in one department who necessarily knew information which should have been kept within the other department. In the event, there was transmission of confidential information as to the claimant's personal affairs within the firm, in particular as to the structure of his personal holdings.

The defendant accountancy firm argued that it had done everything reasonable to preserve the confidentiality of the claimant's information. However, Lord Millett, speaking for a unanimous House of Lords, held that the defendant's obligation was not a mere obligation to do all that was reasonable; rather, it was an absolute duty to ensure that there was no breach of confidence. Thus there was no defence for the defendant on the basis that the defendant had sought to do everything reasonable in the circumstances. His Lordship held that in relation to solicitors acting for their clients:[445]

> the duty to preserve confidentiality is unqualified. It is a duty to keep the information confidential, not merely to take all reasonable steps to do so. Moreover, it is not merely a duty not to communicate the information to a third party. It is a duty not to misuse it, that is to say, without the consent of the former client to make any use of it or to cause any use to be made of it by others otherwise than for his benefit.

That the duty is 'unqualified' means that the fiduciary has no defence if the duty is breached and the beneficiary suffers some loss from that breach. Further, however, the fiduciary is under a duty not to misuse the information generally and therefore the fiduciary would be liable to be subjected to an injunction to prevent the misuse of the property and not simply to account for the benefit in the event that the misuse caused some loss to the beneficiary.

Indeed, if the business at issue is of such confidentiality and of such significance to one client's business, then it may be that the court will consider that it would not be possible to put effective barriers in place and so enjoin the advisor from acting for both clients.[446] So, in *Marks & Spencer plc v Freshfields Bruckhaus Deringer*,[447] a firm of solicitors acquired a great deal of confidential information about their client's logistical arrangements and supply chain. The client, Marks & Spencer, was in the process of restructuring these core elements

---

445 [1999] 2 AC 222, 232, [1999] 1 All ER 517, 527, *per* Lord Millett.
446 *Marks & Spencer plc v Freshfields Bruckhaus Deringer* [2004] 3 All ER 773.
447 [2004] 3 All ER 773, [2004] EWHC 1337 (Ch). Applying *Young v Robson Rhodes (A Firm)* [1999] 3 All ER 524; *Baron Investments (Holdings) Ltd (In Liquidation)* [2000] 1 BCLC 272; *Baird Textiles Holdings Ltd v Marks & Spencer plc* [2002] 1 All ER (Comm) 737.

of their business: as a nationwide high street retailer, this sort of information was vital to their business. The solicitors then sought to act at the same time for a consortium which was seeking to take over Marks & Spencer. It was held that the principles as to Chinese walls were not restricted to confidential information in one transaction but would apply in relation to information which might be passed across different transactions. An injunction was granted to prevent the solicitors from acting for both clients so that the risk of confidential information being passed would be avoided.[448]

In *Bolkiah v KPMG* itself, the House of Lords held that there was a difference between acting as a solicitor and acting as an accountant who provides audit services. The solicitor acts throughout the duration of her retainer in a fiduciary capacity for the client, but that fiduciary obligation comes to an end when the relationship ceases, so that the solicitor may thereafter act against the former client. However, in relation to information relating to the time when the solicitor was acting for the client, the solicitor remains in a fiduciary relationship forever, or else the client could have no practical protection against the solicitor's breach of duty. Auditors, by contrast, frequently provide accountancy services to people who may be in conflict in the future or who may even be in conflict at the time of providing the services. Significantly, the basis for the fiduciary's duty is the need to avoid any conflict of interest between the fiduciary's personal capacities and the obligations owed to the beneficiary.[449]

8.5 LIMITATION OF THE TRUSTEES' DUTIES

Trustees are entitled to have their liabilities for breach of trust and for the commission of any tort limited by the terms of the trust instrument. Such liability exclusion clauses are equitable devices and not contractual provisions. Trustees can limit their liability for negligence and gross negligence, but it appears that they may not limit their liability for dishonesty or fraud. There is a division in the authorities between a permissive approach to such exclusion clauses and an approach which prefers to limit them.

8.5.1 The validity of exclusion of liability clauses under case law

The trustees' right to exclude their liabilities by express provision in the trust instrument

The trustees' liability for breach of trust may be excluded completely or limited by an express provision to that effect in the trust instrument.[450] Such exclusion of liability provisions takes effect as equitable provisions and not as contractual provisions.[451] A number of different

---

448   See also *Koch Shipping Inc v Richards Butler (A Firm)* [2002] EWCA Civ 1280, [2002] 2 All ER (Comm) 957.
449   [1999] 2 AC 222, 232, [1999] 1 All ER 517, 527, *per* Lord Millett.
450   *Armitage v Nurse* [1998] Ch 241; *Taylor v Midland Bank Trust Co* (2000) 2 ITELR 439; *Bogg v Raper* (1998) *The Times,* 22 April; *Wight v Olswang* (1999) *The Times,* 18 May. This approach has also been followed in pensions law, with the following cases all concerned with the interpretation of trustee exemption provisions: *Elliott v Pensions Ombudsman* [1998] OPLR 21; *Woodland-Ferrari v UCL Group Retirement Benefits Scheme* [2002] EWHC 1354 (Ch), [2003] Ch 115; *Seifert v Pensions Ombudsman* [1997] 4 All ER 947; *Duckitt v Pensions Ombudsman* [2000] OPLR 167; *Alexander Forbes Trustee Services Ltd v Halliwell* [2003] EWHC 1685 (Ch), [2003] Pens LR 269.
451   *Re Duke of Norfolk Settlement Trusts* [1982] Ch 61, 77.

expressions are used in this context to describe effectively the same material. Strictly, 'exclusion of liability' clauses seek completely to prevent the trustees from bearing any liability for any breach of trust; whereas 'limitation of liability' or 'exemption of liability' clauses usually seek only to prevent trustees from being liable for breach of trust for particular acts or omissions. Commonly, however, all of these terms are used as though they are synonymous and concerned with attempting to limit the liability of trustees for breach of trust for identified categories of behaviour, such as negligence or carelessness or mistake. There are also clauses which seek to exclude the trustees' liabilities by extending their powers such that anything which might otherwise be a breach of trust falls under the trustees' impliedly extended powers so as not to constitute a breach of trust at all. Similar in effect are 'duty modification' clauses which alter the extent of the trustees' duties so as effectively to exclude liability for breach of trust. In this discussion the term 'exclusion of liability' clause shall be used to refer to all of these intentions, except where the context requires otherwise.

Technically it is the settlor who provides for the trustees' exclusion of their liabilities when the settlor creates the trust instrument and declares the trust. However, in practice it will be professional trustees who will either be solicitors responsible for drafting the trust instrument who will therefore include an exclusion of liability provision in that instrument, or else they will insist that whoever does draft the trust instrument includes such an exclusion of liability provision.[452] Therefore, while the settlor technically grants this immunity from liability for breach of trust to the trustees, in practice it is more likely to be the trustees themselves who ensure that it happens and who dictate the terms on which it takes effect.

Trustees are permitted therefore to elude liability for breach of trust if there is a provision in the trust instrument which excludes their liability for the particular type of breach which is complained of. Liability for breach of trust, as described in Chapter 18 in detail, may otherwise arise on breach of an express provision of the trust instrument, or on breach of some provision of the Trustee Act 2000, or on breach of some obligation imposed by the case law. It is the trust instrument which must exclude liability for breach of trust for present purposes, as opposed to the various defences to actions of breach of trust which excuse liability as opposed to preventing it arising in the first place. Thus, by way of example, liability based on a negligent breach of trust will only be excluded if the trust instrument is drafted so as to exclude liability for negligent acts by the trustees.

The decision in Armitage v Nurse

The leading case in this area is the decision of the Court of Appeal in *Armitage v Nurse*[453] which held that a clause excluding a trustee's personal liability in all situations, including loss caused by the trustee's own gross negligence, except in cases of the trustee's own dishonesty, would be valid.[454] Consequently, that trustee would not have been held liable for breach of

---

452 See, however, *Bogg v Raper* (1998/99) 1 ITELR 267, 281 – a case in which the trustees were permitted to rely on the exclusion clause which they had drafted. See also Law Commission, 'Trustee Exemption Clauses' (2006), para 2.13.

453 [1998] Ch 241.

454 Under a Guernsey statute, a trustee is entitled to rely on an exclusion of liability clause (in relation to a trust created under that system of law) to exclude liability for her own gross negligence: *Spread Trustee Ltd v Hutcheson* [2010] WTLR 315, Guernsey Court of Appeal, as affirmed by the majority of the Privy Council [2011] UKPC 13, as considered below.

trust even if he had caused loss to the beneficiaries through his own grossly negligent breach of trust. In that case the claimant was a beneficiary under a trust which held agricultural land among the trust property. The trustees of that settlement were also directors of a company which farmed the land which was held on trust. The value of the land had fallen substantially, it was alleged, on the basis of the negligence of the trustees in their management of it. The trustees, therefore, sought to rely on their exclusion of liability clause to prevent any liability for breach of trust on grounds of this alleged negligence. The Court of Appeal held that the trustees could rely on the exclusion of liability clause. The exclusion of liability clause in that settlement provided that no trustee would be liable for any loss or damage caused to the trust fund unless it was caused by any trustee's 'own actual fraud'. It was held that this exclusion clause would be effective even where it purported to limit that trustee's liability for gross negligence. Millett LJ held that while it was permissible for a trustee to exclude her liability for all defaults including gross negligence, a trustee could not exclude her own liability for breach of trust if that breach of trust was caused by her own fraud or dishonesty. Earlier authorities which had suggested that gross negligence could not be excused were not followed.[455] On the *Armitage v Nurse* approach to this area of law, a trustee exemption clause will be effective in relation to the matters for which it seeks to exclude the trustee's liability for breach of trust, in the words of Millett LJ,[456] 'no matter how indolent, imprudent, lacking in diligence, negligent or wilful he may have been, so long as he had not acted dishonestly'.

Interpretation of the trust instrument

It was held in *Armitage v Nurse* that the older case of *Wilkins v Hogg*[457] had established the principle that a settlor was able to limit the liabilities of her trustees if she so wished and provided that such an intention to exclude the trustees' liabilities was set out in the trust instrument.[458] An exclusion of liability clause will be interpreted so as to give that clause its natural meaning, but the settlor's intention to exclude the trustees' liabilities must nevertheless be plain.[459] The court's role when faced with an exclusion clause is that the court 'must construe the words of the exemption clause in light of the conduct complained of and decide whether liability has been excluded by the terms of the clause. In carrying out this exercise the clause must be construed fairly according to the natural meaning of the words used'.

Therefore, a trustee will not necessarily have her liabilities for breach of trust excluded entirely, unless the appropriate clause in the trust instrument envisaged the exemption of liability for the particular fault complained of.

Dishonesty

A trustee may not exclude her liability for dishonesty, as considered above. The question of what constitutes 'dishonesty' is complex in this context. The meaning of 'dishonesty' in

---

455 See *Pass v Dundas* (1880) 43 LT 665, as held by Millett LJ at [1998] Ch 241, 256.

456 Followed in *Barraclough v Mell* [2005] EWHC 3387 (Ch), [2006] WTLR 203, [90].

457 (1861) 31 LJ Ch 41.

458 *Armitage v Nurse* [1998] Ch 241, 255, where it was required that the settlor make her intention plain.

459 *Armitage v Nurse* [1998] Ch 241, 255. See also *Midland Bank Trustee (Jersey) Ltd v Federated Pension Services Ltd* [1996] PLR 179, 192; *Bogg v Raper* (1998/99) 1 ITELR 267, 280; *Wight v Olswang (No 2)* (1999/2000) 2 ITELR 689 on this point.

relation to the law on dishonest assistance is considered in detail in section 20.2. In relation to liability for breach of trust, the Court of Appeal in *Walker v Stones*[460] was asked to consider whether or not a solicitor had been dishonest. The question arose whether or not a solicitor could be dishonest if he did not subjectively appreciate that he was being dishonest because he believed that he was acting in the best interests of the trust. It was held by Nourse LJ that a solicitor could not escape a finding of dishonesty in this fashion if no reasonable solicitor acting as trustee would have considered it to be honest to act in that way. In *Armitage v Nurse*, Millett LJ held that 'actual fraud', as described in the trust instrument in that case, meant simply 'dishonesty'.[461] Where trustees will be liable for breach of trust if they act dishonestly, then the appropriate test for identifying dishonesty here has been held by Millett LJ to require '. . . at the minimum an intention of the part of the trustee to pursue a particular course of action, either knowing that it is contrary to the interests of the beneficiaries or being recklessly indifferent whether it is contrary to their interests or not'.[462]

This subjective approach to dishonesty, based on the defendant's knowledge, is at odds with the objective test for dishonesty set out in *Royal Brunei Airlines v Tan*[463] as considered in Chapter 20 in relation to dishonest assistance.[464] It is suggested, in consequence, that the approach in *Walker v Stones* is to be preferred.

An intentional breach of trust is not necessarily a dishonest breach of trust; wilful default

It has been held that an intentional breach of trust is not necessarily a dishonest breach of trust.[465] The clearest example of this initially surprising proposition is that in which a trustee deliberately embarks on a course of action which she knows to be in breach of trust but which she genuinely believes will be in the best interests of the beneficiaries ultimately.[466] It is not dishonest because it is done out of benign motives. This would still be a breach of trust but it would not be dishonest. Consequently, if the trustee's liability were excluded by a provision in the trust instrument, which nevertheless did not exclude liability for dishonesty, then that trustee could rely upon that exclusion of liability clause even if her breach of trust had been deliberate because it would not necessarily be dishonest. So, in *Woodland-Ferrari v UCL Group Retirement Benefits Scheme*[467] two trustees of a pension fund were removed from office having committed breaches of trust which caused the trust a shortfall in excess of £870,000. The trustees claimed to be entitled to rely on an exclusion of liability clause contained in the trust instrument. The question arose as to whether or not there had been a 'fraudulent breach of trust' for the purposes of s 281 of the Insolvency Act 1986. It was

---

460 [2001] QB 902.

461 [1998] Ch 241, 251.

462 This approach is followed in *Gwembe Valley Development Co v Koshy* [2004] 1 BCLC 131, 170; *Newgate Stud Company v Penfold* [2004] EWHC 2993 (Ch), [249], *per* David Richards J. Cf *Isaac v Isaac* [2004] All ER (D) 71.

463 [1995] 2 AC 378.

464 See section 20.2 generally.

465 *Armitage v Nurse* [1998] Ch 241, 250; *Taylor v Midland Bank Trust Co Ltd* [1999] All ER (D) 831, *per* Ratte J in the Court of Appeal; *Woodland-Ferrari v UCL Group Retirement Benefits Scheme* [2002] EWHC 1354 (Ch), [2003] Ch 115.

466 This was the example used by Millett LJ in *Armitage v Nurse* [1998] Ch 241, 250.

467 [2002] EWHC 1354 (Ch), [2003] Ch 115.

found that the word 'fraudulent' in this context would require 'dishonesty'. On the facts, not enough information had been pleaded in detail before the Pensions Ombudsman to disclose a finding of dishonesty, nor even of wilful default. It was found that even though the trustees had caused the trust assets to be invested in investments in which they also had interests, nevertheless it had not been proven that there had been anything 'dishonest' about their breach of trust on the facts. The test for 'dishonesty' combined references to *Armitage v Nurse* and *Walker v Stones*. Consequently, the finding of the Pensions Ombudsman that a statutory demand be levied against the trustees was to be set aside because a 'fraudulent breach of trust' had not been proved on the facts. What emerges from this case, nevertheless, is the proposition that a 'deliberate breach of trust' is not necessarily a 'fraudulent' nor a 'dishonest' breach of trust, relying on *Armitage v Nurse*. Therefore, a trustee's breach of trust may be excluded even if it has been deliberate, but provided that it was not dishonest.

Nevertheless, as for 'wilful default' on the part of a trustee, Millett LJ held in *Armitage v Nurse* that it may not be excluded by a provision in the trust instrument on the following basis:[468]

> A trustee is said to be accountable on the footing of wilful default when he is accountable not only for money which he has in fact received but also for money which he could with reasonable diligence have received. It is sufficient that the trustee has been guilty of a want of ordinary prudence.[469] In the context of a trustee exclusion clause, however, such as s 30 of the Trustee Act 1925, it means a deliberate breach of trust.[470] The decision has been criticised, but it is in line with earlier authority.[471] Nothing less than conscious and wilful misconduct is sufficient. The trustee must be—
>
> > 'conscious that, in doing the act which is complained of or in omitting to do the act which it said he ought to have done, he is committing a breach of his duty, or is recklessly careless whether it is a breach of his duty or not'.[472]
>
> A trustee who is guilty of such conduct either consciously takes a risk that loss will result, or is recklessly indifferent whether it will or not. If the risk eventuates he is personally liable. But if he consciously takes the risk in good faith and with the best intentions, honestly believing that the risk is one which ought to be taken in the interests of the beneficiaries, there is no reason why he should not be protected by an exemption clause which excludes liability for wilful default.

Lord Clarke agreed in *Spread Trustee Company Ltd v Hutcheson* with the argument that under English law a trustee's liability cannot be excused for wilful default.[473]

---

468 [1998] Ch 241 at 252.
469 See eg, *Re Chapman, Cocks v Chapman* [1896] 2 Ch 763, [1895–9] All ER Rep 1104.
470 *Re Vickery, Vickery v Stephens* [1931] 1 Ch 572, [1931] All ER Rep 562.
471 See *Lewis v Great Western Rly Co* (1877) 3 QBD 195, [1874–80] All ER Rep Ext 1793, *Re Trusts of Leeds City Brewery Ltd's Debenture Stock Trust Deed, Leeds City Brewery Ltd v Platts* [1925] Ch 532n, and *Re City Equitable Fire Insurance Co Ltd* [1925] Ch 407, [1924] All ER Rep 485.
472 *Re Vickery, Vickery v Stephens* [1931] 1 Ch 572 at 583, [1931] All ER Rep 562 at 567], *per* Maugham J.
473 [2011] UKPC 13, [2012] 1 All ER 251, at [55].

Cases after Armitage v Nurse

The *Armitage v Nurse* approach has been approved in four subsequent cases. First, in *Bogg v Raper*[474] the Court of Appeal considered a claim that trustees had failed to exercise sufficient control over the trust property which comprised a controlling shareholding in a private limited company. In such circumstances trustees would ordinarily be required to ensure that they exercised sufficient scrutiny of the company's activities because the shareholding granted them control enough to do so. The trust instrument, however, excluded the trustees' liability for 'any loss' provided that they acted in good faith. The court held that the exclusion of liability clause meant that the trustees bore no liability for breach of trust in this context. The Court of Appeal also rejected an argument to the effect that the trustees, being the solicitors and accountants to the trust, should not be permitted to rely on language in the trust instrument which they had drafted and included. It was held that this was not a benefit conferred on the trustees but rather simply defined the extent of their liabilities.[475]

Secondly, *Wight v Olswang (No 2)*[476] followed the underlying principle in *Armitage v Nurse* in theory. However on the precise facts of that case there were two clauses which were contradictory. One of those clauses purported to exclude the trustees' liabilities for breach of trust, whereas the other did not. It was held that the trustees could not rely on the purported exemption of liability provision because it was not clear that it disclosed an intention on the part of the settlor, when read with the other clause, to exclude their liabilities in the manner for which they contended. Therefore, while no doubt is cast on the *Armitage v Nurse* principle in the abstract, it may not be relied upon if it is not clear that the settlor intended to exclude the trustees' liability for breach of trust in the relevant circumstances.

Thirdly, in *Barraclough v Mell*[477] there was a clause in a will trust which provided that the trustee's liability for breach of trust was to be excluded 'unless the same shall have happened through his own personal act done by him either with the knowledge that it was wrongful or without any belief that it was rightful and not caring whether or not it was wrongful'. This case therefore addresses a lacuna in the law as described by Millett LJ in *Armitage v Nurse*. Strictly speaking, on the basis that Millett LJ in *Armitage v Nurse* permitted exclusion of liability for negligence but not for dishonesty, it was therefore unclear whether or not a breach of trust caused by the trustee's own recklessness – falling somewhere between gross negligence and dishonesty, it is suggested – could be excluded by an exclusion of liability clause in the trust instrument. This exemption of liability provision in *Barraclough v Mell* considers just such a provision based on recklessness in that the trustee need not care whether or not the breach was wrongful. Judge Behrens QC appeared to accept that this provision would be enforceable, without any point being taken on whether or not 'recklessness' in general terms should be considered to fall on the permissible or impermissible exemption clause side of the line. Instead Judge Behrens QC proceeded on the evidence to consider whether or not the trustee had acted wrongfully in making payments out of the trust fund

---

474   (1998/99) 1 ITELR 267.
475   It has been suggested that, not only did this confer a benefit by permitting the trustees to exclude themselves from liability in a manner which they had engineered in advance, but also that this constituted a benefit in that it saved the trustees the insurance premiums necessary to protect themselves against liability otherwise: see Hayton & Mitchell, 2005, 9–311.
476   (1999/2000) 2 ITELR 689.
477   [2005] EWHC 3387 (Ch), [2006] WTLR 203.

which she was not authorised to make under the terms of the trust. It was found that the trustee had not known of the wrongfulness of her actions and that she had acted immediately to seek to recover the money when the true nature of her actions was brought to her attention: therefore, it was found that she was entitled to rely on the exclusion of liability provision and so was not liable for breach of trust.

It is respectfully suggested that this sort of approach to exclusion of trustees' liability is precisely the sort of approach which will lead trustees to be lazy in working out the extent of their powers and the nature of their actions: if trustees know that they will not be liable in any event (whether they understand the nature of their actions or not) then they are unlikely to be suitably diligent in working out the nature of their duties. Why go to the effort of finding out if you will not be liable in any event? It is, to quote concepts from Chapter 18 on breach of trust, likely to be an opiate on the diligence of the trustees.[478]

Fourthly, in *Baker v JE Clark & Co (Transport) UK Ltd*[479] a widow brought a claim against a trustee of a company pension scheme for failing to make a payment out of the trust after her husband, who was an employee of the company, had died. The trust instrument contained an exclusion of liability provision to the effect that:

> None of the trustees shall be liable for the consequence of any mistake or forgetfulness ... or for breach of duty or trust whatsoever, whether by commission or omission unless it shall be proved to be made, given, done or omitted in personal conscious or bad faith of the trustees or any of them.

Thus, the exclusion of the trustees' liability was intended to be total, except for breaches of trust committed knowingly in bad faith. On the facts it was not proved that the trustee had acted in bad faith. Therefore, it was held that the trustee was entitled to rely on the exemption clause and therefore bore no liability for breach of trust. The trustee had not brought the exemption of liability clause to the attention of the beneficiaries when they had contributed to the pension fund (as settlors, therefore) but that was not considered by the Court of Appeal to be any objection to the effectiveness of the exemption of liability clause.[480]

Gross negligence in Spread Trustee Company Ltd v Hutcheson

The Privy Council has considered the law relating to the exclusion of liability of trustees in an appeal from Guernsey in *Spread Trustee Company Ltd v Hutcheson*.[481] A statute enacted in 1989 in Guernsey permitted liability to be excluded for negligence and gross negligence but not for fraud nor for wilful default; uninterestingly for our purposes this case considered the law in Guernsey before and after that statute came into effect, but interestingly with a

---

478 Sentiments expressed in *Bahin v Hughes* (1886) 31 Ch D 390, at 398, *per* Frey LJ. See section 18.2.4.
479 [2006] EWCA Civ 464.
480 A further point was alluded to by Tuckey LJ, which impacts on the discussion at para 21.2.4 concerning the overlap between contract law and trusts law which, by extrapolation, suggests that even if a trust were to be interpreted as being based on the principles of contract law then trustee exemption clauses required by the trustees could be ineffective by dint of the Unfair Contract Terms Act 1977.
481 [2011] UKPC 13, [2012] 1 All ER 251. See generally Matthews, 1989, which is referred to extensively by the Privy Council.

consideration of the English law position and its possible effect as an aid to the interpretation of the law in Guernsey. It was accepted by Lord Clarke (speaking for the majority) that there were instances in which English law does differentiate between ordinary negligence and 'gross negligence';[482] although Millett LJ in *Armitage v Nurse* had considered that to be only a difference of degree (i.e. slightly negligent running through to very negligent) as opposed to a qualitative difference between two different types of negligence.[483] Nevertheless, it was accepted that under English law, since *Armitage v Nurse* certainly, liability could be excluded for gross negligence.[484]

Lady Hale in a spirited dissenting speech noted that the Supreme Court has yet to have the opportunity to consider the judgment of Millett LJ in *Armitage v Nurse* and also doubted that the law in England and Wales (let alone Scots law, which was also in issue in that appeal) had always been clear about the treatment of grossly negligent breaches of trust. Her lady-ship made the point that cases such as *Re City Fire and Equitable Insurance*[485] and *Re Trusts of Leeds City Brewery Debenture*[486] did not in fact consider the point whether or not trustees were entitled to exclude their liabilities. Her ladyship referred to arguments in Parliament relating to the Trustee Act 2000 (on investment of trusts, discussed in Chapter 9) that profes-sional trustees should bear a different test from other trustees (to the effect that professional trustees seeking to exclude their liability should be subject to the same test as for contractual exclusion of liability clauses under the Unfair Contract Terms Act 1977).[487] However, it is Lord Kerr who really hit the nail on the head in his dissenting judgment when his lordship held the following:

> If, as I suggested at the beginning of this judgment, the placing of reliance on a responsible person to manage property so as to promote the interests of the beneficiaries of a trust is central to the concept of trusteeship, denying trustees the opportunity to avoid liability for their gross negligence seems to be entirely in keeping with that essential aim.[488]

A trustee ought not to be able to exclude liability for gross negligence. A trustee is a fiduciary who is required to act selflessly in the interests of her beneficiaries, or to take proper advice where that is not otherwise possible. It is not too high a standard to set for that person to avoid grossly negligent performances of those duties. It is not being said that that person cannot still avoid liability for being negligent or careless; all that is being suggested is that when that negligence is so severe as to be 'gross', then liability for it ought not to be excluded by the trust instrument. Lord Kerr pointed out that the claimant in *Armitage v Nurse* was a 17-year-old girl, Paula, something which otherwise escapes our notice. Professional trustees who were expected to care for Paula's remainder interest in land were entitled to escape liability for their grossly negligent acts, provided that they had not been dishonest in so

482   See [2011] UKPC 13, [2012] 1 All ER 251, at [50].
483   [1998] Ch 241 at 253–4.
484   Cf. Matthews, 1989 and *Midland Bank Trust Co (Jersey) Ltd v Federated Pension Services* [1995] JLR 352.
485   [1925] Ch 407.
486   [1925] Ch 532n.
487   [2011] UKPC 13, [2012] 1 All ER 251, at [136].
488   *Ibid., Ibid.* at [180].

doing. In the meantime they would have charged their fees to the trust while at the same time they would have been shielded from any liability for their gross carelessness by a provision placed in the trust instrument for their sole benefit by other professionals, the solicitors who drafted that trust instrument. There is something very wrong in this. The decision in *Armitage v Nurse* is both an opiate on the professionalism of trustees and an opiate on their consciences.

The nature of trustees' obligations if they are limited by exclusion clauses

Trustees' exclusion of liability clauses raise important questions as to the nature of the obligations of a trustee in general terms. There are two ostensibly competing lines of authority. The first line of authority, in short, holds that any express provision in a trust deed, or some collateral contract, which purports to limit the liability of the trustees will be given full force and effect by the courts.[489] The most important recent case in this line is that of *Armitage v Nurse*[490] (decided before the enactment of the Trustee Act 2000).[491] In explaining the limit of the trustee's obligations, Millett LJ had the following to say:

> [T]here is an irreducible core of obligations owed by the trustees to the beneficiaries and enforceable by them which is fundamental to the concept of a trust. If the beneficiaries have no rights enforceable against the trustees there are no trusts. But I do not accept the further submission that their core obligations include the duties of skill and care, prudence and diligence. The duty of trustees to perform the trusts honestly and in good faith for the benefit of the beneficiaries is the minimum necessary to give substance to the trusts, but in my opinion it is sufficient . . . a trustee who relied on the presence of a trustee exemption clause to justify what he proposed to do would thereby lose its protection: he would be acting recklessly in the proper sense of the term.

His Lordship acknowledged the notion that there is a minimum content beneath which the office held is not the office of a trustee. Nevertheless, a trustee who excludes her liability for all loss caused by breach of trust (except losses caused by her own actual fraud) will not be subject to any liability for breach of trust. Thus, while it is accepted that one does not have an arrangement which can properly be defined as being a trust if the obligations imposed on the fiduciary are too slight, almost all of the liabilities ordinarily associated with being a trustee can be excluded. The result would be that, in practice, a trustee with the protection of an exclusion of liability of clause will face almost no liabilities for breach of trust, provided she is not actually dishonest. However, merely requiring someone not to be dishonest does not put too much strain on their conscience. Nor does it make it seem as though there is anything very special about a trust.

The question of course remains: what is the minimum content beneath which one will not be a trustee at all? Denying the existence of any duty of care and skill is at odds with the general duty of care provided in s 1(1) of the Trustee Act 2000 (enacted after the decision of

---

489   *Armitage v Nurse* [1998] Ch 241; *Taylor v Midland Bank Trust Co* (2000) 2 ITELR 439; *Bogg v Raper* (1998) *The Times*, 22 April; *Wight v Olswang* (1999) *The Times*, 18 May.
490   [1998] Ch 241, [1997] 2 All ER 705: adopting the language of DJ Hayton.
491   Considered in para 9.3 below.

the Court of Appeal in *Armitage v Nurse*) which requires that a trustee 'must exercise such care and skill as is reasonable in the circumstances', thus imposing a partial duty to take care and to exercise skill if that provision is not expressly excluded in the trust instrument. Nevertheless, the approach of the court in *Armitage v Nurse* was to pitch that minimum content at merely requiring the trustee to act honestly; the court would have held differently if the trustees had acted dishonestly or fraudulently because in such a situation the exclusion clause would have had no effect. To demonstrate that there has been fraud would be difficult to prove in a situation in which the trustee did not take any direct, personal benefit.[492] The duties of acting honestly and in good faith are seemingly not capable of being excluded. By way of further example, the trustees' duty to account[493] to the beneficiaries cannot be excluded by the trust instrument because it is one of the core obligations of trusteeship.[494]

The test for dishonesty which was applied by Millett LJ required:

> at the minimum an intention of the part of the trustee to pursue a particular course of action, either knowing that it is contrary to the interests of the beneficiaries or being recklessly indifferent whether it is contrary to their interests or not.[495]

This is, it is suggested, a predominantly subjective approach to dishonesty, being based on the defendant's knowledge, is at odds with the objective test for dishonesty set out in *Royal Brunei Airlines v Tan*[496] as considered in Chapter 20.[497] The weakness with Millett LJ's approach is that one can escape liability simply by claiming that subjectively you see nothing wrong in what you have done.

Nevertheless, in general terms, to find that the office of trusteeship equates to a requirement merely of acting honestly and of rendering accounts does not appear to make the office of trustee different in quality from many other, non-fiduciary relationships. Millett LJ even adopted the words of Sir Nathaniel Lindley MR to the effect that as 'my old master, the late Selwyn LJ, used to say "The main duty of a trustee is to commit *judicious* breaches of trust"'.[498] That is, not to get caught, not to commit breaches for which liability is not excluded, and not to commit breaches which will cause loss. The effect of these *dicta* is that the trustees' duties are not to avoid breaches of trust but rather a trustee will still be obeying the letter of the law in performing her duties if she only commits breaches of trust which are excused within the precise terms of her trusteeship. In truth, what the Court of Appeal was doing in *Armitage v Nurse* was recognising the preference for professional trustees to be able to restrict their liabilities by means of careful drafting of the trust instrument. The exclusion clause in that case was upheld as being valid because to have done otherwise might be to rob

---

492   This issue is considered at para 9.5.2 below in relation to investment of trust funds.
493   As considered in para 8.4.8 above. See Thomas and Hudson, 2004, 358, para 10.130.
494   *Armitage v Nurse* [1998] Ch 241, 253, *per* Millett LJ.
495   This approach is followed in *Gwembe Valley Development Co v Koshy* [2004] 1 BCLC 131, 170; *Newgate Stud Company v Penfold* [2004] EWHC 2993 (Ch), [249], *per* David Richards J. Cf *Isaac v Isaac* [2004] All ER (D) 71.
496   [1995] 2 AC 378.
497   See section 20.2 generally.
498   [1998] Ch 241, 250, [1997] 2 All ER 705, 709, quoting *Perrins v Bellamy* [1899] 1 Ch 797, 798, *per* Sir Nathaniel Lindley MR.

professional trustees of the protection of wide-ranging exclusion clauses in the future with the result that they may refuse to act as trustees. The principal objection to this approach is that the fiduciary nature of the trust relationship is thus transformed into something akin to a merely contractual relationship between settlor and trustee. If exclusion clauses can displace many of the trustee's obligations to act in the utmost good faith, not to permit conflicts of interest, and to invest as though managing the property of someone for whom the trustee felt morally bound to provide, then the nature of trusteeship fails to have any particular resonance. It is like being a party to an ordinary contract and not like being someone who is subject to fiduciary duties.

More specifically, the decision in *Walker v Stones*[499] took a subtly but significantly (I would suggest) different tack to the decision in *Armitage v Nurse*. The issue in *Armitage v Nurse*, strictly put, was to decide whether or not the trustees had acted dishonestly within the meaning of the exclusion clause in that case. A similar provision was contained in the trust deed in *Walker v Stones*. The trustees of a discretionary trust in this case, who were solicitors, were exempted from all liability except 'wilful fraud or dishonesty'. The Court of Appeal in *Walker v Stones* took the view that the proper test to be applied in deciding whether or not a trustee had acted dishonestly was that applied by the Privy Council in *Royal Brunei Airlines v Tan*[500] to the effect that one should consider whether or not the trustee had acted as an honest trustee would have acted in the circumstances. The consequences of such a test is that the court does not look to see whether or not the trustee has acted deceitfully, but rather considers the objective notion of whether she failed to do what an honest person would have done. This latter, objective approach is far broader than asking the question whether or not the trustee knew that she was being deceitful. In relation specifically to exclusion of liability clauses, the court in *Walker v Stones* was of the view that if the trustee took the view unreasonably that her actions were honest then the exclusion clause could not be relied upon. Therefore, the notion of honesty which was bound up in the precise terms of these particular exclusion clauses is broadened here again to make trustees liable for any breach of their duties which they could not reasonably have considered to be honest exercises of their duties. Consequently, it was not open to the solicitors acting as trustees in that case to argue that they did not realise that their behaviour would have been considered to have been dishonest by an objective person nor that they considered their actions (though objectively dishonest) to have been in the interests of the beneficiaries.

The issue could be considered in the following manner. The trustee would argue that she only agreed to act as a trustee on the basis that her liability was limited to the extent of the exclusion of liability clause. Therefore, the trustee would not be acting in bad conscience by insisting that she should not be liable for any default beyond that specified in the exclusion of liability clause because she did not agree to be bound by anything else. Thus, on the one hand it could be said on behalf of the trustees that they did not agree to act as trustees unless their liabilities were excluded by the trust instrument. Alternatively, it might be said that if someone agrees to act as a trustee then she must be taken to accept the general obligations of good conscience and good management required of a trustee and therefore that to allow

499   [2001] QB 902. This case has been doubted in relation to its findings on the issue of reflected loss in *Gardner v Parker* [2004] BCLC 554 in the wake of the decision of the House of Lords in *Johnson v Gore-Wood* [2002] AC 1, [2001] 1 All ER 481, *Giles v Rind* [2002] 4 All ER 977, [2003] 1 BCLC 1.

500   [1995] 2 AC 378. See now also *Twinsectra v Yardley* [2002] 2 WLR 802, [2002] 2 All ER 377.

extensive exclusion clauses to be effective subverts the necessary stringency of the office of trustee. Thus, on the other hand, it could be argued that acting as a trustee should be deemed necessarily to incorporate a range of obligations which include liability to account for breach of trust which cannot be excluded at all if the obligations which are owed by trustees are to remain special and unique to the particular office of being a trustee. There is no perfect answer to this debate: either the trustees escape liability and impose a loss on the beneficiaries, or the trustees are forced to bear liabilities which they had not agreed to bear.

This issue is considered further in Chapter 21.[501]

Statutory restrictions on limitation of liability

There are important categories of trustee who are not permitted to exclude their liabilities for breach of trust. The restrictions on exclusion of liability are all provided for by statute as part of public policy. So, pension fund trustees are not permitted to exclude their liabilities;[502] trustees of unit trusts are not permitted to exclude their liabilities;[503] and trustees of debenture trusts are not permitted to exclude their liabilities.[504]

The oddity of the commercial trusts

It seems to me that what Millett LJ was seeking to do in *Armitage v Nurse, inter alia*, was to make the trust more attractive to commercial people. More specifically, it seems that Millett LJ was seeking to make the office of trustee more attractive to commercial, professional people who will wish to act as trustee but who will not want to assume the very broad liabilities which ordinarily come with that office. In consequence, to make trusts law seem commercially astute, Millett LJ held that trustees should be able to restrict their liabilities by insisting on the inclusion of an express provision to that effect in the trust instrument – an approach which was approved of expressly in *Bogg v Raper*, as considered above. However, while the trusts case law is seeking to make itself appear to be more commercial, the most commercial aspects of financial law are moving in the opposite direction. As set out in the immediately preceding section there are three categories of trustees, who are involved in the most advanced investment structures in the modern economy, who are not permitted to exclude their liabilities. They are not permitted to exclude their liabilities because public policy recognises that the imposition of stringent fiduciary duties on trustees, including full liability for breach of trust, is essential if those trustees are to be held in check and required to act in the most professional manner possible. This, it is suggested, is a standard of behaviour which should be required of all trustees in all circumstances.

The paradox in the law on exemption clauses

The present organisation of the law on trustee exemption clauses contains one tremendous paradox, namely that the more professional a trustee is, the more likely she is to have a term

---

501 See para 21.2.4.
502 Pensions Act 1995, s 33.
503 Financial Services and Markets Act 2000, s 253.
504 Companies Act 2006, s 750.

included in the trust instrument which governs her actions so as to exclude her liability when she acts negligently in the discharge of her fiduciary duties; whereas, a non-professional trustee who would probably not know that such a provision could be included in a trust instrument would therefore be held fully liable for breach of trust if she causes some loss to the trust despite never having held herself out as being a professional trustee in the first place. Thus, the qualified and experienced professional trustee escapes liability for causing loss completely, whereas the non-qualified and inexperienced trustee will bear full liability. There is something intuitively wrong with that, I would suggest.

The Law Commission's reform proposals

The Law Commission has made proposals for an extra-statutory change to the law dealing with the exclusion of trustees' liabilities in its paper 'Trustee Exemption Clauses'.[505] The somewhat toothless proposal that was made in this paper was to avoid legislation imposing duties on trustees and instead to rely on a statement of best practice whereby professional trustees should be required to bring any exclusion clause to the attention of the settlor at the time of creating the trust and to ensure that the settlor understands its effect. Thus, a welcome distinction is drawn between professional and non-professional trustees. However, there is no meaningful obligation – certainly no legal obligation – to be placed on trustees to control their use of exclusion clauses.

8.5.2 Disclaimer, release and extinguishment of powers

Disclaimer

Once a person has accepted the office of trustee, any fiduciary power such as the office of trustee may be disclaimed in accordance with s 156 of the Law of Property Act 1925. Such a disclaimer must be a complete disclaimer and may not simply disclaim a part of the power.[506] The fiduciary is not capable of exercising that power once it has been disclaimed. Alternatively, the beneficiaries could agree by deed[507] to release the trustee from her obligations in whole or in part.[508]

Release

In circumstances in which the beneficiaries agree formally to release the trustee from any liability, the equitable doctrine of release will operate so as to protect that trustee from any liability arising from her breach of trust.[509] However, that does not prevent the

---

505 Law Commission, *Trustee Exemption Clauses*, Law Com No 301 (Cmnd 6874).
506 *Re Eyre* (1883) 49 LT 259; *Saul v Pattinson* (1886) 34 WR 561; *Re Lord and Fullerton's Contract* [1986] 1 Ch 228, 233.
507 Law of Property Act 1925, s 155(1).
508 Conveyancing Act 1881, s 52. Cf *Weller v Kerr* (1866) LR 1 Sc&D 11, whereby a power coupled with a trust or a collateral power could not be released in this fashion under the general law, although this position was reversed by the Law of Property Act 1925, s 155.
509 *Lyall v Edwards* (1861) 6 H & N 337; 158 ER 139; *Ecclesiastical Commissioners for England v North Eastern Railway Co* (1877) 4 Ch D 845; *Turner v Turner* (1880) 14 Ch D 829.

beneficiaries from seeking equitable relief in respect of any factor which was not made known to them at the time of granting the release or which arises outside the terms of that release.[510] Therefore, in a situation in which employees signed a release form in respect of any breach of duty by their employer, it was held that this would not prevent a claim for relief in relation to any stigma caused to their careers when it subsequently emerged that their employer bank had been dealing dishonestly.[511]

8.6 CONTROL OF THE TRUSTEES

The trustees may be controlled by the beneficiaries by means of an application to the court. The court has an inherent jurisdiction to make orders in relation to the adminis-tration of a trust. The court may make orders by way variously of (a) giving directions, (b) assuming administrative control, (c) judicial review (in a private law sense) of the trustees' actions, or (d) setting aside any decision of a trustee made by taking into account irrelevant considerations or failing to take into account relevant considerations.

8.6.1 Control of the trustees by the beneficiaries

This section considers the ways in which beneficiaries are able to exert control over the administration of the trust, generally by application to the court. It should be recalled that the logic of the law of express trusts is that there must be some person in the role of beneficiary in whose favour the court can decree performance of the trust.[512] Therefore, it is of the essence of a trust that the beneficiaries are able to petition the court in relation to the actions or omissions of trustees[513] and that the court has an inherent jurisdiction to supervise the administration of a trust.[514] This right to petition the court rests with objects of a discre-tionary trust as much as beneficiaries with vested rights under a bare trust.[515] Typically, control will be exercised by petition to the court seeking a declaration as to the manner in which the trustees are required to act. The most complete form of control for absolutely entitled, *sui juris* beneficiaries acting together is that they are able to terminate the trust by directing that the trustees deliver the trust property to them.[516]

What is less clear is the basis on which the trustees can be controlled during the life of the trust, that is, without calling for the termination of the trust by delivery of the property to the beneficiaries. It is clear that the trustee cannot decide the terms of the trust.[517] Therefore, the trustee is necessarily bound by the terms of the trust, entitling the beneficiary to petition the court to have the trust property administered in accordance with the terms of the trust. In *Re Brockbank*,[518] it was held that where the court is unable to interfere in the selection of

---

510 *BCCI v Ali* [2000] 3 All ER 51.
511 *Ibid.* Cf *Malik v BCCI* [1997] 3 All ER 1.
512 *Morice v Bishop of Durham* (1805) 10 Ves 522.
513 *Ibid.* See section 4.2 above.
514 *Schmidt v Rosewood Trust Ltd* [2003] 2 WLR 1442.
515 See, eg, *Re Ralli's WT* [1964] 2 WLR 144.
516 *Saunders v Vautier* (1841) 4 Beav 115.
517 *Re Brooks' ST* [1939] 1 Ch 993.
518 [1948] 1 All ER 287.

trustees, the beneficiaries are similarly unable to act. The case of *Tempest v Lord Camoys*[519] illustrates the principle that the court will not interfere in the appointment of a new trustee, provided that is done in accordance with the terms of the trust and not in contravention of public policy. Furthermore, it is not clear how this interacts with the s 26(3) of the Law of Property Act 1925 duty to consult with beneficiaries under a trust for sale, now under s 11 of the Trusts of Land and Appointment of Trustees Act 1996.

8.6.2 Control of the trustees by the court

The mode of control of the trustees by the court is dependent on the nature of the power

The extent of the court's control of the trustees will depend upon the precise nature of the trust, and whether the power given to the trustee is a personal power or a fiduciary power. Trustees are required to consider the exercise of trust powers: they cannot exercise them entirely capriciously.[520] A trustee can act however she likes where it is a personal power.[521] In this latter circumstance, the court will not interfere with the *bona fide* exercise of the power. Where trustees have a power of appointment, they are required to consider the exercise of their discretion and the range of the objects of their power.[522] The nature of the trustees' general duties under the various forms of power were considered in detail in section 3.5 above.

Directions

Trustees are entitled at any stage to petition the court for guidance as to the proper performance of their duties. Trustees are entitled to seek guidance as to the nature and extent of their duties,[523] as to the effect of trust documents,[524] and generally to ensure that they do not commit a breach of trust.[525] The Civil Procedure Rules contains the means for making such an application in Part 64.[526] Equally, the beneficiaries may make an application to prevent or require the doing of some act.[527]

Administration

When the functioning of the trust has become impossible or the disputes between the parties have reached an insurmountable obstacle, an application may be made to the court asking the court to direct the proper administration of the trust.[528] The court in such a circumstance may

---

519 (1882) 21 Ch D 571.
520 *Re Hay's ST* [1981] 3 All ER 786.
521 *Ibid.*
522 *Ibid; Turner v Turner* (1978) 122 SJ 696, CA.
523 *Re Buckton* [1907] 2 Ch 406, 414; *McDonald v Horn* [1995] 1 All ER 961, 970. A protector of a trust may make a similar application: *Re Omar Family Trust* [2000] WTLR 713; *Re Hare Trust* (2001) 4 ITELR 288, as may a beneficiary.
524 *Re Berens* [1888] WN 95; *Re Freme's Contract* [1895] 2 Ch 256.
525 *Ibid.*
526 CPR Pt 64, r 64.2(1).
527 *Suffolk v Lawrence* (1884) 32 WR 899.
528 *Talbot v Earl of Radnor* (1834) 3 My & K 252; *Re Gyhon* (1885) 29 Ch D 834; *Re Blake* (1885) 29 Ch D 913.

make an order for the replacement of some or all of the trustees or make a declaration as to the probity of the course of action which some or all of the trustees had proposed to take.[529]

Judicial review of trustees' actions[530]

Trustees have obligations under trusts and they may also have a range of discretionary trust or fiduciary mere powers. Any failure to perform an obligation under a trust may be the subject of an action for breach of trust if there is any loss or an application for directions if no loss is suffered. As to powers, a further question may arise as to the beneficiaries' rights to challenge the exercise of a power. The question then arises as to the extent to which the court will consider itself empowered to intervene to compel the exercise of some power, or alternatively to declare that a decision has been reached inappropriately. It was stated by Lord Truro in *Re Beloved Wilkes's Charity*[531] that:

> the duty of supervision on the part of the Court will thus be confined to the question of the honesty, integrity, and fairness with which the deliberation has been conducted, and will not be extended to the accuracy of the conclusion arrived at, except in particular cases.

Therefore, the form of judicial review at issue here is concerned with the honesty, integrity and fairness of the trustees' decisions or actions, but will not revisit the content of any such decision. In other words, it is for the trustees to make their own decisions about the management of the trust (always provided that there has been no breach of trust), whereas the court will only consider the probity of such decisions in relation to honesty, integrity and fairness.

Trustees also owe a large number of obligations under general trusts law beyond the limitations of the basis for judicial review of trustees' actions set out immediately above. It may be, therefore, that the breach of any such principle may give rise to such a judicial review. For example, in general terms, trustees are required to act prudently,[532] and also to exercise their powers in a responsible manner according to the purpose of that power.[533] So, if a trustee of a discretionary trust chose to advance the whole of the income from a trust fund to an object of the trust to whom she was engaged to be married so that they could pay for improvements to their home, then the question would arise whether or not the trustee had acted honestly and it would be open to the other objects of the discretionary trust to seek a judicial review of that trustee's decisions. Alternatively, if the trustee had exercised her power so as to advance the whole of the trust income equally between the objects of a discretionary trust, while excluding herself despite being one of the objects of the trust, then there would be no suggestion that a question as to her honesty, integrity or fairness arose. Thus, judicial review is limited to circumstances in which an issue of honesty, integrity or fairness would arise.

In the ordinary exercise of a discretionary trust power it has been held that the court will not interfere with or review the accuracy of a decision in relation to a power which has been

---

529   See generally *Re Cabburn* (1882) 46 LT 848.
530   In general terms, see Thomas and Hudson, 2004, Chapter 20.
531   (1851) 3 Mac & G 440, 448.
532   *Learoyd v Whiteley* (1887) 12 App Cas 727; *Eaton v Buchanan* [1911] AC 253.
533   *McPhail v Doulton* [1971] AC 424, 449, *per* Lord Wilberforce.

exercised in good faith.[534] It has been held, exceptionally, that a power (which is not expressed to be uncontrollable in a trust instrument) may be interfered with by the court even if there has not been any bad faith: for example, where applications of trust property for the maintenance of children by means of their education were deemed by the court not to be in the beneficiaries' best interests.[535] It seems that the courts are more inclined to interfere with the trustees' actions where the beneficiaries are children and the powers being exercised are for the maintenance of such children, particularly where the trustees have acted capriciously in the exercise of their powers,[536] or have acted on the basis of manifestly improper reasons.[537] More generally, courts have interfered with a trustees' discretions in circumstances in which the trustees have failed to examine the contents of deeds before signing them,[538] or have acted in a way which was so unreasonable as to appear vexatious.[539] Where a power of appointment was expressly specified to be exercisable only before a given date, the court would not interfere with the trustees' power so as to force them to exercise it given that it was a mere power of appointment drafted in permissive form.[540] Therefore, there had not been any unconscionable act simply in the trustees failing to exercise that power, nor could any proceedings be begun on the basis of breach of trust on this basis: in either case, the trustees were permitted not to exercise that power.

Where a company has a power[541] to distribute the surplus of an employee pension fund (where that fund is actually held by a trust company), the company has a fiduciary duty which governs the manner in which it distributes the proceeds of that pension fund.[542] This power is incapable of review by the court unless it is exercised capriciously or outside the scope of the trust.[543] In *Mettoy Pension Fund Trustees Ltd v Evans*,[544] because the power was held to be a fiduciary power, it was held that it could not be released or ignored by the fiduciary. This meant that the company was always trustee of that power and that it had no beneficial interest in the fund. Therefore, when the company went into insolvency, the liquidator could not take possession of the contents of the trust fund and use it to pay off ordinary creditors of the company because the employee-contributors to the fund were not volunteers but rather beneficiaries under a trust.[545]

---

534 *Gisborne v Gisborne* (1877) 2 App Cas 300, 305, *per* Lord Cairns; *Re Schneider* (1906) 22 TLR 223, 226, *per* Warrington J. In circumstances in which the trustees' discretionary powers are expressed to be 'absolute' powers, there is a difficult question as to whether or not those powers are justiciable at all. An absolute power, assuming it to be a fiduciary power and not a personal power, cannot in principle be beyond the control of the court. If the power-holder is a fiduciary, then those obligations considered above in section 8.3, requiring that the trustees refrain from conflicts of interest and so forth, must necessarily be capable of being applied by the court.

535 *Tabor v Brooks* (1878) 10 Ch D 273, *per* Malins VC. Cf, however, *Re Schneider* (1906) 22 TLR 223.

536 *Re Hodges* (1878) 7 Ch D 754; *Tabor v Brooks* (1878) 10 Ch D 273.

537 *Klug v Klug* [1918] 2 Ch 67.

538 *Turner v Turner* (1978) 122 SJ 696.

539 *Re Chapman* (1895) 72 LT 66.

540 *Breadner v Granville-Grossman* [2001] Ch 523; applying *Cooper v Martin* (1867) LR 3 Ch App 47 and *Re Hastings-Bass* [1975] Ch 25, CA.

541 Whether a fiduciary mere power or a power under a discretionary trust.

542 *McPhail v Doulton* [1970] 2 WLR 1110, *per* Lord Wilberforce; *Mettoy Pensions Fund* [1990] 1 WLR 1587.

543 *Mettoy Pensions Fund* [1990] 1 WLR 1587, *per* Warner J.

544 *Ibid.*

545 See Chapter 24 on this issue.

Trustees must give informed consideration to the exercise of their discretion. For example, the trustees may need to have reference to actuarial principles to come to such a decision.[546] The exercise of the decision of the trustees in *Stannard v Fisons*[547] was found by Dillon LJ to be capable of review where such knowledge 'might materially have affected the trustees' decision'. One further argument in this context would be that a beneficiary is entitled to see documents with reference to the trust as part of the trustee's duty to account to the beneficiary of the trust, as considered above.

8.6.3 Setting aside trustees' decisions for taking into account irrelevant considerations or for failing to take into account relevant considerations

The trustees' decisions may be set aside if they have taken into account irrelevant considerations or if they have failed to take into account relevant considerations. This part of the courts' armoury, known as the principle in *Re Hastings-Bass*,[548] was considered in detail at para 8.3.13 above. It is suggested that, as well as being a part of the trustees' general duties, it may also be thought of as a way in which the beneficiaries, through the courts, can police the manner in which the trustees exercise their powers. Broadly put, the courts' power is a power to set aside trustees' decisions for taking into account irrelevant considerations or for failing to take into account relevant considerations. The complexities associated with this analysis are considered at para 8.3.13 as aforesaid.

---

546 *Stannard v Fisons* [1992] IRLR 27.
547 *Ibid.*
548 *Re Hastings-Bass* [1975] Ch 25.

Chapter 9

The investment of trusts

OVERVIEW

*The trustee's general duties of investment can be summarised in the following principles:
to act prudently and safely; to act fairly between beneficiaries; to do the best for the
beneficiaries. The best interests of the beneficiaries are generally taken to be their financial interests. Therefore, non-financial considerations must not be taken into account
when deciding what to invest in, except in the exceptional circumstances where all the
actual or potential beneficiaries are adults with strict moral views on particular matters.*

*The Trustee Act 2000 sets out the statutory code relating to the investment of trust funds
and the delegation of the trustees' duties to agents, custodians and nominees. Of particular
significance are the duty to act with skill and care, the duty to act reasonably, the duty to
take proper advice, and the duty to observe the standard investment criteria that one must
both invest suitably and in an appropriately diversified manner. The Trustee Delegation
Act 1999 deals with enduring powers of attorney relating to trustees' obligations.*

9.1 THE USE OF TRUSTS AS INVESTMENT VEHICLES

9.1.1 The scope of this chapter[1]

The trust has a complex provenance: its progenitors emerged in English history as early as the
13th century as a means of recognising that a number of people might have simultaneous
rights of use over land and other property.[2] The rules which sustain the modern trust were

---

1   This chapter follows the structure of previous editions of this text combined with the impression of Alastair
    Hudson, *The Law of Finance*, Sweet & Maxwell, 2009, Chapters 8 and 9.
2   On the general roots of uses and trusts, see Chapter 2 above.

developed in the mid-17th and mid-19th centuries, principally in relation to family trusts which allocated rights in the wealth of landed families.[3] From these beginnings the trust became ever more institutional (that is, founded on a series of strictly observed formalities)[4] despite its heritage as a tool of the courts of equity in recognising entitlements to property beyond the common law.[5] By the end of the 20th century, the most visible caucus of litigation relating to the use of trusts was concerned with its application to commercial situations.[6] In the 1990s, the moral heritage of the trust as a creature of 'conscience' was reclaimed by the courts in the complex matter of applying concepts generated for family law situations to the commercial context.[7] These questions are central to the operation of the trust as an investment structure. The intervention of the Trustee Act (TA) 2000 demonstrates that the principles generated over the centuries by these various aspects of the trust do not meet the complexities of modern investment practice, the use of professional investment managers in the investment of trust funds, and the difficulties associated both with wanting trustees to be careful with trust property while also wanting them to generate the best available return for the beneficiaries.

The focus of this chapter is therefore on three facets of the trust as an investment tool. First, the issues surrounding the moral foundations of the trust and its application to the commercial context. Secondly, the rules of trusts law relating specifically to the investment of ordinary trust funds, the obligations of trustees in such situations, and the concomitant rights of beneficiaries, particularly as understood differently by the case law and the TA 2000. Thirdly, an analysis of the developing categories of investment trust. It will be important to bear in mind some of the mismatches between judge-made obligations on trustees and standard commercial practice, in particular those relating to professional trustees' contractual limitation of their liability, the structure of investment trust funds, and differences between 'professional-commercial' and 'informal' trusts.[8]

9.1.2 The utility of private trusts for investment purposes

As we have considered throughout this Part 3, the office of trustee places an onerous task on the person who accepts that office. Bound up with this set of obligations are duties in relation

---

3 The importance of such arrangements to the upper middle classes is evident from great literary works of the period such as Jane Austen's *Sense and Sensibility* and Charles Dickens's *Bleak House*, in which the reduced circumstances of the main protagonists are caused by a fee entail and chancery litigation over a will respectively.
4 In particular rules as to certainty of subject, object and intention (eg, *Knight v Knight* [1925] Ch 835); the perpetuities rules (eg, *Re Wood* [1949] 1 All ER 1100); and rules as to completely constituted trusts (*Milroy v Lord* (1862) 4 De GF & J 264).
5 Maitland, 1936, Chapter 1; Hanbury, 1934, 55 *et seq*.
6 A plethora of banking law cases concerning the imposition of constructive and resulting trusts, including: *Agip v Jackson* [1990] Ch 265, 286, *per* Millett J, CA; [1991] Ch 547; *Barlow Clowes International Ltd (In Liquidation) v Vaughan* [1992] 4 All ER 22; *Bishopsgate v Homan* [1995] 1 WLR 31; *Boscawen v Bajwa* [1996] 1 WLR 328; *Chase Manhattan Bank NA v Israel-British Bank (London) Ltd* [1981] 1 Ch 105; *Re Goldcorp* [1995] 1 AC 74; *Guinness Mahon v Kensington & Chelsea RLBC* [1998] 2 All ER 272; *Kleinwort Benson v Sandwell Borough Council* [1994] 4 All ER 890, *per* Hobhouse J; *Kleinwort Benson v South Tyneside MBC* [1994] 4 All ER 972, *per* Hobhouse J; *MacJordan Construction Ltd v Brookmount Erostin Ltd* [1992] BCLC 350; *Macmillan v Bishopsgate (No 3)* [1996] 1 WLR 387; *Westdeutsche Landesbank v Islington LBC* [1996] AC 669, HL.
7 *Target Holdings v Redferns* [1996] 1 AC 421, [1995] 3 WLR 352, [1995] 3 All ER 785; *Westdeutsche Landesbank v Islington LBC* [1996] AC 669, HL.
8 Which could be rendered as being similar to the distinction between *conscious express trusts* and *unconscious express trusts*.

to the treatment of the trust fund.[9] Thus far we have seen negative obligations requiring the trustee not to act outwith the terms of the trust nor to treat the beneficiary or the trust property otherwise than in accordance with those terms. A different context arises in relation to the investment of the trust fund. In that context, as we shall see, there are positive obligations on the trustee to generate the best return on the property which is reasonable in the circumstances. As will emerge below, there is a mixture of case law and statute in this area. What is readily apparent is the surprising level of restriction in the law before 2000 as to the nature of investments that may be made and the nature of the obligations imposed on the trustee. Historically, this stringency can be attributed to the fact that the rules on investment of trusts were devised for family trusts in which the duty of the trustee was to preserve the trust fund for future generations while also ensuring that current generations would receive suitable incomes.

Those rules will cover a number of very different circumstances. A trust can be used specifically for investment purposes. Unit trusts (equivalent to the US mutual funds) or investment vehicles like hedge funds (occasionally structured as trusts, rather than companies or partnerships) are based on the ordinary principles of trust. In such a situation, the trustees will be investment professionals with suitable expertise to choose between the available investment options. The terms of the trust will be set out in the terms of the contract under which the trustees agree to offer their services. Typically, this will take the form of a Conduct of Business letter constructed to comply with Financial Services Authority regulatory rules.[10] Alternatively, the trustee may be someone who has no expertise in financial markets but who is responsible for the trust fund. The question will therefore be as to the comparative levels of obligation to generate the best possible return from the trust. Evidently, the nature of the trust property itself will have an impact on the extent of that obligation in any particular circumstance.

The bulk of the case law considered in this chapter concerns investment in financial market securities.

9.2 INTRODUCTION TO THE PRINCIPLES OF THE TRUSTEE ACT 2000

9.2.1 The scope of the Trustee Act 2000

The Trustee Act 2000 ('TA 2000') introduces a code of provisions which relate primarily to the appointment of agents, nominees and custodians by trustees and particularly introduces provisions in relation to the investment of trust funds.[11] The TA 2000 does not apply generally to pension funds[12] nor to authorised unit trusts,[13] both of which have statutory and regulatory regimes of their own. That it was considered necessary to introduce a statute to govern the investment of trust funds is interesting in itself, particularly when taken together with the statutory codes which already govern pension funds and unit trusts, because it illustrates the

---

9   See section 8.3 above.
10 Financial Services and Markets Act 2000, s 1.
11 See generally Hicks, 2001.
12 TA 2000, s 36; considered in Chapter 24.
13 *Ibid*, s 37.

perception that the general law of trusts was not sufficient to protect the beneficiaries from the misfeasance of trustees. In relation to professional trustees authorised under the Financial Services and Markets Act 2000 to sell financial instruments, as with trustees of pension funds and unit trusts, there is a statutory regulator created which regulates the activities of such trustees and shortcuts the need for the beneficiary to rely on the general law of trusts when making a complaint.

Significantly, the TA 2000 provides a form of statutory long-stop and does not set out mandatory rules for the administration and investment of trusts: that is, it is possible for the provisions of a trust instrument to exclude the operation of the Act either by express provision or by inference from the construction of any such provisions.[14] The TA 2000 provides that, for example, 'the duty of care [imposed on trustees][15] does not apply if or in so far as it appears from the trust instrument that the duty is not meant to apply'.[16] Thus, settlors have the freedom to create whatever arrangements they wish without the interference of mandatory, legal rules which might prohibit certain forms of action. The role of the TA 2000 is therefore to supply trust provisions where otherwise there would be a gap in the trusts provisions.

9.2.2 The meaning of 'trustee' in this context

What remains unclear within the terms of the TA 2000 is what exactly is meant by the term 'trustee' itself. The legislation itself makes general reference only to a 'trustee', but does not make clear whether or not that is to apply only to express trustees (that is, trustees who have accepted the office possibly subject to a detailed trust instrument) or whether it refers also to constructive trustees, trustees of resulting trusts, or trustees of implied trusts like that in *Paul v Constance*[17] – the common feature between all those latter forms of trust being that the trustees may not know of their trusteeship until the court order which confirms it. Therefore, it is possible that there are trustees who do not know of their obligations and who are in breach of the positive obligations in the TA 2000 which apply in the absence of an exclusion clause – such as to produce a policy statement for the investment of trust funds and so forth.[18] The structure of the Act, and its references to exclusion of liability in the trust instrument, indicate that the legislative draftsperson was focused on such express trusts formed by way of an instrument.[19]

9.2.3 The repeal of the Trustee Investment Act 1961

The Trustee Investment Act 1961 is repealed by the TA 2000.[20] The 1961 Act had previously obliged trustees to split the trust fund in half and to hold each half in very conservative forms of investment as specified by that Act. The principal purpose of the 2000 Act is to permit

---

14 See eg *ibid*, Sched 1, para 7 and other provisions referred to in the text to follow.
15 Considered below at para 9.2.2.
16 TA 2000, Sched 1, para 7.
17 [1977] 1 WLR 527; considered above at para 3.3.1.
18 TA 2000, s 4.
19 Eg *ibid*, ss 9, 22, Sched 1, para 7, all of which make reference to existing trust instruments or provisions.
20 TA 2000, s 7(3).

trustees to act as though the absolute owners of the property and to invest in whatever investments they consider appropriate within the terms of their investment powers as set out in the
trust instrument.[21]

9.2.4 A map of the law on the investment of trusts

*The correct method with which to approach a question relating to the
investment of a trust*

This chapter is concerned with identifying the extent of the trustees' obligations when investing
the trust fund and consequently with considering the circumstances in which the trustees will
be liable for breach of trust if those obligations are breached. The discussion to follow may
seem to be quite complex unless we introduce the various sources of the law on the investment
of trusts. This short section gives you an outline of the questions you should ask – and the order
in which you should ask them – when considering a problem relating to trustees' obligations
in relation to the investment of the trust fund. It is suggested that you use these lists of principles as a check-list when considering any set of facts to see which issues are significant.

There are three places from which you will find the trustees' investment obligations in the
following order, to see whether or not there has been a breach of trust:

1   The trust instrument.
2   The provisions of the Trustee Act 2000.
3   The case law on trustees' investment duties.

Then you should consider:

4   Any other obligations of the trustees under case law.
5   Defences to breach of trust.
6   Liability and remedies for breach of trust.

Each of these sources of the law on investment of trusts should be considered in that order.

(1) Breach of the terms of the trust instrument

If the trust instrument imposes an obligation on the trustee, then any breach of that obligation
will constitute a breach of trust,[22] as discussed in Chapter 8.[23] In such a situation the trustee
would be reliant on one of the defences to a claim for breach of trust, as discussed in section
18.4 below, such as the defence in s 61 of the Trustee Act 1925 that she ought to be excused
by the court on the basis that she acted honestly and reasonably in the circumstances.

If a trustee wants to be excused from such a *prima facie* breach of the terms of the trust
instrument, then she will need to demonstrate that she has acted appropriately within the

---

21   See section 9.3 following.
22   *Clough v Bond* (1838) 8 LJ Ch 51.
23   Section 8.3.2.

terms of the TA 2000 or under the case law principles. Alternatively, if the trust instrument has no investment obligations provision or if there is such a provision but it omits to cover something important, then the trustee's obligations will also fail to be judged by reference to the terms of the TA 2000 or the case law principles.

(2) The structure of the Trustee Act 2000

The TA 2000 should be considered next because it was enacted after the case law and because legislation is sovereign over case law principles. At the time of writing there have been no cases on the investment provisions of the Trustee Act 2000. As is explained below, the entirety of the TA 2000 or any part of it may be expressly excluded by the trust instrument if the settlor wants to impose different types of obligation on the trustees.[24] However, assuming that there is no such provision in the trust instrument, the significant requirements of the TA 2000 are as follows:

1   The trustees have the power to act as though they were the absolute owners of the trust property themselves: that is, without any restriction (unless there is some restriction included in the trust instrument) (s 3(1)), except for investments in land (s 3(3)).
2   The trustees have a duty to exercise such skill and care as is reasonable in the circumstances (s 1(1)).
3   The trustees must have regard to the standard investment criteria when making investments (s 4).
    a   The first standard investment criterion is the need to ensure that the proposed investments are suitable for a trust of the type that the trustees are managing.
    b   The second standard investment criterion is the need to ensure that the trust's investment are sufficiently well diversified for a trust of that type.
4   The trustees must take proper advice as to the investment of the trust (s 5).

The first provision grants the trustees a power to act. Provisions numbered 2 to 4 in this list impose obligations on the trustees. If the trustees fail to obey these obligations they will have committed a breach of trust. If the trust suffers a loss as a consequence of that breach of trust then the trustees will be personally liable to account for that loss to the beneficiaries of the trust.

(3) The case law principles

At the time of writing there have been no cases on the interpretation of the TA 2000 and therefore it is suggested that the old case law may be used by the courts as a guide to interpretation, including those situations in which the Act is different in principle from the case law. Also there will be situations in which the TA 2000 has been excluded by the terms of the trust instrument or situations in which the issue at hand is outwith the scope of the Act: in either of these situations the case law will be decisive of the extent of the trustees' obligations. The principal obligations are:

24 TA 2000, s 6.

1   The duty to act as though a prudent person of business acting on behalf of someone for whom one feels morally bound to provide.
2   The duty to make the best available financial return.
3   The duty to manage risk through the use of portfolio management strategies.
4   The duty to manage a controlling interest in a company.

(4) Any other obligations under the case law

There were 13 principal trustee obligations identified in Chapter 8. All or any of those obligations may be applicable in relation to any given trustee. Of particular significance in relation to the investment of trusts, aside from those obligations already mentioned, are:

1   The duty to act evenly between different classes of beneficiaries.
2   The duty to control delegates.

(5) Defences to breach of trust

The defences to breach of trust in general terms are considered in detail in section 18.4. In relation to breach of obligations relating to the investment of the trust fund, the principal defences are:

1   Acting as other market participants acted in relation to similar trust funds.[25]
2   Having the court excuse the trustees for having acted honestly and reasonably further to s 61 of the Trustee Act 1925.

There are two other significant doctrines which were considered in Chapter 8 which are important in excusing trustees' liability in relation to breach of trust:

3   An express provision of the trust instrument excluding or limiting the liability of the trustees for breach of trust.[26]
4   Set aside of the exercise of a power or discretion of the trustees on the grounds that they took into account an irrelevant factor or that they failed to take into account a relevant factor.[27]

Thus, even if a *prima facie* breach of trust is established, it may be necessary to consider the extent of the statutory and of the case law interpretations of the trustees' general obligations when investing the trust fund, lest any of these defences should apply.

---

25 *Nestlé v National Westminster Bank plc* [2000] WTLR 795.
26 *Armitage v Nurse* [1998] Ch 241; *Galmerrow Securities Ltd v National Westminster Bank plc* [2002] WTLR 125.
27 *Re Hastings-Bass* [1975] Ch 25.

(6) Liability and remedies for breach of trust

The nature of liability for breach of trust is considered below in section 9.9; and in detail in Chapter 18. In essence the trustees will be liable to return any specific property taken from the trust, or to account personally for any loss suffered by the trust so as to restore the trust to its previous worth before the breach of trust.[28]

9.3 THE GENERAL POWER OF INVESTMENT

9.3.1 The scope of the general power of investment

In general terms

In comparison with the formalism previously imposed by the Trustee Investment Act 1961, the TA 2000 provides that 'a trustee may make any kind of investment that he could make if he were absolutely entitled to the assets of the trust': this is referred to in the legislation as the 'general power of investment'.[29] Therefore, the trustee is not constrained as to the investments which are made by reason only of his trusteeship.[30] It should be remembered that the trust instrument may impose restrictions on the trustees' powers to make investments and financial regulation may in effect preclude certain types of investment by persons who are considered to be insufficiently expert to make them.[31] There remain restrictions on the power of trustees to make investments in land unless by way of loans secured on land (such as mortgages).[32]

In creating a general power of investment, the TA 2000 also provides that that power is both in addition to anything set out in the trust instrument but also capable of being excluded by any such trust instrument.[33] Therefore, the settlor could preclude the trustees from making particular forms of investment or otherwise qualify the trustees' powers of investment. In contradistinction to the 1961 code, this means that the trustee is presumed to be free to make any suitable investments in the absence of any express provision to the contrary, whereas the trustee was previously presumed to be capable only of making a limited range of investments in the absence of any provision to the contrary.[34] Therefore, the purpose of the 2000 Act is to supplement the powers of trustees in the event that the trust instrument does not deal with the matter.

---

28 *Target Holdings v Redferns* [1996] 1 AC 421.
29 TA 2000, s 3(1).
30 Before the late 18th century, trustees were frequently conceived of as being the absolute owner of the trust property and subject only to equitable duties to account to the beneficiaries. It was during the 18th century that it was recognised that trustees could only exercise powers granted to them by a trust instrument, as opposed to treating the trustee as the absolute owner of the trust property: see, for example, *Holmes v Dring* (1788) 2 Cox Eq Cas 1. The law of trusts then developed a means of understanding the trustee as being hemmed in by obligations and of the beneficiary as having equitable proprietary rights. The TA 2000 could be considered in this sense as returning to a very old understanding of the rights of the trustee.
31 Financial Services and Markets Act 2000, Part I.
32 TA 2000, s 3(3).
33 *Ibid*, s 6(1).
34 The 1961 code is now replaced by the TA 2000 in this regard: *ibid*, s 7(3).

9.3.2 The meaning of 'investment'

The term 'investment' is not defined for the purposes of s 3 of the TA 2000. Its meaning in the general law of trusts has transformed from simply a consideration of income yield,[35] into a broader notion of the enhancement of capital value in parallel with increase in income,[36] and also into the desirability of the diversity of investment risk by means of portfolio investment strategies.[37] The Financial Services and Markets Act 2000 defines 'investment' in more categorical terms. That statute defines the term 'investment' by means of a list of broadly-defined market activities,[38] including dealings in shares or debt securities, government and public securities, warrants, certificates representing securities, units in collective investment schemes, financial derivatives and contracts for differences generally, contracts of insurance or participation in Lloyd's syndicates, bank deposits, loans secured on land, or any right in an investment.[39] The expansion of trustees' investment powers signalled by the TA 2000 makes no explicit reference to the enactment of the Financial Services and Markets Act 2000 even though that latter statute has effected wide-ranging change in the substantive law and regulation of financial services in the UK and may be used as a means of defining that term in the future.

9.4 THE TRUSTEES' STANDARD OF CARE WHEN MAKING INVESTMENTS

9.4.1 The statutory duty of care

The TA 2000 provides for a statutory duty of care which imposes a duty of 'such skill and care as is reasonable in the circumstances' in s 1 in the following terms:[40]

(1) Whenever the duty under this subsection applied to a trustee, he must exercise such care and skill as is reasonable in the circumstances, having regard in particular –
  (a) to any special knowledge or experience that he has or holds himself out as having, and
  (b) if he acts as trustee in the course of a business or profession, to any special knowledge or experience that it is reasonable to expect of a person acting in the course of that kind of business or profession.
(2) In this Act the duty under subsection (1) is called 'the duty of care'.

Therefore, this 'duty of care'[41] is relative to the context in which the trustee is acting. In subsection (1) it should be noted that the courts are not limited to the matters set out in paras (a) and (b) when deciding the extent of the trustees' liabilities. The matters set out in those paragraphs, however, operate in the following way. Where the trustee has, or holds herself out as having, any particular 'special knowledge or experience', then the

---

35 *Re Somerset* [1894] 1 Ch 231, 247; *Re Wragg* [1919] 2 Ch 58, 65.
36 *Cowan v Scargill* [1985] Ch 270, 287; *Harries v Church Commissioners* [1992] 1 WLR 1241, 1246.
37 See discussion below at para 9.6.4.
38 Financial Services and Markets Act 2000, s 22. See Alastair Hudson, *The Law of Finance*, Sweet & Maxwell, 2009, paras 9–06 *et seq*.
39 *Ibid*, Sched 2, Pt II.
40 TA 2000, s 1(1).
41 *Ibid*, s 1(2).

trustee's duty of care will be inferred in the light of those factors.[42] Consequently, if the trustee pretends to have experience which she does not have, then she will be treated as though she did have that level of experience. To do otherwise would be to allow a deceitful or overly boastful trustee to induce the beneficiaries into using her services on the basis that she was capable of acting, and then to excuse that person from causing loss to the trust because they had misled the beneficiaries and was in truth incompetent. Further, if the duties of trustee are performed 'in the course of a business of profession', then the duty of care is applied in the context of any special knowledge or experience which such a professional could be expected to have.[43] It is worth considering what would happen, for example, in relation to an inexperienced stockbroker advising on a trust's investment policy: would that stockbroker be able to plead her lack of experience so as to avoid liability for breaching this duty of care? The statute reads so as to say that the level of special knowledge or experience is a level which 'it is reasonable to expect of a person acting in the course of that kind of business of profession': thus we must consider 'a person' acting in such a professional capacity, and not 'a person in the defendant's particular circumstances', with the result, it is suggested, that all professionals shall be held to the same standard appropriate for members of that profession or participants in that sort of business without permitting any kind of defence based on the defendant's own lack of experience. Thus the risk of liability for any losses and the burden of acting appropriately is borne by anyone who acts in the course of a business, as opposed to being borne by the beneficiaries. This is appropriate, it is suggested, because the trust will be employing a trustee on the basis of that trustee's professionalism and therefore it would be unfortunate if the trustee were able to avoid liability for failing to act as a professional in that sort of business ought to act.

It should be remembered that the provisions of the TA 2000 can be expressly or impliedly displaced by the trust instrument.[44] In consequence, this duty of care may be limited by the express provisions of the trust, or even by a construction of those provisions, which suggests that the settlor's intention was to exclude such a liability.[45]

The duty of care is not expressed by the 2000 Act to be a general duty in the form of an all-encompassing statutory tort; rather, the Act provides that the duty will apply in certain limited circumstances.[46] It is instead a form of limited equitable wrong. The principal instance in which the statutory duty of care applies[47] is in relation to a trustee exercising a 'general power of investment'[48] under the Act or any other power of investment 'however conferred'.[49] Alternatively, the duty of care applies when trustees are carrying out obligations under the Act in relation to exercising or reviewing powers of investment.[50] The duty

---

42 *Ibid*, s 1(1)(a).
43 *Ibid*, s 1(1)(b).
44 *Ibid*, Sched 1, para 7.
45 Cf section 8.5 above.
46 *Ibid*, s 2.
47 *Ibid*, Sched 1, para 1.
48 As defined by *ibid*, s 3(2) and considered below.
49 With the effect that this provision may be only mandatory provision in the legislation because it appears to apply to powers of investment in general and not simply to that set out in s 3(2). However, the Act does permit an express exclusion in the trust to obviate the operation of any of the provisions in the Act and therefore it would appear possible to circumscribe the operation of this provision: Sched 1, para 7.
50 TA 2000, ss 4, 5.

of care also applies in relation to the acquisition of land,[51] which would logically appear to cover the use of appropriate advice and appropriate levels of care in selecting the land, contracting for its purchase and insuring it.[52] It applies in general terms in relation to the appointment of agents, custodians and nominees:[53] this would include the selection of reasonable agents with appropriate qualifications for the task for which they were engaged.

9.4.2   The possible meanings of 'reasonable' care in this context

The governing adjective which qualifies the care which must be exercised by the trustee is 'reasonable'. The inclusion of this adjective ensures a great potential scope for the development of the duties of trustees. By contrast, the word 'prudent' has been used in the case law since the 19th century,[54] suggesting that caution was more important than other concerns. The underlying purpose of the TA 2000 is to liberate trustees from the overriding objective to be prudent in their investment activities to the exclusion of all else. If a trustee is required to act prudently then that means that the trustee must avoid investments which present any significant degree of risk of loss; whereas if a trustee is required to act 'reasonably' then that permits a trustee to make investments which take a level of risk which is appropriate for the particular trust in question. Prudence therefore limits the trustees' choices. After all, all investment involves risk.[55] Thus if a trustee is required to act prudently then many ordinary investments may be beyond that trustee's powers. By contrast a reasonable trustee, particularly one with a broad portfolio of investments, would take some risks so as to make a reasonable level of profit for the beneficiaries. The precise phrasing of s 1(1) of TA 2000 is important, however, because it requires that a trustee 'exercise such care and skill as is reasonable in the circumstances'. Therefore, it is not simply that a trustee must act 'reasonably' but more precisely that that trustee must do three things: first, exercise skill and care; secondly, exercise that skill and care reasonably; and, thirdly, do so in a way which is appropriate to the circumstances. That a trustee must exercise skill and care requires that the trustee act skilfully and furthermore that she also act with care: thus we might consider that there remains a remnant of the old case law requirement of prudence in this requirement of care. The second element, though, is significant in that the level of care required is not absolute prudence at all times – which would suggest caution on the part of the trustee – but rather the level of care which is to be taken should be a level of care which is reasonable in the circumstances. If the requirement was for absolute caution then if the trustee took any hazardous risk at all she would be liable for breach of trust if a loss resulted; however, if a trustee is permitted to act reasonably then she may be excused liability for breach of trust if the risk she took was reasonable in the circumstances. For example, if the trust was created by a billionaire with the express purpose that the trustees invest a large sum of money so as to make as much profit as possible, then it would be reasonable for the trustees to invest in complex and risky investments because they would be expected to generate the highest levels of profit; whereas it would not be reasonable to take such risks if the trustees were

---

51   *Ibid*, Sched 1, para 2.
52   *Ibid*, Sched 1, para 5; TA 1925, s 19.
53   *Ibid*, Sched 1, para 3.
54   *Learoyd v Whiteley* (1887) 12 App Cas 727.
55   A point accepted explicitly by Lord Nicholls in *Royal Brunei Airlines v Tan* [1995] 2 AC 378.

investing only a few thousand pounds in relation to a bare trust the only beneficiary of which was an elderly widow with no other source of income and whose trustees would therefore need to be more careful not to lose the trust fund.

The upshot of this movement from 'prudence' to 'reasonableness' is that trustees may be expected to seek to generate greater profit for the trust now that they are imbued with a general investment power by the TA 2000[56] and now that trustees providing investment advice as part of a business are regulated by the Financial Services Authority ('FSA'). With the increased participation of many ordinary citizens in financial market activity (whether directly through share acquisitions in public limited companies, or indirectly through participation in unit trusts or occupational pension funds), it is suggested that the culture in which trustees are investing should require a transformation in the standard expected of trustees when exercising their investment powers. That transformation should be a change from the caution which has been required historically into a power to incur a level of investment risk which is commensurate with the nature of the trust which they are administering. So, non-professional trustees' investment of a family trust would require greater care and lower levels of investment risk than professional fund managers investing a commercially-marketed unit trust or pension fund. Under the TA 2000 regime, it is of central significance that the nature of the duty of care[57] is relative to the context in which the trustee is acting.

The most significant form of trustee in relation to investment powers will be the professional trustee who is retained to act as trustee precisely because he is a professional. It is precisely such trustees, ironically, who will generally not be covered by the TA 2000 in practice because they will generally agree to act as trustees only if the trust instrument specifies their powers, their obligations, and the precise manner in which their fees will be calculated.[58] When considering the standard of care appropriate for a professional trustee, it would be appropriate to ascertain the standard of her obligations by reference to standard market practice and by reference to standard market regulation.[59] An appropriate, objective measurement of the obligations of such professional trustees would be the provisions of the FSA's regulatory Conduct of Business Sourcebook ('COBS').[60] That rulebook describes the manner in which such organisations and their employees are expected to behave, on penalty of sanction by the FSA, and therefore the appropriate rulebook constitutes a code of principles by which both professional trustee and beneficiary can reasonably expect the trustee to be judged.

It is by reference to non-professional trustees that the most difficult problems arise. Two conflicting points of principle collide at this juncture. The first concerns the level of expectation expressed by the settlor and by the beneficiaries, and the reasonableness of their reliance on the particular trustee; the second is the protection of the trustee in relation to liabilities which he may not have understood he was assuming or which he may not have considered himself sufficiently skilled to assume. The question for the courts will be whether they choose to measure reasonableness by reference to the need to compensate the beneficiary for any loss occasioned by the trustee's action or omission, or whether the courts choose to measure reasonableness by reference to the justice of holding the individual trustee only to

56 Unless that power has been expressly excluded by the trust instrument: TA 2000, s 6.
57 *Ibid*, s 1(2).
58 See, for example, *Armitage v Nurse* [1998] Ch 241.
59 See, for example, *Bankers Trust v Dharmala* [1996] CLC 252.
60 See the discussion of this FSA Conduct of Business rulebook at para 9.8.3.

obligations which he assumed voluntarily and in full cognisance of their ramifications.[61] The courts have been reluctant to hold trustees to account if they have acted as other trustees would have acted in the circumstances, even if that has resulted in a poor investment return for the beneficiaries:[62] however, in relation to inexpert trustees, it will be difficult to adduce evidence of what other trustees would have done in the same context because such information will not be as readily available as it would be in relation to professional investment managers.

The case law relating to the investment of trust funds dealt with different concepts – in particular the requirement of 'prudence'[63] – which are analysed below in section 9.6. If that case law is used by the courts to measure the obligations of trustees then, it is suggested, that would be to return to a mode of thought which prioritised care and caution over the modern approach of balancing the need to take risks with the return that the trustees are expected to generate for the beneficiaries. More recent cases have, however, begun to prioritise the standards of 'modern portfolio investment theory'[64] over the more traditional notions of prudence.[65]

9.5 THE PROCESS OF MAKING INVESTMENT DECISIONS

9.5.1 The statutory duty of care in the process of making investment decisions

The TA 2000 creates a statutory duty of care to which trustees are subject when making investment decisions. The detail of the duty of care is considered below.[66] This section of this chapter is concerned with the statutory principles governing the mechanism by which trustees make investment decisions. The duties which those trustees bear in the investment-making process are subject always to the statutory duty of care (unless the trust instrument provides to the contrary),[67] whether in relation to the general power of investment or their obligations to review the fund's investments, as considered immediately below. Therefore, the trustees' liability for any malfeasance or loss occasioned through their investment decisions will fall to be assessed in accordance with the duty of care and with the principles of breach of trust under the general law of trust. The following paragraphs will consider the investment decision process before turning to the detail of the statutory duty of care.

9.5.2 Standard investment criteria

The TA 2000 requires that the trustees have regard to something described in the statute as the 'standard investment criteria'[68] when exercising their investment powers: that is, it is suggested,

---

61 Cf *Armitage v Nurse* [1998] Ch 241.
62 *Nestlé v National Westminster Bank plc* [2000] WTLR 795.
63 *Learoyd v Whiteley* (1887) 12 App Cas 727.
64 *Nestlé v National Westminster Bank plc* [2000] WTLR 795.
65 See para 9.6.3.
66 See the discussion at para 9.6.3.
67 TA 2000, Sched 1, para 1(b).
68 *Ibid*, s 4(1).

whether making new investments or considering their existing investments.[69] The 'standard investment criteria' to which the trustees are to have regard comprise two core principles of prevailing investment theory which relate, first, to the need to make 'suitable' investments and, secondly, to the need to maintain a diverse portfolio of investments to spread the fund's investment risk. We shall take each of these in turn. The trustees are required to consider under s 4(2):

(a) the suitability to the trust of investments of the same kind as any particular investment proposed to be made or retained and of that particular investment as an investment of that kind, and

(b) the need for diversification of investments of the trust, in so far as is appropriate to the circumstances of the trust.[70]

The term 'suitability' is one familiar to investment regulation specialists[71] which requires that, in general terms, investment managers are required to consider whether or not the risk associated with a given investment is appropriate for the client proposing to make that investment. In consequence, the investment manager could not sell, for example, complex financial derivatives products to inexpert members of the general public who could not understand the precise nature of the risks associated with such a transaction. Under the terms of the TA 2000, the trustee is required to consider whether the trust fund for which she is making an investment would be dealing in a suitable manner in making the proposed investment. It is presumed that the trustee would be liable for breach of trust in the event that an unsuitable investment were made which caused loss to the trust.[72] The FSA Conduct of Business regulations might give us some guidance as to what suitable behaviour would involve, remembering always that the steps which are required of any service provider:

will vary greatly, depending on the needs and priorities of the private customer, the type of investment or service being offered, and the nature of the relationship between the firm and the private customer and, in particular, whether the firm is giving a personal recommendation or acting as a discretionary investment manager.[73]

Having categorised each client in this manner, the service provider is then required to treat them in a manner which is commensurate with their expertise and also to ensure that the investments sold to them are suitable for their purposes. Therefore, the requirement under s 4(2)(a) of the TA 2000 that the trustee is required to consider whether the trust fund for which she is making an investment would be dealing in a suitable manner in making the proposed investment will differ depending on the nature of the trust. Where the trust is a small family trust with a comparatively weak risk appetite, the investments to be made should be safe, whereas investments made on behalf of a trust fund created by two corporations who are expert in financial services (a not uncommon structure for highly-leveraged hedge funds) could be considerably more adventurous, and so intended to take greater risks.

---

69 *Ibid*, s 4(2).
70 *Ibid*.
71 See para 9.8.3 below for a discussion of this term. See Alastair Hudson, *The Law of Finance*, Sweet & Maxwell, 2009, paras 10–46 *et seq*.
72 *Target Holdings v Redferns* [1996] 1 AC 421, [1995] 3 WLR 352, [1995] 3 All ER 785.
73 FSA, Conduct of Business Rules, para 5.3.4.

It is presumed that the trustee would be liable for breach of trust in the event that an unsuitable investment were made which caused loss to the trust.[74]

Secondly, the trustees must pay heed to 'the need for diversification of investments of the trust, in so far as is appropriate to the circumstances of the trust'.[75] Two points arise from this provision. First, the question as to the amount of diversification necessary is dependent on the nature of the trust. For example, a trust which requires the trustees to hold a single house on trust for the occupation of a named beneficiary does not require that the trustees make a range of investments: rather, the trustees are impliedly precluded from making a range of investments. Secondly, a trust with only a small amount of capital could not afford to buy a large number of investments.

Therefore, the need for diversification itself is bound up with need to dilute the risk of investing in only a small number of investments. This is frequently referred to as 'portfolio theory'[76] and is predicated on the theory that if an investor invests in a number of investments in different markets, the impact of any individual market or investment suffering from a fall in value is balanced out by the investments made in other markets which will not have suffered from that particular fall in value. Let us imagine a trust with a general power of investment. If that trust fund was comprised of £10 million, diversification would require that the trustees do not simply invest in shares in a single company. Equally, diversification would require that the trustees do not invest in a number of companies which all deal in the same market, for example computer manufacture, because if there were a fall in that market then the entire value of the trust would fall. Therefore, diversification would involve acquiring shares in a number of companies in a number of different markets. However, diversification would also require investment in a number of different types of investments – for example, bonds, derivatives, land, foreign exchange and commodities, as well as shares – so that if there were a fall in UK share markets then the investments in other markets would balance out the fall in the trust's investment in shares. The assumption is that in modern marketplaces there will be volatility in all investment markets and therefore that this volatility – meaning that investments may increase and decrease greatly in value over comparatively short periods of time – carries with it the risk of investments falling in value. Investment professionals rely on volatility to generate profits: if different investments within markets, as well as the markets generally, rise and fall in value then a skilful investment professional will take advantage of opportunities to buy investments when they are cheap and to sell them when they have risen in value. In previous centuries it was generally supposed that investments would move slowly in value and therefore that prudence was an appropriate approach to investment; this assumption fell away in the late 20th century. Thus we come to the requirement expressed by judges such as Hoffmann J[77] that trustees should take account of 'modern portfolio theory' when making investments so that a range of different investments will insulate the trust against the fall in any individual market or investment.[78]

74 *Target Holdings v Redferns* [1996] 1 AC 421, [1995] 3 WLR 352, [1995] 3 All ER 785.
75 TA 2000, s 4(2)(b).
76 Considered below at para 9.6.4.
77 *Nestlé v National Westminster Bank plc* [2000] WTLR 795.
78 The point made about portfolio investment by Warren Buffett of Berkshire Hathaway (possibly the world's most successful investor) is that it is a poor short-term strategy because it assumes that some investments will fail, as opposed to selecting successful, long-term investments carefully on the basis of strong fundamentals and good management.

However, when thinking about the appropriate level of diversification it is also important to consider the size and nature of the trust. As was considered above, if the trust instrument clearly requires that the trustee invest in only a limited form of investments, then the trustee would be in breach of trust if she sought to diversify the trust's investments into any other forms of investments which were not permitted by the precise terms of the trust instrument. If the settlor's intention that, for example, a trust was invested only in 'technology companies in the UK' failed to anticipate a period in which technology companies lost lots of money due to changes in the technology marketplace, then it would seem illogical to require that the trustee continue to obey the terms of the trust instrument and thus lose the trust a lot of money. Instead, s 33 of the Trustee Act 1925, as discussed in Chapter 18, might give the trustees an 'excuse' for committing a technical breach of trust so as better to protect the trust fund. The trustee should ideally seek a variation under the Variation of Trusts Act 1958 or under s 57 of the Trustee Act 1925. Nevertheless, if the trust fund were comprised of only £10,000 in free cash, then it would be unreasonable to expect that a trustee would be able to diversify the trust's investment portfolio as broadly as a trust containing £10 million because clearly the larger trust can afford many more different types of investment and can better afford the fees involved with buying that number of investments. Therefore, diversification in relation to the trust fund containing £10,000 will necessarily require the trustees to diversify only to the extent that the trust can afford to do so. Thus a trust fund comprising £10 million may include hundreds of different investments in its portfolio, whereas a trust fund including only £10,000 may have only six or seven different, carefully-selected investments in different markets. These questions are impossible to decide in the abstract. Rather, they must be considered on a case-by-case basis by reference to these principles.

9.5.3 The obligation to take professional advice

Trustees are under a positive obligation to take professional advice on the investments which they propose to make on behalf of the trust.[79] It is the TA 2000 which imposes this positive obligation on the trustees to seek out professional advice on the investments to be made.[80] This obligation is set out in s 5 of TA 2000 in the following terms:

> (1) Before exercising any power of investment, whether arising under this Part or otherwise, a trustee must (unless the exception applies) obtain and consider proper advice about the way in which, having regard to the standard investment criteria [set out in the preceding section], the power should be exercised.
> (2) When reviewing the investments of the trust, a trustee must (unless the exception applies) obtain and consider proper advice about whether, having regard to the standard investment criteria, the investments should be varied.

Thus, under subsection (1), before the trustees make any investment they are required to seek 'proper advice'. This advice must be taken before the exercise of any investment power.[81] Similarly, under subsection (2), when considering whether or not to vary the investments which the trust has made, the trustees are also required to take qualified investment

---

79 TA 2000, s 5(1).
80 *Ibid*, s 5(1).
81 TA 2000, s 5(4).

advice,[82] unless it appears reasonable to the trustees in the circumstances to dispense with such advice.[83] The type of advice which the trustee must acquire is 'proper advice': that is, advice from someone whom the trustee reasonably believes is qualified to give such advice.[84] There may, therefore, be interesting questions as to the sort of advice which qualifies as being 'proper advice'. It is suggested that consulting a professional in the field in which the investment is to be made would definitely constitute 'proper advice' if the professional was consulted on ordinary business terms and paid in the ordinary manner.

There may be more difficult questions, for example, if a trustee sought to take advice from a professional one weekend at a barbecue in a mutual friend's garden when both had been drinking and neither party had had a chance to discuss the matter in a normal professional manner. It is suggested that this might not constitute 'proper advice' if the professional were not able to consider all of the necessary issues in a professional manner as would ordinarily be expected of someone in her profession; whereas asking a professional, for example, what sort of investments had been recommended for a particular type of client in the previous week might come closer to being proper advice because that professional would not necessarily need to consider any other matters before dispensing that sort of advice. So, if, for example, the professional was a land management professional then a question as to the time at which pruning was conducted on valuable trees on trust land would not require the estate manager necessarily to do a large amount of investigative work in advance of giving advice. By contrast, in relation to the investment of a pension fund of £10 million, an investment professional would need to comply with FSA regulation as to the terms on which the advice was given, the current nature of the trust's portfolio and so forth: thus off-the-cuff advice would not be appropriate in that context. The requirement of taking 'proper advice' would, it is suggested, not be satisfied by simply reading a newspaper article if the decision being made was how to invest millions of pounds in financial markets without taking specific advice as to the needs of the particular trust. Again, by contrast, if the trustees were simply researching a simple question – such as the manner in which a speedboat held on trust should be moored – then reading an article in an appropriate journal or consulting the internet might be sufficient. Nevertheless, best practice for trustees would be to seek professional advice from a professional advisor (or from a number of professional advisors) on ordinary commercial terms such that the advisor was able to assess all of the relevant information and to give sufficiently well-considered advice.

Once the advice has been obtained, the trustees are required to consider it and its bearing on the manner in which their investment power should be exercised.[85] There is no statutory obligation on the trustees to follow the advice which they receive and so it is open to them to follow whichever path they consider appropriate. Consequently, trustees may well seek advice from different professionals before making up their own minds as to which course of action they consider to be most appropriate for the trust. Different stockbrokers might, for example, suggest different courses of action for a trust seeking to invest its cash. The trustees may have their own views as to the need to conserve the trust's capital for its infant beneficiaries as opposed to seeking profits in a hurry by means of taking big risks. Thus, the

---

82 *Ibid*, s 5(2).
83 *Ibid*, s 5(3).
84 *Ibid*, s 5(4).
85 *Ibid*.

trustees may reject advice given to them by aggressive stockbrokers and instead prefer to take the advice of more cautious stockbrokers who fit in with the trust's general ethos. So, taking advice does not necessarily mean that that advice must be followed slavishly. Megarry VC held the following in relation to the trustees' obligations in relation to the advice they receive:

> Although a trustee who takes advice on investments is not bound to accept and act on that advice, he is not entitled to reject it merely because he sincerely disagrees with it, unless in addition he is acting as an ordinary prudent man would act.[86]

There is nothing in the statute to preclude trustees from taking advice from a number of sources, or to take advice from one source as to a range of different investment decisions which could be taken, before then selecting the strategy which most appeals to them in the context of their fiduciary responsibilities.

9.5.4 Investment in land

Trustees are empowered to acquire freehold and leasehold land for any purpose.[87] The TA 2000 provides that the acquisition can be for the purposes of investment or for the occupation of a beneficiary, but also provides that it may be made for 'any other reason':[88] the purpose of listing the two specific contexts is to avoid any doubt that those two reasons are permissible. The trustee has the powers of 'the absolute owner in relation to the land'.[89] This presumably means that the trustee is free to deal with the land on behalf of the trust in terms of conveying it, securing it and so forth. However, it is not supposed that this could be taken to mean that the trustee is entitled to ignore the equitable interests of any beneficiaries in that land when held on trust.

In line with the general scheme of the 2000 Act, the legislation provides for additions to any terms of any trust instrument so that there are default provisions if a trust should lack them.[90] However, it is open to the settlor to exclude the operation of the statute in any particular circumstances, reinforcing the point yet again that the Act does not impose mandatory rules as to the behaviour of trustees.

9.6 CASE LAW ON THE TRUSTEES' DUTIES IN THE INVESTMENT OF TRUSTS

9.6.1 The interaction of the Trustee Act 2000 and the old case law

This chapter has considered the general principles of trust investment. It should be borne in mind that these principles apply generally to ordinary, private trusts but that there are specific

---

86 *Cowan v Scargill* [1985] Ch 270, 289.
87 These particular powers do not apply to land that was settled land before 1996: *ibid*, s 10.
88 *Ibid*, s 8(1).
89 *Ibid*, s 8(3).
90 *Ibid*, s 9.

principles which apply to the specialist forms of trust which are considered elsewhere: pension fund trusts[91] and unit trusts.[92]

The trustee's general duties of investment can be summarised as being bound up in the following three obligations: to act prudently and safely;[93] to act fairly between beneficiaries;[94] and to do the best for the beneficiaries.[95] This ties in with the preceding discussion and the understanding in the case law of the trust as being an equitable doctrine operating on the conscience of the trustee rather than the more formal institution which investors and investment managers typically have in mind when creating a trust for commercial purposes. However, the case law has taken a mercenary turn in considering the standard of investment management expected of trustees in even the most rudimentary of trusts and so the best interests of the beneficiaries are generally considered to be their financial interests.[96] Therefore, non-financial considerations must not be taken into account when deciding what to invest in, except in the exceptional circumstances where the trust instrument permits only particular types of investment or where all the actual or potential beneficiaries are adults with strict moral views on particular matters.[97] The source of this principle is in the conception of trusts in the 19th century as a means of protecting family wealth over a number of generations and the need to maximise the family's total income from long-term investments.

Otherwise the law is concerned with negative duties on the trustees to refrain from making unauthorised personal profits[98] and from committing breaches of trust more generally.[99] Therefore, there is a mixture of negative obligations dealing with the prevention of breach of trust and there are positive obligations in relation to the investment of trusts requiring the trustee to generate the best available return on the property in the circumstances.

9.6.2 The duty to make the best available return

The issue then arises: to what extent is a trustee obliged to realise the maximum reasonable return? There are three different senses in which this duty could be said to operate. The first, simply put, would be to require the trustees to seek the highest possible market return on the trust's capital. It is suggested that such an approach would require the trustees to seek the most risky available investments so as to acquire as high a return as possible. The second approach, subtly different from the first, would be to require the trustees, when choosing between a range of available investments, to select that investment which offered the highest available yield made possible by the investment criteria which the trustees have created for the trust. In this situation, the trustees would not be seeking investments which promised a high return at a potentially unacceptable level of risk, but rather, once a field of suitable

91 Chapter 24.
92 See Thomas and Hudson, 2004, Chapter 51, and the essay on unit trusts on www.alastairhudson.com.
93 *Ibid.*
94 *Nestlé v National Westminster Bank plc* [1994] 1 All ER 118.
95 *Cowan v Scargill* [1985] Ch 270.
96 *Ibid.*
97 *Ibid*, as considered below.
98 *Boardman v Phipps* [1967] 2 AC 46; see section 12.5 below.
99 *Target Holdings v Redferns* [1996] 1 AC 421; see section 18.1 below.

investments had been identified, the trustees would be required to choose the most remunerative of those suitably low-risk investments. The third approach would be to recognise that non-financial considerations ought not to be taken into account. This third approach would therefore suggest that trustees ought not to allow ethical or other considerations to sway their financial decisions.

The relevant principle is probably more elegantly expressed as an obligation to make the optimum return for trust. This issue arose in the case of *Cowan v Scargill*,[100] in which the defendant was one of the trustees of the miners' pension fund and also President of the National Union of Mineworkers. The board of trustees was divided between executives of the trade union and executives from the Coal Board. The most profitable investments identified by the trustees were in companies working in oil and also in South Africa. The defendant refused to make such investments on the grounds that it was ethically wrong for the fund to invest in apartheid South Africa and also contrary to the interests of the beneficiaries to invest in an industry which competed with the coal industry, in which all the beneficiaries worked or had worked previously.

Megarry VC held that: 'When the purpose of the trust is to provide financial benefits for the beneficiaries, the best interests of the beneficiaries are their best financial interests.' Therefore, the duty of the trustees to act in the best interests of the beneficiaries is to generate the best available return on the trust fund regardless of other considerations. The scope of the duty of investment was summarised by his Lordship as the need to bear in mind the following: 'The prospects for the yield of income and capital appreciation both have to be considered in judging the return from the investment.'

His Lordship therefore focused on the objections which the defendant trustee had raised in respect of the particular form of investment which had been suggested. He held that while 'the trustees must put on one side their own personal interests and views . . .', and later that '. . . if investments of this type would be more beneficial to the beneficiaries than other investments, the trustees must not refrain from making the investments by reasons of the views that they hold'. The irony is that, in relation to the moral nature of the obligations on the trustee to deal equitably with the trust fund, the trustee is not permitted to bring decisions of an ethical nature to bear on the scope of the investment powers. As his Lordship put it: 'Trustees may even have to act dishonourably (though not illegally) if the interests of their beneficiaries require it.'

Thus, there is a positive duty to invest regardless of ethics and yet Megarry VC was expressly prepared to accept that a *sui juris* set of beneficiaries with strict views on moral matters (for example, condemnation of alcohol) would be entitled to prevent the trustees from investing in companies involved in the production of alcohol; thus suggesting that ethics can control investment powers. The question which comes to mind is whether Megarry VC simply did not agree with the particular form of political belief advanced by an avowedly Marxist leader of the trade union, in this case Arthur Scargill.[101] For example, why should refusing to invest in apartheid-controlled South Africa not be considered as valid an exercise of a trustee's discretion as a decision in favour of beneficiaries who all formed part of a Methodist temperance movement to refrain from investing in a whisky distillery? What is

---

100 [1984] 3 WLR 501.
101 Scargill appeared in person the High Court.

not clear from the judgment is what the court's approach would have been if the trust had expressly excluded investment in South Africa. It must be the case that such an express provision would have had to be enforced.

Megarry VC decided that the argument that the oil industry competed with coal was not well-founded. His principal objection was that many of the beneficiaries under the pension trust fund had retired and therefore that their income was no longer dependent on the comparative performance of coal over oil. That the communities in which these people lived were dependent entirely on the coal industry eluded his Lordship. It was therefore held that the trustees could not refuse to invest in an industry which competes with the interest of some of the pension fund members. Therefore, of the three possible senses of the duty to realise the optimum return for the trust, the third sense (not to take into account non-financial considerations) will be generally applicable except in limited situations. As will emerge in the next section, however, it is the second sense (to make the optimum return taking only suitable risks) which applies too.

9.6.3 The standard of care of the prudent businessperson

The duty to invest as though a prudent businessperson acting for someone for whom one feels morally bound to provide

Having established that there is an obligation to avoid hazardous investments, there is a counter-balancing duty in the old case law on the trustee to generate the best possible return from the trust property in the circumstances. The trustee's general duties of investment can be summarised in the following three core principles: to act prudently and safely;[102] to act fairly between beneficiaries;[103] and to do the best for the beneficiaries financially.[104] Evidently, there is a contradiction in these principles between acting prudently and making the maximum possible return on the property. In most cases, there will be an increased element of risk required in seeking to generate a higher investment return. The general encapsulation of this obligation is that the trustee bears a duty to invest as though she were a prudent businessperson acting for someone for whom she felt morally bound to provide.[105]

Under the old authority of *Learoyd v Whiteley*,[106] when the trustee is investing trust property, she must not only act as a businessperson of ordinary prudence, but must also avoid all investments of a hazardous nature. The difficulty with this approach is that all investment necessarily involves some risk and therefore it is impossible for the trustees to make investments which are completely risk-free. A trustee can invest in less risky securities, or other property, such as deposit bank accounts, but that is still not entirely free of the risk, for example, that the bank would go into insolvency. Therefore, the old approach was modified slightly in *Bartlett v Barclays Bank*,[107] in which a distinction was drawn between a prudent

102 *Learoyd v Whiteley* (1887) 12 App Cas 727.
103 *Bartlett v Barclays Bank* [1980] Ch 515.
104 *Cowan v Scargill* [1984] 3 WLR 501.
105 *Learoyd v Whiteley* (1887) 12 App Cas 727.
106 *Ibid*.
107 [1980] Ch 515.

degree of risk and something which amounted to 'hazard'. The former, prudently taken risk, would be acceptable, whereas to put the trust fund in hazard would be unacceptable.

As this concept was put by Megarry VC, the trustees are required to:

> take such care as an ordinary prudent man would take if he were minded to make an investment for the benefit of other people for whom he feels morally bound to provide.[108] This duty includes the duty to seek advice on matters which the trustee does not understand, such as the making of investments, and, on receiving that advice, to act with the same degree of prudence. Although a trustee who takes advice on investments is not bound to accept and act on that advice, he is not entitled to reject it merely because he sincerely disagrees with it, unless in addition he is acting as an ordinary prudent man would act.[109]

The approach taken here is that the trustees are to focus primarily on the protection and maintenance of the trust fund, whilst also allowing it to grow steadily. The modern expectation of perpetual growth in investments, which has shored up the market in personal pensions and the UK housing market, suggests a contrary expectation.

The irony behind this search for the perfect conceptualisation of the trustee's investment obligations is that it will only be possible to know whether or not an investment is a good one when it has expired: until then, all is quite literally speculation. Furthermore, the trustees were required to take advice where necessary. Under s 6 of the Trustee Investments Act 1961, there was a statutory duty to consider the suitability of particular investments, especially in the light of the need for diversification: see now section 9.2 above for the general investment power created by the TA 2000. What is clear is that a trustee will not be allowed to invest in anything in which she has a personal interest.[110]

The duty to act fairly between beneficiaries

The duty to act fairly between the beneficiaries is primarily a product of the history of these trusts as family settlements in which the life tenant and the remainderman would both want to ensure that the trustees dealt equally as between income generation and the protection of capital under the trust. This rule is still observed in the modern case law, as in *Nestlé v National Westminster Bank plc*,[111] where it was held that a trustee must act fairly where there are different classes of beneficiaries. As between life tenant and remainderman, the trustee must be aware of the interests of the remainder beneficiary. However, it was held that 'it would be an inhuman rule which required trustees to adhere to some mechanical rule for

---

108 A rendering of the concept of prudence in relation to trustees in Guernsey, a Francophile system of law based on Norman law at root, is put somewhat more lyrically as an obligation to act 'en bon père de famille': or, to put that into English, to act as though a good parent acting for his family. With all of the time-bound, gendered notions to one side, that gives a flavour of the trustee acting for someone for whom he or she felt morally bound to provide.

109 [1985] Ch 270, 289.

110 *Re David Feldman Charitable Foundation* (1987) 58 OR (2d) 626.

111 (1988): [2000] WTLR 795, *per* Hoffmann J; [1994] 1 All ER 118 CA. (This case was reported at first instance only some years after it was heard.)

preserving the real value of the capital when the tenant for life was the testator's widow who had fallen upon hard times and the remainderman was young and well-off'.

In the case of *Nestlé v National Westminster Bank plc*,[112] the court held that the trustees were entitled to invest cautiously in a way which would not simply generate high levels of income but which would also maintain the fund's capital. In that instance, it appeared in evidence that the value of the fund after 60 years of management by the trustees was worth about a quarter of the prevailing market investment rate.[113] Nevertheless, the trustees were able to demonstrate that their careful investment strategy was the sort of investment strategy which was adopted by most professional trustees when managing family trusts with an eye to the maintenance of the capital value of the fund for future generations and to the avoidance of risk so far as possible. Hoffmann J held that:

> A trustee must act fairly in making investment decisions which may have different consequences for differing classes of beneficiaries. . . . The trustees have a wide discretion. They are, for example, entitled to take into account the income needs of the tenant for life or the fact that the tenant for life was a person known to the settlor and a primary object of the trust whereas the remainderman is a remoter relative or stranger. Of course, these cannot be allowed to become the overriding considerations but the concept of fairness between classes of beneficiaries does not require them to be excluded. It would be an inhuman rule which required trustees to adhere to some mechanical rule for preserving the real value of capital when the tenant for life was the testator's widow who had fallen upon hard times and the remainderman was young and well-off.[114]

In consequence, the rule permitted some reference to the precise issues which faced the trustee in the context of his own trust obligations and did not simply require that the trustees live up to an objective standard of proper performance. Ordinarily, then, the trustees and the life tenants are responsible to prevent the trust fund from falling into disrepair with the aim that the value of the trust fund be maintained for remainder beneficiaries. There are circumstances in which the preservation of the capital value of the asset may not depend upon the life tenant and the trustee maintaining that property if, for example, in the case of real property, the real value of the capital asset is bound up in the development potential of the land and not in the state of repair of a house on that land occupied by the life tenant.[115] Therefore, it does appear that there is some flexibility in the operation of this principle.[116]

---

112 [2000] WTLR 795.
113 This case is considered in greater detail in the next paragraph.
114 *Nestlé v National Westminster Bank plc* [2000] WTLR 795, 802.
115 On the facts of an Australian case, it was held that where the life tenant had allowed a house on a large piece of land to fall into disrepair, there was no need to consider whether or not the life tenant was obliged to maintain the property so as to preserve its value for the capital beneficiaries, on the basis that the property's value rested on the development potential of the land rather than on the condition of the house on that land. Therefore, on these facts the life tenant's failure to maintain the property had caused no loss to the remainder beneficiaries: *Perpetual Trustees WA Ltd v Darvell* [2002] WTLR 1349.
116 *Re Pauling's ST* [1964] Ch 303.

9.6.4 The management of risk through portfolio investment strategies

The courts have begun to accept the need to adapt to the manner in which financial markets and finance professionals operate in the modern context; that is, that such professionals will typically only agree to be retained for a fee, in accordance with existing regulation of financial services, and on the terms of conduct of business letters entered into between the advisor and the lay client. In this way, principles of equity relating to the investment powers and obligations of trustees have altered. So, in *Nestlé v National Westminster Bank plc*,[117] the beneficiaries alleged that the trustees who had managed the investment of a family trust between 1922 and 1986 had failed to generate sufficient profit. It was alleged that while the trust amounted to £269,203 in 1986, if properly invested over that same period, it should have amounted to over £1 million; even if it had risen only in line with the cost of living, then it would have amounted to £400,000. The trustee bank defended its management of the trust on the basis that it had generated a broadly similar return on capital for its clients as other banks investing large family trusts had generated for theirs. On these facts the judge at first instance had found that the bank had done no less than what had been expected of a trustee in managing such a fund. However, it was also found that the trustee would have been able to generate a much healthier return if it had realised that the fund would not have been subject to estate duty (such that the capital did not need to be maintained in the manner it was) and if it had realised that it should have switched a number of the investments into gilts (government index-linked securities). Importantly, the Court of Appeal held that there was no default committed by the trustees; rather, the plaintiff was contending that there had been a failure to do better, which is not the same thing. If the plaintiff could have demonstrated some misfeasance in the management of the trust, then liability would have been easier to demonstrate. However, the trustee could not be shown to have acted wrongly in a manner which caused loss, only to have acted less profitably, which did not cause loss so much as it failed to generate a larger return.

In effect, the trustee bank was able to demonstrate that its management of the trust was broadly in line with the management policies of other trustees of private, family trusts (in which the risk appetite is usually small) and therefore that it had acted perfectly properly. Hoffmann J, in delivering judgment in *Nestlé v National Westminster Bank plc* at first instance, held that:[118]

> Modern trustees acting within their investment powers are entitled to be judged by the standards of current portfolio theory, which emphasises the risk level of the entire portfolio rather than the risk attaching to each investment taken in isolation.[119]

In pursuing this point, his Lordship found that a trustee is required to act fairly between all the beneficiaries of the trust fund which he was empowered to invest. However, the reference back to the behaviour of trustees acting in the context of the modern financial markets

---

117 [1993] 1 WLR 1260, [1994] 1 All ER 118.
118 [2000] WTLR 795, approved at [1993] 1 WLR 1260; see also Thomas and Hudson, 2004, 1609; Underhill and Hayton, 2002, 598.
119 A discretionary portfolio manager is someone who is given freedom to decide what investments are made and what risks are taken – see generally Hudson, 1999:1.

indicates the appropriateness of trustees balancing their investments between different types of product to even out risk, as well as taking into account the necessary risk required to make the maximum return for the trust.

The position which the trustee is placed in by equity – that is, to achieve the highest return possible at the lowest reasonable level of risk – appears to be a deeply invidious one, unless some reference is made to common market practice; that is, unless the trustee is able to rely on the fact that comparable investors had adopted similar investment strategies. Otherwise, at every crash in a financial market, all trustees would be *prima facie* liable for failing to generate a high investment return.[120] The duty to act evenly between different categories of beneficiaries requires a difficult balancing act between generating short-term return and protecting the integrity of the long-term fund. High-risk, short-term investments are necessary to satisfy the requirements of the rule to make the maximum possible return for the trust.[121] However, within that doctrine of maximum gain there is a requirement to act as a prudent person of business would act specifically with reference to someone for whom the trustee felt morally bound to provide (that is, over and above dealings in that person's own affairs).[122] The types of transaction available for the trustee's investment without stricture may be limited by the trust instrument[123] and by common law (aside from the requirement of prudence, there are prohibitions on lending on personal security).[124]

The trustee is similarly required to supervise professionals to whom delegation of the investment function is made. The principle in *Learoyd v Whiteley*[125] indicates that the trustee when investing trust property must not only act as a businessperson of ordinary prudence, but must also avoid all investments of a hazardous nature; whereas in *Bartlett v Barclays Bank*,[126] a distinction was drawn between a prudent degree of risk and unacceptable hazard: the former would be acceptable whereas the latter would not. In consequence, it is difficult to establish liability for a trustee who fails to generate a large return on the trust's capital. It is only in circumstances in which the trustee can be shown to have made some mistake or to have acted wrongly that there will seem to be any liability.

This reflection of current portfolio theory in the 2000 Act underlines the need for the trustee to walk a narrow line between modern practice and long-established equitable obligations. In this field, perhaps as in no other, the particular nature of the trust is important. The trust occupies a place somewhere between rules of property and rules of personal obligation. Whereas equity operates on the property that is held as the trust fund by means of proprietary principles, there are also a raft of personal claims against the trustee in connection with the manner in which the function of managing and safeguarding the trust fund is carried out.[127] There are obligations for a trustee making too little profit, making profits for

---

120 See immediately above the discussion of *Nestlé v National Westminster Bank plc* [1993] 1 WLR 1260 in relation to 'current portfolio theory'.
121 *Cowan v Scargill* [1985] Ch 270.
122 *Speight v Gaunt* (1883) 22 Ch D 727.
123 *Bartlett v Barclays Bank Trust Co Ltd* [1980] Ch 515.
124 *Holmes v Dring* (1788) 2 Cox Eq Cas 1; *Khoo Tek Keong v Ch'ng Joo Tuan Neoh* [1934] AC 529.
125 (1887) 12 App Cas 727.
126 [1980] Ch 515.
127 As to the nature of trusteeship in this context, see Hayton, 1996, 47, emphasising the core of the nature of the trust being the ability of the beneficiary to enforce the trust by personal obligations enforceable against the trustee.

herself which were not open to the trust,[128] and taking risks to make greater profit which then caused loss to the trust.[129]

9.6.5 Liability in accordance with standard market practice

Liability where the profit is too small can be defended if in accordance with standard market practice

The beneficiaries may seek to complain that while the trustees may have generated a profit, the profit is nevertheless too small. This particular line of attack was taken in *Nestlé v National Westminster Bank plc*,[130] in which the beneficiaries argued not that the trustees had lost them money, but rather that the trustees' surfeit of caution had caused a much reduced return on their capital than average market investment would have realised. Hoffmann J held that the trustees were entitled to have their actions measured in accordance with current portfolio theory and, furthermore, that they were entitled to have their actions compared with other market professionals. On the basis that the trustees had spread the investments and invested in the same manner as other market professionals, they were held not to have breached their duties. In this manner, the objectivity of the case law is fixed by reference to the activities or opinions not of any one trustee, but rather by reference to the practice of the market. Consequently, the trustees were held not to be liable for breach of trust on the basis that they had acted as other trustees in the same position would have acted. Similarly in *Galmerrow Securities Ltd v National Westminster Bank plc*,[131] trustees had invested in the UK property market in relation to an investment fund created specifically to invest in that market. Therefore, the investments which the trustees made were investments which were of a type which was specifically envisaged when the trust was created. The market fell in value and the beneficiaries sued the trustees for breach of trust. It was held, *inter alia*, that the trustees would not be liable for breach of trust because all participants in the marketplace had lost money and because the investments for which the trust had been set up were simply a type of investment which had the risk of loss inherent in them.[132]

In a contradiction of the old requirement of prudence, it has been held that a failure to diversify a holding of government bonds into shares would itself be a breach of trust which would make the trustees liable to pay equitable compensation to the beneficiaries.[133] Identifying the level of compensation payable would be a difficult matter. It has also been suggested that one might look to the average return which would have been obtained by a reasonable investment professional over the same period of time.[134]

---

128 *Cowan v Scargill* [1985] Ch 270. See section 12.5 also.
129 *Bartlett v Barclays Bank* [1980] Ch 515.
130 [2000] WTLR 795.
131 [2002] WTLR 125.
132 See para 9.9.3 for further discussion of this case.
133 *Guerin v The Queen* [1984] 2 SCR 335, (1984) 13 DLR (4th) 321; cited with approval in *Nestlé v National Westminster Bank plc* [1993] 1 WLR 1260, 1268, *per* Dillon LJ.
134 *Nestlé v National Westminster Bank plc* [1993] 1 WLR 1260, at 1268, *per* Dillon LJ and at 1280, *per* Staughton LJ.

The difficulty with identifying the 'market' with which to effect comparison

Attempting to defend oneself against a charge of failing to make insufficient profit based on an assertion that the entire market had acted in the same way raises the problem of identifying the market in question. If the trustee is a professional fund manager, then it may be possible to demonstrate in evidence the sorts of investment return which had been realised by similar market professionals, governed by the same regulation and dealing in very similar investments. However, there will not be such a market in relation to non-professional trustees. Even when considering professional trustees, it may be difficult to know whether to take as a comparator the entire investment market, or only professionals dealing in a defined market (such as shares quoted on the London Stock Exchange) but acting for all sorts of clients, or whether to consider only professionals dealing on such a market who were advising only trusts of the type in question. The answer which may be received for different market segments may be very different. Even if the market segment were limited, what variable ought to be included for pure chance: that is, what account does one take of the fact that one company may have gone into bankruptcy due to circumstances which were unforeseen (such as a fire at one of its factories) and so unbalance the investment portfolio when compared to other investment portfolios? The courts have, as yet, given no guidance on these questions and instead it will be a matter of adducing evidence and seeking to convince the court in each circumstance.

In relation to *Nestlé v National Westminster Bank plc* itself, the evidence suggested that this process of measuring the trustees against the average market performance would not, however, be an entirely objective matter: rather, the court would look to other trustees investing on behalf of a similar type of risk-averse, family trust rather than taking as a comparator the entire equities market. It is suggested that such a process then becomes entirely circular. In deciding the question 'what sort of investment professionals should be taken as a comparator for the trustees in this instance?', the court will necessarily be asking the general question: 'is the investment performance of these trustees to be measured against the market generally or against a risk-averse, specialist investment community which would have performed as weakly as this particular trust?' It is the general question which needs to be addressed first because the more specific question is dependent upon it.[135] A large part of this question involves identifying the appropriate market: is it the entire stock market? Or is it just the market of private trustees investing on behalf of trusts of the sort at issue? Or is it to be measured by reference to some external market index? Once the court in *Nestlé v National Westminster Bank plc* decided to limit its survey to trustees of the same type as the defendants, that necessarily produced the answer that the defendants had not acted inappropriately nor in breach of their investment duties. If any objective market index had been taken then the defendants would have seemed to be far behind the average. One other point remains: if

---

135   The further point mentioned in *Nestlé v National Westminster Bank plc* is that if the trustees choose investments which lose money from a selection of investment possibilities of which other possibilities would have made gains, the trustees will not be liable for a breach of trust provided that their investment decisions were reasonable in the context. The alternative view was advanced in *Robinson v Robinson* (1851) 1 De GM & G 247 to the effect that trustees could be liable for breach of trust if they selected the wrong investments. It is suggested that this goes too far and means that trustees could, in effect, become liable for breach of trust in any circumstance in which their investment choices lead to a loss without the trustees having acted negligently or inappropriately. It would replace a fault-based liability with a nearly strict liability.

the measurement is taken by reference to an average, then by definition there are likely to be as many people below the average as there were people above the average; and therefore that does not really answer the question whether or not there was a breach of trust, just whether or not the trustees underperformed approximately one half of other people in the market.

9.7 EXPRESS INVESTMENT POWERS

9.7.1 Priority of express powers of investment over statutory principles

An express power on a trustee to make an investment may be general, giving the trustees power to invest in whatever they wish, or limited to specific types of investment. The trustee will nevertheless be subject to certain limitations. Although in *Re Harari's ST*,[136] it was held that such a power would not be interpreted restrictively, the case of *Re Power's WT*[137] established that the word 'invest' implied a yield of income and, thus, non-income producing property would not be permissible as an investment. Therefore, while there is a permissive approach to interpreting investment clauses, it is important that it is 'investment' which is taking place. In *Re Power*, the trustee was relying on the investment provision to justify the acquisition of a house for the beneficiaries to live in. It was held that this acquisition did not include the necessary element of income generation for the trust. Thus, in *Re Wragg*,[138] it was permitted to acquire real property on the basis that that property was expected to generate income. It should be remembered that the trustee will have powers of investment both under any express power and under the TA 2000, as considered above at section 9.2.

9.7.2 Strict construction of powers of investment

The authorities are inconclusive on the manner in which powers of investment are to be construed. In general terms, provisions which have sought to enlarge the trustees' powers of investment have tended to be construed strictly,[139] whereas other forms of trust power have not always been construed restrictively.[140]

9.7.3 Power to confer investment powers on the trustees

Section 57 of the TA 1925 gives the court power to confer investment powers on the trustees. That section provides that:

> Where in the administration of any property vested in trustees [any investment] is in the opinion of the court expedient, but the same cannot be afforded by reason of the absence of any power for that purpose vested in the trustees by the trust instrument, if any, or by law, the court may by order confer upon the trustees, either generally or in any particular instance, the necessary power for the purpose.

136 [1949] 1 All ER 430.
137 [1951] Ch 1074; distinguishing *Re Wragg* [1919] 2 Ch 58.
138 [1919] 2 Ch 58.
139 *Re Maryon-Wilson's Estate* [1912] 1 Ch 55; *Re Harari's Settlement Trusts* [1949] WN 79.
140 *Re Peczenik's Settlement Trusts* [1964] 1 WLR 720.

Therefore, the court is entitled to permit investments of a broad range, from mortgages and loans through to purchase or sales of assets generally, where the court considers it to be expedient. There are cases which have suggested that that power can be exercisable on a one-off basis or can almost be by way of an effective variation of the terms of the trust. However, recent authority has been concerned to prevent any alteration in the nature or scope of the beneficial interests under a trust by way of a s 57 application, precisely because the Variation of Trusts Act 1958 exists for that purpose.[141] Such transactions must be for the benefit of all of the beneficiaries and not for any particular beneficiary.[142] In cases involving large funds, the court may permit a large expansion of the trust investment powers to enable the retention of a professional fund investment manager. Thus, in *Anker-Peterson v Anker-Peterson*,[143] the investment powers of the trustees of a fund containing £4 million were expanded in this way so that the investment manager would be able to invest the fund in a commercially reasonable manner. Each case must be treated on its own merits, something which may be necessary even after the TA 2000 if the trust instrument had some express restriction on investment.[144] This provision is considered in greater detail at section 10.4.5 below.

9.8 TRUSTEES AS AUTHORISED PERSONS UNDER THE FINANCIAL SERVICES AND MARKETS ACT 2000

9.8.1 The purpose of the Financial Services and Markets Act 2000

The Financial Services and Markets Act 2000 ('FSMA 2000') is the principal legislation concerning the regulation of financial activity in the UK. By that Act, the Financial Services Authority ('the FSA') was created as the single principal regulator for financial activity in the UK. The objectives of the FSA, as established by that legislation, are to promote 'market confidence, public awareness, the protection of consumers, and the reduction of financial crime'.[145] For the purposes of this discussion, we are concerned with those circumstances in which trustees will be required to acquire authorisation from the FSA to sell investments to their beneficiaries (through the medium of the trust) whether in the form of a necessarily regulated structure like a unit trust or through a private express trust arrangement. On the concepts of finance law see Alastair Hudson, *The Law of Finance* generally.[146] The Financial Services Bill 2012 is intended to amend the FSMA 2000 and to replace the FSA with various subsidiary entities of the Bank of England,[147] although the regulatory rules for the most part will continue in effect under the stewardship of the new entities in the same form because that form was dictated by EU directives. Therefore, the following outline of the regulatory principles will continue to hold good as to their fundamentals.

---

141 *Southgate v Sutton* [2011] EWCA Civ 637.
142 *Re Craven's Estate* [1937] Ch 431.
143 (1991) LS Gaz 32.
144 *Trustees of the British Museum v Attorney-General* [1984] 1 WLR 418.
145 FSMA 2000, s 2(2).
146 Alastair Hudson, *The Law of Finance*, Sweet & Maxwell, 2009.
147 Various aspects of the FSA's work will be divided between the Financial Conduct Authority, the Prudential Regulatory Agency and also the Serious Fraud Office.

9.8.2 Regulated activities of trustees and authorisation

The scope of the regulation of trustees by the FSA

Any person who carries on a regulated activity in the UK is required to obtain authorisation to do so from the FSA.[148] Therefore, one is not entitled to carry on investment activity as a business without authorisation,[149] nor is one entitled to advertise the sale of any investment without FSA authorisation,[150] nor is one entitled (in effect) to do any preparatory or inchoate act connected with engaging in investment activity.[151] The penalties for acting without authorisation vary from the unenforceability of any agreements formed by an unauthorised person[152] to criminal penalties for the breach of the code prohibiting financial promotion and advertisement.[153]

In this discussion we shall first consider the case law on what it means to conduct investment activities by way of business such that one falls within the regulatory ambit of the FSA; and secondly we shall consider the terms of the Regulated Activities Order (RAO), which specifies which forms of trustee activity will be excluded from regulation and, by inference, which will not.

Trustees will be regulated under the FSMA 2000 by the FSA in circumstances in which they are conducting 'regulated activities'[154] of a specified kind[155] and always providing that they do so 'by way of business'.[156] The meaning of 'activities carried on by way of business' is defined by Treasury regulation, further to s 419 of the FSMA 2000, such that it applies to persons who deal in investments either as principal or as agent, including those safeguarding or administering investments, as well as those advising on investments within the context of the RAO.[157] However, the appropriate regulation is very vague about the content of 'business' for these purposes,[158] providing only that it applies to those dealing in investments either as principal or as agent, or safeguarding or administering investments, or advising on investments within the context of the Regulated Activities Order. The FSA rulebooks are similarly non-committal as to the meaning of the term 'business'.[159] The only case in which the meaning of 'business' was considered within the financial services context was (in relation to s 63 of the old Financial Services Act 1986) in the case of *Morgan Grenfell & Co v Welwyn Hatfield DC*.[160] In that case, Hobhouse J suggested that there was no reason to impose a narrow meaning on that term for these purposes and that 'it should not be given a technical construction but rather one which conformed to what in ordinary parlance would be described as a business transaction as opposed to something personal or casual'.[161]

---

148 FSMA 2000, s 19.
149 *Ibid.*
150 *Ibid*, s 21.
151 *Ibid*, s 26.
152 *Ibid*, s 26.
153 *Ibid*, ss 21, 23.
154 *Ibid*, s 22(2), giving effect to s 22(1) by way of Sched 2.
155 That is, those listed in *Ibid*, Sched 2, as considered below.
156 *Ibid*, s 22(1).
157 The Financial Services and Markets Act 2000 (Regulated Activities) Order 2001 (SI 2001/544).
158 The Financial Services and Markets Act 2000 (Carrying on Regulated Activities by Way of Business) Order 2001, para 3.
159 FSA, *AUTH Module*, Block 3, Chapter 2 (Regulatory Processes).
160 [1995] 1 All ER 1.
161 *Ibid.*

This has been the tenor of most of the case law considering the meaning of the term 'business' in other contexts.[162] The frequency of the investment activity might be a guide to, but not conclusive of, the question whether or not a business of investment is being carried on.[163] While many of the decided cases on the meaning of the term 'business' have emphasised the frequency with which the activity must be carried on to constitute a business, there are three other factors which must be of importance: whether or not the trustee takes a personal benefit beyond any fee ordinarily accruing to her under the terms of the trust, the amount of money involved in the trust fund, and the quantity and sophistication of the investment choices made.[164] Therefore, it is suggested that there are four general badges of business in this context: time,[165] volume,[166] profit[167] and quality.[168]

The excluded categories of trustee activity under the Regulated Activities Order (RAO)

A rough rule of thumb would operate as follows: trustees will be covered by FSA regulation (under FSMA and the RAO) if they fall within any of the specified activities in the RAO; unless they benefit from any one of the six categories of exclusion (set out below) *and* provided they are not remunerated for their activities.

Trustees will be liable to regulation under FSMA 2000 if they carry on an activity which falls within the RAO. Trustees' liability to regulation will be excluded, however, if they fall within any of the exclusions provided by Article 66 of the RAO, dealing with 'Trustees, nominees and personal representatives'. In outline, those categories of person are fivefold. First, bare trustees (who are not acting as a principal in the transaction) will not fall within FSA regulation for the purposes of Article 25 of the RAO (dealing with making deals in investments on behalf of another), provided that such a bare trustee does not hold himself out as providing a service of buying and selling investments.[169] Secondly, a trustee will not be subjected to FSA regulation in relation to a transactions carried out in the administration of testamentary trusts.[170] Thirdly, a trustee will not be caught under Article 37 of the RAO

---

162 *American Leaf Blending Co Sdn Bhd v Director General of Inland Revenue* [1979] AC 676.
163 *Morgan Grenfell & Co v Welwyn Hatfield DC* [1995] 1 All ER 1.
164 *Re Brauch* [1978] 1 Ch 316, in which case it was accepted that for a business to be conducted, the defendant would need to be acting on behalf of other people. Cf *R v Wilson* [1997] 1 All ER 119, in which to be carrying on an insurance business one had to be acting for one's own benefit and not for the benefit of others.
165 *Smith v Anderson* (1880) 15 Ch D 247 (speculative activity carried on frequently and over a long period of time is likely to indicate a business); *Re Debtor ex p Debtor (No 490 of 1935)* [1936] Ch 237. See also *American Leaf Blending Co Sdn Bhd v Director General of Inland Revenue* [1979] AC 676 (occasional dealings with capital assets may nevertheless indicate a business is the underlying purpose); *Morgan Grenfell & Co v Welwyn Hatfield DC* [1995] 1 All ER 1.
166 *Re Griffin ex p Board of Trade* (1890) 60 LJ QB 235; *CIR v Marine Steam Turbine Co Ltd* [1920] 1 KB 193 (where an activity is conducted only rarely it is unlikely to be a business, whereas regular repetition of activity is more likely to indicate a business).
167 *Rolls v Miller* (1884) 27 Ch D 71 (pleasure is not business); *R v Crayden* [1978] 1 WLR 604 (the generation of profit ordinarily indicates a business).
168 Eg, *Calkin v IRC* [1984] 1 NZLR 1, in which the New Zealand Court of Appeal considered that the term 'business' concerned 'the nature of the activities carried on including the period over which they are engaged in, the scale of operation and the volume of transactions, the commitment of time, money and effort, the pattern of activity and the financial results'.
169 The Financial Services and Markets Act 2000 (Regulated Activities) Order 2001, art 66(1).
170 *Ibid*, art 66(2).

(in relation to managing investments) unless 'he holds himself out as providing a service' or the assets are held as part of an occupational pension scheme.[171] Fourthly, a trustee will not be caught under Article 40 of the RAO (in relation to safeguarding and administering investments) unless 'he holds himself out as providing a service' in that regard.[172] Fifthly, a trustee will not be caught by FSA regulation under Article 45 of the RAO (in relation to sending dematerialised instructions) provided that the instruction relates to an investment held by him as trustee or as personal representative.[173] Sixthly, a trustee will be excluded from FSA regulation for the purposes of Article 53 of the RAO (advising on investments) if the advice is given to a fellow trustee or to a beneficiary.[174]

However, there is an important limitation on these exclusions. In general terms, except for the first exclusion relating to bare trustees, none of these exclusions from regulatory oversight will apply so as to exclude that trustee from FSA regulation if the trustee is remunerated for supplying these services over and above any remuneration for acting as trustee in the ordinary way: that is, it would seem, if he is acting by way of business in relation to the investments.[175]

It should be remembered that, under English law, many forms of trustee will not be caught by FSA regulation because their ordinary activities do not involve investment of the sort envisaged by the RAO: for example, trustees of land holding that land for the occupation of the beneficiaries. Only trustees involved in investment of the trust property will potentially fall within FSA regulation, in the manner considered above. The central question will therefore be whether or not a trustee, aside from these exemptions, falls within the scope of the business activities which are covered by the RAO.

9.8.3 Conduct of business regulation

If a professional trustee conducts business which falls within FSA regulation, then that trustee will be required to obey the Conduct of Business Sourcebook ('COBS'), which is the regulatory rulebook published and created by the FSA.[176] COBS implements the principles in the Markets in Financial Instruments Directive (MiFID). Specifically, COBS sets out the manner in which financial institutions are required to deal with their customers. The watchword of conduct of business regulation is 'suitability': that is, the trustee must deal with the customer in a suitable manner and the investments which are provided for the customer must be suitable for that customer's purposes. Therefore, as considered thus far in this chapter, the trustee will be held to the context in which she operates: so, complex investment activities will be inappropriate for risk averse family trusts and so forth. The trustee faces regulatory penalties and liability in tort for failure to sell appropriate investments to the trust, as well as potential liabilities as considered thus far for failure to perform the obligations of trustee properly.

---

171 *Ibid*, art 66(3).
172 *Ibid*, art 66(4).
173 *Ibid*, art 66(5).
174 *Ibid*, art 66(6).
175 *Ibid*, art 66(7).
176 FSA Handbook, *Conduct of Business Sourcebook* ('COBS') was introduced in 2007 to account for the Markets in Financial Instruments Directive (MiFID).

Under COBS, regulated trustees are required, *inter alia*, to act 'honestly, fairly and professionally in accordance with the best interests of their clients',[177] which is referred to as the 'client's best interests' rule; the trustees are required to classify the level of expertise of the client against the regulatory categories and to treat the customer accordingly; [178] the trustees are required to ensure 'best execution' of each transaction for the customer, including obtaining the best available price.[179] The general requirement which underpins COBS is that when the seller communicates information to a customer, it must do so in a way which is 'clear, fair and not misleading'. The regulations provide that the seller must have regard to the level of knowledge which the buyer has of the transaction at issue when making written or oral communications. Further, the seller must ensure that its officers do not take any inducements or 'soft commissions' in effecting transactions. At the outset, the seller must provide a private customer with its terms of business before any designated business is conducted,[180] whereas intermediate customers must only be so informed within a reasonable period of the beginning of designated business being conducted.[181] Those terms of business should include mention of the commencement of the terms of business, the applicable regulator, the investment objectives, any restrictions on the relevant designated business, which services will be provided, how payment for services will be effected, disclosure of any polarisation, whether the seller is to act as investment manager, any conflicts of interest, and whether or not the client has a right to withdraw.[182] Conduct of business regulation imposes active obligations on regulated trustees above and beyond any in the trust instrument or in general trusts law.

9.8.4 Control of misfeasance by financial regulation

Market abuse

The market abuse code was introduced by the FSMA 2000 in order to expand the powers of the FSA to prosecute any market participants for any misfeasance in financial dealings. The importance of this regime is that it carries punitive penalties but that it does not replicate all of the protections and rights which are characteristic of the criminal law.[183] The market abuse regime relates to 'qualifying investments' traded on LIFFE, the London Stock Exchange and other markets[184] where the behaviour in question would be regarded by 'a regular user of that market' as a failure 'to observe the standard of behaviour reasonably expected of a person in. . . . their position in relation to the market'.[185] A 'regular user' is

---

177 MiFID, art 19(1).
178 MiFID, art 19(4).
179 MiFID, art 21.
180 Except where the client is habitually resident outside the UK.
181 COB, 4.2.5.
182 COB, 4.2.15.
183 This in itself may cause difficulties in relation to Art 6 of the European Convention on Human Rights and its guarantees of a right to a fair trial. Its legislative purpose was therefore to make successful prosecutions for market abuse easier to obtain than had been the case under the pre-existing criminal law.
184 FSMA 2000, s 118(1).
185 *Ibid*, s 118(3).

someone who is a 'reasonable person who regularly deals on that market in investments of the kind in question'; the term 'regular user' appears frequently in this code.[186] More specifically, the behaviour in question must exhibit three further features. First, it must be based on information which is 'not generally available to those using the market' but which would be considered by a 'regular user' of the market to be 'relevant' to entering into transactions on that market.[187] Secondly, it must be 'likely to give a regular user of the market a false or misleading impression' as to the supply of, demand for and value of the investments in question.[188] Thirdly, the behaviour must be of a kind that would be 'likely. . . . to distort the market' in question.[189] To supplement this statutory code, there is a code of conduct (referred to as 'MAR 1' in the FSA Handbook)[190] which is required to be created by the FSA under the auspices of the FSMA 2000.[191]

Making misleading statements

The offence of making misleading statements is contained in s 397 of the FSMA 2000.[192] That offence is committed in one of three circumstances. First, where a person makes a statement, promise or forecast which 'he knows to be misleading, false or deceptive in a material particular'.[193] What is not made clear in this context is what will constitute knowledge; that is, whether one can be taken to 'know' a statement is misleading only if they have actual knowledge, or whether it would be sufficient to have constructive notice of its misleading nature, or whether it would be sufficient that one has wilfully and recklessly failed to make the inquiries which an honest and reasonable person would have made in that context.[194] Secondly, where such a person 'dishonestly conceals any material facts' in relation to a statement, promise or forecast.[195] Again, it is unclear whether dishonesty in this context would require actual fraud or whether it could be established in circumstances in which the defendant fails to act as an honest person would have acted in the circumstances.[196] It is suggested that the latter would accord most closely with the 'reasonable user' test within the market abuse code more generally. Thirdly, where such a person 'recklessly makes (dishonestly or otherwise) a statement, promise or forecast which is misleading, false or deceptive in a material particular'.[197]

Money laundering

The development of money laundering is significant in relation to trusts because trusts are an otherwise unregulated means by which ownership of assets can be hidden or obfuscated. The

---

186 *Ibid*, s 118(10).
187 *Ibid*, s 118(2)(a).
188 *Ibid*, s 118(2)(b).
189 *Ibid*, s 118(2)(c).
190 Published under the Financial Services Authority, Market Conduct Sourcebook Instrument 2001 (MAR 1).
191 FSMA 2000, s 119.
192 Cf *R v De Berenger* (1814) 3 M & S 66.
193 FSMA 2000, s 397(1)(a).
194 Eg, *Re Montagu's Settlement* [1987] Ch 264.
195 FSMA 2000, s 397(1)(b).
196 Eg, *Royal Brunei Airlines v Tan* [1995] 2 AC 378.
197 FSMA 2000, s 397(1)(c).

regulation of institutions, such as professional trustees, which operate accounts includes money-laundering regulation. In the UK, the Proceeds of Crime Act 2002 ('POCA 2002') seeks to make provision for the treatment of the proceeds of criminal activity and the Terrorism Act 2000 makes provision for the treatment of funds which it is suspected will be applied for the purposes of terrorism. The POCA 2002 criminalised two principal activities: first, the receipt of any benefit from 'criminal property';[198] and, secondly, 'tipping off' a money launderer. A third, and significant, purpose of the Act and regulations created in relation to it is to require the disclosure of specified types of dealing to the authorities. Sections 330, 331 and 332 of the POCA 2002 provide for a range of criminal offences in the event that there is a failure to disclose instances of money laundering, where the defendant knows or is suspicious of, or if the defendant has reasonable grounds to believe that money laundering offences have taken place.

For financial institutions which operate as trustees of complex trusts, there is a strict regulatory framework governing their activities to seek out money laundering. The Money Laundering Regulations 2007 ('MLR 2007')[199] implemented the EC Third Money Laundering Directive 2005.[200] These regulations are then implemented and supplemented by the FSA in its *Money Laundering Sourcebook* in relation to regulated firms. The MLR 2007 impose standards of behaviour on financial institutions governing 'know your client' regulation in relation to customers. The entities which are governed by these regulations are the sorts of entities through which large or small amounts of cash, or in some cases securities, could be passed and so laundered more efficiently than in other contexts. The 'know your client' regulation at issue here is a requirement that the regulated entities confirm the identity of their customers and keep records in an appropriate fashion through their appropriately trained staff. The intention, in effect, is to erect a structure for observing client conduct so that a documentation trail will be prepared for any subsequent prosecution or investigative activity. The heart of the regulations is the set of obligations imposed on regulated persons to keep records and to report certain types of action. The regulated persons are required to conduct due diligence in relation to their customers. This must be done by using documents or other information which has been acquired from a reliable source. Regulated persons are required to ensure that they keep appropriate records of their dealings with their customers. This in turn requires that the regulated persons have staff who are suitably trained in their responsibilities to maintain such records.

Insider dealing

The legislative code on insider dealing was established under Part V of the Criminal Justice Act 1993 and is intended to deal with any situation in which a market participant abuses

---

198 The principal offences under s 327 of POCA 2002 apply where a person either conceals, disguises, converts or transfers 'criminal property', or removes it from the jurisdiction. There are therefore five offences contained within this subsection, all of which relate to 'criminal property'. Criminal property is defined as being 'a person's benefit from criminal conduct or it represents such a benefit' or if 'the alleged offender knows or suspects that it constitutes or represents such a benefit' (Proceeds of Crime Act 2002, s 340(3)). There is a separate offence under s 328 of POCA 2002 for any person who 'enters into or becomes concerned in an arrangement' which she 'knows or suspects facilitates (by whatever means) the acquisition, retention, use or control of criminal property by or on behalf of another person'. There is a further offence under s 329(1) of POCA 2002 if 'a person . . . (c) has possession of criminal property'.

199 SI 2007/2157.

200 Directive 205/60/EC of 2005, which came into effect on 26 October 2005.

price-sensitive information which she acquires when acting as an insider when dealing in price-affected securities.[201] Further to the enactment of the FSMA 2000, the FSA has the power to prosecute any allegations of insider dealing.[202]

9.9 BREACH OF TRUST AND INVESTMENT

9.9.1 The concept of 'loss' and breach of trust

Breach of trust in general terms

The leading case of *Target Holdings v Redferns*,[203] discussed in detail in Chapter 18, sets out the nature of the trustee's liability for breach of trust. *Target Holdings* identifies three categories of liability: the liability to replace the trust fund; the liability to replace a cash equivalent to the value of the trust fund; and a liability to provide equitable compensation to the beneficiaries.[204] In relation to investment, however, more complex questions arise as to whether or not there has been a loss suffered at all, for example, if an investment has been made in unauthorised investments when authorised investments might have realised a larger profit, or where another investment strategy altogether might have realised a greater profit. In such circumstances, it is not evidently an out-of-pocket loss but rather a loss of opportunity which has been suffered.

Investment in unauthorised investments

The core issue arising in this context revolves around the following problem: what if a trustee invests in something which is outside the scope of his authority? The question is whether or not the trustee should be required to replace the trust fund. In the context of investments in financial securities, the issue is whether the trustees are required to replace the stock which they have sold in breach of trust, or simply repay the cash equivalent of the sale. The answer suggested by the case of *Re Massingberd*[205] is that the trustees should replace the stock that is sold and not simply provide a mere cash equivalent. This appears to coincide with the general right of the beneficiary in the property held in the trust and not simply an interest in an amount of value, which is dependent on the market value of the securities at any particular time, thus returning us to the core debate considered in Chapter 18 as to whether this area of law is concerned with rights in specific property or rights merely in relation to a given value attaching to different property from time to time.

Where unauthorised investments made a profit but a lesser profit than authorised investments

The issue nevertheless remains as to the value of unauthorised investments which must be replaced by authorised investments, particularly in circumstances in which the unauthorised

201 Criminal Justice Act 1993, s 52.
202 FSMA 2000, s 402. See Alastair Hudson, *The Law of Finance*, Sweet & Maxwell, 2009, Chapter 14.
203 [1996] 1 AC 421, [1995] 3 WLR 352, [1995] 3 All ER 785.
204 *Ibid.*
205 (1890) 63 LT 296.

investments generated a profit but arguably a lesser profit than authorised investments would have done. Usually, the trustee's duty is to restore the trust to the value it contained before the breach of trust,[206] in which case the acquisition of an unauthorised investment which made a smaller profit than might have been made by an authorised investment would not disclose any loss. That is the first possible analysis. However, there is another possible analysis. The trustee might be held liable to account to the trust for the difference between the profit which was actually made from the unauthorised investments and the profit which would have been made by authorised investments on the basis that the trust lost the opportunity to make the larger profit. It has long been held that trustees can offset gains made, even through breaches of trust, against losses made through the same breach of trust, and therefore it is only for the difference in amounts of profit for which the trustee could be liable.[207]

It has been suggested in Australia that it would be open to the beneficiaries to surcharge the trustees' accounts for the failure to acquire the return on appropriate investments.[208] The requirement on the trustee is that the trust fund be placed in the position it would have been in but for the trustees' breach of trust.[209] In that sense, the trust would have been in possession of a greater profit but for the trustees' breach of trust and therefore that the trustees be required to fund the difference between those two amounts.

The practical difficulty would be in demonstrating as a matter of fact that the trustees would have been compelled to acquire a particular set of investments, which would have realised the profit contended for, from among the range of possible investments which would otherwise have been possible.[210] Suppose that within the class of authorised investments, investment x would have generated a larger profit than the unauthorised investments actually acquired, but that investment y from the class of authorised investments would have made a lower profit. How can the beneficiaries demonstrate that they have suffered an opportunity loss? After all, it is unlikely that *all* of the possible investments from the class of authorised investments would have generated the same level of profit and therefore the opportunity loss to the fund would be equally difficult to prove. Where some authorised investments would have generated a profit and others a loss, it is suggested that it would be impossible to prove as a matter of fact that the trust did in fact suffer a loss through the unauthorised investments.

9.9.2 Measurement of liability in accordance with standard market practice

As was considered above at para 9.6.5, to establish that a trustee – in particular a professional trustee – has acted in breach of her general duties to invest the trust property, it is often necessary to demonstrate that that trustee has acted differently from the rest of the

---

206 *Nocton v Lord Ashburton* [1914] AC 932, 952, *per* Lord Haldane LC.
207 *Wiles v Gresham* (1854) 2 Drew 258, 271; *Fletcher v Green* (1864) 33 Beav 426; *Vyse v Foster* (1872) 8 Ch App 309, affirmed at (1874) LR 7 HL 318; *Re Deare* (1895) 11 TLR 183.
208 *Glazier v Australian Men's Health (No 2)* [2001] NSW SC 6.
209 *Re Dawson* [1966] 2 NSWLR 211.
210 If the unauthorised investments were in bonds, whereas the class of authorised investments was limited exclusively to share markets, it would be difficult to prove that the trustees would have acquired shares which made a profit as opposed to shares which made a loss. Furthermore, it would be impossible to know precisely which shares would have been acquired and, because different shares would make different levels of profit, it would be impossible to demonstrate with exactitude the extent of the trust's loss. Alternatively, a broadbrush approach would be to use an index of bonds against an index of equities to estimate the loss.

investment market. Or, to put the point more precisely, the trustee will frequently be able to defend any suggestion that she has failed to act in accordance with her general duties of investment by demonstrating that her investment strategy was similar in its material respects with the rest of the investment market investing trust funds of a similar kind.[211]

9.9.3 The validity of exclusion clauses under case law

Exclusion clauses in general terms

A provision in a trust instrument, or a contractual provision entered into between a trustee and some person employed to act on behalf of the trust, which restricts the liability of either the trustee or that other person will be valid unless it purports to limit that person's liability for dishonesty. Ordinarily, professional trustees will not agree to act unless their obligations are limited by contract. Paradoxically, this has the result that in the former situation, the trustee is punished for a lack of expertise if the trust does not generate a reasonable return, whereas in the latter, the professional trustee is absolved from any failure to generate a profit precisely by virtue of her expertise.[212] The case of *Armitage v Nurse*[213] (decided before the enactment of the TA 2000, discussed above) held that a clause excluding a trustee's personal liability would be valid even where it purported to limit that trustee's liability for gross negligence. In explaining the limit of the trustee's obligations, Millett LJ had the following to say:

> [T]here is an irreducible core of obligations owed by the trustees to the beneficiaries and enforceable by them which is fundamental to the concept of a trust. If the beneficiaries have no rights enforceable against the trustees there are no trusts. But I do not accept the further submission that their core obligations include the duties of skill and care, prudence and diligence. The duty of trustees to perform the trusts honestly and in good faith for the benefit of the beneficiaries is the minimum necessary to give substance to the trusts, but in my opinion it is sufficient . . . a trustee who relied on the presence of a trustee exemption clause to justify what he proposed to do would thereby lose its protection: he would be acting recklessly in the proper sense of the term.

The approach of the court would have been different if the trustees had acted dishonestly or fraudulently: in such a situation, the exclusion clause would have had no effect in the opinion of the court. To demonstrate that there has been fraud would be difficult to prove in a situation in which the trustee did not take any direct, personal benefit. The more likely ground for any claim brought by the beneficiaries would be that the trustee had breached a duty to act fairly between the beneficiaries or to do the best possible for the beneficiaries within the limits of current portfolio theory, all of which were considered above.[214] This area of law was analysed in detail in section 8.5.

---

211 *Nestlé v National Westminster Bank plc* [1993] 1 WLR 1260.
212 *Armitage v Nurse* [1998] Ch 241.
213 *Ibid.*
214 See para 9.5.2 above.

Exclusion of liability where there is negligence in the management of investments

The issue of the exclusion of liability in an investment contract was considered in *Galmerrow Securities Ltd v National Westminster Bank plc*,[215] a case in which the fiduciaries in a unit trust scheme, here the National Westminster Bank, had expressly excluded their liability for the exercise of their investment obligations except in cases of negligence or fraud. The beneficiaries contended that the scheme managers had been negligent in their investment of the bulk of the fund in the real property market. The scheme managers contended that it would have been impossible to have amended their investment powers so as to have avoided the investment objectives of the unit trust and to have extracted the fund's investments from the real property market before it collapsed. The court held that:

> The venture was a speculation and like all speculations carried with it the risk of failure. It would not be right to visit the consequences of that misjudgment of the market upon NatWest which is not shown to have had any power open to it which would remedy or mitigate the consequence . . . it is not negligent to fail to act where no alternative course of conduct to the continuance of the present arrangement is proved to have been available to the person who has a power to act.

Therefore, the circumstances precluded the trustees from suffering liability because there was no other course of action open to them. The trust's objective of speculating on the property market was, quite simply, a speculation which failed. It was, perhaps, a result of the intractability of the terms of the trust and of the requirement that those terms be sufficiently rigid to attract the approval of the fund's regulators that this speculation could not be undone.

9.9.4 Different levels of liability for different types of trustee

A trust can be used specifically for investment purposes. Unit trusts, pension funds (considered in Chapter 24) or even investment vehicles like hedge funds (occasionally structured as trusts, rather than companies or partnerships) are all based on the ordinary principles of trust. In such a situation, the trustees will be investment professionals with suitable expertise to choose between the available investment options. The terms of the trust will incorporate specific provisions (forming a contract with those professional trustees) under which the trustees agree to offer their services. As considered above, this contractual limitation in investment situations generally takes the form of a 'conduct of business' letter constructed to comply with the FSA's regulatory rules.

Alternatively, the trustee may be someone who has no expertise in financial markets but who is responsible for the trust fund. The question will therefore be as to the comparative levels of obligation to generate the best possible return from the trust. In considering unit trusts and pension funds, there are particular regulatory and statutory regimes which cover those particular entities over and above the general rules of trustee liability. Evidently, the nature of the trust property itself will have an impact on the extent of that obligation in any particular circumstance: land has different investment qualities from financial securities

---

215 [2002] WTLR 125, at 155.

from valuable oil paintings. Necessarily different forms of property will necessitate subtly different forms of investment obligation.

What is complex about the investment trust is that the beneficiary is frequently only interested in the return which the investment promises and not particularly interested in establishing meaningful ties of ownership with the property which comprises the trust. In relation to trusts over a house which the beneficiaries occupy as their home,[216] there will necessarily be close ties of ownership such that the beneficiaries will be particularly concerned to ensure that the trustees maintain the home for their benefit and also for their occupation. By contrast, participants in a unit trust scheme are comparatively uninterested in forging emotional bonds with the scheme property and instead are almost entirely concerned with the profit which the scheme manager (or, for our purposes, trustee) can generate on their behalf. Participants in a unit trust are beneficiaries and the scheme property is held on trust for them, but there is also an investment contract between the scheme manager and the participants which is the core of their relationship *in commercial terms*. Therefore, the topic of investment of trust funds cuts to the heart of the nature of trusteeship because the manner in which the fund is invested and the property maintained will differ markedly from context to context. The standard of behaviour expected from a professional investment manager acting as a trustee therefore ought to reflect both its expertise and the parties common intention in generating the maximum possible profit; by contrast, family trusts relating to land will be concerned to maintain the land and family trusts over money and will generally wish to take less risk in their investment portfolio than commercial parties would.[217]

9.9.5 Limitation of liabilities arising under statute

Liabilities under the Trustee Act 2000

The provisions of the TA 2000 can be expressly or implied displaced by the trust instrument.[218] In consequence, this duty of care may be limited by the express provisions of the trust, or even by a construction of those provisions which suggests that the settlor's intention was to exclude such a liability. The duty of care is not expressed by the 2000 Act to be a general duty in the form of an all-encompassing statutory tort. Rather, the Act provides that the duty will apply in certain limited circumstances.[219] The principal instance in which the statutory duty of care applies[220] is in relation to a trustee exercising a 'general power of investment'[221] under the Act or any other power of investment 'however conferred'.[222] Alternatively, the duty of care applies when trustees are carrying out obligations under the

---

216 Considered in Chapter 16.
217 Cf para 22.4.3 below.
218 TA 2000, Sched 1, para 7.
219 *Ibid*, s 2.
220 *Ibid*, Sched 1, para 1.
221 As defined by *ibid*, s 3(2) and considered below.
222 With the effect that this provision may be only mandatory provision in the legislation because it appears to apply to powers of investment in general and not simply to that set out in the TA 2000, s 3(2). However, the Act does permit an express exclusion in the trust to obviate the operation of any of the provisions in the Act and therefore it would appear possible to circumscribe the operation of this provision: TA 2000, Sched 1, para 7.
223 TA 2000, ss 4, 5.

Act in relation to exercising or reviewing powers of investment.[223] The duty of care also applies in relation to the acquisition of land,[224] which would logically appear to cover the use of appropriate advice and appropriate levels of care in selecting the land, contracting for its purchase and insuring it.[225] It applies in general terms in relation to the appointment of agents, custodians and nominees:[226] which would include the selection of reasonable agents with appropriate qualifications for the task for which they were engaged.

Authorised persons under the Financial Services and Markets Act 2000

The principles relating to the trustees' ability to exclude or limit their liability by contract were considered in Chapter 8.[227] In relation to trustees who are regulated by the FSA, there are regulations as to the conduct of investment business which prevent the regulated (or, authorised) person from relying on contractual provisions which are inappropriate for that type of customer, as described under the conduct of business regulations.[228]

9.10 THE SELECTION AND MANAGEMENT OF PARTICULAR TYPES OF INVESTMENT

9.10.1 The duty in general terms

The extent of the trustee's obligation to intervene in the investments held by the trust is illustrated starkly by *Bartlett v Barclays Bank*[229] in which, despite a near-total shareholding, the trustees failed to be forewarned about a disastrous property speculation made by the company in which the trustees had invested. The questions arose as to the scope of the duty of the trustee; the extent to which the trustee bank had been in breach of that duty; whether any such breach of duty had caused the loss suffered by fund; and the extent to which the trustee bank was liable to make good that loss.

It was held that the standard of observation and control in relation to the investments was the 'same care as an ordinary prudent man of business would extend towards his own affairs'. That left the question as to the nature of the obligation: it was held that 'the duty rather is to take such care as an ordinary prudent man would take if he were minded to make an investment for the benefit of other people for whom he felt morally bound to provide'. Therefore, the trustee's obligation is to treat the beneficiaries as though they were effectively dependant children for whom the trustee would be required to provide. The trustee would be permitted to take risks but not to expose the beneficiaries to hazard within the scope of that investment policy.

Given that the trustees in that case had been investing in a private company, the trustees' obligation was to 'ensure an adequate flow of information in time to make use of controlling interest'. In other words, in some situations the trustee will be required to intervene and ensure

---

224 *Ibid*, Sched 1, para 2.
225 *Ibid*, Sched 1, para 5; TA 1925, s 19.
226 *Ibid*, Sched 1, para 3.
227 See para 8.5.1 above.
228 See generally Thomas and Hudson, 2004, 1505 *et seq*.
229 [1980] Ch 515.

that she is able to amass sufficient information to manage the investment. All that can be said in summary of this area of the law is that it will depend on the context; where the trustee has access to some control of a company, then the trustee would be expected to procure some control in return for that significant investment, whereas a trustee holding only a small investment in a large public company would not have such control (unless a trustee of a particularly large pension fund, for example) and therefore would not be expected to exert such control.

9.10.2 When the trust property includes a controlling interest in a company

The application of these general principles to the situation in which trust property includes a controlling interest in a company was considered in *Re Lucking's WT*.[230] It was said that the trustee should not simply consider the information she receives as shareholder, but should, in some way, ensure that she is represented on the board. The extent of such representation will depend upon the circumstances: she may be required to act as managing director or she may only need to ensure that she has a nominee on the board who can report back. This principle was interpreted more liberally in *Bartlett v Barclays Bank*,[231] in which it was said that the trustee need not always be represented on the board if the circumstances did not require this, provided that the trustee retained a sufficient flow of information from the company in accordance with the size of the shareholding. Other methods of control over the company's affairs may be sufficient depending on the context.

9.10.3 When the trust property includes a mortgage

There has been much discussion as to whether power to invest in mortgages allows investment in equitable and second mortgages. In view of the objections to the latter put forward in *Chapman v Browne*,[232] it seems unlikely that the latter, at least, are permissible notwithstanding the removal of the objection concerning protection by the Land Charges Act 1972.

Section 8 of the TA 1925 provides guidelines for a trustee investing in a mortgage to follow. If she does so, she will not subsequently be liable if the security later proves to be insufficient, in line with the following: the trustee must invest on the basis of a report prepared by an able and independent surveyor or valuer as to the value of property;[233] the amount of the loan must not exceed two-thirds of the value as stated in the report;[234] and the report expressly advises the loan, in which case the trustee is entitled to presume that this advice is correct.[235]

If the only aspect of non-compliance with s 8 is the amount loaned, s 9 of the TA 1925 still offers some protection in that the trustee will only be liable for the difference between the amount in fact lent and the amount which should have been lent. In addition to following the general principles, a trustee must limit the investments to those authorised either by the trust instrument or by statute.

230 [1968] 1 WLR 866.
231 [1980] Ch 515.
232 (1801) 6 Ves 404.
233 TA 1925, s 8(1)(a).
234 *Ibid*, s 8(1)(b).
235 *Ibid*, s 8(1)(c); *Shaw v Cates* [1909] 1 Ch 389.

9.10.4 Duty to control delegates under the case law

In section 9.2, the specific context of the delegation of trustee powers was considered in relation to the TA 2000. It is possible to exclude those provisions expressly in the trust instrument. This discussion considers the way in which the case law has developed principles to
govern the manner in which trustees are to be held responsible for any failure to control the
actions of anyone to whom their powers are delegated. In the context of delegating authority
to investment, the classic statement of the trustee's obligation is set out in *Speight v Gaunt*[236]
in the decision of Lord Jessel MR:

> It seems to me that on general trust principles a trustee ought to conduct the business of
> the trust in the same manner that an ordinary prudent man of business would conduct his
> own, and that beyond that there is no liability or obligation on the trustee.

Exceptionally in *Re Vickery*,[237] where a trustee had given money to solicitor who absconded
with it, Maugham J considered the central issue to be whether the trustee was negligent in
employing the solicitor or permitting money to remain in his hands. It was held that there
was no liability on the trustee unless there had been some 'wilful default' by him, being
something more than a mere lack of care. This test has come in for much academic criticism,[238] being based on *Re City Equitable Fire Insurance*,[239] which was a company law case
looking at the obligations of company directors and auditors in the context of specific articles of association.

Jones contends that the better test is one based on 'want of reasonable care' rather than
'wilful default'. It is said by some commentators that the test for trustees ought to be higher.
Similarly, Hayton argues that there are problems with delegation to market makers or to
finance professionals who will deal on their own account, as well as providing financial
products for their clients; that is, market makers sell their clients securities which the market
maker already owns rather than going to buy securities on the open market to the client's
order. Consequently, there is a conflict of interest between such market makers' desire to
offload at a profit securities which they have already bought instead of focusing entirely on
identifying securities in the broader marketplace which might have been more advantageous
to the client. In his suggestion, it would be better to subject this area to control by established
market regulators such as the FSA.

The core issue appears to be whether or not the law should recognise that the beneficiaries
(ultimately) have to rely on market professionals to do things which trustees cannot do.
Within that recognition must be some recognition of the role of market regulators and the
shortcomings of regulation. The requirement of equity that beneficiaries under trusts should
be insulated from risk of market movement and personnel default (whether by trustees or

236 (1883) 9 App Cas 1.
237 [1931] 1 Ch 572.
238 Jones, 1968; Hayton, 1990:2.
239 [1925] Ch 407.

market professionals) in making investment decisions does not accord with the basis upon which financial professionals are prepared to enter into terms of business. The client is required to accept the risk of loss as well as the possibility of gain. In this context, equity must also consider how to balance the need to make best profit against requirement not to lose trust money. One solution might be to grant an automatic trustee indemnity where the trustee is able to obtain an indemnity from the market professional, thus freeing trustees from the need to control that which they cannot control in generally standard form 'terms of business' letters.

The context of risk is therefore problematic in equity. The courts have imposed near strict liability in the context of fiduciaries.[240] The decision of the Privy Council in *Royal Brunei Airlines v Tan*[241] indicates a growing acceptance of reckless risk-taking as part of the unconscionable behaviour against which equity will act.[242] However, the attitude of the House of Lords in *Westdeutsche Landesbank v Islington*[243] (for example) failed to accept the commercial context of risk management as something which ought similarly to be encompassed in granting remedies. The context of equitable proprietary remedies remains outwith the ambit of these developing principles, except for the protection of beneficiaries.

---

240 *Bartlett v Barclays Bank* [1980] Ch 515; *Nestlé v National Westminster Bank plc* [1993] 1 WLR 1260, [1994] 1 All ER 118.
241 [1995] 2 AC 378.
242 See Chapter 12.
243 [1996] AC 669.

Chapter 10

The powers of trustees and the variation of trusts

10.1 GENERAL POWERS OF TRUSTEES

10.1.1 The nature of trustees' powers

This chapter is concerned with trustees' powers, whereas the previous two chapters have focused primarily on the trustees' obligations and only considered their powers in relation to the investment of the trust property. There are two contexts in which trustees have powers.[1] The first context was considered in Chapter 3 in relation to the powers granted to trustees or other fiduciaries in relation to the administration of property: that is, the distinction between trust obligations, discretionary trust powers, fiduciary mere powers and personal powers. The second context relates to the inherent capabilities of trustees in general terms, beyond any specific provision in a trust instrument. This chapter is concerned with this second form of power.[2] The trustee is the legal owner of the trust property and as such must have a number of powers to use that property, beyond any rights or powers set out in the trust instrument. General powers granted by the law of trusts supplement the trust instrument,[3] where those powers are not expressly excluded by the trust instrument or are not inconsistent with the terms of that instrument.[4] Of particular importance in practice are the powers of maintenance and advancement, considered in section 10.2 below, and the power to delegate, considered in section 10.3.

10.1.2 Power to give receipts

Trustees have an implicit power to give receipts. The question is then as to the ability of such receipts to discharge third parties from any liability owed to the trust. Under statute, however, the giving of a receipt is a sufficient discharge from liability for the misapplication of trust property for anyone dealing with a trust.[5]

10.1.3 Power to compromise

Trustees are empowered under statute to compromise in litigation. Two trustees or a trust corporation may reach such a compromise; a sole trustee may only do so as permitted by statute generally (and so may not accept sale proceeds in relation to land for example).[6] The trustees personally will incur no liability provided that they have acted with due care as required by the duty of care under s 1(1) of the TA 2000.[7] There may be an adequate

---

1 The discussion in this chapter draws both on previous editions of this work and also on the discussion variously in Thomas and Hudson, 2004. The section on powers draws also on Thomas, 1998 generally.
2 It was during the 18th century that it was recognised that trustees could only exercise powers granted to them by a trust instrument, as opposed to an earlier understanding of the trust which conceived of the trustee as the absolute owner of the trust property: *Holmes v Dring* (1788) 2 Cox Eq Cas 1. The doctrine of powers is a means of understanding the trustee as having capabilities limited to the particular rights granted to them by the settlor and then as seeing the trustee as having capabilities rather than being hemmed in by obligations.
3 TA 1925, s 69(2).
4 *IRC v Bernstein* [1961] Ch 399, 412, *per* Lord Evershed MR.
5 TA 1925, s 14(1).
6 *Ibid*, s 15(1).
7 *Ibid*. Previously, before the 2000 Act, the trustee had been required to act prudently and in good faith: *Re Owens* (1882) 47 LT 61.

compromise if the trustees would, for example, resolve a long-standing dispute, even if the compromise did not in itself achieve equal financial benefits between all of the interested parties.[8] Thus, a suitable compromise may be one which is suitable in all the circumstances and not simply in the best financial interests of the beneficiaries (provided that no unnecessary loss is suffered).[9] The trustees therefore have a complete discretion to act as they see fit, provided that they can justify their actions.[10]

10.2 POWERS OF MAINTENANCE AND ADVANCEMENT

The issues considered in this section concern the powers of trustees to deal flexibly with the trust fund so that they can best meet the needs of their beneficiaries. It must be remembered that the trustees are required to carry out the terms of the trust, or face liability for breach of trust. Furthermore, the trustees will be liable (as considered further below) to act without favour or prejudice between all the beneficiaries so that no particular individual or class receives preferential treatment, again on pain of liability for breach of trust. However, those precise trusts provisions may prove too rigid in circumstances in which the settlor had not anticipated that beneficiaries may, for example, suffer hardship in the short term as a result of a trust provision which requires the trustees to accumulate income rather than pay it out immediately to beneficiaries. Therefore, it is necessary to examine the powers which trustees have under general trusts law to apply trust property for the maintenance of beneficiaries. The issue of the variation of trusts to protect vulnerable beneficiaries is considered in section 10.4 below.

10.2.1 Powers of maintenance in relation to infant beneficiaries

Trusts created for the maintenance of particular beneficiaries attract a specific statutory regime. Sections 31 and 32 of the TA 1925 give trustees wide powers to use income and capital for the maintenance of infant beneficiaries and for the advancement and benefit of all beneficiaries. These principles apply provided that the trust instrument shows no contrary intention. The following discussion divides between general entitlement to income, entitlement to income in particular situations and entitlement to capital.

Income under a trust held for infant beneficiaries

In the absence of any express power, income under a trust can be used for the benefit of a beneficiary who is not in receipt of such income under s 31 of the TA 1925. Alternatively, such an order may be made under the court's inherent jurisdiction. The statutory power provides as follows:

   (1) Where any property is held by trustees in trust for any person for any interest whatsoever, whether vested or contingent, then, subject to any prior interests or charges affecting that property –

8 *Re Earl of Stafford* [1980] Ch 28, 33, *per* Megarry VC.
9 See, eg, *Re Ridsdel* [1947] Ch 597.
10 *Ibid*, and *Partridge v Equity Trustees Executors and Agency Co Ltd* (1947) 75 CLR 149.

(i) during the infancy of any such person, if his interest so long continues, the trustees may, at their sole discretion, pay to his parent or guardian, if any, or otherwise apply for or towards his maintenance, education, or benefit, the whole or such part, if any, of the income of that property as may, in all the circumstances, be reasonable, whether or not there is –
(a) any other fund applicable to the same purpose; or
(b) any person bound by law to provide for his maintenance or education.[11]

Clearly, therefore, this provision grants great largesse to the trustees in relation to infant beneficiaries. The courts have accepted that even though a settlor has postponed the beneficiaries' rights to property, it is nevertheless open to the courts to infer an intention on the settlor's part to provide for the maintenance of any children.[12] It has been accepted that this is the only situation in which a court will interfere with a testator's intention as set out in her will.[13] The potential issue for the trustee is the need to demonstrate that the decision taken was indeed reasonable. This may raise issues concerning the need to deal evenly between different beneficiaries. Section 31 continues to consider the position of minors to income:

(ii) if such person on attaining the age of eighteen years has not a vested interest in such income, the trustees shall thenceforth pay the income of that property and of any accretion thereto ... to him, until he either attains a vested interest therein or dies, or until the failure of his interest.[14]

Therefore, trustees are able to circumvent restrictions on entitlement to income being precluded before the beneficiary reaches the age of majority. In general terms, it is provided that '... the trustees shall have regard to the age of the infant and his requirements and generally to the circumstances of the case ...'.[15] The power under s 31 is covered by a proviso in the following terms:

Provided that, in deciding whether the whole or any part of the income of the property is during a minority to be paid or applied for the purposes aforesaid, the trustees shall have regard to the age of the infant and his requirements and generally to the circumstances of the case, and in particular to what other income, if any, is applicable for the same purposes; and where trustees have notice that the income of more than one fund is applicable for those purposes, then, so far as practicable, unless the entire income of the funds is paid or applied as aforesaid or the court otherwise directs, a proportionate part only of the income of each fund shall be so paid or applied.[16]

The principal function of s 31 'appears to be to supply a code of rules governing the disposal of income, especially during a minority, in cases where a settlor or testator has made dispositions of capital and either (a) being an unskilled draftsman has not thought about income, or

---

11 TA 1925, s 31(1)(i).
12 *Re Collins* (1886) 32 Ch D 229, 232, *per* Pearson J.
13 *Chapman v Chapman* [1954] AC 429, 456, *per* Lord Morton.
14 TA 1925, s 31(1)(ii).
15 *Ibid*, s 31(1)(i).
16 *Ibid*, s 31(1).

(b) being a skilled draftsman, has been content to let the statutory code apply'.[17] The trustees can use the income for the 'maintenance, education or benefit' of an infant beneficiary under a trust whose interest carries 'intermediate income', as defined below.

Section 31 can be ousted where there is an express or implied contrary intention in the trust instrument. Such provisions are generally interpreted strictly, and therefore such a provision will not be effected where that would be inconsistent with the purposes of the trust instrument.[18] In *Re Delamere's ST*, an appointment of income to six minors 'in equal shares absolutely' was held to reveal an intention that each was to take an indefeasible share even if dying before reaching the age of 18.

To the extent that it is not so used, the income must be accumulated and added to the capital of the trust fund.[19] If the infant dies before reaching the age of 18 or marrying, her estate will not be entitled to these accumulations even if her interest is vested.[20] At the age of 18, or if there is a marriage at an earlier age, the income (but not the accumulated income) will be paid to the beneficiary.[21] The beneficiary becomes entitled to the accumulation when she becomes entitled to the capital.

It is necessary to make a time apportionment when there is an alteration in the class of income beneficiaries. The case of *Re Joel*[22] concerned a fund which was held upon trust for the testator's grandchildren contingent on their attaining 21, and where the gift carried the intermediate income, which could be applied for the benefit of the grandchildren. Goff J held that each time a member of the class died under the age of 21, or a new grandchild was born, the income of the trust ought to be apportioned so that each member of the class enjoyed only that part of the income attributable to the period for which she was alive.

Application of income during the infancy of the beneficiary

It is provided in s 31(2) of the TA 1925 that during a beneficiary's infancy the property is to be accumulated in the following manner:

> During the infancy of any such person [as mentioned in s 31(1) above], if his interest so long continues, the trustees shall accumulate all the residue of that income by investing it, and any profits from so investing it, from time to time in authorised investments, and shall hold those accumulations as follows –
>
> (i) If any such person –
>
>   (a) attains the age of eighteen years, or marries under that age, and his interest in such income during his infancy or until his marriage is a vested interest; or
>
>   (b) on attaining the age of eighteen years or on marriage under that age becomes entitled to the property from which such income arose in fee simple . . . or for an entailed interest;

---

17 *Re Delamere's ST* [1984] 1 WLR 813.
18 *Ibid.*
19 TA 1925, s 31(2).
20 *Re Delamere's ST* [1984] 1 WLR 813.
21 *Ibid.*
22 [1943] Ch 311.

the trustees shall hold the accumulations in trust for such person absolutely, but without prejudice to any provision with respect thereto contained in any settlement by him made under any statutory powers during his infancy, and so that the receipt of such person after marriage, and though still an infant, shall be a good discharge; and

(ii) In any other case the trustees shall, notwithstanding that such person had a vested interest in such income, hold the accumulations as an accretion to the capital of the property from which such accumulations arose, and as one fund with such capital for all purposes, and so that, if such property is settled land, such accumulations shall be held upon the same trusts as if the same were capital money arising therefrom;

but the trustees may, at any time during the infancy of such persons if his interest so long continues, apply those accumulations, or any part thereof, as if they were income arising in the then current year.

Thus, the trustees are obliged to accumulate income during the beneficiary's infancy in the context set out above.

'Maintenance, education or benefit'

The trustees are empowered to employ trust property for the maintenance, education or benefit of a beneficiary – consequently, it is important to know what these words mean. Generally, they are given a broad meaning.[23] The property may be applied directly to the benefit of the beneficiary or held on trust for that beneficiary absolutely,[24] or held contingently on the beneficiary's majority.[25] When deciding whether to use the income for such purposes, the trustees must consider the age and requirements of the infant, whether other income is available for her maintenance and the general circumstances of the case. If the discretion is exercised in good faith, the court will not interfere.[26] The trustee is required to consider what use of the property would be in the best interests of the beneficiary. This will include a consideration, in many circumstances, of the circumstances of the infant's parents, as set out in the following *dicta*:

In considering [the benefit of the infant], they should take into account that the father is not of sufficient ability properly to maintain his child, and that it is for her benefit not merely to allow him enough to pay her actual expenses, but to enable him to give her a better education and a better home. They must not be deterred from doing what is for her benefit because it is also a benefit to the father, though, on the other hand, they must not act with a view to his benefit apart from her.[27]

On reaching the age of majority, an accumulated, unapplied income then passes to the formerly-infant beneficiary.[28]

---

23 *Re Heyworth's Contingent Reversionary Interest* [1956] Ch 364, 370.
24 *Re Vestey's Settlement* [1951] Ch 209.
25 *Pilkington v IRC* [1964] AC 612.
26 *Bryant v Hickley* [1894] 1 Ch 324.
27 *Re Lotfhouse* (1885) 29 Ch D 921, 932, *per* Cotton LJ.
28 *Stanley v IRC* [1944] 1 KB 255, 261, *per* Lord Greene MR.

'Intermediate income'

A vested gift will always carry intermediate income, whereas, ordinarily a contingent gift will not. A gift will carry intermediate income, and thus s 31 of the TA 1925 will apply in the following circumstances. First, under s 175 of the Law of Property Act (LPA) 1925, a specific gift of realty or personalty or a residuary gift of freehold land will carry intermediate income. Secondly, a gift of residuary personalty carries intermediate income.[29] Thirdly, if the settlor stands *in loco parentis* to the infant beneficiary and the contingency is attaining the age of 18 or earlier marriage, the gift will carry intermediate income. Fourthly, where the gift is directed in the instrument to be set aside. Fifthly, if the instrument shows an intention that the income should be used for the maintenance of an infant beneficiary.[30]

The court's inherent jurisdiction

Under the court's inherent jurisdiction, a court order may allow income to be used for an infant's maintenance.[31] The court's inherent jurisdiction can also be used to enable the trustees to provide for the maintenance even when the beneficiary is not an infant, where the court considers that to be just.[32]

Capital

In the absence of any express power, trust capital can be used for the benefit of a beneficiary who is not yet entitled to such capital, as considered in the following section.[33]

10.2.2 Powers of advancement

The power of advancement refers to the power in the trustees to advance capital to a beneficiary, that is to pay out amounts of capital rather than holding them intact to generate income. Where the trust contains an express power permitting the trustees to advance the capital of the trust fund to specified beneficiaries, that express power will be decisive of the matter. In the absence of an express power, s 32 of the TA 1925 makes provision for powers of advancement, as follows:

> Trustees may at any time or times pay or apply any capital money subject to a trust, for the advancement or benefit, in such manner as they may, in their absolute discretion, think fit, of any person entitled to the capital of the trust property or any share thereof, whether absolutely or contingently on his attaining any specified age or on the occurrence of any other event.[34]

29 *Green v Ekins* (1742) 2 Atk 473.
30 *Re Selby-Walker* [1949] 2 All ER 178.
31 *Wellesly v Wellesly* (1828) 2 Bli (NS) 124.
32 *Revel v Watkinson* (1748) 27 ER 912.
33 TA 1925, ss 32, 53.
34 *Ibid*, s 32(1).

It should be noted that s 32 does not apply to Settled Land Act 1925 settlements.[35] The particular parts of this provision are considered below.

A contingent future gift carries with it the intermediate income.[36] There is a need to distinguish between gifts which are immediate specific gifts and gifts which are future specific property.[37] Where the gift is, for example, a testamentary bequest of personal property held over as residue, all the intermediate income passes with that gift. However, where that income is expressly deferred to a date in the future, the income does not pass with the gift. There may, however, be an incongruity if an order under s 175 of the LPA 1925 allows immediate rights in the case of contingent future gifts against the settlor's wishes.

'Advancement or benefit'

The expression applying money for the 'advancement or benefit' of the beneficiaries has been explained by the courts as connoting setting up the beneficiary in life.[38] Within the compass of setting the beneficiary up in life falls the discharge of the beneficiary's debts and a resettlement of capital to avoid tax. There are restrictions on the power of advancement set out in s 32 of the TA 1925. The trustees must ensure that the advancements are applied for the purposes for which they are made.[39] The restrictions are as follows. First, the trustees must not advance more than half of the beneficiary's presumptive or vested share or interest.[40] Secondly, when the beneficiary becomes absolutely entitled to their interest the advancement must be taken into account.[41] Thirdly, an advancement must not be made if it prejudices a prior interest unless the person with such an interest gives consent to the advancement. If the life tenant under a protective trust gives consent, the protective trust will not be determined under s 33 of the TA 1925.[42]

In *Re Pauling's ST*,[43] the bankers Coutts & Co were trustees of a fund which was held on trust for a wife for her life, with remainder on her death to her children. The trust instrument contained an express power for the trustees to advance to the children up to one-half of their share, with the consent of their mother. The husband of the life tenant, who was the father of the children, lived beyond his means and sought to obtain part of the trust moneys by means of advancements to his children. A series of advancements were made, nominally to the children, but the money was used for the benefit of their father or generally for the family. The Court of Appeal held that:

> the power of advancement can be exercised only if it is for the benefit of the child or remoter issue to be advanced or, as was said during argument, it is thought to be a 'good

---

35 *Ibid*, s 32(2).
36 LPA 1925, s 175.
37 *Re McGeorge* [1963] 2 WLR 767.
38 *Pilkington v IRC* [1964] AC 612. In *Southgate v Sutton* [2011] EWCA Civ 637 it was held that there may be a re-settlement of the trusts applicable to part only of the trust which is partitioned, in accordance with *Pilkington v IRC*.
39 *Re Pauling's ST* [1964] 3 WLR 742.
40 TA 1925, s 32(1)(a).
41 *Ibid*, s 32(1)(b).
42 *Ibid*, s 32(1)(c).
43 [1964] 3 WLR 742.

thing' for the advanced person to have a share of capital before his or her due time. . . .
[A] power of advancement [can] be exercised only if there was some good reason for it.
That good reason must be beneficial to the person to be advanced; the power cannot be
exercised capriciously or with some other benefit in view.

Therefore, to obtain advancements other than for the benefit of the beneficiaries would not
be a proper advancement. There is also a need to distinguish between a beneficiary seeking
an advancement and a trustee stipulating the form of the advancement. To leave the payee
free to decide how it should be applied may lead to a misapplication of trust property. Unless
the trust makes a specific stipulation as to the use of the money once advanced to the beneficiary, it may be difficult to prevent such a misuse.

Power to make loans

Ordinarily trustees may not lend money, unless the trust instrument contains such a power or
unless such a power can be implied in relation to a trust which conducts a business in relation
to which such a power would be normal.[44]

Inherent jurisdiction of the court

There is a statutory jurisdiction for the court to exert a power of advancement and maintenance also. Under s 53 of the TA 1925, the court has power to order the use of capital for an
infant's maintenance where the infant is 'beneficially entitled to any property'. This, it is
submitted, is in addition to the court's inherent jurisdiction to make orders in relation to the
treatment of the trust property.

10.3 DELEGATION OF TRUSTEES' DUTIES

10.3.1 The appointment of agents, custodians and nominees by the trustees

Frequently, the trustees will wish to appoint professionals to act on their behalf. The trustee
will seek to delegate to such professionals their trusteeship responsibilities. The question
will then arise as to any liability for breach of trust, or failure to achieve the best possible
results for the trust, when the trustees' powers were being carried out by delegates: whether
agents, custodians or nominees. The trustees can only appoint agents, nominees or custodians in one of the following circumstances:[45] if those appointees carry on business in that
capacity, or if the appointee is a body corporate (such as an ordinary company) controlled by
the trustees themselves,[46] or the delegates are a body corporate recognised under s 9 of the
Administration of Justice Act 1985.[47] Charitable trustees are required to seek the guidance

---

44 *Re A Trust Ltd* [2008] WTLR 377.
45 TA 2000, s 19(1).
46 As defined by analogy with the Income and Corporation Taxes Act 1988, s 840: TA 2000, s 19(3).
47 TA 2000, s 19(2).

of the Charity Commissioners in this context.[48] It is open to the trustees to decide on the remuneration of such delegates.[49]

10.3.2 Agents

An agent is a form of fiduciary officer who acts, subject to principles of contract, on behalf of a principal. The TA 2000 provides that the trustees are permitted to 'authorise any person to exercise any or all of their delegable functions as their agent'.[50] The functions which are capable of being delegated to an agent are expressed as being any trustee functions except:[51] a decision as to the distribution of trust assets; the power to decide whether fees should be payable out of income or capital; any power to appoint some person to be a trustee; or any power to delegate trustee responsibilities. Therefore, the statute carves out a list of functions which are considered to be the core powers which a trustee is not entitled to delegate to someone acting as their agent: in other words, the trustee must remain responsible for them. In relation to charitable trusts, the trustees are entitled to appoint agents in relation to raising funds (which does not include the conduct of a trade which forms the primary purpose of the trust), any function which involves a decision which the trustees have taken, or any function involving the investment of the trust's funds.[52]

The trustees can appoint one of the trustees to act on their behalf.[53] The trustees are not entitled to authorise a beneficiary to act as their agent.[54] This last provision is clearly in accordance with principle where there is more than one beneficiary, because if one beneficiary could act as the trustee's agent, it would be possible for that beneficiary to advantage herself at the expense of the other beneficiaries. However, there is no general rule of trusts law to preclude a trustee from being a beneficiary. Similarly, under the rule in *Saunders v Vautier*,[55] an absolutely entitled beneficiary would be able to direct the trustees how to act with the property.

One significant provision of the 2000 Act is that the agent is to be subject to the same duties as the trustees when the agent is exercising those powers.[56] However, these powers can be excluded by the terms of the trust instrument, as considered above. Further, the trustees are empowered to decide on the level of the agent's remuneration.[57]

In relation to 'asset management functions', the trustees are only entitled to appoint agents if the terms of the agency are 'evidenced in writing'.[58] The 'asset management functions' of the trustees relate to the investment of assets under the trust, the acquisition of property to be held on trust and the management of interests in property held on trust.[59] Further to the obligation to detail the agency in writing, the trustees are required to prepare a written[60] 'policy

---

48 *Ibid*, s 19(4).
49 *Ibid*, s 20.
50 *Ibid*, s 11(1).
51 *Ibid*, s 11(2).
52 *Ibid*, s 11(3).
53 *Ibid*, s 12(1).
54 *Ibid*, s 12(3).
55 (1841) 4 Beav 115.
56 TA 2000, s 13.
57 *Ibid*, s 14(1).
58 *Ibid*, s 15(1).
59 *Ibid*, s 15(5).
60 *Ibid*, s 15(4).

statement' which guides the agent as to how to exercise the powers which are delegated to them.[61] The agent must then be obliged under the terms of the agency to act in accordance with the terms of the policy statement. The difficulty with this provision is that the trustees themselves are not required to have a policy statement for their own cognisance and therefore the trustees would be required to develop their own such policy statement from scratch, requiring the agent to act in 'the best interests of the trust'.[62]

10.3.3 Nominees and custodians

The trustees are empowered to appoint a nominee, or bare trustee, to act in relation to any of the assets of the trust as they determine.[63] Similarly the trustees have a power to appoint a custodian to take custody of any trust assets they may consider appropriate for such treatment.[64] If the trust acquires bearer securities[65] then it is mandatory that those securities be deposited with a custodian.[66]

What is not immediately apparent is the difference between a nominee and a custodian within the terms of the 2000 Act. Neither term is expressly defined. A 'nominee' could refer to a person who assumes all of the rights of the trustee. Alternatively, a nominee could be a person who holds title in the trust property on behalf of the trustees, in which case, it would be difficult to distinguish them from a custodian. A 'custodian' could be a form of trustee required to hold, and possibly to maintain, the trust assets in the exercise of some trust discretion as to the manner in which those assets are maintained. In this sense, a custodian is someone who is responsible for protecting the trust property from theft, fraudulent conversion or other harm, as with bearer securities considered immediately above.[67] Alternatively, a custodian may be simply a bailee of the trust property with no fiduciary powers over that property other than holding the property for safekeeping[68] – a little like a warehouse.

10.3.4 Powers of attorney

Trustees are empowered to delegate their powers by means of a power of attorney.[69] The donor of the power (for example, the trustee transferring the power) is liable for acts of the donee (that is, the attorney acting on behalf of the trustee) as though they were his own acts.[70]

---

61   *Ibid*, s 15(2).
62   *Ibid*, s 15(3).
63   *Ibid*, s 16(1).
64   *Ibid*, s 17(1).
65   Ie, securities for which the holder of the security document is entitled to receive payment and which are, consequently, always vulnerable to theft and conversion into cash by the thief without much difficulty (a little like a banknote).
66   TA 2000, s 18(1).
67   Perhaps in the sense of a 'custodian trustee' within the Public Trustee Act 1906.
68   An expression used in relation to unit trusts and open-ended investment companies.
69   Trustee Delegation Act 1999, s 5; by amendment to the TA 1925, s 25.
70   Trustee Delegation Act 1999, s 5(7).

10.3.5 Liability for the acts of delegates

The TA 2000 provides for a code to decide the allocation of liability in circumstances in which agents, nominees or custodians have been appointed validly under the terms of the Act. The trustees are required to 'keep under review' the arrangements under which the delegate acts and to consider any 'power of intervention' which they may have.[71] Such a power of intervention includes a power to revoke the delegate's authorisation or a power to give directions to the delegate.[72] If the trustees decide that there is a need to intervene, then they are required to intervene.[73]

A trustee will not be liable for 'any act or default of the agent, nominee or custodian unless he has failed to comply with the duty of care applicable to him'.[74] Therefore, the trustee is in general terms not liable for any breach of duty carried out by the delegate unless the trustee failed to comply with his duty of care in relation to the appointment of suitable agents considered in section 9.5.[75]

10.3.6 The applicable standard of care for trustees under the case law

The question is therefore the notion of when a trustee will be acting in good faith. The leading case is that of *Speight v Gaunt*,[76] in which cheques were given to a broker (who had been retained by the trustees as an agent) in return for a bought note. The broker misappropriated the funds and absconded. The question arose whether or not there would be an action against the trustee. The trustee contended that he could not be fixed with responsibility on the basis that a prudent man of business would have treated the broker in exactly the manner that the trustee had. Lord Jessel MR considered the appropriate test to be as follows:

> It seems to me that on general trust principles a trustee ought to conduct the business of the trust in the same manner that an ordinary prudent man of business would conduct his own, and that beyond that there is no liability or obligation on the trustee.

Therefore, the trustee will not be liable when acting in the ordinary manner of the business being conducted. On the facts, the trustee could demonstrate that business was normally conducted in this manner and that the trustee was not required to comply with any higher set of principles.

10.3.7 An alternative approach

A different approach was adopted in *Re Vickery*, which was decided on the basis of the old s 23 of the TA 1925.[77] The trustee gave money to a solicitor in the course of trust business.

---

71 TA 2000, s 22(1).
72 *Ibid*, s 22(4). Interestingly, the 2000 Act does not require that such powers be expressly included in the documentation required for any effective delegation.
73 *Ibid*, s 22(1).
74 That is, the duty of care under the TA 2000, Sched 1, para 3.
75 *Ibid*, s 23(1).
76 (1883) 9 App Cas 1.
77 [1931] 1 Ch 572.

The solicitor absconded with the money. The question arose whether or not there was a valid claim against the trustee on behalf of the beneficiaries to recover the loss suffered by the trust. Maugham J defined the issue as being whether or not the trustee had been negligent in employing the solicitor or permitting money to remain in the solicitor's hands. The appropriate test for the presence or absence of good faith was found to have been whether or not there had been 'wilful default' on the part of the trustee.[78]

To set the test as high as 'wilful default' is evidently a higher standard than 'mere lack of care'. His Lordship's understanding of the appropriate duty was either a consciousness of negligence or breach of duty on the part of the trustee, or a recklessness in the trustee in the performance of a trust duty. Maugham J adopted the decision in the company law case of *Re City Equitable Fire*,[79] which had been based on the consideration of the specific articles of association of the company in question, rather than on general principles of trusts law.

The decision in *Re Vickery* has been criticised by much of the academic literature. It has been argued that the better test would be a more general 'want of reasonable care' rather than the restrictive 'wilful default'.[80] It is argued that the *Re Equitable Fire* case was decided very much on its own facts and therefore should not have been applied to this area of trustee discretion. Consequently, it is said that the test for trustees ought to be higher. To apply a general test of 'want of reasonable care' would require trustees to act more carefully, whereas a test of 'wilful default' would permit a greater number of examples of mismanagement by trustees to pass without remedy for the beneficiaries.

There remains the more general issue of the manner in which ordinary trustees are to be expected to control the activities of professionals to whom they delegate their powers. By definition, trustees will appoint professionals to perform functions which the trustees are unable to perform themselves. As such, the delegate has all the applicable expertise. This concern would favour the *Re Vickery* approach in that it would only make trustees liable if the trustees themselves had exhibited some wilful default. After all, the trustees would still be able to sue the delegate for negligence, fraud or breach of contract for failure to perform its functions properly. This issue is considered further in Chapter 9.

10.3.8   The devolution of powers or trusts

Where a trust power is given to trustees as joint tenants of that power, in the event of the death of one of those trustees, the survivor is entitled to exercise that power alone.[81] Where one trustee dies, the personal representatives shall exercise their powers. Where there is some failure of *inter vivos* transfer, the property reverts to the settlor, or remains in the personal representatives of the settlor, to be held upon the trusts of the settlement or the will as the case may be.[82]

---

78   This was a case relating to the TA 1925, s 23: in relation to liability for delegates in dealing with trust property, the trustee only bears liability for losses occurring by reason of the trustee's 'own wilful default'. It is important to bear in mind that s 23 refers to general delegations of responsibility, whereas s 30 refers to receipts for trust property comprising money and securities.

79   *Re City Equitable Fire Insurance* [1925] Ch 407.

80   Jones (1968) 84 LQR 474.

81   TA 1925, s 18.

82   *Mallott v Wilson* [1903] 2 Ch 494.

The alternative analysis is that a disclaimer of the transfer to a trustee should make the transfer void and the trust should fail. Alternatively, one may choose to treat this as a constructive trust where all has been done that ought to have been done.[83]

10.4 VARIATION OF TRUSTS

The Variation of Trusts Act 1958 gives discretion to the court to sanction variations of trust in relation to infant beneficiaries, incapacitated beneficiaries, and others whose beneficial rights have not vested in them, provided that the applicant will not derive any unjust benefit from the variation. Other statutory discretions permit variations for the maintenance of infant beneficiaries, and for the extension of trustees' powers where it is expedient.

Under common law, the court has inherent jurisdiction to sanction variation in relation to the maintenance of, and accumulation of capital for, infant beneficiaries, as considered below. Alternatively, the principle in Saunders v Vautier *enables absolutely-entitled beneficiaries to call for delivery of the absolute title to the trust property, effectively terminating the trust.*

10.4.1 Variation of trusts

When a trust is created, its terms become binding on the subsequent actions of the trustees in relation to the trust property. That trust, once created, remains set in stone, unless there is some provision in the trust which permits an alteration in the manner of its exercise.[84] However, there may be occasions when it becomes advantageous to the parties to alter the terms of the trust. For example, suppose that the tax treatment of a particular trust structure was changed by legislation, so rendering the structure originally selected by the settlor less appropriate than it had seemed. In such circumstances the beneficiaries and the trustees would consider it advantageous to vary the terms of the trust to reflect this change in the law. A well-drafted trust would permit variations to accommodate exactly this form of alteration.

There is a distinction to be made between slight variations to a trust and actions which are equivalent to the creation of a completely new trust. What is envisaged in this section are changes which constitute mere variations to the trust. What is not envisaged are attempts to introduce changes which are so fundamental to the operation of the trust that they amount, in truth, to a resettlement of property (that is, the transfer of the trust fund onto effectively new trusts).[85] It is clearly difficult to set out hard-and-fast rules, given that it will be necessary to examine each trust to consider its underlying motivation and the extent to which the proposed alteration goes to the heart of that issue.

83 *Re Rose* [1952] Ch 499, [1952] 1 All ER 1217.
84 *Paul v Paul* (1882) 20 Ch D 742.
85 *Vandervell v IRC* [1967] 2 WLR 87.

10.4.2 Duty not to deviate from the terms of the trust

The general principle

The fundamental duty of the trustees is to observe the terms of the trust and not to deviate from those terms. As considered below in Chapter 18, any deviation from the terms of the settlement constitutes a breach of trust which exposes the trustees personally to liability to restore the property, or to restore the financial equivalent of the trust property lost through equitable compensation. It is therefore important to understand the extent to which the trustees are entitled to tinker with those fundamental terms. Given this central principle, the statutes and case law considered below constitute, in reality, exceptions from the rule that trustees are not permitted to deviate from the terms of the trust.

The court's inherent jurisdiction to permit a deviation

There remains an inherent power in the court to permit departure from the precise terms of the trust, in contradistinction to the general rule just set out.[86] The purpose and extent of this inherent jurisdiction is to enable the court and the trustees to manage 'emergencies'[87] which arise in the administration of the trust. 'Emergencies' include anything which is not provided for, or catered for, in the terms of the trust but which is necessary to ensure its proper administration. Therefore, a trust provision which permits investment only in a particular type of share may be deviated from (with the sanction of the inherent power of the court) to permit the trustees to invest in shares which are issued to replace those specified in the terms of the trust. As such, the court's inherent power will not be of general application but rather is limited to situations which cut to the heart of the proper administration of the trust.

The exceptions in Chapman v Chapman

The decision of the Court of Appeal in *Chapman v Chapman*[88] set out four exceptions to the general principle that the trustee cannot deviate from the terms of the trust. First, cases in which the court has effected changes in the nature of an infant's property (for example, by directing investment of his personalty in the purchase of freeholds). Secondly, cases in which the court has allowed the trustees of settled property to enter into some business transaction which was not authorised by the settlement. Thirdly, cases in which the court has allowed maintenance out of income which the settlor or testator directed to be accumulated. Fourthly, cases in which the court has approved a compromise on behalf of infants and possible after-born beneficiaries.

These four categories clearly constitute narrow contexts in which variations are to be permitted. The issue of compromise is one which is to be distinguished from the *Saunders v Vautier*[89] principle, although there are hints of the latter in the former. Thus in *Allen v Distillers Co (Biochemicals) Ltd*,[90] a case arising out of the thalidomide drugs tragedy, the

---

86 *Re New* [1901] 2 Ch 534.
87 *Ibid, per* Romer LJ.
88 [1954] AC 429.
89 (1841) 4 Beav 115.
90 [1974] QB 384.

courts were able to order the postponement of a payment to a beneficiary even though that beneficiary had reached the age of majority, on the basis of a compromise reached between all the potential beneficiaries as to the manner in which the indisposed beneficiary ought best to be treated. Similarly, compromise has been achieved in relation to pension funds which have sought wider investment powers to enable a substantial capital fund to provide greater benefits for its members.[91]

Otherwise the court retains a case law power to act in cases of emergency to sanction the alteration of the terms of the trust. An example of the use of this power was in *Re Jackson*,[92] where buildings were on the brink of collapse. The court ordered variation so that trust property could be applied to save the buildings from final collapse. The power has also been used in *Re New* to permit the reconstruction of a company's share capital and to empower the trustees to take newly allotted shares.[93] Subsequently, *Re New* was described as the furthest extent to which this jurisdiction will stretch.[94]

10.4.3 The Variation of Trusts Act 1958

Introduction

The role of the Variation of Trusts Act 1958 is to permit variations of trusts in relation to specific types of beneficiaries which are identified in the statute itself.[95] The court's jurisdiction is then limited to variations and revocations to the extent that they interact with those categories of persons.

Scope of persons covered

The scope of persons covered by the 1958 Act is set out in s 1(1):

> Where property, whether real or personal, is held on trusts arising, whether before or after the passing of this Act, under any will, settlement or other disposition, the court may if it thinks fit by order approve on behalf of –
>
> (a) any person having, directly or indirectly, an interest, whether vested or contingent, under the trusts who by reason of infancy or other incapacity is incapable of assenting, or
>
> (b) any person (whether ascertained or not) who may become entitled, directly or indirectly, to an interest under the trusts as being at a future date or on the happening of a future event a person of any specified description or a member of any specified class of persons, so however that this paragraph shall not include any person who would be

---

91 *Mason v Fairbrother* [1983] 2 All ER 1078.
92 (1882) 21 Ch D 786; *Conway v Fenton* (1888) 40 Ch D 512; *Re Montagu* [1897] 2 Ch 8.
93 [1901] 2 Ch 534.
94 *Re Tollemache* [1903] 1 Ch 457, *per* Kekewich J.
95 *D (A Child) v O* [2004] 3 All ER 780 (life insurance policies held on trust for miners in equal shares fell within the 1958 Act).

of that description, or a member of that class, as the case may be, if the said date had fallen or the said event had happened at the date of the application to the court, or

(c) any person unborn, or

(d) any person in respect of any discretionary interest of his under protective trusts where the interest of the principal beneficiary has not failed or been determined,

any arrangement . . . varying or revoking all or any of the trusts, or enlarging the powers of the trustees of managing or administering any of the property subject to the trusts.

Therefore, the focus of the legislation is on infants and incapacitated persons (for example, those suffering from mental health problems, as considered below). It also includes those people who might yet become beneficially entitled under the trust fund (either because their interest has not yet been awarded to them under some fiduciary discretion, or because they have not yet been born). With reference to these categories of person, the court has a discretion to permit variations of trust. However, other questions do arise.

The nature of the court's jurisdiction

The term 'arrangement' is used in the final paragraph of the section deliberately to connote a very broad range of methods of dealing with the trust, to enable the broadest range of proposals to be put into action if the court deems them suitable.[96] However, as Wilberforce J made plain in *Re T's Settlement Trusts*,[97] the court will not be permitted to sanction a proposed arrangement which constitutes a resettlement of the trust property rather than a mere variation of its terms.

Megarry J has held on the same subject that 'if an arrangement, while leaving the substratum, effectuates the purpose of the original trust by other means, it may still be possible to regard that arrangement as merely varying the original trusts, even though the means employed are wholly different, and even though the form is completely changed'.[98] Therefore, it will clearly be necessary to examine the true purpose of the trust (or its 'substratum') and identify whether or not that is changed to such an extent as to constitute *a resettlement on new terms*. Thus, in *Goulding v James*,[99] a proposal to re-effect trusts such that the great-grandchildren who took interests only in remainder ought to be entitled to a settlement of 10% of the capital was considered to be contrary to the stated intention of the settlor at the time of the creation of the settlement.

The approach to variation is explained by Lord Reid in *Re Holmden's ST*[100] as being a consent given by the beneficiaries to the variation, rather than something imposed on them by the court. Beneficiaries not of full age at the time of the variation are bound by such variations, it is said, because the court was empowered by the 1958 Act to take action on their behalf. Otherwise, a beneficiary will not be bound by a variation where she did not accede to it as a *sui juris* beneficiary. This explanation appears to locate the notion of the variation made under

96 *Re Steed's WT* [1960] Ch 407.
97 [1964] Ch 158, 162.
98 *Re Holt's ST* [1969] 1 Ch 100, 111.
99 [1997] 2 All ER 239, *per* Mummery LJ. Merely adding another life interest has been considered to be acceptable, however: *Ridgwell v Ridgwell* [2008] WTLR 527.
100 [1968] AC 685, [1968] 1 All ER 148.

the 1958 Act as being orientated around the consensus of the beneficiaries and therefore as a cousin to the *Saunders v Vautier*[101] principle. Under that principle, considered at section 4.1 all the beneficiaries acting together can call for the delivery of the trust and thus terminate it. As Lord Reid considered the matter in *Re Holmden's ST*,[102] the beneficiaries have a right of veto such that no variation is capable of being enforced against them without their consent.[103]

One point which remains[104] is the interaction between such a change in beneficial interest and the provisions of s 53(1)(c) of the Law of Property Act 1925 – in short, the question is whether or not such a variation constitutes a disposition of an equitable interest requiring signed writing. There is some confusion. In the light of *Neville v Wilson*,[105] it appears that there is an argument that the variation takes effect by way of an implied trust outwith the scope of s 53(1)(c). However, it seems equally valid to look to the mischief of the 1958 Act as being a statute necessarily permitting variations of trusts without the need for any further formality than that contained in the statute. Consequently, the statute ought properly to be considered as an exception to the rule in s 53(1)(c), otherwise it would be of comparatively limited utility and invalid on its own internal logic. The real answer must be that no one considered the point when drafting the 1958 Act.

Precluding the applicant's own benefit

The class of variations and persons in s 1(1) of the 1958 Act is subject to a proviso, also contained in s 1(1), which seeks to ensure that the applicant for the variation will not benefit unjustly from it:

> Provided that except by virtue of paragraph (d) of this subsection [in relation to protective trusts] the court shall not approve an arrangement on behalf of any person unless the carrying out thereof would be for the benefit of that person.

Therefore, where it is the case that such a variation or revocation would benefit any person involved in a protective trust, created to ring-fence property in favour of a susceptible beneficiary, it shall not be granted by the court. The term 'benefit' has been given a broad meaning beyond simply financial benefit, to include moral and social benefit too.[106]

10.4.4 The general principle governing identification of a variation as opposed to a resettlement

There is, as stated above, a clear problem with deciding whether a trust has been merely varied, or whether it has been effectively terminated and new trusts declared. Clearly, the beneficiaries acting together do have the power to resettle the trust. As Megarry J has stated

---

101   (1841) 4 Beav 115.
102   [1968] AC 685, [1968] 1 All ER 148.
103   See *Goulding v James* [1997] 2 All ER 239, *per* Mummery LJ.
104   Pettit, 1997, 473.
105   [1996] 3 All ER 171, [1996] 3 WLR 460.
106   *Re Holt's ST* [1969] 1 Ch 100, *per* Megarry J.

this proposition[107] in relation to the ability of beneficiaries using the rule in *Saunders v Vautier*[108] to re-arrange the terms of a trust:

> If under a trust every possible beneficiary was under no disability and concurred in the re-arrangement or termination of the trusts, then under the doctrine in *Saunders v Vautier* those beneficiaries could dispose of the trust property as they thought fit; for in equity the property was theirs. Yet if any beneficiary was an infant, or an unborn or unascertained person, it was held that the court had no general inherent or other jurisdiction to concur in any such arrangement on behalf of that beneficiary.

The case of *Re Holt*[109] is instructive in this regard. An originating summons was served under the 1958 Act by which the settlor's daughter sought to surrender her life interest in one half of the income of the trust so that she could both reduce her own liability to surtax and increase the entitlement of her children to the life interest. However, she sought ('not surprisingly' in the opinion of Megarry J) to restrict the ability of her children to access the capital of the fund before reaching the age of 25 because, in her own words, '. . . I believe it to be most important that young people should be reasonably advanced in a career and settled in life before they are in receipt of an income sufficient to make them independent of the need to work'. The principal issue which arose was whether the trust was varied automatically by the order of the court (other issues are considered elsewhere in this book).

The doctrine in *Re Hambleden's Will Trusts*,[110] as set out by Wynn-Parry J, stated that the order of the court *ipso facto* altered the trust. This reversed the decision in *Re Joseph's Will Trusts*,[111] where Vaisey J had held that it was necessary for the judge to include words in the court order permitting the trustees to alter the trusts, rather than acknowledging that the court order necessarily had that effect automatically without anything more. While this may appear to be of little immediate importance, it was held in *Re Holt* that the automatic nature of the court order obviated the need for the trustees to perform any formality to secure the variation. For example, the surrender by the settlor's daughter in *Re Holt* constituted a disposition of her equitable interest to her children which, in line with *Grey v IRC*,[112] would have required some signed writing before it could have been effected. However, the automatic nature of the order, accepted in *Re Hambleden*,[113] meant that the equitable interest passed to the disponor's children without the need for signed writing.

The court must be satisfied that the proposal made to it is an 'arrangement', and not a complete resettlement of the entire trust fund. It was held in *Wyndham v Egremont*[114] that an alteration to the perpetuity period in a trust did not constitute a resettlement of that trust. Nor did alterations to the line of future beneficiaries. This particular trust related to an estate

---

107 *Ibid*, 111.
108 (1841) 4 Beav 115.
109 *Re Holt's ST* [1969] 1 Ch 100.
110 [1960] 1 WLR 82.
111 [1959] 1 WLR 1019.
112 [1960] AC 1.
113 [1960] 1 WLR 82.
114 [2009] EWHC 2076 (Ch), 12 ITELR 461.

which included Petworth House in Sussex, which is still the home of the Wyndham family[115] in spite of that splendid, stately pile being made over to the National Trust in 1947.[116] The perpetuity period was the death of 'the last survivor of the issue of George V',[117] who was the Princess Alexandra, aged 72 at the time of this case. Mr Wyndham, son of the current Lord Egremont, would have taken the property absolutely on the death of Princess Alexandra, but preferred that the trust continue in existence not least because of the tax charges which would have fallen on the family[118] (hence the change in the perpetuity provision) and that the property should continue to pass in future with the male heir as opposed to passing in default absolutely to his lordship's son or grandson. It was held by Blackburne J that the change to ensure that the property pass with the male heir was not a complete resettlement of the trust, but rather only a variation of that trust.

10.4.5 There must be a benefit in the variation

The court must be satisfied that the proposal will be beneficial to the beneficiaries. This benefit may not be apparent at first but it must be demonstrable that there will be some benefit in time. So in *Re RGST Settlement Trust*[119] it was held that a proposal to vary the trusts so as to provide for a life interest for a spouse would appear to disadvantage the interests of any children whose interests might therefore appear to be delayed, but the court was convinced that this proposal provided for greater flexibility for the trustees when making advancements to the children (and to any children as yet unborn), and for more coherent inheritance tax and capital gains tax planning for the trust as a whole, and for the prospect of cheaper life insurance in future, all of which Judge Behrens considered would be to the long-term benefit of the beneficiaries. While the 'benefit" ' which is ordinarily sought is a financial benefit,[120] the mitigation of tax is taken to fall within this sort of benefit.[121]

When considering whether or not a benefit would have been conferred upon a child, Rory (a 'minor'), Norris J gave us the following insight in *Wright v Gater*[122] as to the subtleties of the judicial thought process:

(a) I approach the task with what Megarry J in *Re Wallace's Settlements*[123] described as 'a fair cautious and enquiring mind'.

(b) What I am doing is not redistributing property according to some wise scheme of which I approve. The Court of Chancery never claimed a power to direct a

---

115 As Blackburne J explained, Mr Wyndham is heir to Lord Egremont and thus to two baronetcies, of Egremont and Leconfield.

116 The house, with its remarkable collection of paintings by Turner and others, its parkland, and the teas and lunches which are provided (at reasonable cost) by the National Trust are enthusiastically recommended. The small town of Petworth itself also repays a visit. But I digress.

117 This was a very common 'royal lives' clause by reference to which perpetuities were often defined.

118 And which would have necessitated the sale of much of the family property.

119 *Re RGST Settlement Trust; Ridgwell v Ridgwell* [2007] EWHC 2666 (Ch), [2008] STC 1883.

120 *Re Drewe's Settlement; Drewe v Westminster Bank Ltd* [1966] 1 WLR 1518 at 1520.

121 *Re Chapman's Settlement Trusts (No 2)* [1959] 1 WLR 372; *Re Holt's Settlement; Wilson v Holt* [1969] 1 Ch 100 at 120–121; and *Re Weston's Settlement* [1969] 1 Ch 223 at 232, *per* Stamp LJ, as accepted in *Re RGST Settlement Trust* [2008] STC 1883.

122 [2011] EWHC 2881 (Ch), [2012] 1 WLR 802.

123 [1968] 1 WLR 711 at 718 H.

settlement of the property of a minor, and the 1958 Act did not alter this: see *Re T's Settlement Trusts*.[124] Rather, I am supplying consent on behalf of Rory: *Re S*.[125] The question to be asked is therefore: 'Should Rory consent to this arrangement?' That question is answered in the sense 'Only if the judge is satisfied that it is for his benefit.' So it is never enough that the proposal does Rory no real harm: to elicit his consent it must always confer on him a real benefit.

(c) 'Benefit' is generally financial in nature: and when it is the Court is will be concerned in 'a practical and business-like consideration of the arrangement, including the total amounts of the advantages which the various parties obtain, and their bargaining strength'.

(d) But 'benefit' need not be financial: and when it is not . . . business-like considerations do not provide a sure guide, though the recognition of risk will still have some part to play. In such cases the assessment of benefit and advantage must be approached with caution (as Wilberforce J recognised in *Re T*[126]) lest the process simply becomes a reflection of the perceptions and preferences of the individual judge. The difficulties inherent in the task are perhaps illustrated by *Re Weston's Settlement*.[127]

(e) One step towards objectifying the assessment of non-financial benefit would be to pose the question (based on that posed under different legislation in *Re Irving*[128]): 'Would a prudent adult, motivated by intelligent self-interest, and after sustained consideration of the proposed trusts and powers and the circumstances in which they may fall to be implemented, be likely to accept the proposal?'

Therefore, the court is acting in the best financial interests of the child in ensuring that the variation is genuinely expected to confer a real benefit on the child. On the facts of that case, a saving in tax of £89,000 was considered to be a benefit for that beneficiary. By contrast with this acceptance of tax avoidance as a motive for effecting variations, the difficulties to which his lordship referred which arose in *Re Weston's Settlement*[129] were that an application was brought to vary a trust which had a child as its beneficiary, *inter alia*, so that those trusts could be exported outside the UK so as to avoid a charge to UK tax.[130] While the avoidance of tax was not unlawful, the Court of Appeal held that when it was the sole purpose of the application for variation then it was entitled to inquire more closely into the trustees' objectives. On those facts, because it was the sole motivation for the application, it was refused. As Lord Denning put it:[131]

Many a child has been ruined by being given too much. The avoidance of tax may be lawful, but it is not yet a virtue. The Court of Chancery should not encourage or support

---

124 [1964] Ch 158, at 161.
125 [2006] WTLR 1461, at para. [16].
126 *Re T* [1964] Ch 158 at 161.
127 [1969] 1 Ch 234.
128 (1975) 66 DLR (3d) 387.
129 [1969] 1 Ch 234.
130 Broadly speaking, a trust is taken to be resident wherever its trustees are resident: therefore, replacing UK resident trustees with non-UK resident trustees is a common mechanism for attempting to avoid UK tax. Tax law in this context is very complex – being a web of charges to tax and anti-avoidance provisions – so generalisations are difficult to make.
131 [1969] 1 Ch 234, at 245.

it – it should not give its approval to it – if by so doing it would imperil the true welfare of the children, already born or yet to be born.

This, I would suggest, is a little closer to the spirit of trusts law being based in conscience; albeit that the conscience on display here is a public conscience rather than a private one. It just serves to show that even in the most unprepossessing areas of the law, in amongst the seemingly dullest of applications, there are still matters of tremendous ethical importance.

10.4.6 Variation of trusts as part of divorce proceedings

One significant context in which trusts may need to be varied is in relation to divorce. The parties may have created a marriage settlement which will need to be unpacked once the married couple divorce, or trusts may have been created during the marriage in relation to which one partner or both partners may have had interests, or trusts may have been created before the marriage in which only one partner has an interest. On divorce it will be important to consider whether those trusts should be considered to be part of the 'matrimonial property' which the court should take into account when settling the terms of the divorce. In this sense it is important to consider whether or not the settlement which is to be varied is a 'nuptial' settlement or a 'non-nuptial' settlement in divorce proceedings. In essence, where the settlement is a nuptial settlement then the property will be considered to be matrimonial property which is capable of being dealt with by way of a variation of the settlement as part of the divorce settlement under the broad powers of the court under the Matrimonial Causes Act 1973. Waite LJ considered that the powers of the court under the 1973 Act were almost 'limitless' in *Thomas v Thomas*.[132] In such circumstances, as for example in *Charman v Charman*[133] and in *Whaley v Whaley*,[134] the court will embark on a detailed examination of the situation of the parties, of the role which the trusts play as part of the parties' matrimonial property, and of the comparative justice between parties of making a variation of the sort suggested by the applicant.[135] The trust must have continued in existence at the time of making the order.[136]

So, in *BJ v MJ (Financial Remedy: Overseas Trust)*[137] after a divorce, Mostyn J considered two trusts in the light of the dispositive powers of the court under the 1973 Act which are 'unfettered and, in theory, unlimited'.[138] In essence, the court is not supposed to interfere

---

132 [1995] 2 FLR 668.
133 [2007] EWCA Civ 503.
134 [2011] EWCA Civ 617. Among the issues in *Whaley v Whaley*, among the various items of property which imposed business liabilities on the parties as well as constituting assets, there were questions about identifying which assets belonged to which of two family trusts where one spouse had never been a beneficiary under one of those trusts. On appeal on the facts of that case it was argued that the judge at first instance erred in including assets as belonging to the husband which had been part of a trust fund in which the husband had no rights. These arguments were not borne out on the facts. There is also the different question as to whether the trustees are likely to observe the wishes of the parties (for example, as to taking property in equal shares) unless an order for a variation of the trust is made.
135 It was also noted in *Charman v Charman* [2007] EWCA Civ 503, Sir Mark Potter P, at para [106] *et seq.* that the impact of the change in divorce law in *Miller v Miller* [2001] 1 AC 596 had been that divorced wives would have expectations of much larger settlements than hitherto.
136 *C v C* [2004] EWHC 742 (Fam), [2004] Fam 141.
137 [2011] EWHC 2708 (Fam).
138 *Ben Hashem v Al Shayif* [2009] 1 FLR 115, *per* Munby J, at [290].

494 Equity and Trusts

with a trust which has been created after a marriage any more than is necessary to do justice between the parties in dividing property on a divorce. Given that this is part of the scheme for dividing property on divorce, it must correlate with any developments in divorce law and so now it 'must be read in the light of the new distributive régime mandated by the House of Lords in *White v White*[139] and *Miller v McFarlane*.[140,141] On these facts it was important to recognise that the settlements created after the marriage had been created for the benefit of future family members and also to be efficient for capital gains tax purposes. Therefore, in relation to the settlements from which the former spouses took some personal benefit there was to be a division in equal shares between the parties on the basis that that property was properly to be considered to be matrimonial property. Variation of the trusts would be effected so as to remove the wife as a beneficiary once the division of property on equal shares had taken place so as to achieve a final settlement between the parties. In relation to non-nuptial settlements it would be a question of fact to consider whether or not either spouse was intended to take a benefit from such a trust, and consequently whether or not that property should be considered to be matrimonial property.[142]

10.4.7 Disagreement between different beneficiaries

What is more difficult to know is how to deal with an application in which not all of the beneficiaries are in agreement, even if the application is not necessarily contested. In particular, what is to happen if the beneficial interests will be altered. Section 57 is important because it allows trusts to be operated appropriately in the best interests of the beneficiaries. The question, necessarily, is whether any particular proposed course of action would indeed be expedient in this sense. In *Southgate v Sutton*[143] Mummery LJ explained s 57 as operating in the following way:

> The court must be satisfied on two main points before it can exercise its discretion to confer the powers requested: first, that the powers sought are for the purpose of a transaction 'in the management or administration of any property vested in trustees'; and, secondly, that the transaction is, in the opinion of the court, 'expedient', meaning that it must be in the interests of the trust as a whole.

The notion of the power being 'expedient' must be read in the context of the management of the trust as a whole. This is different from the variation of trusts, where an application must be made under the Variation of Trusts Act (discussed above), because the purpose of s 57 is not to alter the beneficial interest under the trusts but rather to allow the trustees to take expedient action. In *Southgate v Sutton* the application was unopposed, which in itself made Mummery LJ 'nervous' because the court prefers in such situations to hear from both sides about whether

---

139   [2001] 1 AC 596.
140   [2006] 2 AC 618.
141   *Ben Hashem v Al Shayif* [2009] 1 FLR 115, *per* Munby J at [290].
142   See generally *Thomas v Thomas* [1995] 2 FLR 668; *Charman v Charman No.1* [2006] 2 FLR 442, CA; *TL v ML* [2006] 1 FLR 1263; *A v A & St George Trustees Ltd* [2007] 2 FLR 467; *Charman v Charman (No 4)* [2007] 1 FLR 1246; *SR v CR* [2009] 2 FLR 1083; *B v B (Ancillary Relief)* [2010] 2 FLR 887; *D v D* [2011] 2 FLR 29 and *Whaley v Whaley* [2011] EWCA Civ 617.
143   [2011] EWCA Civ 637.

or not the application is indeed expedient and proper; although it might be thought that if an application was unopposed because it was uncontroversial that that might reassure the court as to the suitability of the trustees' proposed course of action. In that case the proposal was to 'appropriate and partition' the trust fund so that, in effect, one group of beneficiaries would in the future only enjoy income from a part of the trust fund as opposed to enjoying income from the entire trust fund: the difference being that it was expected that the total amount of income which they would receive in cash terms would the same as the amount they had enjoyed previously. The court was concerned that this would effectively change the beneficial interests, even though the position in cash terms would remain much the same.[144] Nevertheless, the Court of Appeal was prepared to make the order which Mann J would not by distinguishing the authorities on which Mann J had relied; by hearing fresh evidence about the administrative problems facing the trustees without this order; and by seeing this as a problem to do with the management of the trusts which effected only an incidental change to the beneficiaries' equitable interests as opposed to being an application to vary those trusts.[145]

10.4.8 Other statutes permitting deviation from terms of the trust

The following are the primary statutory exceptions to the trustees' obligation to perform, slavishly, the terms of the trust, outside the Variation of Trusts Act 1958.

The maintenance of infants

Section 53 of the TA 1925 provides that the court may make orders for the benefit of infants. This may involve the variation of a trust.

Section 57(1) of the Trustee Act 1925

Section 57 empowers the court to make orders which enable the trustees to act in a way which is 'expedient' in the management of the trust but without varying the terms of the beneficiaries' equitable interests in any meaningful way.[146] Section 57(1) of the TA 1925 provides as follows:

> Where in the management or administration of any property vested in trustees any sale, lease, mortgage, surrender, release, or other disposition, or any purchase, investment,

---

144 These concerns had been voiced at first instance by Mann J in *Southgate v Sutton* [2009] EWHC 3270 (Ch), consequently Mann J had not made the order which had been requested.

145 Mann J had relied at [2009] EWHC 3270 (Ch), *inter alia*, on the decision of Goff LJ in *Re Freeston's Charity* [1978] 1 WLR 741, which had related to an application under s 57 TA 1925 in relation to a perpetual trust dating from 1597 in favour of two charities (one of which was University College, Oxford) and which had not actually proposed a split in the capital of that trust on the same basis and there would have been an impact of the equitable interests of the beneficiaries, and therefore that case was considered to be distinguishable by the Court of Appeal in *Southgate v Sutton*. Reference was made in the Court of Appeal to the decision in the Grand Court of the Cayman Islands in *MEP v Rothschild Trust Cayman Limited* (Cause Nos 128 of 2009 and 576 of 2005) in which a similar order on very similar facts had been made. Mann J had also not considered *Re Downshire* [1953] Ch 218, relating as it did to variation of trusts.

146 *Southgate v Sutton* [2011] EWCA Civ 637.

acquisition, expenditure, or other transaction, is in the opinion of the court expedient, but the same cannot be effected by reason of the absence of any power for that purpose vested in the trustees by the trust instrument, if any, or by law, the court may by order confer upon the trustees, either generally or in any particular instance, the necessary power for the purpose, on such terms, and subject to such provisions and conditions, if any, as the court may think fit and may direct in what manner any money authorised to be expended, and the costs of any transaction, are to be paid or borne as between capital and income.

This provision was considered in section 9.7.3 with reference to investment powers, although clearly it extends further than that. In relation to the categories of property and power set out in s 57, the court is empowered to extend such powers of the trustees to deal with that property. The only explicit criterion for the exercise of that discretion is that it be 'expedient', although, clearly, that expediency would have to be within the general terms and purposes of the trust.

One significant context in which such powers may be sought is in relation to a re-organisation of the trust fund so as to manage it better or to meet the competing needs of different classes of beneficiaries.[147]

Miscellaneous exceptions

Section 96 of the Mental Health Act 1983 gives the Court of Protection the power to vary trusts created in relation to persons falling within its ambit. Section 96(1)(d) gives that court power to make a settlement in relation to the property of a patient falling within the 1983 Act. The powers of variation relate, primarily, to instances in which incorrect information has been supplied in connection with a settlement created under the Act, where the circumstances of the patient have changed substantially. The power of variation itself is a broad one, permitting the court to make any variation it sees fit in the circumstances.

There are also powers in the Matrimonial Causes Act 1973 to alter trusts in cases of divorce or separation.[148] These powers relate to institutions such as ante-nuptial and post-nuptial settlements.[149] Thus, in *Brooks v Brooks*,[150] a variation to a postnuptial settlement was permitted to allow for the creation of a pension for a wife in such a relationship. That case constituted a slightly exceptional circumstance, relating as it did to a pension trust under which the husband was the sole member. The variation permitted the diminution of the husband's entitlement as beneficiary in favour of his wife, by way of a new pension for her benefit. It is clear that the court was prepared to permit this variation only on the basis that there were no other beneficiaries who would be affected by it. In relation to the broader context of pension funds, see Chapter 24 below and the provisions of the Family Law Act 1996.

There are provisions under the Settled Land Act 1925 which relate to variations as between life tenant and other beneficiaries. It is not proposed to deal with those provisions in detail. These provisions are unaffected by the 1958 Act. Section 64(1) of the 1925 Act permits

---

147   *Re Thomas* [1930] 1 Ch 194.
148   See also *Jones v Jones* [1972] 1 WLR 1269.
149   Matrimonial Causes Act 1973, s 24(1)(c), (d).
150   [1996] 1 AC 375.

variations in relation to settled land 'which in the opinion of the court would be for the benefit of the settled land, or any part thereof, or the persons interested under the settlement', such that the tenant for life is able to enter into a transaction which could be validly effected by the absolute owner.

10.5 LIMITS ON THE EXERCISE OF POWERS

10.5.1 Excessive exercise of a power

In general terms, where a power is exercised properly and then also exercised to excess, the proper exercise of the power is valid but the excessive portion is void.[151] This is so unless it is impossible to distinguish between the proper and the excessive portion of the exercise. Suppose a power exists to advance £1,000 out of a fund from which the fiduciary advanced £1,100: it would be possible to separate the excessive £100 from the proper advancement of the £1,000. However, suppose a power exists to transfer a house to two or more of a class of objects: if the house were advanced only to one of the objects, then it would be impossible to segregate the valid from the void portion of the exercise of the power and so the entire exercise of the power would be void.

10.5.2 Fraud on a power

A fraud on a power does not require that the power-holder acts fraudulently, but rather that that person acts deliberately beyond the terms of the power.[152] Where dishonesty or fraud is present, then a fiduciary holding the power will be liable to account for any loss to the beneficiaries of the power and to account for unauthorised profits earned from that act, as considered in Chapter 12.

---

151 Thomas, 1998, 434. See *Alexander v Alexander* (1755) 2 Ves Sen 640; *Re Holland* [1914] 2 Ch 595.
152 *Vatcher v Paull* [1915] AC 372, 378, *per* Lord Parker.

Trusts implied by law

Chapter 11

Resulting trusts

OVERVIEW

*Resulting trusts arise in favour of Y beneficially in the following situations: where Y has
purported to create an express trust but has failed to identify the person for whom that*

property is to be held;[1] *where Y has provided part of the purchase price of property with an intention to take an equitable interest in that property;*[2] *where X has acquired property intended beneficially for Y using money provided by Y.*[3]

There are other situations in which presumptions of advancement operate to deem that rights in property have passed by way of gift between husband and wife, and between father and child.[4] *A resulting trust will arise in favour of the donor where that presumption of advancement can be rebutted on the facts.*[5]

No resulting trust will arise over property in favour of a person who has committed an illegal act in relation to that property.[6] *However, a person who has committed an illegal act can nevertheless take beneficially under a resulting trust where she does not have to rely on the illegal act itself to assert beneficial title in the property.*[7]

Resulting trusts are of particular importance in relation to the acquisition of rights in the home; a topic considered in detail in Chapter 15.

11.1 INTRODUCTION – WHAT IS A RESULTING TRUST?

11.1.1 Beginnings

There are circumstances in which the ownership of property will not be clear because a transfer of property has failed or is incomplete, or because a group of people have contributed to the acquisition of that property without allocating title clearly. In such situations, the doctrine of resulting trusts operates to resolve those questions of ownership. Resulting trusts arise in two quite different contexts: either to restore the equitable interest in property to its original beneficial owner in circumstances in which a transfer of that property has failed;[8] or to recognise the equitable proprietary rights of someone who has contributed to the purchase price of property with an intention that she take some property rights in that property.[9] While the most satisfactory definition of the resulting trust remains a subject for debate, it is suggested that the resulting trust is best thought of as being limited to these two categories.[10] It is suggested that, by extrapolation from the majority judicial opinion,[11] these contexts should be recognised as being in truth two very different forms of trust within the blanket expression 'resulting trust'.

The term 'resulting' itself may seem a little obscure. Professor Birks suggests that the term '*resulting* trust' is derived from the Latin '*resalire*', meaning to 'jump back' – that is, the equitable interest in property 'jumps back' to its original beneficial owner.[12] This is a convenient explanation of that form of resulting trust which arises when a transfer has failed,

1 *Vandervell v IRC* [1967] 2 AC 291.
2 *Dyer v Dyer* (1788) 2 Cox Eq Cas 92.
3 *Ibid.*
4 *Bennet v Bennet* (1879) 10 Ch D 474.
5 *Fowkes v Pascoe* (1875) 10 Ch App Cas 343. See now *Stack v Dowden* [2007] UKHL 17.
6 *Tinsley v Milligan* [1994] 1 AC 340; *Tribe v Tribe* [1995] 3 WLR 913.
7 *Ibid.*
8 *Vandervell v IRC* [1967] 2 AC 291, HL; *Air Jamaica Ltd v Charlton* [1999] 1 WLR 1399, PC.
9 *Dyer v Dyer* (1788) 2 Cox Eq Cas 92.
10 *Westdeutsche Landesbank Girozentrale v Islington LBC* [1996] AC 669.
11 *Ibid.*
12 Birks, 1989, 62.

but is less obviously a complete explanation of that form of resulting trust which arises by means of a contribution to the purchase price of property. These distinctions will be explored in detail in the discussion to follow.

This chapter will do two things. First, it will consider the decided cases dealing with resulting trusts and will attempt to categorise those decisions. Secondly, it will examine the competing academic and judicial explanations of the underlying rationales of resulting trusts which veer broadly between one view asserting a broadly restitutionary role for resulting trusts and another which seeks to limit the resulting trust to those few categories set out in the decided cases. Before considering the decided case law it will be useful to consider the general statements made by Lord Browne-Wilkinson in the House of Lords in the leading case of *Westdeutsche Landesbank Girozentrale v Islington LBC*[13] as to the different types of resulting trust.

11.1.2 Resulting trusts in *Westdeutsche Landesbank v Islington LBC*

Two categories of resulting trust

The leading speech of Lord Browne-Wilkinson in *Westdeutsche Landesbank Girozentrale v Islington LBC*[14] set out the two situations in which his Lordship considered that a resulting trust would arise. This section sets those categories out; later sections will consider how desirable these categories are. The first category of resulting trusts relates to situations in which a person makes a contribution to the purchase price of property, and the second category relates to situations in which the settlor has failed to explain the allocation of equitable interests in property.[15]

Purchase price resulting trusts

Purchase price resulting trusts arise so as to recognise that a person who has contributed to the purchase price of property acquires an equitable interest in that property in proportion to the size of her contribution. That equitable interest is held on resulting trust for the contributor. Lord Browne-Wilkinson expressed the first category as follows:

> (A) where A makes a voluntary payment to B or pays (wholly or in part) for the purchase of property which is vested either in B alone or in the joint names of A and B, there is a presumption that A did not intend to make a gift to B: the money or property is held on trust for A (if he is the sole provider of the money) or in the case of a joint purchase by A and B in shares proportionate to their contributions. It is important to stress that this is only a *presumption*, which presumption is easily rebutted either by the counter-presumption of advancement or by direct evidence of A's intention to make an outright transfer.[16]

13 [1996] AC 669.

14 [1996] 2 All ER 961, [1996] AC 669.

15 In *Elsen v Elsen* [2011] BCCA 314, 14 ITELR 133 the issue arose as to whether a resulting trust could be implied so as to reverse the effect of an express trust for which the beneficiary had given no consideration. It was held that a resulting trust could not operate in this way; and that the express trust, once its existence had been found, would continue in existence. Ordinarily, a resulting trust would only be implied in circumstances in which there were otherwise no proprietary rights in existence.

16 Hayton, 1995, 317 *et seq; White v Vandervell Trustees Ltd* [1974] Ch 269, 288 *et seq.*

This first category affirms the long-standing principle in *Dyer v Dyer*[17] that where a person contributes to the acquisition of property, that person receives a corresponding proportion of the total equitable interest in that property on resulting trust. This resulting trust is said to be a *presumed resulting trust* because it will not always be clear that the contributor is intended to acquire an equitable interest in the purchased property: all that equity is doing, when ownership of the property is contested, is presuming that joint contribution to the purchase price constitutes all of the contributors equitable owners of the property. It is an important part of the operation of this form of resulting trust that the claimant has contributed to the purchase price with an intention that she should acquire proprietary rights in that property. Otherwise people such as mortgagees lending money for the acquisition of property might seem to acquire ownership in equity of the mortgaged property instead of merely the rights of a secured creditor. In short, equity presumes that there is a resulting trust, although that presumption can be rebutted if it can be proved that the contributor intended something other than the acquisition of property rights.

For example, if A Bank lends money to B so that B can buy a car, it will typically be the case that A Bank will have a loan contract with B entitling A Bank to a personal claim to repayment but not for A Bank to acquire any proprietary right in the car.[18] When there is a loan the lender does not acquire a right in any property bought with that money; rather the lender is entitled to a chose in action entitling her to a personal claim for the repayment of the debt (in the form of the repayment of the loan in cash).[19] However, if A and B are husband and wife, and A contributes 50% of the purchase price for the acquisition of the matrimonial home, it will be presumed by equity that A should acquire 50% of the total equitable interest in that matrimonial home because a couple's intention is more likely to be that both acquire equitable title in the home. On this specific point see also the discussion of *Stack v Dowden* in section 15.9.

Resulting trust where no adequate disposal of the equitable interest

The other form of resulting trust arises where there is a 'gap' in the equitable title. For example, if S declares a trust over property but fails to explain who will be the beneficiary

---

17 (1788) 2 Cox Eq Cas 92.

18 Somewhat unsatisfactorily in *Blue Sky One Ltd v Blue Airways LLC* [2009] EWHC 3314 (Comm) at [255] Beatson J suggested that a contract of loan does not exclude the possibility of there being a trust in equity by relying on *Barclays Bank v Quistclose*, even though his lordship was considering the point that a purchase price resulting trust and a loan are usually taken to be opposites. Of course, his lordship had elided very different concepts in this unfortunate remark. A *Quistclose* trust (considered below) is a means of taking security by inserting a term providing for the specific use of loan moneys into a loan contract; whereas a purchase price resulting trust is a presumption which arises from the use of a person's money to acquire property to the effect that they are to take an equitable interest in that property. The circumstance in which a purchase price resulting trust will not arise is a circumstance in which the parties intended the contributor of the purchase price to be making a loan as opposed to taking an equitable interest in the property. A loan contract creates a contractual right at common law to be repaid capital and interest, unless something else is specified; whereas a resulting trust acquires a proprietary right in equity in the property.

19 Thus a mortgagee or chargee over property has only a personal right to receive a sum of money in the first instance, and it is only in default of payment that the chargee's right to possession of the charged property crystallises: the chargee does not take a vested equitable interest in the property in the same way as a beneficiary under a bare trust.

under that trust then the property will be held on resulting trust for S. The underlying rationale for the law of trusts declaring such an *automatic resulting trust* is the underlying policy of English property law that there cannot be property which does not have an owner. Equity abhors a vacuum and therefore will fill any gap in the title with a declaration that the property is held for its previous owner on resulting trust. As a matter of public policy it would be unfortunate if the owners of property could simply refuse to be bound by any obligations to maintain their property once it became burdensome to them. Suppose, for example, that a bicycle was held on trust but that it became rusty and valueless, such that the trustees and the beneficiaries decided that it should be thrown in the canal and abandoned: English property law would consider that the trustees and the beneficiaries retained all of the benefits and the burdens of the ownership of that property thus preventing them from denying responsibility for the bicycle. More significantly, perhaps, the owners of factories which were found to be generating harmful pollutants might otherwise be able to disclaim any obligations to remedy the effects of the pollution they had caused if it were not for this rule.

Lord Browne-Wilkinson explained this second category of resulting trust in the following terms:

> (B) Where A transfers property to B *on express trusts*, but the trusts declared do not exhaust the whole beneficial interest.[20]

This form of resulting trust is considered below at para 11.1.4 in the section headed '*Automatic resulting trust*', particularly in relation to the decision in *Vandervell v IRC*.[21] What is also considered below is the appropriateness of the reference to this resulting trust giving effect to the 'common intention' of the parties. As considered immediately below, this division of the resulting trust into two halves was significantly different from the division set out by Megarry J in *Vandervell (No 2)*[22] which had held sway previously.

The foundations of resulting trusts

Lord Browne-Wilkinson used his leading speech in *Westdeutsche Landesbank Girozentrale v Islington LBC*[23] as an opportunity to state his judicial view not only of the law but also of the underlying foundations of the law of trusts. His Lordship explained the ideology behind the resulting trust in the following terms, in a passage which followed on immediately from those set out above:

> Both types of resulting trust [as set out above] are traditionally regarded as examples of trusts giving effect to the common intention of the parties. A resulting trust is not imposed by law against the intentions of the trustee (as is a constructive trust) but gives effect to his presumed intention.

---

20 [1996] 2 All ER 961, 990–91; Hayton, 1995, 317 *et seq; White v Vandervell Trustees Ltd* [1974] Ch 269, 288 *et seq; Barclays Bank Ltd v Quistclose Investments Ltd* [1970] AC 567.

21 [1967] 2 AC 291.

22 [1974] Ch 269, [1974] 1 All ER 47.

23 [1996] AC 669.

There are some difficulties with this explanation. First, as Dr Chambers points out, it is difficult to see how the resulting trust arises in all cases to enforce the *common* intention of the parties: that is, the intentions not only of the settlor but also of the trustees.[24] In *Vandervell v IRC*,[25] for example, there is only the intention of Mr Vandervell which can have been remotely important when Mr Vandervell decided to settle a parcel of valuable shares on trust for the Royal College of Surgeons and subject to an unallocated option to reacquire those shares in the future.[26] It is the titleholder in property who decides how that property is to be treated – it cannot be the intention of the recipient which is important.[27] In a case like *Westdeutsche Landesbank Girozentrale v Islington LBC*,[28] where there is a vitiated commercial contract between two parties acting at arm's length, it might seem appropriate to talk of a common intention, but that is not true of *all* cases. Secondly, it is difficult to see what business it is of the *trustee* to decide the terms of the trust; it is the settlor's intention alone which is significant.[29] Thirdly, that the trust is said not to be enforced against the intentions of the trustee indicates merely that it is the constructive trust which arises by operation of law irrespective of the intentions of the parties where the defendant has performed some unconscionable act (as considered in Chapter 12). That indicates that the resulting trust is a limited category of trust which relates only to the two situations indicated by his Lordship and to no other. These issues are discussed in more detail below.[30]

11.1.3 Common intention in resulting trusts

The reference to 'common intention' in the creation of a resulting trust is a commonly used one. Its meaning is that a resulting trust is a mixture of the intention of the settlor and the trustee's own knowledge that she is not intended to take the property beneficially. The idea is expressed as follows by Peter Gibson J in *Carreras Rothmans Ltd v Freeman Mathews Treasure Ltd*:[31]

> The principle in all these cases is that the equity fastens on the conscience of the person who receives from another property transferred for a specific purpose only and not, therefore, for the recipient's own purposes, so that such person will not be permitted to treat the property as his own or to use it for other than the stated purpose . . . if the common intention is that property is transferred for a specific purpose and not so as to become the property of the transferee, the transferee cannot keep the property if for any reason that purpose cannot be fulfilled.

It is suggested that this understanding of the resulting trust, framed in the context of *Quistclose* trusts (considered at section 11.3 below), renders it almost indistinguishable from

---

24 Chambers, 1997, Chapter 1.
25 [1967] 2 AC 291.
26 Discussed in detail at para 5.7.3 above.
27 This is so particularly if the recipient is a volunteer. In the event that the recipient has given consideration, the law of contract and the principle of specific performance are applicable.
28 [1996] AC 669.
29 *Re Brooks' ST* [1939] 1 Ch 993.
30 The various theories of resulting trusts are discussed by the New Zealand Court of Appeal in *Re Reynolds: Official Assignee v Wilson* [2007] NZCA 122, (2007–08) 10 ITELR 1064.
31 [1985] Ch 207, 217.

the broad-ranging constructive trust set out by Lord Browne-Wilkinson in *Westdeutsche Landesbank Girozentrale v Islington LBC*,[32] considered in Chapter 12, and is therefore an inadequate explanation of all forms of resulting trust. What sets the resulting trust apart from other forms of trust is that the equitable interest in property reverts to the settlor on resulting trust on the basis that the settlor did not have sufficient intention, or did not perform formally necessary acts, to transfer that property beneficially to some other person in the first place. The concept of 'common intention' in relation to resulting trusts is useful, it is suggested, only in relation to purchase price resulting trusts in relation to which two or more people have evinced an intention to hold the equitable interest in property in common, regardless of who is expressed to be the owner of the legal title in that property.

The assertion made by Peter Gibson J that the resulting trust effects the common intention of the parties does not provide a suitable explanation of the *Vandervell v IRC*[33] form of automatic resulting trust, considered below. Such automatic resulting trusts come into existence because of the settlor's failure to transfer an equitable interest effectively. The intention of the trustee is meaningless because the trustee, in her capacity merely as a trustee, has no entitlement to decide how the owner of property should deal with that property.[34] The only issue is the original titleholder's intention as to the ownership of the equitable interest. That problem is resolved by returning the title to the settlor on resulting trust.

11.1.4 The division between 'automatic' and 'presumed' resulting trusts

The alternative statement of the categorisation of types of resulting trust, and one which had seemed to hold sway up to 1996, was found in the judgment of Megarry J in *Vandervell (No 2)*.[35] Megarry J divided resulting trusts between '*automatic resulting trusts*' and '*presumed resulting trusts*'. In his judgment, he began with a consideration of the manner in which a resulting trust might come into existence. There is no better way to examine these issues than to read the relevant portion of that judgment in detail. In *Re Vandervell (No 2)*, Megarry J explained the law on resulting trusts as operating as follows (each of the points made are commented on in turn):

(1) If a transaction fails to make any effective disposition of any interest it does nothing. This is so at law and in equity, and has nothing to do with resulting trusts.[36]

This first point is straightforward. If the settlor has failed to transfer away any interest in the property which forms the trust fund then the situation remains exactly the same: the settlor remains absolute beneficial owner of all of the property sought to be settled on trust:

(2) Normally the mere existence of some unexpressed intention in the breast of the owner of the property does nothing: there must at least be some expression of that intention before it can effect any result. To yearn is not to transfer.[37]

---

32   [1996] AC 669.
33   [1967] 2 AC 291.
34   *Re Brooks' ST* [1939] 1 Ch 993.
35   [1974] Ch 269, 294, [1974] 1 All ER 47, 64.
36   *Ibid.*
37   *Ibid.*

So, as considered in Chapter 5, it is necessary for the settlor to make a declaration of trust before any express trust will come into existence. Similarly, before there is any transfer of any right in property, the transferor must perform the necessary act to effect that transfer, whether that requires vesting legal title in the property in the trustee or delivering physical possession of a chattel to its donee in the case of a gift:

> (3) Before any doctrine of resulting trust can come into play, there must at least be some effective transaction which transfers or creates some interest in property.[38]

Therefore, for there to be any question of a resulting trust coming into existence (that is, *returning* property rights to the settlor), it is necessary that those rights must have passed away from the settlor in the first place. The question then is, as considered in the following passage, what form of events will lead to the creation of a resulting trust once a transfer of some proprietary rights has been effected.

Presumed resulting trust

Presumed resulting trusts constitute a means by which equity will supplement unclear factual circumstances by presuming that the equitable interest in property results (or jumps back) to its previous owner. That means that, in a case where the evidence adduced by the witnesses will not conclusively support one or other of the parties such that the court cannot know which party to believe, the court will rely on one of its case law presumptions to imply an answer. Those presumptions operate in the following manner:

> (4) Where A effectually transfers to B (or creates in his favour) any interest in any property, whether legal or equitable, a resulting trust for A may arise in two distinct classes of case . . . (a) The first class of case is where the transfer to B is not made on any trust. If, of course, it appears from the transfer that B is intended to hold on certain trusts, that will be decisive, and the case is not within this category; and similarly if it appears that B is intended to take beneficially. [. . .] The question is not one of the automatic consequences of a dispositive failure by A, but one of presumption: the property has been carried to B, and from the absence of consideration and any presumption of advancement B is presumed not only to hold the entire interest on trust, but also to hold the beneficial interest for A absolutely. The presumption thus establishes both that B is to take on trust and also what that trust is. Such resulting trusts may be called 'presumed resulting trusts'.[39]

This first category of presumed resulting trust arises where no trust is created. Rather, there are a number of situations in which the case law raises a presumption that property passes between prescribed categories of individual. The example which arises most frequently is the situation in which property is transferred from father to child. The presumption which the law applies is that the father intends to make an outright gift of that property to the child.[40]

38 *Ibid.*
39 *Ibid.*
40 *Bennet v Bennet* (1879) 10 Ch D 474.

Therefore, in a case in which a father has transferred property to his child such that the child claims that this was an intended gift, but where the father claims that he transferred the property only for some other purpose, the court will not know whom to believe and consequently will revert to its presumption that in any case where a father transfers property to a child the father can be deemed to have intended to make a gift in the child's favour.[41] This presumption can be displaced by evidence that that was not the father's intention. Where such rebuttal of the presumption takes place, the child holds the property on resulting trust for the father. These resulting trusts are considered at section 11.4 below.

Automatic resulting trust

The second category of resulting trust is the automatic resulting trust, which arises (as its name suggests) automatically on the happening of a suitable set of circumstances. Megarry J expressed the category as obtaining in the following circumstances:

> (b) The second class of case is where the transfer to B is made on trusts which leave some or all of the beneficial interest undisposed of. Here B automatically holds on a resulting trust for A to the extent that the beneficial interest has not been carried to him or others. The resulting trust here does not depend on any intentions or presumptions but is the automatic consequence of A's failure to dispose of what is vested in him. Since *ex hypothesi* the transfer is on trust, the resulting trust does not establish the trust but merely carries back to A the beneficial interest that has not been disposed of. Such resulting trusts may be called 'automatic resulting trusts.[42]

The automatic resulting trust operates, in fact, on the basis of the equitable principle that equity abhors a vacuum. In practice this means that property rights must belong to some person; they cannot exist in a vacuum. Where there is no other equitable owner, those equitable rights are deemed to result automatically to the settlor: this appears sensible in principle given that the settlor was the last person to own those proprietary rights.

11.1.5 Doubting the automatic/presumed categorisation

This discussion has presented the arguments of both Megarry J and Lord Browne-Wilkinson because Lord Browne-Wilkinson takes issue with the categorisation set out by Megarry J. Lord Browne-Wilkinson, in his speech in *Westdeutsche Landesbank Girozentrale v Islington LBC*,[43] doubted that the division set out by Megarry J between automatic and presumed resulting trusts could be said to be correct in all circumstances:

> Megarry J in *Re Vandervell's Trusts (No 2)*[44] suggests that a resulting trust of type (B) does not depend on intention but operates automatically. I am not convinced that this is

---

41   See the discussion of *Tribe v Tribe* [1995] 4 All ER 236, [1995] 3 WLR 913, [1995] 2 FLR 966, at para 11.4.6 below for just such a situation.
42   *Re Vandervell's Trust (No 2)* [1974] Ch 269, 294.
43   [1996] AC 669.
44   [1974] Ch 269.

right. If the settlor has expressly, or by necessary implication, abandoned any beneficial interest in the trust property, there is in my view no resulting trust: the undisposed-of equitable interest vests in the Crown as *bona vacantia*.[45]

Lord Browne-Wilkinson is therefore taking issue with the categorisation of some resulting trusts as being 'automatic'. His Lordship considers that where the settlor has sought to divest himself absolutely of his right, there should not be a resulting trust in favour of the settlor. There are two issues which arise here. The first is that English property law has never expressly recognised that it is possible to 'abandon' rights in property.[46] English law has taken the view that one cannot dispose of property other than by transferring or terminating rights in it. What is generally considered to be impossible is simply to say that those rights of ownership which continue to exist belong to no one. The one principal exception to this could be said to operate in relation to the division of assets held by moribund unincorporated associations.[47] Therefore, Lord Browne-Wilkinson is either altering the principle that it is impossible to abandon rights in property, or is suggesting that where rights are purportedly disposed of it is incorrect to apply a resulting trust analysis to those rights. Secondly, it is not clear why those rights ought to revert to the Crown in preference to the original titleholder (or her estate) recovering any title in property which was not adequately disposed of. The intervention of rights of the Crown here is a remedy of convenience rather than a logical outcome in property law terms in the modern era – it does remind us, though, of the roots of English property law in the medieval assertion that all land and other property belonged ultimately to the Crown, and therefore that title in unclaimed property necessarily ought to revert to the Crown in recognition of this fundamental, 'reversionary' title.

11.1.6 Structure of this chapter

This chapter will nevertheless follow the division identified by Megarry J in broad terms, because that was the basis on which much of the case law considered in this chapter was decided. In what follows there is a consideration first of automatic resulting trusts and then of presumed resulting trusts. It should be borne in mind that this layout is itself controversial in the wake of the decision in *Westdeutsche Landesbank Girozentrale v Islington LBC*. The discussion to follow will differ slightly from the arrangement suggested by Megarry J, in that *Quistclose* trusts are considered separately from the other forms of presumed resulting trusts. One further change is a separation out of the treatment of mistake in the cases from the remainder of resulting trusts.

11.2 AUTOMATIC RESULTING TRUSTS

This category of resulting trust arises automatically by operation of law. Where some part of the equitable interest in property is unallocated by the settlor after transferring property to

45   See *Re West Sussex Constabulary's Widows, Children and Benevolent (1930) Fund Trusts* [1971] Ch 1.
46   AH Hudson, 1993.
47   *Re West Sussex Constabulary's Widows, Children and Benevolent (1930) Fund Trusts* [1971] Ch 1; see para 11.2.4 below.

the trustee, the equitable interest automatically results back to the settlor. So, for example, if S purported to transfer 100% of the equitable interest in land on which three houses were built to T to hold on trust, but S failed to declare a trust over one of those houses, the equitable interest in that one house would be held by T on resulting trust for S. This is the simplest form of resulting trust. The broad range of examples of automatic resulting trusts are considered below. Automatic resulting trusts are, it is suggested, to be considered to be a part of the law of property in that they seek to fill any gaps in the title by restoring that title to the previous owner of the property. This form of resulting trust is not restitutionary in that there is no requirement for there to have been an unjust factor in the transfer of the property to the resulting trustee. It could be considered to fall under the general notion that trusts arise on the basis of conscience, in that it would be unconscionable for any person who was not so intended to take beneficial title in the property to seek to act as such and so that person is required to act as resulting trustee of the property for the benefit of the settlor in the event that the settlor's intended disposition of the property fails for whatever reason. The well-understood categories of automatic resulting trust follow.

11.2.1 No declaration of trust, by mistake

The most straightforward form of resulting trust is that which arises when a settlor seeks to create a trust but does not declare the manner in which all of the property at issue is to be held on trust. Therefore, there is some property in relation to which no express trust has been declared. In this situation, the equitable interest in that property is said to be held on resulting trust for the settlor. The case of *Vandervell v IRC*,[48] which was considered in detail in Chapter 5, is authority for this proposition.

In *Vandervell v IRC*, Mr Vandervell sought to benefit the Royal College of Surgeons (RCS). The way in which Vandervell decided to benefit the RCS was by means of a transfer of shares to the RCS, such that the annual dividend on those shares would be paid to the RCS. Vandervell wanted to recover the shares after the dividend had been paid to the RCS. Therefore, Vandervell reserved an option for his trust to repurchase the shares from the RCS on payment of £5,000. The option constituted a form of equitable interest in those shares.[49] However, the owner of this equitable interest was not identified. In line with one of the core equitable principles identified in Chapter 1, the reader will recall that equity abhors a vacuum – which means that someone must be the owner of each equitable interest; that interest cannot exist in a vacuum, instead someone must own it. The equitable interest represented by the option to repurchase the shares could not exist in a vacuum. Consequently, it was said that the unallocated equitable interest personified by the option to repurchase the shares must be held on resulting trust for Vandervell.

This is the clearest example of an automatic resulting trust arising on the decided cases. There are further contexts in which this same principle could arise. Where the equitable interest in property has not been disposed of properly, in accordance with the formalities for transfer appropriate to that form of property, that equitable interest will be held on resulting

---

48 [1966] Ch 261, [1967] 2 AC 291.

49 All options contracted with the owner of property to buy specific property constitute proprietary interests in that property in equity.

trust for the settlor. Therefore, it is assumed that a valid declaration of trust has been effected but that the necessary formality to transfer the equitable interest on trust has not been effected. The principle is therefore akin to that in *Vandervell* considered above, in that the settlor would be deemed to be the beneficiary under a resulting trust over that property.

11.2.2 Failure of trust

Where a trust fails for any reason the equitable interests purportedly allocated by the failed trust must pass to someone, on the basis that equity abhors a vacuum in the equitable owner-ship. A trust may fail because some condition precedent fails – for example, that the benefi-ciaries must marry but they do not – or because some condition subsequent in the trusts fails – for example, that the beneficiaries must remain married but they do not. In such situations where the trust fails, the equitable title in the trust fund passes automatically on resulting trust to the previous beneficial owner.[50]

It was said in Chapter 5 that once an express trust is created, that trust cannot be undone by the settlor.[51] However, there may be some trusts which come into existence only for a given reason: where that reason is not fulfilled it may be that the trust is deemed ineffective. For example, in the situation where a couple had intended to marry and to have certain prop-erty held on the terms of a marriage settlement, but where the marriage never took place in spite of the fact that the couple lived together and had children, it was held that the marriage settlement must fail because there was no marriage.[52] The property purportedly held on the terms of the marriage settlement passed back to the couple on resulting trust.[53] In conse-quence, it can be seen that where the trust fails for any reason, the property intended to be held on trust will be held by the trustees on resulting trust instead. This principle can be distinguished from that in *Paul v Paul*,[54] on the basis that the marriage took effect in *Paul v Paul* and therefore the trusts did not fail even though the marriage subsequently did.

This principle is illustrated in *Re Cochrane's Settlement Trusts*,[55] in which a marriage settlement was created. Both of the parties to the marriage brought property to the marriage settlement. Under the terms of the marriage settlement, the income of the trust was to be paid to the wife provided that she continued to reside with her husband. In the event that either of them should die, the trust provided that the survivor acquired the entirety of the property in the fund beneficially. The wife left her husband who died subsequently. The issue therefore arose whether the wife would be entitled to succeed to the entirety of the trust fund, or whether her interest ceased once she left her husband. It was held that the wife received the equitable interest in the property which she had contributed to the marriage settlement on resulting trust, but that the property which the husband had contributed to the marriage settlement passed to his estate on resulting trust after his death. The basis for this decision was the failure of the purpose of the marriage settlement (that is, that they should stay together) giving rise to a return of the property to the original settlor on resulting trust.

---

50 *Vandervell v IRC* [1967] 2 AC 291; *Chichester Diocesan Fund v Simpson* [1944] AC 341; *Re Ames' Settlement* [1964] Ch 217.
51 *Paul v Paul* (1882) 20 Ch D 742.
52 *Essery v Cowlard* (1884) 26 Ch D 191.
53 *Ibid.*
54 (1882) 20 Ch D 742.
55 [1955] Ch 309.

Similarly, in *Re Ames' Settlement*,[56] a marriage was declared null and void. The question arose as to the treatment of property held on a marriage settlement. The marriage settlement itself provided for beneficiaries to whom the property should pass on failure of the marriage and so forth. On the basis that the marriage was held to have been void *ab initio* – that is, treated as though it had never taken place – the marriage settlement was treated as having failed. On the basis that the marriage was never valid it was held that the marriage settlement was similarly never in existence, and therefore that no term of the marriage settlement as to default beneficiaries could be effective. In consequence Vaisey J found that the property held on the terms of that marriage settlement was held on resulting trust.

The traditional rule relating to gifts made to charity in circumstances in which that charitable purpose fails is that any property purportedly passed under such a failed gift is held on resulting trust for the donor.[57] Where the gift itself is found to be worded so as not to disclose a charitable purpose (for example, where it is expressed to be for a 'benevolent or charitable purpose' and therefore not a purely charitable purpose) then again that property is held on resulting trust for the donor.[58] In similar fashion, if a gift is purportedly made to someone who is not able to receive that gift on grounds of her own incapacity to act, that gift will be held on resulting trust for the donor.[59]

11.2.3 Surplus property after performance of trust

What happens once the purpose of the trust has been performed and there is still property left over? Many of the cases in this area have already been considered in Chapter 4 in relation to the distinction between purpose trusts and trusts for the benefit of people. Related issues arose: should the property be distributed among potential human beneficiaries, or does it fall instead to be held for the donor of the property on resulting trust? The general rule is that such property will be held on resulting trust for the settlor,[60] unless the court can find an intention to benefit specific individuals instead.[61]

Thus, in *Re Trusts of the Abbott Fund*,[62] a trust fund was created in favour of two elderly ladies, and subscriptions were sought from the public. The aim underlying the trust was not fully performed before the two ladies died. It was held that the trust property remaining undistributed at the time of death should be held on resulting trust for the subscribers. A similar approach was taken in *Re Gillingham Bus Disaster Fund*[63] in considering a subscription fund for which money was raised from the public in the wake of a bus crash. The victims of the crash did not require all of the money raised. The issue arose as to treatment of the surplus money raised from the public but not needed by the victims of the disaster. The court held that the surplus should be held on resulting trust for the subscribers.[64] Had the money

---

56 [1964] Ch 217.
57 *Chichester Diocesan Fund v Simpson* [1944] AC 341.
58 *Morice v Bishop of Durham* (1805) 10 Ves 522.
59 *Simpson v Simpson* [1992] 1 FLR 601.
60 *Re Trusts of the Abbott Fund* [1900] Ch 326.
61 *Re Osoba* [1979] 2 All ER 393.
62 [1900] Ch 326.
63 [1958] Ch 300.
64 *Re Hillier* [1954] 1 WLR 9; affirmed in part [1954] 1 WLR 700.

been held on a charitable trust then it could have been applied *cy-près* (as considered in Chapter 25).

The rule in *Hancock v Watson*,[65] however, will prevent a resulting trust in any event if an absolute gift is made to a person subject to a trust which fails. Instead, the absolute gift takes effect without the trust to the exclusion of any residuary beneficiary.[66]

The rule may be summarised in the following way. If a trust's objectives are performed but there is still money remaining to be held on trust by the trustees, that property is to be held on resulting trust for the people who subscribed it in the first place. Suppose, for example, that S created a trust over a sum of money so that his daughter B's fees for dance lessons could be paid out of the trust. If the fees were paid in full but there was still money left over, there would be two theoretical possibilities: either the surplus money could pass to B absolutely, or that surplus money could be returned to S. The case law has taken the view that the surplus money should pass back to S on resulting trust. There are two alternative principles to consider. First, could B invoke the rule in *Saunders v Vautier*[67] as the absolutely-entitled beneficiary so that the property became vested in her absolutely? In principle there is no reason why this rule should not operate, unless S structured the trust so that B took no vested right in the trust property but was entitled only to the benefit of the dance lessons acquired with the trust money. Secondly, on a different point, the rules set out below in relation to unincorporated associations suggest that where money is given to such an association it will not pass back to the settlor on resulting trust.[68] Instead, that property will be distributed according to the terms of the contract between the members of that association.

11.2.4 Upon dissolution of unincorporated association

The context of the unincorporated association was considered in Chapter 4 in relation to purpose trusts. In that chapter an unincorporated association was defined as an association of people which does not itself have legal personality – thus raising problems as to the manner in which property subscribed to such an association is to be treated by the law. A particular problem arises on the dissolution of an unincorporated association as to the ownership of such property formerly held for the purposes of that association. There are two competing approaches: first, that the property should be held on resulting trust for the people who subscribed it; or, secondly, that the contract executed between the members of the association ought to be decisive of the manner in which that property is then distributed.

The classical view emerges from the decision in *Re West Sussex, etc Fund Trusts*,[69] which held that there may be situations in which a resulting trust will be imposed where money has been raised from the public. In that case it was held that, in relation to large donations attributable to identified individuals, such gifts should be held on trust for their donors. However, in relation to property in respect of which it would be difficult or impracticable to trace its donor, the classical view was that the property should pass *bona vacantia* to the Crown.[70]

---

65 [1902] AC 14.
66 This rule was considered in detail at para 3.4.4 above.
67 (1841) 4 Beav 115.
68 *Re Bucks Constabulary Benevolent Fund* [1978] 1 WLR 641, [1979] 1 All ER 623.
69 *Re West Sussex Constabulary's Widows, Children and Benevolent (1930) Fund Trusts* [1971] Ch 1.
70 *Westdeutsche Landesbank Girozentrale v Islington LBC* [1996] AC 669.

Re West Sussex must be considered to be of doubtful authority in the light of the development of a more modern view.[71] In relation to other contributions, such as payment for entertainments or participation in raffles, the approach has been taken that the contract between the donors and the association for the provision of the entertainment disposed of any right which the donors might claim to have had in the property – on the basis that they had got what they paid for.[72]

On older authority, in circumstances in which the donor could not be said to have retained any equitable interest on the basis that her intention had been to make an outright transfer, it has been held that any property left in the hands of a moribund association would not be held on resulting trust for that donor but rather would pass *bona vacantia* to the Crown.[73] This approach was accepted as being conceivable still in *Westdeutsche Landesbank*. However, the notion of a donor ceasing to have any title in property once that property has been transferred, for example, under the terms of a contract, finds its resolution in a more modern view.

This modern view, propounded by Walton J in *Re Bucks Constabulary Fund*,[74] is that the dissolution of a society and the distribution of property held for its purposes is a matter purely of contract. Therefore, it is the contract between the members which should decide how the property is to be distributed without the need for the intervention of any equitable doctrines (like resulting trust). Where there are specific contractual provisions dealing with the distribution of the property, those provisions would be decisive; whereas if there were no specific provisions, the property should be divided among the members in equal shares.[75] In *Davis v Richards & Wallington Industries Ltd*,[76] this approach led to the finding that where a pension trust deed provided that any surplus in the pension fund belonged to the employer, when the pension fund was wound up the surplus passed to the employer rather than being held on resulting trust for the pensioners who had contributed funds to the pension trust. This solution was reached on the basis that it would enforce the contractual intention bound up in the deed: another example of the primacy of contract law over property law.[77]

This alteration in approach indicates two things. First, it demonstrates the important role played by contract in English law in allocating rights in property – an issue probed further in Chapter 21 on the relationship between commercial contracts and trusts. Secondly, it demonstrates that where a person intends to make a gift of property to another person, that donor retains no further property in the gift because the intention to make a gift itself terminates those property rights in the hands of the donor if the gift is completely constituted.

However, the *bona vacantia* principle in relation to property held on moribund trusts or for the purposes of moribund associations was upheld, albeit by way of *obiter dictum* in the speech of Lord Browne-Wilkinson in the House of Lords in *Westdeutsche Landesbank v Islington LBC*,[78] a subsequent decision of the Privy Council has taken a different approach. So, in *Air Jamaica v Charlton*,[79] a provision had been inserted in the trust instrument over an

---

71 *Re Bucks Constabulary Benevolent Fund* [1978] 1 WLR 641.
72 *Ibid.*
73 *Cunnack v Edwards* [1896] 2 Ch 679; *Braithwaite v Attorney-General* [1909] 1 Ch 510.
74 [1979] 1 All ER 623.
75 *Ibid*; see also *Re GKN Sports Club* [1982] 1 WLR 774.
76 [1990] 1 WLR 1511.
77 See para 2.4.1 above.
78 [1996] AC 669.
79 [1999] 1 WLR 1399.

occupational pension fund which provided expressly that no moneys were to be returned to the company in any circumstances. The purpose of that provision had been to preserve the company from any liability for tax arising from an inference that the company might otherwise have appeared to have been beneficially entitled to that trust fund. The trust was subsequently held to have been void for offending the rule against perpetuity. The question then arose whether or not property held on the terms of the void trust should result back to the company or whether that property should pass *bona vacantia* to the Crown. Given the provision of the trust which denied any right in the trust property to the company, it was argued that no sums could result to the company. In spite of the express term in the trust instrument, Lord Millett held that the surplus in the pension fund could be treated as belonging in equity to the company and the members of the pension fund scheme on resulting trust principles. Consequently, the funds remaining in the pension trust would not be treated as *bona vacantia* such that they would have passed to the government of Jamaica. The finding of a resulting trust instead provided that the company and the members of the scheme took title in them in accordance with the size of their contributions to the scheme. This approach accords more closely with the idea that property is privately held by private citizens and is not held simply at the will of the state.

11.3 *QUISTCLOSE* TRUSTS

> *A* Quistclose *trust is imposed over loan moneys if those moneys were lent subject to a condition that they were to be used only for a specified purpose but the borrower misapplied those loan moneys.*

11.3.1 The *Quistclose* trust in outline

This short section is intended only to give an outline of the nature of *Quistclose* trusts, whereas Chapter 22 considers these complex trusts in much greater detail.[80] The reader is referred to that discussion for a closer analysis of the issues surrounding this notoriously intricate aspect of trusts law. The following sections consider the case law's general assertion that these trusts are properly considered to be a form of automatic resulting trust (although it should be remembered that that categorisation is in itself controversial in the eyes of many commentators).

Quistclose trusts, like any idea, can be made simple first. In short, a *Quistclose* trust[81] arises in a situation in which a lender lends money to a borrower subject to a condition that the borrower will use that money only for a specified purpose provided in the loan contract. If the loan moneys are used for some other purpose in breach of that condition, equity deems that a trust has been created over the loan moneys in favour of the lender. The lender's rights under that trust will defeat the rights of any third person to whom the borrower may have transferred those moneys in breach of that condition. This trust has been categorised in two House of Lords decisions as being a form of automatic resulting trust such that the equitable interest in the loan moneys passes back automatically on resulting trust to the lender as soon

---

80 See sections 22.3 and 22.4.
81 *Barclays Bank v Quistclose Investments Ltd* [1970] AC 567.

as those moneys are misapplied.[82] As will emerge, the proper categorisation of this form of trust is a matter for debate.

First, a worked example might be useful. Suppose Laura agrees to lend money to Bill. Bill is facing personal bankruptcy. His business is the manufacture and sale of modern, metal furniture. Bill has been unable to sell enough of his furniture but he thinks that if he were able to adapt his machinery to manufacture a particular type of fashionable furniture then he would be able to move back into profit. Laura therefore agrees to lend Bill £10,000 on the condition that the money is only to be used to adapt that machine.[83] The money is transferred to Bill. The next week, Bill is declared insolvent and his trustee in bankruptcy seeks to divide up the £10,000 among Bill's creditors. The *Quistclose* trust means that the £10,000 is held on trust for Laura because the loan contract specified that the money should be used only to adapt the machine: therefore, the loan money does not form part of Bill's estate for insolvency purposes. Consequently, Laura will be able to recover the loan money (and using the rule in *Saunders v Vautier*, as the sole beneficiary under the *Quistclose* trust, she will be able to compel the trustee to transfer the money to her absolutely).

11.3.2 The decision in *Barclays Bank v Quistclose*

The first modern statement of the above proposition arose in the decision of the House of Lords in *Barclays Bank v Quistclose*[84] and which therefore gives its name to that trust. Much of the difficulty in relation to *Quistclose* trusts revolves around the search for a satisfactory explanation of the working of these trusts which fit uneasily into any categorisation as express trust, or resulting trust, or even constructive trust. While these trusts are commonly known as *Quistclose* trusts their source can be traced to the older principle established in *Hassall v Smither*[85] that equitable title vests in a lender where conditions are attached to the use of loan moneys by their borrower.

In *Barclays Bank v Quistclose* a contract was formed by which Quistclose lent money to a company for a specific purpose, and then sought to recover its loan after the borrower's insolvency on the basis that the purpose had not been carried out. Memorably, Harman LJ described the company as being 'in Queer Street' – referring to the fact that the company had already exceeded its overdraft limit on its general bank account with Barclays Bank and was clearly in financial difficulties. The specific purpose for the loan, after negotiation between Quistclose and the company, was to enable the company to pay a dividend to its preferred shareholders but was subject to an express contractual provision that the loan moneys were not to be used for any other purpose. Importantly, then, the loan was made solely for use for payment of the dividend. It transpired that that purpose could not be performed because the company went into insolvency before paying the dividend to shareholders. At the same time, the company had a large overdraft with Barclays Bank on its general bank account. The loan

---

82 *Twinsectra Ltd v Yardley* [1999] Lloyd's Rep Bank 438; *R v Common Professional Examination Board ex p Mealing-McCleod* (2000) *The Times*, 2 May.

83 Let us suppose that Laura believes that if the money is used for this purpose then Bill will make profits and therefore this is the most likely way that the loan capital and interest will be paid.

84 [1970] AC 567, [1968] 3 All ER 651, [1968] 3 WLR 1097.

85 (1806) 12 Ves 119.

moneys had been paid into the company's share dividend bank account with Barclays Bank and therefore segregated from its general assets.

Subsequently, the company went into liquidation and Quistclose sought to recover the loan money. Barclays Bank contended that the money held in the share dividend account with Barclays should be set off against the company's overdraft with the bank in its general account on the basis that the money belonged beneficially to the company. Quistclose, therefore, needed to demonstrate that it had a proprietary interest in the loan moneys or else the money would be used to discharge the company's overdraft with the bank.

It was held that the loan money, held separately in a share dividend bank account, should be treated as having been held on resulting trust for the lender. The House of Lords held unanimously that the money in the share dividend account was held on trust for Quistclose on the basis that the specified purpose of the loan had not been performed.

Lord Wilberforce upheld the resulting trust in favour of Quistclose on the basis that it was an implied term of the loan contract that the money be returned to the lender in the event that it was not used for the purpose for which it was lent. Lord Wilberforce found that there were two trusts: a primary trust (to use the money to pay the dividend) and a secondary trust (to return the money to the bank if it was not used to pay the dividend). As his Lordship held:

> In the present case the intention to create a secondary trust for the benefit of the lender, to arise if the primary trust, to pay the dividend, could not be carried out, is clear and I can find no reason why the law should not give effect to it.

The principle has been alternatively stated in *Carreras Rothmans Ltd v Freeman Mathews Treasure Ltd* to be that:[86]

> equity fastens of the conscience of the person who receives from another property transferred for a specific purpose only and not therefore for the recipient's own purposes, so that such person will not be permitted to treat the property as his own or to use it for other than the stated purpose.

However, this second description of the trust could be taken to be authority for one of three competing understandings of the *Quistclose* arrangement, considered in section 22.4. As considered in *Westdeutsche Landesbank v Islington*, to define the *Quistclose* trust as operating solely on the conscience of the recipient of the money is merely to place the situation within the general understanding of the trust as part of equity, rather than to allocate it to any particular trust categorisation.

Categorising Quistclose trusts

The principal problem in this context is identifying the proper analysis of the *Quistclose* trust. This weighty task is undertaken in detail in sections 22.3 and 22.4. The real problem is explaining the nature of the rights of the lender, the rights of the borrower and the time at which those rights come into existence, and the form of trust which best explains these features.

---

86   [1985] Ch 207, 222.

Acquiring commercial security other than under a Quistclose arrangement

The rights created under a *Quistclose* trust appear to be similar to the *Romalpa* clause[87] at common law under which a person who transfers property to another for the purposes of a contract expressly retains title in that property during the life of the contract. Indeed, this is the analysis which was advanced by Lord Millett in *Twinsectra Ltd v Yardley*.[88]

These issues are considered in detail in Chapter 22, as mentioned above.

11.4 PRESUMED RESULTING TRUSTS

11.4.1 Introduction

Presumptions of advancement and resulting trusts

As considered above, there are situations in which English law presumes that particular personal relationships give rise to outright gifts when property passes between people in those relationships. The situations in which a presumption is important are those cases in which neither party is able to prove to the court's satisfaction what their true intentions were. Suppose two people, S and T, who are not related to one another. In a situation in which S hands his watch to T there are a number of possible explanations of the parties' intentions. It may be that S is making a gift of the watch to T. Alternatively, it may be that S has asked T to look after his watch while S goes swimming. Yet again, it may be that S has asked T to be trustee of the watch for S for life and then for his children after S's death. If the parties fall out and the matter comes to court, it will be very difficult for the judge to decide what S intended in respect of the watch: T may well insist that S made a gift of the watch, whereas S may argue that T was only to have it for safekeeping. In such situations, equity has developed presumptions as to what the parties intended. That means that if neither party can prove conclusively what was intended, the court will go back to its presumption and deem that that is what happened. In the case of S and T, equity would presume that S did not intend to make a gift of the valuable watch to T because T is not a person for whom S would usually be expected to provide.[89] Therefore, T would hold that watch on resulting trust for S.

The presumptions are a default setting which the courts fix on in cases of uncertainty. A little like a computer which, when you exit all of the software packages, returns to its default setting at the log-on screen. It is the result which the court plumps for when it cannot know on the evidence which is the correct result. As Lord Upjohn held in *Vandervell v IRC*:[90] 'in reality the so-called presumption of a resulting trust is no more than a long-stop to provide an answer where the relevant facts and circumstances fail to reach a solution.'

Suppose that S and T are husband and wife and therefore fall within one of the categories covered by the presumptions.[91] Where S transfers property to T, the presumption is that S intended to make a gift of that property to T. This process of assuming an intention to make

---

87 *Aluminium Industrie Vaassen BV v Romalpa Aluminium Ltd* [1976] 1 WLR 676.
88 [2002] 2 All ER 377.
89 *Bennet v Bennet* (1879) 10 Ch D 474.
90 [1967] 2 AC 291, 313.
91 *Bennet v Bennet* (1879) 10 Ch D 474.

a gift when a husband passes property to his wife is known as 'the presumption of advancement'. The other relationship which gives rise to a presumption of advancement is the situation between father and child. However, suppose that S and T are not married, and do not fall within any of the categories of presumption; where S transfers property to T without intending T to take that property beneficially (because there is no presumption of advancement) there will be a *presumed resulting trust* over that property in favour of S on the basis that S is not presumed to intend to make a gift of that property to T.

In more modern cases, even where a presumption of advancement exists, the courts are likely to accept evidence to disprove (or rebut) any such intention to make an advancement of the property. The court would often prefer to find a conclusive answer on the facts and the evidence given by witnesses rather than simply have recourse to the presumption. In such a case, where there is sufficient evidence, the presumption of a gift between S and T would be rebutted. In its place, a resulting trust comes into existence, because T holds the legal title in the property after the transfer in circumstances in which T was never intended to take that property beneficially.

Before discussing the detailed rules in this area, it is worth considering the social context of these principles. The operation of presumptions in English law is problematic. There are situations established by case law in which it is presumed that a transfer of property manifests an intention to create a gift of that property. The two more usual presumptions are in the cases of transfer from father to child and from husband to wife. This use of presumptions in the modern age is possibly questionable. There is no logic to assume that transfers between father and child should necessarily have a presumption of advancement attached to them where there is no such presumption in the case of transfers between mother and child. In the times when the presumptions were created it was usual for the court to assume that a man would be obliged to provide for his wife and his children. Therefore, it was presumed that any transfer of property to a wife or a child was an act undertaken as part of this obligation to maintain them. The presumption did not operate in relation to a transfer by a wife to her husband because women did not usually have much property of their own, husbands and wives being considered to be one person such that the wife was merely the 'shadow of her husband'.[92]

The importance of the resulting trust in this context is that if the presumption does not operate to transfer property between the purported donor and donee, the principle of resulting trust provides that the equitable interest in the property is held on resulting trust for the donor. The cases which we will examine in the following sections therefore consider whether a presumption applies, or whether that presumption can be rebutted so that a resulting trust arises. In short, where S transfers legal title to T, S will want to rebut any presumption that a gift has been made and demonstrate that the property should be held on resulting trust for S.

Purchase price resulting trusts

Purchase price resulting trusts have been considered to fall within the category of presumed resulting trusts. They do not in fact correspond to the presumed resulting trust category. The

---

92 See *Caunce v Caunce* [1969] 1 WLR 286.

basis on which purchase price resulting trusts should be understood is that it would be unconscionable for the person in whose name the legal title is placed to deny the beneficial interests of the other people who have contributed to the purchase price of the property. This principle is considered below at para 11.4.4.

11.4.2 Presumption of advancement – special relationships

This section considers some of the specific relationships which the case law considers give effect to deemed outright transfers of property in the absence of evidence to the contrary, by way of presumption. The presumption of advancement will be removed by statute for the future, and has been overruled in relation specifically to cases involving the home. This brief survey is useful to understand much of the case law on resulting trusts which were affected by the presumption of advancement.

The abolition of the presumption of advancement for the future

The Equality Act 2010 has abolished the presumption of advancement prospectively. So, under s 199 of that Act it is provided that 'the presumption of advancement is abolished' but that abolition applies only to 'anything done' after the Act has come into effect. Under s 198 of the Act it is provided that '[t]he rule of common law that a husband must maintain his wife is abolished'. The reference to an obligation to 'maintain' a wife meant an obligation to provide her with all of the material things in life which she required (and a presumption to that effect) and not an obligation to 'maintain' her physically as one might 'maintain' the brickwork of an old house.[93] Furthermore, in relation to ownership of the home, the Supreme Court has held in *Jones v Kernott*[94] that the presumption of advancement should not apply in that context, but that the Equality Act will have the effect of removing it in any event.

Father and child

Where a father transferred property to a child, it was presumed that the father intended to make an outright gift of that property to that child.[95] In the absence of any cogent evidence to rebut this presumption of advancement, no resulting trust would be imposed on the property in favour of the father.[96] The presumption was that a father would want to care for his child and therefore would make transfers of property to that child for the purposes of its

---

93   A weak joke perhaps but it does capture something of the oddness of an idea of a human being needing to be maintained as though a chattel or a building. Unlike Dickens in *A Christmas Carol* I cannot see wisdom in this metaphor and, while we can all take some pleasure in the gendered assumptions in these case law rules having been removed at last, I think we must think about what was hidden in this idea of a wife needing to be kept as though something decorative or something owned, rather than being enabled to live a useful life as a human being.

94   [2011] 3 WLR 1121.

95   *Bennet v Bennet* (1879) 10 Ch D 474; *Re Roberts* [1946] Ch 1; *Lavelle v Lavelle* [2004] EWCA Civ 223 Cf *Re Cameron* [1999] 3 WLR 394, 409, suggesting that perhaps mothers ought also to be included.

96   Rebuttal of the presumption is considered at para 11.4.5 below.

maintenance.[97] The relationship of mother and child did not give rise to a presumption of advancement because there was no necessary implication that a mother was required to provide for the financial well-being of the child.[98] (In Australia, the presumption has been held to apply equally to mothers as to fathers.)[99] There was another presumption which arose where the donor stood *in loco patris* to the child (that is, as though the child's father).[100]

However, it has been held in Canada that the presumption of advancement will apply only in relation to transfers made by parents to minor children and not to transfers to adult children. This accords with the understanding that the presumption of advancement applies where fathers are expected to take care of their children, which is not the same position when those children are adults.[101]

Husband and wife

Where a husband made a transfer of property to his wife, the presumption was that the husband intended to make an outright gift of such property.[102] In determining title to property, a transfer made on the breakdown of a relationship would frequently create the following type of conflict between them: one party would assert a resulting trust over the property, whereas the other would wish to argue that the property was the subject of an outright gift. Usually a combination of their conflicting evidence and the fact that few couples would have recorded in writing their true intentions would have meant that the court would be hard-pressed on the facts to decide conclusively how the property should be treated. The husband would seek to argue that he intended the property to be held on resulting trust for him, whereas his wife would have argued that the presumption of advancement should apply to the effect that she took the property as a result of an outright gift. The husband's reasons for effecting a transfer not meant as a gift might be to avoid creditors (as discussed immediately below) or to avoid tax. The rules relating to divorced couples applied equally to couples who were previously engaged.[103]

The clearest modern application of the presumption of advancement between husband and wife was in the decision of the Court of Appeal in *Tinker v Tinker*.[104] Mr Tinker transferred

97 The question arises in relation to the presumption of advancement as to how far it extended. In *Sansom v Gardner* [2009] EWHC 3369 (QB) it was argued that a man who stood *in loco parentis* to a younger man (but who was not actually his biological nor his adoptive father) should be subject to the presumption of advancement. It was held that in theory it was possible. The difficulties here were in demonstrating that the older man had assumed a responsibility to support the younger man and the persistence of such a relationship. However, it is suggested that the presumption does not rest on the assumption of a responsibility but rather on innate presumption that there was a type of relationship which automatically called such a duty into existence: therefore, if the relationship between the men was not of a type which automatically called the existence of the presumption into play, but rather if it was one which depended upon the assumption of that role by the older man, then it did not fall within the presumption of advancement but rather within the ambit of equitable estoppel or the law of contract.
98 *Bennet v Bennet* (1879) 10 Ch D 474.
99 *Brown v Brown* (1993) 31 NSWLR 582, 591.
100 *Re Paradise Motor Company Ltd* [1968] 2 All ER 625.
101 *Pecore v Pecore* [2007] WTLR 1591, Supreme Court of Canada.
102 *Tinker v Tinker* [1970] P 136.
103 Law Reform (Miscellaneous Provisions) Act 1970, s 2(1).
104 [1970] P 136.

land into the name of Mrs Tinker, avowedly to put the land out of the reach of the creditors of his garage business. Mr Tinker then sought to recover the property from his wife when their relationship broke down. Lord Denning held that Mr Tinker could not argue against his wife that the property was held on resulting trust for him while also arguing against his creditors that the property was vested in his wife. Lord Denning found, therefore, that the presumption fell to be applied that the transfer was intended to effect an outright advancement in favour of Mr Tinker's wife. It was clear on the evidence before the Court of Appeal that the wife was intended to acquire the beneficial interest under the transfer and that the husband sought to avoid the rights of his creditors as a priority.

Despite the application of the presumption as set out in *Tinker*, the modern view is to move away from its automatic application, particularly in respect of the family home, even in the case law and not even in the statute. In *Pettitt v Pettitt*,[105] Lord Diplock held that:

> It would in my view be an abuse of the legal technique for ascertaining or imputing intention to apply to transactions between the post-war generation of married couples 'presumptions' which are based upon inferences of fact which an earlier generation of judges drew as the most likely intentions of the earlier generations of spouses belonging to the propertied classes of a different social era.[106]

Similarly, in *Gissing v Gissing*,[107] it was held that the principles determining equitable ownership of the family home as between the respective contributions of husband and wife, raised different concerns from the application of the age-old presumptions. (The details of the rules concerning implied trusts in respect of the family home are considered in Chapter 15.) The foregoing principles were applied by Goff J in *Re Densham*,[108] where a husband was convicted of theft from his employers and made bankrupt. The issue arose as to whether or not his wife would acquire an equitable interest in the property on the basis that their joint savings had been put towards the purchase. Goff J held that the wife did acquire an equitable interest on resulting trust principles given that her money had been applied in the purchase.

No presumption of resulting trust in relation to the home; presumption instead that equitable ownership follows the legal title

Following the decision of the House of Lords in *Stack v Dowden*,[109] the Supreme Court in *Jones v Kernott*[110] has held that the presumption of a resulting trust in relation to the equitable ownership of the home is not to be applied in future. Instead, equitable ownership of the home, in the absence of an express trust, will be presumed to follow the allocation of the legal title. As with all presumptions, the presumption that the equitable ownership follows the legal title can be rebutted by sufficient evidence of a different intention on the part of the parties, resolving itself into a question as to the identification of the 'objectively inferred

---

105 [1970] AC 777.
106 *Ibid*, 824.
107 [1971] AC 886.
108 [1975] 3 All ER 726.
109 [2007] 2 WLR 831.
110 [2011] 3 WLR 1121.

intention' of the parties, or else into doing what the court considers to be fair in the circumstances. In a dissenting judgment in the House of Lords in *Stack v Dowden*, Lord Neuberger had followed the traditional methodology of allocating the equitable interest by reference to a resulting trust following contributions to the purchase price, and then using constructive trust principles to accommodate subsequent changes of intention, but this analysis was rejected by the other members of the House of Lords. On the current state of the authorities, the resulting trust will not apply to cases involving the family home. These issues are considered in detail in Chapter 15.

11.4.3 Voluntary gift

The first applicable category of presumption is where one party makes a gift voluntarily. That is, without any consideration having been provided by the donee.

Personal property

The presumption in respect of personalty is that a voluntary transfer gives rise to a resulting trust. By way of example, the case of *Re Vinogradoff*[111] concerned a grandmother who had a war loan for £800 in her name. (A war loan was in effect a security or bond, whereby the subscriber lent money to the government for the war effort and received a payment of interest and a future promise of repayment to whoever held the security at the time of redemption.) The grandmother transferred the war loan into the joint names of herself and her granddaughter. Unfortunately, she did not make plain her reasons for doing this. In consequence, it was unclear whether the grandmother continued to own the war loan outright, or whether she was now a joint tenant of it with her granddaughter. The grandmother continued to receive the dividends from the war loan until her death. When the grandmother died the issue arose whether or not the war loan formed part of the dead woman's estate or belonged to her granddaughter beneficially. Farwell J held that the property should be presumed to be held on resulting trust for the grandmother. His reasoning was that she did not fall within the usual category of the presumptions because she was not the child's father but only her grandmother. Furthermore, the fact that she continued to receive the dividends on her own without passing any of them to her granddaughter suggested that she had not intended to make a gift in her granddaughter's favour such that her granddaughter could claim the war loan absolutely on her grandmother's death.

Aside from the tortured logic of these presumptions, there are a number of possible objections to this decision in principle. First, the granddaughter was a minor at the time of the purported transfer, and therefore could not have acted as a trustee in any event because she was under-age. Secondly, it is not clear how this resulting trust can be said to accord with the intention of the settlor. Her intention in transferring the war loan into their joint names was ostensibly to benefit her granddaughter in some form. A resulting trust did not achieve that objective because it returned all of the equitable interest to the grandmother. While the testamentary rules of the Wills Act 1837 had not been observed (thus preventing a testamentary gift), it is not clear why there could not have been an *inter vivos* gift of rights in the property

---

111 [1935] WN 68.

by means of the creation of a joint tenancy,[112] or a trust in favour of the grandmother and the granddaughter in remainder.

In *Westdeutsche Landesbank Girozentrale v Islington LBC*,[113] Lord Browne-Wilkinson explained *Re Vinogradoff*[114] and related cases as operating in circumstances where there was no intention to make an immediate gift. His Lordship held that the conscience of the recipient is affected when she discovers the intention of the settlor not to create any personal benefit in the recipient's favour. The resulting trust is said to be imposed at the moment of the acquisition of this knowledge. As such, the resulting trust comes closer to the constructive trust set out by Lord Browne-Wilkinson in that same case – discussed below in Chapter 12. As Martin points out, it is difficult to see how *Vinogradoff* supports this analysis given the infancy of the resulting trustee at all times during the case.[115]

Real property

Prior to the enactment of s 60(3) of the Law of Property Act 1925, it was necessary to specify a particular use governing the land in the conveyance. Where no such use was specified, the property was subject to a resulting trust in favour of the transferor. Section 60(3) provides that: 'In a voluntary conveyance a resulting trust for the grantor shall not be implied merely by reason that the property is not expressed to be conveyed for the use or benefit of the grantee.' As a result, there is no automatic resulting trust on the ground that no use is specified. However, this does not prevent the possibility of resulting trust (as in *Hodgson v Marks*, below). Rather, it restricts the automatic imposition of such a resulting trust.

The case of *Hodgson v Marks*[116] is generally taken to have imposed a resulting trust over land where the intention of the transferor was not effected.[117] Mrs Hodgson was an elderly woman who had a lodger, Evans. Evans was a rogue of the old school. Readers may be reminded of the bounders played by the actor Terry-Thomas in films like *School for Scoundrels*, in Ungoed-Thomas J's description of him as 'a very ingratiating person, tall, smart, pleasant, self-assured, 50 years of age, apparently dignified by greying hair and giving the impression . . . of a retired colonel'. Evans put it about that Mrs Hodgson's nephew disapproved of Evans and that the nephew wanted to throw the lodger out. As we shall discover, Mrs Hodgson would have been well advised to have done so. Mrs Hodgson, however, developed an affection for Evans and transferred her freehold interest in the house to him so that he would be protected from her nephew's purported plan to evict Evans. The transfer was accompanied by an oral agreement that Mrs Hodgson would remain beneficial owner of the property. Evans became the registered proprietor of the property. The nephew's concerns were borne out. Evans sold the freehold to Marks, a *bona fide* purchaser for value without notice of Mrs Hodgson's rights.

The question was whether or not Mrs Hodgson was protected against the purchaser, Marks. The Court of Appeal held that Mrs Hodgson had an overriding interest under s 70(1)

---

112 *Fowkes v Pascoe* (1875) 10 Ch App Cas 343.
113 [1996] AC 669.
114 [1935] WN 68.
115 Martin, 1997, 246.
116 [1971] Ch 892.
117 *Ibid, per* Russell LJ; Birks, 1992, 335 and Chambers, 1997, 25.

(g) of the Land Registration Act 1925. Further, although Mrs Hodgson could not have claimed a declaration of an ordinary express trust under s 53(1)(b) of the Law of Property Act 1925 in the oral agreement, that agreement did prove Mrs Hodgson's intention in respect of the equitable interest and therefore formed 'a resulting trust of the beneficial interest to the plaintiff, which would not, of course, be affected by section 53(1)'.[118]

Hodgson v Marks is an adventurous application of the resulting trust, which might now be covered by the constructive trust as explained by Lord Browne-Wilkinson in *Westdeutsche Landesbank* (considered in Chapter 12). Its basis is that Mrs Hodgson did not intend to transfer the whole of the equitable interest, which she held previously beneficially, to Evans. Rather, she intended to reserve some of those rights to herself during her lifetime. Consequently, it was said that those rights ought to be restored to her by means of resulting trust when Evans breached their arrangement. It is suggested that the court was beguiled by the symmetry of the resulting trust and its rhetoric of returning rights to their original owner. However, the constructive trust appears to fit more comfortably with the facts of that case, given that *Hodgson* does not accord with the usual categories of resulting trust but rather with the underlying aim of the constructive trust to do justice on a broad scale.

An alternative analysis of this case has been advanced by Swadling.[119] Swadling argues that the statement of Russell LJ that the trust was a resulting trust is in fact an *obiter dictum*. Rather, it is contended that *Hodgson v Marks* is predicated on the doctrine in *Rochefoucauld v Boustead*,[120] which provides that statute cannot be used as an engine of fraud. Therefore, it is accepted by the Court of Appeal in *Hodgson v Marks* that Evans could not have relied on s 53(1)(b) of the Law of Property Act 1925 to argue that no trust was created over the land which bound Evans, because that would be to permit Evans to benefit from his own fraud on Mrs Hodgson. Swadling argues that the form of trust created in *Rochefoucauld* was an express trust and therefore that the trust in *Hodgson v Marks* ought to have been found to be an express trust in the same way, which Mrs Hodgson created in her discussion with Evans and from which Evans would be prevented from resiling when selling the property to Marks.[121]

11.4.4 Contribution to purchase price

The clearest form of presumed resulting trust, accepted both by Lord Browne-Wilkinson in *Westdeutsche Landesbank Girozentrale v Islington LBC*[122] and by Megarry J in *Vandervell (No 2)*,[123] is the situation in which a person contributes to the acquisition price of property and is therefore presumed to take a corresponding equitable interest in that property. The core principle in respect of purchase cases can be identified from the judgment of Eyre CB in *Dyer v Dyer*,[124] where his Lordship held that:

118   *Ibid*, 933, *per* Russell LJ.
119   Swadling, 2000, 61.
120   [1897] 1 Ch 196; considered at para 1.4.18 above and also para 5.2.2.
121   As considered at para 5.2.2 above.
122   [1996] AC 669.
123   [1974] Ch 269.
124   (1788) 2 Cox Eq Cas 92.

> The clear result of all the cases, without a single exception, is that the trust of a legal estate, whether freehold, copyhold or leasehold; whether taken in the names of the purchasers and others jointly, or in the names of other without that of the purchaser; whether in one name or several; whether jointly or successive – results to the man who advances the purchase money.

Where a contribution to the purchase price is intended to acquire some property right for the contributor then that contributor receives an equitable interest proportionate to the size of her contribution in the property on resulting trust. However, where the financial contribution is not directed at the acquisition of the property, that contribution will not ground an equitable interest under resulting trust.[125]

In relation to real property constituting a home, a number of specific rules have been developed. Some of those adaptations for that context include an understanding of the nature of the contribution which will give rise to a resulting trust. Therefore, contributions to the mortgage will suffice to create some equitable interest for the contributor[126] in proportion to the size of the contribution relative to the total value of the land,[127] whereas contributions only to domestic expenses will not.[128] These particular principles are considered in Chapter 15. In that chapter it will emerge that the arithmetical certainties generally associated with resulting trusts will often be disturbed in line with some greater notion of justice.[129] It has been suggested that the presumptions of advancement should not have any part to play in decisions as to rights in the family home, where other considerations such as the rights of children come into play.[130]

It is a pre-requisite for the establishment of such a resulting trust that the claimant demonstrates that the contribution to the purchase price is not made for any purpose other than acquisition of a right in the property. For example, where it could be demonstrated that the contributor intended only to make a loan to some other person for the purpose of buying a house, that would not acquire the lender any rights in the property. Similarly, an intention to make a gift of money to someone so that they could buy a house would not grant the donor any right in the property. Thus, in *Sekhon v Alissa*,[131] a mother transferred title in a house into her daughter's name with the intention of avoiding capital gains tax. It was held that she had no intention to benefit her daughter; rather, she had the intention of tax avoidance (or, evasion on those facts) which rebutted the presumption of intention to benefit the daughter. Therefore, whereas the property had been transferred into the name of her daughter, a resulting trust over the property was necessarily said to arise in favour of the mother on the basis of the true, demonstrable intentions of the parties.

125 *Winkworth v Edward Baron* [1987] 1 All ER 114, 118.
126 *Lloyds Bank v Rosset* [1990] 1 All ER 1111.
127 *Springette v Defoe* [1992] 2 FLR 388.
128 *Burns v Burns* [1984] 1 All ER 244; *Nixon v Nixon* [1969] 1 WLR 1676.
129 Swadling, 2000, 61.
130 *Pettitt v Pettitt* [1970] AC 777; *Gissing v Gissing* [1971] AC 886; *Calverley v Green* (1984) 155 CLR 242.
131 [1989] 2 FLR 94.

It will always be a question of proving that both parties are intended to take beneficial interests in the property.[132] This can lead to odd results. Few are odder than *Elithorn v Poulter*,[133] where Madeline put up all of the money for the purchase of a house to be occupied by Madeline and Alick as their home in Oxford. That house was put into joint names because Madeline believed that Alick would sell his house in London and pay her back for having paid the full purchase price upfront. Rimer LJ interpreted this as being a loan relationship between Madeline and Alick whereby Alick was to pay Madeline back in due course.[134] In essence, it was found that she was lending him the money to acquire his half-share, and not that she was acquiring the entire interest for herself. It was held by Rimer LJ, relying on the facts as found by the judge at first instance, that the proper interpretation to be put on the fact that both parties were intended ultimately to contribute half of the purchase price of the property was that the parties had intended to own the property jointly beneficially under resulting trust principles.[135] So, in spite of paying the entire purchase price, she acquired only half of the equitable interest. (Interestingly, throughout this case Madeline is referred to as 'Madeline' by Rimer LJ and Alick is referred to as 'Dr Elithorn', which somewhat diminishes her by reducing her to her first name and elevates him to the level of his medical qualification. That is not the least satisfactory aspect of this case.)

11.4.5 Rebutting the presumption

Given the judicial reluctance to apply the ancient presumptions to cases involving family homes, this section considers the situations in which courts have found that the presumptions have been successfully rebutted.

Generally

The application of the presumptions is clearly capable of outcomes which bear little or no relation to the intentions of the parties. Therefore, the courts have frequently sought to rebut the presumptions. In the old authority of *Finch v Finch*,[136] Lord Eldon suggested that the court should not accept a rebuttal of the presumption unless there was sufficient evidence to

---

132 In *Close Invoice Finance Ltd v Abaowa* [2010] EWHC 1920 (QB) it was found that when the claimant contributed the amount of a deposit to the purchase price of property then the claimant was entitled to an equitable interest on resulting trust principles in proportion to the size of that deposit relative to the total purchase price. On those facts it was found that the parties' intention had been for ownership in common and not that this deposit had been a loan. The remainder of the equitable interest was therefore owned by the defendant who had paid for the remainder of the purchase price.

133 [2008] EWCA Civ 1364.

134 There was much confusion as to the facts because Alick appeared in person and so the process was somewhat irregular.

135 Madeline died, and therefore the case was litigated between Alick and Madeline's other relatives. Let us suppose, however, that Madeline still lives: if that were the case, what rights does she have? The upshot would be that Madeline awaits payment from Alick for his half share, although this loan appears to be unsecured and therefore it is unclear whether she can sell the property and have recourse to the sale proceeds to satisfy Alick's obligation to her. Her recourse ultimately, it is suggested, would be either to seek specific performance of this loan contract whereby Alick is obliged to sell his house and forward to her the sale proceeds, or for Madeline to sell the Oxford property and then to set off the amount to which Alick is entitled from those sale proceeds against the loan repayment which he owes to her, as in *Owen v Wilkinson* (1858) 5 CB(NS) 526.

136 (1808) 15 Ves Jr 43.

justify such rebuttal. The more modern approach, indicated by cases like *McGrath v Wallis*,[137] is to accept a rebuttal of the presumption of advancement in family cases on the basis of comparatively slight evidence – even in a situation where an unexecuted deed of trust was the only direct evidence indicating the fact that a father intended a division of the equitable interest rather than an outright transfer when conveying land into his son's name.[138]

The presumption of resulting trust, which arises when a person has contributed to the purchase price of property, can be rebutted by interpretation of the surrounding circumstances. So, when a couple from different religious backgrounds started a relationship which later collapsed, the court rebutted a presumption of resulting trust to the effect that they were co-owners of a house which the couple had bought when together on the basis that one party collected and kept rents on the property for himself, that the parties had formed separate romantic relationships, and that the parties had never lived together in the property.[139] It was decided by the court that the inference to be drawn was that the parties had never intended that the property be held on resulting trust for them both to be used as their joint home.[140]

The clearest general statement of principle surrounding rebuttals of the presumptions was made by James LJ in *Fowkes v Pascoe*,[141] where his Lordship held as follows: 'Where the Court of Chancery is asked, as an equitable assumption of presumption, to take away from a man that which by the common law of the land he is entitled to, he surely has a right to say: "Listen to my story as to how I came to have it, and judge that story with reference to all the surrounding facts and circumstances."'[142] In that case, Mrs B had purchased shares in the names of herself and her grandson S. There was no personal nexus which would have brought S (although her grandson) within the ambit of the usual presumption of advancement. Therefore, the usual presumption in such a case as this would have been that the property was held on resulting trust for the settlor. Nevertheless, the court illustrated English law's occasional willingness to infer such presumptions of advancement. On the facts the Court of Appeal was prepared to hold that Mrs B's intention must have been to make a gift to S of half of the value of those shares. Therefore, the presumption of a resulting trust in favour of Mrs B would be rebutted.

Bank accounts

Where property is paid into a bank account by a husband with the intention that that property shall be held on a joint tenancy basis by the husband and his wife, the account is so held on joint tenancy and will pass absolutely to the survivor of the two.[143] Similarly, property acquired with funds taken from that joint bank account would belong to them both as joint tenants,[144] unless they were expressly taken in the name of one or other of them.[145] The

---

137 [1995] 2 FLR 114.
138 *Ibid.*
139 *Vajpeyi v Yusaf* [2003] EWHC 2339 (Ch).
140 It is suggested that this decision puts the horse before the cart. That the parties' subsequent behaviour did not demonstrate that they had clung to an intention to remain a couple and to occupy a house together is not evidence that at the time the property was acquired, their common intention was not that it be owned jointly beneficially.
141 (1875) 10 Ch App Cas 343; *Abrahams v Trustee in Bankruptcy of Abrahams* (1999) *The Times*, 26 July.
142 (1875) 10 Ch App Cas 343, 349.
143 *Marshall v Crutwell* (1875) LR 20 Eq 328; *Re Figgis* [1969] Ch 123.
144 *Jones v Maynard* [1951] Ch 572; *Rimmer v Rimmer* [1952] 2 All ER 863.
145 *Re Bishop* [1965] Ch 450.

difficulty arises either in situations where the intentions of the husband are not made clear, or in situations in which the husband transfers the bank account into the joint names of himself and his wife but continues to use the account for his own personal use. In the latter circumstance it would appear that the presumption of advancement is to be rebutted.[146] These same factual issues would arise in relation to any purported joint tenancy over a bank account, but the question of the presumption of advancement will arise only in relation to jointly-held bank accounts between husband and wife or father and child.

It has been held possible for a husband to rebut the presumption of advancement to his wife in circumstances where he agreed merely to guarantee her bank account.[147] For the wife it would be contended that such a guarantee was to be interpreted as an advancement made by the husband for the wife's benefit. The husband would argue that this was merely a guarantee, that no money had actually been transferred until the wife's account fell into arrears, and any money spent in that way was intended to be returned to the husband in any event. In a decided case the court accepted that the husband could recover the amount of the guarantee from his wife when it was called in because there had been no intention to make a gift of the sum to her.[148]

The case of bank accounts is generally a difficult one to assess. Where accounts are opened in joint names with the intention that money is to be used jointly, or even jointly and severally, the owners of the account will be joint tenants. In *Re Figgis*,[149] Megarry J was called on to consider joint bank accounts which had been held for 50 years. The accounts were both a current account and a deposit account. Megarry J held that a current account might be held in common for the sake of convenience so that bills and ordinary expenditure could be paid out of it. The deposit account was a different matter, because money in that account would usually be held for a longer period of time and only used in capital amount for specific purposes. It would, however, be possible for either type of account to be deemed at a later stage to have become an advancement in favour of the wife if the circumstances of the case suggested that that was the better inference. Megarry J therefore held that the presumption of advancement should operate in the wife's favour even though the account had been operated by the wife only during the First World War and during her husband's final illness. A different result was reached in *Marshall v Crutwell*,[150] where the account was opened merely for the sake of convenience and contained only money provided by the husband.[151]

Tax avoidance

Tax avoidance is an expression encapsulating the lawful organisation of a person's tax affairs so as to reduce liability to tax. Frequently, it may be that a taxpayer will transfer property to a family member so as to reduce his own liability to tax. Subsequently, he may seek to have that property retransferred to him once the revenue authorities have been satisfied. The family member may refuse to retransfer the property, thus requiring the

146   *Young v Sealey* [1949] Ch 278.
147   *Anson v Anson* [1953] 1 QB 636.
148   *Ibid*.
149   [1969] Ch 123.
150   (1875) LR 20 Eq 328.
151   Cf *Re Harrison* [1918] 2 Ch 59.

taxpayer to come to court alleging that the property is held on resulting trust. In *Sekhon v Alissa*,[152] a mother transferred property into her daughter's name with the intention to evade or avoid liability to capital gains tax. The mother sought to argue that the property should be held on resulting trust for her because she had no intention to benefit her daughter by the transfer. The mother, in the event, did not have to carry out any illegal action in evading liability to tax in respect of the transfer. Therefore, it was held that the mother was entitled to rely on her intention to rebut any argument that she intended to transfer the money outright to her daughter and thus demonstrate that the equitable interest in the house should remain with her on resulting trust. It remains unclear whether there is a presumption of gift in cases involving mother and daughter which mirrors the established rule in cases between father and child. It would appear that there remains a distinction in relation to the operation of the presumptions between transfers from fathers and those from mothers which is difficult to explain in the modern context.

In *Shephard v Cartwright*,[153] where a father divided shares in his successful companies between his three children, the issue arose as to whether those transfers of shares constituted advancements or whether the father was entitled to rely on his intention to divide them between his children so as to reduce the amount of tax payable on dividends declared over those shares. In that context Viscount Simonds held that the father could not pray in aid his subsequent treatment of the shares and the dividends; neither could he rely on the fact that the children signed documents at their father's instruction plainly without understanding what those documents meant. In consequence, the father's executors were required to hold the shares on trust for the children to give effect to the presumed advancement.

The decision in *Shephard* can be contrasted with that in *Warren v Gurney*,[154] in which a father bought a house which was conveyed into his daughter Catherine's name prior to her marriage. The father retained the title deeds to the property (which title deeds Morton LJ accepted were 'the sinews of the land', adopting Coke's phrase), and this the court took to indicate that the father did not intend to part with all of the rights in the house in favour of Catherine; rather, the father had written a document headed 'my wish' which purported to have the house divided equally between his three daughters. The court took the retention of the title deeds and the document together to rebut any presumption of advancement in favour of Catherine. In consequence, Catherine was deemed to hold the house on resulting trust for her father. The difference between these two cases is difficult to isolate in the abstract. Rather it is only on the facts of each individual set of facts that one can consider them and one must put oneself in the position of the judge deciding that particular case on the basis of the evidence presented to him.

The situation of tax avoidance should now be considered in the light of the doctrine in *Furniss v Dawson*,[155] whereby the court will ignore artificial steps which form part of a scheme designed solely to avoid tax. The courts' reluctance to support tax avoidance schemes is also evident from the decision in *Vandervell v IRC*.[156]

152   [1989] 2 FLR 94.
153   [1955] AC 431.
154   [1944] 2 All ER 472.
155   [1984] AC 474.
156   [1967] 2 AC 291.

11.4.6 Illegality and resulting trust

The law concerning illegal transfers of property was clear before the decision of the majority in the House of Lords in Tinsley v Milligan[157] that equity would not intervene to find an equitable interest on resulting trust in favour of a person who had transferred property away in furtherance of an illegal purpose.

This area of the law has undergone a radical overhaul in recent years. In short, the problem is this: where a person seeks to rebut the presumption of advancement but is required to rely on some illegal or unlawful act to demonstrate the intention that there be a resulting trust, will that illegality preclude the operation of the equitable resulting trust? Suppose, for example, that a husband had transferred property to his wife with the intention of putting that property unlawfully beyond the reach of his creditors; could the husband claim that the presumption of advancement should be rebutted in favour of a resulting trust? It is a core principle that one who comes to equity (for example, to prove a resulting trust) must come with clean hands. In consequence, equity would not find a resulting trust in circumstances in which the claimant was required to rely on an illegal act to prove the existence of that resulting trust. Therefore, the presumption of advancement would apply, or else the common law title would be decisive of the question.[158] That rule subsists in a subtly different form.

The long-established principle is illustrated by *Gascoigne v Gascoigne*,[159] where the court automatically effected the presumption of advancement in connection with the transfer of property by a husband to his wife with the intention of avoiding creditors. The plaintiff had leased land and built a house on it using his own money. The property was transferred into the name of his wife with the intention of eluding creditors. This transfer raised the presumption of advancement, which the plaintiff was required to rebut to demonstrate that his wife was intended to hold the property on resulting trust for the plaintiff. The only reference to actual fraud in the judgment of Lush J was that the plaintiff had refused to pay taxes in respect of the land on the basis that it belonged equitably and in law to his wife, the defendant. It was held, however, that the court would not allow a transferor to rely on an illegal or fraudulent purpose to rebut the presumption of advancement and establish an entitlement to the imposition of an equitable interest under a resulting trust. This approach was adopted as an instinctive response by the courts in these types of case. This principle can be traced back into older cases such as *Holman v Johnson* where in the words of Lord Mansfield: 'No court will lend its aid to a man who founds his cause of action upon an immoral or an illegal act.'[160]

A new direction

The long-established principles of equity in this context were subtly redrawn by the House of Lords in the case of *Tinsley v Milligan*.[161] The appeal concerned a lesbian couple who had

157 [1994] 1 AC 340, [1993] 3 All ER 65, [1993] 3 WLR 126.
158 *Muckleston v Brown* (1801) 6 Ves 52.
159 [1918] 1 KB 223. See also *Collier v Collier* [2002] EWCA Civ 1095.
160 (1775) 1 Cowp 341, 343, *per* Lord Mansfield CJ; as applied by Lord Goff in *Tinsley v Milligan* [1994] 1 AC 340. See also *Roberts v Roberts* (1818) Dan 143, 150; and *Ayerst v Jenkins* (1873) LR 16 Eq 275, 283, *per* Lord Selborne.
161 [1994] 1 AC 340.

concocted a fraudulent scheme to ensure that one of them would receive state benefits to which she would not otherwise have been entitled. Milligan and Tinsley used the house as a lodging house which they ran as a joint business venture. This business provided the bulk of both parties' income. The property was registered in the sole name of Tinsley, although both parties accepted that the property was owned jointly in equity. The purpose for the registration in Tinsley's sole name was to enable Milligan to claim state benefits with Tinsley's full knowledge and assent. The relationship broke down and Tinsley moved out. Tinsley claimed absolute title to the house. Milligan claimed that the house was held on trust for the parties in equal shares. Tinsley argued that Milligan would be required to rely on her illegal conduct to establish this claim and that equity should not therefore operate to give Milligan the benefits of her wrongdoing. It was held that Milligan was entitled to an equitable interest in the property on resulting trust in proportion to her contribution to the purchase price.[162] In short, the rationale for this decision was that Milligan was able to prove that her interest arose from the contribution to the purchase price (a lawful act) and not from the fraud on the social security system (an unlawful act). That thinking requires some closer examination.

In *Tinsley v Milligan*, Lord Browne-Wilkinson held that the following were the core applicable principles:

(a) Property in chattels and land can pass under a contract which is illegal and therefore would have been unenforceable as a contract.
(b) A claimant can at law enforce property rights so acquired, provided that he does not need to rely on the illegal contract for any purpose other than providing the basis of his claim to a property right.
(c) It is irrelevant that the illegality of the underlying agreement was either pleaded or emerged in evidence: if the claimant has acquired legal title under the illegal contract, that is enough.

His Lordship considered the long-standing principle of Lord Eldon in *Muckleston v Brown*,[163] that in cases where the claimant seeks to rely on illegality to establish a trust, the proper response is to say 'Let the estate lie where it falls' with the owner at common law rather than holding it on resulting trust. However, his Lordship found that the earlier cases also showed that the claimant ought to be entitled to rely on a resulting trust where she did not have to rely on her illegality to prove it. Relying on principles of trusts of homes set out in *Gissing v Gissing*[164] and *Lloyds Bank v Rosset*[165] (considered in Chapter 15), Milligan was able to argue that she had acquired an equitable interest in the property. The illegality was raised by Tinsley in seeking to rebut Milligan's claim. Milligan did not have to rely on her own illegality because she was entitled to an equitable share in the property in any event since she had contributed to the purchase price. The illegality was therefore not the *source* of her equitable rights; rather, her contribution to the purchase price was the source of those rights.

Lord Browne-Wilkinson did describe the cases on trusts of homes as establishing the rule that the 'creation of such an equitable interest does not depend upon a contractual obligation

---

162 *Dyer v Dyer* (1788) 2 Cox Eq Cas 92.
163 (1801) 6 Ves 52, 68–69.
164 [1971] AC 886.
165 [1991] 1 AC 107.

but on a common intention acted upon by the parties to their detriment'. The form of trust which his Lordship appeared to have in mind is a common intention constructive trust (considered in Chapter 15) rather than a resulting trust as normally understood. It is submitted that the appropriate form of trust on the facts was a purchase price resulting trust arising from Milligan's contribution to the acquisition of the property. To return to the earlier discussion of the nature of resulting trusts, it does appear that his Lordship was seeking to develop a resulting trust based on 'the common intention of the parties' rather than one which, *strictu sensu*, gives effect to the intention of the settlor alone. The whole drift of the law on resulting trust is therefore moving towards the establishment of resulting trusts in accordance with technical property law rules as opposed to being based on purely discretionary principles. In *Tinsley v Milligan*, Lord Browne-Wilkinson focused carefully on the source of the claimant's rights – in the contribution to the purchase price of the property – as opposed to the unconscionability of the claimant's entire course of dealing in relation to the property – particularly the illegal claim for social security benefits. This marks a movement away from traditional, moral principles towards a more modern and scrupulous approach based on the protection of validly-acquired property rights. However, Lord Keith and Lord Goff dissented in the House of Lords in terms which rehearsed the traditional approach, as is considered in the next section.

The dissenting view

The dissenting speech of Lord Goff in *Tinsley v Milligan* cited a number of authorities,[166] including *Tinker v Tinker*[167] and *Re Emery*,[168] as establishing the proposition that equity will not assist someone who transfers property to another in furtherance of a fraudulent or illegal design to establish an interest in the property disposed of. This approach is founded primarily on the ancient equitable maxim that 'he who comes to equity must come with clean hands'[169] and the fear that an extension of the principle propounded by Lord Browne-Wilkinson would 'open the door to far more unmeritorious cases'. While there is a moral attraction to this approach, it does not deal with the fundamental property law issue, 'who else can assert title to the property?'[170] Where the recipient has knowledge of the illegality bound up in the transfer, there would appear to be no objection to removing any proprietary rights transferred on purely moral grounds. However, where there was no intention to transfer rights absolutely to the recipient, it would appear to cut to the heart of the nature of the resulting trust if the intentions of the settlor are not to be observed. Indeed, the distinction between Lords Goff and Browne-Wilkinson is that the former prefers a moral approach to the law whereas the latter prefers an approach based on an amoral intellectual rigour.

---

166 Among the older authorities were (1775) 1 Cowp 341, 343, *per* Lord Mansfield CJ; *Roberts v Roberts* (1818) Dan 143, 150; and *Ayerst v Jenkins* (1873) LR 16 Eq 275, 283, *per* Lord Selborne.

167 [1970] 2 WLR 331.

168 [1959] Ch 410.

169 Following *Groves v Groves* (1829) 3 Y&J 163, 174, *per* Lord Chief Baron Alexander; *Tinker v Tinker* [1970] P 136, 143, *per* Salmon LJ.

170 Furthermore, Tinsley would have acquired complete title in this property despite being a conspirator in Milligan's illegal actions, thus making it equally undesirable that Milligan's rights be ignored.

The judgment of Nicholls LJ in the Court of Appeal in *Tinsley v Milligan* was particularly interesting in considering the nature of equity.[171] It was argued by Nicholls LJ that there ought to be a 'public conscience' test in cases such as *Tinsley v Milligan*. A public conscience test would mean that the judge could decide whether, in all the circumstances, that particular judge thought that the defendant's behaviour was sufficiently unconscionable to justify denying the award of property. This conscience would be equity in its purest sense: without reference to precedent or statute, the judge would be able to balance, in the words of Nicholls LJ, 'the adverse consequences of granting relief against the adverse consequences of refusing relief'.[172] Even Lord Goff, however, was not prepared to extend equity this far so as to allow the judge to act entirely as she thought fit on a case-by-case basis. One final point, on the facts of *Tinsley v Milligan*, however: we might want to observe that if Lord Goff had spoken for the majority, then surely the result would have been that one of the parties to the criminal conspiracy would have become the absolute owner of the property whereas her fellow conspirator would have received nothing despite having contributed to the purchase price. This would not seem to have generated a fairer result on the facts, even if it would have produced the satisfaction of having refused equitable relief to someone who had committed a criminal act.[173]

The question of intention

The decision of the majority in *Tinsley v Milligan* therefore marked a new departure in the law relating to illegality and the availability of equitable doctrines such as resulting trust: this new departure relied on a technical identification of the source of the claimant's property rights. Subsequently, in *Tribe v Tribe* the Court of Appeal also took into account the claimant's intention. In *Tribe v Tribe*,[174] T owned 459 out of a total of 500 shares in a family company. He was also the tenant of two leases used by the family company as licensees for the conduct of its business. The lessor served a notice of dilapidations on T which, it appeared at the time, would have required T to meet the cost of extensive works on the properties. T was advised that the costs of these works could lead him to lose the assets of the business and would cause him to go into bankruptcy. To avoid liability to his creditors, T purported to sell his shares in the family business to his son for £78,030. To put your assets beyond the reach of creditors in expectation of bankruptcy in this way was an illegal act. T transferred the shares to his son. In the event, no money was actually paid by the son in consideration for the transfer of the shares. Meanwhile, the lessor agreed to a surrender of the lease, which meant that T was not required to sell any assets to repair the property or to satisfy his creditors. T then sought to recover his shares once he knew that his creditors would not need access to them, but T's son refused to retransfer the shares to his father.

The issue arose whether the shares were held on resulting trust for T, or whether the presumption of advancement should lead the court to find that equitable ownership had been passed to T's son. T was therefore required to plead his own illegal act (that is, intentionally

---

171   [1992] Ch 310.
172   [1992] Ch 310, 319.
173   To do justice to Lord Goff, he does mention this point in his speech but nevertheless considers that he is obliged to follow the traditional principles.
174   [1995] 4 All ER 236, [1995] 3 WLR 913, [1995] 2 FLR 966.

putting his assets beyond the reach of his creditors) to rebut the presumption of advancement.

The Court of Appeal held that T was entitled to a resulting trust in his favour because his illegal purpose had not been carried into effect. The lessor had not required T to pay for refurbishment works which would have put T into insolvency, and therefore T had not had any creditors on insolvency to deceive. Therefore, despite T doing acts in the full expectation that they would turn out to be illegal acts, T was entitled to rebut the presumption of advancement to his son because by staying solvent he had not actually carried through his illegal purpose.

The current status of the law is set out in the judgment of Millett LJ in *Tribe v Tribe*:[175]

(1) Title to property passes both at law and in equity even if the transfer is made for an illegal purpose. The fact that title has passed to the transferee does not preclude the transferor from bringing an action for restitution.

(2) The transferor's action will fail if it would be illegal for him to retain any interest in the property.

(3) Subject to (2) the transferor can recover the property if he can do so without relying on the illegal purpose. This will normally be the case where the property was transferred without consideration in circumstances where the transferor can rely on an express declaration of trust or a resulting trust in his favour.

(4) It will almost invariably be so where the illegal purpose has not been carried out. It may be otherwise where the illegal purpose has been carried out and the transferee can rely on the transferor's conduct as inconsistent with his retention of a beneficial interest.

(5) The transferor can lead evidence of the illegal purpose whenever it is necessary for him to do so provided that he has withdrawn from the transaction before the illegal purpose has been wholly or partly carried in to effect. It will be necessary for him to do so (i) if he brings an action at law or (ii) if he brings proceedings in equity and needs to rebut the presumption of advancement.

(6) The only way in which a man can protect his property from his creditors is by divesting himself of all beneficial interest in it. Evidence that he transferred the property in order to protect it from his creditors, therefore, does nothing by itself to rebut the presumption of advancement; it reinforces it. To rebut the presumption it is necessary to show that he intended to retain a beneficial interest and conceal it from his creditors.

(7) The court should not conclude that this was his intention without compelling circumstantial evidence to this effect. The identity of the transferee and the circumstances in which the transfer was made would be highly relevant. It is unlikely that the court would reach such a conclusion where the transfer was made in the absence of an imminent and perceived threat from known creditors.

This statement of the law relating to resulting trusts and illegality still applies the principle in *Gascoigne v Gascoigne*[176] that a claimant cannot rely on an illegal act in seeking to establish a resulting trust. What is important to rebut the finding of a resulting trust is that there is

175   [1995] 4 All ER 236, 257.
176   [1918] 1 KB 223.

a direct link between the interest sought under the resulting trust and the illegal act. What is plain is that the equitable principle here is being drawn very tightly. The ancient principle that 'he who comes to equity must come with clean hands' is being eschewed in favour of Lord Browne-Wilkinson's more focused approach in *Tinsley* on identifying the source of the interest under resulting trust and seeing if that flows directly from an illegal act. Lord Goff favoured a more broad-brush approach which required action in good faith throughout, in line with the classical understanding of the principles of equity. Indeed, that the older principle is being displaced is evident from the decision in *Tribe v Tribe* in which Mr Tribe clearly intended to commit an illegal act and did all the acts preparatory to its commission: it was down primarily to good fortune that he did not have to carry his illegal purpose through. From this tendency in the cases it is evident that any strict attention to the principle of requiring good conscience from the defendant has been replaced by a more formalistic thinking which promotes technical precision over the broad sweep of ancient equitable principle. This was evident in *Tinsley v Milligan* precisely in the distinction between the speeches of Lords Browne-Wilkinson and Goff, where the former preferred a careful analysis of the sources of the parties' property rights and the latter a general view based on morality. A litigant will be required to rely on her illegal act and will therefore be prevented from relying on a resulting trust in circumstances in which, for example, an unmarried couple put their home in the woman's sole name in an effort to hide the man's equitable interest from his wife in matrimonial proceedings;[177] or where a father transferred title in his business premises to his daughter so as to avoid a claim for costs in litigation by making himself seem less wealthy;[178] or where a bankrupt sought to conceal property from his trustee in bankruptcy in insolvency proceedings.[179] In each of these cases the defendant's illegal act was the reason for the purported transfer of property to another person or the purported creation of a trust. It is only when in cases like *Tinsley v Milligan* where the illegal act is not bound up in the transfer of property that the defendant will be entitled to rely on an equitable remedy.[180] In cases of unlawful tax evasion, a claimant may be restrained from claiming an equitable remedy (such as resulting trust or proprietary estoppel) if the source of her rights is in truth an agreement to transfer property in a manner designed unlawfully to deceive HM Revenue and Customs ('HMRC'): so, by falsely completing a tax return to conceal an interest in property, as part of a scheme concocted by an old man with his adult children, an illegal act is performed which precludes the taxpayer from relying on a resulting trust in his favour.[181] However, if a tax evasion scheme is concocted but never carried out (because the false documents were never shown to HMRC) then there would be no illegal act committed which would preclude the finding of a trust,[182] just as in *Tribe v Tribe*.

---

177 *Lowson v Coombes* [1999] Ch 373, [1999] 1 FLR 799.

178 *Collier v Collier* [2002] EWCA Civ 1095, [2002] BPIR 1057.

179 *Barrett v Barrett* [2008] EWHC 1061 (Ch), [2008] BPIR 817.

180 See also *21st Century Logistic Solutions Ltd (in liquidation) v Madysen Ltd* [2004] EWHC 231 (QB), [2004] STC 1535, where an attempt was made to defraud HMRC of VAT payments: the judge held that creating a contract to sell computer parts (on which it was intended not to account ultimately for the VAT) as a preparatory part of that scheme was not an illegal act, but that an illegal act would be performed when a false return was submitted to HMRC.

181 *Q v Q* [2008] EWHC 1874 (Fam), [2009] 1 P & CR D12 (also sub nom *S v R*).

182 *Painter v Hutchison* [2007] EWHC 758 (Ch), [2008] BPIR 170.

The ethics of the resulting trust in cases of illegality

Mr Tribe had, of course, intended to carry out this illegal act in that he had performed all of the actions necessary to make his act illegal, but was fortunate not to have been forced into insolvency. Imagine an assassin on a cold rooftop looking through a telescopic sight on a high calibre rifle at his 'target'. You will be familiar with this scene from American films like *JFK* or Matt Damon's *Bourne* series of movies.[183] The assassin shifts his position, feels the heft of the rifle butt against his shoulder, flexes his fingers around the trigger, and settles his breathing. He is looking at his target standing on the street below on the edge of the kerb. The target seems to be looking absent-mindedly for a taxi. The assassin knows that the target is deaf, old and slow-moving. There is no hope that he can save himself if the assassin takes the shot. The street is clear for a moment. There is nothing to interrupt the assassin's view. He takes the first pressure on the trigger as he squeezes slightly. By increasing the pressure just a little more he will loose a bullet across the street. It is a clear day with no wind. The target steps forwards from the kerb but is still in the centre of the rifle's sights. The assassin squeezes the trigger and the bullet shoots from the rifle barrel. But before the bullet can reach its target, a No.19 bus, travelling at terrific speed, hits the target with tremendous force and kills him instantly. The bullet lands harmlessly in the side of the bus. The bullet would otherwise have hit the target full in the forehead. I would suggest that Mr Tribe is morally in exactly the same position as this assassin in one very important sense. The assassin intended to kill the target and did everything necessary for him to do to kill the target. However, by chance, a bus arrived at the right moment and killed the target instead. Mr Tribe had done everything necessary for him to have committed the illegal act of putting property beyond the reach of his creditors, and it was a little good fortune which meant that all of his actions did not ultimately constitute an illegal act. Morally, however, Mr Tribe was in the same position as the assassin pulling the trigger: he willed the outcome but circumstances intervened to save him from performing the *actus reus* of an illegal act. It seems odd, as a result, that Millett LJ should decide to use an equitable doctrine to come to the aid of Mr Tribe. The only explanation is that his son was also a party to the conspiracy to put property beyond the reach of creditors and therefore was morally in no better position than Mr Tribe, and therefore did not deserve to take title in the property in preference to his father.

Illustrations of the principle in action

There have been a number of more recent cases which have illustrated the basic principle that a person may rely on a resulting trust, in spite of there having been some incidental illegality, providing that the illegality was not the source of the property right claimed by way of resulting trust or alternatively that the illegal act was not in the event performed. There have also been cases in which the claimant has committed an illegal act in an attempt to conceal assets from third parties and so has been prevented from relying on a resulting trust or prevented from denying a proprietary interest by way of resulting trust. The denial of rights in property is a feature of cases involving insolvency or divorce or litigation seeking to impose liabilities over a proportion of the defendant's wealth: in each case, the approach

---

183 Someone looks down through a rifle sight at someone in all of these films. I am thinking particularly of Jason
Bourne looking at Pamela Landy from the roof of a building opposite her office in *The Bourne Ultimatum*.

has been the same as in *Midland Bank v Wyatt* in that the courts have sought, in effect, to prevent the defendant from denying title to property unconscionably. In *Lowson v Coombes* an unmarried couple put their home in the woman's sole name in an effort to hide the man's equitable interest from his wife in matrimonial proceedings but it was held that this was an illegal act and that equity required that the man could not purport to dispose of this property.[184] In *Collier v Collier*, a father faced a large bill for costs arising from litigation and so sought to make himself appear less wealthy by transferring title in his business premises to his daughter, but it was held that the property rights would result back to him nevertheless.[185] In *Barrett v Barrett*, a bankrupt sought to conceal property from his trustee in bankruptcy in insolvency proceedings but was treated as still having those assets as part of his estate for the purposes of the insolvency proceedings.[186] In each of these cases the defendant's illegal act was the reason for the purported transfer of property to another person, or the purported creation of a trust, and therefore the defendant was prevented from being able to rely on his illegal act either to retain or dispose of rights in property. It is only in cases like *Tinsley v Milligan* where the illegal act is not bound up in the transfer of property that the defendant will be entitled to rely on an equitable doctrine like resulting trust, or alternatively the equitable doctrine of resulting trust will operate so as to the bring property back to the defendant so that the claimant can recover it in bankruptcy or other proceedings so as to prevent the defendant putting assets illegally beyond the reach of his creditors.

A large number of cases involve schemes to defraud HMRC, raising the question of at what stage an illegal act has been performed. So, in *21st Century Logistic Solutions Ltd (in liquidation) v Madysen Ltd*[187] a taxpayer hatched a plan to defraud HMRC of VAT payments which involved, as one of its preparatory stages, the creation of a contract to sell computer parts on which the VAT should have been payable. The taxpayer had no intention of paying VAT on those contracts but it was held that simply creating that contract was not in itself an illegal act; instead an illegal act would only be committed when a false VAT return was submitted to HMRC.[188] In cases of unlawful tax evasion, a claimant may be restrained from claiming an equitable remedy (such as resulting trust or proprietary estoppel) if the source of his rights is in truth an agreement to transfer property in a manner designed unlawfully to deceive HMRC. Consequently, where an old man falsely completed a tax return to conceal an interest he held in property as part of a scheme which he had concocted with his adult children, it was held that an illegal act had been performed which precluded the taxpayer from relying on a resulting trust over that property in his favour.[189] However, if a tax evasion scheme is concocted but never carried out (because the false documents were never shown to HMRC) then there would be no illegal act committed which would preclude the finding of a trust,[190] just as in *Tribe v Tribe*.

---

184 [1999] Ch 373, [1999] 1 FLR 799.
185 [2002] EWCA Civ 1095, [2002] BPIR 1057.
186 *Barrett v Barrett* [2008] EWHC 1061 (Ch), [2008] BPIR 817.
187 [2004] STC 1535.
188 *21st Century Logistic Solutions Ltd (in liquidation) v Madysen Ltd* [2004] EWHC 231 (QB), [2004] STC 1535.
189 *Q v Q* [2008] EWHC 1874 (Fam), [2009] 1 P & CR D12 (also sub nom *S v R*).
190 *Painter v Hutchison* [2007] EWHC 758 (Ch), [2008] BPIR 170.

11.4.7 Illegality, the Insolvency Act 1986 and resulting trust

Resulting trust, shams and illegality

One of the more common forms of illegality in this context is the avoidance of creditors when the transferor fears bankruptcy, insolvency or receivership (all varying forms of bankruptcy which occur to different classes of legal person in different circumstances). Under s 423 of the Insolvency Act 1986, the court is empowered to reverse any action which puts assets beyond the reach of creditors with the intention of avoiding or weakening their claims. The section also covers sales at an undervalue in this context. The decision in *Midland Bank v Wyatt*[191] confirmed the decision in *Re Butterworth*,[192] that the creditors need not be creditors at the time of the transaction – it is sufficient that they become creditors after the transfer or sale at an undervalue. Therefore, even transfers carried into effect some time before bankruptcy will be covered by this principle, provided that they are carried out in the expectation of bankruptcy to defeat the interests of creditors. The creditors can be creditors of the insolvent personally, or of a company which he intends to create. There is no need that the transaction be dishonest – it is sufficient that there was a demonstrable intention to put assets out of the reach of creditors.

Midland Bank v Wyatt[193] is an important case on the scope of s 423 of the Insolvency Act 1986 and on the ability of persons to transfer assets out of the reach of their creditors. The case illustrates the difficult line between organising your affairs legitimately so that the failure of a business does not mean losing your house and personal property, and creating unlawful arrangements to outwit your creditors once you have realised that your business is on the brink of insolvency. This case also indicates the ability of the court to look behind sham transactions where necessary in this context.

Mr Wyatt had decided to set up a textile business. The family home had been bought in 1981 and registered in the joint names of Mr and Mrs Wyatt, and was subject to a mortgage in favour of Midland Bank. Mr Wyatt considered this new business venture to be commercially risky and therefore created an express trust in 1987, on advice from his solicitor, under which his family home was held by him on trust for his wife and two daughters. Mr Wyatt was subsequently divorced from his wife in 1989. The business went into receivership in 1991.

Mr Wyatt had used the house as security for a number of loans for his ailing business after 1987. All the lenders and creditors were unaware of the trust, thinking that the equitable interest was held by both Mr and Mrs Wyatt. Interestingly, Mrs Wyatt's solicitors were not made aware of the express trust when preparing the divorce arrangements.

Midland Bank sought a charging order over the family home against Mr Wyatt's interest in the house. Mr Wyatt argued that the house was held on the terms of the express trust declared in 1987 and that the bank could not therefore realise its purported security. The bank contended that the trust was either void as a sham, or voidable further to s 423 of the Insolvency Act 1986. It was held that it was not necessary to establish a fraudulent motive

---

191 [1995] 1 FLR 697, [1995] 3 FCR 11. Also *Agricultural Mortgage Corporation v Woodward* (1995) 70 P & CR 53. Cf *Choithram International v Pagarani* [2000] 1 WLR 1.
192 (1882) 19 Ch D 588.
193 [1995] 1 FLR 697.

to show that there is a sham. Neither was it necessary to show that the declaration of trust should have no effect. It would be enough to set aside the purported express trust that, acting on mistaken advice, the transaction was not in substance what it appeared to be on its face. On the facts, it was clear that at the time of creating the trust Mr Wyatt had no intention of endowing his wife or the children with his interest in the house. This was demonstrated by the fact that Mr Wyatt continued to treat the house as being entirely his own when borrowing money against it, and by the fact that his wife's solicitors were unaware of the purported express trust. Rather, the purpose of the transaction was to provide a safeguard against the commercial risk of the business. The transaction was therefore not what it purported to be. As such it must be held to have been a sham. Consequently, the express trust was held to have been void and unenforceable.

Under s 423 of the 1986 Act, the transaction was also capable of being rendered void because it sought to transfer the property gratuitously to Mrs Wyatt and the children with the purpose of avoiding creditors. The shortcoming with this second point is that there were no specific creditors which were to have been avoided. It is not evident how one could draw the line between a lawful arrangement of one's affairs and an unlawful avoidance of hitherto unknown, potential creditors. In applying the rule in *Re Butterworth*,[194] it was held not necessary to show that the sole motive of the settlement was the avoidance of creditors. It was sufficient that such motive was one of a number of identifiable motives. It would appear that all is to be presumed against the bankrupt and in favour of the creditors in an insolvency situation.

In relation to a claim to establish a resulting trust, it is possible to set aside a transfer as a sham transfer and establish a resulting trust instead. From the point of view of a creditor in a bankruptcy, the creditor will be entitled to any property held in the bankrupt's estate. It is consequently in the creditor's best interests to demonstrate that the bankrupt has property held on resulting trust for him, because a bankrupt is required to transfer to the creditors any property in which the bankrupt has beneficial title under resulting trust or otherwise. Using s 423 of the Insolvency Act 1986, the court has power to recognise that property may continue to be vested in the bankrupt's estate so that it can be realised in the administration of the bankruptcy in satisfaction of the creditor's rights.

So, in general terms, where a trust is created without any intention that the beneficiaries take any equitable interest in the settled property but rather in circumstances in which the settlor is simply seeking to hide her ownership of that property, then that trust may be void on the grounds that it is simply a sham.[195] A sham is any situation in which the parties' documentation and other devices are a 'pretence' or are merely 'dressing up' their true intentions to appear to be something else[196] so as to give 'the appearance of creating between the parties legal rights and obligations different from the actual legal rights and obligations (if any) which the parties intended to create'.[197] The result will be either that the settled property will

194 (1882) 19 Ch D 588.

195 *Yorkshire Railway Wagon Co v Maclure* (1882) 21 Ch D 309; *Stoneleigh Finance Ltd v Phillips* [1965] 2 QB 537; *Snook v London & West Riding Investments Ltd* [1967] 2 QB 786, [1967] 1 All ER 518; *Midland Bank v Wyatt* [1997] 1 BCLC 242; applied in *Minwalla v Minwalla* [2004] EWHC 2823 (Fam); *Re Yates, Carman v Yates* [2004] All ER (D) 373.

196 *National Westminster Bank plc v Jones* [2001] 1 BCLC 98, para [36], *per* Neuberger J, and *Re Yates* [2004] All ER (D) 373, para [217] *et seq*, applying *AG Securities v Vaughan* [1990] 1 AC 417.

197 *Snook v London & West Riding Investments Ltd* [1967] 2 QB 786, 802, *per* Diplock LJ.

pass back to the settlor on resulting trust[198] or, it is suggested more accurately, that no equitable interest will be deemed to have been created in that property on the basis that no trust ever came into existence.

The scope of s 423 of the Insolvency Act 1986

As considered, even if the resulting trust analysis were not available, the court has the power under s 423 of the Insolvency Act 1986 to set aside transactions entered into at an undervalue with a view to defrauding creditors.[199] Section 423 provides that:

(1) This section relates to transactions entered into at an undervalue; and a person enters into such a transaction with another person if –

    (a) he makes a gift to the other person or he otherwise enters into a transaction with the other on terms that provide for him to receive no consideration.[200]

This provision would include a gift of property or a declaration of trust over property in either case in which there would be no consideration paid for the transfer of property. That sub-section then also covers the situation in which:

    (c) he enters into a transaction with the other for a consideration the value of which, in money or money's worth, is significantly less than the value, in money or money's worth, of the consideration provided by himself.

This provision would cover either a declaration of trust or a transfer in relation to which there is no contractual consideration at all or a transfer in which any contractual consideration which is given is significantly less than the value of the property. It is not a requirement that the avoidance of creditors was the sole purpose of the transaction provided that putting assets beyond the reach of creditors was one of the purposes of the transaction.[201] So, where a defendant transferred his matrimonial home to his wife and claimed that she had already held an equitable interest in the property under constructive trust, it was held that he nevertheless had an intention to put property beyond the reach of his creditors and therefore the transfer was capable of being set aside under s 423 of the 1986 Act.[202] The court nevertheless recognised that the wife had a 50% share in the home as a result of her substantial financial contributions on repairs and improvements to the property.

The court's powers are then to make 'such order as the court sees fit'[203] for the purpose of:

(2) (a) restoring the position to what it would have been if the transaction had not been entered into, and

    (b) protecting the interests of the persons who are the victims of the transaction.

---

198 *Midland Bank v Wyatt* [1997] 1 BCLC 242.
199 *Moon v Franklin* [1996] BPIR 196, 205; *Trowbridge v Trowbridge* [2003] 2 FLR 231; *Re Yates* [2004] All ER (D) 373.
200 Insolvency Act 1986, s 423(1).
201 *Kubiangha v Ekpenyoung* [2002] EWHC 1567 (Ch), [2002] 2 BCLC 597, [2003] BPIR 623. See also *Re Schuppan (No 2)* [1997] 1 BCLC 256; *IRC v Hashmi* [2002] EWCA Civ 981, [2002] 2 BCLC 489.
202 *Ibid.*
203 Insolvency Act 1986, s 423(2).

The court's power to make these orders are limited to the following circumstances where the transaction 'was entered into for the purpose':[204]

    (3) (a) of putting assets beyond the reach of a person who is making, or may at some time make, a claim against him.

Thus, the court may make an order to set aside the transaction if, for example, the defendant's creditors are in the process of making a claim against the defendant or even if in general terms they may at some point make such a claim. It was held by the Court of Appeal in *IRC v Hashmi*[205] that for a purpose to fall within s 423(3) it does not have to be the sole nor the predominant purpose of the transaction, but rather it is sufficient if it is one of the purposes of the transaction. A purpose in this sense was taken to be an objective of the transaction rather than a collateral outcome of the transaction: put another way, it must be a 'real substantial purpose and not merely a consequence of the transaction'.[206] It is the reason for entering into the transaction, rather than the transaction itself, which constitutes the purpose.[207]

This provision is very broadly drafted indeed and gives the court a seemingly open-ended power to reverse such transactions. So, in *Trowbridge v Trowbridge*,[208] where a husband made regular payments of money to his wife, purportedly in recognition of the money which she had spent in supporting him, it was held that the payments had in fact been made with the intention of putting large amounts of money beyond the reach of his creditors and further that they were payments made for no consideration under s 423(1).[209] Equally, even though his wife had contributed to the purchase price of the property, it was held that his purpose in allowing the house to be put into his wife's sole name was an attempt to put the house beyond the reach of creditors.[210] Beneficial ownership of the home would be apportioned according to the parties' respective cash contributions to it.[211]

The difficulty of organising one's affairs so as to minimise the risk of insolvency

One ramification of the *Midland Bank v Wyatt* decision is the difficulty of arranging one's affairs before starting a business by having that property held on trust without subsequently having that trust declared to be a sham and thus avoided. What is particular to the *Wyatt* case, of course, is the clear evidence that Mr Wyatt had no real intention to settle his interest in the family home on trust for his wife and daughters, whereas a genuine intention to settle property on trust for third parties would not be so treated. However, if the third parties who are benefited are related to or connected with the settlor then there will remain the possibility

---

204 *Ibid*, s 423(3).
205 [2002] BCC 943, [2002] 2 BCLC 489. See also *Beckenham MC Ltd v Centralex Ltd* [2004] 2 BCLC 764, [2004] BPIR 1112; *Barnett v Semenyuk* [2008] 2 P&CR DG 18; *Hill v Spread Trustee* [2005] EWHC 336, [2006] WTLR 1009; *Papanicola v Fagan* [2008] EWHC 3348 (Ch), [2008] BPIR 320; *4 Eng Ltd v Harper* [2009] EWHC 2633 (Ch).
206 *Papanicola v Fagan* [2008] EWHC 3348 (Ch), [31].
207 *Hill v Spread Trustee* [2005] EWHC 336, [2006] WTLR 1009.
208 [2003] 2 FLR 231, [2004] FCR 79, [2003] BPIR 258.
209 *Trowbridge v Trowbridge* [2003] 2 FLR 231, [2004] FCR 79, [2003] BPIR 258.
210 *Ibid.*
211 *Ibid.*

that the court will interpret the trust as being a sham and so ineffective. Interestingly, then, this area of the law sees through the technical formalism which is accepted in the *Tinsley* decision: insolvency, as ever, prompts the law of property to develop more stringent rules.

11.4.8 A summary of these principles

This section aims to set out a summary of the principles which have been discussed in this section. If a transfer of property is made by Father to his daughter Susan or to his wife Honoria, then the presumption is that Father intended to make a gift to Susan or to Honoria. (He is called 'Father' in this example to underline the fact that only transfers by men on the old authorities attract this presumption in English law.) So, if there is a dispute subsequently as to the ownership of that property, then the court will presume that the property was to be advanced by Father to Susan or Honoria: that is, the court presumes he intended to make a gift of the property to them. However, it is open to Father to seek to rebut that presumption of advancement by arguing that he was only passing the property to Susan or to Honoria, for example, for safekeeping. The effect of this rebuttal, if successful, would be that Susan and Honoria would hold that property on resulting trust for Father.

The one problem which Father could face, however, would be if his rebuttal depended on adducing evidence of some illegality which he had committed, or which he intended to commit. So, like *Tinsley v Milligan* and *Tribe v Tribe*, the resulting trust would not be available to Father if he was committing an illegal act because he would be coming to equity with unclean hands. The illegality would not matter if Father acquired the property otherwise than through the illegal act – for example, if he had bought it legitimately, but not if he had stolen it – or if Father did not actually carry his illegal intention into effect, for example by avoiding going into insolvency. So, if Father transferred property to Susan which he had just stolen so as to avoid the police, then this would be an illegal act and he could not recover the property from Susan by means of a resulting trust. However, if Father did not commit an illegal act in acquiring the property – for example, if it had been given to him – then he could rely on the resulting trust.

Matters are different, however, if Father went into insolvency. It would be an illegal act to seek to put property beyond the reach of one's creditors. Therefore, ordinarily Father could not rely on a resulting trust because Father would have committed an illegal act by avoiding his creditors. However, the law on insolvency would want Father to recover the property so that it could be distributed among his creditors. Consequently, it would be held that under s 423 of the Insolvency Act 1986 that the transfer could be undone and the property recovered by Father, or it could be held that the transfer was a sham so that the property would be recovered by Father: in either of these alternatives the property would be returned to Father so that it could be distributed among his insolvency creditors.

11.5 MISTAKE AND RESULTING TRUST

11.5.1 Recovery of property on grounds of mistake

Where property is transferred under a mistake, the transferor will wish to argue that that property should be held on trust by the transferee for the benefit of the transferor. In such a circumstance the transferor would seek to establish a resulting trust in her favour. Suppose the following situation: W makes an outright transfer of money to I under a contract which is subsequently found to be void because it was beyond I's powers. W and I were operating under a mistake as to the validity of the contract. (Essentially, those were the facts in *Westdeutsche Landesbank Girozentrale v Islington LBC.*)[212] W will seek to recover that payment. The House of Lords has held, unanimously on this point, that the payment is not held on resulting trust for W because W had intended to make an outright transfer to I. The question therefore arises in what circumstances a mistake will found a claim for resulting trust.[213]

There are instances in which property has been transferred by mistake and the court has declared the recipient to be a trustee for the transferor.[214] Those cases have tended not to be explicit about the nature of the trust in this situation.[215] In many such cases it has been held that when the transferee has knowledge of the mistake, that transferee holds the property on constructive trust for the transferor rather than on resulting trust.[216] In two cases, though, the trust was expressly identified as a resulting trust.[217]

The question therefore is: on what basis does someone recover property which originally belonged to her beneficially? As Millett J held in *El Ajou*:

> It would, of course, be an intolerable reproach to our system of jurisprudence if the plaintiff were the only victim who could trace and recover his money. Neither party before suggested that this is the case; and I agree with them. But if the other victims of the fraud can trace their money in equity it must be because, having been induced to purchase the shares by false and fraudulent misrepresentations, they are entitled to rescind the transaction and revest the equitable title to the purchase money in themselves, at least to the extent necessary to support an equitable tracing claim . . .
>
> *But, if this is correct, as I think it is, then the trust which is operating in these cases is not some new model remedial constructive trust, but an old-fashioned institutional resulting trust.*[218]

The point being made is that, in contradistinction to the issues of tracing title in property (considered in Chapter 19), perhaps the manner in which property ought to be considered as being returned to its original (or its traceable) owner is by means of a resulting trust. Millett J's opinion supports Birks's view that the resulting trust operates in a restitutionary way and that a situation such as the return of money to a person defrauded of that money is essentially a restitutionary response: a view rebutted in the *Westdeutsche* case.

---

212 [1996] AC 669.

213 *Ibid.*

214 *Chase Manhattan Bank NA v Israel-British Bank (London) Ltd* [1981] Ch 105; *Leuty v Hillas* (1858) 2 De GF & J 110; *Craddock Brothers v Hunt* [1923] 2 Ch 136, CA; *Blacklocks v JB Developments (Godalming) Ltd* [1982] Ch 183.

215 On this see Chambers, 1997, 23, where the argument is made that the trusts ought to be considered to have been resulting trusts because the equitable interest in property is being returned to its original equitable owner.

216 *Westdeutsche Landesbank Girozentrale v Islington LBC* [1996] AC 669 in considering *Chase Manhattan Bank NA v Israel-British Bank (London) Ltd* [1981] Ch 105.

217 *El Ajou v Dollar Land Holdings* [1993] 3 All ER 717; *Clelland v Clelland* (1945) 3 DLR 664, BCCA.

218 [1993] 3 All ER 717, 734, emphasis added.

11.5.2 Common intention and resulting trust in cases of mistake

The difficulty with the view that the resulting trust is essentially restitutionary is the decision of the House of Lords in *Westdeutsche Landesbank Girozentrale v Islington LBC*. Lord Browne-Wilkinson, speaking extra-judicially, has expressed his conception of the resulting trust as operating in the following way:

> A resulting trust arises in order to give effect to the intention of the parties. Where there is an express declaration of trust which does not exhaust the whole beneficial interest in the property Equity presumes an intention that the trust property is to revert to the original settlor, ie is held on a resulting trust ... A resulting trust then depends on presumed intention ... Under a resulting trust, the existence of the trust is established once and for all at the date on which the property is acquired [by the resulting trustee].[219]

The difficulty with Lord Browne-Wilkinson's model of the resulting trust is that he sees it as arising on the basis of the *common* intentions of the parties, rather than applying the intentions solely of the original owner of the property rights. Chambers confronts this problem in the following way:[220]

> It is clear that a common intention is not a requirement for a resulting trust, which can arise even though one of the parties is unaware of the transfer.[221] Lord Browne-Wilkinson's speech in *Tinsley v Milligan*[222] indicates that he is mixing the requirements for resulting trusts with those for constructive trusts in the context of family home ownership. That case involved a resulting trust based on the common intention of the parties. Both parties had contributed to the purchase of a house and their intentions were relevant as providers. However, his Lordship did not distinguish between the resulting trust based on their contributions and the constructive trust based on a 'common intention acted upon by the parties to their detriment'.[223]

As considered in Chapter 15, in relation to the *Lloyds Bank v Rosset*[224] form of common intention constructive trust, what is not clear is the extent to which the courts will seek to give effect to the common intention of the parties. As Chambers points out, it is similarly uncertain whether such common intention can be said to fall properly within a resulting trust arising from the contribution to the acquisition of an asset or from a constructive trust imposed by reference to the knowledge of the defendant of some factor which is said to affect his conscience. The remodelling of the resulting trust by Lord Browne-Wilkinson does appear to capture the common intention trust by encompassing situations in which the

---

219 1995 Holdsworth Lecture.
220 Chambers, 1997, 37.
221 *Ryall v Ryall* (1739) 1 Atk 59; *Birch v Blagrave* (1755) Amb 264; *Lane v Dighton* (1762) Amb 409; *Childers v Childers* (1857) 1 De G & J 482; *Williams v Williams* (1863) 32 Beav 370; *Re Vinogradoff* [1935] WN 68; *In Re Muller* [1953] NZLR 879.
222 [1994] 1 AC 340.
223 *Ibid*, 371.
224 [1991] 1 AC 107.

parties must be presumed to have intended that the claimant would acquire an interest in the applicable property.

The position in English law relating to recovery on grounds of mistake has been greatly expanded by the decision of the House of Lords in *Kleinwort Benson v Lincoln CC*,[225] which reversed the old rule that there could be no recovery on grounds of mistake of law. It is now clear that recovery can take place as a result of a mistake of law as well as a mistake of fact. The question remains whether that recovery will take place on the facts of the particular case on grounds of resulting trust, constructive trust, or simply under a common law claim for money had and received.

225   [1998] 4 All ER 513.

Chapter 12

Constructive trusts

OVERVIEW

*Constructive trusts arise by operation of law. In general terms, a proprietary construc-
tive trust will be imposed on a person who has knowledge of some unconscionable factor
in relation to her dealing with property.*[1] *All constructive trusts can be understood as
arising on the basis of this central principle, even though there are many different sub-
species of constructive trust. It is important that the trustee has knowledge of the unconscionability of her actions or omissions in relation to that property before a constructive
trust will be imposed. For the imposition of a proprietary constructive trust, the legal
owner of property will be liable if she has knowledge of some factor which affects the
conscionability of asserting beneficial title to that property.*[2] *Constructive trusts will also
arise in a number of contexts in which equitable doctrines such as 'equity shall not be
used as an engine of fraud'*[3] *or 'equity looks upon as done that which ought to have
been done'*[4] *operate so as to prevent rights in property being acquired on the basis of
unconscionable conduct. Among the various types of constructive trust, the following
categories are the most significant.*

---

1 *Westdeutsche Landesbank Girozentrale v Islington LBC* [1996] AC 669.
2 *Ibid.*
3 *Rochefoucauld v Boustead* [1897] 1 Ch 196; *Paragon Finance v Thakerar* [1999] 1 All ER 400.
4 *Lysaght v Edwards* (1876) 2 Ch D 499; *Attorney-General for Hong Kong v Reid* [1994] 1 AC 324; *Jerome
   v Kelly* [2004] 2 All ER 835.

A trustee or fiduciary will be constructive trustee of any unauthorised profits made from her fiduciary office, even where she has otherwise acted in good faith.[5] The purpose of this principle is to prevent a fiduciary from taking any profit from a conflict between her personal interests and her fiduciary duties. The rule is a strict rule that no profit can be made by a trustee or fiduciary which is not authorised by the terms of the trust.[6] A fiduciary who profits from that office will be required to account for those profits.[7] There is no defence of good faith in favour of the trustee.

Where a person committing an unlawful act and/or receiving a bribe is in a fiduciary position during the commission of such an act, the fiduciary is required to hold that bribe or any substitute property acquired with that bribe on proprietary constructive trust for the beneficiaries of the fiduciary duty.[8] That proprietary constructive trust requires that any profits made are also to be held on constructive trust. Similarly, any losses made as a result of investing the bribe will be required to be made good by the constructive trustee.[9]

Where a person receives trust property in the knowledge that that property has been passed in breach of trust, the recipient will be personally liable to account to the trust for the value of the property passed away.[10] The requirement of knowledge in this context has been expressed in different cases as a test of actual or constructive knowledge;[11] as a test of failing to act as an honest person would have acted;[12] or as acting unconscionably.[13] It is a defence to demonstrate the receipt was authorised under the terms of the trust, or that the recipient has lawfully changed his position in reliance on the receipt of the property.

Where a person dishonestly assists another in a breach of trust, that dishonest assistant will be personally liable to account to the trust for the value lost to the trust.[14] 'Dishonesty' in this context requires that the defendant has acted otherwise than as an honest person in her situation would have acted in the circumstances, a test which includes fraud, lack of probity or reckless risk-taking.[15] It also requires that the defendant understands that her conduct would have been considered to be dishonest by

---

5 *Boardman v Phipps* [1967] 2 AC 46. See section 12.5 below.
6 *Ward v Brunt* [2000] WTLR 731.
7 *Ibid.*
8 *Attorney-General for Hong Kong v Reid* [1994] 1 AC 324; *Daraydan Holdings Ltd v Solland International Ltd* [2004] 3 WLR 1106.
9 *Ibid.*
10 *Re Montagu* [1987] Ch 264; *Polly Peck International v Nadir (No 2)* [1992] 4 All ER 769; *Twinsectra Ltd v Yardley* [1999] Lloyd's Rep Bank 438.
11 *Re Montagu* [1987] Ch 264; *Baden v Société Générale pour Favoriser le Developpement du Commerce et de l'Industrie en France SA* [1992] 4 All ER 161; [1993] 1 WLR 509.
12 *Twinsectra Ltd v Yardley* [1999] Lloyd's Rep Bank 438, CA.
13 *Houghton v Fayers* [2000] 1 BCLC 571.
14 *Royal Brunei Airlines v Tan* [1995] 2 AC 378; *Smith New Court v Scrimgeour Vickers* [1997] AC 254; *Corporacion Nacional Del Cobre De Chile v Sogemin Metals* [1997] 1 WLR 1396; *Fortex Group Ltd v MacIntosh* [1998] 3 NZLR 171; *Dubai Aluminium v Salaam* [1999] 1 Lloyd's Rep 415; *Wolfgang Herbert Heinl v Jyske Bank* [1999] Lloyd's Rep Bank 511.
15 *Ibid.*

other reasonable people.[16] *It is not necessary that any trustee of the trust is dishonest, simply that the dishonest assistant is dishonest.*[17]

12.1 INTRODUCTION

12.1.1 Fundamentals of constructive trusts

In English law, a constructive trust arises by operation of law. It is imposed whenever the defendant knows that she has dealt with the property in an unconscionable manner. Thus, a person who steals property will have dealt unconscionably with it;[18] a person who receives a bribe in the conduct of a fiduciary office will have dealt unconscionably with the property representing that bribe;[19] a person who takes property by means of fraud will have dealt unconscionably with it;[20] and so on: in each of these situations, and many others considered in this chapter, the defendant is held to be a constructive trustee of that property because she has knowingly dealt with that property in an unconscionable manner. The statement in the opening sentence indicates two things. First, that the constructive trust is imposed by a court in accordance with established principle and not purely at the court's own general discretion. This English constructive trust is dubbed an 'institutional' constructive trust, which means that a constructive trust comes into existence automatically from the date of the defendant's knowledge of her unconscionable act, and that the court is merely recognising its existence as opposed to creating it out of some general discretion.[21] Secondly, a constructive trust is imposed regardless of the intentions of the parties involved. While there are circumstances in which constructive trusts are enforced in accordance with the intentions of one or other of the parties, but without the necessary intention or formality to create an express trust, in many circumstances the constructive trust is imposed on a defendant without the need for her consent so as to prevent the defendant from acting unconscionably. In that sense, the constructive trust may be imposed contrary to the parties' intentions. The term 'constructive trust' itself arises from the fact that the court *construes* that the defendant is to be treated as a trustee of property. It is in this sense that we can say that a constructive trust does not accord with the intentions of the parties because it may be imposed by the court contrary to what the parties may otherwise have wished if the court considers that to be an appropriate response to the defendant's unconscionable behaviour.[22]

There are a great many examples of the constructive trust. This chapter isolates the most important forms of constructive trust, attempts to allocate them to general categories for ease

---

16 *Twinsectra v Yardley* [2002] 2 All ER 377, HL.
17 *Royal Brunei Airlines v Tan* [1995] 2 AC 378; *Smith New Court v Scrimgeour Vickers* [1997] AC 254; *Corporacion Nacional Del Cobre De Chile v Sogemin Metals* [1997] 1 WLR 1396; *Fortex Group Ltd v MacIntosh* [1998] 3 NZLR 171; *Twinsectra Ltd v Yardley* [2002] 2 All ER 377 [1999] Lloyd's Rep Bank 438; *Dubai Aluminium v Salaam* [1999] 1 Lloyd's Rep 415; *Wolfgang Herbert Heinl v Jyske Bank* [1999] Lloyd's Rep Bank 511; *Dubai Aluminium v Salaam* [2003] 1 All ER 97.
18 *Westdeutsche Landesbank v Islington* [1996] AC 669.
19 *Attorney-General for Hong Kong v Reid* [1994] 1 AC 324.
20 *Westdeutsche Landesbank v Islington* [1996] AC 669.
21 The institutional constructive trust arises by comparison with the discretionary (or 'remedial') constructive trust used in the USA. This nomenclature arises from Maudsley, 1959, 237, drawing on Pound, 1920, 421.
22 *Soar v Ashwell* [1893] 2 QB 390.

of comprehension, and seeks to identify the themes that are common to each category.[23] It is suggested that the best method for analysing constructive trust problems is to allocate the factual situation to one of these categories and then to follow the applicable principles set down for cases falling within that category.

The general approach of this book to the trust is that it is a creature of equity which has developed specific principles of its own beyond the general principles of equity. The core purpose of equity was established by Lord Ellesmere in the *Earl of Oxford's Case*[24] to be to correct men's consciences.[25] In this sense, the constructive trust operates so as to prevent a benefit being taken from unconscionable conduct and to protect the rights of other people in property. The constructive trust is a form of trust most akin to those general principles of equity which prevent a person benefiting from fraud or some other unconscionable action.[26] In what will follow, there is a tension between those constructive trusts which are concerned to protect rights in property,[27] those constructive trusts which are imposed to prevent a benefit being taken from a conflict of interest,[28] those so-called constructive trusts which provide the claimant with only a right in money in the form of compensation for a loss caused by a breach of trust,[29] and those constructive trusts which appear to be penalties for wrongs which the defendant has committed which have proprietary consequences.[30] These subtly different approaches between categories make the area of constructive trusts both interesting and complex. Careful distinction between the categories is, it is suggested, the key.

It is worth beginning with the words of Edmund-Davies LJ in *Carl Zeiss Stiftung v Herbert Smith & Co* that 'English law provides no clear and all-embracing definition of a constructive trust. Its boundaries have been left perhaps deliberately vague so as not to restrict the court by technicalities in deciding what the justice of a particular case might demand'.[31] This statement indicates the essential truth that the constructive trust is not a certain or rigid doctrine. Rather, its edges are blurred and the full scope of its core principles is difficult to define. As considered below, the constructive trust grew rapidly in the latter part of the 20th century and is likely to continue to generate new forms of itself in the future. Some commentators have become so bewildered by it that they have recommended that the constructive trust in its current form should simply be abandoned.[32]

In *Paragon Finance plc v DB Thakerar & Co*,[33] Millett LJ did attempt a general definition of the doctrine of constructive trust:

---

23 See *Martin v Myers* [2004] EWHC 1947 (Ch) in relation to the application of the Limitation Act 1980 to the various forms of constructive trust, considering the various approaches in *Paragon Finance v Thakerar* [1999] 1 All ER 400 and in *James v Williams* [1999] 3 All ER 309.
24 (1615) 1 Ch Rep 1.
25 As discussed in section 1.1 of this book.
26 *Westdeutsche Landesbank Girozentrale v Islington LBC* [1996] AC 669.
27 Eg, *Westdeutsche Landesbank Girozentrale v Islington LBC* [1996] AC 669; *Boardman v Phipps* [1967] 2 AC 46.
28 Eg, *Boardman v Phipps* [1967] 2 AC 46; *Bolkiah v KPMG* [1999] 1 All ER 517.
29 Eg, *Polly Peck International v Nadir (No 2)* [1992] 4 All ER 769; *Royal Brunei Airlines v Tan* [1995] 2 AC 378.
30 *Attorney-General for Hong Kong v Reid* [1994] 1 AC 324.
31 [1969] 2 Ch 276, 300.
32 See, eg, Millett, 1995.
33 [1999] 1 All ER 400.

A constructive trust arises by operation of law whenever the circumstances are such that it would be unconscionable for the owner of property (usually but not necessarily the legal estate) to assert his own beneficial interest in the property and deny the beneficial interest of another.[34]

This breadth of principle explains why the constructive trust is likely to continue to grow because, as is considered below in relation to the decision of the House of Lords in *Westdeutsche Landesbank Girozentrale v Islington LBC*,[35] the constructive trust will arise in *any* situation in which the titleholder of property unconscionably denies or interferes with the rights of another. As such, it is clearly a principle of potentially very broad application. However, it is suggested that even this definition will not capture the depth or variety of constructive trusts recognised in equity.

12.1.2 The distinction between proprietary and personal claims

It is vital to distinguish between personal and proprietary rights. That distinction is one which will be familiar to all students of property law and has been explored in this book already.[36] A proprietary constructive trust will give a right to the beneficiary in specifically identifiable property: that is, a right in the property held by the constructive trustee which is enforceable against any other person. The alternative is merely an *in personam* right against a constructive trustee to make that trustee personally liable for any loss suffered by the beneficiary: that is, a right to recover an amount of money from the constructive trustee equivalent to the value of the property at the time when the constructive trust came into existence, but not any right in any identified property. The forms of trust considered in sections 12.2 to 12.8 will be concerned with proprietary claims, although some in section 12.9 may have features which we will associate with personal claims.

In this context it is best to think of the office of trustee under a constructive trust being imposed on a person who has acted unconscionably. The way in which equity may deal with that constructive trustee may differ in different circumstances. Equity may require that the defendant hold specific property on the terms of a proprietary constructive trust or alternatively it may require that the defendant is simply made personally liable to account for some loss suffered by the beneficiaries, depending on the type of constructive trust at issue. The constructive trusts considered in section 12.9 and in Chapter 18 – known as the doctrines of dishonest assistance and of knowing receipt – are referred to by the courts as 'constructive trusts' but are in truth claims giving only a personal liability to account. The obligation imposed on the defendant in this context will be to make payment of money to the trust for the benefit of the beneficiaries. Professor Hayton has dubbed this form of claim the imposition of 'constructive trustee*ship*': that is, an obligation to compensate the beneficiaries' loss as though an express trustee liable to account for a breach of trust. Usually there will be no specific property capable of being held on trust, only a requirement to make a payment of money. This

---

34 Similarly in *James v Williams* [1999] 3 WLR 451, 458 [1999] 3 All ER 309, *per* Aldous LJ: 'As a general rule a constructive trust attaches by law to property which is held by a person in circumstances where it would be inequitable to allow him to assert full beneficial ownership of the property.'

35 [1996] AC 669.

36 Particularly in section 2.5 above. *Ord v Upton* [2000] Ch 352.

form of personal liability to account is the subject of Chapter 20. Otherwise, the constructive trusts on which we shall focus in this chapter are mainly proprietary constructive trusts.

12.1.3 Constructive trust – institutional in nature

It was said in the opening paragraph of this chapter that a constructive trust is 'institutional' in nature. That means both that the constructive trust arises by operation of law without the discretion of the court and also that a constructive trust has retrospective effect. In consequence, when a court finds that a constructive trust exists, it is in truth recognising that that trust has existed ever since the unconscionable action of the trustee which brought it into effect: the constructive trust does not come into existence from the date of the court order onwards.

The importance of the date of creation of the constructive trust is especially pronounced in the case of insolvency. For example, if it is found that a constructive trust ought to have arisen in January, but the constructive trustee goes into insolvency in March and a court makes an order recognising that proprietary constructive trust only in May, the order recognising the constructive trust will declare that the constructive trust came into existence automatically in January, and therefore that the proprietary rights of the beneficiaries pre-date the insolvency in March. If the constructive trust operated in the same manner as proprietary estoppel, that is prospectively from the date of the court order, granting whatever remedy the court considered appropriate in its discretion (as considered in Chapter 15), then it could not protect the beneficiaries against the constructive trustee's insolvency because such a right would come into existence only in May.[37] The form of remedial constructive trust deployed in the USA operates on a broadly similar basis to proprietary estoppel in this sense.

12.1.4 Fiduciary obligations under constructive trust

In general terms, the office of trustee under a constructive trust is necessarily different from that under an express trust. The parties will not necessarily know with certainty whether or not a constructive trust exists until a court declares that such a trust does in fact exist. What is suggested here is that *in the real world* the very existence of a constructive trust will often be contested until the court makes an order declaring that it does exist. What is therefore at issue is the liability which ought to attach to the constructive trustee for the period between the time when the constructive trust came into existence and the time at which the court made the order confirming its existence.[38] We do know that in theory the office of trustee will arise as soon as the trustee has knowledge of some factor affecting her conscience because constructive trusts are institutional trusts.[39] What remains unclear is the extent to which a constructive trustee would be liable, for example, for a failure to make the best possible return on a trust investment and so forth, as would be required of a trustee under an express trust. As Millett J put the matter in *Lonrho v Fayed (No 2)*:[40] '. . . it is a mistake to suppose that in every situation in which a constructive trust arises the legal owner is necessarily subject to all the fiduciary obligations and disabilities of an express trustee.'

---

37 The precise answer to this question will be addressed in para 12.2.2 below.
38 *Westdeutsche Landesbank Girozentrale v Islington LBC* [1994] 4 All ER 890, *per* Hobhouse J, CA; and reversed on appeal [1996] AC 669, HL.
39 *Westdeutsche Landesbank Girozentrale v Islington LBC* [1996] AC 669.
40 [1992] 1 WLR 1, [1991] 4 All ER 961.

The obligations to be imposed on a constructive trustee will depend on the context of the case. They will generally extend to stewardship and maintenance of the property to the beneficiary's account, but will probably not extend to impose positive obligations as to investment of the fund in all circumstances – particularly given that there will not be any detailed, written provisions of such a trust.

12.2 CONSTRUCTIVE TRUSTS AT LARGE

In broad terms a proprietary constructive trust will be imposed on a person who knows that her actions in respect of specific property are unconscionable.[41] It is important that the trustee has knowledge of the unconscionability of the treatment of that property. For the imposition of a proprietary constructive trust, the legal owner of property will be liable if she has knowledge of some factor which affects the conscionability of asserting an equitable interest in that property.

12.2.1 The general potential application of the constructive trust

This section considers the manner in which constructive trusts may be said to come into existence in general terms, and not necessarily only the limited categories considered in the remainder of this chapter. That is to say, the constructive trust will arise in general terms to enforce the conscience of a defendant in relation to either that defendant's treatment of the claimant's property, or the abuse of some fiduciary duty owed to the claimant.

Section 53(2) of the Law of Property Act 1925 provides that 'implied resulting or constructive trusts' do not require formalities in their creation. Rather, the constructive trust is recognised as coming into existence by operation of law. It is therefore important to recognise the principles upon which such constructive trusts may come into existence in general terms.

12.2.2 Constructive trusts are based on the knowledge and the conscience of the trustee

The most important recent statement of the core principles in the area of trusts implied by law was made by Lord Browne-Wilkinson in *Westdeutsche Landesbank Girozentrale v Islington LBC*,[42] where his Lordship went back to basics, identifying the root of any form of trust as being in policing the good conscience of the defendant. The first of his Lordship's 'Relevant Principles of Trust Law' was identified as being that:

---

41 *Westdeutsche Landesbank Girozentrale v Islington LBC* [1994] 4 All ER 890, *per* Hobhouse J, CA; and reversed on appeal [1996] AC 669, HL.

42 [1996] AC 669, [1996] 2 All ER 961, 988; see also *Allied Carpets Group plc v Nethercott* [2001] BCC 81. In *Martin v Myers* [2004] EWHC 1947 (Ch), para [37], Strauss QC (sitting as a Deputy Judge of the High Court), it is suggested, however, that simply knowing or suspecting that the property is held on trust for someone else is not sufficient because there must also be some relationship between the parties to make retention of that property unconscionable: it is suggested that this assertion is wrong because it is enough on the authorities that one knows of another's rights to render one liable as a constructive trustee and it is not a further requirement that one must necessarily be in a pre-existing fiduciary relationship to the claimant (although that would certainly found a constructive trust). So, for example, in *Ashburn Anstalt v Arnold* [1989] 1 Ch 1, a contractual licence to occupy property will not constitute a constructive trust unless the conscience of the defendant has been affected: applied in *Baybut v Eccle Riggs Country Park Ltd* [2006] All ER (D) 161, para [60], Pelling QC.

(i) Equity operates on the conscience of the owner of the legal interest. In the case of
     a trust, the conscience of the legal owner requires him to carry out the purposes for
     which the property was vested in him (express or implied trust) or which the law
     imposes on him by reason of his unconscionable conduct (constructive trust).

As considered in Chapter 2, this notion of the conscience of the legal owner is said to
underpin all trusts. In relation to the constructive trust it arises as a result of the unconscionable conduct of the legal owner. His Lordship continued with his second principle:

(ii) Since the equitable jurisdiction to enforce trusts depends upon the conscience of the
      holder of the legal interest being affected, he cannot be a trustee of the property if
      and so long as he is ignorant of the facts alleged to affect his conscience, ie until he
      is aware that he is intended to hold the property for the benefit of others in the case
      of an express or implied trust, or, in the case of a constructive trust, of the factors
      which are alleged to affect his conscience.

As a result of the requirement that the conscience of the holder of the legal interest is affected,
'he cannot be a trustee of the property if and so long as he is ignorant of the facts alleged to
affect his conscience'. Therefore, the defendant must have knowledge of the factors which are
suggested to give rise to the constructive trust.[43] Let us suppose a simple, everyday example.
Nicholas is queuing at the till in his local supermarket. He has not bought very many goods
and therefore his bill comes to a little less than £10. He pays with a £10 note. Mistakenly, the
person working on the till thinks that Nicholas has proffered her a £20 note and so gives him
change as though from a £20 note: that is, she hands him a £10 note and coins. The question
would be as to Nicholas's obligations in relation to the £10 note which he has mistakenly
received from the till operative. There can be little doubt that in good conscience Nicholas
ought to inform the till operative of her mistake and return the £10 note to her.[44]
    The important question for the law relating to constructive trusts is the time at which
Nicholas realises that he has been given £10 more than he is entitled to receive. If he realises
at the moment when the till operative hands him the £10 note that she has made a mistake,
and he runs from the shop laughing at his good fortune, he would be a constructive trustee
of that £10 for the supermarket as beneficiary from the moment of its receipt. If he absent-
mindedly received and pocketed the note (thus taking it into his possession) without realising the error, and did not ever subsequently realise that he had £10 more than he should
have had, then he would never be a constructive trustee of that banknote. If he absent-
mindedly pocketed the £10 note without realising the mistake but was accosted by an
employee of the supermarket who informed him for the first time of the mistake, then from

43 Unless, that is, you are an anti-capitalism protester who considers retention of that £10 to be striking a blow for
    redistributing the wealth of corporate supermarkets, in which case your views of good conscience may be
    different. The question in relation to 'conscience' is then whether we ought to permit such moral relativism, or
    simply apply objective standards of good conscience. This so-called 'Robin Hood' defence was rejected,
    however, in *Walker v Stones* [2000] 4 All ER 412, 414; considered at para 18.4.5 below.
44 What is more complex is the following: suppose the clerk mistakenly charged Nicholas £10 too little and
    Nicholas then paid by credit card in full knowledge of the mistake – there would not be any money to hold on
    trust because Nicholas paid by credit card, and therefore the supermarket's claim would be purely a personal
    claim against him for money had and received, unless some portion of the goods acquired could be held on
    constructive trust.

the moment he was informed by that employee he would be a constructive trustee – but not before. That is the importance of the statement in *Westdeutsche Landesbank* that there cannot be liability as a constructive trustee until the defendant has knowledge of the facts said to affect his conscience.[45]

12.2.3 Rights in property and merely personal claims

One further issue arises: does the constructive trust take effect by granting proprietary rights over specific property, or (given that equity acts *in personam*) does it simply impose a personal obligation on a person who has dealt with the property? While we may come to doubt the proposition later in this chapter, the case law is clear that the beneficiary acquires proprietary rights in the property held on constructive trust – except in relation to cases where the defendant is made personally liable to account for dishonest assistance and so forth.[46] In this respect, the third fundamental principle identified by Lord Browne-Wilkinson in *Westdeutsche Landesbank Girozentrale v Islington LBC* operated as follows:

> (iii) In order to establish a trust there must be identifiable trust property. The only apparent exception to this rule is a constructive trust imposed on a person who dishonestly assists in a breach of trust who may come under fiduciary duties even if he does not receive identifiable trust property.

It is trite law that the identity of the property to be held on an express trust must be certain or else the trust will be void.[47] There had been a question whether the property which is the subject of the constructive trust must be certain in the same way. Older authorities consider that the property must be certain under a constructive trust.[48] This older view is upheld by Lord Browne-Wilkinson in *Westdeutsche Landesbank*, although his Lordship still accepts one exception to this principle in relation to 'personal liability to account', considered below at section 12.9.

The fourth fundamental principle sets out the manner in which the proprietary rights of the beneficiaries operate under a proprietary constructive trust:

> (iv) Once a trust is established, as from the date of its establishment the beneficiary has, in equity, a proprietary interest in the trust property, which proprietary interest will be enforceable in equity against any subsequent holder of the property (whether the original property or substituted property into which it can be traced) other than a purchaser for value of the legal interest without notice.

The constructive trust comes into effect at the date this knowledge is acquired and 'as from the date of its establishment the beneficiary has, in equity, a proprietary interest in the trust property'. So the proprietary interest is 'enforceable in equity against any subsequent holder of the property'. This is a concept which will be explored in Chapter 19 to the effect that the beneficiary can literally 'trace' those property rights through into any property which can be

---

45 See section 12.9 below. The claimant must be able to prove that the defendant had knowledge of the mistake alleged to give rise to a constructive trust at the material time or else the court would not even hear the claim for a constructive trust: *Deutsche Bank AG v Vik* [2010] EWHC 551 (Comm).

46 *Re Goldcorp* [1994] 3 WLR 199.

47 *Re Barney* [1892] 2 Ch 265, 273.

48 *Chase Manhattan v Israel-British Bank* [1980] 2 WLR 202.

demonstrated to derive from the trust property. That is so in relation to 'the original property or substituted property into which it can be traced'. The only category of defendant who will not be liable in this way is equity's darling (or the 'purchaser for value of the legal interest without notice'). The role of equity's darling is considered below.

The *Westdeutsche Landesbank* case itself concerned a number of interest rate swaps which required the plaintiff to pay a lump sum to the defendant local authority. The bank sought to prove the existence, *inter alia*, of a constructive trust so that it would be entitled to receive compound interest on the money paid to the authority under the void contract. The House of Lords was unanimous (on this point) in holding that none of the amounts paid to the authority by the bank was to be treated as having been held on constructive trust because, at the time when the authority had dissipated the money, the authority had no knowledge that the contract had been void. In consequence, the authority had no knowledge of any factor which required it to hold the property as constructive trustee for the bank before that money was spent. And once the money had been spent, there was no property left which could have been held on constructive trust.

A further example cited by Lord Browne-Wilkinson in the *Westdeutsche* appeal was that of *Chase Manhattan v Israel-British Bank*,[49] in which a decision of Goulding J to impose a constructive trust was re-interpreted by his Lordship. In the *Chase Manhattan v Israel-British Bank* case, a payment was made by Chase Manhattan to Israel-British Bank, and then that same payment was mistakenly made a second time. After receiving the second, mistaken payment, Israel-British Bank went into insolvency. The question arose whether it was entitled to have that second payment held on constructive trust for it (thus making Chase Manhattan a secured creditor), or whether Chase Manhattan was merely an unsecured creditor owed a mere debt. Goulding J found a trust on the basis of a mixture of equitable principles and restitution of unjust enrichment. This decision was overruled by Lord Browne-Wilkinson. His Lordship explained that this case was an axiomatic example of a constructive trust: where it could be shown that Israel-British Bank had had knowledge of the mistake before its own insolvency, then it would be bound in good conscience to hold that payment on constructive trust for Chase Manhattan from the moment it had realised the mistake, not from the moment of receipt of the second payment. In this way we can see that the constructive trust is capable of arising in a range of general situations which are to do with the conscience of an individual defendant and not with any larger principle. The remainder of this chapter will consider particular situations in which constructive trusts have arisen – although it is suggested that the following sub-categories of constructive trust are necessarily to be read in the light of the foregoing general principles.

12.2.4 The significant case of *Westdeutsche Landesbank v Islington*

A summary of the decision of the House of Lords in *Westdeutsche Landesbank v Islington* would be useful at this early stage because it underpins so much of the law in this area. The facts of *Westdeutsche Landesbank v Islington* were perfect as an arena for the debate which was at the heart of trusts law at the time. The issue was this: when Westdeutsche Landesbank ('WDL') paid money to Islington on the basis of a contract which unbeknownst to either party was void, on what basis could WDL recover its money? It was held that because

---

49 [1980] 2 WLR 202.

Islington did not know that the contract was void before all of the money was spent, then Islington's conscience had not been affected. Because a trust will only come into existence once the legal owner's conscience is affected, there was no trust (whether constructive or resulting) over the money before it was spent. (As is discussed in Chapter 19, WDL could not trace after the money passing into other people's hands because it was not possible to prove where the money went after it was paid into the authority's general bank account.) Therefore, the House of Lords held that the only recourse which WDL could have was to a personal claim at common law for 'money had and received': this meant that WDL was entitled to be paid an amount by Islington equal to its original payment to Islington. Because it was a personal action, if Islington had gone into insolvency in the meantime then WDL would have had only a personal claim against an insolvent person which would have amounted to nothing in practice: fortunately, Islington was still solvent.[50] In reading the case, it is apparent that the only issue remaining in front of the House of Lords was whether WDL was entitled to compound interest or simple interest on its money. It was held by the majority of the House of Lords that under the law at the time, compound interest would only be available to the bank if it still had some proprietary interest in the money.[51] For a discussion of the issues arising before Hobhouse J and the Court of Appeal, and for a full discussion of the issues raised by each member of the House of Lords, see Alastair Hudson, *Swaps, Restitution and Trusts*.[52]

There had been an argument put forward by Prof Birks of the University of Oxford to the effect that if a person like Islington had been unjustly enriched (for example by receiving money under a contract that was actually void) then the payer (WDL) should be able to assert a proprietary claim on the basis of a massively enlarged conception of what constitutes a resulting trust over the money. This argument had a number of academic supporters. This writer is not one of them. The argument was rejected by the House of Lords. The weakness in the argument is that it does not account for the unfairness of entitling the payer to have a property right in money which will put it at an advantage when compared to the payee's other unsecured creditors. Furthermore, if the money has been spent then a resulting trust would not answer the question 'which property are you claiming now it's gone?'. What the majority of the House of Lords did was to re-establish our understanding of equity as being based on

---

50 In permitting a claim at common law, the House of Lords overruled the earlier House of Lords decision in *Sinclair v Brougham* [1914] AC 398 which had decided that no claim for money had and received should stand at common law in relation to a contract which had been void *ab initio* because that would have been to give effect to the void contract. This argument is fallacious: the void contract is not being effected but rather the parties are being returned to the position they occupied previously, in cash terms, as a result of the total failure of consideration and their mistake as to the capacity of both parties when making payment between themselves. This was Lord Browne-Wilkinson's position in *Westdeutsche Landesbank* in a nutshell. And yet in *Haugesund Kommune v Depfa ACS Bank* [2010] EWCA Civ 579 Aikens LJ considered the extent to which Lord Browne-Wilkinson in *Westdeutsche Landesbank v Islington* had intended to overrule *Sinclair v Brougham*. Quite why so much time was lavished by Aikens LJ on this issue, in particular by reference to minority judgments in the House of Lords, is unclear. In the House of Lords in *Westdeutsche Landesbank v Islington* none of their lordships had expressed the view that no such common law claim should be allowed, with the majority overruling the decision in *Sinclair v Brougham* explicitly. This, in essence, was the decision to which the Court of Appeal came in *Haugesund Kommune v Depfa ACS Bank*.

51 The law on interest has changed significantly by virtue of a subsequent decision of the House of Lords in *Sempra Metals Ltd v IRC* [2008] Bus LR 49.

52 Alastair Hudson, *Swaps, Restitution and Trusts*, Sweet & Maxwell, 1999.

conscience. Among the other problems with Birks's argument were the following two issues: first, that it was predicated on a fallacious idea that it was based on Roman law but overlooked the fact that Roman law itself relied on a broadly-based equity ('aequitas'); and, secondly, that it was based on an elderly English case, *Moses v Macferlan*,[53] which was in fact based on equity and not on some Romanist model of unjust enrichment. So, *Westdeutsche Landesbank v Islington* is important because it is the most recent House of Lords case on trusts law which takes the trouble to explain the basics of English trusts law as being based on a central concept of 'conscience', and because it resolved a key academic debate of its day.

12.3 UNCONSCIONABLE DEALINGS WITH PROPERTY

Where the legal owner of property deals with that property knowingly in a manner which denies or interferes with the rights of some other person in that property, the legal owner will hold that property on constructive trust for that other person.

12.3.1 Knowledge and unconscionability in general

This category develops from the general principle set out above in section 12.2. In that paragraph the explanation given for the decision in the *Chase Manhattan* case by Lord Browne-Wilkinson in *Westdeutsche Landesbank Girozentrale v Islington LBC*[54] revealed the potential ambit of this principle. It was said that in *Chase Manhattan*, the unconscionable act which led to the imposition of a constructive trust was the knowledge of the recipient of a payment that the payer had made a mistake and would therefore require repayment. Conscience here does not require that there has been some dishonesty or theft practised by the defendant, only that there be some treatment by the defendant of property in which the claimant has rights which is considered to be wrong, unconscionable or unethical in a broad sense.

12.3.2 Constructive trusts in relation to land

Constructive trusts in relation to land in general terms

Constructive trusts may arise in relation to land in three principal ways. First, by means of a common intention constructive trust, where the parties either form some agreement by means of express discussions, or demonstrate a common intention by their conduct in contributing jointly to the purchase price or mortgage over a property.[55] This category is considered below at para 12.6.1.

Secondly, by entering into a contract for the transfer of rights in land, there is an automatic transfer of the equitable interest in that land as soon as there is a binding contract in effect.[56] That contract would have to be in writing in one document signed by the parties which contained all the terms of the contract.[57] However, proprietary estoppel will now offer a means of evading this statutory requirement in circumstances in which the transferor made assurances to the transferee that the transferee would receive title in this land and where that

53 (1760) 2 Burr 1005, *per* Lord Mansfield CJ.
54 [1996] AC 669.
55 *Lloyds Bank v Rosset* [1990] 1 All ER 1111.
56 *Lysaght v Edwards* (1876) 2 Ch D 499; *Jerome v Kelly* [2004] UKHL 25; [2004] 2 All ER 835.
57 Law of Property (Miscellaneous Provisions) Act 1989, s 2.

transferee acted to her detriment in reliance on those assurances.[58] This category is considered below at para 12.6.2.

Joint ventures in relation to land

The third context in which a constructive may come into existence in relation to land is in relation to parties entering into negotiations for a joint venture to exploit land and subsequently seeking to exploit that land alone when those negotiations had precluded the claimant from exploiting any interest in that land.[59] As is discussed in section 12.3.3 following, a constructive trust will be imposed in circumstances in which the claimant has refrained from exploiting some commercial opportunity in reliance on some agreement or pre-contractual understanding reached with the defendant. This doctrine is known as 'the equity in *Pallant v Morgan*'[60] and has been accepted as being the basis of the constructive trust considered in this section in relation to unconscionable actions between parties to joint ventures. The most significant recent example of this doctrine arose in *Banner Homes Group plc v Luff Development Ltd*,[61] where two commercial parties entered into what was described as a 'joint venture' to exploit the development prospects of land in Berkshire. It was held that no binding contract had been formed between the parties when the defendant sought to exploit the site alone without the involvement of the claimant. Extensive negotiations were conducted between the claimant and the defendant and their respective lawyers with reference to documentation to create a joint venture partnership or company. The defendant continued the negotiations while privately nursing reservations about going into business with the claimant. The defendant decided, however, that it should 'keep [the claimant] on board' unless or until a better prospect emerged. It was held that the defendant could establish a constructive trust even in the absence of a binding contract to the effect that the claimant and defendant would exploit the land jointly, if the defendant had refrained from exploiting any personal interests in that land in reliance on the negotiations being conducted between the claimant and the defendant.

Significantly, there had been sufficient agreement between the parties for the claimant to have relied on the arrangement as founding some right under a constructive trust. It was enough that there had been extensive negotiations so that the claimant could reasonably have relied on the parties' common intention to enter into a joint venture agreement.[62] The constructive trust would not have arisen if there had been no evidence of any agreement between the parties or no evidence that the claimant had made any contribution to the purchase price of property or no evidence that he had suffered any meaningful detriment.[63]

---

58 *Yaxley v Gotts* [2000] Ch 162; [1999] 3 WLR 1217. Cf. *Cobbe v Yeoman's Row* [2008] 1 WLR 1752 below.

59 *Pallant v Morgan* [1953] Ch 43.

60 [1952] 2 All ER 951. See the cases considered in the next section.

61 [2000] Ch 372, [2000] 2 WLR 772. Applied in *Kilcarne Holdings Ltd v Targetfollow (Birmingham) Ltd* [2004] EWHC 2547 (Ch).

62 A joint venture agreement may give rise to a constructive trust where a suitable relationship of trust and confidence is found to have arisen and one of the fiduciaries then seeks to make an unauthorised personal profit from the subject matter of that joint venture: *Murad v Al-Saraj* [2004] EWHC 1235 (Ch), Etherton J; *Button v Phelps* [2006] EWHC 53 (Ch), Englehart QC.

63 It is significant, however, that the parties had reached sufficient agreement to make out the constructive trust. Where the parties have reached no agreement at all on which the claimant could have relied in good conscience, then there will not be a constructive trust: *Kilcarne Holdings Ltd v Targetfollow (Birmingham) Ltd* [2004] EWHC 2547 (Ch); *Popely v Heltfield Properties Ltd* [2005] All ER (D) 287; *Kirker v Ridley* [2008] All ER (D) 179.

So, where the parties are in mid-negotiation and the only documentation refers to the trans-actions as being 'subject to contract'[64] or in 'draft only',[65] then the circumstances may dictate that the parties were not yet in agreement such that the constructive trust under *Banner Homes* would not apply. It should be noted, however, that there was not a 'no contract' provision in the agreement in the *Banner Homes* case itself. Nevertheless in that case it was found that there had been sufficient agreement between the parties on which the claimant could form a reasonable expectation that there would be a formal contract entered into between them in the future.

By contrast, at first instance in *Kilcarne Holdings Ltd v Targetfollow (Birmingham) Ltd*,[66] it was the parties' legal advisors who had deliberately provided in the draft documentation which passed between the parties that there was no contract then in effect between them so that no expectation could reasonably be formed between the parties that such an agreement was then in existence. In *Banner Homes*, so the court considered, there was no equivalent provision included by the parties' legal advisors. Consequently, if well-advised, the parties' expression that there is no contract nor any form of enforceable agreement between them will be binding, whereas if the parties' advisors do not make such a position clear (or if the parties are not advised in this way) then it may be reasonable to form an impression that there is such an agreement on which the claimant can rely so as to give rise to the *Banner Homes* constructive trust.[67]

On appeal to the Court of Appeal in *Kilcarne Holdings Ltd v Targetfollow (Birmingham) Ltd*,[68] approving the decision at first instance, it was accepted that in relation to the '*Pallant v Morgan*' equity in such cases 'the principle required, first, that there be an arrangement or understanding between the parties that A will acquire the property and that if he does so B will obtain some interest in it; and, secondly, that B must act in reliance on that arrangement or understanding'.[69] On the facts of this case the Court of Appeal agreed with the judge at first instance that there had never been any such agreement, arrangement or understanding between the parties precisely because the parties' legal advisors had made it clear that nego-tiations between the parties were always 'subject to contract' such that no contract was yet in place.

Other, more recent cases illustrate the same points. In *Thames Cruises Ltd v George Wheeler Launches*[70] the parties had an informal understanding that they would apply together for a licence to operate cruise boats on the Thames. However, the defendant formed a rival consortium to bid for the licence and that consortium was in time granted the licence. It was held by Peter Smith J that there had not been a legally-binding partnership formed between the parties,[71] merely a non-binding understanding, and therefore the constructive trust did

---

64 *London and Regional Investments Ltd v TBI plc* [2002] EWCA Civ 355, [2002] All ER (D) 369.
65 *Kilcarne Holdings Ltd v Targetfollow (Birmingham) Ltd* [2004] EWHC 2547 (Ch).
66 *Ibid.*
67 The principle in these cases was followed in *Van Laetham v Brooker* [2005] EWHC 1478 (Ch).
68 [2005] EWCA Civ 1355.
69 Adopting the submissions of Edward Nugee QC at [2005] EWCA Civ 1355 at para [21].
70 [2003] EWHC 3093 (Ch).
71 A partnership in legal terms is an undertaking in common with a view to profit under s 1 of the Partnership Act 1890 and therefore constitutes a very particular kind of legal relationship which is very different from an informal understanding.

not arise as it had done in *Banner Homes v Luff*.[72] In *Button v Phelps*[73] it was held that this equity was based on the equity in *Pallant v Morgan* (on which see the next section) and that it was a doctrine similar to proprietary estoppel. Therefore, if the parties had not suffered any detriment in reliance on an understanding between them, it was held that a constructive trust would not come into existence based on *Banner Homes v Luff*. So where the parties had formed an understanding that they might bid to acquire the nightclubs operated by an insolvent company, there would be no constructive trust if the defendant withdrew before any of the other parties had performed any detrimental acts in reliance on that putative understanding. The formulation of the test which was accepted by the Court of Appeal in *Kilcarne Holdings Ltd v Targetfollow (Birmingham) Ltd*[74] (which was quoted above) is indeed very similar to proprietary estoppel and to the common intention constructive trust[75] in *Lloyds Bank v Rosset*[76] in its reference[77] to 'agreement, arrangement or understanding'.[78]

In relation to all of these categories of constructive trust over land, there is a superficial similarity between the constructive trust and proprietary estoppel in that the claimant has generally suffered detriment in reliance on an understanding that there is a formal contract or some similar informal agreement between the parties. The common feature in all of these claims (where estoppel can be defined as a claim) is that the claimant must have suffered some detriment to found its claim.[79] These differences will be probed further later in this chapter.

The effect of the decision in Cobbe v Yeoman's Row

The case of *Cobbe v Yeoman's Row*[80] concerned negotiations between two parties to develop land whereby the claimant spent a large amount of money gaining planning permission to develop the land with the knowledge of the defendant while negotiations towards a contract were proceeding between them; but once planning permission was acquired the defendant reneged on the parties' non-binding understanding that they would develop the land together. The House of Lords held that the claimant was not entitled to any rights based on constructive trust nor on proprietary estoppel. In essence, their Lordships considered that two experienced commercial people like the claimant and the defendant should have known that the fact that there was no enforceable agreement between them meant that neither of them had

---

72 In *Powell v Benney* [2007] EWCA Civ 1283. See also *McGuane v Welch* [2008] EWCA Civ 785, where it was held that the claimant's alleged detriment in relation to assisting an elderly man in his premises would not found rights on 'constructive trust or proprietary estoppel' principles, because there had not been any clear 'bargain' between the parties to the effect that the claimant would perform any detrimental acts nor that those detrimental acts were intended to acquire the claimant any interest in the property.

73 [2006] EWHC 53 (Ch).

74 Adopting the submissions of Edward Nugee QC at [2005] EWCA Civ 1355 at para [21].

75 Which is itself suggested by Lord Bridge in that case to be of a piece with proprietary estoppel.

76 [1991] 1 AC 1.

77 See para 15.4.2.

78 *Grant v Edwards* [1986] Ch 638.

79 *Chattock v Miller* (1878) 8 Ch D 177; *Pallant v Morgan* [1952] 2 All ER 951; *London and Regional Investments Ltd v TBI plc* [2002] EWCA Civ 355; [2002] All ER (D) 369; *Kilcarne Holdings Ltd v Targetfollow (Birmingham) Ltd* [2004] EWHC 2547 (Ch). See also *Pridean Ltd v Forest Taverns Ltd* (1996) 75 P & CR 447, where this concept was argued on the basis of proprietary estoppel.

80 [2008] 1 WLR 1752.

any rights against the other in constructive trust; nor were there any rights in proprietary estoppel because the defendant was not strictly alleging that any true fact was not the case (here, that she was not denying the existence of enforceable rights for the claimant because no such enforceable rights had been created). This decision is discussed in detail at para 13.3.5 in relation to proprietary estoppel. Importantly, the House of Lords retreated from the idea that proprietary estoppel should be based solely on unconscionability, where for example a defendant knowingly allows a claimant to spend large amounts of money before resiling from their common understanding. This decision throws into shadow many of the cases considered above given the lack of enthusiasm in the House of Lords for finding unconscionability sufficient to grant proprietary rights in a commercial arrangement. In relation specifically to constructive trusts, Lord Scott held that:[81]

> If two or more persons agree to embark on a joint venture which involves the acquisition
> of an identified piece of land and a subsequent exploitation of, or dealing with, the land
> for the purposes of the joint venture, and one of the joint venturers, with the agreement
> of the others who believe him to be acting for their joint purposes, makes the acquisition
> in his own name but subsequently seeks to retain the land for his own benefit, the court
> will regard him as holding the land on trust for the joint venturers. This would be either
> an implied trust or a constructive trust arising from the circumstances . . .

However, Lord Scott considered that, on the facts of *Cobbe*, there would not be a constructive trust on the same manner as *Banner Homes v Luff Development* because the property in question had been owned for some years before the negotiations for the joint venture began;[82] furthermore that '[d]espite the unconscionability of the appellant's behaviour in withdrawing from the inchoate agreement immediately planning permission had been obtained, this seems to me a wholly inadequate basis for imposing a constructive trust over the property in order to provide Mr Cobbe with a remedy for his disappointed expectations';[83] and that the parties agreement had not been sufficient to constitute a contract.

The subsequent decision of the House of Lords in *Thorner v Major*[84] has been significant in explaining how the *Cobbe* decision should be understood. Lord Walker suggested that *Cobbe* should be understood as merely reminding us all of the need for 'certainty of interest'. Lord Walker and Lord Rodger effectively suggested in *Thorner v Major* that the result of *Cobbe* was simply to reinforce the need for certainty as to the content of the representation and as to the property in question.

Indeed, it is not entirely clear that the decision in *Cobbe* has had a profound effect on the subsequent decisions of the lower courts.[85] Those courts have focused on the equity in *Pallant v Morgan* and the decision in *Banner Homes* instead. The agreement or understanding between the parties does not need to be as precise as a carefully drafted contract but it must be based on something more than merely the conduct of the parties. So, in *Baynes Clarke v Corless*[86] a property development in which two houses had been built in the grounds

81 [2008] 1 WLR 1752, at [30].
82 *Ibid*, at [33].
83 *Ibid*, at [36].
84 [2009] 1 WLR 776.
85 However, *Cobbe* was followed in *Kirker v Ridley* [2008] All ER (D) 179 (Dec) and in *Qayyum v Hameed* [2009] EWCA Civ 352, [2009] 3 FCR 545.
86 [2009] EWHC 1636 (Ch).

of a larger house in Haywards Heath in West Sussex had led to disputes about the access road to all three properties.[87] The claimants contended that the access road and adjoining land should be treated as being held on constructive trust for them by the defendants, but it was held by Proudman J that there had never been any formal agreement about that and that the claimant's contentions were therefore based merely on their impression of the parties' conduct.[88] Therefore, there was insufficient agreement between the parties to form a constructive trust. It was further held that while unconscionability is a necessary element for a constructive trust based on *Pallant v Morgan*, by itself unconscionability is insufficient to create a constructive trust.[89] There would also need to be some reliance on the agreement between the parties but on these facts there was neither an agreement nor evidence of reliance upon such an agreement.[90]

Similarly, in *Crossco No 4 Unlimited v Jolan Ltd*[91] the Court of Appeal held that where there is no clear agreement between the parties then the principle in *Banner Homes* will not apply so as to create a constructive trust. The issues arose out of negotiations for the ownership and exploitation of a lease over a large retail building in central Manchester.[92] During the negotiations for a complex demerger of the entity which owned that building, the defendant sought to exercise a break clause under the lease. The claimant contended that it had not known of that break clause in the lease and therefore contended it was unconscionable for the defendant to activate the break clause such that a constructive trust should bind the defendant in this regard. It was found that there was no fiduciary duty in this context which had been breached by the defendant. Etherton LJ, in a very full judgment, held that *Banner Homes* continued to be good law in this context after the decision in *Cobbe v Yeoman's Row*, and more significantly his lordship identified the source of the principle in *Banner Homes v Luff Development* and the equity in *Pallant v Morgan* as being based ultimately on a breach of fiduciary duty. Such a breach of fiduciary duty could not be demonstrated on these facts. Therefore, no constructive trust would be available.

However, Arden LJ in *Crossco No 4 Unlimited v Jolan Ltd*, having agreed with the conclusion reached by Etherton LJ, then went to the effort of disagreeing with him as to the source of the *Banner Homes* doctrine and identified it instead as being a 'common intention constructive trust'.[93] There was also some suggestion that this principle might be limited to domestic circumstances and would need to be interpreted in the light of the decision of the Supreme

---

87 Originally, the parties had intended to own the land through a development company but dissatisfaction with the managing director of that company emerged later, and a breakdown of the ordinary cordialities between neighbours later still. The disputes at issue had arisen late in the process when the defendants had decided not to transfer title in the access road to the claimants nor to undertake to maintain that road for more than three years. This case was a classic of its type: neighbours becoming involved in a petty squabble over common land which escalates into aggression, allegations, solicitors being instructed and ultimately a hearing before the High Court. There was even a dispute about a single screw affixed by one party to another party's fence, with which his lordship dealt with great calmness, at para [85].

88 [2009] EWHC 1636 (Ch), at [22] and as explored at para [25] *et seq*.

89 *Ibid*, at [23].

90 *Ibid*, at [24].

91 [2011] EWCA Civ 1619.

92 As Morgan J had observed at first instance, there was an irony in a 15-minute discussion between two business-people giving rise ultimately to a 35-day trial, [2011] EWHC 803 (Ch).

93 [2011] EWCA Civ 1619, at [129] *et seq*.

Court in *Jones v Kernott*.[94] All of this suggestion by Arden LJ is simply wrong.[95] As Etherton LJ correctly pointed out, in disagreeing with Arden LJ, the doctrine 'common intention constructive trust' arose specifically in relation to trusts of homes in *Pettit v Pettit* and *Gissing v Gissing*, and as such had no part to play in the equity in *Pallant v Morgan* (which pre-dated it by seventeen years) nor the decision in *Banner Homes*.[96] This was an unhelpful intervention by Arden LJ, unfortunately followed by McFarlane LJ, and it should be ignored in the future.[97]

12.3.3 Constructive trusts to 'keep out of the market'

A constructive trust will be imposed in circumstances in which the claimant has refrained from exploiting some commercial opportunity in reliance on some agreement or pre-contractual understanding reached with the defendant. This doctrine is known as 'the equity in *Pallant v Morgan*'.[98] In general terms, this is referred to as the claimant 'keeping out of the market'. The basis of the trust is that the claimant will have suffered detriment by failing to exploit a commercial opportunity. The conscience of the defendant is affected where the claimant's decision not to exploit that commercial opportunity is based on some under-standing reached with the defendant, or some assurance made by the defendant that they would reach some other agreement: the defendant must then exploit that opportunity in some way in contravention of the parties' understanding. The trust bites on any property which the defendant realises from exploiting the opportunity. This constructive trust will bind a purchaser of property who had previously procured the claimant's agreement not to bid for property at auction on the basis that the defendant would sell part of that land to the claimant;[99] or bind a purchaser of land at auction who had previously agreed with the claimant not to bid against the claimant for part of that land at auction;[100] or would bind a defendant who acquired development land on its own account where it had reached an understanding with the claimant that that land would be exploited as a joint venture with the claimant.[101]

94   [2011] UKSC 53.
95   See also *Herbert v Doyle* [2010] EWCA Civ 1095, *per* Arden LJ.
96   As this writer has pointed out elsewhere, it would be possible to take the non-commercial doctrine of the common intention constructive trust and to change it so that it could be made to fit commercial situations, such as *Banner Homes*, in which commercial people have come to some 'agreement, arrangement or under-standing', as the concept is described in part in *Lloyds Bank v Rosset* [1992] 1 AC 1.
97   Arden LJ has worked through some interesting and previously unknown concepts in trusts law. Examples are: the use of subjective ideas to apply an objective concept of 'dishonesty' in *Abou-Rahmah v Abacha* [2006] EWCA Civ 1492, [16]; in *Murad v Al-Saraj* [2005] EWCA Civ 939 at paras [82–83] the idea that the principle in *Boardman v Phipps* could be tempered by a modern court, which was clearly contrary to the approach of the English senior courts, and doubted by Sir Peter Gibson in *Wrexham AFC Ltd v Crucialmove Ltd* [2006] EWCA Civ 237, para [51]; the decision in *Pennington v Waine*; in *Charter plc v City Index Ltd* [2008] 2 WLR 950, [64] the idea that 'damages' are payable for breach of trust; and the notion that a trust takes effect 'over the legal title' in property.
98   [1952] 2 All ER 951. See the cases considered in the next section.
99   *Chattock v Miller* (1878) 8 Ch D 177.
100 *Pallant v Morgan* [1952] 2 All ER 951.
101 *Banner Homes v Luff Development* [2000] Ch 372, [2000] 2 WLR 772. Cf *Edwin Shirley Productions v Workspace Management Ltd* [2001] 2 EGLR 16.

12.3.4 Statute cannot be used as an engine of fraud: *Rochefoucauld v Boustead*

It was accepted by Millett LJ in *Paragon Finance v Thakerar*[102] that 'well-known examples' of constructive trusts which are 'coloured from the first by the trust and confidence by means of which the trustee obtained the property' include the doctrine in *Rochefoucauld v Boustead*.[103] This doctrine was considered in detail at para 5.2.2 above. In the *Rochefoucauld* case itself, the trustee was empowered to acquire property for the claimant but the trust was improperly recorded. It was held that for the defendant trustee to have relied on the statutory formalities for the creation of a trust in land would have been to perpetrate a fraud on the claimant for whose benefit that property had been acquired. Similarly, in *Lyus v Prowsa*,[104] a mortgagor sought to deal with property in contravention of the mortgage on the basis that the mortgagee had failed to register the mortgage. It was held that the mortgagor held the property on constructive trust for the mortgagee nevertheless, because the mortgagor had undertaken in the mortgage contract to respect the rights of the mortgagee.[105]

While the *Rochefoucauld* doctrine could be said to operate on the basis of a general equitable principle that statute will not be used as an engine of fraud, Millett LJ in *Paragon Finance* included it four-square within the head of constructive trust, an approach which is in line with cases like *Lyus v Prowsa*.[106] It is one of the core motivations of equity to balance out injustices in the literal application of common law and statutory rules. In such circumstances, there is no intention to create an express trust over the property in question.[107] Therefore, on the basis that a trust has been imposed by the courts to require the legal owner of that property to deal with it in a particular manner for the benefit of the beneficiary, the only viable explanation of the nature of that trust is that it forms a constructive trust in order to regulate the conscience of that common law owner which arises by operation of law.[108] Aspects of this doctrine relating generally to fraud are considered further below at para 12.4.4.

In essence, then, no common law or statutory rule may be used so as to defraud or take unconscionable advantage of another person.[109] This principle, however, conflicts with the basic principle of modern real property law that in statutorily defined circumstances no proprietary right can take effect over any other right if it is not registered. So, in *Midland Bank Trust Co Ltd v Green*,[110] a father had granted his son an option to purchase his farm, which was unregistered land. This right should have been registered under the Land Charges Act 1972 for it to be protected, but the son failed to register his option. With a view to defeating his son's option to purchase, the father sold the farm at an undervalue to his wife. It was held that even though this sale was effected so as to defeat the son's right, the son nevertheless had no rights in equity to prevent the defeat of his option. The purpose of this decision was to protect the integrity of the system of registration. By contrast, in *Peffer v*

---

102 *Paragon Finance plc v Thakerar & Co* [1999] 1 All ER 400; *Lloyd v Dugdale* [2002] 2 P & CR 13.
103 [1897] 1 Ch 196.
104 [1982] 1 WLR 1044.
105 See also *IDC Group v Clark* (1992) 65 P & CR 179.
106 [1982] 1 WLR 1044.
107 As considered in section 2.1 of this book.
108 See Oakley, 1997, 53 *et seq*.
109 *Rochefoucauld v Boustead* [1897] 1 Ch 196.
110 [1981] AC 513.

Rigg,[111] Mr and Mrs Peffer and Mr and Mrs Rigg bought a property, which was registered land, together. When the Riggs separated, the property was purportedly passed to Mrs Rigg who sought to dispose of the property entirely for her own benefit. The Peffers had not protected their rights by registration as required by statute. It was held by Graham J that Mrs Rigg was a constructive trustee for the Peffers because she had had knowledge of their rights and therefore could not purport to defeat those rights simply on the basis that they had not been registered. Thus, there is a clear tension on the cases between the statutory policy which requires that no unregistered right will be protected and the equitable principle which requires that a person who knows of another's rights cannot rely on another person's failure to register their rights so as to defeat them. As was considered above, *Cobbe v Yeoman's Row* throws doubt on the utility of 'unconscionability' as a basis for constructive trusts in commercial transactions; although it is suggested that 'fraud' is of a different order of magnitude.

12.3.5 'Doing everything necessary': *Re Rose*

A more contentious form of constructive trust is derived from the case of *Re Rose*,[112] in which it was accepted that where the absolute owner of property intends to transfer title in that property to another person, a trust will arise in favour of the intended recipient once the transferor has completed all of the necessary formalities required of the transferor personally to effect transfer. It has been accepted by some of the commentators that this form of trust constitutes a constructive trust primarily because it does not satisfy the formalities for the creation of an express trust because no title has been vested in a trustee.[113] Further, it is to be doubted whether this could be considered to be an express trust at all, given that the transferor had no intention to create a trust: rather, he intended in *Re Rose* to make a gift of the property. As such, the trust is being imposed against the intentions of the parties, and therefore can only be described as taking effect by operation of law as a constructive trust. This equitable doctrine was considered in detail at para 5.4.3 above.[114]

In the case of *Re Rose*,[115] Mr Rose had intended to transfer one block of shares to his wife beneficially and another to his wife and another woman on trust for them both. He had completed the appropriate transfer forms. The only formality which remained to be performed was the acceptance by the company of the transfer of ownership: this was an action outside Mr Rose's own control. It was held that Mr Rose had succeeded in transferring the equitable interest in the shares to his wife when he had completed all the formalities required of him.

The classification of this trust is not straightforward. It cannot be deemed to be an express trust because there was no intention on the part of Mr Rose to create express trusts over all of the shares. Nor does the equitable interest result back to Mr Rose. Rather, it must be said that the equitable interest passes as a result of a constructive trust by operation of law. Lord Evershed MR based his judgment not on trust, but rather on the basis of an intention to make

---

111 [1977] 1 WLR 285.
112 [1952] Ch 499, considered at para 5.4.3 above. Cf *Re Trustee of the Property of Jan Yngre Pehrsson (A Bankrupt)* (1999) 2 ITELR 230. See Youdan, 1984.
113 Oakley, 1997.
114 See now also *Scribes West Ltd v Relsa Anstalt* [2004] EWCA Civ 1744.
115 [1952] Ch 499.

a gift such that it would have been inequitable for Mr Rose to have, for example, sought to retain for himself any dividend paid in respect of these shares between the time that Mr Rose completed all of the formalities required of him and the ultimate acceptance by the company's board of directors to validate the transfer. Hence the inclusion of this principle as a form of unconscionable dealing with property: it is accepted by the Court of Appeal in *Re Rose* that the rights of the transferee are based on the unconscionability of the transferor refusing to recognise that a transfer of title in equity has taken place.

The importance of this form of constructive trust is that the formalities for the creation of a trust or the formalities required for the transfer of property can be circumvented where all the formalities required of the transferor have been completed. The problem remains the decision of Turner LJ in *Milroy v Lord*,[116] which provided that 'the settlor must have done everything which, according to the nature of the property comprised in the settlement, was necessary to be done in order to transfer the property'. As provided by s 53(2) of the Law of Property Act 1925, the categorisation of this trust as a constructive trust absolves the settlor of the need to satisfy any formalities.

12.3.6 A constructive trust over a separate fund created to protect pre-payments for goods or services against a company's insolvency

There have been a number of cases in relation to companies which have gone into insolvent administration and which have received money from customers in a situation in which their officers know that the company has ceased to trade and that in consequence those customers will not receive the goods or services for which they have pre-paid. The argument based on constructive trust is that it would be unconscionable for the company to keep those pre-payments when the company's directors know that the company has ceased to trade and therefore that the pre-payments should be held on constructive trust for the customers. There are two difficulties in this area. First, the principal case on these facts, *Nestle Oy v Barclays Bank*,[117] was decided on the basis of a remedial constructive trust – an approach which has been overruled by Lord Browne-Wilkinson in the House of Lords in *Westdeutsche Landesbank v Islington*.[118] Secondly, it is difficult to square the conscionability of holding the money on trust for the customers with the *pari passu* principle in insolvency law that no unsecured creditor should be given an advantage over any other unsecured creditor. These issues are considered below, after we have considered the appropriate cases.

In *Nestle Oy v Barclays Bank*[119] a company, which acted as a shipowner's agent, ceased trading shortly before receiving a payment for future services which it was not going to perform. Bingham J held that it would have been 'contrary to any ordinary notion of fairness' for the company to have kept the money and that in ordinary circumstances when the directors knew that it would not perform these services then the company's directors would have organised a repayment of that amount. Thus, it was held that the company could not have 'in good conscience' retained this payment and that 'accordingly a constructive trust is to be inferred'. Bingham J had therefore awarded what was effectively a remedial constructive trust. The particular concern being that the constructive trust in those circumstances was

116 (1862) 4 De GF & J 264.
117 [1983] 2 Lloyds Rep 658.
118 [1996] AC 669.
119 [1983] 2 Lloyds Rep 658.

being used on a remedial basis, as opposed to the institutional basis on which constructive trusts operate in English law.

A clear, recent example of this issue arose in *Re Farepak Food and Gifts Ltd*,[120] a case in which the directors of Farepak Food and Gifts Ltd ('Farepak') sought to protect customers who had made pre-payments for goods or services. Farepak's directors had decided to cease trading on 11 October 2006. Farepak went into insolvent administration on 13 October 2006. By putting these pre-payments into a separate bank account Farepak's directors intended that the customers' pre-payments would be held on trust and consequently that they would be held outside the assets which were to be distributed in the company's insolvency. Farepak's directors knew that the company would cease to trade as from 11 December and the scheme involving the separate bank account was intended to operate in relation to moneys received from customers after that date. The claimant customers[121] sought to rely on the remedial constructive trust approach in *Nestle Oy v Barclays Bank*, an approach which had been overruled by the House of Lords in *Westdeutsche Landesbank v Islington*,[122] as acknowledged by Mann J in *Re Farepak*. Consequently, Mann J held that he could not impose the constructive trust which had been asked for because the claimants had sought to rely on *Nestle Oy* which had been overruled. The decision in *Nestle Oy* had been predicated on the confused mixture of unjust enrichment and constructive trust which was found in *Chase Manhattan Bank NA v Israel-British Bank (London) Ltd*[123] and which had in turn been explicitly overruled latterly by Lord Browne-Wilkinson in *Westdeutsche Landesbank v Islington*.[124]

I think, however, we can slice through the Gordian knot in which those involved in *Re Farepak Food and Gifts Ltd* allowed themselves to become embroiled in two ways. The first cut uses the law on constructive trusts; the second cut is based on *Re Kayford* in the law of express trusts (which is discussed in section 3.3.1).[125] So, then, constructive trusts. The basis on which constructive trusts, in the ordinary case of events, come into existence after the decision in *Westdeutsche Landesbank v Islington* is that a constructive trust will be imposed on someone who deals unconscionably with property with knowledge of the unconscionability of her actions. Therefore, the only issue in *Re Farepak* was whether or not the directors knew at the time that Farepak received moneys from its customers (via the agents which collected on Farepak's behalf) that the company was no longer trading and that therefore it would be unconscionable to receive and take absolute title over money from those customers when the company's directors knew that none of the services for which the customers were paying would be provided. The directors knew on 11 December – the date that the company's directors decided that the company should cease to trade – that Farepak was ceasing to trade and that it was going into insolvent administration. In *Nestle Oy* Bingham J held that to accept money from customers in such a situation could not be done 'in good conscience'. To that extent, the *result* in *Nestle Oy* seems unremarkable: the directors knew that they were receiving money unconscionably (in that no service would ever be provided in consideration

---

120 [2006] All ER (D) 265 (Dec).
121 Strictly speaking, it was a single test case brought to question the nature and extent of the customers' rights.
122 [1996] AC 669.
123 [1981] Ch 105.
124 [1996] AC 669. This reasoning was accepted in *Box v Barclays Bank* [1998] Lloyds Rep Bank 185, *per* Ferris J and in *Shalson v Russo* [2005] Ch 281, 320, *per* Rimer J.
125 See para 3.3.1, 'The commercial context'.

for that payment) and therefore the requirement of 'knowledge plus unconscionability', set out by Lord Browne-Wilkinson in *Westdeutsche Landesbank v Islington*, was satisfied. It was the reasoning which was at issue. Consequently, in *Re Farepak* it would have been sufficient to find a constructive trust to recognise that the directors knew of the unconscionable factor: which they did from 11 December because they had already decided that the company would cease to trade from that date.[126]

12.4 PROFITS FROM UNLAWFUL ACTS

Where a person committing an unlawful act and/or receiving a bribe is in a fiduciary position during the commission of such an act, the fiduciary is required to hold any property resulting from that unlawful act on proprietary constructive trust for the beneficiaries of the fiduciary duty. That proprietary constructive trust requires that any profits made are also to be held on constructive trust. Similarly, any losses made as a result of investing the bribe will be required to be made good by the constructive trustee.

This section progresses from a general category of unconscionable acts into a first category of the more specific contexts of acts which are unlawful in the sense that they are illegal under the criminal law, or that they are contrary to some norm of regulation or mandatory legal principle. In short, equity takes a particularly strict line in relation to property acquired as a result of unlawful activities. The approach of equity in this context could be said to be based on the proposition that 'no system of jurisprudence can with reason include among the rights which it enforces rights directly resulting to the person asserting for the crime of that person':[127] or, in other words, a criminal cannot be permitted to retain the fruits of her criminal activities. Equity has held since *Bridgman v Green*[128] that the profits of crime will be held on what is now known as a constructive trust. Two themes emerge. First, equity will seek to recover for the victim of the unlawful act full compensation for the effects of that unlawful act, both by means of proprietary constructive trust and also by means of additional personal liability to account in excess of the value of the property held on constructive trust. Secondly, this proprietary constructive trust will be ineffective against a *bona fide* purchaser for value of that property without knowledge of the unlawful act.

12.4.1 Profits from bribery

Introduction

The principle considered in this section is that any bribe (or other profit from an unlawful activity) taken by a fiduciary will be held on constructive trust by that fiduciary for the beneficiaries of her fiduciary office. On the decided cases, this principle has meant that a

---

126 The more difficult question at that stage would be whether or not the property to be held on trust – that is, the money received after the company had gone into administration – could be sufficiently identifiable so as to constitute the subject matter of a trust. The issue of certainty of subject matter is considered below. It is only if there is no identifiable trust property but nevertheless a constructive trust were imposed so as to provide a remedy that there would be the sort of 'frontier' development of the law on constructive trust which concerned Mann J. This issue is considered in Chapter 3.

127 *Cleaver v Mutual Reserve Fund Life Association* [1892] 1 QB 147, 156.

128 (1755) 24 Beav 382.

person acting in a fiduciary position who commits an unlawful act, such as receiving a bribe to breach her duty, will be required to hold any property received on constructive trust for the beneficiary of that fiduciary duty, and similarly to hold any property acquired with that bribe on constructive trust also. A good illustration of this principle is found in *Reading v Attorney-General*,[129] a case concerning a British Army sergeant stationed in Cairo who received payments to ride in uniform in civilian lorries carrying contraband so that those lorries would not be stopped at army checkpoints. It was held by the Court of Appeal that the sergeant occupied a fiduciary position in relation to the Crown in respect of the misuse of his uniform and in respect of his position as a soldier in the British Army. Therefore, it was held that any money paid to him for riding in the lorry in breach of his fiduciary duty was held on constructive trust for the Crown by way of an account of his profits.

The fundamental conceptual problem with this principle is that profits made from, for example, bribes will not have been the property of the beneficiary before they were received by the fiduciary. Furthermore, the fiduciary duties recognised by the court in *Reading v Attorney-General* and in *Attorney-General for Hong Kong v Reid*[130] (considered below and relating to a Director of Public Prosecutions who took bribes not to prosecute certain criminals) are not classically understood categories of fiduciary duty. Rather, the duties of a fiduciary are imposed on the defendant to punish her unlawful act and not to vindicate some pre-existing property right. Consequently, it can be difficult to justify in principle the reallocation of title in such bribes to the beneficiaries on constructive trust. What perhaps emerges here is that the court is as concerned to punish the wrongdoer as to protect rights in property. The court will require that the property be held on constructive trust on the basis that the fiduciary should be required to come to equity with clean hands. One who commits an unlawful act will be treated as having acted *prima facie* unconscionably.

Old authorities: when bribes did not lead to a constructive trust

Until 1994, it was an accepted, but much-contested,[131] facet of English law that a fiduciary who received bribes was liable only to a personal claim to pay the cash equivalent of the bribe to the beneficiary of that fiduciary duty and not to account for any profits made on that bribe as a trustee. In the formerly leading case of *Lister v Stubbs*,[132] the defendant was a buyer for the plaintiff, the company which employed him, who accepted bribes in return for placing orders with particular suppliers. The defendant invested the bribes successfully in land and securities. Therefore, the employee had more valuable property than the bribes in his possession by the time of trial. He had generated great profits from the bribes, with the result that the plaintiff wanted to establish a proprietary claim to the profitable investments which the defendant had acquired with the bribes rather than simply the cash equivalent of the original bribes. The plaintiff sought an order from the court to stop the defendant from dealing with his investments and to hold them instead on constructive trust for the plaintiff. The issue arose whether the defendant was a constructive trustee of the bribe.

129 [1951] 1 All ER 617.
130 [1994] 1 AC 324.
131 See, eg, Millett, 1993.
132 (1890) 45 Ch D 1.

The Court of Appeal held that to allow the order would be to confuse the plaintiff's entitlement to the cash amount of the bribes with ownership of the investments. The logic of the property law rules was followed closely: the plaintiff had never had any proprietary right in the bribes and therefore could not claim title to the property acquired with the bribes. However, it was held that the plaintiff was entitled to require the defendant to account to the plaintiff for the value of the original bribes to prevent the fiduciary from making unauthorised profits from his office. The plaintiff was therefore entitled to an amount of cash which was equivalent to the bribes, but not to a proprietary right in the investments acquired with those bribes which had subsequently increased in value. The claim was considered to be only a personal claim between debtor and creditor for a sum of money equal to the bribes. It was held by the court that, strictly, one could not say entitlement to one form of property (an amount of cash) could be translated into rights in another form of property (the investments) in favour of a plaintiff who had never had title to that money.[133] This decision has been greatly criticised for creating a different scheme of rules from the secret profits cases considered below at section 12.5.[134] This approach will still be applied in cases where the parties' relationship is purely that of debtor and creditor, as in situations where the defendant is contractually obliged to collect fees for the claimant but where the defendant does not hold any such sums on trust,[135] or where their contract excludes the possibility of any form of express or implied trust being imposed.[136] It is suggested, however, that any further extension of such a principle would militate against the idea that constructive trusts arise by operation of law, regardless of the intentions of the parties.

The modern view: receipt of bribes leads to constructive trust

A different approach was taken by the Privy Council in *Attorney-General for Hong Kong v Reid*.[137] The former Director of Public Prosecutions for Hong Kong had accepted bribes not to prosecute certain individuals accused of having committed crimes within his jurisdiction. The bribes which he had received had been profitably invested. The question arose, similarly to *Lister v Stubbs*,[138] whether or not the property bought with the bribes and the increase in value of those investments should be held on constructive trust for the Director of Public Prosecutions's employer, or whether the Director of Public Prosecutions owed only an amount of cash equal to the bribes paid to him originally. Lord Templeman, giving the leading opinion of the Privy Council, overruled *Lister v Stubbs* and took a very much stricter view of the law. He held that a proprietary constructive trust is imposed as soon as the bribe is accepted by its recipient. This means that the employer is entitled in equity to any profit generated by the cash bribe received from the moment of its receipt. Similarly, Lord

---

133 This approach has been approved in Birks, 1989, 386; Virgo, 1999, 543; Burrows, 2002, 500, on the basis that there is no proprietary basis on which to impose a constructive trust because the property has never belonged to the claimant at any time and therefore, it is said, the only action which the claimant can have is a personal action based on debt at common law.

134 These approaches are summarised in *Daraydan Holdings Ltd v Solland International Ltd* [2004] EWHC 622 (Ch), para [75] *et seq*. See also, eg, Goff and Jones, 1998, 85.

135 *Ansys Inc v Lim* [2001] ECDR 34.

136 *Wallace v Shoa Leasing (Singapore) PTE Ltd, Re Japan Leasing* [2000] WTLR 301, [1999] BPIR 911.

137 [1994] 1 AC 324, [1994] 1 All ER 1.

138 (1890) 45 Ch D 1.

Templeman held that the constructive trustee is liable to the beneficiary for any *decrease* in value in the investments acquired with the bribe, as well as for any increase in value in such investments. As Lord Templeman has expressed this principle:[139]

> A bribe is a gift accepted by a fiduciary as an inducement to him to betray his trust. A fiduciary is undoubtedly accountable for a secret benefit which consists of a bribe. In addition a person who provides the bribe and the fiduciary who accepts the bribe may each be guilty of a criminal offence. In the present case the first respondent was clearly guilty of a criminal offence.

The fiduciary is thus liable to account to the beneficiaries for the receipt of the bribe. The moral underpinnings of the imposition of a constructive trust on such a bribe emerges from the following passage which continues on from the passage just quoted:

> Bribery is an evil practice which threatens the foundations of any civilised society. In particular bribery of policemen and prosecutors brings the administration of justice into disrepute. Where bribes are accepted by a trustee, servant, agent or other fiduciary, loss and damage are caused to the beneficiaries, master or principal whose interests have been betrayed. The amount of loss or damage resulting from the acceptance of a bribe may or may not be quantifiable. In the present case the amount of harm caused to the administration of justice in Hong Kong[140] by the first respondent in return for bribes cannot be quantified.

Lord Templeman's policy motivation is clear: to punish the wrongdoer, particularly a wrongdoer in public office. He considered bribery to be an 'evil practice which threatens the foundations of any civilised society'. As such, the imposition of a proprietary constructive trust was the only way in which the wrongdoer could be fully deprived of the value of his malfeasance. This, it is suggested, is less 'restitution' than 'retribution':[141] there is no proprietary right in the loss on the investments; rather there is a policy motivation both to disgorge the wrongdoer's profits and to impose punitive remedies. This is neither compensation nor restitution, rather it is control of the defendant's conscience.

The manner in which Lord Templeman constructed his proprietary remedy is perhaps not straightforward. It accords, however, with the underlying theme of this book that equity acts *in personam* against the defendant, even when awarding a proprietary remedy.[142] Lord Templeman held that equity looks upon as done that which ought to have been done (which is one of the core equitable principles discussed in Chapter 1) and that Reid should have given the bribes to his employer at the moment they were received: therefore, because equity looks upon as done that which ought to have been done, equity would deem that the bribes had actually been given to the employers and thereby the employers would acquire an equitable proprietary interest in the bribes. This equitable proprietary interest takes the form of a

---

139   [1994] 1 AC 324, 330–31; [1994] 1 All ER 1, 4–5.
140   By virtue of the respondent having been Director of Public Prosecutions in Hong Kong and having taken bribes from criminals not to prosecute them.
141   Jaffey, 2000.
142   See section 1.1 of this book.

constructive trust. This knotty train of thought requires some careful deconstruction. Lord Templeman started from the premise that equity acts *in personam*. The defendant had acted unconscionably in accepting the bribe in breach of his fiduciary duty. In consequence of that breach of duty, it was held that the bribe should have been deemed to pass to the beneficiary of the fiduciary power at the instant when it was received by the wrongdoer. Given that equity considers as done that which ought to have been done, it was held that the bribe should have been considered to have been the property of the beneficiary from the moment of its receipt. The means by which title passes to the beneficiary in equity in such circumstances is a proprietary constructive trust. As such, the bribe, any property acquired with the bribe and any profit derived from such property fell to be considered as the property of the person wronged by virtue of being held for that person's benefit on constructive trust.[143] In this circuitous way, Lord Templeman justified the imposition of a proprietary remedy in *Reid*[144] as opposed to the personal claim upheld in *Lister v Stubbs*.[145] It has been held latterly that the reason for the constructive trust in *Reid* was that it would have been 'as a fiduciary unconscionable for him to retain the benefit of it';[146] even though that was not the precise rationale used by Lord Templeman.

Identifying people who will be fiduciaries

Whether or not a person will be considered to be a fiduciary will depend upon the context. There are identified categories of fiduciary office – trustee, company director, business partner and agent – in which such duties will always arise.[147] However, there are also other situations in which a person may be liable as a fiduciary in particular contexts. So, in *Attorney-General for Hong Kong v Reid*, the Director of Public Prosecutions was found to be a fiduciary in relation to the administration of justice in that territory, just like an army sergeant assisting smugglers through army checkpoints by using his rank and uniform.[148] Neither category has previously been held to be a category of fiduciary office, but the misuse of their powers in particular circumstances rendered the defendant in each case a fiduciary. Within companies it is usually only the directors who will owe fiduciary duties – beyond their contract of employment – to the company. However, there may be circumstances in which less senior employees may be considered to be fiduciaries. For example, in circumstances in which a security guard received a bribe to disclose and effectively disarm the claimant's security arrangements to a gang of armed robbers, he was held to be constructive trustee of the bribe as a fiduciary.[149] Ordinarily a security guard would not owe fiduciary duties to his employer because he does not occupy a role of sufficient seniority within a company. However, in relation to the security precautions taken by that company at its warehouses, a security guard would be held to be in a fiduciary capacity.[150] The notion of

---

143 This approach has been followed in *Corporacion Nacional Del Cobre De Chile v Interglobal Inc* (2003) 5 ITELR 744, [2002] CILR 298. See also *Sumitomo Bank v Thahir* [1993] 1 SLR 735.
144 [1994] 1 AC 324, [1994] 1 All ER 1.
145 (1890) 45 Ch D 1.
146 *Yugraneft v Abramovich* [2008] EWHC 2613 (Comm), [2008] All ER (Comm) 299, para [373], *per* Clarke J.
147 See section 14.2 below.
148 *Reading v Attorney-General* [1951] 1 All ER 617.
149 *Brinks v Abu-Saleh (No 3)* [1996] CLC 133.
150 *Ibid.*

fiduciary responsibility is considered in detail in Chapter 14. Equally, in context, a solicitor advising clients as to their legal affairs will be a fiduciary and will be a trustee *de son tort* if she interferes with the running of a trust.[151]

The nature of the constructive trust in Attorney-General for Hong Kong v Reid

What is remarkable about the decision in *Reid* is that there is no requirement of any pre-existing proprietary right in the claimant for the establishment of a constructive trust. Instead it is the fiduciary relationship of good faith which means that the defendant is deemed to hold any property received in breach of that duty as a constructive trustee. In *Reid* itself, it is not difficult to see why on policy grounds the court would wish to impose a constructive trust so as to recover the proceeds of his unlawful act from the defendant, although it is notable that the position of Director of Public Prosecutions[152] and of an army sergeant[153] do not ordinarily fall within the ambit of fiduciary relationships. In both of these contexts, it is difficult to identify the beneficiaries of these trusts other than 'the state' or 'the Crown'.[154] Instead, the principles underpinning these decisions are moral principles.

The super-added personal liability to account for any diminution in the value of the property

A second very important issue arises from the judgment in *Reid*. Lord Templeman held that the defendant's liability does not stop with holding the bribe and any property bought with it on constructive trust, but also includes a liability to make good any diminution in the value of those investments from the constructive trustee's own pocket. By holding that the fiduciary is obliged not only to hold the bribes or any substitute property on constructive trust, but also to account to the beneficiaries for any diminution in the value of those investments, the decision in *Attorney-General v Reid* reaches far beyond the simple rules of property law. The additional personal liability to account which is imposed on the malfeasant fiduciary places this particular claim in the category of a wrong for which the defendant is liable to account to the claimant akin to a claim for breach of trust. As considered below in Chapter 18, trustees are liable not only to replace trust property when they commit a breach of trust, but also to account personally to the beneficiaries for any further, outstanding loss. This constructive trust has been explained in terms of requiring the fiduciary to avoid all conflicts between her personal interests and her fiduciary responsibilities,[155] just as the constructive trust considered below in relation to fiduciaries earning unauthorised profits operates.[156] It is certainly concerned with accounting for an equitable wrong.

---

151 *Boardman v Phipps* [1967] 2 AC 46.
152 *Attorney-General for Hong Kong v Reid* [1994] 1 AC 324, [1994] 1 All ER 1. See generally in this regard early discussions such as Sealy, 1962; Jones, 1968, and more recently Worthington, 1999:2.
153 *Reading v Attorney-General* [1951] 1 All ER 617.
154 Although in *Petrotrade Inc v Smith* [2000] 1 Lloyd's Rep 486, the claimant was not able to impose a constructive trust on employees of a shipping agent who had paid bribes to a port authority to obtain the post of port agents, so causing the claimant loss. The constructive trust was not imposed, in effect, because no fiduciary relationship existed between the parties.
155 Millett, 1993, 20.
156 See para 12.5.2 below.

Whether or not this judgment accords with the basis of constructive trusts in conscience

The constructive trust imposed in *Attorney-General v Reid* clearly accords in broad terms with the speech of Lord Browne-Wilkinson in *Westdeutsche Landesbank Girozentrale v Islington LBC*,[157] that a trustee is a person required by good conscience to hold property on trust for another. However, Lord Templeman reached his conclusion by a different route: his Lordship relied on the operation of the equitable principle that 'equity looks upon as done that which ought to have been done' rather than simply declaring the defendant's behaviour to have been unconscionable. What is unclear is the extent to which Lord Templeman's vitriolic, morally-grounded contempt for 'the evil practice' of receiving bribes should be considered to be limited to cases involving bribery and similarly criminal practices, or whether his model of the constructive trust (and in particular the personal liability to account for any reduction in the value of the property acquired with such bribes) should be applied to all constructive trusts, or whether it can be understood as an extreme example of the central principle that constructive trusts arise on the basis of unconscionable behaviour.

Examples of this constructive trust in operation

The approach of the Privy Council in *Attorney-General for Hong Kong v Reid*[158] has been applied in a number of High Court cases.[159] Two of those cases are considered here. First, in *Tesco Stores v Pook*,[160] Mr Pook had tendered invoices in an aggregate amount of about £500,000 for services which had not in fact been rendered. Out of these amounts, the case concerned a total sum of £323,749 which had allegedly been paid as a bribe indirectly to Pook, who had been appointed as a manager in Tesco's e-commerce business in South Korea, by third parties. Pook claimed that the money had been paid to him as a loan to help him start up in business. It was held by Peter Smith J that these payments should be taken to have been a bribe because they were documented by the payer by means of false invoices and a fraudulent VAT claim, rather than as an ordinary loan. His Lordship applied the decision in *Attorney-General for Hong Kong v Reid*[161] to the effect that this bribe should be held on constructive trust.[162] He approved the idea both that the bribe is held on constructive trust and also that when there is any decrease in the value of any property acquired with the bribe then the fiduciary 'is required to make up the difference'.[163] On these facts, because the bribe

157 [1996] AC 669.
158 [1994] 1 AC 324, [1994] 1 All ER 1.
159 *Ocular Sciences Ltd v Aspect Vision Care Ltd* [1997] RPC 289; *Fyffes Group Ltd v Templeman* [2000] 2 Lloyd's Rep 643 (where this case was *obiter*); *Dubai Aluminium Company Ltd v Alawi* [2002] EWHC 2051 (Comm); *Tesco Stores Ltd v Pook* [2003] EWHC 823 (Ch); *Daraydan Holdings Ltd v Solland International Ltd* [2004] EWHC 622 (Ch). In relation to interlocutory relief, such as Mareva injunctions, the *Lister v Stubbs* approach has also been displaced in favour of the approach in *Attorney-General v Reid: Mercedes Benz AG v Leiduck* [1996] AC 284, 300. This approach has not been followed in *Attorney-General v Blake* [1997] Ch 84, 96, *per* Sir Richard Scott VC; *Halifax Building Society v Thomas* [1996] Ch 217, 229, preferring the approach in *Lister v Stubbs*.
160 [2003] EWHC 823 (Ch).
161 [1994] 1 AC 324, [1994] 1 All ER 1.
162 [2003] EWHC 823 (Ch), paras [45] and [69].
163 *Ibid*, para [69].

had been made by means of a false invoice together with a fraudulent claim for recovery of VAT (that is, a claim for recovery of VAT which had purportedly been paid under this false invoice for a service rendered), it was held that the value of the bribe which should be accounted for was the amount of the invoice falsely rendered together with the VAT amount. Thus, any value received as part of the transaction comprising the bribe will be deemed to be held on constructive trust.

Secondly, in *Daraydan Holdings Ltd v Solland International Ltd*,[164] a married couple, the Sollands, who were directors of a company which was involved in the refurbishment of property in London, connived in the appropriation of a secret commission which was procured by arbitrarily increasing the budget for a refurbishment project by 10% and then diverting that extra 10% so as to pay 'kickbacks'[165] to Khalid. It was found as a fact that Khalid was employed by the person who ultimately controlled a group of organisations which included the company, and thus was acting as a fiduciary. The secret commission, or 'kickback', of 10% was held to have been equivalent to a bribe in this case.[166] Lawrence Collins J began his judgment by quoting that sentence from Lord Templeman in *Reid* to the effect that '[b]ribery is an evil practice which threatens the foundations of any civilised society'.[167] It was held that an agent ought not to put himself into a situation in which his duty and his personal interest conflict. Thus, the constructive trust here was based on avoidance of conflict of interest[168] as well as the need to deal with the 'evil practice' of bribery. It was explained that the constructive trust in this case was further justified because the bribes were drawn from the claimant's property (being the payments for the refurbishment) and also on the basis that the bribes were paid as part of a fraudulent misrepresentation exercised by the Sollands. It was held further that where, as on these facts, a bribe has been paid here by an employee (the Sollands) to a third party (Khalid), and when that third party is acting in a fiduciary capacity, then both parties are required to account jointly and severally for the receipt of that bribe.[169] Consequently, the bribe was deemed to have been held on constructive trust, just as in *Reid*.

Secret commissions

There are occasions on which the principles relating to 'bribes' are treated together with 'secret commissions'. A secret commission is in many cases synonymous with a bribe, in that a person is in receipt of money covertly. Whereas Lord Templeman suggested that an undisclosed commission would not necessarily be treated in the same way as a bribe, it is not always clear what is meant by a 'commission' in this context because the judges have not

---

164   [2004] EWHC 622 (Ch), [2004] 3 WLR 1106; [2005] Ch 1.
165   As described in evidence: [2004] EWHC 622 (Ch), [2004] 3 WLR 1106, para [63].
166   It was found that the employee, Solland, was assisting the agent, Khalid, by permitting him to withhold a 10% secret commission. Khalid was deemed to be a fiduciary on the basis that his contractual link to the organisation was taken to have rendered him an employee of that organisation: [2004] EWHC 622 (Ch), [2004] 3 WLR 1106, para [74]. The defence to the bribe rested in part on an assertion that the bribe was a necessary inducement which had to be paid to third parties as part of the creation of the development contracts.
167   [1994] 1 AC 324, 330.
168   Considered below in section 12.5 in relation to *Boardman v Phipps* [1967] 2 AC 46, the liability for fiduciaries earning unauthorised profits.
169   [2004] EWHC 622 (Ch), [2004] 3 WLR 1106, para [54].

defined their terms. A commission like the 'kickback' in *Daraydan v Solland* which is undisclosed to the beneficiary of the fiduciary arrangement was found to be equivalent to a bribe. Whereas Lord Templeman suggested in *Attorney-General for Hong Kong v Reid* that an undisclosed commission would not necessarily be treated in the same way as a bribe, it is not always clear what is meant by a 'commission' in this context because the judges have not always defined their terms. It is suggested that a secret commission is a payment which is made to a fiduciary unbeknownst to its principal which is usually made by a person. There have been two approaches in the cases.

The older cases took the view that secret commissions occupied a different category. That approach seemed to be followed by the Court of Appeal in *Imageview Management Ltd v Jack*,[170] in which it was held that an agent would be required to account for profits taken from secret commissions on the basis set out in the older cases.[171] In that case a footballer's agent had taken a commission directly from the club for which his principal, a goalkeeper, had signed over-and-above his fee from his principal and without disclosing the commission to his principal. It was held that the agent's commission should be forfeited by the agent accounting to his principal for the amount of the commission. The core principle was that set out in *Boston Deep Sea Fishing and Ice Co v Ansell* where Bowen LJ held as follows:[172]

> Now, there can be no question that an agent employed by a principal or master to do business with another, who, unknown to that principal or master, takes from that other person a profit arising out of the business which he is employed to transact, is doing a wrongful act inconsistent with his duty towards his master, and the continuance of confidence between them. He does the wrongful act whether such profit be given to him in return for services which he actually performs for the third party, or whether it be given to him for his supposed influence, or whether it be given to him on any other ground at all; if it is a profit which arises out of the transaction, it belongs to his master, and the agent or servant has no right to take it, or keep it, or bargain for it, or to receive without bargain, unless his master knows it.

This approach can be understood in line with *Attorney-General for Hong Kong v Reid* in that the principal is deemed to acquire ownership of the commission from the moment of its receipt.[173]

It is clear that agents acting for their principals must avoid conflicts of interest in the form of undisclosed commissions. Agents acting for their clients must avoid conflicts of interest in the form of undisclosed commissions. So, in *Hurstanger Ltd v Wilson*, where an agent was retained to act as broker for a cohabiting couple in relation to the mortgage over their home, he was acting as a fiduciary in that context and would be treated as having acted on a conflict of interest where he acquired a mortgage for the couple based in part on the commission

---

170 [2009] Bus LR 1034.

171 *Boston Deep Sea Fishing and Ice Co v Ansell* (1888) 39 Ch D 339, CA; *Andrews v Ramsay & Co* [1903] 2 KB 635, DC; *Rhodes v Macalister* (1923) 29 Com Cas 19, CA.

172 (1888) 39 Ch D 339, 363.

173 Applied in *Imageview Management Ltd v Jack* [2009] Bus LR 1034 (although doubting the usefulness of the concept of fraud in this context) without citing *Att-Gen v Reid* but relying in part on *Boardman v Phipps*.

which he stood to earn from that mortgage.[174] Therefore, he would be required to account for that commission and for any profits derived from that commission. The onus was on the agent to make full disclosure of the commission which he stood to earn to the customer. In this instance an award of equitable compensation was considered sufficient to right the agent's breach of fiduciary duty. Usually the purpose of such a transaction would be to induce the recipient to act in a corrupt manner. An example of patterns of secret commissions are set out in *Pakistan v Zadari*,[175] a case which – at a purely interlocutory stage – relates to allegations that unauthorised payments were made at the behest of the husband of a former Prime Minister of Pakistan through a series of companies to acquire a 350-acre estate in Surrey and in connection with a variety of other transactions. While it was not necessary to dispose of the facts at this interlocutory stage in the proceedings, in the event that it could be proved that the estate was acquired with secret commissions or bribes then Lawrence Collins J indicated that that estate would be held on constructive trust for the state of Pakistan.

The approach in Sinclair Investment v Versailles Trading – *doubting* Reid

The unfortunate decision of the Court of Appeal in *Sinclair Investments (UK) Ltd v Versailles Trading Ltd*[176] has cast doubt on the *Reid* principle. There has been a long line of cases dealing with the failure of the Versailles Trading group which comprised companies set up by Carl Cushnie which were intended to operate a fraudulent Ponzi scheme.[177] In essence, the Versailles companies took investments from 'traders' and borrowed huge amounts of money from banks on the promise that those borrowings would be invested in a commercial activity known as 'factoring' goods.[178] In truth, the borrowed moneys were simply passed around in complex circles – a process known as 'cross-firing' – so as to make it appear that the companies were engaging in a large number of transactions, when in truth the companies did nothing.[179] As a result, when the fraud was uncovered, Cushnie and others were convicted of criminal offences. This particular case involved a claim over shares which had been bought through the scheme by Cushnie, then sold, and the proceeds used to buy a valuable

---

174 *Hurstanger Ltd v Wilson* [2007] EWCA Civ 299, [2007] 1 WLR 2351.

175 [2006] EWHC 2411 (Comm), [2006] All ER (D) 79 (Oct).

176 [2011] 3 WLR 1153.

177 A Ponzi scheme is a scheme in which a shyster takes investments from investors, pools those investments, and then pays the investors a portion of their capital investment back periodically so as to make it appear that they have made a profit on their investment, while in the meantime living off the rest of the capital themselves. Such a scheme needs a constant flow of new investors to keep the scheme's capital high. Such schemes fail when no new investors can be found or when too many of the investors take their capital back at once. The best-known example of such a scheme in recent times was the Madoff organisation which collapsed in the wake of the 2008 financial crisis in what was dubbed a '$60 billion Ponzi scheme' in the Press.

178 In essence, buying and selling debts, or packaging lots of rights to receive money together and selling those debts off as a package.

179 In JK Galbraith's seminal book *The Great Crash 1929*, 1955, Prof Galbraith described how investment institutions made themselves appear to be larger than they were by using 'leverage', which meant the same small initial loan was invested back and forth several times by companies in the same group so as to make it appear that those companies had a huge amount of capital. Versailles Trading did the same thing in effect through cross-firing payments between companies. This also made it appear that the company was engaged in lots of trading activity, just as the Madoff enterprises had done.

house in Kensington. In essence, the claimant wanted to establish a proprietary constructive trust over the Kensington house. In the meantime, the companies and people involved in the scheme were insolvent and therefore the counter-argument was put that there should not be any such proprietary rights over that Kensington house so that it could be divided up among the unsecured creditors in the various insolvencies. The Court of Appeal held, *inter alia*, that there should not be such a constructive trust in this case.[180] In essence the reason for that decision was to maximise the assets available to the unsecured creditors in general, but the rationale used for that decision is important in relation to the *Reid* principle.

Lord Neuberger presented three arguments in his judgment for not following *Reid*, and not one of them is convincing in itself. First, it is said that the Court of Appeal should follow the decisions of previous Courts of Appeal as opposed to decisions of the Privy Council – and that instead it should be left to the Supreme Court to overrule those Court of Appeal judgments if it so chooses. This means that in this case decisions which were over one hundred years old were to be preferred to the judgments of House of Lords judges sitting only fifteen years previously in the Privy Council. This ignoring of decisions of the Privy Council as a matter of law is anachronistic. Second, it was said that there is a greater weight of journal literature in favour of *Lister v Stubbs* than *Reid*. However, Lord Neuberger does not consider the arguments in any of those articles; instead his lordship simply lists them. He also noted that the trusts law textbooks are generally in agreement with the decision in *Reid* (as this textbook has always been) and failed to note two things: first, textbook writers take a view of the entire topic of trusts law whereas, secondly, many journal articles are written by academics seeking deliberately to take a contrarian point of view in relation to the decided cases so as to make it more likely that their article will be published. It easier for an academic to criticise a judgment in an article than to support it.

Third, and the only substantive argument, Lord Neuberger considered it significant that if a proprietary constructive trust were imposed in favour of the claimant then the assets which were held on trust would not be available to be distributed among the other creditors. This is the heart of the judgment and the real reason for it. The point is simple. If Insolvent takes a bribe in spite of the fiduciary duties which it owes to Beneficiary, and if that bribe and the profits earned with that bribe are held on constructive trust for Beneficiary, then those profits are not be available to be distributed among the unsecured creditors of Insolvent. What Lord Neuberger prefers is that the amount of the bribe should be considered to be a debt, akin to *Lister v Stubbs*, so that the claimant becomes an unsecured creditor and so that the profits generally form part of the insolvent person's estate so that they can be distributed *pari passu* among the unsecured creditors. Instead, it was held that a claimant could only claim a proprietary interest in a bribe if that bribe had involved property which had previously been held on trust by the insolvent person for the claimant. Therefore, the *Reid* constructive trust would only work if there had been a pre-existing trust and if the bribe or similar payment involved property held on that pre-existing trust.

The situation was different in *Reid* because in *Reid* the defendant was not insolvent and therefore there were no insolvency creditors seeking access to assets so as to meet their

---

180 The approach in *Sinclair v Versailles Trading* was followed in *Cadogan Petroleum plc v Tolly* [2011] EWHC 2286 by Newey J; and remarks as to the extent of fiduciary duties were recognised in *Horn v Commercial Acceptances Ltd* [2011] EWHC 1757 (Ch) by Smith J.

claims; whereas in *Sinclair* the opposite is true. The fact of insolvency is therefore making the legal principle here.[181] It is suggested that it would be more satisfactory to establish the most appropriate equitable principle and then to consider how to deal with cases of insolvency. In essence, there is a sense that the Court of Appeal in *Sinclair* thinks that the imposition of the constructive trust is too tenuous to justify taking valuable assets (such as a property in Kensington) out of the insolvent person's estate so as to ring-fence for the purposes of this constructive trust.

The nub of the decision in *Sinclair Investments (UK) Ltd v Versailles Trade Finance Ltd*[182] was set out in the judgment of Lord Neuberger MR where his lordship held that:[183]

> [I]t seems to me that there is a real case for saying that the decision in *Reid* . . . is unsound. In cases where a fiduciary takes for himself an asset which, if he chose to take, he was under a duty to take for the beneficiary, it is easy to see why the asset should be treated as the property of the beneficiary. However, a bribe paid to a fiduciary could not possibly be said to be an asset which the fiduciary was under a duty to take for the beneficiary. There can thus be said to be a fundamental distinction between (i) a fiduciary enriching himself by depriving a claimant of an asset and (ii) a fiduciary enriching himself by doing a wrong to the claimant. Having said that, I can see a real policy reason in its favour (if equitable accounting is not available), but the fact that it may not accord with principle is obviously a good reason for not following it in preference to decisions of this court.

This, it is suggested, is a poor argument. In essence, it is said that because the fiduciary should not have received the bribe then it should not be held on trust. This has the effect that if the fiduciary invests that bribe successfully then she is able to keep the profits for herself because she is not obliged to hold those profits on constructive trust but rather, under *Lister v Stubbs*, only to account for the cash value of the bribe to the beneficiary. This allows fiduciaries to keep the fruits of their unconscionable actions, which is clearly inequitable. Of course, bad people should not do bad things; but if those bad people do bad things then equity and the common law should not conspire to allow them to keep the fruits of their actions. The common law is simply not equipped to punish the malfeasing fiduciary because, as *Lister v Stubbs* shows, the bribe is treated simply as a debt to be paid to the beneficiary. The judgment of Lord Templeman in *Reid*, however, demonstrates that classical equitable principles based on constructive trust are ideally suited to this role of taking the bribe from the wrongdoing fiduciary and of taking a proprietary right in any profits derived from that bribe. The judgment of the Court of Appeal should be disapplied in the future because it is bad in principle.

There are several other difficulties with Lord Neuberger's judgment. First, it is unclear which part of this transaction constitutes a bribe, and why *Reid* needs to be considered at all.

---

181 One must be careful with this argument: it is the basis of the judgment in *Westdeutsche Landesbank v Islington* [1996] AC 669 in rejecting the argument posited by Professor Birks that resulting trusts should operate so as to effect restitution of payments made under a mistake.

182 [2011] EWCA Civ 347, [2011] 3 WLR 1151. The approach in *Sinclair v Versailles Trading* was followed in *Cadogan Petroleum plc v Tolly* [2011] EWHC 2286 by Newey J; and remarks in *Sinclair* as to the extent of fiduciary duties were recognised in *Horn v Commercial Acceptances Ltd* [2011] EWHC 1757 (Ch) by Smith J.

183 [2011] EWCA Civ 347, [2011] 3 WLR 1151, at [80].

In future, it should be considered that these remarks were *obiter dicta* in relation to *Reid*. It is settled authority that *Boardman v Phipps*, considered below, established a principle that a constructive trust is imposed in cases of conflicts of interest by a fiduciary, as was the case here, and therefore the conclusion which is based on a merely partial consideration of the authorities by Lord Neuberger should be ignored in the future. Second, several High Court cases have followed *Reid*, but none of those reasoned judgments was considered by the Court of Appeal. Third, one of the more objectionable facets of Lord Neuberger's judgment is that he did not consider the most important part of Lord Templeman's speech in which he identified the reason for imposing a constructive trust. In essence the argument advanced by Lord Templeman was that if there were an express trust in place, then there would be no doubt that the bribe and any profits would also be held on the terms of that trust, and thus be beyond the reach of any unsecured creditors. Therefore, the only argument is whether or not a constructive trust could be imposed in these circumstances where there was no such express trust. To that, Lord Templeman would say that a constructive trust is appropriate here because the receipt of the bribe was wrong, and therefore because equity requires that the fiduciary must account for any unauthorised payment received in the course of her duties then that profit should be deemed to have been accounted for by means of a constructive trust. On that basis, between solvent parties, the constructive trust is unobjectionable. Under trusts law there should be a proprietary constructive trust. Therefore, as part of trusts law the same analysis should apply between parties one of whom is insolvent. The only issue is whether *as part of insolvency law* there should be a different analysis. This argument is objected to in *Lister v Stubbs* but the reasons for that disagreement are not set out.

In truth, this is the longest-running argument in English law between commercial lawyers – who generally want insolvencies to be played out in an orderly way so that unsecured creditors receive the maximum volume of assets to meet their claims against the insolvent person – and property lawyers – who typically want to operate property concepts the same in relation to solvent and insolvent parties. For commercial lawyers, insolvency is the context which trumps all other concerns. There are no right or wrong answers, just polarised points of view. Do we protect property rights created under the general principles of trusts law, as in *Reid*, or do we limit the means by which property rights can be acquired so as to increase slightly the pool of assets available to the unsecured creditors? What is missing from this debate is any meaningful research into the volume of assets which would be made available to the unsecured creditors as a proportion of their total claims. In large-scale frauds as in *Sinclair Investment v Versailles Trading*, or the similar but much larger Madoff collapse, it is questionable whether the Court of Appeal disturbing well-established trusts law will actually have a meaningful effect on the position of those unsecured creditors in cash terms.

The obligations of company directors in relation to bribes under statute

The Companies Act 2006 introduced a statutory code of directors' general duties for the first time.[184] The directors' duties in the Act are 'based on certain common law rules and equitable principles'[185] and moreover those statutory duties 'shall be interpreted and applied in

---

184 Companies Act 2006, s.170 *et seq.*
185 Companies Act 2006, s.170(3).

the same way as common law rules or equitable principles'.[186] The statutory duties are then to be interpreted in the future in accordance with the development of those case law principles.[187] The principles in relation to bribes are predicated on the equitable doctrines relating to bribes (as in *Attorney-General for Hong Kong v Reid*).[188]

Consequently, there are specific statutory rules relating to company directors, as distinct from trustees. Section 176(1) of the Companies Act 2006 provides (in relation to bribes set out in *Reid*) that 'a director of a company must not accept a benefit from a third party conferred by reason of (a) his being a director, or (b) his doing (or not doing) anything as director'. In this context the term 'third party' 'means a person other than the company, an associated body corporate or a person acting on behalf of the company or an associated body corporate'.[189] Furthermore, under s 176(3) it is provided that '[b]enefits received by a director from a person by whom his services (as a director or otherwise) are provided to the company are not regarded as conferred by a third party'. Section 176(4) provides, however, that 'this duty is not infringed if the acceptance of the benefit cannot reasonably be regarded as likely to give rise to a conflict of interest'. In effect, both of these provisions grant defences to directors for actions which otherwise attracted almost strict liability in equity. The authors of *Lewin on Trusts* have taken the view that the principle in *Sinclair v Versailles Trading* may apply only to company directors and not to trustees.[190]

12.4.2 Profits from killing

It is a well-established principle of equity that killing another person will make the killer a constructive trustee of any property acquired as a result of that killing. This principle applies in general terms to all forms of killing which constitute a criminal offence.[191] In consequence, a person guilty of murder will fall within the principle,[192] as will a person convicted of inciting others to murder her husband[193] and (controversially, because it does not require intention) causing death by reckless driving.[194] It has been held that the principle will not cover involuntary manslaughter where there was no intention to kill,[195] or killing for which there is a defence such as insanity.[196] It is not necessarily a pre-requisite of the application of this principle that there have been criminal proceedings to establish the guilt of the defendant, provided that the criminal activity is proved at the civil proceedings to the criminal standard of proof.[197]

A murderer will not be entitled to take good title in property which is acquired solely by murdering its previous owner. Therefore, in the stuff of crime fiction, when the assassin despatches the victim so as to gain access to her personal wealth, equity will intervene and

186 Companies Act 2006, s.170(4).
187 Companies Act 2006, s.170(4).
188 Companies Act 2006, s.178.
189 Companies Act 2006, s176(2).
190 Lewin on Trusts, 2011, 2nd supplement, para 20–28A and B.
191 *Gray v Barr* [1971] 2 QB 554.
192 *In the Estate of Crippen* [1911] P 108.
193 *Evans v Evans* [1989] 1 FLR 351.
194 *R v Seymour (Edward)* [1983] AC 493.
195 *Re K (Deceased)* [1986] Ch 180; *Re H (Deceased)* [1990] 1 FLR 441.
196 *Re Holgate* (1971) unreported; Criminal Procedure (Insanity) Act 1964, s 1.
197 *Re Sigsworth* [1935] 1 Ch 89.

hold that the murderer holds any property so acquired as a constructive trustee for the victim's estate. In general terms, a murderer, as with a thief (considered at para 12.4.3 below), will not acquire good title in property acquired by way of murder.[198]

However, two problems emerge. First, what if the proceeds of crime are said to be passed to a third person? In the case of *In the Estate of Crippen*,[199] the infamous Dr Crippen had murdered his wife Cora Crippen.[200] Crippen had intended to flee the country with his mistress but was, equally famously, captured on a boat while in flight by virtue of the comparatively new invention of wireless telegraphy when a description of Crippen was wired to the ship. The *Crippen* appeal itself considered the question whether or not property which would ordinarily have passed to Crippen as his wife's next-of-kin ought to pass to his mistress as Crippen's intended legatee. It was held that, given the context of the murder, no rights would transfer to the mistress because Crippen was deemed to hold them on constructive trust for his wife's estate and therefore could not pass them to his mistress beneficially.

The murderer becomes constructive trustee of all rights and interests in property which would have vested in him under the deceased's will,[201] or even as next-of-kin in relation to a deceased who did not leave a will.[202] The criminal will not acquire rights under any life assurance policy which has been taken out over the life of the deceased.[203] Similarly, a murderer will not be entitled to take a beneficial interest under the widow's pension entitlements of his murdered wife.[204]

Secondly, what of the murderer who would have received that property in any event and only hastened its acquisition by killing its previous owner? The point is that the killer would not be acquiring property in which he would not otherwise have had any interest at all (as, for example, with the situation where a murderer steals property from the victim), but rather would be acquiring property in which he would have acquired that interest in the fullness of time in any event. Suppose, for example, that a joint tenant would have been entitled to an absolute interest on the victim's death in any event, but that she killed the victim so as to acquire that interest at an earlier date. It has been held that in such a situation, the killer would acquire the entire legal interest on the survivorship principle, but would hold that equitable interest on constructive trust for herself and for the representatives of the deceased as tenants in common.[205] It has been suggested *obiter* that where a remainder beneficiary killed the life tenant, that remainder beneficiary should be prevented from taking the entire beneficial interest until such period as suggested by actuarial estimate would have been the time when the life tenant would probably have died.[206] What emerges from *Crippen*[207] is that

---

198 Oakley, Parker and Mellows, 1998, 356.

199 [1911] P 108.

200 In the published transcript of the trial it becomes clear that Cora had been unfaithful to her husband many times and he had been driven to extreme jealousy, so had decided to kill her and (hypocritically enough) to flee with his own mistress. It was said of Cora, by reference to her faithlessness, that she was a woman 'the path to whose affections was both easy of access and well-trodden'. Never was such an insult put so beautifully nor has a woman been so hypocritically treated by male commentators.

201 *Re Sigsworth* [1935] 1 Ch 89.

202 *In the Estate of Crippen* [1911] P 108.

203 *Cleaver v Mutual Reserve Fund Life Association* [1892] 1 QB 147.

204 *R v Chief National Insurance Commissioner ex p Connor* [1981] 1 QB 758.

205 *Re K (Deceased)* [1986] Fam 180.

206 *Re Calloway* [1956] Ch 559.

207 *In the Estate of Crippen* [1911] P 108.

the murderer will be deprived of such an interest where he would otherwise have taken that very interest if, for example, the victim had been knocked down accidentally on the day of the planned murder by a No 19 bus before the assassin had carried out his plan. Therefore, Crippen could not have argued that he would have received the interest later anyway if his wife had died of natural causes.[208]

One issue which should be borne in mind is that the courts do not have any principled argument based on property law to justify this principle.[209] Suppose, for example, that the murderer could prove she would have received an interest anyway: an amoral code of property law would have to recognise the murderer's property rights. However, because equity has a moral base, it denies those property rights. The courts, it is suggested, are concerned with the punishment of the defendant. The punishment here is clearly different from that exerted by the criminal law in that there is no incarceration nor any formal power to fine the defendant. However, in the example of the defendant who acquired rights in property earlier than she would otherwise have been entitled, it is clear that if the court refuses to recognise property rights in the defendant which the defendant would otherwise have received, then the court is taking property from the defendant and so performing an act tantamount to punishment: after all, where is the practical distinction between ordering that a person is to be denied access to property which would otherwise have been hers, and fining her?

Exceptionally, in the case of *Re K (Deceased)*, a wife, who had been the victim of domestic violence, picked up a shotgun during an attack on her by her husband which went off accidentally, killing him. Under the Forfeiture Act 1982, the court exercised its discretion to make an order not to oblige the wife to hold property received as a result of her husband's death on constructive trust. The underlying purpose of this principle, which has been accepted in Commonwealth jurisdictions, is that the criminal should simply not benefit from her wrong, as has been held in Canada,[210] South Africa,[211] Australia[212] and New Zealand.[213] But the case of *Re K*[214] demonstrates that the killer may be excused from liability where the killing was not wholly intentional. The purpose of the constructive trust in these circumstances is to prevent a murderer – in the popular imagination perhaps the worst kind of criminal – from taking a benefit from that crime. This is, as said above, to do with retribution and not restitution.

12.4.3 Profits from theft

The further issue with reference to cases of theft is as follows: what are the obligations of a thief in relation to the original owner of the stolen property? The proper answer, drawing on *Attorney-General for Hong Kong v Reid*,[215] would appear to be that the thief is liable as a constructive trustee to hold the property for the victim of the crime. That the thief holds the

---

208 Compare this approach with the amorality in *Tribe v Tribe* (in section 11.4.6) where an unconscionable intention did not prevent the finding of a resulting trust.
209 Youdan (1973) 89 LQR 235.
210 *Schobelt v Barber* [1967] 59 DLR (2d) 519 (Ont).
211 *Re Barrowcliff* [1927] SASR 147.
212 *Rosmanis v Jurewitsch* (1970) 70 SR (NSW) 407.
213 *Re Pechar* [1969] NZLR 574.
214 [1986] Fam 180.
215 [1994] 1 AC 324, [1994] 1 All ER 1.

stolen property on constructive trust has been upheld, albeit *obiter*, in England,[216] and also in Australia[217] and Canada.[218] In consequence, the victim of the crime acquires an equitable interest against the thief and therefore is able to establish a common law tracing claim to recover the stolen property[219] and an equitable tracing claim in any substitute property,[220] as considered in Chapter 19.

It might be thought that this constructive trust resembles a resulting trust, but there is no suggestion that the victim of a theft could have voluntarily transferred any title to the thief: the trust must be one which is imposed by operation of law regardless of the wishes of the parties, in particular, contrary to the wishes of the thief. Indeed, it is suggested that the preferable explanation of the property law treatment of stolen property would be to find that the property rights in the stolen goods never leave the victim of crime, because it is only the original owner of property who can transfer title in that property and clearly a victim of crime does not consent to the transfer of title to a thief. In this sense, it is contended that the proper approach is for the court to make a declaration vindicating the property rights of the victim of the crime regardless of the claims of any other person.[221]

The more difficult context arises when the stolen property has been transferred to a third party. If the property were passed to someone who had notice of the fact that it was stolen, there would clearly be an offence of handling stolen goods,[222] and that wrongful recipient of those goods must hold them on constructive trust for their original owner.[223] So, money stolen from a bank account can be traced in equity through other bank accounts.[224] The complication arises when the thief then purports to sell that property to an innocent third party. There are two competing equitable principles at play. First, the innocent purchaser would claim to be a *bona fide* purchaser for value without notice and therefore entitled to the protection of equity as being equity's darling. This approach was accepted by Lord Browne-Wilkinson in *Westdeutsche Landesbank v Islington LBC*.[225] It is a principle which operates to protect free markets in property by assuring the recipient of property that she can acquire good title in that property regardless of the root of title of that property, always provided that the purchaser does not have notice of the theft.

Imposing a constructive trust on the thief has the ostensibly odd result of seeming to confer legal title in the stolen property on her as constructive trustee.[226] Given that the victim

---

216 *Lipkin Gorman v Karpnale* [1991] 2 AC 548, *per* Lord Templeman; *Westdeutsche Landesbank Girozentrale v Islington LBC* [1996] AC 669, *per* Lord Browne-Wilkinson. Cf the Proceeds of Crime Act 2002 in relation to the recovery of the proceeds of organised crime through a statutory agency.

217 *Black v S Freedman & Co* (1910) 12 CLR 105.

218 *Lennox Industries (Canada) Ltd v The Queen* (1987) 34 DLR 297.

219 *Jones (FC) & Sons v Jones* [1996] 3 WLR 703.

220 *Bishopsgate v Homan* [1995] 1 WLR 31; *Ghana Commercial Bank v C* (1997) *The Times*, 3 March.

221 See *Foskett v McKeown* [2000] 3 All ER 97.

222 Theft Act 1968, s 22.

223 *Attorney-General for Hong Kong v Reid* [1994] 1 AC 324, [1994] 1 All ER 1.

224 *Bankers Trust Co v Shapira* [1980] 1 WLR 1274, 1282.

225 [1996] AC 669.

226 *Shalson v Russo* [2003] EWHC 1637 (Ch), [110], *per* Rimer J, where his Lordship opined that the thief cannot ordinarily be understood to acquire any proprietary interests in stolen property. Nevertheless, he was prepared to find that, in accordance with *Banque Belge pour l'Etranger v Hambrouk* [1921] 1 KB 321, 332, *per* Atkin LJ, the victim of fraud ought to be able to trace after property appropriate from him as part of the fraudulent scheme. See also *Box, Brown & Jacobs v Barclays Bank* [1998] Lloyd's Rep Bank 185, 200, *per* Ferris J in the same vein.

of crime does not consent to the transfer of title to the thief, it would be better to find that no title can be said to pass to the purchaser from the thief so that thief would have no title to give. That would be to reinforce the principle of *caveat emptor* (that is, 'let the buyer beware'). The benefit of the constructive trust is that it enables the victim of the theft to use equitable principles to recover the value of the stolen property. What is particularly useful about the constructive trust in such circumstances is that it provides the victim of crime with a right to trace in equity (as the beneficiary under a constructive trust) so as to recover the traceable proceeds of the stolen property. For example, if the stolen property were used to buy a car, then that car could be subjected to the constructive trust. This issue is pursued in greater detail in Chapter 19.

A difficult case arising in criminal law was that of *Attorney-General's Reference (No 1 of 1985)*,[227] which related to a publican who leased premises from a brewery under an obligation to sell only the brewery's products but who nevertheless used the brewery's equipment (their pumps and so forth) to sell beer which he had bought on his own account. The question asked of the court was whether or not the publican had committed an offence under the Theft Act:[228] to make out this offence, it would have been necessary to show that the money received by the publican from this venture was the property of the brewery on the basis that the money should have been held on constructive trust for the brewery. It was held that there was no proprietary constructive trust which would found liability for the criminal offence and instead that the publican was only obliged to account in civil law to the brewery for his secret profits.[229] This decision is, it is suggested, wrong in so far as it relates to trusts law. The court's *ratio decidendi* was that there were no property rights to show that the publican had stolen the brewery's money: that may well be correct as a question of criminal law. As regards trusts law, however, the publican was found expressly to have been a fiduciary and expressly to be liable to account to the brewery for his profits: therefore, there is no possible conclusion on principle other than that he ought to have been required to account as a constructive trustee.[230]

On a further point of criminal law relating to the recovery of property lost due to theft, the Proceeds of Crime Act 2002 has created the Assets Recovery Agency which is empowered to confiscate property from criminals which has been used in relation to a criminal lifestyle.[231] However, it is suggested that this Act casts little light on the civil liabilities for the recovery of stolen property except that it demonstrates that participation in money laundering is also an unlawful activity. The amount recoverable from the defendant under the 2002 Act is an amount equal to the benefit which the criminal took from his criminal lifestyle.[232]

227 [1986] QB 491.
228 Theft Act 1968, s 5(3).
229 See Archbold's *Criminal Pleading, Evidence and Practice*, 2005, paras 21–69 and 21–70, which still refers to *Lister v Stubbs* and to *R v Governor of Pentonville Prison ex p Tarling* (1978) 70 Cr App R 77, HL, but not to *Attorney-General for Hong Kong v Reid*, as considered above.
230 *Boardman v Phipps* [1967] 2 AC 46, considered at 12.5.2 below.
231 Proceeds of Crime Act 2002, s 6. The elements of such a lifestyle under Sched 2 to the Act include drug trafficking, money-laundering and directing terrorism.
232 *Ibid*, s 7(1).

12.4.4 Profits from fraud

Constructive trust in relation to fraud

The principle that a statute or a rule of common law cannot be used as an engine of fraud was considered above in para 12.3.4. Similarly to that principle, where a criminal, or a person not convicted of a criminal offence, acquires interests in property by means of fraud, the fraudster will be required to hold the property so acquired on constructive trust for the original owner of that property.[233] Under general principles of constructive trust, it would be unconscionable for the fraudster to retain property acquired by fraud[234] unless the victim acquiesced in the fraud.[235] Fraudulent conduct in this equitable context will include representing to the occupant of a cottage that she will be entitled to live in that cottage for the rest of her life and then seeking to evict her.[236] At the other end of the spectrum there are forms of fraud which will constitute criminal offences, such as obtaining pecuniary advantage by deception which will also be recognised by equity. A defendant is not prevented from relying on his rights where, for example, the interest is not registered as required by some rule of formality,[237] unless there is some unconscionability in that action.[238] In consequence, this equitable notion of fraud is more akin to unconscionable behaviour generally, as opposed to the more formalistic requirement at common law that fraud requires that the defendants either have known that their actions were deceitful or were reckless as to whether or not such was the case.[239]

In cases of fraud, a constructive trust will therefore be imposed over any property acquired further to that fraud. So, in *Bank of Ireland v Pexxnet Ltd*[240] the defendants presented forged instruments at a branch of the claimant bank which caused the bank to credit the defendants' accounts with approximately €2.4 million before the forgery was discovered. It was held that this constituted an unconscionable act which, further to *Westdeutsche Landesbank v Islington*,[241] meant that that money was to be held on constructive trust by the accountholders for the bank.[242] This was held to be a 'classic case' of the constructive trust in *Westdeutsche Landesbank v Islington*. Those defendants who could be proved to have known of the fraud would therefore be required to hold property on constructive trust. Some of the money had been transferred to a third party, which meant that an equitable tracing claim in respect of that money could be commenced. Similarly, in *Glen Dimplex Home Appliances Ltd v Smith*[243] the first defendant committed a straightforwardly fraudulent act by diverting £2.8

---

233 *Rochefoucauld v Boustead* [1897] 1 Ch 196.
234 *Westdeutsche Landesbank Girozentrale v Islington LBC* [1996] AC 669; *Kuwait Oil Tanker Co SA*K *v Al Bader (No 3)* (1999) *The Independent*, 11 January.
235 *Lonrho plc v Fayed (No 2)* [1992] 1 WLR 1.
236 *Bannister v Bannister* [1948] 2 All ER 133; *Neale v Willis* (1968) 110 SJ 521; *Binions v Evans* [1972] Ch 359.
237 *Midland Bank Trust Company v Green* [1981] AC 513.
238 *Peffer v Rigg* [1977] 1 WLR 285.
239 *Peek v Gurney* (1873) LR 6 HL 377.
240 [2010] EWHC 1872.
241 Especially the passage in the speech of Lord Browne-Wilkinson at [1996] AC 669, 715. Briggs J also referred to the summary of the law given by Lawrence Collins J in *Commerzbank AG v IMB Morgan plc* [2004] EWHC 2771 (Ch), [2005] 1 Lloyd's Rep 298 rather than primarily on the decision of the House of Lords in *Westdeutsche Landesbank v Islington*, and also on *Trustor v Smallbone (No 3)*, unreported, to the same effect.
242 [2010] EWHC 1872, [55]–[57].
243 [2011] EWHC 3392 (Ch).

million from her employer into bank accounts in the name of her husband and her daughter (the second and third defendants). The fraud was discovered when she was away from work. The issues concerned the second and third defendants.[244] The money was clearly impressed with a constructive trust. Following *Royal Brunei Airlines v Tan*[245] it was held that it would be dishonest to fail to ask questions about the money in the account and to close one's eyes. It was held that the second defendant had been dishonest on this basis; however, it was not proven that the third defendant had appreciated that the money had been acquired by fraud. Nevertheless, the third defendant would have no defence to an equitable tracing action (further to the constructive trust imposed over those moneys) brought to recover the money held in her bank account.

In general terms, then, with the exception of fraudulent misrepresentation,[246] the commission of fraud will constitute a form of unconscionable behaviour which will found a constructive trust. As was held by Lord Browne-Wilkinson in *Westdeutsche Landesbank v Islington*:[247]

> when property is obtained by fraud, equity places a constructive trust on the fraudulent recipient.

In line with the general principle underpinning constructive trusts, then, a fraudulent act must be an unconscionable act such that any profits acquired from that fraud ought to be held on constructive trust for the victim of the fraud. This approach has been applied in four cases in the High Court,[248] but it has not been followed in two other High Court decisions on the basis that fraudulent misrepresentations are ordinarily voidable at the election of the victim of the fraud and therefore ought not to give rise to a constructive trust automatically.[249] First, we shall consider two cases which have applied this principle and then, in the next section, we shall consider the counter-argument based on the voidability of fraudulent misrepresentations.

So, in *Collings v Lee*,[250] an estate agent purported to take a transfer of a house from the vendors in favour of a non-existent, arm's length purchaser, but in fact procured a transfer of the land into a name which was an alias of his own. Subsequently, he refused to pay the purchase price to the vendors, claiming not to be the transferee of the property. It was held that the estate agent was constructive trustee of the property in favour of the vendors so that

---

244 The claimant sought an order for summary judgment – which means an order finding that the facts and liability are so clear that there is no need for a full trial. In fraud cases that requires it to be obvious that there was dishonesty, which was the case on these facts: *Wrexham Association Football Club Ltd v Crucialmove Ltd* [2008] 1 BCLC 508 and *Antonio Gramsci Shipping Corporation v Recoletos Ltd* [2010] All ER (D) 241 (May) were applied in this regard.

245 [1995] 3 All ER 97.

246 Considered immediately below.

247 [1996] AC 669, 716. Applied in *Twinsectra v Yardley* [2000] WTLR 527, 567; and *Niru Battery Manufacturing Co v Milestone Trading Ltd* [2002] EWHC 1425 (Comm), [2002] All ER (Comm) 705, 722, *per* Moore-Bick J.

248 *Twinsectra v Yardley* [2000] WTLR 527, 567, *per* Moore-Bick J; *Collings v Lee* (2001) 82 P & CR 27; *JJ Harrison (Properties) Ltd v Harrison* [2002] 1 BCLC 162; [2001] WTLR 1327; *Niru Battery v Milestone Trading* [2002] EWHC 1425 (Comm).

249 *Box, Brown & Jacobs v Barclays Bank* [1998] Lloyd's Rep Bank 185, *per* Ferris J. See generally *Sinclair Investment Holdings SA v Versailles Trade Finance Ltd* [2004] All ER (D) 158, *per* Strauss QC (sitting as a Deputy Judge in the High Court) considering the conflicting authority but, in interlocutory proceedings, only needing to decide that there was a triable issue.

250 (2001) 82 P & CR 27.

the vendors retained an overriding interest in that property.[251] Similarly, in *JJ Harrison (Properties) Ltd v Harrison*,[252] a director of a company procured the transfer of land owned by the company to himself personally. The transfer was made at an undervalue and therefore constituted a breach of the director's duties to the company. It was held that whereas a director of a company is not ordinarily a trustee of the company's property (because the company is the absolute owner of its own property), in circumstances in which a director has unconscionably procured the transfer of the company's property to himself in breach of his fiduciary duties, then that director will be a constructive trustee of that property in favour of the company.[253] There are also instances of fraudulent conduct which have led to the imposition of a constructive trust over the proceeds received from the fraud: so, procuring secret commissions as a result of defrauding an employer by artificially inflating the size of a budget for a property development project would lead to those commissions (the proceeds of the fraud) being held on constructive trust.[254]

No constructive trust in relation to fraudulent misrepresentation

It is not the case, however, that a contract procured by way of fraudulent misrepresentation will found a constructive trust over any property passed under that contract.[255] In *Lonrho v Al Fayed (No 2)*,[256] Millett J held:

> A contract obtained by fraudulent misrepresentation is voidable, not void, even in equity. The representee may elect to avoid it, but until he does so, the representor is not a constructive trustee of the property transferred pursuant to the contract, and no fiduciary relationship exists between him and the representee. It may well be that if the representee elects to avoid the contract and set aside a transfer of property made pursuant to it, the beneficial interest in the property will be treated as having remained vested in him throughout, at least to the extent necessary to support any tracing claim.[257]

Thus, because the transaction procured by means of the fraudulent misrepresentation may be affirmed by the victim of the fraud, it is held that there ought not to be a constructive trust imposed over the proceeds of the fraud because that would preclude the right to affirm the transaction.[258] So, applying this principle in *Re Ciro Citterio Menswear plc (In*

251 Land Registration Act 1925, s 70(1)(g).
252 [2002] 1 BCLC 162, [2001] WTLR 1327.
253 Applying *Russell v Wakefield Waterworks Co* (1875) LR 20 Eq 474, 479, *per* Lord Jessel MR; *Belmont Finance Corporation v Williams Furniture Ltd and Others (No 2)* [1980] 1 All ER 393, 405, *per* Buckley LJ.
254 *Daraydan Holdings Ltd v Solland International Ltd* [2004] EWHC 622 (Ch), para [88], *per* Lawrence Collins J.
255 *Daly v Sydney Stock Exchange Ltd* (1986) 160 CLR 371, 387. Cf *Collings v Lee* (2001) 82 P& CR 3, although the opposite was accepted, without close analysis, in *Daraydan Holdings Ltd v Solland International Ltd* [2004] EWHC 622 (Ch), para [88], *per* Lawrence Collins J.
256 [1992] 1 WLR 1, [1991] 4 All ER 961.
257 *Ibid*, 11; 971.
258 However, as considered below, it is not necessary that the imposition of a constructive trust should preclude affirmation of the transaction because, being a bare trust, the beneficiary can terminate the trust using the principle in *Saunders v Vautier* and affirm the transaction instead.

Administration),[259] two directors acquired land for which they paid about £250,000 with funds supplied by the company. This transfer of money was in breach of the rules in s 330 of the Companies Act 1985 (see now s 197 of the Companies Act 2006) governing loans to company directors. The company subsequently went into insolvent administration. It was held that a director would not automatically be constructive trustee of moneys loaned to her by the company in breach of the statutory code because such a loan could be made for proper purposes. The effect of the Companies Act prohibiting such loans was merely to make them voidable and not void: therefore, the loan would not found a constructive trust automatically because the company may choose such to affirm the loan subsequently. There may be other factors which would justify the imposition of a constructive trust, for example, if the director was also committing criminal offences relating to insider dealing collateral to the loan contract, as in *Guinness plc v Saunders*.[260]

Whether profits from fraudulent misrepresentation ought to be held on proprietary constructive trust

At first blush, the principle that profits from a fraudulent misrepresentation will not be held on constructive trust would appear to contradict the principle set out by Lord Browne-Wilkinson in *Westdeutsche Landesbank v Islington LBC*, as quoted above, that a person who perpetrates a fraud will be required to hold any property acquired by virtue of that fraud on constructive trust for the representee.[261] The distinction is made in *Lonrho v Al Fayed (No 2)*, however, between cases of theft and fraud where there has not been any consensual transfer on the one hand, and cases where there is an underlying transaction which is voidable on grounds of misrepresentation on the other hand.[262] The logic of this distinction is that a voidable transaction (such as one involving a fraudulent misrepresentation) might be affirmed by the representee, and that it would therefore be contrary to principle for the equitable interest to be held on trust given that that person may subsequently choose to affirm it for the representee. The right to rescind the transaction is a mere equity and not an equitable interest.[263] So, someone who acquires loan moneys under a mortgage contract by way of fraudulent misrepresentation would not be required to hold any surplus proceeds from the sale of the mortgaged property on constructive trust for the mortgagee.[264] However, it is suggested that

259 [2002] 2 All ER 717.
260 [1990] 1 All ER 652.
261 This approach has not been followed, for example, in *Halifax Buildings Society v Thomas* [1996] Ch 217; *Box, Brown & Jacobs v Barclays Bank* [1998] Lloyd's Rep Bank 185, *per* Ferris J; *Shalson v Mimran* [2003] WTLR 1165, 1200, *per* Rimer J, (*sub nom Shalson v Russo* [2003] EWHC 1637 (Ch), para [106]) for the reasons given in the main text to follow. See *Sinclair Investment Holdings SA v Versailles Trade Finance Ltd* [2004] All ER (D) 158 and *Shalson v Russo* [2003] EWHC 1637 (Ch), para [106] for considerations of the conflicting positions.
262 *Bristol & West Building Society v Mothew* [1998] Ch 1, 23; *Twinsectra Ltd v Yardley* [1999] Lloyd's Rep Bank 438.
263 *Ibid.*
264 *Halifax Building Society v Thomas* [1996] Ch 217. It is suggested that this decision is difficult to reconcile with the approach of the Privy Council in *Attorney-General for Hong Kong v Reid* to the effect that one who acquires property unconscionably should be construed to hold that original property on trust for the claimant from the moment of its receipt, such that any profits derived from that property are similarly held on constructive trust for the claimant.

this is no reason to absolve the representor of his fraud; instead, the constructive trust could be terminable at the instance of the representee in the same way that the transaction itself is capable of being affirmed.[265] Indeed, there have been cases in which the acquisition of property by fraud had led to the imposition of a constructive trust. So, as considered above, in *Collings v Lee*,[266] where an estate agent defrauded clients by transferring land to himself acting under an alias, it was held that there had been no intention to transfer the property to the agent and further that the agent had been in breach of his fiduciary duties so as to constitute him a constructive trust of the property. Similarly, as considered above, in *JJ Harrison (Properties) Ltd v Harrison*,[267] a director of a company was held to be a constructive trustee of property which he had fraudulently obtained from the company.[268]

This picture is complicated by the following *dicta* of Millett LJ in *Paragon Finance v Thakerar*[269] relating to frauds in which the fraudster is not an express trustee:

> Equity has always given relief against fraud by making any person sufficiently implicated in the fraud accountable in equity. In such a case he is traditionally though I think unfortunately described as a constructive trustee and said to be 'liable to account as constructive trustee'.

This form of liability is, it is suggested, a reference to liability to account as a constructive trustee for knowing receipt of property in breach of trust and dishonest assistance in a breach of trust: these heads of liability are considered in detail in Chapter 20. In neither circumstance is the defendant liable to hold any property on trust; rather, the defendant is liable to account to the beneficiaries for any loss they suffered as a result of the fraud as though she was an express trustee. This, it is suggested, is a means of providing for equitable relief in a way that is different from holding any particular property and any profits derived from that property on trust:[270] rather, the defendant's liability here is to make good any loss suffered by the beneficiaries from the fraud. So, if £10,000 is taken from the trust property by fraud, then the beneficiaries' loss and the defendant's personal liability is £10,000, whereas if the fraudster earned £5,000 profit from that £10,000, then a proprietary constructive trust would have netted the beneficiaries a total of £15,000.

In accordance with the decision in *Attorney-General for Hong Kong v Reid*,[271] considered above, it would be in line with judicial policy to prevent the fraudster from keeping the £5,000 profits earned by using the trust's money by holding that the entire £15,000 be held on constructive trust. The obstacle to such a proprietary constructive trust is said to be that a fraudulent misrepresentation should give rise to a voidable contract which the beneficiaries

---

265 Such an argument was raised before the Court of Appeal in *Twinsectra Ltd v Yardley* [1999] Lloyd's Rep Bank 438, building on the general principle set out in *Westdeutsche Landesbank Girozentrale v Islington LBC* [1996] AC 669, but rejected by the court: [1999] Lloyd's Rep Bank 438, 461, *per* Potter LJ.
266 (2001) 82 P & CR 27.
267 [2002] 1 BCLC 162, [2001] WTLR 1327.
268 See also *Russell v Wakefield Waterworks Co* (1875) LR 20 Eq 474, 479, *per* Lord Jessel MR.
269 [1999] 1 All ER 400, 408.
270 *Selangor United Rubber Estates Ltd v Craddock (No 3)* [1968] 1 WLR 1555, 1582, [1968] 2 All ER 1073, 1097, *per* Ungoed-Thomas J; approved in *Kilcarne Holdings Ltd v Targetfollow (Birmingham) Ltd* [2004] EWHC 2547 (Ch), para [259], *per* Lewison J.
271 [1994] 1 AC 324, [1994] 1 All ER 1.

may choose to affirm. This policy in favour of allowing the beneficiaries to affirm the transaction should not be taken to be an objection to the imposition of a proprietary constructive trust. It is suggested that the equitable doctrine of election[272] should be applied by the court so that the beneficiaries may elect either to affirm a proprietary constructive trust over the fraudster's profits or to affirm the fraudulent transaction. In this way, the twin policies of holding unconscionable profits on proprietary constructive trust and of permitting the beneficiaries to choose to affirm contracts can be satisfied.

Constructive fraud and undue influence

Property acquired by means of a 'constructive fraud', such as duress or undue influence, will not vest in equity in the person committing that fraud.[273] The remedy applied in this instance is the remedy of setting aside the transaction effected by virtue of the fraud.[274] Where a transaction, which denied the claimant rights in property to which she would otherwise have been entitled, was set aside on the basis of undue influence, the property was held on constructive trust for the claimant in the proportions to which she was otherwise entitled.[275] Clearly, exerting duress or undue influence over a person will be unconscionable conduct and therefore, it is suggested, that any benefit taken from such duress or undue influence should be held on constructive trust for the victim of that behaviour.[276]

12.5 FIDUCIARY MAKING UNAUTHORISED PROFITS

A trustee or fiduciary will be a constructive trustee of any personal profits made from that office, even where she has acted in good faith. The rule is a strict rule that no profit can be made by a trustee or fiduciary which is not authorised by the terms of the trust. A fiduciary who profits from that office will be required to account for those profits. There is no defence of good faith in favour of the trustee.

12.5.1 The development of the principle that a fiduciary may not make unauthorised profits

If a fiduciary earns unauthorised, personal profits from her fiduciary office then she will be obliged to account for those profits: in the first place by means of a constructive trust imposed over those profits; or if, the profits cannot be identified, by means of a personal account to the trust.[277] The purpose of this principle is to prevent fiduciaries from permitting any conflict

---

272 See Chapter 31.

273 *Barclays Bank v O'Brien* [1993] 3 WLR 786.

274 As considered in Chapter 20.

275 *Humphreys v Humphreys* [2004] EWHC 2201 (Ch), making reference to the defendant's morally reprehensible behaviour and *dicta* of Lord Templeman in that regard in *Boustany v Pigott* (1995) 95 P & CR 298, at 302.

276 This argument was attempted in *Hansen v Barker-Benfield* [2006] EWHC 1119 (Ch), but on the facts of that case it was not proved that a testator's second wife had exerted undue influence over her husband so as to induce him to change his will. The argument was being run by the claimant, who was the testator's daughter, that if there had been undue influence then the will was to be set aside and therefore that any property received by the second wife under the will was to be held on constructive trust.

277 *Sinclair Investment Holdings SA v Versailles Trade Finance Ltd (No 3)* [2007] EWHC 915; *CMS Dolphin Ltd v Simonet* [2001] 2 BCLC 704.

between their personal interests and their fiduciary duties. The rule that a fiduciary cannot take an unauthorised, personal benefit from her fiduciary office emerges from the old case of *Keech v Sandford*,[278] in which the benefit of a lease with rights to receive profits from a market was settled on trust for an infant. The trustee sought to renew the lease on its expiry, but his request was refused on the grounds that an infant could not be bound by such a lease. Therefore, the trustee sought to renew the lease in his own name with the intention that its benefit could then be passed on to the infant. As such, the trustee was benefiting personally although purporting to act in the interest of the beneficiary by use of a right not available to the beneficiary or the trust. An application was made on behalf of the infant to the court for the benefit of the lease to be held on trust for him. The Lord Chancellor held that the lease must be held by the trustee for the infant. While there had been no allegation of fraud in that case, the Lord Chancellor considered that the principle that a trustee must not take an unauthorised profit from a trust should be 'strictly pursued' because there were risks of fraud in allowing trustees to take, for example, the benefit of renewed leases which they had previously held on trust.

This form of trust is said to be a constructive trust here because the renewed lease is in fact a different lease from the old one, and therefore is a different piece of property from that originally held on trust: consequently, the infant's trust would be acquiring rights in this particular lease for the first time. Given that the trust referred only to the original piece of property, a trust which attaches to a separate piece of property must be a constructive trust arising by operation of law and by order of the court, not strictly by the action of a settlor in creating a trust. It is possible to avoid a constructive trust in these circumstances only where the individual renewing the lease can demonstrate that he does not hold a fiduciary duty in respect of that property.

As this principle was expressed by Lord Herschell in *Bray v Ford*:[279]

> It is an inflexible rule of the court of equity that a person in a fiduciary position . . . is not, unless otherwise expressly provided [in the terms of that person's fiduciary duties], entitled to make a profit; he is not allowed to put himself in a position where his interest and duty conflict. It does not appear to me that this rule is, as had been said, founded upon principles of morality.[280] I regard it rather as based on the consideration that, human nature being what it is, there is danger, in such circumstances, of the person holding a fiduciary position being swayed by interest rather than by duty, and thus prejudicing those whom he was bound to protect. It has, therefore, been deemed expedient to law down this positive rule.

So, the rule is considered to be a strict rule, as will emerge from the case of *Boardman v Phipps*, considered in detail in the next section. As Lord King held:[281]

> This may seem hard, that the trustee is the only person of all mankind who might not have [the trust property]: but it is very proper that rule should be strictly pursued, and

---

278 (1726) 2 Eq Cas Abr 741.
279 [1896] AC 44, at 51; [1895–99] All ER Rep 1009, at 1011.
280 Although see, eg, Parker LJ in *Bhullar v Bhullar* [2003] 2 BCLC 241, para [17] referring to the 'ethic' in these cases.
281 *Keech v Sandford* (1726) Sel Cas Ch 61.

not in the least relaxed; for it is very obvious what would be the consequence of letting trustees have the lease.[282]

Its base is the avoidance of conflicts of interest between a fiduciary's personal and fiduciary capacities, and is not dependent on proof of bad faith. As Lord Cranworth expressed this principle:[283]

> it is a rule of universal application that no one having such duties to discharge shall be allowed to enter into engagements in which he has or can have a personal interest conflicting or which possibly may conflict with the interests of those whom he is bound to protect.

Nevertheless, it is important that the defendant be shown to have been acting in a fiduciary capacity for this principle to take effect. As emerges from Lord Cranworth's *dicta*, it is necessary that the defendant had appropriate duties. So, in *Re Biss*,[284] a son was entitled to take possession of a renewed lease where, acting in good faith, he had sought a renewal in his own name of a lease which had formerly been held by his father's business, after his father had died intestate. It was held that the son did not occupy a fiduciary position in respect of his father's business, unlike the trustee in *Keech v Sandford*,[285] who clearly occupied the fiduciary position of trustee in relation to the infant's settlement. Therefore, the son in *Re Biss* would not be subject to a constructive trust over the renewed lease in his own name. So, if those profits were not earned in a fiduciary capacity, then an account for the profits earned will not be ordered.[286] While the decision in *Keech v Sandford* relates specifically to leases, its *ratio* has been broadened out into a more general principle that fiduciaries cannot profit personally from their office. This principle was considered in relation to the duties of trustees in para 8.3.9 above.

12.5.2 The application of this principle

The principle that a fiduciary making unauthorised profits founds a constructive trust: Boardman v Phipps

The continued rigour of this rule against fiduciaries taking unauthorised benefits from their offices is best illustrated by the decision of the House of Lords in *Boardman v Phipps*.[287] The respondent, Boardman, was solicitor to a trust: the 'Phipps family trust'. As such he was not a trustee, but he was held to be in a fiduciary capacity as advisor to the Phipps family trust.

---

282 Ie, the trustee would abscond with the valuable property.
283 *Aberdeen Railway Co v Blaikie Bros* (1854) 1 Macq 461, 471; [1843–60] All ER Rep 249, 252.
284 [1903] 2 Ch 40.
285 (1726) 2 Eq Cas Abr 741.
286 *Experience Hendrix LLC v PPX Enterprises Inc* [2003] EWCA Civ 323, [2003] 1 All ER (Comm) 830, [2003] EMLR 515, where royalties had not been paid to a musician further to a contract, but in circumstances in which the defendant was not in a fiduciary relationship to the claimant, there was a right to contractual recovery of money but no equitable accounting.
287 [1967] 2 AC 46, 67. See also *Blair v Vallely* [2000] WTLR 615; *Ward v Brunt* [2000] WTLR 731.

The trust fund included a minority shareholding in a private company. While making inquiries as to the performance of the company on behalf of the trust, Boardman and the one active trustee learned of the potential for profit in controlling the company through confidential information which they obtained at a general meeting of this private company. The company being a private company, Boardman would have been unable to find out this information or to acquire shares in the company without the initial introduction given to him as solicitor to the trustees of the Phipps family trust. Boardman and the trustees considered that the Phipps family trust would benefit if the trust controlled the company by acquiring a majority shareholding in it. The trust was not able to acquire these extra shares itself, both because the trustees did not consider the trust was in sufficient funds for the purpose and because the trust would have required the leave of the court to make such an acquisition. Therefore, Boardman and one of the trustees, Fox, decided to acquire the shares personally. Boardman informed the active trustees that he intended to do this. However, it was held that Boardman had not provided them with enough information to be able to rely on the defence of their consent to his plans.

Together with the Phipps family trust's shareholding, Boardman and the trustees were able, in effect, to control the company. With a great amount of work on Boardman's part, the company generated a large profit for the trust, and for Boardman personally, as shareholders. The issue arose as to whether Boardman was entitled to keep the profit on his own shares, or whether he was required to hold the profit on constructive trust for the beneficiaries of the trust.

The majority of the House of Lords held that Boardman should hold the profits on constructive trust for the beneficiaries of the existing trust. The minority, Viscount Dilhorne and Lord Upjohn, dissented on the basis that Mr Boardman had not acted in bad faith and therefore that he ought not to be subjected to a constructive trust. Mr Boardman was entitled to some compensation (known as 'equitable accounting') for his efforts in spite of the imposition of the constructive trust.[288] All of their Lordships agreed on the principles; they disagreed only as to their application to the particular facts of this case. As Lord Upjohn held:

> Rules of equity have to be applied to such a great diversity of circumstances that they can be stated only in the most general terms and applied with particular attention to the exact circumstances of each case. The relevant rule for the decision of this case is the fundamental rule of equity that a person in a fiduciary capacity must not make a profit out of his trust which is part of the wider rule that a trustee must not place himself in a position where his duty and his interest may conflict. [His Lordship then quoted the passage from *Bray v Ford* which was quoted in the previous section in support of this contention.]

These *dicta* contained the central statement of principle which can be found in the speeches of all of their Lordships to the effect that the constructive trust in this case is predicated on the need to prevent conflicts of interest. Nevertheless, four issues arise: What is the basis of the constructive trust in this context? In what way can authorisation be acquired? To whom are the fiduciary's duties owed? What is the nature of the remedy?

---

288   As considered at para 12.5.3 below.

The basis of the constructive trust in this context: avoidance of conflict of interests

The first issue, then, is as to the basis of the constructive trust in this context. The House of Lords in *Boardman v Phipps* held that it was a principle of strict application that a trustee or fiduciary could not be permitted to allow a conflict between her personal capacity and her fiduciary duties.[289] Consequently, if a fiduciary does act on her own account so as to generate personal profits from her fiduciary office, then she will be required to account to the beneficiaries of her fiduciary duties for those profits. The effect of finding that the fiduciary is required to account for those personal profits is that the fiduciary is required to account for those profits, and thus in the first place to hold those profits on constructive trust for the beneficiaries of her fiduciary duties. This constructive trust will be imposed over the fiduciary's personal profits in any situation in which a fiduciary acquires a profit in the commission of her office regardless of whether or not she acts in bad faith.[290]

The principle will emerge from the following example. If a trustee were to take property from the trust fund, without authorisation under the terms of the trust to do so, and then to invest that property so that she could keep the profits for herself personally, she would be required to hold those profits on constructive trust for the beneficiaries of the trust. The effect of the profits being held on constructive trust is that any property acquired with those profits will similarly be held on constructive trust. If that property were to increase in value, then the constructive trust would continue to bite on the property even though it has become more valuable.[291] This is the effect of a proprietary constructive trust: it bites on whatever property is held on trust from time to time. The trustee's liability is therefore not restricted to a personal remedy equal in value to the profits made, but rather is a proprietary remedy which takes effect over the traceable proceeds of this property.[292] Clearly, this would have been a breach of trust and therefore it is unsurprising that the trustee is required to account for the personal profits realised from the transaction.

To change the example slightly, as we have seen from *Boardman v Phipps*, this liability will take effect over someone who is not an express trustee if that person interferes with the running of the trust so as to become a trustee *de son tort*[293] (that is, a form of constructive trustee who has meddled sufficiently with the trust so as to be deemed to be an express trustee). Mr Boardman was a trustee *de son tort* because, even though he began as a solicitor advising the trustees rather than an express trustee, he took over the management of the trust's affairs. Even though Boardman only used his own money to acquire the shares, it was held that because he permitted a conflict of interest between his personal and his fiduciary interests, he should hold profits earned from his own shareholding on trust for the Phipps family trust. In this situation it is clear that there is no requirement that the trustee have acted

---

289   See also, establishing this point: *Keech v Sandford* (1726) 2 Eq Cas Abr 741; *Ex p Grace* (1799) 1 Bos & P 376; *Rawe v Chichester* (1773) Amb 715; *Aberdeen Railway Co v Blaikie Bros* [1843–60] All ER Rep 249, 252, *per* Lord Cranworth; *Bray v Ford* [1895–99] All ER Rep 1009, at 1011; [1896] AC 51; *Bhullar v Bhullar* [2003] EWCA Civ 424, para 268, *per* Parker LJ. See more recently *FHR European Ventures LLP v Mankarious* [2011] EWHC 2308 (Ch), Simon J.

290   In accordance with the discussion of the general constructive trust considered at the beginning of this chapter, we might consider that the acquisition of an unauthorised profit from a fiduciary office is necessarily to be deemed to constitute unconscionable behaviour suitable to found a constructive trust.

291   *Attorney-General for Hong Kong v Reid* [1994] 1 AC 324, [1994] 1 All ER 1.

292   See Chapter 19 for a discussion of the law on tracing.

293   Considered below at section 12.8.

unconscionably or knowingly in bad faith;[294] rather, it is sufficient that some personal profit has been earned in circumstances in which there was some conflict of interest.

To change the example once more, if a trustee invested trust property in an investment fund managed by Xavier because Xavier offered the trustee £10,000 to invest the property with Xavier rather than some other investment, then that £10,000 would be held on constructive trust on the basis either that it would have been an unauthorised profit from her fiduciary office[295] or that it would have been a bribe.[296] Self-evidently, there would have been a breach of trust here and unconscionable behaviour. However, suppose that Xavier sent the trustee an unexpected Fortnum & Mason hamper of food at Christmas[297] as thanks for investing in Xavier's fund: would this be an unauthorised personal profit? It would certainly be a profit. It is clear from *Boardman v Phipps* that there need not have been any bad faith on the part of the fiduciary for the profits to be held on constructive trust; all that is required is that there has been a conflict of interest. There might be a conflict of interest if we consider that the trustee might now continue to invest in Xavier's fund rather than any other fund out of gratitude, even though the gift was unsolicited. Applying the *Keech v Sandford* principle strictly, the hamper of food should be held on constructive trust for the beneficiaries.

An alternative basis of the constructive trust: misuse of trust property?

The clear view of the House of Lords in *Boardman v Phipps* (and on this point there Lordships were unanimous and speaking in support of *Keech v Sandford*) is that the constructive trust in these circumstances is based on the avoidance of conflict of interests,[298] as discussed immediately above. However, there is also a further explanation for this constructive trust suggested by Lords Hodson and Guest who found that, not only was there a danger of conflict of interest, but also that Boardman should be considered to have misused trust property on the basis that the confidential information obtained while on trust business should be considered to be the property of the Phipps family trust. Consequently, the profit which was generated for Boardman personally was said to be derived from trust property (the confidential information) and therefore ought to have been considered to be the property belonging to the trust.[299] Given that these two judges were of the view that Mr Boardman had used trust property, in the form of the confidential information learned at the company meeting, to earn profits for himself, it was open to their Lordships to hold that it was the misuse of trust property which justified the imposition of a proprietary constructive trust.

If the constructive trust is to be based on vindicating the property rights of the Phipps family trust, then the first problem would be identifying the precise property which Boardman

---

294 *Regal v Gulliver* [1942] 1 All ER 378, 386A, *per* Lord Russell (approved in *Boardman v Phipps* [1967] 2 AC 46, *per* Lord Guest): 'The liability arises from the mere fact of a profit having, in the stated circumstances, been made.'
295 *Boardman v Phipps* [1967] 2 AC 46.
296 *Attorney-General for Hong Kong v Reid* [1994] 1 AC 324, [1994] 1 All ER 1.
297 Fortnum & Mason is a shop, by Royal Appointment, on Piccadilly in London famous, *inter alia*, for the hampers they sell at Christmas full of salmon, champagne and so forth.
298 *Bhullar v Bhullar* [2003] 2 BCLC 241, para [27], *per* Parker LJ.
299 Cf *Satnam Investments Ltd v Dunlop Heywood & Co Ltd* [1999] 3 All ER 652: where confidential information held by S was disclosed to third parties leading to the acquisition of a development site by those third parties, it was held that there was no constructive trust over the defendant because he was not in a fiduciary position in relation to S; applied in *Brisby v Lomaxhall* (2000) unreported.

was to hold on trust for the Phipps family trust. Boardman had acquired his shares in a personal capacity: they had never belonged to the Phipps family trust. Rather, it is suggested, because Lords Hodson and Guest found that trust property had been misused, it was intellectually more satisfying for them to find that Boardman owed a proprietary remedy (in the form of a constructive trust) to the beneficiaries because they considered that he had used trust property to earn himself those profits. Otherwise, it would have to be acknowledged that Boardman acquired his shares with his own money and not with trust money, and therefore it would be intellectually more difficult to justify the imposition of a proprietary remedy on Boardman.

Therefore, we might consider that the constructive trust in *Boardman v Phipps* arises both on the basis of property law, stemming from the confidential information owned by the trust (given the approach of Lords Hodson and Guest), and on the basis of an equitable wrong associated with permitting a conflict between a fiduciary duty and one's personal interest (as is the opinion of the majority). That some of their Lordships held that the trust was founded on this proprietary nexus between the information and the profit, rather than simply finding that the status of fiduciary required that the property be held on trust,[300] suggests that they understood the law on constructive trusts as being a part of property law rather than purely a part of the law of personal, equitable obligations imposed on fiduciaries. We could understand this decision as being based, therefore, on an understanding that it is unconscionable for a fiduciary to earn an unauthorised profit and therefore operating in accordance with *Westdeutsche Landesbank v Islington LBC*, an approach which is particularly attractive if we consider that Mr Boardman had misused trust property;[301] otherwise we would have to think that the constructive trust in this situation is based entirely on a personal obligation borne by fiduciaries based on duties owed by the fiduciary to the beneficiaries.

Nevertheless, in the Court of Appeal in *Bhullar v Bhullar*,[302] the principle has been reasserted that the constructive trust in this context is not dependent on any interference with trust property, but rather is based on the avoidance of conflicts of interest. An Australian decision has similarly held that this form of constructive trust is based on the fiduciary's obligation to permit no conflict between his personal benefit and his duties to others,[303] which again suggests an emphasis on fiduciaries' general obligations as opposed to the protection of rights in property necessarily. If the test is based on the avoidance of conflict of interest by fiduciaries, then it would not matter whether or not trust property was misused; rather, it would be enough that there had been some conflict of interest without trust property ever having been used. Thus, as Lord Cohen also held in *Boardman v Phipps*, 'an agent is, in my opinion, liable to account for profits which he makes out of the trust property if there is a possibility of conflict between his interest and his duty to his principal'. The nature of this constructive trust could therefore be characterised as being a proprietary institution or it could arise simply out of a conflict of duty and be imposed *in personam* in relation to that fiduciary's unconscionable conduct.

300   As in *Attorney-General for Hong Kong v Reid* [1994] 1 AC 324, [1994] 1 All ER 1, considered above at para 12.4.1.
301   As considered in section 12.1.
302   [2003] 2 BCLC 241, para [27], *per* Parker LJ.
303   Deane J in *Chan v Zachariah* (1984) 154 CLR 178.

The dissenting view in Boardman v Phipps

Lord Upjohn and Viscount Dilhorne dissented from the conclusion of the majority in *Boardman v Phipps*. Their Lordships agreed that there was a principle that fiduciaries must not permit a conflict of interest. However, in their opinions, Mr Boardman had neither acted in bad faith nor unconscionably during these transactions and furthermore they considered that Boardman's use of his own money to acquire shares meant that there had not been any conflict of interest on these facts. Lord Upjohn's view was based on the proposition that a solicitor ought to be able to act separately on her own account and on her client's account without the need to impose a constructive trust over any profits realised, provided that she does not allow any conflict of interest to develop between her fiduciary duties to her client and her own desire for personal profit. As such, his Lordship held, there ought to have been no objection to Boardman making some personal profit from these transactions.[304] Furthermore it was accepted by Viscount Dilhorne that Mr Boardman's agency, acting on behalf of the Phipps family trust, ended after the first meeting of the company's shareholders which he attended, and therefore that he bore no further duties than that. It is suggested, however, that Mr Boardman is better thought of as being a trustee *de son tort* (as discussed in section 12.8) due to his interference with the management of the trust and consequently that his fiduciary duties extended throughout the entire time of his interaction with the trust and were not confined simply to his attendance at one particular shareholders' meeting. Furthermore, Boardman was a solicitor dealing as a fiduciary (for which he was paid) and therefore ought to have known that he was not entitled to take profits without the informed consent of the beneficiaries.

No requirement that the profit be made directly from the fiduciary office

It has been held that there is no need to demonstrate that the profit was earned 'from the fiduciary office' as opposed to being made in general terms in a manner which caused a conflict between the fiduciary's personal interest and her fiduciary duties.[305] So, as Morritt VC has put this point:[306]

> If there is a fiduciary duty of loyalty and if the conduct complained of falls within the scope of that fiduciary duty as indicated by Lord Wilberforce in *NZ Netherlands Society v Kuys*[307] then I see no justification for any further requirement that the profit shall have been obtained by the fiduciary 'by virtue of his position'. Such a condition suggests an element of causation which neither principle nor the authorities require. Likewise it is not in doubt that the object of the equitable remedies of an account or the imposition of

---

304   In other contexts, it has been suggested by Arden LJ in *Murad v Al-Saraj* [2005] EWCA Civ 939 at paras [82–83] that equitable principle in relation to the liability of fiduciaries could be tempered by a modern court. This is an obiter remark which is clearly contrary to the approach of the English senior courts, and it was doubted by Sir Peter Gibson in *Wrexham AFC Ltd v Crucialmove Ltd* [2006] EWCA Civ 237, para [51].

305   *United Pan-Europe Communications NV v Deutsche Bank* [2000] 2 BCLC 461; *Button v Phelps* [2006] EWHC 53 (Ch).

306   *United Pan-Europe Communications NV v Deutsche Bank* [2000] 2 BCLC 461, para [47]; approved in *Button v Phelps* [2006] EWHC 53 (Ch), para [66].

307   [1973] 1 WLR 1126.

a constructive trust is to ensure that the defaulting fiduciary does not retain the profit; it is not to compensate the beneficiary for any loss.

Therefore, if, for example, a trustee took some advice from the stockbrokers advising a trust that there was only one remaining parcel of shares in a company which were expected to realise a massive profit, and if the trustee acquired those shares for herself rather than for the trust, it would not be open to the trustee to argue that she acquired the shares on her own account and not while working for the trust. Otherwise it would be too simple for fiduciaries to argue that they were acting in a different capacity when taking direct or indirect advantage of their office. Instead, the strict principle in *Keech v Sandford* and *Bray v Ford* is to be enforced so that no possible conflict of interest can be allowed to exist. This, it is suggested, is the reason for supporting the decision of the majority of the House of Lords in *Boardman v Phipps*: if Boardman had been permitted to retain his profits, then the purity of the principle derived from *Keech v Sandford* and from *Bray v Ford* would have been fatally compromised.

It is not necessary for the defendant to occupy one of the traditional fiduciary categories for this principle to apply. So, in *Cobbetts LLP v Hodge*[308] a 'salaried partner' within a solicitors' firm, which meant that he was an employee working for a limited liability partnership who was not himself a full partner, was held to owe fiduciary duties to the firm because his role was as a 'senior lawyer', albeit not a partner, whose duties included bringing investors and business into the firm. That employee had, however, diverted a private placement of shares issued by a client of the firm to himself while purportedly on the firm's business. Therefore, Floyd J held that the defendant employee would be liable to hold any profits from this unauthorised activity on constructive trust for the benefit of the firm. It was found that the defendant had not made a full disclosure of the share placement and its terms to anyone at the firm, but rather had made only partial and misleading disclosures: therefore, the defence of authorisation was not open to him.

The defence of authorisation

The second issue arising from the appeal in *Boardman v Phipps* surrounds the possibility of Boardman being relieved of any liability under constructive trust if he had made it known to the trustees and beneficiaries that he would be acquiring shares on his own behalf on the basis that the Phipps family trust could not and would not acquire those shares. Some of their Lordships indicated that they would have been prepared to find for Boardman if he could have demonstrated that he had made it clear to the trustees that he was acting on his own behalf, even though he had first acquired the confidential information as a fiduciary of the Phipps family trust. There is, as will emerge from the discussion to follow, a defence to an action for constructive trust on grounds of making personal profits that the fiduciary had authorisation so to do. On the facts of *Boardman v Phipps*, Mr Boardman did not disclose his purpose to all of the trustees: on the facts, one of the trustees was extremely ill and therefore such disclosure would have been impossible. Furthermore, the detail of the scheme had not been disclosed to all of the beneficiaries so that they could have given informed consent to the plan so as to release Boardman from his fiduciary duties in that regard. The majority

308   [2009] EWHC 786 (Ch), [2010] 1 BCLC 30.

of the House of Lords proceeded, as a result, on the basis that there was no authorisation given on the facts by the trustees nor that there was any release of liability nor assent given by the beneficiaries.

In the Privy Council decision in *Queensland Mines v Hudson*,[309] the defendant had been managing director of the plaintiff company and had therefore been in a fiduciary relationship to that company. The defendant had learned of some potentially profitable mining contracts. The board of directors of that company decided not to pursue these possibilities after having been made aware of all the relevant facts. The company was not able to pursue the opportunity and the board of directors decided not to do so, knowing that the managing director intended to do so on his own account. Importantly, then, one director received the informed decision of the remainder of the board that this opportunity would not be pursued by the company, thus impliedly giving that individual director the authorisation to pursue the opportunity on his own account. The managing director resigned and pursued the business possibilities offered by the contracts on his own account, taking great personal risk in so doing. The company sought to recover the profits generated by the contract from the director. The court held that the repudiation of the contracts by the company meant that the director was entitled to pursue them on his own account without a conflict with his fiduciary responsibility to the company, even though the opportunity had come to the managing director by means of the fiduciary office.

The mainstream English law has remained rigidly on course, however. In similar circumstances to *Queensland Mines v Hudson*, in *Industrial Development Consultants Ltd v Cooley*,[310] a managing director was offered a contract by a third party. The offer was made expressly on the basis that the third party would deal only with the managing director, not with his employer company. Without disclosing this fact to the company and claiming to be in ill-health, the managing director left his employment and entered into a contract with the third party within a week of his resignation. It was held that the managing director occupied a fiduciary position in relation to his employer company throughout. He was therefore required to disclose all information to the company and to account for the profits he made under the contract under constructive trusteeship. Equally, if a director sought to tempt a client away from her employers, it has been held that that would constitute a breach of fiduciary duty with the effect that any profits so earned would have to be accounted for by way of constructive trust to the employer company.[311]

This rule is clearly set out in a number of contexts other than simply in relation to trusts and trustees. In *Regal v Gulliver*,[312] which was approved by the House of Lords in *Boardman v Phipps*, it was held that directors of companies are fiduciaries and therefore similarly liable to account for profits made in the conduct of their duties. In *Regal*, four directors of the plaintiff company subscribed for shares in another company which the board of directors had intended to be acquired by the plaintiff company itself. The directors had acquired the shares personally because the company was not able to afford them, even though it did have the legal capacity to have acquired them. It was held that the directors' profits on these shares were profits made from their offices as directors. Therefore, they were required to account

---

309 (1977) 18 ALR 1. See also *Framlington Group plc v Anderson* [1995] BCC 611.
310 [1972] 2 All ER 162.
311 *Item Software (UK) Ltd v Fassihi* [2002] EWHC 3116 (Ch), [2003] 2 BCLC 1.
312 [1942] 1 All ER 378.

for them to the company. The four directors were not able to rely on their purported grant of authorisation to themselves to pursue this opportunity on their own account. Equally, if a director seeking authorisation from the other directors fails to make sufficiently full disclosure of all the relevant facts, then that director will not be taken to have acquired authorisation to earn personal profits.[313]

The defence of authorisation is considered in greater detail below concerning the 'corporate opportunity doctrine' in relation to which most of the decided cases on authorisation have arisen. The distinction between companies cases and trusts cases in this context has been that the director of a company may not divert a corporate opportunity to herself, whereas such commercial concerns do not arise in relation to ordinary trusts which do not carry on a trade. The principal distinction between trusts and companies is as follows: if a board of directors makes an informed decision not to pursue a business opportunity suggested to them by one solitary director (providing they have been given all of the available information without deceit or concealment), then that decision has been made by adults with commercial experience and access to legal and other professional advice,[314] whereas when beneficiaries under a family trust make such decisions, they may not have the experience or knowledge to make informed decisions, particularly if they do not have impartial, professional advice to help them to reach their decisions as to their personal affairs in relation to the trust. Therefore, it will be easier to suggest that a single company director had authorisation to act, whereas a trustee will find it more difficult to prove that she had proper authorisation from the beneficiaries of a family trust.

To whom are the fiduciary's duties owed?

The third issue is: to whom does the fiduciary owe this duty of disclosure before the profits can be authorised? There appear to be three possibilities. The duty of the solicitor to a trust could be said to be owed to the trustees, or simply to all of the beneficiaries, or to those beneficiaries affected by the profit-making. In *Boardman*, there appeared to be an assumption on the part of the House of Lords that this obligation was owed by the fiduciary to the trustees, and that it was the relationship primarily with the active trustee that was of most importance. In *Queensland Mines v Hudson*, the assumption was that consent could be acquired from the other directors (although it was the case that the two majority shareholders were represented on that board in any event). Now, s 170 of the Companies Act 2006 provides that directors owe their duties to the company (on which see below).

Only the strict application of *Regal v Gulliver* appears to suggest that fiduciaries cannot simply rely on the permission of other fiduciaries. In consequence, the duty of disclosure would be a duty to disclose to the shareholders of a company or to the beneficiaries of a trust respectively. This was the approach taken in the New Zealand decision in *Equiticorp Industries Group Ltd v The Crown*,[315] which held that it was the shareholders of a company

---

313   *IDC v Cooley* [1972] 1 WLR 443; *Gwembe Valley Development Co Ltd v Koshy (No 3)* [2004] 1 BCLC 131, where the managing director of a company formed to farm in Zambia failed to disclose his personal interest in activities in which the company was engaged and therefore was held to be liable to account to the company for the profits which he had made.
314   As in *Queensland Mines v Hudson* (1977) 18 ALR 1.
315   [1998] 2 NZLR 485.

who were competent to authorise a fiduciary making such profits on a personal basis. However, even where no authorisation is given, if the fiduciary takes their benefit in a different capacity (for example, as a beneficiary under a will), there will be no liability to account. So, where, for example, a partner in a farming partnership was offered the chance, in the capacity of a beneficiary under the reversioner's will, to acquire the reversion over the agricultural tenancy held by the partnership, she was not liable to account because she was found to be benefiting from her status as a beneficiary and not exploiting her fiduciary office.[316]

Therefore, it would appear that a fiduciary acting in her fiduciary capacity must seek authorisation from the beneficiaries: any other point of view would open itself up to abuse. If the trustees had delegated their authority to a particular fiduciary, then there may be grounds for suggesting that the duty is owed primarily to those trustees. This situation might arise in circumstances in which a solicitor is appointed as in *Boardman*, or where a fund manager is appointed for the delegation of investment obligations. The risk with this approach is that fiduciaries may make decisions in their own interests and thus grant one another permission to act in certain circumstances, without necessarily concerning themselves with the interests of the beneficiaries. As Hayton suggests, the primary relationship of the trust is that between trustee and beneficiary, so that trustees must be considered to owe their duties primarily to the beneficiaries.[317] As such, any fiduciary role in respect of a trust ought to be centred on an obligation ultimately owed to the beneficiaries. Therefore, if duties ought properly to be owed to the beneficiaries, it should be the beneficiaries who authorise any activities which are beyond the powers granted to the trustees under the trust instrument.

The appropriate equitable response

The fourth issue is the nature of the trust which should be enforced against the fiduciary pursuant to the previous discussion of the nature of the trust. It is clearly accepted that a fiduciary making a personal profit from her fiduciary office will hold those profits on constructive trust for the beneficiaries of that fiduciary duty.[318] However, on the decided cases, some issues have arisen as to exactly how that trust operates. This section considers those issues.

If the fiduciary had used trust property to generate a profit, that profit would be said to derive from that property. As such, the trust would be entitled to a proprietary remedy against the fiduciary. That much seems uncontroversial.[319] The Privy Council in *Attorney-General for Hong Kong v Reid*[320] took the view that, where a bribe is received in the course of employment, all profits connected to that property are held on proprietary constructive trust by the fiduciary for the employer.[321] Therefore, in relation to the rule against profit-making

---

316 *Ward v Brunt* [2000] WTLR 731; *Hancock Family Memorial Foundation Ltd v Porteous* [2000] WTLR 1113
      (Sup Ct (WA)).
317 Hayton, 1996.
318 As in *Attorney-General for Hong Kong v Reid* [1994] 1 AC 324.
319 The liability for breach of trust in this context is considered in Chapter 18.
320 [1994] 1 AC 324, [1994] 1 All ER 1.
321 As discussed above at para 12.4.1.

by fiduciaries, the profit ought to be held on proprietary constructive trust for the trust by the fiduciary. Whether or not there is identifiable property of the trust involved is not important, by analogy with *Reid*.[322]

The nature of the remedy of account for unauthorised profits

The proper approach to the nature of the remedy when a fiduciary acquires an unauthorised profit is set out by Rimer J in *Sinclair Investment Holdings SA v Versailles Trade Finance Ltd (No 3)*[323] and by Lawrence Collins J in *CMS Dolphin Ltd v Simonet*,[324] as set out variously below.[325] The remedy has always been generally described by the courts on the basis that the fiduciary is liable to hold the profits on constructive trust or (where no such property remains) that the fiduciary is 'liable to account' to the beneficiaries for the unauthorised profit. The question then is: what is meant by the obligation to account? It could relate either to a proprietary right in relation to the profits themselves or simply a personal obligation to pay an amount of money equal to the profits earned.

Rimer J has explained this doctrine accurately in *Sinclair Investment Holdings SA v Versailles Trade Finance Ltd (No 3)*[326] in the following terms:

> . . . any identifiable assets acquired by fiduciaries in breach of their fiduciary duty are, and can be declared to be, held upon constructive trust for the principal (*Boardman v Phipps, AG Hong Kong v Reid, Daraydan Holdings Ltd v Solland*) . . . There will in practice often be no identifiable property which can be declared by the court to be held upon such a constructive trust, in which case no declaration will be made and the principal may at most be entitled to a personal remedy in the nature of an account of profits. In *Boardman's* case the court made a declaration that the shares that had been acquired by the fiduciaries were held on constructive trust (a proprietary remedy), and directed an account of the profits that had come into their hands from those shares (a personal remedy). *Boardman's* case can be said to have been a hard case as regards the fiduciaries, whose integrity and honesty was not in doubt; and it well illustrates the rigours of the applicable equitable principle. The recovery by the trust of the shares was obviously a valuable benefit to it; and equity's softer side was reflected in the making of an allowance to the fiduciaries for their work and skill in obtaining the shares and profits. On the very different facts of *Reid's* case, there was no question of any such allowance being made.

---

322 Professor Burrows has argued that this doctrine ought to be considered to be restitutionary (Burrows, 2002, 409), although this form of constructive trust is more usually expressed as being a proprietary trust arising on the basis of good conscience. Burrows's viewpoint is based on the premise that the fiduciary is unjustly enriched by making an unauthorised profit. The potential weakness with considering this constructive trust to be restitutionary is that there is no restitution, in the sense of some restoration, of property to the beneficiaries because the beneficiaries would have had no pre-existing rights in the property aside from the chimerical confidential information. As set out by Lord Templeman in *Attorney-General for Hong Kong v Reid*, the constructive trust arises on the basis of equitable principle and not unjust enrichment.

323 [2007] EWHC 915, 10 ITELR 58.

324 [2001] 2 BCLC 704.

325 This discussion is set out below at the end of this section in relation to the 'corporate opportunity doctrine' in company law.

326 [2007] EWHC 915, 10 ITELR 58.

Therefore, the position is clear: the primary remedy is for a proprietary constructive trust over the personal profits; the secondary remedy (if there is no property over which the constructive trust can take effect) is for a personal remedy in the form of an account of profits; and thirdly the court may make some equitable accounting to reduce the amount of any such account if the court considers the circumstances to be appropriate for the equitable relief of such a defendant.[327]

The primary form which the liability to account takes is in the form of a constructive trust, whereby a proprietary right is imposed over those profits such that the fiduciary becomes a constructive trustee over those profits. Because the claimant-beneficiary[328] acquires a propri-etary right over the profits, that beneficiary also has a proprietary right over any property that is acquired with those profits. This constructive trust right also means that even if those profits are mixed with other money, then the beneficiary acquires a right to trace into that mixture or into any substitute property and to impose a proprietary right over it, as discussed in Chapter 19 *Tracing*. The secondary form which the liability to account takes is predicated on the idea either that the profits cannot be traced or that the property substituted for the profits can be traced but has become worthless. In such a situation, the proprietary right would be worthless. In this second context, the fiduciary's liability is to account for the amount of the unauthorised profits personally by paying money or money's worth to the trust equal to the amount of the profits. This chapter focuses primarily on the constructive trust.

However, perhaps the easiest way to understand how this head of liability works is to think about what it means to be a 'constructive trustee'. A 'constructive trust' is a trust which the court 'construes' or 'constructs' in circumstances in which the legal owner of property has behaved unconscionably in relation to property. Thus, a "constructive trustee" is a person who is construed to be a trustee. There is an important distinction between a fiduciary's liability to account for unauthorised profits and the liability of an express trustee to account for breach of trust (where the latter liability is based on the decision of the House of Lords in *Target Holdings v Redferns*[329]). An express trustee is liable to reconstitute the trust fund and to compensate the beneficiaries for any loss which flows from a breach of trust; whereas a fiduciary's liability to account for unauthorised profits does not require that the benefici-aries have suffered a loss. So, in the leading case of *Boardman v Phipps*[330] the beneficiaries had suffered no loss but were nevertheless entitled to force Boardman to account for his unauthorised profits. Consequently this is not a restitutionary remedy because the fiduciary need not have earned her profits at the beneficiaries' expense, as the theory of restitution of unjust enrichment requires. Instead, it is enough that the equitable wrong of earning unau-thorised profits from a fiduciary office has been committed. The basis of this liability is predicated on an actual or even a potential conflict between the fiduciary's personal interests and her fiduciary office.[331] The fiduciary must then account for those profits by means of a constructive trust or secondarily by means of a personal liability to account.

---

327 See also *Markel International Insurance Co Ltd v Surety Guarantee Consultants Ltd* [2008] EWHC 1135 (Comm) illustrating the principle that secret profits made by a fiduciary must be accounted for.

328 The 'claimant-beneficiary' in relation to fiduciary duties generally is a general reference to whoever takes the benefit of that fiduciary relationship, whether a beneficiary under a trust or the company in relation to a director, and so forth.

329 [1996] 1 AC 421.

330 [1967] 2 AC 46.

331 Eg *Boardman v Phipps* [1967] 2 AC 46.

The precise nature of the remedy was subtly differently expressed by some of their Lordships. Lord Cohen held that the fiduciary should be 'accountable to the respondent for his share of the net profits which they derived from the transaction', which could theoretically be explained as being either a proprietary or a personal remedy. Lord Guest was clear, however, that he had 'no hesitation in coming to the conclusion' that the profits were to be held on constructive trust. Lords Hodson and Guest were bolstered in their decisions in finding *inter alia* that the confidential information obtained by Boardman was the property of the Phipps family trust, thus justifying the existence of a constructive trust. What is also clear was that the House of Lords was asked specifically on the appeal whether or not the profits were to be held on constructive trust, and therefore their Lordships can be understood as having found a proprietary constructive trust, just as Wilberforce J had done at first instance.

Other possible approaches would be simply to make good the amount lost to the trust in money terms. This would not amount to a proprietary remedy necessarily.[332] By contrast, an alternative argument might be that in circumstances in which the fiduciary had made a profit in advising the trust without using trust property, any harm which resulted to the beneficiaries could be resolved by a personal claim against the fiduciary for the money received by way of equitable compensation. In *Target Holdings v Redferns*,[333] Lord Browne-Wilkinson identified three possible remedies in connection with trustees' liability for a breach of trust. The first was equitable compensation; the second was the reinstatement of the trust fund, a proprietary remedy; and the third was a payment of money to the trust equal to the value of the amount lost by the trust fund.

The corporate opportunity doctrine

Many of the cases discussed this far relate specifically to company law and therefore it may be useful to identify some of the differences between company law and trusts law in this regard. There are three circumstances in which a company director may earn personal profits: first, if she has authorisation to do so; secondly, if she has resigned from her employment before commencing the activities which led to the profit; and, thirdly, if the director had no powers at all to act as a director in practice before then making those personal profits. Each of these approaches is then taken in turn. First, the complex question of the acquisition of authorisation in relation to companies. Before considering this question in detail, it is important to understand the subtle differences between companies and trusts.

The modern company grew out of trusts in the late 19th century. The principal difference between the two institutions is that companies have distinct legal personality,[334] whereas trusts do not.[335] Therefore, a company is absolute owner of its own property; the directors of the company take no title in the company's property and are therefore not trustees in that sense of the term.[336] Directors are nevertheless fiduciaries. Directors owe their fiduciary

---

332 So, in Canada, the appropriate award has been held to be damages for breach of duty rather than an account of profits or a constructive trust: *Canadian Aero Service Ltd v O'Malley* (1973) 40 DLR (3d) 371.

333 [1996] 1 AC 421, [1995] 3 WLR 352, [1995] 3 All ER 785.

334 *Saloman v A Saloman & Co Ltd* [1897] AC 22.

335 *Smith v Anderson* (1880) 15 Ch D 247.

336 Although the courts in company law cases do occasionally express the role of company directors as being akin to that of a trustee on occasion: eg, *Re Lands Allotment Co* [1894] 1 Ch 616; *Re Duckwari plc* [1999] Ch 253, [1998] 2 BCLC 315.

duties to the company, but do not owe fiduciary duties to the shareholders of the company in the same way that trustees owe duties to their beneficiaries. Significantly, whereas beneficiaries are the equitable owners of the property held on trust, shareholders are not recognised as having any equitable ownership of the company's property. Rather, any rights of ownership which the shareholders might have are restricted to ownership of their individual shares in the company and to any rights they may have to the company's property under the company's constitution if the company is wound up. It is worth noting also that a business partner[337] who earns unauthorised, personal profits in relation to a partnership's property or commercial opportunities, will also be required to account as a constructive trustee to her fellow partners for those profits.[338] Thus, we will need to make a division here broadly between commercial situations, for example those involving company directors and business partners, and non-commercial situations, for example those involving family trusts. The principle in the abstract remains the same – a fiduciary may not permit a conflict of interest – but, as we shall see, that principle may operate slightly differently in commercial situations.

Given that company law is based historically in trusts law, there is no surprise that the *Keech v Sandford*[339] doctrine has been extended to preclude company directors from making unauthorised profits in the same way as trustees.[340] One principal difference between company law and trusts law is that the trustees would, it appears, be required to seek authorisation from the beneficiaries as equitable owners of the trust fund, whereas company shareholders do not have equivalent equitable title in the company's property and therefore the directors' duties are not owed to the shareholders in the same way that trustees owe their duties to beneficiaries.[341] Consequently, for company directors to seek authorisation requires that to acquire authorisation they approach either the board of directors – as the organ of management in the company – or the company's shareholders in general meeting. This bifurcation in control of the company is a complex feature of modern company law. The directors are taken to be the management of the company with control of its day-to-day affairs, but the Companies Act 2006 retains a variety of powers, including the power to remove individual directors from office,[342] for the company's shareholders in general meetings or extraordinary general meetings.

Consequently, the complex issue in *Regal v Gulliver*[343] (considered above) was whether or not the directors could be said to have given authority to themselves as private individuals to pursue a business opportunity in their own names. On the one hand, the directors were solely responsible for the management of the company and therefore it could have been said that they were perfectly competent to grant this authorisation. However, the House of Lords was concerned, amongst other things, to prevent the management from perpetrating a fraud on the

---

337 Under English law, a partnership is an undertaking in common with a view to profit (Partnership Act 1890, s 1) and therefore English law partnerships always involve commercial activity of necessity. Partnerships are not companies, however, and have no legal personality. Partners owe each other fiduciary duties in English law in general terms.

338 *Lindsley v Woodfull* [2004] 2 BCLC 131

339 (1726) Sel Cas Ch 61.

340 *Cook v Deeks* [1916] 1 AC 554.

341 *Percival v Wright* [1902] 2 Ch 421. Cf *Allen v Hyatt* (1914) 30 TLR 444, where the directors undertook exceptionally to act as the agents of the shareholders as well as in the capacity of directors of the company.

342 See Morse, Hudson, *et al, Guide to the Companies Act 2006*, Sweet & Maxwell, 2006, generally.

343 [1942] 1 All ER 378.

shareholders by diverting a business opportunity to themselves which ought properly to have been exploited on behalf of the company. Company law has, in consequence, developed a concept known as the 'corporate opportunity' doctrine whereby the directors will be liable to hold any profits on constructive trust for the company if those profits were made from an opportunity which the company could have exploited or which the company would have exploited but for the actions of the directors in diverting the opportunity for their own, personal benefits. Contrariwise, it is suggested by the corporate opportunity doctrine that if the director were not diverting a maturing business opportunity to herself, then there will be no liability to hold any personal profits on constructive trust for the company. That means, that if the director took advantage of commercial activity which the company itself did not intend to exploit, then it would not be a breach of the director's fiduciary duties if she took advantage of it.

Therefore, in *Queensland Mines v Hudson*,[344] the managing director sought authorisation to develop this business opportunity for his own benefit only once it had become clear that the company would not be able to pursue the opportunity and further that the board of directors had decided that it was not an opportunity which the company would then pursue, knowing of the managing director's personal interest in the transaction. The rejection of the opportunity by the board of directors meant that Hudson was not appropriating a corporate opportunity for his own purposes, precisely because the board of directors had decided that it would not be an opportunity which the company should have pursued. If the board of directors has given informed consent to a director to exploit a business opportunity on her own account, then the director will be absolved from liability as constructive trustee.[345] Provided that the company has not been misled,[346] the board of directors may release a director from liability as a constructive trustee.[347] By contrast, in *Regal v Gulliver*, even though there is a suggestion that the directors considered the company to be unable to procure the requisite finance to pursue the opportunity, the court nevertheless decided that the opportunity was one which the company would have wanted to pursue and therefore that it was a corporate opportunity. That the directors in *Regal v Gulliver* sought to give themselves permission to pursue an opportunity on their own account was evidently too self-serving to constitute a valid release of liability; on the decided cases, there is only authorisation when the majority of the board of directors has made a decision not to pursue an opportunity in the face of the suggestion made by a minority of directors who subsequently leave their employment to pursue the opportunity which the remainder of the board of directors had not wished the company to pursue.

Recent cases in company law have suggested that this corporate opportunity doctrine will be pursued so that a director may be absolved from liability for secret profits if the company is not intending to pursue the opportunity.[348] So, in *Island Export Finance Ltd v Umunna*,[349] the company had a contract with the government of Cameroon to supply the government with post boxes. Mr Umunna resigned from the company once the contract was completed, having worked on that contract and acquired a great deal of expertise in that particular

---

344 (1977) 18 ALR 1.
345 *Peso Silver Mines Ltd v Cropper* (1966) 58 DLR (2d) 1, Supreme Court of Canada.
346 See *IDC Ltd v Cooley* [1972] 1 WLR 443 considered below.
347 *New Zealand Netherlands Society 'Oranje' Inc v Kuys* [1973] 1 WLR 1126, [1973] 2 All ER 1222, PC.
348 See generally Lowry and Edmonds, 2002.
349 [1986] BCC 460.

activity. The company ceased pursuing this line of business and after his resignation Mr Umunna entered into a similar contract on his own behalf. The company sued him for the personal profits which he made for himself under this second contract. The court held that Mr Umunna's fiduciary obligations towards the company did not cease once he resigned from its employment. This makes sense: if it were not the case, then no fiduciary could ever be bound by their fiduciary office if they had the good sense to resign immediately before breaching their duties. However, in this instance, the court found that the company had not been seeking to develop this sort of business opportunity at the time Mr Umunna had done so and therefore he had not interfered with a corporate opportunity.

Secondly, we should consider the position of directors who have resigned from their employment. In *Balston v Headline Filters Ltd*,[350] a director had resigned from a company and leased premises with a view to starting up in business on his own account before a client of the company approached him and asked him to work for the company. Falconer J held that there was no breach of duty in these circumstances because there was nothing wrong with a director leaving his employment and setting up in business on his own account and, furthermore, there had not been any maturing business opportunity in this case which the director had diverted to himself. Therefore, in company law, it has been held that company directors may, assuming nothing in their contracts to the contrary prohibiting such an action under contract law, resign from their posts and on the next day begin activities which would previously have been in breach of their fiduciary duties.[351] Although, a director may not, even after resigning from her post, use either the company's property or information which she had acquired while still a director of the company to generate personal profits.[352] Clearly, if such behaviour were possible then it would constitute all too easy a method for eluding the principle against fiduciaries earning unauthorised profits: one could learn commercially useful information at work on Monday, resign on Tuesday, and make a huge personal profit on Wednesday from that information. Instead, the law of contract permits a person to leave one employment and begin work elsewhere, but the law on constructive trust prevents that person also taking advantage of a conflict between her personal interests and her fiduciary office for that previous employer.

Thirdly, we must consider the position of directors who have no effective powers to act as a director. In the case of *In Plus Group Ltd v Pyke*[353] Mr Pyke was a director of a company, In Plus Ltd, but he had 'fallen out with his co-director' and in consequence he had been 'effectively excluded from the management of the company'. Mr Pyke decided to set up a company on his own while he was still a director of In Plus Ltd. So, he set up his own company and that company entered into contracts on its own behalf with a major customer of In Plus Ltd. Remarkably, the Court of Appeal held that Mr Pyke was not in breach of his fiduciary duties to In Plus Ltd because he had not used any property belonging to In Plus Ltd

---

350 [1990] FSR 385.
351 *CMS Dolphin v Simonet* [2001] 2 BCLC 704 (Lawrence Collins J); *Quarter Master UK Ltd v Pyke* [2005] 1 BCLC 245, 264 (Mr Paul Morgan QC) and *British Midland Tool Ltd v Midland International Tooling Ltd* [2003] 2 BCLC 523 (Hart J).
352 *Ultraframe UK Ltd v Fielding* [2005] EWHC 1638 (Ch), [2005] All ER (D) 397, *per* Lewison J.
353 [2002] 2 BCLC 201; considered in *Ultraframe UK Ltd v Fielding* [2005] EWHC 1638 (Ch), [2005] All ER (D) 397.

and also because he had not made any use of any confidential information which he had acquired while he was a director of In Plus Ltd. As Sedley LJ held:

> Quite exceptionally, the defendant's duty to the claimants had been reduced to vanishing point by the acts (explicable and even justifiable though they may have been) of his sole fellow director and fellow shareholder Mr Plank. Accepting as I do that the claimants' relationship with Constructive was consistent with successful poaching on Mr Pyke's part, the critical fact is that it was done in a situation in which the dual role which is the necessary predicate of [the claimants'] case is absent. The defendant's role as a director of the claimants was throughout the relevant period entirely nominal, not in the sense in which a non-executive director's position might (probably wrongly) be called nominal but in the concrete sense that he was entirely excluded from all decision-making and all participation in the claimant company's affairs. For all the influence he had, he might as well have resigned.

It is suggested that this is an exceptional decision and it is difficult to square with the strictness of the approach in cases such as *Regal v Gulliver*. Had Mr Pyke been a non-executive director of In Plus it would still have been difficult to see how he could have used information acquired while on company business for his personal gain without there being some suggestion that there was at the very least a conflict between his personal interests and the fiduciary duties which he owed to the company.

This case does raise a more general point which is of importance in relation to company law – and one which is little discussed in the cases: how should equity deal with people who are directors of more than one company? If a director is a director of X Ltd and also a director of Y Ltd – something which is common in practice – then that director may learn information while acting for one company which would be beneficial to the other company. Is the director to be precluded from passing on that information learned while working for X Ltd to her fellow directors of Y Ltd? On the one hand, she owes a duty to X Ltd to keep its confidential information secret. On the other hand, it may be said that she owes another duty to Y Ltd to bring all her knowledge to bear so as to make profits for Y Ltd. If she is not required to do so then she owes little duty to Y Ltd; but if she is required to do so then this effectively destroys her duties of confidentiality to X Ltd. Where the information is confidential then it is suggested that she would be obliged to keep that information confidential and to say nothing to anyone at Y Ltd. If the rule were a different one then money-laundering regulation and insider dealing regulation would be at odds with the case law because confidential information could be passed at law, even if it was required to be dealt with differently by statute.

The more difficult situation would revolve around information which was not confidential. Suppose that the fiduciary attended training paid for by X Ltd and learned of a new method for earning money: would that general knowledge be something which she could use when working for Y Ltd? If it is not confidential, then why not? If she learned a marketplace rumour while working for X Ltd and then went to Y Ltd and shared that non-confidential information with co-workers, could that constitute an abuse of her fiduciary duty? It is difficult to see why if that information was not confidential to X Ltd, although she might be helping Y Ltd, a competitor, to make profits which otherwise X Ltd might have been able to corner a market in. These questions are difficult to answer with complete certainty, they are little discussed in the cases on constructive trusts, and yet they arise frequently in the commercial world.

In practice such matters would be dealt with by a well-drafted contract of employment for that director or by the company's constitutional documents (in the form of its articles of association) and so may not be a question for equity to resolve necessarily. The question is still likely to arise in practice. In part it is resolved by the law relating to constructive trusts in relation to confidential information, which is considered below, whereby a fiduciary is bound by duties of confidentiality and therefore ought to respect the confidence of the company on whose business that confidential information was learned. It is still difficult, however, for a human being to forget confidential information and to act in relation to the second company as though she did not know it. Suppose the information were 'confidential' in the sense that it constituted know-how learned on a training course as to a means of constructing a new type of successful investment portfolio: if that director used that new-found know-how when working for a company which had not paid for the training course, or which had not provided that information, then would it be a breach of duty? How could this director forget her new-found knowledge and pretend to act less knowledgeably when working for the second company?

The maintenance of the strict approach in company law cases

The company law cases considered in the previous section seemed to suggest a weakening of the principle against conflict of interests. This is not the case, on the basis of the cases considered in this section, including some more recent cases. Furthermore, as considered below, a new statutory code has been introduced for company directors in the Companies Act 2006. Nevertheless, the stricter approach derived from *Keech v Sandford* considered above still appears to hold sway for the most part in England.[354] There will only be a defence to liability for constructive trust in exceptional cases where either the director has acquired authorisation from the board of directors, without the board acting in bad faith in so doing,[355] or where the company is not pursuing the opportunity in question. This defence will not be available to any fiduciary who can be demonstrated to have been acting in bad faith.[356] So, in *IDC Ltd v Cooley*,[357] a managing director of an architectural practice failed to win a construction contract for the company but was subsequently offered the contract in his personal capacity. The clients had not wanted to offer the work to that consultancy but did want to use the defendant personally. The defendant then left his employment with the company, lying to them that he was in ill-health, and then pursued the contract on his own account. Roskill J held that the defendant should be liable to account to the company for the whole of his personal profits. Here the defendant had deliberately misled his employer while attempting

---

354 *IDC Ltd v Cooley* [1972] 1 WLR 443; *Carlton v Halestrap* (1988) 4 BCC 538.
355 As in *Regal v Gulliver* [1942] 1 All ER 378; [1967] 2 AC 134n.
356 Although cases such as *IDC Ltd v Cooley* [1972] 1 WLR 443 indicate a continued affection for the stricter approach.
357 [1972] 1 WLR 443.

to divert a business opportunity to himself.[358] Similarly, in *Crown Dilmun v Sutton*,[359] the controlling mind of a company learned of an opportunity to develop a football ground which he exploited on his own account once his contract of employment had been terminated. It was found that he had not made full disclosure to the claimant company of the extent of the opportunity. Consequently, he was liable to account to the claimant for the personal profits realised from the transaction. Company law may alter its direction now that s 175 of the Companies Act 2006 has introduced a general duty for company directors not to permit conflicts of interest: the courts may interpret this in accordance with the corporate opportunity doctrine or may return to the stricter approach in *Boardman v Phipps*.

Three more recent cases have reverted to the traditional approach after *Foster v Bryant, Murad v Al-Saraj* (considered below) and *In Plus Ltd*. So, the Court of Appeal in *Re Allied Business and Financial Consultants Ltd*[360] returned to the traditional 'no conflict' principle in *Aberdeen Railway* and *Regal v Gulliver* to the effect that company directors owe an undivided loyalty to the company akin to the obligations of a trustee. Here a director had diverted a business opportunity to an undertaking under his control when it had been difficult to interest any of the company's clients in investing in the opportunity. The strictness of the traditional principle was nevertheless upheld.

A comparatively straightforward case of diverting business opportunities away from a company arose in *Berryland Books Ltd v BK Books Ltd*.[361] However, this is not simply a case involving diversion of a business opportunity, but rather it also involved the use of the company's assets. The defendant director managed the UK operation of an international publishing company. The director then set up a new company which took over the first company's business opportunities and solicited its staff to work for the new company. In essence, the defendant used all of the first company's assets and staff under a new company name, even to the extent of using the first company's resources to set up competing websites and to market the new company's products at industry conferences. It was held that the defendant had breached the 'fundamental duty of loyalty' bound up with being a director.

In *PNC Telecom plc v Thomas (No 2)*[362] it was held that there would be a conflict of interest when the defendant director voted in a situation where there was a clear conflict of interest: the vote related to a proposal for a change in control of the company which would affect whether or not that director was removed as a director. It was held that the conflict of interest principle still applied, even though this was clearly the sort of case on exclusion from participation in the management of the business which had motivated Rix LJ in *Foster v Bryant*.

---

358   The contentious element of this case is the suggestion that the client would not have used the company but only the defendant personally. The deceit involved appears to have been significant in this instance. It is suggested, however, that that would be to look at the wrong aspect of the case. That an employee seeks to resign her employment and even that she misleads the employer as to her reasons for doing so is not in itself a reason for the imposition of a constructive trust. What is significant is whether or not the fiduciary is trying to divert to herself an opportunity which ought to have been exploited for the benefit of the company. The good or bad faith of the fiduciary cannot matter if the principle is to be strictly applied in any event. It cannot be the purpose of this doctrine that it be used so as to punish lies in the abstract: its purpose is to prevent the shareholders of a company and the company itself from having business opportunities filched from them by venal or by otherwise faithful fiduciaries.

359   [2004] 1 BCLC 468.

360   [2009] 2 BCLC 666.

361   [2009] 2 BCLC 709.

362   [2008] 2 BCLC 95.

In reading each of these cases, it is clear that the judges could have adopted the trend established by Sedley, Arden and Rix LJJ in *Foster v Bryant* and *In Plus Ltd*, as discussed above. In each case, it could possibly have been argued that the directors had been excluded from the management of the business or that they had sought to leave the directorship before exploiting an opportunity. Alternatively, Rix LJ might even have considered that the defendant in *Berryland Books* was a 'false fiduciary'. However, the important point is that in each case the courts returned to the leading cases and to the strict version of the rule.

Another illustration of a return to the strict approach to this principle (and referring to the principle as set out in the Companies Act 2006) appears in the Court of Appeal in *Towers v Premier Waste Ltd*[363] where a director of a waste management company accepted a free loan of machinery from a customer which he used in the renovation of a dilapidated farmhouse and outbuildings belonging to himself and his wife. Mummery LJ took a particularly strict line in holding that the company had a right to consider whether or not it considered this transaction to be a diversion of an opportunity away from the company, and thus to require an account from the director. Under the Companies Act 2006, the director owed a duty of loyalty to the company, which included an obligation to avoid conflicts of interest and a duty not to make unauthorised profits. In consequence, the director's contentions that this was a purely private matter between himself and the customer which had no bearing on his relationship with the company that employed him did not find favour with the Court of Appeal. It signals a return to the strict interpretation of this principle. It was difficult to see what the company was losing by the director's use of machinery owned by a customer which was in bad repair so as to refurbish his own property. In essence, the court considered that the company was owed the opportunity to assess the potential benefits which the company could have taken from the transaction. The trial judge had found that the director should account to the company for the hire charge which the customer would have charged the company itself for the hire of this machinery. This is clearly in the form of holding the director strictly to his duties to the company because it is not actually a loss suffered by the company, nor could the director be shown to have acted in bad faith. Instead, the amount for which the director had to account was not even a profit which the director had earned (although perhaps it could be thought of as a cost which he had avoided, which comes to the same thing). Nevertheless, the opportunity which is diverted away from the company in this situation is difficult to identify.

The nature of the remedy as discussed in company law

The company law texts have a tendency to overlook the precise nature of the equitable remedies which are imposed over company directors.[364] As is discussed in Chapter 21, company directors owe a range of duties to the company. We shall focus on the obligations of directors as fiduciaries not to earn unauthorised profits. The way in which Lawrence Collins J conceived of the liability of directors under company law in *CMS Dolphin Ltd v Simonet*[365] was explicitly by way of analogy with the law of trusts. So, in *CMS Dolphin Ltd v Simonet*[366] Simonet

---

363 [2011] EWCA Civ 923, [2011] IRLR 73.
364 See for example Gower and Davies, *Modern Company Law* (2008) 577, which omits to mention constructive trust or account at all.
365 [2001] 2 BCLC 704.
366 *Ibid.*

left a company, an advertising agency, after a falling-out with his co-founder of that agency, Ball. Both men had been directors of that company. Simonet established a rival agency and attracted clients from his former employer. The first advertising agency claimed that Simonet was in breach of his fiduciary duties as a director in diverting business opportunities from the first advertising agency to his new agency. Lawrence Collins J upheld Simonet's liability for diverting a corporate opportunity and so made him liable to account as a constructive trustee for the profits that had been earned from this activity. What is particularly important for present purposes is that manner in which Lawrence Collins J concluded his judgment by explaining the operation of this doctrine, as his Lordship saw it:

> In my judgment the underlying basis of the liability of a director who exploits after his resignation a maturing business opportunity of the company is that the opportunity is to be treated as if it were property of the company in relation to which the director had fiduciary duties. By seeking to exploit the opportunity after resignation he is appropriating for himself that property. He is just as accountable as a trustee who retires without properly accounting for trust property. In the case of the director he becomes a constructive trustee of the fruits of his abuse of the company's property, which he has acquired in circumstances where he knowingly had a conflict of interest, and exploited it by resigning from the company.

The context of the trust may be very different in practice, however. For example, it will be easier to demonstrate that one has the informed consent and authorisation of other company directors – who are likely to be commercial people whom a court will believe will have understood the necessary risks – than it will be to demonstrate that ordinary people who are the beneficiaries of a family trust were able to give similarly informed consent for the activities of trustees. Even if a trustee calls a meeting of the beneficiaries and tries to explain the situation, it may be difficult to demonstrate that the beneficiaries understood what they were being told so that they could be said to have given *informed* consent, as opposed to the sort of well-meaning but uninformed consent a dog might give when you suggest the word 'walk' or the word 'biscuit' to it.[367] By contrast, company directors could be expected to form a meaningful understanding of the circumstances much more easily as in *Queensland Mines v Hudson*, as could commercial people acting on behalf of corporate beneficiaries. So much will depend upon the context. Nevertheless, the general principle is evident from cases like *Boardman v Phipps*,[368] in which everything will be assumed against the trustee to ensure the protection of the beneficiaries. However, it remains to be seen whether or not in the future the courts may yet come to treat family trusts differently from commercial, investment trusts.

---

367 While a dog will happily respond to the word 'walk' or 'biscuit' that is not because the dog necessarily understands everything that the word involves – rather, it remembers the pleasant associations which accompanied those words on the previous occasions on which they were mentioned. I am aware now that I have strayed into large philosophical and epistemological questions as to what dogs can be taken to know and not know, as well as whether or not they truly *understand* all that is being said. If you have a dog of your own, you will doubtless believe (or probably feel you *know*) that your little friend understands everything you say. I think I will leave this footnote just as it is, even though it might be more prudent to change the analogy in the text given all the philosophical problems it raises, because I have enjoyed this little patch of time we have spent together quite so much.

368 [1967] 2 AC 46.

The trust in *Boardman v Phipps* was a family trust in relation to which it might be inappropriate to think in terms of the trust having any 'corporate purpose' and making informed decisions as to which opportunities it will pursue and not pursue. Nevertheless, the Phipps family trust was investing in private companies. Indeed, in many such trusts, the trustees are necessarily making decisions whether or not to invest in one opportunity or another on behalf of the beneficiaries. In relation to pension funds, the Pensions Act 1995 requires the trustees to draw up investment strategies and the TA 2000[369] requires ordinary trustees to have regard to 'standard investment criteria'[370] and to the diversification of investments.[371]

In consequence, different types of trustees are already required by statute to choose between opportunities which they wish to pursue and those which they do not. In relation to unit trust structures and similar structures which are created solely for speculation and investment of capital, the gap between trusts and companies carrying on trading activities is narrower than the gap between family trusts created simply to maintain assets like real property and trading companies. Therefore, one might be tempted to suggest that the advances in company law in relation to the *Keech v Sandford* principle could be adopted into trusts law in relation to commercial trusts structures, particularly given the suggestion that trusts law might yet come to differentiate between commercial trusts and traditional trusts.

For the moment it appears, however, that the *Boardman v Phipps* principle will continue to apply across the whole of trusts law. In consequence, it would appear that profits can only be authorised either in the terms of the trust itself or by the agreement of all of the beneficiaries. This position mirrors that for a trustee's liability for breach of trust whereby the only defences available in the case law refer to the acquiescence of the beneficiaries in the trustee's actions.[372] To draw parallels between breach of trust and liability as a constructive trustee for secret profits also highlights the link between these two areas as species of equitable wrong:[373] that is, imposing liability on the defendant on account of the defendant's unconscionable action in breaching a trust or making unauthorised profits respectively.

The importance of restrictions on the freedom of fiduciaries, in spite of dissentient rumblings in recent cases relating to directors' duties

In two other recent cases there have been signals that the Court of Appeal is reluctant to persist with the strict approach of the principle against secret profits being made by fiduciaries. This section considers the reasons behind those decisions and demonstrates that they are ill-founded. The principal concern among these judges has been the perceived strictness of the test. Nevertheless, it is suggested, fiduciaries may not earn secret profits from their fiduciary duties nor may they permit any possible conflict between their personal interests and their fiduciary duties: that is central to being a fiduciary. It is common to consider that the decision in *Boardman v Phipps* was harsh in its treatment of an honest and hard-working solicitor who risked his own money; however, the long-standing point of fiduciary duties is

---

369 See para 9.2.1 above.
370 TA 2000, s 4(1).
371 *Ibid*, s 4(2).
372 *Lyall v Edwards* (1861) 6 H & N 337; *BCCI v Ali* [2000] 3 All ER 51; para 18.2.5.
373 The expression 'equitable wrong' used, for example, by Lord Nicholls in discussing personal liability to account as a constructive trustee in *Dubai Aluminium v Salaam* [2003] 1 All ER 97, para 9.

that they must be carried out selflessly in the interests of the beneficiaries. Professional fiduciaries like Boardman are entitled to organise the trust instrument (or the company's articles of association) so that they are paid, their expenses covered and their liabilities limited (as in *Armitage v Nurse*[374]): but in the absence of such limitations, it is simply prohibited for fiduciaries to take personal profits from any activity even indirectly connected to their fiduciary duties so as to ensure that all fiduciaries carry out their fiduciary duties entirely faithfully and selflessly. Boardman earned profits in the performance of his fiduciary duties, and therefore there was a conflict between those two interests because he was not acting entirely selflessly in the interests of the beneficiaries, but rather also in his personal capacity.

Nevertheless, in *Murad v Al-Saraj*[375] Arden LJ chose to cast doubt on the suitability of the doctrine in *Boardman v Phipps* to the extent that that doctrine imposed liability to hold property on constructive trust on people who had not been demonstrated to have acted wrongly. She expressed a preference for liability being based on some fault by the defendant. However, speaking in the Court of Appeal she acknowledged that it was not open to her to overrule *Boardman v Phipps*.[376] It should be noted that the majority in *Boardman v Phipps* were all-too-aware that they were imposing a constructive trust on a person who had acted in good faith. Rix LJ in *Foster v Bryant*[377] was similarly equivocal to Arden LJ about the inflexibility of the test in *Boardman v Phipps*. His Lordship, with respect, became overly concerned in his survey of the cases with the notion that the defendant must be misusing trust (or company) property in some way so as to be liable to hold his profits on constructive trust, and thus overlooked the central point of the principle reiterated by Lord Upjohn in *Boardman v Phipps* that its purpose was to prevent both conflicts of interest and even the possibility that there was a conflict of interest. The purpose of that principle is to provide that once one acts in a fiduciary capacity it is simply impossible to take personal profits from a transaction in which the trust (or company) has or may have a direct or an indirect interest.

In *Foster v Bryant*[378] the defendant director of a company was effectively forced to resign by his co-director (who was also the majority shareholder of the company). The defendant resigned from the company after his co-director 'truculently' made the defendant's wife redundant. The defendant was found to have been excluded from the operation of the business, just like the defendant in *In Plus* above. One of the company's principal clients wanted to retain the services of both directors. Before the defendant's resignation came into effect (that is, while he was still technically a director but after he had tendered his resignation) the client began to talk to the defendant about the way in which the defendant could work with this client. Importantly, the defendant had resigned at this stage. When the defendant's resignation took effect, he began to work for the client. The company sued the defendant on the basis that he had been a director of the company when the business opportunity came to light and therefore it was

---

374   See section 8.5.
375   [2005] EWCA Civ 959.
376   In that case, the Murad sisters entered into a joint venture with Al-Saraj to buy a hotel but Al-Saraj did not disclose that he stood to earn personal profits in the form of a commission from the vendor for setting up the transaction. It was found that he had committed fraudulent misrepresentations in relation to the Murad sisters and furthermore that he had stood in a fiduciary capacity in relation to them. The profits had been earned from his fiduciary office without authorisation. Accordingly, he was held liable to account to the Murad sisters for his profits. On the facts, the principle was not one which was at all harsh.
377   [2007] Bus LR 1565.
378   *Ibid.*

argued that any profits earned from that opportunity should be subject to an account in favour of the company. While it was the company which brought the action, in practice it was the majority shareholder (who was also the defendant's co-director) who was driving the litigation. It was the same person who had driven the defendant to resign his directorship. Consequently, the sympathy of Rix LJ was evidently with the defendant. He sought to distinguish the decided cases on the basis severally that they concerned a misuse of the company's property, that many of them concerned 'faithless fiduciaries' who took wrongful or deceitful advantage of their employers (as in *Cooley*), or that they were diversions of maturing business opportunities by the fiduciary. Rix LJ did not doubt that a director needed to deal in good faith with the company nor that a fiduciary could not earn profits in secret from her office from an opportunity which belonged to the company or for which the company was negotiating. However, those principles must be applied in a 'fact-sensitive' way – considering the ripeness of the business opportunity, the specificity of the opportunity, and thus whether the director had diverted the specific opportunity open to the company. It was held that the position changed in this company after the defendant's resignation such that he was excluded from the business and thus had only to act honestly in his role as director, and therefore that he was not required to account for his subsequent profits. Importantly, while agreeing with Rix LJ, Buxton LJ pointed out that just because a fiduciary had not sought to create a conflict of interest that did not necessarily mean that there was no conflict of interest. Furthermore, the fiduciary is required to account for profits in general terms even if no loss is suffered by the company.

Three points emerge, however, it is suggested. First, when one is a fiduciary then one may not take an unauthorised profit from one's fiduciary capacity: end of story. We live in a world where we expect to be able to take whatever we want, to earn quick profits, and to please ourselves. The idea of fiduciary duty comes from the idea that in some contexts people should be required to act selflessly for others, especially where they have voluntarily accepted that office and are being paid for it (like directors of trading companies). As Moses LJ put it in *Foster v Bryant*,[379] the need to take a 'fact-sensitive' approach to each case might almost 'make one nostalgic for the days in when there were inflexible rules, inexorably enforced by judges who would have shuddered at the reiteration of the noun-adjective [fact-sensitive]'. One such inflexible rule is the rule that a fiduciary may not take an unauthorised profit in circumstances in which there may possibly be a conflict between her personal interests and her fiduciary duties. Secondly, this rule is not so strict as all that. Equity does have an ability to relieve a worthy defendant (as in *Boardman v Phipps*) by requiring some account to be given to her. Thirdly, for those who argue that equity is too uncertain for commercial use, it is not open to them to criticise the ancient doctrine which was put to work in *Boardman v Phipps* which unquestionably has the virtue of predictability about it.

Furthermore, in understanding what equity takes 'unconscionability' to mean, it is simply the case that equity considers it to be unconscionable for a fiduciary to permit even the possibility of a conflict between her personal and her fiduciary capacities by taking an unauthorised profit from that office. Just as we might think that murder or theft are examples of things which are unconscionable in almost all circumstances, equity takes the same prudent attitude to fiduciaries taking personal profits from their offices. If you are acting in a fiduciary capacity, then you are obliged to work selflessly for the company and for your contractually

---

379 [2007] Bus LR 1565, 1598.

agreed salary. In *Umunna*, in *Foster v Bryant* and in *In Plus* the judges were convinced that on the facts before them there was no interest belonging to the company which the fiduciary had diverted away from it. By contrast in *Cooley* there had been deceit and in *Regal v Gulliver* there had clearly been a diversion of an opportunity to the directors personally. Where the context suggests that there is no risk of a conflict of interest, then the doctrine does not apply to the duties of those directors. Such a distinction between the obligations of a trustee would be more difficult to prove than in relation to a trading company where one would expect all of the parties to be clearer about their respective rights and duties.

The duties of directors under the Companies Act 2006

The Companies Act 2006 introduced a statutory code of directors' general duties for the first time.[380] The underlying purpose of the legislation was to improve the understanding of directors' legal duties among directors generally. The directors' duties set out in the Act are 'based on certain common law rules and equitable principles'[381] and moreover those statutory duties 'shall be interpreted and applied in the same way as common law rules or equitable principles'.[382] The statutory duties are therefore to be interpreted in the future in accordance with the development of those case law principles.[383] Therefore, the statutory code should be thought of as being a statutory expression of the developing case law principles and will develop as the case law develops in the future. These duties are owed to the company, not to its shareholders.[384] Those duties on each director in outline are: a duty to act within the terms of her powers under the company's constitution;[385] a duty to promote the success of the company as the director sees it in good faith;[386] a duty to exercise independent judgment;[387] a duty to exercise reasonable care, skill and diligence;[388] a duty to avoid conflicts of interest;[389] a duty not to accept benefits, such as bribes and secret commissions;[390] and a duty to declare interests in transactions.[391] These last three remedies are predicated on the equitable doctrines relating to prevention of conflicts of interest (as in *Boardman v Phipps*) and bribes (as in *Attorney-General for Hong Kong v Reid*) as discussed already in this chapter. The 2006 Act expressly incorporates these long-standing equitable doctrines to provide remedies to breach of these director's duties.[392]

Section 175 of the Companies Act 2006 deals specifically with the duties of directors in relation to conflicts of interest. The purpose of this provision is to codify the existing case law principles discussed above in this chapter, and to develop in parallel to those same

---

380 Companies Act 2006, s 170 *et seq.*
381 *Ibid*, s 170(3).
382 *Ibid*, s 170(4).
383 *Ibid*, s 170(4).
384 *Ibid*, s 170(1).
385 *Ibid*, s 171.
386 *Ibid*, s 172.
387 *Ibid*, s 173.
388 *Ibid*, s 174.
389 *Ibid*, s 175.
390 *Ibid*, s 176.
391 *Ibid*, s 177.
392 *Ibid*, s 178.

principles. Section 175(1) provides that 'a director of a company must avoid a situation in which he has, or can have, a direct or indirect interest that conflicts, or possibly may conflict, with the interests of the company'.[393]

Section 175(2) goes further and provides that:

(2)   This applies in particular to the exploitation of any property, information or opportunity (and it is immaterial whether the company could take advantage of the property, information or opportunity).

The principle is therefore not limited to the use of corporate opportunities, as the case law had tended to suggest. This duty does not relate to 'a conflict of interest arising in relation to a transaction or arrangement with the company' on the part of the director.[394] There are then two means of eluding this provision, as set out in s 175(4):

This duty is not infringed–

(a)   if the situation cannot reasonably be regarded as likely to give rise to a conflict of interest; or
(b)   if the matter has been authorised by the directors.

Therefore, the first means of avoiding liability under the *Boardman v Phipps* principle for a company director is if 'the situation cannot reasonably be regarded as likely to give rise to a conflict of interest'.[395] It is suggested that the case law does not give much guidance on what this provision may mean, although cases like *Balston v Headline Filters* would seem to satisfy it.

Section 175(4) provides that there is no breach of this principle if either the profit is authorised or 'if the situation cannot reasonably be regarded as likely to give rise to a conflict of interest'. In relation specifically to the defence of authorisation for a director, authorisation may be given by the directors under statute now:[396] therefore, directors may explicitly now rely on authorisation being given by the board of directors, provided that the meeting which does so is quorate and that the votes of any directors with such a conflict of interest are discounted.[397] The second means depends upon 'authorisation'. This concept was considered earlier in this chapter, although the statute does provide a more formal means of showing authorisation than does the case law: s 175(5) provides that:

Authorisation may be given by the directors–

(a)   where the company is a private company and nothing in the company's constitution invalidates such authorisation, by the matter being proposed to and authorised by the directors; or

---

393   *Ibid*, s 177 provides also that: 'If a director of a company is in any way, directly or indirectly, interested in a proposed transaction or arrangement with the company, he must declare the nature and extent of that interest to the other directors.'
394   Companies Act 2006, s 175(3).
395   It is provided in Companies Act 2006, s 175(7) that '[a]ny reference in this section to a conflict of interest includes a conflict of interest and duty and a conflict of duties'.
396   Companies Act 2006, s 175(5).
397   *Ibid*, s 175(6).

(b) where the company is a public company and its constitution includes provision enabling the directors to authorise the matter, by the matter being proposed to and authorised by them in accordance with the constitution.

Therefore, depending on the nature of the company, the matter must be authorised by the directors in accordance with the articles of association. Section 175(6) provides that the directors are only deemed to have given authorisation in the following circumstances:

(6) The authorisation is effective only if–
   (a) any requirement as to the quorum at the meeting at which the matter is considered is met without counting the director in question or any other interested director, and
   (b) the matter was agreed to without their voting or would have been agreed to if their votes had not been counted.

Therefore, directors may explicitly now rely on authorisation being given by the board of directors, provided that the meeting which does so is quorate and that the votes of any directors with such a conflict of interest are discounted.[398]

The obligations of agents

The principles relating to unauthorised profits taken as part of the fiduciary's discharge of her duties applies to agents as it applies to all other forms of fiduciary. So, in *Imageview Management Ltd v Jack*[399] Kelvin Jack, the goalkeeper for Trinidad and Tobago, engaged Mr Berry, a football agent and the controlling mind of the Imageview agency, to secure him a transfer to a UK football club. Jack agreed to pay the agency 10% of his salary in return. A transfer was agreed with Dundee United Football Club further to the agency arrangement. However, Mr Berry also negotiated a secret fee of about £3,000 for the agency from Dundee United to obtain a work permit for Jack which Jack required to play in the UK. This fee was not disclosed to Jack. When Jack learned of the secret fee which had been paid to the agency he sought an account from the agency for the amount of that fee. The agency was acting as a fiduciary for Jack. In essence, the agency argued that the fee arrangement was 'none of Jack's business', that it was unconnected to its agency for Jack, and therefore that it was not accountable for it. Jacob LJ noted that the law imposes high standards on fiduciaries like agents,[400] and that those standards even apply to football agents.[401] Throughout the discussions with Dundee United, Berry had been working for Jack and therefore there was a potential conflict of interest between the agency's own interests and its obligations to Jack. There was also evidence that Berry had lied to Jack about the entirety of his dealings with Dundee United, which prompted his lordship to wonder why there would be a need to lie if there was nothing to hide. Jacob LJ applied the strict principle, and noted that it was not as harsh as it

---

398 Companies Act 2006, s 175(6).
399 [2009] Bus LR 1034.
400 In reliance on, and with praise for, *Boston Deep Sea Fishing v Ansell* (1888) 39 Ch D 339 and *Rhodes v Macalister* (1923) 29 Com Cas 19: see also the praise lavished on them by Mummery LJ at [64].
401 [2009] Bus LR 1034, at [6]. There could be no doubt that football agents are to be treated the same as any other agent, but I rather like the ironic sense one gets from this part of the judgment as to the legendary disconnection which some people in football have from ordinary commercial mores.

may otherwise appear given that all Berry would have needed to do to escape the liability to account for the secret fee was to have told Jack about it. Disclosure in this instance would have caused the fee to have been authorised.

12.5.3 Equitable accounting

In circumstances in which a fiduciary is considered entitled to some recompense for work done for the beneficiaries, in spite of being held liable as a constructive trustee for unauthorised profits, it will be possible for the fiduciary to acquire some equitable accounting. This doctrine of account permits a court of equity in its discretion to adjust any amount owed by one party to another, or provides in relation to a proprietary constructive trust in favour of the beneficiaries for those beneficiaries to pay some amount to that fiduciary. The House of Lords in *Boardman v Phipps*[402] was conscious of the hard work done by Boardman to generate a windfall profit for the beneficiaries. Therefore, the court ordered that there ought to be some equitable accounting by the trust in recognition of the work done by the fiduciary. It was held that Boardman was entitled to be compensated on a 'liberal scale' for the work and skill involved in acquiring the shares for the Phipps family trust and turning the private company into profit. The precise amount of that recognition was something left to be ascertained after the hearing of the appeal.

By way of contrast, in *Guinness v Saunders*,[403] a director of Guinness plc, Ernest Saunders, had made personal profits from criminal insider dealing in connection with a takeover bid for the company in breach of his fiduciary duty. The company sought to recover the payments made to Saunders amongst other issues as to Saunders' criminal activities in relation to a takeover bid. The company sought to recover the profits made by Saunders from his fiduciary office on constructive trust principles. Saunders, however, sought to suggest that his work for the company over the period of his directorship had enriched the shareholders such that his liability as a constructive trustee in relation to unauthorised or unlawful profits ought to take into account the broader context of his work for the company. Therefore, Saunders claimed entitlement to a *quantum meruit*, or entitlement to some equitable accounting in recognition of his services.

As to the issue of liability as constructive trustee of the profits, it was held that the appropriate remedy was the imposition of a 'restitutionary constructive trust' over the wrongfully-acquired profits made by Saunders from his fiduciary duty. As to the question of equitable accounting for the work done as a director, Lord Templeman was not prepared to allow Saunders to take any personal benefit from such wrongful acts. Indeed, this accords with the core equitable principle that a claimant must come to equity with clean hands.[404] Therefore, it is clear that equitable accounting will only be made available for defendant fiduciaries like Boardman who have acted in reasonably good faith to generate profits for the beneficiaries.

The defendant in *Cobbetts LLP v Hodge*[405] had sought an accounting (an 'equitable allowance'[406]) for the work he had done in acquiring a private placement of shares for himself.

---

402 [1967] 2 AC 46, 67.
403 [1990] 2 AC 663.
404 Saunders' hands, as evidenced by his subsequent criminal trial, were dirty.
405 [2009] EWHC 786 (Ch), [2010] 1 BCLC 30.
406 *Ibid*, at [113].

However, this was not allowed because the defendant had misled the firm and therefore would not receive equitable assistance. His failure to make a disclosure constituted unclean hands.

12.5.4 The self-dealing principle

The foregoing paragraphs have considered the obligations of fiduciaries when making unauthorised profits from their office in general terms. The material in this section was considered in greater detail in para 8.3.9 above regarding the obligations of fiduciaries when dealing with the beneficiaries of their power as a third party,[407] for example, where a trustee seeks to buy property from the trust. In that instance the trustee would be acting on behalf of the trust as well as on her own behalf. Such a transaction bears the risk that the trustee will acquire the property from the trust at an advantageous price and thus exploit the beneficiaries. By the same token, it might be that the price which the trustee obtains would have been the same price which the beneficiaries would have obtained on the open market. The basis of this principle is expressed in the following *dicta* of Lord Cranworth in *Aberdeen Railway Co v Blaikie Bros*:[408]

> it is a rule of universal application, that no one, having such [fiduciary] duties to discharge, shall be allowed to enter into engagements in which he has, or can have, a personal interest conflicting, or which possibly may conflict, with the interests of those whom he is bound to protect.

The self-dealing principle entitles the beneficiary to avoid any such transaction on the basis, set out in the *Keech v Sandford*[409] rule, that even the possibility of fraud or bad faith being exercised by the trustee is to be resisted.[410] Megarry VC in *Tito v Waddell (No 2)*[411] enunciated the self-dealing principle in the following terms: 'If a trustee purchases trust property from himself, any beneficiary may have the sale set aside *ex debito justitiae*, however fair the transaction.' The right of the beneficiary is therefore to set aside the transaction. There is no defence against the exercise of such a right that the transaction was entered into as though between parties at arm's length. The same principle applies to purchases by directors from their companies,[412] although most articles of association in English companies expressly permit such transactions.[413] Where the beneficiary acquiesces in the transaction, that beneficiary is precluded from seeking to have that transaction set aside.[414]

The trustee will not be able to avoid this principle simply by selling to an associate or a connected company or similar person – although the authorities on this point relate primarily

---

407 This issue was considered in detail in relation to trustees' general duties.
408 (1854) 2 Eq Rep 1281.
409 (1726) 2 Eq Cas Abr 741.
410 *Ex p Lacey* (1802) 6 Ves 625; see *Hollis v Rolfe* [2008] EWHC 1747. See, however, the more liberal Australian approach in *Beale v Trinkler* [2008] NSWSC 347, 11 ITELR 53.
411 [1977] Ch 106. Cf *Prince Jefri Bolkiah v KPMG* [1999] 1 All ER 517 – with reference to 'Chinese walls'.
412 *Aberdeen Railway Co v Blaikie Brothers* (1854) 1 Macq 461.
413 See Jaffey, 2000.
414 *Holder v Holder* [1968] Ch 353.

to sales to relatives,[415] the trustee's children[416] and the trustee's spouse.[417] It is suggested that in any event, such a transaction would be a sham transaction and therefore capable of being set aside,[418] or treated as an attempt to effect a fraud on the power.[419]

12.5.5 The fair dealing principle

The fair dealing principle is similar to the self-dealing principle considered immediately above, and is also considered at para 8.3.9 in greater detail.[420] The fair dealing principle validates acquisitions by trustees of the interests of their beneficiaries and finds that they will be enforceable provided that the trustee does not acquire any advantage attributable to his fiduciary office: otherwise, any unconscionable profits will be held on constructive trust.[421] This principle also applies to fiduciary relationships such as acquisitions by agents of the interests of their principals.[422] To demonstrate that the transaction was not procured as a result of any abuse of position, the trustee will be required to demonstrate that no details were concealed, that the price obtained was fair and that the beneficiary was not required to rely entirely on the trustee's advice.[423] The fair dealing principle is necessarily less strict than the self-dealing principle, because the trustee is able to seek justification of the former by demonstrating that the transaction was not procured in bad faith. It is an unconscious aspect of the principle nevertheless that the beneficiaries are required to authorise the transaction rather than permitting the trustee to act entirely alone: this accords with the principles on authorisation considered above at para 12.5.3. Where the beneficiary is an infant, the trustee will not be able to demonstrate that the beneficiary made an informed decision.[424]

12.6 CONSTRUCTIVE TRUSTS AND AGREEMENTS RELATING TO PROPERTY

The constructive trusts considered in this section arise not contrary to the intentions of the parties, but rather in accordance with their common intention (either express or implied) by operation of law. The common intention constructive trust properly so called arises only in relation to trusts of homes by fastening either on an agreement of the parties, or on the conduct of the parties. This form of trust is considered in great detail in Chapter 15. The other form of constructive trust considered in this section is one which arises in relation to contracts (constituting the common intention of the parties that property be transferred between the contracting parties). Equity recognises that title passes automatically on the

---

415 *Coles v Trecothick* (1804) 9 Ves 234 – which may be permitted where the transaction appears to be conducted as though at arm's length.
416 *Gregory v Gregory* (1821) Jac 631.
417 *Ferraby v Hobson* (1847) 2 Ph 255; *Burrell v Burrell's Trustee* 1915 SC 333.
418 Cf *Street v Mountford* [1985] 2 WLR 877; *Midland Bank v Wyatt* [1995] 1 FLR 697.
419 *Rochefoucauld v Boustead* [1897] 1 Ch 196.
420 This issue was considered in detail in relation to trustees' general duties.
421 *Chalmer v Bradley* (1819) 1 J & W 51; *Tito v Waddell (No 2)* [1977] Ch 106. Cf *Clay v Clay* [2001] WTLR 393.
422 *Edwards v Meyrick* (1842) 2 Hare 60.
423 *Coles v Trecothick* (1804) 9 Ves 234.
424 *Sanderson v Walker* (1807) 13 Ves 601.

creation of the contract without the need for further formality, irrespective of the position at common law or under statute.

12.6.1 Common intention constructive trusts and the home

The nature of the common intention constructive trust is considered in detail in Chapter 15 *Trusts of homes*. The common intention constructive trust has been held to exist only in relation to the family home. The decision of the House of Lords in *Gissing v Gissing*[425] held that when deciding which members of a household should have which equitable interests in the home, the court should consider the common intention of the parties. This marked a profound change in the law relating to rights in the family home, which had previously operated on the basis of the rules relating to presumptions of resulting trust and the unenforceability of agreements between husband and wife.

The later House of Lords decision in *Lloyds Bank v Rosset*[426] provided a more rigid statement of the nature of this common intention constructive trust. It arises in two circumstances. First, where the parties can adduce evidence of express discussions to establish common intention by means of an agreement formed, usually, before the date of acquisition of the property.[427] Secondly, where the parties demonstrate a common intention by dint of those claiming an equitable interest having contributed to the purchase price or to the mortgage repayments in respect of the land. In both cases, the claimant would be required to demonstrate detriment. The second form of constructive trust appears to be identical to that form of resulting trust accepted in *Dyer v Dyer*.[428]

Further, in *Lloyds Bank v Rosset*, Lord Bridge clearly intended to compact constructive trust and proprietary estoppel together in this single doctrine: an approach which is criticised at section 15.3 below. The common intention constructive trust grants the successful claimant an equitable proprietary right in the home which will be calculated as a proportion of the total equity which corresponds to the claimant's financial contribution to the property.[429]

While the common intention constructive trust applies only in relation to the home, it might be argued that such a trust could be developed so as to apply similarly in relation to commercial contracts where the parties necessarily formulate an intention as to the allocation of title in property. In commercial contracts, it is more likely, even if the contract is not fully valid, that the parties will have applied their minds more closely to issues of title in property than is commonly the case in family home situations.[430] So, in *Lloyd v Pickering*,[431] the *Lloyds Bank v Rosset* common intention constructive trust was used by Blackburne J to decide whether or not an alleged agreement to co-own a gymnasium business granted the claimant an equitable interest under a constructive trust in that business. Thus, the *Rosset* approach has indeed been used in a commercial, as opposed to a domestic, context.

---

425 [1971] AC 886.
426 [1991] 1 AC 107. See now *Stack v Dowden* [2007] UKHL 17.
427 Always presuming that there is no express intention to the contrary: *Robinson v Reeve* [2002] EWHC 1179 (Ch).
428 (1788) 2 Cox Eq Cas 92; *Mollo v Mollo* [2000] WTLR 227.
429 *Huntingford v Hobbs* [1993] 1 FLR 736. Cf *Stockert v Geddes* (2000) 80 P & CR 11.
430 Hudson, 2000:2; Hudson, 1999:1.
431 [2004] EWHC 1513 (Ch).

Commonwealth jurisdictions have turned against the common intention constructive trust in relation to the home, precisely because it requires the court to try to find a common intention which has frequently never been considered at all by the parties.[432] The difficulty involved with proving such an intention in many cases has caused the English Court of Appeal to favour allocating equal shares in circumstances in which the home has been held by a family for a long period of time – particularly when the litigation is commenced by mortgagees seeking to enforce their security and dispossess the family.[433]

12.6.2 On conveyance of property

Where a contract is effected for the sale or transfer of property, that contract will operate so as to transfer equitable interest in that property from the original owner to the other contracting party.[434] The transfer of the equitable interest takes effect by means of a constructive trust.[435] Similarly, an unexecuted court order for the transfer of property creates a constructive trust over that property until the time of transfer.[436] The rationale behind the operation of this principle is as follows. Once the contract is formally created, the contracting parties acquire rights of specific performance to force the other party to perform its part of the bargain. On the basis that each party has a right in equity to specific performance, and on the basis further that the contract is one to transfer title in property, it is said that the party so entitled acquires a right to the entire equitable interest in that property.[437] Therefore, once such a binding contract has been formed for the transfer of property, it is said that the equitable interest in that property passes to the buyer automatically on the creation of the contract.[438] The automatic vesting of the equitable interest is said to arise due to the equitable principle that equity looks upon as done that which ought to have been done: therefore, equity considers that because the contract requires transfer of title, transfer of title must be deemed to have taken place automatically.[439]

For this constructive trust to be effective, it is necessary that the contract is capable of being specifically enforced, as considered in Chapter 26. On the basis that equity would award specific performance, equity will recognise as done that which ought to have been done. Therefore, if the transfer ought to have been specifically enforced, equity will recognise the transferor as holding the property on constructive trust for the transferee until the transfer is actually enforced.[440] The constructive trust arises from this equitable principle on the basis that it would be unconscionable for one of the contracting parties to refute its specifically enforceable obligation to transfer title to the other party.[441]

---

432 As considered at section 15.8 below.
433 See *Midland Bank v Cooke* [1995] 4 All ER 562.
434 *Lysaght v Edwards* (1876) 2 Ch D 499; *Oughtred v IRC* [1960] AC 206; *Neville v Wilson* [1997] Ch 144.
435 *Chinn v Collins* [1981] AC 533; *Neville v Wilson* [1997] Ch 144.
436 *Mclurcan v Mclurcan* (1897) 77 LT 474; *Mountney v Treharne* [2002] EWCA Civ 1174, [2002] BPIR 1126.
437 *Ibid.*
438 *Chinn v Collins* [1981] AC 533.
439 *Walsh v Lonsdale* (1882) 21 Ch D 9.
440 *Ibid.*
441 *Neville v Wilson* [1997] Ch 144.

Contract for the sale of land

This rule that a contract for the sale of property transfers an equitable interest in that property applies to land in the same way that it applies to other items of property,[442] provided that the contract is in writing containing all of the terms of the agreement in one document which is signed by all the parties.[443] Once that contract has been created, the equitable interest in the land is deemed to have transferred automatically to the purchaser of that interest.[444] This constructive trust comes into operation, as considered above, by extension of the equitable principle that 'Equity looks upon as done that which ought to have been done', such that a specifically enforceable obligation by contract to transfer rights in land is deemed in equity to effect an automatic transfer of those rights.[445] The vendor holds the property on constructive trust for the purchaser until completion of the sale or transfer.[446] Furthermore, in the period of time between the formation of a contract for the sale of land and the registration of the buyer as proprietor on the land register, the former proprietor holds the interests which are the subject of the sale on constructive trust for the buyer until re-registration. Similarly, a contract to grant a lease creates leasehold rights which will be recognised by equity.[447]

There are competing authorities as to whether this trust comes into existence on execution of the contract of sale[448] or on completion of the contract of sale.[449] Similarly, there is authority to effect that the vendor of the property is a trustee *sub modo* rather than a constructive trustee, given (it was suggested) that the contract might not be effected even after an agreement for sale has been reached.[450] However, in the modern context, a contract for sale of land is only effective if it complies with s 2 of the Law of Property (Miscellaneous Provisions) Act 1989 and at that stage should be capable of specific performance. At the point that the contract is capable of specific performance, it is suggested, the constructive trust comes into existence and the vendor becomes a constructive trustee. In *Jerome v Kelly*,[451] Lord Walker considered the dispute on the authorities as to the precise nature of the trustee's obligations under such a constructive trust. It has been suggested that a trustee in such a situation is a peculiar kind of trustee (as considered below) because she has a personal interest, in its colloquial sense, in the property at issue[452] and that the true essence of the

---

442 *Lysaght v Edwards* (1876) 2 Ch D 499; *Rayner v Preston* (1881) 18 Ch D 1.

443 Law of Property (Miscellaneous Provisions) Act 1989, s 2.

444 *Lysaght v Edwards* (1876) 2 Ch D 499. No similar obligation is owed to a further subpurchaser: *Berkley v Earl Poulett* (1977) 242 EG 39. Although a purchase by another person would require the vendor to hold the sale proceeds on trust for the initial purchaser under contract: *Lake v Bayliss* [1974] 1 WLR 1073; *Shaw v Foster* (1872) LR 5 HL 321.

445 *Lysaght v Edwards* (1876) 2 Ch D 499; *Walsh v Lonsdale* (1882) 21 Ch D 9. See also *Kinane v Mackie-Conteh* [2004] EWHC 998 (Ch); [2004] 19 EGCS 164.

446 This operates in parallel, it is suggested, to the doctrine which provides that the vendor acts as trustee of the fee simple absolute in possession over land between the time of completion of sale and the re-registration of the proprietorship of that land in the name of the purchaser.

447 *Parker v Taswell* (1858) 27 LJ Ch 812; *Walsh v Lonsdale* (1882) 21 Ch D 9.

448 *Paine v Meller* (1801) 6 Ves 349; 31 ER 1088, *per* Lord Eldon; *Broome v Monck* (1805) 10 Ves 597, 32 ER 976.

449 *Shaw v Foster* (1872) LR 5 HL 321.

450 *Wall v Bright* (1820) 1 Jac & W 494 at 501, 37 ER 456 at 459, *per* Lord Plumer MR.

451 [2004] 2 All ER 835, [2004] UKHL 25.

452 *Shaw v Foster* (1872) LR 5 HL 321, 338, *per* Lord Cairns; *Lysaght v Edwards* (1876) 2 Ch D 499, 506, *per* Lord Jessel MR.

arrangement is the contract between the parties.[453] Nevertheless, the existence of a contract is the essence of this form of constructive trust and therefore the fiduciary obligations associated with such a constructive trust will take effect in any event: the question is as to the terms of those fiduciary obligations.

The precise nature and scope of this constructive trust is worthy of closer examination. The constructive trust in these circumstances frequently grants more complex powers to the trustee than an ordinary bare trust, although the rights of the beneficiary are typically limited to those of a beneficiary under a bare trust. The limited notion of the constructive trust in these circumstances arises from cases such as *Lloyds Bank v Carrick*,[454] in which the defendant vendor contracted with his sister-in-law to sell a lease over a residential property to her. The transaction required the sister-in-law to sell her own home, to pay those sale proceeds to the defendant, and then to move into property over which the defendant was lessee, at which time he would assign his interest in the lease to her. The defendant took out a charge with the plaintiff bank without informing his sister-in-law. The question turned on whether or not the sister-in-law had a right under a merely bare trust, such that her right did not require registration and so could not be unenforceable against the bank for want of registration. It was held that the contract became specifically enforceable when the sister-in-law began to perform her obligations under the contract by entering into possession of the lease and paying the purchase price.[455] Consequently, it was held that the sister-in-law's interest arose by virtue of the specific enforceability of the contract and therefore was void as against the bank for want of registration.[456] Her right was the right of a person under a bare trust in relation to that interest in property for which she had contracted. Thus, the right is said to be a limited right: the trustee simply holds the property as nominee for the purchaser. This right would, however, grant a priority right in the vendor's insolvency.[457]

The fiduciary obligations of the vendor are limited. The ordinary model of this constructive trust is limited to equity transferring the equitable interest in the property which has been contracted to be sold and does not impose greater obligations on the trustee than that. However, as considered in the next section, it may be that the parties' contract is entered into as part of a more complex network of commercial obligations, such that the vendor does not agree simply to transfer her property rights without some action of the vendor or some condition precedent being performed. After all, if the contract were not performed by the purchaser, then the vendor would wish to recover absolute title to the land without the purchaser acquiring rights for which she has not paid. So, if the purchase price for the property remains unpaid, it does not constitute the vendor a constructive trustee in general terms of, for example, all rents and other income received in relation to that property before the purchase price is actually paid.[458] Furthermore, the vendor is entitled to protect her interests

---

453   *Chang v Registrar of Titles* (1976) 137 CLR 177, 189, *per* Jacob J.

454   [1996] 4 All ER 630.

455   Significantly, however, this particular contract remained executory at the time that the charge was created in favour of the bank: *ibid*, 637.

456   *Ibid*.

457   *Freevale Ltd v Metrostore (Holdings) Ltd* [1984] 1 All ER 495; *Re Coregrange Ltd* [1984] BCLC 453; subject always to any statutory power to disclaim contracts *inter alia* as a fraud on the creditors of the insolvent person.

458   *Rayner v Preston* (1881) 18 Ch D 1, 6, *per* Cotton LJ. The precise point in that case having been altered by the Law of Property Act 1925, s 47. Also *J Sainsbury plc v O'Connor (Inspector of Taxes)* [1991] STC 318. Cf *Paine v Meller* (1801) 6 Ves J 349.

in the property prior to sale, and therefore is not obliged to act only in the best interests of the purchaser, as would be the case with an ordinary trustee.[459] Indeed, the vendor in such circumstances has been described as being a mere 'quasi-trustee' as a result, *inter alia*, of these limitations on her obligations.[460] So, the vendor, as constructive trustee, is entitled to protect her own position and rescind the contract if some condition precedent has not been performed, just as the purchaser could rescind the contract if some condition precedent had not been performed (such as the acquisition of planning permission to develop the land).[461] This point is taken up in the next section.

Nature and the time of the creation of the constructive trust in relation to sale of land

The process of selling land involves a lengthy contractual process in which the parties usually create an oral understanding which will not be a contract,[462] following which written contracts are exchanged which usually constitute a binding contract, although the contract is not completed until a later date specified in the contract, and then the new proprietor's interest is ultimately registered on the Land Register. In the House of Lords in *Jerome v Kelly*,[463] the question arose as to the point in time at which the constructive trust came into existence during such a complex contractual arrangement.[464] There are a number of times at which the constructive trust could possibly arise. It might be that it is when contracts are exchanged that the equitable interest passes, alternatively it could be when sale is completed, or it could be (under the Land Registration Act 2002) when the new proprietor's interest is registered on the Land Register.[465] It is important to know, as in *Jerome v Kelly*, when the equitable interest passes because that is the time at which capital gains tax becomes payable on the disposal of the equitable interest.[466]

The answer posited by Lord Walker to the question 'when does the equitable interest pass?' was that it depends upon the circumstances and the terms of the contract. So, on the facts of *Jerome v Kelly* itself, the purchaser's acquisition of the property was dependent on the acquisition of planning permission to develop the land and, therefore, if planning permission was not obtained, the contract of sale could have been rescinded by the purchaser.[467] On

---

459   *Shaw v Foster* (1872) LR 5 HL 321, 338, *per* Lord Cairns. See also *Royal Bristol and Permanent Building Society v Bomash* (1887) 35 Ch D 390.

460   *Cumberland Consolidated Holdings Ltd v Ireland* [1946] KB 264, 269, *per* Lord Greene MR; *Berkley v Poulett* (1977) 242 EG 39.

461   *Jerome v Kelly* [2004] UKHL 25, [2004] 2 All ER 835.

462   Law of Property (Miscellaneous Provisions) Act 1989, s 2.

463   [2004] UKHL 25, [2004] 2 All ER 835.

464   The particular point in that case related to the defendants' liability to capital gains tax in relation to a contractual arrangement (which it appears had been organised to minimise liability to tax) whereby the vendor and the purchaser of the land did not contract directly such that it was unclear when or whether a '*Lysaght v Edwards* model' constructive trust came into existence.

465   The position in land law is now that registration constitutes the transfer of title at law, whereas *Jerome v Kelly* concerned itself only with execution, exchange of contracts and completion, missing out the vital stage under the Land Registration Act 2002 that there be registration before there is a complete transfer of absolute title.

466   The argument, for capital gains tax purposes, was raised on behalf of the taxpayer that until the date of completion of the contract, the property should be considered to remain absolutely the property of the vendor so that no chargeable disposal of any interest had been made for tax purposes.

467   [2004] UKHL 25, para [36], *per* Lord Walker.

this basis, the purchaser would not wish to have an equitable interest in the property, nor would the vendor wish to have transferred any equitable interest in the property if the contract of sale was ultimately to be rescinded. Thus, it would have been unsatisfactory to have held that the entire equitable interest must pass to the purchaser on exchange of contracts between the parties, so that the vendor became constructive trustee. In the older case of *Lysaght v Edwards*,[468] it had been held that the equitable interest passed when the contract was executed. However, questions were raised in subsequent cases as to the nature of the trusteeship in such circumstances given that the vendor has a right in the land up to the time of transfer which she is entitled to protect.[469] Consequently, this is not the ordinary sort of constructive trusteeship in which the trustee has no personal interests which can conflict with her fiduciary duties;[470] it is not a situation in which the vendor is simply obliged to hold the property solely for the benefit of the beneficiary. Rather, the purpose of the constructive trust here is to ensure equitable protection for the purchaser's contractual rights until the transfer is formally completed by means of registration.

The principal problem which Mason J identified in *Chang v Registrar of Titles*[471] with the *Lysaght v Edwards* approach was that the purchaser may not have the money to complete the purchase or the vendor may not have valid title which can be transferred to the purchaser. In such a situation, the obligations of the constructive trustee would have to be called into question because the trustee, in her capacity as vendor of the property, would wish to exercise her rights to rescind the contract and to recover any damages from the purchaser (if appropriate), whereas ordinarily a trustee would be required to act entirely in the best interests of the beneficiary. Consequently, Mason J suggested, as was accepted by Lord Walker in *Jerome v Kelly*,[472] that the trustee is not a constructive trustee under an ordinary bare trust but rather must be accepted as having a very particular kind of trusteeship which will differ from circumstance to circumstance. The further dimension not considered by the courts in these cases is the *Banner Homes* form of constructive trust considered above, whereby one or other of the contracting parties may also have performed acts to their detriment in reliance on the contract and therefore there may be further liabilities to equitable compensation even if the contract is rescinded.[473]

It is suggested that the best approach to this form of trusteeship is as follows. The vendor holds whatever interest she validly owns and which she purports to transfer to the purchaser on constructive trust for the purchaser from the moment when the contract of sale is specifically enforceable. That is usually on exchange of contracts. If the vendor transpires not to have sufficient title to effect the transfer for which the parties have contracted, then the vendor owes the purchaser damages for breach of contract for the difference between the interest contracted for and the interest actually transferred. If the contract fails, for whatever reason, then in equity there is no conscionable basis on which the vendor is required to continue to hold any part of the equitable interest in the property on constructive trust for the

---

468   (1876) 2 Ch D 499, 506, *per* Sir George Jessel MR.
469   See *Shaw v Foster* (1872) LR 5 HL 321, 338, *per* Lord Cairns; *Rayner v Preston* (1881) 18 Ch D 1, 6, *per* Cotton LJ.
470   This ordinary form of fiduciary obligation was considered in para 8.3.9 of this book.
471   (1976) 137 CLR 177, 184.
472   [2004] UKHL 25, para [31].
473   See para 12.3.2 above.

purchaser. The purpose of the constructive trust is to protect the rights of the purchaser to the extent that the vendor may not act in breach of the contract of sale – while such a contract for sale continues in existence – so as to transfer the rights which are to be sold to some third person or to perform some other act which would reduce the effective value of those rights.[474] The constructive trust does not necessarily transfer the entirety of the equitable interest immediately if the parties' contract, for example, contains provisions which suggest that the contract is not to be immediately enforceable due to some condition precedent. The constructive trust here is therefore a form of equitable protection of the purchaser's rights under the contract for sale until that contract is completed by means of the registration of the rights of the new proprietor of that property. That protection is achieved by means of a transfer of some equitable interest in the land to the purchaser, albeit that that interest will lapse if the contract fails for some reason.

It is suggested, therefore, that the better answer is that the equitable interest passes at whatever time the contract becomes specifically enforceable. After all, it is the specific enforceability of the contract which causes the equitable interest to pass (on the basis that equity looks upon as done that which ought to have been done): therefore, it should be by reference to the specific enforceability of the contract that one should decide when the equitable interest passes by means of constructive trust. On the facts of *Jerome v Kelly*, if the parties' contract was subject to a condition precedent (express or implied) that the contract would only be effective if the purchaser acquired planning permission to develop the property, then there would not be a specifically enforceable contract until that condition precedent was satisfied and therefore the constructive trust would come into effect at that time. This is what Sir George Jessel MR meant, it is suggested, when he held that 'the moment you have a valid contract for sale the vendor becomes in equity a trustee for the purchaser of the estate sold, and the beneficial ownership passes to the purchaser'.[475] As soon as the contract is specifically enforceable, the purchaser becomes an equitable owner of the property by means of a constructive trust.

Contract for the sale of personalty

The basis of the doctrine is that an automatic transfer of the equitable interest occurs where otherwise the former owner of that title would seek to renege on her obligations under contract. However, the notion of automatic transfer has been used particularly in tax planning to effect automatic transfers of the equitable interest in property – and thereby the most valuable part of the absolute title in that property – without the need to effect transfer by means of any documentation or other act which might trigger liability to tax or stamp duty before the more valuable part of the title had been disposed of. This reversal of the core understanding of the *Walsh v Lonsdale*[476] principle into an offensive rather than a defensive mechanism has the weight of authority. Thus, in *Oughtred v IRC*,[477] a mother and son wished to exchange title in valuable shareholdings so that the mother could consolidate a larger shareholding in one particular company. Both sets of shares were held on trust for the mother

---

474   This is recognised by Lord Walker at [2004] UKHL 25, para [37].
475   *Lysaght v Edwards* (1876) 2 Ch D 499, 506.
476   (1882) 21 Ch D 9.
477   [1960] AC 206.

and son respectively. To have effected the documentary transfers of the shares necessary to transfer legal title would have attracted liability to stamp duty. The parties' intention was to transfer their interests without the need for the documentary transfers, and further by avoiding the need for signed writing under s 53(1)(c) of the Law of Property Act 1925 necessary to dispose of their equitable interests in the shares to one another.[478] Therefore, the mother and son created a contract between them by which they agreed to exchange their respective shareholdings. It was held that such a specifically enforceable contract was sufficient to constitute an automatic transfer of their shareholdings. That this structure has been held[479] to effect an automatic transfer of the equitable interest means that the stamp duty levied on the document of transfer of the legal title is levied on a nil amount on the basis that all of the value in the shareholdings moves with the equitable interest and in turn the equitable interest moves as soon as there is a specifically enforceable contract in place between the parties.[480] Until the document transfers legal title to the intended recipient, the *legal* owner is constituted a constructive trustee of the equitable interest in that property.[481]

12.7 VOLUNTARY ASSUMPTION OF LIABILITY

The categories of constructive trust assembled in this section are said to arise on the basis of voluntary assumption of liability, where a person is deemed to be a constructive trustee because of some relationship or some course of dealing into which she entered voluntarily.

12.7.1 Secret trusts

The subject of secret trusts was considered in detail in Chapter 6. Secret trusts arise in circumstances in which, for whatever reason, a testator decides to leave ostensible legacies to someone whom the testator really wants to act as trustee for an intended but undisclosed beneficiary of that legacy.[482] Frequently this is done so as to benefit mistresses or illegitimate children after the testator's death in a way that does not require them to be disclosed in the will. The nature of secret trusts is complicated and falls, on the cases, into two kinds. The fully secret trust is not mentioned on the face of the will at all, whereas the existence of a half-secret trust is revealed on the face of the will, although its precise terms remain undisclosed. Fully secret trusts are frequently identified as constructive trusts,[483] whereas half-secret trusts are often considered to be a species of express trust because they are disclosed on the face of the will.[484] There is some debate between the commentators as to this.[485]

---

478 See also *Neville v Wilson* [1997] Ch 144.
479 The leading speech of Lord Radcliffe in *Oughtred v IRC* [1960] AC 206 itself was somewhat elliptic on this point. His Lordship's intention was to find the taxpayers liable to stamp duty under the then-applicable stamp duty legislation at the least, although he did appear to concede that the equitable interest in the shares did pass on the creation of the contract, even if that had no effect on the stamp duty position ultimately.
480 See *Chinn v Collins* [1981] AC 533; *Neville v Wilson* [1997] Ch 144.
481 *Ibid.*
482 Provided always that the obligation is a trust obligation and not a merely moral obligation: *Kasperbauer v Griffith* [2000] 1 WTLR 333.
483 Oakley, 1997, 260; Martin, 1997, 162.
484 Martin, 1997, 162.
485 See section 6.6 above. [1997] 2 WTLR 333.

The argument raised in Chapter 6 was that all secret trusts ought to be considered to be constructive trusts effected to provide an exception to the Wills Act 1837 and thus prevent a legatee under a will from asserting an unconscionable beneficial title to property. A secret trust is a trust not properly constituted by the settlor but the substance of which was communicated to persons who are named as legatees under the settlor's will. As such, the enforcement of the settlor's promise could not be an express trust because the settlor retains the right to change her will, something which would not be permitted if an express trust had already been created over that property. The only viable trusts law analysis is therefore that the secret trust must be a form of constructive trust. One other possible rationale for the enforcement of secret trusts by the courts is based on the equitable principle that statute and common law should not be used as an engine of fraud, which is presented as a form of constructive trust in this chapter in any event.[486]

12.7.2 Mutual wills

As with secret trusts, equity is prepared to effect testamentary arrangements which do not comply *strictu sensu* with English probate law and s 9 of the Wills Act 1837. The doctrine of mutual wills applies to wills created by two or more people in a particular form with the intention that the provisions of those wills shall be irrevocably binding. Ordinarily a will would be capable of amendment or repeal; mutual wills are subtly different because the parties intend that their wills be binding. When the first of the parties to the mutual wills dies, the arrangement becomes binding on any surviving parties. In the event that any survivor should have attempted to change her will or to break the mutual will arrangement, her personal representatives after her death would be required to hold her estate as constructive trustees subject to the terms of the mutual wills. Lord Camden expressed the doctrine in the following way in *Dufour v Pereira*: '. . . he, that dies first, does by his death carry the agreement on his part into execution. If the other then refuses, he is guilty of a fraud, can never unbind himself, and becomes a trustee of course. For no man shall deceive another to his prejudice.'[487] On this model, the essence of the doctrine is the prevention of a fraud being committed by the survivor in failing to comply with the terms of the mutual will arrangement.[488] A mutual will arrangement is dependent on there being clear and satisfactory evidence of a contract between two testators to the effect that each would make wills in a particular form and that neither party would revoke that will without informing the other testator.[489] The doctrine of mutual wills operates in such a way that 'the conscience of the survivor's executor' is bound by a trust which arises out of 'the agreement between the two testators not to revoke their wills'.[490] That trust comes into effect when the first of the two dies without having revoked her will.[491] For example, a husband and wife may agree that the

---

486 See para 12.3.4 above.

487 (1769) 1 Dick 419. Cf *Birch v Curtis* [2002] 2 FLR 847.

488 The principles governing mutual wills, and the indemnification of the personal representatives, was considered in *Shovelar v Lane* [2011] EWCA Civ 802, [2011] 4 All ER 669.

489 *Olins v Walters* [2009] 2 WLR 1. See also *Birmingham v Renfrew* (1937) 57 CLR 666.

490 *Thomas and Agnes Carvel Foundation v Carvel* [2007] EWHC 1314 (Ch), [2007] 4 All ER 81; and *Olins v Walters* [2009] 2 WLR 1, 10, *per* Mummery LJ.

491 *Ibid.*

survivor be obliged to leave all the matrimonial home to their only child absolutely. Thus, if the husband were to predecease his wife, and if his wife were to have a further child by a subsequent marriage and purport to leave the home after her death on trust for her two children in equal shares, her personal representatives would be obliged to hold that property on constructive trust for the child of her first marriage.

A mutual wills arrangement takes effect by means of a constructive trust in that the arrangement between the two testators by reference to which neither of them alters their will operates on the conscience of the surviving testator once that arrangement has been made, as the Court of Appeal has confirmed in *Olins v Walters*.[492] This understanding of the mutual wills doctrine is generally taken from the judgment of Deane J in *Birmingham v Renfrew*:[493]

> . . . a contract between persons to make corresponding wills gives rise to equitable obligations when one acts on the faith of such an agreement and dies leaving his will unrevoked . . . the doctrines of equity attach the obligation to the property. The effect is, I think, that the survivor becomes a constructive trustee and the terms of the trust are those of the will he undertook would be his last will.

The basis of this doctrine in contract and in constructive trust is therefore clear.

An important case relating to mutual wills with a slightly novel twist came in front of the Court of Appeal in *Olins v Walters*.[494] It concerned an agreement entered into in 1998 between an elderly married couple that they would create mutual wills. The arrangement had been explained to them (correctly) by their grandson, who was a solicitor, to the effect that they agreed not to alter their wills from the form into which they had been amended by codicil in 1998 without the agreement of the other person. When the wife died, after the relationship between the parties had deteriorated, the widower did not wish to be bound by the terms of their agreement. He contended that he had no recollection of the agreement formed in 1998. At first instance,[495] Norris J found on the facts that on the balance of probabilities[496] the parties had formed an agreement between themselves which constituted a mutual wills arrangement. Relying on the documents and on two grandsons' memories of the meeting in 1998, his lordship found that that had been the arrangement. The novel twist in this case was that it was one of the parties to the mutual wills arrangement which was contesting its validity, and even its existence;[497] whereas usually it would be other family members who would be protesting about this after both parties had died.

Olins v Walters was appealed to the Court of Appeal on two grounds: first, that there was insufficient evidence of a mutual wills arrangement and, secondly, that the terms of the 'contract' between the parties were insufficiently clear. The appeal was framed in terms of

---

492   [2009] 2 WLR 1, at [37], *per* Mummery LJ.
493   (1937) 57 CLR 666, 683.
494   [2009] 2 WLR 1.
495   [2007] EWHC 3060, [2008] WTLR 339.
496   Which is the standard of proof applicable to private law questions of this sort.
497   Mummery LJ explained that no case on the authorities had involved a surviving party to the agreement seeking to repudiate it.

'contract'[498] and the Court of Appeal tended to adopt that language, although Mummery LJ in delivering the only judgment of the court did identify very clearly that the doctrine is based on constructive trust.[499] Mummery LJ found that Norris J had had sufficient material on the facts to find that the parties had created a mutual wills arrangement on the balance of probabilities. His lordship also corrected the misapprehension on behalf of the appellant that this area of law was based on contract law and therefore that there must be a contract capable of specific performance. Instead, Mummery LJ explained that this was an equitable obligation imposed on the surviving testator not to alter his will:

> It arises by operation of law on the death of the first testator to die so as to bind the conscience of the surviving testator in relation to the property affected.[500]

The keynote of this doctrine is therefore the impact on the conscience of the surviving testator which imposes a constructive trust over the property to be left by him,[501] which in practice prevents him from altering his will without the agreement of the other testator.

It is frequently the case that mutual wills are effected with the intention that X shall benefit Y and that Y shall benefit X, no matter who dies first. In effect, they are 'mutual' in the sense that they are mutually beneficial and not simply mutually binding. However, in the wake of the decision in *Re Dale*,[502] it was held that there was no requirement that each party to the arrangement take a personal benefit. Rather, it is possible that there be benefits to third parties.

The question is how this intention to create mutual wills would arise. In *Re Hagger*,[503] a husband and wife made separate wills, but both of those wills contained recitals that the parties had agreed to the disposal of their property in accordance with those wills and that they intended their wills to be irrevocable. It was held that this constituted sufficient intention to create mutual wills. That case should be juxtaposed with *Re Oldham*,[504] in which a husband and wife created substantially similar wills with identical treatment of their

---

498 The appellant argued, *inter alia*, that there should not be a mutual wills arrangement found on these facts because not all of the terms of that contract were known and because there was no contract which could have attracted specific performance. As Mummery LJ held, however, all that is required is an agreement between the parties that neither should be entitled to alter their wills after the death of the other such that their wills and the property referenced in them are to be held on constructive trust. It is suggested that any property which was not within the terms of the will (because it was outside the wills as drafted or because it came into the hands of a testator at a later stage and was not referenced in the will) could be disposed of differently. All turns on the terms of the will. That does not mean that the contract is incomplete, but rather it means that the contract refers only to the property referenced in the two wills which are the subject matter of the mutual wills arrangement. The language of contract in this context tends only to divert attention away from the real focus of this doctrine, which is a constructive trust which prevents the surviving testator from purporting to alter his or her will. The language of contract also tends to cause claimants to argue that they were not parties to this contract and therefore that its terms cannot bind them; whereas in truth it is the constructive trust over the property covered by the will which binds the world, and not the contractual agreement itself.
499 [2009] 2 WLR 1, at [37].
500 *Ibid.*
501 *Ibid.*
502 [1994] Ch 31.
503 [1930] 2 Ch 190.
504 [1925] Ch 75; approved in *Gray v Perpetual Trustee Company* [1928] AC 391 and *Birmingham v Renfrew* (1937) 57 CLR 666.

property, but those wills were not expressed as being irrevocable, nor was there any evidence of such an intention, and therefore it was held that these were not mutual wills. Similarly, in *Birch v Curtis*,[505] it was found that a couple could not be proved to have intended to make their wills irrevocable and therefore the doctrine of mutual wills was held not to apply.

In cases of mutual wills it may often happen that one party is on her death bed when the wills are created and therefore the question will arise whether or not that testator had the requisite capacity to make a valid will. In *Baker v Baker*[506] the testator in question was dying in hospital and suffering with hepatic encephalopathy. One of the doctors expressly recorded in the patient's medical notes that in the doctor's opinion he did not have the requisite capacity to make a will. Consequently, it was held that the patient's will would not be admitted to probate and therefore that the mutual will arrangement failed. On the facts, an argument based on proprietary estoppel (to the effect that the other party had created her will in reliance on the death-bed will) was rejected, in part, so as not to give effect to a will which could not have been properly created.

The most important aspects in establishing a mutual will arrangement are an intention expressed by the parties that their wills be irrevocable[507] and that the parties considered that their wills would be binding on one another after death.[508] This is so even if a literal reading of the terms of the wills indicates something other than a mutual will. There will be a mutual will arrangement where evidence from the couple's solicitor indicates that their true intention was to bind one another irrevocably.[509] In general terms, the court is entitled to infer such an intention from the general circumstances of the case.[510]

The mutual wills do not become binding, as intimated above, until one of the parties dies, because the arrangement can be broken up to that moment by all the parties in any event.[511] Where the parties terminate the agreement before the death of any of them, all of the parties are relieved of their obligations under it.[512] Until the death of one of the parties, the arrangement takes effect simply as a contract between the parties and has no effect in equity.[513] In the event that the first to die did not leave property as she was obliged to under the agreement, the survivor is entitled to damages for breach of contract from the deceased's estate.

The obligations of the survivor under the arrangement will clearly depend on the terms of the will and on the parties' intention under the mutual wills arrangement. It is generally assumed that the survivor acquires the property as its absolute owner during her lifetime, subject to a fiduciary duty to settle the property by will in accordance with the arrangement after her death.[514] In this respect, the obligation of the survivor is a form of 'floating' trust,[515]

---

505 [2002] 2 FLR 847.
506 [2008] 2 FLR 767.
507 *Re Green* [1951] Ch 158; *Re Cleaver* [1981] 1 WLR 939.
508 *Re Goodchild (Deceased)* [1996] 1 WLR 694.
509 *Ibid*.
510 *Dufour v Pereira* (1769) 1 Dick 419; *Stone v Hoskins* [1905] P 194.
511 Martin, 1997, 308.
512 *Stone v Hoskins* [1905] P 194.
513 *Robinson v Ommanney* (1883) 23 Ch D 285.
514 *Birmingham v Renfrew* (1937) 57 CLR 666; *Re Cleaver* [1981] 1 WLR 939; *Goodchild v Goodchild* [1996] 1 WLR 694.
515 Hayton, 1992.

or one that is 'in suspense':[516] that is, it will not become fully binding until death. The weakness in this arrangement is that it will not be binding on *bona fide* purchasers without notice of the mutual will arrangement.[517] In creating the wills as part of a mutual wills arrangement, it is of course important that the wills themselves are properly executed. The Court of Appeal in *Gill v Woodall*[518] considered a mutual will arrangement in which it was contended that the wife suffered from a nervous anxiety disorder[519] which would have meant that when the will was drafted and the mutual wills arrangement created that she would not have understood its meaning and that as a result she would have been unduly influenced into making it. It was held by the Court of Appeal that, on these facts, the will had been drafted by a solicitor and read to the wife such that it could be inferred that she had understood the terms of the will and the arrangement, that she had given her knowledge and approval to it, and that there was a 'strong presumption'[520] on these facts that that will constituted her 'testamentary intentions'[521] at the moment of executing it. Therefore, the mutual wills arrangement stood, and in consequence the claimant charity[522] which stood to benefit from the mutual wills arrangement being invalidated took nothing.

12.8 TRUSTEES *DE SON TORT* AND INTERMEDDLERS AS CONSTRUCTIVE TRUSTEES

This section examines situations in which people interfere with the activities of an express trust to such an extent that they are deemed to be trustees themselves. On the basis that these people are not expressly declared by the settlor to be trustees but rather are deemed to be trustees by operation of law on account of their meddling with trust affairs, it is argued that they are constructive trustees.[523]

This doctrine is comparatively straightforward to state. Where a person who has not been officially appointed as a trustee of an express trust interferes with or involves herself in the business of the trust so as to appear to be acting as a trustee, that person shall be deemed to be a trustee. Smith LJ stated the nature of this form of constructive trust in the following way:

> If one, not being a trustee and not having authority from a trustee, takes upon himself to intermeddle with trust matters or to do acts characteristic of the office of trustee, he may therefore make himself what is called in law trustee of his own wrong – ie, a trustee *de son tort*, or, as it is also termed, a constructive trustee.[524]

---

516   *Ottaway v Norman* [1972] Ch 698.

517   *Pilcher v Rawlins* (1872) LR 7 Ch App 259.

518   [2011] 3 WLR 85.

519   Stemming from a fear of her husband's temper, this manifested itself in agoraphobia and a 'panic disorder to a serious degree', which meant that she would rarely go outside and would not attend social events: at [40].

520   In several cases it had been held that a 'grave and strong presumption' arose that a will constituted the testamentary intentions of the testator if it had been read over to or by the testator: *Fulton v Andrew* (1875) LR 7 HL 448, 469, *per* Lord Hatherley; and in particular in *In re Morris, decd* [1971] P 62, 77, *per* Hill J. This approach was approved in *Fuller v Strum* [2002] 1 WLR 1097 and in *Perrins v Holland* [2011] 2 WLR 1086.

521   The expression is culled from *Fuller v Strum* [2002] 1 WLR 1097, at [59], *per* Chadwick LJ.

522   One of the wills had provided that unallocated property should be held for the RSPCA as residuary legatee.

523   Harpum, 1994.

524   *Mara v Browne* [1896] 1 Ch 199, 209.

Therefore, a trustee *de son tort* is a trustee who intermeddles with trust business. What does not emerge from that statement is the usual pre-requisite that the trustee *de son tort* must have trust property in her possession or control before this form of constructive trust will obtain.[525] If the property were not vested in the defendant, then the appropriate form of liability would be that considered in para 12.9.3 below: that of a dishonest assistant. A dishonest assistant is one who assists in a breach of trust in a manner in which an honest person would not have acted, or who was reckless as to some risk being caused to the trust fund.[526] The liability is a personal liability to account for any loss suffered by the trust fund.[527] A constructive trustee (that is, in this context, as trustee *de son tort*), on the other hand, will be responsible for the maintenance of the trust property in her possession, as well as personally liable for loss to the trust arising from a breach of trust.

So, in *Blyth v Fladgate*,[528] Exchequer bills had been held on trust by a sole trustee. That trustee had deposited the bills in the name of a firm of solicitors, thus putting the bills within the control of the solicitors. The trustee died and, before substitute trustees had been appointed, the solicitors sold the bills and invested the proceeds in a mortgage. In the event, the security provided under the mortgage was insufficient, and accordingly the trust suffered a loss. It was held that the firm of solicitors had become constructive trustees by dint of their having dealt with the trust property then within their control.[529] As such, they were liable to account to the beneficiaries for the loss occasioned to the trust.

Similarly, where a manager of land continued to collect rents in respect of that land after the death of the landlord, without informing the tenants of their landlord's death, that manager was held to be a constructive trustee of those profits which had been held in a bank account.[530] Similarly, in relation to *Boardman v Phipps* considered earlier in this chapter,[531] where a solicitor interferes with the management of a trust, then we could consider him to be a trustee *de son tort*: that is, a constructive trust as a result of his assumption of control of the management of the trust.

While the responsibilities of constructive trustees will not always equate to those of an express trustee, it has been held that because a trustee *de son tort* acts as though an express trustee, she is to be treated as bearing all the obligations of an express trustee.[532]

12.9 PERSONAL LIABILITY TO ACCOUNT AS A CONSTRUCTIVE TRUSTEE

12.9.1 Introduction and scope of this discussion

What follows is only a truncated discussion of personal liability to account as a constructive trustee for knowing receipt or dishonest assistance. The full discussion of this material takes place in Chapter 20. Nevertheless, there is a brief mention of these doctrines here because it is clear that the courts do describe liability for knowing receipt and dishonest assistance as

---

525 *Re Barney* [1892] 2 Ch 265.
526 *Royal Brunei Airlines v Tan* [1995] 2 AC 378.
527 *Barnes v Addy* (1874) 9 Ch App 244.
528 [1891] 1 Ch 337.
529 *Re Bell's Indenture* [1980] 1 WLR 1217.
530 *Lyell v Kennedy* (1889) 14 App Cas 437; see also *English v Dedham Vale Properties* [1978] 1 WLR 93.
531 Section 12.5.
532 *Soar v Ashwell* [1893] 2 QB 390.

being constructive trusts.[533] The reason for that is perfectly clear: in such cases, the defendants are deemed to be trustees because of their involvement in breaches of trusts, and thus are described as constructive trustees because the court is 'construing' them to be liable to account to the beneficiaries as though they were trustees. Significantly, the defendants will hold no property on trust; rather, their liability is a personal liability to make good any loss suffered by the beneficiaries as though they were trustees who had committed a breach of trust (as discussed in Chapter 18).[534] This section also includes a fuller discussion of the liabilities of a person who makes herself a trustee *de son tort*, as considered in the preceding section, by interfering with the running of the trust such that she effectively assumes the powers of the trustees.

There are two distinct categories of liability in this context: strangers who *receive* trust property transferred in breach of trust; and strangers who do *not receive* trust property but merely assist its transfer in breach of trust. Evidently there is a narrow line between the categories of claim. The claims for 'unconscionable receipt' and 'dishonest assistance' are personal claims for money brought on behalf of the beneficiaries and predicated on the notion that the original trust property cannot be recovered.[535] However, it may be the case that the beneficiaries of the trust will seek a proprietary claim in respect of the lost property, as well as personal claims against those involved in transferring that property in breach of trust.

12.9.2 Unconscionable receipt

> *Where a person receives trust property in the knowledge that that property has been passed in breach of trust and acts unconscionably in so doing, then, the recipient will be personally liable to account to the trust for the value of the property passed away. It is a defence to demonstrate that the receipt was authorised under the terms of the trust, or that the recipient has lawfully changed her position in reliance on the receipt of the property.*

Unconscionable receipt concerns people who are not trustees but who nevertheless receive trust property beneficially when it has been paid away in breach of trust; and where that person receives the trust property knowing that that property has been passed to her in breach of trust.[536] Whether or not there has been receipt will generally be decided by asking whether or not the defendant had the trust property in her possession or under her control at any time after the breach of trust and after she had the requisite knowledge.[537] The only available defences against a claim for knowing receipt are *bona fide* purchaser for value without notice,[538] change of position,[539] or potentially passing on.[540]

---

533   *Dubai Aluminium v Salaam* [2002] 3 WLR 1913; [2003] 1 All ER 97.
534   *Target Holdings v Redferns* [1996] 1 AC 421; [1995] 3 All ER 785, HL.
535   See Chapter 19 on this point.
536   *Polly Peck International v Nadir (No 2)* [1992] 4 All ER 769, 777, *per* Scott LJ.
537   *El Ajou v Dollar Land Holdings* [1993] BCLC 735; and below in Chapter 19.
538   *Westdeutsche Landesbank Girozentrale v Islington LBC* [1996] AC 669.
539   *Lipkin Gorman v Karpnale* [1991] 3 WLR 10.
540   *Kleinwort Benson v Birmingham CC* [1996] 4 All ER 733, CA.

12.9.3 Dishonest assistance

Where a person dishonestly assists another in a breach of trust, that dishonest assistant will be personally liable to account to the trust for the value lost to the trust. 'Dishonesty' in this context does require that there be some element of fraud, lack of probity or reckless risk-taking. It is not necessary that any trustee of the trust is dishonest; simply that the dishonest assistant is dishonest.

Dishonest assistance concerns the liability of strangers who assist in a breach of trust or in the transfer of property away from a trust. The distinction from knowing receipt is that there is no requirement for the imposition of liability that the stranger has had possession or control of the property at any time. Therefore, some commentators have doubted whether or not this form of liability should really be described as a 'constructive trust' in any event.[541] However, the courts have continued to use the terminology of constructive trust and the imposition of constructive trusteeship despite this conceptual problem.[542]

Liability for dishonest assistance in a breach of trust arises in situations when there has been a breach of trust and in which the defendant's involvement has been dishonest. Lord Nicholls in *Royal Brunei Airlines v Tan* held that a breach of trust by a trustee need not have been a dishonest act *on the part of the trustee*.[543] Rather, it is sufficient that some accessory acted dishonestly for that accessory to be fixed with liability for the breach. The test set out by Lord Nicholls was an objective test which requires the court to consider what an honest person would have done in the circumstances. If the defendant has failed to do what an honest person would have done, then the defendant is deemed to have been dishonest under this objective test. In the subsequent decision of the House of Lords in *Twinsectra v Yardley*,[544] the House of Lords seemed to suggest that the defendant must also have realised that an honest person would have considered the defendant's actions to have been dishonest. This approach imported a level of subjectivity to the test. However, Lord Nicholls in *Dubai Aluminium v Salaam* reinforced the purely objective nature of this test, as confirmed by the Privy Council in *Barlow Clowes v Eurotrust*.[545]

12.9.4 Interaction of these remedies with the doctrine of trustee *de son tort*

As considered in section 12.8, where a person intermeddles with trust property in such a way that she begins to act in fact as a trustee, and that person causes a loss to the trust, that person is held liable to the trust as a trustee *de son tort*.[546] The expression means, literally, a trustee as a result of one's own wrong. Such a person will be treated as a constructive trustee.[547] That person differs from the two categories of personal liability to account considered

---

541 Oakley, 1997, 186 *et seq.*

542 *Agip (Africa) v Jackson* [1991] Ch 547; *Polly Peck International v Nadir (No 2)* [1992] 4 All ER 769; *Westdeutsche Landesbank Girozentrale v Islington LBC* [1996] AC 669.

543 [1995] 2 AC 378; applied in *Dubai Aluminium v Salaam* [2003] 1 All ER 97.

544 [2002] 2 All ER 377.

545 See section 32.2 below.

546 *Selangor United Rubber Ltd v Craddock (No 3)* [1968] 1 WLR 1555; *Rowe v Prance* [1999] 2 FLR 787; *James v Williams* [1999] 3 All ER 309.

547 *Mara v Browne* [1896] 1 Ch 199, 209; *Carl Zeiss Stiftung v Herbert Smith (No 2)* [1969] 2 Ch 276, 289; see also *Dubai Aluminium v Salaam* [2003] 1 All ER 97, *per* Lord Millett.

immediately above because her intermeddling relates to the treatment of the trust property or some interference with the business of the trust: her treatment as a *de facto* trustee arises from the fact that she acts as though she is a trustee – it is not simply that she has committed a wrong in relation to the trust fund. The latter state of affairs applies to personal liability to account as a knowing recipient or as a dishonest assistant.

This pairing of equitable claims which oblige third parties to trusts (that is, people who are neither trustees nor beneficiaries) to account to the beneficiaries of a trust for their part in a breach of trust differs from the liability of intermeddlers considered in section 12.8 above in two ways. First, the liability is a personal liability to account and not a proprietary liability to hold any specific property on trust. Secondly, the third parties (or strangers) are not deemed to be trustees who have meddled with the trust's business. Rather, they are strangers who have either received property with knowledge that that was done in breach of trust, or dishonestly assisted in a breach of trust with receiving any trust property.[548] In short, this is a form of equitable wrong which those strangers have committed, or to which they have been party. It is important to distinguish this form of liability from the proprietary forms of constructive trust which have been considered hitherto in this chapter.

12.10 ISSUES WITH CONSTRUCTIVE TRUSTS

12.10.1 Is the doctrine of constructive trust a coherent one?

It has been suggested that constructive trusts may serve only to confuse the law because it is not clear on what basis they arise, because they are sometimes personal and sometimes proprietary, and because they do not constitute a coherent doctrine.[549] I disagree with the idea that constructive trusts cause confusion: on the contrary, I think that constructive trusts offer a vital means for English private law judges to ensure that justice is done on the facts before them as they see it – having listened to the witnesses and examined the evidence – on the basis of preventing unconscionable conduct. That, it seems to me, is not to impose constructive trusts on a random basis: rather, it is to ensure that an ethical notion of good conscience is maintained in English law. The weakness of the competing doctrine of restitution on grounds of unjust enrichment, advanced by some academics, is precisely that it has no mechanism for achieving just conclusions but instead seeks to bind the courts into narrow, technical rules.[550]

Nevertheless, the question as to whether or not constructive trusts are a coherent doctrine is an interesting one. There are two possible points of view, it seems to me. The first point of view would argue that constructive trusts do not arise on a coherent basis. The point is this. If one looks at all of the various types of constructive trust considered in this chapter, and also looks at the doctrines of dishonest assistance and knowing receipt (which arise on the basis of constructive trusteeship) in Chapter 20, and also the common intention constructive trusts in Chapter 15, then it is plain that they are not identical. The constructive trust in *Boardman v Phipps* arises so as to prevent conflicts of interest; the constructive trust in *Attorney-General for Hong Kong v Reid* arises on the basis of equity looking upon as done

548   Birks, 1993:1, 318; Gardner, 1996, 56.
549   Birks, 1989, 89.
550   See section 31.3, and www.alastairhudson.com/trustslaw/restitutionofunjustenrichment.pdf.

that which ought to have been done so as to take possession of a bribe; the common intention constructive trust in *Lloyds Bank v Rosset* arises so as to effect mutual understandings or in relation to conduct in the form of contributions to the purchase price of property; the constructive trust in *Jerome v Kelly* arises as a trust *sub modo* in relation to a contract to transfer property; the personal 'constructive trusteeship' in *Royal Brunei Airlines v Tan* arises in response to dishonesty. All of these cases are at the House of Lords or Privy Council level and do not include the many decisions of more junior courts: and yet it is apparent that they do not arise on exactly the same basis. These various courts do not even refer to each other – rather they seem to be deciding points which are specific to their own particular form of constructive trust. The key words they use in reaching their judgments – conscience, dishonesty, conflict of interest, that which ought to be done, and so forth – are different. Therefore, we could say that constructive trusts lack a little coherence.

The second point of view would require us to return to another House of Lords decision: *Westdeutsche Landesbank v Islington*. As was discussed at the beginning of this chapter, Lord Browne-Wilkinson reminded us that equity has always operated on the basis of conscience; since the *Earl of Oxford's Case* in 1615 this has been the case, as considered at the very beginning of this book.[551] Constructive trusts are therefore said to arise on the basis of the defendant knowing of some factor which affects her conscience in relation to property. That is a perfectly viable, underpinning principle on which to base a legal concept like the constructive trust. The challenge is then to set out the circumstances in which the court will consider there to have been unconscionable behaviour. Looking at the House of Lords and Privy Council cases listed in the previous paragraph it would be possible to stand back from them slightly and say that, while they do not use exactly the same terminology all of the time, all of their principles operate on a set of concepts which are very similar to saying that the defendant has acted unconscionably. That is so whether the test applied is one of allowing a conflict of interest, or acting dishonestly, or seeking to deny someone rights in a home for which they have paid in part, or seeking to renege on a contractual obligation to transfer property: each of these tests could be understood as responding at root to a requirement that the defendant act in good conscience, just as *Westdeutsche Landesbank v Islington* and the *Earl of Oxford's Case* required.

Either you are convinced that this area is sufficiently explicable on the basis of a deep, underpinning notion of conscience – as discussed in detail in section 32.2 of this book and on-line[552] – or you consider it to be based on no valid organising concept and instead comprised of a scattering of unconnected doctrines. This issue receives lengthy consideration on the companion websites to this book.[553]

12.10.2 Sympathy is not conscience

It is perhaps a trite point but nevertheless one that is worth making: imposing trusts on the basis of conscience does not mean that the court should in some way feel sorry for every claimant who feels that she has been hard done by. There is a tendency among some academics to think that there is something deficient in an area of law which they think

551 See para 1.1.
552 See www.alastairhudson.com/equity/conscience.pdf
553 See www.alastairhudson.com/trustslawindex.htm

operates randomly on the basis of 'right and wrong' or a general notion of 'conscience'; there is a different tendency among some students to think that equity is simply about giving the claimant whatever she wants if she thinks she has been mistreated in some indefinable way. Equity, as should have become clear already in this book, is a fascinating hybrid of technical, intricate principles of law combined with a very stylised notion of conscience which falls into well-understood categories. A good example of equity insisting on technical entitlement to property, and not simply deciding on the basis of sentiment, arose in *Re Farepak Food and Gift Ltd*[554] a case which arose very shortly before Christmas 2006. A large number of predominantly low income families had contributed monthly amounts of money to a Christmas club which was run, commercially, by Farepak Food and Gift Ltd ('F'). The contributors were entitled to receive food hampers and vouchers with which to buy Christmas presents from F and its various suppliers. F went into insolvent administration in October 2006 and, as was reported at length in the national press, the customers were not going to receive their Christmas parcels at all. In the eyes of the national press this seemed like a sob story in which Christmas was being ruined for thousands of ordinary families. Mann J heard an application for a distribution of F's remaining assets to identified classes of customers at great speed shortly before Christmas, and held the following:[555]

> There is no doubt whatsoever that the customers of Farepak deserve an enormous amount of sympathy, and as far as I am concerned they have it. They are also entitled to all the assistance which the court can properly give them, in terms of procedural matters and assistance in having their proper claims speedily determined, including some at least of some of the corner-cutting that has occurred in the present application. That is doubtless why Briggs J ordered that this matter should come on so quickly, and why representative creditors have agreed to be joined and why they and their representatives have acted so expeditiously. Mr Lopian [counsel on behalf of Her Majesty's Revenue and Customs] quite properly made it clear that HMRC was not advancing its points with any enthusiasm, but they were points which had to be made. However, at the end of the day their claims have to be based in law, not sympathy. I have to be satisfied that their claims have been made out to a sufficient level at this stage. If I am not then no amount of sympathy can entitle them to be paid moneys to which they are not, or may not be, legally entitled. There are a large number of insolvencies in respect of which various creditors have to be treated with sympathy, but in all cases it is legal claims which have to rule the day.

The law on constructive trusts, as with all of equity, is not based on some anti-intellectual or emotional sense of 'nice' and 'nasty'. Instead it is a very particular and subtle way of thinking about law. It requires jurists – whether judges, academics or practitioners – to understand the nuances which inform the general principles of equity and to apply them appropriately to individual cases. It is not a form of legal thinking which sets out concrete rules in advance and permits of no exceptions – as some might caricature the common law[556] – but it is no less

---

554   [2006] All ER (D) 265 (Dec).

555   *Ibid*, para [28].

556   Although see the thesis in Cotterrell, *The Politics of Jurisprudence*, 2005, as to the flexible basis of the common law.

scrupulous a way of thinking about law for that. The general idea of conscience is considered in detail in section 32.2.

12.10.3 The possibility of a remedial constructive trust

Usually a remedial constructive trust is taken to be a constructive trust the terms of which are decided by the judge at the date of trial so that the successful claimant acquires a property right in the manner described by the trust from that time forwards. It was held by Lord Browne-Wilkinson in *Westdeutsche Landesbank v Islington*[557] that remedial constructive trusts do not form part of English law, although his Lordship conceded that they might become part of English law in the future.[558] In a dissenting judgment in the House of Lords in *Thorner v Major*,[559] Lord Scott suggested that cases like *Thorner v Major* should be decided by using a 'remedial constructive trust'. His Lordship did not deign to define what he meant by this term. Lord Scott suggested that proprietary estoppel should be limited to circumstances in which 'the representations relied on relate to the acquisition by the repres-entee of an immediate, or more or less immediate, interest in the property in question'[560] such that the representor is 'estopped from denying that the representee has the proprietary interest that was promised'.[561] By contrast it is said that a remedial constructive trust should be used where 'the representation has related to inheritance prospects' because those cases are 'difficult . . . to square with proprietary estoppel' and instead should be understood as relating to the common intention of the parties as in cases like *Gissing v Gissing*. It is suggested that this is a distinction without a meaningful difference. The facts in *Thorner v Major* fit the matrix of representation, reliance and detriment perfectly neatly; whereas the common intention cases relate more specifically to situations in which the parties intend to co-own property as opposed to one party intending to bequeathe the property to another. It is suggested that Lord Scott's approach ought not to be favoured. Proprietary estoppel has long been understood as arising on the basis of a representation (or assurance), reliance and detriment, and not simply on the antique notion that it involves denying the truth of a state-ment (as explained in section 13.1 and the rest of that chapter) as Lord Scott asserted. The remedial constructive trust adds nothing here.

12.10.4 Constructive trusts are like the English language

As was discussed in Chapter 7,[562] studying equity is very like learning the English language. At first blush, it seems that every rule has an exception and that most of the language is an entirely random collection of separate idioms and ideas. In fact, to a native Englishman the English language is made up of a very large number of strict grammatical rules and idiomatic structures which, if broken, really do jar on the ear. It is suggested that the doctrine of

---

557 [1996] AC 669.
558 The law continues to be set against the remedial constructive trust after *Westdeutsche Landesbank v Islington: Clarke v Meadus* [2010] EWHC 3117 (Ch).
559 [2009] 1 WLR 776.
560 [2009] 1 WLR 776, para [20].
561 *Ibid.*
562 Section 7.1.1.

constructive trusts is similar. While it may seem at first glance that this area is comprised of doctrines moving in entirely random motion, in truth each species of constructive trust is based on its own well-understood principles. The principle of conscience, identifiable in equity from the *Earl of Oxford's Case* through to *Westdeutsche Landesbank* and beyond, operates as a high-level principle around which all of these constructive trusts revolve. There is in truth nothing more English than a constructive trust, along with the novels of PG Wodehouse, long games of cricket on June afternoons, and the English language itself.

Chapter 13

Equitable estoppel

13.1 INTRODUCTION

The expression 'equitable estoppel' has been used by the judges in a number of leading cases in this area (on which see *Gillett v Holt*[1] and *Yaxley v Gotts*[2]) and so I am content to adopt it here as a general title for this chapter. In truth, though, there is no such thing as a single 'estoppel' on the decided cases: rather, there are a number of different estoppels which operate in different contexts both at common law and in equity.[3] This chapter will tease out

---

1 [2000] 2 All ER 289.
2 [2000] 1 All ER 711.
3 There are other cases in which the expression has been dismissed as being meaningless because it discloses no particular kind of estoppel. This simply discloses a difference in opinion as to whether there is a single doctrine of estoppel in equity revolving around a single concept of good conscience, or whether there are still to be many different kinds of estoppel operating on different bases. That point is considered in greater detail through this chapter.

some of the commonalities and some of the differences between some of the more significant forms of estoppel.[4]

The word 'estoppel' itself comes from the French '*estouppail*' and '*estoupper*', which are also the source of the English word 'stop'; both have a stem in the Latin '*stuppa*' which relates to tallow or flax used to plug a hole (itself the rarer usage of the English word 'stop'). Quite simply, an estoppel is something which stops a defendant from doing some act, just as a plug prevents liquid from escaping through a hole. Wilken and Villiers[5] quote the words of Coke on estoppel in describing the legal doctrine as being based on the following proposition: '. . . a man's owne act or acceptance stoppeth or closeth his mouth to alleage or plead the truth.' Therefore, an estoppel was aimed at preventing a defendant who had asserted that *x* was the case from relying on the truth which subsequently transpired that *y* was really the case. The defendant was still required to do *x* if that is what the claimant had been led to believe. Many judges were concerned that this doctrine would mean that the truth would be ignored.[6] This literal sense of the word is in effect the sense in which Lord Scott used it in *Cobbe v Yeoman's Row*.[7] Despite this initial misgiving in the case law, latterly judges have come to recognise that estoppel in its many forms is 'perhaps the most powerful and flexible instrument to be found in any system of court jurisprudence'.[8] The reason for this enthusiasm is a recognition that estoppel enables the court to prevent injustice being suffered by individual claimants regardless of the precise legal relations which might otherwise have been created between the parties.

13.2 A SINGLE DOCTRINE OF ESTOPPEL?

The doctrinal position as to the impossibility of the recognition of a single doctrine of estoppel, based on the decided cases, can be simply stated.[9] There is no single doctrine of estoppel; nor would it be possible to create one out of the existing categories, despite some suggestions to the contrary by Lord Denning.[10] First, there is a distinction between the common law and equity, and estoppel is recognised at common law as well as in equity,

---

4 Some of those discussions have taken place at paras 3.4.2 (certainty in the creation of trusts); 5.4.3 (informal creation of equitable interests); 12.3.2 (comparison with constructive trusts); 12.6.1 (within common intention constructive trusts); 15.7 generally (operation of proprietary estoppel within the law on trusts of homes); 21.4.4 (estoppel and the *nemo dat* principle in commercial law).

5 Wilken and Villiers, 1999, 103.

6 The doctrine was considered 'odious' by Bramwell LJ precisely because it gave a claimant a remedy even though the facts on which that claimant relied were not true; *Baxendale v Bennet* (1878) 3 QBD 578.

7 [2008] 1 WLR 1752.

8 *Canada and Dominion Sugar Company Ltd v Canadian National (West Indies) Steamships Ltd* [1947] AC 46, 56 quoting Sir Frederick Pollock.

9 Lord Walker referred to the following sources on the possibility of a single doctrine of equitable estoppel in *Thorner v Major* [2009] 1 WLR 776, at [67], while refusing to comment definitively on the question: 'The index to the first (1923) edition of George Spencer Bower's *Law Relating to Estoppel by Representation* contains in its index the entry "EQUITABLE ESTOPPEL", a meaningless expression', a view which is developed at length in the text, with Lord Selborne LC attracting particular criticism (at p 14) that 'a jurist so nice and discriminating in his phraseology' should have used the expression in *Citizens' Bank of Louisiana v First National Bank of New Orleans* (1873) LR 6 HL 352 at 360.

10 *Amalgamated Investment & Property Co Ltd (In Liquidation) v Texas Commerce International Bank Ltd* [1982] 1 QB 84. A view which also appealed to other judges: eg, *Hiscox v Outhwaite (No 1)* [1992] 1 AC 562, 574, *per* Lord Donaldson; *John v George and Walton* (1996) 71 P & CR 375, 385, *per* Morritt LJ.

where it is based on principles of commercial propriety (as considered in Chapter 21) Therefore, there cannot simply be an equitable estoppel which accounts for all forms of estoppel.

Secondly, there is no single explanation for the manner in which all estoppels operate. Estoppel in all its forms is based on a variety of underlying conceptions, varying from honesty[11] to common sense[12] to common fairness.[13] What emerges just from this short list is that common principles underpinning all estoppel can be identified only at the most rarefied levels – that of fairness, justice and so forth.[14] Some academics argue that estoppel arises on the basis of 'unconscionability',[15] but acknowledge elsewhere that there is nevertheless a distinction between those forms of proprietary estoppel (let alone the others) which arise variously on the basis of avoidance of detriment,[16] enforcement of promise,[17] or on grounds of mistake.[18] There are various forms of estoppel with boundaries so thin that arguments have been led in the cases for their amalgamation.[19]

Nevertheless, despite this doctrinaire position, there has been a powerful argument put by Professor Elizabeth Cooke for the establishment of a single doctrine of estoppel predicated on a concept of good conscience.[20] In general terms, Cooke considers the doctrine of estoppel to be a means of preventing a person from changing her mind in circumstances in which it would be unconscionable so to do.[21] What might be problematic in this conception of estoppel, as Cooke discusses, is deciding on the range of acts and omissions which might be thought 'unconscionable' and so render otherwise ordinary, non-actionable examples of people changing their minds into those sorts of changes of mind which are actionable by estoppel. That point can be made in the following way. If estoppels arise on the basis of unconscionability, then there is only a narrow class of acts of what might be ordinarily recognised as unconscionable behaviour which is legally actionable. Therefore, if you promise to telephone me but know when you make the promise that you really do not want to telephone me and that you probably never will telephone me, we might consider that action to have been unconscionable, in that your lying to me is not the act of a completely honest person, but it is unlikely that we would consider it to be legally actionable. Here there is a disjunction between our notion of 'good conscience' and our notion of 'good conscience which is legally actionable'. The fundamental weakness of purporting to base these doctrines on the abstract notions of 'justice' or 'fairness' is that none of the jurists actually intends to

11   *Re Exchange Securities & Commodities Ltd* [1988] Ch 46, 54, *per* Harman J.

12   *London Joint Stock Bank Ltd v Macmillan* [1918] AC 777, 818, *per* Lord Haldane.

13   *Lyle-Meller v A Lewis & Co* [1956] 1 WLR 29, 44, *per* Morris LJ.

14   The arguments for an all-embracing estoppel are based on such concepts: see, eg, the various *dicta* of Lord Denning in *Amalgamated Investment & Property Co Ltd v Texas Commerce International Bank Ltd* [1982] 1 QB 84; *Lyle-Meller v A Lewis & Co* [1956] 1 WLR 29; *Moorgate Mercantile Co Ltd v Twitchings* [1976] 1 QB 225.

15   Mee, 1999; Cooke, 2000.

16   *Lim v Ang* [1992] 1 WLR 113.

17   *Pascoe v Turner* [1979] 2 All ER 945.

18   *Wilmot v Barber* (1880) 15 Ch D 96.

19   *Crabb v Arun DC* [1976] Ch 179, 193, *per* Lord Scarman; *Taylor Fashions Ltd v Liverpool Victoria Trustees Co Ltd* [1982] 1 QB 133, 151, *per* Oliver J.

20   Cooke, 2000 generally.

21   Eg, *Amalgamated Investment and Property Co Ltd v Texas Commerce International Bank Ltd* [1982] 1 QB 84, 104, *per* Robert Goff J.

capture all unconscionable behaviour: only unconscionable behaviour which falls into established legal and equitable categories.[22]

The tension here between the historical truth that there are many forms of estoppel and the nagging sense nevertheless that they are all based on similar notions of conscionability is encapsulated in Lord Denning's apparent shift in emphasis when in 1980 he likened the many forms of this doctrine to 'a big house with many rooms' where 'each room is used differently from the others',[23] and then in 1981 when his Lordship suggested that while 'the doctrine of estoppel . . . has evolved during the last 150 years in a sequence of separate developments . . . [a]ll these can now be seen to merge into one general principle shorn of limitations'.[24] It is this drift from separation between many technical forms of estoppel towards the recognition of a central operating principle which Cooke observes. In common with the project of this book in examining the roots of a principle of 'good conscience' in much of equity, a principle which draws on the role of the Lords Chancellor as keepers of the monarch's conscience and from procedural notions of *conscentia* in early courts of equity, there is a pleasing symmetry in identifying a form of estoppel which can be grounded in the notion that the defendant should be prevented from asserting that *y* is the case in any circumstance in which it would be unconscionable to deny that *x* was what the defendant had led the claimant to believe was the case, thus causing the claimant detriment, loss or harm.

In common among the various forms of estoppel is the notion of detrimental reliance: that is, some reliance by the claimant on some act, representation or similar assurance of the defendant. The requirement for reliance is weaker in promissory estoppel than in proprietary estoppel. In both of these doctrines, there is some requirement that the defendant has acted unconscionably in some way.[25] The idea that all of estoppel ought to be understood as responding to a general notion of 'unconscionability' (even if the various forms of estoppel cannot be collapsed into one general doctrine) does, however, have some senior judicial support. As Lord Goff put it: 'In the end, I am inclined to think that the many circumstances capable of giving rise to an estoppel cannot be accommodated within a single formula, and that it is unconscionability which provides the link between them.'[26] The principal difference between the doctrines is that of the belief required of the claimant. In promissory estoppel the claimant must have been led to believe by the defendant that her rights will not be enforced: proprietary estoppel requires the claimant to believe that she will acquire some right in property. Estoppel by representation,[27] which is generally merely a rule of evidence,[28] issue estoppel,[29] and estoppel by convention,[30]

---

22 Cooke, 2000, 2.
23 *McIlkenny v Chief Constable of the West Midlands* [1980] 1 QB 283, 317.
24 *Amalgamated Investment and Property Co Ltd v Texas Commerce International Bank Ltd* [1982] 1 QB 84, 122.
25 Cooke, 2000, 54 *et seq. Wilson v Truelove* [2003] WTLR 609.
26 *Johnson v Gore Wood & Co (No.1)* [2002] 2 AC 1, [2001] 2 WLR 72, [2001] BCC 820 at 842, *per* Lord Goff.
27 *Jorden v Money* (1854) 5 HLC 185, (1854) 10 ER 868: a doctrine recognised both by common law and by equity.
28 *Oliver v Bank of England* [1902] 1 Ch 610.
29 This form of estoppel prevented the same claim being brought twice between the same parties in *R (Coke-Wallis) v Institute of Chartered Accountants* [2011] 2 WLR 103.
30 *Co-operative Bank v Tipper* [1996] 4 All ER 366; *Wilson v Truelove* [2003] WTLR 609. In *Trustee Solutions Ltd v Dubery* [2006] EWHC 1426 (Ch) it was held that where there had been no common, shared misunderstanding between members of a pension scheme trust that the terms of the trust would necessitate a change after a ruling of the European Court of Justice as to equal retirement dates between the sexes: because there was no common misunderstanding there could not be estoppel by convention.

likewise a rule of evidence,[31] require the claimant to believe that a given state of affairs exists.[32] It is not sufficient, for example, for a defendant to contend that the simple payment of money to her constituted a representation that it was owed – particularly where a contract between the parties provided expressly to the contrary – unless there was some other factor which justified the claimant's belief in that state of affairs.[33]

Thirdly, there is a distinction between those estoppels which operate only in relation to the past and those which make actionable some representation about the future. Promissory and proprietary estoppel will reflect on future conduct, whereas estoppel by deed and others will relate only to past conduct. In relation to those estoppels which take into account the future there is then the issue of whether or not the defendant's promise will be enforced. Promissory estoppel is a shield which will protect the claimant only from the effects of the detriment caused by the defendant's representation. There is a line carefully drawn between equity's prevention of uncompensated detriment and the enforcement of contract: the former is the sole interest of promissory estoppel, but never the latter.[34] A promise as to future conduct is enforceable only as a contract, and then only if consideration is present.[35] Proprietary estoppel, however, enforces representations as to the future, provided that they are linked specifically to rights in property and not generally as to performance of something akin to a contract. However, it is clear that the various forms of estoppel are combining, at least in the modern judicial mind, ever more closely into a single estoppel based on a notion of good conscience.[36]

The one fly in the ointment here is the decision of the House of Lords in *Cobbe v Yeoman's Row*[37] which is discussed in detail below, which suggests that unconscionability alone is not enough. This is, it is suggested, completely in line with the earlier decided cases if what is meant is that the claimant must also demonstrate for proprietary estoppel that there has also been a representation, reliance and detriment, coupled with unconscionability on the part of the defendant. Lord Scott returned to the notion in *Ramsden v Dyson* that estoppel is based on preventing a person from alleging that something was the case when it was not, and so if no such allegation of fact was made, no claim in estoppel lies. Lord Walker and Lord Rodger effectively suggested in *Thorner v Major*[38] that the result of *Cobbe* was simply to reinforce the need for certainty as to the content of the representation and as to the property in question.

13.3 PROPRIETARY ESTOPPEL

First we shall consider the most significant form of estoppel: proprietary estoppel. This doctrine is also considered in the context of trusts of homes in Chapter 15.[39] In general terms,

---

31 *Lokumal v Lotte Shipping* [1985] Lloyd's Rep 28.
32 *Scottish Equitable v Derby* [2000] 3 All ER 793.
33 *Philip Collins v Davis* [2000] 3 All ER 808.
34 *Jorden v Money* (1854) 5 HLC 185, 10 ER 868.
35 *Ibid.*
36 Eg, *Amalgamated Investment and Property Co Ltd v Texas Commerce International Bank Ltd* [1982] 1 QB 84, 122; *Yaxley v Gotts* [2000] 1 All ER 711; *Gillett v Holt* [2000] 2 All ER 289.
37 [2008] 1 WLR 1752.
38 [2009] 1 WLR 776.
39 See section 15.7 below.

the earliest forms of estoppel were not intended to constitute a cause of action; rather, they were intended to prevent a defendant from reneging on some form of representation on which the claimant had placed detrimental reliance. However, the growth of the proprietary estoppel doctrine has seen the establishment of something which is now akin to a claim, in that the court will frequently award the claimant an interest in property which that claimant would not otherwise have held.[40] Therefore, this is a sword and not merely a shield: it now creates new rights as a distinct cause of action. The doctrine is still avowedly based on the avoidance of detriment,[41] and therefore it would be possible to explain these far-reaching proprietary remedies as being concerned with the avoidance of detriment and not with the establishment of a positive claim.[42] It is true to say that the claimant will acquire any rights under proprietary estoppel only if there has been some assurance, reliance and detriment,[43] but it is suggested that there is only a scintilla of difference between that and a doctrine which actively creates new rights.

13.3.1 Proprietary estoppel and mistake

The doctrine of proprietary estoppel was first most clearly observed in the speeches of the House of Lords in *Ramsden v Dyson*.[44] This approach is not usually applied in modern estoppel cases, as will emerge in the next section. In the speech of Lord Cranworth, the doctrine was stated as operating on the basis of some mistake being formulated in the claimant's mind by the defendant such that the claimant acts detrimentally in reliance on it. So:

> if a stranger begins to build on my land supposing it to be his own, and I, perceiving his mistake, abstain from setting him right, and leave him to persevere in his error, a Court of Equity will not allow me afterwards to assert my title to the land on which he had expended money on the supposition that the land was his own.[45]

The doctrine is here based exclusively on the mistake which the defendant knowingly permits the claimant to nurture. So in the restatement of this approach in *Wilmot v Barber*,[46] those *dicta* are distilled into the 'five probanda' of Fry J:

(a) the claimant must have made a mistake as to his legal rights;

(b) the claimant must have expended some money or done some act on the faith of his mistaken belief;

(c) the defendant must know of the existence of his own right which is inconsistent with the right claimed by the claimant;

(d) the defendant must know of the claimant's mistaken belief in his right; and

---

40 *Wayling v Jones* (1993) 69 P & CR 170; *Pascoe v Turner* [1979] 2 All ER 945.

41 *Lim Teng Huan v Ang Swee Chuan* [1992] 1 WLR 113, PC; *Walton Stores v Maher* (1988) 164 CLR 387.

42 As, eg, with *Ramsden v Dyson* (1866) LR 1 HL 129, *per* Lord Cranworth, and subsequently *Wilmot v Barber* (1880) 15 Ch D 96, in which the doctrine is based on the mistake on which the claimant acted and not with any substantive, pre-existing property right.

43 *Re Basham* [1986] 1 WLR 1498.

44 (1866) LR 1 HL 129.

45 *Ibid*, 140.

46 (1880) 15 Ch D 96.

(e) the defendant must have encouraged the claimant in the expenditure of money, or in the other acts which he has done, either directly or by abstaining from asserting his legal right.

In short, this 'mistake approach' was based on the avoidance of fraud, whereas the more modern approach considered below is focused on the avoidance of detriment being suffered by the claimant. The presence of fraud is said to exist when the defendant attempts to benefit from the mistake which he knows that the claimant is making.[47] Where the mistake doctrine therefore differs in detail from the form of proprietary estoppel considered below is that it does not account for the situation in which the claimant is led to believe that something will be the case in the future – for example, that the claimant will acquire rights in the defendant's property if she nurses him through an illness[48] – where there has been no mistake acted on by the claimant. If the claimant is not mistaken as to her rights but is merely disappointed in her expectation, she would have no *prima facie* claim under *Wilmot v Barber*.[49] While this approach had gone out of fashion in the modern law of estoppel, it was somewhat controversially exhumed by Lord Scott in *Yeoman's Row v Cobbe*,[50] as considered below.

13.3.2 The various approaches in modern proprietary estoppel

The following sections consider the differing goals which the courts appear to have been trying to achieve in modern estoppel cases. These goals vary between: dealing with frustration of expectation, enforcing the promise, compensating the detriment suffered by the claimant, and the prevention of unconscionability. The courts have not announced any sea-changes in their approaches: rather, the shifts between these differing goals can be observed from a close reading of the cases. Then, in paragraph 13.3.3 we shall consider the modern test for estoppel based on representation, reliance and detriment.

Frustration of expectation

Most of the modern cases are concerned with frustration of an expectation which the defendant permitted the claimant to form by means of either an express representation or some implied assurance that she would acquire rights in property.[51] The remedy is addressed to compensate the claimant for any detriment which was suffered in reliance on that representation or assurance. Indeed, proprietary estoppel is best understood as requiring, first, that the claimant prove entitlement to the estoppel and then, secondly, that the appropriate remedy be identified to fit the circumstances. The source of this 'expectation approach' is

---

47 This approach was broadly followed in *Coombes v Smith* [1986] 1 WLR 808.
48 As in *Re Basham* [1986] 1 WLR 1498.
49 See, eg, Mee, 1999, 96. See now *Cobbe v Yeoman's Row* [2008] 1 WLR 1752 below.
50 See the discussion below.
51 The principal modern authorities identifying this broad reading of the proprietary estoppel doctrine, not requiring proof of the five probanda, are as follows: *Taylor Fashions v Liverpool Victoria Trustees Co Ltd* [1982] QB 133; *Habib Bank Ltd v Habib Bank AG Zurich* [1981] 1 WLR 1265; *Re Basham (Deceased)* [1986] 1 WLR 1498; *John v George* (1996) 71 P & CR 375; *Lloyds Bank v Carrick* [1996] 4 All ER 630; *Jones v Stones* [1999] 1 WLR 1739; *Gillett v Holt* [2001] Ch 210; *Jennings v Rice* [2003] 1 P & CR 100. Cases which have suggested that this approach need not be followed include *Swallow Securities Ltd v Isenberg* [1985] 1 EGLR 132, 134, *per* Cumming-Bruce LJ; *Matharu v Matharu* (1994) 68 P & CR 93, *per* Roch LJ.

typically identified with the speech of Lord Kingsdown in *Ramsden v Dyson*,[52] where his Lordship referred to a situation in which the claimant:

> under an expectation, created or encouraged by [the defendant], that he shall have a certain interest . . . upon the faith of such promise or expectation, with the knowledge of the landlord . . . lays out money upon land, a Court of Equity will compel the landlord to give effect to such promise or expectation.

These *dicta* are generally taken to be the root of the modern doctrine of proprietary estoppel, as formalised in the cases which are discussed in the following sections. There are three different bases on which proprietary estoppel might be said to operate: either to give effect to the promise contained in the representation, to compensate the detriment suffered by the claimant, or to prevent unconscionable behaviour. Each of these approaches – all of which have some support on the decided cases – are considered in turn in the sections which follow.

Giving effect to the promise

If the estoppel was concerned to give effect to the representation or promise made by the defendant, then the court's purpose would be to identify the property rights which the claimant was expected to receive. Consequently, this conception of the doctrine refers to a remedy aimed at giving 'effect to such promise' rather than at allowing the detriment suffered by the claimant to pass without compensation. An early formulation of this understanding of the doctrine was set out in *Taylor Fashions v Liverpool Victoria Trustees Co Ltd*[53] by Oliver J such that:

> it would be unconscionable for a party to be permitted to deny that which, knowingly or unknowingly, he has allowed or encouraged another to assume to his detriment.[54]

So, in the case of *Pascoe v Turner*,[55] a woman had been promised that she would be entitled to live in a house for the rest of her life. In reliance on that promise, she expended a small amount of money on decorating the property. The representor failed to leave her an interest in the property. The court found that there was no way of protecting the right of her continued occupation under ordinary land law principles. It was held that she had acted to her detriment in reliance on the representation. The only remedy which would protect her reliance on the promise was a transfer of the freehold interest in the property to her. Similarly, in *Re Basham*,[56] a woman had been promised that a house would be left to her in the proprietor's will. In reliance on that representation, she performed a number of acts to her detriment which were connected to the property and in the expectation that she would receive a right in that property. When the proprietor died without leaving the property to her by will, it was held that she would be entitled to the interest which she had expected to receive. The case of

52 (1866) LR 1 HL 129, 170.
53 [1982] QB 133.
54 *Ibid*, 151.
55 [1979] 2 All ER 945.
56 [1986] 1 WLR 1498.

Wayling v Jones[57] demonstrated a similar tendency. The plaintiff had been in a relationship with the proprietor of a hotel and, in reliance on the understanding that he would be left the property in the proprietor's will, worked for the proprietor for low wages in the proprietor's business. This detrimental act of working for lower wages than otherwise he would have received led to the Court of Appeal awarding the claimant the right in the hotel which he had expected to receive. In each of these cases, it is suggested, the court was giving effect to the claimant's expectation by means of granting the claimant what she had been promised.

Compensating the detriment suffered by the claimant

The alternative approach is not to grant the claimant whatever the claimant may have been promised – particularly where this would result in the transfer of the absolute title in property when only a small amount of detriment had been suffered – but is rather to identify the detriment which the claimant has suffered and to provide equitable compensation for that amount.[58] So, as quoted above, in *Taylor Fashions v Liverpool Victoria Trustees Co Ltd*,[59] Oliver J preferred to focus on the detriment suffered by the plaintiff as opposed to some 'formula serving as a universal yardstick for every form of unconscionable behaviour'.[60] This approach has received general approbation[61] in preference to those few cases which have sought to apply the probanda based on proof of fraud and mistake as set out in *Wilmot v Barber*.[62] The clearest example of a court looking to compensate the detriment suffered by the claimant was in *Baker v Baker*,[63] where the Court of Appeal was asked to consider the position of an elderly man who had been induced to give up his home and to contribute to the purchase price of a house together with his son and daughter-in-law. Evidently the elderly man was entitled to an equitable interest in the house because he had contributed to the purchase price. When the court came to consider how best to conceive of the elderly man's rights, it was decided that the man needed sufficient monetary compensation to buy him sheltered accommodation for the rest of his life, due to his age and infirmity, rather than a declaration that he owned a given percentage of the equity in the house. Thus, the court may seek to identify both the claimant's detriment and his needs as a result.

An example might serve to highlight the distinction. Suppose that a promise was made by Peter to Mary that if Mary paid for renovation works on Peter's house, Peter would leave the freehold interest in the house to Mary in his will. Suppose further that the renovation works cost £10,000 and that the house cost £250,000. If the court is concerned with the claimant's detriment, then the court's approach is to measure the value of the detriment. So, Mary might only receive compensation of £10,000 in cash. By contrast, if the court were concerned to

---

57   (1995) P & CR 170.
58   *Walton Stores v Maher* (1988) 62 AJLR 110; *Lim v Ang* [1992] 1 WLR 113, 117, *per* Lord Browne-Wilkinson.
59   [1982] QB 133.
60   *Ibid.*
61   *Habib Bank Ltd v Habib Bank AG Zurich* [1981] 1 WLR 1265, CA; *Amalgamated Investment & Property Co Ltd v Texas Commerce International Bank* [1982] QB 84, CA; *Attorney-General of Hong Kong v Humphrey's Estate (Queen's Gardens) Ltd* [1987] 1 AC 114, PC; *Lim Teng Huan v Ang Swee Chuan* [1992] 1 WLR 113, PC; *Lloyds Bank v Carrick* [1996] 4 All ER 630, CA.
62   *Coombes v Smith* [1986] 1 WLR 808; *Matharu v Matharu* (1994) 68 P & CR 93; also *Orgee v Orgee* (1997) unreported, 5 November.
63   (1993) 25 HLR 408.

carry out the promise, then Mary would receive the freehold interest in the house. It might be that if Peter was still alive but had changed his mind, then compensating Mary might be appropriate,[64] whereas if Peter had died intestate then granting Mary the freehold might be the more appropriate means of providing her with the minimum equity necessary in the context.[65]

Preventing unconscionable behaviour

A third, alternative basis on which one might understand the operation of proprietary estoppel is to prevent unconscionable benefit being taken from the detrimental reliance of a person on a representation made to her.[66] The aim of the equity in this context might be said, on existing authority, to do the minimum necessary[67] in the light of the unconscionability of allowing the defendant to benefit or the claimant to suffer from the claimant's uncompensated detrimental reliance on the defendant's representation.[68] So, in the Court of Appeal in *Jennings v Rice*,[69] it was held that the aim of the estoppel was 'to do justice' between the parties.[70] This third basis for the estoppel, however, does not help us to know whether the remedy is intended to fulfil the promise or to compensate the detriment suffered. A general notion of unconscionability has always been contained in modern explanations of the doctrine. By way of example, the doctrine of proprietary estoppel was explained in *Taylor Fashions v Liverpool Victoria Trustees Co Ltd*[71] by Oliver J such that:

> it would be unconscionable for a party to be permitted to deny that which, knowingly or unknowingly, he has allowed or encouraged another to assume to his detriment.[72]

However, rather than base proprietary estoppel on a general notion of unconscionability, Oliver J preferred to focus on the detriment suffered by the claimant as opposed to some 'formula serving as a universal yardstick for every form of unconscionable behaviour'.[73] It is a difficult matter to know how the principle of unconscionability would operate as a single form of proprietary estoppel.

As considered at the beginning of this chapter, there is no single explanation for the manner in which all estoppels operate given that estoppel is based on a range of bases varying from honesty[74] to common sense[75] to common fairness.[76] It is only possible to identify

---

64 *Baker v Baker* (1993) 25 HLR 408. It might also be important to know whether or not Mary had alternative accommodation and whether or not she required further compensation to replace the home which she had expected to have once Peter died.

65 *Re Basham* [1986] 1 WLR 1498.

66 *Sledmore v Dalby* (1996) 72 P & CR 196.

67 *Crabb v Arun DC* [1976] 1 Ch 179; *Pascoe v Turner* [1979] 1 WLR 431; *Bawden v Bawden* [1997] EWCA Civ 2664, *per* Robert Walker LJ.

68 *Jennings v Rice* [2002] EWCA Civ 159.

69 [2002] EWCA Civ 159.

70 *Jennings v Rice* [2002] EWCA Civ 159, para 36, *per* Aldous LJ.

71 [1982] QB 133.

72 *Ibid*, 151.

73 *Ibid*.

74 *Re Exchange Securities & Commodities Ltd* [1988] Ch 46, 54, *per* Harman J.

75 *London Joint Stock Bank Ltd v Macmillan* [1918] AC 777, 818, *per* Lord Haldane.

76 *Lyle-Meller v A Lewis & Co* [1956] 1 WLR 29, 44, *per* Morris LJ.

common principles underpinning all forms of estoppel at the most general levels,[77] perhaps on the basis of unconscionability or fairness.[78] That 'the essence of the doctrine of proprietary estoppel is to do what is necessary to avoid an unconscionable result' was asserted by Walker LJ in *Jennings v Rice*[79] and accepted by the Privy Council in *Knowles v Knowles*.[80] What is significant about the development of a principle of unconscionability in this area is that it is difficult to know in advance the nature of the remedy which will be awarded in response to a claim for proprietary estoppel: in general terms, it seems that this approach enables the court to calculate an amount of compensation entirely in the abstract which is appropriate to meet merits of the case. An example of this tendency is *Jennings v Rice*,[81] as considered in detail below, where the judge decided on the round sum of £200,000 entirely in the abstract as meeting the merits of the case without necessarily quantifying any particular amount of unpaid wages, or money spent, or opportunities lost which were required to be compensated. Therefore, we are left with the question, considered below, as to how the appropriate remedy should be identified. First, we shall turn our attention to the three requirements for demonstrating proprietary estoppel.

13.3.3 The three elements of the modern test for proprietary estoppel

The three elements of proprietary estoppel

The court upheld the threefold test for proprietary estoppel which has become familiar in the cases: that there be a representation (or assurance), reliance and detriment.[82] These three elements were set out most cogently by Edward Nugee QC in *Re Basham*[83] as being set out in circumstances in which:

> one person, A, has acted to his detriment on the birth of a belief, which was known to and encouraged by another person, B, cannot insist on his strict legal rights if to do so would be inconsistent with A's belief . . . where the belief is that A is going to be given a right in the future, it is properly to be regarded as giving rise to a species of constructive trust, which is the concept employed by a court of equity to prevent a person from relying on his legal rights where it would be unconscionable for him to do so. The rights to which proprietary estoppel gives rise, and the machinery by which effect is given to them, are similar in many respects to those involved in cases of secret trusts, mutual wills, and other comparable cases in which property is vested in B on the faith of an understanding that it will be dealt with in a particular manner . . . In cases of proprietary

---

77 The argument to the effect that all forms of estoppel could be understood as being based on a single notion of unconscionable was set out by Professor Cooke (Cooke, 2000).

78 The arguments for an all-embracing estoppel are based on such concepts: see, eg, the various *dicta* of Lord Denning in *Amalgamated Investment & Property Co Ltd (In Liquidation) v Texas Commerce International Bank Ltd* [1982] 1 QB 84; *Lyle-Meller v A Lewis & Co* [1956] 1 WLR 29; *Moorgate Mercantile Co Ltd v Twitchings* [1976] 1 QB 225.

79 [2002] EWCA Civ 159, para [56].

80 [2008] UKPC 30, para [27], *per* Sir Henry Brooke (reading the judgment of the entire court).

81 [2002] EWCA Civ 159.

82 *Taylor Fashions Ltd v Liverpool Victoria Trustees Co Ltd* [1982] 1 QB 133; *Re Basham (Deceased)* [1986] 1 WLR 1498; *Wayling v Jones* (1993) 69 P & CR 170; *Gillett v Holt* [2000] 2 All ER 289.

83 [1986] 1 WLR 1498.

estoppel the factor which gives rise to the equitable obligation is A's alteration of his position on the faith of a similar understanding.

Each of those elements is considered in the sections which follow.

The first element of the estoppel: assurance or representation

The first requirement for the demonstration of proprietary estoppel is that there has been a representation made by the defendant to the claimant.[84] It is important that the assurances of the representor have been intended by their maker to lead the claimant to believe that he would acquire rights in property. So, for example, it would not be sufficient that the representor was merely toying with the claimant without either of them forming a belief that the claimant would in fact acquire any rights in property. For, as Robert Walker LJ put it, 'it is notorious that some elderly persons of means derive enjoyment from the possession of testamentary power, and from dropping hints as to their intentions, without any question of any estoppel arising'.[85] In other words, representations may be made which the defendant does not intend to be relied upon by the claimant. The clearest example of a representation would be a single promise made by one party to another which can be proven in court. More often in the cases, there have been a pattern of assurances made by one party to another over a period of time. The claimant's contention will be that the aggregation of these assurances amounted to a representation. So, in *Re Basham*,[86] the claimant had made representations that she would receive a house on the proprietor's death made to her frequently over time.

The breadth of the doctrine of proprietary estoppel in this context was demonstrated by the Court of Appeal in *Gillett v Holt*.[87] That case concerned a friendship between a farmer, Mr Holt, and a young boy of 12, Gillett, which lasted for 40 years, during which time the boy worked for the farmer. Gillett left his real parents and moved in with Holt when aged 15: there was even a suggestion that the farmer would adopt the boy at one stage. On numerous occasions, the claimant, Gillett, was assured by Holt that he would inherit the farm. The claimant's wife and family were described as being a form of surrogate family for the farmer. In time a third person, Wood, turned Holt against Gillett which led to Gillett being removed from Holt's will.[88] Robert Walker LJ held that there was sufficient detriment by Gillett in the course of their relationship over 40 years evidenced by the following factors: working for Holt and not accepting other job offers, performing actions beyond what would ordinarily

---

84 In *Sinclair v Sinclair* [2009] 926 EWHC (Ch) the point was re-affirmed that there cannot be a remedy under proprietary estoppel principles unless a representation can be demonstrated. So, where in that case the claimant could not demonstrate that a representation had been made to him that he would acquire any rights of ownership in a yard, Proudman J did not find an estoppel in his favour even though the claimant had spent a lot of money on the yard in the hope of acquiring such a right. Similarly, in *Walsh v Singh* [2009] EWHC 3219 (Ch), [2010] 1 FCR 177 the claimant could not demonstrate that any clear representation had been made to her that she was to acquire rights in property, even though she had made contributions to the work of finding a property and of renovating it. Consequently her detriment, in leaving the Bar, could not have been said to have been suffered on the basis of a clear representation that she would acquire rights in the property.

85 *Gillett v Holt* [2000] 2 All ER 289, 304.

86 [1986] 1 WLR 1498.

87 [2000] 2 All ER 289. This case was followed in *Van Laetham v Brooker* [2005] EWHC 1478 (Ch), para [61].

88 The nature of their relationship is a fascinating matter for conjecture.

have been expected of an employee, taking no substantial steps to secure for his future by means of pension or otherwise, and spending money on a farmhouse (which he expected to inherit) which had been almost uninhabitable at the outset. The combination of these factors over such a long period of time were considered by the Court of Appeal to constitute ample evidence of detriment sufficient to found a proprietary estoppel. On the facts of *Gillett v Holt*,[89] it was clear that the assurances had been repeated frequently and were sincerely meant when made at various family celebrations and so forth. Thus, the courts will infer a representation from the circumstances, even over a long period of time, without the need for there necessarily to have been a single representation made. Similarly, in *Thorner v Curtis*[90] in front of the Court of Appeal the claimant had worked on the deceased's farm for many years for no wages and had an expectation that he would inherit the farm. The claimant's work had increased its value greatly. The deceased had created a will bequeathing the farm to the claimant but that will was destroyed before the deceased died intestate. It was held that the claimant had formed the impression that he would inherit the farm over time and furthermore that it would have been unconscionable to deny the claimant rights on proprietary estoppel principles. This decision was appealed to the House of Lords, under the name *Thorner v Major*.

Thorner v Major followed only shortly after the decision in *Cobbe v Yeoman's Row*. The claimant contended that a representation had been made to him over time by the deceased to the effect that the claimant would become the owner of the deceased's farm after the deceased's death; however, the deceased died without leaving the farm by will to the claimant. The facts were these. Jimmy and Peter were cousins, and David was Jimmy's adult son. David worked for no pay for 29 years on Peter's farm, as well as working for no pay on Jimmy's farm. David's lifestyle was one of hard physical work for about sixteen hours a day for seven days a week. While it is remarkable to work in this way for another person, that does not in itself entitle that worker to ownership of the other person's property. It was held that what is required under proprietary estoppel principles is a representation which suggests a promise of ownership of that property together with clear identification of the property involved.[91] In this case, the evidence was unclear. One day in 1990, Peter gave David a document relating to insurance policies over Peter's life, which David took as an indication that he was intended to become the future owner of Peter's property including the farm after Peter's death. Otherwise the pair did not tend to say much to one another about anything despite working together for so much time. Their Lordships, especially Lords Walker and Rodger, made much of the fact that was found by the trial judge that farmers in this part of Somerset could be naturally taciturn, that these two men in particular spoke very few words to one another about anything, and therefore that the absence of any more explicit representation should not necessarily be read as denying the presence of a suitable understanding between these parties that the claimant's work was being done (to his evident detriment because he received no pay) in reliance on that understanding. Ironically, the court in *Thorner v Major* found that a representation was impliedly made even though nothing, by definition, was said between two parties too taciturn to discuss their respective rights.

89 *Ibid.*
90 [2008] WTLR 155.
91 [2009] 1 WLR 776, para [61] *et seq, per* Lord Walker.

The House of Lords held that on the facts of *Thorner v Major* there had been a sufficient assurance made by Peter to David on which it was reasonable for David to have formed the impression in these circumstances that he would become the owner of Peter's farm after his death, in reliance on which he worked to his detriment on Peter's farm. As Lord Rodger put it, there does not need to be a 'signature event' on which a clear representation was made.[92] Instead it is sufficient, for Lord Rodger[93] and Lord Walker,[94] that the 'relevant assurance' which was made was 'clear enough' in the context. Lord Hoffmann and Lord Neuberger concurred in general terms with Lord Walker. So, if the representor was 'standing by in silence' aware that the claimant was acting to his detriment on the belief that he was thus acquiring a right in the property, then that would be enough to grant him rights on the basis of proprietary estoppel.[95] (The House of Lords was unanimous in finding the existence of a right on these facts, although Lord Scott dissented in part on the basis that this case should have been decided on the basis of a remedial constructive trust, and not proprietary estoppel, as is discussed in Chapter 12.) It is suggested that *Cobbe* is to be understood as being limited to commercial joint ventures as a result of *Thorner v Major*.

It is clear that in general terms, it will be sufficient if the defendant makes an express representation to the defendant,[96] but it would also be sufficient to establish an estoppel if some implied assurance were made in circumstances in which the defendant knew that the claimant was relying on the impression she had formed.[97] That an implied assurance will constitute a representation is, in any event, in line with the older form of proprietary estoppel which is based on mistake: that is, to lead someone mistakenly to believe that she will receive some property by means of implied assurances would satisfy either form of estoppel.[98] It has been suggested that there need not be a clear representation at all provided that a common understanding arose between the parties that one of them would acquire rights of some kind if the other acted to her detriment.[99] What is important is that the defendant intended the claimant to rely on the representation, assurance or understanding and that the defendant knew that the claimant was so relying.[100] While the courts may infer

---

92 [2009] 1 WLR 776, para [24].

93 *Ibid*, para [26].

94 *Ibid*, para [56]. Relying on Hoffmann LJ in *Walton v Walton*, [1994] CA Transcript No 479 (unreported) to the effect that: 'The promise must be unambiguous and must appear to have been intended to be taken seriously. Taken in its context, it must have been a promise which one might reasonably expect to be relied upon by the person to whom it was made.'

95 [2009] 1 WLR 776, para [55], *per* Lord Walker.

96 *Taylor Fashions Ltd v Liverpool Victoria Trustees Co Ltd* [1982] 1 QB 133; *Re Basham (Deceased)* [1986] 1 WLR 1498; *Wayling v Jones* (1993) 69 P & CR 170; *Gillett v Holt* [2000] 2 All ER 289.

97 *Crabb v Arun DC* [1976] Ch 179.

98 *Ramsden v Dyson* (1866) LR 1 HL 129, *per* Lord Cranworth; *Wilmot v Barber* (1880) 15 Ch D 96; *Coombes v Smith* [1986] 1 WLR 808.

99 *John v George* (1996) 71 P & CR 375; *Gillett v Holt* [2001] Ch 210. Although in *Kellwark Properties Ltd v Waller* [2002] EWCA Civ 1076, [2002] 48 EG 142, a long-standing practice between landowners in relation to the renewal of leases at a ground rent was not taken to have constituted such a common understanding capable of founding a representation. In *Kastner v Jason* [2004] EWCA Civ 1599, para [2], it was suggested that a representation or understanding that one would abide by an arbitration award would give rise to 'proprietary estoppel, itself amounting to a constructive trust' (the point was not necessary for the dismissal of the issues in that case which was primarily concerned with conflict of laws).

100 *Crabb v Arun DC* [1976] Ch 179, 188, *per* Lord Denning; *JT Developments v Quinn* (1990) 62 P & CR 33, 46, *per* Ralph Gibson LJ; *Barclays Bank v Zaroovabli* [1997] Ch 321, 330, *per* Scott VC.

representations from the facts of a case, nevertheless a general promise to support the claimant financially in the future would not give rise to proprietary estoppel if the promise was not explicitly connected to some property in relation to which the claimant would acquire proprietary rights in the event that she acted to her detriment in reliance on the promise.[101] General promises as part of a romantic relationship will not in themselves suppose that rights in property will be created if those promises made no reference to any property.

An interesting illustration of this last principle arose in *Lissimore v Downing*[102] when a very rich rock musician started a relationship 'on the rebound' with a married woman after they met in a pub one evening. They began a very casual, sexual relationship in which she was cheating on her husband. He had taken her to a gate at the edge of his large country estate worth millions of pounds and said to her, words to the effect of 'how would you like to be lady of this estate?' She claimed that she had interpreted this to be a representation that she would acquire an equitable interest in this property, particularly when this was taken in common with the couple's comparatively shortlived, ensuing relationship. However, the court noted the fact that she had continued living with her husband after this statement had been made to her, that she had maintained her job working in a chemist's shop, and considered it unlikely in the circumstances that the rock musician would have intended to give her a share of his hard-earned country estate. Taking all of these circumstances into account, the court held that no representation had been made to the effect that she would acquire proprietary rights in the rock musician's country estate. So, common sense will be applied so that not every slip of the tongue accidentally grants rights in property.

Similarly, it is not enough to acquire an interest in her mother's house that a daughter who was educationally challenged believed she would have a house bought for her by her mother when there was no other evidence to suggest that that had been her mother's intention.[103] Instead, in that case, it appeared that the mother had simply been placating her daughter and not purporting to make her any legally-binding promises. It was held that there had not been any binding representation made which would entitle the daughter to take absolute title in the house after her mother's death when her mother had left the house by will to her third husband. So, for example, where a father promises his son that the son will acquire an equitable interest in a house owned by his father and in reliance on that promise (and with the agreement of his father) the son sells his house so as to pay for renovation works on his father's house, there would be a representation, reliance and detriment (where the detriment was in the form of selling the house to pay for the renovations) sufficient to found a claim for proprietary estoppel.[104]

A claimant cannot argue that she has relied on a representation by performing an action which she was contractually obliged to perform in any event, and furthermore if it would be unreasonable to purport to have relied on a representation then no estoppel will be found.[105]

---

101 *Lissimore v Downing* [2003] 2 FLR 308.
102 *Ibid.*
103 *Turner v Jacob* [2006] EWHC 1317 (Ch).
104 *S v R* [2008] EWHC 1874 (Fam), [2009] 1 P & CR D12 (also sub nom *Q v Q*). In those circumstances, however, the judge expressed himself as finding that the events gave rise to a 'constructive trust' in the son's favour, after some inconclusive discussion about whether 'proprietary estoppel and constructive trust' should be treated as the same doctrine or as two separate doctrines: at para 115.
105 *Hunt v Soady* [2007] EWCA Civ 366.

662   Equity and Trusts

The decision of the Court of Appeal in *Jennings v Rice*[106] demonstrates, in tandem with *Gillett v Holt*, that there need not be a clear representation made at any particular time nor that the representor be proved to have understood that she was making a binding representation; rather, it is sufficient that a 'representation' appears to emerge over time. In *Jennings v Rice*, Mr Jennings began working for Mrs Royle, a widow, as a gardener (for 30 pence an hour) in 1970 on Saturdays and for three evenings per week in summer. Over time Mr Jennings' duties expanded so that he carried out maintenance work, took Mrs Royle shopping and starting running errands for her. By the late 1980s, Mrs Royle had stopped paying Mr Jennings, but he continued with the work. In 1993, Mrs Royle was burgled and Mr Jennings took to sleeping every night at Mrs Royle's house on a sofa in the living room so that she would not be alone in the house, something she feared after the burglary. From the 1970s onwards, the amount of time which Mr Jennings spent at Mrs Royle's house had caused problems with his wife, Mrs Jennings. Before Mrs Royle's death in 1997, Mrs Jennings had begun to help care for the old woman with her husband. There was no evidence that Mrs Royle had ever made a clear representation in the form of a binding contract with Mr Jennings that he would acquire a right in her house, although it was suggested that there were occasions when she said words to the effect 'this will all be yours one day'. It was found that the pattern of the parties' relationship was such that Mrs Royle would be deemed to have made sufficient representation to Mr Jennings over time to found a right under proprietary estoppel. As discussed below, it was not considered that the circumstances would justify granting Mr Jennings the entire interest in the house, but Mr Jennings was entitled to a payment of £200,000 as the minimum equity necessary in the circumstances. It is unclear precisely why that amount of money was appropriate in the circumstances other than that the Court of Appeal wanted to prevent unconscionability and wanted to do the minimum equity which it considered necessary in the circumstances.

Thus, the representation can be divined from the circumstances. In *Gillett v Holt* and in *Jennings v Rice*, there was behaviour over a long period of time which the court (principally Robert Walker LJ) considered would give rise to an unconscionable treatment of the claimant if it were uncompensated. In these cases, as considered in more detail below, the court considered it appropriate to make an award of compensation which, it is suggested, was concerned to compensate the claimant's detriment. By contrast, in *Lissimore v Downing*, there was also only a vague representation, but the court considered that the claimant could not have considered that in such a short relationship (compared to the decades which had passed in *Gillett v Holt* and in *Jennings v Rice*) she could have placed any reasonable reliance on the representation as having been meant seriously. It is suggested that the short, casual relationship in *Lissimore v Downing*, taken together with the comparative lack of detriment (compared to a rent-free life with a rock musician in a huge house), simply did not convince the court that the circumstances were sufficient to justify an award under proprietary estoppel. In effect, the courts have come to focus on the general fairness of the circumstances and whether or not the defendant would be taking an unconscionable advantage of the claimant.

Equitable estoppel will also be available where the defendant would take an unconscionable benefit from the claimant's mistake as to the defendant's representation. So, in relation to the right to seek rectification of a contract on grounds of mistake, it has been held that

106 [2002] EWCA Civ 159.

where one party to the transaction knows of the mistake and nevertheless allows the other party to enter into transactions in reliance on those mistaken assumptions, then equitable estoppel will prevent the defendant from resisting a claim for rectification.[107] It is sufficient for the operation of this form of estoppel that the defendant recklessly shut her eyes to the fact that a mistake has been made – it is not necessary that actual knowledge of the mistake be demonstrated.[108] This latter principle accords with equity's general purpose to avoid unconscionable behaviour[109] and dishonesty in a broad sense.[110] There is no need for an active representation: it is enough to know that the other person is relying on a mistake that would have been obvious to someone who has not refrained from making reasonable inquiries. Furthermore, it is not a requirement that the representation have been an irrevocable representation. So, contrary to earlier authority,[111] the representation does not have to constitute, for example, a binding contract between the parties nor does it have to be an irrevocable representation.[112] Rather, it is sufficient that the representation was one on which the claimant could reasonably rely to her detriment in the manner considered in the following sections.[113] Thus, in *Sutcliffe v Lloyd*[114] where the defendants made representations to the claimant that they would participate jointly in the acquisition and development of disused petrol stations with him, such that the defendant acted to his detriment in reliance on their negotiations, it was no defence to argue that the representations had not themselves constituted binding, contractual or similar obligations in the documentation between the parties. Rather it was enough that they constituted representations on which the claimant could have relied to his detriment such that it would be unconscionable to deny him a remedy based on equitable estoppel.

The second element of the estoppel: reliance on the representation or assurance

The court will look to the context to decide whether or not it was reasonable for the claimant to have relied on the particular representor in relation to that particular representation.[115] This is expressed variously as being 'mutual understanding' between the parties that the actions of the claimant were a *quid pro quo* in relation to the promise made.[116] It is essential that the claimant be able to demonstrate a nexus between the actions which were performed and the representations which were made. Therefore, where a claimant can demonstrate that she worked for lower wages than her trade would ordinarily have attracted with a view to acquiring rights in property, then she would be entitled to a remedy based on proprietary estoppel, whereas if she had accepted lower wages out of love for her employer who was

---

107 *Whitley v Delaney* [1914] AC 132; *Monaghan CC v Vaughan* [1948] IR 306; *A Roberts & Co Ltd v Leicestershire CC* [1961] Ch 555; *Thomas Bates and Sons Ltd v Wyndham's (Lingerie) Ltd* [1981] 1 WLR 505.
108 *Commission for New Towns v Cooper* [1995] Ch 259; *Templiss Properties v Hyams* [1999] EGCS 60.
109 *Riverlate Properties Ltd v Paul* [1975] Ch 133.
110 Cf *Royal Brunei Airlines v Tan* [1995] 2 AC 378; *Twinsectra Ltd v Yardley* [1999] Lloyd's Rep Bank 438.
111 *Kinane v Mackie-Conteh* [2005] EWCA Civ 45, at para [29], *per* Arden LJ.
112 *Sutcliffe v Lloyd* [2007] EWCA Civ 153, para [38], *per* Wilson LJ.
113 *Ibid.*
114 [2007] EWCA Civ 153.
115 *Gillett v Holt* [2000] 2 All ER 289, 306. So, false reliance or reliance on false information will not make out the estoppel: *Willis v Willis* [1986] 1 EGLR 62; *Gonthier v Orange Contract Scaffolding Ltd* [2003] EWCA Civ 873.
116 *Re Basham (Deceased)* [1986] 1 WLR 1498.

also her partner, then she would not.[117] The greater difficulty is those situations in which the claimant suffers only personal detriment, such as moving house, and therefore finds it difficult to demonstrate that the agreement to move house was based on the representation that she would acquire rights in property and was not simply based on love and affection.[118]

The third element of the estoppel: detriment suffered by the claimant

It is necessary that the claimant has suffered some detriment for there to be a proprietary estoppel because equity will not assist a mere volunteer who has neither given consideration nor suffered detriment.[119] The question is then as to the type of behaviour which will constitute detriment, and how restrictively this requirement of detriment will be interpreted. The Court of Appeal in *Gillett v Holt*[120] explained the principle of proprietary estoppel as being based on preventing unconscionable behaviour. The court refused to accept that proprietary estoppel should be seen as confined to narrow categories, preferring instead to recognise that it is based on that underlying concept of good conscience.[121] Similarly, it was suggested that there was no requirement that detriment be considered in a narrow, technical fashion. Rather, different types of representation or assurance could connote different forms of detriment which would stretch beyond spending money.[122] Therefore, it had been suggested that in assessing detriment, one should look in the round at the circumstances of the parties. Lawrence Collins J held in *Van Laetham v Brooker* that:

> [d]etriment is not a narrow or technical concept. The detriment need not consist of the expenditure of money or other quantifiable financial detriment, so long as it is something substantial. The requirement must be approached as part of a broad inquiry as to whether repudiation of an assurance is or is not unconscionable in all the circumstances.[123]

Nevertheless, in spite of the statements made in recent cases to the effect that proprietary estoppel should be understood as arising on a broad basis, it has also been suggested that the detriment on which the claimant seeks to rely must be something substantial. So, spending money will be a clear demonstration of detriment,[124] unless it is expenditure (relating to the acquisition of rights in the home) which is indirectly related to the property such as paying for household bills.[125] Also accepted as constituting detriment will be settling a boundary dispute relating to the property at issue,[126] giving up alternative accommodation in reliance

---

117 *Wayling v Jones* (1993) 69 P & CR 170.
118 *Coombes v Smith* [1986] 1 WLR 808; *Watts v Storey* (1983) 133 NLJ 631, [1983] CA Transcript 319. Cf *Grant v Edwards* [1986] Ch 638.
119 In *Re Basham (Deceased)* [1986] 1 WLR 1498, it was suggested that merely the existence of unconscionable behaviour, without a correlative suffering of detriment, would not make out the estoppel.
120 [2000] 2 All ER 289.
121 See also *Jennings v Rice* [2002] EWCA Civ 159 in this regard.
122 *Grant v Edwards* [1986] Ch 638. Cf *Coombes v Smith* [1986] 1 WLR 808.
123 [2005] EWHC 1478 (Ch), [2006] 2 FLR 495, [74].
124 Even if it is not a large amount of money: *Pascoe v Turner* [1979] 2 All ER 945.
125 *Burns v Burns* [1984] Ch 317; *Lloyds Bank v Rosset* [1991] 1 AC 107.
126 *Re Basham* [1986] 1 WLR 1498.

on the availability of the property at issue,[127] working for reduced wages in reliance on the acquisition of some right in the property at issue,[128] providing unpaid services in the defendant's home in reliance on the acquisition of some rights in the property,[129] and continuing to work unpaid for someone who had previously made payment for gardening work in reliance on a promise that the gardener would inherit the property.[130] Paying for extensive building work on the property will constitute detriment,[131] although merely supervising building work will not.[132] In each of these instances it can be seen that the detriment suffered was connected in some way to the acquisition of rights in the property.

By contrast, there is the more difficult question as to whether suffering detriment which is purely personal – as opposed to financial – will constitute detriment sufficient to found proprietary estoppel. There are competing authorities, for example, on the question whether leaving one romantic relationship to begin another, on the basis that one might expect some property rights in the home established in that second relationship: some cases taking the view that this would not constitute detriment because it was purely personal,[133] whereas other cases have considered this to be detriment when there were children involved because the children also had to move home.[134] Similarly, in *Gillett v Holt*,[135] it was accepted that a combination of otherwise minor acts of detriment could amount to a suitable basis for the estoppel: so, deciding not to continue with schooling, working on the renovation of a building, and working generally on a farm (albeit for a wage) in the expectation of acquiring some rights in property, would cumulatively constitute detriment. A typically erudite discussion of the authorities is set out by Sir Peter Gibson in *Powell v Benney*.[136] In that case, the claimant's alleged detriment simply on the basis of assisting an elderly man in his premises was contended to have awarded them some rights in those premises on 'constructive trust or proprietary estoppel' principles. It was held by the Court of Appeal, however, that there had not been any clear 'bargain' between the parties to the effect that the claimant would perform any detrimental acts nor that those detrimental acts were intended to acquire the claimant any interest in the property, and so no right to an estoppel was found.

---

127   *Ibid.* See also *Jones v Jones* [1977] 1 WLR 438; *Maharaj v Shand* [1986] AC 898, where accommodation was given up so that the plaintiff could live closer to the proprietor of the land in question.

128   *Wayling v Jones* (1995) 69 P & CR 170. Also where the duties were beyond the ordinary course of employment: *Gillett v Holt* [2001] Ch 210.

129   *Greasley v Cooke* [1980] 1 WLR 1306; *Re Basham* [1986] 1 WLR 1498; *Campbell v Griffin* [2001] EWCA Civ 990.

130   *Jennings v Rice* [2003] 1 P & CR 100. The claimant in this case also gave up a large amount of his spare time to sit with the elderly lady who had previously paid him for his gardening work.

131   *Inwards v Baker* [1965] 2 QB 29; *Griffiths v Williams* (1977) 248 EG 947. A small amount of money spent on decoration has even been held to constitute detriment: *Pascoe v Turner* [1979] 1 WLR 431.

132   *Lloyds Bank v Rosset* [1991] 1 AC 107.

133   *Coombes v Smith* [1986] 1 WLR 808. This approach, in general terms, was also taken in *Lissimore v Downing* [2003] 2 FLR 308 to the effect that actions which formed the ordinary part of behaviour within a relationship would not in themselves constitute detriment for the purposes of establishing rights under proprietary estoppel.

134   *Grant v Edwards* [1986] Ch 638.

135   [2001] Ch 210.

136   [2007] EWCA Civ 1283. See also *McGuane v Welch* [2008] EWCA Civ 785.

13.3.4 Identifying the appropriate remedy for proprietary estoppel

The court's discretion: ranging from proprietary remedies to financial compensation

Proprietary estoppel is best thought of as a two-step process: the first step in the process is to establish whether or not the estoppel can be demonstrated on the facts of the case; the second step in the process is to establish the most appropriate remedy to fit those circumstances. Whereas constructive trusts, considered in Chapter 12, were said to arise on an institutional basis (that is, retrospectively from the time of the unconscionable act and automatically without any discretion on the part of the court), proprietary estoppel arises on a remedial basis (that is, prospectively from the date of the court order with the precise nature of the remedy being at the court's discretion).[137] Even though the constructive trust appears to be a flexible doctrine, its avowedly institutional nature does not match the scope of remedy permitted by proprietary estoppel.[138] What has become clear is that proprietary estoppel will give a claimant a substantive form of action with which to acquire rights in property which she had not had before and that it will not operate like promissory estoppel merely so as to defend that claimant from suffering detriment as the hands of the defendant.[139]

What is most significant is that the court will have complete freedom to frame its remedy once it has found that an estoppel is both available and appropriate.[140] Thus the two-stage process develops: first, find whether or not there is an estoppel and, second, decide on the most appropriate and proportionate remedy in the context both in the light of the assurance made and the most effective method of compensating the claimant's detriment.[141] The nature of the remedies available in cases of proprietary estoppel can range from the award of the entire interest in the property at issue[142] to a mere entitlement to equitable compensation.[143] They may be enforceable not only against the person who made the assurance but also against third parties, thus underlining the proprietary nature of such remedies in circumstances where the court considers such a remedy appropriate.[144] This indicates the nature of estoppel as a pure form of equity: the court is entirely at liberty to grant personal or proprietary awards which operate only against the defendant or also against third parties (as proprietary rights ought to).[145]

---

137 See recent cases such as *Gillett v Holt* [2001] Ch 210, 235; *Jennings v Rice* [2003] 1 P & CR 100. See Moriarty (1984) 100 LQR 376, suggesting that estoppel merely perfects and imperfect gift; although Thompson [1986] Conv 406 suggests that Moriarty's suggestion is contrary to principle and that the cases advocate a variety of remedies from context to context.

138 As illustrated by *Sledmore v Dalby* (1996) 72 P & CR 196, *per* Roch J. See also *Campbell v Griffin* [2001] EWCA Civ 990, [2001] WTLR 981.

139 See, eg, *Hearn v Younger* [2002] WTLR 1317 in particular, as well as the cases considered in this section in general whereby claimants establish rights in property which had not previously been vested with them.

140 An approach approved as long ago as *Lord Cawdor v Lewis* (1835) 1 Y & C Ex 427, 433; *Plimmer v Wellington Corp* (1884) 9 App Cas 699, 713. Gardner, 'The Remedial Discretion in Proprietary Estoppel' (1999) 115 LQR 438; Gardner, 'The Remedial Discretion in Proprietary Estoppel – again' (2006) 122 LQR 492.

141 See, eg, *Gillett v Holt* [2001] Ch 210, 235; *Jennings v Rice* [2003] 1 P & CR 100, para 56.

142 *Pascoe v Turner* [1979] 2 All ER 945; *Re Basham (Deceased)* [1986] 1 WLR 1498.

143 *Baker v Baker* (1993) 25 HLR 408, CA; *Sledmore v Dalby* (1996) 72 P & CR 196; *Gillett v Holt* [2001] Ch 210, CA; *Campbell v Griffin* [2001] EWCA Civ 990, [2001] WTLR 981; *Jennings v Rice* [2002] EWCA Civ 159; and also *Raffaele v Raffaele* [1962] WAR 29.

144 *Hopgood v Brown* [1955] 1 WLR 213; *Inwards v Baker* [1965] 2 QB 29.

145 See para 31.2.2.

One example of the range of remedies available would arise where a claimant was assured that she would have a home available for her occupation for the rest of her life. Proprietary remedies will be awarded where that is required to do the minimum equity necessary between the parties.[146] Where it was considered impossible to protect the rights of the claimant to occupy the property for the remainder of her life without transferring the entire fee simple to her, the court decided to award her the entire fee simple.[147] Alternatively, the court may award an irrevocable licence to occupy where that would have been considered indefeasible by any other person to protect a claimant who was considered entitled to occupy property for the remainder of her life.[148] Yet further, where the court was concerned to ensure that an elderly or infirm claimant be provided with appropriate accommodation in her twilight years, it was held that she should receive compensation calculated at a level sufficient to provide her with appropriate accommodation.[149] Compensation can be based on the actual cost of improvements together with interest.[150] Alternatively, where a person has performed detrimental acts in relation to leased premises in the hope of acquiring the lease, the court may order a charge on the lease compensating him for his expenditure in respect of the property.[151]

That proprietary estoppel permits non-proprietary remedies reflects the difficulties which may face a court in deciding the most appropriate method for dealing with any given case. As an example of this phenomenon in *Cobbe v Yeoman's Row Management Ltd*[152] at first instance (subsequently reversed by the House of Lords) the claimant had spent a large amount of money applying for planning permission for the development of land in reliance on the defendant's representation that she would acquire the development land from the claimant. It was held that there had been representation, reliance and detriment and therefore that the estoppel was proved. However, there were difficulties with the remedy. Lewison J considered it inappropriate to make a proprietary award because the claimant's expectation had only been that he would subsequently enter into a contract, after appropriate negotiations, with the defendant and therefore the precise rights which the claimant stood to receive had always been open to negotiation and change. Nevertheless, it was held that the defendant had taken unconscionable advantage of the claimant in allowing the claimant to make the application for planning permission. Consequently, the appropriate remedy was held to be a lien in favour of the claimant equal to half the value of the land once planning permission had been granted.[153] This approach followed the decision of Goff J in *Holiday*

146 *Crabb v Arun DC* [1976] Ch 179. See *Dent v Dent* [1996] 1 All ER 659, the court will consider the appropriateness of awarding a right of occupation in all the circumstances. See generally *Dillwyn v Llewelyn* (1862) 4 De GF & J 517 on the award of the fee simple, or alternatively *Griffiths v Williams* (1977) 248 EG 947 on the award of a lease; or *Plimmer v Mayor of Wellington* (1884) 9 App Cas 699, *Dodsworth v Dodsworth* (1973) 228 EG 1115; *Re Sharpe (A Bankrupt)* [1980] 1 WLR 219 on the award of a perpetual licence to occupy the property.
147 *Pascoe v Turner* [1979] 2 All ER 945.
148 *Greasley v Cooke* [1980] 1 WLR 1306. This will be particularly so where the claimant has contributed substantially to the mortgage repayments in reliance on representations made as to the acquisition of rights in the property by the defendant: *Sleebush v Gordon* [2004] All ER (D) 148.
149 *Baker v Baker* (1993) 25 HLR 408; *Burrows & Burrows v Sharpe* (1991) 23 HLR 82.
150 *Morris v Morris* [1982] 1 NSWLR 61. Cf *Re Whitehead* [1948] NZLR 1066.
151 *McGuane v Welch* [2008] EWCA Civ 785.
152 [2005] All ER (D) 406 (Feb).
153 A lien is a right to possession of the land until such time as the amount of money was paid.

Inns Inc v Broadhead[154] where, after considering a question of withdrawal from a transaction once planning permission was awarded, his Lordship had ordered equal division of the equity. Thus, the claimant's right was a right to money and not to any particular right in property. On similar facts, in *Pridean Ltd v Forest Taverns Ltd* a publican had begun development work on a pub in expectation of the fulfilment of a joint venture agreement with the other party being solemnised in the form of a contract.[155]

This case was appealed to the Court of Appeal in *Yeoman's Row Management Ltd v Cobbe*.[156] Mummery LJ held that the first two and the final grounds of appeal did not raise any meaningful argument on these facts. On the third ground of appeal the judge at first instance had not relied on this being a binding contract, and the second agreement was not in any event expressed as being subject to contract. On the fourth ground, Mummery LJ held that the judge at first instance was entitled to hold that the appellant's behaviour had been unconscionable, particularly given the timing of the withdrawal from the transaction when the property had increased markedly in value. Mummery LJ then considered the nature of the remedy which should be made here. He relied on an article by Dr Gardner[157] and on the judgment of Goff J in *Holiday Inns Inc v Broadhead*[158] where after considering a question of withdrawal from a transaction once planning permission was awarded his Lordship had ordered equal division of the equity as the only feasible means of dealing with the case. It was held by Mummery LJ that where it is not clear what the claimant's expectations would have been, as in this case because it could not be known what level of profit could have been anticipated, then the remedy could not be concerned to meet that person's expectations. Equally, on these facts it was held that it would have been inadequate merely to have reimbursed Cobbe's expenses in the application for planning permission because that would not have taken into account the great increase in the value of the property after planning permission was awarded in which he would have expected to share. Mummery LJ held that Lewison J at first instance had reached an appropriate conclusion on the facts of that case in dividing the equity in the property equally between the parties, as Goff J had done in *Holiday Inns Inc v Broadhead*. This again demonstrates the remedial nature of proprietary estoppel. Dyson LJ agreed with Mummery LJ, focusing on the principle that 'the court must look at the circumstances in each case to decide in what way the equity can be satisfied'.[159] Dyson LJ pointed out that '[t]he courts often do not explain why one remedy is adopted rather than another':[160] this is very true, and therefore we have had to map those different approaches in this chapter.[161]

As *Cobbe v Yeoman's Row Management Ltd* indicates, recent cases have taken a broader approach than simply awarding rights in property, preferring instead to award both a right in some property and also some compensation in cash terms as considered necessary to meet the unconscionability exerted over the claimant. The Courts of Appeal in *Yeoman's Row v Cobbe* and in *Jennings v Rice* were concerned to look at all of the circumstances and then to reach an appropriate, equitable result. This is the way of modern proprietary estoppel. The

---

154   (1974) 232 EG 951.
155   *Pridean Ltd v Forest Taverns Ltd* (1996) 75 P & CR 447.
156   [2006] EWCA Civ 1139.
157   See Gardner, 'The Remedial Discretion in Proprietary Estoppel' (1999) 115 LQR 438.
158   (1974) 232 EG 951.
159   Taken from *Plimmer v Mayor of Wellington* (1884) 9 App Cas 699, 714.
160   [2006] EWCA Civ 1139, para [121].
161   This approach has been followed by the Court of Appeal in *Sutcliffe v Lloyd* [2007] EWCA Civ 153.

House of Lords in *Cobbe v Yeoman's Row*,[162] as considered below, has taken a less expansive approach in relation to commercial contracts; although the subsequent decision of the House of Lords in *Thorner v Major*[163] appears to have returned matters to their previous condition in other circumstances.

The decision in *Cobbe* aside, the different approaches of the courts indicate a general equitable jurisdiction. As Lord Denning put it, 'equity is displayed at its most flexible' in relation to proprietary estoppel.[164] Thus, in *Gillett v Holt*, the claimant, who had worked on the defendant's farm and who had been promised to inherit the farm, was awarded the freehold in a farmhouse, 42 hectares of farmland and £100,000. In *Jennings v Rice*, it was suggested by Robert Walker LJ that the appropriate methodology was 'to do what was necessary to avoid an unconscionable remedy' by means of a proportionate remedy and consequently the claimant was awarded £200,000 in response to about 27 years of casual labour and care for the deceased woman.[165] In *Campbell v Griffin*,[166] the claimant's detrimental reliance was held to entitle him to a payment of £35,000 instead of granting him a right in the property which would 'hold up the administration of the estate for a generation',[167] thus considering the needs and rights of all of the people involved in a case and not just the claimant and defendant. This general approach is similar to Sir Arthur Hobhouse's *dicta* to the effect that the court should 'look at the circumstances in each case to decide in what way the equity can be satisfied'.[168] It is suggested that the more that the cases come to focus on the detriment suffered by the claimant, the more likely it is that the courts will seek to compensate that detriment by payment of money. This approach has the advantage of meeting the needs of the claimant (as in *Baker v Baker*) while ensuring that other people who might be entitled to inherit property from the representor do not lose those rights (as in *Campbell v Griffin*). So, at one end of the spectrum the claimant may acquire the entire absolute interest in the property, while at the other end she may only receive equitable compensation in the form of a personal right to money.

Normal service in the application of proprietary estoppel to domestic situations in the wake of *Thorner v Major* has been resumed (after the decision of the House of Lords in *Cobbe v Yeoman's Row*[169]). For example, in *Porntip Stallion v Albert Stallion Holdings*[170] Porntip Stallion claimed that she had been promised that she could live in premises owned by her former husband, Albert. After Albert died, his subsequent wife, Lilibeth, became his executrix in relation to a will which left no such rights to Porntip. After their divorce, Porntip had continued to live in that property with Albert and Lilibeth. Following *Thorner v Major*,[171] Judge Asplin QC found[172] that 'on the balance of probabilities' such representations

---

162 [2008] 1 WLR 1752.
163 [2009] 1 WLR 776.
164 *Crabb v Arun DC* [1976] Ch 179, 189F.
165 [2003] 1 P & CR 100, para 56.
166 [2001] EWCA Civ 990, [2001] WTLR 981.
167 *Ibid*, at 991, *per* Robert Walker LJ.
168 *Plimmer v Wellington Corporation* (1884) 9 App Cas 699, 714; approved by Robert Walker LJ in *Gillett v Holt* [2001] Ch 210, 235.
169 [2008] 1 WLR 1752.
170 [2009] EWHC 1950 (Ch), [2010] 1 FCR 145.
171 [2009] UKHL 18.
172 [2010] 1 FCR 145, [110] *et seq*.

had been made to Porntip[173] and that Porntip had relied upon those representations to her detriment in agreeing not to contest the divorce nor to acquire the protection of a financial settlement in court. It was ordered that Porntip would be entitled to occupy the property rent-free for the remainder of her life. There was, however, an important caveat to the effect that Porntip would not be granted exclusive possession of the property, but rather she would be required to occupy the property in common with Lilibeth (and Lilibeth's new husband and daughter).[174] On the facts it was found that the parties would be able to live together in tolerable harmony given their history of cohabitation.[175] This demonstrates the remarkable flexibility which is available in cases of proprietary estoppel.[176]

An illustration of the continued affection for older authorities like *Crabb v Arun DC*[177] arises in the decision in *Ashby v Kilduff*.[178] The court considered whether or not the claimant was entitled to rights on constructive trust or estoppel principles in a flat he had previously shared with the defendant. While citing both *Stack v Dowden* and *Thorner v Major*, Judge Livesey QC nevertheless turned ultimately to the much-quoted principle in the estoppel case of *Crabb v Arun DC*[179] that 'the claim is to be satisfied by the minimum award necessary to do justice'.[180] On that basis it was held that 'it seems to me that the court has a discretion to determine how the equity can best be satisfied in order to avoid the unconscionable result which would otherwise prevail'.[181]

173 The judge spends some time on the respective levels of credibility of the various witnesses, who contradict themselves and one another greatly in giving their evidence. As is common in trusts of homes cases, the witnesses are generally impassioned and partial, and occasionally incredible.
174 [2010] 1 FCR 145, [137] and [138]. Porntip had given evidence that they had lived under the same roof 'but separately' before.
175 As the judge held at para [138]: 'In this regard, I appreciate that it is an unusual step to create a situation in which the equity requires a claimant to continue to live in premises with the defendant. However, in this case, Porntip and Lilibeth appear to have done so for a considerable time both before and after Albert's death.' With respect, one cannot help but think that the surprising element is not that claimant and defendant will continue to live together but rather that the former wife and the widow would be expected by the High Court to live together. In that sense it is a very 'modern', even 'progressive' judgment; and a testament to the inherent flexibility of the doctrine of proprietary estoppel.
176 A female friend whom I was boring with an account of this, and other cases, wondered whether the fact that the judge was a woman might have led to this interesting judgment on the facts of this case, and its acceptance of an alternative mode of organising the parties' living arrangements.
177 [1976] Ch 179.
178 [2010] EWHC 2034 (Ch). A married Conservative MP, Ashby, had entered into a homosexual relationship with Kilduff which became the subject of a story in *The Sunday Times*, which in turn was the subject of an unsuccessful libel action on the part of Ashby in 1995. Mrs Ashby had given evidence against her husband at that trial. The two men had lived in flats one on top of the other so as to appear to be merely neighbours while carrying on a relationship. Mr Ashby decided to 'put his flat into the name of' Kilduff by means of a purported sale of that flat. Kilduff purported to sever any joint tenancy over these properties, which prompted Ashby to secure ownership of what had been his former flat. Up until that point, the two men had been living together in one of the two flats. The issues arose whether or not this was a genuine sale or if that flat should be deemed to be held on resulting or constructive trust for Ashby.
179 [1976] Ch 179.
180 *Ibid* at 198.
181 [2010] EWHC 2034 (Ch), at para [73]. It was a complex business to understand the context in which the two men had organised their property rights in the context of concealing their relationship during a libel trial and in the shadow of the possibility that Mrs Ashby would seek to divorce her husband. Disappointingly, Judge Livesey QC decided to leave it until after judgment was delivered to hear written evidence on the appropriate allocation of property rights between the parties.

A vitiating doctrine ensuring the conscionable application of statute

Proprietary estoppel underlines one of the key tenets of equity: that it can do justice between the parties where the ordinary rules of the common law or of statute would have been unfair or unconscionable. While some commentators seek to restrict proprietary estoppel to cases involving land,[182] its remit is much broader. Proprietary estoppel will operate in relation to any form of property in relation to which the defendant has made assurances to the claimant that the claimant will acquire interests in that property and in reliance on which the claimant acts to her detriment.

Moreover, proprietary estoppel will operate to subvert ostensibly mandatory rules of law[183] in some situations. An example of this broader sweep of proprietary estoppel is provided by *Yaxley v Gotts*,[184] in which a joint venture was formed for the acquisition of land. The joint venture did not comply with the requirement in s 2 of the Law of Property (Miscellaneous Provisions) Act 1989 that the terms of any purported contract for the transfer of any interest in land being in writing. The defendant therefore contended that the claimant could have acquired no right in contract to the land because there was no writing in accordance with the formal requirements of the statute. However, the court was prepared to uphold that between the parties there had been a representation that there would be a joint venture between the parties in reliance on which the claimant had acted to its detriment. It was held by the Court of Appeal that a constructive trust had arisen between the parties on the basis of their common intention – and that this constructive trust was indistinguishable in this form from a proprietary estoppel.[185] The doctrine of constructive trust is therefore outwith the ambit of s 2 of the 1989 Act.[186]

The general issue arose as to whether or not the general public policy underpinning the statutory formalities ought to be rigidly adhered to so as to preclude the activation of any estoppel on the basis that it was a principle of fundamentally important social policy.[187] It was held that in deciding whether or not a parliamentary purpose was being frustrated, one should 'look at the circumstances in each case and decide in what way the equity can be satisfied'.[188]

The court is able to apply the doctrine of proprietary estoppel where it was necessary to do the minimum equity necessary between the parties.[189] In effect, this opens the way for the return of the part performance doctrine[190] in the guise of proprietary estoppel and

---

182 See Mee, 1999, 99.

183 That is, civil law rules which preclude the validity of certain acts or which require a certain action in certain circumstances. Although those rights can be overreached: *Birmingham Midshires Mortgage Services Ltd v Sabherwal* (2000) 80 P & CR 256.

184 [2000] 1 All ER 711; L Smith, 2000; Tee, 2000. The principles in this case were applied in *Kinane v Mackie-Conteh* [2005] EWCA Civ 45, [2005] 2 P & CR D9, [25], *per* Arden LJ. See also *S v S* [2006] EWHC 2892 (Fam), Sumner J.

185 *Ibid*, 721 *et seq, per* Robert Walker LJ.

186 *Kilcarne Holdings Ltd v Targetfollow (Birmingham) Ltd* [2004] EWHC 2547 (Ch), para [219], *per* Lewison J.

187 *Kok Hoong v Leong Cheong Kweng Mines Ltd* [1964] AC 993; *Godden v Merthyr Tydfil Housing Association* [1997] NPC 1.

188 *Plimmer v Mayor of Wellington* (1884) 9 App Cas 699, 714, *per* Sir Arthur Hobhouse.

189 *Crabb v Arun DC* [1976] Ch 179, 198, *per* Scarman LJ. It is interesting to note that their Lordships are prepared to find a means of eluding straightforwardly mandatory norms of statute to give effect to some higher purpose contained in the case law.

190 Whereby any contract which had been partly performed would be perfected by equity.

constructive trust. While the doctrine of the creation of equitable mortgages by deposit of title deeds was deemed to have been removed by the 1989 Act,[191] the equitable doctrine of proprietary estoppel remained intact,[192] even where it would appear to offend the principle that an ineffective contract ought not to be effected by means of equitable doctrine.[193]

Given that proprietary estoppel is an equitable doctrine, it is a requirement that the claimant be entitled to an equitable remedy. So, where a claimant has fabricated evidence to make it appear that she had suffered detrimental reliance on a purported representation, the court will hold that that claimant has not come to equity with clean hands and therefore will not be entitled to proprietary estoppel.[194] Where a first mortgagee acquiesces in the detriment of a second mortgagee in relation to property, the doctrine of proprietary estoppel may operate so as to relegate the priority of that first mortgage behind the rights of the second mortgagee.[195]

A difficulty arose with this doctrine as a result of the judgment of Lord Scott in *Cobbe v Yeoman's Row*.[196] Lord Scott suggested that it was not the role of proprietary estoppel to avoid legislation, as had happened in *Yaxley v Gotts*. The decisions in *Herbert v Doyle*[197] and in *Whittaker v Kinnear*[198] have indicated that the *dicta* of Lord Scott in *Yeoman's Row v Cobbe* relating to the extent of s 2 of the Law of Property (Miscellaneous Provisions) Act 1989 were *obiter dicta* and that proprietary estoppel should continue to operate so as to prevent detrimental reliance being unconscionably overlooked just as it did in *Yaxley v Gotts*. Given the more relaxed approach taken to proprietary estoppel by the House of Lords in *Thorner v Major*,[199] this optimism may be well placed. These issues are considered in the next section.

Similarly, Warren J has held in *Clarke v Meadus*[200] that proprietary estoppel can operate so as to deal with detrimental reliance on a representation beyond the rights which are set out in an express trust. As Warren J put it: 'it is clear that the express trusts declared in the [deed of appointment] are capable of being overridden by a proprietary estoppel in favour of [the claimant] as a result of promises and representations made after' the deed was executed.[201] In essence, the claimant had given up her home in Kent and moved to a property in Turners Hill, West Sussex in reliance on a representation that it would be left to her. *Goodman v Gallant* took the approach that the express trust would be definitive of the parties' interests, but the distinction in *Clarke v Meadus* is that representations were made after the deed was executed and so could be said to constitute an entirely new claim separate from the deed which created that express trust.

191 *United Bank of Kuwait plc v Sahib* [1997] Ch 107.
192 *King v Jackson* [1998] 1 EGLR 30; and *McCausland v Duncan Lawrie Ltd* [1997] 1 WLR 38.
193 *Westdeutsche Landesbank v Islington LBC* [1996] AC 669; *Kleinwort Benson v Sandwell BC* [1994] 4 All ER 890.
194 *Gonthier v Orange Contract Scaffolding Ltd* [2003] EWCA Civ 873.
195 *Scottish & Newcastle plc v Lancashire Mortgage Corporation Ltd* [2007] EWCA Civ 684.
196 [2008] 1 WLR 1752.
197 [2010] EWCA Civ 1095.
198 [2011] EWHC (QB) 1479, *per* Bean J.
199 [2009] 1 WLR 776.
200 [2010] EWHC 3117 (Ch).
201 *Ibid*, at [56].

13.3.5 Proprietary estoppel in commercial joint ventures: *Cobbe v Yeoman's Row*

The decision in Cobbe v Yeoman's Row

The decision of the House of Lords in *Cobbe v Yeoman's Row*[202] has, however, disturbed the emerging understanding of proprietary estoppel as being based on the prevention of unconscionability – an idea which had been accepted by the High Court and by the Court of Appeal in that case (as considered above).[203] However, since the subsequent decision of the House of Lords in *Thorner v Major*, it is suggested that *Cobbe v Yeoman's Row*, which is an unfortunate decision for many reasons which are considered here, should be understood as being limited to cases involving commercial development transactions. I would ask you to imagine that a woman called Mrs Lisle-Mainwaring and a man called Mr Cobbe had discussions about developing a property such that Cobbe spent a huge amount of money in reliance on their 'agreement in principle', with Mrs Lisle-Mainwaring's knowledge, on getting planning permission, engaging architects and so on; imagine then that Mrs Lisle-Mainwaring refused to go ahead with their putative arrangement once planning permission for the development was granted. It was found by the judge at first instance as a fact that Mrs Zipporah Lisle-Mainwaring had encouraged Cobbe to believe that the transaction would go ahead and it was consequently found as a fact that she had taken unconscionable advantage of him. Would you think that Cobbe would have some sort of remedy against Mrs Lisle-Mainwaring, particularly a remedy based on proprietary estoppel, in these circumstances? If your answer is 'yes', then you might be surprised to find that the House of Lords did not agree with you.

It was held that the parties had not formed a binding contract and therefore that Cobbe could not make out a claim for proprietary estoppel precisely because the Lisle-Mainwaring was not asserting something that was not the truth in arguing that she was not bound any pre-contractual negotiations with Cobbe. The House of Lords held that it is not enough to make out a claim for proprietary estoppel simply to allege that the defendant's action was unconscionable. Rather there needs to be some fact as to the rights of the parties which the defendant could be estopped from denying. (This proposition is considered below in more detail.) Lord Scott held that it is inappropriate for estoppel to be used to subvert formal requirements of statute simply on the basis of unconscionability (such as s 2 of the Law of Property (Miscellaneous Provisions) Act 1989 requiring that all contracts transferring an interest in property must be in writing). The case of *Cobbe v Yeomans Row* concerned a situation in which the parties had not created a binding contract between them, but rather had merely entered into detailed negotiations sufficient for Cobbe to commence work and employ expensive professional services.[204] Lord Walker considered that it would introduce too much uncertainty to commercial contracts if parties who had refrained from finalising a formally valid contract were found to have given effect to their negotiations by means of proprietary estoppel. One can see his Lordship's point: if we have rules as to when contracts are binding, then those rules ought to be enforced. However, we do also have another set of rules which say that a defendant may not unconscionably rely on the formal rules of common law (such as contract law) so as to take advantage of, for example, the £2 million worth of

---

202 [2008] 1 WLR 1752.
203 Applied in *Brightlingsea Haven Ltd v Morris* [2008] EWHC 1928 (QB).
204 *Cobbe* was followed in *Qayyum v Hameed* [2009] EWCA Civ 352, [2009] 3 FCR 545.

work which a person has invested in a project with the defendant's knowledge in reliance on the understanding that they will both deal in that property together in the future, even if that understanding is not contractually binding. That Lord Walker and Lord Scott, two chancery specialists, should come to the conclusion that they did is frankly staggering.

Difficulties with the decision in Cobbe v Yeoman's Row

Let us recap. The purpose of equity, from Aristotle onwards, has been to ensure that strict legal rules, whether formal rules as to the creation of land contracts or contract law generally, will not act as smokescreen behind which one person will be able to take unconscionable advantage of another. Etherton J was clear at first instance that that was what Mrs Lisle-Mainwaring had done in relation to Cobbe; and the Court of Appeal agreed with Etherton J. We might have thought that the judge in *Gillett v Holt* and *Jennings v Rice*, Lord Walker, would have upheld the notion that a claimant would be entitled to proprietary estoppel in a situation in which large payments increasing the value of the property by up to £2 million on the mooted project were purportedly ignored by a defendant who sought to renege on the parties' formative understanding that they would enter into a contract in the future. Cobbe was instead forced to learn a lesson on behalf of commercial people everywhere: do not start to do preparatory work unless you have a formally valid contract.

Lord Scott's speech is littered with surprising comments on the nature of proprietary estoppel. First, it is said that proprietary estoppel is a claim to a remedy constituting a proprietary right in property.[205] This is not so. There have been many cases in which the remedy received by the successful claimant was merely a right in money (that is, equitable compensation as in *Campbell v Griffin*) to compensate the claimant for her detriment. Therefore, Cobbe could have been awarded compensation on the basis of proprietary estoppel. This would also have overcome the objection that Cobbe would otherwise have been achieving the enforcement of the never-finalised contract by the back door. Second, as set out at the start of this chapter, the term 'estoppel' is based etymologically on the notion of 'stopping' a person from denying that something is the case: however, this is not a notion of estoppel which has been used in the English case law for decades and therefore for Lord Scott to unearth it seems a little out-of-step.

Thirdly, proprietary estoppel is said to be a 'sub-set' of promissory estoppel.[206] No authority is given for this surprising proposition. Unless we accept, as Lord Scott does not, that all forms of estoppel are based on a single form of equitable estoppel, then these two estoppels are not linked in this way. Fourthly, estoppel is said by Lord Scott to be based on 'some fact or facts, or, sometimes, something that is a mixture of fact and law, that stands in the way of some right claimed by the person entitled to the benefit of the estoppel'.[207] This fits in with the definition of 'estop' given at the beginning of this chapter. It was the absence of such a fact that was being denied by the defendant which lost the claimant any right: that is, because there was no binding contract between the parties there was no fact of there being a contract which the defendant was denying and from which she should have been estopped. Older cases on estoppel (such as *Crabb v Arun DC* and *Taylor Fashions*) were distinguished

---

205   *Ibid*, para [4].
206   *Ibid*, para [14].
207   *Ibid*.

on the basis that they concerned a defined interest whereas Cobbe had no such defined interest because no contract had been completed nor any such defined right agreed between the parties. Instead reliance was placed on the old (and generally discarded) form of estoppel in *Ramsden v Dyson* which was based on a wrongful denial of an interest (considered earlier in this chapter). In cases like *Gillett v Holt* and *Jennings v Rice* there was no defined right claimed by the claimant but the Court of Appeal nevertheless awarded proprietary estoppel and used the estoppel's remedial reach to design an appropriate remedy. Lord Scott's approach is in truth at odds with most of the estoppel case law for twenty years: something which, it is suggested, required closer attention in his Lordship's speech.

Fifthly, a claim based on unconscionable conduct in the negotiation of a contract is said not to give rise to a constructive trust and so is said to be 'misconceived': but, interestingly, no explanation as to why it was misconceived was given (except for the repetitious discussion of the non-enforceability of uncertain contracts set out before). Sixthly, in relation to unjust enrichment it is said by Lord Scott that no value in the property is created by the acquisition but rather that its value was unlocked. This is syllogistic misdirection. While there is no planning permission there is no development value in the land: just as until the existing buildings are demolished and new buildings constructed, there will be no development profit. Whether the acquisition of planning permission created or unlocked the land's development value, there can be no doubt that Cobbe spent money on acquiring that permission and therefore that it was Cobbe's expenditure and work which in fact increased the value of the land: it was money which someone had to spend to realise that value, whether that person was Cobbe or not. After all, there is no point in saying that Geoff Hurst deserves no credit for scoring in the 1966 World Cup Final because someone else could have scored: because it was after all Geoff Hurst who scored. Similarly, it was Cobbe who did this work with the knowledge of Lisle-Mainwaring. Therefore Cobbe deserves credit for having done that work on these facts.

A better approach to the decision of this case might have been as follows. Cobbe received assurance from Lisle-Mainwaring (in word, and in deed in the form of her allowing him to do all of this work and spend all that money) in reliance on which he relied to his detriment in spending large amounts of money on the property. The combination of representation, reliance and detriment on the basis of the decision in *Re Basham* and the other modern cases on proprietary estoppel should have given rise to an estoppel in favour of Cobbe. It is to be hoped in time that this decision is seen as being limited to the specific question of whether or not contracts in negotiation may give rise to proprietary estoppel and that it is not extended to other contexts, for example the acquisition of rights in the family home. Otherwise the purpose of proprietary estoppel as it has been developed since *Crabb v Arun DC* will be ruined.

The purpose of equitable estoppel

Lord Walker had the following to say about the nature and purpose of the doctrine of equitable (not proprietary) estoppel:[208]

> My Lords, equitable estoppel is a flexible doctrine which the court can use, in appropriate circumstances, to prevent injustice caused by the vagaries and inconstancy of

---

208 *Ibid*, para [46].

human nature. But it is not a sort of joker or wild card to be used whenever the court disapproves of the conduct of a litigant who seems to have the law on his side. Flexible though it is, the doctrine must be formulated and applied in a disciplined and principled way. Certainty is important in property transactions.

One is tempted to wonder why. If it is indeed a general *equitable* estoppel, as opposed to narrow proprietary estoppel, then why should not the courts impose a remedial set of responses to circumstances in which there has been representation, reliance and detriment which is deemed to be unconscionable? The reference to *equitable* estoppel, it is suggested, has itself been advanced by academics such as Prof Cooke who have sought to transform this doctrine into a single principle and away from being the splintered plethora of doctrines which have existed historically in equity and at common law. On the facts of *Cobbe*, the fact that both of the parties were experienced in property development is a factor which caused the House of Lords to think that ultimately there was no harm here because both parties should have realised that neither of them had any specific contractual rights while the documentation was in negotiation between them.

The subsequent decision of the House of Lords in *Thorner v Major*[209] has been significant in understanding how the *Cobbe* decision should be understood. Lord Walker's speech effectively dampened speculation in the academic commentary on *Cobbe* that the doctrine of proprietary estoppel had been effectively gutted.[210] Instead, Lord Walker suggested that *Cobbe* should be understood as merely reminding us all of the need for 'certainty of interest': that is, proprietary estoppel remains unchanged, except that we are reminded of the need for the representation and the right which is to be acquired being identified with sufficient certainty by the parties. It is difficult to see how the requirements of certainty are promoted in that judgment by finding a representation where none was ever made expressly. Instead, it is suggested, this decision is closer to a doctrine of unconscionability, of the sort identified by Walker LJ (as he then was) in *Jennings v Rice*, whereby the claimant's extensive detriment would have caused an unconscionable benefit to have been bestowed on the farm and on the deceased man, as well as an unconscionable and unrewarded burden being imposed on the claimant. This appears, in truth, to be a doctrine concerned with the avoidance of unconscionability and uncompensated detriment, as opposed to a doctrine predicated on certainty. In truth, *Thorner v Major* has seen proprietary estoppel function on far more traditional principles than *Cobbe* might have suggested.

13.4 ESTOPPEL LICENCES: FROM CONTRACT TO PROPERTY RIGHTS

The doctrine of proprietary estoppel has been used in many situations to attempt to elevate purely personal claims into proprietary claims. One clear example of this tendency relates to estoppel licences – another project of Lord Denning in the field of estoppel. Within the general development of the new model constructive trust, Lord Denning sought to award proprietary remedies to those claimants who had been given only licences (purely personal rights against the licensor) and therefore had no protection against eviction. Lord Denning's particular concern was in situations in which the licensed premises were the licensee's home.

---

209   [2009] 1 WLR 776.
210   See Macfarlane and Robertson, 'The Death of Proprietary Estoppel' [2008] LMCLQ 449.

His Lordship contended that a contract which granted a licence to the licensee constituted a representation that the licensee would acquire rights effectively equivalent to a leasehold interest for the duration of the licence.[211] The general application of this rule – seeking to enlarge licences to the status of leases – was roundly rejected by the Court of Appeal[212] in favour of a more traditional test which asserted that the licensee might be able to acquire rights by virtue of proprietary estoppel or constructive trust.

So, for example, where a person entered into a verbal agreement with a landlord in which the landlord assured that person that she would be granted an interest in the land, such that she expended money in reliance on that assurance, that person would acquire rights in the land under estoppel.[213] It is important that any detriment suffered, or money expended, must have been in the expectation of receiving some right in the property of which the landlord was aware.[214] It is also important that the landlord acquiesced in the claimant's actions, and not merely that the claimant acted without the landlord's knowledge.[215] There is a drift in the cases which focuses on the unconscionable act of the defendant in more general terms concerning the promise of some interest in the property,[216] and even being based on a principle of unjust enrichment.[217] In short, a licensee may acquire estoppel rights against property where a rightholder in that property has made some assurance to that licensee that she would acquire some rights in the property, whether by way of a lease or otherwise.

The remedy available to a claimant is effectively drawn on the same canvas as for proprietary estoppel – as considered above. This may lead to the acquisition of limited rights of secure occupation. Where a licensee had spent £700 on improvements to a bungalow in reliance on representations made to them that they would be able to remain in occupation, the court held that they could remain in secure occupation until their expenditure had been reimbursed[218] or generally 'for as long as they wish to occupy the property'.[219] Alternatively, the claimant may simply be entitled to an amount of money to compensate her for her detriment.[220] In exceptional cases, a transfer of the entire fee simple has been ordered to protect the claimant from suffering detriment:[221] this may be because the contribution was so large that a transfer of the fee simple was the only suitable remedy,[222] or because that would be the only means of securing the claimant's occupation in the light of a representation that she could occupy in perpetuity.[223] What is most significant is that the court will have complete freedom to frame its remedy once it has found that an estoppel is both available

211 *Errington v Errington* [1952] 1 QB 290.
212 *Ashburn Anstalt v Arnold* [1988] 2 WLR 706.
213 *Ramsden v Dyson* (1866) LR 1 HL 129, 170, *per* Lord Kingsdown.
214 *Western Fish Products Ltd v Penwith DC* [1981] 2 All ER 204; *Brinnand v Ewens* [1987] 2 EGLR 67.
215 *Jones v Stones* [1999] 1 WLR 1739.
216 *Taylor Fashions Ltd v Liverpool Victoria Trustees Co Ltd* [1982] QB 133; *Elitestone Ltd v Morris* (1995) 73 P & CR 259; *Lloyds Bank v Carrick* [1996] 4 All ER 630.
217 *Sledmore v Dalby* (1996) 72 P & CR 196, 208, *per* Hobhouse LJ.
218 *Dodsworth v Dodsworth* (1973) 228 EG 1115; *Burrows and Burrows v Sharpe* (1991) 23 HLR 82.
219 *Inwards v Baker* [1965] 2 QB 29.
220 *Baker v Baker* (1993) 25 HLR 408.
221 *Pascoe v Turner* [1979] 1 WLR 431; *Voyce v Voyce* (1991) 62 P & CR 290.
222 *Dillwyn v Llewelyn* (1862) 4 De GF & J 517.
223 *Pascoe v Turner* [1979] 1 WLR 431.

and appropriate.[224] Thus, whereas Lord Denning sought originally to raise personal rights in contract to the status of rights in property, the possibilities for contractual licences to constitute rights in property now rest on ordinary principles of proprietary estoppel.

13.5 PROMISSORY ESTOPPEL

The foundation of the contractual doctrine of promissory estoppel can be found in *Hughes v Metropolitan Railway*,[225] in which case a landlord had been negotiating with his tenant for the renewal of a lease. The lease provided for a specified time within which the tenant would be entitled to serve notice of an intention to renew. The negotiations were continuing during that period until the landlord unilaterally stopped negotiations and sought to terminate the lease. The court held that the landlord would be estopped from terminating the lease on the basis that he had led the tenant to believe that their negotiations would lead to the novation of the lease in any event. The more modern root of this doctrine was in a decision of Lord Denning in *Central London Property Trust Ltd v High Trees House Ltd*,[226] in which his Lordship held that an agreement not to renegotiate the level of rental payments under a lease for the duration of the 1939–45 war estopped the landlord from seeking to rely on a term in the lease that he could rely on at a higher level of rent during that period after a rent review.

The principle which emerges from this vague doctrine is that a party to a contract will be estopped from reneging on a clear promise where it would be inequitable to do so and where the other party has altered its position in reliance on the promise. The promise is required to be clear,[227] but it can be implied from the conduct or words used by the parties.[228] In terms of the inequitability of the action, it is within the court's discretion to decide whether it would be conscionable for the defendant to insist on her strict contractual rights.[229] The alteration of position is broadly equivalent to the detriment required in proprietary estoppel, and would include a party waiving her strict legal rights in reliance on a promise by another person that she would similarly waive her own rights.[230]

What promissory estoppel will not do is replace the doctrine of consideration and lead to the creation of contracts without such consideration.[231] The concern would be that, even though there were no valid consideration, X could claim that Y had made a promise to X in reliance on which X had altered her position, thus entitling her to rely on promissory estoppel. Promissory estoppel will not be used as a sword: that is, it will not create new rights but will only protect the claimant's existing rights. This is different from proprietary estoppel which appears to grant entirely new rights to the claimant – for example, rights in property which the claimant had not previously held – and adds to the assertion made at the beginning of this

---

224 An approach approved as long ago as *Lord Cawdor v Lewis* (1835) 1 Y & C Ex 427, 433; *Plimmer v Wellington Corporation* (1884) 9 App Cas 699, 713.

225 (1877) 2 App Cas 439; *Birmingham and District Land Co v L & NW Railway* (1888) 40 Ch D 268.

226 [1947] KB 130.

227 *Scandinavian Trading Tanker Co AB v Flota Petrolera Ecuatoriana* [1983] QB 549; *Youell v Bland Welch & Co Ltd* [1990] 2 Lloyd's Rep 423.

228 *Attorney-General for Hong Kong v Humphrey's Estate* [1987] 1 AC 114.

229 *D & C Builders v Rees* [1966] 2 QB 617.

230 *Société Italo-Belge v Palm and Vegetable Oils* [1982] 1 All ER 19.

231 *Combe v Combe* [1951] 2 KB 215; *Brikom Investments Ltd v Carr* [1979] QB 467.

chapter that there cannot be a single doctrine of estoppel, without some alteration to existing doctrine, in spite of the initial similarities between the many forms of estoppel recognised both in equity and at common law.[232]

13.6 OTHER FORMS OF ESTOPPEL IN COMMERCIAL CONTEXTS

13.6.1 Common law estoppel and the *nemo dat* principle

Estoppel operates both in common law and in equity. Those forms of estoppel considered thus far have been primarily equitable.[233] The common law has long had a notion of estoppel *in pais*,[234] whereby a person who 'wilfully causes another to believe a certain state of things, and induces him to act on that belief, so as to alter his own previous position, . . . is [prevented from suggesting that] a different state of things existed at the same time'.[235] One example of a common law estoppel is considered in Chapter 21, and arises in relation to sale of goods contracts. The common law estoppel is based on *dicta* of Ashurst J in *Lickbarrow v Mason*,[236] that 'wherever one of two innocent persons must suffer by the acts of a third, he who has enabled such third person to occasion the loss must sustain it'.[237] In truth, this estoppel should be considered as an exception to the *nemo dat* principle which arises in circumstances in which there is an express or an implied representation made by an agent that she has authority from the owner to sell goods as the agent of that owner.[238] In cases involving hire purchase agreements, the estoppel has been invoked in circumstances in which a person has purported to sell a vehicle to a car dealer (the seller) and then sought to purchase it back under a hire purchase agreement, while both purchaser and seller have represented to the finance company that the seller had a good title to the vehicle.[239] Where a shyster purported to buy a car on hire purchase from C, thus entitling him to take the car away, and then sold that same car to another dealer, M, and where M then sold the car to U, it was held that C was not precluded from denying the shyster's authority to sell by virtue of its own *prima facie* negligence in giving the car's document of registration to the shyster.[240]

13.6.2 Estoppel by representation

Estoppel by representation has been enforced both at common law and in equity.[241] However, recent applications of the principle have demonstrated that its basis is one of good conscience

---

232 *Crabb v Arun DC* [1976] Ch 179; *Amalgamated Investment & Property Co Ltd v Texas Commerce International Bank Ltd* [1982] 1 QB 84; *Williams v Roffey Bros & Nicholls (Contractors) Ltd* [1991] 1 QB 1.
233 Although it is not always possible to draw such clear distinctions in the modern law of estoppel: Cooke, 2000, 57 *et seq*.
234 *Ibid*, 16.
235 *Pickard v Sears* (1837) 6 A & E 469, 474. See also *Freeman v Cooke* (1848) 2 Exch 654 and *Heane v Rogers* (1829) 9 B & C 576. I am grateful to Elizabeth Cooke for these references.
236 (1787) 2 TR 63.
237 Commercial lawyers treat this statement with some contempt; Professor Bridge describes it as a 'worn *dictum*': Bridge, 1996, 101.
238 *Henderson v Williams* [1895] 1 QB 521; *Farquharson Bros & Co v King & Co* [1902] AC 325.
239 *Eastern Distributors Ltd v Goldring* [1957] 2 QB 600.
240 *Central Newbury Car Auctions Ltd v Unity Finance Ltd* [1957] 1 QB 371.
241 *Jorden v Money* (1854) 5 HLC 185, (1854) 10 ER 868.

and fairness. In *National Westminster Bank plc v Somer International*,[242] the bank mistakenly credited a payment of US$76,708 to Somer when that amount had been intended for another of its account holders with a similar name. In reliance on the receipt of the money, Somer shipped £13,180 worth of goods to a client from which it had been expecting a payment in a similar amount. The bank sought to recover the mistaken payment. Somer argued that it was entitled to an estoppel by representation because the bank had represented to it that the money belonged to Somer, that Somer had acted to its detriment in reliance on that representation, and that it was therefore entitled to retain the whole of the moneys paid to it by the bank. In a reversal of previous authority suggesting that Somer could have retained the entire payment,[243] the Court of Appeal held that the doctrine of estoppel by representation would prevent retention of the entire sum where that would have been unconscionable. Therefore, on these facts, Somer could retain only an amount equal to the value of the goods which it had shipped in reliance on the representation.[244]

The similarities between proprietary estoppel and estoppel by representation are clear: both operate to prevent unconscionable retention of a benefit and both operate (arguably) to prevent the suffering of uncompensated detriment.[245] It would therefore be easy to see how a unified equitable estoppel could be achieved. The familiar triptych of representation, reliance and detriment is common to both doctrines, and therefore it would be possible, without doing too much violence to either doctrine, to subsume them within a general equitable estoppel. Nevertheless, there are differences between these doctrines. Estoppel by representation has been both a common law and an equitable doctrine, and therefore cannot be said to operate currently solely on the basis of equitable principles of good conscience. Furthermore, estoppel by representation appears to operate primarily as a defence, whereas proprietary estoppel grants property rights as a claim. Estoppel by representation is generally taken to function as a rule of evidence, whereas proprietary estoppel is acquiring a personality of its own as a substantive doctrine.

13.7 IN CONCLUSION

Estoppel achieves justice by preventing a person from going back on her word. The difference between an ordinary promise and a promise giving rise to an estoppel is that it is a requirement of the latter that the claimant must have suffered some detriment in reliance on that promise. Where that estoppel is unfortunate is where it is deployed so as to enable the courts to overturn the mandatory rules set out by Parliament in legislation – from the Statute of Frauds to the Law of Property (Miscellaneous Provisions) Act 1989. At some level there must be a concern that this permits the courts to overrule Parliament.

This discretionary power is in common with the fundamental tenets of equity that it should do justice between the parties in individual cases. In that sense, equitable estoppel is in line with the doctrine in *Rochefoucauld v Boustead*[246] and doctrines like secret trusts. It accords

---

242 [2002] QB 1286, CA.
243 *Avon County Council v Howlett* [1983] 1 WLR 605.
244 *Scottish Equitable v Derby* [2001] 3 All ER 818 applied.
245 Cf *First National Bank plc v Thompson* [1996] Ch 231, 236, where Millett LJ contrasts species of estoppel by representation with the common law principle that a grantor is precluded from disputing the validity of her own grant.
246 See para 5.2.2 above.

with Aristotle's attitude to 'equity' in that it achieves a better result than abstract rules of common law in cases where it is applied between the parties. As with many equitable doctrines, its shortcoming is that it sees the actionable detriment as being focused primarily on expenditure of money and less often on 'detrimental' acts which have no pecuniary effect.

Importantly, estoppel need not be restitutionary. It is not necessary that the defendant has been enriched at the expense of the claimant. All that is required is that the claimant has suffered some detriment. So in cases like *Grant v Edwards*[247] the detriment suffered by the claimant is directed simply at the personal inconvenience of leaving settled accommodation to live with the defendant and the personal inconvenience of undertaking to have a family with the defendant. It is not possible to say that there has been an 'enrichment' there in the financial sense usually required by restitution. In the Canadian sense of enrichment we might consider that the defendant has taken some general 'benefit' from the parties' life history together, but that is not the usual English restitutionary approach. Restitution lawyers have been slow to turn their attention to the family homes cases precisely because there are messier questions at issue than the certainties of restitution of unjust enrichment, the precisions of tracing and the neatness of subrogation will permit.

247 [1986] Ch 638.

Chapter 14

Essay – Thinking about the law on fiduciaries

14.1 THE ROLE OF THE FIDUCIARY

This short essay aims to pull together some of the threads relating to fiduciary responsibility so as to put the subject into a little more focus. What is perhaps most worthy of mention at the outset is the fact that more and more classes of claimant are seeking to argue that they are the beneficiaries of fiduciary relationships. The reason for this mooted expansion of the category is that the remedies available to the beneficiaries of fiduciary relationships are more wide-ranging than the remedies generally available for tort law or contract law claims, in the ways considered in this essay.

A further benefit to be derived from imposing fiduciary liability on another person is that the person thus classified as a fiduciary acquires a different status from that which they held previously. They acquire a recognition from the legal system that they ought to be considered as holding a particular set of rights as a mark of their own social significance. So, for example, if employers were accepted as being fiduciaries in relation to the employment contracts created with employees, that would reverse the power relation which would otherwise exist between employer and employee: the employer would cease to be simply the 'master' in a master-and-servant relationship (the precursor of what we now call 'employment law' or 'labour law') and instead would become a person owing duties to the employee which would also carry wide-ranging legal consequences.

14.2 A QUESTION OF DEFINITION

The word 'fiduciary' is itself a rarely used word in ordinary speech, let alone its very particular definition in legal usage. I can do no better than to quote Professor Ian Kennedy, when he describes the problem of definition in the following terms: 'Of ancient pedigree, and somewhat shrouded in mystery, it cannot be an overstatement that the fiduciary relationship is a legal concept of indistinct features and defining characteristics.'[1] So, we begin by acknowledging that the term fiduciary is difficult to define despite being familiar to lawyers for some centuries. A little like an elephant, we think we would know one when we saw one but find it difficult to describe in the abstract.

A dictionary definition of the word fiduciary, beyond a coy reference to the legal sense, is 'relating to or based on a trust' – but the etymology of the word is more enlightening: 'Late 16th century, via Latin *fiduciarius* "(holding) in a trust" from, ultimately, *fides* "trust".'[2] In this sense the word 'trust' has a link in the Latin with 'faith: *fides*' which is also the root of the English word 'confide', literally to have faith in someone or to have confidence in someone. There is therefore a clear connection between the ordinary use of the word 'fiduciary' with notions of 'faith', 'belief', 'confidence' and 'trust'.

To return to one of the key points in Chapter 2 above, the use of the word 'trust' in English law reverses the way in which that word is ordinarily understood.[3] To trust someone is usually to have faith in them, or to have a belief that they can be trusted. A fiduciary is someone who is believed to be faithful in this sense. Consequently, the common law and equity have developed strict rules to govern the behaviour of those who are fiduciaries precisely to protect those who place such simple faith in others and to ensure that their trust is not abused. The result of this legal development has been a subjugation of the fiduciary to the legal rights of the beneficiary, such that the beneficiary appears to be the powerful one and the fiduciary to be the bearer of weighty obligations.

The question at issue is whether or not a given person ought to be deemed to act as a fiduciary for some other person. The logically subsequent question is then as to the content of those fiduciary duties. First things first, though: who will be a fiduciary?

14.3 ESTABLISHED CATEGORIES OF FIDUCIARY RELATIONSHIP

There are four established categories of fiduciary relationship: trustee and beneficiary, company directors, partners *inter se* (within the terms of the 1890 Partnership Act), and principal and agent.[4] The nature of fiduciary responsibility was considered in Chapter 2[5] and the detailed nature of the obligations of trustees as fiduciaries were considered in detail in Chapter 8.[6] Examples of other situations in which fiduciary relationships have been found are as follows:[7] where a solicitor acts on behalf of his client[8] when advising that client as to

---

1 Kennedy, 1996.
2 *Encarta World Dictionary*, 1999.
3 Cotterrell, 1993:1.
4 The nature of fiduciary duties is considered in Thomas and Hudson, 2004, para 25.15 *et seq*.
5 See para 2.3.3.
6 See the introduction to section 8.1 for an outline of the many specific obligations.
7 These examples have arisen primarily in England and Wales, whereas other jurisdictions have accepted that a doctor may own fiduciary duties to his patient (*McInerney v MacDonald* (1992) 93 DLR (4th) 415) and that a parent who has abused his child is taken to have breached fiduciary duties to that child (*M(K) v M(H)* (1993) 96 DLR (4th) 449; *H v R* [1996] 1 NZLR 299).
8 *Nocton v Lord Ashburton* [1914] AC 932; *McMaster v Byrne* [1952] 1 All ER 1363; *Brown v IRC* [1965] AC 244; *Boardman v Phipps* [1967] 2 AC 46; *Maguire v Makaronis* (1997) 144 ALR 729. By contrast, the Law Society owes no fiduciary duties to the solicitors whom it represents: *Swain v Law Society* [1983] 1 AC 598.

the client's affairs within the scope of the solicitor's retainer;[9] in relation to senior employees holding sensitive positions with reference to their employers,[10] or where any employee exploits his office to generate a personal profit by way of a bribe;[11] between the promoter of a company and the company itself;[12] in relation to those who occupy public office whether as members of the secret service,[13] or as members of the armed forces using their rank to obtain passage for contraband through army roadblocks,[14] or a Director of Public Prosecutions in particular when taking a bribe not to prosecute an alleged criminal.[15]

The following definition of a fiduciary suggests that a range of duties to avoid conflicts of interest[16] and so forth flow from any situation in which a person is in a position of loyalty and confidence in relation to another person:

> A fiduciary is someone who has undertaken to act for or on behalf of another in a particular matter in circumstances which give rise to a relationship of trust and confidence. The distinguishing obligation of a fiduciary is the obligation of loyalty. The principal is entitled to the single-minded loyalty of his fiduciary. The core liability has several facets. A fiduciary must act in good faith; he must not make a profit out of his trust; he must not place himself in a position where his duty and his interest may conflict; he may not act for his own benefit or the benefit of a third person without the informed consent of his principal. This is not intended to be an exhaustive list, but it is sufficient to indicate the nature of fiduciary obligations. They are the defining characteristics of the fiduciary.[17]

What emerges from this definition of a fiduciary is that the categories of fiduciary are open. So, while there are four clear categories of fiduciary office, as set out at the beginning of this section, it is always possible to find that fiduciary duties exist in new contexts on a case-by-case basis. If we understand that the number of fiduciary offices is potentially infinite, and that the category of fiduciary relationships is therefore an elastic one, it should be recognised

---

9 *Marks & Spencer plc v Freshfields Bruckhaus Deringer* [2004] 3 All ER 773, [2004] EWHC 1337; *Bolkiah (Prince Jefri) v KPMG* [1999] 2 AC 222. This limitation has two senses, it is suggested. First, that the fiduciary obligations terminate when the retainer terminates: *Bolkiah v KPMG*. Secondly, that the solicitor is obliged to observe the obligations of a fiduciary in relation to the client's legal affairs but not as to his choice of socks, where the latter falls outwith the scope of the duties forming a part of his retainer.

10 *Canadian Aero-Services Ltd v O'Malley* (1973) 40 DLR (3d) 371 at 381, *per* Laskin J; *Sybron Corporation v Rochem Ltd* [1984] Ch 112 at 127, *per* Stephenson LJ; *Neary v Dean of Westminster* [1999] IRLR 288. However, this does not relate to ordinary employees and does not form a necessary part of the employment contract: *Nottingham University v Fishel* [2000] IRLR 471.

11 *Attorney-General for Hong Kong v Reid* [1994] 1 AC 324.

12 *Erlanger v New Sombrero Phosphate Company* (1878) 3 App Cas 1218. See Hudson, 'Capital issues', in Morse (ed), *Palmer's Company Law*, para 5–113.

13 A contentious category whereby it was accepted in *Attorney-General v Guardian Newspapers Ltd (No 2)* [1990] 1 AC 109 that such a person would be a fiduciary (in that case, when publishing his memoirs), but in *Attorney-General v Blake* [1998] 1 All ER 833, CA, [2000] 4 All ER 385, HL, it was considered that such a person would not always be fiduciary of necessity, although his position may be akin to that of a fiduciary.

14 *Reading v Attorney-General* [1951] 1 All ER 617.

15 *Attorney-General for Hong Kong v Reid* [1994] 1 AC 324.

16 Considered in detail in section 12.5 above and in relation to the obligations of trustees specifically in para 8.3.9 above.

17 *Bristol and West Building Society v Mothew* [1998] Ch 1 at 18, *per* Millett LJ.

that the obligations befitting a fiduciary will differ from circumstance to circumstance. As Lord Browne-Wilkinson has held:

> the phrase 'fiduciary duties' is a dangerous one, giving rise to a mistaken assumption that all fiduciaries owe the same duties in all circumstances. That is not the case. Although so far as I am aware, every fiduciary is under a duty not to make a profit from his position (unless such profit is authorised), the fiduciary duties owed, for example, by an express trustee are not the same as those owed by an agent.[18]

So it is with the precise obligations borne by a constructive trustee:[19] the precise obligations of the trustee will fall to be defined from context to context.

The office of fiduciary can be imposed in addition to other legal obligations. So, for example, partners have contractual obligations between them as set out in their partnership agreement. Similarly, agents stand in a contractual relationship to their principals. However, both partners and agents bear fiduciary obligations above and beyond their contractual bonds. A trustee of an occupational pension fund, as considered in Chapter 24, will often be a professional investment manager acting as a trustee on the basis of a contract with the employer who has created the scheme, but she also owes fiduciary duties over and above any contractual obligations. As will be discussed, the precise nature of many of the fiduciary obligations owed by that trustee will be defined by that contract. A professional trustee will only agree to act if sufficient limitations on her potential liability for breach of duty are included in the contract.[20] In consequence, the professional trustee will be authorised to take a commission from the management of the fund and the trustee's general obligations to achieve the best possible return for the fund will be circumscribed by a contractual variation on the usual legend 'this investment may go down as well as up'. In all of the situations, there will also be another kind of obligation owed beyond that of contract.

In consequence, when considering the nature of fiduciary obligations, it will frequently be necessary to examine the context to decide precisely what those fiduciary obligations mean in that particular situation. Such an atomisation of fiduciary obligations into particular factual circumstances contributes to our difficulty in defining precisely what is meant by labelling someone as a fiduciary. We return to the general ideas of good faith and loyalty outlined above for a more general understanding of what it means to be a fiduciary. A beneficiary is entitled (in the legal sense of having a 'right') to expect that the fiduciary will not permit that beneficiary to suffer loss. So, where does that insight take us? It means that the fiduciary responsibility is something greater than either contractual or tortious liability, even though the content of the fiduciary liability may be limited by the fiduciary's express contractual refusal to adopt certain forms of liability. To be a fiduciary attracts liability for all loss suffered by the beneficiary and is not restricted simply to contractually anticipated forms of loss or even to the tests of causation and remoteness of damage under the duty of care in the tort of negligence. The following section examines the particular benefits which result from successfully identifying a defendant as owing fiduciary duties to a claimant.

---

18 *Henderson v Merrett Syndicates* [1995] 2 AC 145 at 206.
19 Whether under a resulting trust or a constructive trust.
20 For the court's willingness to accept the efficacy of such provisions, see *Armitage v Nurse* [1998] Ch 241.

14.4 THE ADVANTAGES OF REMEDIES BASED ON FIDUCIARY RESPONSIBILITY

The responsibilities of the fiduciary are based on a standard of utmost good faith in general terms. The older case law took the straightforward attitude that if there were any loss suffered by a beneficiary then the fiduciary would be strictly liable for that loss.[21] This attitude has been promulgated by the decisions in *Regal v Gulliver*[22] (concerning directors of a company) and *Boardman v Phipps*[23] (concerning a solicitor advising trustees), which imposed strict liability for all unauthorised gains made by the fiduciaries deriving, however obliquely, from their fiduciary duty.

The company directors in *Regal* were prevented from making a profit from a business opportunity which it was felt by the court ought to have been exploited on behalf of the company rather than on behalf of the directors personally. At one level this personal gain for the directors constituted a fraud on the shareholders, who might otherwise have benefited in increased dividends from the investment in question. In *Boardman*, the obligations of fiduciary office were extended to a solicitor using his own money to exploit an opportunity which the trust could not have taken and which the solicitor himself realised – the only nexus with the trust was the fact that he learned of the possibility while attending a meeting on behalf of his clients,[24] the trustees. Despite the tenuous link between the solicitor's personal profits and the proprietary rights of the beneficiaries (who had all benefited directly from the solicitor's skills), the court held that the strict rule against fiduciaries profiting from their office should be upheld. When a court of Equity asks for good faith it really does mean good faith.

We should also consider the instructive example of *Attorney-General for Hong Kong v Reid*,[25] in which a public official was required to hold property on constructive trust for an unestablished category of beneficiaries in circumstances in which that property had never belonged to any person who could possibly have been considered to be a claimant. The money used to bribe the Director of Public Prosecutions had only ever belonged to those whom the Director of Public Prosecutions had refused to prosecute. In some general sense the bribes were held on trust for the people or the government of Hong Kong. The niceties of trusts – that is, the need for title in property and for identified beneficiaries – were overlooked in the court's enthusiasm to find a justification for taking the proceeds of the bribes off the defendant.

There are two possible bases for this decision: disgorging an enrichment from the defendant who had clearly acted in bad faith, and punishing a wrong committed by that defendant which the criminal law in itself cannot punish sufficiently (that is, that the law of property is required to recover the proceeds of this particular crime). The difficulty remains that the enrichment disgorged from the defendant did not make restitution to the claimant for some direct proprietary loss suffered by the claimant. The bribes were not taken from the claimant (who was the succeeding Attorney-General suing on behalf of Hong Kong). The claimant's loss was as a victim of crime – the defendant's criminal refusal to prosecute criminals who paid him bribes. There is no properly restitutionary basis for this decision.

---

21 *Keech v Sandford* (1726) Sel Cas Ch 61.
22 [1967] 2 AC 134n.
23 [1967] 2 AC 46.
24 Together with the use of confidential information.
25 [1994] 1 AC 324, [1993] 3 WLR 1143.

Rather, the decision is to do with equity's moral condemnation of the defendant's unconscionable actions and with the nature of the fiduciary duty which the defendant owed to the people of Hong Kong.

The case of *Attorney-General for Hong Kong v Reid*,[26] considered at length in Chapter 12, demonstrates two important facts of fiduciary responsibility. First, liability as a fiduciary can be imposed in entirely novel circumstances; there is no need to demonstrate a close analogy with any existing category of fiduciary. In *Reid*, there was no prior case law relating to the position of an Attorney-General, although there were cases relating to people in public office more generally defined (for example, the army sergeant in *Reading v Attorney-General*).[27] It would be disingenuous to suggest that *Reid* broke entirely new territory: rather, it resolved the long-running skirmish in the academic journals in relation to the legal treatment of bribes.[28] That a constructive trust was imposed was a novel departure for the law – albeit one well-trailed in the scholarly literature. That constructive trust was founded on equity's determination that that which ought to have been done is looked upon as having been done: in other words, that the bribes once received ought to have been held on trust from the moment of their receipt.

Secondly, the liability imposed on a trustee is not necessarily linked to any pre-existing relationship but may arise in relation to some subsequent act and relate only to that act. The liability imposed on the defendant in *Reid* was imposed not only in relation to property used in breach of the fiduciary duty, but also in relation to an obligation to make good any loss on the investment of such property. The strict nature of fiduciary liability was observed once again. Beyond any precise contractual obligations owed by the Director of Public Prosecutions to the government which employed him, there were the fiduciary obligations of a constructive trust in the receipt of the bribes alone – that action of receipt of a bribe generated fiduciary obligations (to hold the bribes on constructive trust) from that moment onwards.[29] *Boardman* was a slightly different situation, because the solicitor was already in a fiduciary relationship to his client before making unauthorised profits; although it could be argued that the constructive trust was a new aspect to those fiduciary obligations once the unauthorised profits had been made.

The beneficiary acquires a range of equitable claims and remedies under the law on fiduciaries. The fiduciary will hold any property received in breach of some duty on trust for the beneficiary. That also grants the beneficiary rights to any property acquired with that original property, whether in the form of an income stream (such as dividends from shares) or in the form of substitute property (that is, a replacement capital asset). The beneficiary is also entitled to be compensated for any loss made by the fiduciary in dealing with property which was held on a constructive trust for the beneficiary as a result of some breach of duty. The beneficiary can acquire compound interest on any judgment received against the fiduciary for breach of duty. Furthermore, the general result of finding that the fiduciary is indeed a fiduciary is that everything is assumed against the fiduciary. This is what *Boardman* and *Regal* indicate: the fiduciary will always be liable for any loss suffered by the beneficiary and also responsible for generating the best possible return for that beneficiary. So one of the principal benefits of imposing fiduciary obligations on a defendant from the perspective of

26 *Ibid.*
27 [1951] 1 All ER 617.
28 Eg, Maudsley, 1959.
29 Cf *Attorney-General v Blake* [2000] 4 All ER 385.

the claimant is the creation of a virtual land of milk and honey in which the fiduciary owes everything to the beneficiary.

So what does this discussion tell us about the nature of established categories of fiduciary relationships? It tells us that fiduciary obligations will be said to arise in prescribed circumstances, but it also tells us that those obligations can be shaped and limited by agreement between the parties. It tells us that fiduciary obligations in the form of trusts implied by law can be imposed on defendants outside those well-established categories – generally with a purpose typically limited to dealings with specific property. It tells us that the courts will protect the interests of the beneficiaries to an extent which removes any possibility of harm being suffered by those beneficiaries or of the fiduciary being enriched. What is most important to note is that the fiduciary duty raises in the court a heightened suspicion of anything which may conceivably benefit the fiduciary without sufficient authorisation under cover of an abstract standard of good faith and loyalty.

The beneficiary rides in an equitable sedan chair borne by the fiduciary, cushioned against every bump in the road. Hence the difficulty in reaching any precise definition of the term 'fiduciary' – it is a deliberately fluid concept permitting of addition and atomisation. As such it is at one with the underlying theory advanced in this book of equity as constituting a means of ensuring fairness in individual cases in mitigation of potential injustices that would otherwise be caused by literal application of the common law.

14.5 SCOPE FOR THE DEVELOPMENT OF NEW CATEGORIES?

So much for the established categories of fiduciary: what of the future? The utility for the beneficiary of the fiduciary concept means that there will always be pressure in a common law system for further categories of fiduciary to be added, or for other relationships to be accepted as being closely analogous to fiduciary duties. Claimants will continue to press for new forms of relationship to be accepted as giving rise to fiduciary duties. The advantages of fiduciary status for the beneficiary have been set out above.

The principal question is: 'how do we add to the categories of fiduciary liability?' Perhaps this may also cause us to ask 'how were the *existing* categories formulated and in what way can future additions be made?' Such a change in the recognition of a particular category of person as a fiduciary for the first time will constitute a paradigm shift in the legal treatment of other defendants occupying the same position, because an entirely new range of remedies and structures become available to the claimant. So, for example, if one employer was accepted as occupying a fiduciary relationship in relation to her employees, that would potentially alter the legal relationship between all employers and all employees by granting employees a new range of remedies against their employers.

However, that is not to suggest that a change in the law will necessarily change the entirety of such a relationship. There will be some aspects of a relationship in which there will be fiduciary responsibilities and other aspects of the same relationship where there are not. An example taken from employment law would be the recognition that non-executive employees owe fiduciary responsibilities to their employers in relation to the treatment of confidential information and in relation to theft of the employer's property, but not in relation to their ordinary duties which do not involve their employer's property or confidential processes.[30]

---

30 *Hivac Ltd v Park Royal Scientific Investments Ltd* [1946] Ch 169.

As considered above, fiduciary obligations may arise only in limited circumstances within any given relationship. A further example might be the recognition that there is a fiduciary obligation imposed on a solicitor in advising a client on matters of law and dealing with that client's money, but an absence of such fiduciary obligations on a solicitor when advising a client on her choice of hat: the former activity is clearly in furtherance of the particularly sensitive relationship between solicitor and client, whereas the latter is a purely personal interaction which bears no relation to their respective fiduciary duties.

Maybe our social mores require that certain forms of activity are recognised as being so important that fiduciary status follows, for example, the sensitive relationship of trustee to beneficiary or directors in relation to their company. That being the case, we must try to identify what forms of social need ought to be accepted in future as establishing fiduciary relationships.

As mentioned earlier, the other advantage of according fiduciary status to any particular relationship is that the relationship is redefined. The fiduciary is subjugated to the legal entitlements of the beneficiary. The fiduciary is obliged to consider the exercise of any of her powers in the light of the obligations generally imposed in favour of a beneficiary. The fiduciary becomes a person in whom the beneficiary is entitled to have faith – with all the delicacy that the law requires from such a simple faith. For example, the fiduciary is not entitled to act in the pursuit of her own interests if she is also a fiduciary for the other person. Rather, the fiduciary is precluded from making any unauthorised personal gain from the relationship. Furthermore, the remedies available to the beneficiary accord with the trust-based and strict liability obligations considered above. Akin to *Reid*, the fiduciary runs the risk of being made liable both to disgorge any enrichment from the relationship and to account for all loss suffered by the beneficiary.

Mortgagee–mortgagor

A mortgagee acquires extensive powers of repossession and sale of mortgaged property, as discussed in Chapter 23. The right of repossession is said to obtain even before the ink is dry on the mortgage contract,[31] whereas the statutory power of sale does not obtain until the mortgagor has been in breach of the mortgage agreement or is in arrears for at least two months on payments of interest.[32] The question which arises in the cases is the precise nature of the obligations, if any, which are imposed on the mortgagee when exercising the statutory power of sale. The common law has long accepted that the mortgagee owes no fiduciary obligations to the mortgagor in exercising this power of sale.[33] The only fiduciary obligation arises when the property has been sold, when the mortgagee is deemed to hold the sale proceeds as trustee to discharge the expenses of the sale, then the mortgage debt and finally to transfer any surplus to the mortgagor.

In a departure from this line of authority it was accepted in *Palk v Mortgage Securities*[34] by Nicholls VC that the mortgagee owes duties which are 'analogous to fiduciary duties' when both refusing to sell the property and dealing with that property prior to any future sale in a manner which is oppressive of the mortgagor. In *Palk*, the mortgagee refused to consent

---

31 *Four Maids v Dudley Marshall* [1957] Ch 317.
32 Law of Property Act 1925, s 103.
33 *Cuckmere Brick v Mutual Finance* [1971] Ch 949.
34 [1993] 2 WLR 415.

to a sale at a time of low property prices until the value of the property rose to match the amount owing to the mortgagee. In consequence the debt owed by the mortgagor, who was unable to repay the mortgage, rose by about £30,000 annually, with no end then in sight given the depressed state of the property market at the time. His Lordship considered this situation to be oppressive of the mortgagor and so ordered a sale of the property.

What is interesting is precisely what Nicholls VC meant by finding that the obligation of the mortgagee was *analogous* to that of a fiduciary. A fiduciary would have been unable to profit from the relationship except in so far as contract permitted. Therefore, the mortgagee would have been entitled to receive interest payments and repayment of the capital but not to make any excess profits. It could be argued that waiting until the value of the house rose to be able to meet the mortgage debt would not have been to generate an *excess* profit but only a profit permitted by the mortgage contract. What the mortgagee would have been obliged to do as a fiduciary would have been to act in the best interests of the mortgagor: that is, to prevent the debt escalating year on year while both parties waited for the property market to improve. Here the obligation on the quasi-fiduciary is focused solely on avoiding taking action that would have been oppressive of the beneficiary of that duty. As such it falls some way short of the sensitivity evident in cases considered hereto.

Doctor–patient

The relationship of doctor and patient (in circumstances in which the doctor is treating the patient for some medical complaint) is one of particular sensitivity. The clearest disparity between the two is that the doctor has all the knowledge of medicine which most patients will not. Consequently, the patient is particularly dependent on the doctor. Furthermore, the patient is usually ill when consulting a doctor, and therefore bears anxieties and weaknesses over and above the usual imbalance of power between a person with technical knowledge and a person without such knowledge.[35]

Bearing that context in mind, the law is confronted by a difficulty when resolving disputes between doctor and patient. The law of tort usually resolves questions to do with misdiagnosis or mistreatment under the heading of medical negligence and through the doctrine of the 'best interests' of the patient.[36] These approaches have a number of shortcomings. In practice such litigation will settle if the doctor has clearly been negligent, but in more marginal cases the individual litigant will have to face the powerful interests of the NHS trusts. That disparity in expertise, knowledge and access to evidence is exacerbated in particular if the claimant cannot obtain legal aid or negotiate a suitable conditional fee arrangement.

The question is then whether the imperfections of the law of tort could be remedied by developing a conception of the doctor as owing fiduciary obligations to the patient. In an insightful survey of this area, Kennedy sets out those common law jurisdictions in North America which accept that the doctor–patient relationship is a fiduciary relationship in some circumstances. In those jurisdictions it is typically in relation to the question whether or not the doctor must give information to the patient that fiduciary obligations are imposed. The rationale for the imposition of fiduciary obligations is that the law of tort will not impose affirmative obligations (for example, an obligation to give information to the patient on

---

35 Kennedy, 1996.
36 *Ibid.*

which informed consent to treatment can be reached) but fiduciary obligations do impose such affirmative obligations.[37]

In English law the doctor–patient relationship is not a fiduciary one.[38] This is so even in relation to confidentiality which would usually connote a fiduciary responsibility,[39] as has been apparently accepted in Canada,[40] although this has been doubted by judges in Australia.[41] As Kennedy explains, these developments in the law relating to confidentiality in the Commonwealth are examples of equity seeking to provide a remedy where none would otherwise exist – that is, for example, in preventing the doctor from disclosing confidential patient information (perhaps by injunction) and by compensating such disclosure.[42] Quoting Sopinka J in *International Corona Resources Ltd v LAC Minerals Ltd*,[43] 'fiduciary obligation must be reserved for situations that are truly in need of the special protection which equity offers'. This is perhaps the acid test for future developments in the field of fiduciary liability.

Employer–employee

In general terms, company directors will owe fiduciary duties to the company not to, for example, make personal profits or divert contracts which the company could have exploited to their own personal gain.[44] The legal treatment of more junior employees is not so straightforward. Clearly, any employee would be liable for assisting in a breach of trust in, for example, diverting assets owned by the employer to a competitor.[45] Employees will also be restricted *qua* fiduciaries from sharing confidential information owned by the employer with competitors or other persons. That liability will attach more easily to expert employees with knowledge of the employer's secret processes or know-how, than to employees without access to such material.[46] This is said to form part of a general duty of fidelity[47] which Lord Greene MR considered to be an implied term of the employment contract,[48] and even extends to preventing an employee from working in her spare time in a manner which would cause harm to her employer. Breach of this duty can be remedied by dismissal of the employee if the action constitutes a sufficiently material breach of the contract of employment[49] over and above the more general remedies considered above. The liability of that employee will depend on the precise terms of that person's employment contract and the general law relating to the employer's ability to restrain the employee's trade by including a term in the contract preventing that employee from working for competitors for a specified period of time.

Beyond these particular contexts, are there fiduciary duties created by the contract of employment *simpliciter*? This raises two issues. First, does the employee owe general duties

37 *Canterbury v Spence* (1972) 464 F 2d 772; *Reibl v Hughes* (1980) 114 DLR (3d) 1.
38 *Sidaway v Governors of Bethlem Royal Hospital* [1984] 1 QB 515.
39 Kennedy, 1996, 123.
40 *McInerney v McDonald* (1992) 93 DLR (4th) 415; *Norberg v Wyrinb* (1992) 92 DLR (4th) 449.
41 *Breen v Williams* (1996) 70 ALJR 772.
42 Kennedy, 1996, 130.
43 (1989) 2 SCR 574, 596.
44 *Regal v Gulliver* [1942] 1 All ER 378, [1967] 2 AC 134n; *Horcal v Gatland* [1983] IRLR 459.
45 *Royal Brunei Airlines v Tan* [1995] 2 AC 378.
46 *Hivac Ltd v Park Royal Scientific Investments Ltd* [1946] Ch 169.
47 *Adamson v B & L Cleaning Services* [1995] IRLR 193.
48 *Hivac Ltd v Park Royal Scientific Investments Ltd* [1946] Ch 169, 174.
49 *Boston Deep Sea Fishing Co Ltd v Ansell* (1888) 39 Ch D 339.

to the employer as a fiduciary always to do the best for the employer? This would extend, in theory, to liability for lost production on each illicitly taken sick-day when not really ill, or for each personal telephone call made from the employer's telephone.[50] In consequence, it would seem that there will be fiduciary liability only in the limited contexts outlined above. Secondly, does the employer owe fiduciary duties to the employee, for example, to safeguard her employment or to make the largest possible profit to pay to her in bonuses? The short answer is: no. The law does not accept a general fiduciary duty owed by the employer to the employee at all. The employer is free to fire the employee at will under the principles attaching to fiduciaries (for example, to do the best for the beneficiary) and is constrained only by the laws on unfair dismissal and so forth which are outside the purview of equity.

Abuser–abused

This particular context relates to the uncomfortable subject of the sexual abuse of children. The question arises whether or not there is any remedy which the law can provide for the victim of such abuse against the abuser. Part of the uncomfortable nature of this topic in this particular context should be examined at the outset. Namely, is it appropriate for the law to seek to provide a remedy based on financial equitable compensation or common law damages in an effort to 'compensate' the victim of such abuse as though money could somehow remove that problem? What is being suggested here is not an apology or a cure-all but rather a form of contribution which the law could make to the activities which the victim may be required to undertake as part of the process of coping with a history of abuse.

First, let us consider the alternative to fiduciary liability. The tort of battery would provide for cash damages in relation to out-of-pocket loss. Similarly, the tort of negligence would require breach of a duty of care. Both remedies would require two things. First, proof that the loss suffered flowed directly from the actions of the defendant. In relation to the possibility of many years of psychiatric treatment, it might not be easy to demonstrate how much of the expenditure constituted a loss flowing directly from the actions of the defendant. Secondly, there would be the problem of estimating the likely future expense from the date of trial.

In relation to the development of fiduciary law into the realm of sexual abuse, it would seem most straightforward to facilitate this development in cases involving parents and their own children, on the basis that equity has accepted a fiduciary responsibility between parent and child from the early development of the presumptions of advancement in *Bennet v Bennet*.[51] Where the provenance of this new form of liability is more problematic is in relation to abuse by persons other than the victim's parents, where those parents were not necessarily in a position to prevent such abuse from occurring. A further issue may be caused by different intensities of abuse, or between contexts in which that abuse has occurred for longer or shorter periods of time. It is contended that if we do accept that fiduciary liability ought to exist between an adult who abuses and a child who suffers that abuse, then the natural flexibility in the law relating to fiduciaries ought to be able to define the particular duties owed and remedies resulting in any set of circumstances.

---

50 The cartoonist Scott Adams has a suitable response for overworked employees in the 21st century when confronted with complaints about making personal phone calls: that is to invoice the employer for all the unpaid overtime usually put in by the employee.
51 (1879) 10 Ch D 474.

Related issues were raised in *Sidaway v Governors of Bethlem Royal Hospital*,[52] in which the Court of Appeal suggested that English law would only use fiduciary liability to protect the economic interests of claimants and not to protect them, for example, from sexual exploitation. The reluctance of English law to develop in this direction will result from the fact, which I freely acknowledge, that this context is far from the paradigm case of the fiduciary: that is, the trustee holding property on the terms of an express trust. What may seem particularly objectionable in this approach is the determination of the courts to protect claimants' property rights and financial interests but not to look to the protection of the claimant's long-term medical, psychiatric and welfare interests by means of identical remedies. Thus, if X was sexually abused by her trustee and also had her trust fund looted by that same trustee, X would have an action in equity for recovery of her lost money but not for the cost of future treatment or any resultant personal difficulties stemming from the abuse. It should be remembered that the criminal law will punish the trustee but it will not make any strides towards compensating X.

The primary advantage of the creation of a fiduciary obligation in English law to cater for such situations would be that equity has a lower threshold of liability in such circumstances. As considered above, the fiduciary becomes almost strictly liable for all loss flowing from his actions once fiduciary liability is accepted. The important corollary is the obligation on the fiduciary 'to do the best possible' for the beneficiary – which offers a broader range of liabilities than that contained within the narrowness of the duty of care.[53] While vulnerability will not in itself found fiduciary liability,[54] it is suggested that a breach of a relationship of trust (in the vernacular sense of that term) should found such a liability. As such, in line with the *dicta* of Sopinka J in *International Corona Resources Ltd v LAC Minerals Ltd*[55] that 'fiduciary obligation must be reserved for situations that are truly in need of the special protection which equity offers', this context could be said to be one in which fiduciary liability would permit a new form of remedy for an aspect of our lives which (while anticipated by the early works of Freud) appears to claim an ever more significant part of our understanding of human biographies.

14.6 CONCLUSIONS – THE TRADITIONAL CONTEXT

In a powerful essay, Professor Hayton suggests that the fiduciary liability provided by equity should not be used simply as a 'firefighter' in cases in which common law principles of contract and tort will not provide sufficient remedy.[56] Rather, it is said that equity and the common law should proceed on principled bases and not in a way that leads to equitable ideas being 'bandied about in common law courts as though the Chancellor still had only the length of his own foot to measure when coming to a conclusion'.[57]

Professor Hayton does end his essay on a forward-looking note by suggesting that 'the "survival of the fittest" mentality of the common law is appropriate for a capitalist society dedicated to economic efficiency but in today's more caring and European-law-influenced

---

52   [1984] 1 QB 515, 519.
53   As considered generally in Chapter 8.
54   *Mabo v Queensland (No 2)* (1992) 175 CLR 1.
55   (1989) 2 SCR 574, 596.
56   Hayton, 1997.
57   *Campbell Discount Co Ltd v Bridge* [1961] 1 QB 445, 459, *per* Harman LJ.

times such mentality needs to change'.[58] In Chapter 17, we will compare human rights thinking (drawing on a European jurisprudence) with the traditional attitudes of equity. What we will see is that the sort of concentration on property rights which has prevented many of the possible developments in the law on fiduciaries may be displaced by other ideological totems, such as the right to a family life and to integrity of the person which are contained in the European Convention on Human Rights. While the Human Rights Act 1998 did not include the usual commitment under the European Convention on Human Rights to ensure that domestic law provides protection for all rights contained in the Convention, it is likely that the angle of attack on the development of equitable principles in areas such as the family, the family home and integrity of the person will switch now to the language of human rights. For that reason, a discussion of the conservative approach to equity-as-firefighter must be postponed until we have examined trusts over the home and human rights to property and a family life in the following chapters.

58 Hayton, 1997.

Part 5

Equity, trusts and the home

Chapter 15

Trusts of homes

OVERVIEW

Where there has been an express trust declared over land, the terms of that trust will be
decisive of the division of the equitable interest in land.[1] *Such a declaration of trust must*
satisfy s 53(1)(b) of the Law of Property Act 1925.

   If there is no express trust declared the courts will look for the common intention of
the parties as to the equitable ownership of the home. The decision of the majority of the
Supreme Court in Jones v Kernott, *as it interpreted the earlier decision of the majority*

---

1 *Goodman v Gallant* [1986] Fam 106; *Re Gorman* [1990] 1 WLR 616; *Harwood v Harwood* [1991] 2 FLR 274.

of the House of Lords in Stack v Dowden, *held that where the legal title is in joint names, there will be a presumption that the equitable interest is similarly held jointly; whereas if the legal title is held in one person's sole name, then the presumption will be that that person is the sole owner of the equitable interest. Either presumption may be rebutted. If the facts do not disclose a clear common intention then the court will seek objectively to infer a common intention from the evidence; but if that evidence is not conclusive then the court will seek to achieve fairness between the parties. Ordinarily, a resulting trust will no longer be used in this regard. The previous case law has not been overruled and therefore will still be significant in relation to establishing a common intention or in establishing what constitutes a fair outcome.*

The position established in Lloyds Bank v Rosset *in the earlier House of Lords' decision was as follows: where the parties have formed an agreement, arrangement or understanding as to the beneficial ownership of the home then the court will give effect to that common intention by means of constructive trust or proprietary estoppel ('common intention constructive trust' by agreement) if the claimant has also suffered detriment.*[2] *The second means, in the absence of an agreement, will be to give effect to the common intention of the parties where the claimant has contributed to the purchase price of the property or to the mortgage instalments, again by way of 'constructive trust or proprietary estoppel' ('a common intention constructive trust by conduct').*[3]

However, this approach in Lloyds Bank v Rosset *had not commanded complete obedience in the lower courts nor did it accord with preceding doctrine. Thus, some Court of Appeal decisions held that where a person contributed to the purchase price of the home, an amount of the total equitable interest proportionate to the size of the contribution would be held on resulting trust for that person.*[4]

Alternative Court of Appeal decisions developed two further approaches. First, a balance sheet approach based on resulting trust which favours a measurement of financial contributions over the life of a relationship to calculate proportionate equitable rights in the home.[5] *Secondly a family assets approach, akin to the approach of a family court in divorce proceedings, which undertakes a survey of the parties' entire course of dealing – thus going far beyond the approach in* Lloyds Bank v Rosset – *which suggested that property should be deemed to be held equally between couples.*[6]

The doctrine of proprietary estoppel will grant an equitable interest to a person who has been induced to suffer detriment in reliance on a representation that she would acquire some rights in the property as a result.[7] *Proprietary estoppel is a remedial doctrine whereby the court may award any one of a number of rights ranging from the entire freehold through to merely equitable compensation in money.*[8]

---

2 *Lloyds Bank v Rosset* [1991] 1 AC 107; *Ivin v Blake* [1995] 1 FLR 70.
3 *Lloyds Bank v Rosset* [1991] 1 AC 107.
4 *Dyer v Dyer* (1788) 2 Cox Eq Cas 92; *Westdeutsche Landesbank Girozentrale v Islington LBC* [1996] AC 669.
5 *Springette v Defoe* [1992] 2 FLR 388; *Huntingford v Hobbs* [1993] 1 FLR 736; *McHardy v Warren* [1994] 2 FLR 338.
6 *Hammond v Mitchell* [1991] 1 WLR 1127; *Midland Bank v Cooke* [1995] 4 All ER 562.
7 *Taylor Fashions Ltd v Liverpool Victoria Trustees Co Ltd* [1982] 1 QB 133; *Re Basham (Deceased)* [1986] 1 WLR 1498; *Wayling v Jones* (1993) 69 P & CR 170; *Gillett v Holt* [2000] 2 All ER 289.
8 *Crabb v Arun DC* [1976] Ch 179; *Baker v Baker* (1993) 25 HLR 408.

A more recent trend in the case law had been to develop an approach based on avoiding unconscionability if the defendant were permitted to deny the claimant an equitable interest in the property.[9] These cases tended to seek first an agreement between the parties and then secondly to undertake a survey of the entire course of dealing between the parties. The ultimate aim is to reach a 'fair' result and to supply the parties with a common intention if that is necessary, an approach which has the tacit approval of Stack v Dowden. *This is an uncomfortable fusion of the preceding doctrines. This approach also seeks to fuse constructive trusts with proprietary estoppel.*

15.1 INTRODUCTION

15.1.1 Understanding the legal treatment of the home

There can be few more psychologically loaded concepts than that of the home. As the anthropology of property law, and indeed the whole sweep of human history, demonstrates there are few things more important to human beings than land. The means by which access to land and protection of rights to use land are provided constitute a central part of all world cultures. Under English law, the legal treatment of trusts of land, specifically in relation to family homes, is particularly vexed: so much so that the subject commands its own individual treatment in this Part 5 of the book. The treatment of the family home is clearly of enormous sociological, political, economic, spiritual and psychological importance in any system of law – that is quite a list.

In any situation in which more than one person occupies a home, there will be an issue as to the equitable and common law rights in that property. It is important to understand the structure of the chapters and of those issues which are considered in this Part. Rather than present the material in one very long chapter, it has been broken down into three sub-divisions. First, in this chapter an analysis of the means by which the common law and equity accept that a person will acquire rights in land by means of express trust, resulting trust, constructive trust and proprietary estoppel. This discussion includes a comparison drawn with the very different approaches taken to these same issues in two Commonwealth jurisdictions: Canada and Australia. This chapter and Chapter 16 also include an analysis of the various forms of estoppel available under English law. What will emerge is a conceptually complex distinction between these modes of trust and of estoppel. Secondly, Chapter 16 considers the specific legislation dealing with family breakdown and the rights of children, including those issues more commonly dealt with only in family law textbooks which entitle claimants to acquire rights to occupy the home, the Trust of Land and Appointment of Trustees Act 1996 dealing with the operation of trusts of land. Thirdly, in Chapter 17 an analysis is given of human rights law in this context and of philosophical concepts of social justice.

The purpose of this threefold division is to juxtapose the very different conceptual underpinnings of trusts law, equitable estoppel and family law in relation to the home. Too little of the literature seriously attempts to deal with these very different areas of law separately. Section 17.5 considers the nature of rights under these various areas of the law from the

---

9 See variously *Jennings v Rice* [2002] EWCA Civ 159; *Oxley v Hiscock* [2004] 3 All ER 703; *Stack v Dowden* [2005] EWCA Civ 857, [2006] 1 FLR 254 and other cases referred to in the chapter below.

perspective of philosophical conceptions of social justice as a means of unpacking their various intellectual differences. Section 17.1 considers the significant developments promised by the Human Rights Act 1998 in relation to the possibility of conceiving of rights in property as specifically human rights in English law for the first time. This will offer a further means of conceiving of the law on the home.

15.1.2 A survey: a taste of what is to come

What will emerge from this discussion is that the treatment of resulting trusts and of constructive trusts in relation to the home is very different from that discussed in Chapters 11 and 12 respectively. Resulting and constructive trusts are said in the cases to arise on the basis of strict principles of law, acting retrospectively and imposing institutional trusts.[10] That strict trusts law approach then falls to be compared with proprietary estoppel, which is a remedial doctrine capable of providing a range of proprietary and personal remedies at the discretion of the court which are prospective and which do not impose institutional trusts.[11] The development of the 'common intention constructive trust' in this area is a unique one which is specific to the socially sensitive treatment of the family home.[12] The common intention constructive trust plays fast and loose with a mixture of concepts borrowed from resulting trusts, constructive trusts and proprietary estoppel.[13]

When considering family law, what will emerge is that the family courts identify the welfare of children as being the paramount consideration,[14] which causes problems when stacked up against the overriding concern of the law of trusts to protect the property rights of the person who paid for the home[15] – usually not a child. In considering human rights, we encounter yet another legal paradigm which asserts both a right to property and a right to a family life simultaneously.[16] What this English law approach does not address is the needs of those persons who do not have independent possessions because they do not have sufficient money of their own, for example, children and cohabitees who do not work. As will emerge, the Commonwealth jurisdictions are taking a very different approach to these issues.[17]

An analysis of family law in Chapter 16 will offer a means of understanding the competing areas of law dealt with in this chapter. The point which will emerge is that a family lawyer would come to consider questions as to rights in the home in connection with those materials considered in Chapter 16, whereas a property lawyer would concentrate on the material in this chapter, a human rights lawyer on the material in Chapter 17, and a social security or housing lawyer on other material entirely.[18]

---

10 *Westdeutsche Landesbank Girozentrale v Islington LBC* [1996] AC 669; considered in Chapters 11 and 12.

11 Considered at section 15.7 below.

12 *Gissing v Gissing* [1971] AC 886; *Lloyds Bank v Rosset* [1990] 1 AC 107.

13 *Lloyds Bank v Rosset* [1990] 1 AC 107.

14 In line with the Children Act 1989, s 1.

15 Contributions must be made with a view to acquiring rights in the property, and made only to the purchase price or to the repayments of mortgage instalments: *Burns v Burns* [1984] Ch 317; *Lloyds Bank v Rosset* [1990] 1 AC 107. Considered at section 15.4 below. Cf *White v White* [2000] 2 FLR 981.

16 Analysed in Chapter 17.

17 See, eg, *Bryson v Bryant* (1992) 29 NSWLR 188.

18 For a completely different perspective on rights in the home see Hudson, 1997:1 and Hudson, 2004: 2.

15.1.3 The social context of the law

The social context

The right to occupy the home is an issue about which everyone has opinions, whether a lawyer or not. With the regular diet of soap operas, kitchen sink dramas and tabloid sensations which occupy our popular culture, we are all aware of the sorts of issues which accompany battles for rights in the home, whether by relationship breakdown, death, birth or otherwise. In dealing with the legal issues which follow in Part 5, we should never lose sight of the human dramas which are played out behind the concepts of the courtroom.

The most common set of circumstances which arises in the cases is that of a couple who have occupied a home and run through the gamut of human experiences: children, redundancy, riches, poverty, and separation. In these situations it is difficult to know who should acquire rights in the home either to prevent third parties from purchasing it, or to prevent mortgagees from repossessing it, or to decide between the couple whether the property should be sold or whether a part of the family unit should continue to live in it. As we shall see, the trust is the legal mechanism used in English law to allocate property rights in the home. Typically, those rights will revolve around the amount of money that is contributed to the purchase of the property, or to its maintenance throughout the relationship. At the back of our minds, it will be important to recognise a central issue as to whether or not it is right that financial contributions are the only form of contribution which ought to count in many circumstances, because that is typically the basis on which such property rights are allocated.[19]

In short, the law relating to the home is an extraordinary mixture of these ingredients. The following chapter will consider the manner in which equity allocates rights in the home, and will also consider the theoretical bases on which that allocation takes place. The case law relating to trusts of homes is very complicated. The many available doctrines are woven one into another in a stream of decided cases which often defy tidy categorisation. The discussion in this chapter follows what is considered by this writer to be a combination of the classical and most comprehensible divisions between the doctrines. At the end of the chapter the academic discussion is drawn together of the law's treatment of rights in the home, and some of the broader questions are introduced.

Cohabitees – a neutral expression

The material considered in this chapter walks a fine line between a number of very different social contexts. Many of the core cases which established this field in the 1970s[20] concerned married couples who had separated, such that one of the former spouses sought an order under the Married Women's Property Act 1882.[21] It is not necessary that the couple be

---

19 *Burns v Burns* [1984] Ch 317; *Lloyds Bank v Rosset* [1990] 1 AC 107.
20 *Pettitt v Pettitt* [1970] AC 777; *Gissing v Gissing* [1971] AC 886.
21 There is little doubt, as will emerge, that the courts will favour married couples because it is easier to find the sorts of common intentions favoured by the courts, as has been the case since *Hyde v Hyde* (1866) LR 1 P& D 130; *Quilter v Attorney-General* [1998] 1 NZLR 523.

married to establish any of the claims considered in this chapter[22] – although the bulk of the cases in Chapter 17 will refer only to marital breakdown.[23] This area of law potentially covers relationships as distinct as married couples; unmarried couples with children in permanent relationships; heterosexual couples who have for the sake of convenience taken to living together, as much out of sexual desire as anything else, but who have no firm intention of establishing a permanent relationship; homosexual couples in similar senses; or people who are simply sharing accommodation which they have bought communally. Between these various core intentions are millions of shades of possible other intentions. Children conceived by accident, couples thrown together out of circumstances, doomed relationships wracked by illness, or poverty or bad luck: all fall to be discussed by the law. Chaos is not so much a feature of the law as of the circumstances on which the court is asked to rule.[24]

This chapter will use 'cohabitees' as a deliberately neutral term which can encapsulate all of the foregoing possible types of relationship.[25] While that neutral terminology will be employed, it should not be forgotten that there are differences in bargaining power between different participants in this rights-in-homes lottery. In many of the decided cases women have been in an economically disadvantageous position because they have been cast in the role of carer and not of breadwinner.[26] In consequence, principles which are based solely on financial contribution to the purchase price of the home will tend to discriminate against people who have contributed by means of services to the family,[27] or by contribution only to general family expenses and not directly to the purchase of the home.[28] Similarly, while equity might appear to have an egalitarian sweep in this context, ignoring the precise nature of the relationship, there is little doubt that the common intention constructive trust considered at section 15.4 below will lead courts to find such property rights more readily in circumstances in which there is a long-standing marriage than in connection to a short-term relationship.[29]

It is not obvious whether there is a benefit to be drawn from the courts being slow to find such common intentions in relation to less formal relationships. On the one hand, it may be that in the context of relationship breakdown, it would be unfair to displace one party from a flat she has owned outright for 10 years because of something said in the heat of passion to a partner about them 'living together for ever', and so giving that other person a property

---

22 *Springette v Defoe* [1992] 2 FLR 388, at para 15.5.3 below; *Wayling v Jones* (1993) 69 P & CR 170. In each case the court will turn to consider the parties' intentions and so forth, as considered below, whether this be as a 'paramour' (*Forgeard v Shanahan* (1994) 18 Fam LR 281); as a 'mistress' – which may connote lack of intention to live together in some circumstances (*Crick v Ludwig* (1994) 117 DLR (4th) 228); as a 'consort' (*Hollywood v Cork Harbour Commissioners* [1992] 1 IR 457); or as a 'concubine'(!) (*Hill v Estate of Westbrook* 95 Cal App (2d) 599 (1950)).

23 The courts are concerned, however, not to make awards of property interests in cases concerning meretricious sexual cohabitation – by which the courts typically mean prostitution – *Marvin v Marvin* 18 Cal (3d) 660 (1976).

24 Dewar, 1998.

25 There is a better term used in the television series *The Beiderbecke Affair*, written by Alan Plater, where the unmarried couple who act as the ironic heroes (played by James Bolam and Barbara Flynn) refer to themselves as 'spousal analogues', by which they mean that they are not married but their relationship is analogous to a marriage.

26 Wong, 1998.

27 *Nixon v Nixon* [1969] 1 WLR 1676; *Burns v Burns* [1984] Ch 317; *Lloyds Bank v Rosset* [1990] 1 AC 107.

28 *Burns v Burns* [1984] Ch 317; *Lloyds Bank v Rosset* [1990] 1 AC 107.

29 An approach which the Court of Appeal took in *Midland Bank v Cooke* [1995] 4 All ER 562.

right when they had lived together for only six months. On the other hand, it may be that the couple are seeking to establish rights against third parties (such as a mortgagee), and therefore to judge the quality of their rights from the comparatively brief nature of their relationship at that point, even though they may intend to have children in the future, would do them great injustice and even harm the viability of that relationship in the future if their home were repossessed.[30] No single answer will fit all cases satisfactorily or evenly.

It is suggested that the complexity in the law relating to the home which is produced in all Commonwealth jurisdictions arises directly out of the impossibility of finding one neat set of rules which will meet all circumstances. It is in the context of trusts of homes that those who would introduce greater rigidity to equity meet their match.

15.1.4 The principles set out in *Stack v Dowden* and in *Jones v Kernott*

If there is no express trust declared the courts will look for the common intention of the parties as to the equitable ownership of the home. The decision of the majority of the Supreme Court in Jones v Kernott, *as it interpreted the earlier decision of the majority of the House of Lords in* Stack v Dowden, *held that where the legal title is in joint names, there will be a presumption that the equitable interest is similarly held jointly; whereas if the legal title is held in one person's sole name, then the presumption will be that that person is the sole owner of the equitable interest. Either presumption may be rebutted. If the facts do not disclose a clear common intention then the court will seek objectively to infer a common intention from the evidence; but if that evidence is not conclusive then the court will seek to achieve fairness between the parties. The foregoing case law has not been overruled and therefore will still be significant in relation to establishing a common intention or in establishing what constitutes a fair outcome.*

There have been two decisions of the highest court in this area in recent years: by the House of Lords in *Stack v Dowden*[31] and by the Supreme Court in *Jones v Kernott*.[32] The decision of *Jones v Kernott* was concerned primarily with interpreting *Stack v Dowden* and attempting to iron out problems which had emerged in the cases which had followed *Stack v Dowden*. This section sets out the key principles from those cases. However, the decision in *Stack v Dowden*[33] has had only a marginal effect on the detail of the law on trusts of homes. Therefore, this section will summarise the key principles set out in *Stack v Dowden* and *Jones v Kernott* – which draw on a variety of concepts from earlier cases and which are a response to those ealier cases – before proceeding through those earlier cases and coming chronologically to *Stack* and to *Kernott*. As will emerge from the discussion to follow, the older authorities will continue to be important because *Stack* and *Kernott* overruled very little previous authority and because their broad principles still leave room for those earlier cases to apply.

---

30 In relation to the difficulty faced by same-sex couples, see *Fitzpatrick v Sterling Housing Association* [1998] Ch 304; *Attorney-General of Canada v Mossop* (1993) 100 DLR (4th) 658.
31 [2007] UKHL 17, [2007] 2 WLR 831. A casenote on the decision of the House of Lords in the case of *Stack v Dowden* is on my personal website (www.alastairhudson.com/trustslawindex.htm).
32 [2011] UKSC 53, [2011] 3 WLR 1121.
33 [2007] UKHL 17, [2007] 2 WLR 831. A casenote on the decision of the House of Lords in the case of *Stack v Dowden* is on my personal website (www.alastairhudson.com/trustslawindex.htm).

There are three core principles which were established in *Stack v Dowden* in the judgment of Lady Hale: the detail of the decision in that case is considered below in section 15.9. First, if there is a valid express trust created over land, then that express trust will be decisive of the parties' equitable interests in that property, assuming that there is no common intention to the contrary between the parties. Secondly, if only one of the parties is entered on the legal title of property, then there is a presumption that the equitable interest in the property is held by that person. Thirdly, if more than one of the parties is entered on the legal title of the property, then there is a presumption that the equitable interest in the property is held by the parties in equal shares. These presumptions can be rebutted by evidence to the contrary that the parties' common intention was something else. To rebut those presumptions, we are required to consider the law before *Stack v Dowden* because the House of Lords in *Stack v Dowden* did not overrule the bulk of those earlier cases. That the presumption can be rebutted by evidence that the ownership of the legal title did not reflect the parties' intentions has been accepted explicitly by the Court of Appeal.[34] The presence of a common intention will be important even where there may otherwise appear to be a good conveyance of a home at common law. Just because someone receives a conveyance of property to herself alone, that will not defeat an agreement between that person and others that some other person is to have an equitable interest in that land.[35] The earlier cases are frequently in contradiction to one another. It was held by Lord Walker and Lady Hale in *Jones v Kernott* that the court should seek to 'objectively infer the intentions of the parties' by reference to the evidence that does exist. If the evidence is not conclusive as to the parties' common intention, then further to the judgment of Lord Walker and Lady Hale in *Jones v Kernott*, the court will consider what would be fair between the parties in the light of the evidence.

The decision of the Supreme Court in *Jones v Kernott*[36] attempted to clarify the judgment of Lady Hale in *Stack v Dowden* (in particular by reference to whether the court could impute or merely infer a common intention from the parties' conduct). Lord Walker and Lady Hale delivered a joint judgment, with each of the other members of the Supreme Court delivering judgments in slightly different terms, as considered below in section 15.9.7. However, Lord Kerr attempted to identify the principles which were agreed between the members of the Supreme Court. That summary is set out here, with the detail of the various judgments being considered in section 15.9.7 below:[37]

> (i)   In joint names cases [where the legal title in the property is put into joint names], the starting point is that equity follows the law [such that the parties are deemed to be joint owners of the equitable interest]. One begins the search for the proper allocation of shares in the property with the presumption that the parties are joint tenants and are thus entitled to equal shares.

This means that where the legal title in the property has been put in the joint names of the parties then it is presumed that parties will own the equitable interest jointly. This presumption can be rebutted on the following terms:

---

34 *Laskar v Laskar* [2008] EWCA Civ 347, [2008] 2 FLR 589. See *Hollis v Rolfe* [2008] EWHC 1747 (Ch) applying the presumptions.
35 *Bannister v Bannister* [1948] 2 All ER 133; *Staden v Jones* [2008] EWCA Civ 936, [2008] 2 FLR 1931.
36 [2011] UKSC 53, [2011] 3 WLR 1121, [2011] 3 FCR 495.
37 [2011] UKSC 53, [2011] 3 WLR 1121, [2011] 3 FCR 495, at [68].

(ii)   That presumption can be displaced by showing (a) that the parties had a different common intention at the time when they acquired the home or (b) that they later formed the common intention that their respective shares would change.

The rebuttal of the presumption can take effect either before purchase or at a later date. Resulting trusts focused on the parties' financial contributions are relegated from their primacy in earlier cases. What is unclear here, significantly, is what sort of common intention would be required to rebut this presumption after the purchase, especially given that the parties are likely to present different evidence at trial if equitable ownership is contested between them. The question then is as to the way in which the common intention is to be identified. There was a great deal of discussion at the hearing (and a lot of discussion in the judgments in the Supreme Court) as to whether the court could impute an intention to the parties or whether the court must simply infer such an intention from the actual intentions of the parties. As his lordship put it:

(iii)   The common intention, if it can be inferred, is to be deduced objectively from the parties' conduct.

This complex idea means that a subjective intention is impossible to prove definitively, and therefore the court must rely on evidence such as documentation, proof of any discussion the parties had as to their equitable rights (whether through e-mail, text or evidence of personal conversations), much of which will be contested between the witnesses, and so forth. Moreover, the ways in which the parties conduct themselves, what each party pays for (including the mortgage and other household outgoings), how the parties organise their living arrangements, and so forth, will all be conduct suggesting their intentions as to the equitable ownership of the property. In that sense, what the parties must have intended is deduced objectively from the parties' conduct because it throws light on what the parties must have intended. In many cases where the evidence is inconclusive, the court will have recourse to the final principle of fairness:

(iv)   Where the intention as to the division of the property cannot be inferred, each is entitled to that share which the court considers fair. In considering the question of what is fair the court should have regard to the whole course of dealing between the parties.

Thus, ultimately, the court will have to have recourse to what is 'fair' between the parties. This will require, it is suggested, that the courts will potentially have recourse to all of the earlier authorities considered in this chapter in deciding what constitutes fairness between the parties. It should be recalled that *Stack v Dowden* overruled very little case law explicitly and the same is true of the decision in *Jones v Kernott*. Therefore, aside from setting out the presumptions above and giving an order to the questions which the courts will ask, these two decisions have effected very little change in circumstances in which the parties are in disagreement and the evidence is inconclusive.

15.1.5 The approach taken in this chapter

The underlying thesis of this chapter is that it is not possible to reconcile the many cases on trusts of homes with one another. The aim of the claimant in each case is to establish as large an equitable interest in the home as possible, either because of a separation from a partner or because of a mortgagee seeking repossession of that home by a mortgagee or some other secured creditor. In line with traditional trusts law, it might have been possible before 1991 to divide between the express trusts law rules on acquisition of rights in the home, then the resulting trust rules, and then the constructive trust rules. However, since the decision of the House of Lords in *Lloyds Bank v Rosset* in 1991, there has been a splintering of the doctrines into many mini-doctrines. The aim of this chapter is to distinguish between them and to help to categorise them for you. Even after the judgments in *Stack v Dowden* and in *Jones v Kernott*, these contradictory currents in the earlier cases remain. There are, I would suggest, six doctrines of importance. This is the order in which they are considered in this chapter.

First, if there has been an express trust created, then that express trust will be enforced. All of the other approaches assume no express trust has been created. If there is no express trust then there are two alternative presumptions: the first assumes that multiple ownership of the legal title presumes equal ownership of the equitable interest; whereas sole ownership of the legal title presumes sole ownership of the equitable interest. However, these presumptions can be rebutted by evidence supporting any of the following approaches.

Secondly, then, the strict, 'common intention' approach in *Lloyds Bank v Rosset* looks either for an agreement between the parties or appropriate conduct to acquire an equitable interest, which means either contribution to the purchase price or payment of the mortgage instalments. This appeared to be a strict test but nevertheless most subsequent cases have refused to apply it scrupulously.

Thirdly, subsequent Court of Appeal cases have relied on resulting trust principles and concerned themselves only with the amount of money which each party has contributed to the property. Exceptionally, these resulting trusts may be adjusted to accommodate later work done on the property. This approach is referred to in this chapter as the 'balance sheet approach'.

Fourthly, a family court judge overlooked the niceties of the *Lloyds Bank v Rosset* test and instead undertook a survey of the parties' entire course of dealing, with the result that the property rights may be frequently divided equally between them. This approach is referred to as the 'family assets approach'. It has been influential on the subsequent cases.

Fifthly, proprietary estoppel is a remedial doctrine which permits the court to award any remedy it chooses (ranging from mere financial compensation through to the grant of the fee simple absolute in possession in the home) if the claimant has acted to her detriment in reliance on some representation made to her by the defendant.

Sixthly, more recent cases have been concerned to avoid unconscionability. In doing so, the Court of Appeal in particular has sought to reconcile all of the preceding approaches. The courts are prepared to 'supply' the parties' common intention, and more generally to seek to achieve a 'fair' result. This is referred to in this chapter as the 'unconscionability approach'.

These approaches are radically different from one another and offer a fascinating study of the way in which a common law legal system can splinter into a number of different principles even when some of the judges are desperately seeking certainty. The decision of the Court of Appeal in *Oxley v Hiscock* attempted unconvincingly to reconcile these many approaches by requiring that the courts should impute a common intention to the parties, where it could not be proved to have been created expressly, by undertaking a survey of the parties' entire course of dealing and by doing what is fair. This approach was influential in *Stack v Dowden* and in *Jones v Kernott*, although not followed dogmatically. All of these cases should now be read in the light of *Jones v Kernott*.

The approach taken in the following discussion is to conduct a broadly chronological survey of the decided cases, but with those cases divided into their appropriate groups. We begin with the simplest case: where an express trust has been declared over the equitable interest in the property.

15.2 EXPRESS TRUSTS OF HOMES

> *Where there has been an express trust declared over land, the terms of that trust will be decisive of the division of the equitable interest in land. Such a declaration of trust must satisfy s 53(1)(b) of the Law of Property Act 1925.*

When attempting to decide which of a number of co-owners is to acquire equitable rights in the home, the most straightforward factual situation is that where there has been an express declaration of trust dealing with the whole of the equitable interest in the land. Such a trust may arise under the terms of the conveyance of the property to the co-owners,[38] or as a result of an express declaration of trust between the parties,[39] or in a situation in which the property is provided for the co-owners under a pre-existing settlement.[40]

The most straightforward authority in this context is the case of *Goodman v Gallant*,[41] where the conveyance of property included the express trust which allocated the entire equitable interest between the parties. The trust provided that the property was to be held on trust for the parties as joint tenants. The issue arose as to what interest each party had on the break-up of the relationship, given their differing financial contributions towards the property up to that time. It was held by the Court of Appeal that the express trust in the deed of conveyance was decisive of all of the interests of all parties to land, and therefore that the wife took a half of the interest in the property as the deed provided.[42] It was held by Slade LJ in *Goodman v Gallant* that:

> If, however, the relevant conveyance contains an express declaration of trust which comprehensively declares the beneficial interests in the property or its proceeds of sale, there is no room for the application of the doctrine of resulting implied or constructive trusts unless and until the conveyance is set aside or rectified; until that event *the declaration contained in the document speaks for itself.*[43]

In short, there is no need to consider any surrounding circumstances in the context in which the equitable interest in the property has been allocated between the parties on express trust. This principle will apply even where the parties to the conveyance had neither read nor

38 *Goodman v Gallant* [1986] Fam 106. This principle was set out in *Pettitt v Pettitt* [1970] AC 777, at 813, *per* Lord Upjohn and *Gissing v Gissing* [1971] AC 886, at 905, *per* Lord Diplock, and has been accepted in cases such as *Painter v Hutchison* [2007] EWHC 758 (Ch), [2008] BPIR 170. An express trust created between parties establishing that the survivor would be absolutely entitled to the proceeds of sale would be enforced between a married couple and against third parties: *Bindra v Chopra* [2008] EWHC 1715, Smith J.

39 *Lloyds Bank v Rosset* [1990] 1 AC 107.

40 *Pettitt v Pettitt* [1970] AC 777.

41 [1986] FLR 513; *Re Gorman* [1990] 1 WLR 616; *Harwood v Harwood* [1991] 2 FLR 274. A solicitor may even be negligent where she does not ensure that she has properly recorded the parties' intentions as to the beneficial interest in property: *Walker v Hall* [1984] FLR 126, 129, *per* Dillon LJ.

42 A deed will bind all parties to that deed: *City of London Building Society v Flegg* [1988] AC 54. It is suggested that the binding nature of the declaration by way of deed is based on the doctrine of estoppel by deed: Mee, 1999, 32.

43 [1986] Fam 106, 110; emphasis added.

necessarily understood it, provided that the declaration was formally valid.[44] The only exception to this rule would be in a situation in which, under the principle in *Saunders v Vautier*,[45] the absolutely entitled beneficiaries under such a trust had directed that the equitable interest be dealt with by the trustees in some other way. Commonwealth attitudes to this principle are less fixated on the necessary decisiveness of the deed of conveyance.[46] There have been English cases in which the courts have held that statements as to the parties' interests in the conveyance which do not reflect the parties' own intentions may be held not to constitute effective declarations of trust at all.[47] The court will therefore be required to consider whether or not there was a sufficient intention to create an express trust.

It should be remembered that in order for there to be a valid declaration of trust over land, the declaration must comply with s 53(1)(b) of the Law of Property Act 1925: '. . . a declaration of trust respecting any land or any interest therein must be manifested and proved by some writing signed by some person who is able to declare such trust or by his will.' Failure to comply with that formality requirement will lead to a failure to create a valid express trust over land. It should also be remembered that under s 53(2), there is no formality requirement in relation to constructive, resulting or implied trusts.

15.3 RESULTING TRUSTS AND THE EMERGENCE OF COMMON INTENTION

Where a person contributes to the purchase price of the home, an amount of the total equitable interest proportionate to the size of the contribution will be held on resulting trust for that person. Alternatively, this might be expressed as a constructive trust based on the mutual conduct of the parties evidenced by their contribution to the purchase price or the mortgage repayments. However, the role of the resulting trust has been doubted in Stack v Dowden *and in* Jones v Kernott.

15.3.1 Traditional resulting trust principles

The core principle in this area was set out in *Dyer v Dyer*,[48] where Eyre CB held that there is a resulting trust in favour of a person who contributes to the purchase price of property in the following terms: 'The clear result of all the cases, without a single exception, is that the trust of a legal estate . . . results to the man who advances the purchase money.'[49] That resulting trust takes effect at the date of its creation and ordinarily cannot be altered after that time.[50]

---

44 *Pink v Lawrence* (1978) 36 P & CR 98; although there is authority to suggest that there is an exception to this principle where cogent evidence could be advanced to demonstrate that the parties' intentions were other than those contained in the deed: *Huntingford v Hobbs* [1993] 1 FLR 736.

45 (1841) 4 Beav 115.

46 Hayton, 1988, 259.

47 See *Harwood v Harwood* [1991] 2 FLR 274; *Huntingford v Hobbs* [1993] 1 FLR 736; *Stack v Dowden* [2005] EWCA Civ 857; [2006] 1 FLR 254, [8]–[9].

48 (1788) 2 Cox Eq Cas 92. See also *Dewar v Dewar* [1975] 1 WLR 1532, 1537; *Tinsley v Milligan* [1994] 1 AC 340, 371, contributing money to the purchase price raises a presumption that you are to acquire an equitable interest in that property.

49 *Ibid*, 93.

50 *Curley v Parkes* [2004] All ER (D) 344. Cf *Huntingford v Hobbs* [1993] 1 FLR 736, considered below at para 15.5.2.

That principle received support in the speech of Lord Browne-Wilkinson in *Westdeutsche Landesbank Girozentrale v Islington LBC*, when his Lordship recognised the purchase price resulting trust as being one of only two forms of resulting trust in existence.[51] As Lord Browne-Wilkinson held in *Tinsley v Milligan*: 'Although for historical reasons legal estates and equitable estates have differing incidents, the person owning either type of estate has a right in property, a right *in rem* and not merely a right *in personam*.'[52] Therefore, where a person contributes to the purchase price of land, that person will be entitled to a proportionate part of the beneficial interest in that land on resulting trust principles: that right is a proprietary right and not merely a personal claim.[53]

The most straightforward rule in situations where there is no express trust over land is that any person who contributes to the acquisition price of property will acquire an equitable interest in that property. That interest will be expressed as a percentage of the total equitable interest in the property, in proportion to the cost of acquiring the total interest in the property. The only exceptions to such a finding would occur in situations in which the contribution to the purchase price was made by way of a gift of money to the purchasers, or by way of a loan to the purchasers, either of which would negate any presumption that the donor was intended to take an equitable interest in the property;[54] otherwise banks lending money under mortgage agreements would acquire equitable interests in property beyond their statutory right to repossession.[55] Similarly, a gift of money involves an outright transfer to the donee but does not entitle the donor to any rights in property acquired with the money.[56] So, a gift of money to a couple on their wedding day to enable them to buy a house would not grant the donor any interest in the house which the couple subsequently bought with that money in circumstances in which the donor had intended to make an outright transfer of that money.[57] It is always important to ascertain the purpose underlying the advancement of money to acquire the property.

The following sections will consider the detail of the rules relating to the operation of resulting trusts in this area, and in particular the form of contribution which will acquire rights in property on resulting trust principles. That discussion will focus on two pivotal decisions in the House of Lords which altered this area of law throughout the Commonwealth.

One of the principal problems with the resulting trust is that it is supposed to take effect at the date of the purchase of the property and to be set in stone from that date. The problem is that this resulting trust cannot take into account changes in the parties' circumstances in the future. For example, if Arthur has agreed to make all of the mortgage repayments while Bertha pays for half of the purchase price in cash, we would suppose that each of these parties would take the equitable interest equally on resulting trust principles. However, if Arthur became ill and was made redundant five years later, then Bertha would be required to assume responsibility for the mortgage repayments. Consequently, it would seem inequitable to deny Bertha an increased share in the equitable interest in the property. However, to

---

51 [1996] AC 669; *IRC v Eversden* [2003] STC 822; [2003] 75 Tax Cas 340.
52 [1994] 1 AC 340.
53 See also *Walker v Hall* [1984] FLR 126, 133, *per* Dillon LJ.
54 *Grant v Edwards* [1986] Ch 638.
55 This would interfere with the equity of redemption necessary in the law of mortgages. For the mortgagee to acquire an equitable interest would mean that the mortgagor would not be able to recover unencumbered possession of his rights. *Samuel v Jarrah Timber Corp* [1904] AC 323, and so forth, considered in Chapter 23.
56 *Westdeutsche Landesbank Girozentrale v Islington LBC* [1996] AC 669.
57 *McHardy v Warren* [1994] 2 FLR 338.

do this will require a different group of principles from those traditionally associated with the resulting trust precisely because the resulting trust is usually considered to be set in stone at the time of the purchase of the property. Primarily, this will require a constructive trust to re-calibrate the resulting trust, as considered below.[58]

15.3.2 The birth of common intention

The decision of the House of Lords in *Pettitt v Pettitt*[59] was the first to begin the process of staking out a modern code of rules to deal with the allocation of equitable interests in the family home under resulting trust principles. In that case, Mrs Pettitt had been bequeathed the entire beneficial interest in a cottage. Her husband performed renovation works on that cottage which cost him £730, and which were agreed to have increased the value of the property by about £1,000. Mr Pettitt contended that he had acquired some equitable interest in the cottage by virtue of those works, and sought an order under s 17 of the Married Women's Property Act 1882 to reflect those contentions. It was argued by Mr Pettitt that the presumption of advancement would require that the wife be deemed to have intended that some equitable interest pass to the husband in return for the work undertaken in the property.[60] On these facts, Mr Pettitt had not contributed to the purchase price of the property because his wife had been bequeathed it. It was held that Mr Pettitt had not performed sufficiently important works to be entitled to an equitable interest in the property: a stream of thought which persists to this day and which denies equitable interests to those who perform only minor works of repair or alteration and who have not contributed directly to the purchase price of the property.

Previously, the law on resulting trusts held that there should be a presumption to the effect that any transaction between husband and wife should raise a presumption that the husband intended to make a gift to his wife. As to the operation of the presumptions of advancement,[61] Lord Reid held that they should be taken to belong to a different era and should not have any place in deciding modern cases concerning the family home. This approach has been supported by the Court of Appeal in *Lavelle v Lavelle*[62] to the effect that the court should instead seek to ascertain the real intention of the transferor of the property. As discussed in Chapter 11, the Equality Act 2010 has abolished the presumption of advancement. However, vestiges of the old outlook continued in *Pettitt v Pettitt*. It was held by Lord Upjohn that: 'Nor can the meaning of the [Married Women's Property Act 1882] have changed merely by reason of a change in social outlook since the date of its enactment; it must continue to bear the meaning which upon its true construction in the light of the

---

58 This was the approach taken in *Huntingford v Hobbs* [1993] 1 FLR 736 and in Australia in *Giumelli v Giumelli* [1999] HCA 10.

59 [1970] AC 777.

60 While criticised in *Pettitt v Pettitt* [1970] 1 AC 777, 793, *per* Lord Reid, the presumption is defended by Lord Upjohn, and considered by Deane J to be too well entrenched to be completely ignored: *Calverley v Green* (1984) 155 CLR 242, 266.

61 It should be recalled from the discussion of resulting trust that a presumption of advancement operates when a husband transfers property to a wife to the effect that the husband is presumed, unless the contrary can be proved, to have intended to make a gift of the property to the wife, as opposed to requiring that his wife hold that property on resulting trust for him or be required to deal with it in some other way: see section 11.4.2.

62 [2004] EWCA Civ 223, *per* Lord Phillips MR. See also *Kyriakides v Pippas* [2004] EWHC 646 (Ch), [2004] 2 P & CR D10; and *Crossley v Crossley* [2005] EWCA Civ 1581, [9], *per* Sir Peter Gibson, CA.

relevant surrounding circumstances it bore at that time.'[63] In other words, in Lord Upjohn's opinion, the statute of 1882 was to be interpreted in accordance with the presumption and the social mores of the time in which it was enacted. For Lord Upjohn it was not enough to argue that the world had changed between 1882 and 1970, and that the courts should treat rights in the home differently as a result.[64]

The presumption of advancement between husband and wife belonged to an era in which men were expected to care for women on the basis that women were not presumed to have property or incomes of their own. It should be recalled that it was only in 1969 that English law accepted, finally, that wives were not to be considered simply as the shadows of their husbands – a development which meant that wives were entitled to have rights in property separate from their husbands for the first time.[65] Lord Reid proposed a more enlightened attitude to rights between spouses in the family home. In *Pettitt v Pettitt*, it was considered that, for the first time, the court should consider all the surrounding circumstances in recognising the existence of rights in the home, even at a time when wives did not acquire rights independent of their husbands.

A number of important questions arose in this appeal. The first issue was whether a spouse could acquire rights in property by doing acts or defraying expenditure which enabled the other spouse to maintain the home. The simple answer was that only expenditure directed at the acquisition of rights in the property at the time of purchase would generate any such equitable interest.[66] Simply paying for repair or maintenance work to the premises would not constitute expenditure directed solely at the acquisition of rights in the property. The focus of this thinking was therefore clearly on the direct acquisition of property rights, and not on any more general question of justice between the parties to a marriage or other relationship.

The second issue was as to the status of agreements between spouses. It had long been a vexed question whether or not spouses could form enforceable contracts between themselves – such contracts having been considered immoral and contrary to the notion that husbands and wives formed one legal unit which could not have rights against one another. However, as Lord Reid decided, just because an agreement may not be enforceable in itself does not mean that the performance of an act undertaken in reliance on such an agreement does not have legal consequences. So, for example, even if husbands and wives could not form contracts between themselves as to the use of their home, their common intentions as to the use of that home might raise rights in equity.

The third issue was therefore the extent to which the parties can reach some agreement as to the allocation of the total equitable interest in the property, without forming a binding contract or a formally valid express trust, and make that agreement binding both between themselves and on third parties. As we will see at para 15.3.3 below in relation to the case of *Gissing v Gissing*,[67] the House of Lords came to accept that such an agreement would be enforceable in equity where it constituted a 'common intention' formed between the parties. The nature of that common intention was said to be either as to the equitable interest which

---

63 *Ibid*, 813.
64 This despite Philip Larkin's lament that the 1960s in particular constituted such a sea change in our social life: 'Sexual intercourse began/In nineteen sixty-three/(Which was rather late for me)/Between the end of the *Chatterley* ban/And the Beatles' first LP.' Larkin, 'Annus Mirabilis', 1974.
65 *Caunce v Caunce* [1969] 1 WLR 286.
66 [1970] AC 777, 794, *per* Lord Reid.
67 [1971] AC 886.

each party would receive ('interest consensus'), or as to the size of the contribution which each party would make to the purchase price of the property ('money consensus'), as conceived of by Bagnall J in *Cowcher v Cowcher*.[68] These various forms of common intention are considered in more detail below.

The final issue is whether or not the law of restitution of unjust enrichment (as formulated in the book *The Law of Restitution* by Goff and Jones shortly before this appeal in 1966) has any part to play in deciding whether or not any person who has expended money ought to be entitled to some equitable interest in return. Briefly put, this claim would have meant that one party to a relationship could have claimed an interest in the home if the other party was unjustly enriched in some way by the first party's actions, for example, where the first party repaired or maintained the property. Lord Reid considered such an action would result only in a 'money claim' in any event: that is, a right to be paid an amount of money to compensate that person for the work done rather than a 'beneficial interest in the property which has been improved'.[69]

On the facts Mr Pettitt's claim failed because the improvements were of a purely ephemeral nature[70] and because 'do-it-yourself' jobs in themselves ought not to ground rights in property.[71] Therefore, it is only contributions to the purchase price of the property, or substantial financial contributions to the property itself, which will grant rights under resulting trust to the contributor. The limitation on the forms of contribution formed part of the judicial concern that insubstantial contributions should not be accepted as creating rights in property. Adopting the words of Coke, Lord Hodson suggested that total judicial discretion in this area would not be appropriate: 'this would be to substitute the uncertain and crooked cord of discretion for the golden and straight metwand of the law.'[72] In other words, the law should always strive for certainty and principle as opposed to permitting judges to do as they thought fit in any case. These words may appear ironic given the complexities which were to follow.

15.3.3 The central text

The leading case in this area still appears to be *Gissing v Gissing*.[73] I say 'appears' because the case law takes a variety of different directions, as we shall see below. While there have been a number of decisions in the House of Lords and Court of Appeal coming after *Gissing*, as well as significant developments in a number of Commonwealth jurisdictions, all those judges have used *Gissing* as a starting-point for judgments which have then tended to contradict one another.[74] As such, this decision has become the central text in this area, which establishes the principle that the common intention of the parties is to be taken as the root of any equitable interest in the property. From that seed equity has taken many different directions.

---

68 [1972] 1 WLR 425.
69 [1970] AC 777, 795, *per* Lord Reid.
70 *Ibid*, 796, *per* Lord Reid.
71 A view expressed variously in cases like *Nixon v Nixon* [1969] 1 WLR 1676; *Burns v Burns* [1984] Ch 317.
72 *Pettitt v Pettitt* [1970] AC 777, 808. I admit I do not know precisely what a 'metwand' is, nor can I find a dictionary definition of it, but I rather like the expression: it indicates an intention that equity in this area should be a straight staff which is principled, reliable and very English.
73 [1971] AC 886, [1970] 3 WLR 255.
74 Cases as different as *Lloyds Bank v Rosset* [1991] 1 AC 107 and *Midland Bank v Cooke* [1995] 4 All ER 562 have all prayed *Gissing* in aid.

Mrs Gissing had worked as a secretary and married in 1935. Her husband could not find work after the 1939–45 war, but she procured him a position with the firm where she worked. Her husband did well and prospered in his new position. The couple bought a house in 1951 which was registered in the husband's name. The purchase price was provided predominantly by a mortgage in the husband's name together with a loan from the couple's employers. Mrs Gissing spent £220 on laying a lawn at the house and on furnishings for the house. Her husband left her in 1961 to live with another woman. The wife sought a declaration that she had some equitable interest in the property.

It was held, unanimously, that Mrs Gissing acquired no beneficial interest in the property on the grounds that she had made no contribution to the purchase price of the property. Expending money on ephemeral items was not the same as contributing to the purchase price. The House of Lords in *Gissing v Gissing* accepted that the common intention of the parties played an important part, but the court was concerned that such common intentions should not be too loosely defined. Lord Diplock, significantly, held that *Pettitt* was not correct to the extent that his Lordship found it impossible to impute a common intention in circumstances where there was no direct evidence of any express agreement between the parties.[75] As a general statement, Lord Diplock acknowledged that: '[The parties'] common intention is more likely to have been concerned with the economic realities of the transaction than with the unfamiliar technicalities of the English law of legal and equitable interests in land.'[76] These *dicta* indicate that the court is to look to the circumstances as the parties saw them and not to restrict the parties to any particular legal formula. This approach recognises that, in the detail of their lives, ordinary people will not tend to be overly formalistic in their dealings with their homes. Consequently, a common intention can be imputed to the parties by reference to the evidence or inferred from their conduct, as well as from direct discussions between the cohabitees.[77]

The importance of the decision in *Gissing v Gissing* is that it breaks out of the mould which restricts the parties only to the acquisition of rights under resulting trusts. Instead of restricting the parties only to rights which flowed directly from a contribution to the purchase price, the focus on the broader common intention of the parties meant that there could be some other factor which would permit the founding of some equitable interest. Significantly, Lord Diplock's *dicta* restricted the possible forms of such common intention. Nevertheless, to permit rights to be formed on the basis of common intention, even if only a narrow range of intentions can be included,[78] does mean that the parties are not limited only to rights founded on the *Dyer v Dyer* principle. As a result, there is less formality required in the creation of such trust arrangements in an attempt to recognise and enforce the genuine, underlying intention which is constituted by the relationship between the parties. The adoption of the language of 'common intention' by Lord Diplock opened the way for the use of the constructive trust for the granting of rights in land, rather than the more mathematical precision of the purchase price resulting trust which would grant them only an equitable interest in proportion to the plaintiff's contribution to the purchase price. This use of the constructive trust has been adopted by the courts in preference to the resulting trust – perhaps, in part, because of the comparatively large discretion which is given to the court.

75 [1971] AC 886, 904.
76 *Ibid*, 906.
77 *Lloyds Bank v Rosset* [1991] 1 AC 107.
78 As considered in section 15.4 below.

15.4 CONSTRUCTIVE TRUSTS – ACQUISITION OF EQUITABLE INTERESTS BY CONDUCT OR AGREEMENT

Where a person contributes to the purchase price of the home, this might be expressed as a constructive trust based on the mutual conduct of the parties evidenced by their contribution to the purchase price or the mortgage repayments ('common intention constructive trust by mutual conduct').

Where there is no such contribution nor an express declaration of trust, the equitable interest in the home will be allocated according to the common intention of the parties by means of constructive trust ('common intention constructive trust by agreement'), based on an express agreement between the parties which need not constitute an express declaration of trust.

15.4.1 Foundations of the common intention constructive trust

Roots of common intention constructive trusts

As considered above, the speeches in the House of Lords in *Gissing v Gissing*[79] created the possibility of looking behind the formal arrangements between the parties to uncover their informal, common intentions as to the allocation of rights in their home. It was held that this common intention ought to be the element which was decisive of the division of equitable interests between them. As mentioned above, the use of the constructive trust gives the court greater leeway in declaring the respective interests of the parties, when compared with the resulting trust which measures their cash contribution without more. However, the problem remains that the intentions of the parties will remain unclear in many cases. The courts are therefore often asked to allocate equitable interests in circumstances in which it is very difficult to discern whether or not the parties ever did manifest or form a common intention. So, bound up in this discussion is a shadow of Lord Hodson's sentiments in *Pettitt v Pettitt*,[80] quoted at para 15.3.2 above, that the law should strive for certainty (to preserve its 'golden metwand') and not permit too much uncertainty so that judges are able to decide cases on an entirely discretionary basis without reference to principle. Therefore, the form of constructive trust which is to be used is an institutional constructive trust as opposed to a remedial constructive trust.[81] Again, we see the perennial to-ing and fro-ing between certainty and flexibility.

Mapping constructive trusts

The decision of Bagnall J in *Cowcher v Cowcher*[82] sought to conceptualise the different possible approaches to the form of constructive trust used in cases of common intention. This approach had not been followed explicitly for some time until the decision of the Court of Appeal in *Midland Bank v Cooke*,[83] where Waite LJ adopted it as a suitable exposition of

---

79 [1971] AC 886.
80 [1970] AC 777.
81 *Westdeutsche Landesbank Girozentrale v Islington LBC* [1996] AC 669 – as considered in Chapter 12.
82 [1972] 1 All ER 948, 948–51, 954–55.
83 [1995] 4 All ER 562.

the principles in *Gissing v Gissing*. It is considered here as a reasonable introduction to the development of the principle of constructive trust in this context. Bagnall J began by explaining that proprietary rights are *not* to be determined simply on the basis of what is considered to be 'reasonable, fair and just in all the circumstances', thus underlining the courts' determination to avoid the development of a remedial constructive trust approach in relation to family homes. That a decision appeared to be 'unfair' did not make it 'unjust'. Consequently, the courts ought not to be concerned to do fairness between the parties, but rather to uncover their real intentions and reflect them through the constructive trust.

It was held, furthermore, that the concepts of resulting and constructive trust could be taken to be synonymous, although the category of constructive trust ought more usually to be reserved for situations in which a fiduciary had sought to benefit from his office. The heart of the analysis is then that the cases resolve into the two basic categories considered at para 15.3.2 above: 'interest consensus' and 'money consensus'. To take each concept one at a time: the *interest consensus* constituted an expression of the common intention of the parties as to the extent of one another's interest in the property regardless of their financial contributions. The interest consensus would therefore be an agreement as to the equitable interest which each party is to receive, which would be derived from the conduct of the parties if no express agreement could be proved. Such conduct need not be evidenced solely at the date of acquisition but could also develop subsequently.[84] The *money consensus* would derive from the parties agreeing how much money each would contribute to the purchase price of the property. The money consensus is not derived from conduct, but rather is based on an express agreement as to the amount of money provided by each party for the purchase of the property.[85]

This form of common intention constructive trust appears to be a mixture of a resulting trust (which measures the parties' contributions to the purchase price of the property) and a constructive trust properly so-called (which would evaluate the conscionability of allowing one party to take an unfair benefit from some understanding reached between the parties as to ownership of the property). The common intention constructive trust is different from the model of constructive trust considered in Chapter 12, in that the leading authority on the operation of the common intention constructive trust, *Lloyds Bank v Rosset*[86] considered immediately below, restricts its operation to a particular form of conduct to do with contribution to the purchase price and does not allow it to operate on the basis of a general test of good conscience (as do the courts in Australia).[87]

15.4.2 *Lloyds Bank v Rosset* – the common intention constructive trust

The context of Lloyds Bank v Rosset

The decision in the House of Lords in *Lloyds Bank v Rosset*[88] both tidied and confused this area of law. The case law surrounding the decision in *Gissing v Gissing* offered a scattered

---

84 Although this is not permitted in *Lloyds Bank v Rosset* [1991] 1 AC 107, it is accepted in cases like *McHardy v Warren* [1994] 2 FLR 338.
85 *Springette v Defoe* (1992) 24 HLR 552, [1992] 2 FLR 388.
86 [1991] 1 AC 107.
87 Considered below at para 15.10.2.
88 [1991] 1 AC 107.

reading of the nature of the constructive trust. The decisions in cases such as *Cowcher v Cowcher*,[89] *Grant v Edwards*[90] and *Coombes v Smith*[91] offered a variety of readings of the concept of 'common intention' which ranged from divisions between the forms of consensus, the need for common intention to be coupled with detriment, and proprietary estoppel respectively. In the light of this welter of contradictory and difficult authority, there was some momentum for rationalisation of the law. Particularly in an area of such great social importance, there was also some momentum for clearing up the difficulties and making the law more straightforward. Just such a rationalisation was set out in the leading speech of Lord Bridge in *Lloyds Bank v Rosset*.[92] Lord Bridge appointed himself the task of setting out the terms on which a claimant may acquire an equitable interest in the home on grounds of 'constructive trust or proprietary estoppel'. It is worth noting that the form of constructive trust set out in this area bears very little relation to the general constructive trust which was set out in *Westdeutsche Landesbank v Islington*[93] to operate in all other contexts.[94]

The facts of *Lloyds Bank v Rosset* were as follows. A semi-derelict farmhouse was put in H's name. The house was to be the family home and renovated as a joint venture. H's wife, W, oversaw all of the building work. W had been led to believe that the property was to be acquired without a mortgage. However, H did acquire the property with a mortgage registered in his sole name. H fell into arrears on the mortgage and the mortgagee bank sought repossession in lieu of money owed by H under the mortgage. W sought to resist an order for sale in favour of the mortgagee, *inter alia*, because of her equitable interest in the property which she claimed granted her an overriding interest on grounds of actual occupation.[95] It was held that W had acquired no equitable interest in the property on the basis that activities like supervising renovation work were too peripheral to acquire an equitable interest. Lord Bridge delivered the only speech in the House of Lords, in which he sought to redraw the basis on which a common intention constructive trust would be formed. The test fell into two halves and therefore created two distinct forms of common intention constructive trust: common intention based on conduct; and common intention based on agreement.

Common intention evidenced by agreement

Building on the advances made in *Gissing v Gissing*,[96] the court accepted that common intention could arise from some agreement between the parties. The issue is therefore as to the form of agreement which the parties must reach to constitute a trust. If that intention needed to be in writing then it might constitute evidence of an express declaration of trust. It is the exceptional case in which the parties have gone to such pains to make their intentions so clear. In most of the cases there will only be evidence as to conversations between the parties, which may or may not have been explicit about their intentions as to rights in the property. On the basis that such an agreement would not be sufficient to constitute an express

---

89 [1972] 1 All ER 948.
90 [1986] Ch 638.
91 [1986] 1 WLR 808.
92 [1991] 1 AC 107.
93 [1996] AC 669.
94 See section 12.1 *et seq*.
95 Land Registration Act 1925, s 70(1)(g); see now the Land Registration Act 2002, Sched 3, para 2.
96 [1971] AC 886.

trust on the ground that it would not satisfy s 53(1)(b) of the Law of Property Act 1925, it would have to be enforced by some form of trust implied by law.[97]

The first limb of the *Rosset* test provided that there would be an agreement between the parties sufficient to constitute a common intention on the following terms, in the words of Lord Bridge:[98]

> The first and fundamental question which must always be resolved is whether, independently of any inference to be drawn from the conduct of the parties in the course of sharing the house as their home and managing their joint affairs, there has at any time prior to acquisition, or exceptionally at some later date, been any agreement, arrangement or understanding reached between them that the property is to be shared beneficially.

This is the court's first inquiry on this model of the common intention principle.[99] The type of situation which is envisaged by Lord Bridge is an occasion on which the couple sat down to discuss how the rights in the property were to be divided between them. Perhaps his Lordship had in mind an intense conversation over dinner one evening, Vivaldi playing on the stereo and the pepper pots strewn across the tabletop to represent the parties' various interests. The issue remains as to the type of conversation or consensus which would be sufficient to constitute such an 'agreement'. It is clear that it need not form a binding contract.[100] In the words of Lord Bridge:[101]

> The finding of an agreement or arrangement to share in this sense can only, I think, be based on evidence of express discussions between the partners, however imperfectly remembered and however imprecise their terms.

Two points are worthy of note. First, the discussions are expected to have been carried out in advance of the purchase. Subsequent discussions between the parties are not important, or at least are of less importance. It is suggested that this approach does not seem to recognise the reality of relationships in which intentions alter over the years with the birth of children, the death of family members, the bane of unemployment and the thousand other shocks that flesh is heir to. Similarly, the agreement is related to each property individually (subject to what is said below about deposits and the use of sale proceeds of previous properties). Suppose a couple buy a house, then sell it and move to a second house: it is not clear to what extent conversations about the second house can override agreements formulated as to title in the first house, although it is clear that the courts will impute intentions relevant to the first house to subsequent purchases.[102]

Secondly, the assumption is that there are express discussions, rather than an emerging but unspoken intention between the parties. For example, where one party ceases work to bring up children, thus interrupting the ability to earn money to be applied to the mortgage instalments, the intention of the parties will be impliedly recalibrated when the other partner assumes the burden of paying off the mortgage. It is unlikely that there will be an express

97   Law of Property Act 1925, s 53(2).
98   [1990] 1 All ER 1111, 1116.
99   *Savill v Goodall* [1993] 1 FLR 755.
100   See now in any event the Law of Property (Miscellaneous Provisions) Act 1989, s 2.
101   [1990] 1 All ER 1111, 1117.
102   *McHardy v Warren* [1994] 2 FLR 338.

discussion as to *rights in the property* which each is intended to receive, although it is likely that the parties will adjust their lifestyle to accommodate the need to meet their household expenses and so forth. The second limb of the test is the only one which permits for this type of flexibility, which is considered immediately below.

An example of such an agreement would be where a husband and wife prepared a transfer form such that the entire interest in the property would be transferred to the wife. In the event the form was not presented to the Land Registry and therefore there was no transfer at common law. However, the court was prepared to find that this was evidence of the parties' intentions to transfer title to the wife.[103] It is presumed that the result would have been different if the failure to present the form was a result of the parties having changed their minds: nevertheless, it would still have constituted evidence that *at one time* their intention was to transfer rights to the wife. It would usually be the case that the intentions of the parties are more difficult to isolate. So where a woman left Poland, thus 'burning her boats', to come and live in England with the defendant, it was held that she had understood that she would have a home for life even though there was no demonstrable intention that all of the rights in the property be transferred to her. Therefore, the woman would be entitled to have the property held on trust for her occupation during her lifetime.[104] In general terms, the courts will be reluctant to draw inferences of such agreements if they are not evident on the facts of the case.[105]

The High Court in *Legder-Beadell v Peach*[106] has, however, held that there was sufficient ground for granting a constructive trust when a house was acquired and put in A's name on the basis that the parties would decide later whether or not other parties who had put up the purchase price would have a beneficial interest in that property and, if so, what form that interest would take.[107] It was held on the facts that it was appropriate to apply a constructive trust, as opposed to a resulting trust in these circumstances, to give effect to the parties' developing intentions. Interestingly, of course, this contravenes the literal force of Lord Bridge's *dicta* in *Rosset* to the effect that this agreement must have been formed before the acquisition of the property: a point which was not considered in the High Court. Instead the court relied on the 'unconscionability approach' case of *Oxley v Hiscock*,[108] as considered in detail below in section 15.8, which permitted a survey of the whole course of the parties' dealings so as to reach a fair result. This is just a hint of the uncertainty which will yet attend the otherwise clear prescriptions of the House of Lords in *Rosset* when describing the common intention constructive trust. A draft trust (which was never executed) setting out the parties' equitable interests has been accepted by the Court of Appeal as being evidence which may be used in establishing the contents of the parties' agreement;[109] although presumably this could only be used if the parties' intentions could not be shown to have changed from the contents of that draft trust.

---

103 *Barclays Bank v Khaira* [1993] 1 FLR 343.
104 *Ungarian v Lesnoff* [1990] Ch 206 – under the Settled Land Act 1925. Also *Costello v Costello* [1996] 1 FLR 805. Cf *Dent v Dent* [1996] 1 All ER 659.
105 '. . . our trust law does not allow property rights to be affected by telepathy', *Springette v Defoe* [1992] 2 FLR 388, 392, *per* Steyn LJ; *Evans v Hayward* [1995] 2 FLR 511. Although the family assets approach is prepared to permit such unspoken intentions to be enforced, as considered at section 15.6 below.
106 [2006] All ER (D) 245.
107 *Ledger-Beadell v Peach* [2006] All ER (D) 245, Nicholas Strauss QC.
108 [2005] Fam 211.
109 *Williamson v Sheikh* [2008] EWCA Civ 990.

Nevertheless, the principal line of cases has required clear evidence of an agreement, arrangement or understanding.[110] So, when a claimant sought an equitable interest in the defendant's home on the basis that she had lent money to the defendant's business, it was held that there had been no agreement, arrangement or understanding that the claimant would acquire any interest in the defendant's home and therefore the claimant acquired no such interest.[111] Equally, if a widowed mother asked her 19-year-old son to co-sign a mortgage over their home, that would not in itself suggest an agreement that the son should have an equitable interest in that home when his signature had only been added to make the mortgage easier to obtain and when he made few or no payments at all towards the property latterly.[112] Evidently, where there is no evidence to substantiate the existence of an agreement, the court will not create one out of thin air.[113]

Common intention evidenced by conduct

The second form of common intention constructive trust arises in the absence of an express agreement or arrangement to share the beneficial ownership. Where there is no such agreement the court will consider the conduct of the parties. In this situation it is payments towards the initial purchase price of the property or towards mortgage instalments 'which justify the inference necessary for the creation of a constructive trust'. As Lord Bridge set out the test:[114]

> In sharp contrast with [the common intention constructive trust by agreement] is the very different one where there is no evidence to support a finding of an agreement or arrangement to share, however reasonable it might have been for the parties to reach such an arrangement if they had applied their minds to the question, and where the court must rely entirely on the conduct of the parties both as the basis from which to infer a common intention to share the property beneficially and as the conduct relied on to give rise to a constructive trust. In this situation direct contributions to the purchase price by the partner who is not the legal owner, whether initially or by payment of mortgage instalments, will readily justify the inference necessary to the creation of a constructive trust. But as I read the authorities it is at least extremely doubtful whether anything less will do.

Thus the parties' conduct in respect of the property is capable of forming a common intention sufficient for the finding of a constructive trust. The type of conduct envisaged by Lord Bridge is, however, very limited. He has in mind 'direct contributions to the purchase price'

---

110 See *Kean v McDonald* [2006] All ER (D) 348 where the parties agreed in 1997 to transfer title in property on payment of £10,000: this agreement was found to constitute a common intention constructive trust, even though the parties seemed to have agreed that there would be an outright transfer of title in the property as opposed to a trust, and even though there had not been a proper conveyance of title at common law (simply a purported payment of money further to the agreement, which would not have constituted a valid contract for a sale of an interest in land). Furthermore, it did not matter to the court (Crystal QC), it seems, that some of the parties were involved in criminal activities and that the Crown Prosecution Service were objecting to the constructive trust. No point was taken by the court as to whether or not the parties here had acted with clean hands.

111 *Koulias v Makris* [2005] All ER (D) 352; *Popely v Heltfield Properties Ltd* [2005] All ER (D) 287; *Lightfoot v Lightfoot-Brown* [2005] All ER (D) 115.

112 *Abbey National v Stringer* [2006] EWCA Civ 338.

113 *Churchill v Roach* [2002] EWHC 3230, [2004] 3 FCR 744.

114 [1990] 1 All ER 1111, 1117.

only. Any other conduct which indicates a common intention to own the property jointly in some way, such as selecting the decorations together or sending out invitations to the house-warming party in joint names, will not be sufficient to demonstrate a common intention.

One further problem arises: most people are not able to afford to buy their homes for cash and are therefore required to take out mortgages which are paid back over a period of (usually) 25 years. In recognition of the reality of those families who finance the purchase of the property by mortgage, rather than by cash purchase, Lord Bridge tells us that it is sufficient for the contributions to be made either 'initially [that is, by cash purchase or cash deposit] or by payment of mortgage instalments'.[115] The limitation of these means of contribution is underlined when Lord Bridge explicitly holds that 'it is at least extremely doubtful whether anything less will do'. It is suggested below that this last sentence is of pivotal importance.

It is assumed, but not explicit in the judgment, that it is possible for B to acquire rights in the property when B begins to pay off the mortgage instalments as a result of A becoming unemployed or taking maternity leave to bring up children.[116] This issue is considered in sections 15.5 and 15.6 below in the 'balance sheet approach' and the 'family assets approach'.

The ghost of this approach, it is suggested, lives on in the line of authority which led to *Oxley v Hiscock* and *Stack v Dowden*: it is clearly antipathetic to the sort of formalism seen in *Lloyds Bank v Rosset*. Nevertheless, the decision in *Jones v Kernott* seems concerned with the same task of introducing order as the court in *Lloyds Bank v Rosset*.

The need for detriment in common intention constructive trust

It was held in *Rosset* that it is also necessary for the claimant to demonstrate that she has suffered detriment before being able to demonstrate a common intention constructive trust. In *Grant v Edwards*,[117] Browne-Wilkinson VC sought to expatiate on the core principles of the common intention constructive trust, set out by Lord Diplock in *Gissing v Gissing*. In his opinion, there were three important principles to be analysed:

(a) the nature of the substantive right, which required that there must be a common intention that the claimant was to have a beneficial interest *and* that the claimant had acted to her detriment;

(b) proof of the common intention, requiring direct evidence or inferred common intention;

(c) the quantification of the size of that right.

The formulation of the principle which was set out by Browne-Wilkinson VC in *Grant v Edwards* was as follows:[118]

If the legal estate in the joint home is vested in only one of the parties ('the legal owner') the other party ('the claimant'), in order to establish a beneficial interest, has to establish a constructive trust by showing that it would be inequitable for the legal owner to claim sole beneficial ownership. This requires two matters to be demonstrated: (a) that there

---

115 [1990] 1 All ER 1111, 1117.
116 *Ibid.*
117 [1986] Ch 638. See now also *Hyett v Stanley* [2003] EWCA Civ 942, [2003] 3 FCR 253; *Lalani v Crump* [2007] EWHC 47.
118 [1986] Ch 638, 654D.

was a common intention that both should have a beneficial interest; (b) that the claimant has acted to his or her detriment on the basis of that common intention.

The requirement for detriment in the context was mirrored in *Midland Bank v Dobson*,[119] where it was held insufficient to create an equitable interest that there be simply a common intention unless there was also some detriment suffered by the claimant.

The importance of detriment was stressed by the Court of Appeal in *Chan Pu Chan v Leung Kam Ho*.[120] In that case, the defendant had promised that he would leave his wife and live with the claimant. He bought a house in Surrey for them both to occupy. The defendant appeared to have promised the claimant shares in both the house and the business. The court had clear difficulty establishing the facts here and the trial judge considered the defendant to be a liar. The claimant agreed to work for the defendant's business projects and latterly acquired a general power of attorney over his affairs while he served a prison sentence for bribery. The mortgage on the property, which had been organised through companies controlled by the defendant such that the legal title of the house was put into the name of one of these companies, was paid off using profits from the business. Subsequently the claimant obtained a court order excluding the defendant from the property on grounds of his violence. The issue arose whether or not she had acquired any rights in the house. It was held that she had acted to her detriment in working to maintain the defendant's businesses and that she had acted in reliance on his promise to marry her. In consequence, she acquired a right in the property seemingly both because her work in the businesses gave her some entitlement through the funds which discharged the mortgage, and also because of her reliance on his statement that she would have an equal share in the property and in the businesses.

In *Grant v Edwards*,[121] which was relied upon heavily in *Chan v Leung*, it was held that there must be an agreement or conduct on the part of the non-property-owning party which could only be explained as being directed at acquiring rights in property. While the claimant in that case had not made a financial contribution directly towards the purchase of the property, the defendant had made excuses to her for not putting her name on the legal title, which was held to indicate an intention that she would otherwise have acquired rights in the property but for the defendant's subterfuge. In short, he had sought to keep her off the title through deceit, indicating that otherwise she would probably have had formal rights.[122]

Further, it was found that her contributions to family expenses were more than would otherwise have been expected in the circumstances and thereby enabled the defendant to make the mortgage payments. It was held that this behaviour could not have been expected unless she understood that she would acquire an interest in the property. Consequently, she acquired an equitable interest by dint of facilitating payment for the house and in accordance with, effectively, an imputed common intention. The roots of the modern approach are discernible in this double-barrelled focus both on any agreement made between the parties and also on an analysis of the parties' conduct in respect of the purchase of the property and on its mortgage repayments.

The somewhat heretical conclusion reached in that case was that it is possible that purely personal acts will be evidence of an intention that a proprietary interest is to be acquired by

---

119   [1986] 1 FLR 171.
120   [2003] 1 FLR 23.
121   [1986] Ch 638; *Lloyd v Dugdale* [2002] 2 P & CR 13.
122   *Eves v Eves* [1975] 1 WLR 1338.

the claimant. However, *Coombes v Smith*[123] took the view that for the claimant to leave her partner to have children with the defendant would not lead to the acquisition of a right in property because that was purely personal detriment, not the sort necessary to acquire rights in property. As considered below, it is generally the case that detriment which is suffered merely as a part of a claimant's personal life (for example, where that person leaves her current partner on the promise that the defendant will give her a right in property) will not be sufficient to grant a right in property. Nonetheless, it must be noted that detriment is an important part of demonstrating rights under a common intention constructive trust – a feature which makes it appear similar to proprietary estoppel.[124]

With an admirable affection for the strict rules of company law, the Court of Final Appeal in Hong Kong has held that where a property is owned by a company then a human being cannot make representations to a woman which will bind the company if that woman suffers detriment in reliance on that representation.[125] That is so even if the representor is a shareholder in that company because under company law the company itself is a person distinct from its shareholders.[126]

15.4.3 Application of the common intention constructive trust concept

Approaches in the wake of Rosset

The courts have not slavishly followed the very clear test set out in *Rosset*.[127] While that test may not be entirely desirable on principle, as discussed at para 15.4.4 below, it does have the merit of greater clarity than many of the other decided cases. The decisions in subsequent cases have tended to favour an approach based on calculation of the proportionate interests acquired by the parties from the cash amounts which they have contributed to the purchase of the property. For example, the decision of the Court of Appeal in *Huntingford v Hobbs*,[128] particularly in the judgment of Sir Christopher Slade, demonstrated an attitude based not on 'an abstract notion of justice' but on a rough approximation of what each party had contributed with adjustments for outstanding obligations: this approach will be dubbed below the 'balance sheet approach', which seeks merely to add up all the contributions made by the various parties to the household and then to calculate them as a proportion of the total expenditure on the property.

In *Huntingford v Hobbs*,[129] there were two contributors to the purchase price of the property: one party had contributed cash, whereas the other had undertaken to pay off the mortgage on the property. In part the Court of Appeal, without express reference to the doctrinal issues considered above, was relying on resulting trust principles to grant interests equivalent to the cash contributions made. However, the court did not restrict itself to resulting trust principles. Rather, it also inferred a common intention from the conduct of the parties that

---

123   [1986] 1 WLR 808.
124   As considered below at section 15.7.
125   *Luo v The Estate of Hui* (2007) 11 ITELR 218.
126   *Salomon v A Salomon & Co Ltd* [1897] AC 22.
127   Although there are cases which have applied *Lloyds Bank v Rosset*: eg, *Ivin v Blake* [1995] 1 FLR 70; *Buggs v Buggs* [2003] EWHC 1538 (Ch) and *McKenzie v McKenzie* [2003] EWHC 601. There are more cases such as *H v M* [2004] 2 FLR 16, which did not cite *Rosset* at all.
128   [1993] 1 FCR 45.
129   *Ibid.*

the plaintiff would be responsible for the mortgage, and therefore that it would accord him with an interest in proportion to the size of that undertaking. This was despite the fact that both parties were legally responsible for the mortgage – that is, while only the person who makes the repayments is awarded the proprietary rights, both are potentially legally liable under the terms of the mortgage contract. The court preferred to concentrate on the parties' agreement as to who should pay off the mortgage, rather than on their respective legal obligations which could have made them liable to the mortgagee to make repayments. It is clear that the court will not consider itself bound simply by the cash contributions made by the parties, but rather will also consider any other understanding reached between them as to the equitable interests which they intended each to receive.[130]

The further issue which arose was the need to account for the amount of the mortgage which had been paid off at that time, and to discount that part of the mortgage which remained to be paid off in the future. It was contended that it would have been unfair for the party responsible for the mortgage payments to claim entitlement to an equitable interest which reflected a part of the mortgage amount not yet paid off. It was held that the plaintiff was to have his interest reduced to account for the amount of the mortgage which remained outstanding and which would be met by the other party. The basis on which this decision was reached is therefore a mixture of the resulting trust and the discretionary features of the common intention constructive trusts.

Huntingford v Hobbs[131] reflects the somewhat scattered approach that the courts have taken to the application of these principles.[132] By contradistinction, in *Midland Bank v Cooke*,[133] it was held that a common intention constructive trust can arise where H and W equally provide a deposit on a house purchased in the name of one or both of them. The dispute arose in circumstances in which H and W acquired property in H's name, and in which W had signed a consent form agreeing to her interests being relegated to those of the mortgagee. W had contributed nothing to the purchase price but contributed the deposit for the purchase of the property equally with H. The question arose whether or not she had any beneficial interest in the property in any event. It was held by Waite LJ that the court is required to survey the whole course of dealing between the parties. Furthermore, it was held that the court is not required to confine its survey to the limited range of acts of direct contribution of the sort that are needed to found a beneficial interest in the first place: which is precisely what *Rosset* did require. If that survey is inconclusive, Waite LJ held that the court should fall back on the maxim 'equality is equity'. It is difficult to know whether these approaches could be used to find sufficient intention to displace the provisions of an express trust in a conveyance,[134] given that the principles of proprietary estoppel, for example, are so

---

130   *Drake v Whipp* [1996] 1 FLR 826 – where a contribution of one-fifth of the purchase price (on a net basis) was enlarged to one-third of the entire equitable interest because the court inferred that to be the parties' underlying intention on the evidence despite their direct proportions to the purchase price; *Killey v Clough* [1996] NPC 38.

131   [1993] 1 FCR 45.

132   Cf *Crisp v Mullings* (1976) 239 EG 119; *Walker v Hall* [1984] FLR 126, CA; *Harwood v Harwood* [1991] 2 FLR 274; *Roy v Roy* [1996] 1 FLR 541, CA.

133   [1995] 4 All ER 562.

134   On the general reluctance to rectify a conveyance to make it reflect the parties' intentions, see *Wilson v Wilson* [1969] 1 WLR 1470, *per* Buckley J; *Pink v Lawrence* (1978) 36 P & CR 98; *Goodman v Gallant* [1986] 1 FLR 513, 524, *per* Slade LJ; *Roy v Roy* [1996] 1 FLR 541.

frequently used to displace a statutory provision.[135] As considered above, it is difficult to reconcile this decision with the other cases in this area such as *Rosset*. However, it does indicate the Court of Appeal's preference to look at the whole range of facts on offer and not to be restricted to direct, financial contributions in all cases. The doctrine of precedent does not appear to apply here – in that the *precise detail* of the very clear tests in *Rosset* are effectively ignored, even though the case was usually cited by the junior courts before the decision in *Stack v Dowden*, and this ignorance of its detail is in spite of *Rosset* being a House of Lords judgment. The flexible approach of the courts to the identification of the parties' common intentions is evident from *Hyett v Stanley*,[136] in which an unmarried couple who had lived together for over 10 years before the death of one of them took out a loan secured over their home for which they were jointly and severally liable, and in consequence the court inferred a common intention to share the equitable interest in the property equally solely from that joint loan. The court did not apply strictly the *dicta* of Lord Bridge in *Rosset* as one would expect having read that admirably clear, if conceptually harsh, speech.

The decision of the Court of Appeal in *Ivin v Blake*[137] did apply the approach of the House of Lords in *Rosset* – and is worthy of note precisely because it is one of very few Court of Appeal cases to apply the *Rosset* tests closely. In *Ivin v Blake*, B had run a pub from the time of her husband's death, in 1953, which became profitable enough for her to buy a house. However, she could not acquire a mortgage in her own name and therefore the mortgage was taken out in the name of her son, T. B's daughter, D, had given up her job to work in the pub full-time to help her mother, also in 1953. D's agreement to come and work in the pub, thus saving B from having to hire more staff, enabled B to cobble together enough money to buy the property and to generate sufficient income to meet the mortgage repayments. The issue arose whether or not T was required to hold the pub on constructive trust (in part) for D on the basis that D's contribution to the pub business had facilitated the acquisition of the house and also the making of mortgage payments over the house.

The court held that there had been no intention at the time of the acquisition of the house that D would acquire any interest in the house, and therefore there could be no constructive trust. Furthermore, there had been no direct contribution by D to the purchase price of the house. Consequently, D had satisfied neither limb of the *Rosset* test. It was held that D acquired no equitable interest. On the basis that B had met all of the cash expenses of the purchase of the house which had not been provided by means of the mortgage, her equitable interest was said to have survived her death and that it fell to be apportioned according to her will with the rest of her estate.[138] As will emerge below in relation to *Oxley v Hiscock*[139] and the other cases referred to as the 'unconscionability approach' cases: while *Rosset* is cited, it is only one of a number of conflicting authorities which the junior courts added to the stew of case law which they use in reaching their decisions.

---

135   *Yaxley v Gotts* [2000] 1 All ER 711.
136   [2003] EWCA Civ 942, [2004] 1 FLR 394, [2003] 3 FCR 253, [2004] Fam Law 23. This case applied *Grant v Edwards* [1986] 2 All ER 426, as well as considering *Lloyds Bank v Rosset* [1991] 1 AC 107.
137   [1995] 1 FLR 70.
138   Further, only occasional contributions to expenses do not acquire rights: *Kowalczuk v Kowalczuk* [1973] 1 WLR 930, 935, *per* Buckley LJ.
139   [2004] 3 All ER 703.

Domestic work or property rights?

In line with *Gissing*, the Court of Appeal in *Burns v Burns*[140] held that a mere contribution to household expenses would not be sufficient to acquire an interest in property. Rather, the claimant would have to demonstrate that her contributions were made to the purchase price of the property with a view to acquiring an interest in that property. A wife who had run the home, cared for the children and paid some household bills (including utility bills and shopping bills) would not acquire rights in the property. This is contrary to the approach in *Midland Bank v Cooke*,[141] and contrary to the more progressive approach taken in Canada.[142] The *Burns v Burns* approach has been applied in a number of cases, including *Lloyds Bank v Rosset* (where mere supervision of building work was not sufficient to found a right in the property) and *Nixon v Nixon*[143] (where contribution to household expenses was again considered inadequate to found a right in property). Therefore, to found a right in property there is a need for some substantive (typically financial) contribution to the property beyond mere work within the normal context of the family, such as housework. Similarly, a temporary contribution to repayments of a mortgage will not, without more, found a right in property; nor will merely providing security for another person's acquisition of property.[144]

Court discretion granted by statute

Statute provides for an example of sufficient detriment to acquire an equitable interest. Section 37 of the Matrimonial Proceedings and Property Act 1970 provides that:

> where a husband or a wife contributes in money or in money's worth to the improvement of real or personal property in which . . . either or both of them has or have a beneficial interest, the husband or wife so contributing shall . . . be treated as . . . having then acquired by virtue of his or her contribution a share . . . in that beneficial interest . . . as may in all the circumstances seem just to any court.

Therefore, under s 37 of the 1970 Act, where a husband or wife contributes to the improvement of property, that contributor will be awarded such equitable interest as appears to the court to be just. It is important to note that this statute is restricted to cases involving spouses as opposed to other forms of relationship.

Under s 23 of the Matrimonial Causes Act 1973, the court is entitled (as part of its powers in relation to financial settlement on divorce) to adjust the beneficial interests of the parties to the former marriage. As part of its powers, the court is required to bear in mind the welfare of any children of the relationship[145] and also the parties' respective financial contributions to the welfare and upbringing of such children.[146] In effect, then, there is a very broad

---

140 [1984] Ch 317.
141 [1995] 4 All ER 562, considered at para 15.11.2.
142 Considered below at para 15.10.1.
143 [1969] 1 WLR 1676.
144 *Carlton v Goodman* [2002] 2 FLR 259.
145 Matrimonial Causes Act 1973, s 25(1).
146 *Ibid*, s 25(2).

discretion on the court to take into account a wide range of issues which properly forms the subject matter of a family law text.[147]

Excuses

There are a number of cases which deal with defendants who have given excuses to claimants for denying them express rights in their homes.[148] The clear inference in these cases was that the claimants would otherwise have had rights in the property but for the excuses they were given. The courts in these cases have found that the claimant is entitled to an equitable interest in her home because of her reliance on the excuse given to her and because to do otherwise would have been unconscionable in the context. Therefore, these cases have developed without the need to show a common intention – given that the parties' motives and intentions here seem to have been diametrically opposed – but rather have been predicated on unconscionability, like the ordinary constructive trusts considered in section 12.1.

Civil partnerships

The Civil Partnership Act 2004 was enacted, *inter alia*, to regularise the proprietary and other rights between unmarried people. In the popular press, this legislation has been associated most clearly with 'gay marriages'. The legislation addressed issues such as succession to property between unmarried people and co-ownership of property. Under s 65 of the Civil Partnership Act 2004, where a partner under a registered civil partnership has made a 'substantial contribution'[149] to 'the improvement of real or personal property'[150] in which one or other of the civil partners has an interest, then the applicant will be deemed to have acquired an enlarged share in the property. This legislation therefore affects the allocation of property rights in the home between unmarried people who have nevertheless gone through a civil partnership in the manner set out in the 2004 Act. The question then arises as to the size of the share which that person would acquire in the property. If the partners have reached an agreement as to their shares in the property, then that agreement will be binding.[151] If there was no agreement between the partners, then the size of that share will be decided by the court in a manner 'as may seem in all the circumstances just'.[152] There is no definition as

---

147   See *Hosking v Michaelides* [2004] All ER (D) 147, [49]. That a person makes an occasional contribution to mortgage repayments will not, in itself, necessarily acquire that person an equitable interest in the home. So, in *Abbey National v Stringer* [2006] EWCA Civ 338 a widowed mother asked her 19-year-old son to co-sign a mortgage over their home, the son lived with his mother but had a girlfriend with whom his mother expected him to live later in life. The son did make very occasional payments towards the mortgage but his signature had been used solely to convince the mortgagee that the money was not being lent solely to a widowed women in middle age. Therefore, the contribution to the mortgage by the son would not in itself constitute conduct sufficient for the son to acquire an equitable interest in the home. This may indicate, as considered with cases later in this chapter, a less than scrupulous attention to the detail in *Lloyds Bank v Rosset*.

148   See, for example, *Oates v Stimson* [2006] EWCA Civ 548, considered below, where one of the parties was made redundant. *Eves v Eves* [1975] 3 All ER 768; *Grant v Edwards* [1986] Ch 638; *Van Laetham v Brooker* [2006] 2 FLR 495.

149   Civil Partnership Act 2004, s 65(1)(b).

150   *Ibid*, s 65(1)(a).

151   *Ibid*, s 65(2)(a).

152   *Ibid*, s 65(2)(b).

to what is meant by an agreement in this sense: therefore it is suggested that the test set out by Lord Bridge in *Lloyds Bank v Rosset* would be the best approach, requiring that some agreement, arrangement or understanding have been reached between the parties, although not necessarily only before the acquisition of property. Where there has been no agreement, it is suggested that the courts would be well advised to apply the ordinary principles considered in this chapter in reaching that decision. After the dissolution of a civil partnership, the partners have three years to bring claims to assert rights to the other partner's property.[153] If the property has been sold then, it is suggested, either civil partner who has not received the share of those sale proceeds to which they were beneficially entitled will be able to make a claim against the other partner in relation to any property no longer in that other partner's possession nor under his control (such as a house which has been sold) on the basis that it is 'money to which, or to a share of which, [she] was beneficially entitled'.[154]

15.4.4 The difficulties with a strict application of the *Rosset* test

An example of substantive unfairness in Rosset

The aim of this section is to consider, in broad terms, the difficulties which are specific to the *Rosset* decision. Much of this thinking is then taken up in the final section of this chapter. Any test which is rigid necessarily creates the possibility for unfairness at the margins. That would appear to be the case in respect of the test for common intention constructive trust in *Rosset*. Suppose the following situation:

> *A and B are a married couple. They acquire a freehold house entirely by means of a mortgage. It is agreed that A will be the sole mortgagor and entirely responsible for the repayments. They have a child who requires special needs education. It is possible for them, let us suppose, to obtain that special needs education only by buying it privately. It is agreed that B will go to work and that she will be entirely responsible for paying for the special needs education. Let us suppose further that the cost of the education matches exactly the cost of the mortgage, and also that it would have been impossible for A to pay both for the education and for the mortgage.*

A strict application of the *Rosset* test would deny B any interest in the property on the basis that B had not contributed directly to the purchase price nor to the mortgage repayments, in line with the decision in *Ivin v Blake* above.[155] All this despite the necessity of B's contribution to familial expenses to make it possible for A to discharge all of the mortgage expenses. B's greatest hope would be to rely on the *dicta* in *Pettit* referring to one party enabling another to make payments to the property, possibly enabling the acquisition of some equitable rights. The 'family assets' approach considered at section 15.6 below may offer greater hope to B of acquiring rights in the property. These equivocal factual situations must form the background to much of the ensuing discussion in this chapter.

---

153 *Ibid*, s 68(3).
154 *Ibid*, s 67(1).
155 [1995] 1 FLR 70; see para 15.4.3. See now *White v White* [2000] 2 FLR 981, where family law has suggested that one should not look solely at the breadwinner's financial contribution to the home.

What Lord Bridge appeared to forget is that people fall in love. And love they sometimes move in together, or get married, or have children. O don't fall in love but they have children and so have to move in together. And on. Hundreds of years of novels, plays and (latterly) films have shown us the perfidie human heart. Similarly, they have shown us (to quote Shakespeare's *King Lear*) fate dea with us cruelly: 'as flies to wanton boys are we to the gods/they use us for their sport.' It is not possible to create a strict test like that in *Rosset* and expect either that people will always sit down calmly in those glorious early days of a relationship and decide who is to have what equitable interest in the home, or that people will be able to form a common intention at the start of their relationship which will work perfectly throughout it without anyone becoming ill, being made redundant, falling out of love, or whatever else. Life is just not like that. It is suggested that it is contrary to the very core of equity's flexible ability to do right on a case-by-case basis to use concepts like that in *Rosset* to attempt to fetter and bind the ability of the courts to see the right result in any particular case and, as with Dworkin's ideal judge Hercules, to act with integrity to isolate the best possible outcome.[156]

Resulting trust, constructive trust or proprietary estoppel?

One issue which emerges from the foregoing discussion is the precise form of the trust created by Lord Bridge. This is considered again below, but is worthy of mention at this stage. On the one hand, Lord Bridge refers in his speech to 'constructive trust or proprietary estoppel' on five occasions. This raises the question as to whether he intends to merge those two doctrines into one composite set of rules as to the acquisition of rights in the home. This could be said to be a constructive trust in that it creates rights for the claimant by operation of law. Alternatively, it could be said to arise by dint of proprietary estoppel, because it creates rights to prevent the claimant suffering detriment.

The hidden motive behind Lord Bridge's speech in *Rosset* may have been an elision of the categories of common intention constructive trust and proprietary estoppel, as mentioned above. The decision of Nourse LJ in *Stokes v Anderson*[157] makes the case for the contrary argument. His Lordship, in following *Rosset* and *Grant v Edwards*, held that the 'court must supply the common intention by reference to that which all the material circumstances have shown to be fair'.[158] At that stage, his Lordship did not see any reason for the elision of the common intention principles of *Gissing* with the doctrine of proprietary estoppel, considered at section 15.7 below. As set out in that discussion, the proprietary estoppel doctrine operates entirely at the discretion of the court and is prospective; whereas the constructive trust is an institutional trust (that is, without any discretion for the court) which operates retrospectively. Any attempt to merge these concepts would have to address these differences.[159]

What is also noticeable is that Lord Bridge did not use the expression 'resulting trust' anywhere in his judgment, and yet the common intention formed by conduct encapsulates precisely the presumed resulting trust set out in *Dyer v Dyer*[160] which comes into existence in circumstances in which the claimant has contributed to the purchase price of the property

---

156 Dworkin, 1986.
157 [1991] 1 FLR 391.
158 *Ibid*, 400.
159 Notwithstanding Hayton, 1990:1, considered below.
160 (1788) 2 Cox Eq Cas 92.

...tary right in that property.[161] As such, the common
..., so-called, in fact straddle the different concepts of
...nd proprietary estoppel. The reasons for recognising
...s are considered in more detail at the end of this chapter.
...1e those Court of Appeal decisions which have evidently
...pproach and categorise them as disclosing a 'balance sheet'
...s' approach – both of which break the taboos set out in the

_ SHEET APPROACH

...t of Appeal decisions have developed a balance sheet approach which
fav~ ...rement of financial contributions over the life of a relationship to calcu-
late pro~ ...nate equitable rights in the home.

15.5.1 Introduction

The doctrine of precedent appears to have been thrown to the four winds in the area of trusts
of homes. There were House of Lords decisions in *Gissing* and in *Pettitt* which redressed the
balance of the rights of spouses to acquire rights in the family home. Subsequently, the
House of Lords decision in *Rosset* set out the very strict test based on the common intention
constructive trust – as set out above. There is also some confusion as to whether or not that
common intention constructive trust doctrine ought to be read as subsuming the doctrines of
proprietary estoppel and resulting trust, as considered above. However, the Court of Appeal
moved in a number of different directions in the 1990s, effectively side-stepping the didactic
test in *Rosset* in favour of a range of flexible, case-by-case approaches. This section considers
the first of the Court of Appeal's approaches; section 15.6 (the family assets approach)
considers a second trend in the Court of Appeal's decisions which leans towards an equal
division of the equitable interest for couples who have terminated a long relationship.

The essence of the 'balance sheet approach' is that the court draws up a list of financial
contributions made by each party towards the property, akin to an accountant preparing a
balance sheet, and calculates each party's proportionate equitable interest in the home
according to that list. What will emerge from the following discussion is that the times at
which these contributions are made need not comply with the requirements set out in *Rosset*
that they be made before the acquisition and that they be directed solely at acquiring interests
in property.

15.5.2 Calculating the size of the equitable interest

The trend towards balance sheet calculation began with the decision of the Court of Appeal
in *Bernard v Josephs*,[162] in which the court considered itself entitled to examine the mathematical equity contributed by each party across the range of transactions contributing to the

---

161 *Re Roger's Question* [1948] 1 All ER 328; *Bull v Bull* [1955] 1 QB 234; *Winkworth v Edward Baron
Development Co Ltd* [1986] 1 WLR 1512; Warburton, 1987, 217.
162 [1982] Ch 391; *Passee v Passee* [1988] 1 FLR 263. 137 See *Trowbridge v Trowbridge* [2003] 2 FLR 231;
[2004] FCR 79.

acquisition of a property.[163] Dealing simply with the issue of contributions made to the purchase at the date of acquisition, it is clear that a contribution can be made in a number of different ways. The following are some of the more common forms of financial contribution:

(a) by cash payment;
(b) by agreeing to pay all or part of the interest payments on the mortgage throughout the life of the mortgage;
(c) by agreeing to pay the whole or part of the capital cost of the mortgage throughout the life of the mortgage;
(d) agreeing to be liable to the lender for the mortgage debt in the event that the mortgagor goes into arrears without actually making any payments;
(e) acting as guarantor or surety for the mortgage;
(f) obtaining a reduction or discount in the acquisition price by exercise of a pre-existing right in the property.

The fourth and fifth solutions do not require that any payment be made at the time of acquisition. Indeed, the second and third options only require that periodic payments are made after the date of acquisition. There are, then, a number of possible means by which contributions could be made after the date of acquisition. There are yet further possibilities:

(g) by undertaking to make only some of the mortgage repayments on an *ad hoc* basis – for example, where a wife undertakes to pay the mortgage for a period of a couple of months while her husband finds work;
(h) by repaying some of the capital cost of the mortgage without acquiring a legal obligation to do so.

All eight of these possibilities (clearly there could be others) assume some level of agreement between the parties: that is, some explicit or implicit understanding that both of them are contributing to the acquisition of the property at the outset or subsequently. Two further issues then arise. First, the situation where there is no express agreement but the parties fall into a pattern of shared expenditure which is dictated by, for example, whether or not they are in employment at any particular time during their joint occupation of the family home. Secondly, the situation where there is a casual agreement that one party will meet expenses related to the mortgage while the other meets 'domestic' expenditure. In this latter situation, it may be that the mortgagor could not make those mortgage repayments unless the other party met the ordinary domestic expenditure: it should be remembered that under a literal application of the test in *Rosset*, those payments for ordinary expenses would not acquire any interest in the property, even though they were necessary to enable the mortgagor to make his mortgage payments.

As considered above, direct contribution will give rise to a resulting trust,[164] or a common intention constructive trust by conduct.[165] The second possibility will give rise to an equitable interest in the cohabitee's favour on resulting or constructive trust, where it can be proved that the cohabitee contributed to the price of the property after the acquisition. The

163 *Ibid.*
164 *Dyer v Dyer* (1788) 2 Cox Eq Cas 92.
165 *Lloyds Bank v Rosset* [1990] 1 AC 107.

size of the interest in such circumstances will be proportionate to the contribution to the total purchase price.[166] The Court of Appeal in *Huntingford v Hobbs* was prepared to look behind the documentation signed by the parties which suggested that they held the equitable interest in the property in equal shares. However, it was held that to look behind such documents there must be 'cogent evidence' that any documentation signed by the parties was not intended to constitute the final statement as to their beneficial interests. Therefore, where a house cost £100,000 and X provides £40,000, where Y procures a mortgage for £60,000, Y is taken to have contributed 60% of the purchase price.[167]

There is also the possibility of equitable accounting to take into account periods of rent-free occupation and so forth by one or other of the parties.[168] So, where, for example, one spouse quits the property until the litigation as to the equitable interest is resolved, it will be possible for such a spouse to recover money from the spouse who remains in residence to defray part of the costs of his own rental obligations. Equity will ensure that an account is taken between the party of the amounts owed between them, such as the inferred rental cost of one person occupying co-owned property alone.[169] Remember it is possible for litigation to take a number of years to resolve, during which time one spouse would have full use of the property while the other party would be required to find the financial wherewithal to live elsewhere. What is clear from this doctrine of equitable accounting is that equity will provide for items to be added to this 'balance sheet' which are outside the strict test in *Rosset*. It is clear that *Rosset* does not paint the full picture. The question of what can be taken into account is considered in further detail below.

15.5.3 What can be taken into account?

Non-cash contributions

What is clear from the preceding discussion is that direct cash contributions to the purchase price, or to the mortgage repayments, will be taken into account in calculating an equitable interest.[170] What is less clear is the extent to which non-cash provisions of value can be taken into account similarly, particularly given that *Rosset* would not allow them. An interesting question arose in *Springette v Defoe*[171] as to whether or not a person who procures a discount on the purchase price of property is entitled to bring that discount (or reduction) on the price of the property into the calculation of her equitable interest in the property. The argument runs that getting a discount on the property constitutes an indirect contribution to the purchase price, being reliant on the use of some other right that person has.[172]

On the facts of *Springette v Defoe*, Miss Springette had been a tenant of the London Borough of Ealing for more than 11 years. She began to cohabit with Mr Defoe and they decided to purchase a house in 1982. Neither party was able to raise the necessary mortgage

---

166 *Huntingford v Hobbs* [1993] 1 FLR 736.
167 *Ibid; Cowcher v Cowcher* [1972] 1 WLR 425.
168 *Bernard v Josephs* [1982] Ch 391; *Huntingford v Hobbs* [1993] 1 FLR 736.
169 *Byford v Butler* [2003] EWHC 1267 (Ch), [2004] 2 FCR 454, [2004] 1 FLR 56; *Pavlou (a bankrupt), Re* [1993] 3 All ER 955, [1993] 1 WLR 1046; *Stack v Dowden* [2007] UKHL 17, [2007] 2 FCR 280, [2007] 1 FLR 1858; *Murphy v Gooch* [2007] 3 FCR 96.
170 *Lloyds Bank v Rosset* [1990] 1 AC 107.
171 (1992) 24 HLR 552, [1992] 2 FLR 388.
172 Cf *Evans v Hayward* [1995] 2 FLR 511, *per* Staughton LJ; *Ashe v Mumford* (2000) *The Times*, 15 November.

because their incomes, either jointly or severally, were not large enough. However, Miss Springette was entitled to a discount of 41% under the applicable right-to-buy legislation on the purchase price of her home from the council, because she had been an Ealing council tenant for more than 11 years. The purchase price was therefore £14,445 with the discount. The parties took out a mortgage for £12,000. There was an agreement between the parties that they would meet the mortgage repayments half each. Mr Defoe provided £180 in cash; Miss Springette provided the balance of £2,526 in cash. Their relationship broke down in 1985. The issue arose as to the proportionate equitable interest which each should have in the house.

The Court of Appeal held that there should be a resulting trust imposed unless there was found to be sufficient specific evidence of a common intention to found a constructive trust. Such a common intention must be communicated between the parties and made manifest between them at the time of the transaction. On the facts of *Springette*, there was no evidence to support the contention that the parties had had any sort of discussion as to their respective interests (within Lord Bridge's test in *Rosset*), nor that they had reached any such agreement.[173] Therefore, the presumption of resulting trust could not be displaced. The court performed a calculation exercise in the following terms, calculating the amount of value which each party had contributed to the purchase price:

Springette		*Defoe*	
£10,045	(discount on property price)		
£6,000	(half of mortgage payments)	£6,000	(half of mortgage payments)
£2,526	(cash contribution)	£180	(cash)
£18,571		£6,180	

Therefore, Springette was taken to have contributed 75% of the equity and Defoe 25% (after rounding).

Effect of merely contributing 'value', not cash

Importantly, the court looked at the *value* contributed and not at the *amount of cash paid* in *Springette v Defoe*. It is interesting to see how this compares to Lord Bridge's insistence in *Rosset* that it is 'at least extremely doubtful whether anything less' than a direct contribution to the mortgage instalments or to the purchase price will do. If it is accepted that procuring a reduction in the purchase price is a sufficient contribution, why should it be impossible to argue that if A pays for the household costs, the car and the children's clothes, thus enabling B to defray the mortgage, that A is not making it possible for B to pay off the mortgage and thus making a financial contribution to the purchase? After all, once you accept that the contribution need not be made in cash but merely by some other form of 'value', at what point is the line to be drawn under the range of non-cash contributions which are possible? For example, could someone with a natural flair for negotiating discounts claim a share in

173 Cf Mee, 1999.

the property simply by virtue of convincing the vendor that he should sell the property for less than would otherwise have been accepted?[174] In *Cox v Jones*,[175] the claimant had acquired a flat on a private basis from the vendor whom she had known personally when occupying a flat in the same block as him: that the property was acquired on a private basis meant that it was cheaper than it would have been if the parties had had to buy it through an estate agent. However, the point was not taken in that case as to whether or not this acquisition of a reduction in the value of the flat constituted an acquisition of an equitable interest in the flat in itself. Rather, it was one of a number of factors which the court took into account when deciding that the claimant should acquire a right in the flat.[176]

It is suggested that what is significant about *Springette v Defoe* is that the contribution which is made by way of the discount on the sale price arises directly from a statutory entitlement: that is, Miss Springette has a right of a given value under statute which is deducted from the acquisition of the property and which makes the purchase possible. Where, for example, a discount on the sale price is negotiated, that is not a contribution of some valuable right of the claimant but rather an alteration in the contractual sale price without the transfer of any valuable rights on the part of the claimant. It is suggested that the former constitutes the contribution of a valuable right which Miss Springette owned, as opposed to the performance of some task of negligible value which did not constitute the transfer of a valuable right.

The nature of the contribution acceptable is complicated even on the facts of *Rosset*. It is accepted that the courts should allow the parties to include contingent or future liabilities, such as the mortgage obligations, as part of the calculation of their respective contributions. Rather than a straightforward application of the principle in *Dyer v Dyer* that such a contribution denotes an interest under resulting trust, the parties are being permitted to include in the calculations amounts which they will have to pay in the future but which they have not paid yet under the mortgage contract. This issue is considered further below.

Unpaid mortgage capital and other issues

Judgment in *Springette* was delivered by the same Court of Appeal and on the same day as *Huntingford v Hobbs*,[177] discussed briefly above. *Huntingford* pursued the issue of the means by which contributions to the acquisition of the property should be calculated and reflected in the equitable interests which were ultimately awarded to the parties. The plaintiff and the defendant lived together but did not marry. The plaintiff was living on social security benefits; the defendant had been recently divorced and was living in her former matrimonial

---

174   See *Evans v Hayward* [1995] 2 FLR 511, *per* Staughton LJ.

175   [2004] 3 FCR 693, [2004] EWHC 1486 (Ch).

176   In that case, the claimant acquired the absolute interest in the flat because it was found on the facts of that case to have been the parties' intention that the defendant would acquire the property as nominee for the claimant because he was the only person who could have obtained the mortgage necessary to effect the purchase. That she had acquired a reduction in the purchase price of the property was held to be one factor among many which justified this conclusion. However, it seems unfair to deny the defendant any right in this flat because he had assumed the legal responsibility for the mortgage and had also contributed half of the deposit on the flat. Granting the claimant the entire interest in the flat, however, was part of a larger settlement in that case in which the defendant was awarded the majority share in a country house in Essex which the couple had bought together. See the discussion of this case in section 15.8 below.

177   [1993] 1 FLR 736.

home. The plaintiff moved in with the defendant but was uncomfortable living in his partner's matrimonial home, and therefore they decided to sell up. The plaintiff wanted to move to Woking where he felt he had a better chance to make money as a music teacher. The parties also wanted to be able to provide a home for the defendant's 21-year-old daughter.

The plaintiff and the defendant bought a property for £63,250 in 1986. The defendant had sold her previous property and put £38,860 towards the purchase of the new property. The remaining £25,000 was provided by way of endowment mortgage. The mortgage liability was undertaken in the names of both plaintiff and defendant. It was agreed between the plaintiff and the defendant that the plaintiff would make the mortgage repayments. In 1988 the plaintiff left the defendant. The plaintiff had paid £5,316.30 in mortgage interest and £1,480.25 in premium payments. The plaintiff spent £2,000 on the construction of a conservatory, but this did not increase the value of the property although it was found on the facts that it did make it easier to sell: the defendant did not have any real income; the plaintiff paid for most income expenses and household bills. The property was valued at £95,000 at the time of the hearing and there remained £25,000 in capital outstanding on the mortgage.

The plaintiff contended that the property was to be held in equity under a joint tenancy on the basis of the terms of the conveyance into the names of both plaintiff and defendant. Therefore, the plaintiff sought an order that the property should be sold and the sale proceeds divided in equal shares between the parties. The Court of Appeal held that the property should be sold, but that the sale should be postponed to give the defendant a chance to buy out the plaintiff. Further, it was found that the plaintiff must have been intended to have some equitable interest in the property.

In terms of establishing the parties' respective balance sheets, the court decided as follows. The defendant should be deemed to have contributed the cash proceeds of sale of her previous home; whereas the plaintiff should be deemed to have contributed the whole amount of the mortgage (because he was to have made the mortgage repayments) and should receive some credit for the cost of the conservatory. The issue then arose: what about the remaining, unpaid capital left on the mortgage? The Court of Appeal held that the plaintiff should have deducted from his equitable interest an amount in recognition of the fact that he had not yet paid off the capital of the mortgage and that it was the defendant who would have to meet that cost, because she had agreed to take on responsibility for the mortgage. Therefore, the Court of Appeal calculated that:

(a) the plaintiff should receive £2,000 (conservatory);
(b) the defendant should receive £25,000 (capital of the mortgage);
(c) the plaintiff should receive 39% (proportion contributed by mortgage);
(d) the defendant should receive 61% (proportion of cash contribution).

Again, the court's approach was to look straightforwardly at the amounts of money contributed by the parties towards the property without taking a literal approach to whether such expenditure took place at the time of acquisition (for example, the money spent on the conservatory was applied after purchase) and whether such expenditure was directed at the purchase price and not merely at more ephemeral matters of building work on the property (for example, the money expended on the conservatory again).

One further, significant aspect emerges from this judgment. The Court of Appeal was prepared to accept that, while the balance sheet approach would be based primarily on resulting trust principles crystallised at the time of the acquisition of the property, it would be possible for the parties to advance cogent evidence of subsequent changes of intention which would be effected by means of constructive trust. On these facts the contribution to the conservatory was made after the date of the acquisition of the property. Similarly, it would be possible to overturn even documentary evidence of the parties' intentions with cogent evidence of other intentions. A hybrid form of resulting and constructive trust is therefore formed – one which enables changes in the relationship between the parties to be accounted for in the equitable interests which the court will recognise as existing between the parties.

The courts have demonstrated themselves to be prepared to examine cogent evidence of the parties' true intentions rather than to consider themselves bound by, for example, contributions made directly to the purchase price at the outset, whether under resulting trust principles or otherwise. Therefore, where a wife had made a contribution of one-fifth of the purchase price of property (on a net basis), the court enlarged her share to one-third of the entire equitable interest because it was prepared to find that that had been the parties' underlying intention on the evidence in place of the size of their direct proportions to the purchase price.[178]

So, in *Drake v Whipp*[179] the Court of Appeal held that where there was evidence of a common understanding having been formed between the parties then that would be preferred to the mathematical strictures of a resulting trust which would have restricted the parties to their proportionate contributions to the purchase price of property. While Peter Gibson LJ did make reference to *Lloyds Bank v Rosset*, his Lordship did not restrict himself to the rigorous two-step test set out by Lord Bridge, which would have required allocation of title between the parties in the exact shares in which they contributed to the purchase price or in exact compliance with their earlier common understanding: instead constructive trust principles were relied upon by the court to give effect to what the court considered to be the justice of the case having regard both to their agreement and to their contributions to the purchase price. Peter Gibson LJ left it unclear precisely on what basis that decision was reached (whether mathematical calculation, a decision based on avoidance of unconscionability, or some other), other than to make it plain that it is a constructive trust which is being applied to re-calibrate the resulting trust on which the claimant had relied at first instance.[180]

Deposits and sale proceeds from previous properties

One of the common shortcomings of English property law is that the rules focus on specific items of property rather than taking into account the range of dealings between individuals which might *impact* on the property but which were perhaps not *directly related* to it. In this way, sales of properties generate capital to acquire further properties, typically after discharge of the mortgage. It is important, therefore, that focus on the particular land in issue does not ignore interests held previously in other properties. So if A and B acquired No 55 Mercer Road with equal cash contributions on the basis of a tenancy in common, that 50:50 division in the equitable interest ought to be carried forward when No 55 Mercer Road is sold and the proceeds used to buy No 1 Acacia Avenue: that is, so that those parties then have a 50:50 share of the equitable interest in No 1 Acacia Avenue.

Similarly, it will typically be the case that individuals buying a home will generate most of the capital to acquire the property by means of mortgage. Those individuals may be required

---

178   *Drake v Whipp* [1996] 1 FLR 826.
179   [1996] 1 FLR 826.
180   See in this sense *Giumelli v Giumelli* [1999] HCA 10 in Australia.

to pay a deposit from their own funds by the mortgagee in order to take out that mortgage, or they may choose to do so to reduce the size of their mortgage debt. Where these deposits are the only cash contributions made by the parties (otherwise than by way of mortgage), their proportionate size may be decisive of the parties' respective equitable interests, or may contribute to their part of the balance sheet, as seen above in relation to *Springette v Defoe* and *Huntingford v Hobbs*, and below in relation to *Midland Bank v Cooke* and *McHardy v Warren*. In short, if A and B each contribute £5,000 separately by way of mortgage deposit, and borrow £90,000 by way of mortgage (making a total acquisition price of £100,000), A and B would acquire half each of the equitable interest in the property – the mortgagee would not acquire any equitable interest in the property because the parties' common intention would have been that the mortgagee acquire only the rights of a secured lender and not those of a beneficiary under a resulting trust. As a consequence, the mortgage deposit will be a significant part of the allocation of the equitable interest in many such cases.

So, in *Midland Bank v Cooke*,[181] it was held that a common intention constructive trust can arise where X and Y equally provide a deposit on a house purchased in the name of one or both of them.[182] W had contributed nothing to the purchase price, but was deemed to have contributed the deposit for the purchase of the property, which had been given to them by way of wedding gift, equally with H. The question arose whether or not she had any beneficial interest in the property in any event. Waite LJ held that the judge must survey the whole course of dealing of the parties. Further, the court is not required to confine its survey to the limited range of acts of direct contribution of the sort that are needed to found a beneficial interest in the first place. If that survey is inconclusive, the court should fall back on the maxim 'equality is equity'. Part of the judgment of Waite LJ was that equal contribution to the original deposit was an indication that the parties intended to split the equitable interest in their home equally between them. However, as considered above, it is difficult to reconcile this focus on equality between the parties with the other cases in this area asserting a strict approach based on direct contributions to the purchase price (for example, *Rosset*), or the balance sheet cases (for example, *Huntingford*) which would consider such an equal division to be inequitable.

On the issue of deposits and subsequently-purchased homes, in *McHardy v Warren*,[183] H's parents had paid the whole of the deposit on the matrimonial home acquired by H and his wife, W. The legal title in the property was registered in H's sole name. The remainder of the purchase price of the property was provided entirely by means of a mortgage. The mortgage was taken out in H's name only. That house was sold and then two subsequent homes were bought (one after the other) out of the sale proceeds of the first home. The mortgagee sought to recover its security by seeking an order for the sale of the house. W sought to resist its claim on the basis that she had an equitable interest in the property too, grounded on the argument that the deposit provided by her father-in-law constituted a wedding gift to them both, and therefore that she had acquired an equitable interest at that stage derived from her share of the wedding present. Consequently, she claimed that she had 50% of the equitable interest in the original property, which translated into 50% of all subsequent acquisitions.

It was contended on behalf of the mortgagee that W had only a right equal to the cash value of W's half of the deposit in proportion to the total purchase price of the house. That is, a right

181 [1995] 4 All ER 562.
182 The facts of this case are considered in greater detail in section 15.6 below in relation to the family assets doctrine.
183 [1994] 2 FLR 338.

to half of the original £650 deposit (£325) out of the total value of the property. The central principle was held to be that the parties must have intended that there be equal title in the property to sustain W's argument. On the facts, the court felt that the only plausible conclusion to be drawn was that the intention of the father in putting up the deposit was to benefit H and W equally, and that their intention must be that the property be held equally in equity. Therefore, the court held that W was entitled to equal share of house with H because W put up the deposit equally with H. In consequence, the building society could not claim that W was entitled merely to £325 and was bound by her half-share in the equitable interest in the property.

Time of the creation of the interest

What emerges from the foregoing discussion is that the contribution does not need to be made before the purchase of the property. Rather, the various forms of contribution accepted in the foregoing cases demonstrate that the manner in which the court will draw up the parties' balance sheet will be by reference to a broad range of contributions and entitlements created at different times after acquisition. The Court of Appeal in *Huntingford v Hobbs*[184] upheld the use of cogent evidence to demonstrate that documentation was not intended to constitute the full extent of the parties' interests. Further, it was held that the resulting trust in that case crystallised on the date of the acquisition of the property. There was also the possibility of equitable accounting to take into account periods of rent-free occupation by one or other of the parties.[185] In contradistinction to the assertion made in *Rosset* that the contribution to the purchase price, or the agreement giving rise to a common intention constructive trust, must occur at the date of the purchase, it has been held that a constructive trust arises from the date of the acts complained of.[186]

Resulting trusts under Jones v Kernott

As discussed in detail below, the doctrine of resulting trusts was not considered by Lord Walker in *Stack v Dowden* or in *Jones v Kernott* to be appropriate in relation to trusts of homes. However, even the decisions on the facts of those cases focused primarily on the cash contributions made by the parties, just like a resulting trust. The dissenting judgment of Lord Neuberger in *Stack v Dowden* began with a resulting trust and, very like *Huntingford v Hobbs*, then allowed the resulting trust to be adjusted to account for subsequent developments. In truth, the only difference between these approaches in practice is the extent to which the initial calculation, based on the parties' financial contributions to the purchase price of the property and to the mortgage instalments, is adjusted to take into account later changes in the parties' intentions.

15.6 THE FAMILY ASSETS APPROACH

> *Alternative Court of Appeal decisions have developed a family asset approach which suggests that property should be deemed to be held equally between couples.*

---

184 [1993] 1 FLR 736.
185 *Bernard v Josephs* [1982] Ch 391; *Huntingford v Hobbs* [1993] 1 FLR 736.
186 *Re Sharpe* [1980] 1 WLR 219.

15.6.1 Explaining the approach

It is common for civil code jurisdictions to take the approach that married couples take all of their property communally – neither having any interest without the other. This concept is similar to the English notion of joint tenancy. In California and in France, for example, there is an ability for married couples to select the legal form of marriage they prefer, and whether or not they agree to take their property communally or separately (joint or several ownership respectively, in effect). This approach has had some currency in occasional English common law decisions relating to equitable ownership of the family home. Most recently, I will argue, it is the decisions of Waite LJ which have propounded a form of family assets doctrine which is avowedly grounded in *Gissing v Gissing*,[187] but which has eschewed the complexity of much of the other case law in favour of dividing property equally between couples terminating a long relationship.

The expression 'family assets' was used by Lord Denning in relation to the division of property on a divorce.[188] The phrase 'family assets' was considered to be a 'convenient short way of expressing an important concept. It refers to those things which are acquired by one or other or both of the parties, with the intention that there should be continuing provision for them and their children during their joint lives, and used for the benefit of the family as a whole'.[189] While this attempt to introduce a new model constructive trust to give effect to family assets was championed by Lord Denning,[190] it did not find universal favour in the law of property and was discarded.[191] Lord Denning sets out his eminently readable view of the cases in which he was involved in this area in his memoir *The Due Process of Law*.[192] He also maps with great clarity the crumbling of the developments which he helped to propound. It is not suggested here that that thinking has been given effect to in the courts in retrospect. Rather, it is suggested that there are similarities in a strain of decisions delivered by family courts in relation to rights in property which have echoes of Lord Denning's approach.[193]

This approach has been rejected in a number of English decisions. It has been held in a range of cases[194] that English law on the home contains no such concept as the 'family assets' doctrine as a result of the decisions of the House of Lords in *Gissing* and *Pettitt*. What is meant by a family assets doctrine in *those cases* is that it is not possible to say that where a purchase is made out of the general assets of a family the equitable interest in the property so acquired should be divided equally among those family members. However, the law of trusts of homes permits a number of seemingly irreconcilable doctrines, as will emerge from the following discussion. The family assets approach considered here is something quite different.

---

187 [1971] AC 886. Cf *White v White* [2000] 2 FLR 981, 989, *per* Lord Nicholls, eschewing concentration solely on the financial contributions of the breadwinner.

188 *Wachtel v Wachtel* [1973] Fam 72, 90.

189 *Ibid.*

190 *Hussey v Palmer* [1972] 1 WLR 1286; *Cooke v Head* [1972] 1 WLR 518; *Eves v Eves* [1975] 1 WLR 1338: imposed wherever 'justice and good conscience require'. *Hazell v Hazell* [1972] 1 WLR 301 – look at all circumstances, including overall contribution to the family budget.

191 *Ivin v Blake* [1995] 1 FLR 70; *MacFarlane v MacFarlane* [1972] NILR 59, 66; and *McHardy v Warren* [1994] 2 FLR 338.

192 Butterworths, 1980, 227 *et seq.*

193 *Hammond v Mitchell* [1991] 1 WLR 1127; *Midland Bank v Cooke* [1995] 4 All ER 562; *Drake v Whipp* [1996] 1 FLR 826; *Rowe v Prance* [1999] 2 FLR 787. Cf *Re B (Child: Property Transfer)* [1999] 2 FLR 418.

194 *Ivin v Blake* [1995] 1 FLR 70; *MacFarlane v MacFarlane* [1972] NILR 59, 66 and *McHardy v Warren* [1994] 2 FLR 338.

15.6.2 Where equality is equity

The confusion which remains at the doctrinal level in these cases is well illustrated by the decision of the Court of Appeal in *Midland Bank v Cooke*.[195] In 1971, a husband and wife purchased a house for £8,500. The house was registered in the husband's sole name. The purchase was funded as follows: the bulk of the purchase price (£6,450) was provided by means of mortgage taken out in the husband's name, although Mrs Cooke was a signatory to a second mortgage subsequently taken out over the property. Mr Cooke made a cash contribution of £950, with the balance being provided by means of a wedding present made to the couple of £1,100. That is:

(a)   £6,450 (by way of mortgage loan);
(b)   £1,100 (wedding gift from H's parents to the couple);
(c)   £950 (H's cash contribution);
(d)   £8,500 (total purchase price).

In 1978, the mortgage was replaced by a more general mortgage in favour of H, which secured the repayment of his company's business overdraft. In 1979 W signed a consent form to subordinate any interest she might have to the bank's mortgage. Subsequently the bank sought forfeiture of the mortgage and possession of the house in default of payment. W claimed undue influence (before the decision in *Barclays Bank v O'Brien*[196]) and an equitable interest in the house to override the bank's claim.

The Court of Appeal, in the sole judgment of Waite LJ, went back to *Gissing* without considering the detail of *Rosset* (although accepting that the test in *Rosset* was ordinarily the test to be applied). Waite LJ had trouble with the different approaches adopted in *Springette v Defoe*[197] and *McHardy v Warren*.[198] The former calculated the interests of the parties on a strictly mathematical, resulting trust basis; whereas the latter looked to the intentions of all the parties as to whether or not the deposit should be considered as a proportionate part of the total purchase price, or as establishing a half-share of the equity in the property. His Lordship claimed to find the difference in these approaches 'mystifying'.

The question then arose as to how the court should address this problem. Waite LJ returned to the speech of Lord Diplock in *Gissing* and to the decision of Browne-Wilkinson VC in *Grant v Edwards*, before holding as follows:

> [T]he duty of the judge is to undertake a survey of the whole course of dealing between the parties relevant to their ownership and occupation of the property and their sharing of its burdens and advantages. That scrutiny will not confine itself to the limited range of acts of direct contribution of the sort that are needed to found a beneficial interest in the first place. It will take into consideration all conduct which throws light on the question what shares were intended. Only if that search proves inconclusive does the court fall back on the maxim that 'equality is equity'.

195   [1995] 4 All ER 562.
196   [1994] 1 AC 180.
197   [1992] 2 FLR 388.
198   *Ibid.*

On these facts, the matter could not be decided simply by reference to the cash contributions of the parties. The court accepted that the parties constituted a clear example of a situation in which a couple 'had agreed to share everything equally'. Facts indicating this shared attitude to all aspects of their relationship included evidence of the fact that Mrs Cooke had brought up the children, worked part-time and full-time to pay household bills, and had become a co-signatory to the second mortgage. This is an approach which echoes family law principles such as the 'clean break' approach in divorce proceedings under s 25A of the Matrimonial Causes Act 1973.[199]

What is not clear is how this decision is to be reconciled with the findings in *Burns v Burns*[200] and *Nixon v Nixon*[201] that activities revolving only around domestic chores could not constitute the acquisition of rights in property. Further, it is not obvious how the decision can be reconciled with the *dicta* of Lord Bridge in *Rosset* that a common intention formed on the basis of conduct must be directed at the mortgage payments and that it 'is at least extremely doubtful that anything less will do'. Returning to *Gissing*, as Lord Pearson held: 'I think that the decision of cases of this kind have been made more difficult by excessive application of the maxim "equality is equity".'[202] Therefore, Waite LJ's approaches in *Cooke* above and in *Hammond v Mitchell*[203] are fundamentally different from those earlier principles. Furthermore, the family assets approach is in line with the possibility of providing for equitable accounting, so that the court can take account of expenditure made on property even if the claimant is not awarded the proprietary interest which she sought.[204] The principles of family law considered in Chapter 17[205] will include those forms of ancillary and substantive relief available to claimants under statute.[206] That the settled patterns of ownership in proportion to contributions to purchase price are not to be followed slavishly has emerged in family law cases, which are more concerned to consider the family's needs in the round.[207]

15.6.3 Communal undertakings

In most cases involving long-term relationships and children, there will be a complicated list of items of property and communal undertakings. Picking between real and personal property, and including matters like the value of voluntary work by one spouse in the other spouse's business, will all confuse the issue whether or not any rights in property have been acquired. There are also further issues as to title in the personal property which a couple will amass during the course of their relationship. One of my favourite cases explores precisely

---

199 Eg, *F v F (Clean Break: Balance of Fairness)* [2003] 1 FLR 847.
200 [1984] Ch 317.
201 [1969] 1 WLR 1676.
202 [1971] AC 886, 903.
203 [1991] 1 WLR 1127.
204 For a discussion of the operation of such equitable accounting in English law, see Cooke, 1995, 391; also *Re Pavlou* [1993] 2 FLR 751, Millett J; *Leake v Bruzzi* [1974] 1 WLR 1528, CA; not following *Cracknell v Cracknell* [1971] P 356; *Suttill v Graham* [1977] 1 WLR 819, CA; *Re Gorman* [1990] 2 FLR 284, *per* Vinelott J.
205 At section 17.4 below.
206 *Bedson v Bedson* [1965] 2 QB 666; *Re John's Assignment Trusts* [1970] 1 WLR 955; *Bernard v Josephs* [1982] Ch 391, 411; *Chhokar v Chhokar* [1984] FLR 313.
207 *Lambert v Lambert* [2002] EWCA Civ 1685; cf *Le Foe v Le Foe* [2001] 2 FLR 970. See Probert, 2004; Barlow, 2004.

this point. *Hammond v Mitchell*[208] was a decision of Waite J (as he then was) in which the question arose as to rights in real property, business ventures and chattels. Hammond was a second-hand car salesman who was aged 40 and who had recently left his wife. He picked up Mitchell when she flagged his car down to ask directions in Epping Forest. She was then a Bunny Girl (or nightclub hostess) at the Playboy club in Mayfair, then aged 21. Very soon after that first meeting they began living together. It was said by Waite J that '[t]hey both shared a zest for the good life'.[209] The relationship lasted 11 years and produced two children. Their partnership was tempestuous, and when it finally ended the issue arose whether or not Mitchell had acquired any interest in any property which, predominantly, was held in Hammond's name.

The history of the equitable interest in their personal and their real property followed a familiar pattern, in that '[t]hey were too much in love at this time either to count the pennies or pay attention to who was providing them'.[210] Hammond had told Mitchell that they would marry when he was divorced. He also told her not to worry about herself and the children because 'everything is half yours'. In time they bought a house in Essex in which they continued to live until the break-up of their relationship. They lived hand-to-mouth, trading in cash and filling their house with movable goods. She worked in his business ventures with him. There were no formal accounts and no formal agreements as to rights in any form of property. Aside from the house and its contents, they both acquired interests in restaurant ventures in Valencia, Spain. Mitchell decided to leave Hammond, and so stuffed the Mercedes he had bought her with lots of movables and moved out of the house when he was abroad. They were briefly reconciled before she left him again, with a large amount of personal property crammed this time into a Jaguar XJS.

Waite J was clear that he considered the question of finding a common intention 'detailed, time-consuming and laborious'.[211] The first question for the court to address was whether there was any agreement. Here there had been discussions as to the house. Echoing Lord Pearson in *Pettitt v Pettitt*, Waite J held that '[t]his is not an area where the maxim "equality is equity" falls to be applied unthinkingly'.[212] However, in the light of all the facts, it was found that Mitchell's share of the house should be one half of the total interest, on the basis that it appeared that the couple had intended to muck in together and thereby share everything equally.

The second question was whether or not there was any imputed intention which should be applied to the parties. It was found that while Mitchell contributed personally to the business which Hammond had set up in Valencia, this did not justify any reallocation of any proprietary rights without more. Her cash investment had not, it was found, been made with an intention to acquire any further property rights in that Spanish property. With reference to the household chattels, it was held that 'the parties must expect the courts to adopt a robust allegiance to the maxim "equality is equity" '.[213] Therefore, everything was divided in accordance with the parties' perceived common intentions much in the manner that a family court judge would have divided the property, it is suggested.

208 [1991] 1 WLR 1127.
209 *Ibid*, 1129.
210 *Ibid*, 1130.
211 *Ibid*.
212 *Ibid*, 1137.
213 *Ibid*, 1138.

The extraordinary facet of the 'family assets doctrine' is that it eschews all of the carefully prescribed rules in *Rosset* and other similar cases. Rather than concern himself with the niceties of the time of contributions and so forth, Waite LJ appears to be either a great realist or a great romantic. He is a great realist in that he acknowledges that life is a chaotic muddle for many people, in which they do not pay careful attention to their property rights when seeking to cope with the many vicissitudes of life. It is the possibility of drawing careful distinctions which is (in the judge's word) mystifying, particularly when those distinctions will not fall easily between an interest consensus and a money consensus on competing authorities. Waite LJ is a great romantic when he acknowledges the passionate confusion personified by Hammond and Mitchell and acknowledges that their real intention was to treat everything as shared between them.

There is one further doctrine which offers even more scope to the judiciary to indulge their desire for the discretion to allocate proprietary rights between one party and another: that is the doctrine of proprietary estoppel, which is considered next.

15.7 PROPRIETARY ESTOPPEL

Exceptionally, the doctrine of proprietary estoppel will grant an equitable interest to a person who has been induced to suffer detriment in reliance on a representation (or some assurance) that she would acquire some rights in the property as a result. Whereas rights based on constructive trust and resulting trust are 'institutional' trusts taking retrospective effect, proprietary estoppel may give a different kind of right.

This section considers the doctrine of proprietary estoppel as it relates to the home. Chapter 13 considers the breadth and scope of equitable estoppel in greater detail. The reader is therefore also referred to that discussion for a more detailed discussion of these principles and of recent cases.

15.7.1 The test underlying the doctrine of proprietary estoppel

The modern understanding of the doctrine of proprietary estoppel was set out most clearly by Edward Nugee QC in *Re Basham*.[214] That case supported the three-stage requirement of representation, reliance and detriment:

> ... where one person, A, has acted to his detriment on the birth of a belief, which was known to and encouraged by another person, B, cannot insist on his strict legal rights if to do so would be inconsistent with A's belief ... where the belief is that A is going to be given a right in the future, it is properly to be regarded as giving rise to a species of constructive trust, which is the concept employed by a court of equity to prevent a person from relying on his legal rights where it would be unconscionable for him to do so. The rights to which proprietary estoppel gives rise, and the machinery by which effect is given to them, are similar in many respects to those involved in cases of secret trusts, mutual wills, and other comparable cases in which property is vested in B on the faith of an understanding that it will be dealt with in a particular manner ... In cases of

214 [1986] 1 WLR 1498.

proprietary estoppel the factor which gives rise to the equitable obligation is A's alteration of his position on the faith of a similar understanding.

In short, proprietary estoppel will arise where the claimant has performed some act (arguably, which must be done in relation to the property) to her detriment in reliance upon a representation made to her by the cohabitee, from whom the claimant would thereby seek to acquire an equitable interest in the property.[215]

It is clear from the cases that the representation made by the defendant need only amount to an assurance, and it can be implied rather than needing to be made expressly.[216] Therefore, it is sufficient that the defendant allowed the claimant to believe that her actions would acquire her property rights; it is not necessary that there be any express, single promise. Therefore, a series of suggestions made at family gatherings over a number of years which caused the claimant to believe that doing work on land for low wages would lead to the acquisition of some interest in the land was sufficient to constitute a representation.[217] However, it must not be the case that the representation was simply being made by a man to impress a woman in the early stages of a casual relationship when it could not reasonably have been intended that that man intended to part with half of the equitable interest in a huge country estate.[218] Similarly, it is not enough to acquire an interest in her mother's house that a daughter who was educationally-challenged believed that she would have a house bought for her by her mother.[219] In that case, it was held that there had not been any binding representation made which would entitle the daughter to take absolute title in the house after her mother's death when her mother had left the house by will to her third husband. Reliance is generally assumed (on an evidential basis) where a representation has been made.[220] The question of what will constitute 'detriment' is considered below.

The decision of the House of Lords in *Thorner v Major*[221] concerned the availability of proprietary estoppel in relation to a farm, and gave a clear idea of just how far the requirement of a representation can be stretched. The claimant had worked seven days a week, often for sixteen hours a day, for many years on the deceased's farm. There was a suggestion that a representation had been impliedly made to the claimant over time by the deceased to the effect that the claimant would become the owner of the deceased's farm after the deceased's death, even though in the event the deceased did not leave the farm by will to the claimant. These two men had never discussed the matter between them, something which was explained by their lordships as involving the legendarily taciturn nature of farmers in that part of Somerset. Remarkably, this meant that a representation was found on the facts even though no words were ever spoken between them. The House of Lords held that on these facts there had been a sufficient assurance made by the deceased to the claimant on which it was reasonable for the claimant to have formed the impression that he would become the owner of the farm after the deceased's death, in reliance on which he worked to his detriment

---

215 *Ibid; In Re Sharpe (A Bankrupt)* [1980] 1 WLR 219.
216 *Crabb v Arun DC* [1976] Ch 179.
217 *Gillett v Holt* [2001] Ch 210.
218 *Lissimore v Downing* [2003] 2 FLR 308.
219 *Turner v Jacob* [2006] EWHC 1317 (Ch).
220 *Lim v Ang* [1992] 1 WLR 113; *Grant v Edwards* [1986] Ch 638.
221 [2009] 1 WLR 776. This case was considered in *Sinclair v Sinclair* [2009] EWHC 926 (Ch) where it was described as being a case 'about what was expressly said by way of assurance': although the case clearly is more nuanced than that.

on the other man's farm. The claimant worked staggeringly long hours on the farm in hard, physical work, and it is difficult not to think that the court was anything other than impressed by that dedication and imputed (or possibly inferred) both an understanding on the part of the claimant that he must have expected a right in the property and an intention on the part of the deceased that the farm would be left to the claimant. In any event, the claim for proprietary estoppel was upheld.[222] Their lordships, especially Lords Walker and Rodger, made much of the fact that was found by the trial judge that farmers in this part of Somerset could be naturally taciturn, that these two men in particular spoke very few words to one another about anything, and therefore that the absence of any more explicit representation should not necessarily be read as denying the presence of a suitable understanding between these parties that the claimant's work was being done to his evident detriment in reliance on that understanding. As Lord Rodger put it, there does not need to be a 'signature event' on which a clear representation was made:[223] which means that there does not need to be a single moment when the representation was made and evidenced and so forth. Instead it is sufficient, as Lord Rodger[224] and Lord Walker[225] held, that the 'relevant assurance' which was made was 'clear enough' in the context. So, if the representor was 'standing by in silence', aware that the claimant was acting to his detriment on the belief that he was thus acquiring a right in the property, then that would be enough to grant him rights on the basis of proprietary estoppel.[226] Lord Hoffmann and Lord Neuberger concurred in general terms with Lord Walker.

It is important that the assurances of the representor have been intended by their maker to lead the claimant to believe that he would acquire rights in property. So, for example, it would not be sufficient that the representor was merely toying with the claimant without either of them forming a belief that the claimant would in fact acquire any rights in property. For, as Robert Walker LJ put it in *Jennings v Rice*, 'it is notorious that some elderly persons of means[227] derive enjoyment from the possession of testamentary power, and from dropping hints as to their intentions, without any question of any estoppel arising'.[228] On the facts of *Gillett v Holt*[229] it was clear that the assurances had been repeated frequently and were sincerely meant when made. It is clear that in general terms it will be sufficient if the defendant makes an express representation to the claimant[230] but it would also be sufficient to establish an estoppel if some implied assurance were made in circumstances

222 The House of Lords was unanimous in finding the existence of a right on these facts, although Lord Scott dissented in part on the basis that this case should have been decided on the basis of a remedial constructive trust, and not proprietary estoppel.

223 [2009] 1 WLR 776, para [24].

224 *Ibid*, para [26].

225 *Ibid*, para [56]. Relying on Hoffmann LJ in *Walton v Walton*, [1994] CA Transcript No 479 (unreported) to the effect that: 'The promise must be unambiguous and must appear to have been intended to be taken seriously. Taken in its context, it must have been a promise which one might reasonably expect to be relied upon by the person to whom it was made.'

226 [2009] 1 WLR 776, para [55], *per* Lord Walker. The House of Lords was unanimous in finding the existence of a right on these facts, although Lord Scott dissented in part on the basis that this case should have been decided on the basis of a remedial constructive trust, and not proprietary estoppel.

227 A 'person of means' is a rich person.

228 [2000] 2 All ER 289, 304.

229 *Ibid*.

230 *Taylors Fashions Ltd v Liverpool Victoria Trustees Co Ltd* [1982] 1 QB 133; *Re Basham (Deceased)* [1986] 1 WLR 1498; *Wayling v Jones* (1993) 69 P & CR 170; *Gillett v Holt* [2000] 2 All ER 289.

in which the defendant knew that the claimant was relying on the impression she had formed.[231]

As *Re Basham* and *Thorner v Major* indicate, a typical situation in which proprietary estoppel claims arise is where promises are made by the absolute owner of land to another person that the other person will acquire an interest in the land if she performs acts which would otherwise be detrimental to her.[232] Typically, then, the person making the promise dies without transferring any right in the property to that other person. This aspect of the doctrine is similar to the law on secret trusts considered in Chapter 6 above, whereby proprietary rights are transferred despite the formal requirements of the Wills Act 1837. For example, in *Re Basham*,[233] the plaintiff was 15 years old when her mother married the deceased. She worked unpaid in the deceased's business, cared for the deceased through his illness, sorted out a boundary dispute for the deceased, and refrained from moving away when her husband was offered employment with tied accommodation elsewhere. All of these acts were performed on the understanding that she would acquire an interest in property on the deceased's death. The deceased died intestate. It was held that the plaintiff had acquired an equitable interest on proprietary estoppel principles. It was found that proprietary estoppel arises where A has acted to his detriment, on the faith of a belief, which was known of and encouraged by B, that he either has or will receive a right over B's property; in which case B cannot insist on strict legal rights so as to conflict with A's belief.

This can be contrasted with *Layton v Martin*,[234] in which a man had promised to provide for his mistress in his will. He died without leaving any of the promised bequests in his will, and therefore the mistress sued his estate claiming rights on constructive trust. Her claim was rejected on the basis that she had not contributed in any way to the maintenance of his assets.[235] At one level it is a decision based on the absence of detriment. This can be compared with the decision in *Re Basham*, in which the claimant was found to have made sufficient contributions to the defendant's assets.[236] Similarly, where a wife contributes to her husband's business activities generally, it may be found that she has suffered detriment which will ground a right in property,[237] particularly if this evidences a common intention at some level which may be undocumented.[238] Other relatives will be entitled to rely on their contributions to the acquisition or maintenance of property where there have been assurances made to them that they would be able to occupy that property as their home.[239] In such situations it is essential that the expenditure is made in reliance on a representation that it will acquire the contributor some right in the property.[240] So, for example, if a father were to promise his son

---

231   *Crabb v Arun DC* [1976] Ch 179.
232   *Gillett v Holt* [2000] 2 All ER 289.
233   [1986] 1 WLR 1498.
234   [1986] 1 FLR 171.
235   See also *Midland Bank v Dobson* [1986] 1 FLR 171 – the wife's claim failed because there was no evidence that she had suffered any detriment.
236   As noted by Martin, 1997, 211; Hayton, 1997, 215; Davey, 1988, 101.
237   *Heseltine v Heseltine* [1971] 1 WLR 342.
238   *Re Densham* [1975] 1 WLR 1519.
239   *Re Sharpe* [1980] 1 WLR 219 – aunt acquires 'constructive trust' right on the basis of contributions to the acquisition of the property based on a promise that she could live there.
240   *Thomas v Fuller-Brown* [1988] 1 FLR 237, *per* Slade LJ – spending money does not, by itself, bring rights in property.

that the son would acquire an equitable interest in a house owned by his father and that in reliance on that promise (and with the agreement of his father) the son were to sell his house so as to pay for renovation works on his father's house, there would have been a representation, reliance and detriment (where the detriment was in the form of selling the house to pay for the renovations) sufficient to found a claim for proprietary estoppel.[241] In those circumstances, however, the judge expressed himself as finding that the events gave rise to a 'constructive trust' in the son's favour, after some inconclusive discussion about whether 'proprietary estoppel and constructive trust' should be treated as the same doctrine or as two separate doctrines.[242]

Another classic example of proprietary estoppel arose in the decision of Lord Denning in *Greasley v Cooke*.[243] There a woman, Doris Cooke, had been led to believe that she could occupy property for the rest of her life. She had been the family's maid, but then had formed an emotional relationship with one of the family and become his partner. In reliance on this understanding, she looked after the Greasley family, acting as a housekeeper, instead of getting herself a job and providing for her own future. The issue arose whether or not she had acquired any equitable interest in the property. It was held by Lord Denning that she had suffered detriment in looking after the family and not getting a job in reliance on the representation made to her. Therefore, it was held that she had acquired a beneficial interest in the property under proprietary estoppel principles, because she had acted to her detriment in continuing to work for the Greasleys in reliance on their assurance to her that she would acquire some proprietary rights as a result. The form of right which Lord Denning granted was an irrevocable licence to occupy the property for the rest of her life.[244] That such a particular remedy was awarded brings us to the more general question: what form of remedy can be awarded under proprietary estoppel principles?

---

241 *S v R* [2008] EWHC 1874 (Fam), [2009] 1 P & CR D12 (also sub nom *Q v Q*). This was a case with a Dickensian range of characters (sons and daughters) involving tremendous familial bitterness in which a widower (aged 98 at the date of the proceedings) railed against his middle-aged son and daughter-in-law, referring to one of his sons as a 'rotter' and in evidence said 'I already cut you off a matter of years ago so unfortunately am denied the satisfaction of doing it again, for you are indeed the prodigal son personified, and deserve the soubriquet as they say "in spades" '. May you burn in Hell.' As such the court had great difficulty in finding facts because of the enmity between the parties. The daughter-in-law faced charges that she was a 'gold digger'; but she, giving as good as she got, suggested that the old man was 'fantastically mean/stingy'. The dispute concerned reorganisation of the family houses and personal property so as to minimise liability to inheritance and capital gains tax; and in particular one house which had fallen into disrepair. This particular house had not been dusted for fourteen years, it needed underpinning work, it was infested with fleas, smelled strongly of dog urine, had old tyres in the loft, the plumbing and wiring were 'pre-war', and 'the garden was a jungle'. It sounds like a palace! The old man exerted influence over his sons by reference to parcelling out his wealth. Some of the family members were wealthy and successful; one other had succumbed to drink: yet at one time the father's affection was for the recovering alcoholic, not the successful son, although affections and alliances had shifted over time. Consequently, trying to establish the agreement (founding the representation) in the context of complex tax planning before the old man moved to Monaco was difficult. However, the summary in the text serves well enough as a digest of the points of principle in the case.

242 *Ibid*, para 115, *per* Black J.

243 [1980] 1 WLR 1306.

244 What is particularly satisfying about this case is that, had Charles Dickens sought to incorporate these events into a novel like *Nicholas Nickleby*, he could have found no better name for the exploitative family than 'the Greasleys'.

15.7.2 The nature of the interest awarded under proprietary estoppel

Proprietary estoppel is very different, in a number of ways, from the institutional resulting and constructive trusts considered above. The aim of proprietary estoppel is to avoid detriment rather than to enforce the promise, whereas the common intention constructive trust appears to be quasi-contractual (in that it enforces an express or implied agreement), estoppel is directed at preventing detriment being caused by a broken promise. In *Walton Stores v Maher*,[245] Brennan J held that:

> The object of the equity is not to compel the party bound to fulfil the assumption or expectation: it is to avoid the detriment which, if the assumption or expectation goes unfulfilled, will be suffered by the party who has been induced to act or to abstain from acting thereon.[246]

In a similar vein, Lord Browne-Wilkinson held in *Lim v Ang*[247] that the purpose of proprietary estoppel is to provide a response where 'it is unconscionable for the representor to go back on the assumption that he permitted the representee to make', that is, to avoid the detriment caused from retreating from that representation. This approach is important, because the court's intention is not merely to recognise that an institutional constructive trust exists between the parties but rather to provide a remedy which prevents the claimant from suffering detriment.[248] The narrow line between proprietary estoppel and the (at the time of writing, heretical) remedial constructive trust is considered at the end of this chapter. The determination of the courts to prevent detriment therefore requires the court both to identify the nature of the property rights which were the subject of the representation and to mould a remedy to prevent detriment resulting from the breach of promise. Typically, this requires the demonstration of a link between the detriment and an understanding that property rights were to have been acquired. Thus, in *Wayling v Jones*,[249] two gay men, A and B, lived together as a couple. A owned an hotel in which B worked for lower wages than he would otherwise have received in an arm's-length arrangement. A promised to leave the hotel to B in his will. The hotel was sold and another acquired without any change in A's will having been made to reflect that assurance. B sought an interest in the proceeds of sale of the hotel. The issue turned on B's evidence as to whether or not he would have continued to work for low wages had A not made the representation as to the interest in the hotel. Initially, B's evidence suggested that it was as a result of his affection for A that B had accepted low wages. Before the Court of Appeal, B's evidence suggested that he accepted low wages from A in reliance on the assurance that B would acquire property rights in the hotel. Consequently, the Court of Appeal held that B was entitled to acquire proprietary rights under proprietary estoppel because his detrimental acts were directed at the acquisition of rights in property and were not merely the sentimental ephemera of their relationship.

In Hayton's view,[250] the court is not here giving effect to pre-existing rights but rather is fitting a remedy to a particular wrong. This remedy may be in the form of a prospective,

245 (1988) 62 ALJR 110.
246 *Ibid*, 125.
247 [1992] 1 WLR 113, 117.
248 *Westdeutsche Landesbank Girozentrale v Islington LBC* [1996] AC 669.
249 (1993) 69 P & CR 170.
250 Hayton, 1990:1, 370; Hayton, 1993, 485.

remedial constructive trust. Indeed, it was held in *In Re Sharpe*[251] that the proprietary estoppel right exists only from the date of the court order. The award appears to be remedial in its effect – providing a remedy for the detriment suffered.[252] However, it is worthy of note that in a number of cases, the court appears to be awarding expectation loss (that is, giving to the claimant rights which the claimant had expected to receive) rather than simply avoiding detriment.[253]

15.7.3 The nature of the remedies awarded under proprietary estoppel

The nature of the remedy is at the discretion of the court. The decision of the Court of Appeal in *Pascoe v Turner*[254] is illustrative of the breadth of the remedy potentially available under a proprietary estoppel claim. The plaintiff and the defendant cohabited in a property which was registered in the name of the plaintiff alone. The plaintiff often told the defendant that the property and its contents were hers – however, the property was never conveyed to her. In reliance on these representations, the defendant spent money on redecoration and repairs to the property. While the amounts were not large, they constituted a large proportion of the defendant's savings. The defendant sought to assert rights under proprietary estoppel when the plaintiff sought an order to remove the defendant from the property.

The decision of the Court of Appeal in *Pascoe v Turner* was that the size of interest applicable would be that required to do the 'minimum equity necessary' between the parties. Therefore, it was decided to award the transfer of the freehold to the defendant, to fulfil the promise that a home would be available to her for the rest of her life, rather than (apparently) merely to avoid the detriment which had actually been suffered in reliance on the representation. It is impossible to grant a larger interest in land than an outright assignment of the freehold. Therefore, the court apparently has within its power the ability to award any remedy which will prevent the detriment which would otherwise be suffered by the claimant or to fulfil the defendant's representation.

However, it is not the case that proprietary estoppel will always lead to an award of property rights.[255] For example, in *Baker v Baker*,[256] the plaintiff was deemed entitled only to compensation in respect of the cost of giving up secure accommodation. The plaintiff was a 75-year-old man with a secure tenancy over a house in Finchley. The defendants were his son and daughter who rented accommodation in Bath. It was agreed that the plaintiff should vacate his flat and that the parties should buy a house together in Torquay. The plaintiff contributed £33,950, in return for which he was entitled to occupy the property rent-free. The defendants acquired the remainder of the purchase price by way of mortgage. The parties decided to terminate the relationship and the plaintiff was re-housed as a secure tenant with housing benefit.

It was not held that there was a resulting trust in favour of the plaintiff (a matter accepted by the court, and presumably the parties, although the reason is not clear from the judgment).

---

251 *In Re Sharpe (A Bankrupt)* [1980] 1 WLR 219.
252 *Lim v Ang* [1992] 1 WLR 113, 117. See also Pawlowski, 1996, generally.
253 *Pascoe v Turner* [1979] 1 WLR 431; *Greasley v Cooke* [1980] 1 WLR 1306; and *Re Basham* [1986] 1 WLR 1498, all considered below.
254 [1979] 2 All ER 945, [1979] 1 WLR 431.
255 *Matharu v Matharu* [1994] 2 FLR 597, criticised by Battersby, 1995, 59.
256 (1993) 25 HLR 408.

Therefore, he sought to establish rights on the basis of proprietary estoppel. It was held that the appropriate equitable response was to provide him with equitable compensation rather than with a proprietary interest in the Torquay house. The amount of compensation was valued in accordance with the annual value of the accommodation he enjoyed, capitalised for the remainder of his life. The amount of the award would then be discounted as an award of a capital sum. Some account was also taken of the costs of moving and so forth. The application of equitable compensation, while a matter of some complexity,[257] does not convey proprietary rights in the land at issue but only a right to receive equity's equivalent to common law damages to remedy the detriment suffered as a result of the failure of the representation. What is remarkable about this decision is that the court was concerned to consider the claimant's needs (here, for sheltered accommodation for the remainder of his life) and not simply to consider whether or not he had acquired rights in property. The strength of proprietary estoppel is that it enables the courts to achieve the most just result between the parties in novel situations.[258]

An excellent example of the flexibility of the award that is possible in proprietary estoppel cases emerges from the remarkable case of *Porntip Stallion v Albert Stallion Holdings (Great Britain) Ltd*[259] Porntip Stallion, who was from the Philippines, came to London to work for Albert Stallion in 1984 and later married him in June 1989. She lived at Stallion's premises at The Cut, Waterloo in London with Albert Stallion from some time in 1991. The couple divorced in 1995. Albert Stallion married Lilibeth Stallion in the Philippines in 1996 before they moved to London together. However, Porntip had continued to occupy the property at The Cut even after the divorce, including intermittent periods during which she occupied that property with Albert and Lilibeth. Albert Stallion died in 2004, leaving Lilibeth as his executrix. The property had been owned by Albert Stallion Holdings (Great Britain) Limited, a company controlled by Albert Stallion.[260] Porntip contended that representations had been made to her by Albert[261] that she would be able to live at the property rent-free for the rest of her life provided that she did not contest the divorce in 1995 and that she did not seek a court order to protect her position.[262] Judge Asplin QC found[263] (following *Thorner v Major*[264]) that 'on the balance of probabilities' such representations had been made[265] and that Porntip had

---

257 Considered below in Chapter 18.
258 On the ability of proprietary estoppel to adapt to novel situations and to meet changing social mores, see
        Matharu v Matharu (1994) 68 P & CR 93; *Sledmore v Dalby* (1996) 72 P & CR 196; Cooke, 2000, 433.
259 [2009] EWHC 1950 (Ch), [2010] 1 FCR 145.
260 The property was a house with a cellar in the Waterloo area of London, which excluded a bookmaker's shop
        located on the ground floor which was leased from the company. Albert was the sole director and owner of
        7,999 out of 8,000 shares in that company. The company conducted its business from these premises, although
        upper floors were given over to a residential home with four or five bedrooms.
261 The representations were made in part by a colleague (who did Albert's 'dirty work') being deputed to ask her
        for a divorce; on one particular night Albert making oral representations to her about her ability to occupy the
        property and then writing them out on the basis that she could occupy the property or be paid £55,000 if she
        was asked to leave it; and then repetition of the representations at later meetings, at which other people were
        present, which were contended to have removed this caveat about the payment of money instead.
262 Porntip claimed exclusive possession of the residential part of the premises but abandoned a claim to the rents
        and profits from the remainder of the property.
263 [2010] 1 FCR 145, [110] *et seq*.
264 [2009] UKHL 18.
265 The judge spends some time on the respective levels of credibility of the various witnesses, who contradict
        themselves and one another greatly in giving their evidence. As is common in trusts of homes cases, the
        witnesses are generally impassioned and partial, and occasionally incredible.

relied upon those representations to her detriment: the detriment being located in her agreement not to contest the divorce nor to acquire the protection of a court order. Illustrating the remarkable flexibility of proprietary estoppel in provided tailor-made remedies, it was held that Porntip would be entitled to occupy the property rent-free for the remainder of her life; although she would not be granted exclusive possession of the property, but rather she would be required to occupy the property in common with Lilibeth (and her new husband and daughter).[266] On the facts it was found that the parties would be able to live together in tolerable harmony.[267] All of which simply goes to show that there is no accounting for the complexity of other people's lives, and the occasionally surprising open-mindedness of English judges.[268]

In conclusion, it is clear that proprietary estoppel will provide an entitlement to a broad range of remedies the application of which is at the discretion of the court. The court's discretion will be exercised so as to prevent the detriment potentially suffered by the claimant. What is more difficult to isolate is the extent to which this remedial jurisdiction equates to restitution of unjust enrichment. The issue is therefore whether proprietary estoppel could be said to be about the reversal of unjust enrichment. The difficulty with any such analysis is that there is no necessary pre-existing proprietary right in the property at issue. Rather, it is sufficient that there is some representation made in relation to that property. Consequently, it is unclear how proprietary estoppel could be said to operate so as to *restore* property rights to their original owner where there was previously no such right.[269]

What is less clear, then, is the basis on which proprietary estoppel arises. The role of estoppel is to prevent a legal owner from relying on common law rights where that would be detrimental to another. Alternatively, proprietary estoppel might be bundled up with the constructive trust notion of preventing unconscionable conduct more broadly, in particular if *Rosset* is taken to have elided the concepts. Some authorities would describe proprietary estoppel as raising a 'mere equity' which is binding only between the parties until the judgment is performed. More difficult explanations are that it provides a cause of action, thus infringing the notion that estoppel can only be a shield and not a sword, or that it operates to perfect imperfect gifts.[270] Both of these readings have some validity on the cases considered. Evidently, in many situations, proprietary estoppel is the only means by which a claimant can sue *and* be awarded rights in land. For example, the award made in *Pascoe* operates in the face of *Rosset*, which would not have awarded any proprietary rights to the claimant for

266 [2010] 1 FCR 145, [137] and [138]. Porntip had given evidence that they had lived under the same roof 'but separately' before.

267 As the judge held at para [138]: 'In this regard, I appreciate that it is an unusual step to create a situation in which the equity requires a claimant to continue to live in premises with the defendant. However, in this case, Porntip and Lilibeth appear to have done so for a considerable time both before and after Albert's death.' With respect, one cannot help but think that the surprising element is not that claimant and defendant will continue to live together but rather that the former wife and the widow would be expected by the High Court to live together. In that sense it is a very 'modern', even 'progressive' judgment; and a testament to the inherent flexibility of the doctrine of proprietary estoppel.

268 A female friend whom I was boring with an account of this, and other cases, wondered whether the fact that the judge was a woman might have led to this interesting judgment on the facts of this case, and its acceptance of an alternative mode of organising the parties' living arrangements.

269 Nor is proprietary estoppel restitutionary in the sense of reversing unjust enrichment because there is no requirement that the defendant has been enriched – simply that the claimant has suffered detriment which was directed at the acquisition of rights in the property.

270 As considered in Chapter 13.

mere decorative work on the building. Consequently, the doctrine has the hallmarks of a *de facto* claim made to preclude unconscionability rather than to deal with the claimant's pre-existing property rights. As to the rule that equity will not perfect an imperfect gift, in any case where there is a representation to transfer rights in property, and where that promise is not carried out, proprietary estoppel is perfecting that imperfect gift on proof of some detriment suffered by the claimant – that is the distinction between the successful claimant and the mere volunteer.

15.8 THE UNCONSCIONABILITY APPROACH

15.8.1 The nature of the unconscionability approach

For some time it appeared that there was a further approach emerging in the cases based on the court considering whether or not there would be any unconscionability in denying the claimant an equitable interest in the property. In Chapter 12, we considered that constructive trusts were imposed wherever the defendant had acted knowing of some unconscionability in her treatment of property;[271] and similarly in Chapter 13, we considered that, further to the decision of the Court of Appeal in *Jennings v Rice*,[272] the doctrine of proprietary estoppel might be metamorphosing into a general doctrine of equitable estoppel which is based on unconscionability in general terms. Consequently, a test based on unconscionability in relation to trusts of homes would bring this area into line with the mainstream principles on constructive trusts. In the developing 'unconscionability approach' in the law on trusts of homes, it is suggested, the courts are looking to consider whether or not it would be unconscionable for the defendant to deny property rights to the claimant. This may yet lead to a fusing of the principles of constructive trust and of proprietary estoppel in this context. This is very similar in form to the test of unconscionability which has been used in Australia for some time, as considered in para 15.10.2 below. It should be noted that identifying the existence of this 'unconscionability approach' is my own theory – collecting together otherwise disparate decisions of differently constituted courts – but it is suggested that it is the best way to understand this drift in the law.

The doctrinal significance of the unconscionability approach is that the courts are allocating equitable interests in the home without needing to base that finding on a common intention. Therefore, unlike the need in *Lloyds Bank v Rosset* to identify a common intention between the parties, the courts are considering whether or not it would be unconscionable to deny the claimant an interest in the home. This finding of unconscionability usually begins with a consideration of whether or not the parties have in fact reached an agreement, but even then the often vague finding of an agreement is usually tempered by a consideration of the entire course of dealing between the parties. Some of these courts have then expressed their intention as being to do what is 'fair' between the parties. Consequently, the doctrine of proprietary estoppel, with its remedial nature, and the general doctrine of constructive trusts, based on institutional and conscionable trusts, appear at first blush to be functioning in very similar fashions.

There are two distinct characteristics of the 'unconscionability approach'. First, it is prepared to merge the doctrines of constructive trust and of proprietary estoppel so that the

---

271 See para 12.2.1 above; see, eg, *Westdeutsche Landesbank v Islington LBC* [1996] AC 669.
272 [2003] 1 P & CR 100; [2002] EWCA Civ 159.

courts will be able to reach the decision which they consider to be most conscionable on the facts of any given case. This is different from the approach in *Lloyds Bank v Rosset* where Lord Bridge sought to merge these doctrines but precisely so that there could not be any such flexibility for the courts. Secondly, the courts are accepting that it will not be possible to generate any single set of principles which will cover all circumstances, primarily because there are so many different forms of relationship, and therefore achieving the most conscionable solution to any given set of facts is considered to be the only feasible means for a court to proceed. Consequently, the courts which have adopted this approach were paying lip-service to the test in *Lloyds Bank v Rosset* while also seeking to use the approach of Waite LJ in *Midland Bank v Cooke* to allow themselves to survey the whole course of dealing between the parties beyond merely financial contributions to the purchase of the property. As Patten J put this matter in *Turner v Jacob*:[273] 'The question of unconscionability requires the court to look at all the relevant circumstances and not at particular factors in isolation.' The cases considered below indicate this drift in the cases clearly.

15.8.2 The consensual approach taken in *Oxley v Hiscock*

The decision in Oxley v Hiscock

The most significant case in this vein at the time of writing appears to be *Oxley v Hiscock*.[274] This decision of the Court of Appeal has become influential on subsequent decisions of the Court of Appeal and the Supreme Court even though, as will emerge, it attempts an uncomfortable elision of most of the cases considered so far in this chapter into one combined test.[275] We shall consider the facts of the case first, and then we shall consider how Chadwick LJ seeks to combine the earlier authorities.

In *Oxley v Hiscock* a woman exercised her statutory right to buy the house over which she had been a secure tenant: to effect the purchase, she used money given by her partner, a man to whom she was not married. The house was bought as a home for the couple and her children by a previous marriage, after he had been released from his confinement as a hostage during the 1990 Gulf War. The property was sold for £232,000 after their relationship broke down and issues arose as to which of them had what equitable interest in the property. Ultimately, the court held that this was a case of pooling resources[276] where Mr Hiscock had contributed £60,000 and Ms Oxley had contributed £36,000 and other outgoings: therefore, the court divided the property in the ratio 60:40 in favour of Mr Hiscock. In reaching this conclusion, the court attempted a survey of the whole of the case law in this area and, even more optimistically, sought to reconcile the various cases. The court considered *Springette v Defoe, Walker v Hall,*[277] *Grant v Edwards, Lloyds Bank v Rosset* and *Midland Bank v Cooke*, broadly in that order. These cases have all been considered already in this chapter.

---

273 [2006] EWHC 1317 (Ch), [84].
274 [2004] EWCA Civ 546, [2004] 2 FLR 669, [2004] Fam Law 569.
275 It has been followed in *Stack v Dowden* [2005] EWCA Civ 857, [2006] 1 FLR 254; *Crossley v Crossley* [2005] EWCA Civ 1581, [2006] BPIR 404; and *Turner v Jacob* [2006] EWHC 1317 (Ch).
276 [2004] 2 FLR 669, para [74].
277 [1984] FLR 126.

The rationale underpinning the decision of Court of Appeal in Oxley v Hiscock

Relying particularly on *Grant v Edwards* as an explanation of *Pettitt v Pettitt* and *Gissing v Gissing*, the court held that the first question which a court must ask itself was whether or not there had been any common intention formed between the parties, either on the basis of direct evidence or inferred from the circumstances. Having identified such a common intention, it was held that one must then quantify the size of the right intended by that agreement. The speech of Lord Bridge in *Lloyds Bank v Rosset* was considered to be an affirmation of the judgment of Browne-Wilkinson VC in *Grant v Edwards*, rather than being a new approach entirely,[278] although Chadwick LJ in *Oxley v Hiscock* did lapse into Lord Bridge's habit of referring in composite terms to 'constructive trust or proprietary estoppel' as though they were the same doctrine.[279] It was said that the remedial techniques of proprietary estoppel can be used so as to alter the size of the share which either party may acquire in the property.[280] The evident differences between *Springette v Defoe* and *Lloyds Bank v Rosset* were explained away on the basis that the former case concentrated solely on the question as to the parties' common intention, whereas the latter required a further question to be answered as to whether or not the parties had reached any agreement.[281] (That one case was concerned with resulting trust and the other with 'constructive trust or proprietary estoppel' was overlooked by Chadwick LJ.) *Midland Bank v Cooke* was considered by Chadwick LJ to have established a different understanding of the law based on a survey of the whole course of dealing, but it was further considered that the decision in *Drake v Whipp*[282] had subsequently reasserted that equitable interests would be based on resulting trust, while also permitting the respective rights of the parties under that resulting trust to be adjusted so as to achieve fairness between them. If one reads the judgment of Peter Gibson LJ in *Drake v Whipp*, however, it is plain that the Court of Appeal chose to base their judgment on constructive trust principles and not to limit themselves to the formulaic mathematics of resulting trusts. However, *Midland Bank v Cooke* was also explained by Chadwick LJ as being a case where Mrs Cooke was accepted as having acquired some interest under trust in the house and that the decision in that case was therefore really focused on quantifying that right. This approach, even if it is correct (which I doubt), does not tell us how Mrs Cooke is said to acquire a right from payment of bills and so forth in a manner which would not have been accepted in *Lloyds Bank v Rosset* as being anything more than a *de minimis* contribution at its highest.[283]

The conclusion to which Chadwick LJ came in *Oxley v Hiscock*[284] was that:

> what the court is doing, in cases of this nature, is to supply or impute a common intention as to the parties' respective shares (in circumstances in which there was in fact no common intention) on the basis of that which, in the light of all the material circumstances (including the acts and conduct of the parties after the acquisition) is shown to

---

278   [2004] 2 FLR 669, para [36].
279   *Ibid*, para [36].
280   *Ibid*, para [44], considering *Stokes v Anderson* [1991] 1 FLR 391.
281   [2004] 2 FLR 669, para [48].
282   [1996] 1 FLR 826.
283   [2004] 2 FLR 669, para [67].
284   *Ibid*, para [66].

> be fair . . . and it may be more satisfactory to accept that there is no difference in cases of this nature between constructive trust and proprietary estoppel.

It is suggested that the 'unconscionability' element of this approach is encapsulated in the notion that the court is looking for an understanding of the parties' common intention which would be 'fair', to quote Chadwick LJ. The court is thus concerned with establishing a fair result, as opposed to giving effect to the pre-existing rights of the parties. This is, it seems to me a very significant point: the court is prepared to 'supply' the parties' common intention, not simply to find it on the facts. That means the court is prepared to make up what the court thinks their common intention would have been, not simply to try to find out what it actually was. This is, therefore, a fiction of sorts. The court is doing what the court thinks is 'fair', not necessarily what the parties agreed to do.[285] The reason for this is that the parties often do not discuss their property rights in advance and so the courts feel compelled to supply an agreement for them. This is, I would suggest, a very long way away from Lord Bridge's clear requirements in *Lloyds Bank v Rosset* that there must have been an agreement, arrangement or understanding reached before the acquisition of the property.

Thus, the approach of Chadwick LJ appears to be remedial, like proprietary estoppel, as opposed to being institutional, like traditional constructive trusts: this means that the court is deciding what the parties' rights ought to be (and thus is in the form of a remedy invented by the court at its discretion) rather than simply seeking to give effect to the parties' pre-existing property rights based on their contributions to the purchase price (as with an institutional constructive trust). What this quasi-remedial, unconscionability approach also does is to fabricate or invent the parties' common intention – by inferring it from the circumstances – and opposed to requiring cogent evidence that that was consciously the actual common intention of the parties. It is this artificiality which has concerned other Commonwealth jurisdictions so much, as is considered below in relation to the New Zealand and Australian cases. Those courts are concerned that the English cases require them to 'supply' the parties' intention, even though the parties may not actually have had that intention consciously. What might be more intellectually satisfying would be for the English courts to accept that they wish to behave like family law courts and simply decide what sort of remedy would be fairest for the parties in all the circumstances, regardless of what they may have done beforehand.

Furthermore, considering the passage just quoted from the judgment of Chadwick LJ, I would suggest that this conclusion is insupportable on the decided cases as they have already been discussed in this chapter. It seems that Chadwick LJ's reference to 'cases of this nature' is a reference to cases in which there has been no agreement, or else *Rosset* would simply require that the agreement be enforced.[286] (Oddly, his Lordship considered this to be limited

---

285 See for example *Akhtar v Arif* [2006] EWHC 2726 (Ch) in which Stuart Isaacs QC, sitting as a deputy judge of the High Court, was faced with contradictory evidence from numerous parties as to what their rights must have been and as to what their intentions must have been. Eventually the court ruled that the parties should be taken to have the equitable interest half each. It is a strange judgment which cites no case law authority at all but in which a judge at first instance can be seen wrestling with contradictory evidence and ending up with the compromise of equal division because there is no 'correct' answer on the facts. Thus the unconscionability approach does anticipate the plight of the ordinary judge in trying to impose a suitable answer on confused circumstances.

286 See the explanation which his Lordship gives at [2004] 2 FLR 669, para [68].

to cases where both parties contributed to the purchase price (ignoring the cases where that did not happen)[287] and where people intended to live together as husband and wife (thus ignoring the cases on same-sex couples and non-romantic home sharers).)[288]

Even if it should be taken to be a reference to all cases on trusts of homes, there is a clear difference between the first category of *Rosset* common intention constructive trusts by agreement, the balance sheet cases and the family assets cases, as discussed earlier in this chapter. *Rosset* was concerned with finding an agreement or inferring a common intention only from payment of the purchase price or the mortgage; it was not concerned with finding a common intention in the abstract. Moreover, *Rosset* and the 'balance sheet cases' are not concerned with a survey of all of the material circumstances, as was *Midland Bank v Cooke*, but rather only with contributions of money. None of the cases have expressed themselves to be concerned simply with 'fairness', except the 'family assets cases'. And, for the reasons given at the end of this section, it is not possible simply to declare that constructive trust and estoppel are the same: if they are to be merged, then the basis on which one or other of the doctrines is to be altered must be explained. Therefore, Chadwick LJ cannot succeed in explaining all of the cases as being in agreement with one another. What must be done instead is to declare some cases correct and other cases incorrect – something which a Court of Appeal cannot do in the wake of a House of Lords judgment. Or better, as in this chapter, one should instead understand the differences between the cases.

The clearest example of Chadwick LJ's attempt to merge together doctrines which simply cannot be merged arises from his Lordship's attempt to reconcile *Lloyds Bank v Rosset* and *Midland Bank v Cooke* in one combined test. In *Lloyds Bank v Rosset*, Lord Bridge set out perfectly clearly that if there was no agreement between the parties then only contributions to the purchase price of the property or to the mortgage instalments would be sufficient to acquire an equitable interest in the land. By contrast, Waite LJ held that the court should 'survey the whole course of dealing' in *Midland Bank v Cooke* when deciding what conduct might be appropriate in the acquisition of an equitable interest in the land. Therefore, Waite LJ was clearly prepared to consider all conduct, even if it stretched beyond contributions to the purchase price of the property or to the mortgage instalments. Waite LJ is clearly taking an approach typical of a family court judge in considering all of the circumstances of the case. So, we come to Chadwick LJ in *Oxley v Hiscock*. His Lordship purported to reconcile these two radically different approaches (and all of the other approaches ranged across the spectrum between them) so that they could be merged into one test. That test would require that the court should look first for an agreement between the parties and only then at 'the whole course of dealing' if no such agreement could be found. This is simply to ignore the fact that the House of Lords in *Rosset* did not intend to permit such a broad survey to be undertaken by the court. Indeed the majority in the House of Lords in *Gissing v Gissing* also expressed themselves to be reluctant to accept the suggestion of Diplock LJ that common intentions could be identified on such a broad scale. It is suggested, therefore, that the exercise which Chadwick LJ undertook in *Oxley v Hiscock* is simply intellectually unsustainable. Nevertheless, this approach has been followed by two differently constituted Courts of Appeal and in essence by the majority in *Stack v Dowden*.

287   Eg, *Hammond v Mitchell* [1991] 1 WLR 1127; *Midland Bank v Cooke* [1995] 4 All ER 562. And the estoppel
      cases like *Re Basham (Deceased)* [1986] 1 WLR 1498 and *Pascoe v Turner* [1979] 1 WLR 431.
288   *Wayling v Jones* (1993) 69 P & CR 170; *Tinsley v Milligan* [1994] 1 AC 340.

Two cases in support of Oxley v Hiscock

In the Court of Appeal in *Stack v Dowden*[289] Chadwick LJ delivered a judgment which took the same approach as his judgment in *Oxley v Hiscock*. In that judgment Chadwick LJ suggested that there is a presumption that each of two parties whose names were put on the legal title of land were to take an equal equitable interest in that land.[290] Furthermore, when deciding the extent of the parties' equitable interests the court should survey the entire course of the parties' dealings so as to reach a 'fair' conclusion. The couple had met when she was 17 and he was 19. She earned more money than him. The parties kept their bank accounts and financial affairs entirely separate throughout their 27-year relationship, and had four children. When they bought their first house, it was bought by her and was put in her sole name. That house was sold and their second house bought. The purchase of the second house came as to 65% from the woman's money (in cash and in the form of the sale proceeds of the first house) and 35% by way of a mortgage taken out by the man. It was held by the Court of Appeal that the property should be divided in the proportions 65:35 in favour of the woman in proportion to their respective financial contributions to the purchase price of the house. This much could have been decided on resulting trust principles – although the court did not limit its judgment to resulting trust, thus following *dicta* of Lord Diplock in *Gissing v Gissing* to the effect that it was unnecessary to decide which form of trust gave rise to the equitable interest on these facts. The complicating factor in this case was that the conveyance of the property had contained a statement to the effect that the parties were to be beneficial owners of the property in equal shares. It was accepted, however, that this did not reflect the parties' true intentions. Consequently, it was held that there was no effective declaration of trust over the property and therefore that the equitable interest in the property ought to be divided in accordance with the parties' common intention. The House of Lords upheld the decision of the Court of Appeal; although the detail of its thinking was different, as is set out below in section 15.9.

In *Crossley v Crossley*[291] the Court of Appeal appeared to perpetuate a tendency in the courts to take the requirement in *Lloyds Bank v Rosset* – that an agreement, arrangement or understanding between the parties be taken to be their common intention – to mean that the court is at liberty to formulate precisely what it considers that understanding ought to be understood to have been, as opposed to insisting that there is precise evidence as to what the parties' understanding actually was. Thus the precision required in *Rosset* seems to have been diluted slightly in these cases. Thus it was considered appropriate for the trial judge to have decided that the parties had agreed merely that the claimant would have some beneficial interest in the property, without needing to find a precise understanding as to the extent and nature of that interest.[292] Here Corinna and Alan acquired the local authority house in which they lived under the right-to-buy legislation. They used a mortgage to acquire the property which was taken out in the name of Corinna, Alan and also their son, Paul. Paul did not make any payments towards the purchase of the property. When Alan died, the question arose whether or not Paul had an equitable interest in the property or whether the entire equitable

---

289 [2005] EWCA Civ 857, [2006] 1 FLR 254.

290 This case has since been the subject of an appeal to the House of Lords. A casenote is available on www. alastairhudson.com.

291 [2005] EWCA Civ 1581, [2006] BPIR 404.

292 [2005] EWCA Civ 1581, [23]–[29], *per* Sir Peter Gibson.

interest passed to Corinna under the survivorship principle. Having found such an intention that the claimant was to have an interest, the trial judge then estimated, without suggesting from where this inference came, that the size of that interest was equal to one-third of the total equity in the property. Similarly, it is suggested, the Court of Appeal proceeded to infer the common intention from the circumstances, based in part on the finding of a common intention that Paul was to have some interest in the property and then, presumably, on the basis that that interest should be an equal share. Thus a broader use is being made of *Rosset* than a literal reading of that case would permit, in favour of general approach based on preventing unconscionability: thus adopting the eclectic approach typified by *Oxley v Hiscock*.

15.8.3 Proprietary estoppel and unconscionability: *Jennings v Rice*

Proprietary estoppel was considered in section 15.7 above, and in much greater detail in Chapter 13. The purpose of this brief section is to correlate recent cases on proprietary estoppel with the 'unconscionability approach'. It was Walker LJ in *Jennings v Rice*[293] who expressed the view that proprietary estoppel is intended to prevent unconscionability. What emerged from the discussion of proprietary estoppel above, and which is observable in the case of *Jennings v Rice* itself, is that a successful claimant may not be awarded property rights to prevent unconscionability. Instead the court may order that, to prevent the claimant suffering the effects of unconscionable behaviour, the claimant should be awarded an amount of money sufficient to compensate her for her detriment. So, in *Jennings v Rice* itself it was held by the Court of Appeal that a man who had helped an old woman around her home for a number of years should be entitled to something to compensate him for his trouble on the basis that she had given rise in his mind to some expectation in reliance on which he had acted to his detriment. The remedy was for an arbitrary sum of money: 'arbitrary' in the sense that it bore no specific relation to any particular detriment which he had suffered nor to any salary he might otherwise have earned. Instead, the court decided that was fair compensation in the circumstances generally. This approach in equitable estoppel is not entirely new, of course, as evidenced by the following passage from Oliver J in *Taylor Fashions v Liverpool Victoria Trustees Co Ltd*[294] to the effect that if an award of proprietary estoppel were not made in that case then:

> it would be unconscionable for a party to be permitted to deny that which, knowingly or unknowingly, he has allowed or encouraged another to assume to his detriment.[295]

Therefore, we can see that proprietary estoppel is increasingly based on the notion of unconscionability, arguably in common with the ordinary test for constructive trusts under *Westdeutsche Landesbank v Islington*.[296]

This proximity between the doctrines of constructive trust and proprietary estoppel is considered in detail in section 15.11.2, where it is suggested that there have always been

---

293   [2002] EWCA Civ 159.
294   [1981] 2 WLR 576, 593. These sentiments were echoed by Oliver LJ in *Habib Bank Ltd v Habib Bank AG* [1981] 2 All ER 650, [1981] 1 WLR 1265, 1285.
295   This approach was followed in *Turner v Jacob* [2006] EWHC 1317 (Ch), [81].
296   [1996] AC 669.

significant differences between the doctrines. However, a semi-conscious elision of the concepts has been accepted in the unconscionability cases because there is a superficial similarity between their shared notions of 'unconscionability'. So, in *Yaxley v Gotts*[297] it was held that both doctrines are 'concerned with equity's intervention to provide relief against unconscionable conduct'. Similarly in *Grant v Edwards*[298] it was suggested by Browne-Wilkinson V-C that 'useful guidance may in future be obtained from the principles underlying the law of proprietary estoppel which in my judgment are closely akin to those laid down in *Gissing v Gissing*'.[299] Thus there is a reasonably long pedigree underpinning the idea that common intention constructive trusts and proprietary estoppel are based on similar principles. Most of these judicial comments do not suggest that the two doctrines should actually be seen as being one. The point is also made in *Van Laetham v Brooker* by Lawrence Collins J that the *remedies* provided in proprietary estoppel and constructive trust are effectively the same in that the courts award whatever rights they consider appropriate in good conscience.[300] So, his Lordship identified an amount of money which the claimant was entitled to receive in that case which reflected her financial and manual contribution to the acquisition and development of various properties, while also taking into account the skilled and larger contributions of the defendant. Thus, instead of arguing that the two doctrines are identical, the courts tend to suggest that there are merely general similarities between them. That they do conceptually remain distinct is considered below at 15.11.2.

15.8.4 Seeking fairness in all the circumstances: *Cox v Jones*

An example of a court seeking to achieve a fair result in the circumstances, without concerning itself overly closely with the niceties of doctrine, is *Cox v Jones*. In *Cox v Jones*[301] two barristers became engaged to be married and set up home together.[302] It was evident that their relationship was in difficulties from the beginning when the couple only managed to cohabit successfully for three months after their engagement.[303] Mr Jones was much older than Miss Cox and his legal practice was much more successful than hers.[304] The couple bought a country house in Essex together for £480,000 in October 1999, but the property was placed in Mr Jones's sole name, with Mr Jones taking out a mortgage in his sole name for £450,000. The property required extensive renovation which Miss Cox supervised but for which Mr Jones paid almost exclusively. Mr Jones raised a mortgage to acquire a flat in Islington which Mr Jones contended was intended to be an investment for him, whereas Miss Cox contended that it was intended to be purchased by him as a nominee for her, with Miss Cox providing just

---

297 [2000] Ch 162, 176, [2000] 1 All ER 711, *per* Walker LJ.
298 [1986] Ch 638, 656, *per* Browne-Wilkinson V-C.
299 [1971] AC 886.
300 [2006] 2 FLR 495, para [263].
301 [2004] 3 FCR 693, [2004] EWHC 1486 (Ch).
302 It should be noted that acquisition of such rights may be considered to have been made conditional on the parties being married and that if they are not, then such rights might not come into existence: *Ottey v Grundy* [2003] EWCA Civ 1176; [2003] WTLR 1253; *Lightfoot v Lightfoot-Brown* [2004] EWCA 840, [2004] All ER (D) 92.
303 Mr Jones lived in a flat in Stone Buildings in Lincoln's Inn and Miss Cox had a large Alsation dog called 'Bootsie' which caused tension due to its ebullient behaviour in a small flat.
304 The couple met, it appears from evidence, in chambers when she was seeking a tenancy and where he was already a long-standing tenant, although their relationship did not start until after she had left that chambers.

over half of the deposit. Miss Cox also owned a Fiat car which Mr Jones used overseas: Mr Jones claimed to have bought the car from Miss Cox, whereas Miss Cox claimed that she had only lent the car to Mr Jones. Mr Jones had bought an engagement ring for Miss Cox for £10,000: their engagement was broken, but there was no agreement about whether the engagement ended in 1998[305] (albeit their relationship continued in some form) or only some years later in 2001. Their relationship ended ultimately in 2001 after the last in a string of situations in which Mr Jones had been physically violent towards Miss Cox.

The claims were as to ownership of the Essex country house, the Islington flat, the car and the engagement ring. As to findings of evidence, it was made clear in the judgment that the facts were found on the judge's impression as to the credibility of each of the witnesses in the witness box.[306] This demonstrates how it is frequently very difficult to arrive at 'the truth' in trusts of homes cases precisely because the parties frequently cannot prove everything they allege, because the parties have frequently fallen out with one another, and because people are frequently poor witnesses when asked to discuss their personal lives. As to the Essex house, Mann J held that the parties' intentions were contained in an agreement (akin to that identified in *Lloyds Bank v Rosset*) whereby the couple had agreed that the house would be held jointly between them and in relation to which Miss Cox had acted to her detriment by supervising the renovation works[307] and by giving up her legal practice to do so.[308] However, because Mr Jones had suffered much greater detriment than Miss Cox, the property would be distributed 75:25 between them as opposed to being divided equally.

What is interesting here is that Mann J did not find any clear agreement as to what interest each person was supposed to have: rather, he found that there was some form of general agreement but felt himself entitled to declare what share should result from it. The court instead looked for a solution which would be 'fair having regard to the whole course of dealing between them in relation to the property'.[309] This is a much more flexible approach than that used in *Lloyds Bank v Rosset*, where the assumption was that the parties must have reached an agreement either as to the shares which each party would have (which the parties had not in this instance) or as to the amount of money which each party would contribute (where Miss Cox had contributed nothing and so would have had to receive no interest at all). So, it was held to be unconscionable to have denied some interest to Miss Cox because the parties had intended the house to be a jointly-held house, whereas it was also considered unconscionable to give Miss Cox a half-share in that house given the size of her contribution.

As to the flat, it was found that the parties' intention was that the flat was intended to have been bought by Mr Jones as nominee for Miss Cox because only he could have obtained the mortgage, whereas she could not have done so (due to his income being larger

---

305   When the couple had an argument and Mr Jones pretended to throw the engagement ring out of the window (although he actually retained the ring and gave it back to Miss Cox the next day).

306   This may seem surprising in itself in that the principal witnesses were barristers whom one might have expected to make competent witnesses. It just goes to show that one often behaves very differently in relation to one's personal affairs when compared to one's business affairs.

307   Interestingly, of course, supervision of building works had been ignored by the House of Lords in *Lloyds Bank v Rosset* itself.

308   Giving up her legal practice, however, would constitute detriment even though supervision of building work would not ordinarily acquire an equitable interest in the property.

309   Quoting Chadwick LJ in *Oxley v Hiscock* [2004] EWCA Civ 546, [2004] 2 FCR 295, para [69].

than hers). Therefore, Miss Cox was found to be entitled to the entire equitable interest in the flat.[310] It was found as a fact that Miss Cox procured the purchase of the flat at a lower price than otherwise it would have been sold because she knew the vendor personally and so convinced him to make a private sale rather than purchasing it at a higher rate through estate agents.[311] She did not acquire an equitable interest on the basis of this reduction in price (by extrapolation from *Springette v Defoe*), but rather it was taken into account as something beneficial to Mr Jones which she had contributed,[312] together with the detriment associated with her not seeking to acquire the flat in her sole name.[313] As to the chattels, it was held that the ring was intended to have been given to Miss Cox absolutely and that Miss Cox had intended to transfer outright the car to Mr Jones; consequently, neither chattel was to be returned.

On the basis of the foregoing discussion, the 'unconscionability approach' requires the court to consider the extent to which it would be unconscionable for the defendant to deny an equitable interest in the property to the claimant. This approach seems content to meld the strict approach in *Lloyds Bank v Rosset*, ostensibly based on constructive trust, with general principles of good conscience as emerge in the general law on constructive trusts[314] and on proprietary estoppel.[315] There are two key difficulties with this approach. First, Lord Bridge's speech in *Rosset* was clearly not intended to be as flexible as it is being portrayed in these cases; rather, it is the more flexible approach in *Grant v Edwards*[316] which is really being applied. It would be more intellectually satisfying, it is suggested, if the courts acknowledged that the tests set out in *Rosset* are inappropriate in this context and so explored more satisfactorily the principles which they wish to apply. Pretending to apply a test which is not really being applied at all (or, at least, applying it improperly) is only likely to cause confusion and to hide the courts' real purpose. Secondly, this approach continues to purport to meld the doctrines of constructive trust and proprietary estoppel together when they operate on very different bases: the former institutional and the other remedial. To meld them together would require that one or other or both of the doctrines be altered significantly: to do this, the courts must analyse what those changes are, or admit that such a synthesis of principle is impossible.[317]

15.8.5 A model of the general constructive trust combined with the common intention constructive trust

What the Court of Appeal was seeking to do in *Oxley v Hiscock* was to combine the general law on constructive trusts with the general principles of proprietary estoppel with the common intention constructive trust. A much more convincing model of this sort of

---

310   It is unclear then whether or not Mr Jones is obliged to pay off the mortgage or whether Miss Cox is obliged to assume liability for the mortgage henceforth.

311   She had lived in a flat in the same block of the vendor and so knew him personally: this was credited with enabling her to obtain a reduction in the purchase price.

312   An odd argument this: she is taken to have given something of benefit whereas, of course, Mr Jones was otherwise buying her a flat so the benefit was a benefit she was really contributing to herself rather than to him.

313   It is unclear how this head of detriment is said to relate to the acquisition of the flat, however, given that she still had the flat acquired for her by Mr Jones's mortgage.

314   As discussed in section 12.1 above.

315   As discussed in section 13.3 above.

316   [1986] Ch 638.

317   See Hudson, 2004:2.

combined approach was attempted in *Van Laetham v Brooker*.[318] In that case Lawrence Collins J incorporated the general understanding of constructive trusts principles into the area of trusts of homes under the sub-heading 'constructive trusts' in the following terms:[319]

A trust arises in connection with the acquisition by one party of a legal title to property whenever that party has so conducted himself that it would be inequitable to allow him to deny to the other party a beneficial interest in the property acquired. This will be so where (i) there was a common intention that both parties should have a beneficial interest and (ii) the claimant has acted to his detriment in the belief that by so acting he was acquiring a beneficial interest . . .

This formulation of the constructive trust is familiar from the material considered in Chapter 12 in relation to constructive trusts in general, but it is combined here with the sort of constructive trust which was applied in *Lloyds Bank v Rosset*. This formulation connects the general notion of good conscience in relation to constructive trusts with the common intention constructive trust.

A differently constituted Court of Appeal in *Oates v Stimson*[320] took a similarly eclectic approach to the law in this area, although on different bases from *Oxley v Hiscock*. In this case two men acquired a house together by means of an endowment mortgage. The couple agreed that they would make equal payments towards the mortgage. Latterly, the claimant was made redundant and the defendant agreed to take on responsibility for all of the mortgage repayments and other outgoings on the house. It was found that the two men had agreed orally that the defendant would take on these added responsibilities in return for a right to acquire the house on payment of an agreed sum. Issues arose as to what rights the parties had. It was held by Sir Christopher Staughton that: 'If there must be a search for the minimum equity to do justice, there is also an obligation to take into account all relevant circumstances including the conduct of the parties.'[321]

This encapsulation of the test combines ideas reminiscent of proprietary estoppel (in the 'search for the minimum equity to do justice' akin to *Crabb v Arun DC*) with the approach in *Midland Bank v Cooke* (the requirement to 'take into account all relevant circumstances') but no reference is made in this judgment to *Lloyds Bank v Rosset* (unless we are supposed to infer it from the reference to 'the conduct of the parties', which seems unlikely in the context). It is thus not at all clear on what doctrinal basis his Lordship reached his decision. What is clear is that on the facts his Lordship considered that the claimant should be bound by the agreement he reached with the defendant to the effect that the defendant would acquire responsibility for the mortgage repayments and surrender to the defendant the rights which he had agreed to sell to him.

By contrast, Auld LJ expressed his conception of the test in the following fashion:

Mr Oates's conduct, in reliance upon which Mr Stimson acted to his detriment and/or changed his position, gave rise to a constructive trust in favour of Mr Stimson rendering

318 [2005] EWHC 1478 (Ch), [2006] 2 FLR 495, [2006] 1 FCR 697.
319 *Ibid*, para [61].
320 [2006] EWCA Civ 548.
321 *Ibid*, para [13].

it unconscionable not to permit him to enforce the oral agreement for [the sale of the property].

This conceptualisation of the test was based expressly on *Lloyds Bank v Rosset* and *Yaxley v Gotts* and is a combination of common intention constructive trust and of proprietary estoppel respectively which bases the 'constructive trust' on 'detriment' and on the unconsionability which would be occasioned if the claimant could not enforce the agreement. It could be that this 'constructive trust' arises on a general basis as with *Westdeutsche Landesbank v Islington*. Keene LJ expressed agreement with Auld LJ rather than Sir Christopher Staughton.

15.8.6 The 'excuses' cases: rights not based on common intention

Oddly, for all of the talk of 'common intention' in this area of law, there have been cases in which constructive trusts have been upheld over the home in flat contradiction of the intention of one of the parties: and thus these cases are definitely not concerned with the *common* intention of the parties. *Van Laetham v Brooker*[322] concerned, *inter alia*, a situation in which the defendant provided an excuse for not putting the land in question in joint names: his excuse was that the woman would have had to pay capital gains tax if the property had been put in her name. Two earlier decisions had considered excuses. In *Eves v Eves*[323] the claimant was told by the defendant that her name could not be put on the legal title of the property until she was 21. It was held that because the defendant had led the claimant to believe that she would acquire a beneficial right in the property by using excuses, when in truth he intended to deny her any rights in the property, the claimant was entitled to an equitable interest in the property. In *Grant v Edwards*[324] the defendant gave an excuse for not putting the claimant on the legal title which, as the Court of Appeal found, suggested that her name would be added to the legal title in the future. Consequently, it was held that the excuse amounted to a representation that she would acquire such a right in the future and therefore it would be unconscionable to deny her a right in the property. It was held by Lawrence Collins J that these cases could be considered to be proprietary estoppel cases and not true common intention constructive trust cases because the very fact that the defendant had made excuses to the claimant suggested that the parties did not have a common intention as to who owned the beneficial interest in the property: that is, the defendant thought the claimant had no rights, whereas the claimant thought that she did.[325] Therefore, rather than the claimant's rights being based on a common intention, those rights are based on the unconscionability of denying a beneficial interest in the property. This is the antithesis of *Rosset*. The excuses cases are based on unconscionability and not on common intention.

15.8.7 Conclusions on the unconscionability approach

The notion of unconscionability is gaining ground across equity generally. It should be recalled that all constructive trusts are based on a notion of good conscience such that a person will be required to hold property on constructive trust whenever she has knowledge

---

322 [2005] EWHC 1478 (Ch), [2006] 2 FLR 495, [2006] 1 FCR 697.
323 [1975] 3 All ER 768, [1975] 1 WLR 1338, 1342, *per* Lord Denning.
324 [1986] Ch 638.
325 [2005] EWHC 1478 (Ch), para [67].

of some factor in relation to that property which affects her conscience, such as having stolen the property or having received it under a mistake. This principle is considered in section 12.1 in relation to the decision of the House of Lords in *Westdeutsche Landesbank v Islington*.[326] In another context, in relation to constructive trusteeship imposed on people who receive trust property further to a breach of trust, the most recent Court of Appeal decisions have found that liability will be based on the defendant having received the trust property in unconscionable circumstances.[327] Consequently, it is only in relation to trusts of homes, oddly, that this notion of unconscionability has been slow to take hold. In this most traditional of contexts, the courts have continued to apply comparatively rigid principles, such as the common intention constructive trust, instead of the general principles of good conscience which have traditionally informed equity. Consequently, it is unsurprising that the courts have begun to develop a means of thinking about rights in the home which is based on fairness. Like grass growing between paving flags, it is a phenomenon which is always likely to re-emerge whether in the form of Lord Denning's family assets doctrine, or Waite LJ's use of family law methodologies to allocate rights in the home, or this general notion of unconscionability.

A note of caution in relation to the unconscionability approach, however. The Court of Appeal in *Stack v Dowden* was required to consider *Huntingford v Hobbs* in relation to the terms of the conveyance in that case. This required Chadwick LJ to quote the following *dicta* from Sir Christopher Slade in the Court of Appeal in *Huntingford v Hobbs*: '. . . the parties' respective beneficial interests in the property fall to be determined not by reference to any broad concepts of justice, but by reference to the principles governing the creation or operation of resulting, implied, or constructive trusts'.[328] Thus, it can be observed that the balance sheet approach did not envisage a general notion of good conscience or justice as has been used by the courts under the unconscionability approach, any more than the House of Lords in *Lloyds Bank v Rosset* or the majority in *Gissing v Gissing* did. Therefore, it cannot be said that the unconscionability approach now constitutes a settled view of the law. Rather it is a trend in the case law used by judges to reach decisions which they consider to be appropriate on their own facts. In the next section we shall turn to consider the decision of the House of Lords in *Stack v Dowden* and then how other Commonwealth jurisdictions have dealt with these ideas, before attempting to correlate some of the conceptual approaches to the case law principles. First, a note on how these cases sometimes work in practice.

15.8.8 An odd case not relying on conscionability

The case of *Kean v McDonald*[329] has not yet made an appearance in the full, printed law reports[330] and I doubt that it ever shall. I make mention of it here only to illustrate a more general point about the way in which English property law operates in practice out there in the murky world beyond the high-minded certainties and decencies of the university seminar room. The parties in this case agreed in 1997 to transfer title in land (seemingly a flat near Southport, Merseyside) on payment of £10,000. That sum of money strikes one as a small

326 [1996] AC 669.
327 *BCCI v Akindele* [2001] Ch 437.
328 [1993] 1 FLR 736, at 744: quoted at [2006] 1 FLR 254, [19].
329 [2006] All ER (D) 348.
330 It is available only on-line.

amount for a transfer of rights in land, even a flat. This agreement was found by Michael Crystal QC, sitting as a deputy High Court judge, to constitute a common intention constructive trust further to *Lloyds Bank v Rosset*. There are a number of oddities, I would suggest, about this decision. A common intention constructive trust was held to exist even though the parties seem to have agreed that there would be an outright transfer of title in the property as opposed to a trust, but no conveyance was ever carried out so as to effect that intention.

Let us take an analogy with the law on express trusts. Under the principle in *Milroy v Lord*,[331] and even though there had not been a proper conveyance of title at common law (simply a purported payment of money further to the agreement, which would not have constituted a valid contract for a sale of an interest in land) we might have thought that no trust could be effected on the basis that equity will not assist a volunteer, or on the basis that there is no equity to perfect an imperfect gift. Of course, consideration (it seems) did pass in this case on payment of £10,000, and therefore the claimant was not a volunteer. But none of these issues of technicality arises in relation to constructive trusts. That is in the nature of constructive trusts under s 53(2) of the Law of Property Act 1925 under which there is no formality required for their existence.

Interestingly, however, the common intention constructive trust seems to arise here regardless of the equity of the case and not only regardless of principles like that in *Milroy v Lord*. Furthermore, it did not matter to the court (Deputy Judge Crystal QC), it seems, that some of the parties were involved in criminal activities and that the Crown Prosecution Service ('CPS') was objecting to the constructive trust. The presence of the CPS is intriguing and not explained fully in the judgment. A number of parties were refused the right to appear before the court; there were references to the criminal records of many or all of the witnesses; the payment of £10,000 is only 'alleged' to have been made; one claimant to a right in the property is, we are told, 'a fugitive from justice'; the property was purportedly, possibly fraudulently (but ultimately unsuccessfully) transferred to a company for a consideration of £1; the CPS contended that much of the evidence was untruthful: and thus one is left with the impression that property is being passed between people suspected by the CPS of involvement in criminal activity so as to put property beyond the reach of the CPS at an undervalue. If this were so, would it not constitute unconscionable behaviour in general terms?

No point was taken by the court as to whether or not the parties here had acted and come to equity with clean hands. In parallel with the decision in *Tinsley v Milligan*[332] the claimant here is entitled to take an equitable interest on the basis that he has paid for that interest and on the basis that its acquisition was not proved to have been directly the result of an illegal act. Had Lord Goff, who dissented in *Tinsley v Milligan*, been deciding *Kean v McDonald* then he might very well have held that the criminal activities in which the parties had been involved, and the clear attempt to transfer this land at an undervalue between them, ought to mean that equity (in the form of a common intention constructive trust) should not have been available to the claimant. In *Kean v McDonald* there was no consideration at all of any authorities other than *Lloyds Bank v Rosset* and *Yaxley v Gotts* (to the effect that an equitable interest may pass on the basis of detrimental reliance without the need to be bound by statutory principles under the Law of Property (Miscellaneous Provisions) Act 1989). It would

---

331 (1862) 4 De GF&J 264.
332 [1994] 1 AC 340.

have been interesting to know whether or not the new judicial enthusiasm for unconsciona-bility would have led to this claimant being denied a right in the property.

This case demonstrates, I would suggest, how many cases are decided before the courts which we would not have known about before the advent of electronic reporting of all deci-sions in the higher courts: it demonstrates how many of those cases are disposed of entirely on their own facts without reference to all of the possible authorities which might be discussed in the textbooks. It demonstrates how many important decisions are made in a rush and under great pressure, with attention only to the precise circumstances in front of our noses. How like life.

15.9 THE PRINCIPLES IN *STACK v DOWDEN* AND *JONES v KERNOTT*

15.9.1 Introduction

The decision of the House of Lords in *Stack v Dowden*[333] made the newspapers and the head-lines on BBC Radio 4 news. A remarkable thing really given that it effected very little real change to the law. It was a great, missed opportunity to tidy up the law relating to trusts of homes. The subsequent decision of the Supreme Court in *Jones v Kernott*[334] presented a guide to the interpretation of the judgment of Baroness Hale in *Stack v Dowden* and, usefully, set out a clear summary of the principles which emerged as a result of it. What emerges, however, is that very little of the previous case law has been overruled, that the previous case law will continue to be significant, and that many of the courts at first instance were not following the approach set out in *Stack v Dowden* in any event[335] – which is perhaps a signal for the future of this area of the law. Each of these cases is considered in turn before a short discussion of some of the key remaining problems is presented.

15.9.2 What the House of Lords decided in *Stack v Dowden*

The majority of the House of Lords agreed that there should be a presumption that if there is more than one person registered on the legal title of the home then those legal owners should be presumed to be the owners of the equitable interest in that home equally; whereas, if there is only one person registered on the legal title of the home then that sole legal owner should be presumed to be the sole owner of the equitable interest in that home. These presumptions are merely presumptions, and can therefore be rebutted by any evidence which suggests that the parties' common intention was something different.[336] Therefore, all of the law before *Stack v Dowden* will still be needed to identify both those situations in which people other than the legal owners can acquire an equitable interest in that property, and also the

---

333   [2007] UKHL 17, [2007] 2 WLR 831.
334   [2011] UKSC 53, [2011] 3 WLR 1752.
335   As is considered in the text, a survey of all of the courts at first instance to have considered these issues since *Stack v Dowden* demonstrates a continuation of the same loose observance of the doctrine of precedent which was the case before *Stack v Dowden* was decided. Judges at first instance seem to pick equally happily from any of the earlier cases, and to use ideas from proprietary estoppel or constructive trust as they please. Most of these cases are unreported and so available only by a careful search of online sources.
336   This tells us nothing, however, about the situation in which the parties do not have an intention in common – for example where one of the parties has made excuses to the other party not to include her on the legal title over the property – about who was intended to be an equitable owner of the property.

circumstances in which the equitable interests of the parties in their home can be greater or less than an equal share in the total equitable interest.

Baroness Hale did suggest approval for the general drift in the law suggested by *Oxley v Hiscock* and those textbook writers who have seen a preference in the courts for taking into account the whole course of dealing between the parties and not simply their financial contributions to the purchase price of the property.[337] However, the majority did express a preference for finding the parties' intention and not simply looking for what is fair. That the courts may simply abandon the search for the parties' common intention and simply replace that with whatever it considers to be 'fair' was considered in *Holman v Howes*[338] to be contrary to the direction signalled by the House of Lords in *Stack v Dowden*.[339] However, it is suggested that Lloyd LJ did stray too far in this regard by stating that the inquiry into what is fair to be 'impermissible':[340] it is suggested that Baroness Hale specified that it should not be the first resort for a court but did not preclude such a consideration outright. The following *dicta* of Baroness Hale have acquired some force in the lower courts to the effect that: "[t]he search is to ascertain the parties' shared intentions, actual, inferred or imputed, with respect of the property in light of their whole course of conduct in relation to it".[341] The decision in *Stack v Dowden* is actually quite retrograde when looked at closely. It has in truth reversed much of the progress that was being made towards giving judges the power to decide what they considered to be 'fair' and instead has returned to a focus on the formalities of conveyancing and the primacy of monetary contributions in allocating rights in the home.[342] Thus the trend suggested in the earlier portions of this chapter in the case decided after *Lloyds Bank v Rosset* appears to have been approved by the majority of the House of Lords; whereas *Lloyds Bank v Rosset* itself did receive some criticism for being too stringent, even if it was not explicitly overruled. This tentativeness can be explained by the preference of the majority of the House of Lords to await Law Commission proposals in this area and potentially statutory guidance as to how such cases should be decided. The approach in *Jones* v *Kernott* qualified this slightly.

The facts in *Stack v Dowden* concerned Ms Dowden, a successful electrical engineer who contributed the majority of the family's finances, and Mr Stack, a self-employed builder and decorator, who began a relationship in 1975 before Ms Dowden bought a house in her sole name in 1983. The couple had four children. The couple sold their first house for three times its purchase price and then bought a second home in their joint names. Ms Dowden provided 65% of the purchase price of the second home, with the balance being provided by way of a mortgage. Ms Dowden paid off about 60% of the capital on the mortgage. Mr Stack paid for the mortgage interest instalments, and the parties separately paid the premiums on separate endowment insurance policies. The couple kept their bank accounts separate, in large part because Mr Stack operated his business accounts separately. Mr Stack had his business correspondence sent to his father's address. The House of Lords upheld the judgment that the equitable interest in the property should be divided 65:35 in favour of Ms Dowden.

---

337   [2007] UKHL 17, [2007] 2 WLR 831, para [61] *et seq.*
338   [2007] EWCA Civ 877, [2007] BPIR 1085, para [29] *et seq., per* Lloyd LJ.
339   The same point was accepted in *Fowler v Barron* [2008] EWCA Civ 377, 11 ITELR 198, 205, [17], *per* Arden LJ.
340   *Ibid*, para [32].
341   [2007] UKHL 17, [2007] 2 AC 432, para [60]. See also *Bindra v Chopra* [2008] EWHC 1715 (Ch); and *Morris v Morris* [2008] EWCA Civ 257.
342   This argument is made by Probert, 'Equality in the Family Home?' (2007) *Feminist Legal Studies*, 341.

Undertaking a survey of the entire course of dealing between the parties, including the extensive work which Mr Stack had performed on both properties, the equitable interests nevertheless closely reflected their financial contributions in fact.

15.9.3 What the House of Lords did not decide in *Stack v Dowden*

So, let us consider what the House of Lords did not decide. First, the House of Lords did not overrule any of the preceding cases. Therefore all of the law before 2007 seemingly continues in full force and effect. The only exception was a suggestion made in *Walker v Hall, Springette v Defoe* and *Huntingford v Hobbs* that there should be different principles in relation to cases where there is only one person on the legal title and cases where there is more than one person on the legal title: this narrow proposition was doubted.[343]

Secondly, and following on from the first point, the House of Lords did not create a new test to replace any of the previous law. In this sense, the decision in *Stack v Dowden* was a great missed opportunity.[344] Therefore, we are left with the problem of applying the various differing approaches considered already in this chapter, once we have applied the presumptions set out above. As legal scholars studying equity and the law of trusts we must observe how those approaches do indeed operate differently. Lord Neuberger, in his dissenting speech in *Stack v Dowden*, did attempt to set out a clear approach to answering a range of questions to do with trusts of homes, but this was not followed by any of the other members of the House of Lords: more of that below.

15.9.4 Who agreed with whom about what in *Stack v Dowden*

The majority

In this section we shall consider what the House of Lords did decide. Lord Hoffmann agreed with the result Baroness Hale came to on the appeal.[345] Lord Hope expressed concurrence with Baroness Hale.[346] Lord Walker expressed concurrence with Baroness Hale and further told us that he had set aside large sections of his own speech (tragically, given his long experience in trusts law matters) having read her account of the sociological problems surrounding trusts of homes.[347] Baroness Hale then set out her speech (in reverse order) disposing of the question on the facts of the case, making some comments about *Oxley v Hiscock* and related cases, and considering some of the issues raised in the family law literature in relation to cohabitees. Lord Neuberger then delivered a dissenting speech which dealt in detail with the law in this area and which suggested a model for answering questions in the future, with which none of the other members of the court concurred.

---

343 [2007] UKHL 17, [2007] 2 WLR 831, para [65].
344 Swadling, 2007.
345 [2007] UKHL 17, [2007] 2 WLR 831, para [1]. Although he did not, strictly, say that he agreed with her views on the law, rather 'for the reasons she gives I too would dismiss the appeal': ie his Lordship agreed with the result but did not strictly express a view as to the law.
346 [2007] UKHL 17, [2007] 2 WLR 831, para [2].
347 [2007] UKHL 17, [2007] 2 WLR 831, para [14].

Lord Hope – the Scots law problem

Lord Hope considered that the most significant question was to identify the correct starting point in cases relating to the home.[348] This he did by dividing between cases in which the legal title is held only in one name and cases in which the legal title is held in joint names:[349] his lordship then referred to Baroness Hale's opinion as to the presumption that multiple ownership of the legal title leads to equal division of the equitable interest, and sole ownership of the legal title leads to a presumption of sole ownership of the equitable interest.[350]

Lord Hope also expressed the hope that English law could come to resemble certain aspects of Scots law.[351] In Scots law, s 27(3) of the Family Law (Scotland) Act 2006 gives the courts the power to disapply the presumption that the family home will be divided equally between parties to a divorce.[352] The real difficulty with suggesting parallels with Scots law is that Scotland does not have equity as part of its jurisprudence. So to suggest a parallel between the two legal systems is extremely unhelpful. When English law decides these questions according to conscience and trust and so forth, then why look for inspiration from a jurisdiction which has none of those ideas in its jurisprudence? If all that is intended is the expression of a hope that Parliament may create a similar statute for England and Wales then that is one thing, but it is pointless for a court to suggest parallels with another jurisdiction where things are done very differently if that same court is not going to effect any meaningful changes to the existing case law principles.

Lord Walker – the trusts law specialist

Lord Walker was the law lord in *Stack v Dowden* with the most experience of trusts law. His judgments in *Jennings v Rice*[353] and other cases had also informed much of the development of the 'unconscionability approach' in recent cases, as considered above. It is therefore something of a tragedy that he decided to delete most of his draft opinion[354] in deference to the opinion of Baroness Hale, particularly given that Baroness Hale approaches much of this issue from the perspective of land law and family law, as opposed to trusts law. Lord Walker expressed his judgment as being merely a footnote to the judgment of Baroness Hale. We do pick up some interesting ideas from Lord Walker nevertheless. First, we are told that the law on trusts of homes will not gravitate towards unjust enrichment law in this context,[355] as it has in Canada for example, nor will it gravitate towards contract law,[356] but rather it will remain a question for trusts law. Lord Walker considered that the court should not make such a change before the Law Commission had published proposals in this area. Secondly, Lord Walker expressed his view to be that there should not be any fusion of constructive trust with proprietary estoppel in this area,[357] given (it is suggested) the institutional nature of the former

---

348   [2007] UKHL 17, [2007] 2 WLR 831, para [3].
349   [2007] UKHL 17, [2007] 2 WLR 831, para [4].
350   [2007] UKHL 17, [2007] 2 WLR 831, para [4].
351   [2007] UKHL 17, [2007] 2 WLR 831, para [6].
352   [2007] UKHL 17, [2007] 2 WLR 831, para [7].
353   [2003] 1 P&CR 100.
354   As we are told at [2007] UKHL 17, [2007] 2 WLR 831, para [14].
355   [2007] UKHL 17, [2007] 2 WLR 831, para [23]. Cf. Lord Hope [2007] UKHL 17, [2007] 2 WLR 831, paras [9]-[11], suggesting that that is the Scots law approach.
356   [2007] UKHL 17, [2007] 2 WLR 831, para [28].
357   [2007] UKHL 17, [2007] 2 WLR 831, para [37].

doctrine and the remedial nature of the latter. The resulting trust was considered to be a doctrine of limited usefulness in this context.[358] (Interestingly, as considered below, even though resulting trusts based solely on financial contributions are disparaged in these recent cases, nevertheless the judgments tend to follow very closely the proportions which the parties would have received if only their financial contributions had been taken into account.)

Thirdly, the decision in *Lloyds Bank v Rosset* was criticised, although not explicitly over-ruled. Lord Walker considered that *Rosset* was in line with some earlier cases but considered that it 'did not take full account of the views . . . expressed in *Gissing v Gissing*'.[359] Lord Walker then suggested that, whether the second common intention constructive trust is correct or not, 'the law has moved on [from *Rosset*], and your Lordships should move it a little more in the same direction, while bearing in mind that the Law Commission . . . may recast the law in this area'.[360] It is suggested that this criticism is not quite the same as over-ruling *Rosset* and is certainly not the same as setting out a new test. Rather, Lord Walker was suggesting that the developments outlined in this Chapter 15 should continue: that is, moving from the strict *Rosset* test towards an approach based on unconscionability and a considera-tion of the whole course of dealing between the parties.

Fourthly, there is some discussion of the tendency in cases like *Pettitt v Pettitt* for the court itself to 'imply' or 'infer' a common intention from the circumstances and thus to impute that court-created intention to the parties, rather than to insist upon explicit evidence of the existence of such an intention.[361] This tallies with the view of Chadwick LJ in *Oxley v Hiscock*[362] that the court can 'supply' the parties' common intention if they did not actually have a conscious common intention.

Other than this, Lord Walker deliberately chose not to consider the 'academic questions' as to the nature of the trust and so forth. This attitude, it is suggested, will not do. The so-called 'academic questions' are very important in practice. First, it is important to know whether or not the common intention must be proven on the facts or whether it can be imputed. If it is to be imputed then it is very important to know what sort of factors will encourage a court to find an intention either to award or to deny a right in the home to someone. Secondly, distinguishing between institutional constructive trusts, remedial constructive trusts and proprietary estoppel is important because it is important to know whether the successful claimant will acquire a right in property (and if so, in what form) or alternatively merely a right to an amount of money (whether the latter is only available under proprietary estoppel). Thirdly, if the successful claimant may only acquire a right to an amount of money, by way of proprietary estoppel, then is that an amount of money to compensate her detriment, to fulfil her expectations, or simply to prevent 'unconscionability' in some general sense?[363] Fourthly, it is very important to know on what basis the court will adjust any original agreement between the parties or any resulting trust allocation of rights to account for changes in the parties' circumstances or intentions in later years. Fifthly, it is

358   [2007] UKHL 17, [2007] 2 WLR 831, para [28]; although see para [32] in relation to quasi-commercial relationships.
359   [2007] UKHL 17, [2007] 2 WLR 831, para [26].
360   [2007] UKHL 17, [2007] 2 WLR 831, para [26].
361   [2007] UKHL 17, [2007] 2 WLR 831, paras [18] *et seq.*
362   [2004] 2 FLR 669, para [66].
363   In that unconscionability may itself seek to prevent a person suffering uncompensated detriment, or it may seek to prevent a person taking some sort of enrichment, or it may seek to prevent reneging on a promise which has induced detrimental reliance from the claimant.

very important to know what the test is supposed to be; and if the test is simply to be a power to prevent unconscionability then to have some idea as to the principles which inform that notion of unconscionability. These are not merely academic questions: rather, they are practical questions on which the lower courts may well be entitled to expect some guidance.

Baroness Hale – a family lawyer's approach

It was Baroness Hale who delivered the leading speech. Her approach is undoubtedly that of a family lawyer, referring as it does to a wealth of family law scholarship[364] but to little trusts law scholarship (of which there is a library's worth). Quite deliberately, Baroness Hale avoided setting out anything as clear as a test or even a set of central principles by reference to which future decisions could be made. Instead there are general preferences for one kind of approach – broadly, that suggested by Chadwick LJ in *Oxley v Hiscock*, in spite of its many flaws – and a hope that the Law Commission will spare all our blushes by generating something which can in time become legislation to decide these difficult questions. There are six principal points to emerge from the speech of Baroness Hale. This judgment is reviewed by Lord Walker and Lady Hale in a joint judgment in the later Supreme Court decision in *Jones v Kernott* which is considered below; but for present purposes it is useful to focus on this judgment in the abstract before considering the way it has been re-interpreted by Lady Hale and Lord Walker later.

First, there is a distinction to be drawn between the personal context and the commercial context.[365] It seems that this, following on from *Pettitt v Pettitt*, may have been a feature in argument in that the court was being asked to consider whether or not to impute a common intention in the same way that a common law court sometimes reads implied terms into contracts. By emphasising the distinction between personal and commercial contexts, we can dilute the whiff of contract law in Lord Bridge's common intention constructive trust in *Lloyds Bank v Rosset*.[366] The distinction between inferring and imputing the parties' common intentions became a very significant part of later cases dealing with *Stack v Dowden*. This issue is considered in detail below.

Secondly, Baroness Hale was betting the farm on the Law Commission generating proposals for legislative intervention in this area, even though the Law Commission has not even produced proposals for reform in this field in its recent consultation papers, and is not intending to include even a draft bill in upcoming publications.[367] In effect, the House of Lords remains where it was in *Pettitt v Pettitt* in 1970: pleading for Parliamentary intervention.[368] That no such intervention was forthcoming (nor is it likely to be) has meant that

---

364 Especially [2007] UKHL 17, [2007] 2 WLR 831, para [45] *et seq.*

365 [2007] UKHL 17, [2007] 2 WLR 831, para [42].

366 Somewhat disingenuously, there was an attempt to suggest that *Lloyds Bank v Rosset* had commented on the law on trusts of homes by way of *obiter dicta*: [2007] UKHL 17, at [63].

367 [2007] UKHL 17, [2007] 2 WLR 831, para [45] *et seq.* Especially, para [47].

368 The experience of the Family Law Act 1996 is instructive here: that was an Act which was passed in the teeth of vituperate opposition from the Catholic Church and the *Daily Mail* on one wing, and the pressure groups representing, for example, victims of domestic violence on the other wing. And even after the careful compromises in that legislation which dealt only with married couples, ensuring that there could not be divorce without a cooling-off period or mediation and so forth, there were still parts of that Act which have not been brought into force. Given how comparatively uncontroversial married life is compared to the many, many

the Supreme Court in *Jones v Kernott* was driven to produce quasi-legislative statements of the law.

Baroness Hale also hoped that the new Land Registry form TR1 will lead to people identifying their common intentions at the outset.[369] There are two problems with this approach. High street solicitors are conspicuously bad at ensuring that these complex niceties are sorted out. Beyond that, rights are not always acquired at the date of acquisition of the property but rather are acquired due to changes in the parties' circumstances in later years. Moreover, the relationships between these people begin casually in circumstances in which there may not be an opportunity to identify who owns what. Baroness Hale's expectation is overly optimistic in this context, as is considered further below. To a divorce lawyer, dealing with married couples, expecting such clarity of thought at one clearly identifiable point in time may seem reasonable. To a property lawyer, exposed to a different take on life, it does not.

Thirdly, there are two new presumptions introduced, as considered above. That passage is repeated here for ease of reference.[370] The majority of the House of Lords agreed that there should be a presumption that if there is more than one person registered on the legal title of the home then those legal owners should be presumed to be the owners of the equitable interest in that home equally; whereas, if there is only one person registered on the legal title of the home then that sole legal owner should be presumed to be the sole owner of the equitable interest in that home. These presumptions are merely presumptions, and can therefore be rebutted by any evidence which suggests that the parties' common intention was something different.[371] Therefore, all of the law before *Stack v Dowden* will still be important to identify both those situations in which people other than the legal owners can acquire an equitable interest in that property, and also the circumstances in which the proportionate shares of the parties in the equitable interest can be greater or less than an equal share in that equitable interest.

Fourthly, Baroness Hale identified, from two sources, a definite drift in the cases which I have already mapped out in this chapter: that is, a drift away from simply looking to see which of the parties has contributed how much money to the purchase price on resulting trust principles,[372] and towards undertaking a survey of the whole course of dealings between the parties.[373] Baroness Hale did not go into the detail of any of the earlier cases nor of the academic commentary in this regard, which is a shame. Her two sources were, broadly, the decision of Chadwick LJ in *Oxley v Hiscock*, which has been criticised in this chapter on a number of grounds, and a book written by Gray and Gray, *Elements of Land Law*.[374] The notion that the court should 'undertake a survey of the whole course of dealing' between the

forms of unmarried relationships (straight, gay, and non-romantic too), it is unlikely that there will be any governmental enthusiasm to support any particular model for legislation if the Law Commission will not even sign up to one. We have already waited 37 years for legislation in this area: there is no reason to suppose that it is coming now.

369 [2007] UKHL 17, [2007] 2 WLR 831, para [52].
370 [2007] UKHL 17, [2007] 2 WLR 831, paras [54] and [56].
371 This tells us nothing, however, about the situation in which the parties do not have an intention in common – for example where one of the parties has made excuses to the other party not to include her on the legal title over the property – about who was intended to be an equitable owner of the property.
372 Presumptions of resulting trust are considered to be merely a matter of 'judicial consensus' rather than a principle of law: [2007] UKHL 17, [2007] 2 WLR 831, para [60].
373 [2007] UKHL 17, [2007] 2 WLR 831, para [61] *et seq*.
374 As discussed [2007] UKHL 17, [2007] 2 WLR 831, paras [61]–[66].

parties in fact comes from *Grant v Edwards* and *Midland Bank v Cooke* and not originally from the Law Commission, even though it is the Law Commission and *Oxley v Hiscock* which are cited as having spawned the idea. This approach suggests a pragmatism which is typical of family law whereby the courts tailor the solution to fit the facts of any given case.

Fifthly, *Oxley v Hiscock* seems to have been approved, although we must be careful with this observation: Baroness Hale does not go through the whole of the troublesome attempt by Chadwick LJ in *Oxley v Hiscock* to reconcile *Lloyds Bank v Rosset* with *Midland Bank v Cooke* and every other case in the canon in this field.[375] Therefore, we can know that *Oxley v Hiscock* is approved to the limited sense in which Baroness Hale uses it: that is, by reference to the passage in Chadwick LJ's judgment (quoted above) which requires that a court be 'fair' and that a court should undertake a survey of the whole course of dealing between the parties, and which consequently does not require that a court restrict itself to the sort of considerations which would have satisfied the test in *Rosset*. Importantly, Baroness Hale was clear that the court should not simply look at what was fair between the parties, although it was unclear whether that was intended to exclude the possibility of considering what was fair or whether it was to prevent the courts from only considering what was fair as opposed to trying to find a common intention. (The standard of fairness as a last resort is, however, adopted explicitly in *Jones v Kernott* by Lord Walker and Lady Hale.) As considered above, *Oxley v Hiscock* presents us with the difficulty that it introduced a general notion of 'fairness' without explaining either its precise provenance or its meaning, that it suggests that courts can 'supply' (or, make up) the common intention of the parties, and that it seeks to reconcile the irreconcilable earlier authorities.

Sixthly, there is a reference to a comment of Lord Hoffmann during argument that, to deal with subsequent changes to the parties' circumstances or common intention, it may be necessary to develop an 'ambulatory constructive trust' which will move and change in parallel with the parties' circumstances.[376] Baroness Hale does not exactly approve this idea but she does seem to acknowledge its usefulness. Care must be taken with this notion though: an ambulatory constructive trust suggests a constructive trust which is constantly capable of change. This is different, strictly speaking, from an institutional constructive trust of the kind set out in *Westdeutsche Landesbank v Islington*[377] which recognises that the parties have rights created at some point before the matter came on to trial when the defendant knew of some factor which affected her conscience. By contrast, a remedial constructive trust (as used in the USA) or proprietary estoppel gives the court complete licence to reach whatever conclusion the court considers to be conscionable and to impose whatever remedy it considers conscionable: however, these rights come into existence from the date of trial onwards for the first time, in this sense a little like a right to common law damages. So, an ambulatory constructive trust (assuming that to mean one that moves over time) is a constructive trust whose precise nature can only be known at the date of trial precisely because its nature changes as the parties' circumstances change. And if its nature is only knowable at the date of trial, then it is more akin to a remedial constructive trust than to a traditional institutional constructive trust precisely because it will be creating new rights at the date of judgment rather than recognising rights which came into existence at the time of some unconscionable act. Up to now, English equity has resisted the remedial constructive trust.

---

375 See the discussion of *Oxley v Hiscock* in section 15.8.2.
376 [2007] UKHL 17, [2007] 2 WLR 831, para [62].
377 [1996] AC 669.

But, as Prof Craig Rotherham suggests, perhaps it has already crept into English equity by stealth.[378]

Lord Neuberger – beyond fairness and back to rigour

Lord Neuberger made a valiant attempt to deal with the various circumstances which might arise in cases relating to trusts of homes. Lord Neuberger, however, delivered a dissenting speech and his approach was out of step with the majority of the House of Lords. There are two notable features of this approach. First, it relied on resulting trusts in the first place[379] – a notion unpopular with Lord Walker – and understands those resulting trusts as being capable of change on constructive trust principles when the circumstances require it.[380] Secondly, it disapproves the idea of 'fairness' or the imputation of rights being used by the courts to allocate the equitable interest in the home because it is too vague and not helpful in letting the parties know in advance what their rights are.[381]

What Lord Neuberger proposed, therefore, was similar to the judgment in *Huntingford v Hobbs*, considered above, where the court would begin with a resulting trusts analysis (predicated therefore primarily on the parties' financial contributions to the property) which would be re-calibrated by constructive trust principles over time to reflect the parties' common intention as it might change during their occupancy of the property. The precise basis on which these constructive trust principles would operate is less clear. Ordinarily, a constructive trust would operate in response to conscience, as in *Westdeutsche Landesbank v Islington*, but the constructive trust at play in trusts of homes cases has always been different from the ordinary model, whether on the basis of *Grant v Edwards* or *Lloyds Bank v Rosset*. This judgment is by some distance the most cogent of those delivered by the House of Lords. What it lacks is a means of accommodating changes in the parties' intentions after the acquisition of the property or to reflect other inputs to the property from the date of acquisition other than merely money; in essence, it lacks a means of taking the needs of 'fairness' or 'good conscience' into account.

15.9.5 The legacy of *Stack v Dowden* and *Jones v Kernott*

A judgment often acquires a life of its own after it has been delivered because later courts will frequently identify specific *dicta* from within that judgment which they will emphasise and to which they will accord a particular meaning over time. Two ideas from the speech of Baroness Hale in *Stack v Dowden* have been accorded great significance in later cases: first, an issue as to whether the courts should 'infer' or rather 'impute' the parties' common intention, where the former requires identifying an intention in the minds of the parties themselves and where the latter involves the court supplying the parties' common intention for them; and, secondly, that the law is still focused on seeking out what the common intention of the parties must have been and 'undertaking a survey of the whole course of dealing' between the parties, but not simply looking for what the court considers to be 'fair'. In expressing the first idea, Baroness Hale held the following:

---

378   Rotherham, 2002, especially Ch.1.
379   [2007] UKHL 17, [2007] 2 WLR 831, para [110], where there are different contributions to the purchase price.
380   [2007] UKHL 17, [2007] 2 WLR 831, para [124].
381   [2007] UKHL 17, [2007] 2 WLR 831, para [125].

There is no need for me to rehearse all the developments in the case law since *Pettitt v Pettitt* and *Gissing v Gissing* . . . The law has indeed moved on in response to changing social and economic conditions. The search is to ascertain the parties' shared intentions, actual, inferred or imputed, with respect to the property in the light of their whole course of conduct in relation to it.[382]

In expressing the second idea, Baroness Hale held the following:

> *Oxley v Hiscock* was, of course, a different case from this. . . . The Claimant [in that case] had first to surmount the hurdle of showing that she had any beneficial interest at all, before showing exactly what that interest was. The first could readily be inferred from the fact that each party had made some kind of financial contribution towards the purchase. As to the second, Chadwick LJ said this, at para 69:
>
> > . . . in many such cases, the answer will be provided by evidence of what they said and did at the time of the acquisition. But, in a case where there is no evidence of any discussion between them as to the amount of the share which each was to have – and even in a case where the evidence is that there was no discussion on that point – the question still requires an answer. It must now be accepted that (at least in this court and below) the answer is that each is entitled to that share which the court considers fair having regard to the whole course of dealing between them in relation to the property. And in that context, the whole course of dealing between them in relation to the property includes the arrangements which they make from time to time in order to meet the outgoings (for example, mortgage contributions, council tax and utilities, repairs, insurance and housekeeping) which have to be met if they are to live in the property as their home.[383]

Oxley v Hiscock has been hailed by Gray and Gray as 'an important breakthrough'.[384] The passage quoted is very similar to the view of the Law Commission in *Sharing Homes*[385] on the quantification of beneficial entitlement:

> If the question really is one of the parties' 'common intention', we believe that there is much to be said for adopting what has been called a 'holistic approach' to quantification, undertaking a survey of the whole course of dealing between the parties and taking account of all conduct which throws light on the question what shares were intended.

That may be the preferable way of expressing what is essentially the same thought, for two reasons. First, it emphasises that the search is still for the result which reflects what the parties must, in the light of their conduct, be taken to have intended. Second, therefore, it does not enable the court to abandon that search in favour of the result which the court itself considers fair. For the court to impose its own view of what is fair upon the situation in which the parties find themselves would be to return to the days

382 *Stack v Dowden* [2007] UKHL 17, [2007] 2 WLR 831, para [60].
383 [2007] UKHL 17, [2007] 2 WLR 831, para [61].
384 K Gray and S Francis Gray, *Elements of Land Law*, Oxford University Press, 2005, 931, para 10.138.
385 Law Commission, *Sharing Homes*, 2002, para 4.27.

before *Pettitt v Pettitt*[386] without even the fig leaf of s 17 of the 1882 [Married Women's Property] Act.

And yet, in spite of decrying the idea of deciding these cases simply by reference to a concept of 'fairness' in *Stack v Dowden*, that is exactly what Lady Hale did (in her joint judgment with Lord Walker) in *Jones v Kernott* (in the fourth stage of their test, set out below). There is no explanation of this *volte face* between the two judgments; nor is there any explanation as to what is meant by the concept of 'fairness' in this context – for example whether it is to be read in accordance with family law concepts of fairness, whether it is to include financial contributions, or whether there are any concepts which should be prioritised over others. What the Supreme Court has succeeded in doing is leaving every court at first instance in its wake entirely without guidance as to what 'fairness' means on the facts in front of it. The result of this failure to introduce clarity is that the whole sorry circus of courts at first instance taking entirely different approaches to the law will begin again (as happened in the wake of the decision in *Lloyds Bank v Rosset*) so that ten years from now we shall be trying to identify the patterns in another spaghetti of case law. The next section considers how differently subsequent decisions of the Court of Appeal treated the dicta of Lady Hale in *Stack v Dowden*, and then we come to the detail of *Jones v Kernott* in the section following that.

15.9.6 The development of the principles in *Stack v Dowden* in subsequent cases

Cases following Stack v Dowden

In spite of the attempt by the House of Lords to bring some conceptual order to this area of law, the academic treatment of their overly general judgments (with the notable exception of the judgment of Lord Neuberger) indicated that too much uncertainty remained.[387] The treatment of *Stack v Dowden* in many of the cases following it highlighted the issue of imputing and inferring intentions, in particular by reference to the *dicta* of Baroness Hale, quoted above, to the effect that '[t]he search is to ascertain the parties' shared intentions, actual, inferred or imputed, with respect to the property in light of their whole course of conduct in relation to it'.[388] Those few words, and the concept of fairness, received more attention in later cases than the rest of the judgment. In discussing *Stack v Dowden*, the Court of Appeal in *Holman v Howes*[389] held that simply launching an inquiry into what is 'fair' between the parties would be 'impermissible'.[390] On the *Holman v Howes* approach, the decision in *Stack v Dowden* has reversed much of the progress that was being made towards giving judges the ability to decide what they considered to be 'fair' and instead has returned to a more limited focus on the primacy of monetary contributions in allocating rights in the home.[391]

---

386   [1970] AC 777.
387   See Gray and Gray, 2009, 7-072; Swadling, 2007; Gardner and Davidson, 2011. See also Cooke, 2011. *Stack v Dowden* was, however, followed in *Attorney-General's Reference (No 2 of 2008)* [2008] EWCA Crim 2953; *Ashby v Kilduff* [2010] EWHC 2034 (Ch); *Thomson v Humphrey* [2009] All ER (D) 280 (Jun).
388   [2007] UKHL 17, [2007] 2 AC 432, para [60]. See also *Bindra v Chopra* [2008] EWHC 1715 (Ch); and *Morris v Morris* [2008] EWCA Civ 257.
389   [2007] EWCA Civ 877, [2007] BPIR 1085, para [29] *et seq.*, *per* Lloyd LJ.
390   *Ibid*, para [32].
391   This argument is made by Probert, 'Equality in the family home?' (2007) *Feminist Legal Studies*, 341.

Sir John Chadwick in the Court of Appeal in *James v Thomas*[392] held that the common intention between the parties can be formed at any time (whether before, during or after acquisition of the property) and accepted that a judgment as to the fairness of the situation cannot be the sole criterion[393] but rather must follow an inquiry into the parties' common intention.[394] The decisions of the Court of Appeal in *James v Thomas*[395] and *Morris v Morris*[396] demonstrated that in the absence of an express agreement after the date of acquisition, the courts will generally be reluctant to infer an intention to vary the parties' pre-acquisition beneficial interests in the home based on their conduct alone. Exactly that point was made in *Mirza v Mirza*.[397] So, in *James v Thomas* it was found to be insufficient that the claimant performed extensive acts of physical labour on the property for her to acquire a right in the property to vary their previous understanding. In that case Ms James 'drove a tipper, dug trenches, picked up materials, laid concrete, tarmac and gravel and generally undertook manual work associated with the business of Mr Thomas' – nevertheless, that was not enough to constitute conduct which altered the parties' previously agreed beneficial interests in the home. In *Morris v Morris*,[398] Peter Gibson LJ explained that the fact that the claimant was starting a riding school business or that the claimant was participating in the farm business was insufficient to suggest that the defendant was representing (either for constructive trust or for proprietary estoppel purposes) that the claimant was intended to acquire any greater beneficial interest in the farm or other property.[399] In *Williams v Lawrence*[400] it was held that simply because a father allowed his son to convert the family home (so that two families could live in it) and to move into it with his partner did not mean that his son had necessarily been granted a beneficial interest in that property. On the facts of *Williams v Lawrence* there had been no discussion nor any agreement to that effect between the parties and, relying on *James v Thomas*, the court was reluctant to infer such an agreement from conduct alone.[401]

That the law remained confused was evident from the decision of the Court of Appeal in *Williams v Parris*,[402] which proceeded primarily on the basis of *Lloyds Bank v Rosset* in

---

392   [2008] 1 FLR 1598.
393   It should be recalled that as Chadwick LJ he had given judgment in *Oxley v Hiscock* and had advocated the approach of using fairness.
394   So, when a woman moved into a house which a man already owned and began to work on the property with him, it would be possible to find a common intention: on those facts, looking at the whole course of the parties' dealings, the man's assurances that their common endeavours 'will benefit us both' were insufficient to constitute a representation that she would acquire a beneficial interest in the property.
395   [2007] EWCA Civ 1212, [2007] 3 FCR 696, [2008] 1 FLR 1598, at [36], *per* Sir John Chadwick.
396   [2008] EWCA Civ 257, at [36], *per* May LJ.
397   [2009] 2 FCR 12, 33.
398   [2008] EWCA Civ 257, at [36], *per* May LJ.
399   [2008] EWCA Civ 257, at [24]. Cf. *Thorner v Major* [2009] 1 WLR 776 where extensive physical labour on a farm was held to be suggestive of a representation that the claimant was to acquire rights under proprietary estoppel in the farm and other related property.
400   [2011] EWHC 2001 (Ch), [2011] WTLR 1455.
401   Where a father promised in *de Bruyne v de Bruyne* [2010] EWCA Civ 519 to settle a farm and shares on trust, and other family members made transfers of property in reliance on that promise, then the father was deemed to hold that property on constructive trust for the children who were intended to be the beneficiaries of the arrangement.
402   [2008] EWCA Civ 1147. In relation to the acquisition of other property, such as a boat, see *The 'Up Yaws'* [2007] EWHC 210 (Admlty), [2007] 2 FLR 444.

finding that there was an agreement sufficient to constitute a common intention constructive trust between people who decided to acquire flats in their block and to let them out for their common benefit. It was held that all that was required, beyond the express discussions which constituted the agreement that each person was to have an equitable interest in the property, was that the parties must have suffered some detriment. It was found that even though the claimant had made no contribution to the purchase price (because he was bankrupt at the time) his 'contribution appears to have been confined to some two days' painting work, plus hance charges' and that that was sufficient to acquire him an equitable interest.[403] Later cases have deviated similarly from the decision in *Stack v Dowden*. It has been held that where the parties agree that one of them will have no interest in the property, his later contribution to the property will not acquire him an equitable interest in that property,[404] unless (it is suggested) the parties can be shown to have changed their common intention. Moreover, it has been held in *Laskar v Laskar*[405] that the principle in *Stack v Dowden* applies only to the home and not to commercial property nor lettings run as a business intended solely to raise income.[406]

Therefore, the lower courts have not simply swung in behind one House of Lords approach or the other. Instead the courts continue to select doctrines and ideas from any or all of the cases decided from *Pettitt v Pettitt* in 1970 through to *Stack v Dowden*[407] in 2007 with all the care of children at a pick-and-mix counter. Just consider the range of different doctrines which have been applied by the cases considered in this chapter. It is as if the doctrine of precedent had become truly optional.[408] For the future, it is suggested that the decision of the Supreme Court in *Jones v Kernott*, as it interpreted *Stack v Dowden*, will be as effective in controlling subsequent behaviour as herding cats. It is well known that if you try to herd more than one cat in the same direction then each one of those cats will immediately separate and scamper off their own way. The High Court and the Court of Appeal appear to react similarly.

---

403 Similarly the High Court in *Samad v Thompson* [2008] EWHC 2809 (Ch) tended to follow *Rosset* with only passing reference to *Stack*.

404 *Griffiths v Cork* [2007] EWHC 1827 (Ch), 10 ITELR 313, where he had executed a deed recognising that he had no interest in the property, and the defendant succeeding in demonstrating that he had been competent to execute that deed at the time even though he was otherwise shown to have been suffering from paranoid schizophrenia.

405 [2008] EWCA Civ 347, [2008] 2 FLR 589.

406 The Court of Appeal in Singapore has nevertheless expressed its view that there is common sense underpinning the presumptions of advancement in certain types of relationship where a gift was a reasonable inference (*Lau Siew Kim v Yeo Guan Chye Terence and Another* [2007] SGCA 54, [2008] 4 LRC 587) and the presumption has been considered by the Supreme Court of British Columbia (*Kerr v Baranow* (2007) BCSC 1863, 10 ITELR 763). Similarly it was held that the equitable ownership should follow the law unless other considerations required (*Ibid.*).

407 It is a significant feature of English law generally that the advent of electronic databases has meant that there are many, many cases available to us all whereas previously only those cases collected in the law reports could expect a broad public. With so many cases available now, it is evident that many courts simply do not follow the doctrine of precedent either slavishly or at all. For example, the decision in *Williams v Parris* suggests that courts may follow the line of authority they think most convenient or expeditious. The decision in *Kean v McDonald* [2006] All ER (D) 348 is a good example of a case on the ownership of a home which pays little attention to the many possible authorities in reaching a conclusion.

408 On which see Duxbury, 2008 generally.

The position after Stack v Dowden

That the law had 'moved on' from *Lloyds Bank v Rosset* was underlined in *Abbott v Abbott*[409] by Baroness Hale in the Privy Council, just as it had been suggested by Baroness Hale in the House of Lords in *Stack v Dowden*; however, there is little judicial guidance as to where the law should go in the future. We are left with the notion that the court should identify the common intention between the parties as to the equitable ownership of their home. What this does not help us to understand is how the court will 'supply' a common intention when the parties had not consciously considered the question at all. The Labour government announced that there would be no legislation in England and Wales to deal with this matter, just as I had predicted,[410] and the Coalition government shows no inclination to broach this topic. So, we were left in a most unsatisfactory condition after *Stack v Dowden* with little judicial guidance as to how we should proceed. It is suggested that in fact (regardless of what Baroness Hale may have said) the courts will ultimately resort to what individual judges consider to be fair in the circumstances if there is no clear evidence as to what the parties did actually intend.[411] The decision in *Jones v Kernott*, with its formalistic attempt to set out clear rules, can be understood as a reaction to that lack of political will to legislate in this area.

15.9.7 The decision in *Jones v Kernott*

The decision on the facts

Ms Jones was a mobile hairdresser; Mr Kernott was a self-employed ice cream salesman who received benefits during the low season for ice cream sales. The couple met in 1980. In 1981, Jones bought a mobile home in her sole name and Kernott moved in with her in 1983. They had two children. In 1985, Jones sold her mobile home and the couple bought a property in on Badger Hall Avenue in Thundersley, Essex. The Badger Hall Avenue property was bought in their joint names. The purchase price of £30,000 was cheap because it had belonged to a relative of a client of Jones.[412] Jones contributed £6,000 in cash by way of deposit on the property, with the remainder coming by way of an endowment mortgage in the parties' joint names. Kernott contributed £100 per week to household expenses, with Jones paying for everything else 'out of joint resources'.[413] The couple took out a joint loan to extend the property, with Kernott and friends doing the building work, with a 50% increase in the value of the property to £44,000.[414] Kernott left in 1993 after a little over eight years of cohabitation. Thereafter, for over 14 years, Ms Jones met all the expenses associated with the property and Kernott made very little contribution to the maintenance of his two children. The parties later cashed in a joint insurance policy so that Kernott could put down a

---

409 [2007] UKPC 53, [2008] 1 FLR 1451.
410 The announcement was made by the government minister Bridget Prentice on 6 March 2008.
411 In *Laskar v Laskar* [2008] EWCA Civ 347, [2008] 2 FLR 589 the Court of Appeal did not simply decide what was 'fair' but did look to ensure that the result of focusing primarily on the parties' discussions and financial contributions did not lead to an unfair result.
412 No point was taken about whether or not Jones should acquire any credit for having obtained a reduction in the price of the property, as in *Cox v Jones* or *Springette v Dafoe*.
413 [2011] 3 WLR 1121, at [38]
414 Thus, it was argued that Kernott's labours increased the value of the property, thus acquiring him an extra share of the equitable interest.

deposit on his own home, something he could afford to do in part because he was not contributing to the maintenance of his children.

The case came on because Ms Jones sought to sell the property at Badger Hall Avenue and Kernott claimed that he had an equitable interest in the property. The judge at first instance found on the facts that the equitable interest in the property should be divided roughly in the proportions 90:10 in favour of Ms Jones, a division which broadly reflected their financial contributions over the nearly 23 years they had held the property and was in line with the evidence as the judge could find it in relation to the parties' intentions. The trial judge had found at first instance, as accepted by Strauss QC on appeal to the High Court, that the parties had changed their intentions especially when Kernott left the property but that Kernott had not intended to abandon any right to the Badger Hall Avenue property. On the facts, taking into account the various contributions, assessing Ms Jones's share at 90% was decided by the judge at first instance to be fair and just, as confirmed by Strauss QC, but without having displaced evidence of the parties' intentions. The majority of the Court of Appeal, unaccountably, held that this was a joint tenancy, which meant that Kernott was entitled to one half of the equitable interest. Quite why 14 years of absence and a complete lack of contribution during that time could not have been taken to constitute a severance of the joint tenancy and a concomitant need to establish the size of the parties' respective equitable interests as tenants in common, is unclear – quite apart from the simple justice of the case which seemed to require that 14 years of contributions on her own should have entitled Ms Jones to the lion's share of the equitable interest. Jacob LJ dissented on the basis that there was no reasonable basis for an appellate court to disturb the decision of the court of first instance which had heard the evidence and drawn sensible conclusions from it.

The Supreme Court reversed the Court of Appeal's decision and restored the judgment at first instance. Interestingly, while the Supreme Court was at pains to consider the niceties relating to inferring or imputing common intention and the residual role of using a standard of fairness when the evidence was otherwise inconclusive, the outcome broadly reflected the parties' financial contributions to the property, with other considerations having very little meaningful effect on those calculations. Interestingly, the standard of 'unconscionability' was not mentioned, even though it might be thought that 14 years without contribution to a property or to the family unit which lived there might have resulted in an unconscionable benefit for Kernott in the Court of Appeal, which could therefore have been reversed by a traditional constructive trust intended to avoid unconscionability being suffered. Having considered the facts of the case, we turn now to the detail of the judgments.

The principles set out by Lord Walker and Lady Hale

Lord Walker and Lady Hale, in their joint judgment, identified what they considered to be the law. Interestingly, rather than leave matters to possible misinterpretation or confusion, as had been the case after *Stack v Dowden*, the later passages in their joint judgment identified the key principles in numbered form, more akin to legislation than a discursive judgment, after having considered *Stack v Dowden* and other issues. We shall begin with this summary of the principles, before considering some of the points which were made in their joint judgment. Lord Walker and Lady Hale divided again between homes in which the legal title is held in joint names and homes held in the name of only one party when they held that:[415]

---

415 [2011] UKSC 53, [2011] 3 WLR 1121, [2011] 3 FCR 495, at [51].

[51] the following are the principles applicable in a case such as this, where a family home is bought in the joint names of a cohabiting couple who are both responsible for any mortgage, but without any express declaration of their beneficial interests:

(1) The starting point is that equity follows the law and they are joint tenants both in law and in equity.

(2) That presumption can be displaced by showing (a) that the parties had a different common intention at the time when they acquired the home, or (b) that they later formed the common intention that their respective shares would change.

(3) Their common intention is to be deduced objectively from their conduct: 'the relevant intention of each party is the intention which was reasonably understood by the other party to be manifested by that party's words or conduct notwithstanding that he did not consciously formulate that intention in his own mind or even acted with some different intention which he did not communicate to the other party' (Lord Diplock in *Gissing v Gissing*[416]). Examples of the sort of evidence which might be relevant to drawing such inferences are given in *Stack v Dowden*.[417]

(4) In those cases where it is clear either (a) that the parties did not intend joint tenancy at the outset, or (b) had changed their original intention, but it is not possible to ascertain by direct evidence or by inference what their actual intention was as to the shares in which they would own the property, 'the answer is that each is entitled to that share which the court considers fair having regard to the whole course of dealing between them in relation to the property': Chadwick LJ in *Oxley v Hiscock*.[418] In our judgment, 'the whole course of dealing . . . in relation to the property' should be given a broad meaning, enabling a similar range of factors to be taken into account as may be relevant to ascertaining the parties' actual intentions.

(5) Each case will turn on its own facts. Financial contributions are relevant but there are many other factors which may enable the court to decide what shares were either intended (as in case (3)) or fair (as in case (4)).

[52] This case is not concerned with a family home which is put into the name of one party only. The starting point is different. The first issue is whether it was intended that the other party have any beneficial interest in the property at all. If he does, the second issue is what that interest is. There is no presumption of joint beneficial ownership. But their common intention has once again to be deduced objectively from their conduct. If the evidence shows a common intention to share beneficial ownership but does not show what shares were intended, the court will have to proceed as at [51] (4) and (5), above.

[53] The assumptions as to human motivation, which led the courts to impute particular intentions by way of the resulting trust, are not appropriate to the ascertainment of beneficial interests in a family home. Whether they remain appropriate in other contexts is not the issue in this case.

---

416 [1970] 2 All ER 780 at 790, [1971] AC 886 at 906.
417 [2007] 2 FCR 280 at [69], [2007] 2 All ER 929.
418 [2004] 2 FCR 295 at [69], [2004] 3 All ER 703.

It is worth noting two things. First, the other members of the Supreme Court did not adopt this list of five principles as being a correct statement of the law in this area. Lord Collins agreed with the reasoning for allowing the appeal but did not express concurrence with the judgment, instead giving a judgment of his own. Lord Wilson disagreed about the desirability, in his view, of imputing a common intention to the parties, as discussed below. Lord Kerr set out his own summary of the principles, in which he identified differences between the judges, as considered below. As a result, whether this list of principles is accepted as being a correct statement of the law by the courts in the future remains to be seen. It is likely to be accepted by courts at first instance as a useful means of proceeding at the very least. Courts at first instance are likely to be eager to adopt this systematic statement of the principles in reaching their decisions because it lends them structure. Therefore, it is likely that these principles will be adopted by courts in the future. Secondly, the difficulty is in knowing what those principles mean, for example in the use of the term 'fairness'. It is in this context that the future case law is likely to return to the case law before *Stack v Dowden* for inspiration.

The approach suggested by Lord Walker and Lady Hale divided between the legal title of properties put in the name of one party and in the parties' joint names, as in *Stack v Dowden*. The presumption is that the parties' beneficial interests are to follow the pattern of their ownership of the legal title – that is, either joint or separate – unless there is evidence to rebut that presumption. Where the equitable ownership is unclear, then the court will engage in a survey of the entire course of dealing between the parties, as was first set out in *Midland Bank v Cooke* and then repeated in *Oxley v Hiscock*. A difficulty with this approach is that, while the joint judgment accepts that the parties' intentions might change,[419] nevertheless locking the presumption into the situation as recorded on the Land Register when the property was acquired initially means that subsequent changes of intention must act as a rebuttal to that presumption. And yet it is not clear what changes of intention count: must they be joint changes of intention, or a unilateral change of intention, or changes in circumstances which would be considered to be material objectively? Or would an aggregate of small changes in intention constitute sufficient for a change in intention? At what time must that change in intention have manifested itself? What if the other party disagreed?

The presumption of resulting trust is removed from the equation, as in *Stack v Dowden*.[420] Interestingly, Lord Walker and Lady Hale seem to disparage the use of presumptions in relation to the family home while, without irony, creating two new presumptions in *Stack v Dowden*. There is no clearer example of a court imputing a common intention to the parties than creating a presumption, albeit a rebuttable one.

What Jones v Kernott *decided about imputation and inference*

The judges in the Supreme Court were agreed as to the outcome of the appeal. However, it is not clear that there was a majority for any given conceptualisation of the legal principle, although there is very little difference between Lord Walker and Lady Hale and Lords Kerr and Collins on the bulk of the propositions, with Lord Wilson being the most obviously at odds with them about his preference for imputing a common intention as opposed merely to inferring it (after all, as Strauss QC put it in relation to fairness, 'that is what courts

---

419 [2011] UKSC 53, at [14].
420 [2011] UKSC 53, at [25], [29] and [53], quoted above.

are for'[421]). Lord Collins thought the distinction between imputation and inference would make little difference in practice (because the court would ultimately have to deal objectively with all of the contradictory evidence in any event); whereas Lords Kerr and Wilson considered that it would be significant in practice (because it would govern the court's approach either to deciding what it thought was fair or alternatively searching for a common intention on the evidence).

Lord Kerr attempted to identify the principles which were agreed between the members of the Supreme Court, which was a useful exercise from the perspective of courts at first instance deciding cases subsequently.[422] Those principles were as follows:

(i)   In joint names cases, the starting point is that equity follows the law. One begins the search for the proper allocation of shares in the property with the presumption that the parties are joint tenants and are thus entitled to equal shares;

(ii) That presumption can be displaced by showing (a) that the parties had a different common intention at the time when they acquired the home or (b) that they later formed the common intention that their respective shares would change;

(iii) The common intention, if it can be inferred, is to be deduced objectively from the parties' conduct;

(iv) Where the intention as to the division of the property cannot be inferred, each is entitled to that share which the court considers fair. In considering the question of what is fair the court should have regard to the whole course of dealing between the parties.

By contrast, the two areas of disagreement which his lordship identified were the following:[423]

(a) Is there sufficient evidence in the present case from which the parties' intentions can be inferred?

(b) Is the difference between inferring and imputing an intention likely to be great as a matter of general practice?

There is a great difference between 'imputing' an intention to the parties and 'inferring' that intention from the parties' conduct and evidence. This particular formulation by Lord Kerr adopts the uncomfortable notion that the court must objectively ascertain the intentions of the parties: meaning that the court must consider all of the evidence to identify as clearly as possible what the parties should be taken to have intended. This issue took up a large part of the hearing in front of the Supreme Court. Lord Kerr considered this to be important, whereas Lord Collins considered that it would make little difference in practice. The philosophical difference is a great one, however.

If a court 'imputes' a common intention then the court is imposing its view of what is 'fair' or appropriate on the parties; whereas, if a court 'infers' a common intention then the court is simply enforcing the parties' own agreement, but not substituting its own views for the parties' intentions. However, as Lord Walker and Lady Hale held, adopting *dicta* of Judge Strauss QC, 'it is not open to a court to impose a solution upon [the parties] in contradiction to those intentions, merely because the court considers that it is fair to do so.'[424]

---

421 [2010] 1 WLR 2401, at [33].
422 [2011] UKSC 53, [2011] 3 WLR 1121, [2011] 3 FCR 495, at [68].
423 [2011] UKSC 53, [2011] 3 WLR 1121, [2011] 3 FCR 495, at [68].
424 [2011] UKSC 53, [2011] 3 WLR 1121, [2011] 3 FCR 495, at [46].

Interestingly, these *dicta* seem to suggest that the parties may have had different intentions from which the court will seek to infer an appropriate arrangement. Nevertheless, this passage suggests that the concept of fairness is to be used only once the evidence as to the parties' common intention is unclear. The court must work with the grain of what the parties can be proved to have intended, perhaps taking an objective stance to interpret what those individual elements of intention can be taken to constitute in the final analysis. For example, suppose Brenda and Robert cohabited in a house which had been acquired entirely by way of a mortgage which Robert had discharged from his salary before being made redundant. In that case, separate strands of evidence that Brenda was to go out to work to supplement the family's income for the first time and that Robert was to continue to pay the mortgage (albeit from a redundancy payment, not from a salary) might reasonably be fused together by the court to infer a common intention that Brenda was to acquire rights in the home for the first time; alternatively, if that evidence was considered inconclusive, the court could take the view that fairness meant that Brenda should acquire a right for the first time, especially if Robert could only make those payments if Brenda paid for everything else.

The choice is between a judge-made approach as to who should own the parties' home, regardless of the parties' own preferences, and an approach which allows freedom of choice for the people involved by creating their own common intention. The difficulty identified by Piska[425] is that it will be difficult in practice to 'access' the parties' subjective intentions; or rather, it will be difficult to unlock the epistemically difficult concept of 'the parties' objective intentions',[426] by which it is suggested is meant 'the arrangement which the parties must have intended, given all the available evidence'. As behavioural psychologists have long said, the subjective thoughts of any person are unknowable.[427] Instead, the courts can only access an approximation of those thoughts through cross-examination in court and any other evidence which can be identified. They will attempt to do this, as Lord Walker and Lady Hale put it, as a result of 'the primary search for what the parties actually intended, to be deduced objectively from their words and their actions'.[428]

It will not always be an easy thing to establish on the evidence at trial what the intentions of the parties were. One party may allege a purely business relationship whereas the other party may allege that there was a sexual relationship between them: the former may indicate absolute ownership of a flat as a business asset by the person who paid for it, whereas the latter may indicate that at the date of purchase there was an intention of common ownership in equity.[429] The judge will be required to form a view of the witnesses and the likelihood of the things they allege. There are several cases considered above in which men have lied to women about the reasons they were not put on the legal title of property, and several cases have made the point that witnesses in these sorts of cases tend to become overwrought and give bad evidence (even if those witnesses are themselves barristers, as in *Cox v Jones*). Therefore, the practical business of finding fact is very difficult indeed. Hence, in practice, it

425 Piska, 2008.

426 *Ibid*, 127.

427 See, for example, the famous lecture delivered by John Watson in 1919, 'Psychology as the Behaviourist Views it', set out in Watson, 1994: 'Society as a whole is under constant endeavour to get the individual to materialise thoughts in overt speech or in deeds. . . . There is no known direct method of detecting whether an individual is lying, notwithstanding the many studies made upon that topic.' The point being that subjective thought processes remain locked inside the mind.

428 [2011] UKSC 53, [2011] 3 WLR 1121 [46].

429 *Favor Easy Management Ld v Wu* [2011] EWHC 2017 (Ch).

is suggested that the concept of fairness will be used far more than the Supreme Court has anticipated to reach the final conclusion in many cases.

Unconscionability: the Voldemort concept

Somewhat oddly, during argument in front of the Supreme Court in *Jones v Kernott*, Lady Hale remarked that 'the law of trusts has no way of producing fairness'. The principal concept which was not mentioned in front of the Supreme Court and which was not mentioned in *Stack v Dowden* nor in *Jones v Kernott* was 'unconscionability'. It has become a Voldemort concept: no one, it seems, can speak its name.[430] *Jones v Kernott* could have been decided on the basis that to have allowed Kernott a half-share would have been unconscionable, just as it would have been unconscionable to have left him with nothing; and in *Stack v Dowden* that good conscience entitled Ms Dowden to a 65% share in the property in that case. The absence of the concept of unconscionability in these cases is all the more surprising given that Lady Hale suggested that the law of trusts had no mechanism for doing justice between the parties. Two points follow from this alarming suggestion. First, equity and trusts law exists to ensure good conscience and therefore they do contain a concept which can generate justice between the parties. Second, as the highest appellate court, which had already taken it upon itself to review the entirety of the law in this area (and not simply to answer the factual problems in front of it), it was open to the Supreme Court in any event to have created a doctrine to produce justice if it had chosen to do so.

15.9.8 Three persistent problems

There are three significant themes which illustrate difficulties with these cases: the nature of real relationships between home sharers that are messier than the courts have accepted; the persistence of relying on financial contributions, for all of the fine talk about the law having 'moved on',[431] which makes it difficult to know what 'fairness' will add; and the difficulties of differentiating between imputing or inferring a common intention. These themes are considered in the sections to follow.

15.9.9 (1) Real property, real relationships and real people

The messy facts of people's lives and the normative judgments in Stack *and* Kernott

What is surprising about the judgments in *Stack v Dowden* is how surprised the judges were about the slightest idiosyncrasy in people's lives. That an unmarried couple with separate occupations maintained separate bank accounts is treated as though it necessarily carries Mr Stack and Ms Dowden outside the norm. The truth is that, particularly when dealing with unmarried couples, everyone is outside the norm. There is no norm any more among

---

430 The reference is, of course, to the character of Lord Voldemort in JK Rowling's Harry Potter books, whose name no one was supposed to speak. I mentioned the metaphor behind this idea to Martin Dixon, (my esteemed fellow author at Routledge, friend, and of the University of Cambridge) over coffee at the Supreme Court on the day *Jones v Kernott* was heard. We agreed this was a good idea and that there would be a race between us to write it down first. It is my idea. I have written it down first. Just so he knows. (For the avoidance of doubt, dear reader, we are only joking.)

431 [2007] 2 AC 432, at [60], *per* Baroness Hale.

unmarried home sharers. As Hans Magnus Enzensberger memorably put it: this standard deviationism is now all part of the ordinary exoticism of everyday life.[432] As opposed to the conformity of the middle of the 20th century, everyone is 'into' something now and they define themselves by reference to it: law student, juggler, Buddhist, lesbian, motorbike enthusiast, actor, grime DJ, Belieber,[433] alternative therapist, blogger, whatever. None of these things defines a whole person but they may be the features which people use to define themselves. People define themselves in their own terms. Everyone wants to be treated as an individual and everyone sees themselves as having something special about them. The same is true of home sharers' relationships, no matter what the glossy magazines try to tell them.[434] None of these relationships conforms to a norm but our highest courts want to pretend that they do. Home sharers and cohabitees, as opposed simply to those in 'intimate relationships', are both categories of people who are governed by these trusts of homes rules but who conform to none of the relationship categories to which Lady Hale referred. The Law Commission report to which she and Lord Walker referred in both judgments makes careful reference to 'home sharers' and not to 'couples'. Home sharers may be new graduates buying and sharing a home after university as they start their careers; home sharers may be a gay couple with no intention of having children; home sharers may be a couple whose relationship has ended but who continue to live in the same home because neither can afford a home in the same neighbourhood on their own and because they want to help raise their children.

The sort of circumstance which is not considered by any of these courts would be the following, which is illustrated by no less a part of our culture than the television programme *Sex and the City*.[435] Suppose that a man (let us call him 'Big'[436]) owns an apartment which he has bought outright, and then a woman (let us call her 'Carrie') moves into that apartment when their relationship becomes increasingly serious. But she does not move in on one particular night after a long conversation, still less does she move in once a TR1 Land Registry form has been completed to decide on her right in the property. Instead, Carrie spends more and more time at his flat, until she begins to leave a few clothes and then an increasing number of toiletries there because it is easier for her to get ready for work when she stays the night. What leaving these few items behind implies for their relationship becomes a micro-crisis in their lives. Over time, let us suppose that Carrie moves in: perhaps because she has to move out of her flat because her lease terminates or because she loses her job, perhaps she becomes pregnant without either of them planning that she would, or

432 Enzensberger, 1992, 179.
433 A 'Belieber' is one who 'believes' in Justin Bieber, a pop singer with an ardent, youthful following. The Monkees should have re-released their song 'I'm a Believer' with the lyrics: 'And I saw his face / Now I'm a Belieber' to capture the phenomenon. Presumably this will all be ancient history by the time of the next edition of this book.
434 There is nothing more 'normalising' than the ideals which glossy lifestyle magazines, weekend newspaper supplements or supermarket freebie magazines try to impose on their readers.
435 This particular micro-crisis began with a hairdryer in *Sex and the City*, 'Evolution', Season 2, Episode 23 (Home Box Office, 1999), written by Darren Star. Carrie wanted to leave things at Big's apartment. Big was threatened by this disturbance to his ordered, minimalist and masculine life. Ironically and tragically, Carrie was delighted to be allowed to leave a hairdryer and other objects, but this only served to demonstrate that she was intended to have no property rights because she needed permission to leave them and as such she had no right to do so.
436 That is a name given to this character in the programme, and not one of my own invention, in case you were confused.

perhaps they just want to spend more and more time together – eventually, however, through force of circumstance Big's flat becomes her permanent home. Let us suppose that ten years later the parties need to decide whether or not she has any rights in the property. In what circumstances might a person like Carrie acquire a right in the home beyond the imaginings of the Supreme Court?

At no point will an ordinary couple identify a particular moment as being so significant that they will need to take legal advice to regularise who has what right in the property. This is why *Stack v Dowden* is so unrealistic. The couple will focus on the first toothbrush to be left in the flat because it says more about their relationship than about their property law rights: becoming a couple who 'live together' rather than two people who 'go out' is the real concern for them, not their equitable interests. Hence the need to interpret their relationship as a court of equity and not to expect that it will respond to rigid legal categories. If Carrie is pregnant then her health and their financial concerns are likely to take control of their minds, not their property law rights. There will be no 'magic moment' in which they formulate a common intention. There may not even be a single moment in which they even have a common intention about all of the things which the courts consider important in this context.[437] This is why the standard of 'fairness' will be important in practice because the courts will have to formulate a rough approximation of what their common intention should have been from the information available.

If Carrie starts to pay the mortgage or the couple clearly start to present themselves as 'spousal analogues'[438] in the way they live their life together then maybe we would begin to say that Carrie should have acquired rights in the home. The issue is which of these two things would actually prompt the judges to grant her rights in the property. For all that the law has 'moved on'[439] from *Lloyds Bank v Rosset* and from money-based resulting trusts, what is noticeable is that the courts in *Stack v Dowden* and in *Jones v Kernott* do not appear, on the facts, to place a specific value on anything which happens between the parties other than their financial contributions. Instead, the courts seem to focus on finding a common intention at the outset and on the parties' financial contributions. The messy facts of most people's lives are much more difficult to quantify. (This point is taken up again below.)

In truth, haute bourgeois judges are simply out of touch with the way in which other people live their lives: for very few people is everything mapped out so comfortably that everyone involved has enough money, self-confidence and legal advice to identify their common intentions in advance of purchase. It will often be the case that the parties privately disagree about their respective rights in the property, and that that is precisely why the matter is never discussed. Because they are English, this will be the last thing they will ever discuss. What they would risk would be the ending of their relationship in a spectacular argument. So, instead they focus on choosing the right colour paint for the back bedroom in a DIY super-store and play out their angst in disagreements over the taps which would work best in the

---

437 It was a staple of 1970s sitcoms, for example, that married men had little control over their domestic arrangements – see for example, *George and Mildred* – and that as a result their 'common intention' about their home life was something which they waited to be told. The idea that a 'common intention' would be 'common' at times seems a little unlikely. An emotionally constipated nation like the English always appeared to be in the 20th century will necessarily find it difficult to discuss their common intentions and so it is improbable in many cases that one will be created without the parties being questioned about it together at one particular time.

438 This is the term which Alan Plater invents in *The Beiderbecke Affair* for the two unmarried schoolteacher heroes to use to define their quasi-marital relationship.

439 [2007] UKHL 17, at [60], *per* Baroness Hale.

guest lavatory.[440] If a couple have children, then it is common for one partner to take the lead role in looking at properties to buy during the week while the other partner is at work, but the roles will commonly be reversed when it comes to solicitors and negotiating the price of the property through estate agents. In these sorts of situations, even if the parties do buy their first home together, there will obviously be power relationships within 'intimate relationships' which prevent the parties either from ever considering who owns what or from making a common intention explicit. The idea of a common intention is therefore often a fabrication.

Sisters doing it for themselves, or just following the money?

What is interesting about *Stack v Dowden* and about *Jones v Kernott* is that both of the women are the successful, higher earners in their relationships who have the property rights at the start of the relationship. This marks a great sea-change from the old-fashioned hearth-and-home wives Mrs Pettitt and Mrs Gissing, let alone those women who had sought 'the deserted wife's equity' before then. The feminist scholarship in this field has always made the sensible central point that in relation to the home it cannot only be financial contributions by men under the old nuclear family model which should acquire rights in property, but rather that other forms of contribution to the home or to the family should be taken into account. What is interesting in the judgments of Lady Hale, as a former family law academic, is that so little account is taken of the things which the men did within their relationships (for example, in working on the home), even though their financial contributions were less significant than those of their partners. What both of those cases have shown, ironically, is that financial contributions will still remain the most significant factor in spite of the law having purportedly 'moved on'.

In *Jones v Kernott* it seems entirely reasonable that a 90% contribution from Ms Jones, with no contribution from Kernott for over 14 years, should result in a 90% equitable interest for her – but there is very little in the judgment which takes account of anything that Kernott may have done beyond a financial contribution estimated at about 10% of the equity.[441] Similarly, Ms Dowden earned more than Mr Stack and so contributed more financially to the home, and the ultimate decision came down broadly in the same proportions as the parties' financial contributions. Notably, that decision also identified equitable interests which were very close to the parties' proportionate financial contributions. The same is true of the decision in *Oxley v Hiscock*. For all of the fine talk about undertaking surveys of the entire course of dealing, of considering what is fair, of inferring common intentions objectively, this seems to make very little difference to the final calculation beyond assessing the parties' financial contributions. Even if these factors are being taken into account, they only appear to make a small difference at the edges to the parties' rights in the property. As yet there is no guidance as to how they could be brought into account. Older judgments like that in *Midland Bank v Cooke* (finding that the equities were equal because there was no clear answer otherwise) and in *Jennings v Rice* (where the shares on estoppel principles were such as to prevent unconscionability) tell us much more about bringing other factors into account. This is what makes the judgment about what is 'fair' after *Jones v Kernott* more difficult because it is not at all clear what weight, if any, is being given *in practice* to any other forms of contribution to the home by the highest courts in recent cases. The solid tug of money appears to be working on the courts too.

---

440 And, yes, I realise it may be bourgeois to have a guest lavatory, which is exactly why I mentioned it.
441 The trial judge does appear to have taken into account Kernott's work on the property but that is supposed to have increased its value by 50%, which is hardly borne out by the 10% ultimate share.

15.9.10 (2) Imputation, inference and judge-made decisions

A large part of the oral argument before the Supreme Court in *Jones v Kernott* involved the question of whether the parties' common intention should be imputed to them or whether it should be inferred from the evidence. In essence, if the court *imputes* a common intention then the court is imposing its view of what is proper or appropriate or fair (where those three things are very different) onto the parties. A judge would always prefer to *infer* a common intention by looking at the evidence and identifying what the parties must have intended their rights to be. As Piska has discussed, it is not possible to identify the true subjective intentions of either party because they are locked inside those parties' minds.[442] Indeed, there would be three problems anyway, even if one could peer into their minds: that party may not have consciously formulated a clear view about all of the significant questions in any event; that party's view may change over time, depending perhaps on the strength of their relationship with their partner, the arrival of children, and so forth; the parties' subjective views may indicate only a fundamental disagreement with one another which they have never voiced out loud. Often there will not be a clear consensus; which has the result that the court will be forced to impose a conclusion on the parties.[443] This is why in *Jones v Kernott* there is an unsatisfactory concept of the court objectively inferring the parties' intentions. What this means is that the court will listen to all the evidence and try to estimate what the parties' subjective intentions probably were, and as a consequence what the most rational common intention must have been in that context. In essence, then, the court will always be imposing a common intention on the parties in truth by dint of selecting which evidence appears to shed a meaningful light on what their intentions must have been.

15.9.11 (3) The last resort: going to the fair

Lord Walker devoted a large part of his judgment in *Stack v Dowden*, which was intended to be merely a 'footnote' to Baroness Hale's judgment, to considering the legacy of the word 'fair' in the cases up to and including *Gissing v Gissing*. The law before *Pettitt* and *Gissing* had seen valiant attempts by Lord Denning and others to introduce a notion of fairness into the law by means of 'the deserted wife's equity', as considered above. Therefore, Lord Diplock's judgments in the Court of Appeal in *Pettitt v Pettitt* and in *Gissing v Gissing* in the House of Lords were delivered in reaction to the difficulties with that concept of the court making an order which was 'fair'. Instead, fairness was considered by Lord Walker to be a large part of the drive to impute common intentions to the parties where the parties were to be taken to have intended what was fair.[444] This, however, is as much discussion as we get from Lord Walker or Lady Hale as to what the idea of fairness may involve. Lady Hale

---

442 Piska, 2008.

443 Indeed, the courts are concerned to identify a consensus too often, whereas in practice there may have been a vague common understanding at one or other time in the relationship (often at times of crisis or stress when there seems to be no alternative) but intentions and sentiment will change over time through a long relationship and identifying the time at which the intention is to be fixed is important: on the date of purchase, on the birth of the first child, on the children leaving home, when the breadwinner lost their job and the other party went out to find work, and so on.

444 It is of course the proof of human rationality to assume that parties to a relationship are always concerned to be fair as opposed to anything else. As Jerry Seinfeld put it, 'If you don't play games [in a relationship], how do you know who is winning?'

excluded the possibility, as was discussed above, of the court simply deciding what was fair in *Stack v Dowden*.[445] However, in *Jones v Kernott* Lord Walker and Lady Hale had decided that the court could do what was fair if the presumption had been rebutted and the evidence was not otherwise conclusive of a common intention.[446]

Ultimately, the courts will be required to ask what is 'fair' on the facts of countless cases at first instance because evidence of the parties' true common intention will be difficult to isolate among the mass of evidence.[447] The higher courts have left us no indication as to what that might mean in recent cases. Therefore, the courts at first instance will have recourse to all of the preceding authority to decide what is fair. It is the last, and necessary, resort of the law in this area but courts at first instance require a little guidance as to how they should approach it, not least to minimise the number of likely appeals. In circumstances which involve 'intimate relationships' it may be sensible to move lock, stock and barrel to adopting family law concepts. What makes judges nervous of doing this is that they do not wish to appear to be producing property law rights out of thin air.[448]

15.10 DIFFERENT APPROACHES ELSEWHERE IN THE COMMONWEALTH

Other Commonwealth jurisdictions have taken a different approach to that developed in English law since the decision in *Gissing v Gissing*. Typically, *Gissing* is seen as the common conceptual root in considering cases concerning trusts of homes in Commonwealth jurisdictions as far flung as Canada, Australia and New Zealand. The common intention constructive trust approach in *Rosset* has not found favour generally across the Commonwealth, and it is at that point that the other jurisdictions have begun to diverge from English law. Each jurisdiction has developed its own approach. There is a much longer discussion of these principles on www.alastairhudson.com/trustslaw.

15.10.1 Canada and 'unjust enrichment'

The test for unjust enrichment

The core of the Canadian approach is the imposition of a proprietary constructive trust 'where a person who holds title to property is subject to an equitable duty to convey it to another on the ground that he would be unjustly enriched if he were permitted to retain it'.[449] The sea-change in the Canadian case law came in *Pettkus v Becker*,[450] in the leading judgment of Dickson J. The parties were an unmarried couple who had lived together for 19 years. The property at issue was the farm in which they had both lived, and a bee-keeping business which had been established through their joint efforts. The woman claimed an entitlement to half of the business and to the land. The court was unanimous in holding that she should be entitled to a constructive trust to prevent any unjust enrichment on the part of her former partner. Dickson J set out the general underpinnings of the Canadian approach:

445 [2007] UKHL 17, at [61].
446 [2011] UKSC 53, at [46] and [47].
447 As acknowledged in general terms at [2011] UKSC 53, at [36].
448 See Rotherham, 2002, Ch10.
449 *Ibid*, 629.
450 (1980) 117 DLR (3d) 257.

... where one person in a relationship tantamount to spousal prejudices herself in the reasonable expectation of receiving an interest in property and the other person in the relationship freely accepts benefits conferred by the first person in circumstances where he knows or ought to have known of that reasonable expectation, it would be unjust to allow the recipient of the benefit to retain it.[451]

In the later case of *Peter v Beblow*,[452] the test is more clearly stated. For there to be an unjust enrichment in the Canadian law relating to equitable rights in the home, it was held that three conditions must be satisfied: '(1) there has been an enrichment; (2) a corresponding deprivation has been suffered by the person who supplied the enrichment; and (3) there is an absence of any juristic reason for the enrichment itself.'[453]

The effect of this test is said to be the creation of a presumption that the 'performance of domestic services will give rise to a claim for unjust enrichment'.[454] The principal driver away from the English common intention constructive trust was that, in the words of Dickson J, the courts were involved in the 'meaningless ritual' of searching for a 'fugitive common intention'.[455] On the facts of *Pettkus* there had been no common intention formed, but the court wished to provide the claimant with a remedy. It was considered that a judgment in money by way of equitable compensation would have been inappropriate to prevent that unjust enrichment, and the court therefore made an order for a constructive trust over the property at issue.

15.10.2 Australia and 'unconscionability'

The development of a test of unconscionability

The modern position in Australian law was established originally in the decision of the High Court of Australia in *Baumgartner v Baumgartner*.[456] The plaintiff and defendant had lived together, sharing all household and other expenses, for a period of four years. They had not married, although the plaintiff had changed her name by deed poll so that it was the same as that of her partner. The couple had one child during this time. The couple sold a home which had been wholly owned by the defendant and sought to construct another one with the sale proceeds of the first and a mortgage taken out in the man's name. The plaintiff worked throughout the relationship, and passed her wage packets to her partner each time she was paid on the basis that he looked after their financial affairs. The plaintiff eventually left her partner with their child and claimed an equitable interest in the property.

It was found that the parties did not form a common intention but that that would not dispose of the matter. The court wanted to provide for a means of acquiring rights in the home which went beyond straightforward financial contribution to the acquisition cost of the home. The court held that a proprietary interest by way of constructive trust would be ordered where failure to do so would have been 'so contrary to justice and good conscience' that it

---

451 (1980) 117 DLR (3d) 257, 274.
452 (1993) 101 DLR (4th) 621. *Egana v Normore* 10 ITELR 813 applied *Peter v Beblow*.
453 *Ibid*, 630, *per* Cory J.
454 Mee, 1999, 192.
455 (1980) 117 DLR (3d) 257, 269.
456 [1988] Conv 259, (1988) 62 ALJR 29, (1987) 164 CLR 137.

could not have been permitted. This approach is best explained as a test based on the issue whether or not the trustee's retention of the beneficial interest would be 'unconscionable'. On these facts it was held that it would be unconscionable for the plaintiff to deny any beneficial interest to the defendant. As the court expressed the position:

> The case is accordingly one in which the parties have pooled their earnings for the purposes of their joint relationship, one of the purposes of that relationship being to secure accommodation for themselves and their child. Their contributions, financial and otherwise, to the acquisition of the land, the building of the house, the purchase of furniture and the making of their home, were on the basis of, and for the purposes of, that joint relationship. In this situation the [defendant's] assertion, after the relationship had failed, that the Leumeah property, which was financed in part through the pooled funds, is his sole property, is his property beneficially to the exclusion of any interest at all on the part of the respondent, amounts to unconscionable conduct which attracts the intervention of equity and the imposition of a constructive trust at the suit of the [plaintiff].

Therefore, the court is prepared to allocate rights on the basis of a general contribution to a joint undertaking between two people as partners. It does not require the application of that money solely to the acquisition cost,[457] neither does it preclude actions of contribution to general household expenses, nor does it require some evident common intention between the parties. This test of unconscionability allows the court, in effect, to impute motives and to judge the justice of the case objectively – that is, without the need to pretend to be able to read the minds of the protagonists. The approach in Australia has therefore been to return to the notion of unconscionable behaviour as a general yardstick for measuring the suitability of an order as to the ownership of the equitable interest in land.

Forms of unconscionability granting rights in the home

In Australia, direct contributions to the purchase price and to the mortgage instalments still count towards an interest in the property.[458] Similarly, work done in repairing the property will afford some equitable interest.[459] Other contributions will also be recognised. Facilitating the payment of the mortgage by paying for other expenses will acquire an equitable interest in the home.[460] More extensively, working unpaid in the family business may acquire rights in the home.[461]

In relation to non-financial contributions – or contributions involving money, such as working unpaid – the Australian approach is less clear. In short, such non-financial contributions will be accounted for by means of an equitable interest if they have facilitated direct

---

457 Which had formerly been the position in *Calverley v Green* (1984) 155 CLR 242.
458 *Atkinson v Burt* (1989) 12 Fam LR 800; *Ammala v Sarimaa* (1993) 17 Fam LR 529; *Harmer v Pearson* (1993) 16 Fam LR 596. Payments towards the mortgage similarly: *Carville v Westbury* (1990) 102 Fed LR 223; *Kais v Turvey* (1994) 17 Fam LR 498.
459 *Miller v Sutherland* (1991) 14 Fam LR 416, 424; *Booth v Beresford* (1993) 17 Fam LR 147; *Kais v Turvey* (1994) 17 Fam LR 498.
460 *Baumgartner v Baumgartner* (1987) 164 CLR 137; *Hibberson v George* (1989) 12 Fam LR 725; *Lipman v Lipman* (1989) 13 Fam LR 1; *Renton v Youngman* (1995) 19 Fam LR 450; *Bell v Bell* (1995) 19 Fam LR 690.
461 *Lipman v Lipman* (1989) 13 Fam LR 1. Cf *Ivin v Blake* [1995] 1 FLR 70; and proprietary estoppel in *Wayling v Jones* (1993) 69 P & CR 170.

financial contributions to the acquisition of the property in some way.[462] In the case of *Bryson v Bryant*,[463] a wife had cared for her husband through a long marriage (of about 60 years) until her death. The couple had built a house together and, while he had been the main bread-winner, she had contributed to the family income during the Depression, becoming the breadwinner for a while. Evidence was limited on their precise contributions. After her death, while her husband was in hospital suffering from senile dementia, their extended family began to argue over the rights in their home. The court held that unconscionability would require that the wife receive a half-share in the property on constructive trust princi-ples. As Kirby P presented their argument:

> It is important that the 'brave new world of unconscionability' should not lead the court back to family property law of twenty years ago by the back door of a preoccupation with contributions, particularly financial contributions . . . Nor should those who have provided 'women's work' over their adult lifetime . . . be told condescendingly, by a mostly male judiciary, that their services must be regarded as 'freely given labour' only or, catalogued as attributable solely to a rather one-way and quaintly described 'love and affection', when property interests come to be distributed.

The question which follows is precisely how far this notion of unconscionability is intended to stretch. Clearly it will encompass things otherwise dismissed by *Rosset* and other English cases as merely 'women's work'.[464] The concept of unconscionability has been pursued in more recent cases such as *Giumelli v Giumelli*[465] and *Killen v Rennie*.[466] These issues are pursued in the next section which conducts a survey of the academics' course of dealing with this subject.

15.11 TRENDS IN THE ACADEMIC DISCUSSION OF TRUSTS OF HOMES

15.11.1 Framing the problem

The issue of rights in the home is a particularly important socio-economic phenomenon. Any property which is co-owned in England and Wales may be affected by these rules – millions of homes and families are affected by this area of law. It is therefore somewhat surprising that every Anglo-centric common law jurisdiction is experiencing such difficulty in formulating suitable legal and equitable principles in this area. The problem with the current English approach to the common intention constructive trust is perhaps summarised best by Dixon J in *Pettkus v Becker*,[467] in his description of the court's role in trusts of homes cases as being '[t]he judicial quest for the fugitive or phantom common intention'. Necessarily the court is required to use some fiction, or impute an intention which the parties had never really consid-ered before coming to court. More to the point, it is impossible for ordinary people to know the nature of their rights in their homes when the law is quite so complex and obscure.

---

462 *Stowe and Devereaux Holdings Pty Ltd v Stowe* (1995) 19 Fam LR 409, 418.
463 (1992) 29 NSWLR 188.
464 See generally the excellent Bryan, 1990, 25.
465 [1999] HCA 10.
466 [2005] NSWCA 392.
467 (1980) 117 DLR (3rd) 257.

15.11.2 Conceptual issues with the common intention constructive trust

The phantom common intention

The criticism of the common intention constructive trust highlighted above was based primarily on its reliance on an implied agreement where no such agreement has ever existed: it has been described as a 'phantom'. For example, the term 'mutual conduct common intention constructive trust', as set out in *Lloyds Bank v Rosset*, is simply self-contradictory. Where there is avowedly no express agreement of any kind between the parties, the court has given itself the power to impute such an intention from the behaviour of the parties. The court supposes that the parties would have reached such and such an agreement if they had thought about it – the whole point being that they did not think about it. Therefore, they are treated as having created an agreement where in reality there was none. That is a legal fiction.

The feminist analysis

There are objections made by feminist theorists which home in on the requirement that there must have been some direct contribution to the mortgage repayments or purchase price[468] rather than any more general contribution to familial expenses or to family life in general.[469] It is suggested that in most of the decided cases the claimant is a woman who does not work because the parties' lifestyle is organised around the woman as carer and the man as breadwinner. The English approach does not give any recognition to the work that is done by women in this circumstance. In Canada, in Australia and in *Midland Bank v Cooke*,[470] there is some recognition of the non-financial contribution of (typically) women in relationships. Similarly, where the woman does contribute financially to the home it is often by means of paying for bills, or paying for other expenses on an *ad hoc* basis or by helping in a family business. The *Rosset* test does not take these forms of contribution into account. Therefore, women not entitled to protection under matrimonial legislation are victims of the affection of English judges for allocating rights in property on the basis of cash contributions.

The changing understanding of women's rights

The position of women under English law before the Married Women's Property Act 1882 was truly disturbing.[471] A wife became 'the shadow of her husband' on marriage with the effect that all of the woman's property passed absolutely to her husband and became in law his property. If you have read Jane Austen's novel *Persuasion* you will have encountered the heroine Anne who must resist the advances of unctuous Mr Elliot who is a gold-digger seeking a rich wife so that his own penury can be remedied by acquiring ownership of all of her money after marrying her. In such circumstances, many women would be abandoned by unscrupulous husbands who spent all of their wives' money and kept mistresses. In this sense equity came to the rescue of these women by holding 'their' property on well-drafted settlements so that roguish husbands could not steal it away from them. Equity was

---

468   *Lloyds Bank v Rosset* [1990] 1 All ER 1111, 1119, *per* Lord Bridge.
469   *Burns v Burns* [1984] Ch 317. Cf *White v White* [2000] 2 FLR 981, 989. See Wong, 1998 and Wong, 2004.
470   [1995] 4 All ER 562.
471   Cretney, *Family Law in the Twentieth Century* Oxford, 2003 at pp. 92 *et seq.*

consequently considered to be a woman's protector. It was not until important decisions in the late 20th century (such as *Williams & Glyn's Bank v Boland*[472]) that wives were recognised as having distinct rights in matrimonial property. Even among the seemingly enlightened judiciary of the 20th century, there were some very patronising and out-dated ideas in play. Lord Denning, who is for many people a sort of judicial saint, considered that:

> No matter how you may dispute and argue, you cannot alter the fact that women are different from men. The principal task in life of women is to bear and rear children: and it is a task which occupies the best years of their lives. The man's part in bringing up the children is no doubt as important as hers, but of necessity he cannot devote so much time to it. He is physically the stronger and she the weaker. He is temperamentally the more aggressive and she the more submissive. It is he who takes the initiative and she who responds . . .[473]

It goes on in that vein for some time. And he is generally thought to be one of the good guys! The recent case law on trusts of homes suggests that we live in more enlightened times now.

The supremacy of money

The other question which falls to be answered is why the focus of so much English law is so determinedly directed at financial contributions to the exclusion of all else. At one level it is clear that restricting the detriment necessary to found a claim to cash payments would make it easier for equity to decide what sort of contribution should count. Unfortunately for proponents of that argument, it is then necessary to include undertakings to make mortgage repayments in the future, and then to include the provision of cash discounts on the property, and so on. Equity is simply ducking the difficult question: in relation to families, what forms of action ought to confer rights in the home?

It is suggested that the better approaches would be the following. At a fundamental level, it should be recognised that labour in the family business or in the home is equivalent in worth to cash contributions in the home. In family contexts, particularly when children are involved, the courts should be mindful of the needs of the parties. By 'needs' is meant the requirement of the children to have a home and their welfare catered for. In the context of couples in long-term relationships without children (married or unmarried, heterosexual or homosexual), the courts should be mindful of the needs of the parties balanced by their deserts. The balance between needs and deserts means that parties should receive such remedy (personal or proprietary) as is appropriate to the nature of their relationship.

Therefore, long-term relationships should allocate equal rights to the parties unless it would be unconscionable to do so, whereas relationships of comparatively short standing should give priority (but not exclusivity) to the deserts of those parties who have contributed through finance or labour to the property. Where the parties do in fact reach an express agreement or found an express trust as to their respective rights, those rights should be enforced in the absence of any supervening factor.

472 [1981] AC 487.
473 Denning, *The Due Process of Law*, Butterworths, 1980 at p.194.

The dangers of bright-line development

There are a number of potential issues arising specifically from the test set out in *Rosset*. In a note, Gardner has described this a part of the 'bright-line' development of the law relating to the family home:[474] that is, a development of a strict test over a number of cases in place of a flexible, discretionary form of equity.[475] Within the bright-line development in *Rosset*, there is a loss of flexibility, which has led to a number of Court of Appeal decisions simply ignoring the rigour of the *Rosset* test. Such uncertainty cannot be useful for a mature system of jurisprudence. Furthermore, it can be argued that *Rosset* ignores the role of the resulting trust like that in *Dyer v Dyer*,[476] with the effect that there is great uncertainty in distinguishing between constructive trust and proprietary estoppel principles.

The core problem is that each system of rules is reliant on a central fiction. For example, the common intention constructive trust depends on there being a 'common intention', even in situations where the parties have come to no agreement at all. In each jurisdiction there are presumptions and assumptions as to the parties' intentions and the appropriate response. Couple these conceptual problems with the changing nature of the family and the higher incidence of family breakdown, and the difficulties facing the law increase.

Distinguishing between constructive trusts and proprietary estoppel

It is important to understand the differences between proprietary estoppel and constructive trust, because those differences are real and significant. Any attempt to unify them, as Lord Bridge attempts in *Rosset*, will require the creation of a new concept which straddles the existing categories. To begin with proprietary estoppel, the estoppel does not require common intention. Further, proprietary estoppel enables the court to tailor the remedy to fit the wrong, and there need not be an impact on third parties unless they have acted unconscionably.[477] Estoppel may reverse detriment but will also give effect to expectations and so perfect imperfect gifts.[478] The scope for remedies is broader: there may be a life interest or co-ownership interest, or a licence or a money judgment under estoppel which may be secured by a charge over the property.[479]

The proprietary constructive trust is a more precise and rigid approach, recognising that there is a difference between proprietary and personal remedies. To compare the constructive trust with estoppel, the institutional constructive trust does not take account of the rights of third parties. With *Rosset*-style constructive trusts, the court gives effect to the whole of

474 (1991) 54 MLR 126.
475 In a number of cases, including *Abbey National v Cann* [1991] 1 AC 56, *City of London BS v Flegg* [1988] AC 54, and *Rosset* [1990] 1 All ER 1111 itself, the House of Lords has favoured a tightening of the tests relating to the family home. This tendency can also be seen in the decisions of the Privy Council in *Re Goldcorp* [1995] 1 AC 74; *Attorney-General for Hong Kong v Reid* [1994] 1 AC 324, and *Royal Brunei Airlines v Tan* [1995] 2 AC 378, where their Lordships have moved towards more concrete tests for equitable responses like the constructive trust. Similarly, the decision of Lord Browne-Wilkinson in *Westdeutsche Landesbank Girozentrale v Islington LBC* [1996] AC 669 started from a restatement of the core principles of trusts law and sought to solidify the basis on which equity operated: similarly *Target Holdings v Redferns* [1996] 1 AC 421.
476 (1788) 2 Cox Eq Cas 92.
477 See Hayton, 1995:1, 386.
478 Eg, *Pascoe v Turner* [1979] 1 WLR 431.
479 Hayton, 1990:1.

the common intention (via express agreement or mutual conduct); whereas with an estoppel-type remedy, preventing unconscionable behaviour can be achieved by a tailor-made remedy varying between personal and proprietary court orders.

A line in the case law has developed to erode the distinction between constructive trusts and proprietary estoppel. It is generally considered that the constructive trust does not have the flexibility to decide what the extent of the interest in any case ought to be, although a slew of recent cases (from *Bernard v Josephs* through to *Huntingford* and the possibly anomalous *Midland Bank v Cooke*) have suggested a more flexible balance sheet approach to the identification and calculation of the equitable interest. In more general terms, it has been accepted in Australia in *Walton Stores v Maher* that equity will come to the relief of the parties simply where there has been 'unconscionable conduct', a more general approach which accords with cases like *Westdeutsche Landesbank v Islington LBC* and *BCCI v Akindele*.[480] The doctrine of constructive trust is thus becoming ever looser, in contradistinction to Lord Bridge's attempt in *Rosset* to rigidify the doctrine.

Thus, classically, where only one party contributes to the mortgage this usually leads straightforwardly to a resulting trust rather than to some more flexible remedy like estoppel. However, in the wake of *Bernard v Josephs* and *Huntingford v Hobbs* there has developed something of a fashion among judges for the use of equitable accounting to determine the size of the equitable interest and to reallocate value where appropriate, rather than a reliance on a straightforward arithmetical resulting trust. So, for example, where the mortgage debt remains outstanding and one party assumes responsibility for the first time for discharging the remaining capital, that person acquires the value of that outstanding capital on her side of the balance sheet: thus equitable accounting permits alteration of the parties' original intentions where appropriate.[481] Consequently, resulting trust and constructive trust have acquired some of the flexibility of estoppel by means of equitable accounting used to level out the unfairness sometimes exerted by trust-based approaches.

Ferguson has argued that it is wrong to merge the doctrines of constructive trust and proprietary estoppel because the courts are maintaining a distinction between the two in practice and because there is a difference in the onus of proof in the two remedies.[482] Further, it is suggested that the doctrine of proprietary estoppel requires the cohabitee to raise a *prima facie* case of representation, reliance and detriment, with the other side then having to rebut that argument, whereas the constructive trust does not have a clear onus of proof. Proprietary estoppel is easier to plead because you know with certainty which three elements to plead in a statement of claim; whereas constructive trusts are more uncertain in that they require a vaguer argument predicated on the conscience of the defendant – unless applying the strict *Rosset* test.

A number of recent cases have taken the view that proprietary estoppel and constructive trust are to be considered as being part of the same doctrine. This process of eliding the two distinct doctrines perpetuates the suggestion made in *Lloyds Bank v Rosset*, where Lord Bridge considered that rights in the home come into existence on the basis of 'constructive

---

480 [2000] 3 WLR 1423.

481 *Huntingford v Hobbs* [1993] 1 FLR 736.

482 Ferguson, 1993. However, her analysis is based on the fact that Lord Bridge in *Rosset* does not join the two concepts *all* the time. Perhaps the better argument would be based on the decision of Nourse LJ in *Stokes v Anderson*, who argues that there *ought* to be a difference between the doctrines.

trust or proprietary estoppel': as though the same doctrine. First, in *Yaxley v Gotts*,[483] it was suggested, when deciding that a partly performed contract should take effect in equity even though it was in breach of s 2 of the Law of Property (Miscellaneous Provisions) Act 1989, that this equity was based on equitable estoppel or constructive trust because the two were effectively indistinguishable. Similarly in *Grant v Edwards*[484] it was suggested that 'useful guidance may in future be obtained from the principles underlying the law of proprietary estoppel which in my judgment are closely akin to those laid down in *Gissing v Gissing*'.[485]

Secondly, in *Oxley v Hiscock*,[486] Chadwick LJ was called upon to consider the equitable interests to the home of an unmarried couple. His Lordship commenced by considering the speech of Lord Bridge in *Lloyds Bank v Rosset*, in part to the effect that equitable interests occurred on the basis of 'constructive trust or proprietary estoppel', before then considering that he was entitled to consider the entire course of dealing between the parties on the basis of the judgment of Waite LJ in *Midland Bank v Cooke*. It has been suggested in this chapter that these two approaches are completely different. His Lordship expressed the opinion that the doctrines of constructive trust and proprietary estoppel were effectively identical. The subtler point is also made in *Van Laetham v Brooker* by Lawrence Collins J that the *remedies* provided in proprietary estoppel and constructive trust are effectively the same: that is, not that the two doctrines are exactly the same but rather that their effects are very similar.[487]

Professor Mark Thompson has expressed the view[488] that this elision of the concepts, as suggested in *Oxley v Hiscock*, is not conceptually possible. The differences which he identifies are as follows. First, estoppel will grant rights such as easements[489] which the doctrine of constructive trust will not grant, whereas constructive trusts are limited to granting proportionate rights in property. Secondly, the two doctrines come into existence on very different bases: constructive trust is based on the prevention of unconscionable conduct, whereas proprietary estoppel is based on detrimental reliance on a representation. Thirdly, constructive trusts are institutional, whereas proprietary estoppel is a remedial doctrine.[490] In conclusion, Professor Thompson suggests that the Court of Appeal was attempting to 'reconcile the irreconcilable',[491] a view which is shared by this writer.[492] What the expression 'reconcile the irreconcilable' means, as considered above in relation to the 'unconscionability approach' is that the various cases which were discussed by Chadwick LJ in that case are so doctrinally different that it is not possible to mix into a combined test. For example, the speech of Lord Bridge, with which the other members of the judicial committee of the House of Lords agreed, was clear that if there was no agreement between the parties then only contributions to the purchase price of the property would be conduct appropriate in the acquisition of an equitable interest in that land. By contrast, Waite LJ held that the court could 'survey the whole course of dealing' in *Midland Bank v Cooke* when deciding what conduct might be

483 [2000] 1 All ER 711.
484 [1986] Ch 638, 656, *per* Browne-Wilkinson V-C.
485 [1971] AC 886.
486 [2004] 3 All ER 703, [2004] EWCA Civ 546.
487 [2006] 2 FLR 495, para [263].
488 Thompson, 2004.
489 *ER Ives Investment Ltd v High* [1967] 2 QB 379; *Crabb v Arun DC* [1976] Ch 179.
490 See, eg, *Ottey v Grundy* [2003] EWCA Civ 1176.
491 Thompson, 2004.
492 See also Gardner (2004) 120 LQR 541, 546.

appropriate in the acquisition of an equitable interest in the land. Chadwick LJ in *Oxley v Hiscock* then purported to say that these two radically different approaches could be merged into one test whereby one looked first for an agreement between the parties and then at 'the whole course of dealing' if no such agreement could be found. This is simply to ignore the fact that the House of Lords in *Rosset* did not intend to permit such a broad survey to be undertaken by the court. Indeed the majority in the House of Lords in *Gissing v Gissing* expressed themselves to be reluctant to accept the suggestion of Diplock LJ that common intentions could be identified on such a broad scale. It is suggested, therefore, that the exercise which Chadwick LJ undertook in *Oxley v Hiscock* is simply intellectually unsustainable.

15.11.3 Answering a problem question on the law on trusts of homes

There are a number of conflicting approaches set out in this chapter and consequently this is fertile ground for writing essays but it can be difficult when it comes to answering problem questions. The key to answering problem questions is to impose a structure on the material. I suggest the following structure for this area. First, if there is no express trust, apply the presumptions set out in *Stack v Dowden* and the fine principles set out in *Jones v Kernott*. Given that *Stack v Dowden* did not overrule any of the preceding law those presumptions can be rebutted by using any of the following principles. You may therefore wish to write in a way which identifies the divisions in the earlier cases. So, secondly, set out the strict test in *Lloyds Bank v Rosset* and apply it to the facts of the question. Come to a conclusion on the application of that test to the facts of the problem. Thirdly, in the alternative, consider whether or not the balance sheet cases would produce a different answer on the facts by means of resulting trust thinking. Fourthly, consider whether or not the family assets approach would lead to yet another answer on the facts – it is likely that 'undertaking a survey of the whole course of dealing' will lead to a different conclusion from that in *Lloyds Bank v Rosset*. Set out the conclusion based on this analysis and reflect on the difference from the *Rosset* approach. Fifthly, consider whether or not the doctrine of proprietary estoppel could lead to yet another conclusion. The principal difference here will be that proprietary estoppel permits a broad range of remedies ranging from absolute title to mere financial compensation, depending on whether or not the court is concerned to effect the promise, or to compensate detriment, or to prevent unconscionability. Finally, the recent unconscionability approach cases (seemingly with the approval of Baroness Hale in *Stack v Dowden*) may permit yet another conclusion based on seeking an agreement between the parties and then undertaking a survey of the whole course of dealing between them. In this way it will be possible both to show an understanding of the different effects of these different approaches and also it will be possible to lend structure to a problem answer. This may resolve itself in a question as to what is 'fair' after *Jones v Kernott*.

An alternative approach would be to consider the facts on the basis of traditional trusts law categories: express trust, then resulting trust, then constructive trust, and then proprietary estoppel. The difficulty with this approach, it is suggested, is that the courts do not appear to be using these categories to mean the same thing, and therefore it may produce a 'wobbly' structure for a problem answer in the context of trusts of homes.

In terms of essay writing this area clearly has a large literature. The key to a strong essay is to have a thesis (one which answers the question being asked . . .) which one either seeks to prove or to disprove. A clear target for an essay in this area would be the unsatisfactory nature of the decision in *Lloyds Bank v Rosset*, and the gaps in *Stack v Dowden* and *Jones v Kernott* or the differences between the approaches of various courts as discussed in this chapter or as seen through one of the lenses set out immediately above or in Chapter 17.

15.11.4 Conclusions – rethinking the law on trusts of homes

The argument raised in Marilyn French's novel *The Women's Room* in favour of an ignored and brutalised wife was that she was entitled to receive from her husband a divorce settlement which recognised her role as housekeeper, mother and sexual partner throughout their relationship. This attitude turns on its head the English approach to rights in the family home, based as it is solely on 'breadwinning' and mortgage payments leading to the acquisition of equitable property rights. The English law is wrestling with its own heritage. On the basis that it began with the idea that wives did not have rights independent of their husbands' rights, Lord Diplock in *Gissing v Gissing* advanced a seemingly radical notion that there might be some other form of common intention created between couples. This rule has transmuted evenly enough to unmarried couples, but remained bound to the proposition that the person who provided the cash flow and the capital would be the only person entitled to have rights in the property. Other forms of commitment or of giving value attracted no similar rights.

The only recognition of the likelihood that many families will disintegrate into divorce rapidly is in the common law relating to sales of the home, in which children may be allowed to remain in the home (with the parent who has custody) until school-leaving age. The problem is in providing sufficient wherewithal for both parties to a relationship to quit that relationship and acquire suitable alternative accommodation. It is obvious that two incomes will provide a better home than only one income. The cases need to recognise the need for flexibility to deal with cases requiring homes to be found for children. This perhaps requires a recognition that equitable rights in property must be granted to the parent who retains custody of the children. By the same token, childless couples perhaps have need of a different test which recognises their lack of dependants (whether children, aged relatives or other persons).

One cannot help but think that the rigidity of the test in *Rosset* is measuring the wrong thing and ensuring that there are a number of cases in which the courts will fail to identify situations in which there ought to be some recognition of the contribution made to a relationship by some party other than the breadwinner. Whether this requires an approach as mercenary as that in Canada remains to be seen. The North American approach assumes not only that there ought to be some accounting for the broader context of a relationship, but also that it is possible to put a monetary value on something as intangible as participation in a relationship. The intellectual shortcoming in that approach is an assumption that the 'breadwinner' is not also entitled to claim some emotional capital invested in the relationship.

Perhaps, then, the prevention of the exploitation of one party at the expense of the other is the most useful foundation for the allocation of equitable interest. However, it does not answer the question how other contexts, such as the welfare of children, should be addressed. In an area of such tremendous social importance, the words of Lord Reid in considering this confused mixture of case law have a great resonance: 'The whole question can only be resolved by Parliament and in my opinion there is urgent need for comprehensive legislation.'[493] The problem with the current state of the case law is that it is both confused and, at times, unsuited to dealing with the thousand natural shocks that flesh is heir to.

---

493 *Pettitt v Pettitt* [1970] AC 777, 797.

Chapter 16

Trusts of land

16.1 INTRODUCTION

The purpose of this chapter is to consider how the law of trusts, equity and land law interact. The first section considers the regime introduced by the Trusts of Land and Appointment of Trustees Act (TLATA) 1996 dealing with trusts of land. This Act deals with issues as disparate as the abolition of the doctrine of conversion, the rights of beneficiaries to occupy the trust property, the obligations and powers of trustees, and the resolution of applications for orders for sale. The second section draws together some of the disparate discussions in this book of the various equitable doctrines which relate to land law. Land law, principally by means of the Law of Property Act (LPA) 1925, rationalised those rights which would be legal estates and legal interests, and those rights which would therefore be equitable interests. These equitable interests suggest situations in which equity is deeming there to be a right in parallel to the formal legal right. Equitable doctrines also suggest that in given situations, a general notion of unconscionability will operate so as to provide rights for the claimants.

16.2 TRUSTS OF LAND

16.2.1 Introduction to the treatment of trusts of land

While this Part 5 has been concerned throughout with the law of trusts as it relates to land, its main focus has been on the trusts implied by law aspect of the allocation of equitable interests in the home. The issues considered in Chapter 15 were concerned with whether or not a particular person is to have equitable rights in the home at all. In this situation we are concerned with situations in which parties have been held to have such equitable interests in land. There may be situations, as in *Goodman v Gallant*,[1] where there is an express trust created over the family home which make clear those persons who are to be considered *prima facie* to have rights in the home. Therefore, in this discussion we are concerned by turns with equitable interests in land by means of constructive trust, resulting trust or possibly by proprietary estoppel, as well as rights under express trusts.

In either situation, there will be a 'trust of land' created in respect of that property, which is now subject to the TLATA 1996 dealing with the administration of that trust. Having decided that there is an equitable interest vested in a claimant, the next question is to understand the nature of the obligations imposed on the person who is to act as trustee of that equitable interest. Typically, litigation as to the respective rights of persons in land is concerned with a desire in one or more of those litigants to dispose of that land, or to evict another person from that land, or possibly to ascertain tax liability or liability in relation to insolvency. Therefore, a claimant will be commencing litigation to establish rights under constructive trust or another form of trust precisely because she wishes to assert her rights to land.

Once the decision is reached that that person does have a right in the property by means of a constructive trust or proprietary estoppel the question necessarily arises: how is that property to be dealt with as a result of the recognition of that trust? If the relationship between the occupants has broken down, should the property be sold and the proceeds divided between them, or should one or other of the parties be entitled to remain in occupation of that property? This section will consider these questions from the perspective of the law of trusts, as opposed to family law. Under the old s 30 of the LPA 1925 (now replaced by s 14 of the TLATA 1996)[2] the applicant would frequently seek a court order for the sale of the property and the division of the proceeds between the equitable interest holders.[3] As a corollary to that, the defendant may wish to assert rights to continue in occupation of that land and to resist any application for a sale of the property. The 1996 legislation sets out the context in which that is done. As to the obligations of the trustee not to permit conflicts of interest and so forth,[4] the general principles of trusteeship will apply to a trustee of a trust of land as to any other trustee of a trust implied by law.

1 [1986] Fam 106.
2 Although most of the decided cases are decided on the basis of the substantively similar LPA 1925, s 30.
3 See, eg, *Jones v Challenger* [1961] 1 QB 176; *Re Citro* [1991] Ch 142 – considered in greater detail below.
4 As considered in Chapter 8.

16.2.2 The Trusts of Land and Appointment of Trustees Act 1996

Technical objectives of the Act

The TLATA 1996 was enacted further to the Law Commission Paper *Transfer of Land: Trusts of Land*.[5] The fundamental technical aim of the TLATA 1996 was to achieve the conversion of all settlements under the Settled Land Act 1925, all bare trusts, and all trusts for sale under the LPA 1925 into a composite form of trust defined to be the 'trust of land'. Within this redrawing of rights in land were some larger objectives concerned with the rights of beneficiaries under trusts of land to occupy the home and an extension of the categories of person whose rights should be taken into account when reaching decisions on applications for the sale of the home.

As part of this technical aim to reform the manner in which land was treated by the 1925 legislation, s 3 of the TLATA 1996 set out the abolition of the doctrine of conversion. The abolition of the doctrine of conversion removed the automatic assumption that the rights of any beneficiary under the trust for sale (under the LPA 1925) were not vested in the property itself but rather were vested in the proceeds of sale. This notion of conversion of rights flowed from the understanding of trusts for sale as being trusts whose purpose was the sale of the trust fund and its conversion into cash. Clearly, this ran contrary to the intention of most people acquiring land for their own occupation in which it was not supposed for a moment that their sole intention was to dispose of the property as though a mere investment (rather, their true intention must be to live in the property). Therefore, the common law developed the notion of a 'collateral purpose' under which the court would resist the obligation to sell the property in place of an implied ulterior objective for families (for example) to retain the property as their home.[6]

16.2.3 The meaning of 'trust of land'

The term 'trust of land' means 'any trust of property which consists of or includes land'.[7] Therefore, any trust will become a trust of land if it includes a parcel of land within a more general portfolio of property, even if the remainder of the trust property is comprised of chattels and intangible property, or alternatively if the trust fund includes money which is intended to be applied for the acquisition of land, in the manner considered below. Trusts of land include not only express trusts but also constructive trusts, resulting trusts, 'implied trusts', bare trusts and trusts for sale: indeed 'any description of trust'.[8] Trusts are caught within the scope of trusts of land whether they were created before or after the 1996 Act came into force.[9] In terms of trusts implied by law, the statute covers any trusts 'arising' before or after the coming into force of the Act, as well as any express trust consciously 'created' before or after the Act.[10] There are two forms of land which fall outwith the Act:

---

5 1989, Law Comm No 181, HMSO.
6 *Jones v Challenger* [1961] 1 QB 176; *Re Citro* [1991] Ch 142.
7 TLATA 1996, s 1(1)(a).
8 *Ibid*, s 1(2)(a). The reference to 'trusts for sale' is to trusts falling under the LPA 1925, a code repealed by the 1996 Act.
9 TLATA 1996, s 1(2)(b).
10 *Ibid*, s 1(2)(b).

land which was settled land under the Settled Land Act 1925 (before the TLATA 1996 came into force) or land to which the Universities and Colleges Estates Act 1925[11] applies.[12]

16.2.4 The functions of the trustees of land

The trustees have general powers to deal with the trust property as though they were the absolute owners of the trust property, as expressed in the following terms:[13]

> For the purposes of exercising their functions as trustees, the trustees of land have in relation to the land subject to the trust all the powers of an absolute owner.

Therefore, akin to the powers of trustees under the TA 2000, the trustees are entitled to deal with the property held under the trust as though its absolute owner.[14] The reference to 'their functions as trustees' in s 6(1) is a reference to the powers and the obligations of the trustees considered in Part 3 of this book and the specific terms of the trust instrument dealing with the powers of the trustees. There are, necessarily, restrictions on the scope of the trustees' powers such that the reference to the trustees being entitled to act as though the 'absolute owner' of the trust property.[15] The trustees are required to act in the best interests of the beneficiaries and to avoid any conflict of interest between their personal and their fiduciary capacities. Within the TLATA 1996, there is also an express restriction to the effect that:[16]

> The powers conferred by [s 6] shall not be exercised in contravention of, or of any order[17] made in pursuance of, any other enactment or any rule of law or equity.

Within the reference to the 'rule of . . . equity' can be supposed to be a reference to the principles limiting the powers of trustees, as considered above in Part 3 of this book generally. In any event, the trustees are expressly required by statute to 'have regard to the rights of the beneficiaries'.[18] Furthermore, the TLATA 1996 provides that the generality of the power does not operate so as to override any restriction, limitation or condition placed on the trustees by any other 'enactment'.[19]

---

11 Where universities, generally bodies corporate, have land held on trust, then this provision is of significance to them. Excluded from the scope of universities and colleges under the 1925 Act are those institutions of further education effected under the Education Reform Act 1988 as higher education or further education corporations.

12 TLATA 1996, s 1(3).

13 TLATA 1996, s 6(1). See also the TA 2000, s 8(3), which grants trustees the power to acquire land for the occupation of beneficiaries or as an investment without the need for the existence of a trust of land.

14 The LPA 1925, s 28, by contrast provided that the trustees had 'all the powers of a tenant for life and the trustees of a settlement under the Settled Land Act 1925'.

15 The Law Commission sought to make the powers of the trustees of land as 'broadly based and as flexible as possible': Law Commission Report No 181, para 10.4.105.

16 TLATA 1996, s 6(6).

17 Whether that be an order of the court or of the Charity Commissioners: TLATA 1996, s 6(7).

18 *Ibid*, s 6(5).

19 *Ibid*, s 6(8). It is suggested that these provisions add nothing which the general law of trusts would not have added in any event. It could not be supposed that trustees would be permitted, simply by virtue of s 6(1) of the TLATA 1996, to circumvent their ordinary fiduciary obligations or any mandatory rules of statute applicable to them. The draftsperson of the TA 2000, which has a similarly broad power of investment for trustees, did not consider it necessary to qualify that power in this manner.

The TLATA 1996 contains two further express powers for trustees. First, provided that all of the beneficiaries under the trust of land are of full age and full capacity, the general powers of the trustees include a power 'to convey the land to the beneficiaries even though they have not required the trustees to do so'.[20] The beneficiaries are then required to do 'whatever is necessary' to ensure that the property vests in them as beneficiaries subject to the possibility that a court may order them so to do.[21] This is, in effect, the inverse of the rule in *Saunders v Vautier*,[22] in that the trustee is able to compel a conveyance of full title in the property to the beneficiaries, as opposed to the beneficiaries calling for a conveyance of that title. Secondly, the trustees have 'power to purchase a legal estate in any land in England or Wales'.[23] The statute is clear to express the breadth of this principle. This power can be exercised by way of investment,[24] to provide land for the occupation of any of the beneficiaries[25] or for any other reason.[26]

16.2.5 The trustees' duty of care

Trustees owe a general duty to exercise reasonable skill and care towards the beneficiaries in the management of their obligations. As considered in detail in Chapter 8, the TA 2000 imposes a duty of care on trustees in the following terms:[27]

> Whenever the duty under this subsection applies to a trustee, he must exercise such care and skill as is reasonable in the circumstances, having regard in particular –
>
> (a) to any special knowledge or experience that he has or holds himself out as having, and
> (b) if he acts as trustee in the course of a business or profession, to any special knowledge or experience that it is reasonable to expect of a person acting in the course of that kind of business or profession.

The effect of this provision is to enlarge the potential liabilities of trustees of land, particularly those acting in furtherance of a business or profession, by imposing an implied duty to exercise reasonable skill and care in the discharge of their fiduciary obligations. The duty of care under the 2000 Act is imposed on trustees of land by means of an amendment to s 6 of the 1996 Act.[28]

16.2.6 Exclusion and restriction of the powers of trustees of land

The provisions of the legislation may be excluded by the terms of the trust instrument. So, even though the powers of trustees under the TLATA 1996 as considered in the preceding paragraphs are extensive,[29] those powers:

---

20 TLATA 1996, s 6(2).
21 *Ibid*, s 6(2)(a) and (b).
22 (1841) 4 Beav 115.
23 TLATA 1996, s 6(3).
24 *Ibid*, s 6(3)(a).
25 *Ibid*, s 6(3)(b).
26 *Ibid*, s 6(3)(c).
27 TA 2000, s 1(1).
28 By means of inserting a provision to that effect in the TLATA 1996, s 6(9).
29 *Ibid*, s 8.

do not apply in the case of a trust of land created by a disposition in so far as provision to the effect that they do not apply is made by the disposition.[30]

Therefore, the powers of the trustees to deal with the land as absolute owner or to partition the land can be excluded by the trust instrument itself, just as the provisions of the TA 1925 and the TA 2000 can be excluded by the terms of the trust instrument. However, the terms of s 8(1) of the TLATA 1996 would appear to have the effect of enabling the settlor to postpone the trustees' right of sale of the property indefinitely.[31] Furthermore, in general terms the trustees are prevented from exercising either of these powers without the consent of the beneficiaries if the consent of the beneficiaries is required.[32]

16.2.7 Delegation of the powers of trustees of land

The TLATA 1996 has given trustees of land much wider powers to delegate their responsibilities than was possible under the TA 1925. Section 9 provides that:[33]

> The trustees of land may, by power of attorney, delegate to any beneficiary or beneficiaries of full age and beneficially entitled to an interest in possession in land subject to the trust any of their functions as trustees which relate to the land.

The trustees are entitled to delegate their functions in relation to the land only when acting collectively; any trustee wishing to delegate his functions individually to some other person must comply with the procedure for so doing in the TA 1925 or the Enduring Powers of Attorney Act 1985. The delegation under s 9 of the TLATA 1996, requiring the trustees to act as a body and not individually, must be agreed unanimously.[34] The delegation must be effected in the form of a deed,[35] but it may be for a definite or an indefinite period of time.[36] Delegation of the trustees' powers to a beneficiary renders that beneficiary a trustee for those purposes under statute.[37] This power, it is suggested, would have been available under the general law of trusts, particularly under the general obligation imposed on a trustee to avoid conflicts of interest on pain of liability to account to the beneficiaries for breach of trust. The trustees nevertheless become jointly and severally liable for the actions of such a beneficiary to whom the trustees' powers have been delegated[38] only to the extent that they have acted without reasonable care in their choice of delegate.[39]

Purchasers of the land dealing with a delegate exercising the powers of the trustees are given protection by s 9. It is assumed that the delegate was someone to whom the functions

---

30 *Ibid*, s 8(1).
31 Provided always that such a provision conformed with the rule against perpetuities.
32 TLATA 1996, s 8(2).
33 *Ibid*, s 9(1).
34 *Ibid*, s 9(3).
35 *Ibid*, s 9(1).
36 *Ibid*, s 9(5).
37 *Ibid*, s 9(7).
38 *Ibid*, s 9(8).
39 *Ibid*, s 9(8).

of the trustees could have been properly delegated provided that a purchaser, or indeed any third party dealing with the delegate, was acting in good faith.[40] This protection is then extended to cover those who acquire trust property in good faith from someone who dealt with the delegate.[41]

16.2.8 The rights of beneficiaries under a trust of land

The meaning of 'beneficiary'

The term 'beneficiary', for the purposes of the TLATA 1996, means:

> a person who under the trust has an interest in property subject to the trust (including a person who has such an interest as a trustee or a personal representative).[42]

In consequence, the definition of 'beneficiary' is very wide-ranging. Falling within this definition are beneficiaries under express trusts, constructive trusts or resulting trusts over the land. That the definition includes any person with a proprietary interest in the land has the effect that mortgagees and trustees in bankruptcy constitute beneficiaries under the terms of the Act. Similarly, trustees and personal representatives are expressly defined as falling within the definition of 'beneficiary'. The purpose behind this extensive definition is to grant *locus standi* to this broad a range of people with interests in the property to be consulted as to dealings with the property or to commence proceedings to seek an order for the sale of that property or some other order from the court. People who acquire rights under the trust by virtue of being trustees or personal representatives[43] or by virtue of being an annuitant[44] are excluded from the definition of 'beneficiary'.

The beneficiaries' power of consent

A trust instrument may seek to protect the rights of the beneficiaries by means of obliging the trustees to seek the consent of the beneficiaries or some other persons to any proposed, specified course of action. For example, this would prevent the trustees from selling the trust property or from encumbering the trust property without such a consent. With this in mind, s 10 of the TLATA 1996 provides as follows:

> If a disposition creating a trust of land requires the consent of more than two persons to the exercise by the trustees of any function relating to the land, the consent of any two of them to the exercise of the function is sufficient in favour of a purchaser.[45]

Thus, such a requirement of consent can be satisfied if two of the beneficiaries (or other specified people) give their consent. This is similar to the principle of overreaching in land

---

40 *Ibid*, s 9(2).
41 *Ibid.*
42 TLATA 1996, s 22(1).
43 *Ibid*, s 22(2).
44 *Ibid*, s 22(3).
45 *Ibid*, s 10(1).

law whereby a good receipt can be given by two trustees.[46] In effect, the statute seeks to simplify the trustees' obligations in relation to obtaining consent from all of the people who might have been required to consent under the terms of the trust instrument.[47] Section 14(2) of the TLATA 1996 permits the trustees to acquire an order from the court to relieve them of the requirement to obtain the consent of any person connected with the operation of the trustees' functions.[48]

The beneficiaries' rights to be consulted by the trustees

In common with the issue considered immediately above in relation to the right of the beneficiaries to give or to withhold consent in relation to the exercise of the trustees' powers, a trust instrument may also provide for the beneficiaries to have the right to be consulted in limited circumstances. More generally, the TLATA 1996 provides for beneficiaries to be consulted by the trustees in relation to the carrying out of any of their powers.[49] Section 11 of the TLATA 1996 provides:[50]

> The trustees of land shall in the exercise of any function relating to land subject to the trust –
>
> (a) so far as practicable, consult the beneficiaries of full age and beneficially entitled to an interest in possession in the land, and
>
> (b) so far as consistent with the general interest of the trust, give effect to the wishes of those beneficiaries, or (in case of dispute) of the majority (according to the value of their combined interests).

Two issues arise from this provision. First, in which circumstances are the trustees obliged to carry out their obligations of consultation? The expansive wording of this provision, particularly the terms 'so far as practicable' and 'so far as consistent', are not qualified in the statute, nor have they received a close analysis in the decided cases. Furthermore, it is not clear what types of trust business might be considered too minor to require consultation with the beneficiaries, nor how far the practicalities of the situation (such as the detrimental effect of delay, difficulties with obtaining responses from individual beneficiaries, and so on) could be taken to absolve the trustees from any claim that they had failed to carry on an effective consultation in deciding to desist from contacting the beneficiaries.

At the first level, matters such as the size of the trust, the extent of its property holdings, and the number of beneficiaries who might need to be consulted will affect both the possibility of the trustees being able to contact those beneficiaries and the range of

---

46 LPA 1925, ss 2, 27.

47 Unless, that is, the trust instrument excludes the operation of the statute.

48 In relation to minors whose consent is required by the trust instrument, the trustees are required to obtain the consent of 'a parent who has parental responsibility for him within the meaning of the Children Act 1989' or of a guardian: TLATA 1996, s 10(3).

49 TLATA 1996, s 11(3). Such a power to be consulted was only available under s 26(3) of the LPA 1925 in relation to trusts for sale implied by law. The new provision extends to all trusts of land. The new provisions apply to all trusts of land created after 1996, but only apply to trusts created before 1997 if there is a provision contained in a deed requiring such consultation.

50 TLATA 1996, s 11(1).

business activities (both large and small) which the trustees may have to manage. Some of the trusts activities may be thought suitably significant to require consultation and others not. For example, a decision to change the bank with which the trust account is held might not be significant enough to require consultation, whereas a decision whether to sell the trust's holding of land to effect a transfer of the trust's investment temporarily into bonds would be sufficiently significant.

The second issue relates to the identification of what will constitute the general interests of the trust. The more complex the trust's holdings, its classes of beneficiaries, and the powers of the trustees, then the more difficult the task of establishing what those interests will be. The greater the number of beneficiaries, the more difficult the task of picking a path between their conflicting interests. While this statutory provision imposes an obligation on the trustees to consult with the beneficiaries, it is suggested that in practice it simply requires that the trustees observe the general duty under trusts law to permit no conflict of interest, to act fairly between the trustees and to refrain from committing any breaches of trust.[51] The effect of this provision is that, in conducting the proper management of a trust of land and, in relation to issues of appropriate significance to the trust, the trustees must first consult with the beneficiaries and then act in accordance with the ordinary principles of the law of trusts and the terms of the trust instrument.

The trustees are not obliged to obey the beneficiaries, merely to consult with them. Nevertheless, failure to consult the beneficiaries at all when required to do so will itself constitute a breach of trust.[52] Moreover, it might be that if the trustees failed to take into account some relevant consideration raised by the beneficiaries, then any decision made on that basis might be capable of being set aside.[53] However, if the trustees can demonstrate that they have consulted an appropriate consultation and then that they have decided to act otherwise than in accordance with the view of one group of beneficiaries, their decision will not necessarily constitute a breach of trust. Rather, under general trusts law the trustees are required to act in the interests of all of the beneficiaries and not to favour any particular group of beneficiaries. So, if the trustees can demonstrate that their decision was reasonable in all the circumstances, even if it did not give effect to the wishes of a simple majority of the beneficiaries, then the trustees would not be liable for any breach of trust to any beneficiaries who formed a part of that majority, always provided that they had conducted the consultation in the first place.

Section 14(2) of the TLATA 1996 permits the trustees to acquire an order from the court to relieve them of the requirement either to consult any person or to obtain the consent of any person connected with the operation of the trustees' functions. The trustees would therefore be well-advised in practice to seek the permission of the court before dispensing with the requirement to consult with the beneficiaries.

The beneficiaries' limited rights of occupation

One of the underlying aims of the changes introduced by the TLATA 1996 was to grant beneficiaries under trusts of land a qualified right to occupy land held on trust for them. The

---

51 See, eg, *Rodway v Landy* [2001] Ch 703.
52 *Re Jones* [1931] 1 Ch 375; *Crawley Borough Council v Ure* [1996] QB 13, [1996] 1 All ER 724.
53 *Re Hastings-Bass* [1975] Ch 25: see para 8.3.13 above.

contexts in which this right of occupation was permitted will, in some circumstances, limit the rights of some beneficiaries to occupy the land at the expense of others. Section 12 of the TLATA 1996 provides that:

A beneficiary who is beneficially entitled to an interest in possession in land subject to a trust of land is entitled by reason of his interest to occupy the land at any time if at that time –

(a) the purposes of the trust include making the land available for his occupation (or for the occupation of beneficiaries of a class of which he is a member or of beneficiaries in general), or

(b) the land is held by the trustees so as to be so available.

Therefore, the 1996 Act provides for a right of occupation for any beneficiary whose interest is in possession at the material time. What is clear is that no beneficiary has a right to occupy the land simply by virtue of being a beneficiary under a trust of land.[54] Rather, the terms of the trust instrument must entitle the beneficiary to go into occupation and, therefore, the trust instrument must not contain provisions which exclude that possibility. The right of occupation, as expressed in s 12, can be exercised at any time and therefore need neither be permanent nor continuous.

Section 12 then contains a number of alternative caveats. The first is that the purposes of the trust include making the land available for a beneficiary such as the applicant. Again, this serves merely to reinforce the purposes of the trust of land, excluding from occupation those beneficiaries who were never intended to occupy and permitting occupation by those beneficiaries who were intended to be entitled to occupy the property. The trustees are nevertheless required to act fairly and evenly between all of the potential occupants.[55]

The second means of enforcing a right to occupy is that the trustees 'hold' the land to make it available for the beneficiary's occupation. The problem is what is meant by the term 'hold' in these circumstances. There are two possibilities: either the trustees must have made a formal decision that the property is to be held in a particular manner, or more generally that it must be merely practicable that the land is made available for the beneficiary's occupation, given the nature and condition of the land. The case law has defined the notion of availability for occupation to be dependent on whether or not the trust instrument provides that the beneficiaries are entitled to occupy that land or that it would be a proper exercise of the trustees' powers as expressed in that trust instrument to make it available for the occupation of the beneficiaries.[56]

Clearly, this second possibility is broader than the first: in effect, the land is available for occupation if there is nothing in the trust instrument to prevent the trustees from allowing beneficiaries to occupy it and if occupation is physically possible in the sense of the property being habitable and vacant. Nevertheless, it has also been held that just because the trustees have a power, as opposed to an obligation, to make the property available for the beneficiaries' occupation, that does not entitle the beneficiaries to go into occupation unless the trustees decide to exercise their power such that any of the beneficiaries are permitted to

54 *IRC v Eversden* [2002] STC 1109, at para 25.
55 *Rodway v Landy* [2001] Ch 703.
56 *IRC v Eversden* [2002] STC 1109.

occupy it.[57] Depending on the terms of the trust instrument, which may contain a provision which explicitly prevents such a course of action, it would be possible for the trustees to sell the trust property and use the sale proceeds to acquire another property which could be made available for the beneficiaries' occupation further to the power contained in s 8(1)(c) of the TA 2000.

The exclusion of beneficiaries from occupation of the property

The more contentious part of the legislation is that in s 13(1) whereby the trustees have the right to exclude beneficiaries in the following circumstances:

> Where two or more beneficiaries are entitled under s 12 to occupy land, the trustees of land may exclude or restrict the entitlement of any one or more (but not all) of them.

The limits placed on this power by the legislation are set out in s 13(2):

> Trustees may not under subsection (1) –
>
> (a) unreasonably exclude any beneficiary's entitlement to occupy land, or
> (b) restrict any such entitlement to an unreasonable extent.

Therefore, the trustees are restricted from excluding any beneficiary unreasonably. In deciding which of the beneficiaries to allow into occupation and which to exclude from occupation, the trustees are required to take into account 'the intentions of the person or persons . . . who created the trust'[58] and 'the purposes for which the land is held . . .'[59] and 'the circumstances and wishes of each of the beneficiaries . . .'.[60] Therefore, all that the s 13 power to exclude achieves is the application of the purposes of the trust, while recognising that the trustees do have the power to exclude beneficiaries.[61] It is submitted that these intentions could be expressed in a document creating the trust or be divined in the same manner as a common intention is located in a constructive trust over a home. It is also possible for the trustees to effect a partition of the property and thereby to require that the beneficiaries occupy different portions from one another, and to require further that the beneficiaries do not intrude on one another's portions.[62] So, in *Rodway v Landy*,[63] two medical practitioners shared trust premises which they used in partnership for their medical practices. One party terminated the partnership and wished to have the property sold. It was found that such a sale would have been unlawful under the National Health Service Act 1977. Consequently, it was held, in place of a sale being made, that the parties would be required to partition the building so that they could carry on their medical practices separately in that building.

---

57 *Ibid*, affirmed at [2003] EWCA Civ 668.
58 TLATA 1996, s 13(4)(a).
59 *Ibid*, s 13(4)(b).
60 *Ibid*, s 13(4)(c).
61 It is suggested that these intentions could be expressed in a document creating the trust or be divined in the same manner as a common intention is located in a constructive trust over a home: as considered in the previous paragraph.
62 *Rodway v Landy* [2001] EWCA Civ 471, [2001] Ch 703.
63 *Ibid*.

The mechanics of the statutory trust in favour of a minor

A statutory trust is automatically created in any situation in which a legal estate is purportedly conveyed to a minor.[64] A question arises as to the operation of that trust when, for example, a lease (which is a legal estate) is purportedly granted to a minor. In *Hammersmith & Fulham LBC v Alexander-David*[65] a 16-year-old girl was granted a tenancy over a local authority flat which, further to Sched 1 of TLATA 1996,[66] the local authority held on trust for her.[67] This raised the interesting problem that the local authority as her landlord could not serve her with a notice to quit for two reasons: first, such a notice to quit should be served on the trustee, not the beneficiary; and, second, the landlord was also trustee and therefore serving the notice to quit would appear to constitute a breach of trust because the trustee would be terminating the trust in so doing. The local authority had nevertheless served a notice to quit on the girl. For the girl it was argued that the notice to quit in this case had been served on the tenant herself rather than on the trustee of the lease, and that it should properly have been served on the trustee under general trusts law. At first instance an order to quit had been made. The tenant appealed.

The Court of Appeal analysed the transaction in the following manner. First, the local authority had not granted an equitable lease but rather had granted a legal tenancy on its ordinary terms. That the tenant was a minor who could not hold a legal estate did not mean that a legal estate had not been granted: rather, such a legal estate was held on trust for the tenant. Second, the agreement between the parties was deemed to have constituted the declaration of the statutory trust under Sched 1 of TLATA 1996. Third, the appeal would be allowed on the basis that the notice to quit had been served on the wrong person, because the notice to quit should have been served by the local authority as lessor on the local authority as trustee, and not on the tenant-beneficiary directly.[68] Of course, this case does have the odd effect that if there is to be a valid notice to quit served then the lessor must serve that notice on itself.

This leaves the further question of whether the service of a notice to quit in any such circumstance constitutes a breach of trust. It was held by Sullivan LJ that 'for so long as the respondent [local authority] held the premises in trust for the appellant, it could not lawfully destroy the subject matter of the trust by serving notice to quit on the appellant'.[69] Quite where this leaves the lessor is unknowable. The primitive conception of the role of a fiduciary used by Sullivan LJ – i.e. as an all-or-nothing office – makes it impossible ever to terminate such a tenancy or to enforce its covenants. However, it has frequently been held

64 Trusts of Land and Appointment of Trustees Act 1996, Sched 1, para 1.
65 [2009] EWCA Civ 259, [2010] Ch 272.
66 Trusts of Land and Appointment of Trustees Act 1996, Sched 1, para 1(1)(b).
67 Typically these applicants, being in 'priority need' further to art 3 of the Homelessness (Priority Need for Accommodation) (England) Order 2002, SI 2002, No. 2051, have applied to the local authority to be housed as a homeless person under the Housing Act 1996; on which see Alastair Hudson, *The Law on Homelessness*, Sweet & Maxwell, 1997.
68 It was held further that it was not sufficient in relation to 16- and 17-year-old tenants to succeed in creating mere licences, as opposed to leases, to provide that their agreements constituted merely licences when they were on the same terms as other agreements, and where they granted exclusive possession to those tenants: in reliance on *Street v Mountford* [1985] AC 809.
69 [2009] EWCA Civ 259, [2009] 3 All ER 1098, at [31]. No comment was made as to what would happen if the local authority as landlord served the notice to quit on itself as trustee in the proper form.

that fiduciary offices are not all identical but rather the nature of each fiduciary office depends upon its own terms.[70] It is suggested that the trustee's obligations in these circumstances should be understood as being in the form of a bare trust (i.e. merely to hold the legal title in the property for the benefit of the tenant) and not as extending so far as to preclude it from exercising the ordinary rights and powers of a lessor if the tenant is in breach of the terms of the lease; these fiduciary obligations should be considered to be distinct from the powers and obligations of a lessor outwith this bare trust. A trustee is obliged, after all, to act in the interests of her beneficiary only to the extent of its fiduciary obligations but no further. Thus, if the fiduciary duties are understood in this context as being in the form of a bare trust, then there would be no overlap with its rights as a lessor.

The effect of these provisions on the unity of possession

The argument has been made that the TLATA 1996 does violence to the concept of unity of possession, reawakening the spectre of *Bull v Bull*,[71] whereby a trustee who is also a beneficiary under a trust of land could abuse her powers as trustee to exclude other persons who were also beneficiaries but not trustees under the trust of land.[72] As to the merits of that argument, it seems that s 12 operates only where it is the underlying purpose of the trust that the claimant-beneficiary be entitled to occupy that property[73] or that the property is otherwise held so as to make that possible, in which case the trustees would be required to observe the terms of the trust in making any such decision.[74] Consequently, the exclusion of beneficiaries under s 13 will only apply where it is in accordance with the purpose of the trust.

Furthermore, an unconscionable breach of the trustees' duty to act fairly as between beneficiaries would lead to the court ordering a conscionable exercise of the power. In any event, there is a power to make an order in relation to the trustees' functions under s 14 to preclude the trustee from acting in flagrant breach of trust or in a manner which was abusive of her fiduciary powers in permitting a personal interest and fiduciary power to come into conflict.[75]

Of course, s 12 of the TLATA 1996 could simply be considered to be a provision which grants a qualified right of occupation, in relation to which it is necessary to protect the trustees from an action for breach of the duty of fairness by means of s 13 if some beneficiaries are protected rather than others. That means that the trustee would deemed to have a power to permit some person to occupy the land under s 12 whilst at the same time protecting the trustee from any action based on breach of trust under s 13 in permitting that occupation.

None of this would be of importance in relation to '*de facto* unions' (marriages, etc)[76] because the purpose of the trust would clearly be to allow all parties to occupy the land as their home. Therefore, it is only in relation to the odd cases where land is acquired with a purpose that only some of them might occupy the property that the *Bull v Bull*[77] problem is of any great concern. It seems that the TLATA 1996 intends to displace the concept of

---

70 Eg *Henderson v Merrett Syndicates* [1995] 2 AC 145 at 206, *per* Lord Browne-Wilkinson.
71 [1955] 1 QB 234.
72 Barnsley, 1998.
73 TLATA 1996, s 12(1)(a).
74 *Ibid*, s 12(1)(b).
75 As considered in Chapter 8.
76 See this expression deployed in *Gillies v Keogh* [1989] 2 NZLR 327.
77 [1955] 1 QB 234.

interests in possession as the decisive factor in the treatment of the home in favour of considering the advantages of permitting some persons to continue to occupy the home.

In the wake of the balance sheet cases[78] and the family assets cases[79] considered in Chapter 15, the courts are more likely to allocate interests between beneficiaries and decide on the parties' respective merits rather than step back to the idea of interests in possession.[80] Therefore, the approach of the courts appears to be more likely to support the underlying purpose of the legislation in granting rights of occupation to beneficiaries under trusts of land. As suggested above the argument has been made that the 1996 Act interferes with the concept of unity of possession, as was considered in *Bull v Bull*,[81] whereby a trustee who is also a beneficiary under a trust of land could abuse her powers as trustee to exclude other persons who were also beneficiaries but not trustees under the trust of land.[82] As to the merits of that argument, it is suggested that s 12 operates only where it is the underlying purpose of the trust that the claimant-beneficiary be entitled to occupy that property[83] or that the property is otherwise held so as to make that possible, in which case the trustees would be required to observe the terms of the trust in making any such decision.[84] Consequently, the exclusion of beneficiaries under s 13 will only apply where it is in accordance with the purpose of the trust.

Furthermore, an unconscionable breach of the trustees' duty to act fairly as between beneficiaries would lead to the court ordering a conscionable exercise of the power. In any event, there is a power to make an order in relation to the trustees' functions under s 14 to preclude the trustee from acting in flagrant breach of trust or in a manner which was abusive of her fiduciary powers in permitting a personal interest and fiduciary power to come into conflict.

The beneficiaries' rights of occupation in the event of a beneficiary's bankruptcy

The preceding sections have considered the rights of any beneficiaries whose interests are in possession to occupy the trust property. However, the rights of the parties to occupy the trust property will be changed in the event that a beneficiary goes into bankruptcy. From the moment of that beneficiary's bankruptcy, that beneficiary's trustee in bankruptcy will seek to take possession of his rights under the trust.[85] At first blush, any spouse of that bankrupt person might seek to assert rights of occupation of that property. However, s 336 of the Insolvency Act 1986 provides that:

(1) Nothing occurring in the initial period of the bankruptcy (that is to say, the period beginning with the day of the presentation of the petition for the bankruptcy order and ending with the vesting of the bankrupt's estate in a trustee) is to be taken as having given rise to any [matrimonial home rights under Part IV of the Family Law Act 1996] in relation to a dwelling house comprised in the bankrupt's estate.

78 *Bernard v Josephs* [1982] Ch 391; *Huntingford v Hobbs* [1993] 1 FLR 736.
79 *Midland Bank v Cooke* [1995] 4 All ER 562.
80 That is, beyond the necessary inclusion in the legislation requiring that the rights must be in possession at the time of the claim.
81 [1955] 1 QB 234.
82 Barnsley, 1998.
83 TLATA 1996, s 12(1)(a).
84 *Ibid*, s 12(1)(b).
85 The right of a beneficiary to a share of a life interest which is defeasible by a power of the trustees will not, however, constitute a basis for possession or sale for a mortgagee: *Skyparks Group plc v Marks* [2001] WTLR 607.

Thus, any rights which might otherwise arise under the Family Law Act 1996 are restricted. Similarly:

(2) Where a spouse's [matrimonial home rights under the Act of 1996] are a charge on the estate or interest of the other spouse, or of trustees for the other spouse, and the other spouse is adjudged bankrupt –
   (a) the charge continues to subsist notwithstanding the bankruptcy and, subject to the provisions of that Act, binds the trustee of the bankrupt's estate and persons deriving title under that trustee, and
   (b) any application for an order under [section 33 of that Act] shall be made to the court having jurisdiction in relation to the bankruptcy.

The powers of the court to make an order are then expressed in the following form:

(4) On such an application as is mentioned in subsection (2) . . . the court shall make such order under [section 33 of the Act of 1996] . . . as it thinks just and reasonable having regard to –
   (a) the interests of the bankrupt's creditors,
   (b) the conduct of the spouse or former spouse, so far as contributing to the bankruptcy,
   (c) the needs and financial resources of the spouse or former spouse,
   (d) the needs of any children, and
   (e) all the circumstances of the case other than the needs of the bankrupt.

Whereas the scope of those rights might seem expansive, and to be similar in form to those in s 15 (as considered below), they are limited by the following significant proviso which requires the court to give priority to the interests of the bankrupt's creditors:

(5) Where such an application is made after the end of the period of one year beginning with the first vesting under Chapter IV of this Part of the bankrupt's estate in a trustee, the court shall assume, unless the circumstances of the case are exceptional, that the interests of the bankrupt's creditors outweigh all other considerations.

Where a beneficiary is entitled to occupy trust property as her residence, there may be claims as to the bankrupt's right to remain in that property. Section 337(2) of the Insolvency Act 1986 provides a right for the bankrupt not to be evicted or, if not already in occupation, to go into occupation, in the following terms:[86]

(2) Whether or not the bankrupt's spouse (if any) has rights of occupation under [matrimonial home rights under Part IV of the Family Law Act 1996] –
   (a) the bankrupt has the following rights as against the trustee of his estate –
      (i) if in occupation, a right not to be evicted or excluded from the dwelling house or any part of it, except with the leave of the court,

---

86 By virtue of s 337(1), this principle 'applies where – (a) a person who is entitled to occupy a dwelling house by virtue of a beneficial estate or interest is adjudged bankrupt, and (b) any persons under the age of 18 with whom that person had at some time occupied that dwelling house had their home with that person at the time when the bankruptcy petition was presented and at the commencement of the bankruptcy'.

> > (ii) if not in occupation, a right with the leave of the court to enter into and
> > occupy the dwelling house, and
>
> (b) the bankrupt's rights are a charge, having the like priority as an equitable
> interest created immediately before the commencement of the bankruptcy, on
> so much of his estate or interest in the dwelling house as vests in the trustee.

Taking into account the foregoing rights of the bankrupt person to make an application to the
court, the court is empowered on such an application to 'make such order under [s 33 of the
Act of 1996] as it thinks just and reasonable having regard to the interests of the creditors, to
the bankrupt's financial resources, to the needs of the children and to all the circumstances
of the case other than the needs of the bankrupt'.[87] Significantly, the court's approach to the
making of any order is made subject to following proviso:[88]

> (6) Where such an application is made after the end of the period of one year beginning
> with the first vesting . . . of the bankrupt's estate in a trustee, the court shall assume,
> unless the circumstances of the case are exceptional, that the interests of the bank-
> rupt's creditors outweigh all other considerations.

Consequently, the core principle of insolvency law that, all else being equal, the rights of
creditors are to be considered to be paramount is maintained.

Section 338 of the Insolvency Act 1986 deals with the possibility that the bankrupt might
argue that payments towards the discharge of the mortgage would vest the bankrupt
with property rights in the following terms:

> Where any premises comprised in a bankrupt's estate are occupied by him . . . on condi-
> tion that he makes payments towards satisfying any liability arising under a mortgage of
> the premises or otherwise towards the outgoings of the premises, the bankrupt does not,
> by virtue of those payments, acquire any interest in the premises.

Therefore, the impact of insolvency law on the ownership of property is prevented from
raising any presumption that a bankrupt person owns property simply because she defrays
some part of the mortgage over that property.

The broader context of the inter-action of human rights law and the provisions of the
Insolvency Act 1986 in this context, and also the circumstances in which an order of sale
may nevertheless be refused, are considered in section 16.2.9.

16.2.9 The powers of the court to make orders, *inter alia*, for the sale of the land

The range of people entitled to petition the court

When there are disputes between the beneficiaries to a trust, or between trustees and some or
all of the beneficiaries, then it is open to the parties to petition the court for an order as to how
they should proceed. The most common form of dispute is between beneficiaries, some of
whom want the land retained and others of whom want the land sold. In a family situation,

---

87 Insolvency Act 1986, s 335A(5).
88 *Ibid*, s 335A(6).

for example, property that is held on the terms of a trust land will be attractive for those beneficiaries who occupy the trust property as their home, but unattractive to beneficiaries who would rather sell the land so that they can take the cash and live elsewhere. Clearly, the wishes of these varying beneficiaries to the trust of land are in conflict and it will be difficult for the trustees to know in which direction to proceed. Consequently, the parties will seek an order of the court further to s 14 of the TLATA 1996. A court which is seised of an application under s 14 of the TLATA 1996 is free to make any order which it sees fit, except in relation to the appointment or removal of trustees.[89] Section 14(1) provides that:

> Any person who is a trustee of land or has an interest in property subject to a trust of land may make an application to the court for an order under this section.[90]

Consequently, occupants of property can only make an application to the court if they have an 'interest in property': that is, if they have a proprietary right in the land held on trust. It is suggested that there are three categories of person with a sufficient interest in the property. First, the trustees may make an application as expressly envisaged by the statute. As considered in the previous sections of this chapter, the trustees may seek directions from the court in circumstances in which they are unable to reach a unanimous decision between themselves, or alternatively in circumstances in which the trustees were required to consult with the beneficiaries but where that consultation did not generate a unanimous view. Secondly, the beneficiaries may make an application (as the archetypal person with 'an interest in property')[91] seeking an order to direct that the trustees deal with the property in a given way. The most common form of application in the decided cases relates to beneficiaries seeking a sale of the property, for example, in the event of a relationship breakdown, and thus seeking an order that the trustees effect such a sale. The respondent to such an application will typically seek either to resist the application in its entirety or to agree to such an order only on terms, for example, as to her right or the right of any children of the relationship to continue in occupation of the home. Thirdly, an application may be made by any other person who has 'an interest in property'[92] such as a mortgagee or other secured creditors with a right secured over the home.

The requirement that an action can be brought only by people with an interest in the property will generally exclude children of the family living in the property or any other relatives occupying the property who do not have a proprietary right in that home. Subject to what is said in relation to s 15 of the TLATA 1996 below, children are entitled to have their interests taken into account when the court considers the form of order it wishes to make, but not to apply to the court in relation to the trustees' treatment of the land.[93]

Section 14 of the TLATA 1996 replaced s 30 of the LPA 1925 which provided that the court was entitled to make any order it saw fit in response to an application. There was an extensive case law on the effect of s 30 of the 1925 Act, particularly in relation to disputes between family members at a time of family breakdown or situations involving a mortgagee seeking

---

89 TLATA 1996, s 14(3).
90 Applications under this section may be made either before or after the commencement of this Act: *ibid*, s 14(4).
91 *Ibid*, s 14(1).
92 *Ibid*.
93 See, eg, the Children Act 1989, s 1, which establishes that the welfare of the child is paramount, as considered below.

repossession or sale of the home further to a mortgage loan contract. The more difficult area in the cases has been the question of whether or not to order a sale of land where the beneficiaries cannot come to a unanimous decision as to whether or not a sale should go ahead. It is suggested that those cases will continue to be important in relation to s 14 applications.

The powers of the court

The scope of any order which the court is entitled to make is set out in s 14(2) of the TLATA 1996[94] in the following terms:

> the court may make any such order –
>
> (a) relating to the exercise by the trustees of their functions (including an order relieving them of any obligation to obtain the consent of, or to consult, any person in connection with the exercise of any of their functions), or
>
> (b) declaring the nature or extent of a person's interest in property subject to the trust, as the court thinks fit.[95]

The two provisions, s 30 of the 1925 Act and s 14 of the 1996 Act which replaced it, operate similarly to the extent that the court is empowered to make any such order as the court 'thinks fit' in relation to the trustees' functions. Section 14 of the TLATA 1996 necessarily makes express reference to the court making orders as to the trustees' obligations to consult the beneficiaries and to obtain consent in circumstances where such consents are necessary: the obligations to obtain consent and to consult, respectively, were considered earlier.

Matters which the court is required to take into account when considering an application

The principal question, then, is as to the matters which the courts are required to take into account when exercising their powers under s 14 of the TLATA 1996: s 15 sets out those matters.[96] The four categories of persons whose interests and preferences are to be considered in relation to an exercise of a power under s 14 are as follows:[97]

(a) the intentions of the persons or persons (if any) who created the trust,
(b) the purposes for which the property subject to the trust is held,
(c) the welfare of any minor who occupies or might reasonably be expected to occupy any land subject to the trust as his home, and
(d) the interests of any secured creditor of any beneficiary.

There is a balancing act to be conducted by the court between these four potentially contradictory considerations. It does not appear that there is any significance in the ranking of these

---

94 Formerly personified in s 30 of the LPA 1925.
95 TLATA 1996, s 14(2).
96 There was no comparable provision in the 1925 Act to s 15, although three of the matters which are identified in s 15 were features of the case law on s 30.
97 TLATA 1996, s 15(1).

matters which the courts are required to take into account: that is, it does not seem to matter that the matters to be taken into account have been listed in this particular order.[98] Each category is considered in turn in the paragraphs to follow.

The purpose of the trust and the settlor's intention

Paragraph (1)(a) of s 15 provides that the underlying purpose of the trust as expressed by its settlor is to be applied by the court in reaching any decision. Therefore, this heading requires that the court consider the settlor's intentions in creating the trust.[99] While the settlor's intentions are to be considered, it is not the case that the settlor's intentions under the general law of trusts are necessarily decisive as to the interpretation of the trust. The rule in *Saunders v Vautier*[100] necessarily accepts that the beneficiaries, acting unanimously, may direct the trustees how to use the trust property or may terminate the trust. An example would be the decision in *Re Bowes,*[101] in which the settlor's original intention, to provide for the maintenance of large gardens on settled land, was overridden by the unanimous direction of the beneficiaries to the effect that the trust property should be applied for their personal benefit as opposed to its use solely for the abstract purpose of the maintenance of parkland. By extrapolation from this principle, the law of trusts does not require the trustees to follow the settlor's intentions slavishly, even if they can be clearly divined from the wording of the trust instrument.

The second matter to be considered, under para (1)(b) of s 15, is the purpose for which the trust was created. This is subtly different from the settlor's stated intentions. If, for example, the settlor created a trust to benefit all of her children, then this might colour the trustees' decisions when those children become adults. While the children were infants, the trustees would be concerned with the maintenance of the children, whereas once the children grow up, the trustees might be more concerned with providing income so that those adults can make their own decisions about the way in which they want to live their lives. Therefore, if there is an underlying purpose to the trust – such as the prosperity of the settlor's children – it might be that a decision to preserve the house as a home for the children while they were minors would be displaced by a decision to sell the house and divide the proceeds between the children once they have become adults with their own homes. It might be that the terms of the trust instrument and the use to which those powers are being put by the trustees might not be capable of easy reconciliation. In such a situation, the attitude of English trusts law to the effect that all of the beneficiaries acting in concert are able to direct the trustees how to deal with the property may trump the settlor's original intentions.[102] Thus, the trust's purposes from time-to-time may differ from the original purposes set out in the trust instrument which are the subject matter of para (1)(a). It has been accepted on the authorities that these 'purposes' may vary from context to context.[103]

---

98   *A v B* (unreported, Family Division, 23 May 1997), *per* Cazalet J.
99   TLATA 1996, s 15(1)(a).
100   (1841) 4 Beav 115.
101   [1896] 1 Ch 507.
102   *Saunders v Vautier* (1841) 4 Beav 115.
103   *Bankers Trust Co v Namdar* [1997] EGCS 20; *Barclays Bank v Hendricks* [1996] 1 FLR 258; *Mortgage Corporation v Shaire* [2000] 1 FLR 973; *Grindal v Hooper* (2000) *The Times*, 8 February.

The rights of children in occupation of the property

The most contentious part of s 15 is para (1)(c), which imports into this area of trusts law the need to consider the rights of children in relation to their homes are to be taken into account.[104] Under ordinary principles of trusts law, children do not have rights in the home under property law principles on the basis that they are unlikely to have made a financial contribution to the acquisition of the property.[105] Consequently, ordinary trusts law would not consider the rights of children in deciding the allocation of rights in the home, as considered in Chapter 15. The inclusion of para (c), therefore, requires that the position of the children be taken into account for the first time.

The case law dealing with s 30 of the LPA 1925 did give peripheral consideration to the place of the children in making an order under that section. For example, in *Re Holliday*,[106] the needs of the children to finish their schooling were taken into account such that the order for sale of the property was made conditional on the children of the relationship reaching school-leaving age. What was obvious, however, was that the rights of a mortgagee[107] or a bankruptcy creditor[108] would always take priority over the needs of the children in those cases.[109] The significance of the introduction of s 15(1)(c) is that the needs of children might be elevated to being of equal significance to the rights of secured creditors and other people.

This provision may lead to the importation of elements of child law and of the case law under the Children Act 1989 to this area, under which the welfare of the child is made paramount.[110] The principles of child law have developed since the principal cases on s 30 were decided: therefore, it is difficult to know how property law courts will deal with concepts developed originally by family courts in disposing of applications seeking the use of the family courts' broad, statutory discretion. Under ss 14 and 15, it would be possible for the court to import child law concepts given the express power for the court to make such order as it sees fit.[111] The interests of children are generally best served by resisting an application for the sale of property so that the children can remain in their home and thus reduce any volatility in their lifestyle which would result from the need to move home. This is particularly true if the family unit intends to stay together and if it is only a secured creditor which is seeking to have the home sold. By contrast, different considerations come into play if the sale is being sought by one of the child's unmarried parents:[112] in this situation, the best interests of the child might be served by living with one parent rather than another in circumstances in which it would not be practicable, possible or even desirable to remain in the original home.

---

104 Cf family law where the welfare of the child is paramount: Children Act 1989, s 1.
105 As required, for example, by *Lloyds Bank v Rosset* [1991] 1 AC 1.
106 [1981] 2 WLR 996.
107 *Lloyds Bank v Byrne* (1991) [1993] 1 FLR 369, (1991) 23 HLR 472.
108 *Re Citro* [1991] Ch 142.
109 One exceptional case was *Re Holliday* [1981] 2 WLR 996, in which the bankruptcy creditor's interests were relegated behind the needs of the family – including the children – to remain in their home: that decision was based on the small size of the debt compared to the value of the home whereby it was considered disproportionate to sell a house to discharge such a small debt.
110 *Bankers Trust Co v Namdar* [1997] EGCS 20; *Barclays Bank v Hendricks* [1996] 1 FLR 258; *Mortgage Corporation v Shaire* [2000] 1 FLR 973; *Grindal v Hooper* (2000) *The Times*, 8 February.
111 TLATA 1996, s 14(2).
112 If the parents were married, then divorce law might decide the question as to which course is most appropriate.

At the time of writing, the jurisprudence in this area is in its infancy. The possibilities are considered below, after the discussion of the rights of secured creditors, which are considered next.

The situation when one of the beneficiaries is bankrupt

The circumstances in which one of the beneficiaries is bankrupt are different from other circumstances. If one of the trustees of land is bankrupt, the trust property will not form a part of that beneficiary's estate simply because she is a trustee. It is only if the trustee also has some beneficial interest in the trust property that the trust property will be brought into account in the bankruptcy proceedings. If it is a beneficiary who is bankrupt, then the trustee in bankruptcy will be entitled to bring an application under s 14 as a person with an interest in the land by dint of the bankruptcy proceedings. Section 335A(1) of the Insolvency Act 1986 overrides the provisions of the 1996 Act providing that:[113]

> Any application by a trustee of a bankrupt's estate under section 14 . . . for an order under that section for the sale of land shall be made to the court having jurisdiction in relation to the bankruptcy.

The application under s 14 is therefore subjugated to the hearing of the bankruptcy petition. That court's powers operate as follows:[114]

> the court shall make such order as it thinks just and reasonable having regard to –
>
> (a) the interests of the bankrupt's creditors;
> (b) where the application is made in respect of land which includes a dwelling house which is or has been the home of the bankrupt or the bankrupt's spouse or former spouse –
>   (i)   the conduct of the spouse or former spouse, so far as contributing to the bankruptcy,
>   (ii) the needs and financial resources of the spouse or former spouse, and
>   (iii) the needs of any children; and
> (c) all the circumstances of the case other than the needs of the bankrupt.

Under this provision, the court may make any order which it considers just and reasonable to make provided that it takes into account considerations which are broadly similar to those under s 15 of the TLATA 1996. However, s 335A(3) provides that, regardless of the ostensible similarity of these provisions to s 15 of the TLATA 1996:

> Where such an application [under section 14 of the 1996 Act] is made after the end of the period of one year beginning with the first vesting . . . of the bankrupt's estate in a trustee, the court shall assume, unless the circumstances of the case are exceptional, that the interests of the bankrupt's creditors outweigh all other considerations.

---

113 Further to the TLATA 1996, s 15(4).
114 Insolvency Act 1986, s 335A(2).

Therefore, regardless of the provisions of s 15 of the TLATA 1996, the court is obliged to assume that the interests of the bankrupt's creditors must be given priority over all other considerations and the rights of other people in relation to the trust property. Consequently, it is assumed that the property is to be sold and the relevant proportion of the proceeds transferred to the trustee in bankruptcy to discharge the creditors' debts.

Whereas the statute does not go further in setting out the principles which the court must bear in mind, it was held in *Harrington v Bennett*[115] that the requirements of s 335A of the Insolvency Act 1986 are fivefold. First, where the application is made more than one year after the vesting of the bankrupt's property in the trustee, the interests of creditors are paramount. Secondly, the court can only ignore the creditors' interests in exceptional circumstances, which circumstances will typically relate to the personal circumstances of the joint owners. Thirdly, the categories of exceptional circumstances are not closed, with the result that it is open to the judge to decide what may constitute exceptional circumstances in future cases. Fourthly, the term 'exceptional circumstances' indicates circumstances 'outside the usual melancholy consequences of debt or improvidence'. Fifthly, that the sale proceeds may be used entirely to discharge the expenses of the trustee in bankruptcy is not an exceptional circumstance which may still benefit the creditors.[116] The term 'exceptional' is to be given 'its ordinary and familiar meaning'[117] which in turn is said to involve the expressions 'out of the ordinary course, or unusual, or special, or uncommon'.[118] This definition includes almost all of the elements of the definition in the *Oxford English Dictionary*. The practice of the courts, however, has been to reserve a finding of exceptional circumstances to a very small and rare category of circumstances indeed, as considered in the discussion to follow. The finding of 'unusual' seems somewhat mild given the attitude of the courts in general.

In the case of an application made by a trustee in bankruptcy under s 14 of the TLATA 1996, different criteria have been applied on the cases under s 30 of the 1925 Act from those considered in relation to the other paragraphs of s 15 of the TLATA 1996 which do not relate to bankruptcy. Regardless of s 335A of the 1986 Act, the court would ordinarily have ordered a sale of the property automatically in a situation in which one of the beneficiaries has been declared bankrupt. So, in the case of *Re Citro,*[119] it was no answer to an application for sale on behalf of the bankrupt's creditors that the loss of the home which was the subject of the trust would require the family to leave the area in which they lived and to uproot their children from their schooling. It was held that a sale of the property would not be refused unless the circumstances were exceptional and that this form of hardship was, in the maudlin and yet lyrical view of the court, merely one of the melancholy features of life. As Nourse LJ put the matter:[120]

> What then are exceptional circumstances? As the cases show, it is not uncommon for a
> wife with young children to be faced with eviction in circumstances where the

115 [2000] BPIR 630.
116 See also *Judd v Brown* [1998] 2 FLR 360; *Re Raval* [1998] 2 FLR 718; *Claughton v Charalambous* [1999] 1 FLR 740; *Re Bremner* [1999] 1 FLR 912.
117 *Nicholls v Lan* [2006] EWHC 1255 (Ch), [2006] All ER (D) 16, [10], *per* Morgan QC.
118 *Hosking v Michaelides* [2004] All ER (D) 147, *per* Morgan QC.
119 [1991] Ch 142.
120 *Ibid*, 157.

realisation of her beneficial interest will not produce enough to buy a comparable house in the same neighbourhood or indeed elsewhere. And, if she has to move elsewhere, there may be problems over schooling and so forth. Such circumstances, while engendering a natural sympathy in all who hear of them, cannot be described as exceptional. They are the melancholy consequences of debt and improvidence with which every civilized society has been familiar.

If everyone wanted proof that this is a cold and heartless world, then those *dicta* are that proof. That is not to say that they are wrong in principle, nor that they are even undesirable in a society in which people are so dependent on debt that the consequences of denying creditors the right to recover their money would mean reduced access to debt for us all. I sense that even Nourse LJ would agree with that.

There have been very few cases in which the courts have resisted an application for sale when one of the beneficiaries has been declared bankrupt. The first situation in which an application for an order for sale was denied was that in *Re Holliday*,[121] a case in which the bankrupt had gone into bankruptcy on his own petition to rid himself of his creditors and one in which the debt was so small in comparison to the sale value of the house that there was thought to be no hardship to the creditors in waiting for the bankrupt's three children to reach school-leaving age before ordering a sale. However, that hardship will be caused to the children or to the family in general as a result of a sale in favour of a trustee in bankruptcy is considered, as mentioned in the preceding paragraphs, to be merely one of the maudlin vicissitudes of life.[122] In *Re Holliday*, however, the circumstances were rare in that the debt owed was very small and constituted only a fraction of the total market value of the house at issue. There have been a few melancholy situations in which sale has not been ordered immediately: where the bankrupt's spouse was terminally ill and had special housing needs,[123] or where the property had been adapted specially to accommodate an occupant's special housing needs.[124] A finding of exceptional circumstances has been made in circumstances in which the bankrupt's spouse has been diagnosed as being a paranoid schizophrenic.[125] Such a finding has been held to justify a one-year suspension of sale.[126] There has also emerged an equity of exoneration whereby the bankruptcy debts of one of a number of co-owners of property are to be met only out of the share of the bankrupt party even if the entire property had purportedly been charged to secure the bankrupt's debts.[127] It should not be forgotten either that cases like *Re Holliday* remain cases out of the ordinary run of the case law themselves and so remain the rare exceptions.[128]

---

121 [1981] 2 WLR 996.
122 *Re Citro* [1991] Ch 142.
123 *Claughton v Charalambous* [1999] 1 FLR 740; *Re Bremner* [1999] 1 FLR 912. Further, *Re Raval* [1998] 2 FLR 718, in which a one-year suspension of the sale was granted due to a diagnosis of paranoid schizophrenia. See also *Skyparks Group plc v Marks* [2001] WTLR 607, in which a mortgagee was denied an order for possession and sale of mortgaged property against a contingent right of a beneficiary under a trust for sale.
124 *Re Gorman* [1990] 1 WLR 616, where this was proposed hypothetically by Vinelott J at 629.
125 *Re Raval* [1998] 2 FLR 718; *Nicholls v Lan* [2006] EWHC 1255 (Ch), [2006] All ER (D) 16.
126 *Re Raval* [1998] 2 FLR 718.
127 *Re Pittortou* [1985] 1 WLR 58, 61; *Judd v Brown* [1998] 2 FLR 360, 362.
128 See *Harman v Glencross* [1986] Fam 81, 95, *per* Balcombe LJ.

The position may be thought of differently where the property is held on an express trust for sale (that is, where the purpose expressly is to sell the property) with a power to postpone the sale. This was the case in *Avis v Turner*[129] during matrimonial proceedings where the husband had been made bankrupt. This was the position in the law before the enactment of the 1996: all trusts over land were deemed to be trusts to sell that land with a power to postpone sale.[130] Section 14(2)(a) of the 1996 Act was taken by Chadwick LJ in that case to empower the court to order the trustees to relax their power to postpone the sale and thus to seek a sale of the property. Ordinarily then a sale of the property will be sought in cases of bankruptcy. It is not surprising that where the property is held on trust for the purpose of seeking a sale with a mere power to delay sale, that a sale will be ordered where bankruptcy has visited one of the parties.

Findings of fact

The job of finding facts in these cases is a matter for the judge at first instance. It will be a rare occasion on which an appellate court will disturb the findings of fact of the trial or on which an appellate court will disturb the trial judge's conclusions as to the balancing act under ss 14 and 15 of TLATA 1996. In *G v G*,[131] in relation to proceedings under the old s 30 of the 1925 Act, Lord Fraser held that:[132]

> the appellate court should only interfere when they consider that the Judge of first instance has not merely preferred an imperfect solution which is different from an alternative imperfect solution which the Court of Appeal might or would have adopted, but has exceeded the generous ambit within which a reasonable disagreement is possible.

This approach has been followed in a number of cases in relation specifically to cases under the 1996 Act.[133] This may involve differences of view as to the significance of medical evidence in deciding whether or not there are exceptional circumstances to justify refusing an immediate order of sale.

The rights of any secured creditor of the beneficiaries

In the cases on s 30 of the LPA 1925, which has been displaced by s 14 of the TLATA 1996, the rights of secured creditors were prioritised over the rights of other people. The result of this prioritisation was that the property would be sold so that the sale proceeds could be used to discharge the debt. Paragraph (1)(d) of s 15 of the 1996 Act requires the court to consider the rights of any creditor of any beneficiary, not requiring that the beneficiary be bankrupt at the time. Therefore, mortgagees will be entitled to have their interests taken expressly into

---

129 [2008] 2 WLR 1.
130 *In re Mayo* [1943] Ch 302, 304, *per* Simonds J; *Jones v Challenger* [1961] 1 QB 176, 181, *per* Devlin LJ.
131 [1985] 1 WLR 647.
132 *Ibid*, 652.
133 *Assicurazioni Generali SPA v Arab Insurance Group: Practice Note* [2003] 1 WLR 577; *Nicholls v Lan* [2006] EWHC 1255 (Ch); *Donohoe v Ingram* [2006] BPIR 417.

account. The courts have indicated that mortgagees ought to be protected with the same enthusiasm as bankruptcy creditors in these contexts.[134] It has been held that the primary interest of secured creditors is taken to be to recover their debt and therefore to seek an immediate sale, ordinarily without the need for further analysis.[135] Therefore, the question for the court usually resolves itself to a question as to whether or not there is any good reason to prevent a sale of the property so as to recover as much of the creditors' debt as possible.

Human rights law and s 335A

Section 335A of the 1986 Act has been held to be in compliance with the human right to a family life of occupants of property under Article 8 of the European Convention on Human Rights.[136] There has been one tentative suggestion that in future the interpretation of this provision might need to be altered so as to ensure compliance with the spirit of Article 8.[137] However, there has been held to be no necessary infraction of Article 8 in relation to considering the sale of a home occupied by a woman who had been diagnosed as being schizophrenic.[138] More generally, it has been held by the House of Lords that Article 8 could not be relied upon to defeat proprietary or contractual rights to possession nor to confer a right to be provided with a home.[139] This approach has been considered as a further reason for denying that s 335A is necessarily in breach of Article 8.[140] In short, a succession of decisions of the High Court have demonstrated a reluctance to take a point based on Article 8 on the basis, it is suggested, that the balancing act which is necessarily a part of hearing a s 14 application under the 1996 Act will consider whether or not it is appropriate to take away the defendant's home by means of a sale.

The interpretative role of the case law decided before 1997

It seems probable that the courts will continue to consider the case law decided under s 30 of the 1925 Act. What is unclear is the extent to which the introduction of s 15 of the TLATA 1996 will render the principles under the 1925 Act inapplicable. The case of *Mortgage Corp v Shaire*[141] has suggested that the TLATA 1996 could be read as intending to alter the manner in which the old case law should be dealt with by the courts. The legislative intention might be taken to create equality between the rights of secured creditors such as mortgagees and the rights of occupants of the property and their families (including children), rather than simply assuming that the rights of creditors should still be treated as being paramount (as

---

134 *Lloyds Bank v Byrne* (1991) 23 HLR 472, [1993] 1 FLR 369.
135 *Re Citro* [1991] Ch 142; *Bank of Ireland Home Mortgages Ltd v Bell* [2001] 2 All ER (Comm) 920, [31] and [38]; *First National Bank Plc v Achampong* [2004] 1 FCR 17, [61]; *Nicholls v Lan* [2006] EWHC 1255 (Ch), [47]–[49].
136 *Jackson v Bell* [2001] EWCA Civ 387.
137 *Barca v Mears* [2004] All ER (D) 153, *per* Strauss QC.
138 *Nicholls v Lan* [2006] EWHC 1255 (Ch).
139 *Harrow LBC v Qazi* [2003] UKHL 43, [2004] 1 AC 983. See also *Price v Leeds CC* [2005] EWCA Civ 289, and now on appeal *Leeds CC v Price* [2006] UKHL 10, [2006] 2 WLR 570.
140 *Donohoe v Ingram* [2006] BPIR 417, [21].
141 [2001] Ch 743, [2001] 4 All ER 364. See also *Bank of Ireland Home Mortgages Ltd v Bell* [2001] 2 All ER (Comm) 920; *First National Bank plc v Achampong* [2004] 1 FCR 17.

considered in the previous paragraph). In the case of *Mortgage Corp v Shaire* itself, only interlocutory questions were considered without any final decision on the merits being reached. Therefore, the High Court did not reach any conclusions as to the proper interpretation of the new legislation. Other, as yet unreported,[142] cases have suggested, however, that the pre-1997 case law will continue to be of significance in interpreting the broadly similar matters to be taken into account under the 1996 Act.[143] It is suggested that the position in relation to bankruptcy will remain as it was before 1997 by virtue of s 335A of the Insolvency Act 1986 and that the remaining case law on s 30 of the 1925 Act will continue to be influential given that the provisions of s 30 of the 1925 Act and s 14 of the 1996 Act are so similar.

16.2.10 The protection of purchasers of the land

When the purchase is contracted with a delegate of the trustees' powers

When a purchase is contracted with someone to whom the trustees have delegated their powers, this raises the possibility that the sale may subsequently be repudiated by the trustees or the beneficiaries. In circumstances in which the purchaser has acted in good faith, the purchase is presumed to be valid.[144] Section 10 of the TLATA 1996 provides that where two or more people are to give their consent in advance of a valid sale, consent being given by any two of them is sufficient to transfer good title to the purchaser.[145]

Overreaching

The doctrine of overreaching provides that if the purchase price for property is paid to two trustees or a trust corporation, then the rights of the purchaser overreach the interests of the beneficiaries under that trust of land.[146] Overreaching will not operate in situations in which there is only one trustee of the trust of land.[147] The particular problem which has arisen in land law is whether an overriding interest[148] in relation to a person in actual occupation of land[149] would take priority over the rights of a purchaser who has paid purchase moneys over that land to two trustees so as to claim a right to overreach the rights of those beneficiaries. The House of Lords has held that an equitable interest acquired by a wife against her husband under an implied trust for sale coupled with actual occupation of that land constituted an overriding interest:[150] however, the doctrine of overreaching was not at issue in that case.[151] A subsequent decision of the House of Lords held that the proper management of the conveyancing system required that the doctrine of overreaching should take priority over an

---

142 In the materials available to me at the time of writing.
143 See *Wright v Johnson* (unreported, Court of Appeal, 2 November 1999), *per* Robert Walker LJ.
144 TLATA 1996, s 9(1).
145 *Ibid*, s 10(1).
146 LPA 1925, s 27.
147 *Williams & Glyn's Bank Ltd v Boland* [1981] AC 487.
148 After the enactment of the Land Registration Act 2002, Sched 3, now rendered as 'interests which override'.
149 The decided cases relate to LRA 1925, s 70(1)(g).
150 That was, under s 70(1)(g) of the 1925 Act.
151 *Williams & Glyn's Bank Ltd v Boland* [1981] AC 487.

equitable interest coupled with actual occupation of the property.[152] The effect of this latter decision was to enhance the protection available to purchasers who pay the purchase moneys for land to two or more trustees, or to a trust corporation, by ensuring that their interests overreach those of any beneficiary in actual occupation of the property under a trust for sale or, latterly, by extension under a trust of land.

16.3 CONCURRENT OWNERSHIP OF LAND

16.3.1 Joint tenancy and tenancy in common

The rules relating to joint tenancies and tenancies in common are also significant in relation to land. Where the parties have acquired the property with unity of time, title, interest and possession, they will be taken to be joint tenants of that property, provided that they had sufficient intention to do so.[153] The result is that neither party takes any individual interest in the property: rather, both acquire the whole of the interest in the property. It is a perfect communist model: together they hold everything; apart they have nothing. The joint tenancy best expresses the traditional legal understanding of marriage (the most common source of joint tenancies) as a unit in which the spouses acquire no rights against one another. Further, the last of them left alive acquires the whole of the rights in the property under the survivorship principle, provided that the joint tenancy was not severed before the death of the penultimate living joint tenant.[154] Severance of the joint tenancy – leading to the creation of a tenancy in common – occurs in a number of ways where the parties evidence sufficient intention to deal with their own share.[155] Severance will occur on service of a notice to that effect by one joint tenant to the others,[156] or by the bankruptcy of one joint tenant,[157] by the mutual conduct of the parties,[158] or by their mutual agreement.[159] Severance on divorce is a more complex business, whereby if death occurs before service of the final order, then severance will not take place,[160] although there are authorities which have held that service of final divorce proceedings will constitute an act of severance,[161] whereas merely seeking the advice of the court as to one's rights as a preparatory step to divorce proceedings will not.[162] The detail of this area of land is considered in detail in textbooks on land law[163]and was considered in the previous chapter in relation to the judgment in *Jones v Kernott*.[164]

---

152 *City of London Building Society v Flegg* [1988] AC 54.
153 See, eg, *Burgess v Rawnsley* [1975] Ch 429 – where a woman went into occupation of property with a man but subject to a misunderstanding about his unrequited love for her: a sad case in which he presents the genteel object of his affection with a rose wrapped in a newspaper.
154 *Re Draper's Conveyance* [1969] 1 Ch 486; *Harris v Goddard* [1983] 1 WLR 1203.
155 *Williams v Hensman* (1861) 1 J & H 546, (1861) 70 ER 862. Eg, by dealing fraudulently with the property: *Ahmed v Kendrick* (1988) 56 P & CR 120, except where that would permit the fraudster to benefit from that fraud – *Penn v Bristol & West Building Society* [1995] 2 FLR 938.
156 *Re 88 Berkley Road* [1971] Ch 648.
157 *Re Gorman* [1990] 2 FLR 284; *Re Pavlou* [1993] 2 FLR 751.
158 *McDowell v Hirschfield Lipson & Rumney and Smith* [1992] 2 FLR 126; *Gore and Snell v Carpenter* (1990) 60 P & CR 456, 462.
159 *Hunter v Babbage* [1994] 2 FLR 806.
160 *Re Palmer (Deceased)* [1994] 2 FLR 609.
161 *Re Draper's Conveyance* [1969] 1 Ch 486.
162 *Harris v Goddard* [1983] 1 WLR 1203.
163 See, eg, Thomas and Hudson, 2004, Chapter 57 generally.
164 [2011] 3 WLR 1121.

16.3.2 Understanding the law's manifold treatment of the family home

There is no single attitude to the home in the common law or in equity, in spite of developments in the legislation since the housing statutes of 1977,[165] the Children Act 1989, and the variety of family law, housing and property legislation passed in 1996.[166] It is submitted that this lack of common principle is true of the various departments of common law and equity, covering the well-established divisions between trusts law, family law, child law, public law and housing law. Rather, each area of law appears to advance its own understanding of the manner in which such rights should be allocated, causing an inability to generate a single legal model which is able either to understand the changing nature of the family or to account for it in the current jurisprudence. Consequently, there is a hotchpotch of rules and regulations coming at the same problem from different directions. A comprehensive legislative code dealing with title to the home, the rights of occupants, the rights of children and the rights of creditors is necessary to reduce the cost and stress of litigation, and to ensure that this problem is given the political consideration that it deserves.

---

165 Ie, the Housing (Homeless Persons) Act 1977, the Protection from Eviction Act 1977 and, of course, the Rent Act 1977.

166 Principally the Family Law Act 1996 and the Housing Act 1996.

Chapter 17

Essay – Family law, human rights law and equity

17.1 INTRODUCTION

17.1.1 Issues of definition

This essay falls into four parts. First, a consideration of the intellectual distinctions between the philosophy of human rights and the philosophy of equity. Secondly, an analysis of the possible applications of human rights law to the norms of trusts law. Thirdly, an analysis of the manner in which family law and child law approach questions as to ownership and occupation of the home differently from trusts law. Fourthly, a consideration of how these various approaches conceive differently of socially just conclusions to the questions which they consider.

Up to now this book has considered two streams of thought in English law. First, the comparatively haphazard development of principle in the Courts of Equity in the Tudor period[1] and, secondly, the development of trusts law since the early 19th century. In Chapter 1, the philosophy underpinning equity was explained as being a means of achieving socially just ends as a counter-balance to the rigidity of the common law. With the enactment of the Human Rights Act 1998, there is a possibility of a very different legal culture in England and Wales. For equity this presents a new challenge. What is not clear is whether the principles which underpin human rights are the same as the principles which underpin equity and trusts law, particularly in relation to rights to property and rights to the home.[2]

At one level equity is simply the product of its own history: a ramshackle bag of ideas which are the product of a culture rather than of a formal ideological programme. That means, equity has developed without any specific programme, and therefore we should not be surprised if at some points the logic appears to break down. In the late 20th century, a tremendous literature was spawned which examined the trust in particular (as opposed to equity in general). In contrast, human rights law is an ideological product of liberal democracies in the wake of the Second World War. This essay will attempt an introduction to some of the fault-lines of the distinction between human rights law[3] and equity: any more ambitious project could only be frustrated in the space available.

Human rights law talks of the right to possessions, the right to a family life and so forth in the European Convention on Human Rights. It is that Convention which is the subject matter of the Human Rights Act 1998. It was drafted in the wake of the horrors of the Second World War and clearly recognises the suffering of the people of Europe at the hands of the Nazis. Equity has an older provenance than human rights thought which deploys expressions like 'conscience', 'the trust' and 'bona fides' dating back into the mists of English jurisprudential history. Those principles were considered in Chapter 1 and their common features are analysed in the final chapter of this book.

17.1.2 The similarities between human rights law and equity, in outline

The argument is simply this: both human rights law and equity sound as if they ought to be concerned to improve the lot of ordinary citizens either by protecting a list of fundamental freedoms, or by generating 'fair' results to litigation. However, it is not clear that their different principles will always lead to the same 'just' result. Both streams of thought are normative systems, in the sense that human rights are committed to protecting the rights of the individual against state action and in the sense that equity is committed to the enforcement of contracts, to the protection of private property rights and to the control of the defendant's conscience. Both are normative. Both are 'streams of *ought*' in this sense. Perhaps one key difference between them is that equity will typically be directed at the application of discretionary principles to individual cases, whereas human rights law will typically erect general, ideologically-grounded norms to fit all cases. There is perhaps a difference between micro- and macro-provision of fair dispute resolution respectively.

---

1 That is, the range of actions which the Courts of Equity have developed from the times of the medieval Lords Chancellor.
2 See generally Douzinas, 2000.
3 Meaning those entitlements which English law will protect and recognise, as opposed to general claims to entitlement which are not necessarily recognised by the law.

17.2 HUMAN RIGHTS LAW AND EQUITY

17.2.1 The theoretical basis of human rights law

The very notion of human rights is an ideological result of Enlightenment thought in Western Europe. The development of humanism in Western thought is key to the political landscape at the beginning of the 21st century. As philosophers moved beyond placing God as the source of all human thought and morality, replacing divine intervention with a theory of self-determination for human beings, those same human beings began the agonising process of conceiving of their own intellectual structures of right and wrong. Through Hobbes and Locke we see natural right replace straightforward observance of religious law developed through the revealed word of God.

The development of secular law (as opposed to religious law or superstitious 'lore') to govern the actions and interactions of human beings itself requires that there be a set of developed principles which underpin this law-making. Given the flimsy, animated sacks of water that we human beings are, desperately trying to keep the hordes of chaos at bay, there should be little surprise that legal systems tend to veer between the creation of rigid rules and a demand for flexible justice. Deep in the philosophy of law is a need to balance discretion with certainty and certainty with discretion. The genesis of human rights was something very different.

Probably the most significant intellectual development in the late 20th century was the primacy acquired by human rights thinking in liberal democracies. In fact, human rights law has become one of the most prolific exports from these liberal democratic countries, despite the difficulty of tracing any neat philosophical source for it. With the onset of globalisation these human rights norms have become common currency, as developing nations seek access to the financial resources and technology of the more developed economies. At the surface level this global commitment to human rights is indicative of a more mature political culture; at another level many commentators worry that it only demonstrates a new economic imperialism.[4] There are three main objections to the development of a human rights law culture: the effects of economic globalisation; constitutional control by the judiciary; and an atomisation of social relations. Each will be examined in turn.

Globalisation is a complex phenomenon of late modernism. At its most conspicuous level, globalisation concerns the generation of brands which are recognised around the world. At another level globalisation signals the victory of one view of liberal democracy over other political ideologies. Bauman points out the shortcomings of this globalisation in two phenomena: first, the new ability offered to multinational corporations to move between markets without needing to feel engaged by the local communities which they affect; and secondly, in a division between a new cosmopolitan elite and the remaining majority of the population excluded from the possibilities offered by this process of globalisation.[5] The fall-out of this development of globalisation is that communities are weakened, with the result that social ties are loosened in favour of an atomisation of society which focuses instead on individual rights as conceived of in human rights thinking.[6] Human rights are becoming the greatest export commodity from the capitalist democracies to the rest of the world – they are

---

4 Eg, Chomsky, 2000.
5 Bauman, 2000.
6 Bauman, 1998; Houellebecq, 2001.

all but boxed up with everything else that is sold.[7] As such, the ideology underpinning human rights as applied in the globalised economy is criticised for seeking above all to secure the rights of Western capitalists through the protection of rights in property: in that sense there is a different goal from property law, but an equal veneration in practice for private property.

Secondly, the generation of human rights norms through law means that judges acquire potentially very large amounts of power to overrule legislation passed by the democratically elected members of the legislature.[8] By introducing a Human Rights Act, there is a danger that liberal constitutionalism takes priority instead, which would mean that the courts could have more power than Parliament, particularly in relation to any legislation which appeared to contravene that human rights legislation.[9]

The same reservations which we might have about human rights law might also beset our consideration of equity. In general terms it has been accepted in this book that it is a good thing for the legal system to provide for a means of achieving fair and flexible responses to particular factual situations. On the other hand it could be asked: who are the judges who are developing these equitable principles? Are the judges sufficiently democratically accountable when they develop and apply these norms? Why are these principles being developed and not others? The passive nature of equity (in that it is only applied to cases which come before the courts) has meant, for example, that equity concentrated primarily on commercial law cases in the 1990s, without extending its gaze to social welfare cases and so forth.

Thirdly, human rights norms assert the rights of the individual over and above social rights and obligations. As such, some socialists have criticised them for being 'atomistic' – that is, for separating human beings off from one another and breaking down social solidarity.[10] It would not be correct to say that all socialists have objected to human rights.[11] Many socialists have seen fit to redraw the socialist project (always a troubled expression) to define their socialism as an essentially moral project which has a sense of right and wrong which is lacking from rightwing, capitalist thought.[12] For many on the left, indeed, human rights became a means of campaigning against the worst excesses they identified in late capitalist society.

Equity-in-theory (that is, the form of philosophical equity set out in Chapter 32)[13] is concerned with ensuring fair results on a case-by-case basis. As such, it could be said to contribute to the atomisation of social relations by considering each case separately. Alternatively it could be said that it ensures that a socialist project both stays true to its

---

7 Chomsky, 1999.

8 Ewing, 1994, 147. This conceptual difficulty faced the Labour government which introduced the Human Rights Act 1998. The point made by Gearty and Tomkins, 2000, 64, is that democratic socialism, properly so called, requires that the democracy has the upper hand and therefore that Parliament is sovereign (although, of course, other socialists would dispense with the term 'sovereignty').

9 This explains the decision by the Labour administration in enacting the Human Rights Act to provide that the courts could merely make a declaration of incompatibility (s 4 of the 1998 Act), so that Parliament remains sovereign and so that the judges are merely enabled to pass comment on legislation and not to overrule it: considered below.

10 See, eg, Sypnowich, 1990, 84 et seq; and Hunt, 1992, 105.

11 The sort of problems which beset the socialists are well expressed by Gearty and Tomkins, 2000. Those two express themselves as being comfortable if human rights norms develop 'the dignity of the individual' (p 66).

12 See, eg, Habermas, 1990, 3.

13 Identified with Aristotle's Ethics, 1955, and parts of Hegel's Philosophy of Right, 1952.

ideology and also prevents it from being blind to the individual suffering of many.[14] Further, the cultural relativism of English equity means that it is able to assimilate the precise ideological components of a common morality (such as a distaste for unconscionable behaviour and fraud) and apply them in individual cases.

In comparing human rights law with English equity the argument can be made that human rights law offers a more forward-looking attitude to the principles on which individual cases could be decided. Equity-in-practice, by contrast, is a collection of parochial, English aphorisms applied by the courts ('he who comes to equity must come with clean hands' and so forth). What human rights law offers is a means of ensuring that the rights of individual people are not overlooked by a legal system as part of the natural tendency which all legal systems exhibit to generate abstract technical models to meet real-world problems. Human rights law is therefore founded in developing cosmopolitan,[15] international norms, in contradistinction to equity which offers merely a stream of case law principle and procedure which has been developed entirely within the historical culture of the English Lord Chancellors and their Courts of Chancery. So, at one level human rights law constitutes a part of a growing, global ideology whereas equity is a parochial product of strictly English culture. But is that to overlook the humane possibilities offered by flexible and responsive equity in contradistinction to political principles drafted in the middle of the 20th century?

17.2.2 A theoretical basis for equity?

Perhaps one of the difficulties which equity faces is that it has not expressly expounded a clear underlying philosophy. The statements to the effect that equity is concerned to preclude unconscionable behaviour do not explain sufficiently what is meant by that *unconscionable* behaviour at the abstract level, or the ways in which it might apply in detailed contexts. As such, it is vulnerable to attack from those who have a philosophy of their own to hand.

For example, the restitution lawyers have been able to deploy civilian concepts of unjust enrichment to meet many of the cases for which equity is currently used.[16] Those restitution lawyers do not, for the most part, advocate the discontinuance of the equitable claims and remedies:[17] instead they call for the acceptance that the reversal of unjust enrichment is the causative factor behind the implementation of many of those equitable remedies. Their underlying philosophy is drawn from Roman law[18] – albeit that they shrink from defining in philosophical terms what they mean by 'unjust'.[19]

The law of restitution has a number of influential judicial supporters, including Lord Goff (in many ways its creator) and Lord Millett. The standard of conscience erected by Lord Browne-Wilkinson in *Westdeutsche Landesbank Girozentrale v Islington LBC*[20] (or the

---

14 Bevan (1952), 1978.
15 A favoured term of Beck, 1992.
16 See in general terms Birks, 1989.
17 Because they do not consider them. However, Beatson, 1991, and Jaffey, 2000, have both called for unjust enrichment to replace equity wholesale – by which they can only be taken to mean replace trusts law and not injunctions, specific performance and the rest.
18 Birks, 1992.
19 Birks, 2000:1, 8.
20 [1996] AC 669.

reliance on the doctrine of notice in *Barclays Bank v O'Brien*)[21] does not help us to identify any more closely equity's underlying philosophical base. After all, one person's conscience is another person's ethical whimsy. Perhaps the truth is that equity is a haphazard product of history more than a carefully crafted creed in the manner of the civil codes in continental Europe.

This book attempts to identify a philosophical root for equity in social justice, in the meaning given to that term in Chapter 32. That is, a social justice based on equality of access for citizens to principles of fairness in recognition of their needs and deserts, which ensures that the legal system is not blind to any injustice suffered by the individual under the common law. Following Aristotle,[22] this form of equity is a flexible means of achieving something different from the justice sought by the general law where fairness demands it; similar sentiments are expressed by Hegel.[23] While that may sound, at first blush, to be a normatively loaded programme, it is no more prescriptive than the loaded terminology of 'conscience' and 'justice' used by the traditional trust lawyers or by the restitution lawyers respectively.

17.2.3 Modelling human rights law

At the time of writing, if we are to be honest with one another, no one is entirely sure how human rights law will impact on ordinary private law. It may be that human rights norms will have a seismic impact on private law – or the judiciary may take the view that existing case law and statute already give the courts a capacity to give effect to the norms embodied in European human rights law without the need for further amendment. However, it is important to recognise that human rights law is as much about a way of thinking, at the time of writing, as about any particular corpus of case law.

Distinguishing between 'rights' and 'freedoms'

There is one fundamental distinction to be drawn in this thinking before we can hope to apply the law relating to the Human Rights Act to equity and the law of trusts. That distinction is between 'human rights' and 'civil liberties'. These terms appear to have been used as synonyms one for the other in the arguments which have grown up surrounding the movement for the adoption of the European Convention on Human Rights (ECHR) into English law. However, there is a very significant difference between them.

A 'human right' suggests something inalienable which attaches to the very humanity of the individual: that is, a right which each individual human being has simply by virtue of being alive. By contrast a 'civil liberty' attaches to the individual's status as a citizen: that is, a freedom conferred only on persons who are citizens, rather (possibly) than those who are asylum seekers or who do not otherwise qualify as being citizens. This second category might include rights to vote, or freedoms from arbitrary arrest which are conferred on citizens but not on others. This distinction is little discussed even in the human rights law literature, and remains a confusing distinction at the heart of this emerging area of law.[24]

---

21 [1994] 1 AC 180.
22 Aristotle, *Ethics*, 1955, 198, para 1137a17, x: see section 1.1 above.
23 Hegel (1821), 1952, 142, para 223.
24 Ewing and Gearty, 2000, 1.

Furthermore, a 'civil liberty' would seem to imply a 'freedom'. The term freedom, itself, can be used here in relation to a '*freedom from*' as well as in relation to a '*right to*'. That means the distinction between protection from an abuse of some inalienable freedom as opposed to a positive permission to perform a given act as a free citizen. Many of the key tenets of ECHR concern freedom *from* torture and other abuses of the rights of the person. In the wake of a traumatic world war it is unsurprising that there would have been some focus on ensuring that ordinary human beings could be protected from such abuses of the liberty of the person by means of torture, false imprisonment, degrading treatment and so forth.

The alternative approach is the 'rights-based' approach which would assert that individuals have '*rights to*'[25] perform certain actions or to enjoy certain attributes. So, for example, in relation to the right to a family life or the right to possessions, we might consider that these rights are *rights* in the sense of positive freedoms to act without let or hindrance. The question then is 'how far should these rights go?' Many would argue for a 'right to strike' or a 'right to equal pay for like work' being enshrined as legal entitlements within a code of *economic* civil liberties. The boundaries are therefore important ones between freedoms from abuse of the person, rights to perform inalienably human activities, and more rarefied political entitlements.

17.3 PRINCIPLES OF HUMAN RIGHTS LAW

17.3.1 The applicable human rights norms

There are two general issues. First, the role of the state in protecting rights enshrined in the European Convention on Human Rights which interact with equity and trusts. Secondly, the potential development of horizontal rights and obligations between private persons in circumstances in which common law rights are developed in accordance with Convention rights.

The position under English law is that with effect from October 2000 the provisions of the Human Rights Act 1998 came into effect. The 1998 Act provides that 'primary legislation and subordinate legislation must be read and given effect in a way which is compatible with the Convention rights'.[26] The aim of the legislation is therefore to secure a form of interpretation of legislation, although that is not intended to 'affect the validity, continuing operation or enforcement of any incompatible primary legislation', with the effect that the courts cannot overrule legislation if it is considered to be in conflict with human rights law.[27] Therefore, legislation may be passed, perhaps in relation to immigration, which may lead to effects which are contrary to a literal application of the Convention rights: but that will not permit a court to declare that legislation ineffective; rather the court is empowered only to make a declaration of incompatibility[28] which will not affect the validity of that provision.[29] The sovereignty of Parliament is thus maintained.

---

25 Or 'freedoms to'.
26 Human Rights Act 1998, s 3(1).
27 *Ibid*, s 3(2)(b).
28 *Ibid*, s 4(2).
29 *Ibid*, s 4(6).

What the 1998 Act has not done is to create a new cadre of legal rules in the nature of a common law of human rights: the precise terms of the Convention have not become mandatory norms of English law. Whether a treaty is to have direct, mandatory effect as part of ordinary English law would depend on the terms of that treaty, and that is not the case here;[30] rather, the Convention rights are, initially, aids to the construction of legislation.[31] What is less clear is how the courts will react to the concomitant possibility that human rights norms might come to influence the common law over time, such that judges come to give effect to human rights norms as part of the common law.[32]

Gearty and Tomkins[33] state that 'what is . . . interesting is the extent to which the Human Rights Act may mould the common law', although the point is controversial as considered by Buxton,[34] in that 'traditional forms of law . . . may well be required in future to evolve in a Convention-compatible way, with this evolution being assisted by the principles to be found in the European Convention'. There had already been case law decided before the Human Rights Act 1998 came into full force and effect on the Convention-compatibility of the reforms to civil procedure, introduced by Lord Woolf, in *General Mediterranean Holdings v Patel*,[35] and more specifically in relation to private law the case of *DPP v Jones*.[36] This demonstrates that private law was beginning to develop in parallel with Convention norms even before the enactment of the Human Rights Act and its full implementation in October 2000. In *Jones*, the comments as to the primacy of private property indicated the straightforwardly capitalist turn which we can expect English property law to take even when applying human rights norms by protecting these rights in property in preference to other competing claims.

17.3.2 The nature of human rights in property

So, the fundamental question in relation to human rights and property law is between (i) a positive right to property and (ii) a negative[37] freedom from abuse of that property. At one level the proprietor of land would argue that she is entitled to use that land without interference by state agencies or others. Yet planning law permits use of land for purposes which may adversely affect a neighbouring proprietor if planning permission is awarded, and also permits compulsory acquisition of land in defined circumstances. The point could be made that this is a loss which is compensated: however, that compensation disavows the core logic of English property law, that the owner of property rights has *proprietary* rights and not simply rights to financial compensation. At one level, then, the entire scheme of planning law appears to run counter to the idea of rights *in* property. However, similar environmental laws regulating the use of land for purposes which pollute other land would appear to benefit the users of neighbouring land while similarly appearing to breach the property rights of the polluter.

---

30 See, eg, cases dealing with maritime treaties: *The Hollandia* [1982] QB 872; *Caltex Singapore Pte v BP Shipping Ltd* [1996] 1 Lloyd's Rep 286.
31 Grosz, Beatson, Duffy, Gearty *et al*, 2000, 7 *et seq*.
32 Hunt, 1998; Phillipson, 1999.
33 Gearty and Tomkins, 2000, 65.
34 Buxton, 2000.
35 [1999] 3 All ER 673.
36 [1999] 2 All ER 257 – a case involving trespass which drew on Convention concepts as to protection of rights to possessions.
37 In Hegelian terms.

What this does is to pull us closer to the centre of the issues discussed in Chapter 31 as to the intrinsic nature of property rights. Is a right to property a right which attaches to its holder as part of that person's fundamental freedoms, or is it a right held by whoever happens to be the owner of that property from time to time which should be deemed to be a mere commodity? By 'commodity' is meant a right with a given value attaching to it from time to time which can be transferred intact from one person to another, without necessarily attaching to that person. So, if I have property rights in *x* but *x* is taken from me in breach of trust and the sale proceeds used to buy *y*, property law will recognise my rights as attaching instead to *y*. What I 'own' is not the property itself (whether *x* or *y*) but rather those rights which attach to different property from time to time.[38] Therefore, it is unimportant for property law in many situations which precise property is at issue: although when seeking to establish an inalienable human right to possessions it would typically be easier to demonstrate that such a right ought to attach to identified property with which the claimant had had some long-standing connection than in relation to property with which there was only a loose relationship. At this level, ordinary property law and human rights law applying to property may have differential applications.

Section 2 of the Human Rights Act 1998 leads to the development of common law norms on the basis of Convention jurisprudence. There are three particular contexts in which this might be important. First, the right to one's 'possessions' in the First Protocol; secondly, the right to respect for one's home and for a family life; and, thirdly, the interaction of these ideas with notions of social justice and of community interest.

17.3.3 The right to family life – Art 8

The most important provision in the European Convention adopted by the 1998 Act for our purposes is the right to family life in Art 8. The Convention has a European method of using general concepts which are then given substance by case law, whereas English statute tends to deal with detail, hiding its philosophy and leaving it to the courts to develop the big ideas. The right to 'family life' is a similarly big idea which is somewhat alien to an English property lawyer's ears. The key issues will be whether the right to a family life will impinge on litigation between couples as to rights in the family home on separation, or in cases involving third parties asserting rights over that family home. In the Convention case of *Sporrong v Sweden*,[39] it was held that:

> the Court must determine whether a fair balance was struck between the demands of the general interest of the community and the requirement of the protection of the individual's fundamental rights. The search for this balance is inherent in the whole of the Convention.

So, in *James v United Kingdom*[40] – a case brought by the Duke of Westminster seeking to show that the provisions of the Leasehold Reform Act 1967 (entitling tenants to extend long leases or compulsorily acquire the freehold of property) were an abrogation of his human rights – it was held by the court that this was not the case, even though (as Cooke and

---

38 As considered in Chapter 31, that would depend on the property and the person in any given context.
39 (1982) 5 EHRR 35, 52.
40 (1986) 8 EHRR 123.

Hayton[41] point out) 'a number of wealthy tenants made a windfall profit by their discounted purchase' and the Duke of Westminster lost many rights in his land as a result. However, it was found by the court that the enactment of the 1967 statute had been 'calculated to enhance social justice', and therefore it served the general interest in a way which overrode those individual rights. We therefore have a principle that notions of social justice can override an individual's human rights. Is social justice to do with equality, or simply to do with personal gain? It is difficult to see on the jurisprudence on the decided cases what is meant by 'social justice' here.

What will be significant in relation to English property law is whether English judges decide that preserving a free market in mortgage services is more important than protecting families against actions brought by mortgagees for sale of mortgaged property. Left to its own devices English property law has always sought to protect the property market[42] and to ensure that a *bona fide* purchaser takes good title in property.[43] A little like the Bible, such broad pronouncements in the European human rights jurisprudence will support any point of view. Professor Gray put the matter in the following way: 'We have made property so central to our society that any thing and any rights that are not property are very apt to take second place.'[44] Perhaps it is that truth which will limit the future development of human rights principles in all areas of English property law.

As Howell has pointed out, there are real problems in relation to the law of adverse possession, which gives an occupier of land for 12 years immunity from any claim to remove her, and also in relation to the law on security of tenure, which prevents a landlord from evicting a tenant arbitrarily. The question is whether these facets of English property law abrogate rights to property, or whether they will be adjudged to achieve a socially useful function which absolves them from such a claim.[45] This is all in contrast to the South African constitution which provides explicitly that the right to housing is a human right.[46]

In another case on Art 8, the applicant contended that the noise generated by an airport close to the applicant's home was an abrogation of his human rights.[47] The court held that this application was ill-founded and did not raise any question of his right to a peaceful family life. A claim in relation to forfeiture of a lease as a result of non-payment by the lessee of a service charge was held to have been similarly ill-founded as a purported claim within Art 8.[48] Similarly, denial of planning permission for Romany people to erect caravans on their own land has been upheld because it was held that the applicants' right to their home must be balanced against the interests of the broader community which were said to favour preventing the establishment of such a gypsy community.[49]

41 Cooke and Hayton, 2000.
42 *City & London BS v Flegg* [1988] AC 54.
43 *Westdeutsche Landesbank Girozentrale v Islington LBC* [1996] AC 669.
44 Gray and Gray, 2001.
45 Howell, 1999, 287.
46 Robertson, 1998, 311.
47 *Powell v United Kingdom* (1987) 9 EHRR 241.
48 *Applicant No 11949/86 v United Kingdom* (1988) 10 EHRR 149.
49 *Buckley v United Kingdom* (1997) 23 EHRR 101.

17.3.4 The right to possessions

Article 1 of the First Protocol to the European Convention on Human Rights provides that 'Every natural or legal person is entitled to the peaceful enjoyment of his possessions' and that 'No one shall be deprived of his possessions except in the public interest and subject to the conditions provided for by law'. Whether there could ever be said to be a human right to trust property seems bound up with who it was who abstracted that property. If it were the trustee or some stranger to the trust, that would appear to be a matter for the law on breach of trust considered in Chapter 18. Alternatively, if it were some state agency or some person liable for breach of human rights then the First Protocol comes into play. With regard to the law of trusts, one context in which it might be useful to talk of human rights would be in relation to trust property taken by the state, or property which the state is alleged to hold on trust for private citizens.

In general terms, claims (that is a right to sue another person or a chose in action) will be recognised by English law as a possession, and therefore the rights of beneficiaries under a trust in general terms should be held as being a possession, being an equitable right in property. The principles established in *Sporrong* and *James* (considered at para 17.3.3 above) have been taken to apply in this context, to the effect that interferences with such rights are permissible only where they are in the public interest. In general terms, a deprivation of property will be required to be a permanent deprivation and not merely a temporary interference with its use.[50] Rights for private persons to take transfers of property rights from other private persons will not be deprivations where there is a public interest in such a transfer, as in *James* concerning enfranchisement of leasehold rights. A feature of a lawful deprivation will be whether or not there is compensation available for the person losing property rights.[51]

17.4 FAMILY LAW AND THE LAW OF THE HOME

17.4.1 The context

It is a regrettable feature of English law that frequently, socially important aspects of our communal life fall between a number of unrelated legal disciplines rather than being dealt with entirely by any one set of coherent rules. By 'unrelated legal disciplines' I mean that the practitioners, judges and academics in such areas are either ignorant of or reluctant to apply the norms developed in other legal disciplines. One good example of this is the law relating to the family home. To read books written by property and trusts lawyers, one would not think that there had been legislation passed in 1989[52] and 1996[53] relating to the primacy of the rights of the child in disputes over the family home. Similarly, in reading the works of family lawyers in such contexts, one would not know that there were bitter divisions between property lawyers relating to unjust enrichment, the classification of trusts implied by law,

---

50 *Handyside v United Kingdom* (1976) 1 EHRR 737 – in which a provisional seizure of obscene publications was not such a deprivation.
51 *James v United Kingdom* (1986) 8 EHRR 123.
52 Children Act 1989.
53 Family Law Act 1996.

and so forth.[54] Typically, legal categories cut across very significant social arenas. That is not to criticise those authors – rather it is merely to recognise the way in which the practise of English law has splintered.[55] The family law statutes relate to the divorce of married couples, whereas the law on trusts of homes (discussed in Chapter 15) relates to any situation in which the co-owners are not married or in which a secured creditor is proceeding against a married couple. So, this observation is not meant as a criticism of those different camps of lawyers: 'family law' is concerned with the divorce of married couples and with child law applications, whereas property law is required to deal with everything else in relation to the home and a family's moveable property. Consequently, the organisation of the legal system means that one cadre of lawyers need not know about the thought processes of the other. However, it does seem to be a somewhat arbitrary place to draw such a hard and fast line between different types of case.

We can draw a significant distinction between the sort of considerations which were set out in Chapter 15 in relation to *Trusts of homes* and two recent decisions on divorce in the House of Lords. In *Miller v Miller, Macfarlane v Macfarlane*[56] the courts responded to the very different culture in family law without a moment's thought as to the manner in which ordinary property law might have considered the same question. The types of concerns which were taken into account are far more reminiscent of Waite LJ in *Midland Bank v Cooke* than the House of Lords in *Lloyds Bank v Rosset*, for example. So, there was no need to follow nor consider *Lloyds Bank v Rosset*. Instead, the House of Lords followed the general prescriptions in *White v White*[57] that one should not give priority to the breadwinner when deciding what rights each party to a divorce should have in the family home, to their personal property, to future income, to pension rights, and so on and so forth. Lord Nicholls suggested that the courts should seek fairness in dividing up rights to property, compensation for any economic disparity in the way that the parties lived out their marriage, and taking into account the equal sharing that is ordinarily a part of married life. The court is generally concerned to achieve a clean break for the parties so that they can put their terminated marriage behind them, although there will frequently still be an obligation for one party to make periodical income payments to the other party, possibly for the maintenance of their children. The court drew a distinction in the abstract between long and short marriages, whereby a longer marriage would more readily justify the inference that the parties should be taken to hold their property equally, whereas a shorter marriage would lead less obviously to that inference if the parties continued to treat some of their property separately. So, the marriage in *Miller* lasted for only two years and nine months and so could be treated differently from the marriage in *Macfarlane* which lasted for 16 years and resulted in three children. Similarly, where one party had made a 'stellar contribution' to their married life, for example by earning an extraordinary amount of money which permitted them to live a luxurious lifestyle, then that stellar contributor may be entitled to a larger share of their property than the party who had contributed much less: this would be particularly so if their marriage had been a short one, whereas a longer marriage might more easily justify the

---

54 Hayes and Williams, 1996; Hoggett, Pearl, Cooke and Bates, 1996. See Hudson, 2004:4.
55 Perhaps this serves to show that while law may itself be a closed social system, many of its sub-sets are similarly autopoietically closed from each other by virtue of the development of separate norms and procedures.
56 [2006] UKHL 24.
57 [2001] 1 AC 596.

conclusion that the other party had assisted the stellar contributor by the provision of a home and so forth. What was particularly clear from the speeches in the House of Lords, particularly those of Baroness Hale and Lord Nicholls, was that none of these principles constituted a hard-and-fast rule. Rather, they were principles for the guidance of subsequent courts when disposing of the precise circumstances before them, but nevertheless principles which provided a sustainable framework for deciding future cases. As Baroness Hale put the matter:

> There is much to be said for the flexibility and sensitivity of the English law of ancillary relief. It avoids the straitjacket of rigid rules which can apply harshly or unfairly in an individual case. But it should not be too flexible. It must try to achieve some consistency and predictability. This is not only to secure that so far as possible like cases are treated alike but also to enable and encourage the parties to negotiate their own solutions as quickly and cheaply as possible.[58]

This encapsulates the entire dilemma of equitable relief, and demonstrates the desire of a judge in a senior court to provide clear guidance for junior courts.

The discussion which follows aims to integrate the trusts law thinking considered hitherto in this Part with family law thinking. It is only in this way that it is possible to understand some of the divisions in the case law between the judges and to understand the complexity and texture of the many debates surrounding the family and the home in modern legal theory.

17.4.2 The Family Law Act 1996

The Family Law Act (FLA) 1996 made significant changes to the legal treatment of relationship breakdown and to the rights of members of relationships to use family property after break-up. This short section aims to summarise the principal statutory provisions affecting this area with the main aim of illustrating the difference between the treatment of family property by a law of trusts which is blind to the context of relationship breakdown, and by a family law which takes a very different approach to the supposed sanctity of rights in property. The concluding section of this chapter will attempt to draw these threads together to explain the philosophically different attitudes both to property and to families in each system.

Matrimonial home rights – rights in property or personal rights

The FLA 1996 introduced the concept of 'matrimonial home rights' in s 30[59] in place of the pre-existing regime of rights of occupation created by the Matrimonial Homes Act 1967. The significance of these matrimonial homes rights is that they apply only to spouses and not to unmarried cohabitants.[60] A matrimonial home right provides a spouse with a registrable interest in the home in the form of a charge, thus affording that spouse better rights than hitherto. The other spouse is entitled to remain in the home unless excluded by an order of the court.[61]

---

58 [2006] UKHL 24, para [122].
59 Derived in part from the Matrimonial Homes Act 1983, s 1.
60 Except in relation to certain tenancies and mortgage possession proceedings which are outwith the parameters of this discussion.
61 *Morris v Tarrant* [1971] 2 QB 143; *Tarr v Tarr* [1973] AC 254.

It is important to stress that the 'matrimonial home rights' under the 1996 Act are provided to spouses and not to unmarried cohabitants.[62] This indicates the push-me-pull-you nature of public policy in this area. Considered below are the areas in which cohabitants will acquire rights against the family home, but the advances made by the matrimonial home rights are expressly reserved for the spousal relationship.[63]

Occupation orders

Under Part IV of the FLA 1996, the courts have powers to make two forms of order to secure the occupation rights of the applicant to the family home: occupation orders and non-molestation orders.[64] This section will focus on occupation orders and the next on non-molestation orders.

Occupation orders entitle the applicant to occupy a dwelling house which has been at some time the family home, or a home with which the applicant is associated.[65] Where applications are made by someone who has some beneficial interest in the home,[66] or some right to occupy the home by virtue of a contract[67] or some statutory provision,[68] or who has matrimonial home rights,[69] the court has the power to declare the nature of the applicant's rights to occupy the property.[70] The applicant does not receive some proprietary right over the home but rather receives, in effect, the court's permission to occupy the property in accordance with the terms of the order. The order may grant rights of exclusive occupation, or it may declare the arrangements by which a number of people are to live together in the property,[71] including details like the use of the furniture and other ephemera of modern living.[72] The powers of the court include the power to make an ouster order which precludes specified people, such as the applicant's former partner, from occupying the property.[73] An ouster order may contain conditions as to whether or not the respondent is entitled to enter the premises, or (for example) impose a boundary line of a given distance from the home within which the respondent is not permitted to come. The court is required to consider the various levels of harm which may be suffered by all family members in considering the order to be made.[74]

Where applications are made by cohabitants without any interest in the property then the courts' powers are different. The court is required to consider the nature of the parties' relationship, and in particular to give weight to the fact that unmarried couples will not have

---

62 FLA 1996, s 30(2); see especially *Windeler v Whitehall* [1990] FLR 505, *per* Millett J, which suggested that there was no power to use matrimonial concepts in non-matrimonial cases.
63 *Ibid.*
64 Adapting the Matrimonial Homes Act 1967 and the Domestic Violence and Matrimonial Proceedings Act 1976.
65 FLA 1996, s 63(1).
66 *Ibid*, s 33(1).
67 *Ibid.*
68 *Ibid.*
69 Qualifying as a 'person entitled': *ibid*, s 30.
70 *Ibid*, s 33(4).
71 *Ibid*, s 33(3).
72 *Ibid.*
73 *Ibid.*
74 *B v B (Occupation Order)* [1999] 1 FLR 715, CA.

established a necessary commitment one to another.[75] This provision has the dual effect of favouring married applicants over unmarried applicants, and also of prioritising the rights of those who have rights in the property over those who have no such rights in the property. Therefore, the 1996 legislation contains broad powers for the courts to grant broadly-based orders taking into account all of the family's circumstances, but it also favours traditional marital relationships – another example of the confusion in the public policy in this area which both seeks to help those in informal relationships while at the same time not wishing to be seen to weaken the institution of marriage. A worrying theme in the case law in this area is the reluctance of even family courts to displace pre-existing property law rights unless there are exceptional circumstances to justify such an order.[76] Therefore, while the statute may give the judiciary large scope to make any orders which they consider fit, the judges are nevertheless likely to lapse into their long-standing affection for the protection of private property rights.

Non-molestation orders

The principal significance of non-molestation orders is that they grant rights to applicants not to be molested in circumstances in which the law would previously not have been satisfied that there was some common law right which had been interfered with: in effect the FLA 1996 plugs the hole left by the absence in English common law of a tort of harassment.[77] Despite judicial attempts to widen the possibilities of injunctive relief for harassment by stalkers,[78] the courts have reinforced the need for the applicant for a non-molestation injunction to have some interest in the property in relation to which relief is sought.[79] In the family context, this disadvantages a person in a relationship who is being molested by her partner but who does not have a right in the home. In consequence, no non-molestation order will be granted to such a person with the effect of excluding the abusive partner from the home. The choice facing the victim of that molestation would therefore be to remain in the home suffering harm, or to leave the home without any certainty as to the chances of being re-housed. There is no duty on a local authority to re-house that person if she leaves the home in circumstances where it appears that she has made herself intentionally homeless.[80] This last point illustrates the need in these situations to consider the social security and the public sector housing law context of cases concerned with relationship breakdown.[81]

---

75 FLA 1996, s 41.
76 *Chalmers v Johns* [1999] 1 FLR 392, 397, CA.
77 *Montgomery v Montgomery* [1965] P 46; *Patel v Patel* [1988] 2 FLR 179; *Hunter v Canary Wharf Ltd* [1997] AC 655.
78 *Khorasandjian v Bush* [1993] QB 727, CA. See now also the Protection from Harassment Act 1997, s 7, which precludes acts intended to cause 'harassment'.
79 *Hunter v Canary Wharf Ltd* [1997] AC 655.
80 See, eg, *R v Wandsworth LBC ex p Nimako-Boateng* (1984) 11 HLR 95; *R v Eastleigh BC ex p Evans* (1984) 17 HLR 515; *R v Purbeck DC ex p Cadney* (1985) 17 HLR 534.
81 Indeed, it could be said that the law of trusts is concerned only with the property-owning middle classes, whereas it is the working classes (and the 'underclass') who are reliant on the regulatory schemata of housing legislation, regulation and practice.

The non-molestation order may be specific as to the conduct prohibited.[82] The term 'molestation' is not defined, although it was explained by the Law Commission[83] as including serious pestering or harassment.[84] The court can make such order as it sees fit in all circumstances, with particular reference to the safety and well-being of any child.[85]

Occupation orders: protection of property rights or discretionary response to needs?

In theory, there is one significant difference in family law applications of this sort in that the court is *not simply* concerned to unearth pre-existing property rights and to give effect to them. Rather, the court is empowered to examine all of the parties' needs and circumstances – together with those of any children[86] – including their housing needs and their income to ensure a result which best serves the family's overall welfare. The task which family law takes on in this context is necessarily a complex one in any particular set of circumstances. Clearly it is not desirable for the family courts to proceed on the basis of the kinds of strict criteria which property law courts will tend to apply in cases like *Lloyds Bank v Rosset,*[87] for fear of introducing too much formalism into an area of law which deals with the most intimate and psychologically-fraught aspects of an individual's life.

In the context of relationship breakdown there is therefore the possibility that property courts and family courts will be acting on the basis not only of very different substantive norms developed by case law or by statute respectively, but also on the basis of very different procedural rules: property law recognising pre-existing rights in land, while family law makes open-ended judgments to address the needs of the family. What is of concern is the Janus-faced nature of the legislation – turning between liberality and traditionalist support for the institution of marriage – and a determination to favour those with property rights over those without. The difficulty with that is that it will frequently be the partner who has raised children who will be disfavoured when rights in property are handed out, because that career break will have meant that she is less likely to have contributed in monetary terms to the costs of maintaining the property. Similarly, a partner who is ill or unable to find work – in effect, the weaker party in the relationship – is generally less likely to be able to contribute financially to the acquisition of the property, and therefore is less likely to be protected on the breakdown of the relationship *if* the courts continue to favour the rights of those persons with pre-existing property rights over the needs of those without.

The theoretical nature of these rights as property rights

One further point about the nature of the property rights which the FLA 1996 offers to applicants for occupation orders is not a right in the property, that is, not a right *in rem*, but rather a right of the use of that property. In Hohfeld's division of these issues this constitutes a right

---

82 FLA 1996, s 42(1).
83 *Domestic Violence and Occupation of the Family Home*, Law Com No 207, 1992, para 3.1.
84 Cf the Protection from Harassment Act 1997, under which there is no definition of the term 'harassment'.
85 FLA 1996, s 42(2).
86 Eg, the FLA 1996, ss 62(2) and 63 are concerned to prevent 'significant harm' being caused to any child.
87 [1990] 1 All ER 1111.

against the respondent to be allowed to occupy the property.[88] It is a property right only in the sense that it affords protection against the respondent in person. The significance of the matrimonial home right is that it offers the applicant a registrable charge which *is* a form of right *in rem* because it will bind all third parties once it is registered. Thus, it operates as a right attaching to the property which is exercisable against the world and not simply as a right against the respondent *in personam*.

17.4.3 The impact of the Children Act 1989

The Children Act (CA) 1989 provides that the welfare of the child is paramount.[89] This provision encapsulated a growing change in English family law by expressly recognising the needs of the child. The 1989 Act drew upon the spirit of a raft of legislation passed in the 1970s[90] and hardened it into a general principle that the welfare of the child is paramount in family proceedings.[91] The Matrimonial Causes Act 1973 required that in making financial orders the court must give 'first consideration' to the welfare of the child.[92] As such, the housing needs of the family are generally considered through this lens.[93]

The legislation in this area has also created a debate as to precisely what is meant by the child's 'welfare' in this context. For the trusts lawyer it is rare that children are ever mentioned, because in trusts law cases the focus is on contributions directly to the purchase price of property or, exceptionally, to general family expenses: it is very rare that a child would ever make such a contribution. In consequence, trusts law and property law would not consider the needs of the child. Property law is concerned to vindicate the rights of adults in the property. It is only in a needs-based system of family law that the place of the children is taken into account in allocating rights in law.[94] Exceptionally, statute has introduced the possibility that the *existence* of children may be considered in property law claims to do with the sale of property[95] – but subject always to the rights of any creditors of the property.[96] It is suggested that, but for that statute, property law would pay children no heed.[97]

The impact of the 1989 Act is therefore to require family courts to consider the place of children and their *needs*. In the FLA 1996, the court is required, when making ouster orders,[98] to make an order which ensures that there is no 'significant harm' suffered by any child.[99]

---

88 Hohfeld, 1919; see para 31.2.2.
89 CA 1989, s 1.
90 Matrimonial Causes Act 1983; Domestic Violence and Matrimonial Proceedings Act 1976; Adoption Act 1976; Domestic Proceedings and Magistrates' Courts Act 1978; Matrimonial and Family Proceedings Act 1984.
91 Except in relation to applications for leave to apply under CA 1989, s 8: *Re A and W (Minors) (Residence Order: Leave to Apply)* [1992] Fam 182, CA; *K v H (Child Maintenance)* [1993] 2 FLR 61.
92 Matrimonial Causes Act 1973, s 25(1); *Waterman v Waterman* [1989] 1 FLR 380.
93 *M v B (Ancillary Proceedings: Lump Sum)* [1998] 1 FLR 53, CA.
94 Ie, rights to use or occupy property under statute.
95 TLATA 1996, s 14, considered at para 16.2.9 above.
96 Whether creditors in a bankruptcy (*Re Citro* [1991] Ch 142) or mortgagees protecting their security (*Lloyds Bank v Byrne* (1991) 23 HLR 472; [1993] 1 FLR 369).
97 See, eg, *Re Citro* [1991] Ch 142.
98 Considered in para 17.4.2 above.
99 FLA 1996, ss 62(2), 63.

17.4.4 Cohabitants and married couples

One of the virtues of the law of trusts as considered in Chapter 15 might be said to be its blindness to whether the couples who claim rights are married or unmarried,[100] of different sexes or the same sex.[101] The law of trusts, however, is preoccupied with financial contributions made by the parties[102] over and above other, less material measurements of their intention.[103] It is family law which has prioritised the needs of the family and the most appropriate means of *using* (rather than *owning*) family property as its guiding principle. Its failing is a need in the public policy motivating legislation to attempt consciously to support the institution of marriage by providing rights only for married couples in many contexts: a trend which is evident in the case law.[104] In general terms the courts have not been willing to extend matrimonial rights to non-married couples.[105] This includes claims brought by mistresses of married people,[106] or by the business partners of married people.[107] The approach of the courts in relation to cohabitants has been to consider their various claims for rights in property to be a matter for contract[108] or agreement[109] between them. This is to be contrasted with the situation in which the rights of children or the rights of children to occupy property are involved.

In relation to married couples, the case law used to be reluctant to enforce contracts between the parties on the basis that marriage constituted the couple as one person in law.[110] Early suggestions of an alteration to this traditional understanding were set forth in landmark decisions such as *National Provincial Bank v Ainsworth*[111] and also *Pettitt v Pettitt*,[112] where it was suggested that spouses could create legally enforceable rights between themselves; as well as *Williams & Glyn's Bank v Boland*,[113] in which a wife acquired a novel right of actual occupation distinct from her marriage to her husband.[114] *Boland* was heralded as a progressive decision precisely because it enlarged the rights of a spouse who had some equitable interest in the matrimonial home – and consequently merely a minor interest protected only if registered as such – to the status of an overriding interest due to the further fact that Mrs Boland was also in actual occupation of the matrimonial home. Previously, it had been

---

100 *Hammond v Mitchell* [1991] 1 WLR 1127.
101 *Wayling v Jones* (1993) 69 P & CR 170; *Tinsley v Milligan* [1993] 3 All ER 65.
102 *Lloyds Bank v Rosset* [1990] 1 All ER 1111.
103 Except in the family assets cases like *Midland Bank v Cooke* [1995] 4 All ER 562.
104 *Windeler v Whitehall* [1990] FLR 505, *per* Millett J.
105 *Ibid; Mossop v Mossop* [1989] Fam 77.
106 *Dennis v MacDonald* [1981] 1 WLR 810, 814, *per* Purchas J.
107 *Harwood v Harwood* [1991] 2 FLR 274: husband's business partner claims rights in the matrimonial home.
108 For rights to be created under contract, the statutory requirements of the Law of Property (Miscellaneous Provisions) Act 1989, s 2(1) would have to be satisfied. A formally ineffective contract would have no effect: *Hemmens v Wilson Browne* [1994] 2 FLR 101; *United Bank of Kuwait plc v Sahib* [1997] Ch 107, *per* Chadwick J; *Pitt v PHH Asset Management Ltd* [1993] 4 All ER 961, CA. Although see now *Yaxley v Gotts* [2000] 1 All ER 711, in which proprietary estoppel was used to avoid the provisions of the 1989 Act.
109 In the forms considered in Chapter 15 as to common intention and so forth.
110 *Hyman v Hyman* [1929] AC 601; *Sutton v Sutton* (1984).
111 [1965] AC 1175.
112 [1970] AC 777.
113 [1981] AC 487.
114 See also *Tanner v Tanner* [1975] 1 WLR 1346; *Layton v Martin* [1986] 2 FLR 227.

doubted whether or not spouses could create such rights *inter se* and, furthermore, use such rights to bind third parties, such as mortgagees.

17.5 SOCIAL JUSTICE AND RIGHTS IN THE HOME

This section takes a different approach to the means by which rights to occupy or to 'own' the home may be acquired. It considers both a theory of social justice and its potential application to this topic, as well as a factual example of the manner in which different legal categories might have different impacts on these problems.

17.5.1 Social justice and the legal treatment of the home

A viable concept of social justice

'Social justice' is a term so commonly used by political scientists, politicians, and even philosophers that its very ubiquity would seem to suggest that it is a term without content: an empty vessel. It is argued that such a suggestion would be mistaken. This section will adopt the definitions of that term considered by Miller[115] to highlight the philosophical differences between the norms exacted by three different sub-systems of law: English property law, English family law, and the Canadian law of unjust enrichment.

As considered in Chapter 1, the term 'justice' has been the subject of complex philosophical debate since the time of Aristotle. 'Social justice' more particularly relates to the applications of these theories of justice to social goods beyond simply claims between individuals. In Miller's analysis the forms of social justice can be divided into two: conservative and ideal. First, *conservative* social justice seeks to apply principles of justice so as to preserve a status quo: such justice may, for example, seek restitution to vindicate the property rights of some person so that the pre-existing division of property rights is maintained.[116] Secondly, *ideal* social justice seeks to change existing social conditions in line with some political ideology – the particular ideology need not matter for that categorisation.[117] This marks out two political philosophies: the radical and the conservative.

Beyond that initial delineation it is said that social justice operates on one or more of the following three bases: rights, deserts, or needs. Social justice based on *rights* is orientated around the vindication of some recognised entitlement to property.[118] Social justice based on *deserts* allocates goods to a person because that person is said to be deserving on account of her talents, her social position, or in recompense for some previous action. Social justice based on *needs* measures neither a pre-existing entitlement nor a deserving case, but rather identifies a category of person who requires a transfer of goods to her so that her lack of such goods can be alleviated. It would be possible to imagine situations in which a person's needs

---

115 Miller, 1976.
116 Such as in *Foskett v McKeown* [2000] 3 All ER 97.
117 This is primarily a radical political agenda, but may also be reflected in doctrines like proprietary estoppel which frequently create rights which had never existed before.
118 There is insufficient space here to consider the ways in which 'rights' may come into existence philosophically – the reader is referred to the discussion of human rights law above.

might give rise to a right under a particular legal system,[119] or where we might argue that to have a right to something means that you are deserving of it under a positivist system of law.

An example of this model in action

The example which Miller gives to tease apart the three forms of social justice[120] relates to two boys who agree to clean my windows on the basis that I will pay them £1 each for the work. I notice that one boy works diligently and performs an excellent job, whereas the other boy is slovenly and cleans the windows poorly. I have the following dilemma: do I pay the boys equally for their unequal work? A *rights* theory would require me to pay them according to our agreement: that is, a contract which entitles each to be paid £1 and which creates common law rights for each boy. A *deserts* theory might suggest that I pay £1.25 to the diligent child and only £0.75 to the slovenly child, on the basis that the diligent boy's personal characteristics and hard work mean that he *deserves* to receive more than the lazy boy. Alternatively, it might require me to reward the diligent boy with an extra £0.25 and to respect the lazy boy's rights to receive his £1. A *needs* theory may make me take into account the possibility that one boy is from a rich home whereas the other is from a poor home – perhaps this would prevent me from refusing to pay the slovenly boy less than I owed him under our contract if he was poor and his apparent slovenliness caused by malnourishment. Alternatively, a *needs* thesis might encourage me to withhold the money from the lazy boy if he was rich and did not need the full £1, so that some of that money could be redistributed to a diligent, poor boy.

Rights, deserts and needs in distinct approaches to trusts of homes

If we consider the manner in which English law deals with the home against these models we will see that there are different concepts of justice at play. English property law provides that on relationship breakdown only a person who has contributed to the purchase price of the property is entitled to take property rights in it.[121] This is a *rights*-based conception of a just conclusion which awards rights in property solely on the basis of some recognised legal entitlement. So it is that the purchase price resulting trust recognises a right as arising from the payment of money: it is this right which gives rise to an equitable interest in property, but it is blind to any question of the needs of the parties.[122] This attitude is similar to contract law which enforces my obligation to the other contracting party on the basis of our freely created contract. It is value-neutral (except to the extent that it supports commercial morality by requiring that a contract once made is inviolate).

The Australian unconscionability approach is founded on concepts from commercial partnership law. In *Muschinski v Dodds*,[123] the analogy developed by Deane J was that those rules 'applicable to regulate the rights and duties of the parties to a failed partnership or joint

119 As evidenced in housing law or the family proceedings considered above.
120 Miller, 1976, 28. See Hudson, 2004:3 for a full analysis of these issues.
121 *Lloyds Bank v Rosset* [1991] 1 AC 107.
122 *Tinsley v Milligan* [1994] 1 AC 340.
123 (1985) 160 CLR 583.

venture' ought to be incorporated into a case in which two people had brought severally their money and their brawn to the development of a piece of land on which they intended to live together until their relationship failed.[124] This is also a *rights*-based conception of a just conclusion which awards rights in property solely on the basis of some recognised pre-existing entitlement. What is concealed is the court's value judgment in preferring expressed, contractarian models to any other. So it is that the purchase price resulting trust recognises a right as arising from the payment of money: it is this right which gives rise to an equitable interest in property but it is blind to any question of the needs of the parties.[125] This attitude, as mentioned above, is similar to contract law in that it is ostensibly value-neutral – but that seems to deny the possibility either that the arrangement was formed on the basis of inequality of bargaining power, or that the parties' circumstances altered significantly subsequently.

Canadian unjust enrichment law takes a more creative approach to rights in the home, by finding that property rights come into existence when a person participates in a relationship such that the other party receives valuable services, albeit not payments in cash. This is an approach based on *deserts* – to contribute to a relationship over a period of time means that the individual acquires some claim to just treatment by way of a transfer of some right in that property.[126] Similarly, the approach taken by Waite LJ in *Midland Bank v Cooke*,[127] in recognition of a wife's contribution to a marriage, accepts that she deserves some right in the property sufficient to defeat the claim of a mortgagee to take possession of that property from her. It could be said that proprietary estoppel is similarly based on deserts.[128] When a right to the fee simple in property is awarded to a claimant who has been promised that she will receive the property in its owner's will, it could be said that she deserved that transfer of title in the light of her acts to her detriment in reliance on the promise made to her.[129] One exceptional decision under the doctrine of proprietary estoppel which is based on needs is that of *Baker v Baker*.[130] In that case, whereas the court could have decided to award an elderly man merely a proprietary right in a house which he shared with relatives and which he had helped to purchase, the court instead decided to make him an order for an amount of money which would satisfy his *need* to pay for sheltered accommodation in his declining years. Simply to have recognised that he deserved a proprietary right would not have met his more immediate need to pay for nursing home care.

---

124 *Ibid*, 618.
125 *Tinsley v Milligan* [1994] 1 AC 340.
126 *Peter v Beblow* (1993) 101 DLR (4th) 621.
127 [1995] 4 All ER 562.
128 It might well be considered that the use of the term 'deserve' here supposes that a beneficent, mostly male judiciary would be handing out gifts of interest in the home as though rewards to female claimants. That is not the sense of 'desert' which Miller, or I, intend. There is, I do not deny, always the problem that when one talks of a 'deserving' claimant that necessarily opens the door to unfortunate value judgments. All cases involving rights in the home already do involve value judgments, but we tend to try to keep them concealed behind a cloak of technicalities, doctrines and legal principles like the common intention constructive trust, proprietary estoppel and so forth. Such value judgments should be made express so that they can be criticised and/or developed: Hudson, 2004:2.
129 *Re Basham* [1986] 1 WLR 1498.
130 (1993) 25 HLR 408.

English family law takes different approaches. The CA 1989 places the welfare of the child as the paramount consideration – in consequence, the legislation takes a *needs* approach to a just conclusion. The child will not have contributed to the purchase price, neither will it necessarily have formed an integral part of the family unit for long enough to deserve property rights (or even occupation rights). Similarly, the Inheritance (Provision for Family and Dependants) Act 1975 provides a power for the court to rewrite a will either on grounds of some overlooked proprietary right, or on grounds of need – an alternative choice of rights and needs respectively.

Property law is directed at the recognition of pre-existing rights. Purely remedial, equitable doctrines such as proprietary estoppel are concerned to ensure both good conscience, and also that someone who has suffered detriment receives her just deserts or that her needs are met. Family law, housing law and social security law are concerned to meet the needs of applicants.[131] Within these subtly different approaches to social justice are the true differences between these various aspects of the English law treatment of the home.

17.5.2 Understanding the difficulties with relationship breakdown

It is one thing to allocate rights in property; it is another to break up a family.[132] However, in the termination of most familial relationships disputes about the two contexts overlap.

Suppose the following situation. A married couple have acquired a house as joint tenants both at law and in equity of the fee simple. Suppose that the husband has decided to leave his wife, and so is trying to borrow as much money as possible before fleeing the jurisdiction by taking out a mortgage and forging his wife's signature on the agreement. The husband then seeks to acquire a mortgage over the property without getting the agreement of his wife. If the husband enters into a fraudulent transaction, that will sever the joint tenancy between husband and wife.[133] However, the rights of the mortgagee will bite on the husband's severed half share in the equitable interest in the house.[134] Therefore, the mortgagee would be entitled to seek an order for the sale of the property and so realise its security to the extent of the husband's half interest in the property.[135] Unless the wife were able to assume her husband's obligations under the mortgage (although she would not have received the capital with which her husband had absconded), she would be required to sell the property and find somewhere else to live with only half (in this example) of the total value of the house which was her home before her husband's fraudulent activities.[136]

The preceding analysis is based on a property law rule. If the same situation were addressed as a question of divorce law before the husband had sought to defraud the mortgage company and desert his wife, she might have a claim to remain in the property (particularly if there

---

131   Although it could be argued that with the possibility of losing entitlement to Job Seeker's Allowance on grounds of failure to attend interviews, such social security provision is now based on a weak form of right which stems from attendance at interviews and not simply from an assessment of needs.

132   See in particular Dewar, 1998.

133   *First National Security v Hegerty* [1985] QB 850.

134   *Ibid; Ahmed v Kendrick* (1988) 56 P & CR 120.

135   *Lloyds Bank v Byrne* (1991) 23 HLR 472; [1993] 1 FLR 369.

136   Her strongest line of defence would be under *Barclays Bank v O'Brien* [1993] 3 WLR 786; *Barclays Bank v Thomson* [1997] 4 All ER 816 on grounds of undue influence or, on these facts, misrepresentation in any agreement to the terms of the mortgage.

were children).[137] The difference is clearly the intercession of the mortgage company asserting the rights of a third party. It is an essential truth of English law that all rules are different where one party goes into bankruptcy: the rights of creditors will always fall to be considered,[138] and under English law they will always be protected.[139] The only exceptions to this rule would be those circumstances in which the rights of the creditor are deemed to have been subjugated to the rights of some other person in equity[140] or on grounds of fraud.[141]

Clearly there are difficulties in deciding between rights in property and the justice to be allocated between family members other than simply by recognition of pre-existing property rights. This is a tension which has expressed itself in a number of cases; as with *Davis v Johnson*[142] considering the Domestic Violence and Matrimonial Proceedings Act 1976 and holding that a court can oust a property owner from his home on grounds of domestic violence. Previously the courts had considered that a property owner could not be removed from the property. In other words, it had been said that morality could not override a person's property rights.[143] Similarly the court in *Dart v Dart*[144] considered s 25 of the Matrimonial Causes Act 1973 in relation to the courts' approach to the redistribution of property rights between spouses in divorce. In that case the specific context was domestic violence, which placed the court in a difficult position between the need to protect a person from domestic violence and the concomitant need to protect another person's pre-existing property rights.

The decision in *Peffer v Rigg*[145] demonstrates the conflict between providing for certainty on the one hand and providing a just result on the other.[146] In that case, Mr Peffer and Mr Rigg had married two sisters. The question arose which of these couples should care for the sisters' mother. It was decided between both families, after some negotiation, that the husbands would buy a home for their mother-in-law, although only Rigg's name appeared on the legal title. All of the parties were aware that Rigg and Peffer had contributed equivalent amounts to the purchase price, and therefore that each had equivalent rights in the property. Each therefore had minor interests in the property as a result, but neither registered their interests. When the Riggs divorced subsequently, they purported as part of their divorce settlement to transfer the entire freehold interest to Mrs Rigg and to ignore Peffer's rights. The Riggs argued that Peffer had no rights because he had failed to register them. However, Graham J held that it would be unconscionable for Mrs Rigg to deny Mr Peffer's rights, and therefore that Mrs Rigg (by then in possession of the entire legal title) held the property on

---

137   FLA 1996, s 30; CA 1989, s 1.
138   TLATA 1996, s 15(1)(d): 'The matters to which the court is to have regard in determining an application for an order under section 14 include – . . . (d) the interests of any secured creditor of any beneficiary.'
139   *Lloyds Bank v Byrne* (1991) 23 HLR 472, [1993] 1 FLR 369. Albeit that those rights may be actionable only against the share of one party in some cases: *First National Security v Hegerty* [1985] QB 850.
140   *Thames Guaranty v Campbell* [1985] QB 210; *Abbey National v Moss* [1994] 1 FLR 307.
141   *Ahmed v Kendrick* (1988) 56 P & CR 120; *Penn v Bristol & West Building Society* [1995] 2 FLR 938.
142   [1979] AC 264.
143   Cooke and Hayton, 2000, 433.
144   [1996] 2 FLR 286.
145   [1977] 1 WLR 285.
146   See also *Prudential Assurance Co v London Residuary Body* [1992] 2 AC 388, [1992] 3 All ER 504. Cf *Midland Bank Trust Co v Green* [1981] AC 513, where failure to register precluded enforcement of similar rights despite *prima facie* unconscionability on the part of the defendants.

constructive trust for Peffer and herself as beneficiaries. This case contrasts significantly with the unregistered land case of *Midland Bank v Green*,[147] in which a father had granted his son a right to buy a farm from him at a price which subsequently appeared to be a good one. This right to buy was an estate contract and could be protected against third parties only if it were registered as a land charge. The son failed to register his right. The father sought to renege on this right by selling the land at an under-value to his son's mother. The mother also had actual knowledge of the right to buy. Whereas the son argued that his parents' actions had been unconscionable, the House of Lords held that the son had not registered his right and therefore that it was not protected against the sale at an under-value to the mother. In *Peffer v Rigg*, the approach is very much in line with traditional equitable thinking, whereas *Midland Bank v Green* is predicated on land law policy.

What must not be allowed to happen is that the concepts of equity are used as though some covert feint to provide an answer to a problem, as in *Peffer v Rigg* where otherwise Peffer would have suffered the loss of his rights due to the formal requirements of statute. Rather, equitable concepts should be accepted as being simply discretionary and applied so as to achieve just results – not as some dodge in a technical game.[148] The difficulty is in attempting to avoid a common law rule while also obfuscating the equitable principle. It would be better for the courts to acknowledge that, in general terms, they are concerned to do justice on the facts of individual cases and not that the certainty of the general law is being called into question.[149]

The role of children was considered above in relation to family proceedings: but the rights of children are not considered in property law disputes. What is significant is that the perception which the British polity has of a 'property-owning democracy' is in truth a 'democracy-owning-property-through-mortgages',[150] in which the reality as perceived by the citizen frequently differs markedly from the reality as exercised through law. The law of property is not the only means of allocating rights in property: there are housing law, social security law (especially housing benefit), family law, equity (especially proprietary estoppel and the availability of injunctions), trusts law and human rights law to be considered too. It is suggested that equity is sufficiently flexible to absorb principles from these other legal fields and to relax its automatic affection for the protection of private property rights. Equity ought not to harden its own principles so that they become just another part of the technical posturing that makes up much commercial litigation.[151]

147 [1981] AC 513.
148 This form of 'covert equity' is evident in *Barclays Bank v O'Brien* [1994] 1 AC 180 and *Bruton v Quadrant Housing Trust* [2000] 1 AC 406.
149 In relation to *Bruton v Quadrant Housing Trust* [2000] 1 AC 406, which found the existence of a lease even though the purported lessor had no interest in the demised property, Hayton and Cooke have said: 'Yes of course we have benefited from reminders in recent years that a lease is primarily contractual but to suggest that a lease might be purely contractual with no need for an estate in land is completely novel': Cooke and Hayton, 2000, 437, thus illustrating the danger of seeking a particular result while using doctrinally difficult methods so to do.
150 To borrow from Lord Diplock in *Pettitt v Pettitt* [1970] AC 777.
151 See, generally, Chapter 21 on this tendency.

Part 6

Breach of trust and related equitable claims

Chapter 18

Breach of trust

18.5   ALLOCATING CLAIMS

OVERVIEW

A trustee will be liable for breach of trust if that breach of trust causes a loss to the beneficiaries. Such a trustee will be liable in the event of a breach of trust either, in the first place, to restore the trust property which was passed away in breach of trust; or if that is not possible to reconstitute the value of the trust fund in cash to its level before the breach of trust, or to pay equitable compensation to the beneficiaries.[1] There is an important distinction to be made here between proprietary liability and personal liability.

Proprietary claims will be considered in relation to specific restitution and to tracing in Chapter 19, whereas personal liability claims are considered in this chapter in relation to compensation,[2] dishonest assistance[3] and knowing receipt.[4] Issues relating to the liability of fiduciaries in respect of making authorised profits from the trust were considered in Chapter 12.

A trustee will be liable in the situation in which the breach of trust has caused some loss to the trust.[5] There will be no liability in respect of a breach of trust where that breach resulted in no loss to the trust.[6] The measurement of compensation will be the actual, demonstrable loss to the trust, rather than some intermediate value of the property lost to the trust.[7]

18.1   INTRODUCTION

18.1.1 The liability of trustees within the context of breach of trust more generally

In this book so far we have considered the means by which express private trusts and trusts implied by law are created and administered. In this Part, the emphasis changes to those situations in which trusts are breached, such that the beneficiaries may seek to bring claims either to recover the original trust property or to recover its equivalent value in cash from the trustees and others. This chapter will focus first on the liability of those who are identified as express trustees. The reader is referred back to the general discussion of the duties of trustees in Part 3 above: those three chapters set out the general obligations of trustees which, if breached, would make a trustee liable for breach of trust.

---

1 *Nocton v Lord Ashburn* [1914] AC 932; *Target Holdings v Redferns* [1996] 1 AC 421, [1995] 3 WLR 352, [1995] 3 All ER 785.
2 See section 18.5 below.
3 See paras 12.9.3 above and 18.4.3 below.
4 See paras 12.9.2 above and 18.4.4 below.
5 *Target Holdings v Redferns* [1996] 1 AC 421.
6 *Ibid.*
7 *Ibid.*

While the discussion of 'breach of trust' in most trusts law textbooks usually refers only to the liability of the trustees themselves for breach of trust, it is important to bear in mind that there are other claims which are of significance to beneficiaries when there has been a breach of trust, such as tracing rights in trust property into substitute property, imposing personal liability to account on people who have received property unconscionably and knowing of the breach of trust, and on people who have dishonestly assisted in that breach of trust. All of these claims are collected into subsequent chapters of this Part 6 of this book. In this chapter we will consider the liability of trustees for any loss suffered by the beneficiaries as a result of a breach of trust. Tracing will be explained in Chapter 19 as being the process by which a beneficiary can claim title either to the original property or to a substitute for that original property[8] in the hands of another person. Unconscionable receipt and dishonest assistance are discussed in Chapter 20, giving rise to a personal liability to account as a constructive trustee for any loss suffered by the trust if the defendant has either received the trust property knowing of the breach of trust[9] or if she has assisted in that breach of trust.[10] This form of liability is also in addition to any liability to account for any profits made out of a breach of trust[11] by holding those profits on constructive trust for the beneficiaries of the trust,[12] as was considered in Chapter 12.[13] Together, all of these claims constitute the potential scope of liability for breach of trust available to beneficiaries.

In this chapter, then, we will consider the context of the liability of the trustees for breach of trust: namely, in what circumstances will a breach arise, and what forms of claim may flow from that?

18.1.2 The nature of liability for breach of trust

The trustees will be liable for any loss caused by a breach of trust. No dishonesty, negligence or other *mens rea* is required to fix a trustee with liability for breach of trust. Rather, for there to be a breach of trust, it is enough that there has been a breach of the terms of the trust or a breach of one of the duties of trustees discussed in Chapters 8 and 9. Where the breach of trust has caused property to pass out of the trust fund then the trustee's principal obligation is to recover that property and to restore it to the trust fund. (This is referred to here as 'specific restitution'.) If that property cannot be recovered, or if the trustee has caused some loss to the trust other than transferring away trust property, then the trustees' liability is to reconstitute the value of the trust fund in cash and to pay equitable compensation for any consequent loss. These principles are clearly established by the decision of the House of Lords in *Target Holdings v Redferns*. The key development in this area of the law of trusts established by that case is the requirement that the trustees' breach of trust must have, in some way, caused the beneficiaries' loss. The purpose of remedies for breach of trust is to compensate the beneficiaries for any loss to the value of the trust fund and to protect the integrity of the trust fund.

---

8 Eg, the sale proceeds of the original property taken in breach of trust.
9 *Re Montagu* [1987] Ch 264.
10 *Royal Brunei Airlines v Tan* [1995] 2 AC 378.
11 *Boardman v Phipps* [1967] 2 AC 46.
12 *Attorney-General for Hong Kong v Reid* [1994] 1 AC 324, [1993] 3 WLR 1143.
13 Section 12.5 above.

18.1.3 What constitutes a breach of trust

Lord Browne-Wilkinson held that:

> The basic right of a beneficiary is to have the trust duly administered in accordance with the provisions of the trust instrument, if any, and the general law.[14]

Therefore, the most obvious example of a breach of trust would be a breach of the terms of the trust instrument[15] or a breach of any obligation imposed on trustees under the general law of trusts. Breaches of trust can take many forms, as Millett LJ made in clear in the following passage from his judgment in *Armitage v Nurse*:[16]

> Breaches of trust are of many different kinds. A breach of trust may be deliberate or inadvertent; it may consist of an actual misappropriation or misapplication of the trust property or merely an investment or other dealing which is outside the trustees' powers; it may consist of a failure to carry out a positive obligation of the trustees or merely of a want of skill and care on their part in the management of the trust property; it may be injurious to the interests of the beneficiaries or be actually to their benefit.

Thus a breach of trust will encompass any failure by the trustees to comply with the obligations which are set out in the trust instrument itself,[17] or which are set out in the Trustee Act 2000 if applicable, or which arise under the case law: all of these obligations were discussed in detail in Chapters 8 and 9 of this book. All that is required is the fact of the trustee having committed a breach of trust which causes loss to the trust:[18] there is nothing equivalent to *mens rea* by which to attach liability to a trustee. The various forms of liability, remedies and defences are considered in detail in this chapter.

18.2 THE BASIS OF LIABILITY FOR BREACH OF TRUST

> *A trustee will be liable for breach of trust if that breach of trust causes a loss to the beneficiaries. Such a trustee will be liable in the event of a breach of trust to restore the very trust property which was passed away in breach of trust, or to provide value equivalent to the value of any property passed away in breach of trust, or to pay equitable compensation to the beneficiaries.[19] There is an important distinction to be made here between proprietary liability and personal liability.*
>
> *A trustee will be liable in the situation in which the breach of trust has caused some loss to the trust. There will be no liability in respect of a breach of trust where that breach resulted in no loss to the trust. The measurement of compensation will be the*

---

14 *Target Holdings v Redferns* [1996] 1 AC 421, 434.
15 *Clough v Bond* (1838) My & Cr 490, (1838) 8 LJ Ch 51, (1838) 40 ER 1016.
16 [1998] Ch 241, 251.
17 *Clough v Bond* (1838) My & Cr 490.
18 *Target Holdings v Redferns* [1996] 1 AC 421.
19 *Ibid.*

actual, demonstrable loss to the trust, rather than some intermediate value of the property lost to the trust.[20]

This section focuses on the leading case in relation to claims for breach of trust, *Target Holdings v Redferns*,[21] and two issues specifically: first, in what circumstances a loss can be remedied by a claim based on breach of trust; and, secondly, how should the loss be valued?

18.2.1 The development of liability for breach of trust

As was considered in detail in Chapter 8, the trustee owes a range of obligations under general trusts law to the beneficiaries beyond any obligations which may be included in any particular trust instrument. So, a breach of trust may arise either on the basis of a breach of an express term of the trust instrument or a breach of an obligation contained in the general law of trusts.

The trustee's principal duty is said to be to account to the trustees both in the sense of providing accounts as to the contents of the trust fund from time to time and also in the sense of justifying their actions to the beneficiaries. So, as Lord Millett explained this matter when writing an article:[22]

> The primary obligation of a trustee is to account for his stewardship [of the trust]. The primary remedy of the beneficiary . . . is to have the account taken, to surcharge and falsify the account, and to require the trustee to restore to the trust estate any deficiency which may appear when the account is taken.

Therefore, the trustee must account to the beneficiaries and the beneficiaries are entitled to recover any loss caused by a breach of the trustees' duties.

The traditional approaches to breach of trust differed in significant ways from the modern approach set out by the House of Lords in *Target Holdings v Redferns*. The modern approach requires that the beneficiaries have suffered a loss and there must have been a causal link between the loss suffered and the trustees' actions. The older approach took a strict deterrent policy in relation to the trustees' liability for breach of trust[23] by making the trustee strictly liable for any loss which resulted from a breach of trust.[24] So, if the trustee made a distribution out of the trust property to a person whom she considered to be entitled to receive that property on the basis of forged documentation or a forged marriage licence, then she would nevertheless be held liable for breach of trust.[25] The trustee was typically responsible not for the replacement of the specific property but for an equivalent amount by way of compensation.[26] So, in *Re Massingberd's Settlement*, it was held that where the trustee had made *unauthorised* investments in breach of trust, he was required to procure *authorised* investments within the terms of the trust and to make good the loss suffered by the trust from

20 *Ibid.*
21 *Ibid.*
22 Millett, 1998.
23 Hayton, 1995, 845.
24 *Clough v Bond* (1838) 3 My & Cr 490, (1838) 8 LJ Ch 51, (1838) 2 Jur 958.
25 *Ashby v Blackwell* (1765) Eden 299; *Eaves v Hickson* (1861) 30 Beav 136. Cf *Re Smith* (1902) 71 LJ Ch 411.
26 *Re Massingberd's Settlement* (1890) 63 LT 296. See also *Knott v Cottee* (1852) 16 Beav 77.

that transaction by reconstituting the trust fund with those authorised investments. Equally, the trustees may be liable for breach of trust in failing to sell the property in sufficient time to make a profit.[27] Notably, it is still not required that the trustee has made any personal profit from the breach of trust to be liable for breach of trust.[28]

The principal duty imposed on the defaulting trustee is one of effecting restitution of the breach of trust.[29] This use of the term 'restitution' in this context means simply the *restoration* of property or its equivalent cash value to its original owner,[30] and not necessarily reversal of an unjust enrichment. The focus here is on compensating the beneficiaries for any loss and on protecting their property rights. This obligation is not limited by common law principles of remoteness of damage.

18.2.2 The modern law on breach of trust: *Target Holdings v Redferns*

The leading decision in this area is that of the House of Lords in *Target Holdings v Redferns*,[31] and it is from this case that the core test is drawn.

Target were seeking to enter into an investment with people who subsequently turned out to be fraudsters. As part of the transaction, Target wanted a mortgage over a piece of land (referred to as 'the Property' from here onwards). To achieve this, they required a valuation of the Property and the legal services of Redferns, a firm of solicitors, to ensure that they would acquire a valid legal charge over the Property. The borrowers were fraudsters. They acquired a fraudulently high valuation over the property which was being put up as security under the mortgage agreement. This over-valuation convinced Target that their loan would be adequately secured. When the fraudsters absconded with the loan moneys, Target found out that the Property was not worth as much as they had been told. As the fraudsters could not be found, Target was required to find someone else to sue.

Target had paid the loan moneys necessary to acquire the mortgage interest to Redferns, the solicitors. The agreement was that the solicitors were to hold the money as trustees on trust in their client account, to be paid out if the security was acquired or to be returned to Target if it was not. Redferns were not a party to the fraudulent valuation. In breach of the trust, however, the solicitors paid the trust fund away in breach of trust in ways not permitted for them to do under the terms of the transaction, principally by advancing money to the borrower before the mortgage security had been created, and also to defray other personal expenses of their solicitors' firm. These breaches of trust were wholly unconnected to the fraudulent valuation of the Property. In time, however, the solicitors paid enough money back into their client account to pay for the acquisition of the mortgage security. This payment was made and Target therefore acquired the mortgage security which they had sought from the outset. However, it was when Target attempted to enforce their security

---

27 *Fry v Fry* (1859) 27 Beav 144.
28 *Dornford v Dornford* (1806) 12 Ves 127, 129; *Adair v Shaw* (1803) Sch & Lef 243, 272; *Lord Mountford v Lord Cadogan* (1810) 17 Ves 485.
29 *Re Dawson* [1966] 2 NSWR 211; *Bartlett v Barclays Trust Co Ltd* [1980] Ch 515; *Bank of New Zealand v New Zealand Guardian Trust Co Ltd* [1999] 1 NZLR 664.
30 *Swindle v Harrison* [1997] 4 All ER 705.
31 [1996] 1 AC 421.

later, when the underlying commercial transaction broke down, that Target realised that they had been given a fraudulently high valuation over the Property.

Consequently, Target began to search for someone they could sue to recover the loss they had made on the transaction. It is important to remember that the loss suffered by Target was the difference between the real value of the Property and the fraudulently high valuation of the Property which Target had been given when creating their mortgage security. Given that the parties to the transaction were not able to make good Target's loss, Target was forced to sue the first solvent person who came within their reach. Therefore, Target sought to sue Redferns, the solicitors, for breach of their trust obligations in respect of the money held in the client account.

Target's arguments fell into two parts: first, that Target were entitled at the date of the trial to have the trust fund restored on a restitutionary basis; and, secondly, that immediately after the moneys had been paid away by Redferns in breach of trust there had been an *immediate* loss to the trust fund which Redferns were required to make good.

It is important to consider these arguments one at a time. The first line of argument would have obliged the trustees to restore the trust fund. The trust fund was made up of the money provided by Target to acquire the mortgage security. Target sought restitution of that fund from Redferns, because it was Redferns who had paid away the property that had formerly been in the trust fund in breach of that express trust. This argument proceeded on the basis that there was a strict liability for a trustee to restore a trust fund in any circumstances in which there had been a misapplication of such property in breach of trust. This raised the second line of argument, under which Target maintained that there was a loss to the trust at the very moment Redferns made the payment of the money away in breach of trust.

Redferns counter-argued that while there had been a breach of trust, the money was restored to the trust fund before Redferns were required to acquire the mortgage security. Target's argument on this form of strict liability was therefore being made irrespective of the fact that Redferns had made good the money taken from the client account before the date of creating the mortgage. Target were in effect not asking for the restoration of the trust fund, but a payment equal to the loss suffered as a result of the Property not being worth the value represented by the fraudulent valuation.

Lord Browne-Wilkinson took the view, to cut a long story short, that the loss suffered by Target had therefore been caused by the fraudulent valuation of the Property and not by Redferns' breach of trust. The breach of trust had been remedied by Redferns acquiring the mortgage security which Target had required from them. Redferns had provided the service which Target had required originally. The loss arose from different circumstances: to whit, the fraud of other people. Therefore, Target would not be entitled to claim compensation for breach of trust against Redferns in respect of the loss caused by the insufficiency of the value of the mortgage security.[32] Having cut the long story short, however, it is important to probe the more detailed elements of the decision.

---

32 *Target Holdings* was applied in *Cherney v Newman* [2011] EWHC 2156 (Ch) by Henderson J in relation to a claim for breach of fiduciary duty in relation to a solicitor acting for its client in relation to property transactions: it was held that the solicitor bore no duties to advise his client as to the commercial aspects of this transaction and therefore that the loss had not flowed from any breach of duty.

18.2.3 Loss as a foundation for the claim

The requirement that there must have been a loss for liability for breach of trust

The underpinning rationale for the decision in *Target Holdings v Redferns*[35] is that there must be a loss suffered as a direct result of the breach of trust, or else there would be beneficiaries who might seek to 'double up' on their damages by suing on a breach of trust even if that technical breach of trust happened to benefit the beneficiaries. This development is contrary to the approach in the older cases which did not permit a trustee to plead some intervening act which allegedly caused the loss.[34] The example given by Lord Browne-Wilkinson in *Target Holdings v Redferns*[35] to illustrate the importance of requiring a causal link was to imagine a situation in which a trustee made unauthorised investments which then turned out to be profitable. The traditional strict liability approach to breach of trust favoured in the older authorities would mean that the beneficiaries would be entitled to sue even if the trust fund had increased in value as a result of something which was technically a breach of the terms of the trust. Suppose, for example, a trust instrument which empowers trustees to invest only in Betamax plc shares but suppose instead that the trustees bought Gotech plc shares, technically in breach of trust. The Gotech plc shares then doubled in value while the Betamax plc shares remained static. If the basis of liability were a strict liability, then the beneficiaries would be able to sue the trustees even though the Gotech plc shares generated a greater profit than the Betamax plc shares. The approach in *Target Holdings v Redferns* instead was that the beneficiaries could only sue for breach of trust if the trustees had caused a loss to the beneficiaries. However, the beneficiaries would be able to require that the trustees replace the Gotech plc shares with the authorised Betamax plc shares.[36]

So, the question then is as to the rights which must be affected to found a claim for breach of trust. Lord Browne-Wilkinson considered the position which would arise in relation to a technical breach of trust by the trustee carried out with the consent of one beneficiary but not the other. His Lordship posed the question whether there could be liability in such circumstances on a strict liability basis even though there had been in fact no loss suffered by the beneficiary who had not consented to the breach. He held:[37]

> A carping beneficiary could insist that the unauthorised investment be sold and the proceeds invested in authorised investments: but the trustee would be under no liability to pay compensation either to the trust fund or to the beneficiary because the breach has caused no loss to the trust fund. Therefore, in each case the first question is to ask what are the rights of the beneficiary; only if some relevant right has been infringed so as to give rise to a loss is it necessary to consider the extent of the trustee's liability to compensate for such loss.

---

33 *Ibid.*
34 Cf *Kellaway v Johnson* (1842) 5 Beav 319; *Magnus v Queensland National Bank* (1888) 37 Ch D 466; *Re Brogden* (1888) 38 Ch D 546.
35 [1996] 1 AC 421.
36 *Re Massingberd's Settlement* (1890) 63 LT 296.
37 [1995] 3 All ER 785, 793.

Therefore, there must be a loss which flows directly from the breach of trust.[38] It is not enough that there is some breach of trust if no loss is actually suffered as a result of it. The sequence of events is also important. For there to have been a breach of trust, a trust must have been formed before the purported breach of duty took place.[39] So, if a financial institution breached its obligations to its customer *before* that money was settled on trust, then the breach of duty would not be a breach of trust, even if a trust was created later (without any further breach of duty taking place then).[40] The loss must also accrue to the claimant personally and not to some other person or company in which the claimant has an interest. So, where a claimant contended that shares were held on trust for him and that the company allegedly suffered a loss due to the defendant director's actions, it was held that the claimant had no action personally on the basis that the loss accrued to the company and not to the claimant personally: thus, a shareholder cannot recover compensation on her own account from a director of the company if the company in which she holds those shares has already recovered damages on its own account from that director in relation to that same loss.[41]

Difficulties with demonstrating loss in relation to investment of a trust

In relation to the investment of a trust fund, it may be difficult to prove that there has been a loss caused to the trust if the trustees have kept the capital value of the trust broadly steady but if they have nevertheless failed to generate any profit on that trust fund or if the capital value of the fund has fallen in real terms.[42] For example, in *Nestlé v National Westminster Bank plc (No 2)*,[43] the bank had acted as trustee of a will trust for 60 years. The plaintiff contended that the bank had generated a rate of return on the trust property which was lower than comparable investment indices. The bank demonstrated that it had acted prudently and in accordance with investment market practice throughout the period of its trusteeship. In consequence, it was not possible to demonstrate that the plaintiff had suffered any particular level of loss, nor that the trustee had breached its fiduciary duties in general terms. In that case, then, it could not be demonstrated that there had been a loss. It was also difficult to

---

38 The beneficiary must be able to prove loss. So, in *Jeffrey v Gretton* [2011] WTLR 809 a beneficiary under a trust over a dilapidated house claimed that she had not been fully informed about a deed of variation in relation to the trust and she claimed further that a sale of the house had been delayed so as to allow another beneficiary to live there and so as to cause her loss. It was found that her claim was not proved: she had been informed sufficiently about the deed; the sale had been delayed while the house was refurbished; and another beneficiary had not been in regular occupation of the property. Oddly, the court only relied upon *Jaffray v Marshall* and not *Target Holdings v Redferns*.

39 *Re BA Peters plc, Moriarty v Atkinson* [2009] BPIR 248, [2010] 1 BCLC 142, [2008] EWCA Civ 1604, [2011] WTLR 1661.

40 *Ibid.*

41 *Shaker v Al-Bedrawi* [2003] Ch 350; [2002] 4 All ER 835, doubting *Walker v Stones* [2001] QB 902, CA on this point. This sort of claim is generally referred to as a claim for 'reflective loss' where the shareholder-beneficiary seeks to recover for a loss already recovered by the company. Furthermore, under company law, the case was disposed of on the basis that a shareholder could not sue on a loss which was a loss properly accruing only to the company in any event: *Prudential Assurance Co Ltd v Newman Industries Ltd (No 2)* [1982] Ch 204, CA.

42 That is, in relation to the reference to 'real terms', if a fund was worth £20,000 in 1960, that would have been a very large fund which could have bought a detached house, but in 2000, the same amount of money would have been worth much less and would have constituted only about 5% of the purchase price of a similar house.

43 [1993] 1 WLR 1260, [1994] 1 All ER 118.

demonstrate that there had been any loss because, even though the beneficiaries were disappointed with the return which had been realised on the trust's investments, it appeared that other banks would have followed a similar investment strategy in relation to that type of trust. So, although there is a small gain, the beneficiaries may seek to argue that there has in fact been a loss. This argument will not succeed if the investment manager can demonstrate that her investment strategy was the same as that which would have been adopted in the marketplace generally.

18.2.4 Allocating liability for breach of trust among a number of trustees

The general rule: joint and several liability of trustees

The question arises whether trustees are to be held liable jointly or whether liability can be imposed on only one of the trustees. So, where there are a number of trustees but when a breach of trust is committed by only one of them, are all of the trustees to be equally liable for the breach of trust or only the blameworthy trustee? Where there is more than one trustee, those trustees are expected to act jointly.[44] Therefore, as a general rule, the trust property is required to be vested in the name of all of the trustees jointly, all of the trustees must receive any trust income, all of the trustees must give a receipt, and so forth. In that sense it would be expected that liability for breach of trust would attach to the trustees jointly and severally,[45] no matter which of them was directly responsible for the breach of trust. The trustees are jointly liable in that each of them is equally liable for any breach of trust, subject to what is said below. That the trustees are jointly *and* severally liable means that if one or more of the trustees were unable to meet their obligations, then the beneficiaries would be able to recover their loss from those trustees who are able to meet their trustees' collective obligations.

The reason for all of the trustees being held to be jointly and severally liable for the breach of trust is that to do otherwise would encourage trustees to take no responsibility for the decisions made in connection with their trusteeship. That is, it would be attractive to individual trustees to take no part in the management of the trust so that they could claim later not to have been responsible for any decision or action. It has been held that encouraging the trustees to act in this way would be an 'opiate on the consciences of the trustees', whereas it is in the interests of the beneficiaries to have all of the trustees taking an active part in the management of the trust so that they exercise control over one another.[46] Thus, all of the trustees are made equally liable for any loss to the trust. However, as considered in the next section, liability may be apportioned between the trustees once the beneficiaries' claim has been satisfied.

There are circumstances in which the trustees need not act jointly and in relation to which there is no requirement that all of the trustees should be jointly and severally liable. For

---

44 *Luke v South Kensington Hotel Co* (1879) 11 Ch D 121; *Re Dixon* (1826) 2 GL & J 114; *Re Hilton* [1909] 2 Ch 548; *Re Whitely* [1910] 1 Ch 600; *Re Butlin's Settlement Trust* [1976] Ch 251. See para 8.2.4 above.

45 'Joint and several' liability means that all of the trustees may be held liable together or that each individual trustee may be separately liable for the whole of the loss, regardless of which was directly responsible in fact for the acts constituting the breach of trust. Thus, the beneficiaries may sue one or all of the trustees to recover any loss suffered. The trustees, as considered in the text, may then seek to recover a contribution to the compensation paid to the beneficiaries from one another.

46 *Bahin v Hughes* (1886) 31 Ch D 390, at 398, *per* Frey LJ.

example, the trust instrument may permit some other means of proceeding without unanimity[47] or necessity may require that assets be registered in the name of only one of the trustees at a given time.[48] Thus, it may be that some of the trustees have their liability limited by the trust instrument: in general terms, limitation of liability clauses will exclude the liabilities of trustees.[49] Therefore, it would seem possible that a trustee whose liability was expressly limited could be excluded from liability, whereas a trustee whose liability was not so limited would not have her liability excluded. In such situations, however, the property must not be left in the hands of one or only a few of the trustees for longer than is necessary.[50] If a trustee is also a beneficiary under that trust, then if the trustee has committed a breach of trust that person cannot take their beneficial interest until they have accounted for their breach of trust.[51]

Apportioning liability between trustees

From the preceding principles, then, the beneficiaries may proceed against any trustee in relation to a loss suffered as a result of some breach of trust because all of the trustees are jointly and severally liable for any breach of trust. Nevertheless, it has been held that no individual trustee will be liable for any default which is the default individually of another trustee.[52] Thus, any individual trustees who have been required to compensate the beneficiaries for a breach of trust may subsequently recover any compensation paid to the beneficiaries from whichever of the other trustees was actually responsible for the acts which constituted the breach of trust. So, the beneficiaries may sue any one or more of the trustees, and then it is for the trustees to sort matters out between themselves afterwards (unless any of them has her liability expressly excluded by the terms of the trust instrument). Trustees may be liable to make contributions alongside the other trustees in situations in which they are liable for a breach of trust in common with those other trustees further to the Civil Liability (Contribution) Act 1978. The 1978 Act displaced the inherent power of the courts of equity to order a trustee to make such a contribution. The Act operates[53] so that any trustee who is made liable to compensate the beneficiaries for any breach of trust is entitled to recover a contribution towards her liability from the other trustees who are also liable for that same breach[54] and whose responsibility, impliedly, is not excluded by the trust instrument or

---

47 TA 2000, s 11. For example, where only one trustee is to receive income on behalf of all of the other trustees: *Townley v Sherbourne* (1633) Bridg 35; 2 W & TLC (9th edn) 577; *Gouldsworth v Knights* (1843) 11 M & W 337.
48 *Consterdine v Consterdine* (1862) 31 Beav 330.
49 See para 8.5.1 above.
50 *Brice v Stokes* (1805) 11 Ves 319; *Re Munton* [1927] 1 Ch 262.
51 *Re Dacre, Whitaker v Dacre* [1916] 1 Ch 344 at 346–7, *per* Lord Cozens-Hardy MR; *Brazzill v Willoughby* [2009] EWHC 1633 (Ch), [2010] 1 BCLC 673.
52 *Townley v Sherbourne* (1633) Bridg 35; 2 W & TLC (9th edn) 577. This principle was enshrined in the now-repealed Trustee Act 1925, s 30(1), whereby trustees were liable only for their own acts and defaults. However, a trustee will be liable for any breach of trust of which she has knowledge or which she conceals or, obviously, in which she knowingly participates in some way: *Boardman v Mosman* (1799) 1 Bro CC 68. There will also be liability for failing to protect the interests of the beneficiaries in such a situation: *Brice v Stokes* (1805) 11 Ves 319; *Gough v Smith* [1872] WN 18.
53 The relevant acts must have occurred after 1978 for the Act to be effective.
54 Civil Liability (Contribution) Act 1978, ss 1(1), 6(1). See *Friends Provident Life Office v Hillier Parker May & Rowden* [1997] QB 85. The trustee must have become a trustee after 1978: Civil Liability (Contribution) Act 1978, s 7(2); *Lampitt v Poole Borough Council* [1991] 2 QB 545.

by contract. The amount of the contribution to be made is such as the court considers to be just and equitable in the circumstances.[55] In assessing the extent of the justice and equity of any trustee making a contribution, the court will look to the fault which would attach to that trustee in regard to the breach of trust.[56] As a result, it is open to the court to absolve the trustee from liability altogether or to require her to provide a complete indemnity to the other trustees or anything in between.[57]

The courts will generally apportion liability evenly between the trustees[58] except in circumstances in which one trustee has acted fraudulently[59] or has demonstrated wilful default.[60] Suppose that one trustee had intentionally defrauded the beneficiaries by taking property from the trust and that the extent of the other trustees' liability was to fail to spot what the fraudulent trustee was doing. In such a situation, the court will typically require that the trustee who is most culpable will bear the larger share of the loss.[61] Similarly, a trustee who takes some personal benefit from the breach of trust will generally be liable to bear a proportionately increased share of the liability,[62] although not necessarily the complete liability.[63] In the event that there has been no loss suffered but there are costs incurred in righting the breach of trust, those costs can be recovered from the trustee against whom the action is to be taken.[64] It has been suggested that the courts will typically take into account the following factors: how large a role each trustee played in causing the loss, the level of moral blameworthiness attaching to each trustee, and the extent to which each trustee had taken some personal benefit from the breach of trust.[65]

Breach of trust by a company acting as trustee

Where the trustee is a company, then the directors of that trustee company will owe their fiduciary duties to the company and it is the company which owes the duties of a trustee to the beneficiaries of the trust.[66] In the event of a breach of trust, the beneficiaries must proceed against the company and then the company must bear any liability and in turn seek to recover its own loss from the director.[67]

---

55 Civil Liability (Contribution) Act 1978, s 2(1).
56 *Ibid. Cf Baker v Willoughby* [1970] AC 467; *Madden v Quirk* [1989] 1 WLR 702.
57 Civil Liability (Contribution) Act 1978, s 2(2). See *Bacon v Camphausen* (1888) 58 LT 851; *Ramskill v Edwards* (1885) 31 Ch D 100.
58 See *Bacon v Camphausen* (1888) 58 LT 851; *Ramskill v Edwards* (1885) 31 Ch D 100.
59 *Charitable Corporation v Sutton* (1742) 2 Atk 400; *Lingard v Bromley* (1812) 1 V & B 114; *Tarleton v Hornby* (1833) 1 Y& C 333; *Attorney-General v Wilson* (1840) Cr & Ph 1.
60 *Scotney v Lomer* (1886) 29 Ch D 535.
61 *Monetary Fund v Hashim* (1994) *The Times*, 11 October; *Dairy Containers Ltd v NZI Bank Ltd* [1995] 2 NZLR 30; *Re Mulligan* [1998] 1 NZLR 481; *Dubai Aluminium Co Ltd v Salaam* [1999] 1 Lloyd's Rep 415.
62 *Lockhart v Reilly* (1857) 25 LJ Ch 697; *Thompson v Finch* (1856) 8 De GM & G 560; *Blyth v Fladgate* [1891] 1 Ch 337; *Re Turner* [1897] 1 Ch 536.
63 *Butler v Butler* (1875) 5 Ch D 554, affirmed on appeal (1878) 7 Ch D 116.
64 *Re Lindsay* [1904] 2 Ch 785.
65 Mitchell, 2000, 211.
66 *Gregson v HAE Trustees Ltd* [2008] EWHC 1006 (Ch), [2008] 2 BCLC 542.
67 This is often referred to in the cases as a 'dog-leg claim'.

18.3 REMEDIES FOR BREACH OF TRUST

18.3.1 The remedies for breach of trust in outline

Having considered the factors that will give rise to a claim for breach of trust, it is important to consider the remedies which flow from such a claim.[68] The following discussion considers those remedies imposed on trustees who have misapplied the trust property. The context of remedies against third parties is considered at section 18.4 below, and claims in relation to title to the trust property itself are examined in Chapter 19.

From Lord Browne-Wilkinson's account of the available claims, the following three equitable remedies can be divined:

(a) a claim ordering the trustee to restore the original property which formed part of the trust fund, referred to here as 'specific restitution of the trust property';[69]

(b) a claim against the trustee to pay money or to provide property of equivalent value to the amount lost to the trust fund if the original assets cannot be recovered; or

(c) a claim for equitable compensation to recover any further loss suffered by the trust.

Even in situations in which the loss or breach of trust was caused by the dishonesty of a third party to the trust, the beneficiary is required to proceed first against the trustee for breach of trust in any event.[70] In this sense the liability of the trustees for any breach of trust is a primary liability. Each of these remedies is considered in turn in the sections to follow.

18.3.2 Specific restitution of the trust property

The first option is to require the trustee to restore the trust fund to its original condition by recovering the very property which was originally held on trust. Where it is a particularly valuable or important item of property that is lost to the trust fund, the principles considered in Chapter 19 will apply to require the trustee to deliver up that specific property if it is in her possession or under her control, or to enable a clean substitute for the trust property to be identified and recovered (common law tracing),[71] or its traceable substitute to be acquired and added to the trust fund (equitable tracing).[72] In relation to a loss caused by a breach of trust, the question is then as to the nature of the remedy necessary to compensate the beneficiary by means of restoration of the trust fund.[73] Specific restitution is the primary remedy because it enforces the trustees' obligation to safeguard the trust property.

Lord Browne-Wilkinson explained the options for remedying breach of trust as being focused on recovery of the original trust property where possible in the first instance. This

---

68 Contrary to Professor Birks's argument that it is not appropriate to talk of 'rights' and 'remedies' but rather only of 'rights' which necessarily imply their remedies (Birks, 2000:1), this is one context in which the rights of the claimant may lead to the realisation of any one of a number of remedies dependent on the context, one of which (equitable compensation) necessarily involves some judicial discretion (see generally Barker, 1998, 319).

69 This claim is *in personam*, as considered below only in that the defendant trustees are judged on the basis of their personally-owed obligations to safeguard the trust property and to observe the terms of the trust.

70 *Target Holdings v Redferns* [1996] 1 AC 421.

71 *FC Jones (A Firm) v Jones* [1996] 3 WLR 703.

72 *Re Diplock's Estate* [1948] Ch 465; *Boscawen v Bajwa* [1996] 1 WLR 328.

73 *Caffrey v Darby* (1801) 6 Ves 488, [1775–1802] All ER Rep 507; *Clough v Bond* (1838) 3 My & Cr 490, (1838) 40 ER 1016; *Nocton v Lord Ashburton* [1914] AC 932.

point emerges from the following extract from his Lordship's speech in *Target Holdings v Redferns*:[74]

> The equitable rules of compensation for breach of trust have been largely developed in relation to such traditional trusts, where the only way in which all the beneficiaries' rights can be protected is to restore to the trust fund what ought to be there. In such a case the basic rule is that a trustee in breach of trust must restore or pay to the trust estate either the assets which have been lost to the estate by reason of the breach or compensation for such loss. Courts of Equity did not award damages but, in acting *in personam*, ordered the defaulting trustee to restore the trust estate.[75]

Compensation for a breach of trust is thus achieved by recovery of the original trust assets (specific restitution) in the first place; and only secondarily by compensation in money. The position in English law remains that the trustee is responsible in the first instance for the restoration of the particular trust property which was lost in the breach of trust, and only if that is not possible for compensation of the beneficiary for loss of the original assets in cash. Typically, therefore, if the trust assets have been dissipated, compensation will have to be made by way of a cash payment from the trustee. What is important to note is that the beneficiaries may, in many circumstances, prefer to recover the specific property that was lost (because it will grant a proprietary right, because it had sentimental value, because it was expected to increase in value, or because it was intrinsically valuable) rather than to receive simply its cash equivalent from the trustee which may not reflect the future profits which might be earned from that property and which will not reflect any value beyond simply its market value in cash. Specific restitution is therefore a proprietary obligation on the trustee to recover the original trust assets.

However, what is important to note is that while tracing revolves around the assertion of proprietary rights either in a specific item of property or in its substitute, Lord Browne-Wilkinson expressed the jurisdiction of equity in this context to be in the form of an action *in personam* against the trustee to recover the trust estate. In parallel with the decision of Lord Templeman in *Attorney-General for Hong Kong v Reid*,[76] the court is providing for an action *in personam* against a particular person who is identified as a trustee, seemingly, acting on the principle that 'equity looks upon as done that which ought to have been done' such that the trustee is required to continue to hold that item of specific property on trust for the beneficiaries (unless the property has passed out of the trustee's control or possession).[77] Where the original trust property has passed out of the trustee's control or possession such that it cannot be recovered, the action converts to a mere action for money to recover the equivalent cash value of the specific assets misapplied in breach of trust, as considered in para 18.3.3 below. The action for specific restitution, however, is not a personal action, but rather an action in relation to specific property which is brought against the trustee. There

---

74 [1996] 1 AC 421, [1995] 3 All ER 785 HL.

75 *Nocton v Lord Ashburton* [1914] AC 932, at 952, 958, *per* Viscount Haldane LC.

76 *Attorney-General for Hong Kong v Reid* [1994] 1 AC 324, [1993] 3 WLR 1143.

77 The distinction between an *in personam* and an *in rem* action in this context is that an action *in personam* in equity binds only the particular defendant, whereas an action *in rem* would bind any successors in title or assignees from the defendant (other than the *bona fide* purchaser for value).

will only be a personal action to account in money if the original trust property cannot be recovered.

In situations in which the trustees have invested in property not permitted by the trust instrument, their obligation will be to replace those unauthorised investments with authorised investments.[78] This is different from providing specific restitution because the trustees are not recovering property which has been passed away from the trust in breach of their duties, but rather the trustees are acquiring the assets of a type which they ought to have acquired beforehand.

It was suggested in *Harris v Kent*[79] that the application of the remedy of specific restitution might be inappropriate in a context in which none of the parties (beneficiaries and trustees) wanted to keep the trust in existence, something which would be done by recovering the original trust property. Therefore, it was considered that the better remedy would be to compensate the beneficiary for the loss she would not have suffered but for the breach of trust.

18.3.3 Equitable compensation to restore the value of the trust fund

If the specific property which comprised the trust fund cannot be recovered, the following course of action arises from the speech of Lord Browne-Wilkinson:

> If specific restitution of the trust property is not possible, then the liability of the trustee is to pay sufficient compensation to the trust estate to put it back to what it would have been had the breach not been committed.[80]

The second course of action is then for restoration (confusingly rendered in the cases as 'restitution')[81] of an amount of money equal to the value of the property lost to the trust fund by the breach of trust.[82] The issue of valuation is considered further at para 18.3.5 below, but in general terms the valuation will be an amount to return the trust to the position it had occupied before the transaction which constituted the breach of trust. As Lord Browne-Wilkinson explained the appropriate valuation, it is that required to 'put [the trust fund] back to what it would have been had the breach not been committed'. In other words, the aim of this second remedy is to calculate the amount of money which is necessary to restore the value of the trust fund. It is important to note that there is a difference between personal compensation for loss suffered as a breach of trust, and compensation equivalent to the value of property lost to the trust as considered in the next section.[83]

---

78 *Re Massingberd's Settlement* (1890) 63 LT 296.
79 [2007] EWHC 463 (Ch), Briggs J.
80 Cf *Caffrey v Darby* (1801) 6 Ves 488, [1775–1802] All ER Rep 507; *Clough v Bond* (1838) 3 My & Cr 490, (1838) 40 ER 1016. See now *Bairstow v Queens Moat Houses* (2001) unreported, 17 May.
81 *Swindle v Harrison* [1997] 4 All ER 705. 'Confusing' in that the trustee will not necessarily have been personally enriched: see section 31.3.
82 The obligation of the fiduciary being to compensate the beneficiaries for the loss caused by the breach of duty, as set out in *Target Holdings v Redferns*, was observed in *Lee v Futurist Developments Ltd* [2010] EWHC 2764 (Ch), [2011] 1 BCLC 653, [49].
83 *Swindle v Harrison* [1997] 4 All ER 705; *Bristol & West Building Society v Mothew* [1996] 4 All ER 698.

It is possible that this restoration of the value of the fund could take a number of forms other than straightforwardly paying cash. For example, it might permit the acquisition of an annuity which would generate similar levels of income to any trust capital misapplied in breach of trust. The level of compensation, as a matter of evidence, must equate to the loss which the beneficiary can demonstrate was caused by the breach of trust such that the trust fund is placed back in the position it would have occupied but for the breach.[84] This might include any loss which the trust would have suffered subsequently as a result of the nature of the trust property – for example, accounting for a large fall in the value of such property subsequently.

18.3.4 Equitable compensation for losses to the trust in general

Introduction to equitable compensation in general terms

The previous section considered liability for equitable compensation in a way that was limited to effecting restoration of the value of the trust fund. Equitable compensation is available more broadly under the general principles of equity for any other losses which may have been suffered by the trust.[85] Suppose that the trustees had incurred expenses in committing a breach of trust such as selling property which ought to have been retained as part of the trust fund. The restoration to the trust fund of the value of the property transferred away should be considered to be separate from the recovery of any other loss consequential to the breach of trust. For example, if the loss to the trust was in the form of a lost opportunity in the future – such as a right to receive a dividend[86] which was lost when shares held as part of the trust fund were sold in breach of trust – then the beneficiaries will wish to recover equitable compensation from the trustees for this lost opportunity to receive a dividend and not simply for the capital value of the shares.

Compensation is an equitable remedy which gives rise to a right which is purely personal in nature, giving no right to any specific property. In relation to breach of trust, some loss has been caused to the trust, and it is that loss which is made good by compensation. The court is therefore awarding a payment of money instead of some proprietary right which relies on the beneficiaries showing that a loss has resulted from the breach of trust. Rather than recognising some proprietary right in the beneficiary and imposing a trust or charge to recognise the right as being proprietary, compensation requires only that the loss to the trust is calculated in cash terms and that that amount is accounted for by the trustee to the trust fund.[87]

There is a need for the beneficiaries to decide, in many cases, whether to proceed in relation to a restitutionary proprietary claim for some property held in the trustee's hands, for a claim equal to the value of some specific property lost to the trust, or for a compensatory claim in relation to the breach of trust *simpliciter*.[88] These are different remedies and the

---

84 *Target Holdings v Redferns* [1996] 1 AC 421.
85 Further to *Gwembe Valley Development Co Ltd v Koshy* [2003] EWCA Civ 1048, [2004] 1 BCLC 131, at para 142 *et seq., per* Mummery LJ, a director who breaches his fiduciary duties to a company in a manner which causes loss to that company will also be liable to pay equitable compensation to the company.
86 A 'dividend' is a right making up part of a shareholder's rights to receive an income payment annually as and when declared by the board of directors to be paid out of the company's profits.
87 *Target Holdings v Redferns* [1996] 1 AC 421.
88 *Target Holdings v Redferns* [1996] 1 AC 421, [1995] 3 WLR 352, [1995] 3 All ER 785.

beneficiary will be required to elect between them to remove the possibility of multiple recovery in respect of the same loss.[89] It is important to note that there is a difference between personal compensation for loss suffered as a breach of trust, and compensation equivalent to the value of property lost to the trust,[90] as considered in the next section.

Distinguishing between 'restorative' and 'compensatory' remedies

The cases have distinguished between remedies which are concerned merely to put the parties back in the position which they occupied before the breach of trust ('restorative' remedies) and remedies which are concerned to compensate the claimant for further losses as well as restoring the parties to the position before the breach was committed ('compensatory' remedies). There is a line to be drawn between compensation in relation to breach of the duty of skill and care, and breach of the general fiduciary duty not to permit conflicts of interest or not to deal with the trust property personally. In relation to the former (breach of the duty of skill and care), the court will import analogous principles to those of causation and remoteness of damage.[91] However, in relation to duties to avoid conflicts of interest and self-dealing, equitable compensation in such circumstances would be awarded in lieu of rescission of the contract which the trustee had entered into in breach of that duty.[92] Compensation in that circumstance would be calculated according to the value of the property lost to the trust, less the price paid to the trustee, plus interest.[93] Thus, the second form of compensation is said to be 'restorative', in that it effects rescission, rather than being generally compensatory, which would deal with all consequent loss.

So, in *Swindle v Harrison*,[94] by way of illustration of compensation for conflict of interest by a fiduciary, the (wonderfully-named) solicitor Mr Swindle failed to disclose all material facts to his client Mrs Harrison in his fiduciary capacity in connection with a purchase of property, such that she lost money in the transaction. Mrs Harrison sought compensation from the solicitor for her loss. The Court of Appeal held that Mrs Harrison was entitled to restorative compensation only, that is, an amount of compensation to put the trust into the position which it had occupied before the transaction. The aim of this restorative remedy was to achieve rescission of the transaction, and so put her back in the position which she would have occupied but for the breach of trust, as opposed to compensating her for any general further loss. The Court of Appeal held that only this restorative remedy was available where the plaintiff had been in some way culpable for her loss; whereas if the plaintiff had been induced into the contract by some fraud or unconscionable act on the part of the fiduciary then a compensatory remedy would be appropriate. On the facts of *Swindle v Harrison*, it was found that Mrs Harrison had decided to enter into the transaction of her own volition, and therefore generally compensatory remedies would not be available.

The measure of compensation here is that of compensation for loss suffered as a result of the breach of trust. It is this measure which makes up the third limb of the test in *Target*

---

89 *Tang v Capacious Investments* [1996] 1 AC 514.
90 *Swindle v Harrison* [1997] 4 All ER 705; *Bristol & West Building Society v Mothew* [1996] 4 All ER 698.
91 *Bristol & West Building Society v Mothew* [1996] 4 All ER 698, *per* Millett LJ.
92 *Ibid.*
93 *Holder v Holder* [1968] Ch 353.
94 [1997] 4 All ER 705.

Holdings v Redferns.[95] The measure of the size of the loss is therefore a measurement of consequential loss only, and is not limited to a measurement of the value of the property which made up the trust fund before the transaction.

The establishment of the liability to pay compensation

The core issue is the measurement of the amount of compensation which is to be paid. As considered above, there is no strict rule of foreseeability, nor of remoteness of damage, in relation to a breach of trust. It is therefore possible that the trustee will be liable in respect of any loss which accrues to the trust. The issue is then the extent to which such common law concerns ought to intrude in deciding exactly how large the loss to the trust fund has been. Lord Browne-Wilkinson held as follows in *Target Holdings v Redferns*:[96]

> At common law there are two principles fundamental to the award of damages. First, that the defendant's wrongful act must cause the damage complained of. Second, that the plaintiff is to be put 'in the same position as he would have been in if he had not sustained the wrong for which he is now getting his compensation or reparation'.[97] Although, as will appear, in many ways equity approaches liability for making good a breach of trust from a different starting point, in my judgment those two principles are applicable as much in equity as at common law. Under both systems liability is fault-based: the defendant is only liable for the consequences of the legal wrong he has done to the plaintiff and to make good the damage caused by his wrong or to pay by way of compensation more than the loss suffered from such wrong.

Compensation for breach is therefore based on fault, rather than on any strict liability of the trustee.[98] The distinction between fault-based common law damages and fault-based equitable compensation is then a further issue. Lord Browne-Wilkinson put it in the following terms:

> The detailed rules of equity as to causation and the quantification of the loss differ, at least ostensibly, from those applicable at common law. But the principles underlying both systems are the same. On the assumptions that had to be made in the present case until the factual issues are resolved (ie that the transaction would have gone through even if there had been no breach of trust), the result reached by the Court of Appeal does not accord with those principles. Redferns as trustees have been held liable to compensate Target for a loss caused otherwise than by the breach of trust.

Therefore, while there remains some distinction between the common law and equity in this context, Lord Browne-Wilkinson does not find it necessary to probe that difference on the facts of *Target Holdings* on the basis that there is no proof that the loss to the trust was caused in any way by the breach of trust itself. As his Lordship considered the matter:

---

95 Considered above at para 18.3.3.
96 [1996] 1 AC 421, [1995] 3 All ER 785, 792.
97 *Ibid*.
98 Pawlowski, 2000.

the common law rules of remoteness of damage and causation do not apply. However, there does have to be some causal connection between the breach of trust and the loss to the trust estate for which compensation is recoverable, viz the fact that the loss would not have occurred but for the breach.[99]

In line with the older authorities in this area, the distinction between the common law and equitable codes would be that the common law will impose liability to pay damages only where there is sufficient proximity and foreseeability, whereas equity will award compensation where the loss can be shown to have been derived from the breach of trust. The difference would therefore be that equitable compensation may be awarded even where the loss was not strictly foreseeable, provided that it did result from the breach of trust.[100]

The nature of compensation as part of equity

A trustee will be liable to compensate the beneficiaries for the loss occasioned by a breach of trust even though the loss may flow unexpectedly from the breach. The genesis of this principle is perhaps rooted in the understanding of trusts as being founded on the conscience of the trustee. Breach of a trust is an unconscionable act imposing liability on trustees to compensate beneficiaries no matter what. That conscience could be said to extend properly to the situation in which the trustee breaches the terms of the trust in such a way that the trustee may have been acting out of the best of motives (perhaps in investing in assets not strictly within her investment powers) but nevertheless caused some loss to the trust.

So, suppose T invested in A plc shares, outwith the investment powers in the trust, on the basis that such shares were expected in good faith to generate a better return for the trust than the authorised investments. Suppose then that A plc fell unexpectedly into insolvency as a result of terrorist activity in their production plants, and that the trust's investment was lost. Under common law, it would be arguable that the terrorist activity was unforeseeable and that no liability should attach to the trustees as a result. However, equity would impose liability for breach of trust regardless. The validity of this liability would be based on T's knowledge that the investment was a breach of trust, even though it was undertaken from the best of motives. The strict rule of trusts law must be enforced: the trustee must not be permitted to do anything which she knows to be contrary to conscience.[101]

However, Lord Browne-Wilkinson explained liability as arising not simply on the occurrence of a breach but rather only when that breach causes a loss to the trust. This approach rests on a positive duty on trustees to protect the trust fund and its value, leading to a concomitant duty on trustees to account to the beneficiaries for any loss in the value of that fund caused by their breach of trust. As Lord Browne-Wilkinson considered the matter in *Target Holdings v Redferns*:[102]

---

99 See also *Re Miller's Deed Trusts* (1978) 75 LS Gaz 454; *Nestlé v National Westminster Bank plc* [1994] 1 All ER 118, [1993] 1 WLR 1260.
100 *Clough v Bond* (1838) 3 My & C 490, (1838) 8 LJ Ch 51, (1838) 2 Jur 958; *Re Massingberd's Settlement* (1890) 63 LT 296.
101 [1967] 2 AC 46.
102 [1996] 1 AC 421, [1995] 3 All ER 785, 793.

The equitable rules of compensation for breach of trust have been largely developed in relation to such traditional trusts, where the only way in which all the beneficiaries' rights can be protected is to restore to the trust fund what ought to be there. In such a case the basic rule is that a trustee in breach of trust must restore or pay to the trust estate either the assets which have been lost to the estate by reason of the breach or compensation for such loss. Courts of Equity did not award damages but, in acting *in personam*, ordered the defaulting trustee to restore the trust estate.[103]

Therefore, the remedy of compensation is available on a personal basis from the trustee to achieve restitution of the loss suffered by the trust fund. Historically, this rule has been developed in relation to family trusts, where the trustees were generally considered to occupy a position of especial tenderness in relation to the beneficiaries. Consequently, the trustees were to be held personally liable if any of the beneficiaries' personal fortunes were lost through the misfeasance of the trustees. It is perhaps questionable whether the same rule ought to apply to commercial situations, where perhaps a claim based on contract might be preferable.

The more difficult situation is where the beneficiaries seek to recover some lost opportunity caused by the breach of trust. While it is commonly said that the trustee will not be liable for such opportunity cost,[104] it might well be the case that the development of a causal link for the liability of trustees[105] will lead to liability for losses which are foreseeable as a result of the breach of trust. Suppose, for example, that a valuable oil painting held on trust was to have been sold to a dealer for £100,000, but the trustee sold it instead in breach of trust for only £75,000; it would be reasonable to suppose that the beneficiary ought to have some claim against the trustee for the lost opportunity of the more valuable sale.[106]

The issue which remains is that compensation will not achieve restitution of specific property; only a payment of money equal to the loss. Lord Browne-Wilkinson continued:

> If specific restitution of the trust property is not possible, then the liability of the trustee is to pay sufficient compensation to the trust estate to put it back to what it would have been had the breach not been committed.[107] Even if the immediate cause of the loss is the dishonesty or failure of a third party, the trustee is liable to make good that loss to the trust estate if, but for the breach, such loss would not have occurred.[108]

Therefore, compensation will be available on an almost strict liability basis, provided that causation can be demonstrated. The trustee is personally liable, even where the source of the misfeasance is with some third party who perhaps induced the trustee to act as she did.

---

103 See *Nocton v Lord Ashburton* [1914] AC 932 at 952, 958, *per* Viscount Haldane LC.

104 *Palmer v Jones* (1862) 1 Ven 144.

105 *Target Holdings v Redferns* [1996] 1 AC 421, [1995] 3 WLR 352, [1995] 3 All ER 785.

106 Mowbray *et al*, 2001, 1194; *Kingdon v Castleman* (1877) 46 LJ Ch 448. Cf *Hobday v Peters (No 3)* (1860) 28 Beav 603.

107 *Caffrey v Darby* (1801) 6 Ves 488, [1775–1802] All ER Rep 507; *Clough v Bond* (1838) 3 My & Cr 490, (1838) 40 ER 1016.

108 [1995] 3 All ER 785, 792. Cf *Re Dawson, Union Fidelity Trustee Co Ltd (No 2)* [1980] 2 All ER 92, [1980] Ch 515.

18.3.5 A comparison of common law damages and equitable compensation

Distinguishing between common law damages and equitable compensation

The third limb of the possible remedies for breach of trust set out in *Target Holdings v Redferns* suggests at first blush an overlap with common law damages[109] and the need for evidence of a link between loss and remedy.[110] The important initial point is that the suit must be brought against the trustee in cases of breach of trust, before the matter is pursued against others who may have orchestrated the breach of trust in fact. As Lord Browne-Wilkinson continued: 'Even if the immediate cause of the loss is the dishonesty or failure of a third party, the trustee is liable to make good that loss to the trust estate if, but for the breach, such loss would not have occurred.'[111]

One of the more complex issues to arise out of the *Target Holdings v Redferns*[112] litigation was the line between equitable compensation and common law damages. In short, Lord Browne-Wilkinson held that there is little difference between the two doctrines. Both are dependent, first, on the fault of the defendant and, secondly, on a nexus between the loss suffered by the claimant and the defendant's wrongdoing. This point emerges from the speech of Lord Browne-Wilkinson in *Target Holdings v Redferns*:[113]

> At common law there are two principles fundamental to the award of damages. First, that the defendant's wrongful act must cause the damage complained of. Second, that the plaintiff is to be put 'in the same position as he would have been in if he had not sustained the wrong for which he is now getting his compensation or reparation' . . . Although, as will appear, in many ways equity approaches liability for making good a breach of trust from a different starting point, in my judgment those two principles are applicable as much in equity as at common law. Under both systems liability is fault based: the defendant is only liable for the consequences of the legal wrong he has done to the plaintiff and to make good the damage caused by his wrong or to pay by way of compensation more than the loss suffered from such wrong. The detailed rules of equity as to causation and the quantification of the loss differ, at least ostensibly, from those applicable at common law. But the principles underlying both systems are the same.

There is close intellectual ground between the two approaches. However, there is a subtle distinction between the evidential burden in cases of equitable compensation in contradistinction to cases involving common law damages. As his Lordship continued:

> Thus the common law rules of remoteness of damage and causation do not apply [in relation to breach of trust]. However, there does have to be some causal connection

---

109   Somewhat oddly there is repeated reference in *Ramzan v Brookwide Ltd* [2011] EWCA Civ 985, at [49] *et seq.* by Arden LJ to 'damages for breach of trust', even though 'damages' are available only at common law (with a voluminous jurisprudence as to their scope) whereas the equitable remedies available in relation to breach of trust were clearly set out by the House of Lords in *Target Holdings v Redferns* as considered above.
110   See also *Bristol & West Building Society v Mothew* [1996] 4 All ER 698.
111   Cf *Re Dawson, Union Fidelity Trustee Co Ltd (No 2)* [1980] 2 All ER 92, [1980] Ch 515.
112   [1996] 1 AC 421.
113   [1996] 1 AC 421, [1995] 3 All ER 785, 792.

between the breach of trust and the loss to the trust estate for which compensation is recoverable, viz the fact that the loss would not have occurred but for the breach.[114]

Significantly, then, there is required to be a causal link between the loss suffered and the breach of trust perpetrated. Thus, Target were held not to be entitled to recover compensation from Redferns for breach of trust. It was not necessary on the facts of that case to inquire into questions of remoteness of damage nor the precise issues of causation to reach that decision in *Target Holdings*. This remains a conceptual difficulty for future cases in understanding the sliver of difference between the common law and the equitable doctrines.

Liability in the tort of negligence in relation to trusts

There are a number of situations in which common law claims, in particular liability in negligence, may be significant in relation to the operation of trusts. Principally, claims in negligence will be available in favour of people who do not have the rights of beneficiaries under trusts, particularly if their hopes of prospective rights were frustrated by someone's negligence. Thus, a lawyer drafting a trust may be liable for common law damages under the tort of negligence if that duty is carried out negligently so as to cause the claimant loss.[115] So, in *White v Jones*[116] a solicitor took so long to draft a will that the intended beneficiary acquired no rights in the client's estate on the client's death intestate some time later. The third party who was intended to have acquired rights under the will which was to have been drafted was held by a majority of the House of Lords to be entitled to recover damages for her loss. While a solicitor would not ordinarily owe duties to someone other than her client, Lord Goff was of the opinion that justice demanded a remedy in this instance because the solicitor's negligence had caused loss to this third party.[117] Equally, failure to warn a testatrix that it would only be possible to dispose of property by will in the manner which she intended if she first severed the joint tenancy on which it was then held, gave rise to liability in negligence to those third parties who would otherwise have acquired beneficial rights in that property under the will.[118] This liability in damages will, however, only be available to people who are intended to be either a beneficiary or a legatee.[119] Liability at common law may also be held to arise on the basis of breach of an implied contractual term. So, a lawyer's failure to protect a client's confidence in a conveyancing transaction was held to give rise to damages for breach of an implied term of the contract between solicitor and client to maintain the confidentiality of the client's affairs.[120] For present purposes, however, the principal claim which will be brought by a beneficiary under the law of trusts would be a claim for breach of trust because there is no need to prove foreseeability nor causation in the common law sense of that term, and the remedies available for breach of trust are broader than those available for breach of a common law duty.

---

114   Cf *Re Miller's Deed Trusts* (1978) 75 LS Gaz 454; *Nestlé v National Westminster Bank plc* [1994] 1 All ER 118, [1993] 1 WLR 1260.

115   See generally Clerk and Lindsell, 2006, para 10–104 *et seq*.

116   [1995] 2 AC 207.

117   *Ibid*, 259.

118   *Carr-Glyn v Frearsons* [1999] Ch 326.

119   *Worby v Rosser* [2000] PNLR 140; *Gibbons v Nelsons* [2000] PNLR 734.

120   *Hilton v Barker Booth & Eastwood* [2005] 1 WLR 567, [2005] UKHL 8.

The fusion fallacy: merging equity with common law in error

There is a phenomenon known as the 'fusion fallacy' by reference to which common lawyers occasionally seek to rely on common law remedies (in particular damages) to impose liability to effect compensation on people who are trustees; whereas they should rely on the law on breach of trust. For example, in a sprawling range of litigation in the linked cases of *Concord Trust v Law Debenture Trust Corporation plc*[121] and *Law Debenture Trust Corporation v Elektrim Finance BV*[122] an investor in a bond issue sought to have a bond agreement terminated: under the terms of that agreement the trustee had a power to terminate the bond agreement in certain circumstances. Issues arose as to whether or not the trustee was liable in tort for activating its powers under the bond agreement improperly and whether or not the trustee was liable for breach of contract. It was held at first instance in *Concord Trust* by Smith J that the trustee had used its powers under the terms of the trust and of the contract properly.[123] It was held that if a trustee who is empowered to terminate a bond agreement does so incorrectly, then that trustee would be liable to the borrower for damages in contract.[124] It was held further that there would not be any liability in tort because the relationship between the parties was based on contract.[125] On these facts, it was held that the trustee bore no liability in tort nor in contract. It is a remarkable thing that the obligations of the trustee were considered to arise entirely at common law in this case, when the liabilities of a trustee lie properly in the law of trusts for breach of trust.

18.3.6 Valuation of the loss to the trust

The methodology for valuing the loss to the trust

A difficult question arises in relation to compensation for breach of trust: at what level should compensation be awarded in respect of property which fluctuates in value between the date of the breach and the date of judgment?

For the beneficiary, it would be preferable to claim the highest value for that property between those two dates. This approach, dubbed 'the highest intermediate balance', was adopted in *Jaffray v Marshall*.[126] Under the principle in *Jaffray v Marshall*, every presumption is to be made against the wrongdoing trustee. Therefore, if there had been an opportunity to realise (or sell) the assets during a continuing breach of trust, this would lead to the quantum of the compensation payable by the trustee imposing an obligation to make good the lost opportunity at its highest point. There was no distinction made in that case between shares and other types of property. The approach in *Jaffray* is based on a strict liability on the part of the trustee for any breach of trust, holding the trustee accountable for the highest possible loss in the circumstances.

---

121 [2005] UKHL 27 arising out of the same facts. This case is discussed in detail in Alastair Hudson, *The Law of Finance*, Sweet & Maxwell, 2009, para 33–41.

122 [2005] EWHC 1999 (Ch).

123 [2004] EWHC 270 (Ch).

124 *Concord Trust v Law Debenture Trust Corporation plc* [2005] UKHL 27, para [41], *per* Lord Scott.

125 *Ibid* at para [38], *per* Lord Scott.

126 [1994] 1 All ER 143, [1993] 1 WLR 1285; see also *Nant-y-glo and Blaina Ironworks Co v Grave* (1878) 12 Ch D 738.

However, Lord Browne-Wilkinson in *Target Holdings* overruled the decision in *Jaffray* as being wrong in principle. As considered above, in *Target Holdings*, the appropriate valuation was found to be that required to 'put [the trust fund] back to what it would have been had the breach not been committed'. The valuation is therefore that required to identify a level of compensation which is capable of restoring the value of the trust fund. Rather than selecting a specific formula, Lord Browne-Wilkinson preferred to leave the issue as a matter of evidence. The claimant beneficiary is therefore required to prove the level of compensation which equates to the loss caused to the trust by the breach of trust. The underlying intention is to return the trust fund to the position that it would have occupied but for the breach.

It has been held more generally by the courts that the measure of compensation for breach of trust would be 'fair compensation', that is to say, the difference between proper performance of the trust obligations and what the trustee actually achieved, not the least that could have been achieved.[127] It has been held that the trustee will not be liable for speculative or unliquidated losses: the beneficiary must be able to demonstrate that amounts have been lost.[128] However, it is not clear how this will interact with the principles of equitable compensation and their potentially broader ambit.[129]

No set-off permitted

The trustees are not permitted to set off a profit in one transaction against a loss in another transaction.[130] So, in *Dimes v Scott*,[131] trustees breached their trust by paying the income of the trust to the testator's widow but their delay in the administration of the trust had permitted them to buy more securities for the trust than would otherwise have been the case: it was held that the commission of the breach of trust was actionable in itself regardless of any profit which the trustees had made in some collateral transaction.[132] Similarly, in *Fletcher v Green*[133] the trustees had committed breaches of trust by lending money under a mortgage to a firm in which one of the trustees had a personal interest. When the mortgage was unwound at a loss and the money paid into court, that money was invested in securities which rose in value. It was held that the trustees should not be permitted to set off the loss which they had caused against the profit made on the acquisition of the securities. However, in *Bartlett v Barclays Bank*[134] the trustee was held liable for breach of trust in failing to supervise the board of directors of a company in which the trust held a controlling shareholding, and Brightman J considered the difficulty of applying this rule in many cases. The directors of the company had made two principal investments, one of which was a success and the other of which was a failure. It was held that in these circumstances it would be permissible to set off the loss on one project against the gain on the other project because, on

---

127 *Nestlé v National Westminster Bank plc* [1994] 1 All ER 118, [1993] 1 WLR 1260, CA.
128 *Palmer v Jones* (1862) 1 Vern 144.
129 Rickett, 2000.
130 *Dimes v Scott* (1828) 4 Russ 195, *per* Lord Lyndhurst. See also *Bartlett v Barclays Bank* [1980] Ch 515, 538; [1980] 1 All ER 139, 155, *per* Brightman J.
131 (1828) 4 Russ 195.
132 See also *Fletcher v Green* (1864) 33 Beav 426.
133 (1864) 33 Beav 426.
134 [1980] Ch 515, 538, [1980] 1 All ER 139, 155.

the facts of that case, the two separate transactions were nevertheless part of the same pattern of wrongful conduct committed by the board of directors.

Exemplary damages

It has been suggested by some commentators that trustees may be liable for exemplary damages if their behaviour in breaching their trust has been 'outrageous'.[135] Under English law, however, it has been held that the court will only impose liability on a trustee to the extent that a trustee has caused a loss through her breach of trust, and that a court will not impose exemplary liability over and above that loss.[136] This approach has also been taken in Australia.[137] The suggestion has been made that the position in England may be susceptible to change with a change in approach to exemplary damages more generally.[138] However, it is suggested that, in line with the approach taken in the rest of this chapter, the liability of the trustees is to account for any loss occasioned by a breach of trust and not to account for anything outwith such a loss.

18.3.7 Some reservations about *Target Holdings v Redferns*

Jaffray v Marshall,[139] considered immediately above, was said to be wrongly decided in principle by Lord Browne-Wilkinson in *Target Holdings*, on the ground that its award of compensation was assessed on the basis of an assumption of a potentially impossible sale (that is, a sale which could not have taken place in practice, even though an open-market value could be estimated for that time). On the contrary, the true purpose of compensation was said in *Target Holdings* to be to make good the loss, even though the right of action based on breach of trust technically arose immediately. This is a possible weakness with the decision in *Target* in that there would have been a valid action against Redferns if such an action had been brought before Redferns had acquired the mortgage security for Target, but that action appeared to dissolve because Redferns had remedied the breach before it came to light.

One further problem with *Target* is that the beneficiary is not able to bring a claim against a trustee for breach of trust unless that beneficiary has suffered some financial loss directly as a result of the breach of trust. There may be other breaches of trust, for example, in a situation in which investments are to be restricted only to ethical investment funds and the trustees contravene those instructions, which will generate no entitlement to compensation or reconstitution of the trust fund unless there has been financial loss. So, if the trustee were to invest in unethical investments in breach of trust but nevertheless made a profit then no action for compensation would lie because compensation is only for financial loss and not

---

135 See Hayton and Mitchell, 2005, 706. This approach has been applied in relation to breaches of fiduciary duty elsewhere in the Commonwealth.
136 *Re Brogden* (1886) 38 Ch D 546, 557, *per* North J. See also *Vyse v Foster* (1872) LR 3 Ch App 309, 333.
137 *Harris v Digital Pulse Pty Ltd* (2003) 56 NSWLR 298, *per* Heydon JA; see also, however, the remarks of Mason P to the contrary.
138 See Hayton and Mitchell, 2005, 706; making reference to *Kuddas v Chief Constable of Leicestershire* [2002] 2 AC 122.
139 [1994] 1 All ER 143, [1993] 1 WLR 1285.

other types of loss. In this example, however, the trustee would be obliged to bear the cost of replacing the unauthorised investments with authorised investments. The appropriate claim against the trustee would be for an injunction, considered in Chapter 27, to prevent continued breach of the trust terms and requiring observance of those terms in future.

The more complex problem might be in circumstances in which property with only senti-mental value is disposed of. Perhaps the property is intrinsically valuable but in a way which the decision in *Target Holdings* does not accept, because *Target* assumes the only significant value to be an open-market value. The requirement to demonstrate loss which can be quan-tifiable in terms of money compensation gives the beneficiary no effective remedy. This approach indicates that the right of the beneficiary is to be measured in terms of re-sale value and not in relation to the intrinsic value of taking a proprietary right over specific, identified trust property.

18.3.8 The claim for breach of trust after termination of the trust

Where property is paid away in breach of trust, the question arises at what point the trust terminates; and furthermore as to the nature of the claim which can be brought when the trust property has been paid away.

When does the trust end?

In deciding whether or not a claim for breach of trust can be brought after termination of a trust, it is important to know when a trust ends. It has been suggested that a trust ends when the trust property is transferred away.[140] However, it is not clear, in the wake of the decision of the House of Lords in *Westdeutsche Landesbank Girozentrale v Islington LBC*,[141] how this position can be maintained on principle. It would appear that the trust, that is, the obliga-tion of the trustee, does not come to an end when the property is transferred away. A trust is not simply title to property but also involves obligations of trusteeship to the beneficiaries which are imposed on the trustee personally. Therefore, the trusteeship must necessarily continue where there is some order either for reconstitution of the fund, or for the payment of compensation. The fact that such an order would be operative on the trustee must imply that obligations which arose by virtue of the trust continue to be operative too. The imposition of any equitable remedy on a trustee, whether personal or proprietary, requires the continuation of the trusteeship.

A trust can be deemed to have been terminated, for example when its purpose has been superseded by another structure and all of the property transferred out of the trust with the intention that the trust will have no further activities. So, in *Southampton City Council v Southampton Median Mosque Trust Ltd*[142] a charitable purpose trust was formed for the creation of a new mosque in Southampton (to obtain planning permission and so forth) but issues arose as to who would be responsible for its construction. Consequently, after meet-ings between all of the parties, a company limited by guarantee was formed for this purpose

---

140 Davern, 1997, 86.
141 [1996] AC 669.
142 [2010] EWHC 2376 (Ch).

and issues arose as to the purpose of the trust. It was held that the trust was deemed to have been terminated and its activities passed to the company instead.

Issues with holding trustees to account

Where there is a *Vandervell*-style[143] trust obligation (where legal and equitable title to the trust fund are transferred together) that is validly performed (that is, there is no equitable claim against trustee), it can properly be said that the trust has ended because the trusteeship has ended. The acid test will always be whether the trustee has acted in any sense in breach of trust in the conduct of that *Vandervell*-style transfer, or whether she breached some contractual warranty concerning the manner in which that transfer was to be performed. Where there is no claim in equity in respect of the trusteeship, it can be said, in hindsight, that the trust has come to an end.

The counter-argument might be that the trust in *Target* terminated at the date of transfer, and therefore there is no need to raise the argument that there be reconstitution of the trust fund, on the basis that there would be no fund to reconstitute in any event.[144] The argument runs that once the trust is dead, it cannot be brought back to life. The issue is then whether the trust had transformed into a chose in action against the trustee personally equal to the value of the trust fund. However, this would be to overlook the fact that equity will still give effect to many of those equitable obligations that made up the trust by means of equitable tracing claims, personal claims for dishonest assistance or knowing receipt, or subrogation claims. It must be the case that property acquired as a result of such a claim must be held on trust in the same manner that the property was held on trust before the unconscionable event which gave rise to the claim. Otherwise, when the fund property is got in, it would not be subject to the terms of that same express trust. It could not be established, on principle, that breach of trust would be remedied by an order to deal with property otherwise than in accordance with the trust that was originally breached.

Further to *Target Holdings v Redferns*, there is no liability to reconstitute to the trust fund where the underlying commercial transaction has been performed. Suppose a situation in which a bank conducts a transaction in a context where it is in a fiduciary position in relation to its client. Suppose the customer invests an amount of capital with that bank with the investment aim of taking a position only on the performance of ordinary shares on the FTSE–100. That bank will be liable to reconstitute the fund placed with it if it takes unacceptable risks with that fund in breach of trust and causes loss to the client, but not if the underlying commercial purpose of the transaction has been performed.[145] Therefore, the bank would not be liable for a fall in price of shares, but it would be liable if it invested in bonds instead of shares which fell markedly in value.

So, in *Target Holdings v Redferns*, obtaining security over property was the commercial purpose of the trust. The loss suffered by the beneficiary did not flow from the technical breach of trust. The issue is therefore whether the appropriate claim is breach of contract, negligence or breach of trust. It is submitted that allocation of risk and not conscionability is

143   *Vandervell v IRC* [1967] 2 AC 291; see section 5.7 above.
144   See Davern, 1997.
145   *Target Holdings v Redferns* [1996] 1 AC 421.

the only useful analysis of this issue in relation to the share dealing transactions considered immediately above.[146] While it is an established principle of equity that the imposition of a fiduciary duty cannot be used to enlarge contractual duties, in the application of rules of equity, it is suggested that there ought to be a conceptual difference between a commercial trust and a traditional family trust, such that non-compliance with instructions becomes really a matter of contract rather than a matter of trust in commercial cases.

18.3.9 Breach of trust in relation to investment of the trust fund

For a detailed consideration of liability for breach of trust as it relates to the investment of the trust property, see para 9.9.1 above.

18.4 DEFENCES TO LIABILITY FOR BREACH OF TRUST

While there are, potentially, a large number of defences to a claim for breach of trust, this section highlights the most significant of them.

18.4.1 Lack of a causal link between breach and loss

The claimant is required to prove a causal link between the loss suffered and the breach of trust.[147] If there is no link between the breach of trust and the loss, then the trustee will not be liable for any loss that is suffered. The discussion of *Target Holdings v Redferns* in this chapter has demonstrated this principle.

18.4.2 Breach committed by another trustee

The alternative defence which an individual trustee may put forward is that the breach of trust was the responsibility of another trustee. One trustee is not held to be liable for the actions or omissions of any other trustee.[148] So, for example, a trustee will be liable for custody of money only where that trustee has given a receipt for that property, and not otherwise.[149] A trustee will only be liable in this context for any wilful default[150] or for a failure to ensure, for example, that money has been properly invested, such that liability will not attach to a trustee who has attempted to ascertain that the other trustee has carried out her obligations properly.[151] There is an obligation on a trustee to take action to protect the beneficiaries in the event that she learns of a breach of trust committed by another trustee,[152] for example, by beginning a claim for restoration of the trust fund.[153]

---

146 Hudson, 1999:1.
147 *Nestlé v National Westminster Bank plc (No 2)* [1993] 1 WLR 1260, [1994] 1 All ER 118.
148 *Townley v Sherborne* (1633) Bridg 35, (1633) W & TLC 577.
149 TA 1925, s 30(1); *Re Fryer* (1857) 3 K & J 317; *Brice v Stokes* (1805) 11 Ves 319.
150 *Re Vickery* [1931] 1 Ch 572, 582.
151 *Thompson v Finch* (1856) 22 Beav 316; *Hanbury v Kirkland* (1829) 3 Sim 265. Cf *Re Munton* [1927] 1 Ch 262.
152 *Brice v Stokes* (1805) 11 Ves Jr 319; *Oliver v Court* (1820) 8 Price 127, 166; *Booth v Booth* (1838) 1 Beav 125; *Gough v Smith* [1872] WN 18.
153 *Earl Powlet v Herbert* (1791) 1 Ves 297.

18.4.3 Failure by the beneficiary to alleviate loss

Failure by the beneficiary to minimise her own loss does not constitute a full defence to a claim for breach of trust, but it may serve to reduce the trustee's liability. Where the beneficiary fails to take straightforward measures to protect herself against further loss, after due notice and opportunity to do so, then the trustee will not be liable for any further loss arising after the beneficiary could have taken action to protect herself.[154]

18.4.4 Release

Where the beneficiaries agree formally to release the trustee from any liability, the equitable doctrine of release will operate so as to protect that trustee from any liability arising from her breach of trust.[155] However, that does not prevent the beneficiaries from seeking equitable relief in respect of any factor which was not made known to them at the time of granting the release or which arises outside the terms of that release.[156] Therefore, where employees signed a release form in respect of any breach of duty by their employer, it was held that this would not prevent a claim for relief in relation to stigma attached to them when it subsequently emerged that their employer bank had been dealing dishonestly.[157]

18.4.5 Trustee exemption clause

Where the trust instrument contains a clause excluding or limiting the trustees' liabilities, that exemption of liability provision will generally be enforced.[158] This position was considered in great detail in section 8.5.1.[159] The question in recent cases has been as to the form of exemption clause which will be enforced. A typical form of exemption clause is one which excludes the trustee's liability except in the event of the trustee's dishonesty. It was held in *Armitage v Nurse*[160] that such an exemption clause would be effective even to exclude liability for the trustees' own negligence in the performance of their duties. Clearly, this approach greatly limits the extent of the trustee's liability if the trustee was sufficiently well-advised to have insisted on such a contractual provision from the outset. Ordinarily, as considered above, the trustee would be liable for all loss resulting from her breach of trust without needing to identify fault or foreseeability: that a breach of trust led to loss would be sufficient to impose liability.[161] A more restricted approach was taken in *Walker v Stones*,[162] in which an exemption clause that sought to exclude the trustee's liability for all actions except dishonesty was held to be effective in general terms, but not so as to exclude liability

---

154 *Corporacion Nacional del Cobre de Chile v Sogemin Metals Ltd* [1997] 1 WLR 1396, 1403; *Canson Enterprises Ltd v Boughton & Co* (1991) 85 DLR (4th) 129, 161.
155 *Lyall v Edwards* (1861) 6 H & N 337, (1861) 158 ER 139; *Ecclesiastical Commissioners for England v North Eastern Railway Co* (1877) 4 Ch D 845; *Turner v Turner* (1880) 14 Ch D 829.
156 *BCCI v Ali* [2000] 3 All ER 51.
157 *Ibid.* Cf *Malik v BCCI* [1997] 3 All ER 1.
158 *Armitage v Nurse* [1998] Ch 241; *Bogg v Raper* (1998) *The Times*, 12 April; *Wight v Olswang* [2000] WTLR 783; *Walker v Stones* [2001] QB 902. Cf *Rothmere Farms Pty Ltd v Belgravia Pty Ltd* (1999) 2 ITELR 159.
159 See para 8.5.1 above.
160 [1998] Ch 241; *Galmerrow Securities Ltd v National Westminster Bank plc* [2002] WTLR 125.
161 *Target Holdings v Redferns* [1996] 1 AC 421.
162 [2001] QB 902.

in circumstances in which the trustee could not reasonably have believed that her actions would be considered to be honest.

Underlying these decisions is a fundamental difference of opinion as to the minimum content of trusteeship. In *Armitage v Nurse*, the court took the view that exclusion clauses ought to be upheld because otherwise professional trustees would have refused to hold the office in question; however, in *Walker v Stones*, the court doubted the breadth of that proposition and preferred instead to look objectively at the probity of the trustee's actions.[163] Nevertheless, the principle is generally accepted that trustee exemption clauses will be effective to limit the trustee's liability; the only exception to that principle will be if the trustee has acted dishonestly. It does appear that liability for acting negligently can be excluded.[164]

18.4.6 Excuses for breach of trust

There is a power for the court in s 61 of the TA 1925 to grant partial or total relief for breach of trust. That section provides that:

> If it appears to the court that a trustee . . . is or may be personally liable for any breach of trust . . . but has acted honestly and reasonably, and ought fairly to be excused for the breach of trust and for omitting to obtain the directions of the court in the matter in which he committed such breach, then the court may relieve him either wholly or partly from personal liability for the same.

Therefore, the question is whether or not a trustee has acted honestly such that the court considers it appropriate to relieve her of her liability. This provision was directed primarily at the perceived harshness of the case law on breach of trust, which tended to hold amateur trustees liable for the whole of any loss suffered by beneficiaries in circumstances in which there was no reason to suppose that those trustees had held themselves out as having any particular competence to manage the trust to any particular standard. So, in *Re Evans (Deceased)*,[165] a daughter acted as administrator in her deceased father's estate, holding that estate on trust for herself and her brother beneficially as next-of-kin under the intestacy rules. When she came to distribute the estate she assumed that her brother was dead because she had not heard from him for 30 years. The defendant bought an insurance policy to pay out half the value of the estate in the event that her brother re-appeared. Her brother did re-appear four years later and claimed that the defendant had breached the trust by taking all of the fund for herself beneficially, and claimed further that the insurance policy would be insufficient to meet his total loss. The judge concluded that the defendant ought to be granted partial relief: her liability was limited to the amount which could be met from the sale of a house forming part of the estate. Otherwise, the approach of the courts has been to take a case-by-case approach to relief under this provision, dependent usually on whether or not the trustee has acted reasonably[166] in the manner in which she might have handled her own

---

163 Cf para 8.5.5 above and para 21.2.4 below. Cf *In Williams WT* (2000) 2 ITELR 313, permitting such clauses in the USA.

164 *Armitage v Nurse* [1998] Ch 241.

165 [1999] 2 All ER 777; Lowry and Edmunds, 2002.

166 *Chapman v Browne* [1902] 1 Ch 785.

property,[167] or whether the trustee acted unreasonably by leaving the trust property in the hands of a third party without good reason[168] or on an erroneous understanding of the law.[169] It has been held that if a trustee has acted grossly negligently in breaching her trust obligations – in that case by paying trust moneys out to people who were not entitled to them on the terms of the trust – then the relief under s 61 would not be available to the trustee.[170]

On this basis, there may be a defence for the trustee where she can demonstrate that there was a good reason for the sale or misapplication of the trust property.[171] Therefore, where a trustee breaches the precise terms of a trust by investing in property outwith the investment powers contained in the trust deed, in circumstances where the trustee is able to demonstrate that the technical breach of trust protected the beneficiaries from losses which they would otherwise have suffered, it will be open to that trustee to maintain that the breach of trust is therefore not actionable. At one level it would be necessary for the beneficiary to demonstrate loss in any event. On the authority of *Nestlé v National Westminster Bank plc*,[172] even if a small loss had been suffered, it is open to a trustee to demonstrate that the investment strategy applied was adopted both for the long-term benefit of the beneficiaries and to guard against future risk to the fund. If proven, such an argument would constitute a good defence to a claim for compensation for breach of trust arising out of such a loss on the basis that it shielded the fund from future loss even if it failed to generate the maximum short-term gain.[173] Evidently, the trustee would be required to prove that the adopted course of action was indeed wellfounded in accordance with market practice, and further that any loss was reasonable to achieve that alternative goal.[174]

18.4.7 Action not in connection with fiduciary duties, or action permitted by the terms of the trust

Most obviously, the trustee will not be liable for breach of trust in circumstances in which either the terms of the trust permit the action complained of[175] or if the action complained of is not connected to the trustee's fiduciary duties.[176] For example, in *Ward v Brunt*,[177] a family farm business was left without anyone to run it after Norman Ward died. Norman had left the farm to be held equally for his grandchildren such that the farm business was to be run by them as partners. Susan, one of the beneficiaries under this arrangement, gave up her work as a teacher to take over the running of the farm because no one else was prepared to do so. Susan was thus a fiduciary in relation to the other partners. Norman's executors offered Susan an option to purchase the freehold over the farm, in accordance with the terms of Norman's will, which Susan subsequently agreed to exercise. Thus, Susan acquired the

---

167 *Re Stuart* [1897] 2 Ch 583; *Re Barker* (1898) 77 LT 712. See also *Perrins v Bellamy* [1898] 2 Ch 521, *per* Kekewich J.
168 *Wynne v Tempest* (1897) 13 TLR 360; *Re Second East Dulwich etc Building Society* (1899) 68 LJ Ch 196.
169 *Ward-Smith v Jebb* (1964) 108 SJ 919.
170 *Barraclough v Mell* [2005] EWHC B17 (Ch), [98], *per* Judge Behrens QC.
171 *Ibid.*
172 *Ibid.*
173 [1993] 1 WLR 1260, [1994] 1 All ER 118.
174 On these issues, see generally Chapter 9 in relation to the investment of trust funds.
175 *Galmerrow Securities Ltd v National Westminster Bank plc* [2002] WTLR 125.
176 *Ward v Brunt* [2000] WTLR 731.
177 *Ibid.*

freehold over the land and Susan personally became landlord to the business which she had agreed to run on behalf of the partnership. In time, Susan decided to serve a notice to quit on the farm business. The other beneficiaries contended that this service of the notice to quit was in breach of Susan's fiduciary duties as manager of the trust's business. It was held that Susan did not breach her fiduciary duties to the partnership in acquiring the freehold of the farm for herself and in consequence she was entitled to exercise all of the rights of a freeholder to serve a notice to quit on tenants of the property. Furthermore, Susan was not liable for the profits which she made from having a freehold with vacant possession after the termination of the lease. Therefore, there is no liability for breach of trust, even if the fiduciary is acting contrary to the interests of the beneficiaries, provided that the powers which the fiduciary is exercising accrue to her in a personal capacity or derive from her beneficial capacity. In this case, Susan's powers accrue to her in a personal capacity and derive from her beneficial ownership of the freehold.

18.4.8 Concurrence by a beneficiary in a breach of trust

If a beneficiary concurs or acquiesces in a breach of trust, then that beneficiary is estopped from seeking to recover compensation for that breach of trust from any trustees to whom that concurrence was proffered.[178] To demonstrate that a beneficiary has concurred in a breach of trust that beneficiary must have had sufficient knowledge of the breach of trust. The principles have been explained in the following manner:[179]

> The ... court has to consider all the circumstances in which the concurrence of the *cestui qui trust* was given with a view to seeing whether it is fair and equitable that, having given his concurrence, he should afterwards turn round and sue the trustees; ... subject to this, it is not necessary that he should know that what he is concurring in is a breach of trust, provided that he fully understand what he is concurring in, and ... it is not necessary that he should himself have directly benefited by the breach of trust.

Therefore, the most significant underlying factor is the fairness and equity in the beneficiary bringing an action for compensation for breach of trust. In essence, one cannot have known of and agreed to something in relation to which one subsequently seeks to recover compensation.

18.4.9 Change of position

There is authority to suggest that the defence of change of position may potentially have been available for claims for breach of trust. This defence is considered in detail in Chapter 19. The only defence which would have been available in *Haugesund Kommune v Depfa*

---

178 *White v White* (1798–1804) 5 Ves 554; *Evans v Benyon* (1888) 37 Ch D 329; *Re Pauling's Settlement Trusts* [1964] Ch 303, at 335, [1962] 1 WLR 86, at 106. Cf *Chillingworth v Chambers* [1896] 1 Ch 685.

179 *Re Pauling's Settlement Trusts* [1962] 1 WLR 86, at 108, *per* Wilberforce J. See also *Re Garnett* (1885) 31 Ch D 1, a case dealing with release but adopted for this purpose; and *Holder v Holder* [1968] Ch 353; *Re Freeston's Charity* [1978] Ch 741, relating specifically to acquiescence. See further *Spellson v George* (1992) 26 NSWLR 666.

ACS Bank[180] was the defence of change of position.[181] It was held that this was a transaction in which the recipient of the payments knew that they would have to be repaid and therefore that the defence of change of position would not apply.[182]

18.5 ALLOCATING CLAIMS

There are two issues considered in short compass in this section. First, how does the claimant decide which of a potentially large number of claims to pursue? Secondly, how does the court decide how liability for loss suffered by the claimant is allocated between a large number of defendants?

18.5.1 Choice between remedies

As considered above, there is a possibility of a number of remedies, ranging from those associated with tracing claims, to those associated with restoration of the value of specific property, to those based on compensation.[183] There is then a question as to the remedy which the beneficiary is required to pursue in all the circumstances. The equitable doctrine of election arises in such situations to provide that it is open to the claimant to elect between alternative remedies.[184] In *Tang v Capacious Investments*, the possibility of parallel remedies arose in relation to a breach of trust, for the plaintiff beneficiary to claim an account of profits from the malfeasant trustee or to claim damages representing the lost profits to the trust. It was held that these two remedies existed in the alternative and therefore that the plaintiff could claim both, not being required to elect between them until judgment was awarded in its favour. Clearly, the court would not permit double recovery in respect of the same loss, thus requiring election between those remedies ultimately.

18.5.2 Allocation of liability between defendants

The manner in which the courts apportion liability between the trustees was considered above.[185] There is a difficulty in deciding which of a number of defendants will be required to make good the claimant's loss. It may be that the first defendant acted deliberately to defraud the claimant, whereas the other defendants would claim to be less culpable because they did not act deliberately, or because the first defendant's actions were the primary factor in causing the loss, or some similar explanation. In such a situation, the court will typically require the defendant who is most culpable to bear the larger share of the loss in fact.[186] It has been suggested that the courts will typically take into account the following factors: how large a role each defendant played in causing the loss; the level of moral blameworthiness

---

180 [2010] EWCA Civ 579.
181 Cf *Goss v Chilcott* [1997] 2 All ER 110, [1996] AC 788.
182 The approach of Pill LJ to change of position was cited with approval in *Ibrahim v Barclays Bank* [2011] EWHC 1897 (Ch).
183 *Target Holdings v Redferns* [1996] 1 AC 421.
184 *Tang v Capacious Investments Ltd* [1996] 1 All ER 193. See Birks, 2000:1, 8.
185 See para 18.2.4 above.
186 *Monetary Fund v Hashim* (1994) *The Times*, 11 October; *Dairy Containers Ltd v NZI Bank Ltd* [1995] 2 NZLR 30; *Re Mulligan* [1998] 1 NZLR 481; *Dubai Aluminium Co Ltd v Salaam* [1999] 1 Lloyd's Rep 415, CA.

attaching to each defendant; and the extent to which each defendant had taken some personal benefit from the breach of trust.[187] Of course, it should not be forgotten that each defendant to a claim for breach of trust is potentially liable for the entire loss if, for example, the other defendants are bankrupt at the time of the trial.

18.5.3 Limitation period

One point which has arisen recently is whether there is any limitation period on an action for account. It has been held that the appropriate period is that for common law fraud, unless there has been a dishonest breach of fiduciary duty, in which case there is no period applicable.[188]

---

187 Mitchell, 2000.
188 *Coulthard v Disco Mix Club Ltd* [2000] 1 WLR 707; *Paragon Finance v DB Thakerar* [1999] 1 All ER 400; *Raja v Lloyds TSB Bank plc* (2000) *The Times*, 16 May; *Cia de Seguros Imperio v Heath (REBX) Ltd* [2001] 1 WLR 112.

Chapter 19

Tracing

OVERVIEW

In situations in which the claimant seeks to identify a specific item of property (or its 'clean' substitute) in the hands of the defendant, the claimant will pursue a common law 'following' claim to require the return of that specific item of property.[1]

The more complex situation is that in which the claimant's property has passed into the hands of the defendant but has been substituted for another item of property in which the claimant has never previously had any proprietary rights. The claimant may pursue either a common law tracing claim,[2] or an equitable tracing claim[3] to assert title to the substitute property as being representative of the claimant's original property. In the event that the original property or the substitute property has been mixed with other property then the claimant will only be able to bring an equitable tracing claim, because common law tracing claims are restricted to situations in which the property against which the claim is brought remains separate from all other property. An equitable tracing claim requires that the claimant had some pre-existing equitable proprietary right in that property[4] – although the validity of this latter rule has been doubted by many commentators.[5]

The particular difficulty arises in relation to money passed through bank accounts. English law treats each payment of money as being effectively distinct tangible property such that, when a bank account containing such money is run overdrawn, that property is said to disappear.[6] Consequently, there can be no tracing claim in respect of property which has ceased to exist.[7]

---

1   *FC Jones (A Firm) v Jones* [1996] 3 WLR 703 – considered below at para 19.2.3.
2   *Ibid.*
3   *Pilcher v Rawlins* (1872) LR 7 Ch App 259; *Westdeutsche Landesbank Girozentrale v Islington LBC* [1996] AC 669; *Boscawen v Bajwa* [1996] 1 WLR 328.
4   *Re Diplock's Estate* [1948] Ch 465; *Boscawen v Bajwa* [1996] 1 WLR 328.
5   Eg, Smith, 1997.
6   Eg, *Westdeutsche Landesbank Girozentrale v Islington LBC* [1996] AC 669.
7   *Roscoe v Winder* [1915] 1 Ch 62.

The process of tracing, and identifying property over which a remedy is sought, is different from the issue of asserting a remedy in respect of that property.[8] *Tracing is simply the process of identifying property against which the claimant may bring a claim; whereas the question as to the form of remedy which the court may award in support of that property right is a separate question. Aside from the loss of the right to trace, remedies in relation to tracing claims may typically include: the establishment of a constructive trust, an equitable charge, a lien, possibly a resulting trust, and subrogation.*[9] *In relation to mixtures of trust and other money held in bank accounts, a variety of approaches has been taken in the courts from the application of the old first-in, first-out principle,*[10] *to the establishment of proportionate shares in any substitute property.*[11]

Defences available in relation to tracing claims include change of position,[12] *bona fide purchase of the property for value,*[13] *estoppel by representation,*[14] *and passing on.*[15]

19.1 TRACING – UNDERSTANDING THE NATURE OF THE CLAIM

19.1.1 Introduction

This chapter considers the law relating to tracing. The function of the law of tracing is to enable the owner of property to recover that property in the event that it is taken from her involuntarily. By 'involuntarily' is meant that the owner has not agreed to any transfer of title in that property to the defendant. It may be that the property has been stolen, or taken in breach of trust, or taken by mistake: whatever the cause, the owner has not consented fully to giving that property up to the defendant.

Tracing operates on three levels. At the first level it might be that all the owner is seeking to do is to recover her original property from the defendant. At the second level, the owner might be seeking to recover both her original property and any profits which have been realised from the defendant's use of the property. At the third level, the owner may not be able to recover her original property because that property has been mixed with other property, or it cannot be found, or some other person has acquired good title to it by virtue, for example, of having purchased it in good faith.[16] In such a situation, the owner may seek to establish property rights against some other property which the defendant has acquired by using the original property. Therefore, the claimant is seeking to assert title to substitute property, which might take the form of sale proceeds received on the sale of the original property, or of property acquired with those sale proceeds, or of some composite property in which the original property has been combined in some way. This substitute property we will refer to as the 'traceable proceeds' of the original property. The reason why we will use the term 'traceable proceeds' is that the owner's rights in the original property are *traced* into the substitute property. This third category of cases is clearly the most difficult and will form the

---

8 *Boscawen v Bajwa* [1996] 1 WLR 328.
9 As considered at section 19.5 below.
10 *Clayton's Case* (1816) 1 Mer 572.
11 *Barlow Clowes International Ltd (In Liquidation) and Others v Vaughan and Others* [1992] 4 All ER 22.
12 *Lipkin Gorman v Karpnale* [1991] 2 AC 548; *Scottish Equitable v Derby* [2001] 3 All ER 818.
13 *Westdeutsche Landesbank Girozentrale v Islington LBC* [1996] AC 669.
14 *National Westminster Bank plc v Somer International (UK) Ltd* [2001] Lloyd's Rep Bank 263.
15 *Kleinwort Benson v Birmingham City Council* [1996] 4 All ER 733, CA.
16 *Westdeutsche Landesbank Girozentrale v Islington LBC* [1996] AC 669.

principal focus of this chapter.[17] A worked example of the issues raised is given below; however, there are other matters which require mention first.

There is an important point of distinction to be made between seeking to establish title in the original item of property which was previously owned, and seeking to establish title to substitute property (or traceable proceeds) which is not the exact property which was previously owned. Clearly, the former case requires the claimant to say 'That property is mine and I want it back'. In many cases this will be a case of fact and proof. Suppose my car is taken from me – a car which I will be able to identify by its registration plates and chassis number – I will wish to have that very car returned to me once I have proved that the car in the defendant's possession bears my number plates and chassis number and is therefore demonstrably my car. However, suppose that my car was taken from me and sold to someone who has moved, such that I cannot now find my car. In that case, I would be forced to bring proceedings against the person who took the car from me to recover the sale proceeds of the car from her: that is, money which had never previously belonged to me but which is clearly derived directly from the sale of my property. To establish such a claim would require me to *trace* my property rights from the car into the cash which the defendant has received. The former situation is clearly a process that recognises my original ownership, whereas the latter situation involves the proposition that it is somehow morally 'correct' for the defendant to give up the money which was received from the wrongful sale of my car. That process of following and tracing rights in property in these ways is our principal focus in this chapter.

The conceptual problem that these issues pose is the difficulty of the claimant trying to establish rights in property in which she had never previously had any rights. For example, if a thief steals my property and sells it to a *bona fide* purchaser, this sale would have the result that the *bona fide* purchaser[18] would take good title in equity to the property.[19] I will wish to argue that I have property rights in the sale proceeds which the thief has realised from the sale of the stolen goods. Of course, I have never had property rights in that particular money before. However, common sense would dictate that I ought to be entitled to take that money from the thief to make good my loss as a victim of crime. This also serves the subsidiary benefit of punishing the thief.[20]

Before launching into the law relating to tracing, it is important to understand the factual problems which generate it. This worked example should illustrate the issues. Suppose the following set of facts:

> Timothy, a trustee, physically removed a painting which formed part of a trust fund in breach of trust. Timothy will therefore bear the liability of breach of trust considered in Chapter 18. Suppose then that the painting was transferred by Timothy to another person, Anne, his accomplice. There are three possible, factual scenarios to consider,

17 The word 'owned' here is an admittedly ugly usage. As will emerge from the ensuing discussion, there are different forms of tracing claim at common law and in equity, as well as claims to vindicate rights in property. The word 'owned' will serve, for the time being, to cover a broad range of possible states of affairs at law and in equity.
18 Ie, a *bona fide* purchaser for value without notice of the victim's rights in the property; or 'Equity's darling'.
19 *Pilcher v Rawlins* (1872) LR 7 Ch App 259; *Westdeutsche Landesbank Girozentrale v Islington LBC* [1996] AC 669.
20 More specific reading in this area is the excellent Smith, 1997.

as set out below, under which the beneficiaries might seek to establish rights in the property.

(1) Identifying the original property

First, suppose that Timothy transferred the painting to Anne, his accomplice, and that Timothy has no money to make good the loss to the trust fund in relation to his liability for breach of trust. Therefore, although the beneficiaries would ordinarily proceed against Timothy for a breach of trust claim,[21] it is clear that that claim will be of no value to them if Timothy has no money to make good their loss. Suppose that Anne still has the painting in her possession at the time of the claim. In that circumstance, all that the beneficiaries would be required to do would be positively to identify the painting as being the one taken in breach of trust, and to have that painting restored to the trust fund. This claim will be considered under the general heading of 'common law tracing' (or, more specifically, 'following') at section 19.2 below.[22] We could describe this claim as simply vindicating the beneficiaries' right in the painting by ordering a retransfer of the painting to the trust fund.[23] Lord Millett has described this notion of following in this fashion: '[f]ollowing is the process of following the same asset as it moves from hand to hand.'[24]

(2) Substitute property

Secondly, suppose that Timothy transferred the painting to Anne but that Anne sells the painting on to a third person. If Timothy had no money to make good the loss to the trust fund then he would not be able to satisfy a judgment based on breach of trust. Suppose further that Anne did not have the painting in her possession at the time of the claim. Rather, the painting had been sold to a *bona fide* purchaser for value without notice of the breach of trust and is now unobtainable (for reasons considered later).[25] Clearly, the beneficiaries cannot now recover the original painting. Suppose, however, that Anne does still have the proceeds of sale of the painting remaining in cash in an envelope under her bed.

The claim on behalf of the beneficiaries is more complex in this second example because the property at issue is not the original property, the painting, which the trustees had previously held on trust for the beneficiaries; rather, it constitutes the sale proceeds received on transfer of that property. This money did not form a part of the trust fund. However, it is clearly identifiable as a substitute for the property which Timothy and Anne took from the trust. If the sale proceeds have been held distinct from all other property then the beneficiaries may be able to bring a common law tracing claim.[26] What the beneficiaries would be required to do here would be properly described as 'tracing', as opposed to merely 'following' as explained below, because the property in Anne's hands is different property acquired as a

---

21 *Target Holdings v Redferns* [1996] 1 AC 421, [1995] 3 WLR 352, [1995] 3 All ER 785.
22 *FC Jones (A Firm) v Jones* [1996] 3 WLR 703.
23 *Foskett v McKeown* [2001] 1 AC 102.
24 *Ibid.*
25 *Pilcher v Rawlins* (1872) LR 7 Ch App 259; *Westdeutsche Landesbank Girozentrale v Islington LBC* [1996] AC 669.
26 *FC Jones (A Firm) v Jones* [1996] 3 WLR 703 – considered below at para 19.2.3.

substitute for the painting.[27] Nevertheless, the claim here is comparatively straightforward because the sale proceeds are clearly a 'clean' substitute for the painting and have not been mixed with any other property.

As will emerge from the discussion which follows, there is authority that a common law tracing claim will allow a claimant to establish rights in property in circumstances in which the original property and any substitute property, or property added to the original property and forming part of it, are kept distinct from all other property.[28] For example, provided that the sale proceeds were kept in a bank account separate from all other moneys, it would be possible for the claimant to establish rights on both the sale proceeds and any interest earned on that money held in the account.[29]

If the sale proceeds had been mixed with other property then the claim becomes more complex because common law tracing does not extend to mixtures of property.[30] The claim to be brought in this latter example would be an 'equitable tracing claim'. This form of claim is considered next.

(3) Mixtures of property

Thirdly, as before, suppose that Timothy has transferred the painting in breach of trust to Anne. Timothy has no money to make good the loss to the trust fund. Suppose that Anne does not have the painting in her possession at the time of the claim. Rather, the painting has been sold and is now unobtainable.[31] Importantly, Anne does hold the proceeds of sale of the painting separately, but rather Anne has paid that money into a bank account along with other money unconnected to the breach of trust. Therefore, the sale proceeds derived from the sale of the painting have been mixed with other property unconnected with the breach of trust.

This situation is similar to example (2) above in that the original trust property has been substituted for money. Therefore, the claim is an equitable tracing claim, seeking to assert that it would be unconscionable for Timothy and Anne to refuse to transfer the money to the trust as a substitute for the painting taken from the trust fund. The added difficulty here is that the money which was substituted for the painting has been irretrievably commingled with other money. The issue considered in detail later in this chapter is how to award a proprietary right to the beneficiaries over such a mixed fund. The cases have taken a number of different approaches. In short, the claimant may be entitled to a charge over the mixed fund,[32] or entitled to proprietary rights in property acquired from that mixed fund,[33] or

---

27 *Foskett v McKeown* [2001] 1 AC 102.

28 *FC Jones (A Firm) v Jones* [1996] 3 WLR 703.

29 *Ibid.*

30 *Taylor v Plumer* (1815) 3 M & S 562; *Agip v Jackson* [1990] Ch 265, 286, *per* Millett J; [1991] Ch 547 CA; *El Ajou v Dollar Land Holdings* [1993] 3 All ER 717. However, see Smith, 1995:2, 240, suggesting that *Taylor v Plumer* in fact turned on questions of equitable tracing.

31 Again, perhaps because it has been sold to a *bona fide* purchaser without notice of the beneficiaries' rights.

32 *Re Diplock's Estate* [1948] Ch 465.

33 Variously calculated in *Clayton's Case* (1816) 1 Mer 572; *Barlow Clowes International Ltd (In Liquidation) and Others v Vaughan and Others* [1992] 4 All ER 22.

entitled to a constructive trust[34] over such property,[35] or entitled to be subrogated to the rights of some person with an interest in that fund.[36] These doctrines are explained fully later.

Comparison with personal liability to account

It is worth remembering that the tracing claims, based on the facts above, will operate in tandem with other principles considered already in this book. Timothy will be liable for breach of trust either to provide compensation, or to reconstitute the trust fund directly.[37] Anne will be liable for knowing receipt of the trust property,[38] and possibly for dishonest assistance in that breach of trust.[39] Personal liability to account is therefore a liability to pay an amount of compensation equal to the loss suffered by the trust. Importantly, personal liability to account is a purely personal claim such that if Timothy or Anne were to go into insolvency, the claimant would have no advantage in that insolvency because the claimant would have no proprietary rights.

By contrast, the focus of the tracing rules is on establishing a claim to specific property. Where that property is particularly valuable, or likely to increase in value, the establishment of a proprietary claim will enable the claimant to claim entitlement to any profits derived from that property.[40] In some circumstances, a proprietary claim will entitle the claimant to recover compound interest (rather than merely simple interest) on the property recovered.[41] Therefore, there are frequently advantages in establishing a proprietary claim.

So, to alter the hypothetical facts slightly: if Anne organises the means by which Timothy can sell that painting through art dealers but does not touch the painting herself, then Anne will face liability for dishonest assistance in a breach of trust.[42] If Bert were to receive the painting and store it prior to selling it on Timothy's behalf, Bert will face liability for knowing receipt of property in breach of trust.[43] As explained in Chapter 20, these actions would impose personal claims for the value of the property passed on to Anne and Bert rather than any proprietary liability in favour of the beneficiaries. However, the focus of this chapter is on the claim brought on behalf of the beneficiaries to assert proprietary rights to recover the painting itself, or any property substituted for the painting. Frequently, all of these claims (whether personal or proprietary) will be pursued simultaneously by the beneficiaries.[44] This is, in truth, the search for a solvent defendant: that is, anyone who will be able to make good the claimant's losses. As such, the issues considered in this chapter will typically form a part only of the web of claims brought in relation to any one set of facts.

---

34 *Westdeutsche Landesbank Girozentrale v Islington LBC* [1996] AC 669.
35 *El Ajou v Dollar Land Holdings* [1993] 3 All ER 717.
36 *Boscawen v Bajwa* [1996] 1 WLR 328.
37 *Target Holdings v Redferns* [1996] 1 AC 421.
38 *Re Polly Peck International* [1992] 3 All ER 769.
39 If the property had not passed through A's hands – *Royal Brunei Airlines v Tan* [1995] 2 AC 378.
40 *Attorney-General for Hong Kong v Reid* [1994] 1 AC 324.
41 *Westdeutsche Landesbank Girozentrale v Islington LBC* [1996] AC 669. Cf. *Sempra Metals v IRC* [2008] Bus LR 49.
42 *Royal Brunei Airlines v Tan* [1995] 2 AC 378.
43 *Re Polly Peck International* [1992] 3 All ER 769.
44 See, eg, *Lipkin Gorman v Karpnale* [1991] 2 AC 548.

19.1.2 The distinction between following, common law tracing and equitable tracing

The distinction between following and tracing has been explained by Lord Millett in the following terms:[45]

> [Following and tracing] are both exercises in locating assets which are or may be taken to represent an asset belonging to the [claimants] and to which they assert ownership. The processes of following and tracing are, however, distinct. Following is the process of following the same asset as it moves from hand to hand. Tracing is the process of identifying a new asset as the substitute for the old.

A *following* claim requires simply that a specific piece of property is followed and identified by its original common law owner, thus being returned to that original owner.[46] In short, following claims appear to have more in common with a principle of vindicating the rights of the original owner in the very property which was taken from him as opposed to the establishment of a derivative claim in other property which is said to represent the property taken.[47] On the other hand, a *tracing* claim concerns the identification of property or value in which the claimant has some pre-existing interest which the court is then asked to recognise – typically because the claimant's original property has been substituted by a wrongdoer for the property claimed.

There is also a distinction between common law tracing and equitable tracing, as suggested above. This chapter will focus on equitable tracing for the most part, after disposing of common law tracing at section 19.2 below. In short, the common law will allow tracing only into the original property which was taken from its original owner. Latterly, this jurisdiction has been extended to include 'clean substitutions', where the original property is substituted by other property but where that substitute property is kept distinct from all other property.[48] Equitable tracing is by far the more extensive jurisdiction because it entitles the claimant to rights not only in property substituted for the original property taken in breach of trust, but also in mixtures into which such property is passed.[49]

19.1.3 Tracing is a process, not a remedy

Tracing is a process. Tracing itself does not provide a remedy.[50] It does nothing more than trace a right in an original piece of property into subsequent items of property or value. Having performed the tracing element, there is then the further issue as to the form of remedy which should be granted or the form of trust which arises. Therefore, the lawyer is required to do two things, one after the other: first, trace into the appropriate property; and, secondly, identify the best remedy to bring against that property. That is why this part is titled *Breach*

---

45 *Foskett v McKeown* [2001] 1 AC 102.
46 See Smith, 1997, 1–14.
47 An issue pursued in Chapter 31.
48 *FC Jones (A Firm) v Jones* [1996] 3 WLR 703.
49 It is a pre-requisite of equitable tracing, on the current understanding of the authorities, that there has been some pre-existing equitable or fiduciary relationship to invoke the equitable jurisdiction, see *Shalson v Russo* [2003] EWHC 1637 (Ch), para [02].
50 *Boscawen v Bajwa* [1996] 1 WLR 328. *Filby v Mortgage Express (No 2) Ltd* [2004] EWCA Civ 759 and *Bracken Partners Ltd v Gutteridge* [2004] 1 BCLC 377. See also Smith, 1997.

of Trust and Related Equitable Claims. The term 'claims' is very important. The legal rules and equitable principles considered in the early sections of this chapter concern only the right of the claimant first, to identify property derived from her property and then secondly, to bring a claim to assert proprietary rights over identified property. For ease of reference, I shall refer to this process and the claim to a remedy as a 'tracing claim' or as a 'tracing action'. The remedy which the court will then impose is a separate issue. If the claimant cannot prove that any given property was derived from her original property, then there will be no right to claim any sort of remedy.[51] As outlined above, the court may make an order for compensation,[52] an order that the property be restored by direct transfer to the original owner,[53] or an order that the property be held on resulting trust[54] or constructive trust,[55] or be subject to a charge.[56] That eventual remedy is a separate issue from the question whether or not the claimant can establish a tracing claim against identified property in the first place.

The distinction is made plain in *Boscawen v Bajwa*[57] in the judgment of Millett LJ, where his Lordship held that:

> Tracing properly so-called, however, is neither a claim nor a remedy but a process . . . It is the process by which the plaintiff traces what has happened to his property, identifies the persons who have handled it or received it, and justifies his claim that the money which they handled or received (and if necessary which they still retain) can properly be regarded as representing his property. He needs to do this because his claim is based on the retention by him of a beneficial interest in the property which the defendant handled or received. Unless he can prove this, he cannot (in the traditional language of equity) raise an equity against the defendant . . .

This is an important first point. Part 9 considers the equitable remedies which may be available; Part 4 has already dealt with constructive trusts and resulting trusts. Common law remedies may be available in relation to common law tracing, encompassing remedies beyond the scope of this book such as the simple common law restitution of property and an action for money had and received.[58] The following discussion will therefore consider the appropriate tracing rules at common law and in equity before moving on to consider the manner in which the courts have used trusts and equitable remedies to address questions of tracing.

19.2 COMMON LAW TRACING

In situations in which the claimant seeks to identify a specific item of property in the hands of the defendant in which the claimant has retained proprietary rights, the

---

51 *Ultraframe UK Ltd v Fielding* [2005] EWHC 1638 (Ch), [2005] All ER (D) 397, [1471].
52 *Target Holdings v Redferns* [1996] 1 AC 421, [1995] 3 WLR 352, [1995] 3 All ER 785.
53 *Foskett v McKeown* [2000] 3 All ER 97.
54 *El Ajou v Dollar Land Holdings* [1993] 3 All ER 717.
55 *Westdeutsche Landesbank Girozentrale v Islington LBC* [1996] AC 669.
56 *Barlow Clowes International Ltd (In Liquidation) and Others v Vaughan and Others* [1992] 4 All ER 22.
57 [1995] 4 All ER 769.
58 Cf *Westdeutsche Landesbank Girozentrale v Islington LBC* [1996] AC 669.

claimant will seek a common law tracing claim to require the return of that specific item of property.

19.2.1 Introduction

Common law tracing permits the claimant to identify that a particular item of property belongs at common law to the claimant. What is required is that the claimant is able to demonstrate that the property claimed is the very property which is to be restored, or that the property claimed has not been mixed with any other property. Therefore, in a situation in which a partner in a solicitors' firm took money from a client account to gamble at a casino, the casino held some money separately in an account for the partner. The partner's firm sought to recover the moneys paid to the casino which had come originally from its client account through, *inter alia*, common law tracing. It was held that there was a right to claim in common law tracing in respect of those amounts of money which were identifiable as having come from that client account.[59] That is, the claimant could establish common law tracing rights against sums of money held by the casino to the partner's account which could be proven to have come from the firm's account and passed to the defendant without being mixed with other moneys. Provided that money in bank accounts was held unmixed with other moneys, it was possible for common law tracing to be effected.[60] Note that it has been held that common law tracing cannot take effect over telegraphic transfers between electronic bank accounts because such insubstantial property will not be clearly identifiable.[61]

In *Agip (Africa) v Jackson*,[62] the defendant accountants arranged that money would be taken from the plaintiff by means of forged payment orders made out in favour of a series of dummy companies. The intention had been to launder the money through the 'shell' companies (that is, companies created solely to carry out the defendants' fraudulent purpose) by means of passing the money through a number of bank accounts in a number of different currencies belonging to a number of different companies, but where those companies were wound up after the money had passed through their accounts.[63] The plaintiffs pursued a number of claims simultaneously against the defendant. One of the claims was for restitution at common law of money taken from them. It was held that for common law tracing to be available it would be necessary for the plaintiff to demonstrate that the money claimed was the very money which had been wrongfully taken from the trust by the defendant's fraud held separately from all other moneys. On the basis that money had been moved through numerous companies, currencies and bank accounts, it was held that it was no longer possible

---

59 *Lipkin Gorman v Karpnale* [1991] 2 AC 548.

60 *Banque Belge pour L'Etranger v Hambrouck* [1921] 1 KB 321.

61 *El Ajou v Dollar Land Holdings* [1993] 3 All ER 717. This approach has been followed in *Nimmo v Westpac Banking Corporation* [1993] 3 NZLR 218; *Bank Tejarat v Hong Kong and Shanghai Banking Corporation (CI) Ltd* [1995] 1 Lloyd's Rep 239. Cf Birks, 1995:3. It has also been accepted that telegraphic transfer does not involve a transfer of property but rather simply an adjustment in the value of the choses in action constituted by the bank accounts: *R v Preddy* [1996] AC 815; considered in Chapter 31. See generally Matthews, 1995:2.

62 [1991] Ch 547, 566, *per* Fox LJ, [1991] 3 WLR 116, [1992] 4 All ER 451.

63 This is standard practice in money laundering. By transferring the money into different accounts, by combining it with other money and by changing it into different currencies, it becomes very difficult to prove where the original money went. The device of running the various companies insolvent means that the tracing process must be conducted through the complexities of such companies' windings up, which adds further problems.

for the original money to be identified. Consequently, common law tracing would not be available to the plaintiff in relation to those sums.[64] So, where property is taken in breach of fiduciary duty and passed through a number of companies, the beneficiary of the original fiduciary duty is entitled to trace her property rights through those successive companies.[65]

19.2.2 Understanding the limitations

As is obvious from the two cases considered immediately above, the common law tracing process is very brittle. If the property becomes unidentifiable, or if it becomes mixed with any other property, then the common law tracing claim will fail. The usual tactic for the money-launderer is therefore to take the original money, to divide it up into randomly-sized portions, pay it into accounts which already contain other money, convert the money into different currencies and move it into accounts in another jurisdiction. This type of subterfuge puts that property beyond the reach of common law tracing. Instead, the claimant would be required to rely on equitable tracing, as considered at section 19.3 below.

It is these limitations which have led many leading academics and judges to recommend that the distinction between common law tracing and equitable tracing should be removed. In *Agip (Africa) v Jackson*, Millett J sought to preclude common law tracing from operation in circumstances where there had been anything other than clean, physical substitutions. Writing extra-judicially he has said:[66] 'A unified and comprehensive restitutionary remedy should be developed based on equitable principles, and attempts to rationalise and develop the common law action for money had and received should be abandoned.' These arguments are considered in more detail at the end of this chapter. However, one more recent decision of the Court of Appeal, in which Millett LJ ironically delivered the leading judgment, suggested that common law tracing may have a broader ambit than had previously been thought.[67]

19.2.3 A new direction

The Court of Appeal decision in *FC Jones & Sons v Jones*[68] concerned an amount of £11,700 which was loaned by a partnership to Mrs Jones, who was the wife of one of the partners. There was no suggestion that this transaction was wrongfully performed. Mrs Jones invested the money in potato futures[69] and made a large profit. Ultimately she held a balance of £49,860: all of the money was held separately in a single bank account. Subsequently, it transpired that the partnership had committed an act of bankruptcy under the Bankruptcy Act 1914 (rendering it technically bankrupt *before* it had made the payment to Mrs Jones), and therefore all of the partnership property was deemed to have passed retrospectively to the Official Receiver. This meant that the Official Receiver was entitled to the £11,700 before it

---

64 *Agip* is considered in greater detail below at para 19.3.3.
65 *El Ajou v Dollar Land Holdings* [1993] 3 All ER 717; *Bracken Partners Ltd v Gutteridge* [2004] 1 BCLC 377.
66 Millett, 1991, 85.
67 *FC Jones (A Firm) v Jones* [1996] 3 WLR 703.
68 [1996] 3 WLR 703, [1996] 4 All ER 721.
69 Ie, a form of derivatives contract traded on the commodities markets which speculates on the value of potatoes in the future.

had been paid to Mrs Jones. Therefore, it was claimed that Mrs Jones had had no title to the original £11,700 and that the Official Receiver should be entitled to trace into Mrs Jones's bank account to recover the money from her.

The question, however, became more complex than that. There was no doubt that the Official Receiver was entitled to the £11,700 before the date of its transfer to Mrs Jones, and that the sum of £11,700 ought to have been recoverable by the Official Receiver. The more difficult problem was to decide whether or not the Official Receiver ought to be entitled to the entire £49,860 which Mrs Jones had generated from that initial £11,700 in her investments in potato futures.

The ordinary understanding of common law tracing would have suggested that the Official Receiver could have recovered the £11,700, being the original property, but that it could not recover any further amounts unless it could demonstrate equitable title in the property (under equitable tracing principles). On these facts there could be no equitable tracing because the partnership firm had retained no equitable interest in the money lent to Mrs Jones. Furthermore, the combination of the conversion of the original £11,700 into options contracts and then its mixture with profits made on those investments would ordinarily have meant that common law tracing would have offered no redress for the Official Receiver winding up the partnership's assets. However, the Court of Appeal held that all of the £49,860 was to be paid to the Official Receiver as part of a common law tracing claim. The rationales behind that decision suggest a significant development in the scope of common law tracing.

Millett LJ was prepared to allow a proprietary, common law claim on the basis that the money at issue in this case was perfectly identifiable in a single bank account. Here the £11,700 originally held and the £49,860 generated in profits ultimately had been held in a single bank account and not mixed with any other moneys. On the facts, there could not have been a claim in equity against Mrs Jones because she had never been in any fiduciary relationship with the Official Receiver nor with the partnership (a necessary pre-requisite of an equitable tracing claim).[70] The nature of the common law tracing right was explained by Millett LJ as being a proprietary right to claim whatever was held in the bank account, whether the amount at the time of the claim was more or less than the original amount deposited. Furthermore, it was held that it was immaterial whether or not those amounts constituted profits on the original money, or simply the original money, or a combination of the two.

For his part, Nourse LJ reached the same conclusion by a different route. His Lordship confusingly mixed personal and proprietary claims. The claim he expressed himself willing to grant was the personal claim for money had and received, but on these facts that was explained as being a right entitling the Official Receiver to a right in property *representing* the original property (which may therefore have been more than the original money) and not merely the original property. Furthermore, his Lordship held that the claim for money had and received was based on conscience, making it seem more like an equitable claim than a common law claim.[71]

Following on from Smith's work on *Taylor v Plumer*,[72] the Court of Appeal accepted that the founding case on common law tracing had in fact used equitable tracing rules. Smith has

70 As considered below at section 19.3.
71 See Davern, 1997, 92.
72 (1815) 3 M & S 562; Smith, 1997, 162 *et seq*.

taken this to be justification for the amalgamation of common law tracing with equitable tracing in the future (considered at the end of this chapter). However, the Court of Appeal held that the principle of common law tracing remained valid separate from equitable tracing nonetheless.[73]

What is perhaps remarkable about the decision of the Court of Appeal in *FC Jones (A Firm) v Jones* is that the court appears to have generated an entirely novel remedy at common law. Common law recognises two remedies principally in this context:[74] common law damages;[75] and a claim for money had and received.[76] The common law does have property law concepts, of which the most obvious in this book has been the legal title held by the trustee of a trust fund. However, those common law concepts have been so little discussed in recent years that it is equitable principles to do with tracing, charges and trust which seem to have displaced them. The remedy awarded in *Jones* has some initial commonsensical attraction: you have my property and I wish you to return my property to me. Therefore, the Court of Appeal ordered Mrs Jones to transfer the £11,700 to the Official Receiver. As a question of *property law* that order is remarkable in itself, even though as a question of *common sense* it seems in keeping with the idea of protecting rights in property. What is even more remarkable is that the profit made on the original £11,700, bringing the total amount held in Mrs Jones's potato futures bank account to £49,860, is also able to be traced at common law. It is a little like the argument that if one owns the tree then one also owns any fruit which grows on that tree.[77] This appears to extend the common law tracing doctrine to include substitute property (that is, the profit on the original property). This remedy is akin to a *vindicatio* under Roman law, under which the court would order a recognition that a person's rights be vindicated. Nevertheless it appears that common law tracing will not permit a claim to pass through inter-bank clearing systems because the original property in such situations is not capable of being identified sufficiently clearly.[78]

19.3   EQUITABLE TRACING

Equitable tracing is the only means by which a claimant can trace into mixtures of property, where a part of that mixture represents or comprises money in which the claimant previously held some equitable proprietary right. Particular difficulties have arisen in relation to money passed through electronically-held bank accounts. English law treats each payment of money as being distinct tangible property such that, when a bank account containing such money is run overdrawn, that property is said to

---

73 See, however, Millett, 1991, 71, in which Millett surprisingly argues for the elimination of common law tracing shortly before extending its ambit greatly in *Jones*.

74 There are other common law principles to do with identification of assets under which mixtures of tangible property will be divided on the basis of the old Roman rules of *commixio* and *confusio* (*Indian Oil Corp Ltd v Greenstone Shipping SA* [1987] 3 All ER 893) provided that they have not become capable of separation, in which case the claimants would become tenants in common of the combined mass (*Buckley v Gross* (1863) 3 B & S 566). See also *Greenwood v Bennett* [1973] QB 195.

75 As provided in relation to breach of contract and to compensate tortious loss.

76 Or 'a personal claim in restitution', *per* Lord Goff in *Westdeutsche Landesbank Girozentrale v Islington LBC* [1996] AC 669.

77 Not that I am suggesting that potatoes grow on trees, either; it is just that that is the metaphor so loved of economists in this area.

78 *FC Jones (A Firm) v Jones* [1997] Ch 159, 168.

disappear. Consequently, there can be no tracing claim in respect of property which has ceased to exist.

19.3.1 Introduction

Tracing in equity (or 'equitable tracing') is a considerably more extensive means of tracing property rights than is available at common law. As will emerge, equitable tracing permits property rights to be traced into mixtures of property so that one of a number of different equitable remedies may be used to reconstitute the claimant's property rights. The fundamental pre-requisite for the bringing of an equitable tracing claim is that the claimant must have had some equitable interest in the property which is to be traced before equity will entertain the claim.[79] That pre-existing equitable interest may be a beneficial interest under an express or a constructive trust. As discussed above, it is important to remember that this is a two-stage process. The first stage is for the detective work of the tracing process to be carried out so that the claimant is able to identify the property which stands as a substitute for her original property and against which she therefore wishes to bring a claim. The second stage, having traced the property, is to identify which equitable remedy should be imposed over that property. These various elements of a tracing claim are considered in turn in the sections to follow.

19.3.2 Need for a prior equitable interest

The traditional rule

It is a pre-requisite for an equitable tracing claim that the claimant had some equitable interest in the original property, or that the person who transferred that property away had some fiduciary relationship to the claimant (such as being a trustee).[80] Therefore, before starting an equitable tracing claim, one must always ensure that there is a pre-existing equitable interest.

An example of the application of this principle was the decision of the Court of Appeal in *Boscawen v Bajwa*[81] that there must be a pre-existing fiduciary relationship which calls the equitable jurisdiction into being. That case concerned a purported contract for the sale of land which was not completed. Bajwa had charged the land by way of a mortgage with a building society (the Halifax Building Society) before then exchanging contracts for the sale of the property with purchasers. In turn, the purchasers had sought a mortgage with the Abbey National. The loan moneys provided by Abbey National were paid to solicitors who were entitled to use the moneys only as part of the purchase. Mistakenly, the solicitors thought that the sale was going ahead properly, but in fact the sale was never completed. This had the result that the solicitors used the Abbey National's money to pay off Bajwa's mortgage with the Halifax, but did not acquire a legal charge in favour of the Abbey National because the purchase did not take place. In turn, however, the solicitors who were holding the purchase moneys went into insolvency and therefore the sale could not be completed.

---

79 *Re Diplock's Estate* [1948] Ch 465
80 *Ibid.*
81 [1995] 4 All ER 769.

The issue arose how the Abbey National was to recover its money, which had been held on express trust for it by the solicitors and then used to pay off Bajwa's debt with the Halifax Building Society. The more precise legal question was whether or not the bank was entitled to trace into the debt with the building society and claim a right in subrogation to the debt owed to the building society.[82] On the facts, it was accepted that the money had been held on trust from the outset. The money could therefore be followed into the solicitors' client account. The issue was whether it could be traced further into the payment to the building society.

In explaining the ability to trace into a mixed fund, Millett LJ held that: '... equity's power to charge a mixed fund with the repayment of trust moneys enables the claimant to follow the money, not because it is his, but because it is derived from a fund which is treated as if it were subject to a charge in his favour.' In *Boscawen v Bajwa*, Bajwa and the solicitors were not dishonest in mixing the bank's money and Bajwa's money. Therefore, Bajwa and the bank could be treated as ranking *pari passu* in the making of payments. The solicitors were clearly fiduciaries. Further, Bajwa must have known that he was not entitled to that money until contracts were completed. As such, Bajwa could not keep the sale proceeds and title to the property. Bajwa could not therefore rely on the favourable tracing rules set out in *Re Diplock*[83] for innocent volunteers, considered below.

Liability to equitable tracing even of innocent volunteers

Significantly the defendant need not have acted unconscionably. Rather, the unconscionability will be in denying the rights of the beneficiary to their property. In *Diplock* the defendants had been the recipients of grants made to them by the personal representatives of a deceased testator in accordance with the terms of a residuary bequest in that will. The gift was afterwards held to have been void in other litigation by the House of Lords on the basis that its charitable purpose failed.[84] The residue was therefore to have passed on an intestacy. The next-of-kin, entitled on intestacy, brought an action to recover the money which had been paid away by the personal representatives. It was found that the recipients of the money had acted in good faith and had every reason to think that it was their property. They were held nevertheless to be subject to the rights of the residuary beneficiaries to trace after the money in equity, even though they had not themselves acted unconscionably. The beneficiaries' property rights were held to bind even 'volunteers provided that as a result of what has gone before some equitable proprietary interest has been created and attaches to the property in the hands of the volunteer'.[85] Therefore, it would not matter that the ultimate recipients were innocent of any breach of trust provided that there had been some preceding breach of an equitable duty by someone else. In effect this approach distinguishes between the source of the property rights in the hands of persons under a fiduciary duty and the further question of the remedy which might then be sought against the volunteers who then held the property. As the matter was put in *Re Diplock*:

> once the proprietary interest has been created by equity as a result of the wrongful or unauthorised dealing by the original recipient of the money, that interest will persist and be operative against an innocent third party who is a volunteer, provided only that the

---

82 The remedy of subrogation is considered in Chapter 30.
83 [1948] Ch 465.
84 *sub nom Chichester Diocesan Board v Simpson* [1944] AC 341.
85 *Ibid*, 530.

means of identification or disentanglement remain. For such purpose it cannot make any difference whether the mixing was done by the original recipient [that is, the fiduciary] or by the innocent third party.[86]

What emerges from these *dicta* is that the court will seek to protect the beneficiary under the original fiduciary duty rather than allow the subsequent innocent volunteer to retain any rights in the windfall which he has received. This approach was applied by the House of Lords in *Foskett v McKeown*,[87] in circumstances in which a trustee took money from the trust and used it to pay the premiums on an insurance policy which was made out in favour of the trustee's children. It was held that the beneficiaries under the trust were entitled to trace in equity into the proceeds of the insurance policy after the trustee's death, thus illustrating that the limitation on the children's rights in the lump sum paid on the maturity of the insurance policy was subject to the beneficiaries' right to trace even though the children had played no part in the breach of trust. Therefore, the innocent volunteer is *prima facie* liable in a tracing claim, with the precise remedy to be decided, as considered below.[88]

The order made in *Diplock* was that the innocent volunteers and the beneficiary claimants should take a *pro rata* share under an equitable charge in the property held in that commingled fund. This principle was encapsulated in the following terms:

> Where an innocent volunteer (as distinct from a purchaser for value without notice) mixes 'money' of his own with 'money' which in equity belongs to another person, or is found in possession of such a mixture, although that other person cannot claim a charge on the mass superior to the claim of the volunteer, he is entitled, nevertheless, to a charge ranking *pari passu* with the claim of the volunteer . . . Such a person is not in conscience bound to give precedence to the equitable owner of the other of the two funds.[89]

Therefore, it is not simply a question of conscience which gives rise to this claim, and the remedy recognises the continued rights of the innocent volunteer only in that part of the fund not derived from the trust. The claim arises to vindicate the property rights of the beneficiaries of the original trust in the items of property which were mistakenly paid away. In that sense, the equitable tracing claim is predicated on the existence of the original equitable relationship – and consequently recognises the original duties of good conscience owed to the claimant–beneficiary – and is merely enforcing that person's property rights by means of equitable tracing.

19.3.3 The benefits of equitable tracing

The benefits

The clear benefits of equitable tracing over common law tracing appear in money-laundering cases like *Agip (Africa) v Jackson*,[90] which upheld the core principle that there must be a

---

86 *Ibid*, 536.
87 [2000] 3 All ER 97.
88 See section 19.5 below.
89 [1948] Ch 465, 524.
90 [1991] Ch 547, 566, *per* Fox LJ, [1991] 3 WLR 116, [1992] 4 All ER 451.

fiduciary relationship which calls the equitable jurisdiction into being. In *Agip*, on instructions from the plaintiff oil exploration company, the Banque du Sud in Tunis transmitted a payment to Lloyds Bank in London, to be passed on to a specified person. The plaintiff's chief accountant fraudulently altered the payment instruction so that the money was in fact passed on to a company called Baker Oil Ltd. Before the fraud was uncovered, Lloyds Bank had paid out under the chief accountant's instruction to Baker Oil before receiving payment from Banque du Sud via the New York payment system. The account was then closed and the money was transferred via the Isle of Man to a number of recipients controlled by the defendants. The defendants were independent accountants who ran a number of shell companies through which the moneys were paid, their intention being to pass the moneys through these companies so that the funds would become, in effect, untraceable in practice, with the ultimate intention that they would keep those moneys. The defendants were clearly rogues of the lowest sort. The issue arose whether or not the value received by Baker Oil constituted the traceable proceeds of the property transferred from Tunis.

It was held that either principal or agent can sue on the equitable tracing claim, and that the role of plaintiff was not restricted to the Banque du Sud in this case. The bank had not paid Baker Oil with 'its own money' but rather on instruction from the plaintiff oil company which was its customer (albeit that they were fraudulent instructions). Further, it was impossible to trace the money at common law where the value had been transferred by 'telegraphic transfer' thus making it impossible to identify the specific money which had been misapplied. On these facts, because the plaintiff's fiduciary (that is, its chief accountant) had acted fraudulently, it was held that it was open to the plaintiff to trace the money in equity through the shell companies and into the defendant's hands. There was also a personal liability to account imposed on those persons who had knowingly received misapplied funds, or who had dishonestly assisted in the misapplication of the funds as discussed in Chapter 20.

This case demonstrates the ability of equity to trace into complex mixtures of property beyond the jurisdiction of the common law. It is also possible for equity to make a variety of awards of trusts and other remedies, as considered below at section 19.5. The equitable jurisdiction makes awards for discovery of documents during litigation to assist in the tracing process, and also provides for injunctions which will prevent a defendant dissipating property after the date of the injunction.[91]

Limitations on the right to trace in equity

The question of loss of the right to trace is considered separately below,[92] but it is useful to dwell on it while looking at the particular problem of electronic bank accounts. In *Bishopsgate Investment Management v Homan*,[93] money was taken by newspaper mogul Robert Maxwell from pension funds under his control. The beneficiaries under those pension funds sought to recover the sums taken from their trusts on the basis of an equitable tracing claim. The money had been passed into bank accounts which had gone overdrawn between the time of the payment of the money into the accounts and the bringing of the claim. On the basis that the accounts had gone overdrawn (and therefore had no property in them), it was held that

---

91 Eg, *Bankers Trust Co v Shapira* [1980] 1 WLR 1274; *In Re DPR Futures Ltd* [1989] 1 WLR 778.
92 See para 19.5.1.
93 [1995] Ch 211, [1995] 1 All ER 347, [1994] 3 WLR 1270.

the beneficiaries had lost their right to trace into those particular accounts because the property had disappeared from them.

The same principle appears in *Roscoe v Winder*,[94] where it was held that beneficiaries cannot claim an amount exceeding the lowest intermediate balance in the bank account after the money was paid in. The claimant will not be entitled to trace into any such property where the account has been run overdrawn at any time since the property claimed was paid into it. It would be possible for the plaintiff to trace into the account into which such money was paid subsequently. However, in practice, if a fraudster who has taken the money belonging beneficially to the claimant pays it into a bank account held in the UK, then removes all of the money from that UK account and pays it into a bank account in another jurisdiction which will not enforce judgments from an English court, the loss of the right to trace into the UK account will effectively signal the loss of any feasible hopes of recovering the claimant's money at all. This principle is considered further below.[95]

19.4 EQUITABLE TRACING INTO MIXED FUNDS

The process of tracing, and identifying property over which a remedy is sought, is different from the issue of asserting a remedy in respect of that property. In relation to mixtures of trust and other money held in bank accounts, a variety of approaches has been taken in the courts, from the application of the old first-in, first-out principle to the establishment of proportionate shares in any substitute property.

As considered in the initial hypothetical situations at the start of this chapter, one of the more problematic issues in equitable tracing claims is that of identifying title in property in funds which are made up both of trust property and other property. Where it is impossible to separate one item of property from another, it will be impossible to effect a common law following claim. Suppose that it was a car, registration number SAFC 1, that had been taken and parked in a car park with other cars. It would be comparatively easy to identify that car and recover it under a common law following claim, as in *Jones* above.[96] However, where the property is fungible, such as money in a bank account, such segregation cannot be easily performed. When my car is parked in a car park there is no meaningful mixture of property because my car can be easily identified. If, however, I bought a bag of Demerara sugar and my sugar was tipped into a sugar bowl with other Demerara sugar, then it would be impossible to identify my sugar in amongst that mixture. In such a situation, equitable tracing and an equitable remedy will be required to identify where my property is deemed to have gone and what recourse I have against the person who is controlling that mixture. It is this sort of situation which will interest us for the remainder of this chapter. Because this sort of litigation can be complex, and therefore expensive in practice, most of the cases are concerned with large amounts of money being mixed in bank accounts[97] or other intangible property (like modern financial instruments or securities) being moved between accounts.

---

94   [1915] 1 Ch 62.
95   See para 19.5.1.
96   *Jones, FC (A Firm) v Jones* [1996] 3 WLR 703, [1997] Ch 159.
97   See Alastair Hudson, *The Law of Finance*, Sweet & Maxwell, 2009, Chapter 21.

19.4.1 Mixture of trust money with trustee's own money

The first factual situation to be considered in the context of equitable tracing into mixed funds is that where the trustee mixes money taken from the trust with property that is beneficially her own. There are a number of conflicting cases in this area, with the result that it is not always clear which approach should be taken in any given situation. The attitude of the courts could be best explained as selecting the approach which achieves the most desirable result for the beneficiaries under the trust which has had its funds misapplied. In short, the courts appear to be seeking to achieve a just result and therefore selecting the approach which gets them there most efficiently.

The honest trustee approach

The problem with commingling the trustee's own money with trust property is deciding whether property acquired with money from that mixture is to be treated as having been taken from the trust or as having been taken from the trustee's own money. On the basis that the trustee is required to invest trust property to achieve the best possible return for the trust,[98] and on the basis that the trustee is required to behave honestly in respect of the trust property, the court may choose to assume that the trustee intended to use trust property to make successful investments and her own money for any inferior investments.

This approach is most clearly exhibited in *Re Hallett's Estate*.[99] Hallett was a solicitor who was a bailee of Russian bonds for one of his clients, Cotterill. Hallett also held securities of that type on express trust for his own marriage settlement (so that he was among the beneficiaries of that marriage settlement). Hallett sold the bonds and paid all the proceeds of sale into his own bank account. Hallett died subsequently. Therefore, it was left to the trustees of the marriage settlement and Cotterill to claim proprietary rights over the remaining contents of Hallett's bank account.

It was held that it could be assumed, where a trustee has money in a personal bank account to which trust money is added, that the trustee is acting honestly when paying money out of that bank account. Therefore, it is assumed that the trustee is paying out her own money on investments which lose money and not the trust money. It was held that: '. . . where a man does an act which may be rightfully performed . . . he is not allowed to say against the person entitled to the property or the right that he has done it wrongfully.' Therefore, it is said that the trustee has rightfully dissipated her own moneys such that the trust money remains intact. The beneficiaries were entitled to claim either equitable title in the assets acquired by the trustee, or a lien over that asset.[100] In the more modern language of the law of trusts we might argue that this recognises the basis of the trust in the conscience of the trustee.[101] Therefore, not only is the court assuming that the trustee was acting honestly but it is also applying the tenets of equity so as to require him to act honestly: that is, by holding that any benefit to

---

98 *Cowan v Scargill* [1985] Ch 270.
99 (1880) 13 Ch D 696.
100 A lien is a right to take possession of property until one is paid what one is owed. It is clear though that the beneficiary will not now be confined to claiming a lien: *Re Tilley's Will Trusts; Burgin v Croad* [1967] Ch 1179, 1186, [1967] 2 All ER 303, 308; *Scott v Scott* (1963) 109 CLR 649; *Foskett v McKeown* [2000] 3 All ER 97, 123, *per* Lord Millett.
101 Cf *Westdeutsche Landesbank Girozentrale v Islington LBC* [1996] AC 669.

derive from the property held would be passed to the beneficiaries. By the same token, it might be said that an investment in successful investments would be deemed to be an investment made out of the trust property.[102]

So to take an example of this approach in operation, imagine that a trustee has taken property from a trust fund and mixed it with her own money in her own bank account. If that mixture of money was then used half to pay for an expensive meal and half to buy shares, the court would assume that the trustee was acting honestly and (based on this convenient fiction) would attribute the valuable shares to the trust fund and the money dissipated on the meal to the trustee's own money. In this way the trust is able to recover the shares from the trustee, and thus recoup the value of the trust fund. One way of thinking of this doctrine is as an extension of the remedy of specific restitution for breaches of trust by trustees whereby the trustee is required to recover the trust's property: *Hallett* is effectively going one step further by allowing the trust[103] to establish an equitable interest in the property acquired with the original trust money.

Beneficiary election approach

By contradistinction to the 'honest trustee approach', there is the 'beneficiary election' approach which appears most clearly in *Re Oatway*.[104] In that case, the trustee held £4,077 in a personal bank account. The trustee then added £3,000 of trust money to this account. Out of the £7,077 held in the account, £2,137 was spent on purchasing shares. The remainder of the money in the bank account was then dissipated. The beneficiaries sought to trace from the £3,000 taken out of the bank into the shares and then to impose a charge over those shares. The shares themselves had risen in value to £2,474. The beneficiaries also sought a further accounting in cash to make up the balance of the £3,000 taken from the trust fund.

It was held that where a trustee has wrongfully mixed her own money and trust money, the trustee is not entitled to say that the investment was made with her own money and that the trust money has been dissipated. Importantly, though, the beneficiaries are entitled to elect either that the property be subject to a charge as security for amounts owed to them by the trustee, or that the unauthorised investment be adopted as part of the trust fund: hence the term 'beneficiary election approach'. It is therefore clear that the courts are prepared to protect the beneficiaries at all costs from the misfeasance of the trustee – re-emphasising the strictness of the trustee's obligations to the beneficiaries.[105] So, on the facts of *Oatway* the beneficiaries were able to elect to have the valuable shares subsumed into the trust as opposed simply to taking rights over money (which was to their advantage because it was considered likely that those shares would increase in value in the future), and also to be able to require the trustee to account in cash for the remaining shortfall in the balance taken from the trust fund (in effect based on the principles of breach of trust spelled out in *Target Holdings* in Chapter 18 requiring a trustee to reconstitute the value of the trust fund).

---

102 See *Re Oatway* [1903] 2 Ch 356, below.
103 Strictly, a trust is not an entity because it has no legal personality, but please excuse this useful shorthand in this context.
104 [1903] 2 Ch 356.
105 See now *Foskett v McKeown* [2000] 3 All ER 97, 123, *per* Lord Millett.

This approach has been expressed as being an exception to the main approach of rateable division of the property in *Foskett v McKeown*[106] by the House of Lords on the basis, in effect, of fault by Lord Millett.[107] His Lordship held that:

> The primary rule in regard to a mixed fund, therefore, is that gains and losses are borne by the contributors rateably.[108] The beneficiary's right to elect instead to enforce a lien to obtain repayment is an exception to the primary rule, exercisable where the fund is deficient and the claim is made against the wrongdoer and those claiming through him.

Lord Millett relied on similar principles which apply in relation to physical mixtures, where it is said that if the mixture is the fault of the defendant then it is open to the claimant to 'claim the goods'.[109] Importantly, even where the defendant is not at fault in the commingling of property, such an innocent volunteer is not entitled to occupy a better position than the person who was responsible simply by reason of her innocence.[110] This issue of innocents caught up in the affairs of others is considered immediately below.

There is one anomalous case, given the general trend in the cases to assume everything against the trustee who acts wrongfully. In *Re Tilley's Will Trusts*,[111] a trustee took money which she held on trust and paid it into her own personal bank account. The trustee made investments on her own behalf from that bank account. The moneys she took from the trust settled her overdraft on that account in part so that she was able to continue her investment activities. The court held that the beneficiaries had no rights to trace into the investments which the trustee had made with the money taken from that account; rather the court was convinced on the facts that the trust money had simply served to reduce her overdraft but not to pay for her investments. An alternative analysis, more in line with *Foskett v McKeown*, would have been to find that if the trust money made the investment possible, the trust should be taken to have contributed traceable funds to the acquisition of those investments.

19.4.2 Mixture of two trust funds or mixture with innocent volunteer's property

General principle

This section considers the situation in which trust property is misapplied in such a way that it is mixed with property belonging to an innocent third party. Therefore, rather than consider the issues which arose in the previous section concerning the obligations of the wrongdoing trustee, it is now necessary to decide how property belonging to innocent parties should be allocated between them. It was held in *Re Diplock*[112] that the entitlement of the beneficiary to the mixed fund should rank *pari passu* (or 'in equal step', or proportionately) with the rights of the innocent volunteer:

---

106 [2000] 3 All ER 97. *Foskett* was followed in *Serious Fraud Office v Lexi Holdings plc* [2008] EWCA Crim 1443, [2009] 1 All ER 586.
107 *Ibid*, 124.
108 Ie, in proportionate shares.
109 *Lupton v White, White v Lupton* (1808) 15 Ves 432, [1803–13] All ER Rep 336; *Sandeman & Sons v Tyzack and Branfoot Steamship Co Ltd* [1913] AC 680, 695; [1911–13] All ER Rep 1013, 1020, *per* Lord Molton.
110 *Jones v De Marchant* (1916) 28 DLR 561; *Foskett v McKeown* [2000] 3 All ER 97.
111 *Re Tilley's Will Trusts, Burgin v Croad* [1967] Ch 1179.
112 [1948] Ch 465, 524.

> Where an innocent volunteer (as distinct from a purchaser for value without notice) mixes 'money' of his own with 'money' which in equity belongs to another person, or is found in possession of such a mixture, although that other person cannot claim a charge on the mass superior to the claim of the volunteer, he is entitled, nevertheless, to a charge ranking *pari passu* with the claim of the volunteer . . . Such a person is not in conscience bound to give precedence to the equitable owner of the other of the two funds.

Therefore, none of the innocent contributors to the fund is considered as taking any greater right than any other contributor to the fund. Rather, each person has an equal charge over that property. This approach has been adopted in *Foskett v McKeown*[113] by Lord Millett:[114]

> The primary rule in regard to a mixed fund, therefore, is that gains and losses are borne by the contributors rateably.[115] The beneficiary's right to elect instead to enforce a lien to obtain repayment is an exception to the primary rule, exercisable where the fund is deficient and the claim is made against the wrongdoer and those claiming through him.

As considered above, Lord Millett relied on similar principles which apply in relation to physical mixtures, where it is said that if the mixture is the fault of the defendant then it is open to the claimant to 'claim the goods'.[116] It was said at that stage that even where the defendant was not at fault in the commingling of property, such an innocent volunteer would not be entitled to occupy a better position than the person who was responsible simply by reason of her innocence.[117] In the case of *Foskett v McKeown* itself, a trustee had been misusing the trust's funds to pay two of the five premiums on a life assurance policy, of about £20,000, which he had taken out in favour of his wife and children. When the trustee committed suicide and the breach of trust was discovered, it was held that the beneficiaries of the trust were entitled to trace into the moneys paid out under the life assurance policy on the basis that their money had been mixed with the trustee's own money to pay for the life assurance policy premiums, which were to pay a lump sum to the trustee's children on the trustee's death. Whereas the Court of Appeal had held that the beneficiaries were entitled only to an amount of money equal to the two premiums, about £20,000, the House of Lords held that they were entitled to a two-fifths share of the lump sum, worth about £400,000.

Opinion differs over the rights and wrongs of this decision.[118] The House of Lords chose to vindicate the property rights of the beneficiaries by means of recognising that the contributions which the trust fund made to the insurance policy premiums enhanced the final lump sum and, significantly, that the comparatively small contributions to those premiums acquired proportionate proprietary rights in the much larger lump sum paid out on the policy's maturity. Thus, a contribution of only £20,000 landed a share of the £1 million policy

---

113   [2000] 3 All ER 97.
114   *Ibid*, 124.
115   That is, in proportionate shares.
116   *Lupton v White, White v Lupton* (1808) 15 Ves 432, [1803–13] All ER Rep 336; *Sandeman & Sons v Tyzack and Branfoot Steamship Co Ltd* [1913] AC 680, 695, [1911–13] All ER Rep 1013, 1020, *per* Lord Molton.
117   *Jones v De Marchant* (1916) 28 DLR 561; *Foskett v McKeown* [2000] 3 All ER 97.
118   Eg, Virgo, 2004 and Rotherham, 2004.

pay-out because that £20,000 constituted two-fifths of all the premiums. An alternative approach, and one which would have recognised the innocence of the children who were expecting to take absolute title in the whole of the lump sum paid out from the insurance policy, would have been to order compensation for the beneficiaries equal to the amount of cash taken from the trust fund to pay the policy's premiums. This approach would have meant that the beneficiaries would not have recovered a proportionate share in the much larger pay-out from the insurance policy. However, what the majority decision in the House of Lords achieves is recognition of the fact that the trustee ought to have been investing the trust fund properly, and therefore that for the beneficiaries simply to have the looted cash returned to them would not give them the return they would otherwise have expected on their capital if the trustee had managed and invested it properly. In effect, what is being suggested is that the children would otherwise have received a windfall (in the form of the size of the insurance policy pay-out) without recognising the beneficiaries' unwitting contribution to their wealth. What makes this case difficult is that it involves two sets of innocent parties fighting over the money that is left after the wrongdoing trustee's death. There is no completely satisfactory answer in that one or other of the parties seems likely to receive less money than that to which they would otherwise feel they were entitled. The logic of the law of tracing suggests that the beneficiaries are entitled to pursue their property rights into any fund of money if the defendant has no defence to a claim for its recovery.[119] Therefore, the law of tracing necessarily requires that if the beneficiaries have involuntarily had their property invested in an insurance policy, those beneficiaries deserve a share in the investment. So, in *Clark v Cutland*,[120] when one of the shareholders organised the diversion of a company's assets into his personal pension fund, it was held that the company was entitled to trace into that pension fund.[121] It was held further that an appropriate proportion of the value taken from the pension fund should be held on constructive trust for the company.

The law of tracing functions by awarding proportionate interests in the fund available. This is so whether the fund decreases or increases in value. Suppose the following situation. Shyster is trustee of a trust over a store of 10,000 Belgian chocolates, which are held in a warehouse, in favour of Bernice as beneficiary. Shyster also owns a store of 10,000 identical chocolates in a neighbouring warehouse beneficially in common with his wife, Innocent. Suppose then that Shyster takes the chocolates which are held on trust for Bernice and has them transferred to the warehouse where he and Innocent hold their own chocolates. Innocent does not know of this event. Due to poor air conditioning it is found that 5,000 of the mixed stock of chocolates are rendered unfit to eat. The question then arises as to who has rights in the remaining chocolates. Even though Innocent knows nothing of Shyster's breach of trust, she will be bound by any rights which Bernice has. Therefore, Bernice would remain entitled to one half of all of the chocolates held in the warehouse, because that was the rateable proportion of chocolates which she contributed to the stock of chocolates held in the warehouse. Therefore, Bernice would be entitled to an equitable interest in 7,500 good chocolates and 2,500 of the worthless, spoiled chocolates (that is, half of the good 15,000 chocolates to account, and forgetting her half of the 5,000 chocolates which have been spoiled) together

119 See section 19.5 below and Virgo, 2003, 203.
120 [2003] 4 All ER 733, [2003] EWCA Civ 810.
121 Applying *Foskett v McKeown* [2001] 1 AC 102; *Allan v Rea Bros Trustees Ltd* [2002] EWCA Civ 85, (2002) 4 ITELR 627.

with a claim against Shyster personally in breach of trust for the value of the spoiled choco-lates,[122] or a lien over the chocolates such that she is repaid their cash value.[123] Innocent is not entitled to resist Bernice's claim solely on the basis that she did not know of Shyster's actions; although she would probably also have a personal claim against Shyster herself for the loss which resulted from the damage to her chocolates. These principles function on the basis of logic and of property law. There is a possibility on the facts of this hypothetical example that a court may have recourse to morality in that the court may order that the spoiled chocolates should be deemed to have belonged beneficially to Shyster on the basis that he was a defaulting trustee and so that none of the innocent parties for whom he was holding chocolates on trust would suffer any loss as a result of his actions.[124]

The more difficult situation is that in which the property cannot be divided between the parties rateably because, for example, it is a garment like a coat which cannot reasonably be cut into pieces and divided. Page Wood VC has held quite simply that:

> if a man mixes trust funds with his own, the whole will be treated as the trust property, except so far as he may be able to distinguish what is his own.[125]

Therefore, suppose that it was money which had been taken from Bernice's trust fund by her trustee Shyster, and further suppose that that money had been used to buy a coat which has now passed into the possession of Innocent and Shyster. A coat could not be sensibly divided up between the parties in the way that the store of chocolates could be divided up. Bernice might have been entitled to recover the entire property as opposed to only having a right to a *pro rata* share or a lien to make good her loss. So, Bernice could take possession of the coat until Shyster pays her in money or in money's worth the value of her right in the coat, instead of seeking to take title in a part of the coat (for example, a sleeve) when the coat was not physically capable of being divided up sensibly in this way. After all, what use would it be to have a mere sleeve from a coat; whereas it would be possible to have a proportionate part of a fund of money or of a physical commodity like salt. It is not surprising to learn that English law will apply subtly different approaches depending on the type of property at issue. This is considered in relation to the remedies for tracing below.

Furthermore, it does not matter what the market value was of the assets contributed to the fund at the time of their contribution: what matters is the value which they constitute as a proportion of the total fund at the time of making the claim. Suppose, for example, that Shyster took 1,000 SAFC plc shares from Bernice at a time when those shares were worth 100p, and later that Innocent added 1,000 shares which were worth only 90p at the time when she contributed them. Suppose further that at the time of making the claim SAFC plc shares were worth 150p. The courts will not take Innocent's contribution to have been £900 (the value of her shares at the time of their contribution) and Bernice's shares £1,000. Rather, each is deemed to have contributed one half of all of the property in the mixed fund of 2,000

---

122 As considered at section 18.5 above; ie, a claim to restitution or compensation – *Target Holdings v Redferns* [1996] 1 AC 421, [1995] 3 WLR 352, [1995] 3 All ER 785.
123 *Re Oatway* [1903] 2 Ch 356; *Foskett v McKeown* [2000] 3 All ER 97.
124 *Re Hallett's Estate* (1880) 13 Ch D 696.
125 *Frith v Cartland* (1865) 2 Hem & M 417, 420, (1865) 71 ER 525, 526; *Foskett v McKeown* [2000] 3 All ER 97, 125.

shares.[126] The approach taken is that the claimants receive rights in property regardless of the precise market value of the property at any time: the purpose of a property court is to vindicate the claimant's property rights first, and it is then for other doctrines such as breach of trust, considered in Chapter 18, to look to the compensation of any of the parties for any loss which remains outstanding.

The question then is as to the range of other remedies which the courts may choose to offer. On the cases relating to money in bank accounts, much has turned on whether or not the claimants can establish rights either to money subsisting in bank accounts or to moneys used to buy assets of substantial value. Typically in the cases involving money in bank accounts, some money has simply been dissipated whereas other money has acquired profitable investments. It is to this type of issue that we now turn.

Payments made through current bank accounts

Different principles apply in relation to tracing payments made through current bank accounts. The rule in *Re Diplock* which was considered at para 19.4.2 above applies satisfactorily to static funds where no property moves in or out. Suppose that the property making up the fund constitutes two cars of equal value contributed one each by the two innocent parties. In that circumstance it is easy to divide the fund between two claimants so that they receive one car each. If the fund were a house which was bought with the aggregate proceeds of the property belonging to the two innocent parties, *Re Diplock* would require that each person take an equal charge over that house.

The more difficult situation, however, is that in which the fund containing the mixed property is used in chunks to acquire separate property. Suppose a current bank account from which payments are made to acquire totally unrelated items of the property. The problem will lie in deciding which of the innocent contributors to the fund ought to take which right in which piece of property. The facts in the following table may illustrate the problem, concerning payments in and out of a current bank account the balance of which stood at zero at the opening of business on 1 June.

Date	Payments in	Payments out
1 June	£1,000 from trust A	
2 June	£2,000 from trust B	
3 June		£500 to buy ICI plc shares
4 June		£1,500 to buy SAFC plc shares
5 June		£1,000 to buy BP plc shares

On these facts £3,000 was in the account at the end of 2 June, being a mixture of money from two separate trusts (A and B). By 6 June, the traceable proceeds of that property had been used to buy ICI shares, SAFC shares, and BP shares. The problem is then to ascertain the title to those shares. There are two possible approaches: either particular shares are allocated

126 *Foskett v McKeown* [2000] 3 All ER 97, *per* Lord Millett.

between the two trust funds, or both funds take proportionate interests in all of the shares.[127] The two scenarios appear in different cases, as considered immediately below.

The first in, first out approach

The long-standing rule relating to title in property paid out of current bank accounts is that in *Clayton's Case*.[128] In relation to current bank accounts, the decision in *Clayton's Case* held that the appropriate principle is 'first in, first out' such that in deciding which property has been used to acquire which items of property it is deemed that money first deposited is used first. The reason for this rule is a rigid application of accounting principles. If money is paid in on 1 June, that money must be deemed to be the first money to exit the account.

Therefore, according to the facts set out above, the deposit made from trust A on 1 June is deemed to be the first money to be paid out. The ICI shares acquired on 3 June for £500 would thus be deemed to have been acquired solely with money derived from trust A. The tracing process consequently would assign rights in the ICI shares to A. By the same token, the SAFC shares would be deemed to have been acquired on 4 June with the remaining £500 from trust A and £1,000 from trust B. The BP shares are therefore acquired with the remaining £1,000 from trust B.

The drawback with the *Clayton's Case* approach is that it would be unfair to trust A if ICI shares were to halve in value while shares in BP were to double in value. That would mean that trust A's £500 investment in ICI would be worth only £250 as a result of the halving in value, whereas trust B's £1,000 investment in BP would then be worth £2,000.

The only way of understanding this rule is to recall that it derives from a case decided early in the 19th century when there was comparatively little litigation concerning intangible property. Rather, this case appears to have its roots in cases regarding tangible property like soft fruit. If we ran a business as wholesalers of soft fruit – oranges, pears and so forth – we would have a large warehouse in which the fruit was stored. When an order came in for a consignment of oranges, we would be foolish to ship out the fruit which had arrived in our warehouse most recently, because that would leave older fruit at the rear of the warehouse at greater risk of rotting. Instead, the first fruit to have arrived in our warehouse would be the first fruit which we would ship out: first in, first out. This way of thinking carried on into elementary book-keeping, in which the assumption was that the first money to be paid into a bank account would similarly be the first money to be paid out. In a world of intangible property, it is an approach which appears anachronistic. Another approach is suggested in the next section.

Proportionate share

The alternative approach would be to decide that each contributor should take proportionate shares in all of the property acquired with the proceeds of the fund. This is the approach taken in most Commonwealth jurisdictions.[129] On the facts in the table on page 913 above,

---

127 The proportionate approach is probably to be preferred now, although, as will emerge, the authorities are not yet clear on this point: *Foskett v McKeown* [2000] 3 All ER 97.
128 (1816) 1 Mer 572.
129 *Re Ontario Securities Commission* (1985) 30 DLR (4d) 30; *Re Registered Securities* [1991] 1 NZLR 545.

each party contributed to the bank account in the ratio 1:2 (in that trust A provided £1,000 and trust B provided £2,000). Therefore, all of the ICI shares, the SAFC shares, and the BP shares would be held on trust one-third for A and two-thirds for B. The result is the elimination of any differential movements in value across this property in circumstances in which it is pure chance which beneficiaries would take rights in which property.

A slightly different twist on this approach was adopted in *Barlow Clowes International v Vaughan*.[130] In that case, investors in the collapsed Barlow Clowes organisation had their losses met in part by the Department of Trade and Industry. The Secretary of State for Trade and Industry then sought to recover, in effect, the amounts which had been paid away to those former investors by tracing the compensation paid to the investors into the assets of Barlow Clowes.

At first instance, Peter Gibson J held that the rule in *Clayton's Case*[131] should be applied. *Clayton's Case* asserts the rule (as considered immediately above) that tracing claims into mixed funds in current bank accounts are to treat the money first paid into the bank account as the first paid out of the account. The majority of the Court of Appeal favoured a distribution between the rights of the various investors on a *pari passu* basis, considering *Clayton's Case* too formalistic and arbitrary. Leggatt and Woolf LJJ approved a 'rolling charge' approach culled from the Canadian cases. This meant that the investors would have to take into account not only the size of their contribution to the fund, but also the length of time for which that money was part of the fund. Clearly, the longer an investment is made, the more money it could be expected to make. Therefore, the attraction of the rolling charge would be to take into account the length of time for which depositors had deposits. In this way they would also share the impact of losses.

It is suggested that this rolling charge approach is the more sensible approximation to the contribution which each good faith investor has made to the total fund. Rather than look to which investors contributed their money first and which last – always a result of chance – it seems a more equitable approach to resort to the resulting trust principle that each should take according to the proportionate size of their contributions. On the facts of *Barlow Clowes*, the process of calculating these separate entitlements would have been particularly complicated given the large number of investors and the huge range of investments made by the funds at issue. The one caveat might then be to recognise that some investors would have had their investments in the fund for longer, and that therefore they should receive some credit for the duration of their investment. Some equitable accounting at that level would appear to be conscionable.

It is clear from decisions in the wake of *Barlow Clowes* that the English courts would prefer to resile from the *Clayton's Case* principle;[132] at the time of writing, however,

130 [1992] 4 All ER 22, [1992] BCLC 910; noted Birks, 1993, 218.
131 (1816) 1 Mer 572.
132 *Barlow Clowes v Vaughan* [1992] 4 All ER 22; *El Ajou v Dollar Land Holdings (No 2)* [1995] 2 All ER 213, 222, Robert Walker J; *Re Lewis's of Leicester* [1995] 1 BCLC 428; *Sheppard v Thompson* (2001) unreported, 3 December; *Russell-Cooke Trust Co v Prentis* [2003] 2 All ER 478; *Commerzbank AG v IMB Morgan plc* [2004] EWHC 2771 (Ch). Commonwealth jurisdictions have long turned their back on *Clayton's Case* (see *Re Ontario Securities Commission* (1988) 52 DLR (4th) 767 (Sup Ct) in Canada and *Re French Caledonia Travel Service Pty Ltd* (2003) 204 ALR 353, *per* Campbell J, in Australia), as have the courts in the USA (see *Re Walter J Schmidt & Co*, 298 F 314, 316 (1923), *per* Learned Hand J).

Clayton's Case has not been formally overruled, merely criticised and distinguished. So, in *Russell-Cooke Trust Co v Prentis*[133] a solicitor conducted an investment scheme and took investments from his clients in return for a guaranteed return of 15% on all investments. All of the investments were paid into the solicitor's client account, which meant that those funds were held on trust for the clients in proportionate shares. The solicitor's practice was the subject of complaints and when the Law Society intervened, a number of irregularities and shortfalls in the operation of the investment fund were discovered. The court was asked whether the more appropriate principle was that in *Clayton's Case* (the 'first-in, first-out' approach) or that in *Barlow Clowes* (the 'rolling charge' approach). Lindsay J held that the *Clayton's Case* approach was still binding but that it was also capable of being distinguished on the facts of any given case. Having suggested that the 'first-in, first-out' approach was the binding principle, it was held that that principle could be displaced in circumstances in which, for example, the parties had demonstrated a contrary intention in their dealings or in which that conclusion would be unfair between the parties. As is considered in the following paragraph, it is frequently the case that the 'first-in, first-out' approach will appear to be unfair to one party or another. As this point was put by Woolf LJ in *Barlow Clowes v Vaughan*:[134]

> There is no reason in law or justice why his depredations upon the fund should not be borne equally between [the parties]. To throw all the loss upon one, through the mere chance of his being earlier in time, is irrational and arbitrary, and is equally a fiction as the rule in *Clayton's Case*. When the law adopts a fiction, it is, or at least it should be, for some purpose of justice. To adopt it here is to apportion a common misfortune through a test which has no relation whatever to the justice of the case.

This approach suggests that the court's purpose – when dealing with mixtures of the property of two innocent people – is to achieve justice between them if there is no obvious fault on the part of one party or the other.[135] Or, to put the same idea in the language of equity, division of property should be made on a *pari passu*[136] basis where the equities between the parties are even.

Latterly, in *Commerzbank AG v IMB Morgan plc*,[137] the same approach to authority of *Clayton's Case* was taken by Lawrence Collins J. A fraudulent investment scheme was operated through a correspondent bank account managed by Commerzbank. Money was taken from the public and mixed in the bank account. It was held that it would have been unjust and impracticable to have applied *Clayton's Case* on these facts: unjust because it would have produced arbitrary results between the investors, and impracticable in that it would have required a difficult exercise to decide which payments in and out of this account were derived from which investors and made in which order.

---

133 [2003] 2 All ER 478.

134 [1992] 4 All ER 22, 44.

135 Cf *Re Eastern Capital Futures Ltd* [1989] BCLC 371, 375, *per* Morritt J, where it was held that the preference should be for even division of the property where the equities were even.

136 '*Pari passu*' meaning 'in equal step', suggesting a division in proportion to contribution without any addition or reduction needing to be made to account for inequitable behaviour.

137 [2004] EWHC 2771 (Ch).

Which approach is to be preferred?

Therefore, the rolling charge approach has been approved but not applied, and the rule in *Clayton's Case* was criticised by Leggatt LJ in *Barlow Clowes* as having 'nothing to do' with tracing property rights through into property. Indeed, it does appear to effect somewhat arbitrary results in many circumstances. Suppose, for example, the following facts. £5,000 is taken from a trust fund and mixed in a bank account with £10,000 belonging to the trustee's mother which was already in that account. Suppose then that £7,500 is taken out of the mixture and used to buy Gotech plc shares which double in value, while the remaining £7,500 is lost on a bet on a three-legged terrier running against greyhounds at White City dog track. If *Clayton's Case* were applied, the money used to buy the valuable shares would be deemed to come entirely from the mother's money. The money wasted on the bet would be deemed to have come as to £2,500 from the mother and £5,000 from the trust. However, if *Barlow Clowes* were applied, the trust would be able to argue that, because it had contributed one-third of the money in the bank account (that is, £5,000 of the total £15,000 in the account), the trust should be entitled to one-third of the valuable shares and one-third of the useless bet in proportion to its total contribution.

The result of these cases is that the English cases will disapply *Clayton's Case* on the slightest indication that to apply *Clayton's Case* would produce injustice in the form of 'irrational and arbitrary' results. Otherwise, *Clayton's Case* has not been formally overruled. Therefore, in deciding tracing claims relating to current bank accounts, it is necessary first to consider the effect of *Clayton's Case* and secondly to consider whether the alternative approach based on *pari passu* or proportionate division would produce more equitable results between the parties or results more in tune with their evident intentions.

The rule in *Clayton's Case* derives from a time when money was considered to be a tangible item of property like cattle, land, and so forth. As mentioned above, the first in, first out rule mimics the way in which goods in a warehouse would be accounted for. In *Clayton's Case*, money is being treated in the same fashion – thus denying that it is in fact intangible – and the application of that rule generates arbitrary results in many circumstances.

19.4.3 Tracing payments made by mistake

Suppose A mistakenly pays money to B, so that B has no true entitlement to it.[138] The question which would arise is whether or not A is entitled to trace that payment and enforce a remedy to recover it from B.

In *Chase Manhattan Bank NA v Israel-British Bank (London) Ltd*,[139] a payment between banks was made twice by mistake. The recipient bank went into insolvency before repaying the second, mistaken payment. The issue arose whether the payer had a proprietary right in the payment so that it could be traced by the payer and deemed to be held on trust for it (thus protecting that payment from the insolvency). It was held by Goulding J that the property should be held on trust for the payer and that the payer could therefore trace into the assets of the recipient bank as a result of the equitable interest founded under the trust. The precise

---

138   That is, suppose the absence of a contract or any other juristic reason entitling B to retain that money.
139   [1981] 1 Ch 105, [1980] 2 WLR 202, [1979] 3 All ER 1025.

basis for the extended fiduciary duty imposed by Goudling J is difficult to identify, being an uncomfortable combination of restitution of unjust enrichment and constructive trust.[140]

The rationale of this judgment was doubted (but its result approved on other grounds) by Lord Browne-Wilkinson in *Westdeutsche Landesbank Girozentrale v Islington LBC*,[141] where his Lordship declared that he was prepared to accept that this decision was correct on the basis that a constructive trust arose at the time when the property had been received *and* the recipient knew of the mistake: it was said that the combination of knowledge of the mistake and the effect on the recipient's conscience would be sufficient to justify the creation of a constructive trust. By the same token, ignorance of the mistake would not have given rise to an equitable proprietary right. In *Lloyds Bank plc v Independent Insurance Co Ltd*,[142] a bank made a mistake in relation to a payment into an account held by one of its clients. However, the bank's mistake was not as to a countermand, but rather as to how much money was paid through its customer's account. It was held (following *Barclays Bank v Simms*)[143] that the bank could not recover against the payee because the payment discharged a debt owed by the bank's customer to the payee.

19.5   LOSS OF THE RIGHT TO TRACE

19.5.1   Loss of the right to trace: the general principle

A claimant in a tracing claim will lose her right to trace if the property into which she is seeking to trace her rights either ceases to exist or cannot be found. The loss of the right to trace is considered in detail below in relation to electronic bank accounts: in that context, by way of example, money is often moved between electronic bank accounts by money-launderers or by thieves in an effort to make it impossible to prove where the money which was derived from the claimant's property has gone. If the trail goes cold, then the tracing claim is lost. So, if a bank account into which the claimant's money was paid subsequently goes overdrawn (that is, if the account is run down to zero) then the claimant will lose her right to claim into that particular bank account because the money which represented her property has clearly passed out of that account by the time the level of that account reached zero.[144] The same point holds true for all forms of property: if the property and its traceable substitute cease to exist, the claimant loses the right to trace.[145] So, in *Ultraframe (UK) Ltd v Fielding*[146] the claimant sought to claim that the defendant had earned profits by misusing the claimant's intellectual property in breach of trust to manufacture high quality double glazing components.[147] Therefore, the claimant argued, *inter alia*, that the defendant's profits had been derived from the claimant's property. However, the claimant could not prove an

---

140 Old editions of Professor Martin's *Modern Equity* have suggested that Goulding J stopped short of adopting the principle of unjust enrichment as the basis for this trust: 13th edn, 1989, 628.
141 [1996] AC 669.
142 [1999] 2 WLR 986, CA.
143 [1980] QB 677.
144 *Westdeutsche Landesbank v Islington* [1996] AC 669.
145 *Roscoe v Winder* [1915] 1 Ch 62; *Boscawen v Bajwa* [1996] 1 WLR 328; *Box v Barclays Bank* [1998] Lloyd's Rep Bank 185.
146 [2005] EWHC 1638 (Ch), [2005] All ER (D) 397.
147 This is a filleted account of a very, very long case which involved a very large number of parties.

unbroken chain of property rights leading from itself to the defendant. Therefore, it was held that where the claimant could not identify any particular item of property as constituting the traceable proceeds of the original trust property, then it would not be possible to trace into any profits which the defendant had made because no link between it and any property taken in breach of trust had been proven. Instead, the claimant could only demonstrate that the defendant had earned a profit from behaviour which had been allegedly unconscionable but could not demonstrate that that profit had been derived from the claimant's property or from its traceable proceeds. The point is that the claimant must be able to demonstrate that property in the defendant's hands constitutes the traceable proceeds of the claimant's property: if there is any break in that chain then the claimant will lose her right to trace into the property in the defendant's hands.

This principle is demonstrated most clearly in *Bishopsgate Investment Management v Homan*.[148] Here, in the aftermath of newspaper mogul Robert Maxwell's death, it transpired that amounts belonging to pension trust funds under his control had been misapplied. The amounts had been paid into accounts held by MCC (a company controlled by Maxwell) and other companies. Those accounts had gone overdrawn since the initial deposit of the money. The pension fund trustees sought an order granting them an equitable charge over all the accounts held by MCC, in line with *dicta* of Lord Templeman in *Space Investments Ltd v Canadian Imperial Bank of Commerce*.[149] It was held, nevertheless, that it is impossible to trace money into an overdrawn account on the basis that the property from which the traceable substitute derives is said to have disappeared.[150]

Further, on the facts of that case it was also held that there could be no equitable remedy enforced against an asset which was acquired before the misappropriation of the money took place. This is because it is not possible to trace into property which had been acquired without the aid of the misapplied property: that is, if Anne buys a car on 1 January, and then subsequently Anne misappropriates cash from a trust fund on 1 February, it cannot be said that that trust property made it possible to acquire the car.

The same principle was upheld by the Court of Appeal in *Serious Fraud Office v Lexi Holdings plc*[151] to the effect that a general charge would not be ordered over all of the assets of a bank on the basis that the claimant could demonstrate that the traceable proceeds of their property had passed into the bank at some point. Rather, the claimant is required to demonstrate into which fund or account that property passed. In essence, it is suggested, the *obiter* remarks of Lord Templeman amount to nothing more than a personal claim against a bank (in that no specific property is identified) for a given amount of money. This point was reinforced by Briggs J in *Re Lehman Brothers (Europe) (No 2)* where client money had been mixed with the bank's own money in such a way that it was impossible to identify any given money flowing from the traceable proceeds of a particular class of claimant and that as a

---

148 [1995] Ch 211, [1995] 1 All ER 347, [1994] 3 WLR 1270; *Law Society of Upper Canada v Toronto Dominian Bank* (1998) 169 DLR (4th) 353 (Ont Ca).

149 *Space Investments Ltd v Canadian Imperial Bank of Commerce Trust Co (Bahamas) Ltd* [1986] 1 WLR 1072, [1986] 3 All ER 75.

150 The loss of the right to trace was also upheld in *Re BA Peters plc, Atkinson v Moriarty* [2008] EWCA Civ 1604, [2010] 1 BCLC 142, [15], *per* Lord Neuberger where it was held that if the property over which proprietary rights were sought had ceased to exist in the hands of the defendant then there could be no proprietary right in the form of a trust against that defendant.

151 [2008] EWCA Crim 1443, [2009] 1 All ER 586, [2009] QB 376.

result it was impossible for them to bring a tracing action, and furthermore that they could not assert a charge over the entire assets of the defendant bank.[152] Such a claim for a general charge over the assets of the bank would offend the anti-deprivation[153] and *pari passu*[154] principles in insolvency law whereby assets may not be taken from the insolvent person's estate nor may one unsecured creditor be advantaged ahead of any other unsecured creditor.

19.5.2 Lowest intermediate balance

The principle set out above does not account for the circumstance which is more generally the case when property is taken away from a mixed fund and new property added subsequently. Suppose that £100 is taken from a trust fund and paid into a bank account which already contains £50; suppose that £130 is spent, leaving only £20 of the original mixture. If £200 is added subsequently, then there is a question as to whether a claimant-beneficiary can recover the whole of her loss from that account or only the £20 which could be said to have represented her property. The question arises whether the claimant ought to be able to trace into any property held in a fund to which her own property has been added, or whether the claimant should be restricted to tracing only into property which can be demonstrated to have derived from the original misappropriated property.

The rule is that the claimant has only a right to claim the lowest intermediate balance of that property.[155] The reference to lowest intermediate balance means that the claimant will be entitled to trace into only the lowest value of the property held between the date of its misapplication and the date of the claim being brought because that is the largest amount which could possibly be said to have resulted from her contribution to the mixture originally. That is, the £20 which represents the last money which the trust could possibly have contributed to that bank account in the example given above. So, by way of illustration, *Roscoe v Winder*[156] concerned money being taken from a trust, paid into a bank account, and mixed with other money such that sums were paid into and out of that account on numerous occasions, causing fluctuating balances in that account over time. The issue would be to ascertain which level in the bank account should be considered to be the one against which the claimant could claim. The court held that, assuming the trust money was the last to be paid out of the account, the claimant could assert a claim only against the lowest level in that account because (by definition) any money paid into the account after that lowest level had been reached could not be said to have been derived from the trust.

Suppose the following, to repeat the example given above: £100 is taken from a trust fund and added to a bank account already containing £50 on 1 January. Then suppose that £130 is taken out of the account on 1 February, before a new £200 unrelated to the trust is paid into the account on 1 March. If a claim were brought on 1 April, the beneficiary would be entitled to trace into only the £20 which was left in the account on 1 February, on the basis that that is the only money which could possibly be said to have derived from the original £100. That

---

152 [2009] EWHC 3228 (Ch), [2010] EWHC 47 (Ch), [2010] 2 BCLC 301.
153 *Belmont Park Investments Pty Ltd v BNY Corporate Trustee Services Ltd* [2011] UKSC 38, [2011] 3 WLR 521.
154 *British Eagle International Airlines Ltd v Cie Nationale Air France* [1975] 1 WLR 758.
155 *Roscoe v Winder* [1915] 1 Ch 62. See also *Campden Hill Ltd v Chakrani* [2005] EWHC 911 (Ch).
156 [1915] 1 Ch 62.

£20 is the lowest intermediate balance of the fund. The £200 paid in subsequently had not come from the trust, by definition, and therefore there could be no claim against it.

The £20 is the lowest intermediate balance against which a claim based on tracing can be established. The claimant would have lost her right to claim into the remaining money once it was paid out of that account – instead, the claimant would have to find out where that money had gone and then seek to trace into the place where that money subsequently came to rest. So, suppose the remaining £80 (out of the original £100 in this example) had moved into bank account No. 100, then the claimant would seek to trace into the first account for £20 and into bank account No. 100 for the remaining £80.

19.5.3 Tracing through electronic bank accounts

One of the most vexed problems in tracing claims then is that of establishing proprietary rights in amounts of money which are held in electronic bank accounts. Most of the cases in this area involve large banking and commercial institutions, for two reasons. First, it is only such wealthy institutions which can afford to pay for the complex and convoluted litigation that is necessary in this field to bring matters to court (involving expensive experts in accountancy and banking, as well as lawyers). Secondly, the nature of electronic bank accounts raises very particular problems for English lawyers, and indeed all legal systems.

Electronic bank accounts are choses in action (that is, debts) between depositor and bank. The bank owes, by way of debt, the amount of money in the account to the depositor (provided that the account is in credit) on the terms of their contract. Therefore, these accounts are not tangible property. Rather, they are debts with value attached to them (that value being the amount of the deposit plus interest). It is consequently surprising that English lawyers continue to think of money (whether held in a bank account or not) as being tangible property. When considering the way in which tracing applies to money held in accounts, conceiving of that money as being tangible rather than being simply an amount of value, creates problems, particularly in relation to the loss of the right to trace.[157]

By way of example, it was held in *Westdeutsche Landesbank Girozentrale v Islington LBC*[158] that the specific property provided by the payer was not capable of identification given that it had been paid into bank accounts which had subsequently been run into overdraft on a number of occasions. The analogy used by Lord Browne-Wilkinson in explaining the nature of equitable proprietary rights was that of 'a stolen bag of coins'. His Lordship was supposing that to identify any money which was being traced, we must imagine that the money was in the form of coins held in a bag which had been stolen, and that the claimant can only trace after the specific coins in that bag but not any other coins which might have been added to the bag subsequently. This metaphor is particularly enlightening, for the reasons given above, because it envisages proprietary rights in electronic bank accounts as being concerned with tangible property and not as the intangible property which it clearly is. Money in an electronic bank account is not in the form of tangible coins in a bag: it is in the form of memory stored in a computer's memory. Therefore, we have to ask whether or not this tangible property metaphor is useful in relation to electronic money.

---

157 See now *Lloyds Bank plc v Independent Insurance Co Ltd* [1999] 2 WLR 986, CA.
158 [1996] AC 669, [1996] 2 All ER 961.

In that eccentric way which English lawyers think about money held in electronic bank accounts, it was said by Lord Browne-Wilkinson that once a bank account goes overdrawn or the money is spent, that money disappears.[159] This is a money-launderer's paradise. Rather than saying 'if money passes out of a computer-held bank account but its value is still held in some form by the owner of that account, therefore we should treat that person as still having the money', English law actually says 'if that electronic money has gone from that account and cannot be traced in its equivalent proprietary form, we must assume it has disappeared'. No wonder the English have such an affection for mediocre TV magicians if they are so easily convinced by these disappearing tricks. In this way, English law retains its determination to understand property in terms of tangible property and not as value which attaches to different items of property (tangible or intangible) from time to time. This is ironic given that the purpose of the law of tracing is straightforwardly to recognise that property rights may continue to exist even though the original property itself is beyond reach.[160]

19.6 CLAIMING: TRUSTS AND REMEDIES

Aside from the loss of the right to trace, remedies in relation to tracing claims will typically include: the establishment of a lien; the establishment of a constructive trust; the establishment of an equitable charge; and subrogation.

Having considered the nature of the tracing process, it is important to consider the types of claim and the forms of remedy which might be imposed as a result of it. The two principal remedies are the charge[161] and the constructive trust;[162] although resulting trust,[163] equitable compensation,[164] lien[165] and subrogation[166] are also possible on the basis of decided cases.[167] The structure is simple: first, the tracing process is carried out in accordance with the principles considered above; then, secondly, having identified the property which is to be the subject matter of the claim, the claimant seeks to impose a trust or some equitable remedy over that property. The various possibilities are considered below. In short, there are no clear rules as to which remedy should be applied in which situation but rather the courts seem to be prepared to impose whichever remedy seems to be most appropriate in the circumstances and whichever remedy provides the most convenient solution for the successful claimant. Therefore, this section will consider all of the principal remedies in turn. First, however, we shall consider in the abstract which form of remedy is likely to be most appropriate in which type of situation: this will make the nature of each remedy easier to understand.

159 For an extended discussion of this idea, see generally Chapter 31.
160 In general see Chapter 31; Hudson, 1999:3, 170.
161 *Re Tilley's Will Trusts* [1967] Ch 1179.
162 *Westdeutsche Landesbank Girozentrale v Islington LBC* [1996] AC 669, at para 19.5.3 below.
163 *El Ajou v Dollar Land Holdings* [1993] 3 All ER 717.
164 *Target Holdings v Redferns* [1996] 1 AC 421, [1995] 3 WLR 352, [1995] 3 All ER 785.
165 *Foskett v McKeown* [2001] 1 AC 102.
166 *Boscawen v Bajwa* [1996] 1 WLR 328. Considered in section 30.7.
167 Contrary to Professor Birks's argument that it is not appropriate to talk of 'rights' and 'remedies' but rather only of 'rights' which necessarily imply their remedies (Birks, 2000:1), this is one context in which the rights of the claimant may lead to the realisation of any one of a number of remedies dependent on the context, one of which (equitable compensation) necessarily involves some judicial discretion; see generally Barker, 1998, 319.

19.6.1 What form of remedy would be most appropriate: a charge, a lien or a constructive trust?

The onus is on the claimant to claim the remedy which is most appropriate in the circumstances. Different types of remedy will be more suitable or more appropriate in different circumstances depending on the nature of the property and whether or not there are innocent third parties involved. Usually this issue resolves itself to a choice between a charge over the traced property, or a possessory lien over the property, or the award of proprietary rights in the form of a constructive trust over the property in favour of the claimant. Each of these remedies is considered in detail below but their basic characteristics can be explained here. First, the charge arises only in equity and entitles the claimant to seize the property and seek a court order to sell it if the defendant does not pay the claimant whatever the claimant is owed under the terms of the charge. Secondly, a lien entitles the claimant to take physical possession of property and to retain that property until the defendant pays the claimant whatever the claimant is owed. Both of these types of remedy are therefore concerned with ensuring that the claimant is paid an amount of money and both require that the property can be identified separately from other property. The third 'remedy'[168] is the constructive trust which entitles the claimant to an equitable proprietary interest in the traced property. In theory such a constructive trust could be constructed so that any third party with rights in the traced property would hold the equitable interest in that property in common with the claimant; more usually a constructive trust will be claimed so that the claimant can become the absolute beneficial owner of property so that she can acquire any future increase in value in that property. A constructive trust is likely to be sought in circumstances in which the property is intrinsically valuable or when it is likely to be of use to the claimant.

So, if the property that was being traced was a cargo of cotton onboard a ship moored at Tilbury Docks in London and if the claimants had no use themselves for a large quantity of cotton, the claimants might seek a charge over the cotton so that they could force payment of an amount equal to the amount of money which was wrongfully taken from their trust fund; if payment was not made, they could use their rights under the charge to sell the cotton. If they feared that the ship might sail away from England, then they could seek a lien so as to take possession of the cotton until they were paid an amount equal to the amount of money taken wrongfully from their trust fund. If the property being traced was a holding of valuable shares, the claimants may prefer to enforce a constructive trust over those shares so that the claimants would become the beneficial owners (and would thus remain the beneficial owners even if they subsequently increased in value).

The decision as to which remedy will be the most appropriate will therefore depend on the circumstances. The nature of the property will be particularly important, as outlined above. So, where the property subject to the tracing claim is capable of being separated from other property so that it could form the subject matter of a trust, a constructive trust may be the most appropriate remedy. If the property were not so segregated, then it would not be possible to impose a trust over that property because the subject matter of that trust would not be separately identifiable.[169] If, for example, the traceable proceeds of the claimant's

---

168   The word 'remedy' here is in inverted commas because, strictly, constructive trusts are *institutional* and not *remedial*.

169   *MacJordan Construction Ltd v Brookmount Erostin Ltd* [1992] BCLC 350.

original property were mixed with property belonging to other innocent parties, the more appropriate approach would be to award a charge to each party in proportion to their contribution to the total fund. Alternatively, the claimant might be awarded a lien in circumstances in which compensation in money would be appropriate, but so that the claimant would have the protection of a lien in the event that payment was not made. Each of these claims is considered further below.

The advantage of the constructive trust is that the claimant acquires equitable title in specific property. However, a fixed charge does grant property rights which will be enforceable in the event of an insolvency by means of granting the claimant a right to be paid an amount of money but, if the debtor defaults, giving the claimant a right to seize the specified property to realise its claim.[170] The shortcoming of a charge is that once the repossessed property is sold, the claimant is entitled only to recover the amount of the debt, not to take absolute title in the property, having to account to the debtor instead for any surplus. Were the claimant to establish a right under a constructuve trust, as considered below, the claimant would be entitled to take equitable ownership of the property and thus take title in any increase in value in that property. So, this raises the question: which remedy should be applied in which circumstances. Lord Millett held the following in *Foskett v McKeown*:[171]

> As Ames pointed out in 'Following Misappropriated Property into its Product' (1906) Harvard Law Review 511, consistency requires that, if a trustee buys property partly with his own money and partly with trust money, the beneficiary should have the option of taking a proportionate part of the new property or a lien upon it, as may be most for his advantage.

The detail of these *dicta* need not detain us at the moment – we shall consider the obligations of trustees shortly. What is significant is the acceptance by Lord Millett here that there is no single remedy which the court is obliged to impose: rather, the court will impose whatever remedy is appropriate bearing in mind the convenience to the claimant. Thus, when I identified the most important remedies as being the constructive trust, the charge and the lien, I was doing so on the basis of what judges have tended to do in practice. At the time of writing there is no clear, single judicial statement of which remedy should be applied in which context and therefore we shall have to formulate an understanding of why judges impose given remedies in given situations for ourselves.

The main principles, it is suggested, are as follows, once the tracing process has been successfully pursued and the target property has been successfully identified, if the original property which was taken from the trust can be identified separately from all other property, then a following claim will be sufficient for the court to declare that that property belongs beneficially to the beneficiaries of the trust.[172] For the other principles we must assume that the original property cannot be identified separately from all other property and that instead that property is mixed with other property. If the property is of a fungible sort – like money in a bank account or salt in a salt cellar – and if the claimant wants the property itself, then

---

170 *Re Tilley's Will Trusts* [1967] Ch 1179; *Paul Davies Pty Ltd v Davies* [1983] 1 NSWLR 440.
171 [2001] 1 AC 102, 127.
172 *Ibid.*

the claimant will seek a constructive trust over the entire fund so that the claimant is beneficially entitled to an appropriate proportion of that fund. Put crudely, she will become the owner of part of that property.

Alternatively, if the property is not property which the claimant would wish to own but if the claimant would prefer to have the cash equivalent of her loss as a beneficiary, then she will prefer to have a charge or a lien over the entire mixture of property. As discussed below, a charge will entitle the claimant to petition the court for seizure of the property if the defendant does not pay her the cash amount required; or alternatively a lien will entitle the claimant to take possession of the property until such time as payment in an amount sufficient to settle the claim is made to her, and if payment is not so made then the claimant will petition the court for seizure of the property. So, if the property acquired with the trust's money was a component in a large industrial machine, the claimant might have no use for that component. Therefore, she would prefer to have a charge over the entire machine to secure her right to money from the defendant, but so that she could insist on the sale of the machine if payment were not made. If the property acquired with the trust's money was something more portable, like an oil painting which is not expected to increase much in value, then the claimant would prefer to take a lien over the painting – such that she would take physical possession of the painting – until such time as she is paid enough money to settle her claim by the defendant. If the defendant does not pay up then the claimant would apply to the court for permission to sell the painting. So, we can see that much will depend on the nature of the property involved as to which remedy is the most appropriate, and also much will depend on whether or not the claimant would have any use for the type of property which the defendant had acquired with the misapplied trust fund.

19.6.2 Constructive trust recognised in response to equitable tracing claims

The basis on which a constructive trust will be used as a remedy in a tracing claim

As considered in the previous section, a constructive trust will be an appropriate response[173] to a tracing claim where there is identified and separate property capable of being held on trust for the claimant as a result of the tracing process. As discussed in Chapter 12, in general terms a constructive trust is imposed in circumstances in which the defendant deals with property knowing of some factor which affects her conscience.[174] Thus, the House of Lords in *Westdeutsche Landesbank v Islington LBC*[175] held that there will not be a constructive trust without the defendant having knowledge of some factor which affects her conscience. For the imposition of a constructive trust as a result of an equitable tracing claim, it is therefore required that there be a pre-existing equitable interest sufficient to ground the equitable tracing claim,[176] that there be identifiable property which can be the subject matter of the trust,[177] and that the defendant have acted unconscionably with knowledge that her actions were unconscionable.[178]

---

173 The term 'response' is used here because, strictly, the word 'remedy' would be inaccurate given that English constructive trusts are *institutional* and not *remedial*.
174 See section 12.1 above.
175 [1996] AC 669, [1996] 2 All ER 961.
176 *Re Diplock* [1948] Ch 465.
177 *Westdeutsche Landesbank v Islington LBC* [1996] AC 669.
178 *Ibid.*

In *Westdeutsche Landesbank v Islington LBC*,[179] a bank paid money to a local authority under an interest rate swap contract which was subsequently found to have been void *ab initio*. The principal question was whether or not the bank could demonstrate that the local authority should be required, by virtue of their common mistake[180] as to the validity of the contract or the failure of consideration when the contract was avoided, to be treated as a constructive trustee of the moneys paid to it such that the bank would be able to trace its money into the local authority's general funds. It was held that the local authority would not be treated as having been a constructive trustee of the moneys paid to it by the bank because, from the time it received the money until the time at which it dissipated those moneys, it had no knowledge that the contract was void *ab initio* and therefore could not have dealt unconscionably with the money.[181] There was no constructive trust, nor any trust of any other kind,[182] and therefore no equitable interest sufficient to found an equitable tracing claim. Furthermore, there could not have been a constructive trust because there was no property over which such a trust could have been imposed, or in relation to which an equitable tracing claim could have been commenced, once the local authority had spent the money paid to it by the bank.[183]

Whether constructive trusts will be imposed in response to a tracing claim to award new rights in property, and whether an equitable base sufficient to found a tracing claim is necessary to found a constructive trust

In the abstract, it is clear in *Westdeutsche Landesbank v Islington LBC* that there was no constructive trust because there was no knowledge of any factor affecting the defendant's conscience. Nevertheless, it should be recognised that in general terms, constructive trusts may arise in two completely different contexts. The first context would be in recognition of a pre-existing proprietary right which is deemed to have been transferred into the traceable proceeds of property taken originally from the claimant. The second context would be to impose an equitable obligation over a defendant in relation to property which the claimant had not previously owned because the defendant is deemed to have acted unconscionably in relation to that property in general terms.

The former type of constructive trust, in the form of a recognition of pre-existing property rights, is evident from the decision in *Westdeutsche Landesbank v Islington LBC*.[184] By contrast, the latter form of constructive trust arises in satisfaction of a form of general, equitable obligation in the manner demonstrated by Lord Templeman in *Attorney-General for Hong Kong v Reid*.[185] In the latter case, Lord Templeman held that a person who receives a bribe in breach of some office holds that bribe on constructive trust from the moment he receives it, with the result that any property which is acquired with that property or any profit

---

179 [1996] AC 669.
180 Or alternatively by virtue of failure of consideration in the form of the void contract.
181 See generally the discussion of this principle at section 12.1.
182 Particularly no resulting trust, as considered at section 11.1.
183 The moneys had been paid into the local authority's general bank accounts and those accounts had subsequently gone overdrawn, this terminating any possible right of tracing, as considered at section 19.3.
184 [1996] AC 669.
185 [1994] 1 AC 324, [1993] 3 WLR 1143.

derived from that property is similarly held on constructive trust.[186] This constructive trust arises over property in which the claimant previously had no proprietary rights but founds equitable proprietary rights by operation of law and consequently a right to commence an equitable tracing claim if the constructive trustee passes that property away or deals with it in some way.

This second type of constructive trust could be imposed simply on the basis of the court's measurement of the conscionability of the defendant's actions. Therefore, it is possible that the claimant might not need to demonstrate a pre-existing equitable interest appropriate to commence an equitable tracing claim, as required by *Re Diplock*,[187] but simply to show that the defendant has behaved unconscionably in general terms. In *Attorney-General for Hong Kong v Reid*,[188] the claimant was entitled to property rights in the defendant's property not because the claimant had had any prior rights in the property or in property through which it was traced, but simply because it is considered equitable to award her such property rights. So, if one thinks carefully about the claim in *Attorney-General for Hong Kong v Reid* the claimant Attorney-General was able to impose a constructive trust over property which had been acquired with bribes without needing to prove that the claimant had any prior equitable interest in the bribes, never mind attempting to prove that any such rights could be traced into the acquired property. Instead, the constructive trust in that case was imposed over substitute property solely on the basis of the defendant's unconscionable behaviour in receiving bribes. Alternatively, the better analysis in keeping with *Diplock*, would be to say that the unconscionable act of, for example, receiving a bribe as in *Reid* is itself the thing which gives rise to the equitable proprietary action, therefore there is no logical gap in this area of the law.

Nevertheless there may be a tension in the nature of constructive trusts between those constructive trusts imposed on a person who deals with property knowing that his actions are unconscionable, and those constructive trusts which are imposed in relation to equitable tracing claims.[189] It has been suggested that even as a result of the speech of Lord Browne-Wilkinson in *Westdeutsche Landesbank v Islington LBC*,[190] there is no need to demonstrate a prior equitable interest in the property to establish a constructive trust. This conclusion results from his Lordship only requiring a defendant to have knowledge of a factor which affects her conscience for there to be a constructive trust imposed.[191] Lord Browne-Wilkinson did, however, mention the need for a pre-existing equitable interest on which an equitable tracing claim should be based and therefore it could be said that his Lordship was not intending to overlook the niceties of the law tracing before the award of a constructive trust in such cases.

---

186 The first constructive trust over the bribe itself arises as a result of equity acting *in personam* against the defendant such that his unconscionable receipt of that property causes him to be deemed to be a constructive trustee of that property for those beneficiaries to whom fiduciary duties were owed. On the basis, then, that equity looks upon that as done which ought to have been done, the property held on trust is to be treated as having been the property of the claimant from the moment when the conscience of the defendant was affected by knowledge that his act was unconscionable, thus giving rise to a proprietary right in equity.

187 [1948] Ch 465.

188 [1994] 1 AC 324.

189 See specifically the discussion of the nature of constructive trusts in equitable tracing claims in Thomas and Hudson, 2004, at para 29–73 *et seq.*

190 [1996] 2 WLR 802, 838–39 in relation to a part of the speech headed 'The stolen bag of coins'.

191 Birks, 1996:2 at 10.

By contrast with ordinary constructive trusts, equitable tracing claims entitle the claimant to a remedy even if the defendant is an innocent volunteer.[192] That means that the defendant need not have acted unconscionably for a constructive trust to be imposed as a response to an equitable tracing claim; rather, such constructive trusts are imposed so as to vindicate the claimant's rights in the traced property. In some circumstances, it may be that the defendant has acted unconscionably in coming into possession of the property but that is not a pre-requisite of the claim. So, in *Re Diplock* there was an equitable tracing claim brought in relation to money paid out of a trust in the belief that the trustees were entitled to pay money to a medical charity, whereas the charitable purpose clause in that will trust was found to be void for not expressing a purely charitable purpose. Therefore, the beneficiaries under the will trust sought to trace into the assets of the charity to recover the property which had been paid to them in good faith by the trustees and which the charity had received in good faith. The beneficiaries' claim to be able to trace into the assets of the charity to recover the trust's money was not prevented by the fact that the charity had not acted unconscionably. Rather, the tracing claim was concerned to recover the beneficiaries' property rights regardless of the conscionability of the defendant's actions, unless the defendant could demonstrate one of the defences considered below. The same point emerges from *Foskett v McKeown* where the defendants had not personally committed any unconscionable act.

However, there are cases where good conscience has been held to be a good reason for not permitting a tracing action in relation to which the claimant was seeking to impose a constructive trust over property. An illustration of this line of authority can be taken by extrapolation from one decided case, *Allan v Rea Brothers Trustees Ltd*.[193] Suppose that property was transferred from one pension trust fund, A, to another pension trust fund, B. Suppose further that it was found that the money had been received by the trustees of the A trust in breach of the terms of the B trust, but that the consciences of the trustees of the A trust were not affected because they did not know that their actions constituted a breach of the terms of the B trust. The question would be whether or not the beneficiaries of trust A could trace into trust B and impose a constructive trust over the moneys which had been paid into trust B. Mainstream constructive trusts law would require that the trustees be shown to have acted unconscionably in relation to the receipt of that money before a constructive trust could be imposed over it. On the basis of this argument it was held in *Allan v Rea Brothers Trustees Ltd* that there would not be any trust over the transferred moneys in favour of the B trust because the trustees had not had knowledge at the material time of any factor which ought to have affected their consciences. However, in that case, it was acknowledged[194] that the property remained in equity the property of the B trust, further to the decision in *Foskett v McKeown*, regardless of the knowledge of the trustees of the B trust.

Clearly, there is a tension here between the question whether or not a person can be held liable to hold property on constructive trust further to an equitable tracing claim so as to vindicate the claimant's property rights in the trust property, or whether such a constructive trust can only come into existence if the defendant's conscience is affected. It is suggested that the courts have taken the approach that a constructive trust will be imposed further to an

---

192   *Re Diplock's Estate* [1948] Ch 465; *Foskett v McKeown* [2001] 1 AC 102, [2000] 3 All ER 97.
193   *Allan v Rea Brothers Trustees Ltd* [2002] EWCA Civ 85, where this issue emerges at para 46.
194   *Ibid*, at para 52, *per* Robert Walker LJ.

equitable tracing claim so as to vindicate the claimant's property rights;[195] just as tracing in general is said to be concerned with vindicating the claimant's property rights in general.

I would suggest that there is a way out of this puzzle as to whether or not the defendant ought to be required to have knowledge of some factor which affects her conscience before a constructive trust can be imposed over property in her possession. In practice, it is suggested that for an equitable tracing claim to be successful, it would be necessary in any event for the defendant to have under her control or in her possession the traceable proceeds of some property belonging in equity to the claimant. Therefore, the commencement of proceedings to assert title to that property and any communications prior to the service of proceedings will have furnished the defendant with sufficient knowledge to be obliged to hold that property on constructive trust for the claimant. Therefore, the start of the litigation would itself constitute the claimant giving the defendant notice of that unconscionable factor, even if the defendant had not known about it beforehand. The defendant would be required to make out a defence either of change of position, or of having purchased that property in good faith, or of estoppel by representation to resist the tracing claim. In this way, it is suggested, the conceptual problem as to whether or not the mooted imposition of a constructive trust in a claim for equitable tracing would be trumped by a lack of sufficient knowledge disappears in practice when the claimant first contacts the defendant. If the property or its traceable proceeds is no longer in the possession of the defendant then the right to trace would have been lost in any event, and so a tracing claim would in any event be inappropriate.[196]

That constructive trusts are institutional, and not remedial, in this context

In the speech of Lord Browne-Wilkinson in *Westdeutsche Landesbank Girozentrale v Islington LBC*,[197] when considering the flawed judgment of Goulding J *Chase Manhattan v Israel-British Bank*,[198] the problem that arose was the use of a seemingly remedial constructive trust by Goulding J with reference to a mistaken payment made by one bank to another. Lord Browne-Wilkinson held that English law will only impose an institutional constructive trust, not a remedial constructive trust. The institutional constructive trust is defined as arising by operation of law so as to protect pre-existing property rights without the scope for discretionary application on a case-by-case basis; a remedial constructive trust, by contrast, would permit the court's discretion as to the terms and nature of that constructive trust.

Under an institutional constructive trust, the trust arises by operation of law as from the date of the circumstances which give rise to it: the function of the court is merely to declare that such trust has arisen in the past. The consequences that flow from such a trust having arisen are also determined by rules of law, not under a discretion. However, in *Chase Manhattan*, Goulding J had suggested that there was no distinction between English and New York law, even though New York law would apply a remedial constructive trust in the following way. As Lord Browne-Wilkinson held, the remedial constructive trust is very different from the institutional constructive trust used in England:

195 *Re Diplock; Diplock v Wintle* [1948] Ch 465; *Foskett v McKeown* [2001] 1 AC 102.
196 *Westdeutsche Landesbank v Islington* [1996] AC 669.
197 [1996] AC 669.
198 [1981] 1 Ch 105.

A remedial constructive trust, as I understand it, is different. It is a judicial remedy giving rise to an enforceable equitable obligation: the extent to which it operates retrospectively to the prejudice of third parties lies in the discretion of the court.[199]

While the institutional constructive trust remains the English law approach, it was held possible by Lord Browne-Wilkinson for the remedial constructive trust to be introduced in the future:

Although the resulting trust is an unsuitable basis for developing proprietary restitutionary remedies, the remedial constructive trust, if introduced into English law, may provide a more satisfactory road forward.

The future of the law of tracing may therefore lie with a constructive trust imposed by the court, perhaps in similar manner to the doctrine of proprietary estoppel, by means of a remedy which is tailor-made for each case as opposed to one which simply recognises pre-existing property rights.

There are two other views of the result in *Chase Manhattan*. The first is that rescission ought to effect automatic revesting of the property in the claimant.[200] As Millett LJ held in *El Ajou v Dollar Land Holdings*, the form of trust involved here could be seen as being based on the resulting trust. However, we must remember that this was the model of restitutionary resulting trust which had been advanced originally by Prof Birks[201] and which had been so roundly dismissed by the House of Lords in *Westdeutsche Landesbank v Islington*, as considered in Chapter 11. The second view, related to the first, is that a remedy based on a tracing claim should exist to prevent unjust enrichment.[202] This is the argument based on Smith's work[203] which was rejected in *Foskett v McKeown* when it was held by Lord Browne-Wilkinson[204] and by Lord Millett that the purpose of tracing is to protect property rights as part of property law, and not to reverse enrichments received by defendants as a result of some unjust factor.[205] The broader impact of the decision in *Westdeutsche Landesbank* in the context of imposing proprietary rights by constructive trust is considered at para 19.6.2 below, and the general nature of such trusts in cases of theft at para 19.5.3.

19.6.3 Charges and liens in tracing

Equitable charges

Equitable charges are considered in detail in Chapter 23.[206] For the purposes of this discussion, a charge will give the claimant a proportionate right in a fund of property equal to a

199 [1996] AC 669, *per* Lord Browne-Wilkinson.
200 *El Ajou v Dollar Land Holdings* [1993] 3 All ER 717.
201 Birks, 1992.
202 Goff and Jones, 2002, 101.
203 Smith, 1997.
204 [2001] 1 AC 102, 109.
205 *Ibid*, 129.
206 See section 23.2 below.

given value, but without the need for the claimant to segregate property within that fund as would be required for the creation of a trust.[207] Charges can be fixed over specific property, or they can float over a pool of property such that the legal owner of that fund can continue to deal with it. Charges take effect only in equity, not at common law.[208] The means of identifying the difference between a fixed and a floating charge is the following one:

> A [fixed, or] specific charge . . . is one that without more fastens on ascertained and definite property or property capable of being ascertained and defined; a floating charge, on the other hand, is ambulatory and shifting in its nature, hovering over and so to speak floating with the property which it is intended to effect until some event occurs or some act is done which causes it to settle and fasten on the subject of the charge within its reach and grasp.[209]

It is more likely that a court would order a fixed charge so as to freeze the fund held by the defendant, with each claimant to a beneficial share of that fund entitled to a specified proportion of it. A charge, then, offers a means of granting a security interest over property to the claimant without the need for the formalities necessary for a trust.[210]

In a tracing action, the benefit of a charge to the claimant would be to grant her a right to be paid whatever amount of money has been awarded by the court further to the tracing action so as to compensate the beneficiaries for their loss, but with the added benefit of a security interest over the charged property which can be seized by order of the court if the defendant fails to make payment. Thus, charges grant a right to seize the charged property in the event that the defendant does not perform her obligations to pay money or to transfer property to the claimant. Importantly, though, a mere charge does not grant the chargee an immediate right in the charged property in the manner that a mortgage grants the mortgagee such an immediate right of ownership in the mortgaged property.[211] As the current authors of *Fisher and Lightwood's Law of Mortgage* put the matter:

> A charge is a security whereby real or personal property is appropriated for the discharge of a debt or other obligation, but which does not pass either an absolute or a special property in the subject of the security to the creditor, nor any right to possession. In the event of non-payment of the debt, the creditor's right of realisation is by judicial process.[212]

---

207 *Re Goldcorp* [1995] 1 AC 74.
208 *Re Coslett Contractors Ltd* [1998] Ch 495. Explained in Gleeson, *Personal Property Law* (FT Law & Tax, 1997) 235, to be the case because title may not be divided at common law.
209 *Illingworth v Houldsworth* [1904] AC 355, 358, *per* Lord Macnaghten.
210 *Clough Mill v Martin* [1984] 3 All ER 982.
211 It should be noted that the judges are not always so discriminating between charges and mortgages, often using the terms synonymously. See, for example, Slade J in *Siebe Gorman v Barclays Bank* [1979] 2 Lloyd's Rep 142, 159 where the terms are used interchangeably in the following passage: '. . . a specific charge on the proceeds of [the book debts] as soon as they are received and consequently prevents the mortgagor from disposing of an unencumbered title to the subject matter of such charge without the mortgagee's consent, even before the mortgagee has taken steps to enforce its security.'
212 Falcon Chambers, *Fisher and Lightwood's Law of Mortgage* (11th edn, Butterworths, 2002) 25.

Thus a chargee has a right to apply to the court to seek a right to seize the charged property and to sell it so as to realise the amount owed to it.[213] Any surplus realised on sale will be held on constructive trust for the chargor.[214] There is no specific formality for the creation of a charge over personalty.[215] Once a court orders the existence of a charge then the chargee – the claimant in a tracing claim – will have a right to receive money in satisfaction of her rights or to enforce the charge as just described.

Liens

A lien is a right to take possession of another person's property until such time as that other person makes payment in satisfaction of a debt or some other obligation. In equity, it is not necessary for the claimant to have possession of the property before seeking permission to seize that property. A lien is a right only to detain property and not a right to sell it.[216] If the claimant wishes to sell the property to recover amounts owed to her by the defendant, then she must apply to the court for permission.[217] Liens can arise both at common law and in equity. Common law liens are frequently annexed to a contractual right in some way. By contrast, in general, equitable liens can be imposed by the courts otherwise than by means of an express contractual provision.[218] Rather, an equitable lien is a right accepted by equity to detain property which then gives rise to an equitable charge,[219] such an equitable charge in turn granting its holder a proprietary right in the manner considered above. So, an equitable lien is really a manifestation of a jurisdiction accepted by courts of equity to detain property by imposing an equitable charge over it.[220] That equitable charge in turn grants the chargee a right to apply to the court for an order for sale of that property by means of a writ in the Chancery Division of the High Court endorsed with a claim to be entitled to an equitable lien,[221] and otherwise in the manner considered above in relation to equitable charges.[222] In a tracing claim the usefulness of a lien is that it enables the claimant to assume physical control of property until the defendant satisfies her obligations to the claimant. Diplock LJ described the lien as a 'primitive remedy'[223] of a 'self-help' variety whereby the claimant has a right exercisable over goods already in her possession (in the case of a common law lien)

213 *Johnson v Shippen* (1703) 2 Ld Raym 982; *Stainbank v Fenning* (1851) 11 CB 51; *Stainbank v Shepard* (1853) 13 CB 418. This doctrine is also considered in the following cases: *Swiss Bank Corporation v Lloyds Bank Ltd* [1982] AC 584 at 595, [1980] 2 All ER 419 at 425, CA, [1982] AC 584, [1981] 2 All ER 449, HL; *Carreras Rothmans Ltd v Freeman Mathews Treasure Ltd* [1985] Ch 207, [1985] 1 All ER 155 at 169; *Re Charge Card Services Ltd* [1987] Ch 150 at 176, [1989] Ch 497 CA; *Re BCCI (No 8)* [1998] AC 214, [1997] 4 All ER 568, HL; *Re Coslett Contractors Ltd* [1998] Ch 495 at 507, *per* Millett LJ.
214 Cf Law of Property Act 1925, s 103.
215 *Cradock v Scottish Provident Institution* (1893) 69 LT 380, affirmed at (1894) 70 LT 718, CA.
216 *Hammonds v Barclay* (1802) 2 East 227.
217 *Larner v Fawcett* [1950] 2 All ER 727.
218 *In Re Welsh Irish Ferries Ltd* [1986] Ch 471.
219 *Ibid; In Re Kent & Sussex Sawmills Ltd* [1947] Ch 177.
220 *Ibid.*
221 *Bowles v Rogers* (1800) 31 ER 957; *Re Stucley* [1906] 1 Ch 67.
222 See Hudson, 2006, para 11–70 *et seq.*
223 Primitive in the sense that it reeks of brute force and the common-sensical notion that if you owe me *x* and I have property of yours in my possession equal to the value of *x*, then I should simply keep your property unless you make payment of *x* to me.

or possibly not in her possession (in the case of an equitable lien) and operates as a defence to the other party's claim for recovery of those goods.[224]

Ordinarily, the courts will award equitable liens in a narrow range of well-established contexts.[225] Examples of equitable liens include an equity to secure the discharge of indebtedness,[226] the solicitor's lien on property recovered,[227] a trustee's lien in relation to her expenses,[228] and in relation to contracts for the sale of land there are the vendor's lien over the purchase money and the concomitant purchaser's lien over any deposit advanced.[229] The equitable lien is predicated on there being some obligation to pay money or to do some similar act. Equity will impose a charge in such circumstances to reflect this obligation.

19.6.4 Subrogation

Subrogation is a powerful equitable remedy in tracing and other situations. It is best explained by means of an example. If Arthur's money was used by Brian to pay off a debt which Brian owed to Colin, then equitable subrogation would permit Arthur to insist that Brian owed that same debt to Arthur. This remedy is particularly useful in tracing claims when the original property has been dissipated or cannot be traced: what the claimant can do is to demand that any obligation which was discharged with the original property is henceforth owed to the claimant instead. The equitable remedy of subrogation is considered in section 30.7. The leading case in this context is *Boscawen v Bajwa*,[230] which was considered above at para 19.3.2, in which the Abbey National Building Society paid mortgage moneys to Bajwa expecting that they would be secured over the land which Bajwa was selling. Due to a mistake by the solicitors acting in this case, the mortgage moneys were paid to Bajwa's account, so that Bajwa's mortgage with the Halifax Building Society was discharged, but the sale of the property did not go through. Therefore, the Abbey National did not acquire the mortgage security it was expecting. The remedy of subrogation meant that the mortgage which Bajwa owed to Halifax was revived and Bajwa owed the mortgage debt instead to Abbey National on the same terms: the Abbey National was thus subrogated to the earlier rights of the Halifax. Abbey National acquired a remedy by way of subrogation in the form of being owed the mortgage debt which had been discharged with their money. Thus a remedy is provided even though the money taken from Abbey National has ceased to be traceable because it has passed into Halifax's general accounts and cannot be identified. In relation to tracing generally, the remedy of subrogation allows the claimant to trace her property into the defendant's possession and then, even if that property has been used to pay off a debt and ostensibly has therefore disappeared, the claimant can become the defendant's creditor for the debt which was discharged.[231]

---

224 *Tappenden v Artus* [1964] 2 QB 185.
225 Not in relation to sales of goods, where a statutory lien applies: Sale of Goods Act 1979, s 41.
226 *Re Bernstein* [1925] Ch 12 at 17; *Re Bond Worth Ltd* [1980] Ch 228 at 251.
227 See *Snell's Equity* (Sweet & Maxwell, 2005), para 42–05.
228 Trustee Act 1925, s 30(2); *Re Beddoe* [1893] 1 Ch 547.
229 *Mackreth v Symmons* (1808) 15 Ves 329 at 340, 33 ER 778 at 782; *Rose v Watson* (1864) 10 HL Cas 672 at 684.
230 [1996] 1 WLR 328. See also para 30.7.3 below. *Ibrahim v Barclays Bank* [2011] EWHC 1897 (Ch) followed *Boscawen v Bajwa*.
231 *Gertsch v Aspasia* (2000) 2 ITELR 342.

19.6.5 Swollen assets theory

There is one anomalous set of *dicta* which suggested a radically different approach to equitable tracing. They appeared in the speech of Lord Templeman in *Space Investments Ltd v Canadian Bank*:[232]

> In these circumstances [where money has passed in breach of fiduciary duty into the assets of the defendant, such that the specific money cannot be traced] it is impossible for the beneficiaries interested in trust money misappropriated from their trust to trace their money to any particular asset belonging to the trustee bank. But equity allows the beneficiaries, or a new trustee appointed in place of an insolvent bank trustee . . . to trace the trust money to all the assets of the bank and to recover the trust money by the exercise of an equitable charge over all the assets of the bank . . . that equitable charge secures for the beneficiaries and the trust priority over the claims of customers . . . and . . . all other unsecured creditors.

The importance of this approach is that it is not necessary to identify specific property over which the tracing claim is to be exercised. On the facts, money was paid by one bank to another as a result of an unjust factor, which would have entitled the payer to recover that property in ordinary circumstances. However, the money passed into the general accounts of the payee, so that it could not be separated from the general assets of the payee. The traditional approach would be to say: 'If the payment cannot be identified among other property, there is no right to trace into that property.'

Lord Templeman's approach suggests that it is possible to say: 'My money went in there, it is still in there somewhere, and therefore I want rights over the whole thing equal to the value of my lost money.' This mirrors the American 'swollen assets theory', which entitles the claimant to impose a charge over the assets of the recipient equal to the value of the property which was misappropriated. Subsequently, these *obiter dicta* have been criticised by academics and judges alike. The criticism of this approach is that it grants advantageous rights to unsecured creditors over the whole of the assets in an entity in the event of that entity's insolvency, particularly when that creditor cannot identify rights in any specific property. Thus, it was held in *Bishopsgate v Homan*[233] by Dillon LJ that the 'swollen assets approach' should not be interpreted in any event to give rights in an overdrawn account by asserting rights over all the assets of the bank. This approach perhaps recognises more accurately the true nature of the sets of property rights represented by electronic bank accounts, as considered above.

It is clear that the 'swollen assets approach' is not English law but rather forms part of *obiter dicta* delivered by Lord Templeman. By contrast, in *Re Goldcorp*,[234] it was held that the rights of claimants to some proprietary tracing claim would be restricted to the situation in which identifiable property was held distinctly and separately for the benefit of those claimants. In part this follows the general English law approach that equitable tracing will be available only where there is some pre-existing equitable or fiduciary relationship which

---

232 [1986] 3 All ER 75, 76–77, [1986] 1 WLR 1072, 1074.
233 [1995] 1 WLR 31.
234 [1995] 1 AC 74.

gives rise to some proprietary rights in the claimant, and in part it is the result of the possibility of the imposition of a trust only in circumstances in which the property held on trust is segregated from other property.[235]

The approach which English law adopts does mean that the availability of equitable tracing and equitable proprietary claims in general is greatly restricted precisely because such claims are said to attach only to identifiable, segregated property. Thus in *Ultraframe (UK) Ltd v Fielding*[236] it was held that where the claimant could not identify any particular item of property as being a substitute for the original trust property, but instead could only demonstrate that the defendant had earned a profit from behaviour which had been allegedly unconscionable, then it was held that it would not be possible to trace into that profit because no link between it and any property taken in breach of trust had been proven. In that case, which was a voluminous piece of litigation, it had been alleged that confidential information relating to the construction of conservatories had been taken in breach of fiduciary duty by employees of a company and then used for their own personal profit. Amongst many other claims, the claimants sought to trace into the profits which had resulted from the use of this information. However, the link had not been proved on the facts: all that could be demonstrated was that there had been profits made but not that any property held on trust had been used to make them. By extrapolation, then, simply identifying a profit in the hands of a defendant will not be sufficient to found a tracing action unless that profit can be demonstrated to constitute a substitute for the original property. The claimant would therefore be required to seek other remedies based on constructive trust in relation to that property.

19.6.6 An oddity with tracing remedies

One of the more unusual factors about the remedies usually applied in relation to tracing actions is that not all of them are ordinarily proprietary. A constructive trust will recognise that the successful claimant has property rights in the traced property. However, a lien is a purely possessory remedy which does not grant a proprietary right but only a right to detain property until an amount of money is paid. It is only if the money is not paid that the claimant is entitled to petition to court to ask that the property be sold so as to realise the amount of money which is owed to the claimant. Similarly, a charge does not grant a proprietary right in the charged property (unlike a mortgage) but rather grants the chargee only a contingent right to seize the property until she is paid the amount of money which she is owed, and if she is not paid that money then she may seek a sale of the property. It is therefore somewhat counter-intuitive that these latter remedies are not strictly concerned with proprietary rights, although they do involve dealings with property to secure a right in money, and yet nevertheless they are commonly used as remedies in tracing actions. In cases involving money, as in *Westdeutsche Landesbank v Islington* or *Foskett v McKeown*, usually the claimants will only be concerned to recover money and may be comparatively unconcerned about the precise legal mechanism which leads to those sums being paid into their bank account.

Lord Millett in *Foskett v McKeown* did suggest that proprietary remedies, like the constructive trust, are the primary form of remedy in relation to mixed funds, with a lien

---

235 See also *Westdeutsche Landesbank Girozentrale v Islington LBC* [1996] AC 669.
236 [2005] EWHC 1638 (Ch), [2005] All ER (D) 397.

being available in the event that a constructive trust is inappropriate. What his Lordship said more precisely was the following:

> The primary rule in regard to a mixed fund, therefore, is that gains and losses are borne by the contributors rateably.[237] The beneficiary's right to elect instead to enforce a lien to obtain repayment is an exception to the primary rule, exercisable where the fund is deficient and the claim is made against the wrongdoer and those claiming through him.

Lord Millett relied on similar principles which apply in relation to physical mixtures where it is said that if the mixture is the fault of the defendant then it is open to the claimant to 'claim the goods'.[238] Nevertheless, it is exactly this sort of loose phraseology about the nature of the remedies in tracing claims which generates confusion. It is suggested that the general approach outlined in section 19.6.1 is the best description of how remedies are to be identified in the absence of a single, clear judicial statement of the principles.

19.6.7 Choice of remedies

Clearly there are a number of remedies potentially available in relation to a tracing claim. No court will permit double recovery in respect of the same loss. Therefore, the equitable doctrine of election arises in such situations to provide that it is open to the claimant to elect between alternative remedies.[239] In *Tang v Capacious Investments*, the possibility of two parallel remedies arose in relation to a breach of trust. It was held that these two remedies existed in the alternative and therefore that the plaintiff could claim both, not being required to elect between them until judgment was awarded in its favour. However, it was held in *Crittenden v The Estate of Charles Albert Bayliss*[240] that it would be an abuse of the process of the court for a claimant to elect not to bring a tracing claim and then at a later stage in litigation to seek to bring that tracing claim in any event.

19.7 DEFENCES

> *Defences available in relation to tracing claims include change of position, estoppel by representation and passing on, in which the defendant will assert that she dealt with the property in reliance on good faith that she had some rights in the property. The further defence would be that the defendant was a bona fide purchaser for value of the property without notice of the claimant's rights.*

While the preceding discussion has considered the contexts in which a claimant will be able to mount a tracing claim, there will be situations in which the recipient of the traceable proceeds of the claimant's property will be able to resist the claim. The following defences

---

237 That is, in proportionate shares.
238 *Lupton v White, White v Lupton* (1808) 15 Ves 432, [1803–13] All ER Rep 336; *Sandeman & Sons v Tyzack and Branfoot Steamship Co Ltd* [1913] AC 680, 695, [1911–13] All ER Rep 1013, 1020, *per* Lord Molton.
239 *Tang v Capacious Investments Ltd* [1996] 1 All ER 193. See Birks, 2000:1, 8.
240 [2005] EWCA Civ 1425.

are apparently available: change of position, passing on, estoppel by representation, and *bona fide* purchaser for value without notice.

19.7.1 Change of position

The basis of the defence of change of position

The defence of change of position will be available to a defendant who has received property and, on the faith of the receipt of that property, suffered some change in her personal circumstances.[241] The most concise judicial statement of the manner in which the defence of change of position might operate can be extracted from the (partially dissenting) speech of Lord Goff in *Westdeutsche Landesbank v Islington LBC*:[242]

> Where an innocent defendant's position is so changed that he will suffer an injustice if called upon to repay or to repay in full, the injustice of requiring him so to repay outweighs the injustice of denying the plaintiff restitution.

Thus, the court is required to consider which outcome would be more unjust: either allowing the defendant to keep the property given the harm that would cause to the claimant, or forcing the defendant to return the property to the claimant if the defendant had acted in some way in reliance on having received that property.[243]

   The doctrine of change of position has grown as part of the doctrine of restitution of unjust enrichment. The outlines of the doctrine of change of position were set out in the following terms by Lord Goff in his speech in the House of Lords in *Lipkin Gorman v Karpnale*.[244] In that case, the defendant casino had received money from a solicitor who had appropriated that money from a law firm's client accounts and gambled it away at the defendant casino. The law firm sought to recover the lost moneys from the casino by means of equitable and common law tracing claims, as well as personal liability to account for participation in a breach of trust. With these facts in mind, Lord Goff described the future development of the defence of change of position in the following way:[245]

> I am most anxious that, in recognising this defence to actions of restitution, nothing should be said at this stage to inhibit the development of the defence on a case by case basis, in the usual way. It is, of course, plain that the defence is not open to one who has changed his position in bad faith, as where the defendant has paid away the money with knowledge of the facts entitling the plaintiff to restitution; and it is commonly accepted that the defence should not be open to a wrongdoer. . . . It is not however appropriate in the present case to attempt to identify all those actions in restitution to which change of position may be a defence. . . . At present I do not wish to state the principle any less broadly than this: that the defence is available to a person whose position has so changed

---

241 *Lipkin Gorman v Karpnale* [1991] 2 AC 548.
242 [1996] AC 669.
243 *Scottish Equitable v Derby* [2000] 3 All ER 793, HC, [2001] 3 All ER 818, CA.
244 [1991] 2 AC 548.
245 *Ibid* at 580.

that it would be inequitable in all the circumstances to require him to make restitution, or alternatively to make restitution in full. I wish to stress however that the mere fact that the defendant has spent the money, in whole or in part, does not of itself render it inequitable that he should be called upon to repay, because the expenditure might in any event have been incurred by him in the ordinary course of things. I fear that the mistaken assumption that mere expenditure of money may be regarded as amounting to a change of position for present purposes has led in the past to opposition by some to recognition of a defence which in fact is likely to be available only on comparatively rare occasions.[246]

The four key themes to emerge from this passage of Lord Goff's speech are as follows.

(1) The open nature of the defence of change of position

First, Lord Goff places no boundaries on the future development of the defence, although his Lordship did not anticipate that it would develop into a defence of very general application. For example, as his Lordship outlined, simply that the defendant has spent money will not in and of itself demonstrate a change of position. At the very least, the expenditure of money would need to be balanced, as with any other detrimental act, against the injustice of permitting the claimant to trace their property rights into the property in the defendant's hands. Thus, the defence will itself arise on technical bases which are to be established in future cases. However, as will be considered below, the very open nature of this defence now makes it doubtful whether change of position is to be understood as a restitutionary defence or whether it is really just another way of understanding equity's role dealing in good conscience with the parties.

(2) Bad faith as a barrier to the defence of change of position

Secondly, 'bad faith' will be a barrier to any reliance on the defence. What constitutes bad faith in such circumstances remains a difficult question. If a commercial person receives money which was paid by mistake, without making any enquiries of the payer, and then uses that money in a way which would otherwise constitute a change of position, it would be doubtful that such a person will be found to have acted in good faith.[247] Equally, if the recipient has said or done something which has encouraged the payer to make that payment, whether innocently or deliberately, then the recipient will be unlikely to make out the defence of change of position successfully.[248] Change of position will be available to the extent that

---

246 In considering the nature of the defence of change of position it was held in *Haugesund Kommune v DEPFA ACS Bank* [2011] 1 All ER 190, [152] by Pill LJ held that: 'The defence [of change of position] is not fixed in stone, and has developed and can be expected to develop further over time on a case-by-case basis. Broadly speaking the defence is available to a person whose position has so changed that it would be inequitable in all the circumstances to require them to make restitution or alternatively to make restitution in full . . . Concepts of relative fault are not applicable; good faith being a sufficient requirement in this context . . . The defence is to be regarded as founded on a principle of justice designed to protect the defendant from a claim to restitution in respect of a benefit received by him in circumstances in which it would be inequitable to pursue that claim or to pursue it in full . . .' This passage was cited with approval in *Ibrahim v Barclays Bank* [2011] EWHC 1897 (Ch).

247 *Niru Battery Manufacturing Co v Milestone Trading Ltd* [2002] EWHC 1425 (Comm), para 135, *per* Moore-Bick J.

248 See *Larner v London County Council* [1949] 2 KB 683 at 688, *per* Lord Denning.

a defendant made payments unknowingly to the fictitious subsidiary company of a third party, as part of a scheme to defraud the defendant and the claimant, but will not be able to rely on that defence in relation to commissions received as part of the process of making those same payments.[249] That the defence of change of position is predicated on the balance of justice between the parties, rather than on proving the fault or deliberate action of either party,[250] suggests that even innocent actions of this sort may cause the defence of change of position to be unavailable. It has been held by Sedley LJ in *Niru Battery Manufacturing Company v Milestone Trading Ltd*[251] that the defence of change of position is not dependent upon the demonstration of an absence of bad faith in equal and opposite manner to the obligation to prove dishonesty in a claim for dishonest assistance.[252] Bad faith in this context is therefore not to be taken to be equivalent to dishonesty.[253]

In *Barros Mattos v MacDaniels Ltd*[254] Laddie J accepted the proposition that the defence of change of position would not be available to someone who had acted illegally. It was held that the defendant could not put up a tainted claim to retention of the property against the claimant's untainted claim for restitution. It was accepted, however, that the illegal act might be so minor that it could be ignored on the *de minimis* principle (that something very small can be ignored) and the defence of change of position could still be available. In this case, a fraudster had stolen money from a Brazilian bank and passed it to the defendant. The defendant had then distributed the money according the defendant's instructions. The defendant sought to resist a claim for knowing receipt and restitution of the amount stolen from the bank on the basis of change of position. Laddie J approved the principle in *Tinsley v Milligan*[255] to the effect that a person who had performed an illegal act could not rely on that illegal act as the basis for rights in property nor could that person, by extension, defend an action for tracing or in knowing receipt. Consequently, the defendant was obliged to account for the entire amount received.[256]

The reliance placed by Laddie J on *Tinsley v Milligan* and the old equitable cases[257] on illegality when denying the defence of change of position demonstrates the strong link between equitable principles and the principles of unjust enrichment outlined in *Lipkin Gorman v Karpnale*.[258] It is suggested that the propinquity of change of position and the

---

249 *Maersk Air Ltd v Expeditors International (UK) Ltd* [2003] 1 Lloyd's Rep 491.

250 See *Dextra Bank and Trust Company Ltd v Bank of Jamaica* [2002] 1 All ER (Comm) 193, para 142.

251 [2003] EWCA Civ 1446.

252 *Ibid*, para 179. In *Niru Battery v Milestone Trading*, Niru had agreed to buy lead ingots from Milestone and so Milestone had obtained financing from CAI to acquire that lead by means of commonly used financial instruments known as 'warehouse warrants'. To pay for the release of the warrants, Milestone in turn acquired further finance from BS and SGS. CAI sold the warrants when it became concerned about the market value of lead and so Milestone was not able to fulfil its obligations to Niru. In proceedings for restitution, it could not be demonstrated that any party had acted dishonestly, with SGS being liable in negligence and CAI liable only in unjust enrichment.

253 *Ibid*, para 182, applying *BCCI v Akindele* [2001] Ch 437, distinguishing *Medforth v Blake* [2000] Ch 86.

254 [2004] 3 All ER 299, [2004] EWHC 1188 (Ch).

255 [1994] 1 AC 340, [1993] 3 All ER 65.

256 It is unclear whether or not the obligation to account was made ultimately on the basis of knowing receipt or on the basis of restitution of unjust enrichment: there is a reliance on *Lipkin Gorman v Karpnale* [1991] 2 AC 548 which suggests the latter, although the matter is not explained clearly because the application was made on an interlocutory basis.

257 See, eg, *Holman v Johnson* (1775) 1 Cowp 341, 343, 98 ER 1120, 1121.

258 [1991] 2 AC 548.

principles of equity mean that the barrier between the two is disappearing in practice. This is particularly so where, as in *Barros Mattos v MacDaniels*, this case could have been disposed of on the basis that a defendant cannot advance the defence of change of position if she has come to equity with unclean hands on the basis of having committed an illegal act.[259]

(3) Measurement of comparative inequity or harm to be caused to each party

Thirdly, the general purpose of the test is to measure the comparative inequity of recovering the property from the defendant or denying such recovery to the claimant if the defendant has changed her position in some way. The manner in which this process has been carried out will emerge from the cases considered in the following sections.

(4) Activity which will constitute a change of position

Fourthly, it is important to attempt to understand what types of behaviour will constitute a change of position. In short, a change of position could be embodied either by taking any steps which would not otherwise have been taken, or by refraining from some action which would otherwise have been taken. The defence of change of position would seem to include all sums expended by the defendant in reliance on any representation or payment made by the claimant, including the cost of financing a proposed transaction between the parties.[260] Furthermore, where the defendant forgoes an opportunity to take a benefit from another source in reliance on the payment received from the claimant, the defendant is entitled to include such a reliance within her defence of change of position.[261] It has been suggested that even receipt of a payment of money in reliance on an agreement not to contest a divorce petition might constitute a change of position.[262] What the defendant cannot do is seek to rely on the benefit of a contract which turned out to have been void,[263] or to have acted in good faith reliance on a payment in circumstances in which they have acquiesced in the action which rendered such payment void.[264] In any event, the defendant is required to have acted in good faith in seeking to assert a defence of change of position.[265] However, if the defendant has had the benefit of money paid to her, for example, in that she has earned interest on that money or has saved herself banking charges by not going overdrawn to the extent of that payment, then the defendant will be required to account for any such benefit in reducing the worth to her of the change of position defence.[266] Where, for example, the defendant received

---

259 See, for example, *Tinsley v Milligan* [1994] 1 AC 340, 355, [1993] 3 All ER 65, 72, *per* Lord Goff; *Barros Mattos v MacDaniel* [2004] 3 All ER 299, 306, *per* Laddie J.

260 *Sanwa Australia Finance Ltd v Finchill Pty Ltd* [2001] NSWCA 466.

261 *Palmer v Blue Circle Southern Cement Ltd* [2001] RLR 137.

262 *X v X (Y and Z Intervening)* [2002] 1 FLR 508, as considered in *Commerzbank v Price* [2003] EWCA Civ 1633, para 68, *per* Munby J.

263 *South Tyneside Metropolitan Borough Council v Svenska International plc* [1995] 1 All ER 545.

264 *Standard Bank London Ltd v The Bank of Tokyo Ltd* [1995] 2 Lloyd's Rep 169.

265 *Lipkin Gorman v Karpnale* [1991] 2 AC 548; *South Tyneside Metropolitan Borough Council v Svenska International plc* [1995] 1 All ER 545; *Euroactividade AG v Moeller* (2001) unreported, 1 February. See also *Lloyds Bank v Independent Insurance* [1999] 2 WLR 986; *Friends Provident v Hillier Parker* [1995] 4 All ER 260.

266 *Pearce v Lloyds Bank plc* [2001] EWCA Civ 1097. Also, if the defendant acquired land with the property, then there will not have been a change of position: *Campden Hill Ltd v Chakrani* [2005] EWHC 911 (Ch).

£10,000 from the claimant and thus earned interest on that £10,000, the claimant will be entitled to reduce the amount which the defendant claims is represented by her change of position to account for that interest earned. Further examples of changes of position are considered in the following sections.

Change of position in relation to mistaken and to windfall payments

Since the decision of the House of Lords in *Lipkin Gorman v Karpnale*,[267] there have been a slew of cases on change of position. In *Scottish Equitable v Derby*,[268] a pensioner received a payment of about £172,400 from a pension fund by mistake. The issue arose as to whether or not the pension fund could recover the mistaken payment from the pensioner. The pensioner sought to defend the pension fund's claim to recover the mistaken payment on the basis that he had changed his position in reliance upon receipt of the money. The pensioner had not taken any steps nor refrained from any action on receipt of the windfall from the pension fund, except for an expenditure of about £9,600 on his family's home. The pensioner contended, however, that to repay the money to the pension fund at a time when he was separating from his wife would cause him great financial hardship. In effect he was arguing that it would have been unfair for him to have repaid the money because he had come to consider that money as belonging to him since his receipt of it. The precise change of position which he hastily alleged was the disappointment this would cause him and his wife who were dividing their property on divorce on the basis that he owned this large windfall. However, it was held in the High Court that because his hardship was not causally linked to the mistaken payment to him (the hardship having resulted from his separation from his wife, whereas the payment was caused by an unrelated administrative error), the pensioner was not entitled to rely on the defence of change of position, except in relation to the £9,600 which he had spent in reliance on his receipt of the money.[269] The Court of Appeal held that the sums claimed by the claimant were so large that they bore no relation to the detriment which the defendant pensioner was claiming he had suffered by way of a change of position.[270] Therefore, the pensioner was not entitled to retain the full £172,400, but he could retain the £9,600 which he had spent in good faith. The Court of Appeal also considered the question of estoppel by representation, which is discussed below.

Similar issues arose in *Philip Collins Ltd v Davis*,[271] where overpayments were made to one of Phil Collins's backing musicians by mistake. The musician sought to retain that money simply on the basis that he thought he was due it, even though his contract provided expressly to the contrary. The employer proposed to recover the money by withholding it from future royalties which would otherwise have been paid to the musician. The musician contended that he had changed his day-to-day lifestyle in reliance on the receipt of the money. It was held that the musician bore the burden of proving that the defence applied to him. On these facts, he was entitled to resist recovery of half of the overpayments, in that he had changed his lifestyle in reliance on having received them. He was entitled to a defence in relation to half of the overpayments because the court considered that in all of the

---

267 [1991] 2 AC 548.
268 [2000] 3 All ER 793.
269 *Ibid.*
270 [2001] 3 All ER 818.
271 [2000] 3 All ER 808.

circumstances, that was an appropriate proportion to which he should be entitled: it was no more sophisticated an analysis than that. Alternatively, it might be suggested that this is a thin premise on which to deny the claimant recovery of money which had been paid mistakenly, to which the defendant had no entitlement, and to which one might have expected the defendant to realise she had no entitlement.[272]

It is not sufficient for the claimant to argue that her expectations in receiving the windfall would be disappointed by return of the money to the payer (in that she would have less money than she had otherwise thought); rather, there must be some change in position linked to the receipt of that money in circumstances in which it could not be alleged by the defendant that she had any good reason to assume that the money was rightfully hers.[273] Therefore, where a payment is made mistakenly without any representation that the defendant was entitled to that money to which she would not otherwise be entitled, and where the sum of money was so large that the defendant ought reasonably to have realised that there had been a mistake, then there should be no defence of change of position.[274] What is required is that the transfer of the property which is being traced should be referable in some way to the change of position.[275]

Change of position as an equitable defence concerned to effect justice

Whereas we have considered the defence of change of position to be primarily a restitutionary defence up to now, it has emerged in more recent cases that it can be understood as being based on a combination of restitution and general equitable principles. Indeed, in Lord Goff's original speech in *Lipkin Gorman v Karpnale*, there were clear references to an understanding of the comparative inequity of requiring that the defendant accede to the claimant's tracing claim.[276] The general principle on which the Court of Appeal in *Niru Battery Manufacturing Co v Milestone Trading Ltd* has recognised the operation of the defence of change of position is by reference to:

> the essential question ... whether on the facts of a particular case it would in all the circumstances be inequitable or unconscionable, and thus unjust, to allow the recipient of money paid under a mistake of fact to deny restitution to the payer.[277]

272   Indeed, this final element – as to the conscionability or reasonableness (where those two terms are taken to be broadly similar in this sense) of the defendant failing to notice that she has received an overpayment – might be considered an important element of this defence in the future. Such an approach would recognise the importance of proof of a link between the conscionability of the change of position, or the hardship that the claimant would suffer, and the receipt of the money. See, for example, *Lloyds Bank v Independent Insurance* [1999] 2 WLR 986; *Home Office v Ayres* [1992] ICR 175.

273   What is not addressed in *Derby* is what would have happened if the pensioner had separated from his wife *because* he had received this money and could therefore support himself with the money received.

274   *State Bank of New South Wales v Swiss Bank Corporation* (1995) 39 NSWLR 350: a case in which a bank received a very large electronic payment transfer from another bank without any clear instruction as to which account or customer that amount was to have been credited – it was held that, while not dishonest, the recipient bank could not credibly claim that it was entitled to rely on the receipt of so large an amount without any identified payee, so as to have changed its position. See also *Philip Collins Ltd v Davis* [2000] 3 All ER 808.

275   *Philip Collins Ltd v Davis* [2000] 3 All ER 808 at p 827f, *per* Jonathan Parker J.

276   [1991] 2 AC 548 at 580.

277   *Niru Battery Manufacturing Co and Another v Milestone Trading Ltd and Others* [2003] EWCA Civ 1446, para 162, *per* Clarke LJ.

Alternatively, Sedley LJ has expressed the same process in terms that:

> courts . . . are not tied to a single rigid standard in deciding whether a defence of change of position succeeds. They are to decide whether it is equitable to uphold the defence. Since the doctrine of restitution is centrally concerned with the distribution of loss among parties whose rights are not met by some stronger doctrine of law, one is by definition looking for the least unjust solution to a residual problem.[278]

What is clear from these *dicta* is that the defence of change of position is capable of being understood on the basis of equitable notions of fairness.[279] References to 'the doctrine of restitution' notwithstanding, there is no explanation of these principles by reference to unjust enrichment on this model. Similarly, in *Dextra Bank and Trust Co v Bank of Jamaica*, the keynote of the defence of change of position has become its transformation into a general, equitable form of defence which is:

> founded on a principle of justice designed to protect the defendant from a claim to restitution in respect of a benefit received by him in circumstances in which it would be inequitable to pursue that claim, or to pursue it in full.[280]

Thus, restitution – in a general conception of recovery or return of property – has become equated with general notions of equity and as such need not be based on restitution of unjust enrichment.[281]

Whether incurring future liabilities can amount to a change of position

Thus far, our focus has been on a defendant who has changed her position after receipt of the traced property but before the action comes to court. What has not been considered so far is the position of a defendant who has changed her position by committing herself to legal liabilities which will take effect only in the future. Suppose, for example, that, in reliance on the receipt of a valuable piece of machinery which was previously held on trust, the defendant entered into a contract to supply electronic components to be made with that machinery. In this example, the defendant would claim to have changed her position on the basis that she will, in the future, be liable to perform the contract and so her position will be changed. The authorities are in conflict as to whether or not such future changes of position are sufficient to found the defence.[282]

The principal authority suggesting that the change of position cannot take effect in the future is the decision of Clarke J in *South Tyneside Metropolitan BC v Svenska International*

---

278 *Ibid*, para 192, *per* Sedley LJ.
279 The same use of words has been applied in *Credit Suisse (Monaco) SA v Attar* [2004] EWHC 374 (Comm), para [98], *per* Gross J.
280 *Dextra Bank and Trust Co v Bank of Jamaica* [2002] 1 All ER (Comm) 193, para 38.
281 That is, the thesis advanced by Professor Smith in *The Law of Tracing* (Smith, 1997) that tracing is always concerned to effect restitution of unjust enrichment is not the sole basis – if indeed it need be any of the bases – on which equitable tracing is awarded.
282 It could be argued, I acknowledge, that a present contractual obligation to perform some act in the future could be considered to be a present liability, albeit that it falls only to be performed in the future.

plc.[283] It was held by Clarke J that the change of position must have taken place after receipt of the property. In this latter case, the bank had entered into hedging transactions in anticipation of amounts which it would receive from the local authority under an interest rate swap contract which was subsequently held to have been void *ab initio*. It was held that the bank could not claim that its hedging policy – involving the creation of financial instruments with third parties, the effect of which was expected to cancel out the effect of any loss suffered under the swap contract with the local authority – could not found a defence of change of position because those hedging contracts were created before its obligation to effect restitution of payments arose. This decision was considered to have been reached on 'exceptional' circumstances by the Privy Council in *Dextra Bank and Trust Co v Bank of Jamaica*.[284]

A future liability has also been held not to amount to a factor sufficient to found the defence of change of position in *Pearce v Lloyds Bank*.[285] In that case, the defendant's bank had set-off amounts in the defendant's bank account against forged payment instructions which it had received from third parties out of that same account. The defendant contended that the bank ought not to have been entitled to set off those amounts because the defendant would have been liable to pay VAT on the payments which had passed in and out of that account. At the time, however, these future liabilities to VAT had not been discharged. It was held that such future liabilities could not found a defence of change of position.

There are two principal authorities suggesting that a future liability can amount to a change of position. In *Lipkin Gorman v Karpnale*,[286] it was accepted without much discussion that such future liabilities would found the defence of change of position. It was in *Dextra Bank and Trust Co v Bank of Jamaica*[287] that the position was given closer consideration. In that case, the Privy Council was prepared to hold that incurring a future liability would constitute a change of position. Dextra had been approached by W who induced it to lend US$3 million to the Bank of Jamaica secured by a note issued by the Bank of Jamaica, although W had no authority to execute this transaction. W in turn convinced the Bank of Jamaica that the money was to be used in a foreign exchange transaction to acquire its equivalent in Jamaican dollars. This was a fraudulent conspiracy. The Bank of Jamaica paid out the equivalent of US$3 million in Jamaican dollars to the conspirators, all the while believing that it was making payment to Dextra. The argument was raised, *inter alia*, that the Bank of Jamaica could have relied on the defence of change of position to Dextra's action in restitution. During the transaction, the Bank of Jamaica had paid Jamaican dollars before Dextra's cheque had cleared into the Bank of Jamaica's accounts and therefore the change of position was in relation to a future payment at that stage. The Privy Council was of the opinion that there was no objection to such a claim. They preferred to permit the defence to be broadly understood, on the following terms:[288]

> It is surely no abuse of language to say, in the second case as in the first, that the defendant has incurred expenditure in reliance on the plaintiff's payment or, as it is

283   [1995] 1 All ER 545.
284   *Dextra Bank and Trust Co v Bank of Jamaica* [2002] 1 All ER (Comm) 193.
285   [2001] EWCA Civ 1097.
286   [1991] 2 AC 548.
287   [2002] 1 All ER (Comm) 193.
288   *Ibid*, para 38.

sometimes said, on the faith of the payment. It is true that, in the second case, the defendant relied on the payment being made to him in the future (as well as relying on such payment, when made, being a valid payment); but, provided that his change of position was in good faith, it should provide, *pro tanto* at least, a good defence because it would be inequitable to require the defendant to make restitution, or to make restitution in full. In particular it does not, in their Lordships' opinion, assist to rationalise the defence of change of position as concerned to protect the security of receipt and then to derive from that rationalisation a limitation on the defence. The defence should be regarded as founded on a principle of justice designed to protect the defendant from a claim to restitution in respect of a benefit received by him in circumstances in which it would be inequitable to pursue that claim, or to pursue it in full.

In principle, it is suggested, there is no objection to allowing a future obligation to be considered to be a change of position. In many ordinary contracts, for example, a person is legally obliged today to perform some act in the future such that that person will incur liabilities in damages or in specific performance immediately there is some refutation of the contractual obligations. Therefore, one could be said to have changed one's position by agreeing to such a future obligation in an immediately legally binding form. Therefore, it is suggested that the approach taken in *Dextra Bank and Trust Company Ltd v Bank of Jamaica* is to be preferred. Once a liability becomes legally enforceable, whether or not it has been discharged, the defendant can be considered to have changed her position in the sense that her balance sheet will show that she owes a liability and not that the assets necessary to discharge that liability constitute free funds.

Whether the change of position can take place before the receipt of the property

A further question is whether or not the change of position on which the defendant seeks to rely can take place before the property which is being traced has been received by the defendant. That a change of position can take place before the property is received has been accepted in *Commerzbank AG v Price*,[289] in which case a merchant banker took the decision not to seek alternative employment on the basis that he would receive a severance payment from the bank which employed him at the time: it was no objection to his reliance on the defence of change of position that his alleged change of position took place before his receipt of the property. So, if Xavier enters into a contract with Yolanda on Monday whereby he promises to deliver a computer to her on Wednesday, then Xavier is under a legal liability on Monday to deliver a computer, albeit that delivery does not take effect until Wednesday: by the same token, Yolanda incurs a debt to make payment for that computer. Both parties' accounts will show a liability respectively for one computer and for payment on Monday, and therefore both parties could be said to have changed their positions on Monday and not only on Wednesday.[290]

---

289   [2003] EWCA Civ 1633.
290   If the contract were cancelled by both parties, then their accounts would be altered from the date of cancellation.

19.7.2 Estoppel by representation

The foregoing section considered the defence of change of position, which was explained by
the Court of Appeal in *Niru Battery v Milestone* as being based on equitable principles.
Another means of defending a tracing action is to rely upon the doctrine of estoppel by representation which is straightforwardly equitable. Estoppel by representation is a defence which
is superficially similar to change of position. An estoppel by representation will be made out
in circumstances in which the defendant to a tracing action can demonstrate that some representation has been made to her, that that representation was deliberately or accidentally
false, that the claimant knew the representation would be acted upon, that the defendant then
acts to her detriment in reliance upon the representation, and that there is no defence to the
estoppel.[291] This estoppel has been recognised both at common law and in equity.[292] The
significant difference between the two defences is that the estoppel is predicated on some
representation being made by the claimant, as opposed to a balancing of the competing equities of the case as suggested by the defence of change of position.[293]

An example of the defence of estoppel by representation in action arose in *National
Westminster Bank plc v Somer International*.[294] Somer held a US dollar account with the
bank into which it paid moneys received from foreign clients. Somer was expecting to
receive a sum of between US$70,000 and US$78,000 from one of its clients and informed
the bank of this. Subsequently, the bank received a payment of US$76,708 which was
intended for another of its account holders but which it mistakenly credited to Somer's US
dollar account. The bank informed Somer that the money had been paid into its dollar
account and Somer assumed that it was the payment which it was expecting to receive from
its own client. In reliance on the receipt of the money, Somer shipped US$13,180 worth of
goods to the client from which it was expecting the payment. Subsequently, the bank sought
to recover the mistaken payment. Somer argued that it was entitled to an estoppel by representation because the bank had represented to it that the money belonged to Somer, that
Somer had acted to its detriment in reliance on that representation and that it was therefore
entitled to retain the whole of the moneys paid to it by the bank.

Previously, the doctrine of estoppel by representation had operated only as a rule of
evidence to the effect that a claimant would have been entitled to retain the whole of a
mistaken payment.[295] The Court of Appeal in *National Westminster Bank plc v Somer
International* held that the doctrine of estoppel by representation operated on equitable
principles such that it was possible to operate outwith any strict rule requiring that the
defendant be entitled to retain the whole of the payment. Rather, where the court considered
the retention of the whole of the payment to be unconscionable, it would be possible to limit
the defendant's entitlement to rely on the estoppel only to the extent that it had suffered
detriment. Therefore, on these facts, Somer could retain only an amount equal the value
of the goods which it had shipped in reliance on the representation.[296] This mooted

---

291   See generally the various forms of estoppel by representation applied in *Jorden v Money* (1854) V HLC 185;
       10 ER 868 and *National Westminster Bank plc v Somer* [2002] QB 1286, CA.
292   *Jorden v Money* (1854) V HLC 185; 10 ER 868.
293   Goff and Jones, 2002, 829.
294   [2002] QB 1286, CA.
295   *Avon County Council v Howlett* [1983] 1 WLR 605.
296   *Scottish Equitable v Derby* [2001] 3 All ER 818 applied.

development is, however, at odds with earlier authority, and the flexibility of the older, purely evidential form of the estoppel by representation consequently awaits confirmation by a higher court.[297]

19.7.3 Passing on

The defence of passing on bears some similarity to the defence of change of position. Passing on requires that the defendant has passed the property on, or that some expense has been incurred such that the value of the property has effectively been passed on to some third person. The defendant will therefore claim that she does not have possession of the property, nor of its traceable proceeds, because that property has been transferred to another person without receipt of any traceable proceeds. Given that tracing is a proprietary claim, it is necessary for there to be some traceable proceeds in the hands of the defendant. Otherwise, to impose a liability on the defendant to account to the claimant with some property which was not the traceable proceed of the claimant's original property would be to impose a personal claim on the defendant rather than a proprietary claim.

The defence of passing on was raised before the Court of Appeal in *Kleinwort Benson v Birmingham CC*.[298] That case concerned an interest rate swap. The bank claimed that the defence of passing on should have been available to it on the basis that the contract with the local authority (which was subsequently held to have been void *ab initio*) had caused the bank to incur extra expense to manage the risk of the transaction. The Court of Appeal held, however, that there was no necessary link between the contract with the local authority and the bank's decision to incur that expense by means of a hedging strategy over which the local authority had no control. Therefore, the passing on defence is available where the property has been passed on, but not where there is no link between the expenditure and the liability incurred.

19.7.4 *Bona fide* purchaser for value without notice

The final problem is the perennial one of deciding between the person who has lost property to a wrongdoing fiduciary, and the person who buys that property in all innocence. Suppose the example of the painting held on trust for beneficiaries which is transferred away in breach of trust by Tim. Suppose then that the painting is purchased by Eve in good faith for its full market price. Eve will necessarily take the view that she has paid an open-market price for property in circumstances in which she could not have known that the property ought properly to have been held on trust. By the same token, the beneficiaries would argue that it is they who ought to be entitled to recover their property from Eve.

From a strict analytical viewpoint, the property lawyer ought to find for the beneficiaries. At no time do the beneficiaries relinquish their property rights in the painting before Eve purchases it. Therefore, those rights ought to be considered as subsisting. Eve cannot acquire good title on the basis that the beneficial title still properly remains in the beneficiaries. The approach of equity, though, is to protect free markets by ensuring that the *bona fide* purchaser

---

297 See *Avon County Council v Howlett* [1983] 1 WLR 605 at 622, *per* Slade LJ.
298 [1996] 4 All ER 733; Hudson, 1997:2, 27.

for value without notice of the rights of a beneficial owner is entitled to assert good title in property in such situations. Such a person is rightly referred to as 'Equity's darling'. Consequently, a good defence to a tracing claim would appear to be an assertion that you are a purchaser acting in good faith without notice of the rights of the beneficiary.[299]

19.7.5 Consensual transfer

The matter is little discussed, but if the original owner of the property either made a perfect gift of the property to the defendant, or entered into a contract to transfer the property to the defendant, the defendant ought to be recognised as having a complete defence to any tracing action. The second proposition is clearly an extension of the *bona fide* purchaser principle, potentially, into cases in which the contract transferring the property might not constitute a contract of sale. The former principle seems to be common sense. In the event that there has been a transfer of absolute title from the claimant to the defendant without any duress or undue influence, the common law would recognise the defendant's ownership of that property. Thus it is possible to sever a claimant's ties with her original property or its traceable proceeds where she can be taken to have agreed to transfer title in it. The only complication here is where there was an intention to transfer that property away which the claimant subsequently sought to disavow, as in *National Westminster Bank v Somer*,[300] in which the claimant appeared to have an intention to transfer property at the outset but subsequently realised a mistake and so sought to reverse that transfer. This issue has been considered in para 19.6.3 above.

19.8 ISSUES WITH TRACING

19.8.1 Does conscience matter in relation to equitable tracing?

Equity, as we have discussed throughout this book, is concerned with good conscience. The law of tracing, however, is not always concerned with good conscience, even in relation to equitable tracing.[301] In *Westdeutsche Landesbank v Islington LBC*, it was held by Lord Browne-Wilkinson that a constructive trust will be imposed whenever the defendant has knowledge of some factor which affects her conscience. Therefore, when a constructive trust is being used as a remedy in relation to a tracing action, it should be the case that that constructive trust is imposed as a response to the defendant's unconscionable behaviour. Thus, the House of Lords held (unanimously on this point) in *Westdeutsche Landesbank Girozentrale v Islington LBC*[302] that there will not be an equitable proprietary right in the form of a trust without there being knowledge of some factor which affects the conscience of the legal owner of property. This is similar to the approach taken by Lord Templeman in *Attorney-General for Hong Kong v Reid*,[303] where his Lordship held that an equitable proprietary right arises as a result of equity acting *in personam* against the defendant such that

---

299 *Westdeutsche Landesbank Girozentrale v Islington LBC* [1996] AC 669, *per* Lord Browne-Wilkinson.
300 [2002] QB 1286, CA.
301 See Gleeson, 1995.
302 [1996] AC 669, [1996] 2 All ER 961.
303 [1994] 1 AC 324, [1993] 3 WLR 1143.

unconscionable dealing with property will cause the defendant to be deemed to be a constructive trustee of that property for those beneficiaries to whom fiduciary duties were owed. On the basis, then, that equity looks upon as done that which ought to have been done, the property held on trust is to be treated as having been the property of the claimant from the moment when the conscience of the defendant was affected by knowledge of an unjust factor, thus giving rise to a proprietary right in equity. On the basis of cases such as *Westdeutsche Landesbank Girozentrale v Islington LBC* and *Attorney-General for Hong Kong v Reid*, it has been argued that this approach means that a constructive trust might be imposed in situations where there has been some general unconscionability, but this leaves at large the question as to whether or not there must be some pre-existing proprietary base for the action.

Indeed, it has been argued that this approach means that a constructive trust might be imposed in relation to a tracing action without the need to establish a prior equitable interest and so forth.[304] In *Re Diplock*,[305] a charity was held liable to account to the claimant beneficiaries for property which had been passed to it under a void charitable purpose clause. The charity in this case had not committed any unconscionable act, but was nevertheless liable under the equitable tracing action. Similarly, in *Foskett v McKeown*,[306] the defendants were the children of a trustee who had committed a breach of trust, but the defendants themselves had committed no unconscionable act. Nevertheless, the defendants were held liable in relation to an equitable tracing action brought by the beneficiaries of the trust. In that case, the basis of the tracing action was explained as being to *vindicate* the property rights of the claimant and therefore the tracing action was not predicated on any unconscionable behaviour. Consequently, we can observe that a tracing action may either relate to some unconscionable behaviour on the part of the defendant; or else it may simply be predicated on a determination in English property law to protect (or vindicate) the claimant's property rights, even if that requires tracing the original property rights into substitute property. If one were determined to argue that tracing in equity is based on conscience, then it could be said that vindicating the rights of the owner of property is a demonstration of a conscience on the part of property law itself.

19.8.2 Tracing as part of equity and property law, not restitution

There is a question as to whether tracing is concerned with subtracting an unjust enrichment from the hands of the defendant, or whether equitable tracing operates on the basis of protecting the claimant's property rights against unconscionable misuse by permitting their recovery even from complex mixtures and changes of form. The language preferred by Smith is that the claimants in tracing cases achieve restitution of that property by means of having property rights in the form of the equitable interest in that property passed back to them to be held on the terms of the original trust.[307] This model of restitution of unjust

---

304 Birks, 1996:1. However, it could be argued, to the contrary, that the unconscionable behaviour brings a proprietary base into existence at the same moment as imposing a remedy by way of constructive trust over the property at issue.

305 *Diplock's Estate, Re* [1948] Ch 465.

306 *Foskett v McKeown* [2000] 3 All ER 97.

307 Smith, 1997, generally.

enrichment is considered in Chapter 31.[308] However, there is now clear authority that tracing does not arise on the basis of restitution of unjust enrichment.[309]

Prof Birks' first model of restitution of unjust enrichment[310] was concerned with the subtraction of enrichments from defendants who had acquired their enrichments at the plaintiff's expense and due to some unjust factor, such as a mistake or undue influence or some such. That the enrichment was 'unjust' meant that it arose on the basis of one of a list of factors suggested by various restitution scholars and not on the basis that it was in some general way 'unconscionable'. The appropriate remedy for the recovery of property by way of restitution was said to be a resulting trust. This theory was dismissed by the House of Lords in *Westdeutsche Landesbank v Islington*.[311] Smith applied this theory to the law on tracing.[312] His contention was that when property is recovered through any tracing action, the tracing process is undertaken further to an unjust factor having arisen so as to transfer the property away from the plaintiff and is then recovered from the defendant by means of restitution in the form, in the original version of this theory, of a resulting trust. The problem with this theory – aside from the rejection of the resulting trust remedy in *Westdeutsche Landesbank v Islington* – was that it did not accord with authority, nor was it entirely clear what its benefit would be (other than a superficial claim to have tidied up the law in some fashion). On the authorities, in cases such as *Re Diplock*, the claimant was entitled to recover her property by means of a tracing action on the basis that that property had belonged to the claimant and that the defendant had no legally-enforceable right to retain it. The courts had not based their decisions on the defendant having been unjustly enriched. Rather, as Lord Millett made clear in *Foskett v McKeown*, tracing operates as a part of property law in protecting the rights of claimants to assert title to property which remains theirs at common law or which is a substitute for property taken from them in breach of trust.

The decision in *Westdeutsche Landesbank Girozentrale v Islington LBC* is remarkable, in part, because it avoids the contract purportedly entered into between the parties while at the same time implicitly accepting that the transfer of property under that void contract is nevertheless valid. So it is that the bank is deemed to have transferred title in the money paid to the local authority even though the contract which purported to transfer that title was itself held to have been void. The alternative view of this context would be that a mistake as to the validity of the contract[313] (or other vitiating factor)[314] would lead to the contract being rescinded at the claimant's election, and thus give rise to a right to trace after that money.[315] *Westdeutsche Landesbank Girozentrale v Islington LBC* held that there is no such right to trace where the intention of the parties was to transfer outright the title in the property[316] and where the money or its traceable proceeds had been dissipated.[317]

308 See section 31.3.
309 *Boscawen v Bajwa* [1995] 4 All ER 769, 776; *Foskett v McKeown* [2001] 1 AC 102, 109 and 129.
310 See Birks, 1992.
311 [1996] AC 669.
312 See Smith, 1997.
313 Now a valid ground for avoidance of a contract: *Kleinwort Benson v Lincoln City Council* [1998] 4 All ER 513.
314 Such as misrepresentation or undue influence: Martin, 1997, 666.
315 *Daly v Sydney Stock Exchange* (1986) 160 CLR 371; *Lonrho plc v Al Fayed (No 2)* [1992] 1 WLR 1; *El Ajou v Dollar Land Holdings* [1993] 3 All ER 717; *Halifax Building Society v Thomas* [1996] Ch 217.
316 Although, necessarily, that intention would not have been present but for the mistake which the parties had made as to the validity of the contract.
317 See also *Re Goldcorp* [1995] 1 AC 74.

19.8.3 Tracing into stolen property

One particular context in which tracing becomes important, other than the straightforward breaches of fiduciary duty considered above, is when property is stolen. This issue was considered at para 2.6.3. Clearly, no system of law will permit a thief to obtain any proprietary rights in the proceeds of the crime. The question is the manner in which the thief is required to deal with the property after the theft, and whether or not the thief ought to be required to hold the stolen property on trust for the victim of the theft as the result of a tracing claim. It has been held that where property is stolen from a pension fund, the thief holds the stolen property on constructive trust for victims of the theft; therefore it is possible to trace into that stolen property and to establish title over it.[318] Similarly, it was held in *Westdeutsche Landesbank Girozentrale v Islington LBC* that by analogy with a hypothetical stolen bag of coins, the thief should hold that stolen property on constructive trust for the victim of the crime.[319] Therefore, equitable tracing is available to the victim of crime because the thief holds the stolen property on constructive trust, with the result that the victim has an equitable interest in the property.

In Chapter 12, the Privy Council decision in *Attorney-General for Hong Kong v Reid* is considered.[320] In that case, the Attorney-General for Hong Kong accepted bribes in return for which he did not prosecute particular criminals. The receipt of those bribes was in itself a criminal offence. It was held by Lord Templeman that from the moment of receipt of the bribes, the defendant held that property on constructive trust for his employers. The consequence of that immediate imposition of a constructive trust was that the defendant also held on constructive trust any profits made from those bribes, or any property acquired with the money representing the bribes. Consequently, a thief (or other criminal obtaining pecuniary advantage from a crime) will hold the stolen property and its traceable substitute on constructive trust for the original owner of the property.

The result of this decision is akin to Lord Browne-Wilkinson's *dicta* in *Westdeutsche Landesbank Girozentrale v Islington LBC* that a constructive trust will be imposed on a person whose conscience is affected by knowledge of a factor which is considered to have affected it. Thus, a thief knows of the unconscionability of stealing property and therefore will be subject to a constructive trust in respect of that property from the moment of the theft. Lord Templeman rendered this principle in a slightly different way in *Reid*. His Lordship held that equity acts *in personam* (as considered in Chapter 1) and also 'looks upon as done that which ought to have been done'. Therefore, the imposition of the constructive trust in *Reid* operates as a 'personal claim'[321] against the defendant, which requires that the defendant is not entitled to deal with the property other than to hold it on trust for the claimant.

The other means of conceiving of the law in this area is that the victim of the crime is the only person who could release her rights in the property which was stolen. Therefore, those rights must be considered to have continued in existence, despite the theft. Consequently, the

---

318 *Bishopsgate v Maxwell* [1993] Ch 1, 70.
319 *Westdeutsche Landesbank Girozentrale v Islington LBC* [1996] AC 669.
320 *Attorney-General for Hong Kong v Reid* [1994] 1 AC 324, [1993] 3 WLR 1143.
321 In the sense discussed in para 1.14.12, that equity is concerned with the conscience of the defendant in general terms and and not simply that the defendant is not necessarily subject to a proprietary claim.

courts should not be concerned to grant new property rights to the claimant under constructive trust, but rather should simply be recognising that those rights have always continued in existence such that the claimant ought to be entitled to a declaration that those rights have continued to exist. The slight conceptual problem with the imposition of a constructive trust on the thief is the apparent recognition that the thief acquired legal title in the stolen property when she acts as trustee of the constructive trust. Indeed, the further problem with *Reid* is that the employer had no pre-existing rights in either the stolen property or its proceeds, and therefore arguably ought only to receive a right *in personam* against the defendant in the manner which Lord Templeman explained it. In both of these situations, equity appears to be acting in a way which punishes the criminal, in effect, and which grants the victim of crime a right to trace her stolen property in equity by granting her an equitable interest in the property by means of the constructive trusts device.[322]

322 Without the grant of a constructive trust, the victim would be considered to have held only an absolute title in the property such that there was no distinct equitable interest capable of founding equitable tracing: *Westdeutsche Landesbank Girozentrale v Islington LBC* [1996] AC 669.

Chapter 20

The liability of strangers to account for involvement in a breach of trust

OVERVIEW

*Where a person dishonestly assists in a breach of trust, that dishonest assistant will be
personally liable to account to the beneficiaries of that trust for the value lost to the trust.
The test for dishonesty is an objective test (although there is authority suggesting a
modicum of subjectivity too) which requires that the court consider what an honest
person would have done in the circumstances, albeit seen through the lens of the personal
characteristics and knowledge of the defendant.[1] 'Dishonesty' in this context encompasses fraud, lack of probity and reckless risk-taking. The liability is predicated on an
equitable wrong and imposes a personal liability to account to the beneficiaries as though
a constructive trustee.[2] It is not necessary that any trustee of the trust is dishonest; simply
that the dishonest assistant is dishonest.[3] The claim for dishonest assistance is one which
has provoked great controversy among academic commentators and has spawned two
Privy Council and two House of Lords decisions, seven decisions of the Court of Appeal
including dishonest assistance claims, and dozens of decisions in the High Court in
recent years. The principal issue is as to the nature of the test for dishonesty and the
precise level of subjectivity which can be admitted to an avowedly objective test.*

*A person who is neither a trustee nor a beneficiary will be personally liable to account
to the trust for any loss suffered in a situation in which she receives trust property
unconscionably with knowledge that the property has been passed to her in breach of
trust.[4] 'Knowledge' in this context includes actual knowledge, wilfully closing one's
eyes to the breach of trust, or failing to make the inquiries which a reasonable person
would have made.[5] Recent cases have recast this test of knowledge so that it is based on
whether or not the defendant had acted unconscionably in receiving the trust property.[6]
Another (short) line of authority had predicated this test on dishonesty.*

---

1   *Royal Brunei Airlines v Tan* [1995] 2 AC 378; *Dubai Aluminium v Salaam* [2002] 3 WLR 1913, [2003] 1 All ER 97.
2   *Royal Brunei Airlines v Tan* [1995] 2 AC 378.
3   *Ibid.*
4   *Re Montagu* [1987] Ch 264; *Agip v Jackson* [1990] Ch 265, 286, *per* Millett J; [1991] Ch 547, CA; *Lipkin
    Gorman v Karpnale* [1991] 2 AC 548; *El Ajou v Dollar Land Holdings* [1993] 3 All ER 717, appealed [1994]
    2 All ER 685.
5   *Re Montagu* [1987] Ch 264.
6   *BCCI v Akindele* [2001] Ch 437; *Charter plc v City Index Ltd* [2008] 2 WLR 950.

20.1 INTRODUCTION

20.1.1 The liability of strangers to the trust in relation to a breach of trust

This chapter considers the circumstances in which people who are neither trustees nor fiduciaries will be liable for any loss suffered by beneficiaries as a result of some breach of trust.[7] The status of the trustee and the fiduciary is easily comprehensible. The rule that a fiduciary cannot profit from that office and that trustees will be liable for any loss caused by a breach of trust are well-established in equity.[8] The more difficult question is: in what circumstances will a person who is neither a trustee nor a beneficiary under a trust be held liable in respect of any loss caused by a breach of that trust? Such a person is referred to in the following sections as a 'stranger' to the trust,[9] having no express position connected to that trust. Equity has always sought to impose fiduciary duties on those who misuse trust property, whether holding an office under that trust or not. This has extended to the imposition of the duties of a trustee onto people who meddle with the trust fund. One of the practical reasons for pursuing this remedy is that the intermeddler is frequently an advisor or a professional who is solvent and therefore capable of making good the money lost to the trust if the trust property itself is lost and if the trustees have no money to make good the loss to the trust in an action for breach of trust.

20.1.2 Understanding the basis of each claim

The receipt claim and the assistance claim

The two sets of applicable principles can be summarised in the following terms. First, a person who is neither a trustee nor a beneficiary will be personally liable to account to the trust for any loss suffered in a situation in which she dishonestly assists the commission of a breach of trust, without receiving any proprietary right in that trust property herself.[10] This liability is referred to as 'dishonest assistance'. The test for 'dishonesty' in this context is a test which asks whether or not the defendant acted as an honest person would have acted in the circumstances.[11] This notion of dishonesty extends beyond straightforward deceit and fraud potentially into reckless risk-taking with trust property.[12]

Secondly, a person who is neither a trustee nor a beneficiary will be personally liable to account to the trust for any loss suffered in a situation in which she receives trust property with knowledge that the property has been passed to her in breach of trust.[13] This form of liability is referred to as 'knowing receipt'(or, unconscionable receipt now). 'Knowledge' in this context includes actual knowledge, wilfully closing one's eyes to the breach of trust, or

---

7 This category of claim was considered in outline in section 12.9 above. Readers should also have reference, when indicated in this chapter, to section 12.8 above in relation to the liability of trustees *de son tort*.
8 See sections 12.5 and 18.1 respectively.
9 The expression 'strangers' is used by Lord Selborne in *Barnes v Addy* (1874) 9 Ch App 244, at 251.
10 *Royal Brunei Airlines v Tan* [1995] 2 AC 378.
11 *Ibid.*
12 *Ibid.*
13 *Re Montagu's Settlements* [1987] Ch 264.

failing to make the inquiries which a reasonable person would have made in these circumstances.[14] Recent cases have suggested that liability for receipt of property in breach of trust should be based on proof that the defendant has acted unconscionably[15] which, it is suggested, would include having knowledge that there had been a breach of trust.

In either case, there must have been loss suffered by the beneficiaries as a result of some breach of trust: the liability of the strangers is then to account to the beneficiaries for that loss, providing that the knowing receipt or dishonest assistance has been demonstrated.[16] Therefore, there must have been a breach of trust before either of these claims could arise. The remedy which is sought is a remedy which will make the defendant liable to account to the beneficiaries *as though they had been trustees*;[17] that is, the defendants are construed by the court (hence the term 'constructive trustees') to have rendered themselves liable to account to the beneficiaries in the same way that trustees would be liable by virtue of their participation in the breach of trust. Therefore, their obligation is to account to the beneficiaries personally (that is, from their own, personal funds) for the full loss suffered by the beneficiaries in the same way that express trustees would have to account to the beneficiaries under the *Target Holdings v Redferns*[18] principle.

These two types of claim should be understood as being related to constructive trusts because the courts have clearly described the liability here as being a form of constructive trusteeship.[19] Equally importantly, however, it is accepted that the defendants do not hold any property on trust. This form of claim is brought in situations in which the claimant is not able to identify the original property nor its traceable proceeds, and where she is unable to recover the whole of the value lost to the trust fund from the trustees alone. In such situations, the claimant will be seeking someone else who can be made liable for the loss to the trust fund, and so will sue people who have either received the trust property during the breach of trust or assisted in the breach of trust without receiving the property, as is considered in the next section.

How dishonest assistance and knowing receipt combine with other claims relating to breach of trust

Claims for dishonest assistance and knowing receipt should be understood as combining with the claims brought against trustees for breach of trust (considered in Chapter 18) and to trace the substitute for the original property taken in breach of trust (considered in Chapter 19). For example, suppose that Tim held a pristine, extremely valuable first edition of Charles Dickens's novel *Oliver Twist* on trust. If Tim were to transfer that book away in breach of trust, then he would be personally liable as a trustee for breach of trust. As discussed in Chapter 18, a trustee (Tim) would be liable to restore the *Oliver Twist* first edition to the

---

14 *Ibid.*

15 *BCCI v Akindele* [2001] Ch 437; *Charter plc v City Index Ltd* [2008] 2 WLR 950.

16 See Thomas and Hudson, 2004, para 30.19 *et seq*. Also on the older position in relation to the liability of strangers, see Harpum, 1986.

17 *Ibid.*

18 [1996] 1 AC 421; see section 18.1 above.

19 See, eg, *Dubai Aluminium v Salaam* [2002] 3 WLR 1913, [2003] 1 All ER 97.

trust fund, or to restore the cash value of the novel to the trust fund, or to pay equitable compensation to the beneficiaries.[20] The beneficiaries would be required to proceed against Tim, as trustee, in the first place.[21]

Given that a first edition of *Oliver Twist* is particularly valuable, it might be that Tim would not be able to compensate the beneficiaries in cash simply because he might not have enough money to do so. Therefore, the beneficiaries would need to find someone else who would be able to make good their loss. Suppose then that Julia, a book dealer, organised the sale of the book to a client overseas for Tim. Julia would then face personal liability for dishonest assistance in a breach of trust: that is, the liability of one who assisted the breach of trust.[22] If Julia organised the sale of the book, she would clearly have assisted the breach of trust. To use language familiar to criminal lawyers, purely by way of illustration: Julia will have committed the *actus reus* necessary for this form of liability. As will emerge from the discussion below, it will be necessary to demonstrate that Julia acted dishonestly when assisting the breach of trust.[23] Therefore, to use criminal law jargon again, it will be necessary to demonstrate that Julia has the appropriate *mens rea* of 'dishonesty' to be liable.[24] The test of 'dishonesty' which equity uses has extended beyond the ordinary meaning of the word 'dishonesty'. The precise nature of Julia's liability would be to make good all of the loss suffered by the beneficiaries *as though Julia had been a trustee*.[25]

Further, suppose that Kramer owns a book depository in which valuable, antique books are stored in airtight conditions and in which they can be displayed for purchasers. If Kramer received the book and stored it prior to selling it on Tim's behalf, then Kramer might face liability for knowing receipt of that book in breach of trust: that is, a potential liability based on the receipt of the book when it comes into his possession. It would be necessary that two things took place: an *actus reus* of receipt of the book and also a *mens rea* of knowledge that Kramer had received the book in breach of trust. The applicable principles surrounding each of these terms are considered below. The significant factor at this stage is that the liability which Kramer faces is based on receipt of the property and not simply on assisting with the breach of trust.[26]

---

20 *Target Holdings v Redferns* [1996] 1 AC 421, [1995] 3 WLR 352, [1995] 3 All ER 785.

21 *Ibid.*

22 *Royal Brunei Airlines v Tan* [1995] 2 AC 378; *Smith New Court v Scrimgeour Vickers* [1997] AC 254; *Corporacion Nacional del Cobre De Chile v Sogemin Metals* [1997] 1 WLR 1396; *Fortex Group Ltd v MacIntosh* [1998] 3 NZLR 171; *Twinsectra Ltd v Yardley* [1999] Lloyd's Rep Bank 438; *Dubai Aluminium v Salaam* [1999] 1 Lloyd's Rep 415; *Wolfgang Herbert Heinl v Jyske Bank* [1999] Lloyd's Rep Bank 511; *Thomas v Pearce* [2000] FSR 718; *Dubai Aluminium v Salaam* [2002] 3 WLR 1913, [2003] 1 All ER 97.

23 *Ibid.*

24 It should be stressed that the courts do not use this criminal law jargon, but it is hoped that these concepts will be familiar to serve by way of analogy.

25 *Royal Brunei Airlines v Tan* [1995] 2 AC 378; *Smith New Court v Scrimgeour Vickers* [1997] AC 254; *Corporacion Nacional del Cobre De Chile v Sogemin Metals* [1997] 1 WLR 1396; *Fortex Group Ltd v MacIntosh* [1998] 3 NZLR 171; *Twinsectra Ltd v Yardley* [1999] Lloyd's Rep Bank 438; *Dubai Aluminium v Salaam* [1999] 1 Lloyd's Rep 415; *Wolfgang Herbert Heinl v Jyske Bank* [1999] Lloyd's Rep Bank 511; *Thomas v Pearce* [2000] FSR 718; *Dubai Aluminium v Salaam* [2002] 3 WLR 1913, [2003] 1 All ER 97.

26 *Grupo Toras v Al-Sabah* (2000) unreported, 2 November, CA.

These claims would impose on Julia and Kramer respectively personal liability to account to the beneficiaries for the value of the property passed and for any consequent loss that the beneficiaries suffer.[27] In either case, liability as a knowing recipient or as a dishonest assistant should be understood as imposing liability as a constructive trustee on the defendant.[28] So, Julia is construed to be a trustee as a result of her unconscionable act of dishonestly assisting a breach of trust such that she bears the liability to make good any loss suffered by the beneficiaries which arises from Tim's breach of trust, and Kramer will be liable to account as a constructive trustee on the basis of his receipt of the book. Significantly, in this example, Julia did not receive the book; rather, her liability is based on her wrongful act of dishonest assistance rather than on any contact with the property itself.

However, it should not be forgotten that in many cases, these claims will form part of a much larger web of claims commenced by beneficiaries. The beneficiaries may also seek to recover the book itself or the traceable proceeds of the book by way of tracing.[29] The first claim would be a proprietary tracing action at common law to recover the very first edition of *Oliver Twist* which was taken from the trust fund.[30] If the book had been sold, they would seek an equitable proprietary tracing action to assert title to the money received for the sale of the book.[31] These claims were considered in Chapter 19. Frequently, all of these claims will be pursued simultaneously by the beneficiaries. As such, the issue considered in this chapter might constitute only one of a number of claims brought in relation to any one set of facts. The beneficiaries will then be able to elect between these two remedies, but not to recover their loss more than once.[32] The many defendants may then sue one another for a contribution to the liability which any one of them might face in relation to the beneficiaries. Liability for personal liability to account under either of these heads will apply specifically in relation to a breach of trust or more generally in relation to any other breach of fiduciary duty, such as a breach of duty by a company director or a business partner or an agent, in exactly the same way as it applies to trustees.[33] However, for ease of reference we shall refer primarily to 'trustees', although the principles will apply in relation to any breach of fiduciary duty.

Three cases will serve to illustrate the combination of claims against trustees and strangers which might follow on from a breach of trust. The first is the decision of the House of Lords

---

27 What remains unclear is the extent to which the equitable remedy of account in these cases will permit the court to hold the defendant liable only to the extent that the defendant is genuinely culpable in the same way that, eg, a common law court would invoke principles of contributory negligence to reduce the defendant's liability.

28 *Dubai Aluminium v Salaam* [2002] 3 WLR 1913, [2003] 1 All ER 97, *per* Lord Nicholls, as considered below. See also Hayton, 1995:2.

29 Considered in Chapter 19.

30 *Jones, FC (A Firm) v Jones* [1996] 3 WLR 703.

31 *Re Diplock's Estate* [1948] Ch 465; *Westdeutsche Landesbank Girozentrale v Islington LBC* [1996] AC 669, HL.

32 *Tang v Capacious Investments* [1996] 1 AC 514.

33 See, eg, *JJ Harrison (Properties) Ltd v Harrison* [2002] 1 BCLC 162, 'where a director who had bought land belonging to the company, without disclosing its development potential, was held to have acquired the property as constructive trustee' as explained in *Ultraframe (UK) Ltd v Fielding* [2005] EWHC 1638 (Ch), [2005] All ER (D) 397, para [1481], *per* Lewison J.

in *Lipkin Gorman v Karpnale*.[34] In that case, a partner in a firm of solicitors frequently drew money from the firm's client account and gambled it away in the defendant's casino. When the firm of solicitors discovered that this money had been taken from accounts which the partnership held on trust for its clients, the firm had to find a means of recovering their client's loss. The partner himself owed his fellow partners a liability as a fiduciary, but he was unable personally to make good the loss to the partnership. Therefore, the firm proceeded against the casino under a range of personal and proprietary claims. Among the personal claims brought by the solicitors' firm were actions against the casino under the tort of negligence, an action for money had and received (or 'personal liability in restitution'), an action for conversion of cheques, an action for conversion of a banker's draft, and an action for knowing receipt in respect of the money taken from their client account. Among the proprietary claims were actions for common law tracing into the casino's bank accounts and for equitable tracing similarly into its bank accounts. The firm also claimed against the bank which held the firm's client account, claiming dishonest assistance, conversion of cheques, conversion of a banker's draft and breach of contract. All of these claims were pursued simultaneously as the firm of solicitors sought to prosecute every possible claim which might recover all or part of their loss.

In the House of Lords, the matter was ultimately settled, in part, on the basis of unjust enrichment on the part of the casino, with an account taken of the casino's change of position on receipt of the moneys – thus establishing the case as a landmark decision among restitution lawyers. The plaintiffs were able to establish proprietary claims with reference to those moneys which the casino had held separately from other of their moneys so as to be identifiable, but were only able to proceed for the remaining moneys under personal claims to the extent that the casino could be demonstrated to have had sufficient knowledge of the source of the partner's moneys or to have been otherwise negligent. The complex web of actions was essential to the firm's claims.

The second case which will serve as an illustration is *Agip (Africa) v Jackson*,[35] in which the defendant accountants arranged that money would be taken from the plaintiffs by means of forged payment orders payable to a series of 'dummy companies'.[36] The intention had been to launder the money through the dummy companies. The plaintiffs pursued a number of claims simultaneously, both personally against the accountants themselves, against their firm, against the companies and the banks which received the money, and also brought proprietary claims against any property which constituted or had been derived from the original moneys taken. This type of web of claims is typical of cases brought in these areas of law – as the claimant seeks for some person (or a sufficient number of people) able to make good its losses.[37] In each case, the claimants sought to recover all of their loss by whatever method against whichever defendant would be successful, and then subsequently to elect which of those claims they wish to enforce.

34   [1991] 3 WLR 10.
35   [1990] Ch 265, 286, *per* Millett J, [1991] Ch 547, CA.
36   'Dummy' or 'shell' companies are companies which do not conduct a trade but which are used solely to hold assets for their shareholders: they are similar to trusts in this sense.
37   What is often referred to as the 'search for the solvent defendant'.

The third illustration is *Primlake Ltd v Matthews*,[38] in which case an architect, Matthews, advised a company, Primlake, on the development of land. Primlake sold an option to acquire the development land in return for three large deposits (totalling about £3 million). Matthews procured payments to himself, in his own name and that of his wife, of about £900,000 in total by giving instructions to a person who controlled those funds to make the payments. While Lawrence Collins J was only appraised of this case at an interlocutory stage, his Lordship made it clear in his concluding passage what his conclusions on the merits of liability for constructive trust and for personal liability to account as a constructive trustee would be. Issues arose as to whether or not Matthews was a director of the payer company – something which it is not necessary for us to resolve for the purposes of this example. It is sufficient to note that Matthews was not entitled to receive the money and it was found to have been paid to him in breach of fiduciary duty. It was held by Lawrence Collins J that Matthews would be liable for dishonest assistance in the breach of fiduciary duty because he had actual knowledge of his lack of entitlement to the money and because he had organised the payments; he could also be liable for knowing receipt of those same moneys because the payments were made into his own bank accounts and because he had actual knowledge of the breach of duty; and he would also be liable to hold those payments or any property acquired with them on constructive trust because he had obtained those moneys unconscionably further to the general principle set out in *Westdeutsche Landesbank v Islington*.[39]

The nature of the remedy of personal liability to account

The form of relief awarded in claims for dishonest assistance or knowing receipt is the imposition of a personal liability to account on the stranger as a constructive trustee.[40] In *Selangor v Craddock (No 3)*,[41] it was held by Ungoed-Thomas J that this form of relief is:

> nothing more than a formula for equitable relief. The court of equity says that the defendant shall be liable in equity, as though he were a trustee.

In short, this is not a trust as ordinarily understood; rather, the explanation of these two claims as imposing constructive trusteeship is, in Ungoed-Thomas J's opinion, really just a means of intellectualising the way in which equity chooses to provide a remedy for the beneficiaries. Neither dishonest assistance nor knowing receipt operates as an ordinary trust because there is no specific property which is held on trust. Rather, this is an example of equity granting a personal remedy to beneficiaries. Indeed, the cases on dishonest assistance were excluded by Lord Browne-Wilkinson from many of the rules which concern express

---

38 [2006] EWHC 1227 (Ch).
39 It should be noted, however, that in his Lordship's conclusion there is a pell-mell finding of liability across the distinct doctrines of resulting trust, constructive trust, money had and received, dishonest assistance and knowing receipt which makes it particularly difficult to know on what precise basis any particular claim was made out.
40 Cf Elliott and Mitchell, 2004.
41 [1968] 1 WLR 1555, 1579.

trusts in *Westdeutsche Landesbank Girozentrale v Islington LBC*,[42] when his Lordship explained that:

> In order to establish a trust there must be identifiable trust property. The only apparent exception to this rule is a constructive trust imposed on a person who dishonestly assists in a breach of trust who may come under fiduciary duties even if he does not receive identifiable trust property.

It does appear that this type of equitable relief is as much in the form of a remedy as an institutional trust. That means dishonest assistance (and, it is suggested, knowing receipt)[43] is as much a form of equitable wrong (organised around a standard of good conscience) as a breach of trust (under which identified property is held on trust for beneficiaries). Each of the two heads of liability to account to the beneficiaries is considered in turn, beginning with dishonest assistance.

20.2 DISHONEST ASSISTANCE

Where a person dishonestly assists in a breach of trust, that dishonest assistant will be personally liable to account to the beneficiaries of that trust for the value lost to the trust. The test for dishonesty is an objective test (although there is authority suggesting a modicum of subjectivity too) which requires that the court consider what an honest person would have done in the circumstances, albeit seen through the lens of the personal characteristics and knowledge of the defendant.[44] 'Dishonesty' in this context encompasses fraud, lack of probity and reckless risk-taking. The liability is predicated on an equitable wrong and imposes a personal liability to account to the beneficiaries as though a constructive trustee.[45] It is not necessary that any trustee of the trust is dishonest; simply that the dishonest assistant is dishonest.[46] The claim for dishonest assistance is one which has provoked great controversy among academic commentators and has spawned two Privy Council and two House of Lords decisions, seven decisions of the Court of Appeal including dishonest assistance claims, and dozens of decisions in the High Court in recent years. The principal issue is as to the nature of the test for dishonesty and the precise level of subjectivity which can be admitted to an avowedly objective test.

20.2.1 Introduction

Liability for dishonest assistance relates to 'strangers' to trusts: that is, someone who is not a trustee of that trust. The elements of that liability can be summed up in the following way:

---

42 [1996] AC 669.
43 There is a tendency to separate out these two claims on the basis that in relation to knowing receipt, there will have been specific property received by the defendant before liability will attach to her; however, the remedy is still a personal remedy and is not dependent upon there still being any property in the defendant's hands which could be held on trust.
44 *Royal Brunei Airlines v Tan* [1995] 2 AC 378; *Dubai Aluminium v Salaam* [2002] 3 WLR 1913, [2003] 1 All ER 97.
45 *Royal Brunei Airlines v Tan* [1995] 2 AC 378.
46 *Ibid.*

A stranger will be personally liable to account as a constructive trustee to the beneficiaries of a trust for any loss caused to the trust by a breach of trust if the stranger assisted
that breach of trust and if the stranger did so dishonestly.[47]

The stranger is described as being a 'constructive trustee' because she will be made liable as
if she had actually been a trustee for the loss caused by the breach of trust: in that sense she
is 'construed' to be a trustee and hence is a 'constructive trustee'. The liability to account to
the beneficiaries is effectively the same as though the stranger had been an express trustee
and required to account under *Target Holdings v Redferns*,[48] as discussed in Chapter 18. The
stranger is '*personally* liable to account' in that she does not hold any property on trust, and
in that sense is not an ordinary, constructive trustee; rather, her liability is to compensate the
beneficiaries of the trust for the loss which was caused by the breach of trust, with that
compensation coming from her own personal property. Ordinarily, the stranger would
account in money for the cash equivalent of the loss. Therefore, this is a personal and not a
proprietary liability. This form of liability is clearly a potentially very large one because the
stranger can be personally liable for the whole of the beneficiaries' loss.[49] The concept of
'assistance' is considered below although there is little case law on exactly what is meant by
that term. It appears that any substantive act or omission which facilitates the breach of trust
will be sufficient. The difficulty in the case law has been in identifying what is meant by
'dishonesty'. That issue will occupy the bulk of the discussion.[50]

---

47   This summary of the test is the author's own, although it is culled from various authorities considered in this
section: *Royal Brunei Airlines v Tan* [1995] 2 AC 378; *Dubai Aluminium v Salaam* [2002] 3 WLR 1913, [2003]
1 All ER 97; *Twinsectra v Yardley* [2002] 2 AC 164; *Barlow Clowes v Eurotrust* [2005] UKPC 37, [2006] 1
WLR 1476; *Abou-Rahmah v Abacha* [2006] EWCA Civ 1492; and the less celebrated decisions in *Goose
v Wilson Sandford & Co* [1998] EWCA Civ 245; *Brinks Mat v Abu-Saleh (No3)* [1999] CLC 133; *Brown
v Bennett* [1999] 1 BCLC 659; *Wakelin v Read* [2000] EWCA Civ 82; *Woodland-Ferrari v UCL Group
Retirement Benefits Scheme* [2002] 3 All ER 670, [2002] EWHC 1354 (Ch D); *Carr v Bower Cotton* [2002]
EWCA Civ 1788; *Manolakaki v Constantinides* [2004] EWHC 749; *Ultraframe (UK) Ltd v Fielding* [2005]
EWHC 1638 (Ch); *AG Zambia v Meer Care & Desai & Others* [2007] EWHC 952 (Ch), on appeal [2008]
EWCA Civ 1007; *Markel International Insurance Co Ltd v Surety Guarantee Consultants Ltd* [2008] EWHC
1135 (Comm); *JD Wetherspoon plc v Van de Berg & Co Ltd* [2009] EWHC 639 (Ch); *Markel International
Insurance Company Ltd v Higgins* [2009] EWCA Civ 790; *Aerostar Maintenance v International Ltd v Wilson*
[2010] EWHC 2032 (Ch); *Independent Trustee Services Ltd v GP Noble Trustees Ltd* [2010] EWHC 1653
(Ch); *Al Khudairi v Abbey Brokers Ltd* [2010] EWHC 1486 (Ch), [2010] PNLR 32; *Dyson Technology Ltd
v Curtis* [2010] EWHC 3289 (Ch); *Starglade v Nash* [2010] EWCA Civ 1314; *Secretary of State for Justice
v Topland Group plc* [2011] EWHC 983 (QB); *Fiona Trust & Holding Corporation v Privalov* [2010] EWHC
3199 (Comm); *Law Society of England and Wales v Habitable Concepts Ltd* [2010] EWHC 1449 (Ch); *Law
Society of England and Wales v Isaac* [2010] EWHC 1670 (Ch); *Apax Global Payment and Technologies Ltd
v Morina* [2011] All ER (D) 185 (Jun); and *Agip (Africa) Ltd v Jackson* [1990] Ch 265.
48   [1996] 1 AC 421.
49   In circumstances in which there are several people who may be responsible in various ways for the breach of
trust, then the Civil Liability (Contribution) Act 1970, as explained in *Dubai Aluminium Company v Salaam*
[2002] 3 WLR 1913, [2003] 1 All ER 97, will allocate responsibility between them.
50   Liability for dishonest assistance differs from claims for unconscionable receipt in that there is no requirement
for the imposition of liability for dishonest assistance that the stranger has had possession or control of the
property at any time, whereas unconscionable receipt is based on the defendant having taken trust property into
her possession. A person who is liable for dishonest assistance in a breach of trust is obliged to account to the
beneficiaries for any loss suffered as a result of that breach of trust. Elliott and Mitchell, 2004.

The principles informing this area of equity were set out in the speech of Lord Selborne LC in *Barnes v Addy*, where his Lordship held that:

> strangers are not to be made constructive trustees merely because they act as the agents of trustees in transactions within their legal powers, transactions, perhaps, of which a Court of Equity may disapprove, unless those agents receive and become chargeable with some part of the trust property, or unless they assist with knowledge in a dishonest and fraudulent design on the part of the trustee.[51]

The decision in *Barnes v Addy* offers us a clear foundation for the modern law on dishonest assistance because it is a decision of the House of Lords which cites no earlier authority: the defendant's liability is based on her dishonest participation in actions which constituted a breach of trust. It is worth noting that the test as set out by Lord Selborne relates to 'knowledge' of a dishonest design on the part of the trustee: indeed, this area of law was known as 'knowing assistance' for most of the 20th century as a result. There were other cases on which the House of Lords in *Barnes v Addy* could have chosen to rely or to build, but they did not.[52] It was in 1995 with the judgment of Lord Nicholls in *Royal Brunei Airlines v Tan*[53] that there was a movement from 'knowing assistance' towards 'dishonest assistance'. The principal effect of this change was a movement away from subjective ideas of what the defendant knew about the breach of trust towards a test based on objectivity which required the court to identify what an honest person would have done in the circumstances. This area of law has subsequently been bedevilled by a see-sawing between preferences for an objective and for a subjective approach to this area. It is suggested that the current state of the law is that the courts are predominantly following the judgment of Lord Nicholls in *Royal Brunei Airlines v Tan*, which established an objective test, but those courts are giving weight to *dicta* from within that judgment which nevertheless admit some subjectivity into the process.[54]

What this section will do is to trace the development of the law chronologically through the cases decided by the Privy Council, the House of Lords and the Court of Appeal (in that order), before coming to a raft of High Court decisions in which the judges at first instance have been faced with the difficult business of identifying one clear test from among all of those authorities. One of the results of the movement towards electronic law reporting of all cases which are decided in the High Court and above in this area is that there are many more cases available to us than was the case when *Royal Brunei Airlines v Tan* was decided. This has the result that the state of the authorities simply becomes more confusing because there are many cases reported with alternative approaches to the law than are published in the mainstream law reports. If one takes a purist's approach to the doctrine of precedent, then this is all very unsatisfactory. Therefore, this section will finish by working through a hypothetical set of facts to demonstrate how the five principal, different approaches in the cases to the test of dishonesty can lead to different results.

---

51 (1874) 9 Ch App 244, 251–2.
52 *Fyler v Fyler* (1841) 3 Beav 550, 49 ER 1031; *Attorney-General v Leicester Corp* (1844) 7 Beav 176, (1844) 49 ER 1031; *Eaves v Hickson* (1861) 30 Beav 136.
53 *Royal Brunei Airlines v Tan* [1995] 3 All ER 97, 102.
54 *Ibid.*

20.2.2 A summary of the cases on the test for dishonesty

This short section sets out a map through the different interpretations of 'dishonesty' in the context of liability for dishonest assistance. In essence, the test for dishonesty is predicated on the judgment of Lord Nicholls in the Privy Council in *Royal Brunei Airlines v Tan*[55] to the effect that the test is an objective one: such that a person is dishonest if she fails to do what an honest person would have done in those circumstances. Nevertheless, in *Twinsectra v Yardley*[56] in the House of Lords, Lord Hutton held that the test for dishonesty required not only an inquiry as to what an honest person would have done in the circumstances but also an inquiry into whether or not the defendant subjectively appreciated that what he had done would have been considered to be dishonest by honest people. The shortcoming in Lord Hutton's version of the test was demonstrated in *Barlow Clowes v Eurotrust*[57] in the Privy Council in which the defendant sought to argue that his personal morality was such that he did not know that honest people would have thought his actions were dishonest and that his personal morality meant that, in effect, he would do whatever his clients wanted with no questions asked. The Privy Council, including Lord Nicholls and judges who had purport-edly support Lord Hutton in *Twinsectra*, held unanimously that the test should be the objec-tive test set out in *Royal Brunei Airlines v Tan*. In the meantime, in *Dubai Aluminium v Salaam* in the House of Lords,[58] it had been held by Lord Nicholls that the appropriate test for dishonesty was the objective test in *Royal Brunei Airlines v Tan*, although *Dubai Aluminium* has rarely been cited in the later cases.

Latterly, the Court of Appeal in *Abou-Rahmah v Abacha*[59] purportedly followed *Barlow Clowes v Eurotrust* (and thus by implication *Royal Brunei Airlines v Tan*). However, they did this by relying on *dicta* in Lord Nicholls's judgment in *Royal Brunei Airlines v Tan* which suggested that reference could be made to the defendant's personal attributes. Subsequent cases[60] have continued to rely on this idea that within the objective test a court can consider the personal attributes, experience and intelligence of the defendant, provided that one does not allow the defendant's personal beliefs to excuse an otherwise dishonest act.

The rationale behind the imposition of liability for dishonest assistance

The rationale for imposing liability on a dishonest assistant in a breach of trust is to protect the beneficiaries from the acts of strangers interfering with the trust in some way such that they assist or facilitate the breach of trust. There may, however, be several people involved in a breach of trust: the trustees, the dishonest assistants, any knowing recipients of the

---

55 *Royal Brunei Airlines v Tan* [1995] 3 All ER 97.

56 *Twinsectra v Yardley* [2002] 2 AC 164. This interpretation was accepted in *Ultraframe (UK) Ltd v Fielding* [2005] EWHC 1638 (Ch), [2005] All ER (D) 397.

57 *Barlow Clowes v Eurotrust* [2005] UKPC 37, [2006] 1 All ER 333.

58 *Dubai Aluminium v Salaam* [2002] 3 WLR 1913.

59 *Abou-Rahmah v Abacha* [2006] EWCA Civ 1492, CA.

60 *AG Zambia v Meer Care & Desai & Others* [2007] EWHC 952 (Ch); *Markel International Insurance Co Ltd v Surety Guarantee Consultants Ltd* [2008] EWHC 1135 (Comm), [2008] All ER (D) 10; *Aerostar Maintenance v International Ltd v Wilson* [2010] EWHC 2032 (Ch); *Starglade v Nash* [2010] EWCA Civ 1314 and others referred to below.

trust property, and anyone innocently or knowingly holding the traceable proceeds of trust property after the breach of trust. Liability for dishonest assistance is a secondary form of liability in that the dishonest assistant will be sued either once the trustee's liability for breach of trust has been established or if the trustee cannot be held liable for breach of trust for some reason. The liability is secondary then to the primary liability of the trustee. It should be recalled that a trustee need not be dishonest to be liable for breach of trust: rather, it is sufficient that there was a breach of trust and that it caused loss to the beneficiaries.[61]

The basis of liability for dishonest assistance in the old case of *Barnes v Addy* was that the defendant participated in or carried out a 'dishonest and fraudulent design'. Today it is sufficient that the assistant was dishonest even if the trustee was entirely unaware of the breach of trust (or if the trustee was a company). In *Dubai Aluminium v Salaam*[62] Lord Nicholls explained this form of liability as being a form of 'equitable wrong'.[63] Nevertheless, what is clear from those 19th-century judgments is the fact that all of the judges use the formula of constructive trust to impose liability *as though the defendant were an express trustee* but not on the basis that property is actually held on trust by the dishonest assistant. That means that the courts are construing someone who is a stranger to the trust to be liable to account to the beneficiaries *as though* she were an express trustee: anyone who is construed to be a trustee is a constructive trustee. This might just be a 'formula for equitable relief', as Ungoed-Thomas J has suggested,[64] but the reason for imposing that equitable relief at all is that the beneficiaries are entitled to expect that their trustees will be able to fulfil their fiduciary duties properly without interference from third parties:[65] this is so whether those third parties procure a breach of trust from gullible trustees, conspire with those trustees to commit a breach of trust, or otherwise assist in the breach of the trustees' obligations. The nature of the modern test emerges in the next section from the decision of the Privy Council in *Royal Brunei Airlines v Tan*, considered next.[66]

20.2.3 The nature of dishonest assistance

The requirement that there has been a breach of trust

The liability of the dishonest assistant is based on fault: the defendant is held liable both for the act of assisting in the breach of trust and also for her fault in doing so dishonestly. The loss for which the stranger must account to the beneficiaries is the loss which stems from

---

61 *Twinsectra v Yardley* [2002] 2 AC 164, 194, *per* Lord Millett.
62 [2002] 3 WLR 1913, [2003] 1 All ER 97.
63 At para [9]. In *Dubai Aluminium v Salaam* Lord Millett focused on Lord Selborne's suggestion that liability may be predicated on the defendant making herself in effect an express trustee *de son tort* by interfering with the running of the trust to such an extent that she is construed by the court to have become a trustee, with the result that she may be held liable for any breach of trust ([2002] 3 WLR 1913, [2003] 1 All ER 97, para 140 *et seq*). Lord Millett, however, is alone in taking this approach.
64 *Selangor v Cradock (No 3)* [1968] 1 WLR 1555, 1579. What Ungoed-Thomas J meant was that the doctrine is really just a convenient mechanism for holding the dishonest assistant liable for the loss suffered by the beneficiaries. I prefer the idea, set out in the text, that it is really a form of equitable wrong which extends the notion of trusteeship to anyone who interferes with the trust sufficiently so as to contribute to the causation of a breach of trust.
65 *Royal Brunei Airlines v Tan* [1995] 3 All ER 97, 103, *per* Lord Nicholls.
66 [1995] 2 AC 378.

her assistance in the breach of trust.[67] Without a breach of trust, there would be no loss for which to account.[68] It is not required that the defendant knows the specifics of the breach of trust; rather, as will emerge, it will be sufficient that the defendant was dishonest and that there was a breach of trust or some other fiduciary duty.[69] It has been held that there is a requirement that the assistance must have had some link to the loss suffered by the claimant. So, in *Brown v Bennett*[70] it was held that: 'if there is no causative effect and therefore no assistance given by the [defendant], on whom it is sought to establish the liability as a constructive trustee, for my part I cannot see that the requirements of conscience require any remedy at all.'[71] Thus the defendant must have genuinely assisted the breach of trust in some way.

Time and nature of the assistance and its relation to the breach of trust

Whereas the trustees will be liable for any loss caused by their breach of trust (referred to as the 'primary liability'), someone who assists in a breach of trust dishonestly will also be liable for that loss (referred to as a 'secondary liability'). As considered below, the trustee need not be dishonest – thus the trustee may have been duped by the dishonest assistant into committing the breach of trust.[72] The dishonest assistant may be a shadowy Moriarty figure[73] who does not come into contact with the trust property but who is in some way, as considered below, responsible for the breach of trust. Alternatively, the assistant may be a conspirator with the trustee who commits the breach of trust. Furthermore, the assistance can take place after the breach of trust; it need not be contemporaneous with it. As Lord Millett held in *Twinsectra v Yardley*:

> The accessory's liability for having assisted in a breach of trust is quite different [from liability for knowing receipt, considered below]. It is fault-based, not receipt-based. The defendant is not charged with having received trust moneys for his own benefit, but with having acted as an accessory to a breach of trust. The action is not restitutionary; the

---

67 *Derksen v Pillar* [2002] All ER (D) 261, [32].
68 So, in *Cattley v Pollard* [2006] EWHC 3130 (Ch) it was held that there could not be a claim for dishonest assistance brought in circumstances in which there had been no pre-existing trust or trusteeship (with, however, unfortunate references to 'knowing assistance'). However, where a solicitor was entrusted with trust moneys by trustees, he acted as their 'fiduciary agent' in taking those moneys and therefore was taken to be 'trustee of them' (*Soar v Ashwell* [1893] 2 QB 390, 394, *per* Lord Esher MR); and so (by extension) misappropriation of those moneys could give rise to actions for breach of trust or dishonest assistance. There must be a breach of trust or a breach of some other fiduciary duty: *Dyson Technology Ltd v Curtis* [2010] EWHC 3289 (Ch).
69 *Agip (Africa) Ltd v Jackson* [1990] Ch 265; *Barlow Clowes v Eurotrust* [2006] 1 WLR 1476; *Abou-Rahmah v Abacha* [2006] EWCA Civ 1492, *per* Rix LJ; *Al Khudairi v Abbey Brokers Ltd* [2010] EWHC 1486 (Ch), [2010] PNLR 32; *Dyson Technology Ltd v Curtis* [2010] EWHC 3289 (Ch).
70 [1999] 1 BCLC 659.
71 Approved in *Yugraneft v Abramovich* [2008] EWHC 2613 (Comm), [2008] All ER (Comm) 299, para [390], *per* Clarke J.
72 *Royal Brunei Airlines v Tan* [1995] 2 AC 378.
73 Moriarty was Sherlock Holmes's nemesis: a man who controlled the London underworld but whose guilt could never be proven.

claimant seeks compensation for wrongdoing.[74] The cause of action is concerned with attributing liability for misdirected funds. Liability is not restricted to the person whose breach of trust or fiduciary duty caused their original diversion. His liability is strict. Nor is it limited to those who assist him in the original breach. It extends to everyone who consciously assists in the continuing diversion of the money. Most of the cases have been concerned, not with assisting in the original breach, but in covering it up afterwards by helping to launder the money.[75]

Thus it may be the case that the assistance takes place at some later date and yet still imposes liability.[76] The most difficult problem, however, as considered in the next section, is in establishing whether or not a person has been dishonest.

The basis of the liability on proof of the stranger's dishonesty

The leading case on, and the clearest illustration of, the test for dishonest assistance is the decision of the Privy Council in *Royal Brunei Airlines v Tan*.[77] In that case, the appellant airline contracted an agency agreement with a travel agency, BLT. BLT was a company. Under that agreement, BLT was to sell tickets for the appellant. BLT held money received for the sale of these tickets on express trust for the appellant in a current account. BLT was therefore the trustee. BLT was contractually required to account to the appellant for these moneys within 30 days. The respondent, Mr Tan, was the managing director and principal shareholder of BLT. From time to time, amounts were paid out of the current account into deposit accounts controlled by Mr Tan. The current account was used to defray some of BLT's expenses, such as salaries, and to reduce its overdraft. This was all in breach of trust. In time, BLT went into insolvency. Therefore, the appellant sought to proceed against Mr Tan personally for 'knowingly assisting'[78] in a breach of trust. The issue between the parties was whether 'the breach of trust which is a pre-requisite to accessory liability must itself be a dishonest and fraudulent breach of trust by the trustee'. On behalf of Mr Tan it was argued

---

74 A restitutionary action would seek recovery of property or the subtraction of an unjust enrichment which the defendant had received – a restitutionary action, properly so called, is not concerned to compensate the defendant but rather only to 'subtract' the enrichment which was received unjustly. The enrichment need not be equal to the size of the claimant's loss.

75 [2002] 2 AC 164, 194.

76 In *Al Khudairi v Abbey Brokers Ltd* [2010] EWHC 1486 (Ch), [2010] PNLR 32 there were two defendants of significance. The first defendant was guilty of procuring a breach of trust and paying moneys away through bank accounts operated by the second defendant. The second defendant's position was more difficult because the second defendant was not directly involved in the commission of the breach of trust but he did make available a bank account through which those moneys were paid and therefore he was held to have assisted the breach of trust. It was held that he had had sufficient knowledge of the circumstances to mean that an honest person in his circumstances would have considered his assistance given to the first defendant to have been dishonest. Reliance was placed on *dicta* of Arden LJ in *Abou-Rahmah v Abacha* to the effect that '[i]t is sufficient if the defendant knows of the elements of the transaction which make it dishonest according to normally accepted standards of behaviour', *Abou-Rahmah v Abacha* [2006] EWCA Civ 1492, at [59].

77 [1995] 2 AC 378.

78 Before the decision in *Royal Brunei Airlines v Tan*, this form of liability was referred to as 'knowing assistance' because the test at that time was a test of knowledge, not dishonesty.

that the trustee, BLT, had not been dishonest and therefore there had not been a dishonest design on the part of the company, as required by *Barnes v Addy*.[79]

The Privy Council held that Mr Tan was personally liable to account for assisting in the breach of trust and that it was unnecessary for the trustee itself to have been dishonest.[80] Rather, it is sufficient that some accessory acted dishonestly for that accessory to be fixed with liability for dishonest assistance. The express trustee's state of mind is unimportant. The scenario posited here is that the express trustee may be honest, but the stranger who is made constructive trustee is dishonest. Where the third party is acting dishonestly, that third party will be liable to account. It is not enough to impose liability on an assistant that the fiduciary was dishonest but that the assistant was not dishonest: the assistant's liability rests on the dishonesty of the assistant.[81]

The decision of the Privy Council was set out in the judgment of Lord Nicholls. That judgment created a test of 'dishonesty' to replace the old test of 'knowledge'. Importantly, Lord Nicholls held that the question of whether or not the defendant was dishonest was one to be assessed by reference to what an honest, reasonable person would have done in the circumstances. The appropriateness of this purely objective test for dishonesty has been an issue in subsequent decisions, and in particular some *dicta* which refer to the court considering what the individual defendant knew in the circumstances. This section will be structured in the following way: first, to analyse the objective test as set out in *Royal Brunei Airlines v Tan*; secondly, to consider the mooted requirement of subjectivity which has been introduced to it by subsequent decisions; and, thirdly, to consider how the law appears to stand now.[82]

20.2.4 The objective test for 'dishonesty'

A note before we begin

It is remarkable what can happen to a judgment after it has been delivered and set free into the world: it can develop a life of its own in the way it is adopted and adapted by subsequent judgments. So it is with the judgment of Lord Nicholls in *Royal Brunei Airlines v Tan*, which is discussed in detail in this section. The courts have focused their discussion of that case onto two passages within a judgment which had as its dual intention, first, to change the test from 'knowledge' to 'dishonesty' and, second, to make that test for dishonesty an objective test. Nevertheless, the courts have tended to rely on two short passages within that judgment which can be interpreted so as to introduce subjectivity into the test and as a result have begun to convert that test effectively back into a test which is in large part concerned with

---

79 This, it is suggested, is dubious. Ordinarily, the knowledge of the controlling mind of a company – here Mr Tan – would be attributed to the company itself: so, the company would be deemed to know everything that Tan knew: *Meridian Global Funds Management Asia Ltd v Securities Commission* [1995] 3 All ER 918, [1995] 2 BCLC 116; *Lebon v Aqua Salt Co Ltd* [2009] UKPC 2, [2009] 1 BCLC 549.

80 Applied in *Statek Corp v Alford* [2008] EWHC 32, Evans-Lombe J.

81 Remarkably an argument to the contrary was attempted before the court in *Wrexham AFC v Crucialmove Ltd* [2006] EWCA Civ 237, before it was batted away by Sir Peter Gibson and the point made in the text was re-affirmed, at para [37].

82 *Twinsectra v Yardley* [2002] 2 All ER 377.

knowledge. This section considers the judgment in *Royal Brunei Airlines v Tan* before later sections consider how that principle has developed in later cases.

The objective test in Royal Brunei Airlines v Tan

In describing the nature of the test for dishonesty in this context in *Royal Brunei Airlines v Tan*, Lord Nicholls held that:

> acting dishonestly, or with a lack of probity, which is synonymous, means simply not acting as an honest person would in the circumstance. This is an objective standard.[83]

Therefore, the question which this test requires the court to ask is not what the defendant thought personally, but rather what an honest person would have done if they had been placed in the same circumstances as the defendant. If the defendant did not act in the way that an honest person would have acted in those circumstances, then the defendant is deemed to have been dishonest. The court will therefore be holding the defendant up to an objective idea of what constitutes honest behaviour. The interesting notion raised by this passage is that dishonesty can be either an *active* state of mind, or alternatively a *passive* 'lack of probity'. The vernacular, ordinary meaning of 'dishonesty' would tend to involve some *active deceit* or lying.[84] However, dishonesty is considered more broadly by the Privy Council to involve failing to do what an honest person would do, such that *passive* dishonesty (such as failing to make inquiries, or to ensure that a proposed investment risk is not too great) is included within the test. This *Tan* test is therefore based on an objective understanding of 'dishonesty'; whereas the claim for knowing receipt, in the judgment of Megarry VC in *Re Montagu*,[85] sets out a subjective test of what the defendant can be taken to have known.[86]

It was found as a fact by the Brunei Court of Appeal that BLT, the travel agency company run by Mr Tan, had not acted dishonestly.[87] The Privy Council took this to mean that it was not established that Mr Tan, as BLT's directing mind, had intended to defraud the airline. The money was held to be lost 'in the ordinary course of a poorly run business with heavy overhead expenses'. Lord Nicholls accepted that Tan 'hoped, maybe expected, to be able to pay the airline':[88] therefore, he was not suggesting that Tan was necessarily acting fraudulently. The test for dishonesty will therefore bite where a business is run incompetently. It was enough that Tan had not done what an honest person would have done.

The basis of Lord Nicholls's decision was that 'Mr Tan had no right to employ the [trust] money in the business at all. That was the breach of trust. The company's inability to pay the airline was the consequence of that breach of trust.'[89] Tan had actual knowledge of this breach of trust on these facts. So, Lord Nicholls found that Tan was not acting as an honest

---

83 *Royal Brunei Airlines v Tan* [1995] 2 AC 378, 386.
84 *R v Ghosh* [1982] 2 All ER 689, [1982] QB 1053; *R v Hicks* [2000] 4 All ER 833.
85 [1987] CL 264.
86 As to the nature of liability for breach of trust, see further at para 18.3.1 above.
87 Although, it is suggested that, on the facts of *Tan*, Mr Tan was the controlling mind in any event.
88 *Royal Brunei Airlines v Tan* [1995] 2 AC 378, 390.
89 *Ibid.*

person would have acted. He was using money in a way that was not permitted. Therefore, he was held to have been dishonest. In bringing a claim, the allegation of dishonesty must be pleaded plainly when bringing proceedings.[90]

The two possible readings of the test in Royal Brunei Airlines v Tan

The case law which has followed *Royal Brunei Airlines v Tan* is among the most interesting in modern equity. It cuts to the very heart of the purpose of equity in reaching judgment in relation to individual defendants. Interestingly, as is considered below, Lord Nicholls was very clear that the new test of dishonesty should not be allowed to collapse into a general test of unconscionability (which, ironically, is exactly what has happened to the doctrine of knowing receipt, which is considered in the second half of this chapter). Instead, Lord Nicholls's judgment requires close analysis. What is clear is that his lordship intended the test for dishonesty to be an objective test, but importantly there are two points in his otherwise very clear and concise judgment in which his lordship muddied the purity of the objective test which he otherwise appeared to be advocating. The most quoted passage from the judgment of Lord Nicholls in later cases is the following:

> Before considering this issue further it will be helpful to define the terms being used by looking more closely at what dishonesty means in this context. Whatever may be the position in some criminal or other contexts (see, for instance, *Reg v Ghosh*[91]), in the context of the accessory liability principle acting dishonestly, or with a lack of probity, which is synonymous, means simply not acting as an honest person would in the circumstances. This is an objective standard. At first sight this may seem surprising. Honesty has a connotation of subjectivity, as distinct from the objectivity of negligence. Honesty, indeed, does have a strong subjective element in that it is a description of a type of conduct assessed in the light of what a person actually knew at the time, as distinct from what a reasonable person would have known or appreciated. Further, honesty and its counterpart dishonesty are mostly concerned with advertent conduct, not inadvertent conduct. Carelessness is not dishonesty. Thus for the most part dishonesty is to be equated with conscious impropriety. However, these subjective characteristics of honesty do not mean that individuals are free to set their own standards of honesty in particular circumstances. The standard of what constitutes honest conduct is not subjective. Honesty is not an optional scale, with higher or lower values according to the moral standards of each individual. If a person knowingly appropriates another's property, he will not escape a finding of dishonesty simply because he sees nothing wrong in such behaviour.

> In most situations there is little difficulty in identifying how an honest person would behave. Honest people do not intentionally deceive others to their detriment. Honest people do not knowingly take others' property. Unless there is a very good and compelling reason, an honest person does not participate in a transaction if he knows it involves

90 *Taylor v Midland Bank Trust Co* [2002] WTLR 95.
91 [1982] QB 1053.

a misapplication of trust assets to the detriment of the beneficiaries. Nor does an honest person in such a case deliberately close his eyes and ears, or deliberately not ask questions, lest he learn something he would rather not know, and then proceed regardless. However, in the situations now under consideration the position is not always so straightforward. This can best be illustrated by considering one particular area: the taking of risks.[92]

Then in that discussion of risk which follows soon after this first passage, Lord Nicholls held that:

when called upon to decide whether a person was acting honestly, a court will look at all the circumstances known to the third party at the time. The court will also have regard to personal attributes of the third party such as his experience and intelligence, and the reason why he acted as he did.[93]

In essence there are two contradictory trends in these passages: on the one hand, the court is simply to look at what an objective, honest person would have done in the circumstances of the case and ask whether or not the defendant did that, but without any reference to the defendant's own belief system; on the other hand, the court is entitled to look at the defendant's personal attributes (thus including subjective factors relating to the defendant) while assessing what an honest person would have done in this circumstance. The latter approach is not a purely objective test, whereas the former test is. Therefore, one's reading of this passage depends entirely upon whether one reads it as a whole and notices the repeated emphasis throughout the judgment (and not just in these passages) that the test is an objective test to be measured by an objective standard, or whether one teases out the two references (one in the long passage and one in the shorter passage) to subjective factors and uses them to justify returning to a test which involves some subjectivity and an assessment of the defendant's knowledge alongside an assessment of what an honest person would have done. Let us consider that in a little more detail.

In the first passage, Lord Nicholls could be understood as doing the following: acknowledging that ordinarily people would expect that the concept of dishonesty would involve subjective factors but making it very plain that in his version of the concept of dishonesty there should be no subjective factors at all. Let us call this the 'pure objective' reading. This pure objective approach would rely on the words 'acting dishonestly, or with a lack of probity, which is synonymous, means simply not acting as an honest person would in the circumstances' and 'these subjective characteristics of honesty do not mean that individuals are free to set their own standards of honesty in particular circumstances. The standard of what constitutes honest conduct is not subjective'. In particular this reading of the test for dishonesty could be encapsulated in a finding that the defendant was 'not acting as an honest person would in the circumstances', without worrying about what the defendant

92 [1995] 2 AC 375, 389.
93 *Ibid*, 391B.

personally thought.[94] An objective test requires that the judge decides what an honest person would have done in the circumstances; or perhaps if there is a formal regulatory code in existence the judge should ask whether the defendant complied with it because such a regulatory code could be taken as a statement of what a regulated person should have done in the circumstances.[95]

There is, however, another possible reading of that first passage whereby Lord Nicholls could be understood as doing the following: identifying that honesty is always a subjective concept at root but that the defendant may not excuse behaviour which honest people would consider to be dishonest by reference to her own personal beliefs. Let us call this the 'primarily subjective' reading. It is only 'primarily subjective' in that Lord Nicholls clearly acknowledges that objective standards can override subjective beliefs. This reading is bolstered by the words 'for the most part dishonesty is to be equated with conscious impropriety' (that is, intentional dishonesty) and in particular by the idea in the second passage that 'the court will also have regard to personal attributes of the third party such as his experience and intelligence, and the reason why he acted as he did'. The idea in the second passage has found particular favour with the High Court[96] and with the Court of Appeal[97] in recent cases.

I must admit to some personal difficulty with this primarily subjective reading of the first passage.[98] If Lord Nicholls had intended us to take the view from the first passage that his lordship intended dishonesty to have a subjective connotation in the application of the test to factual circumstances, then why would he have held that 'this is an objective standard' before discussing subjectivity, and why would he have concluded those six sentences ruminating on the fact that this objective approach may seem 'surprising' by saying 'however' (indicating a switch in the argument away from support for subjectivity), individuals may not set their own standards, the standard of honest conduct is not subjective, and honesty is not an optional scale. In the first passage, I would suggest, Lord Nicholls was acknowledging that instinctively one might think of dishonesty as involving subjectivity but that that was not his lordship's intention in this instance. Nevertheless, this passage has been taken, for example by Arden LJ,[99] to suggest a slightly subjective slant to the otherwise objective test.

---

94 The proof of how strictly objectivity can be interpreted is perhaps demonstrated by *Markel International Insurance Company Ltd v Higgins* [2009] EWCA Civ 790 where the suggestion that the defendant was suffering from the early stage of Alzheimer's disease was insufficient to avoid a finding of dishonest assistance as having been overwhelming on the facts: subjectively it might clearly have been possible to have failed to consider something dishonest, whereas here dishonesty could only be based on the objectivity of the dishonesty being proven.

95 See Alastair Hudson, *The Law of Finance*, Sweet & Maxwell, 2009, Ch 3.

96 Those cases include *AG Zambia v Meer Care & Desai & Others* [2007] EWHC 952 (Ch), on appeal [2008] EWCA Civ 1007; *Fiona Trust & Holding Corporation v Privalov* [2010] EWHC 3199 (Comm), at [1437], *per* Andrew Smith J.

97 *Starglade v Nash* [2010] EWCA Civ 1314.

98 I prefer to acknowledge my own prejudices and views explicitly in the text rather than to present a partial account of the cases while keeping my views secret. Let us be transparent and expose our opinions to the disinfectant properties of daylight. I hope too that presenting these arguments on the basis of disagreement between human beings, rather than as entirely abstract ideas, will make them easier to understand for student readers in particular.

99 *Abou-Rahmah v Abacha* [2006] EWCA Civ 1492, considered in detail below.

The second passage is, of course, harder to explain away. Two points do present themselves. First, it is not part of the *ratio decidendi* in that Lord Nicholls was dealing here with risk-taking in investment transactions and therefore he was no longer considering the test for dishonesty which should be applied specifically to Mr Tan. Second, it is one sentence out of a twelve page judgment which otherwise sticks doggedly to the line that honesty should be objective. Other than that, of course, it is impossible to correlate the idea that the court should consider the personal attributes, experience and intelligence of the defendant specifically while still pursuing an exclusively objective test. A pure objective reading of the first passage requires that the court sit in judgment – in a literal and a metaphorical sense of that term – not by questioning the personal motivations or beliefs of the defendant, but rather in an abstract way by deciding what an honest person would have done in those circumstances and then simply asking whether or not on the facts of the case the defendant had behaved in that way. Clearly, as soon as a judge is entitled to ask what the defendant's 'personal attributes' were, whether she was intelligent enough to have understood the situation or whether her experience would have led her to a particular course of action, then the objective idea of dishonesty is clearly compromised. It is suggested that by including a reference to the subjective characteristics of the defendant in the test that this shatters the pure objectivity of that test. The idea of dishonesty and honesty being an objective standard cannot co-exist with an examination of the defendant's personal characteristics. In fact, its very inconsistency with the idea of an objectively honest person as being the test is the third argument for refusing to accord this second passage any particular weight. Lord Nicholls cannot have intended the test to be both an objective test and also one which permitted this level of subjectivity.

As will emerge from the analysis of the cases to follow – especially *Twinsectra v Yardley* and *Barlow Clowes v Eurotrust* – this debate is continued by the judges themselves. However, before coming to those cases, we will briefly consider the question of what constitutes an 'honest person' in this test.

Who is the 'honest person'?

Thus far I have advanced a pure objective reading of *Tan*, while acknowledging that other people prefer a primarily subjective reading. That does not mean that I consider the pure objective reading to be without difficulties. The principal difficulty is in identifying what is meant by an honest person. I have certainly never met one. After all, what does it mean to be an honest person? What attributes does an honest person have? There are many activities which cannot sensibly be said to be capable of being conducted 'honestly': for example, how does a person eat a sandwich 'honestly', or open curtains 'honestly'? Clearly, there are some activities in which the concept of dishonesty has no meaningful part to play. Therefore, it is suggested, when deciding what constitutes an honest person the court must necessarily focus on those actions or omissions which call a standard of honesty or dishonesty into play. This means considering the circumstances of the case to identify what would constitute honesty in that particular context. For example, a sandwich could be eaten dishonestly if it had been stolen from a sandwich shop and if the person eating it then pretended to have paid for it. However, it is not the eating itself which is done dishonestly – presumably the mastication and digestion would have taken place in a usual, if possibly furtive, manner – but rather it is the context of appropriating the sandwich and then lying about having paid for it which makes it dishonest. Therefore, the court would need to identify which circumstances throw a light on whether or not a hypothetical, honest person would have acted in one way or another.

It is at that point that the question arises whether or not the defendant's own characteristics are to be used to identify the context in which honesty is measured. It is suggested that all an objective test for dishonesty requires is that the court identify the *facts* which were known to the defendant – so that the hypothetical, honest person can be taken to know those facts – but not the defendant's *characteristics* – such as a tendency to lie, or to be garrulous, or to be easily fooled. The second passage from Lord Nicholls, quoted above, clearly admits 'personal attributes' but the first passage clearly excludes personal moral codes and beliefs which would excuse an action which would otherwise be considered to be dishonest. So, there are very few personal attributes which can be admitted into the analysis. In essence, what the court must do is to postulate a hypothetical person who had access to the same facts as the defendant who has to act honestly in the situation in which the defendant found herself. Ultimately, it is likely that this will mean that the judge will probably be asking what they think that they ought to have done if they had found themselves in that situation. What prevents this from being an entirely subjective measurement on the part of the judge as to what she would have done herself, however, is the requirement that the judge identify an objectively honest person's conduct and be able to justify the finding that this is behaviour which would have been expected of anyone. These theoretical questions will emerge again in the later cases.

20.2.5 Introducing a modicum of subjectivity to the test of 'dishonesty'

Ordinarily one cannot rely on one's own, subjective opinion of what is honest: the 'Robin Hood defence'

It was clear in Lord Nicholls's leading opinion in the Privy Council in *Royal Brunei Airlines v Tan* that his Lordship did not intend the test of dishonesty to be subjective. This means that his Lordship did not want the question 'has this person acted dishonestly?' to be answered by reference to whether or not the defendant herself considered her actions to have been dishonest, or whether or not she knew that other people would have considered them to be dishonest. This view emerges from the following passage, already quoted above:

> . . . subjective characteristics of dishonesty do not mean that individuals are free to set their own standards of honesty in particular circumstances. The standard of what constitutes honest conduct is not subjective. Honesty is not an optional scale, with higher or lower values according to the moral standards of each individual. If a person knowingly appropriates another's property, he will not escape a finding of dishonesty simply because he sees nothing wrong in such behaviour.[100]

---

100 [1995] 2 AC 375, [1995] 3 All ER 97, 106. Cf *Walker v Stones* [2001] QB 902. The last sentence contains an unfortunate reference to 'appropriation', whereas it is not necessary for the operation of the assistance liability that the defendant receive the property into his possession: the term 'appropriation' here should be read as referring to participation in the act of appropriation of property from the trust fund without passing possession or control of it to the defendant.

This approach to the notion of dishonesty is very different from that in the criminal law, whereby conviction for a crime of dishonesty will require that the defendant personally knew that her actions were dishonest, which is sometimes referred to as the 'Robin Hood' defence.[101] In the context of the criminal law, we might consider it unsurprising if the courts require that a person not be convicted of a crime without knowing that they had committed some act which they knew to involve a criminal *mens rea* because ignorance of the loss is no defence to conviction of a crime against the state, whereas some wrong committed against another private person is typically treated by English law as a matter of a different order.[102]

The distinction between subjective and objective bases of law in the jurisprudence of equity

So, we have established that ordinarily equity will not permit a defendant to avoid liability to account to the beneficiaries on the basis that she personally did not consider her actions to have been dishonest, even though criminal law frequently uses subjective tests. Given the general principle that 'ignorance of the law is no defence', this might lead us to suppose that the defendant ought not to be permitted to rely on a defence that she did not know her actions would be considered to be dishonest by other people. Indeed, this takes us to the very heart of debates about the purpose of law in society. If, as positivists claim, the law operates as a series of commands given by a sovereign (the law) to ordinary people, there is no reason to deny the power of the law to ascertain objective notions of what constitutes honest or dishonest behaviour. Citizens can consequently expect to be subject to those value judgments through the courts. Alternatively, even if law is to be based on natural law principles (founded on some moral grundnorm)[103] there is no reason to suppose that the law ought to be shy when deciding whether or not a person has acted dishonestly. If the law gives effect to an objective morality, it could be said that there is no objection to the courts establishing objectively the nature of that morality and therefore the nature of dishonest conduct. What the law appears to have done instead in the House of Lords in *Twinsectra v Yardley*, after *Royal Brunei Airlines v Tan*, is to take an alternative approach which suggests that in deciding what constitutes an objective notion of dishonest conduct one must nevertheless consider whether or not the defendant herself knew that her conduct would be considered to be dishonest by other people.

What none of the courts since *Twinsectra v Yardley* has accepted is that the defendant can rely on a defence that her own moral code did not consider her wrongdoing to have been dishonest. The idea that the defendant might seek to defend herself on the basis that subjectively she considered her actions to be honest is frequently referred to as the 'Robin Hood defence' on the basis that the defendant might suggest that she considered robbing from the rich to be acceptable if it was done to give money to the poor, as Robin Hood did in the legend.[104] It has been held that:

---

101 *R v Ghosh* [1982] QB 1053.
102 In *AAH Pharmaceuticals v Birdi* [2011] EWHC 1625 (Ch), at [34], Coulson J took the view that the *Ghosh* test for dishonesty in theft was the same as the test in *Tan* which has 'a connotation of subjectivity'. This, it is suggested, is simply wrong.
103 A 'grundnorm' is, to borrow from the jurisprudential theorist Kelsen, a notion that there is some central point from which the law and morality is said to flow and from which it draws its legitimacy.
104 *Walker v Stones* [2000] 4 All ER 412.

A person may in some cases act dishonestly, according to the ordinary use of language, even though he genuinely believes that his action is morally justified. The penniless thief, for example, who picks the pocket of the multi-millionaire is dishonest even though he genuinely considers the theft is morally justified as a fair redistribution of wealth and that he is not therefore being dishonest.[105]

Thus, dishonesty is said to be based on objective principles because to measure dishonesty on a subjective basis would permit an unacceptable level of moral relativism whereby each defendant would seek to excuse behaviour which is objectively dishonest. The suggestion that subjectivity should be required in assessing dishonesty arises in the judgments considered in the next section.

The suggestion that the defendant must be both objectively and subjectively dishonest

A combined subjective and objective approach emerged from the decision of the House of Lords in *Twinsectra Ltd v Yardley*.[106] In that case, Yardley sought to borrow money from Twinsectra to acquire property. It was a term of the loan agreement that the money was to be used solely for that purpose. It was a further part of the agreement that the money would be paid to Sims, a solicitor acting on behalf of Yardley, such that Sims would hold the loan money on trust with a power to spend it only for the acquisition of the property. Furthermore, Sims gave a solicitor's undertaking as to the proper repayment of the loan. The terms of the trust here were slightly unusual in that they took the form of a solicitor's undertaking that the money would be used only for the prescribed purpose, although Yardley was entitled to use the loan moneys as collateral for other transactions. However, Sims was replaced as Yardley's solicitor in this transaction by Leach. Yardley assured Sims that the money could be passed to Leach on the basis that Leach would now act as solicitor under the agreement. The money was misapplied by Yardley and the loan was not repaid. Twinsectra brought proceedings, *inter alia*, against Leach, contending that Leach had dishonestly assisted in a breach of Sims's trust obligations. Leach's defence was that he considered himself to have been entitled to use the money for whatever purposes Yardley directed him to use it, and in consequence that he did not consider that he had done anything dishonest. The majority of the House of Lords (with Lord Millett dissenting) appeared to agree with the speech of Lord Hutton which held that liability for dishonest assistance required *both* that the actions would have been considered dishonest by honest and reasonable people and *also* that the defendant himself realised that the actions would have been considered dishonest by honest and reasonable people. After reviewing the authorities, Lord Hutton gave the following exposition of the test:

> There is, in my opinion, a further consideration [beyond deciding whether the test is one of knowledge or dishonesty as set out by Lord Nicholls] which supports the view that for liability as an accessory to arise the defendant must himself appreciate that what he was doing was dishonest by the standards of honest and reasonable men. A finding by the judge that a defendant has been dishonest is a grave finding, and it is particularly

---

105 *Ibid*, 444, *per* Sir Christopher Slade.
106 [2002] 2 All ER 377.

grave against a professional man, such as a solicitor. Notwithstanding that the issue arises in equity law [*sic*] and not in a criminal context, I think that it would be less than just for the law to permit a finding that a defendant had been 'dishonest' in assisting in a breach of trust where he knew of the facts which created the trust and its breach but had not been aware that what he was doing would be regarded by honest men as being dishonest.[107]

This version of the test, therefore, clearly adds an important second, subjective element to the test of dishonesty. Significantly, though, the second limb of the test is whether or not the defendant realised that *other people* would have considered her actions to have been dishonest and not simply that *the defendant herself* thought that the action was dishonest.

An example might help to illustrate the point. Suppose that I have been renting a flat from someone while they were abroad on business. Suppose further that I had a lot of difficulties with the flat and so consider that the rent I had to pay was far too high for the trouble I suffered when occupying it. On the day of my departure I decide that it would be nice to have some memento of my time in that flat, and I see an old edition of a novel I have always wanted to read. I decide that, in the light of the trouble I have been caused and the huge rent I have paid for the flat, I deserve to take that novel and keep it for myself, even though I know it belongs to my landlord. At that moment I may be able to justify my conduct to myself and so convince myself that it is not dishonest in the context for me to take that book. However, it must be the case that I know, somewhere at the back of my mind, that *other people* would think 'the book does not belong to you and therefore it is dishonest for you to take it'. This is the distinction here between realising that other people consider an act to be dishonest and considering it to be dishonest oneself. What this strange 'combination test' in *Twinsectra v Yardley* achieves is the addition of a modicum of subjectivity to the law, but it does not turn its back entirely on objective notions of what honest and reasonable people would think of one's actions.[108] It was, in truth, a hybrid test.

The issue is then as to the efficacy of the test set out by Lord Nicholls in *Royal Brunei Airlines v Tan*. Lord Hutton explained the issue in the following way:

> It would be open to your Lordships to depart from the principle stated by Lord Nicholls [in *Royal Brunei Airlines v Tan*] that dishonesty is a necessary ingredient of accessory liability and to hold that knowledge is a sufficient ingredient. But the statement of that principle by Lord Nicholls has been widely regarded as clarifying this area of the law and, as he observed, the tide of authority in England has flowed strongly in favour of the test of dishonesty. Therefore, I consider that the courts should continue to apply that test and that your Lordships should state that dishonesty requires knowledge by the defendant that what he was doing would be regarded as dishonest by honest people, although he should not escape a finding of dishonesty because he sets his own standards of honesty and does not regard as dishonest what he knows would offend the normally accepted standards of honest conduct.[109]

---

107 *Ibid*, 387.
108 More generally, this would be an ineffective argument on my part on the basis of the Robin Hood defence criticised in *Walker v Stones* [2000] 4 All ER 412.
109 [2002] 2 All ER 377.

So, Lord Nicholls's original test in *Royal Brunei Airlines v Tan* is to continue in existence, albeit in a hybrid form. This combination of an alteration of that *Tan* test and yet a purported approval of it by the House of Lords is slightly awkward in the abstract. The utility of the dishonesty test and its growing popularity are cited as the reasons for its retention. Furthermore, it is unfortunate that the gloss which Lord Hutton put on that test, by way of a subjective element, is expressed as requiring 'knowledge' that what the defendant was doing would be considered dishonest: this is unfortunate because the test of dishonesty was developed precisely to move away from tests of knowledge.[110]

The effect, it is suggested, is to leave the law in a confused state. Neither is it entirely clear with which parts of Lord Hutton's analysis the other members of the judicial committee of the House of Lords were agreeing. Lord Steyn concurred with both Lord Hutton and Lord Hoffmann. Lord Slynn concurred with Lord Hoffmann at the beginning of his short speech, but then expressed concurrence also with Lord Hutton, although it is not entirely clear with which parts of that judgment he proposed to concur. Lord Hoffmann disposed of the matter first by analysing the terms of the undertaking given by Sims. Lord Hoffmann then appeared to express agreement with Lord Hutton that 'a dishonest state of mind' is to be conceived of as 'consciousness that one is transgressing ordinary standards of honest behaviour', but then proceeded in the next paragraph to express agreement with Lord Nicholls in *Tan*, who was against any such subjectivity in relation to one's own moral code, and then to express regret that the trial judge used subjective-sounding expressions such as 'the defendant shut his eyes to the obvious' (considered below).[111] Lord Millett dissented by focusing primarily on the nature of this arrangement as a *Quistclose* trust, and his analysis of the concept of dishonesty was predicated on a close analysis of Lord Nicholls's leading opinion in *Tan*. In Lord Millett's view, Leach knew all of the facts which caused his action to be considered wrongful and therefore could be considered to have acted dishonestly. It is suggested that Lord Millett's analysis is the most cogent on the facts of this case: the solicitor was supposed to a professional, he had possession of all of the facts necessary to show to an ordinarily honest person that his actions were wrong, and therefore he was to be held to have been dishonest.

Another example of this tendency towards subjectivity, it is suggested, arises in *Brinks Ltd v Abu-Saleh (No 3)*[112] where a security guard's wife would have been held liable for assisting her husband's breach of his fiduciary duties to his employer – after her husband had helped armed robbers to steal gold bullion from his employer – when she helped him to transport the cash proceeds of the robbery overseas. The reason she was not held to be

110 This is an interesting combination of the subjective and objective elements bound up in a notion of conscience. Whereas the conscience might be thought of as being a necessarily personal thing and therefore subjective, it would clearly be impossible for the law to concern itself solely with whether or not the defendant considered that she ought or ought not to be liable. The work of phenomenological philosophers and of ethical philosophers like Emmanuel Levinas suggest that notions of good and bad conscience exist outside the individual. Theorists like Norbert Elias point out that all human beings, from their first weaning as infants through their schooling and their adult life, are surrounded and shaped by external inputs to their individual psyches. Consequently, it is suggested that the law need not be quite so shamefaced at the notion of erecting entirely objective notions of conscience in such cases. This question is considered in greater detail in the final chapter of this book in section 32.2. See also Hudson, 2004:2, 23.
111 [2002] 2 All ER 377, 383. This approach was applied without comment by Peter Smith J in *Manolakaki v Constantinides* [2004] EWHC 749 (Ch), [167].
112 [1999] CLC 133.

liable on the facts was that she had not known of the robbery and had instead assumed that her help had been sought on the basis that her husband was involved in some tax evasion scam, as opposed to disposing of the fruits of an armed robbery: her ignorance of the true nature of their dealings meant that she was held not to have been assisting her husband dishonestly. As we have seen, however, the court's reliance on her subjective lack of appreciation of the circumstances does not square with the objectivity required by *Tan*: an objective test would require the court to ask what an honest person would have done in the defendant's circumstances, and not what she herself knew or did not know.

The re-establishment of a purely objective test for dishonesty, and of personal liability to account as being an equitable wrong giving rise to 'constructive trusteeship'

A subsequent decision of the House of Lords in *Dubai Aluminium v Salaam*[113] has re-established the test for dishonesty as being purely objective and has reaffirmed that personal liability to account as a dishonest assistant is an equitable wrong giving rise to 'constructive trusteeship'. Unfortunately, however, this important case is rarely cited in the discussions about dishonest assistance, seemingly because it relates to a case of assistance in a breach of a different kind of fiduciary duty. This case involved a fraudulent scheme whereby Dubai Aluminium Co Ltd paid out US$50 million in a sham consultancy agreement. One of the fraudsters, Salaam, was a client of a firm of solicitors, Amhurst Brown.[114] It was claimed by Dubai Aluminium that Mr Amhurst, a partner of the Amhurst Brown firm of solicitors, had been a dishonest assistant in the fraud, in that Mr Amhurst had advised Salaam throughout his various activities. The House of Lords was able to proceed on the basis that the Amhurst Brown partners were innocent of the fraud and to recognise that no fraud had been proved against Mr Amhurst himself because all of the parties had agreed to settle. The remaining question was as to the liability of the Amhurst Brown partnership under the Civil Liability (Contribution) Act 1978 and, consequently, whether Mr Amhurst's liability was for the equitable wrong of dishonest assistance as opposed to a common law liability under tort, because equitable and common law liabilities received different treatment under the 1978 Act. Lord Nicholls gave a leading speech in *Dubai Aluminium v Salaam*[115] with which Lord Slynn concurred. Lord Millett gave a speech in slightly different terms. Lord Hutton concurred with both Lord Nicholls and Lord Millett. Lord Hobhouse gave a speech, without concurring with any of the others, focusing on the role of the 1978 Act and, *inter alia*, its use in providing 'restitutionary remedies for unjust enrichment at the expense of another'.[116]

Lord Nicholls described liability for dishonest assistance as being the 'equitable wrong of dishonest assistance in a breach of trust or fiduciary duty'.[117] This form of liability was further described by Lord Nicholls as being for a 'wrongful act' whereby if a partnership were held liable for fraudulent misrepresentation then it would be 'remarkable' if the

---

113   [2002] 3 WLR 1913, [2003] 1 All ER 97.
114   In fact, Amhurst were two successive partnerships but they were treated by the House of Lords as being one partnership.
115   [2002] 3 WLR 1913, [2003] 1 All ER 97.
116   *Ibid*, para 76.
117   *Ibid*, para 9.

members of the partnership were not also vicariously liable for an individual partner's 'dishonest participation . . . in conduct directed at the misappropriation of another's property'.[118] Lord Nicholls described the liability as being that of a 'constructive trustee'[119] whose 'misconduct . . . gives rise to a liability in equity to make good resulting loss'.[120] This analysis was predicated both on Lord Nicholls's own decision in *Royal Brunei Airlines v Tan*[121] and on the older judgment in *Mara v Browne*,[122] where a partnership was held liable for a breach of fiduciary duty committed by one of the partners.[123] No mention was made in his Lordship's speech of the approach taken in *Twinsectra v Yardley*, which purported to introduce a subjective element to the objective notion of dishonesty in *Royal Brunei Airlines v Tan*. Instead the test for dishonesty was again centred on an objective conception of dishonesty, as discussed above in relation to *Tan*.

By contrast, in Lord Millett's speech, the particular facts of this case were not disposed of by reference to dishonest assistance principles alone, but rather they were disposed of by reference to old principles imposing vicarious liability on a partnership for the equitable wrongdoing of any one partner[124] as contrasted with vicarious liability in tort.[125] As to the roots of the dishonest assistance claim in cases such as *Mara v Browne*,[126] Lord Millett placed this claim in the context of trusteeship having become 'more professional. Clients no longer look to their trustees to be philosophers, guides and friends . . .', with the effect that we do not need to consider the usage of 'constructive trust' and 'constructive trustee' in *Mara v Browne* as denoting a trust of identifiable property[127] and that we should recognise that 'meanings have changed over time'. Lord Millett suggested that we should consider the form of constructive trusteeship in *Mara v Browne* as equivalent to liability as a trustee *de son tort*.[128] The impact of such a definition of the liability for dishonest assistance would be to predicate it solely on the fault of the defendant for intermeddling with the operation of the trust or rendering herself an 'actual trustee',[129] and not simply by means of assisting in a breach of that trust without seeking to take over its management. What Lord Millett sought to make of this understanding on the facts before him was the proposition that no partnership can accept that any individual partner is entitled to breach her fiduciary duties to a client and therefore the partnership cannot be said to accept any liability for the actions of an individual partner who acts dishonestly. Therefore, Amhurst Brown could not be liable as a trustee *de son tort* in relation to Mr Amhurst's actions because it had never accepted any liability for Mr Amhurst acting outside the scope of his fiduciary duties.

---

118   *Ibid*, para 11.
119   *Ibid*, para 40.
120   *Ibid*.
121   [1995] 2 AC 378.
122   [1896] 1 Ch 199, 208, *per* Lord Herschell.
123   Cf *In Re Bell's Indenture* [1980] 1 WLR 1217, 1230, *per* Vinelott J.
124   *Brydges v Branfill* (1842) 12 Sim 369.
125   *Credit Lyonnais Bank Nederland NV v Export Credits Guarantee Department* [2000] 1 AC 486.
126   [1896] 1 Ch 199.
127   *Paragon Finance plc v DB Thakerar & Co* [1999] 1 All ER 400, 408; *Coulthard v Disco Mix Club Ltd* [2000] 1 WLR 707, 731.
128   [2002] 3 WLR 1913, [2003] 1 All ER 97, paras 135 and 138. Cf *Taylor v Davies* [1920] AC 636; *Clarkson v Davies* [1923] AC 100, 110.
129   *Taylor v Davies* [1920] AC 636, 651, *per* Viscount Cave.

However, it is suggested that Lord Millett's approach overlooks the broader explanation of this liability in *Barnes v Addy*[130] given by Lord Selborne, to the effect that the defendant would be liable not only for rendering himself a trustee *de son tort*, but also by 'actually participating in the fraudulent conduct of the trustee to the injury of the *cestui que trust*'[131] in committing a breach of trust. Therefore, the history of this claim has been predicated on a form of constructive trusteeship which undoubtedly involves assistance in a breach of trust, or where 'they assist with knowledge in a dishonest and fraudulent design on the part of the trustees',[132] and not control of the trust by the defendant. The whole purpose of the dishonest assistance claim is that it is imposed on the defendant due to her wrongdoing and not due to her acceptance of liability as such: in this regard, Lord Millett's comments must be taken to relate solely to the partnership aspects of this case. The correct approach to this remedy is that the wrongdoing dishonest assistant is made 'accountable in equity' for the loss which her dishonesty has caused to the beneficiaries.[133]

The position after Twinsectra v Yardley

According, *inter alia*, to the decision of Lewison J in *Ultraframe (UK) Ltd v Fielding*,[134] the effect of the decision of the House of Lords in *Twinsectra v Yardley* was that the test for dishonesty in this context had changed subtly but significantly to the effect that the defendant must be shown to have understood that she had acted dishonestly and not simply that an honest person would not have acted as she had done. Oddly the courts had tended to overlook the *dicta* in *Dubai Aluminium v Salaam* relating to dishonesty. However, the Privy Council in *Barlow Clowes v Eurotrust*,[135] considered next, has suggested a movement back to a purely objective test. Being a Privy Council decision, however, it is of purely persuasive authority. This decision has been approved by the Court of Appeal in *Abou-Rahmah v Abacha*,[136] although that decision is not without its difficulties as will be considered in the next section but one.

The facts in Barlow Clowes v Eurotrust

The movement back towards a straightforwardly objective test for 'dishonesty' in this context is suggested by the decision of the Privy Council in *Barlow Clowes v Eurotrust*.[137] The facts relate to the collapse of Barlow Clowes International Ltd ('Barlow Clowes'). Barlow Clowes had attracted approximately £140 million, principally from private British investors. The bulk of that money was dissipated by Peter Clowes and his associates both on other business ventures and on 'extravagant living'.[138] Peter Clowes was convicted and

---

130 (1874) 9 Ch App 244.
131 *Ibid*, 251.
132 *Ibid*, 252.
133 *Selangor United Rubber Estates Ltd v Cradock (No 3)* [1968] 1 WLR 1555, 1582, *per* Ungoed-Thomas J.
134 [2005] EWHC 1638 (Ch), [2005] All ER (D) 397, para [1481].
135 [2005] UKPC 37, [2006] 1 WLR 1476, [2006] 1 All ER 333.
136 *Ibid.*
137 *Ibid.*
138 *Barlow Clowes v Eurotrust* [2006] 1 WLR 1476, [2006] 1 All ER 333, [1].

imprisoned for offences relating to the eventual collapse of the Barlow Clowes investment scheme.

This particular case related to funds which were paid through a company called International Trust Corporation (Isle of Man) Ltd ('ITC'). ITC provided financial services and, in time, was to act as a management company for a range of other companies where those other companies were the vehicles through which much of the Barlow Clowes money was dissipated. At first instance, this action related to the liability of ITC and two of its principal directors, Henwood and Sebastian, in dishonestly assisting Peter Clowes and his associate Cramer in misappropriating investors' funds from Barlow Clowes and related companies. Of particular significance were four sums paid away between June and November 1987 of £577,429, £6 million, £205,329, and £1,799,603 respectively, although there were as many as 15 payments considered at first instance. It was found that there was no commercial purpose for these transactions other than to spirit them out of the Barlow Clowes group.

The appeal brought before the Privy Council related to Henwood's claim that he had not acted dishonestly. Henwood appealed against the Acting Deemster's finding[139] at first instance that he had dishonestly assisted Peter Clowes and Cramer on the basis that there was insufficient evidence to support such a finding. It is this appeal which is the centre of our concerns.

The facts relating to Henwood's involvement with the Barlow Clowes organisation are set out in summary form in Lord Hoffmann's judgment: they can be understood as follows. Henwood and ITC were first involved with Cramer and payments from the Barlow Clowes organisation[140] in May 1986. In the Spring of 1987, as Lord Hoffmann told the tale, Henwood's business relationship with Cramer and Peter Clowes grew close and the possibility arose that Henwood might go into a 'virtual partnership' with these two men in relation to a reverse takeover of another company, JFH. We are told that it was at this stage that Henwood 'began to take a lively interest in their business'.[141] It was in the summer of 1987 that the first of the relevant transactions took place by means of transfer from the Barlow Clowes organisation through ITC. Henwood approved the transfer of the money from ITC to Cramer so that Cramer could pursue personal business interests. The judge at first instance found that Henwood 'knew enough about the origins of the money to have suspected misappropriation and that he acted dishonestly in assisting in its disposal'.[142] The judge further found that after June 1987 Henwood 'strongly suspected'[143] that the monies passing through ITC had come from private British investors. Consequently it was held that no honest person could have assisted Peter Clowes and Cramer if those suspicions were correct. Henwood, we are told, had 'consciously decided not to make inquiries because he preferred in his own interest not to run the risk of discovering the truth'.[144]

---

139 The Acting Deemster was the judge at first instance in the Isle of Man.
140 We are not given specific information as to which company paid money to ITC and therefore I will simply refer to 'the Barlow Clowes organisation' to represent the payer in these transactions.
141 *Barlow Clowes v Eurotrust* [2006] 1 WLR 1476, [7].
142 *Ibid*, [8].
143 *Ibid*, [11].
144 *Ibid*, [11].

The decision of the Privy Council in Barlow Clowes v Eurotrust

Lord Hoffmann delivered the unanimous judgment of the Privy Council in the following, unequivocal terms: 'Their Lordships consider that by ordinary standards such a state of mind is dishonest'.[145] Therefore Henwood's claim that he had simply followed his clients' instructions without asking any questions was considered to have been dishonest. In support of this statement, Lord Hoffmann considered the argument raised at first instance that Henwood lived by a different moral code and that by his own moral standards obeying instructions from his clients, Peter Clowes and Cramer, took priority in a way that excluded all other moral claims to his attention. In the words of the Acting Deemster, Henwood had an:

> exaggerated notion of dutiful service to clients, which produced a warped moral approach that it was not improper to treat carrying out clients' instructions as being all important.[146] Mr Henwood may well have thought this to be an honest attitude, but, if so, he was wrong.[147]

The argument advanced by Henwood's counsel was as follows. Lord Hutton in *Twinsectra v Yardley* had suggested that for a person to be dishonest, his actions must not only be considered to be dishonest by an objectively honest person but the defendant himself must also be aware that his actions would be considered to be dishonest by such a person.[148] Consequently, counsel for Henwood argued that Henwood had not appreciated that his actions would be considered to be dishonest and therefore that Henwood could not be a dishonest assistant. The court of appeal in the Isle of Man, known as the Staff of Government Division, considered that the Acting Deemster had drawn inferences of dishonesty from Henwood's evidence and had based her judgment on those inferences. This court of appeal considered that, just because Henwood knew the general nature of Cramer and Peter Clowes's business, it did not follow that Henwood would necessarily have formed the view that the monies paid through ITC were necessarily taken in breach of trust from Barlow Clowes's private investors. Consequently, the court of appeal found that there was insufficient evidence of dishonesty on Henwood's part. This finding of a lack of dishonesty, then, relied on Lord Hutton's explanation of what 'dishonesty' meant in *Twinsectra v Yardley*.

The Privy Council overturned the decision of the court of appeal. As to the facts of the case, Lord Hoffmann considered that it was the Acting Deemster who had heard six days of evidence from Henwood and others and who was therefore in a good position to judge whether or not Henwood had acted dishonestly. His Lordship was unconvinced by the court of appeal's argument that a trial judge 'drawing inferences from inferences' was likely to lead to injustice, for the same reason. Instead, his lordship was prepared to rely on the Acting Deemster's findings of fact and her impression that Henwood had been dishonest in the circumstances.

---

145   *Ibid*, [12].
146   That is, Henwood argued that he considered his loyalty to Cramer and Clowes, his clients, as being more important than the rights or interests of any other person.
147   *Barlow Clowes v Eurotrust* [2006] 1 WLR 1476, [2006] 1 All ER 333 [12].
148   [2002] 2 AC 164, 174.

Re-establishing the objective test for 'dishonesty'; explaining Twinsectra v Yardley

As to the appropriate legal principles, there are three significant issues. First, Lord Hoffmann held that neither he nor Lord Hutton, when both gave judgment in *Twinsectra v Yardley*, had intended the test for dishonesty to be understood as having a subjective requirement (that one appreciate that other people would consider one's behaviour to have been dishonest) added to it.[149] Instead, the purely objective test in *Royal Brunei Airlines v Tan* should be understood to be the governing test. Consequently, Henwood would not be able to rely on his own moral code to absolve him of liability and therefore he was held liable as a dishonest assistant.

However, this argument seems a little thin given that Lord Hutton had held the following in *Twinsectra v Yardley* in purportedly (we had previously thought) adding a subjective dimension to the test for 'dishonesty':

> There is, in my opinion, a further consideration [than deciding whether the test is one of knowledge or dishonesty as set out by Lord Nicholls] which supports the view that for liability as an accessory to arise the defendant must himself appreciate that what he was doing was dishonest by the standards of honest and reasonable men. A finding by the judge that a defendant has been dishonest is a grave finding, and it is particularly grave against a professional man, such as a solicitor. Notwithstanding that the issue arises in equity law [*sic*] and not in a criminal context, I think that it would be less than just for the law to permit a finding that a defendant had been 'dishonest' in assisting in a breach of trust where he knew of the facts which created the trust and its breach but had not been aware that what he was doing would be regarded by honest men as being dishonest.[150]

This form of the test, therefore, clearly did add an important second, subjective element to the test of dishonesty. Significantly, though, the second limb of the test is whether or not the defendant realised that *other people* would have considered his actions to have been dishonest and not that *the defendant himself* thought that the action was dishonest. Consequently, on this basis, Henwood's argument (had his evidence been credible) would in theory have been successful if he could have shown, even though an honest person would not have acted as he had acted, that he did not himself appreciate that other people would have considered his actions to have been dishonest.

The key passage from Lord Hoffmann's judgment in *Barlow Clowes v Eurotrust* in this context is in paragraph [10], as follows:

> The judge stated the law in terms largely derived from the advice of the Board given by Lord Nicholls of Birkenhead in *Royal Brunei Airlines v Tan*. In summary, she said that liability for dishonest assistance requires a dishonest state of mind on the part of the person who assists in a breach of trust. Such a state of mind may consist in knowledge that the transaction is one in which he cannot honestly participate (for example, a misap- propriation of other people's money), or it may consist in suspicion combined with a

---

149 *Barlow Clowes v Eurotrust* [2006] 1 WLR 1476, [2006] 1 All ER 333 [15]–[16] and [18].
150 *Twinsectra v Yardley* [2002] 2 All ER 377, 387.

conscious decision not to make inquiries which might result in knowledge: see *Manifest Shipping Co Ltd v Uni-Polaris Insurance Co Ltd.*[151] Although a dishonest state of mind is a subjective mental state, the standard by which the law determines whether it is dishonest is objective. If by ordinary standards a defendant's mental state would be characterised as dishonest, it is irrelevant that the defendant judges by different standards. The Court of Appeal held this to be a correct state of the law and their Lordships agree.

So, what results is a re-affirmation that the test is an objective test. However, whereas Lord Nicholls suggested considering what an honest person would have done and measuring the defendant's actions against the hypothetical actions of this honest person, Lord Hoffmann suggests that 'ordinary standards' will be the standard against which the court will decide whether or not the defendant's actions had been dishonest. It is suggested that asking what an honest person would have done is almost a counsel of perfection (but not in the pejorative sense in which people often use that term). Asking what an honest person would have done means identifying an almost ideal course of conduct untainted by any moral impropriety. An objective set of standards may, however, permit some level of 'moral ambiguity' between things which are deemed 'honest' and things which are deemed to be 'dishonest'. There is therefore a sliver of difference between the approach expressed by Lord Hoffmann in *Barlow Clowes v Eurotrust* and the approach set out by Lord Nicholls in *Royal Brunei Airlines v Tan*.

What Lord Hutton should be taken to have meant in Twinsectra v Yardley

Secondly, Lord Hoffmann explained in *Barlow Clowes v Eurotrust* that Lord Hutton should not have been interpreted as adding a level of subjectivity to the test. Rather, their Lordships in *Barlow Clowes v Eurotrust* took Lord Hutton in *Twinsectra v Yardley* to have meant that the defendant's:

> knowledge of the transaction had to be such as to render his participation contrary to normally acceptable standards of conduct. It did not require that he should have had reflections about what those normally acceptable standards were.[152]

However, there are two problems with this attempt to 'spin'[153] Lord Hutton's *dicta*. The first problem is that Lord Nicholls's objective approach in *Royal Brunei Airlines v Tan* does not *require* that the defendant realise that his actions would be dishonest by ordinary standards (although if that could be proved it would clearly show dishonesty): rather the court measures what an honest person would have done and then asks whether or not the defendant acted in that way. The second problem is that Lord Hutton is a criminal lawyer and criminal law's notion of dishonesty is subjective: it requires that the defendant know that his actions

---

151   [2003] 1 AC 469.
152   *Barlow Clowes v Eurotrust* [2006] 1 WLR 1476, [2006] 1 All ER 333 [15].
153   'Spin' is the art used in modern political activity of presenting an account of events in such a way as to make them seem less embarrassing, damaging or unfortunate.

986 Equity and Trusts

would be considered to be dishonest.[154] Thus it is perfectly probable that a criminal lawyer would have taken this attitude to questions of dishonesty.[155]

Lord Hoffmann then gave an explanation of his own speech in *Twinsectra v Yardley*, which had expressed concurrence with Lord Hutton. Lord Hoffmann, however, made clear that his comment in that case to the effect that the defendant must have exhibited 'consciousness that one is transgressing ordinary standards of honest behaviour'[156] does not require subjective reflection on what those standards are: rather, it was intended to be an objective requirement of dishonesty. This attempt by Lord Hoffmann to spin his own earlier judgment, particularly when the facts of *Eurotrust* had indicated why that test would not work, does seem a little disingenuous.

The correct approach to Henwood's evidence

Thirdly, what emerged from Lord Hoffmann's recitation of the court's opinion was that the judge at first instance was right to listen to the defendant's evidence and have regard to 'the lies which Mr Henwood told in evidence'.[157] The trial judge here considered that there may be a number of reasons why Henwood lied in evidence as to the time when he learned about the Barlow Clowes business – either to conceal his guilt or out of fear that he would not be believed – and it was considered right by Lord Hoffmann, given that there is 'no window into another mind', to draw inferences from the circumstances and what was said in evidence.[158] What is happening here reflects Scott LJ's *dicta* in *Polly Peck v Nadir (No 2)*[159] that no matter which test is used the question boils down to the trial judge asking herself, 'Ought the defendant to have been suspicious [as to whether or not this property is derived from a breach of trust] in these circumstances?'[160] So, we are told by Lord Hoffmann in *Barlow Clowes v Eurotrust*[161] that it is not necessary that the defendant should have known

---

154 *R v Ghosh* [1982] 2 All ER 689, [1982] QB 1053; *R v Hicks* [2000] 4 All ER 833.
155 One understanding of this case is that Lord Hutton had previously run the 'Diplock courts' in Northern Ireland. These special criminal courts heard cases involving terrorist and similar organisations without juries. The system had been introduced because the intimidation of juries had been such a problem. Consequently, the judges in Diplock courts had to act as both judge and jury. Jackson and Doran, 1995 found somewhat counter-intuitively that these judges were doing a good job in difficult circumstances of compensating for the absence of a jury in the conduct of these trials, in spite of the self-evident civil liberties implications. (For a contrary view, see Greer and White, 1986.) What this means for our purposes is that Lord Hutton spent a very long time becoming used to seeking proof that a defendant knew herself that she had been dishonest both as judge and as jury. Therefore, his attitude in *Twinsectra v Yardley* was entirely consistent with those beliefs. This also explains the Hutton Inquiry into the death of David Kelly and the start of the Iraq War: in spite of intense media scrutiny when Tony Blair gave evidence that he had not thought himself to have been dishonest, Lord Hutton would not have considered him dishonest because his own test was a subjective one; whereas when BBC journalists admitted that they had said they had checked facts in stories when they had not, then they were held to have been subjectively dishonest. The selection of Lord Hutton – with his steely determination and experience of intense outside pressure, and with his preference for a subjective test – was a stroke of genius by those who appointed him if their goal was to have the Prime Minister exonerated by that report for any dishonesty.
156 *Twinsectra v Yardley* [2002] 2 AC 164, [20].
157 *Barlow Clowes v Eurotrust* [2006] 1 WLR 1476, [2006] 1 All ER 333 [23].
158 *Ibid*, [26].
159 [1992] 4 All ER 769.
160 See the discussion at section 20.3.4 below.
161 *Barlow Clowes v Eurotrust* [2006] 1 WLR 1476, [2006] 1 All ER 333 [28].

that the monies came from a breach of trust but rather it would be sufficient that 'he should have entertained a clear suspicion that this was the case'.[162] On these facts, it was not necessary that Henwood know the detail of all of Peter Clowes and Cramer's transactions but rather it would be enough that he had 'grounds to suspect'[163] that they were misappropriating the money. The *dicta* of Rimer J in *Brinks Ltd v Abu-Saleh*[164] to the effect that the defendant must know either of the existence of the trust or of the facts giving rise to the trust, were disapproved of by Lord Hoffmann.[165]

The decision of the Acting Deemster was therefore restored on the basis that the Privy Council considered that there was sufficient evidence to support the Acting Deemster's findings.[166]

The decision of the Court of Appeal in Abou-Rahmah v Abacha

The Court of Appeal in *Abou-Rahmah v Abacha*[167] has *prima facie* approved the approach of the Privy Council in *Barlow Clowes v Eurotrust*. However, as is explained below, there are serious difficulties with the detail of the judgments of Rix LJ and Arden LJ in that case. The facts in *Abou-Rahmah v Abacha* were as follows. The claimants were contacted by the second defendant to ask the claimants to assist the first defendant with some financial problems. Briefly put, the claimants were offered a share in a trust fund of US$65 million which the first defendant claimed he was trying to get out of Benin. To gain access to this money, or so the claimants were told, it was necessary to make a number of payments, totalling US$1.375 million, to various government agencies purportedly to acquire regulatory permission to move the target money and to meet VAT liabilities. The claimants paid the amounts which were purportedly required to access the target money. These arrangements were a scam intended to take money from the claimants. In time, after the payments had been made, the defendants absconded with the money. The claimants sought to recover their losses from a variety of third parties who had been involved with this scam in various ways. This particular piece of litigation concerned a claim brought by the claimants against a bank into which two payments totalling US$625,000, which had been taken from the claimants as part of the scam, had been paid. While a number of claims were made at first instance, only questions relating to dishonest assistance and to the change of position defence were made in front of the Court of Appeal.

At first instance, Treacy J followed the hybrid subjective–objective test for dishonesty in *Twinsectra v Yardley*: the decision in *Barlow Clowes v Eurotrust* was reached after the trial had ended, although Treacy J had accepted skeleton arguments on the nature of the test.[168] On appeal, Rix LJ stated the principles underpinning dishonest assistance in the following terms:

162   *Ibid.*
163   *Ibid.*
164   [1996] CLC 133, 151.
165   *Barlow Clowes v Eurotrust* [2006] 1 WLR 1476, [2006] 1 All ER 333 [28].
166   *Ibid*, [29] and [32].
167   [2006] EWCA Civ 1492, [2007] Bus LR 220.
168   [2005] EWHC 2662 (QB), [2006] 1 Lloyd's Rep 484.

It would seem that a claimant in this area needs to show three things: first, that a defendant has the requisite knowledge; secondly, that, given that knowledge, the defendant acts in a way which is contrary to normally acceptable standards of honest conduct (the objective test of honesty or dishonesty); and thirdly, possibly, that the defendant must in some sense be dishonest himself (a subjective test of dishonesty which might, on analysis, add little or nothing to knowledge of the facts which, objectively, would make his conduct dishonest).[169]

However, this passage, it is suggested, is simply a misunderstanding of the debate which has followed *Royal Brunei Airlines v Tan* – a debate which his Lordship sought to essay in those parts of his judgment which followed the passage quoted above and which dealt with dishonest assistance. What is a misunderstanding, it is suggested, is the inclusion of the first and second requirements: what was required by Lord Nicholls in *Royal Brunei Airlines v Tan* was an objective test to decide whether or not the defendant had been 'dishonest', not the old test which had considered the defendant's 'knowledge'. The third element of the test is very wide of the mark. Therefore, this test cannot really be considered as being an application of the *Tan* test as set out in *Barlow Clowes v Eurotrust* as it purports to be. Here knowledge is put ahead of dishonesty by Rix LJ, and not in the nuanced way in which Lord Nicholls mentioned it briefly in *Tan*. *Royal Brunei Airlines v Tan* did not create a test of what the defendant knew; rather it is only a question of what an honest person would have done in the circumstances and whether or not the defendant lived up to that standard of honesty. Failure to be honest in this sense renders a person dishonest. It was Lord Hutton's now discredited suggestion in *Twinsectra v Yardley* – that the defendant must *also* be proved to have appreciated that other people would have considered her behaviour to have been dishonest – which brought in this element of subjective dishonesty to the previously entirely objective test of dishonesty. However, as Rix LJ recognised, the unanimous decision of the Privy Council in *Barlow Clowes v Eurotrust* sought to return the test to its purely objective state in *Royal Brunei Airlines v Tan*. Therefore, the reference to knowledge which Rix LJ makes should not be made if, as Rix LJ claimed to be doing, the law is to be returned to its purely objective state in *Royal Brunei Airlines v Tan*. What Rix LJ has achieved instead, ironically enough, is an affirmation of the hybrid subjective–objective test for dishonesty in *Twinsectra v Yardley* or a test for subjective knowledge.

Also in *Abou-Rahmah v Abacha*, Arden LJ set out the following summary of the principles relating to dishonest assistance:

In *Barlow Clowes International Ltd (in liquidation) v Eurotrust International Ltd*,[170] the Privy Council considered the case law of England and Wales on the issue of the element of dishonesty necessary for liability under this head. Its interpretation of that case law was that it is unnecessary to show subjective dishonesty in the sense of consciousness that the transaction is dishonest. It is sufficient if the defendant knows of the elements of the transaction which make it dishonest according to normally accepted standards of behaviour. This is the first opportunity, so far as I am aware, that this Court has had an

169   [2006] EWCA Civ 1492, [16].
170   [2006] 1 All ER 333.

opportunity of considering the decision of the Privy Council, and in my judgment this court should follow the decision of the Privy Council.[171]

What Arden LJ should be taken to mean here, in following the test in *Barlow Clowes v Eurotrust*, is that the *Eurotrust* test for dishonesty would definitely be made out on any given set of facts if the defendant 'knows of the elements of the transaction which make it dishonest according to normally accepted standards of behaviour'. If the defendant knew that her behaviour would be considered to be dishonest according to normal standards of behaviour then that would mean that the defendant would be held to have been dishonest on any formulation of the dishonesty test. However, to be liable under *Tan* or *Eurotrust* it would not have been necessary to prove such subjective knowledge: rather, merely identifying that in the circumstances an honest person would not have behaved as the defendant behaved would have been sufficient. The defendant would not be found to have been dishonest because she realised the nature of her actions would have been considered to have been dishonest by other people, but rather because her actions offended the normal standards of behaviour. This formulation by Arden LJ blurs that point.

Arden LJ laid great emphasis on the following idea from the opinion of Lord Nicholls:

> As Lord Nicholls said in the *Royal Brunei* case, honesty has 'a strong subjective element in that it is a description of a type of conduct assessed in the light of what a person actually knew at the time, as distinct from what a reasonable person would have known or appreciated.'[172]

But this passage is being taken totally out of context. It is a discussion of *honesty* – not *dishonesty* – and refers to *dishonesty* as being 'its counterpart' immediately after the passage which Arden LJ has quoted. The key passage emerges immediately before the sentence which Arden LJ has quoted. That passage in Lord Nicholls's opinion in the Privy Council in *Royal Brunei Airlines v Tan* read:

> Whatever may be the position in some criminal or other contexts . . ., in the context of the accessory liability principle acting dishonestly, or with a lack of probity, which is synonymous, means simply not acting as an honest person would in the circumstance. This is an objective standard.[173]

Then Lord Nicholls held 'This may seem surprising', and *only then* did he speak the words quoted by Arden LJ above. In other words his Lordship was pointing out that his insistence on a purely objective test may seem counter-intuitive at first – and that honesty may seem to connote subjective notions – but that in truth objectivity was nevertheless the keynote. After the passage quoted by Arden LJ, and references to a common understanding of there being some subjectivity in discussions of honesty and dishonesty, Lord Nicholls then changed tack completely and held the following, focusing on pure objectivity and speaking out clearly against form of subjectivity:

---

171 [2006] EWCA Civ 1492, [59a].
172 *Ibid*, [66].
173 [1995] 2 AC 378, 386.

However, these subjective characteristics of honesty do not mean that individuals are free to set their own standards of honesty in particular circumstances. The standard of what constitutes honest conduct is not subjective. Honesty is not an optional scale, with higher or lower values according to the moral standards of each individual. If a person knowingly appropriates another's property, he will not escape a finding of dishonesty simply because he sees nothing wrong in such behaviour.[174]

It could not be plainer. Lord Nicholls was demanding a test which could not enable the defendant to use subjective standards of morality to excuse her from liability for conduct which would have been held to be dishonest by reference to objective standards of honesty.[175] It is only in the second passage quoted from *Tan* earlier in this chapter that Lord Nicholls unequivocally allowed a reference to personal attributes, intelligence and experience to be included in the court's analysis of the facts. Arden LJ appears to be engaging in the primarily subjective" reading of this passage but without reference to the remainder of the paragraph from which it is taken. This, it is suggested, is a good example of how a short phrase, or a sentence or a single concept in a judgment can acquire a life of its own through the work of judges in later cases, and often the entire context in which that concept was developed in the judgment is lost as a result.

20.2.6 The difficulty for judges at first instance in the light of the current state of the authorities

The different strands of authority: five different tests

As a result of the foregoing mass of authority, it is not an easy matter for a judge at first instance to decide a case relating to dishonest assistance. The instinct of any judge at first instance is to identify the facts: it must be remembered that the hearing at first instance is the trial and that any appellate court will rely on the facts which the trial judge finds by reference to the evidence submitted in court. Ordinarily, it is only the trial judge who hears the witnesses and who sees examination and cross-examination on their evidence. Therefore, a trial judge will tend to devote a large amount of her judgment to a finding of fact, but this in turn tends to mean that in dishonest assistance cases a large amount of attention is lavished on evidence as to the subjective motivations, beliefs, intelligence, experience and actual knowledge of the defendant. In relation to a strictly objective test, where all that one should consider is what an honest person would have done and not at all what the defendant subjectively thought or knew, this is largely irrelevant. As discussed above, what makes that

---

174 *Ibid*; [1995] 3 All ER 97, 106. Cf *Walker v Stones* [2001] QB 902.The last sentence contains an unfortunate reference to 'appropriation', whereas it is not necessary for the operation of the assistance liability that the defendant receive the property into his possession: the term 'appropriation' here should be read as referring to participation in the act of appropriation of property from the trust fund without passing possession or control of it to the defendant.

175 Arden LJ was therefore quoting a passage entirely out of the context of the opinion of Lord Nicholls in *Royal Brunei Airlines v Tan*, an approach which has been approved by the Privy Council in *Barlow Clowes v Eurotrust* and notionally even by Arden LJ. It cannot be acceptable that a person escapes liability for dishonesty simply by claiming that she did not think what she did was dishonest. That may be sufficient to keep someone out of prison in the criminal law, but it is insufficient when a court is called upon to decide whether or not an objectively dishonest person should be required to compensate the victim of her actions in equity.

formulation of the objective test complicated, however, is that Lord Nicholls in *Tan* did refer (as considered above) to the defendant's knowledge, personal attributes and experience, which has sent judges in subsequent cases scurrying off to consider what the defendant's knowledge was, even though this is only a three-word construct in a much fuller judgment which otherwise was remarkably clear about its focus on objectivity.

Nevertheless, on the state of the authorities there are five possible, contradictory things that a trial judge may be looking for by reference to the current authorities. The following range of possibilities are suggested, *inter alia*, by Judge Strauss QC at first instance in *Starglade v Nash*.[176] This also serves as a useful summary of the foregoing discussion of the authorities:

(1)   In *Royal Brunei Airlines v Tan*, Lord Nicholls identified the test as being what an honest person would have done in the circumstances (where the circumstances are to be identified by reference to the *facts* available to the defendant[177]). As is generally forgotten, the House of Lords in *Dubai Aluminium v Salaam* agreed with this approach.

(2)   In *Twinsectra v Yardley* in the House of Lords, Lord Hutton required both that the defendant's behaviour was dishonest by the standards of honest people and also that the defendant must be shown to have appreciated that her behaviour contravened ordinary standards of conduct (that is, that an honest person would have considered her behaviour to have been dishonest).

(3)   In *Barlow Clowes v Eurotrust* in the Privy Council, the Privy Council speaking through Lord Hoffmann explicitly re-interpreted Lord Hutton's speech (but it is not strictly open to the Privy Council to overrule the House of Lords) and found that a person may not escape liability for dishonesty by reference to some personal code of morality (and thus a failure to appreciate that her actions would have been considered to have been dishonest by reference to the standards of honest people). Instead, liability was to be decided by reference to the objective standards of honest people.

(4)   In *Abou-Rahmah v Abacha*, Arden LJ purported to accept the judgment of Lord Nicholls in *Tan* (after *Twinsectra* and *Eurotrust*) as constituting English law, although it is not clear that the rest of the Court of Appeal agreed with her as to the details, and it was not clear therefore whether Rix and Pill LJJ should be taken to have required a subjective knowledge of one's own dishonesty.

(5)   In *Royal Brunei Airlines v Tan*, Lord Nicholls also referred to the defendant's personal attributes, experience and intelligence (in the second passage quoted above in the discussion of *Tan*) which was taken by Lord Clarke and by Smith J in *A-G for Zambia v Mesai Care* to elevate the examination of the defendant's knowledge, personal attributes, experience, intelligence and so forth (all of which are clearly subjective characteristics) to the same level in the analysis as an objective examination of what an honest person would have done. This approach has been followed in numerous other High Court and Court of Appeal cases which are considered in this section. What is difficult is that the second passage from the judgment of Lord Nicholls in *Royal Brunei Airlines v Tan* has been elevated to the same status as the objective test in the remainder

---

176   [2009] EWHC 148 (Ch), [2010] WTLR 1267.

177   By 'available' is meant things which were actually known and things which ought to have been known to someone who was not shutting her eyes to the obvious or who was not failing to make the inquiries which an honest person would have made.

of the judgment. The concept of objective dishonesty is identified most clearly in these cases with the idea that a defendant may not escape liability by reference to a subjective moral code or other set of beliefs.

Each of these tests is clearly subtly but importantly different. I really do empathise with trial judges in this context. In the following sections I consider some High Court cases decided since *Abou-Rahmah v Abacha* and the ways in which they have dealt with these difficulties. It is suggested, ultimately, that the approach which was accepted by the House of Lords in *Dubai Aluminium v Salaam* – approving *Tan* – should be accepted as the leading case: that approach is considered after the survey of these cases. First, however, to illustrate the differences, let us consider a hypothetical example and apply each of the five preceding approaches to it.

> *Eric overhears Stan and Kyle, two investment bankers, talking in loud, drunken voices about a 'secret deal' they will do the next day. They think they are alone in the train carriage. The deal is the announcement of a takeover of one company by another which no one in the market will know about before the next day at 10.00am. The share price of both companies will rise sharply when the news becomes public. Eric was brought up by his mother with one single motto, which she even wrote on his bedroom wall as a boy: 'Take any opportunity which comes along, no matter what the risk.' He had little formal education, little contact with other people, and had always been considered to be a liar at school. Eric's mother is also in need of an operation which can be performed quickly, so as to ease her suffering, only if Eric obtains £20,000. Eric buys shares in both companies at 9.00am the following day and then sells them at 11.00am and makes £20,000 profit.*
>
> *Is Eric dishonest? Would your answer differ if you knew that Eric's actions would be a criminal offence under insider dealing legislation?*

Let us take each of the five analyses one at a time.

(1) Lord Nicholls in *Tan* would ask us to take the perspective of an honest person in this context. If Lord Nicholls took the view that profiting from a secret conversation like this was not something that an honest person would do, then Eric would be dishonest because he did not do what an honest person would have done.[178]

---

178 In January 2012, the Financial Services Authority handed down a record £7.2 million fine for 'market abuse' violations (a regulatory penalty based on misuse of 'inside information' akin to insider trading) to David Einhorn, the manager of American hedge fund Greenlight Capital (worth $7 billion at the time), for selling more than 11.6 million shares in a company over four days after he had been told by a stockbroker advising that company the confidential information (which should not have been disclosed nor dealt on under market abuse regulation) that the company was going to issue a large number of new shares (which would have reduced the value of Einhorn's own shares). Einhorn protested that he had not understood the law in the UK (which is remarkable for a market professional of his experience), that the FSA had taken an odd interpretation of the regulations (even though there had been no change in the FSA's policy or regulations), and that Einhorn was in fact considered by people who worked with him to be a very ethical person. He launched a public relations offensive (in many senses of that term) in the press to recover his reputation: see, for example, 'The outsider who has run foul of the FSA', *The Financial Times*, 27 January 2012. Even a well-established market professional like Einhorn will seek to plead ignorance and innocence in relation to an activity which involves straightforwardly unethical conduct. See the many reports on this story at www.ft.com.

(2) Lord Hutton in *Twinsectra* would require that Eric understood that honest people would consider his behaviour to have been dishonest. Here, Eric would say that his moral code (in the form of the motto given to him by his mother) led him to take this advantage and that he did not know what other people would think of his actions. In consequence, in spite of this being a criminal offence, he would escape liability for dishonesty.

(3) The Privy Council in *Barlow Clowes v Eurotrust* would not allow Eric to rely on his own moral code to escape liability. It would also be necessary to show that ordinary standards of behaviour required Eric to have behaved differently. On that basis he would be likely to escape liability.

(4) The Court of Appeal in *Abou-Rahmah v Abacha* would have required some subjective knowledge and awareness of his own dishonesty (on the formulation advanced by Rix LJ) before Eric would have been considered to be dishonest. Arden LJ would have followed *Eurotrust* but with an element of considering Eric's own knowledge.

(5) The High Court decisions to follow would consider Eric's personal attributes (deceitfulness, concern for his mother), his experience (limited schooling, little contact with other people), and his intelligence, and bring those factors to bear alongside a consideration of ordinary standards of honest behaviour, although Eric would not be able to rely on his personal motto or other beliefs. Clearly, while this approach has an element of sounding like the test in *Tan*, it tends to bring into account a number of subjective factors (which Lord Nicholls did mention, once, in his own judgment). The decision in *Starglade Properties Ltd v Nash*[179] considered the defendant's lack of education and lack of understanding of legal concepts as being important. This last approach is considered in the discussion to follow.

The sections that follow consider some more recent decisions in the wake of *Abou-Rahmah v Abacha* which have experienced problems with the application of the various approaches set out above. There is one last point before turning to the many decisions which have come in the wake of *Abou-Rahmah* and which display a variety of these five analyses: the definition of concepts which are popularly known as 'sociopathology' (more formally encompassing antisocial personality disorders, and some bipolar disorder) in any authoritative reference work on psychiatry or psychopathology will define those terms as including such a person having no understanding of common standards of behaviour or social mores, and indeed as involving 'a pervasive pattern of disregard for the rights of others'.[180] Sociopaths are often charming and often driven towards achieving their goals, but they exhibit a disconnect from the feelings or beliefs of other people, and from social norms in general. It is suggested that any subjective test of dishonesty allows the defendant to escape liability on the basis that she did not understand that other people would consider her behaviour to run contrary to the generally accepted standards of conduct in society. Such a subjective test is therefore more likely to absolve sociopaths from liability. This is not meant to be a flippant point. There is nothing at all amusing about mental illness. However, the sort of behaviour which is excused by subjective tests for dishonesty would appear at face to encompass these sorts of disorders. It is too easy for a defendant to escape liability simply by saying that she

179 [2010] EWCA Civ 1314.
180 See Carr and McNulty, 2006, for example.

had not realised that reasonable people would consider her actions to have been dishonest. In this way, the more immoral a defendant is, the less likely she is to be found dishonest because she will claim she was unaware of ordinary people's morality. The point that is being made here, at root, is that subjective tests seem to have lost their moral centre in that the defendant is to be judged only by reference to her own standards as opposed to objective standards which the law sets down. Objective tests maintain the moral status of the law in this area: to judge our actions.

AG Zambia v Meer Care & Desai: what to make of experience and knowledge?

A formulation of the test for dishonesty, which draws heavily on the second passage quoted earlier from the judgment of Lord Nicholls in *Royal Brunei Airlines v Tan*, has been suggested by Sir Anthony Clarke MR in an article to the effect that the test is an objective one but that nevertheless the court should take into account the circumstances in which the defendant was acting and the level of experience which the defendant had. His lordship suggested in that article as follows:

> The test is an objective one, but an objective one which takes account of the individual in question's characteristics, experience, knowledge, etc.[181] . . . It is a test which requires a court to assess an individual's conduct according to an objective standard of dishonesty. In doing so, a court has to take account of what the individual knew, his experience, intelligence and reasons for acting as he did. Whether the individual was aware that his conduct fell below the objective standard is not part of the test.[182]

This approach is necessarily inserting some subjectivity into the test.[183] What is one supposed to do having decided that the defendant is 'experienced' and 'intelligent'? Presumably, an intelligent or experienced person is to be held liable because of their experience and intelligence, whereas the stupid and inexperienced are to escape liability because of their stupidity and inexperience, even if their actions would have been considered to be dishonest by honest and reasonable people.

The purpose of this area of law is to protect the position of beneficiaries of fiduciary arrangements: therefore the risk of the stupidity of third parties dealing with the trust is thrown onto the beneficiaries. That has never been the approach of equity. Nevertheless, in *AG Zambia v Meer Care & Desai & Others*[184] Peter Smith J held that this was the proper approach, and this approach was followed in *Markel International Insurance Co Ltd v Surety Guarantee Consultants Ltd*.[185] In reliance on Lord Clarke's article Peter Smith J constructed a peculiar test for dishonesty in *Attorney General of Zambia v Meer Care &*

181 It should be noted that these two things are mutually exclusive: how can an objective test consider subjective characteristics?

182 Clarke, 'Claims against professionals: negligence, dishonesty and fraud' [2006] 22 *Professional Negligence* 70–85.

183 This approach was followed by Peter Smith J in other judgments in *JD Wetherspoon plc v Van de Berg & Co Ltd* [2009] EWHC 639 (Ch), Peter Smith J, and *Independent Trustee Services Ltd v GP Noble Trustees Ltd* [2010] EWHC 1653 (Ch), Peter Smith J.

184 [2007] EWHC 952 (Ch).

185 [2008] EWHC 1135 (Comm), [2008] All ER (D) 10.

Desai[186] to the effect that it 'is essentially a question of fact whereby the state of mind of the Defendant had to be judged in the light of his subjective knowledge but by reference to an objective standard of honesty'[187] and that '[t]he test is clearly an objective test but the breach involves a subjective assessment of the person in question in the light of what he knew at the time as distinct from what a reasonable person would have known or appreciated'. However, if the test is an objective test then it definitively does *not* require questioning the defendant's subjective state of mind. What Smith J's test produces is a situation in which one asks whether or not the defendant was consciously (that is, subjectively) dishonest and then whether or not that can correlate with an objective standard of honesty. Quite how these subjective and objective concepts are to be brought together is unclear because they appear to be opposites.

If one nevertheless wants this sort of hybrid test to be the test in English law then one must stop pretending that one is applying an objective test of the sort set out by Lord Nicholls in *Royal Brunei Airlines v Tan* or in *Dubai Aluminium v Salaam*, or by the Privy Council in *Barlow Clowes v Eurotrust*, as considered above. On appeal, the Court of Appeal in *Attorney General of Zambia v Meer Care & Desai*[188] observed Smith J's use of this odd test in relation to dishonest assistance but did not cite any of the House of Lords, Privy Council or even Court of Appeal decisions considered thus far in its own deliberations as to the nature of the liability, which is really quite odd. There are decisions of the High Court which purport to be using an objective test but which nevertheless cannot stop themselves from delving into the subjective state of the defendant's own attitudes, knowledge and beliefs. One such is *Markel International*, considered next.

Markel International Insurance Co Ltd v Surety Guarantee Consultants Ltd

In *Markel International Insurance Co Ltd v Surety Guarantee Consultants Ltd* the defendant contended that he was not dishonest because of the circumstances in which he was acting. Those circumstances were that he asked the experienced bond traders with whom he was dealing whether or not all was well with a series of bond transactions and contended that he was entitled simply to rely on their answers without considering the matter further himself. After all, they were the experts and he had asked their professional advice, and then acted on it. The defendant contended therefore that he had not been dishonest because he had relied on the answers given to his questions by the professionals whom he was entitled to trust with those transactions. It is suggested that the court's deliberations should be restricted to a question as to whether or not in those circumstances an honest person would have acted as the defendant acted. After *Barlow Clowes v Eurotrust*, it is definitively not a question as to whether or not the defendant subjectively appreciated that her own behaviour was dishonest according to social mores. Therefore, it is suggested that this should not be considered to be a third approach to the question of dishonesty at all, but rather that it should be considered to be necessarily a part of the question as to whether or not the defendant was dishonest by the lights of honest and reasonable people, as required by Lord Nicholls in *Tan*.

---

186   [2007] EWHC 952 (Ch).
187   *Ibid*, para [334].
188   [2008] EWCA Civ 1007, para [151] *et seq*. The Court of Appeal ultimately failed to find any dishonesty on the facts of the case.

Nevertheless, in *Markel* the judge, Tearse J, spent a large amount of the latter stages of his judgment considering what *the defendant* honestly thought and did not think, as opposed to deciding *objectively* what the judge considered an honest person would have thought. So, despite his Lordship's analysis of the law, his approach lapsed almost absent-mindedly into a subjective examination of the defendant's own state of mind.[189] In that judgment many pages were spent on analysing the appropriate objectivity of the test for dishonesty and then, remarkably enough, many more pages considering the evidence as to what the defendant subjectively thought. If the test is one of objective dishonesty, then it cannot matter at all what the defendant thought subjectively because objective dishonesty (as set out in *Tan*) requires asking only what an honest and reasonable person would have done in the circumstances.

Starglade v Nash: the dilemma of triangulating between objective standards and subjective qualities

The decision of Judge Strauss QC at first instance in *Starglade Properties Ltd v Nash*[190] is another not entirely satisfactory exposition of this test, which was in turn overturned as to its treatment of the facts of the case by the Court of Appeal.[191] What emerges clearly from this case is that the position under English law remains confusing for judges at first instance: it is unclear whether *Twinsectra* in the House of Lords is to be followed or *Eurotrust* in the Privy Council which re-interprets *Twinsectra*; it is unclear whether Arden LJ in *Abou-Rahmah* was speaking alone, and whether the judgments of Rix and Pill LJJ constitute the majority; and it is unclear whether references in the cases to the defendant's 'knowledge' are references to her general knowledge, intelligence and experience, or whether it is a reference only to a knowledge of the facts available to her at the time. Therefore it is unclear to what extent the 'knowledge' of the defendant should be included in the judge's survey of the facts.

In *Starglade*, Larkstore bought land from Starglade. Starglade had had an expert report prepared into the condition of the soil at the site from Technotrade: that report was negligently prepared and there was subsequently a landslide at the site after Larkstore had begun to develop it. Consequently, Larkstore was sued by third parties whose properties had been damaged by the landslide. Larkstore negotiated with Starglade that Starglade would assign the benefit of its contract with Technotrade to Larkstore so that Larkstore could recover the cost of compensating those third parties from Technotrade. Starglade drove a hard bargain and convinced Larkstore to agree to pay one half of any compensation acquired from Technotrade to Starglade. An agreement was drawn up to this effect, with a specific provision that all money received from Technotrade would be held on trust and then divided in

---

189 See, for example, *ibid,* para [209]: 'For these reasons I have reached the conclusion that he did not honestly
    believe that his conduct in signing bonds in excess of the stated limits was justifiable' and more generally the
    defendant's motive in taking this role that he wanted 'a quiet life': none of this can matter because all that
    matters is what an honest person would have done in the circumstances. Elsewhere in the same case, where
    two other defendants were demonstrated to have assisted a breach of a company's fiduciary duties dishonestly
    (without there being any real question that they had been dishonest on any basis), then those two defendants
    were held liable for 'knowingly assisting' [*sic*] the beneficiary of that fiduciary relationship; see para [237].
190 [2009] EWHC 148 (Ch), [2010] WTLR 1267. This case was followed in *Adelaide Partnerships Ltd v Danison*
    [2011] All ER (D) 01 (Mar).
191 [2010] EWCA Civ 1314.

equal shares. However, when this money (over £300,000) was received, Larkstore paid it out to its ordinary creditors and did not pay anything to Starglade. Among the creditors who received money was Mr Nash. Mr Nash had seen the terms of the agreement between Starglade and Larkstore but it was found by Strauss QC that he was not an educated man, that he had not understood what a trust was, that he had thought that a company was entitled to use its money to pay its creditors in any way that it wished,[192] and that therefore he had not known that there was a trust. Nevertheless, Starglade sued Mr Nash for dishonest assistance in the breach of trust committed by Larkstore in paying money out of a trust fund to people who were not entitled to it.

Judge Strauss QC considered himself caught between the competing authorities, as set out above. Nevertheless, his lordship spent the entirety of the judgment before the fifty-fourth paragraph dealing with entirely subjective characteristics of Mr Nash's personality, experience, intelligence and attitude to the transaction in front of him. It is only in that fifty-fourth paragraph that Strauss QC addressed the notion of what ordinary mores would have required of Mr Nash, before deciding that what Mr Nash had done in this context, given that most people would not have known that a company could not pay its creditors in any order it saw fit, did not traduce ordinary standards of behaviour. His lordship then held that in his view Mr Nash had not considered that ordinary people would have considered his behaviour to have been dishonest. Of particular interest is Strauss QC's elision of Lord Nicholls's idea of the defendant's knowledge with the more general idea expressed by Lord Clarke and Smith J that the defendant's knowledge includes his subjective knowledge, intelligence and experience. Oddly, Strauss QC considers these to be 'part of the same' concept of knowledge, even though the latter form is clearly subjective whereas the former was avowedly objective.

On appeal, in *Starglade v Nash* in the Court of Appeal,[193] the Chancellor held the following:

> There is a single standard of honesty objectively determined by the court. That standard is applied to specific conduct of a specific individual possessing the knowledge and qualities he actually enjoyed.[194]

This clearly takes the objective standard and makes it subjective in effect by limiting the 'objectively honest person' to a person who is subjectively the same as the defendant. Then the Chancellor held further that:

> There is no suggestion in any of the speeches in *Twinsectra Ltd v Yardley* that the standard of dishonesty is flexible or determined by any one other than by the court on an objective basis having regard to the ingredients of the combined test explained by Lord Hutton.[195]

---

192   Strauss QC admitted that he believed this to be the case, even though there is clear authority to the contrary, and entirely overlooking the fact that a company acting as trustee cannot pay trust property to third parties without committing a breach of trust.

193   [2010] EWCA Civ 1314, at [25]. Followed in *Secretary of State for Justice v Topland Group plc* [2011] EWHC 983 (QB), King J. See also *Fiona Trust & Holding Corporation v Privalov* [2010] EWHC 3199 (Comm), at [1437], *per* Andrew Smith J.

194   *Starglade v Nash* [2010] EWCA Civ 1314, [25]. Followed in *Secretary of State for Justice v Topland Group plc* [2011] EWHC 983 (QB), King J.

195   *Starglade v Nash* [2010] EWCA Civ 1314, [28].

Therefore, the law is returned to the position under *Twinsectra*, in spite of the decision in *Barlow Clowes v Eurotrust*. His lordship then held:

> The relevant standard, described variously in the statements I have quoted, is the ordinary standard of honest behaviour. Just as the subjective understanding of the person concerned as to whether his conduct is dishonest is irrelevant so also is it irrelevant that there may be a body of opinion which regards the ordinary standard of honest behaviour as being set too high. Ultimately, in civil proceedings, it is for the court to determine what that standard is and to apply it to the facts of the case.[196]

What we have, ultimately, then, is a recognition that it is a question for the court to decide on a case-by-case basis what the appropriate standard is, while triangulating between the need to understand the inflexible 'ordinary standards of honest behaviour' and the need to ignore 'the subjective understanding" of the defendant while nevertheless considering his 'knowledge and qualities'. All of this is conceptually incoherent unless one takes a pure objective approach to the root concepts in *Tan* and in *Eurotrust*.

Aerostar Maintenance International Ltd v Wilson: *standing in the defendant's shoes*

The following useful summary of the principles has been set out in *Aerostar Maintenance v International Ltd v Wilson* by Morgan J:

> The test as to dishonesty, distilled from the above authorities,[197] is as follows. Dishonesty is synonymous with a lack of probity. It means not acting as an honest person would in the circumstances. The standard is an objective one. The application of the standard requires one to put oneself in the shoes of the defendant to the extent that his conduct is to be assessed in the light of what he knew at the relevant time, as distinct from what a reasonable person would have known or appreciated. For the most part dishonesty is to be equated with conscious impropriety. But a person is not free to set his own standard of honesty. This is what is meant by saying that the standard is objective. If by ordinary objective standards the defendant's mental state would be judged to be dishonest, it is irrelevant that the defendant has adopted a different standard or can see nothing wrong in his behaviour.[158]

In that case the defendant had expressed his view in e-mails that he considered his actions in 'doing the dirty' on a woman to be acceptable because she in turn had 'done the dirty' on someone else: as such, he considered his behaviour to have been justifiable. Nevertheless, it was held that his behaviour had been objectively dishonest and therefore his actions, even if

196 *Ibid*, [32].
197 Those authorities were: the decision of the Privy Council in *Royal Brunei Airlines v Tan* [1995] 2 AC 378, the decision of the House of Lords in *Twinsectra Ltd v Yardley* [2002] 2 AC 164 and the decision of the Privy Council in *Barlow Clowes International Ltd v Eurotrust International Ltd* [2006] 1 WLR 1476. And in his lordship's opinion, correctly, 'the two decisions of the Privy Council represent the law to be applied in this jurisdiction: see *Abou-Rahmah v Abacha* [2007] 1 All ER (Comm) 827 at [66]–[70]'.
198 [2010] EWHC 2032 (Ch), at [184].

justifiable subjectively in his own mind, were dishonest.[199] That much is unobjectionable. What is difficult, however, is the concept suggested by Morgan J of 'putting oneself in the shoes of the defendant'. This is a concept about which one must be careful. By definition one person's shoes will not fit everyone in the world: fitting into a person's shoes is a very subjective activity – given the idiosyncrasies of length and width of foot, and taste in shoes – and is the antithesis of an objective approach where one size must necessarily fit all. To assess the situation while standing in the defendant's shoes necessarily involves a large amount of subjectivity. The objective test set out in *Royal Brunei Airlines v Tan* requires, it is suggested, that one must consider the circumstances in which that reasonable person must be acting (for example, that they were a solicitor of 30 years' experience who had received a suspicious e-mail) but not about any of that person's own moral code (for example, that they believed their clients were all liars and so were ripe for being the victims of theft). After all, in *Barlow Clowes v Eurotrust* it was held that:

> The reference to 'what he knows would offend normally accepted standards of honest conduct' meant only that his knowledge of the transaction had to be such as to render his participation contrary to normally acceptable standards of honest conduct.[200]

And further:

> Although a dishonest state of mind is a subjective mental state, the standard by which the law determines whether it is dishonest is objective. If by ordinary standards a defendant's mental state would be characterised as dishonest, it is irrelevant that the defendant judges by different standards.[201]

Therefore, even though the question of whether or not a person is being dishonest can only be proved with absolute certainty from within that person's mind, the law can only judge a person's actions objectively from the standpoint of what a person ought to have done in the circumstances of any given case. The court ought not to be standing in the defendant's shoes.[202]

20.2.7 Dishonesty, the provision of professional services and negligence

The distinction between dishonesty and negligence in Royal Brunei Airlines v Tan

In his judgment in *Royal Brunei Airlines v Tan*,[203] Lord Nicholls recognised that there is only a thin line between dishonest assistance and negligence, particularly in contexts in which the trustees are professionals, tendering their services under contract. In such a situation, it is possible that the same person might be liable for breach of contract, for breach of a duty of

---

199 *Ibid*, [185].
200 [2006] 1 WLR 1476, [15].
201 *Ibid*, [10].
202 It is often said that, so as to empathise with another person's situation, you should 'walk a mile in their shoes'. The only difficulty with that idea being that you will be a mile away and they will not have any shoes.
203 [1995] 3 All ER 97, 108.

care (that is, the tort of negligence) and for breach of trust in a situation in which there has been a breach of a trust. However, liability in equity rests on the dishonesty of the assistant, and it is not enough that they have been negligent or that they have breached a contract. Given what has been said thus far in this section, it is still somewhat surprising that in *Twinsectra Ltd v Yardley*[204] a solicitor was able to contend that he did not consider his actions to be dishonest even though those actions constituted a breach of trust and a breach of the original solicitor's undertaking. There is only a narrow line here between common law negligence and dishonesty sufficient to found liability for an equitable wrong. The solicitor would appear to have been negligent in considering that paying money to Yardley which was only to have been used for the purpose of acquiring good title in property was something which could have been done lawfully. Potentially, Leach's liability at common law might also have been a tortious procuring of a breach of Sims's undertaking to Twinsectra.

The jump to liability for dishonest assistance is a significant one. One might have thought that the professional nature of a solicitor's role and the reliance placed by Twinsectra on the undertakings given to it by the solicitor Sims might raise the presumption that an honest person would have expected a solicitor in Leach's position to consider properly the nature of his obligations both to his client, Yardley, and to the lender, Twinsectra, who had paid the loan moneys into trust subject to a solicitor's undertaking. The solicitor, Leach, is considered by the House of Lords to be entitled to restrict his liability to common law claims in tort on the basis that his own lack of diligence as a solicitor failed to bring to his conscious mind the self-evident fact that if he paid the money to Yardley, he would be breaching the fiduciary obligations owed by Sims to Twinsectra – particularly given that those fiduciary obligations could be said to have been passed to him when he assumed Sims's role as Yardley's solicitor. This, it is suggested, weakens markedly the nature of a solicitor's fiduciary duties and also returns us to that form of thinking so evident in cases like *Armitage v Nurse*,[205] whereby trustees are ever more capable of reducing their liabilities as trustees by reference to contractual exemption clauses, or the terms of their retainers, or (it appears) their own ignorance of their responsibilities under professional transactions.

By contrast, in *Walker v Stones*[206] it was held that where a trainee solicitor committed a breach of trust which no reasonable trainee solicitor could have considered to have been in the interests of the beneficiaries, that trainee solicitor should be deemed to have acted dishonestly. It is suggested that this approach demonstrates a more sensitive appreciation of the nature of the reliance which is placed not only upon a solicitor's good faith, but also upon her competence and her observance of the regulatory norms which bind her legal practice. Where such a solicitor, even during training, commits a breach of trust which is not in the interests of the beneficiaries of a trust, the proper approach must be that that person owes a duty to account to those beneficiaries who suffer a loss as a result of that breach of trust.

---

204   [2002] 2 All ER 377.
205   [1998] Ch 241; see para 21.2 below.
206   [2001] QB 902, at 903.

The meaning of 'dishonesty' in other contexts relating to professionals

In *Bryant v Law Society*[207] an interesting example of the test of 'dishonesty' arose before the Divisional Court in relation to two solicitors who were involved, in contravention of the Law Society's regulatory system on money laundering and other fraudulent transactions, in what was allegedly professional misconduct involving dishonesty. The solicitors' clients organised for large payments to be made through their solicitors, instead of through a bank as the parties' contracts required, without the solicitors asking any questions of their clients. The circumstances of the payments bore all the hallmarks of money laundering and were exactly the sort of transactions described as being prohibited in the relevant Law Society circulars. The criminal law test of dishonesty set out famously in *R v Ghosh*[208] requires first that one identifies what is objectively dishonest, and secondly that one asks whether or not the defendant was aware that her conduct was dishonest. In *Bryant v Law Society* one of the solicitors in question suggested that he honestly believed that what he was doing was honest and reasonable. The court considered that the test of 'dishonesty' to be applied by the tribunal was a test which took into account the solicitor's own perspective on what was honest. The solicitors were found, on the application of the subjective test, nevertheless to have committed professional misconduct.

The question remains as to the operation of this test in the abstract. As with *Barlow Clowes v Eurotrust*, what of the situation in which the professional contends that her behaviour was subjectively reasonable and honest? The concern must be that because the defendant was so anti-social as to have an inappropriate sense of the proprieties of life and thus to have a personal morality which meant that she considered her objectively dishonest behaviour to be subjectively honest, then she would escape liability. What the court should have found in *Bryant* was that because this person (by his own admission) had failed to observe the requirements of proper behaviour then he should be held liable for dishonesty. In *Twinsectra v Yardley* the majority of the House of Lords excused a solicitor from liability on the basis that it was a serious thing to condemn a professional man for dishonesty if he had not appreciated subjectively that that would be considered to be the case; in *Bryant v Law Society* the court expressed concern at the notion that a solicitor might otherwise be subjected to liability when he might not have realised that his actions would have been considered to have been dishonest by honest people. A better approach, it is suggested, would be to hold professional people (above all others) to an objective standard of honest behaviour. Professional people acting in their professional capacity should be expected to be rational and compliant with the appropriate professional ethics and regulatory rulebooks in the conduct of their duties. To excuse them on the basis of their imperfect understanding of what other people expect is for the law to demonstrate a sort of moral cowardice.

In essence, *Bryant* and *Twinsectra* are cases involving professionals who have been accused of dishonesty in breaches of their fiduciary duties and whom the courts have sought to excuse from liability on the basis that the effects of a finding of dishonesty on such a professional would be profoundly damaging to their careers, instead of recognising that professionals ought properly to be held to a higher standard or at least to the standards

---

207 [2009] 1 WLR 163.
208 [1982] QB 1053.

contained in any professional regulations which bind them; and by inquiring into evidence as to what the defendant must subjectively have believed in the context, as opposed to focusing solely on what an honest person would have done objectively in those circumstances.

This urge to protect professional people on account of their own moral weakness must stop. Leaving the criminal context aside for a moment, the question for private law is to identify what the law considers to be honest in the abstract (that is, objectively) and then to measure individual defendants up against that standard. One of the principal roles of law is to judge. Another role (of property law and contract law in particular) is to offer models to the citizenry by reference to which they can organise their communal activities. In either event, the role of the law is to judge which structures and activities are worthy of the support of law and which are not. Therefore, the law does not need to pander to the subjective standards of honesty and dishonesty of any individual defendant. Instead, the law stands in judgment over them. It is a matter for the criminal law to decide how squeamish it is about criminalising people who did not realise that ordinary decent people would have considered their behaviour to be dishonest, but there is no reason why anyone (solicitor or not) should escape liability to compensate a claimant under private law simply because they were similarly unconscious of the standards of the society around them. Ignorance of the law is generally considered to be no defence; so why should ignorance of the standards of honest conduct be a defence? This urge to require that the defendant must realise that what she was doing was contrary to social mores is weak-kneed liberalism of the most obvious kind. Liberalism is tolerant and open-minded; it is therefore weak when it is confronted by people who simply refuse to play the game, to recognise ordinary standards of common decency, and so forth. So, instead of condemning people who would be thought dishonest by the reasonable person, liberalism of this weak sort excuses them from liability if they had failed to notice what was evident to honest people and apologises for having troubled them. Our private law should condemn such people so as to protect those objective standards simply for the ethical imperative of preventing unconscionable benefit being taken from inappropriate behaviour and also *pour encourager les autres*.

20.2.8 Investment, risk-taking and dishonesty

Lord Nicholls expanded his discussion of 'dishonesty' to consider the taking of risk. Risk is expressly encompassed within the new test. Lord Nicholls held:

> All investment involves risk. Imprudence is not dishonesty, although imprudence may be carried recklessly to lengths which call into question the honesty of the person making the decision. This is especially so if the transaction serves another purpose in which that person has an interest of his own.[209]

Therefore, an investment advisor who is employed by the trust could be liable for 'dishonesty' if she advises the trust to take a risk which is considered by the court to have been a reckless risk. The thinking is that if X advises the trustees to take a risk which is objectively

209 *Royal Brunei Airlines v Tan* [1995] 2 AC 378, 387.

too great, then X could be considered to have been dishonest in giving that advice. Lord Nicholls also considered that if that advisor took a fee or had some other stake in the transaction, then the likelihood of being found to have been dishonest increases. The basis of liability is that a third party 'takes a risk that a clearly unauthorised transaction will not cause loss . . . If the risk materialises and causes loss, those who knowingly took the risk will be accountable accordingly'.[210] For these purposes it is said that 'fraud includes taking a risk to the prejudice of another's rights, which risk is known to be one which there is no right to take'.[211] Therefore, there is enormous potential liability in respect of advisors who advise trustees in any matter to do with investment or the treatment of their property.

There is a difference where there is doubt whether the risk is authorised or not. In situations where an investment advisor retained by the trustees is unsure whether or not an investment is encompassed by the investment powers of the trust, the issue arises whether or not the investment advisor is acting dishonestly. The question is then how to deal with matters of degree relating to the authority of trustees and third parties.

In Lord Nicholls's opinion, it will be obvious in most cases whether or not a proposed transaction would offend the normal standards of honest conduct. It is suggested that this does not help us towards an understanding of how far this new test for dishonesty extends. Similarly, it does not help us to understand how a test for dishonesty is necessarily more certain than a test based on unconscionability, as suggested by Lord Browne-Wilkinson in *Westdeutsche Landesbank Girozentrale v Islington LBC*.[212]

Lord Nicholls's position can be criticised on two levels. The first is that the test for 'dishonesty' relies upon an artificial rendering of the word 'dishonesty' which is not necessarily comprehensible to a third party or a trustee. The second is that it does not cover the situation where the investment decision being made is in itself risky. An investment decision taken to achieve the best return for the trust will necessarily involve a higher level of risk than an investment which restricts its exposure to a risk level and a rate of return which is below the market average. There is no obvious distinction here between a risky investment which is authorised and an equally risky investment which is probably unauthorised.[213]

Dishonesty therefore encompasses a level of risk which the court considers to be too great. Thus, an accessory may be liable where the risk taken was in furtherance of a contractual obligation to invest property and manage its level of risk. The court might consider that risk to be too great. Whereas the market might consider a particular investment to be standard practice, and even advisable in many circumstances, a court may nevertheless decide subsequently that the very fact that such an investment caused a large loss meant that the risk posed by that investment must have been too great. On the basis that it is the court's decision on the level of risk that counts, it is therefore difficult to counsel an investment advisor as to the approach to be taken to the investment of trust property.

It is not a failure to ascertain whether or not the investment is in breach of trust which is decisive of the matter, but rather whether or not the *level of risk* assumed is in breach of trust. His Lordship tells us that 'honesty is an objective standard'. Therefore, it is for the court to

210 *Ibid.*
211 *Ibid.*
212 [1996] AC 669.
213 See Alastair Hudson, *The Law of Finance*, Sweet & Maxwell, 2009, Ch 8.

measure the level of risk and, consequently, the honesty of the third party. The outcome would seem to depend upon 'the circumstances known to the third party at the time', which necessarily imports a subjective element. However, recklessness as to the ability of the trust to invest must similarly be a factor to be taken into account in deciding on the honesty of the third party investment manager.

It does appear that the range of matters brought within the ambit of dishonest assistance (dishonesty, recklessness, inappropriate risk-taking and fraud) points towards the creation of a general test of unconscionability, despite Lord Nicholls's express assertion that this was not the case. The example of an investment advisor who is 'dishonest' on this technical meaning, while only actually being reckless as to the form of the investment, could be described as acting unconscionably, given the nature of his client. The test for 'dishonesty' that covers such a context, to use Lord-Nicholls's own words, 'means something different' from the natural use of 'dishonesty'. A better approach, it is suggested, might be to admit that the test is really one of unconscionability, and thus to bring the issue back within the more formal ambit of constructive trusts as defined by Lord Browne-Wilkinson in *Westdeutsche Landesbank Girozentrale v Islington LBC*.[214] See the discussion in section 20.3.5 on a similar issue.

Procedural questions in relation to pleading dishonest assistance

There have been cases in which the courts have been prepared to accept that a claim for dishonest assistance may be made out even if imperfectly pleaded if the pleaded facts disclose a sufficient suggestion of dishonest assistance.[215]

20.2.9 The nature of the remedy

The defendant will be personally liable to account as a constructive trustee to the benefici-aries for any loss suffered by the breach of trust. This liability is based on the defendant's dishonesty in assisting the breach of trust. It is based on compensating the beneficiaries' loss. It is not concerned to subtract an unjust enrichment from the defendant. The nature of the remedy is considered in further detail below in section 20.7.1.

An argument that there is a proprietary claim arising from dishonest assistance

The remedy for dishonest assistance has been expressed by some judges as being either compensation for a loss caused as a result of a breach of trust or as a requiring an account for any profit made by the defendant.[216] This is a confusion into which we must not allow ourselves to fall. A remedy based on an account of profits will only ever be applicable in cases in which profits have been made; otherwise the remedy of personal liability to account as a dishonest assistant is predicated on the need to compensate a beneficiary for a loss

---

214 *Ibid.*

215 *Caring Together Ltd (in liquidation) v Bauso* [2006] EWHC 2345 (Ch), Briggs J.

216 *Yugraneft v Abramovich* [2008] EWHC 2613 (Comm), [2008] All ER (Comm) 299, para [392], *per* Clarke J: citing *Fyffes Group v Templeman* [2000] Lloyd's Rep 643; *Ultraframe (UK) Ltd v Fielding* [2005] EWHC 1638.

resulting from a breach of trust, and so is not predicated on the defendant having earned profits. If the defendant was a fiduciary and if she earned unauthorised profits, then she would be required to account for those profits by holding those profits on constructive trust, as was discussed in Chapter 12.[217] This is a proprietary claim. By contrast, claims for dishonest assistance in a breach of trust are focused on a personal liability to account for the loss suffered by the beneficiaries as a result of the breach of trust with which the defendant assisted dishonestly. It may be that the same set of facts may give rise both to a remedy for dishonest assistance and to a proprietary constructive trust based on the unconscionable action of the defendant, demonstrated by her dishonesty, in relation to the trust property. This proprietary constructive trust could be based either on an action in tracing (considered in Chapter 19) or on the imposition of a constructive trust further to the general principle in *Westdeutsche Landesbank v Islington*[218] against unconscionable misuse of property or on the basis that the defendant became trustee *de son tort*: but that constructive trust will only arise if the defendant still has some identifiable property in her possession. The remedy of personal liability to account as a result of dishonest assistance is a personal liability to account for the loss caused by the breach of trust (that is, a liability to compensate the beneficiaries for their loss flowing from the breach of trust). Therefore, the remedy stemming from dishonest assistance is a personal claim, and therefore any proprietary claim must be based on the principles set out under those other doctrines in other chapters of this book.

So, while dishonest assistance clearly does give rise to a purely personal remedy, the jargon of 'constructive trusteeship' causes confusion for some people. In the decision of Rimer J in *Sinclair Investment Holdings SA v Versailles Trade Finance Ltd (No 3)*[219] issues arose as to the precise nature of dishonest assistance as the result of a complex fraud. In essence, the claimant was induced to investment money in V Ltd as a result of fraudulent misrepresentations made by Cushnie and others as the directing minds of V Ltd to people who advised the claimant. V Ltd was a company which was part of the Versailles group of companies comprising many of the defendant companies. Fraud was found on the part of Cushnie and others in earlier litigation.[220] The issue in this instance was whether or not the claimant could establish a proprietary right over a house in Kensington acquired by the defendants' group of companies which was occupied by Cushnie. Cushnie was alleged to have been a dishonest assistant in a breach of fiduciary obligations by V Ltd in yet more, earlier litigation (*Sinclair v Versailles Trade Finance Ltd (No 2)*).[221] In the current litigation, two points were found. First, on the facts, Cushnie did not ever form a fiduciary relationship with the claimant because he did not deal directly with or for the claimant (but that is not a key issue here). Secondly, (which is an issue here) the claimant sought to argue that if Cushnie was a dishonest assistant then he ought to be required to hold property bought for him by companies in the Versailles group of companies on constructive trust for the claimant. It was held by Rimer J that being a dishonest assistant meant that one was responsible for paying 'equitable compensation' to the claimant beneficiary of the fiduciary arrangement,

---

217   Section 12.5.
218   [1996] AC 669.
219   [2007] EWHC 915 (Ch), 10 ITELR 58.
220   On the course of the litigation, see [2005] EWCA Civ 722, [2006] 1 BCLC 60 where the Court of Appeal refused to strike this case out as disclosing no cause of action with a reasonable prospect of success.
221   [2006] EWHC 573 (Ch).

but that did not mean that one became a trustee of any property for the claimant. The purpose of the remedy of account as a constructive trustee for dishonest assistance is only to make the dishonest assistant personally liable to compensate the beneficiaries for the loss which they have suffered as a result of the breach of trust.

There may be an argument for saying that, if the defendant had the traceable proceeds of trust property in her possession, then she should be liable to hold that property on constructive trust for the claimant. However, importantly, a dishonest assistant is not required to have trust property nor its traceable proceeds in her possession at any stage to be liable as a dishonest assistant: rather, the liability is based entirely on the wrong of assisting the breach of trust. So dishonest assistance is not a proprietary remedy.

When it is said that one is a 'constructive trustee' that does not mean that one becomes a trustee of any property; instead it means that one is treated as being liable to the beneficiaries to account to the beneficiaries for the loss suffered by the trust, just as if one were an express trustee liable under *Target Holdings v Redferns*. Therefore, one is not construed to be the trustee of identified property; rather, one is construed to be personally liable in the same way that an express trustee would have been personally liable for the breach. Hence Edmund-Davies LJ's view that this is really just 'a formula for equitable relief' (that is, this is a justification for imposing liability on a person who assists the breach of trust). Therefore, we could say that it is an actionable wrong in equity for a person to assist a breach of trust.

20.3 UNCONSCIONABLE RECEIPT

Where a person receives trust property in the knowledge that that property has been passed to her in breach of trust, the recipient will be personally liable to account to the trust for the value of the property passed away. A person is taken to have received property when it comes under her possession or control. The test for whether or not a defendant had the requisite knowledge requires that the defendant had one of the following three states of mind: actual knowledge of the breach of trust, or a wilful failure to make the inquiries which an honest and reasonable person would have made, or having wilfully shut her eyes to the obvious. A recent line of cases has required that the defendant will be liable for knowing receipt only if she has received property unconscionably, and therefore the detailed test of knowledge is being qualified. There was also a line of cases which suggested that the test should be a test of dishonesty. It is a defence to demonstrate the receipt was authorised under the terms of the trust, or that the recipient has lawfully changed his position in reliance on the receipt of the property.

20.3.1 Introduction

The second category of personal liability to account concerns strangers who receive some trust property when it has been transferred away in breach of trust. This has been described as a receipt-based claim analogous to equitable compensation.[222] This doctrine was referred to as 'knowing receipt' throughout the 20th century, although a line of cases in the 21st century has inserted a requirement that a defendant's behaviour in relation to the receipt of

---

222 *El Ajou v Dollar Land Holdings* [1993] 3 All ER 717; appealed [1994] 2 All ER 685.

property must have been 'unconscionable' into the doctrine, and in consequence the doctrine is referred to here as 'unconscionable receipt'. Such unconscionability, as will emerge from the discussion to follow, will involve knowledge of the circumstances surrounding the breach of trust. In essence, the doctrine operates as follows:

> Where a person knowingly receives trust property which has been transferred away from the trust or otherwise misapplied, and where that person has acted unconscionably, then that person will incur a personal liability to account as a constructive trustee to the beneficiaries of that trust for the amount of their loss.[223]

As Morritt V-C put it: '[a] claim for "knowing receipt" is parasitic on a claim for breach of trust in the sense that it cannot exist in the absence of the breach of trust from which the receipt originated.'[224] Once a breach of trust has been proved, it is incumbent on the claimant to demonstrate that the defendant had the requisite knowledge[225] and that the defendant acted unconscionably.[226] Whether or not there has been receipt will generally be decided in accordance with the rules for tracing claims.[227]

The current case law on unconscionable receipt is set out in the discussion to follow in the following structure. First, a consideration of the competing authorities on what constitutes 'receipt'. Second, because the concept of unconscionable receipt still includes a concept of 'knowledge', there is an examination of the authorities on knowledge. Third, an analysis of the change effected to the law by the introduction of the concept of 'unconscionability'. Fourth, a consideration of a line of cases applying a test of dishonesty to the receipt-based claim, and an explanation of how those cases correlate with the concept of unconscionable receipt.

20.3.2 The nature of 'receipt'

The first question is what actions will constitute 'receipt' under this category. In the decision of Millett J in *Agip v Jackson*,[228] it was held that: '. . . there is receipt of trust property when a company's funds are misapplied by any person whose fiduciary position gave him control of them or enabled him to misapply them.' Therefore, a person receives trust property if she takes that property under her control or takes it into her possession. The cases are not precise in defining the manner in which the property must be 'received'. Seemingly, it is enough that the property passes through the stranger's hands, even if the stranger never had the rights of an equitable or common law owner of the property. Lack of proof of receipt will prevent a claim for knowing receipt being commenced, such a claim will be struck out.[229] For example, a bank through which payments are made appears to be capable of being accountable for

---

223 This summary is the author's own. It is culled from the principles set out in the cases to follow in the text.
224 *Charter plc and another v City Index Ltd* [2006] EWHC 2508 (Ch), [2007] 1 WLR 26.
225 *Polly Peck International v Nadir (No 2)* [1992] 4 All ER 769, 777, *per* Scott LJ.
226 *Charter plc and another v City Index Ltd* [2006] EWHC 2508 (Ch), [2007] 1 WLR 26.
227 *El Ajou v Dollar Land Holdings* [1993] BCLC 735, [1993] 3 All ER 717 and also in Chapter 19.
228 *Agip v Jackson* [1990] Ch 265, 286, *per* Millett J, [1991] Ch 547, CA.
229 *Fraser v Oystertec* [2004] EWHC 2225 (Ch); see also *Compagnie Noga D'Importation et D'Exportation v Abacha* [2004] EWHC 2601 (Comm).

knowing receipt of money paid in breach of trust.[230] Once money is paid into a person's bank account, then the owner of that bank account will have received that money; or alternatively the bank may be considered to 'own' the money, subject to a debt in that amount owed to the account holder.[231] Equally, using another person's property to pay off one's own debts constitutes receipt of that other person's property.[232] More evidently, where consignments of hazelnuts, which had been appropriated in breach of trust, were delivered to the defendant and placed knowingly in storage by the defendant, that would constitute receipt.[233]

Issues with the notion of 'receipt'

A much cited test for what constitutes 'receipt' in this context is that set out by Hoffmann LJ in *El Ajou v Dollar Land Holdings*:[234] but it was in different terms from that set out by Millett J (above) because it included taking trust property or the traceable proceeds of the trusts property into one's possession or under one's control:

> For this purpose the plaintiff must show, first, a disposal of his assets in breach of fiduciary duty; secondly, the beneficial receipt by the defendant of assets which are traceable as representing the assets of the plaintiff; and thirdly, knowledge on the part of the defendant that the assets he received are traceable to a breach of fiduciary duty.

A number of problems arise with this formulation. First, the circumstances of the receipt do not require 'a disposal of his assets in breach of fiduciary duty' but rather there must have been property (not necessarily an 'asset'[235]) passed away in breach of fiduciary duty. The action need not be brought by the *owner* of the asset, for example the action may be brought by a beneficiary under an open-ended discretionary trust or by a shareholder bringing a derivative action on behalf of a company may be the plaintiff: neither would necessarily be said to be acting in relation to 'his assets' as an owner because the company owns its own property and the object of an open-ended discretionary trust may not have any proprietary rights until property is appointed to her. Secondly, interestingly, on Hoffmann LJ's formulation the defendant does not need to receive the original trust property but rather may receive other property provided that that other property constitutes the traceable proceeds of trust property. So, for example, if a painting was held on trust and that painting was sold in breach of trust, then receipt of the sale proceeds would constitute receipt of the traceable proceeds of the breach of trust because that money was derived from the original painting. Thirdly, it is problematic that there must be 'beneficial receipt' of the property because that would be to suggest that the recipient must become the owner of the property in equity; whereas the formulation by Millett J (quoted at the start of this section) is founded on the basis that the

230 *Polly Peck International v Nadir (No 2)* [1992] 3 All ER 769.
231 *Ibid*; *Versailles Trade Finance Ltd v Artagent Ltd* [2004] All ER (D) 318.
232 *MT Realisations Ltd v Digital Equipment Co Ltd* [2003] 2 BCLC 117.
233 *Bank of Tokyo-Mitsubishi Ltd v Baskan Gida* [2004] EWHC 945 (Ch), [2004] 2 Lloyd's Rep 395.
234 [1994] 2 All ER 685, 700; cited with approval in *Charter plc v City Index Ltd* [2007] 1 WLR 26, 31, *per* Morritt C.
235 One can, after all, own a tax loss, or own a chose in action which is currently generating a loss but which may yet show a profit (as with an interest rate swap).

defendant need only take the property under her control or into her possession. Acquiring control or possession or property does not make a person the owner of that property necessarily. This latter approach has the advantage of broadening the scope of liability to include people who knowingly pass property between themselves but in a way that ensures that they never acquire property rights in it.

Thus, it is suggested, Millett J correctly extended the ambit of liability to any person who commits the equitable wrong of taking property into her possession, for example as part of a money laundering scheme where property is put beyond the reach of its true beneficial owner. It is only under Millett J's formulation that *all* persons 'knowingly' and 'unconscionably' involved in the breach of trust can be held liable for knowing receipt. Strictly, if property were stolen from a trust and passed to the defendant, then the defendant could not become *beneficially* entitled to the stolen trust property[236] and so on Hoffmann LJ's formulation could never strictly found liability for knowing receipt, which cannot be correct.

In *Uzinterimpex JSC v Standard Bank plc*[237] the authorities relating to knowing receipt of money paid through a bank account were considered. On the facts it was held that when money was paid into an account, the entity holding that account had no knowledge of any breach of duty which would have made it unconscionable to deal with that money in accordance with the terms of its contractual obligations and therefore that it was not liable to account for knowing receipt. It was important to know whether or not the defendant had received the property. One key distinction which was made on those facts was whether or not the person holding the account was acting merely as an agent for others (that is, that it was acting in a 'ministerial capacity') or whether it had received the property in a beneficial capacity: it was held that holding the property simply as an agent would have suggested that the defendant ought not to be liable for knowing receipt because there would not have been appropriate receipt of the property because the receipt was only as agent.[238] However, it is suggested that if the test for receipt is simply whether or not property has passed into the defendant's possession or control then it ought not to matter whether or not the defendant acquired beneficial rights in that money or took it under his control merely as an agent: instead, the focus should be on whether or not that receipt was coupled with the appropriate knowledge of the breach of trust.

20.3.3 The nature of 'unconscionability' in unconscionable receipt

The concept of unconscionability

The evolution of the doctrine of 'knowing receipt' into a doctrine predicated more generally on 'unconscionability' emerged from the decision of the Court of Appeal in *Bank of Credit and Commerce International v Akindele*[239] in which it was held that, for a defendant to be liable in unconscionable receipt, it is enough to establish that he knew or ought to have known of the breach of trust or fiduciary duty. The model for unconscionability in this

---

236 Because that property would be treated as being held on constructive trust (and thus beneficially) for the victim of the crime: *Westdeutsche Landesbank v Islington* [1996] AC 669.
237 [2008] EWCA Civ 819, [2008] Bus LR 1762, para [37] *et seq.*, *per* Moore-Bick LJ.
238 *Ibid* at [39]. See Bryan, 1998.
239 [2000] 4 All ER 221.

context, it is suggested, can be found most clearly in the judgment of Nourse LJ in *Bank of Credit and Commerce International v Akindele*[240] when his lordship held as follows, doubting the efficacy of a categorisation based on knowledge:

> What then, in the context of knowing receipt, is the purpose to be served by a categorisation of knowledge? It can only be to enable the court to determine whether, in the words of Buckley LJ in *Belmont Finance Corpn Ltd v Williams Furniture Ltd (No 2)*,[241] the recipient can 'conscientiously retain [the] funds against the company' or, in the words of Sir Robert Megarry V-C in *In re Montagu's Settlement Trusts*,[242] '[the recipient's] conscience is sufficiently affected for it to be right to bind him by the obligations of a constructive trustee'. But, if that is the purpose, there is no need for categorisation. All that is necessary is that the recipient's state of knowledge should be such as to make it unconscionable for him to retain the benefit of the receipt.
>
> For these reasons I have come to the view that, just as there is now a single test of dishonesty for knowing assistance, so ought there to be a single test of knowledge for knowing receipt. The recipient's state of knowledge must be such as to make it unconscionable for him to retain the benefit of the receipt. A test in that form, though it cannot, any more than any other, avoid difficulties of application, ought to avoid those of definition and allocation to which the previous categorisations have led. Moreover, it should better enable the courts to give commonsense decisions in the commercial context in which claims in knowing receipt are now frequently made . . .[243]

Therefore, the defendant is taken to have acted unconscionably if his knowledge was such that (to borrow from Nourse LJ) it would be unconscionable for him to retain any benefit taken from the receipt of the property, or (preferably, it is suggested) it would cause the beneficiaries uncompensated loss without the defendant having a good defence or an absence of knowledge.[244] The significance of this model is the approximation of 'unconscionability' to the pre-existing test of 'knowledge'. The ostensible uncertainty in the word 'unconscionability' is removed by equating that word to the clear test of knowledge to emerge after *Re Montagu's Settlements*, a case which is considered in detail below. What remains unclear, however, are those categories of things which may be considered to be 'unconscionable' but which are beyond the test of knowledge.

The effect of using a concept of 'unconscionability' in the cases has been a likelihood that the defendant will escape liability. So, in *Bank of Credit and Commerce International v Akindele*[245] itself Chief Akindele, the defendant, was a client of a bank, BCCI, which later collapsed amid systematic fraud among many of that bank's officers.[246] The defendant had

---

240 [2001] Ch 437, [2000] 4 All ER 221.
241 [1980] 1 All ER 393, 405.
242 [1987] Ch 264, 273.
243 [2001] Ch 437, 455.
244 It is suggested that Nourse LJ's formulation presents the difficulty that it focuses on the defendant having taken a benefit and thereby strays too close to rendering this doctrine a restitutionary doctrine concerned with the reversal of an unjust enrichment, whereas the purpose of this doctrine is to compensate the beneficiaries for any loss occasioned by a breach of trust.
245 [2000] 4 All ER 221.
246 See, for example, Adams and Frantz, 1992.

effectively been promised a very high return on his investments by the bank's officers and those bank officers sought in breach of their fiduciary duties to the bank to procure the defendant that return on his investments even though his investments had not performed nearly so well. The question at issue was whether in relation to a series of payments to the defendant he had at any time had knowledge of the breaches of fiduciary duty involved. It was found on the facts that the defendant had heard rumours about goings-on inside the bank. Under the test for knowledge set out in *Baden v Société Générale*, it might have been enough to demonstrate knowledge to show that the defendant had had knowledge of factors which would have put an honest and reasonable man on inquiry as to the propriety of the actions of the bank's officers. However, Nourse LJ held that in general terms there was nothing on the facts to demonstrate that the defendant had acted unconscionably in general terms and therefore it was held that the defendant would not be liable for knowing receipt. Thus, even though he would have been treated as having had constructive knowledge of the fraud, because he was not found to have acted unconscionably he was not liable under the receipt claim. The effect of the notion of unconscionability was to permit the court to reach the conclusion which it wanted to reach on the facts: that is, to absolve the defendant of liability even when a stricter test may have made him liable to account to the bank because he had had knowledge of factors which might have put a reasonable person on inquiry.

Carnwath LJ took a similar approach to Nourse LJ in the Court of Appeal in *Charter plc v City Index Ltd*.[247] Carnwath LJ (with whom Mummery LJ agreed) took the view that the test of unconscionability in *BCCI v Akindele* is now to form part of the appropriate test in cases of receipt of property in breach of trust.[248] As his lordship put it:

> liability for 'knowing receipt' depends on the defendant having sufficient knowledge of the circumstances of the payment to make it 'unconscionable' for him to retain the benefit or pay it away for his own purposes.

The notion of unconscionability is therefore linked to the requirement of knowledge. On this model of the test, it is not that the defendant has acted unconscionably in general terms which imposes liability, but rather it is a question as to whether or not the defendant had such knowledge of the circumstances so as to make his retention or dealing with the property unconscionable. Thus, having knowledge which would satisfy the test for constructive knowledge that the property was passed to him in breach of trust, as in *Re Montagu*, would also constitute an unconscionable circumstance for the defendant to have received that property.[249] However, Carnwath LJ focused on the benefit being retained by the defendant. If the benefit had been retained, then there would *prima facie* be a tracing claim available into that benefit. That is not the purpose of liability for knowing (or, unconscionable) receipt: liability for unconscionable receipt is predicated on the defendant being liable to compensate the

---

247 *Charter plc v City Index Ltd* [2008] 2 WLR 950.
248 *Ibid*, [31].
249 For example, where there has been fraud in the movement of money from an account held for the benefit of the claimant to an account held by the defendant then there will have been an unconscionable receipt of that money by the defendant, as in *Papamichael v National Westminster Bank plc* [2003] EWHC 164 (Comm), [2003] 1 Lloyd's Rep 341.

beneficiaries for any loss occasioned to the trust by the breach of trust, as a result of his unconscionability.

The court in *Criterion Properties Ltd v Stratford UK Properties*[250] applied the unconscionability test in circumstances relating particularly to ostensible authority in relation to the capacity of a company to enter into transactions including a joint venture agreement seeking to fend off a takeover. In *Criterion Properties plc v Stratford UK Properties LLC*[251] the Court of Appeal approved the flexibility of the notion of 'conscionability'[252] in relation to a claim brought on behalf of shareholders to the effect that the directors of a company had knowingly committed breaches of duty by entering into arrangements which would prevent a takeover of that company by third parties. The Court of Appeal in *Niru Battery Manufacturing Co v Milestone Trading Ltd*[253] expressed its support for the test of unconscionability.[254]

The organisation of this discussion

The foregoing has established two things. First, that the concept at play here is 'unconscionable' receipt and not simply 'knowing' receipt; and, secondly, the concept of 'knowledge' in the cases remains significant as the primary concept to be identified in fixing a defendant with liability for unconscionable receipt, prior to inquiring whether or not she also acted unconscionably.

20.3.4 The nature of 'knowledge'

The fundamental question is what constitutes 'knowledge' in this context. As Lord Browne-Wilkinson held in *Westdeutsche Landesbank Girozentrale v Islington LBC*:

> If X has the necessary degree of knowledge, X may himself become a constructive trustee for B on the basis of knowing receipt.[255] But unless he has the requisite degree of knowledge he is not personally liable to account as trustee.[256] Therefore, innocent receipt of property by X subject to an existing equitable interest does not by itself make X a trustee despite the severance of the legal and equitable titles.[257]

It is important to note that the test in this area is one of 'knowledge' and not 'notice'. Rather than depend on the imputed notice as used in conveyancing law or in relation to undue

---

250   [2003] 1 WLR 218, CA.
251   [2003] 2 BCLC 129. Carnwath LJ, having been the trial judge in *BBCI v Akindele*, acknowledged that the Court of Appeal had overruled his own preference for a test of dishonesty at first instance: [2001] Ch 437, 455, *per* Nourse LJ.
252   [2003] 2 BCLC 129, [33].
253   [2004] 2 WLR 1415, [2004] 1 Lloyd's Rep 344, para 188, *per* Sedley LJ.
254   The following High Court cases have also followed *Akindele: Independent Trustee Services Ltd v GP Noble Trustees Ltd* [2010] EWHC 1653 (Ch), *per* Peter Smith J; *Law Society of England and Wales v Habitable Cocnepts Ltd* [2010] EWHC 1449 (Ch), *per* Norris J.
255   [1996] AC 669.
256   *Re Diplock* [1948] Ch 465 and *Re Montagu's Settlement Trusts* [1987] Ch 264.
257   [1996] 2 All ER 961, 990.

influence, the courts have focused instead on whether or not the defendant has knowledge of material factors. If the defendant is to be fixed with personal liability to account, then it is thought that the defendant must be demonstrated to *know* those factors which will attach liability to her. The further question, however, is what a person can be taken to 'know'. The most significant judicial explanation of the various categories of knowledge was that set out by Peter Gibson J in *Baden v Société Générale*,[258] as follows:

(a) actual knowledge;[259]
(b) wilfully shutting one's eyes to the obvious;[260]
(c) wilfully and recklessly failing to make inquiries which an honest person would have made;
(d) knowledge of circumstances which would indicate the facts to an honest and reasonable man;
(e) knowledge of circumstances which would put an honest and reasonable man on inquiry.

The fourth and fifth categories are the most interesting, given that they are potentially the broadest. The first three categories of knowledge are taken to indicate forms of actual knowledge of the circumstances.[261] The actual knowledge categories encompass situations in which the defendant knew the material facts, regardless of whether or not she tried to ignore them. The last two, it is suggested, are really indicators of constructive knowledge.[262] However, these five categories were whittled down to the first three for the purposes of liability for knowing receipt in *Re Montagu*.[263] The three are thus as follows:

(a) actual knowledge;
(b) wilfully shutting one's eyes to the obvious;
(c) wilfully and recklessly failing to make inquiries which an honest person would have made.

The reason for this restriction was that they included a necessary element of wilful or deliberate behaviour on the part of the defendant who cannot be proved to have actually

---

258 *Baden v Société Générale pour Favoriser le Developpement du Commerce et de l'Industrie en France SA* [1993] 1 WLR 509. For a discussion of categories of knowledge relating to commercial law, see *Manifest Shipping Co Ltd v Uni-Polaris Shipping Co Ltd* [2003] 1 AC 469; *Seb Trygg Holding Aktiebolag v Manches* [2005] EWHC 35 (Comm), para [128] *et seq.*

259 Where there is proof that a defendant actually knew, then that will be sufficient to make out the claim: *Bank of Tokyo-Mitsubishi Ltd v Baskan Gida* [2004] EWHC 945 (Ch), [2004] 2 Lloyd's Rep 395. In *Dyson Technology Ltd v Curtis* [2010] EWHC 3289 (Ch) it was held that because the amounts which were paid into the defendant's hands were so large she would be considered to have had actual knowledge of the breach of fiduciary duty which underpinned those payments. There was also reference there to 'personal and proprietary claims against the second defendant in knowing receipt', which cannot be correct because such a claim is purely personal in nature, at [190].

260 See *Manifest Shipping Co Ltd v Uni-Polaris Shipping Co Ltd* [2003] 1 AC 469.

261 Cf *White v White* [2001] 1 WLR 481 – 'knowledge' in relation to knowledge as to whether or not a vehicle was uninsured.

262 *Agip v Jackson* [1989] 3 WLR 1367, 1389, *per* Millett J.

263 [1987] Ch 264.

known of the facts which were alleged.[264] As considered below in relation to *Re Montagu* itself, Megarry VC preferred to exclude the fourth and fifth categories because they did not require wilfulness on the part of the defendant, and therefore if a defendant claimed to have forgotten the knowledge which previously she had had, then she would be held liable for knowing receipt. Megarry VC preferred to exclude such liability. It is tempting then to approach this test of knowledge as creating rigid categories, although, as Scott LJ held in *Polly Peck*, these categories are not to be taken as rigid rules and 'one category may merge imperceptibly into another'.[265] These categories were rendered slightly more memorably by counsel in *Baden* as 'actual knowledge', 'Nelsonian knowledge',[266] and 'naughty knowledge' respectively.[267]

The issue is stated most clearly in Lord Selborne LC's *dicta* in *Barnes v Addy*[268] distinguishing between 'knowing receipt' and 'knowing assistance'. This is rendered as the difference between two things: first, the liability of a person as 'recipient' of trust property or its traceable proceeds constitutes knowing receipt; whereas, secondly, the liability of a person as 'accessory' to a trustee's breach of trust constitutes dishonest assistance.

20.3.5 The acid test for knowledge – 'should you have been suspicious?'

The acid test

The third category of knowledge in *Baden v Société Générale* quoted above is difficult to define because it deals with situations in which the defendant could have been expected to have asked more questions or investigated further the source of the property. This form of constructive knowledge is best explained by Scott LJ in *Polly Peck International v Nadir* (No 2),[269] where he held that the acid test in such situations was whether or not the recipient of the property 'ought to have been suspicious' that the property had been acquired in breach of trust.[270] This rule of thumb, it is suggested, gives a clear indication of the manner in which judges will approach the witnesses in cases of this sort: if it is difficult to prove one way or another what the recipient knew or did not know, what the recipient had asked or ought to have asked, the trial judge will instead ask herself 'ought the recipient to have been suspicious as to the source of this property?'.[271]

---

264 See *Imobilari Pty Ltd v Opes Prime Stockbroking Ltd* [2008] FCA 1920, (2009) 252 ALR 41, at [27]: 'knowledge of facts that would put an honest and reasonable person on notice (but not merely inquiry) of a real and not remote risk that the transfer was in breach of trust or fiduciary duty or involved the misapplication of trust property'.

265 *Polly Peck International v Nadir (No 2)* [1992] 3 All ER 769.

266 Although see *Twinsectra Ltd v Yardley* [2002] 2 All ER 377, 383, *per* Lord Hoffmann, criticising the image which this nomenclature summons up of Admiral Nelson at Copenhagen.

267 Hayton, 1995:2, 412.

268 (1874) 9 Ch App 244, 251–52.

269 [1992] 4 All ER 769.

270 *Eagle Trust v SBC (No 2)* [1996] 1 BCLC 121; *Hillsdown plc v Pensions Ombudsman* [1997] 1 All ER 862.

271 In this sense the definition of knowledge in knowing receipt cases appears to be slightly broader than in dishonest assistance cases. In the latter, as considered below, the court has tended to concentrate on the categories of actual knowledge.

Similarly, in *Macmillan v Bishopsgate*,[272] it was held that account officers were not detectives and therefore not to be fixed with knowledge which they could only possibly have had if they had carried out extensive investigations, in a situation in which they had no reason to believe that there had been any impropriety in passing money from companies controlled by the late Robert Maxwell. It was held that they were 'entitled to believe that they were dealing with honest men' unless they had some suspicion raised in their minds to the contrary. In *El Ajou v Dollar Land Holdings*,[273] Millett J held that liability for knowing receipt would attach 'in a situation in which any honest and reasonable man would have made inquiry'. In short, the issue is whether or not the circumstances are such as to require a person to be suspicious, so that their conscience would encourage them to make inquiries. If there is nothing about the circumstances to make the recipient suspicious, then they will not be held to have had knowledge under the third category of knowledge. Where there is something about the context which should make the recipient suspicious, then the recipient should make reasonable inquiries; if those inquiries produce no information or if the recipient is deceived when making those inquiries, then she will be absolved from having knowledge of those circumstances. Therefore, recipients of property such as banks should make reasonable inquiries.

Knowledge may depend on context

The case of *Polly Peck v Nadir (No 2)*[274] is a useful illustration of the principle in action. The facts related to the actions of Asil Nadir in respect of the insolvency of the Polly Peck group of companies. This particular litigation referred to an action brought by the administrators of the plaintiff company against a bank controlled by Nadir, IBK, and the Central Bank of Northern Cyprus. It was alleged that Nadir had been responsible for the misapplication of substantial funds in sterling which were the assets of the plaintiff company. It was claimed that the Central Bank had exchanged the sterling amounts for Turkish lire either with actual knowledge of fraud on the plaintiff company or in circumstances in which the Central Bank ought to have been put on inquiry as to the source of those funds. The plaintiff claimed against the Central Bank personal liability to account as a constructive trustee as a result of knowing receipt of the sterling amounts which had been exchanged for lire.

The Central Bank contended that it had no such knowledge, actual or constructive, of the source of the funds. It argued that large amounts of money passed through its systems as a central bank on a regular basis, and that as such it should not be on notice as to title in every large amount. The Court of Appeal held that there was no requirement to prove a fraudulent misapplication of funds to found a claim on knowing receipt. It was enough to demonstrate that the recipient had the requisite knowledge both that the funds were trust funds and that they were being misapplied. On the facts of this case, it was held that the simple fact that the plaintiff company was exchanging amounts of money between sterling and lire via IBK was not enough to have put the Central Bank on suspicion that there had been a breach of trust.

In deciding whether or not the Central Bank ought to have been suspicious, Scott LJ preferred to approach the matter from the point of view of the 'honest and reasonable

---

272 [1996] 1 WLR 387. See also *United Mizrahi Bank Ltd v Doherty* [1998] 1 WLR 435; *Bank of Scotland v A Ltd* (2001) *The Times*, 6 February.
273 *El Ajou v Dollar Land Holdings* [1993] 3 All ER 717, appealed [1994] 2 All ER 685.
274 [1992] 4 All ER 769.

banker',[275] although he did express some reservations that this was not necessarily the only test.[276] It does appear, however, that the reasonableness of the recipient's belief falls to be judged from the perspective of the recipient itself. On the facts, it was held that there was no reason for suspicion because large amounts of money passed through the Central Bank's accounts regularly, and there was nothing at the time of this transaction to cause the bank to be suspicious of this particular transaction.

Knowledge is subjective and therefore knowledge can be forgotten

The tests of knowledge have been demonstrated to have been subjective in the decision of Megarry VC in *Re Montagu's Settlement*,[277] in which the 10th Duke of Manchester was a life tenant beneficiary under a settlement created by the 9th Duke. On the terms of the settlement, the trustees considered themselves to have a power to appoint chattels to the 10th Duke, which meant that the trustees considered that they were able to transfer absolute title in those items of property to the 10th Duke rather than holding them on trust during his life and then for his successor in title after his death. Thus, it was in breach of trust that the 10th Duke and the trustees lapsed into the habit of treating all of the valuable chattels held on trust as belonging absolutely beneficially to the 10th Duke. The Duke took a variety of chattels including a very valuable portrait by the Dutch master Van Dyck and an historic antique in the form of a trunk belonging to Katherine of Aragon. Auctions of trust property took place at the family's castle and at the London auctioneers Christie's. After the 10th Duke's death, the issue arose whether or not the 10th Duke's estate should have been held liable for knowing receipt of these chattels in breach of trust.

Megarry VC took the view that there had been 'an honest muddle' in this case. It was found as a fact that the 10th Duke had undoubtedly had actual knowledge of the terms of the trust at one stage in part because explicit references were made to the relevant provisions of the settlement in correspondence between the parties. Nevertheless, his Lordship accepted that the Duke might have forgotten the detailed terms of the settlement over time. Consequently, it was held that a defendant does not have the requisite knowledge on which to base a claim for knowing receipt if the defendant has genuinely forgotten the relevant factors.[278] Because the three categories of knowledge applied in *Re Montagu* were all predicated on wilful behaviour or actual knowledge, having forgotten information would absolve a person from having had knowledge of that information at the material time.

The counter-argument was made that the solicitors knew the terms of the settlement throughout and that the Duke should be imputed with the knowledge of his solicitors. However, Megarry VC held, in support of the idea that one should be liable for knowing receipt only if one had knowledge of the relevant factor, that the knowledge of a trustee-solicitor or other agent should not be imputed to the defendant. That is, you do not 'know' something simply because your agent knows it. Thus, the distinction is drawn with the

---

275 [1992] 4 All ER 769, 778–80; *Finers v Miro* [1991] 1 WLR 35.
276 *Ibid*, 778.
277 [1987] Ch 264.
278 *Re Montagu* was followed on the question of forgetting negativing knowledge in *MCP Pension Trustees Ltd v AON Pension Trustees Ltd* [2010] EWCA Civ 377, [2011] 1 All ER (Comm) 228, at [14], *per* Elias LJ.

doctrine of notice under which notice can be imputed from agent to principal.[279] Therefore, while the Duke had forgotten the terms of the trust, he was not to be imputed with his lawyers' knowledge that for him to treat the property as his own personal property would have been in breach of trust.

The categories of knowledge set out in *Baden v Société Générale* were five, including failure to make the inquiries which an honest person would have made without the need that failure to make those inquiries had been wilful. If the defendant was not required to have acted wilfully or intentionally, then it would be easier to fix the defendant with knowledge than in circumstances in which the claimant was required to prove that the defendant had acted intentionally in failing to make reasonable inquiries as to the source of the property which he had received. Thus, Megarry VC narrowed the scope of the knowledge test to the first three categories of knowledge set out in *Baden v Société Générale*, thus incorporating acts which the defendant conducted wilfully or deliberately, or facts of which he had actual knowledge. Consequently, no liability for knowing receipt attached to the 10th Duke nor to his estate.

Misuse of confidential information and trust property

In a different case, the question arose whether or not misuse of confidential information could lead to knowing receipt. In *Satnam Investments Ltd v Dunlop Heywood*,[280] Satnam's agents (DH) had passed on confidential information to the claimant's business rival, Morbaine. Morbaine then relied upon this information in acquiring a development site which Satnam had wanted to buy. The Court of Appeal rejected an argument that Morbaine held the site on constructive trust for Satnam. It was argued, *inter alia*, that Morbaine had been the recipient of trust property in that, it was said, the confidential information itself should have been deemed to have been property of the trust. Nourse LJ held:

> Clearly, DH and Mr Murray can be regarded as trustees of the information and, clearly, Morbaine can be regarded as having been a knowing recipient of it. However, even assuming, first, that confidential information can be treated as property for this purpose and, secondly, that but for the disclosure of the information Morbaine would not have acquired the Brewery Street site, we find it impossible, in knowing receipt, to hold that there was a sufficient basis for subjecting the Brewery Street site to the constructive trust for which Satnam contends. The information cannot be traced into the site and there is no other sufficient nexus between the two.

The problem which the court encountered here was in interpreting this transmission of confidential information as being causally linked to Morbaine's subsequent acquisition of the development site which Satnam had wanted to acquire itself.[281] The problem with this approach is that, if Morbaine acted knowing of Satnam's intentions and knowing that the

---

279   See Chapter 29 on the doctrine of notice.
280   [1999] 3 All ER 652.
281   This passage was approved in *Ultraframe (UK) Ltd v Fielding* [2005] EWHC 1638 (Ch), [2005] All ER (D) 397.

information was treated as being confidential, then Morbaine would have exploited valuable commercial information to its own benefit and thus to the detriment of Satnam. Therefore, Morbaine's gain was made unconscionably – assuming the presence of knowledge – at Satnam's expense.

Difficulty with the approach in *Satnam Investments Ltd v Dunlop Heywood* was expressed in *Rockbrook Ltd v Khan*[282] where Mr Khan had talked two other people out of investing in land and had instead sought to exploit the land on his own account, contrary to an alleged agreement between the parties to the contrary. On the facts no 'dishonesty' was proved.[283] The judge's difficulty in *Rockbrook* was that Nourse LJ had continued on from the passage quoted above to suggest that a claim for dishonest assistance would have been appropriate if Morbaine could have been demonstrated to have been dishonest: the difficulty being in explaining why liability for dishonest assistance should arise in a situation in which no nexus between the information and the acquisition of the site could be demonstrated which would have been sufficient to impose liability for knowing receipt.

Knowing receipt in complex commercial fraud

It seems useful to present an example of the type of complex commercial fraud which is often at the root of knowing receipt claims. The case of *El-Ajou v Dollar Land Holdings*[284] is a good example of a complex commercial fraud involving knowing receipt of property. Three Canadians, who operated two Dutch 'shell' companies,[285] bribed a Swiss investment manager in Geneva to invest the plaintiff's funds through those shell companies as part of a fraudulent share selling scheme. These shell companies held no other assets and carried on no trade. Their existence was solely to hold assets for the Canadians. The Canadians then passed the profits of their share selling scheme through a range of different locations – including Geneva, Gibraltar and Panama – in an attempt to launder their money. Money laundering in this sense is the process by which a shyster tries to hide the source of money by paying it through a number of bank accounts in a number of jurisdictions, by winding up the companies which own those bank accounts, by mixing those moneys with other moneys, by changing these moneys into different currencies, and so on until the original money because unidentifiable or very difficult to identify indeed. Some of the moneys which the Canadians had moved around the world were invested in a property company, called 'DLH', in London. When the plaintiff discovered the original fraud in Geneva, he brought proceedings against DLH for knowing receipt on the basis, first, that property had been taken from the plaintiff in breach of trust and passed to DLH so that DLH had received it, and, secondly, that DLH had received the property with knowledge of the breach of trust. It was held by the Court of Appeal that the chairman of DLH, even though he played no part in the ordinary management of DLH, had been the person who organised for the investment to pass into DLH. Therefore, in this context the chairman had been 'the directing mind and will' of the

---

282   [2006] EWHC 101 (Ch).

283   *Ibid*, para [42].

284   [1994] 2 All ER 685, [1994] 1 BCLC 464, [1994] BCC 143.

285   A shell company being a company, for these purposes, which carries on no trading or other activities, and which therefore exists solely to hold assets for the human beings who control it or to act as a front for those human beings.

company and therefore any knowledge which he had had as to the source of these funds would be attributed to the company. It was held that the chairman had had sufficient knowledge of the manner in which the investment had been acquired to constitute knowledge of the fraud and breach of fiduciary duty, and therefore that knowledge would be attributed to DLH. Consequently, DLH was held to be liable for knowing receipt of these moneys.[286]

20.3.6 Dishonesty in unconscionable receipt

The alternative test of 'dishonesty'

In the Court of Appeal in *Twinsectra Ltd v Yardley*[287] Potter LJ made it clear that, in his opinion, the applicable test for both knowing receipt and dishonest assistance was one of 'dishonesty' as set out in *Royal Brunei Airlines v Tan*, considered above. This confirmation of the position of English law[288] indicates a movement away from knowledge as the basis for the receipt-based claim. It is clear that the same test was being used by Potter LJ both for dishonest assistance and knowing receipt (even though he acknowledged that one claim was receipt-based and the other was not).

In his judgment, Potter LJ made frequent references to the old knowledge-orientated ideas of the defendant 'shutting his eyes to the obvious'.[289] However, the Court of Appeal in *Twinsectra*, followed by the High Court in *Bank of America v Arnell*[290] and the Court of Appeal in *Heinl and Others v Jyske Bank*,[291] used the established *Baden* categories within which to analyse the mental state of the defendant (for example, wilfully shutting your eyes to the obvious), but were concerned with whether or not that person was *honest* or dishonest, as opposed to whether or not that person had *knowledge* of some breach of trust. Therefore, a number of Court of Appeal decisions have focused on asking whether or not the defendant had been dishonest when she received property in breach of trust.

Whichever test is used, there remains the problem of witness credibility for the judge. In that sense, the question which the judge will continue to ask himself, regardless of which test

---

286 On the facts of *Uzinterimpex JSC v Standard Bank plc* [2008] EWCA Civ 819, [2008] Bus LR 1762, para [37] *et seq.*, *per* Moore-Bick LJ, even though the defendant was not acting simply as an agent (but rather was acting in part as trustee and in part in relation to its own rights) it was nevertheless found that there was insufficient proof of knowledge to make the defendant liable for knowing receipt. The defendant was acting as the agent of a number of banks who had acted as a syndicate in lending money to the claimant. The role of the agent in syndicated lending is to ensure proper payment by the borrower, to ensure the lenders and borrower obey the terms of their contract, and to supervise both property put up as security and to transmit payments between the parties (on which see Alastair Hudson, *The Law of Finance*, Sweet & Maxwell, 2009, Chapter 34). The complex loan contract provided that the defendant was to act as trustee of some property put up as security for the syndicate banks and to act as agent in relation to other obligations. Nevertheless, there was no evidence of knowledge of a breach of duty and therefore the defendant could not be fixed with liability for knowing receipt.

287 See, for example, Nicholls, 1998.

288 *Tan* was a Privy Council decision.

289 There is mention of ' "not dishonest", he [the judge at first instance] was referring to the state of conscious [*sic*], as opposed to "Nelsonian" dishonesty . . .': *ibid*, 462, col 2.

290 [1999] Lloyd's Rep Bank 399.

291 [1999] Lloyd's Rep Bank 511.

is used, is: 'do I believe that this witness acted like an honest person?' Beyond that, there will clearly be an important distinction at the edges as to whether or not the defendant should also have realised that other people would have considered her actions to have been dishonest.

Perhaps there appears to be only a marginal shift between a test of *knowledge* and a test of *dishonesty*, but it is suggested that it could make a significant difference in borderline cases. A test based on knowledge is concerned with the state of mind of the defendant and seeks to establish precisely what that particular defendant knew. In that sense, a test of knowledge is in line with the core equitable principle that the court is concerned with the state of mind of the defendant as part of an *in personam* action. A test based on dishonesty (in the definition given to that term by Lord Nicholls) is a test not solely concerned with the particular mental state of the defendant, but rather primarily with what an honest person would have done in the defendant's place: that is, the court will attempt to establish what an objective, reasonable person would have done in those circumstances. There is therefore a partial shift here in the *Twinsectra v Yardley* decision in the Court of Appeal: the trigger for liability is 'what an objective, honest person would have done' rather than 'what did the defendant know?'[292]

Subsequently, the Court of Appeal in *Niru Battery Manufacturing Co v Milestone Trading Ltd*[293] has doubted that dishonesty is a requirement of liability for knowing receipt, relying on the decision in *Belmont Finance Corp Ltd v Williams Furniture Ltd*.[294] A preference for a test of unconscionability, which expressly disavows a test of dishonesty in this context, was upheld in *Criterion Properties plc v Stratford UK Properties LLC*.[295] The Court of Appeal in this case preferred the flexibility of the notion of 'conscionability',[296] albeit in relation to a claim brought on behalf of shareholders that the directors of a company had knowingly committed breaches of duty in entering into arrangements which would have prevented a takeover of that company by third parties.

Difficulties with some of the judicial explanations of knowing receipt, and errors based on unjust enrichment

The judgment of Arden LJ in *Charter plc v City Index Ltd*, with which neither of the other members of the Court of Appeal agreed, requires some criticism because it suggests some fundamental misconceptions about the notion of knowing receipt. As was the case with the judgment of Arden LJ in *Abou Rahmah v Abacha*, much of the judgment is somewhat elliptically expressed. The following points can, however, be made. First, Arden LJ favours us with the following explanation of the principles:

---

292   *Twinsectra v Yardley* [1999] Lloyd's Rep Bank 438, 464, col 2, *per* Potter LJ, quoting Lord Nicholls in *Royal Brunei Airlines v Tan* [1995] 2 AC 378.

293   [2004] 2 WLR 1415, [2004] 1 Lloyd's Rep 344, para 188, *per* Sedley LJ.

294   [1980] 1 All ER 393. Similarly, *Polly Peck International plc v Nadir (No 2)* [1992] 4 All ER 769, 777, *per* Scott LJ and *Eagle Trust plc v SBC Securities Ltd* [1993] 1 WLR 484, 497, *per* Vinelott J have held that proof of fraud is not a pre-requisite of a claim for knowing receipt.

295   [2003] 2 BCLC 129. Carnwath LJ, having been the trial judge in *BBCI v Akindele*, acknowledged that the Court of Appeal had overruled his own preference for a test of dishonesty at first instance: [2001] Ch 437, 455, *per* Nourse LJ.

296   [2003] 2 BCLC 129, [38].

The expressions 'constructive trust' and 'liable to account' are portmanteau expressions that can be used to define the remedies for different sorts of causes of action, including breach of trust, and different types of relief. Despite this, it is important in the context of the question at issue on this appeal to distinguish between a claim that a person should pay damages to make good the claimant's loss and a claim that a person should account for profits which he has made by the use of the claimant's property.[297]

A number of points arise. As emerged in Chapter 12, constructive trusts are not limited to cases of breach of trust. Furthermore, neither liability to hold property on constructive trust nor liability to account for involvement in a breach of trust involve 'damages'. Damages are limited to actions at common law and involve questions as to foreseeability, formal questions of causation, proximity, and so forth:[298] all of which were elements which are excluded from liability to account in relation to losses caused by a breach of trust by the House of Lords in *Target Holdings v Redferns*.[299] Disastrously the headnote in the Weekly Law Reports refers to this doctrine as the '*tort* of knowing receipt' which cannot possibly be correct because that would constitute another example of the fusion fallacy whereunder common law and equitable doctrines are incorrectly bundled together. Furthermore, liability for knowing receipt, which is a personal remedy, is separate from the proprietary constructive trust which is imposed over the receipt of secret profits by a fiduciary. Secondly, liability for receipt of trust property is somewhat uncomfortably divided between 'claims for unjust enrichment based on the wrongful conduct of the defendant (known as knowing receipt) and claims for unjust enrichment based on innocent receipt (often called claims for money had and received)' by Arden LJ.[300] Knowing receipt is not predicated on unjust enrichment. By definition, a defendant will be liable to account for knowing receipt if she has received trust property knowing of the breach of trust and has since disposed of the property without earning any profit from the transaction. Thus, the defendant need not be enriched to be liable for knowing receipt. Liability is based on the need to compensate the beneficiaries' loss. This is why we must understand the liability as being based on the wrong of knowing and unconscionable receipt of trust property. A claim for money had and received is generally understood as arising at common law when the defendant has acquired an enrichment at the claimant's expense as the result of some unjust factor. Thirdly, Arden LJ suggested that the purpose of the doctrine of knowing receipt 'is imposed to deter trustees'; whereas it is suggested that the liability is in fact imposed to compensate the loss suffered by the beneficiaries as a result of the breach of trust. It is suggested in consequence that Arden LJ's remarks are unhelpful.

---

297 *Charter plc v City Index Ltd* [2008] 2 WLR 950, [64]. They are not really 'portmanteau' expressions: the dictionary definition of the term 'portmanteau' is a composite word formed by fusing two words together as in 'smog' which is a portmanteau combination of 'smoke' and 'fog'.
298 A point which Arden LJ acknowledges at *ibid* at [74].
299 [1995] AC 421.
300 *Charter plc v City Index Ltd* [2008] 2 WLR 950, [62].

The present state of the law: a viable model of 'unconscionable receipt'

At the time of writing, the preponderance of recent judicial opinion in variously constituted Courts of Appeal is that the test is a test of 'unconscionability'.[301] That means that the court must ask itself whether or not the manner in which the defendant came to receive the property was unconscionable. It is suggested, adapting the *dicta* of Carnwarth LJ in *Charter plc v City Index plc*, that the approach should be to ask first whether or not the defendant had one of the requisite types of knowledge from *Montagu*. If there is such knowledge then this may demonstrate unconscionability, or that may need to be proved separately as in *Akindele*. Alternatively, in the absence of proof of the requisite categories of knowledge, the court should consider whether or not there was something unconscionable about the circumstances of the case more generally. The notion that this area of the law should be based on a loose notion of unconscionability has been criticised.[302] It is suggested that this need not be a problem if the concept of unconscionability in this context is filled in appropriately. If the court considers that an honest person could not have considered the transaction to be honest or reasonable in the circumstances, then the court is likely to find that that person had knowledge, or that she was dishonest, or that she had acted unconscionably – whichever form of the test is applied.[303] Therefore, the concept of 'unconscionability' can be understood as being satisfied if unconscionability is based on the long-standing tests of knowledge or of dishonesty (as discussed already in this chapter), and only if those tests are not satisfied should unconscionability be based on some more general idea that the defendant has acted unconscionably in the circumstances.

This last conception of unconscionability is, it is suggested, an entirely appropriate development of equitable doctrine to prevent the beneficiaries suffering loss as a result of the equitable wrong of receiving trust property knowing of a breach of trust or in any other circumstance in which the court considers that receipt of property to have been dishonest or unconscionable. The most useful way forward through this thicket, it seems to me, is to remind ourselves of Scott LJ's comment in *Polly Peck v Nadir (No 2)* that whatever the test that is to be applied the judge is ultimately always called upon to decide whether or not the defendant 'ought to have been suspicious'[304] as to the provenance of the property in the circumstances by the lights of honest people. In that sense it is suggested that, regardless of the niceties of the tests, in the bulk of cases the court will need to decide whether or not the individual defendant ought to have realised that property was being passed to her in breach of trust. The test of 'unconscionability' should be understood in that light; and if it is, then it is not too vague to be useful in this context.

20.3.7 The nature of the remedy

The defendant will be personally liable to account as a constructive trustee to the beneficiaries for any loss suffered by the breach of trust. This liability is based on the defendant's

---

301 *BBCI v Akindele* [2001] Ch 437, 455, per Nourse LJ; *Niru Battery Manufacturing Co v Milestone Trading Ltd* [2004] 2 WLR 1415; [2004] 1 Lloyd's Rep 344, para 188, *per* Sedley LJ; *Criterion Properties plc v Stratford UK Properties LLC* [2003] 2 BCLC 129; *Charter plc v City Index Ltd* [2008] 2 WLR 950.

302 *Crown Dilmun v Sutton* [2004] EWHC 52 (Ch), para [23].

303 *Ali v Al-Basri* [2004] EWHC 2608, [195].

304 *Polly Peck International v Nadir (No 2)* [1992] 4 All ER 769.

unconscionability, dishonesty or knowing actions when receiving property further to the breach of trust. It is based on compensating the beneficiaries' loss. It is not concerned to subtract an unjust enrichment from the defendant, even though the property had passed through the defendant's hands at some time. The nature of the remedy is considered in further detail below in section 20.7.1.

20.4 DEFENCES

20.4.1 *Bona fide* purchaser for value without notice of the breach of trust

Among the only available defences against a claim for knowing receipt are, first, that the defendant was a *bona fide* purchaser for value without notice of the claimant's rights. Where the defendant can demonstrate that she purchased the property in good faith (which would in any event cancel out a claim for knowing receipt in that the requirement of *bona fides* would require an absence of knowledge or dishonesty).[305] This defence is considered in greater detail in section 19.6 above.

20.4.2 Change of position

In circumstances in which the defendant can demonstrate a change of position in good faith in reliance on receipt of trust property, the defendant would be entitled to resist the claim for personal liability to account.[306] The court will measure the comparative justice and injustice of requiring the defendant to account for knowing receipt of property, when the defendant had changed her position in reliance on receipt of that property, measured against the injustice of denying the claimant an account from the defendant equal to her loss. This defence would be unavailable where the defendant is demonstrated to have had sufficient knowledge of the breach of trust, or to have acted dishonestly. So, for example, in *Barros Mattos v MacDaniels Ltd*,[307] where the defendant had knowingly received money which had been stolen from a bank, and where the defendant was consequently found to have committed an illegal act itself, the defence of change of position would not be available. Therefore, it is unlikely that the defence would be available if the *mens rea* were satisfied, unless the defendant could demonstrate that the purchase or the change of position took place before the defendant had acquired the requisite knowledge. This defence is considered in detail in section 19.6 and the reader is therefore referred to that discussion.

20.4.3 Release

The defendant will be able to defend a claim to dishonest assistance or knowing receipt on the basis that she has been released from liability by the beneficiaries. This defence is considered in greater detail in section 19.6 above.

---

305 *Westdeutsche Landesbank Girozentrale v Islington LBC* [1996] AC 669.
306 *Lipkin Gorman v Karpnale* [1991] 3 WLR 10.
307 [2004] 3 All ER 299, [2004] EWHC 1188 (Ch).

20.5 THE PARTICULAR QUESTION OF LIABILITY TO ACCOUNT IN CORPORATE CONTEXTS

20.5.1 The personal liability to account of employees of companies, and the liability of that company for personal liability to account

Liability for dishonest assistance may attach to anyone who provides advice to trustees or who otherwise advises trustees as to the management of the trust property. In such situations it may be difficult to know whether liability attaches to the individual who gives that advice or whether liability can attach to a company or partnership which employs the advisor. The clearest example of such liability would arise in relation to advice given to trustees as to the investment of the trust fund where the advisor is dishonest in the provision of the advice which is given to the trustees. It is not required, in relation to dishonest assistance, that the trustees be dishonest, and therefore it would be sufficient to establish liability to account if the advisor can be shown to have been dishonest.[308] If the individual advisor receives a personal commission from the transaction which caused the breach of trust, then that would increase the likelihood of her being proved to have acted dishonestly.[309] The further question is whether or not the company which employs the advisor would also be fixed with any knowledge or dishonesty of the advisor. In general terms, if the advisor were a controlling mind of the company, then that company can itself be held to have had the same *mens rea* as the individual advisor.[310] So, the Chief Executive Officer of a company may be its controlling mind or the managing director of a division within a large company may be part of its controlling mind, but a junior employee or a mere branch manager in a nationwide supermarket chain would not be.

Liability for dishonest assistance will also attach to any person who assists a breach of a fiduciary duty by a director of a company who breaches her duties to that company.[311] So, if a defendant dishonestly procured the transfer of property away from a company so that it was passed, for example, to a competitor company in breach of the director's duties to the first company, that would make the defendant liable to the first company to account as a constructive trustee for any loss which it suffered as a result of that breach of duty.[312]

The same analysis holds in relation to the knowledge which is required to be proved in relation to a claim for knowing receipt. So, in *Crown Dilmun v Sutton*,[313] the controlling mind and managing director of a company learned of an opportunity to develop a football ground which he should have exploited for the benefit of that company: instead, he created a new company (the second defendant) to exploit that opportunity on his own account. It was

---

308 *Royal Brunei Airlines v Tan* [1995] 2 AC 378.
309 *Ibid.*
310 *Tesco Supermarkets v Nattrass* [1972] AC 153.
311 *Brown v Bennett* [1999] 1 BCLC 649, [1999] BCC 525; *Natural Extracts Pty Ltd v Stoller* (1997) 24 ACSR 110. See also *Consul Development Pty Ltd v DPC Estates Pty Ltd* (1975) 132 CLR 373, 396, *per* Gibbs J. *Royal Brunei Airlines v Tan* related to a breach of trust, as opposed to a breach of a director's duty to its company.
312 Cf section 12.5.
313 [2004] 1 BCLC 468. This decision applies *Satnam Investments Ltd v Dunlop Heywood & Co Ltd* [1999] 1 BCLC 385, [1999] 3 All ER 652; *Criterion Properties Ltd v Stratford UK Properties plc* [2003] 2 BCLC 129, [2003] 1 WLR 218.

held that the knowledge of the director would be transferred to the second defendant because the director was the controlling mind of the second defendant also. Therefore, the receipt of profits from the development of the football ground which passed through the second defendant's bank accounts led to the second defendant being liable for knowing receipt of those profits (further to the constructive trust imposed over those personal profits further to *Boardman v Phipps*).[314] To be able to fix the company with liability has the advantage of providing a defendant which is more likely to be able to make good the beneficiaries' loss than an individual employee.[315]

The controlling mind of a company is not necessarily the same person as the person who carries on the management of that company. However, it is important to consider from case to case and transaction to transaction who is the controlling mind of the company in that context. So in *El-Ajou v Dollar Land Holdings*[316] the plaintiff had been defrauded of his money in Geneva by an investment manager who diverted that money into companies controlled by two men who had bribed him to do so. The plaintiff's money was moved around the world in an attempt to disguise its source before the traceable proceeds of that money were ultimately invested in a London property company called 'DLH'. The investment had come to DLH through its chairman, a man who ordinarily took no part in the day-to-day management of the company. It was found that only the chairman had sufficient knowledge of the manner in which the money had come to be invested in DLH, but not any of the other directors of DLH. It was held at first instance by Millett J that while it was possible to trace the moneys into the hands of DLH, it was nevertheless not possible to prove that DLH had knowledge of the fraud because only the chairman, who did not participate in the ordinary management of the company, had had the requisite knowledge. The matter was then appealed to the Court of Appeal. It was confirmed that the test for demonstrating that a company has knowledge of something is that 'the controlling mind' or 'the directing mind and will' of the company had knowledge of whatever has been alleged. On these facts, there were different people within DLH who acted as the directing mind and will of DLH in different contexts. In that case, it was necessary to identify the person who was the directing mind and will in the particular context in relation to the act or omission which was the basis of the complaint. On these facts, even though the chairman of the company ordinarily played no part in the day-to-day management of the company, he had been the person who had organised the investment by the Canadians in DLH and he had acted without any of the requisite resolutions of the board of directors in so doing: these factors suggested that the chairman was the directing mind and will in this particular context because he had assumed managerial control of this transaction. Therefore, any knowledge which the chairman had about these transactions could be attributed to DLH. On the facts it was therefore held that the chairman and consequently DLH had had the requisite knowledge of the circumstances which had led to the Canadians making the investment in DLH. By contrast, a person who was merely the chairman of a company, but who never carried out the day-to-day management of that company nor took control of *any* given transaction, would not be the controlling

---

314 [1967] 2 AC 46.
315 An employee will also be personally liable for any fraud which she commits in the course of her employment, over and above any liability attaching to her employer: *Standard Chartered Bank v Pakistan National Shipping Corp* [2003] 1 AC 959.
316 [1994] 2 All ER 685, [1994] 1 BCLC 464, [1994] BCC 143.

mind of that company. Therefore, sometimes one must look for the person or people who actually control the company, and not simply look at the people who are installed as figureheads.[317]

The same principle as that in *El Ajou* was applied by the Privy Council in *Lebon v Aqua Salt Co Ltd*.[318] In the Privy Council in *Meridian Global Funds Management Asia Ltd v Securities Commission*[319] it was held that when deciding the obligation of a company which traded in securities to report that it held a given number of a particular type of share so as to comply with securities regulation, the knowledge which should be attributed to the company would be the knowledge of the people who were authorised to acquire those shares on behalf of the company. This approach is not limited to a single person or to a small group of people who run the entire organisation – which would tend to make it difficult to demonstrate knowledge in relation to a large organisation where a function like acquiring shares might be conducted at a much lower level within the company – but rather identifies knowledge in the hands of the individuals who could bind the company in those transactions. Where information comes to the attention of one director of a company, that may be treated as knowledge held by the company even if that director did not inform other board directors of the facts.[320]

20.5.2 The personal liability to account of financial advisors and financial institutions

The particular context of investment advice

There are particular problems associated with financial advice. In the previous paragraph, we considered the general problem of fixing liability both on employees of companies and on the companies themselves. The further dimension which applies to financial or investment advice raises three issues. First, we should observe that all investment involves risk and therefore any investment advisor who gives advice to a trustee will be advising that trustee to take a risk. As was considered by Lord Nicholls in *Royal Brunei Airlines v Tan*, if an advisor is advising the taking of reckless risks, then this might call into question the honesty of the defendant.[321] Secondly, investment advisors are regulated by the Financial Services Authority under the auspices of the Financial Services and Markets Act 2000, and therefore their case law liabilities are supplemented by regulatory requirements. Thirdly, 'investment advisors' may either be financial institutions (which are companies or banks or partnerships) or the employees of such financial institutions. Typically, the financial institution will enter into contracts with clients and the financial institution will receive property from clients, although it is the employee who will make all of the decisions and will give all of the advice. Each of the heads of liability is considered in the following paragraphs.

317 See now also *Stone & Rolls Ltd v Moore Stephens* [2008] Bus LR 1579.
318 [2009] UKPC 2, [2009] 1 BCLC 549; also applied in *Meridian Global Funds Management Asia Ltd v Securities Commission* [1995] 3 All ER 918, [1995] 2 BCLC 116; and in *Jafari-Fini v Skillglass Ltd* [2007] EWCA Civ 261.
319 [1995] 3 All ER 918, [1995] 2 BCLC 116.
320 *Jafari-Fini v Skillglass Ltd* [2007] EWCA Civ 261.
321 [1995] 2 AC 378, 387.

Dishonest assistance by investment advisors

Lord Nicholls applied his test for 'dishonesty' in *Royal Brunei Airlines v Tan* to the particular context of investment advisors in the following manner:

> All investment involves risk. Imprudence is not dishonesty, although imprudence may be carried recklessly to lengths which call into question the honesty of the person making the decision. This is especially so if the transaction serves another purpose in which that person has an interest of his own.[322]

It may be that an investment advisor will be liable to account to the beneficiaries of her trustee customer for any loss caused by an investment strategy which is both a breach of trust and one which is considered to have been recklessly imprudent in that context. Furthermore, there are contexts in which modern market practice permits stockbrokers not to acquire securities for their clients in the open market, but rather those stockbrokers – referred to as 'market makers' in the market jargon – sell securities *which they already own* to their clients (including trustees) and so have a conflict between their personal interests in selling those securities and the interests of their clients. The advisor will therefore stand to make a profit from the transaction by way of commission and will thus increase the likelihood that she will be held to have been 'dishonest' in the sense identified in the passage quoted above. The basis of this form of liability is that the investment advisor:

> takes a risk that a clearly unauthorised transaction will not cause loss. . . If the risk materialises and causes loss, those who knowingly took the risk will be accountable accordingly.[323]

Thus, an investment advisor may be liable in circumstances in which the risk taken in acquiring a particular financial instrument if the court considers the risk associated with that instrument to have been too great.[324] In general terms, a person who is 'guilty of commercially unacceptable conduct in the particular context' of the transaction at issue is likely to be held to have acted dishonestly;[325] this is particularly so where that behaviour also contravenes the requirements of financial regulation.[326] So, where an investment advisor procured investments for beneficiaries in a market – here, a short-lived market in insurance and reinsurance losses – which was considered always to have been unsustainable by financial regulators, that advisor would have been a dishonest assistant in a breach of trust due to the level of risk involved.[327] The regulator found that the risk management procedures across the

---

322   *Ibid.*

323   [1995] 2 AC 378, 387.

324   If the FSA's Conduct of Business rulebook required a particular level of treatment for a particular type of client and the investment advisor failed to observe those obligations, then the likelihood that the advisor will be held to be have acted 'dishonestly' in this sense is all the greater.

325   *Cowan de Groot Properties Ltd v Eagle Trust plc* [1992] 4 All ER 700, at 761, *per* Knox J, approved by Lord Nicholls in *Royal Brunei Airlines v Tan* [1995] 2 AC 378, at 390.

326   See also *Heinl v Jyske Bank Ltd* [1999] Lloyd's Rep Bank 511, at 535, *per* Colman J; and *Bank of Scotland v A Ltd* [2001] 3 All ER 58; *Tayeb v HSBC Bank plc* [2004] 4 All ER 1024.

327   *Sphere Drake Insurance Ltd v Euro International Underwriting Ltd* [2003] EWHC 1636 (Comm).

investment advising firm were 'well below what would have been expected' from professional advisors in that general marketplace.[328]

It will also be important to consider the comparative expertise of the advisor and the
person who was the victim of the breach of trust, in line with FSA regulation, which requires
such measurement of the client's expertise. Where the client is inexpert and the advisor
encourages the taking of a risk which is incommensurate with that client's level of expertise,
then a finding of dishonest assistance is all the more likely.[329] So, where an investment
advisor advised complex investments in real property in the UK through offshore companies, when the client had originally wished only to acquire accommodation for a child who
was to study in the UK, and where that client had expertise only in running a successful business selling pottery but not in financial investments, then these factors would support a
finding of dishonesty.[330] Further, where the defendant ignored regulatory guidance as to the
manner in which clients should be treated, and particularly where the defendant back-dated
documents and prepared documents containing untrue statements, dishonesty would be
clearly demonstrable on the facts.[331] By contrast, the absence of any likelihood of a personal
profit being realised by the defendant would tend to argue against dishonesty.[332]

Unconscionable receipt of property by investment advisors

Among the positive obligations which are imposed on regulated investment advisors and
other financial institutions are requirements that they act in the client's best interests in all
circumstances. Thus, each investment firm is required to act 'honestly, fairly and professionally in accordance with the best interests of its client'.[333] Further, they are required to ensure
the 'best execution' of client transactions such that they acquire the best available price
'investment firms take all reasonable steps to obtain, when executing orders, the best possible
result for their clients taking into account price, costs, speed, likelihood of execution and
settlement, size, nature or any other consideration relevant to the execution of the order.'[334]
These, it is suggested, impose positive fiduciary obligations on regulated 'investment
firms'.[335] Banks also face statutory obligations to report transactions where there are suspicions of money laundering or other criminal activity.[336]

In circumstances in which a person receives trust property in the knowledge that that
property has been passed in breach of fiduciary duty, the recipient will be personally liable
to account to the trust for the value of the property passed away.[337] In relation to investment

---

328   Ibid.
329   Manolakaki v Constantinides [2004] EWHC 749 (Ch).
330   Ibid. On the facts of this case, only procedural matters were at issue and no definitive finding was made on the
       facts of the case.
331   Ibid. See generally A S Hudson, 'The liability of trusts service providers in international finance law', in
       J Glasson and G W Thomas (ed) The International Trust, 2nd ed, Jordans, 2006, 638; Alastair Hudson, The
       Law of Finance, Sweet & Maxwell, 2009, Chapter 3.
332   Ibid.
333   MiFID, art 19(1); COBS. 2.1.1R.
334   COBS, 11.2.1R, et seq.
335   See Alastair Hudson, The Law of Finance, Sweet & Maxwell, 2009, paras 10–16 et seq., and 10–41 et seq.
336   The procedure for making disclosure and acquiring consent is set out in Proceeds of Crime Act 2002, ss 335
       and 338: see Alastair Hudson, The Law of Finance, para 15–42.
337   Per Scott LJ in Polly Peck International plc v Nadir (No 2) [1992] 4 All ER 769.

advice, the advisor must therefore be demonstrated to have received by that advisor for her to be liable for knowing receipt. Frequently, an investment advisor (particularly if that advisor takes funds from the client and invests on their behalf) will maintain accounts for its customers so that the advisor will organise that the money which it holds to its customer's account is invested in the requisite investments. In such a situation, the advisor will receive the trust property and so be liable for knowing receipt.

The more difficult question is: who is it who receives the trust property? Typically, the individual who provides investment advice will be employed by a financial institution and it will be that institution which holds the client's account and which will receive the trust property. Consequently, it will be necessary to show that the financial institution which receives the trust property had the requisite knowledge to justify the imposition of liability to account as a constructive trustee. The categories of knowledge applicable in this context are actual knowledge of the breach of trust; wilfully shutting one's eyes to the obvious fact that the property was paid away in breach of trust; and wilfully and recklessly failing to make inquiries which an honest person would have made so as to discover that the property was passed away in breach of trust.[338] As Scott LJ held in *Re Polly Peck plc v Nadir (No 2)*,[339] these categories are not to be taken as rigid rules and 'one category may merge imperceptibly into another'.[340] In that case, it was held that there was no requirement to prove a fraudulent misapplication of funds to found a claim on knowing receipt; rather, it was enough to demonstrate that the recipient had had the requisite knowledge both that the funds were trust funds and that they were being misapplied. Scott LJ approached the liability of commercial people from the perspective, in a case involving the liability of a bank, of an 'honest and reasonable banker'.[341] In that sense, it is important to look to regulatory norms to consider how a commercial person in the circumstances of the defendant might have been expected to act in any particular market because, it is suggested, such regulatory norms will supply an objective statement of how such a person should have behaved in the circumstances, *inter alia*, with reference to the inquiries which they should have made as to the source of the property which they received.[342]

20.5.3 An issue in relation to bank accounts

On the cases decided before *Royal Brunei Airlines v Tan*,[343] the primary distinction between knowing receipt and dishonest assistance was expressed to be that dishonest assistance required that there be some fraud in the misapplication of trust funds.[344] The primary difference between dishonest assistance and knowing receipt since *Tan* is the introduction of a radical distinction between a test for dishonesty and a test for knowledge respectively. That distinction is often difficult to make in the case of banks. Where X Bank allows a cheque

---

338 The original five categories are restricted to three by *Re Montagu* [1987] Ch 264.
339 *Per* Scott LJ in *Polly Peck International plc v Nadir (No 2)* [1992] 4 All ER 769.
340 *Per* Millett J in *Agip (Africa) Ltd v Jackson* [1989] 3 WLR 1367, 1389.
341 *Polly Peck International plc v Nadir (No 2)* [1992] 4 All ER 769, 778–80.
342 It does appear however, that the reasonableness of the recipient's belief falls to be judged from the perspective of the recipient itself.
343 [1995] 2 AC 378.
344 See Vinelott J in *Eagle Trust plc v SBC Securities Ltd* [1992] 4 All ER 488, 499; Scott LJ in *Re Polly Peck* [1992] 3 All ER 769, 777.

drawn on a trust account to be paid to a third party's account, the bank may be liable for dishonest assistance. Where the third party's account was overdrawn, the credit of the cheque will make the bank potentially liable for knowing receipt where the funds are used to reduce the overdraft, because in the latter instance the bank receives the money in discharge of the overdraft loan. Similarly, where the bank charges any fees in connection with the transfer, then some part of the trust property will have been received.[345] However, in *Polly Peck International v Nadir (No 2)*,[346] Scott LJ held that the bank was liable only for dishonest assistance because it had acted only as banker. The risk for the bank is that a remedy based on dishonest assistance will require the bank to pay over funds which it has never received.

20.6 THE PERSONAL REMEDY IN *RE DIPLOCK*

Where a beneficiary under a will has been underpaid or unpaid, that beneficiary may bring a personal action against any beneficiary who has been overpaid from the assets of the will trust. The remedy is a personal remedy against that overpaid person for the amount of the overpayment. This remedy emerges from the decision of the Court of Appeal in *Re Diplock*.[347] It is unclear whether or not this remedy is available in relation to a trust which was created *inter vivos*, or whether it is only available in relation to will trusts as in *Diplock* itself. Commentators such as the editors of *Lewin on Trusts* are of the view that there is no principled reason for denying the general applicability of this remedy in relation to ordinary trusts just as it is available in relation to recovery under will trusts or to recovery against next of kin in relation to intestacy proceedings.[348]

20.7 QUESTIONS AS TO THE NATURE OF THE LIABILITY OF STRANGERS

20.7.1 A question as to the extent of the remedy of personal liability to account

Will liability be limited according to fault?

There is one key problem with the remedy of personal liability to account. The liability attaches to the defendant either for receipt or for assistance, provided that the relevant *mens rea* of knowledge or dishonesty has been satisfied. The defendant is then liable for the whole of the loss suffered by the beneficiaries, the remedy appearing to be an all-or-nothing remedy on the decided cases. The only defences would appear to be those available to express trustees, considered above at section 20.5, including the beneficiaries' acquiescence in the defendant's actions. However, there is a different sense in which the defendant's liability might be reduced: that is, to recognise that the defendant is possibly not culpable for the whole of the loss. There is no equitable defence comparable to the common law defence

---

345   See Oakley, 1997, 186 *et seq*.
346   [1992] 4 All ER 769.
347   *Re Diplock* [1948] Ch 465; approved in general terms by the House of Lords in *Ministry of Health v Simpson* [1951] AC 251. See also *Re Leslie Engineering Co* [1976] 1 WLR 292, 299, *per* Templeman J who considered the application of this remedy in relation to wrongly paid out assets in a corporate liquidation.
348   Lewin, 2000, 1334.

available to the defendant in the form of the defence of contributory negligence in relation to the law of tort, in which the defendant can admit liability but nevertheless demonstrate that the claimant's loss was not due entirely to the defendant's actions. The defendant to a claim for liability to account in equity has not been awarded such a defence in the cases considered here. It would seem, in general terms, possible for a court of equity to exercise its discretion so as to measure the extent of the defendant's culpability for the loss suffered by the beneficiaries.

Suppose, for example, that the defendant was secretary to a fiduciary who intended to defraud the trust by transferring all of the trust's money into his personal bank account and then to disappear to a new life in the South of France. Suppose further that the fiduciary told the secretary of his entire plan one evening in the office and asked her to go out and buy him three large Samsonite suitcases in which he could conceal the cash. If the secretary was uneasy as to whether or not her boss was joking, and agreed to buy her boss's suitcases and then watched her boss fill the suitcases with the cash he had drawn from the bank that morning, we would have to say that she assisted the breach of trust in the broadest possible sense. We might also say that she was dishonest for not doing what an honest person would have done[349] – perhaps to have asked her boss outright whether or not he had in fact stolen that cash from the trust's bank account. Nevertheless, she has no actual knowledge that a crime is taking place and she is not directly involved in the commission of the crime.

An easier situation would be that in which the secretary agreed to have the money paid into bank accounts which she opened under false names at her boss's instruction so that her boss would not be suspected of having taken the money from the bank accounts. Here we might consider that the secretary was more dishonest than before because she had undertaken dishonest acts – opening the bank accounts under a false name – which assisted the breach of trust. Consequently, the secretary's level of liability would appear to be much higher in this circumstance than in the preceding example where she was possibly innocently caught up in someone else's fraud. In this situation, an honest person would have asked why she was being asked to open bank accounts in false names, at the very least. In either situation, theoretically, the secretary may be held to be liable for acting dishonestly on an objective test like that in *Royal Brunei Airlines v Tan*.

The question arises whether her liability ought to be the same in both factual situations. In the first example, she would be able to claim that she was only partly responsible for the loss suffered by the beneficiaries because, while perhaps not entirely honest, she was not after all the person who stole the money. Nevertheless, if her boss absconded so that he could not be found so as to be sued, the claim based on personal liability to account may impose liability on the secretary for the entirety of the loss,[350] whereas in the second example the secretary would clearly be far more culpable for the loss suffered by the trust and yet there is nothing, as yet, on the cases to indicate that her liability would be any greater than in the first example. It is suggested in such a situation that a court of equity ought to measure the extent to which that secretary was liable and require her to account to the beneficiaries only to that extent. The court ought to impose liability to an extent commensurate only with the extent of the defendant's culpability for the loss suffered by the breach of trust.

---

349 The test laid down by Lord Nicholls for 'dishonesty' in *Royal Brunei Airlines v Tan* [1995] 2 AC 378.
350 *Ibid.*

Causation and loss

What is unclear is the extent to which a dishonest assistant is liable only for losses which flow directly from her assistance or for the whole of the losses flowing from the breach of trust if those losses are larger than those caused by the assistance.[351] Suppose there is a breach of trust whereby four oil paintings, which were held on trust, were taken from the trust fund and sold. If the assistant assisted only with the appropriation of one of the four paintings – perhaps because she was a security guard in the gallery where that one painting was stored – then it would seem reasonable to find that the defendant be liable for the loss stemming from the loss of that one painting rather than from all four. Otherwise, the question is the same question as in the preceding section: that is, to what extent can liability be reduced if one contributes only in part to a larger conspiracy which causes a large loss to the beneficiaries? So, if I am one of four conspirators, should I be liable for only one quarter of the total loss suffered by the beneficiaries, as a defendant to a negligence claim might be *mutatis mutandis*? Alternatively, assuming I am a security guard over an art gallery, if my dishonest assistance was intended to cause a single oil painting to be vulnerable to thieves (perhaps by switching off a single circuit on the alarm) but if I could not have conceived that the thieves would thus be able to steal the three further works of art at the same time, should I be liable for the entire loss or only for the loss which I anticipated as a result of my assistance? On the basis of the liability imposed on express trustees by *Target Holdings v Redferns*,[352] it is not necessary to demonstrate causation or foreseeability; rather, liability will attach for the entire loss once there is some general causal connection between the action and the loss.

20.7.2 The distinction between the receipt-based and the assistance-based claim

Clearly there is a distinction to be drawn between receipt-based liability (knowing receipt) and fault-based liability (dishonest assistance). The latter claim is based solely on the wrong committed by the defendant in dishonestly assisting the breach of trust. As highlighted in section 20.2 above, the potential liability of advisors extends beyond those who are actively deceitful to those who take reckless risks in relation to property held on trust. In practice, this means that an advisor who advocates an investment which later loses the beneficiaries a large amount of money may be considered to have advocated a reckless risk and so be potentially liable for dishonesty.[353]

The difference between the two claims was stated in the following terms by the Court of Appeal in *Grupo Toras v Al-Sabah*:[354]

> The basis of liability in a case of knowing receipt is quite different from that in a case of dishonest assistance. One is a receipt-based liability which may on examination prove to be either a vindication of persistent property rights or a personal restitutionary claim based on unjust enrichment by subtraction; the other is a fault-based liability as an accessory to a breach of fiduciary duty.

---

351 *Derksen v Pillar* [2002] All ER (D) 261, [32]. This case raised these issues but, being an interlocutory hearing, did not need to dispose of them.

352 [1996] 1 AC 421.

353 *Royal Brunei Airlines v Tan* [1995] 2 AC 378.

354 (2000) unreported, 2 November, CA.

The suggestion made here is that knowing receipt is a property law claim that seeks to vindicate the property rights of the claimant. The form of vindication is not a restoration of the original property to the claimant, but rather a cash payment equivalent to the value of that lost property to the beneficiary. It is said by some that the claim is based on reversal of unjust enrichment:[355] but this is simply not a tenable position. It is said by those people that the unjust enrichment takes effect by way of subtraction of the enrichment: however, the measure of liability here is the loss to the beneficiaries and not the enrichment gained by the defendant. It may well be that the defendant received property worth £10,000 but was enriched by only £500 (for example, by way of a commission): in that circumstance, the claimant would be entitled to only £500 by way of subtraction of the unjust enrichment, whereas the remedy of knowing receipt entitles the beneficiaries to recover their entire loss, that is, £10,000, from the defendant and not merely the extent of her enrichment. Similarly, the claim for dishonest assistance realises a remedy equal to the loss suffered by the beneficiaries.

Nevertheless, it has been suggested that the knowing receipt claim is restitutionary in many contexts.[356] There is another basis on which a suggestion that knowing receipt is restitutionary can be rejected. Knowing receipt is predicated on the knowledge of the defendant that there has been some breach of trust. In consequence, knowing receipt is not concerned to impose liability to return property to the claimant – because that would form a tracing claim – but rather to compensate the beneficiaries for the loss which they suffered in part because of the defendant's receipt of property in breach of trust. That liability is faced not because the defendant retains some traceable proceeds of that trust property in her hands, but rather because her knowledge of the breach of trust constituted that receipt a wrongful act. Where alternative tests of dishonesty or of unconscionability are imposed, rather than one of knowledge, that merely underlines the assertion that the claim is fault-based, and so not within the restitutionary canon. The requirement that the defendant must have acted unconscionably only underlines this point. There may be circumstances in which the defendant looks to be effecting restitution where the loss is equal to the value of the property received, but it is perfectly possible that the liability for which the defendant is liable as though a trustee is greater than the value of the property received in breach of trust. Therefore, the liability is a liability in equity, which was recognised as long ago as *Barnes v Addy* as imposing liability for the defendant's participation in a breach of trust. The form of equitable compensation for which trustees may be liable in relation to breach of trust was considered in section 18.3.

The further point relates to that made at section 12.9 above as to the possibility of the court deciding that the defendant was only liable in part for the loss suffered by the beneficiaries, and therefore that she would be liable only for the loss which could be said to have been caused by her act. It is suggested that an equitable remedy of liability to account should permit a flexible obligation on the part of the defendant to account to the extent to which she is culpable for the loss. This would be broadly in line with the remedy for a person who was expressly appointed as a trustee, for whom there is liability only where there is some causal connection between the breach of trust and the loss.[357]

---

355 See also Millett, 1998:2, 399: arguing for replacing constructive trusteeship by restitution. Also Fox, 1998, 391: considering what form of 'notice' is required in knowing receipt, and Smith, 1999, 294.

356 Birks, 2002:2.

357 *Target Holdings v Redferns* [1996] 1 AC 421.

Part 7

Commercial uses of trusts

Chapter 21

Commerce, international trusts law and dealing with property

21.1 INTRODUCTION

This chapter considers the way in which trusts are used in commercial transactions. One of the themes in many of the later sections of this book is the difficulties which ensue when disputes arising from the real-world activities of the parties to litigation – for example, the financial transactions at issue in the local authority swaps cases – are dealt with by the courts according to the long-established norms of legal categories like contract law, trusts law and so on. What happens frequently is that the lawyers translate issues from the language of finance and commerce into the language of law. Sometimes this can lead to the courts dealing with the parties' dispute in ways which they did not expect. This is mainly because law uses its own language and its own concepts when thinking about disputes. Law is primarily all language.[1] In studying this subject of equity and trusts, the reader has had to learn a new language in which ordinary English words like 'demise', 'trust' and 'interest' have been given technical meanings by lawyers. This process of translation arises in all litigation. This chapter will consider the particular context of commercial transactions – replete with their own technical language, their own norms and their own objectives – when they come into contact with equity. As we shall see, commercial people tend to be very suspicious of the use of the sort of discretionary judicial remedies considered in this book, although they have been eager to exploit express trusts, floating charges and the early trust-based company

---

1 See generally Goodrich, 1990.

models developed by equity. The use of equitable concepts by commerce has been a complex process.

In this Part of this book we are considering differences in approach from commercial law, equity, the law of property, partnership law and company law. It seems a little counter-intuitive that cases decided ultimately by the same members of the House of Lords and Court of Appeal[2] can nevertheless generate different legal rules depending on the question that is put to them. Nevertheless, it is true. As will emerge from the discussion to follow, commercial law has developed different forms of estoppel (at common law) and different forms of rules as to proprietary rights in mixed funds in some contexts. So in this chapter we will see that commercial lawyers have adopted a different approach to title in mixtures of property from that in the law of trusts. An example of this phenomenon is the requirement in the law of trusts that property be segregated for there to be a possibility of asserting proprietary rights over it,[3] which is met by some commercial law cases and statute on the basis that the claimants may be considered to be tenants in common of a mixed fund without the need for identification of their segregated share.[4] We will observe a number of contexts in which the approaches of other areas of law to problems long-decided by judges in relation to the law of trusts have taken different and anomalous paths.

In many situations, the reasons for this difference in path will be a desire among commercial lawyers for commonsensical approaches to business questions. So in commercial law we will first examine an impatience with the niceties of equity before exploring the detail of particular rules which show a difference in the thinking of trusts lawyers and commercial lawyers – as though equity were something which can be taken up or left at will. In effect, we will observe that there is frequently one rule for commercial people and a different rule for everyone else.[5]

What is perhaps also surprising is the notion that lawyers are not omni-capable, but rather prefer to specialise in a narrow group of rules which are unique to their own field of speciali-sation. Naively, one might think that any 'lawyer' ought to know of all the rules of property and apply them evenly in the contexts of commerce, intellectual property and so forth, as one would in relation to an ordinary land dispute.[6] In truth, lawyers in practice tend to become specialised in particular areas of law and so do not have such a breadth of knowledge. Perhaps it is a feature of our rapidly changing world that it is impossible to know everything that relates to all areas of law; instead we are separated into our own ghettoes of special competence.[7] It is only if those, at one time, globalising and fragmenting processes are observed that we can hope to understand how commercial law could ever succeed in sepa-rating its own norms from the ordinary norms of equity.

2 Much of the difference, of course, rests with the different divisions of the High Court.
3 *Re Goldcorp* [1995] 1 AC 74, considered at section 3.4 above.
4 Sale of Goods (Amendment) Act 1995.
5 A phenomenon which I have referred to elsewhere as the privatisation of law by commercial people: meaning that commercial people, through arbitration and other devices, are able to hide their disputes from the ordinary processes of law and are able to convince the courts that their particular economic context requires special treatment.
6 Hudson, 2004:4.
7 Elias, 1990; Hudson, 2004:4.

21.2 EQUITY AND COMMERCE

21.2.1 Keeping equity out of commercial transactions

One of the principal interactions between commercial law and equity has been a desire on the part of commercial lawyers to keep equity out of commercial cases.[8] The thinking is this: the law dealing with commercial contracts requires certainty so that commercial people can transact with confidence as to the legal treatment of their activities. Consequently, it is said, discretionary remedies and equitable doctrines are likely to disturb commercial certainties and therefore should be avoided. However, what this thinking fails to admit is the need for some ethical norms to govern commercial life in the same way that they govern non-commercial life. This is accepted to some extent by commercial lawyers in any event: the laws on fraud, on restitution of mistaken payments and so forth impose a morality as to the legal treatment of such phenomena. Furthermore, the whole edifice of the regulation of financial markets, codes of practice for many business activities and so on also indicate an acceptance by policymakers and by commercial people that commercial activity cannot exist in a state of complete anarchy. What the commercial lawyers are keen to avoid is any further discretion on the part of judges to interfere with the terms of their carefully crafted contractual documentation and also, in some markets, the well-understood conventions on which such transactions are carried out.

Many commercial markets develop their own legal norms which they seek to protect because their users consider them to be efficient, or because there is a settled understanding between those users as to how they operate so that they control the amount of risk involved in their business activities. The standard market documentation and the jargon used in financial derivatives markets are very good examples of this phenomenon of the conflict between legal norms and commercial norms.[9] The local authority swaps cases, such as *Westdeutsche Landesbank Girozentrale v Islington LBC*,[10] were the first to bring derivatives (in the form of interest rate swaps) before a court. Before then, the lawyers advising the investment banks had formed a settled, common view that such transactions would cause no problems when conducted with local authorities. In such a situation, in theoretical terms, the closed world of the derivatives markets – a small community of investment bankers specialising in structuring these highly complex financial instruments for large corporate clients, serviced by specialist lawyers in the major commercial law firms – met the closed world of the legal system – with its notions of proprietary rights, of restitution of money, and of the limited powers of local authorities – with the result that their norms clashed.[11] The investment banks had thought that their contracts were valid, whereas the courts held that they were void.[12] The investment banks then thought that the complex contracts used to document derivatives transactions[13] would govern the manner in which those transactions were unwound, with the result, *inter alia*, that they would receive compound interest on the moneys which had been transferred to the local authorities under those transactions; whereas

---

8 Millett, 1998; Goode, 1998.
9 Hudson, 2002, 93; Hudson, 2006.
10 [1996] AC 669.
11 Hudson, 1999:1, which is an analysis of these cases generally; Hudson, 2000:2, on the systemic irritation (to use the theoretical jargon) between principles of finance and principles of law.
12 *Hazell v Hammersmith & Fulham* [1992] 2 AC 1.
13 Hudson, 2002, 379, Hudson, 2006.

the courts held, first, that where the contracts were beyond the powers of the local authority the terms of those contracts were ineffective[14] and, secondly, that there was no entitlement to compound interest in circumstances in which the claimant retained no title in the property transferred, whether under trust or otherwise.[15] It is this kind of conflict between the law – principally equity – and commercial practice which makes commercial people and their advisors nervous of equity. Equally, however, for those not bound in such markets, our concerns might equally well be with ensuring the power of the law and of equity in controlling commercial activities which contradict such norms.

This suspicion of the role of equity in commercial disputes is not restricted to the horny-handed practising lawyers but also is a commonplace of judicial thinking. In considering the types of trusts and remedies which equity leaves open to judges, the judges tend to consider it unsurprising that commercial lawyers, industrialists and bankers do not want to entrust their well-being to complicated ideas like equitable tracing, equitable compensation, and constructive trusts. As Mason put it:[16]

> there is strong resistance, especially in the United Kingdom, to the infiltration of equity into commercial transactions . . . [arising] from apprehensions about the disruptive impact of equitable proprietary remedies, assisted by the doctrine of notice, on the certainty and security of commercial transactions.

It is in response to these fears that many distinct, commercial marketplaces have sought to develop standardised contractual documentation which allocates risks and imposes responsibilities in the event of a number of specified occurrences in an effort, primarily, to exclude the need to resort to general legal principles in relation to their shared contracts.

So it is that the shipping community has devised the Hague-Visby Rules and the Hamburg Rules in relation to carriage of goods by sea. Similarly, the construction industry has developed the JCT 500 contract not only to standardise the legal provisions of ordinary transactions, but also to arrive at a common understanding of the risks which are to be borne by the contracting parties. In both cases what we see is an autopoietic[17] closure of the legal norms and the commercial goals of those parties: that is, an attempt to separate off the legal treatment of that activity from other areas of human activity.[18]

On a slightly different model, many areas of international banking practice have sought to develop standard form contracts both for well-established areas of activity like commodities trading and also for more anarchic and less well-understood areas like financial derivatives. The aim is to reduce the risk associated with these markets by standardising the contracts which market participants sign, and also to create the impression that there are standard conventions governing the conduct of such business. It is also hoped by its participants that the international derivatives market can be sealed off (or autopoietically closed) from general

14 *Westdeutsche Landesbank Girozentrale v Islington LBC* [1994] 4 All ER 890, CA.
15 *Westdeutsche Landesbank Girozentrale v Islington LBC* [1996] AC 669, HL.
16 Mason, 1997/98, 5; *Lonrho Exports Ltd v Export Credits Guarantee Department* [1999] CL 158, 182.
17 Autopoiesis being a theory based on the science of biology considering how closed cells are able to ingest and excrete material: in the same way social systems are said to become closed off from one another, leading social scientists to study the ways in which information, norms and communications are exchanged between such systems. See Teubner, 1994.
18 Hudson, 1999:4; and Hudson, 2000:2.

legal norms. The assumptions blithely made by the parties are that, first, it is a desirable thing for bankers to be permitted to generate their own norms without outside agencies (like the courts) having the right to intervene and, secondly, that the norms of ordinary private law ought not to be permitted to comment on the probity of the actions of participants in such markets. In effect, the bankers want to be hermetically sealed off from the ordinary law because they consider that there is something different and special about commercial life.[19]

These marketplaces are therefore attempting to close themselves off from censure by the outside world. The aim of the commercial or finance lawyer is generally to remove the need to rely on litigation or the application of the courts' discretion. A reasonable expression of these concerns can also be found in the words of Lord Browne-Wilkinson: '. . . wise judges have often warned against the wholesale importation into commercial law of equitable principles inconsistent with the certainty and speed which are essential requirements for the orderly conduct of business affairs.'[20] These principles are derived from older authorities such as *Barnes v Addy*,[21] as well as being discernible in more modern ones such as *Scandinavian Trading Tanker Co AB v Flota Petrolera Ecuatoriana*.[22] For finance lawyers, maintaining the distance between the counterparties and the courts is the primary element in their risk management functions. The advising lawyer's role is primarily a prophylactic one.

This issue of certainty is typically linked by the judiciary to a need to protect the integrity of commercial contract and not to allow other considerations to intrude unless absolutely necessary. The problem is said to be the intervention of some legal principle outwith the expectation of the parties. As Robert Goff LJ has said:[23]

> It is of the utmost importance in commercial transactions that, if any particular event occurs which may affect the parties' respective rights under a commercial contract, they should know where they stand. The court should so far as possible desist from placing obstacles in the way of either party ascertaining his legal position, if necessary with the aid of advice from a qualified lawyer, because it may be commercially desirable for action to be taken without delay, action which may be irrecoverable and which may have far-reaching consequences. It is for this reason, of course, that the English courts have time and again asserted the need for certainty in commercial transactions – the simple reason that the parties to such transactions are entitled to know where they stand, and to act accordingly.

The essence of commercial certainty is therefore said to be the minimal use of discretionary remedies. See, for example, Leggatt LJ in the Court of Appeal in *Westdeutsche Landesbank Girozentrale v Islington LBC*,[24] who was moved by similar concerns and cited his own words from the earlier case of *Scandinavian Trading Tanker Co AB v Flota Petrolera Ecuatoriana*:[25]

---

19 Hudson, 2000:1, Chapter 1.
20 *Westdeutsche Landesbank Girozentrale v Islington LBC* [1996] AC 669, 695.
21 (1874) 9 Ch App 244.
22 [1983] 2 WLR 248.
23 *Ibid*, 257.
24 [1994] 4 All ER 890.
25 [1983] 2 WLR 248, 258.

Tempting though it may be to follow the path which Lloyd J was inclined to follow in *The Afovos*,[26] we do not feel that it would be right to do so. The policy which favours certainty in commercial transactions is so antipathetic to the form of equitable intervention invoked by the charterers in the present case that we do not think it would be right to extend that jurisdiction to relieve time charterers from the consequences of withdrawal.

However, it might also be argued that equity offers a particularly valuable means by which our social mores and culture can express affirmation or disapprobation of certain forms of commercial activity.

21.2.2 Developing the commercial trust

The issue is therefore whether a particular form of trust is called for which would satisfy the needs of commercial people, and if so, what the fundamentals of such a trust would be. The ordinary trust developed as a means of enabling land to be vested in one person but held 'to the use of another'. The trust evolved, as considered in Chapter 2, to deal with all forms of property, from land through choses in action to assets like non-transferable milk quotas.[27] A more modern statement of the nature of the trust delivered by Lord Browne-Wilkinson identified it as being founded solely on the regulation of the conscience of the trustee.[28] The fact cannot be avoided that the trust is an ethical response to the knowledge and the conscience of the common law owner of property.

The argument would be that these foundations are insufficient to sustain the precise needs of commercial people in a global market economy; that there ought to be trusts developed which cater specifically for commercial situations. For example, the role of the *Quistclose* trusts fits, for some writers, into a stream of discussion about retention of title in commercial contracts generally – see Chapter 22 below[29] – the argument being that equity is responding to the needs of commercial people and using the trust structure to fit into that context. Similarly, in the local authority swaps cases, complex subject matter from the world of global finance intruded into a seismic debate about the structure and future legal treatment of personal and proprietary rights to property.[30]

It is this writer's opinion that the law should not pander to those wishes but that it should generate principles which are suitable for deciding such cases in the abstract. Evidently, that is a proposition which requires some expansion: the line between 'pandering' and 'acting suitably' may appear to be paper thin. The core of the problem is that the traditional rules relating to the availability of proprietary remedies sit uneasily in the commercial context. Principles which were created with family trusts in mind do not respond well to the requirements and challenges of commercial contracts. As Lord Browne-Wilkinson said in *Target Holdings v Redferns*:[31]

---

26 [1980] 2 Lloyd's Rep 469.
27 *Don King Productions v Warren* [1998] 2 All ER 608; affirmed [1999] 2 All ER 218; *Re Celtic Extraction Ltd (In Liquidation); Re Bluestone Chemicals Ltd (In Liquidation)* [1999] 4 All ER 684; *Swift v Dairywise Farms* [2000] 1 All ER 320 (milk quotas are property, even if nontransferable).
28 *Westdeutsche Landesbank Girozentrale v Islington LBC* [1996] AC 669, HL.
29 Worthington, 1996; Moffat, 1999.
30 Hudson, 2000:2, 62.
31 [1996] AC 421.

In the modern world the trust has become a valuable device in commercial and financial dealings. The fundamental principles of equity apply as much to such trusts as they do to the traditional trusts in relation to which those principles were originally formulated. But in my judgment it is important, if the trust is not to be rendered commercially useless, to distinguish between the basic principles of trust law and those specialist rules developed in relation to traditional trusts which are applicable only to such trusts and the rationale of which has no application to trusts of quite a different kind.[32]

As his Lordship said, there is a need for equity to winnow out those principles which are of use only in family and similar situations. Similarly, equity must ensure that it does develop specialist rules which are appropriate to the deciding of commercial cases. It is perhaps somewhat ironic that Lord Browne-Wilkinson both set out this call for the possible need for equity to adopt a new approach in the commercial context and then delivered the leading speech in the House of Lords in *Westdeutsche Landesbank Girozentrale v Islington LBC*,[33] in which the existing rules are consolidated in contradistinction to laying the groundwork for the development of such new commercial principles.

There are a number of problems for the Chancery courts in considering commercial transactions. The first is that it is often possible for the courts to interfere with freedom to contract only where there has been some unconscionable behaviour which amounts to provable fraud. The other is the difficulty of intruding on freedom of contract by replacing the precise terms of the agreement with some standard arrived at by applying principles according to conscionability – for example, by judges fixing the price of the contract.

For example, how is equity to respond to a situation in which someone contends that a commercial contract was unjust on the basis that, *ex post facto*, the claimant has suffered greater losses than that person had expected? One approach would be to leave the parties to reap what they have sown – that is, you entered into the contract, you must bear its consequences. That might appear to be a suitable approach where the parties are of equal bargaining strength.[34] Alternatively, we might take the approach that some transactions necessarily place one person in a position of strength as against another person. An example would be as regards a mortgage over residential property, in which the mortgagee will typically have greater expertise than the mortgagor.[35] In many circumstances, statute will intervene to protect the inexpert party from an unconscionable bargain.[36]

In his book *The Rise and Fall of Freedom of Contract*, Professor Atiyah addressed precisely this difficulty of legal intervention in contracts which proved ultimately to be to the disadvantage of one party or another.[37] As he put it:

> A person who indulges in a foolish speculation is apt to feel, after the speculation has failed, that it was an unfair arrangement. Of course, the same is true of any transaction which necessarily involves some element of risk, though that is not nearly so obvious to the parties involved.

32 See Nolan, [1996] LMCLQ 161.
33 [1996] AC 669.
34 *Multiservice Bookbinding v Marden* [1979] Ch 84, *per* Browne-Wilkinson J.
35 *Fairclough v Swan Brewery* [1912] AC 565; cf *Knightsbridge Estates Trust v Byrne* [1938] Ch 741.
36 See, eg, Consumer Credit Act 1974, s 137.
37 Atiyah, 1979, 174.

So, the person who suffers such a loss is likely to argue that there was unconscionable behaviour in the dealing which led to the creation of the arrangement in the first place. In the 18th century, the South Sea Bubble crisis produced a litany of litigation. For example, there were a number of decisions which set aside contracts on the basis that they were 'against natural justice', in the words of the court in *Stent v Baillie*,[38] simply because the losses which they generated were considered by the judges of the time to be so extraordinarily large. In *Stent v Baillie*, shares had been sold at a vastly inflated price at the height of speculative fever and the courts were not prepared to enforce the contracts. Similarly, inflated house prices were not enforced by the courts where the purchaser had lost money after the South Sea Bubble burst, even though he had already contracted for the purchase of the property.[39] The Lord Chancellor held in *Savile v Savile*[40] that the property 'would appear dear sold and consequently a bargain not fit to be executed by this court'. As Professor Atiyah saw it, there was a clash of moralities between the 'paternal, protective Equity' of the old school and 'the newer individualism, stressing risk-taking, free choice, rewards to the enterprising and sharp, and devil take the hindmost'.[41] What better summary of the role of equity in the context of commercial markets? What we need not do, however, is to abandon the notion of conscience, because that is a sufficiently flexible idea to be applied in commercial and in non-commercial contexts: a notion considered again in Chapter 32.[42] The parallel with contract law, however, is one which has been developed further by some commentators, as considered next.

21.2.3 The interaction between trusts law and contract law

The contractarian argument

By contrast with the problems identified above in equity's perceived uncertainty, contract law is often considered to offer a haven of dependability for commercial lawyers. Consequently, in commercial practice there is a drive to displace the perceived uncertainties of trusts law, and in particular the beneficiary principle, in favour of the more familiar territory of the law of contract. The chief advocate of this view has been Professor Langbein. Langbein is determined that every trust is part of a larger contract, and therefore that there is no need to consider the nature of the trust in isolation from the contractual matrix of which it forms a part.[43] The argument proceeds as follows. All trusts are said to be based on a contract between the settlor and the trustee such that the prevailing code of law governing that relationship is to be considered to be the law of contract rather than the law of property. In most commercial situations, this analysis-opening assertion will frequently – but not always[44] – be correct. Commercial parties will receive advice from lawyers and others as to

---

38 (1724) 2 P Wms 217.
39 *Savile v Savile* (1721) 1 P Wms 745, (1721) 24 ER 596. Also *Keen v Stuckley* (1721) Gilb Rep 155, (1721) 25 ER 109.
40 *Savile v Savile* (1721) 1 P Wms 745, (1721) 24 ER 596, 597.
41 Atiyah, 1979.
42 See section 32.2 below.
43 Langbein, 1995, 625.
44 See *Re Kayford* [1975] 1 WLR 279, considered in para 3.3.1 above, a commercial situation involving a mail order company's dealings with its customers where the trust was unconscious.

the creation of their trust. The trustees will often be professionals who, as professionals, will agree to act as trustees only if their duties and liabilities are controlled by contract.[45] Consequently, Langbein considers this contract to be the heart of the trust because it sets out the precise ambit of the trustees' obligations. This would not mean, *inter alia*, that it would be necessary for there to be any beneficiary able to satisfy the beneficiary principle,[46] but rather it would be sufficient to establish a trust if there were a contract demonstrating an intention to create a trust. Such a view means that all questions as to the enforceability of the trust fall to be considered by reference to the law of contract rather than the law of trusts.

Before continuing any further with this analysis it is worth pointing out that this fundamental assertion is wrong. Many trusts are not bound up with a contract. In relation to commercial practice, it is true that there will commonly be a commercial contract which uses a trust as a device to hold security for payment, or a contract for services whereby some person will be limiting his liability and identifying his fee in return for acting as trustee. To that extent there will be a contract; and to that extent the Court of Appeal has held that this contract ought to limit even trustees' liability for breach of trust if the terms of the contract require that – even where the trustee has been guilty of gross negligence.[47] However, many express trusts arise without a contract in will trusts and in situations like those in *Paul v Constance*[48] or *Re Kayford*,[49] where the courts imply that the parties have created something akin to a trust but which the parties themselves did not realise was a trust. These sorts of 'unconscious express trusts' may occur naturally in the wild in great profusion but they are unlikely to have enough at stake to reach the Chancery courts: that is, there are probably many of them in the world but very few of them will ever be litigated upon. Self-evidently, constructive trusts and resulting trusts do not depend upon a contract for their existence. Langbein does acknowledge that there are a few exceptional cases, such as will trusts, but he does not include the very common examples of resulting, constructive, unconscious express and implied trusts in that list. It is not true to say that trusts are built on contracts in all cases: consequently, I would suggest that we should treat with caution any argument that the principles of express trusts law be overthrown in favour of contractarian or other obligations-based theories.[50]

To return to the central argument of Langbein's essay: trusts should be considered as being contracts at root and therefore it should not matter that there is or is not a beneficiary who can satisfy the beneficiary principle. This is particularly important for a range of vehicles used to hold assets for tax avoidance purposes, whereby those who contribute to a fund might wish to appear to have no beneficial interest in that fund for tax purposes but nevertheless be able to rely on the assistance of a discretionary trustee looking favourably upon them when the time comes to distribute the fruits of the fund. It is important that no individual be identifiable as a beneficiary for two reasons. First, so that no revenue authority can identify any profit-generating property in any of the participants. Secondly, so that no individual can claim entitlement to the fund in the absence of any other person and so establish a beneficial

45 See para 8.5.1 above.
46 See section 4.1 above.
47 *Armitage v Nurse* [1998] Ch 241.
48 [1977] 1 WLR 527.
49 [1975] 1 WLR 279.
50 Matthews, 2002, 144.

claim to the fund ahead of the participants. This second feature means that there is no beneficiary capable of satisfying the beneficiary principle.

Trusts in investment contracts

In this book we have already considered the interaction of trusts and contract on a number of occasions. First, when seeking to define a trust by explaining that it imposed fiduciary duties on a trustee such that it was different from an ordinary contract which would not impose duties of that quality. Secondly, when considering the ability of trustees to exclude their own liability for dishonesty by means of an exclusion clause in the contract for their professional services.[51] Thirdly, when considering the common intention constructive trust which awarded rights in the home in situations, *inter alia*, in which couples had entered into quasi-contractual agreements, arrangements or understandings as to the equitable ownership of the home.[52] It was also considered in that discussion that the rules which equity was developing appeared to be more rigid and so more akin to common law doctrines than to classically equitable ones.[53] In each of these situations it was evident that contractual thinking was creeping into the law of trusts.

It was in a fourth context, however, that the key to the similarities between trust and contract emerged. In relation to trusts used for investment purposes – whether occupational pension funds or unit trusts – the role of the contract is important. There are a number of circumstances in which investment managers use trust structures for investment funds. Pension funds, insurance company-managed investment funds and unit trusts are all structured as trust funds. Also of importance in corporate finance are eurobond trustees and debenture trustees, both of which are required by applicable regulation to oversee securities issues in those contexts. There is a tension at the heart of each fund: on the one hand the parties' principal concerns are the performance of the fund's investments and the performance of their investment contract, whereas the legal analysis of their relationship is that of trustee and beneficiary. It has been suggested by some commentators that, for example, unit trusts ought to be considered to be in truth contracts rather than trusts (given that that is the parties' fundamental purpose)[54] with the result that the ordinary principles of the law of trusts would not apply to their arrangements.[55]

In unit trusts, the investment manager and the investor enter into a contract for the investment of money in which the existence of a trust fund to hold the pooled investment capital appears to be secondary to the underlying commercial purpose of investment.[56] In the occupational pension fund it is clear that the management of the fund will require consideration of the pensioner's contract of employment as well as the scheme rules in many situations.[57] Therefore, in both of these contexts, the existence of a trust used to manage the capital is collateral to some underlying contractual purpose. The result of this observation might be

51 See para 8.5.1 above: *Armitage v Nurse* [1998] Ch 241. Cf *Walker v Stones* [2000] 4 All ER 412.
52 See para 15.4.2 above.
53 See para 15.9.2 above.
54 Sin, 1997.
55 Hudson, 2000:1, generally.
56 See Thomas and Hudson, 2004, Chapter 51.
57 See para 26.1.1 below.

that we would consider such arrangements to be contractual in nature and so apply the rules of the law of contract to their analysis, rather than stricter trusts law rules as to fiduciary obligations and so forth. However, that there are contracts in place in these situations does not displace the existence of trusts in parallel. It is true to say that the contract might contain many of the terms governing the trustees' obligations, but that is no different, it is suggested, from those trusts obligations being contained in a trust deed in the same terms. The more important factor is that there are trusts in both of these contexts, and that trusts were selected by Parliament in the Pensions Act 1995 and in the Financial Services and Markets Act 2000[58] as being the most appropriate vehicle for the management of the capital in both. Therefore, the role of the trust outwith the terms of the contract remains important. Trustees are obliged to obey those provisions in the pensions and in the unit trusts legislation which prevent the wholesale limitation of their liabilities in many circumstances.[59] Legislative policy was to maintain the duties of trustees as fiduciaries over these scheme managers as opposed to defining their obligations as being governed entirely by contract. Consequently, while we might identify a contractual, commercial purpose at the root of these funds, there is no doubt that the legal norms which govern them are trusts-based norms. The principles of trusts law are not intended to be limited in such situations. Rather, the trust continues to be used here precisely because it is something different from a contract: in particular because it is a mechanism by which those who manage property on behalf of others can be held to account.

The next two sections consider the ways in which the contractarian basis of trusts has been applied to trusts in other jurisdictions for the avoidance of taxation and other regulatory rules. Discussions of the investment models considered in this section can be found at www.alastairhudson.com/trustslaw.

21.2.4 Exclusion of liability through the trust instrument or through contract

One further context in which this contractarian argument is significant is in relation to the obligations of trustees. As was discussed in great detail in Chapter 8,[60] the Court of Appeal has held that trustees are able to limit their liabilities by including a provision in their contract of appointment which excludes liability for a range of defaults, including gross negligence, but not dishonesty.[61] It is significant that the courts have found that a trustee's obligations are not mandatory in the sense that they are not enforced strictly in the abstract. Rather, a trustee can escape liability for gross negligence on the basis that he has contracted with the settlor to have his liability so excluded. This disturbs the ordinary understanding that a trustee's obligations are owed principally to the beneficiaries and that the settlor drops out of the picture *qua* settlor once the trust has been properly constituted.[62] The alternative view would have been to say that, as a fiduciary, the trustee owes certain duties of competence and good faith to the beneficiaries which cannot be excluded by contract. That the law does not presently take that view is a serious abrogation of the principle that the trustees must do the best possible for the beneficiaries in all circumstances. The rationale behind this rule is easy to

---

58   Both of which continued the policies of earlier legislation in this respect.
59   See Thomas and Hudson, 2004, Chapter 51.
60   See para 8.5.1 above.
61   *Armitage v Nurse* [1998] Ch 241.
62   *Paul v Paul* (1882) 20 Ch D 742.

identify of course: if the trustee could not rely on such contractual protection she might have refused to act as trustee at all, and therefore it would be wrong to expose her to liabilities which she had not voluntarily assumed. The great irony is that it will only be professional trustees who will be sufficiently knowledgeable to have such an exclusion clause included in their conduct of business agreement; non-professionals acting as trustees will not know that they ought to include such a provision to limit their liabilities. In consequence, the professional trustees will escape liability for failing properly to perform the actions for which they are being paid large fees and on the basis of which they have forged their professional reputations; amateur trustees will face liability for exactly the same sorts of defaults when they have never held themselves out as being professional trustees at all.

The development of these quasi-contractual exclusion clauses for the liabilities of trustees does appear to be – even if only for those trusts where there are contracts for services in place with the trustees – a limitation on the liabilities of the trustees imposed entirely by the law of contract. It could be suggested that this indicates that the obligations of the trustee are therefore personal obligations owed to the beneficiaries and not proprietary duties.[63] The alternative argument is that this development of exclusion clauses does no violence to the trust concept at all: the contract merely stands for the expression of the trustees' duties which could have been contained in a trust deed but which were included instead in a contract for services or a conduct of business agreement. The real question is a more essential one than that, however.

The real question is: if the trustees' duties are limited to such an extent, do they fall to be categorised as trustees' duties at all? The heart of the law on express trusts – remember, these questions do not arise in relation to constructive or resulting trusts – is that where the trust has been consciously created by the settlor in circumstances in which the legal owner of property is impressed with obligations of good conscience towards another person in relation to that property, there will be a trust. It is open to the settlor to limit the liabilities of that trustee as to her competence and so forth in the management of that property. The case law has never contained a quasi-statutory list of positive obligations which are borne by the trustee; rather, those obligations have tended to be negative: thou shalt not make secret profits;[64] thou shalt not permit conflicts of interest;[65] thou shalt not favour one beneficiary over another.[66] Positive obligations would require the trustees to perform given obligations to a given standard. The only senses in which the case law has imposed such obligations are in the limited contexts of generating the maximum feasible return in line with market practice,[67] investing as though for someone for whom one felt morally bound to provide,[68] and providing the beneficiaries with information as to the manner in which the trustees have managed the trust.[69] Therefore, there is, in truth, little that is added to trusts law by accepting that if the settlor agrees to limit the trustees' liabilities from the outset then the terms of that trust can be depended upon.

---

63 Penner, 2002.
64 *Boardman v Phipps* [1967] 2 AC 46.
65 *Ibid.*
66 *Nestlé v National Westminster Bank plc* [1993] 1 WLR 1260, [1994] 1 All ER 118.
67 *Ibid.*
68 *Speight v Gaunt* (1883) 22 Ch D 727.
69 *Re Beloved Wilkes Charity* (1851) 3 Mac & G 440.

What is new, perhaps, is the idea that the trustee need act only honestly, but not necessarily competently, in the performance of her office as trustee. The root of the trust is identified in the speech of Lord Browne-Wilkinson in *Westdeutsche Landesbank Girozentrale v Islington LBC* (see para 21.2.2 above) as being concerned with the conscience of the legal owner of property. Therefore, provided that the trustee does not act in bad faith – through fraud, dishonesty, or similarly acting otherwise than as an honest person would have acted in those circumstances – then this accords with a restricted reading of that central principle. It is not to restrict the liabilities of the trustee to those of a mere party to an ordinary contract, because such a person would not ordinarily be liable, for example, to hold unauthorised profits from that contract on constructive trust for the beneficiaries, nor to provide for equitable compensation in the event that the beneficiaries suffered any loss from any breach of duty, nor (most significantly) to acquire a priority in that person's insolvency. There are enormous benefits to identifying someone as a trustee, even if the liability of such a trustee can be limited by contract. One problem which would be created if trusts were deemed to be a species of contract would be that trustee exemption clauses demanded by professional trustees might be considered to be unfair contract terms and might be unenforceable.

The courts have apparently accepted the notion that there is nothing wrong in principle with restricting one's liabilities as a trustee by means of contract, even in cases such as *Walker v Stones*,[70] in which the Court of Appeal otherwise expressed a nervousness at the idea that trustees should be able to use contractual exclusion clauses as a shield in all cases. There is nothing wrong in principle, of course, with the suggestion that my conscience is not affected if I undertake to manage your investments as a trustee entirely on the basis that I will do so only provided that I do not undertake any liability to you in the event that I act negligently. Suppose I make this stipulation because I am not a financial expert and therefore do not want to be held to account as though I was one. In such a situation, if the settlor agrees to my stipulation from the outset, I cannot be said to have acted in bad conscience if I do make negligent investments and seek not to be liable for the losses which those investments cause to you. Rather, our concern is with professional trustees who take large fees based on their assumed professional competence but who then seek to hide behind exclusion of liability clauses in the event that they turn out to be less adept than they had at first suggested. At first blush, the same argument applies to them: they have only agreed to act based on stipulations as to the limits of their liability, and consequently they are entitled to rely on them because otherwise they would not have entered into the contract. In such a situation, the question of conscience is a different one, as the House of Lords accepts in *Twinsectra v Yardley*.[71] In that case, the test for dishonesty – at issue in *Armitage v Nurse*[72] and *Walker v Stones*[73] – was expressed to be both an objective question as to how an honest person would have behaved in the circumstances and a subjective question as to whether or not the defendant realised that her behaviour would be considered to have been dishonest. In relation to a professional trustee, particularly one regulated under the Financial Services and Markets Act 2000, it is suggested that any failure to observe the standards of financial regulation ought to constitute unconscionable behaviour on this subjective standard: that is, a

70 [2000] 4 All ER 412.
71 [2002] 2 All ER 377.
72 [1998] Ch 241.
73 [2000] 4 All ER 412.

professional trustee subject to such regulation cannot be permitted to act otherwise than in accordance with the diktat of such regulation. Thus, it is possible to impose 'external' constraints based on conscionability by courts of Equity while also observing the 'internal' limitations on liability imposed by any contract between trustee and settlor. In this way the notion of conscience, properly understood, can be adapted to apply effectively to commercial and to non-commercial situations. This issue is considered in greater detail in Chapter 32.[74]

21.2.5 Themes in international trusts law

There are two principal themes in international trusts law which are dealt with in outline here. The first is the Hague Convention on the Recognition of Trusts, which concerns the recognition of the trusts law of some jurisdictions in other jurisdictions. The second is the pressure to adopt the contractarian approach to trusts law, outlined in para 21.2.3 above, brought to bear by offshore 'tax havens' to support the central place of trusts services in their economies.

Recognition of trusts

The Hague Convention on the recognition of trusts (that is, the Hague Convention on the Law Applicable to Trusts on their Recognition 1985) was incorporated into English law by the Recognition of Trusts Act 1987. There is not space here to consider this legislation in great detail.[75] Briefly put, the purposes of the Convention are threefold. First, to permit the settlor to provide for the governing law of a trust. That means that the system of rules which governs any disputes as to the trust can be selected by the settlor and therefore might not be English law. This raises the problem (in the next section) as to whether or not English law would recognise the analysis placed on a trust dispute by the chosen governing law if some question of English law – most probably revenue law – were raised. Secondly, a trust created in that manner is to be recognised in other signatory jurisdictions. Thirdly, the Convention seeks to preclude any signatory state through its trusts law seeking to disapply the more favourable rules of another state.

The Convention applies to trusts which are created voluntarily, and therefore does not apply to trusts implied by law.[76] Also outwith the scope of the Convention are testamentary trusts and lifetime settlements of foreign immovables and movables, in which cases ordinary rules of conflict of laws will apply. The choice of law in relation to a trust which does fall within the Convention is effective only if the system of rules chosen recognises the trust concept.[77] However, significantly, it is not necessary for the system of law chosen to have any connection with the trust, so that, for example, a trust declared in England by an English settlor with English trustees can theoretically have a different system of law from English law. It is possible to select different systems of law to govern different parts of a trust.

---

74 See section 32.2 below.
75 The reader is referred to Harris, 2002, generally.
76 Hague Convention, Art 6.
77 *Ibid.*

Where no express choice of law is made, the 'law with which it is most closely connected' will be the governing law of the settlement.[78] Therefore, the court will look at all the circumstances, including the jurisdiction where the settlor, trustees and beneficiaries are resident, the locus of the property and so forth. Weighing those factors, it will identify the jurisdiction with which the settlement has the closest connection.

Significantly, however, where there are overriding rules of the forum seised of the question, the Convention provides that that forum so seised is entitled to decide, if the trust has such a weak connection with the jurisdiction of its governing law, that the mandatory rules of the jurisdiction hearing the question should be applied instead.[79] This provision would be the Achilles heel for tax avoidance schemes which seek to select an artificial system of law as the governing law of the trust.

However, many commentators have suggested that these mandatory rules are limited to rules of conflict of laws and of international comity.[80]

Offshore trusts services

The central question for offshore trusts service providers is whether or not the trust should be considered by English law to be equivalent in all material respects to the contract such that the beneficiary principle could be done away with. The clearest explanation of these offshore trusts structures is provided by Lord Walker in *Schmidt v Rosewood*[81] in the opening paragraph of his opinion in the following terms:

> It has become common for wealthy individuals in many parts of the world (including countries which have no indigenous law of trusts) to place funds at their disposition into trusts (often with a network of underlying companies) regulated by the law of, and managed by trustees resident in, territories with which the settlor (who may be also a beneficiary) has no substantial connection. These territories (sometimes called tax havens) are chosen not for their geographical convenience (indeed face-to-face meetings between the settlor and his trustees are often very inconvenient) but because they are supposed to offer special advantages in terms of confidentiality and protection from fiscal demands (and sometimes from problems under the insolvency laws, or laws restricting freedom of testamentary disposition, in the country of the settlor's domicile). The trusts and powers contained in a settlement established in such circumstances may give no reliable indication of who will in the event benefit from the settlement. Typically it will contain very wide discretions exercisable by the trustees (sometimes only with the consent of a so-called protector) in favour of a widely-defined class of beneficiaries. The exercise of those discretions may depend upon the settlor's wishes as confidentially imparted to the trustees and the protector. As a further cloak against transparency, the identity of the true settlor or settlors may be concealed behind some corporate figurehead.

---

78 *Ibid*, Art 7.
79 *Ibid*, Art 16.
80 Mowbray *et al*, 2001, 297.
81 [2003] UKPC 26, [2003] 2 AC 709. *Charman v Charman* [2005] EWCA Civ 1606, [2006] 2 FLR 422, considers these issues in relation to ancillary relief proceedings in a matrimonial dispute.

Such trusts can be used simply to shelter assets from regulatory oversight, or to achieve objectives which are impossible in the settlor's home jurisdiction, or simply to hold the assets, or to hide assets from family members and others. While these structures are executed as trusts, they often also support investment arrangements between the service provider and the settlor-investor. The trust in such circumstances is merely a vehicle to make the investment possible. The parties' principal intention will be the investment contract between them. By reducing the trust from the level of a proprietary relationship, as traditionally understood in the English tradition in cases such as *Saunders v Vautier*, to that of a mere contract as Langbein suggests,[82] the trust can be used as an investment device without the investors being recognised for tax purposes as having proprietary rights in the trust fund. Those jurisdictions commonly referred to as 'tax havens' have generally altered their own trusts law codes to accept as trusts such devices where there is no equitable, proprietary title for the beneficiary.[83] The concern of practitioners in such jurisdictions is that if English courts will not accept such structures as being trusts (and therefore consider the client-taxpayer to be still the absolute owner of the property on resulting trust principles),[84] then a so-called 'limping trust' is created[85] which would be accepted as being validly constituted in their jurisdiction but not in England. The argument is advanced by others[86] that there is no need to enforce the beneficiary principle strictly if there is some other person (typically dubbed a 'protector' or 'enforcer' in such a jurisdiction) who can sue as though a beneficiary under the trust, so satisfying the beneficiary principle by other means.

Trusts are problematic for financial regulators and law enforcement agencies generally because trusts can be created casually and trustees are not obliged to post accounts with any central agency (unlike companies in most jurisdictions). Consequently, trusts structures are frequently used by people who want to launder money associated with drug trafficking, arms dealing, or funding terrorism, as well as by people who more generally want to keep their financial affairs beyond the knowledge of financial regulators or tax authorities. The suggestion that English law should dispense with the beneficiary principle is therefore a proposal that, beyond trusts being used for these purposes, the beneficial owner of the property held on trust need not even have any proprietary right in the property which is, in reality, being held at her direction and for her benefit. The trust without the beneficiary principle would therefore make it easier for drug traffickers, arms dealers and terrorists to conceal their financial affairs in England and Wales, let alone in tax havens. Given the global climate at the time of writing, it is suggested that this is a development which should self-evidently be resisted.

In short, the matter is this: the trusts service providers in the tax havens want English trusts law to be fundamentally changed so that their clients can avoid liability to tax, or so that their clients can put assets beyond the reach of financial services and other regulatory authorities. While I am confident that this may be an exciting notion to many revenue law practitioners, I consider this to be a conspicuously bad reason to change English trusts law. These clients should simply pay their tax and give themselves up to regulation; English trusts law need not change.

---

82   As it is increasingly understood in the USA, with the possible exception of Nebraska.
83   For a discussion of these structures see the opening section of Lord Walker's judgment in *Schmidt v Rosewood Trust Ltd* [2003] UKPC 26, [2003] 3 All ER 76.
84   *Vandervell v IRC* [1967] 2 AC 291, HL.
85   Waters, 2002.
86   Hayton, 2001.

Protectors

Protectors do not exist formally in English trusts law in the sense that the term 'protector' has no technical meaning in English law, and yet protectors are used frequently. That may seem to be an impossible paradox but it is a fair representation of the position in practice. It is commonly the case that someone – we shall call them a 'protector', although sometimes to term 'enforcer' is used, sometimes 'appointor' – is appointed under the terms of a trust to look after the interests of the beneficiaries by controlling some of the trustees' functions or by ensuring that the settlor's intentions are put into effect. This may be done by giving the protector a right to veto the actions or decisions or exercises of discretion by the trustees, or by giving the protector the right to appoint trust property for specified purposes, or by giving the protector the right to appoint or remove trustees, or by giving the protector the right to negotiate and to settle trustees' fees and other commissions.[87] This needs to be done, for UK tax purposes, in such a way that the trustees do not appear to have their freedom to manage the trust's affairs controlled by the protector.[88]

The question arises as to the proper analysis of the protector's role under English trusts law. It is important to remember that in the English trusts lexicon there is no single definition of what is meant by the term 'protector'. Under many other systems of trusts law – particularly in offshore jurisdictions – specific legislation has been drafted to specify the role and purpose of such protectors. In England and Wales, however, no such legislation nor any such case law principles exist. Thus the following analysis is predicated entirely on argument, rather than on authority. For many practitioners in the international trusts law world protectors are so commonplace that the discussion to follow may dismay them.

The first possibility is that protectors are in fact trustees themselves. The careful structuring of the tax avoidance specialist will seek to have the protector occupy no trustee-like role; however, if the protector is able to veto the decisions of trustees and so forth then the issue must arise whether or not the protector is in truth acting as some sort of trustee. If the trustees decide to invest in *x* and the protector intervenes to prevent an investment in *x*, how are we to understand the power of this protector? This person has the right to gainsay the decisions of trustees and therefore she must be acting with a power equivalent to that of trustees. Could this protector act capriciously in so doing? The answer must be 'no'. If the protector is able to overturn the decisions of the trustees, then the protector is empowered to act in relation to another person's right in property, namely the beneficiaries. This must constitute a fiduciary role if it involves control of the decisions of the trustees themselves. Given that the protector's actions will have direct effects on the rights of the beneficiaries to the trust fund, it must be the case that the protector is occupying a fiduciary capacity in deciding whether or not to gainsay the decisions of the trustees. Taking control of the decisions of the trustees in this manner means that the protector is able to take control of the rudder of the trustees' actions and decisions. I would suggest that if this person were not named 'protector' in the trust instrument already then any person who took control of the trust in this fashion would be considered to be a trustee *de son tort* and so be construed to be a trustee.[89] That is, 'if one, not being a trustee . . . takes upon himself to intermeddle with

---

87 See Venables, *Non-resident Trusts*, Key Haven Publications, 1999.
88 Venables, 1999.
89 See para 12.8.

trust matters or to do acts characteristic of the office of trustee, he may therefore make himself what is called in law trustee of his own wrong.'.[90] Either way, the protector is acting *in loco* trustee and so must be considered to be a species of trustee with control over certain aspects of the trust property.

The second possibility relates to the preceding section whereby the protector exists so that there need not be any beneficiary with vested proprietary rights which might attract liability to tax. The trustees' aim is to seek investors who will contribute to the trust fund in the expectation that the presence of a protector will replace the need for the beneficiaries to have any vested proprietary rights in that trust fund – if the investors retain no proprietary rights then it is hoped that there will be no tax payable on any profits their investments realise and furthermore the protector's presence will also enable them to supervise the activities of the trustees on behalf of the beneficiaries.[91] The difficulty, as explained in the previous paragraph, is that English law does not permit a trust to come into existence without a beneficiary.[92] Thus, even if an offshore jurisdiction were to enact legislation permitting a trust to exist without investors needing to have equitable proprietary rights, there would be the problem that such a trust would not be recognised as being valid in England and Wales, and therefore the investor would be treated as continuing to hold an equitable interest in her investment on resulting trust principles. For this English law analysis not to apply to an offshore trust the protector would be required actually to have the equitable interest in the property vested in it. That would be something which the investor may not wish to countenance, particularly given that the purpose of the transaction would be to transfer the profits to the investors so that the protector would not really be intended to hold the equitable interest. The consequence of pretending that the protector owned the equitable interest when in reality it would be treated as though it remained the property of the investor would be that the trust would be treated as being a sham and the equitable interest treated by English law as belonging to the investors. The sham doctrine is considered briefly in the section after next. The next section will consider another structure which frequently causes problems of sham trusts: revocable trusts.

Revocable trusts

The preceding section considered, in its later stages, the problem of some protector arrangements being deemed to be shams. Another structure which is frequently used in tax avoidance arrangements – whether within England and Wales, or cross-border – is that of the revocable trust. In an effort to avoid liability to tax stemming from equitable ownership of the profits derived from a trust fund, the owner of profit-generating property may settle that property on trust on terms that she shall henceforth have no rights in the property but so that

---

90 *Mara v Browne* [1896] 1 Ch 199, 209, *per* Smith LJ.

91 Now protectors are nothing new. There are protectors in English law, albeit in different forms. They are principally regulators, like the FSA and Pensions Regulator, or ombudsmen. These regulators are different from the protector in that they do not have a simulacrum of the property rights of a beneficiary at their disposal to entitle them to sue trustees for breach of trust, but they do have statutory powers of investigation, scrutiny and censure. Accordingly, it is suggested that there are already models in the UK for the protection of investor-beneficiaries which are already applied to unit trusts, pension funds and even trustees in Eurobond transactions.

92 As discussed in section 4.2 in detail.

the trust instrument contains a power for the settlor to cancel or revoke the trust and recover the property once the tax bill has been settled. If done correctly this would mean that the trust would pay a lower rate of tax than the settlor. The danger is that this revocable trust would be deemed to be a sham whereby the settlor was seeking to pull the wool over the eyes of HM Revenue and Customs. Consequently, the profits from that sham trust would be deemed to belong absolutely to the settlor so that she would have to pay the tax on any attributable profits. This sort of arrangement is ordinarily organised as a discretionary trust in practice – so as to avoid simply having a taxable, revocable trust which returns the entire interest to the settlor – with the result that the trustees have a very large class of objects to whom they may transfer the trust property, one of whom is the settlor. Needless to say, in carrying out the settlor's plan, the trustees then exercise their discretion so as to transfer the property back to the settlor. The dangers for the settlor are whether or not that trust will be treated as a sham, and whether or not under revenue law the settlor will be deemed still to be the absolute owner of the property for tax purposes in any event. The detail of revenue law is outside the scope of this book; whereas the principles relating to sham trusts are outlined below.

Sham trusts

As considered in the two preceding sections there is a risk that a number of trusts structures which are used in international trusts law practice and in tax avoidance practice may be held to be shams and so held to be of no effect such that the trust property is deemed to be held on resulting trust for the settlor. In defining what is meant by a 'sham', Diplock LJ held that a sham constitutes:[93] 'acts done or documents executed by the parties to the "sham" which are intended by them to give to third parties or to the court the appearance of creating between the parties legal rights and obligations different from the actual legal rights and obligations (if any) which the parties intended to create.'

Therefore, a sham is a scheme of action or a pattern of documentation which seeks to create the impression that the state of affairs is one thing when in fact it is something else. An example would be the purported creation of a trust to make it appear that the settlor had divested herself of property, whereas in fact the property is still to be held for her use and enjoyment in fact such that it could be said that she still owns it outright.[94] It is a requirement of finding a transaction to be a sham that the parties to that sham intended to deceive other people as to the nature of their true rights.[95] The principles surrounding sham trusts were considered in detail in section 3.3.3. International trusts law practice is thus concerned with structuring arrangements so as to permit regulatory or tax avoidance across borders, always with the worry that English law would consider a structure involving a UK resident to be a sham or to be taxable or to be subject to UK regulatory control.

21.2.6 The nature of equitable remedies in company law

There are two principal forms of equitable remedy in company law: the first relates to the rights of shareholders to prevent unfairly prejudicial conduct being exerted over them, and

---

93 *Snook v London and West Riding Investments Ltd* [1967] 2 QB 786, 802.
94 *Minwalla v Minwalla* [2004] 7 ITELR 457.
95 *Scott v Federal Commissioner of Taxation (No 2)* (1966) ALJR 265, 279, *per* Windeyer J.

the second relates to the obligations of directors to the company generally.[96] To begin with the directors' duties, ss 170 *et seq.* of the Companies Act 2006 introduced a statutory code of directors' general duties. These duties are 'based on certain common law rules and equitable principles'[97] and 'shall be interpreted and applied in the same way as common law rules or equitable principles'.[98] The three duties which are more obviously based on equitable fiduciary doctrines are: the duty to avoid conflicts of interest;[99] the duty not to accept benefits, such as bribes and secret commissions;[100] and the duty to declare interests in transactions[101] The 2006 Act expressly incorporates these long-standing equitable doctrines to provide remedies for breach of these director's duties[102] There is no doubt about the connection here between mainstream company law and the principles of equity.

Shareholders have a range of rights expressed in the company's constitution (its articles of association) and generally under the Companies Act 2006. For the most part, control of the company is exercised by the company's management in accordance with the powers given to them by the articles of association, and otherwise are exercised by the majority of shareholders voting in the company's general meetings. This power of the majority shareholders (that is, shareholders together holding more than 50% of the voting rights in the company) is expressed in the decision in *Foss v Harbottle*,[103] which provides that the decision of the majority shareholders will not be displaced by the court because the majority will be able to enforce or ratify their wishes through a vote at the general meeting in any event. There are four exceptions to this principle, however: two of which are important for present purposes.[104]

First, further to s 994 of the Companies Act 2006, a shareholder has an action where the affairs of the company have been conducted in a way that is unfairly prejudicial to her. In relation to the s 994 action, there has been the most confusion in relation to the nature of equitable doctrine. Lord Hoffmann held in *O'Neill v Phillips*[105] that:

> In [s 994] Parliament has chosen fairness as the criterion by which the court must decide whether it has jurisdiction to grant relief. It is clear from the legislative history . . . that it chose this concept to free the court from technical considerations of legal right and to

96 For a more detailed discussion of shareholders' rights and directors' duties see Alastair Hudson, *Understanding Company Law*, Routledge-Cavendish, 2010, and Girvin, Hudson and Frisby, *Charlesworth's Company Law*, 18th edn, Sweet & Maxwell, 2010.

97 Companies Act 2006, s 170(3).

98 *Ibid*, s 170(4).

99 *Ibid*, s 175.

100 *Ibid*, s 176.

101 *Ibid*, s 177.

102 *Ibid*, s 178.

103 (1843) 2 Hare 461.

104 First, where a shareholder (even a minority shareholder) has a personal right (for example, under contract). Secondly, where the shareholder brings a derivative action further to s 260 *et seq* of the Companies Act 2006. A derivative action is one in which the shareholder brings litigation in the name of the company seeking a remedy against the directors 'arising from an actual or proposed act or omission involving negligence, default, breach of duty or breach of trust by a director of the company' (Companies Act 2006, s 260(3)). Thirdly, further to s 994 *et seq* on the basis of conduct which was unfairly prejudicial to the claimant shareholder. Fourthly, where the company is wound up on the 'just and equitable' ground under s 122 of the Insolvency Act 1986.

105 [1999] 2 All ER 961.

confer a wide power to do what appeared just and equitable. But this does not mean that the court can do whatever the individual judge happens to think fair. The concept of fairness must be applied judicially and the content which it is given by the courts must be based upon rational principles.

This is an unreconstituted common lawyer's approach to a doctrine in which the court has been given an express statutory power to do what is 'just and equitable' so as to prevent 'unfairness'. (Nothing could be more equitable than that!) Furthermore, it supposes that this general statutory power must necessarily be limited by a judicial gloss with principles which are necessarily not contained in the statute. Quoting Warner J in *Re JE Cade & Son*,[106] Lord Hoffmann returned to the common lawyer's view that 'the court . . . has a very wide discretion, but it does not sit under a palm tree'. In particular, his Lordship wishes to focus on the nature of companies as businesses in which the applicable notions of fairness would have to be interpreted in accordance with the parties' commercial purposes Therefore, it is held that 'unfairness' can only be demonstrated if it is contrary to the terms of the company's articles of association. This is a serious restriction on the courts' powers. For example, if the majority shareholders voted to limit the payment of dividends only to the majority shareholders under a power contained in the company's constitution (that is, its articles of association), this would be unfair on the minority shareholders because it would prevent them from taking any profit from the company, but the effect of Lord Hoffmann's approach would be that simple unfairness would be insufficient to allow the minority shareholders to seek to have that decision set aside on grounds of unfairness.

Section 122 of the Insolvency Act 1986 grants the court the power to wind up a company where it appears to the court to be 'just and equitable' to do so. It was held by Lord Wilberforce in the leading case of *Ebrahimi v Westbourne Galleries*[107] that when exercising this power 'as equity always does, to enable the court to subject the exercise of legal rights to equitable considerations; considerations, that is, of a personal character arising between one individual and another, which may make it unjust, or inequitable, to insist on legal rights, or to exercise them in a particular way'. This approach is different to the approach taken by Lord Hoffmann in *O'Neill v Phillips* in that it accepts that the court may take a generally equitable view of the circumstances by considering whether or not the exercise of a person's legal rights are equitable in the specific circumstances. That the directors owe fiduciary duties to the company and that the Companies Act 2006 grants the shareholders rights to proceed against the company (and thus indirectly the other shareholders) should be taken to mean that it is appropriate to apply equitable doctrines in deciding whether or not the affairs of the company are being operated suitably.

21.2.7 Equity as a risk

Equity itself is said to constitute a risk, as considered in para 12.2.2. A risk, that is, of disturbing the commercial certainty of the parties to a transaction. The economic impact of

---

106   [1992] BCLC 213 at 227.
107   [1972] 2 All ER 492 at 500, [1973] AC 360 at 379.

equity intruding in such circumstances is taken for granted: it is assumed that it could only be bad. Many members of the English judiciary take the approach that well-understood components of contract law should govern the availability of equitable remedies in these situations. The approach of Lord Woolf in *Westdeutsche Landesbank v Islington LBC* is particularly instructive in this context. In his Lordship's view, the availability of equitable proprietary remedies in commercial transactions ought to be predicated on whether or not either party could reasonably have foreseen that in the ordinary course of things the loss was likely to occur.[108]

As Atiyah has explained the interaction of the risk and the use of contract:[109]

> In the market, parties were expected to calculate rationally the various risks, whether of past or of future events, which might affect the value of the contract. Provided that there was no fraud, and provided that the bargaining process was itself fair, the result must be deemed to be fair. Unexpected events, unknown factors, whether occurring before or after the contract was made, were not to be allowed to upset the resultant bargains. In principle all such risks were capable of being perceived and evaluated; in practice, not everybody succeeded in doing so. Or doing it very well . . . The whole point of the free market bargaining approach was to give full rein to the greater skill and knowledge of those who calculated risks better. . . . He who failed to calculate a risk properly when making a contract would lose by it, and next time would calculate more efficiently.

On the other hand, in Atiyah's conception, the purpose of the contract is to evaluate the risks between commercial parties and, even more broadly, to identify a policy underpinning the law of promoting greater economic efficiency by requiring commercial people to become better at evaluating such risks before forming contracts. It is suggested that this goes too far and blithely accepts that markets and free acceptance of risk necessarily constitute the most efficient economic solution: particularly given that it has no strategy for ensuring equity between contracting parties (in the sense that an economist would understand that term as meaning something akin to 'fairness') nor any explicit conception of what constitutes an efficient solution in any particular circumstance.[110]

21.2.8 In defence of equity

As considered below, this commercial detestation for equity masks two things. First, at a technical level, it overlooks the important role which equity has played in developing commercial concepts. The secured interest would be impossible without the trust, and a more flexible form of secured interest over a changeable fund of property would have been impossible without equity's development of the floating charge. Secondly, at a more general level, it would not be enough for commerce to be left to its own devices outwith the normative reach of the legal system. Whether a positivist (believing that law operates as a sovereign over its subjects, like Austin) or a natural law enthusiast (believing that law draws on some greater principle of what is 'right', like Fuller), the reader must agree that law operates

---

108 [1996] 2 All ER 961, 1016; citing, with approval, Mann, 1985, 30.
109 Atiyah, 1979, 437.
110 See Le Grand, 1991, 20 *et seq*; Le Grand, 1982, especially 1–19; Evans, 1998, especially 17 *et seq*.

on the basis of enforcing some very general conception of right and wrong. So it is that equity has tended to limit itself to the prevention of fraud and the enforcement of good conscience. For commercial law to seek to avoid equity would be to allow commerce to escape the norms of the legal system which are nevertheless enforceable against all ordinary citizens. This would be a particularly pernicious development which would permit the already powerful corporate and commercial interests to set up their own legal system: in effect, it would be to produce one law for them and another law for the rest of us.

Nothing in this discussion should be taken to support the view that commercial practice ought to be able to develop its own distinct rules and norms. Rather, it is suggested that norms and rules should be developed which take into account the very particular context in which commerce operates: an approach which may require that commercial organisations (like pension funds perhaps) are required to act in a way which is particularly sensitive to the needs of their clientele, instead of permitting commercial practice to set out its own contractual norms. What is suggested is that equity should consider the context of commercial activity in the same way that it considers all cases in their own contexts; what cannot be acceptable is that commercial people are able to pick and choose which laws they wish to be bound by and which they wish to ignore.[111]

---

111 For a consideration of the development of a form of capitalism which operates outwith national, legal boundaries and the pernicious effects which that may have, see Klein, 2000 and Bauman, 2000.

Quistclose trusts

OVERVIEW

A Quistclose *trust comes into existence in relation to a loan contract when the intention of the parties is that the borrower is required to use the loan moneys for a specified purpose. In the event that the borrower goes into insolvency, the loan moneys are deemed to have been held on trust for the lender. The issue is as to the basis on which this trust comes into existence. In* Barclays Bank v Quistclose, *Lord Wilberforce held that a primary trust took effect over the loan moneys until they were used for their assigned purpose, and a secondary trust came into existence so as to carry the equitable interest back to the lender. This was interpreted by many commentators as being a resulting trust. Lord Wilberforce himself expressed this as a combination of common law and equitable principles such that an equitable remedy granted property rights to the lender in the event that the terms of the contract were not performed. In* Twinsectra v Yardley, *Lord Millett considered that this was a resulting trust which operated so that sufficient title was transferred to the borrower to carry out the terms of the loan contract but that the lender otherwise retained the equitable interest in the loan moneys.*

22.1 INTRODUCTION

The most significant overlap between commercial activity and the law of trusts (as commonly understood by commercial lawyers in terms of sale of goods, loan contracts and so forth) relates to taking title in goods and to the acquisition of security as part of a transaction. Typically, the issue is as follows: in creating a commercial contract, how do the parties acquire or retain title (as appropriate) in property which is used or transferred for the purposes of that contract? This chapter considers the manner in which contract law and the law of trusts variously deal with these questions.

There are three issues considered here. First, the manner in which a titleholder in property may seek to retain title in that property even though it is being used for the purposes of a contract. The titleholder would wish, in an ideal world, to remain the absolute owner of that property. This will be possible where the property is, for example, plant or machinery which remains entirely separate from all other property. The more difficult situation arises when the property is mixed with other property so that it is impossible to identify that property in its original form. For example, where sugar is used to manufacture chocolate: once the chocolate has been manufactured it will not be possible to identify the sugar separately as sugar. Consequently, the titleholder would want to acquire some rights in the chocolate which are distinct from the rights of any other contracting party. Secondly, in a contract of loan, there are issues as to the forms of security which the lender could acquire. The lender may take a charge or mortgage over property owned absolutely by the borrower as security for the performance of the loan (as considered in Chapter 23 in relation to mortgages). Alternatively (and the third issue), the lender may impose a condition on the purposes for which the loan moneys can be used so that those loan moneys are held under a *Quistclose* trust for the lender.[1] The options for the lender vary between retaining title in the loan moneys before they are spent, acquiring rights over a mixed fund of property, or acquiring that form of right identified with the *Quistclose* trust. This chapter will consider these various possibilities, but its principal focus will be on the nature of *Quistclose* trusts.

There are then two final sections which consider in outline the manner in which trusts structures are used in relation to debt securities: eurobonds and debentures. Securities in this sense are financial instruments which can be traded on the open market which evidence a debt. They differ from an ordinary loan contract in that such a contract is created privately between the lender and the borrower; and whereas the benefit of a loan contract could be transferred to another person, it is not traded on an open exchange in the same way as a bond. In relation to both of these debt securities, a trustee is used as a regulatory device to ensure that the company issuing the bond or the debenture performs its obligations properly. The trustee is entitled to sue on behalf of the bondholders or the debenture holders in the event of

---

1 *Barclays Bank v Quistclose Investments Ltd* [1970] AC 567.

default. A trust is used in these circumstances for two reasons. First, the presence of the trustee ensures, it is hoped, the proper performance of the debtor's obligations but, secondly, there is also the utility of the notion of 'trust' which operates to reassure investors that their acquisition of bonds is not entirely unprotected. These two contexts serve to round off this chapter's analysis of the interaction of commercial trusts with commercial lending.

What will emerge from this discussion is another example of concepts of contract and of property mixing to allocate rights in assets used as part of commercial transactions. The techniques are the same: can the parties demonstrate that they still have title in assets, or can they assert title to some assets in the event that the counterparty to the contract fails to perform?

22.2 RETENTION OF TITLE AND PLEDGE

This short section summarises the legal treatment of contractual provisions relating to retention of title in property, and the opposite position where title is transferred outright to the counterparty to a contract by way of a pledge. These two structures will throw into relief the uses of trusts later in this chapter and the use of charges and equitable mortgages considered in Chapter 23. The purpose of these short outlines, then, is to set out the manner in which the laws of property and contract deal with those questions in contrast to the main discussion point of this chapter: the *Quistclose* trust.[2]

22.2.1 *Romalpa* clauses – right in specific property

A *Romalpa* clause is a contractual provision which enables the titleholder to property to retain common law rights in that property.[3] In relation to a contract in which property is to be used as part of the contractual purpose, that property will remain the property of the provider both at common law and in equity,[4] unless that property becomes mixed with other property so as to be indistinguishable, leaving only rights in equity for the claimant.[5] In the latter situation, it would be a matter for construction of the contract as to the rights which the provider of the property was intended to acquire. It is likely that that would disclose a floating charge in many instances. In general a retention of title under a *Romalpa* clause would prevent another party to that contract from passing good title to a third party under the *nemo dat* principle (considered in Chapter 21), although a third party with notice of the contract would be precluded from taking good title in any event.[6]

22.2.2 Transfer of title and pledge

The trust transfers only equitable title to the beneficiaries of the trust arrangement subject to the limitations and provisions of the trust itself. Typically the trust will make the rights

2 *Ibid.*
3 *Aluminium Industrie Vaassen BV v Romalpa Aluminium Ltd* [1976] 1 WLR 676.
4 *Ibid.*
5 *Clough Mill v Martin* [1984] 3 All ER 982.
6 *De Mattos v Gibson* (1858) 4 De GF & J 276, (1858) 45 ER 108.

of the parties contingent on their performance under the terms of any commercial contract. A pledge, as ordinarily understood,[7] would involve the owner of property parting with possession of the property by delivering it to the secured party, without giving that secured party the right to deal with that property as though its absolute owner.[8] The secured party is prevented from dealing with the property as its absolute owner until such time as its proprietary rights do crystallise. In the event that those rights crystallise, thus vesting almost absolute title in the secured party, the secured party is entitled to sell the pledged asset to make good the counterparty's failure in performance of the principal contract.[9] The pledgee's rights are to apply the property to discharge the pledgor's obligations and are not a transfer of absolute title because such a transfer of title would entitle the pledgee to retain any surplus in the value of the property over the debt owed to the pledgee.[10]

The precise rights of the secured party will turn on the manner in which they are expressed by the pledge agreement. A pledge agreement may provide, quite simply, that the secured party is entitled to absolute title in the pledged assets in the event of non-performance by its counterparty, thus establishing a different case to that set out immediately above. More commonly, a contract would provide that the secured party is entitled to take absolute title in the pledged assets only up to the value of any amount owed to it by its counterparty. Within this second analysis, the pledge contract might provide that the pledgee takes no proprietary title until some default of the pledgor identified in the agreement, and has merely a possessory interest until that time. As witness to this analysis, it was held in *The Odessa*:[11]

> If the pledgee sells he does so by virtue of and to the extent of the pledgor's ownership, and not with a new title of his own. He must appropriate the proceeds of the sale to the payment of the pledgor's debt, for the money resulting from the sale is the pledgor's money to be so applied.

It is suggested that that analysis must necessarily be contingent on the precise terms of the pledge agreement and the form of rights which they purport to the grant to the secured party.[12] There are then two options: either the secured party is entitled to take title in the assets themselves, or it is entitled only to sell the assets and take such proportion of those sale proceeds as is required to offset the counterparty's outstanding obligations. In deciding which is applicable, recourse must be had to the precise terms of the pledge agreement.

---

7 The most common example of a pledge would be an arrangement with a pawnbroker.
8 *The Odessa* [1916] 1 AC 145.
9 The secured party will be trustee, it is suggested, of any such surplus between the time it is received and its payment to the counterparty. Where the surplus has not been segregated from the amount which the secured party is entitled to retain in discharge of the counterparty's failure to pay, the entire sale proceeds of the pledged assets are held on trust by the secured party in proportion to the amount to which each party is entitled: *Re Goldcorp* [1995] 1 AC 74, at sections 3.4 and 21.1 above.
10 *Re Hardwick, ex p Hubbard* (1886) 17 QBD 690. Cf *Carter v Wake* (1877) 4 Ch D 605; *Fraser v Byas* (1895) 11 TLR 481.
11 [1916] 1 AC 145, 159.
12 See generally Palmer and Hudson, 1998.

22.3 THE FUNDAMENTALS OF *QUISTCLOSE* TRUSTS

22.3.1 *Quistclose* trusts in outline

A general definition of the Quistclose *trust*

Commercially-speaking, a *Quistclose* trust is a means by which a lender of money can retain a 'security interest' in loan moneys by inserting a clause into the loan contract which provides that the borrower may use those loan moneys only for specified purposes. If the borrower uses the money for some other purpose, then a trust is imposed on the moneys in the lender's favour. This form of trust is particularly significant as a means of protecting the lender against the borrower's insolvency because the loan moneys are treated as being held on trust for the lender and therefore are not distributed in the insolvency proceedings as part of the insolvent borrower's estate. Even if the borrower remains solvent after lending the money then the lender has a right under the *Quistclose* trust to recover the loan moneys or to trace those loan moneys into the hands of any third party who has received them in breach of the loan contract.

While this will serve as an adequate description of the commercial usefulness of a *Quistclose* trust a number of complex legal questions arise.[13] First, it will be important to identify precisely what sort of 'security interest' the lender acquires. Secondly, it will be important to know whether the lender 'retains' a right in the original loan moneys throughout the life of the loan contract, or whether that right only comes into existence for the first time when the borrower disobeys the terms of the loan contract, or whether the right comes into existence in some other way. Thirdly, it will be important to know what form of trust – express trust, resulting trust, constructive trust, or some other construct – best explains the *Quistclose* trust. Fourthly, while all of the preceding issues have generated a complex legal literature in the abstract, it may be important to consider how the precise terms of any loan contract alter the appropriate analysis on the facts of any given case. Before turning to these questions, however, we should consider chronologically the cases which have given rise to the modern *Quistclose* trust concept.

The source of Quistclose *trusts*

The *Quistclose* trust takes its name from the decision of the House of Lords in *Barclays Bank v Quistclose*.[14] The principle in *Barclays Bank v Quistclose* in turn derives from a number of earlier decisions including *Hassall v Smither*.[15] In short, where a transferor transfers property subject to a contractual provision that the transferee is entitled only to use that property for limited purposes, then the transferee will hold the property on trust for the transferor in the event that the property is used for some purpose other than that set out in the contract. Significantly, in the event that the transferee purports to transfer rights to some third party in breach of that contractual provision, the transferor is deemed to have retained its rights under a trust which will preclude the transferee from acquiring rights in that property. At present

---

13 See, for example, Thomas & Hudson, 2004, 292 *et seq*; Priestley, 1987, 217; Ricketts, 1991; Bridge, 1992; Payne, 2000; Chambers, 1997, Ch 3; Worthington, 1996, Ch 3; Thomas, 1998, 260; and more generally Swadling (ed), 2004.

14 [1970] AC 567.

15 (1806) 12 Ves 119; *Toovey v Milne* (1819) 2 B & Ald 683, (1819) 106 ER 514.

the *Quistclose* arrangement has been applied only to loan moneys but, as Worthington suggests, there is no reason in principle why it should apply only to money and not to other forms of property.[16] This issue is discussed below.[17] The following discussion will examine the *Quistclose* decision and the various explanations for the nature of the trust created.

22.3.2 The decision in *Barclays Bank v Quistclose*

The decision in Barclays Bank v Quistclose *itself*

In *Barclays Bank v Quistclose*[18] a loan contract was formed by which Quistclose lent money to Rolls Razor Ltd on the condition that the loan moneys were to be used solely for the payment of dividends to its preferred shareholders. That money was held in a share dividend bank account separate from all other moneys. Memorably, Harman LJ described Rolls Razor as being 'in Queer Street' at the time – referring to the fact that the company had already exceeded its overdraft limit with the bank on its general bank account and was clearly in financial difficulties. The specific purpose for the loan, after negotiation between Quistclose and the company, was to enable the company to pay a dividend to an identified category of shareholders but it was a condition of this arrangement that the loan money was not to be used for any other purpose. In the event Rolls Razor went into insolvency before the dividend was paid. Therefore, the loan money rested in a bank account held with Barclays Bank without being paid in fulfilment of the term of the loan contract. Rolls Razor's bank accounts with Barclays Bank were in overdraft: an overdraft is, in effect, a loan made by a bank to the person who is entitled to draw on the overdraft. Therefore if a bank uses money to pay down an overdraft then it is using that money to pay off a loan owed to it. Once Rolls Razor had become insolvent, Barclays Bank was concerned to pay off the overdraft which it had provided to Rolls Razor. Consequently, Barclays Bank argued that it should be entitled to set off the money held in the share dividend account against the overdraft which Rolls Razor had with the bank. Quistclose contended that the money in the share dividend account was held on trust for Quistclose and therefore that the bank was not entitled to set that money off against the outstanding overdraft on Rolls Razor's other account.

The House of Lords decided that the loan money held separately in the share dividend bank account should be treated as having been held on trust for Quistclose. The trust was said to have come into existence on the basis that the specified purpose of the loan had not been performed and that the loan moneys were purportedly being used for a non-authorised purpose. Furthermore, the House of Lords held unanimously that the money in the share dividend account was held on resulting trust for Quistclose.

Lord Wilberforce upheld the resulting trust in favour of Quistclose on the basis that it was an implied term of the loan contract that the money be returned to the Quistclose in the event that it was not used for the purpose for which it was specifically lent. Lord Wilberforce found that there were two trusts: a 'primary trust' (which empowered Rolls Razor to use the money to pay the dividend) and a 'secondary trust' (which required Rolls Razor to hold the money on resulting trust for the bank if it was not used to pay the dividend). As his Lordship held:

---

16 Worthington, 1996, 63. See now also *Farepak Food & Gift Ltd* [2006] All ER (Dec) 265 (D).
17 Section 22.4.9.
18 *Barclays Bank v Quistclose Investments Ltd* [1970] AC 567.

In the present case the intention to create a secondary trust for the benefit of the lender, to arise if the primary trust, to pay the dividend, could not be carried out, is clear and I can find no reason why the law should not give effect to it.

From this proposition we can derive the general principle that *Quistclose* trusts take effect as resulting trusts by means of this two-level, primary/secondary trust structure. We will probe this idea in greater detail below.

Examples of Quistclose trusts

The case of *Twinsectra v Yardley*[19] gives us another factual example of circumstances in which a *Quistclose* trust might arise. In that case moneys were lent by Twinsectra to Yardley. Twinsectra wanted the security of knowing that the loan moneys would only be used for specified purposes which were specified in the loan contract. Yardley's solicitor was also required to give a formal undertaking to Twinsectra as to the proper use of the money. The first solicitor was replaced by a second solicitor, Leach, who paid away the loan moneys in accordance with Yardley's instructions: those instructions were in breach both of the terms of the loan contract and also of the terms of the undertaking which the first solicitor had given and by which Leach had agreed to be bound. The loan money was spent and Yardley was unable to repay the loan, so Twinsectra sought to recover their loss. This case is discussed in detail in section 20.2.5 in relation to Leach's potential liability for the misuse of the loan money. Lord Millett, in a minority speech, held that this arrangement had also created a *Quistclose* trust because there was a contractual limitation on the use of the loan moneys. None of the other law lords expressed a view on the detail of the *Quistclose* trust question in their speeches. The precise nature of the *Twinsectra* trust suggested by Lord Millett is considered below; for the present we are simply trying to understand the sort of factual bases on which a *Quistclose* trust will come into existence.

In similar fashion to *Twinsectra v Yardley*, a solicitor's undertaking was given in *Global Marine Drillships Ltd v Landmark Solicitors LLP*[20] to the effect that money had been placed by Global Marine with its solicitors, Landmark, and a Ms Jones so that it was to be held on trust by them and so that it was to be used for the purpose identified in the solicitor's undertaking. This arrangement was held to constitute a *Quistclose* trust.[21] In essence, the moneys had been passed by Ms Jones and Landmark to third parties after they had been put under pressure by them to do so; in consequence, Henderson J held that the *Quistclose* trust principle applied to those moneys, which would permit Global Marine to trace after them.

Another example of a *Quistclose* trust arose in *Templeton Insurance Ltd v Penningtons Solicitors LLP*,[22] a case in which money was lent by Templeton to clients of Penningtons, a firm of solicitors, to purchase a 'brown-field' development site. These moneys were lent on the condition that the loan moneys would be held by Penningtons subject to a solicitor's undertaking that the money was to be used to complete the purchase of that land or, in the event that the sale could not be completed, on the condition that the loan money would be

---

19   [2002] 2 AC 164.
20   [2011] EWHC 2685, Henderson J.
21   These proceedings were summary proceedings (that is, they were brought seeking to terminate the litigation without the need for a full trial) and therefore did not need to pursue matters to a conclusion.
22   [2006] EWHC 685 (Ch).

held in Pennington's client bank account on trust for the lender. It was held that this constituted a *Quistclose* trust in favour of Templeton.

There are numerous other examples on the cases. Most of the cases require that the loan
contract identify a single, specific use of the loan moneys. In *Re Northern Developments
Holdings Ltd*,[23] the loan money was paid for 'the express purpose of providing money for the
subsidiary's unsecured creditors over the ensuing weeks and for no other purpose' and
consequently a *Quistclose* trust was upheld. In *Re EVTR*[24] the loan money was advanced 'for
the sole purpose of buying new equipment', with the same result. Similarly, in *General
Communications Ltd v Development Finance Corporation of New Zealand Ltd*[25] the loan
money was paid 'for the express purpose' of purchasing new equipment, with the result that
a *Quistclose* trust was found.

Outright transfers of the loan moneys mean there is no Quistclose *trust*

A *Quistclose* trust requires that the loan moneys are transferred subject to a specific obligation to use the moneys only for a specified purpose. There will not be a *Quistclose* trust if the
loan moneys are transferred outright to the borrower, as would be the case in an ordinary
loan contract, without any obligation to use the loan moneys only for a specified purpose
being imposed on the borrower.[26] Otherwise, there is a tendency for claimants who have had
their property misused to seek to claim that the defendant *ought* to have used that property
for such-and-such a purpose, and so that a *Quistclose* trust should be taken to have arisen
over the property, even though there was no contractual provision which required such a use
of that property.[27]

It must be proved, of course, that it was the intention of the parties that these loan moneys
were to be used for identified purposes and were not simply loans made in the ordinary way
whereby the borrower can use the money as he or she so chooses.[28] The same point arose
before the High Court of the Isle of Man in *Du Preez Ltd v Kaupthing Singer & Friedlander
(Isle of Man) Ltd*,[29] where a customer of a bank argued that when it had instructed that bank
to transfer moneys through its accounts to a third party then that constituted a *Quistclose*
trust over those moneys which bound the bank to that purpose. (It should be remembered
that money held in a bank account is not held on trust by the bank unless a trust is expressly
created over it.[30]) The reason for arguing for the existence of such a trust was that the bank
had gone into insolvency and therefore the customer sought to argue that those moneys were
impressed with a trust so that they would not simply be distributed among the unsecured

23 Unreported, 6 October 1978, *per* Megarry V-C.
24 [1987] BCLC 646.
25 [1990] 3 NZLR 406, 432.
26 *Abou-Rahmah and Others v Abacha and Others* [2005] EWHC 2662 (QB), [2006] 1 Lloyd's Rep 484.
27 *Re Farepak Food and Gift Ltd* [2006] All ER (D) 265 (Dec).
28 *Soutzos v Asombang* [2010] EWHC 842 (Ch), [2010] BPIR 960, Newey J.
29 [2011] WTLR 559, (2010) 12 ITELR 943. See the same point at first instance in *Habana Ltd v Kaupthing
    Singer & Friedlander (Isle of Man) Ltd* [2011] WTLR 275, (2009–10) 12 ITELR 736. Reference was made to
    the Isle of Man case *Magenta Finance & Trading Co v Savings and Investment Bank (In Liquidation)* [1985]
    Fin LR 237 where a tracing order was refused to a customer in relation to moneys which had already been
    distributed as part of the bank's settlement of its debts.
30 *Foley v Hill* (1848) Cas 28, 9 ER 1002. On these facts there had not been even an express trust created over
    these moneys by the customer at any time, as was found at first instance.

creditors of the bank. However, there was no proof that the parties had had any such intention, and therefore no *Quistclose* trust was found. This was simply a transfer of moneys between bank accounts and therefore there was nothing about the circumstances, and certainly no discussions between the parties, to the effect that those moneys were intended to be held on trust.[31]

So much for the precise facts of the decisions which have illustrated the decision in *Barclays Bank v Quistclose*: the issue now is to identify what type of a trust a *Quistclose* trust is. To do this we will need to examine a range of different analyses which have been proposed in cases after the decision of the House of Lords in *Quistclose*. As we identify each different analysis we will pause to consider whether or not each argument is watertight before moving on to the next analysis. Therefore, we shall consider arguments for resulting trust, express trust and constructive trust in that order. As will emerge below, the speech of Lord Millett in *Twinsectra v Yardley*[32] has received a great deal of support although,[33] it is suggested, there are some gaps in its logic: this approach is considered last.

22.4 CATEGORISING THE *QUISTCLOSE* TRUST

22.4.1 The issue

Categorising the *Quistclose* trust within the pantheon of established forms of trust is problematic. The real problem is explaining the nature of the rights of the lender, the rights of the borrower and the time at which those rights come into existence. This two-layered trust structure used by Lord Wilberforce in *Barclays Bank v Quistclose* (combining a primary and a secondary trust) is unique to the case law in this area – although it would be possible to create a complex express trust which mimicked it. What is significant is that the *Quistclose* trust will be imposed in circumstances in which the parties to a loan contract have been silent as to the precise construction which is to be placed on their contract. The courts have not yet considered a contract which expressly imposed a categorisation on its trust: the suggestion which is made below is that such an express categorisation would be decisive of the question. For present purpose we shall have to consider this question in the abstract. It should be recalled that the House of Lords in *Barclays Bank v Quistclose* has used the expression 'resulting trust' to describe this arrangement.[34] It is with this analysis that we shall begin.

---

31 A poor argument was raised in *Annabel's (Berkeley Square) Ltd v Revenue and Customs Commissioners* [2009] 4 All ER 55, at [31] to the effect that in a tronc arrangement for tips in a nightclub and restaurant, the tronc-master who held the tips should be considered to have done so under a primary trust for the employees and a secondary trust for the employer based on *Quistclose v Barclays Bank*. Two points arise. First, this argument did not deal with the obvious point that hitherto the authorities which have considered this area of law properly have recognised that it relates solely to loan contracts, not arrangements which clearly constitute express trusts in general terms. Second, there is no good reason why the employer should take beneficial rights in a tronc when any surplus funds should clearly be distributed proportionately among the wait staff for whom they were intended by the customers.

32 [2002] 2 AC 164.

33 See for example, Underhill and Hayton, 2002 and *Templeton Insurance Ltd v Penningtons Solicitors LLP* [2006] EWHC 685 (Ch).

34 *Ibid*, and *Westdeutsche Landesbank v Islington* [1996] AC 669, *per* Lord Browne-Wilkinson.

22.4.2 Resulting trust

The argument for resulting trust: are there two different types of resulting trust here?

The first explanation of the nature of a *Quistclose* trust, which was accepted by Lord Wilberforce in *Barclays Bank v Quistclose*, is that the *Quistclose* trust transfers the equitable interest in the loan moneys back to the lender on resulting trust. This analysis suggests that title in the loan moneys passes away from the lender to the borrower, under Lord Wilbeforce's 'primary trust', before then bouncing back to the lender on resulting trust when the 'secondary trust' comes into existence at the moment when the borrower has breached the terms of the loan contract. It should not be forgotten that the lender also retained rights to sue at common law for breach of contract, if the defendant were solvent. Lord Wilberforce held that it was clearly the 'mutual intention' of the parties on these facts that the loan moneys should not become part of the assets of Rolls Razor Ltd but rather that those moneys were to be used to pay the dividend.[35] Indeed, his Lordship held that this was 'the essence of the bargain'.[36]

By contrast, as is considered in greater detail below, Lord Millett in the House of Lords in *Twinsectra v Yardley*[37] recognised that this sort of trust is a resulting trust[38] but Lord Millett's explanation of the resulting trust form of *Quistclose* trust was that the lender retained ownership of the equitable interest in the loan moneys throughout the life of the transaction.[39] Therefore, this resulting trust would not really involve any property 'jumping back' to the lender (as a resulting trust, taken literally, is supposed to do[40]): instead the resulting trust would be recognising that the lender had had some equitable ownership of the loan moneys until the borrower used them for their proper purpose. If the loan moneys were not used for their proper purpose, then the resulting trust would recognise the continued equitable ownership on the part of the lender. (There are, however, difficulties with the way in which Lord Millett expresses this idea, as considered below at para 22.4.5.)

The *Quistclose* approach can be distinguished from the transaction at issue in *Westdeutsche Landesbank v Islington*[41] (which denied the existence of any proprietary rights on resulting trust to effect restitution of unjust enrichment in general terms) on the basis that the moneys paid in that case were transferred outright without any condition being placed on their use – although it should be remembered that Lord Browne-Wilkinson did expressly accept that a *Quistclose* trust is a form of resulting trust. The *Quistclose* trust, by distinction, operates only in circumstances in which there is a condition attached to the purpose for which the loan moneys are to be used. The principle reason for supporting a resulting trust in favour of the lender appears to be that, if the court held otherwise, it would permit the borrower to affirm the transaction in part (by taking the loan moneys and passing that money to creditors on insolvency) but to refuse to be bound by the condition that the property could only be used for a specified purpose.[42]

---

35 *Barclays Bank v Quistclose* [1970] AC 567, 580.
36 *Ibid.*
37 [2002] 2 AC 164.
38 *Ibid*, para [100].
39 See Thomas and Hudson, 2004, 293.
40 See 11.1, where the expression resulting trust is said to derive from the Latin 'resalire' meaning to 'jump back'.
41 [1996] AC 669.
42 *Re Rogers* (1891) 8 Morr 243, 248, *per* Lindley LJ.

Therefore, on this analysis, the *Quistclose* trust would appear to operate such that the borrower has title to the money at common law and is entitled to dispose of it in the way provided for in the contract subject to the fact that equity prevents the borrower from using that money for any purpose other than the purpose set out in the loan agreement. Consequently, the lender retains an interest in the money on resulting trust principles throughout the life of the transaction which entitles the lender to recover that property if the purpose is not carried out. The fact that this interest appears to be continuous throughout the transaction is the element which gives rise to the argument that this trust is a resulting trust, rather than a new constructive trust imposed by the court when the borrower seeks to act unconscionably.

On this analysis the *Quistclose* right appears to be similar to the *Romalpa* clause under which a person who transfers property to another for the purposes of a contract expressly retains title in that property during the life of the contract. As such, it should properly be said that the right comes into existence at the time that the contract is created. Therefore, the lender should be treated as holding that right in the property from the moment of the creation of that contract.

Against a resulting trust: the equitable interest comes into existence too late

The principal problem with Lord Wilberforce's model of the *Quistclose* trust is explained by reference to the diagram set out immediately below. That problem concerns the fact that a resulting trust will only come into existence once the loan moneys have been misused and therefore the lender's security interest is created only after there has been a breach of contract. Therefore, it is suggested, this security interest will come into existence too late to be of use in many circumstances. The time sequence in a *Quistclose* transaction should be understood as operating in the following way:

Day 1: Loan contract entered into between lender and borrower, including a provision that the borrower use the money only for a specific purpose.	**Day 2**: Loan moneys transferred at common law to borrower.	**Day 3**: Borrower breaches the term in the loan contract by using the money for an unspecified purpose.	**Day 4**: Lender seeks to recover the loan moneys as a result of the breach of the term in the loan contract.

It is not necessary in practice that these events take place on different 'days'; and so you may prefer to think of them as 'stages'; although I do think that breaking them out into different 'days' makes the explanation easier. So, to consider the table. The loan moneys are transferred outright to the borrower on Day 2. The borrower is the absolute owner of the loan moneys on Day 2. The loan moneys are then paid away by the borrower on Day 3. Lord Wilberforce's resulting trust analysis says that the secondary trust only comes into existence once the moneys have been misused. Therefore, the resulting trust will only be able to bite if the loan moneys are still separately identifiable on Day 3, or on the day when the claim is brought.

The question as to the categorisation of *Quistclose* trusts is therefore as follows: does the lender retain some equitable interest in the loan moneys from Day 1, or are all rights given up on Day 2 with the transfer of the loan moneys, or does the lender only re-acquire rights in the money on Day 3? For there to have been a trust it cannot be that the lender acquires rights in the loan moneys only on Day 4 because that would be to make the trust remedial, something which is not possible at English law.[43] The principal problem with having the resulting trust come into existence on Day 3 is that there is only a security interest for the lender *after* the breach of contract has been committed. By the time that the lender's interest comes into existence the money will have disappeared and the borrower may already be insolvent. The most satisfying approach would be one which imposes a property right in favour of the lender from Day 1, as suggested below in relation to the use of express trusts. It is true that even such a structure runs the risk that the borrower will still misuse the money in practice, but at least the property right will have pre-dated any insolvency of the borrower.

It might be possible to analyse Lord Wilberforce's model differently. It could be argued that the purpose of the primary trust is to impose a trust over the loan moneys throughout the life of the loan contract. However, this would be an express trust – as is considered below – and it would seem illogical to have a resulting trust come into existence on Day 3 which superseded the primary, express trust.

Lord Millett's verson of the resulting trust could be understood as meaning that there is a retention of an equitable interest in favour of the lender throughout the loan contract too – although, again, it is difficult to see how this differs from an express trust, as considered below.[44] The better analysis might be to think of this form of *Quistclose* trust as being an express trust, which Lord Millett does not do, which is imposed from the outset in the loan contract on Day 1 and which grants the borrower a power to use the money for the contractually specified purpose. Significantly, if the trust comes into existence on Day 1, then the lender has her security interest before the breach of contract. If the purpose is contravened then the express trust provides that the money is held on trust by the borrower for the lender absolutely from that time onwards.

Against a resulting trust: retention, not transfer

In advancing the argument that a *Quistclose* trust is a resulting trust, it is commonly said that the trust imposed on the borrower when seeking to use the property for an unauthorised purpose does have the hallmarks of a resulting trust properly so-called because it returns equitable title in property to its original owner once that original owner had transferred title away. Alternatively, in rebutting the contention that a *Quistclose* trust is a resulting trust, it could again be argued that the retention of rights by the original owner constitutes a *creation* of an equitable interest and not a *recovery* of an equitable interest after some transfer away on a typical resulting trust model. After all, the secondary trust could be said to have created the equitable interest for the first time, as opposed to returning it to the lender.

The principal weakness of a resulting trust analysis, from a security interest perspective, is the time at which the lender acquires its proprietary rights. The resulting trust is said by Lord Wilberforce in *Barclays Bank v Quistclose* to come into existence in the form of a secondary trust only at the time at which the borrower misuses the loan moneys. If the loan moneys were received on Monday before the borrower went into insolvency on the Tuesday before the loan moneys were misused contrary to the terms of the contract on the Wednesday, then the resulting trust would only come into existence *after* the borrower had gone into insolvency. Therefore, the lender would not have a proprietary right, on this analysis, before

---

43 *Westdeutsche Landesbank v Islington* [1996] AC 669.
44 Hackney, 1987, 154; Payne, 2000.

the insolvency and would therefore not be a secured creditor. The risk for the lender is that there is no resulting trust over the loan moneys between the time of transfer to the borrower and the misuse of the money.

In the manner this form of resulting trust is explained by Lord Millett in *Twinsectra v Yardley*, there is a retention of title by the lender. However, a trust in which the beneficiary 'retains' rights from the outset is not a resulting trust. A *Quistclose* trust, significantly, does not arise on the basis of a transfer of property away from the lender which is then returned to the lender. As such it could not be a resulting trust, as a resulting trust is ordinarily described.[45] If there were an outright transfer of the loan moneys from the lender to the borrower, as ordinarily happens in loan contracts, the lender would cease to have any title in the property which could be held on resulting trust.[46] So, Worthington juxtaposes the *Quistclose* trust with a transfer in the sale of goods context in which the seller gives up title to the buyer as part of the sale contract and therefore does not retain rights in the property.[47] Rather, an alternative conceptualisation of this structure would be that the lender transfers the loan moneys to the borrower on the basis that the borrower is entitled to use those moneys for the contractually specified purpose. If that purpose is carried out the lender is bound by the contract to release any proprietary rights in the loan moneys; if the purpose is not carried out the lender does not release those proprietary rights. The equitable interest in the loan money does not leave the lender – it would be, in fact, an express trust contained in the contract. The express trust analysis and the reasons for preferring it are considered next.

22.4.3 Express trust

The express trust analysis

The analysis of the *Quistclose* trust as a form of express trust would proceed as follows. The lender enters into a contract of loan with the borrower. That contract does not conform to the ordinary presumption of a loan contract that the lender intends to transfer outright all of the interest in the loan moneys but rather contains an express contractual provision which precludes the borrower from using the money for any purpose other than that provided for in the contract. The contract could be understood as containing an express trust for the benefit of the lender on the following terms: the loan moneys will be advanced to the borrower as trustee with a power to pay away that money for the purposes specified in the loan contract and for no other purpose; otherwise the loan moneys are held on trust for the lender by the borrower until the loan moneys are used for the contractual purpose. Those terms would continue: if the borrower purports to use the loan moneys for any other purpose then the borrower will be acting in excess of her power, such that the exercise of the power will be void, and those loan moneys would continue to be held on trust for the benefit of the lender. The lender would be able to trace the loan moneys into the hands of any third party and so recover them, as considered in Chapter 19. The borrower would be liable to account to the lender for any breach of trust, as considered in Chapter 18.

The lender's rights under the express trust would come into existence from the moment that the loan contract was created. The lender's security interest would therefore be in

45 *Ibid.*
46 *Westdeutsche Landesbank v Islington* [1996] AC 669.
47 Worthington, 1996, 44.

existence from the date of the creation of the contract. What would be required would be sufficient certainty of intention to create an express trust from that moment as opposed to transferring absolute title in the loan money to the borrower, as is more usual in relation to loan contracts.

What is perhaps difficult about this analysis is that, first, it has not been upheld in an English case yet, although it has been upheld in Australia;[48] and secondly, it is perhaps sufficiently complex to require drafting explicitly in a loan contract, otherwise a court may be reluctant to infer its existence. It is clearly the most advantageous analysis of a *Quistclose* arrangement, it is suggested, because it offers the neatest protection for the lender of the money throughout the life of the loan contract by not relying on the commission of a breach of contract before the trust comes into existence for the first time.

More frequently the cases have turned on contracts in which it is not clear what the parties intended. Such contracts may nevertheless disclose an express trust (such intention being capable of imputation by the court as an unconscious express trust).[49] As contended in the diagram in para 22.4.2, the lender does not part with equitable title in a *Quistclose* situation: rather, the lender retains equitable title in the loan moneys. That retention of title in which the borrower acquires legal title (and thus the ability to pay the loan moneys into its own bank account) coupled with the retention of the equitable title by the lender and the contractual limitation on the use of the property, constitutes this *Quistclose* trust as a form of express trust.[50] It is suggested that it would have been preferable if Lord Millett had referred to his trust in *Twinsectra v Yardley* as being an express trust rather than a resulting trust, as considered below. What his Lordship did not do was to explain the nature of the borrower's power to use the loan moneys.

An example of the express trust analysis

The Australian case of *Re Australian Elizabethan Theatre Trust* has held that there is no need for a separate analysis of the *Quistclose* trust and that, instead, ordinary principles of express trust law are sufficient to explain the appropriate property law principles.[51] Thus, it is said,[52] there is an express trust with two limbs: one granting a power to the borrower to use the loan moneys for the contractually-specified purpose and the second which provides that any misuse of the loan moneys causes the entire equitable interest to be held for the lender.[53] In *Templeton Insurance Ltd v Penningtons Solicitors LLP*[54] there was a suitable factual matrix to permit this analysis. Templeton wanted to lend money to J for the purposes of buying an identified plot of land for development. The loan contract was structured so that Templeton did not pay the money to J but rather paid it to Penningtons, J's solicitors, subject to a solicitor's undertaking on Penningtons' part that Penningtons would keep the money in its client account only to be used to acquire the absolute title in the development land, or else to be held in an identified account so as to collect interest for Templeton. Whereas Lewison J analysed

48 *Re Australian Elizabethan Theatre Trust* (1991) 102 ALR 681, 691, *per* Gummow J.
49 As in *Paul v Constance* [1977] 1 WLR 527.
50 Thomas, 2000.
51 *Re Australian Elizabethan Theatre Trust* (1991) 102 ALR 681, 691, *per* Gummow J.
52 *Ibid*. See Thomas and Hudson, 2004, para 9.84.
53 *General Communications Ltd v Development Finance Corporation of New Zealand Ltd* [1990] 3 NZLR 406, 432.
54 [2006] EWHC 685 (Ch).

this transaction on the basis of *Twinsectra v Yardley* – a resulting trust analysis – it would have been possible to say that Penningtons held the money as trustee under an express trust which could be inferred from the circumstances of paying the money into a client account[55] and that Penningtons had a limited power as trustee to advance the loan moneys to complete the purchase of the development land. If Penningtons had breached the terms of the trust then it would have acted in excess of that power and in breach of its obligations as trustee.

Against the express trust

The principal argument against the express trust model, it is suggested, is not a theoretical objection but rather a practical one: in *Barclays Bank v Quistclose* and in *Twinsectra v Yardley*, two differently-constituted Houses of Lords have not found that there was an intention to create an express trust. Perhaps after Lord Wilberforce's *dicta* in *Barclays Bank v Quistclose* the courts have become locked into a resulting trust analysis which has prevented them from seeing the trust in any other way. Lord Wilberforce's 'primary trust' does suggest the existence of some form of trust from the time of the creation of the loan contract and, it is suggested, this could be understood as being an express trust in relation to which the borrower has a power to advance the money for the purposes identified in the loan contract. Equally, Lord Millett's retention of title could be understood as being a retention of title on the basis of an express trust, which would have been a more comfortable analysis than a resulting trust where that resulting trust would ordinarily be understood as coming into existence at some time after the loan contract had been created. That is, if the lender is taken to have retained some interest in the loan money from the creation of the contract, then it could have been said that that interest takes the form of an equitable interest under an express trust. Nevertheless, the express trust analysis does not have the support of English authority at present.

To return to the diagram at para 22.4.2 above, the finding of an express trust would require that that trust be created on Day 1 at the same time as the loan contract is created. Thus, when the loan moneys are transferred to the borrower, they are transferred to the borrower as trustee. This would need to be made clear on the terms of the loan contract. In this sense the lender would be retaining an equitable interest in the money. This goes against the ordinary mechanism of a loan contract whereby the lender transfers absolute title to the borrower, as opposed merely to the legal rights of a trustee.

22.4.4 Constructive trust

The argument in favour of a constructive trust

The third explanation of the nature of these trusts would be that the *Quistclose* trust could be considered to be a constructive trust on the general basis that it would be unconscionable for the lender to assert title to that money if it was not used for the purpose for which it was lent. The *Quistclose* trust principle was stated in *Carreras Rothmans Ltd v Freeman Mathews Treasure Ltd*[56] to be that:

---

55 As was the case in *Target Holdings v Referns* [1996] AC 421 and in *Boscawen v Bajwa* [1996] 1 WLR 328.
56 [1985] Ch 207, 222.

equity fastens of the conscience of the person who receives from another property transferred for a specific purpose only and not therefore for the recipient's own purposes, so that such person will not be permitted to treat the property as his own or to use it for other than the stated purpose.

This statement could be taken to be authority for one of three competing understandings of the *Quistclose* arrangement. At first blush, the reference to the 'conscience' of the recipient equates most obviously to a constructive trust, although these *dicta* are capable of multiple analyses. This judgment was given immediately at the end of the trial, whereas it is more usual for a judge to retire to reflect on his judgment at the end of a complex trial, and therefore some commentators[57] have suggested that this expression should not be relied upon too closely as requiring any particular analysis of the *Quistclose* trust. In line with the general theory of trusts advanced in *Westdeutsche Landesbank v Islington*, to define the *Quistclose* trust as operating solely on the conscience of the recipient of the money is merely to place the situation within the general understanding of the trust as part of equity, rather than to categorise it necessarily as any particular type of trust.

Against a constructive trust

The principal argument against the imposition of a constructive trust is that the equitable interest of the lender appears to exist *before* the borrower seeks to perform any unconscionable act in relation to the property. As the speech of Lord Browne-Wilkinson in *Westdeutsche Landesbank v Islington*[58] reminds us, a constructive trust only comes into existence when the trustee has knowledge of some factor which affects her conscience. In the context of a *Quistclose* arrangement the rights of the lender arise under the contract and therefore pre-date the transfer of the loan moneys. A constructive trust would seem to require that the borrower misapply the loan moneys before her conscience could be affected so as to create a constructive trust. It is not the court imposing a constructive trust to grant rights, nor to restore pre-existing rights, to the lender. Rather, the lender appears to have retained its proprietary rights throughout the transaction. So, if the contract is created on Day 1 and the loan moneys are transferred to the borrower on Day 2, it is not until Day 3, when the borrower misuses the money contrary to the terms of the contract, that any constructive trust could come into existence because it is only on Day 3 that there is any unconscionable action in the form of the misuse of the loan moneys. If the borrower had gone into insolvency on Day 2 then there would be no effective proprietary rights in favour of the lender over the loan money because the insolvency would have occurred before those constructive trust rights came into existence.

One further shortcoming with the analysis of this form of trust as a kind of constructive trust is that it really avoids the question of what form of trust is a *Quistclose* trust: bracketing it off as being something imposed by operation of law is to ignore the structure used by the parties and the two-tier trust accepted by the courts in *Quistclose*. Its strength is that is recognises that, where the parties have failed to create a conscious express trust, it is

---

57 Thomas and Hudson, 2004, 292 *et seq.*
58 [1996] AC 669.

necessarily equity which intervenes to allocate title between the parties. That intervention is to police the conscience of the borrower as trustee in the manner in which she deals with the loan moneys.

22.4.5 The *Quistclose* trust as a retention of title: the *Twinsectra* model

The nature of the Twinsectra *model*

An alternative analysis of the *Quistclose* trust, as considered in outline above, was advanced by Lord Millett in his minority speech in the House of Lords in *Twinsectra Ltd v Yardley*.[59] The approach advanced there was that the *Quistclose* trust should be considered to be akin to a retention of title by the lender whereby the lender effectively retains an equitable interest in the property throughout the transaction. In that case a solicitor permitted loan moneys to be used by his client in breach of the express terms of a loan contract. On this analysis, a *Quistclose* trust enables a party to a commercial contract to retain their equitable interest in property provided as part of a commercial agreement. There is a similarity between *Quistclose* trusts in equity and *Romalpa* clauses at common law (as considered in section 22.2 above) to the extent that the original titleholder is able to retain rights in property: in *Romalpa* clauses it is the absolute title which is retained whereas in *Quistclose* trusts it is the equitable interest which is retained. Lord Millett took the view that the solicitor's undertaking to use the money only for a limited purpose gave rise to a *Quistclose* trust. His Lordship took the opportunity to ventilate the following understanding of a *Quistclose* trust:

> The *Quistclose* trust is a simple, commercial arrangement akin . . . to a retention of title clause (though with a different object) which enables the borrower to have recourse to the lender's money for a particular purpose without entrenching on the lender's property rights more than necessary to enable the purpose to be achieved. The money remains the property of the lender unless and until it is applied in accordance with his directions, and in so far as it is not so applied it must be returned to him. I am disposed, perhaps predisposed, to think that this is the only analysis which is consistent both with orthodox trust law and with commercial reality.[60]

The lender could therefore be taken to retain the equitable interest in the loan moneys throughout the life of the contract.[61] However, a closer reading of Lord Millett's words, quoted above, and in particular the expression 'the money remains the property of the lender', could be read so as to suggest that the property remains absolutely the property of the lender: that is, the entire title, both legal and equitable, could be said to remain with the lender. It is suggested, however, that this analysis would mean that there was no trust of any sort at all because no title would have passed to the borrower so as to constitute a trust of any sort. Instead, the lender would have remained the outright, absolute owner of the

---

59 [2002] 2 All ER 377. See also Lord Millett in *Re Crown Forestry Rental Trust; Latimer v Commissioner of Inland Revenue* [2004] 4 All ER 558, [2004] STC 923 and Millett, 1985. For an analysis of this approach see Penner, 2004.

60 [2002] 2 All 377, 398–99.

61 *Ibid*, 398, para 80. This approach was followed in *Re Margaretta Ltd, Freeman v Customs and Excise* [2005] All ER (D) 262, *per* Crystal QC (sitting as a Deputy Judge in the High Court), para [15] *et seq*.

money. This is not how loan contracts operate: ordinarily the borrower becomes absolute owner of the money. Perhaps the use of the vague term 'property' by Lord Millett here is unfortunate. Maybe, the lender would remain the owner of all of the property rights in the borrowed money and the borrower would be merely the bailee of the borrowed money until such time as it was applied for the contractually-specified purpose:[62] again this seems unlikely on most loan contracts. It is suggested that Lord Millett's expression 'the money remains the property of the lender' should be interpreted to mean that it is merely all of the *equitable* interest in the money which remains vested in the lender, and that the borrower is vested either with the legal title in that money so as to be entitled to use it for the purpose identified in the loan contract as a trustee, or else with a power to advance that money for the contractually-specified purpose. Consequently, the lender's equitable interest must be defeasible by the borrower's proper use of the money, with the result either that the borrower has the power as trustee of the money to defeat the lender's rights in that money or alternatively that the borrower itself has an equitable interest in the money which is contingent on the borrower's proper use of the loan moneys. This last analysis would suggest that the lender does not hold all of the equitable interest, but rather holds all of the equitable interest except for that part represented by the borrower's contingent rights; or alternatively that the borrower has a mere power to use the money subject to the lender's outright title.

It is suggested, then, that the least satisfactory analysis of a *Quistclose* trust would be that the lender retains absolute title in the money because that would deny the existence of a trust. It would be the case that the lender retained absolute title in the loan moneys if the loan contract provided that the borrower had merely a facility with the lender such that the borrower could instruct the lender to make payment of the loan moneys to a third party identified in the loan agreement (in a manner similar, perhaps, to a letter of credit facility).[63] In such a situation, however, there would be no trust but rather merely a contractual right to instruct the lender to transfer the money at the borrower's instruction in the manner provided for in the loan agreement. In accordance with commercial reality, this mimics a retention of title clause with title in the money only passing once the money is used for its specified purpose. Similarly, the borrower does not acquire full title in the property because that would defeat the purpose of the arrangement if the borrower were found to have an entirely free use of the money.[64] However, for there to be a trust at all there must be a declaration of a trust such that there is a division between the ownership of the legal and of the equitable interests in the loan moneys between two or more people. As considered earlier in this chapter, the commercial purpose of a *Quistclose* trust – that the borrower be prevented from using borrowed moneys for some purpose other than that agreed between borrower and lender – can be achieved by a number of devices by which the lender retains some proprietary rights in the loan moneys and thus makes those moneys available to the borrower but without vesting absolute title in the loan moneys in the borrower. It is suggested that deciding which of those models has been used will depend upon a proper analysis of the terms of the individual loan contract.

62 As Lord Browne-Wilkinson reminded us in *Westdeutsche Landesbank v Islington* [1996] AC 669: if there is no separation of the equitable title from the legal title such that a trustee or trustees hold the equitable title for identified beneficiaries, then there is no trust: rather, absolute title remains with the outright 'owner' of the property – the person whom civilian lawyers would consider to have dominium in the property.
63 See Millett, 1985.
64 *Twinsectra v Yardley* [2002] 2 All ER 377, 399, para 81.

There is one other problem with Lord Millett's formulation, which falls into two parts. First, the *Twinsectra* trust is said by Lord Millett to be a resulting trust. Secondly, despite it being a resulting trust the lender is said to retain her interest in the loan property. A resulting trust operates by the property 'jumping back' to the beneficiary of that resulting trust. In the example of a *Quistclose* arrangement, as under the diagram set out in para 22.4.2 above, this would necessitate that the resulting trust could only come into existence on Day 3 when the trust money is misused and, in any event, only once the interest in the property has been transferred away to the borrower. This does not sit well, however, with the notion that the lender has retained an interest in the loan money. The lender has either relinquished her rights in the money so that a resulting trust can come into existence later, or else the lender has retained an equitable interest in the loan money as from Day 1 in which case that equitable interest cannot be said to jump *back* to the lender because she has retained it throughout. Alternatively, we would have to re-write our understanding of a resulting trust as a doctrine which returns ownership to its beneficiary. It is suggested that there is no need for that, however, because this is simply a confusion between an inappropriate resulting trust and a more useful express trust which is to be inferred from the circumstances.

Thus Lord Millett has only served to raise as many questions as he has answered. The commercial difficulties with Lord Millett's model of the *Quistclose* trust are considered at para 22.4.8 below.[65]

22.4.6 Analysing the key decisions closely

We can only understand the arguments about the nature of a *Quistclose* trust if we focus in detail on the precise formulations used by the courts. In that vein, let us bore down a little more deeply into the detail of the *dicta* of Lord Wilberforce in *Barclays Bank v Quistclose*. The main argument advanced by Barclays Bank was that there was only a loan contract between Quistclose and Rolls Razor, and under banking law there is a clear principle that loan contracts and contracts for bank accounts in themselves do not create a trust relationship.[66] Lord Wilberforce, however, was prepared to imply the existence of a trust on the facts in line with earlier cases like *Re Rogers* where the existence of the trust was predicated on the important fact that the loan contract contained a statement of a limited purpose for which the loan money could be used.[67] It is important to dwell a little on the precise words which Lord Wilberforce used. His Lordship held that: '[i]t is not difficult to establish precisely upon what terms the money was advanced . . . to Rolls Razor Ltd. There is no doubt that the loan was made specifically in order to enable Rolls Razor Ltd. to pay the dividend . . . and for no other purpose'.[68] The parties' contractual purpose was clear: the money was to be used only for a limited purpose.

Lord Wilberforce continued:

---

65 See also GW Thomas and AS Hudson, *The Law of Trusts*, 2004, para 49–14 *et seq* for a more detailed discussion of *Quistclose* trusts in general.

66 See Alastair Hudson, *The Law of Finance*, Sweet & Maxwell, 2009, para 30–4. See *Foley v Hill* (1848) 2 HL Cas 28, 9 ER 1002, 1005, *per* Lord Cottenham LC.

67 [1970] AC 567, 581.

68 Ibid.

There is surely no difficulty in recognising the co-existence in one transaction of legal and equitable rights and remedies: when the money is advanced, the lender acquires an equitable right to see that it is applied for the primary designated purpose:[69] when the purpose has been carried out (that is, the debt paid) the lender has his remedy against the borrower in debt: if the primary purpose cannot be carried out, the question arises if a secondary purpose (that is, repayment to the lender) has been agreed, expressly or by implication: if it has, the remedies of equity may be invoked to give effect to it, if it has not (and the money is intended to fall within the general fund of the debtor's assets) then there is the appropriate remedy for recovery of a loan.[70]

This passage means that there is no problem both with having obligations at common law (that is, to repay the loan) and also obligations in equity (that is, to hold the money on trust until it is used for the specified purpose). Thus, if the purpose is performed then the lender has rights against the borrower at common law under the terms of the contract (that is, 'has his remedy in debt'). The 'secondary obligation' arises in equity either on the express terms of the contract or impliedly from the circumstances. The 'remedies of equity' in this context are the 'secondary trust' which requires that the loan money is held on trust if it is not used for the specified purpose. Interestingly, though, Lord Wilberforce expressed this in terms of being a general 'equitable right' rather than explicitly a resulting trust: an idea to which we shall return below. A similar formulation has been used by Lord Millett in *Twinsectra v Yardley*,[71] and approved by Evans-Lombe J in *Cooper v PRG Power Ltd*,[72] to the effect that 'when the money is advanced, the lender acquires a right, enforceable in equity, to see that it is applied for the stated purpose, or more accurately to prevent its application for any other purpose': again, it is an equitable ability to prevent misuse of the money. As Lord Wilberforce continued:

I can appreciate no reason why the flexible interplay of law and equity cannot let in these practical arrangements, and other variations if desired: it would be to the discredit of both systems if they could not. In the present case the intention to create a secondary trust for the benefit of the lender, to arise if the primary trust, to pay the dividend, could not be carried out, is clear and I can find no reason why the law should not give effect to it.

Therefore, the *Quistclose* trust arises from the interplay of the ordinary principles of the contract of loan at common law and the equitable principles which prevent ownership of the loan money being passed to a third party if it is misused. The manner in which the *Quistclose* trust arises is then by means of a 'secondary trust' coming into existence for the benefit of the lender if the 'primary trust . . . cannot be carried out'. Three points emerge. First, this trust was based on that interaction of primary and secondary trusts being the intention of the parties, an idea which has been approved in subsequent cases.[73] For example, in

---

69 *In re Rogers*, 8 Morr. 243, *per* both Lindley LJ and Kay LJ.
70 *Barclays Bank v Quistclose* [1970] AC 567, 581–2.
71 [2002] 2 AC 164, para [69].
72 [2008] BCC 588, para [13].
73 *Re Niagara Mechanical Services International Ltd (in admin)* [2001] BCC 393; *Shalson v Russo* [2003] EWHC 1637 (Ch), [2005] Ch 281; *Cooper v PRG Power* [2008] BCC 588.

Abou-Rahmah v Abacha[74] it was held that there could not be a *Quistclose* trust if the parties' intentions were that money was paid 'unconditionally' from one to the other. Secondly, this does not require that the borrower must have misused the money; instead, it only requires that the purpose 'cannot be carried out' for whatever reason, whether because of the borrower's insolvency or some other event. Thirdly, this form of trust must be a resulting trust because the equitable interest arises for the first time once the primary purpose cannot be carried out. Moreover, because the House of Lords was asked specifically in this appeal whether or not a resulting trust came into existence, we must assume that they are therefore upholding the existence of a resulting trust on this appeal even though the expression 'resulting trust' is not used by Lord Wilberforce.

It is this last conceptualisation of the *Quistclose* trust which we should pursue into the model advanced by Lord Millett in *Twinsectra v Yardley*. Lord Millett upheld the theory of the *Quistclose* trust being a resulting trust, but explains its nature differently from Lord Wilberforce in the *Quistclose* case. We shall focus on two passages in particular from his Lordship's speech. First, paragraph 81 of the judgment, which was considered in outline above, which reads as follows:

> On this analysis, the *Quistclose* trust is a simple commercial arrangement akin . . . to a retention of title clause (though with a different object) which enables the borrower to have recourse to the lender's money for a particular purpose without entrenching on the lender's property rights more than necessary to enable the purpose to be achieved. The money remains the property of the lender unless and until it is applied in accordance with his directions, and insofar as it is not so applied it must be returned to him. I am disposed, perhaps pre-disposed, to think that this is the only analysis which is consistent both with orthodox trust law and with commercial reality. . . .

The second sentence is very problematic: 'The money remains the property of the lender unless and until it is applied in accordance with his directions, and insofar as it is not so applied it must be returned to him.' There is a clear contradiction in terms here: if the money *remains* the property of the lender then how can it possibly be *returned* to him? If I retain property then I cannot possibly ask you to return it to me later because I have kept it. Imagine that you ask to borrow my umbrella because it is raining and I refuse to lend it to you,[75] if I were then to come to you the next day and demand that you return my umbrella you would say 'well, you kept your umbrella so how can you possibly have it returned to you?' It is the same problem with Lord Millett's formulation here: if the lender retains the money, it cannot logically be returned to him. What we might take Lord Millett to mean is that *ownership* of the money in equity remains with the lender even if *possession* of the money is passed to the borrower, such that the borrower has to return *possession* of the money to the lender. Similarly, Lord Millett's reference to 'the property' is unclear because we cannot know if it means retention of absolute title (which would negate the possibility of there being a trust) or whether it is supposed to mean only retention of an equitable interest under a trust.

74 [2005] EWHC 2662 (QB), [2006] 1 Lloyd's Rep 484.
75 I can be capricious like that, especially with umbrellas because you never get them back.

The following paragraph from Lord Millett's speech also presents problems; it is paragraph 100:

> As Sherlock Holmes reminded Dr Watson, when you have eliminated the impossible, whatever remains, however improbable, must be the truth. I would reject all the alternative analyses, which I find unconvincing for the reasons I have endeavoured to explain, and hold the *Quistclose* trust to be an entirely orthodox example of the kind of default trust known as a resulting trust. The lender pays the money to the borrower by way of loan, but he does not part with the entire beneficial interest in the money, and in so far as he does not it is held on a resulting trust for the lender from the outset. Contrary to the opinion of the Court of Appeal, it is the borrower who has a very limited use of the money, being obliged to apply it for the stated purpose or return it. He has no beneficial interest in the money, which remains throughout in the lender subject only to the borrower's power or duty to apply the money in accordance with the lender's instructions. When the purpose fails, the money is returnable to the lender, not under some new trust in his favour which only comes into being on the failure of the purpose, but because the resulting trust in his favour is no longer subject to any power on the part of the borrower to make use of the money. Whether the borrower is obliged to apply the money for the stated purpose or merely at liberty to do so, and whether the lender can countermand the borrower's mandate while it is still capable of being carried out, must depend on the circumstances of the particular case.

Again, as with paragraph 81, there is a problem in that we are told that the money 'remains throughout in the lender' and yet that 'the money is returnable to the lender'. Furthermore, the *Quistclose* trust is held explicitly to be a resulting trust, even though ownership of the money is said to *remain* with the lender. Therefore, this is not a resulting trust as Prof Birks has explained it because a resulting trust ordinarily requires that equitable ownership of the property has passed away and that it then 'jumps back'[76] to the lender. That cannot happen if the lender *retains* equitable ownership of the loan money throughout the loan contract. Alternatively, we must reject Prof Birks's analysis of a resulting trust and instead accept that Lord Millett has established that resulting trusts are merely a 'default trust' in which a court of equity simply recognises that when there is a question as to the ownership of property then we should recognise that the last owner of that property is still its owner. This is the analysis which is advanced in Chapter 11 of this book of resulting trusts in general: an automatic resulting trust operates in circumstances in which it is unclear who is the owner of property so as to declare that the property is held on trust for the last person who was undoubtedly the owner of that property.

We are told that the borrower has merely a power to use the money for the described purpose (just like the powers discussed in Chapter 3). The money is said 'to be returnable to the lender' (oddly even though the lender has nevertheless retained equitable ownership of it) because the power disappears (apparently) once it is not performed. In the final sentence, Lord Millett acknowledges that the precise nature of the parties' obligations will depend upon the precise terms of the contract between them. Therefore, we have a very stylised form

---

76 See section 11.1 of this book.

of resulting trust in the speech of Lord Millett. This model is necessary for Lord Millett's analysis and yet Lord Millett delivered a dissenting speech in the House of Lords, and as such it is difficult to know what the force of this model is in English trusts law. What is important to note is that subsequent cases have supported it, and thus have lent it some gravitas. It is nevertheless suggested that the better analysis would be to infer the existence of an express trust (just as in *Re Kayford*[77]) from the circumstance.

22.4.7 The nature of the *Quistclose* trust is dependent on the terms of the loan contract

The effect of the terms of the loan contract

While the preceding analysis of the *Twinsectra* model[78] of the *Quistclose* device might appear to present a step towards a settled understanding of the *Quistclose* trust, it is suggested nevertheless that the precise nature of any given *Quistclose* arrangement will depend upon the structure of the loan agreement which the parties have effected. It might of course be that the loan moneys are not to be advanced to the borrower until the contractually-specified object has been performed or under terms whereby the bank insists on a payment facility which can only be used for the completion of that specified purpose, such as by way of a banker's draft in favour of the third party who is specified in the loan contract. The use of the loan moneys might be made available to the borrower subject to a trust arrangement made explicit in the loan contract that the funds were to be held by some custodian subject only to a power to use them for the contractually specified purpose. In consequence, the commercial objective of a *Quistclose* trust would be achieved without the use of either a traditional *Quistclose* model (with its primary and secondary trust) or the *Twinsectra* model (with the retention of rights in the property by the lender). In *Mundy v Brown*[79] it was considered particularly significant, in reliance upon the dicta of Lord Millett in *Twinsectra v Yardley*, that the moneys had not been left at the free disposal of the recipient, but rather that the intentions of the parties were that the recipient was obliged to use those moneys only for a specified purpose. This is, in effect, just another way of looking at the recipient's obligation being to observe the purpose specified in the contract.

Alternatively then, as discussed above, a *Quistclose* trust could be conceived of on the basis that the loan moneys are subject to an express trust under which the borrower acts as trustee with a power to use the trust property for the purpose specified in the contract, but for no other. The benefit of such a structure would be that the borrower, as trustee, would bear personal liability for the breach of any trust as well as an obligation to reconstitute the trust fund in the event that the moneys were transferred away for some purpose other than that specified in the contract. For such an express trust analysis to be viable in any given circumstance, it would be necessary for there to be sufficient intention on the part of the contracting parties for the borrower to hold the loan moneys on trust from the outset of the transaction, and not simply that the trust is enforced by the court subsequently to prevent the borrower unconscionably from seeking to apply those moneys otherwise than for the contractually agreed purpose. In other words, the loan contract would need to make this express trust

---

77 [1975] 1 WLR 279.
78 [2002] 2 All ER 377, 398–399.
79 [2011] EWHC 377 (Ch).

explicit on its face. This analysis of a loan contract does not conform to the ordinary presumption of a loan contract that the lender intends to transfer outright all of the interest in the loan moneys but rather contains an express contractual provision which precludes the borrower from using the money for any purpose other than that provided for in the contract. A well-drafted contract may well provide that the borrower shall hold the loan moneys on trust for the lender until such time as the contractually stipulated purpose is performed. At that time the borrower would be obliged to transfer the money outright. Such a contract would clearly contain an express trust. More frequently the decided cases have considered loan contracts in which it is not clear what the parties intended. Such contracts may nevertheless suggest the existence of an express trust (such intention being capable of imputation by the court in an unconscious express trust).[80] The question is to identify the most secure method of structuring a *Quistclose* trust arrangement to protect against these uncertainties.

22.4.8 The safest commercial approach to controlling borrowed moneys

If a lender is seeking to protect itself against either the misbehaviour of the borrower or the insolvency of the borrower, then it is suggested that, instead of using a *Quistclose* trust, the following structure would be the safest approach: the lender should remain the absolute owner of the loan moneys and never transfer them to the 'borrower' but rather should merely grant a facility to the borrower to instruct the lender when to make payment such that it is the lender itself who transfers the loan moneys for the contractually specified purpose at the borrower's order. The lender, then, should not transfer legal title nor indeed any title to the borrower. Rather, the lender should pay the loan moneys into a separate bank account which is held in the lender's sole name without any declaration of trust in favour of the borrower. The borrower should then have a mandate, granted by contract, to direct the bank when the appropriate time has arisen to make the payment to the person or for the purpose identified in the loan contract. Thus, the borrower cannot acquire title in the loan moneys should it become insolvent, nor can the borrower use the money for any purpose other than that specified in the contract.

The workings of the *Quistclose* trust, in the wake of Lord Millett's speech in *Twinsectra v Yardley*, are explained by Thomas and Hudson as operating in the following way:

> Akin to a retention of title clause (though with a different object) [the *Quistclose* trust] enables the borrower to have recourse to the lender's money for a particular purpose without entrenching on the lender's property rights more than necessary to enable the purpose to be achieved. The money remains the property of the lender unless and until it is applied in accordance with his directions, and in so far as it is not so applied it must be returned to him, notwithstanding the borrower's insolvency. It is therefore a form of asset protection.[81]

It is suggested that this is the clearest description of the best means of using a *Quistclose* trust. It avoids the ambiguity in Lord Millett's formulation[82] in which Lord Millett refers to the trust as arising as a 'resulting trust', suggesting that title had passed to the borrower only

---

80 *Paul v Constance* [1977] 1 WLR 527.
81 Thomas and Hudson, *The Law of Trusts*, Oxford University Press, 2004, 292.
82 *Twinsectra v Yardley* [2002] 2 AC 164, 187–193.

to jump back on resulting trust when the borrower breaches the term of the contract. It is possible that Lord Millett intended the trust to come into existence at the same time as the loan contract but the reference to a resulting trust makes this unclear. Therefore, the contested forms of *Quistclose* trust should not be used. After all, no commercial client would be content to take a troubled form of equitable interest over money instead of the retention of *absolute* title which I am advocating here.

In my suggested structure, the assets remain the property of the lender throughout the life of the transaction but the borrower has a power to direct the use of that money. This structure would achieve three things. First, the lender would retain proprietary rights in the loan moneys. Secondly, the lender itself would be able to vet the purposes for which the moneys are intended to be used rather than rely on the good faith of the borrower under an ordinary outright transfer of loan moneys. Thirdly, the moneys retained in the account would constitute an identifiable fund which could be subjected to a trust without confusion as to its identity.

I have suggested in the passage before the quotation from Thomas and Hudson above a further refinement to the effect that the lender should limit the borrower's power to spend the money without the lender's prior consent. This change would require that there is no trust created at all: instead the lender should retain absolute title in the money and instead simply agree contractually to transfer it directly to the third party identified in the loan contract at a time when the borrower may direct. By controlling the borrower's use of the money by preventing the borrower from having any property right in it, the lender is protected against the borrower's insolvency and should be able to protect itself against misapplication of the money by its own clerks ensuring that the moneys are being advanced for the contractually specified purpose before paying them away themselves on behalf of the lender.

22.4.9 The *Quistclose* trust as a form of purpose trust

The argument has been raised that a *Quistclose* trust is a form of abstract purpose trust whereby the trust comes into existence for the purpose of retaining title in money. However, it is suggested that it is not a purpose trust, which ought properly to be void due to its lack of a beneficiary, but rather there will always be a beneficiary of the trust arrangement, whether the lender or the borrower, who can take an immediate interest in the loan money. Which of them takes that interest from time to time is dependent on whether or not it has been used in accordance with the terms of the loan contract. Therefore, this form of trust will be valid because there is some person who has an equitable interest in the property, such that the beneficiary principle is satisfied. In truth there are many 'purpose trusts' of some sort which are given effect in English law, provided that there is also some beneficiary of the trust. So, there is no objection to a trust for the benefit of identified persons also containing a statement of a purpose for which the trust property is to be used. The trust is valid because there are beneficiaries and what is more the trustees have a clear statement of their goals as trustees in the form of their obligations and powers.

22.4.10 Two different commercial contexts in which *Quistclose* trusts are significant

The Quistclose *trust in the abstract*

There are two different practical contexts in which a *Quistclose* trust may be important. The first is that in which the borrower of the money goes into insolvency. The purpose of the

Quistclose trust will be to keep the loan moneys separate from the borrower's estate which will be divided up among the borrower's unsecured creditors. The second context is that in which the borrower has transferred the loan money to some third party so that the lender will have difficulty in recovering it. The discussion of *Quistclose* trusts in the cases and amongst the commentators has tended to focus on their advantages in protecting against insolvency and has therefore simply assumed that the loan money would be separately identifiable in a bank account so that it could form the subject matter of a trust without undue complication. However, what if the loan money has been paid away and it is not separately identifiable in a way which satisfies the requirement of certainty of subject matter in trusts law?

In addressing these different contexts we should begin by reminding ourselves of the example used in para 11.3 to describe a *Quistclose* trust. It went as follows:

> Suppose Laura agrees to lend money to Bill. Bill is facing personal bankruptcy. His business is the manufacture and sale of modern, metal furniture. Bill has been unable to sell enough of his furniture but he thinks that if he were able to adapt his machinery to manufacture a particular type of fashionable furniture then he would be able to move back into profit. Laura therefore agrees to lend Bill £10,000 on the condition that the money is only to be used to adapt that machine. The money is transferred to Bill. The next week, Bill is declared insolvent and his trustee in bankruptcy seeks to divide up the £10,000 among Bill's creditors.

In dealing with the first context in which *Quistclose* trusts are used – to guard against the borrower's insolvency – this hypothetical example was explained as being analysed legally in the following manner:

> The *Quistclose* trust means that the £10,000 is held on trust for Laura and therefore does not form part of Bill's estate for insolvency purposes. Consequently, Laura will be able to recover the loan money (and using the rule in *Saunders v Vautier*, as the sole beneficiary under the *Quistclose* trust, she will be able to compel the trustee to transfer the money to her absolutely).

However, instead of Bill going into insolvency and leaving the £10,000 easily identifiable, suppose that Bill had used the money in the following way:

> In breach of the contractual condition, Bill decides to use the money to pay one of his suppliers of leather, Caroline. Caroline has paid the money into her general bank account and mixed it up with her other money.

In this changed set of facts it is not possible simply to impose a trust over 'the loan money' because the loan money has ceased to exist separately from the other money in Caroline's bank account. It could be said that the *Quistclose* trust could not be imposed because of lack of certainty of subject matter.[83] However, in this context, the utility of the *Quistclose* trust – as is discussed in detail in Chapter 19 – is in giving Laura the equitable foundation to trace

---

83 *MacJordan v Brookmount* [1992] BCLC 350.

her loan money into Caroline's general bank account and to impose an equitable remedy (such as a charge or a lien) over that general bank account so as to recover her money. To trace her money into a mixed account like this, Laura would be required to demonstrate that she had had an equitable interest, such as an interest under a trust, in the loan money before it was misapplied.[84] The *Quistclose* trust grants Laura such an interest and so permits her to trace her money into this mixed account. This second use of *Quistclose* trusts is the main focus of this section after we have outlined the applicable principles of insolvency law which are important in this context.

Insolvency

If a person – whether a human being or a company – goes into bankruptcy or insolvency, liquidation or administration, then that person is not at liberty to dispose of its property as it may otherwise wish. Frequently, trusts are used as shelters against insolvency of all of the types just mentioned by providing that the person whom it is feared might go into insolvency is merely the trustee of property which would otherwise be considered to be her own property and which would consequently fall to be divided up among her creditors on her insolvency. *Quistclose* trusts are one means of shielding money against a borrower's insolvency in loan transactions. However, sham trusts are often used so as to give the mere appearance of separating property from the insolvent person's assets whereas the insolvent person continues to use the property as though it remains entirely her own.[85] The Insolvency Act 1986 gives the court the power to unpick transactions – such as the settling of property on trust – which are done in an attempt to elude the effects of personal bankruptcy or corporate insolvency. In relation to a personal bankruptcy, if the bankrupt had entered into any transaction with anyone at an undervalue then the trustee in bankruptcy may apply to the court, *inter alia*, to have the transaction set aside and any property transferred or settled on trust restored to the position it was previously.[86] Similarly, if a bankrupt has given a 'preference' to anyone then that transaction may be treated in the same manner.[87] If a transaction is undertaken at an undervalue so as to defraud the insolvent person's then creditors or future creditors, then the court may order the return of the position to the *status quo ante* as though the transaction had not taken place.[88] This statutory power is considered in detail at para 11.4.7. By providing that the lender retains or re-acquires (depending on whether it is an express or a resulting trust) title in the loan moneys, a *Quistclose* trust provides that the lender has a beneficial interest in those loan moneys which she will retain even if the borrower goes into insolvency.

Quistclose *trust as an equitable device enabling tracing where the loan moneys have been put beyond reach*

Much of the debate surrounding *Quistclose* trusts proceeds on the basis of an abstract intellectual analysis of the structure itself. Primarily, the question has been put as to whether

---

84   *Westdeutsche Landesbank v Islington* [1996] AC 669.
85   See section 3.3.
86   Insolvency Act 1986, s 339.
87   *Ibid*, s 340.
88   *Ibid*, s 423.

a *Quistclose* trust is truly a resulting trust, or an express trust or simply a different form of trust altogether.[89] For the purposes of this section, however, the more important question is as to the manner in which a contractual provision sets out to achieve the general aim of a *Quistclose* trust: that is, to provide security for the lender in relation to loan moneys which were to have been used only for a specified purpose. The assumption made by many of the judges when dealing with *Quistclose* trusts is that the borrower is obliged to keep the money separate from all other moneys, so as to use that money for the contractually-specified purpose, and that consequently there will be some identifiable fund over which the *Quistclose* trust can take effect in a way that will avoid it being declared to be invalid under the principle that there be sufficient certainty of subject matter.[90] The principal difficulty, it is suggested, with the operation of *Quistclose* trusts is that the borrower who breaches the stipulation in the loan contract that the loan moneys be used only for a specified purpose will necessarily have paid those moneys away such that there may not be a fund over which such a trust can take effect. To put it crudely: the money will have gone, so what use is the *Quistclose* trust? That problem is considered in this section.

It is suggested that the central issue in the design of a *Quistclose* structure is that it ought properly to be ineffective in the event that the loan moneys or their traceable equivalent are not identifiable in the hands of the borrower. Suppose, for example, that a loan is made to a borrower subject to an express contractual provision that the loan moneys are to be used solely to discharge sums owed to identified trade creditors. If those loan moneys were in fact dissipated by the borrower on general expenses otherwise than for those identified trade creditors, such that the moneys had passed into a general current account which had subsequently gone overdrawn, then it would be impossible to identify property which could be the subject matter of a trust in that general current account. In theory, the *Quistclose* trust would exist because of its inclusion in the loan contract. However, where there is no identifiable subject matter of a trust, that trust will fail.[91]

As considered briefly above, that is not the principal strength of the *Quistclose* trust in these circumstances, however. What the lender will need to do in such circumstances is to trace after the loan moneys to seek to take title over whatever substitute property has been acquired with the loan moneys or to take title over whichever bank account comes to be the moneys last resting place. Only equitable tracing can trace loan moneys through mixtures: such as bank accounts in which the loan moneys have been mixed with other money (see section 19.4). Equitable tracing can only be begun if the claimant had an equitable interest,

---

89 Yet another explanation would be that the *Quistclose* trust is properly to be considered as a constructive trust on the basis that it would be unconscionable for the lender to assert title to that money if it was not used for the purpose for which it was lent, on which see the *dicta* from *Carreras Rothmans Ltd v Freeman Mathews Treasure Ltd* [1985] 1 Ch 207 reproduced above. The principal shortcoming with the analysis of this form of trust as a kind of constructive trust is that the equitable interest of the lender appears to exist *before* the borrower seeks to perform any unconscionable act in relation to the property. In the context of a *Quistclose* arrangement the rights of the lender arise under the contract and therefore pre-date the transfer of the loan moneys. A constructive trust would seem to require that the borrower misapply the loan moneys before her conscience could be affected so as to create a constructive trust: *Westdeutsche Landesbank v Islington LBC* [1996] AC 669. It is not the court imposing a constructive trust to grant rights, or restore pre-existing rights, to the lender. Rather, the lender would ordinarily appear to have retained its proprietary rights throughout the transaction.

90 See para 3–01.

91 See para 3–01 *et seq.*

such as an interest under a trust, in those loan moneys: simply having absolute title in the loan moneys would not be enough to commence an equitable tracing claim.[92] What the *Quistclose* trust analysis would provide is exactly such an equitable interest on the basis of which the lender could seek to trace those funds in equity through other bank accounts.[93] This is a very important strength of the *Quistclose* trust.

Can a Quistclose *trust arise in situations not connected to loan contracts?*

Quistclose trusts have arisen only in relation to loan contracts thus far on the decided cases. It has been suggested by Sarah Worthington that this need not necessarily be the case because there seems to be nothing about the *Quistclose* technique *per se* which means that the trust could only take effect over money and only when that money is being loaned.[94] In the High Court in *Re Farepak Food and Gifts Ltd*,[95] Mann J considered the availability of a *Quistclose* trust over moneys which had been pre-paid in the expectation of being exchangeable for goods in the future. There was no contract of loan. The point that *Quistclose* trusts had only previously arisen in relation to loan contracts was not taken by Mann J. No such trust was found on the facts because it was not found to have been within the contemplation of the parties. However, had the facts been different, there was nothing in the judgment to suggest that that trust would not have been imposed by Mann J.

The reason why Mann J found that there was no *Quistclose* trust was because it would have made no business sense on the facts for Farepak to have been intended to put all of the moneys received to one side subject to a *Quistclose* trust. It is not clear from the judgment on what basis a *Quistclose* trust was being argued for by counsel: there was no contract of loan and therefore this would have been a novel type of *Quistclose* trust; and it is not clear what the purported use of the money should have been to lead to the inference of a *Quistclose* trust in these circumstances. Therefore, it is difficult to know against what Mann J was arguing. His Lordship held as follows:

> I have already held that the money is taken by the Agents as agent for Farepak. That of itself does not militate against the existence of a *Quistclose* trust. However, there is no suggestion that the Agent was expected to keep the money separate from other money (or indeed his or her own), and it is indeed known that it was mixed with the money of others and paid over to Farepak with the money of others. Again, that of itself it not inconsistent with a *Quistclose* trust, but it does not help.[96]

However, normal service appears to have been resumed as his Lordship carried on in the following manner:

> But crucially, there is no suggestion that the money ought to have been put on one side by Farepak pending the transmutation from credited money to goods or vouchers. If

92 *Westdeutsche Landesbank v Islington* [1996] AC 669.
93 *Ibid*, para 33–97.
94 Worthington, 1996.
95 [2006] All ER (D) 265 (Dec).
96 *Ibid*, [34].

there were a *Quistclose* trust then that obligation would have been inherent in it, but the business model would have made no sense. It would have required Farepak to have kept all the customer moneys in a separate account from January until November, untouched until the time when the goods or vouchers were acquired and then sent out. That is completely implausible. It would turn Farepak into a very odd savings organisation. Even banks do not have to do that.[97]

There is, however, nothing to prevent the finding of a *Quistclose* trust that the trustees were permitted to use the property subject to the *Quistclose* trust in the approved manner – that is, subject to a power to use the property otherwise held on trust – but such that any breach of the conditions on which the property was to be used would cause the imposition of the *Quistclose* trust to prevent the misuse and/or to permit the beneficiaries to begin a tracing claim to recover their property. Therefore, it is suggested, Mann J could have held that the moneys were subject to an express trust such that Farepak could use the money for appropriate purposes in the running of the Christmas fund but so that a *Quistclose* trust would be imposed in the event that they purported to misuse any of the property.

In the interesting case of *Cooper v PRG Power Ltd*[98] an employee of a company was provided with a Mercedes car. The car was acquired by means of the employee entering into a hire purchase finance contract with the supplier and the company then paid all of the amounts owed by its employee under the contract. The employee left his employment but wanted to keep the car. However, there were amounts left unpaid on the finance agreement, so the company agreed to contribute £3,000 to the lump sum which the employee had to pay under that contract so as to acquire absolute title in the car. For reasons of administrative convenience (because the company had made all of the payments thus far) the company agreed to make the full lump sum payment to the car supplier but required its former employee to pay his part of the lump sum (£34,239) to it first. The employee duly paid the money to the company but the company went into insolvency. As a result the cheque was dishonoured (that is, it 'bounced'). The employee therefore wanted to show that the amount of £34,239 was held on *Quistclose* trust for him because it was intended to be used only for the limited purpose of acquiring absolute title in the car. It was held by Evans-Lombe J that there was a *Quistclose* trust over the money because the parties' intention was that the money was to be used only for that limited purpose such that the employee would retain equitable ownership of it until it was used for that purpose. (Somewhat unfortunately this was described as being a 'purpose trust'.)

Three important points arise as a result of the decision in *Cooper v PRG Power Ltd*. First, interestingly, there was no loan between the employee and the company unlike ordinary *Quistclose* trusts. Therefore, strictly this should not have been a *Quistclose* trust and instead should have been an ordinary express trust – as in *Re Kayford* – whereby money was intended to be kept separate from all other money and used for an identified objective. (Indeed in recent cases many barristers seem content to argue for *Quistclose* trusts in many circumstances in which a better knowledge of ordinary express trusts law would lead them to argue for an ordinary express trust.) Secondly, importantly, it was held that the money to be subjected to the *Quistclose* trust does not need to be held separately from all other money.

---

97 *Ibid.*
98 [2008] EWHC 498, [2008] BCC 588.

Therefore, the lender's equitable interest exists even if the money disappears into a general bank account such that there is no certainty of subject matter. However, the importance of Lord Millett's analysis in *Twinsectra v Yardley* was that the payer of the money retained an equitable interest in the money throughout the transaction. Therefore, coming to the third point, the payer is able to trace in equity into the mixed bank account which contains the misused money and establish an equitable remedy over that mixed bank account equal to the amount of money to which the payer is entitled. (Tracing of this sort was discussed in Chapter 19.)

22.4.11 The rights of third parties to the loan moneys

It has been suggested in one decided case[99] that, if the loan contract required that the borrower pay the loan moneys to X then X would acquire an equitable interest in the loan moneys before they were even paid to him. It is suggested that such an analysis could only be possible if the third party's acquisition of such rights were demonstrably within the contemplation of the parties.

22.4.12 Conclusion

As the playwright and diarist Alan Bennett once said, when writing one wonders if one has merely succeeded in adding to the number of words in the world, rather than adding anything of significance. Given the sheer volume of discussion of the *Quistclose* trust this is perhaps just another opinion tossed into the ether. However, it does appear to me that a *Quistclose* trust is properly to be considered to be a form of commercial express trust contained in a contract which retains an equitable interest for the lender of money until such time as that interest is discharged by the application of the loan moneys for their contractually-stipulated purpose.

---

99 *Re Northern Developments (Holdings) Ltd*, 6 October 1978 (unreported).

Chapter 23

Mortgages, charges and taking security

This chapter is available on the author's website at www.alastairhudson.com/trustlaw/ mortgages.pdf

Mortgages, charges and taking security

Part 8

Welfare uses of trusts

Chapter 24

Occupational pension funds

This chapter is available on the author's website at www.alastairhudson.com/trustlaw/
pensions.pdf

Chapter 25

Charities

OVERVIEW

*The case law on charitable trusts has always divided between trusts for the relief of
poverty; trusts for the advancement of education; trusts for the advancement of religion;
and trusts for other purposes beneficial to the community. However, the enactment
of the Charities Act 2011 has had the effect of expanding the categories of 'charitable
purpose' beyond those categories set out by the case law. The first three categories –
the prevention and relief of poverty, the advancement of religion and the advancement of
education – remain, but the fourth category has been replaced by a statutory list of
purposes. That statutory list includes: the advancement of health or the saving of lives; the
advancement of citizenship or community development; the advancement of the arts,
culture, heritage or science; the advancement of amateur sport; the advancement of human*

rights, conflict resolution or reconciliation or the promotion of religious or racial harmony or equality and diversity; the advancement of environmental protection or improvement; the relief of those in need by reason of youth, age, ill-health, disability, financial hardship or other disadvantage; the advancement of animal welfare. Consequently, the bulk of this chapter deals with the long-established case law categories of charitable purpose first before turning to consider the various statutory categories later on.

Trusts for the relief of poverty must relieve the poverty of some person. 'Poverty' means 'something more than going short' but does not require absolute destitution. It is apparently the case that it need not be a broad section of the community which stands to benefit from the trust. Rather, trusts for the relief of poverty are presumed to have a generally altruistic motivation and are therefore enforceable as being charitable. There have been subtle but significant alterations to the poverty charities in the Charities Act 2011 which call into question trusts for the relief of the poverty of only a small number of people.

Trusts for the advancement of education require that there is some institution of education benefited, or that the purpose of the trust is to generate research which will be published for the public benefit. Trusts for the pursuit of sport fall within the charitable head provided they are annexed to some institution of education. In many cases, educational charitable trusts have been used as fronts for the provision of benefits to a private class of individuals. Consequently, the courts have developed a requirement that there be a sufficient public benefit, which requires that there is no 'personal nexus' between the people who stand to benefit and the settlor of the trust.

Trusts for the advancement of religion are required to have a sufficient public benefit, such that, for example, the works done and the prayers said by a cloistered order of nuns, though religious, would not be charitable in legal terms. Religion is concerned with 'man's relations with God' and therefore excludes many modern new age religions and cults.

Other purposes beneficial to the community require sufficient public benefit. A community must be more than a mere fluctuating body of private individuals (such as employees of a small company). 'Benefit' will accrue from the maintenance of public buildings, the provision of facilities for the disabled within a community, but under case law will not be said to accrue from mere recreation or social events (subject to statute). Political purposes promoting a change in legislation will not be charitable.

25.1 INTRODUCTION

25.1.1 Context

The law relating to charities is a subject in itself, separate from the ordinary law of trusts and commanding its own distinct treatment in the practitioners' treatises and in textbooks.[1] The law relating to charities does not itself conform neatly with the law on express trusts which we have already considered in Part 2. That the law of charities forms part of trusts law is an accident of history. Charities were originally overseen by the ecclesiastical courts and, as will emerge, retain many of the seeds of their religious heritage in the modern law. This part of the ecclesiastical jurisdiction was subsumed by the Courts of Chancery, in particular by those Lords Chancellor who were themselves bishops, and charities were consequently administered in a manner broadly similar to express trusts. A charity is an institution which acts in

---

1 Tudor, 2003; Picarda, 2007.

the public benefit, especially (in the words of the Oxford English Dictionary) to relieve need or distress, or to provide for the communal services more generally. Charities do not seek to earn profits for any purpose other than their charitable purposes. It will be the principal focus of this chapter to explore precisely what English law considers a charitable purpose to be.

Charities form an essential part of social welfare provision in many Western countries. The charitable sector in the USA stands in place of a welfare state in many contexts, relying on corporations and private individuals to shore up areas of social endeavour by donation or annuity. In the UK, the 'third sector' (as it has become known) provides important support in particular areas of social need by raising funds from the public, or by means of corporate or other donation. Charities are referred to as the 'third sector' because they are neither part of the public sector, because they are not run by the state, but nor are they entirely private bodies. While the charitable third sector, operating somewhere between the public sector and the private sector, does provide important services and support, it has not been admitted historically by any governmental administration that it is meant to act as a replacement for the welfare state, although there are signs that the Labour government and the Conservative Party are both interested in enhancing the role of the charitable sector in providing services which would otherwise have to be provided by government. The principal problem with this approach, it is suggested, is that charities are not democratically accountable in the way that governments are, and therefore it may be difficult to control the decisions of charitable bodies.

Consequently, the charitable sector occupies a difficult middle ground between the private and public sectors. There are issues of public law (or, administrative law) which centre on the equivocal nature of charities as institutions aimed at providing good public works by entities which are not publicly accountable in the way that central or local government are. Therefore, it is unclear how these bodies ought to be controlled. Responsibility for charities lies with The Charity Commission, a public body created originally by the Charities Act 2006. A perception of widespread mismanagement, and possibly corruption, in the charitable sector had previously led to the enactment of the Charities Acts of 1960 and 1993, with the purpose of creating regulatory bodies which would scrutinise and regulate the affairs of charities more closely than before. Shortcomings were said to include irregular keeping of accounts by charities and a lack of control on the part of the Charity Commissioners to ensure that money was being applied as required by the charities' own purposes. The Charities Act 2006 has changed the Charities Commissioners into The Charity Commission in an attempt to renew the regulation of charities yet again.

25.1.2 The structure of this chapter: the changes effected by the Charities Act 2011

The Charities Act 2011 has consolidated nearly all of the earlier charities legislation into a new Act. In particular, the important developments in the old Charities Act 2006 have been transposed into the 2011 Act without substantive change.

The Charities Act 2006 effected some important changes on this topic. The principal purpose of this chapter is to consider the law relating to deciding which purposes will be charitable and which purposes will not be charitable. There is a huge case law on the question which purposes are or are not charitable. The up-shot of that case law was that there were three clear 'heads' (or, categories) of charitable purpose: the relief of poverty, the advancement of religion and the advancement of education. There was a fourth, catch-all category: 'other purposes beneficial to the community'. If one could not demonstrate that one's purpose fell within one or other of the first three heads of charity, then one attempted to argue that it fitted under this fourth, general head. Much of the case law related to the extent of this fourth category. One of the main effects of the Charities Act 2011 has been to extend the heads of charity into areas which the case law had previously refused to acknowledge as being charitable. So, what I have done in re-writing this chapter to reflect the Charities Act 2011 is to retain the discussion of the first three heads of charity (because the 2006 Act leaves them largely unaffected[2]); then to consider in outline how the case law on the fourth head divided itself because the courts may yet decide to retain that category regardless of the Act; and then finally to consider each of the new heads of charity created originally by the 2006 Act in turn, reflecting particularly on how some of these new heads of charity impact on the old case law.

The remainder of the chapter then considers two issues: first, the new regulatory structure for the administration of charities by The Charity Commission and, secondly, the *cy-près* doctrine. The chapter ends with an analysis of the important 'public benefit test' in charities law.

25.1.3 Categories of charitable trust under the case law

The aim of this introduction is to give some explanation of the importance and context of charities law. However, it is difficult to understand modern charities law without some notion of its history.

The roots of the law of charity

The law of charities has its roots in the legislation of 1530 dealing with paupers. While this statute has been long-since repealed, its effect was to regularise the provision of alms to the poor. It is clearly demonstrable that, for example, the case law surrounding the Housing Act 1996 dealing with the rights of homeless people to be housed is still grounded in the Poor Law and, I would suggest, this 16th century statute. The statute passed in 1530 aimed to license begging and to 'outlaw vagabondage by the imposition of severe punishments'. The medieval laws dealing with the poor were used in part to organise casual labour in agricultural communities and provide occasional subsistence living for the poor. The responsibility for controlling such people was placed on their local parishes. The penalties for unlicensed begging and homelessness were criminal punishments. The Vagrancy Acts of 1824 and 1935 remain unrepealed and similarly make it a criminal offence to beg or, effectively, to be part of the indigent poor.

The New Poor Law of the 19th century continued to deal with the issue of homelessness as primarily a criminal matter. The workhouses brought to life in Dickens' *Oliver Twist*, and his own experiences of debtors' prisons, were the reality of the treatment of the poor by the law. The spirit of Christian utilitarianism, and the enforced links between the homeless and the parishes from which they came originally, were key features of the treatment of the indigent poor. In a nation which was organised around religious conflict during the 16th century, the division of the country into parishes was the principal means of allocating responsibility for the treatment of the impoverished. Thus, for example, in terms of the law on homelessness, it is still necessary for the applicant to demonstrate a local connection with the local authority which is alleged to be responsible for the accommodation of that person.[3] Such

---

2   There are, however, some important, subtle changes introduced by the Charities Act 2011.
3   Hudson, 1997.

organised, if harsh, benevolence has been replaced by the hostels and pavements of today. There is still a reliance on good works and charity running drop-in centres and soup kitchens, to deal with the most obvious symptoms of a crisis in the social provision of accommodation and subsistence levels of income. The earliest charities law, then, was the statute of 1601 (considered immediately below) which was bound up with this treatment of the poor as both a threat to public order (and so subject to criminal punishments) and also as the object of pity to be cared for by the church in their local parishes. It was these local churches which, in time, became responsible for schooling the people of its parish as well as dispensing an eleemosynary ministry. Consequently, the case law developed three principal categories of charitable purpose: the relief of poverty, the advancement of religion and the advancement of education.

The context of this discussion

The placing of this discussion of the law of charities within a general examination of the welfare uses of trusts is intended to identify precisely the role of charities as a means of providing for welfare services otherwise than through government spending. Charitable trusts are considered by the law and by policymakers to be desirable institutions and therefore they attract many benefits not afforded to ordinary trusts or ordinary companies.[4] This has led to a great deal of abuse, which is considered towards the end of this chapter. More generally, this Part 8 *Welfare uses of trusts* argues for a coherent set of principles to be developed in relation to the fiduciary obligations of public and welfare trusts generally (including institutions as apparently diverse as pension funds and NHS trusts, as well charities) in recognition of the place of such trusts in the economic life of England and Wales.

The preamble to the Statute of Elizabeth 1601

In the development of the law controlling the giving of alms to the poor, the welter of common practice dealing with the dispossessed was eventually crystallised in the 1601 Statute of Elizabeth.[5] The aim of the 1601 statute appears to have been to reduce the obligations for the care of paupers which had been placed on parishes. The creation of charities in this way permitted philanthropic assistance to be given to charitable aims in a way that would reduce demand on the coffers of each parish.

The preamble to the 1601 statute set out a number of categories of activity which would be considered to be charitable, as follows:

> The relief of aged, impotent and poor people, the maintenance of sick and maimed soldiers and mariners, schools of learning, free schools and schools in universities, the repair of bridges, ports, havens, causeways, churches, sea-banks and highways, the

---

4   That charitable companies are companies with all of the formal difficulties of operating an ordinary company is illustrated by *Seray-Wurie v Charity Commissioners* [2007] 1 WLR 3242, in which the claimant contended that he was a director of this charity as a result of some acrimonious divisions between members of the management committee of the East End Citizens Advice Bureau. Richards J held that the matter was something which the Charity Commission was competent to resolve further to s 26 of the Charities Act 1993 (now Charities Act 2011).

5   43 Eliz I, c 4, 1601, more commonly known as the Charitable Uses Act 1601.

education and preferment of orphans, the relief, stock or maintenance for houses of correction, the marriage of poor maids, the supportation, aid and help of young tradesmen, handicraftsmen and persons decayed, the relief or redemption of prisoners or captives and the aid or ease of any poor inhabitants concerning payment of fifteens, setting out of soldiers and other taxes.

While this statute was repealed by the Mortmain and Charitable Uses Act 1888, its spirit lived on in the common law and by virtue of s 38(4) of the Charities Act 1960. Despite confusion over the effect of the 1888 Act and the Charities Act 1960 (under neither of which was it entirely clear whether or not the Preamble to the 1601 statute was intended to have been repealed *in toto*), it is clear that the courts have incorporated the practice of allocating charitable status to purposes analogous to the Preamble of 1601 into common law. In *Scottish Burial Reform and Cremation Society v Glasgow City Council*[6] the House of Lords accepted that the case law flowing from the preamble should be accepted as keeping 'the law of charities moving as new social needs arise or old ones become obsolete or satisfied'.[7] In that case a trust for the maintenance of a crematorium was found to have been a charitable purpose.

Therefore, it has been accepted that a purpose will be charitable if it can be shown to fall within the Preamble to the 1601 statute or where it ranks by analogy with one of the purposes set out in that preamble. So in *Incorporated Council of Law Reporting for England and Wales v Attorney-General*[8] the dissemination of law reports was found to be a purpose beneficial to the community. Typically, the court will refer to the case law as to the definition of a 'charitable purpose' rather than grappling expressly with the preamble itself. Therefore, the four categories of charity considered in this chapter are those followed by the courts, as considered immediately below.

The roots of the case law on charities

The starting point for much of the case law on the definition of a 'charitable purpose' is *Pemsel's Case*.[9] It was in that decision that Lord Macnaghten set out the four categories of charity which are recognised by the case law on charities today:

(1) the relief of poverty;
(2) the advancement of education;
(3) the advancement of religion; and
(4) other purposes beneficial to the community.

The first three categories, with some oddities, form comparatively straightforward tests for whether or not a trust's purpose is a valid charitable purpose, whereas the fourth offers greater scope for interpretation. In short, before the Charities Act 2006, the lawyer was

---

6 [1968] AC 138; *Re Hummeltenberg* [1923] 1 Ch 237 (training mediums). Cf *Funnell v Stewart* [1996] 1 WLR 288 (faith healing).
7 *Ibid*, 154, *per* Lord Wilberforce.
8 [1972] Ch 73, 88.
9 *Commissioners for the Purposes of Income Tax v Pemsel* [1891] AC 531.

concerned to decide in the first place whether or not the trust purpose in question fell within one of the first three charitable purposes: if not, attention then turned to whether or not it could fall within the fourth, general head. In the next section we consider the effect of the Charities Act 2011 on these categories of charitable purpose.

25.1.4 The definition of 'charitable purposes' in the Charities Act 2011

The meaning of 'charity' as disclosing a 'charitable purpose'

A 'charity' is defined in the Charities Act 2011 as being 'an institution', which can be a trust or a company under English law, 'which is established for charitable purposes only' and 'falls to be subject to the control of the High Court in the exercise of its jurisdiction with respect to charities'.[10] Thus, to know whether or not a trust purpose will constitute a charity we must establish whether or not that purpose can be defined as being a 'charitable purpose', as considered in the next section.

The definition of 'charitable purposes' in the Charities Act 2011

A charitable purpose is one which fulfils two requirements. First, it must fall within the list of purposes set out in s 3(1) of the 2011 Act, as considered in the remainder of this section; and, secondly, it must satisfy the public benefit test, considered in the next section. The definition of 'charitable purposes' in the Charities Act 2011 is found in s 3(1) in the following manner. There are thirteen categories, of which the first three and the last one refer back to the pre-existing case law on the definition of a charitable purpose.

(a) the prevention or relief of poverty;
(b) the advancement of education;
(c) the advancement of religion.

These first three categories are therefore very similar to the initial three case law categories of charitable purpose; whereas the following categories are new:

(d) the advancement of health or the saving of lives;
(e) the advancement of citizenship or community development;
(f) the advancement of the arts, culture, heritage or science;
(g) the advancement of amateur sport;
(h) the advancement of human rights, conflict resolution or reconciliation or the promotion of religious or racial harmony or equality and diversity;
(i) the advancement of environmental protection or improvement;
(j) the relief of those in need by reason of youth, age, ill-health, disability, financial hardship or other disadvantage;
(k) the advancement of animal welfare;
(l) the promotion of the efficiency of the armed forces of the Crown, or of the efficiency of the police, fire and rescue services or ambulance services;

10 Charities Act 2011, s 1(1).

(m) any other purposes within subs (4) [that is categories of charitable purpose which are already accepted under the case law on charities].

Each of these new categories of charitable purpose is considered in turn later in this chapter in section 25.6, after a discussion of the existing heads of charity set out in the first three categories in the statutory list. The importance of the new categories is that they either give validity to some purposes which the case law refused to recognise as being charitable, or that they bring novel purposes under the umbrella of charitable purposes as part of government policy. Among the purposes which are now included in the list of charitable activities which might otherwise have been excluded from being charitable by the old case law are purposes such as animal welfare, campaigning for human rights and environmental protection. The detail of these changes is considered later in the chapter. Before that we need to introduce some more of the essential features of charities law.

The reduced significance of the Preamble to the Statute of 1601

The Charities Act 2011 seeks to displace the importance of the Preamble to the 1601 Statute in defining the meaning of 'charitable purposes'. Thus any references to the Preamble of the 1601 Act in any documents constituting a charitable trust or company are now to be read as references to the Charities Act 2011, so that it is the new Act which now governs the validity of charities.[11] This objective was somewhat over-emphasised because the case law on the meaning of 'charitable purpose', as considered in the remainder of this chapter, has developed regardless of the Preamble in most circumstances, with only older cases on the fourth head of charity being closely concerned with defining 'charitable purpose' by analogy with the contents of that Preamble.

The continued validity of charitable purposes accepted in the old case law

What is particularly important is that categories of charity which have been accepted in the old case law continue to be valid under the 2011 Act. Thus, it is provided in s 3(1)(m)(iii) of the 2011 Act that any purposes which are 'recognised as charitable purposes under existing charity law', for example under the old case law, will continue to be recognised as charitable purposes regardless of whether or not they appear in the list of charitable purposes in s 3(1) of the 2011 Act. Consequently, it is still important to consider those categories of charitable purpose which have been upheld by the pre-2011 case law because the 2011 Act maintains their validity.

The statutory test of 'public benefit'

As considered above, it is a pre-requisite of a trust purpose being held to be a charitable purpose that it is 'for the public benefit' under s 2(1)(b) of the 2011 Act. This statutory requirement of public benefit is expressly stated to be a public benefit as currently understood under the case law in the law of charities,[12] as discussed in this chapter. So, it is

---

11 *Ibid*, s 1(2).
12 *Ibid*, s 3(3).

important to consider what the case law has defined a 'public benefit' to be. You are referred to the lengthy discussions later in this chapter of the concept of 'public benefit' in relation to the case law on educational purposes and on religious purposes. In the following section is a rough rule of thumb as to what will constitute a 'public benefit' and in the section after that it is suggested that the case law, however, did not require that charities for the relief of poverty need be for the public benefit and therefore it will remain a complex matter knowing what constitutes a public benefit in this context.

A rough rule of thumb as to 'public benefit' in the case law

The test for a public benefit is ordinarily understood negatively by considering what will *not* constitute a public benefit. So, in the House of Lords in *Oppenheim v Tobacco Securities Trust*[13] Lord Simonds held that there could not be a public benefit if there was a nexus between the people who established the charity and the people who were intended to benefit such that the people who stood to benefit could not be said to constitute a section of the public. In that case, where a company sought to establish a trust to pay for the school fees of the children of its employees, it was held that there was no *public* benefit because there was a nexus between the children who were to benefit and the company which was establishing the trust. The children of employees did not constitute a section of 'the public' and therefore there was no 'public' benefit. In relation to charities which are created for general purposes, it was suggested by Russell LJ in *ICLR v Attorney-General*[14] that where a trust purpose removes the need for statutory or governmental action by providing a service voluntarily, the organisation providing that service should be deemed to be acting for the public benefit and so to be acting charitably. However, there have been recent cases, particularly relating to the advancement of religion, which have suggested that if a purpose could possibly be interpreted so as to be for the public benefit, or even if it could not be so interpreted but nevertheless if the trustees would operate the trust so that there would be a public benefit in practice, then that purpose can be considered to be for the public benefit.[15] These principles are considered in greater detail in the various discussions of 'public benefit' in relation to the case law heads of charity elsewhere in this chapter.

The requirement for a public benefit: distinguishing two lines of authority on the decided cases

The law of charities teems with case law: there are many hundreds of decisions relating to the validity of individual trusts as charitable purposes. Many of those cases are difficult to reconcile in the abstract because they are so dependent on their own facts. However, it is possible to identify some key themes in relation to judicial attitudes to charitable purposes. There is one very important division which can be made between cases which apply a technical 'public benefit' requirement and other cases which are satisfied if there is some genuine charitable intention on the settlor's part. The purpose of this short section is to draw out one key area of debate. It is suggested, therefore, that there has been a general

---

13 [1951] AC 297.
14 [1972] Ch 73.
15 See, eg, *Re Hetherington* [1990] Ch 1.

division in the courts' attitudes to purportedly charitable trusts over the years into two conflicting approaches:

(1) a requirement that the applicant only needs to show a genuine charitable intention for there to be a valid charitable purpose trust (see *Dingle v Turner*[16] below), or
(2) a requirement that the applicant demonstrate that there is no personal nexus between the settlor and the class of people to be benefited, but rather that there is a sufficiently public benefit from the trust's purpose before it can be a valid charitable purpose (see *Re Compton*[17] below).

This theme of conflict between these two approaches will be followed in the large amount of case law considered below. The point is this. There is a significant difference between establishing, first, that there is something intrinsically charitable in the creation of a trust, compared with, second, a merely evidential question of demonstrating that there is a predominantly public rather than a private benefit in the purposes of that particular trust. The former approach considers the intrinsic merits of the trust purpose which is proposed. Thus, even if only a small number of people will take a benefit from the trust, the court may still find that it is a valid charitable trust if the settlor's intentions are genuinely charitable. By contrast with such examples of a genuine charitable intention, there have been a number of cases in which settlors have sought to win the tax breaks which charitable trusts attract by pretending to create charitable trusts which are in truth intended only to benefit people who are closely linked to the settlor personally. It is because of this sort of abuse that the second approach was developed. The second approach therefore looks to see how the trustees are actually running the trust and whether or not they are achieving sufficiently public, charitable effects. Thus, defeating this sort of abuse of charitable status has prompted some courts to require the existence of a public benefit to demonstrate that the settlor is not simply trying to achieve tax breaks.

The Charities Act 2011 has extended the requirement of 'public benefit' to all forms of charity in the manner discussed below (in that there are now some questions as to exactly how it will apply to trusts for the relief and prevention of poverty). The cases which created the public benefit approach were more concerned with demonstrating that the settlor's intention is to benefit a sufficiently broad category of the public rather than to attract the tax benefits of charitable status to something which is in truth a trust intended to benefit a private class of beneficiaries. This is particularly true in relation to some of the educational charities considered below in which companies sought to acquire tax benefits for paying for the school fees of their employees' children.[18] In those cases, the issue resolves itself to a question of whether or not the company can prove that a sufficiently large proportion of the public will benefit from the trust.

There is one further theme which is worthy of mention at this stage. The courts are eager to find a charitable trust valid wherever possible.[19] I would suggest that this line of cases can be understood as fitting into the approach which seeks to validate genuine charitable

16 [1972] AC 601.
17 [1945] Ch 123.
18 *Oppenheim v Tobacco Securities Trust Co Ltd* [1951] AC 297.
19 *Re Hetherington* [1990] Ch 1; *Guild v IRC* [1992] 2 AC 310.

purposes. This approach goes beyond any of the tendencies in the case law relating to private trusts to interpret such trusts so as to make them valid. Clearly this underscores the policy addressed at granting advantages to charities which are not available to other forms of institution, such as private trusts or trading companies. Therefore, in practice the courts have tended to try to validate genuine charitable purposes whenever they are convinced that the settlor's motives are genuinely charitable and not directed, for example, at the achievement of some undeserved relief from tax.

25.2 THE SPECIAL FEATURES OF CHARITIES

25.2.1 The trusts law advantages of charitable status

Are charities 'trusts' at all?

In the early law of charities, the admission of trust purposes to charitable status and the general, legal treatment of charities were the responsibility of individual parishes and therefore fell under the ecclesiastical courts' jurisdiction. Over time, the Courts of Chancery acquired responsibility for charities organised as trusts and thus the jurisprudence of charities and the jurisprudence of trusts have come to sit uneasily one beside the other.[20]

There are a number of interesting features of the charitable trust. Primarily, the trustee/beneficiary structure is somewhat more complicated in the case of a charitable (or public) trust than in a private trust. The triangle of settlor-trustee-beneficiary does not apply in the case of public trusts such as charities. There is necessarily a requirement of an intention to create a trust, requiring some person to act as settlor, and there are also trustees appointed to oversee the trust property and to promote the objectives of the trust. However, there is no nexus between trustee and beneficiary precisely because there are no individual beneficiaries. This is because the Attorney-General sues in place of beneficiaries to enforce the purposes of the charity against the trustees. While charities will seek to benefit individuals or groups of people, those people are not beneficiaries in the trusts law sense because they do not acquire proprietary rights in the property held on trust for the charitable purpose. Therefore, the powers of trustees are *de facto* more wide-ranging because they are not susceptible to the direct control of any beneficiary: only regulation by The Charity Commission and litigation brought by the Attorney-General *in loco cestui qui trust* (or, as though a beneficiary).

As will be clear from the discussion in this chapter, there is a requirement that a charitable trust take effect for the public benefit (with the exception of some cases to do with relief of poverty) and therefore there cannot be individual beneficiaries capable of enforcing the trust by definition. Indeed, it is this writer's view that charitable trusts are not properly trusts at all, but rather a form of quasi-public body in which the officers have fiduciary duties which are overseen by a regulatory structure made up of the Attorney-General and The Charity Commission.

Charitable companies

Charities can also be organised as companies. They need not be trusts. Strictly, the law on companies is outside the scope of this book. Whereas companies are ordinarily organised so

---

20 Matthews, 1996.

that they have shareholders who own shares in the company, it is more usual for charitable companies to be organised as 'companies limited by guarantee' which do not have share-holders nor a share capital. This form of company limited by guarantee is thus closer to the American notion of a 'not-for-profit' company in relation to which the company limited by guarantee does not have to make profits so as to be able to pay dividends to its shareholders. Instead, its purposes are limited to the pursuit of its charitable goals. In Australia charities law was changed so that charities can only be organised as companies and not as trusts. The purpose behind this change was to limit the possibilities for fraud and mismanagement of charitable trusts. A company will be required to publish accounts annually and its internal structure will be more formalised than the looseness of structure which trusts law ordinarily permits. The downside to the refusal of charitable trusts is that it is comparatively easy for small communities or for people who have little money and little legal expertise to create socially useful charitable trusts; whereas the creation and operation of a charitable company involves a large amount of formality and complexity which in turn requires a large amount of professional expertise. This chapter, however, shall continue to consider only charitable trusts, and the general principles relating to charitable purposes which are applicable thereto.

Formalities

There are a number of advantages in applying charitable status to a trust. As seen in the preceding Part 2 *Express trusts* there are a number of formalities and issues of certainty to be satisfied before a trust will be valid. For the most part, charitable trusts are exempted from these pre-requisites. Some of the most obvious advantages of charitable status are the following.

First, the rules as to perpetuities do not apply to charitable trusts. The rules against inalien-ability and remoteness of vesting do not apply to charitable trusts, therefore endowment capital and income can be tied up indefinitely.[21] Clearly, a charitable purpose would be expressed by a purpose such as 'to accumulate capital to relieve poverty in the East End of London'. If that were an ordinary private trust, it would be potentially void as a purpose trust and also void on the ground that it would make the property inalienable. However, the aim of charities is to amass large amounts of money, know-how and property to achieve socially-desirable objectives. Therefore, it is important that ordinary principles of trusts law are not allowed to operate so that these charitable intentions are frustrated.

Consequently, trust objects are valid despite being for abstract purposes provided that those purposes are charitable purposes. As will emerge in this chapter, the term 'charitable purpose' has a very specific legal meaning beyond any vernacular definition. The explana-tion for the relaxation of this core rule of the law of trusts is that the trust will be overseen by the Attorney-General and/or the Charity Commission in any event. Similarly, there is no need to satisfy the certainty of objects rule so long as there is a general charitable intention. The *cy-près* doctrine, considered at the end of this chapter, governs the application of assets where the precise objects of any charitable trust are uncertain or impossible to ascertain.

There are also differences in the manner in which the trust is organised in that the trustees do not need to act unanimously, rather they need only act by majority. This relaxation of the

---

21   *Christ's Hospital v Grainger* (1849) 1 Mac & G 460.

rules for the administration of trusts, as considered in Part 3, again is aimed at facilitating the use of trusts for charitable purposes. There is a question, in any event, as to why it is that trusts are used as a structure for charitable purposes. Recent developments in Australia have seen the company be designated as the only possible means for carrying out a charitable purpose.[22] The aim of that reform is to restrict the use of charities and to ensure that proper accounts are filed, as required for all companies.

However, the focus on using the company as the only form of charitable body loses some of the informality which is possible where a charity is created on a cottage-industry basis. A trust can be created with comparative informality without the need for the complexity and expense of producing accounts, keeping detailed minutes of meetings, maintaining a share register, and so forth which are required by company law. One of the keynotes of the English law charity is that it can be created with great informality: the applicant need only declare a trust over property and then fill in the forms demonstrating charitable intention, trustee structure and so forth which are required by The Charity Commission before granting registration. This means that comparatively small sums of money and low levels of expertise will not prevent community groups from setting up local charities for the general, public benefit just as effectively as national charities managing millions of pounds and employing professional staff. This informality, it is suggested, is characteristic of the English law charity as a result of its roots in local parish care for the poor. Through the Victorian era much charitable activity was dependent on the (sometimes stern) philanthropy of men like Gradgrind in Dickens's *Hard Times* who gave of their time and their money in the betterment of their fellow men and women. Such altruism relied in large part on the ability of such people to create their own charities and to administer them with some level of informality.

25.2.2 The tax advantages of charitable status

Advantages to charities

The primary benefit of charitable status (beyond the altruistic benefits of being empowered to do good works) is freedom from most of the taxes paid by individuals and corporations. Charities are free from the income taxes paid by both individuals and trusts. They are similarly free from corporation tax paid by companies and unincorporated associations. In terms of chargeable gains resulting from the disposal of capital assets, whereas individuals, private trusts and corporations would pay capital gains tax in ordinary circumstances, charitable trusts are free from capital gains tax. Similarly, aside from central governmental taxes, charities are also free from council tax and other local taxes. However, charities are subject to value-added tax (VAT) which is chargeable on any person who supplies goods or services to other persons. In circumstances in which charities are providing such goods or services, there is no reason in principle why they should be free from such a tax.

The freedom from tax means, in terms, that other taxpayers are subsidising the charitable sector (through higher rates of tax than would otherwise be necessary) by freeing charities from liability to tax. The most tax-efficient structure for a charitable trust is frequently to organise itself as a charitable company, rather than as a trust, which will be liable for all the

---

22 Bryan, 1999.

trustees' fiduciary duties and which would then covenant to pay all of its profits to the charity, thus attracting tax relief.

Advantages to third persons

It is not only charities who benefit from the removal of liability to tax from charities. Individuals who make deeds of covenant in favour of charities (under which they pay regular sums to charity) typically have the covenanted amount treated as part of the charity's income for tax purposes. Similarly, companies can have some of the tax they pay recouped by giving gifts to charity (see, for example, the discussion below on companies' educational charities). This ability which charities have to recover the tax paid by donors led to a spate of tax avoidance schemes in the 1960s and 1970s when the highest income tax rates in the UK remained above 60% for some time. Taxpayers falling into super-tax brackets would covenant money to charities. The charity would then be able to recover the tax paid by the taxpayer from the Inland Revenue. In many circumstances, the charity would then pay the tax deducted back to the taxpayer (typically offshore) as part of a complex tax avoidance arrangement.

Suppose the following situation in illustration of this scheme.

> The charity would receive a donation (say, £40,000 after tax had been deducted) and recovered the tax paid by the taxpayer (£60,000 at a 60% tax rate) and then paid the recovered tax covertly to the taxpayer (£60,000). Consequently, the taxpayer earned more money through this route than through paying tax in the ordinary way. When some tax rates rose to 98% under super-tax, the taxpayer could (on £100,000 income) pay £2,000 to charity and have the charity recover £98,000 from Her Majesty's Revenue and Customs.

In the 1990s, developments in legislation and case law made these types of simple schemes impossible by ignoring any 'artificial steps' in such transactions.[23] More recent case law on tax avoidance has removed the presumption against artificiality in favour of an approach which subjects each taxing statute to ordinary principles of statutory interpretation.[24]

25.3 FACTORS WHICH MAY NEGATE A FINDING OF CHARITABLE STATUS: THE NEED FOR A CHARITABLE INTENTION, BUT NO POLITICAL PURPOSES

25.3.1 Sufficient intention to create a charitable trust

In general terms

The settlor must have had an exclusively charitable intention in creating her trust for it to be a valid charitable purpose. The courts have tended to disallow ostensibly charitable purposes if there has been some failure to disclose a purpose which is exclusively charitable. This chapter will consider the detail of each of the heads of charity. The structure of that analysis will be to examine each of those heads and then to consider those factors which will deprive

---

23 *Ramsay v IRC* [1982] AC 300, *Furniss v Dawson* [1984] 2 WLR 226.
24 *Barclays Mercantile Business Finance Ltd v Mawson* [2004] UKHL 51, [2005] 1 AC 684, [2005] 1 All ER 97.

an institution of charitable status, even if it is *prima facie* charitable. So, if a settlor has two purposes behind his trust, one charitable and the other not, then the trust may not be held to be a valid charity. By the same token, however, some courts will seek to validate a genuinely charitable purpose wherever they find one.[25] Evidently, as with all forms of trust, there is a requirement that there be sufficient intention to create a charitable trust on the part of the settlor before that trust will be deemed to be charitable. Thus, in *Re Koeppler*,[26] Slade LJ looked to the general charitable intention of a testator who had sought to leave money for the furtherance of a charitable project on which he worked. It was held that, even where a gift is expressed in vague terms, it would be interpreted as having been charitable. It is clear from the decided cases that the court will tend to find trusts with a genuine charitable intention valid wherever possible.[27] This theme is considered further in relation to the *cy-près* doctrine at the end of this chapter. At this stage it is sufficient to point out that the courts will give effect to a genuine charitable intention wherever they find one.

Need for exclusivity of charitable intention

It is important that the settlor's purpose be exclusively charitable. That means the settlor will not be able to confuse a charitable with a non-charitable purpose and hope to have the trust recognised as being charitable. The case law has taken a very strict approach to this question in many cases.[28] If the settlor were to declare that property be held on 'charitable *or* other purposes', then the trust would not be a valid charitable trust because that could potentially be applied by its trustees for a charitable purpose or alternatively for a non-charitable purpose.[29] The uncertainty introduced by the word 'or' is crucial. The rationale for disallowing such trusts from being charitable trusts is that it is possible for the trustees to apply the property either for charitable purposes or potentially for some other purpose which is not charitable. However, there have been cases in which the use of the disjunctive '*or*' in these circumstances has been coupled with a purpose which the court has been able to accept as being almost charitable: such as 'charity, or any other public objects in the parish of Farringdon'[30] and '[charity] or some similar purpose in connection with it'[31] because in those circumstances the court was prepared to interpret that provision as meaning that the trustees were still required to use the trust property for purposes which were charitable, even if they may have some other features as well as their charitable nature.

Cases in which the settlor has provided that property be settled for a 'charitable *and* other purpose' have tended to receive a more generally benign construction where the court has been able to interpret the word '*and*' as connoting an intention either that the trustees must

---

25 *Re Hetherington* [1990] Ch 1.
26 [1984] 2 WLR 973.
27 *Incorporated Council for Law Reporting v Attorney-General* [1972] Ch 73; *Guild v IRC* [1992] 2 AC 310.
28 *Blair v Duncan* [1902] AC 37 (charitable or public purposes); *Chichester Diocesan Board of Finance v Simpson* [1944] AC 341 (charitable or benevolent purposes); *Re Coxen* [1948] Ch 747 (quantification of separable charitable and non-charitable elements). Cf *Re Best* [1904] 2 Ch 354 ('charitable and benevolent'); *Attorney-General v National Provincial and Union Bank of England* [1924] AC 262 ('such patriotic purposes or objects and such charitable institution or institutions or charitable object or objects. . .'); Charitable Trusts (Validation) Act 1954.
29 *Re Macduff* [1896] 2 Ch 451; *Blair v Duncan* [1902] AC 37; *Houston v Burns* [1918] AC 337.
30 *Re Bennett* [1960] Ch 18.
31 *Guild v IRC* [1992] 2 AC 310.

administer the trust in a charitable manner even if some other, incidental purpose is also to be achieved, or that the other purpose must be also be charitable – or at least not detract from the underlying charitable purpose.³² However, where that provision is interpreted to mean that the trust need have charitable purposes only as part of its core goals, then it will be invalid as a charitable trust: for example, 'benevolent, charitable and religious purposes' where charity was found to be only one of three purposes in which 'benevolent' does not mean 'charitable',³³ and similar situations where purposes were grouped so as to make them appear to be in the alternative.³⁴

It is suggested that, in the wake of more benignant constructions like that in *Guild v IRC*³⁵ and *Re Hetherington*³⁶ in recent years, that the courts are less likely to invalidate trusts on the basis of lack of exclusivity of purpose than was the case in many of the preceding decisions. However, that does not mean that the courts will accept as charitable those trusts which are not exclusively charitable. Rather, they will be prepared to accept both that the underlying intention can be *construed* as being charitable and that the trustees will *in practice apply* the trust property so as to make it operate as a charitable trust: that is, by applying the property only for strictly 'charitable' purposes and not also for more generally 'benevolent' but non-charitable purposes.

In *Re Harding*³⁷ Lewison J applied this notion of validating charitable, testamentary gifts wherever possible in relation to a purpose which in itself was so broadly drafted that it could not have disclosed an exclusively charitable purpose. The bequest was to the effect that property was to be held 'in trust for the black community of Hackney, Haringey, Islington and Tower Hamlets'. Lewison J held that this purpose should be interpreted so as to make it valid. However, it is suggested that that bequest was so broadly drafted that it did not disclose a charitable purpose but nor did it make clear what the trustees would or would not be permitted to do with the property. Remarkably, Lewison J held that to comply with s 34(1) of the Race Relations Act 1976 the specific ethnic limitation in the bequest should be treated as having been removed – so in the end, the bequest was simply 'for the benefit of the people' of four large London boroughs. Other than the notion that this is to be for the benefit of those people (more than a million in all probability), there is nothing either to tell us when the trustees have performed or not performed their duty, nor that this is necessarily a charitable use. As Lewison J put it, cryptically enough, in the final substantive sentence of his judgment '[t]he precise nature of the trusts can be dealt with by a scheme'³⁸ – in other words, the trustees will be required to generate a scheme for using the property which would satisfy the Charity Commission and/or the courts.

25.3.2 Political purposes

The theoretical outline

The notion of charity has been taken by English law to exclude any attempt to promote political purposes, even where the end-goal of such a political policy is aimed at the benefit

32 *Blair v Duncan* [1902] AC 37, *supra*; *Re Sutton* (1885) 28 Ch D 464; *Re Best* [1904] 2 Ch 354.
33 *Williams v Kershaw* (1835) 5 Cl & F 111; also *Morice v Bishop of Durham* (1805) 10 Ves 522.
34 *Re Eades* [1920] 2 Ch 353; *Attorney-General v National Provincial and Union Bank of England* [1924] AC 262; *Attorney-General for the Bahamas v Royal Trust Co* [1986] 1 WLR 1001.
35 [1992] 2 AC 310.
36 [1990] Ch 1.
37 [2008] 2 WLR 361.
38 *Ibid*, para [27].

of a community. Where a goal is avowedly political, the courts will not uphold it as a valid charitable purpose.[39] The stated reason for this principle is that it would be beyond the competence of the court to decide whether or not that purpose would be for the benefit of the community.

Furthermore, Lord Simonds in *National Anti-Vivisection Society*[40] cited with approval the argument that the court must assume the law to be correct and therefore could not uphold as charitable any purpose which promotes a change in the law. This jurisprudential approach does appear to be a little thin. Given that judges contentedly take it upon themselves to interpret, limit and extend statutes (as well as occasionally recommending the creation of new statutes to shore up the common law), it is peculiar to see judges so coy in the face of an argument being advanced that legislation might be changed.

Clearly, there will be factual circumstances in which a charitable purpose is advanced for political ends. For example, a charitable purpose to care for the elderly may also serve as a vehicle for pressuring central government into changing its policy on the treatment of elderly people. It is common for charities to campaign for the advancement of their cause as a collateral object to the charitable purpose. As a general rule of thumb, the courts will consider activities as being political if they involve campaigning for a change in the law. However, there will necessarily be a large range of activities which fall short of such campaigning but which go beyond the pursuit of the charitable objective. So, for example, the Royal Society for the Prevention of Cruelty to Animals (RSPCA) has as one of its many objectives the goal of a change in the law relating to testing on animals: this is something which is ordinarily a void political purpose (as is considered in the next section) but which does not call the charitable status of the RSPCA into question because it is merely one of its minor objectives.

The strict rule

The leading case of *National Anti-Vivisection Society v IRC*[41] before the House of Lords considered the question whether or not the society's political campaigning for the banning of vivisection[42] would prevent its purposes from being defined as being charitable. The type of political campaigning undertaken was to procure a change in the law so that vivisection would be banned outright. Lord Simonds considered the society's aims to be too political to qualify as a charity on the basis that an aim to change legislation is necessarily political. Consequently, the society was found not to be charitable and therefore not exempt from income tax. It is suggested that this approach creates a strict rule for charitable status. In applying the approach of Lord Simonds, it must be the case that to advance a change in the law as a core aim of the trust will be to take outwith the definition of charity necessarily.[43]

There is a theoretical problem as to whether or not the court could decide that the benefit of one side of a political argument (for example, banning vivisection) outweighs another.

---

39 *National Anti-Vivisection Society v IRC* [1940] AC 31.
40 *Ibid.*
41 *Ibid.*
42 'Vivisection' means animal experimentation.
43 Even though animal welfare is now one of the statutory heads of charity, as discussed below, if this society continued to campaign for a change in the law then that would mean that it would still be pursuing a non-charitable, political purpose.

Suppose for example a trust with a purpose to advance the medical utility of experiments on animals in the search for a cure for cancer. By admitting the medical trust to charitable status the law is impliedly accepting that side of the political argument. Clearly, the argument in defence of the current position is that the law is outside politics. However, it is clear that the effect of the law is to favour some political points of view over others.

As with all trusts law issues, the question is to use the correct structure for the statement of aims. The RSPCA is registered as a charity, even though it works to stop vivisection in some contexts. The reason why it is upheld as being charitable despite its attempts to stop vivisection are that the anti-vivisection attitudes it holds are only a part of its activities. Similarly, in *Bowman v Secular Society*,[44] Lord Normand held that a society whose *predominant* aim was not to change the law, could be charitable even though its campaign for a change to legislation was merely a subsidiary activity. It is a question of degree whether a society seeks to change the law as its main focus, or whether it espouses ends which incidentally require a change in the law. It is unclear where the law of charities draws that particular line.

Arguments for flexibility

If the approach in *National Anti-Vivisection Society v IRC*[45] were to be followed to its logical conclusion, it would mean that housing charities like Shelter would be able to research into improving housing conditions while helping the homeless, but that it would not be able to publish its results for fear that they would be recommending a change in the law. In *McGovern v Attorney-General*,[46] the human rights campaigning organisation Amnesty International was held not to be charitable, despite its good works, because it campaigned for changes in the laws of many nations. The court held that it was not for the court to decide whether or not the changes in the law which it sought would be in the public interest or not. However, the Charity Commissioners have suggested that an organisation may supply information to the government regarding changes in the law without forfeiting its charitable status. Without this flexibility being built into the law, many charities would not be able to disseminate the important information which only they are able to amass.

On the cases it is clear that a trust for the discussion of political ideas is not itself void under the rule in the *National Anti-Vivisection* case.[47] For example, it is not an invalid activity under the law of charities for a university students' union to discuss political matters[48] but it is not a charitable purpose to campaign on a political issue or to apply funds to an organisation formed to change the law or public policy. So in *Webb v O'Doherty*[49] a students' union wanted to pay funds to a national committee of students which sought to apply pressure to stop the conflict in the Persian Gulf in 1991 but the union was not able to uphold this purpose as a charitable purpose because it was found to be politically motivated. As Lewison J put it: 'there is a distinction between the purposes or objects of a charity and the means by

---

44 [1917] AC 406.
45 [1940] AC 31.
46 [1982] 2 WLR 222.
47 [1940] AC 31.
48 *Attorney-General v Ross* [1986] 1 WLR 252; *Re Koeppler's WT* [1986] Ch 423.
49 (1991) *The Times*, 11 February.

which it promotes those purposes or objects'.[50] Thus, a court may consider the fact that an organisation does in fact pursue political objectives and so deny that organisation charitable status, or contrariwise look to the charitable means by which it promotes its objectives.

25.3.3 A note before we proceed

For the student of trusts law, charities can offer a comparatively welcome relief from the complexities of forming express private trusts, as considered in Part 2, and from implied trusts in Parts 4, 5 and 6, or the many equitable remedies in Part 9. The central question with reference to charities for our purposes is to decide in what circumstances a trust will be held to be charitable. In any charities problem, the subject matter should be divided clearly between the various different categories of charitable trust: trusts for relief of poverty, trust for educational purposes, trusts for religious purposes and trusts for other purposes beneficial to the community as listed in s 3(1) of the Charities Act 2011. Sections on charities in trusts law textbooks are capable of being extremely long, given the enormous variety of the case law. However, it is proposed in this chapter to concentrate on the leading cases in each of the four categories and then tease out some of the inconsistencies among some of the other decisions. This may then prove to be a banker at exam time.

25.4 RELIEF AND PREVENTION OF POVERTY

Trusts for the relief of poverty must relieve the poverty of some person. 'Poverty' means something more than simply 'going short' but does not require absolute destitution. It is apparently unnecessary that a broad section of the community stand to benefit from the trust. Rather, trusts for the relief of poverty are presumed to have a generally altruistic motivation and are, therefore, enforceable as being charitable. There is no need for a 'public benefit' – a factor which has led to the anomalous trusts for the benefit of relatives which appear, prima facie, *to be private trusts, although the Charities Act 2011 may call the validity of these trusts into question. Furthermore, the 2011 Act has introduced the new concept of 'the prevention of poverty' to that head of charity.*

25.4.1 Introduction

The first category of charitable purpose under the case law is that of the relief of poverty. This is the clearest category of charitable purposes in many ways. Having considered the birth of the law on charities in terms of a development of the legislation dealing with the poor above, poverty is the most straightforward illustration of a charitable intention. The Charities Act 2006 has amended this category slightly by providing that the trust should be created for 'the *prevention* or relief of poverty'. The effect of this slight change is considered below. For present purposes, however, we shall consider the leading case on trusts for the relief of poverty which was decided before the Act came into force, on the basis that it is provided in s 4(3)of the Charities Act 2011 that any purposes which are 'recognised as charitable purposes under existing charity law', for example under the old case law, will

---

50 *Hanchett-Stamford v Attorney-General* [2008] 4 All ER 323, para [17].

continue to be recognised as charitable purposes. We will, however, need to consider some old cases known as the 'poor relatives' cases more carefully in the light of the 2011 Act.

The leading case in relation to the relief of poverty is the decision of the House of Lords in *Dingle v Turner*,[51] which forms the centrepiece of this section. Characteristic of the approach of the courts in this area is the 'purposive' decision of Lord Cross. Of further interest is the historical context of cases on the creation of trusts expressed to be for the relief of impoverished relatives, whether they should properly have been considered to be charitable given the nexus between settlor and beneficiary, and the suitability of such trusts in the modern context.

The trust in *Dingle v Turner* concerned a bequest of £10,000 to be applied 'to pay pensions to poor employees of E Dingle & Company'. Those arguing that the bequest be held invalid sought to rely on *Oppenheim v Tobacco Securities Trust*,[52] and also *Re Compton*,[53] which had held that a trust could not be charitable if 'the benefits under it are confined to the descendants of a named individual or company'.[54] It was contended, further, that the poor relations cases were simply an anomaly in the development of this core principle and that the *Dingle* trust could not be validated by analogy to those cases.[55]

Lord Cross did not allow this appeal. He explained that the rule in *Re Compton* was not one of universal application in the law of charities, particularly in relation to trusts for the relief of poverty. His speech had two main points: first, that the *Compton* principle was intellectually unsound in itself and, second, that trusts for the relief of poverty required a different test from other forms of charitable trust which did not require a public benefit.

As to the first strand of his Lordship's decision, the approach taken by Lord Cross was to say that the meaning of the term 'public' in the public benefit test was itself a difficult one. The expression which was frequently used in previous cases to contrast with the term 'public' was the term 'a mere fluctuating body of private individuals', by which the courts meant that if the people who would benefit from a trust purpose would be merely a fluctuating body of private individuals then they could not constitute a sufficiently large section of the public to constitute a charity. However, Lord Cross in *Dingle v Turner* pointed out that logically the public was itself just such a fluctuating body of private individuals: that is, the total population may be 60 million private individuals in the UK but it was still a fluctuating body of private individuals. Therefore, this was an insufficient rendering of the difference between the terms 'private' and 'public' class. Lord Cross explained that the residents of a particular London borough could be both a section of the public and a fluctuating body of private individuals. There would be no doubt that 'all of the residents of the Royal London Borough of Kensington and Chelsea' would constitute a valid section of the public for the purposes of the law of charity. Nevertheless, logically, the total number of inhabitants of Kensington and Chelsea would be a fluctuating body of private individuals: that is, some will be born and some will die, some will move into the area and some will move out of it (such that their identities will fluctuate), and each of those inhabitants is a private citizen, even though collectively they constitute a section of the public. Similarly, to talk of 'the blind' would be

---

51 [1972] AC 601.
52 [1951] AC 297.
53 [1945] Ch 123.
54 *Oppenheim* is a case relating to educational purpose trusts, considered below at para 27.3.3.
55 Considered below at para 27.3.

to define a section of the public, even though its members have a common characteristic which binds them together. That means the law of charities will accept that a trust for the benefit of the 'blind in the UK' will be a valid charitable purpose, although logically again this class constitutes a group of private individuals with a link between them and so, logically again, it ought to fail on a literal application of the *Compton* test. Therefore, Lord Cross sought to demonstrate that the *Compton* test was not logically appealing and so Lord Cross chose not to follow it in relation to trusts for the relief of poverty.

His Lordship then turned to the question of the validity of a trust for the benefit of employees of a company, and the argument that such a class would be a private class (and so arguably invalid under charities law) on the basis that the people who were to benefit from the trust were bound together by a common factor. It was held that, even when considering gifts to employees of a large company, it might be that a particular corporation would employ many thousands of people and therefore constitute a numerically larger class than were resident in a particular borough. It would be illogical to consider the former to be a void private class, whereas the latter would be a valid section of the public, when the former is a numerically larger class than the latter. For example, the Post Office employs hundreds of thousands of sorting staff and delivery staff in the UK and so a trust 'for the benefit of employees of the Post Office' would fail a literal application of the *Compton* test (because all of the people who would benefit worked for the same organisation) even though the class which could benefit would constitute a statistically significant proportion of the population. By contrast a trust for the benefit of the inhabitants of a small town would pass the literal application of the *Compton* test but oddly the people who stood to benefit from the trust would be numerically smaller than in the Post Office example. Lord Cross suggests that the Post Office trust could be valid, provided that the settlor's intention was a genuinely charitable one. It is the settlor's intention which is said to be vital in *Dingle v Turner*. In the words of Lord Cross:

> *Much must depend on the purpose of the trust.* It may well be that, on the one hand, a trust to promote some purpose, *prima facie* charitable, will constitute a charity even though the class of potential beneficiaries might fairly be called a private class and that, on the other hand, a trust to promote another purpose, also *prima facie* charitable, will not constitute a charity even though the class of potential beneficiaries might seem to some people fairly describable as a section of the public.

It is suggested that the opening words of these *dicta* (with this author's own italics) sum up the approach of the House of Lords in *Dingle* most accurately in this area. This encapsulates Lord Cross's second line of argument. The court is prepared to adopt a purposive approach to charitable purposes genuinely concerned with the relief of poverty. To put it crudely, if you are genuinely acting with a charitable purpose in the relief of poverty, then your trust will be valid.

The point of distinction from the *Compton* and *Oppenheim* line of cases was said to be the fact that those cases involved trusts whose purpose was to acquire 'an undeserved fiscal immunity'. In short, the court would be prepared to support a genuinely charitable motive, although in the absence of such a motive the court would refuse to find the trust charitable. It is suggested that charitable motives are more obviously demonstrated in relation to the relief of poverty (provided those receiving the benefits can be shown to be genuinely impoverished), unlike cases in which companies are seeking to acquire tax benefits for their directors and other employees by setting up educational trusts which benefit only the children of their own employees. Lord Cross described this as the 'practical justification . . . if not the historical explanation' for the distinction between trusts for the relief of poverty and other trusts.

It is possible to return to the earlier distinction between decisions based on finding an underlying charitable intention on the one hand, and seeking a sufficient public benefit on the other hand. *Dingle v Turner* is clearly demonstrative of the line of cases which are concerned with the identification of an underlying charitable motive for the trust. Lord Cross considered this to be more important than seeking to address a purely evidential question as to whether or not a sufficient section of the public will be benefited by the operation of the trust.

Having considered the leading case, it is worth exploring the requirements for a charitable trust for the relief of poverty. There are two core questions concerned with the relief of poverty: first, what is 'poverty', and second, what is 'relief'? These two questions will be considered in turn.

25.4.2 What is 'poverty'?

There is a perennial discussion between political scientists as to the meaning of the term 'poverty'. In forming public policy there is a temptation to set an absolute measurement of poverty, bound to income levels, health and housing requirements perhaps. Once an individual reaches that absolute measurement, that individual ceases to be poor. There are two principal problems with this approach. First, the setting of such levels would necessarily cause disagreement as to what constitutes a level of poverty. Second, there is the issue of general social enrichment which might render such standards obsolete over time, such that an income level for poverty set in the 1960s would now be meaningless as a result of inflation and the greater distribution of consumer goods amongst the whole population. (On this issue see generally the work of Townsend.[56])

The contrary argument is that there should not be absolute standards of poverty set because the question of impoverishment is something which should always be relative to standards of living at any period of time in any social context. However, the counter-argument is that it becomes impossible to eradicate poverty if the measurements are allowed to shift in this way.

On the cases, there are precious few clear statements on the meaning of 'poverty'. In *Mary Clark Homes Trustees v Anderson*,[57] Channell J held that poverty was a relative term which would consider someone to be poor if he is in 'genuinely straitened circumstances and unable to maintain a very modest standard of living for himself and the persons (if any) dependent upon him'.[58] Even this approach does not require destitution. Nor is there any sense of the length of time for which those who are to benefit from the trust are required to be in straitened circumstances: presumably that must last for more than one or two days. What is interesting about this approach is that it focuses on the poverty of individuals benefiting from the munificence of the charity and not on the framing of the charity's objects

---

56 Townsend, 1979, and the work of the Child Poverty Action Group generally.
57 [1904] 2 KB 745.
58 Quotation taken from Tudor, 1995, 29; see also *Re Clarke* [1923] 2 Ch 407; *Re De Carteret* [1933] Ch 103; *Shaw v Halifax Corp* [1915] 2 KB 170; see also Cross (1956) 72 LQR 182.

to apply solely to people in general terms as though that category must be sufficiently impoverished. This chimes in with the acceptance in *Dingle v Turner*[59] that the trust need not be demonstrated to be for the public benefit. Given the all-encompassing nature of the case law definitions, the meaning of poverty can be most clearly demonstrated by examples, as set out in the following sections.

Examples of poverty

The difficulty for the courts is then to establish a test for deciding in any case whether or not a particular trust is sufficiently directed at the relief of poverty. To be honest, there is no very clear definition of 'poverty' in the law of charities. The cases have taken the view that poverty does not necessitate proof of outright destitution, rather it can encompass which exceeds simply 'going short'.[60] There are a number of examples of situations in which the courts have held cases of financial hardship, rather than grinding poverty, to be within the technical definition of 'poverty'. For example, a trust for 'ladies of limited means' has been held to be charitable[61] together with the (gloriously expressed) trust for the benefit of 'decayed actors'.[62] It is difficult to know exactly what a '*decayed* actor' is, but I think it is a wonderful idea. In the 17th century this term 'decayed' had as one of its meanings 'to have declined in prosperity':[63] so, again, it did not require that the person benefiting had become entirely destitute but rather simply that they were in greatly straitened circumstances. Significantly, that we cannot know exactly what a decayed person is, despite its inclusion in the 1601 Statute of Elizabeth (and assuming it is not meant literally as someone decomposing), does not stop the purpose from being a valid charitable purpose. It is an illustration of the type of vague trusts provision which courts are prepared to admit as valid in the context of charitable trusts for the relief of poverty whereas they would never satisfy the tests for conceptual certainty for express private trusts considered in Chapter 3 *The creation of express trusts*. Another example is a trust for the benefit of members of a club who have 'fallen on evil days', which would have been too vague an expression for ordinary private trusts purposes.[64]

Poverty and the preamble

There was an argument raised as to notion of poverty in the preamble to the 1601 statute in the case of *Joseph Rowntree v Attorney-General*.[65] It was argued that the expression 'aged, impotent and poor' in the preamble to the 1601 Statute should be read so as to require the class forming the charitable purpose to be all three of those things, such that someone who

59 [1972] AC 601.
60 *Re Coulthurst's Will Trusts* [1951] Ch 661, at 666 (more than 'going short'); *Re Cottam* [1955] 3 All ER 704 (flats at 'economic rents'); *Joseph Rowntree Memorial Trust Housing Association Ltd v Attorney-General* [1983] 1 All ER 288 (special housing for the elderly; 'alleviation' of poverty constitutes 'relief').
61 *Re Gardom* [1914] 1 Ch 662.
62 *Spiller v Maude* (1881) 32 Ch D 158.
63 See, for example, the definition of the word 'decay' in the Shorter Oxford English Dictionary, which contains this sense among numerous others.
64 *Re Young* [1951] Ch 344.
65 [1983] 1 All ER 288.

was not (for example) aged would not fall within the test. It was held that the three terms should be considered disjunctively so that a beneficiary need only fit one of these descriptions.[66] Therefore, if the beneficiary is aged and impotent but not poor, then the trust will be held to be valid.[67] It has been held that a person aged 50 was 'aged' (although that was in a decision in 1889 when life expectancies were shorter).[68] After the enactment of the Charities Act 2006, the role of the 1601 Preamble will nevertheless be limited.

Poverty and social class

There have been cases in which the largesse of the courts has been pushed to its limits. A number of charitable purposes have been expressed to be for the relief of the poverty of the 'working classes'. It was held in *Re Sanders' WT*[69] that the 'working class' do not constitute a section of the poor. It is necessary to define in some way those in poverty, as opposed to those who could be merely expressed to be working class. However, in *Re Niyazi's WT*[70] it was held that a gift for the construction of a working men's hostel in an area of extreme poverty in Cyprus created a valid charitable trust for the relief of poverty on the basis that the class of persons described could be considered, in all the circumstances, to be suitably impoverished.

The latter case of *Niyazi* illustrates the acceptance of the courts that there is a need, with reference to charitable trusts, to look to the manner in which the money is to be used in fact to determine whether or not there is sufficient charitable intention. This has tended to be the approach of the courts in situations in which it would be possible for both rich and poor people to benefit from a particular trust on the face of the trust. Therefore, in *Re Gwyon*[71] a trust for the provision of clothing for boys was held to be invalid on the basis that there was no necessary requirement that the boys in question be in poverty. Rather, the court accepted that the money would be applied *de facto* by the trustees for the benefit of poor boys only. This purposive approach has led to the validity of a number of charitable trusts for the relief of poverty which would otherwise have appeared to have been uncertain in their charitable intent.

25.4.3 What is meant by 'relief' and by 'prevention'?

The relief of poverty

The term 'relief' is not intended to lead to resolution of the poverty experienced by those who receive the benefits of the trust. Rather, it is sufficient that there be some alleviation of the poverty as a result of the activities of the trust.[72] Therefore, a trust for the relief of poverty of millionaire food merchants by means of food parcels, would not be a valid charitable trust for

---

66 *Re Resch's Will Trusts* [1967] 1 All ER 915.
67 *Re Glyn's WT* (1950) 66 TLR 510; *Re Bradbury; Re Robinson* [1951] Ch 198; *Re Cottam* [1955] 3 All ER 704; and *Re Lewis* [1955] Ch 104.
68 *Re Wall* (1889) 42 Ch D 510.
69 [1954] Ch 265.
70 [1978] 1 WLR 910.
71 [1930] 1 Ch 255.
72 *Joseph Rowntree Memorial Trust Housing Association Ltd v Attorney-General* [1983] 1 All ER 288.

the *relief* of poverty as there is no poverty which would actually be relieved by such a trust because the recipients are already millionaires. However, it would appear that a genuine charitable intention to relieve poverty by opening a soup kitchen which also occasionally provided food to people who were not impoverished would not be invalid, provided that the poverty of others who were impoverished was being relieved. So, it is said, it cannot be a trust for the *relief* of poverty if the soup kitchen provides millionaires with food because millionaires would not be in need of such soup to relieve any poverty. Whereas, a soup kitchen for the benefit of the genuinely impoverished will be a valid charity for the relief of poverty.[73]

The prevention of poverty

The Charities Act 2011, s 3(1)(a) adds the notion of the 'prevention' of poverty to this category. The principal effect of this change would be to remove the requirement that the people who are to be helped must already be in poverty. Thus it would be a valid charitable purpose if someone anticipated that a person was going to fall into poverty and so took some action by constituting a trust to prevent that state of affairs arising. This could clearly be open to abuse. Suppose two examples. First, if a trust was created to provide a hostel for young people in London who found themselves with no home then that would be preventing those people from falling into poverty by dint of giving them somewhere to live, especially so if the trust also helped them to find work or gave them enough money to afford food and clothing. Second, suppose that a trust was created for the benefits of the permanent inhabitants of Marlow in Buckinghamshire, one of the richest towns in the country, in case any of its permanent inhabitants should possibly fall into poverty. Suppose further that the settlor's real objective was to achieve the tax benefits of charitable status so that all of the money which he gave to the charity received tax relief but was never paid out to any impoverished people and instead was used to pay for dinners for himself and his millionaire friends at the golf club. In this example, whereas the trust appears to be worded so as to prevent poverty, in fact it is not being so used. The difficulty with the notion of prevention is that it supposes action before poverty has necessarily arisen. However, it is suggested that Lord Cross's test in *Dingle v Turner* remains the best one in this context because it will deny charitable status only to those trusts which do not disclose a genuine charitable intention: something which exists in the first of my examples but not the second.

25.4.4 Limits on the class of people taking a benefit

It is a peculiarity with reference to the rules for charitable trusts for the relief of poverty that the settlor can validly define a limited group of people who are entitled to benefit from the trust, and can even show a nexus the intended beneficiaries.

Is there a need for a public benefit?

It was held in *Dingle v Turner*[74] that a trust for the relief of poverty does not have to be shown to be for the general public benefit, as long as it does go beyond the relief of the

---

73 *Biscoe v Jackson* (1887) 35 Ch D 460.
74 [1972] AC 601.

poverty of a single, individual beneficiary. Therefore, the applicant would be required to show that the trust was more than a private trust for the benefit of a fixed class of beneficiaries which merely sought to attract the fiscal advantages of charitable status. However, it is acceptable for the people who will actually benefit from the trust to be related, or otherwise linked, to the settlor (as considered immediately below). Thus in *Dingle v Turner* a trust for the relief of poverty of poor employees was upheld as a valid, charitable purpose, despite the link between the settlor and the intended class of beneficiaries as employer and employees.

Consequently, it has been held that a trust for the purpose of establishing a home for elderly Presbyterians was held to be a sufficiently broad public benefit, even though the category of people who could have benefited was limited.[75] In that case there was sheltered accommodation provided by a company (Joseph Rowntree Memorial Housing Association Ltd) which both charged occupants for their accommodation and which made that accommodation available only to a limited number of people. It was held by Peter Gibson J that neither of these factors disqualified the purpose from qualifying as a charitable purpose. Just as in *Re Neal*,[76] Goff J had upheld a trust which charged occupants of an old persons' home as being charitable; similarly Buckley J in *Re Payling's WT*.[77] In such cases, where there is an intention to provide for 'succouring and supplying the needs of old persons because they were old persons' was sufficient to found a charitable intention to relieve poverty – provided also that these old persons were in need of the help that they were given. An organisation which had assumed responsibility for the maintenance and management of many properties from a local authority was held not to have exclusively charitable purposes because it conferred private benefits on individual tenants as part of its activities.[78]

The Charities Act 2011 requires that any charitable purpose both be on the list of charitable purposes – as the prevention and relief of poverty is under s 3(1)(a) – and also be 'for the public benefit'. There is no exception, it seems, from the requirement of a public benefit for poverty trusts, even though the effect of *Dingle v Turner* was that there would not need to be a public benefit in trusts for the relief of poverty. Therefore, we must consider whether poverty trusts now do require a public benefit to be valid, or whether the old case law approach which did not require such a public benefit still lives on. We must consider the effect of s 4(3) of the 2011 Act which provides that the 'reference to the public benefit is a reference to the public benefit as that term is understood for purposes of the law relating to charities'. This provision should, it is suggested, be understood to mean that the requirement for a public benefit under the statute is to be interpreted in accordance with the understanding of the term public benefit as applied in the case law on charities before 2006 (when the statutory concept was first introduced). The understanding of the public benefit requirement before the Act came into force was that that public benefit requirement did not apply to poverty trusts. Thus, s 4(3) should be interpreted so as to mean that no public benefit is required in relation to a trust for the prevention or relief of poverty. To do otherwise would be to overrule a long line of cases, including *Dingle v Turner*, which have granted charitable status to trusts for comparatively small numbers of people provided that there was a genuine charitable intention to relieve poverty involved. The alternative reading would be to take this provision to mean that a public benefit

75 *Joseph Rowntree Memorial Trust Housing Association Ltd v Attorney-General* [1983] 1 All ER 288.
76 (1966) 110 SJ 549.
77 [1969] 1 WLR 1595; cf *Re Martin* (1977) 121 SJ 828.
78 *Helena Housing Ltd v Revenue and Customs Commissioners* [2011] STC 1307, TCC.

test must apply to poverty trusts as well, and that that public benefit test should be the same as the public benefit test applied on the authorities in charities law generally. As considered below in relation to the 'poor relations cases', such as *Re Scarisbrick*,[79] there are some cases in which the link between the settlor and her own relatives does make the finding of a charitable purpose somewhat eccentric. Those cases can only be explained as demonstrating a genuine charitable intention to relieve the poverty of people for whom one is not morally bound to provide. Otherwise, I must confess to a personal preference for the *Dingle v Tuner* formulation of the test for charitable status over the formulaic 'public benefit' test because it does ensure that genuine charitable intentions are not frustrated simply because the settlor is considered to be relieving too little poverty to constitute a benefit to the public at large.

Charging for services

It is not an objection to its charitable status that a charity charges generally for the services which it provides[80] nor that it receives rent for accommodation provided.[81] Similarly, charities can trade in general terms without necessarily threatening their charitable status under trusts law principles.[82]

This permission granted to charities to trade and to charge those who benefit from its services is in spite of the general statement by Rowlatt J that charity is to be provided by way of 'bounty and not bargain'.[83] However, that ideal was limited to its own facts in that case by Peter Gibson J in *Joseph Rowntree* where it concerned the obligation on a mutual society (that is, a society providing benefits for its own members on the basis of contract) which sought to acquire charitable status in circumstances in which it charged those same members for its services. It has even been held that the making of loans to poor people may be charitable purposes.[84]

Links to the settlor – trusts for the benefit of poor relatives

Following on from the issue of the breadth of public benefit necessary to create a valid trust for the relief of poverty, is the question of the closeness of the links between settlor and the people who are to be benefited. For charitable purposes other than the relief of poverty, it is important that the class of purposes to be benefited must not be defined by reference to their proximity to the settlor. In terms of trusts for charitable purposes, it stands to reason that a settlor could not create a settlement 'for the benefit of my two poor children' and then claim that it is a charitable trust for the relief of poverty. Such a trust would clearly be an express private trust in relation to which the children were intended to be beneficiaries. It would stretch the credulity of the court to suppose that a parent could permit her children to live in poverty

---

79 [1951] Ch 622.
80 *Re Cottam* [1955] 1 WLR 1299; *Re Resch's WT* [1967] 1 All ER 915; *Abbey Malvern Wells v Ministry of Local Government and Planning* [1951] Ch 728.
81 *Re Estlin* (1903) 72 LJ Ch 687; *Joseph Rowntree Memorial Trust Housing Association Ltd v Attorney-General* [1983] 1 All ER 288.
82 *Incorporated Council for Law Reporting v Attorney-General* [1972] Ch 73.
83 *IRC v Society for the Relief of Widows and Orphans of Medical Men* (1926) 11 TC 1.
84 *Re Monk* [1927] 2 Ch 197. The reader is referred to the essay on www.alastairhudson.com/trustslaw on *Co-operatives, Friendly Societies and Trusts* for a discussion of mutual societies.

and then to be entitled to charitable tax breaks in supporting them. However, it has been held that to define a charitable purpose for the relief of poverty of the settlor's poor relations would not affect its validity as a charitable bequest.[85] So in *Re Scarisbrick*[86] a testatrix provided that property be held on trust 'for such relations of my said son and daughters as in the opinion of the survivor of my said son and daughters shall be in needy circumstances'. It was held by the Court of Appeal that this was a valid charitable trust for the relief of the poverty of such persons.[87] It is from this line of decisions that trusts for the benefit of poor relations have been upheld as being valid charitable trusts. This line of cases would be overruled if the public benefit test in s 2(1)(b) of the 2011 Act were interpreted as applying to trusts for the relief of poverty because there is clearly a nexus between the settlor and the people who are intended to benefit from the trust. But for the poverty of the relations involved, such trusts would clearly be private express trusts. Notably, there can be no presumption that a purpose is for the public benefit, as expressed by s 4(2), which overrides s 4(3) (as set out in s 4(4)).

25.5 TRUSTS FOR THE ADVANCEMENT OF EDUCATION

Trusts for the advancement of education require that there is some institution of education benefited or that the purpose of the trust is to generate research which will be published for the public benefit. Trusts for the pursuit of sport fall within the educational head of charity, provided that they are annexed to some institution of education. In many cases, educational charitable trusts have been used as sham devices for the provision of tax and other benefits to a private class of individuals. Consequently, the courts have developed a requirement that there be a sufficient public benefit which requires that there be no 'personal nexus' between the people who stand to benefit and the settlor of the trust.

25.5.1 Introduction

The discussion in this section considering the nature of charitable educational trusts falls into two halves. The first half will consider the decision in *IRC v McMullen*[88] (a decision of the House of Lords which offers the most accessible entry point to the concept of education) and other cases which define what is meant by the term 'education' in this context. The second half will consider the tax avoidance cases in which corporations sought to benefit their employees by using sham charities. These cases demonstrate the extent to which it is necessary to demonstrate some public benefit to be classified as a truly charitable trust.

25.5.2 What is 'education'

Education in general terms

The first issue is to decide what exactly is meant by the term 'education' in the context of the law of charities. Clearly trusts purposes involving schools and universities fell within the

---

85 *Re Scarisbrick* [1951] Ch 622.
86 *Ibid.*
87 Following *Attorney-General v Price* (1810) 17 Ves 371; *Gibson v South American Stores* [1950] Ch 177; *Re Cohen* [1973] 1 WLR 415; see also *Re Segelman* [1995] 3 All ER 676.
88 [1981] AC 1.

cases analogous to the preamble of the 1601 statute; however, the case law has developed a more sophisticated understanding of what constitutes an educational purpose, as considered below. The contexts in which there is greater confusion surround trusts set up for the study of more esoteric subjects, or even simply to advance an ideological position, which are not annexed to any accepted educational institution.

What is clear is that 'education' in the charitable sense is not limited to teaching activities in schools and universities. Rather, education can involve activities not in the classroom such as sport[89] or the establishment of a choir[90] or the payment of staff in educational establishments.[91] It will also involve the establishment of companies to provide education, subject to the proviso that they must not seek to make a profit (of the sort which would be distributed among shareholders like a trading company).[92]

Research, as considered below, will also be a valid educational purpose in many circumstances[93] as will the educational advancement of the works of a renowned classical composer.[94] Gifts to established museums will also be charitable as being educational purposes.[95] In *Re Holburne*[96] an art museum was founded and held to be of public utility for the purposes of education. By contradistinction keeping a collection of eclectic *objets d'art* (some described in evidence as being 'atrociously bad') intact for the benefit of the National Trust will not be charitable if it is impossible for the court to establish any merit in the objects nor any public utility in the gift.[97]

Provided that there is a genuine charitable intention evident in the words, the courts will be prepared to validate such a trust wherever possible.[98] The main caveats are that there must be sufficient public utility and sufficient public benefit (which terms might be synonymous, depending on the context) in the purpose.

The reason why the allocation of charitable status to these purposes is important is that it frees them from liability to pay tax on their ordinary activities. A number of the key areas of controversy are considered in the sections which follow.

Research, teaching and ideology

One leading case in this context is that of *Re Hopkins*[99] under which a bequest had been made to the Francis Bacon Society. The aim of the society was to prove that Bacon was in fact the author of the works generally attributed to William Shakespeare. The court held that this purpose was educational because it was 'of the highest value to history and to literature'. The

---

89 *IRC v McMullen* [1981] AC 1; *London Hospital Medical College v IRC* [1976] 1 WLR 613 (sport in universities).
90 *Royal Choral Society v IRC* [1943] 2 All ER 101.
91 *Case of Christ's College, Cambridge* (1757) 1 Wm Bl 90.
92 *Abbey Malvern Wells Ltd v Ministry of Local Government and Planning* [1951] Ch 728; *Re Girl's Public Day School Trust* [1951] Ch 400.
93 *McGovern v Attorney-General* [1982] Ch 321.
94 *Re Delius* [1957] Ch 299.
95 *British Museum Trustees v White* (1826) 2 Sm & St 594.
96 (1885) 53 LT 212; (1885) 1 TLR 517.
97 *Re Pinion* [1965] Ch 85; following *Re Hummeltenberg* [1923] 1 Ch 237. Cf *Funnell v Stewart* [1996] 1 WLR 288.
98 *Re Koeppler's WT* [1986] Ch 423.
99 [1965] Ch 699; Shapiro, 2010 which presents the case that Shakespeare wrote his own work, albeit occasionally in collaboration with others, very cogently.

contention had been made in favour of the purpose being found to be charitable that the Society would tend to publish its work. Consequently, the court held that the fact that the research would be made public would lean towards finding of charitable status, thus illustrating the requirement that there be some *public* benefit resulting from the gift.

A case reaching a different conclusion was that of *Re Shaw*.[100] The trust at issue in that case concerned a bequest made by the great socialist playwright and man of letters George Bernard Shaw. Shaw had left money to be applied towards research to create a new alphabet. Ultimately, it was hoped that this research would have led to the creation of a new common language, in line with Shaw's humanist philosophy, so that his works could be comprehensible to all nations no matter what their mother tongue and so that peace might be founded through this common language. It was held by Harman J (never the most liberal of judges) that this purpose was not a charitable purpose because it involved propaganda.

The two cases of *Shaw* and *Hopkins* deserve a little comparison. In *Hopkins* it was held that there could be a valid, charitable purpose based on an ideological commitment to the idea that the son of a Midlands glove-maker could not have written *Hamlet, King Lear*, or the rest of the staples of the English literary canon. Instead, the Francis Bacon Society seem to take the view that it must have been the university-educated Bacon who produced such works of genius. On the other hand, a determination that war and conflict could be reduced if different nations spoke a common language (made possible by the development of a new alphabet) was held not to be a charitable purpose. The latter purpose clearly has, at its root, a commitment to the public benefit. (What could be more beneficial to the public than the prevention of war?) Therefore, it is not that element which explains the difference between the decisions. Rather, it is a murkier thread in the case law that there are certain activities which judges are prepared to accept are beneficial to the public in the manner which the judiciary chooses to interpret that term.

The decision in *Hopkins*, delivered by Wilberforce J, considered *Shaw* and sought to expand the definition of 'education' used by Harman J to extend beyond a necessity that there be teaching. Rather, it would be sufficient that research be carried out either for the benefit of the researcher or with the intention that it be published. Provided that there was some element of publication, and thereby public benefit, that would qualify as a charitable purpose.

Slade J set out the principles on which a court would typically find that research work would be held charitable in *McGovern v Attorney-General*:[101]

> (1) A trust for research will ordinarily qualify as a charitable trust if, but only if, (a) the subject matter of the proposed research is a useful subject of study; and (b) it is contemplated that knowledge acquired as a result of the research will be disseminated to others; and (c) the trust is for the benefit of the public, or a sufficiently important section of the public. (2) In the absence of a contrary context, however, the court will be readily inclined to construe a trust for research as importing subsequent dissemination of the results thereof. (3) Furthermore, if a trust for research is to constitute a valid trust for the advancement of education, it is not necessary either (a) that a teacher/pupil relationship should be in contemplation, or (b) that the persons to benefit from the knowledge to be

---

100 [1958] 1 All ER 245, confirming [1957] 1 WLR 729. See also *Re Shaw's WT* [1952] Ch 163.
101 [1982] Ch 321: see also that judge in *Re Besterman's Will Trusts* (1980) *The Times*, 21 January.

acquired should be persons who are already in the course of receiving 'education' in the conventional sense.

Therefore, the term 'education' will encompass research carried out outside schools or universities, provided that there is an intention to publish that research or to make its benefits available to the public. Beyond academic research, the courts have also been prepared to find that the practice of high quality craftsmanship will also be of educational value to the public in charitable terms.[102]

Sport and education

In the leading case of *IRC v McMullen*,[103] the House of Lords considered the charitable status of a trust created to promote the playing of Association Football and the playing and coaching of other sports, provided that it is done within schools or other educational establishments. The contention was made that the playing of sport ought properly to be considered a part of education, in the same way that sitting in a classroom is generally supposed to be educational. The leading speech was delivered by Lord Hailsham, who held that this purpose was indeed educational because sport was essential to the development of young persons.

However, sporting purposes will not, in themselves, be charitable. A trust to provide a cup for a yachting competition was not held to be charitable[104] and the same was held in relation to a cricket competition.[105] It does appear that the link to formal education is a necessary one, in the terms that Lord Hailsham described in *McMullen*, as was decided in *Re Mariette*[106] a case in which a trust for the conduct of sport in a school was found to have been charitable. Trusts in relation to the conduct of sports and cultural activities at university have also been held to be charitable purposes.[107] (In this writer's opinion, all this supposes that drinking while wearing a rugby shirt counts as either a sport or culture.)

Where to draw the line at the extent of charitable purposes in this area is a difficult issue. In *Re Dupree's Deed Trusts*[108] Vaisey J was uneasy about the limits on this charitable educational purpose. When validating a trust to provide funds for an annual chess tournament for young men under the age of 21, his Lordship sensed that:

> one is on rather a slippery slope. If chess, why not draughts? If draughts, why not bezique, and so on, through to bridge and whist, and by another route, to stamp collecting and the acquisition of birds' eggs? Those pursuits will have to be dealt with if and when they come up for consideration.

Therefore, there will come practical limits on the types of pursuits which will be genuinely charitable – although the cases will not give us hard-and-fast principles on which to make such decision in advance.

---

102 *Commissioners of Inland Revenue v White* (1980) 55 TC 651.
103 [1981] AC 1.
104 *Re Nottage* (1985) 2 Ch D 649.
105 *Re Patten* [1929] 2 Ch 276.
106 [1915] 2 Ch 284.
107 *London Hospital Medical College v IRC* [1976] 2 All ER 113; *Attorney-General v Ross* [1985] 3 All ER 334.
108 [1945] Ch 16, 20.

Business and charity

Many charities carry on trading activities to support their underlying charitable purposes. As considered above, it is not an objection to its charitable status that a charity charges generally for the services which it provides[109] nor that it receives rent for accommodation provided.[110] By the same token, charities can trade without the carrying on of the trade itself calling their charitable status into question under trusts law principles.[111]

Therefore, the fact that a purpose involves trading with the public will not preclude the organisation involved from being a charity. In this way in *Incorporated Council for Law Reporting v Attorney-General*,[112] the ICLR had been permitted registration as a charity. It was held that, because the law reports are essential for the study of law, they must be considered to be educational and also valid as a purpose beneficial to the community under the fourth head of charity. Therefore, the publication of law reports and all other attendant activities fall within the head of education in relation to their research function and their contribution to education ordinarily so-called in universities.[113]

An important note for students of law

As a service to law teachers around the world I will also tarry briefly over the following words of Buckley LJ in *ICLR v Attorney-General* as to the importance of reading cases:

> In a legal system such as ours, in which judges' decisions are governed by precedents, reported decisions are the means by which legal principles (other than those laid down by statutes) are developed, established and made known, and by which the application of those legal principles to particular kinds of facts are illustrated and explained. Reported decisions may be said to be the tissue of the body of our non-statutory law . . . *In a system of law such as we have in this country this scholarship can only be acquired and maintained by a continual study of case law.* [Emphasis added]

It is perhaps ironic that in a textbook such as this I belabour the importance of reading cases. What this book aims to do is to give you, dear reader, a flavour of the many impulses behind those decisions and their practical effects on the world in which we live. But there is no substitute for going out and reading that material for yourself and for living that life for yourself. In the words of Dickens in *David Copperfield*, this book seeks only to be 'guide, philosopher and friend' – it cannot be a replacement for your own reading, thought and effort.

---

109   *Re Cottam* [1955] 1 WLR 1299; *Re Resch's WT* [1967] 1 All ER 915; *Abbey Malvern Wells v Ministry of Local Government and Planning* [1951] Ch 728.
110   *Re Estlin* (1903) 72 LJ Ch 687; *Joseph Rowntree Memorial Trust Housing Association Ltd v Attorney-General* [1983] 1 All ER 288.
111   *Incorporated Council for Law Reporting v Attorney-General* [1972] Ch 73.
112   [1972] Ch 73.
113   See also on similar points *Beaumont v Oliviera* (1864) 4 Ch App 309; *Re Lopes* [1931] 2 Ch 130; *Royal College of Surgeons v National Provincial Bank* [1952] AC 631; *Re British School of Egyptian Archaeology* [1954] 1 All ER 887; provided that the objects are exclusively charitable: *Royal College of Nursing v St Marylebone Corporation* [1959] 3 All ER 663.

25.5.3 The 'public benefit' requirement

In this chapter we have already considered trusts for the relief of poverty. In that context it was found unnecessary to demonstrate a public benefit to qualify as a charity. The rationale given in the old case law was that giving property for the relief of poverty will typically constitute a charitable purpose in and of itself. That discussion was contrasted with tax avoidance cases in which corporations have sought to gain tax advantages for themselves and their employees by creating trusts which had the form of charitable purposes but which were in substance private trusts for the benefit of employees and their families. In consequence, it has become important in the context of educational trusts to look beyond the apparent purpose of the trust to require some evidence that the trust is intended to be run as a *de facto* charity. Therefore, the requirement of sufficient public benefit has emerged. All charities must be for the public benefit.[114] The requirement for a public benefit was always a part of charities law relating to the advancement of education. It is provided in s 4(3) of the Charities Act 2011 that any purposes which are 'recognised as charitable purposes under existing charity law', for example under the old case law, will continue to be recognised as charitable purposes. Consequently it is supposed that the old case law will continue in effect for the application of the public benefit test to purposes for the advancement of education.

The problem

Suppose the following facts. MegaCorp plc, employers of 200,000 people in the UK, decide to set up a trust which has only one purpose – 'to provide educational opportunities for young people in the UK', giving the trustees unfettered discretion to receive applications for grants and to apply the money as they see fit. On its face, that purpose looks straightforwardly charitable. However, suppose that all of the money is distributed only to defray the school fees of children of the board of directors. In that situation, the trust would be one run simply as a private trust. Therefore, it would fall to be taxed as an ordinary trust would. Alternatively, if the money was paid out over a ten-year period to children who had no family connection with the company, the trust would be a charitable trust. It depends on whether or not the trust is run for the public benefit.

   The difficulty would come if money was given out for the benefit of children of the 200,000 ordinary employees (otherwise than on the basis of their poverty). One argument might be that such children formed a sufficiently large section of the public to enable the trust to be considered to be a charitable one.[115] Alternatively, it could be said that the trust remains a private trust *de facto* because money is only applied to those with a nexus to the settlor.[116] The trustees may, for form's sake, pay 10% of the available money to children entirely outside any nexus to the company. In such a situation, the argument would still appear to be that the trust is predominantly a private trust.[117] The question would then be: what if the trustees paid 50% to those outwith any nexus with the company, and 50% to those who were the children of employees? These issues are considered in the sections to follow.

---

114   Charities Act 2006, s 2(1)(b).
115   Cf *Dingle v Turner* [1972] AC 601.
116   *Oppenheim v Tobacco Securities Trust Co Ltd* [1951] AC 297.
117   *IRC v EGA* [1967] Ch 123 below; *Re Koettgen* [1954] Ch 252 below.

The 'personal nexus' test

The leading case is that of *Oppenheim v Tobacco Securities Trust*[118] in which the House of Lords considered a trust which held money from which the income was to be applied for the education of the children of employees of British-American Tobacco Co Ltd. That company was a very large multi-national company employing a large number of people. The trust would have been void as a private trust on the basis that it lacked a perpetuities provision. It was argued, however, that the purpose was charitable and therefore that no perpetuities provision was necessary. Lord Simonds followed *Re Compton*[119] in holding that there was a requirement of public benefit to qualify as an educational charity.

The phrase that was used by the court to encapsulate the test was whether or not those who stood to benefit from the trust constituted a sufficient 'section of the community'. Lord Simonds held that:

> A group of persons may be numerous, but, if the nexus between them is their personal relationship to a single *propositus* or to several *propositi*, they are neither the community not a section of the community for charitable purposes.

Therefore, it was held that the trust at issue could not be a charitable trust because of the nexus between those who stood to benefit from the trust and the *propositus* (the company) which was settlor of that trust.

The in-between cases

The heading for this section (the 'in-between cases') is not intended to suggest that there are cases which seek to apply different tests. Rather, there are cases which indicate that the court, and HM Revenue and Customs, will take flexible approaches to charitable trusts in some cases. For example, the court in *IRC v Educational Grants Association*[120] supported the core principle that where a trust is for the benefit of private persons it cannot be a charitable trust. In that case, however, there was a trust created with the apparently charitable purpose of holding property on trust 'for the education of the children of the UK'. In fact the trust was actually operated predominantly by the trustees to provide funds for the education of children of employees of the company Metal Box. This application for the employees of the company and their children accounted for 80% of the trust fund. The remaining 20% was applied for ostensibly charitable purposes. It was held that there could be no permissible exemption from tax on the grounds of charitable status on these facts because the trust was being run as a *de facto* private trust.

The older case of *Re Koettgen*,[121] a decision of Upjohn J, upheld a trust as charitable where the assets were applied 75% as a private trust and only 25% for the public benefit. This decision was rationalised in *IRC v EGA* as being properly considered as a trust for a public class, with a direction to the trustees to give preference to a private class who fell within the

118 [1951] AC 297.
119 [1945] Ch 123.
120 [1967] Ch 123.
121 [1954] Ch 252.

definition of that public class. Thus in *Koettgen* the trustees were required by the terms of the trust to give money to the public, but also directed to prefer that part of the public which also had a nexus with the settlor. Clearly, therefore, this was a *de facto* private trust which was masquerading as an entirely charitable trust for the public benefit. Consequently, in practice here, charitable tax relief was allowed only to the extent that the trustees could demonstrate that the property had in fact been applied for the public benefit; that is only for 25% of the fund.

The status of independent schools as charities

One perennial problem in the law of charities has, for decades, been the status of independent, fee-paying schools (of which the best-known examples are referred to, for historical reasons,[122] as 'public schools') as charities. Such schools charge high fees for pupils to attend, they are consequently apparently available only to a narrow range of people who can afford those fees, and yet they are treated as charities (with all the attendant tax benefits attached to that status) in spite of the absence of any meaningful public benefit in their activities. The tax benefits which these schools receive mean that the fees which they charge are lower than they otherwise would be, and are vital to the solvency of many of them.[123] As a result of the Charities Act 2006 these schools have put on a show of specious activities intended to demonstrate a public benefit, such as providing bursaries to some students (whether competitive scholarships, which would not in themselves suggest a charitable purpose because they are not based on relieving any need, or scholarships based solely on need, which would suggest a charitable purpose because they are based on relieving poverty or similar need), or allowing pupils from state schools to attend some classes or to use some facilities at the independent school.

In *Independent Schools Council v Charity Commission*[124] the Upper Tribunal considered whether or not such independent schools were charities concerned with the advancement of education in the public benefit. It was held that a public benefit was required to be something which was both of benefit to the community and directed at a sufficiently large section of the community.[125] That a purpose was educational did not necessarily mean that it was of benefit to the community nor that it was directed at a sufficiently large section of it. So, in deciding whether or not a sufficient section of the community was benefiting, the Commission would

---

122 Before there was a school system in the UK, when the children of the nobility had private tutors, there were schools created nominally for 'the public' which over time became fee-paying private schools, although the counter-intuitive name 'public school' stuck with them.

123 Their critics suggest that if their charitable status was abolished and their fees increased as a result then that would mean the children of middle-class families moving into the state school system with a concomitant benefit to that state system of intelligent children and highly motivated parents. It would also have the political effect of creating greater equality in education and provide a rise in standards and resources for the state school system. Moreover, the taxes of people who cannot afford private school fees would no longer be used to subsidise the tax breaks enjoyed by public schools and the concomitant lowering of their fees for rich parents.

124 [2012] 2 WLR 100, [2012] 1 All ER 127, [2011] UKTT 421 (TCC).

125 *Jones v Williams* (1767) Amb 651, *Income Tax Special Purposes Comrs v Pemsel* [1891–4] All ER Rep 28, *Re Hummeltenberg, Beatty v London Spiritualistic Alliance Ltd* [1923] All ER Rep 49, *Gilmour v Coats* [1949] 1 All ER 848, *Williams' Trustees v IRC* [1947] 1 All ER 513 and *Oppenheim v Tobacco Securities Trust Co Ltd* [1951] All ER 31.

have to consider the number of people who would be able to pay the fees charged by that school and then consider whether or not that suggested a charitable purpose. The core issue for the Upper Tribunal which heard this case was whether or not independent schools provided a benefit which was directed at a sufficiently wide section of the community so as to constitute a 'public benefit'. It was considered that schools which charged fees for pupils to attend them could not be charities because they excluded poor people and their children from their educational services.[126] By contrast, a school which admitted students no matter what their ability to pay the fees (whether by making bursaries available to the families of pupils who required them or otherwise) could be a charity because it was available to the community in general.

Interestingly, the tribunal considered that any school established as a charity before the Charities Act 2006 would be taken to have been established for the public benefit. This point cannot be correct. It is possible that the assessment of its provision of a public benefit was incorrect, or that its operation of its activities after its registration as a charity did not comply with its public benefit obligations, or that the understanding of the meaning of 'public benefit' in the case law would develop so that the school no longer fell within that categorisation, or that the requirement of public benefit was considered to apply to independent schools literally for the first time with the establishment of a new regulator of charities, or that a charity could have its charitable status withdrawn.

Concluding themes

Returning to the themes identified at the beginning of this chapter, it is clear that the approach taken by the authorities in the educational trusts cases is one of requiring the person contending that the trust is charitable to prove that the trust will operate for the benefit of the public. Therefore, the onus is, in reality, to disprove the existence of a personal nexus (such as ties of blood, or an employment contract) between the settlor and those who stand to benefit from the trust. This approach contrasts with that of the House of Lords in *Dingle v Turner*[127] where the court focused on seeking out a truly charitable intention, rather than proving or disproving any relationship between the parties. It is suggested that the context of tax avoidance is the distorting factor here. Generally, in genuinely seeking to relieve poverty, there is not such a problem of motive; by contrast the provision of free education would have been capable of being provided as a tax-free perk if the courts had not acted as they did.

The principle to be taken away from *Oppenheim v Tobacco Securities*[128] is that a trust will not be accorded charitable status where the purpose fails the 'personal nexus' test. The purpose of the trust must be to benefit a 'section of the community'. Therefore, where there is a personal nexus between those who stand to benefit from the trust (for example, where they are employed by the same company) and the settlor, those 'beneficiaries' cannot constitute a requisite 'section of the community'. By way of contrast with *Dingle v Turner*, where the court did not follow the personal nexus test, one should look to the substance of the trust

126 *Jones v Williams* (1767) Amb 651, *Re Macduff, Macduff v Macduff* [1895–9] All ER Rep 154 applied; *Taylor v Taylor* (1910) 10 CLR 218 and *Le Cras v Perpetual Trustee Co Ltd, Far West Children's Health Scheme v Perpetual Trustee Co Ltd* [1967] 3 All ER 915 adopted.
127 [1972] AC 601.
128 [1951] AC 297.

and evaluate its effects (although this comment is possibly *obiter*). In *Oppenheim*, however, a majority of the House of Lords said that fiscal matters should not be taken into account as a determining factor in deciding whether or not a purpose is charitable.

The question then is as to the applicability of the *Oppenheim* decision across the law of charities. Lord Cross held in *Dingle* that no distinction ought to be drawn between different types of trusts for the relief of poverty. Deciding on whether or not a group forms a section of the public is a matter of degree in which 'much must depend upon the purpose of the trust'. Whereas the issues in *Oppenheim* were decided very much on the basis that the trust would attract an undeserved fiscal advantage if it were found to be charitable.

25.6 TRUSTS FOR RELIGIOUS PURPOSES

Trusts for the advancement of religion are required to have a sufficient public benefit, such that the works done and the prayers said by a cloistered order of nuns (for example), though religious, would not be charitable in legal terms. Religion in the case law is concerned with 'man's relations with God' and, therefore, excludes many modern New Age religions and cults. The Charities Act 2011 has changed this position. The definition of 'religion' for the purposes of allocating charitable status requires a public benefit and will not necessarily include all purposes which might be considered by a layperson to be 'religious'.

25.6.1 Introduction

This section considers the third of Lord Macnaghten's heads of charity: religion. The concept of religion has a very particular form in the cases – if not in the Charities Act 2011. In the case law, religion is considered to be concerned with the worship of a deity. Indeed, in these times of growing New Age cults, crystals and baubles, the attitude taken to charitable religious purposes in the cases has been limited to the presence of a public benefit from a deistic form of religion,[129] and has not embraced any of the so-called New Age belief systems. However, the effect of the Charities Act 2011 has been to expand the concept of religion beyond the case law focus on systems of belief which believe in a god and into any 'religion which does not involve belief in a god'.[130] This significant change is considered below in section 25.6.2. It is also a requirement, as underlined by the 2011 Act, that there must be a public benefit from the religious purpose. Indeed, the requirement of public benefit has even caused bequests in favour of orders of contemplative nuns in *Gilmour v Coats*[131] to be held not charitable on the basis that contemplative religious communities cannot benefit the public because they are cloistered away from the public. Therefore, a lifetime's religious devotion will not necessarily be enough to convince an English court that a purported charitable trust created to further your observance ought properly to be considered a valid religious, charitable purpose, unless that purpose also confers a palpable public benefit.[132]

---

129 *Re South Place Ethical Society* [1980] 3 All ER 918, below.
130 Charities Act 2006, s 2(3)(a)(ii).
131 [1949] AC 426.
132 *Gilmour v Coats* [1949] AC 426; *Leahy v Attorney-General for NSW* [1959] AC 457.

The reason for the presence of this head of charity results from the historical administration of alms to the poor and of education in local parishes by the church – in consequence, the English conception of charity has long been bound up with religious devotion.

25.6.2 What is a 'religion' in charities law?

The structure of this discussion

It is important to understand that the case law on the meaning of 'religion' was limited to belief in god, whereas the Charities Act 2006 explicitly seeks to extend that definition into religions which do not involve a belief in a god. It is unclear at the time of writing where the new legislation will take this area of the law. Therefore, this section will, first, consider the old case law in detail before, secondly, considering how the new legislation may impact on that case law. First, then, a consideration of the case law definition of 'religion'.

The old case law definition of 'religion'

In *Re South Place Ethical Society*,[133] Dillon J gave a taste of the meaning of the concept of a 'religious purpose' in the law of charity: 'religion, as I see it, is concerned with man's relations with God.' Therefore, on the facts of *South Place*, the study and dissemination of ethical principles was held not to constitute religion. In the words of Dillon J, 'ethics are concerned with man's relations with man'. He continued: 'It seems to me that two of the essential attributes of religion are faith and worship: faith in a god and worship of that god.' The focus is therefore on a system of belief in a god or the promotion of spiritual teaching connected to such religious activity.[134] The leading case of *Gilmour v Coats*[135] in the House of Lords took the view that mere religious observance was insufficient to constitute a charitable purpose unless there was some demonstrable public benefit. So, simply arguing that the prayers of a cloistered order of nuns would be for the benefit of mankind was not considered to be a valid charitable purpose for the advancement of religion. Other forms of spiritual observance are not included in this category by the case law. Therefore, beliefs in crystals or in the majesty of Sunderland Football Club would not constitute religion (no matter how fervent the devotion to the cause).

Similarly, the activities of the Scientologists have not been held to constitute religious purposes.[136] The approach of the courts to Scientology has been vitriolic. In *Hubbard v Vosper*[137] Lord Denning described Scientology as 'dangerous material'. Whereas Goff J described it as 'pernicious nonsense' in *Church of Scientology v Kaufman*.[138] The beliefs of the Unification Church (popularly known as the 'Moonies') have been accepted as disclosing

---

133 [1980] 3 All ER 918.

134 *Keren Kayemeth Le Jisroel Ltd v IRC* [1931] 2 KB 465.

135 [1949] AC 426.

136 In essence, the Scientologists believe in the writings of L Ron Hubbard, a science fiction novelist, to the effect that human beings were placed on Earth by aliens millions of years ago and that, through a process of auditing themselves, they make themselves ready for the return of said aliens.

137 [1972] 2 QB 84, 96.

138 [1973] RPC 635, 658.

a valid charitable religious purpose in spite of their popular presentation in tabloid newspapers as a dangerous cult. The distinction is that the former does not involve an element of worship of a god or gods whereas the latter does. Freemasonry is not a religion for similar reasons.[139] The effect of the 2011 Act, however, will be that henceforth the presence of a 'god' will not necessarily be the definitive question.

The effect of the Charities Act 2011 on the meaning of 'religion' in charities law

The effect of s 3(2)(a) of the Charities Act 2011 will be significant in relation to trusts for the advancement of religion. Under s 3(2)(a)(i), the charities law practice of accepting major world religions, such as Hinduism, which include belief in more than one god, has been given statutory effect. That paragraph provides that a religion for the purposes of charities law will include 'a religion which does not involve belief in a god'. Thus it is clear that religions such as Hinduism will constitute religions (although that particular example was always accepted by the old Charity Commissioners as constituting a religion for charities law purposes in any event).[140]

A more complex idea is contained in s 3(2)(a)(ii) of the Charities Act 2011. That paragraph further provides that the term 'religion' includes 'a religion which does not involve belief in a god'.[141] This latter extension to the concept of religion will be more problematic. Previously, charities law had separated religions off from other forms of belief by reference to the existence of a belief in a god or gods. It is suggested that the principal purpose behind this provision was to confirm that Buddhism would be a religion for charitable purposes without needing to show belief in a god or gods. However, more generally, now that there is no need for the presence of a god, how will a religion be distinguished from, for example, a merely ethical system of belief, or a belief in the existence of hobbits, or a belief in Spider Man as the ultimate power for good in the universe? In the last census in the UK, thousands of people identified their religion as being 'Jedi Knight', as in the Star Wars films. So, we need to consider what might constitute a 'religion' for these purposes. The Shorter Oxford English Dictionary defines 'religion', from the Middle English period onwards, as involving a:

> belief in or sensing of some superhuman controlling power or powers, entitled to obedience, reverence, and worship, or in a system defining a code of living, esp. as a means to achieve spiritual or material improvement.

There are, it is suggested, two very different senses of 'religion' bound up in this definition. First, the requirement for some 'superhuman being' and, secondly, 'a code of living'. I shall deal with each in turn. The requirement that there be a 'superhuman being' clearly accords with the need for a god at one level. The Canadian authorities have identified a 'belief in the supernatural' as being one of the main indicia of a charitable purpose for the advancement of religion.[142] This was the approach in the old case law. Literally, of course,

---

139   *United Grand Lodge of Ancient Free and Accepted Masons of England v Holborn Borough Council* [1957] 3 All ER 281.
140   Charities Act 2006, s 3(2)(a)(i).
141   *Ibid*, s 3(2)(a)(ii).
142   *Church of the New Faith v Commissioner of Pay-roll Tax* [1982–1983] 154 CLR 120, 174, *per* Wilson and Deane JJ.

the reference to a 'superhuman being' could also include a belief in the powers of the comic book superhero Spider Man, but that would not necessarily include the notion of Spider Man having an entitlement to reverence or worship. It is not a requirement that one be able to prove the existence of one's god, but it would seem reasonable that one would genuinely have to believe that one's 'superhuman being' did have the powers which one revered.

The second sense of religion in this definition is interesting and potentially much broader. Of course being an exhaustively trained samurai warrior or an elite soldier on special operations or a dedicated swimmer who trains every morning at 5am is involved in a 'code of living . . . as a means to achieve . . . material improvement', but none of these activities necessarily involves any sort of belief in a higher power or a controlling energy in the universe. However, membership of an organisation which the tabloid newspapers might refer to as a 'cult' would involve a code of living seeking spiritual improvement if, for example, the adherents live in a commune, devote themselves to good works and contemplation, and seek spiritual enlightenment without believing there is a god in the universe. It is suggested that such a code of living would be easier to demonstrate in relation to groups of individuals, either living communally in the context of their shared beliefs or coming together in some form of religious activity, than it would be for individuals who adhered to entirely individual beliefs on their own. This would be so because charities law requires a public benefit which would be easier to achieve for groups of people reaching larger sections of the community, whereas a lone individual would find it more difficult to demonstrate a credible belief system. So, if I were to erect a religion on my personal belief in the holy nature of the 'stuff I keep under my bed', then it would be unlikely that charities law would accept that as being a religion and it would be difficult to prove that I genuinely believed in it as a religion. Of course, if I were able to gather many other adherents, then my claim to a religion relating to the 'stuff under my bed' would take on a new credence. However, taken literally, the presence of a 'belief system' of some sort ought to constitute a religion if it defines the manner in which the adherent or adherents live.

On this basis, the activities of groups like the Scientologists may now become valid charitable purposes because they live communally and pursue a system of belief. The Scientologists' system of belief (to the extent that I understand it) relates both to a belief that the aliens whom they believe put us here millions of years ago will return at some point in the future, and to a belief in personal development through a number of 'courses' of 'auditing' which resemble one-on-one counselling sessions. There is no god in which adherents believe – the aliens apparently constituting neither gods nor immortal beings. Nevertheless, it would be difficult for charities law to accept Scientology as being a charitable purpose given the opprobrium which has been heaped on it in previous, decided cases, as mentioned earlier in the preceding section. Scientology has been described judicially as 'pernicious nonsense': it would be interesting to see how the judges would explain such 'pernicious nonsense' as being a religion which is entitled to the state's support in the form of relief from taxation and so forth. The reason why the Charity Commissioners, before 2006, refused to accept the Scientologists as being a charitable purpose was that their activities were conducted in private and therefore did not constitute a public benefit. More 'New Age' religions which have a belief in spiritualism as opposed to a god might therefore constitute religious charitable purposes, if they involve a belief system and a code of living. However, the ethical, humanist society in *Re South Place Ethical Society* is unlikely still to be a religion because humanism generally constitutes a form of atheism, and is therefore almost the opposite of a religious purpose which may be considered to lack the presence of a code of belief or a code of living because it does not involve any single system of belief, but rather an 'unbelief'.

25.6.3 The requirement of public benefit

Drawing distinctions

All charities must be for the public benefit.[143] The requirement for a public benefit was always a part of charities law relating to the advancement of religion. It is provided in s 3(1) (m)(i) of the Charities Act 2011 that any purposes which are recognised as charitable purposes under the old case law will continue to be recognised as charitable purposes. Consequently it is supposed that the old case law will continue in effect for the application of the public benefit test to such purposes. In *Thornton v Howe*[144] the question at issue was the validity as a charitable purpose of a trust created to secure the publication of the writings of one Joanna Southcott, who had claimed to have been impregnated by the Holy Ghost and to have been pregnant with the new Messiah. It was held that the publication of such works would be for the public benefit. By definition, the root of the word 'publication' is 'public' – thus the former implied a benefit to the latter necessarily.

In contrast to publication of such spiritual works, the trust at issue in *Gilmour v Coats*[145] was a trust created for the benefit of an order of contemplative Carmelite nuns. The trust was held not to have been charitable on the basis that the order contemplated in private, thus failing to communicate any benefit to the public. The court dismissed an argument that the nuns' contemplation would have helped society in a spiritual sense, on the basis that it would not have been enough to constitute charitable help to society. Lord Simonds required tangible proof that the works of the trust would convey a benefit to the public, as opposed simply to the adherents' belief that the power of prayer would necessarily be of benefit to the public. This point has been accepted in a number of cases.[146] In *Dunne v Byrne*[147] the point is made that such activities of nuns in a convent would be accepted as being 'religious' in a general sense but not 'charitable' in the legal sense.

Which types of activities constitute a 'public benefit'?

The courts are concerned with the advantages of charitable status being given to certain activities. Therefore, English law ought to state clearly that it is not awarding badges of honour to certain types of activity, nor judging their merits. Rather, it is concerned to accord the precise benefits attached to charitable status (principally tax relief and excusal from private trusts law formalities) to particular forms of approved activity like the relief of poverty and doing good works in the community. As has already been seen, a trust for the benefit of a contemplative order of nuns will not be valid because there is no public benefit

---

143 Charities Act 2011, s 2(1)(b).
144 (1862) 31 Beav 14.
145 [1949] AC 426.
146 *Cocks v Manners* (1871) LR 12 Eq 574; *Re White* [1893] 2 Ch 41; and also *Leahy v Attorney-General for NSW* [1959] AC 457.
147 [1912] AC 407.

resulting from that cloistered observance.[148] Religious observance or activity is generally not a public matter but to deny it charitable status is not to criticise it.

The courts have begun to adopt increasingly relaxed approaches to the interpretation of such charitable purposes. In *Neville Estates v Madden*[149] the issue arose whether a trust to benefit members of the Catford Synagogue could be a charitable purpose. The central issue was whether the members of that synagogue could be considered to be a sufficient section of the population for 'public benefit'. It was held that, because the religious observance practised in the synagogue was (in theory) open to the public, the requirement of public benefit would be satisfied.[150]

In *Re Hetherington*[151] there was a trust to provide income for the saying of masses in private. On the facts it was found that it was not susceptible of proof in these circumstances that there would be a tangible benefit to the public. Nevertheless, Browne-Wilkinson V-C was prepared to construe the gift as being a gift to say masses in public (and therefore as a charitable purpose) on the basis that to interpret the transfer as such a trust would be to render it valid and that it was open to the court to interpret a transfer as being an intention to create a charitable trust so as to make that trust valid. Therefore, Browne-Wilkinson V-C is underscoring a straightforwardly purposive approach to the treatment of charitable trusts by the courts. On those facts it was therefore possible that the masses be heard in public and a further benefit in that the funds provided by the trust would relieve church funds in paying for the stipends of more priests.

This purposive approach indicates the attitude of the courts to validate charitable trusts wherever possible, in contradistinction to the stricter interpretation accorded generally to express private trusts. However, it worth noting that Browne-Wilkinson V-C in *Hetherington* was careful to rely on authorities like *Gilmour v Coats*,[152] *Yeap Cheah Neo v Ong*[153] and *Hoare v Hoare*[154] in relation to the need for a public benefit, and *Re Banfield*[155] in relation to the exclusion of non-charitable purposes. This decision also illustrates a generational approach by judges like Lords Wilberforce, Goff and Browne-Wilkinson (when in the High Court) to upholding the validity of trusts wherever possible, in contrast to the approaches of judges like Viscount Simonds and Harman J to invalidating trusts in circumstances in which there was some apparent incongruity in their creation.

Some conclusions on religion

This sub-heading does seem a little overly portentous as written ('some conclusions on religion') – it does not intend to draw theological conclusions on the meaning of religion. Rather, its aim is limited to an examination of the types of activity which English law will accept as being charitable, religious purposes. A charitable religious purpose requires some

148   *Gilmour v Coats* [1949] AC 426.
149   [1962] Ch 832.
150   See also *Attorney-General v Bunce* (1868) LR 6 Eq 563; *Bunting v Sargent* (1879) 13 Ch D 330.
151   [1990] Ch 1.
152   [1949] AC 426.
153   (1875) LR 6 PC 381.
154   (1886) 56 LT 147.
155   [1968] 2 All ER 276.

public action or benefit. The question then is what type of action. It does appear that the courts have in mind religious observance which involves classically English activities such as jumble sales and gymkhanas which will have a public benefit. As will be discussed below in *Other purposes beneficial to the community*, political action to improve the housing conditions of the impoverished by religious groups will not be *charitable* actions under the head of religious purpose. Their only possible salvation[156] in the law of charities for this type of purpose is as a trust for the relief of poverty or under one of the new statutory heads of charity.

Similarly, religious observance itself is insufficient – it must be available to the public. However, the notion of religion is that it has adherents (or members) and therefore excludes others. Necessarily, religions, and religious observance will exclude sections of the public as well as offering others spiritual succour. The point is that seeking a public benefit in relation to religious purposes appears to be, at some level, counter-intuitive.

Indeed the general approach to religion is a rather parochial Anglican approach to religion and spirituality. It might be asked, in these pluralistic times, why New Age spiritual awareness or druidism should not be allowed registration as religious charitable trusts. In a patch of purple prose in *Re South Place Ethical Society*,[157] Dillon J explained his requirements for qualification as a charitable religious purpose in the following terms:

> If reason leads people not to accept Christianity or any known religion, but they do believe in the excellence of qualities, such as truth, beauty and love, or believe in the platonic concept of the ideal, their beliefs may seem to them to be the equivalent of a religion, but viewed objectively they are not a religion.

In other words, if you do not believe in what I believe in (or in what established religions believe in) in the way that I believe in them, then you do not have a religion at all. That is far from the approach in *Dingle v Turner*[158] whereby the court would look to whether or not there is an underlying charitable or altruistic purpose to the trust. Instead an ideological approach to religion emerges in relation to the availability of the fiscal and other advantages of charitable status.

25.7 OTHER PURPOSES BENEFICIAL TO THE COMMUNITY

> *Other purposes beneficial to the community require that there be a sufficient 'public benefit'. A 'community' in this sense must be something more than a mere fluctuating body of private individuals (such as employees of a small company). The term 'benefit' will be found to exist in relation to purposes providing for the maintenance of public buildings, the provision of facilities for the disabled within a community, but will not apply under the case law in relation to mere recreation or social events (subject to certain statutory exceptions). These principles will be subject to certain general exclusions from the category of charitable purposes. After the Charities Act 2011, the*

---

156 No pun intended.
157 [1980] 3 All ER 918.
158 [1972] AC 601.

forms of charity which are accepted as being valid under this head will continue to be valid, although the fourth head itself as a means of categorisation is likely to be of no further use now that there are new statutory heads of charity.

25.7.1 Introduction

This fourth category of charitable purpose under the case law is clearly broader in scope than the other three heads of charity under the old case law, acting as a reservoir for a number of the miscellaneous trusts which had struggled to qualify as being charitable despite their seemingly benevolent aim. The category is culled from those parts of the 1601 preamble which do not fit into those already considered and the cases which have argued by analogy, or more generally, that they disclose purposes beneficial to the community. It appears that many of the new charitable purposes which were approved by the Charity Commissioners before the passage of the old 2006 Act have fallen under this head rather than under any of the three more specific purposes. In many of the decided cases, applicants have sought to argue that they fell within one of the three specific heads of charity and have then argued that, in the alternative, they fell within the fourth head. Therefore, the fourth head can often be seen as a catch-all or residuary category for purposes which could not otherwise be characterised as being charitable.

This category no longer exists intact as a result of the passage of the 2011 Act. Rather, a number of the categories of purpose which used to fall under this head are now listed in s 3(1) of the 2011 Act. However, any purposes which were formerly valid under the pre-2006 case law,[159] whether or not they are now listed in that Act, will continue to be valid.[160] Therefore, it is still important to know how the fourth head under *Pemsel's Case* operates because any case which would have been valid under it will still be valid in the future, whether or not it appears in the list in s 3(1) of the 2011 Act. Furthermore, a number of the issues considered in this section relating to the nature of a benefit or to the scope of the community which is to be benefited will continue to be important even after the enactment of the 2011 Act. For the purposes of this discussion, this category of other purposes beneficial to the community will still be referred to as 'the fourth head'.

25.7.2 The nature of the fourth head: other purposes beneficial to the community

To fall under this head the trust has to show that its purpose is either analogous with the examples cited in the preamble to the statute of 1601 or with the principles deriving from its decided cases: as held by Lord Macnaghten in *Pemsel's Case*.[161] As considered above, while the 1601 preamble was repealed by the Charities Act 1960, the effect of the preamble on the common law was retained by the decision in *Scottish Burial v Glasgow Corporation*.[162] Importantly, in that same decision Lord Reid held that a trust ought not to be deprived of its charitable status simply because it charges fees or conducts a trade with the public;[163]

---

159 Charities Act 2006, s 2(8).
160 *Ibid*, s 2(4)(a), by dint of s 2(2)(m).
161 [1891] AC 531.
162 [1968] AC 138.
163 See the discussion of *Joseph Rowntree Memorial Trust Housing Association Ltd v Attorney-General* [1983] 1 All ER 288; *ICLR v Attorney-General* [1972] Ch 73, considered above.

provided that the profits derived from such fees or trade are applied for the purposes of the charity and not paid out to individuals. In this way, schools which charge fees have been accepted as being charitable provided that they are either non-profit making or that any profits are applied for the benefit of the school. It is of course questionable whether the fiscal advantages of charity ought to be accorded to charitable entities which trade. Any other person who makes a profit will be *prima facie* liable to some form of taxation.

25.7.3 The requirement of a public benefit

The fourth head includes a requirement that the purpose be 'beneficial to the community'. It is therefore important to unpack this notion of 'community'. In terms of education and religion, the requirement of public benefit has been adapted to cope with the particular types of trust which have generated litigation. With reference to educational purposes, the focus has been on the extent to which the fund has been applied for people outwith any personal nexus to the settlor, and in relation to religion the public benefit has come to include a notion of access to religious service. The conception of 'beneficial to the community' is slightly different. It can be best summarised as requiring that some identifiable section of the community can derive a real benefit from the purpose. The roots of the case law are established in the *dicta* of Sir Samuel Romilly in *Morice v Bishop of Durham*[164] making reference to a requirement of 'general public utility' to satisfy this fourth head.

The notion of 'benefit'

The existence of some benefit is important. The people who are intended to take a benefit from the trust must actually be shown to benefit in some tangible fashion. Thus, for example, a trust of a small amount of money for the benefit of aged and blind millionaires would not qualify on the basis that such people would not derive any further benefit from such a trust, given their existing wealth.[165] However, a charitable purpose for the care of the blind which will provide real benefits to the blind people within a given area would be charitable because those people who were intended to benefit would actually be taking a tangible benefit.[166]

As a general rule of thumb it was suggested in *ICLR v Attorney-General*[167] by Russell LJ that where a trust purpose removes the need for statutory or governmental action by providing a service voluntarily, the organisation providing that service should be deemed to be charitable. However, that permissive approach is not adopted in all cases. In *Re South Place Ethical Society*[168] Dillon J suggested that to say that a purpose is of benefit to the community and therefore charitable, is to put the cart before the horse – the two ideas are not mutually inclusive. Just because a purpose may be of benefit to the community does not necessarily mean that it is charitable. The only rational approach for the student of this subject is to consider each case in turn to decide whether or not there appears to be sufficient benefit provided by the particular trust purpose.

---

164 (1805) 10 Ves 522.
165 As considered in *Rowntree Memorial Trust Housing Association v Attorney-General* [1983] Ch 159, 171.
166 *Re Lewis* [1955] Ch 104.
167 [1972] Ch 73.
168 [1980] 3 All ER 918.

The notion of 'community'

There is a necessary requirement that there be sufficient benefit to the community. The term 'community' is a particularly vexed one for political scientists and sociologists as well as for lawyers. A community could be said to be defined by reference to a geographical area. The obvious question would be what size of geographic area would be necessary to constitute a community. To define that area as being 'people in my back garden' or 'the monsters under my bed' would clearly be too small a geographic area. But would the settlor be required to identify an area as populous as 'London' or as geographically large as 'Yorkshire'? In *Verge v Somerville*[169] Lord Wrenbury held that:

> The inhabitants of a parish or town or any particular class of such inhabitants, may, for instance, be the objects of such a gift, but private individuals, or a fluctuating body of private individuals cannot.

Therefore, the community must be more than a fluctuating body of private individuals – precisely the concept which was criticised in *Dingle v Turner*[170] as being a reasonable definition of a group as large as the inhabitants of a London borough, as discussed above.

The further question with reference to charity would be whether a defined class of people (such as 'the elderly', or 'six-year-old footballers') within that geographic area would be sufficiently 'communal'. In some cases, the class may be a broad enough section of the community – such as 'the elderly'. Whereas others may appear to be too narrow and overly selective – such as 'six-year-old footballers'. There are arguments raised by the political scientists that the millions of people who watch *Big Brother* on Channel 4 constitute a community, or that people who share a physical ailment or a religious or political belief should all be considered as examples of virtual (rather than tangible) communities.

The question is then as to the approach which English law does in fact take. Evidently, a purpose which provides a benefit to a private class sharing a personal nexus with the settlor will not be a valid charitable purpose.[171] The notion of limiting the class extends further than the personal nexus test used in *Oppenheim*[172] for educational purpose trusts. Thus in the leading case of *IRC v Baddeley*[173] the settlor purported to create a charitable trust to provide facilities for 'religious services and instruction and for the social and physical training and recreation' of Methodists in the West Ham and Leyton area of east London. It was held by Viscount Simonds that the charitable purpose would fail because the class of those who could benefit was too narrowly drawn. His Lordship held that 'if the beneficiaries are a class of persons not only confined to a particular area but selected from within it by reference to a particular creed' it cannot fall under the fourth head of charity. Therefore, to restrict the class of people who can benefit from the purpose too narrowly will fail the requirement of a benefit to the community. In the words of Viscount Simonds, those who are expressed as

---

169   [1924] AC 496.
170   [1972] AC 601.
171   *Re Hobourn Aero Components Ltd's Air Raids Disaster Fund* [1946] Ch 194 – in which the mooted benefit was restricted to the employees of a particular company.
172   [1951] AC 297.
173   [1955] AC 572.

being entitled to benefit from the purpose must be an 'appreciably important class of the community'.

Benefiting individuals within a community

The courts have accepted a variety of defined classes as being suitably charitable. Trusts for the relief of the aged have been held to be charitable. Thus, in *Re Dunlop*[174] a trust to provide a home for elderly Presbyterians was upheld as being a valid charitable purpose, as was sheltered accommodation providing for fee-paying patients in *Rowntree Memorial Trust Housing Association v Attorney-General*.[175] As considered above, despite the charging of fees, trusts will be upheld as being for valid charitable purposes when they are for the care of the elderly, or the sick, or the disabled. It appears that these cases are adopting the *Dingle v Turner* approach of seeking out an underlying charitable purpose, rather than relying simply on the applicant to prove that a sufficient constituency of the public will be benefited by the trust.

Benefiting the civic amenities of a community

Aside from demonstrating that charitable assistance will be given to people, it is sufficient that the trust fulfils a purpose not directed at specific individuals but providing for some civic amenity. Trusts for the maintenance of a town's bridges, towers and walls have been upheld as valid charitable purposes[176] as has a trust for the support of a crematorium.[177] In these cases there are no specific individuals who stand to benefit directly, rather the community in general receives some indirect benefit in the quality of their civic life.

The notion of community, and of municipal services, is greatly extended by some of the case law. Included within the idea of 'benefit to the community' is the resettlement of criminal offenders and the rehabilitation of drug users.[178] Similarly, trusts for the support of firefighting services[179] and lifeboats[180] have been upheld as charitable purposes. It is suggested that this development, and understanding of the civic context of the 'community' is a very welcome development for the law. The fiscal and other advantages of charitable status ought to be bestowed on socially useful activities. The way forward for the charitable sector is in the support of the welfare state and local government in the development of such amenities and in the support of local initiatives within which communities develop their own shared space.

As a slight development to one side of those issues of civic amenity, trusts for the moral improvement or instruction of the community have been upheld as being charitable purposes. Thus, a trust, *inter alia*, to 'stimulate humane and generous sentiments in man towards lower animals' has been upheld as a charitable purpose attached to the

---

174 [1984] NI 408.
175 [1983] Ch 159; *Re Resch's WT* [1969] 1 AC 514.
176 *Attorney-General v Shrewsbury Corp* (1843) 6 Beav 220.
177 *Scottish Burial Reform and Cremation Society v Glasgow Corp* [1968] AC 138.
178 *Attorney-General for Bahamas v Royal Trust Co* [1986] 1 WLR 1001.
179 *Re Wokingham Fire Brigade Trusts* [1951] Ch 373.
180 *Johnston v Swann* (1818) 3 Madd 457.

establishment of an animal refuge.[181] Even trusts for 'the defence of the realm' have been upheld as being charitable.[182]

The question of the provision of recreation grounds and sporting or leisure amenities was covered by the Recreational Charities Act 1958, before the introduction of s 5 of the Charities Act 2011, in the wake of the *Baddeley* decision considered above. Decisions in which such amenities have been upheld as charitable have now been dismissed as being anomalous and outwith the operation of the statute.[183] In *Williams v IRC*[184] a trust was established for 'the benefit of Welsh people resident in London'. In delivering the leading speech, Lord Simonds held that 'a trust must be of a public character' and not restricted to individuals. The trust failed as a charitable purpose trust on the basis that the trust's purpose was solely social and recreational, and not strictly charitable. This particular decision, it is suggested, must now be considered to be have been overruled by s 3(1) in relation to the playing of amateur sport and potentially some of the other categories as well.

25.7.4 The remaining purposes beneficial to the community under the Charities Act 2011

The principal effect of the Charities Act 2011 in relation to the definition of 'charitable purpose' has been to break out a number of the key, contested categories of 'other purposes beneficial to the community' in an attempt to make clear that they should now be considered to be valid heads of charity in their own right. What is unclear at the time of writing is whether or not the courts will attempt to perpetuate their case law categorisations of charitable and non-charitable purposes regardless of the statute on the basis that the statute is drafted in only the most general language. Significantly head (m) in s 3(1) of the Charities Act 2011 preserves all charitable purposes which were previously valid under the case law, as set out in s 3(1)(m)(i) of that Act. Also contained in that provision is a reference to the validity of recreational charities, given that under the old case law the courts effectively chose to ignore the Recreational Charities Act 1958 which had been passed to overturn a decision of the House of Lords which had sought to perpetuate long-standing principles of the case law disallowing charitable status to recreational activities. It is to be hoped that the courts will react to the spirit of the statute which is clearly to expand the categories of charitable purposes to include activities which the case law had previously refused to recognise as being charitable. Those purposes, and the old case law which previously dealt with them, are considered in turn in the following section of this chapter.

The decision of Lewison J in *Hanchett-Stamford v Attorney-General*[185] threatens to limit the effect of the Act quite remarkably by taking the position that (in relation specifically to animal welfare) if the charitable purpose was potentially valid under the old case law then the Act should not be taken as having any effect in broadening that category of charitable purpose. This would mean that the Parliamentary intention of modernising and expanding the categories of charitable purpose would be frustrated by the courts. This case is considered below at para 25.8.9.

---

181 *Re Wedgwood* [1915] 1 Ch 113.
182 *Re Stratheden* [1895] 3 Ch 265; *Re Corbyn* [1941] Ch 400.
183 *Williams Trustees v IRC* [1947] AC 447.
184 *Ibid.*
185 [2008] EWHC 330 (Ch), [2008] 4 All ER 323.

25.8 THE NEW CATEGORIES OF CHARITABLE PURPOSE UNDER THE CHARITIES ACT 2011

25.8.1 An introduction to the Act

It is difficult to write much on the terms of this new Act immediately in the wake of it receiving the Royal Assent because there is no case law to explain the extent of the new heads of charity and because the manner in which those categories are expressed is very general indeed. Therefore, what follows is a discussion of each of the new statutory heads of charity in turn with a reference to previous problems in the case law where appropriate and otherwise with a suggestion as to their possible future applications. There is a division between these new statutory heads of charitable purpose: first, those heads which have been the subject of litigation and which the statute now seeks to resolve; and, secondly, those heads which are new governmental initiatives without any history in the old case law.

25.8.2 The advancement of health or the saving of lives

The reference to the advancement of health includes the 'prevention or relief of sickness, disease or human suffering'.[186] Research into medical procedures would ordinarily have fallen under educational purposes under the research category in any event, in the manner considered earlier in this chapter in relation to the advancement of education. Therefore, it is to be supposed that this category is aimed at other purposes. The '*advancement* of health' could encompass activities which promote healthy eating – such as celebrity chef Jamie Oliver's campaigning for the improvement of dinners in schools – or public information campaigns promoting sexual health. Campaigning for the advancement or improvement of public health would in itself be a charitable activity, although if that campaigning took to advocating a change in the law then it would fall foul of the principle in *National Anti-Vivisection v IRC*[187] that no charitable purpose may campaign for changes in the law. It may also include the advancement of alternative health therapies. The 'saving of lives' could encompass anything from medical care to lifeboat services which save lives at sea.[188]

25.8.3 The advancement of citizenship or community development

Category (e) in s 3(1) deals with 'the advancement of citizenship or community develop-ment'. At first blush, this category is very much in line with the rhetoric of the current government and is fairly meaningless as drafted. The Act contains a gloss to the effect that it includes 'rural or urban regeneration' and 'the promotion of civic responsibility, volunteering, the voluntary sector or the effectiveness or efficiency of charities'.[189] What is not clear is what is meant by 'citizenship'. It could be linked to whatever is taught in schools as part of the national curriculum under 'citizenship'. There are references elsewhere in s 3(1) to religious or racial harmony and equality,[190] although the reference to 'community

---

186 Charities Act 2011, s 3(2)(b).
187 [1940] AC 31.
188 *Thomas v Howell* (1874) LR 18 Eq 198; *Re David* (1889) 43 Ch D 27.
189 Charities Act 2011, s 3(2)(c).
190 *Ibid*, s 3(1)(h).

development' could include the organisation of youth groups, and other activities which are directed at harmony. What is difficult to see is how these intangible – but important – improvements in social life will tally with the judges' historical aversion to services or activities which do not lead to any tangible benefit to identifiable groups of people. For example, recreational charities were always avoided in the case law because mere social activities had no direct effect on the quality of people's lives. Therefore, the judges would need to expand their understanding of a charitable activity in this sense to incorporate a range of intangible activities, which must extend beyond those categories of purpose which have already been accepted under the old case law and which will continue to be effective in the future.[191]

25.8.4 The advancement of the arts, culture, heritage or science

This category refers to 'the advancement of the arts, culture, heritage or science'. Each of these four elements should be considered separately. None of these terms is defined in the Act and therefore we must develop our own understandings of these provisions and guess as to the future. First, 'the arts'. It is suggested that the reference to 'the arts' in the plural is not a reference simply to 'art'. Thus, it is a reference to activities which ordinarily constitute a part of 'art' in the singular and so refers to painting, to sculpture and so forth; but it could also be said to refer to theatre performances, opera, classical music and so forth which all generally fall under the rubric of 'the arts' generally. The advancement of art, in the singular, could include not only the display of artworks[192] and the maintenance of museums,[193] but its advancement might also refer to the funding of future artworks provided the Charity Commission can accept that it is genuinely of sufficient artistic merit.[194] The general reference to 'heritage' suggests the maintenance of historic land, gardens and buildings, and also monuments and so forth beyond artworks. Heritage need not be purely physical: there are, for example, a large number of folk music societies whose work is concerned with the preservation and conservation of cultural heritage items like songs, poems and so forth. This last item might be said to merge into 'culture'. The meaning of the term 'culture' is one which is hotly contested among social theorists and could encompass almost any aspect of human interaction.[195] In the context of these four categories, culture would certainly include literature, theatre, classical music and opera, in the sense, that is, of what is commonly referred to as 'high culture'. However, ceremonies or festivals which are particular to specific geographic communities or ethnic communities – such as religious festivals, or the Durham Miners' Gala, or festivals of popular music – could certainly fall within a broader definition of 'culture'. The advancement of science need not be limited to scientific research because that is already included under 'education' – therefore it can be assumed that this purpose is supposed to stretch further than research. The advancement of science could include the establishment or support of institutes which bring scientists together or which popularise science among the population generally.

191 *Ibid*, s 3(1)(m)(i).
192 *Abbott v Fraser* (1874) LR 6 PC.
193 *Trustees of the British Museum v White* (1826) 2 Sim & St 594; *Re Holburne* (1885) 53 LT 212.
194 See Charity Commission, *RR10: Museums and Art Galleries*, paras 7–12 and Annex A.
195 Taken literally, of course, 'culture' could refer to mould or fungus.

25.8.5 The advancement of amateur sport

This category refers to 'the advancement of amateur sport'. Under the old case law the mere advancement of sport did not in itself constitute a charitable purpose: thus paying for a cup for a yachting competition and to promote yachting was not held to be a charitable purpose,[196] nor was the promotion of cricket.[197] Recreational charities have been held valid under the old case law as charitable purposes only if they improved the conditions of life of the people using them and either if they are available to all members of the population without discrimination or if they are made available by reason of their users' 'youth, age, infirmity, disability, poverty or social and economic circumstances': all terms which were contained in the Recreational Charities Act 1958 and now s 5 of the Charities Act 2011, which is considered in detail below in section 25.8.12. Most of the key cases on recreational charities related to combined sports and social clubs. Thus the inclusion of this category in the list of charitable purposes will require the judges to accept the charitable nature of amateur sports clubs or the raising of money, for example, for the training of amateur athletes for the 2012 London Olympic Games. What the judges will need to accept is that it is not necessary for the participation in sport to alleviate some lack in the sportsperson's life. (It should be recalled that the chance to earn money from sport will not count in this instance because the category refers strictly to *amateur* sport.) The Charity Commission has, however, changed its view and decided that it will accord charitable status to 'the promotion of community participation in healthy recreation by providing facilities for playing particular sports'.[198] Consequently, in practice there are unlikely to be any further cases on this topic because the Charity Commission will not challenge genuine trusts set up to achieve these goals. The terms of the new Act have only confirmed this approach, it is suggested. The remaining questions relating to recreational charities, discussed below, may similarly be disposed of by this regulatory development.

25.8.6 The advancement of human rights, conflict resolution or reconciliation or the promotion of religious or racial harmony or equality and diversity

This category deals with 'the advancement of human rights, conflict resolution or reconciliation or the promotion of religious or racial harmony or equality and diversity'. Purposes of this kind would previously have run the risk of being held to be void purposes on the basis that they sought a change in the law or that they were more generally political purposes.[199] As considered above, political purposes will not be enforced by the courts. The pretext for refusing to enforce such purposes is that it might be considered to be tantamount to the courts expressing support for one political ideology over another and that it would be impossible for a court to weigh purely political arguments given that judges (purportedly) merely put the law into effect but do not make it.[200] The old case law had not recognised the pursuit of better relations between groups or nations – such as the British and the Boers after the Boer War – as being charitable.[201] The Charity Commission, however, doubtless

196 *Re Nottage* (1885) 2 Ch D 649.
197 *Re Patten* [1929] 2 Ch 276.
198 Charity Commission, *RR 11: Charitable Status and Sport* (2003).
199 See *National Anti-vivisection Society v IRC* [1940] AC 31.
200 However, in a common law system where the bulk of the law has been made by a judge at some point this argument has always struck this writer as being facile in the extreme.
201 See *Re Strakosch* [1949] Ch 529.

emboldened now by the new Act, has expressed its view that promoting good race relations ought to be considered to be a charitable purpose in the future and as being self-evidently for the public benefit.

25.8.7 The advancement of environmental protection or improvement

This category is concerned with 'the advancement of environmental protection or improvement'. The environment can be taken to refer to particular items of flora and fauna, at one end of the spectrum, right the way through to combating climate change or global warming at the other end. Thus the protection of sites of special scientific interest or the maintenance of areas of outstanding natural beauty – particularly areas which have been classified as such under planning law – would constitute environmental protection at what we might consider the 'micro' end of the spectrum. Research into climate change or activities relating to global environmental threats might be considered to be the 'macro' end of this spectrum. Both, it is suggested, should constitute charitable purposes. It is suggested that such activities can be demonstrated to be for the public benefit if it is accepted, as the Act seems to suggest by the very inclusion of this category in s 3(1), that protection or improvement of the environment is necessarily in the public good.

25.8.8 The relief of those in need by reason of youth, age, ill-health, disability, financial hardship or other disadvantage

The contents of this category are 'the relief of those in need by reason of youth, age, ill-health, disability, financial hardship or other disadvantage', of which references to 'the relief of aged impotent and poor people' were contained in the Preamble to the statute of 1601. At first blush, it is difficult to see how this category extends far beyond the category for the relief and prevention of poverty: the focus would need to be on the 'other disadvantage' which persons might suffer to extend it beyond mere poverty. It is easiest to see how suffering connected to ill-health or old age or disability could be assisted by charitable donation or services. These ideas were encapsulated in the Preamble to the Statute of 1601, as set out earlier in this chapter. What one needs to demonstrate is a 'need' which would be met by that charitable service. Need in relation to youth could involve after-school care if there is no parent or other adult able to care for a child before her parents finish work or recover from a medical condition. Activities involving the National Society for the Prevention of Cruelty to Children have been upheld as being charitable purposes,[202] as has the provision of a children's home.[203] Otherwise, this category seems to enact a part of the old fourth head under the case law and the Preamble.

25.8.9 The advancement of animal welfare

The advancement of animal welfare under statute

This category relates to 'the advancement of animal welfare'. This would encompass the good works of the Royal Society for the Prevention of Cruelty to Animals or the Royal

---

202 See *D v NSPCC* [1978] AC 171.
203 *Re Sohal's WT* [1958] 1 WLR 1243.

Society for the Protection of Birds, it is suggested, as organisations committed to the care of animals. Equally, the provision of hospices for animals or even the provision of veterinary services may be charitable purposes. What is significant is that under the old case law the thread which appeared to run through those cases (for the most part) was that there was a public benefit in animal welfare if, and only if, there could be shown to be some moral improvement to the human community by dint of treating animals better.[204] It remains to be seen whether or not the courts will consider the express inclusion of this category in the legislation as signalling a need to accept that promoting or procuring better animal welfare was in itself for 'the public benefit' without any anthropomorphic or humanist concerns about showing some moral improvement in the human community. It is suggested that a civilised human society only truly achieves a higher level of civilisation when it is capable of treating all creatures humanely, just as it looks after human beings incapable of caring for themselves. Thus, it is suggested, the advancement of animal welfare should be considered to be a good in itself. However, it may be that a trust to provide for the welfare of the settlor's only dog would not constitute a public benefit because the only benefit would be felt within the settlor's own home. Therefore, the trust would need to achieve some advancement of animal welfare which had a broader effect, but without needing to show that human beings in particular were benefiting. The old – and frequently unsatisfactory – case law is considered in the next section.

The pre-2006 case law on benefiting animals

It is frequently said that the British are a nation of animal lovers and that they become more concerned about harm being caused to animals than to people (that is probably because animals cannot tell you what they are thinking and that is clearly a cause to like anyone). There are frequently attempts to create trusts for the maintenance of animals. Typically this would not constitute a valid private trust if it were for the benefit of specific animals.[205] The argument might be that a trust for the benefit of a broadly defined class of animals would constitute a charitable purpose. On the basis that such a purpose directed at the prevention of cruelty to animals would contribute to public morality, the Court of Appeal held that the trust would be a valid charitable trust.[206] In *Re Moss*[207] a trust for a specified person to use 'for her work for the welfare of cats and kittens needing care and attention' was held to be a valid charitable purpose by Romer J.[208] Similarly, a trust, *inter alia*, to 'stimulate humane and generous sentiments in man towards lower animals' has been upheld as a charitable purpose attached to the establishment of an animal refuge.[209]

However, the Court of Appeal in *Re Grove-Grady*[210] held that a will providing for a residuary estate to be use to provide 'refuges for the preservation of all animals or birds' was not a charitable purpose because there was no discernible benefit to the community. It that

---

204 *Re Wedgwood* [1915] 1 Ch 113.
205 *Re Lipinski* [1976] Ch 235, *infra; Re Endacott* [1960] Ch 232.
206 *Re Wedgwood* [1915] 1 Ch 113.
207 [1949] 1 All ER 495.
208 An approach applied generally in *University of London v Yarrow* (1857) 21 JP 596; *Tatham v Drummond* (1864) 4 De GJ & Sm 484; *Re Douglas* (1887) 35 Ch D 472; and *Re Murawski's WT* [1971] 2 All ER 328.
209 *Re Wedgwood* [1915] 1 Ch 113.
210 [1929] 1 Ch 557.

case, Russell LJ held that there was no general rule that trusts for the preservation and care of animals would necessarily be of benefit to the community: rather, each case should be considered on its own merits.

The protection of animals could also be expressed in terms of protection of the environment (and thereby of benefit to the community)[211] or as an educational purpose in some circumstances. Interestingly in *Re Lopes*[212] Farwell J held that 'a ride on an elephant may be educational'. The trouble with that statement is that it would seem to make circuses potentially charitable, particularly if linked specifically to a research or straightforwardly educational activity.

Case law on the 2006 Act

In spite of the express inclusion of a category of animal welfare in the Charities Act 2006 (now consolidated into the Charities Act 2011) for the first time, Lewison J chose to limit the future possible development of charitable animal welfare purposes in *Hanchett-Stamford v Attorney-General*.[213] In that case a couple had long maintained an unincorporated association ('The Performing and Captive Animals Defence League') which sought to achieve a change in the law so as to ban the use of performing animals: the association had been denied charitable status on the basis that it sought to effect a change in the law. Lewison J held, correctly it is suggested, that the Charities Act 2006 had not effected any change in the law on preventing charities from seeking a change in the law. In relation specifically to animal welfare, however, the claimants argued that the inclusion of the category of animal welfare into the Charities Act 2006 when taken together with the provisions of the Animal Welfare Act 2006 (which created offences of causing distress to animals) had effected a significant change in the law. Lewison J held that animal welfare purposes had been valid under the case law prior to the 2006 Act and therefore that the Act should not be interpreted as having changed the scope of that position under charities law. This is a surprisingly narrow interpretation of the legislation. It is clear that the prior case law had taken a very equivocal attitude to animal welfare whereby many purposes linked to animals had been held invalid, whereas the 2011 Act explicitly includes 'animal welfare' within the list of valid charitable purposes without any qualification: therefore, it is suggested that the purpose of the 2011 Act should be interpreted to be an intention to permit all animal welfare purposes as being valid charitable purposes beyond the limited categories which were permitted previously. To take Lewison J's position further would be to suppose that if any of the other statutory categories had been validated even partially under the old case law then the Act would not be permitted to extend in any way the categories of charitable purpose and therefore the purpose of the Act would be straightforwardly frustrated.

25.8.10 The promotion of the efficiency of the armed forces of the Crown

This category was a late addition to the legislation and covers 'the promotion of the efficiency of the armed forces of the Crown'. It had previously been the case that trusts to promote national defence through the armed forces would be considered to be for the public

---

211 *Re Verrall* [1916] 1 Ch 100.
212 [1931] 2 Ch 130.
213 [2008] EWHC 330 (Ch), [2008] 4 All ER 323.

benefit.[214] The armed forces refer clearly to the Army, the Royal Air Force and the Royal Navy, and all attendant services. The statute focuses on the 'efficiency' specifically of these forces. This could have two senses. The first sense might include an economic measure of efficiency. The second sense could be taken to mean the 'effectiveness' of the armed forces, perhaps including activities such as the physical fitness of soldiers, or the ability of armed services personnel to use modern technology. If this second sense were taken to its extremes then it could even include the acquisition of military equipment which would make the armed services more effective or efficient. It would, however, be an odd notion of charity which extended to the acquisition of weapons.

25.8.11 The promotion of the efficiency of the police, fire rescue and ambulance services

This category covers 'the promotion of the efficiency of the police, fire rescue and ambulance services'. It had previously been the case that trusts to promote the services provided by the three emergency services were considered to be charitable.[215] The statute focuses on the 'efficiency' specifically of these forces. As with the previous provision, this could have two senses. The first sense might include an economic measure of efficiency or the ability of those services directly to carry out their functions. The second sense could be taken to mean the 'effectiveness' of these services, perhaps including activities such as the physical fitness of police officers, the ability of ambulance personnel to use modern technology, and so forth. Importantly the old case law had held that a trust for the recreation of police officers was not a charitable purpose.[216] It is suggested, however, that a distinction should be drawn between circumstances in which police officers are merely being provided with social club facilities such as a pool table which cannot improve the discharge of their official duties, and circumstances in which the fitness or other equipment which is being provided would enable those officers to discharge their official duties more effectively. Thus, put at its crudest, a fitter policeman is more likely, one might say, to be able to cope with arresting fit young criminals if she has fitness equipment made available to her. In that sense all of the emergency services would become more 'efficient' if recreational and other equipment were put at their disposal. It is in this direction which the legislation ought, it is suggested, to develop in its application.

25.8.12 Recreational charities

Introduction

Recreational charities have long been contentious in the law of charities. Under the old case law charitable status was not given to social clubs or sports clubs which did not alleviate any material lack in the lives of a section of the public. That much was outlined in relation to the new purpose of the advancement of amateur sport above, and is considered in detail in the next section. Recreational charitable purposes under s 1 of the Recreational Charities Act 1958 remain effective further to s 5 of the Charities Act 2011. Section 5 of the Charities Act

---

214   The 'setting out of soldiers' was included in the 1601 Preamble.
215   *Re Wokingham Fire Brigade Trusts* [1951] Ch 373.
216   *IRC v Glasgow City Police* [1953] AC 380.

2011 makes provision for the effectiveness of some recreational purposes as charities. This part of this chapter considers the case law and then the material terms of the 1958 Act.

The old case law

In the wake of the *IRC v Baddeley*[217] decision, which held that recreation for a restricted class of people in a specific geographic area would not be charitable, the Recreational Charities Act 1958 was introduced to bring such purposes within the heads of charity. It had long been a part of the common law that a generally expressed trust for recreation would not be a charitable trust.[218] Similarly in *IRC v Glasgow City Police*[219] it had been held that the provision of facilities for the recreation of police officers would not be a charitable purpose and that in *Williams v IRC*[220] a trust established for 'the benefit of Welsh people resident in London' and the development of 'Welshness' would not be considered to be charitable.[221] So it has been held that 'general welfare trusts' seeking to provide in general terms for the welfare of the community were not charitable trusts because their purposes would be too indistinct.[222] This is particularly so where the community whose welfare the purposes sought to secure was either too narrow a class or related to too limited a geographic area.[223]

The Recreational Charities Act 1958 established a 'public benefit test' to legitimise recreational charities as charitable trusts.[224] However, the facilities must be provided with the intention of improving the conditions of life of the person benefiting.[225] There are two further, alternative requirements that either[226] those persons must have a need of those facilities on grounds of their social and economic circumstances or that the facilities will be available to both men and women in the public at large.[227] Section 5 of the 2011 Act, re-enacting in substantially similar language the provisions of the 1958 Act, provides that:

(1) It is charitable (and is to be treated as always having been charitable) to provide, or assist in the provision of, facilities for

   (a) recreation, or

   (b) other leisure-time occupation,

if the facilities are provided in the interests of social welfare.

(2) The requirement that the facilities are provided in the interests of social welfare cannot be satisfied if the basic conditions are not met.

---

217 [1955] AC 572.
218 *Guild v IRC* [1992] 2 All ER 10, [1992] 2 AC 310, [1992] 2 WLR 397; *Re South Place Ethical Society* [1980] 1 WLR 1565.
219 [1953] AC 380.
220 [1947] AC 447.
221 See generally: *IRC v City of Glasgow Police Athletic Association* [1953] AC 380 (police efficiency); *Re Wokingham Fire Brigade Trusts* [1951] Ch 373 (fire brigade); *Re Resch's Will Trusts* [19691 1 AC 514 (hospitals); *Joseph Rowntree Memorial Trust Housing Association Ltd v Attorney-General* [1983] 1 All ER 288 (special housing for the elderly).
222 *Attorney-General Cayman Islands v Wahr-Hansen* [2000] 3 All ER 642, HL.
223 *Ibid.*
224 Recreational Charities Act 1958, s 1(1).
225 *Ibid*, s 1(2)(a).
226 *Ibid*, s 1(2)(b)(i).
227 *Ibid*, s 1(2)(b)(ii).

(3) The basic conditions are –
    (a) that the facilities are provided with the object of improving the conditions of life for the persons for whom the facilities are primarily intended, and
    (b) that –
        (i) those persons have need of the facilities because of their youth, age, infirmity or disability, poverty, or social and economic circumstances, or
        (ii) the facilities are available to members of the public at large or to male, or to female, members of the public at large.

Thus it is a charitable purpose under the Act to provide recreational facilities provided that those facilities both improve the 'conditions of life' of those who will use them and that the facilities are generally available to the public or they are needed by certain people who will use them because of their youth or disability and so forth. On a lenient interpretation it could be said that improving the conditions of someone's life might include simply providing recreational facilities which otherwise they did not have; or else one could take a restrictive view that one must be suffering from some lack or poverty and that the mere provision of recreational facilities will not necessarily be making good such lack or poverty and so should not be protected by the Act. In explaining the ambit of the 1958 Act, the majority of the House of Lords in *IRC v McMullen*[228] held that it was only if the persons standing to benefit from the trust were in some way deprived at the outset that their conditions of life could be said to have been improved. Therefore, their Lordships took the more restrictive view of the Act. On the facts of that case the promotion of the playing of organised football among young people by the Football Association, by providing facilities for the playing of football by people at school or university, could not be said to 'improve the conditions of life' of the persons who would benefit because it would not remedy any identifiable deprivation in those people.[229] The minority were of the view that the test ought to be relaxed so that a very broad interpretation could be given to social and economic circumstances requisite for the application of the 1958 Act: effectively the lenient view set out above. The minority would have allowed this promotional activity to be validated by the 1958 Act. If these activities were carried on in a school then they would be valid as an educational charity.

    A more liberal interpretation was taken by a differently constituted House of Lords in *Guild v IRC*[230] in relation to a bequest 'to the town council of North Berwick for the use in connection with the sports centre in North Berwick or some similar purpose in connection with sport'. It was accepted that this sports centre would be available to the general public as required by s 1(2)(b) of the Act. The principal question was whether or not this sports centre could be said to be connected with 'social welfare' as required by s 1(1) of the Act (now s 5(2)). Lord Keith made it plain that he was prepared to adopt a 'benignant construction' of the bequest in this case. It was a bequest which demonstrated that the testator's intention was to benefit a sports centre the facilities of which were available to the public at large. Consequently, it was held that this constituted a valid charitable purpose under s 1(1) and (2) of the 1958 Act.

228 [1981] AC 1.
229 By extrapolation from the London Welsh case, then, the establishment of a 'London Scottish' centre for the recreation of Scottish people living in London could not be said to 'improve the conditions of life' of the persons who would benefit because it would not remedy any identifiable deprivation in those people in spite of the passage of the Act.
230 [1992] 2 AC 310, [1992] 2 All ER 10.

To reinforce the status of charities as welfare trusts, there is a specific provision in s 2 of the 1958 Act which provides for the validity as charitable trusts of trusts provided for the social welfare activities set out in the Miners' Welfare Act 1952, which relates to miners' welfare funds. Those trusts must have been declared before 17 December 1957. Otherwise, such a fund would not necessarily have been a charitable purpose given the nexus between the members and the possibility that the fund was a mutual fund organised on the basis of contract rather than as a charity.

The effect of s 5 of the Charities Act 2011

Section 5(2) of the Charities Act 2011 introduces two 'basic conditions' to the Recreational Charities Act 1958, namely that the recreational facilities must be provided on the same terms as under s 1(2) of the 1958 Act as previously in effect, except that the material in paragraphs (a) and (b) are now pre-conditions for the validity of the charitable purpose. What has not been dealt with in the 2011 Act is the restrictive interpretation which has been put on the 1958 Act by the House of Lords in *IRC v McMullen*, as considered in the previous section.

25.9 CY-PRÈS DOCTRINE

The cy-près *doctrine gives the courts a power to re-constitute the settlor's charitable intentions so as to benefit charity if the original purposes cannot be achieved, for whatever reason. The Charities Act 1960 (as amended in 1993) provided for broader powers to apply property* cy-près *than was available under the case law. Those principles are now consolidated in s 61 et seq of the Charities Act 2011. The case law itself drew a distinction between impossibility of achieving those objectives before the trust came into effect, and impossibility arising at a later date.*

The central difference between public charitable trusts and express private trusts is exemplified by the *cy-près* doctrine. As considered in Chapter 3 the certainties requirements for express private trusts are extremely stringent. A failure to satisfy these requirements leads to the invalidity of the trust. Where the objects of an express private trust are uncertain, the trust will be void. In relation to a charitable trust, however, where the charitable objects do not exist or are uncertain, the court has the power to order an application of the trust fund for alternative charitable purposes which are in accordance with the settlor's underlying intentions. This alternative application is referred to as the *cy-près* doctrine. The best book on this particular doctrine is that by Prof Rachael Mulheron, *The Modern Cy-Près Doctrine*.[231]

25.9.1 The case law position

Before the enactment of the Charities Act 1960 the case law provided that the *cy-près* doctrine could only be invoked if it was either impossible or impracticable to perform the purposes of the trust. The aim of the 1960 Act was to widen the powers of the court to reconstitute a charitable trust if its terms were merely inconvenient or unsuitable, as opposed to being genuinely impossible. Those principles now appear in Part 6 of the Charities Act 2011.

---

231 Mulheron, 2005.

Impossibility at the commencement of trust

If the trust is impossible to perform from the outset, the property settled on trust passes on resulting trust back to the settlor's estate.[232] In *Re Rymer*,[233] a legacy to the rector of an identified seminary from time to time failed when the seminary ceased to exist. It was held that the bequest was so specific to that seminary that it did not disclose a general charitable intention. A further example is found in *Re Good's Will Trusts*[234] in which the settlor intended the erection of rest homes on identified land but that specific land could not be acquired: no general charitable intention could be found beyond the building of the specific rest homes on that site. Where the specified charity or object existed at the time of the creation of the trust, it is frequently held that the settlor did not intend there to be a general charitable intention.[235]

An exception to this general rule would apply where the trust disclosed a general charitable intention beyond an intention merely to benefit the identified charity. In *Biscoe v Jackson*[236] the settlor sought to create a soup kitchen 'in the parish of Shoreditch . . . and a cottage hospital'. When the intended land could not be acquired, the Court of Appeal held that the settlor had disclosed a general charitable intention such that the fund could be applied *cy-près*. In such cases where no specific charity is identified or where there is a long list of potential charities, then the courts are more likely to find that there was a general charitable intention beyond the benefit of any one charity.[237] So in *Re Harwood*[238] it was considered by Farwell J that where there was a specific charity identified by the settlor that would mitigate against the finding of a general charitable intention, whereas the *cy-près* doctrine would be applied where the settlor had prepared a long list of possible charities without demonstrating a clear intention to benefit only particular charities.[239] A gift for an identified *purpose* (rather than for a particular existing, charitable *institution*) follows similar principles[240] – although, logically, it could be said a trust for a general purpose (for example, 'the relief of poverty in the East End of London') is more likely to disclose a general charitable intention than a trust provision for an identified charitable organisation (for example, 'for the homelessness charity Shelter').

Alternatively, the charity may have continued in another form and so the courts may apply the *cy-près* doctrine to benefit the successor entity.[241] A distinction is drawn on the cases between unincorporated and incorporated charities. Transfers to unincorporated charities (such as unincorporated associations or purpose trusts) will generally constitute a purpose trust and be capable of being applied *cy-près*,[242] whereas a transfer to an incorporated entity (such as a company) will not necessarily constitute a general charitable intention where that specific entity is identified by the settlor.[243]

232   *Re Rymer* [1895] 1 Ch 19; *Re Wilson* [1913] 1 Ch 314; *Re Packe* [1918] 1 Ch 437. Cf *Bath and Wells Diocesan Board of Finance v Jenkinson* (2000) *The Times*, 6 September.
233   [1895] 1 Ch 19.
234   [1950] 2 All ER 653.
235   *Re Davis* [1902] 1 Ch 876.
236   (1887) 35 Ch D 460.
237   *Re Davis* [1902] 1 Ch 876.
238   [1936] Ch 285.
239   *Re Stimson's WT* (1970).
240   *Re Spence* [1979] Ch 483.
241   *Re Faraker* [1912] 2 Ch 488; *Re Finger's WT* [1972] 1 Ch 286.
242   *Re Vernon WT* [1972] Ch 300.
243   *Re Harwood* [1936] Ch 285; *Re Meyers* [1951] Ch 534; *Re Finger's WT* [1972] 1 Ch 286.

Where the gift was intended for an organisation which was not a charity there will not usually be a *cy-près* application for charitable purposes. So in *Re Jenkin's WT*[244] a settlor sought to create a trust for the benefit of an anti-vivisection charity which was not a charitable purpose. A decision indicating the pragmatism of the courts on this basis was that in *Re Satterthwaite's WT*[245] in which an excitable testator declared that she hated the entire human race and so sought to benefit in her will only animal charities which she plucked at random from a telephone directory. Of the nine bequests made, none were to identified charities and one was to an anti-vivisection society (which was not a charitable purpose). The Court of Appeal held that eight-ninths of the testatrix's estate could be applied *cy-près* to animal hospitals and to animal charities, and that only the ninth which had been intended to pass to the non-charitable purpose would lapse into residue.[246]

Impossibility after the commencement of the trust

Different principles apply if the charitable purpose fails after the trust has come into operation – that is, from the date of its operation rather than the date of its declaration. There are two possibilities for *cy-près* distribution. First, on the basis that the settlor had a general charitable intention.[247] In the event that the settlor intended to benefit a specific, existing charity this means of distribution will not be available to the court. This principle is in line with the discussion of these questions in the previous section.

Second, on the basis that property had passed to a charity before its ceasing to exist, whether or not it has been benefited as a specifically named institution without a general charitable intention as considered above, there may be grounds for *cy-près* distribution in any event. The question in relation to this latter example is whether the property has passed effectively to a named charity so as to have become the property of that charity requiring *cy-près* application. So, for example, where a testator left a specific pecuniary legacy to an orphanage which was in existence at the date of declaration of the trust, but which ceased to exist just after the testator's death but before the legacy could be paid to it, it was held that this legacy could be applied *cy-près* because it became on the testator's death the property of the orphanage and with the dissolution of the orphanage that property fell to be distributed by the Crown for some analogous purpose.[248] The power of the Crown to divide such property for analogous purposes in relation to charities which have ceased to exist was contained

---

244   [1966] Ch 249.

245   [1966] 1 WLR 277.

246   In *Catholic Care v Charity Commission* [2010] 4 All ER 1041 the Charity Commission refused to consent to a change of objects (ie the purposes for which the charity had been created) by a charity which acted as an adoption agency and which provided support to adoptive parents on the basis that the charity wanted only to offer support to heterosexual couples. This proposed change of objects was refused, *inter alia*, on the basis of the principle against discrimination on grounds of sexual orientation in the provision of services further to the Equality Act (Sexual Orientation) Regulations 2007 which were made further to the Equality Act 2006. Briggs J considered the role of reg 18 of those regulations in providing an exemption for charities from the requirements of the regulations, and ultimately remitted the matter to the Commission to decide on the appropriateness of this proposed amendment in this context.

247   *Re Slevin* [1891] 2 Ch 236, *infra*; *Re King* [1923] 1 Ch 243.

248   *Re Slevin* [1891] 2 Ch 236.

in older cases such as *Attorney-General v Ironmongers' Co*[249] and *Wilson v Barnes*.[250] This thinking was applied in *Re Wright*[251] where the application of funds to the construction of a convalescent home became impracticable but it was unclear whether the test for impracticability applied at the date of the testatrix's death or at the date at which the funds were available: it was held that the applicable date was the date of the testatrix's death.

25.9.2 Exclusivity of purpose

It is required that the underlying purpose of the settlor was exclusively charitable, as can be seen from cases like *Chichester Diocesan Fund v Simpson*.[252] In relation to finding a charitable purpose this is a pre-requisite of deciding that a purpose is charitable – as considered above. That requirement of charitable purpose is equally important in relation to the operation of the *cy-près* doctrine. The courts will, in certain circumstances, give a permissive interpretation to trusts where the issue is as to the charitable status of that trust. In *Simpson* the testator left property for 'charitable or benevolent purposes'. The word 'benevolent' was held not to be a synonym for the technical term 'charitable' and therefore it was held that the testator had not evidenced an unequivocal intention to settle property on exclusively charitable purposes. However, in *Guild v IRC* the House of Lords held that the words 'some similar purpose in connection with sport' in a settlement could be interpreted as connoting a charitable intention on the part of the settlor.[253]

Alternatively, it is open to the court to apportion a trust fund between valid charitable purposes and other objects. It is possible that non-charitable objects will fail but that the charitable objects will be severed from those other provisions and validated separately, as was held in *Re Clarke*.[254] This division may take place even if the settlor had not expressed a division of the property. The division between the potential beneficiaries in this context is affected on the basis that 'equality is equity' and that therefore each of those objects should take the property in equal amounts.[255] However, where it is impossible to separate property between valid charitable trusts objects and other, invalid objects, then the whole trust must fail.[256]

25.9.3 The mechanics of the *cy-près* doctrine under statute

The provisions in outline

The Charities Act 1960 sought, *inter alia*, to expand the operation of the *cy-près* doctrine: the provisions of the 1960 Act have been re-enacted in the Charities Act 2011, Part 6. The principal change was to extend the operation of the doctrine beyond requirements of mere impossibility or impracticability into other situations in which the trustees may prefer to apply the funds for other (charitable) purposes than those identified by the settlor.

---

249 (1834) 2 My & K 526.
250 (1886) 38 Ch D 507.
251 [1954] Ch 347.
252 [1944] AC 341.
253 *Guild v IRC* [1992] 2 AC 310.
254 [1923] 2 Ch 407.
255 *Salusbury v Denton* (1857) 3 K & J 529; *Re Douglas* (1887) 35 Ch D 472.
256 *Re Coxen* [1948] Ch 747.

The key provision in this context is s 62 of the Charities Act 2011 which sets out the following situations in which a *cy-près* application can be made. They are as follows:

(1) it must be demonstrated that there is a general charitable intention; and either
(2) where the purposes have been 'as far as may be fulfilled';
(3) where the purposes cannot be carried out as directed or within the spirit of the gift;
(4) where the purpose provides a use for only part of the gift;
(5) where the property can be more usefully applied along with other property applied for similar purposes;
(6) where the area of the original purpose is no more; or
(7) where the original purposes are adequately provided-for purposes such as statutory services, or are harmful to the community, or useless to the community, or are no longer an effective use of the property.

Attention must also be paid to the spirit of the gift and to the social and economic circumstances at the time of altering the purposes of the trust when making the decision about a *cy-près* application.[257]

The detail of the provisions

To take each of these provisions in turn. First, it remains a requirement that the settlor's intention be generally charitable beyond an intention to benefit only a single, named institution as considered above.

Second, where the purposes have been 'as far as may be fulfilled'.[258] This builds on case law dating before the 1960 legislation in which it was found that the purposes for which the charitable trust was created no longer continued in existence. For example, it was considered that there were no more 'infidels' in Virginia requiring conversion to Christianity in *Attorney-General v City of London*[259] and that there were no more slaves in Turkey requiring redemption in *Ironmongers' Co v Attorney-General*:[260] in both cases the funds were applied *cy-près*. More generally this will apply to circumstances in which the original charitable objectives have no further use of the funds to achieve the purposes set out in the trust.

Third, where the purposes cannot be carried out as directed or within the spirit of the gift.[261] Considering older authorities, whether or not the spirit of the gift can be carried out will depend upon the context. So in *Re Robinson*[262] it was held that a stipulation that a preacher wear a particular item of clothing (a black gown) while preaching would alienate the congregation and thus defeat the core objective of bringing people into the congregation. A slightly wider approach was taken in *Re Dominion Students' Hall Trusts*[263] in which a charitable company was established to create and maintain a hostel for students in London.

---

257 Charities Act 2011, ss 61 and 62.
258 Charities Act 2011, s 62(1)(a)(i).
259 (1790) 3 Bro CC 121.
260 (1844) 10 Cl & F 908.
261 Charities Act 2011, s 62(1)(a)(ii).
262 [1921] 2 Ch 332.
263 [1947] Ch 183.

It was a part of that company's objects that non-white students be excluded from the hostel. It was held by Evershed J that this provision should be deleted – a decision, again, on the case law requirement of impossibility which was more stringent even than the statutory code. *Re Lysaght*[264] considered a similar point to *Re Dominion Students' Hall*[265] when a testatrix provided for a bequest in favour of the Royal College of Surgeons which that College sought to repudiate on the basis that it contained a proviso that no funds be applied for the benefit of women, Jews or Catholics.[266] Buckley J approved a deletion of that paragraph which both achieved the settlor's underlying objectives while also placating the College. It has been held that the court is entitled to alter the size of payments made under a trust.[267]

Fourth, where the purpose provides a use for only part of the gift.[268] In this situation, where the purposes expressed by the settlor will only find a use for a part of the gift and leave a surplus, the court may choose to apply the surplus *cy-près* for similar charitable purposes (an idea accepted in the case law in *Re North Devon and West Somerset Relief Fund*).[269]

Fifth, where the property can be more usefully applied together with 'other property applicable similar purposes can be more effectively used in conjunction and to that end can suitably, regard being had to the spirit of the gift, be made applicable to common purposes'.[270] The question of amalgamation of one fund with another fund to achieve common charitable purposes was accepted in principle in *Re Harvey*.[271] In general terms, this provision will permit such an amalgamation of funds where both the charitable objectives are sufficiently similar and the amalgamation of those funds will be more effective than the status quo.

Sixth, 'where the original purposes were laid down by reference to an area which then was but has since ceased to be a unit for some other purpose, or by reference to a class of persons or to an area which has for any reason since ceased to be suitable, regard being had to the spirit of the gift, or to be practical in administering the gift'.[272] In short, if the underlying rationale for the original purpose has ceased to exist, then this ground for the use of the *cy-près* doctrine may be applicable. It is sufficient that the area has ceased to be 'suitable' – which involves a potentially broader category of circumstances including a decision by the trustees that the continued application of the funds for the identified purpose is no longer in accordance with the spirit of the settlor's intention. So in *Peggs v Lamb*[273] it was held that there be an amendment of the class of persons entitled to benefit from the work of a charity in circumstances in which the potential class of persons benefiting had dwindled to 15 and their income from the charitable bequest had risen far in excess of the testator's original intention.

Seventh, a more general provision justifying *cy-près* application on the following bases: where the original purposes are adequately provided for by other means, or where those

---

264 [1966] 1 Ch 191.

265 [1947] Ch 183.

266 Remarkably, however, the court objected only on the basis that the purpose discriminated against Jews and Catholics but voiced no objection to the discrimination against women.

267 *Re Lepton's Charity* [1972] Ch 276.

268 Charities Act 2011, s 62(1)(b).

269 [1953] 1 WLR 1260.

270 Charities Act 2011, s 62(1)(c).

271 [1941] 3 All ER 284.

272 Charities Act 2011, s 62(1)(d).

273 [1994] Ch 172.

purposes are adequately provided for by statutory or governmental services, or are harmful to the community, or useless to the community, or are no longer an effective use of the property.[274] In relation to services already provided, there is an explicit understanding that the voluntary, third sector will often mimic the work of the welfare state and that such duplication would not be a useful application of charitable funds. Rather, it would be better to use those funds for purposes not provided for by the state. In all circumstances, the *cy-près* application is required to refer to the original spirit of the gift[275] as applied by the trustees from time to time.[276] For example, the 'original purposes' of a trust may be altered from the provision of specified playing fields to enable trustees to sell those playing fields to acquire better facilities for a similar charitable purpose.[277] Such a *cy-près* application will more generally be denied where the proposed scheme is contrary to the 'original purposes' of the charitable trust.[278]

Problems with the identification of the alternative charity

It can be a difficult question to know whether a *cy-près* application should be required to pursue the goals of the settlor or whether the court should simply seek to identify a similar charitable purpose in the abstract, regardless of the precise personal attitudes of the settlor. So, in *Kings v Bultitude*[279] a testatrix made a bequest in favour of a particular religious charity which was a splinter organisation from the Roman Catholic Church. She had devoted a large amount of her life to that organisation, even conducting its religious services after her husband's death (where he had previously served as its primate). After her death, however, the organisation disbanded. When that organisation ceased to exist the question arose as to whether or not the bequest could be applied *cy-près* to other religious charitable purposes. Proudman J found that the testatrix had not had a general charitable intention but rather only an intention to benefit that particular organisation, and therefore the bequest could not be applied *cy-près*. Clearly, Proudman J was motivated by the clear objectives of the testatrix in leaving money to that specific organisation to which she had devoted so much of her time and energy.

By contrast, in *White v Williams*[280] Briggs J considered an application to apply property (in the form of one of three buildings used for worship) from one moribund religious order, BT, *cy-près* for the purposes of another order (BC UK) from which BT had split previously. The trustees of BT considered that an application of the property for the purposes of BC UK would be an application for essentially the same religious purposes as BT (in the sense that their religious beliefs were in common) in spite of the earlier split between those organisations. Therefore, Briggs J allowed the *cy-près* application.[281] At one level it could have been said that when these organisations (indeed, the people who made up the congregations for each church) had split one from another then that might have led to the same conclusion as

274 Charities Act 2011, s 62(1)(e).
275 *Ibid*, s 62(1)(e)(iii).
276 *Ibid*, s 62(3).
277 *Oldham Borough Council v Attorney-General* [1993] Ch 210.
278 *Re JW Laing Trust* [1984] Ch 143.
279 [2010] EWHC 1795 (Ch).
280 [2010] EWHC 940 (Ch).
281 Cf *Varsani v Jesani* [1998] 3 All ER 273.

in *Kings v Bultitude*. However, Briggs J looked more generally at the abstract charitable purposes of the congregations and saw a continuity of purpose in the second organisation which had previously been joined to the moribund organisation which had received the bequest and which served the same community in Lewisham in south London. Finding a continuity of purpose in *White v Williams*, where in *Kings v Bultitude* the congregation had simply dissolved away, appears to be the key difference on the facts, although there is also a difference of principle here.

Application cy-près *where the objects fail*

Under s 63 of the 2011 Act, where property is given for specific charitable purposes which fail, there may be a *cy-près* application where the settlement was made either by a donor who cannot be found or by a donor who executed a written disclaimer of his rights. This section therefore provides for a general power in the court to order *cy-près* applications of property if the trusts have straightforwardly failed. The spectre of the settlor's intention hangs heavily over this area – even though the role of the *cy-près* doctrine is to subvert that intention. What is important to note is that a specific doctrine is needed to carry out that subversion and also that the settlor must have had a charitable intention at the outset before this doctrine could apply: the words of the settlor ring on. Section 63 supplements the position in circumstances in which the settlor is effectively no longer in existence (either through death, absence, or repudiation of responsibility) and replaces the role of the settlor to some extent by precluding any notion of resulting trust. Once the money is in the charitable sector, the *cy-près* doctrine keeps it there.

Small charities

There were also statutory provisions in the Charities Act 1993 dealing with charities which had an annual turnover (that is, gross income) of less than £5,000 and which did not hold land as part of their assets. The trustees of such charities could resolve that the assets of their charity were transferred to another charity (or be divided between other charities) or that the purposes of the charity were altered to other charitable purposes.[282] Similarly, in relation to charities which were organised as endowments (that is, funds whose capital is required to be kept intact and used solely to generate income) but whose capital generated less than £1,000 in any given financial year, the trustees were empowered to resolve that the restriction in the charity's constitutive documents dealing with the treatment of the capital be altered.[283] Section 75 contained no provision as to the alternate purpose at which those capital assets must be directed; s 74 contained no requirement that the transferee charity be carrying on a similar charitable purpose – although it had to be carrying on a charitable purpose of some kind.

The future for the cy-près *doctrine*

In her book on this topic, Prof Mulheron suggests that the *cy-près* doctrine could have a more general application in relation to the validation of non-charitable purpose trusts than

---

282   Charities Act 1993, s 74.
283   *Ibid*, s 75.

being restricted to the law of charities as it is at present.[284] It is suggested that many void private trusts could usefully be maintained if the courts were able to order the application of the trust property for equivalent purposes so as to make them valid. Of course, as was considered in sections 4.2.3 and 4.2.4 in relation to cases such as *Re Barlow*,[285] *Re Denley*[286] and *Re Lipinski*,[287] it often happens that judges seek to give effect to the settlor's true intentions by means of benignant constructions of the trust instrument. For example, in *Re Barlow's WT* Browne-Wilkinson J was prepared to permit the trustees to carry out a bequest (which might otherwise have been void for uncertainty of objects) partly on the basis of proposed scheme of distribution which his Lordship considered would give effect to the spirit of the testator's intentions.[283] It could be said that this operates as a sort of distant cousin to the *cy-près* doctrine in private law terms in that the precise words used by the settlor are interpreted by the court so as to achieve an equivalent result which is valid under private trusts law. While the *cy-près* doctrine has always been limited to the law of charities in England and Wales there is no reason why an expansion of the doctrine, if thought desirable in the manner in which Prof Mulheron makes clear in Chapter 10 of her book,[289] should be considered impossible in perpetuity.

25.10 THE REGULATION OF CHARITIES

Charities are regulated by the Charity Commission,[290] which maintains the register of charities.[291] Mindful of the intermittent concerns expressed about the abuse of charities, the Charity Commission has five key objectives:[292]

(1) The public confidence objective is to increase public trust and confidence in charities.
(2) The public benefit objective is to promote awareness and understanding of the operation of the public benefit requirement.
(3) The compliance objective is to increase compliance by charity trustee with their legal obligations in exercising control and management of the administration of their charities.
(4) The charitable resources objective is to promote the effective use of charitable resources.
(5) The accountability objective is to enhance the accountability of charities to donors, beneficiaries and the general public.

These regulatory objectives do not create legal rights in the hands of the people who are mentioned in the text of the objectives, but rather anticipate that the Charity Commission will consider the interests of those people when exercising their regulatory function. The

---

284 R Mulheron, *The Modern Cy-près Doctrine*, UCL Press, 2006, Chapter 6 and Chapter 10.
285 [1979] 1 WLR 278.
286 [1969] 1 Ch 373.
287 [1976] Ch 235.
288 Otherwise, his Lordship was also prepared to give effect to this bequest by interpreting it to be a gift as opposed to a trust.
289 R Mulheron, *The Modern Cy-près Doctrine*, UCL Press, 2006, 304 *et seq*.
290 Charities Act 2011, ss 13–16.
291 *Ibid*, s 29.
292 *Ibid*, s 14.

general functions of the Commission are then to decide whether or not purposes are chari-table, to encourage better administration of charities, to investigate mismanagement in the administration of charities, to determine the suitability of public collections certificates, and to disseminate information about its activities and to advise government ministers.[293] A Charity Appeal Tribunal has been created in relation to the activities and decisions of the Commission, with appeal to the High Court.[294]

There are detailed alterations made to the administration of charities. Changes are to be made to the *cy-près* doctrine to the effect that the Commission must bear in mind the spirit of the original gift, the desirability of applying the gift for purposes similar to the original purpose, and the need for the charity to be able to make a significant social or economic impact.[295] Changes are also to be made to the removal of the trustees of charities[296] and the power of the Commission to direct the application of the charities' property.[297]

25.11 A BRIEF SURVEY OF THE PUBLIC BENEFIT TEST IN THE LAW OF CHARITIES

This short section considers the extent of the notion of public benefit in the law of charities. It is suggested that, prior to the enactment of the Charities Act 2011, it was a rule honoured more in the breach than in the observance, unless the settlors were seeking to use their charity solely or primarily for the avoidance of tax. As was suggested in the final part of section 25.1 above, there are two lines of authority in relation to 'public benefit'. On the one hand we have the *Re Compton* line of cases which require that there must be no personal nexus between the people who will benefit from the charitable trust and the settlor of that trust. Thus, the benefit must be available to a sufficiently large section of the public outwith any direct connection to the settlor. This, it is suggested, does not tell us much about the nature of the trust – it only tells us that the settlor must be acting selflessly in the provision of some communal benefit. This brings us neatly to the alternative line of authority, that propounded by Lord Cross in *Dingle v Turner*. His Lordship identified a number of short-comings with the *Compton* approach. First, that approach is predicated on cases which were attempting to avoid tax by means of applying the benefit of the trust to a narrow group of people. This means that the approach of those courts was necessarily skewed towards seeking an open-ended public benefit. Secondly, the *Compton* approach requires that a large section of the public be able to take a benefit even if the funds which are to be raised by charity are likely to be small and so no general benefit of this sort can be attained. Suppose a charity for sufferers from a particularly rare disease. The people who will take a benefit may be small, even if the benefit stemming from the charity may be theoretically available to the entire population. Thirdly, Lord Cross identified a logical problem with the *Compton* test to the effect that there may be a nexus between the settlor and those who will take a benefit, but nevertheless the number of people who will take a benefit would be a sufficiently large section of the population. For example, the largest employer of non-skilled labour in

293 Charities Act 2011, s 14.
294 *Ibid*, s 315.
295 *Ibid*, s 61.
296 *Ibid*, s 76 et seq.
297 *Ibid*, ss 69 et seq.

the country is the Post Office: a trust for the benefit of the employees of the Post Office would be of benefit to a significant proportion of the population but a literal application of the *Compton* test would find that that trust was void. Similarly, the expression used in *Oppenheim*, that the class of people taking a benefit be 'more than a mere fluctuating body of private individuals', would itself be a description of the entire general public: the general public is a fluctuating body of private individuals. So the *Compton* test tells us nothing. The core point instead, as suggested by Lord Cross, is that there must be some genuine charitable intention on the part of the settlor. Thus trusts for the relief of poverty may be valid, even if there are only a few people who will take a benefit from the trust, provided that there is a genuine intention to relieve poverty. As the distinction between these two approaches was expressed above: Lord Cross's approach requires that there is something intrinsically charitable in the creation of a trust, compared with the *Compton* approach which is concerned with a merely evidential question of demonstrating that there is a predominantly public rather than a private benefit in the purposes of that particular trust. The former approach considers the intrinsic merits of the trust purpose which is proposed; whereas the latter looks instead to see how the trustees are actually running the trust and whether or not the practical approach achieves suitably public, charitable effects.

There are two other doctrines which have an effect on the free operation of the *Compton* test as applied to all charities other than charities for the relief of poverty. First, the intention disclosed in *Re Hetherington* and in *Guild v IRC* to validate genuine charitable intentions wherever possible, even if that means effectively altering the purpose of the trust or requiring the trustees to undertake to manage the trust in accordance with the court's directions so as to make it compliant with charities law. Thus a trust need not be drafted so as to disclose a public benefit because the court may well order that the trust be performed in a compliant manner. Thus trusts such as that in *Re Koettgen* may be validated for tax purposes to the extent that they were operated in compliance with charities law. Secondly, the *cy-près* doctrine enables the court to give effect to otherwise invalid or impossible purposes and thus, again, validates a trust which is performed in accordance with charities law. On the one hand it could be said that these two doctrines enhance the public benefit requirement by interpreting trust powers so as to fit in with charities law; on the other hand they tend to show that a settlor need not have drafted a charitable purpose which was compliant with the public benefit because the court will find a way to render it valid wherever possible. What these two doctrines illustrate is that, for all the apparent rigidity of the *Compton* test, the law of charities operates on a far more flexible basis. The basis for this flexibility is the general understanding that charities are a good thing, and that in consequence a genuinely charitable intention should be supported wherever possible.

Part 9

Equitable remedies

Chapter 26

Specific performance

OVERVIEW

Specific performance operates in personam *by imposing a personal obligation on the defendant to perform specific contractual obligations. It is not necessary for there to have been a pre-existing breach of contract for the award of an order for specific performance.*

Specific performance will be available in relation to contracts where the particular subject matter of the contract has some significance. Therefore, a contract for the sale of particular parcel of land will be specifically enforceable. Such an order will be made in relation to chattels only where a particularly significant chattel, which is not reasonably capable of being substituted with another chattel, is concerned.

Specific performance will typically not be available in circumstances where the contract is illegal or immoral; where there is no consideration; where the contract involves the exercise of some particular skill by the defendant (on grounds that the court could not administer such performance); where the contract involves mere payment of money (on grounds that common law damages would be sufficient remedy); where the contract is for an insubstantial interest; where the contract requires supervision; or where the contract is not mutually binding.

Defences to specific performance include: lack of an enforceable contract; absence of some formality; misrepresentation; undue influence or unconscionable bargain; mistake; lapse of time; or sufficiency of damages as a remedy.

26.1 THE NATURE OF SPECIFIC PERFORMANCE

26.1.1 Introduction

Specific performance is an equitable remedy in relation to the enforcement of contracts. An award of specific performance compels the defendant to perform her contractual obligations. As with all equitable remedies, its award depends on common law remedies, such as an award of damages, being insufficient in the circumstances.[1] The role of specific performance as a residual, discretionary remedy applied where damages are inappropriate was explained by Lord Hoffmann in *Cooperative Insurance v Argyll*:[2]

> Specific performance is traditionally regarded in English law as an exceptional remedy, as opposed to the common law remedy of damages to which a successful plaintiff is entitled as of right . . . specific performance was part of the discretionary jurisdiction of the Court of Chancery to do justice in cases in which the remedies available at common law were inadequate.

Specific performance relates to the performance of contracts. As considered below, the aim of the remedy is to require the parties to carry out their contractual obligations. The remedy is in the discretion of the court and may be displaced in situations in which such performance is impracticable, or in relation to specified categories of contract set out below.

26.1.2 Specific performance acts *in personam*

As considered in Chapter 1, equity acts *in personam* in the sense that an order made by a Court of Equity is made in respect of a particular person in relation to some factor which is said to affect that person's conscience. Therefore, an award of specific performance operates on that person as an order made, originally, by the Lord Chancellor requiring that person to act.

---

1   *Wilson Northampton and Banbury Junction Railway Co* (1874) 9 Ch App 279.
2   [1997] 3 All ER 297, [1998] AC 1.

Furthermore, the equitable remedy is discretionary. Equity operates in contradistinction to the common law, where the common law will enable a claimant to enforce her rights regardless of the justice of the situation. This also means, however, that a court of equity will not award specific performance in favour of those who have committed fraud or equitable wrongs (that is, those who have come to equity with unclean hands), or to those who have delayed before bringing a claim for specific performance, or to those whose consciences have been adversely affected. In this sense, specific performance falls into line with constructive trust, rescission and injunctions (considered elsewhere in this book) as a truly equitable remedy. To this extent, the defences considered in section 26.4 illustrate the contexts in which the courts will refuse to exercise their discretion to make an award for specific performance.

26.1.3 No requirement of breach

It is important to note that specific performance is an order which is made to require the performance of contractual obligations in certain circumstances. Consequently, the order requires only the performance of those obligations and does not rest on there having been some breach of contract, for example a transgression of an obligation not to perform some act.

26.2 CONTRACTS WHERE SPECIFIC PERFORMANCE IS AVAILABLE

Specific performance will be available in relation to contracts where the particular subject matter of the contract has some significance. Therefore, a contract for the sale of particular parcel of land will be specifically enforceable. Such an order will be made in relation to chattels only where a particularly significant chattel, which is not reasonably capable of being substituted with another chattel, is concerned.

For specific performance to be ordered, it is necessary that the circumstances of the contract require the performance of the particular contractual obligation as opposed to a mere payment of money damages. As will be seen below, the situations in which specific performance will not be ordered divide into two broad categories: cases in which payment of cash damages would be sufficient compensation for non-performance of the bargain; and cases in which the nature of the contract would make it impossible for the court to supervise performance of the obligation.

26.2.1 Specific performance in relation to land

The underlying principle in relation to real property is that each parcel of land is unique, so that an award of damages would be insufficient compensation for a failure to transfer a specified piece of land.[3] Therefore, the buyer of land may be able to impose an award of specific performance on the seller to compel the transfer of land as required by the terms of the contract. However, for the seller of land, damages will generally be adequate compensation when all that the seller sought from the contract was a cash payment in any event.

---

3 *Sudbrook Trading Estate Ltd v Eggleton* [1983] 1 AC 444.

As Sir John Leach VC held in *Adderley v Dixon*:[4]

> Courts of Equity decree the specific performance of contracts not upon any distinction between realty and personalty, but because damages at law may not in the particular case afford a complete remedy. Thus a Court of Equity decrees performance of a contract for land, not because of the real nature of the land, but because damages at law, which must be calculated upon the general money value of land, may not be a complete remedy to the purchaser to whom the land may have a peculiar and special value.

In accordance with this determination that specific performance will not depend on any difference between personalty and realty, the remedy will be available in respect of purely personal rights in land, such as a licence to occupy.[5] Therefore, the focus is on land as the subject matter of a contract, rather than on the need for the acquisition of proprietary rights *per se*.

26.2.2 Specific performance in relation to chattels

The underlying principle in relation to contracts for the transfer of chattels is that specific performance will be ordered in circumstances in which the chattel has a particular intrinsic value such that it would not be readily possible to acquire a substitute chattel. The possibility of acquiring a substitute chattel would mean that an award of damages would be sufficient. Suppose that A, a person seeking to establish a Sunderland Football Club museum of memorabilia, entered into a contract with B to acquire the very football with which Ian Porterfield scored the winning goal for Sunderland in the 1973 FA Cup Final, for a consideration of £10,000. A would seek specific performance on the basis that it would not be sufficient remedy that B merely pay an amount of money to A by way of general compensation for failure to perform the contract, because the chattel involved was so intrinsically valuable that equity would require transfer of the particular chattel specified in the contract.

To continue the quotation from Sir John Leach VC in *Adderley v Dixon*[6] (see above):

> . . . a Court of Equity will not, generally, decree performance of a contract for the sale of stock or goods, not because of their personal nature, but because damages at law, calculated upon the market price of the stock or goods, are as complete a remedy to the purchaser as the delivery of the stock or goods contracted for; inasmuch as with the damages, he may purchase the same quantity of the like stock or goods.

The issue is therefore as to the ability to acquire substitute goods elsewhere. A distinction could be drawn between a contract for the sale of shares easily obtained on the Stock Exchange (in respect of which damages would be sufficient remedy) and shares in a private company which could not otherwise be acquired (in respect of which specific performance would be ordered).[7] Similarly, where the chattel at issue is a particularly rare antique vase,

---

4 (1824) 1 Sim & St 607.
5 *Verrall v Great Yarmouth BC* [1981] QB 202.
6 (1824) 1 Sim & St 607.
7 *Neville v Wilson* [1997] Ch 144.

and therefore of particular value, specific performance will be awarded in respect of a contract of sale over that property.[8]

26.3 CONTRACTS WHERE SPECIFIC PERFORMANCE IS UNAVAILABLE

Specific performance will typically not be available in circumstances where the contract is illegal or immoral; where there is no consideration; where the contract involves the exercise of some particular skill by the defendant (on grounds that the court could not administer such performance); where the contract involves mere payment of money (on grounds that common law damages would be sufficient remedy); where the contract is for an insubstantial interest; where the contract requires supervision; or where the contract is not mutually binding.

Specific performance will be ordered, necessarily, in relation to contracts only where the context requires that the contracting parties carry out the particular obligations contained in the contract. There are two broad categories in which specific performance will not be awarded. First, as considered above, that common law damages would have been sufficient remedy will lead a Court of Equity to refuse to order specific performance. Secondly, specific performance will be refused on the basis that specific performance of the particular contract is inappropriate, perhaps because it would be contrary to public policy, that it could not be supervised properly by the court or that the circumstances in general make specific perform-ance impracticable. The following categories rehearse, with some exceptions, the structure of this subject in *Snell's Equity*.[9]

26.3.1 Illegal or immoral contracts

Clearly it would be contrary to public policy to order specific performance of a contract which would be either illegal or immoral. For example, a contract for payment for prostitu-tion would not be enforced by specific performance because equity will not act in favour of those who do not have 'clean hands'.

26.3.2 No consideration

For there to be specific performance, it is logical to pre-suppose that there must be an enforceable contract. It is a trite part of English contract law that there must be consideration before there can be a valid contract. Therefore, in situations in which there is no considera-tion, a Court of Equity will not enforce that contract by means of specific performance. More significantly, equity will not assist a volunteer, and therefore the court will not order specific performance to assist a person who has not provided consideration in relation to a contract.[10]

That rule has been extended, however, beyond cases of no general consideration to include those contracts which are effected by deed (and therefore do not require consideration to be valid contracts) to refuse specific performance on the basis that the claimant has nevertheless

---

8 *Falcke v Gray* (1859) 4 Drew 651.
9 McGhee, 2005.
10 *Cannon v Hartley* [1949] Ch 213.

failed to provide any consideration.[11] This rule is perhaps slightly more surprising than the principles considered hitherto, given that a contract under a deed is a valid contract. Perhaps the easiest way of understanding this principle is to see it as being in line with the core principle that equity will not assist a volunteer. Furthermore, it would appear to correlate with the roots of the English law contract as a principle founded on reciprocal bartering arrangements entered into between contractual parties which require consideration, rather than being based on the enforcement of mere promises as contracts.

26.3.3 Contracts involving personal skill

Contracts involving the personal skill of one of the parties are frequently the clearest example of contracts which will not be specifically enforced on the basis that an order of specific performance would be inappropriate in the circumstances.[12]

An example illustrating this principle was discussed by Megarry J in *CH Giles & Co Ltd v Morris*[13] as follows. Suppose that the contract was for an opera singer to perform at the Royal Opera House. If the court were to order specific performance that would mean that the singer would be required to exercise her skill as provided in the contract. An order for specific performance carries with it the threat of holding the defendant in contempt of court (a criminal offence) if the defendant fails to heed the order. However, it would be impossible for the court to supervise the singing performance, because in such a circumstance it would be too complicated a matter to rule whether or not the singer had performed adequately when forced to sing at the opera house. Suppose that the singer sang flat or otherwise under par. It would not be possible to know whether this inadequate performance was a genuine personal shortcoming, or a refusal to perform under the contract in defiance of the court order. Therefore, the court will not make an order for specific performance in such circumstances where it would be impracticable for the court to supervise the proper performance of the contractual obligation.

Matters of skill are generally beyond the ability of the court to supervise them in this way. Consequently, the discretionary nature of the remedy of specific performance is reinforced by demonstrating that the court will refuse such an order where it is inconvenient to enforce the order. However, Megarry J did hold that it is possible that there are contracts involving personal skill which would not be equivocal in this way. For example, where a builder contracts to build a wall suitable to support a roof, if that wall does not support the roof, there has clearly been a failure to perform the contract.

26.3.4 Specific performance in money transactions

The importance of the equitable remedy of specific performance in the commercial context is its availability only in respect of circumstances in which damages are not an appropriate remedy.[14] Therefore, specific performance will not usually be available for an executory

---

11 *Jefferys v Jefferys* (1841) Cr & Ph 138; *Cannon v Hartley* [1949] Ch 213.
12 *CH Giles & Co Ltd v Morris* [1972] 1 WLR 307.
13 *Ibid.*
14 *Hutton v Watling* [1948] Ch 26, [1948] Ch 398.

contract simply to pay an amount of money.[15] This is because damages are invariably an adequate remedy for a cash-settled contract. The authorities with reference to a contract to pay a loan satisfy the proposition that courts will not exercise their discretion to grant specific performance where damages would be an adequate remedy. Therefore, specific performance will not be appropriate for cash-settled contracts. However, in respect of a transaction in which physical delivery of a chattel or security is required, specific performance will be available where damages would not be a sufficient remedy.[16]

The general rule in relation to contracts for the payment of money is that common law damages will typically be a sufficient remedy. Therefore, a stream of cases in relation to contracts for loan witnessed a denial of specific performance on the basis that an award of damages would be adequate compensation for the lender. However, in *Beswick v Beswick*,[17] an uncle agreed to transfer his business as a coal merchant to his nephew, provided that his nephew would retain him as a consultant and pay an annuity to his uncle's widow. The nephew refused to make this payment to his aunt in the event. Therefore, his aunt sought an order for specific performance in her capacity as administratrix of her husband's estate. Even though the award was only an award for money, it was held that damages would be an insufficient remedy (being only nominal damages on the facts of that case) because it would have been impossible to predict the value of an annuity in the future and thus inappropriate to seek to reduce it to an award of damages. Therefore, we can see from this case that there are situations in which contracts for the payment of money will be specifically enforceable.

The issue may then turn on whether or not it would be a feasible remedy to make an order for cash damages, on the basis that the claimant could then obtain a substitute for the property forming the subject matter of the contract without too much difficulty. So, where it *is* relatively easy to acquire a replacement transaction in the market, specific performance will not be ordered,[18] whereas the unavailability of a replacement transaction will make specific performance appropriate.[19] A possible approach in circumstances where only a part of the property specified in the contract can be supplied by the defendant, might be for an order either for rescission or for specific performance of the contract to be coupled with damages.

26.3.5 Contracts for insubstantial interests

Where the right which the claimant wishes to enforce is insubstantial, the court will not seek to reinforce it by means of an order for specific performance. It should be emphasised that the court is not seeking to ascertain the value of the right in this context. Rather, it is attempting to ascertain its nature. One example of a right falling within this category would be a tenancy at will which occurs, typically, at the effluxion of a fixed-term lease at a time when the landlord permits the tenant to continue in occupation of the property.[20] The right exists only while the landlord continues to grant his permission to the tenant to occupy the property. In the event that the landlord activated the procedure for terminating the lease, the

---

15 *South African Territories Ltd v Wallington* [1898] AC 309; *Beswick v Beswick* [1968] AC 58.
16 *Cohen v Roche* [1927] 1 KB 169.
17 [1968] AC 58.
18 *Cuddee v Rutter* (1720) 5 Vin Abr 538.
19 *Duncruft v Albrecht* (1841) 12 Sim 189; *Kenney v Wexham* (1822) 6 Madd 355; *Sullivan v Henderson* [1973] 1 WLR 333.
20 *Glasse v Woolgar and Roberts (No 2)* (1897) 41 SJ 573.

rights under the tenancy at will would have no substance, and therefore it is said that there should be no specific performance of the contract.

This principle is to be doubted, however, in the light of the *dicta* of Roskill LJ in *Verrall v Great Yarmouth BC*,[21] which granted specific performance of a contract for occupation of land which granted a mere licence. On the basis that courts of common law are reluctant to ensure that consideration is sufficiently valuable (or that it constitutes a market value) in the formation of a contract, it appears undesirable that courts of equity would retain the power to themselves to decide whether or not a right is of sufficient substance to be enforceable. It is suggested that if the right is a valid contractual right it should be enforced to the extent that that is possible on its own terms.

26.3.6 Contracts requiring supervision

In common with contracts requiring the personal skill of the parties to perform them, a contract which requires the supervision of one party by another will typically not be specifically enforced by a Court of Equity.[22] In *Ryan v Mutual Tontine Westminster Chambers Association*,[23] the contractual provision at issue was an undertaking to provide a porter for a block of flats. It was held that the court would not order specific performance given that, if the court was to ensure that the order was being complied with, it would be necessary to check on a regular basis that a porter was present. Such a course of action would be impractical for the court, and therefore it was considered that no order for specific performance should be made in the circumstances. The rationale behind this principle is the difficulty for the court in overseeing proper performance of such a contract, given that such oversight would require constant monitoring by the court. It is accepted that oversight in such circumstances would be by means of a series of court rulings, rather than by hands-on supervision, but it would be so undesirable due to these practical difficulties in any event that specific performance would not be awarded.[24]

There are situations, however, in which such contracts may be specifically enforceable. The situations in which the rule will be circumscribed are where the contractual obligation requires regular activities which can be monitored.[25] The rationale for this principle is that it is comparatively easy for the court to observe whether or not regular duties have been performed adequately. Therefore, in relation to a contractual obligation to provide portering services in relation to a block of flats, it was held that the obligations to maintain central heating and to remove refuse would be capable of specific performance.[26] The distinction from the decision in *Ryan* was that these particular activities could be ordered to be specifically performed and could be controlled without the need for unacceptable levels of superintendence by the court, unlike the obligation to have a porter posted permanently on the premises.

Within this principle, there is an exceptional category in relation to construction contracts. Construction contracts will typically require supervision of sub-contract workers. Given that

---

21 [1981] QB 202.
22 *Ryan v Mutual Tontine Westminster Chambers Association* [1893] 1 Ch 116.
23 *Ibid*.
24 *Co-operative Insurance v Argyll Stores (Holdings) Ltd* [1997] 3 All ER 297, [1998] AC 1.
25 *Tito v Waddell (No 2)* [1977] Ch 106.
26 *Posner v Scott-Lewis* [1987] Ch 25.

element of supervision, it would appear likely that specific performance would not be ordered. However, given the specificity of construction work, it would be possible for the court to consider the completed work, with the aid of expert evidence. Consequently, it is possible for the court to consider the condition of the completed work and therefore to make an order for specific performance of those obligations without the need for unacceptable levels of superintendence.[27]

26.3.7 Contracts not mutually binding

It is important that the contract be binding on all parties to the contract. It must not be the case that only one party is unilaterally obliged to perform under the contract. The logic of this principle is that there must have been a contract which imposes equivalent obligations on all parties. However, a modern view has not sought to apply this principle rigidly on the basis that there may be contracts imposing unequal obligations on the parties in respect of which justice nevertheless requires that specific performance be ordered. Therefore, in relation to an obligation on a landlord to repair demised premises, it was held that specific performance could be ordered on the basis that no hardship would be caused to the landlord by the order.[28]

26.4 DEFENCES TO A CLAIM FOR SPECIFIC PERFORMANCE

Defences to specific performance include: lack of an enforceable contract; absence of some formality; misrepresentation; undue influence or unconscionable bargain; mistake; lapse of time; or sufficiency of damages as a remedy.

There are a number of circumstances in which a defendant will be able to rebut a claim for specific performance.

26.4.1 No enforceable contract

Before ordering specific performance of a contract, it is a logical pre-requisite that the contract be valid in the first place. Therefore, the requirements of offer, acceptance, consideration and an intention to affect legal relations must all be shown to have been in existence, or else that the contract has been created by deed. Similarly, the contract must not have become void, for example, on grounds of fraud or *ultra vires*.[29]

26.4.2 Absence of writing

There are contracts which have formal requirements for their creation. As considered above, it is necessary that the contract be enforceable, and therefore those formalities must have been complied with. An example of perhaps the most common formality arises under s 2 of the Law of Property (Miscellaneous Provisions) Act 1989. That section provides that:

---

27 *Wolverhampton Corp v Emmons* [1901] 1 KB 515.
28 *Price v Strange* [1978] Ch 337.
29 *Cannon v Hartley* [1949] Ch 213.

(1)   A contract for the sale or other disposition of an interest in land can only be made
       in writing and only by incorporating all the terms which the parties have expressly
       agreed in one document or, where contracts are exchanged, in each.

The 1989 statute repealed the doctrine of part performance (previously contained in s 40 of
the Law of Property Act 1925) whereby beginning performance of the contract would itself
have created an equitable right in the performing party to enforce the contract against its
counterparty.

26.4.3 Misrepresentation

In cases where the claimant has exerted a misrepresentation over the defendant which has
induced the defendant to enter into the transaction, the court will not make an order for
specific performance in favour of the claimant. The reason for this approach is that, in line
with the principle that she who comes to equity must come with clean hands, a person who
makes a misrepresentation to induce another into a contract should not be entitled to rely on
her own wrongdoing to force the defendant to perform the contract.

   In circumstances of misrepresentation inducing a claimant to enter into a contract, that
claimant will be entitled to rescind that contract, as considered in Chapter 28. This right to
rescission will therefore constitute a defence to a claim for specific performance.

   For the purposes of rescission based on misrepresentation, there is an important distinction to be made between fraudulent misrepresentation and innocent misrepresentation. A
fraudulent misrepresentation will render a contract void where that misrepresentation was
made with an intention that it should be acted upon by the person to whom it was made.[30]
The type of fraud required is that sufficient to found a claim in the tort of deceit, that is a
misrepresentation made knowingly, or without belief in its truth, or with recklessness as to
whether or not it was true.[31] At common law, an innocent misrepresentation will found a
claim provided that it has become a term of the contract. Section 1 of the Misrepresentation Act 1967 provides further that rescission will be available in cases of innocent misrepresentation in a situation in which that misrepresentation has induced the other party to enter into
the contract. Therefore, a party to a contract who had made an innocent misrepresentation
would give the other party to the contract a good defence to a claim for specific performance
of that contract.

26.4.4 Undue influence and unconscionable bargains

The problem of undue influence is considered in Chapter 29, particularly in relation to setting
aside mortgage contracts in situations in which the mortgagee had constructive notice of
some undue influence or misrepresentation having been exercised over a co-signatory by a
mortgagor to such a mortgage transaction. Furthermore, it was also considered that where
one party to a transaction exerts undue influence over the other party to that contract, the
victim of the undue influence will be entitled to have that contract rescinded.[32] Alongside

---

30 *Peek v Gurney* (1873) LR 6 HL 377.
31 *Derry v Peek* (1889) 14 App Cas 337.
32 *Barclays Bank v O'Brien* [1993] 3 WLR 786.

undue influence are the other categories of equitable wrongs and those issues which will be categorised as unconscionable bargains. Any such wrong would constitute a good defence to a claim for specific performance of that contract.

26.4.5 Mistake

In line with cases of misrepresentation, where there has been a mistake which has operated to induce a defendant to enter into a contract, it would be inequitable in many circumstances to entitle the claimant to enforce that contract against the defendant.

Aside from the instances considered above of actual fraud, misrepresentation and constructive fraud, it is possible that contracts will be rescinded in situations in which there is an operative mistake between both parties to a contract. Such rescission, again, will constitute a good defence to a claim for specific performance. The rule in relation to mistake is, strictly, that a mistake made by both parties (common mistake) in entering into a transaction will enable that contract to be rescinded.

However, where only one party to a contract is acting under a mistake (unilateral mistake), the contract, typically, will not be rescinded.[33] Where only one party is acting under a mistake it is not the case that the entire contract has been founded on a misconceived basis. Indeed, the limits of a rule which permitted unilateral mistake would be difficult to apply in all circumstances. There is a conceptual problem, however, as to what will constitute a mistake and what will constitute merely a lack of knowledge. Suppose a contract between two traders. Where one party to the investment contract knows that its approach will generate a greater income for it as a result of its superior research into the market, it could be argued that if the other party were acting under a mistake as to the profitability for it of the investment it is making, then the more knowledgeable party could be said to be exploiting the other party. It would be difficult to say that the party which loses money on its investment due to its failure to understand the market properly was acting under a legally actionable mistake. Consequently, it would be difficult to suggest that it should be entitled to rescission, whereas the other party ought to be entitled to specific performance of the contract to realise the profit which arose from its superior research and market knowledge. There would be, however, a fine line to be drawn between a situation in which the party making a profit is simply better informed and circumstances in which it takes advantage both of its own knowledge of the market and of its counterparty's comparative lack of knowledge. A little like the conjuror on the street corner who knows that the Queen of Spades playing card is concealed up his sleeve rather than on the table in front of his customer, the winning trader might be thought to be exploiting his counterparty. In the banking context specifically there is a regime of financial regulation which requires each financial institution to categorise its counterparties' expertise and to deal with them accordingly. This would mean that dealings at arm's length with another expert trader would prevent the losing trader from claiming it was operating under a mistake when it was suffering instead from a lack of market knowledge or experience. The situation would be different, however, if the trader had sold an inappropriate financial instrument to an elderly widow who had no knowledge of financial markets at all.

One significant development in this context is that which provides that parties are entitled to rely on a mistake of law in seeking to rescind their contracts, upheld by the House of

---

33 *Riverlate Properties Ltd v Paul* [1975] Ch 133.

Lords in *Kleinwort Benson v Lincoln CC*.[34] Whereas previously it was only possible to rely on a mistake of fact, as considered in the foregoing discussion, it is now possible to contend that one's mistake was a mistake as to the substance of the law at any particular time. This case considered the contention led by investment banks that the derivatives market had had a settled understanding that UK local authorities were capable of entering into interest rate swap contracts when it transpired subsequently that they were not. This mistake was one which could be used as a ground for restitution of moneys paid under such a void swap contract. The difficult issue, however, is whether or not, at a time before a court declares the law in any particular area (such as the capacities of local authorities), it is possible to say that there was a mistake at all, because arguably there is no law before a court delivers its opinion on a novel question.

Questions of equity and of restitution

Thus the issue of mistake feeds directly into questions of restitution, as well as into questions of specific performance. The question is as to the role of equity in this context. On the one hand, equity is applying age-old principles concerned with the rights of parties to enforce the full effect of their bargains. On the other hand, equity appears to be operating to prevent the unjust enrichment of one contracting party at the expense of the other party where there is some unjust factor (such as mistake or misrepresentation) involved in the generation of that enrichment.

26.4.6 Lapse of time

In common with other equitable remedies, a court of equity will require that the claimant seek to protect her rights with sufficient speed. The proper approach is to consider the subject matter of the contract and to decide on that basis whether or not specific enforcement of the contract has justly to be denied as a result of the parties' delay.[35] Thus, where a party fails to act under its rights under a rent review clause within reasonable time, it will be unable to require its landlord to carry out its obligations to demand only a lesser rent in the meantime.[36]

26.4.7 Damages in lieu of specific performance

Specific performance operates as an equitable remedy supporting the common law of contract. The interaction between those two systems of law is important in the understanding of specific performance. The context of the equitable remedy of injunctions is considered in Chapter 27, where the point is made that an injunction will not be awarded where a common law remedy would dispose adequately of the issues between the parties. This is a feature common to a number of the equitable remedies discussed in Part 9. It has already been considered that an equitable remedy will be made if no common law remedy would provide a suitable resolution to the dispute.

---

34 [1998] 4 All ER 513.
35 *Lazard Bros & Co Ltd v Fairfield Properties Co (Mayfair) Ltd* (1977) 121 SJ 793; *United Scientific Holdings Ltd v Burnley BC* [1978] AC 904.
36 *United Scientific Holdings Ltd v Burnley BC* [1978] AC 904.

However, there is also a long-standing power in the court to award damages either in tandem with, or in place of, the equitable remedies of injunction and specific performance. Section 50 of the Supreme Court Act 1981 provides that: 'Where the Court of Appeal or the High Court has jurisdiction to entertain an application for an injunction or specific performance, it may award damages in addition to, or in substitution for, an injunction or specific performance.' Therefore, the court has a statutory discretion to decide that on the facts in front of it, while specific performance might ordinarily be available, an award of cash damages would be a sufficient and suitable remedy for the harm which the applicant would suffer by reason of the respondent's failure to perform its specific obligations under the contract.

Chapter 27

Injunctions and confidences

OVERVIEW

The courts have a broad inherent jurisdiction to award injunctions in any circumstances, and the ability of the courts to award new forms of injunction continues to manifest itself in relation to freezing orders, search orders and super-injunctions. The power to award injunctions may also be granted by statute in particular circumstances but those statutory powers are beyond the scope of this chapter.

An injunction will be awarded either on an interim or a permanent basis, either in a mandatory or prohibitory form. It is necessary that no common law remedy would be sufficient in the circumstances; the applicant must come with clean hands; there must not have been delay on the applicant's part; some right of the applicant must be affected; and the respondent must not suffer undue harm as a result of the injunction.

Injunctions divide between those which require some action from the respondent (mandatory injunctions), those which require the respondent to refrain from some action (prohibitory injunctions), and those which seek to prevent some action which it is feared may be performed in the future.

Interim (formerly interlocutory) injunctions are awarded on an interim basis during litigation. Their award is based on a balance of convenience between the potential harm suffered by the applicant if no injunction were awarded, and the potential inconvenience caused to the respondent if the injunction were to be awarded. The universal application of this approach has been doubted in some more recent cases. The applicant must therefore demonstrate a strong, prima facie *case.*

Freezing injunctions are awarded to prevent the respondent from removing assets from the English jurisdiction before the completion of litigation to avoid settlement of a final judgment. The applicant is required to demonstrate three things: a good arguable case; that there are assets within the jurisdiction; and that there is a real risk of the dissipation of those assets which would otherwise make final judgment nugatory.

The search order is a form of injunction which entitles the applicant to seize the defendant's property to protect evidence in relation to any future litigation. The order will be made on the satisfaction of three criteria: there must be an extremely strong prima facie *case; the potential or actual damage must be very serious for the applicant; and there must be clear evidence that the defendants have in their possession incriminating documents or things with a real possibility that they may destroy such material before an application could be made to the court.*

An injunction will not be ordered in circumstances in which damages would be sufficient remedy.

The equitable doctrine of confidence has an ancient pedigree. Since at least the 17th century English courts have had the power to award injunctions to prevent 'breaches of trust, confidences and contract'. While this appears to be a general jurisdiction to award injunctions on an interim or permanent basis, there are particular contexts in which such injunctions have been awarded: to protect property rights, including the protection of intellectual property rights; in cases of husband and wife; to protect private, confidential information; to protect breaches of contract; and generally to protect 'secrets' in the old language. In recent years, this equitable doctrine has been superseded by the tort of misuse of private information and the freedom of speech and protection of privacy provisions of the Human Rights Act, but the equitable doctrine still subsists in rude health in the other contexts.

The power of the court to award super-injunctions has been particularly newsworthy in recent years. A 'super-injunction' is an injunction which prevents the reporting of legal proceedings and also the reporting of the existence of such an injunction; whereas an 'anonymised injunction' prevents the reporting of the identity of any of the parties or any information which would enable their identities to become known. Anonymised injunctions are used broadly in family law and criminal law cases, and latterly their use in privacy cases has increased. A super-injunction is ordinarily ordered on the basis of a balancing act between the need for open justice and freedom of speech on the one hand, and the need to respect the privacy of litigants on the other.

27.1 NATURE OF INJUNCTIONS

An injunction will be awarded either on an interim (formerly interlocutory) or a permanent basis, either in a mandatory or prohibitory form. It is necessary that no common law remedy would be sufficient in the circumstances; the applicant must come with clean hands; there must not have been delay on the applicant's part; some right of the applicant must be affected; and the respondent must not suffer undue harm as a result of the injunction.

27.1.1 Introduction

This chapter considers the equitable remedy of injunctions. The first half of this chapter is concerned with the general principles governing the award of various types of injunction before trial (so-called 'interim injunctions') and injunctions awarded after trial (so-called 'permanent injunctions'). The second half of this chapter then focuses in detail on the equitable doctrine of confidence (which is ordinarily supported by the award of an injunction) and its role in the particular context of 'super-injunctions', which are a form of interim injunction which have become particularly important and been particularly newsworthy in the period running from 2010 through 2012.

27.1.2 The breadth of the power of the courts to grant injunctions

The injunction is an equitable remedy. It is at the discretion of the court to make an order to either party to litigation, or by way of a final judgment, to take some action or to refrain from some action. The broadest discretion of the court is required at this point. Injunctions can be used in a broad range of factual situations, from family law disputes to commercial litigation. Sometimes the injunction forms a part of the relief sought by one or other of the parties in parallel to claims for damages and other remedies, whereas at other times the injunction is the sole remedy required by the claimant. Section 37(1) of the Supreme Court Act 1981 provides that:

> The High Court may by order (whether interlocutory or final) grant an injunction . . . in all cases in which it appears to the court to be just and convenient to do so.

As Spry has pointed out,[1] the court's jurisdiction towards injunctions operates 'without limits, and can be exercised either in support of any legal right, or in the creation of a new equitable right, as the court thinks fits in the application of equitable principles'.[2] Lord Nicholls set out the breadth of the power of the courts to grant injunctions in the following terms in the House of Lords in *Mercedes Benz AG v Leiduck* to the effect that:

> the jurisdiction to grant an injunction, unfettered by statute, should not be rigidly confined to exclusive categories by judicial decision. The court may grant an injunction against a party properly before it where this is required to avoid injustice . . . The court habitually grants injunctions in respect of certain types of conduct. But that does not mean that the situations in which injunctions may be granted are now set in stone for all time. . . . The exercise of the jurisdiction must be principled, but the criterion is injustice. Injustice is to be viewed and decided in the light of today's conditions and standards, not those of yester-year.[3]

Therefore, under statute and further to that decision of the House of Lords, the courts have a very broad, inherent power to grant injunctions in any sort of case in the interests of avoiding injustice. Nevertheless, as will emerge from the discussion in this chapter, the courts have tended to develop strict principles governing the situations in which injunctions will be awarded in certain types of case (for example, interim injunctions granted before a full trial is held). Rather than strict rules governing the grant of injunctions, these will tend to be broad principles to which the court will ordinarily be expected to have regard when awarding injunctions in particular types of case. Therefore, in practice it will be important to bear in mind the criteria which the courts are required to take into account when deciding whether or not to grant an injunction, and the precise terms of the injunction. The court will be required to take into account specified types of factors before addressing the precise circumstances of the parties and the most suitable means for resolving the issues between them. The verb which runs with the expression 'the grant of an injunction' is 'to enjoin': thus a court enjoins a person from continuing with an action.

27.1.3 Distinguishing injunctions from common law remedies

It is important to underline the role of the equitable remedy of injunction as a remedy which will be applied only where the common law will not achieve justice between the parties. Frequently there will be a fine line between granting a common law remedy and providing an injunction.

---

1 Spry, *Principles of Equitable Remedies*, 8th edn, Sweet & Maxwell, 2010, 331.
2 *Ibid.*
3 [1996] AC 284, at 308.

A most useful case on final injunctions generally is the decision of the Court of Appeal in *Jaggard v Sawyer*.[4] The facts revolved around restrictive covenants effected between freeholders of land in a residential, cul-de-sac development. The covenants prevented the freeholders from using any undeveloped land adjoining their plots, or made part of their plots, for any purpose other than as domestic gardens. The respondent acquired a plot neighbouring his land and, operating under some misapprehension as to the status of the land, built an access road across it to his house. A neighbour, the applicant, sought an injunction to prevent the respondent from maintaining this road, on the basis that it was in breach of covenant and that it required the respondent to trespass on the applicant's land. The applicant had commenced, but not pursued, proceedings when the development started but had sought injunctive relief once the development had been completed. The issues arose, *inter alia*, as to whether the applicant ought to be entitled to the injunctive relief sought and whether in fact damages would have been a sufficient remedy.

In giving his judgment, Sir Thomas Bingham MR considered the four probanda relevant for the grant of an injunction as set out in *Shelfer v City of London Electric Lighting Co*.[5] There are four requirements which must be satisfied before a court will award damages instead of an injunction in circumstances where an injunction might otherwise be awarded:

(a) the harm suffered by the applicant must have been comparatively slight;
(b) the harm suffered must be capable of being quantified in financial terms;
(c) the harm suffered must be such that it can be compensated adequately by payment of damages; and
(d) it must have been oppressive to the respondent to have granted the injunction sought.[6]

Millett LJ considered the question whether damages for the tort of trespass (common law) ought to be held sufficient such that there would be no requirement for an award of an injunction. He held that 'the common law remedy of damages in cases of continuing trespass is inadequate not because the damages are likely to be small or nominal but because they cover the past only and not the future'. Therefore, it is possible to contend that, where there is the likelihood of future harm if the respondent is not enjoined from continuing past behaviour, an injunction will necessarily be a valid adjunct to common law damages. This argument proceeds on the basis that common law damages will remedy the applicant's loss for the past, whereas an injunction will provide a remedy for what would otherwise be future loss. The two can validly run together without doing violence to the underlying rationale of either remedy.

In the alternative, his Lordship did recognise that this principle would not apply in all cases. While the main rule is that equity and the common law should seek to provide remedies in parallel, Millett LJ did acknowledge the utility of an award of damages to guard against potential future loss when he held that a court 'can in my judgment properly award damages "once and for all" in respect of future wrongs because it awards them in substitution for an injunction and to compensate for those future wrongs which an injunction would have prevented'.

4 [1995] 1 WLR 269, [1995] 2 All ER 189.
5 [1895] 1 Ch 287.
6 *Ibid, per* AL Smith LJ.

There is also a further issue which arises from Millett LJ's judgment in *Jaggard v Sawyer*[7] which refers to the nature of an injunction and damages as being either compensatory or restitutionary. If these remedies are to be compensatory, that would require measuring the loss suffered by the applicant and providing for a remedy which adequately compensates the applicant for her loss. Alternatively, a restitutionary remedy is concerned to take from the respondent the gain which the respondent has made by passing that gain to the applicant. Therefore, the restitutionary remedy would not necessarily require a calculation of the loss suffered by the applicant, but would instead be concerned to take from the respondent the gain made at the applicant's expense.[8]

27.1.4 General equitable principles governing injunctions

Injunctions are important for two reasons in the general argument of this book. First, injunctions are a particularly significant remedy in almost all areas of law and therefore require special attention. Secondly, injunctions demonstrate the application of some central equitable principles, as discussed in Chapter 1.

Damages, or other common law remedies, must not be an adequate remedy

One of the core equitable principles appropriate to awards of injunctions is that it must not be sufficient to provide a remedy for the applicant that the respondent make a payment of cash damages, or settle the matter satisfactorily by application of some other common law remedy.[9] This harks back to the role of equity as a code of principle which existed to shore up shortcomings in the common law in achieving justice between the parties. Therefore, while equity will take priority over common law, it is important to establish first that common law will not adequately dispose of the matter. However, where the court feels that, while damages are available, they would not be an adequate remedy, an equitable remedy (such as an injunction) will be awarded.[10]

The applicant must come to equity with clean hands

This venerable equitable principle finds its echo in Lord Browne-Wilkinson's explanation of the trust relationship as being built on the conscience of the trustee in dealing with the trust property.[11] It is a key part of any equitable remedy that the applicant is not seeking that remedy to advance some inequitable purpose.[12]

The applicant must not delay in seeking the remedy

The injunction is generally a remedy which seeks to remove immediate risk of harm from the applicant. Therefore, it is said that the applicant ought to lose that right where the

---

7 [1995] 1 WLR 269, [1995] 2 All ER 189.
8 This issue is considered in section 31.3.
9 *London and Blackwall Railway Co v Cross* (1886) 31 Ch D 354.
10 *Beswick v Beswick* [1968] AC 58.
11 *Westdeutsche Landesbank Girozentrale v Islington LBC* [1996] AC 669.
12 *Tinsley v Milligan* [1994] 1 AC 340, *per* Lord Goff.

applicant has delayed unreasonably in seeking the remedy. As Millett LJ held in *Jaggard v Sawyer*: 'If the applicant delays proceedings until it is no longer possible for him to obtain an injunction, he destroys his own bargaining position and devalues his right.'[13] As considered in Chapter 1, avoiding delay is one of the core equitable principles.[14] Delay will typically be taken as a sign of acquiescence in the actions of the defendant and thus disqualify the claimant from obtaining an injunction[15] and from damages in connection with any such injunction.[16]

Equity will not act in vain

Where it is impossible to undo the harm done to the applicant by the respondent, the court will not make an order for an injunction, on the basis that such an order would achieve nothing. Therefore, the applicant will be required to demonstrate that he stands to suffer some substantial harm which outweighs the harm which would be caused to the respondent by the award of the injunction. However, as a corollary to that, the injunction must contribute to the avoidance of some measure of harm to the applicant and will not be awarded simply because harm may be suffered, as considered below.

Some right of the applicant must be affected

This principle harks back to the notion of *locus standi*: that an applicant cannot sue on an issue unless that applicant has some right which is affected by the suit. While the point is made above that s 37(1) of the Supreme Court Act 1981 provides that the courts have the power to 'grant an injunction . . . in all cases in which it appears to the court to be just and convenient to do so', there is nevertheless a restriction placed on the seeming generality of that principle by the common law to the effect that the applicant for the injunction must show some effect on a right which it holds. Therefore, in *Paton v British Pregnancy Advisory Service Trustees*,[17] it was held by Sir George Baker P that 'the first and basic principle is that there must be a legal right enforceable in law or in equity before the applicant can obtain an injunction from the court to restrain an infringement of that right'. In line with the principle that equity will not act in vain, considered immediately above, is an extension that the applicant must not only suffer harm but similarly must have some legal right affected. Therefore, the injunction is required, at root, to support some existing right of the applicant and will not be awarded generally to prevent harm in the abstract.

The injunction must not cause undue hardship to the respondent

As will be seen in relation to the specific forms of injunction considered below, it is important that the court be convinced that the grant of the injunction will not cause disproportionate hardship to the respondent. The issue for the court will typically be resolved in a comparison of the comparative hardship to the applicant if the injunction is not granted, and

---

13   [1995] 1 WLR 269, [1995] 2 All ER 189.
14   *Gafford v Graham* [1999] 41 EG 157.
15   *Ibid*.
16   *Ibid*.
17   [1979] QB 276.

the likely hardship to the respondent if the injunction is granted. In *Jaggard v Sawyer*,[18] Sir Thomas Bingham MR pointed out that 'the test is one of oppression, and the court should not slide into the application of a general balance of convenience test'. Furthermore, the material time which the court must consider in deciding whether or not that oppression exists is at the time the court is asked to consider whether or not to grant an injunction.

27.2   CLASSIFICATION OF INJUNCTIONS

Injunctions divide between those which require some action from the respondent (mandatory injunctions), those which require the respondent to refrain from some action (prohibitory injunctions), and those which seek to prevent some action which it is feared may be performed in the future.

There is a need to distinguish between the various types of injunctions. As mentioned above, the power of the court to grant an injunction is broad-ranging, and therefore it is important to be able to classify how different types of injunction might operate.

27.2.1 Mandatory injunctions

The mandatory injunction requires that the defendant take some action. For example, where a defendant's negligence has caused water to leak onto another person's property, the court may seek to order that defendant to take some action which will stop the water leakage. One means of doing this would be by way of mandatory injunction to require the defendant to take action to mend the leak, as well as other actions in respect of damages and so forth. There is a degree of overlap between the mandatory injunction and specific performance (considered in the previous chapter), in that both obligations may seek to force the defendant to perform an action. Specific performance refers specifically to contractual obligations, whereas a mandatory injunction has broader application outside specific performance and gives the court greater leeway to impose conditions on its performance.

27.2.2 Prohibitory injunctions

The prohibitory injunction requires the defendant to refrain from an action. For example, injunctions may be issued in the family law context to prevent person A from passing within a given radius of person B's home. Alternatively, where the defendant's negligent use of land is causing water to leak onto another person's land, the court may make an order by way of prohibitory injunction to require the defendant to stop the activity which is causing water to escape onto the other person's land.

27.2.3 Injunctions *quia timet*

A *quia timet* injunction is one which is ordered to protect the applicant from an action which it is feared may be committed in the future, on the basis that some right of the applicant will otherwise be infringed.[19] Literally, the term '*quia timet*' means 'he who fears', that is, he

---

18 [1995] 1 WLR 269, [1995] 2 All ER 189.
19 *Redland Bricks Ltd v Morris* [1970] AC 652.

who fears that he will suffer some harm. Clearly, this category of injunction stands out from the general principles of equity above which required that there be some right of the applicant affected. The *quia timet* injunction does not require that some right of the applicant has been affected, only that there is a risk of its being affected. Therefore, the grant of this type of injunction is typically limited to situations in which there is a real risk of detriment to the applicant. As Lord Buckmaster held in *Graigola Merthyr Co Ltd v Swansea Corp*,[20] 'a mere vague apprehension is not sufficient to support an action for a *quia timet* injunction. There must be an immediate threat to do something'.

It must be demonstrated that the respondent intends to, or is likely to, participate in the act complained of. Where the respondent demonstrates a disinclination to participate in the action then the injunction will not be granted.[21]

27.3 INTERIM INJUNCTIONS

Interim injunctions (formerly interlocutory injunctions) are awarded on an interim basis during litigation. Their award is based on a balance of convenience between the potential harm suffered by the applicant if no injunction were awarded, and the potential inconvenience caused to the respondent if the injunction were to be awarded. The universal application of this approach has been doubted in some more recent cases. The applicant must therefore demonstrate a strong, prima facie *case.*

27.3.1 Introduction

The interim injunction is an injunction made during litigation, which is binding on the parties only up to the date of final judgment. This is opposed to the permanent injunctions considered immediately above, which are binding on the parties from the date of judgment in perpetuity (or until the judge expresses them to expire, or until a successful appeal against the injunction).

Consider the following example:

Suppose that Ben, a member of a class of beneficiaries under a discretionary trust, has commenced litigation against T, the trustee of that trust, claiming that T had breached the terms of the trust by deciding to pay trust income to other beneficiaries and wind up the trust. Ben will therefore be seeking a declaration that the payments would be in breach of trust. However, in the meantime, Ben will want to ensure that T does not make those payments before the completion of the litigation. Therefore, Ben will seek an injunction against T which will prevent T making any such payments before the litigation is completed. Such an injunction, binding only up to the date of judgment, would be an interim injunction.

Clearly, the court has subtly different issues at stake here from the final injunctions considered above. In relation to a final injunction, the court will have heard full evidence from all relevant parties and will have conducted a full trial of all relevant issues. In that context, the

---

20 [1929] AC 344, 353.
21 *Celsteel Ltd v Alton House Holdings Ltd* [1986] 1 WLR 512.

court is able to reach an informed decision on the most suitable means for disposing of the differences between the parties. In the case of an interim injunction, there will not have been a trial of the issues between the parties. Therefore, the court will not have had the opportunity to form an opinion on the merits of the case. To award an injunction in favour of one party (the applicant) will prevent the other party (the respondent) from acting as they otherwise would. It is possible that the respondent would win the trial and therefore would have suffered detriment for the period of the injunction. However, if the respondent were permitted to continue to act freely, and then lost at trial, this might cause even greater loss to the applicant.

Therefore, in the example given above, if the court ultimately held that Ben was correct in his interpretation of the trust, it would have been unjust to deny an injunction to prevent the trustee from paying the money away. However, in the opposite scenario, if T was held to have been correct, then it would have been to the detriment of the other beneficiaries if the injunction had been granted in favour of Ben such that no money was paid out until final judgment.

27.3.2 The core test – 'balance of convenience'

The classic test for the availability of an interim injunction was contained in *American Cyanamid v Ethicon Ltd.*[22] In the words of Lord Diplock, 'The court must weigh one need against another and determine where "the balance of convenience" lies.' Therefore, in considering the mutual benefits and burdens that may result from the award of an interim injunction, the court is required to consider, in all the circumstances, whether it would be more convenient on balance to award or deny the award.

There are four elements to the test:

(a) that the balance of convenience indicates the grant of an award;
(b) *semble*, that the applicant can demonstrate a good *prima facie* case;
(c) that there is a serious question to be resolved at trial; and
(c) that there is an undertaking for damages in the event that the applicant does not succeed at trial.

The need for a strong, prima facie *case*

Lord Diplock also indicated the importance of the applicant showing not only a likelihood of suffering loss if the injunction is not granted, but also a likelihood that the applicant would succeed at full trial:

> To justify the grant of such [an interim injunction] the applicant must satisfy the court first that there is a strong *prima facie* case that he will be entitled to a final order restraining the defendant from doing what he is threatening to do, and secondly that he will suffer irreparable injury which cannot be compensated by a subsequent award of damages in the action if the defendant is not prevented from doing it between the date of the application for the [interim] injunction and the date of the final order made on trial of the action.[23]

22 [1975] AC 396, [1975] 1 All ER 504.
23 [1975] AC 295, 360.

However, his Lordship also pointed out that it is impossible for the court at an interim stage to reach a firm conclusion as to the merits of the case.[24] Therefore, the requirement to show a *prima facie* case will always stop short of requiring the applicant to go as far as proving the entire case. The court will, however, consider the relative strength of each party's case as it appears from affidavits deposed by each party's witnesses.[25] These approaches appear to be difficult to reconcile. The explanation proffered by Laddie J[26] is that Lord Diplock must have required the court to consider the comparative strengths of the parties' cases but without needing to resolve any difficult issues of fact or law. His Lordship's conviction is that, in most cases, it will be apparent which party is more likely to win at trial.

Is the balance of convenience test applicable in all circumstances?

However, subsequent cases have cast doubt on the breadth of the applicability of *American Cyanamid*.[27] In *Cambridge Nutrition Ltd v British Broadcasting Association*,[28] in a dissenting judgment, Kerr LJ held that the *American Cyanamid* principle is not a principle of universal application. This is in spite of the approach which was adopted by Lord Diplock which suggested that *American Cyanamid* was proposing a principle of universal application. The reason why *Cambridge Nutrition* was considered to operate on a different footing was that the interlocutory injunction sought, to prevent the transmission of a current affairs television programme, would have been equivalent to the award of a final injunction, not an interim injunction, in those circumstances. It was in the nature of this particular programme that to prevent its transmission at that time would effectively mean that the programme could never have been shown. Therefore, Kerr LJ held that this application for interlocutory relief was different in character to *American Cyanamid* because it would dispose of the matter without the need for a full trial. The majority of the Court of Appeal continued to follow *American Cyanamid*.

27.3.3 Relationship with common law remedies

As with final injunctions, where the applicant would be adequately compensated by an award of damages the injunction will not be granted. So, if the applicant would suffer only financial loss up to the date of trial, the court will typically not award an interim injunction. The issue which arises, then, is as to the solvency of the respondent. It is all very well to say, 'let's not award an interim injunction because damages would be a sufficient remedy' if the respondent would not be able to pay the damages owed to the applicant. It is thus common practice to require an undertaking as to the ability to pay damages. Alternatively, if the applicant is granted an interim injunction but does not subsequently win at trial, the respondent may well be entitled to damages. In such circumstances, the respondent will also require an undertaking as to ability to pay damages from the applicant. The court will typically require that such undertakings are made, and that an ability to pay damages is demonstrated.

24 Cf *Hoffmann La Roche & Co v Secretary of State for Trade and Industry* [1973] AC 295; *Evans Marshall & Co Ltd v Bertola SA* [1973] 1 WLR 349.
25 *Series 5 Software v Clarke* [1996] 1 All ER 853, *per* Laddie J.
26 *Ibid.*
27 [1975] AC 396, [1975] 1 All ER 504.
28 [1990] 3 All ER 523.

27.4 FREEZING INJUNCTIONS

Freezing injunctions are awarded to prevent the respondent from removing assets from the English jurisdiction before the completion of litigation to avoid settlement of a final judgment. The applicant is required to demonstrate three things: a good arguable case; that there are assets within the jurisdiction; and that there is a real risk of the dissipation of those assets which would otherwise make final judgment nugatory.

27.4.1 Introduction

The freezing injunction was formerly known as the 'Mareva injunction' on account of the case in which it first appeared.[29] This form of equitable relief has developed into one of the most powerful tools in the armoury of private international litigation. The risk addressed specifically by the freezing injunction is that a defendant in litigation will remove all of its assets from England and Wales, so that it will be impossible for the applicant to find any assets within the jurisdiction against which it could enforce the final judgment.

See the following example:

Suppose that A, a Venezuelan art dealer, had sold a painting, which A represented was an original version of Dali's 'Girl at a Window', to B, an English company, for £3 million. In the event it turns out that the painting is a fraud and was painted by an art student from Bermondsey. Although a good likeness, it is worth only £5,000. Assuming the art student to have no money, B would sue A for repayment of the £3 million on grounds of breach of warranty and fraud. The risk is that A will remove all of her assets from the jurisdiction by emptying her English bank accounts and selling all other property held in England. The remedy which B will want up to the date of judgment, and until judgment is satisfied, is an injunction preventing A from removing any assets from the jurisdiction. In effect, all A's assets would be frozen. This would be a freezing injunction.

The dilemma for the court is the same as in relation to any interim injunction. There is a risk of prejudice to A if it transpires that A was not guilty of fraud or misrepresentation. Alternatively, B's judgment will be useless where A has no assets against which the judgment for £3 million could be enforced.

Given the risk of the defendant removing property from the jurisdiction before the court order is made, the hearing is usually held *ex parte* (that is, without the defendant being present). This enables the applicant to bind the defendant before the defendant can spirit assets out of the reach of the courts: a jurisdiction which may be used by the police or the Serious Fraud Office as well as by private parties to litigation.[30]

27.4.2 The nature of the freezing injunction

The potentially very broad ambit of the freezing injunction has been limited by the courts. As Kerr LJ held in *Z Ltd v A–Z*:[31]

---

29 *Mareva Compania Naviera SA v International Bulk Carriers SA* [1975] 2 Lloyd's Rep 509. It is now referred to as an 'asset freezing order' in the reforms to the Rules of the Supreme Court.
30 *Bank of Scotland v A Ltd* [2001] All ER (D) 81.
31 [1982] QB 558, 585.

Mareva injunctions should be granted . . . when it appears to the court that there is a combination of two circumstances. First, when it appears likely that the applicant will recover judgment against the defendant for a certain or approximate sum. Secondly, when there are also reasons to believe that the defendant has assets within the jurisdiction to meet the judgment, in whole or in part, but may well take steps designed to ensure that these are no longer available or traceable when judgment is given against him.

Therefore the applicant must prove a combination of a likelihood of success at trial, akin to search (or *Anton Piller*) orders,[32] and that the defendant has some assets within the jurisdiction of the court to meet that judgment. However, a freezing injunction will not be awarded where such an injunction would displace remedies which might be ordered at full trial of the issue.[33] There is consequently a 'high duty' to be borne by the lawyers for the applicant on the basis that these injunctions are being sought on an *ex parte* basis without the other side being notified.[34] The lawyers are required to ensure that any unusual features are brought to the court's attention and to ensure that there is a 'full, fair and accurate disclosure of material information to the court'.[35]

27.4.3 The core test

There are three requirements for the grant of a freezing injunction:

(a) that the applicant has a good case;
(b) that the applicant has satisfied the court that there are assets within the jurisdiction; and
(c) that there is a real risk of dissipation or secretion of those assets which would make a judgment nugatory.[36]

The freezing injunction requires that there is 'a good arguable case'. This requires the applicant to declare all matters relevant to the applicant's claim to the court, so that a rational decision can be made by the court.[37] The test differs from the standard test for interim injunctions precisely because of the effect which a freezing injunction will have on the defendant in circumstances in which the defendant is typically not present in court at the original application. A 'good, arguable case' connotes a higher standard than merely a '*prima facie* case'. This is a particularly important element of the application process given that the hearing is usually *ex parte*, and the court requires some evidence that the applicant is likely to succeed at trial. If the applicant is subsequently shown to have withheld important information from the court, the freezing injunction will generally be discharged.[38]

---

32 Considered below at section 27.5.
33 *Derby & Co v Weldon (Nos 3 and 4)* [1990] Ch 65, 76.
34 *Memory Corporation Plc v Sidhu (No 2)* [2000] 1 WLR 1443, 1460, *per* Mummery LJ.
35 *Ibid.*
36 *Re BCCI SA (No 9)* [1994] 3 All ER 764; *Derby & Co v Weldon (Nos 3 and 4)* [1990] Ch 65. See now *JSC BTA Bank v Solodchenko* [2010] EWCA Civ 1436, [2011] 1 WLR 888.
37 *Third Chandris Shipping Corp v Unimarine SA* [1979] QB 645; *Memory Corporation Plc v Sidhu (No 2)* [2000] 1 WLR 1443.
38 *Ali & Fahd v Moneim* [1989] 2 All ER 404; *Dubai Bank Ltd v Galadari* [1990] 1 Lloyd's Rep 120.

The applicant is also required to give an undertaking in damages to the effect that, if the applicant is unsuccessful at trial, the applicant will be able to compensate the defendant adequately.[39] This is an undertaking made to the court, rather than to the defendant (given the *ex parte* nature of the procedure).[40]

27.4.4 The requirement of commencement of substantive proceedings

A freezing injunction will be ordered whether or not substantive proceedings to which it relates have already been instituted.[41] The traditional view was that a Mareva injunction was an interlocutory order which is awarded only to keep assets which are the subject of main proceedings within the reach of the claimant, assuming the test set out in the preceding section is satisfied. Therefore, an applicant could not be awarded a freezing order in the abstract without bringing substantive proceedings at the same time. By contrast, cases involving anti-suit injunctions had suggested that injunctions might nevertheless be awarded in general terms in situations in which 'it is appropriate to avoid injustice', on the basis more generally that 'the width and flexibility of equity are not to be undermined by categorization'.[42] This broader basis for injunctions was predicated on the applicant demonstrating either that the respondent has invaded or threatens to invade a legal or equitable right of the applicant, or that the respondent has behaved or threatened to behave unconscionably.[43] Therefore, a freezing order may be made either once proceedings have been served or before substantive proceedings have been instituted.[44] Nevertheless, the court will not make an order for a freezing injunction if it would place a greater burden on the respondent than would be just and convenient.[45] The present position is set out by the House of Lords in *Fourie v Le Roux*.[46]

The applicant before the House of Lords in *Fourie v Le Roux*[47] was involved in litigation concerning the respondent individuals and companies in South Africa. Through various forms of deception, assets against which the applicant might have brought a claim had been moved to England. The applicant therefore sought a freezing order over those assets in England. The basis on which the order was resisted was that the applicant had not yet brought any substantive proceedings against the respondents and therefore that the court had no jurisdiction to make a freezing order. Lord Scott held that the trial judge had had jurisdiction to make an order in the strict sense that the assets and the parties were properly parties before an English court. The issue remained whether or not the jurisdiction of the court specifically to make freezing orders was dependent upon the issue of substantive proceedings which were being protected by the freezing order.

---

39 *Third Chandris Shipping Corp v Unimarine SA* [1979] QB 645.
40 *Balkanbank v Taher* [1994] 4 All ER 239.
41 *The Siskina* [1979] AC 210; *Channel Tunnel Group Ltd v Balfour Beatty Construction Ltd* [1993] AC 334.
42 *Castanho v Brown & Root (UK) Ltd* [1981] AC 557, 573, *per* Lord Scarman.
43 *South Carolina Insurance Co v Assurantie NV* [1987] 1 AC 24, 40, *per* Lord Brandon.
44 *Fourie v Le Roux* [2007] UKHL 1, [32], *per* Lord Scott.
45 *Ibid.*
46 [2007] UKHL 1.
47 *Ibid.*

27.4.5 The worldwide freezing injunction

Extraordinarily, the English courts have decided that, in some circumstances, they have the jurisdiction to grant freezing injunctions over assets held outside England and Wales: the so-called worldwide freezing injunction. The power is said to arise further to s 37(1) of the Supreme Court Act 1981 and to obtain in the event that the defendant is properly before the court.[48] In *Derby v Weldon*,[49] the Court of Appeal was of the view that the defendants were a corporation with sufficient know-how to put assets beyond the reach of the applicant even if the applicant was successful at trial. Therefore, the Court of Appeal held, exceptionally, that the freeze on the defendants' assets would be required to be global in scope for the applicant to be certain of receiving adequate compensation in the event of success at trial.

In one of the cases arising out of the BCCI collapse, Rattee J awarded a worldwide freezing injunction on the basis that, in the context of 'the complex international nature of the financial dealings' concerned in a case in which neither respondent was resident in England and Wales, it was necessary to make the injunction similarly international.[50] In a comparative relaxation of the principle, the Court of Appeal in *Credit Suisse Fides Trust v Cuoghi*[51] held that the worldwide freezing injunction can be granted in circumstances in which 'it would be expedient', rather than being limited to a situation in which exceptional circumstances justify the order. However, it remains the case that the applicant is required to demonstrate a likelihood of assets being put beyond its reach in circumstances in which the respondent is both able and likely to act in that way. Many of the cases in which the injunction has been granted with worldwide effect have therefore involved financial institutions for which movements of assets around the world are logistically comparatively straightforward.

Evidently, this extension of the principle constitutes a large expansion of the accepted jurisdiction of the English courts, with the possibility of particularly onerous results for the respondents. One of the particular features of this form of litigation is the risk of a proliferation of proceedings in a number of jurisdictions where assets are held. Clearly, the respondent will wish to be able to continue to dispose of and to use assets held in jurisdictions outside England and Wales. While this raises questions of conflict of laws outside the scope of this book, there are consequences for the conduct of litigation under the freezing injunction. For example, the undertaking required from the applicant will be comparatively onerous, and may extend to an undertaking not to commence parallel proceedings in other jurisdictions.[52]

27.5 SEARCH ORDERS

The search (formerly Anton Piller*) order is a form of injunction which entitles the applicant to seize the defendant's property to protect evidence in relation to any future litigation. The order will be made on the satisfaction of three criteria: there must be an extremely strong* prima facie *case; the potential or actual damage must be very serious for the applicant; and there must be clear evidence that the defendants have in their*

---

48   *Derby & Co Ltd v Weldon (Nos 3 and 4)* [1990] Ch 65, 93, *per* Neill LJ.
49   *Ibid.*
50   *Re Bank of Credit and Commerce International SA (No 9)* [1994] 3 All ER 764.
51   [1997] 3 All ER 724.
52   *Practice Direction* [1994] 4 All ER 52.

*possession incriminating documents or things with a real possibility that they may
destroy such material before an application could be made to the court.*

27.5.1 Introduction

A further weapon in the litigator's arsenal is the search order, which entitles the successful
applicant to seize property belonging to the defendant to protect evidence for any future trial.
It is this legal procedure which most resembles an episode of the 1970s television programme
The Sweeney, in which lawyers and hired hands appear at the defendant's premises in the
early morning, brandishing copies of the court order, and proceed to impound property or,
more likely, to load it onto vans to take it away to secure storage.

Typically the order will be obtained *ex parte* (without the defendant being aware of the
hearing) to enable the applicant to exercise it before the defendant realises the risk of having
property seized.[53] In many cases, a freezing injunction and a search order are obtained at
once in respect of the same defendant and over the same property: a case of 'freeze' and
'seize'. See the following example:

> *Suppose that Supplier has sold electronic components to Techno Ltd under contract,
> taking proprietary rights in specified computers manufactured by Techno Ltd. At the
> relevant time, Supplier is owed £100,000. Supplier will sue Techno Ltd for payment
> under specific performance or breach of contract. However, Supplier may have a genuine
> concern that Techno Ltd is about to destroy evidence of their contract or deny that the
> identifiable electronic components were ever delivered to Techno Ltd by destroying them.
> Supplier may then seek a court order permitting it to seize electronic components used by
> Techno Ltd to manufacture computers to ensure that it will be able to enforce its propri-
> etary rights over the computers. Such an order would be a search order.*

The courts became worried that search orders were being granted too readily. Recent decisions have emphasised that such an order ought to be a remedy of last resort given that the
impact on the respondent is potentially enormous. In *Anton Piller KG v Manufacturing
Processes Ltd*,[54] Lord Denning MR held that such an order should be made 'only in an
extreme case where there is grave danger of property being smuggled away or of vital
evidence being destroyed'.

27.5.2 The requirements for grant of a search order

The core test is set out most clearly in the original case of *Anton Piller KG v Manufacturing
Processes Ltd* by Ormrod LJ:

> There are three essential pre-conditions for the making of such an order . . . First, there
> must be an extremely strong *prima facie* case. Secondly, the damage, potential or actual,
> must be very serious for the applicant. Thirdly, there must be clear evidence that the
> defendants have in their possession incriminating documents or things, and that there is

---

53 *Universal Thermosensors Ltd v Hibben* [1992] 3 All ER 257. See also *Emmanuel v Emmanuel* [1982] 1 WLR
   669; *Burgess v Burgess* [1996] 2 FLR 34: injunction awarded to prevent destruction of evidence.
54 [1976] Ch 55, 61.

a real possibility that they may destroy such material before any application *inter partes* can be made.[55]

A decision of Hoffmann J in *Lock plc v Beswick*[56] emphasised that this three-point test must still be applied but that it is not to be assumed to be the case that a person in possession of evidence will necessarily seek to destroy that evidence. In many circumstances it may be appropriate to make an interim order in the usual way, requiring delivery of that evidence to the other side's solicitors in the usual way. The search order should not be made where there is insufficient evidence to constitute a strong *prima facie* case.[57]

27.6 INTERACTION WITH THE COMMON LAW

An injunction will not be ordered in circumstances in which damages would be suffi-cient remedy.

Some other issues arise peripherally to the question of obtaining an injunction. First, in what circumstances will a court decide that it would be preferable to award damages rather than an injunction; and, secondly, in what circumstances will there be difficulties in enforcing the injunction?

27.6.1 Damages in lieu of injunction

It has been considered already that an injunction will not be awarded where a common law remedy would dispose adequately of the issues between the parties. However, there is also a long-standing power in the court to award damages either in tandem with, or in place of, the equitable remedies of injunction and specific performance. Section 50 of the Supreme Court Act 1981 provides that: 'Where the Court of Appeal or the High Court has jurisdiction to entertain an application for an injunction or specific performance, it may award damages in addition to, or in substitution for, an injunction or specific performance.' *Jaggard v Sawyer*,[58] considered above, discussed the common law relating to this principle, which had formerly been contained in Lord Cairns' Act.[59]

The common law permits awards of damages in two contexts, in the application of the statutory discretion. The first category of awarding damages is as a means of providing compensation to the applicant for the respondent's previous actions, while also granting an injunction to restrain future behaviour. The underlying concern here is that if damages were not awarded at the same time as the injunction, the applicant might be precluded from suing for damages in relation to a set of facts on which a court has already reached a conclusion. This rule against suing a second time on identical facts and issues is the *res judicata* rule.[60]

The second category of awarding damages is *in place of* the grant of an injunction. As considered at para 27.1.1 above, there are four requirements which must be satisfied before

55 *Ibid*, 62
56 [1989] 1 WLR 1268.
57 *Ibid*.
58 [1995] 1 WLR 269, [1995] 2 All ER 189.
59 Chancery Amendment Act 1858, s 2.
60 *Jaggard v Sawyer* [1995] 1 WLR 269, 286, *per* Millett LJ.

a court will award damages instead of an injunction in circumstances where an injunction might otherwise be awarded:

(a) the harm suffered by the applicant must have been small;
(b) the harm suffered must be capable of being quantified in financial terms;
(c) the harm suffered must be capable of adequate compensation by damages; and
(d) it must have been oppressive to the respondent to have granted the injunction sought.[61]

Furthermore, the award of an injunction may be denied on the basis of delay or acquiescence, as considered above.

27.6.2 The measure of damages

The measure of damages is held not to be the same as under common law but rather on the basis of compensation.[62] Therefore, in circumstances where no loss can be demonstrated by the applicant, it is possible for the applicant to recover substantial damages nevertheless on the basis of an amount necessary to compensate that applicant for loss of rights not calculable in financial terms. Clearly, the line between common law damages (based on calculable financial loss) and compensation (based on the broader context of harm caused to the applicant) is a narrow one. However, as with personal injury general damages in tort, there may be elements of harm (pain and suffering) which are recoverable as well as financial loss (such as lost earnings).

It appears that it is not necessary for a claim for damages to be pleaded by the applicant – rather, the court can make an award without such a claim being included in the statement of claim.[63]

27.7 THE EQUITABLE DOCTRINE OF CONFIDENCE

27.7.1 Introduction

This section and the section to follow consider the legal background to a particularly significant debate in the Press at the start of the 21st century: namely, the ability of the Press to publish private details about the lives of celebrities, politicians and ordinary members of the public, and the ability of those celebrities, politicians and ordinary members of the public to use injunctions to prevent the publication of those things. The reason that this discussion is contained in the chapter on injunctions is that ultimately the equitable remedy which is most important in relation to breach of confidence is the injunction, and furthermore (for the purposes of this book on equity more generally) the law on confidence and confidential information is rooted in equitable principles. Consequently, in legal terms, what we shall be considering is the ancient equitable doctrine of confidence. It was a general equitable doctrine relating to breach of confidence which always provided a right to an injunction or to compensation in identified types of case, principally those relating to confidential commercial information, contracts restraining the use of information, and secrets between husband

61 *Shelfer v City of London Electric Lighting Co* [1895] 1 Ch 287, *per* AL Smith LJ.
62 *Jaggard v Sawyer* [1995] 1 WLR 269, [1995] 2 All ER 189; *Wrotham Park v Parkside Homes* [1974] 1 WLR 798.
63 *Jaggard v Sawyer* [1995] 1 WLR 269, [1995] 2 All ER 189, *per* Millett LJ.

and wife. Indeed, much of the 19th-century case law in this area was concerned with what the judges referred to as 'secrets' and 'confidences'.[64] The development of mass literacy and the Press as we know it today (let alone the internet) moved this area of the law into a new context beyond the sort of 'secrets' which might be overheard by servants in the grand houses of the aristocracy. The next section of this chapter will consider the comparatively recent development of the tort of misuse of private information using concepts taken from human rights law and the use of 'super-injunctions' by celebrities and others to protect their private lives from public scrutiny; however, this section is concerned with the general equitable doctrine, which still continues in existence in even the most recent case law.

27.7.2 The traditional equitable doctrine of breach of confidence

The ancient roots of the principle

The precise source of the equitable principles relating to the maintenance of 'confidences' is lost in the mists of equitable time. However, a judgment of the Lord Chancellor Sir Thomas More in the 16th century is often cited as the foundation of our understanding of the doctrine, and in particular the following idea:

> Three things are apt to be helpt in Conscience: Fraud, Accident and things of confidence.[65]

Therefore, even in the 16th century the protection of 'confidences' was a key part of equity. The reference to 'Conscience' here is a reference to the Courts of Equity and these *dicta* identify the three things which equity was particularly astute to address. The most obvious examples of confidence in equity relate to particular categories of relationship of 'trust and confidence'. The clearest examples of relationships of trust and confidence relate to fiduciaries duties such as trusteeship. The ancient rules against trustees permitting conflicts of interest (as considered in Chapter 12, for example in *Boardman v Phipps*[66]) are a clear example of the confidences which trustees were obliged to observe.[67]

A neat encapsulation of how this seemingly discretionary doctrine operates in a principled way can be derived from Story's *Equity Jurisprudence*, in which Judge Story suggested that while a doctrine might revolve around the discretion of the court, it is nevertheless 'not of arbitrary or capricious discretion, dependent upon the mere pleasure of the Judge, but of that sound, and reasonable discretion, which governs itself, as far as it may, by general rules and principles'.[68] So, the seemingly open-ended idea of protecting confidences is actually circumscribed by more detailed equitable principles. One of the key cases to identify those principles is the remarkable case of *Prince Albert v Strange*,[69] which is considered next.

---

64 The word 'confidence' itself is derived from the Latin '*fides*' meaning faith, and literally means having faith with another person (as suggested by the prefix 'con-'). Similarly, the word 'fiduciary' is also derived from the Latin '*fides*'.

65 Quoted by Megarry J in *Coco v AN Clark (Engineers) Ltd* [1969] RPC 41, 46.

66 [1967] 2 AC 46.

67 See generally the discussion in section 12.5.

68 Story, *Equity Jurisprudence*, Vol 2, 25–6.

69 (1849) 41 ER 1171, *per* Lord Cottenham LC.

The roots of the equitable treatment of confidences: the principle in
Prince Albert v Strange

Queen Victoria, her husband Prince Albert, her family and her intimate circle made paintings and sketches of each other, their pets and so forth, going about their private lives.[70]
Those artworks were transformed into etchings and those etchings were passed to a printer
for the printer to create prints from them which would be passed between members of that
intimate family circle.[71] Someone created copies of those prints, contrary to the wishes of the
Queen and her husband, Prince Albert. It was not clear how this had been done. It seems
most likely that the prints were obtained either by a member of the royal household or
somehow by means of the printer who was engaged to prepare a limited number of prints
from the etchings, although that question was never answered entirely satisfactorily.
Significantly, it was never demonstrated nor argued conclusively that they had been taken in
breach of contract.[72] In any event, those prints were passed to the defendant, Strange, who
decided to mount an exhibition of them and to charge the public to see these representations
of their monarch and her family relaxing at home. Strange also produced a catalogue of the
prints, which he proposed to sell: this is important because it is the catalogue which becomes
the centre of the case. In essence, Prince Albert wanted to stop all of this. So, a claim was
brought by Prince Albert seeking an injunction against the publication of the catalogue
which reproduced the etchings; it was not even an issue before the court that the exhibition
could not go ahead as planned. The basis on which the injunction was sought was that this
would be a publication of confidential information. As Lord Cottenham noted, this case
turned on a question of privacy: and that is how his lordship's decision has been interpreted
in many cases latterly.[73]

It was accepted by the defendant before the hearing of the action before the House of
Lords that he could not exhibit the etchings, and therefore the injunction imposed at first
instance was not objected to on those grounds. Instead, the issue before the House of Lords
focused more specifically on the defendant's right to publish and sell *the catalogue* which
described those etchings.[74] The subject matter of the decision of the House of Lords was
therefore not about the treatment of etchings which were stolen physically from the Royal
household and then exploited commercially; instead, the subject matter of that decision was
whether or not the dissemination of a catalogue which merely described those etchings could
have been enjoined by the court. Ironically, of course, by describing the etchings (albeit

---

70 No information is given as to the intrinsic artistic merits of these items, of course, but I shall refer to them as
'the artworks' in the text for ease of reference. If I were to produce pictures of my family at home then my
principal concern would be embarrassment as the quality of my draughtsmanship. In the modern world, I
suppose, we would be more likely to take digital photographs and 'put them' on Facebook; or, in the case of the
modern Royal family, appoint an official photographer to distribute them to the Press. How times have changed.
71 Prince Albert was well-known for having brought this *Gemächlichkeit* culture to the British Royal family from
Germany, with its emphasis on Romantic music, literature and art.
72 That is, if the printer had taken them then that might have been a breach of contract; or it might similarly have
been a breach of contract if it had been someone in the Royal household. However, these etchings might have
been purloined by a third party without any contractual link to the esteemed creators of these etchings.
Significantly, as becomes clear in the text, this case was decided on the basis of privacy in any event by Lord
Cottenham.
73 *Argyll v Argyll* [1967] Ch 302; *Stephens v Avery* [1988] Ch 449.
74 As Lord Cottenham held: 'The only question I have to decide is, whether, this right being so established and
admitted, the defendant is to be permitted to publish the catalogue in question.'

briefly) in the report of the case, much of the same material is being made publicly available through the good offices of the law reporters.[75]

The House of Lords found unanimously, as expressed in the speech of Lord Cottenham, the Lord Chancellor, that an injunction should be granted so as to prevent publication of the catalogue. However, the precise ratio of the judgment is more difficult to identify. In truth, one will search in vain for a clear encapsulation of Lord Chancellor Cottenham's point in the judgment itself.[76] Lord Cottenham saw the question as to the propriety of awarding an injunction to restrain publication and circulation of the catalogue in the interests of privacy as falling into two parts: first, on the basis of a property right to the etchings which were described in the catalogue (but without identifying their owners on the facts of this case); and then, secondly, on a more general basis that an injunction should be available in equity to enjoin dealings with confidential information where that was done in 'breach of trust, confidence, or contract'. It is this second branch of the judgment which is most commonly cited in subsequent cases as constituting three grounds for the award of an injunction in this context, although the idea appears in Lord Cottenham's judgment without careful analysis or explanation. In truth, the inevitability of the claimant being successful is suggested by the opening words of Lord Cottenham's judgment where his lordship held that:

> The importance which has been attached to this case arises entirely from the exalted station of the Plaintiff, and cannot be referred to any difficulty in the case itself.[77]

In other words, the niceties of the jurisprudence rank second behind the need to find for this very important individual.

It has been held in the Court of Appeal in *Imerman v Tchenguiz*[78] by Lord Neuberger latterly that this decision was predicated on Prince Albert being the owner of the materials (both at common law and in relation to their intellectual property rights which include the right to make copies of them) which were transformed into the etchings, and in consequence that this right to confidentiality therefore turned on a property right. Importantly, however, when one looks closely at the facts of *Prince Albert v Strange*, the creators of the artworks are the Queen and other members of the family: therefore, Prince Albert was not the owner

75 This difficulty of reporting cases without giving away too much private information remains an issue today in relation to super-injunctions, as considered below. Presumably in 1849 it was not thought likely that many people would have access to the report of this decision. Interestingly, though, there do not appear to have been any reporting restrictions imposed in this case, other than Lord Cottenham's own delicacy in relation to the information which he was prepared to relate in his judgment. Indeed, it is from the arguments of counsel that most of the facts emerge in this report.

76 Much of the discussion is couched in terms of property rights in the etchings themselves, even though his Lordship never took the point that the particular plaintiff here (in the person of Prince Albert) had no property rights in some at least of the etchings. Nor did Lord Cottenham distinguish between different creators of different etchings. Nor did Lord Cottenham take the point (except possibly obliquely in argument, according to the elliptical report of the argument) that the catalogue would have described some etchings belonging to the plaintiff personally and therefore that the catalogue would necessarily have described his own etchings as well as those belonging to his wife.

77 In truth, it is a poorly constructed judgment in many ways and is clearly influenced by the fact that the House of Lords would always have found for the Royal family in any event. The case revolves around an enraged husband, Prince Albert, seeking to protect his family. In consequence, the rationale for the judgment would have been less important in 1849 than the inevitability of the claimant's success.

78 [2011] 2 WLR 592.

of the intellectual property rights in all of the artworks. Rather, this principle should be understood as resting on a traditional equitable concept of preventing an unconscionable breach of another's confidence. Here, the idea of a confidence is not limited to its colloquial meaning of a secret which is told to you confidentially by the person who would be harmed by its misuse, but rather an interference with the confidential or private information relating to any person whether they know you have access to it or not. If this were not the appropriate meaning of the term 'confidence' in this context then thieves would not be prevented from stealing secrets without the claimant's knowledge. The sort of information which is covered by this idea of confidential information includes commercial secrets[79] and intellectual property as well as personal or intimate information relating to an individual.

If we pause for a moment, in the Victorian era, long before British royalty decided to become 'the Royal Family' and thus to open themselves up to publicity and press coverage of their every movement,[80] it would have been completely unacceptable for the general populace to be allowed to gawp at pictures of their betters sitting at home. Consequently, the outcome of *Prince Albert v Strange* was never in doubt. What is of interest is the way in which those principles were explained. Two points of fact are important to isolate at the start. First, it was not proved that Prince Albert, who was the plaintiff, had been the creator of all of these etchings. Indeed, it was contended by the defence (and not disproved or even contested in argument) that many of the etchings had been produced by other people, including the Queen herself. Therefore, Prince Albert was not the owner of those etchings. Second, it is not suggested that there was anything sexual, obscene or similarly embarrassing about these etchings. Far from it. They seem (although the judges are, of course, far too delicate to describe any of the etchings in detail) to be entirely innocent representations of royalty at home. The issue relates to the essentially private nature of this material, which is possibly mixed with the idea that even to consider the idea of royalty playing the piano or sitting reading a book or playing with a pet dog would be remarkable. While to a modern ear all of this talk of the private lives of royalty hints at something salacious, undoubtedly the mundane truth is that those etchings will have presented the blameless domesticity of the monarch, her consort, her family circle and her pets relaxing in their private apartments. And that was precisely what was considered to have been private about them. To a modern ear, it could not have been remarkable to learn that the monarch had pets – indeed our Queen is well known for keeping corgis – but at the time even the publication of that tit-bit of information, seemingly the subject of one of the artworks, would have been an invasion of privacy.

While *Prince Albert v Strange* is often taken as being the source of the law on confidence, Lord Cottenham cited many of the earlier authorities which also dealt with the concept, not least the judgment of Lord Eldon and decisions such as the *Duke of Queensbury v Shebbeare*.[81] Relying on *Tipping v Clarke*,[82] Lord Cottenham drew an analogy with clerks in a counting house being under an implied contract not to make public any information

---

79 This can include logistical information held by a supermarket as to how it manages to distribute its stock efficiently, something which is at the very heart of a supermarket's profitability by controlling its cost base and maximising its ability to meet customer demand quickly: *Marks & Spencer v Freshfield Bruckhaus Deringer* [2004] EWHC 1135 (Comm), [2004] 3 All ER 773.

80 Some would say this began an inevitable decline in the way in which royalty in Britain would be perceived by the public.

81 (1758) 2 Eden 329.

82 4 Burr 2379.

which they obtain during the performance of their duties. It is left to us to assume that what this survey of the cases means is that somebody somewhere (either in the Royal household or at the printers or somewhere in-between) breached an express or implied contractual duty or breached their confidential obligations to the Royal family. The niceties of demonstrating exactly what sort of obligation was breached, by whom, how and when are overlooked.

If this area of law were based on property rights, then that would mean that photographs taken by third parties at a distance of somebody engaging in a private act would constitute a criminal offence but would not give a right to an injunction or damages for someone who was not the owner of the photograph. That the law on confidence is drawn more broadly so as to relate to 'breach of trust, confidence and contract' makes it better suited to dealing with the modern age. When property rights are interfered with, then that should constitute a right to a proprietary remedy and/or to an injunction and/or to compensation or damages. That it is a general equitable principle based on conscience makes it more adaptable to modern circumstances. The maturity of that equitable principle, and its roots in ideas of conscience, are considered in the next section.

The development of the equity of confidence: a single doctrine or a number of doctrines?

The obsession with privacy and with confidentiality is a modern one. The old textbooks on equity devoted little time to 'confidence' among all of the other equitable doctrines and remedies which abounded at the time. The principles did exist, but they were not as important as they appear today in our media age, where everyone with a computer and a broadband connection can become a 'citizen journalist'. So, for example, Judge Story in his excellent *Equity Jurisprudence*, published originally in 1839, gave only one paragraph to injunctions which are used to 'restrain the party from making a disclosure of secrets communicated to him in the course of a confidential employment'.[83] Ashburner in his *Principles of Equity*, which was published originally in 1903, devoted a mere two pages[84] to the prevention of breaches of confidence under the headings of: 'protection of unpublished manuscripts', which are described as the earliest forms of action in equity to restrain breaches of confidence;[85] 'private letters';[86] and 'lectures delivered without notes'.[87] Ashburner was very clear that this doctrine was not a proprietary doctrine, such that there was no requirement that the confidential information in question be shown to have been the property of the plaintiff:[88]

> It is misleading to base the jurisdiction, as is often done even now, upon the protection of a common law rights of property in the author of an unpublished manuscript. The

---

83 Story, 1839, 621.
84 In all honesty, it was only in the seventh edition of this book that an extended discussion of this doctrine was presented, having previously been limited to the approach of the cases on constructive trusts to confidential information (in Chapter 12) and the trustees' obligations in relation to information (in Chapter 8).
85 *Webb v Rose* (1732), cited in 4 Burr 2330; *Duke of Queensbury v Shebbeare* (1758) 2 Eden 329.
86 A staple of Sherlock Holmes stories (for example, 'The Adventure of Charles Augustus Milverton' in A Conan Doyle, *The Return of Sherlock Holmes*, first published in 1904) and much Victorian fiction, where these purloined letters were used for purposes of blackmail. Even youthful expressions of love in a letter could be used at the time to blackmail a woman when she was about to marry. See for example *Gee v Prichard* (1818) 2 Sw 402, *per* Lord Eldon.
87 *Abernethy v Hutchinson* (1825) 3 LJ Ch 209.
88 Browne, *Ashburner's Principles of Equity*, 2nd edn, Butterworth & Co, 1933, 373.

right has never been recognised or protected but by proceedings in equity. . . . And it is obvious that property in these cases is something quite different from property in tangible things. An injunction may be granted although the manuscript wrongfully reproduced is safe in the author's desk, or although it belongs (as in the case of a letter) to the person restrained, or although there is no manuscript in existence.

Therefore, this is an equitable doctrine which exists 'at large' rather than in support of a specific property right. Much more recently, the judgment of Lord Neuberger MR in the Court of Appeal in *Imerman v Tchenguiz*[89] has re-emphasised the distinction between equity and the common law in cases of confidence. The development of a tort of misuse of private information, based both on Art 8 of the European Convention on Human Rights (ECHR) and on principles of tort law (considered in the next section of this chapter), are distinct from the equitable doctrine of confidence. Lord Neuberger was very clear that that distinction remains in effect.[90] In *Imerman v Tchenguiz*, prior to divorce proceedings beginning in earnest, a wife's brothers accessed her husband's confidential computer files held on a computer server which her husband used as part of a business in common with her brothers. The information held on the files which the brothers accessed may well have been information which would have been disclosed at the discovery stage in divorce proceedings, but nevertheless those files were held to constitute the husband's confidential information. Moreover, he was not required to identify documents which would be considered confidential to him: instead, his rights of confidence simply existed at large. Importantly, while the case could have proceeded on the basis that those files were in some way the property of the husband and that it was his property which had been interfered with, the Court of Appeal nevertheless focused on the general jurisdiction of equity to grant injunctions in cases in which a person's confidential information was at risk.

It is difficult to know whether the law on confidence should be understood as proceeding in relation to a general principle or whether it should be understood as proceeding on the basis of analogies with the distinct categories already established in the cases. One example of a clear category which has arisen in the cases is that of confidences between husband and wife.[91] So, perhaps most famously, the decision of Ungoed-Thomas J in *Duchess of Argyll v Duke of Argyll*[92] dealt with newspaper stories which had been fed by the Duke of Argyll to *The People* newspaper which disclosed confidential information about his own wife. Indeed, these tabloid revelations – to the limited extent they are explained in the law reports – related to confidences which had passed between husband and wife. (By modern standards these particular allegations appear to be thin gruel: he made allegations about her attitudes to sexual fidelity in marriage, and she made counter-allegations about his drug use and his financial situation.)[93] His Lordship held that it was a part of the equitable jurisdiction to

---

89 [2011] 2 WLR 592.
90 Applying *dicta* of Lord Phillips MR in *Douglas v Hello! Ltd (No 3)* [2006] QB 125, [96]. See also *White v Withers LLP* [2009] 1 FLR 383, Eady J.
91 See more recently *Hirschfield v McGrath* [2011] EWHC 249 (QB), Tugendhat J.
92 [1967] Ch 302.
93 The truth is that the Duchess is reputed to have led a particularly salacious lifestyle, even by modern standards. She was the subject of a flattering line in the libretto of a popular musical comedy of her day, written by a very famous novelist whose work is still in print; and was reputedly the woman involved in a particularly infamous sex scandal in the 1960s (which became a staple of the Sunday newspapers for a while) for which a very

award injunctions in these categories of case, and thus it was not any part of a common law doctrine of tort.[94]

Interestingly, then, one specific context in which confidences were considered to be particularly important were in relation to marriage. The principle in cases of husband and wife is one of 'preserving the confidence of the conjugal relation'. It is clear that this is an equitable doctrine, which is necessarily subject to all of the usual doctrines of equity. So, it was held that:

> A person coming to Equity for relief – and this is equitable relief which the plaintiff seeks – must come with clean hands; but the cleanliness required is to be judged in relation to the relief that is sought.[95]

As to the distinction between a proprietary basis for law on confidence and a truly personal basis of that law, his Lordship held as follows:

> Injury to property can be far less serious than other forms of injury such as, for example, injury to reputation, and I see no rational ground whatsoever in distinguishing between injury to property and other forms of injury, nor was any suggested.[96]

Therefore, the basis of equitable relief in relation to cases of confidence is not necessarily proprietary. Instead the relief may be based on protecting a person's reputation.

The open-textured nature of the equitable doctrine of confidence

As will have become apparent through the course of this book, there are two types of lawyer in the world: those who demand certainty, order and taxonomy from their law, and those who prefer to apply general, high-level principles to each particular factual circumstance. A 'taxonomy' is a way of ordering material which is common among scientists, particularly biologists, who organise all living things into species, genus, families and so forth so as to identify common or distinct characteristics of various animals, plants and so on. There is a certain type of lawyer who demands that law should be organised by reference to this sort of order.[97] However, as is well known, there is another species of scientist, in particular the theoretical physicist, who recognises that in many instances it is impossible to produce tidy taxonomies because too many phenomena are inexplicable or unpredictable. As the theoretical physicists' theory of Schrödinger's cat demonstrates, it is not even possible to know

---

well-known judge was deputed to organise an inquiry to find out the identities of the people involved. Rather than tell you all of this information, I will give you the pleasure of an internet-based quiz to identify: (a) the author of the libretto; (b) the musical comedy in which the line appears; (c) the nickname given to the unknown man participating in that scandal; and (d) the identity of the judge who led the inquiry. All of the information you need to begin the search is contained in the law report of the case.

94   Interestingly, the authors of *Meagher, Gummow and Lehane's Equity: Doctrines and Remedies* consider that the first two decisions of the English Court of Appeal which deal plainly and exclusively with an equitable duty of confidence are as recent as the 1960s: *Saltman Engineering Co Ltd v Campbell Engineering Co Ltd* (1948) 65 RPC 203 and *Seager v Copydex Ltd* (1967) RPC 349, [1967] 2 All ER 415.
95   [1967] Ch 302, 332.
96   [1967] Ch 302, 344.
97   See Birks and Chambers, 1997 for an example.

whether a cat is alive or dead or both at any given moment, let alone how black holes operate. Therefore, there will be situations in which all one can do is to understand the 'high-level principles' by which one operates – such as: one must act in good conscience, one must not cause harm to others, and so forth – and then (legally speaking) develop a jurisprudence which makes clear how those principles operate in some circumstances.

That the equitable doctrine of confidence is still understood as operating by reference to a high-level principle of good conscience is demonstrated by Brooke LJ, who held the following in *Douglas v Hello! Ltd*:[98]

> For a very long time the judges of the Court of Chancery exercised an equitable jurisdic-
> tion to restrain freedom of speech in circumstances in which it would be unconscionable
> to publish private material. If information is accepted on the basis that it will be kept
> secret, the recipient's conscience is bound by that confidence, and it will be unconscion-
> able for him to break his duty of confidence by publishing the information to others.

Here, the doctrine is clearly based on the idea that it is the confidentiality and the secrecy of the information, and the defendant's awareness of that, which bind that person's conscience so as to invoke the equitable doctrine of confidence and an injunction to prevent publication. Similarly, it is suggested, any profits taken in such a situation should be held on constructive trust due to this combination of a breach of conscience and knowledge of that fact in the circumstances.

27.7.3 The modern equitable doctrine of confidence

The central principles

The core of the equitable doctrine of confidence is, in reality, a concern to seek injunctions to prevent the disclosure of confidential information in the majority of cases. In other cases, the injured party may seek compensation for a confidence which has been broken. Most of the cases in this area relate to confidential information. The clearest exposition of those principles arose in *Coco v AN Clark (Engineering) Ltd*[99] in which Megarry J held as follows:

> In my judgment, three elements are normally required if, apart from contract, a case of
> breach of confidence is to succeed. First, the information itself, in the words of Lord
> Greene, MR in the *Saltman* case on page 215,[100] must 'have the necessary quality of
> confidence about it'. Secondly, that information must have been imparted in circum-
> stances importing an obligation of confidence. Thirdly, there must be an unauthorised
> use of that information to the detriment of the party communicating it.

Therefore, there are three requirements: that the information must be confidential information; that the circumstances in which that information was passed to the defendant should

---

98 [2001] QB 967, at [65].

99 [1969] RPC 41, at 47.

100 *Saltman Engineering Co Ltd v Campbell Engineering Co Ltd* (1948) 65 RPC 203. His lordship also relied on
      Terrapin Ltd v Builders' Supply Co (Hayes) Ltd [1960] RPC 128 and *Seager v Copydex Ltd* [1967] 1 WLR
      923, [1967] RPC 349.

have suggested that it was confidential; and that the use of the information must have been unauthorised. This demonstrates Megarry J in his common role of identifying with as much clarity as possible the principles on which an equitable doctrine should operate, as opposed to leaving a doctrine like that of confidence in its open-textured state[101] operating by reference to a general principle of good conscience and of preventing confidences being breached in general terms.

However, Megarry J also made further delineations in the topic. He divided between marital and commercial situations, and between contractual and non-contractual cases.[102] Where there is a contract between the parties which requires that a confidence be maintained then the terms of that confidence are as set out by the contract; whereas if there is no contract then the parties are thrown back on the general law to define their relationship. What is special about marital situations is that a special relationship of trust and confidence is thought to exist between husband and wife. This has a lot to do with the essentially private nature of what goes on within a marriage that is not open to the public gaze, although there is no reason (it is suggested) for that to be limited only to married couples.[103]

When is information 'confidential'?

As will be apparent from the discussion so far, for a pragmatic equity specialist like Megarry J – that is, one who needs to see principle and not simply open-ended discretion before giving effect to an equitable doctrine – the doctrine of confidence was a little open-ended about its detail. As Megarry J put it: 'From the authorities cited to me, I have not been able to derive any very precise idea of what test is to be applied in determining whether the circumstances import an obligation of confidence.'[104] Indeed, the judgment of Megarry J is generally taken by intellectual property law specialists as the starting point for identifying when confidential information is to be treated as intellectual property deserving of protection precisely because his lordship sought to introduce some more rigid principles here.

So, in the opinion of Megarry J, when considering confidential information, there needs to be something about it which transforms it from being mere tittle-tattle into having that quality of being unknown to the outside world and thus intrinsically valuable in commercial terms to become an item of property. Clearly, this is only a commercial understanding of what will constitute information as property, whereas the equitable doctrine of confidentiality applies to non-commercial information too. Megarry J conceived of the line between confidential and non-confidential information in the following terms:

> . . . the information must be of a confidential nature. As Lord Greene said in the *Saltman* case at page 215, 'something which is public property and public knowledge' cannot *per se* provide any foundation for proceedings for breach of confidence. However confidential the circumstances of communication, there can be no breach of confidence in revealing to others something which is already common knowledge. But this must not be taken too far. Something that has been constructed solely from materials in the public

---

101   That is to say, not bound by rigid rules but rather operating by reference only to general, high-level principles such as good conscience.
102   All on [1969] RPC 41, at 46 and 47.
103   See, for example, the discussion of *Argyll v Argyll* [1967] Ch 302 immediately above.
104   [1969] RPC 41, at 48.

domain may possess the necessary quality of confidentiality: for something new and confidential may have been brought into being by the application of the skill and ingenuity of the human brain.

These general principles, of course, give us little practical guidance; although the concept behind equitable doctrines of this sort is that the court has great latitude to act in applying general principles to the facts in front of it. In *Coco v Clark*, the case concerned a design for an engine for a moped which the claimants sought to protect by means of an interim injunction against the defendants. The question was whether or not there was confidential information in relation to this engine which was at risk without an interim injunction being awarded. His lordship used the 'officious bystander' test as a yardstick here to the effect that, when considering whether or not the context in which the information was passed to the defendant was confidential, one should consider whether or not the parties would have responded to the officious bystander's question 'Is this confidential?' with a testy 'Of course'.[105] Thus, in commercial situations, the context in which the parties are interacting will be considered to be important in deciding whether or not the information is confidential, and not simply the nature of the information itself. On the facts, it was held that the information was not of a sufficiently confidential nature.

27.7.4 Contexts in which confidential information has already been considered in this book

There are two contexts in which confidential information has already been considered in this book: in relation to constructive trusts over unauthorised profits and in relation to Chinese walls.

Constructive trusts and confidential information

When confidential information is taken to constitute a trust fund, for example, then misuse of that confidential information will lead to any unauthorised profits being taken from the use of that information by a fiduciary being held on constructive trust by that fiduciary.[106] This idea was considered in detail in Chapter 12.

Chinese walls and confidential information

The other principal context in which confidential information has been considered to give rise to rights in equity is in relation to Chinese walls. The most significant context in which Chinese walls have arisen in the cases is in relation to a single firm of solicitors or accountants representing both sides to a dispute and mismanaging confidential information so that it passed internally, to the detriment of one of their clients. The Chinese wall refers to the arrangement which that firm would put in place to attempt to maintain the confidentiality of all information held during the dispute. As Lord Millett held in *Bolkiah v KPMG*,[107] the duty on the firm to maintain that confidentiality is an absolute duty – such that any breach of

---

105 *Ibid*, at 50.
106 *Boardman v Phipps* [1967] 2 AC 46.
107 [1999] 2 AC 222.

confidentiality is actionable in equity, no matter what the circumstances – and not merely a duty to do their best to maintain it.

The trustees' obligation in relation to confidential information

In Chapter 8, the case law on the trustees' general lack of obligation to disclose confidential information about the operation of the trust even to the beneficiaries was considered. Information which is considered to relate to only one part of the trust, and not to others, need not be disclosed to beneficiaries with an interest only in that other part of the fund.[108] In general terms, where the confidential information in question is itself the property of the trust, then the trustee is obliged to maintain and safeguard it just as she would be obliged to maintain any other part of the trust fund, on pain of liability for breach of trust.

27.7.5 Equity, confidence and the development of a law of privacy

The remainder of this chapter is concerned with the development of a law of privacy from a combination of these equitable principles and the new human rights law which was created by the Human Rights Act 1998 in the UK. This section considers how the roots of the law of privacy have been identified by the highest courts in the equitable principle of confidence and good conscience, and how human rights law has come to displace those concepts in the separate branch of law that relates to the 'tort of misuse of private information' which is the most visible part of privacy law today. Nevertheless, the equitable principle of confidence continues in existence, and the equitable principles relating to injunctions are considered below too.

The modern equitable principle of confidence is based on conscience

Much of the debate relating to the law of privacy has been concerned with the development of a tort of 'misuse of private information',[109] but as this chapter has made clear there has always been a part of equity which has been concerned with the protection of 'confidences'. This equitable principle is applied by the law of injunctions as everything from private family photographs to secret commercial processes have been protected against the effects of publication. The doctrine of breach of confidence has a long pedigree in equity. As it was summarised by Lord Hoffmann in *Campbell v MGN Ltd*:[110]

> Breach of confidence was an equitable remedy and equity traditionally fastens on the conscience of one party to enforce equitable duties which arise out of his relationship with the other.

The precise juristic nature of this area of the law has always been difficult to identify, it is suggested, because it was predicated ultimately on a general equitable principle of conscionability, as Lord Hoffmann identified, but earlier judges such as Megarry J in *Coco v A N*

---

108 *Re Londonderry* [1965] Ch 918. See also the important judgment of Briggs J in *Breakspear v Ackland* [2008] 3 WLR 698.
109 As it was described by Lord Nicholls in *Campbell v MGN* [2004] 2 AC 457, at [13]–[14].
110 [2004] 2 AC 457, 471, at [44].

Clark (Engineers) Ltd[111] were determined to generate more concrete principles. In truth, the equitable doctrine of confidence was necessarily a fluid one, just like the equitable principles on injunctions more generally. The different strains of authority and the different shades of principle which gave rise to this area of equity were identified by Sir George Turner VC in *Morison v Moat*[112] in the following terms:

> That the court has exercised jurisdiction in cases of this nature does not, I think, admit of any question. Different grounds have indeed been assigned for the exercise of that jurisdiction. In some cases it has been referred to as property, and others to contract, and in others, again, as founded upon trust or confidence, meaning, as I conceive, that the court fastens the obligation upon the conscience of the party, and enforces it against him in the same manner as it enforces against a party to whom a benefit is given the obligation of performing a promise on the face of which the benefit has been conferred; but, upon what other grounds this jurisdiction is founded, the authorities have no doubt as to the exercise of it.

On that basis, the jurisdiction should be understood as being founded on a general equitable principle. In consequence, confidential information in the circumstances may be property or it may not, but that will not affect the power of the court to award an injunction or not as the circumstances require. As Lord Neuberger held in *Imerman v Tchenguiz*:[113]

> A claim based on confidentiality is an equitable claim. Accordingly, the normal equitable rules apply. Thus, while one would normally expect a court to grant the types of relief we have been discussing, it would have a discretion whether to refuse some or all such relief on familiar equitable principles. Equally, the precise nature of the relief which would be granted must depend on all aspects of the particular case: equity fashions the appropriate relief to fit the rights of the parties, the facts of the case, and, at least sometimes, the wider merits. But, as we have noted, whether confidential information has been passed by the defendants to a third party, the claimant's rights will prevail as against the third party, unless he was a bona fide purchaser of the information without notice of its confidential nature.

In summary then, the law on confidence is subject to general equitable principles (meaning discretion as to whether to award an injunction where there has been delay, or where the claimants has come with clean hands, and so forth). What the courts have done ever since the decision of the House of Lords in *Prince Albert v Strange*[114] is to recognise that injunctions and other equitable relief may be awarded without the need to identify that the confidential information in question is property. As Lord Cottenham held, it is sufficient that there has been some breach of trust, breach of confidence, or breach of contract to find a claim based on confidence. Therefore, the question remains at large in what circumstances confidential information should be treated as being property as opposed to simply entitling the claimants to equitable relief or to claim damages at common law.

111 [1969] RPC 41, 47–8.
112 (1851) 9 Hare 241, 255.
113 [2011] 2 WLR 592, [74].
114 (1849) 41 ER 1171.

27.7.6 The modern principle of breach of confidence giving way to the tort of misuse of private information

The traditional equitable doctrine of confidence has given way, in many contexts, to a newly developing 'tort of misuse of private information'[115] (which is often referred to simply as a 'tort of privacy') which is based on principles of human rights law more than on principles of confidence. The clearest explanation of the development of this area of the law is that set out by Lord Nicholls in typically clear fashion in the House of Lords in *Campbell v MGN Ltd* in the following terms:

> The common law or, more precisely, courts of equity have long afforded protection to the wrongful use of private information by means of the cause of action which became known as breach of confidence. A breach of confidence was restrained as a form of unconscionable conduct, akin to a breach of trust. Today this nomenclature is misleading. The breach of confidence label harks back to the time when the cause of action was based on improper use of information disclosed by one person to another in confidence. To attract protection the information had to be of a confidential nature. But the gist of the cause of action was that information of this character had been disclosed by one person to another in circumstances 'importing an obligation of confidence' even though no contract of non-disclosure existed: see the classic exposition by Megarry J in *Coco v A N Clark (Engineers) Ltd*.[116] The confidence referred to in the phrase 'breach of confidence' was the confidence arising out of a confidential relationship.
>
> This cause of action has now firmly shaken off the limiting constraint of the need for an initial confidential relationship. In doing so it has changed its nature. In this country this development was recognised clearly in the judgment of Lord Goff of Chieveley in *Attorney General v Guardian Newspapers Ltd (No 2)*.[117] Now the law imposes a 'duty of confidence' whenever a person receives information he knows or ought to know is fairly and reasonably to be regarded as confidential. Even this formulation is awkward. The continuing use of the phrase 'duty of confidence' and the description of the information as 'confidential' is not altogether comfortable. Information about an individual's private life would not, in ordinary usage, be called 'confidential'. The more natural description today is that such information is private. The essence of the tort is better encapsulated now as misuse of private information.[118]

However, it is suggested that this does not dispose of the equitable doctrine of confidence. Rather, the tort of privacy relates only to actions for injunctions and for damages in relation to private information of this sort. The traditional equitable doctrine will continue to operate outside the scope of that tort. So, in the judgment of Lord Neuberger MR in the Court of Appeal in *Imerman v Tchenguiz*[119] his lordship underlined the continuing distinction between equity and the common law in cases of confidence. The development of a right to privacy based both on Art 8 of the ECHR and on a tort of privacy are historically distinct from the

---

115 As it was described by Lord Nicholls in *Campbell v MGN* [2004] 2 AC 457, at [13]–[14].
116 [1969] RPC 41, 47–8.
117 [1990] 1 AC 109, 281.
118 *Campbell v MGN* [2004] 2 AC 457, at [13]–[14].
119 [2011] 2 WLR 592.

equitable jurisdiction in relation to claims predicated on confidence, and Lord Neuberger was very clear that that distinction remains in effect.[120] (This case was considered above.) Equally important, as considered above, the equitable doctrine of confidence relates to non-proprietary claims as well as to proprietary claims. What is clear, however, is that in recent litigation concerning super-injunctions (as considered below in detail) it is the tort of privacy in alliance with human rights law which has become the focus for the protection of confidences at the beginning of the 21st century.

27.8 SUPER-INJUNCTIONS AND THE TORT OF MISUSE OF PRIVATE INFORMATION

27.8.1 Introduction[121]

This section is a sequel to the previous section on the 'Equitable Doctrine of Confidence'. This section traces the development of the 'tort of misuse of private information' and the concomitant development of so-called 'super-injunctions' to prevent misuse of private information. (The emergence of the tort from the equitable doctrine was explained, in a passage quoted from Lord Nicholls in *Campbell v MGN Ltd*[122] set out immediately above.) The tort has developed from the equitable principle of confidence and from the general principles relating to interim injunctions (considered earlier in this chapter), which have been adapted for use as 'super-injunctions'. This section considers those principles, and thus returns our discussion to the principles governing the award of interim injunctions which were considered earlier in this chapter, albeit principally in the context of the prevention of the publication of information (primarily by the newspapers and other media). This section relates to equity in that the law considered here builds on the equitable principles relating to interim injunctions and demonstrates a development of the law of privacy which began with the equitable principle of confidence.

However, because this topic is likely to generate lively debate in the seminar room, and because so much of the public debate around so-called super-injunctions has been carried on in (possibly wilful) ignorance of the true, legal position surrounding super-injunctions, we shall begin with an overview of the public debate about 'super-injunctions', 'hyper-injunctions' and 'anonymised injunctions', before turning to consider the legal principles in detail. The internet abounds with commentary and argument about press freedom, freedom of speech, the super-injunctions issue specifically, and of course the lives of celebrities. This introduction to the public debate is not intended to be anything more than a taster plate of some of the issues, before we turn to the legal principles for the award of injunctions in this context.

---

120 Applying *dicta* of Lord Phillips MR in *Douglas v Hello! Ltd (No 3)*[2006] QB 125, [96]. See also *White v Withers LLP* [2009] 1 FLR 383, Eady J.

121 This new section has been added to this book because it became clear to me than many university courses were exploring newsworthy aspects of the law on interim injunctions – in particular 'super-injunctions' – even though these issues are more closely related to the law of tort and the law of human rights than traditional equitable concepts, as is explained in the text by reference to the speech of Lord Nicholls in *Campbell v MGN* set out immediately above in the text.

122 [2004] 2 AC 457, at [13]–[14].

Definition of terms: 'super-injunction' and 'anonymised injunction'

The term 'super-injunction' has been bandied around in the Press so as to cover a number of different legal devices. From a lawyer's perspective, it is important to distinguish between a 'super-injunction' and an 'anonymised injunction', and other forms of injunction. The Report of the Committee on Super-Injunctions defines a super-injunction as being:

> an interim injunction which restrains a person from:
>
> (i)   publishing information which concerns the applicant and is said to be confidential or private; and,
> (ii) publicising or informing others of the existence of the order and the proceedings (the 'super' element of the order).

By contrast, an anonymised injunction is defined as being:

> an interim injunction which restrains a person from publishing information which concerns the applicant and is said to be confidential or private where the names of either or both of the parties to the proceedings are not stated.

As is considered in the text to follow, it is not unusual to have anonymised proceedings in criminal and in family law matters. Similarly, the principles governing interim injunctions generally apply to super-injunctions with the addition of certain principles considered below. It is in relation to the area of privacy in particular that super-injunctions have acquired their own peculiar lustre.

The public debate about 'super-injunctions'

The law on injunctions became front-page news in 2010 and 2011 as part of a media storm about the media's own treatment of the privacy of celebrities and ordinary civilians.[123] This furore gave rise to the 'Leveson Inquiry into the Culture, Practice and Ethics of the Press', chaired by Leveson LJ,[124] which was created in large part as a response to invasions into the private lives of celebrities and civilians by the tabloid press and others. Nevertheless, a legal technique which began to attract particular importance in this debate was the so-called 'super-injunction'. In essence, a 'super-injunction' is an injunction which not only prevents

---

123   I use the word 'civilians' to refer to non-celebrities who have been unwittingly caught up in the war between the media (in particular the tabloid press) and the celebrities on whose misery they feed. A short documentary film by Adam Curtis (shown as part of BBC4's *Charlie Brooker's 2011 Wipe*, transmitted on 30 December 2011) is very interesting about the way in which the tabloid press sought to undercut the Establishment in Britain both by writing about the Royal Family as an ordinary family (and not the sort of revered royalty whose private pastimes were at issue in *Prince Albert v Strange*, considered above) and also by elevating celebrities to a remarkable status. The treatment of celebrities as being flawed individuals is then fed back to the readership as a pablum of 'current affairs' (pun intended) in the 'public interest'.

124   The inquiry website can be found at www.levesoninquiry.org.uk. This inquiry in itself generated litigation as to the ability of witnesses to give evidence to it, to the effect that journalists would be permitted to give evidence to the inquiry anonymously so as to avoid suffering 'career blight' (on the grounds that it was an inquiry and not a criminal trial so that different questions of natural justice arose): *R (ex p Associated Newspapers Ltd) v The Rt Hon Lord Justice Leveson* [2012] EWHC 57 (Admin).

the media from reporting the detail of any legal proceedings but also prevents the media from reporting the very existence of the injunction itself. Furthermore, these injunctions are often reinforced by an order that the parties are only allowed to be referred to in the court lists by anonymous names (usually in the form of three entirely random initials). As the media presented these injunctions, they were straightforwardly an infringement of the freedom of the press to print news, and therefore they were presented as infringements of freedom of speech contrary to Art 10 of the ECHR. In truth, these sorts of injunctions are common in family law and criminal law proceedings; but in relation to the debate about the privacy of celebrities and of civilians whose lives had become a short-term enthusiasm for the Press, they were treated as though they were a novel incursion into the right of Press to write about (and publish photographs of) whatever it chooses. The subjects of this new coverage argued that their right to privacy under Art 8 of the ECHR would be infringed without injunctions to protect both their privacy and thus private, confidential information about them.

The ways in which super-injunctions have been circumvented in practice (although not in law) have involved the disclosure of the identity of the parties involved in such injunctions on websites, via Twitter, or in Parliament in reliance on the principle of Parliamentary privilege. It was said, as discussed below, that there were even attempts to bring 'hyper-injunctions' to prevent discussion in Parliament of matters which were before the courts. At this point, the law on injunctions threatened to turn into a very difficult constitutional question concerned with the relationship between the House of Commons and the courts. Sedley LJ, writing an excellent article in *The London Review of Books*, argued (against the tide of journalistic and political opinion) that it was Parliamentarians who should stop publishing information which was subject to court injunctions by debating it in Parliament under cover of Parliamentary privilege. Sedley LJ argued that this was harmful to justice and harmful to the independence of the judiciary.[125] It was said that justice dictates that when judges have undertaken a careful analysis of the facts of a case and ordered that certain information be kept secret until trial then Parliament should not interfere with that operation of the law. Contrariwise, it was argued in general terms that this would make it possible for the judges to maintain secrecy in relation to very serious matters which ought to be made public, such as the dumping of toxic waste[126] or political skulduggery.

Clearly there are very important political and constitutional arguments behind these legal principles: whether individuals should have their privacy, or whether the Press should benefit from freedom of speech to maintain our democracy; and whether or not orders of the courts to preserve confidentiality should be allowed to be circumvented by Parliamentary debate. This section of this chapter considers the law on injunctions as it applies to super-injunctions, which will deflate some of the rhetoric which has tended to be attached to this issue in the media's treatment of it, but first it considers some of the public debate which is likely to enliven discussion in the seminar room.

---

125 Stephen Sedley, 'The Goodwin and Giggs Show', (2011) 33 *London Review of Books*, 16 June 2011, p 3. Accessible at www.lrb.co.uk [accessed 8 February 2012].

126 See, for example, the *Trafigura* case (*RJW & SJW v The Guardian newspaper & Person or Persons Unknown* (Claim no HQ09)) in relation to which Paul Farrelly MP asked a question in Parliament about allegations of the dumping of toxic waste by a company – an issue which was subject to an anonymised injunction at the time. This case is considered below.

The media furore over super-injunctions and phone-hacking

The media is never more excited than when talking about the media, and about media freedom of speech. In consequence in 2010 and in 2011 in particular there was a media storm about two issues: first, super-injunctions used by celebrities to keep their private lives out of the newspapers; and, second, allegations that tabloid newspaper journalists had hacked into the voicemails of celebrities, politicians and others. These two issues tended to become fused together in debates about the state of the Press. However, it was only when it became clear that journalists and/or private investigators hired by tabloid newspapers had hacked into the voicemail[127] on young murder victim Milly Dowler's mobile telephone that the debate changed gear because it became clear that ordinary citizens were at risk here and not simply the sort of celebrities who might be thought to pander to those same media organisations whom they were now seeking to sue.[128] This furore led to the closure of the Sunday tabloid newspaper the *News of the World* in 2011, for decades a part of the sewer in newsprint form which runs under the edifice of British culture, because that was the newspaper which was first proved to have engaged in 'phone-hacking'. Against that background, celebrities such as Steve Coogan and Hugh Grant took to the television studios to argue against press intrusion and in favour of super-injunctions to protect their privacy.[129] It was precisely this furore which gave rise to the 'Leveson Inquiry into the Culture, Practice and Ethics of the Press', which is still hearing evidence at the time of writing.

Another step-change in this story came with the outing of footballer Ryan Giggs via the online instant messaging site Twitter[130] as a seeker of super-injunctions[131] to maintain the privacy of an adulterous relationship with a reality TV personality.[132] In spite of the existence of an injunction maintaining the confidentiality of those proceedings, several tens of thousands of 'tweets' purportedly revealed that it was Giggs who was the famous footballer

---

127   This practice was known as 'phone-hacking', in which journalists would call the mobile phone number of their victim and, assuming that the owner would not have set a password, they would be able to open the victim's voicemail. This is a criminal offence and was, for a while at least, a common feature of tabloid journalism practice.

128   In a particularly cruel development for Milly Dowler's parents at a time when her whereabouts were unknown, her mobile phone was hacked and her voicemails deleted – this led her parents to believe that she was still alive and had accessed her voicemail.

129   You will be able to find their interviews on BBC 2's *Newsnight* and other forums online. See, for example, http://news.bbc.co.uk/1/hi/programmes/newsnight/9487491.stm [accessed 8 February 2012].

130   I feel the need to explain what Twitter is because there is always a chance that it will have been superseded by some other online service before the next edition of this book is published.

131   Other seekers of super-injunctions had been outed before then: including footballer John Terry (see *Terry v Persons Unknown* [2010] 1 FCR 659), and former journalist and now TV presenter Andrew Marr. The latter case attracted opprobrium because as a former left-of-centre newspaper journalist Andrew Marr would previously have argued strenuously for freedom of the press instead of hypocritically seeking to silence them by means of an injunction. He argued that he had sought the injunction, not unreasonably perhaps, to give his family time to adapt to the news that he had had an adulterous affair.

132   Reported ad nauseam in the British Press: see for example: www.telegraph.co.uk/technology/twitter/8532001/Ryan-Giggs-unmasked-as-gagging-order-footballer.html [accessed 8 February 2011] or through any search engine. In all these sorts of revelations about celebrity infidelities, one is reminded of the ironic question addressed to anyone – one thinks of the short-sighted actions of Michael Douglas's character in the film *Fatal Attraction* – who is unfaithful, in spite of having a perfectly lovely partner at home, in terms such as: 'Why eat hamburger when you've got steak at home?' and answering: 'Well, sometimes I just really fancy a hamburger.' It is precisely because of this sort of irrational human response to life that equity is required in the first place.

legendarily (according to long-standing internet rumour[133]) at the heart of the super-injunction furore. While each of these tweets was technically in contempt of court (and therefore each was a criminal offence) their sheer volume prevented any action being taken against their publishers.[134] The publication of this information was supported on the basis that it was in the public interest. This cuts to the heart of that debate: it is commonly said to be 'in the public interest' if something is sufficiently prurient to interest the public. Indeed, even the courts tend to accept that tittle-tattle about celebrities is notionally in the public interest, even on the slightest suggestion that contradictions in their real lives with things said in interviews constitute hypocrisy which should be exposed by newspaper stories to that effect.[135] The story at issue in *JIH v Newsgroup Newspapers Ltd*[136] was about a footballer who was alleged to have had an extra-marital affair. From Giggs's perspective it was about protecting his family life. In *JIH v Newsgroup Newspapers* and *CTB v News Group Newspapers Ltd*[137] allegations that the famous footballer in that case had been blackmailed were also made. From the young woman's perspective this prevented her both from protecting herself by launching a public relations offensive[138] of her own and from mone-tising her experiences by selling her story.[139]

If any of the detail of this sort of gossip interests you then, I would respectfully suggest, you need to look to yourself. If you do not like football, then this can be of little interest to you; if you do like football then, unless you are personally acquainted with the Giggs family, what Ryan Giggs does off the pitch or outside the training ground can be of little genuine interest to you either. By contrast, it is worth remembering that in France, the French President François Mitterand conducted an extra-marital affair with a woman (with whom he had a child) for many years in a context in which the affair was well known in political and journalistic circles but was never made public knowledge: this is always taken to demon-strate an entirely different cultural appreciation in France of what constitutes newsworthy information about someone's private life, as opposed to private information which should be published so as to expose any differences between a person's private life and their public pronouncements. Allegations of hypocrisy are commonly used to justify publication of private information, such as covert photographs of a supermodel leaving a Narcotics Anonymous meeting after she had given interviews denying that she had used drugs.[140] Nevertheless, the argument has been made that super-injunctions were mainly sought by powerful, rich men to silence women from talking about their interaction with those men,

---

133 In truth, internet rumour had identified dozens of sports personalities as the person involved. As Andy Hamilton put it in his Radio 4 sitcom *Old Harry's Game*: internet rumour spreads by word of mouse.

134 It has been estimated that there were as many as 75,000 tweets and blogs exposing Giggs as the person who had obtained a super-injunction. (It is unclear whether someone who publishes a tweet is to be referred to as a tweeter, a twitterer or a twit.)

135 See eg, *Campbell v MGN Ltd* [2004] UKHL 22 where it could simply have been held that it is no one's busi-ness what a supermodel gets up to when she is not on the catwalk or in front of a fashion photographer's lens. Instead, that someone makes their living from their public profile seems to make press reporting of their lives an inevitability, as opposed to a contested right.

136 *JIH v News Group Newspapers Ltd* [2011] EWCA Civ 42, [2011] 2 FCR 95.

137 [2011] EWCA Civ 42, [2011] 2 FCR 95.

138 Never was the term 'offensive' better used than in relation to public relations.

139 See *JIH v News Group Newspapers Ltd* [2011] EWCA Civ 42, [2011] 2 FCR 95 for a case involving just such a famous sports personality. Even if the identity of the personality involved was now considered to be common knowledge, it is not clear that the injunction has been lifted, even if it is no longer of any effect.

140 *Campbell v MGN Ltd* [2004] UKHL 22.

and therefore that that is an argument against permitting them.[141] However, there have been several cases in which it has been women who have been seeking to protect themselves against disclosure of information about their private lives, including the supermodel Naomi Campbell and the author JK Rowling. The cases in which it has been argued that the ability of women to speak out is being denied by these sorts of injunctions have tended to involve kiss-and-tell stories about footballers and pop stars in many cases, and in cases such as *JIH v News Group Newspapers Ltd*,[142] *CTB v News Group Newspapers Ltd*[143] and *TSE v News Group Newspapers Ltd*[144] (all relating to an unfaithful footballer or footballers) there have been allegations of blackmail exerted by these women as well.[145] The argument that this area of the law is necessarily stacked against women does not necessarily hold water; instead, this area of the law is necessarily stacked against those who do not have sufficient money to afford the sort of expensive legal advice which is necessary either to obtain or to resist these sorts of injunctions, which may of course involve women in many circumstances.

The editor of the satirical bi-weekly magazine *Private Eye*, Ian Hislop, gave his own perspective on super-injunctions in a number of media forums with words to the effect that this is all really just about 'footballers and slappers', but one day it might actually be about something important.[146] Now, that language is more than a little distasteful[147] but nevertheless Hislop put his finger on an important point: this particular furore about celebrity gossip was unimportant, but the legal principles which it engendered were potentially very worrying for our democracy *when those principles are employed in relation to important news stories* such as misdeeds in government or the dumping of toxic waste. For example, consider the effect of the use of super-injunctions if they had been used by MPs to prevent *The Daily Telegraph* from publishing details of their abuses of the Parliamentary expenses system (for which three of them were later jailed).[148] The MPs' expenses scandal went to the heart of our democratic system and the probity of our representative politicians in their offices.[149] If super-injunctions could be used more broadly, then possibly it is this sort of genuinely important news story which could be hidden from public scrutiny.

The principal shortcoming in Hislop's point, from the perspective of an equity specialist, is that there have been much more important issues addressed in the decided cases than mere celebrity gossip. There is a tendency in the media to assume that only the issues which have

---

141 See, for example, www.guardian.co.uk/lifeandstyle/the-womens-blog-with-jane-martinson/2011/apr/26/superinjunction-andrew-marr-women [accessed 8 February 2012].

142 [2011] EWCA Civ 42, [2011] 2 FCR 95.

143 [2011] EWHC 1232 (QB).

144 [2011] EWHC 1308 (QB).

145 This is made explicit in *CTB v News Group Newspapers Ltd* [2011] EWHC 1232 (QB).

146 This second formulation was used on the BBC2 satirical, current affairs television programme *Have I Got News for You*, although the first half of the remark was also used on BBC Radio 4's *Today* programme.

147 For example, *Have I Got News For You*, broadcast on 22 April 2011 on BBC1. The distasteful element, as ventilated online, is of course the reference to the women involved as being 'slappers'. Why a woman attracts this derogatory reference, when the man involved is referred to by reference to his job as opposed to his status in relation to his wife, is both appalling and commonplace. What Hislop meant at root was that this sort of story was unimportant gossip. Possibly, for him, 'footballer' is also a mild insult. If so, it is still a less unpleasant and less gendered term than 'slapper'.

148 The story was broken by *The Daily Telegraph*, and the information is available at: www.telegraph.co.uk/news/newstopics/mps-expenses/ [accessed 8 February 2012].

149 Much more information is now publicly available. See, for example: www.parliament.uk/mps-lords-and-offices/members-allowances/ [accessed 8 February 2012].

appeared in front of their noses have been discussed in court in the real world. In the real world there have been important cases relating to the issues revolving around super-injunctions (in particular bans on reporting details of a case and the anonymity of the participants) which have not concerned footballers or their sexual imbroglios: notably the decision of the House of Lords in *In re S*[150] which concerned the very sensitive issue as to whether or not the identity of the very young brother of an infant murder victim could be reported and whether or not the identity of the woman who was to stand trial for the murder of that infant could be reported: the woman in question was the mother of both children. As Lady Hale pointed out in *Campbell v MGN*[151] the issue in *S* was clearly of greater significance than the publication of stories relating to supermodel Naomi Campbell.[152] Of course, such injunctions are commonplace in criminal trials to protect the identity of victims or innocent third parties caught up in criminal acts. Equally, any student of family law will know that a very large number of cases relating to families and most cases relating to children are referred to by initials and not by the names of the parties – in that sense, anonymised injunctions are normal in child law. The courts have great discretion in these areas to decide which facts can and cannot be reported in the interests of justice. So, in our consideration of the law relating to 'super-injunctions' it is important to recall that many of the principles at issue are already dealt with frequently in our courts. Indeed the things which are referred to in the Press as 'super-injunctions' and the things which are referred to in law as interim injunctions, anonymised injunctions and so forth are very different things. (The detail of the law, as opposed to media speculation about the law, on super-injunctions is considered below.)

What is considered to be particularly significant about the super-injunction cases which revolve around privacy and around celebrities is that the media is being prevented from performing a vital role in a democratic society of exposing hypocrisy and uncovering scandal,[153] and that the interests of justice require that trials themselves are held in public so that justice can be seen to be done and so that the courts are not able to make decisions in secret. However, in *Campbell v MGN*[154] the hypocrisy which was said to be at issue was a supermodel's use of drugs after she had said in interviews that she did not take drugs: this was used to justify publishing photographs of her leaving a Narcotics Anonymous meeting. This is hardly hypocrisy of the same order as going to war without a genuine reason to do so, or MPs misusing their expenses as part of dishonest property dealings, or the dumping of large quantities of toxic waste.

Another issue which emerges from the case law on super-injunctions, however, is that these cases have been made available in the form of law reports in the ordinary way, and (with the exception of the identity of the parties and information which might reveal their identities being withheld by court order) the thought processes, the objectives and the

---

150 [2004] 4 All ER 683.
151 [2004] 2 All ER 995.
152 See also *W v M* [2011] EWHC 1197 (COP), [2011] 4 All ER 1295, CA, concerning a right to privacy in relation to mental health applications in the Court of Protection on the basis that the first respondent was no longer competent to make decisions about her continued medical treatment and that her family considered that she would not wish to continue living in a 'minimally conscious state'. The court awarded the order as to her right to privacy and to her family life, *inter alia*, against an application from Times Newspapers to be allowed to report the story.
153 It is perhaps unfortunate that a large amount of what is 'exposed' is naked, celebrity flesh and what is 'uncovered' is similarly salacious. The MPs' expenses scandal is an important exception to this pattern.
154 [2004] 2 All ER 995.

decisions of the judges have been made public in the ordinary way. Indeed, Eady J and Tugendhat J[155] have taken the unusual step of using their judgments to correct some common Press misapprehensions about the way in which they have reached their decisions. As will emerge in the discussion of the law to follow, the truth may be very different from the hype.

The legal issues considered here

It is important to distinguish between four different legal issues in this context. First, the issue in human rights law of balancing freedom of speech on the one hand (which would allow the media to write and talk about whatever they like) and a right to privacy and to a family life on the other (which would prevent the media from writing and talking about whatever they like). Second, the development of a tort of misuse of private information (a 'tort of privacy' in effect) at common law which would sound in damages for any harm caused by a breach of that right. Third, the effect on the law relating to injunctions of the use of court orders to prevent the reporting of the existence of legal proceedings and to preserve the anonymity of the parties. Fourth, the impact on the ancient equitable principle of confidence of these issues, which is most commonly used to claim injunctions to prevent publication of confidential information. The first and second issues are beyond the scope of this book; the third and fourth issues are considered here. As will emerge, the use of super-injunctions has been quite narrow (even if the media reporting of the issue has been expansive). The principles which apply to super-injunctions, and which apply to all forms of interim injunction, will prevent many of the concerns which are commonly voiced in the public debate from becoming real.

27.8.2 The law on super-injunctions

Introduction

Now that we have sketched in the public debate, it is important to close the door on all that excitement and consider the legal principles which govern the award of injunctions. One point is particularly important: super-injunctions are interim injunctions, which means that they are only temporary. Newspapers argue that an item may only be newsworthy for a short period of time and that in consequence a temporary injunction can have the same effect as a permanent injunction on that basis; however, this is no different from the same issue in relation to general interim injunctions as considered above. It is important to look beneath the hype in this area. So-called 'super-injunctions' are in fact just interim injunctions, and so they are governed by the same principles as other interim injunctions, as considered immediately above, with the following principles specific to this context.

The core principle relating to the award of super-injunctions

The core test was set out in *In re S (A Child) (Identification: Restrictions on Publication)*[156] by Lord Steyn in the following terms:

---

155 *TSE v News Group Newspapers Ltd* [2011] EWHC 1308 (QB).
156 [2005] 1 AC, 603, *per* Lord Steyn.

The interplay between articles 8 and 10 has been illuminated by the opinions in the House of Lords in *Campbell v MGN Ltd.*[157] ... What does, however, emerge clearly from the opinions are four propositions. First, neither article has *as such* precedence over the other. Secondly, where the values under the two articles are in conflict, an intense focus on the comparative importance of the specific rights being claimed in the individual case is necessary. Thirdly, the justifications for interfering with or restricting each right must be taken into account. Finally, the proportionality test must be applied to each. For convenience I will call this the ultimate balancing test. This is how I will approach the present case.

Therefore, there are four core principles. The first principle is that Art 8 and Art 10 of the ECHR have equal weight, and therefore both must be applied to facts. As will emerge below, in relation to the other principles, the way in which the courts have approached these questions is to consider whether the right to privacy under Art 8 applies at all on the facts of any given case (because if it does not apply then there is no case to answer), before then considering whether or not Art 10 shall be taken to supersede the right to privacy in the circumstances.[158]

As identified above, the new tort on misusing private information has emerged in tandem with Art 8 of the ECHR relating to a private and family life. Article 8 provides that:

(1) Everyone has the right to respect for his private and family life, his home and his correspondence.
(2) There shall be no interference by a public authority with the exercise of this right except such as is in accordance with the law and is necessary in a democratic society in the interests of national security, public safety or the economic well-being of the country, for the prevention of disorder or crime, for the protection of health or morals, or for the protection of the rights and freedoms of others.

The countervailing right in this context is that set out in Art 10. Article 10 provides that:

(1) Everyone has the right to freedom of expression. This right shall include freedom to hold opinions and to receive and impart information and ideas without interference by public authority and regardless of frontiers. This article shall not prevent States from requiring the licensing of broadcasting, television or cinema enterprises.
(2) The exercise of these freedoms, since it carries with it duties and responsibilities, may be subject to such formalities, conditions, restrictions or penalties as are prescribed by law and are necessary in a democratic society, in the interests of national security, territorial integrity or public safety, for the prevention of disorder or crime, for the protection of health or morals, for the protection of the reputation or the rights of others, for preventing the disclosure of information received in confidence, or for maintaining the authority and impartiality of the judiciary.

As is made clear by the Court of Appeal in *Donald v Ntuli,*[159] one of the key effects of Art 10 is that it modifies the general principles which cover the award of interim injunctions because of the importance which it accords to freedom of expression for the first time and

---

157 [2004] 2 All ER 995.
158 *Murray v Express Newspapers* [2009] Ch 481.
159 [2010] EWCA Civ 1276.

the need for it to be balanced with the other elements relating to the award of such an interim injunction under the general law.[160]

The two-step process in considering an application for an injunction relating to private information: the balancing act

The law on privacy in United Kingdom is shaped by Art 8 of the ECHR, which provides that a person has a right to privacy and to a family life, and also by Art 10 of the Convention, which provides for freedom of expression for the Press amongst others. The approach taken by the courts is to recognise that a balancing act must be conducted between these two articles once the court been convinced that a question of privacy has arisen in the first place. As Lord Hope held in *Campbell v MGN Ltd*,[161] exactly that sort of balancing act had been a part of English law at least since the decision in *Attorney General v Guardian Newspapers Limited (No 2)*.[162]

The case of *Murray v Express Newspapers plc*[163] concerned covert photographs which were taken off the author JK Rowling and her child. Sir Anthony Clarke MR established a two-stage process for deciding whether or not an injunction relating to private information should be awarded, which drew in turn on the *Campbell* case. Sir Anthony Clarke held the following:

> The first question is whether there is a reasonable expectation of privacy. This is of course an objective question. The nature of the question was discussed in *Campbell v MGN Ltd*. Lord Hope emphasised that the reasonable expectation was that of a person who was affected by the publicity.[164]

If there is a reasonable expectation of privacy, then it is said that 'Article 8 is engaged'.[165] In *Hutcheson v News Group Newspapers Ltd*[166] it was held that, because the applicant would be unlikely to conceal the existence of his second family in any event, that his reasonable expectation of privacy had gone. Therefore, the first question had not been answered in the affirmative, and the Court of Appeal considered that there was no further question to answer in effect. However, in cases in which the Art 8 right to privacy is considered to be relevant, then the court will proceed to consider whether or not the Art 10 right should supersede it. This is referred to as a balancing act between those two articles. What makes it difficult in understanding this as an objective test is that the reasonable expectation is to be assessed from the perspective of the person who was affected by the publicity, which adds at the very least a large amount of subjectivity to this test. It seems as though the test is actually one of deciding whether or not we think it is reasonable for that person in those circumstances to expect her privacy to be protected.

Only if the first question is answered in the affirmative does the court move on to the second question. The second question is 'whether in all the circumstances the interest of the

---

160 *Ibid*, at [33].
161 [2004] UKHL 22, [2004] 2 AC 457, at [106].
162 [1990] 1 AC 109, *per* Lord Goff.
163 [2009] Ch 481.
164 *Ibid*, at [35].
165 *Ibid*, at [37].
166 [2011] EWCA Civ 808.

owner of the information must yield to the right to freedom of expression conferred on the publisher by article 10'.[167]

Another illustration of the balancing act which must be conducted in relation to an application for a super-injunction arose in *CTB v News Group Newspapers Ltd*[168] in which a famous footballer had had an adulterous relationship with Imogen Thomas, a reality television star, in which the footballer contended that he had been blackmailed in effect, and that he therefore offered the woman money. She contended that anonymity should be lifted in relation to him because no anonymity had been ordered to cover her: however, this somewhat disingenuous argument failed to recognise that she was the one attempting to sell her story to the newspapers. Eady J observed the two-stage process. His Lordship held that the claimant would be likely to obtain a permanent injunction to maintain the confidentiality of this information, as a married man with children, although subsequently the claimant was in fact outed on the internet.

The leading case in general terms is that of *Campbell v MGN Ltd*[169] before the House of Lords. In that case the internationally famous fashion model Naomi Campbell had denied in interviews that she took drugs and yet someone tipped off the newspapers that she was attending Narcotics Anonymous meetings: consequently, she was photographed outside one of them and a story about her addiction was published. The House of Lords was divided on this issue with Lord Nicholls and Lord Hoffmann dissenting on the basis that they considered, with great misgivings, that publication should be permitted. Lord Hope held that the information was confidential. The five elements that constituted the information were the fact that she was a drug addict, the fact she was receiving treatment, the identity of the organisation providing that treatment, details of her treatment, and a photograph of her leaving the place where that treatment was provided. Lord Hope considered that this was confidential in the sense that it was analogous to information about a medical condition.[170] His Lordship held further that there must be some interest of a private nature which the claimant wished to protect: something he was prepared to find in this context.[171] Similarly, her very attendance at these meetings was held to constitute private information which imported the duty of confidence in itself.[172] In considering the Art 10 right, his Lordship balanced the interest in publication with the serious harm that it could cause to Miss Campbell. The combination of text and photographs in this instance caused his Lordship to find that the balance weighed in favour of Miss Campbell's rights to privacy.

In a lively judgment, in which she described this case as involving 'a prima donna celebrity against a celebrity-exploiting tabloid newspaper' which intended to show that she had feet of clay,[173] Baroness Hale came to the same conclusion. As Baroness Hale pointed out, it has been accepted that the *Mirror* newspaper was entitled to publish the fact that Miss Campbell was taking drugs and was having therapy, but it was argued that what could not be disclosed was that it was with Narcotics Anonymous that she was having treatment. Her ladyship pointed out that while these were clearly private issues relating to Miss Campbell,

---

167 [2009] Ch 481, at [27].
168 [2011] EWHC 1232 (QB).
169 [2004] UKHL 22, [2004] 2 AC 457.
170 *Ibid*, at [91].
171 *Ibid*, at [92].
172 *Ibid*, at [95].
173 *Ibid*, at [143].

at the same time she earned her living from her participation in public life and by maintaining her public profile in the newspapers. Again the balance was found to lie in favour of Miss Campbell. Lord Carswell agreed. Naomi Campbell was therefore awarded damages, as opposed to an injunction on those facts, because the article had already been published.

The potentially harmful effect on children

The potentially harmful effect on children, as in the case of *Murray*, is often important in these cases. However, those children do not need to be directly involved with the circumstances. For example, Eady J was concerned in *CDE v MGN Ltd*,[174] in relation to a relationship between a television personality and 'a single mother in receipt of disability benefits' which took place primarily by electronic messages between them, involving 'a good deal of flirtation and sexual innuendo', that publication of these facts would be likely to prove distressing to the claimant's children.

The likelihood of success at trial

An issue clearly exists, as with all interim injunctions, as to the extent to which the applicant seeking an injunction must be able to demonstrate that she would be likely to be successful at trial. Lord Nicholls held in *Cream Holdings Ltd v Banerjee*[175] that the court must consider 'what degree of likelihood makes the prospect of success "sufficiently favourable". The general approach should be that courts will be exceedingly slow to make interim restraint orders where the applicant is not satisfied the court that he will probably ("more likely than not") succeed at trial.'

The question as to what sorts of speech are appropriate here under Article 10

There is clearly a question as to the sorts of information which ought to engage the right under Art 10. The courts have been very broad-minded in accepting that what may be in the public interest is an elastic concept. Indeed there are many things which they are prepared to accept as being in the public interest which one might rightly think are of no genuine interest to public debate at all. Baroness Hale set out the following conceptualisation in *Campbell v MGN Ltd*:[176]

> There are undoubtedly different types of speech, just as there are different types of private information, some of which are more deserving of protection in a democratic society than others. Top of the list is political speech. The free exchange of information and ideas on matters relevant to the organisation of the economic, social and political life of the country is crucial to any democracy. Without this, it can scarcely be called a democracy at all. This includes revealing information about public figures, especially those in elective office, which would otherwise be private but is relevant to their participation in public life. Intellectual and educational speech and expression are also important in a democracy, not least because they enable the development of an individual's

174   [2010] EWHC 3308 (QB).
175   [2005] 1 AC 253, [2004] UKHL 44, at [22].
176   [2004] AC 457, at [158].

potential to play a full part in society and in our democratic life. Artistic speech and expression is important for similar reasons . . .

In the same case, Lord Hoffmann held that in general terms 'the press is free to publish anything it likes', subject to the laws on defamation, no matter 'how trivial, spiteful or offensive the publication may be'.[177] His Lordship recognised that this is only problematic when that right to freedom of expression comes into contact with a right to privacy. Nevertheless, the House of Lords was prepared to accept that in principle the supposed hypocrisy of a supermodel claiming in an interview that she had not taken drugs while in fact she was attending Narcotics Anonymous meetings was something which was in the public interest. It might be thought, of course, that this is merely gossip of interest to the public as opposed to important information which genuinely *serves* the public interest.

In *CTB v News Group Newspapers Ltd*[178] in which a famous footballer had had an adulterous relationship with Imogen Thomas, a reality television star, Eady J observed that 'as in so many "kiss and tell" cases, it seems to me that the answer, in stage two, is not far to seek. Indeed, it was not even argued [in that case] that publication would serve the public interest'.[179] Indeed mere gossip of this sort cannot be said to *serve* the public interest in the same way that the exposure of corruption by politicians would necessarily *serve* the public interest; as opposed to being of merely titillating interest to the public.

An application to set a super-injunction aside

It will frequently happen that an applicant will seek to beef up an injunction which she has been awarded, or that a respondent will seek to have an injunction set aside. The question then is as to the basis on which an appellate court should set aside such an injunction. Sir Anthony Clarke MR has held that the test for setting aside an injunction of this sort would depend upon the applicant seeking to have the injunction set aside demonstrating that the judge at first instance had 'erred in principle or reached a conclusion that was plainly wrong'.[180]

The Court of Appeal in the case of *Donald v Ntuli*[181] considered just such an appeal from a judgment of Eady J which had granted an anonymised injunction to a member of the 'boy band' Take That in relation to another musician with whom he had had a relationship. She had sent him a text message which, in terms, suggested that she was about to sell her story to the newspapers. The claimant sought an interim injunction to restrain publication. He did so on the basis that publication would have made public knowledge private and confidential information about his life. The respondent argued that the injunction was too vague in its reference to any intimate or sexual activity between the parties amongst other things. The claimant sought to rely on Art 8 and the respondent sought to rely on a right to freedom of expression under Art 10. The Court of Appeal relied on *Campbell v MGN* and on the case of

177 *Ibid*, at [56].
178 [2011] EWHC 1232 (QB).
179 *Ibid*, at [26].
180 *Lord Browne of Madingly v Associated Newspapers Ltd* [2008] QB 103, [2007] EWCA Civ 295, at [45].
181 [2010] EWCA Civ 1276. Followed in *MNB v News Group Newspapers Ltd* [2011] EWHC 528 (QB), *per* Sharp J in *XJA v News Group Newspapers Ltd* [2010] EWHC 3174 (QB), *per* Sharp J, and in *KJH v HGF* [2010] EWHC 3064 (QB), *per* Sharp J.

In re S, and the four-stage test set out by Lord Steyn. The respondent argued that she did not intend to publish any sexually explicit details of her relationship with the claimant, given that sexual information was something which Lord Hoffmann had identified in *Campbell v MGN* as being the sort of information which would ordinarily be considered is to be private. The claimant contended that the court of first instance should have gone further and prohibited any mention of the relationship at all. The question therefore was whether in *Donald* there were any substantial arguments for publication of this information in the public interest. It was held that on these facts 'the mere fact of this past relationship which, on any view, was not entirely secret, does not carry with it a particularly grave adverse consequences'. Therefore, it was held that the judge had not erred in principle. Nor had the threshold in the case of *Browne* been reached in that it could not be demonstrated that the judge had reached a conclusion which was plainly wrong.

In the case of *Goodwin v NGN Ltd*,[182] an application was made to vary an injunction so as to permit more information about a story involving the former chief executive of the Royal Bank of Scotland and a female employee of that bank to be published by the *Sun* newspaper. The newspaper contended that it did not intend to publish any sexual or salacious information, nor to publish any photographs of the woman involved nor any members of her family. The respondent sought to resist these variations to the order. The woman contended that publication of her name by the *Sun* newspaper would be a very serious intrusion into private and family life further to Art 8. The court used the familiar two-step process, the first step being whether or not it was a reasonable expectation of privacy in the context, and the second step only being relevant if the answer to the first is in the affirmative. It was held that while the details of a sexual relationship are confidential and private, that does not necessarily mean that the 'bare fact [i.e. the existence] of a sexual relationship is private'. On the facts of the case, the parties had put forward very little evidence indeed about the nature of their relationship, and as such they failed to convince the court that there was anything about it which was specifically confidential and private. Indeed, Tugendhat J accepted a distinction between confidentiality on the one hand and press intrusion on the other, where the mere fact of intrusion by the tabloid press does not necessarily mean that the information which they uncover is confidential. Similarly, criticism in the press, no matter how robust it is, does not necessarily constitute unreasonable conduct nor harassment. In relation to the woman it was held that her name should not be published because that would be likely to precipitate a significant intrusion into their private and family life from which she was considered to be entitled to be protected. In making that award, his Lordship was concerned not to make an award which would be futile, and in this regard he recognised expressly that the woman's name might be published on the internet and in consequence that the injunction would be of no worth. Nevertheless, it was ordered that the woman's name could not be published but that her job description could be published.

The terms of a super-injunction

The report sets out a model format for a super-injunction. The central principle on the decided case law is that an injunction should be 'to the highest degree clear and precise so that no publisher would be in any doubt whether he was infringing it or not'.[183]

---

182   [2011] EWHC 1437 (QB).
183   *Times Newspapers Ltd v MGN Ltd* [1993] EMLR 443 at 447, *per* Sir Thomas Bingham MR.

27.8.3 The Report of the Committee on Super-Injunctions

The principal contribution to this debate, which is so thorough that it almost makes a text-book treatment of this topic unnecessary, is the *Report of the Committee on Super-Injunctions* ('the Report') which was prepared under the leadership of the Master of the Rolls, Lord Neuberger, and which is available online.[184] The Report is divided between the following six issues:

(1) The principle of 'open justice';
(2) The law relating to super-injunctions and anonymised injunctions (and, in essence a defence of the current position in the light of extensive media criticism of it;
(3) Procedural issues (considered here only in outline);
(4) Issues concerning data collection (considered here only in outline);
(5) Communication between the courts and Parliament (considered here only in outline);
(6) The problem of Parliamentary privilege and hyper-injunctions.

That structure will be used in the discussion to follow.

(1) The principle of 'open justice'

The Report extols the virtues of the principle of 'open justice'. This is expressed as being 'an essential aspect of our constitutional settlement'.[185] So far as the Report is concerned, the principal objections to super-injunctions relate to those injunctions being an obstacle to open justice. The Report observes that ever since the case of *Prince Albert v Strange* in 1849, and indeed much earlier than that (as considered in the preceding section of this chapter), English law has dealt with questions of confidence by means of equitable principles, both in relation to commercial secrets and private, confidential information. When the Human Rights Act 1998 passed through Parliament, Parliamentarians were at great pains to point out that they hoped that the freedom of the press would be strengthened by that legislation and that it would not be subordinated behind a right to privacy. As Spry has pointed out in his book *Principles of Equitable Remedies*,[186] the court's jurisdiction towards injunctions operates 'without limits, and can be exercised either in support of any legal right, or in the creation of a new equitable rights, as the court thinks fits in the application of equitable principles'.[187] The principle of open justice as it is deployed in the Report is based on cases such as *Scott v Scott*[188] where it was described by Lord Shaw as being 'a sound and very sacred part of the constitution of the country and the administration of justice' and that open justice is of great constitutional importance because it is 'on the whole, the best security for the pure, impartial, and efficient administration of justice, the best means for winning its public confidence and respect'.[189] *Scott v Scott* itself was a somewhat earthy proceeding in relation to a petition for divorce on grounds of a husband's impotence (in relation to which by

---

184 The *Report of the Committee on Super-Injunctions* is accessible at the following address: www.judiciary.gov. uk/Resources/JCO/Documents/Reports/super-injunction-report-20052011.pdf [accessed 8 February 2012].
185 *Report of the Committee on Super-Injunctions*, para 1.36.
186 Spry, *Principles of Equitable Remedies*, 8th edn, Sweet & Maxwell, 2010, 331.
187 The slight amendments to this quotation are taken from the Report at p 4.
188 [1913] AC 417.
189 *Report of the Committee on Super-Injunctions*, para 1.17.

medical examination it was confirmed that the wife remained a virgin). An order had been granted that the proceedings were to remain confidential but the wife had three copies of the official shorthand writer's[190] note of the proceedings made and circulated to members of the husband's family. The issue arose whether or not this was in contempt of court. It was held that these proceedings (which did not include the medical examination) did not need to be held *in camera* (that is, in secret) and that the evidence at issue could have been given in open court on the basis, as emphasised by the Earl of Halsbury, that the principle of open justice was significant.

While this principle of open justice is undoubtedly important, it is interesting that it is thought to apply to the most mundane of matters, whereas it might be thought that calls for open justice were more redolent of preventing pogroms and anti-democratic revolutions with courts operating in secret. To prevent such a situation ever developing – in the manner of the old Court of Star Chamber (discussed in Chapter 1) – then open justice is to be understood as an absolute principle. It opens justice up, to coin an old phrase, to the disinfectant properties of daylight. In general terms, it is hoped in the Report that litigants will seek less drastic remedies than super-injunctions. The Report considers that the award of a super-injunction will be appropriate when it is a 'necessity'.[191] In relation to the Civil Procedure Rules, r39.2, the Report takes the view that it is not a question of a court having a discretion to award a super-injunction, but rather a court has to award such an injunction as a 'matter of obligation' if it is justified.[192] This is interesting: the court is obliged to make such an order in appropriate circumstances; although appropriate circumstances will generally be exceptional circumstances. That makes the question as to whether or not the circumstances are appropriate for a super-injunction all the more critical because, as the Report makes clear, the award of a super-injunction is anything but a routine matter.

(2) The legal context of super-injunctions

One of the principal issues in the press coverage of the super-injunctions question was the frequency with which the courts seemed to award such super-injunctions. However, the Report lists all of the super-injunctions of which its authors were aware and thus compiles a list of only 18 cases in which the award of a super-injunction had even been considered by the courts. In each of these 18 cases, there had been a 'reasoned judgment' published, *inter alia*, over the internet. In very few of these cases had it been deemed appropriate to award a super-injunction. This survey of the decided cases does tend to undermine the press speculation that super-injunctions were common in practice. The legal principles governing the award of super-injunctions were set out above.

(3) Procedural issues

The Report sets out guidance for the procedural elements of an application for a super-injunction and the form which an order should take. As with all injunctions, there are

---

190 Those remarkable individuals would sit in court, typically with head bowed, making remarkably fast notes of the proceedings which constituted an official record of all court proceedings.

191 *Report of the Committee on Super-Injunctions*, p 11. *Pink Floyd Music Ltd v EMI Records Ltd* [2010] EWCA Civ 794; *Ntuli v Donald* [2010] EWCA Civ 1276.

192 *Report of the Committee on Super-Injunctions*, para 1.33.

questions as to whether the injunction should be awarded *ex parte*[193] so as to facilitate speed, or whether other people involved should be permitted to make representations from the outset.[194] Super-injunctions are primarily a procedural device and so their correlation with the Civil Procedure Rules (which govern civil applications in the higher courts) is necessary.

(4) Data collection

The purpose of the report in large part was to refute Press speculation about the nature and content of super-injunctions, as well as to regularise the position. To this end, the report recommended a new effort to collate and maintain data on these forms of injunction.

(5) Communication between the courts and Parliament

The difficulty of MPs and the courts coming to cross-purposes – where the former wishes to discuss or publicise an issue, and where the latter has ordered that some part of that information remain confidential – is partly one of communication. In theory, the office of the Speaker of the House of Commons and those maintaining the court lists would be able to identify matters which were *sub judice* and so prevent confidential material being debated in Parliament as a matter of comity between those two branches of the constitution. However, the fact that some parties are anonymised in litigation has meant that there have been questions raised inadvertently in Parliament about matters which had been kept confidential by court order but the Speaker's Office had not been able to find out about that litigation because the parties' identities had been anonymised.[195] The Report therefore recommends that new mechanisms for ensuring appropriate communication between officials in Parliament and in the courts are identified.

(6) The problem of Parliamentary privilege and hyper-injunctions

The difficulties of correlating the freedom of Parliament in a democratic society to debate any issue it pleases with the independence of the judiciary to make any lawful order it sees fit were considered above. This issue has become particularly acute in circumstances in which a judge has ordered that a matter be kept confidential when a Parliamentarian wants to discuss it openly in Parliament. There is also the matter of debates in Parliament being freely reported in a democratic society, which is really at the heart of the publication of such material. In the bulk of the cases which are in the public domain, the issues have revolved around information relating to private individuals being capable or being incapable of being reported by journalists.

---

193 That is, without the other parties being present.

194 Typically, even if an order is made from the outset *ex parte*, the other people involved will be able to petition the court for an alteration of the order or for its removal. There is always a judge nominated to hear applications out of hours simply because such urgent injunction requests arise in all sorts of contexts.

195 See in particular the *Trafigura* case (*RJW & SJW v The Guardian Newspaper & Person or Persons Unknown* (Claim no HQ09)) in relation to which Paul Farrelly MP asked a question on 19 October 2009 which was allowed to be tabled by the Table Clerks Office. Farrelly had known of the injunction but not the full anonymous title accorded to it, and so it had eluded the clerks and had been tabled. His asking of his question in relation to allegations of dumping toxic waste became a *cause célèbre* among those who extolled the virtues of freedom of speech in this context and suggested that Parliament offered a means of eluding such injunctions.

In response to this problem, judges have been asked to consider the award of so-called 'hyper-injunctions', which are injunctions which purport to enjoin specific MPs from discussing particular issues relating to a specific case in Parliament so as to preserve the confidentiality of information bound up in those proceedings. Similarly, there have been applications for injunctions '*contra mundum*' (that is, 'against the world') which are intended to bind everyone in the world to preserve the confidentiality of any given proceedings.

The Report is clear that the courts should not interfere with the freedom of Parliamentarians to discuss whatever they please, except that there should be some communication between the officers of Parliament and those running the court lists to identify sensitive litigation. This is clearly a difficult issue to resolve in the abstract. The right of the courts to order confidentiality on an interim basis is an unstoppable object, whereas the rights of Parliamentarians to discuss any issue they consider appropriate is an immovable post: and those two things cannot logically co-exist in the same universe – either the unstoppable object is stopped when it hits the immovable post, or the immovable post will move.

Chapter 28

Rescission and rectification

28.1 INTRODUCTION

This chapter considers two separate equitable remedies: rescission and rectification. The two remedies have been grouped together because they are concerned with issues surrounding the termination of contracts or the alteration of their terms. Rescission constitutes complete termination (or avoidance) of a contract, whereas rectification entails the alteration of its terms and possibly the termination of a given aspect of a contract as a result.

In terms of our understanding of the principles of equity, these subjects indicate the means by which equity has come to interfere with the exclusive competence of the common law in relation to contracts. Whereas a contract might be validly formed under common law, and whereas common law provides for payment of damages in situations in which there has been some misrepresentation by one party which induces the other party to enter into the contract, equity provides a means of terminating or altering contracts where to do otherwise would be against conscience.

The concept of 'conscience' is used here, again, as a summary of what the courts appear to be doing, rather than as an accurate description of the principles at work. However, it is plain that it is only in relation to the usual array of fraud, misrepresentation, mistake and equitable wrongs (such as undue influence, considered in Chapter 29) that the doctrines of rescission and rectification will be available. That is, in situations in which it would be inequitable to permit the common law to enforce the precise terms of those agreements.

28.2 RESCISSION

Rescission is an equitable remedy used to set aside contracts and to restore the parties to the positions which they had occupied previously.

In cases of fraudulent misrepresentation, the claimant will be entitled to rescind the contract to prevent the wrongdoer from benefiting from its wrongdoing. The position in relation to innocent misrepresentations is more equivocal (as considered below). Contracts requiring utmost good faith will necessarily imply a misrepresentation where such disclosure is not made.

Rescission will be generally available in cases of unconscionable bargains, or in cases of some undue influence which induces one party to enter into the contract.

A material mistake made by both parties to a contract will enable that contract to be rescinded. Unilateral mistake may lead to rescission only where there has been some unconscionability in the formation of the contract. Mistakes of law and of fact may both give good grounds for rescission.

The right to rescind will be lost where it is impossible to return the parties to the positions they occupied previously, where the contract has been affirmed, or where there has been delay.

The form of rescission that is considered in this chapter is the general equitable power to achieve a *restitutio in integrum*; that is, to restore parties to the position which they had occupied originally. The most common form of rescission is observable in the law of contract, in which parties to a purported contract are returned to their original positions by having their contract set aside. In short, rescission will be awarded in cases of mistake, misrepresentation, or to set aside an unconscionable bargain.[1]

The important point to make about rescission is that it is an equitable remedy available on application to a court of equity at the discretion of such court. The parameters of that remedy are considered below. It is, however, clear that rescission applies only to contracts which are voidable. Where a contract is void *ab initio*, there is no question of rescission on the basis that such a contract is taken never to have existed.[2] There is only a question as to the rescission of a contract if that contract is capable of being affirmed by either party. This chapter will consider rescission in its strict sense of setting aside contracts which are merely voidable, that is, capable of being declared void but not void *ab initio*.

28.2.1 The scope of equity

It is important to note that equity will not interfere with the general rule of contract that the parties should be entitled to freedom of contract. The only exception to that principle is that equity will act to prevent unconscionable behaviour in cases of bargains formed through misrepresentation, mistake, fraud or constructive fraud. Therefore, there is no claim in equity

---

1 *TSB v Camfield* [1995] 1 WLR 430.
2 *Westdeutsche Landesbank Girozentrale v Islington LBC* [1994] 4 All ER 890, *per* Leggatt LJ, CA.

to set aside a bargain in which one party is aware that the contract will be more profitable to it than to its counterparty. English law is not based on morality but rather on trade. The growth of common law and equitable principles is centred on facilitating freedom of commercial dealings. It is only in cases of the most flagrant breaches of commercial ethics (such as fraud or misrepresentation) that the courts will intervene to ensure fair play.

28.2.2 Misrepresentation

In cases of fraudulent misrepresentation, the claimant will be entitled to rescind the contract to prevent the wrongdoer from benefiting from its wrongdoing. The position in relation to innocent misrepresentations is more equivocal (as considered below). Contracts requiring utmost good faith will necessarily imply a misrepresentation where such disclosure is not made.

In circumstances where there has been a misrepresentation inducing a claimant to enter into a contract, that claimant will be entitled to rescind that contract, as considered below. There is, however, an important distinction to be made between fraudulent misrepresentation and innocent misrepresentation from the outset.

Fraudulent misrepresentation

A fraudulent misrepresentation will render a contract voidable where that misrepresentation was made with an intention that it should be acted upon by the person to whom it was made.[3] The type of fraud required is that sufficient to found a claim in the tort of deceit, that is, a misrepresentation made knowingly, or without belief in its truth, or with recklessness as to whether or not it was true.[4] The rationale for permitting rescission of contracts made on the basis of fraudulent misrepresentation is that it would be inequitable to permit a person with such a fraudulent motive to profit from their common law rights.[5] As such, it is a principle which is easy to reconcile with the underlying tenets of equity.

Innocent misrepresentation

Aside from fraudulent misrepresentations, there is then the issue as to which forms of misrepresentations made without a fraudulent motive will also entitle a claimant to claim rescission of a contract created in reliance on such a representation. Absent the motive of fraud, which will clearly act to prevent a fraudster from benefiting from her own wrong-doings, there is the further question whether mere negligence or innocent misstatements ought, in equity, to permit a contract to be set aside.

At common law, an innocent misrepresentation will found a claim for rescission of the contract provided that the matter which made up the representation has become a term of the contract.[6] Section 1 of the Misrepresentation Act 1967 provides further that rescission will

---

3 *Peek v Gurney* (1873) LR 6 HL 377; *County NatWest Bank Ltd v Barton* (1999) *The Times*, 29 July.
4 *Redgrave v Hurd* (1881) 20 Ch D 1; *Derry v Peek* (1889) 14 App Cas 337.
5 *Redgrave v Hurd* (1881) 20 Ch D 1, *per* Lord Jessel MR.
6 *Derry v Peek* (1889) 14 App Cas 337; *Low v Bouverie* [1891] 3 Ch 82. Cf *William Sindall v Cambridgeshire CC* [1994] 1 WLR 1016, 1035, *per* Hoffmann LJ.

be available in cases of innocent misrepresentation in a situation in which that misrepresentation has induced the other party to enter into the contract.[7] Furthermore, in equity, that a person had made an innocent misrepresentation would give the other party to the contract a good defence to a claim, for specific performance of that contract.[8] The court has power to order that a contract continue to subsist in spite of the innocent misrepresentation where it would be equitable to do so.[9] In general terms, any term[10] in the contract which purports to exclude the right to rescind on the basis of misrepresentation will be of no effect unless it is considered equitable to give effect to that term.[11]

Contracts uberrimae fidei

Aside from the two categories of misrepresentation considered above, there is a further important category of contracts which have a standard of utmost good faith (or *uberrimae fidei*) read into them by law. The most common example of this type of contract is the contract of insurance. Utmost good faith connotes an obligation on parties to such contracts to make full disclosure of all material facts. Therefore, there is an obligation not to conceal any matter which might be of importance. For insurance contracts, this means that the insured is required to make full disclosure to the insurer so that there is no matter of which the insurer is ignorant.

The significance of such contracts in the context of misrepresentation is that it is not possible for a defendant to fail to disclose information and then seek to claim that there was no misrepresentation on the basis that silence ought not to be considered a representation at all.[12] In situations in which there is a requirement of utmost good faith, silence as to a material factor which ought to have been disclosed will be considered to be tantamount to a misrepresentation.

There may also be factual situations in which concealing facts, perhaps in response to a direct question, might amount to a misrepresentation even though based on silence. Suppose an investor was seeking to buy shares in Sunderland AFC plc and asked the board of directors 'tell me now if you are intending to release world-class manager Roy Keane; if not I will invest in the club's shares'. If the board of directors were to sit in silence and let him purchase a shareholding as a result, knowing that they had already accepted Roy Keane's resignation and retirement from football, that silence would be a misrepresentation in the same way that a verbal denial would have been a misrepresentation.[13]

28.2.3 Undue influence and unconscionable bargains

> *Rescission will be generally available in cases of unconscionable bargains, or in cases of some undue influence which induces one party to enter into the contract.*

7 See also *Bannerman v White* (1861) 10 CB 844; *Heilbut Symons & Co v Buckleton* [1913] AC 30.
8 *Walker v Boyle* [1982] 1 WLR 495; *Smelter Corporation of Ireland Ltd v O'Driscoll* [1977] IR 305.
9 Misrepresentation Act 1967, s 2(2).
10 *Walker v Boyle* [1982] 1 WLR 495; *South Western General Property Co v Marton* (1982) 263 EG 1090.
11 Misrepresentation Act 1967, s 3.
12 *Gordon v Gordon* (1821) 3 Swans 400; *Harvey v Cooke* (1827) 4 Russ 34; *Roberts v Roberts* [1905] 1 Ch 704.
13 Roy Keane has since left. (This footnote, and indeed this example, is the legacy of earlier editions and I have not the heart to change it. The arrival of Martin O'Neill is a new cause for optimism, however.)

The problem of undue influence is considered in Chapter 29, particularly in relation to setting aside mortgage contracts in situations in which the mortgagee had constructive notice of some undue influence or misrepresentation having been exercised over a co-signatory by a mortgagor to such a mortgage transaction. Furthermore, it was also considered that where one party to a transaction exerts undue influence over the other party to that contract, the victim of the undue influence will be entitled to have that contract rescinded.[14] Alongside undue influence are the other categories of equitable wrongs and those issues which will be categorised as unconscionable bargains.

28.2.4 Mistake

A material mistake made by both parties to a contract will enable that contract to be rescinded. Unilateral mistake may lead to rescission only where there has been some unconscionability in the formation of the contract. Mistakes of law and of fact may both give good grounds for rescission.

Unilateral and common mistake

The rule in relation to mistake is, strictly, that a mistake made by both parties (common mistake) in entering into a transaction will enable that contract to be rescinded.[15] However, where only one party to a contract is acting under a mistake (unilateral mistake), the contract, typically, will not be rescinded[16] unless the party who was not operating under a mistake was aware that the other party was so operating.[17]

Thus, in *Cooper v Phibbs*,[18] parties to a lease had created the lease agreement on the mistaken assumption that the purported lessee did not already have an equitable interest in the demised property. On discovering the existence of this equitable interest, the lessee sought to rescind the lease contract on the ground that both parties to it had been operating under a common mistake as to the lessee's property rights. The House of Lords held that the contract could be rescinded on the basis of the parties' common mistake.

Furthermore, it does appear that the mistake must have been operative on the minds of the contracting parties and must have induced them to enter into the contract.[19] Thus, in *Oscar Chess v Williams*,[20] where two parties contracting for the sale of a car in circumstances in which some unknown third party had altered the log book's entry as to the date the car was manufactured, the contract was not rescinded for mistake because neither party had sought to rely on that date in the creation of the contract.

---

14 *Barclays Bank v O'Brien* [1993] 3 WLR 786. Aside from the examples, considered above, of actual fraud, misrepresentation and constructive fraud, it is possible that contracts will be rescinded in situations in which there is an operative mistake between both parties.
15 *Cundy v Lindsay* (1878) 3 App Cas 459.
16 *Riverlate Properties Ltd v Paul* [1975] Ch 133.
17 *Webster v Cecil* (1861) 30 Beav 62; *Hartog v Colin & Shields* [1939] 2 All ER 566. See also *Clarion Ltd v National Provident Institution* [2000] 1 WLR 1888.
18 (1867) LR 2 HL 149.
19 *Bell v Lever Bros* [1932] AC 161.
20 [1957] 1 WLR 370.

The scope of equity in relation to mistake

Lord Denning had argued for a broader equitable discretion to permit rescission of contracts where there was a fundamental mistake which led to the creation of the contract, even in circumstances in which the common law would not permit such an action based on mistake.[21] This approach has been followed in subsequent decisions. However, it is difficult to reconcile with the House of Lords decision in *Bell v Lever Bros*.[22] What is at issue is the extent to which equity can, and should, operate to set aside contracts on the basis that the mistake is so fundamental to the contract that the contract cannot be said to reflect the real intentions of the parties at the time of its creation.

This book is not able to consider the detailed ramifications of this dilemma for the law of contract. In applying general principles of equity, the correct approach to a case of unilateral mistake appears to be to measure the extent to which the defendant is acting unconscionably in seeking to rely on a mistake to the detriment of the claimant. Where neither party was aware of the mistake at the time that the contract was created, neither party's conscience can be said to be affected. Therefore, there ought properly to be no equity to rescind such a transaction. The loss must lie where it falls, with the party who was in error.

There is also the position in relation to a common mistake between both contracting parties. On the one hand, it is difficult to assert that there is an unjust factor at work in a situation in which both parties are innocent in the mistake that they have made in the formation of their contract. However, there would be no common intention to effect the transaction in the manner it turns out, where there was a mistake in the minds of both parties about something fundamental to the contract.

It is suggested that this latter argument cuts to the heart of the nature of a contract, being a bargain between two or more people that they will transact on agreed terms in the expectation that certain matters are the case and will enable their agreement to proceed in the manner expected. Matters extraneous to the contract, such as market movements or war, which make the anticipated performance of the contract impossible (or the situation so different from the parties' original expectations as to be virtually impossible) would appear to fall within the doctrine of frustration where they can be shown to be so fundamental to the proper functioning of the agreement. Common mistake as to a fact or as to law, on the other hand, will mean that there is no agreement between those parties at all.

That is different, it is suggested, from the situation in which there is unilateral mistake because the world-view which created the common intention of the contracting parties is not affected; rather, one party is insufficiently informed as to the true state of affairs. In such situations, the conscience of the party who gains will be affected, in terms of equity, only if that party has unduly influenced the losing party or made a misrepresentation to the loser, or exerted some fraud over the loser. In the former case, however, no one's conscience is affected; only the commercial acumen of the party acting under a mistake. While there is no apparent morality in this approach (maybe where one party exploits another's ineptitude), that is the business of capitalism. The approach of English law is to intercede only to prevent unconscionability, but never to interfere with the profit motive of commercial people in the absence of such unconscionability.

---

21 *Solle v Butcher* [1950] 2 QB 507.
22 [1932] AC 161; *Hartog v Colin & Shields* [1939] 2 All ER 566.

Mistakes of fact and mistakes of law

Where the parties have made a mistake as to some material fact in the creation of their contract, that contract will be capable of being rescinded. That parties are entitled to rely on a mistake of law in seeking to rescind their contracts has been upheld by the House of Lords in *Kleinwort Benson v Lincoln CC*.[23] The facts of *Kleinwort Benson v Lincoln CC* are those common to the local authority swaps, as in *Westdeutsche Landesbank Girozentrale v Islington LBC*,[24] in which a bank was seeking to recover moneys paid to the respondent local authority under interest rate swap agreements which the House of Lords in *Hazell v Hammersmith & Fulham*[25] had held to be beyond the powers of the local authority and therefore void *ab initio*. The claim for recovery of payments was based on a contention that those payments had been made under a mistake of law: that is, the assumption that local authorities could enter into interest rate swaps.

Lord Goff held that there could be restitution of money paid under a mistake of law (thus repealing the long-established common law rule to the contrary). One interesting argument raised by the appeal was whether a mistake of law must be a mistake as to decided case law or legislation, or whether it was sufficient that there was a mistaken belief embodied in a common perception in a marketplace that the law would give effect to a particular rule if such a matter was ever brought before a court. Thus, it was argued that the swaps market had generally believed that local authorities could enter into swaps agreements even though a subsequent decision of the House of Lords established that they could not. The House of Lords held that payments made under a settled understanding of the law among market participants, which is subsequently departed from by judicial decision, are irrecoverable on grounds of mistake of law.

There remains a large amount of uncertainty as to precisely those factors which will constitute a mistake of law. The very fact that common law and equity develop on a case-by-case basis means that it is impossible to be certain as to the law in any given case. Consequently, it is important to know precisely what types of mistake of law will be permissible in the future, but there is no definitive, detailed judicial guidance at the time of writing.

Questions of equity and of restitution

Thus the issue of mistake feeds directly into questions of restitution as well as into questions of rescission. The question is, again, as to the role of equity in this context. On the one hand, equity is applying age-old principles concerned with the rights of parties to escape their bargains. On the other hand, equity appears to be operating to prevent the unjust enrichment of one contracting party at the expense of the other party where there is some unjust factor (such as mistake or misrepresentation) involved in the generation of that enrichment. Aside from the entitlement to rescission, it is also open to the claimant to seek common law damages for breach of contract[26] and keep any deposit in lieu of damages.[27]

---

23 [1998] 4 All ER 513.
24 [1996] AC 669.
25 [1992] 2 AC 1, [1991] 2 WLR 372, [1991] 1 All ER 545.
26 *Johnson v Agnew* [1980] AC 367.
27 *Dewar v Mintoft* [1912] 2 KB 373; *Damon Compania Naviera SA v Hapag-Lloyd International SA* [1985] 1 WLR 435.

28.2.5 Loss of the right to rescind

The right to rescind will be lost where it is impossible to return the parties to the positions they occupied previously, where the contract has been affirmed, or where there has been delay.

While the preceding sections have considered those situations in which rescission will be available, it must be remembered that rescission is a discretionary, equitable remedy. Therefore, it is possible that a court may hold that any given set of circumstances may appear to fall within entitlement to rescission but that the applicant will not be entitled to rescind a contract where it would be inequitable to do so, perhaps in circumstances in which the applicant has begun to perform the contract in full knowledge of the factor which is relied on to support the claim for rescission. In such circumstances, it is said to be inequitable to allow the applicant to set aside a contract which its conduct has indicated that it intends to honour.

Possibility of restitutio in integrum

It is necessary for an award of rescission that it is possible to return the parties to the position which they occupied before the creation or performance of the contract: an inability to do so would negate the possibility of rescission.[28] The process of restitution may be resorted to such that it is not necessary to restore any specific property passed under the agreement, provided that the value of that property can be restored by means of equitable compensation.[29] It may be the case that in some instances it will be impossible to restore the parties to the position which they had occupied originally because the property which was passed (perhaps sensitive information or know-how) is not capable of being compensated by financial restitution. However, the general proposition remains true that rescission will be effected if appropriate value can be restored.[30] Furthermore, it is possible for the court to award damages rather than rescission in cases of misrepresentation under s 2(2) of the Misrepresentation Act 1967, which provides that:

> Where a person entered into a contract after a misrepresentation has been made to him otherwise than fraudulently, and he would be entitled, by reason of the misrepresentation, to rescind the contract . . . the court . . . may declare the contract subsisting and award damages in lieu of rescission.

Therefore, a contract can be affirmed by a court where it appears that damages would provide adequate remedy and make rescission unnecessary.

Affirmation

In a situation in which the claimant has affirmed the transaction in full knowledge of the factor which is subsequently relied upon to make out a claim for rescission, that claimant

---

28 *Erlanger v New Sombrero Phosphate Co* (1873) 3 App Cas 1218; *Clarke v Dickson* (1859) EB & E 148; *Lagunas Nitrate Co v Lagunas Syndicate* [1899] 2 Ch 392; *Steedman v Frigidaire Corp* [1932] WN 248; *Thorpe v Fasey* [1949] Ch 649; *Butler v Croft* (1973) 27 P & CR 1. Cf *Urquhart v Macpherson* (1878) 3 App Cas 831.

29 *Mahoney v Purnell* [1996] 3 All ER 61.

30 *Newbigging v Adam* (1886) 34 Ch D 582; *Spence v Crawford* [1939] 3 All ER 271.

will not be entitled to claim rescission of the contract.[31] In *Peyman v Lanjani*,[32] the defendant had carried out a fraudulent impersonation of someone else to obtain a leasehold interest in a restaurant. The claimant knew of the fraud, but did not know that it gave him a right to rescission, when he agreed to become the defendant's manager. It was held that the claimant could not rely on rescission in these circumstances where he had known of the fraud but nevertheless entered knowingly into the transaction. In such circumstances, the claimant is deemed to have waived his rights in respect of the claim for rescission.[33]

Suppose a situation in which Sunderland AFC contracted to acquire a footballer on the basis of an innocent representation that the footballer was predominantly left-footed and therefore capable of playing on the left wing. Sunderland AFC would be entitled to rescind that contract on the basis of a fundamental misrepresentation if it transpired that the player was, in fact, only capable of playing effectively on the right wing. However, if Sunderland AFC, in full knowledge of their right to rescind, agreed to buy the player and to play him anyway, they would be deemed to have affirmed the contract and therefore lost their right to rescind.

Delay and acquiescence

In a number of circumstances, affirmation can take the form of implied affirmation. Therefore, affirmation can take the form of an express agreement to waive the right of rescission, or it can be merely implied from the circumstances.[34] It is possible for a sufficient delay in activating the right of rescission to raise the inference of affirmation of the contract. Alternatively, that delay, or some action performed in furtherance of the contract, might be deemed to constitute acquiescence in the continued validity of the transaction. As above, it would be important that the claimant had knowledge both of the factor giving rise to the claim for rescission and of the right to rescind at the time of affirmation.

There is a further possibility for loss of the right to rescind in the situation in which a third party acquires rights in the subject matter of the transaction.[35] However, the third party must acquire those rights for valuable consideration and not be merely a volunteer.[36]

28.3 RECTIFICATION

Rectification is available to amend the terms of a contract better to reflect the true intentions of the contracting parties. Rectification will be available in circumstances of common mistake. Rectification will be available in relation to a unilateral mistake only in cases of fraud or similar unconscionable behaviour. Rectification may also be available in respect of voluntary settlements to reflect the settlor's evident intention. Alternatively, the court may order the delivery and cancellation of documents, or in relation to 'ne exeat regno'.

---

31 *Peyman v Lanjani* [1985] Ch 457.
32 *Ibid.*
33 *Clough v London & North Western Railway Co* (1871) LR 7 Ex Ch 26.
34 Lapse of time will not necessarily preclude this application: *Life Association of Scotland v Siddal* (1861) 3 De GF & J 58; *Charter v Trevelyan* (1844) 11 Cl & F 714; *Leaf v International Galleries* [1950] 2 KB 86.
35 *Oakes v Turquand* (1867) LR 2 HL 325.
36 *Re Eastgate* [1905] 1 KB 465.

28.3.1 The nature of the remedy of rectification

The purpose of rectification is not to set a contract aside, but rather to amend its terms to reflect the real intention of the parties.[37] It is restricted to situations in which there is a written document which fails to reflect the true intention of the parties.[38] The order effects an alteration in the written document itself.[39] However, what rectification does not do is alter the agreement itself, on the basis that equity will not intervene in the contractual freedom of the parties.[40] Rather, rectification recognises that the parties have made a mistake in a written document which requires alteration to reflect their true contractual intention. Rectification is a discretionary remedy,[41] but will generally be ordered provided that some substantive right of the parties is at issue rather than a mere fiscal advantage which is sought by means of the rectification.[42] Rectification will not be ordered where there is some sufficient, alternative remedy available, such as common law damages,[43] or where the matter forming the subject matter of the application could be dealt with by a simple correction of, for example, a clerical error.[44] As considered above in relation to rescission, there is a need to distinguish between cases of common mistake and cases of unilateral mistake.

28.3.2 Common mistake between parties

Rectification will be available in circumstances of common mistake.

Where there is a common mistake between two parties to a contract, and it is possible to ascertain their true contractual intention, the court is able to order rectification of the written document.[45] The common intention of the parties to the contract must be demonstrable so as to support the claim for rectification.[46] Therefore, it is necessary to demonstrate that an agreement was formed before the document was created, and that the document mistakenly contradicted the common intention set out in that agreement.[47]

28.3.3 Unilateral mistake

Rectification will be available in relation to a unilateral mistake only in cases of fraud or similar unconscionable behaviour.

Despite the general principle of contract law that mistake must be a common mistake of contracting parties, there may be situations in which unilateral mistake will found a successful

---

37 *M'Cormack v M'Cormack* (1877) 1 LR Ir 119; *Frederick E Rose (London) Ltd v William H Pim Jr & Co Ltd* [1953] 2 QB 450.
38 *Racal Group Services v Ashmore* [1995] STC 1151 – requiring that the mistake must have been made in the writing.
39 *Craddock Bros Ltd v Hunt* [1923] 2 Ch 136.
40 *Mackenzie v Coulson* (1869) LR 8 Eq 368.
41 *Whiteside v Whiteside* [1950] Ch 65, 71, *per* Lord Evershed MR.
42 *Ibid.*
43 *Ibid; Walker Property Investments (Brighton) Ltd v Walker* (1947) 177 LT 204.
44 *Wilson v Wilson* (1854) 5 HLC 40.
45 *Murray v Parker* (1854) 19 Beav 305; *Mackenzie v Coulson* (1869) LR 8 Eq 368.
46 *Frederick E Rose (London) Ltd v William-Pim Jr & Co Ltd* [1953] 2 QB 450. See also *Crane v Hegeman-Harris Co Inc* [1939] 1 All ER 662; *Joscelyne v Nissen* [1970] 2 QB 86.
47 *Gilhespie v Burdis* (1943) 169 LT 91.

claim for rectification.[48] The first situation in which such rectification may be awarded is where the defendant was guilty of fraud in permitting the claimant to enter into the contract under a mistake.[49] The second is where the defendant knew that the claimant considered the mistaken element to be a term of the contract.[50] Both of these scenarios are clearly proximate to the general equitable principle that a party will not be permitted to rely on its common law rights in the context of fraud or unconscionable behaviour. In both of these cases, the defendant would be knowingly allowing the claimant to suffer a loss or detriment as a result of some mistake of law or mistake of fact. Buckley LJ considered this principle to turn on the issue whether or not the conscience of the defendant was affected by failing to draw the mistake to the claimant's attention in circumstances in which the defendant knew that it would benefit from the claimant entering into the contract under the influence of that mistake.[51]

Alternatively, where one party to the transaction knows of the mistake and nevertheless allows the other party to enter into the transactions, a form of equitable estoppel will prevent that person from resisting a claim for rectification.[52] It is sufficient for the operation of this form of estoppel that the defendant recklessly shut his eyes to the fact that a mistake had been made – it is not necessary that actual knowledge of the mistake be demonstrated.[53] This latter principle accords with equity's general purpose to avoid unconscionable behaviour[54] and dishonesty in a broad sense.[55]

28.3.4 Rectification of voluntary settlements

Rectification may also be available in respect of voluntary settlements to reflect the settlor's evident intention.

The last situation in which rectification may be important, particularly in relation to the law of trusts, is in relation to settlements. It is possible to effect rectification of a will where it can be demonstrated that the will as drafted did not express the clear intention of the testator (for example, where names are mistakenly transposed).[56] With reference to *inter vivos* settlements, it is possible to achieve rectification also at the instance of the settlor,[57] or potentially at the instance of a beneficiary.[58] However, cases in which such rectifications have been made are rare and turn on very specific evidence of an intention to provide something

---

48 The doctrine of unjust enrichment may provide a useful analysis of this area as being concerned to preclude enrichment being derived from an unjust factor: that is, knowledge of the other person's mistake. Clearly, however, there is a narrow line between knowing that someone is making a mistake of fact or law in entering into a contract and knowing that the other person is unlikely to make a profit from a transaction, where the latter is permitted under more general law of contract.
49 *Ball v Storie* (1823) 1 Sim & St 210; *Hoblyn v Hoblyn* (1889) 41 Ch D 200.
50 *A Roberts & Co Ltd v Leicestershire CC* [1961] Ch 555.
51 *Thomas Bates & Son Ltd v Wyndham's (Lingerie) Ltd* [1981] 1 All ER 1077.
52 *Whitley v Delaney* [1914] AC 132; *Monaghan CC v Vaughan* [1948] IR 306; *A Roberts & Co Ltd v Leicestershire CC* [1961] Ch 555; *Thomas Bates & Son Ltd v Wyndham's (Lingerie) Ltd* [1981] 1 WLR 505.
53 *Commission for New Towns v Cooper* [1995] Ch 259; *Templiss Properties v Hyams* [1999] EGCS 60.
54 *Riverlate Properties Ltd v Paul* [1975] (Ch) 133.
55 Cf *Royal Brunei Airlines v Tan* [1995] 2 AC 378; *Twinsectra Ltd v Yardley* [1999] Lloyd's Rep Bank 438.
56 Administration of Justice Act 1982, s 20.
57 *Re Butlin's ST* [1976] Ch 251.
58 *Thompson v Whitmore* (1860) 1 John & H 268.

different in the settlement, such as by means of a letter of instructions to a trustee.[59] The unilateral mistake of the settlor is sufficient to ground a claim for rectification of the settlement, provided that the settlement is not part of a bargain between the settlor and the trustees (in which case common mistake must be proved).[60]

28.3.5 Delivery up and cancellation of documents

A separate, but similar, remedy in relation to documents is that of delivery up and cancellation. Rather than rectify a document to reflect the true intentions of the parties, the court will order the cancellation of that document in circumstances in which a document has been declared void and where it is considered by the court that it would be inequitable for one party to remain in possession of a document which appears, on its face, to be valid.[61] The remedy is available even if the document is void at common law,[62] although there must be some ground of inequity to invoke the equitable jurisdiction.[63] Similarly, where a contract is voidable and has been declared void, the remedy of delivery up may be ordered.[64] The remedy will not obtain where the contract is not wholly avoided, however.[65]

The purpose behind this remedy is to prevent the inequity of allowing one party to a purported transaction to retain an apparently valid document when the transaction has been declared void.[66] Clearly, there would be a risk to the other party that the document could be used purportedly to grant rights to third parties acting in good faith, despite the invalidity of the underlying transaction creating the document. Therefore, in relation to a deed of conveyance, for example, which had been procured by fraudulent misrepresentation (and therefore held to have been void *ab initio*), the risk would be that the fraudster would seek to transfer the benefit of the deed to a *bona fide* purchaser for value without notice.[67] The innocent party to the void transaction would therefore face the difficulty of establishing rights in the subject matter of the deed against the purchaser. The remedy of delivery up and cancellation requires that the fraudster, in this example, deliver the document to the innocent party and that the document then be cancelled.

As with many of the equitable principles which have been considered, the remedy will not be available where a remedy at common law would be sufficient.[68]

Similarly, the court may order the remedy on terms to achieve justice between the parties.[69] For example, a borrower under a loan agreement effected by means of a document which was held void may be entitled to cancel the document subject to a requirement to repay the moneys borrowed so that the borrower would not be unjustly enriched.[70]

---

59 *Weir v Van Tromp* (1900) 16 TLR 531.
60 *Re Butlin's ST* [1976] Ch 251.
61 *Davis v Duke of Marlborough* (1819) 2 Swan 108.
62 *Ryan v Macmath* (1789) 3 Bro CC 15.
63 *Simpson v Lord Howden* (1837) 3 My & Cr 97.
64 *Duncan v Worrall* (1822) 10 Price 31.
65 *Onions v Cohen* (1865) 2 H & M 354; *Ideal Bedding Co Ltd v Holland* [1907] 2 Ch 157.
66 *Jervis v White* (1802) 7 Ves 413; *Wynne v Callender* (1826) 1 Russ 293; *Earl of Milltown v Stewart* (1837) 3 My & Cr 18.
67 *Peake v Highfield* (1826) 1 Russ 559; *Burton v Gray* (1873) 8 Ch App 932.
68 *Brooking v Maudslay, Son and Field* (1888) 38 Ch D 636.
69 *Kasumu v Baba-Egbe* [1956] AC 539.
70 *Lodge v National Union Investment Co Ltd* [1907] 1 Ch 300.

28.3.6 *Ne exeat regno*

The writ of *ne exeat regno* is rarely deployed in modern litigation. Literally, it is an order that the defendant should not leave the kingdom. It entitles the successful applicant to arrest a debtor such that the debtor is required to provide security for a debt. The writ is available only in circumstances in which there is a good cause action for at least £50, where there is a 'probable cause' to believe that the debtor would leave the jurisdiction unless arrested, and that it would be to the material prejudice of the applicant if the debtor were outside the jurisdiction.[71] This remedy is typically sought in support of an application for a freezing injunction to prevent a debtor from leaving the jurisdiction.

---

71 *Felton v Callis* [1969] 1 QB 200, *per* Megarry J.

Doctrine of notice and undue influence

OVERVIEW

Where there has been undue influence or a misrepresentation exercised by a mortgagor over a signatory to a mortgage contract, or over a surety of a mortgage transaction, and if the mortgagee has not taken reasonable steps to ensure that that signatory or surety has received independent legal advice as to the nature of the transaction, the mortgagee will be taken to have had constructive notice of the undue influence or misrepresentation. In such a situation, the signatory/surety can set the mortgage aside against the mortgagee.[1] Whereas previously it was necessary to demonstrate that there was some manifest disadvantage to the signatory/surety in the transaction, such that the mortgagee would be fixed with notice of the undue influence or misrepresentation, that is no

---

1 *Barclays Bank v O'Brien* [1994] 1 AC 180; *Royal Bank of Scotland v Etridge* [1998] 4 All ER 705, CA.

longer a requirement.[2] However, there must be something about the transaction which would cause the mortgagee to be put on notice.[3] An example of a situation in which there will generally be something about the transaction which ought to put the mortgagee on notice is where the claimant was acting as a surety.[4]

There are two categories of undue influence: actual undue influence and presumed undue influence. Actual undue influence requires evidence of some influence exercised over the claimant. Notice of presumed undue influence will arise (seemingly) in situations in which there is a manifest disadvantage to the claimant, or where there is a special relationship between the claimant and the mortgagor which ought to put the mortgagee on notice.[5] In circumstances in which the transaction is ostensibly unremarkable and to the financial advantage of the claimant, no claim would stand against the defendant third party.[6]

The mortgagee will not be bound by any undue influence or misrepresentation where the mortgagee has taken 'reasonable steps' to find out the signatory's rights.[7] 'Reasonable steps' will be said to exist in circumstances in which the claimant has received, or even just signed a certificate asserting that she has received, independent legal advice as to the effect of the mortgage or surety she is signing.[8]

In circumstances in which the claimant had knowledge of a part of the mortgage or surety but did not know the full amount of the liability, the claimant will nevertheless be entitled to have the mortgage set aside in toto.[9] The only exception to that principle will be where the claimant has nevertheless taken some benefit from the transaction – in which case, the claimant will be required to account to the defendant for that benefit.[10]

The doctrines of undue influence and misrepresentation have long formed part of the equitable doctrine of constructive fraud. The scope of these doctrines has been enlarged by recent decisions relating to the creation of mortgages, in which some person is forced into signing a mortgage contract or agreeing to act as a surety for a mortgage contract as a result of undue influence or misrepresentation as to its terms. In this chapter the discussion will focus on the application of the general doctrines of constructive fraud and the doctrine of notice to the particular context of the law of mortgages: the lesser here stands for the greater.

29.1 THE DOCTRINE OF NOTICE

The doctrine of notice has seen something of a resurgence in recent years, after it had been consigned to the footnotes of many land law courses. The reason for this resurgence was a series of decisions of the House of Lords in which Lord Browne-Wilkinson placed the

---

2 *Royal Bank of Scotland v Etridge (No 2)* [2002] AC 773, HL.

3 *Ibid.*

4 *Perry v National Provincial Bank* [1910] 1 Ch 464; *Royal Bank of Scotland v Etridge (No 2)* [2002] AC 773, HL; *Greene King plc v Stanley* [2002] BPIR 491.

5 *Barclays Bank v O'Brien* [1994] 1 AC 180; *CIBC v Pitt* [1993] 3 WLR 802 – in the manner considered below.

6 *CIBC v Pitt* [1993] 3 WLR 802; *Leggatt v National Westminster Bank* [2000] All ER (D) 1458, CA.

7 *Barclays Bank v O'Brien* [1994] 1 AC 180.

8 *Midland Bank v Massey* [1995] 1 All ER 929; *Banco Exterior Internacional v Mann* [1995] 1 All ER 936; *Halifax Mortgage Services Ltd v Stepsky* [1996] Ch 1; *Barclays Bank v Coleman* [2000] 1 All ER 385.

9 *TSB Bank v Camfield* [1995] 1 All ER 951; *Castle Phillips Finance v Piddington* (1995) 70 P & CR 592.

10 *Midland Bank v Greene* [1994] 2 FLR 827; *Dunbar Bank plc v Nadeem* [1997] 2 All ER 253.

doctrine of notice 'at the heart of equity'.[11] As considered already in this book, the core decision in *Westdeutsche Landesbank Girozentrale v Islington LBC*[12] reaffirmed the core principles on which a constructive trust will be imposed – placing knowledge of the unconscionability of the action at its centre: as considered in Chapter 12. This approach has demonstrated a theme in the case law of retreating to the core principles on which equitable institutions work. As part of this notion of conscience, Lord Browne-Wilkinson also turned to the importance of the role of the doctrine of notice in his leading speech in *Barclays Bank v O'Brien*,[13] a case concerning the rights of co-owners to set aside mortgages, examined later in this chapter. In that decision, Lord Browne-Wilkinson asserted that the doctrine of notice is at the heart of equity, in that notice of (or, in terms of constructive trusts, knowledge of) another's rights will preclude a defendant from seeking to defeat that person's rights.

The role of the doctrine of notice in most land law courses is limited to the issue of protecting equitable interests in unregistered land as centred on a number of cases on the rights of persons in actual occupation.[14] The purpose of the doctrine is to make persons bound by the rights of others in circumstances in which they have notice of those same rights. It is important to note that this doctrine refers to 'notice' of those rights, rather than to 'knowledge' of them. It is not required, in all cases, that the defendant actually *know* of the rights in question; instead, it is sufficient if there has been some series of events by which the defendant is deemed to have had those rights brought sufficiently to her attention such that she ought to be bound by them.

The ambit of the doctrine of notice is set out most clearly in the case of *Hunt v Luck*.[15] There are three strands to the doctrine: actual notice, imputed notice, and constructive notice. The defendant will be said to have notice of the claimant's rights in any of these three situations. The first, actual notice, refers to the situation in which the rights have been brought directly to the attention of the defendant such that she does know of the existence and nature of those rights.

The second, imputed notice is the strand which arises most often in the case law. Imputed notice arises when some person has notice of the claimant's rights in circumstances in which the defendant ought to be bound by the notice of that third person; for example, the third person may be the defendant's agent, as in *Kingsnorth Finance v Tizard*.[16] In *Tizard*, the finance company employed a surveyor (therefore, the finance company's agent) to inspect a property before entering into a mortgage agreement with the legal owner of that property. It was held that the surveyor had notice of the rights of the legal owner's wife due to his failure to inspect the property sufficiently closely and because of the finance company's failure to spot discrepancies in the information provided to it by the legal owner. The court held that, because the agent/surveyor had notice of these rights, the principal/finance company ought similarly to have constructive notice of everything of which the agent had notice.

The third category, constructive notice, arises when a person knows of certain facts which put him on inquiry as to the possible existence of the rights of another person, and that

11 *Barclays Bank v O'Brien* [1994] 1 AC 180, [1993] 3 WLR 786.
12 [1996] AC 669.
13 [1994] 1 AC 180.
14 *Midland Bank Trust Co Ltd v Green* [1981] 2 WLR 28; *Kingsnorth Finance v Tizard* [1986] 2 All ER 54; *Bristol & West Building Society v Henning* [1985] 1 WLR 778; *Abbey National v Cann* [1991] 1 AC 56.
15 [1902] 1 Ch 428.
16 [1986] 2 All ER 54.

person fails to make such inquiry or take such other steps as are reasonable in the circumstances. Failure to make such inquiries will lead to a finding that such a person has constructive notice of the other person's right and therefore takes subject to it. Thus, constructive notice operates to bring within its ambit situations in which the defendant does not have actual notice but is deemed to have notice, potentially, through the failure of another person to identify reasonably ascertainable information.

The doctrine of notice had become of peripheral importance in situations concerning land as a result of the introduction of the registered land system and land charges. Similarly, the growth of tests of knowledge in the area of constructive trusts and equitable claims, such as *Barlow Clowes*[17] and *Re Montagu*[18] (considered in Chapters 20 and 19) have meant that the long-standing doctrine of notice had become of less importance. In many cases, such as *Tizard*, the test of notice had transformed from an issue surrounding factors of which the agent could be said to have notice, into a test asserting those things which the agent ought to have looked for. This is to be contrasted with cases like *Henning v Bristol and West Building Society*,[19] in which the court looked for matters of which the defendant (or its agent) actually had notice, rather than prescribing issues which they ought to have investigated. Thus, the doctrine of notice had become uneven in its application.

Indeed, in the more recent case of *O'Brien*, it is questionable whether Lord Browne-Wilkinson was seeking to measure matters of which the defendant could be said to have notice, or was in fact creating a menu of issues which are to be investigated to prevent a finding that there is constructive notice arising from a failure to ask certain prescribed questions.

29.2 UNDUE INFLUENCE

There are two categories of undue influence: actual undue influence and presumed undue influence. Actual undue influence requires evidence of some influence exercised over the claimant. Notice of presumed undue influence will arise (seemingly) in situations in which there is a manifest disadvantage to the claimant, or where there is a special relationship between the claimant and the mortgagor which ought to put the mortgagee on notice.

The doctrine of undue influence is a long-established equitable principle which prevents a person from relying on her common law rights where those rights were created as a result of some undue influence being exercised over another person. Before coming to the modern law on undue influence in relation to the law of trusts and of property, it is as well to consider the doctrine of undue influence as it has been classically applied, and its particular relationship with the law of contract.

29.2.1 A species of constructive fraud

The legal textbooks, before the decision of the House of Lords in *Barclays Bank v O'Brien*, considered undue influence to be one part of the equitable rules against 'constructive

---

17 *Barlow Clowes International Ltd (In Liquidation) and Others v Vaughan and Others* [1992] 4 All ER 22.
18 *Re Montagu* [1987] Ch 264.
19 *Henning v Bristol & West Building Society* [1985] 1 WLR 778.

fraud'.[20] To that extent, the doctrine was considered to be of only restricted importance alongside three other equitable wrongs making up constructive fraud. Given the proximity of undue influence to notions of fraud, there are shades of the doctrine in *Rochefoucauld v Boustead*[21] in this area to the effect that equity will not permit a person to use her common law rights to perpetrate a fraud. The place of misrepresentation and other equitable wrongs in this area is considered below.

The doctrine of notice is found by Lord Browne-Wilkinson in *O'Brien* to lie at the heart of undue influence and this form of equity as a means of resisting constructive fraud on the following basis:

> if the party asserting that he takes free of the earlier rights of another knows of certain facts which put him on inquiry as to the possible existence of the rights of that other and he fails to make such inquiry or take such other steps as are reasonable . . . he will have constructive notice of such other right and take subject to it.

Therefore, the issue arises as to the notice on the part of a third party of undue influence between two other people. As Lord Browne-Wilkinson extended the point:

> if the creditor bank has notice, actual or constructive, of the undue influence exercised by the husband (and consequentially of the wife's equity to set aside the transaction) the creditor will take subject to that equity and the wife can set aside the transaction against the creditor (albeit a purchaser for value) as well as against the husband.

29.2.2 Two classes of undue influence

The following test for the application of the doctrine of undue influence was derived from *Bank of Credit and Commerce International SA v Aboody*[22] and is that applied in the House of Lords in *O'Brien*:

> Class 1: actual undue influence . . . Class 2: presumed undue influence . . . the complainant only has to show, in the first instance, that there was a relationship of trust and confidence between the complainant and the wrongdoer of such a nature that it is fair to presume that the wrongdoer abused that relationship.

Therefore, the doctrine of undue influence divides into two: first, situations in which there has been *de facto* undue influence; and, secondly, circumstances in which undue influence is presumed. These two classes are considered in turn below.

Actual undue influence

Actual undue influence requires that there is some influence exerted on another person to make a gift or to enter into a transaction. It has been equated with common law duress.[23]

---

20 See McGhee, 2005.
21 [1897] 1 Ch 196.
22 [1992] 4 All ER 955.
23 Beatson, 1989, 278.

Clearly, the line between permissible pressure and undue influence will be a difficult one to draw in many circumstances. For example, it is clear that where a person is induced to enter into a mortgage to avert the prosecution of his son in relation to the forgery of bills held by the mortgagee, that mortgage will be set aside on grounds of undue influence.[24] Other cases have involved a demonstration of *de facto* control of one person by another in circumstances of religious observance,[25] or simply where an older man has control over a younger man.[26]

Therefore, influence need not be physical, but it must be unjustified in that it seeks a benefit for the person exercising the influence which would not otherwise have been agreed to. The purpose behind the application of the principle is to prevent a person from relying on his common law rights where those rights have arisen as a result of some fraud or wrongful act on the part of that person. In the old cases it was necessary to demonstrate both that there was some benefit to the defendant[27] and some manifest disadvantage to the plaintiff.[28] The removal of these elements as being pre-requisites of the claim is considered at para 29.4.4 below.[29]

Presumed undue influence

The second category of undue influence is more difficult to pin down. The first category of actual undue influence turns on a question of fact – whether or not there has been any express influence which is considered to be 'undue'. The presumed undue influence category advances a more difficult proposition – that there are certain relationships which ought to warn third parties that some undue influence might be possible, such that those persons are deemed to have constructive notice of the undue influence. The aim of equity in this context is to provide particular protection for parties in one of the prescribed relationships. The problem then is to identify those relationships which ought to put the other party on notice, because '[a]t least since the time of Lord Eldon, equity has steadfastly and wisely refused to put limits on the relationships to which the presumption can apply'.[30]

Typically it is required that there is a suitable degree of trust and confidence between the parties such that it could be presumed that one party would tend to rely on the other. It is not sufficient to demonstrate that one party is in a fiduciary relationship with that other.[31] This is because fiduciary relationships arise in a variety of situations, some of which would not necessarily include the possibility of undue influence. For example, a doctor would not necessarily be in a position to exert undue influence to force a patient to sign a mortgage, but might be able to exert some undue influence over them to buy private healthcare services. It is important to look at the facts to decide whether or not there ought to be a presumption of undue influence in any particular case.[32]

Thus, in the case of *Lloyds Bank v Bundy*,[33] Lord Denning held that an elderly bank customer who was cajoled into incurring injurious debts to the bank on the advice of the

24 *Williams v Bayley* (1866) LR 1 HL 200.
25 *Morley v Loughman* [1893] 1 Ch 736.
26 *Smith v Kay* (1859) 7 HLC 750.
27 *Allcard v Skinner* (1887) 36 Ch D 145.
28 *Bank of Credit and Commerce International SA v Aboody* [1990] QB 923.
29 *Royal Bank of Scotland v Etridge (No 2)* [2002] AC 773.
30 *Goldsworthy v Brickell* [1987] Ch 378, 401, *per* Nourse LJ.
31 *Re Coomber* [1911] 1 Ch 723; *Goldsworthy v Brickell* [1987] Ch 378.
32 *National Westminster Bank v Morgan* [1985] AC 686.
33 [1975] QB 326.

bank manager was entitled to rely on a presumption of undue influence between banker and a customer in the position of that particular customer. Lord Denning was concerned to protect the interests of a person who was vulnerable and who was in a situation in which he would tend to rely on the advice given to him by the bank. However, Lord Denning's formulation of the appropriate principles has been much criticised, as will emerge below. Instead, the tighter formulation of the *O'Brien* principle has been favoured over Lord Denning's concern to achieve the right result first and then to explain the intellectual arguments justifying it second.

On the older authorities pre-*O'Brien* there was no presumption of undue influence in cases between husband and wife simply as a result of that relationship.[34] The reason for this principle was that such a presumption being made in every case would render married life intolerable because husband and wife would not be able to deal together with any other person without such a presumption operating. However, the progress that *O'Brien* makes is to presume such a conflict in every situation about which there is some evidently unfavourable aspect (formerly expressed in the legal requirement of manifest disadvantage) from the perspective of the spouse, cohabitee or surety in a sufficiently close relationship. What this achieves is a slightly back-to-front means of imposing an obligation on mortgagees to inquire into the information which has been given to the surety before consenting to the arrangement which is said to have resulted from some undue influence.

In a more recent case, the Court of Appeal upheld the finding of a county court judge that in a situation in which a man in his mid-forties convinced his parents, then in their seventies, to put their house up as security for a loan the son was taking out to acquire an interest in a public house, there would be a relationship of trust and confidence between the son and the parents.[35] The most significant factor in that context was the comparative business experience and acumen of the son and the naivety of his parents, such that the transaction ought to have been evidently unfavourable to the parents who ran this risk of losing their home if their son's business failed.

More recently still in the Privy Council, a member of the elite military unit the Special Air Service (SAS) contended that he had been put under undue influence by the regiment to sign a confidentiality agreement to the effect that he would not publish any memoirs relating to his service in the SAS.[36] The soldiers were offered an ultimatum to the effect that either they signed the agreement, or they would be required to leave the regiment and return to their previous regiment – something which for such soldiers would be considered equivalent to an humiliating demotion. The claimant pointed to the hierarchy found in the regiment and the fact that the officer who required the soldiers to sign the agreements was the claimant's commanding officer and someone for whom the claimant had formed soldierly respect. Lord Hoffmann in the Privy Council held that:[37]

> Certain relationships – parent and child, trustee and beneficiary, etc – give rise to a presumption that one party had influence over the other. . . . if the transaction is one which cannot reasonably be explained by the relationship, that will be *prima facie* evidence of undue influence. Even if the relationship does not fall into one of the

34   *Howes v Bishop* [1909] 2 KB 390.
35   *Greene King plc v Stanley* [2002] BPIR 491.
36   *R v Attorney-General* (2003) unreported, 17 March (Privy Council Appeal No 61 of 2002).
37   *Ibid*, para 21 *et seq*.

established categories, the evidence may show that one party did in fact have influence over the other.

In this case the soldiers had been required to sign confidentiality agreements specifically without seeking independent legal advice but with the benefit of a brief, written explanation of the terms of the agreement: the claimant contended that this means of procuring his signature constituted undue influence. Lord Hoffmann went on to say that the presence or absence of independent legal advice 'may or may not be a relevant matter according to the circumstances' and that there will be circumstances in which denying a person independent legal advice will not necessarily connote undue influence. On these facts, the Privy Council formed the view that the soldier would have realised 'with a moment's thought'[38] that he would be precluded from publishing his memoirs; therefore the taking of legal advice would have made no difference to his decision. It was held that the soldier had not been subject to undue influence in procuring his signature to the agreement, but rather that he had agreed to sign the agreement because he wished to remain in the regiment.[39]

The issue therefore is in what circumstances a presumption will arise that there could be undue influence and thus place liability on a third party to the undue influence itself. As will be seen below, the onus of proof falls on the defendant to disprove that there was any undue influence in line with the presumption. The result is that the defendant is bound by any undue influence which arises in such a situation.[40] The relationships in which presumed undue influence arises most frequently in the recent cases are that of parent and child,[41] trustee and beneficiary,[42] doctor and patient,[43] and even between religious advisor and devotee.[44] It was held in *Curtis v Curtis*[45] that where a man had begun to attend a spiritual healing centre, he had been unduly influenced by people at the centre to settle property on trust for the benefit of the centre. The trust could be set aside on the basis that it had been created as a result of undue influence.

There have also been cases where a presumption of undue influence has been held possible depending on the circumstances of the particular situation. Two such situations are those of husband and wife[46] and employer and employee,[47] provided that there is something about the transaction itself which ought to raise that presumption in the mind of the other party.[48] In relation to husband and wife, Lord Browne-Wilkinson in *O'Brien* made reference to the relationship of special tenderness which makes it possible to manipulate emotional and sexual ties to exert undue influence in many cases. Similarly, it would be possible in some

---

38 *Ibid*, para 27.
39 Alternatively it could be argued that this was in itself a threat which constituted undue influence: either you give up some right you currently hold (to publish memoirs of your time with the regiment), or else you will be humiliated by being forced to leave the regiment.
40 *Barclays Bank v O'Brien* [1994] 1 AC 180.
41 *Bainbrigge v Browne* (1881) 18 Ch D 188. There may be undue influence exerted by an adult child on a vulnerable parent: *Abbey National v Stringer* [2006] EWCA Civ 338.
42 *Beningfield v Baxter* (1886) 12 App Cas 167.
43 *Mitchell v Homfray* (1881) 8 QBD 587.
44 *Huguenin v Baseley* (1807) 14 Ves Jun 273; *Allcard v Skinner* (1887) 36 Ch D 145; cf *Nel v Kean* [2003] WTLR 501.
45 [2011] EWCA Civ 1602.
46 *Barclays Bank v O'Brien* [1994] 1 AC 180; *CIBC v Pitt* [1993] 3 WLR 802.
47 *Credit Lyonnais Nederland NV v Burch* [1996] NPC 99.
48 *CIBC v Pitt* [1993] 3 WLR 802.

cases for employers to exert pressure on employees through the bond of the contract of employment. These issues are considered more closely below.

Understanding this division within undue influence

Lord Hobhouse in *Royal Bank of Scotland v Etridge (No 2)*[49] identified the source of this division in the following manner:

> The division between presumed and actual undue influence derives from the judgments in *Allcard v Skinner*. Actual undue influence presents no relevant problem. It is an equitable wrong committed by the dominant party against the other which makes it unconscionable for the dominant party to enforce his legal rights against the other. It is typically some express conduct overbearing the other party's will. It is capable of including conduct which might give a defence at law, for example, misrepresentation.

Interestingly, here his Lordship sees undue influence as forming part of the long equitable tradition to do with the treatment of unconscionable behaviour, and also identifies undue influence as being 'an equitable wrong' whereby the reason for the setting aside of the contract is the wrongful action of the defendant. In consequence, it is not founded on any notion of restitution of unjust enrichment, a doctrine which has application without any need to find fault on the part of the defendant.[50]

Undue influence and wills

Claims of undue influence arise most commonly in relation to wills, whereby it is often alleged that a person unduly influenced a testator to change their will so as to benefit that person. The bulk of this chapter is concerned with the large amount of litigation concerning undue influence in relation to mortgages in recent years: however, undue influence in relation to wills is a serious problem in practice too. Where there has been 'a form of coercion, or pressure exerted so as to overpower the will without convincing the judgment of the testator',[51] then the bequest in question may be set aside.[52] It must be proved that the pressure was both 'improper pressure' and that the bequest must have resulted from that pressure.[53] The burden of proving these factors falls on the party alleging that there has been undue influence.[54] What has to be proved, precisely, is that 'the circumstances of the will are consistent with the hypothesis that it was obtained by undue influence, and inconsistent with a contrary hypothesis'.[55] This latter element is troublesome: what has to be proved is not that there definitely was undue influence – presumably because once the testator has died there may only have been two people present at the time of the undue influence and therefore that

---

49 [2002] AC 773, para 103.
50 See *Smith v Cooper* [2010] EWCA Civ 722.
51 This form of words was used in *Abbott v Richardson* [2006] EWHC 1291 (Ch), [197], *per* Strauss QC, adapting expressions from earlier cases.
52 *Hall v Hall* (1868) LR 1 P&D 481; *Wingrove v Wingrove* (1885) 11 PD 81; 50 JP 56.
53 *Ibid; Abbott v Richardson* [2006] EWHC 1291 (Ch), [197].
54 *Ibid.*
55 *Re Cooper* [2005] EWHC 2389, [53]; applied in *Abbott v Richardson* [2006] EWHC 1291 (Ch), [197].

proof may be impossible in most cases – but rather it must simply be proved, in effect, that the only reasonable explanation for the bequest was that there must have been undue influence exerted over the testator.

29.3 MISREPRESENTATION AND EQUITABLE WRONGS

29.3.1 Misrepresentation in equity

Misrepresentation is included in this chapter as a principle which might lead to a transaction being set aside as a result of the decision in *O'Brien*. In that case, it was held by Lord Browne-Wilkinson that notice of a misrepresentation made to the claimant appears to be capable of founding an equitable right in the claimant to prevent the defendant from relying on his equitable rights.

This strand of analysis is separate from the issue of undue influence. As considered above, in relation to undue influence, there is a question as to whether or not the pressure imposed on B by A was tantamount to undue influence. In relation to misrepresentation, it is sufficient for B to set aside the transaction if B can demonstrate that a material misrepresentation perpetrated on B by A induced B to enter into the transaction.

A number of problems arise with the development of this principle, as arose with undue influence. The primary issue is that of imputing constructive notice of a misrepresentation to a person who had no part to play in that misrepresentation. It is suggested that the problems in relation to undue influence and misrepresentation are similar. More exactly, the problem is in setting aside a transaction between A and C on grounds of misrepresentation, when the misrepresentation was perpetrated by A on B to make B consent to the transaction or to stand as surety for it.[56] C may have had no knowledge or notice of that misrepresentation.

29.3.2 Equitable wrongs

Having understood misrepresentation as being an addition to the development of undue influence, there is also a need to explore what is meant by the expression 'equitable wrongs' as used by Lord Browne-Wilkinson in *O'Brien*. In seeing undue influence as one of the traditional categories of constructive fraud, it is to be supposed that by the term 'equitable wrong' Lord Browne-Wilkinson intended to refer to the other three recognised categories of equitable wrongs: abuse of conscience, unconscionable bargains, and frauds on a power.

The category of misrepresentation added by *O'Brien* is probably best understood as fitting into the pattern of these wrongs. If their common link is taken to be their proximity to fraud, then misrepresentation (in its narrow sense of 'an intention to deceive') clearly fits this pattern in relation to civil wrongs such as fraudulent misrepresentation. Where the problem becomes more complex is in relation to the other potential forms of misrepresentation. Innocent misrepresentation would not seem to import any notion of fraud, unless it arose in relation to a defendant who occupied a position in which any assurances or statements would necessarily be relied upon by the recipient. That comes closer to the form of negligent misstatement in *Hedley Byrne v Heller*.[57] Indeed, it brings the matter closer to

---

56 *Barclays Bank v O'Brien* [1994] 1 AC 180.
57 [1964] AC 465.

negligent misrepresentation, under which the defendant exhibits negligence as to the misleading nature of an assurance or statement. It is not clear that negligence necessarily imports an impact on the conscience such that equitable relief would necessarily be required.

Equity will operate, therefore, to protect a party to a transaction from suffering the effects of some wrong committed by the other party. However, equity will not operate to rescue a person from a bad bargain which she has entered into in full cognisance of the facts.[58] Therefore, where a person agreed to invest in a particular pension mistakenly believing that that pension would be more profitable than ultimately it proved to be, it was not open to that person to have the agreement set aside because the seller of the pension had not acted unconscionably so as to induce him to enter into the contract.[59]

29.4 SETTING MORTGAGES ASIDE – THE PRINCIPLE IN *BARCLAYS BANK v O'BRIEN*

The stream of cases following O'Brien *has permitted individuals, who were not necessarily parties to mortgages, to prevent the mortgagee from relying on a statutory right to repossession or sale of the property on the basis that those individuals had been the victim of a misrepresentation or some undue influence by the mortgagor. The essence of this power to set aside the mortgage against the mortgagee is that the mortgage created is in circumstances in which the mortgagee is taken to have notice of the misrepresentation or undue influence. The most significant case now is the decision of the House of Lords in* Royal Bank of Scotland v Etridge.

There are two categories of undue influence: actual undue influence and presumed undue influence. Actual undue influence requires evidence of some influence exercised over the claimant. Notice of presumed undue influence will arise (seemingly) in situations in which there is a manifest disadvantage to the claimant, or where there is a special relationship between the claimant and the mortgagor which ought to put the mortgagee on notice.[60]

The mortgagee will not be bound by any undue influence or misrepresentation where the mortgagee has taken 'reasonable steps' to find out the signatory's rights.[61] *'Reasonable steps' will be said to exist in circumstances in which the claimant has received, or even just signed a certificate asserting that she has received, independent legal advice as to the effect of the mortgage or surety she is signing.*[62]

In circumstances in which the claimant had knowledge of a part of the mortgage or surety but did not know the full amount of the liability, the claimant will nevertheless be entitled to have the mortgage set aside in toto.[63] *The only exception to that principle will be where the claimant has nevertheless taken some benefit from the transaction – in which case the claimant will be required to account to the defendant for that benefit.*[64]

---

58   *Clarion Ltd v National Provident Institution* [2000] 2 All ER 265.
59   *Ibid.* Cf *Torrance v Bolton* (1872) LR 8 Ch App 118; *Solle v Butcher* [1949] 2 All ER 1107.
60   *Barclays Bank v O'Brien* [1994] 1 AC 180; *CIBC v Pitt* [1993] 3 WLR 802 – in the manner considered below.
61   *Barclays Bank v O'Brien* [1994] 1 AC 180.
62   *Midland Bank v Massey* [1995] 1 All ER 929; *Banco Exterior Internacional v Mann* [1995] 1 All ER 936; *Halifax Mortgage Services Ltd v Stepsky* [1996] Ch 1; *Barclays Bank v Coleman* [2000] 1 All ER 385.
63   *TSB Bank v Camfield* [1995] 1 All ER 951; *Castle Phillips Finance v Piddington* (1995) 70 P & CR 592.
64   *Midland Bank v Greene* [1994] 2 FLR 827; *Dunbar Bank plc v Nadeem* [1997] 2 All ER 253.

29.4.1 Context

One particularly important area in which the doctrine of notice has come into recent promi-
nence has been that of undue influence in the law of mortgages.[65] A difficult issue which is
being faced by more and more solicitors is the ability of, typically, a spouse to claim priority
to a mortgagee bank or building society to the matrimonial home in the event of failure to
make repayments under the charge. It is as well to understand the context behind this development in the case law as expressed in the leading case *Barclays Bank v O'Brien*[66] before the
House of Lords, in which the leading speech was delivered by Lord Browne-Wilkinson. The
problem was stated to be:

> whether a bank is entitled to enforce against a wife an obligation to secure a debt owed
> by her husband to the bank where the wife has been induced to stand as surety for her
> husband's debt by the undue influence or misrepresentation of the husband ... The
> large number of cases of this type coming before the courts in recent years reflects the
> rapid changes in social attitudes and the distribution of wealth which have recently
> occurred. Wealth is now more widely spread. Moreover a high proportion of privately
> owned wealth is invested in the matrimonial home.

Bound up with this desire to develop the principle of undue influence is a modern understanding of the way in which properties acquired under mortgage are to be held. His Lordship
continued:

> In parallel with these financial developments, society's recognition of the equality of the
> sexes has led to a rejection of the concept that the wife is subservient to the husband in
> the management of the family's finances. A number of the authorities reflect an unwill-
> ingness in the court to perpetuate law based on this outmoded concept.

The nature of the decision is therefore set out as being policy-based, with a specific aim of
providing a defence to wronged spouses and others in relation to the mortgage over their homes.

The law of mortgages provides straightforwardly that the mortgagor is liable to make good
periodical amounts due under the mortgage agreement. Failure to make good the periodical
payments results in the mortgagee's ability to take possession of the property provided as security for the mortgage. That much is trite law. The complexity relates to the rights of the mortgagor and others to resist repossession and sale, as introduced by the important House of Lords
decisions in *Barclays Bank v O'Brien*[67] and in *CIBC v Pitt*[68] (the latter appeal having been heard
by the same House of Lords and in which judgment was delivered on the same day).

29.4.2 *Barclays Bank v O'Brien*

The facts revolved around a misrepresentation and alleged undue influence exercised by a
husband over his wife. The husband was a shareholder in a manufacturing company which

---

65 These principles apply to re-mortgages just as they apply to the original mortgage: *Yorkshire Bank v Tinsley*
   [2004] 3 All ER 463.
66 [1993] 3 WLR 786.
67 *Ibid.*
68 [1994] 1 AC 200.

had a substantial, unsecured overdraft. The husband arranged with the manager of the respondent bank for an overdraft facility for which the husband agreed to secure the company's indebtedness. The husband provided security by means of a second charge over the matrimonial home owned jointly by the husband and the appellant, his wife.

The bank prepared the necessary documentation, which included a guarantee to be provided by the husband and a charge to be signed by both the husband and the wife. Although the respondent's manager had instructed that the couple should take independent legal advice and that the couple should be advised on any aspect of the transaction which they did not understand, the respondent's staff responsible for effecting the transaction did not ensure that such advice had been obtained by the couple prior to signing the documents. Indeed, Lord Browne-Wilkinson found that the respondent's manager had made a note that the appellant, Mrs O'Brien, might pose a problem and also that 'if [the couple] are in any doubt they should contact their solicitors before signing'. The husband signed the documentation without reading it, and the appellant was taken to the bank by her husband to sign the documents which made her a surety for the overdraft.

It is important to note that Mrs O'Brien was a guarantor of the overdraft provided for her husband's business. She took no direct benefit from the guarantee which she signed (although it might be said that she benefited indirectly from the continued solvency of her husband's business). Significantly, Mrs O'Brien was not advised as to her own, personal liabilities if the overdraft was not maintained and the guarantee called in. Furthermore, her husband had lied to her about the size of the overdraft and, therefore, about the size of the guarantee she was signing. While Mrs O'Brien knew that she was creating a charge over the matrimonial home in favour of the respondent bank, she believed that it was for £60,000 rather than £135,000 and that it would last for only three weeks.

In time, the company's indebtedness increased above the agreed overdraft limit and the respondent bank sought to take its security by forcing a sale of the O'Briens' house. The appellant, Mrs O'Brien, argued that her husband had exercised undue influence over her and that he had misrepresented the effect of the charge which she had signed. The problem was stated to be: '... whether a bank is entitled to enforce against a wife an obligation to secure a debt owed by her husband to the bank where the wife has been induced to stand as surety for her husband's debt by the undue influence or misrepresentation of the husband.'

It is important to note that, while Lord Browne-Wilkinson undertook a general survey of the law in this area, Mrs O'Brien's successful appeal turned ultimately on the argument that she had been the victim of misrepresentation. The question of undue influence on the facts of *O'Brien* was unproven.

The nature of undue influence

The definition of undue influence divided into two parts, as set out at para 29.2.2 above, and was derived from *Bank of Credit and Commerce International SA v Aboody*:[69]

> Class 1: actual undue influence ... Class 2: presumed undue influence ... the complainant only has to show, in the first instance, that there was a relationship of trust and confidence between the complainant and the wrongdoer of such a nature that it is fair to presume that the wrongdoer abused that relationship.

69   [1992] 4 All ER 955.

Therefore, Lord Browne-Wilkinson held that in cases involving husband and wife, the wife can demonstrate that there was a relationship of 'trust and confidence' between them such that there is a presumption of undue influence. Importantly, in *CIBC v Pitt*, Lord Browne-Wilkinson held that this presumption will arise only in circumstances in which there is some manifest disadvantage to that cohabitee. On the facts of *O'Brien*, it was held that because Mrs O'Brien was acting as surety in a transaction under which she took no direct, personal benefit, it must be presumed that she might have been the subject of some undue influence. It is suggested that this must be correct, or else all mortgagees would be required to enquire into the detail of the relationship between each married couple seeking to take out mortgages with them.

The foundation for this constructive notice is the most difficult aspect of the decision in *O'Brien*, because it is said by Lord Browne-Wilkinson to arise as a result of some 'agency' between the person effecting the undue influence and the mortgagee, as considered next.

Agency

The difficulty in setting aside a mortgage against a mortgagee in a case of undue influence between a married couple is the logical problem of establishing that the mortgagee ought to be bound by something which occurs entirely between that couple. There is a possibility not only that there has been undue influence, but also that the husband was acting as the creditor's agent, or that the creditor had actual or constructive notice. Suppose that the bank had suggested a particular course of action to one of the parties and had instructed that person to convince the cohabitee to consent to that transaction: in such a situation, any undue influence exerted by the mortgagor on the cohabitee might lead to the mortgagor being considered to be the bank's agent in exerting that undue influence. Such a relationship of agency would, *prima facie*, fix the bank with notice of everything of which their agent had notice.[70]

The importance of the agency principle underpinning undue influence was applied to the facts of *O'Brien* in the following way:

> If the wrongdoing husband is acting as agent for the creditor bank in obtaining the surety from the wife, the creditor will be fixed with the wrongdoing of its own agent and the surety contract can be set aside as against the creditor . . . Similarly, in cases such as the present where the wife has been induced to enter into the transaction by the husband's misrepresentation, her equity to set aside the transaction will be enforceable against the creditor if either the husband was acting as the creditor's agent or the creditor had actual or constructive notice.

On the facts in *O'Brien*, the creditor was held to have been put on inquiry in that the transaction was to the financial disadvantage of Mrs O'Brien and that there is a substantial risk in transactions of that kind that the husband has committed a legal or equitable wrong in procuring the wife's agreement to act as surety. Alternatively, where the mortgagor is found to have been acting as the agent of the bank in procuring the agreement of another person to the transaction, the bank will be fixed with notice of any undue influence which that person had perpetrated. The suspicion of agency in *O'Brien* arose from the fact that it was the bank

---

70 *Kingsnorth Finance v Tizard* [1986] 2 All ER 54.

which had proposed the surety arrangement to support the problem of an overdraft for Mr O'Brien's company.

It is to be noted that the agency here is a deemed agency between the mortgagor and the mortgagee, as opposed to the form of agency which will be attached to the advising solicitor, as discussed at para 29.4.7 below.

The argument based on misrepresentation

The argument based on misrepresentation is far more straightforward. It is sufficient to show that there has been a misrepresentation effected by the mortgagor against the co-signatory which induced that person to sign the agreement. Again, where the mortgagee has failed to ensure that the co-signatory has received independent advice as to the effect of the transaction, the mortgagee will be fixed with constructive notice of that misrepresentation. Consequently, the co-signatory will be entitled to set aside the mortgage against the mortgagee.[71]

29.4.3 Comparison with *CIBC v Pitt*

Concentration in the profession in practice has focused on *O'Brien*, which is unsurprising given the power shift it suggests in favour of the mortgagor – allowing cohabitees generally to set aside the mortgage. However, *CIBC v Pitt*[72] makes for sobering reading in the majority of circumstances. Whereas *O'Brien* was a surety case, in which it was held that there was evidence to establish an agency relationship between the misrepresentor and the financial institution, *CIBC v Pitt* concerned a straightforward mortgage over property rather than the provision of a guarantee by a cohabitee.

The essential difference

The case of *O'Brien* is explicitly distinguished by Lord Browne-Wilkinson on the basis that there is a difference between a case of a joint advance under a mortgage and a case of a surety. In the case of a surety:

> there is not only the possibility of undue influence having been exercised but also the increased risk of it having been exercised because . . . the guarantee by a wife of her husband's debts is not for her financial benefit. It is the combination of the two factors that puts the creditor on enquiry.

Mr Pitt had told the appellant that he wished to borrow money on the security of the house to finance speculation on the stock market. The appellant, Mrs Pitt, was unhappy with this suggestion and expressed these reservations to her husband. Mr Pitt imposed undue influence on Mrs Pitt to agree to the loan. Mrs Pitt did not read any of the documentation and saw only the first and last pages of it. The solicitors who acted for the couple were also solicitors for the bank. The appellant did not receive any independent advice as to the transaction. The

---

71 Subject to the extent of that person's reliance on the representations: *Barclays Bank v Rivett* [1999] 1 FLR 730. See also *Habib Bank Ltd v Tufail* [2006] EWCA Civ 374.
72 [1993] 4 All ER 433.

appellant alleged that she had entered into the transaction as a result of her husband's undue influence and by her husband's false representation. The trial judge found that there had been undue influence but no misrepresentation.

What the appellant could not demonstrate on the facts was that the financial institution was affected by the undue influence of the husband. There is no causal link necessarily between there being undue influence and an ability on the part of the wronged spouse to resist the chargee's claim for possession. Therefore, the pleadings setting out the parties' arguments in the litigation must explore the link between the undue influence and agency between the wrongdoing spouse and the financial institution. On the facts in *Pitt*, there was nothing to indicate that there was anything other than a normal loan secured by a charge between husband and wife.[73] It was held that, unlike the facts in *O'Brien* where Mrs O'Brien was acting to her manifest disadvantage as a surety, there was no factor which ought necessarily to raise a presumption of undue influence in *Pitt* given that the bank was found to have been extending money on an ordinary secured loan transaction which indicated no necessary disadvantage to Mrs Pitt. This approach received the approbation of a differently constituted House of Lords in *Royal Bank of Scotland v Etridge (No 2)*, considered next.

29.4.4 Some factor sufficient to call the arrangement to the mortgagee's attention

The issue

Following on from the above, it is clear that there is a need for there to be some factor which will call the transaction to the mortgagee's attention: that is, there must be something which would indicate to the mortgagee that the signatory in this case was more likely to have been placed under undue influence. What emerges most clearly from the decision of the House of Lords in *Royal Bank of Scotland v Etridge (No 2)*[74] is that transactions where some person is required to act as a surety will be an example of a situation in which such a person might have been the victim of some undue influence or misrepresentation, because she is guaranteeing another person's performance of the transaction without taking any direct benefit herself *qua* surety.

The old approach – manifest disadvantage

Before the decision in *Royal Bank of Scotland v Etridge (No 2)*, it was unclear whether or not it was necessary for the claimant to have established that the transaction necessitated 'manifest disadvantage' to her, such that the defendant must necessarily have been put on notice.[75] In *CIBC v Pitt*, Lord Browne-Wilkinson held that if a plaintiff could prove actual undue influence there was no requirement to demonstrate that the transaction was manifestly disadvantageous to the plaintiff. Rather, there would be an entitlement to have the transaction set aside as of right. That is the rule to be divined from *Pitt*. There is, however, some potential confusion, in that the reason why the House of Lords did not permit Mrs Pitt to set aside the mortgage transaction against the mortgagee was that there was no manifest

---

73 *Leggatt v National Westminster Bank* [2000] All ER (D) 1458.
74 [2002] AC 773.
75 *National Westminster Bank v Morgan* [1985] AC 686; *Goldsworthy v Brickell* [1987] Ch 378, 401, *per* Nourse LJ.

disadvantage which ought to have put the bank on notice as to her predicament. Therefore, in *CIBC v Pitt*, even though there was found to have been actual undue influence, his Lordship suggested that proof of manifest disadvantage was not required, whereas in *Barclays Bank v O'Brien*, he had suggested that it was. However, it is important to bear in mind that the deciding factor in *CIBC v Pitt* was the lack of any obvious manifest disadvantage in the transaction which led to Mrs Pitt failing to set the mortgage aside.

In other cases, such as *Cheese v Thomas*,[76] a finding of manifest disadvantage was made where an elderly man parted with all of his savings to enter into a purchase of a property with his great-nephew. In the alternative, there will be no manifest disadvantage where the contracting party has an interest in the subject matter of the transaction such as shares in a company repackaging a loan.[77] In such cases of manifest disadvantage, the courts have considered the mortgagee to be on notice of any presumed undue influence. An absence of any such evident disadvantage to the claimant, on the other hand, has caused the courts to deny a remedy setting aside the transaction. While the *dicta* have proved equivocal on this issue, it is clear that the presence of such demonstrable disadvantage in the transaction will lead the courts to order setting aside, whereas they have tended not to do so if it is absent.

The requirement of manifest disadvantage has been criticised on a number of grounds. The first is that, in line with the more general development of a principle of restitution of unjust enrichment in English law, manifest disadvantage is a requirement which perverts the doctrine from requiring simply the proof that undue influence has been exercised into a further evidential requirement that the disadvantage which it will cause the cohabitee is manifest. However, it is difficult to see why the doctrine of undue influence should necessarily be required to fall into line with doctrines such as mistake and misrepresentation in that sense.

A further point is that the modern use of the term 'manifest disadvantage' (as used initially by the House of Lords in *National Westminster Bank v Morgan*)[78] is a development of the principle set out by Lindley LJ in *Allcard v Skinner*,[79] that the principle was satisfied by 'a gift so large as not to be reasonably accounted for on the ground of friendship, relationship, charity or other motives on which ordinary men act'.[80] The test adopted in *Morgan* is a more brutal rendition of the *Allcard* principle, which proceeded on the basis of transactions which were out of the ordinary course of transactions between such persons. That something is required to be 'manifest' connotes something which would be 'obvious to any independent and reasonable persons who considered the transaction at the time with knowledge of all relevant facts'.[81] There is an important change of emphasis here between an objective understanding of something being out of the ordinary, and a more subjective assessment of whether or not someone involved in the transaction would have found the facts to be demonstrably obvious.

In fact the courts have tended to consider each case on its own merits. In some cases, such as *Burch* where a junior employee was required to provide her small flat as security for her employer's debt, the disadvantage would indeed be obvious. However, in cases such as *Bank*

---

76 [1994] 1 WLR 129.

77 *Bank of Scotland v Bennett* [1997] 1 FLR 801; *Goode Durrant Administration v Biddulph* [1994] 2 FLR 551; *Britannia Building Society v Pugh* [1997] 2 FLR 7.

78 [1985] AC 686.

79 (1887) 36 Ch D 145.

80 O'Sullivan, 1998, 50.

81 *Bank of Credit and Commerce International SA v Aboody* [1990] QB 923, 964, *per* Slade LJ.

of Scotland v Bennett[82] and *Mahoney v Purnell*,[83] the courts have tended to look closely at the precise structure of the transaction, rather than relying on matters to be obvious from afar.[84]

The new approach – Royal Bank of Scotland v Etridge (No 2)

Lord Nicholls suggested in *Royal Bank of Scotland v Etridge (No 2)*[85] that the test of manifest disadvantage was no longer required but that the suggestion made in *Barclays Bank v O'Brien* that there be some notion of fixing mortgagees with notice in circumstances in which a cohabitee stands to suffer some financial disadvantage would remain an important factor. The approach in *CIBC v Pitt*, long championed in earlier editions of this textbook, was therefore approved. The question remains somewhat at large, however, as to what it is exactly that will put the mortgagee on notice as to the cohabitee's position.[86] Whereas the House of Lords is concerned to make the test clearer than it was previously,[87] there is an implicit admission in the speech of Lord Nicholls that it is not possible to define in advance all of the circumstances in which such a right to set aside a contract will arise, particularly when his Lordship suggests in practice that the mortgagee insist that the cohabitee is separately advised 'to be safe'.[88] What emerges also is that the principal focus of Lord Nicholls' speech is on the position of sureties in particular, and not signatories to mortgages in general.

Lord Hobhouse was generally supportive of the approach taken by Lord Browne-Wilkinson in *Barclays Bank v O'Brien*, but was critical of the use of the constructive notice test on the basis that it would be necessary to apply this test differently in different situations.[89] For example, a case involving a wife acting as surety would require very little to fix the mortgagee with notice, whereas situations in which there appeared to be nothing out of the ordinary with the transaction would make it much more difficult to fix the mortgagee with notice of the undue influence. Lord Hobhouse does suggest that it might be better to set aside unconscionable bargains in the manner that the Australians do, rather than to fix the mortgagee with notice. The Australian approach would mean that it would be possible for the court simply to identify there being some unconscionability in binding a claimant to a contract to which she had given her consent only under undue influence, and to set that contract aside due to the presence of the unconscionability, without needing to ascertain whether or not the mortgagee could be said to have had notice of that unconscionability.

Lord Scott's approach was somewhat different again. He focuses more clearly on the cohabitee failing to give free consent to a contract if she has acted under undue influence or some misrepresentation. The approach taken here is more akin to a contract lawyer's approach to the possibility of setting aside a contract between two people where one has unduly influenced the other. The injustice of enforcing such a contract *between those two people* is self-evident. However, the property lawyer faces a more complex job when seeking to set aside a right to repossess the cohabitee's home because of some undue influence exercised over her

---

82 [1997] 1 FLR 801.
83 [1996] 3 All ER 61.
84 *Barclays Bank v Coleman* [2000] 1 All ER 385, [2001] 1 QB 20.
85 [2002] AC 773, [2001] 4 All ER 449.
86 *Ibid*, 466.
87 *Ibid*, 475.
88 *Ibid*, 467.
89 *Ibid*, 484.

by a third party, such that the contract between the mortgagee and the third party should be set aside *in toto*. The addition of the third person to the matrix complicates the neat contractual theory of free consent. The further question asked by Lord Scott to deal with this question of fixing the mortgagee with responsibility (in the form of losing its proprietary rights to repossession) for a private wrong committed between the mortgagor and his cohabitee is that of asking whether or not the mortgagee had knowledge of that wrong. The test of knowledge requires the mortgagee to have been fixed with direct knowledge itself – although it is not made clear whether or not that includes constructive knowledge, where the bank is taken to have known of any factors which it would have discovered but for wilfully and recklessly failing to make the enquiries which a reasonable bank would have made, or but for wilfully closing its eyes to the obvious – and not simply that it has constructive notice or imputed notice of the undue influence via some agent.[90] Lord Scott does, however, agree with Lord Nicholls' core assumption that if there is some special feature in the transaction which ought to bring the risk that there has been some undue influence to the mortgagee's attention then that will fix the mortgagee bank with knowledge of any undue influence.[91]

Briefly put, that three of their Lordships weigh in with lengthy speeches, each of which sets out lengthy summaries of the applicable tests in slightly different terms, does not help to introduce the certainty which they had desired.[92] In effect, the law stays much the same as it was under the *O'Brien* principle, except that the requirement of manifest disadvantage has been removed. There is, however, a reinforcement of the principles, considered below, that independent legal advice ought to be addressed to ensuring that the cohabitee understands the agreement before agreeing to become a co-signatory to it, or before agreeing to act as a surety.

29.4.5 The burden of proof

The mortgage cases still require a high level of proof and expertly prepared pleadings to sustain successful claims. Following on from the preceding discussion, there are a number of issues surrounding the question of the burden and standard of proof. This is particularly so in relation to questions of proving manifest disadvantage in relation to presumed undue influence. The onus of proving the undue influence lies with the claimant alleging such behaviour to support setting aside the mortgage.[93] This authority appears to contradict *dicta* of Lord Browne-Wilkinson in *CIBC v Pitt*, although that case was not strictly concerned with the onus of proof. As Lord Nicholls put the question of proof:[94]

> Whether a transaction was brought about by the exercise of undue influence is a question of fact. Here, as elsewhere, the general principle is that he who asserts a wrong has been committed must prove it. The burden of proving an allegation of undue influence rests upon the person who claims to have been wronged. This is the general rule. The evidence required to discharge the burden of proof depends on the nature of the alleged undue influence, the personality of the parties, their relationship, the extent to which the

---

90 *Ibid*, 509.
91 *Ibid*.
92 This case has been followed in all subsequent cases: eg, *Sanders v Buckley* [2006] All ER (D) 307 (Dec) where the claimant was unable to prove that undue influence had actually been exerted.
93 *Barclays Bank v Boulter* [1999] 1 WLR 1919, HL. See also *Sanders v Buckley* [2006] All ER (D) 307 (Dec).
94 *Royal Bank of Scotland v Etridge (No 2)* [2002] 2 AC 773, 775.

transaction cannot readily be accounted for by the ordinary motives of ordinary persons in that relationship, and all the circumstances of the case.

Whether or not undue influence has been proved by the claimant is therefore a question dependent on the circumstances of the case. While there is a presumption of undue influence in some cases, as considered above, this is a presumption which may be rebutted on the circumstances of any particular case.[95] So in *Wadlow v Samuel (No 1)*[96] it was held that the court should first consider whether or not there was a relationship of trust and confidence; secondly, it must be proved that the transaction in question was one that called for an explanation; and then, if the presumption of undue influence arose, whether or not it could be rebutted on the facts of the particular case. Thus, in *Wadlow v Samuel*, the claimant (a singer) had been persuaded to enter into transactions at the behest of the defendant (his first manager) in circumstances in which the claimant took his advice from the defendant. Even though the defendant had ensured that the claimant took independent advice, nevertheless after that advice had been taken the defendant cajoled the claimant into the transaction by reminding him of all that he owed the defendant for his help and support in the past. This cajoling was held to trump the procuring of independent advice and it was therefore held that the defendant had failed to rebut the presumption of undue influence which was found to have arisen from the outset in this case. This facts in this case are considered again below[97] where the claimant claimed that this undue influence had also infected a further agreement they entered into five years later: but it was held by the Court of Appeal in that second case that their relationship had changed sufficiently by that time for there to have been no undue influence still in existence between the parties: this was demonstrated by the very fact that the singer had terminated their business relationship and acquired a new manager demonstrating that he was clearly no longer in the thrall of his first manager. Thus the court will need to be convinced on the facts of each case that there has genuinely been undue influence in commercial transactions. So, in *Ellse v Hill-Pickford*,[98] for example, the trial judge watched all of the parties in the witness box and expressed himself unconvinced that the claimant was the sort of person who could have been unduly influenced by the defendants in the circumstances.

29.4.6 Mortgagee's means of discharging this duty

As Lord Browne-Wilkinson held in *Barclays Bank v O'Brien*, the mortgagee can be discharged from constructive notice where the mortgagee had taken 'reasonable steps' and not acquired actual notice of the matters complained of. The most important question on the cases has therefore become that of delineating the circumstances in which the mortgagee is able to restrict its own liability by means of taking 'reasonable steps'. In general terms, this has been approved by the House of Lords in *Royal Bank of Scotland v Etridge (No 2)*.[99]

---

95 *Royal Bank of Scotland v Etridge (No 2)* [2002] 2 AC 773, paras [219–221], *per* Lord Scott. Applied in *Wadlow v Samuel* [2006] EWHC 1492 (QB).
96 [2006] EWHC 1492 (QB).
97 *Wadlow v Samuel (No 2)* [2007] EWCA Civ 155, under the sub-heading 'Whether undue influence in relation to one document can be transmitted to another document'.
98 [2006] EWHC 3293 (Ch).
99 [2002] AC 773.

In *Massey v Midland Bank*,[100] Miss Massey had been persuaded by her partner to charge her property as security for his overdraft with the mortgagee. The bank interviewed them together, but Miss Massey was advised by the mortgagee to seek independent advice. This advice was given to Miss Massey in her partner's presence. The Court of Appeal held that the mortgagee was required only to see that advice was sought by the spouse, not to ensure that the advice was properly given. As Steyn LJ held: 'In these circumstances *nothing more was required of the bank than to urge or insist* that Miss Massey should take independent advice [emphasis added].'

This is an incredibly significant restriction on the underlying principle set out by Lord Browne-Wilkinson in *O'Brien*. In that case it was held that there will be presumed undue influence where the transaction is to the manifest disadvantage of the cohabitee, and that the mortgagee will have constructive notice of any misrepresentation or undue influence exercised over that person unless it has advised that person to seek independent advice. In *Massey*, the Court of Appeal reduces the obligation on the mortgagee markedly. Now the mortgagee is required only to 'urge or insist' that independent advice is taken – the corollary appears to be that there is no comeback for the bank if that advice is not actually taken.

From the judgment of Steyn LJ, the two questions which must be considered are:

(a) was the mortgagee put on inquiry as to the circumstances in which the cohabitee agreed to provide the security; and
(b) if so, did the mortgagee take reasonable steps to ensure that the agreement of the cohabitee to the charge was properly obtained?

This test was followed by a differently constituted Court of Appeal in *Banco Exterior Internacional v Mann*[101] and was the approach taken in *Bank of Boroda v Rayarel*.[102]

Providing a certificate that advice has been taken

Banking practice has developed to require the co-signatory, cohabitee, or surety to sign a certificate attesting to the fact that she has taken independent advice. In *Banco Exterior Internacional v Mann*, the issue arose where the solicitor appeared both for the borrower and for the company for which the loan was sought, and it was unclear whether or not the cohabitee had received separate advice. Morritt LJ held that the position must be considered from the point of view of the mortgagee at the time. On the facts of *Mann*, the mortgagee had been shown a certificate that the cohabitee had received legal advice, and therefore regarded this to be sufficient demonstration of the cohabitee's agreement to the charge. It was held irrelevant to take into account a relationship between the cohabitee and a person who could not have exercised undue influence over her: or, in other words, the only relationships which ought to be taken into account are those in which undue influence would be possible.

Therefore, the cohabitee need not have actually received any such advice. Rather, it is enough for the mortgagee to demonstrate that the cohabitee has attested that such advice has been taken. It is suggested that this rule must be subject to the principle that the mortgagee has no actual notice of the cohabitee not having received such advice, nor notice via an agent

100 [1995] 1 All ER 929.
101 [1995] 1 All ER 936.
102 [1995] 2 FLR 376.

that the cohabitee has been influenced into signing the certificate itself. Indeed, the rule in *Mann*, if followed to its logical conclusion, would seem to circumvent the initial thrust of *O'Brien* that the mortgagee is required to look into certain matters where there is presumed undue influence.

Lord Scott agreed in his summary of the law in this area in *Royal Bank of Scotland v Etridge (No 2)*[103] that a solicitor should give advice to the cohabitee together with written confirmation that such advice has been given to enable the mortgagee to form a reasonable belief that the signatory or surety understands the effect of the transaction. Lord Hobhouse similarly placed much reliance on there being 'true independent advice' given by a solicitor which would lead to 'real consent' to the contract.[104] Lord Nicholls suggested that the bank should obtain in every case a written confirmation from the solicitor that the solicitor had explained the transaction to the cohabitee armed with the 'necessary financial information' supplied to it by the mortgagee.[105]

Cases involving vulnerable people

In cases of undue influence it is clearly the case that the more vulnerable the mortgagor happens to be, the easier it will be for someone to exert undue influence over them. Therefore, the courts have developed a line of cases in which the mortgagor's vulnerability has been a factor in suggesting that the mortgagee should have realised that there was some remarkable feature of this transaction which ought to have put them on notice as to the possibility of undue influence. The vulnerability in these cases has frequently revolved around the mortgagor being unable to understand English, and so being unable to appreciate the effect of the transaction; or the vulnerability has occasionally revolved around some frailty of the mortgagor, such as extreme old age or serious illness. So, in *National Westminster Bank v Amin*,[106] the House of Lords created an exception to the *Mann* principle in relation to a couple who spoke no English and who were given advice by a solicitor who was also advising the mortgagee. The court remitted the matter for trial to ascertain more clearly than had been done whether or not the nature of the transaction had been explained sufficiently to the wife who was seeking to have the mortgage set aside. The court would not accept that just because a certificate had been signed, the mortgagee should be entitled to automatic protection against having the transaction set aside. On these facts, the court was particularly concerned that the bank knew the couple spoke no English and were therefore especially vulnerable to exploitation. This case could possibly be confined to its facts but it does also appear to correlate with Lord Nicholls' requirement in *Etridge* that the claimant has been properly advised by the solicitor. A similar approach was taken by the Court of Appeal in *Abbey National v Stringer*[107] where a widowed mother in her mid-fifties took out a mortgage over her own home to secure business loans in favour of her son's new business venture. The mother spoke very little English and so did not understand the effect of the transction – having been born in Italy and despite having lived in England for some time – and therefore, relying on *Etridge*,[108] it was

---

103   *Royal Bank of Scotland v Etridge (No 2)* [2001] 4 All ER 449, 509 *et seq.*
104   *Ibid*, 489.
105   *Ibid*, 473.
106   [2002] 1 FLR 735.
107   [2006] EWCA Civ 338.
108   Oddly, *Amin* was not referred to by the court.

held that the woman was in a vulnerable position and that the mortgagee should have been put on notice that there was something different about this transaction because the mortgage was being used as collateral for loans to a business in which the mortgagor had no personal interest. Consequently the mortgage was set aside on grounds of undue influence.

Where a person is physically vulnerable in some way, this may make it more likely that there will be a finding of undue influence. So, in *Goodchild (by his litigation friend) v Bradbury*[109] an elderly man was reliant on his great-nephew with whom he lived on a farm. The old man wanted to grant a piece of land of one acre to his great-nephew as a wedding present, with permission to build six dwelling houses on it. A solicitor attended the house to organise the transaction and the solicitor took the old man into a room on his own to explain the transaction to him. The solicitor gave evidence that he had had to compete with the noise of the television for the old man's attention but that nevertheless the solicitor was reassured that the old man knew what he was doing. Latterly, the old man had a stroke before the completion of the transfer. By the time of trial the old man was too ill to attend court and had had to move out of his house. The old man's 'litigation friend' interceded on behalf of the old man to complain that the transfer had been procured by means of undue influence. It was held by the Court of Appeal that in these circumstances there was a relationship of dependence in which undue influence was a possibility and that the transfer of the property was not of the sort that would be expected between a great-uncle and great-nephew: therefore the transaction was set aside. This decision does strike one as being a little unfortunate. The old man had agreed to the transaction and had received a separate interview with a solicitor, even though the judge at first instance had held that the old man had not received 'independent advice': therefore it could be said that the old man had formed informed consent before the transaction was commenced. While this transaction was not ordinary for a great-uncle and great-nephew, it was nevertheless not entirely unexceptional for people who live together as a family.[110] Consequently, it could have been said that the old man had formed his intention with some legal advice before his incapacity.

The most celebrated case on undue influence involving an elderly man was a decision of Lord Denning in *Lloyds Bank v Bundy*[111] in which Mr Bundy had been induced by employees of the bank to invest his life savings in a transaction suggested to him by the bank. It was held that the bank had therefore unduly influenced this elderly man into a transaction which stood to lose him everything and therefore that the transaction would be set aside. The undue influence here appeared to be more direct. Significantly, also, in relation to the principles of banking law, it was the officers of the bank themselves who were responsible for the unjust enrichment, as opposed to being fixed with notice of some undue influence exerted by some third party.

Whether undue influence in relation to one document can be transmitted to another document

It is possible that undue influence exerted over a person in relation to one document can be transmitted to the execution of another document if the court is convinced that the execution of that second document was predicated on a continuance of the undue influence. So, if Agnes agrees to sign a second document because she is still in fear of Arthur after the threats

---

109 [2006] All ER (D) 247.
110 See, for example, *Gillett v Holt* [2001] Ch 210.
111 [1975] QB 326.

which Arthur made to her before forcing her to sign the first document, then Agnes may still rely on that undue influence in relation to that second document. So in *Yorkshire Bank v Tinsley*[112] it was held that a wife was still entitled to rely on the undue influence exerted over her by her former husband when the bank required her to sign a second mortgage agreement over a new home after her separation from her husband. Sir Peter Gibson expressed the view that the 'conscience of the bank' had been effected in a manner which infected the discharge of the first mortgage and the creation of this second mortgage. It was held by Longmore LJ in that case that:

> A substitute contract will often come into existence in a different factual context from an earlier contract, and that factual context may show that the second contract is not a true substitute for the first. But if the factual situations are materially similar, and if it is a condition of the rescission or release of the original void or voidable bargain that the parties enter into a new bargain, that new bargain must be as open to attack as the old one.

So, in *Wadlow v Samuel (No 2)*[113] a singer entered into a management agreement with his first manager, which it was accepted had been created under undue influence. A later settlement agreement was effected between those same parties when the singer sought to end his relationship with the first manager and to enter into an agreement with a new manager. The question was whether or not these two agreements, which were entered into about five years apart, were infected by the same undue influence which had affected the first agreement. It was held that on these facts the first undue influence had not effected the second (settlement) agreement, even though the settlement agreement had imported language from the management agreement. On these facts it was held that a sufficient amount of time had passed for the relationship between the parties to have altered such that the claimant had been exercising his own free will in entering into the settlement agreement. The fact that the parties' relationship was terminated by the settlement agreement was an indication of this fact. Indeed, the settlement agreement had greatly reduced the defendant's entitlement to payments from the singer's albums.

29.4.7 The liability of the solicitor

Shifting liability from the home towards the solicitor

All that is required for the mortgagee to do in the wake of *Massey* is to 'urge' the proposed surety to seek independent advice. What is not clear is the role of the mortgagee if that advice is not taken as urged. Where advice is taken, the mortgagee is not responsible for the advice that is given. That 'is a matter for the solicitor' professional judgment and a matter between him and his client'. As was said in *Midland Bank v Serter*, any deficiencies in this advice are the responsibility of the solicitor on general tortious principles. The effect of the decision of the House of Lords in *Royal Bank of Scotland v Etridge (No 2)*[114] is that their Lordships have thrown their weight behind a procedure whereby it is the responsibility of a solicitor to give independent advice to the cohabitee. The ramification of this drift in the law,

---

112 [2004] EWCA Civ 816, [2004] 1 WLR 2380.
113 [2007] EWCA Civ 155, [2007] All ER (D) 370 (Feb).
114 [2002] AC 773.

as considered below, is that the cohabitee's principal claim in the event of any undue influence or misrepresentation will be to sue the solicitor for failing to give proper advice, rather than to resist any claim to repossession brought by the mortgagee by means of setting aside the mortgage contract: the effect of that change is that the cohabitee's rights are predicated in the tort of negligence and not in the law of property.

The solicitor's role – advising more than one party

In *Midland Bank v Serter*,[115] the Court of Appeal held that where the solicitor had represented the mortgagee, mortgagor and the cohabitee, the mortgagee was not bound by constructive notice of any undue influence where the cohabitee had signed a certificate acknowledging receipt of legal advice. Even in circumstances in which it is the mortgagee which directs the solicitor to advise the cohabitee, the solicitor acts as solicitor to the cohabitee, owing that person all of the duties of a solicitor.[116]

The bank is then entitled to rely on the advice which the solicitor gives to the cohabitee, even if the solicitor in fact breaches the obligation to the cohabitee and favours the mortgagee or the mortgagor instead by not passing information as to the nature of the transaction to the cohabitee.[117] Where the solicitor undertakes the task of advising the cohabitee, the solicitor is deemed to be independent and the mortgagee is entitled to rely on the appropriate advice having been given by the solicitor.[118] In fact, what has happened is that the obligation on the mortgagee to ensure that there is no constructive notice of any misrepresentation or undue influence has transferred to a liability in negligence on the solicitor in providing advice to the cohabitee, as considered below.

In the Court of Appeal decision in *Barclays Bank v Thomson*,[119] the bank obtained a mortgage over T's family home, lending the money to T's husband. The bank instructed a solicitor to act on its behalf in the mortgage transaction, including giving advice to T. The solicitors had explained to T the effect of the mortgage on the family home in the husband's absence. It was held that the bank was entitled to rely upon the solicitor's assurance that T had been properly advised. As a result, the bank was not to be imputed with any notice of any undue influence or misrepresentation which was active on T. Therefore, it was found that the bank was able to remove constructive notice by receiving a representation that T had received legal advice. The onus has therefore shifted from the mortgagee making enquiries as to whether or not there are rights in some cohabitee, to ensuring that a cohabitee certifies that some independent legal advice has been given.[120]

It is only Hobhouse LJ, in *Banco Exterior v Mann*,[121] who, in delivering a dissenting judgment, pointed out that a solicitor can only be truly independent if, in a case of undue influence or misrepresentation, that solicitor straightforwardly advises the cohabitee not to co-sign the mortgage agreement if that agreement would be potentially disadvantageous. In reality, it is said that a solicitor will not act with such impunity in a situation in which

---

115 [1995] 1 FLR 367.
116 *Ibid; Banco Exterior v Mann* [1995] 1 All ER 936.
117 *Halifax Mortgage Services Ltd v Stepsky* [1996] 2 All ER 277.
118 *Banco Exterior v Mann* [1995] 1 All ER 936.
119 [1997] 4 All ER 816.
120 Cf *Halifax Mortgage Services Ltd v Stepsky* [1996] 2 All ER 277.
121 [1995] 1 All ER 936.

she is acting as solicitor for the mortgagee and the mortgagor simultaneously. And yet the court in *Halifax BS v Stepsky*[122] was prepared to absolve the mortgagee from any responsibility to procure truly independent advice in such circumstances. This tortious remedy of suing the solicitor in negligence for damages will only generate a right to cash from the solicitor (assuming the solicitor is solvent or suitably insured); it will not protect the claimant's right to remain in occupation of the home which was put up as security for the mortgage loan.

Clearly, though, where the solicitor is obviously involved in a conflict of interest in acting for the bank, for the mortgagor and for the cohabitee, then the solicitor will not be able to give independent advice on which the mortgagee can rely to discharge its liability.[123] Therefore, where the solicitor is advising the bank as to a complex financial transaction and is found to have placed improper pressure on the mortgagor to agree to that transaction, it was held that that cannot be suitable to discharge the bank's obligation to take reasonable steps.[124]

What this development in the law has done is to shift responsibility from the bank to make inquiries onto the solicitor giving advice. As such the claimant acquires rights to sue the solicitor in the event that advice is negligently given under the tort of negligence. From the perspective of the cohabitee that will be an inferior form of remedy compared to the possibility of a quasi-proprietary remedy[125] which sets aside the entirety of the mortgage:[126] the claim in negligence is a purely personal claim to receive common law damages which will not in itself protect the claimant's rights in her home.

29.4.8 Setting aside in part or in whole

Understanding the problem

One important issue which remains outstanding is whether or not a mortgage obtained by means of some undue influence (for which the lending institution is found to be liable in part) should be set aside *in toto*, or whether that mortgage should be partially enforced.

Suppose the following set of facts:

> *A cohabitee consents to a mortgage up to a value of £15,000, and the mortgagor secures the family home in return for loan moneys of £30,000. Should the cohabitee's interests be subject to the mortgage to the extent of £15,000, or is the cohabitee to elude liability altogether by having the mortgage set aside* in toto?

The position under the case law

In *TSB v Camfield*,[127] a husband and his business partner requested a £30,000 overdraft from the plaintiff bank. The overdraft was agreed to, provided that the plaintiff bank was

---

122 [1996] 2 All ER 277.
123 *National Westminster Bank plc v Breeds* [2001] All ER (D) 5.
124 *Ibid.*
125 The nature of which is considered immediately below.
126 See para 29.4.8 below.
127 [1995] 1 WLR 430.

able to take a charge over each of their houses. The bank manager responsible stipulated that the mortgagors' wives should receive independent, separate legal advice. Contrary to the assurance given by the solicitors involved, neither wife was advised separately from her husband. It was found that, owing to the husband's innocent misrepresentation, the wife was induced to stand as surety for double the amount that she believed she was securing. She had consented to an obligation of £15,000, whereas the charge was secured as to £30,000.

The dispute concerned the extent of the wife's remedy. At first instance it was held that the mortgage should be set aside only to the extent that the cohabitee had not consented to it. Therefore, the charge would be enforceable as to £15,000. However, Nourse LJ in the Court of Appeal followed Ferris J in *Allied Irish Bank v Byrne*[128] and set the mortgage aside *in toto*. He concurred with the *dicta* of Ferris J that 'to set aside a transaction is an all or nothing process'.

Eight days later, Robert Walker QC in *Bank Melli Iran v Samadi-rad*[129] decided on similar facts without the benefit of Ferris J's judgment in *Byrne*. Again that case dealt with the question of total or partial enforcement of a charge which had been obtained as a result of some undue influence. The mortgage was partially enforced on the basis that the cohabitee had been induced to enter into a transaction to the extent of £60,000. Robert Walker QC held that equity could force her, as a condition of relief, to recognise the security as good for that limited sum to which she had consented.

While acknowledging the force of Robert Walker QC's argument, Nourse LJ followed *Byrne*. Nourse LJ held:

> If this claim is upheld, the court seeks to put that party into the position in which he would have been if the representation had not been made. This involves ascertaining what the position would have been if the transaction had not taken place. *It does not involve reforming the transaction to accord with the representation.*[130]

Accordingly the mortgage was set aside *in toto*. As his Lordship continued: 'The wife's right to have the transaction set aside *in toto* as against the husband is no less enforceable against the mortgagee.' Therefore, a mortgagee in this type of case cannot be in a better position than any other third party who has notice of the cohabitee's equitable rights.

The *TSB v Camfield* approach has been followed in *Castle Phillips Finance v Piddington*[131] in the Court of Appeal. In that case a husband used money lent on security against the matrimonial home to secure an overdraft. The cohabitee had been informed that the money was being used for roof repairs. It was found that there had been undue influence exerted over the cohabitee to consent to the charge. Further, it was found that the mortgagee had not established whether or not the cohabitee had taken independent legal advice. The judge at first instance set aside the mortgagee's charge in part only. Peter Gibson LJ, giving the leading judgment in the Court of Appeal, held that the mortgage must be set aside *in toto*.

---

128 [1995] 1 FCR 430.
129 [1993] 2 FLR 367.
130 Emphasis added. See also *Redgrave v Hurd* (1881) 20 Ch D 1.
131 (1995) 70 P & CR 592. See also *Goode Durrant v Biddulph* (1994) 26 HLR 625; *Bank of Cyprus v Markou* [1999] 2 All ER 707.

Other approaches

There have been cases in which the court has refused to set aside the transaction where that would have been inequitable to the mortgagee. Thus, in *Midland Bank v Greene*,[132] loan moneys had been extended in the context of undue influence exercised by a husband on his wife, but the wife had subsequently benefited from improvements to the property and the enlargement of her equitable interests from rights in a lease to rights in the freehold. The court ordered that accounts be taken of the comparative value of the interests of the parties, such that the mortgagor and plaintiff wife be required to account to the mortgagee for the benefits received by use of the loan moneys. The court explained that it was giving equitable relief on terms rather than setting aside the transaction or rewriting the agreement between the parties. In *Dunbar Bank v Nadeem*,[133] it was held that a wife's rights to rescission of the mortgage agreement under the *O'Brien* principle were contingent on the wife accounting to the bank for the amount of money lent by the mortgagee and used to acquire her half share in the leasehold interest in property. The creditor may acquire a charge against the husband's interest in any event, and thus seek a sale of the property, as considered in section 16.2.[134]

Some problems with the Camfield *approach*

The approach of the Court of Appeal in *TSB v Camfield* and of the High Court in *Castle Phillips Finance v Piddington* is in marked contrast to that of the Court of Appeal in *Equity Home Loans v Prestidge*.[135] In the former cases, the cohabitee's equitable rights in the property are enforced against the mortgagee such that the mortgage is discharged completely. In *Prestidge*, the mortgagor gained the agreement of the cohabitee to the original mortgage for the purchase of property. The mortgagor then sought a remortgage on more onerous terms. This remortgage was completed without the consent of the cohabitee. The issue arose whether the remortgage was binding against the cohabitee.

It was held by the Court of Appeal that the remortgage was made against the background of the cohabitee's consent to the original mortgage for the purchase of the house. She had consented to the original mortgage and therefore she was taken to have given imputed consent to the remortgage being replaced only on the terms of the original mortgage. The Court of Appeal held that her imputed consent to the remortgage applied whether or not she knew of the creation of the remortgage, provided it did not prejudice her equitable interest further than she had already agreed. To do justice to the mortgagee and the cohabitee, it was held that the substitute mortgage ranked ahead of the cohabitee's beneficial interest to the extent of (but no further than) the consent which was to be imputed to her.

In *TSB v Camfield*, the cohabitee had knowledge of the further mortgage. Therefore, she had an opportunity to seek advice on the full extent of her obligations which had not been available in *Prestidge*. Similarly, in *TSB v Camfield*, the cohabitee had an opportunity to take legal advice on the effect of the charge. The Court of Appeal held that the cohabitee was not bound by the mortgage at all – as a result of the undue influence – even to the extent to which she had agreed to the borrowing. However, in *Prestidge*, the cohabitee had no knowledge of

132 [1994] 2 FLR 827.
133 [1997] 2 All ER 253, [1998] 3 All ER 876, CA.
134 *Zandfavid v BCCI* [1996] 1 WLR 1420; *Alliance & Leicester plc v Slayford* (2000) *The Times*, 19 December.
135 [1992] 1 All ER 909.

the remortgage but was, nevertheless, held to have agreed to it to the extent of her consent to the original mortgage.

The conceptual difference between these two cases appears to be that there was undue influence in the former but not in the latter. However, the practical difference between the two is more difficult to fathom. In both instances, the cohabitee has been the victim of some wrong on the part of the mortgagor seeking to raise unauthorised capital on the matrimonial home. It is contended, therefore, that the *Prestidge* decision cannot be supported in the light of the cases following *O'Brien*.

Chapter 30

Miscellaneous equitable remedies

30.1 INTRODUCTION

The equitable jurisdiction has been considered in this book, thus far, as being concerned with a philosophical notion of achieving fair results in the circumstances of individual cases, with substantive principles (such as the trust), and now with procedural principles.[1] Equity has developed, significantly, ever since the medieval period by means of a series of different forms of writ developed by the Lords Chancellor. We have already considered injunctions, specific performance, rescission and rectification as examples of equitable remedy. In this chapter, we shall consider a collection of lesser equitable remedies, some of which have already been considered in earlier chapters (such as account and subrogation). This chapter is not an exhaustive list of all of the available remedies to which equity will give effect, but rather it is a compilation of the most common general remedies.

30.2 ACCOUNT

30.2.1 The various senses of account

The principal remedy available to beneficiaries against trustees is the right to demand an account from those trustees.[2] It is in that context that we have considered 'account' thus far. 'Account' has two senses which are of importance here. The first sense of 'account' is that the fiduciary is obliged to provide accounts to the beneficiary as to the value and condition of property held on trust. Where the documentary accounts are inadequate or incorrect in some way, the beneficiaries are entitled to 'falsify' those accounts and demand a proper reckoning from the fiduciary. By contrast, the second sense of 'account' is an obligation to make good any losses disclosed by those accounts. This is more akin to one of the alternative, vernacular meanings of the verb 'account', meaning to explain or justify oneself.

In essence, the equitable remedy of account is then a factual matter of identifying a loss caused by a breach of duty and requiring the fiduciary to make good that loss.[3] In truth, however, 'account' does not tell us the nature of the remedy which will be imposed on the defendant. So, in relation to breach of trust by a trustee (considered in Chapter 18 in detail), the trustee may be liable to make specific restitution of the original trust property where that is appropriate, or else to compensate the beneficiaries in financial terms if that property cannot be recovered. The making of awards by way of monetary compensation is referred to as 'equitable compensation'.

However, we encountered the notion of 'account' in other contexts in this book. For example, when a fiduciary (whether a trustee or not) earns an unauthorised profit from her fiduciary office, she will be liable to account to beneficiaries for those profits by way of a constructive trust being imposed over the profits[4] or their traceable proceeds.[5] By contrast, a person who dishonestly assists in a breach of trust or who receives property with knowledge that that property has been sourced from a breach of trust will be liable to account to the beneficiaries for any loss caused by the breach of trust.[6] The liability as a dishonest assistant[7] or as a knowing recipient[8] is a personal liability to account, as opposed to the proprietary constructive

1 As 'equity' was defined in section 1.1 of this book.
2 Millett, 1998.
3 *Target Holdings v Redferns* [1996] 1 AC 421.
4 *Boardman v Phipps* [1967] 2 AC 4.
5 *Attorney-General for Hong Kong v Reid* [1994] 1 AC 324.
6 See Chapter 20 for a full discussion of these claims.
7 *Royal Brunei Airlines v Tan* [1995] 2 AC 378.
8 *Re Montagu* [1987] Ch 264

trust awarded in relation to fiduciaries earning unauthorised profits;[9] hence the suggestion that 'account' covers both giving an explanation (requiring a proprietary remedy in some contexts) and making good any loss (generally by monetary compensation in the alternative).

30.2.2 The categories of equitable liability to account

Few of the books on equity have a consideration of 'account' as a separate topic for two reasons: first, it has become subsumed into other doctrines so that it is difficult to identify distinct principles underpinning this area as a field in its own right and, secondly, it is a practical matter on a case-by-case basis to identify what has been lost and therefore equity has not developed detailed principles to cover 'account' as a distinct field. Only *Meagher, Gummow and Lehane's Equity: Doctrines and Remedies* give this topic a separate discussion.[10] The authors of the current edition of that book explain how the equitable doctrine of account was more straightforward than that at common law and that it had consequently assumed primacy by 1760.[11] The equitable doctrine of account is described there as arising in eight contexts, and that division of the material is adopted here together with two additional categories considered in this book already.

The eight circumstances are as follows. First, where the parties have mutual, agreed accounts such that the court is really concerned only to effect an equitable set-off between the parties of the amounts owed between them.[12] Secondly, where the parties are in a fiduciary relationship with one another – such as where one is trustee for the other.[13] Thirdly, on dissolution of a partnership (in which context the partners will stand in a fiduciary relationship to one another) such that joint debts of the partnership will be paid out of jointly held accounts in accordance with the partnership agreement;[14] by contrast, separate creditors of separate partners will not be entitled to an account from all of the partners, particularly if they are insolvency creditors of a bankrupt partner with no claim against the partnership.[15] Fourthly, in circumstances in which common law accounting could not provide an account, to identify the obligation to account in entangled accounts.[16] In this way, equity had greater flexibility to allocate claims between the partner's severally in their personal contexts and jointly in their partnership contexts.[17] Fifthly, to prevent waste, a claimant can seek an account in equity together with an injunction to prevent the waste taking effect.[18] Sixthly, in passing off and patent infringement cases.[19] Seventhly, accounts ordered to ensure that the claimant received payment of amounts which the defendant had prevented accruing to the claimant.[20] Eighthly, as considered above, to prevent the earning of unauthorised profits in a

9 *Boardman v Phipps* [1967] 2 AC 4; see para 12.5.2 above.

10 Meagher, Heydon and Leeming, 2002, 869 *et seq.* See also Pettit, 2001, 669.

11 *Ibid*, 869; *Ex p Bax* (1751) 2 Ves Sen 388.

12 *Phillips v Phillips* (1852) 9 Hare 471, 68 ER 596; *Anglo-American Asphalt Co v Crowley Russell & Co* [1945] 2 All ER 324, 331, *per* Romer J.

13 Eg, *Target Holdings v Redferns* [1996] 1 AC 421; *Warman International Ltd v Dwyer* (1995) 182 CLR 544.

14 *Re Budgett* [1894] 2 Ch 557.

15 See *Lacey v Hill* (1872) LR 8 Ch App 441, 444, *per* James LJ.

16 Eg, *O'Connor v Spaight* (1804) 1 Sch & Lef 305.

17 *Ibid*, 309, *per* Lord Redesdale.

18 *Duke of Leeds v Lord Amherst* (1843) 12 Sim 459, 60 ER 178.

19 See *Colbeam Palmer v Stock Affiliates Pty Ltd* (1968) 122 CLR 25.

20 *McIntosh v Great Western Railway Co* (1850) 2 Mac & G 74, 42 ER 29.

fiduciary capacity.[21] Where those profits were not earned in a fiduciary capacity, then a full account of profits will not be ordered.[22] Equitable accounting will also be available to compensate a fiduciary for the effort or cost involved in earning unauthorised profits (provided that there has been no breach of any other equitable obligation).[23] To this eighth category should be added a ninth, referred to above, relating to personal liability to account for dishonest assistance in a breach of trust or knowing receipt of property derived from a breach of trust. And to this list should be added a tenth category relating to the obligation of express trustees to account to their beneficiaries, which was considered in detail in section 8.4 above.[24] These liabilities of trustees are considered, *inter alia*, in the next two sections in the context of general equitable remedies.

30.3 SPECIFIC RESTITUTION

The remedy of specific restitution,[25] as we have considered it thus far in this book, relates to the obligation of an express trustee who commits a breach of trust involving the transfer of trust property out of the trust fund. It is a proprietary remedy. That trustee is obliged to restore the original trust property to the trust fund.[26] Where that property has been sold to a *bona fide* purchaser for value without notice of the beneficiaries' rights, the trustee will generally not be able to recover that property,[27] nor will it be possible to recover that property from a recipient who has changed her position substantively in reliance on the receipt of the property.[28] It is suggested that this remedy is based on the same principles as following or common law tracing[29] whereby a person recovers property in which the recipient has no better proprietary right.[30] In the event that specific restitution is not possible – for example, because the original property has been inextricably mixed with other property or has been passed to a person who has a good defence to the restitution claim – then the beneficiaries would have either to seek a personal claim against the trustee or some third party culpable in that breach of trust[31] or an equitable tracing claim into the mixture.[32]

Specific restitution is also available to restore property which belongs in equity to a person to that person.[33] So, where a valuable heirloom held on the terms of a strict settlement was

---

21 *Boardman v Phipps* [1967] 2 AC 46 (trustee *de son tort* earning unauthorised personal profit in conflict of interest); *Attorney-General v Blake* [2001] AC 268 (in relation to treasonable profits from an office in the secret service).

22 *Experience Hendrix LLC v PPX Enterprises Inc* [2003] EWCA Civ 323, [2003] 1 All ER (Comm) 830, [2003] EMLR 515, where royalties had not been paid to a musician further to a contract, but in circumstances in which the defendant was not in a fiduciary relationship to the claimant, there was a right to contractual recovery of money but no equitable accounting.

23 *Boardman v Phipps* [1967] 2 AC 46.

24 See section 8.4 above, where this head of liability to account is considered in detail.

25 A term used in *Swindle v Harrison* [1997] 4 All ER 705.

26 *Target Holdings v Redferns* [1996] 1 AC 421; see section 18.3 above.

27 *Westdeutsche Landesbank v Islington LBC* [1996] AC 669.

28 *Lipkin Gorman v Karpnale* [1991] 2 AC 548; see para 19.6.1 above.

29 Considered in section 19.1 above.

30 See *Foskett v McKeown* [2000] 3 All ER 97.

31 In the form of dishonest assistance or knowing receipt considered in Chapter 20.

32 Section 19.4 of this book.

33 See generally Meagher, Gummow and Lehane, 2002, 823 *et seq.*

taken from the fund, the court may order the restoration of that property.[34] This power relates to property which has intrinsic (rather than resale) value to the claimant. As before, defences of change of position and of *bona fide* purchase for value would be available to the defendant. Specific delivery of chattels is also available in equity further to an award of specific perform-ance whereby a court which has ordered specific performance of a contract for the transfer of property will order that that property be transferred as required by the contract.[35]

30.4 EQUITABLE COMPENSATION

This book gives over this short section to a consideration of equitable compensation as a distinct remedy in the light of its growing importance in the equitable canon after *Target Holdings v Redferns*.[36] Equitable compensation, as it relates to breach of trust, was consid-ered in detail at para 18.3.4 above. The aim of this section is to explore the underpinnings of compensation as a general equitable remedy in line with other remedies such as subrogation, specific performance, rescission, rectification and injunction. More controversially, it should also be ranged among equitable institutions such as proprietary estoppel, constructive trust and resulting trust as a means of preventing detriment being suffered by the claimant.[37]

The central importance of equitable compensation is that it stands as a parallel to the common law remedy of damages. Equitable compensation is not dependent, however, upon common law standards of causation nor of foreseeability,[38] particularly in relation to breach of fiduciary duty.

30.5 EQUITABLE DAMAGES

30.5.1 The inherent jurisdiction to award equitable damages after the Judicature Act 1873

The principal monetary award which is made by equity is in the form of equitable compensa-tion, as considered in the previous section.[39] However, ever since the Judicature Act 1873, the courts of equity have also had the power to make awards of damages,[40] although this power is rarely used.[41] It is usual, of course, to consider the common law as awarding damages and therefore to consider that equity makes an award of compensation or some other form of monetary award. Indeed, the current edition of *Snell's Equity*[42] subsumes much of this material within a discussion of 'personal monetary claims', whereas Spry's *Equitable Remedies*[43] uses the expression 'equitable damages' throughout: the latter is used here, to

---

34   *Duke of Somerset v Cookson* (1735) 3 P Wms 390, 24 ER 1114. Cf *Pusey v Pusey* (1684) 1 Vern 273, 23 ER 465.
35   *Neville v Wilson* [1997] Ch 144: see section 12.6 above.
36   [1996] 1 AC 421, [1995] 3 WLR 352, [1995] 3 All ER 785.
37   See, eg, *Baker v Baker* (1993) 25 HLR 408.
38   *Target Holdings v Redferns* [1996] 1 AC 421, considered at para 18.3.4 above. See suggestions to the contrary in McGhee, 2005, para 18–14.
39   This general sense of the doctrine is not considered by McGhee, 2005.
40   See Spry, 2001, Chapter 7.
41   *Sefton v Tophams Ltd* [1965] Ch 1140, 1169, which suggests that this jurisdiction should only be exercised in a 'special case'.
42   McGhee, 2005, Chapter 18.
43   Spry, 2001, Chapter 7.

distinguish this remedy from the other forms of personal monetary claim already considered in this chapter, such as equitable compensation, personal liability to account as a dishonest assistant or as a knowing recipient of property in a breach of trust, and so forth.

On the decided cases, equity has the power to make an award of damages in circumstances in which the common law would not do so (for example, due to a deficiency in the pleadings),[44] or in which it is more convenient to seek damages from a court of equity in which the same proceedings have already been commenced (for example, where the damage suffered will result from an equitable concept such as breach of trust or in connection with specific performance)[45] rather than sending the claimant to seek her damages in fresh proceedings at common law before a common law court.[46] So, where a claimant sued in equity for specific performance of a contract, the claimant would be required to pursue her claim for damages in the equitable court where the claim for damages was linked to the claim for specific performance.[47] If the harm or loss suffered is small, if it can be valued in monetary terms, and if any other equitable remedy would be oppressive of the defendant, then an award of equitable damages can be made.[48] Alternatively, there is an equitable discretion to award equitable damages as opposed to specific equitable relief, if awarding other equitable relief would be unreasonable in the circumstances.[49]

30.5.2 Equitable damages under statute

Damages may be awarded under s 50 of the Supreme Court Act 1981, as considered already in this book in relation to injunctions[50] and to specific performance,[51] in 'addition to or in substitution for such injunction or specific performance'.[52] This jurisdiction to award damages was originally contained in s 2 of the Chancery Amendment Act 1858 (commonly referred to as 'Lord Cairns's Act'). Thus, in any case in which there is a power to award an injunction or to award specific performance, the court may order damages instead, as considered in the preceding section in relation to the court's inherent jurisdiction, provided that specific performance would otherwise have been available (and not precluded by any of the matters considered in Chapter 27).[53] Similarly, under s 2 of the Misrepresentation Act 1967, the court may displace its power to award rescission with an award of damages.

30.6 COMPOUND INTEREST

The issue considered in this section is whether or not courts of equity have an inherent power to award compound interest on awards of damages at common law.[54] Compound interest

---

44 *Phelps v Prothero* (1855) 7 De GM & G 722; 44 ER 280; *Eastwood v Lever* (1863) 4 De GJ & S 114, 128, *per* Turner LJ.
45 See the explanation in Spry, 2001, 623.
46 *Ferguson v Wilson* (1866) LR 2 Ch App 77, at 88, *per* Turner LJ.
47 *Phelps v Prothero* (1855) 7 De GM & G 722, at 734, 44 ER 280, at 285, *per* Turner LJ.
48 *Shelfer v City of London Electric Lighting Co* [1895] 1 Ch 287, 322, *per* Smith LJ.
49 *Wedgwood v Adams* (1843) 6 Beav 600, at 605, *per* Lord Langdale. Also *Keenaway v Thompson* [1981] QB 88.
50 See Chapter 27 above.
51 See para 26.4.7 above.
52 Supreme Court Act 1981, s 50. See *Jaggard v Sawyer* [1995] 1 WLR 269.
53 *Lavery v Pursell* (1888) 39 Ch D 508, 519, *per* Chitty J.
54 Compound interest is interest calculated on awards of interest as well as on capital.

will be awarded in one of four situations.[55] First, where a contract or common commercial practice provides for compound interest. Secondly, where the claimant has a proprietary right under trust in the property which is the subject matter of the claim for loss. Thirdly, by way of special damages relating to compound interest as a result of a defendant's wrongful act or omission. Fourthly, in arbitration cases. Only the second and third categories are of significance here. In general terms, it has been accepted that courts of equity have the power to make awards of simple interest as ancillary relief in relation to equitable remedies.[56]

There is an issue as to whether compound interest will only be awarded when there are fiduciary duties owed such that the fiduciary owes obligations to account,[57] or whether compound interest can only be awarded (other than in relation to an express contractual provision) in cases where there has been fraud.[58] The basis of this jurisdiction to award compound interest is to prevent a fiduciary from taking any profit from any breach of fiduciary duty.[59] In *Westdeutsche Landesbank v Islington LBC*,[60] it was held by the majority of the House of Lords that compound interest would not be available where a bank acquired damages at common law further to a claim for money had and received because the bank had no proprietary rights under a trust in the property which formed the source of the common law claim. Compound interest would have been available had the bank had a proprietary interest under trust in the property. This position was changed by the House of Lords in *Sempra Metals v IRC*[61] to the effect that compound interest could be awarded whenever the court thinks it appropriate in cases of money had and received at common law, whether the claimant has a proprietary interest or not.

It had been thought that equity had a power to award compound interest on damages awarded at common law where those damages are awarded for fraud.[62] However, a closer examination of the authorities has led courts more recently to suggest that there was no such general jurisdiction expressly accepted on the older authorities.[63]

30.7 SUBROGATION

30.7.1 The nature of subrogation

Subrogation is an equitable remedy which arises when a defendant has received a benefit at the claimant's expense and which also enables one claimant to be replaced with another so as to prevent one person taking a benefit at the expense of another person.[64] The claimant

---

55 See the Law Commission's Consultation Paper No 167, 31 July 2002.
56 *President of India v La Pintada Compania Navigacion SA* [1985] AC 104, 115, *per* Lord Brandon; [1984] 2 All ER 733.
57 *Westdeutsche Landesbank v Islington LBC* [1996] AC 669, 701, *per* Lord Browne-Wilkinson.
58 *Clef Aquitaine SARL v Laporte Minerals (Barrow) Ltd* [2002] QB 488, 506, *per* Simon Brown LJ. This issue is raised in *Black v Davies* [2004] EWHC 1464 (QB).
59 *Wallersteiner v Moir (No 2)* [1975] QB 373, [1975] 1 All ER 849.
60 [1996] AC 669, 701, *per* Lord Browne-Wilkinson. See now also *Sempra v IRC* [2005] EWCA Civ 389.
61 [2007] 3 WLR 354.
62 See, eg, suggestions to this effect in *Armory v Delamire* (1723) 1 Str 505; *Johnson v R* [1904] AC 817.
63 *Black v Davies* [2004] EWHC 1464 (QB), [13]; relying on *Burdick v Garrick* (1870) LR 5 Ch App 233, 241, *per* Lord Hatherly; *Attorney-General v Alford* (1885) 4 D & GM 843 and *Westdeutsche Landesbank v Islington LBC* [1996] AC 669. Cf *Hungerfords v Walker* (1989) 171 CLR 125, considering *Hadley v Baxendale* (1854) 9 Ex 341.
64 *Banque Financière de la Cité v Parc (Battersea) Ltd* [1999] 1 AC 221; *Liberty Mutual Insurance Co (UK) Ltd v HSBC Bank plc* [2001] All ER (D) 72.

who is entitled to the remedy of subrogation is put 'in the shoes' of the defendant so that the claimant acquires whatever rights the defendant previously had.[65] Subrogation arises in a number of contexts, as will be considered in this section. Two examples will illustrate the simple and reviving forms of subrogation.[66] So, if Insure Ltd had insured Betty against the costs of any motoring accident and Charlie had driven into Betty, then Insure Ltd would be obliged to pay Betty the amount of her loss, but would also be entitled to be subrogated to Betty's rights to sue Charlie in the tort of negligence: that is, Insure Ltd sues Charlie as though Insure Ltd were Betty to recover the amount it paid to Betty.[67] Alternatively, if Alex involuntarily confers a benefit on Betty (for example, by paying her money), Alex may be entitled to a remedy against Betty where it would be inequitable for Betty to retain that benefit. So, where Alex's money was used by Betty to pay off a debt which Betty owed to Charlie, then, assuming that Betty had no conscionable excuse for using that money for that purpose, then Betty would owe that debt to Alex instead.[68] In either case, one person is subrogated to the rights of another.

Subrogation is an equitable remedy.[69] As has been considered in this book, there is a tension between the traditional doctrines of equity and the principle of restitution of unjust enrichment.[70] A number of cases in the 1990s held that subrogation is used to reverse the unjust enrichment of the defendant.[71] So, the remedy of subrogation will be available in circumstances in which it can be shown that the defendant has been enriched at the claimant's expense in circumstances in which that enrichment was unjust. Recent cases have suggested that there is no practical difference, however, between doctrines which are concerned with avoiding unconscionability (such as equity) and doctrines which are concerned with avoiding injustice (such as restitution of unjust enrichment).[72] In one case which proposed the restitution of unjust enrichment understanding of subrogation, *Boscawen v Bajwa*,[73] it was nevertheless held that:

> The equity arises from the conduct of the parties on well-settled principles and in defined circumstances which made it unconscionable for the defendant to deny the proprietary interest claimed by the plaintiff. A constructive trust arises in the same way.

---

65 See, eg, *Re National Permanent Benefit Building Society ex p Williamson* (1869) 5 Ch App 309, 311, *per* Giffard LJ; *Boscawen v Bajwa* [1996] 1 WLR 328.

66 To use Mitchell's vocabulary: Mitchell, 1994.

67 *Burnand v Rodocanachi* (1882) 7 App Cas 333.

68 *Boscawen v Bajwa* [1996] 1 WLR 328.

69 Traditionally considered to be a 'right': *Castellain v Preston* (1883) 11 QBD 380, 390, *per* Brett LJ; although this doctrine is now properly understood to be a 'remedy': *Boscawen v Bajwa* [1996] 1 WLR 328, 335, *per* Millett LJ; James (1971) 31 MLR 149, 154; Mitchell, 1995, 71–74; Goff and Jones, 2002, 121.

70 See the essay taken from the third edition of this book on 'restitution of unjust enrichment' at www.alastairhudson.com/trustslaw/trustslawindex.htm

71 *Boscawen v Bajwa* [1996] 1 WLR 328, [1995] 4 All ER 769, 777, *per* Millett LJ; *Banque Financière de la Cité v Parc (Battersea) Ltd* [1999] 1 AC 221, [1998] 1 All ER 737, 749, *per* Lord Hoffmann. See now *Anfield (UK) Ltd v Bank of Scotland plc* [2010] EWHC 2374, [2011] 1 WLR 2414.

72 See, eg, *Cheltenham & Gloucester plc v Appleyard* [2004] EWCA Civ 291, para [49], *per* Neuberger LJ; *Filby v Mortgage Express (No 2) Ltd* [2004] EWCA Civ 759, para [56], *per* May LJ: where both Courts of Appeal suggested that the decision of the House of Lords in *Banque Financière de la Cité v Parc (Battersea) Ltd* arose in relation to such a unique set of circumstances that it should not be considered to require the court to 'apply that decision like a straitjacket' in future cases.

73 [1996] 1 WLR 328, [1995] 4 All ER 769, 777, *per* Millett LJ.

From these *dicta*, it is clear that the basis of subrogation remains equity, which seeks to identify whether or not activity is unconscionable, and which arises in a manner similar to a constructive trust. Therefore, it is suggested that the basis of subrogation is an equitable notion of good conscience.[74] The earliest understandings of this equity in English law were that it was 'the plainest equity that could be'[75] and based on a 'principle of natural justice'.[76] Thus, to consider subrogation as being a part of general equity is entirely justifiable on the established authorities, whereas the suggestion that it is based on unjust enrichment is a comparatively recent one.[77]

30.7.2 Forms of subrogation

The neatest example of subrogation arises when Betty takes Alex's money to discharge a debt which Betty owes to Charlie, with the result that Alex is subrogated to Charlie's rights so that Betty owes that debt to Alex instead.[78] However, while that is an example of subrogation, it is not a description of the whole of subrogation. Here are some other examples in which subrogation has been permitted. Where Alex is a surety for Betty's debts and pays off Betty's debts owed to Charlie, Alex is entitled to any securities which Betty has deposited with Charlie to secure that debt by way of subrogation.[79] Where Betty borrowed money from Alex to acquire property from Charlie, Alex should be entitled to a charge by way of subrogation against the purchased property.[80]

The established categories of people entitled to the remedy of subrogation are:[81] sureties discharging the debts of their principals[82] have a right of subrogation against the principal;[83] people who endorse bills of exchange and who then pay the bill in full have a right of subrogation against the acceptor;[84] insurers suing to recover amounts paid out under a contract of insurance;[85] creditors of a business carried on by a trustee such that the creditor is subrogated to the right of indemnity which the trustee has against the trust fund;[86] mortgagors who use a third person's property to discharge their mortgage (or other secured) debt with the

---

74 *Lord Napier and Ettrick v RF Kershaw Ltd* [1993] AC 713, 738, *per* Lord Templeman.

75 *Randal v Cochran* (1748) 1 Ves Sen 98; *Burnand v Rodocanachi* (1882) 7 App Cas 333, 339, *per* Lord Blackburn.

76 *Craythorne v Swinburne* (1807) 14 Ves 160, 162, *per* Sir Samuel Romilly.

77 Beginning with Professor Mitchell, 1995 and then being picked up in subsequent cases, eg, *Banque Financière de la Cité v Parc (Battersea) Ltd* [1999] 1 AC 221, [1998] 1 All ER 737, 749, *per* Lord Hoffmann; *Crantrave Ltd v Lloyds Bank plc* [2000] QB 917, [2000] 4 All ER 473.

78 *Boscawen v Bajwa* [1995] 4 All ER 769, [1996] 1 WLR 328.

79 *Aldrich v Cooper* (1803) 8 Ves 382, 389, *per* Lord Eldon.

80 *Orakpo v Manson Investments Ltd* [1977] 1 WLR 347, 357, *per* Buckley LJ.

81 For a fuller discussion of these categories, see Goff and Jones, 2002, 139 *et seq.*

82 Provided that the agent has the authority to discharge that debt: *In Re Cleadon* [1939] Ch 286; *Crantrave Ltd v Lloyds Bank plc* [2000] QB 917, [2000] 4 All ER 473. Cf *B Liggett (Liverpool) Ltd v Barclays Bank Ltd* [1928] 1 KB 48.

83 *Aldrich v Cooper* (1803) 8 Ves 382; *Craythorne v Swinburne* (1807) 14 Ves 160. Cf *Banque Financière de la Cité v Parc (Battersea) Ltd* [1999] 1 AC 221; *Cheltenham & Gloucester plc v Appleyard* [2004] EWCA Civ 291.

84 *Ex p Bishop, re Fox, Walker & Co* (1880) 15 Ch D 400, 411, *per* James LJ.

85 *Lord Napier and Ettrick v RF Kershaw Ltd* [1993] AC 713, where the appropriate remedy may be a lien over a defined fund.

86 *Dowse v Gorton* [1891] AC 190, 203, *per* Lord Macnaghten.

mortgagee such that the third party is subrogated to the rights which were previously owed to the mortgagee;[87] lenders may be subrogated to an unpaid vendor's lien which the borrower acquires over another's property if acquired by means of the borrowed money.[88] In each case, the remedy entitles the claimant to assume the rights of the defendant in circumstances in which it would be unconscionable for the defendant to deny the claimant those rights.

30.7.3 Subrogation and tracing

Tracing is a process which offers both some striking similarities with, and differences from, the remedy of subrogation. Equitable tracing claims are based on a breach of trust which results in the original property rights of the claimant being pursued into substitutes for that property or into mixtures of that property with other property. Equitable tracing constitutes the substitution of one piece of property for another, whereas subrogation constitutes the substitution of one claimant for another.[89] Subrogation may operate as a remedy to a tracing claim. For example, in *Boscawen v Bajwa*,[90] Bajwa (B) had charged land to a building society (the Halifax) before then exchanging contracts for the sale of the property with purchasers. In turn, the purchasers had sought a mortgage with Abbey National. The loan moneys provided by Abbey National were used to pay off the Halifax, thus redeeming that mortgage. In turn, however, the solicitors who were holding the purchase moneys went into insolvency and therefore the sale could not be completed. The issue arose how Abbey National was to recover its money, which had been held for it by the solicitors, and then used to pay off B's debt with the building society. The more precise legal question was whether or not the bank was entitled to trace into the debt with the building society and claim a right in subrogation to the debt previously owed to the Halifax before it had been redeemed. It was held that there must be a fiduciary relationship which calls the equitable jurisdiction into being. It was accepted that the money had been held on trust from the outset. The money could therefore be followed into the solicitors' client account. The issue was whether it could be traced further into the payment to the building society. It is not clear on the facts whether the money was held in a separate, designated account or whether it was paid into a general, mixed bank account.

In explaining the ability to claim into a mixed fund, Millett LJ held that:

> Equity's power to charge a mixed fund with the repayment of trust moneys enables the claimant to follow the money, not because it is his, but because it is derived from a fund which is treated as if it were subject to a charge in his favour.

Here, B and the solicitors were not dishonest in a mixture of bank's money and B's money. Therefore, B and the bank could be treated as ranking *pari passu* in the making of payments.

---

87 *Boscawen v Bajwa* [1995] 4 All ER 769, [1996] 1 WLR 328. See also the survey of this area of the law conducted by May LJ in *Filby v Mortgage Express (No 2) Ltd* [2004] EWCA Civ 759, para [31] *et seq*, where the approach in *Boscawen* was followed.

88 *Thurstan v Nottingham Permanent Benefit Building Society* [1902] 1 Ch 1, [1903] AC 6; *Burston Finance Ltd v Speirway Ltd* [1974] 3 All ER 735, [1974] 1 WLR 1648; *Boodle Hatfield & Co v British Films Ltd* [1986] PCC 176.

89 The best case considering the two areas is *Boscawen v Bajwa* [1996] 1 WLR 328.

90 [1995] 4 All ER 769, [1996] 1 WLR 328.

The solicitors were clearly fiduciaries. B must have known that he was not entitled to that money until contracts were completed. B could not keep the sale proceeds and title to the property. B could not therefore rely on the favourable trac'.ng rules set out in *Re Diplock*[91] for innocent volunteers.

On a similar note, in *Wenlock v River Dee Co*,[92] the issue arose as to whether or not the plaintiff's property had been used to pay creditors of the defendant, which would entitle the plaintiff to be subrogated to the rights of the creditors. Some creditors had been paid by the defendant's bank, which thereby acquired a debt owing from the defendant; then, the money being traced was paid to the bank in discharge of this debt. It was held[93] that there was no difficulty in tracing this money to the payments received by the creditors.

30.8 RECEIVERS

The power to appoint receivers is the power to appoint a person to take control of property and then to administer and distribute that property appropriately. The principal purpose of a receiver is to preserve property while litigation as to the ownership or use of that property is settled, although receivers may be appointed to preserve property even in the absence of pending litigation.[94] Thus, the receiver's goal is to preserve the property 'in a state of security pending litigation'.[95] So, a receiver may be appointed to take control of property where otherwise there is no owner who will take such control.[96] Alternatively, a receiver may be appointed to prevent a party who is in possession of the property from misusing the property, but this power will only be used if the circumstances dictate that this is desirable.[97] Otherwise, the courts would be slow to interfere with pre-existing property rights. However, in circumstances in which one object under a discretionary trust was in possession of the trust property and it was feared that that person would dissipate that property before the trustees could deal with it, it would then be reasonable to appoint a receiver to prevent that person from misusing the trust property.

There are three contexts in which receivers are appointed regularly.[98] First, mortgagees may appoint receivers over mortgaged property under their statutory power of sale.[99] Secondly, the power to appoint receivers may be exercised in favour of a person's creditors,[100] although freezing injunctions are more commonly used to prevent assets being removed.[101] Thirdly, a receiver will be appointed when a partnership is close to termination so that the assets of the partnership can be sold as a going concern and so forth.[102]

---

91 [1948] Ch 465.
92 (1887) 19 QBD 155. Cf *Cantrave Ltd v Lloyds Bank* [2000] 4 All ER 473 – no subrogation where the money lent by a bank to a customer did not discharge any debt of that customer.
93 *Ibid*, 166.
94 *Re Oakes* [1917] 1 Ch 230.
95 *Free v Hindle* (1827) 2 Sim 7 at 11, *per* Hart VC.
96 *Owen v Homan* (1853) 4 HLC 997, 1032, *per* Lord Cranworth.
97 *John v John* [1898] 2 Ch 573.
98 There are other contexts, on which see McGhee, 2005, 431 *et seq*.
99 Law of Property Act 1925, ss 101, 109. This power applies to equitable mortgages: *Re Crompton & Co Ltd* [1914] 1 Ch 954.
100 *Cummins v Perkins* [1899] 1 Ch 16.
101 Section 27.4 above.
102 *Smith v Jeyes* (1841) 4 Beav 503; *Pini v Roncoroni* [1892] 1 Ch 633; *Taylor v Neate* (1888) 39 Ch D 538.

30.9 DELIVERY AND CANCELLATION OF DOCUMENTS

A court of equity may order that documents be delivered and cancelled in a number of circumstances. Broadly, those circumstances relate to situations in which: an ostensibly valid document is void or voidable,[103] where an ostensibly valid document may cause a false claim to be made,[104] where an ostensibly valid document may cause some party to rely on it thinking its contents to be true,[105] or where it would otherwise be contrary to public policy.[106] The documents will not be cancelled entirely in the abstract, but rather the court may require equitable relief to be provided on the part of any other person involved. So, if a loan were cancelled by cancellation of the loan document, then the borrower would be required to repay the capital borrowed under the loan and may not simply rely on the cancellation of the loan to vest her with title in the loan moneys.[107] Evidently, not to provide for reciprocal equitable relief may contravene the equitable principle that she who seeks equity (in the form of the cancellation of documents) must also do equity (in the form of providing reciprocal relief) in given circumstances.

30.10 EQUITABLE DOCTRINES MODIFYING EXISTING RIGHTS

The doctrines considered in this section function as part of the general equitable motivation to interfere with legal rights so as to ensure justice between the parties.

30.10.1 Conversion

The equitable doctrine of conversion deems, in any circumstances in which there is a binding obligation to sell property, that rights in that property are converted into rights in the proceeds of sale.[108] This doctrine is an extension of the equitable principle that equity looks upon as done that which ought to have been done. This doctrine has been abolished in so far as it relates to trustees of land holding that land for the purpose of sale.[109] The significance of the doctrine before 1925 related to property which passed to the next-of-kin on death, but those technicalities were abolished by the 1925 reforms of land law.[110]

30.10.2 Election

If a person takes a transfer of property, made by will or by deed, and is bound by the terms of that transfer to perform some other act in consideration for that receipt, then she is not entitled in good conscience to the former without electing to be bound by the latter.[111]

---

103 *Davis v Duke of Marlborough* (1819) 2 Swans 108.
104 *Wynne v Callender* (1826) 1 Russ 293 (where a negotiable instrument might have been used for an improper purpose).
105 *Cooper v Joel* (1859) 1 De GF & J 240 (where a guarantee was procured by misrepresentation); *Peake v Highfield* (1826) 1 Russ 559 (where a false conveyance may have induced a third party to seek to acquire the property).
106 *W v B* (1863) 32 Beav 574 (where a contract was formed for an immoral purpose).
107 *Earl of Aylesford v Morris* (1873) 8 Ch App 484.
108 *Fletcher v Ashburner* (1779) 1 Bro CC 497, 499, *per* Sir Thomas Sewell MR; *Re Richerson* [1892] 1 Ch 379, 383.
109 Trusts of Land and Appointment of Trustees Act 1996, s 3.
110 Administration of Estates Act 1925, ss 33, 45.
111 *Re Mengel's WT* [1962] Ch 791, 797, *per* Buckley J.

30.10.3 Performance

Equity imputes an intention to fulfil an obligation.[112] Therefore, when a person is obliged (principally under covenant on the decided cases) to perform a duty, any act which is taken is deemed to be in partial performance of that duty.[113] So, if one contracts to buy a large area of land as agent for another person, and then one buys a parcel of that land, it is assumed that one has performed that contract in part.[114] Alternatively, if a person covenanted to leave property to identified people by will after her death, if she then died intestate, anything which passes to those identified people would be deemed to have passed in partial performance of that covenant.[115] Thus, performance deems actions to be done in performance of one's obligations, thus reducing them *pro tanto*, provided that they can reasonably be construed as being performance of the same. The importance of this doctrine is that if the action can be deemed to be performance of the obligation, then the defendant's obligation will be reduced by the amount of the performance.

30.10.4 Satisfaction

Satisfaction will be available if a person was obliged to do act *x* and instead does act *y* and if *y* can be considered to be a replacement for the performance of *x* which satisfies the defendant's obligation to perform *x*. So, if the defendant leaves a legacy to the claimant, then any action for debt which the claimant has against the defendant's estate may be reduced by the amount of the legacy if the legacy can be deemed to have been in satisfaction of the debt.[116] The legacy will be deemed to be in satisfaction of the debt if there is no intention to the contrary, if the legacy is equal to or greater than the debt, and if the legacy is equally beneficial as repayment of the debt.[117]

30.11 MERE EQUITIES

Mere equities are a difficult category to describe in the abstract precisely because they arise on a case-by-case basis, usually as a procedural device, in circumstances in which the courts think it necessary to do justice between the parties.[118] Mere equities will run with land or other property, rather than being simply of a personal nature. So, an equity to have a transaction set aside for fraud[119] or to have an instrument rectified for mistake[120] may be ancillary to property and may pass with the property to a successor in title.[121] The only category of person who will escape a mere equity will be a *bona fide* purchaser of the relevant property

---

112 *Sowden v Sowden* (1785) 1 Bro CC 582.
113 *Lechmere v Lady Lechmere* (1735) Cas t Talb 80.
114 *Ibid.*
115 *Garthshore v Chalie* (1804) 10 Ves 1.
116 *Talbott v Duke of Shrewsbury* (1714) Prec Ch 394, 395, *per* Trevor MR.
117 *Re Stibbe* (1946) 175 LT 198; Snell, 2005, 132 *et seq.*
118 See, for example, *Shiloh Spinners v Harding* [1973] AC 691, 721, referring to Snell, currently 2005, para 2–05.
119 *Ernest v Vivian* (1863) 33 LJ Ch 513.
120 *Smith v Jones* [1954] 2 All ER 823; *Re Colebrook's Conveyance* [1972] 1 WLR 1397.
121 Law of Property Act 1925, s 63; *Boots the Chemist Ltd v Street* [1983] EGD 251.

for value without notice of the claimant's rights.[122] With the enactment of the Land Registration Act 2002, mere equities take effect over successors in title from the moment at which the equity comes into existence.[123] A mere equity may take effect in relation to land as an overriding interest[124] if the rightholder is in actual occupation of the property or by the entry of a notice on the Land Register.[125]

30.12 MUTUAL BENEFIT AND BURDEN

An equitable doctrine of mutual benefit and burden has been used in the law relating to easements where it would be unconscionable for someone who takes the benefit of a right to refuse to accept a correlative burden.[126] An extreme example of this doctrine arose in the case of *Ives (ER) Investment Ltd v High*,[127] in which the original covenanting parties had agreed that in consideration for developers being allowed to have the foundations for their building encroaching on the other party's land, that other party was permitted access across the developer's land. Successors in title from the developers sought to deny access to the other party's successors in title. It was held by Lord Denning, *inter alia*, that the doctrine of mutual benefit and burden precluded the defendants from continuing to take the benefit of having their foundations encroaching on the claimant's land while seeking to deny themselves the burden of suffering the claimant's access across their land. The breadth of the principle is uncertain, perhaps arising in circumstances of unconscionable denial of another's rights rather than as a general rule of law.[128]

122 *National Provincial Bank Ltd v Ainsworth* [1965] AC 1175, 1238; *Westminster Bank Ltd v Lee* [1956] Ch 7; *Westdeutsche Landesbank v Islington LBC* [1996] AC 669; *Malory Enterprises Ltd v Cheshire Homes Ltd* [2002] Ch 216.

123 Land Registration Act 2002, s 116. See *Blacklocks v JB Developments (Godalming) Ltd* [1982] Ch 183.

124 Land Registration Act 2002, Sched 3, para 2(c).

125 In relation to a mortgage, the mere equity may be overreached: *Birmingham Midshires Mortgage Services Ltd v Sabherwal* (2000) 80 P & CR 256, noted at (2000) Conv 256, (2000) 116 LQR 341.

126 *Halsall v Brizell* [1957] Ch 169, 182; *Tito v Waddell (No 2)* [1977] Ch 106, 292C, 305H, *per* Megarry VC.

127 [1967] 2 QB 379.

128 *Government Insurance Office (NSW) v KA Reed Services Pty Ltd* [1988] VR 829, 840, *per* Brooking J; *Rhone v Stephens* (1993) 67 P & CR 9, 15, *per* Nourse LJ. Cf *Green v Lord Somerleyton* [2004] 1 P & CR 520 at para 103, suggesting a modern breadth to this principle beyond the old law on deeds.

Theoretical questions relating to equity and trusts

Theoretical questions relating to equity and trusts

Chapter 31

The nature of property in equity and trusts

31.1 QUESTIONS OF PROPERTY AS THEY APPLY TO TRUSTS

31.1.1 The component legal aspects of a trust

There is much in this book which has had to do with commerce and much which has had to do with property. The development of the principles of equity in England and Wales has interacted closely with commercial developments – the company, the floating charge, the trust itself – and also with the law of property – the trust of land, family settlements, and so forth. The historical competition between the courts of common law and the courts of equity saw responsibility for much of these areas move between the two jurisdictions. The courts of equity became amenable to commercial goals such as the control of contractual obligations through specific performance,[1] rectification and rescission,[2] as well as to disputes over the use of land through equitable easements,[3] the enforceability of the burden of negative covenants,[4] and the equity of redemption in mortgages.[5] There is no reason in the abstract why the courts of common law could not have developed means of achieving the same goals. After all, common law developed its own notion of fraud and could therefore have made the

---

1 See chapter 26.
2 See chapter 28.
3 *ER Ives Investment Ltd v High* [1967] 2 QB 379.
4 *Tulk v Moxhay* (1848) 18 LJ CL 88.
5 See chapter 23 above.

small leap to a notion of unconscionability too. Throughout its complex history, however, the common law failed to develop procedural rules to allow such concepts to be developed in its own courts once they had been manufactured in equity. Amongst all of these developments it is the trust which has demonstrated itself to be the most versatile and wide-ranging technique in equity's armoury. The modern equity which is visible to us today is the product of this history by means of which equity has both developed and discarded many forms of action, many procedural rules and many substantive concepts. But it is not just equity which has changed; the world with which equity is confronted has changed radically too over time. This chapter considers the change in the nature of the property with which equity has had to deal. Most of the discussion will focus on the trust institution, being equity's most important tool in property disputes.

We might think of the law of trusts as being a mixture of concepts derived from the law of property (as to ownership of the trust fund, as to tracing property rights, and so forth) and also from the law of obligations, loosely defined (as to the liability of the trustee for breach of trust, the potential liability of third parties for losses suffered by the trust, and so forth). Between express trusts and trusts implied by law, the nature of those property rights and those obligations may differ markedly from context to context. The trust has also been presented in this book as an offshoot from equity which developed from the powers of the Courts of Chancery as a means of regulating the conscience of the common law owner of property by recognising that the beneficiary also has rights in that property. Nevertheless, the modern express trust has hardened into an institution which is built on certainty[6] and formal rules,[7] and so has appeared to move away from its general, equitable roots as a means of controlling the conscience of the trustee.[8] In tandem with the growing debate about the nature of trusts implied by law, it is suggested that the time has come to recapture those equitable roots and to understand trusts as being the kith and kin of equitable remedies like specific performance, injunctions and so forth. Only then will the potentially broad social application of equitable concepts become apparent.

Bound up with this reclaiming of the trust's roots is a need to understand some of the logical problems which trusts law faces, primarily because its ancient methods of understanding property as being necessarily something tangible and readily identifiable do not mesh easily with the sorts of disputes which have come before it in recent years concerning intangible property of a very different sort. Furthermore, this chapter will consider how theories of the legal nature of property impact on the law of trusts. In particular it will question the binary division between explanations of property rights as either attaching *to a thing*, or as constituting rights *against other persons*. It is suggested that the logic of that form of property law which was developed to deal with land has been applied uncomfortably to intangible, movable property. The treatment of issues concerning electronic money and other choses in action with those same rules has generated a large number of additional problems.

---

6 See Chapter 3.
7 See Chapters 4 and 5.
8 *Westdeutsche Landesbank Girozentrale v Islington LBC* [1996] AC 669.

31.1.2 Problems with the logic of express trusts

The rapid growth of the importance of the express trust in every context, from testamentary trusts to modern pensions funds, has meant that the logic of the rudimentary trusts has been bent out of shape. With the earliest trusts over land it was easy to see why, if Richard left England for a number of years and entrusted his lands to John for safekeeping in the interim, Richard should be recognised by equity as retaining effective title in that land until his return. Equity would recognise Richard's rights even if common law title over that land had been transferred to John to facilitate his role of keeper of Richard's lands. So far so good.

However, that logic only works for property like land which does not change its essential nature and which is difficult to mix with other property. It is a logic which does not apply so neatly to situations in which money held in an electronic bank account is transferred into another electronic bank account and mixed in a way which is impossible to untangle by restoration of the property. The rules which have been developed, for example as to the need for the segregation of property, have sought to extend principles developed in relation to land into disputes concerning other forms of property. The result is that those rules have begun to seem increasingly unsuited to the cases they are supposed to resolve.

The following logical problem arises with even the simplest express trust. Suppose that Simon leaves £10,000 to be held by Tina on trust for Brian and Betty in equal shares. There is no suggestion that that trust would be invalid if the £10,000 is identifiable, if Brian and Betty are identifiable and if Simon clearly intends to create a trust. What is more difficult is the suggestion that Brian and Betty have rights *in* the trust fund. We cannot know in which property each of them has their rights. As a matter of common sense we could say: 'Well, Tina would simply have to divide that property into two equal halves.' We could also say: 'It's only money after all – what could it matter who gets which notes provided that they get the correct *value*?' That is the key: Brian and Betty do not have rights *in* the trust fund; rather, they have rights *against the trustee* as to the treatment of that property, and they have rights *against the rest of the world* to prevent any third party from interfering with the fund held on trust for them. To that extent they have proprietary rights: to that extent they are able to direct the trustee to transfer title them under the rule in *Saunders v Vautier*. But they do not have rights *in* the trust moneys in the same way that we might have said that Richard, in the previous example, ought to be recognised as having rights *in* the land. Richard's rights attached to clearly identifiable property in the form of his land; whereas Brian and Betty have rights of a given value to a share in a fund of money. Nevertheless, the difference which I shall attempt to establish is that the logic of trusts law applies unevenly in relation to different kinds of property.

Even if the property were land held on trust by Tina such that Brian and Betty were to have rights to occupy the land, trusts law would say that Brian and Betty have equitable interests *in* the land even though neither of them has any right to remove any of that land or to deal with it separately from the other beneficiary. The only way in which they could deal with it separately would be to sell the land and to divide the sale proceeds between themselves.[9] Even then, they would have no right *in* any specific money received for the sale until Tina had separated it and transferred it to them: up to that moment their so-called *proprietary* right would have been a right only to control the manner in which Tina dealt

---

9 As considered in Chapter 16.

with that property. Their more useful right, in real life, is more likely to be the right to occupy the property – that is, a right to *use* the property. The most significant rights which Brian and Betty would have would be their rights to control Tina's treatment of the property and the right to prevent others from occupying the land. Their most significant rights are therefore rights operative *against* other people and not rights *in* the land.

31.1.3 Rights having value – not identity

The traditional English lawyer's approach to property law as enforcing rights against an identified item of property is an insufficient explanation of the broad potential range of features of those rights, for example, in relation to the proportionate rights which the beneficiary acquires against a mixed fund. English law recognises the beneficiary as having proprietary rights against that fund even though no particular property need be segregated for the use of an individual beneficiary in circumstances where property is held, for example, 'on trust equally for A and for B'. Rather, it is said that A and B have property rights in proportion to half of the fund. In truth what they have is a claim against the trustee in relation to *a value equivalent to* half of the value of the fund. The claim, while described as being proprietary, is effectively, if not technically, a personal claim against the trustee which will *result in a transfer of property* – that is, half of the property held on trust provided that constitutes half of the value of the fund.

The so-called proprietary claim is nothing more than a *personal claim with proprietary consequences* in this context: that is, a right to control another person's treatment of property so that the use of that property is affected. This is qualitatively different from saying that the proprietary right attaches only to the property itself.

A claim to a mixed fund is therefore also substantively different from a claim for the freehold of land which is a proprietary claim relating undoubtedly to identifiable property (the land itself). The certainty of that claim, as a claim relating only to that particular land, can be compared with the comparative vagueness of a claim to a part share of a bank account containing a mixture of different moneys. Typically, the legal analysis of money held in an electronic bank account is such that the property involved is commonly accepted as being susceptible to treatment by the rules for tangible property despite the fact that it is in truth only evidence of a debt owed by a bank to its customer. A bank account is merely a chose in action: a contractual recognition by the bank that the account-holder has deposited money with it and that the bank is required to return that money to the customer in accordance with the terms of their contract. It is not true to say that there is money *in* a bank account. Rather, the bank account is an acknowledgment of a claim in favour of the account-holder with a given value attached to it. Therefore, to claim an equitable proprietary right over 'money in a bank account in equal shares' with another beneficiary is to present a logical fallacy: the claim is merely a claim to an amount of value owed by the bank to the account-holder (or trustee in this example). There is no identified property available: only value.

To pursue this point a little further, even if we were to bring a claim in relation to an amount of money in cash, rather than in a bank account, that money is itself only currency.[10] It is tempting to think of notes and coins as being tangible property. In fact, notes and coins

---

10 As defined later, currency is itself only evidence of a personal liability on the part of a central bank to meet a claim based on any banknote or coin.

are merely tangible evidence of a personal claim against the Bank of England in the form of the legendary 'promise to pay the bearer on demand' the face value of the banknote. The property held in a bank account is accepted as being property *in legal practice* because that is the only way of maintaining the logic of modern capitalist society: that is, that a promise by a bank to repay a deposit is equivalent to a property right. It is accepted as being property *in theory* on the basis that it constitutes a set of transferable rights and obligations.[11] Property theorists argue that because this account is capable of being transferred to another person or has a particular value, it should be treated as though it were property. In this chapter, those rights which are transferable encapsulations of merely personal rights are referred to as being 'quasi-property'. The ensuing discussion of property and of the nature of money in this chapter teases apart these arguments and apparent contradictions.

31.2 THEORIES OF PROPERTY IN LAW

The core contention of the following section is that even the sophisticated distinctions in modern legal theory fail to account fully for mutual, collectivist forms of property ownership and also fail to give an account of the nature of personal claims (such as bank accounts held in electronic form) which is sufficiently coherent. This section considers the nature of property as understood by law and also the extent to which property as understood by law involves rights.

31.2.1 The ordering of property theory

In this discussion I want to do two things. First, I want to establish (at least in outline terms) that the legal conception of property law cannot be categorised *either* as simply rights in things *or* as rights between people. Rather, I shall attempt to demonstrate that there are times when rights in property are best expressed as rights in a thing and at other times as rights between people. However, I shall also seek to establish that there are two other positions which need to be recognised: contexts in which property rights are established by democratic control over property; and contexts in which quasi-proprietary rights are supported in law in relation to purely personal claims.

Therefore, I am arguing for a fourfold division in the understanding of property in law. The thread running through these four divisions is that property rights can only be understood as *rights with a value attached* and that the law will give a variety of remedies in different contexts to the four different forms of rights: in short, many of theories of property in law confuse the nature of the remedy with the nature of the right it supports. For example, to conceive of a number of beneficiaries as each having separate proprietary rights in a fund of money held on trust for them equally is to confuse the beneficiary's right against a proportion of the fund with the remedy of delivery up of property of a given value. Suppose the beneficiary seeks to enforce a right to be delivered her share of the total fund in a manner permitted by the terms of the trust. The beneficiary does not have any right to *the particular property* paid over by the trustee until it is actually paid over by the trustee: up to that time the beneficiary had merely a right to *some property of that value* to be paid to her by the trustee. To call the right of the beneficiary 'proprietary' is to elide the claim with the remedy.

---

11 Penner, 1997, 105.

Many so-called property rights of this kind have in fact nothing to do with property and everything to do with rights which can only be exercisable between two particular people and no one else, for example in relation to transferable debts where property is owed only between debtor and creditor (whoever that happens to be from time to time, given that those rights can be transferred). Consequently, the conception of property currently accepted by English law is so vacuous as to be meaningless, because it does not differentiate systematically between property rights constituting an entitlement to an identified item of property and those constituting an entitlement to be paid an amount of money from a trust fund: both are described as being 'proprietary'. That is not to deny that English law accepts such rights as being property rights; rather, it is to question the logic behind such a position. What is argued for in this chapter is a recognition of different forms of rights in relation to property, or different forms of rights with a value attached arising in different contexts.

31.2.2 Four forms of property rights

(1) Property rights as 'rights in a thing'

The simplest property right is the right to the use of a 'thing'. The simplest form of rights in a thing arises in relation to ownership of land. In this conception of property, the homeowner has rights in her land, whether in the form of rights to prevent others from using that land, rights to deal with the land, or rights to adapt the land (within the confines of planning law). The simplest example of this phenomenon in relation to investment would be a nominee relationship under which an investment manager held property for an individual investor on bare trust. If that property were to be invested so as to generate an income stream without the capital being passed to any other person (like an ordinary bank deposit), then it could be said that the investor retained rights in the very property which was passed into the control of the investment manager. However, once the investment manager is permitted to dispose of the original capital to acquire other investments (perhaps securities), the investor's rights transfer from the original capital into the securities which are acquired by the trustee. The rights of the investor have therefore transferred from one item of property to another.

Once the trustee is entitled to take the investor's capital and mix it with other investors' capital, the rights of the investor become qualitatively different in property law terms. The investor has personal rights against the trustee as provided for in their contractual arrangements. The property rights which the investor holds will similarly be subject to the terms of that contractual arrangement. If the trustee is bound to acquire securities on behalf of those investors, to hold those securities and any income stream on trust for the investors, and then to sell the securities on a given date and divide the proceeds *pro rata* between the investors, the investor would be said to acquire an equitable proprietary interest in the investment fund. The value of that equitable interest would be proportionate to the fraction of the total fund which each investor contributed at the outset.

Here there is a logical leap in property law. As pointed out above, that mixed fund is said to be held on trust for *all* of those investors even though no single investor would be able to identify which securities within the general pool were the particular property of that investor. However, the law of trusts recognises a proportionate right in each investor provided that the entire fund is segregated from other entire funds. There is no particular problem with this in commonsensical terms. What is interesting, however, is that the law of property is prepared to elide the concepts of separate property and of value. Whereas the investor contributes property A (the investment stake), that right is said automatically to transfer to property B (the securities) and property C (the income stream from the securities). The elision occurs when the law says that the investor does not have to have its own investment held distinct from the remainder of the pool, but rather that the law will recognise that each investor has made an investment of a given proportion of the total value of the fund.

Thus, *property* becomes *value* for all practical purposes: one stands for the other. It is of no interest to the investor which securities are segregated for her, provided that she receives their cash return. This has ramifications for the legal treatment of unit trusts,[12] eurobonds,[13] pension funds[14] and shareholdings in ordinary companies.[15] What is important to note is that the 'rights in a thing' thesis is easily diluted in the practice of property law to connect to value rather than necessarily to any single, particular thing.

(2) Property rights as 'rights against people'

The property rights as a 'rights against people' thesis, identified most commonly with Hohfeld, is predicated on the following notion: property rights should not be considered as rights which attach to a thing, but rather as rights which protect the rights of the owner against the actions and rights of other persons.[16] Therefore, an example of this form of right would be a freehold covenant in favour of a plot of land, Blackacre, which prevents the owner of neighbouring land, Whiteacre, from building above a certain height so that the owner of Blackacre can grow vegetables in open sunlight rather than in the shadow of Whiteacre's buildings. The right could be said to be a right which is exercisable by the owner of Blackacre against the owner of Whiteacre to enable her personally to grow vegetables, and therefore as a right activated between persons and not necessarily which attaches to Blackacre, because a subsequent owner of the land might not want to grow vegetables. Alternatively, under the rights-in-a-thing thesis, this could be said to be a right which necessarily attaches to Blackacre and would have no sense nor any efficacy in relation to any other land. The law of freehold covenants requires that for the covenant to run with Blackacre, it must touch and concern that land.[17] A right to prevent a neighbouring landowner from building above a given height would clearly be of benefit to the land, but that does not mean that the motivation for creating that right was not predicated on the covenantee having a personal need to ensure sunlight, not shadow, passing to Blackacre across Whiteacre. That the covenant must touch and concern the land is not doubted: what is asked is whether such covenants are better thought of as rights in the thing, or as rights between persons affecting their use of that land. In relation to freehold covenants, that they are attached to specific land and would make no sense if the covenantee purported to transfer them to the owner of different land means that they will generally be considered as attaching to the thing.

Nevertheless, in civil code jurisdictions, it is only the equivalent of the fee simple absolute in possession which would be considered to be a property right; all other rights would be merely personal rights. Thus, a covenant would be considered to be merely a personal right,

---

12 Thomas and Hudson, 2004, Chapter 51.
13 See section 22.5 above. Thomas and Hudson, 2004, Chapter 50.
14 Chapter 24.
15 See section 25.1 above.
16 Eleftheriadis, 1996.
17 *Spencer's Case* (1583) 5 Co Rep 16.

and the means of its running with the land a matter of some complexity. In English law, even, there is a logical contrast between a fee simple and a mere covenant against the fee simple. A covenant or an easement clearly affects the nature of the property rights which make up the fee simple over the servient tenement because it means that the freeholder does not have a right, for example, to build above a given height within his bundle of property rights. So, in *Rhone v Stephens*,[18] it was accepted by the House of Lords that negative covenants were property concepts because they had this subtractive effect on the quality and content of the owner's property rights.

However, the trust, constitutes a very different form of property right. When we suggest that the beneficiary has rights in the trust fund, they are not absolute rights of ownership but equitable interests. If the property held on trust is money in a bank account, the beneficiaries' names will not even appear on the cheque book and they will not be empowered to spend that money to acquire securities to be held on trust: such tasks are the preserve of the trustee. The property rights of the beneficiary are rights to demand that the trustee adhere to the terms of the trust set down by the settlor, or to refrain from permitting conflicts of interests or the preferential treatment of one beneficiary over another. It is only the principle in *Saunders v Vautier* which permits the beneficiaries to direct the trustees how to deal with the property. Otherwise, the position of the beneficiary is passive: reactive always to the good conscience of the trustee. The property right here is therefore not simply in the sense of dominium, or simple ownership, as understood by civil code jurisdictions. Instead, the property right is embodied in a right to *control* the activities of the trustee, rather than simply the right to *own* the property.

The evolution of more sophisticated forms of property has necessarily required more ethe-real forms of rights in property than were necessary in relation to straightforward ownership of land. The example of the freehold covenant suggests a more complex form of property right than simple ownership of the fee simple. Discretionary trusts taken over bank accounts or over copyrights do not constitute such self-evident effects on the quality of the property which is the subject of the trust. It is suggested that there needs to be a further category of property right which recognises that the power of control of property is in itself a form of property right. With the increasing importance of community-based initiatives, such as co-operatives, it will be important for the law to facilitate them by developing legal struc-tures that recognise such democratic control as being equivalent to proprietary rights in such entities. Even in company law it is suggested that the understanding of the share as simply a 'bundle of rights' constituting property is insufficient to explain the complex web of rela-tionships which exist in a company and which constitute both effective *entitlements* and also *assertions* of rights against the assets of the company.

(3) Quasi-property rights – 'transferable personal claims'

Property law does recognise as property some phenomena which in truth constitute only personal claims: this relates to the 'quasi-property' mentioned above. Their status as prop-erty is said to rest primarily on their transferability or 'separability'.[19] As set out above, in a mixed trust fund the beneficiaries are all said to have proprietary rights even though there

---

18 [1994] 2 AC 310.
19 The latter is the argument considered by Penner, 1997, 105.

need be no particular part of the fund segregated for their use: thus, their claim of a certain value can generate a remedy which does grant them rights in a particular thing, but where that thing can be identified only after judgment. For example, a single beneficiary within a beneficial class of 10 people who are entitled in equity to a fund of £10,000 which is held on trust for them 'in equal shares' has a right to one-tenth of the total fund, but does not own any specific £1,000 outright until that amount is paid to her by the trustee. Until the trustee effects payment, the beneficiary has, in truth, only a right of a given value against the trustee. It is tempting then to talk of such beneficiaries' rights as being in truth merely personal claims.[20] Nevertheless, English trusts lawyers talk of the beneficiary's one-tenth share in the total fund as being a property right, with the result that the beneficiary can sell that right to another person, or borrow money against it, or be recognised as a secured creditor in the event of the trustee's insolvency. Beyond that assertion as an example of the mutable logic of the law of property, the more general point made in this short section is that some things which are recognised as being property by English law are in fact only personal claims.

The most common example of this phenomenon is the chose in action. The chose in action is a claim which attaches to one person and is exercisable over another. The chose in action is accepted in English law as being itself an item of property capable of transfer at law and having a value of its own. It is this transferability and this possibility of distinct value which imbue such personal claims with the status of property. So it is that money held in an electronic bank account is treated as being property and the bank account itself (being a chose in action owed by the bank to its customer) is also property. What is peculiar about this form of property is that ownership of the right does not in itself give rise to any right in any identifiable property. Rather, it is a claim which entitles the holder of the right to be given some property of a given type and value – here, sterling – when she calls for it. The important factor here is not the identity of the property but rather its value: to put it crudely, it does not matter which pound coins are handed over provided that they have the same value total as the value of the claim. The transferable personal claim is therefore property with no identifiable proprietary base.

The upshot of the foregoing discussion is that there is a profound, two-step logical difficulty in English law's understanding of choses in action and similar claims as being property. First, there is something illogical in saying that a claim which is only a personal claim in itself ought to be considered to be property in the same way that, for example, rights attaching exclusive title in immovable property like land are considered to be property. Secondly, given that there is only a narrow distinction to be drawn between an ordinary personal claim and the possibility of transferring a personal claim, there is a weakness in a system of property law which supports completely different rights and remedies in relation to one form of personal claim from the other.

At the edge of the law of property there is an awkward distinction drawn between those claims which are considered to be property and those claims which are not. The following section advances the argument that there is a further category of relationship which ought to be considered to be proprietary given English law's attachment to conceiving of transferable personal claims as being property: that is, the status of democratic control over property as being a form of property right.

---

20 Penner, 2002.

(4) Control as a property right – property which cannot be owned

Ben Elton's play *Gasping* is a satire of the Thatcherite policy of privatising essential services like water and electricity: it assumes an attempt to privatise and to market air. Part of the central conceit of the play is the illogicality of suggesting that any person owns the air we breathe so that it could be privatised and sold off. The logical problem which arises with the privatisation of such services is this: how can water and air be privatised if they do not belong to anyone in the first place? Of course, part of the answer might be that it is *service* of providing drinkable water to millions of citizens which was being privatised. Nevertheless, the point remains: to what extent can all matter be owned?

In another book I posited the example of Essex Road in Islington and a different way of thinking about 'ownership' of that road.[21] Essex Road is 'owned' by the Crown in some way that we know to be true as part of constitutional law but which has little practical relevance: it is not suggested that the Queen would ever choose to picnic in the middle of Essex Road. Rather, Essex Road is administered by government, through the Highways Agency and the local authority, through whose jurisdiction it passes. There are powers to close the road for maintenance, to legislate for the speed and manner in which people may use it, and so forth, but that does not capture the essence of the ownership of Essex Road, because Essex Road is just a foul-smelling, congested strip of tarmac which connects Islington Green with Newington Green. It is lined with shops, houses and residential estates. It is not really 'owned' by anyone. For some it is a route to work or school, for others it is the place where they live, for others it is simply another part of London. In this context, *use* is far more important than *ownership*. Co-operatives hold money for the common purposes of the members of the co-operative: no single person has ownership; rather, all members have ownership and rights of use. So it is with Essex Road: it is available and it is used. It is not useful to think of it as being owned.

This idea that property exists and is shared is very useful in relation to the law of trusts. As explained at the outset of this chapter, there are problems with thinking of beneficiaries under a trust as having rights *in* the trust property where there is more than one beneficiary; rather, those individuals have rights against the trustees and protective rights against the rest of the world to prevent interference with the trust property. As between the beneficiaries there is merely a right to use, or a right to receive, some value derived from that fund. For the member of a co-operative there is a right to receive value or benefit from the co-operative; for the member (or shareholder) of a company there is a right to receive a benefit from the company in the form of a dividend.

The common link between all of these various forms of belonging (whether as beneficiary, member or shareholder) is a benefit of a given value. The only difference is the manner in which English law recognises the nature of those rights. A beneficiary under a trust is said to have rights in the property under *Saunders v Vautier*[22] in accordance with the terms of the trust; a member of a co-operative has rights based on the core constitution of the co-operative based on the law of contract; and the shareholder has rights based on company law to receive property on the winding up of the company or otherwise to be benefited in accordance with the constitution of the company. In each situation, a form of contractual thinking

21   Hudson, 2000:1, 50.
22   (1841) 4 Beav 115.

applies the principles contained in the constitutive documents of each entity[23] (trust, co-operative or company) as binding the rights and obligations of the members *inter se*. What this establishes is a form of democracy between those members, in which the shareholders can vote to take control of the company, the members of the co-operative can control their common undertaking, and the beneficiaries acting together can call for delivery of the trust property.

The purposes of this diversion into the respective statuses of beneficiaries, members of co-operatives and shareholders are twofold. First, to explain one frequently overlooked commonality between these different legal categories: that democratic action between right-holders may have the same effect as the exercise of what is commonly accepted as being a property right. Secondly, to demonstrate that in a hyper-complex world it is not a straight-forward question 'what is the nature of property in law?' because the rights of individuals and companies differ from context to context between rights to use property, rights to the exclusive possession of property, rights to prevent others from using property, and rights to derive a benefit from property.

31.2.3 The modern forms of property

Tangible money theory

One important aspect of property law cases in the last decade of the 20th century was the unsuitability of applying concepts formulated originally to deal with disputes over land to complex commercial disputes involving claims to money held in electronic bank accounts.[24] 'Tangible money theory' is the term used in this section to encapsulate this phenomenon.

For example, in the appeal in *Westdeutsche Landesbank Girozentrale v Islington LBC*,[25] the principal focus of the House of Lords was on the proprietary rights attaching to a capital amount of (in total) £2.5 million which had been transferred by the bank to a local authority at the outset of a transaction which was subsequently held to have been void *ab initio*. The bank was said to have lost its right to trace into the bank account to which the £2.5 million was transferred because that account had gone overdrawn between the time of receipt of the payment and the commencement of the action for restitution of the £2.5 million. The consequence of the House of Lords' unanimous finding (on that point at least) was that the money at issue was seen to have 'disappeared' once it passed from that bank account. What this means is that 'money' in this context is tangible (once the account has gone overdrawn, the money is said to have disappeared)[26] rather than being considered to be an amount of value which has passed into the possession of its recipient (which would not necessarily be said to have disappeared when the account ran overdrawn).[27]

Therefore, a transaction involving the transfer of money between an account in the name of A, held with X Bank, to an account in the name of B, held with Y Bank, constitutes the

---

23 It is acknowledged that a trust is not technically an 'entity' – although see Hudson, 2000:1, 67.
24 Hudson, 1999:3.
25 [1996] AC 669.
26 *Bishopsgate v Homan* [1995] 1 WLR 31.
27 An approach taken by Lord Templeman, *obiter*, in *Space Investments Ltd v Canadian Imperial Bank of Commerce Trust Co (Bahamas) Ltd* [1986] 1 WLR 1072, [1986] 3 All ER 75. However, this approach has been much doubted.

satisfaction of an undertaking between A and B to transfer amounts between them, and also constitutes a re-correlation of the debts between A and X Bank, and between B and Y Bank. Those transactions can be considered in two ways. First, as a transfer of property from A's account to B's account. This is the English law approach. It is an approach built on two premises: initially that physical currency would move between A and B, and latterly that the book entries used to record those transfers were themselves a recognition of a transfer of tangible property. The second analysis would be that no property has passed.[28] The property has not passed from A to B because A retains its rights against X Bank in the form of its bank account, only in relation to a smaller cash value. What has actually taken place is an alteration in the size of the debts which are owed between the respective banks and their customers. That is, value has passed from A's account and equivalent value has been added to B's account. No identifiable property has passed at all.[29]

It is no accident that the word 'pecuniary' comes from the Greek 'pecus' meaning cow; and that the word 'chattel' has the same stem as 'cattle'. In both instances, once human beings had moved on from assigning rights in land between one another, they looked to their livestock as the next form of matter over which they wanted to create proprietary rights. In short, property law as 'rights in a thing' works well when dealing with 'my land' or 'my cow', but does not translate to situations in which the property is intangible. For example, the loss of the right to trace rule[30] is necessarily orientated around the notion of property being tangible.[31] Thus we continue to speak of all property using language which has its roots specifically in the world of tangible property.

The lightness and the softness of modern property

It has long been the case that there are some who have much property and some who have little. Typically, this inequality in property ownership has meant that life is comparatively easy for some and hard for others. What is observable in the modern world is that our attitudes towards property have changed profoundly, even if the inequalities have remained broadly the same. It has been observed by the sociologist Richard Sennett that the most successful entrepreneurs and business leaders of our age treat their business assets not as property to be guarded and maintained but rather as simply assets which can be sold and turned to account without sentiment.[32] The relationship of commercial people to their property has consequently become 'light'. Where once the industrialist owned a factory, employed labour from the local community and therefore established ties with that community, now manufacturers are less likely to own their own factories, preferring instead to exploit commercial brands and to grant franchises to third party factory owners to produce their goods for them. The principal consequence of such arrangements is that the brand

28 Hudson, 1999:2.
29 Eg, in *R v Preddy* [1996] AC 815, where accusations of theft were dismissed in the context where a telegraphic transfer from one bank account to another was held not to involve the transfer of 'property' for the purposes of the Theft Act 1968 but rather only an alteration in the value of those choses in action. This case led to the enactment of the Theft (Amendment) Act 1996, which created the new offence of theft of a money transfer: *Re Holmes* [2005] 1 All ER 490; Theft Act 1968, s 15A.
30 See section 19.8 above.
31 Cf *Re Goldcorp* [1995] AC 74; section 3.4 above.
32 Sennett, 1998, 61.

owner has no direct connection with the workforce. The only property involved is the trade mark imprinted on the trainers, on the coffee cup or on the sweatshirt. This has been expressed as granting the industrialist 'lines of flight' from the use of any given workforce or geographic location, because production can be shifted to another factory or another manufacturer without any profound consequences for the industrialist because the industrialist has no direct ties to the workforce or to the communities dependent on that industrialist's business.[33] The involvement with this property is consequently light. The metaphor for our age is software: soft links between people and places.

It is not just the wealthy industrialists who have this sense of only soft links with their property. Our culture encourages us to be fashionable. Instead of developing ourselves through thought, reflection and study, we are encouraged to shop for our identities. We can buy clothes, music, cars, cosmetics and films to shape ourselves. When they go out of fashion, we abandon them and buy some more. We have become consumers rather than producers.[34] Of course, for those who are not very wealthy there are still the problems of maintaining their property by paying their mortgages, their credit card bills and so on. For them, property is less light – instead it is burdensome.[35]

In parallel with the increasing intangibility of the property which equity is asked to deal with, our social attitudes to property are also becoming softer. The metaphor used, for example, in relation to the law of tracing, even in relation to complex financial transactions like the interest rate swap in *Westdeutsche Landesbank Girozentrale v Islington LBC*,[36] is of 'a stolen bag of coins', as though we can only think of such property as though it were represented in tangible form such that its face value was the same as its intrinsic value in gold. This fails to deal adequately with the softness of this form of property as it passes through the computerised records of the bank which holds the accounts. As the world becomes ever more virtual – through e-mail, websites, telephone call centres – our property law is failing to keep pace. The complexities caused by the issues considered in this chapter are the result of adapting ancient principles to very modern forms of property.

The fragility of our understanding of property

What this tells us is that the current state of our property law is the product of its history. That the earliest forms of property law were generated over land and livestock has given rise to a code of rules which are predicated on the presence or absence of that property. Another approach to property law would be to focus on the value represented by the property rights rather than on the identification of the specific property claimed. Foucault focuses on '*les choses dites*'[37] as constituting the genesis of many of our social customs and laws. His point is that things are only the way they are because we say they are.[38] In other words, if we said that these things were to be different, then they would be different. Our property law is organised in the way that it is because we accept that it ought to be. Any student of English law or equity should understand them both as being the product of things that are said

---

33 Hardt and Negri, 2000.
34 Bauman, 2001.
35 Hudson, 2004:1.
36 [1996] AC 669.
37 That is, 'things said'.
38 Foucault (1969), 1972.

(principally by lawyers and judges): our law is the product of texts and of speeches in the form of statutes and law reports. All of this law is the product of things which are said. Therefore, this law is capable of change simply by virtue of different things being said. As the ordinary lives of ordinary people are undergoing change we need to learn to talk differently about our law. One different form of discourse already considered in Chapter 17 is that of human rights. A modernised concept of equity is considered in Chapter 32. Before that however, we turn to consider the technocratic conservatism of the principle of restitution of unjust enrichment in the next section.

31.3   THE DISTINCTION BETWEEN EQUITY AND RESTITUTION OF UNJUST ENRICHMENT

This short section is intended simply to gather together in one place a discussion of the distinction between restitution of unjust enrichment and equity.[39] Equity, as discussed in Chapter 1, is based on the principles developed by the English courts of equity since the *Earl of Oxford's Case*,[40] in which Lord Ellesmere described equity as being concerned 'to correct men's consciences' and to 'mollify the extremity of the [common] law'. In turn, it is suggested that equity fits into a larger philosophical tradition concerned to deal justly with individual circumstances.[41] From these roots have grown the range of equitable doctrines and remedies considered in this book. The full range of these remedies have no comparator elsewhere in English law, nor have the bulk of them been addressed by restitution specialists.

In recent years, there has grown a view among some commentators that 'equity' should be displaced, in particular to replace equity with restitution of unjust enrichment in a number of circumstances. What none of these commentators do, however, is to explain how the full range of equitable doctrines and remedies – including injunctions, express trusts, constructive trusts and so on – should be replaced by other doctrines. Instead they have focused on only a few doctrines, such as subrogation, tracing, and resulting trusts. There are three models of unjust enrichment in the English context which have been suggested by the work of Professor Birks. The first version suggested that the purpose of restitution was to identify circumstances in which the defendant has received an enrichment (such as a payment of money) unjustly (such as by means of a mistake in the payer) at the claimant's expense.[42] It was suggested that it should have been a resulting trust which was the device to transfer the enrichment back to the claimant: an argument which was rejected by the majority of the House of Lords in *Westdeutsche Landesbank v Islington LBC*.[43]

Two things should be understood about this model of restitution. First, restitution is concerned not to compensate the claimant for whatever loss she has suffered, but rather it is concerned to take from the defendant whatever enrichment she has realised. Equitable

---

39 See the essay taken from the third edition of this book on 'restitution of unjust enrichment' at www. alastairhudson.com/trustslaw/trustslawindex.htm.

40 (1615) 1 Ch Rep 1.

41 However, it is acknowledged that the courts do not tend to base their principles explicitly on such principles. However, it is suggested that knowledge, for example, of Aristotle, would have been a part of the classical education of the early judges at least. Therefore, it is suggested that it should come as no surprise that there are similarities between the doctrines.

42 Birks, 1989.

43 [1996] AC 669.

compensation, by contrast, measures the loss suffered by the claimant and requires the defendant to make good that amount. Secondly, the notion of 'injustice' in this context is not a general notion of injustice, but rather is limited to a contested list of technical examples of injustice (such as mistake, failure of consideration and undue influence). Therefore, restitution is limited to primarily commercial situations according to a list of doctrines where those doctrines are already accounted for elsewhere in English law and where the precise contents of the list are contested.[44]

The second version of restitution came after the rejection of the proprietary model of the concept in *Westdeutsche Landesbank v Islington LBC*.[45] This model suggested that the enrichment gained by the defendant should be considered to remain the property of the claimant throughout the transaction if that enrichment had been gained unjustly.[46] The focus of the doctrine was on reversing unjust enrichments in general terms and not on making restitution to the claimant by means of resulting trust. The third version focused on unjust enrichments which are analogous to a mistake: thus, it is suggested, limiting the doctrine even further and offering little prospect of displacing the full range of equitable doctrines.[47]

The intellectual distinction between equity and restitution is as follows. The restitution lawyers prefer the idea of a positivist, clearly-defined legal system in which each area of law is set out on the basis of a neat model. So, Professor Birks's work contains talk of 'taxonomy' (a term used by scientists when they categorise different phenomena from the natural world) and diagrams in the form of grids which set out how the legal system should be divided between consent, wrongs and unjust enrichment. By contrast, equitable principles are open-textured and based on natural law principles of right and wrong. It is suggested that while the former approach may seem harder-nosed and tidier, it is, in fact, the latter which is more realistic because no rigid rules will ever cope (without more) with the natural chaos of the world, as considered in Chapter 32.

---

44 Compare, eg, Birks and Chambers, 1997 with Virgo, 1999 and with Goff and Jones, 2002, where each has a different number of unjust factors.
45 See Hudson, 1999:1.
46 Birks, 1996:2.
47 Birks, 2003.

Chapter 32

Equity, chaos and social complexity

32.1 MAPPING THE SOCIAL ROLE OF EQUITY

The purpose of this chapter is both to justify the continued use of equity by English law and also to give some indication of its particular relevance to the world at the beginning of the 21st century. The following are the principles on which I would rest a defence of equity: the remainder of this essay will pursue each of them in greater detail. At section 32.2 there is an attempt to explain how we might understand the notion of conscience as used in equity.

32.1.1 In defence of equity

(1) Society has become particularly complex[1] – creating insecurity and fear for individuals.[2] This idea of complexity – explored most comprehensively in particle physics[3] – engenders a form of social chaos in which individuals have become atomised[4] and the paths to social solidarity obfuscated.[5] The scientific model of complexity theory is useful in relation to social theory.[6] It is suggested that a legal system must be able to cater for this complexity in a way that is both principled and sensitive to context.

(2) Human beings crave order and are fearful of chaos.[7] This tendency expressed itself in law-making by means of an instinct for formalism and certainty.[8] In a world that is fundamentally chaotic, the classical model of equity considered in this book permits sufficiently flexible claims and remedies to address this chaos and this social complexity.

(3) 'Equity' is a concept recognised across the social sciences: by leftist economists as a means of introducing fairness in opposition to efficiency;[9] by American social theorists under cover of 'equity theory' to justify some inequality in society;[10] by classical philosophers as a counterpoint to rigid systems of rules;[11] and by business theorists to describe ownership of corporations.[12] The commonalities between these conceptions of equity are that they contain a sense of a social morality put into effect in individual cases, and a sense of worth or value. A developed concept of equity enables the legal system to communicate more effectively with other social institutions and systems of thought.

(4) Equity's role is both cultural and political. This conception of equity permits an understanding of the legal system as being something owned by the citizens and not as something either positivist or based on an external morality: the two preeminent theories in the jurisprudential canon. Equity is cultural as an expression of 'Englishness and Welshness'; equity is political in that it facilitates a discourse about the practice of justice. Equity is political also to the extent that it lends power to the judiciary: to this extent, the study and description of equitable doctrine are themselves political acts in that they shape and describe citizens' rights. A conception of equity as being a dynamic agent of cultural and political discourse would be inclusive of citizens in a way that classical jurisprudence does not seek to be.

(5) Equity is necessary to achieve a number of socially desirable goals: to protect the liberties and rights of the individual;[13] to ensure fairness through conscionable behaviour;[14] and to ensure equal access to justice.[15]

---

1 Byrne, 1998.
2 Giddens, 1991; Bauman, 2001, 83.
3 Cohen and Stewart, 1994.
4 Houellebecq, 2001.
5 Cotterrell, 1995.
6 Byrne, 1998; 1999.
7 Freud, 1930.
8 As considered in Chapter 7.
9 Le Grand, 1982.
10 Della Fave, 1980.
11 Eg, Aristotle and Hegel, as considered in section 1.1 above.
12 Brealey and Myers, 1998.
13 See section 1.1 above and the discussion of Aristotle and Hegel.
14 Rawls, 1971 and 1985: discussion of justice through fairness as a principle of 'fair play'.
15 Hudson, 1999:2, 256 *et seq.*

32.1.2 The nature of equity

In the modern world, each circumstance is different from every other, and each person demands to be recognised as a unique individual[16] – one set of rules will not satisfy all situations; rather, it is necessary to decide what is suitable in each context. What is a suitable standard of behaviour for a pension fund trustee may not be so for a trustee of a family home, or for a trustee in a eurobond transaction. To suggest that all of these situations can be met by the same, ever-hardening equitable and common law rules is folly. It is a spurious attempt to impose order on what is necessarily chaotic. While some writers identify order and certainty as being the first virtue of most legal systems, what is equally true is that chaos and uncertainty are the common characteristics of most disputes brought before them.[17] The resolution of disputes and the generation of legal norms must be sensitive to their context and to the principle that law is *of the people* and not something which is simply used to control them. What is important instead is to conceive of the principles that we wish to apply to various situations. The development of human rights law is just such a process of establishing immutable, general principles,[18] whereas the hardening of equitable principles into rigid tests is its antithesis.

In its English legal practice, equity has evolved a wide range of writs from its genesis as a means of petitioning the King as early as the 12th century,[19] via the broad principles enunciated in *Snell's Equity*,[20] into an ever more concrete set of rules.[21] For example, the acquisition of an interlocutory injunction has continued to be an ever more institutional remedy with the continued development of the *American Cyanamid*[22] principles, whereas otherwise one might have expected this to be an area which would have demonstrated a strong judicial discretion.[23] The creation of the express trust has continued to be an increasingly formalised procedure reliant on compliance with statutes on perpetuities, certainties principles and other rules of formalities.[24] The suspicion of the use of equity in commercial contexts has added to this policy of applying equitable remedies and trusts only in situations in which those more concrete rules are satisfied.

At first blush, the *Westdeutsche Landesbank Girozentrale v Islington LBC*[25] litigation looked to have reclaimed the heritage of the trust as a creature responsive to the conscience of a person entitled to property at common law.[26] However, Lord Browne-Wilkinson, in speaking for the majority, denied the equitable remedy of compound interest on the basis of general justice which had been sought by the minority. The general principles of trust, while founded on the very mutable notion of 'good conscience', were set out with clinical precision but without any clear idea of what is meant by the term 'conscience' itself in that context. The recasting of the decision in *Chase Manhattan v Israel-British Bank*[27] was a

---

16 Hudson, 2004:2.
17 Oakley, 1997, 27.
18 See para 17.2.1 above.
19 A general jurisdiction described in Maitland, 1936, 1–11.
20 McGhee, 2005.
21 As considered in Chapters 7 and 14 in particular.
22 [1975] AC 396.
23 See para 27.3.2 above.
24 See Chapter 7 above.
25 [1996] AC 669.
26 This jurisdiction being described by Maitland, 1936, 8, as a combination of 'rules of equity and good conscience'.
27 [1981] 1 Ch 105.

good example of greater rigidity of principle at work even in the otherwise flexible area of constructive trust.[28] This notion of conscience is considered next.

32.2 THE LEGAL NOTION OF CONSCIENCE

32.2.1 The paradox within equity

What I hope to do in this section is to confront one of the central paradoxes which lies unspoken within equity.[29] Equity operates through judicial discretion against the conscience of the individual defendant and yet it is based on formally-generated, juristic principles. Thus, equity is at one and the same time a means of ensuring justice in individual cases whilst also constituting a code of abstract, technical rules which are applied by judges carefully in accordance with case law precedent. So, equity is free and yet constrained. The key to this apparent paradox, it is suggested, lies in a fuller understanding of the nature of 'conscience' in this context and in understanding that equity is, in truth, a mosaic of doctrines, principles and patterns of justice provision.

Equity, it is said, is a doctrine based on conscience. What appears little in the modern literature on the juristic concept of equity is any discussion of what this notion of conscience means. It is suggested that conscience has a stylised meaning particular to its use in equity. Therefore, we must consider the nature of equity, then consider what conscience connotes in its more general sense, before attempting to assess the interaction of the two terms.

The trust, used here as an example of an equitable device, is responsive to the conscience of the legal owner of property. This may manifest itself by means of express trusts through the claim for breach of trust which compels the trustee to permit no conflict of interest, no loss to the beneficiaries nor any deviation from the terms of her trusteeship, or it may manifest itself by means of trusts implied by law which seek to prevent the legal owner of property or some other person from taking a benefit unconscionably from that property. The express trust suggests a formalised equity which has been rigidified to achieve specific legal and non-legal goals: the protection of beneficiaries, certainty in relation to title over property and so forth. The trusts implied by law suggest responses to factual situations which appear to be contrary to conscience or demanded by fairness more generally. These latter manifestations of equity display a much broader use of judicial discretion to achieve goals which we might consider to be broadly moral or ethical, but which are nevertheless established in accordance with principle to a large extent and with precedent to a lesser extent. In this sense, 'principle' refers to that body of equitable principles such as 'you must come to equity with clean hands', whereas 'precedent' is used here to suggest a slavish application of rules in earlier cases with a lesser use of discretion in any individual case which is more clearly associated with the common law.

28 It is acknowledged that doctrinally this decision is said to create more uncertainty than it clears up (see perhaps Birks, 1996:2, 3) – the reference here is to the attempt to introduce clarity in the first place.
29 This contradiction is evident from the growing gap between books in this area which deal with 'Equity' (frequently in Australia) and books which deal only with 'The Law of Trusts and Equitable Remedies' and yet which are in truth dealing with the same subject matter. The key distinction between the two approaches is that the former type of book typically begins with Aristotle's *Ethics* and its ancient conception of equity as rectifying formal rulemaking, whereas the latter begins with the formalities necessary to create express trusts to give effect to commercial transactions, marriage settlements and wills.

Still, equity is said to be based on conscience. The principle within the equitable canon which best encapsulates the notion of conscience intended is the principle that 'equity acts *in personam*'. This principle means that the court's concern is to look to the conscience of the individual defendant and to respond to that defendant's actions and omissions. At first blush, this would suggest that the court will inquire into the individual's own conscience. As such, it would be expected that equity would prefer subjective tests to objective tests. However, that is to misunderstand the manner in which equity operates. Historically, equity is, in theory at least, the embodiment in legal principle of the monarch's conscience expressed through the powers delegated to the Lords Chancellor, or alternatively a development of the procedural notion of 'conscentia' whereby judges would seek to give effect to the correct decision even if all of the facts could not be proved objectively. A more modern under-standing of that concept would be to recognise equity as being an embodiment of an objec-tive ethics to which the individual is intended to aspire and by reference to which her deeds and misdeeds will be judged by the civil courts. In that sense, there might be broad parallels between the role of equity in the civil law and the role of the criminal law more generally: a marriage which is suggested by the expression that the old Court of Star Chamber was concerned with 'criminal equity'.

32.2.2 Thinking about conscience within ethical philosophy

Nevertheless, this troublesome term 'conscience' remains. If equity were said to act on the basis of 'a public morality expressed through the courts', then that would not lead to the uncomfortable muddle generated by the modern usage which suggests that equity is concerned with the individual defendant's conscience rather than with the embodiment of the sovereign's conscience through the actions of her officials and delegates. The term 'conscience' suggests a subjectivity at first blush. However, matters are perhaps not so easy. To suggest that conscience is something entirely within the individual and is something other than a public ethic expressed through legal principle is to suggest that the individual conscience and the consciousness to which it is both etymologically and metaphysically connected are not socially constructed at some level. This notion is beautifully expressed by the playwright Luigi Pirandello in his play *Each in His Own Way*, when the character Diego challenges the other characters who are talking about giving Catholic confession to a priest (itself that classical objectification of the conscience) and claiming that their self-contained consciences are clear:

> But what is this conscience? It is the voice of others inside you.[30]

What this idea suggests is that conscience is formed by our interactions with other people and is not something which we develop inside our own heads in a vacuum. This raises a range of important philosophical questions. At root, perhaps, it reflects those debates about whether or not the law should operate objectively or subjectively.

---

30 Pirandello, *Each in His Own Way*, spoken by Diego in Act 1, trans Firth, *Pirandello – Collected Plays*, 1992, Calder, London, Vol 3, 71. Also rendered in other versions as 'Don't you see that blessed conscience of yours is nothing but other people inside you!' for example, in Williams, *The Wimbledon Poisoner*, London: Faber & Faber, 1990, 169.

The distinction between subject and object is, of course, problematic. To talk of the subject meaningfully, one must mean an individual and particular person. As soon as discussion turns to the similarities between subjects or of an idealised subject, then one immediately begins to objectify that subject.[31] The conscience is most easily recognised as that still, small voice within us individually which speaks to us primarily of shame. For equity to seek to judge the conscience in accordance with decided principle is necessarily to seek to objectify that conscience. To judge the conscience even on the basis of total judicial discretion is to objectify it; it is to take it outside the subject and to use it as a lens through which to view those acts or omissions for which the defendant is on trial.

This perception of the vernacular sense of conscience is still troublesome. Is it correct to think of the conscience as a *still*, small voice? Or is the conscience something which moves, which grows and which develops? Further, is the conscience a still, *small* voice? If the individual is formed socially, at least in part, then the conscience is potentially a particularised rendering of a massive, public morality which is produced within the individual as an amalgam of socially-broadcast messages about right and wrong, of the products of interactions with other individuals (from immediate family, to work-mates to school-friends), and of more subtle phenomena like law, environment and so forth which shape expectations and attitudes more subliminally still. In Elias's view, individuals are necessarily socially constructed as we learn language from others, learn a basic sense of right and wrong from parents and teachers, and so continue throughout our lives to form our views of the world by interaction with other people.[32] The internal world of the particular individual can therefore be considered to be objectively formed at some level.

At a further level, Levinas locates the essence of morality in a respect for other people. In this sense, equity might sensibly be said to operate on the externally-exhibited morality of the individual rather than on the internally-situated morality of that same person. Equity is responsive to the external manifestation and not inquisitive as to the contents of the internal morality. This is always assuming that the individual is *conscious* of her own internal morality until external factors challenge that individual, causing her *conscience* to speak for the first time 'out loud', even to herself about her own attitudes to particular ethical challenges. At this level, therefore, it is possible that the conscience remains dormant and unexplored in many of us until something in the outside world calls it unexpectedly to our conscious perception (our true feelings about strawberry yoghurt, an aversion to blue food dye, a thrill at the smell of warm road tar, a suspicion of sewing needles, a fear of accidentally chewing the tin foil wrapper on a Kit-Kat).[33] Conscience, that automatic censor, is therefore not only externally created in part, but the process of its generation in terms of our realisation of what our conscience likes and dislikes is frequently dependent on external stimuli.

All that can be said is that the conscience is *privately situated*. This suggests that the individual hosts her conscience. What remains at large are both the *contents* of that conscience and the *process* by which the conscience is formed. The contents of that conscience are prey to constant change and adaptation. Furthermore, the contents of that conscience at any particular time will be objective material, even if passed through ostensibly subjective filters.

---

31 Adorno, 1978.
32 Elias, 2001.
33 Another brand name which is automatically familiar to my spell-checker.

In conclusion, it is suggested that the conscience on which equity purports to act is necessarily a partly objective phenomenon in any event. Indeed, the most striking example of the
action of public morality on the privately-situated conscience would be a judgment from a
court of equity that a particular action breaches that equitable code. Law exists to measure
the behaviour of individuals against the objective conscience of society as expressed through
law – therefore, equity is simply expressing that general dynamic.

32.2.3 A future for equity in public law?

This very short section is simply intended to plant the seed of an idea. There is some suggestion that the law on legitimate expectations in relation to judicial review is akin to estoppel
in that a public body making a decision which leads another person to believe that its decision will be x, such that that other person reasonably forms the impression that x will indeed
be the state of affairs, will have a decision y judicially reviewed if her legitimate expectations have been disappointed. It is said that this is broadly akin to equitable estoppel in
private law which seeks to prevent detriment or unconscionability if one person makes a
representation to another in reliance on which that other relies to her detriment.

However, equity does not apply in public law. Nor does equity apply in quasi-public areas
of law such as public sector housing law. Equity only applies in areas relating to bourgeois
private property or commercial property law, or in relation to injunctions and commercial
transactions concerned with equitable remedies in contract law. This may seem surprising
given that Aristotle's conception of equity, and indeed many of the discussions of equity
since then, were expressed in terms of *all* legislation or *all* law. Indeed, much of subjects like
housing law and social security law, which lie somewhere between public law and private
law, have simply not been subjected to the weight or type of scrutiny that has been lavished
on private law or on judicial review down the centuries, let alone to the tender affections of
equity. These areas have tended to be creatures of statute and of regulation instead.

My suggestion is that these areas of law could easily and usefully adopt principles of
equity which are similar to the economists' notion of equity, as discussed above, which is
concerned to ensure equal and fair access to public goods. An example of what I have in mind
emerges from *Arun DC v First Secretary of State*[34] in which a woman received planning
permission for an extension to her home on the condition that the extension remained part of
a single dwelling. Instead, the woman began to use the extension as a separate dwelling.
However, the manner in which the legislation had been drafted meant that, even though this
woman deliberately flouted the terms on which planning permission had been granted to her
originally, because she had committed this particular breach by changing the use of the extension four years after the permission was granted, therefore the ordinary rules as to breach of
planning permission conditions did not apply. Sedley LJ in a short judgment held that:

> the discovery that Mrs Brown has – not to put too fine a point on it – cheated on a condi-
> tional grant of permission, to the detriment of her neighbours and of planning control,
> may well be a matter of time and chance [because this particular type of breach has a
> different statutory limitation period from other such breaches].[35]

---

34 [2007] 1 WLR 523.
35 *Ibid*, 532, para [36].

Now, my suggestion would be that the courts could develop a notion of equity even in relation to quasi-public law contexts like this in which a statute has, effectively, been used as an engine of fraud. In a private law context it would be possible to say that the defendant was taking unconscionable advantage of the statute and therefore that equity should be entitled to disapply the advantage which the defendant would otherwise receive, as was the case in *Rochefoucauld v Boustead*[36] and in relation to proprietary estoppel in *Yaxley v Gotts*.[37] After all, as Sedley LJ pointed out in this instance, the defendant had 'cheated' on the conditions on which she had been granted planning permission and clearly the Court of Appeal was reluctant to find that she could benefit from a mismatch in the drafting of the legislation relating to the limitation period applicable to this sort of planning grant. It would, it is suggested, be only a short step to introduce general notions of equity and of unconscionability in this sort of context.[38] For the future, then, it would be a larger question whether or not the discussion of 'equity' in the other social sciences, relating to fairness and equality of treatment, can be developed by English public law.

32.3 SOCIAL COMPLEXITY

32.3.1 Social complexity

Society has become particularly complex in the modern and postmodern era.[39] The old structures and certainties have broken down. The increased level of globalisation through the internet, through the power of multinational enterprises, and the shrinkage in the power of the nation state have all contributed to a changed society. For some this manifests itself in a new cosmopolitanism[40] in which an international elite crosses borders and cultural boundaries, while a new lumpen proletariat of people who have been overlooked by the new technologies is left behind.[41] For others, this offers a new possibility for legal structures like trusts in applying the techniques developed in English trusts law to specific jurisdictions like the Cayman Islands,[42] or more generally in international commercial transactions.[43] Similarly, the enhanced status of women as economic actors, as cultural actors and simply as human beings has complicated the nature of the family.[44] The examples of such phenomena are legion.

The old certainties are breaking down: the advent of mass unemployment has meant that there is no longer certainty about employment patterns; the increase in global income disparity (the 358 top global billionaires have the same income as the poorest 2.3 billion people in the world)[45] enhances the insecurities of those both with and without money; and

---

36 [1897] 1 Ch 196. See section 5.2.2 above.
37 [2000] Ch 162. See section 13.3.4.
38 It should be recalled that Sedley LJ has already made significant pronouncements on the role of equity and the treatment of injustice in relation to the formerly purely restitutionary defence of change of position in *Niru Battery Manufacturing Co v Milestone Trading* [2003] EWCA Civ 1446, para [152], as was discussed section 19.6.1.
39 Byrne, 1998.
40 Beck, 1992; Bauman, 1998.
41 Virilio, 2000.
42 Hayton and Cooke, 2000.
43 Eg, Hudson, 1998, 265, in relation to the use of collateral in financial derivatives transactions.
44 Gauthier, 1996.
45 Bauman, 2001, 85.

the environmental concerns evident in the deterioration of the global environment are all indicative of change. The upshot of these trends is an increase in insecurity and fear for individuals.[46] Rather than replacing one set of certainties with a new set, these changes have generated uncertainty and complexity. This complexity – mirrored in advanced physics[47] – engenders a form of social chaos in which individuals have become atomised[48] and the paths to social solidarity obfuscated.[49] The metaphor for chaos is one familiar to family lawyers:[50] it encapsulates the impossibility of creating a model to which family rules can be applied identically in all circumstances and recognises the need for principles which can be applied in a way that is sensitive to context.

Instead, the challenge for the English legal system is to recognise the changes which are occurring in society and to generate models which will deal effectively with this new complexity. Not that the norms need necessarily to change simply because society is going through observable change – although in socially sensitive areas such as labour and social security, legislative change is bound to be required by alterations in public policy. Rather, the legal system needs to recognise a different understanding of itself: not as a system of positivist rules which dictate behaviour to citizens, but rather as a system of rules, norms and structures which *belong to* those citizens – that is, a system of statute, common law and equity which presents means of resolving disputes between citizens and also offers them techniques which they can deploy for socially useful activities, such as the creation of co-operatives[51] or other unincorporated associations,[52] by manipulating concepts of contract and property. The goal for a legal system must be to cater for this level of social complexity in a way that is both principled and sensitive to context.

I suggest that equity offers a means of achieving this.

32.3.2 Borrowing from the science of complexity

As with the development of quantum physics, it is possible to identify simple events arising from an accumulation of unrelated episodes. Examples given are the well-known butterfly flapping its wings in Beijing and beginning a chain reaction which causes rain in New York. Other examples are the dripping tap which, despite the maintenance of a steady flow of water, lets water fall at occasionally irregular intervals as a result of random and chaotic factors outwith the control of the scientist-observer.[53] In short, an accumulation of simple events can lead to complex and unexpected conclusions.[54]

Similarly, scientists point to the idea of complexity. In scientific terms, complexity considers the way in which simple phenomena can lead to complex results. The theory of complexity is a useful understanding of how a reactive, responsive justice system can operate

46 Giddens, 1991; Bauman, 2001, 83.
47 Cohen and Stewart, 1994.
48 Houellebecq, 2001.
49 Byrne, 1998.
50 Dewar, 1998.
51 Hudson, 2000:1, 276.
52 Chapter 4.
53 Gleick, 1988.
54 Capra uses this metaphorical trick to explain a post-Cartesian, Zen account of social relations and the need to adopt holistic approaches to everything from medicine to social relations: Capra, 1983.

in the context of a hyper-complex society. One frequent starting analogy is the simple phenomenon of wind leading a complex and unpredictable pattern of waves crashing onto land. Complexity is said to indicate the natural tendency for physical and biological systems to take this complexity and nevertheless produce regular patterns from it.[55] In short, a tendency for plants and animals to generate order out of chaos. The interaction of chaos and complexity theories illustrates the dialectic between pattern and disorder which we can observe in the social sciences as well as the natural sciences.[56]

The production of just results out of a mixture of common law and equity perhaps responds to this metaphor. A complex and largely unpredictable mass of litigation comes to court and leads to a complex web of judicial decisions. However, those decisions are not entirely responsive solely to the dispute brought before the tribunal, but rather by reference to an overarching structure of decided case law. A semblance of order is thus made of the chaos: what will not happen is that the chaos and the complexity of our social relations will be removed.

32.4 EQUITY AND CHAOS

32.4.1 The psychology of order and chaos: common law and equity

The core argument is this: human beings crave order and are fearful of chaos.[57] In a world that is fundamentally chaotic, equity permits sufficiently flexible claims and remedies to address this chaos. Having suggested that the world is more complex than ever it was, we turn now to consider how a legal system should address that added complexity and the extraordinary diversity of claims over which it will be required to sit in judgment.

Freud creates one of the most famous dialectics in modern thought: that between the ego and the id in the human psyche. A well-balanced psyche will achieve its equilibrium through a synthesis of the conscious and unconscious represented by ego and id respectively. This metaphor is reminiscent of the manner in which the English legal system seeks to arrive at the 'right answer' in civil law cases by balancing the common law with equity.[58] Freud also posits the tendency of human beings to seek certainty as an instinct. This is said to be located in the awkward adaptation of human instincts (or human nature) to the cultural constraints of civilisation.[59] The tendency then is to focus the rational mind on the pursuit of certainty in law-making and in other activities so that chaotic and anarchic forces are repressed.[60] The balance is between order/ego and chaos/id: both are forces in the human psyche. Effective law-making would require a balance between formalism and flexibility; creating standards while accepting difference; synthesising common law and equity.

---

55 Lewin, 1993.
56 Cohen and Stewart, 1994, 6, who refer to this dialectic in terms of 'simplexity and complicity'.
57 Freud, 1930.
58 Although it is true to say that not all legal problems will require that both common law and equity be put to work; but not all psychological issues necessarily require psychoanalysis either.
59 Freud, 1930, especially 288 et seq.
60 So with Weber, for example, the development of rationality is expected to remove the need for casuistic decision-making, permitting instead a bureaucratic formalism to hit upon the 'right answer' every time.

32.4.2 Reconstituting equity as a tool of social justice

Much has been made in this book of the uncertain world which has been created by the onward march of globalisation and a greater social complexity. What is apparent is that equity is applied (albeit carefully) in commercial cases and in cases involving homes more often than it is ever applied in cases involving social or personal welfare. The fiduciary categories of company director, agent, business partner and trustee are far more mature than are the comparable fiduciary duties in relation to the operation of public sector services. Equity has become a tool of commerce in the recent case law. Due to the inaccessible nature of the English legal system to most ordinary citizens,[61] it is a head of claim deployed to prevent unconscionable behaviour between commercial people. In the discussion of express trusts in Chapter 7, it was pointed out that most of the major cases over the last 10 years have involved financial institutions. Aside from trusts of homes, few other cases involving trusts reach the High Court. The conscious express trust has all but extracted itself from mainstream equity; its terms are interpreted like a contract, as are the duties of its trustees.

The next stage for the law is to identify the way in which it can respond to the increased social complexity of the risk society. This book has argued for an understanding of law as a facilitator of communal and communicative action,[62] in the manner suggested by Durkheim.[63] The models identified in this book can enable communities to act together. What is lacking is a clearly defined understanding of the fiduciary duties at issue here. The issue is that of a different context from the well-understood family trusts and the sophisticated structures of commercial investment entities. Each context is significantly different. A one-size-fits-all approach to the legal treatment of these structures will not be sufficient. Rather, our new, more complex society requires the development of legal principles which will allow the courts to be responsive to context and to the needs of the human beings involved in legal disputes.

32.4.3 Equity out of chaos in a risk society

The global economy is organised around risk: risk in terms of financial speculation; risk in terms of the broader range of decisions and choices which face most of our citizens; and risk in terms of the increased hazard posed by the activities of international corporations. Social change is visible in the changed roles of women over the latter half of the 20th century; the decline of the institution of marriage in many Western societies, and the greater appreciation of post-Cold War environmental catastrophe through ecological risk. Mass unemployment and deterioration in structures of belief in common goals and organised religion are the flipside of income mobility, broader national and international career opportunities, and a greater tolerance of a plurality of belief. For Chomsky, these developments have occurred at great cost to the spiritual welfare of individuals, with a late-capitalist economy generating the illusion of lifechances as a mask for the multinational corporate power which has assumed a morally ambiguous control over world politics.[64] For Beck, the increase in social

---

61   As a result of cost and the inaccessibility of legal aid for most citizens: see Hudson, 1999:2, 19.
62   Habermas (1981), 1984.
63   Durkheim (1894), 1994.
64   Chomsky, 1999.

risk has derived from an increase in choices and has also caused a displacement of politics from its traditional arenas to more localised forums and groups.[65] Thus risk offers both opportunity and threat. For Giddens, the creation of what he terms 'institutional reflexivity' indicates both greater power in the hands of institutions and more profound existential problems associated with requiring individuals to make ever more complex life choices.[66] For all three there is a common link in their observation that the world has thrown greater risk on the individual citizen by means of an increasingly powerful global economy facilitating new connections, new industries and new sources of social power outwith the control of national governments.

For sociologists like Giddens, globalisation is something broader than the operation of financial markets across geographic boundaries.[67] Globalisation refers to a systematic change in social relations. The range of options produced creates problems for the individual in a way which a lack of choice never did.[68] It requires the individual to become bound up in investment activity through the structures discussed in this book in a number of ways – either through quasi-compulsory pensions arrangements,[69] or through a decision to invest personal capital, or (more fundamentally) simply by reliance on public services which are provided by quasi private sector investment structures like the PFI (private finance initiative) scheme or NHS trusts.[70] The techniques, in the best postmodern tradition, are both simple and very complex. This analysis of the variety of treatments of trusts has shown English law to be caught between very simple, intuitive ideas and subject matter too complex to analyse easily. The role of equity is to address itself to that form of social realignment: to provide justice in a more difficult and more complicated world than the one which produced trusts and other equitable doctrines originally.

This is a world of increased risk of many kinds: opportunity and choice, hazard and danger. The legal treatment of trusts must recognise that – whether involved in social investment (as with charities, co-operatives and so forth), or private welfare through investment (as with pension funds, unit trusts and so forth). Investment is a means of speculating on the hazard and volatility inherent in the global economy. Investment is a modish form of public policy which reduces the burden on central taxation and places it instead on the enthusiasm of venture capitalists for infrastructural projects underwritten by government. Investment is also, however, a means of expressing a commitment to each other and to our communal welfare by means of co-operative activity.[71] It constitutes a profoundly humane understanding of the need to nurture our most precious resource: the talents and the aspirations of ordinary people.[72]

65 Beck, 1992.
66 Beck, Giddens and Lash, 1994.
67 Giddens, 1994.
68 Giddens, 1991.
69 That is, not compulsory private pensions schemes but schemes which the citizen is ever more likely to have to acquire because of the phased reduction in the level and availability of the state pension.
70 Hudson, 2000:1, 309.
71 Maloney, Smith and Stoker, 2000, 212.
72 Sentiments associated with John Smith, 1994: 'The scourges of poverty, unemployment and low skills are barriers, not only to opportunities for people, but to the creation of a dynamic and prosperous society. It is simply unacceptable to continue to waste our most precious resource – the extraordinary skills and talents of ordinary people.'

32.5 EQUITY, CULTURE AND POLITICS

32.5.1 Equity in the culture

Equity's role is both cultural and political. This section will consider the cultural place of equity. It is said that a definition of 'culture' is one of the most complex issues in the humanities.[73] The roots of property have been explained[74] as being planted in allocation of rights in land, growing in part out of human beings taking to agriculture. The roots of the term 'culture' are in 'coulter', meaning to cultivate – again, drawn from agriculture.[75] The word 'culture' itself can be juxtaposed with 'nature': human society transforms the natural into the cultural by civilising it and by ordering it. The cultural possibility of equity is contained in the series of lyrical core principles of equity set out in Chapter 1.[76] The morality evident in those core principles is primarily commercial, echoing the trade-based principles considered in Chapter 2.[77]

To expose this commercial underbelly one needs only to probe some of the core equitable claims considered hitherto. For example, proprietary estoppel will be available only where the claimant has suffered some detriment broadly equivalent to consideration in contract;[78] equity will not assist a volunteer in general terms, even where that would enable a defendant to go back on an ordinary promise made to the claimant, thus underlying an amorality in the absence of some form of contract;[79] and equity will not permit unreasonable delays even where the merits of the case would otherwise have permitted a remedy.[80] The upshot is a form of equity which has developed historically to the benefit of commercial activities, thus expressing a cultural tendency in the law (alongside the requirement of consideration in the law of contract) to promote certainty in trade before any more common morality. In Chapter 3, we considered in detail the difference between obligations which would be enforced by equity as trusts and obligations which were merely moral duties not enforceable in equity.[81]

This conception of equity permits an understanding of the legal system as being something owned by the citizens and not something either positivist or based on an external morality. Equity is cultural as an expression of 'Englishness and Welshness'. Equity is political in that it facilitates a discourse about the practice of justice. Equity is political also to the extent that it gives power to the judiciary: to this extent, the study and description of equitable doctrine are themselves political acts in that they shape and describe citizens' rights. These cultural and political dynamics are potentially inclusive of citizens where they present a means by which citizens can shape the content of notions like 'good conscience' through litigation and dispute resolution.

---

73 Eagleton, 2000, 1.
74 See section 31.1 above.
75 Eagleton, 2000, 1.
76 See section 1.4 above.
77 See section 2.1 above.
78 *Coombes v Smith* [1986] 1 WLR 808: consideration itself demonstrating that contract law enforces only bargains but does not enforce mere promises made to volunteers.
79 See section 1.2 above.
80 See section 1.4 above.
81 See section 3.3 above.

32.5.2 Equity as something quintessentially English

Maitland remarks in his *Essays on Equity* that equity is quintessentially English.[82] It seems to me that that is a very interesting attitude to equity. The point has already been made in section 31.3 that this comment of Maitland can be juxtaposed with the Roman law roots of the ideas asserted by the restitution lawyers.[83] But perhaps the more interesting aspect to this remark is identifying precisely what is meant by 'Englishness'[84] on this model. What does it mean to say that equity is in some way English?[85]

   The notion of Englishness is a profoundly complex one, particularly at the time of writing. At the first level it is unclear what is meant by 'English' as opposed to 'British'. Frequently, Englishness is identified with the world depicted by Evelyn Waugh, PG Wodehouse and EM Forster – that is, a world set in either Victorian or Edwardian England in which the confidence of Empire and economic expansion is relaxing into the promise of the early 20th century. Much of this attitude to Englishness finds its expression in historical hagiographies of the English, like Winston Churchill's *History of the English Speaking Peoples*, on which Margaret Thatcher drew for a vision of the English as suffused with Viking blood and mixing doughty pragmatism with an indomitable island spirit.

   When Maitland talks about the English, it should be remembered that his best-known work is in relation to legal history – a field which, it might be said, occasionally overlooks social history in favour of an approach based on 'common law through the ages'. Maitland's own attitude to history (and that of other 'Whig' historians) is criticised by Davies in his history of Britain and Britons, *The Isles*,[86] in the following terms:

> FW Maitland (1824–97), Downing Professor of Law at Cambridge, whose *History of English Law* (1895) took the narrative up to the critical reign of Henry III. Despite their immense erudition, and their enormous services to the subject, all these scholars positively crowed with nationalistic self-satisfaction . . . As for Maitland, the legalist par excellence, he saw an unbreakable bond between the Common Law and 'our land and race'; and he eulogised the judges of Henry III's reign . . . History in the hands of lawyers will always turn lawyers into heroes.

While the historians like Maitland identify something marvellous in their history of England, for the most part they ignore the real facts about England at the time. For example, Richard the Lionheart is generally presented as the saviour of a nation in Robin Hood films. In fact England was ruled by the Plantagenets (like Richard I) who were French by birth and the language of the law and of the court was French until the time of Henry VIII. England was nothing more than an occupied territory within a larger kingdom. The king would turn his attention to England only if there were occasionally wars of subjugation to be fought. The

---

82 Maitland, 1936, 1.
83 Hackney, 1997.
84 Wrapped up in this phrase, 'English' in this context is necessarily a notion of 'Welshness' given that the jurisdiction is that of England and Wales. The reader will please excuse a lack of reference to Welshness given the comments which are made below about the manner in which an idea of Englishness is played out in the literature.
85 Or Welsh.
86 Davies, 1999.

attentions of these kings were generally turned outwards from France; towards the Middle East.[87] The official language of the English Royal Court was French; the kings spoke French and not English; English itself did not exist as a single, formal language at the time.[88] And yet the development of a system of common law by the Norman kings and subsequently by the Plantagenets was eulogised as being part of the creation of the indomitable English spirit.

The English were ruled from overseas. Even the term 'Anglo-Saxon' acknowledges that the native English were ruled by the Angles and the Saxons after the Romans had left. The only parts of the British Isles peopled solely by 'native' Britons were Wales and Scotland. The term 'Briton' itself is thought to derive from Brutus, son of Aeneas, who was believed to have settled in England after the fall of Troy and founded London.[89] Then came the Norman Conquest to replace the work of Alfred the Great in attempting to forge a coherent culture for the tribes over which he had authority. The ensuing history of England up to the Reformation, although frequently presented as a seamless narrative by historians, was in fact a history of rule by the French and internecine strife between members of a variety of French royal families (for example, the accession of Stephen to the throne in 1135).[90]

It is with the Reformation, during which Henry VIII replaced the Catholic church with the Church of England as the dominant creed, that the churches were dispossessed and replaced by English customs which drew heavily on the pre-existing traditions but with the king replacing the Pope as head of the church and Defender of the Faith. Tudor England grew as a trading nation, with London, in particular, flourishing. This spirit of self-confidence continued in the reign of Elizabeth I and founded much of the modern enthusiasm among the English for their adopted Englishness. Only under Victoria was there to be a similarly enthusiastic expression of Englishness in the form of the 'British' character and the British Empire.

So what does this tell us about Maitland's determination that equity is somehow English? Throughout the Tudor period, the Lords Chancellor became more powerful. Ever more writs were served by the Lord Chancellor, and more and more forms of action were generated during that period. The generation of equity therefore grew out of the increasing political power of the Chancery and the power of men like Thomas More and Thomas Cromwell – as depicted gloriously in Robert Bolt's play *A Man for All Seasons*. And yet the legal principles which were adopted by the Courts of Chancery at this time developed a series of propositions (outlined in Chapter 1 above) which Snell was able to record at the turn of the 19th century in his book on *Equity*.[91] Those principles were an expression of morality which gave way over time to rigid rules dealing with trusts, injunctions and so forth.[92] Equity is therefore cultural in that it is part of English history – part of a nation's attempt to forge its own identity under Henry VIII and Elizabeth I. It is the culture of a powerful, emerging bureaucracy under the Lord Chancellor, who (at the time of writing) remains a great constitutional anomaly with a presence in the executive, the judiciary and the legislature. The practice of equity emerged from the politics of the 16th century. It is part of our culture and, for good or ill, part of our island's story.

---

87 Richard, Coeur de Lion, for example, spent only six months of his 10-year reign as King of England actually in England.

88 Davies, 1999.

89 Ackroyd, 2000.

90 Even the taking of the name 'Stephen' by the king concealed the fact that his birth-name was 'Etienne'.

91 See section 1.4 above.

92 Gardner, 1996.

What is plain is that the nature of equity as something English has developed with time – and that equity will continue to develop. The argument was made in section 31.3 that restitution is almost an unnecessary adjunct to equity – beyond the valuable, technical work done by restitution lawyers on the frequent incoherence identifiable in the law of trusts. Some of the frequent objections made to the introduction of a code of restitution are based on restitution's place as a part of Roman law and not as a part of English law.[93] As such, that part of the argument is based on a preference for something English over something European on a civil code model – those continental European jurisdictions being based on Roman law.[94]

However, it is not clear that modern European thinking is necessarily tied up with Roman law; rather, a different set of principles based on proportionality, freedom of movement and so forth has been developed. These freedoms seem to work at two levels: economic liberties within the European Economic Community; and principles of procedural justice such as proportionality. These ideas have already permeated public law, but private law has been much more reluctant to adopt them. There are perhaps broad comparators between concepts like equitable estoppel in private law and concepts like legitimate expectations in public law.[95] Alternatively, perhaps equity offers a means of meeting the new social complexity and of achieving a measure of *social* justice. This issue is considered next.

32.6 THE GOALS OF EQUITY

So why should equity be retained? Is it not simply another example of the British theme-park constitution which ought to be discarded? I think not. Equity is necessary to achieve a number of socially desirable goals: to protect the liberties and rights of the individual;[96] to ensure fairness through conscionable behaviour;[97] and to ensure equal access to justice.[98] To take each in turn. The liberties of the individual are capable of being protected only if a system of dispute resolution and justice recognises that there is a need to consider individual cases on their own merits. Individual liberties can also be protected at a political, as well as at a legal, level by means of accepting those rights as being human rights. As considered in Chapter 17, there are differences between the philosophies of human rights and equity: the former being avowedly political in nature, while the latter are primarily juristic.

The role of the Lord Chancellor was to act as Keeper of the Sovereign's Conscience – sometimes being an ecclesiastic and at other times being a secular lawyer. Thus the concept of conscience came to inhabit the remit of the Courts of Chancery. The courts therefore developed a principle of acting *in personam* in relation to the behaviour of the individual defendant. Protecting the liberties of the citizenry through equity meant ensuring that as a matter of private law no one person could act unconscionably in relation to any other person.

---

93 See section 31.3 above.

94 Given the membership of the United Kingdom in the European Union, perhaps there is an argument that equity ought to adopt more Roman principles to bring English law more in line with European thinking: Hayton, 2000.

95 As expressed in *R v North and East Devon Health Authority ex p Coughlan* [2000] 3 All ER 850 in the development of a principle by which an applicant can seek an order in public law for the efficacy of some representation or assurance made to them forming a legitimate expectation in their mind.

96 See section 1.1 and the discussion of Aristotle and Hegel.

97 Rawls, 1971 and 1985: discussion of justice through fairness as a principle of 'fair play'.

98 Hudson, 1999:2, 91.

The maintenance of equitable behaviour through litigation is dependent on all citizens being able to access the courts, and thus being equal before the law as a matter of practice. Such a discussion clearly takes us into issues as to the structure of the legal system, the availability of legal aid and so forth. It is this writer's view, expressed elsewhere, that the Woolf reforms[99] and the limping modernisation of the English legal system do not amount to the provision of an equally-accessible, citizen-orientated public service.[100] Again, the role of equity is to ensure equality: two words ('equity' and 'equality') sharing a common etymological root – to be free and to be equally free.[101]

In a world in which technology enables us to talk intimately and instantaneously with people in other parts of the world, when many of us live in cities where we hardly know our next door neighbours, we are in danger of overreaching the individual. As Virilio shows us, technology enables cars to hurtle past us, aeroplanes and faxes to pass over us, and our own selves to shrink within the power of the machines that move us, help us and watch us.[102] As part of this late modernity there is a need for people to communicate one with another to shape the norms which drive our lifeworld.[103] To maintain the social legitimacy of our institutions it is important that people are connected and feel an ownership of the means of dispute resolution through the justice system.[104] Now is not the place to engage with such a broad debate about the good and ill of the justice system. However, one thing can be said in the context of this book. By maintaining a system of equity we give individuals a chance to speak and to have their concerns heard outwith the rigidities of the common law. Equity enables our individual voices to be heard in the tempest of technological innovation.

32.7 IN CONCLUSION

There is something remarkably humane, in this writer's opinion, in the development of equity. This final essay has sought to capture something of the passion bound up in the historical development of equity – from the early days of the burgeoning numbers of writs served by the Lords Chancellor, to equity's troubled transition from heraldic artefact to standard bearer of social justice in the 21st century.[105] Beyond that there is in equity a possibility of providing for justice on its own terms on a case-by-case basis. Within the positivist demands of the common law there is a need to create a space in which private law can give effect to a basic morality to do with achieving fair results in individual cases. Under the umbrella of such a jurisdiction, human beings can be recognised as individuals with their own very personal motivations, commitments and beliefs, and not simply be dealt with just as litigants against whom abstract rules are to be enforced. We have little difficulty in accepting that there is something different in each human being[106] but, yet, in our law-making we assume too often that all cases can be resolved by reference to the same norms.[107] It is

---

99 Hudson, 1999:2, 167.
100 *Ibid*, 256.
101 Rawls, 1985.
102 Virilio, 1986 and 2000.
103 Habermas (1981), 1984.
104 Habermas, 1972.
105 See section 17.5 above.
106 Hudson, 2004:2.
107 Habermas (1992), 1996, 151 *et seq*, 222 *et seq*.

suggested that those norms must always be flexible enough to permit of individual difference, to leave sufficient room for fair application.

What is needed is a structure within which justice can be generated by the establishment
of rules by which each citizen is required to live. This is the external morality which is
created in part by equity's notion of conscience. What is also required is a means of ensuring
that the advancement of the many does not allow the casual oppression of the individual.
This balancing act is achieved supremely well by the juxtaposition of common law and
equity as classically understood. Consequently, any attempt to rigidify equity is to be
resisted. What modern thought has achieved through the philosophy of Nietzsche, as adopted
by the post-structuralists like Foucault and Derrida and the existentialists like Sartre and
Camus, is an innate suspicion of any assertion to fundamental truth or any claim to legitimacy. In such terms, to claim that the uncertain world which is policed by equity can be
reduced to a series of tightly prescribed rules is entirely to ignore the one true advance in
human thought in the wake of the Second World War – that there can never be such
unthinking confidence in our assumptions again.

As Freud has told us, there is much in the make-up of the individual psyche which, while
conforming to some general patterns, will be made up of impulses as individual as dreams,
personal mythologies and individual experience.[108] For Jung, there is much store to be placed
in the spiritual interactions between the personal space and the collective unconscious.[109] In
either case, the exchange of impulses between the one and the many is sophisticated and
intricate. What Freud and Marx also did for human thought was to open up the possibility of
reasoning by deductive logic and ideology, without necessarily needing every assertion to be
capable of empirical proof.[110] From such epistemological advances we can recognise in law-
making a desire to achieve order through law, and in our society a concomitant desire to
achieve social justice: that is, to balance a desire for simplicity in the order of our social relations with an appreciation of the complexity necessarily bound up in the lives of millions of
individuals.[111] So, in delineating the respective spaces of common law and equity, it is
important to ensure that a balance is maintained between the two – that the willowy suppleness of equity is not displaced by a brittle demand for common law certainty.[112]

It is only through equity that our machines of justice can appreciate and meet the intrinsic
chaos in our social relations. That is the only way in which we can extricate the human being
from the impersonal machinery of the legal system. The flexibility of equity brings equilibrium to our private law in balance with the certainties of common law. Through this synergy
we can achieve harmony. We must resist the temptation to impose too much order on what
will remain a fundamentally chaotic universe.

108 Freud, 1923.
109 Jung, 1927.
110 Geuss, 1981.
111 Cohen and Stewart, 1994.
112 As suggested by the model of restitution advanced, *inter alia*, by Beatson, 1991.

Bibliography

Ackroyd, P, *London: Biography of a City*, 2000, London: Chatto & Windus

Adams, J, (1975) 39 Conv 94

Adams, J and Frantz, D, *A Full Service Bank: How BCCI stole billions around the world*, *A Full Service Bank: How BCCI stole billions around the world*, London: Simon & Schuster

Adorno, T, 'Subject and object', in Arato, A and Gerbhardt, E (eds), *The Essential Frankfurt School Reader*, 1978, New York: Continuum

Allen, 'Bribes and constructive trusts: *A-G Hong Kong v Reid*' (1995) 58 MLR 87

American Law Institute, *Restatement of the Law of Restitution*, 1937, St Paul, Minn: ALI

American Law Institute, *Restatement of Trusts*, 2nd edn, 1959, St Paul, Minn: ALI

Annetta, V, 'Priority rights in insolvency – the doctrinal basis for equity's intervention' (1992) 20 ABLR 311

Arendt, H, *The Human Condition*, 2nd edn, 1958, Chicago: Chicago University Press

Aristotle, *The Nicomachean Ethics*, 1955, Thomson (trans), Harmondsworth: Penguin

Arora, A, 'The bank's liability as a constructive trustee' [1990] JBL 217

Arrowsmith, S, 'Ineffective transactions and unjust enrichment: a framework for analysis' (1989) 9 LS 121

Atiyah, P, *The Rise and Fall of Freedom of Contract*, 1979, Oxford: Clarendon

Atiyah, P, *Essays on Contract*, 1986, Oxford: Clarendon

Auchmuty, R, 'The fiction of equity', in Scott-Hunt, S and Lim, H (eds), *Feminist Perspectives on Equity and Trusts*, ed., 2001, London: Cavendish, 1

Austin, R, 'Constructive trusts', in Finn, P (ed), *Essays in Equity*, 1985, Sydney: LBC, 196

Bainham, M, *Children: The Modern Law*, 1998, Bristol: Family Law

Baker, P and Langan, P, *Snell's Principles of Equity*, 29th edn, 1990, London: Sweet & Maxwell

Bamforth, N, 'Unconscionability as a vitiating factor' [1995] LMCLQ 538

Barker, K, 'Rescuing remedialism in unjust enrichment law: why remedies are right' [1998] CLJ 301

Barlow, A, 'Rights in the family home: time for a conceptual revolution?', in Hudson, AS (ed), *New Perspectives on Property Law, Human Rights and the Home*, 2003, London: Cavendish Publishing, 53

Barnsley, DG, 'Co-owners' rights to occupy trust land' [1998] CLJ 123

Bartlett, R, 'When is a "trust" not a trust? The National Health Service Trust' [1996] Conv 186

Battersby [1995] CFLQ 59

Bauman, Z, *Postmodernity and its Discontents*, 1997, Cambridge: Polity

Bauman, Z, *Globalisation*, 1998, Cambridge: Polity

Bauman, Z, *Community*, 2000, Cambridge: Polity

Bauman, Z, *The Individualised Society*, 2001, Cambridge: Polity

Beatson, J, 'Restitutionary remedies for void and ineffective contracts' (1989) 105 LQR 179

Beatson, J, *Use and Abuse of Unjust Enrichment*, 1991, Oxford: Clarendon

Beatson, J, 'The relationship between regulations governing the financial services industry and fiduciary duties under the general law', in McKendrick, E, *Commercial Aspects of Trusts and Fiduciary Obligations*, 1992, Oxford: Clarendon, 55

Beck, U, *The Risk Society*, 1992, London: Sage

Beck, U, Giddens, A and Lash, S, *Reflexive Modernization*, 1994, Cambridge: Polity

Benjamin, J, *The Law of Global Custody*, 1996, London: Butterworths

Benjamin, J, *Interests in Securities*, 2000, Oxford: Oxford University Press

Bevan, A, *In Place of Fear* (1952), 1978, London: Quartet

Birks, P, *Introduction to the Law of Restitution*, 1989, Oxford: Clarendon (1989:1)

Birks, P, 'Misdirected funds' (1989) 105 LQR 258 (1989:2)

Birks, P, 'The English recognition of unjust enrichment' [1991] LMCLQ 473

Birks, P, 'Mixing and tracing' (1992) 45(2) CLP 69

Birks, P, 'Restitution and resulting trusts', in Goldstein (ed), *Equity: Contemporary Legal Developments*, 1992, Jerusalem, 335

Birks, P, 'Persistent problems in misdirected money' [1993] LMCLQ 218 (1993:1)

Birks, P, 'No consideration: restitution after void contracts' (1993) 23 UWALR 195 (1993:2)

Birks, P, 'Establishing a proprietary base' [1995] RLR 83 (1995:1)

Birks, P, 'Overview: tracing, claiming and defences', in Birks, P (ed), *Laundering and Tracing*, 1995, Oxford: Clarendon, 289 (1995:2)

Birks, P, (1995) 9 Trusts Law International 91 (1995:3)

Birks, P, 'Equity in the modern law: an exercise in taxonomy' (1996) 26 UWALR 1

Birks, P, 'Inconsistency between compensation and restitution' (1996) 112 LQR 375 (1996:1)

Birks, P, 'Trusts raised to avoid unjust enrichment: the *Westdeutsche* case' [1996] RLR 3 (1996:2)

Birks, P, 'Tracing, subrogation and change of position' (1996) 8 Trusts Law International 2 (1996:3)

Birks, P, 'On taking seriously the difference between tracing and claiming' (1997) 11 Trusts Law International 2

Birks, P, 'Definition and division: a meditation on *Institutes* 313', in Birks, P (ed), *The Classification of Obligations*, 1997, Oxford: Clarendon, 1 (1997:2)

Birks, P, 'The burden on the bank', in Rose, F (ed), *Restitution and Banking Law*, 1998, Oxford: Mansfield, 189 (1998:1)

Birks, P, 'Misnomer', in Cornish, W, Nolan, R, O'Sullivan, J and Virgo, G (eds), *Restitution, Present and Future: Essays in Honour of Gareth Jones*, 1998, Oxford: Hart, 1 (1998:2)

Birks, P, 'Rights, wrongs and remedies' (2000) OJLS 1 (2000:1)

Birks, P, 'Epilogue', in Birks, P and Rose, F (eds), *Resulting Trusts and Equitable Compensation*, 2000, London: Mansfield, 261 (2000:2)

Birks, P, (ed), *Private Law*, 2000, Oxford: Oxford University Press (2000:3)

Birks, P, 'The content of fiduciary obligations' (2002) 16 Trusts Law International 34

Birks, P, 'Receipt', in Birks, P and Pretto, A (eds), *Breach of Trust*, 2002, Oxford: Hart (2002:2)

Birks, P, 'Knowing receipt', in Birks, P and Pretto, A (eds), *Breach of Trust*, 2002, Oxford: Hart (2002:3)

Birks, P, *Unjust Enrichment*, 2003, Oxford: Oxford University Press

Birks, P and Chambers, R, *Restitution Research Resource*, 1997, Oxford: Mansfield, 1–6 (1997:1)

Birks, P and Pretto, A (eds), *Breach of Trust*, 2002, Oxford: Hart (2002:1)

Black, J, *Rules and Regulators*, 1997, Oxford: Clarendon

Blair, A, *The Third Way: New Politics for the New Century*, Fabian Pamphlet 588, 1998, London: The Fabian Society

Blair, W, Allison, A, Morton, G, Richards-Carpenter, P, Walker, G and Walmsley, N, *Banking and Financial Services Regulation*, 3rd edn, London: Butterworths, 2003

Bostock, C, *Aristotle's Ethics*, 2000, Oxford: Oxford University Press

Bottomley, A, 'Our property in trust: things to make and do', in Scott-Hunt, S and Lim, H (eds), *Feminist Perspectives on Equity and Trusts*, 2001, London: Cavendish Publishing

Brealey, RA and Myers, SC, *Principles of Corporate Finance*, 5th edn, 1996; 6th edn, 1998, Toronto: McGraw Hill

Bridge, M, *Personal Property Law*, 2nd edn, 1996, London: Blackstone

Bryan, M, 'The conscience of equity in Australia' (1990) 106 LQR 25

Burn, E, *Cheshire and Burn's The Law of Real Property*, 15th edn, 1994, London: Butterworths

Burrows, A (ed), *Essays in the Law of Restitution*, 1991, Oxford: Clarendon (1991:1)

Burrows, A, 'Public authorities, *ultra vires* and restitution', in Burrows, A (ed), *Essays in the Law of Restitution*, 1991, Oxford: Clarendon (1991:2)

Burrows, A, *The Law of Restitution*, 1993; 2nd edn, 2002, London: Butterworths

Burrows, A, *Remedies in Contract and Tort*, 2nd edn, 1994, London: Butterworths

Burrows, A, 'Swaps and friction between common law and equity' [1995] RLR 15

Burrows, A, 'Understanding the law of restitution: a map through the thicket', in *Understanding the Law of Obligations*, 1998, Oxford: Hart, 45

Burrows, A, 'Proprietary restitution: unmasking unjust enrichment' (2001) 117 LQR 412

Burrows, A, 'We do this at common law but that in equity' (2002) 22 OJLS 1

Burrows, A and McKendrick, E, *The Law of Restitution*, 1997, Oxford: Oxford University Press

Buxton, R, 'The Human Rights Act and private law' (2000) 116 LQR 48

Byrne, D, *Complexity Theory and the Social Sciences*, 1998, London: Routledge

Byrne, D, *Social Exclusion*, 1999, Buckingham: Open University Press

Campbell, D, 'Facism and legality' (1946) 62 LQR 141

Capra, F, *The Turning Point*, 1983, London: Fontana

Carr, A and McNulty, M, *The Handbook of Clinical Adult Psychology*, 2006, London: Routledge

Chambers, R, 'Restitution, trusts and compound interest' (1996) 20 Mel UL Rev 848

Chambers, R, *Resulting Trusts*, 1997, Oxford: Clarendon

Chambers, R, 'Constructive trusts in Canada', Pt 1 (2001) 15 Trusts Law International 214; and Pt 2 (2002) 16 Trusts Law International 2

Cheshire, GC and Burn, EH, *The Law of Real Property*, 16th edn, 2000, London: Butterworths

Chesterman, M, 'Foundations of charity law in the new Welfare State' (1999) 62 MLR 333

Chitty on Contracts, 27th edn, 1994, London: Sweet & Maxwell

Chomsky, N, *Profit Over People*, 1999, New York: Seven Stories

Chomsky, N, *The New Military Humanism*, 2000, London: Pluto

Clapham, N, *Human Rights in the Private Sphere*, 1993, Oxford: Clarendon

Clark, JB, *Theobald on Wills*, 15th edn, 1993, London: Sweet & Maxwell, 646

Clarke, A, 'Property law' (1995) 48 CLP 117

Cohen, J and Stewart, I, *The Collapse of Chaos – Discovering Simplicity in a Chaotic World*, 1994, Harmondsworth: Penguin

Collins, L, *Dicey and Morris on the Conflict of Laws*, 12th edn, 1993, London: Sweet & Maxwell

Conaglen, M, 'Equitable compensation for breach of fiduciary dealing rules' (2003) 119 LQR 246

Cooke, A and Hayton, D, 'Land law and trusts', in Hayton, D (ed), *Law's Futures*, 2000, Oxford: Hart, 433

Cooke, E, 'Equitable accounting' [1995] Conv 391

Cooke, E, *The Modern Law of Estoppel*, 2000, Oxford: Clarendon

Cooke, E, 'In the wake of *Stack v Dowden*: the tale of TR1' [2011] Fam Law 1142

Cotterrell, R, *Sociology of Law*, 1993, London: Butterworths (1993:1)

Cotterrell, R, 'Trusting in law: legal and moral concepts of trust' (1993) 46(2) CLP 75 (1993:2)

Cotterrell, R, *Law's Community*, 1995, Oxford: Clarendon

Cotterrell, R, *Emile Durkheim – Law in a Moral Domain*, 1999, Edinburgh: Edinburgh University Press

Cowan, D, 'Banks, swaps, restitution and equity' [1993] LMCLQ 300

Cowan, D, *Housing Law and Policy*, 1999, London: Macmillan

Crane, R, 'After the deserted wife's licence', (1965) 29 *The Conveyancer*, 254

Cranston, R, *Principles of Banking Law*, 1997, Oxford: Oxford University Press

Cretney, S, *Family Law in the Twentieth Century: A History*, 2005, London: Sweet & Maxwell

Cretney, S and Masson, J, *Principles of Family Law*, 1997, London: Sweet & Maxwell

Croft, C, 'Lord Hardwicke's use of precedent in equity' (1989) Aust Bar Rev 29

Cross (1956) 72 LQR 182

Davern, R, 'The problem with bare trusts in contractual contexts' (1997/98) 8 KCLJ 86

Davern, R, 'Common law tracing, profits and the doctrine of relation back' [1997] RLR 92

Davey, N, (1988) 8 LS 92

Davies, N, *The Isles*, 1999, London: Macmillan

Deakin, S and Morris, G, *Labour Law*, 1998, London: Butterworths

Della Fave, R, 'The meek shall not inherit the earth' (1980) 45 American Soc Rev 955

Denning, *The Due Process of Law*, 1980, London: Butterworths

Dewar, J, 'The development of the remedial constructive trust' (1982) 60 Can BR 265

Dewar, J, *Law and the Family*, 2nd edn, 1992, London: Butterworths

Dewar, J, 'The normal chaos of family life' (1998) 61 MLR 467

Dixon, M, 'The never-ending story: co-ownership after *Stack v Dowden*' (2007) 71 Conv 456

Douzinas, C, *The End of Human Rights*, 2000, Oxford: Hart

Durkheim, E, *The Division of Labour* (1894), 1994, London: Macmillan

Duxbury, N, *The Nature and Authority of Precedent*, 2008, Cambridge: Cambridge University Press

Dworkin, R, *Law's Empire*, 1986, Cambridge, Mass: Harvard University Press

Eagleton, T, *The Idea of Culture*, 2000, Oxford: Blackwell

East, R, *Social Security Law*, 1999, London: Macmillan

Eleftheriadis, P, 'The analysis of property rights' (1996) OJLS 31

Elias, G, *Explaining Constructive Trusts*, 1990, Oxford: Clarendon

Elias, N, *The Society of Individuals*, 2001, New York: Continuum

Elliott, S and Mitchell, C, 'Remedies for dishonest assistance' (2004) 67 MLR 16

Emery, C, 'The most hallowed principle – certainty of beneficiaries of trusts and powers of appointment' (1982) 98 LQR 551

Encarta World Dictionary, Hudson (ed), 'Law', 1999, London: Bloomsbury

Enzensberger, HM, *Mediocrity and Delusion, Collected Diversions*, 1992, London: Verso

Esping-Andersen, G, *Three Worlds of Welfare Capitalism*, 1990, Cambridge: Polity

Etzioni, A, *The Spirit of Community*, 1993, New York: Crown Publishers

Evans, J, 'Economic globalisation: the need for a social dimension', in Foden, D and Morris, P (eds), *The Search for Equity*, 1998, London: Lawrence and Wishart

Evans, S, 'Rethinking tracing and the law of restitution' (1999) 115 LQR 469

Ewing, K, 'Democracy or juristocracy in Britain?', in Ewing, K, Gearty, C and Hepple, B (eds), *Human Rights and Labour Law*, 1994, London: Mansell, 147

Ewing, K and Gearty, C, *The Struggle for Civil Liberties*, 2000, Oxford: Oxford University Press

Ferguson, P, 'Constructive trusts: a note of caution' (1993) 109 LQR 114

Finn, P (ed), *Fiduciary Obligations*, 1977, Sydney: LBC

Finn, P (ed), *Essays in Equity*, 1985, Sydney: LBC

Finn, P (ed), *Equity and Commercial Relationships*, 1985, Sydney: LBC (1985:1)

Finn, P (ed), *Essays on Restitution*, 1990, Sydney: LBC

Finn, P, 'Fiduciary law in the modern commercial world', in McKendrick, E (ed), *Commercial Aspects of Trusts and Fiduciary Obligations*, 1992, Oxford: Clarendon

Ford, H, 'Public unit trusts', in Austin, RP and Vann, R (eds), *The Law of Public Company Finance*, 1986, Sydney: LBC, 400

Ford, H and Lee, W, *The Law of Trusts*, 3rd edn, 1996, Sydney: LBC

Foucault, M, *The Archaeology of Knowledge* (1969), 1972, London: Tavistock

Foucault, M, *The History of Sexuality* (1976), 1979, London: Allen Lane

Foucault, M, *Power/Knowledge: Selected Interviews and Other Writings 1972–1977*, Gordon (ed), 1981, London: Routledge

Fox, D, 'Constructive notice and knowing receipt: an economic analysis' [1998] CLJ 391

Freedland, 'Public and private finance' [1998] PL 288

Freud, S, *Beyond The Pleasure Principle*, 1923, Harmondsworth: Penguin

Freud, S, *Civilisation and its Discontents*, 1930, Harmondsworth: Penguin

Fridman, 'The reach of restitution' (1991) 11 LS 304

Fried, C, *Contract as Promise*, 1981, Oxford: Clarendon

Friedmann, D, (1991) 11 LS 304

Friedmann, D and Cohen, N, *The International Encyclopaedia of Comparative Law*, 1991, Lancaster, 24n 177

Fukuyama, F, *The End of History and the Last Man*, 1992, New York: Free Press

Fukuyama, F, *Trust*, 1995, London: Hamish Hamilton

Fuller, L, *The Morality of Law*, 1964, New Haven: Yale University Press

Gardner, S, *Introduction to the Law of Trusts*, 1990, Oxford: Clarendon

Gardner, S, 'Rethinking family property' (1993) 109 LQR 263

Gardner, S, 'Rethinking family property' (1996) 112 LQR 56

Gardner, S and Davidson, K, 'The future of *Stack v Dowden*' (2011) 127 LQR 13

Garton, J, 'The role of the trust mechanism in the rule in *Re Rose*' [2003] Conv 364

Gauthier, AH, *The State and the Family*, 1996, Oxford: Clarendon

Gearty, C and Tomkins, A, 'Constitutional and human rights law', in Hayton, D (ed), *Law's Futures*, 2000, Oxford: Hart

Getzler, J, *Rationalizing Property, Equity and Trusts*, 2003, London: LexisNexis

Geuss, R, *The Idea of a Critical Theory*, 1981, Cambridge: Cambridge University Press

Giddens, A, *Modernity and Self-Identity*, 1991, Cambridge: Polity

Giddens, A, *Beyond Left and Right*, 1994, Cambridge: Polity

Giddens, A, *The Third Way: The Renewal of Social Democracy*, 1998, Cambridge: Polity

Gleeson, S, 'The involuntary launderer: the banker's liability for deposits of the proceeds of crime', in Birks, P (ed), *Laundering and Tracing*, 1995, Oxford: Clarendon, 115

Gleick, J, *Chaos: Making a New Science*, 1988, London: Heinemann

Glover, J, 'Bankruptcy and constructive trusts' (1991) 19 ABLR 98

Goff, R and Jones, G, *The Law of Restitution*, 6th edn, 2002, London: Sweet & Maxwell

Goode, R, (1983) 3 LS 283

Goode, R, 'Ownership and obligation in commercial transactions' (1987) 103 LQR 433

Goode, R, 'Property and unjust enrichment', in Burrows, A (ed), *Essays on Restitution*, 1991, Oxford: Clarendon, Chapter 9

Goode, R, 'Charges over book debts: a missed opportunity' (1994) 110 LQR 592

Goode, R, *Principles of Corporate Insolvency Law*, 2nd edn, 1997, London: Sweet & Maxwell (1997:1)

Goode, R, *Commercial Law*, 2nd edn, 1997, Harmondsworth: Penguin (1997:2)

Goode, R, *Commercial Law in the Next Millennium – The Hamlyn Lectures 1998*, 1998, London: Sweet & Maxwell

Goodrich, P, *The Language of Law*, 1990, London: Weidenfeld & Nicholson

Goulding, S, 'Equity and the money-launderers' [1992] Conv 367

Grantham, R, 'Doctrinal bases for the recognition of proprietary rights' (1996) OJLS 561 (1996:1)

Grantham, R, 'Restitution, property and ignorance – a reply to Mr Swadling' [1996] LMCLQ 463 (1996:2)

Grantham, R and Rickett, C, 'Trust money as an unjust enrichment: a misconception' [1988] LMCLQ 514

Grantham, R and Rickett, C, 'On the subsidiarity of unjust enrichment' (2001) 117 LQR 273

Gravells, N, 'Public purpose trusts' (1977) 40 MLR 397

Gray, K, 'Equitable property' [1994] CLP 157

Gray, K and Gray, F, *Elements of Land Law*, 3rd edn, 2001, London: Butterworths

Gray, K and Gray, F, *Elements of Land Law*, 6th edn, 2009, London: Butterworths

Grbich, Y, 'Baden: awakening the conceptually moribund trust' (1974) 37 MLR 643

Green, B, 'The dissolution of unincorporated non-profit associations' (1980) 43 MLR 626

Green, B, '*Grey, Oughtred* and *Vandervell* – a contextual reappraisal' (1984) 47 MLR 385

Greer, S and White, A, *Abolishing the Diplock Courts*, 1986, London: Cobden Trust

Griffiths, G, 'Missed or misguided? Formality, land contracts and the statute of frauds', in Hudson, AS (ed), *New Perspectives on Property Law, Obligations and Restitution*, 2003, London: Cavendish Publishing

Grosz, S, Beatson, J, Duffy, P, Gearty, C et al, *Human Rights*, 2000, London: Sweet & Maxwell

Grubb, A, 'Powers, trusts and classes of objects' [1982] Conv 432

Gummow J, 'Unjust enrichment, restitution and proprietary remedies', in Finn, PD (ed), *Essays on Restitution*, 1990, Sydney: LBC, Chapter 3

Habermas, J, *Theory of Communicative Action* (1981), 1984, Boston: Beacon

Habermas, J, *Legitimation Crisis* (1973), 1988, Cambridge: Polity

Habermas, J, 'The rectifying revolution' (1990) 183 New Left Rev 3

Habermas, J, *Beyond Facts and Norms* (1992), 1996, Cambridge: Polity

Hackney, J, *Understanding Equity and Trusts*, 1987, London: Fontana

Hackney, J, 'A trace of the old philosophy', in Birks, P (ed), *The Classification of Obligations*, 1997, Oxford: Clarendon

Ham, R, 'Trustees' liability' (1995) 9 Trusts Law International 21

Hammond (1990) 106 LQR 207

Hanbury, HG, *Essays in Equity*, 1934, Oxford: Clarendon

Hanbury, HG, *Modern Equity*, 1st edn, 1935, London: Stevens

Hanbury, HG and Martin, J, *Modern Equity*, 13th edn, 1993, London: Sweet & Maxwell

Hardt, M and Negri, A, *Empire*, 2000, Cambridge: Harvard University Press

Hardy Ivamy, ER, *Underhill's Principles of the Law of Partnership*, 12th edn, 1986, London: Butterworths

Harpum, C, 'The stranger as constructive trustee' (1986) 102 LQR 114

Harpum, C, 'Overreaching, trustee's powers, and the reform of the 1925 legislation' (1990) 49 CLJ 277

Harpum, C, [1991] CLJ 409

Harpum, C, 'The basis of equitable liability' in Birks, P (ed), *The Frontiers of Liability, Vol 1*, 1994, Oxford: Oxford University Press, 9

Harpum, C, 'Knowing assistance and knowing receipt: the basis for equitable liability', in Birks, P (ed), *The Frontiers of Liability*, 1994, Oxford: Clarendon (1994:1)

Harpum, C, 'Accessory liability for procuring or assisting a breach of trust' (1995) 111 LQR 545

Harpum, C, *Megarry and Wade's Law of Real Property*, 6th edn, 2000, London: Sweet & Maxwell

Harris, J, 'Trust, power, or duty' (1971) 87 LQR 31

Harris, J, (1975) 38 MLR 557

Harris, J, *Variation of Trusts*, 1975, London: Sweet & Maxwell (1975:1)

Harris, J, *Property and Justice*, 1996, Oxford: Oxford University Press

Harris, T, *The Hague Trusts Convention*, 2002, Oxford: Hart

Hayes, M and Williams, C, *Family Law: Principles, Policy and Practice*, 1996, London: Butterworths

Hayton, D, 'Constructive trusts' (1985) 27 Malaya L Rev 313

Hayton, D, 'Remedial constructive trusts of homes; an overseas view' [1988] Conv 259

Hayton, D, 'Constructive trusts: is the remedying of unjust enrichment a satisfactory approach?', in Youdan (ed), *Equity, Fiduciaries and Trusts*, 1989, Zurich: Carswell

Hayton, D, 'Equitable rights of cohabitees' [1990] Conv 370 (1990:1)

Hayton, D, 'Investment management problems' (1990) 106 LQR 89 (1990:2)

Hayton, D, 'Equitable rights of cohabitees', in Goldstein (ed), *Equity and Contemporary Legal Developments*, 1992, Jerusalem

Hayton, D, 'Constructive trusts: a bold approach' [1993] LQR 485

Hayton, D, 'Equity's identification rules', in Birks, P (ed), *Laundering and Tracing*, 1995, Oxford: Clarendon, 6–19 (1995:2)

Hayton, D, 'The irreducible core content of trusteeship', in Oakley, A (ed), *Trends in Contemporary Trust Law*, 1996, Oxford: Oxford University Press, 47

Hayton, D, 'Fiduciaries in context', in Birks, P (ed), *Privacy and Loyalty*, 1997, Oxford: Clarendon

Hayton, D (ed), *Modern International Developments in Trust Law*, 1999, The Hague: Kluwer

Hayton, D, 'Developing the obligation characteristic of the trust' (2001) 117 LQR 96

Hayton, D (ed), *Extending the Boundaries of Trusts and Similar Ring-fenced Funds*, 2002, Hague: Kluwer Law International

Hayton, D, Matthews, P and Mitchell, C, *Underhill and Hayton's Law of Trusts and Trustees*, 18th edn, 2010, London: Butterworths

Hayton, D and Cooke, E, 'Land law and trusts', in Hayton, D (ed), *Law's Futures*, 2000, Oxford: Hart, 433

Hayton, D and Marshall, *Cases and Commentary on the Law of Trusts and Equitable Obligations*, 11th edn, 2001, London: Sweet & Maxwell

Hayton, D, Kortmann, S and Verhagen, H (eds), *Principles of European Trusts Law*, 1999, The Hague: Kluwer

Hedley, S, 'Unjust enrichment as the basis of restitution – an overworked concept' (1985) 5 LS 56

Hedley, S, 'The taxonomy of restitution', in Hudson, AS (ed), *New Perspectives on Property Law, Obligations and Restitution*, 2003, London: Cavendish Publishing

Hegel, GWF, *Philosophy of Right* (1821), trans Knox, 1952, Oxford: Oxford University Press

Hicks, A, 'The Trustee Act 2000 and the modern meaning of "investment" ' (2001) 15 *Trusts Law International* 203

Hobsbawm, E, *The Age of Capital: 1848–1875*, 1975, London: Weidenfeld & Nicolson

Hodge, D, 'Secret trusts: the fraud theory revisited' [1980] Conv 341

Hoggett, B, Pearl, D, Cooke, E and Bates, P, *The Family, Law and Society*, 4th edn, 1996, London: Butterworths

Hohfeld, WN, *Fundamental Legal Conceptions as Applied in Judicial Reasoning*, Cook (ed), 1919, London: Yale University Press

Holdsworth, Sir W, *A History of English Law*, vol iv, 1945, London: Sweet & Maxwell

Holland (1945) 9 CLJ 17

Honoré, A, 'Trusts: the inessentials', in Getzler, J (ed), *Rationalizing Property, Equity and Trusts*, 2003, London: LexisNexis

Hopkins, J, 'Certain uncertainties of trusts and powers' [1971] CLJ 68

Houellebecq, M, *Atomised*, 2001, London: Vintage; 1999, Paris: Flammarion

Howell, J, 'Land and human rights' [1999] Conv 287

Hudson, AH, 'Abandonment', in Palmer, N and McKendrick, E (eds), *Interest in Goods*, 1993, London: Lloyd's

Hudson, AS, *The Law on Homelessness*, 1997, London: Sweet & Maxwell (1997:1)

Hudson, AS, 'Proprietary rights in financial transactions' (1997) *Amicus Curiae*, 2 November, 27 (1997:2)

Hudson, AS, 'Justice in a reasonable period' (1997–98) KCLJ 8, 133–36

Hudson, AS, 'Void interest swaps: restitution not reinforcement' (1998) 19(6) Company Lawyer 181–82 (1998:2)

Hudson, AS, *Swaps, Restitution and Trusts*, 1999, London: Sweet & Maxwell (1999:1)

Hudson, AS, *Towards a Just Society: Law, Labour and Legal Aid*, 1999, London: Pinter (1999:2)

Hudson, AS, 'Money as property in financial transactions' (1999) 14:06 JIBL, 170–77 (1999:3)

Hudson, AS, 'The regulatory aspect of private law in financial transactions', in Hudson, AS (ed), *Modern Financial Techniques, Derivatives and Law*, 1999, London: Kluwer (1999:4)

Hudson, AS, 'Assessing mistake of law in derivatives transactions' [1999] 14:03 JIBL 1–5 (1999:5)

Hudson, AS, 'Seller liability in credit derivatives', in Hudson, AS (ed), *Credit Derivatives*, 1999, London: Sweet & Maxwell (1999:6)

Hudson, AS, 'Termination and restitution of credit derivatives', in Hudson, AS (ed), *Credit Derivatives*, 1999, London: Sweet & Maxwell (1999:7)

Hudson, AS, *The Law on Investment Entities*, 2000, London: Sweet & Maxwell (2000:1)

Hudson, AS, 'Law of finance', in Birks, P (ed), *Lessons from the Swaps Cases*, 2000, London: Mansfield (2000:2)

Hudson, AS, 'The unbearable lightness of property', in Hudson, AS (ed), *New Perspectives on Property Law, Obligations and Restitution*, 2004, London: Cavendish Publishing, 1 (2004:1)

Hudson, AS, 'Equity, individualisation and social justice', in Hudson, AS (ed), *New Perspectives on Property Law, Human Rights and the Home*, 2004, London: Cavendish Publishing, 1 (2004:2)

Hudson, AS, 'Rapporteur: between morality and formalism in property, obligations and restitution', in Hudson, AS (ed), *New Perspectives on Property Law, Obligations and Restitution*, 2004, London: Cavendish Publishing (2004:3)

Hudson, AS, 'Rapporteur: differentiation in property and obligations', in Hudson, AS (ed), *New Perspectives on Property Law, Human Rights and the Home*, 2004, London: Cavendish Publishing (2004:4)

Hudson, AS (ed), *New Perspectives on Property Law, Obligations and Restitution*, 2004, London: Cavendish Publishing (2004:5)

Hudson, AS (ed), *New Perspectives on Property Law, Human Rights and the Home*, 2004, London: Cavendish Publishing (2004:6)

Hudson, AS, with Thomas, GW, *The Law of Trusts*, 2004, Oxford: Oxford University Press

Hudson, AS, 'The liability of trusts service providers in international finance law', in Glasson J and Thomas GW (eds), *The International Trust*, 2006, Bristol: Jordans (2006:2)

Hudson, AS, 'The regulation of trustees', in Dixon and Griffiths (eds), *Developments in Contemporary Property Law*, 2007, Oxford: Oxford University Press

Hudson AS, *Securities Law*, 2008, London: Sweet & Maxwell

Hudson AS, *The Law of Finance*, 2009, London: Sweet & Maxwell

Hudson, AS, with Thomas, GW, *The Law of Trusts*, 2nd edn, 2010, Oxford: Oxford University Press

Hudson, AS, *Understanding Company Law*, 1st edn, 2011, London: Routledge

Hudson, AS, 'Trusts and Finance Law', in Hayton D (ed), *The International Trust*, 3rd edn, 2012, Bristol: Jordans, Chapter 12

Hudson, AS, 'Asset Protection Trusts', in Hayton D (ed), *The International Trust*, 3rd edn, 2012, Bristol: Jordans, Chapter 6

Hudson, AS, *The Law on Financial Derivatives*, 5th edn, 2012, London: Sweet & Maxwell

Hudson, AS, *Understanding Equity & Trusts*, 4th edn, 2012, Oxford: Routledge

Hughes, D and Lowe, S, *Social Housing Law and Policy*, 1995, London: Butterworths

Hughes, D and Lowe, S, *Public Sector Housing Law*, 2000, London: Butterworths

Hunt, A, 'A socialist interest in law' (1992) 192 New Left Rev 105

Hunt, M, 'The "horizontal effect" of the Human Rights Act' [1998] Public Law 423

Ibbetson, D, *A Historical Introduction to the Law of Obligations*, 1999, Oxford: Oxford University Press

Jackson, J and Doran, S, *Judge without Jury: Diplock Trials in the Adversary System*, 1995, Oxford: Clarendon

Jaffey, P, 'Restitutionary damages and disgorgement' [1995] RLR 30

Jaffey, P, [1996] RLR 92

Jaffey, P, *The Nature and Scope of Restitution*, 2000, Oxford: Hart

Jameson, F, *Postmodernism – or the Cultural Logic of Late Capitalism*, 1991, London: Verso

Jennings, *Jarman on Wills*, 8th edn, 1951, London: Sweet & Maxwell

Jones, G, (1968) 84 LQR 474

Jones, G, 'Unjust enrichment and the fiduciary's duty of loyalty' (1968) 84 LQR 472

Jones, G, 'Remedies for the recovery of money paid by mistake' (1980) 39 CLJ 275

Jones, G, *Restitution in Public and Private Law*, 1991, London: Sweet & Maxwell

Jones, G, [1996] CLJ 432

Jung, C, 'Structure of the psyche' (1927), in Storr (ed), *Essential Jung*, 1998, London: Fontana

Kant, I, *The Metaphysics of Morals*, 1996 (1758), Cambridge: Cambridge University Press

Keeton, R, 'Conditional fault in the law of torts' (1959) 72 Harv L Rev 401

Kennedy, I, 'The fiduciary relationship – doctors and patients', in Birks, P (ed), *Wrongs and Remedies in the 21st Century*, 1996, Oxford: Clarendon

Klein, N, *No Logo*, 2000, London: Flamingo

Langbein, J, 'The new American trust-investment Act' (1994) 8 Trusts Law International 123

Langbein, J, 'The contractarian basis of the law of trusts' (1995) 105 Yale LJ 625

Langbein, J and Posner, R, 'Social investing and the law of trusts' (1980) 79 Michigan Law Review 72

Larkin, P, *High Windows*, 1974, London: Faber & Faber

Law Commission, *Fiduciary Duties and Regulatory Rules*, 1992, 124

Law Commission, *Restitution: Mistakes of Law and Ultra Vires Public Authority Receipts and Payments*, Law Com No 227, 1994

Law Commission, *Fiduciary Duties and Regulatory Rules*, Law Com No 236, 1995

Law Commission, *Sharing Homes*, Law Com No 278, 2002

Law Commission, *Cohabitation: The Financial Consequences of Relationship Breakdown*, Law Com No 307, 2007

Law Commission, *Illegality Defence*, Law Com Consultation Paper No 189, 2009

Le Grand, J, *A Strategy for Equality*, 1982, London: George Allen & Unwin

Le Grand, J, *Equity and Choice*, 1991, London: HarperCollins

Lewin, R, *Complexity*, 1993, London: Phoenix

Lewin, T, *A Practical Treatise on the Law of Trusts and Trustees*, 1837, London: Maxwell

Leyden, W von, *Aristotle on Equality and Justice: His Political Argument*, 1985, London: Macmillan

Lim, H, 'The waqf in trust', in Scott-Hunt, S and Lim, H (eds), *Feminist Perspectives on Equity and Trusts*, 2001, London: Cavendish Publishing.

Litman, MM, 'The emergence of unjust enrichment as a cause of action and the remedy of constructive trust' (1988) 26 Alberta LR 407

Lomnicka, E, *Modern Banking Law*, 2nd edn, 1994, Oxford: Oxford University Press

Loughlan, P, 'The historical role of equitable jurisdiction', in Parkinson, P (ed), *The Principles of Equity*, 2nd edn, 2003, Sydney: LBC

Lowe, N and Douglas, G, *Bromley's Family Law*, 8th edn, 1998, London: Butterworths

Lowry, J and Edmunds, R, 'Excuses', in Birks, P and Pretto, A (eds), *Breach of Trust*, 2002, Oxford: Hart, 269

Lupoi, M, *Trusts: A Comparative Study*, 2000, Cambridge: Cambridge University Press

McCormack, G, [1989] LMCLQ 198

McCormack, G, 'Assisting in a breach of trust: principles of accessory liability' (1995) TLI 102 (1995:1)

McCormack, G, *Reservation of Title*, 2nd edn, 1995, London: Sweet & Maxwell (1995:2)

McCormack, G, 'Mistaken payment and proprietary claims' [1996] Conv 86 (1996:1)

McCormack, G, 'The eye of equity: identification principles and equitable tracing' [1996] JBL 225 (1996:2)

McCormack, G, 'Fiduciary obligations in a changing commercial climate', in Rider, B and Andenas, M (eds), *Developments in European Community Law*, 1996, London: Kluwer, Vol 1, 33 (1996:3)

McCormack, G, (1998) 19(2) The Company Lawyer 39

McGhee, J, *Snell's Equity*, 31st edn, 2005, London: Sweet & Maxwell

McGregor, H, 'Restitutionary damages', in Birks, P (ed), *Wrongs and Remedies in the 21st Century*, 1996, Oxford: Clarendon, 203

McKendrick, E, 'Tracing misdirected funds' [1991] LMCLQ 378

McKendrick, E, *Commercial Aspects of Trusts and Fiduciary Obligations*, 1992, Oxford: Clarendon

McKendrick, E, 'Local authorities and swaps: undermining the market?', in Cranston, R (ed), *Making Commercial Law: Essays in Honour of Roy Goode*, 1997, Oxford: Clarendon

Maitland, FW, *Equity – A Course of Lectures*, 2nd edn, 1936, Cambridge: Cambridge University Press

Maloney, W, Smith, G and Stoker, G, 'Social capital and human capital revisited', in Baron, S, Field, J and Schuller, T (eds), *Social Capital*, 2000, Oxford: Oxford University Press, 212

Mann, F, 'On interest, compound interest and damages' (1985) 101 LQR 30

Mann, F, *The Legal Aspect of Money*, 5th edn, 1992, Oxford: Oxford University Press

Martin, J, 'Tracing, fraud and *ultra vires*' [1993] Conv 370

Martin, J, 'Certainty of subject matter: a defence of *Hunter v Moss*' [1996] Conv 223

Martin, J, *Hanbury and Martin, Modern Equity*, 15th edn, 1997, London: Sweet & Maxwell

Marx, K and Engels, F, *Critique of the Gotha Programme*, 1959, Harmondsworth: Penguin

Mason, A, 'Equity's role in the twentieth century' (1997/98) 8 KCLJ 1

Matthews, P, 'The true basis of the half-secret trust?' [1979] Conv 360

Matthews, P, 'The efficacy of trustee exemption clauses in English law' [1989] Conv 42

Matthews, P, 'A problem in the construction of gifts to unincorporated associations' [1995] Conv 302 (1995:1)

Matthews, P, 'The legal and moral limits of common law tracing' in Birks, P (ed) *Laundering and Tracing*, 1995, Oxford: Clarendon (1995:2)

Matthews, P, 'The new trust: obligations without rights?' in Oakley, A (ed), *Trends in Contemporary Trusts Law*, 1996, Oxford: Oxford University Press, 1

Matthews, P, 'From obligation to property, and back again? The future of the noncharitable purpose trust', in Hayton, D (ed), *Extending the Boundaries of Trusts and Similar Ring-fenced Funds*, 2002, Hague: Kluwer Law International

Maudsley, R, 'Proprietary remedies for the recovery of money' (1959) 75 LQR 234

Maurice, 'The office of custodian trustee' (1960) 24 Conv 196

Meagher, R and Gummow, WMC, *Equity: Doctrines and Remedies*, 3rd edn, 1992, Sydney: Butterworths

Meagher, R, Heydon, D and Leeming, M, *Meagher, Gummow and Lehane's Equity: Doctrines and Remedies*, 4th edn, 2002, Sydney: Butterworths

Mee, J, [1992] Conv 202

Mee, J, *The Property Rights of Cohabitees*, 1999, Oxford: Hart

Miller, D, *Social Justice*, 1976, Oxford: Oxford University Press

Millett, P, 'The *Quistclose* trust: who can enforce it?' (1985) 101 LQR 269

Millett, P, 'Tracing the proceeds of fraud' (1991) 107 LQR 71, 85

Millett, P, 'Bribes and secret commissions' [1993] RLR 7

Millett, P, (1995) 7 Trusts Law International 35

Millett, P, 'Equity's place in the law of commerce; restitution and constructive trusts' (1998) 114 LQR 214

Millett, P, 'Restitution: taking stock', delivering the Society of Advanced Legal Studies Lecture, Institute of Advanced Legal Studies, London, 23 July 1998 (1998:1)

Millett, P, 'Restitution and constructive trusts' (1998) 114 LQR 399 (1998:2)

Mitchell, C, *The Law of Subrogation*, 1994, Oxford: Oxford University Press

Mitchell, C, 'Apportioning liability for trust losses', in Birks, P and Rose (eds), *Restitution and Equity, Vol 1*, 2000, Oxford: Mansfield, 211

Mitchell, C, 'Assistance', in Birks, P and Pretto, A (eds), *Breach of Trust*, 2002, Oxford: Hart

Moffat, *Trusts Law*, 3rd edn, 1999, London: Butterworths

Monbiot, G, *The Captive State: Corporate Takeover of Britain*, 2000, London: Macmillan

Moriarty, 'Tracing, mixing and laundering', in Birks, P (ed), *Laundering and Tracing*, 1995, Oxford: Clarendon, 73

Morrison, W, *Jurisprudence – From the Greeks to Postmodernism*, 1995, London: Cavendish Publishing

Morse, G, *Partnership Law*, 4th edn, 1998, London: Blackstone

Morse, G *et al*, *Palmer's Company Law*, 26th edn, successive updates, London: Sweet & Maxwell

Mowbray, J *et al*, *Lewin on Trusts*, 32nd edn, 2010, London: Sweet & Maxwell

Mulheron, R, *The Modern Cy-Près Doctrine*, 2006, London: UCL Press

Murphy, T and Roberts, S, *Understanding Property Law*, 3rd edn, 1998, London: Sweet & Maxwell

Lord Nicholls, 'Trustees and their broader community: where duty, morality and ethics converge' (1995) 9 Trusts Law International 71

Lord Nicholls, 'Knowing receipt: the need for a new landmark', in Cornish, W (ed), *Restitution: Past, Present and Future*, 1998, Oxford: Hart

Nolan, R, 'How knowing is knowing receipt?' [2000] CLJ 421

Nolan, R, *'Vandervell v IRC*: a case of overreaching' [2002] CLJ 169

Nolan, R, 'Property in a fund' (2004) 120 LQR 108

Oakley, A, 'The pre-requisites of an equitable tracing claim' (1975) 28 CLP 64

Oakley, A, [1995] CLJ 377

Oakley, A, *Constructive Trusts*, 3rd edn, 1997, London: Sweet & Maxwell

Oakley, A, Parker and Mellow, *The Modern Law of Trusts*, 7th edn, 1998, London: Sweet & Maxwell

O'Donovan, K, *Family Law Matters*, 1993, London: Pluto

Oliver, P, 'New model trusts' (1997/98) 8 KCLJ 147

O'Sullivan, J, 'Undue influence and misrepresentation after *O'Brien*', in Rose, F (ed), *Restitution and Banking Law*, 1998, London: Mansfield

Paciocco, DM, 'The remedial constructive trust: a principled basis for priorities over creditors' (1989) 68 Can BR 315

Panesar, S, *General Principles of Property Law*, 2001, London: Longman

Parkinson, P, 'Reconceptualising the express trust' [2002] CLJ 657

Pawlowski, M, *The Doctrine of Proprietary Estoppel*, 1996, London: Sweet & Maxwell

Pawlowski, M, 'Equitable wrongs: common law damages or equitable compensation?' (2000) 6(9) T & T 20

Payne, J, *'Quistclose* and resulting trusts', in Birks, P and Rose, F (eds), *Resulting Trusts and Equitable Compensation*, 2000, Oxford, Mansfield

Pearce, 'A tracing paper' (1976) 40 Conv 277

Penner, J, *The Idea of Property in Law*, 1997, Oxford: Oxford University Press

Penner, J, 'Exemptions', in Birks, P and Pretto, A (eds), *Breach of Trust*, 2002, Oxford: Hart, 241

Penner, J, *The Law of Trusts*, 4th edn, 2004, London: Butterworths

Penner, J, 'Lord Millett's analysis', in Swadling, W (ed), *Quistclose Trusts*, 2004, Oxford: Hart, 41

Pennington, RR, *The Law of the Investment Market*, 1990, Oxford: Blackwell

Pennington, RR, *Company Law*, 8th edn, 2001, London: Butterworths

Pettit, P, *Equity and Trusts*, 9th edn, 2001, London: Butterworths

Phillipson, G, 'The Human Rights Act, "horizontal effect" and the common law: a bang or a whimper?' (1999) 62 MLR 824

Picarda, H, *The Law and Practice Relating to Charities*, 4th edn, 2007, London: Butterworths

Piska, N, 'Intention, fairness and the presumption of resulting trust after *Stack v Dowden*' (2008) 71 MLR 120

Pollard, D, *'Schmidt v Rosewood*' (2003) 17 Trusts Law International 90

Pollock, Sir F and Maitland, FW, *History of English Law*, 1895, vol ii

Pound, R, 'The progress of law' (1920) 33 Harv L Rev 420

Probert, R, 'Family law and property law: competing spheres in the regulation of the family home', in Hudson, AS (ed), *New Perspectives on Property Law, Human Rights and the Home*, 2003, London: Cavendish Publishing, 37

Probert, R, 'Equality in the family home?' (2007) *Feminist Legal Studies*, 341

Rajani, S, 'Equitable assistance in the search for security', in Rajak, H (ed), *Insolvency Law: Theory and Practice*, 1993, London: Butterworths, Chapter 2

Rawls, J, *Theory of Justice*, 1971, Oxford: Oxford University Press

Rawls, J, 'Justice as fairness: political not metaphysical' (1985) 14 Philosophy & Public Affairs 223

Rayden, W and Jackson, J, *Divorce and Family Matters*, 1999, London: Butterworths, supplement on Human Rights Act 1998

Raz, J, *The Morality of Freedom*, 1986, Oxford: Clarendon

Riches (1997) PCB 5

Rickett, C, (1979) 38 CLJ 260

Rickett, C, (1991) 107 LQR 608

Rickett, C, 'The remedial constructive trust in Canadian restitution law' [1991] Conv 125

Rickett, C, 'Compensating for loss in equity', in Birks, P and Rose, F (eds), *Restitution and Equity, Vol 1*, 2000, Oxford: Mansfield, 172

Rickett, C, 'Completely constituting an *inter vivos* trust: property rules?' [2001] Conv 515

Rickett, C and Grantham, R, 'Resulting trusts – a rather limited doctrine', in Birks, P and Rose, F (eds), *Restitution and Equity, Vol 1*, 2000, Oxford: Mansfield, 39

Rider, B, 'The fiduciary and the frying pan' [1978] Conv 114

Rider, B, Abrams, N and Ashe, M, *Guide to Financial Services Regulation*, 3rd edn, 1997, Oxford: CCH

Robertson, 'Land and post-apartheid South Africa', in Bright, S and Dewar, J (eds), *Land Law: Themes and Perspectives*, 1998, Oxford: Oxford University Press, 311

Rose, F, 'Gratuitous transfers and illegal purposes' (1996) 112 LQR 386

Rose, F (ed), *Restitution and Banking Law*, 1998, Oxford: Mansfield

Rotherham, C, *Proprietary Remedies in Context*, 2002, Oxford: Hart

Rotherham, C, 'Property and unjust enrichment: a misunderstood relationship', in Hudson, AS (ed), *New Perspectives on Property Law, Obligations and Restitution*, 2003, London: Cavendish Publishing

Rutherford [1996] Conv 260

Scott, AW and Fratcher, WF, *The Law of Trusts*, 3rd edn, 1967, Boston: Little, Brown

Scott-Hunt, S and Lim, H (eds), *Feminist Perspectives on Equity and Trusts*, 2001, London: Cavendish

Sennett, R, *The Corrosion of Character: the Personal Consequences of Work in the New Capitalism*, 1998, New York: WW Norton

Sealy, L, 'Fiduciary relationships' [1962] CLJ 69

Shapiro, J, *Contested Will: Who Wrote Shakespeare*, 2010, Faber

Sherrin, CH, Barlow, RFD and Wallington, RA, *Williams's Law Relating to Wills*, 6th edn, 1987, London: Butterworths, Vol 1, 326

Sherwin, E, 'Constructive trusts in bankruptcy' [1989] University of Illinois L Rev 297

Shipwright, A and Keeling, E, *Revenue Law*, 1998, London: Blackstone

Sin, KF, *The Legal Nature of the Unit Trust*, 1997, Oxford: Clarendon (1997:1)

Sin, KF, 'Enforcing the unit trust deed among unitholders' (1997) 15 ACSR 292 (1997:2)

Smith, J, 'Foreword' to *Strategies for National Renewal*, 1994, London: Vintage

Smith, J, 'Preface' to *Strategies for Renewal*, 1994, London: Vintage

Smith, L, 'Presents, principles and trusts principles' [1982] Conv 352

Smith, L, 'Tracing into the payment of a debt' [1995] CLJ 290 (1995:1)

Smith, L, 'Tracing in *Taylor v Plumer*: equity in the Court of King's Bench' [1995] LMCLQ 240 (1995:2)

Smith, L, *The Law of Tracing*, 1997, Oxford: Clarendon

Smith, L, 'Tracing and electronic funds transfer', in Rose, F (ed), *Restitution and Banking Law*, 1998, Oxford: Mansfield, 120

Smith, L, 'Constructive trusts and constructive trustees' [1999] CLJ 294

Smith, L, 'Unjust enrichment, property, and the structure of trusts' (2000) 116 LQR 412

Smith, R, 'Oral contracts for the sale of land' [2000] 116 LQR 11

Snaith, I, *The Law on Co-operatives*, 1984, London: Waterlow

Snaith, I, 'Mutuals and co-operatives: property, obligations, business and dedicated assets', in Hudson, AS (ed), *New Perspectives on Property Law, Obligations and Restitution*, 2003, London: Cavendish Publishing, 345

Snell, *Equity*, 1868, 1st edn

Sparkes, P, *A New Land Law*, 1999, Oxford: Hart

Spry, I, *Equitable Remedies*, 8th edn, 2010, Sydney: LBC

Spry, I, *The Principles of Equitable Remedies*, 8th edn, 2010, London: Sweet & Maxwell

Stephenson, 'Co-trustees or several trustees?' (1942) 16 Temple ULQ 249

Stevens, 'Election between alternative remedies' [1996] RLR 117

Stewart, A, *Rethinking Housing Law*, 1996, London: Sweet & Maxwell

Story, J, *Commentaries on Equity Jurisprudence*, 1839, Boston: Little and Brown

Story, J, *Commentaries on Equity Jurisprudence*, 13th edn, ed. Bigelow, 1886, Little and Brown

Swadling, W, [1994] All ER Rev 259 (1994:1)

Swadling, W, [1994] RLR 195 (1994:2)

Swadling, W, 'A new role for resulting trusts?' (1996) 16 LS 110

Swadling, W, 'Property and conscience' (1998) 12 Trusts Law International 228

Swadling, W, 'A hard look at *Hodgson v Marks*', in Birks, P and Rose, F (eds), *Resulting Trusts and Equitable Compensation*, 2000, Oxford: Mansfield, 61

Swadling, W, *Quistclose Trusts*, 2004, Oxford: Hart

Swadling, W, 'The common intention constructive trust in the House of Lords: an opportunity missed' (2007) 123 LQR 511

Sypnowich, C, *The Concept of Socialist Law*, 1990, Oxford: Clarendon

Tee, L, 'A merry-go-round for the millennium' [2000] CLJ 23

Tennekoon, R, *The Law and Regulation of International Finance*, 1991, London: Butterworths

Tennekoon, R, *Legal Aspects of International Finance*, 1992, London: Butterworths

Tettenborn, A, [1980] CLJ 272

Tettenborn, A, *The Law of Restitution in England and Ireland*, 2nd edn, 1997, London: Cavendish Publishing

Tettenborn, A, 'Misnomer: a response', in Cornish, W, Nolan, R, O'Sullivan, J and Virgo, G (eds), *Restitution, Present and Future: Essays in Honour of Gareth Jones*, 1998, Oxford: Hart, 31

Teubner, G, *Law as an Autopoietic System*, 1994, Oxford: Blackwell

Thomas, G, 'James I, equity and Lord Keeper John Williams' (1976) English Historical Rev 506

Thomas, G, *Taxation and Trusts*, 1981, London: Sweet & Maxwell

Thomas, G, *Powers*, 1998, London: Sweet & Maxwell

Thomas, G, *Powers*, 2nd edn, 2012, Oxford University Press

Thomas, GW and Hudson, AS, *The Law of Trusts*, 2nd edn, 2010, Oxford: Oxford University Press

Thompson, EP, *The Making of the English Working Class*, 1963, London: Victor Gollancz; references are to the Penguin 1968 edition

Thompson, M, 'Constructive trusts, estoppel and the family home' [2004] Conv 1

Tiley, J, *Revenue Law*, 4th edn, 2001, Oxford: Hart

Townsend, P, *Poverty in the United Kingdom*, 1979, Harmondsworth: Penguin

Tudor, OD, *Tudor on Charities*, 9th edn, 2003, London: Sweet & Maxwell

Underhill, A, *A Practical and Concise Manual of the Law Relating to Private Trusts and Trustees*, 3rd edn, 1889, London: Butterworths

Underhill, A and Hayton, D, *The Law of Trusts and Trustees*, 16th edn, 2002, London: Butterworths

Van Parijs, P, *Real Freedom For All*, 1995, Oxford: Oxford University Press

Venables, R, *Non-Resident Trusts*, 5th edn, 1999, London: Key Haven

Venables, R, *The Taxation of Trust Post Finance Act 2006*, 2006, Oxford: Key Haven Publications

Vernon, S, *Social Work and the Law*, 1998, London: Butterworths

Virgo, G, 'Undue influence and misrepresentation after *O'Brien*', in Rose, F (ed), *Restitution and Banking Law*, 1998, London: Mansfield, 70

Virgo, G, *Principles of the Law of Restitution*, 1999, Oxford: Oxford University Press

Virgo, G, 'Vindicating vindication: *Foskett v McKeown* reviewed', in Hudson, AS (ed), *New Perspectives on Property Law, Obligations and Restitution*, 2003, London: Cavendish Publishing

Virilio, P, *Vitesse et politique: essai de dromologie*, 1977, Paris: Galilee

Virilio, P, *Speed and politics*, 1986, New York: Semiotext(e)

Virilio, P, *La bombe informatique*, 1998, Paris: Galilee

Virilio, P, *Information Bomb*, 2000, Verso: London

Walsh, 'Unit trusts', in Grbich, YFR, Munn, GD and Reicher, H, *Modern Trusts and Taxation*, 1978, Melbourne: Butterworths Australia, 36

Warburton, J, [1987] Conv 217

Waters, D, *The Constructive Trust*, 1964, London: Athlone

Waters, D, 'Reaching for the sky – taking trusts laws to the limit, in Hayton, D (ed), *Extending the Boundaries of Trusts and Similar Ring-fenced Funds*, 2002, Hague: Kluwer Law International, 59

Watson, J, *Psychology from the Standpoint of the Behaviourist*, (1919), 1994, London: Routledge

Watts, P, (1996) 112 LQR 219

Weil, S, 'Human Personality', reproduced in Miles, S (ed), *Simone Weil – An Anthology*, 2005, London: Penguin, 69 (originally published by Virago Press, 1985)

Wilken, S and Villiers, T, *Waiver, Variation and Estoppel*, 1999, London: John Wiley

Wong, S, 'Constructive trusts over the family home: lessons to be learned from other Commonwealth jurisdictions' (1998) 18 LS 369

Wong, S, 'When trust(s) is not enough: an argument for the use of unjust enrichment for home-sharers' (1999) 7(1) FLS 47

Wong, S, 'Rethinking *Rosset* from a human rights perspective', in Hudson, AS (ed), *New Perspectives on Property Law, Human Rights and the Home*, 2003, London: Cavendish Publishing, 79

Wood, P, *Law and Practice of International Finance*, 1980, 1995, London: Sweet & Maxwell

Woodward, L, *The Age of Reform: England 1815–1870*, 2nd edn, 1962, Oxford: Oxford University Press

Wooldridge [1987] JBL 329

Worthington, S, *Proprietary Interests in Commercial Transactions*, 1996, Oxford: Clarendon

Worthington, S, 'Reconsidering disgorgement for wrongs' (1999) 62 MLR 218 (1999:1)

Worthington, S, 'Fiduciaries: when is self-denial obligatory?' [1999] 58 CLJ 500 (1999:2)

Youdan, T, 'Formalities for trusts of land, and the doctrine in *Rochefoucauld v Boustead*' [1984] 43 CLJ 306

Youdan, TG (ed), *Equity, Fiduciaries and Trusts*, 1989, Toronto

Zimmerman, *The Law of Obligations: Roman Foundations of the Civilian Tradition*, 1996, Oxford: Oxford University Press

Index